D0744577

PRENTICE HALL MATHEMATICS

GEOMETRY

Laurie E. Bass
Randall I. Charles
Art Johnson
Dan Kennedy

PEARSON
Prentice
Hall

Boston, Massachusetts
Upper Saddle River, New Jersey

Authors

Series Authors

Dan Kennedy, Ph.D., is a classroom teacher and the Lupton Distinguished Professor of Mathematics at the Baylor School in Chattanooga, Tennessee. A frequent speaker at professional meetings on the subject of mathematics education reform, Dr. Kennedy has conducted more than 50 workshops and institutes for high school teachers. He is co-author of textbooks in calculus and precalculus, and from 1990 to 1994 he chaired the College Board's AP Calculus Development Committee. He is a 1992 Tandy Technology Scholar and a 1995 Presidential Award winner.

Randall I. Charles, Ph.D., is Professor Emeritus in the Department of Mathematics and Computer Science at San Jose State University, San Jose, California. He began his career as a high school mathematics teacher, and he was a mathematics supervisor for five years. Dr. Charles has been a member of several NCTM committees and is a former Vice President of the National Council of Supervisors of Mathematics. Much of his writing and research has been in the area of problem solving. He has authored more than 75 mathematics textbooks for kindergarten through college.

Dorling Kindersley (DK) is an international publishing company that specializes in the creation of high-quality, illustrated information books for children and adults. Dorling Kindersley's unique graphic presentation style is used in this program to motivate students in learning about real-world applications of mathematics. DK is part of the Pearson family of companies.

ISBN 0-13-062560-4

19 20 09 08 07 06

Geometry Authors

Laurie E. Bass is a classroom teacher at Fieldston, the grades 7–12 division of the Ethical Culture Fieldston School in Riverdale, New York. Ms. Bass has a wide base of teaching experience, ranging from grades 6 and 7 through Advanced Placement Calculus. She was the recipient of a 2000 Honorable Mention for the RadioShack National Teacher Awards. She also has been a contributing writer of a number of publications, including software-based activities for the Algebra 1 classroom. Among her areas of special interests are cooperative learning for high school students and geometry exploration on the computer.

Art Johnson, Ed.D., is a mathematics educator with 32 years of public school teaching experience. Dr. Johnson is a frequent speaker and workshop leader, and the recipient of a number of awards, including the Tandy Prize for Teaching Excellence in 1995 and a 1992 Presidential Award for Excellence in Mathematics Teaching. He was profiled by the Disney Corporation in the American Teacher of the Year Program. Dr. Johnson is currently a professor of mathematics education at Boston University.

Algebra 1 and Algebra 2 Authors

Allan E. Bellman
Lecturer/Supervisor in the School of Education at the University of California
Davis, California

William G. Handlin, Sr.
Department Chairman of Technology Applications
Spring Woods High School
Houston, Texas

Sadie Chavis Bragg, Ed.D
Professor of Mathematics and Vice President of Academic Affairs
Borough of Manhattan Community College of the City University of New York
New York, New York

Reviewers

Algebra 1 Reviewers

Mary Lou Beasley
Southside Fundamental Middle School
St. Petersburg, Florida

Blanche Smith Brownley
Washington, D.C., Public Schools
Washington, D.C.

Joseph Caruso
Somerville High School
Somerville, Massachusetts

Belinda Craig
Highland West Junior High School
Moore, Oklahoma

Jane E. Damaske
Lakeshore Public Schools
Stevensville, Michigan

Stacey A. Ego
Warren Central High School
Indianapolis, Indiana

Earl R. Jones
Formerly, Kansas City Public Schools
Kansas City, Missouri

Jeanne Lorenson
James H. Blake High School
Silver Spring, Maryland

John T. Mace
Hibbett Middle School
Florence, Alabama

Ann Marie Palmieri-Monahan
Director of Mathematics
Bayonne Board of Education
Bayonne, New Jersey

Marie Schalke
Woodlawn Middle School
Long Grove, Illinois

Julie Welling
LaPorte High School
LaPorte, Indiana

Sharon Zguzenski
Naugatuck High School
Naugatuck, Connecticut

Geometry Reviewers

Marian Avery
Great Valley High School
Malvern, Pennsylvania

Mary Emma Bunch
Farragut High School
Knoxville, Tennessee

Karen A. Cannon
K–12 Mathematics Coordinator
Rockwood School District
Eureka, Missouri

Johnnie Ebbert
Department Chairman
DeLand High School
DeLand, Florida

Russ Forrer
Math Department Chairman
East Aurora High School
Aurora, Illinois

Andrea Kopco
Midpark High School
Middleburg Heights, Ohio

Gordon E. Maroney III
Camden Fairview High School
Camden, Arkansas

Charlotte Phillips
Math Coordinator
Wichita USD 259
Wichita, Kansas

Richard P. Strausz
Farmington Public Schools
Farmington, Michigan

Jane Tanner
Jefferson County International Baccalaureate School
Birmingham, Alabama

Karen D. Vaughan
Pitt County Schools
Greenville, North Carolina

Robin Washam
Math Specialist
Puget Sound Educational Service District
Burien, Washington

Algebra 2 Reviewers

Josiane Fouarge
Landry High School
New Orleans, Louisiana

Susan Hvizdos
Math Department Chair
Wheeling Park High School
Wheeling, West Virginia

Kathleen Kohler
Kearny High School
Kearny, New Jersey

Julia Kolb
Leesville Road High School
Raleigh, North Carolina

Deborah R. Kula
Sacred Hearts Academy
Honolulu, Hawaii

Betty Mayberry
Gallatin High School
Gallatin, Tennessee

John L. Pitt
Formerly, Prince William County Schools
Manassas, Virginia

Margaret Plouvier
Billings West High School
Billings, Montana

Sandra Sikorski
Berea High School
Berea, Ohio

Tim Visser
Grandview High School
Cherry Creek School District
Aurora, Colorado

Content Consultants

Courtney Lewis
Mathematics
Prentice Hall Senior National Consultant
Baltimore, Maryland

Deana Cerroni
Mathematics
Prentice Hall National Consultant
Las Vegas, Nevada

Kimberly Margel
Prentice Hall National Consultant
Scottsdale, Arizona

Sandra Mosteller
Mathematics
Prentice Hall National Consultant
Anderson, South Carolina

Rita Corbett
Mathematics
Prentice Hall Consultant
Elgin, Illinois

Cathy Davies
Mathematics
Prentice Hall Consultant
Laguna Niguel, California

Sally Marsh
Mathematics
Prentice Hall Consultant
Baltimore, Maryland

Addie Martin
Mathematics
Prentice Hall Consultant
Upper Marlboro, Maryland

Rose Primiani
Mathematics
Prentice Hall Consultant
Brick, New Jersey

Loretta Rector
Mathematics
Prentice Hall Consultant
Foresthill, California

Charlotte Samuels
Mathematics
Prentice Hall Consultant
Lafyette, Pennsylvania

Margaret Thomas
Mathematics
Prentice Hall Consultant
Indianapolis, Indiana

Contents in Brief

Chapter 1

Tools of Geometry

Student Support

Reasoning and Proof

Student Support

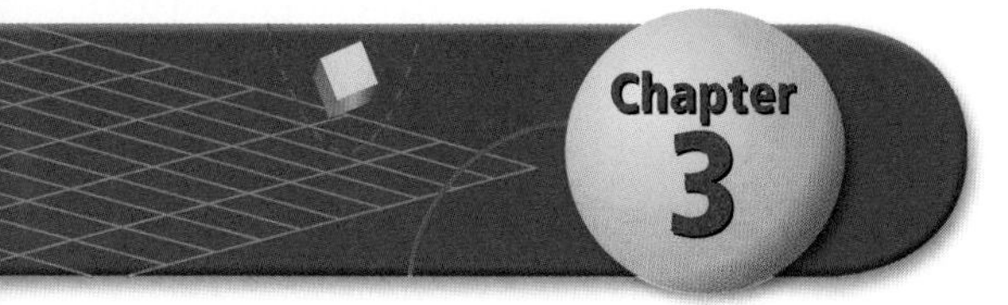

Parallel and Perpendicular Lines

Student Support

Congruent Triangles

Student Support

Instant Check System

Reading Math

Standardized Test Prep

Real-World Connections

Relationships Within Triangles

Student Support

Quadrilaterals

Student Support

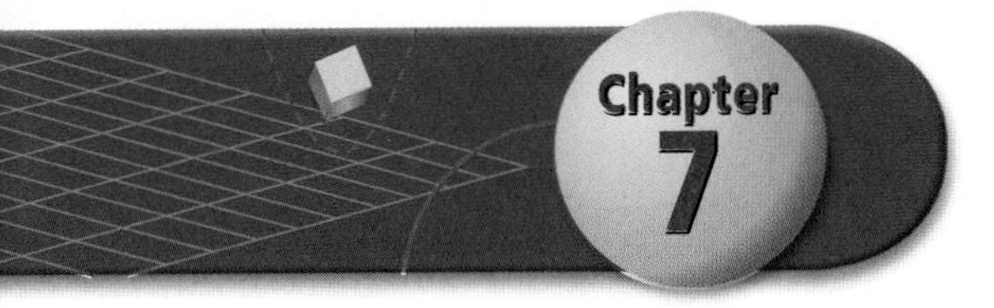

Area

Student Support

Chapter 8 Similarity

Student Support

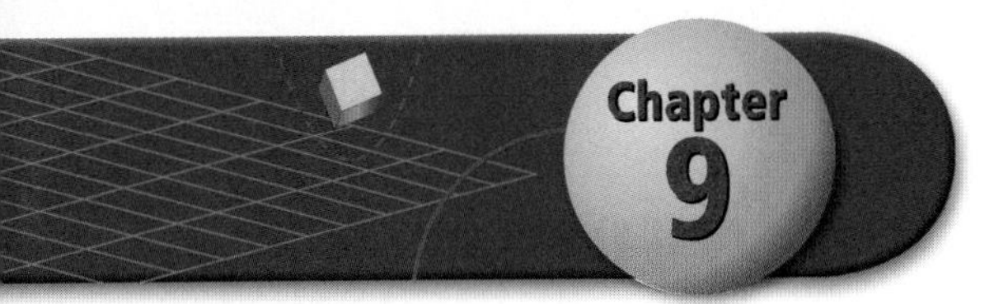

Right Triangle Trigonometry

Student Support

Surface Area and Volume

Student Support

Instant Check System

Reading Math

Standardized Test Prep

Real-World Connections

Circles

Student Support

Transformations

Student Support

Take It to the Net

Throughout this book you will find links to the Prentice Hall Web site for *Geometry*. Use the Web Code provided with each link to gain direct access to online material.

For a complete list of online features, use Web Code afk-0099

Here's how to **Take It to the Net:**

- Go to **PHSchool.com**.
- Enter the Web Code.
- Click Go!

Lesson Quiz Web Codes

There is an online quiz for each lesson. Access these quizzes with Web Codes afa-0101 through afa-1209 for Lesson 1-1 through Lesson 12-9. *See page 9.*

78 Lesson Quizzes
Web Code format: afa- 02 04 02 = Chapter 2 04 = Lesson 4

Chapter Resource Web Codes

Chapter	Vocabulary Quizzes *See page 61.*	Chapter Tests *See page 64.*	Dorling Kindersley Real-World Snapshots *See pages 110–111.*	Chapter Projects
1	afj-0151	afa-0152		afd-0161
2	afj-0251	afa-0252	afe-0253	afd-0261
3	afj-0351	afa-0352		afd-0361
4	afj-0451	afa-0452	afe-0453	afd-0461
5	afj-0551	afa-0552		afd-0561
6	afj-0651	afa-0652	afe-0653	afd-0661
7	afj-0751	afa-0752		afd-0761
8	afj-0851	afa-0852	afe-0853	afd-0861
9	afj-0951	afa-0952		afd-0961
10	afj-1051	afa-1052	afe-1053	afd-1061
11	afj-1151	afa-1152		afd-1161
12	afj-1251	afa-1252	afe-1253	afd-1261
End-of-Course		afa-1254		

Additional Resource Web Codes

Data Updates Use Web Code afg-2041 to get up-to-date government data for use in examples and exercises. *See page 389.*

Geometry at Work For information about each Geometry at Work feature, use Web Code afb-2031. *See page 40.*

A Point in Time For information about each A Point in Time feature, use Web Code afe-2032. *See page 88.*

Graphing Calculator Procedures There are 27 procedures available online. Use Web Code afe-2100 for an index of all the procedures, or Web Codes afe-2101 through afe-2127 to access individual procedures. *See page 57.*

Using Your Book for Success

Welcome to Prentice Hall *Geometry*. There are many features built into the daily lessons of this text that will help you learn the important skills and concepts you will need to be successful in this course. Look through the following pages for some study tips that you will find useful as you complete each lesson.

Instant Check System™
An *Instant Check System™*, built into the text and marked with a ✔, allows you to check your understanding of skills before moving on to the next topic.

✔ Diagnosing Readiness
Complete the *Diagnosing Readiness* exercises to see what topics you may need to review before you begin the chapter.

✔ Check Skills You'll Need
Complete the *Check Skills You'll Need* exercises to make sure you have the skills needed to successfully learn the concepts in the lesson.

New Vocabulary
New Vocabulary is listed for each lesson so you can pre-read the text. As each term is introduced, it is highlighted in yellow.

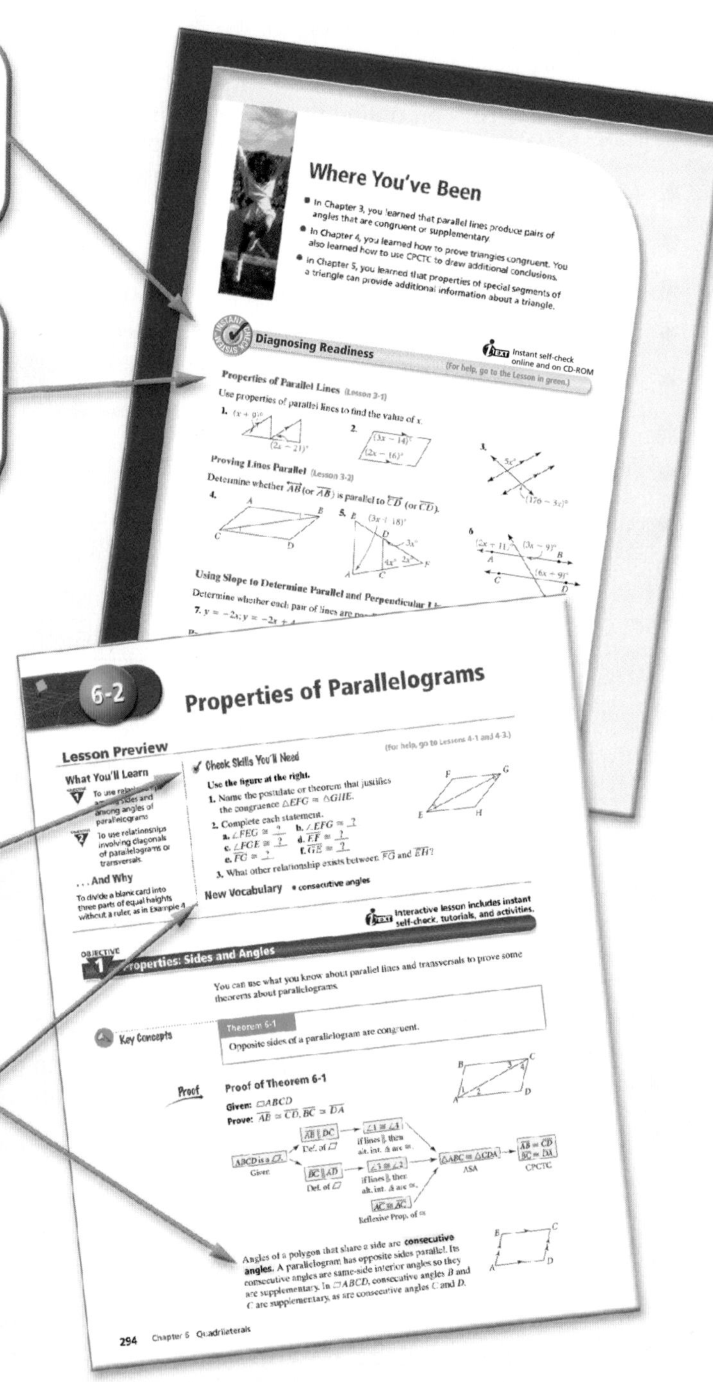

Where You've Been

- In Chapter 3, you learned that parallel lines produce pairs of angles that are congruent or supplementary.
- In Chapter 4, you learned how to prove triangles congruent. You also learned how to use CPCTC to draw additional conclusions.
- In Chapter 5, you learned that properties of special segments of a triangle can provide additional information about a triangle.

Diagnosing Readiness

Instant self-check online and on CD-ROM

(For help, go to the Lesson in green.)

Properties of Parallel Lines (Lesson 3-1)

Use properties of parallel lines to find the value of x.

Proving Lines Parallel (Lesson 3-2)

Determine whether $\overline{AB}$ (or $\overleftrightarrow{AB}$) is parallel to $\overline{CD}$ (or $\overleftrightarrow{CD}$).

Using Slope to Determine Parallel and Perpendicular L...

6-2 Properties of Parallelograms

Lesson Preview

What You'll Learn

To use relationships involving diagonals of parallelograms or transversals

... And Why

To divide a blank card into three parts of equal heights without a ruler, as in Example 4

✔ Check Skills You'll Need (For help, go to Lessons 4-1 and 4-3.)

Use the figure at the right.

1. Name the postulate or theorem that justifies the congruence $\triangle EFG \cong \triangle GHE$.
2. Complete each statement.
3. What other relationship exists between $\overline{FG}$ and $\overline{EH}$?

New Vocabulary • consecutive angles

Interactive lesson includes instant self-check, tutorials, and activities.

Objective 1 Properties: Sides and Angles

You can use what you know about parallel lines and transversals to prove some theorems about parallelograms.

Key Concepts

Theorem 6-1

Opposite sides of a parallelogram are congruent.

Proof

Proof of Theorem 6-1

Angles of a polygon that share a side are **consecutive angles.** A parallelogram has opposite sides parallel. Its consecutive angles are same-side interior angles so they are supplementary. In $\square ABCD$, consecutive angles B and C are supplementary, as are consecutive angles C and D.

294 Chapter 6 Quadrilaterals

Reading Math

The *Reading Math* hints help you to use mathematical notation correctly, understand new mathematical vocabulary, and translate mathematical symbols into everyday English so you can talk about what you've learned.

Check Understanding

Every lesson includes numerous *Examples,* each followed by a *Check Understanding* question that you can do on your own to see if you understand the skill being introduced. Check your progress with the answers at the back of the book.

Need Help?

Need Help? notes provide a quick review of a concept you need to understand the topic being presented. Look for the green labels throughout the text that tells you where to "Go" for help.

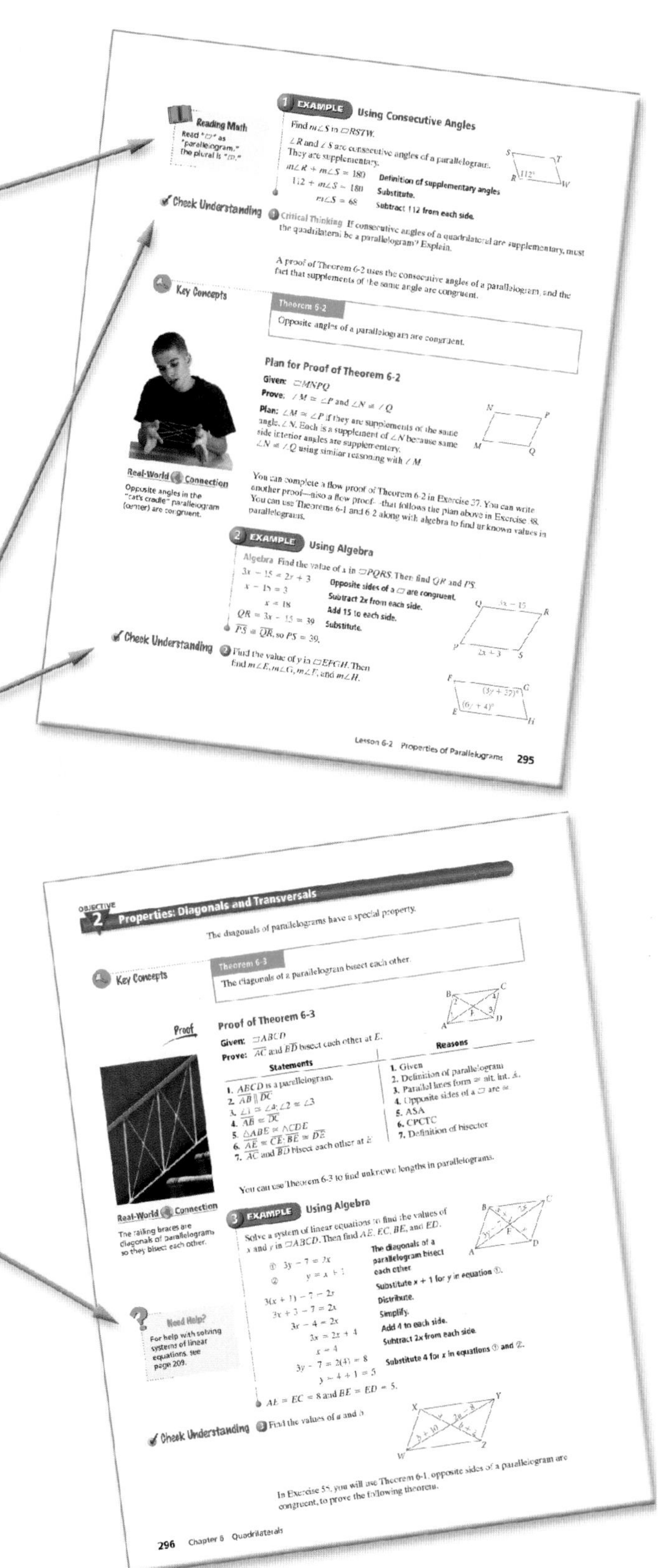

Exercises
There are numerous *Exercises* in each lesson that give you the practice you need to master the concepts of the lesson. Each practice set includes the following sections.

A: Practice by Example
The *A: Practice by Example* exercises refer you back to the Examples in the lesson, in case you need help with completing these exercises.

B: Apply Your Skills
The *B: Apply Your Skills* exercises combine skills from earlier lessons to offer you richer skill exercises and multi-step application problems.

C: Challenge
The *C: Challenge* exercises give you an opportunity to solve problems that extend and stretch your thinking.

Standardized Test Prep
Standardized Test Prep exercises give you daily practice with the types of test question formats that you will encounter on state and national tests.

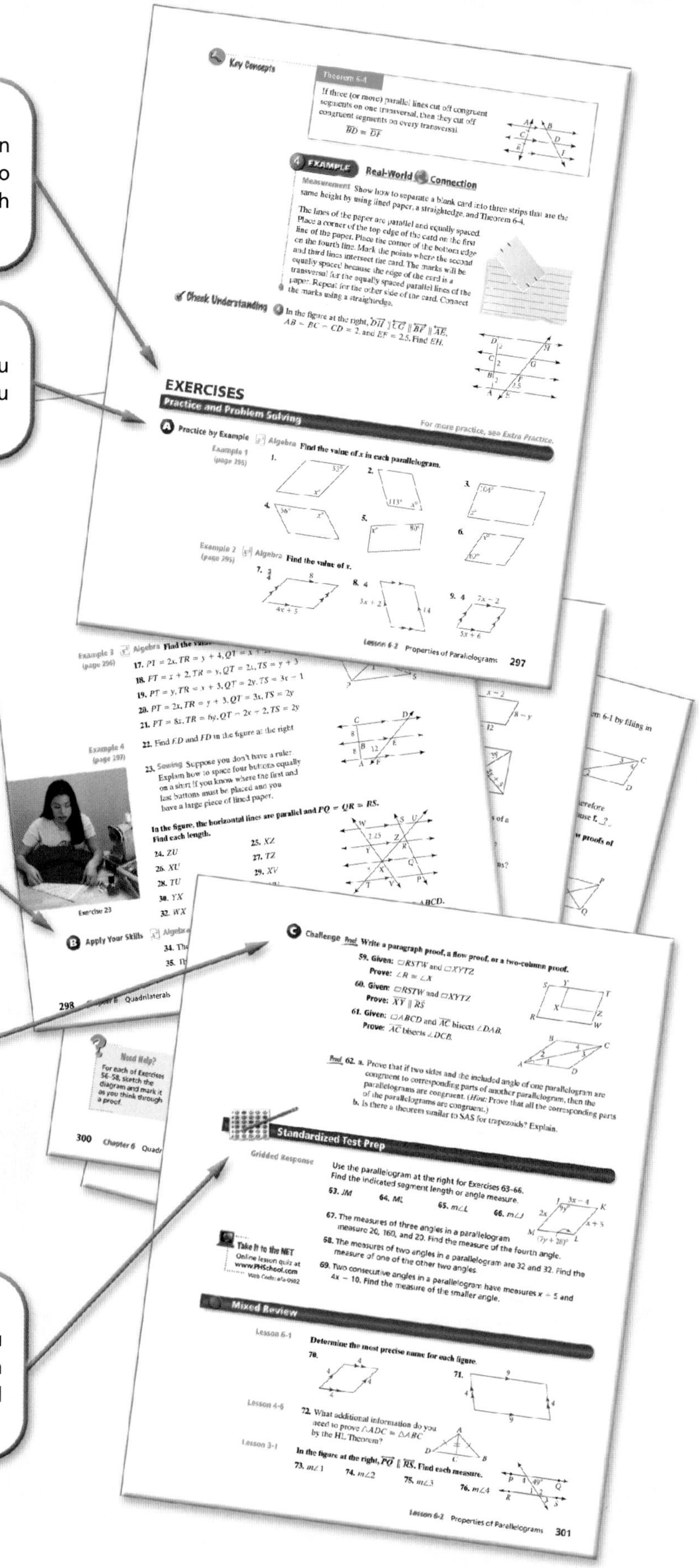

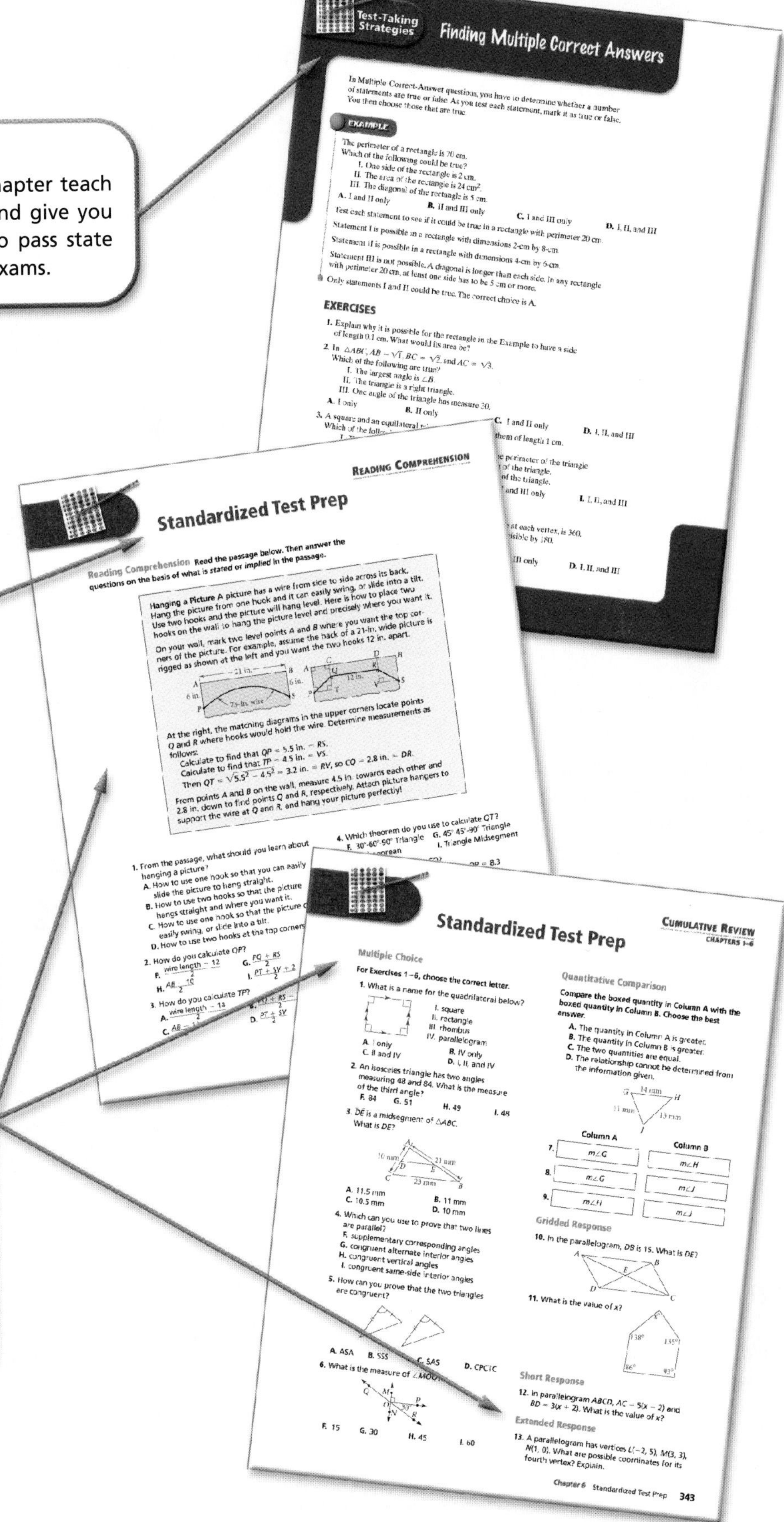

Test-Taking Strategies
Test-Taking Strategies in every chapter teach you strategies to be successful and give you practice in the skills you need to pass state tests and standardized national exams.

Standardized Test Prep
Standardized Test Prep pages in every chapter give you more opportunities to prepare for the tests you will have to take.

Test Item Formats
The *Standardized Test Prep* exercises in your book give you the practice you need to answer all types of test questions.

- *Multiple Choice*
- *Quantitative Comparison*
- *Gridded Response*, for which you write your answer in a grid
- *Short Response*, which are scored using a rubric
- *Extended Response*, which are scored using a rubric
- *Reading Comprehension*

Reading to Learn

In addition to the Reading Math hints shown on page xxi, your *Geometry* text provides even more ways for you to develop your ability to read mathematically so that you are successful in this course and on state tests.

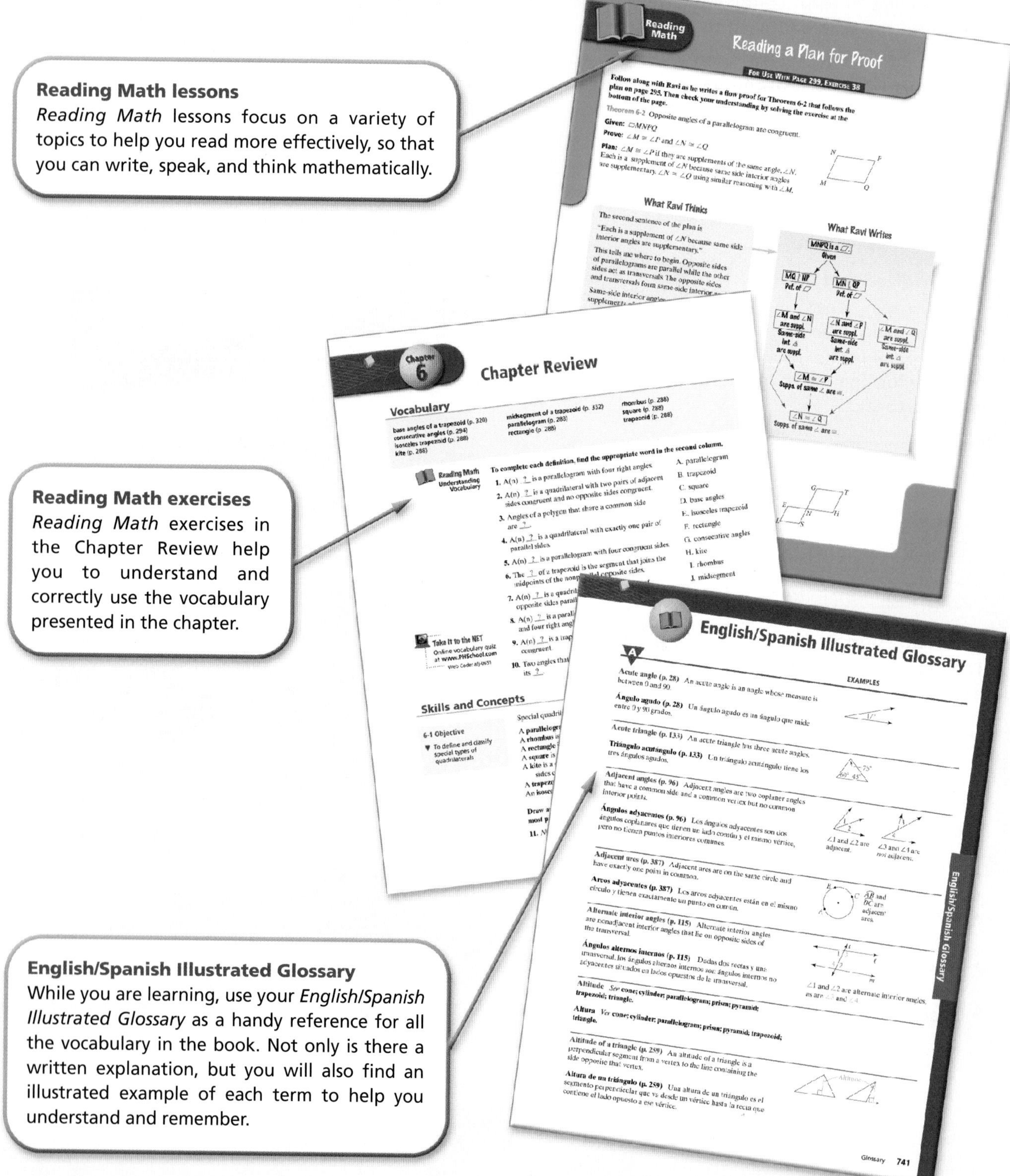

Reading Math lessons
Reading Math lessons focus on a variety of topics to help you read more effectively, so that you can write, speak, and think mathematically.

Reading Math exercises
Reading Math exercises in the Chapter Review help you to understand and correctly use the vocabulary presented in the chapter.

English/Spanish Illustrated Glossary
While you are learning, use your *English/Spanish Illustrated Glossary* as a handy reference for all the vocabulary in the book. Not only is there a written explanation, but you will also find an illustrated example of each term to help you understand and remember.

Dorling Kindersley (DK) Real-World Snapshots

Dorling Kindersley (DK) is an international publishing company that specializes in the creation of high-quality, illustrated information books for children and adults. DK is part of the Pearson family of companies.

Real-World Snapshots
The *Real-World Snapshots* feature applies the exciting and unique graphic presentation style found in Dorling Kindersley books to show you how mathematics is used in real life.

Activities
Using data from these pages and data that you gather, complete the hands-on *Activities* to apply the mathematics you are learning in real-world situations.

Take It to the Net
Enter the Web Code for online information you can use to learn more about the topic of the feature.

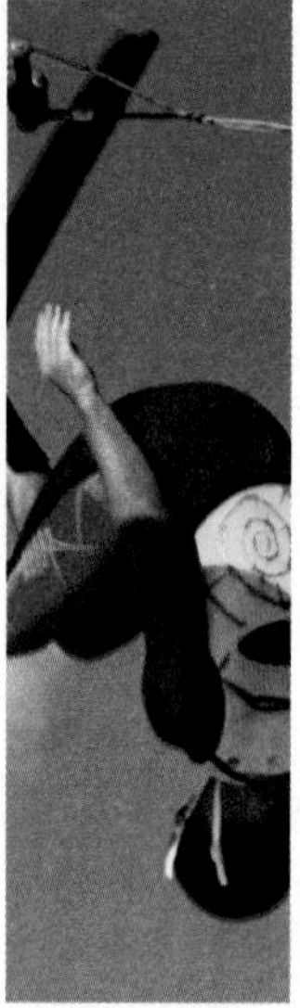

Where You've Been

In previous courses, you learned

- to apply your knowledge of arithmetic to the study of algebra. You also learned about the real number system, including operations on rational and irrational numbers.
- to write algebraic expressions, and equations to represent relationships.
- to use a variety of techniques to solve equations and inequalities with one or more variables.

iTEXT Instant self-check online and on CD-ROM

Diagnosing Readiness

(For help, go to the Skills Handbook.)

Squaring Numbers (Skills Handbook page 715)

Simplify.

1. 3^2 **2.** 4^2 **3.** 11^2

Simplifying Expressions (Skills Handbook page 716)

Simplify each expression. Use 3.14 for π.

4. $2 \cdot 7.5 + 2 \cdot 11$ **5.** $\pi(5)^2$ **6.** $\sqrt{5^2 + 12^2}$

Evaluating Expressions

Evaluate the following expressions for $a = 4$ and $b = -2$.

7. $\frac{a + b}{2}$ **8.** $\frac{a - 7}{3 - b}$ **9.** $\sqrt{(7 - a)^2 + (2 - b)^2}$

Finding Absolute Value (Skills Handbook page 719)

Simplify each absolute value expression.

10. $|-8|$ **11.** $|2 - 6|$ **12.** $|-5 - (-8)|$

Solving Equations (Skills Handbook page 720)

x^2 **Algebra** Solve each equation.

13. $2x + 7 = 13$ **14.** $5x - 12 = 2x + 6$ **15.** $2(x + 3) - 1 = 7x$

Tools of Geometry

Chapter 1

Where You're Going

- In this chapter, you will learn how to make plausible conclusions based on patterns you observe.
- You will learn the foundation blocks for the structure of geometry.
- These foundations will provide you with ways to measure segments and angles.
- You will also learn to use constructions and the coordinate plane to represent geometric figures.

Real-World Connection Applying what you learn, you will do activities involving parallel lines and planes on pages 18 and 19.

LESSONS

Key Vocabulary

- acute angle (p. 28)
- angle bisector (p. 36)
- collinear points (p. 11)
- congruent angles (p. 29)
- congruent segments (p. 25)
- conjecture (p. 5)
- coordinate (p. 25)
- coplanar (p. 11)
- counterexample (p. 5)
- inductive reasoning (p. 4)
- obtuse angle (p. 28)
- parallel lines (p. 18)
- parallel planes (p. 18)
- perpendicular bisector (p. 35)
- perpendicular lines (p. 35)
- plane (p. 11)
- postulate (p. 12)
- ray (p. 17)
- right angle (p. 28)
- segment (p. 17)
- skew lines (p. 18)
- straight angle (p. 28)

1-1 Patterns and Inductive Reasoning

Lesson Preview

What You'll Learn

To use inductive reasoning to make conjectures

. . . And Why

To predict future sales for a skateboard business, as in Example 4

✓ Check Skills You'll Need

(For help, go to the Skills Handbook page 715.)

Here is a list of the counting numbers: 1, 2, 3, 4, 5, . . .
Some are even and some are odd.

1. Make a list of the positive even numbers.
2. Make a list of the positive odd numbers.
3. Copy and extend this list to show the first 10 perfect squares.
   $1^2 = 1, 2^2 = 4, 3^2 = 9, 4^2 = 16, \ldots$
4. Which do you think describes the square of any odd number?
   It is odd. It is even.

New Vocabulary • inductive reasoning • conjecture • counterexample

Interactive lesson includes instant self-check, tutorials, and activities.

OBJECTIVE 1

Using Inductive Reasoning

Real-World Connection

You can predict growth of the chambered nautilus shell by studying patterns in its cross sections.

Inductive reasoning is reasoning that is based on patterns you observe. If you observe a pattern in a sequence, you can use inductive reasoning to tell what the next terms in the sequence will be.

1 EXAMPLE Finding and Using a Pattern

Find a pattern for each sequence. Use the pattern to show the next two terms in the sequence.

a. 3, 6, 12, 24, . . .

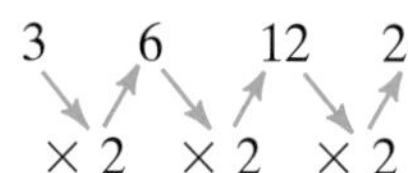

Each term is twice the preceding term. The next two terms are $2 \times 24 = 48$ and $2 \times 48 = 96$.

b.

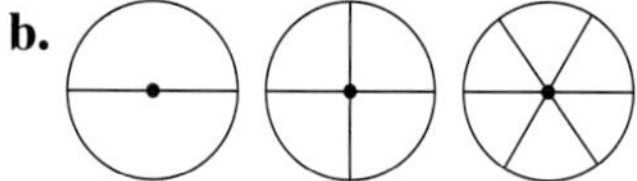

Each circle has one more segment through the center to form equal parts. The next two figures:

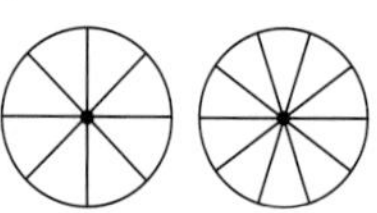

✓ Check Understanding

1 Write the next two terms in each sequence.

a. 1, 2, 4, 7, 11, 16, 22, . . .

b. Monday, Tuesday, Wednesday, . . .

c.

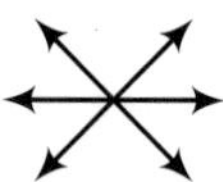

A conclusion you reach using inductive reasoning is called a **conjecture.**

2 EXAMPLE Using Inductive Reasoning

Make a conjecture about the sum of the first 30 odd numbers.

Find the first few sums. Notice that each sum is a perfect square.

$1 = 1 = 1^2$

$1 + 3 = 4 = 2^2$

$1 + 3 + 5 = 9 = 3^2$

$1 + 3 + 5 + 7 = 16 = 4^2$

The perfect squares form a pattern.

Using inductive reasoning, you can conclude that the sum of the first 30 odd numbers is 30^2, or 900.

Check Understanding 2 Make a conjecture about the sum of the first 35 odd numbers. Use your calculator to verify your conjecture.

Not all conjectures turn out to be true. You can prove that a conjecture is false by finding one counterexample. A **counterexample** to a conjecture is an example for which the conjecture is incorrect.

3 EXAMPLE Testing a Conjecture

When points on a circle are joined by as many segments as possible, nonoverlapping regions are formed inside the circle as shown below.

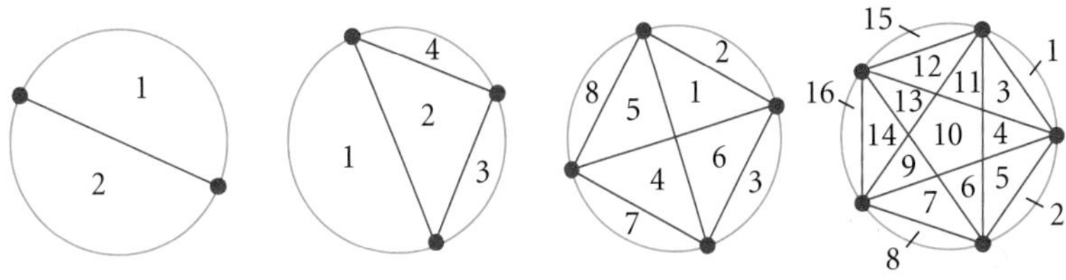

The table at the right shows the number of regions for 2, 3, 4, and 5 points. You might conjecture that the number of regions doubles at each stage. Find a counterexample to show that this conjecture is false.

Points	Regions
2	2
3	4
4	8
5	16

Make a diagram showing a circle with 6 points. This diagram shows that only 31 regions are possible. You have found a counterexample that shows your "doubling" conjecture is false.

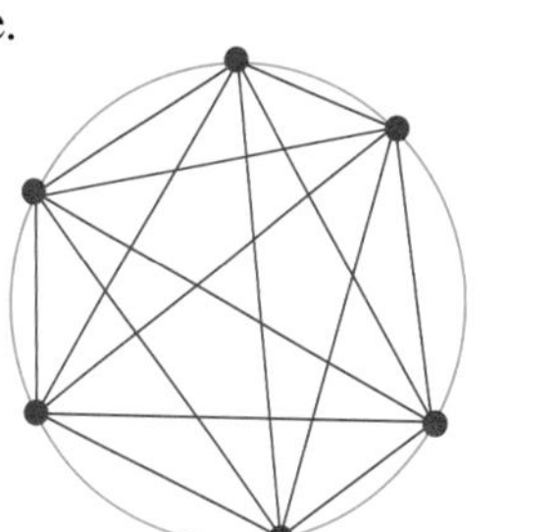

Check Understanding 3 **Critical Thinking** Some products have 5 as a factor, as shown. Make two conjectures based on these products, one that you believe is true and one that you know is false.

$5 \times 7 = 35$	$5 \times 13 = 65$
$5 \times 3 = 15$	$5 \times 9 = 45$
$5 \times 11 = 55$	$5 \times 25 = 125$

4 EXAMPLE Real-World Connection

Business Sales A skateboard shop finds that over a period of five consecutive months, sales of small-wheeled skateboards decreased.

Use inductive reasoning. Make a conjecture about the number of small-wheeled skateboards the shop will sell in June.

The graph shows that sales of small-wheeled skateboards is decreasing by about 3 skateboards each month. By inductive reasoning you might conclude that the shop will sell 42 skateboards in June.

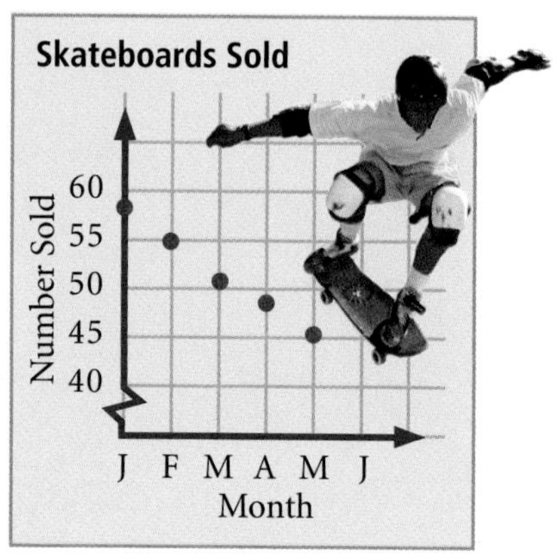

 **Check Understanding** 4 **a.** Make a conjecture about the number of small-wheeled skateboards the shop will sell in July.

b. **Critical Thinking** How confident would you be in using the graph to make a conjecture about sales in December? Explain.

EXERCISES

For more practice, see *Extra Practice.*

Practice and Problem Solving

A Practice by Example

Example 1 (page 4)

Find a pattern for each sequence. Use the pattern to show the next two terms.

1. 5, 10, 20, 40, . . .
2. 3, 33, 333, 3333, . . .
3. 1, −1, 2, −2, 3, . . .
4. $1, \frac{1}{2}, \frac{1}{4}, \frac{1}{8}, \ldots$
5. 15, 12, 9, 6, . . .
6. 81, 27, 9, 3, . . .
7. O, T, T, F, F, S, S, E, . . .
8. J, F, M, A, M, . . .
9. 1, 2, 6, 24, 120, . . .
10. 2, 4, 8, 16, 32, . . .
11. $1, \frac{1}{4}, \frac{1}{9}, \frac{1}{16}, \frac{1}{25}, \ldots$
12. $1, \frac{1}{2}, \frac{1}{3}, \frac{1}{4}, \ldots$
13. George, John, Thomas, James, . . .
14. Martha, Abigail, Martha, Dolley, . . .
15. George, Thomas, Abe, Alexander, . . .
16. Aquarius, Pisces, Aries, Taurus, . . .

Draw the next figure in each sequence.

17. 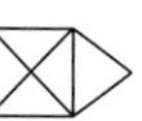 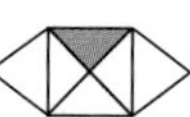 

18.  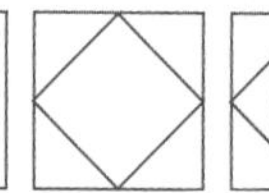 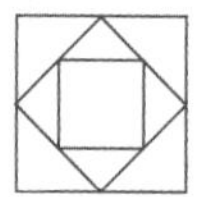

Example 2 (page 5)

Use the table and inductive reasoning. Make a conjecture about each value.

19. the sum of the first 6 positive even numbers

20. the sum of the first 30 positive even numbers

21. the sum of the first 100 positive even numbers

2	$= 2 = 1 \cdot 2$
2 + 4	$= 6 = 2 \cdot 3$
2 + 4 + 6	$= 12 = 3 \cdot 4$
2 + 4 + 6 + 8	$= 20 = 4 \cdot 5$
2 + 4 + 6 + 8 + 10	$= 30 = 5 \cdot 6$

22. Use the pattern in Example 2 to make a conjecture about the sum of the first 100 odd numbers.

Predict the next term in each sequence. Use your calculator to verify your answer.

23. $12345679 \times 9 = 111111111$
$12345679 \times 18 = 222222222$
$12345679 \times 27 = 333333333$
$12345679 \times 36 = 444444444$
$12345679 \times 45 = ■$

24. $1 \times 1 = 1$
$11 \times 11 = 121$
$111 \times 111 = 12321$
$1111 \times 1111 = 1234321$
$11111 \times 11111 = ■$

Example 3 (page 5)

Find one counterexample to show that each conjecture is false.

25. The sum of two numbers is greater than either number.

26. The product of two positive numbers is greater than either number.

27. The difference of two integers is less than either integer.

28. The quotient of two proper fractions is a proper fraction.

Example 4 (page 6)

29. **Weather** The speed with which a cricket chirps is affected by the temperature. If you hear 20 cricket chirps in 14 seconds, what is the temperature?

Chirps per 14 Seconds

5 chirps	45°F
10 chirps	55°F
15 chirps	65°F

30. **Physical Fitness** Dino works out regularly. When he first started exercising, he could do 10 push-ups. After the first month he could do 14 push-ups. After the second month he could do 19, and after the third month he could do 25. Predict the number of push-ups Dino will be able to do after the fifth month of working out. How confident are you of your prediction? Explain.

B Apply Your Skills

Find a pattern for each sequence. Use the pattern to show the next two terms.

31. 1, 3, 7, 13, 21, . . .

32. 1, 2, 5, 6, 9, . . .

33. 0.1, 0.01, 0.001, . . .

34. 2, 6, 7, 21, 22, 66, 67, . . .

35. 1, 3, 7, 15, 31, . . .

36. $0, \frac{1}{2}, \frac{3}{4}, \frac{7}{8}, \frac{15}{16}, \ldots$

37. M, V, E, M, . . .

38. AL, AK, AZ, AR, . . .

39. H, He, Li, Be, . . .

40. **Writing** Choose two of the sequences in Exercises 31–36 and describe the patterns.

41. Draw two parallel lines on your paper. Locate four points on the paper, each an equal distance from both lines. Describe the figure you get if you continue to locate points, each an equal distance from both lines.

Real-World Connection

Points along the yellow line are equal distances from both sides of the bike trail (Exercise 41).

Draw the next figure in each sequence.

42.

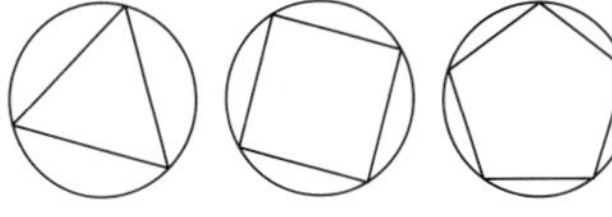

43.

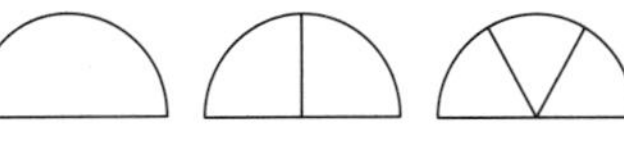

44.

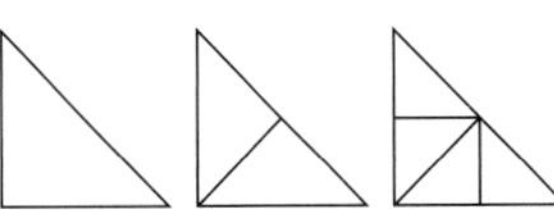

45.

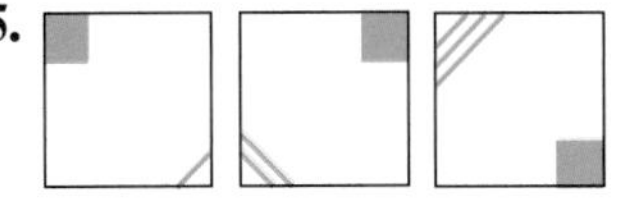

46. Use inductive reasoning. Find the perimeter when 100 triangles are put together in the pattern shown. Assume that all triangle sides are 1 cm long.

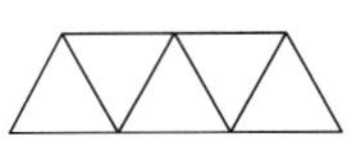

47. Math in the Media Read this exerpt from a news article.

> **Top female runners** have been improving about twice as quickly as the fastest men, a new study says. If this pattern continues, women may soon outrun men in competition!
>
> The study is based on world records collected at 10-year intervals, starting in 1905 for men and in the 1920s for women. If the trend continues, the top female and male runners in races ranging from 200 m to 1500 m might attain the same speeds sometime between 2015 and 2055.
>
> Women's marathon records date from 1955 but their rapid fall suggests that the women's record will equal that of men even more quickly, perhaps by 2005.

a. What conclusion was reached in the study?
b. How was inductive reasoning used to reach the conclusion?
c. Explain why the conclusion that women may soon be outrunning men may be incorrect. For which race is the conclusion most suspect? For what reason?

48. Communications The table shows the number of commercial radio stations in the United States for a 50-year period.
a. Make a line graph of the data.
b. Use the graph and inductive reasoning to make a conjecture about the number of radio stations in the United States in the year 2010.
c. How confident are you about your conjecture? Explain.

Number of Radio Stations

Year	Stations
1950	2,835
1960	4,224
1970	6,519
1980	7,871
1990	9,379
2000	10,577

SOURCE: Federal Communications Commission

49. Open-Ended Write two different number-pattern sequences that begin with the same two numbers.

50. Error Analysis For each of the past four years, Paulo has grown 2 in. every year. He is now 16 years old and is 5 ft 10 in. tall. He figures that when he is 22 years old he will be 6 ft 10 in. tall. What would you tell Paulo about his conjecture?

Need Help?
For Exercise 51, you may want to review "Coordinates of a point" in the Glossary.

51. Coordinate Geometry You are given x- and y-coordinates for 14 points.
$A(1, 5)$ $B(2, 2)$ $C(2, 8)$ $D(3, 1)$ $E(3, 9)$ $F(6, 0)$ $G(6, 10)$
$H(7, -1)$ $I(7, 11)$ $J(9, 1)$ $K(9, 9)$ $L(10, 2)$ $M(10, 8)$ $N(11, 5)$
a. Graph each point.
b. Most of the points fit a pattern. Which points do not?
c. Describe the figure that fits the pattern.

52. History Leonardo of Pisa (about 1175–1258), also known as Fibonacci (fee buh NAH chee), was born in Italy and educated in North Africa. He was one of the first Europeans known to use modern numerals instead of Roman numerals. The special sequence $1, 1, 2, 3, 5, 8, 13, \ldots$ is known as the Fibonacci sequence. Find the next three terms of this sequence.

53. Time Measurement Leap years have 366 days.
a. The years 1984, 1988, 1992, 1996, and 2000 are consecutive leap years. Look for a pattern in their dates. Then, make a conjecture about leap years.
b. Of the years 2010, 2020, 2100, and 2400, which do you think will be leap years?
c. Research Find out whether your conjecture for part (a) and your answer for part (b) are correct. How are leap years determined?

Challenge

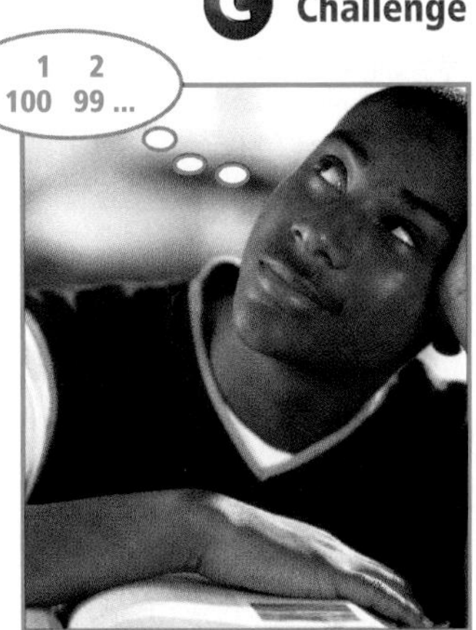

54. **History** When he was in the third grade, German mathematician Karl Gauss (1777–1855) took ten seconds to sum the integers from 1 to 100. Now it's your turn. Find a fast way to sum the integers from 1 to 100; from 1 to n. (*Hint:* Use patterns.)

55. **a. Algebra** Write the first six terms of the sequence that starts with 1, and for which the difference between consecutive terms is first 2, and then 3, 4, 5, and 6.
   b. Evaluate $\frac{n^2 + n}{2}$ for $n = 1, 2, 3, 4, 5,$ and 6. Compare the sequence you get with your answer for part (a).
   c. Examine the diagram at the right and explain how it illustrates a value of $\frac{n^2 + n}{2}$.
   d. Draw a similar diagram to represent $\frac{n^2 + n}{2}$ for $n = 5$.

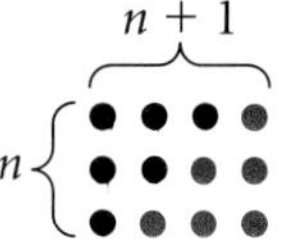

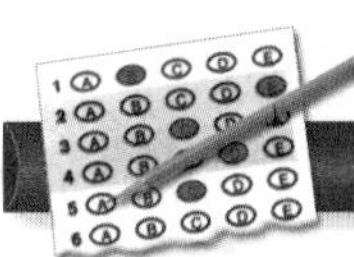

Standardized Test Prep

Multiple Choice

56. The sum of the numbers from 1 to 10 is 55. The sum of the numbers from 11 to 20 is 155. The sum of the numbers from 21 to 30 is 255. Based on this pattern, what is the sum of numbers from 91 to 100?
   A. 855 **B.** 955 **C.** 1055 **D.** 1155

57. Which of the following conjectures is false?
   F. The product of two even numbers is even.
   G. The sum of two even numbers is even.
   H. The product of two odd numbers is odd.
   I. The sum of two odd numbers is odd.

Short Response

58. **a.** How many dots would be in each of the next three figures?
   b. Write an expression for the number of dots in the nth figure.

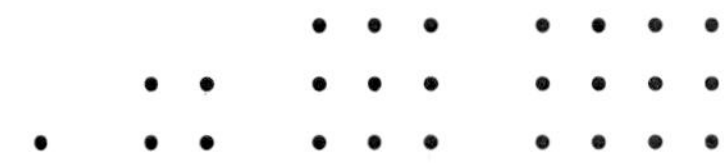

Extended Response

59. **a.** Describe the pattern. List the next two equations in the pattern.
   b. Guess what the product of 181 and 11 is. Test your conjecture.
   c. State whether the pattern can continue forever. Explain.

$(101)(11) = 1111$
$(111)(11) = 1221$
$(121)(11) = 1331$
$(131)(11) = 1441$
$(141)(11) = 1551$

Take It to the NET
Online lesson quiz at **www.PHSchool.com**
Web Code: afa-0101

Mixed Review

Previous Course

Graph each point.

60. $Y(-5, -8)$ **61.** $B(7, -10)$ **62.** $M(9, 12)$ **63.** $Q(-3, 2)$

64. $G(-6, 0)$ **65.** $F(-4, -5)$ **66.** $C(-7, 10)$ **67.** $N(0, -5)$

Classify the points in Exercises 60–67 as described below.

68. in Quadrant IV **69.** on the y-axis **70.** on the x-axis

Points, Lines, and Planes

Lesson Preview

What You'll Learn

To understand basic terms of geometry

To understand basic postulates of geometry

. . . And Why

To explain why a photographer uses a tripod, as in Exercise 45

Check Skills You'll Need

(For help, go to the Skills Handbook page 722.)

x^2 **Algebra** **Solve each system of equations.**

1. $y = x + 5$
   $y = -x + 7$
2. $y = 2x - 4$
   $y = 4x - 10$
3. $y = 2x$
   $y = -x + 15$
4. Copy the diagram of the four points A, B, C, and D. Draw as many different lines as you can to connect pairs of points.

$A\bullet$ $\bullet B$ $C\bullet$ $\bullet D$

New Vocabulary • point • space • line • collinear points • plane • coplanar • postulate • axiom

Interactive lesson includes instant self-check, tutorials, and activities.

OBJECTIVE 1

Basic Terms of Geometry

Investigation: How Many Lines Can You Draw?

Many constellations are named for animals and mythological figures. It takes some imagination to join the points representing the stars to get a recognizable figure such as Leo the Lion. How many lines can you draw connecting the 10 points in Leo the Lion?

- Make a table and look for a pattern to help you find out.

1. Mark three points on a circle. Now connect the three points with as many (straight) lines as possible. How many lines can you draw?
2. Mark four points on another circle. How many lines can you draw to connect the four points?
3. Repeat this procedure for five points on a circle and then for six points. How many lines can you draw to connect the points?
4. Use inductive reasoning to tell how many lines you can draw to connect the ten points of the constellation Leo the Lion.

In geometry, some words such as *point*, *line*, and *plane* are undefined. In order to define these words you need to use words that need further defining. It is important however, to have general descriptions of their meanings.

You can think of a **point** as a location. A point has no size. It is represented by a small dot and is named by a capital letter. A geometric figure is a set of points. **Space** is defined as the set of all points.

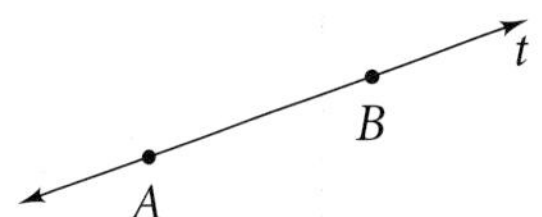

> **Reading Math**
> $\overleftrightarrow{AB}$ and $\overleftrightarrow{BA}$ name the same line.

You can think of a **line** as a series of points that extends in two opposite directions without end. You can name a line by any two points on the line, such as $\overleftrightarrow{AB}$ (read "line AB"). Another way to name a line is with a single lowercase letter, such as line t (see above). Points that lie on the same line are **collinear points.**

1 EXAMPLE Identifying Collinear Points

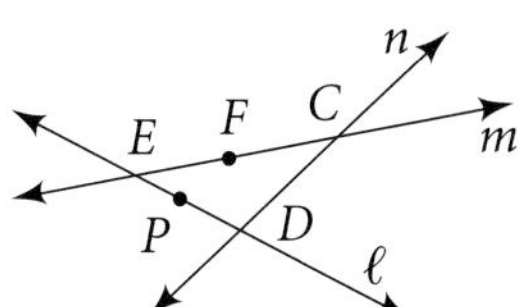

a. Are points E, F, and C collinear? If so, name the line on which they lie.

Points E, F, and C are collinear. They lie on line m.

b. Are points E, F, and D collinear? If so, name the line on which they lie.

Points E, F, and D are not collinear.

✓ Check Understanding 1 **a.** Are points F, P, and C collinear?
b. Name line m in three other ways.
c. **Critical Thinking** Why do you think arrowheads are used when drawing a line or naming a line such as $\overleftrightarrow{EF}$?

A **plane** is a flat surface that has no thickness. A plane contains many lines and extends without end in the directions of all its lines. You can name a plane by either a single capital letter or by at least three of its noncollinear points. Points and lines in the same plane are **coplanar.**

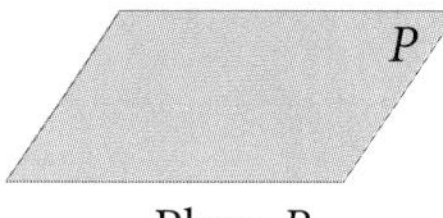

Plane P

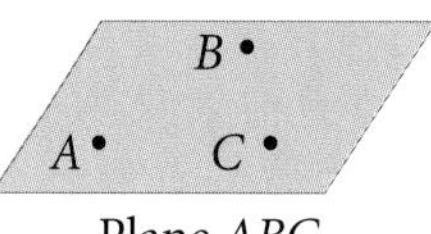

Plane ABC

2 EXAMPLE Naming a Plane

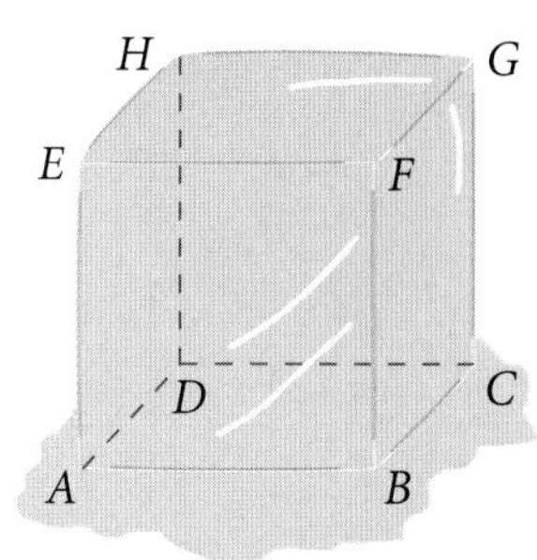

Each surface of the ice cube represents part of a plane. Name the plane represented by the front of the ice cube.

You can name the plane represented by the front of the ice cube using at least three noncollinear points in the plane. Some names are plane AEF, plane AEB, and plane $ABFE$.

✓ Check Understanding 2 List three different names for the plane represented by the top of the ice cube.

OBJECTIVE 2

Basic Postulates of Geometry

A **postulate** or **axiom** is an accepted statement of fact.

You have used some of the following geometry postulates in algebra. For example, you used Postulate 1-1 when you graphed an equation such as $y = -2x + 8$. You plotted two points and then drew the line through those two points.

Key Concepts

Postulate 1-1

Through any two points there is exactly one line.

Line t is the only line that passes through points A and B.

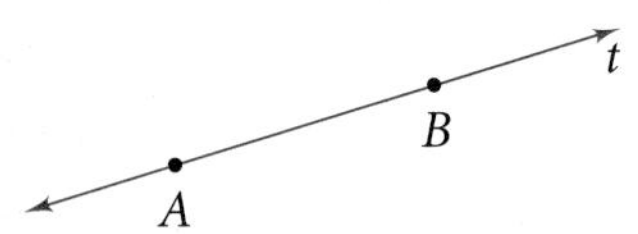

Reading Math

There is exactly one means "there is one and there is no more than one."

In algebra, one way to solve a system of two equations is to graph the two equations. As the graphs of

$$y = -2x + 8$$

$$y = 3x - 7$$

show, the two lines intersect at a single point, (3, 2). The solution to the system of equations is (3, 2).

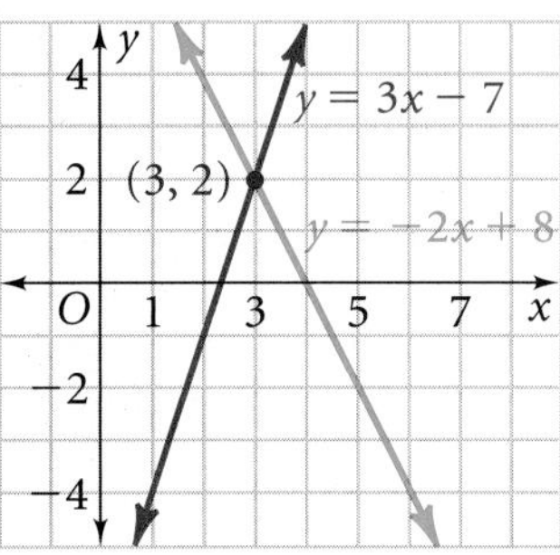

This illustrates Postulate 1-2.

Key Concepts

Postulate 1-2

If two lines intersect, then they intersect in exactly one point.

$\overleftrightarrow{AE}$ and $\overleftrightarrow{BD}$ intersect at C.

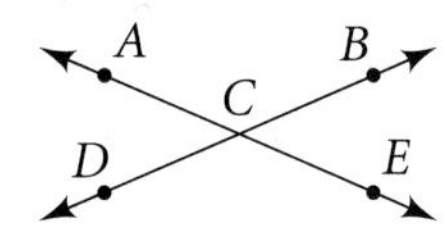

There is a similar postulate about the intersection of planes.

Key Concepts

Postulate 1-3

If two planes intersect, then they intersect in exactly one line.

Plane RST and plane STW intersect in $\overleftrightarrow{ST}$.

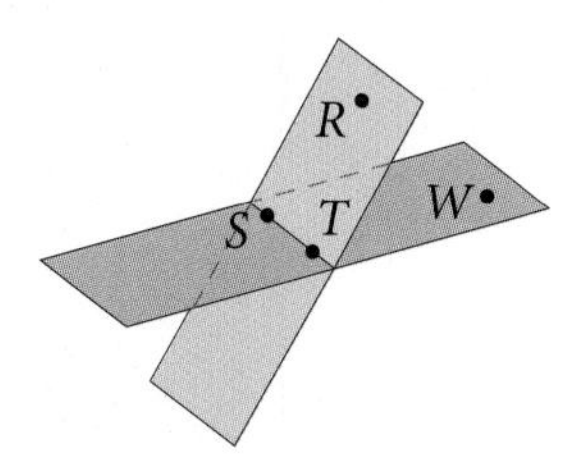

When you know two points in the intersection of two planes, Postulates 1-1 and 1-3 tell you that the line through those points is the line of intersection of the planes.

3 EXAMPLE Finding the Intersection of Two Planes

What is the intersection of plane *HGFE* and plane *BCGF*?

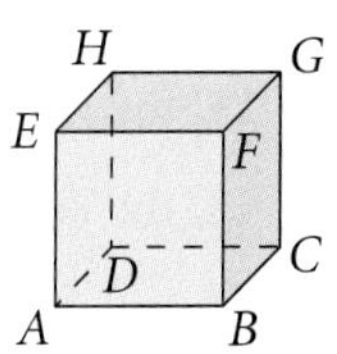

Plane *HGFE* and plane *BCGF*, intersect in $\overleftrightarrow{GF}$.

✔ Check Understanding 3 Name two planes that intersect in $\overleftrightarrow{BF}$.

A three-legged stand will always be stable. As long as the feet of the stand don't lie in one line, the feet of the three legs will lie exactly in one plane.

This illustrates Postulate 1-4.

Key Concepts

Postulate 1-4

Through any three noncollinear points there is exactly one plane.

4 EXAMPLE Using Postulate 1-4

a. Shade the plane that contains *A*, *B*, and *C*.

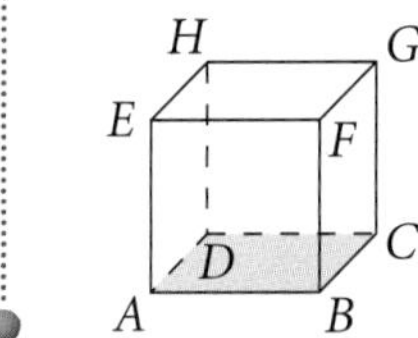

b. Shade the plane that contains *E*, *H*, and *C*.

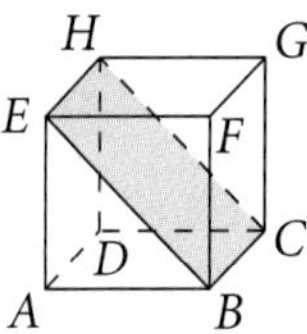

✔ Check Understanding 4 **a.** Name another point that is in the same plane as points *A*, *B*, and *C*.

b. Name another point that is coplanar with points *E*, *H*, and *C*.

EXERCISES

For more practice, see *Extra Practice*.

Practice and Problem Solving

A Practice by Example

Example 1 (page 11)

Are the three points collinear? If so, name the line on which they lie.

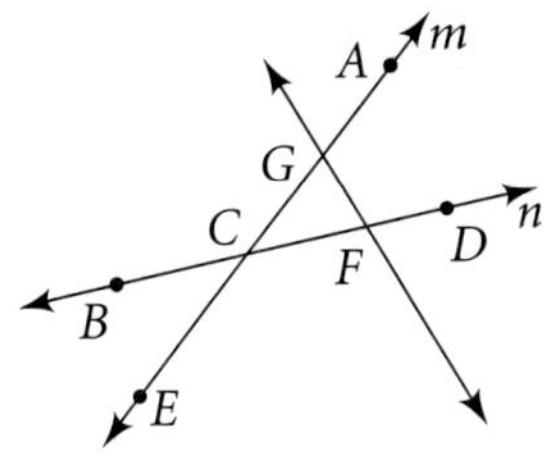

1. *A*, *D*, *E* **2.** *B*, *C*, *D*

3. *B*, *C*, *F* **4.** *A*, *E*, *C*

5. *F*, *B*, *D* **6.** *F*, *A*, *E*

7. *G*, *F*, *C* **8.** *A*, *G*, *C*

9. Name line *m* in three other ways.

10. Name line *n* in three other ways.

Example 2 (page 11)

Name the plane represented by each surface of the box.

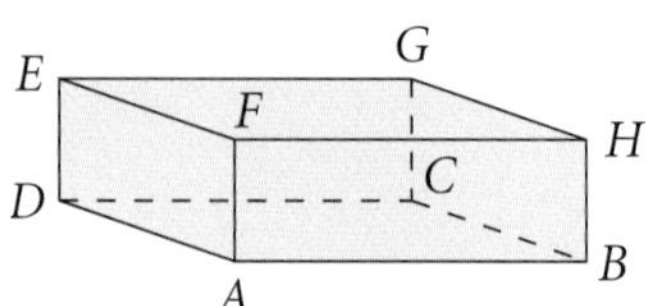

11. the bottom **12.** the top

13. the front **14.** the back

15. the left side **16.** the right side

Example 3 (page 13)

Use the figure at the right for Exercises 17–37.
First, name the intersection of each pair of planes.

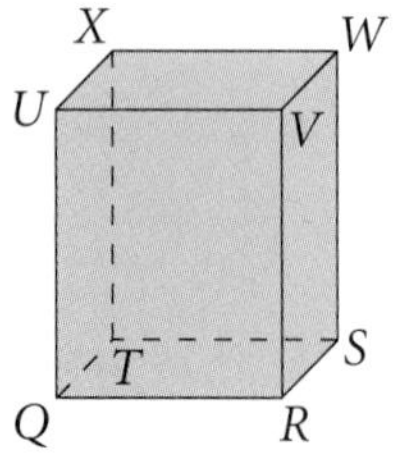

Exercises 17–37

17. planes QRS and RSW **18.** planes UXV and WVS

19. planes XWV and UVR **20.** planes TXW and TQU

Name two planes that intersect in the given line.

21. $\overleftrightarrow{QU}$ **22.** $\overleftrightarrow{TS}$ **23.** $\overleftrightarrow{XT}$ **24.** $\overleftrightarrow{VW}$

Example 4 (page 13)

Copy the figure. Shade the plane that contains the given points.

25. R, V, W **26.** U, V, W **27.** U, X, S **28.** T, U, X **29.** T, V, R

Name another point in each plane.

30. plane RVW **31.** plane UVW **32.** plane UXS **33.** plane TUX **34.** plane TVR

Is the given point coplanar with the other three points?

35. point Q with V, W, S **36.** point U with T, V, S **37.** point W with X, V, R

B Apply Your Skills

Postulate 1-4 states that any three noncollinear points lie in one plane. Find the plane containing the first three points listed, then decide whether the fourth point is in that plane. Write *coplanar* or *noncoplanar* to describe the points.

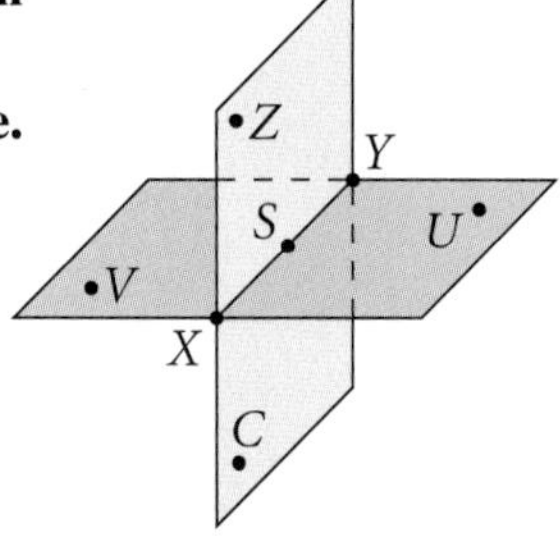

38. Z, S, Y, C **39.** S, U, V, Y

40. X, Y, Z, U **41.** X, S, V, U

42. X, Z, S, V **43.** S, V, C, Y

44. Describe two intersecting planes in your classroom. Describe their intersection.

45. **Photography** Photographers and surveyors use a tripod, or three-legged stand, for their instruments. Use one of the postulates to explain why.

46. Which postulate is sometimes stated as "Two points determine a line"?

47. **Open-Ended** Draw a figure with points $B, C, D, E, F,$ and G that shows $\overleftrightarrow{CD}$, $\overleftrightarrow{BG}$, and $\overleftrightarrow{EF}$, with one of the points on all three lines.

If possible, draw a figure to fit each description. Otherwise write *not possible.*

48. four points that are collinear **49.** two points that are noncollinear

50. three points that are noncollinear **51.** three points that are noncoplanar

Real-World Connection

Careers The photographer uses a tripod to help assure a clear picture.

Coordinate Geometry **Graph the points and state whether they are collinear.**

52. $(0, 0), (0, 2), (0, 4)$ **53.** $(0, 0), (3, 0), (5, 0)$ **54.** $(0, 0), (0, 2), (3, 0)$

55. $(2, -2), (2, 2), (2, 3)$ **56.** $(3, -3), (2, -3), (-3, 1)$ **57.** $(2, 2), (-2, -2), (3, 2)$

58. $(2, -2), (-2, -2), (3, -2)$ **59.** $(-3, 3), (-3, 2), (-3, -1)$

Use *always, sometimes,* or *never* to make a true statement.

60. Intersecting lines are _?_ coplanar.

61. Two planes _?_ intersect in exactly one point.

62. Three points are _?_ coplanar.

63. A plane containing two points of a line _?_ contains the entire line.

64. Four points are _?_ coplanar.

65. Two lines _?_ meet in more than one point.

Need Help?

In Exercise 66, segments of the given lines are shown in the diagram.

66. How many planes contain each line and point?

a. $\overleftrightarrow{EF}$ and point G **b.** $\overleftrightarrow{PH}$ and point E

c. $\overleftrightarrow{FG}$ and point P **d.** $\overleftrightarrow{EP}$ and point G

e. **Make a Conjecture** What do you think is true of a line and a point not on the line?

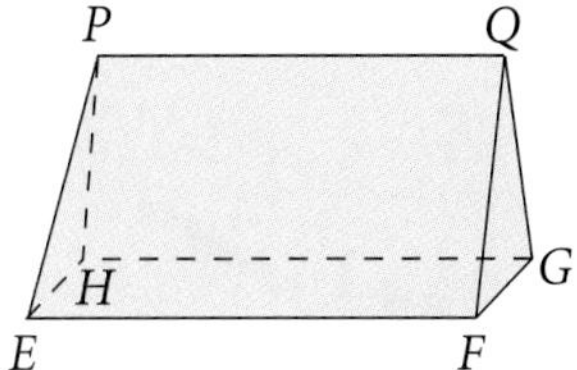

In Exercise 67 and 68, sketch a figure for the given information. Then name the postulate that your figure illustrates.

67. The noncollinear points A, B, and C are all contained in plane N.

68. Planes LNP and MVK intersect in $\overleftrightarrow{NM}$.

69. **Optical Illusions** The diagram (right) is an optical illusion. Which three points are collinear: A, B, and C or A, B, and D? Are you sure? Use a straightedge to check your answer.

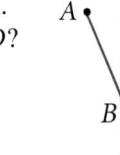

Writing **Use postulates to explain each situation.**

70. A land surveyor can always find a straight line from the point where she stands to any other point she can see.

71. A carpenter knows that a line can represent the intersection of two flat walls.

72. A furniture maker knows that a three-legged table is always steady, but a four-legged table will sometimes wobble.

Coordinate Geometry **Graph the points and state whether they are collinear.**

73. (1, 1), (4, 4), (−3, −3) **74.** (2, 4), (4, 6), (0, 2) **75.** (0, 0), (−5, 1), (6, −2)

76. (0, 0), (8, 10), (4, 6) **77.** (0, 0), (0, 3), (0, −10) **78.** (−2, −6), (1, −2), (4, 1)

Challenge

79. How many planes contain the same three collinear points? Explain.

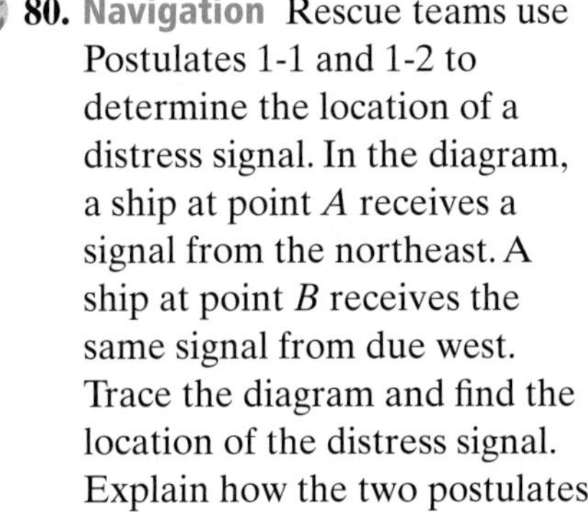

80. **Navigation** Rescue teams use Postulates 1-1 and 1-2 to determine the location of a distress signal. In the diagram, a ship at point A receives a signal from the northeast. A ship at point B receives the same signal from due west. Trace the diagram and find the location of the distress signal. Explain how the two postulates help locate the distress signal.

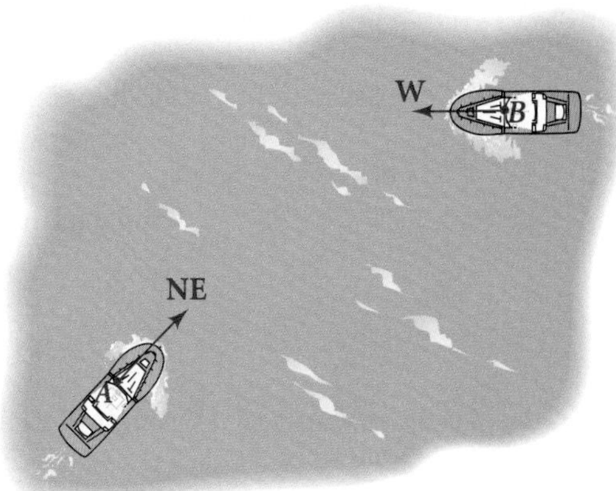

81. a. **Open-Ended** Suppose two points are in plane P. Explain why it makes sense that the line containing the points would be in the same plane.

b. Suppose two lines intersect. How many planes do you think contain both lines? You may use the diagram and your answer in part (a) to explain your answer.

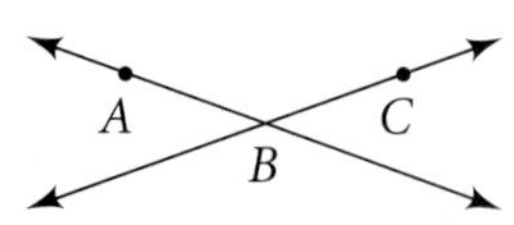

Probability **Points are picked at random from A, B, C, and D, which are arranged as shown. Find the probability that the indicated number of points meet the given condition.**

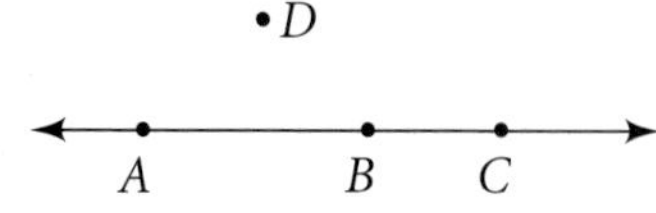

82. 2 points, collinear **83.** 3 points, collinear **84.** 3 points, coplanar

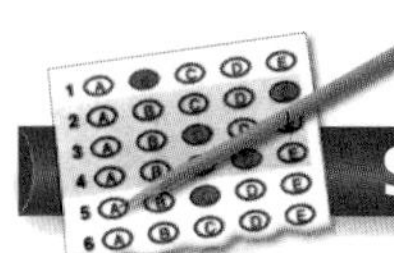

Standardized Test Prep

Multiple Choice

85. In the figure at the right, which points are collinear with C and H?

A. B, F
B. E, F, G
C. A, D, G, I
D. A, D, E, H

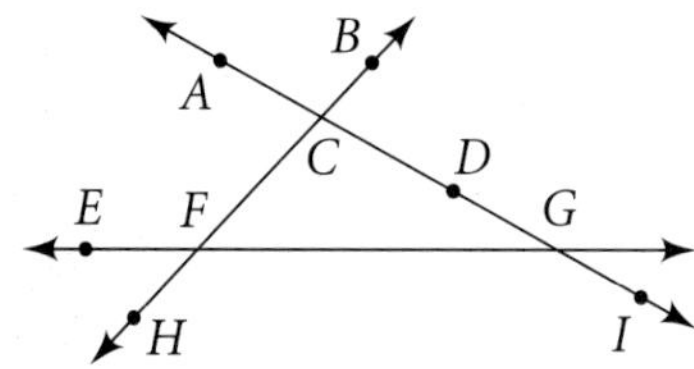

86. A solid chunk of cheese is to be cut into 4 pieces. What is the least number of slices needed?

F. 5 G. 4 H. 3 I. 2

Take It to the NET
Online lesson quiz at
www.PHSchool.com
Web Code: afa-0102

87. Ronald is making a table. What is the least number of legs that the table should have so that it will not wobble?

A. 4 B. 3 C. 2 D. 1

88. At most, how many lines can contain pairs of the points P, Q, and R?

F. 1 G. 2
H. 3 I. 4

Short Response

89. Use the figure at the right.

a. Name all the planes that form the figure.
b. Name all the lines that intersect at D.

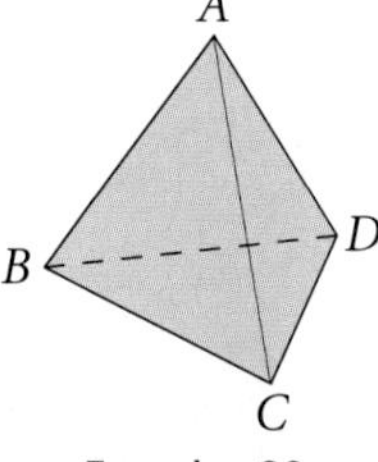

Exercise 89

Mixed Review

Lesson 1-1

90. **Reasoning** What is the last digit of 3^{45}? To answer, make a table, look for a pattern, and use inductive reasoning. Explain the pattern.

Find a pattern for each sequence. Use the pattern to show the next two terms.

91. A, C, E, G, . . . **92.** 2, 6, 12, 20, 30, . . .

93. 4, 16, 64, 256, . . . **94.** 100, 95, 85, 70, 50, . . .

Previous Course

x^2 **Algebra** **Evaluate each expression for the given values.**

95. $a^2 + b^2$ for $a = 3$ and $b = -5$ **96.** $\frac{1}{2}bh$ for $b = 8$ and $h = 11$

1-3 Segments, Rays, Parallel Lines and Planes

Lesson Preview

What You'll Learn

To identify segments and rays

To recognize parallel lines

. . . And Why

To identify compass directions that can be represented by opposite rays, as in Exercise 49

✓ Check Skills You'll Need

(For help, go to Lesson 1-2.)

Judging by appearances, will the lines intersect?

1. 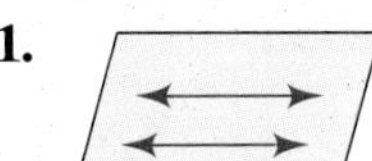

2. 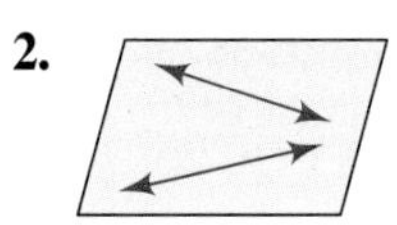

3. 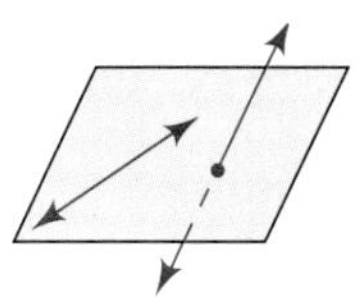

Name the plane represented by each surface of the box.

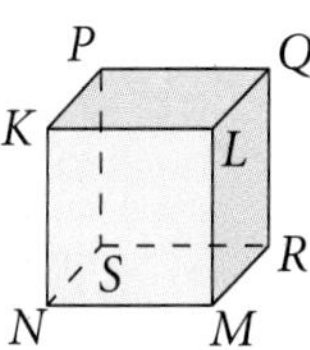

4. the bottom **5.** the top

6. the front **7.** the back

8. the left side **9.** the right side

New Vocabulary • segment • ray • opposite rays • parallel lines • skew lines • parallel planes

 Interactive lesson includes instant self-check, tutorials, and activities.

OBJECTIVE 1 Identifying Segments and Rays

Real-World Connection

A sunbeam models a ray. The sun is its endpoint.

Many geometric figures, such as squares and angles, are formed by parts of lines called segments or rays. A **segment** is the part of a line consisting of two endpoints and all points between them.

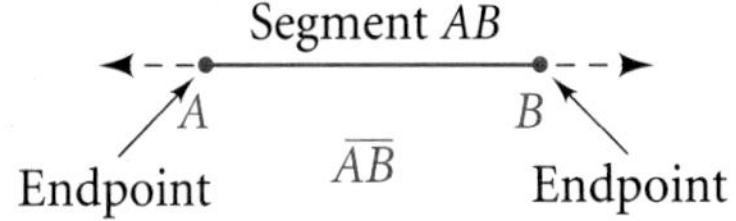

A **ray** is the part of a line consisting of one endpoint and all the points of the line on one side of the endpoint.

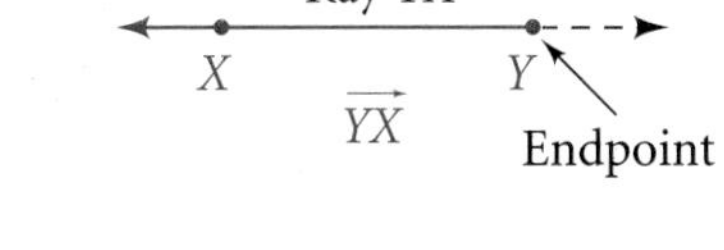

Opposite rays are two collinear rays with the same endpoint. Opposite rays always form a line.

Q R S

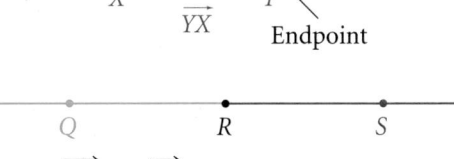

$\overrightarrow{RQ}$ and $\overrightarrow{RS}$ are opposite rays.

1 EXAMPLE Naming Segments and Rays

Name the segments and rays in the figure at the right.

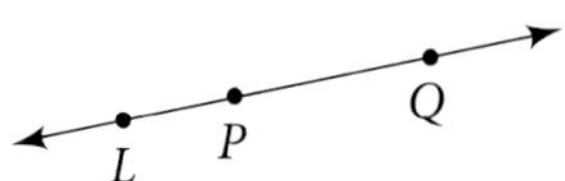

- The three segments are $\overline{LP}$, $\overline{PQ}$, and $\overline{LQ}$.
- The four rays are $\overrightarrow{LP}$ or $\overrightarrow{LQ}$, $\overrightarrow{PQ}$, $\overrightarrow{PL}$, and $\overrightarrow{QP}$ or $\overrightarrow{QL}$.

✓ Check Understanding **1** **Critical Thinking** $\overrightarrow{LP}$ and $\overrightarrow{PL}$ form a line. Are they opposite rays? Explain.

OBJECTIVE 2

Recognizing Parallel Figures

Lines that do not intersect may or may not be coplanar.

Parallel lines are coplanar lines that do not intersect. **Skew lines** are noncoplanar; therefore, they are not parallel and do not intersect.

Reading Math

You read $\overleftrightarrow{AB} \parallel \overleftrightarrow{EF}$ as line *AB* is parallel to line *EF*.

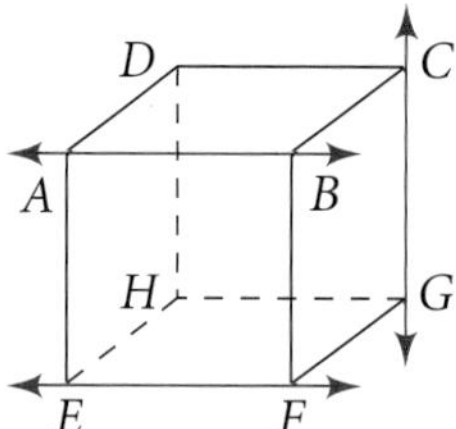

$\overleftrightarrow{AB} \parallel \overleftrightarrow{EF}$

$\overleftrightarrow{AB}$ and $\overleftrightarrow{CG}$ are skew.

Segments or rays are parallel if they lie in parallel lines. They are skew if they lie in skew lines. $\overline{AB}$ and $\overline{CG}$ are skew because $\overleftrightarrow{AB}$ and $\overleftrightarrow{CG}$ are skew.

2 EXAMPLE Identifying Parallel and Skew Segments

a. Name all labeled segments that are parallel to $\overline{DC}$.

$\overline{AB}$, $\overline{GH}$, and $\overline{JI}$ are parallel to $\overline{DC}$.

b. Name all labeled segments that are skew to $\overline{DC}$.

$\overline{NJ}$, $\overline{GJ}$, and $\overline{HI}$ are skew to $\overline{DC}$.

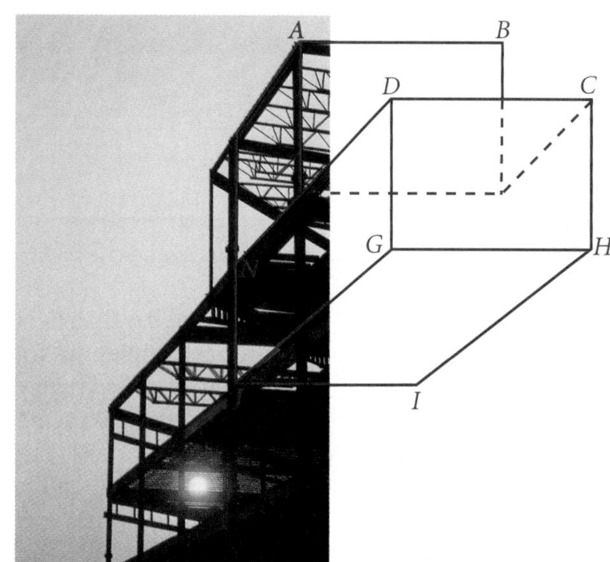

Check Understanding 2 Use the diagram in Example 2.

a. Name all labeled segments that are parallel to $\overline{GJ}$.

b. Name all labeled segments that are skew to $\overline{GJ}$.

c. Name another pair of parallel segments; of skew segments.

Parallel planes are planes that do not intersect.

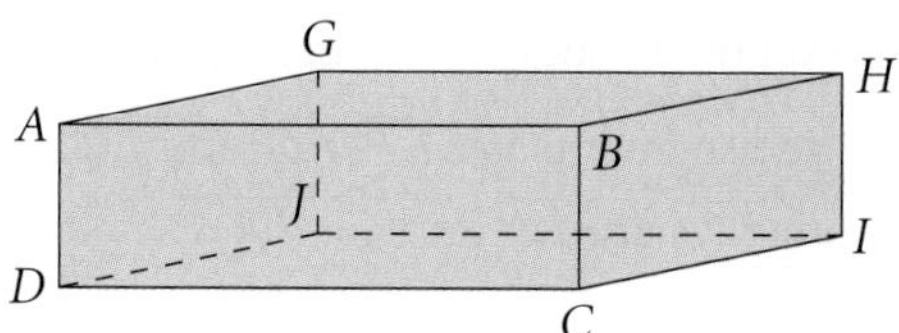

Plane *ABCD* $\parallel$ Plane *GHIJ*

3 EXAMPLE Identifying Parallel Planes

The planes of the front and back are parallel. Name two other pairs of parallel planes in the figure.

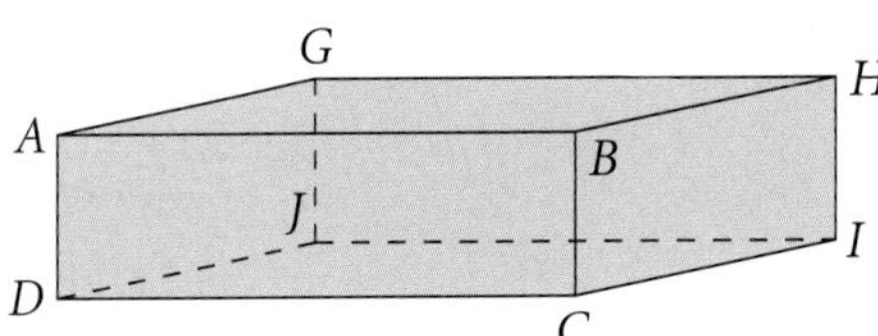

Plane $ABHG \parallel$ plane $DCIJ$; plane $ADJ \parallel$ plane BCI.

3 Use the diagram at the right to name the figures.

a. three pairs of parallel planes

b. a line that is parallel to $\overleftrightarrow{PQ}$

c. a line that is parallel to plane $QRUV$

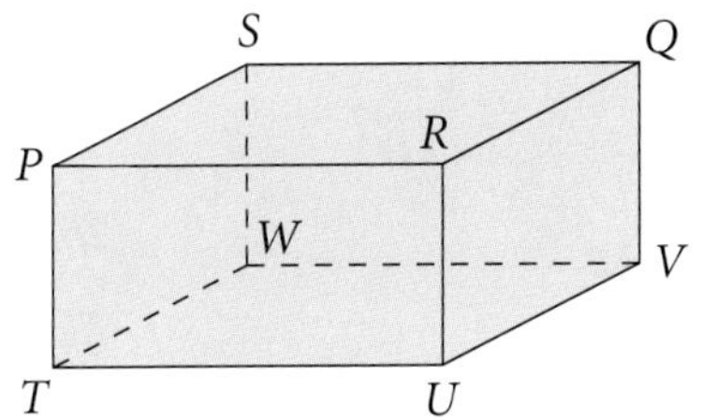

EXERCISES

For more practice, see *Extra Practice*.

Practice and Problem Solving

Practice by Example

Example 1 (page 17)

Sketch each of the following.

1. $\overline{AB}$ **2.** $\overrightarrow{AB}$ **3.** $\overrightarrow{BA}$ **4.** $\overleftrightarrow{BA}$

Use the figure at the right for Exercises 5–10.

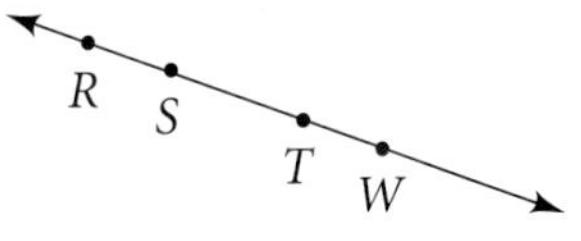

Exercises 5–10

5. Name all the labeled segments.

6. Name all the labeled rays.

7. a. Name a pair of opposite rays with T as an endpoint.

b. Name another pair of opposite rays.

Copy the line pictured above. On your copy mark a different point, *Y*. How many of each type of figure are there with *Y* as an endpoint? Name them.

8. segments **9.** rays

10. Critical Thinking Are there any new rays you can name (see Exercise 6) using R, S, T, or W as the endpoint and Y as the second point? If *yes*, name them.

Example 2 (page 18)

In the diagram, name all segments shown that are parallel to the given segment.

11. $\overline{AC}$ **12.** $\overline{EF}$ **13.** $\overline{AD}$

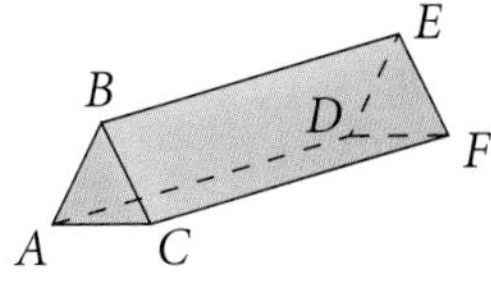

Exercises 11–20

In the diagram, name all segments shown that are skew to the given segment.

14. $\overline{AC}$ **15.** $\overline{EF}$ **16.** $\overline{AD}$

Example 3 (page 19)

Use the diagram above and name a pair of figures to match each description.

17. parallel planes **18.** parallel lines **19.** skew lines

20. a line and a plane that are parallel

Use the figure at the right to name the following.

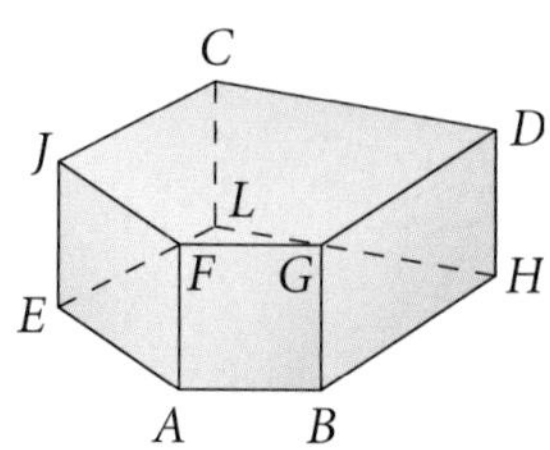

21. all lines that are parallel to $\overleftrightarrow{AB}$

22. two lines that are skew to $\overleftrightarrow{EJ}$

23. all lines that are parallel to plane $JFAE$

24. the intersection of plane FAB and plane FAE

B Apply Your Skills

In Exercises 25–32, describe the statement as true or false. If *false*, explain.

25. $\overleftrightarrow{CB} \parallel \overleftrightarrow{HG}$

26. $\overleftrightarrow{ED} \parallel \overleftrightarrow{HG}$

27. plane $AED \parallel$ plane FGH

28. plane $ABH \parallel$ plane CDF

29. $\overleftrightarrow{AB}$ and $\overleftrightarrow{HG}$ are skew lines.

30. $\overleftrightarrow{AE}$ and $\overleftrightarrow{BC}$ are skew lines.

31. $\overleftrightarrow{CG}$ and $\overleftrightarrow{AI}$ are skew lines.

32. $\overleftrightarrow{CF}$ and $\overleftrightarrow{AJ}$ are skew lines.

Are the two figures the same? Explain.

33. $\overline{XY}$ and $\overline{YX}$

34. $\overrightarrow{XY}$ and $\overrightarrow{YX}$

35. $\overleftrightarrow{XY}$ and $\overleftrightarrow{YX}$

36. The following steps show how to draw planes A and B intersecting in $\overleftrightarrow{FG}$.

Step 1

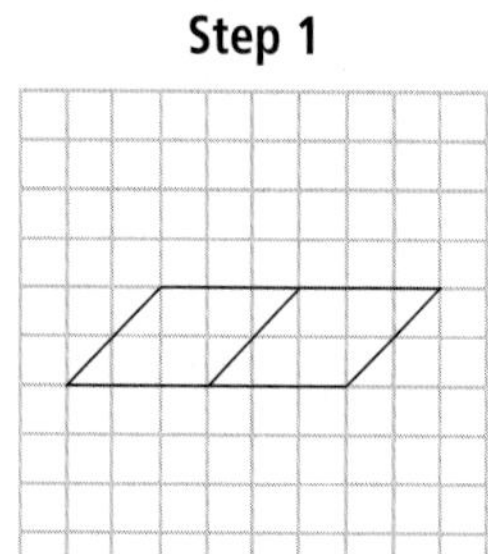

Step 2

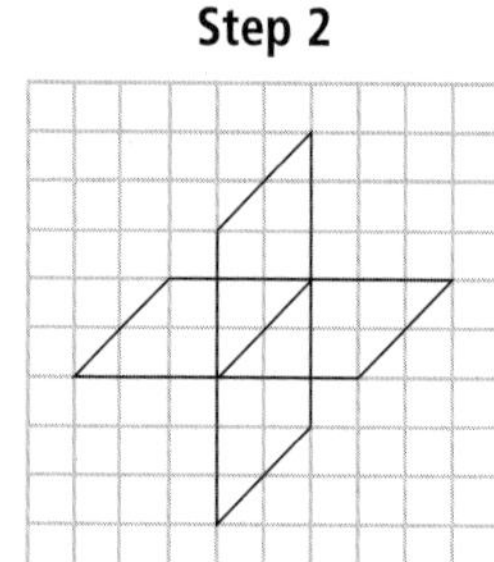

Step 3

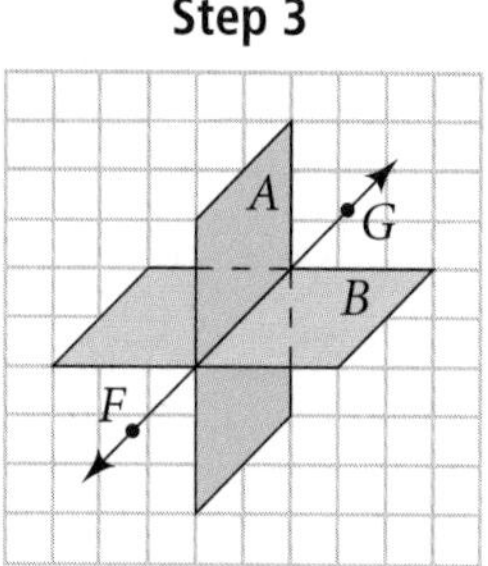

Use similar steps to draw plane DFE and plane DFJ intersecting in $\overleftrightarrow{DF}$.

Reading Math

"Always," "sometimes," and "never" refer to all possible cases, not to intervals of time.

Complete Exercises 37–47 with *always*, *sometimes*, or *never* to make a true statement.

37. Two parallel lines are __?__ coplanar.

38. Two skew lines are __?__ coplanar.

39. Two opposite rays __?__ form a line.

40. $\overleftrightarrow{TQ}$ and $\overleftrightarrow{QT}$ are __?__ the same line.

41. $\overrightarrow{GH}$ and $\overrightarrow{HG}$ are __?__ the same ray.

42. $\overrightarrow{JK}$ and $\overrightarrow{JL}$ are __?__ the same ray.

43. $\overline{AX}$ and $\overline{XA}$ are __?__ the same segment.

44. Two lines in the same plane are __?__ parallel.

45. Two planes that do not intersect are __?__ parallel.

46. Two lines that lie in parallel planes are __?__ parallel.

47. Two lines in intersecting planes are __?__ skew.

48. **Coordinate Geometry** $\overrightarrow{AB}$ has endpoint $A(2, 3)$ and contains $B(4, 6)$. Give possible coordinates for point C so that $\overrightarrow{AB}$ and $\overrightarrow{AC}$ are opposite rays. Graph your answer.

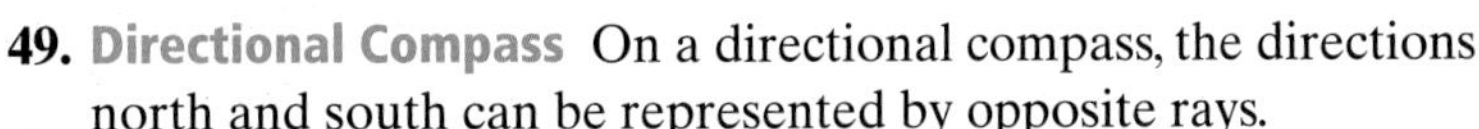

49. Directional Compass On a directional compass, the directions north and south can be represented by opposite rays.

a. Name two other compass directions that can be represented by opposite rays.

b. What other pairs of opposite directions, if any, can you find?

50. Open-Ended Summarize the three ways in which two lines may be related. Give examples from the real world that illustrate the relationships.

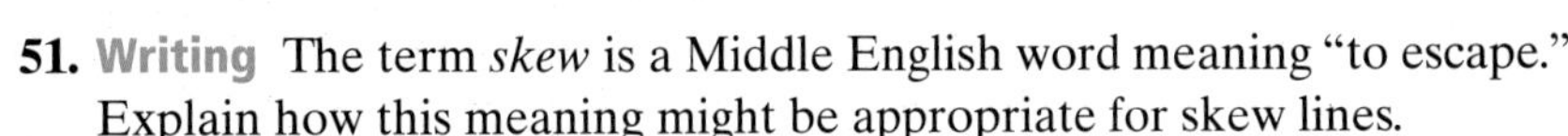

51. Writing The term *skew* is a Middle English word meaning "to escape." Explain how this meaning might be appropriate for skew lines.

Describe each figure using geometric terms.

52. S T U V

53. Z Y R X W

54.

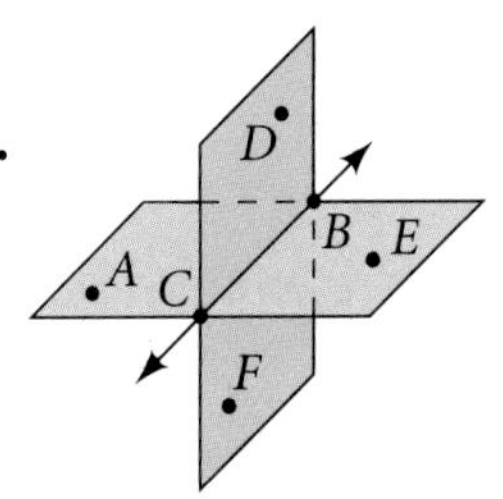

55. Critical Thinking Suppose two parallel planes A and B are each intersected by a third plane C.

a. Make a conjecture about the intersection of planes A and C and the intersection of planes B and C.

b. Find examples in your classroom.

C Challenge

56. Chemistry In diamond, each carbon atom bonds to four other carbon atoms in a three-dimensional network. In graphite, each carbon atom bonds to three carbon atoms in the same plane. The "sheets" or planes of graphite are parallel. Find out how these structures affect the properties of diamond and graphite.

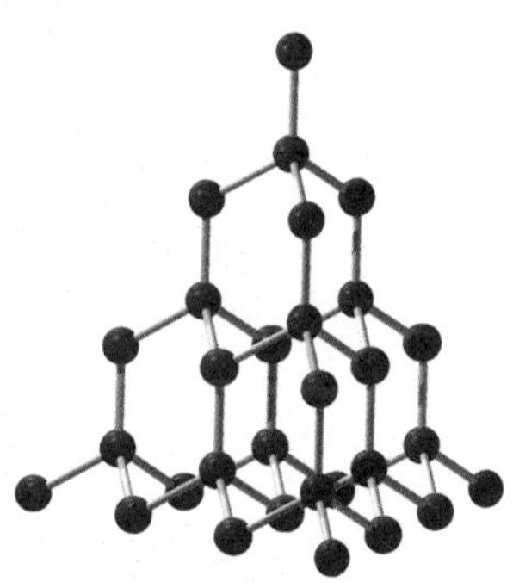

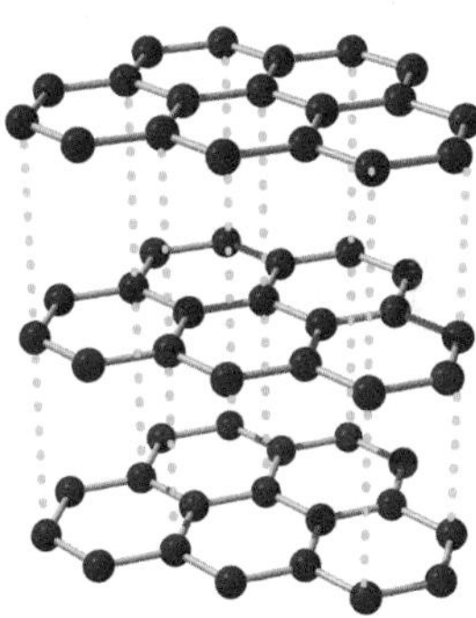

57. a. Draw a line. Draw points E and F on the line. How many different segments do points E and F determine? Name the segments.

b. Draw another line. Draw points E, F, and G on the line. How many segments do points E, F, and G determine? Name them.

c. Continue to draw lines, labeling one more point each time. Make a table showing the number of points and the number of segments determined. Look for and describe a pattern in the data.

d. Use your pattern to find how many segments are determined if you label 10 points on a line.

e. If you label n points on a line, how many segments can you name?

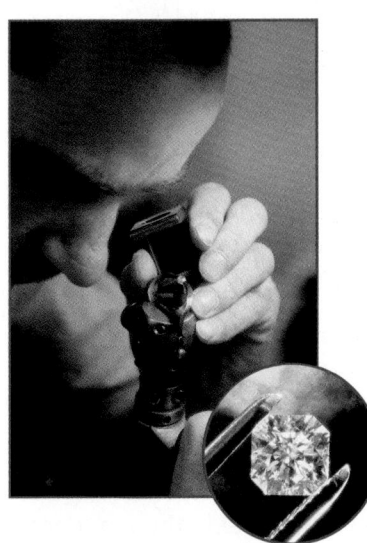

Real-World Connection

Careers Because of the diamond's atomic structure, a diamond cutter can split a diamond in four directions parallel to the octahedral crystal faces.

Use the figure at the right for Exercises 58 and 59.

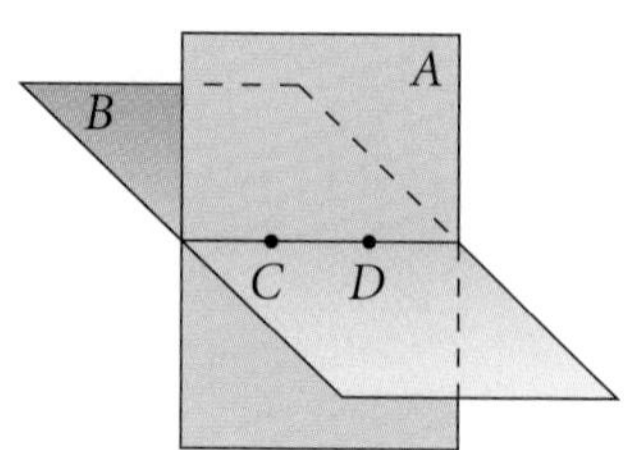

58. Do planes A and B have other lines in common that are parallel to $\overleftrightarrow{CD}$? Explain.

59. **Visualization** Are there planes that intersect planes A and B in lines parallel to $\overleftrightarrow{CD}$? Draw a sketch to support your answer.

The figure at the right is a pyramid.

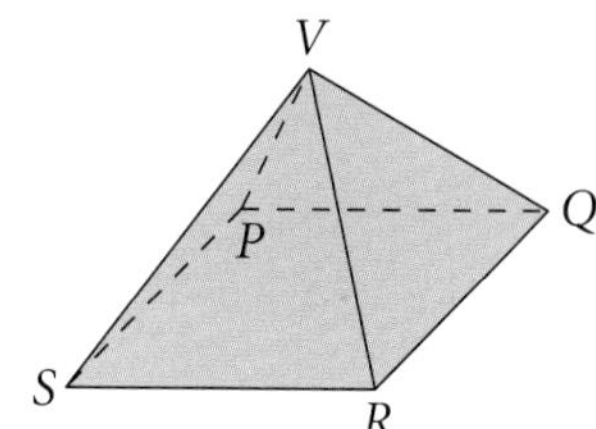

60. Name three lines that intersect at one point.

61. What line could be parallel to $\overleftrightarrow{PS}$?

62. **Visualization** Consider a plane through V that is parallel to plane $PQRS$. Can a line in that plane be parallel to $\overleftrightarrow{SR}$? Can it intersect $\overleftrightarrow{SR}$? Can it be skew to $\overleftrightarrow{SR}$? Explain each answer.

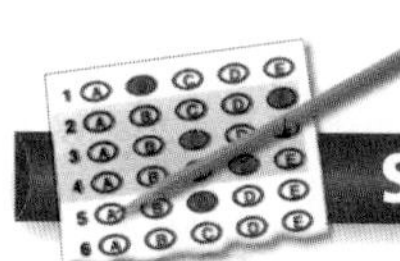

Standardized Test Prep

Use the figure at the right for Exercises 63–65.

A B C D E

Multiple Choice

63. How many labeled segments are in the figure?
A. 1 **B.** 4 **C.** 6 **D.** 10

64. Which ray is opposite $\overrightarrow{BC}$?
F. $\overrightarrow{BE}$ **G.** $\overrightarrow{BD}$ **H.** $\overrightarrow{BA}$ **I.** $\overrightarrow{AB}$

65. What is another name for $\overrightarrow{CA}$?
A. $\overrightarrow{AC}$ **B.** $\overrightarrow{CB}$ **C.** $\overrightarrow{CE}$ **D.** $\overrightarrow{DC}$

66. Which figure could be the intersection of two planes?
F. line **G.** ray **H.** point **I.** segment

Quantitative Comparison

Compare the boxed quantity in Column A with the boxed quantity in Column B. Choose the best answer.

A. The quantity in Column A is greater.
B. The quantity in Column B is greater.
C. The two quantities are equal.
D. The relationship cannot be determined from the information given.

	Column A	Column B
67.	the next number in the sequence 1, 3, 5, 7, . . .	the next number in the sequence 2, −4, 6, −8, . . .
68.	the number of lines determined by two points	the number of points determined by two intersecting lines
69.	the number of segments that can be named using points A, B, and C	the number of lines determined by three points, A, B, and C

Take It to the NET
Online lesson quiz at
www.PHSchool.com
Web Code: afa-0103

Short Response

70. a. Use the diagram to explain how parallel lines and skew lines are alike and how parallel lines and skew lines are different.

b. Does the diagram suggest other lines that are parallel to $\overleftrightarrow{JM}$, besides $\overleftrightarrow{KL}$, $\overleftrightarrow{QR}$, and $\overleftrightarrow{PS}$? Explain.

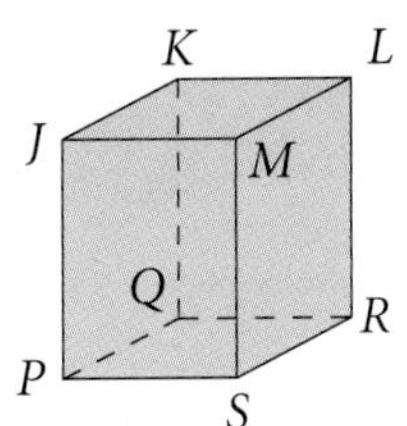

Mixed Review

Lesson 1-2

Use the diagram for Exercises 71–78 and name each geometric figure.

71. a line

72. a point

73. the intersection of $\overline{DC}$ and $\overleftrightarrow{CG}$

74. two planes that intersect in $\overleftrightarrow{EF}$

75. the plane represented by the top of the box

76. the plane represented by the front of the box

77. the intersection of planes EFG and DFG

78. another point in plane CGH

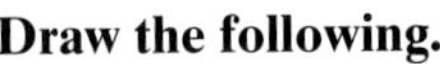

Draw the following.

79. $\overleftrightarrow{TR}$

80. $\overline{PQ}$

81. $\overrightarrow{NV}$

Lesson 1-1

Find the next two terms in each sequence.

82. 1, 1.08, 1.16, 1.24, 1.32, . . .

83. −1, −2, −4, −7, −11, −16, . . .

84. AB, BC, CD, DE, EF, . . .

85. A, D, G, J, M, . . .

86. **Reasoning** Raven conjectured: "If you subtract a number from a given number, the result is always less than the given number." Is her conjecture true? Explain.

Checkpoint Quiz 1 — Lessons 1-1 through 1-3

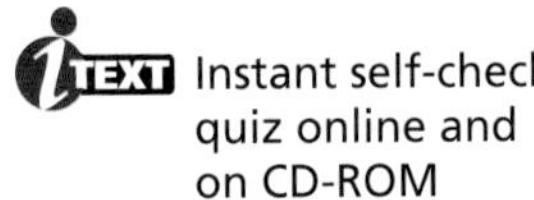

Instant self-check quiz online and on CD-ROM

Find the next two terms in each sequence.

1. 19, 21.5, 24, 26.5, . . .

2. 3.4, 3.45, 3.456, 3.4567, . . .

3. **Writing** Describe the pattern of each sequence in Exercises 1 and 2.

Use the diagram for Exercises 4–10. In Exercises 4–7, do the points appear to be coplanar? If *yes*, name the plane. If *no*, explain.

4. Points A, E, F, and B

5. Points D, C, E, and F

6. Points H, G, F, and B

7. Points A, E, B, and C

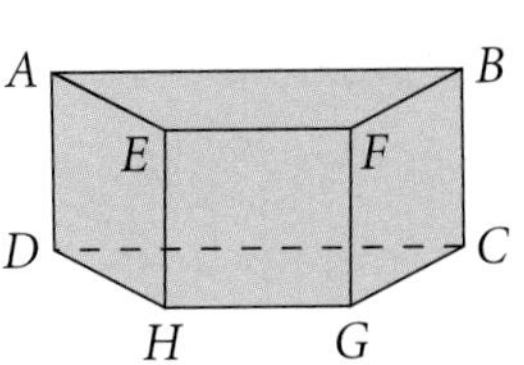

8. Name all the segments parallel to $\overline{HG}$.

9. Name a pair of skew lines.

10. What is the intersection of plane $EFGH$ and $\overleftrightarrow{DH}$?

Algebra 1 Review

Solving Linear Equations

For Use With Lesson 1-4

Sometimes you need to combine like terms to solve a linear equation.

1 EXAMPLE

Solve $(5x + 8) - (2x - 9) = 38$.

$(5x + 8) - (2x - 9) = 38$	
$(5x + 8) + (-1)(2x - 9) = 38$	**$-(2x - 9) = (-1)(2x - 9)$**
$(5x + 8) + (-1)2x + (-1)(-9) = 38$	**Use the Distributive Property.**
$5x + 8 - 2x + 9 = 38$	**Simplify.**
$3x + 17 = 38$	**Combine like terms.**
$3x = 21$	**Subtract 17 from each side.**
$x = 7$	**Divide each side by 3.**

To solve an equation with the variable on *both* sides, first convert the equation to one with the variable on *only one* side.

2 EXAMPLE

Solve $4x - 9 = 7x - 15$.

$4x - 9 = 7x - 15$	
$-9 = 3x - 15$	**Subtract 4*x* from each side.**
$6 = 3x$	**Add 15 to each side.**
$2 = x$	**Divide each side by 3.**

EXERCISES

Solve.

1. $10n + 12 = 14n - 12$

2. $(4w - 28) + (11w + 13) = 180$

3. $(7a + 3) + (-a - 5) = -16$

4. $7y + 44 = 12y + 11$

5. $(7t - 21) + (t + 4) = 15$

6. $8x - 4 - 2x = -10$

7. $(8t + 30) + (-2t - 16) = -22$

8. $6x + 17 = 9x + 2$

9. $(3y - 5) + (5y + 20) = 135$

10. $(11x - 37) + (5x + 59) = 54$

11. $3x - 35 = 9x - 59$

12. $9x - 3 = 8x - 7$

13. $(5w + 24) + (2w + 13) = 156$

14. $(3x + 10) - 5x = 6x - 50$

15. $8y + 12 = 2y - 18$

16. $7t - 8t + 4 = 5t - 2$

17. $13c + 40 = 9c - 20 + c$

18. $(6a - 54) - (5a + 27) = 23$

19. $(2 + 4y) - (y + 9) = 26$

20. $(12c + 35) - (5c - 11) = -2$

1-4 Measuring Segments and Angles

Lesson Preview

What You'll Learn

To find the lengths of segments

To find the measures of angles

. . . And Why

To find distance using a highway number line, as in Exercise 36

✓ Check Skills You'll Need

(For help, go to the Skills Handbook pages 719 and 720.)

Simplify each absolute value expression.

1. $|-6|$ **2.** $|3.5|$ **3.** $|7 - 10|$

4. $|-4 - 2|$ **5.** $|-2 - (-4)|$ **6.** $|-3 + 12|$

x^2 **Algebra** **Solve each equation.**

7. $x + 2x - 6 = 6$ **8.** $3x + 9 + 5x = 81$ **9.** $w - 2 = -4 + 7w$

New Vocabulary • coordinate • congruent segments • midpoint • angle • acute angle • right angle • obtuse angle • straight angle • congruent angles

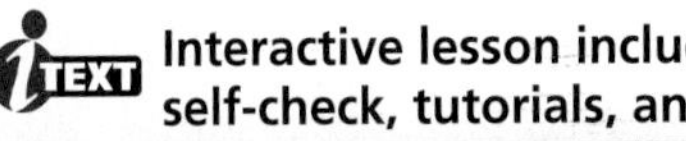
Interactive lesson includes instant self-check, tutorials, and activities.

OBJECTIVE 1 Finding Segment Lengths

The distance between points C and D on the ruler is 3. You can use the Ruler Postulate to find the distance between points on a number line.

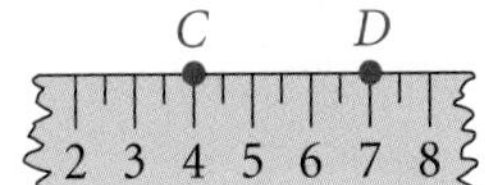

Key Concepts

Postulate 1-5 **Ruler Postulate**

The points of a line can be put into one-to-one correspondence with the real numbers so that the distance between any two points is the absolute value of the difference of the corresponding numbers.

the length of $\overline{AB}$

$$AB = |a - b|$$

coordinate of A coordinate of B

Reading Math

The congruence symbol (≅) shows that two figures are equal (=) in size and similar (~) in shape.

Two segments with the same length are **congruent (≅) segments.** In other words, if $AB = CD$, then $\overline{AB} \cong \overline{CD}$. You can use these statements interchangeably.

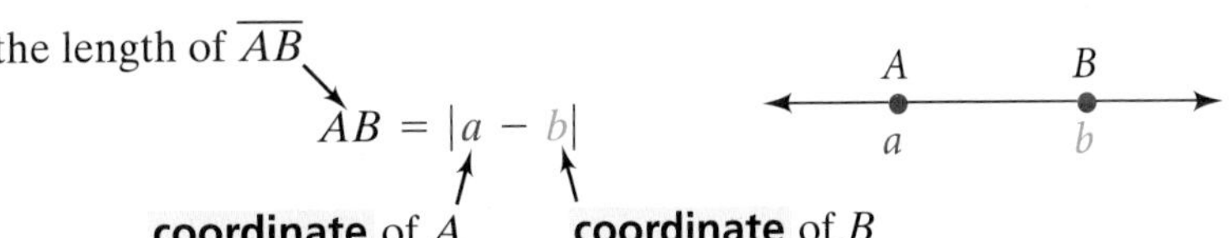

As illustrated above, segments can be marked alike to show they are congruent.

1 EXAMPLE Comparing Segment Lengths

Find AB and BC.

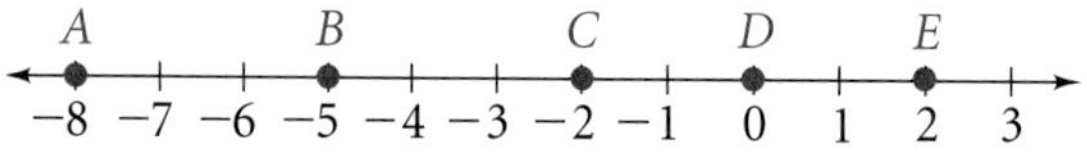

$AB = |-8 - (-5)| = |-3| = 3$
$BC = |-5 - (-2)| = |-3| = 3$
$AB = BC$ or $\overline{AB} \cong \overline{BC}$

✓ Check Understanding **1** **a.** Compare CD and DE.
b. Critical Thinking To find AB in Example 1, suppose you subtract -8 from -5. Do you get the same result? Why?

Examine the lengths of $\overline{AB}$ and $\overline{BC}$ in Example 1. Notice that $AB + BC = 6$. Notice that $AC = 6$. This suggests the following postulate.

Key Concepts

Postulate 1-6 Segment Addition Postulate

If three points A, B, and C are collinear and B is between A and C, then $AB + BC = AC$.

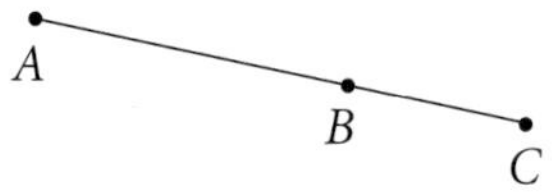

2 EXAMPLE Using the Segment Addition Postulate

Algebra If $DT = 60$, find the value of x. Then find DS and ST.

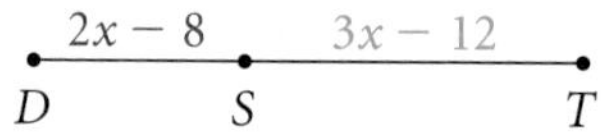

$DS + ST = DT$	**Segment Addition Postulate**
$(2x - 8) + (3x - 12) = 60$	**Substitute.**
$5x - 20 = 60$	**Simplify.**
$5x = 80$	**Add 20 to each side.**
$x = 16$	**Divide each side by 5.**
$DS = 2x - 8 = 2(16) - 8 = 24$	**Substitute 16 for *x*.**
$ST = 3x - 12 = 3(16) - 12 = 36$	

✓ Check Understanding **2** $EG = 100$. Find the value of x. Then find EF and FG.

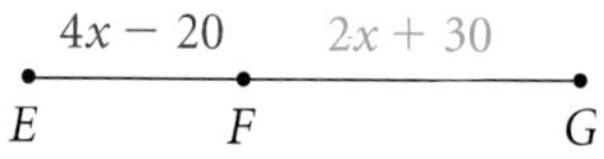

A **midpoint** of a segment is a point that divides a segment into two congruent segments. A midpoint, or any line, ray, or other segment through a midpoint, is said to *bisect* the segment.

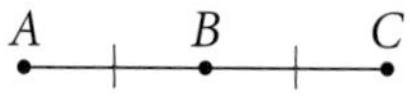

$\overline{AB} \cong \overline{BC}$

3 EXAMPLE Finding Lengths

Algebra C is the midpoint of $\overline{AB}$. Find AC, CB, and AB.

$2x + 1$ $3x - 4$

A C B

$AC = CB$	**Definition of midpoint**
$2x + 1 = 3x - 4$	**Substitute.**
$2x + 5 = 3x$	**Add 4 to each side.**
$5 = x$	**Subtract 2*x* from each side.**
$AC = 2x + 1 = 2(5) + 1 = 11$ $CB = 3x - 4 = 3(5) - 4 = 11$	**Substitute 5 for *x*.**

AC and CB are both 11, which is half of 22, the length of $\overline{AB}$.

Check Understanding 3 Z is the midpoint of $\overline{XY}$, and $XY = 27$. Find XZ.

OBJECTIVE

2 Finding Angle Measures

Reading Math

You may also refer to the angle suggested by the two *segments* $\overline{BT}$ and $\overline{BQ}$ as $\angle TBQ$.

An **angle** ($\angle$) is formed by two rays with the same endpoint. The rays are the *sides* of the angle. The endpoint is the *vertex* of the angle. The sides of the angle shown here are $\overrightarrow{BT}$ and $\overrightarrow{BQ}$. The vertex is B. You could name this angle $\angle B$, $\angle TBQ$, $\angle QBT$, or $\angle 1$.

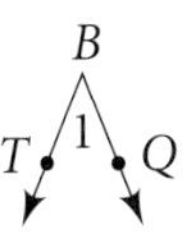

4 EXAMPLE Naming Angles

Name $\angle 1$ in two other ways.

$\angle AEC$ and $\angle CEA$ are other names for $\angle 1$.

Check Understanding 4 **a.** Name $\angle CED$ two other ways.
b. **Critical Thinking** Would it be correct to name any of the angles $\angle E$? Explain.

One way to measure an angle is in degrees. To indicate the size or degree measure of an angle, write a lowercase m in front of the angle symbol. The degree measure of angle A is 80. You show this by writing $m\angle A = 80$.

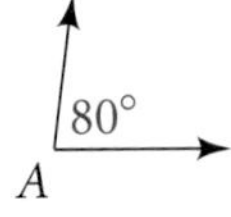

Key Concepts

Postulate 1-7 **Protractor Postulate**

Let $\overrightarrow{OA}$ and $\overrightarrow{OB}$ be opposite rays in a plane. $\overrightarrow{OA}$, $\overrightarrow{OB}$, and all the rays with endpoint O that can be drawn on one side of $\overleftrightarrow{AB}$ can be paired with the real numbers from 0 to 180 so that

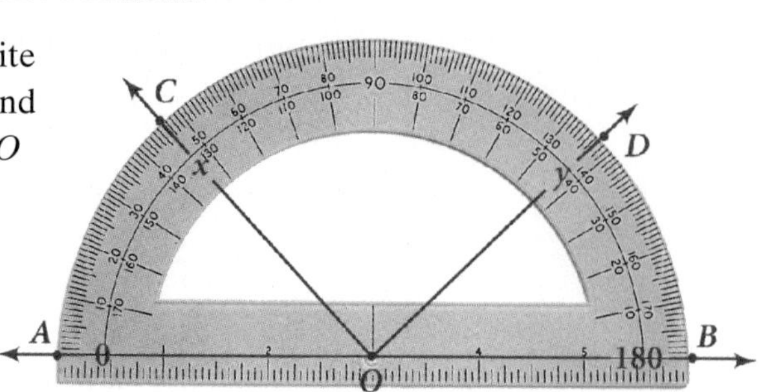

a. $\overrightarrow{OA}$ is paired with 0 and $\overrightarrow{OB}$ is paired with 180.

b. If $\overrightarrow{OC}$ is paired with x and $\overrightarrow{OD}$ is paired with y, then $m\angle COD = |x - y|$.

Reading Math

This symbol indicates a right angle.

You can classify angles according to their measures.

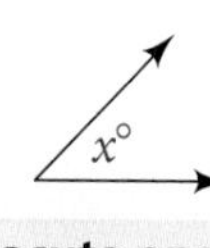

acute angle
$0 < x < 90$

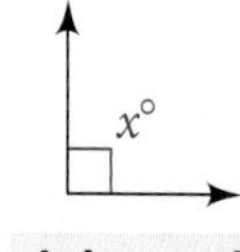

right angle
$x = 90$

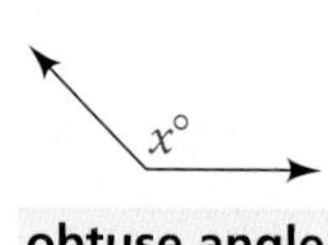

obtuse angle
$90 < x < 180$

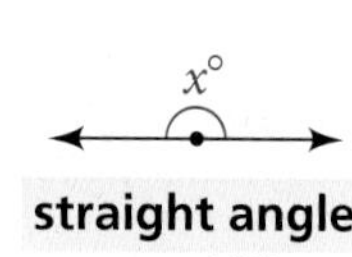

straight angle
$x = 180$

5 EXAMPLE Measuring and Classifying Angles

Find the measure of each angle. Classify each as *acute*, *right*, *obtuse*, or *straight*.

a.

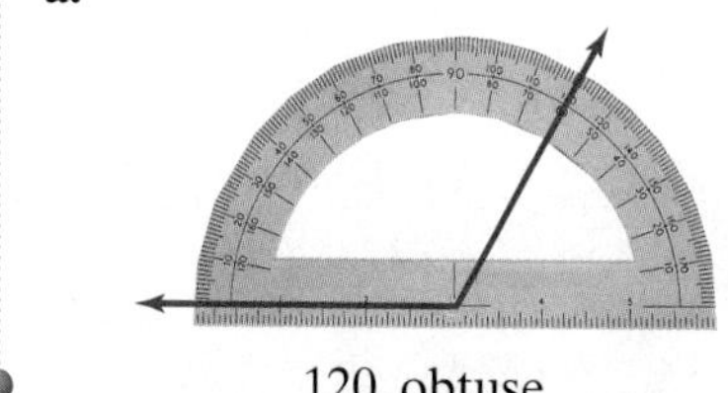

120, obtuse

b.

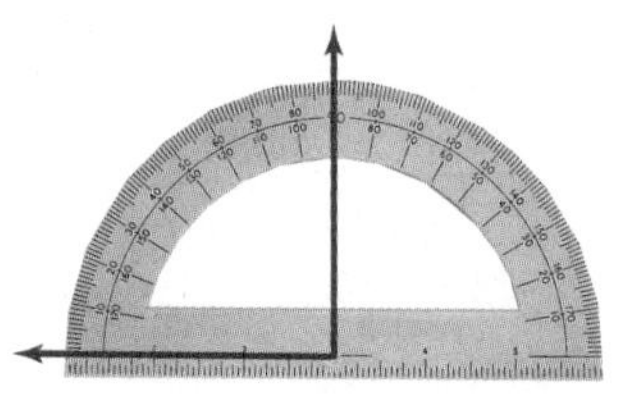

90, right

Check Understanding 5 Find the measure of each angle. Classify each as *acute*, *right*, *obtuse*, or *straight*.

a.

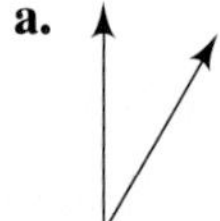

b.

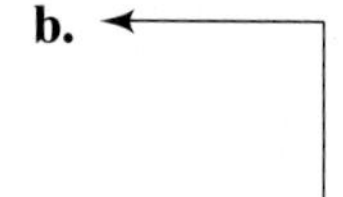

c.

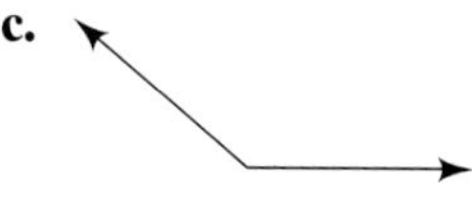

The Angle Addition Postulate is similar to the Segment Addition Postulate.

Key Concepts

Postulate 1-8 **Angle Addition Postulate**

If point B is in the interior of $\angle AOC$, then $m\angle AOB + m\angle BOC = m\angle AOC$.

A B O C

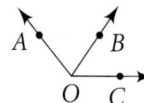

If $\angle AOC$ is a straight angle, then $m\angle AOB + m\angle BOC = 180$.

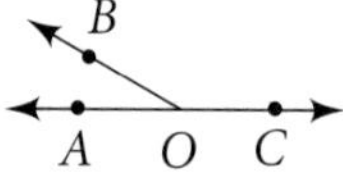

6 EXAMPLE Using the Angle Addition Postulate

What is $m\angle TSW$ if $m\angle RST = 50$ and $m\angle RSW = 125$?

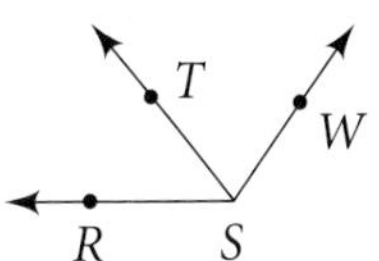

$m\angle RST + m\angle TSW = m\angle RSW$	**Angle Addition Postulate**
$50 + m\angle TSW = 125$	**Substitute.**
$m\angle TSW = 75$	**Subtract 50 from each side.**

✓ Check Understanding 6 If $m\angle DEG = 145$, find $m\angle GEF$.

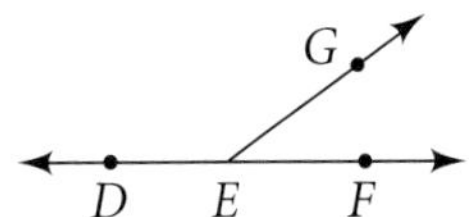

Angles with the same measure are **congruent angles.** In other words, if $m\angle 1 = m\angle 2$, then $\angle 1 \cong \angle 2$. You can use these statements interchangeably.

Angles can be marked alike to show that they are congruent, as in this photograph of the Air Force Thunderbirds precision flying team.

EXERCISES

For more practice, see *Extra Practice.*

Practice and Problem Solving

Find the length of each segment. Tell whether the segments are congruent.

1. $\overline{AC}$ and $\overline{BD}$
2. $\overline{BD}$ and $\overline{CE}$
3. $\overline{AD}$ and $\overline{BE}$
4. $\overline{BC}$ and $\overline{CE}$

A B C D E
−8 −6 1 3 7

Example 1 (page 26)

On a number line, the coordinates of X, Y, Z, and W are –7, –3, 1, and 5, respectively. Compare the lengths of the two segments.

5. $\overline{XY}$ and $\overline{ZW}$
6. $\overline{ZX}$ and $\overline{WY}$
7. $\overline{YZ}$ and $\overline{XW}$

Example 2 (page 26)

Use the figure at the right for Exercises 8–11.

R S T

8. If $RS = 15$ and $ST = 9$, then $RT = ■$.
9. If $ST = 15$ and $RT = 40$, then $RS = ■$.
10. a. **Algebra** If $RS = 3x + 1$, $ST = 2x - 2$, and $RT = 64$, find the value of x.
    b. Find RS and ST.
11. a. **Algebra** If $RS = 8y + 4$, $ST = 4y + 8$, and $RT = 15y - 9$, find the value of y.
    b. Find RS, ST, and RT.

Example 3 (page 27)

12. **Algebra** A is the midpoint of $\overline{XY}$.
   a. Find XA.
   b. Find AY and XY.

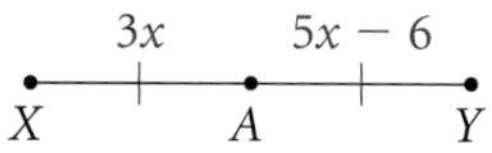

$3x$ $5x - 6$
X A Y

Algebra In Exercises 13–15, use the figure and find *PT*.

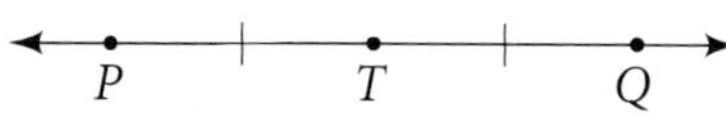

13. $PT = 5x + 3$ and $TQ = 7x - 9$
14. $PT = 4x - 6$ and $TQ = 3x + 4$
15. $PT = 7x - 24$ and $TQ = 6x - 2$

Example 4 (page 27)

Name each angle in three ways.

16.

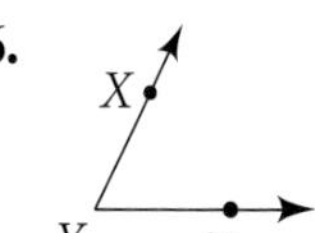

17.

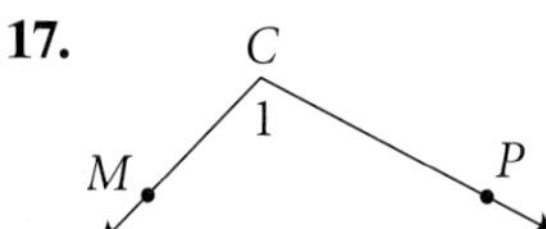

Use the figure at the right. Name the indicated angle in two different ways.

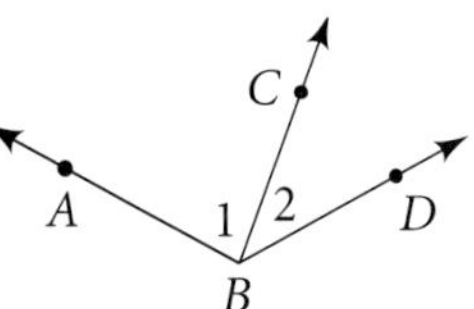

18. $\angle 1$
19. $\angle 2$

Example 5 (page 28)

Draw and label a figure to fit each description.

20. an obtuse angle, $\angle RST$
21. an acute acute, $\angle BCD$
22. a straight angle, $\angle EFG$
23. a right angle, $\angle GHI$

Measure and classify each angle.

24.

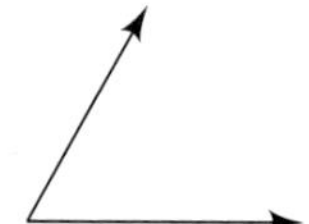

25.

26.

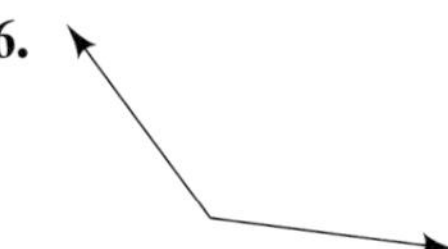

Example 6 (page 29)

27. Find $m\angle CBD$ if $m\angle ABC = 45$ and $m\angle ABD = 79$.

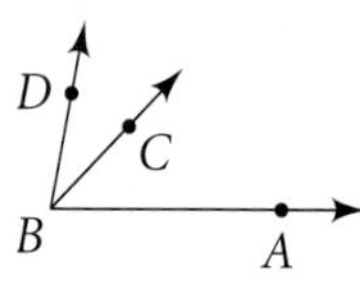

28. Find $m\angle GFJ$ if $m\angle EFG = 110$.

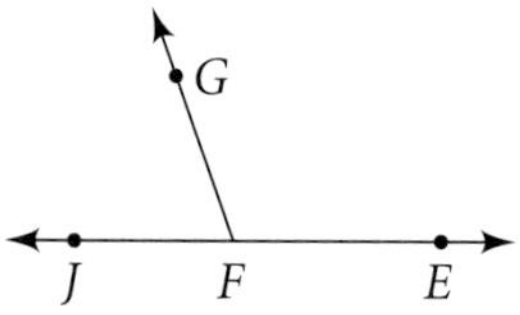

G
J F E

B Apply Your Skills

Use the figure at the right for Exercises 29–32.

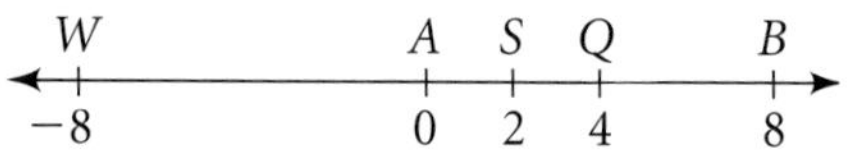

W A S Q B
−8 0 2 4 8

29. Find the midpoint of $\overline{AB}$.
30. What is the coordinate of the midpoint of $\overline{QB}$?
31. What is the coordinate of the midpoint of $\overline{WA}$?
32. What is the coordinate of the midpoint of the segment formed by the two points you found in Exercises 30 and 31?

Suppose the coordinate of *A* is 0 and *AR* = 5 and *AT* = 7 in the figure above. What are the possible coordinates of the midpoint of the given segment?

33. $\overline{AR}$
34. $\overline{AT}$
35. $\overline{RT}$

36. Mileage Highways and the mile markers along their sides suggest a number line. You can find the distance between mile markers in the same way that you find distance on a number line.

a. Michael sees mile marker 237 when he enters the highway and mile marker 159 when he exits. How far did he travel?

b. Open-Ended Give another real example of finding distance using a number line.

Visualization **Without using your ruler, sketch a segment with the given length. Then use your ruler to see how well you did.**

37. 3 cm **38.** 3 in. **39.** 6 in. **40.** 10 cm **41.** 65 mm

Need Help?

For Exercise 43 you are to decide whether the distance *BD is less than* the distance *CD*.

In Exercises 42–45, describe the statement as *true* or *false*. Explain.

A B C D E

−8 −6 1 3 7

Exercises 42–46

42. $\overline{AB} \cong \overline{CD}$ **43.** $BD < CD$

44. $AC + BD = AD$ **45.** $AC + CD = AD$

46. Suppose $EG = 5$. Find the possible coordinate(s) of point G.

In the diagram, $m\angle ACB = 65$. Find each of the following.

47. $m\angle BCD$ **48.** $m\angle ECD$

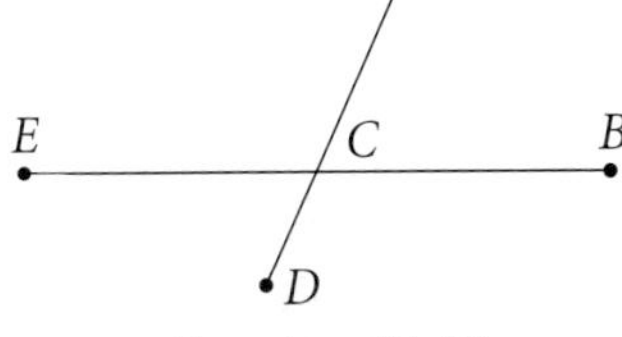

Exercises 47–48

49. Coordinate Geometry $A(3, 0)$ is an endpoint of $\overline{AB}$. If $AB = 12$, give four possible coordinates for point B.

Visualization **Without using your protractor, sketch an angle with the given measure. Then use your protractor to see how well you did.**

50. 45 **51.** 60 **52.** 90 **53.** 120 **54.** 135

55. Skiing Use a protractor on the photograph to measure the angle formed by the two skis.

Open-Ended **Name two times of the morning when the hands of a clock form each type of angle.**

56. right **57.** obtuse **58.** straight

Estimation **Estimate the measure of the angle formed by the hands of a clock at each time.**

59. 6:00 **60.** 7:00 **61.** 11:00

62. 4:40 **63.** 5:20 **64.** 10:40

Use this figure for Exercises 65–69.

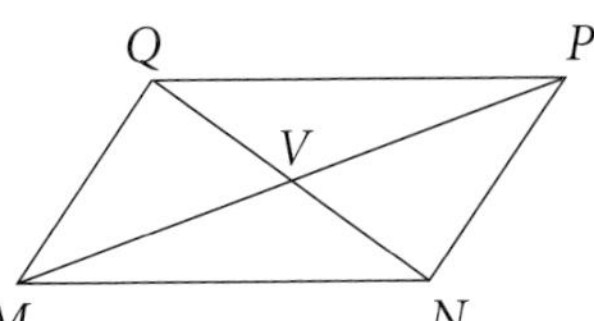

65. If $m\angle MQV = 90$ and $m\angle VQP = 35$, what is $m\angle MQP$?

66. If $m\angle MVQ = 55$, what is $m\angle QVP$?

Judging by appearance in the diagram above, name each of the following.

67. two acute angles **68.** two obtuse angles **69.** two right angles

70. **a.** **Algebra** Solve for x if $m\angle RQS = 2x + 4$ and $m\angle TQS = 6x + 20$.
b. What is $m\angle RQS$? $m\angle TQS$?
c. Show how you can check your answer.

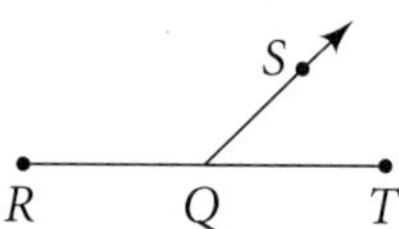

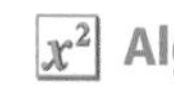 **Use the diagram at the right for Exercises 71 and 72.**

71. If $AD = 12$ and $AC = 4y - 36$, find the value of y. Then find AC and DC.

72. If $ED = x + 4$ and $DB = 3x - 8$, find ED, DB, and EB.

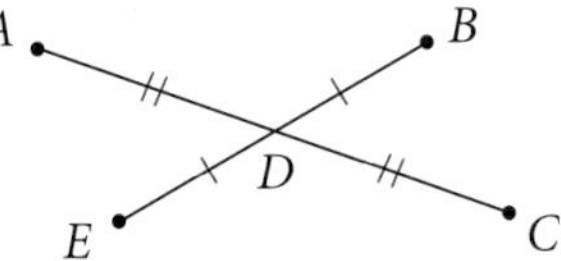

73. **Writing** The word *acute* can mean "sharp" in conversational English.
a. Explain why this meaning describes an acute angle.
b. Use "acute" in a sentence.

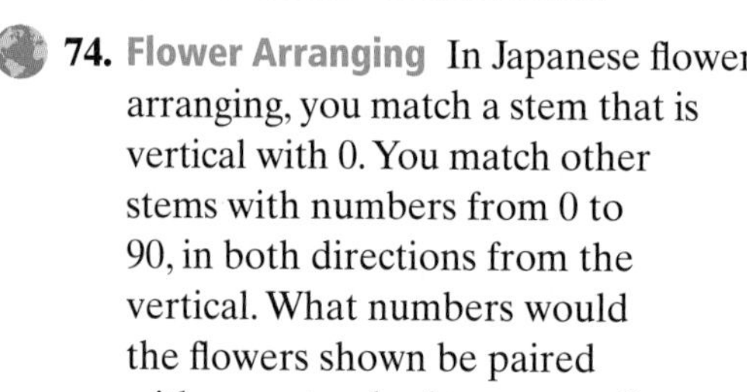

74. **Flower Arranging** In Japanese flower arranging, you match a stem that is vertical with 0. You match other stems with numbers from 0 to 90, in both directions from the vertical. What numbers would the flowers shown be paired with on a standard protractor?

Real-World Connection

Japanese flower arranging makes precise use of angles to create a mood.

Algebra **Use the diagram, below right, for Exercises 75–78. Solve for x. Find the angle measures to check your work.**

75. $m\angle AOC = 7x - 2$, $m\angle AOB = 2x + 8$, $m\angle BOC = 3x + 14$

76. $m\angle AOB = 4x - 2$, $m\angle BOC = 5x + 10$, $m\angle COD = 2x + 14$

A, B, C, D, O diagram

77. $m\angle AOB = 28$, $m\angle BOC = 3x - 2$, $m\angle AOD = 6x$

78. $m\angle AOB = 4x + 3$, $m\angle BOC = 7x$, $m\angle AOD = 16x - 1$

 **Challenge**

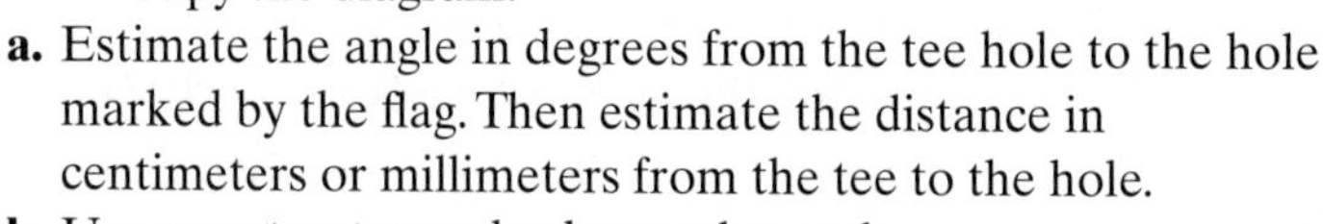

79. C is the midpoint of $\overline{AB}$, D is the midpoint of $\overline{AC}$, E is the midpoint of $\overline{AD}$, F is the midpoint of $\overline{ED}$, G is the midpoint of $\overline{EF}$, and H is the midpoint of $\overline{DB}$. If $DC = 16$, find GH.

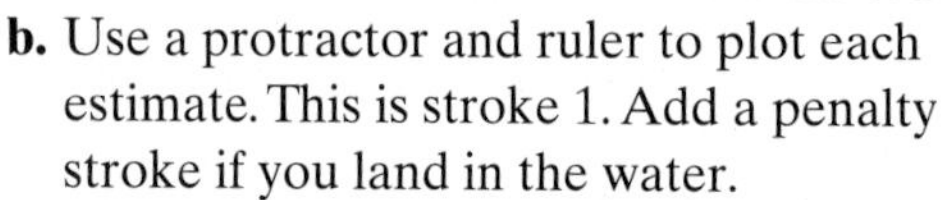

80. **Golf** Copy the diagram.
a. Estimate the angle in degrees from the tee hole to the hole marked by the flag. Then estimate the distance in centimeters or millimeters from the tee to the hole.
b. Use a protractor and ruler to plot each estimate. This is stroke 1. Add a penalty stroke if you land in the water.
c. Continue until you are at most 5mm from the hole marked by the flag. What is your score?

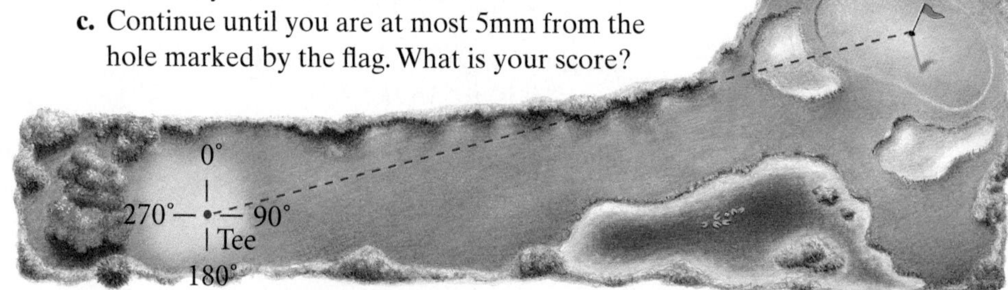

81. **Technology** Leon constructed an angle. Then he constructed a ray from the vertex of the angle to a point in the interior of the angle. He measured all the angles formed. Then he moved the interior ray. What postulate do the two pictures support?

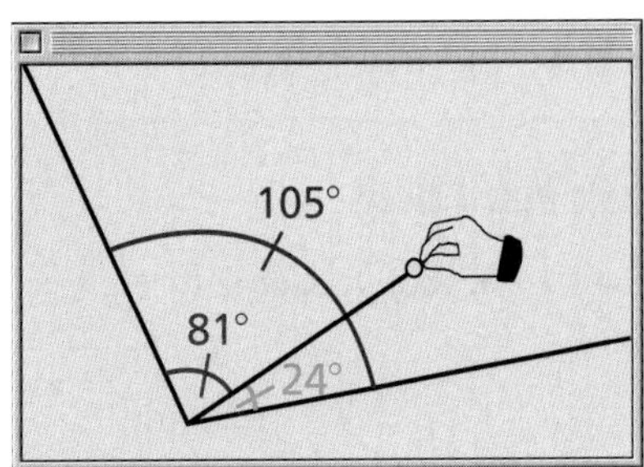

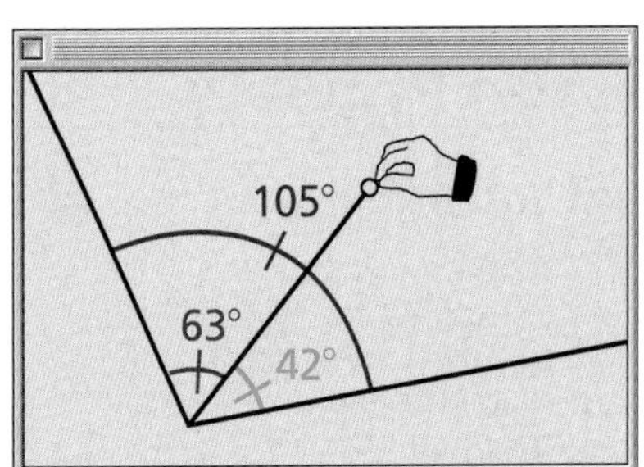

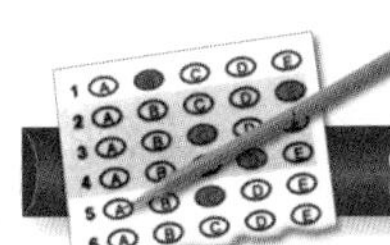

Standardized Test Prep

Multiple Choice

2x + 10   4x + 1
K   C   N
Exercises 82–84

82. If $KC = 31$, what is KN?

A. 43   B. 62   C. 74   D. 82

Take It to the NET
Online lesson quiz at **www.PHSchool.com**
Web Code: afa-0104

83. If $KN = 29$, what is CN?

F. 13   G. 14.5   H. 15.5   I. 16

84. If C is the midpoint of $\overline{KN}$, what is KC?

A. 4.5   B. 9   C. 18   D. 19

85. When 15 is subtracted from the measure of an angle, the result is the measure of a right angle. What is the measure of the original angle?

F. 75   G. 85   H. 105   I. 115

Short Response

86. You are given that $m\angle ABD + m\angle DBC = m\angle ABC$.

a. Draw a diagram to show the above.

b. If $m\angle ABD = 12$ and $\angle ABC$ is obtuse, what are the least and greatest whole number measures possible for $\angle DBC$? Explain.

Mixed Review

Lesson 1-3

Complete each statement with *always*, *sometimes*, or *never* to make a true statement.

87. Skew lines are _?_ coplanar.

88. Skew lines _?_ intersect.

89. Opposite rays _?_ form a line.

90. Parallel planes _?_ intersect.

Lesson 1-2

91. Three points are _?_ coplanar.

92. Two points are _?_ collinear.

93. The intersection of two planes is _?_ a line.

94. Intersecting lines are _?_ parallel.

Lesson 1-1

Find the next two terms in each sequence.

95. 5, 10, 15, 20, . . .

96. 5, 25, 125, 625, . . .

97. 14, 18, 22, 26, . . .

Basic Constructions

Lesson Preview

What You'll Learn

OBJECTIVE 1 To use a compass and a straightedge to construct congruent segments and congruent angles

OBJECTIVE 2 To use a compass and a sraightedge to bisect segments and angles

. . . And Why

To construct the bisector of an angle to illustrate angles of incidence and reflection, as in Exercise 18

✔ Check Skills You'll Need

(For help, go to Lessons 1-3 and 1-4.)

In Exercises 1–6, sketch each figure.

1. $\overline{CD}$ **2.** $\overrightarrow{GH}$ **3.** $\overleftrightarrow{AB}$

4. line m **5.** acute $\angle ABC$ **6.** $\overline{XY} \parallel \overline{ST}$

7. $DE = 20$. Point C is the midpoint of $\overline{DE}$. Find CE.

8. Use a protractor to draw a 60° angle.

9. Use a protractor to draw a 120° angle.

New Vocabulary • construction • straightedge • compass • perpendicular lines • perpendicular bisector • angle bisector

Interactive lesson includes instant self-check, tutorials, and activities.

OBJECTIVE 1

Constructing Segments and Angles

Need Help?
You may use a ruler as a straightedge, but you may not use its markings.

In a **construction** you use a straightedge and a compass to draw a geometric figure. A **straightedge** is a ruler with no markings on it. A **compass** is a geometric tool used to draw circles and parts of circles called arcs.

Four basic constructions involve constructing congruent segments, congruent angles, and bisectors of segments and angles.

1 EXAMPLE Constructing Congruent Segments

Construct a segment congruent to a given segment.

Given: $\overline{AB}$

Construct: $\overline{CD}$ so that $\overline{CD} \cong \overline{AB}$

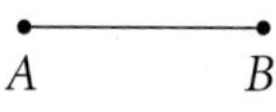

Step 1
Draw a ray with endpoint C.

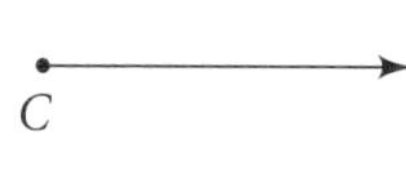

Step 2
Open the compass to the length of $\overline{AB}$.

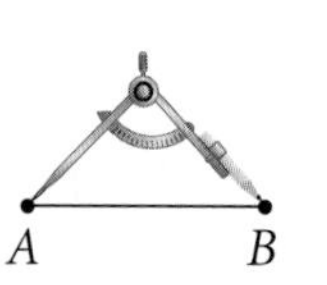

Step 3
With the same compass setting, put the compass point on point C. Draw an arc that intersects the ray. Label the point of intersection D.

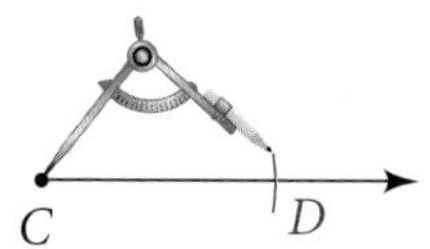

$\overline{CD} \cong \overline{AB}$

✔ Check Understanding 1 Use a straightedge to draw $\overline{XY}$. Then construct $\overline{RS}$ so that $RS = 2XY$.

2 EXAMPLE Constructing Congruent Angles

Construct an angle congruent to a given angle.

Given: $\angle A$
Construct: $\angle S$ so that $\angle S \cong \angle A$

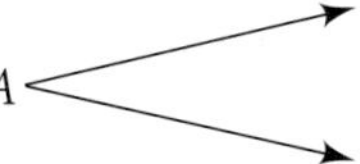

Step 1
Draw a ray with endpoint S.

Need Help?
In Step 2, make your arc big enough to swing the compass easily, but small enough to intersect both sides.

Step 2
With the compass point on point A, draw an arc that intersects the sides of $\angle A$. Label the points of intersection B and C.

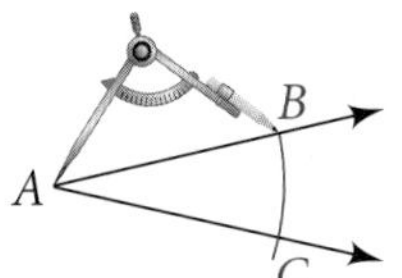

Step 3
With the same compass setting, put the compass point on point S. Draw an arc and label its point of intersection with the ray as R.

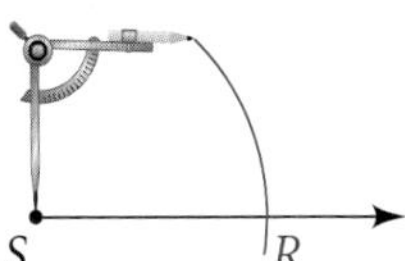

Step 4
Open the compass to the length BC. Keeping the same compass setting, put the compass point on R. Draw an arc to locate point T.

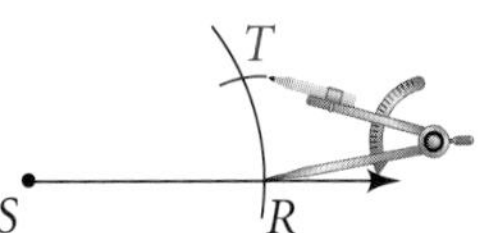

Step 5
Draw $\overrightarrow{ST}$.

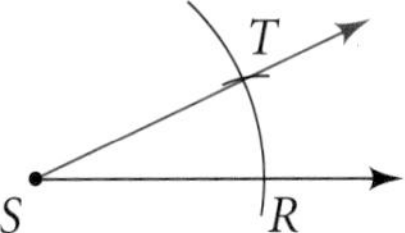

$\angle S \cong \angle A$

Check Understanding 2 Construct $\angle F$ with $m\angle F = 2m\angle B$.

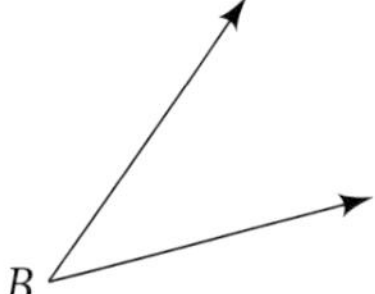

OBJECTIVE

2 Constructing Bisectors

Perpendicular lines are two lines that intersect to form right angles. The symbol $\perp$ means "is perpendicular to." In the diagram at the right, $\overleftrightarrow{AB} \perp \overleftrightarrow{CD}$ and $\overleftrightarrow{CD} \perp \overleftrightarrow{AB}$.

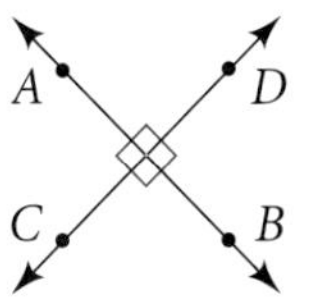

A **perpendicular bisector** of a segment is a line, segment, or ray that is perpendicular to the segment at its midpoint, thereby bisecting the segment into two congruent segments.

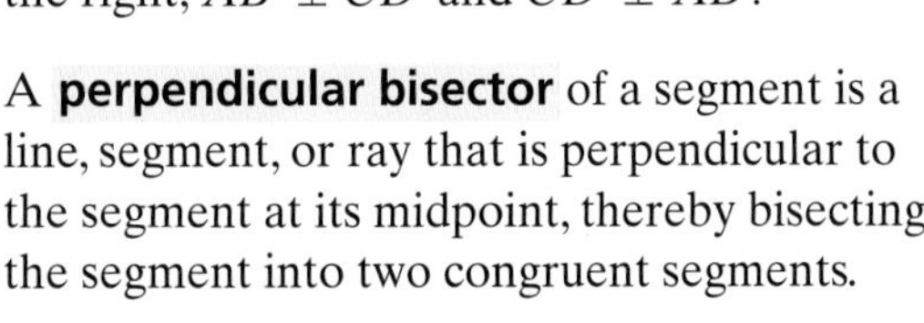

Real-World Connection
Perpendicular hands signal "Time out."

As you will learn in Chapter 5, there is just one line that is the perpendicular bisector of a segment in a given plane. Here is a way to construct the perpendicular bisector.

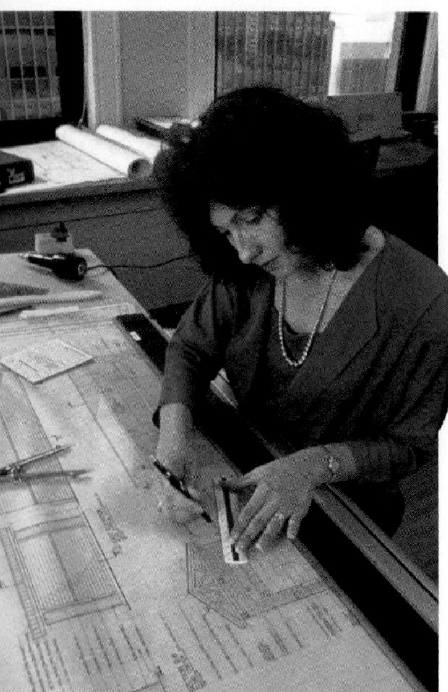

Real-World Connection

Careers Architects use construction tools to work with their designs.

3 EXAMPLE Constructing the Perpendicular Bisector

Construct the perpendicular bisector of a segment.

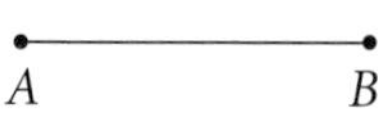

Given: $\overline{AB}$
Construct: $\overleftrightarrow{XY}$ so that $\overleftrightarrow{XY} \perp \overline{AB}$ at the midpoint M of $\overline{AB}$.

Step 1
Put the compass point on point A and draw a long arc as shown. Be sure the opening is greater than $\frac{1}{2}AB$.

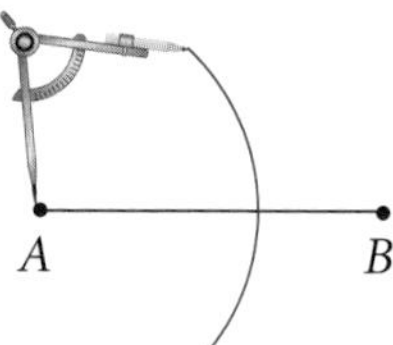

Step 2
With the same compass setting, put the compass point on point B and draw another long arc. Label the points where the two arcs intersect as X and Y.

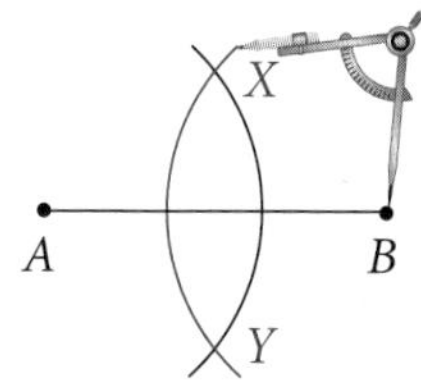

Step 3
Draw $\overleftrightarrow{XY}$. The point of intersection of $\overline{AB}$ and $\overleftrightarrow{XY}$ is M, the midpoint of $\overline{AB}$.

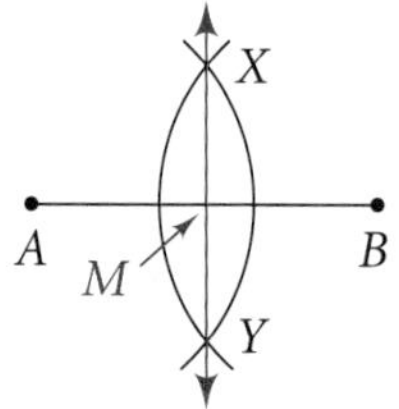

$\overleftrightarrow{XY} \perp \overline{AB}$ at the midpoint of $\overline{AB}$, so $\overleftrightarrow{XY}$ is the perpendicular bisector of $\overline{AB}$.

Check Understanding **3** Draw $\overline{ST}$. Construct its perpendicular bisector.

An **angle bisector** is a ray that divides an angle into two congruent coplanar angles. Its endpoint is at the angle vertex. Within the ray, a segment with the same endpoint is also an angle bisector. You may say that the ray or segment *bisects* the angle.

4 EXAMPLE Finding Angle Measures

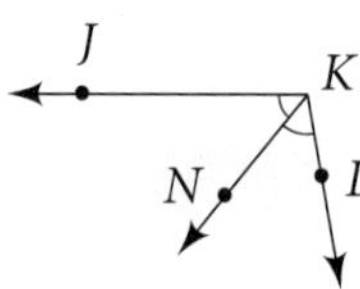

Algebra $\overrightarrow{KN}$ bisects $\angle JKL$ so that $m\angle JKN = 5x - 25$ and $m\angle NKL = 3x + 5$. Solve for x and find $m\angle JKN$.

$m\angle JKN = m\angle NKL$	**Definition of angle bisector**
$5x - 25 = 3x + 5$	**Substitute.**
$5x = 3x + 30$	**Add 25 to each side.**
$2x = 30$	**Subtract 3*x* from each side.**
$x = 15$	**Divide each side by 2.**
$m\angle JKN = 5x - 25 = 5(15) - 25 = 50$	**Substitute 15 for *x*.**

$m\angle JKN = 50$

Check Understanding **4** Find $m\angle NKL$ and $m\angle JKL$

5 EXAMPLE Constructing the Angle Bisector

Construct the bisector of an angle.

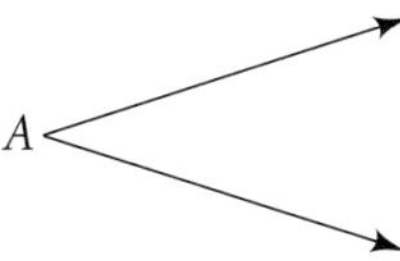

Given: $\angle A$

Construct: $\overrightarrow{AX}$, the bisector of $\angle A$

Step 1
Put the compass point on vertex A. Draw an arc that intersects the sides of $\angle A$. Label the points of intersection B and C.

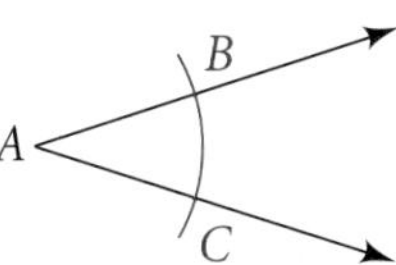

Step 2
Put the compass point on point C and draw an arc. With the same compass setting, draw an arc using point B. Be sure the arcs intersect. Label the point where the two arcs intersect as X.

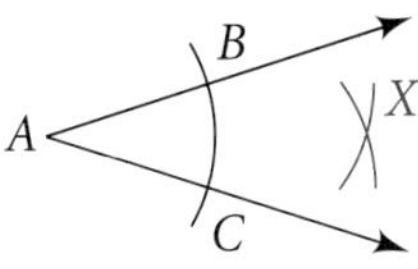

Step 3
Draw $\overrightarrow{AX}$.

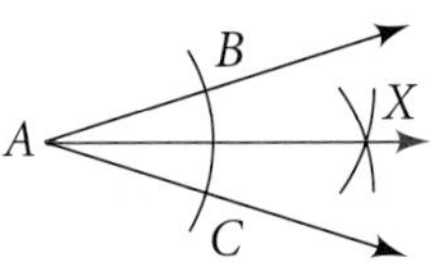

$\overrightarrow{AX}$ is the bisector of $\angle CAB$.

5 **a.** Draw obtuse $\angle XYZ$. Then construct its bisector $\overrightarrow{YP}$.
b. Explain how you can use your protractor to check your construction.

EXERCISES

For more practice, see *Extra Practice*.

Practice and Problem Solving

A Practice by Example

In Exercises 1–8, draw a diagram similar to the given one. Then do the construction. Check your work with a ruler or a protractor.

Example 1 (page 34)

1. Construct $\overline{XY}$ congruent to $\overline{AB}$.
2. Construct $\overline{VW}$ so that $VW = 2AB$.

3. Construct $\overline{DE}$ so that $DE = TR + PS$.
4. Construct $\overline{QJ}$ so that $QJ = TR - PS$.

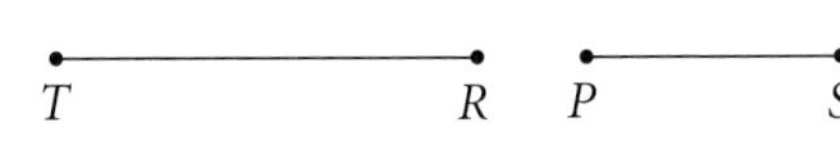

Example 2 (page 35)

5. Construct $\angle D$ so that $\angle D \cong \angle C$.
6. Construct $\angle F$ so that $m\angle F = 2m\angle C$.

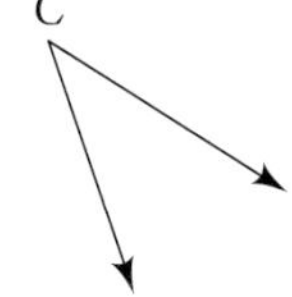

Example 3 (page 36)

7. Construct the perpendicular bisector of $\overline{AB}$.
8. Construct the perpendicular bisector of $\overline{TR}$.

Example 4 (page 36)

x^2 9. **Algebra** $\overrightarrow{GH}$ bisects $\angle FGI$.
a. Solve for x and find $m\angle FGH$.
b. Find $m\angle HGI$.
c. Find $m\angle FGI$.

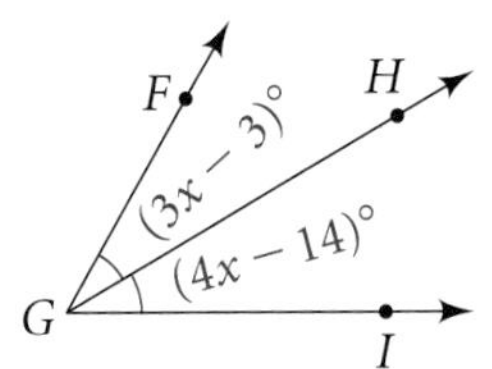

x^2 **Algebra For Exercises 10–12, $\overrightarrow{BX}$ bisects $\angle ABC$. Solve for x and find $m\angle ABC$.**

10. $m\angle ABX = 5x, m\angle XBC = 3x + 10$

11. $m\angle ABC = 4x - 12, m\angle ABX = 24$

12. $m\angle ABX = 4x - 16, m\angle CBX = 2x + 6$

Example 5 (page 37)

13. Draw acute $\angle PQR$. Then construct its bisector.

14. Draw right $\angle TUV$. Then construct its bisector.

B Apply Your Skills

15. Use your protractor and draw $\angle W$ with $m\angle W = 120$. Construct $\angle Z \cong \angle W$. Then construct the bisector of $\angle Z$.

Sketch the figure described. Explain how to construct it. Then do the construction.

16. $\overleftrightarrow{XY} \perp \overleftrightarrow{YZ}$

17. $\overrightarrow{ST}$ bisecting right $\angle PSQ$

18. Optics A beam of light and a mirror can be used to study the behavior of light. Light that strikes the mirror is reflected so that the angle of reflection and the angle of incidence are congruent. In the diagram, $\overline{BC}$ is perpendicular to the mirror and $\angle ABC$ has a measure of 41°.

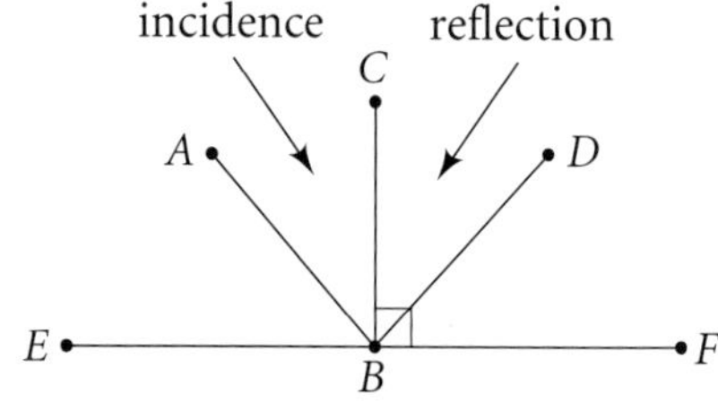

a. Name the angle of reflection and find its measure.

b. Find $m\angle ABD$.

c. Find $m\angle ABE$ and $m\angle DBF$.

19. Use a straightedge and protractor.

a. Draw a mirror and a light beam striking the mirror and reflecting from it.

b. Construct the bisector of the angle formed by the incoming and reflected light beams. Label the angles of incidence and reflection.

PEANUTS® by Charles M. Schulz

20. Open-Ended Snoopy can draw squares with his compass. You can only draw circles. You can, however, construct a square. Explain how to do this. Use sketches if needed. Then do the construction.

21. Answer these questions about a segment in a plane. Explain each answer.

a. How many midpoints does the segment have?

b. How many bisectors does it have? How many lines in the plane are its perpendicular bisectors?

c. How many lines in space are its perpendicular bisectors?

For Exercises 22–24, copy $\angle 1$ and $\angle 2$.

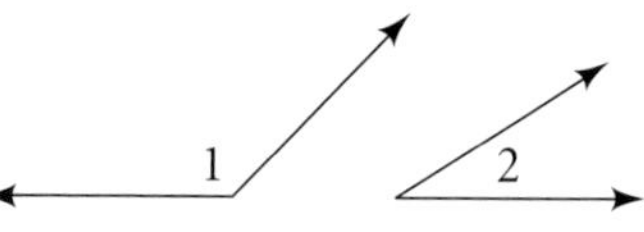

22. Construct $\angle B$ so that $m\angle B = m\angle 1 + m\angle 2$.

23. Construct $\angle C$ so that $m\angle C = m\angle 1 - m\angle 2$.

24. Construct $\angle D$ so that $m\angle D = 2m\angle 2$.

25. **Reasoning** When $\overrightarrow{BX}$ bisects $\angle ABC$, $\angle ABX \cong \angle CBX$. Lani claims there is always a related equation, $m\angle ABX = \frac{1}{2}m\angle ABC$. Denyse claims the related equation is $2m\angle ABX = m\angle ABC$. Which equation is correct? Explain.

26. **Writing** Describe how to construct the midpoint of a segment.

27. Construct a 45° angle.

Need Help?

In Exercise 28a, your construction may suggest something but be slightly off. If so, test your conjecture very carefully in part (b).

28. a. Draw a large triangle with three acute angles. Construct the bisectors of the three angles. What appears to be true about the three angle bisectors?
    b. Repeat the constructions with a triangle that has one obtuse angle.
    c. **Make a Conjecture** What appears to be true about the three angle bisectors of any triangle?

Use a ruler to draw segments of 2 cm, 4 cm and 5 cm. Then construct each triangle, if possible. If not possible, explain.

29. with 4-cm, 4-cm, and 5-cm sides
30. with 2-cm, 5-cm, and 5-cm sides
31. with 2-cm, 2-cm, and 5-cm sides
32. with 2-cm, 2-cm, and 4-cm sides

33. a. Draw a segment, $\overline{XY}$. Construct a triangle with sides congruent to $\overline{XY}$.
    b. Measure the angles of the triangle.
    c. **Writing** Describe how to construct a 60° angle; a 30° angle.

34. **Art** You can create daisy designs with a compass.
    a. Construct a circle. Keeping the same compass setting, put the compass point on the circle and construct an arc within the circle. The endpoints of the arc should be on the circle.
    b. Keeping the same compass setting, put the compass point on each endpoint of the first arc and draw two new arcs.
    c. Continue to make arcs around the circle using the endpoints of previously drawn arcs until you get a six-petal daisy.

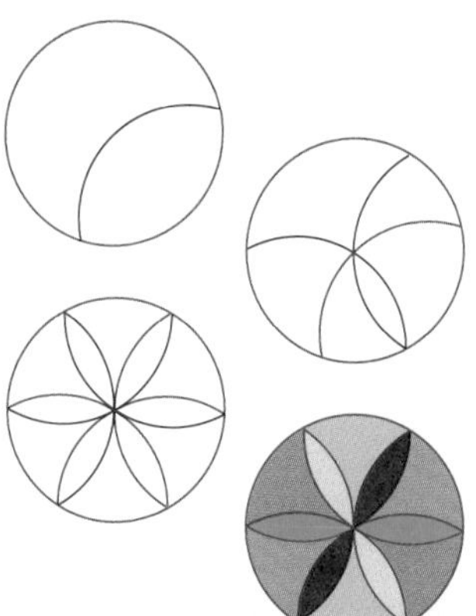

Challenge

35. a. Use your compass to draw a circle. Locate three points A, B, and C on the circle.
    b. Construct the perpendicular bisectors of $\overline{AB}$ and $\overline{BC}$.
    c. **Critical Thinking** Label the intersection of the two perpendicular bisectors as point O. Make a conjecture about point O.

36. Study the figures. Complete the definition of a line perpendicular to a plane:

    A line is perpendicular to a plane if it is _?_ to every line in the plane that _?_.

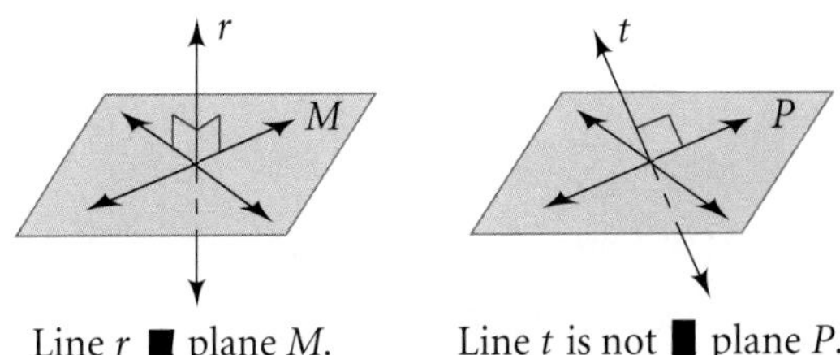

Line r ⊥ plane M. Line t is not ⊥ plane P.

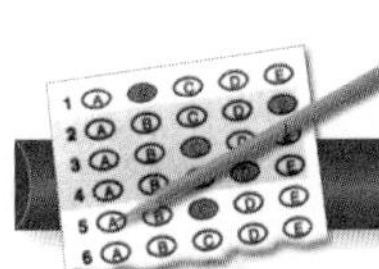

Standardized Test Prep

Multiple Choice

37. What must you do to construct the midpoint of a segment?
    A. Measure half its length.
    B. Measure twice its length.
    C. Construct an angle bisector.
    D. Construct a perpendicular bisector.

38. Which of these is the first step in constructing a congruent segment?

F. Draw a ray.
G. Draw a line.
H. Label two points.
I. Measure the segment.

Short Response

39. Explain how to do each construction using a compass and a straightedge.
   a. Draw an acute angle, $\angle ABC$. Construct an angle congruent to $\angle ABC$.
   b. Construct an angle whose measure is twice that of $\angle ABC$.

Extended Response

40. Explain how to do each construction using a compass and a straightedge.
   a. Divide a segment into two congruent segments.
   b. Divide a segment into four congruent segments.
   c. Construct a segment that is 1.25 times as long as a given segment.

Take It to the NET
Online lesson quiz at **www.PHSchool.com**
Web Code: afa-0105

Mixed Review

Lesson 1-4

Use the number line at the right. Find the length of each segment.

41. $\overline{AC}$
42. $\overline{AD}$
43. $\overline{CD}$
44. $\overline{BC}$

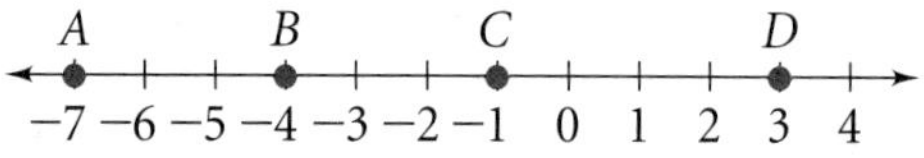

45. Use a protractor to draw a 72° angle.

46. $\angle DEF$ is a straight angle. $m\angle DEG = 80$. Find $m\angle GEF$.

47. $m\angle TUV = 100$ and $m\angle VUW = 80$. Find possible values of $m\angle TUW$.

Lesson 1-3

48. Draw $\overleftrightarrow{RS}$.

Use your drawing from Exercise 48. Answer and explain.

49. Are $\overrightarrow{RS}$ and $\overrightarrow{SR}$ opposite rays?

50. Are $\overline{RS}$ and $\overline{SR}$ the same segment?

Geometry at Work

Cabinetmaker

Cabinetmakers not only make cabinets but all types of wooden furniture. The artistry of cabinetmaking can be seen in the beauty and uniqueness of the finest doors, shelves, and tables. The craft is in knowing which types of wood and tools to use, and how to use them.

The carpenter's square is one of the most useful of the cabinetmaker's tools. It can be applied to a variety of measuring tasks. The figure shows how to use a carpenter's square to bisect $\angle O$.

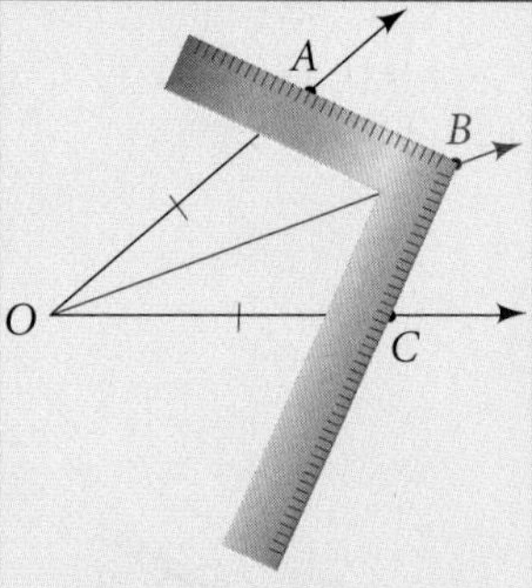

First, mark equal lengths OA and OC on the sides of the angle. Then position the square so that $BA = BC$ to locate point B. Finally, draw $\overrightarrow{OB}$. $\overrightarrow{OB}$ bisects $\angle O$.

Take It to the NET For more information about cabinetmaking, go to **www.PHSchool.com**.
Web Code: afb-2031

Exploring Constructions

For Use With Lesson 1-5

Points, lines, and figures are created in geometry software using Draw tools or Construct tools. A figure created by Draw has no constraints. When the figure is manipulated, it moves or changes size freely. A figure created by Construct is dependent upon an existing object. When you manipulate the existing object, the constructed object similarly moves or resizes.

In this activity you will explore the difference between Draw and Construct. Before you begin, familiarize yourself with the tools of your software.

Draw and Construct

- Draw $\overline{AB}$ and Construct the perpendicular bisector $\overleftrightarrow{DC}$.
- Draw $\overline{EF}$ and Construct G, any point on $\overline{EF}$. Draw $\overleftrightarrow{HG}$. Find EG, GF, and $m\angle HGF$. Try to drag G so that $EG = GF$. Try to drag H so that $m\angle HGF = 90$. Were you able to draw the perpendicular bisector of $\overline{EF}$? Explain.

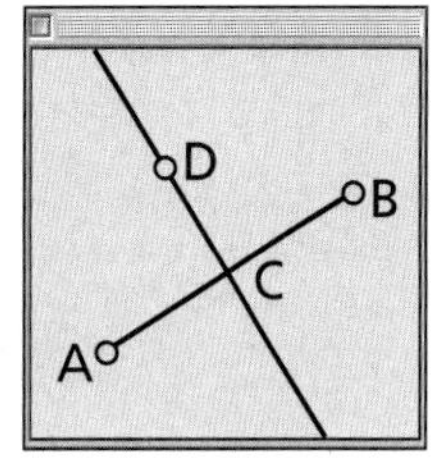

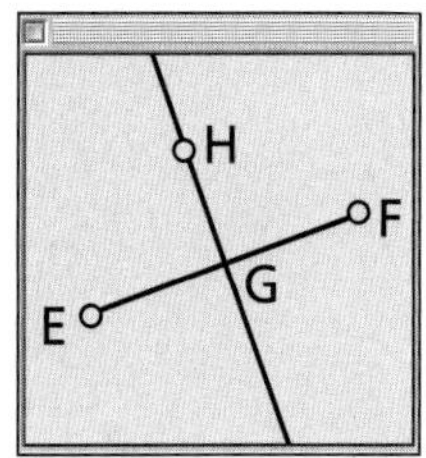

Investigate

- Drag A and B. Observe AC, CB, and $m\angle DCB$. Is $\overleftrightarrow{DC}$ always the perpendicular bisector of $\overline{AB}$ no matter how you manipulate the figure?
- Drag E and F. Observe EG, GF, and $m\angle HGF$. How is the relationship between $\overline{EF}$ and $\overleftrightarrow{HG}$ different from the relationship between $\overline{AB}$ and $\overleftrightarrow{DC}$?

EXERCISES

1. a. Write a description of the general difference between Draw and Construct.
b. Use your description to explain why the relationship between $\overline{EF}$ and $\overleftrightarrow{HG}$ differs from the relationship between $\overline{AB}$ and $\overleftrightarrow{DC}$.

2. a. Draw $\angle JKL$.
b. Construct its angle bisector, $\overrightarrow{KM}$.
c. Manipulate the figure and observe the different angle measures. Is $\overrightarrow{KM}$ always the angle bisector of $\angle JKL$?

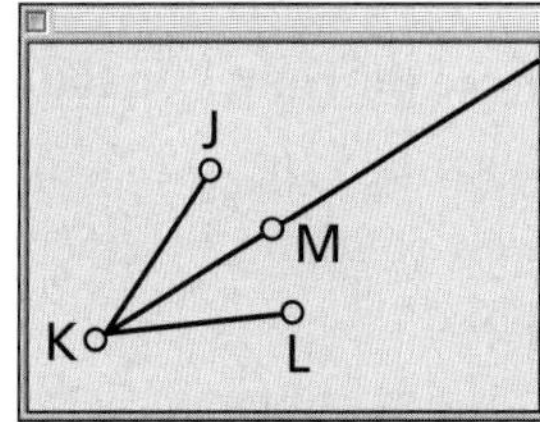

3. a. Draw $\angle NOP$. Draw $\overrightarrow{OQ}$ in the interior of $\angle NOP$. Drag Q until $m\angle NOQ = m\angle QOP$.
b. Manipulate the figure and observe the different angle measures. Is $\overrightarrow{OQ}$ always the angle bisector of $\angle NOP$?

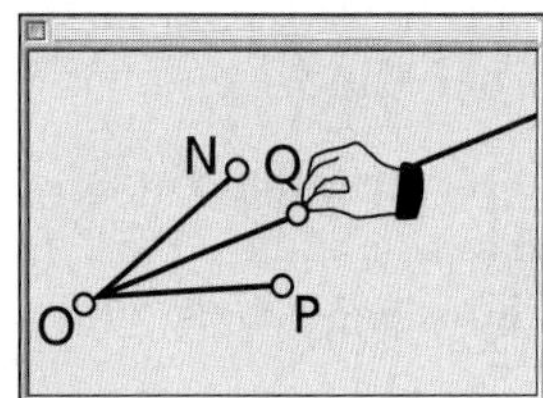

Investigation

Distance in the Coordinate Plane

FOR USE WITH LESSON 1-6

Much of Manhattan is laid out in a rectangular grid, as shown in this map. In general, the streets are parallel running east and west. The avenues are parallel running north and south.

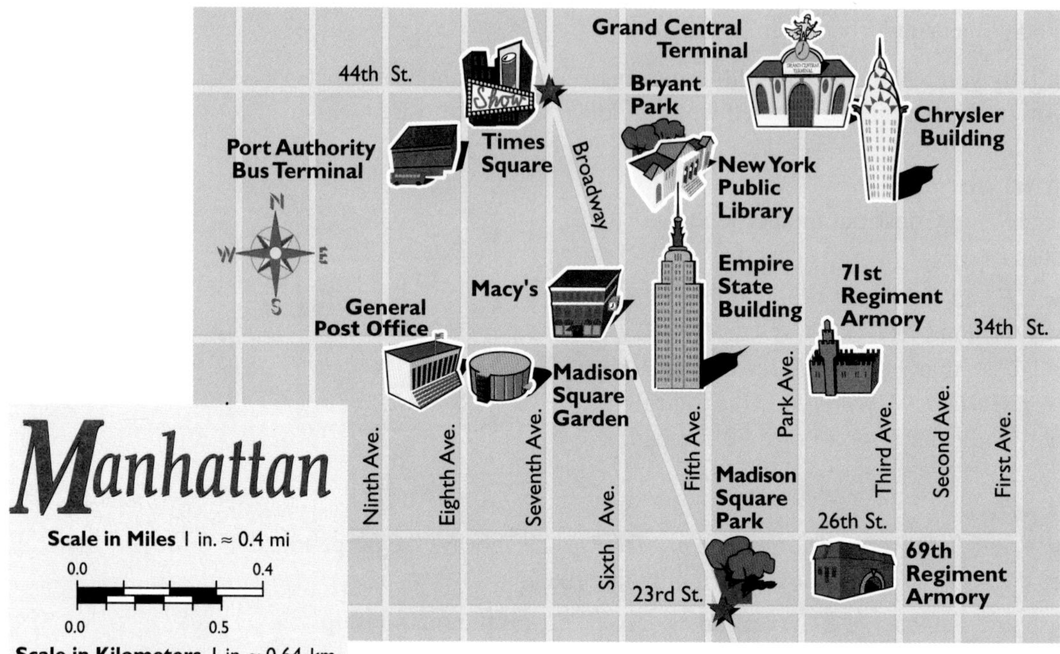

Yvonne's family is at the corner of 44th Street and 7th Avenue. They plan to walk to Madison Square Park at 23rd Street and 5th Avenue. There are several possible routes they can take.

EXERCISES

Use tracing paper to trace the routes on the map. Answer the following questions.

1. Yvonne's father wants to walk east on 44th Street until they reach 5th Avenue. He then plans to walk south on 5th Avenue to Madison Square Park. About how long is his route?

2. Yvonne's mother wants to walk south on 7th Avenue until they reach 23rd Street. She then plans to walk east on 23rd Street to Madison Square Park. About how long is her route?

3. Yvonne notices on the map that Broadway cuts across the grid of streets and leads directly to Madison Square Park. She suggests walking all the way on Broadway. About how long is her route?

4. Whose route is the shortest? Explain.

5. Whose route is the longest? Explain.

1-6 The Coordinate Plane

Lesson Preview

What You'll Learn

OBJECTIVE 1: To find the distance between two points in the coordinate plane

OBJECTIVE 2: To find the coordinates of the midpoint of a segment in the coordinate plane

. . . And Why

To find the distance between two points on a map, as in Example 2

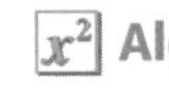 Check Skills You'll Need

(For help, go to the Skills Handbook pages 715 and 716.)

Find the square root of each number. Round to the nearest tenth if necessary.

1. 25 **2.** 17 **3.** 123

Algebra **Evaluate each expression for $m = -3$ and $n = 7$.**

4. $(m - n)^2$ **5.** $(n - m)^2$ **6.** $m^2 + n^2$

Algebra **Evaluate each expression for $a = 6$ and $b = -8$.**

7. $(a - b)^2$ **8.** $\sqrt{a^2 + b^2}$ **9.** $\frac{a + b}{2}$

Interactive lesson includes instant self-check, tutorials, and activities.

OBJECTIVE 1 Finding Distance on the Coordinate Plane

You can think of a point as a dot, and a line as a series of points. In coordinate geometry you describe a point by an ordered pair (*x*, *y*), called the *coordinates of the point.*

Need Help?

To help review terms shown here, see "Coordinate plane" in the Glossary.

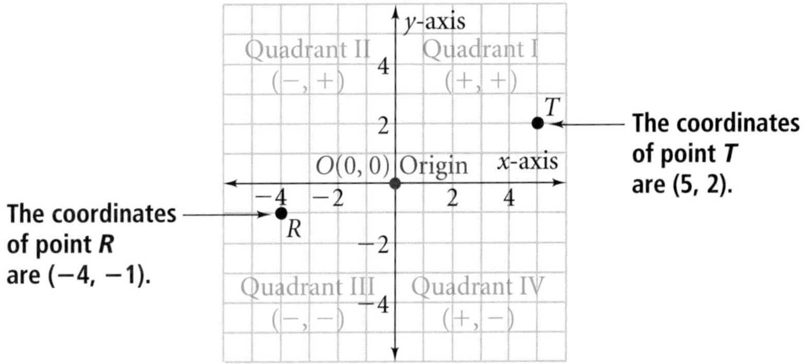

You can use the Ruler Postulate to find the distance between two points if the points are on a horizontal line or a vertical line. To find the distance between two points that are not on a horizontal or vertical line, you can use the Distance Formula.

Key Concepts

Formula **The Distance Formula**

The distance d between two points $A(x_1, y_1)$ and $B(x_2, y_2)$ is

$$d = \sqrt{(x_2 - x_1)^2 + (y_2 - y_1)^2}.$$

You will verify this formula in Chapter 7.

1 EXAMPLE Finding Distance

Reading Math
For help with reading Example 1, see p. 50.

Find the distance between $T(5, 2)$ and $R(-4, -1)$ to the nearest tenth.

Let $(5, 2)$ be (x_1, y_1) and $(-4, -1)$ be (x_2, y_2).

$d = \sqrt{(x_2 - x_1)^2 + (y_2 - y_1)^2}$ **Use the Distance Formula.**

$d = \sqrt{(-4 - 5)^2 + (-1 - 2)^2}$ **Substitute.**

$d = \sqrt{(-9)^2 + (-3)^2}$ **Simplify.**

$d = \sqrt{81 + 9} = \sqrt{90}$

90 [√] 9.4868330 **Use a calculator.**

To the nearest tenth, $TR = 9.5$.

Check Understanding 1 **a.** $\overline{AB}$ has endpoints $A(1, -3)$ and $B(-4, 4)$. Find AB to the nearest tenth.
b. **Critical Thinking** In Example 1, suppose you let $(-4, -1)$ be (x_1, y_1) and $(5, 2)$ be (x_2, y_2). Do you get the same result? Why?

2 EXAMPLE Real-World Connection

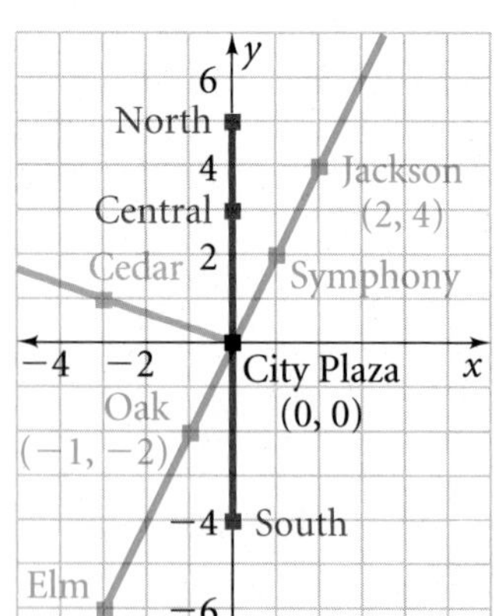

Travel Each morning Juanita takes the "Blue Line" subway from Oak Station to Jackson Station. As the map at the left shows, Oak Station is 1 mile west and 2 miles south of City Plaza. Jackson Station is 2 miles east and 4 miles north of City Plaza. Find the distance Juanita travels between Oak Station and Jackson Station.

Let Oak$(-1, -2)$ be (x_1, y_1) and Jackson $(2, 4)$ be (x_2, y_2).

$d = \sqrt{(x_2 - x_1)^2 + (y_2 - y_1)^2}$ **Use the Distance Formula.**

$d = \sqrt{(2 - (-1))^2 + (4 - (-2))^2}$ **Substitute.**

$d = \sqrt{3^2 + 6^2}$ **Simplify.**

$d = \sqrt{9 + 36} = \sqrt{45}$

45 [√] 6.7082039 **Use a calculator.**

Juanita travels about 6.7 miles between Oak Station and Jackson Station.

Check Understanding 2 **a.** Find the distance between Elm Station and Symphony Station.
b. Maple Station is located 6 miles west and 2 miles north of City Plaza. Find the distance between Cedar Station and Maple Station.

OBJECTIVE

2 Finding the Midpoint of a Segment

To find the coordinate of the midpoint of a segment on a number line, find the *average* or *mean* of the coordinates of the endpoints. The coordinate of the midpoint of a segment with endpoints a and b is $\frac{a + b}{2}$.

You can extend this process (see next page) to find the coordinates of the midpoint of a segment in the coordinate plane.

Real-World Connection

A well-made seesaw balances (without riders) at its midpoint.

Study the diagram of $\overline{TS}$ with endpoints $T(4, 3)$ and $S(8, 5)$. $\overline{TR}$ is a horizontal segment and $\overline{SR}$ is a vertical segment. The coordinates of R are $(8, 3)$.

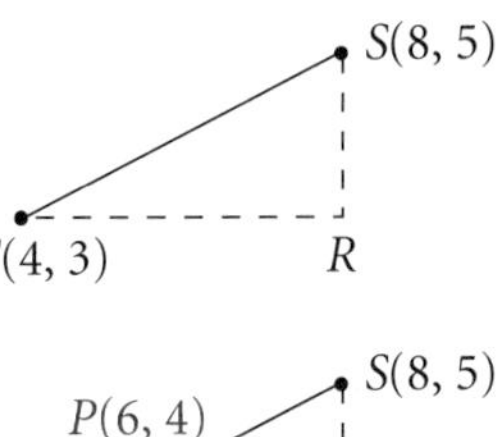

The coordinates of M, the midpoint of $\overline{TR}$, are $(6, 3)$. The coordinates of N, the midpoint of $\overline{SR}$, are $(8, 4)$. A vertical line through M and a horizontal line through N meet at P, the midpoint of $\overline{TS}$.

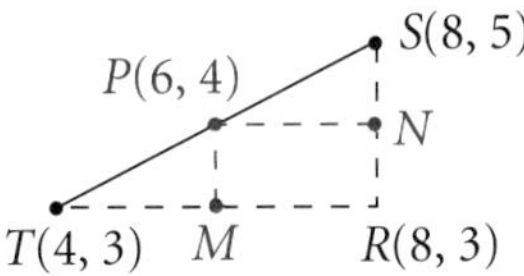

The coordinates of P are $(6, 4)$.

Thus, you find the coordinates of the midpoint of a segment by averaging the x-coordinates and averaging the y-coordinates of the endpoints.

Key Concepts

Formula **The Midpoint Formula**

The coordinates of the midpoint M of $\overline{AB}$ with endpoints $A(x_1, y_1)$ and $B(x_2, y_2)$ are the following:

$$M\left(\frac{x_1 + x_2}{2}, \frac{y_1 + y_2}{2}\right)$$

3 EXAMPLE Finding the Midpoint

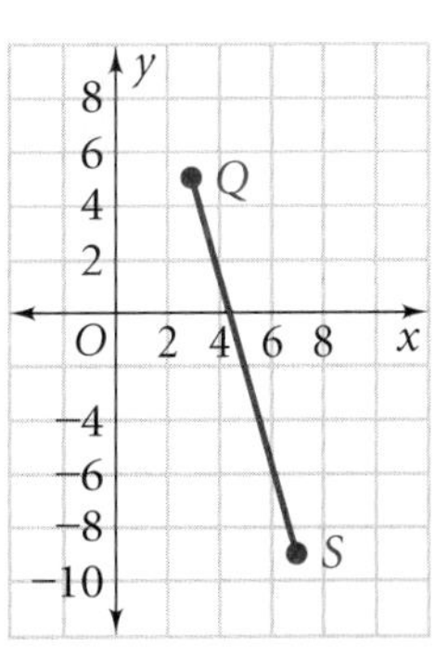

Algebra $\overline{QS}$ has endpoints $Q(3, 5)$ and $S(7, -9)$. Find the coordinates of its midpoint M.

Let $(3, 5)$ be (x_1, y_1) and $(7, -9)$ be (x_2, y_2).

$$x\text{-coordinate of } M = \frac{x_1 + x_2}{2} = \frac{3 + 7}{2} = \frac{10}{2} = 5$$

$$y\text{-coordinate of } M = \frac{y_1 + y_2}{2} = \frac{5 + (-9)}{2} = \frac{-4}{2} = -2$$

The coordinates of midpoint M are $(5, -2)$.

✓ Check Understanding 3 Find the coordinates of the midpoint of $\overline{XY}$ with endpoints $X(2, -5)$ and $Y(6, 13)$.

4 EXAMPLE Finding an Endpoint

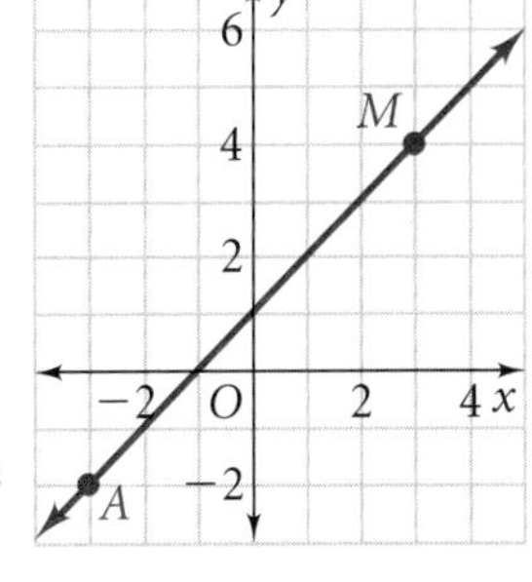

Algebra The midpoint of $\overline{AB}$ is $M(3, 4)$. One endpoint is $A(-3, -2)$. Find the coordinates of the other endpoint B.

Use the Midpoint Formula. Let the coordinates of B be (x_2, y_2).

$3 = \frac{-3 + x_2}{2}$	← **Midpoint Formula** →	$4 = \frac{-2 + y_2}{2}$
$6 = -3 + x_2$	← **Multiply each side by 2.** →	$8 = -2 + y_2$
$9 = x_2$		$10 = y_2$

The coordinates of B are $(9, 10)$.

✓ Check Understanding 4 The midpoint of $\overline{XY}$ has coordinates $(4, -6)$. X has coordinates $(2, -3)$. Find the coordinates of Y.

EXERCISES

For more practice, see *Extra Practice.*

Practice and Problem Solving

A Practice by Example

Example 1 (page 44)

Find the distance between the points to the nearest tenth.

1. $J(2, -1), K(2, 5)$
2. $L(10, 14), M(-8, 14)$
3. $N(-1, -11), P(-1, -3)$
4. $A(0, 3), B(0, 12)$
5. $C(12, 6), D(-8, 18)$
6. $E(6, -2), F(-2, 4)$
7. $Q(12, -12), T(5, 12)$
8. $R(0, 5), S(12, 3)$
9. $X(-3, -4), Y(5, 5)$

Example 2 (page 44)

Use the map in Example 2 on page 44. Find the distance between the stations.

10. North and South
11. Oak and Symphony
12. City Plaza and Cedar

Use the map at the right. Find the distances between the stations to the nearest tenth.

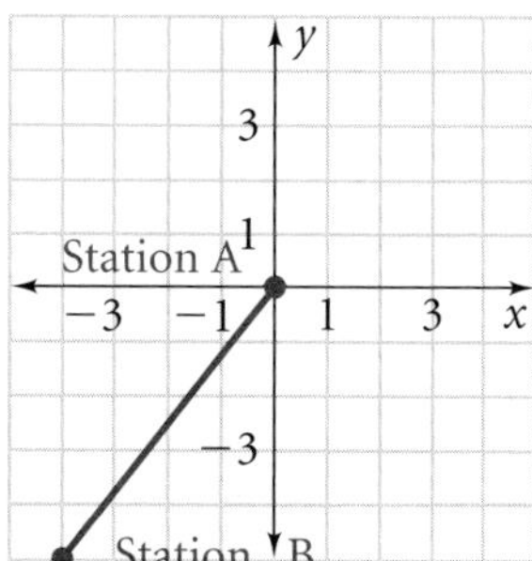

13. Station A and Station B
14. Station B and Station C located at (5, 8)
15. Station B and Station D located at (1, 10)
16. Station E at (2, 12) and Station F at (5, 16)
17. List the stations B, C, D, E, and F in the order of least to greatest distance from Station A.

Example 3 (page 45)

x^2 Algebra **Find the coordinates of the midpoint of $\overline{HX}$.**

18. $H(0, 0), X(8, 4)$
19. $H(-1, 3), X(7, -1)$
20. $H(13, 8), X(-6, -6)$
21. $H(7, 10), X(5, -8)$
22. $H(-6.3, 5.2), X(1.8, -1)$
23. $H\left(5\frac{1}{2}, -4\frac{3}{4}\right), X\left(2\frac{1}{4}, -1\frac{1}{4}\right)$

Example 4 (page 45)

x^2 Algebra **The coordinates of point T are given. The midpoint of $\overline{ST}$ has coordinates $(5, -8)$. Find the coordinates of point S.**

24. $T(0, 4)$
25. $T(5, -15)$
26. $T(10, 18)$
27. $T(-2, 8)$
28. $T(1, 12)$
29. $T(4.5, -2.5)$

An endpoint and a midpoint are given. Find the coordinates of the other endpoint.

30. endpoint (2, 6), midpoint (5, 12)
31. endpoint (2, 3), midpoint (3, −4)

B Apply Your Skills

Find (a) PQ to the nearest tenth and (b) the coordinates of the midpoint of $\overline{PQ}$.

32. $P(3, 2), Q(6, 6)$
33. $P(0, -2), Q(3, 3)$
34. $P(-4, -2), Q(1, 3)$
35. $P(-5, 2), Q(0, 4)$
36. $P(-3, -1), Q(5, -7)$
37. $P(-5, -3), Q(-3, -5)$
38. $P(-4, -5), Q(-1, 1)$
39. $P(2, 3), Q(4, -2)$
40. $P(4, 2), Q(3, 0)$

41. The midpoint of $\overline{TS}$ is the origin. Point T is located in Quadrant II. What quadrant contains point S?

42. Graph the points $A(2, 1)$, $B(6, -1)$, $C(8, 7)$, and $D(4, 9)$. Draw quadrilateral $ABCD$. Use the Midpoint Formula to find the midpoints of $\overline{AC}$ and $\overline{BD}$. What appears to be true?

Need Help?

In Exercise 43, you can compare lengths in radical form and not need a calculator.

43. The coordinates of S, T, V, and W are given below. Graph the points and draw segments to join them in order. Draw $\overline{WS}$. Are the lengths of the four sides of quadrilateral $STVW$ the same? Show your work.

$S(-6, 2)$ $T(-3, 5)$ $V(-6, 6)$ $W(-9, 5)$

For each graph, find (a) AB to the nearest tenth and (b) the coordinates of the midpoint of $\overline{AB}$.

44. 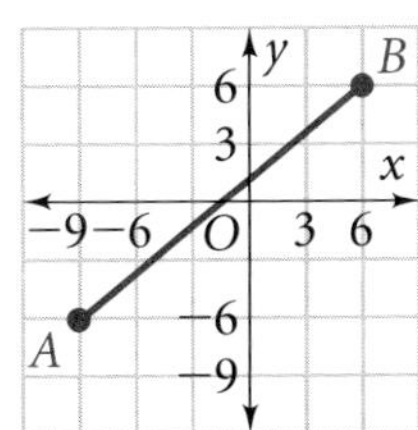

45. 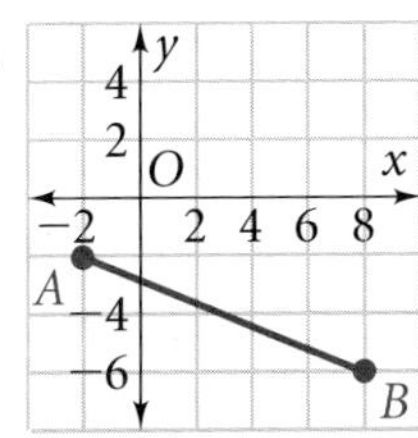

46. 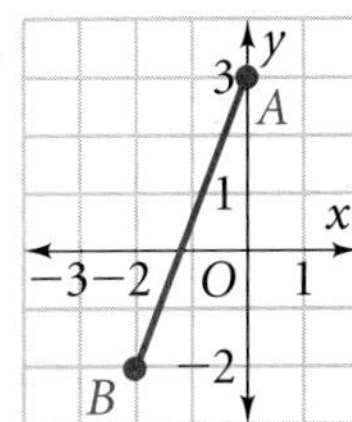

 **47. Navigation** A boat at $X(5, -2)$ needs to travel to $Y(-6, 9)$ or $Z(17, -3)$. Which point is closer? What is the distance to the closer point?

 **48. Writing** An airplane at $T(80, 20)$ needs to fly to both $U(20, 60)$ and $V(110, 85)$. What is the shortest possible distance for the trip? Explain.

Communications The cell phone screen at the right shows coordinates of six cities from a grid placed on North America by a long-distance carrier. The carrier finds distance by the Distance Formula. Each grid unit equals $\sqrt{0.1}$ mile. Find the distance between each pair of cities to the nearest mile.

49. Houston and Chicago

50. Denver and New Orleans

51. Boston and San Francisco

52. New Orleans and Houston

San Francisco (8495, 8720)
Chicago (5985, 3439)
New Orleans (8448, 2625)
Denver (7490, 5881)
Houston (8936, 3542)
Boston (4422, 1241)

SOURCE: Peter H. Dana

Real-World Connection

Teens average about 7 hours on the phone each week.

Graph $X(-2, 1)$, $Y(2, 3)$, $A(-1, 4)$, $B(0, 2)$, and $C(4, 2)$. For each point described below, give two sets of possible coordinates if they exist. Otherwise, write *exactly one point* and give the coordinates, or *not possible* and explain.

53. point D so that $\overleftrightarrow{AD} \parallel \overleftrightarrow{XY}$

54. E so that $\overleftrightarrow{EC} \parallel \overleftrightarrow{XY}$

55. point F so that $\overleftrightarrow{FB} \perp \overleftrightarrow{XY}$

56. point G so that $\overleftrightarrow{GC} \perp \overleftrightarrow{XY}$

C Challenge

57. point H so that $\overleftrightarrow{HX} \parallel \overleftrightarrow{AY}$, and $\overleftrightarrow{HA} \parallel \overleftrightarrow{XY}$

58. point J so that $\overleftrightarrow{JB} \perp \overleftrightarrow{XY}$, and $\overleftrightarrow{JC} \perp \overleftrightarrow{CY}$

59. Open-Ended In a coordinate plane, draw any $\overline{AB}$. Draw another segment that is both congruent and parallel to $\overline{AB}$. Label the new segment $\overline{CD}$ in such a way that $ABCD$ is a quadrilateral.

a. Find BC and AD. What do you notice?

b. Write a conjecture that generalizes the result you found in part (a).

c. Find the midpoint of $\overline{AC}$ and the midpoint of $\overline{BD}$. What do you notice?

d. Write a conjecture that generalizes the result you found in part (c).

e. Find the midpoint E of $\overline{AD}$ and the midpoint F of $\overline{BC}$. Find EF and AB. What do you notice?

f. Write a conjecture that generalizes the result you found in part (e).

Exercise 60

Geometry in 3 Dimensions **You can use three coordinates (x, y, z) to locate points in three dimensions. Point P has coordinates $(6, -3.5, 9)$.**

60. Give the coordinates of points $A, B, C, D, E, F,$ and G.

61. Draw three axes like those shown. Then graph $R(4, 5, 9)$.

Distance in 3 Dimensions **In a three-dimensional coordinate system, the distance between two points (x_1, y_1, z_1) and (x_2, y_2, z_2) can be found using this extension of the Distance Formula.**

$$d = \sqrt{(x_2 - x_1)^2 + (y_2 - y_1)^2 + (z_2 - z_1)^2}$$

Find the distance between each pair of points to the nearest tenth.

62. $P(2, 3, 4), B(-2, 4, 9)$

63. $Q(0, 12, 15), Y(-8, 20, 12)$

Standardized Test Prep

Multiple Choice

64. What are the coordinates of the point that is halfway between (4, 1) and (−22, 8)?
A. (−9, 3.5) **B.** (−9, 4.5) **C.** (−18, 9) **D.** (13, 4.5)

65. Which point lies the farthest from the origin?
F. (0, −7) **G.** (5, 1) **H.** (−4, −3) **I.** (−3, 8)

Quantitative Comparison

Compare the boxed quantity in Column A with the boxed quantity in Column B. Choose the best answer.

A. The quantity in Column A is greater.
B. The quantity in Column B is greater.
C. The two quantities are equal.
D. The relationship cannot be determined from the information given.

	Column A	Column B
66.	distance from (2, −3) to (0, 19)	distance from (−12, 6) to (−4, −10)
67.	distance from (−31, −17) to (−23, −16)	distance from (8, 0) to (0, −1)
	A segment has endpoints at (14, −5) and (6, 14).	
68.	the x-coordinate of the midpoint of the segment	the y-coordinate of the midpoint of the segment

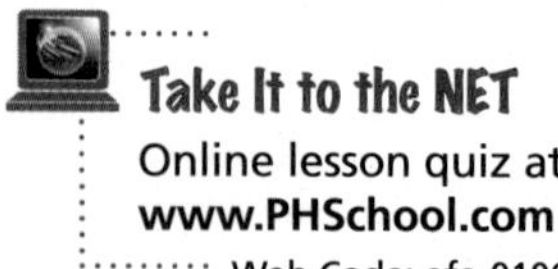

Take It to the NET
Online lesson quiz at **www.PHSchool.com**
Web Code: afa-0106

Short Response

69. a. Points $P(-4, 6)$, $Q(2, 4)$, and R are collinear. One of the points is the midpoint of the segment formed by the other two points. What are the possible coordinates of R?

b. $RQ = \sqrt{160}$. Does this information affect your answer to part (a)? Explain.

Mixed Review

Lesson 1-5 **Use a straightedge and compass.**

70. Draw $\overline{AB}$. Construct $\overline{PQ}$ so that $PQ = 2AB$.

71. Draw $\overline{LK}$. Construct the perpendicular bisector of $\overline{LK}$.

72. Draw an obtuse $\angle B$. Construct $\angle C$ so that $m\angle C = m\angle B$.

73. Draw an acute $\angle RTS$. Construct the bisector of $\angle RTS$.

Lesson 1-4 **74. Algebra** The length of $\overline{AC}$ is 45. If $AB = x + 8$ and $BC = 3x - 3$, find the value of x.

75. Find AB if the coordinate of A is 5 and the coordinate of B is -5.

76. Algebra C is the midpoint of $\overline{EF}$. Find EF.

77. Name $\angle A$ two other ways.

78. $m\angle PQR = 60$. What is $m\angle RQS$?

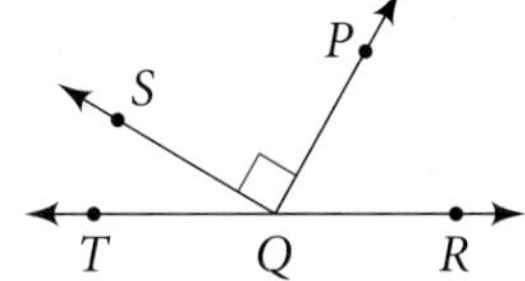

Checkpoint Quiz 2 — Lessons 1-4 through 1-6

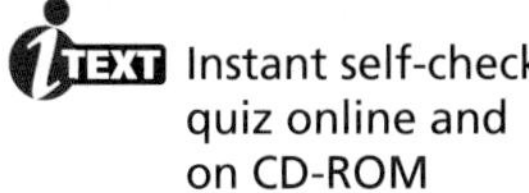
Instant self-check quiz online and on CD-ROM

Use the figure for Exercises 1–3.

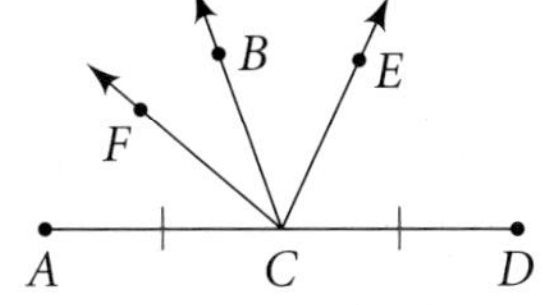

1. If $AC = 4x + 5$ and $DC = 3x + 8$, find AC.

2. If $m\angle BCE = 45$ and $m\angle ECD = 65$, find $m\angle BCD$.

3. If $m\angle FCA = 40$, find $m\angle FCD$.

4. $\overleftrightarrow{AX}$ is the perpendicular bisector of $\overline{QS}$ at M.
   a. What is $m\angle AMS$?
   b. If $QM = 30$, what is QS?

5. $\overrightarrow{PT}$ is the bisector of $\angle APR$. Name two congruent angles.

6. $\overrightarrow{OR}$ is the bisector of right $\angle TOS$. Find $m\angle TOR$.

Use a straightedge to draw three figures like the ones shown at the right. Then do each construction.

7. Construct $\overline{FG}$ so that $FG = CD + RT$.

8. Construct $\angle HSK$ so that $m\angle HSK = \frac{1}{2}m\angle LSK$.

$\overline{AB}$ has endpoints $A(-4, 5)$ and $B(6, -2)$.

9. Find AB to the nearest tenth.

10. Find the coordinates of the midpoint of $\overline{AB}$.

Reading Math

Reading an Example

For Use With Page 44, Example 1

In this text, every lesson has two or more worked-out examples. Examples show you how to use the concepts taught in each lesson. In each example, a problem is stated, then solved. Each step in the solution is in the left-hand column, and an explanation of each step is in **bold** at the right.

Before you read an example, be sure to read the material that comes before it. There you will often find important information about the concept illustrated by the example.

EXAMPLE Finding Distance

Find the distance between $T(5, 2)$ and $R(-4, -1)$ to the nearest tenth.		This is the statement of the problem.
Let $(5, 2)$ be (x_1, y_1) and $(-4, -1)$ be (x_2, y_2).		This is the first step in the solution. It assigns the numbers in the example to the variables in the Distance Formula.
$d = \sqrt{(x_2 - x_1)^2 + (y_2 - y_1)^2}$	**Use the Distance Formula.**	This is the next step. The text in **bold** explains what is being done.
$d = \sqrt{(-4 - 5)^2 + (-1 - 2)^2}$	**Substitute.**	Variables and their corresponding values are shown in color to help you see the substitutions.
$d = \sqrt{(-9)^2 + (-3)^2}$ $d = \sqrt{81 + 9} = \sqrt{90}$	**Simplify.**	Check the calculations yourself to verify that the expression is simplified correctly.
90 [√] 9.4868330	**Use a calculator.**	The input and the keystroke for one type of calculator is given, followed by the calculator output. Try it yourself on your calculator, using, of course, the keystroke(s) appropriate for it.
To the nearest tenth, $TR = 9.5$.		The solution is written as a sentence.

EXERCISE

You will see this Check after every example. The Check Understanding exercise will help you check your understanding of the mathematics in each example. Try the one on page 44 under Example 1, as shown below.

a. $\overline{AB}$ has endpoints $A(1, -3)$ and $B(-4, 4)$. Find AB to the nearest tenth.

b. **Critical Thinking** In Example 1, suppose you let $(-4, -1)$ be (x_1, y_1) and $(5, 2)$ be (x_2, y_2). Do you get the same result? Why?

Perimeter, Circumference, and Area

Lesson Preview

What You'll Learn

To find perimeters of rectangles and squares, and circumferences of circles

To find areas of rectangles, squares, and circles

. . . And Why

To find the amount of fencing material needed to build a fence, as in Example 1

✓ Check Skills You'll Need

(For help, go to Skills Handbook page 719 and Lesson 1-6.)

Simplify each absolute value.

1. $|4 - 8|$ **2.** $|10 - (-5)|$ **3.** $|-2 - 6|$

Find the distance between the points to the nearest tenth.

4. $A(2, 3), B(5, 9)$ **5.** $K(-1, -3), L(0, 0)$

6. $W(4, -7), Z(10, -2)$ **7.** $C(-5, 2), D(-7, 6)$

8. $M(-1, -10), P(-12, -3)$ **9.** $Q(-8, -4), R(-3, -10)$

Interactive lesson includes instant self-check, tutorials, and activities.

OBJECTIVE 1

Finding Perimeter and Circumference

Need Help?

You can think of the *perimeter* of a polygon as the distance around it and the *area* as the number of square units it encloses.

Investigation: Finding Perimeter and Area

Draw each figure on centimeter grid paper.

- a rectangle with length 5 cm and width 3 cm
- a rectangle with length 8 cm and height 2 cm
- a rectangle with each side 4 cm

1. To find the perimeter of each rectangle, find the sum of the lengths of the sides. Record the perimeter of each rectangle.
2. To find the area of each rectangle, count the number of square centimeters in its interior. Record the area of each rectangle.
3. Do rectangles with equal perimeters have the same area?
4. Do rectangles with the same area have the same perimeter?

The perimeter P of a polygon is the sum of the lengths of its sides. The area A of a polygon is the number of square units it encloses. For special figures such as squares, rectangles, and circles, you can use formulas for perimeter (called circumference in circles) and area.

Some formulas for perimeter and area are given in the chart at the top of the next page. You will also find the chart on pages 726 and 727 to be useful at times.

Key Concepts

Summary **Perimeter and Area**

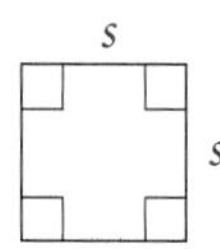

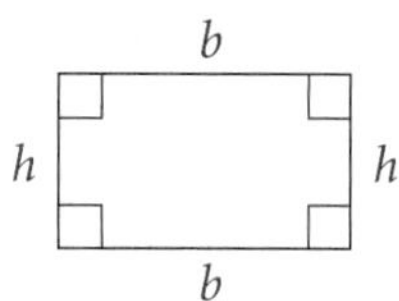

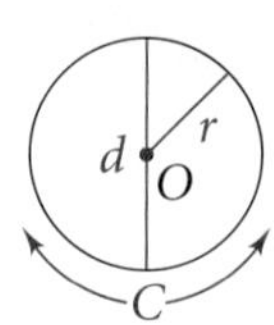

Square with side length s	Rectangle with base b and height h	Circle with radius r and diameter d
Perimeter $P = 4s$	Perimeter $P = 2b + 2h$	Circumference $C = \pi d$, or $C = 2\pi r$
Area $A = s^2$	Area $A = bh$	Area $= \pi r^2$

The units of measurement for perimeter and circumference include inches, feet, yards, miles, centimeters, meters, and kilometers. When measuring area, use square units such as square inches (in.^{2}), square centimeters (cm^2), square meters (m^2), and square miles (mi^2).

1 EXAMPLE Real-World Connection

Fencing Your pool is 15 ft wide and 20 ft long with a 3-ft wide deck surrounding it. You want to build a fence around the deck. How much fencing will you need?

3 ft
20 ft
15 ft

To find the perimeter of the pool with the deck, first find the width and length of the pool with the deck.

Width of pool and deck $= 15 + 3 + 3 = 21$

Length of pool and deck $= 20 + 3 + 3 = 26$

Perimeter of a rectangle $= 2b + 2h$ **Use the formula for the perimeter of a rectangle.**

$P = 2(21) + 2(26)$ **Substitute.**

$P = 42 + 52$ **Simplify.**

$P = 94$

You will need 94 ft of fencing.

Need Help?
For a rectangle, "length" and "width" are sometimes used in place of "base" and "height."

Check Understanding

1 Suppose you want to frame a picture that is 6 in. by 7 in. with a $\frac{1}{2}$-in. wide frame.
a. Find the perimeter of the picture.
b. Find the perimeter of the outside edge of the frame.

Notice that the formulas for a circle involve π. Since the number π is irrational,

$$\pi = 3.1415926\ldots,$$

you cannot write it as a terminating decimal. For an approximate answer, you can use 3.14 or $\frac{22}{7}$ $\left(3.14 \approx \frac{22}{7}\right)$ for π. You can also use the rounded decimal you get by pressing π on your calculator. For an exact answer leave the result in terms of π.

2 EXAMPLE Finding Circumference

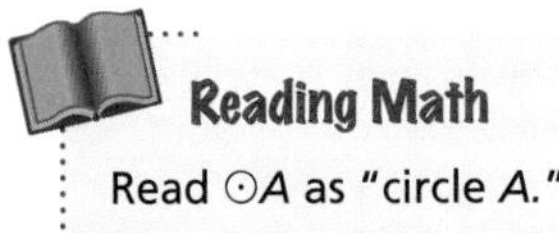

Reading Math

Read ⊙*A* as "circle *A*."

Find the circumference of ⊙*A* in terms of π. Then find the circumference to the nearest tenth.

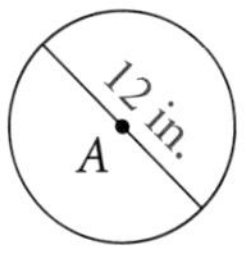

(Figure: circle with center A and diameter 12 in.)

$C = \pi d$

$C = 12\pi$ **This is the exact answer.**

12 [×] [π] [=] 37.699112 **Use a calculator.**

$C \approx 37.7$

The circumference of the circle is 12π in., or about 37.7 in.

Check Understanding 2 **a.** Find the circumference of a circle with a radius of 18 m in terms of π.
b. Find the circumference of a circle with a diameter of 18 m to the nearest tenth.

3 EXAMPLE Finding Perimeter in the Coordinate Plane

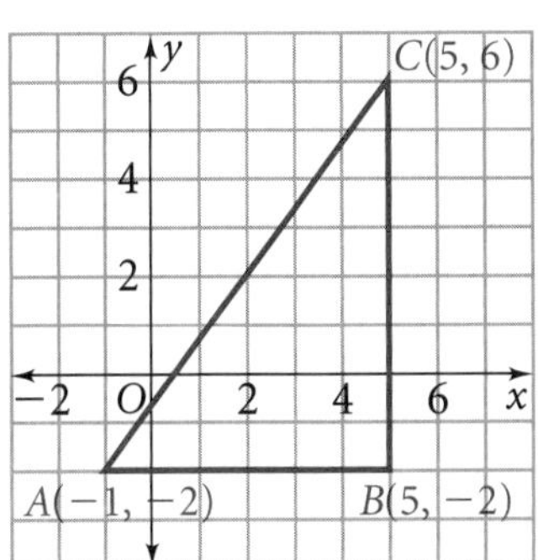

Algebra Find the perimeter of $\triangle ABC$.

Find the length of each side. Add the lengths to find the perimeter.

$AB = |5 - (-1)| = 6$ **Use the Ruler Postulate.**

$BC = |6 - (-2)| = 8$

$AC = \sqrt{(5 - (-1))^2 + (6 - (-2))^2}$ **Use the Distance Formula.**

$= \sqrt{6^2 + 8^2} = \sqrt{100} = 10$

$AB + BC + AC = 6 + 8 + 10 = 24$

The perimeter of $\triangle ABC$ is 24 units.

Check Understanding 3 Graph quadrilateral *KLMN* with vertices $K(-3, -3)$, $L(1, -3)$, $M(1, 4)$, and $N(-3, 1)$. Find the perimeter of *KLMN*.

OBJECTIVE

2 Finding Area

To find area, you should use the same unit for both dimensions.

4 EXAMPLE Finding Area of a Rectangle

You are designing a rectangular banner for the front of the museum. The banner will be 4 ft wide and 7 yd high. How much material do you need?

7 yd = 21 ft **Change yards to feet using 1 yd = 3 ft.**

Area = bh **Use the formula for area of a rectangle.**

$A = 4(21)$ **Substitute 4 for *b* and 21 for *h*.**

$A = 84$

The area of the banner is 84 square feet (ft^2). You need at least 84 ft^2 of material.

Check Understanding 4 Find the area of the banner in Example 4 by first changing all units to yards. Compare your answer to the one in Example 4. How do they compare?

5 EXAMPLE Finding Area of a Circle

The diameter of a circle is 10 in. Find the area in terms of π.

$\text{radius} = \frac{10}{2}$ or 5 $\quad r = \frac{d}{2}$

$\text{Area} = \pi r^2$ **Use the formula for area of a circle.**

$A = \pi(5)^2$ **Substitute 5 for *r*.**

$A = 25\pi$

The area of the circle is 25π in.^{2}.

Check Understanding 5 The diameter of a circle is 5 ft.

a. Find the area in terms of π.

b. Find the area to the nearest tenth.

The following postulates are useful in finding areas of figures with irregular shapes.

Key Concepts

Postulate 1-9

If two figures are congruent, then their areas are equal.

Postulate 1-10

The area of a region is the sum of the areas of its nonoverlapping parts.

Example 6 applies Postulate 1-10 by summing the areas of the parts of a figure.

6 EXAMPLE Finding Area of an Irregular Shape

Find the area of the figure at the right.

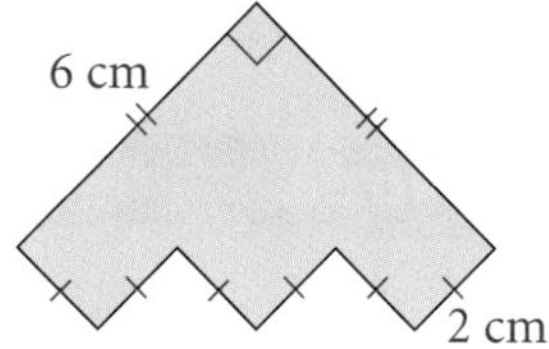

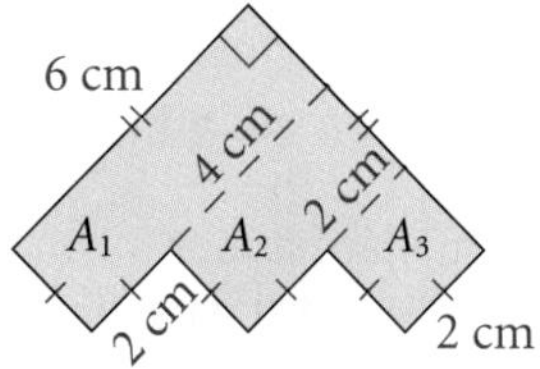

Separate the figure into rectangles.

$\text{Area} = bh$ **Use the formula for the area of a rectangle.**

$A_1 = 6 \cdot 2 = 12$ **Find the area of each rectangle.**

$A_2 = 4 \cdot 2 = 8$

$A_3 = 2 \cdot 2 = 4$

$\text{Total Area} = 12 + 8 + 4 = 24$ **Add the areas.**

The area of the figure is 24 cm^2.

Check Understanding 6 Copy the figure in Example 6. Separate it in a different way. Find the area.

EXERCISES

For more practice, see *Extra Practice.*

Practice and Problem Solving

Practice by Example

Example 1 (page 52)

Find the perimeter of each figure.

1. 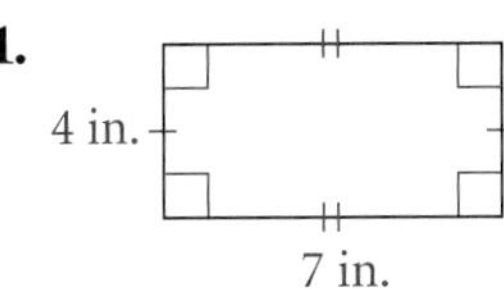

2. 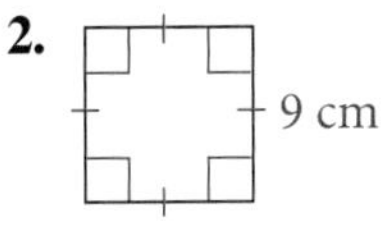

Find the perimeter of each rectangle with the given base and height.

3. 21 in., 7 in. **4.** 16 cm, 23 cm **5.** 24 m, 36 m

6. **Framing** A rectangular certificate 8 in. by 10 in. will have a frame $1\frac{1}{2}$ in. wide surrounding it. What is the perimeter of the outside edge of the frame?

7. **Fencing** A garden that is 5 ft by 6 ft has a walkway 2 ft wide around it. Find the amount of fencing needed to surround the walkway.

Example 2 (page 53)

Find the circumference of each circle in terms of π.

8. 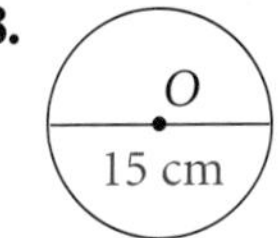

9. 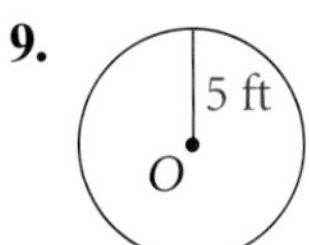

10. 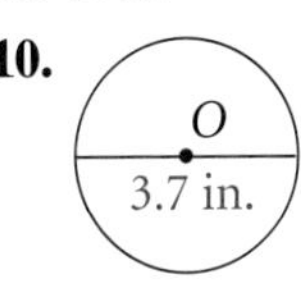

11. 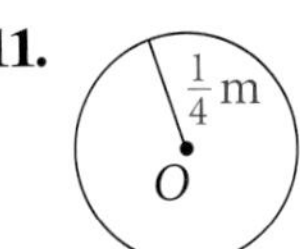

Find the circumference of the circle to the nearest tenth.

12. $r = 9$ in. **13.** $d = 7.3$ m **14.** $d = \frac{1}{2}$ yd **15.** $r = 56$ cm

Example 3 (page 53)

Draw each figure in the coordinate plane. Find the perimeter.

16. $X(0, 2), Y(4, -1), Z(-2, -1)$ **17.** $A(-4, -1), B(4, 5), C(4, -2)$

18. $L(0, 1), M(3, 5), N(5, 5), P(5, 1)$

19. $S(-5, 3), T(7, -2), U(7, -6), V(-5, -6)$

Example 4 (page 53)

Find the area of each rectangle with the given base and height.

20. 4 ft, 4 in. **21.** 30 in., 4 yd **22.** 2 ft 3 in., 6 in.

23. 40 cm, 2 m **24.** 3 m, 190 cm **25.** 240 cm, 5 m

26. Find the area of a section of road pavement that is 20 ft wide and 100 yd long.

Example 5 (page 54)

Find the area of each circle in terms of π.

27. 20 m

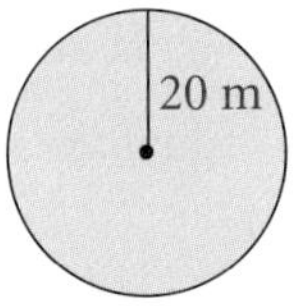

28. 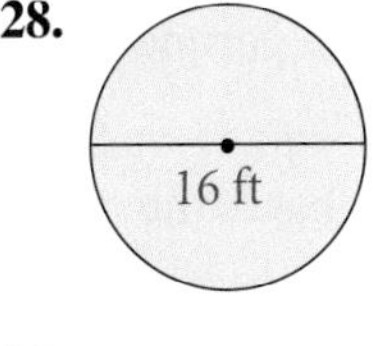

29. 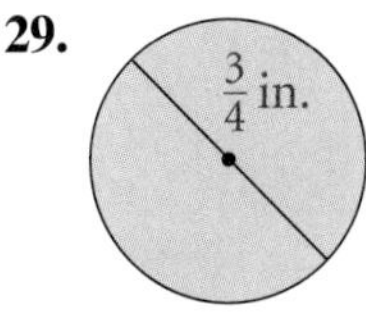

30. 0.5 m

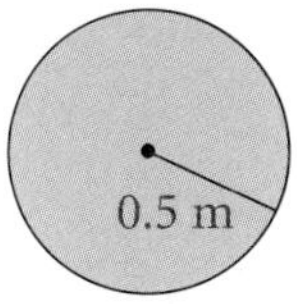

31. 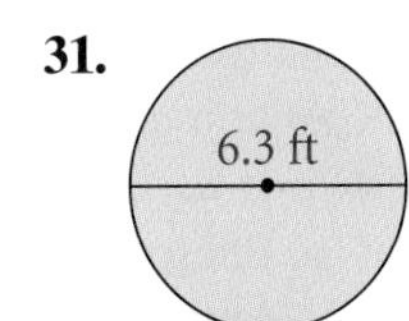

32. 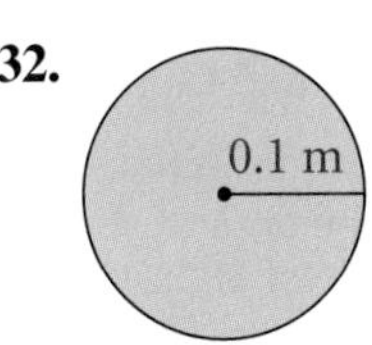

Find the area of each circle to the nearest tenth.

33. $r = 7$ ft **34.** $d = 8.3$ m **35.** $d = 24$ cm **36.** $r = 12$ in.

Example 6 (page 54)

Find the area of the shaded region. All angles are right angles.

37.

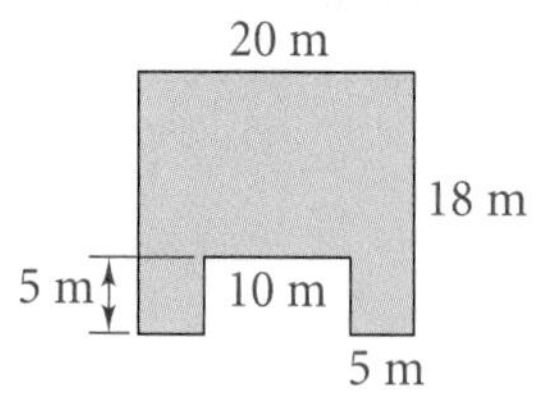

38.

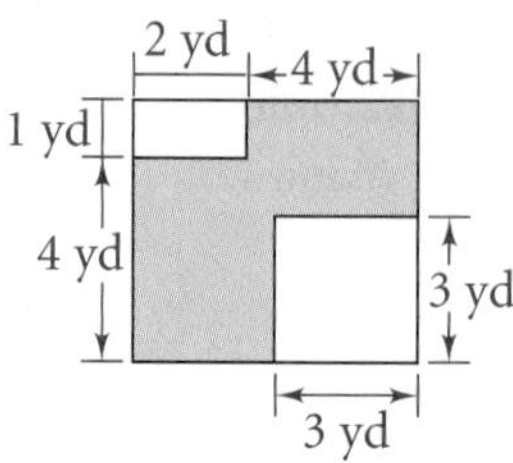

39.

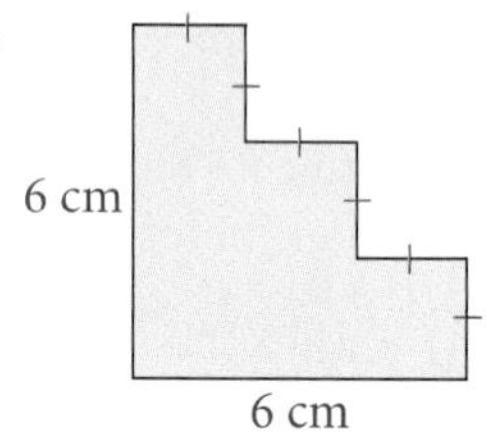

40.

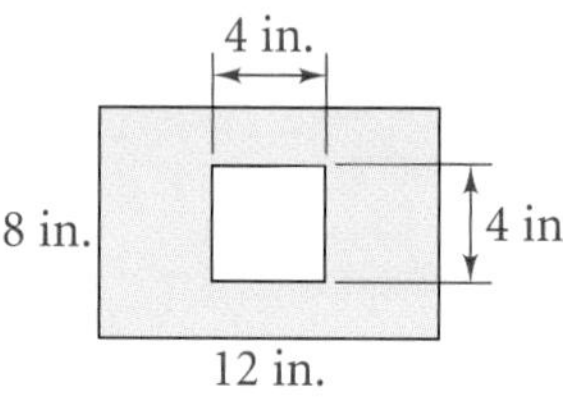

B Apply Your Skills

41. a. What is the area of a square whose sides are 12 in. long?
b. What is the area of a square whose sides are 1 ft long?
c. **Reasoning** How many square inches are in a square foot? Explain.

42. a. Count squares to find the area of the polygon outlined in blue.
b. Use a formula to find the area of each square outlined in red.
c. How does the sum of your results in part (b) compare to your result in part (a)? Which postulate does this support?

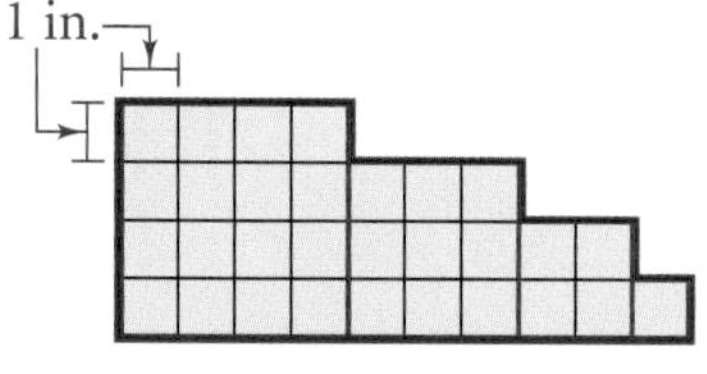

43. Estimation On a postcard from Mexico, Ky sketched the "footprint" of the pyramid known as El Castillo in the ancient Mayan city Chichen Itza. He said he estimated the three different lengths on each side to be 22 m, 6 m, and 11 m. Use those estimates to estimate the area of El Castillo's footprint.

El Castillo
Chichen Itza, Mexico

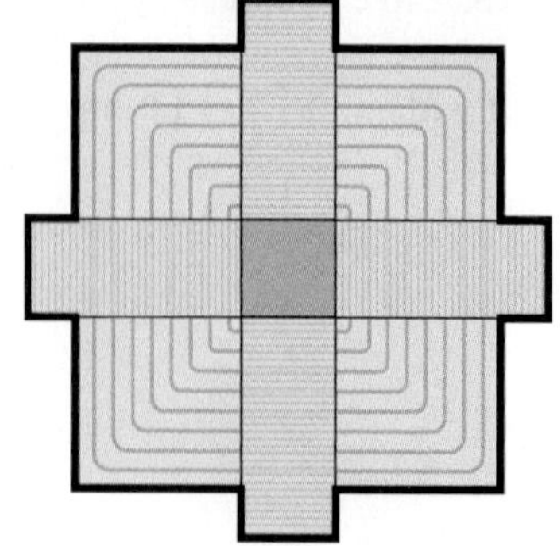

Real-World Connection

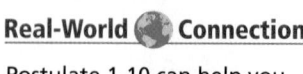

Postulate 1-10 can help you estimate the area of the "footprint," of El Castillo.

Estimation **Estimate the perimeter and area of each object.**

44. the front cover of this book **45.** the front cover of your notebook

46. a classroom bulletin board **47.** the top of your desk

48. Writing Choose one exercise from Exercises 44–47 and explain why you chose your unit of length.

49. The area of an 11-cm wide rectangle is 176 cm^2. What is its length?

50. The perimeter of a rectangle is 40 cm and the base is 12 cm. What is its area?

51. A square and a rectangle have equal area. The rectangle is 64 cm by 81 cm. What is the perimeter of the square?

52. a. **Critical Thinking** Can you use the formula for the perimeter of a rectangle to find the perimeter of any square? Explain.
b. Can you use the formula for the perimeter of a square to find the perimeter of any rectangle? Explain.
c. Use the formula for the perimeter of a square to write a formula for the area of a square in terms of its perimeter.

Real-World Connection

Four 6 in.-by-6 in. tiles will cover 1 ft^2.

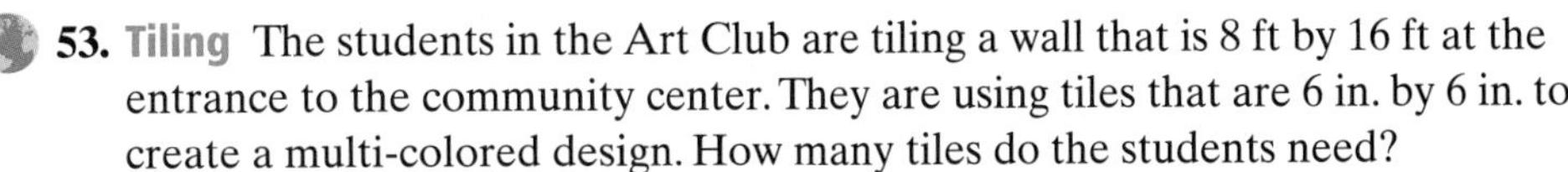

53. **Tiling** The students in the Art Club are tiling a wall that is 8 ft by 16 ft at the entrance to the community center. They are using tiles that are 6 in. by 6 in. to create a multi-colored design. How many tiles do the students need?

Algebra **Draw each rectangle in the coordinate plane. Find its perimeter and area.**

54. $A(-3, 2), B(-2, 2), C(-2, -2), D(-3, -2)$

55. $A(-2, -6), B(-2, -3), C(3, -3), D(3, -6)$

Coordinate Geometry **On graph paper, draw polygon $ABCDEFGH$ with vertices $A(1, 1)$, $B(10, 1)$, $C(10, 8)$, $D(7, 8)$, $E(7, 5)$, $F(4, 5)$, $G(4, 8)$, and $H(1, 8)$.**

56. Find the perimeter of the polygon.

57. Divide the polygon into rectangles. Find the area of the polygon.

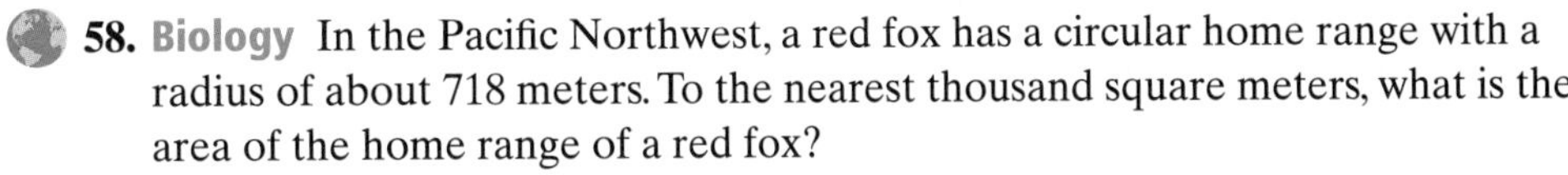

58. **Biology** In the Pacific Northwest, a red fox has a circular home range with a radius of about 718 meters. To the nearest thousand square meters, what is the area of the home range of a red fox?

59. A circle has area 225π m^2. What is the diameter of the circle?

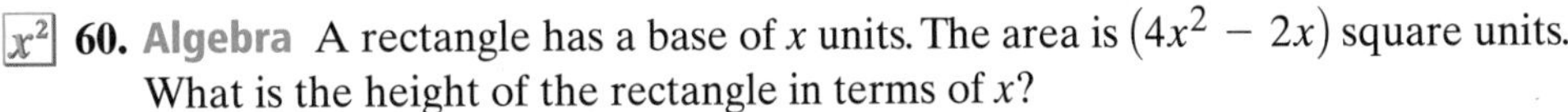

60. **Algebra** A rectangle has a base of x units. The area is $(4x^2 - 2x)$ square units. What is the height of the rectangle in terms of x?

Home Maintenance **To determine how much of each item to buy, tell whether you need to know area or perimeter. Explain your choice.**

61. wallpaper for a bedroom

62. weatherstripping for a door

63. fence for a garden

64. paint for a basement floor

65. **Coordinate Geometry** The endpoints of a diameter of a circle are $A(2, 1)$ and $B(5, 5)$. Find the area of the circle in terms of π.

C Challenge

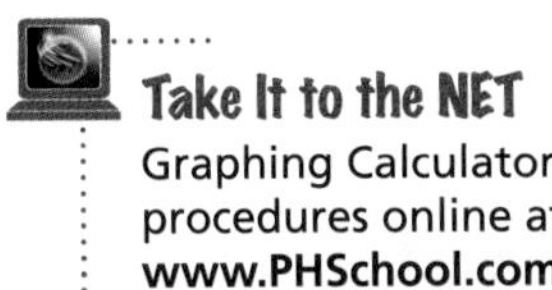

Take It to the NET
Graphing Calculator procedures online at **www.PHSchool.com**
Web Code: afe-2104

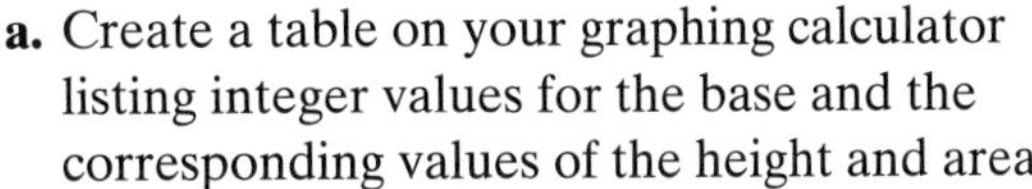

66. **Graphing Calculator** You want to build a rectangular corral by using the side of a barn for one side and 100 ft of fencing for the other three sides.
   a. Create a table on your graphing calculator listing integer values for the base and the corresponding values of the height and area.
   b. Make a graph using your table values. Graph the base on the horizontal axis and area on the vertical axis.
   c. What are the dimensions of the corral with the greatest area?

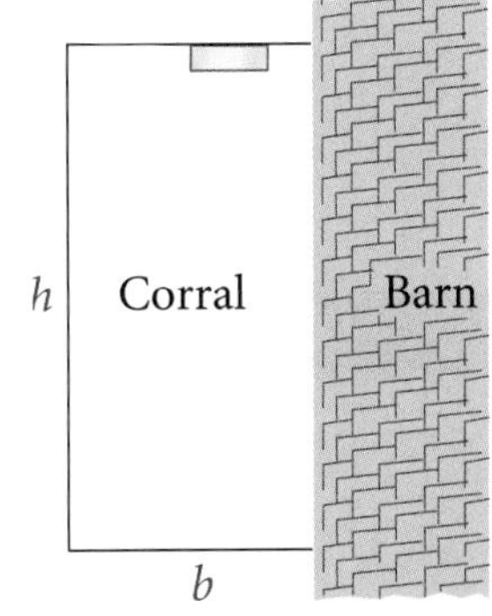

67. How many circles with the given radius are needed for the sum of their areas to equal the area of a circle with the second given radius?
   a. 1 in., 3 in.
   b. 2 in., 6 in.
   c. 3 in., 9 in.
   d. **Make a Conjecture** How many circles with a radius of n in. are needed for the sum of their areas to equal the area of a circle with a radius of $3n$ in.?

Algebra **Find the area of each figure.**

68. a rectangle with side lengths of $\frac{2a}{5b}$ units and $\frac{3b}{8}$ units

69. a square with perimeter $10n$ units

70. a square with side lengths of $(3m - 4n)$ units

71. Open-Ended The area of a 5 in.-by-5 in. square is the same as the sum of the areas of a 3 in.-by-3 in. square and a 4 in.-by-4 in. square. Find two or more squares whose total area is the same as the area of an 11 in.-by-11 in. square.

72. Track An athletic field is a rectangle, 100 yards by 40 yards, with a semicircle at each of the short sides. A running track 10 yards wide surrounds the field. Find the perimeter of the outside of the running track to the nearest tenth of a yard.

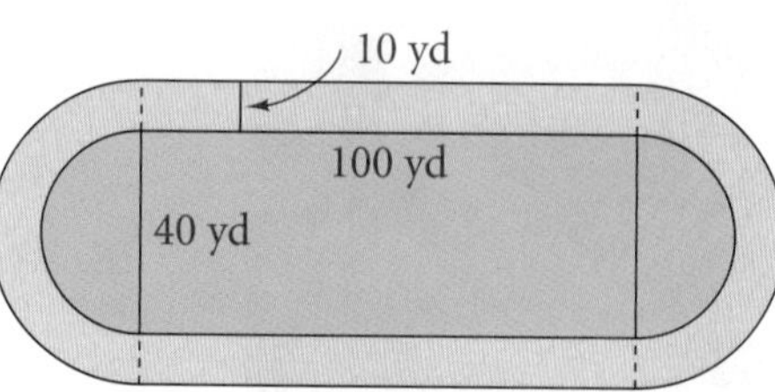

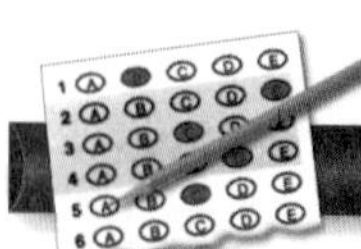

Standardized Test Prep

Gridded Response

For Exercises 73 and 74, a rectangular garden has a rectangular walkway around it. The width of the walkway is 8 ft.

73. How many feet greater than the perimeter of the garden is the outside perimeter of the walkway?

74. If the garden is a square with a perimeter of 260 ft, what is the area of the walkway in square feet?

Take It to the NET
Online lesson quiz at **www.PHSchool.com**
Web Code: afa-0107

75. You need to tile a 12 ft-by-15 ft floor. The color you want allows you the choices found in the table at the right. How many dollars would it cost to tile the floor with 12 in.-by-12 in. tiles?

Size of Tiles	Cost
12″ × 12″	$3/ft^2
11″ × 11″	$3/ft^2
10″ × 12″	$4/ft^2
6″ × 8″	$4.50/ft^2

76. How many tiles would cover the 12 ft-by-15 ft floor if you choose the 10 in.-by-12 in. tiles?

77. How many dollars would it cost to cover the 12 ft-by-15 ft floor with the tiles that are 6 in. by 8 in.?

Mixed Review

Lesson 1-6

78. The midpoint of $\overline{CD}$ has coordinates (5, 6). Point *C* has coordinates (−5, −1). Find the coordinates of point *D*.

Find (a) *AB* to the nearest tenth and (b) the coordinates of the midpoint of $\overline{AB}$.

79. $A(4, 1), B(7, 9)$ **80.** $A(0, 3), B(3, 8)$ **81.** $A(9, 2), B(-3, 9)$

82. $A(0, 1), B(-4, 6)$ **83.** $A(4, 10), B(-2, 3)$ **84.** $A(-1, 1), B(-4, -5)$

Lesson 1-5

$\overleftrightarrow{BG}$ is the perpendicular bisector of $\overline{WR}$ at point *I*.

85. What is $m\angle BIR$? **86.** Name two congruent segments.

87. $\overline{WR}$ has length 124. What is the length of $\overline{IR}$?

Lesson 1-4

For the given coordinates, find *PQ*.

88. *P*: 12, *Q*: −6 **89.** *P*: 3, *Q*: 9 **90.** *P*: −23, *Q*: 10

Technology Comparing Perimeters and Areas

FOR USE WITH LESSON 1-7

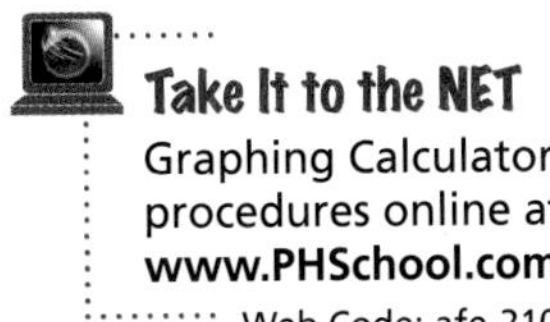

Take It to the NET
Graphing Calculator procedures online at **www.PHSchool.com**
Web Code: afe-2104

You can use a graphing calculator or spreadsheet technology to find maximum and minimum values for area and perimeter problems.

You have 32 yards of fencing. You want to make a rectangular pen for the calf you are raising as a 4-H project. What dimensions will give the maximum area? What is the maximum area?

Investigate

Draw some possible rectangular pens and find their areas.

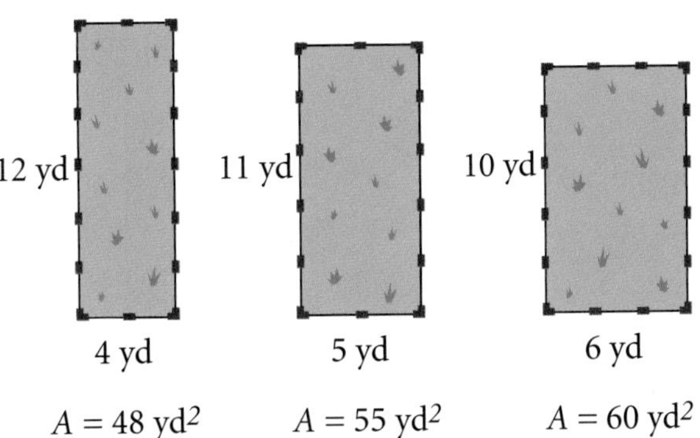

$A = 48\text{ yd}^2$ $\quad A = 55\text{ yd}^2$ $\quad A = 60\text{ yd}^2$

Create a graphing calculator table to find area. Let X represent values for the base. The height then is 16 − X, and the area is X(16 − X). Enter Y1 = 16 − X and Y2 = X(16 − X). Set the table so that X starts at 1 and changes by 1.

Scroll down the table. Area is maximum when X (or b) is 8. When $b = 8, h = 8$ and $A = 64$.

You can confirm this result by graphing Y1 = X(16 − X). Trace on the graph to find the maximum area.

A square pen with sides of 8 yd will give maximum area for your calf. The maximum area is 64 yd^2.

X	Y_1	Y_2
4	12	48
5	11	55
6	10	60
7	9	63
8	8	64
9	7	63
10	6	60

X=4

Y2=X(16-X)

X=8 Y=64

X min = 0 Y min = 0
X max = 18 Y max = 70
X scl = 2 Y scl = 7

EXERCISES

1. **Make a Conjecture** For a fixed perimeter, what rectangular shape will result in a maximum area?
2. Consider that the pen is not restricted to polygon shapes. Determine the area of a circular pen if the circumference is 32 yd. How does this result compare with the maximum square area of 64 yd^2 found in the investigation?
3. You want to make a rectangular garden with an area of 900 ft^2. You want to use a minimum amount of fencing to keep the cost low.
   a. List some possible dimensions for the rectangular garden. Find the perimeter of each rectangle.
   b. Create a graphing calculator table. Use integer values of the base b, and the corresponding values of the height h, to find values for P, the perimeter. What dimensions will give you a garden with the minimum perimeter?

Test-Taking Strategies

Writing Gridded Responses

Some tests include gridded-response questions. You find a numerical answer. Then you write the answer at the top of the grid and fill in the corresponding bubbles below. You have to be sure that you use the grid correctly.

1 EXAMPLE

What is the x-coordinate of the midpoint of the segment with endpoints $H(5, 1)$ and $K(12, 2)$?

By the Midpoint Formula, you can find that the coordinates of the midpoint are $\left(\frac{17}{2}, \frac{3}{2}\right)$.

The answer to the question is $\frac{17}{2}$.

You can write the answer as 17/2 or 8.5.

The grids at the right show two ways to enter the answer.

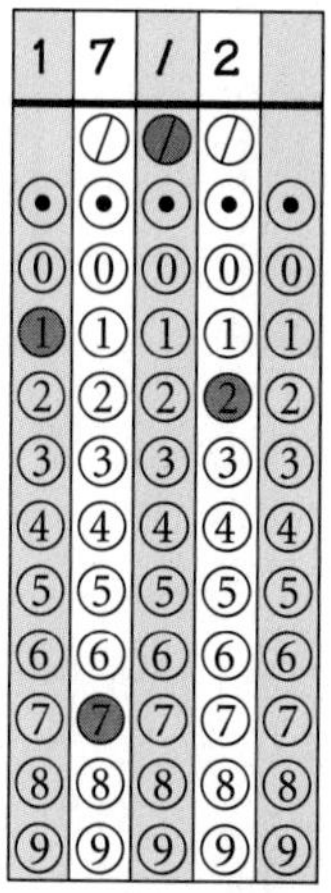

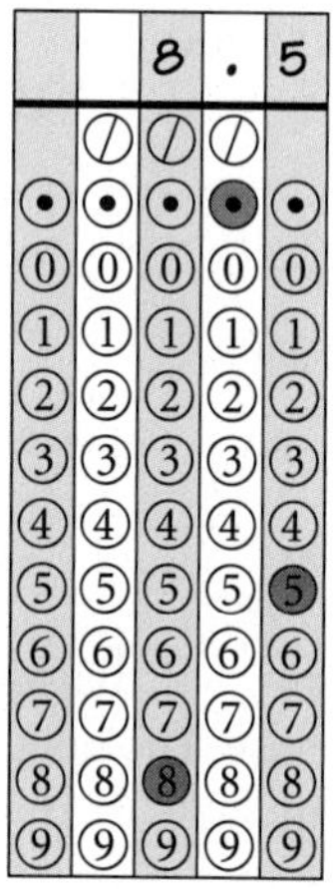

Certain tests may have specific directions for entering answers in grids.

If your answer doesn't fit, then you may have misread the directions or the problem itself, or you made a calculation error. Go back and check.

2 EXAMPLE

What is the distance between the points $A(0, 0.14)$ and $B(0.1, 0.2)$? Round your answer to the nearest hundredth.

The answer is 0.12. You grid this as .12 or as 0.12.

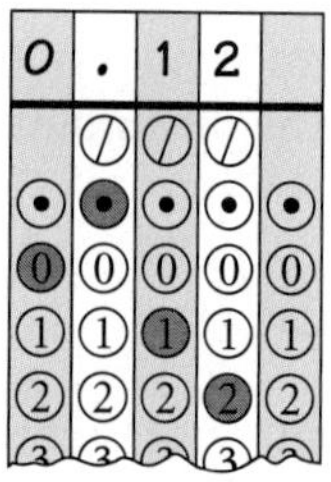

EXERCISES

Write what you would grid for each answer.

1. What is the y-coordinate of the midpoint of a segment with endpoints $C(0, -1)$ and $D(-6, 12)$?
2. What is the diameter, in centimeters, of a circle with circumference 0.5π cm?
3. What is the distance between $L(0, 0)$ and $M(0.3, 0.4)$?
4. The endpoints of a diameter of a circle are $R(3, 5)$ and $T(12, 5)$. What is the area of the circle? Round your answer to the nearest hundredth.
5. What is the radius of a circle whose area is 10π cm^2? Round your answer to the nearest hundredth of a centimeter.

Chapter Review

Vocabulary

acute angle (p. 28)
angle (p. 27)
angle bisector (p. 36)
axiom (p. 12)
collinear points (p. 11)
compass (p. 34)
congruent angles (p. 29)
congruent segments (p. 25)
conjecture (p. 5)
construction (p. 34)
coordinate (p. 25)
coplanar (p. 11)
counterexample (p. 5)
inductive reasoning (p. 4)
line (p. 11)
midpoint (p. 26)
obtuse angle (p. 28)
opposite rays (p. 17)
parallel lines (p. 18)
parallel planes (p. 18)
perpendicular bisector (p. 35)
perpendicular lines (p. 35)
plane (p. 11)
point (p. 11)
postulate (p. 12)
ray (p. 17)
right angle (p. 28)
segment (p. 17)
skew lines (p. 18)
space (p. 11)
straight angle (p. 28)
straightedge (p. 34)

Understanding Vocabulary

Choose the correct term to complete each sentence.

1. Figures that are in the same plane are _?_.

2. A(n) _?_ is the part of a line consisting of two endpoints and all points between them.

3. Two segments with the same length are _?_.

4. A(n) _?_ of a segment is the point that divides the segment into two congruent segments.

5. A(n) _?_ is a ray that divides an angle into two congruent angles.

6. A conclusion based upon inductive reasoning is sometimes called a(n) _?_.

7. A(n) _?_ is an accepted statement of fact.

8. _?_ are coplanar lines that do not intersect.

9. A(n) _?_ is an angle whose measure is between 90 and 180.

10. A(n) _?_ of a segment is a line, segment, or ray that is perpendicular to a segment at its midpoint.

Take It to the NET
Online vocabulary quiz at **www.PHSchool.com**
Web Code: afj-0151

Skills and Concepts

1-1 Objectives

▼ To use inductive reasoning to make conjectures

You use **inductive reasoning** when you make conclusions based on patterns you observe. A **conjecture** describes a conclusion reached using inductive reasoning. A **counterexample** to a conjecture is an example for which the conjecture is incorrect.

Find a pattern for each sequence. Describe the pattern and use it to show the next two terms.

11. 40, 35, 30, 25, . . .
12. 5, –5, 5, –5, . . .
13. 34, 27, 20, 13, 6, . . .
14. 6, 24, 96, 384, . . .
15. 2, 4, 8, 16, 32, . . .
16. 1, 2, 5, 6, 9, . . .

17. Draw the next figure in the sequence.

1-2 and 1-3 Objectives

- To understand basic terms and postulates of geometry
- To identify segments and rays
- To recognize parallel lines

Points that lie on the same line are **collinear points.** Points and lines in the same plane are **coplanar. Segments** and **rays** are parts of lines.

Lines that are coplanar and do not intersect are **parallel lines.** Lines in space that are not parallel and do not intersect are **skew.** Planes that do not intersect are **parallel planes.**

A **postulate** or **axiom** is an accepted statement of fact.

Use the figure at the right for Exercises 18–23.

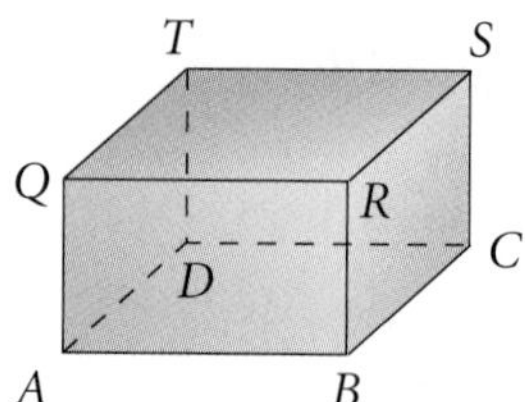

18. Name two intersecting lines.

19. Name a pair of skew lines.

20. Name three noncollinear points.

21. Name four noncoplanar points.

22. Name a pair of parallel planes.

23. Name three lines that intersect at D.

Complete with *always, sometimes,* or *never* to make a true statement.

24. A line and a point are __?__ coplanar.

25. Two segments are __?__ coplanar.

26. Skew lines are __?__ coplanar.

27. Parallel lines are __?__ skew.

28. Two points are __?__ collinear.

29. Parallel lines are __?__ coplanar.

1-4 Objectives

- To find the lengths of segments
- To find the measures of angles

Segments with the same length are **congruent segments.** The **midpoint** of a segment divides a segment into two congruent segments.

Two rays with the same endpoint form an **angle.** Angles are sometimes measured in degrees. Angles can be classified as acute, right, obtuse, or straight. Angles with the same measure are **congruent angles.**

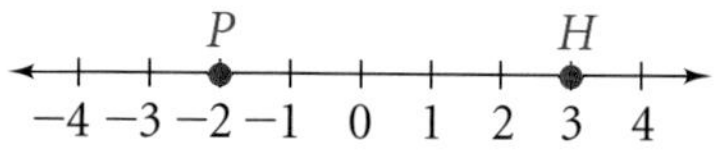

30. Find two possible coordinates of Q so that $PQ = 5$.

31. Find the coordinate of the midpoint of $\overline{PH}$.

x^2 Algebra **Find the value of each variable.**

32.

33.

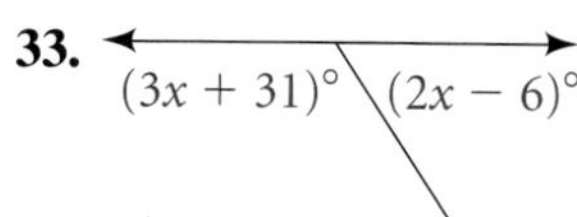

34. Name the congruent segments.

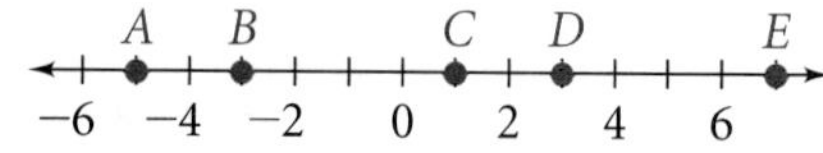

35. Name ∠1 and ∠2 two other ways.

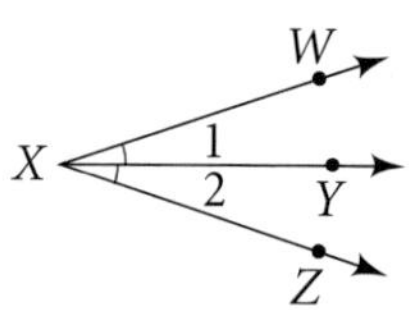

1-5 Objectives

- To use a compass and a straightedge to construct congruent segments and congruent angles
- To use a compass and a straightedge to bisect segments and angles

Construction is the process of making geometric figures using a **compass** and a **straightedge.** Four basic constructions involve constructing congruent segments, congruent angles, and bisectors of segments and angles.

Perpendicular lines intersect at right angles. A **perpendicular bisector** of a segment is perpendicular to the segment at its midpoint, and bisects it into two congruent segments. An **angle bisector** is a ray that divides an angle into two congruent angles.

36. Use a protractor to draw a 64° angle. Then construct an angle congruent to your 64° angle.

37. Use a ruler and draw $\overline{PQ}$.

a. Construct $\overline{AB} \cong \overline{PQ}$.

b. Construct the perpendicular bisector of $\overline{AB}$.

P •———————• Q

1-6 Objectives

- To find the distance between two points in the coordinate plane
- To find the coordinates of the midpoint of a segment in the coordinate plane

The x-axis and the y-axis intersect at the origin $(0, 0)$ and determine a coordinate plane. You can find the coordinates of the midpoint M of $\overline{AB}$ with endpoints $A(x_1, y_1)$ and $B(x_2, y_2)$ using the **Midpoint Formula.**

$$M = \left(\frac{x_1 + x_2}{2}, \frac{y_1 + y_2}{2}\right)$$

You can find the distance d between points $A(x_1, y_1)$ and $B(x_2, y_2)$ using the **Distance Formula.**

$$d = \sqrt{(x_2 - x_1)^2 + (y_2 - y_1)^2}$$

Find the distance between the points to the nearest tenth.

38. $A(-1, 5), B(0, 4)$

39. $C(-1, -1), D(6, 2)$

40. $E(-7, 0), F(5, 8)$

$\overline{GH}$ has endpoints $G(-3, 2)$ and $H(3, -2)$.

41. Find the coordinates of the midpoint of $\overline{GH}$.

42. Find GH to the nearest tenth.

1-7 Objectives

- To find perimeters of rectangles and squares, and circumferences of circles
- To find areas of rectangles, squares, and circles

The perimeter P of a polygon is the sum of the lengths of its sides. The area A of a polygon is the number of square units it encloses.

Formulas:	Square	Rectangle	Circle
	$P = 4s$	$P = 2b + 2h$	$C = \pi d$ or $C = 2\pi r$
	$A = s^2$	$A = bh$	$A = \pi r^2$

Find the perimeter and the area of each figure.

43. 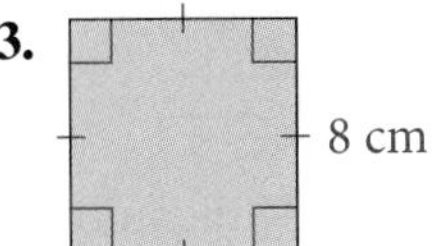

44. 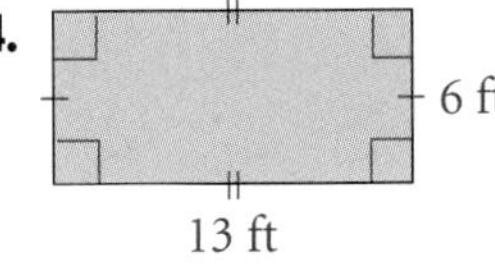

45. 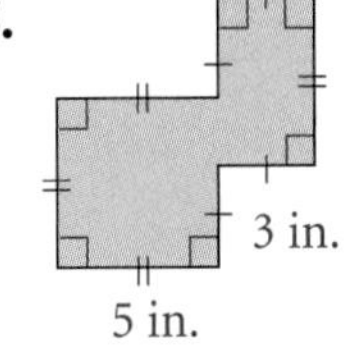

Find the circumference and the area of each circle to the nearest hundredth.

46. $r = 3$ in.

47. $d = 15$ m

48. $r = 26$ m

Chapter Test

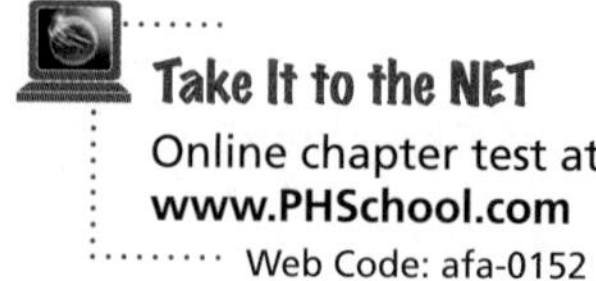

Take It to the NET
Online chapter test at
www.PHSchool.com
Web Code: afa-0152

Describe each pattern and find the next two terms of each sequence.

1. 8, −4, 2, −1, . . .

2. 0, 2, 4, 6, 8, . . .

3. S R Q P

4. Open-Ended Write two different sequences whose first three terms are 1, 2, 4. Describe each pattern.

Use the figure for Exercises 5–9.

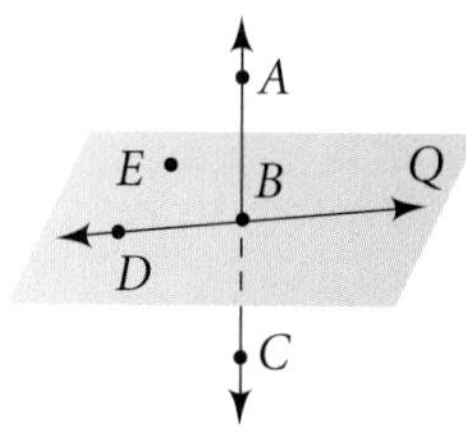

5. Name three collinear points.

6. Name four coplanar points.

7. Name four noncoplanar points.

8. What is the intersection of $\overleftrightarrow{AC}$ and plane Q?

9. How many planes contain each line and each point?

a. $\overleftrightarrow{BD}$ and point A **b.** $\overleftrightarrow{AB}$ and point C

c. $\overleftrightarrow{BE}$ and point C **d.** $\overleftrightarrow{BD}$ and point E

10. Track The running track is a rectangle with a half circle on each end. If $\overline{FI}$ and $\overline{GH}$ are diameters, find the area inside the track to the nearest tenth.

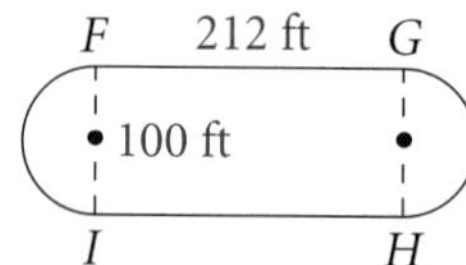

Complete with *always, sometimes,* or *never* to make each statement true.

11. $\overrightarrow{LJ}$ and $\overrightarrow{TJ}$ are __?__ opposite rays.

12. Four points are __?__ coplanar.

13. Skew lines are __?__ coplanar.

14. Two segments that lie in parallel lines are __?__ parallel.

15. The intersection of two planes is __?__ a point.

16. Algebra $JK = 48$. Find the value of x.

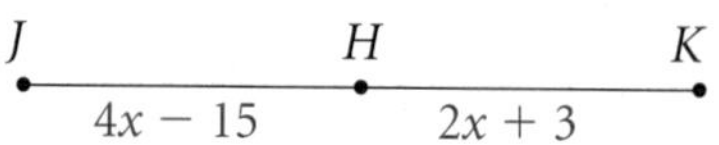

17. Algebra $M(x, y)$ is the midpoint of $\overline{CD}$ with endpoints $C(5, 9)$ and $D(17, 29)$.

a. Find the values of x and y.

b. Show $MC = MD$.

18. To the nearest tenth, find the perimeter of $\triangle ABC$ with vertices $A(-2, -2)$, $B(0, 5)$, and $C(3, -1)$.

For the given dimensions, find the area of each figure to the nearest hundredth.

19. rectangle
$b = 4$ m
$h = 2$ cm

20. square
$s = 3.5$ in.

21. circle
$d = 9$ cm

Algebra **Find the value of each variable in Exercises 22 and 23.**

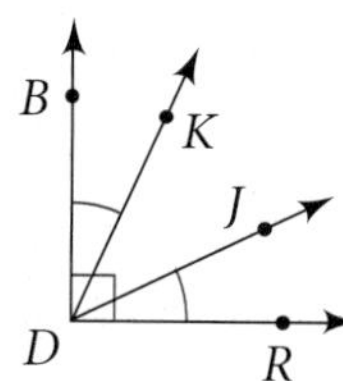

22. $m\angle BDK = 3x + 4$, $m\angle JDR = 5x - 10$

23. $m\angle BDJ = 7y + 2$, $m\angle JDR = 2y + 7$

24. Writing Why is it useful to have more than one way of naming an angle?

25. Draw an obtuse $\angle ABC$. Use a compass and straightedge to bisect the angle.

Use the figure to complete Exercises 26–30.

26. $\overline{VW}$ is the __?__ of $\overline{AY}$.

27. $EW + EV =$ __?__

28. If $EY = 3.5$, then $AY =$ __?__.

29. $\frac{1}{2}$ __?__ $= AE$

30. __?__ is the midpoint of __?__.

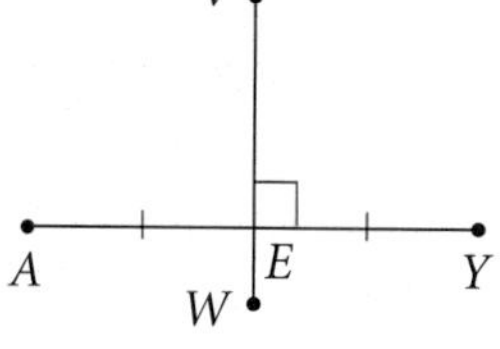

31. Carpeting How many square yards of carpet are needed to carpet a room that is 15 ft long and 20 ft wide?

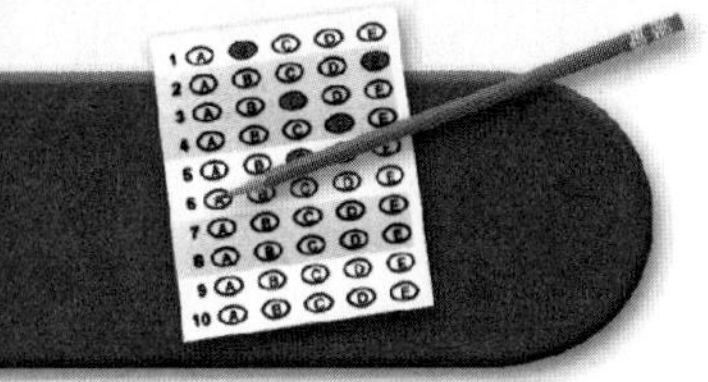

Standardized Test Prep

Reading Comprehension **Read the passage below, then answer the questions on the basis of what is *stated* or *implied* in the passage.**

Instructions for Building the Rainbow Toy Chest

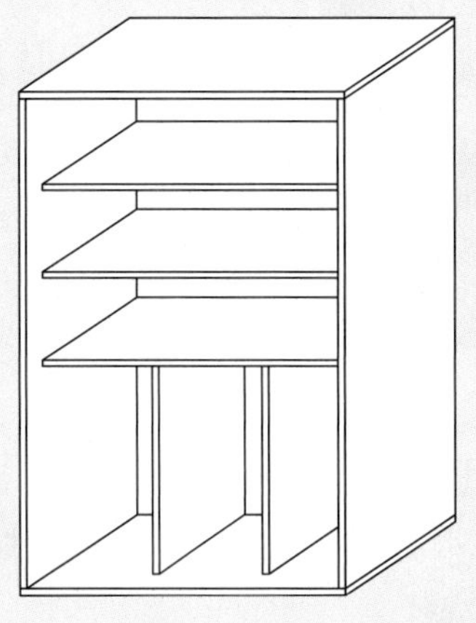

Use $\frac{3}{4}$-in.-thick plywood.

- Cut the top and bottom 18 in. by 42 in. Paint the top red and the bottom violet.

Use $\frac{1}{2}$-in.-thick plywood.

- Cut the two sides 18 in. by 60 in. Paint: left side brown, right side white.
- Cut the three shelves 15 in. by 41 in. Paint: top orange, middle yellow, bottom green.
- Cut the two dividers 24 in. by 15 in. Paint: left blue, right indigo.

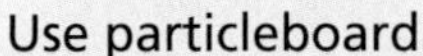

Use particleboard.

- Cut the back 41 in. by 60 in. Paint the back gray.

Assemble the painted pieces using nails and glue.

1. How many pieces must be cut to make the chest?
   A. 5 **B.** 7 **C.** 9 **D.** 10
2. What is the shape of each piece?
   F. square **G.** rectangular
   H. round **I.** cannot be determined
3. Which uses thicker wood, a divider or the top?
   A. divider **B.** top
   C. same thickness **D.** cannot be determined

Assume that the toy chest has been assembled.

4. Take the top of the bookshelf as the first horizontal surface and count downward. What is the color of the fourth surface down?
   F. white **G.** yellow **H.** green **I.** blue
5. Which corners are NOT coplanar?
   A. the four corners of the right side
   B. the two top corners of the left side and the two front corners of the bottom
   C. the two top corners of the right side and the two bottom corners of the left side
   D. the two front corners of the top and the two back corners of the bottom
6. Where do the violet board and the particleboard meet?
   F. the front edge of the violet board
   G. the back edge of the left side
   H. the right edge of the bottom
   I. the bottom edge of the back
7. Which edge is skew to the front edge of the orange board?
   A. the left edge of the orange board
   B. the top edge of the white board
   C. the back edge of the yellow board
   D. the front edge of the middle shelf
8. What are the colors of two boards that are NOT perpendicular?
   F. blue and gray **G.** indigo and violet
   H. blue and white **I.** yellow and brown
9. How tall is the toy chest?
10. What is the area of the top?
11. What is the perimeter of the front?
12. The back edge of each shelf touches the back of the chest. How far "recessed" is the front edge of a shelf from the front edge of a side?

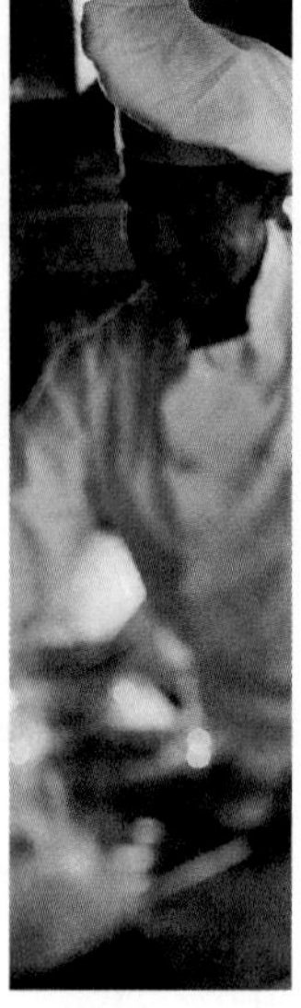

Where You've Been

In Chapter 1, you learned

- many of the basic terms and assumptions used in geometry.
- to measure angles and segments, do basic constructions, and use the coordinate plane to find the midpoint of a segment and the distance between two points.
- to find the area of and the distance around rectangles and circles.

Instant self-check online and on CD-ROM

Diagnosing Readiness

(For help, go to the Lesson in green.)

Evaluating Expressions (Skills Handbook page 716)

Algebra Evaluate each expression for the given value of x.

1. $9x - 13$ for $x = 7$ **2.** $90 - 3x$ for $x = 31$ **3.** $\frac{1}{2}x + 14$ for $x = 23$

Solving Equations (Algebra 1 Review, page 24)

Algebra Solve each equation.

4. $2x - 17 = 4$

5. $3x + 8 = 53$

6. $(10x + 5) + (6x - 1) = 180$

7. $(x + 21) + (2x + 9) = 90$

8. $3x + 4 = 2x - 1$

9. $3(x + 8) = 12$

10. $2(x + 4) = x + 13$

11. $7x + 5 = 5x + 17$

12. $14x = 2(5x + 14)$

13. $2(3x - 4) + 10 = 5(x + 4)$

Segments and Angles (Lesson 1-4)

Use the figure at the right.

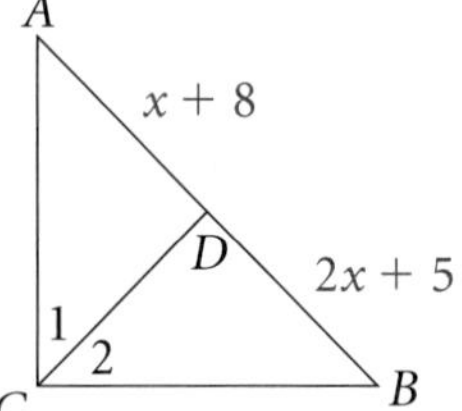

14. Name $\angle 1$ in two other ways.

15. Name the vertex of $\angle 2$.

16. If D is the midpoint of $\overline{AB}$, find x.

17. If $m\angle ADC$ and $m\angle BDC$ have a sum of 180, name the straight angle.

18. If $\angle 1 \cong \angle 2$, name the bisector of $\angle ACB$.

19. If $m\angle 2 = 45$ and $\angle ACB$ is a right angle, find $m\angle 1$.

20. If $\angle ACB$ is a right angle, $m\angle 1 = 4x$ and $m\angle 2 = 2x + 18$, find $m\angle 1$ and $m\angle 2$.

Reasoning and Proof

Chapter 2

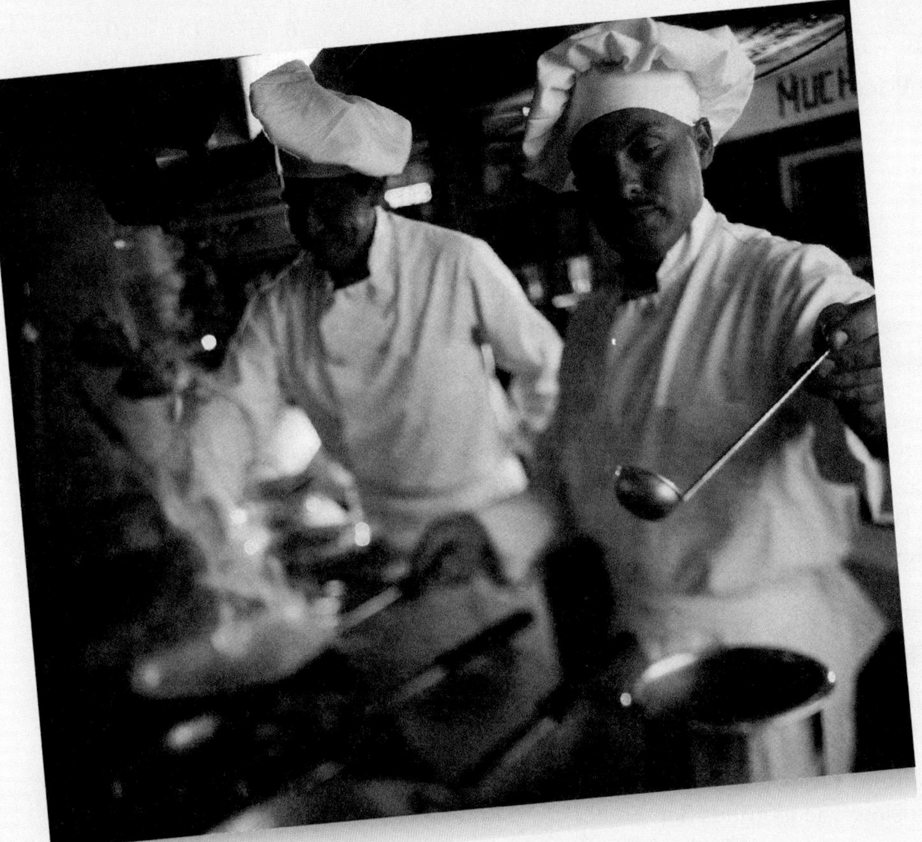

Where You're Going

- In this chapter, you will learn how to write special types of statements known as conditionals, biconditionals, and definitions.
- You will use such statements and deductive reasoning to conclude that other statements are true.
- Understanding how deductive reasoning works, you will apply it to form conclusions using algebra.
- You will also use it to study elementary proofs and form your first significant conclusions about geometric relationships.

Real-World Snapshots Applying what you learn, you will do activities involving food on pages 110 and 111.

LESSONS

Key Vocabulary

- adjacent angles (p. 96)
- biconditional (p. 75)
- complementary angles (p. 96)
- conclusion (p. 68)
- conditional (p. 68)
- converse (p. 69)
- deductive reasoning (p. 82)
- hypothesis (p. 68)
- Law of Detachment (p. 82)
- Law of Syllogism (p. 83)
- hypothesis (p. 68)
- reflexive (p. 91)
- supplementary angles (p. 96)
- symmetric (p. 91)
- theorem (p. 98)
- transitive (p. 91)
- truth value (p. 69)
- vertical angles (p. 96)

2-1 Conditional Statements

Lesson Preview

What You'll Learn

To recognize conditional statements

To write converses of conditional statements

. . . And Why

To help you read critically, as in Example 7

✔ Check Skills You'll Need

(For help, go to the Skills Handbook pages 719 and 720.)

x^2 Algebra **Solve each equation.**

1. $y + 1 = 0$ **2.** $|x| = 2$ **3.** $17 = 15 + z$

4. $x + 4 = 0$ **5.** $|n| = 0$ **6.** $m - 9 = -10$

New Vocabulary • conditional • hypothesis • conclusion • truth value • converse

Interactive lesson includes instant self-check, tutorials, and activities.

OBJECTIVE 1

Conditional Statements

You have heard *if-then* statements such as this one:

If you are not completely satisfied, then your money will be refunded.

Another name for an *if-then* statement is a **conditional.** Every conditional has two parts. The part following *if* is the **hypothesis,** and the part following *then* is the **conclusion.**

1 EXAMPLE Identifying the Hypothesis and the Conclusion

Identify the hypothesis and the conclusion of this conditional statement:

If today is the first day of fall, then the month is September.

Hypothesis: Today is the first day of fall.

Conclusion: The month is September.

✔ Check Understanding 1 Identify the hypothesis and the conclusion of this conditional statement:

If $y - 3 = 5$, then $y = 8$.

You can write many sentences as conditionals.

2 EXAMPLE Writing a Conditional

Write each sentence as a conditional.

a. A rectangle has four right angles.
If a figure is a rectangle, then it has four right angles.

b. A tiger is an animal.
If something is a tiger, then it is an animal.

✔ Check Understanding 2 Write each sentence as a conditional.

a. An integer that ends with 0 is divisible by 5.

b. A square has four congruent sides.

A conditional can have a **truth value** of *true* or *false*. To show that a conditional is true, show that every time the hypothesis is true, the conclusion is also true. To show that a conditional is false, you need to find only one counterexample for which the hypothesis is true and the conclusion is false.

3 EXAMPLE Finding a Counterexample

Show that this conditional is false by finding a counterexample:
If it is February, then there are only 28 days in the month.

To show that this conditional is false, you need to find one counterexample that makes the hypothesis true and the conclusion false.

February in the year 2008 is a counterexample. Because 2008 is a leap year, the month of February has 29 days.

The conditional is false because February 2008 is a counterexample.

✓ Check Understanding 3 Show that this conditional is false by finding a counterexample:
If the name of a state contains the word *New*, then the state borders an ocean.

You can use a Venn diagram to better understand true conditional statements.

4 EXAMPLE Using a Venn Diagram

Draw a Venn diagram to illustrate this conditional:
If you live in Chicago, then you live in Illinois.

The set of things that satisfy the hypothesis lies inside the set of things that satisfy the conclusion.

✓ Check Understanding 4 Draw a Venn diagram to illustrate this conditional:
If something is a cocker spaniel, then it is a dog.

OBJECTIVE 2 Converses

The **converse** of a conditional switches the hypothesis and the conclusion.

5 EXAMPLE Writing the Converse of a Conditional

Write the converse of the following conditional.

Conditional
If two lines intersect to form right angles, then they are perpendicular.

Converse
If two lines are perpendicular, then they intersect to form right angles.

✓ Check Understanding 5 Write the converse of the following conditional.
If two lines are not parallel and do not intersect, then they are skew.

In Example 5, both the original conditional and its converse are true. It is possible for a conditional and its converse to have different truth values.

6 EXAMPLE Finding the Truth Value of a Converse

Consider this true conditional statement. Write the converse and determine its truth value.

Conditional
If a figure is a square, then it has four sides.

Converse
If a figure has four sides, then it is a square.

The converse is *not* true. You can use any rectangle that is not a square as a counterexample to show that the converse is false.

Check Understanding 6 Write the converse of each conditional statement. Determine the truth value of the conditional and its converse. (*Hint*: One of these conditionals is *not* true.)

a. If two lines do not intersect, then they are parallel.
b. If $x = 2$, then $|x| = 2$.

7 EXAMPLE Real-World Connection

This is an illustration by John Tenniel for *Alice's Adventures in Wonderland.*

Literature In Lewis Carroll's *Alice's Adventures in Wonderland*, the Mad Hatter states: "Why you might just as well say that 'I see what I eat' is the same thing as 'I eat what I see'!" Explain why the Mad Hatter is wrong.

The statement "I see what I eat" can be rewritten as a conditional.
"If I eat it, then I see it."

The statement "I eat what I see," can be rewritten as a conditional.
"If I see it, then I eat it."

The two statements are converses of each other. A statement and its converse do not always have the same meaning or the same truth value. The Mad Hatter is wrong to suggest that you can use one just as well as the other.

7 In *Alice's Adventures in Wonderland*, the Dormouse states:
"... that 'I breathe when I sleep' is the same thing as 'I sleep when I breathe'!"
Use conditionals to explain why this statement is wrong.

You can use symbolic form to represent a conditional and its converse. In symbolic form, the letter p stands for the hypothesis and the letter q stands for the conclusion.

Key Concepts

Summary Conditional Statements and Converses

Statement	Example	Symbolic Form	You Read It
Conditional	If an angle is a straight angle, then its measure is 180.	$p \rightarrow q$	If p, then q.
Converse	If the measure of an angle is 180, then it is a straight angle.	$q \rightarrow p$	If q, then p.

EXERCISES

For more practice, see *Extra Practice.*

Practice and Problem Solving

Practice by Example

Example 1 (page 68)

1. Identify the hypothesis and the conclusion in the cartoon.

FRANK AND ERNEST By BOB THAVES

Identify the hypothesis and conclusion of each conditional.

Reading Math

Some conditionals may omit *then*. You can insert it mentally if you wish.

2. If you want to be fit, then get plenty of exercise.

3. Algebra If $x + 20 = 32$, then $x = 12$.
4. "If you can see the magic in a fairy tale, you can face the future." — Danielle Steel, novelist
5. "If somebody throws a brick at me, I can catch it and throw it back." — Harry S Truman
6. "If you can accept defeat and open your pay envelope without feeling guilty, you're stealing." — George Allen, former NFL coach

7. "If my fans think that I can do everything I say I can do, then they're crazier than I am."— Muhammad Ali

8. ". . . if I could paint that flower in a huge scale, you could not ignore its beauty." — Georgia O'Keeffe, artist

Example 2 (page 68)

Write each sentence as a conditional.

9. Glass objects are fragile.

10. Algebra $3x - 7 = 14$ implies that $3x = 21$.
11. Whole numbers that have 2 as a factor are even.
12. All obtuse angles have measure greater than 90.
13. Good weather makes a picnic enjoyable.
14. Two skew lines do not lie in the same plane.

Example 3 (page 69)

Show that each conditional is false by finding a counterexample.

15. If it is not a weekday, then it is Saturday.

16. Odd integers less than 10 are prime.

17. If you live in a country that borders the United States, then you live in Canada.

18. If you play a sport with a ball and a bat, then you play baseball.

Example 4 (page 69)

Draw a Venn diagram to illustrate each statement.

19. If you live in New England, then you live in the United States.

20. If you play the flute, then you are a musician.

21. If an angle has measure 40, then it is acute.

22. Carrots are vegetables.

Example 5 (page 69)

Write the converse of each conditional statement.

23. If you eat your vegetables, then you grow.

24. If a triangle is a right triangle, then it has a 90° angle.

25. If two segments are congruent, then they have the same length.

26. If you do not work, you do not get paid.

Examples 6 and 7 (page 70)

Write the converse of each conditional statement. Determine the truth values of the original conditional and its converse.

27. If you travel from the United States to Kenya, then you have a passport.

28. Coordinate Geometry If a point is in the first quadrant, then its coordinates are positive.

29. Chemistry If a substance is water, then its chemical formula is H_2O.

30. Probability If the probability that an event will occur is 1, then the event is certain to occur.

31. If you are in Indiana, then you are in Indianapolis.

32. If two angles have measure 90, then the angles are congruent.

B Apply Your Skills

Write a conditional statement that each Venn diagram illustrates.

33.

Athletes

Olympians

34.

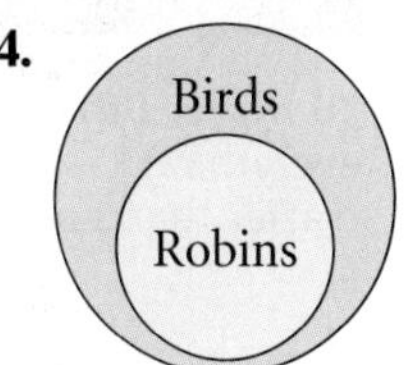

35.

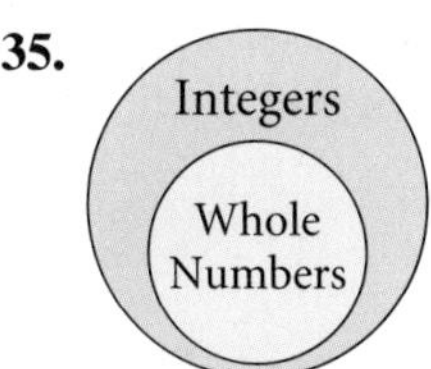

36. Error Analysis Ellen claims that both this conditional and its converse are true.

If x is an integer divisible by 3, then x^2 is an integer divisible by 3.

a. Write the converse of the conditional.

b. Only one of the statements is true. Determine which statement is false and provide a counterexample to support your answer.

Open-Ended **Write a conditional statement and its converse (different from others in this lesson) as described below.**

37. Both are true. **38.** One is true; one is false. **39.** Both are false.

Jeanette Rankin was one of nine women among 435 members of Congress at the start of World War II.

Write each statement as a conditional.

40. "We're half the people; we should be half the Congress."— Jeanette Rankin, former U.S. Congresswoman, calling for more women in office

41. "A great work is made out of a combination of obedience and liberty." — Nadia Boulanger, orchestra conductor and musical mentor

42. "A problem well stated is a problem half solved." — Charles F. Kettering, inventor

Algebra **Write the converse of each statement. If the converse is true, write *true*; if not true, provide a counterexample.**

43. If $x - 3 = 15$, then $x = 18$.

44. If y is negative, then $-y$ is positive.

45. If $x = -6$, then $|x| = 6$.

46. If $x < 0$, then $x^2 > 0$.

47. If $x = 2$, then $x^2 = 4$.

48. If $x < 0$, then $x^3 < 0$.

49. Advertising Al sees an ad that states, "You want to look good at the beach this summer. Join GoodFit Health Club." Al figures, "I am going to join GoodFit Health Club, so that I will look good at the beach."

a. Write the statement in the ad as a conditional.

b. Write Al's statement as a conditional.

c. Writing Explain why the statement in the ad does not have the same meaning as Al's statement.

Reading Math **Let p represent the statement "A figure is a square." Let q represent the statement "A figure has four congruent angles." Write the words for the symbolic statement shown. Determine the truth value of the statement. If it is false, provide a counterexample.**

50. $p \rightarrow q$

51. $q \rightarrow p$

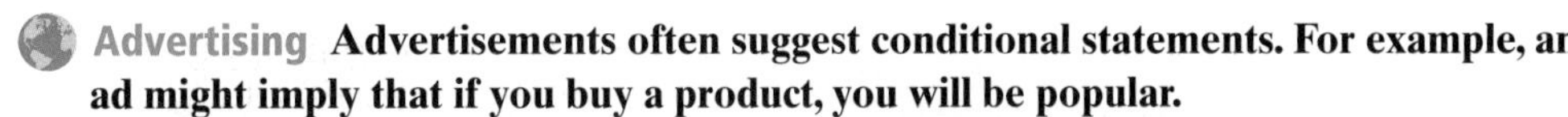

Advertising **Advertisements often suggest conditional statements. For example, an ad might imply that if you buy a product, you will be popular.**

52. What conditional is implied in the ad at the right?

53. Open-Ended Find an ad in which a conditional is used or implied.

For a few extra bucks, you could've had
TREADMASTERS.
TREADMASTER TIRES

Need Help?

Try identifying the conclusion first.

Write each postulate as a conditional statement.

54. Two intersecting lines meet in exactly one point.

55. Two intersecting planes meet in exactly one line.

56. Two congruent figures have equal areas.

57. Through any two points there is exactly one line.

58. Through any three noncollinear points there is exactly one plane.

Challenge Write a statement beginning with *All*, *Some*, or *No* to match each Venn diagram.

59. 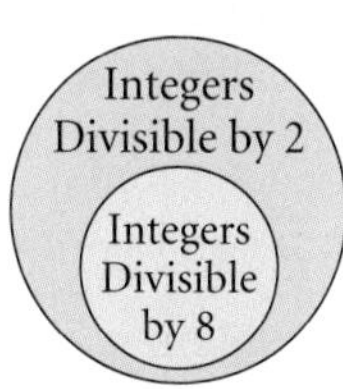

60. 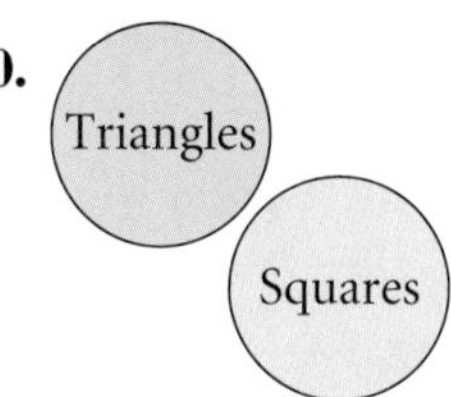

61. 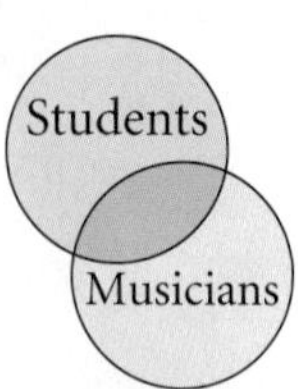

62. **Critical Thinking** You can write many statements that begin with *All* or *No* as conditionals. Give an example of each. (*Hint:* See Exercises 59–61.)

63. Let a represent an integer. Consider the five statements r, s, t, u, and v:
r: a is even. s: a is odd. t: $2a$ is even. u: $2a$ is odd. v: $2a + 1$ is odd.
How many statements of the form $p \rightarrow q$ can you make from these five statements? Decide whether each of the statements is true or false.

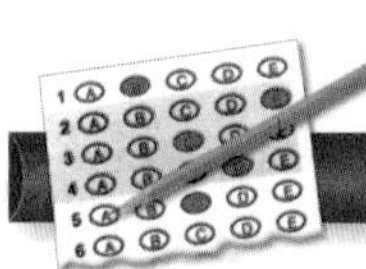

Standardized Test Prep

Multiple Choice

64. Which is the hypothesis of the following statement?
If $4 < k < 6$, then $-4 > -k > -6$.
A. $4 < k < 6$ **B.** $4 > k > 6$ **C.** $-4 > -k > -6$ **D.** $-4 < -k < -6$

65. Which is the converse of this statement?
If you can sing, then you can go with Sarah.
F. You can't sing, then you can't go with Sarah.
G. If you can't go with Sarah, then you can sing.
H. If you can't sing, then you can go with Sarah.
I. If you can go with Sarah, then you can sing.

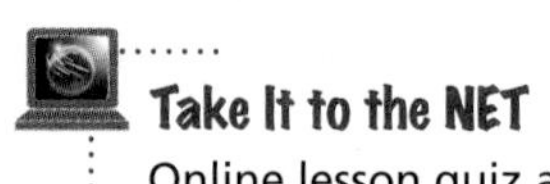
Take It to the NET
Online lesson quiz at **www.PHSchool.com**
Web Code: afa-0201

66. Which statement has a true converse?
A. If a vehicle is a car, then it has four wheels.
B. If you go to Asia from the United States, then you cross an ocean.
C. If you own a dog, then your pet is furry.
D. If you can stand up, then you can walk.

Short Response

67. Write the converse of the following statement. Determine its truth value.
If Marta is five years old, then she is too young to vote.

Mixed Review

Lesson 1-7 Find the perimeter of each rectangle with the given base and height.

68. 6 in., 12 in. **69.** 3.5 cm, 7 cm **70.** $1\frac{3}{4}$ yd, 18 in. **71.** 11 m, 60 cm

72. Find the area of a circle with diameter 10 in. Leave your answer in terms of π.

Lesson 1-6 Find the distance between the points. Round each answer to the nearest tenth.

73. $A(1, 2), B(4, -2)$ **74.** $M(-5, 1), N(0, 5)$ **75.** $R(0, -6), T(2, 3)$

Lesson 1-1 Find the pattern for each sequence. Use the pattern to show the next two terms.

76. $4, 2, 1, \frac{1}{2}, \ldots$ **77.** $5, 2, -1, -4, \ldots$ **78.** N, M, L, K, . . .

2-2 Biconditionals and Definitions

Lesson Preview

What You'll Learn

OBJECTIVE 1 To write biconditionals

OBJECTIVE 2 To recognize good definitions

. . . And Why

To evaluate definitions of letters used in the American Manual Alphabet, as in Exercises 36–40

✓ Check Skills You'll Need

(For help, go to Lesson 2-1.)

Identify the hypothesis and the conclusion of each conditional statement.

1. If $x > 10$, then $x > 5$.

2. If you live in Milwaukee, then you live in Wisconsin.

Write each statement as a conditional.

3. Squares have four sides.

4. All butterflies have wings.

Write the converse of each statement.

5. If the sun shines, then we go on a picnic.

6. If two lines are skew, then they do not intersect.

7. If $x = -3$, then $x^3 = -27$.

New Vocabulary • biconditional

Interactive lesson includes instant self-check, tutorials, and activities.

OBJECTIVE 1 Writing Biconditionals

When a conditional and its converse are true, you can combine them as a true **biconditional.** This is the statement you get by connecting the conditional and its converse with the word *and*. You can write a biconditional more concisely, however, by joining the two parts of each conditional with the phrase *if and only if*.

1 EXAMPLE Writing a Biconditional

Reading Math

Connect the conditional and its converse with *and*. Then compare with the *if and only if* form.

Consider this true conditional statement. Write its converse. If the converse is also true, combine the statements as a biconditional.

<u>Conditional</u>
If two angles have the same measure, then the angles are congruent.

<u>Converse</u>
If two angles are congruent, then the angles have the same measure.
The converse is also true.

Since both the conditional and its converse are true, you can combine them in a true biconditional by using the phrase *if and only if*.

<u>Biconditional</u>
Two angles have the same measure if and only if the angles are congruent.

✓ Check Understanding

1 Consider this true conditional statement. Write its converse. If the converse is also true, combine the statements as a biconditional.

<u>Conditional</u>
If three points are collinear, then they lie on the same line.

You can write a biconditional as two conditionals that are converses of each other.

2 EXAMPLE Separating a Biconditional Into Parts

Algebra Write two statements that form this biconditional about whole numbers:
A number is divisible by 3 if and only if the sum of its digits is divisible by 3.

Here are the two statements. They are converses of each other.

If a number is divisible by 3, then the sum of its digits is divisible by 3.

If the sum of a number's digits is divisible by 3, then the number is divisible by 3.

Check Understanding 2 Write two statements that form this biconditional about integers greater than 1:
A number is prime if and only if it has only two distinct factors, 1 and itself.

Key Concepts

Summary **Biconditional Statements**

A biconditional combines $p \rightarrow q$ and $q \rightarrow p$ as $p \leftrightarrow q$.

Statement	Example	Symbolic Form	You Read It
Biconditional	An angle is a straight angle if and only if its measure is 180.	$p \leftrightarrow q$	p if and only if q.

OBJECTIVE 2

Recognizing Good Definitions

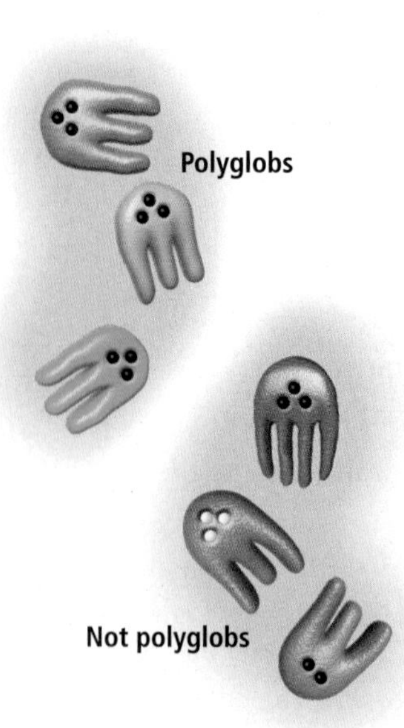

Investigation: Writing a Definition

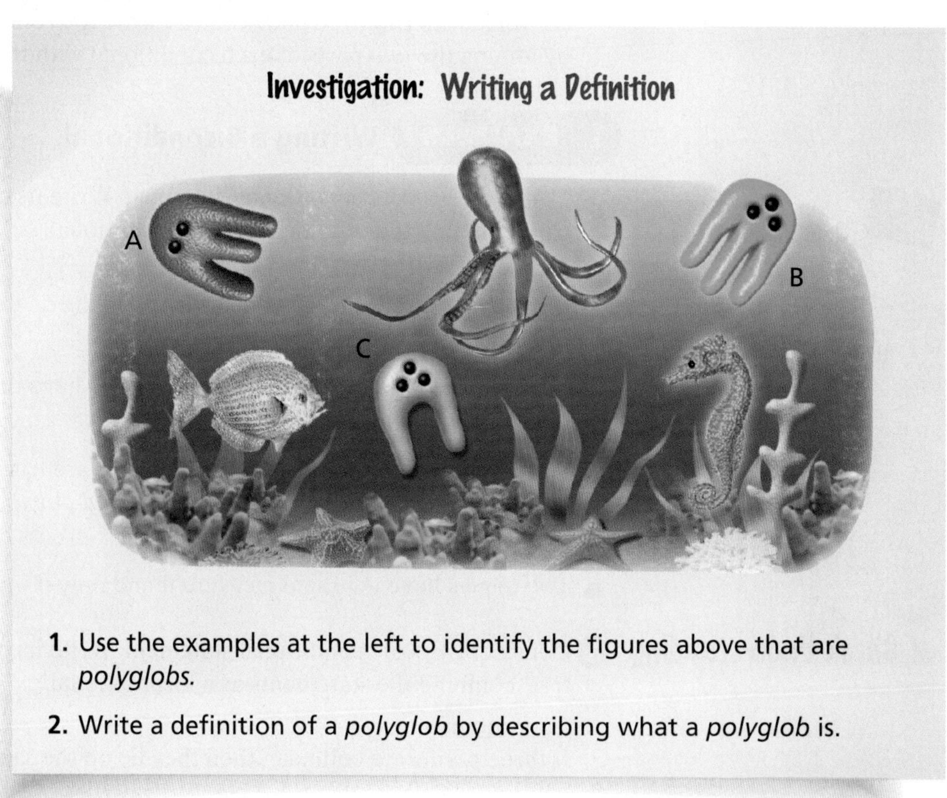

1. Use the examples at the left to identify the figures above that are *polyglobs*.
2. Write a definition of a *polyglob* by describing what a *polyglob* is.

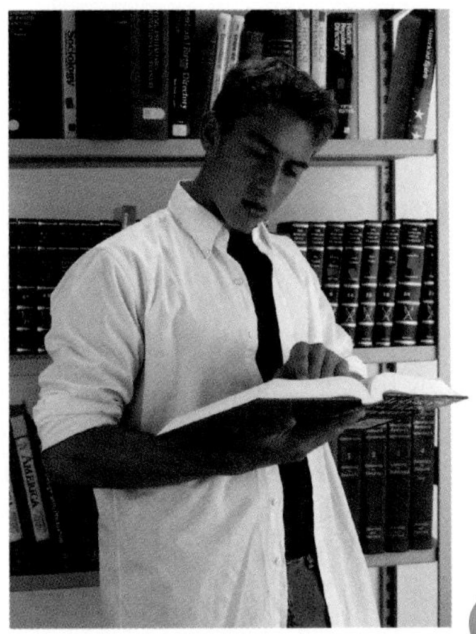

Real-World Connection

The definitions in a dictionary have to be "good definitions."

In geometry you start with undefined terms such as point, line, and plane whose meanings you understand intuitively. Then you use those terms to define other terms such as collinear points.

A good definition is a statement that can help you identify or classify an object. A good definition has several important components.

- ✔ A good definition uses clearly understood terms. The terms should be commonly understood or already defined.
- ✔ A good definition is precise. Good definitions avoid words such as *large*, *sort of*, and *some*.
- ✔ A good definition is reversible. That means that you can write a good definition as a true biconditional.

3 EXAMPLE Writing a Definition as a Biconditional

Show that this definition of *perpendicular lines* is reversible. Then write it as a true biconditional.

Definition
Perpendicular lines are two lines that intersect to form right angles.

Conditional
If two lines are perpendicular, then they intersect to form right angles.

Converse
If two lines intersect to form right angles, then they are perpendicular.

The two conditionals—converses of each other—are true, so the definition can be written as a true biconditional.

Biconditional
Two lines are perpendicular if and only if they intersect to form right angles.

Check Understanding 3 Show that this definition of *right angle* is reversible. Then write it as a true biconditional.

Definition
A right angle is an angle whose measure is 90.

One way to show that a statement is *not* a good definition is to find a counterexample.

4 EXAMPLE Real-World Connection

Need Help?
Think about the Venn diagram for "An airplane is a vehicle that flies."

Language Arts Is the given statement a good definition? Explain.

a. An airplane is a vehicle that flies.

The statement is not a good definition because it is not reversible. A helicopter is a counterexample. A helicopter is a vehicle that flies, but a helicopter is not an airplane.

b. A triangle has sharp corners.
The statement is not a good definition because it uses the imprecise word *sharp*, and it is not reversible.

Check Understanding 4 Is the following statement a good definition? Explain.
A square is a figure with four right angles.

EXERCISES

For more practice, see *Extra Practice.*

Practice and Problem Solving

Practice by Example

Example 1 (page 75)

Each conditional statement below is true. Write its converse. If the converse is also true, combine the statements as a biconditional.

1. If two segments have the same length, then they are congruent.

2. **Algebra** If $x = 12$, then $2x - 5 = 19$.

3. If a number is divisible by 20, then it is even.

4. **Algebra** If $x = 3$, then $|x| = 3$.

5. In the United States, if it is July 4th, then it is Independence Day.

6. **Algebra** If $x = -10$, then $x^2 = 100$.

Example 2 (page 76)

Write the two statements that form each biconditional.

7. A line bisects a segment if and only if the line intersects the segment only at its midpoint.

8. An integer is divisible by 100 if and only if its last two digits are zeros.

9. You live in Washington, D. C., if and only if you live in the capital of the United States.

10. Two lines are parallel if and only if they are coplanar and do not intersect.

11. Two angles are congruent if and only if they have the same measure.

12. **Algebra** $x^2 = 144$ if and only if $x = 12$ or $x = -12$.

Example 3 (page 77)

Test each statement below to see if it is reversible. If so, write it as a true biconditional. If not, write *not reversible*.

13. A perpendicular bisector of a segment is a line, segment, or ray that is perpendicular to a segment at its midpoint.

14. Parallel planes are planes that do not intersect.

15. A Tarheel is a person who was born in North Carolina.

16. A rectangle is a four-sided figure with at least one right angle.

17. A midpoint of a segment is a point that divides a segment into two congruent segments.

Example 4 (page 77)

Is each statement below a good definition? If not, explain.

18. A cat is an animal with whiskers.

19. A dog is a good pet.

20. A segment is part of a line.

21. Parallel lines do not intersect.

22. A square is a figure with two pairs of parallel sides.

23. An angle bisector is a ray that divides an angle into two congruent angles.

Apply Your Skills

24. **Language Arts** Is the following a good definition? Explain.
An obtuse angle is an angle whose measure is greater than 90.

25. **Open-Ended** Choose a definition from a dictionary or from a glossary. Explain what makes the statement a good definition.

26. **Writing** Write a definition of *a line parallel to a plane.*

Need Help?

For Exercise 27, complete this sentence: Two angles are a linear pair if and only if. . .

27. Writing Use the figures below to write a good definition of *linear pair.*

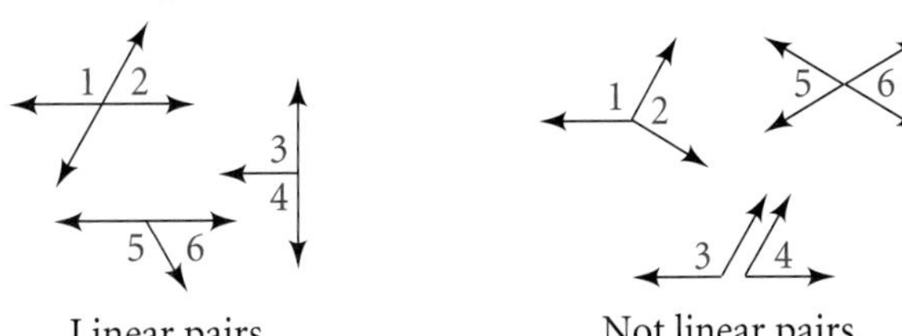

Linear pairs   Not linear pairs

Do angles 1 and 2 form a linear pair? Explain. (*Hint:* See Exercise 27.)

28. **29.** **30.** **31.**

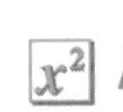

Algebra **Each conditional statement is true. If the converse is true, write a biconditional. If not, provide a counterexample to show that the converse is false.**

32. If $x = 19$, then $2x - 3 = 35$.

33. If $x = 3$, then $x^2 = 9$.

34. If $x > 0$, then $|x| > 0$.

35. If $x = 5$, then $x^3 = 125$.

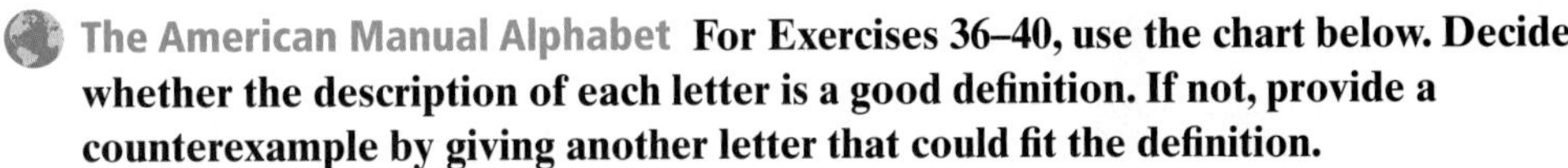

The American Manual Alphabet **For Exercises 36–40, use the chart below. Decide whether the description of each letter is a good definition. If not, provide a counterexample by giving another letter that could fit the definition.**

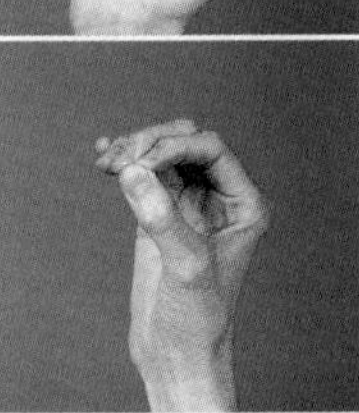

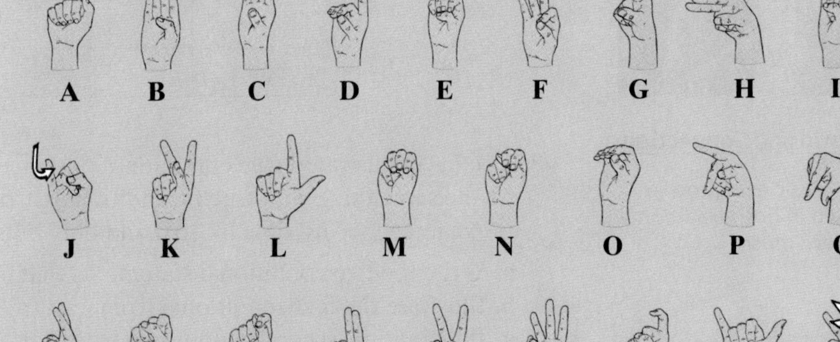

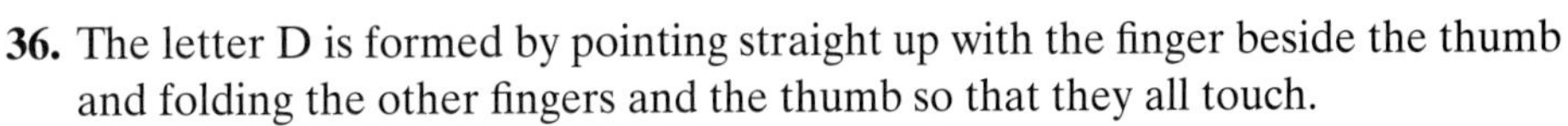

36. The letter D is formed by pointing straight up with the finger beside the thumb and folding the other fingers and the thumb so that they all touch.

37. The letter K is formed by making a V with the two fingers beside the thumb.

38. You have formed the letter Y if and only if the thumb and one finger are pointing up and the other fingers are folded into the palm of your hand.

39. You have formed the letter I if and only if the smallest finger is sticking up and the other fingers are folded into the palm of your hand with your thumb folded over them, and your hand is held still.

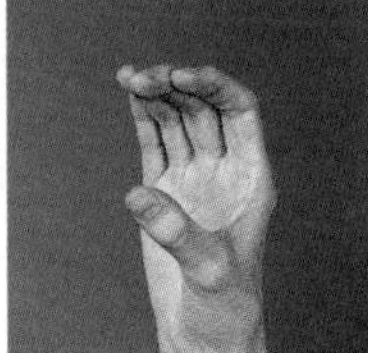

Real-World Connection

The five letters above form a word to think about.

40. You form the letter B by holding all four fingers tightly together and pointing them straight up while your thumb is folded into the palm of your hand.

Write each statement as a biconditional.

41. Congruent angles are angles with equal measure.

42. When the sum of the digits of an integer is divisible by 9, the integer is divisible by 9 and vice versa.

43. The whole numbers are the nonnegative integers.

Reading Math

The expression *vice versa* is a synonym for *conversely*.

Reading Math **Let p be the statement "$\angle A$ is an acute angle." Let q be the statement "$\angle A$ has measure between 0 and 90." Substitute for p and q and write each statement the way you would read it.**

44. $p \rightarrow q$

45. $q \rightarrow p$

46. $p \leftrightarrow q$

Challenge

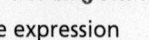

47. Reasoning In a band, Amy, Bob, and Carla are the drummer, guitarist, and keyboard player. Use the clues to find the instrument that each one plays.

Carla and the drummer wear different-colored shirts.
The keyboard player is older than Bob.
Amy, the youngest band member, lives next door to the guitarist.

You can solve this type of logic puzzle by eliminating possibilities. Copy the grid below. Put an X in a box once you eliminate it as a possibility.

Instrument	Amy	Bob	Carla
Drums			
Guitar			
Keyboard			

Real-World Connection

Careers Music educators are well-versed in both traditional and modern music.

48. You have illustrated true conditional statements with Venn diagrams. You can do the same thing with true biconditionals. Consider the following statement.

An integer is divisible by 10 if and only if its last digit is 0.

a. Write the two conditional statements that make up this biconditional.
b. Illustrate the first conditional from part (a) with a Venn diagram.
c. Illustrate the second conditional from part (a) with a Venn diagram.
d. Combine your two Venn diagrams from parts (b) and (c) to form a Venn diagram representing the biconditional statement.
e. What must be true of the Venn diagram for any true biconditional statement?
f. Reasoning How does your conclusion in part (e) help to explain why a good definition can be written as a biconditional?

49. Reasoning Alan, Ben, and Cal are seated as shown with their eyes closed. Diane places a hat on each of their heads from a box they know contains 3 red and 2 blue hats. They open their eyes and look forward.

Alan says,
"I cannot deduce what color hat I'm wearing."
Hearing that, Ben says, "I cannot deduce what color I'm wearing, either."
Cal then says, "I know what color I'm wearing!"

How does Cal know the color of his hat?

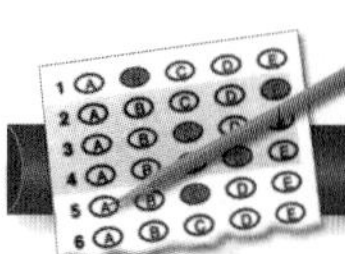

Standardized Test Prep

Multiple Choice

50. Which statement is a good definition?
A. Skew lines are lines that do not intersect.
B. Parallel lines are lines that do not intersect.
C. A square is a rectangle with four congruent sides.
D. Right angles are angles formed by two intersecting lines.

51. Which statement is NOT true?
F. If two lines are parallel, then they lie in one plane and do not intersect.
G. Two lines lie in one plane if and only if the lines are parallel.
H. If two coplanar lines do not intersect, then the lines are parallel.
I. Two lines lie in one plane and do not intersect if and only if the two lines are parallel.

Take It to the NET
Online lesson quiz at **www.PHSchool.com**
Web Code: afa-0202

52. Which statement is NOT true?
A. If $x = 1$, then $x^2 = 1$. **B.** If $x^2 = 1$, then $x = 1$.
C. If $x = -1$, then $x^2 = 1$. **D.** $x^2 = 1$ if and only if $x = 1$ or $x = -1$.

Short Response

53. Write the two conditionals that form this biconditional:
You can go to the movies if and only if you do your homework.

Extended Response

54. Here is a true conditional statement:
If a person is 18 years old, that person is old enough to vote.
a. Write the converse.
b. Determine whether the converse is true or false.
c. If the converse is false, give a counterexample to show that it is false. If the converse is true, combine the original statement and its converse by writing a biconditional.

Mixed Review

Lesson 2-1

Write each statement as a conditional.

55. Whole numbers that end in zero are even.

56. When $x = -5, x^2 = 25$.

57. Sunday is a weekend day.

58. All prime numbers greater than 2 are odd.

Lesson 1-5

59. Draw a segment $\overline{XY}$. Construct a bisector of $\overline{XY}$.

60. Draw an acute angle, $\angle 1$. Construct an angle congruent to $\angle 1$.

61. Draw an obtuse angle, $\angle CAD$. Construct the bisector of $\angle CAD$.

Lesson 1-2

Use the figure at the right to name each of the following.

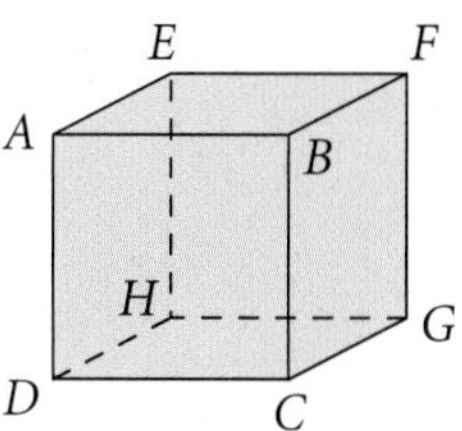

62. two intersecting lines **63.** two skew lines

64. two parallel lines **65.** two parallel planes

66. three coplanar points **67.** two intersecting planes

68. a plane that contains H

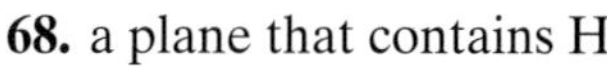

69. the intersection of two planes

2-3 Deductive Reasoning

Lesson Preview

What You'll Learn

To use the Law of Detachment

To use the Law of Syllogism

. . . And Why

To use deductive reasoning to conclude that the Nile River is the longest river in the world, as in Example 5

✓ Check Skills You'll Need

(For help, go to Lesson 2-1.)

Write the converse of each statement.

1. If you don't sleep enough, then your grades suffer.

2. If you want to arrive on time, then you must start early.

Write each statement as a conditional.

3. Leap years have 366 days.

4. Students who do not complete their homework will have lower grades.

5. Two lines that are perpendicular meet to form right angles.

6. Every sixteen-year-old is a teenager.

New Vocabulary
- deductive reasoning
- Law of Detachment
- Law of Syllogism

Interactive lesson includes instant self-check, tutorials, and activities.

OBJECTIVE

1 Using the Law of Detachment

Real-World Connection

Careers An auto mechanic uses deductive reasoning as in Example 1.

In Chapter 1 you learned that inductive reasoning is based on observing what has happened and then making a conjecture about what will happen. In this lesson, you will study deductive reasoning.

Deductive reasoning (or logical reasoning) is the process of reasoning logically from given statements to a conclusion. If the given statements are true, deductive reasoning produces a true conclusion.

Many people use deductive reasoning in their jobs. A physician diagnosing a patient's illness uses deductive reasoning. A carpenter uses deductive reasoning to determine what materials are needed at a work site.

1 EXAMPLE Real-World Connection

Auto Maintenance An auto mechanic knows that if a car has a dead battery, the car will not start. A mechanic begins work on a car and finds the battery is dead. What conclusion can she make?

The mechanic can conclude that the car will not start.

✓ Check Understanding

1 **Critical Thinking** Suppose that a mechanic begins work on a car and finds that the car will not start. Can the mechanic conclude that the car has a dead battery? Explain.

In Example 1 the mechanic is using a law of deductive reasoning called the **Law of Detachment.**

Key Concepts

Property **Law of Detachment**

If a conditional is true and its hypothesis is true, then its conclusion is true.

In symbolic form:
If $p \rightarrow q$ is a true statement and p is true, then q is true.

Reading Math

You can read $p \rightarrow q$ as "p implies q."

2 EXAMPLE Using the Law of Detachment

For the given true statements, what can you conclude?

Given: If M is the midpoint of a segment, then it divides the segment into two congruent segments.
M is the midpoint of $\overline{AB}$.

You are given that a conditional and its hypothesis are true. By the Law of Detachment, you can conclude that M divides $\overline{AB}$ into two congruent segments, or $\overline{AM} \cong \overline{MB}$.

Check Understanding 2 If a baseball player is a pitcher, then that player should not pitch a complete game two days in a row. Vladimir Nuñez is a pitcher. On Monday, he pitches a complete game. What can you conclude?

3 EXAMPLE Real-World Connection

Does the following argument illustrate the Law of Detachment?

Given: If it is snowing, then the temperature is less than or equal to 32°F.
The temperature is 20°F.

You conclude: It must be snowing.

You are given that a conditional and its conclusion are true.
You cannot apply the Law of Detachment and conclude that the hypothesis is true.
You cannot come to any conclusion about whether it is snowing from the information given.

Check Understanding 3 If possible, use the Law of Detachment to draw a conclusion. If it is not possible to use this law, explain why.

Given: If a road is icy, then driving conditions are hazardous.
Driving conditions are hazardous.

OBJECTIVE

2 Using the Law of Syllogism

Another law of deductive reasoning is the Law of Syllogism. The **Law of Syllogism** allows you to state a conclusion from two true conditional statements when the conclusion of one statement is the hypothesis of the other statement.

Key Concepts

Property **Law of Syllogism**

If $p \rightarrow q$ and $q \rightarrow r$ are true statements, then $p \rightarrow r$ is a true statement.

4 EXAMPLE Using the Law of Syllogism

Need Help?

2 is a repeated factor of 12 because it appears more than once in the prime factorization of 12.

$12 = 2 \cdot 2 \cdot 3$

Algebra Use the Law of Syllogism to draw a conclusion from the following true statements.

If a number is prime, then it does not have repeated factors.
If a number does not have repeated factors, then it is not a perfect square.

You have two true conditionals where the conclusion of one is the hypothesis of the other. You can use the Law of Syllogism to draw the following conclusion:

If a number is prime, then it is not a perfect square.

Check Understanding 4 If possible, state a conclusion using the Law of Syllogism. If it is not possible to use this law, explain why.

a. If a number ends in 0, then it is divisible by 10.
If a number is divisible by 10, then it is divisible by 5.

b. If a number ends in 6, then it is divisible by 2.
If a number ends in 4, then it is divisible by 2.

You can use both the Law of Detachment and the Law of Syllogism to draw conclusions.

Real-World Connection

Over 99% of Egypt's people live close to the Nile River.

5 EXAMPLE Real-World Connection

Geography Use the Law of Detachment and the Law of Syllogism to draw conclusions from the following true statements.

If a river is more than 4000 mi long, then it is longer than the Amazon.
If a river is longer than the Amazon, then it is the longest river in the world.
The Nile is 4132 mi long.

You can use the first two statements and the Law of Syllogism to conclude:
If a river is more than 4000 mi long, then it is the longest river in the world.

With this, the fact that the Nile is 4132 mi long, and the Law of Detachment, you can also conclude:
The Nile is the longest river in the world.

Check Understanding 5 Use the Law of Detachment and the Law of Syllogism to draw conclusions.

The Volga River is in Europe.
If a river is less than 2300 mi long, it is not one of the world's ten longest rivers.
If a river is in Europe, then it is less than 2300 mi long.

EXERCISES

For more practice, see *Extra Practice*.

Practice and Problem Solving

A Practice by Example

Examples 1 and 2 (pages 82 and 83)

Use the Law of Detachment to draw a conclusion.

1. If a student gets an A on a final exam, then the student will pass the course.
Felicia gets an A on the music theory final exam.

2. If a student wants to go to college, then the student must study hard.
Rashid wants to go to the University of North Carolina.

3. If two lines are parallel, then they do not intersect.
Line ℓ is parallel to line m.

4. If there is lightning, then it is not safe to be out in the open.
Marla sees lightning from the soccer field.

Example 3 (page 83)

If possible, use the Law of Detachment to draw a conclusion. If not possible, write *not possible.*

Real-World Connection

Hockey wing Nadine Muzerall is a Golden Gopher (Exercise 9).

5. If a figure is a rectangle, then it has two pairs of parallel sides.
Figure $ABCD$ is a rectangle.

6. **Algebra** If n is a prime number greater than 2, then n^2 is an odd number.
9^2 is an odd number.

7. If three points are on the same line, then they are collinear.
Points X, Y, and Z are on line m.

8. If an angle is obtuse, then it is not acute.
$\angle XYZ$ is not obtuse.

9. If you are a Golden Gopher, you've attended the University of Minnesota.
(See photo.)

Example 4 (page 84)

Use the Law of Syllogism to draw a conclusion.

10. **Zoology** If an animal is a red wolf, then its scientific name is *Canis rufus*.
If an animal is named *Canis rufus*, then it is endangered.

11. If two planes intersect, then they intersect in a line.
If two planes are not parallel, then they intersect.

12. If you read a good book, then you enjoy yourself.
If you enjoy yourself, then your time is well spent.

13. If you are studying biology, then you are studying a science.
If you are studying botany, then you are studying biology.

Example 5 (page 84)

Geography **Use the Law of Detachment and the Law of Syllogism to draw conclusions from the following statements.**

14. If a mountain is the highest in Alaska, then it is the highest in the United States.
If an Alaskan mountain is over 20,300 ft high, then it is the highest in Alaska.
Alaska's Mount McKinley is 20,320 ft high.

15. If you live in Little Rock, then you live in Arkansas.
Levon lives in Little Rock.
If you live in Arkansas, then you live in the 25th state to enter the Union.

B Apply Your Skills

For Exercises 16–21, assume that the following statements are true.

A. If Maria drinks juice, then it is breakfast time.
B. If it is lunchtime, then Kira drinks milk and nothing else.
C. If it is mealtime, then Curtis drinks water and nothing else.
D. If it is breakfast time, then Julio drinks juice and nothing else.
E. Maria drinks juice.

Use only the information given above. For each statement, write *must be true*, *may be true*, or *is not true*. Explain your reasoning.

16. Julio drinks juice. 17. Curtis drinks water. 18. Kira drinks milk.

19. Curtis drinks juice. 20. Maria drinks water. 21. Julio drinks milk.

Real-World Connection

Average ocean temperature in Key West is about 80°F, a good snorkeling temperature.

For each of the following, write the first statement as a conditional. If possible, use the Law of Detachment to make a conclusion. If not possible, write *not possible.*

22. All national parks are interesting.
Mammoth Cave is a national park.

23. Weather The temperature is always above 32°F in Key West, Florida.
The temperature is 62°F.

24. Every high school student likes music.
Ling likes music.

25. All squares are rectangles.
ABCD is a square.

26. Writing Give an example of a rule used in your school that could be written as a conditional. Explain how the Law of Detachment is used in applying that rule.

For Exercises 27–31, use the cartoon and deductive reasoning to answer *yes* or *no*. If *no*, explain.

27. Is a person with a red car allowed to park here on Tuesday at 10:00 A.M.?

28. Is a man with a beard allowed to park here on Monday at 10:30 A.M.?

29. Is a woman with a wig allowed to park here on Saturday at 10:00 A.M.?

30. Is a person with a blue car allowed to park here on Tuesday at 9:05 A.M.?

31. Is a person with a convertible with leather seats allowed to park here on Sunday at 6:00 P.M.?

32. Reasoning Assume that the following statements are true.

If Anita goes to the concert, Beth will go.
If Beth goes to the concert, Aisha will go.
If Aisha goes to the concert, Ramon will go.

Only two of the four students went to the concert. Who were they?

33. Critical Thinking Consider the following given statements and conclusion.

Given: If an animal is a fish, then it has gills.
A turtle does not have gills.

You conclude: A turtle is not a fish.

This argument does not use the Law of Syllogism or the Law of Detachment, but it does use good deductive reasoning.

a. Draw a Venn diagram to illustrate the given information.

b. Use the Venn diagram to help explain why the argument uses good reasoning.

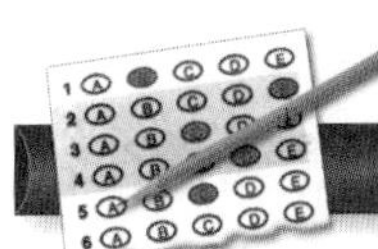

Standardized Test Prep

Multiple Choice

34. What conclusion can you draw from the following two statements?

If a person does not get enough sleep, that person will be tired.
Evan does not get enough sleep.

A. Evan will get enough sleep.
B. Evan will not be tired.
C. Evan should get enough sleep.
D. Evan will be tired.

35. What conclusion can you draw from the following two statements?

If you have a job, then you have an income.
If you have an income, then you must pay taxes.

F. If you have a job, then you must pay taxes.
G. If you don't have a job, then you don't pay taxes.
H. If you pay taxes, then you have a job.
I. If you have a job, then you don't have to pay taxes.

Short Response

36. Carl reads anything Andrea chooses to read. Bert reads what Carl chooses to read and Carl reads what Bert chooses. Andrea reads whatever Darla chooses to read.

a. Carl is reading *Hamlet*. Who else, if anyone, must also be reading *Hamlet*?
b. Exactly three people are reading *King Lear*. Who are they? Explain.

Extended Response

37. Harold, Clara, and Mark each chose a different lunch from three categories: soup, salad, and sandwiches. Each ordered a different drink. Clara will not eat sandwiches. Mark won't eat salad or bread. The person who had the soup also had the iced tea. The person who had the sandwich also had the milk.

a. Who drank the milk? How do you know?
b. One person ordered mineral water. What food did the water go with? Explain.

Take It to the NET
Online lesson quiz at
www.PHSchool.com
Web Code: afa-0203

Mixed Review

Lesson 2-2

Is each statement a good definition? If not, find a counterexample.

38. An angle is a figure formed by two rays.

39. A ray is an angle bisector if and only if it divides an angle into two congruent angles.

Lesson 2-1

Show that each conditional is false by finding a counterexample.

40. Geography If the name of a state contains the word *North*, then the state borders Canada.

x^2 **41.** Algebra If you square a fraction, then the result is always greater than the original fraction.

Lesson 1-3

Complete with *always*, *sometimes*, or *never* to make a true statement.

42. Two lines that do not intersect are __?__ parallel.

43. Two lines that intersect are __?__ skew.

44. Two segments that intersect are __?__ coplanar.

Checkpoint Quiz 1 — Lessons 2-1 through 2-3

Instant self-check quiz online and on CD-ROM

1. Identify the hypothesis and the conclusion of this conditional statement:
   If $x > 5$, then $x^2 > 25$.
2. Write this statement as a conditional: Roses are beautiful flowers.

For Exercises 3 and 4, use this conditional statement:
If an integer ends with 0, then the integer is divisible by 2.

3. Write the converse of the statement.
4. Find a counterexample to show that the converse is *not* true.
5. Write the two conditionals that make up this biconditional:
   An angle is an acute angle if and only if its measure is between 0 and 90.
6. Rewrite this definition as a biconditional:
   Points that lie on the same line are collinear.
7. Find a counterexample to show that the following statement is *not* a good definition:
   A computer is a machine with a keyboard and a memory.

Use the Law of Detachment or the Law of Syllogism to draw a conclusion from each pair of statements. If not possible, write *not possible.*

8. If a student is on the basketball team, then that student has passing grades.
   Theresa is on the basketball team.
9. If a student studies geometry, the student studies mathematics.
   If a student studies mathematics, the student's mind is expanded.
10. If you miss the bus, then you will be late for school.
    You are late for school.

A Point in Time

1500 1600 1700 1800 1900 2000

Hercule Poirot as played by David Suchet, 1989–1997.

Most people are not detectives, but as a young woman, the English writer Agatha Christie (1890–1976) correctly deduced that many people would like to be. In 1920 she published her first book, a detective novel entitled *The Mysterious Affair at Styles* in which she introduced the eccentric and ultra-logical Belgian detective Hercule Poirot. In this and in many subsequent novels, Poirot solves mysteries not with guns or car chases but with logical reasoning.

Take It to the NET For more information about Agatha Christie, go to **www.PHSchool.com**.
Web Code: afe-2032

2-4 Reasoning in Algebra

Lesson Preview

What You'll Learn

To connect reasoning in algebra and geometry

. . . And Why

To justify steps in a logical argument, as in Example 1

✓ Check Skills You'll Need

(For help, go to Lesson 1-4.)

For Exercises 1–5, use the figure at the right.

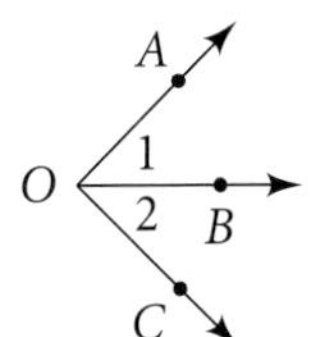

1. Name $\angle 1$ in two other ways.
2. Name the vertex of $\angle 2$.
3. If $\angle 1 \cong \angle 2$, name the bisector of $\angle AOC$.
4. If $m\angle AOC = 90$ and $m\angle 1 = 45$, find $m\angle 2$.
5. If $m\angle AOC = 90$, name two perpendicular rays.

New Vocabulary • Reflexive Property • Symmetric Property • Transitive Property

Interactive lesson includes instant self-check, tutorials, and activities.

OBJECTIVE 1

Connecting Reasoning in Algebra and Geometry

In geometry you accept postulates and properties as true. You use deductive reasoning to prove other statements. Some of the properties that you accept as true are the properties of equality from algebra. They are listed below in terms of any numbers a, b, and c.

Key Concepts

Summary Properties of Equality

Addition Property	If $a = b$, then $a + c = b + c$.
Subtraction Property	If $a = b$, then $a - c = b - c$.
Multiplication Property	If $a = b$, then $a \cdot c = b \cdot c$.
Division Property	If $a = b$ and $c \neq 0$, then $\frac{a}{c} = \frac{b}{c}$.
Reflexive Property	$a = a$
Symmetric Property	If $a = b$, then $b = a$.
Transitive Property	If $a = b$ and $b = c$, then $a = c$.
Substitution Property	If $a = b$, then b can replace a in any expression.

You also assume that other properties from algebra are true.

Key Concepts

Property The Distributive Property

$a(b + c) = ab + ac$

You use deductive reasoning every time you solve an equation. You can justify each statement that you make with a postulate, a property, or a definition. When you solve problems involving angle measures, you can use the Angle Addition Postulate.

1 EXAMPLE Justifying Steps in Solving an Equation

Algebra Solve for x and justify each step.

Given: $m\angle AOC = 139$

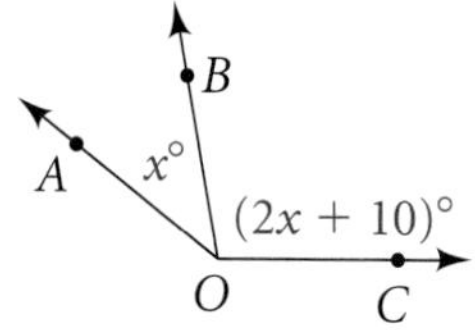

Need Help?
To review the Angle Addition Postulate, go to p. 28.

$m\angle AOB + m\angle BOC = m\angle AOC$	**Angle Addition Postulate**
$x + 2x + 10 = 139$	**Substitution Property**
$3x + 10 = 139$	**Simplify.**
$3x = 129$	**Subtraction Property of Equality**
$x = 43$	**Division Property of Equality**

✓ Check Understanding **1** Fill in each missing reason.

Given: $\overrightarrow{LM}$ bisects $\angle KLN$.

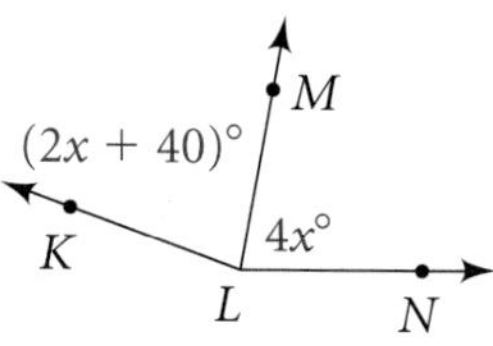

$\overrightarrow{LM}$ bisects $\angle KLN$.	**Given**
$m\angle MLN = m\angle KLM$	**Definition of angle bisector**
$4x = 2x + 40$	?
$2x = 40$	?
$x = 20$	?

You can use the Segment Addition Postulate to justify statements about lengths of segments.

2 EXAMPLE Justifying Steps in Solving an Equation

Algebra Solve for y and justify each step.

Given: $AC = 21$

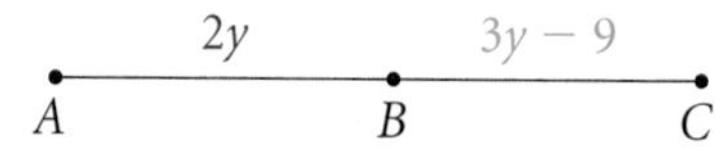

Need Help?
To review the Segment Addition Postulate, go to p. 26.

$AB + BC = AC$	**Segment Addition Postulate**
$2y + (3y - 9) = 21$	**Substitution Property**
$5y - 9 = 21$	**Simplify.**
$5y = 30$	**Addition Property of Equality**
$y = 6$	**Division Property of Equality**

✓ Check Understanding **2** Find AB and BC by substituting $y = 6$ in the expressions in the diagram above. Check that $AB + BC = 21$.

The Reflexive, Symmetric, and Transitive Properties of Equality have corresponding properties of congruence. You can use properties of congruence to justify statements.

Summary	Properties of Congruence
Reflexive Property	$\overline{AB} \cong \overline{AB}$ $\angle A \cong \angle A$
Symmetric Property	If $\overline{AB} \cong \overline{CD}$, then $\overline{CD} \cong \overline{AB}$. If $\angle A \cong \angle B$, then $\angle B \cong \angle A$.
Transitive Property	If $\overline{AB} \cong \overline{CD}$ and $\overline{CD} \cong \overline{EF}$, then $\overline{AB} \cong \overline{EF}$. If $\angle A \cong \angle B$ and $\angle B \cong \angle C$, then $\angle A \cong \angle C$.

3 EXAMPLE Using Properties of Equality and Congruence

Name the property of equality or congruence that justifies each statement.

a. $\angle K \cong \angle K$
Reflexive Property of Congruence

b. If $2x - 8 = 10$, then $2x = 18$.
Addition Property of Equality

c. If $\overline{RS} \cong \overline{TW}$ and $\overline{TW} \cong \overline{PQ}$, then $\overline{RS} \cong \overline{PQ}$.
Transitive Property of Congruence

d. If $m\angle A = m\angle B$, then $m\angle B = m\angle A$.
Symmetric Property of Equality

Check Understanding **3** Name the property of equality or congruence illustrated.

a. $\overline{XY} \cong \overline{XY}$

b. If $m\angle A = 45$ and $45 = m\angle B$, then $m\angle A = m\angle B$.

EXERCISES

For more practice, see *Extra Practice*.

Practice and Problem Solving

A Practice by Example

Examples 1 and 2 (page 90)

x^2 Algebra **Fill in the reason that justifies each step.**

1. Solve for x.

$m\angle CDE + m\angle EDF = 180$ **a.** ?

$x + (3x + 20) = 180$ **b.** ?

$4x + 20 = 180$ **c.** ?

$4x = 160$ **d.** ?

$x = 40$ **e.** ?

2. Solve for n.

Given: $XY = 42$

$XZ + ZY = XY$ **a.** ?

$3(n + 4) + 3n = 42$ **b.** ?

$3n + 12 + 3n = 42$ **c.** ?

$6n + 12 = 42$ **d.** ?

$6n = 30$ **e.** ?

$n = 5$ **f.** ?

x^2 **Algebra** **Give a reason for each step.**

3. $\frac{1}{2}x - 5 = 10$ Given
$2\left(\frac{1}{2}x - 5\right) = 20$ a. ?
$x - 10 = 20$ b. ?
$x = 30$ c. ?

4. $5(x + 3) = -4$ Given
$5x + 15 = -4$ a. ?
$5x = -19$ b. ?
$x = -\frac{19}{5}$ c. ?

Example 3 (page 91)

Name the property that justifies each statement.

5. $\angle Z \cong \angle Z$
6. $2(3x + 5) = 6x + 10$
7. If $12x = 84$, then $x = 7$.
8. If $\overline{ST} \cong \overline{QR}$, then $\overline{QR} \cong \overline{ST}$.
9. If $m\angle A = 15$, then $3m\angle A = 45$.
10. $XY = XY$
11. If $3x + 14 = 80$, then $3x = 66$.
12. If $KL = MN$, then $MN = KL$.
13. If $2x + y = 5$ and $x = y$, then $2x + x = 5$.
14. If $AB - BC = 12$, then $AB = 12 + BC$.
15. If $\angle 1 \cong \angle 2$ and $\angle 2 \cong \angle 3$, then $\angle 1 \cong \angle 3$.

B Apply Your Skills

Use the given property to complete each statement.

16. Addition Property of Equality
If $2x - 5 = 10$, then $2x = \underline{\ ?\ }$.
17. Subtraction Property of Equality
If $5x + 6 = 21$, then $\underline{\ ?\ } = 15$.
18. Symmetric Property of Equality
If $AB = YU$, then $\underline{\ ?\ }$.
19. Symmetric Property of Congruence
If $\angle H \cong \angle K$, then $\underline{\ ?\ } \cong \angle H$.
20. Reflexive Property of Congruence
$\angle PQR \cong \underline{\ ?\ }$
21. Distributive Property
$3(x - 1) = 3x - \underline{\ ?\ }$
22. Substitution Property
If $LM = 7$ and $EF + LM = NP$, then $\underline{\ ?\ } = NP$.
23. Transitive Property of Congruence
If $\angle XYZ \cong \angle AOB$ and $\angle AOB \cong \angle WYT$, then $\underline{\ ?\ }$.
24. Multiplication Property of Equality
If $\frac{1}{3}TR = UW$, then $\underline{\ ?\ }$.

Need Help?
For Exercise 25, you may want to review naming segments and angles (pp. 18 and 27).

25. **Writing** Jero claims that the statements $\overline{LR} \cong \overline{RL}$ and $\angle CBA \cong \angle ABC$ are both true by the Reflexive Property of Congruence. Explain why Jero is correct.
26. Use what you know about transitive properties to complete the following:

The Transitive Property of Falling Dominoes:

If domino A causes domino B to fall, and domino B causes domino C to fall, then domino A causes domino $\underline{\ ?\ }$ to fall.

27. Algebra Fill in the reason that justifies each step.

Given: C is the midpoint of $\overline{AD}$.

$4x$ $2x + 12$

A C D

C is the midpoint of $\overline{AD}$.	**a.** ?
$AC = CD$	**b.** ?
$4x = 2x + 12$	**c.** ?
$2x = 12$	**d.** ?
$x = 6$	**e.** ?

Reading Math

For help with reading and solving Exercise 28, see p. 95.

 **28. Algebra** In the figure at the right, $KM = 35$.

a. Solve for x. Justify each step.

b. Find the length of $\overline{KL}$.

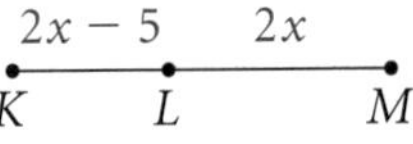

29. Algebra In the figure at the right, $m\angle GFI = 128$.

a. Solve for x. Justify each step.

b. Find $m\angle EFI$.

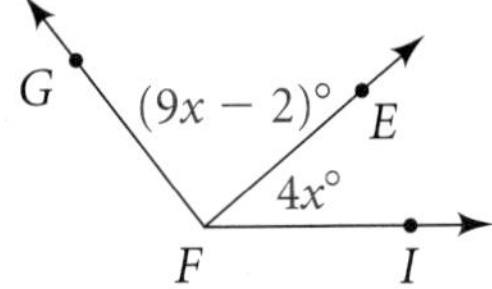

30. Algebra Fill in the reason that justifies each step.

Given: $\overrightarrow{BC}$ bisects $\angle ABD$.

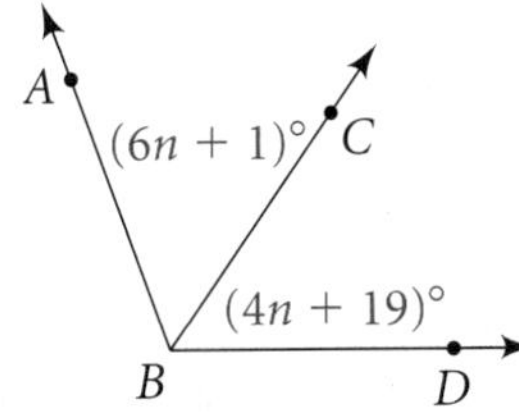

$\overrightarrow{BC}$ bisects $\angle ABD$.	**a.** ?
$m\angle ABC = m\angle CBD$	**b.** ?
$6n + 1 = 4n + 19$	**c.** ?
$2n = 18$	**d.** ?
$n = 9$	**e.** ?

Challenge

31. Error Analysis The steps below "show" that $1 = 2$. Find the error.

Given: $a = b$

$a = b$	Given
$ab = b^2$	Multiplication Property of Equality
$ab - a^2 = b^2 - a^2$	Subtraction Property of Equality
$a(b - a) = (b + a)(b - a)$	Distributive Property
$a = b + a$	Division Property of Equality
$a = a + a$	Substitution Property
$a = 2a$	Simplify.
$1 = 2$	Division Property of Equality

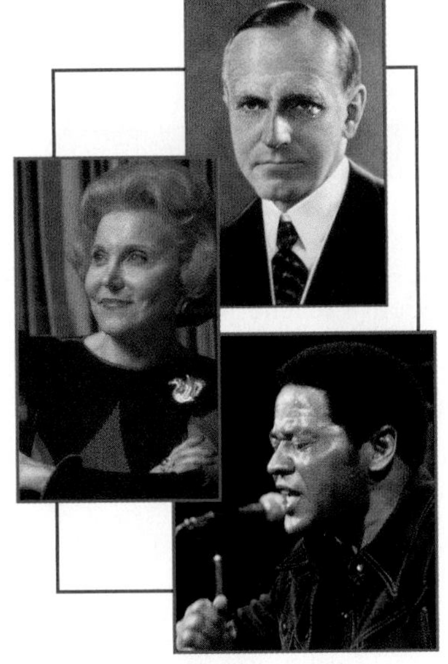

Real-World Connection

President Calvin Coolidge, advice columnist Ann Landers, and musician Bill Withers were all born on the Fourth of July. Each one of them "has the same birthday as" either one of the others.

Relationships You know that the relationships "is equal to" and "is congruent to" are reflexive, symmetric, and transitive. In a later chapter, you will see that this is also true for the relationship "is similar to." Consider the following relationships among people. State whether each relationship is reflexive, symmetric, transitive, or none of these.

Sample: The relationship "is younger than" is transitive. If Sue is younger than Fred and Fred is younger than Alana, then Sue is younger than Alana. The relationship "is younger than" is not reflexive because Sue is not younger than herself. It is also not symmetric because if Sue is younger than Fred, Fred is not younger than Sue.

32. has the same birthday as

33. is taller than

34. lives in the same state as

35. lives in a different state than

36. is the same height as

37. is a descendant of

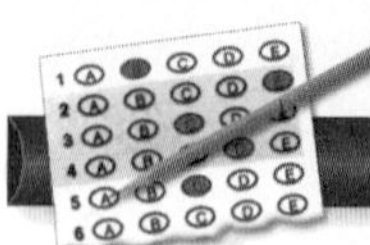

Standardized Test Prep

Multiple Choice

38. Which property justifies this statement?

If $4x = 16$, then $16 = 4x$.

A. Multiplication Property of Equality
B. Transitive Property of Equality
C. Reflexive Property of Equality
D. Symmetric Property of Equality

Quantitative Comparison

Compare the boxed quantity in Column A with the boxed quantity in Column B. Choose the best answer.

A. The quantity in Column A is greater.
B. The quantity in Column B is greater.
C. The two quantities are equal.
D. The relationship cannot be determined from the information given.

	Column A	Column B
39.	area of a circle with diameter 6 cm	area of a circle with radius 6 cm
40.	perimeter of a square with 4-in. sides	perimeter of a rectangle with a pair of 4-in. sides
41.	area of a rectangle with base 12 cm and height 5 cm	area of a square with 6 cm sides

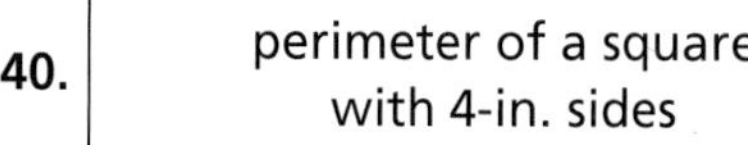

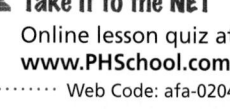

Take It to the NET
Online lesson quiz at **www.PHSchool.com**
Web Code: afa-0204

Short Response

42. In the diagram, $x = 2y + 15$ and $x + y = 120$.
a. Use a Property of Equality to explain why $3y + 15 = 120$.
b. Solve for y. Justify each step. Then find the value of x.

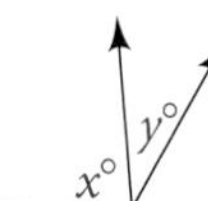

Mixed Review

Lesson 2-3

Reasoning **Use logical reasoning to draw a conclusion.**

43. If a student is having difficulty in class, then that student's teacher is concerned. Elena is having difficulty in history class.

44. If a person has a job, then that person is earning money. If a person is earning money, then that person can save money each week.

Lesson 1-4

Use the diagram at the right and find each measure.

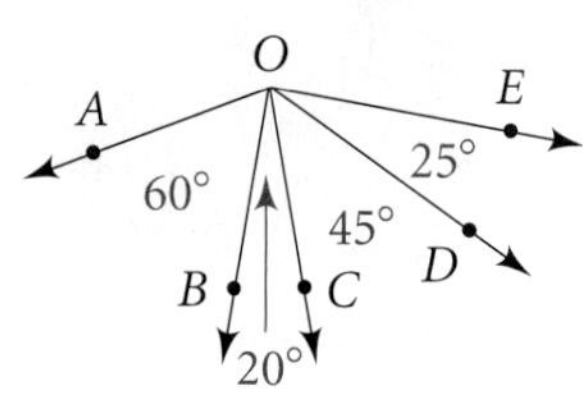

45. $m\angle AOC$ **46.** $m\angle AOD$

47. $m\angle DOB$ **48.** $m\angle BOE$

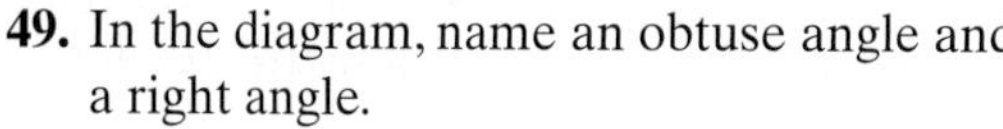

49. In the diagram, name an obtuse angle and a right angle.

Lesson 1-1

Find the next two terms in each sequence.

50. 19, 21.5, 24, 26.5 **51.** 3.4, 3.45, 3.456, 3.4567

52. −2, 6, −18, 54 **53.** 8, −4, 2, −1

Reading Math

Reading for Problem Solving

FOR USE WITH PAGE 93, EXERCISE 28

Read the problem below and then follow along with what Larissa thinks as she solves the problem. Check your understanding by solving the exercise at the bottom of the page.

 **Algebra** In the figure at the right, $KM = 35$.

a. Solve for x. Justify each step.

b. Find the length of $\overline{KL}$.

$2x - 5$ $2x$
K L M

What Larissa Thinks	What Larissa Writes	
What information am I given?	Given: KM = 35, KL = 2x − 5, LM = 2x	
Points K, L, and M are collinear. I can use the Segment Addition Postulate to write an equation.	1. KL + LM = KM	1. Segment Addition Postulate
Now I will substitute for KL, LM, and KM. I get an equation that I can solve for x.	2. (2x − 5) + 2x = 35	2. Substitute.
I simplify the left side.	3. 4x − 5 = 35	3. Simplify.
I add 5 to each side.	4. 4x = 40	4. Addition Property of Equality
I divide each side by 4.	5. x = 10	5. Division Property of Equality
Part (b) asks me to find KL. The diagram shows that $KL = 2x - 5$. I know $x = 10$, so I'll substitute to find KL.	KL = 2x − 5 = 2(10) − 5 = 20 − 5 = 15	
Now, I'll write my answer.	The length of $\overline{KL}$ is 15.	

EXERCISE

Algebra $\angle 1$ and $\angle 2$ are supplementary; $m\angle 1 = 4y + 15$ and $m\angle 2 = 7y - 11$.

a. Solve for y. Justify each step.

b. Find $m\angle 2$.

Proving Angles Congruent

Lesson Preview

What You'll Learn

To identify angle pairs

To prove and apply theorems about angles

. . . And Why

To find the measures of angles formed by the legs of a director's chair, as in Exercise 36

Check Skills You'll Need

(For help, go to Lesson 1-4.)

x^2 Algebra **Find the value of each variable.**

1.

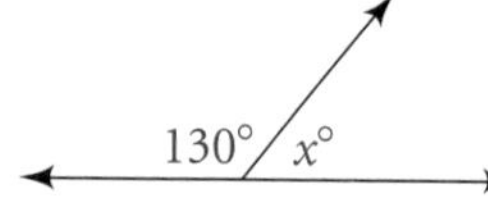

2.

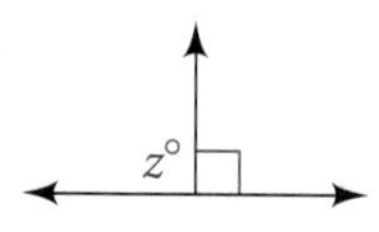

3.

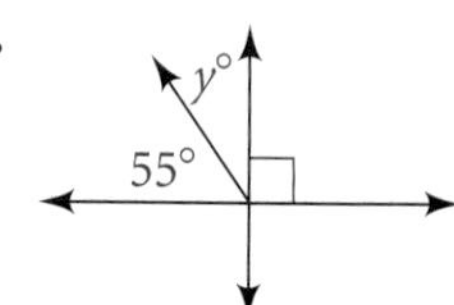

Fill in each blank.

4. Perpendicular lines are two lines that intersect to form __?__.
5. An angle is formed by two rays with the same endpoint. The endpoint is called the __?__ of the angle.

New Vocabulary
- vertical angles
- adjacent angles
- complementary angles
- supplementary angles
- theorem
- paragraph proof

OBJECTIVE

Interactive lesson includes instant self-check, tutorials, and activities.

In this lesson, you will learn about important angle pairs that have special names.

X	Helvetica Condensed
X	Times Roman
X	Eurostile Extended
X	MarkerFelt Thin

In each font, a capital X suggests vertical angles.

vertical angles

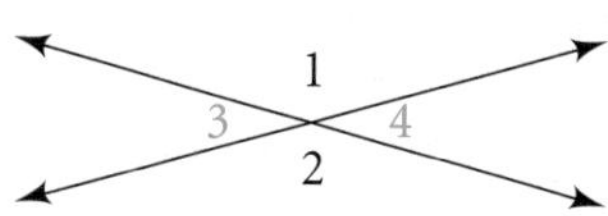

two angles whose sides form two pairs of opposite rays

adjacent angles

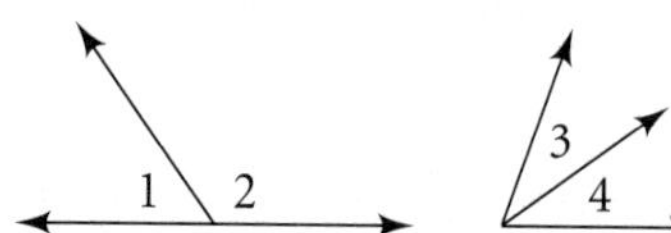

two coplanar angles with a common side, a common vertex, and no common interior points

complementary angles

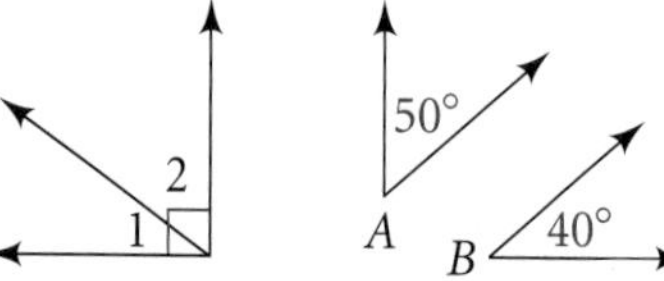

two angles whose measures have sum 90

Each angle is called the *complement* of the other.

supplementary angles

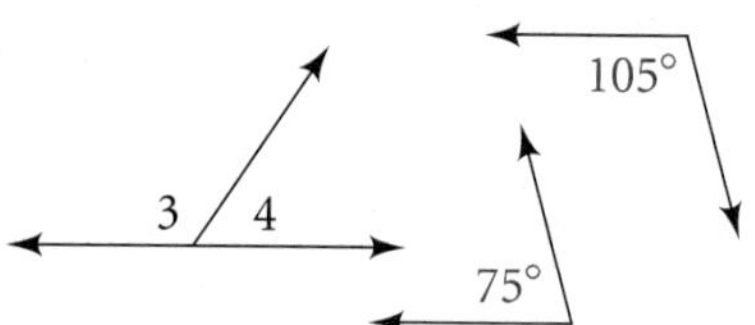

two angles whose measures have sum 180

Each angle is called the *supplement* of the other.

1 EXAMPLE Identifying Angle Pairs

In the diagram identify pairs of numbered angles that are related as follows:

a. complementary
$\angle 2$ and $\angle 3$

b. supplementary
$\angle 4$ and $\angle 5$; $\angle 3$ and $\angle 4$

c. vertical
$\angle 3$ and $\angle 5$

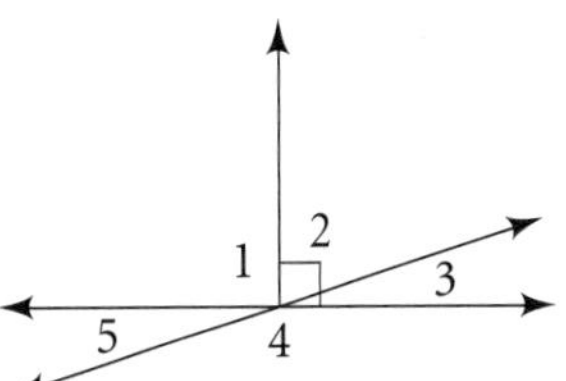

Check Understanding 1 **a.** Name two pairs of adjacent angles in the photo below.
b. If $m\angle EFD = 27$, find $m\angle AFD$.

When entering the roadway, turn and look for oncoming traffic regardless of what you see in the rear-view mirror.

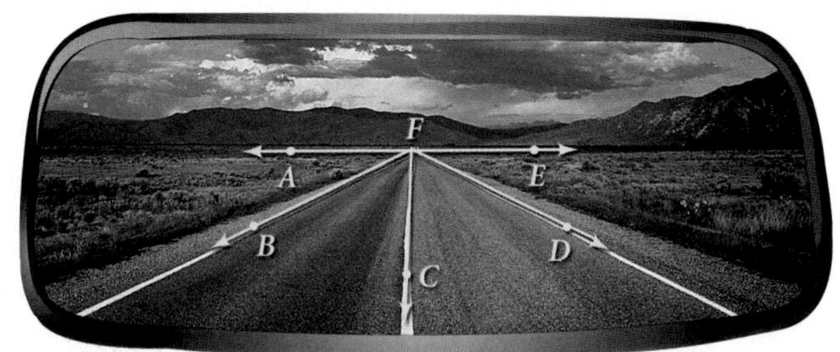

Whether you draw a diagram or use a given diagram, you can make some conclusions directly from the diagrams. You *can* conclude that angles are

- adjacent angles
- adjacent supplementary angles
- vertical angles

Unless there are marks that give this information, you *cannot* assume

- angles or segments are congruent
- an angle is a right angle
- lines are parallel or perpendicular

2 EXAMPLE Making Conclusions From a Diagram

What can you conclude from the information in the diagram?

- $\angle 1 \cong \angle 2$, by the markings.
- $\angle 2$ and $\angle 3$, for example, are adjacent angles.
- $\angle 4$ and $\angle 5$, for example, are adjacent supplementary angles,
or $m\angle 4 + m\angle 5 = 180$ by the Angle Addition Postulate.
- $\angle 1$ and $\angle 4$, for example, are vertical angles.

2 Can you make each conclusion from the information in the diagram? Explain.

a. $\overline{TW} \cong \overline{WV}$ **b.** $\overline{PW} \cong \overline{WQ}$

c. $\overline{TV} \perp \overline{PQ}$ **d.** $\overline{TV}$ bisects $\overline{PQ}$.

e. W is the midpoint of $\overline{TV}$.

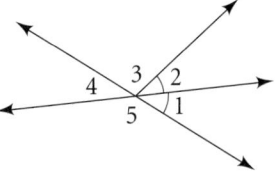

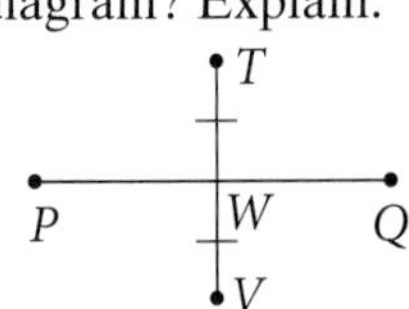

OBJECTIVE 2

Theorems About Angles

Investigation: Vertical Angles

- Draw two intersecting lines. Number the angles as shown.
- Fold the sides of ∠1 onto ∠2.
- Fold the sides of ∠3 onto ∠4.
- Make a conjecture about vertical angles.

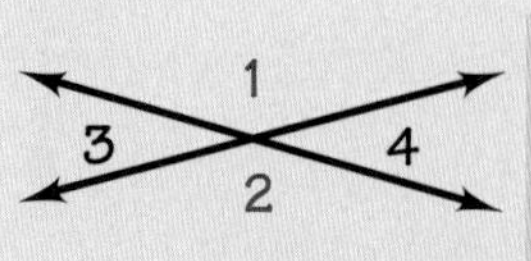

You can use deductive reasoning to show that a conjecture is true. The set of steps you take is called a proof. The statement that you prove true is a **theorem.** The Investigation above leads to a conjecture that becomes the following theorem.

Key Concepts

Theorem 2-1 **Vertical Angles Theorem**

Vertical angles are congruent.

$\angle 1 \cong \angle 2$ and $\angle 3 \cong \angle 4$

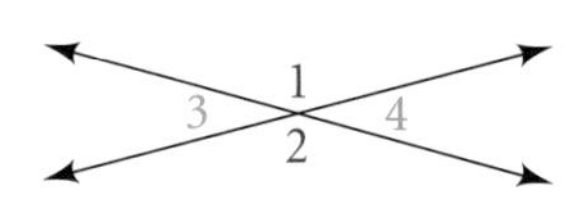

In the proof of a theorem, a "Given" list shows you what you know from the hypothesis of the theorem. You prove the conclusion of the theorem. A diagram records the given information visually.

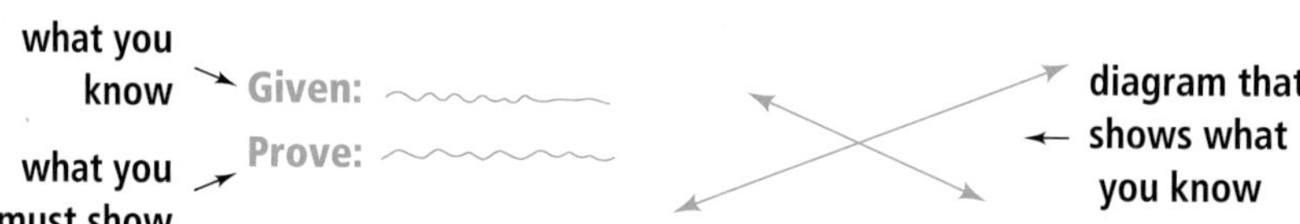

There are many forms of proofs. A **paragraph proof** is written as sentences in a paragraph. Here is a paragraph proof of Theorem 2-1.

Proof

3 EXAMPLE Proving Theorem 2-1

Study what is Given, what you Prove, and the diagram. Write a paragraph proof.

Given: ∠1 and ∠2 are vertical angles. ← what you know →

Prove: $\angle 1 \cong \angle 2$ ← what you show

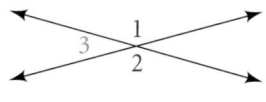

Paragraph Proof: By the Angle Addition Postulate, $m\angle 1 + m\angle 3 = 180$ and $m\angle 2 + m\angle 3 = 180$. By substitution, $m\angle 1 + m\angle 3 = m\angle 2 + m\angle 3$. Subtract $m\angle 3$ from each side. You get $m\angle 1 = m\angle 2$, or $\angle 1 \cong \angle 2$.

Check Understanding 3 **Critical Thinking** Does the size of the angles in the diagram affect the proof? Would the proof change if ∠1 and ∠2 were acute rather than obtuse? Explain.

You can use the Vertical Angles Theorem to solve for variables and find the measures of angles.

4 EXAMPLE Using the Vertical Angles Theorem

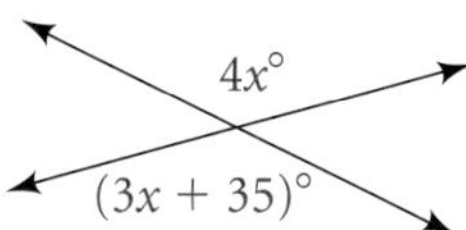

Algebra Find the value of x.

$4x = 3x + 35$ **Vertical angles are congruent.**

$x = 35$ **Subtract $3x$ from each side.**

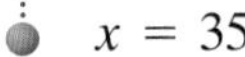

✓ Check Understanding 4 **a.** Find the measures of the labeled pair of vertical angles in the diagram above.
b. Find the measures of the other pair of vertical angles.
c. Check to see that adjacent angles are supplementary.

The Vertical Angles Theorem is actually a special case of the following theorem. A proof of this theorem is shown below. You can write a proof of another form of this theorem in Exercise 55.

Key Concepts

Theorem 2-2	Congruent Supplements Theorem
If two angles are supplements of the same angle (or of congruent angles), then the two angles are congruent.	

Proof

Proof of Theorem 2-2

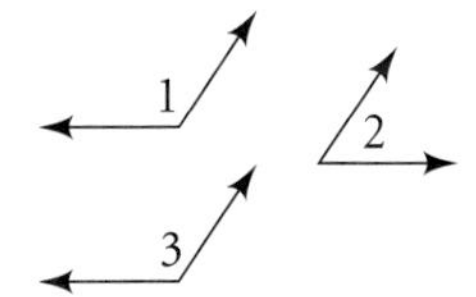

Given: $\angle 1$ and $\angle 2$ are supplementary.
$\angle 3$ and $\angle 2$ are supplementary.

Prove: $\angle 1 \cong \angle 3$

Proof: By the definition of supplementary angles, $m\angle 1 + m\angle 2 = 180$ and $m\angle 3 + m\angle 2 = 180$. By substitution, $m\angle 1 + m\angle 2 = m\angle 3 + m\angle 2$. Subtract $m\angle 2$ from each side. You get $m\angle 1 = m\angle 3$, or $\angle 1 \cong \angle 3$.

Theorem 2-3 is like the Congruent Supplements Theorem. You can demonstrate its proof in Exercises 19 and 56.

Key Concepts

Theorem 2-3	Congruent Complements Theorem
If two angles are complements of the same angle (or of congruent angles), then the two angles are congruent.	
Theorem 2-4	
All right angles are congruent.	
Theorem 2-5	
If two angles are congruent and supplementary, then each is a right angle.	

You can complete proofs of Theorems 2-4 and 2-5 in Exercises 31 and 35, respectively.

EXERCISES

For more practice, see *Extra Practice.*

Practice and Problem Solving

A Practice by Example

Example 1 (page 97)

Name an angle or angles in the diagram described by each of the following.

1. supplementary to $\angle AOD$

2. adjacent and congruent to $\angle AOE$

3. supplementary to $\angle EOA$

4. complementary to $\angle EOD$

5. a pair of vertical angles

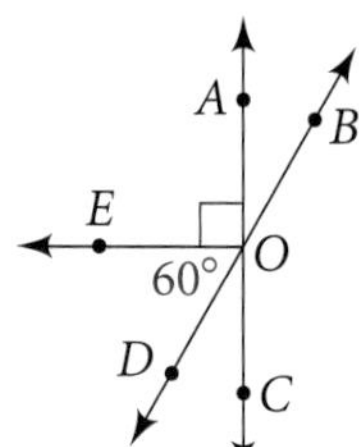

In the diagram above, find the measure of each of the following angles.

6. $\angle EOC$ **7.** $\angle DOC$ **8.** $\angle BOC$ **9.** $\angle AOB$

Example 2 (page 97)

Can you make each conclusion from the information in the diagram? Explain.

10. $\angle J \cong \angle D$

11. $\angle JAC \cong \angle DAC$

12. $\angle JAE$ and $\angle EAF$ are adjacent and supplementary.

13. $m\angle JCA = m\angle DCA$

14. $m\angle JCA + m\angle ACD = 180$

15. $\overline{AJ} \cong \overline{AD}$

16. C is the midpoint of $\overline{JD}$.

17. $\angle EAF$ and $\angle JAD$ are vertical angles.

18. $\overrightarrow{AC}$ bisects $\angle JAD$.

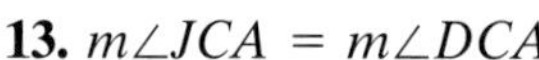

Example 3 (page 98)

19. Developing Proof Complete this proof of one form of Theorem 2-3 by filling in the blanks.

If two angles are complements of the same angle, then the two angles are congruent.

Given: $\angle 1$ and $\angle 2$ are complementary.
$\angle 3$ and $\angle 2$ are complementary.

Prove: $\angle 1 \cong \angle 3$

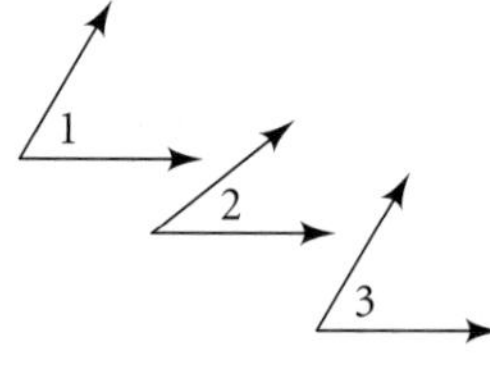

Proof: By the definition of complementary angles, $m\angle 1 + m\angle 2 =$ **a.** _?_ and $m\angle 3 + m\angle 2 =$ **b.** _?_. Then $m\angle 1 + m\angle 2 = m\angle 3 + m\angle 2$ by **c.** _?_. Subtract $m\angle 2$ from each side. You get $m\angle 1 =$ **d.** _?_.

Example 4 (page 99)

x^2 **Algebra Find the value of each variable.**

20.

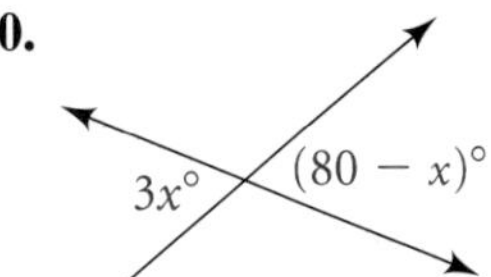

21.

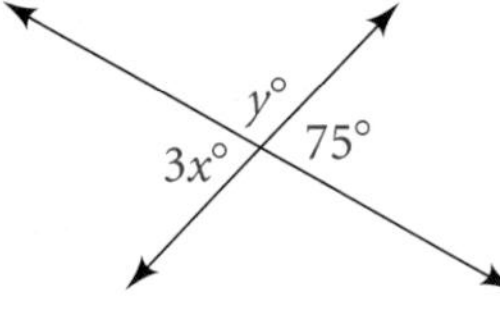

22.

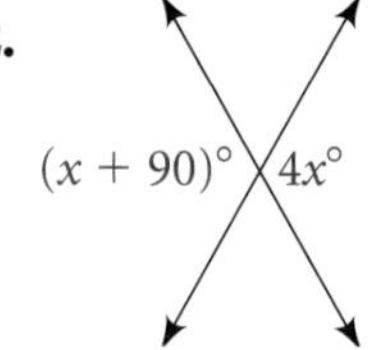

Find the measures of the labeled angles in each exercise.

23. Exercise 20 **24.** Exercise 21 **25.** Exercise 22

B Apply Your Skills

26. **Writing** How is a theorem different from a postulate?

27. **Open-Ended** Give an example of vertical angles in your home.

28. **Reasoning** Explain why this statement is true:
If $m\angle 1 + m\angle 2 = 180$ and $m\angle 3 + m\angle 2 = 180$, then $\angle 1 \cong \angle 3$.

x^2 **Algebra** **Find the value of each variable and the measure of each labeled angle.**

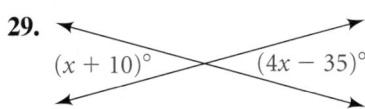

29. 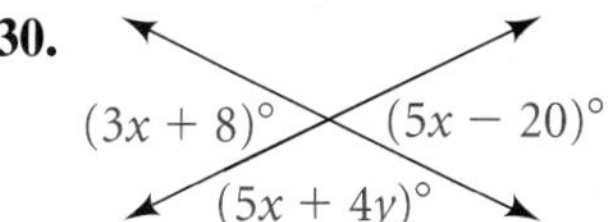

30. 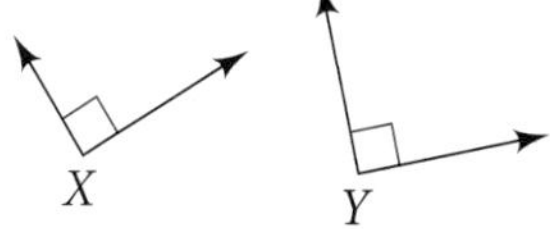

31. **Developing Proof** Complete this proof of Theorem 2-4 by filling in the blanks.

All right angles are congruent.

Given: $\angle X$ and $\angle Y$ are right angles.

Prove: $\angle X \cong \angle Y$

X Y

Proof: By the definition of **a.** __?__, $m\angle X = 90$ and $m\angle Y = 90$.
By the Substitution Property, $m\angle X =$ **b.** __?__, or $\angle X \cong \angle Y$.

Name two pairs of congruent angles in each figure. Justify your answers.

32. 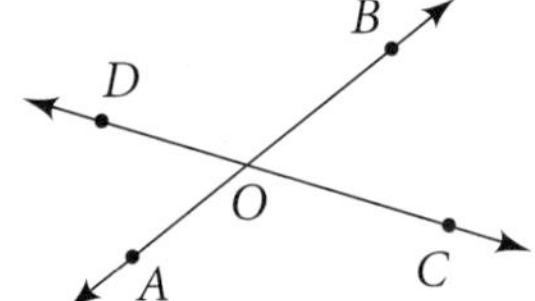

33. 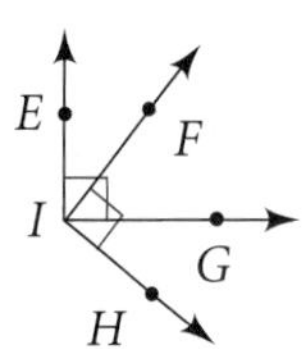

34. 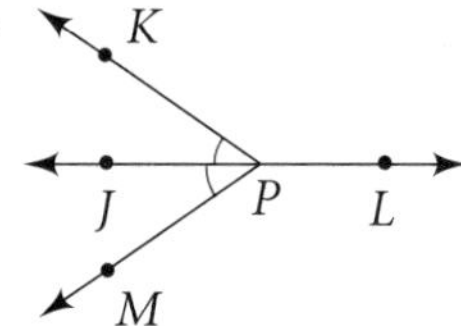

35. **Developing Proof** Complete this proof of Theorem 2-5 by filling in the blanks.

If two angles are congruent and supplementary, then each is a right angle.

Given: $\angle W$ and $\angle V$ are congruent and supplementary.

Prove: $\angle W$ and $\angle V$ are right angles.

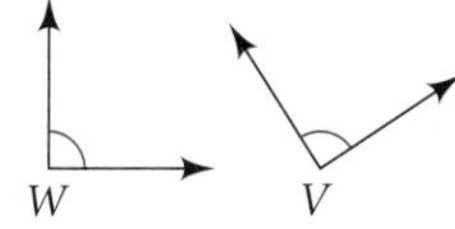

Proof: $\angle W$ and $\angle V$ are congruent, so $m\angle W = m\angle$ **a.** __?__.
$\angle W$ and $\angle V$ are supplementary so $m\angle W + m\angle V =$ **b.** __?__.
Substituting $m\angle W$ for $m\angle V$, you get $m\angle W + m\angle W = 180$, or $2m\angle W = 180$.
By the **c.** __?__ Property of Equality, $m\angle W = 90$.
Since $\angle W \cong \angle V, m\angle V = 90$, too. Then both angles are **d.** __?__ angles.

Exercise 36

36. **Design** The two back legs of the director's chair pictured at the left meet in a 72° angle. Find the measure of each angle formed by the two back legs.

37. **Coordinate Geometry** $\angle AOX$ contains points $A(1, 3)$, $O(0, 0)$, and $X(4, 0)$.
    a. Find the coordinates of a point B so that $\angle BOA$ and $\angle AOX$ are adjacent complementary angles.
    b. Find the coordinates of a point C so that $\overrightarrow{OC}$ is a side of a different angle that is adjacent and complementary to $\angle AOX$.

38. **Coordinate Geometry** $\angle DOE$ contains points $D(2, 3)$, $O(0, 0)$, and $E(5, 1)$. Find the coordinates of a point F so that $\overrightarrow{OF}$ is a side of an angle that is adjacent and supplementary to $\angle DOE$.

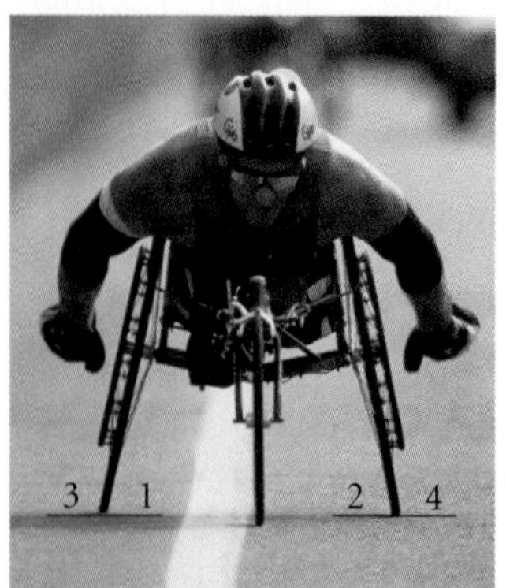

Exercise 43

Algebra **Find the value of each variable and the measure of each labeled angle.**

39.

54°
4x°

40.

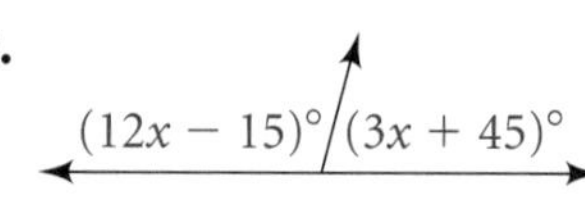

41.

3x°
2x°

42.

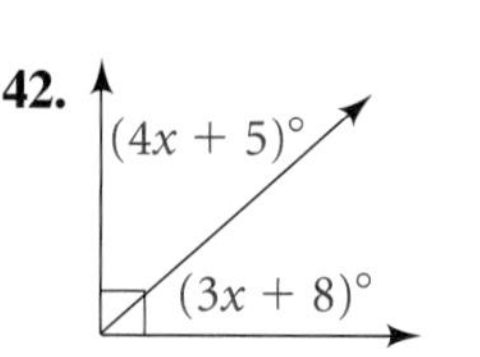

43. Sports In the photograph, the wheels of the racing wheelchair are tilted so that $\angle 1 \cong \angle 2$. What theorem can you use to justify the statement $\angle 3 \cong \angle 4$?

Critical Thinking **If possible, find the measures of the angles described. If it is not possible, explain why.**

44. congruent adjacent supplementary angles

45. congruent adjacent complementary angles

46. congruent vertical angles

Algebra **Find the measure of each angle.**

47. $\angle A$ and $\angle B$ are complementary. $m\angle A = 3x + 12$ and $m\angle B = 2x - 22$.

48. $\angle A$ and $\angle B$ are supplementary. $m\angle A = 3x + 12$ and $m\angle B = 2x - 22$.

49. $\angle A$ is twice as large as its complement, $\angle B$.

50. $\angle A$ is half as large as its complement, $\angle B$.

51. $\angle A$ is twice as large as its supplement, $\angle B$.

52. $\angle A$ is half as large as twice its supplement, $\angle B$.

53. The measure of $\angle B$, the supplement of $\angle A$, is four times the measure of $\angle C$, the complement of $\angle A$.

54. The measure of $\angle B$, the complement of $\angle A$, is one-sixth the measure of $\angle C$, the supplement of $\angle A$.

C **Challenge** Proof **55.** Write a paragraph proof for this form of Theorem 2-2.

If two angles are supplements of congruent angles, then the two angles are congruent.

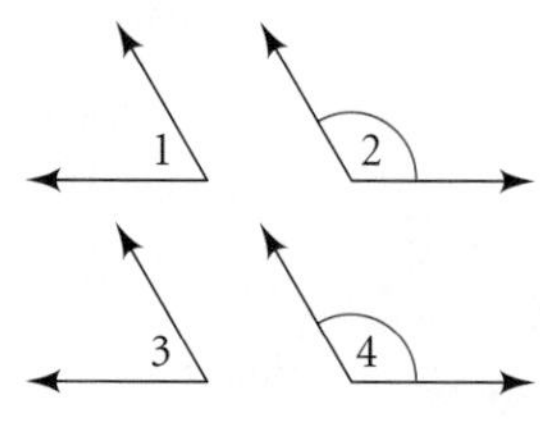

Given: $\angle 1$ and $\angle 2$ are supplementary.
$\angle 3$ and $\angle 4$ are supplementary.
$\angle 2 \cong \angle 4$

Prove: $\angle 1 \cong \angle 3$

Proof **56.** Write a paragraph proof for this form of Theorem 2-3.

If two angles are complements of congruent angles, then the two angles are congruent.

1
2
3
4

Given: $\angle 1$ and $\angle 2$ are complementary.
$\angle 3$ and $\angle 4$ are complementary.
$\angle 2 \cong \angle 4$

Prove: $\angle 1 \cong \angle 3$

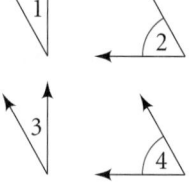

x^2 **Algebra** **Find the value of each variable and the measure of each labeled angle.**

57.

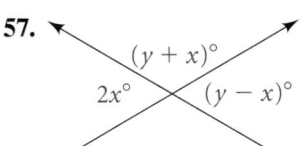

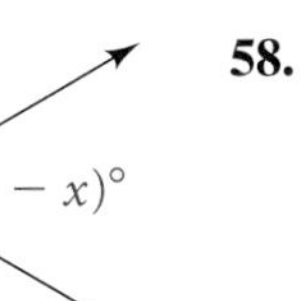

58.

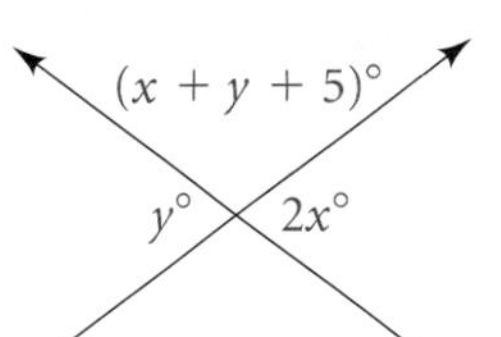

59.

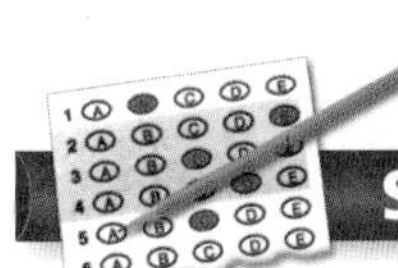

Standardized Test Prep

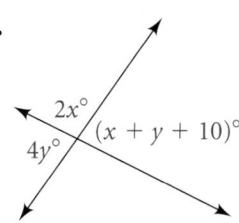

Gridded Response

Find the measure of each angle.

60. an angle with measure 8 less than the measure of its complement

61. one angle of a pair of complementary vertical angles

62. an angle with measure three times the measure of its supplement

Take It to the NET
Online lesson quiz at
www.PHSchool.com
Web Code: afa-0205

Use the diagram at the right to find the measure of each of the following angles.

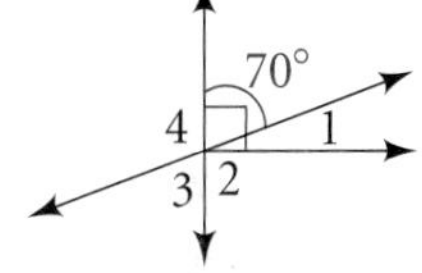

63. $\angle 1$ 

64. $\angle 2$

65. $\angle 3$

66. $\angle 4$

Mixed Review

Lesson 2-4 **Use the given property to complete each statement.**

67. Subtraction Property of Equality
If $3x + 7 = 19$, then $3x = \underline{\ ?\ }$.

68. Reflexive Property of Congruence
$\overline{AB} \cong \underline{\ ?\ }$

69. Substitution Property
If $MN = 3$ and $MN + NP = 15$, then $\underline{\ ?\ }$.

Lesson 2-3 **Use deductive reasoning to draw a conclusion. If not possible, write *not possible.***

70. If two lines intersect, then they are coplanar.
Lines m and n are coplanar.

71. If two angles are vertical angles, then they are congruent.
$\angle 1$ and $\angle 2$ are vertical angles.

Lesson 2-2 **Each conditional statement below is true. Write its converse. If the converse is also true, combine the statements as a biconditional.**

72. If $y + 7 = 32$, then $y = 25$.

73. If you live in Australia, then you live south of the equator.

74. If $n > 0$, then $n^2 > 0$.

Test-Taking Strategies

Writing Short Responses

Short-response questions are usually worth 2 points. To get full credit you must demonstrate a thorough understanding and knowledge of mathematical concepts and techniques.

EXAMPLE

Name a pair of adjacent angles in the diagram at the right. Use the definition of adjacent angles to explain why your angles are adjacent.

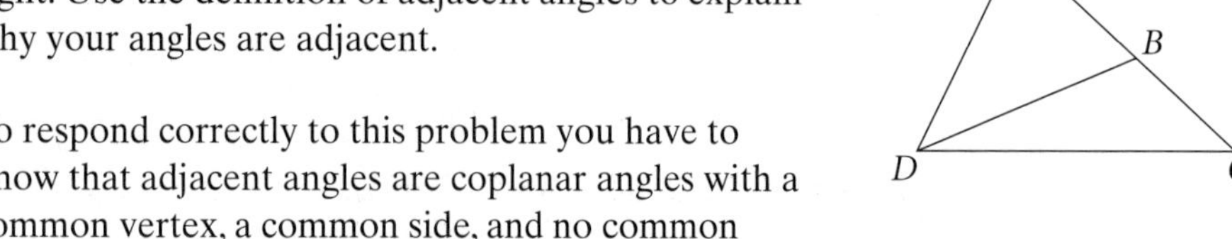

To respond correctly to this problem you have to know that adjacent angles are coplanar angles with a common vertex, a common side, and no common interior points. You have to pick a pair of angles that are adjacent and then use the definition to explain why your angles are adjacent.

2 points	1 points	0 points
∠ABD is adjacent to ∠CBD. They have a common vertex, a common side, and no common interior points.	∠ABD is adjacent to ∠CBD. They don't overlap each other.	∠ABD and ∠ABC

A 2-point response has a correct pair of adjacent angles and an explanation that uses the definition. This 1-point response has a correct pair but an incomplete definition. (An incorrect pair with an explanation that uses the definition is also worth 1 point.) The 0-point response has an incorrect pair and no explanation.

EXERCISES

Score each response to the exercise in the Example above. Explain your reasoning.

1. ∠DBC and ∠ABD are adjacent because they are next to each other and don't overlap.

2. ∠BAD and ∠BCD They aren't next to each other.

3. ∠DBA and ∠DBC Adjacent angles share a vertex and a side and have no interior points in common.

Write a 2-point response to each exercise. Refer to the diagram in the Example.

4. Name a pair of supplementary angles. Use the definition of supplementary angles to explain why your angles are supplementary.

5. $\angle ABD$ and $\angle BDC$ are complementary, $m\angle ABD = 6x$, and $m\angle BDC = 2x + 2$. Use the definition of complementary to explain what x must be.

Chapter Review

Vocabulary

adjacent angles (p. 96)
biconditional (p. 75)
complementary angles (p. 96)
conclusion (p. 68)
conditional (p. 68)
converse (p. 69)
deductive reasoning (p. 82)
hypothesis (p. 68)
Law of Detachment (p. 82)
Law of Syllogism (p. 83)
paragraph proof (p. 98)
Reflexive Property (pp. 89 and 91)
supplementary angles (p. 96)
Symmetric Property (pp. 89 and 91)
theorem (p. 98)
Transitive Property (pp. 89 and 91)
truth value (p. 69)
vertical angles (p. 96)

Reading Math
Understanding Vocabulary

Choose the correct vocabulary term to complete each sentence.

1. The statement "$\angle A \cong \angle A$" is an example of the __?__ Property of Congruence.

2. In a conditional statement, the part that directly follows *if* is the __?__.

3. Two coplanar angles with a common side, a common vertex, and no common interior points are __?__.

4. "If $\angle A \cong \angle B$ and $\angle B \cong \angle C$, then $\angle A \cong \angle C$" is an example of the __?__ Property of Congruence.

5. If the sum of the measures of two angles is 90, the angles are __?__.

6. When a conditional and its converse are true, they may be written as a single true statement called a __?__.

7. Two angles whose sides are opposite rays are __?__.

8. The __?__ of a conditional switches the hypothesis and the conclusion.

9. "If $\angle A \cong \angle B$, then $\angle B \cong \angle A$" is an example of the __?__ Property of Congruence.

10. If the sum of the measures of two angles is 180, the angles are __?__.

Take It to the NET
Online vocabulary quiz at **www.PHSchool.com**
Web Code: afg-0251

Skills and Concepts

2-1 and 2-2 Objectives

- To recognize conditional statements
- To write converses of conditional statements
- To write biconditionals
- To recognize good definitions

An *if-then statement* is a **conditional.** The part following *if* is the **hypothesis.** The part following *then* is the **conclusion.** You find the truth value of a conditional by determining whether it is true or false. The symbolic form of a conditional is $p \rightarrow q$.

The **converse** of a conditional switches the hypothesis and the conclusion. The symbolic form of a converse is $q \rightarrow p$.

When a conditional and its converse are true, you can combine them as a true **biconditional.** To write a biconditional, you join the two parts of each conditional with the phrase *if and only if.* The symbolic form of a biconditional is $p \leftrightarrow q$.

For Exercises 11–13, (a) write the converse and (b) determine the truth value of the conditional and its converse. (c) If both statements are true, write a biconditional.

11. If you are a teenager, then you are younger than 20.

12. If an angle is obtuse, then its measure is greater than 90 and less than 180.

13. If a figure is a square, then it has four sides.

14. Write the following sentence as a conditional: All flowers are beautiful.

A good definition is precise. A good definition uses terms that have been previously defined or are commonly accepted.

15. Rico defines a *book* as something you read. Explain why this is not a good definition.

16. Write this definition as a biconditional:
An *oxymoron* is a phrase that contains contradictory terms.

17. Write this biconditional as two statements, a conditional and its converse:
Two angles are complementary if and only if the sum of their measures is 90.

2-3 Objectives

- ▼ To use the Law of Detachment
- ▼ To use the Law of Syllogism

Deductive reasoning is the process of reasoning logically from given statements to a conclusion. If the given statements are true, deductive reasoning produces a true conclusion.

The following are two important laws of deductive reasoning:
Law of Detachment: If $p \rightarrow q$ is a true statement and p is true, then q is true.
Law of Syllogism: If $p \rightarrow q$ and $q \rightarrow r$ are true statements, then $p \rightarrow r$ is true.

Use the Law of Detachment to make a conclusion.

18. If you practice table tennis every day, you will become a better player. Lucy practices table tennis every day.

19. Line ℓ and line m are perpendicular. If two lines are perpendicular, they intersect to form right angles.

20. If two angles are supplementary, then the sum of their measures is 180. $\angle 1$ and $\angle 2$ are supplementary.

Use the Law of Syllogism to make a conclusion.

21. If Kate studies, she will get good grades. If Kate gets good grades, she will graduate.

22. If a, then b. If b, then c.

23. If the weather is wet, the Huskies will not play soccer. If the Huskies do not play soccer, Nathan can stop at the ice cream shop.

2-4 Objective

- ▼ To connect reasoning in algebra and geometry

In algebra, you use deductive reasoning and properties to solve equations. In geometry, each statement in a deductive argument is justified by a property, definition, or postulate. Some of the properties you need are listed below.

Properties of Equality

Addition Property	If $a = b$, then $a + c = b + c$.
Subtraction Property	If $a = b$, then $a - c = b - c$.
Multiplication Property	If $a = b$, then $a \cdot c = b \cdot c$.
Division Property	If $a = b$ and $c \neq 0$, then $\frac{a}{c} \neq \frac{b}{c}$.
Substitution Property	If $a = b$, then b can replace a in any expression.
Distributive Property	$a(b + c) = ab + ac$

Properties of Congruence

Reflexive Property	$\overline{AB} \cong \overline{AB}$ $\angle A \cong \angle A$
Symmetric Property	If $\overline{AB} \cong \overline{CD}$, then $\overline{CD} \cong \overline{AB}$. If $\angle A \cong \angle B$, then $\angle B \cong \angle A$.
Transitive Property	If $\overline{AB} \cong \overline{CD}$ and $\overline{CD} \cong \overline{EF}$, then $\overline{AB} \cong \overline{EF}$. If $\angle A \cong \angle B$ and $\angle B \cong \angle C$, then $\angle A \cong \angle C$.

24. Algebra Fill in the reason that justifies each step.

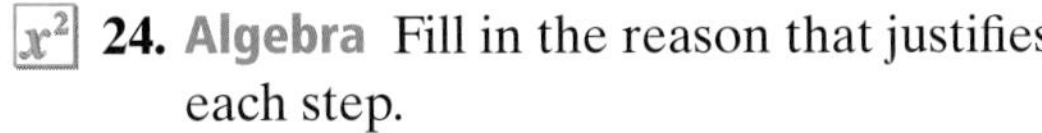

Given: $QS = 42$

$QR + RS = QS$	**a.** ?
$x + 3 + 2x = 42$	**b.** ?
$3x + 3 = 42$	**c.** ?
$3x = 39$	**d.** ?
$x = 13$	**e.** ?

Use the given property to complete each statement.

25. Addition Property of Equality
If $x = 5$, then $x + 3 = \underline{\ ?\ }$.

26. Division Property of Equality
If $2(AX) = 2(BY)$, then $AX = \underline{\ ?\ }$.

27. Reflexive Property of Equality
$m\angle Y = \underline{\ ?\ }$

28. Symmetric Property of Equality
If $XY = RS$, then $\underline{\ ?\ }$.

29. Transitive Property of Equality
If $x = 5$ and $5 = y$, then $x = \underline{\ ?\ }$.

30. Distributive Property
$2(4x + 5) = 8x + \underline{\ ?\ }$

31. Distributive Property
$3p - 6q = 3(\underline{\ ?\ })$

32. Reflexive Property of Congruence
$\overline{NM} \cong \underline{\ ?\ }$

2-5 Objectives

- To identify angle pairs
- To prove and apply theorems about angles

Special relationships exist between some angle pairs. For example, **vertical angles** are congruent. The sum of the measures of **complementary angles** is 90. The sum of the measures of **supplementary angles** is 180.

Algebra Find the value of each variable.

33.

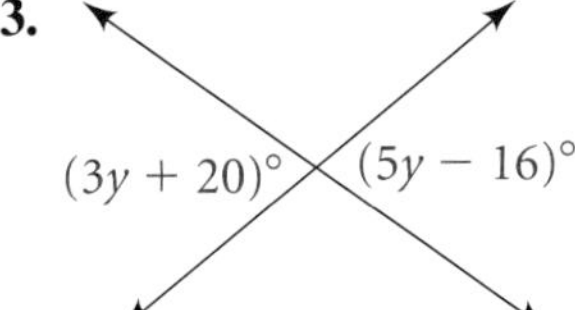

34.

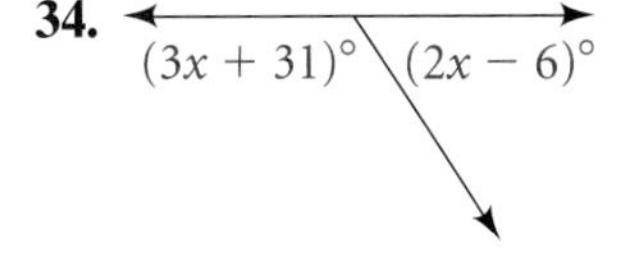

35.

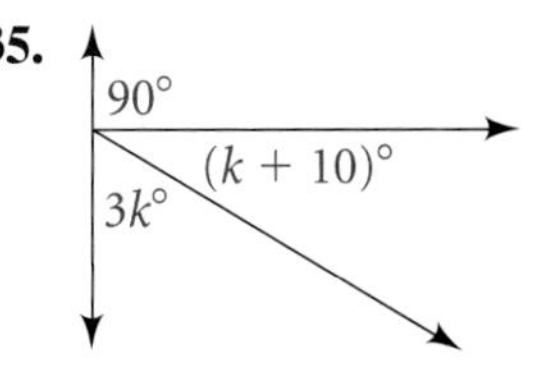

What can you conclude from each diagram? Justify your answers.

36.

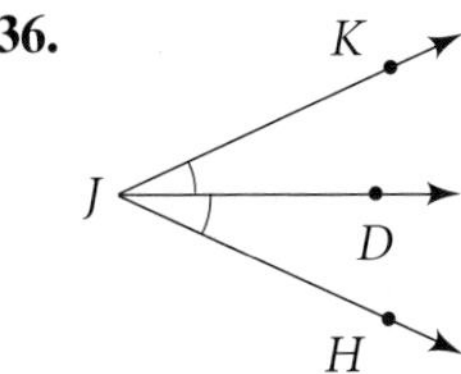

37.

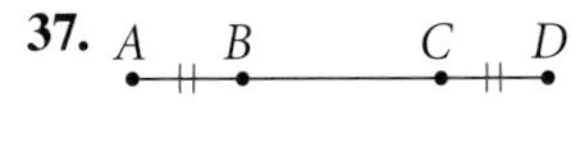

38.

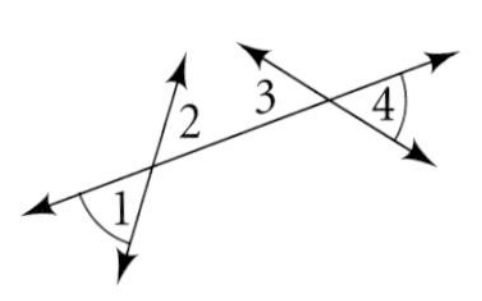

Chapter Test

1. Identify the hypothesis and conclusion:

If $x + 9 = 11$, then $x = 2$.

2. Write this statement as a conditional.

All babies are cute.

3. Find a counterexample to show that this statement is *not* true.

If two angles are complementary, then they are not congruent.

For each statement, (a) write the converse and (b) decide whether the converse is true or false.

4. If a figure is a rectangle, then it has two right angles.

5. If two lines intersect, then they lie in the same plane.

6. If it is snowing in South Carolina, then it is not summer.

Writing Explain why each statement is *not* a good definition.

7. A pencil is a writing instrument.

8. Complementary angles are angles that form a right angle.

9. Vertical angles are angles that are congruent.

For Exercises 10–14, name the property that justifies each statement.

10. If $UV = KL$ and $KL = 6$, then $UV = 6$.

11. If $m\angle 1 + m\angle 2 = m\angle 4 + m\angle 2$, then $m\angle 1 = m\angle 4$.

12. $\angle ABC \cong \angle ABC$

13. If $\frac{1}{2}m\angle D = 45$, then $m\angle D = 90$.

14. If $\angle DEF \cong \angle HJK$, then $\angle HJK \cong \angle DEF$.

15. Find the measure of each angle.

a. $\angle CDM$ **b.** $\angle KDM$

c. $\angle JDK$ **d.** $\angle JDM$

e. $\angle CDB$ **f.** $\angle CDK$

16. The measure of an angle is $2z$. What is the measure of its supplement?

17. The measure of an angle is 52 more than the measure of its complement. What is the measure of the angle?

Give two conclusions you can make from each diagram. Justify your conclusions.

18.

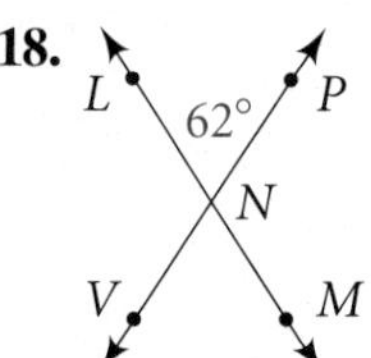

19.

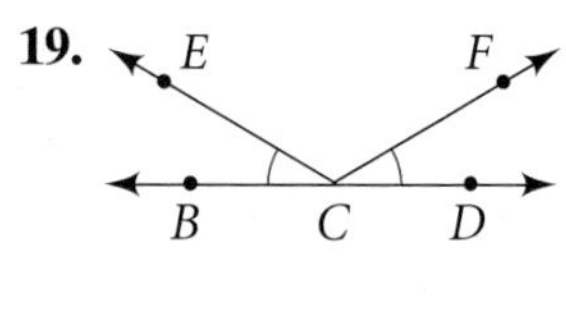

20. Rewrite this biconditional as two conditionals.

A fish is a bluegill if and only if it is a bluish, freshwater sunfish.

21. Complete this statement.

If two angles are complements of congruent angles, the angles are ___?___.

For Exercises 22–26, use the Law of Detachment and the Law of Syllogism to make any possible conclusion. Write *not possible* if you cannot make any conclusion.

22. People who live in glass houses shouldn't throw stones. Lindsay shouldn't throw stones.

23. James wants to be a chemical engineer. If a student wants to be a chemical engineer, that student must graduate from college.

24. $p \rightarrow q$ and $q \rightarrow r$ are true statements.

25. $p \rightarrow q$ and p are true statements.

26. $p \rightarrow q$ and q are true statements.

27. **Developing Proof** Complete this proof by filling in the blanks.

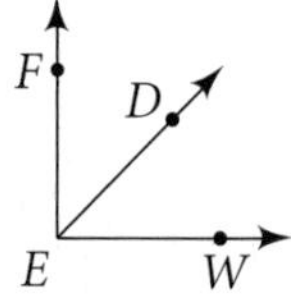

Given: $\angle FED$ and $\angle DEW$ are complementary.

Prove: $\angle FEW$ is a right angle.

Proof: By the definition of complementary angles, $m\angle FED + m\angle DEW =$ **a.** ___?___.
$m\angle FED + m\angle DEW = m\angle FEW$ by the **b.** ___?___.
$90 = m\angle FEW$ by the **c.** ___?___ Property of Equality.
Then, $\angle FEW$ is a right angle, by the **d.** ___?___.

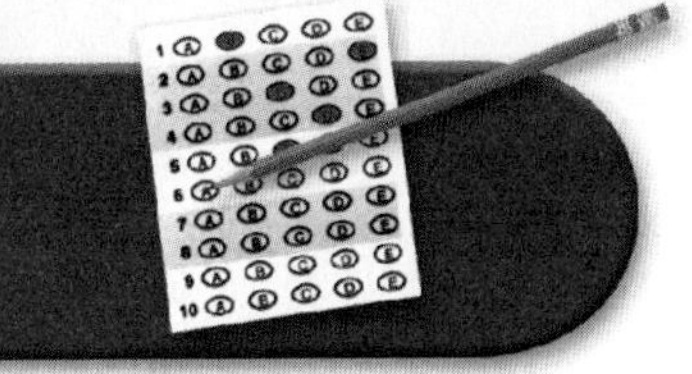

Standardized Test Prep

Multiple Choice

For Exercises 1–10, choose the correct letter.

1. What is the converse of the statement, "If a strawberry is red, then it is ripe"?
   A. If a strawberry is not red, then it is not ripe.
   B. If a strawberry is ripe, then it is red.
   C. A strawberry is ripe if and only if it is red.
   D. If a strawberry is red, then it is ripe.

2. Which is the intersection of two planes?
   F. a point **G.** a line
   H. a plane **I.** a ray

3. Which property justifies this statement?
   If $4AB = 8CD$, then $AB = 2CD$.
   A. Division Property of Equality
   B. Reflexive Property of Equality
   C. Substitution Property of Equality
   D. Distributive Property

4. Which point lies the farthest from the origin?
   F. $(0, -7)$ **G.** $(-3, 8)$
   H. $(-4, -3)$ **I.** $(5, 1)$

5. What is the length of the segment with endpoints $A(1, 7)$ and $B(-3, -1)$?
   A. $\sqrt{40}$ **B.** 8 **C.** $\sqrt{80}$ **D.** 40

6. What is the next number in the pattern?
   $1, -4, 9, -16,$
   F. -35 **G.** -25 **H.** 25 **I.** 35

7. If the measure of an angle is 78 less than the measure of its complement, what is the measure of the angle?
   A. 6 **B.** 12 **C.** 51 **D.** 84

8. $\angle A$ and $\angle B$ are supplementary and vertical angles. What is $m\angle B$?
   F. 45 **G.** 90 **H.** 135 **I.** 180

9. What is the midpoint of a segment with endpoints $(0, -4)$ and $(-4, 7)$?
   A. $(-4, \frac{3}{2})$ **B.** $(-2, 3)$
   C. $(-2, \frac{3}{2})$ **D.** $(2, -3)$

10. The measure of an angle is 12 less than twice the measure of its supplement. What is the measure of the angle?
    F. 28 **G.** 34 **H.** 64 **I.** 116

Quantitative Comparison

Compare the boxed quantity in Column A with the boxed quantity in Column B. Choose the best answer.

A. The quantity in Column A is greater.
B. The quantity in Column B is greater.
C. The two quantities are equal.
D. The relationship cannot be determined from the information given.

	Column A	Column B
	Perimeter of square $RSTV = 12x$	
11.	VT	$3x$
	$\angle A$ is the complement of $\angle B$.	
12.	$m\angle A$	$m\angle B$
13.	$m\angle A + m\angle B$	180
14.	$m\angle B$	90
15.	$m\angle A$	measure of the supplement of $\angle B$

Gridded Response

16. The area of a circle is 10π cm^2. What is the circle's diameter? Round to the nearest hundredth of a centimeter.

17. The measure of an angle is one third the measure of its supplement. What is the measure of the angle?

Short Response

18. $\overline{AB}$ has endpoints $A(3, 6)$ and $B(9, -2)$ and midpoint M. Justify each response.
    a. Find the coordinates of M.
    b. Find AB.

Extended Response

19. Construct a right triangle. Then construct the bisectors of two of its angles.

Real-World Snapshots

The Delicious Side of Division

Applying Reasoning Splitting dessert evenly among brothers and sisters sometimes causes arguments. In some families, one child divides the dessert and another has first choice among the pieces. This encourages the divider to be very, very careful!

Activity 1

Dividing a square cake into an even number of pieces that are alike can be relatively simple. Dividing a square cake into seven same-size pieces is more challenging.

One method is to divide the perimeter of the cake by 7. Then mark the perimeter in seven equal lengths. (Some lengths may go around a corner.) Cut segments from the center of the cake to the marks on the perimeter. This splits the cake into the seven same-size pieces.

Show why this method works.

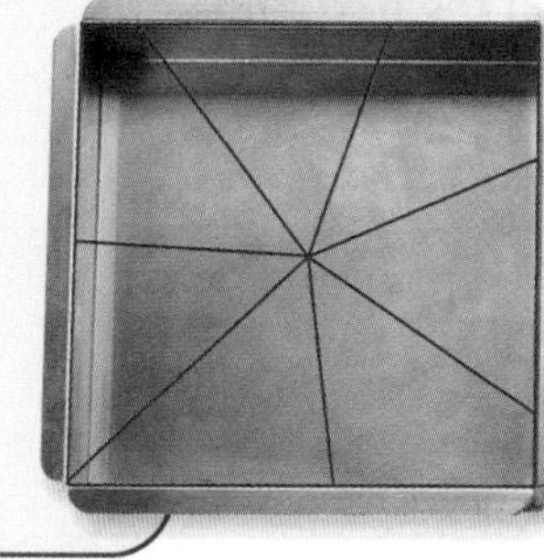

Ground mace

Powdered cocoa

Cooking with Spices

Mace comes from the kernel of an apricot-like fruit that grows mainly in Indonesia. Cocoa comes from the fruit of the cacao tree. Finely ground, both spices add flavor to baked goods.

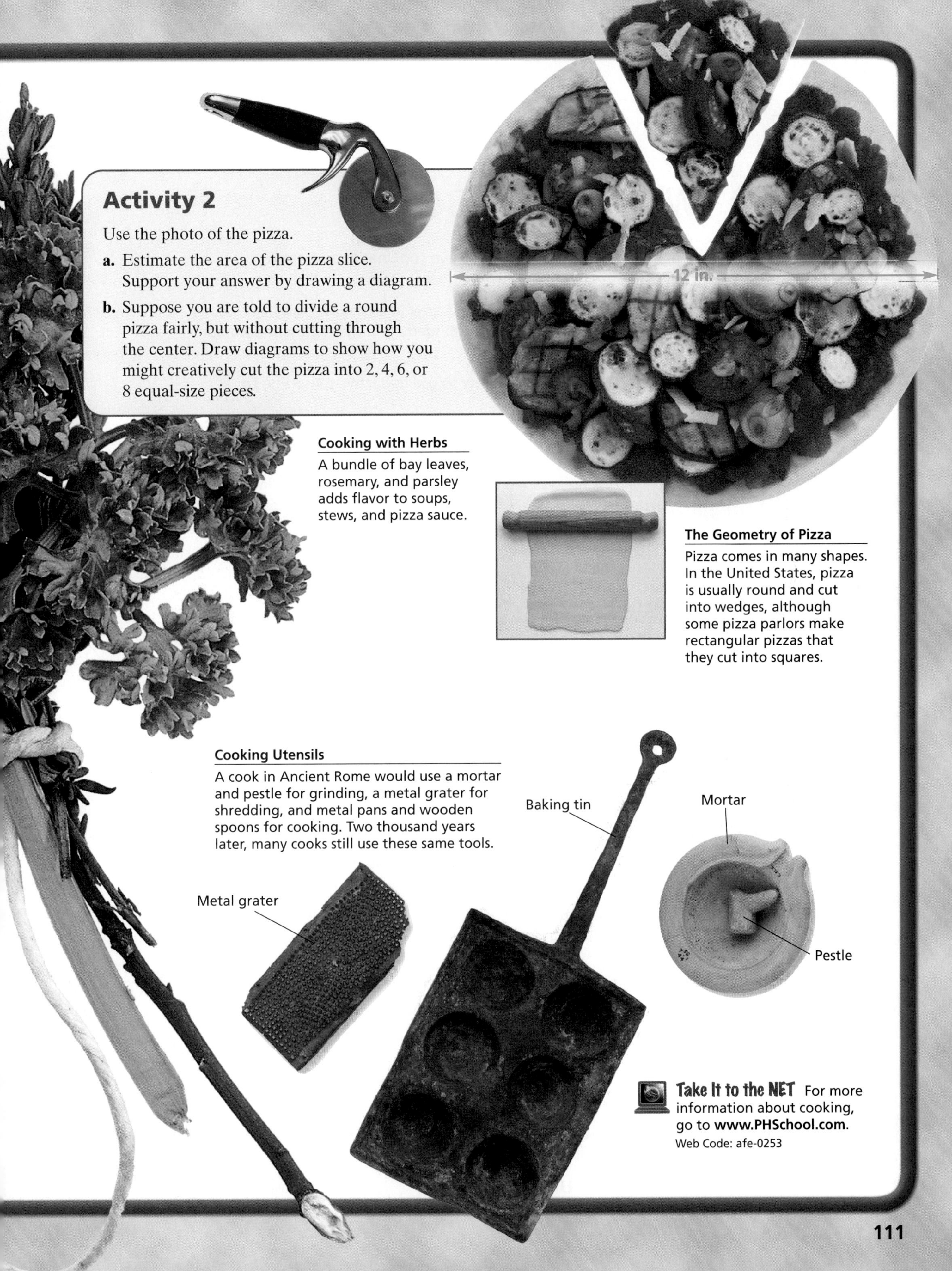

Activity 2

Use the photo of the pizza.

a. Estimate the area of the pizza slice. Support your answer by drawing a diagram.

b. Suppose you are told to divide a round pizza fairly, but without cutting through the center. Draw diagrams to show how you might creatively cut the pizza into 2, 4, 6, or 8 equal-size pieces.

Cooking with Herbs

A bundle of bay leaves, rosemary, and parsley adds flavor to soups, stews, and pizza sauce.

The Geometry of Pizza

Pizza comes in many shapes. In the United States, pizza is usually round and cut into wedges, although some pizza parlors make rectangular pizzas that they cut into squares.

Cooking Utensils

A cook in Ancient Rome would use a mortar and pestle for grinding, a metal grater for shredding, and metal pans and wooden spoons for cooking. Two thousand years later, many cooks still use these same tools.

Take It to the NET For more information about cooking, go to **www.PHSchool.com**.
Web Code: afe-0253

Where You've Been

- In Chapter 1, you learned that two coplanar lines that do not intersect are parallel.
- In Chapters 1 and 2, you learned how to measure angles, recognize congruent angles, and identify angles whose measures have sum 180.
- In Chapter 2, you learned how to use deductive reasoning to draw conclusions.

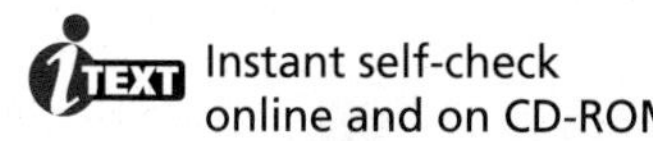

Instant self-check
online and on CD-ROM

Diagnosing Readiness

(For help, go to the Lesson in green.)

Evaluating Algebraic Expressions (Skills Handbook page 716)

x^2 **Algebra** Evaluate each expression for the given value of n.

1. $\frac{360}{n}; n = 5$ **2.** $(n - 2)180; n = 9$ **3.** $(n - 2)180; n = 17$

Solving Equations (Algebra 1 Review page 24)

x^2 **Algebra** Solve each equation.

4. $3x + 11 = 7x - 5$ **5.** $(2x + 5) + (3x - 10) = 70$ **6.** $(3x + 2) - (2x - 3) = -19$

Writing and Solving an Equation (Skills Handbook page 720)

Write an equation and solve the problem.

7. The sum of the measures of three angles is 180. One measure is twice the size of each of the other two. Find the measure of each angle.

8. The sum of the measures of three angles is 180. One measure is half the size of each of the other two. Find the measure of each angle.

Drawing Parallel and Perpendicular Lines (Lesson 1-3)

9. Draw a picture of a rectangular box and label its eight corners A through H. Name two lines in your picture that appear to be parallel. Name two lines that appear to be perpendicular.

Drawing and Measuring Angles (Lesson 1-4)

Use a straightedge and draw the given type of angle as best you can. Estimate its measure, and then find its measure with a protractor.

10. acute **11.** right **12.** obtuse

Parallel and Perpendicular Lines

LESSONS

Key Vocabulary

- alternate interior angles (p. 115)
- concave polygon (p. 144)
- convex polygon (p. 144)
- corresponding angles (p. 115)
- equiangular triangle (p. 133)
- equilateral triangle (p. 133)
- exterior angle of a polygon (p. 133)
- flow proof (p. 123)
- isosceles triangle (p. 133)
- polygon (p. 143)
- regular polygon (p. 146)
- remote interior angles (p. 133)
- same-side interior angles (p. 115)
- scalene triangle (p. 133)
- transversal (p. 115)

Where You're Going

- In this chapter, you will use deductive reasoning to make conclusions about parallel and perpendicular lines.
- You will use parallel lines to learn about angle measures in triangles and other polygons.
- You will also learn ways to think about parallel and perpendicular lines in a coordinate plane.

Real-World Connection Applying what you learn, you will make conclusions about airport runways on pages 116 and 177.

Technology

Parallel Lines and Related Angles

FOR USE WITH LESSON 3-1

Construct

Use geometry software to construct two parallel lines. Check that the lines remain parallel as you manipulate them. Construct a point on each line. Then construct the line through these two points. This line is called a transversal.

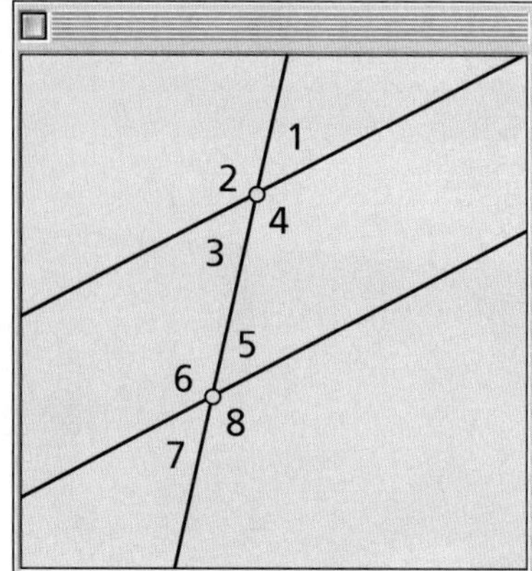

Investigate

Measure each of the eight angles formed by the parallel lines and the transversal. Record the measurements. Manipulate the lines and record the new measurements. What relationships do you notice?

EXERCISES

1. When a transversal intersects two parallel lines, what are the relationships among the angles formed? Make as many conjectures as possible.

Extend

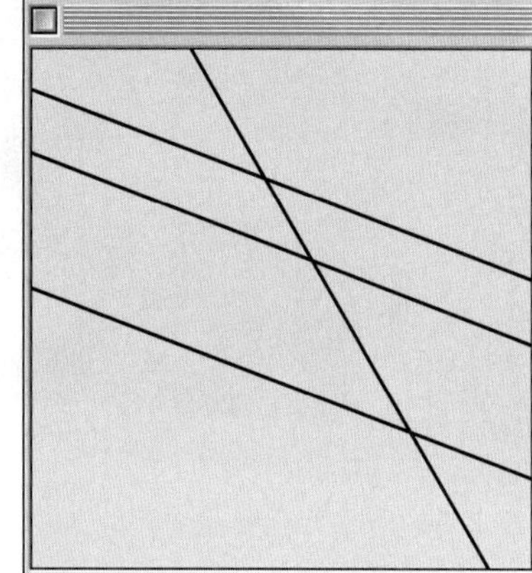

2. Use your software to construct three or more parallel lines. Construct a line that intersects all three lines.
   a. What relationships exist among the angles formed?
   b. How many different angle measures are there?
3. Construct two parallel lines and a transversal perpendicular to one of the parallel lines. What angle does it make with the second parallel line?
4. Using geometry software, construct two lines and a transversal, making sure that the two lines are *not* parallel. Locate two angles that are on alternate sides of the transversal and in the interior region between the other two lines. Manipulate the lines so that these angles have the same measure.
   a. Make a conjecture as to the relationship between the two lines.
   b. How is this conjecture different from the conjecture(s) you made in Exercise 1?
5. Again, draw two lines and a transversal, making sure that the two lines are *not* parallel. Locate two angles that are on the same side of the transversal and in the interior region between the two lines. Manipulate the lines so that these angles are supplementary.
   a. Make a conjecture as to the relationship between the two lines.
   b. How is this conjecture different from the conjecture(s) you made in Exercise 1?

Properties of Parallel Lines

Lesson Preview

What You'll Learn

OBJECTIVE 1 To identify angles formed by two lines and a transversal

OBJECTIVE 2 To prove and use properties of parallel lines

. . . And Why

To describe angles formed by an airport runway that crosses two parallel runways, as in Example 2

 Check Skills You'll Need

(For help, go to page 24 or Skills Handbook page 720.)

x^2 Algebra **Solve each equation.**

1. $x + 2x + 3x = 180$ **2.** $(w + 23) + (4w + 7) = 180$

3. $90 = 2y - 30$ **4.** $180 - 5y = 135$

Write an equation and solve the problem.

5. The sum of $m\angle 1$ and twice its complement is 146. Find $m\angle 1$.

6. The measures of two supplementary angles are in the ratio 2 : 3. Find their measures.

New Vocabulary
- transversal
- alternate interior angles
- same-side interior angles
- corresponding angles
- two-column proof

Interactive lesson includes instant self-check, tutorials, and activities.

OBJECTIVE 1

Identifying Angles

A **transversal** is a line that intersects two coplanar lines at two distinct points. The diagram shows the eight angles formed by a transversal t and two lines ℓ and m.

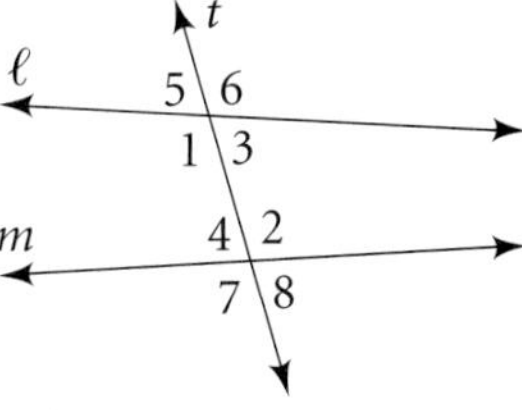

Pairs of the eight angles have special names as suggested by their positions.

Reading Math

Corresponding objects are related in a special way. Here, corresponding angles are angles that are in similar positions on the same side of a transversal.

$\angle 1$ and $\angle 2$ are **alternate interior angles.**

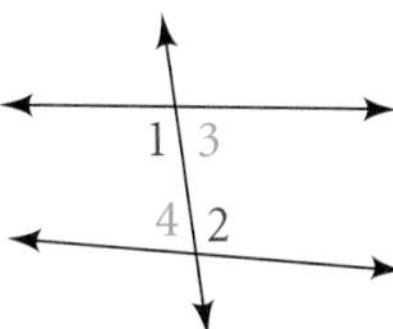

$\angle 1$ and $\angle 4$ are **same-side interior angles.**

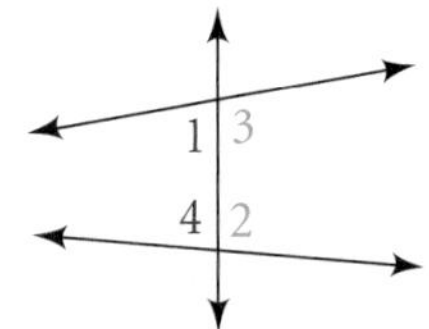

$\angle 1$ and $\angle 7$ are **corresponding angles.**

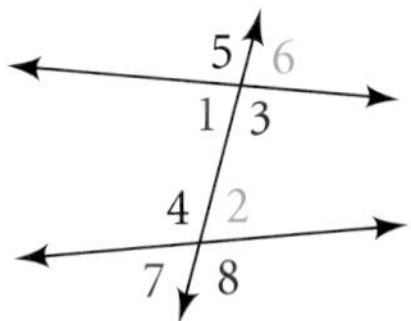

1 EXAMPLE Identifying Angles

Use the diagrams above. Name another pair of alternate interior angles and another pair of same-side interior angles.

$\angle 3$ and $\angle 4$ are alternate interior angles. $\angle 2$ and $\angle 3$ are same-side interior angles.

Check Understanding 1 Name three other pairs of corresponding angles in the diagrams above.

2 EXAMPLE Real-World Connection

Aviation In the diagram of Lafayette Regional Airport, the black segments are runways and the gray areas are taxiways and terminal buildings. Classify ∠1 and ∠2 as alternate interior angles, same-side interior angles, or corresponding angles.

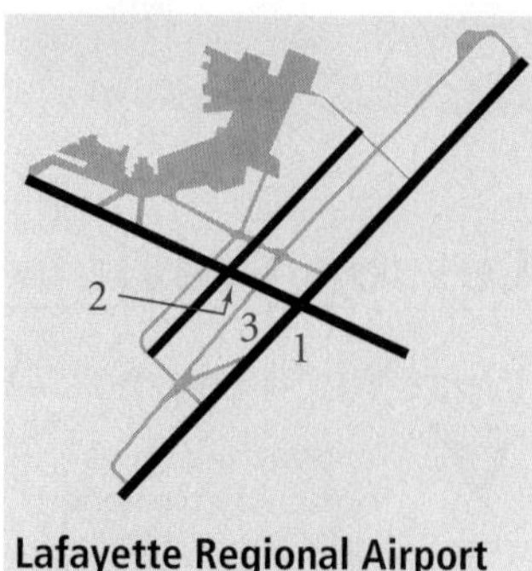

Lafayette Regional Airport
Lafayette, Louisiana

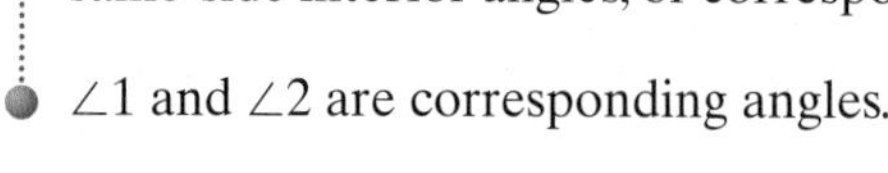

∠1 and ∠2 are corresponding angles.

✓ Check Understanding 2 Classify ∠2 and ∠3 as alternate interior angles, same-side interior angles, or corresponding angles.

OBJECTIVE

2 Properties of Parallel Lines

In the photograph, the vapor trail of the high-flying aircraft suggests a transversal of the parallel trails of the low-flying aircraft.

The same-size angles that appear to be formed by the vapor trails suggest the postulate and theorems below.

Key Concepts

Postulate 3-1 **Corresponding Angles Postulate**

If a transversal intersects two parallel lines, then corresponding angles are congruent.

∠1 ≅ ∠2

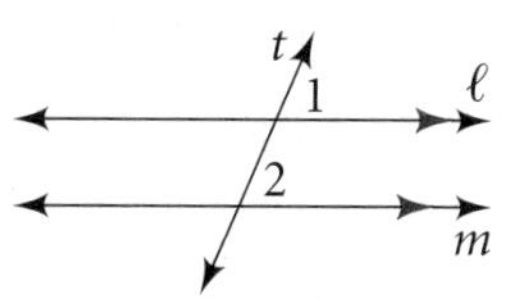

Key Concepts

Theorem 3-1 **Alternate Interior Angles Theorem**

If a transversal intersects two parallel lines, then alternate interior angles are congruent.

∠1 ≅ ∠3

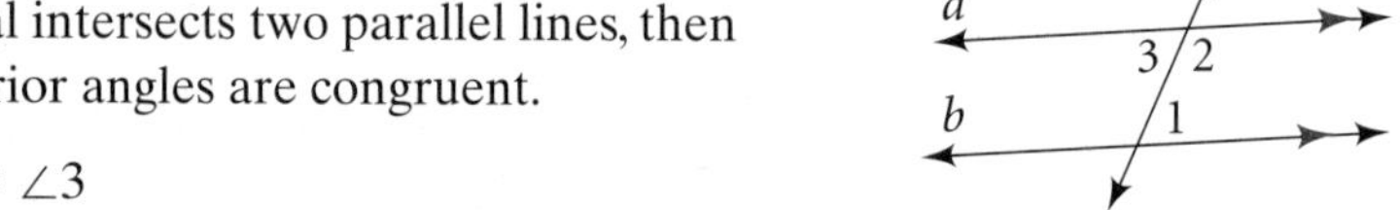

Theorem 3-2 **Same-Side Interior Angles Theorem**

If a transversal intersects two parallel lines, then same-side interior angles are supplementary.

$m\angle 1 + m\angle 2 = 180$

You can display the steps that prove a theorem in a **two-column proof.**

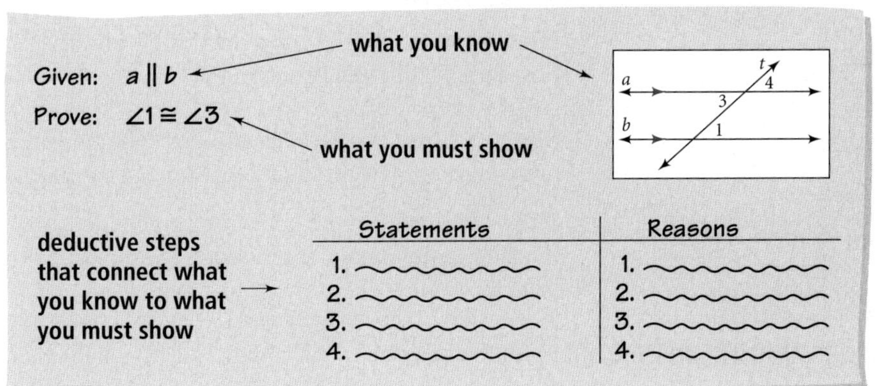

Proof

Two-Column Proof of Theorem 3-1

If a transversal intersects two parallel lines, then alternate interior angles are congruent.

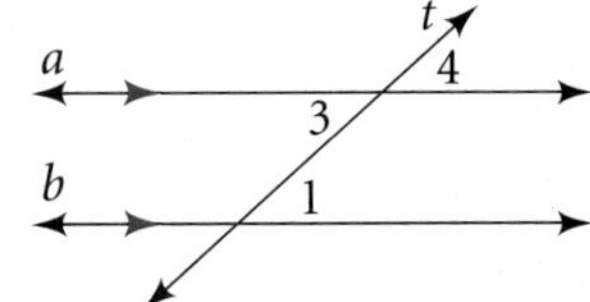

Given: $a \parallel b$

Prove: $\angle 1 \cong \angle 3$

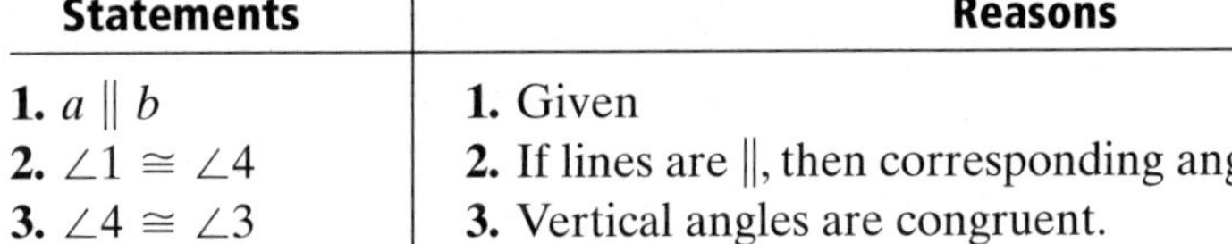

Statements	Reasons
1. $a \parallel b$	**1.** Given
2. $\angle 1 \cong \angle 4$	**2.** If lines are $\parallel$, then corresponding angles are congruent.
3. $\angle 4 \cong \angle 3$	**3.** Vertical angles are congruent.
4. $\angle 1 \cong \angle 3$	**4.** Transitive Property of Congruence

Reading Math

These symbols indicate lines *a* and *b* are parallel.

a b a || b

To write a proof, you may find it helpful to first write a plan for the proof. In a plan, you write key statements that connect what you prove to what is given.

Proof

3 EXAMPLE Planning a Proof

Developing Proof For Theorem 3-2 below, study what is given, what you are to prove, and the diagram. Then write a plan for a proof.

If two lines are parallel and cut by a transversal, then same-side interior angles are supplementary.

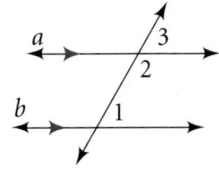

Given: $a \parallel b$

Prove: $\angle 1$ and $\angle 2$ are supplementary.

Plan: To prove that $m\angle 1 + m\angle 2 = 180$, show that $m\angle 3 + m\angle 2 = 180$. Then show that $m\angle 1 = m\angle 3$ and substitute $m\angle 1$ for $m\angle 3$.

a b 3 2 1

✓ Check Understanding 3 Use the plan to write a two-column proof.

When you see two parallel lines and a transversal, and you know the measure of one angle, you can find the measures of all the angles. This is illustrated in Example 4.

4 EXAMPLE Finding Measures of Angles

Find $m\angle 1$, and then $m\angle 2$. Which theorem or postulate justifies each answer?

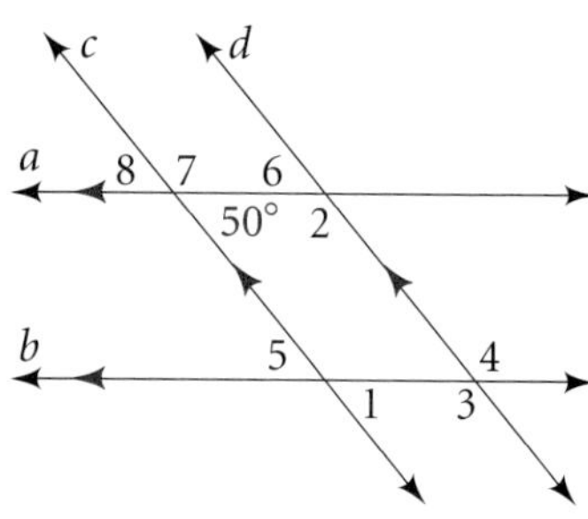

Since $a \parallel b, m\angle 1 = 50$ because corresponding angles are congruent (Corresponding Angles Postulate).

Since $c \parallel d, m\angle 2 = 130$ because same-side interior angles are supplementary (Same-Side Interior Angles Theorem).

Check Understanding 4 Find the measure of each angle. Justify each answer.

a. $\angle 3$ **b.** $\angle 4$ **c.** $\angle 5$
d. $\angle 6$ **e.** $\angle 7$ **f.** $\angle 8$

Sometimes you can use algebra to find angle measures.

5 EXAMPLE Using Algebra to Find Angle Measures

Algebra Find the values of x and y.

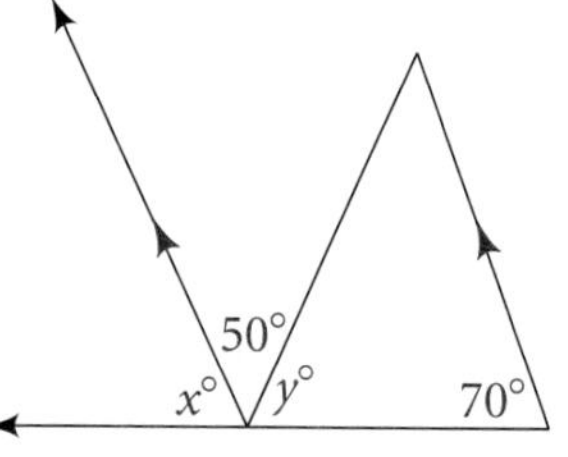

$x = 70$ **Corresponding angles of parallel lines are ≅.**

$70 + 50 + y = 180$ **Angle Addition Postulate**

$y = 60$ **Subtraction Property of Equality**

Check Understanding 5 Find the values of x and y. Then find the measures of the angles.

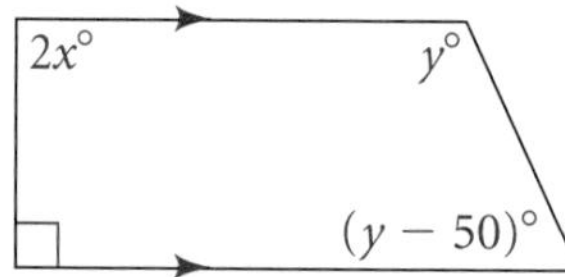

EXERCISES

For more practice, see *Extra Practice*.

Practice and Problem Solving

A Practice by Example

Examples 1, 2 (pages 115, 116)

Name the two lines and the transversal that form each pair of angles. Then classify the pair of angles.

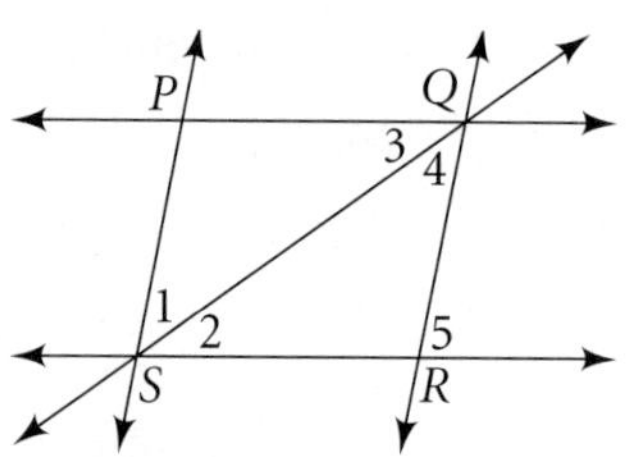

1. $\angle 2$ and $\angle 3$
2. $\angle 1$ and $\angle 4$
3. $\angle SPQ$ and $\angle PQR$
4. $\angle 5$ and $\angle PSR$

Classify each pair of angles labeled in the same color as *alternate interior angles*, *same-side interior angles*, or *corresponding angles*.

5.

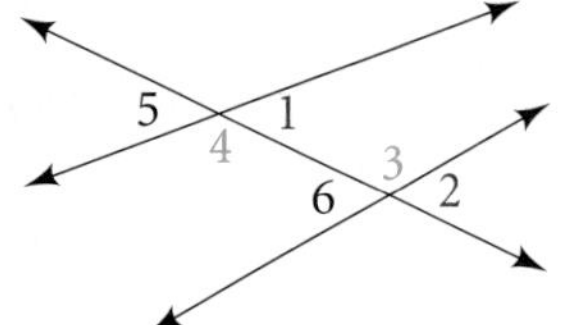

6.

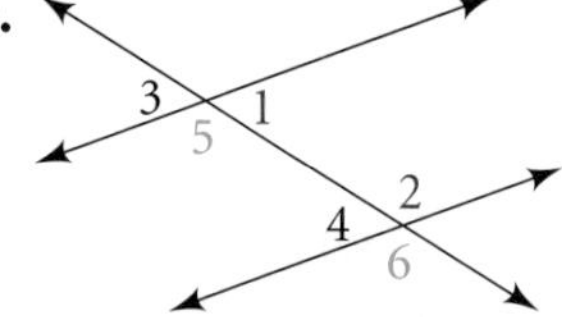

7.

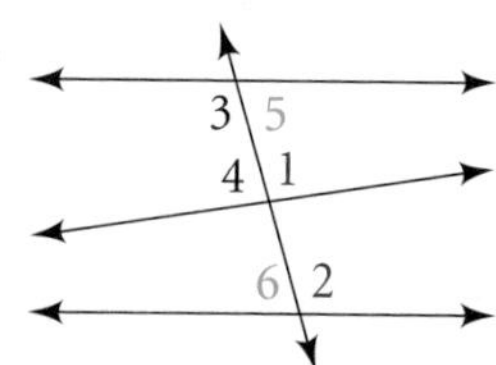

8. The boards securing this barn door suggest two parallel lines and a transversal. Classify $\angle 1$ and $\angle 2$ as alternate interior angles, same-side interior angles, or corresponding angles.

Example 3 (page 117)

9. **Developing Proof** Complete the plan for a proof of the following statement.

If two lines are parallel and one of them is perpendicular to a transversal, then so is the other.

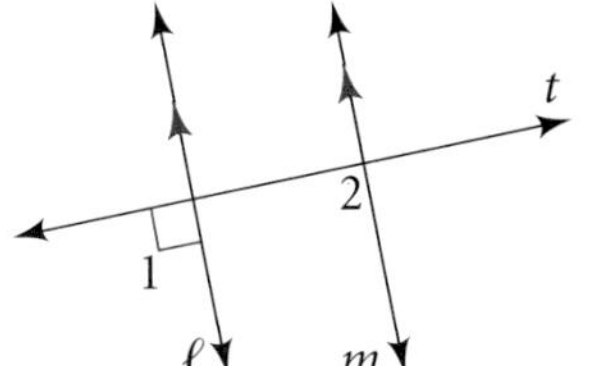

Given: $\ell \parallel m, \ell \perp t$

Prove: $m \perp t$

Plan: To prove $m \perp t$, show that **a.** $\angle$ _?_ is a right angle. $\angle 2$ is a right angle if it is congruent to **b.** $\angle$ _?_. $\angle 2 \cong \angle 1$ because $\ell \parallel m$ and **c.** _?_ angles are congruent.

10. **Developing Proof** Supply the missing reasons in this two-column proof.

In a plane, if a line is perpendicular to one of two parallel lines, then it is perpendicular to the other.

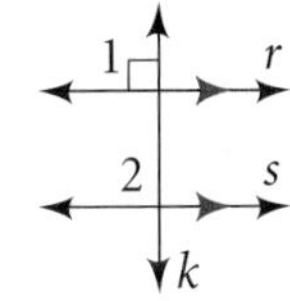

Given: $k \perp r, r \parallel s$

Prove: $k \perp s$

Statements	Reasons
1. $k \perp r$	1. Given
2. $\angle 1$ is a right angle.	a. _?_
3. $m\angle 1 = 90$	b. _?_
4. $r \parallel s$	4. Given
5. $m\angle 2 = m\angle 1$	c. _?_
6. $m\angle 2 = 90$	d. _?_
7. $\angle 2$ is a right angle.	e. _?_
8. $k \perp s$	f. _?_

Example 4 (page 118)

Find $m\angle 1$, and then $m\angle 2$. Justify each answer.

11.

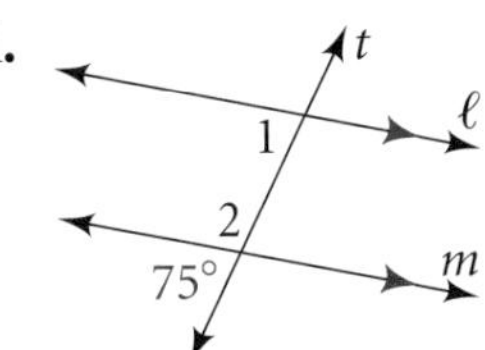

12.

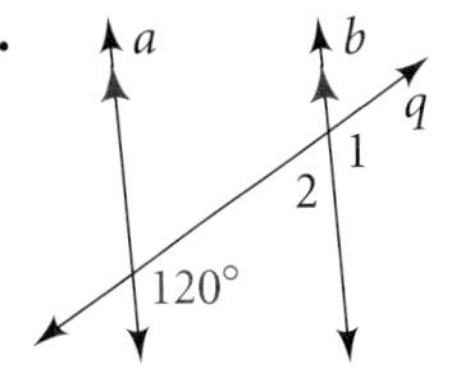

13.

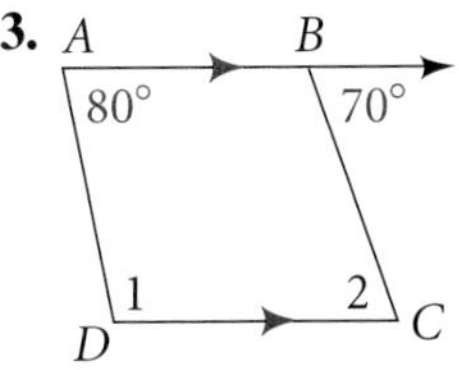

Example 5 (page 118)

x^2 **Algebra** **Find the value of x. Then find the measure of each labeled angle.**

14.

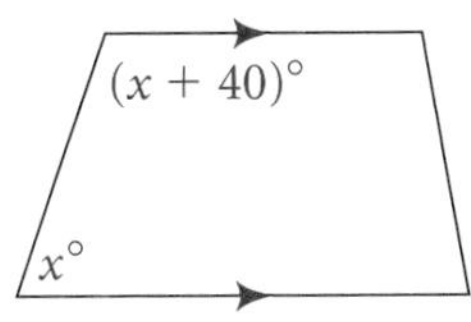

15.

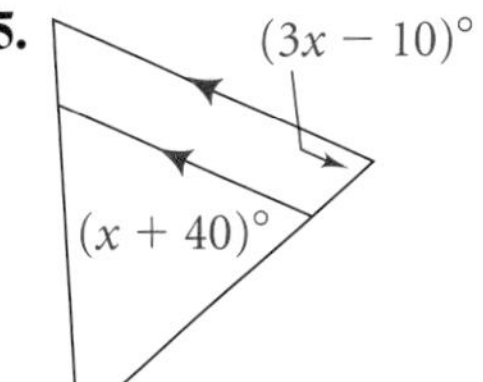

16.

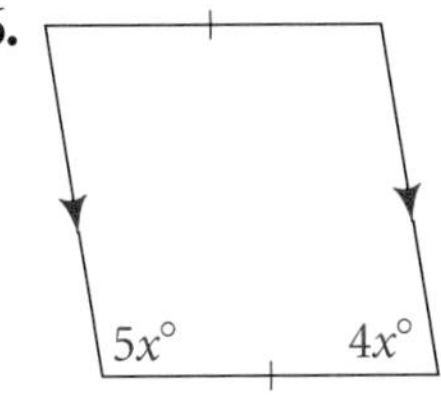

B **Apply Your Skills**

17. In the figure at the right, $f \parallel g$ and $m \parallel n$. Find the measure of each numbered angle.

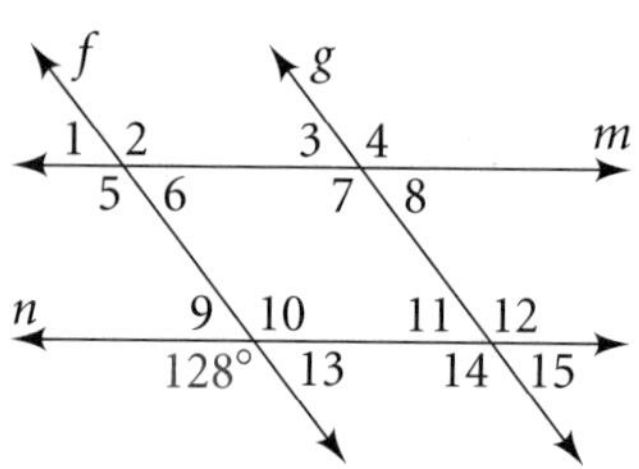

18. Two pairs of parallel segments form the "pound sign" on your telephone keypad. To find the measures of all the angles in the pound sign, how many angles must you measure? Explain.

Two lines and a transversal form how many pairs of the following?

19. alternate interior angles

20. corresponding angles

21. same-side interior angles

22. vertical angles

Need Help?

In Exercise 24, turn your book so the other two parallel lines appear horizontal.

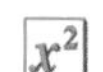 **Algebra** **Find the values of the variables.**

23. $(3p - 6)°$

24.

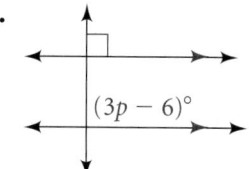

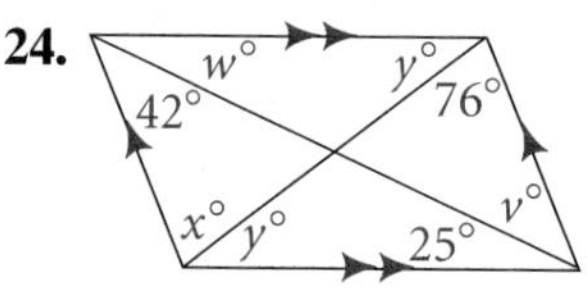

25.

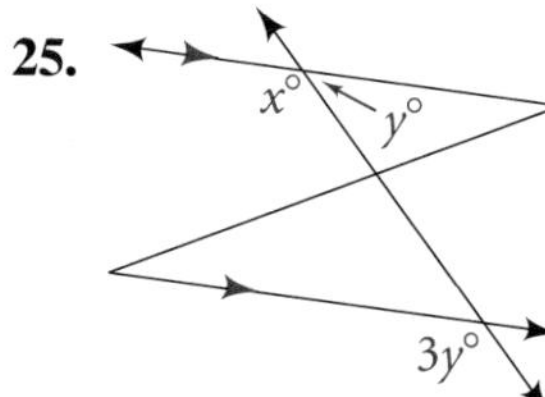

26. **Error Analysis** The diagram at the right contains contradictory information. What is it? Why is it contradictory?

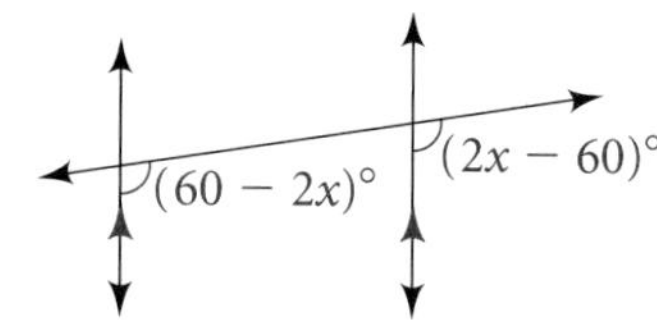

27. **Writing** Look up the meaning of the prefix *trans*. Explain how the meaning of the prefix relates to the word *transversal*.

28. **Open-Ended** The letter Z illustrates alternate interior angles. Find at least two other letters that illustrate the pairs of angles presented in this lesson. Draw the letters, mark the angles, and describe them.

29. **History** About 220 B.C., Eratosthenes estimated the circumference of Earth. He achieved this remarkable feat by using two locations in Egypt. He assumed that Earth is a sphere and that the sun's rays are parallel. He used the measures of $\angle 1$ and $\angle 2$ in his estimation.
   a. Classify $\angle 1$ and $\angle 2$ as alternate interior, same-side interior, or corresponding angles.
   b. How did Eratosthenes know that $\angle 1 \cong \angle 2$?

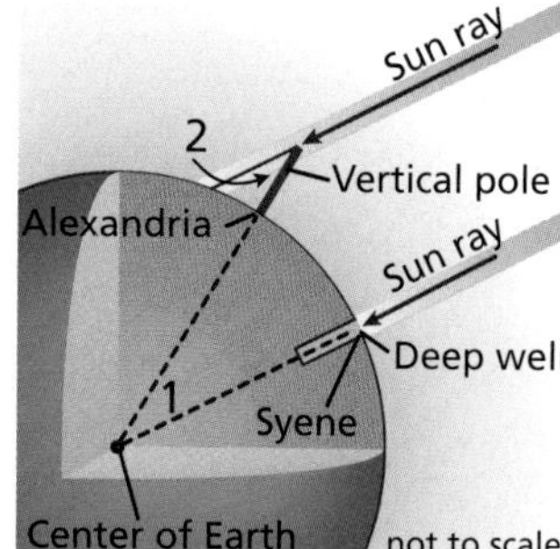

30. **Engineering** Engineers are laying pipe below ground on opposite sides of the street as shown here. To join the pipe, workers on each side of the street work towards the middle.
   a. If one team lays pipe at the angle shown, what should the other team use for $m\angle 1$?
   b. Are these two angles alternate interior, same-side interior, or corresponding angles?

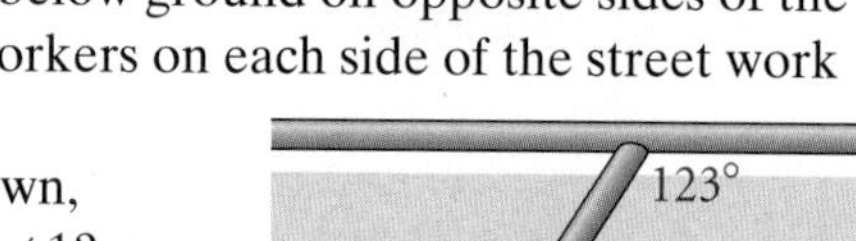

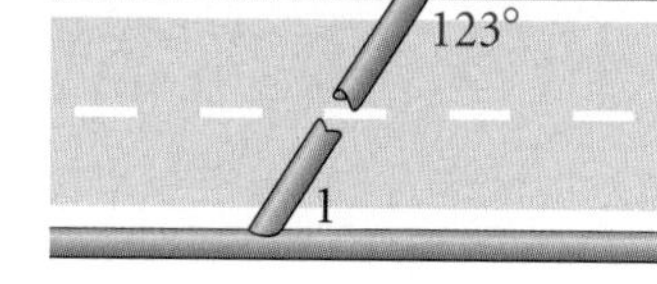

C **Challenge**

31. **Critical Thinking** $\angle 4$ and $\angle 5$ are same-side exterior angles.
   a. Make a conjecture about same-side exterior angles formed by two parallel lines and a transversal.
   Proof b. Prove your conjecture or show a counterexample.

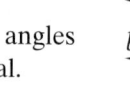

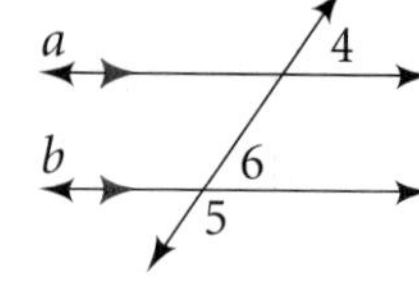

32. **Developing Proof** $\angle 1$ and $\angle 3$ are alternate exterior angles. Follow the plan for a proof and write a two-column proof of the following statement.

If a transversal intersects two parallel lines, then alternate exterior angles are congruent.

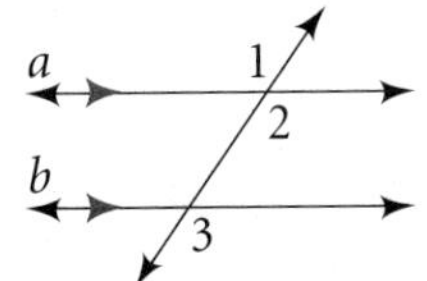

Given: $a \parallel b$

Prove: $\angle 1 \cong \angle 3$

Plan: To prove that $\angle 1 \cong \angle 3$, show that $\angle 1 \cong \angle 2$ and $\angle 2 \cong \angle 3$. $\angle 1 \cong \angle 2$ because vertical $\angle$s are congruent. $\angle 2 \cong \angle 3$ because corresponding $\angle$s are congruent. Thus, $\angle 1 \cong \angle 3$ by the Transitive Property of Congruence.

Line *m* is in plane *A* and line *n* is in plane *B*. Planes *A* and *B* are parallel. Complete each statement with *sometimes, always,* or *never.* Justify each answer.

33. Lines m and n __?__ intersect.

34. Lines m and n are __?__ coplanar.

35. Lines m and n are __?__ parallel.

36. Lines m and n are __?__ skew.

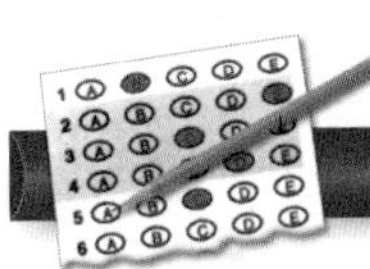

Standardized Test Prep

A fence on a hill uses vertical posts L and M to hold parallel rails N and P. Use the diagram for Exercises 37–41.

Multiple Choice

37. $\angle 10$ and $\angle 14$ are alternate interior angles. Which is the transversal?

A. L **B.** M **C.** N **D.** P

38. If $m\angle 1 = 115$, what is $m\angle 16$?

F. 35 **G.** 65 **H.** 85 **I.** 115

Take It to the NET
Online lesson quiz at **www.PHSchool.com**
Web Code: afa-0301

39. If $m\angle 10 = x - 24$, what is $m\angle 7$?

A. $156 + x$ **B.** $204 + x$ **C.** $156 - x$ **D.** $204 - x$

40. If $m\angle 1 = 6x$ and $m\angle 12 = 4x$, what is $m\angle 5$?

F. 54 **G.** 60 **H.** 72 **I.** 108

Short Response

41. a. Describe a plan for showing that $\angle 1 \cong \angle 5$.
b. Explain why $\angle 1 \cong \angle 5$. Justify each step.

Mixed Review

Lesson 2-5

Find the measure of each angle if $m\angle YDF = 121$ and $\overrightarrow{DR}$ bisects $\angle FDI$.

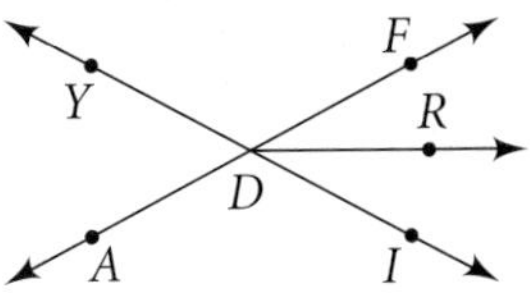

42. $\angle IDA$ **43.** $\angle YDA$ **44.** $\angle RDI$

Lesson 1-6

Coordinate Geometry **Find the coordinates of the midpoint of $\overline{AB}$.**

45. $A(0, 9), B(1, 5)$ **46.** $A(-3, 8), B(2, -1)$ **47.** $A(10, -1), B(-4, 7)$

Lesson 1-1

Find a pattern for each sequence. Use the pattern to show the next two terms.

48. 4, 8, 12, 16, . . . **49.** 1, −2, 4, −8, . . . **50.** 23, 16, 9, 2, . . .

3-2 Proving Lines Parallel

Lesson Preview

What You'll Learn

To use a transversal in proving lines parallel

To relate parallel and perpendicular lines

. . . And Why

To show why opposite sides of a picture frame are parallel, as in Example 5

✓ Check Skills You'll Need

(For help, go to page 24 and Lesson 2-1.)

x^2 Algebra **Solve each equation.**

1. $2x + 5 = 27$

2. $8a - 12 = 20$

3. $x - 30 + 4x + 80 = 180$

4. $9x - 7 = 3x + 29$

Write the converse of each conditional statement. Determine the truth value of the converse.

5. If a triangle is a right triangle, then it has a 90° angle.

6. If two angles are vertical angles, then they are congruent.

7. If two angles are same-side interior angles, then they are supplementary.

New Vocabulary • flow proof

Interactive lesson includes instant self-check, tutorials, and activities.

OBJECTIVE 1

Using a Transversal

On window blinds like those shown here, you move the tilt bar to let in or shut out the light.

When you move the bar, the slats tilt at the same angle. This keeps them parallel and illustrates the converse of the Corresponding Angles Postulate.

Key Concepts

Postulate 3-2 **Converse of the Corresponding Angles Postulate**

If two lines and a transversal form corresponding angles that are congruent, then the two lines are parallel.

$\ell \parallel m$

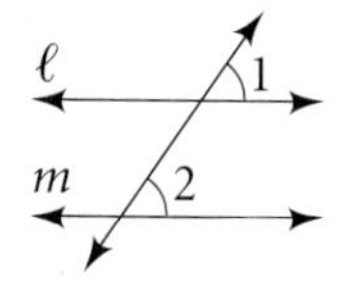

In Lesson 3-1, you proved two theorems based on the Corresponding Angles Postulate. You can also prove theorems that are based on its converse. In fact, Theorems 3-3 and 3-4 happen to be converses of the two theorems from Lesson 3-1, Theorems 3-1 and 3-2.

Key Concepts

Theorem 3-3 **Converse of the Alternate Interior Angles Theorem**

If two lines and a transversal form alternate interior angles that are congruent, then the two lines are parallel.

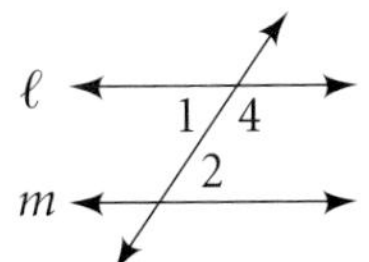

If $\angle 1 \cong \angle 2$, then $\ell \parallel m$.

Theorem 3-4 **Converse of the Same-Side Interior Angles Theorem**

If two lines and a transversal form same-side interior angles that are supplementary, then the two lines are parallel.

If $\angle 2$ and $\angle 4$ are supplementary, then $\ell \parallel m$.

You have seen two forms of proof—paragraph and two-column. In a third form, called **flow proof,** arrows show the logical connections between the statements. Reasons are written below the statements.

Proof

1 EXAMPLE Proving Theorem 3-3

Developing Proof For Theorem 3-3, study what is given, what you are to prove, and the diagram. Then write a flow proof.

If two lines and a transversal form alternate interior angles that are congruent, then the two lines are parallel.

Given: $\angle 1 \cong \angle 2$

Prove: $\ell \parallel m$

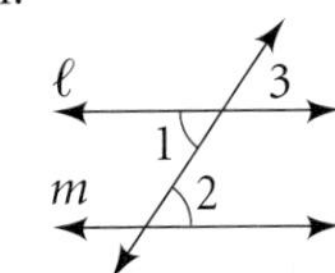

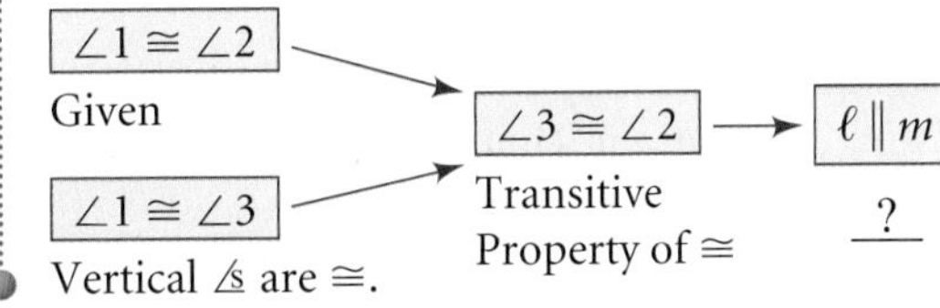

Check Understanding 1 Supply the missing reason in Example 1.

You will write a flow proof of Theorem 3-4 in Exercise 47. Theorems 3-4, 3-3, and Postulate 3-2 now provide you with three ways to prove that two lines are parallel.

2 EXAMPLE Using Theorem 3-4

Developing Proof Which lines, if any, must be parallel if $\angle 1 \cong \angle 2$? Justify your answer with a theorem or postulate.

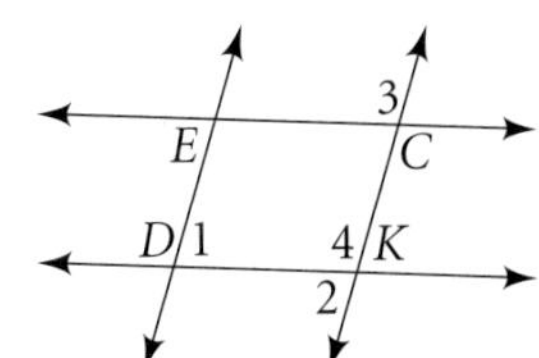

$\overleftrightarrow{DE} \parallel \overleftrightarrow{KC}$ by Theorem 3-3, the Converse of the Alternate Interior Angles Theorem: If alternate interior angles are congruent, then the lines are parallel.

Check Understanding 2 Which lines, if any, must be parallel if $\angle 3 \cong \angle 4$? Explain.

OBJECTIVE 2

Relating Parallel and Perpendicular Lines

The two diagrams suggest ways to draw parallel lines. You can draw them (a) parallel to a given line, or (b) perpendicular to a given line. Theorems 3-5 and 3-6 guarantee that the lines you draw are indeed parallel.

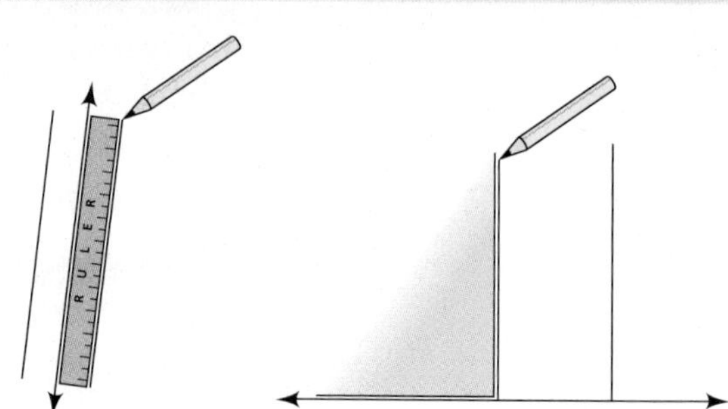

Key Concepts

Theorem 3-5

If two lines are parallel to the same line, then they are parallel to each other.

$a \parallel b$

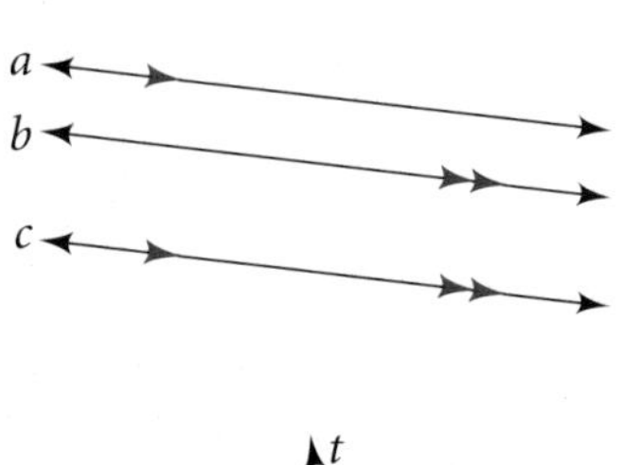

Theorem 3-6

In a plane, if two lines are perpendicular to the same line, then they are parallel to each other.

$m \parallel n$

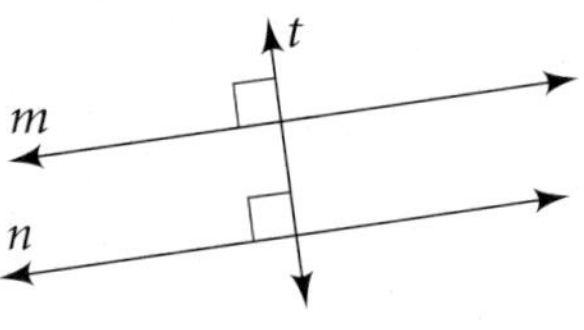

Need Help?

Three lines that meet in the corner of a room show why Theorem 3-6 is not true in space.

Theorem 3-6 includes the phrase *in a plane*. On the other hand, Theorem 3-5 is true for any three such lines, whether they are coplanar (Exercise 26) or noncoplanar.

3 EXAMPLE Proof of Theorem 3-6

Developing Proof Study what is given, what you are to prove, and the diagram. Then write a paragraph proof.

Given: $r \perp t, s \perp t$

Prove: $r \parallel s$

Proof: $\angle 1$ and $\angle 2$ are right angles by the definition of perpendicular, so they are congruent. Since corresponding angles are congruent, $r \parallel s$.

Check Understanding 3 **Critical Thinking** In a plane, if two lines form congruent angles with a third line, must the lines be parallel?

You may need algebra to find values in problems with parallel lines.

4 EXAMPLE Using Algebra

Algebra Find the value of x for which $\ell \parallel m$.

The two angles are corresponding angles.
$\ell \parallel m$ when $2x + 6 = 40$.

$2x + 6 = 40$

$2x = 34$ **Subtract 6 from each side.**

$x = 17$ **Divide each side by 2.**

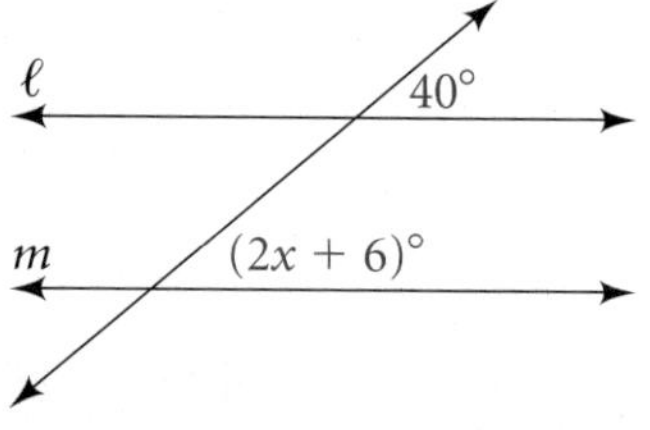

Check Understanding 4 Find the value of x for which $a \parallel b$. Explain how you can check your answer.

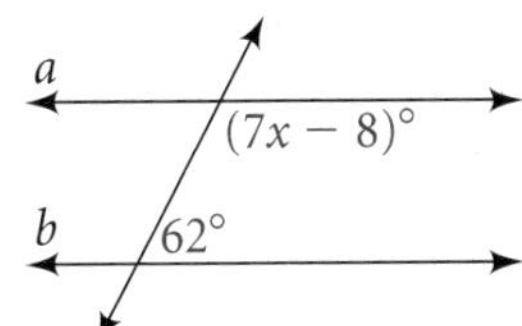

5 EXAMPLE Real-World Connection

Woodworking To make a frame for a painting, a miter box and a backsaw are used to cut the framing at 45° angles. Explain why cutting the framing at this angle ensures that opposite sides of the frame will be parallel.

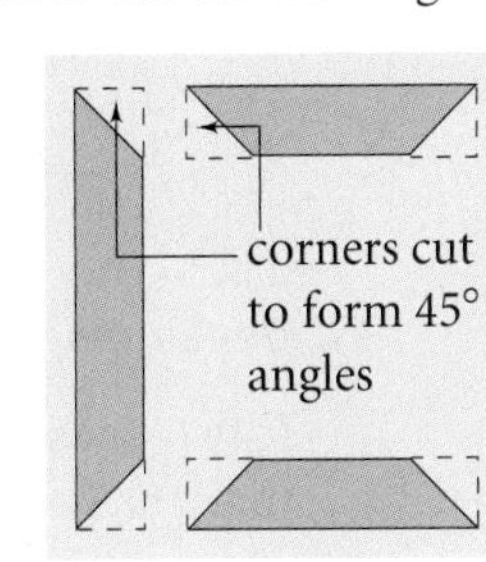

Two adjacent 45° angles form a 90° angle. Two 90° angles are supplementary. By the Converse of the Same-Side Interior Angles Theorem, opposite sides of the frame are parallel.

Check Understanding 5 Explain how you would use the Converse of the Same-Side Interior Angles Theorem to justify the following statement:

In a plane, two lines perpendicular to the same line are parallel.

EXERCISES

For more practice, see *Extra Practice*.

Practice and Problem Solving

Practice by Example

Example 2 (page 123)

Developing Proof **Which lines or segments are parallel? Justify your answer with a theorem or postulate.**

1.

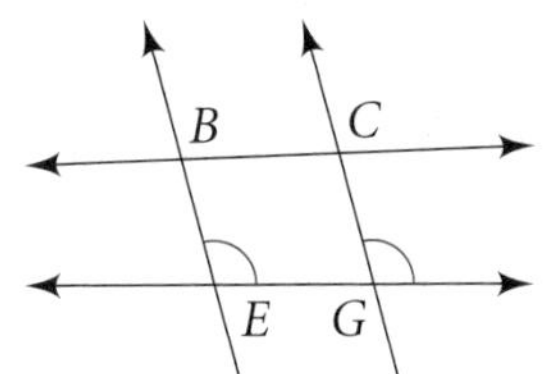

2.

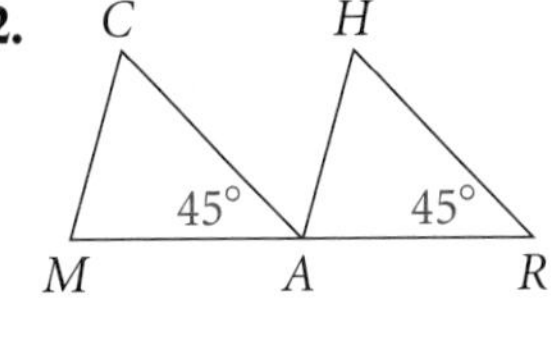

3.

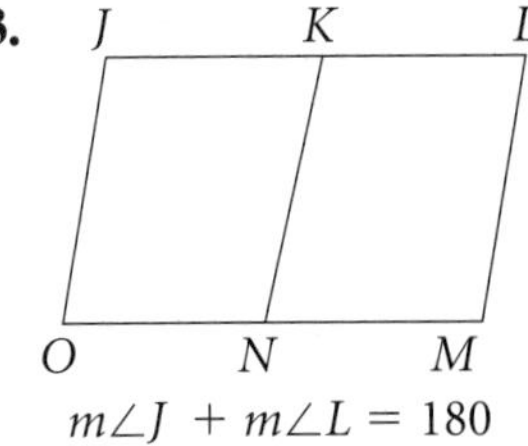

$m\angle J + m\angle L = 180$

Developing Proof **Using the given information, which lines, if any, can you conclude are parallel? Justify each conclusion with a theorem or postulate.**

4. $\angle 2$ is supplementary to $\angle 3$.

5. $\angle 6$ is supplementary to $\angle 7$.

6. $\angle 4$ is supplementary to $\angle 8$.

7. $m\angle 7 = 70, m\angle 9 = 110$

8. $\angle 1 \cong \angle 3$

9. $\angle 9 \cong \angle 12$

10. $\angle 3 \cong \angle 6$

11. $\angle 2 \cong \angle 10$

12. $\angle 1 \cong \angle 6$

13. $\angle 8 \cong \angle 6$

14. $\angle 11 \cong \angle 7$

15. $\angle 5 \cong \angle 10$

Examples 1, 3 (pages 123, 124)

Real-World Connection

The ladder rungs are perpendicular to each side. Therefore, the rungs are parallel to each other.

16. Developing Proof Complete this flow proof of Theorem 3-6.

In a plane, if two lines are perpendicular to the same line, then they are parallel to each other.

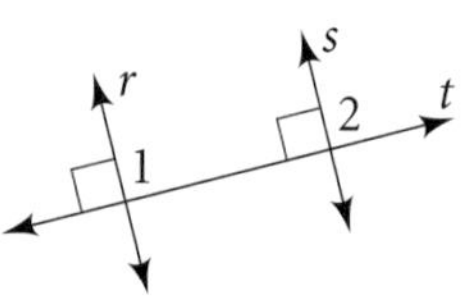

Given: $r \perp t, s \perp t$

Prove: $r \parallel s$

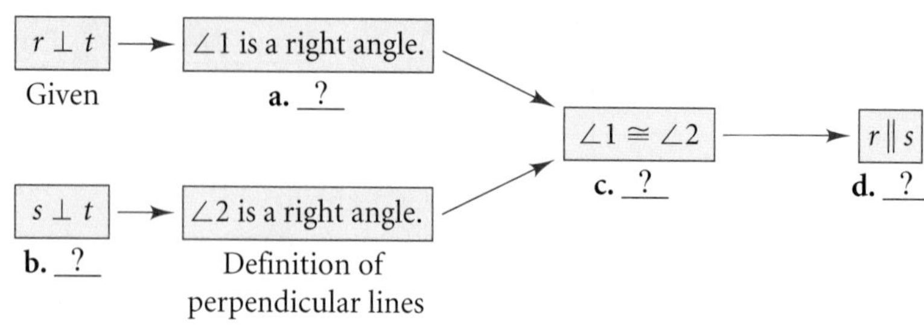

17. Developing Proof Complete this paragraph proof of Theorem 3-4.

If two lines and a transversal form supplementary same-side interior angles, then the two lines are parallel.

Given: $\angle 1$ and $\angle 2$ are supplementary.

Prove: $\ell \parallel m$

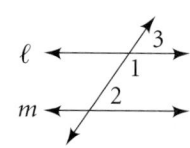

Proof: $\angle 2$ is a supplement of **a.** __?__ and $\angle 3$ is a supplement of **b.** __?__. Since supplements of the same angle are congruent, **c.** __?__ $\cong$ **d.** __?__. Since $\angle 2$ and $\angle 3$ are also corresponding angles, $\ell \parallel m$ by the **e.** __?__ Postulate.

Example 4 (page 124)

x^2 **Algebra Find the value of x for which $\ell \parallel m$.**

18.

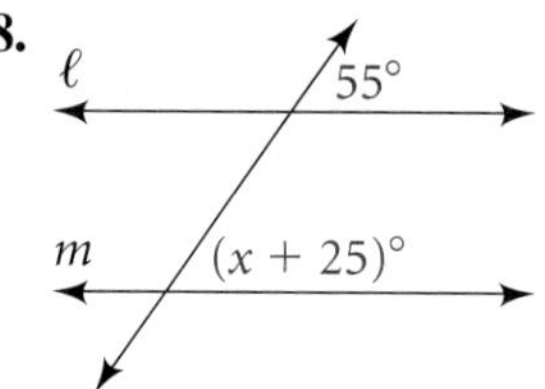

19.

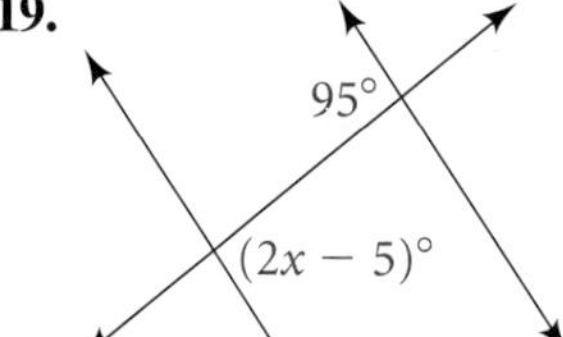

20.

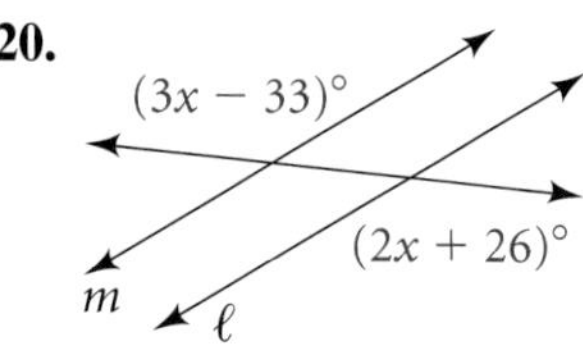

21.

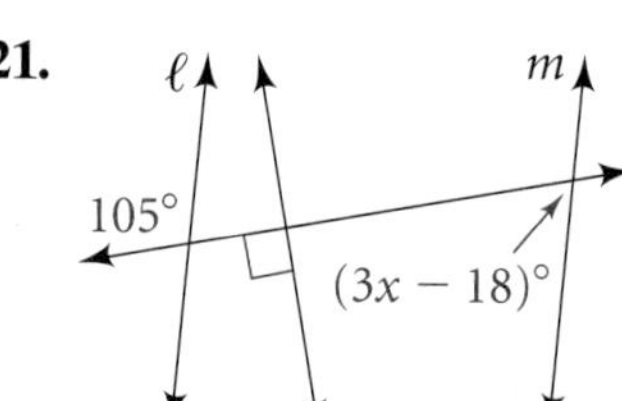

22.

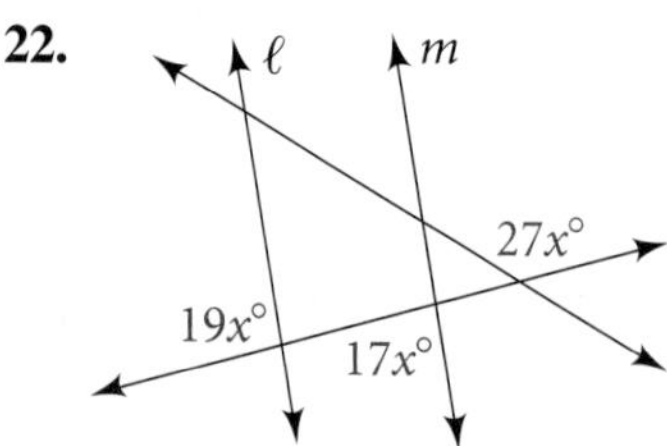

23.

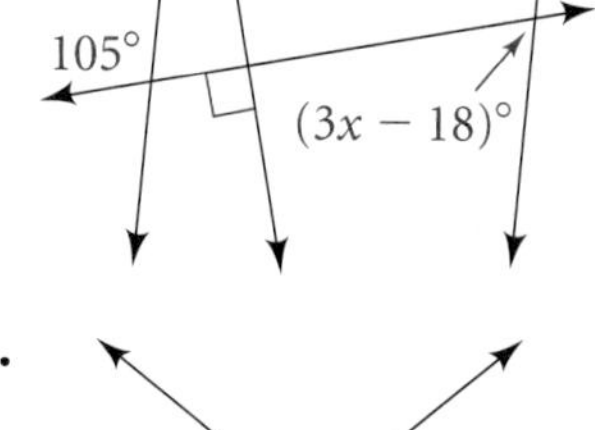
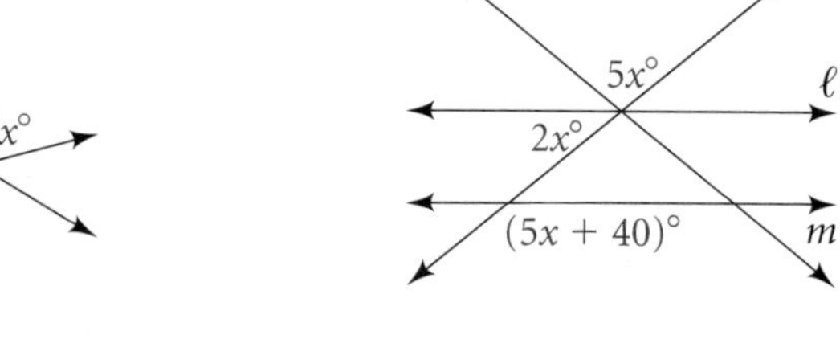

Example 5 (page 125)

24. The top and bottom of a frame are cut from the narrower piece of wood. The sides are cut from the wider piece of wood. Explain why the opposite sides of the frame will be parallel.

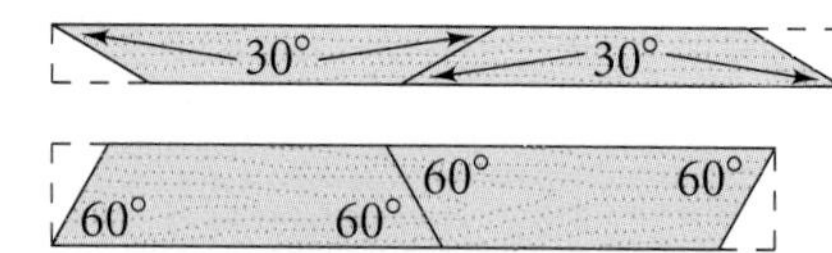

25. **Drafting** An artist uses the drawing tool in the diagram at the right. The artist draws a line, slides the triangle along the flat surface, and draws another line. Explain why the drawn lines must be parallel.

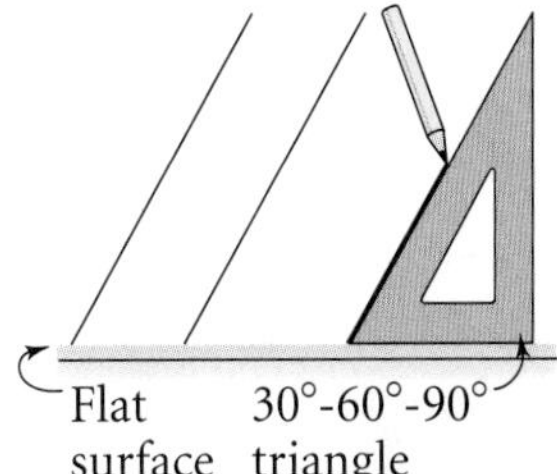
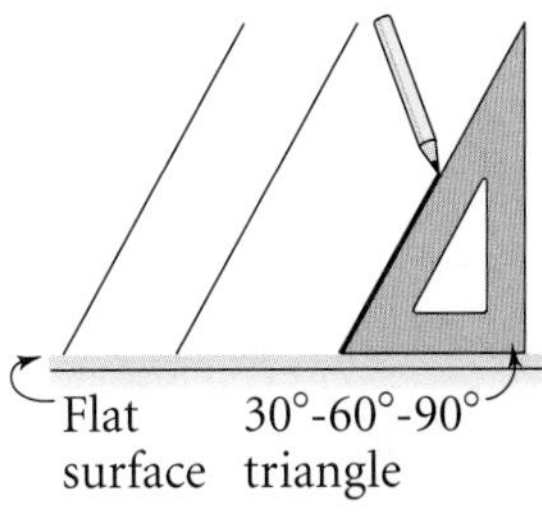
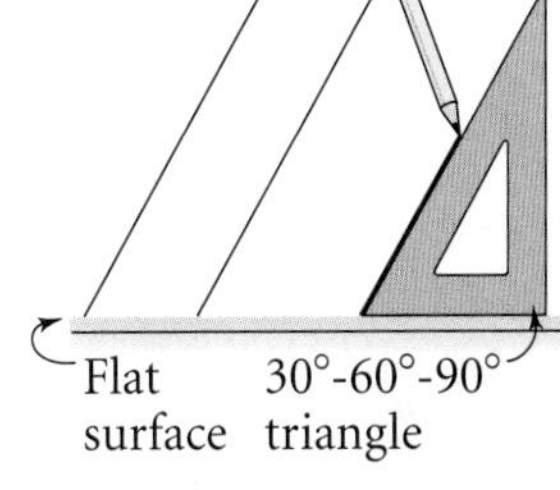

B **Apply Your Skills**

Proof 26. **Developing Proof** Copy and complete the paragraph proof of Theorem 3-5 for three coplanar lines.

Reading Math

For help with reading and solving Exercise 26, see p. 130.

If two lines are parallel to the same line, then they are parallel to each other.

Given: $\ell \parallel k$ and $m \parallel k$

Prove: $\ell \parallel m$

Proof: $\ell \parallel k$ means that $\angle 2 \cong \angle 1$ by the **a.** _?_ Postulate. $m \parallel k$ means that **b.** _?_ $\cong$ **c.** _?_ for the same reason. By the Transitive Property of Congruence, $\angle 2 \cong \angle 3$. By the **d.** _?_ Postulate, $\ell \parallel m$.

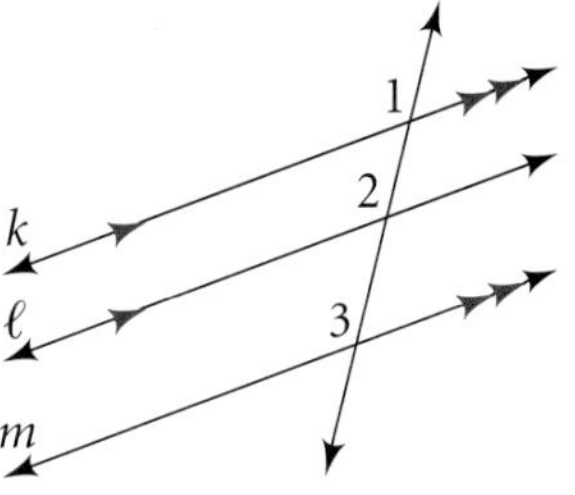

Algebra **Determine the value of x for which $r \parallel s$. Then find $m\angle 1$ and $m\angle 2$.**

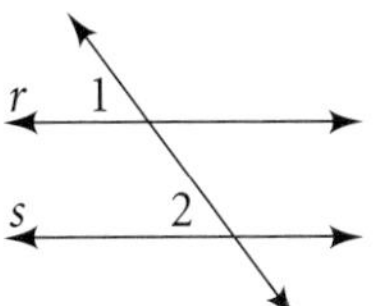

27. $m\angle 1 = 80 - x, m\angle 2 = 90 - 2x$

28. $m\angle 1 = 60 - 2x, m\angle 2 = 70 - 4x$

29. $m\angle 1 = 40 - 4x, m\angle 2 = 50 - 8x$

30. $m\angle 1 = 20 - 8x, m\angle 2 = 30 - 16x$

Real-World Connection

Careers A carpenter must draw angles precisely to ensure good fit.

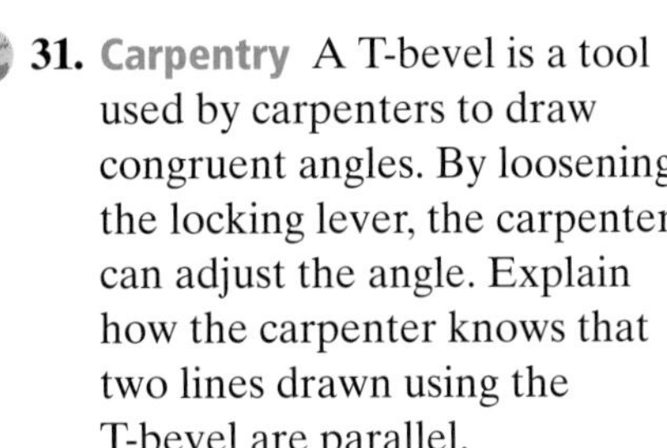

31. **Carpentry** A T-bevel is a tool used by carpenters to draw congruent angles. By loosening the locking lever, the carpenter can adjust the angle. Explain how the carpenter knows that two lines drawn using the T-bevel are parallel.

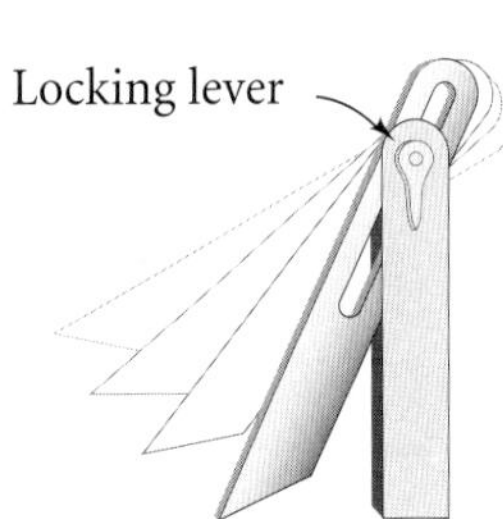

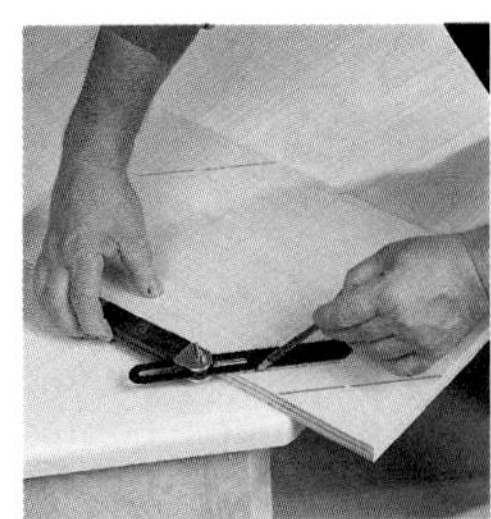

Which sides of quadrilateral $PLAN$ must be parallel? Explain.

32. $m\angle P = 72, m\angle L = 108, m\angle A = 72, m\angle N = 108$

33. $m\angle P = 59, m\angle L = 37, m\angle A = 143, m\angle N = 121$

34. $m\angle P = 67, m\angle L = 120, m\angle A = 73, m\angle N = 100$

35. $m\angle P = 56, m\angle L = 124, m\angle A = 124, m\angle N = 56$

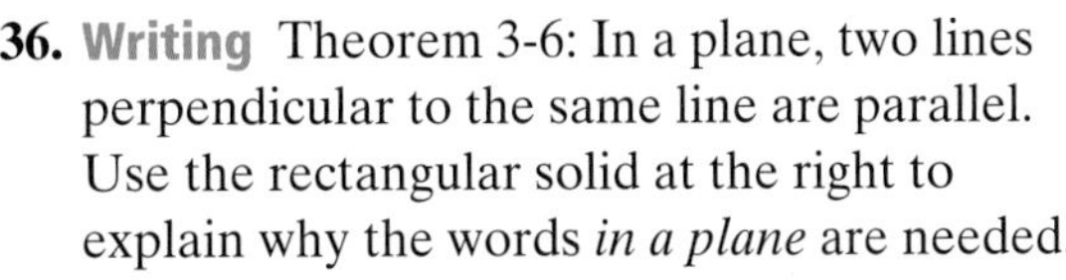

36. **Writing** Theorem 3-6: In a plane, two lines perpendicular to the same line are parallel. Use the rectangular solid at the right to explain why the words *in a plane* are needed.

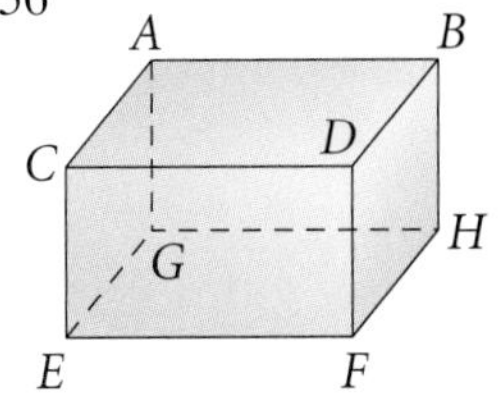

Critical Thinking **The Reflexive, Symmetric, and Transitive Properties for Congruence ($\cong$) are listed on page 91.**

37. Write reflexive, symmetric, and transitive statements for "is parallel to" ($\parallel$). State whether each statement is true or false and justify your answer.

38. Repeat Exercise 37 for "is perpendicular to" ($\perp$).

Exercise 39

39. Crew If the rowing crew at the left strokes in unison, the oars sweep out angles of equal measure. Explain why the oars on each side of the shell stay parallel.

Open-Ended In each exercise, information is given about the figure below. State another fact about $\angle 1$, $\angle 2$, $\angle 3$, or $\angle 4$ that will guarantee two lines are parallel. Tell which lines will be parallel and why.

40. $\angle 1 \cong \angle 3$

41. $m\angle 8 = 70, m\angle 9 = 110$

42. $\angle 5 \cong \angle 11$

43. $\angle 11$ and $\angle 12$ are supplementary.

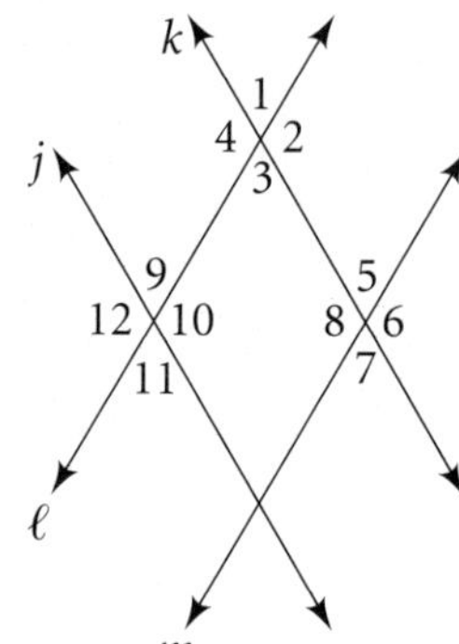

44. Reasoning If $\angle 1 \cong \angle 7$ in the diagram, what two theorems or postulates can you use to show that $\ell \parallel m$?

Challenge

Developing Proof For Exercises 45 and 46, use the diagram at the right and this plan for a proof.

Given: $\ell \parallel m, \angle 12 \cong \angle 8$

Prove: $j \parallel k$

Plan: To prove that $j \parallel k$, show that $\angle 12 \cong \angle 4$. It is given that $\angle 12 \cong \angle 8$, so $\angle 12 \cong \angle 4$ if $\angle 4 \cong \angle 8$. But $\angle 4 \cong \angle 8$ because $\ell \parallel m$ and corresponding angles are congruent.

45. Write a paragraph proof.

46. Write a flow proof.

47. Developing Proof Rewrite this paragraph proof of Theorem 3-4 as a flow proof.

If two lines and a transversal form supplementary same-side interior angles, then the two lines are parallel.

Given: $\angle 1$ and $\angle 2$ are supplementary.

Prove: $\ell \parallel m$

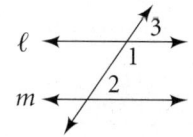

Proof: It is given that $\angle 1$ and $\angle 2$ are supplementary. $\angle 1$ and $\angle 3$ are also supplementary, so $\angle 2 \cong \angle 3$. Since $\angle 2$ and $\angle 3$ are corresponding angles, $\ell \parallel m$.

Need Help?

To show $\angle 1$ and $\angle 3$ are supplementary in Exercise 47, use the Angle Addition Postulate.

Proof For Exercises 48 and 49, write a flow proof.

48. Given: $a \parallel b, \angle 1 \cong \angle 2$

Prove: $\ell \parallel m$

49. Given: $\ell \parallel m$, $\angle 1$ is supplementary to $\angle 3$.

Prove: $a \parallel b$

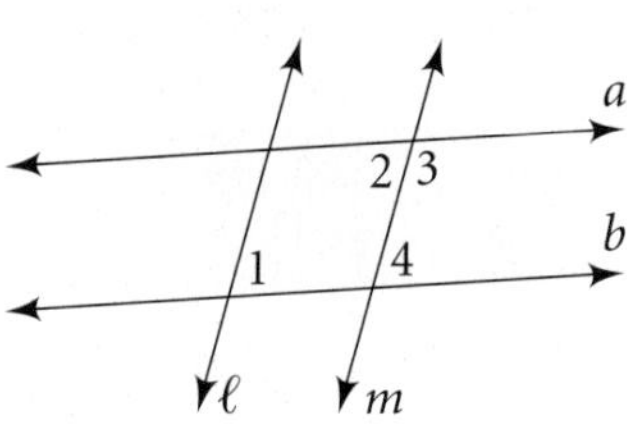

Proof 50. Prove the following statement is true by following the steps below:

If a transversal intersects two parallel lines, then the bisectors of two corresponding angles are parallel.

a. Draw and label a diagram on paper.
b. State what is given and mark the diagram to keep track of the information.
c. State what you are to prove.
d. Write a plan for proof.
e. Follow your plan and write the proof.

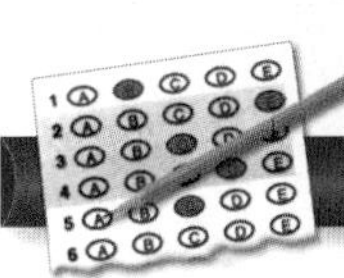

Standardized Test Prep

Multiple Choice

51. If *a*, *b*, *c*, and *d* are coplanar lines and $a \parallel b$, $b \perp c$, and $c \parallel d$, then which statement must be true?

A. $d \perp c$ **B.** $c \parallel a$ **C.** $d \perp a$ **D.** $d \parallel b$

Use the diagram for Exercises 52–54.

52. For what value of *x* is $c \parallel d$?

F. 21 **G.** 23
H. 43 **I.** 53

53. If $c \parallel d$, what is $m\angle 1$?

A. 24 **B.** 44
C. 136 **D.** 146

Short Response

54. Suppose $a \parallel b$ in the diagram above.

a. Write and solve an equation to find the value of *x*.
b. Write and solve an equation to find whether $c \parallel d$. Explain your answer.

Extended Response

Take It to the NET
Online lesson quiz at
www.PHSchool.com
Web Code: afa-0302

55. Two lines, *a* and *b*, are cut by a transversal *t*. $\angle 1$ and $\angle 2$ are any pair of corresponding angles. $\angle 1$ and $\angle 3$ are adjacent angles. $m\angle 1 = 2x - 38$, $m\angle 2 = x$, and $m\angle 3 = 6x + 18$.

a. Draw and label a diagram for the figure described.
b. Determine whether lines *a* and *b* are parallel. Justify your answer.

Mixed Review

Lesson 3-1

Find $m\angle 1$, and then $m\angle 2$. Justify each answer.

56.

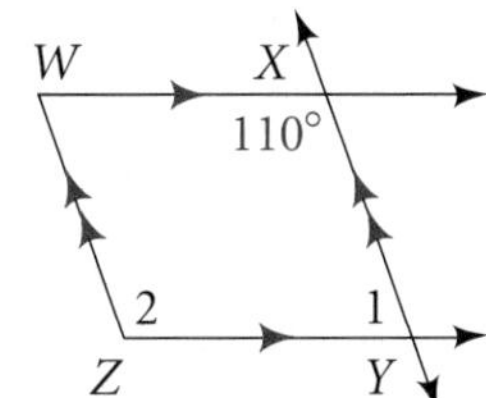

57.

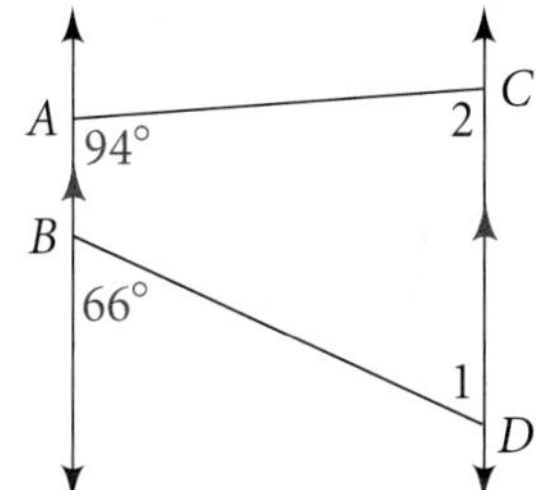

Lesson 2-1

Write the converse of each conditional statement. Determine the truth values of the original conditional and its converse.

58. If you are in Nebraska, you are west of the Mississippi River.

59. If a circle has a diameter of 8 cm, then it has a radius of 4 cm.

60. If a line intersects a pair of parallel lines, then same-side interior angles are supplementary.

61. If you add *ed* to a verb, you form the past tense of a verb.

62. If it is raining, then there are clouds in the sky.

Lesson 1-7

Find the area of each circle. Round to the nearest tenth.

63. $r = 8$ in. **64.** $d = 6$ cm **65.** $d = 9$ ft **66.** $r = 5$ in.

67. $d = 2.8$ m **68.** $r = 1.2$ m **69.** $d = 4.75$ ft **70.** $r = 0.6$ m

Reading for Developing Proof

For Use With Page 127, Exercise 26

Read the problem below and then follow along with what Collin thinks as he solves the problem. Check your understanding by solving the exercise at the bottom of the page.

Copy and complete the paragraph proof of Theorem 3-5 for three coplanar lines.

If two lines are parallel to the same line, then they are parallel to each other.

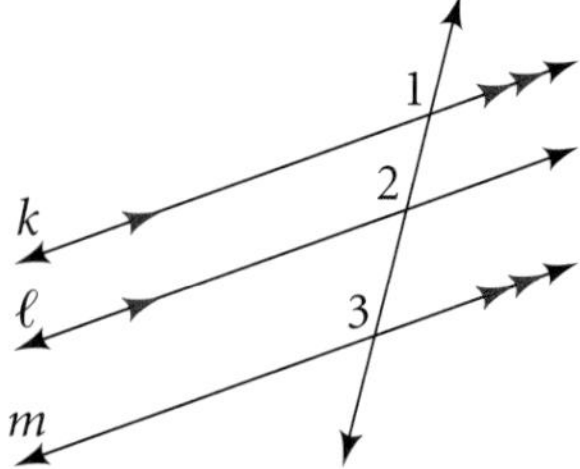

Given: $\ell \parallel k$ and $m \parallel k$

Prove: $\ell \parallel m$

Proof: $\ell \parallel k$ means that $\angle 2 \cong \angle 1$ by the **a.** _?_ Postulate. $m \parallel k$ means that **b.** _?_ $\cong$ **c.** _?_ for the same reason. By the Transitive Property of Congruence, $\angle 2 \cong \angle 3$. By the **d.** _?_ Postulate, $\ell \parallel m$.

What Collin Thinks	What Collin Writes
Let's see. $\angle 1$ and $\angle 2$ are corresponding angles. If $\ell \parallel k$, then $\angle 1 \cong \angle 2$ by Postulate 3-1 on page 116.	**$\ell \parallel k$ means that $\angle 2 \cong \angle 1$ by the a. Corresponding Angles Postulate.**
Now I will use the fact that $m \parallel k$. So I'll ignore line ℓ. That leaves me with $\angle 1$ and $\angle 3$ to consider. These also are corresponding angles.	**$m \parallel k$ means that b. $\angle 1 \cong$ c. $\angle 3$ for the same reason.**
Now, $\angle 2 \cong \angle 3$ and they are corresponding angles. This fits the postulate in which the hypothesis is "corresponding angles are congruent." By Postulate 3-2 on page 122, I can conclude "the lines are parallel."	**By the Transitive Property of Congruence, $\angle 2 \cong \angle 3$. By the d. Converse of the Corresponding Angles Postulate, $\ell \parallel m$.**

EXERCISE

Copy and complete this paragraph proof of Theorem 3-5 for three coplanar lines.

If two lines are parallel to the same line, then they are parallel to each other.

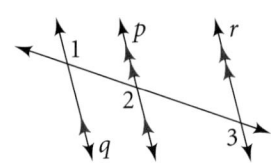

Given: $q \parallel p$ and $p \parallel r$

Prove: $q \parallel r$

Proof: $q \parallel p$ means that $\angle 1 \cong \angle 2$ by the **a.** _?_ Theorem. $p \parallel r$ means that **b.** _?_ $\cong$ **c.** _?_ by the Corresponding Angles Postulate. By the Transitive Property of Congruence, $\angle 1 \cong \angle 3$. By the **d.** _?_ Theorem, $q \parallel r$.

Parallel Lines and the Triangle Angle-Sum Theorem

Lesson Preview

What You'll Learn

To classify triangles and find the measures of their angles

To use exterior angles of triangles

. . . And Why

To find the reclining angle of a lounge chair, as in Example 5

✔ Check Skills You'll Need

(For help, go to Lesson 1-4.)

Classify each angle as *acute, right,* or *obtuse.*

1. 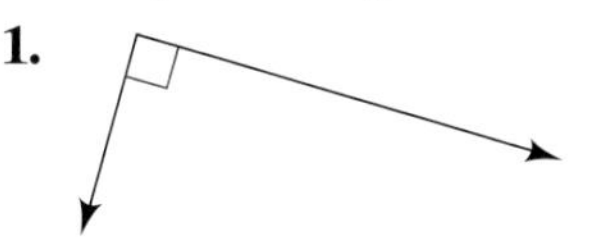
2. 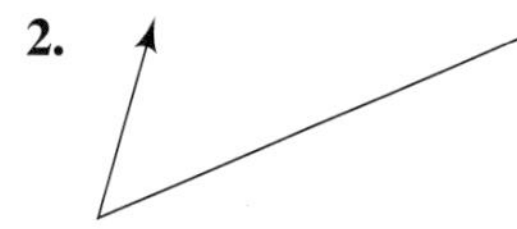
3. 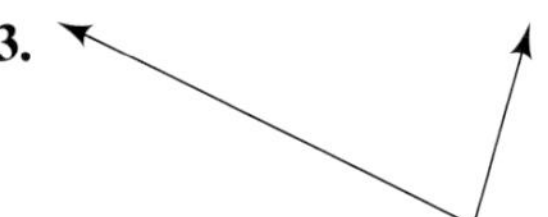

x^2 Algebra **Solve each equation.**

4. $30 + 90 + x = 180$

5. $55 + x + 105 = 180$

6. $x + 58 = 90$

7. $32 + x = 90$

New Vocabulary
- acute triangle
- right triangle
- obtuse triangle
- equiangular triangle
- equilateral triangle
- isosceles triangle
- scalene triangle
- exterior angle of a polygon
- remote interior angles

Interactive lesson includes instant self-check, tutorials, and activities.

OBJECTIVE 1

Finding Angle Measures in Triangles

Investigation: The Sum of Three Angle Measures

- Draw and cut out a large triangle.
- Number the angles and tear them off.
- Place the three angles adjacent to each other to form one angle as shown in the figure at the right.

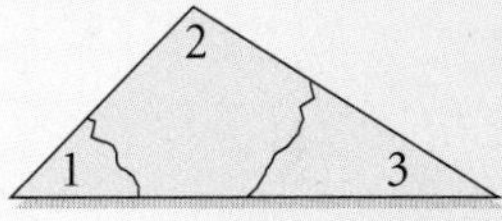

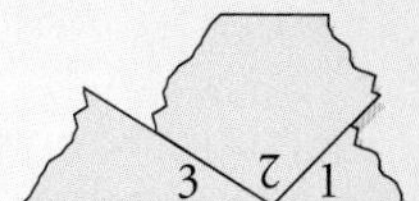

1. Compare your results with others. Write your observations.
2. Make a conjecture about the sum of the measures of the angles of a triangle.

The diagrams in the Investigation suggest the Triangle Angle-Sum Theorem.

Key Concepts

Theorem 3-7 **Triangle Angle-Sum Theorem**

The sum of the measures of the angles of a triangle is 180.

$$m\angle A + m\angle B + m\angle C = 180$$

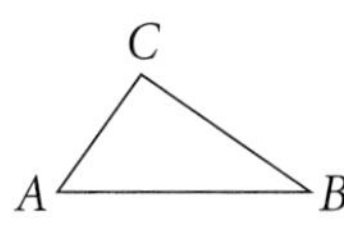

The following proof of Theorem 3-7 relies on the idea that through a point not on a given line you can draw a line parallel to the given line.

Proof

Proof of Theorem 3-7

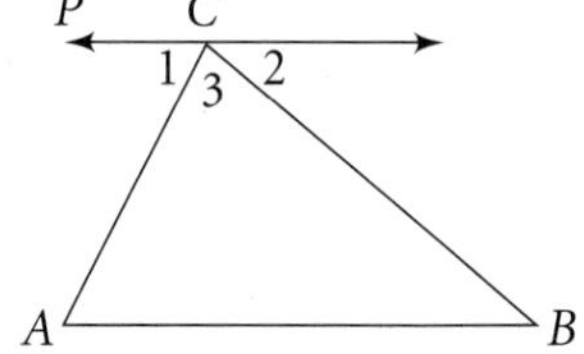

Given: $\triangle ABC$

Prove: $m\angle A + m\angle B + m\angle 3 = 180$

Proof: By the Protractor Postulate, you can draw $\overrightarrow{CP}$ so that $m\angle 1 = m\angle A$. Then, $\angle 1$ and $\angle A$ are congruent alternate interior angles, so $\overleftrightarrow{CP} \parallel \overline{AB}$. $\angle 2$ and $\angle B$ are also alternate interior angles, so by the Alternate Interior Angles Theorem, $m\angle 2 = m\angle B$. By substitution, $m\angle A + m\angle B + m\angle 3 = m\angle 1 + m\angle 2 + m\angle 3$, which is equal to 180 by the Angle Addition Postulate.

Need Help?
Apply the Angle Addition Postulate twice to get $m\angle 1 + m\angle 2 + m\angle 3 = 180$.

1 EXAMPLE Applying the Triangle Angle-Sum Theorem

Find $m\angle 1$.

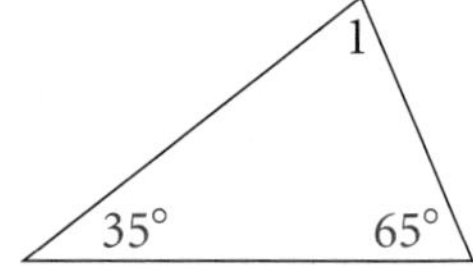

$m\angle 1 + 35 + 65 = 180$	**Triangle Angle-Sum Theorem**
$m\angle 1 + 100 = 180$	**Simplify.**
$m\angle 1 = 80$	**Subtract 100 from each side.**

Check Understanding 1 **a.** $\triangle MNP$ is a right triangle. $\angle M$ is a right angle and $m\angle N$ is 58. Find $m\angle P$.
b. Reasoning Explain why this statement must be true:
If a triangle is a right triangle, its acute angles are complementary.

2 EXAMPLE Using Algebra

Algebra Find the values of x, y, and z.

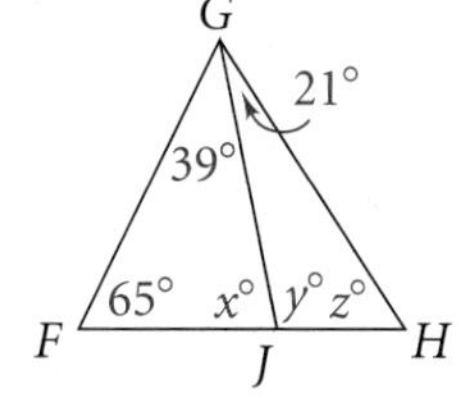

To find the value of x, use $\triangle GFJ$.

$39 + 65 + x = 180$	**Triangle Angle-Sum Theorem**
$104 + x = 180$	**Simplify.**
$x = 76$	**Subtract 104 from each side.**

To find the value of y, look at $\angle FJH$. It is a straight angle.

$m\angle GJF + m\angle GJH = 180$	**Angle Addition Postulate**
$x + y = 180$	**Substitute.**
$76 + y = 180$	**Substitute 76 for *x*.**
$y = 104$	**Subtract 76 from each side.**

To find the value of z, use $\triangle GJH$.

$21 + 104 + z = 180$	**Triangle Angle-Sum Theorem**
$125 + z = 180$	**Simplify.**
$z = 55$	**Subtract 125 from each side.**

Check Understanding 2 **Critical Thinking** Describe how you could use $\triangle GFH$ instead of $\triangle GJH$ to find the value of z.

In Chapter 1, you classified an angle by its measure. You can classify a triangle by its angles and sides.

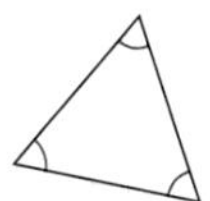
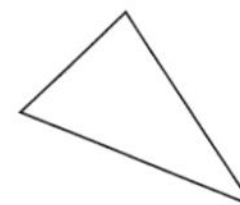
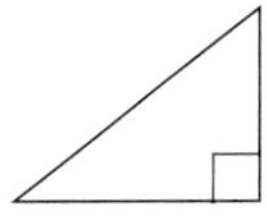
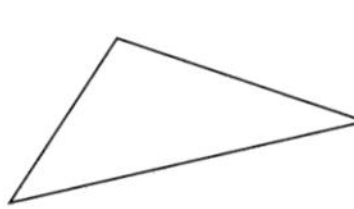

Equiangular	**Acute**	**Right**	**Obtuse**
all angles congruent	all angles acute	one right angle	one obtuse angle

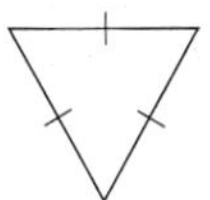
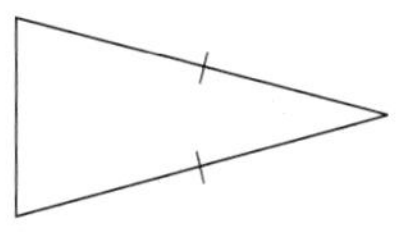
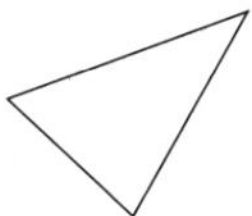

Equilateral	**Isosceles**	**Scalene**
all sides congruent	at least two sides congruent	no sides congruent

Real-World Connection

Four isosceles triangles cap the Smith Tower in Seattle.

3 EXAMPLE Classifying a Triangle

Classify the triangle by its sides and its angles.

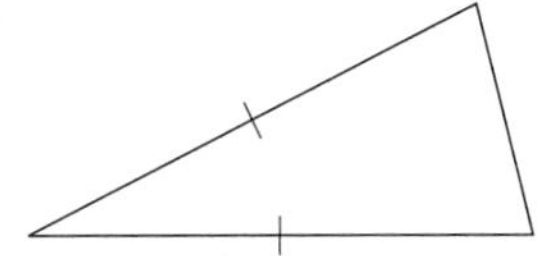

At least two sides are congruent, so the triangle is isosceles. All the angles are acute, so the triangle is acute.

The triangle is an acute isosceles triangle.

Check Understanding 3 Draw and mark a triangle to fit each description. If no triangle can be drawn, write *not possible* and explain why.

a. acute scalene **b.** isosceles right **c.** obtuse equiangular

OBJECTIVE

2 Using Exterior Angles of Triangles

Reading Math

"Interior angle of a triangle" means the same as "angle of a triangle."

An **exterior angle of a polygon** is an angle formed by a side and an extension of an adjacent side. For each exterior angle of a triangle, the two nonadjacent interior angles are its **remote interior angles.**

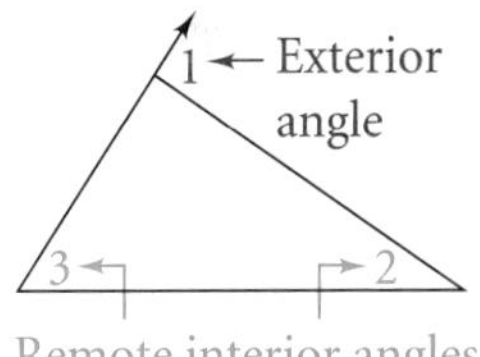

The diagram at the right suggests a relationship between an exterior angle and its two remote interior angles. Theorem 3-8 states this relationship. You will prove this theorem in Exercise 49.

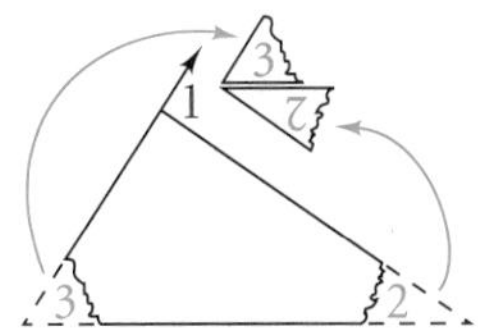

Key Concepts

Theorem 3-8 **Triangle Exterior Angle Theorem**

The measure of each exterior angle of a triangle equals the sum of the measures of its two remote interior angles.

$$m\angle 1 = m\angle 2 + m\angle 3$$

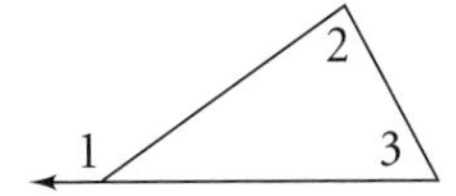

4 EXAMPLE Using the Exterior Angle Theorem

Algebra Find each missing angle measure.

a.

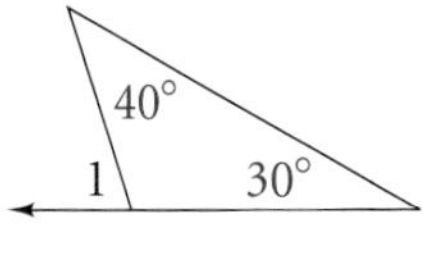

$m\angle 1 = 40 + 30$

$m\angle 1 = 70$

b.

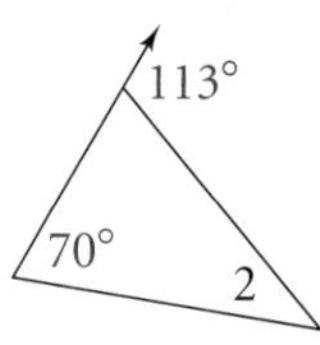

$113 = 70 + m\angle 2$

$43 = m\angle 2$

✓ **Check Understanding** **4** **a.** Find $m\angle 3$.

b. **Critical Thinking** Give the converse of the statement in Check Understanding 1(b). State whether the converse is true. Explain.

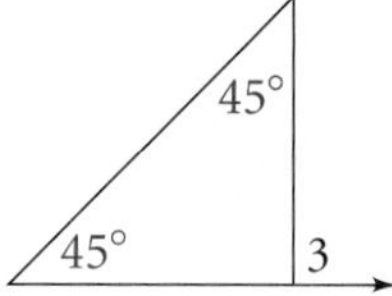

5 EXAMPLE Real-World Connection

Furniture Design The lounge chair has different settings that change the angles formed by its parts. Suppose $m\angle 2$ is 32 and $m\angle 3$ is 81. Find $m\angle 1$, the angle formed by the back of the chair and the arm rest.

$m\angle 1 = m\angle 2 + m\angle 3$	**Exterior Angle Theorem**
$m\angle 1 = 32 + 81$	**Substitute.**
$m\angle 1 = 113$	**Simplify.**

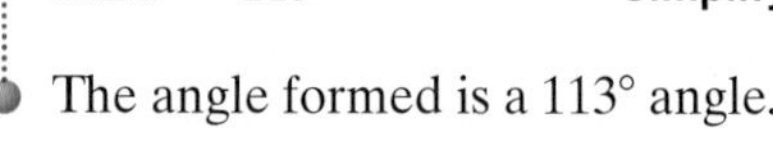

The angle formed is a 113° angle.

✓ **Check Understanding** **5** **a.** Change the setting on the lounge chair so that $m\angle 2 = 33$ and $m\angle 3 = 97$. Find the new measure of $\angle 1$.

b. Explain how you can find $m\angle 1$ *without* using the Exterior Angle Theorem.

EXERCISES

For more practice, see *Extra Practice*.

Practice and Problem Solving

A Practice by Example

Example 1
(page 132)

Find $m\angle 1$.

1.

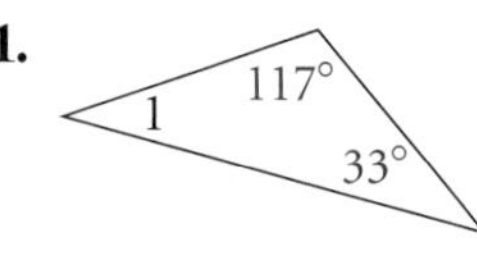

2.

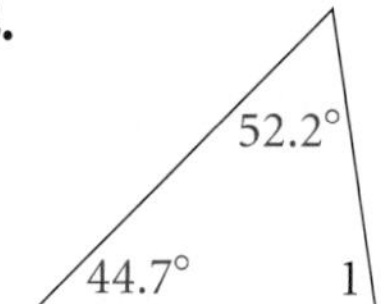

3.

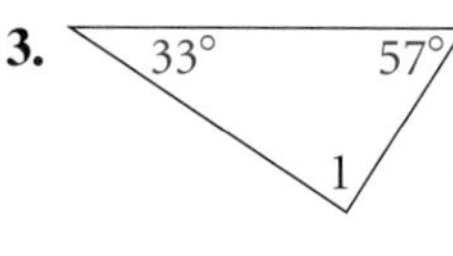

4. $\triangle RGT$ is a right triangle. $\angle G$ is a right angle and $m\angle R = 19$. Find $m\angle T$.

5. $\triangle TNL$ is a right triangle. $\angle N$ is a right angle. Find $m\angle T + m\angle L$.

Example 2 (page 132) x^2 **Algebra** **Find the value of each variable.**

6. 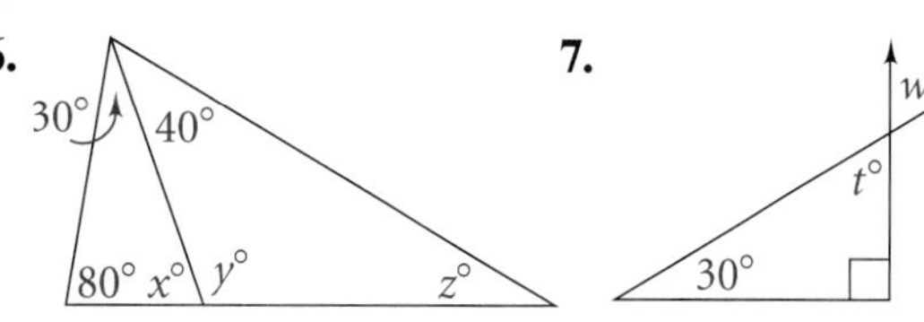

7.

8. 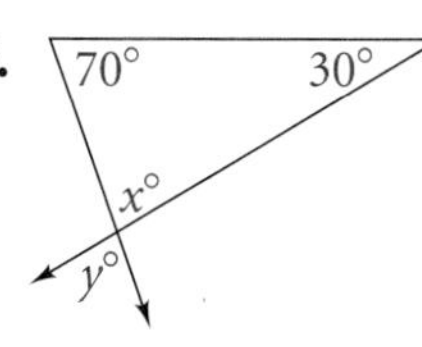

9. 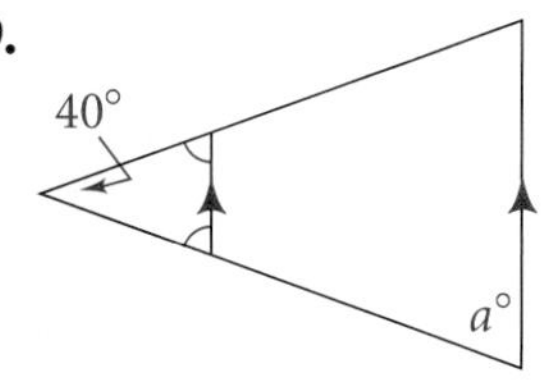

10. 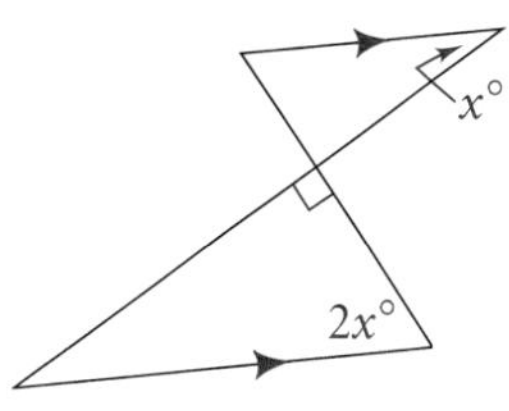

11. 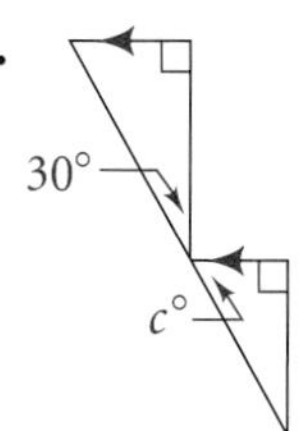

Example 3 (page 133) **Use a protractor and a centimeter ruler to measure the angles and the sides of each triangle. Classify each triangle by its angles and sides.**

12. 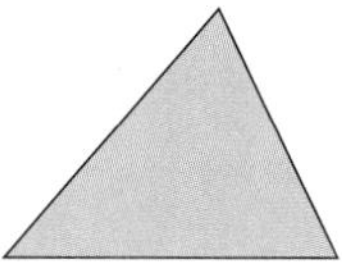

13. 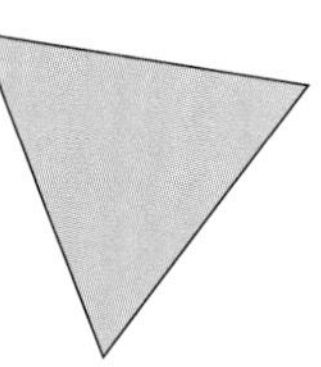

14. 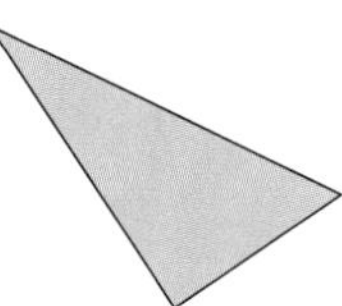

15. 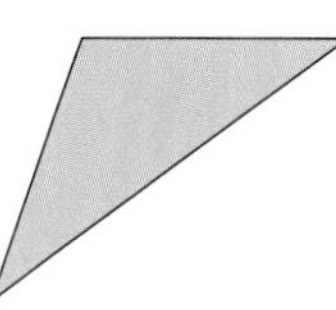

If possible, draw a triangle to fit each description. Mark the triangle to show known information. If no triangle can be drawn, write *not possible* and explain why.

16. acute equilateral

17. equilateral right

18. obtuse scalene

19. obtuse isosceles

20. scalene right

21. acute isosceles

22. isosceles right

23. scalene acute

Example 4 (page 134)

24. a. Which of the numbered angles at the right are exterior angles?
b. Name the remote interior angles for each.
c. How are exterior angles 6 and 8 related?

25. a. How many exterior angles at the right are at each vertex of the triangle?
b. How many exterior angles does a triangle have in all?

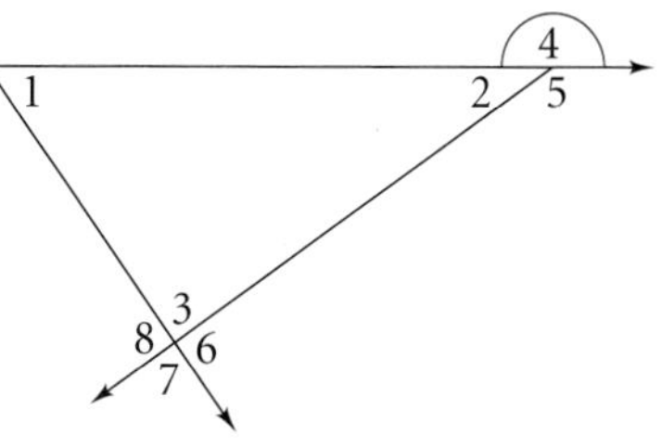

x^2 **Algebra** **Find each missing angle measure.**

26. 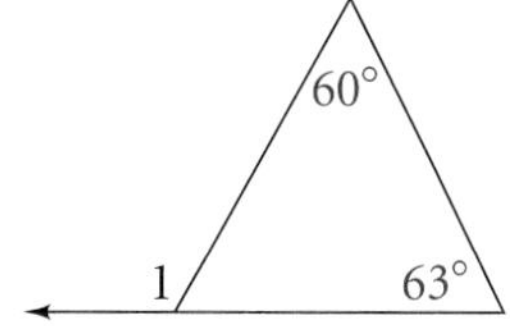

27. 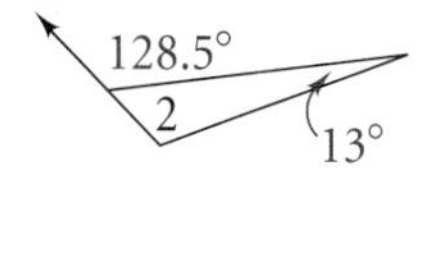

28. 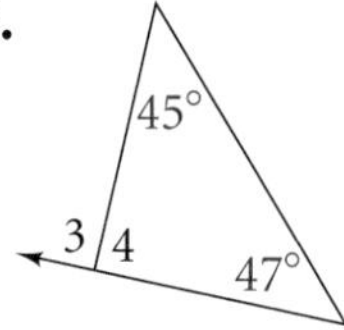

Example 5 (page 134)

29. **Music** The lid of a grand piano is held open by a prop stick whose length can vary, depending upon the effect desired. The longest prop stick makes angles as shown. What are the values of x and y?

30. A short prop stick makes the angles shown below. What are the values of a and b?

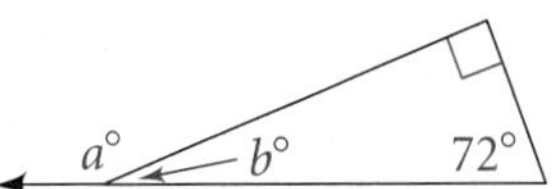

B Apply Your Skills

x^2 **Algebra** **Find the values of the variables and then the measures of the angles. Classify each triangle by its angles. Note that some figures have more than one triangle.**

31.

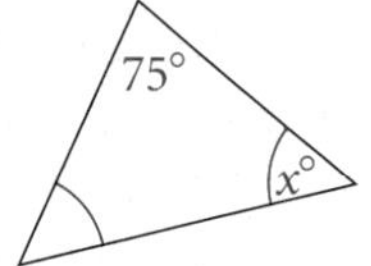

32.

$(8x - 1)°$

$(4x + 7)°$

33.

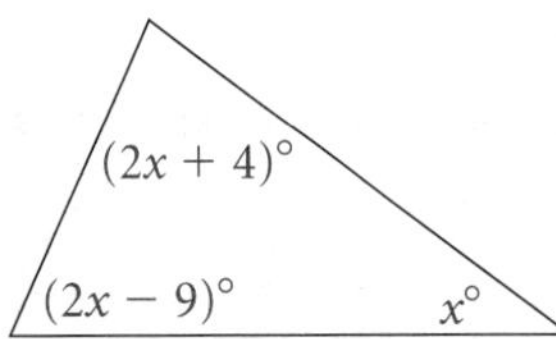

34.

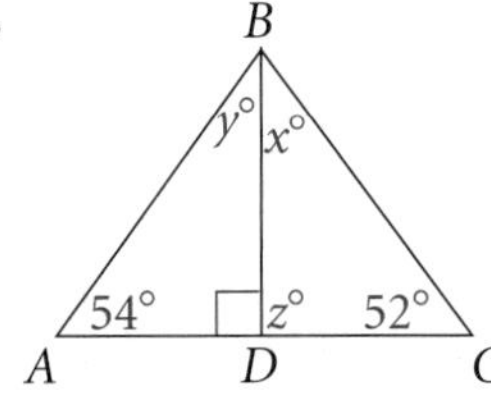

35.

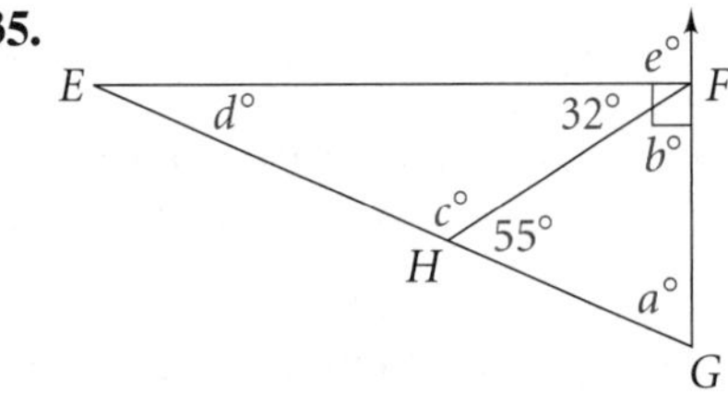

36.

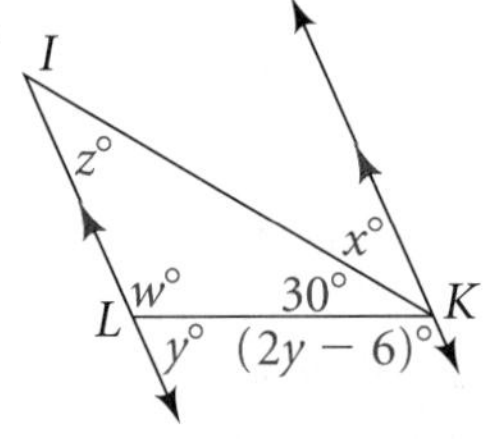

37. **Reasoning** What is the measure of each angle of an equiangular triangle? Explain.

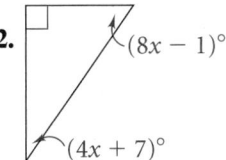

38. **Writing** Is every equilateral triangle isosceles? Is every isosceles triangle equilateral? Explain.

Reading Math

In Exercise 39, two triangles are the same if you can move one onto the other.

39. **Visualization** The diagram shows a triangle on a 3-by-3 geoboard. How many different triangles can be made on this geoboard? Classify each triangle by its sides and angles.

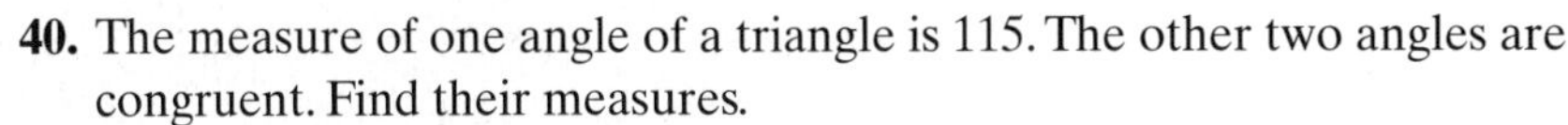

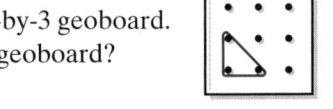

40. The measure of one angle of a triangle is 115. The other two angles are congruent. Find their measures.

41. Draw any triangle. Label it $\triangle ABC$. Extend both sides of the triangle to form two exterior angles at vertex A. Use the two exterior angles to explain why it does not matter which side of a triangle is extended to form an exterior angle.

Need Help?

In Exercise 42, use x and $2x$ for the angle measures. In Exercise 43, use $2x$, $3x$, and $4x$.

x^2 **42. Algebra** A right triangle has acute angles whose measures are in the ratio 1 : 2. Find the measures of these angles.

x^2 **43. a. Algebra** The ratio of the angle measures in $\triangle BCR$ is 2 : 3 : 4. Find the angle measures.

b. What type of triangle is $\triangle BCR$?

Use the figure at the right for Exercises 44–47.

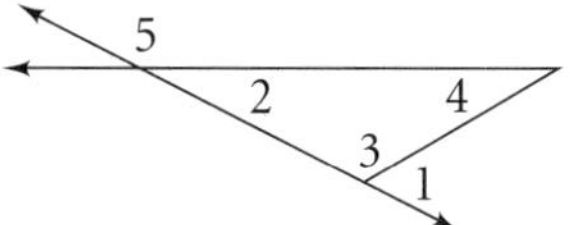

44. Find $m\angle 5$ if $m\angle 3 = 130$ and $m\angle 4 = 30$.

45. Find $m\angle 3$ if $m\angle 5 = 130$ and $m\angle 4 = 30$.

46. Find $m\angle 1$ if $m\angle 5 = 142$ and $m\angle 4 = 65$.

47. Find $m\angle 2$ if $m\angle 3 = 125$ and $m\angle 4 = 23$.

Proof **48. Developing Proof** Complete the paragraph proof of the following statement.

The acute angles of a right triangle are complementary.

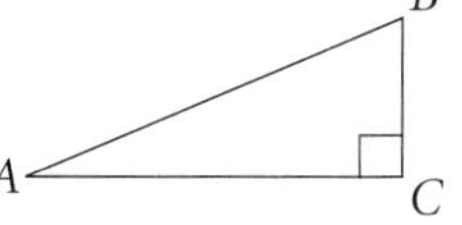

Given: $\triangle ABC$ with right angle C

Prove: $\angle A$ and $\angle B$ are complementary.

Proof: By the definition of right angle, $m\angle C =$ **a.** _?_.
By the Triangle Angle-Sum Theorem, $m\angle A + m\angle B + m\angle C =$ **b.** _?_.
Subtracting 90 from each side gives $m\angle A + m\angle B =$ **c.** _?_, so $\angle A$ and $\angle B$ are **d.** _?_ by the definition of **e.** _?_.

49. Developing Proof Complete this proof of the Triangle Exterior Angle Theorem by filling in the blanks.

Given: $\angle 1$ is an exterior angle of the triangle.

Prove: $m\angle 1 = m\angle 2 + m\angle 3$

a. $m\angle 1 + m\angle 4 = 180$ by the _?_ Postulate.

b. $m\angle 2 + m\angle 3 + m\angle 4 = 180$ by the _?_ Theorem.

c. $m\angle 1 + m\angle 4 = m\angle 2 + m\angle 3 + m\angle 4$ by the _?_ Property of Equality.

d. $m\angle 1 = m\angle 2 + m\angle 3$ by the _?_ Property of Equality.

50. Reasoning Two angles of a triangle measure 64 and 48. Find the measure of the largest exterior angle. Explain.

51. Open-Ended Study the design in the Navajo weaving below. Make a design of your own that makes repeated use of isosceles triangles.

Real-World Connection

Patricia Watson Tsinnie often uses isosceles triangles in her rug designs.

Need Help?

In Exercise 52(a), the solution of $\sqrt{x} = 9$ is not $x = 3$.

52. The measures of the angles of $\triangle RST$ are $5\sqrt{x}, 7\sqrt{x}$, and $8\sqrt{x}$.

a. Find the value of x.

b. Give the measure of each angle.

c. What type of triangle is $\triangle RST$?

Find the measure of an angle formed by the bisectors of the indicated angles.

53. two angles of an equiangular triangle

54. the acute angles of a right triangle

55. two same-side interior angles formed by two parallel lines and a tranversal

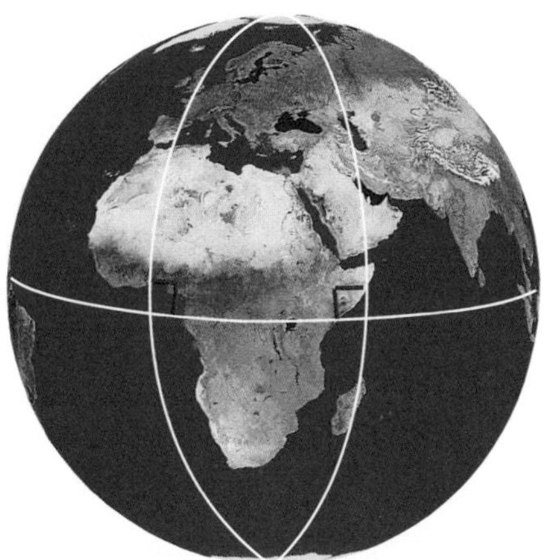

Challenge

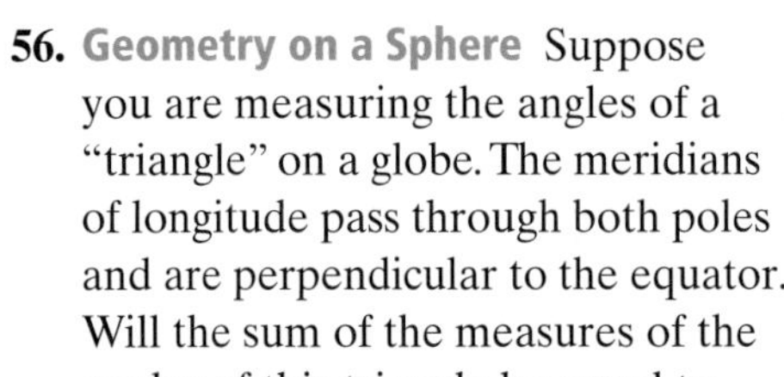

56. Geometry on a Sphere Suppose you are measuring the angles of a "triangle" on a globe. The meridians of longitude pass through both poles and are perpendicular to the equator. Will the sum of the measures of the angles of this triangle be equal to, greater than, or less than 180? Explain.

Probability In Exercises 57–61, you know only what is given about the measures of the angles of a triangle. Find the probability that the triangle is equiangular.

57. Each is a multiple of 30.

58. Each is a multiple of 20.

59. Each is a multiple of 60.

60. Each is a multiple of 12.

61. One is an obtuse angle of measure x.

62. In the figure at the right, $\overline{CD} \perp \overline{AB}$ and $\overline{CD}$ bisects $\angle ACB$. Find $m\angle DBF$.

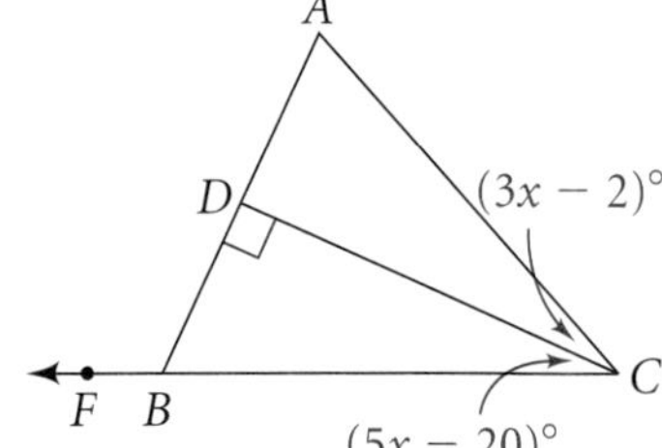

63. What can you conclude about the bisector of an exterior angle of a triangle if the remote interior angles are congruent? Justify your response.

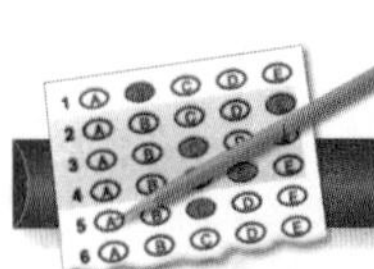

Standardized Test Prep

Multiple Choice

64. The measures of the angles of four triangles are shown. Which angle measures are *not* whole numbers?

A. $a, 3a, 2a$ **B.** $b, 3b, 4b$ **C.** $c, 3c, 5c$ **D.** $d, 3d, 6d$

Use the diagram at the right for Exercises 65–67.

65. $m\angle M = 25$ and $m\angle L = 43$. What is $m\angle JKM$?

F. 18 **G.** 68 **H.** 117 **I.** 162

66. $m\angle M = 4x$, $m\angle L = 5x$, and $m\angle MKL = 6x$. What is $m\angle JKM$?

A. 72 **B.** 108 **C.** 120 **D.** 132

67. $m\angle JKM = 15x - 48$, $m\angle L = 5x + 12$, and $m\angle M = 40$. What is $m\angle MKL$?

F. 9 **G.** 57 **H.** 78 **I.** 97

Short Response

68. A residential block is in the shape of a triangle. First Avenue, a side of the triangle, forms an exterior angle of measure $2x$ with one of the other sides. The remote interior angles measure $2x - 40$ and $x - 15$.

a. Sketch and label the figure with the information in the problem.

b. Write and solve an equation to determine the value of x. Then find the measures of the three interior angles.

Take It to the NET
Online lesson quiz at **www.PHSchool.com**
Web Code: afa-0303

69. $\triangle FYM$ is an obtuse triangle. $m\angle F = 21$ and $\angle M$ is acute.

a. What is the sum of $m\angle Y$ and $m\angle M$? Explain.

b. What is the range of whole numbers for $m\angle M$? Justify your answer.

Mixed Review

Lesson 3-2 x^2 **Algebra** **Determine the value of x for which $a \parallel b$.**

70.

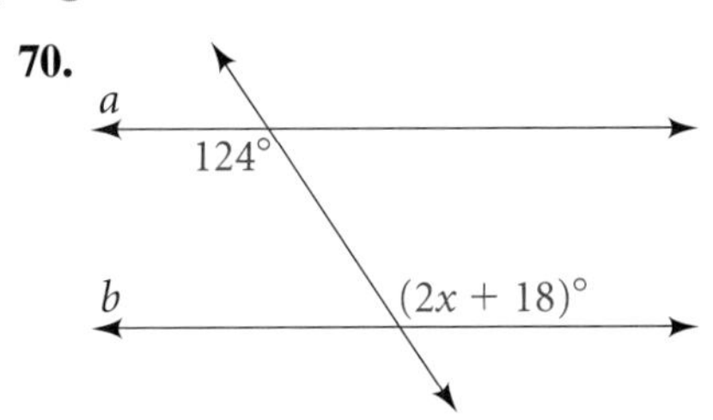

71.

a, b, $(3x - 2)°$, 44°

Lesson 1-4 x^2 **72. Algebra** In the figure at the right, $m\angle AOB = 3x + 20$, $m\angle BOC = x + 32$, and $m\angle AOC = 80$. Find the value of x.

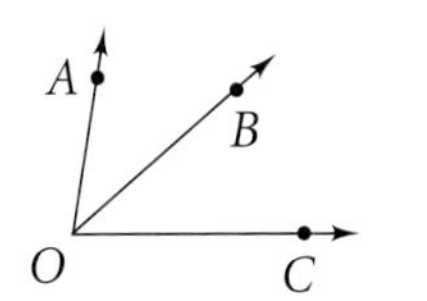

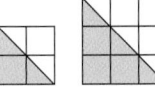

Lesson 1-1 **Draw the next figure in each sequence.**

73.

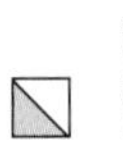
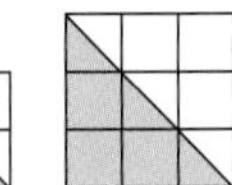

74.

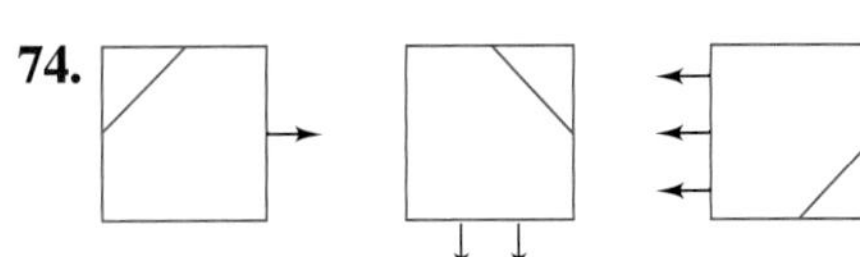

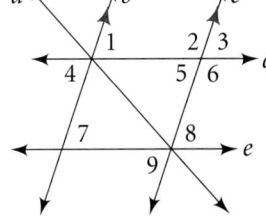

Checkpoint Quiz 1 — Lessons 3-1 through 3-3

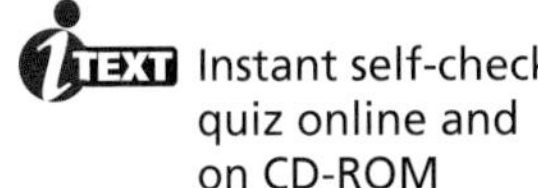

Instant self-check quiz online and on CD-ROM

Use the diagram at the right for Exercises 1–9. State the theorem or postulate that justifies each statement.

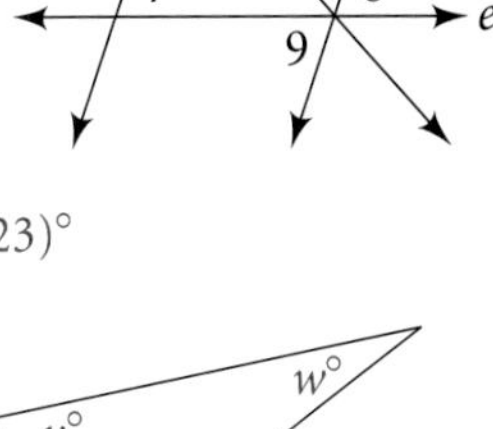

1. $\angle 1 \cong \angle 3$

2. If $\angle 5 \cong \angle 9$, then $d \parallel e$.

3. $m\angle 1 + m\angle 2 = 180$

4. If $\angle 4 \cong \angle 7$, then $d \parallel e$.

5. $\angle 1 \cong \angle 4$

6. $\angle 7 \cong \angle 9$

7. If $\angle 3 \cong \angle 8$, then $d \parallel e$.

8. $\angle 4 \cong \angle 5$

9. If $m\angle 8 + m\angle 6 = 180$, then $d \parallel e$.

10. Find the measures of the angles of each triangle. Classify each triangle by its angles.

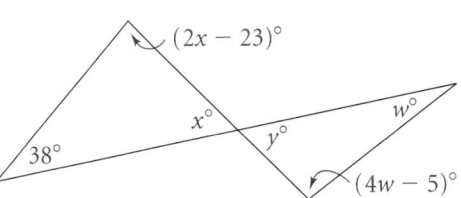

$(2x - 23)°$, $x°$, $y°$, $w°$, 38°, $(4w - 5)°$

Extension

Exploring Spherical Geometry

For Use With Lesson 3-3

Euclidean geometry is the basis for high school geometry courses. Euclidean geometry is the geometry of flat planes, straight lines, and points. In spherical geometry a "plane" is the curved surface of a sphere and a "line" is a great circle. (A *great circle* is the intersection of a sphere and a plane that contains the center of the sphere.)

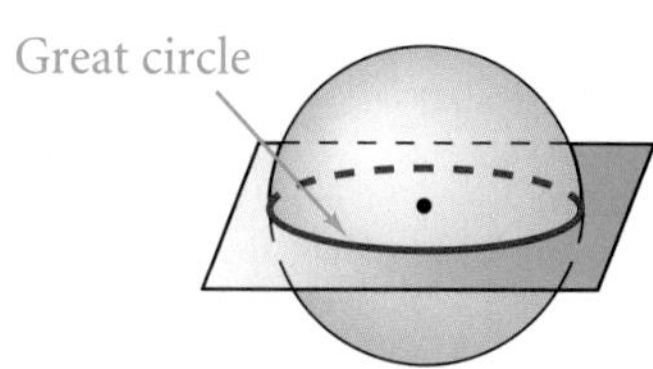

1 EXAMPLE

Lines of latitude and longitude are used to identify positions on Earth. Which of these lines are great circles?

All lines of longitude are great circles. The equator is the only line of latitude that is a great circle. All other lines of latitude are circles smaller than a great circle.

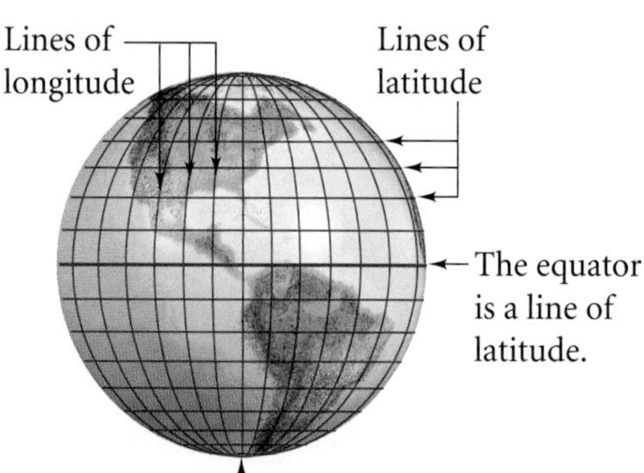

The lines of longitude all pass through the North and South Poles.

In Euclidean geometry,

Through a point not on a line, there is one and only one line parallel to the given line.

This statement is sometimes called Euclid's Parallel Postulate. Since only great circles are lines in spherical geometry, two lines always intersect. In spherical geometry, the Parallel Postulate is quite different:

Through a point not on a line, there is no line parallel to the given line.

2 EXAMPLE

The diagram at the right shows that any two lines on a sphere intersect at *two* points. What are the points of intersection of lines of longitude on Earth? What is special about these points?

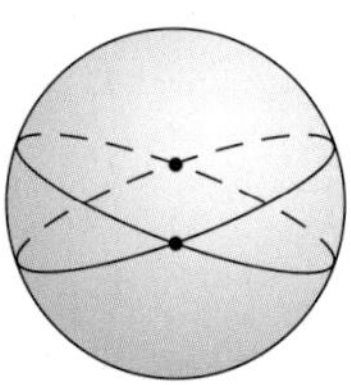

Lines of longitude intersect at the North and South Poles. The poles are on a line that passes through the center of Earth. Thus, the poles lie on Earth's axis and are the endpoints of a diameter of Earth.

One result of Euclid's Parallel Postulate is the Triangle Angle-Sum Theorem of Lesson 3-3. Something quite different happens in spherical geometry as a result of the spherical-geometry Parallel Postulate.

3 EXAMPLE

If you hold a string taut between any two points on a sphere, you obtain an arc that is part of a great circle. Three such arcs form a triangle on the sphere. Determine the sum of the measures of the angles of each of the three triangles shown below.

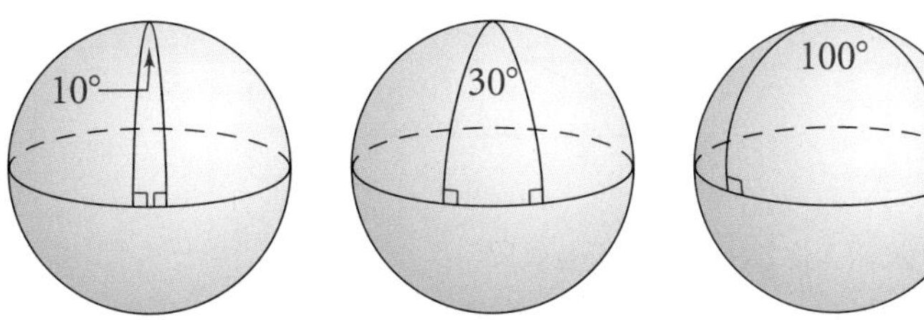

In the first triangle, the sum of the angle measures is 190. In the second triangle, it is 210, and in the third triangle the sum is 280.

EXERCISES

Draw a sketch to illustrate each property of spherical geometry. How does each property compare to what is true in Euclidean geometry?

1. There are pairs of points on a sphere through which more than one line can be drawn.

2. A triangle can have more than one right angle.

3. You can draw two equiangular triangles such that they have different angle measures.

In Exercises 4 and 5, draw a counterexample to show that each of these properties of Euclidean geometry is *not* true in spherical geometry.

4. Two lines that are perpendicular to the same line do not intersect.

5. If two angles of one triangle are congruent to two angles of another triangle, then the third angles are congruent.

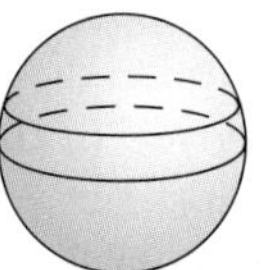

6. The figure at the right appears to show parallel lines on a sphere. Explain why this is not so.

7. Explain why a piece of the top circle in the figure is *not* a line segment. (*Hint:* What must be true of line segments in spherical geometry?)

Each of the following statements is true in Euclidean geometry. Does it seem to be true in spherical geometry? Make figures on a globe, ball, or balloon to support your answer.

8. Vertical angles are congruent.

9. Through a point on a line ℓ there exists one and only one line perpendicular to ℓ.

Technology Exterior Angles of Polygons

For Use With Lesson 3-4

Construct

Use geometry software. Construct a polygon similar to the one at the right. Extend each side as shown. To measure the exterior angles you will need to mark a point on each ray.

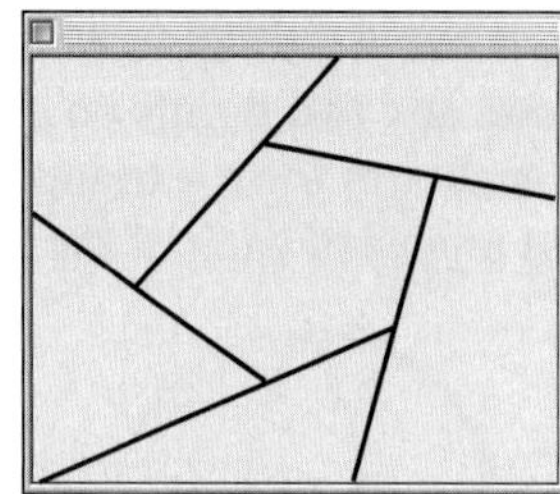

Investigate

- Measure each exterior angle.
- Calculate the sum of the measures of the exterior angles.
- Manipulate the polygon. Observe the sum of the measures of the exterior angles.

EXERCISES

1. Write a conjecture about the sum of the measures of the exterior angles (one at each vertex) of a convex polygon.
2. Test your conjecture with another polygon.

Extend

3. The figures below show a polygon that is decreasing in size until finally it becomes a point. Describe how you could use this to justify your conjecture in Exercise 2.

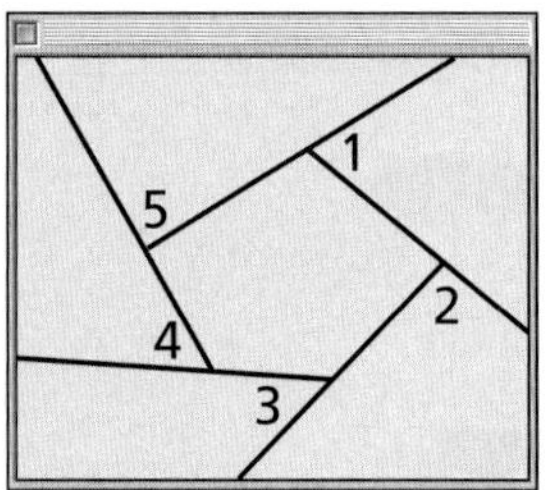

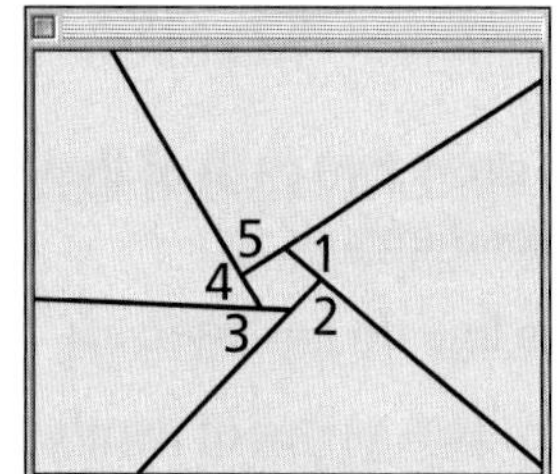

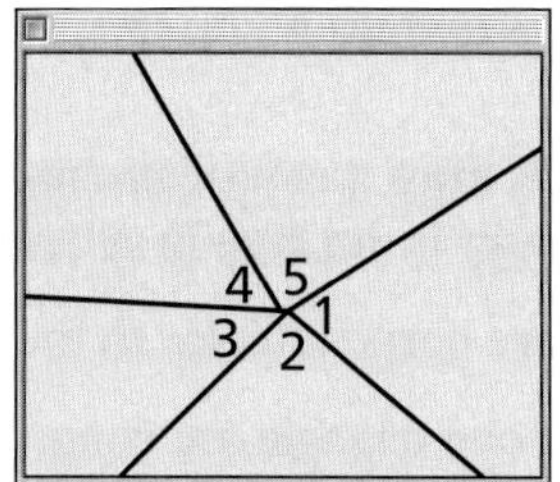

4. The figure at the right shows a square that has been copied several times. Notice that you can use the square to completely cover, or tile, a plane, without gaps or overlaps.
   a. Using geometry software, create several copies of other regular polygons with 3, 5, 6, and 8 sides. Regular polygons have sides of equal length and angles of equal measure.
   b. Which of the polygons you created can tile a plane?
   c. Measure *one* exterior angle of each polygon (including the square).
   d. Write a conjecture about the relationship between the measure of an exterior angle and your ability to tile a plane with a regular polygon.
   e. Test your conjecture with another regular polygon.

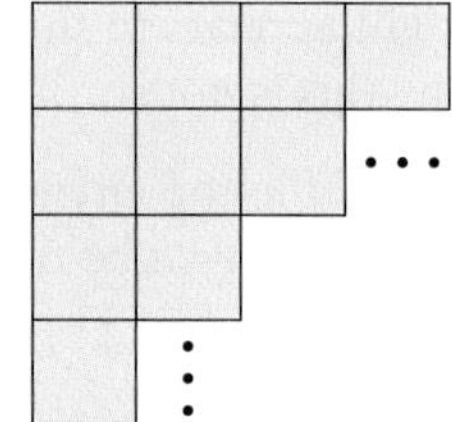

3-4 The Polygon Angle-Sum Theorems

Lesson Preview

What You'll Learn

To classify polygons

To find the sums of the measures of the interior and exterior angles of polygons

. . . And Why

To find the measure of an angle of a triangle used in packaging, as in Example 5

✓ Check Skills You'll Need

(For help, go to Lessons 1-4 and 3-3.)

Find the measure of each angle of quadrilateral $ABCD$.

1. 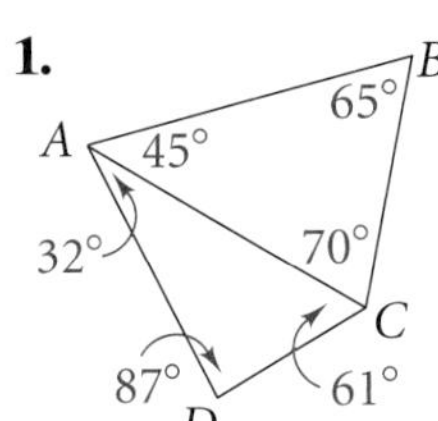

2. 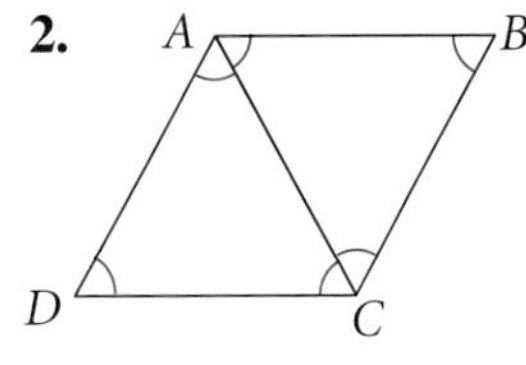

3. 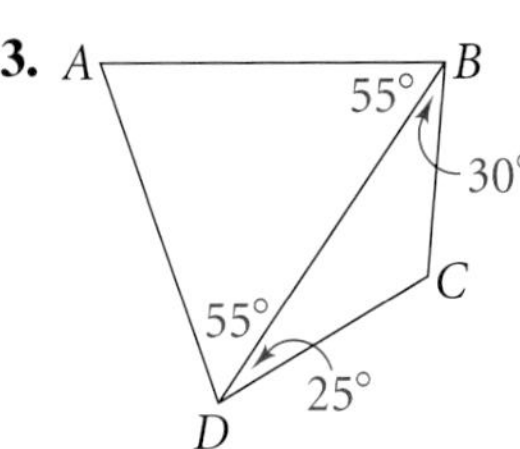

New Vocabulary
- polygon
- convex polygon
- concave polygon
- equilateral polygon
- equiangular polygon
- regular polygon

Interactive lesson includes instant self-check, tutorials, and activities.

OBJECTIVE 1

Classifying Polygons

Real-World Connection

Polygons create striking designs on a soccer ball.

A **polygon** is a closed plane figure with at least three sides that are segments. The sides intersect only at their endpoints, and no adjacent sides are collinear.

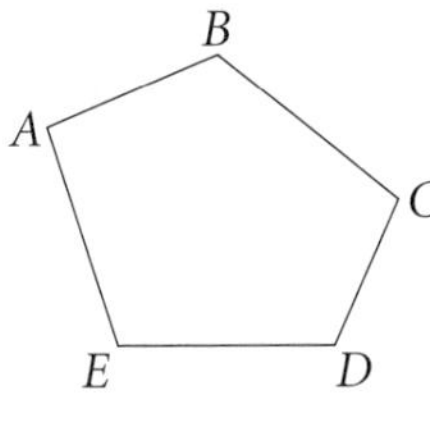

A polygon

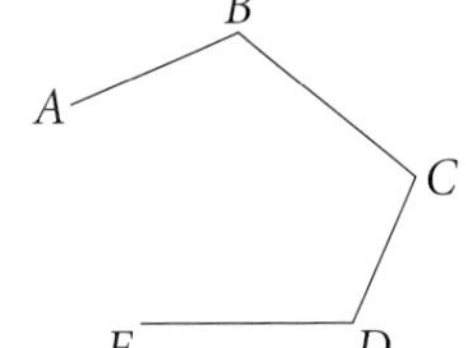

Not a polygon; not a closed figure

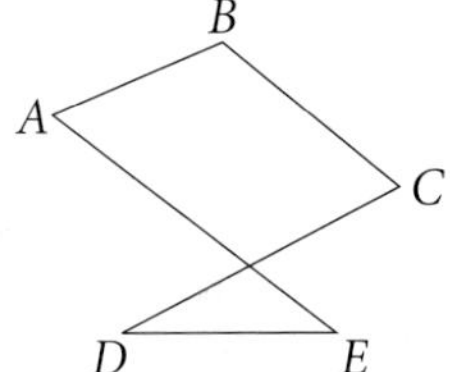

Not a polygon; two sides intersect between endpoints.

To name a polygon, start at any vertex and list the vertices consecutively in a clockwise or counterclockwise direction.

1 EXAMPLE Naming Polygons

Name the polygon. Then identify its vertices, sides, and angles.

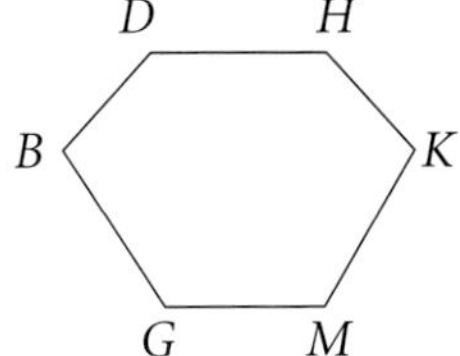

Two names for this polygon are $DHKMGB$ and $MKHDBG$.

vertices: D, H, K, M, G, B

sides: $\overline{DH}, \overline{HK}, \overline{KM}, \overline{MG}, \overline{GB}, \overline{BD}$

angles: $\angle D, \angle H, \angle K, \angle M, \angle G, \angle B$

✓ Check Understanding

1. Three polygons are pictured at the right. Name each polygon, its sides, and its angles.

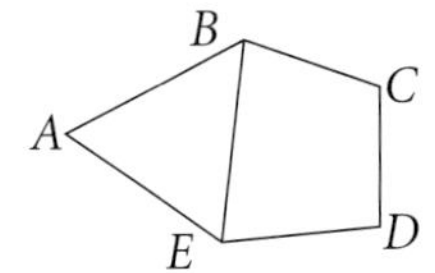

You can classify a polygon by the number of sides it has. The table at the right shows the names of some common polygons.

Sides	Name
3	triangle
4	quadrilateral
5	pentagon
6	hexagon
8	octagon
9	nonagon
10	decagon
12	dodecagon
n	n-gon

Polygons are classified as convex or concave.

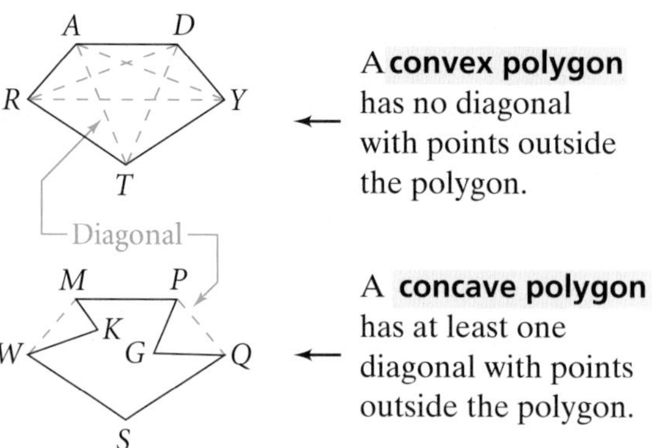

A **convex polygon** has no diagonal with points outside the polygon.

A **concave polygon** has at least one diagonal with points outside the polygon.

Need Help?
A diagonal of a polygon is a segment that connects two nonconsecutive vertices.

In this textbook, a polygon is convex unless stated otherwise.

2 EXAMPLE Real-World Connection

Tilework The tilework in the photo is a combination of different polygons that form a pleasing pattern. Classify the polygon outlined in red by using the table above. Then classify the polygon as convex or concave.

The polygon outlined in red has 6 sides. Therefore, it is a hexagon.

No diagonal of the hexagon contains points outside the hexagon. The hexagon is convex.

Check Understanding 2 Classify each polygon by its sides. Identify each as convex or concave.

a.

b.

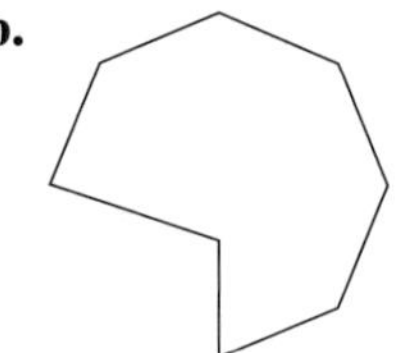

c. the 12-pointed star at the center of the tilework pictured above

OBJECTIVE 2

Polygon Angle Sums

Investigation: The Sum of Polygon Angle Measures

You can use triangles and the Triangle Angle-Sum Theorem to find the sum of the measures of the angles of a polygon. Record your data in a table like the one begun below.

Polygon	Number of Sides	Number of Triangles Formed	Sum of the Interior Angle Measures
(quadrilateral)	4	■	■ • 180 = ■

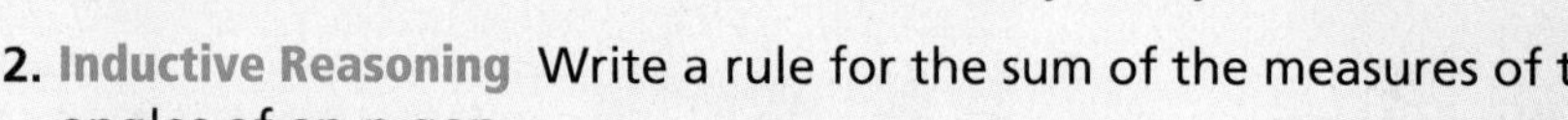

- Sketch polygons with 4, 5, 6, 7, and 8 sides.
- Divide each polygon into triangles by drawing all diagonals that are possible from one vertex.
- Multiply the number of triangles by 180 to find the sum of the measures of the angles of each polygon.

1. Look for patterns in the table. Describe any that you find.
2. **Inductive Reasoning** Write a rule for the sum of the measures of the angles of an n-gon.

Reading Math

An n-gon is a polygon with n sides, where n can be 3, 4, 5, 6, . . .

By dividing a polygon with n sides into $n - 2$ triangles, you can show that the sum of the measures of the angles of any polygon is a multiple of 180.

Key Concepts

Theorem 3-9 **Polygon Angle-Sum Theorem**

The sum of the measures of the angles of an n-gon is $(n - 2)180$.

3 EXAMPLE Finding a Polygon Angle Sum

Find the sum of the measures of the angles of a 15-gon.

For a 15-gon, $n = 15$.

Sum $= (n - 2)180$ **Polygon Angle-Sum Theorem**

$= (15 - 2)180$ **Substitute.**

$= 13 \cdot 180$ **Simplify.**

$= 2340$

The sum of the measures of the angles of a 15-gon is 2340.

✓ Check Understanding 3 **a.** Find the sum of the measures of the angles of a 13-gon.

b. **Critical Thinking** The sum of the measures of the angles of a given polygon is 720. How can you use Sum $= (n - 2)180$ to find the number of sides in the polygon?

You will sometimes use algebra with the Polygon Angle-Sum Theorem to find measures of polygon angles.

4 EXAMPLE Using the Polygon Angle-Sum Theorem

Algebra Find $m\angle Y$ in pentagon $TVYMR$ at the right. Use the Polygon Angle-Sum Theorem for $n = 5$.

$m\angle T + m\angle V + m\angle Y + m\angle M + m\angle R = (5 - 2)180$

$90 + 90 + m\angle Y + 90 + 135 = 540$ **Substitute.**

$m\angle Y + 405 = 540$ **Simplify.**

$m\angle Y = 135$ **Subtract 405 from each side.**

Check Understanding 4 Pentagon $ABCDE$ has 5 congruent angles. Find the measure of each angle.

You can draw exterior angles at any vertex of a polygon. The figures below show that the sum of the measures of the exterior angles, one at each vertex, is 360. This can be proved as a theorem in a way suggested in Exercise 46.

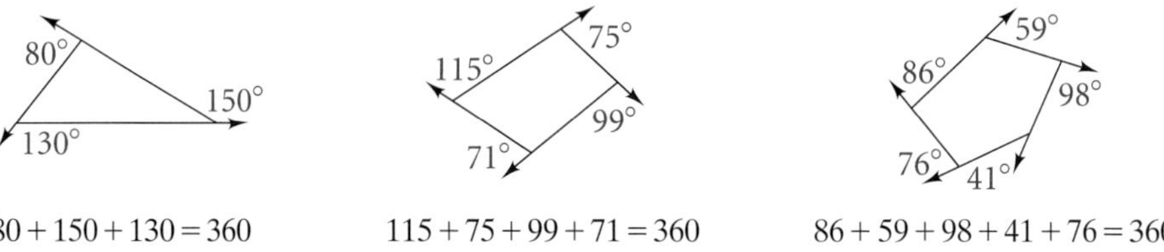

Key Concepts

Theorem 3-10 **Polygon Exterior Angle-Sum Theorem**

The sum of the measures of the exterior angles of a polygon, one at each vertex, is 360.

For the pentagon,
$m\angle 1 + m\angle 2 + m\angle 3 + m\angle 4 + m\angle 5 = 360.$

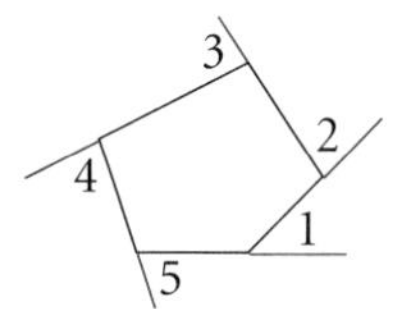

An **equilateral polygon** has all sides congruent. An **equiangular polygon** has all angles congruent. A **regular polygon** is both equilateral and equiangular.

5 EXAMPLE Real-World Connection

Packaging The game board at the left has the shape of a regular hexagon. It is packaged in a rectangular box outlined beneath it. The box uses four right triangles made of foam in its four corners. Find $m\angle 1$ in each foam triangle.

Method 1 Find the measure of an angle of the hexagon first.

- A regular hexagon has 6 sides and 6 congruent angles.
  The sum of the measures of the interior angles $= (6 - 2)180$, or 720.
- The measure of one interior angle is $\frac{720}{6}$, or 120.
- The measure of its adjacent exterior angle, $\angle 1$, is $180 - 120$, or 60.

Method 2 Find the measure of an exterior angle directly.

- The sum of the measures of the exterior angles is 360.
- The measure of one exterior angle, $\angle 1$, is $\frac{360}{6}$, or 60.

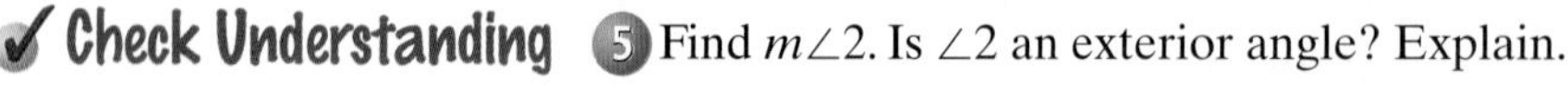

Check Understanding 5 Find $m\angle 2$. Is $\angle 2$ an exterior angle? Explain.

EXERCISES

For more practice, see *Extra Practice.*

Practice and Problem Solving

Practice by Example

Example 1 (page 143)

Is the figure a polygon? If not, tell why.

1. 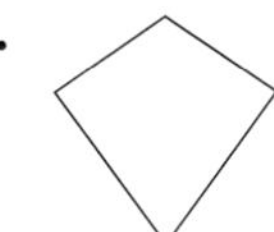

2. 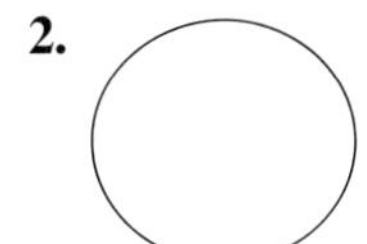

3. 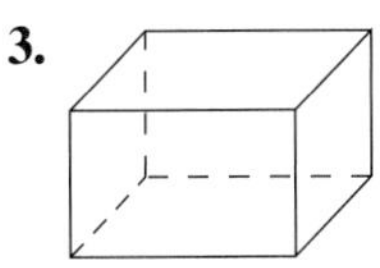

4. 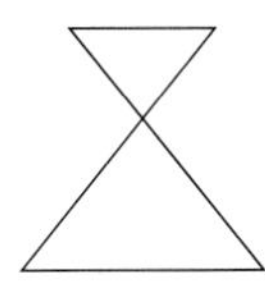

Name each polygon by its vertices. Then identify its sides and angles.

5. 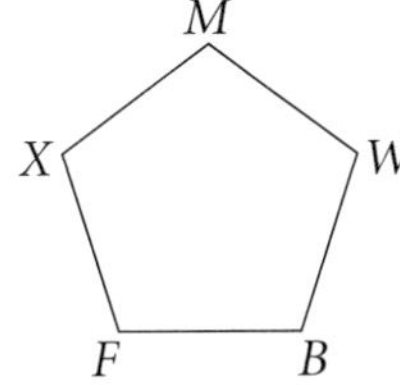

6. 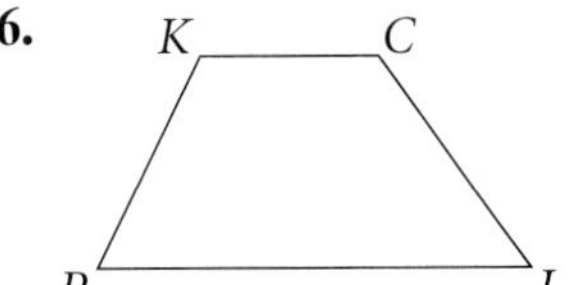

7. 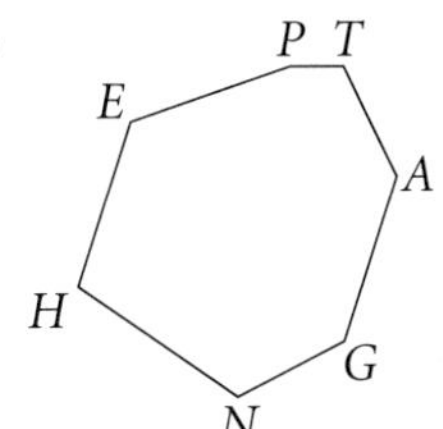

Example 2 (page 144)

Find a polygon in each photograph. Classify the polygon by its number of sides. Tell whether the polygon is convex or concave.

8. 

9.   

10. 

Example 3 (page 145)

Find the sum of the measures of the angles of each polygon.

11. 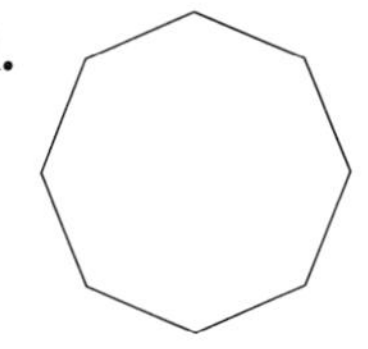

12. dodecagon

13. decagon

14. 20-gon

15. 1002-gon

Example 4 (page 146)

x^2 Algebra **Find the missing angle measures.**

16. 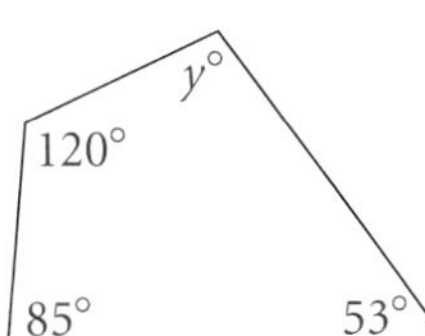

17. 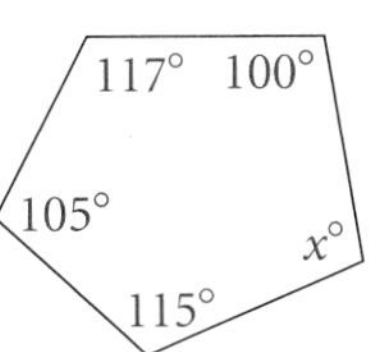

18. 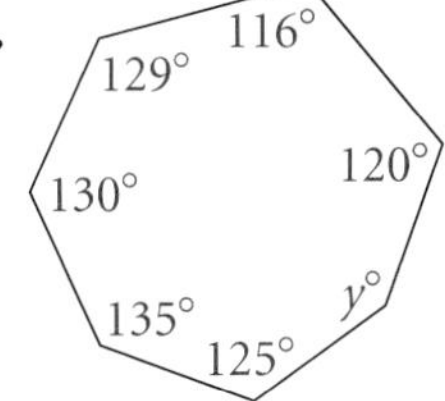

19. 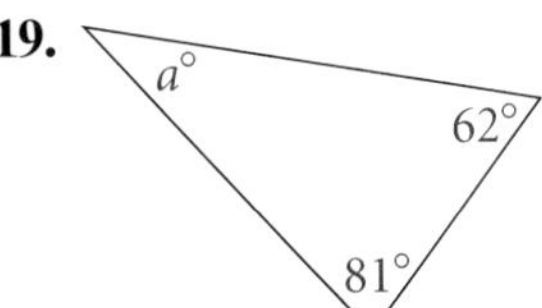

20. 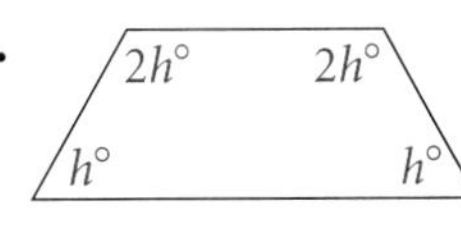

21. 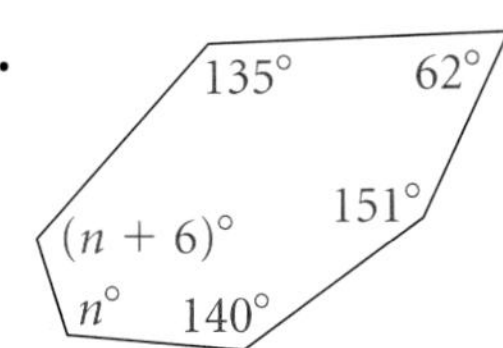

Example 5 (page 146)

Find the measures of an interior angle and an exterior angle of each regular polygon.

22. pentagon

23. dodecagon

24. 18-gon

25. 100-gon

Packaging The nut container at the right has the shape of a regular octagon. It fits in a square box. A cheese wedge fills each corner of the box.

26. Find the measure of each angle of a cheese wedge.

27. Critical Thinking Show how to rearrange the four pieces of cheese to make a regular polygon. What is the measure of each angle of the polygon?

B Apply Your Skills

Use a protractor. Sketch each type of regular polygon.

Sample: dodecagon

Use the protractor to equally space 12 points around a circle. ($360° \div 12 = 30°$, so mark a point every 30°.) Connect these points to form a regular dodecagon.

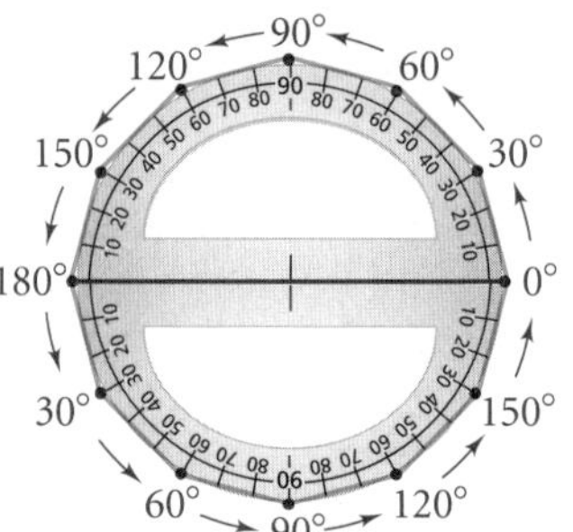

28. triangle **29.** quadrilateral

30. hexagon **31.** octagon

The sum of the measures of the angles of a polygon with n sides is given. Find n.

32. 180 **33.** 1080 **34.** 1980 **35.** 2880

36. To name each figure below, use as many of the letters $A, B, C, \ldots,$ as you need, in order, starting with A. For each figure, how many letters do you need? With this labeling, how many different ways can you name the figure?

a. a triangle **b.** a quadrilateral **c.** a pentagon

37. Stage Design The diagram at the right shows platforms constructed for a theater-in-the-round stage. Describe the largest platform by the type of regular polygon it suggests. Find the measure of each numbered angle.

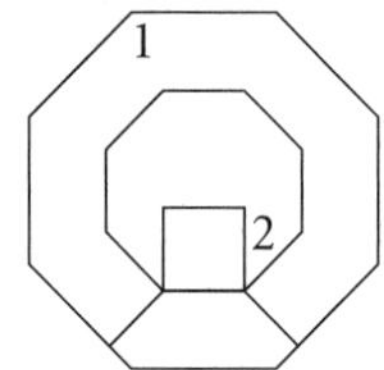

38. Error Analysis Miles said that he measured an angle of a regular polygon to be 130°. Explain why this result is impossible.

39. Critical Thinking A triangle has two congruent angles and an exterior angle with measure 100. Find two possible sets of measures for the angles of the triangle.

Real-World Connection

At a theater-in-the-round, seats are arranged so the audience surrounds the stage.

The measure of an exterior angle of a regular polygon is given. Find the measure of an interior angle, and find the number of sides.

40. 72 **41.** 36 **42.** 18 **43.** 30 **44.** x

45. Probability Find the probability that the measure of an angle of a regular n-gon is a positive integer if n is an integer and $3 \leq n \leq 12$.

46. Algebra A polygon has n sides. An interior angle of the polygon and an adjacent exterior angle form a straight angle.

a. What is the sum of the measures of the n straight angles?

b. What is the sum of the measures of the n interior angles?

c. Using your answers above, what is the sum of the measures of the n exterior angles?

d. What theorem do the steps above lead to?

x^2 **Algebra** **Find each missing angle measure. Then name the polygon.**

47. 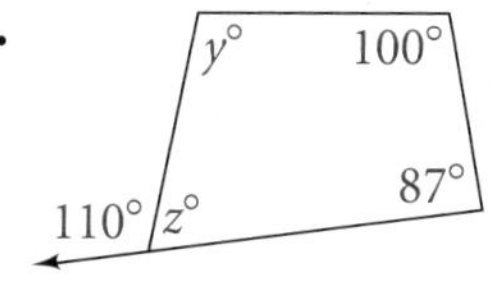

48. 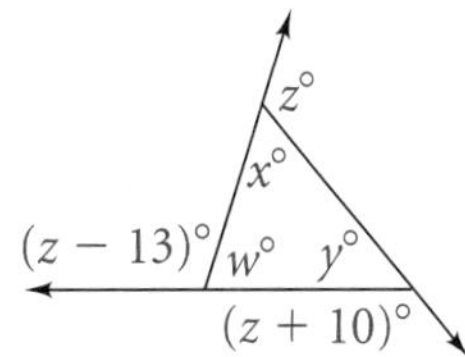

49. 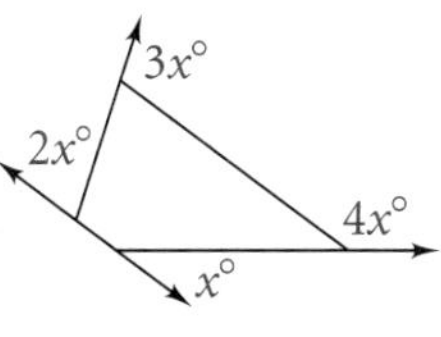

Open-Ended **Sketch each figure described in Exercises 50–53.**

Need Help?
In Exercises 51-53, sketch a figure to meet the first condition. Then adjust it to meet the second condition.

50. a quadrilateral that is not equiangular

51. an equiangular quadrilateral that is not regular

52. an equilateral polygon that is not equiangular

53. an equiangular polygon that is not equilateral

54. **Critical Thinking** Ellen says she has another way to find the sum of the measures of the angles of a polygon. She picks a point inside the polygon, draws a segment to each vertex, counts the number of triangles, multiplies by 180, and then subtracts 360. Does her method work? Explain.

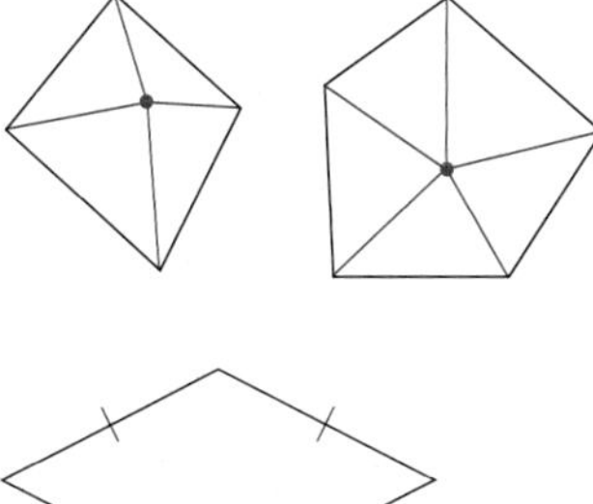

55. **Writing** Tell what you know about the figure at the right.

56. The measure of an interior angle of a regular polygon is three times the measure of an exterior angle of the same polygon. What is the name of the polygon?

 **Challenge**

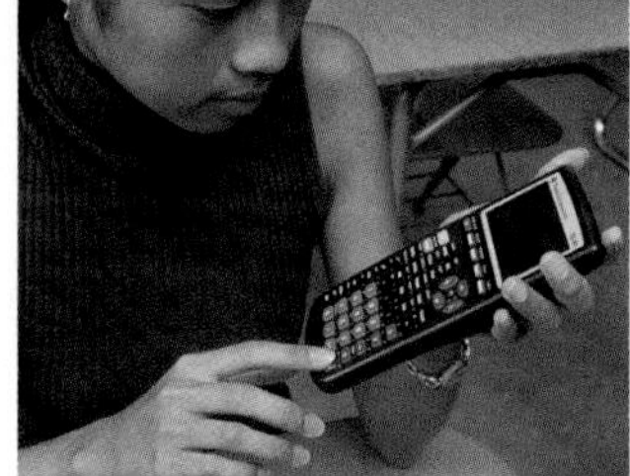

To graph the ordered pairs, use STAT and **STAT PLOT** on your graphing calculator.

57. a. **Graphing Calculator** Find the measure of an angle of a regular n-gon for $n = 20, 40, 60, 80, \ldots, 200$. Record your results to the nearest tenth as ordered pairs in the form (n, measure of each angle).

Xmin = 0 Ymin = 160
Xmax = 200 Ymax = 184
Xscl = 20 Yscl = 4

b. Plot the ordered pairs using a window like the one shown at the right.

c. **Data Analysis** Based on the graph from part (b), make a statement about the measure of an angle of a regular 1000-gon.

d. Is there a regular n-gon with an angle of 180°? Explain.

58. a. Explain why the measure of an angle of a regular n-gon is given by the formulas $\frac{180(n-2)}{n}$ and $180 - \frac{360}{n}$.

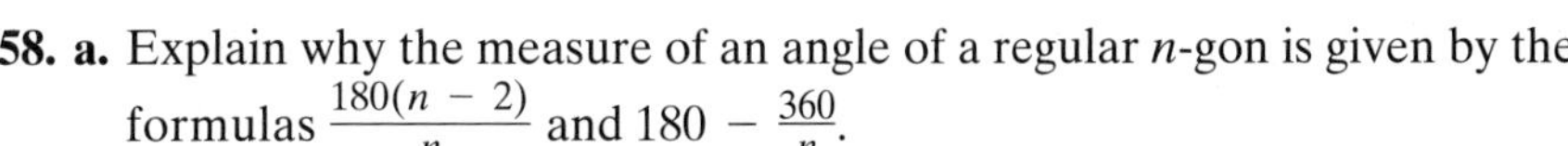

b. Use the second formula to explain what happens to the measures in the angles of regular n-gons as n becomes a large number. Explain also what happens to the polygons.

59. Two rays bisect two consecutive angles of a regular decagon and intersect in the decagon's interior. Find the measure of the acute angles formed by the intersecting rays.

Take It to the NET
Graphing Calculator procedures online at **www.PHSchool.com**
Web Code: afe-2120

Draw, if possible, the concave quadrilateral described. If not possible, explain.

60. with two pairs of congruent adjacent sides

61. with two pairs of congruent opposite sides

62. with three congruent sides

63. with four congruent sides

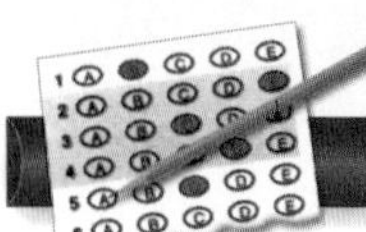

Standardized Test Prep

Gridded Response

For Exercises 64–70, you may need the formula $(n - 2)180$ for the sum of the angle measures in a polygon with n sides.

64. What is the sum of the measures of the angles of a 25-gon?

65. A company is manufacturing a gear that has the shape of a regular polygon. The measure of each angle of the gear is 162. How many sides does the gear have?

66. The car at each vertex of a Ferris wheel holds a maximum of 5 people. The sum of the measures of the angles of the Ferris wheel is 7740. What is the maximum number of people that the Ferris wheel can hold?

67. What is the sum of the measures of the exterior angles, one at each vertex, of an octagon?

68. Exactly four angles of a hexagon are congruent. The other two angles are complementary. What is the measure of one of the four congruent angles?

69. The sum of the measures of the angles of a regular polygon is 4500. How many sides does the polygon have?

70. What is the measure of an exterior angle of a regular polygon with 36 sides?

Take It to the NET
Online lesson quiz at
www.PHSchool.com
Web Code: afa-0304

Mixed Review

Lesson 3-3 x^2 **Find each missing angle measure.**

71. $35°$, $(y - 15)°$, $3y°$

72. $(x + 23)°$, $(x + 13)°$

73. $(2y - 1)°$, $x°$, $(x - 28)°$, $y°$

Lesson 2-4 **Name the property that justifies each statement.**

74. $4(2a - 3) = 8a - 12$

75. If $b + c = 7$ and $b = 2$, then $2 + c = 7$.

76. $\overline{RS} \cong \overline{RS}$

77. If $\angle 1 \cong \angle 4$, then $\angle 4 \cong \angle 1$.

78. If $2r = 18$, then $r = 9$.

79. If $AB = BC$ and $BC = 1$, then $AB = 1$.

Lessons 1-3, 1-4 **Identify the following in the diagram.**

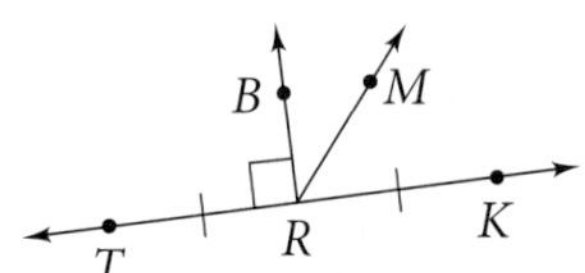

80. a pair of opposite rays

81. two right angles

82. two segments

83. an acute angle

84. an obtuse angle

85. a straight angle

86. a midpoint

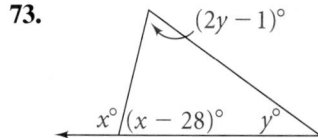

Algebra 1 Review

Slope

For Use With Lesson 3-5

The *slope* of a line is the ratio of the vertical change (rise) to the horizontal change (run) between any two points (x_1, y_1) and (x_2, y_2) of the line.

$$\text{slope} = \frac{\text{vertical change}}{\text{horizontal change}} = \frac{\text{rise}}{\text{run}} = \frac{y_2 - y_1}{x_2 - x_1}$$

The slope of a line indicates the line's steepness and whether it rises or falls from left to right. Line ℓ has slope 1 and rises from left to right. Line r has slope -1 and falls from left to right. Both form a 45° angle with the x-axis.

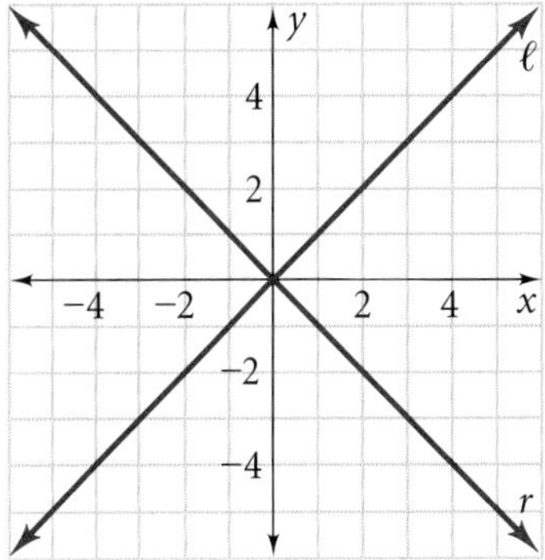

1 EXAMPLE

Find the slope of $\overleftrightarrow{AB}$, which passes through $A(-2, 4)$ and $B(1, -3)$.

Method 1 Use the formula.

$$\text{slope} = \frac{y_2 - y_1}{x_2 - x_1} = \frac{-3 - 4}{1 - (-2)} = \frac{-7}{3}, \text{ or } -\frac{7}{3}$$

Method 2 Use the graph.

$$\text{slope} = \frac{\text{vertical change (rise)}}{\text{horizontal change (run)}} = \frac{-7}{3}, \text{ or } -\frac{7}{3}$$

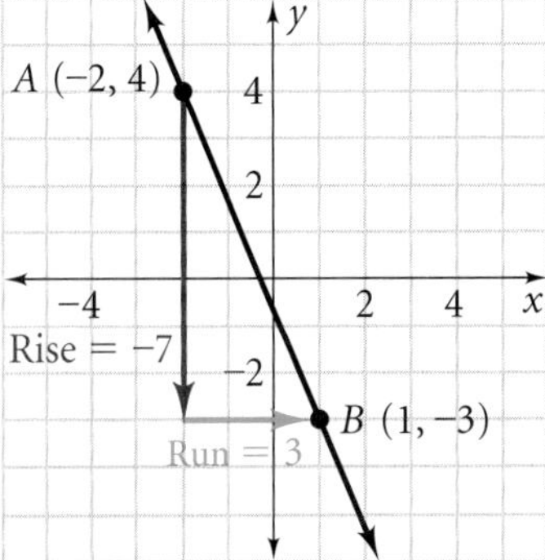

2 EXAMPLE

Compare the rise or fall and the steepness of $\overleftrightarrow{AB}$ in Example 1 with that of line ℓ or r at the top of the page.

The slope of $\overleftrightarrow{AB}$ is negative, so $\overleftrightarrow{AB}$ falls from left to right, the same as line r with slope -1. The slope of $\overleftrightarrow{AB}$ has absolute value $\frac{7}{3}$, which is greater than 1, so $\overleftrightarrow{AB}$ is steeper than line r whose slope has absolute value 1.

EXERCISES

Find the slope of $\overleftrightarrow{AB}$. Compare its rise or fall and its steepness with that of line ℓ or r at the top of the page.

1. $A(4, -6), B(7, 2)$

2. $A(7, -6), B(-5, -8)$

3. $A(-3, 7), B(-1, 4)$

4. $A(-2, -5), B(1, -7)$

5. $A(0, 4), B(4, 0)$

6. $A\left(-3\frac{1}{2}, 3\right), B\left(-7, 2\frac{1}{2}\right)$

7. $A(-1.4, -3.7), B(-2.4, 1.3)$

8. $A(3, -2), B(-6, -2)$

9. $A(5, 9), B(5, -6)$

Open-Ended **Predict how a line with the given slope m will compare with line ℓ or r at the top of the page. Graph such a line.**

10. $m = \frac{1}{3}$

11. $m = -1.7$

12. $m = 37$

13. $m = 0$

ALGEBRA

Lines in the Coordinate Plane

Lesson Preview

What You'll Learn

To graph lines given their equations

To write equations of lines

. . . And Why

To determine whether a wheelchair ramp complies with the law, as in Exercise 52

✔ Check Skills You'll Need

(For help, go to page 151.)

Find the slope of the line that contains each pair of points.

1. $A(-2, 2), B(4, -2)$
2. $P(3, 0), X(0, -5)$
3. $R(-3, -4), S(5, -4)$
4. $K(-3, 3), T(-3, 1)$
5. $C(0, 1), D(3, 3)$
6. $E(-1, 4), F(3, -2)$
7. $G(-8, -9), H(-3, -5)$
8. $L(7, -10), M(1, -4)$

New Vocabulary
- slope-intercept form
- standard form of a linear equation
- point-slope form

Interactive lesson includes instant self-check, tutorials, and activities.

OBJECTIVE 1

Graphing Lines

Need Help?

The *y*-intercept is the *y*-coordinate of the point where a line crosses the *y*-axis. The *x*-intercept is the *x*-coordinate of the point where a line crosses the *x*-axis.

In algebra, you learned that the graph of a linear equation is a line. The **slope-intercept form** of a linear equation is $y = mx + b$, where m is the slope of the line and b is the *y*-intercept. Each line at the right has slope 2, but the lines have *y*-intercepts of 3, −1, and −4.

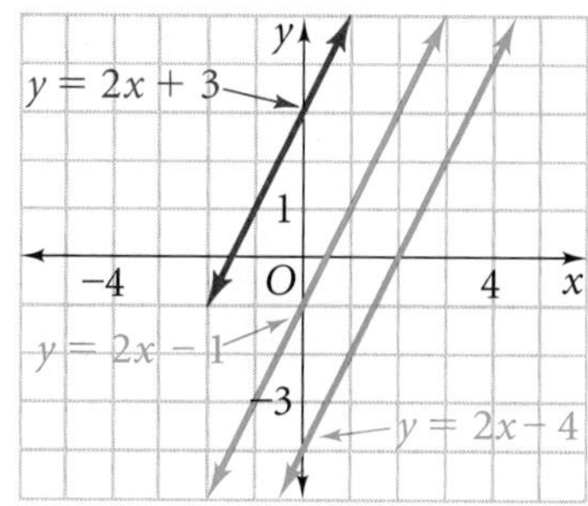

By Postulate 1-1 (two points determine a line), you need only two points to graph a line. The *y*-intercept gives you one point. You can use the slope to plot another.

1 EXAMPLE Graphing Lines in Slope-Intercept Form

Graph the line $y = \frac{3}{4}x + 2$.

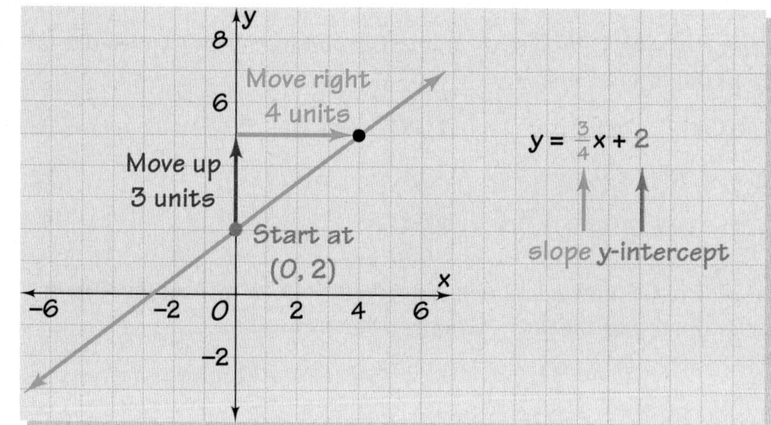

✔ Check Understanding **1** Graph the line $y = -\frac{1}{2}x - 2$.

Reading Math

In the "standard form," A, B, and C are constants. In Example 2, $6x + 3y = 12$ is in standard form with $A = 6$, $B = 3$, and $C = 12$.

The **standard form of a linear equation** is $Ax + By = C$, where A, B, and C are real numbers and A and B are not both zero. To graph an equation written in standard form, you can readily find two points for the graph by finding the x- and y-intercepts.

2 EXAMPLE Graphing Lines Using Intercepts

Algebra Graph $6x + 3y = 12$.

Step 1 To find the y-intercept, substitute 0 for x; solve for y.

$$6x + 3y = 12$$
$$6(0) + 3y = 12$$
$$3y = 12$$
$$y = 4$$

The y-intercept is 4.
A point on the line is $(0, 4)$.

Step 2 To find the x-intercept, substitute 0 for y; solve for x.

$$6x + 3y = 12$$
$$6x + 3(0) = 12$$
$$6x = 12$$
$$x = 2$$

The x-intercept is 2.
A point on the line is $(2, 0)$.

Step 3 Plot $(0, 4)$ and $(2, 0)$. Draw the line containing the two points.

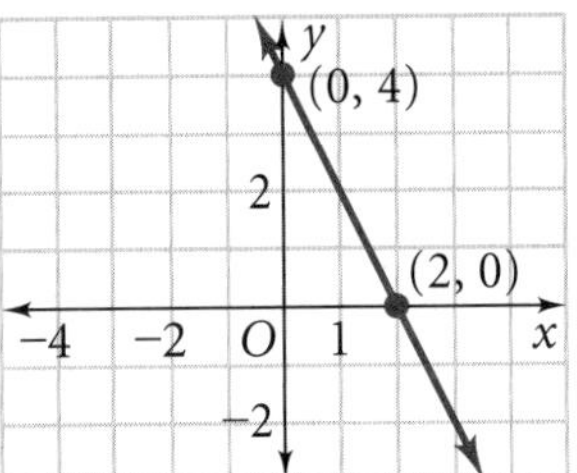

✓ Check Understanding **2** Graph $-2x + 4y = -8$.

As an alternative, you can graph an equation in standard form by transforming it into slope-intercept form. Knowing the slope and y-intercept beforehand can give you a good mental image of what the graph should look like.

3 EXAMPLE Transforming to Slope-Intercept Form

Algebra Graph $4x - 2y = 9$.

Step 1 Transform the equation to slope-intercept form.

$$4x - 2y = 9$$
$$-2y = -4x + 9$$
$$\frac{-2y}{-2} = \frac{-4x}{-2} + \frac{9}{-2}$$
$$y = 2x - \frac{9}{2}$$

The y-intercept is $-4\frac{1}{2}$ and the slope is 2.

Step 2 Use the y-intercept and the slope to plot two points and draw the line containing them.

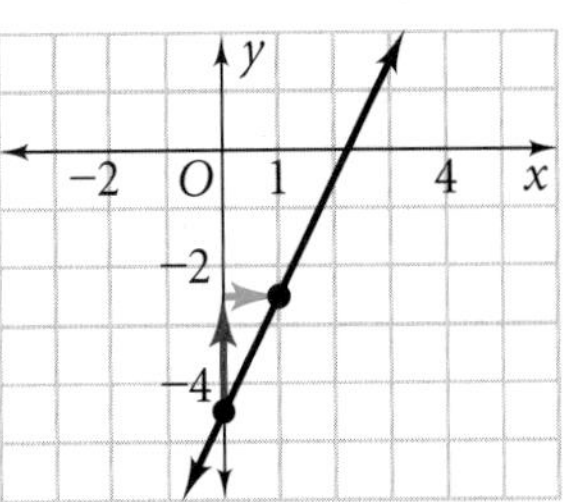

✓ Check Understanding **3** Graph $-5x + y = -3$.

OBJECTIVE 2

Writing Equations of Lines

A third form for an equation of a line is **point-slope form.** The point-slope form for a nonvertical line through point (x_1, y_1) with slope m is $y - y_1 = m(x - x_1)$.

4 EXAMPLE Using Point-Slope Form

Algebra Write an equation of the line through point $P(-1, 4)$ with slope 3.

$y - y_1 = m(x - x_1)$ **Use point-slope form.**

$y - 4 = 3[x - (-1)]$ **Substitute 3 for m and $(-1, 4)$ for (x_1, y_1).**

$y - 4 = 3(x + 1)$ **Simplify.**

Check Understanding 4 Write an equation of the line with slope -1 that contains point $P(2, -4)$.

By Postulate 1-1, you need only two points to write an equation of a line.

5 EXAMPLE Writing an Equation of a Line Given Two Points

Algebra Write an equation of the line through $A(-2, 3)$ and $B(1, -1)$.

Step 1 Find the slope.

$m = \frac{y_2 - y_1}{x_2 - x_1}$

$m = \frac{-1 - 3}{1 - (-2)}$ **Substitute $(-2, 3)$ for (x_1, y_1) and $(1, -1)$ for (x_2, y_2).**

$m = -\frac{4}{3}$ **Simplify.**

Step 2 Select one of the points. Write an equation in point-slope form.

$y - y_1 = m(x - x_1)$

$y - 3 = -\frac{4}{3}[x - (-2)]$ **Substitute $(-2, 3)$ for (x_1, y_1) and $-\frac{4}{3}$ for the slope.**

$y - 3 = -\frac{4}{3}(x + 2)$ **Simplify.**

Check Understanding 5 Write an equation of the line that contains the points $P(5, 0)$ and $Q(7, -3)$.

Recall that the slope of a horizontal line is 0 and the slope of a vertical line is undefined. Thus, horizontal and vertical lines have easily recognized equations.

6 EXAMPLE Equations of Horizontal and Vertical Lines

Write equations for the horizontal line and the vertical line that contain $P(3, 2)$.

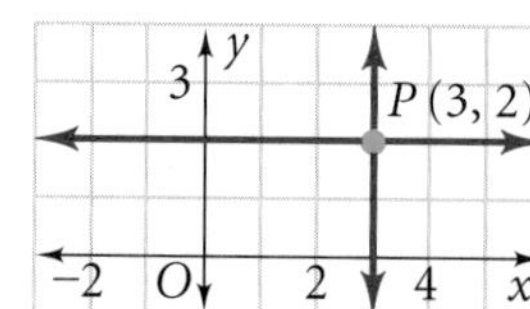

Every point on the horizontal line through $P(3, 2)$ has a y-coordinate of 2. The equation of the line is $y = 2$. It crosses the y-axis at $(0, 2)$.

Every point on the vertical line through $P(3, 2)$ has an x-coordinate of 3. The equation of the line is $x = 3$. It crosses the x-axis at $(3, 0)$.

Check Understanding 6 Write equations of the horizontal and vertical lines that contain the point $P(5, -1)$.

EXERCISES

For more practice, see *Extra Practice*.

Practice and Problem Solving

A Practice by Example

Examples 1, 2 (pages 152, 153)

Algebra **Graph each line.**

1. $y = x + 2$ **2.** $y = 3x + 4$ **3.** $y = \frac{1}{2}x - 1$ **4.** $y = -\frac{5}{3}x + 2$

Algebra **Graph each line using intercepts.**

5. $2x + 6y = 12$ **6.** $3x + y = 15$ **7.** $5x - 2y = 20$

8. $6x - y = 3$ **9.** $10x + 5y = 40$ **10.** $1.2x + 2.4y = 2.4$

Example 3 (page 153)

Algebra **Write each equation in slope-intercept form and graph the line.**

11. $y = 2x + 1$ **12.** $y - 1 = x$ **13.** $y + 2x = 4$

14. $8x + 4y = 16$ **15.** $2x + 6y = 6$ **16.** $\frac{3}{4}x - \frac{1}{2}y = \frac{1}{8}$

Example 4 (page 154)

Algebra **Write an equation in point-slope form of the line that contains the given points and has the given slope.**

17. $P(2, 3)$, slope 2 **18.** $X(4, -1)$, slope 3 **19.** $R(-3, 5)$, slope -1

20. $A(-2, -6)$, slope -4 **21.** $V(6, 1)$, slope $\frac{1}{2}$ **22.** $C(0, 4)$, slope 1

Example 5 (page 154)

Write an equation in point-slope form of the line that contains the given points.

23. $D(0, 5), E(5, 8)$ **24.** $F(6, 2), G(2, 4)$ **25.** $H(2, 6), K(-1, 3)$

26. $A(-4, 4), B(2, 10)$ **27.** $L(-1, 0), M(-3, -1)$ **28.** $P(8, 10), Q(-4, 2)$

Example 6 (page 154)

Write equations for (a) the horizontal line and (b) the vertical line that contain the given point.

29. $A(4, 7)$ **30.** $Y(3, -2)$ **31.** $N(0, -1)$ **32.** $E(6, 4)$

B Apply Your Skills

Graph each line.

33. $x = 3$ **34.** $y = -2$ **35.** $x = 9$ **36.** $y = 4$ **37.** $y = 6$

38. Telephone Rates The equation $C = \$.05m + \$4.95$ represents the cost (C) of a long distance telephone call of m minutes.
a. What is the slope of the line?
b. What does the slope represent in this situation?
c. What is the y-intercept (C-intercept)?
d. What does the y-intercept represent in this situation?

39. Error Analysis A classmate claims that having no slope and having a slope of 0 are the same. Is your classmate correct? Explain.

40. a. What is the slope of the x-axis? Explain.
b. Write an equation for the x-axis.

41. a. What is the slope of the y-axis? Explain.
b. Write an equation for the y-axis.

Real-World Connection

NASA's Advanced Communications Technology Satellite has a capacity for 250,000 phone calls.

Identify the form of each equation. To graph the line, would you use the given form or change to another form? Explain.

42. $-5x - y = 2$ **43.** $y = \frac{1}{4}x - \frac{2}{7}$ **44.** $y + 2 = -(x - 4)$

Need Help?

When you give examples as in Exercises 45 and 46, choose ones that are easy to work with.

Critical Thinking Graph three different lines having the given property. Describe how the equations of these lines are alike and how they are different.

45. The lines have slope 2.

46. The lines have y-intercept 2.

47. Graphing Calculator Graphing calculators use slope-intercept form (rather than standard form or point-slope form) to graph lines. Choose either Exercise 45 or Exercise 46 and write three equations for the lines you graphed. Use the Y= window of your graphing calculator to enter your equations. Press GRAPH. Do the graphs on the screen confirm the description you wrote previously?

Graph each pair of lines. Then find their point of intersection.

48. $y = -4, x = 6$ **49.** $x = 0, y = 0$ **50.** $x = -1, y = 3$ **51.** $y = 5, x = 4$

52. Building Access By law, the maximum slope of a ramp in new construction is $\frac{1}{12}$. The plan for the new library shows a 3-ft height from the ground to the main entrance. The distance from the sidewalk to the building is 10 ft. Can you design a ramp for the library that complies with the law? Explain.

Real-World Connection

To visualize a slope of $\frac{1}{12}$, think "one foot over, one inch up."

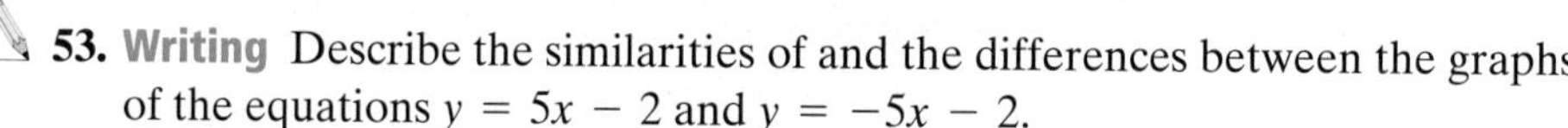

53. Writing Describe the similarities of and the differences between the graphs of the equations $y = 5x - 2$ and $y = -5x - 2$.

54. Open-Ended Write equations for three different lines that contain the point $(5, 6)$.

55. Critical Thinking The x-intercept of a line is 2 and the y-intercept is 4. Use this information to write an equation for the line.

56. The vertices of a triangle are $A(0, 0)$, $B(2, 5)$, and $C(4, 0)$.
a. Write an equation for the line through A and B.
b. Write an equation for the line through B and C.
c. Compare the slopes and y-intercepts of the two lines.

Challenge

Do the three points lie on one line? Justify your answer.

57. $A(5, 6), B(3, 2), C(6, 8)$

58. $D(-2, -2), E(4, -4), F(0, 0)$

59. $G(5, -4), H(2, 3), I(-1, 10)$

60. $J(-2, 9), K(1, -1), L(4, -11)$

A line passes through the given points. Write an equation for the line in point-slope form. Then, rewrite the equation in standard form with integer coefficients.

61. $R(-2, 2), S(0, 8)$

62. $T(5, 5), W(7, 6)$

63. $X(2, 6), Y(5, 8)$

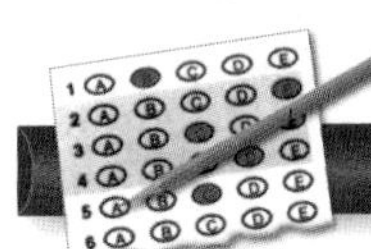

Standardized Test Prep

Multiple Choice

64. Which equation is equivalent to $15x + 3y = 10$?

A. $y = 5x + \frac{10}{3}$ **B.** $y = -5x - \frac{10}{3}$ **C.** $y = 5x - \frac{10}{3}$ **D.** $y = -5x + \frac{10}{3}$

65. Which pair of points $A(-2, 5)$, $B(-1, -2)$, $C(4, -5)$, and $D(7, 0)$, lie on the line with y-intercept closest to the origin?

F. A and B **G.** A and C **H.** B and C **I.** B and D

Quantitative Comparison

Compare the boxed quantity in Column A with the boxed quantity in Column B. Choose the best answer.

A. The quantity in Column A is greater.
B. The quantity in Column B is greater.
C. The two quantities are equal.
D. The relationship cannot be determined from the information given.

	Column A	Column B
66.	the y-intercept of $3x - 8y = 60$	the y-intercept of $3x + 60 = 8y$
67.	the slope of $4y = -10$	the slope of $y = 5$
68.	the slope of the line that passes through $(0, -9)$ and $(-4, -11)$	the slope of the line that passes through $(18, 0)$ and $(4, -7)$

Short Response

69. The slope of line a is $\frac{3}{2}$ and its y-intercept is 12. Line b passes through $(4, 1)$ and $(7, -3)$.

a. Write an equation for each line.

b. Graph both lines on the same coordinate plane. From the graph, what is their point of intersection?

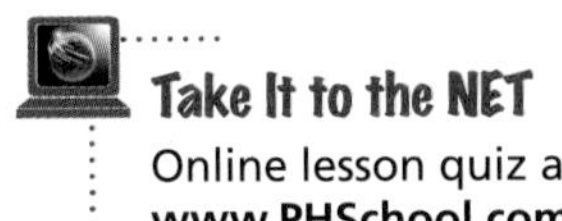

Online lesson quiz at **www.PHSchool.com**
Web Code: afa-0305

Mixed Review

Lesson 3-4 **Find the sum of the measures of the angles of each polygon.**

70. a nonagon **71.** a pentagon **72.** an 11-gon **73.** a 14-gon

Lesson 2-2 **Is each statement a good definition? If not, find a counterexample.**

74. A quadrilateral is a polygon with four sides.

75. Skew lines are lines that don't intersect.

76. An acute triangle is a triangle with an acute angle.

Lesson 1-5 x^2 Algebra **For Exercises 77–80, $\overrightarrow{PQ}$ is the bisector of $\angle MPR$. Solve for a and find the missing angle measure.**

77. $m\angle MPQ = 3a, m\angle QPR = 2a + 5, m\angle MPR = \blacksquare$

78. $m\angle MPQ = 7a, m\angle QPR = 4a + 12, m\angle MPR = \blacksquare$

79. $m\angle MPQ = 8a - 8, m\angle QPR = 5a - 2, m\angle QPR = \blacksquare$

80. $m\angle MPQ = 2a + 9, m\angle QPR = 4a - 3, m\angle MPQ = \blacksquare$

Slopes of Parallel and Perpendicular Lines

ALGEBRA

Lesson Preview

What You'll Learn

To relate slope and parallel lines

To relate slope and perpendicular lines

. . . And Why

To write an equation that models part of a leaded glass window, as in Example 6

✓ Check Skills You'll Need

(For help, go to page 151 and Lesson 3-5.)

Find the slope of the line through each pair of points.

1. $F(2, 5), B(-2, 3)$ **2.** $H(0, -5), D(2, 0)$ **3.** $E(1, 1), F(2, -4)$

Find the slope of each line.

4. $y = 2x - 5$ **5.** $x + y = 20$ **6.** $2x - 3y = 6$

7. $x = y$ **8.** $y = 7$ **9.** $y = \frac{2}{3}x + 7$

Interactive lesson includes instant self-check, tutorials, and activities.

OBJECTIVE 1

Slope and Parallel Lines

The relationship between slope and parallel lines is summarized below and proved in Lesson 8-3.

Key Concepts

Summary **Slopes of Parallel Lines**

If two nonvertical lines are parallel, their slopes are equal.

If the slopes of two distinct nonvertical lines are equal, the lines are parallel.

Any two vertical lines are parallel.

Real-World  Connection

The ramp and rails are parallel because they have the same slope.

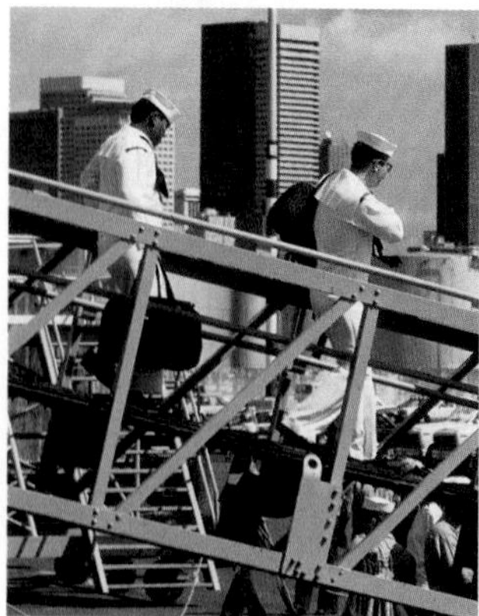

You can test whether nonvertical lines are parallel by comparing their slopes.

1 EXAMPLE Checking for Parallel Lines

Are lines ℓ_1 and ℓ_2 parallel? Explain.

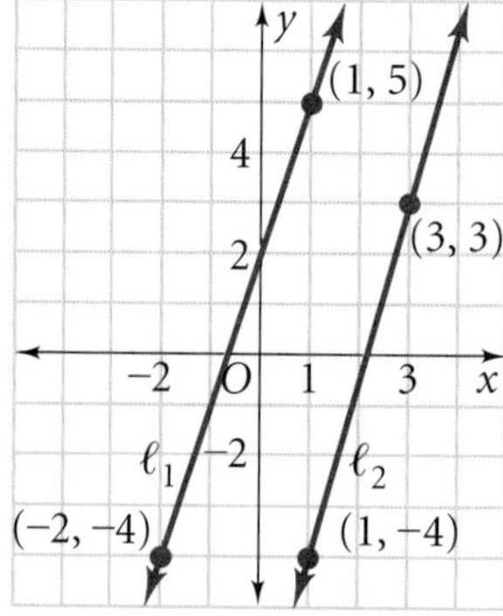

Find and compare the slopes of the lines.

$$\text{slope of } \ell_1 = \frac{5 - (-4)}{1 - (-2)} = \frac{9}{3} = 3$$

$$\text{slope of } \ell_2 = \frac{3 - (-4)}{3 - 1} = \frac{7}{2}$$

Lines ℓ_1 and ℓ_2 are not parallel because their slopes are not equal.

✓ Check Understanding

1 Line ℓ_3 contains $A(-4, 2)$ and $B(3, 1)$. Line ℓ_4 contains $C(-4, 0)$ and $D(8, -2)$. Are ℓ_3 and ℓ_4 parallel? Explain.

Slope-intercept form allows you to compare slopes easily in order to decide whether lines are parallel.

2 EXAMPLE Determining Whether Lines are Parallel

Algebra Are the lines $4y - 12x = 20$ and $y = 3x - 1$ parallel? Explain.

Write $4y - 12x = 20$ in slope-intercept form.

$4y - 12x = 20$

$4y = 12x + 20$ **Add 12*x* to each side.**

$y = 3x + 5$ **Divide each side by 4.**

Each line has slope 3. The y-intercepts are -1 and 5. The lines have the same slope and different y-intercepts. They are distinct lines, so they are parallel.

Check Understanding 2 Are the lines parallel? Explain.

a. $y = -\frac{1}{2}x + 5$ and $2x + 4y = 9$

b. $y = -\frac{1}{2}x + 5$ and $2x + 4y = 20$

You can write an equation for a line parallel to a given line.

3 EXAMPLE Writing Equations of Parallel Lines

Write an equation for the line parallel to $y = -4x + 3$ that contains $(1, -2)$.

Step 1 Identify the slope of the given line.

$y = -4x + 3$

↑ slope

Step 2 Use point-slope form to write an equation for the new line.

$y - y_1 = m(x - x_1)$

$y - (-2) = -4(x - 1)$ **Substitute -4 for *m* and $(1, -2)$ for (x_1, y_1).**

$y + 2 = -4(x - 1)$ **Simplify.**

Check Understanding 3 Write an equation for the line parallel to $y = -x + 4$ that contains $(-2, 5)$.

OBJECTIVE 2 Slope and Perpendicular Lines

The relationship between perpendicular lines and their slopes is summarized below. These statements will be proved in Lessons 6-6 and 6-7.

Key Concepts

Summary **Slopes of Perpendicular Lines**

If two nonvertical lines are perpendicular, the product of their slopes is -1.

If the slopes of two lines have a product of -1, the lines are perpendicular.

Any horizontal line and vertical line are perpendicular.

You can test whether lines are perpendicular by first noting whether either line is vertical or horizontal. If not, check their slopes. If the product of the slopes is −1, the lines are perpendicular.

4 EXAMPLE Checking for Perpendicular Lines

Algebra Lines ℓ_1 and ℓ_2 are neither vertical nor horizontal. Are they perpendicular? Explain.

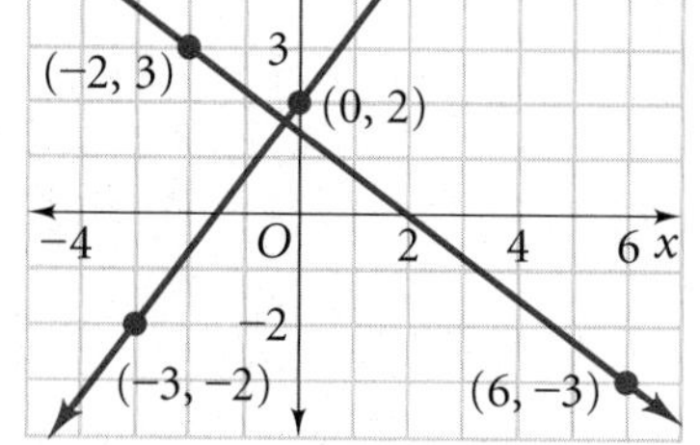

Step 1 Find the slope of each line.

$$m_1 = \text{slope of } \ell_1 = \frac{-2-2}{-3-0} = \frac{-4}{-3} = \frac{4}{3}$$

$$m_2 = \text{slope of } \ell_2 = \frac{3-(-3)}{-2-6} = \frac{6}{-8} = -\frac{3}{4}$$

Step 2 Find the product of the slopes.

$$m_1 \cdot m_2 = \frac{4}{3} \cdot -\frac{3}{4} = -1$$

Lines ℓ_1 and ℓ_2 are perpendicular because the product of their slopes is −1.

✓ Check Understanding 4 Are ℓ_3 and ℓ_4 perpendicular? Explain.

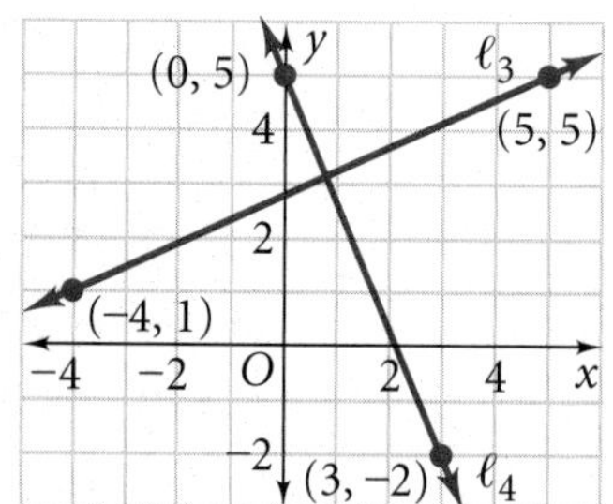

You can write an equation for a line perpendicular to a given line. If the given line is horizontal, write an equation for a vertical line. If the given line is vertical, write an equation for a horizontal line.

5 EXAMPLE Writing Equations for Perpendicular Lines

Write an equation for the line perpendicular to $y = -3x - 5$ that contains $(-3, 7)$.

Step 1 Identify the slope of the given line.

$$y = -3x - 5$$

↑ slope (−3)

Step 2 Find the slope of the line perpendicular to the given line.
Let m be the slope of the perpendicular line.

$-3m = -1$ **The product of the slopes of perpendicular lines is −1.**

$m = \frac{1}{3}$ **Divide each side by −3.**

Step 3 Use point-slope form to write an equation for the new line.

$y - y_1 = m(x - x_1)$

$y - 7 = \frac{1}{3}[x - (-3)]$ **Substitute $\frac{1}{3}$ for m and $(-3, 7)$ for (x_1, y_1).**

$y - 7 = \frac{1}{3}(x + 3)$ **Simplify.**

Need Help?

Numbers with product −1 are opposite reciprocals. In Example 5, the opposite reciprocal of −3 is $\frac{1}{3}$.

✓ Check Understanding 5 Write an equation for the line perpendicular to $5y - x = 10$ that contains $(15, -4)$.

6 EXAMPLE Real-World Connection

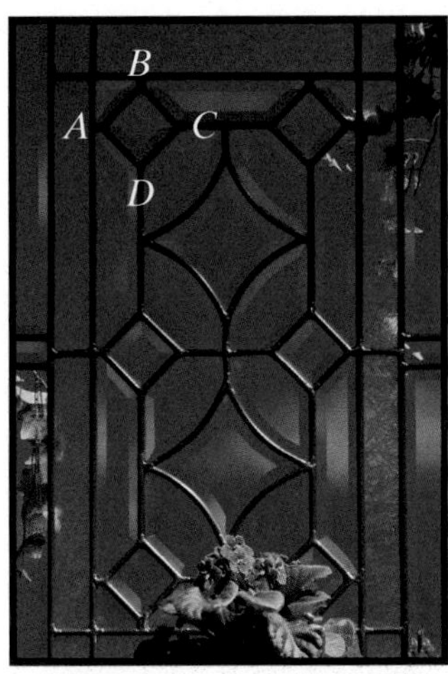

The window at the left includes some perpendicular lead strips. The line that contains $\overline{BC}$ has equation $y = -x + 10$. $\overline{AB}$ is perpendicular to $\overline{BC}$. Write an equation for $\overleftrightarrow{AB}$, the line that contains $\overline{AB}$ and point $(-1, 5)$.

The line that contains $\overline{BC}$ has slope -1. Let m be the slope of $\overleftrightarrow{AB}$.

$-1m = -1$ **The product of the slopes is −1.**

$m = 1$

$\overleftrightarrow{AB}$ has slope 1 and can be written in the form $y = 1x + b$, or $y = x + b$.

$y = x + b$ **$\overleftrightarrow{AB}$ has slope 1.**

$5 = -1 + b$ **Substitute 5 for y and −1 for x.**

$6 = b$ **Add 1 to each side.**

The equation for $\overleftrightarrow{AB}$ is $y = x + 6$.

Check Understanding 6 If the equation for a line containing a lead strip on a different window is $y = -\frac{2}{3}x + 15$, write an equation for the line perpendicular to it that contains $(2, 8)$.

EXERCISES

For more practice, see *Extra Practice*.

Practice and Problem Solving

A Practice by Example

Example 1 (page 158)

In Exercises 1–5, are lines ℓ_1 and ℓ_2 parallel? Explain, using slope.

1.

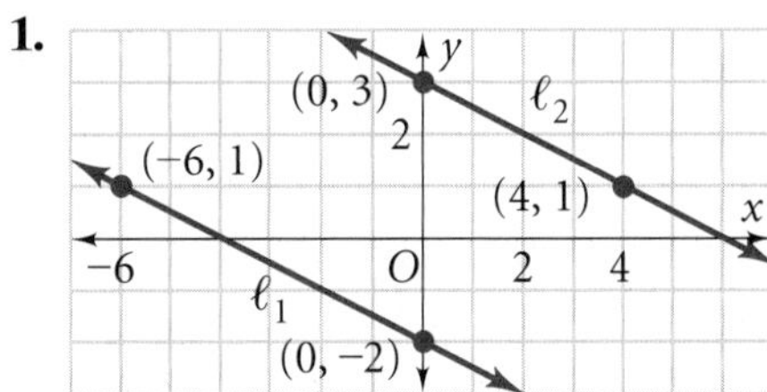

2.

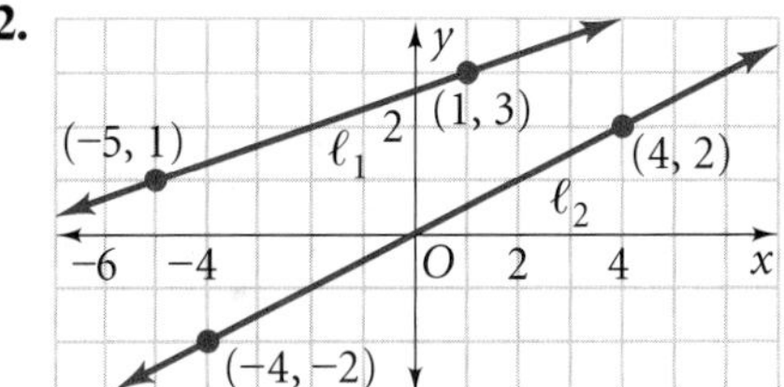

3.

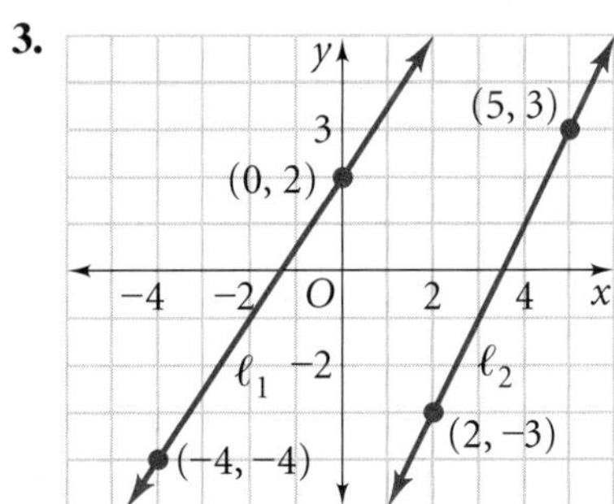

4.

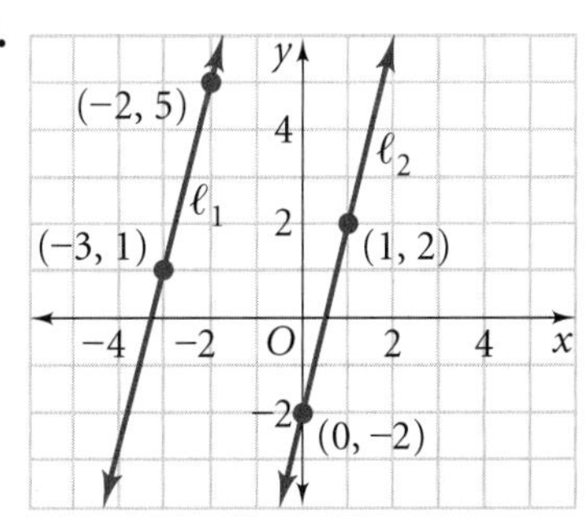

5. Line ℓ_1 contains $A(-3, 6)$ and $B(2, 6)$, and line ℓ_2 contains $C(0, 0)$ and $D(7, 0)$.

Example 2 (page 159)

x^2 Algebra **Are the lines parallel? Explain.**

6. $y = 2x + 5$
   $y = 2x$

7. $y = \frac{3}{4}x - 10$
   $y = \frac{3}{4}x + 2$

8. $y = -x + 6$
   $x + y = 20$

9. $y - 7x = 6$
   $y + 7x = 8$

10. $3x + 4y = 12$
    $6x + 2y = 6$

11. $2x + 5y = -1$
    $10y = -4x - 20$

Example 3 (page 159)

Write an equation for the line parallel to $\overleftrightarrow{AB}$ that contains point C.

12. $\overleftrightarrow{AB}: y = -2x + 1, C(0, 3)$

13. $\overleftrightarrow{AB}: y = \frac{1}{3}x, C(6, 0)$

14. $\overleftrightarrow{AB}: -x + 2y = 4, C(-2, 4)$

15. $\overleftrightarrow{AB}: 3x + 2y = 12, C(6, -2)$

Example 4 (page 160)

x^2 **Algebra** **Are lines ℓ_1 and ℓ_2 perpendicular? Explain using slope.**

16.

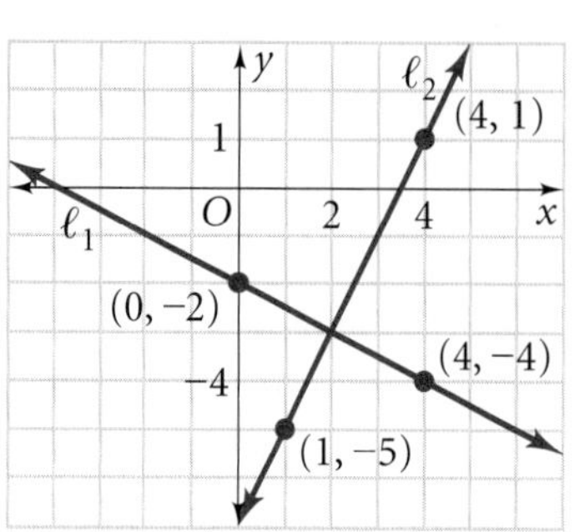

17.

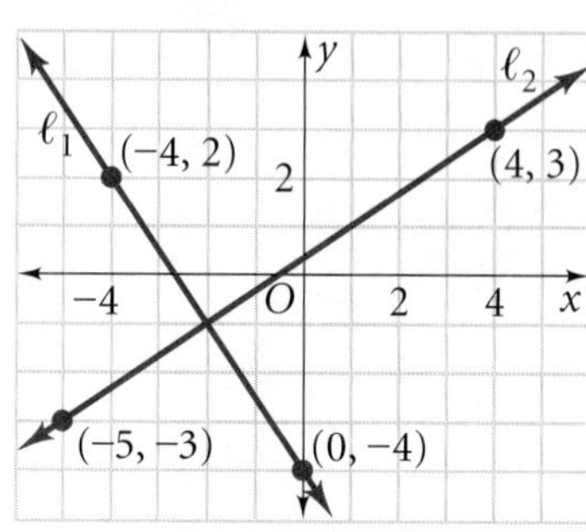

18.

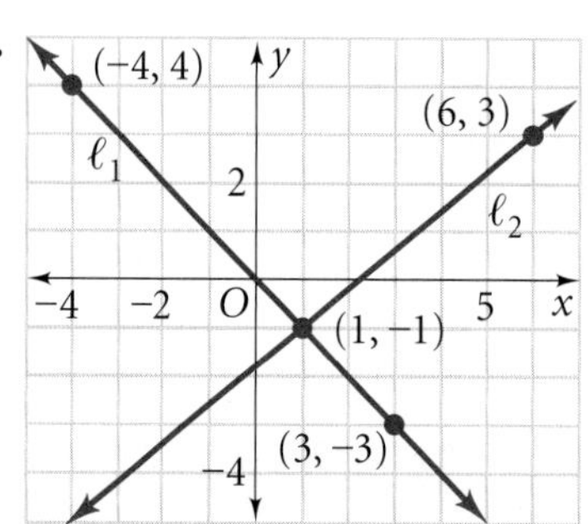

19.

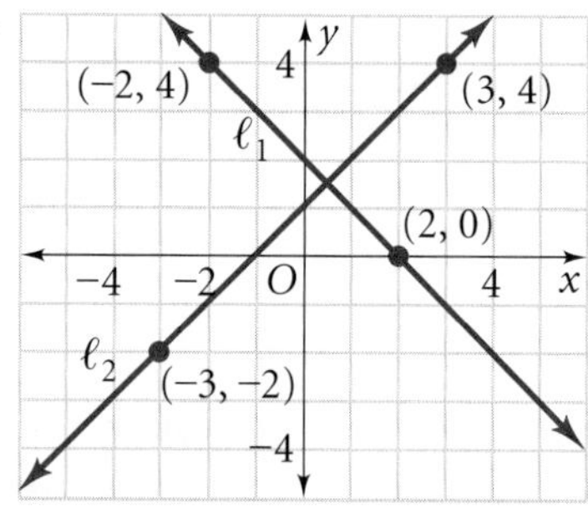

Example 5 (page 160)

Write an equation for the line perpendicular to $\overleftrightarrow{MN}$ that contains point P.

20. $\overleftrightarrow{MN}: y = \frac{2}{3}x, P(6, 6)$

21. $\overleftrightarrow{MN}: y = \frac{1}{2}x - 5, P(4, 0)$

22. $\overleftrightarrow{MN}: y + 2x = -8, P(4, 4)$

23. $\overleftrightarrow{MN}: 4y + 5x = 20, P(0, 0)$

Example 6 (page 161)

24. Highway Construction Highway planners want to construct a road perpendicular to Route 3 at point O. An equation for the Route 3 line is $y = \frac{2}{3}x$. Find an equation for the line for the new road.

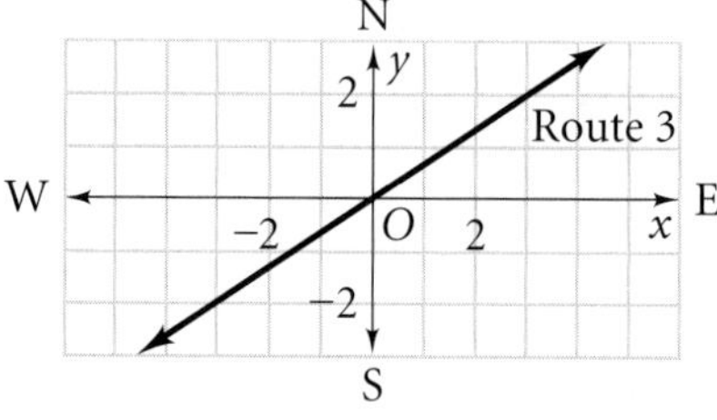

B Apply Your Skills

x^2 **Algebra** **Are the lines perpendicular? Explain.**

25. $y - \frac{1}{2}x = 0$
$y - 2x = -1$

26. $y = -x - 7$
$y - x = 20$

27. $y = 3$
$x = -2$

28. $3y + 2x = 12$
$y + 3x = -2$

29. $2x + 3y = 6$
$6x - 4y = 24$

30. $2x - 7y = -42$
$4y = -7x - 2$

Use slopes to find whether the opposite sides of quadrilateral $ABCD$ are parallel.

31. $A(0, 2), B(3, 4), C(2, 7), D(-1, 5)$

32. $A(-3, 1), B(1, -2), C(0, -3), D(-4, 0)$

33. $A(1, 1), B(5, 3), C(7, 1), D(3, 0)$

34. $A(1, 0), B(4, 0), C(3, -3), D(-1, -3)$

35. Open-Ended Write equations for two perpendicular lines that have the same y-intercept and do not pass through the origin.

36. Writing Can the y-intercepts of two parallel lines be the same? Explain.

37. Use slope to show that the opposite sides of hexagon $RSTUVW$ at the right are parallel.

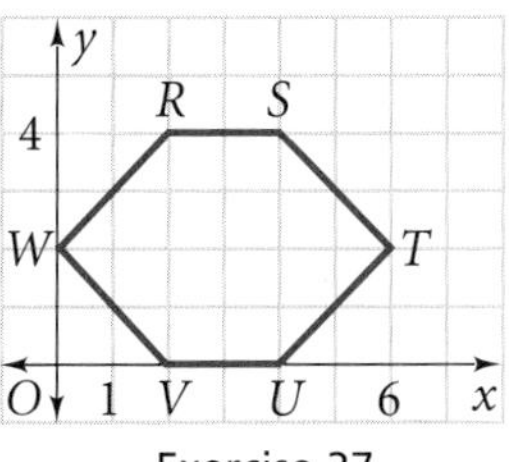

Exercise 37

38. Use slope to determine whether a triangle with vertices $G(3, 2)$, $H(8, 5)$, and $K(0, 10)$ is a right triangle. Explain.

Proof **Developing Proof** **Use slope to explain why each theorem is true for three lines in the coordinate plane.**

39. Theorem 3-5: If two lines are parallel to the same line, then they are parallel to each other.

40. Theorem 3-6: In a plane, if two lines are perpendicular to the same line, then they are parallel to each other.

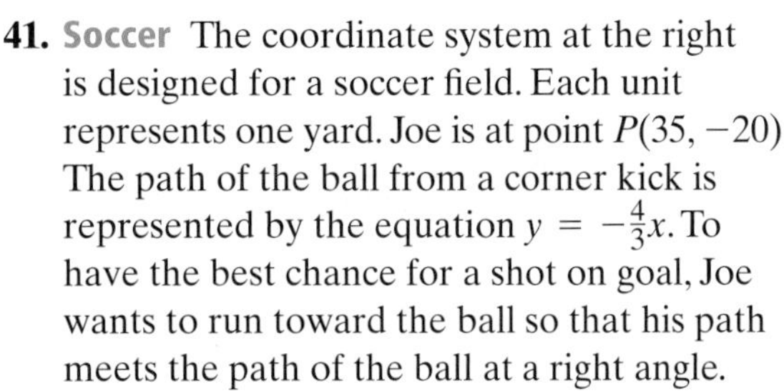

41. Soccer The coordinate system at the right is designed for a soccer field. Each unit represents one yard. Joe is at point $P(35, -20)$. The path of the ball from a corner kick is represented by the equation $y = -\frac{4}{3}x$. To have the best chance for a shot on goal, Joe wants to run toward the ball so that his path meets the path of the ball at a right angle.

a. Find an equation for the line on which Joe should run.

b. Critical Thinking Why is point-slope form the best choice for the equation?

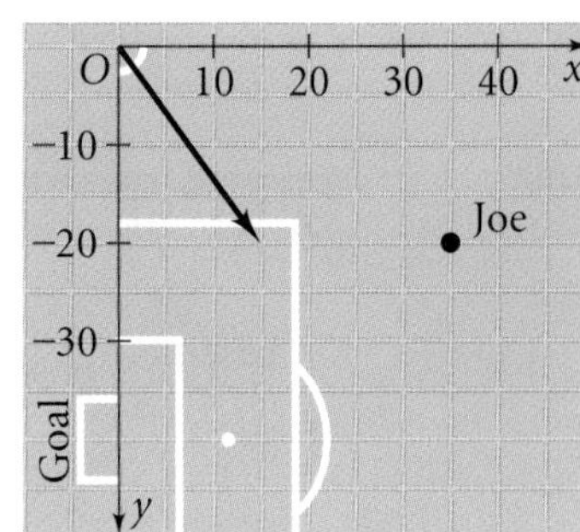

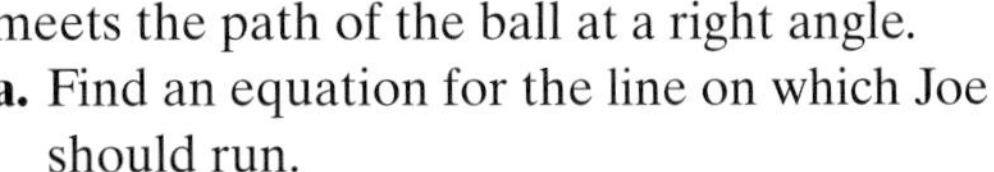

Real-World Connection

For a corner kick, the ball is placed within a quarter circle of radius 1 yd.

Determine whether $\overleftrightarrow{AB}$ and $\overleftrightarrow{CD}$ are *parallel, perpendicular,* or *neither.*

42. $A\left(-1, \frac{1}{2}\right), B(-1, 2), C(3, 7), D(3, -1)$

43. $A(-2, 3), B(-2, 5), C(1, 4), D(2, 4)$

44. $A(2, 4), B(5, 4), C(3, 2), D(0, 8)$

45. $A(-3, 2), B(5, 1), C(2, 7), D(1, -1)$

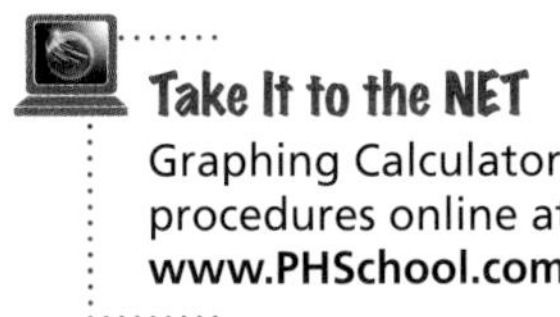

Take It to the NET
Graphing Calculator procedures online at **www.PHSchool.com**

46. Graphing Calculator Use your graphing calculator to find the slope of $\overleftrightarrow{AB}$ in Exercise 45. Enter the x-coordinates of A and B into the L_1 list of your list editor. Enter the y-coordinates into the L_2 list. In your STAT CALC menu select LinReg $(ax + b)$. ENTER to find the slope a. Repeat to find the slope of $\overleftrightarrow{CD}$. Are $\overleftrightarrow{AB}$ and $\overleftrightarrow{CD}$ parallel, perpendicular, or neither?

Challenge

47. Show that the diagonals of the figure at the right are congruent.

48. Show that the diagonals of the figure at the right are perpendicular bisectors of each other.

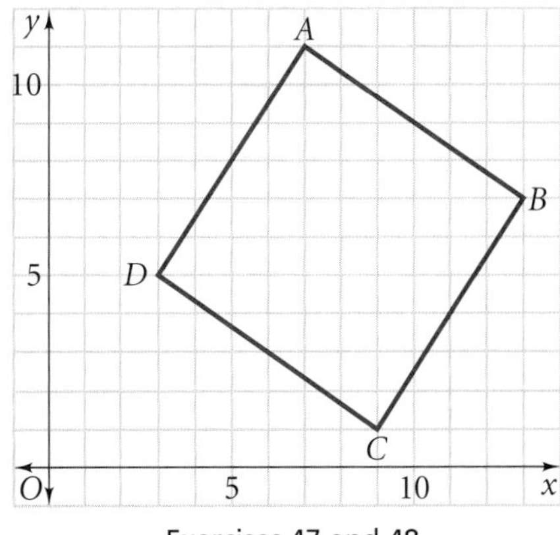

Exercises 47 and 48

49. a. Graph the points $P(2, 2)$, $Q(7, 4)$, and $R(3, 5)$.

b. Find the coordinates of a point S that, along with points P, Q, and R, will form the vertices of a quadrilateral whose opposite sides are parallel. Graph the quadrilateral.

c. Repeat part (b), finding a different point S and graphing the new quadrilateral.

50. A triangle has vertices $L(-5, 6)$, $M(-2, -3)$, and $N(4, 5)$. Write an equation for the line perpendicular to $\overline{LM}$ that contains point N.

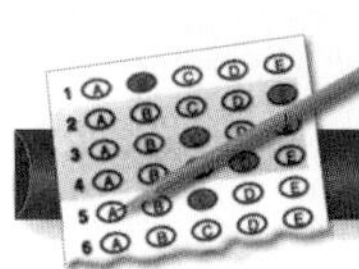

Standardized Test Prep

Multiple Choice

51. What is the slope of a line parallel to the line $6x - 4y = 12$?
A. $-\frac{3}{2}$ B. $\frac{3}{2}$ C. $\frac{4}{3}$ D. $-\frac{4}{3}$

52. The slope of a line is 6. What is the slope of a line perpendicular to it?
F. 6 G. -6 H. $\frac{1}{6}$ I. $-\frac{1}{6}$

Take It to the NET
Online lesson quiz at **www.PHSchool.com**
Web Code: afa-0306

53. Line f contains the points $(5, -4)$ and $(4, -6)$. What is the slope of a line perpendicular to it?
A. 2 B. $\frac{1}{2}$ C. $-\frac{1}{2}$ D. -2

Short Response

54. Line c contains the points $(2, -2)$ and $(-4, 1)$.
a. What is the slope of a line perpendicular to line c?
b. What is the y-intercept of the line perpendicular to line c that contains $(1, 2)$?

Mixed Review

Lesson 3-5 x^2 Algebra **Write an equation for the line containing the given points.**

55. $A(0, 3), B(6, 0)$ 56. $C(-4, 2), D(-1, 7)$ 57. $E(3, -2), F(-5, -8)$

Lesson 2-4 **Name the property that justifies each statement.**

58. $\angle 4 \cong \angle 4$

59. If $m\angle B = 8$, then $2m\angle B = 16$.

60. $-3x + 6 = 3(-x + 2)$

61. If $\overline{RS} \cong \overline{MN}$, then $\overline{MN} \cong \overline{RS}$.

Lesson 2-3 **Use the Law of Syllogism to draw a conclusion.**

62. If you are in geometry class, then you are in math class. If you are in math class, then you are at school.

63. If you travel to Switzerland, then you travel to Europe. If you travel to Europe, then you have a passport.

Checkpoint Quiz 2 — Lessons 3-4 through 3-6

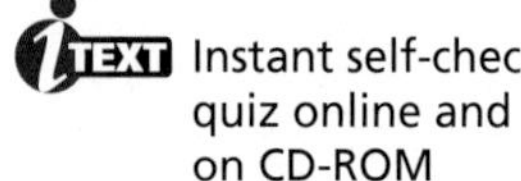

Instant self-check quiz online and on CD-ROM

Use the number of sides to name the polygon. Then find the value of each variable.

1. 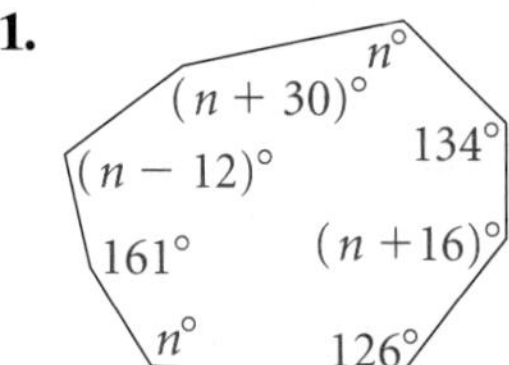

2. 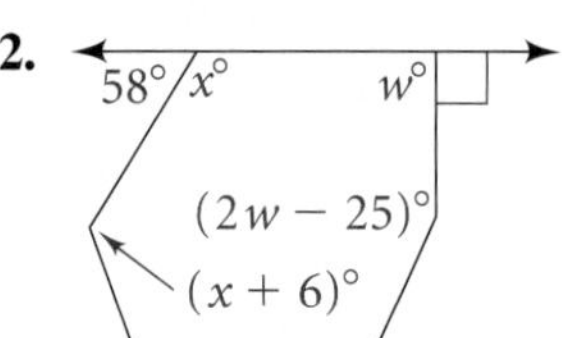

3. 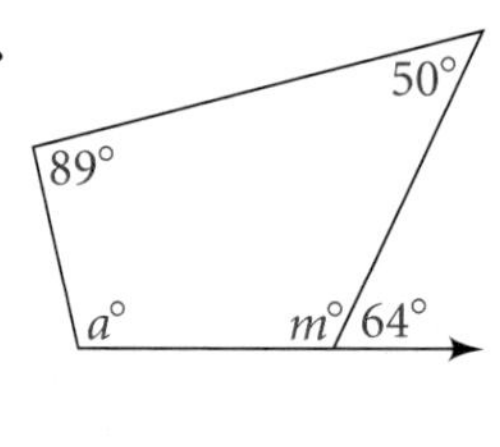

x^2 Algebra **Graph each line using intercepts.**

4. $4x + y = -8$ 5. $-2x + 3y = 12$ 6. $3x + 5y = 30$

Find the slopes of $\overleftrightarrow{RS}$ and $\overleftrightarrow{TV}$. Then determine whether $\overleftrightarrow{RS}$ and $\overleftrightarrow{TV}$ are parallel, perpendicular, or neither. Explain.

7. $R(-2, 6), S(3, 4), T(3, 5), V(0, 0)$

8. $R(6, -1), S(7, 0), T(3, -4), V(0, -1)$

9. $R(9, 1), S(5, 6), T(3, 8), V(-2, 4)$

10. $R(5, -7), S(-4, -9), T(6, 2), V(-3, 0)$

Constructing Parallel and Perpendicular Lines

Lesson Preview

What You'll Learn

To construct parallel lines

To construct perpendicular lines

. . . And Why

To construct the shortest segment from a point to a line, as in Example 4

✓ Check Skills You'll Need

(For help, go to Lesson 1-5.)

Use a straightedge to draw each figure. Then use a straightedge and compass to construct a figure congruent to it.

1. a segment **2.** an obtuse angle **3.** an acute angle

Use a straightedge to draw each figure. Then use a straightedge and compass to bisect it.

4. a segment **5.** an acute angle **6.** an obtuse angle

Interactive lesson includes instant self-check, tutorials, and activities.

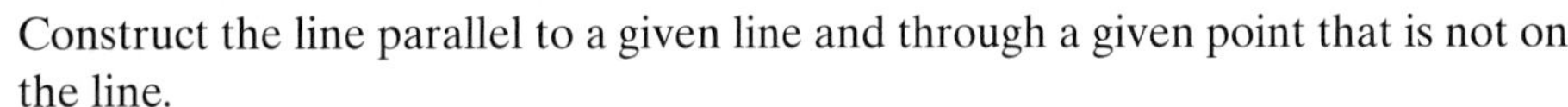

OBJECTIVE 1 Constructing Parallel Lines

You can use what you know about parallel lines, transversals, and corresponding angles to construct parallel lines.

1 EXAMPLE Constructing $\ell \parallel m$

Construct the line parallel to a given line and through a given point that is not on the line.

Given: line ℓ and point N not on ℓ

Construct: line m through N with $m \parallel \ell$

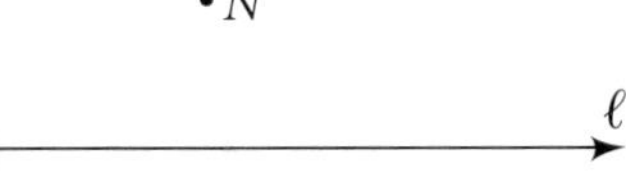

Step 1
Label two points H and J on ℓ.
Draw $\overleftrightarrow{HN}$.

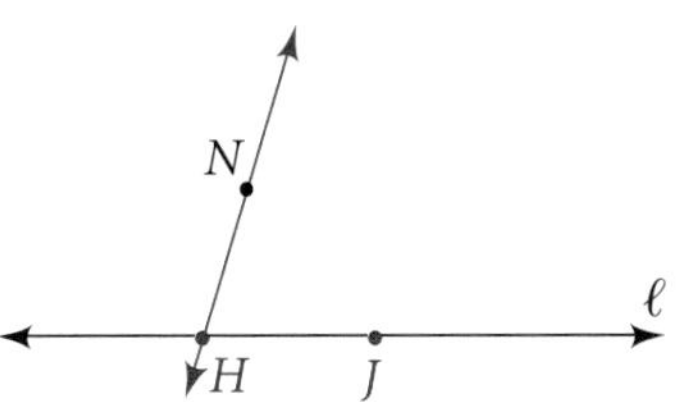

Step 2
Construct $\angle 1$ with vertex at N so that $\angle 1 \cong \angle NHJ$ and the two angles are corresponding angles. Label the line you just constructed m.

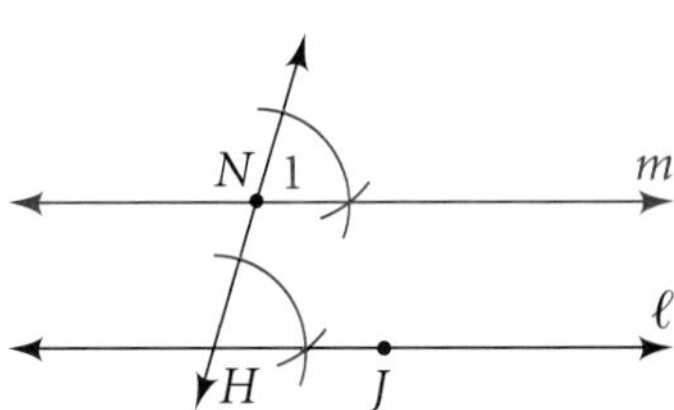

$m \parallel \ell$

Real-World Connection

Careers Architects construct parallel and perpendicular lines when they build models of the buildings they design.

✓ Check Understanding 1 Critical Thinking Explain why lines ℓ and m must be parallel.

For many constructions, you will find it helpful to first visualize or sketch what the final figure should look like. This will often suggest the construction steps. In Example 2, a sketch is shown at the left of the example.

2 EXAMPLE Constructing a Special Quadrilateral

Need Help?

First, draw a sketch of the figure.

Construct a quadrilateral with one pair of parallel sides of lengths a and b.

Given: segments of lengths a and b

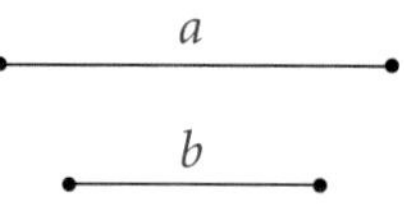

Construct: quadrilateral $ABYZ$ with $AZ = a, BY = b$, and $\overline{AZ} \parallel \overline{BY}$

Step 1
Construct $\overline{AZ}$ with length a.

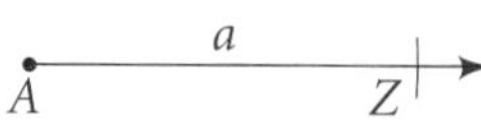

Step 2
Draw a point B not on $\overleftrightarrow{AZ}$. Then draw $\overrightarrow{AB}$.

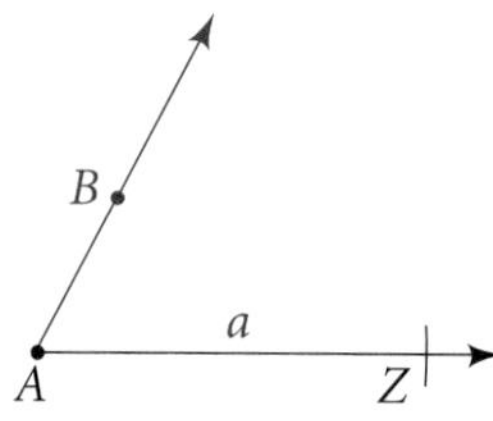

Step 3
Construct a ray parallel to $\overleftrightarrow{AZ}$ through B.

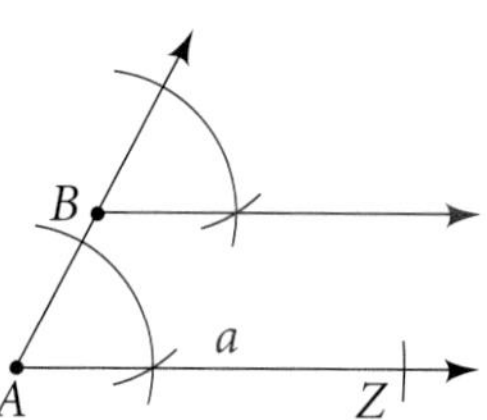

Step 4
Construct Y so that $BY = b$. Then draw $\overline{YZ}$.

Quadrilateral $ABYZ$ has $AZ = a, BY = b$, and $\overline{AZ} \parallel \overline{BY}$.

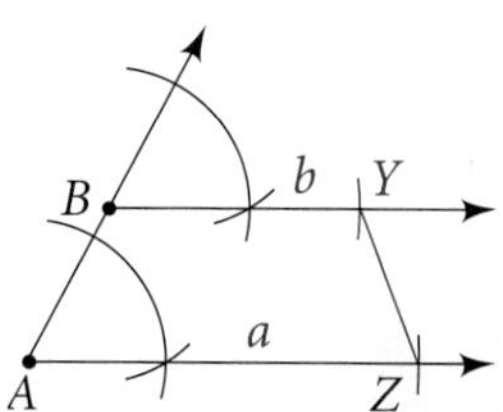

Check Understanding **2** Draw two segments. Label their lengths c and d. Construct a quadrilateral with one pair of parallel sides of lengths c and $2d$.

OBJECTIVE

2 Constructing Perpendicular Lines

You can construct perpendicular lines using a compass and a straightedge.

3 EXAMPLE Perpendicular at a Point on a Line

Construct the perpendicular to a given line at a given point on the line.

Given: point P on line ℓ

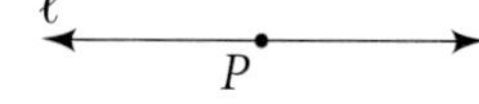

Construct: $\overleftrightarrow{CP}$ with $\overleftrightarrow{CP} \perp \ell$

Step 1
Put the compass point on point P. Draw arcs intersecting ℓ in two points. Label the points A and B.

Step 2
Open the compass wider. With the compass tip on A, draw an arc above point P.

Step 3

Without changing the compass setting, place the compass point on point B. Draw an arc that intersects the arc from Step 2. Label the point of intersection C.

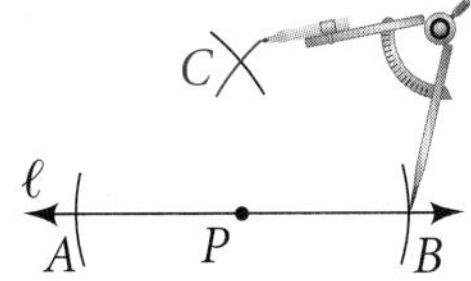

Step 4

Draw $\overleftrightarrow{CP}$.

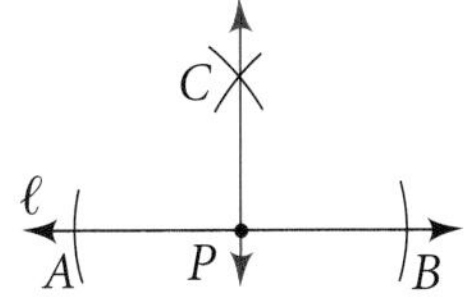

$\overleftrightarrow{CP} \perp \ell$

✓ Check Understanding 3 Use a straightedge to draw $\overleftrightarrow{EF}$. Construct $\overleftrightarrow{FG}$ so that $\overleftrightarrow{FG} \perp \overleftrightarrow{EF}$ at point F.

You will prove in Chapter 5 that the perpendicular segment is the shortest segment from a point to a line. Here is its construction.

4 EXAMPLE Perpendicular From a Point to a Line

Construct the perpendicular to a given line through a given point not on the line.

Given: line ℓ and point R not on ℓ

Construct: $\overleftrightarrow{RG}$ with $\overleftrightarrow{RG} \perp \ell$

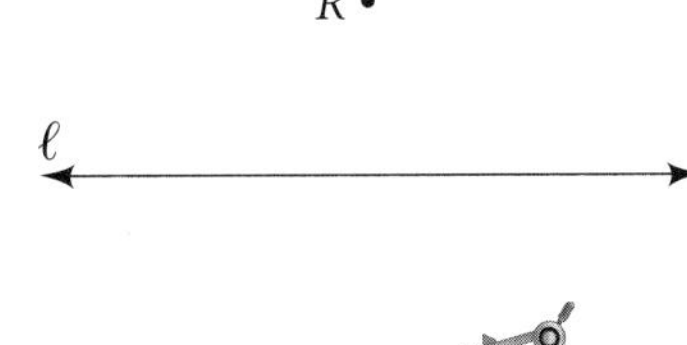

Step 1

Open your compass to a size greater than the distance from R to ℓ. With the compass point on point R, draw an arc that intersects ℓ at two points. Label the points E and F.

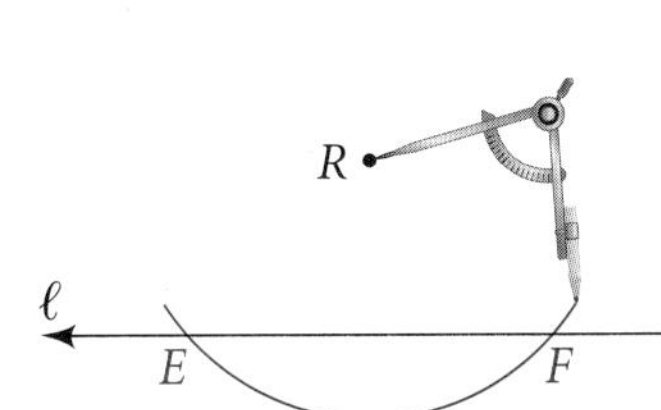

Step 2

Place the compass point on E and make an arc.

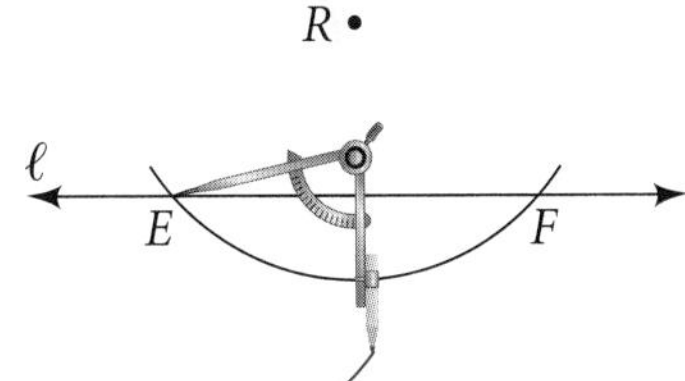

Step 3

Keep the same compass setting. With the compass tip on F, draw an arc that intersects the arc from Step 2. Label the point of intersection G.

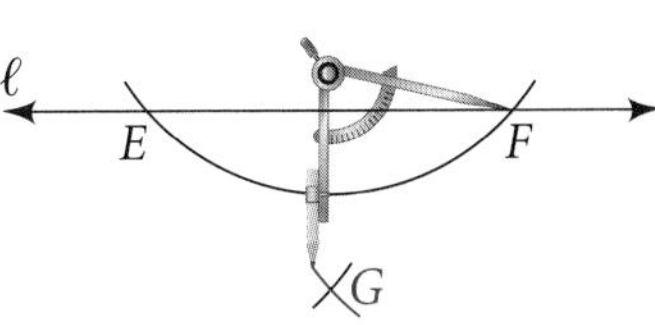

Step 4

Draw $\overleftrightarrow{RG}$.

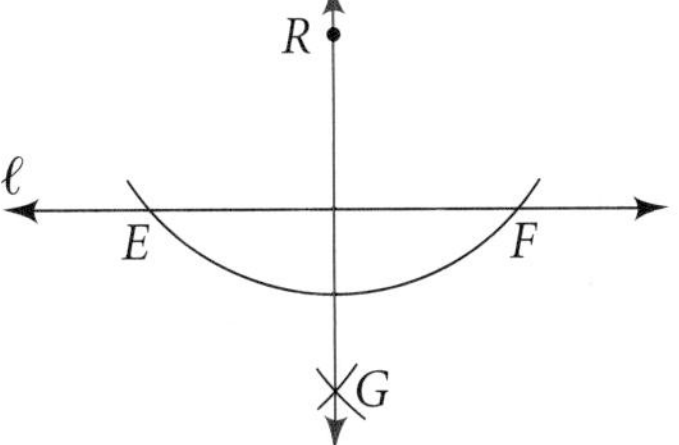

$\overleftrightarrow{RG} \perp \ell$

Real-World Connection

You can draw large circles using a simple, large compass.

✓ Check Understanding 4 Draw a line $\overleftrightarrow{CX}$ and a point Z not on $\overleftrightarrow{CX}$. Construct $\overleftrightarrow{ZB}$ so that $\overleftrightarrow{ZB} \perp \overleftrightarrow{CX}$.

EXERCISES

For more practice, see *Extra Practice.*

Practice and Problem Solving

A Practice by Example

Example 1 (page 165)

In Exercises 1–4, draw a figure like the given one. Then construct the line through point *J* and parallel to $\overleftrightarrow{AB}$.

1. •*J*

A *B*

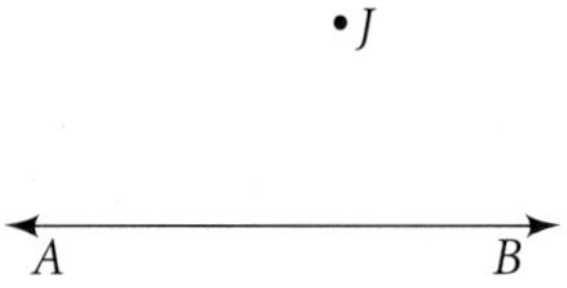

2.

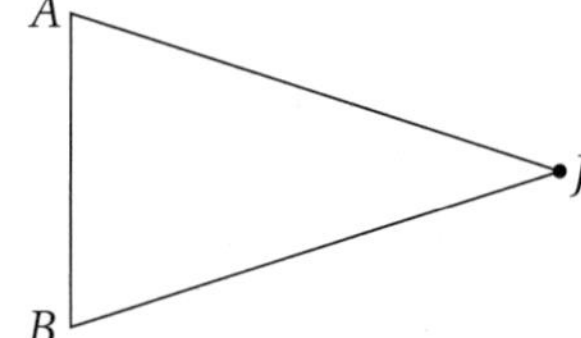

3.

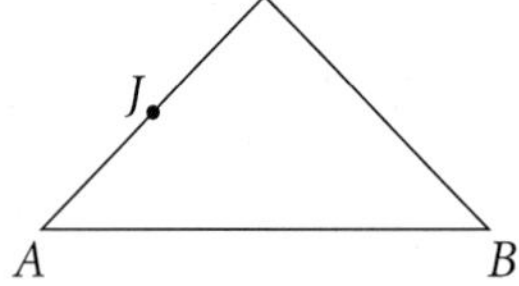

4.

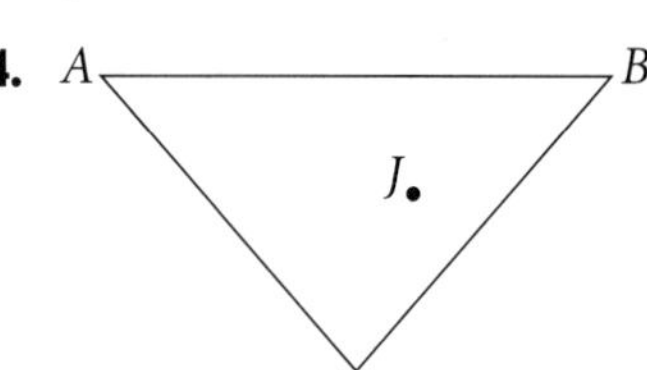

Example 2 (page 166)

For Exercises 5–7, draw two segments. Label their lengths *a* and *b*. Construct a quadrilateral with one pair of parallel sides as described.

5. The sides have lengths *a* and *b*.

6. The sides have lengths 2*a* and *b*.

7. The sides have lengths *a* and $\frac{1}{2}b$.

Example 3 (pages 166, 167)

In Exercises 8–9, draw a figure like the given one. Then construct the line perpendicular to $\overleftrightarrow{AB}$ at point *P*.

8.

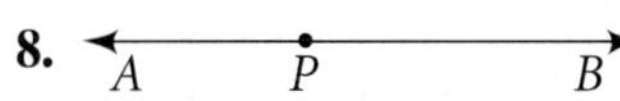

9.

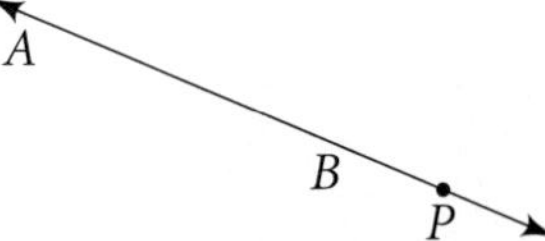

Example 4 (page 167)

In Exercises 10–13, draw a figure like the given one. Then construct the line through point *P* and perpendicular to $\overleftrightarrow{RS}$.

10.

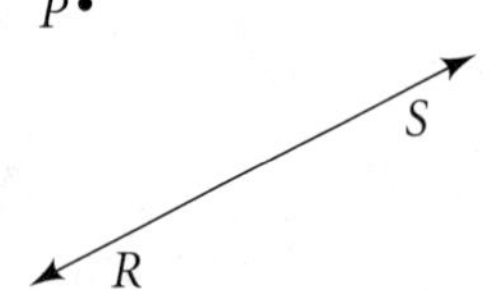

11.

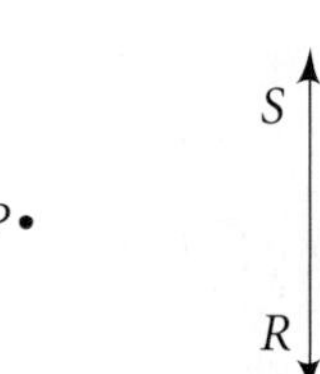

12.

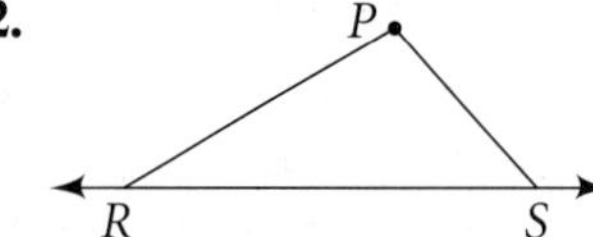

13.

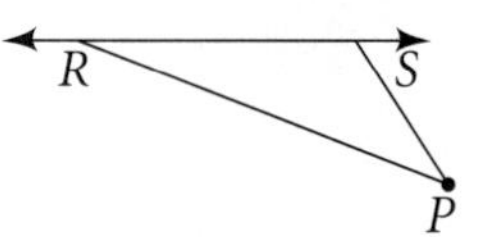

B Apply Your Skills

14. Draw an acute angle. Construct an angle congruent to your angle so that the two angles are alternate interior angles. (*Hint:* Think of the letter Z.)

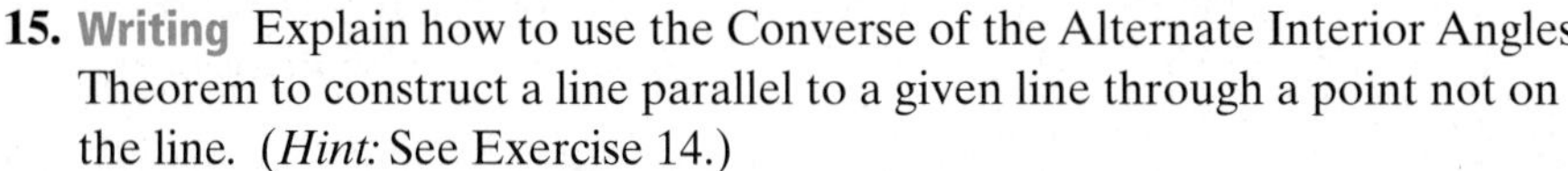

15. **Writing** Explain how to use the Converse of the Alternate Interior Angles Theorem to construct a line parallel to a given line through a point not on the line. (*Hint:* See Exercise 14.)

16. Draw obtuse $\triangle ABC$ with obtuse $\angle B$.
   a. Construct line ℓ through point A so that $\ell \parallel \overline{BC}$.
   b. Construct line m through point C so that $m \parallel \overline{AB}$.

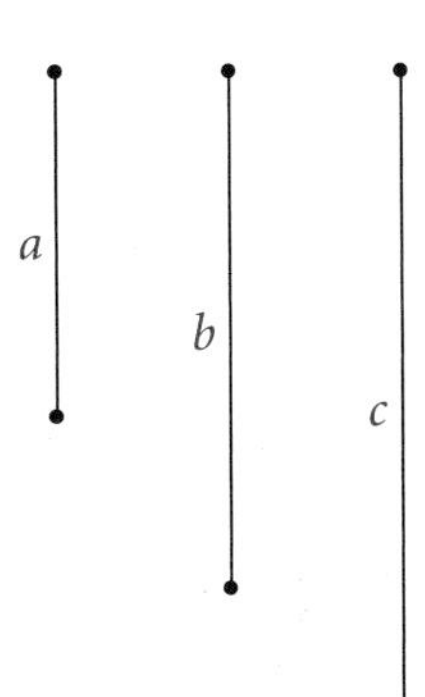

Exercises 17–25

For Exercises 17–25, use the segments at the left.

17. Draw a line m. Construct a segment of length b that is perpendicular to line m.

18. Construct a rectangle with base b and height c.

19. Construct a square with sides of length a.

20. Construct a rectangle with one side length a and a diagonal length b.

21. a. Construct a quadrilateral with a pair of parallel sides of length c.
   b. **Make a Conjecture** What appears to be true about the other pair of sides in the quadrilateral you constructed?
   c. Use a protractor, a ruler, or both to check the conjecture you made in part (b).

22. Construct a right triangle with legs of lengths a and b.

23. Construct a right triangle with legs of lengths b and $\frac{1}{2}b$.

24. a. Construct a triangle with sides of lengths a, b, and c.
   b. Construct a quadrilateral with sides of lengths a, b, and c.
   c. **Writing** How many different triangles could you construct in (a)? Explain. How many different quadrilaterals could you construct in (b)? Explain.

25. a. Construct a triangle with sides of lengths a, b, and c.
   b. Construct the midpoint of each side of the triangle.
   c. Form a new triangle by connecting the midpoints.
   d. **Make a Conjecture** How do the sides of the smaller triangle and the sides of the larger triangle appear to be related?
   e. Use a protractor, a ruler, or both to check the conjecture you made in part (d).

26. **Paper Folding** You can use paper folding to create a perpendicular to a given line through a given point. Fold the paper so that the line folds onto itself and the fold line contains the given point.

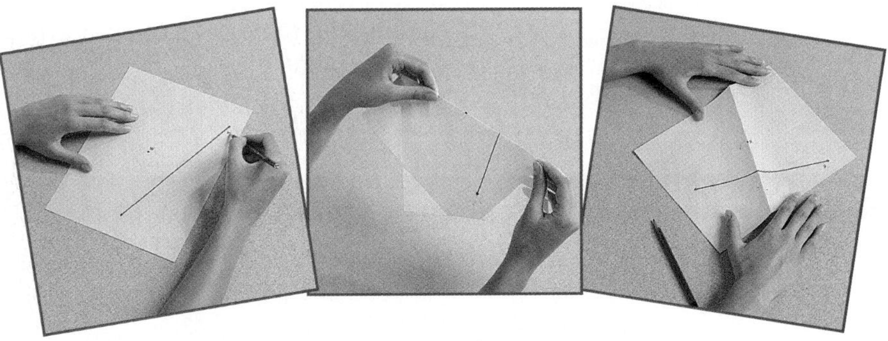

   a. Draw a line m and a point W not on the line. Use paper folding to create the perpendicular to m through W. Label this fold line k.
   b. Next, fold the line perpendicular to k through W. Label this fold line p.
   c. What is true of p and m? Justify your answer.

Challenge

Draw a segment, $\overline{DG}$. Construct a quadrilateral whose diagonals are both congruent to $\overline{DG}$, bisect each other, and meet the additional condition given below. Describe the quadrilateral that you get.

27. The diagonals are not perpendicular.

28. The diagonals are perpendicular.

Construct a rectangle whose side lengths *a* and *b* meet the given condition.

29. $b = 2a$ **30.** $b = \frac{1}{2}a$ **31.** $b = \frac{1}{3}a$ **32.** $b = \frac{2}{3}a$

Construct a triangle whose side lengths *a*, *b*, and *c* meet the given conditions. If such a triangle is not possible, explain.

33. $a = b = c$ **34.** $a = b = 2c$ **35.** $a = 2b = 2c$ **36.** $a = b + c$

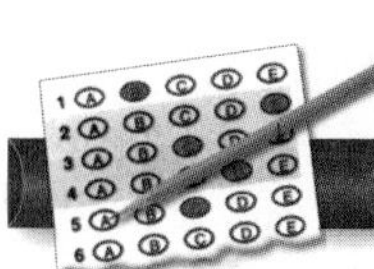

Standardized Test Prep

Multiple Choice

37. In the construction shown at the right, the two arcs with centers A and B have the same radius. What must be true of $\overline{PQ}$?

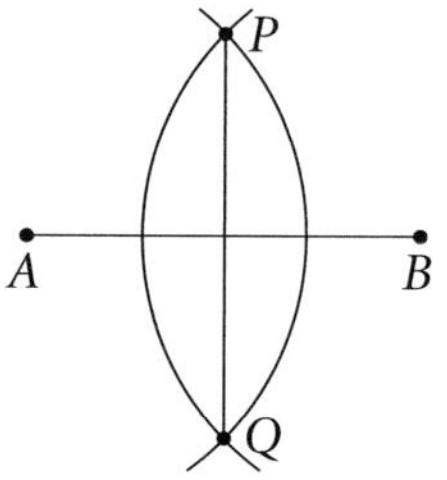

A. $\overline{PQ}$ bisects $\overline{AB}$. **B.** $\overline{PQ} \parallel \overline{AB}$

C. $\overline{PQ} \cong \overline{AB}$ **D.** $\overline{PQ} \cong \overline{AQ}$

38. Suppose you construct lines ℓ, m, and n so that $\ell \perp m$ and $\ell \parallel n$. Which of the following is true?

F. $m \parallel n$ **G.** $m \parallel \ell$ **H.** $n \perp \ell$ **I.** $n \perp m$

Short Response

39. Use a compass and straightedge to construct the following figure.

a. Draw a line ℓ and a point G not on ℓ. Construct an arc centered at point G to intersect ℓ in two points. Label the points R and T. Draw $\overline{GR}$ and $\overline{GT}$.

b. Classify $\triangle RGT$. Justify your response.

40. These pictures show steps for constructing a line parallel to a given line, but they are not necessarily in order.

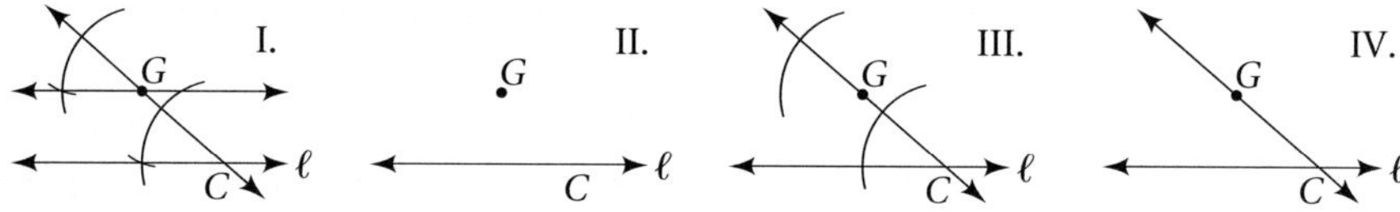

a. List the construction steps in the correct order.

b. For any step that uses a compass, describe the location(s) of the compass point.

Take It to the NET

Online lesson quiz at **www.PHSchool.com**

Web Code: afa-0307

Mixed Review

Lesson 3-6 **Are the lines parallel? Explain.**

41. $y = -4x - 3$
$y = 4x + 3$

42. $y = \frac{1}{2}x + 1$
$y = -2x - 1$

43. $x + 3y = -6$
$4x + 12y = -6$

Lesson 1-6 **Find the distance between the points to the nearest tenth.**

44. $W(8, -2)$ and $Z(2, 6)$

45. $W(-4.5, 1.2)$ and $Z(3.5, -2.8)$

Lesson 1-2 **Name the intersection of the planes.**

46. plane ABE and plane $EBCD$

47. plane $AFDE$ and plane FCD

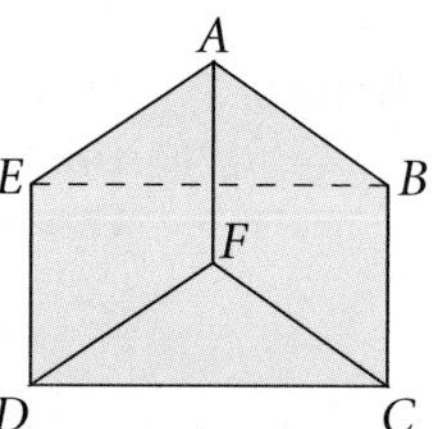

Technology

Using Tables and Lists

FOR USE WITH CHAPTER 3

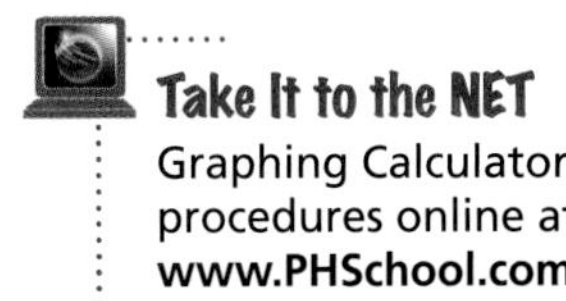

Take It to the NET
Graphing Calculator procedures online at **www.PHSchool.com**
Web Code: afe-2104

Tables and lists on your graphing calculator allow you to study relationships both numerically and graphically. The first example reminds you how to build a table.

1 EXAMPLE

Display a table showing the sums of the measures of the angles of a polygon.

X	Y_1	
3	180	
4	360	
5	540	
6	720	
7	900	
8	1080	
9	1260	

X=3

Use the **Y=** screen and write the polygon angle-sum formula in the form $Y_1 = 180(X - 2)$. Use the **TBLSET** feature so that X starts at 3 and changes by 1.

Use the **TABLE** feature to see the table of n-gon angle sums.

The second example suggests a powerful way to use lists. First, press **Y=** **CLEAR**.

2 EXAMPLE

List and plot four ordered pairs for the line $y = 2x - 1$.

On your home screen generate four values for x in list L_1 as follows.

seq(X, X, −2, 4, 2) **STO▶** L_1 **ENTER**.

Enter the corresponding values for y in list L_2 as follows.

$2\,L_1 - 1$ **STO▶** L_2 **ENTER**.

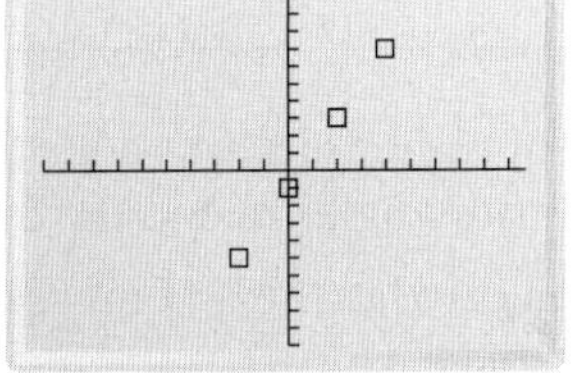

Access **STAT PLOT**, press 1, and turn "On" Plot 1. Check that your **Xlist** is L_1 and your **Ylist** is L_2. Then **GRAPH** in a standard viewing window as shown at the right.

EXERCISES

1. Use lists to plot ordered pairs (x, y) for the relationship $y = 180(x - 2)$. Use the command seq(X, X, 3, 12) to generate L_1 values. Store $180(L_1 - 2)$ into an L_2 list of Y values. Graph the points in an appropriate viewing window.

2. The relationship $y = 180(n - 2)/n$ or $Y_1 = 180(X - 2)/X$ gives the measure of one angle of a regular polygon for each value of n or X.
   a. Display a table of regular-polygon angle measures. Use TblStart = 3.
   b. Scroll down your table. What happens to the angle measures as X gets large?
   c. Create L_1, L_2 lists of (n, y) pairs for $n = 3$ to 20.
   d. Plot the (n, y) points. What happens to the angle measures as n gets large?

3. The formula $y = 360/n$ gives an exterior-angle measure for a regular n-gon. Create L_1, L_2 lists of (n, y) values and plot points. What happens to exterior-angle measures as n gets large?

Test-Taking Strategies Writing Extended Responses

An extended-response question is usually worth a maximum of 4 points and has multiple parts. To get full credit, you need to answer each part and show all your work or justify your reasoning.

EXAMPLE

Algebra Use the triangle at the right.

a. Write an equation that you can use to find the value of x.

b. Show how to solve the equation for x.

c. Find the measure of the smallest interior angle of the triangle.

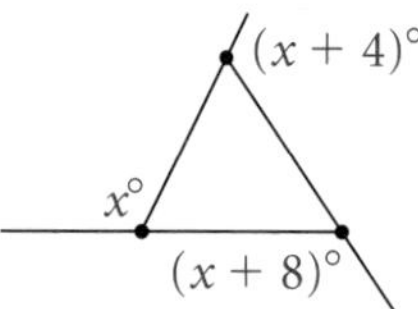

Below are two responses and the amount of credit each received.

4 points	3 points
$x + (x + 4) + (x + 8) = 360$ $3x + 12 = 360$ $3x = 348$ $x = 116$ Exterior angles are 116°, 120°, and 124°. Interior angles are 64°, 60°, 56°. The smallest interior angle has measure 56.	$180 = 180 - x + 180 - (x + 4) + 180 - (x + 8)$ $180 = 540 - 3x + 12$ $-372 = -3x$ $x = 124$ Ext. angles: 124°, 128°, 132° Int. angles: 56°, 52°, 48° The smallest int. angle is 48°.

The 4-point response shows a correct equation and solution. The student examined all the interior angles to find the one with the smallest measure.

There is an error in the 3-point response, but the student completed the problem and answered each part.

If you make an error, you can still get some credit. It is important that you complete each part of the problem or explain how you could do the problem.

EXERCISES

Use the Example above to do each exercise.

1. Where did the student make an error in the 3-point response?

2. When answering an extended-response question, you can describe how you are going to do the problem and then carry out the steps. For the Example exercise, begin with the following observation and write a 4-point response.

The largest exterior angle has measure $x + 8$, and the smallest interior angle is a supplement of that angle.

Chapter Review

Vocabulary

acute triangle (p. 133)
alternate interior angles (p. 115)
concave polygon (p. 144)
convex polygon (p. 144)
corresponding angles (p. 115)
equiangular triangle (p. 133)
equiangular polygon (p. 146)
equilateral triangle (p. 133)
equilateral polygon (p. 146)
exterior angle of a polygon (p. 133)
flow proof (p. 123)
isosceles triangle (p. 133)
obtuse triangle (p. 133)
point-slope form (p. 154)
polygon (p. 143)
regular polygon (p. 146)
remote interior angles (p. 133)
right triangle (p. 133)
same-side interior angles (p. 115)
scalene triangle (p. 133)
slope-intercept form (p. 152)
standard form of a linear equation (p. 153)
transversal (p. 115)
two-column proof (p. 117)

Reading Math
Understanding Vocabulary

Choose the correct vocabulary term to complete each sentence.

1. In a triangle, an angle is right, obtuse, or __?__.
2. A(n) __?__ angle has a measure between 90 and 180.
3. When two coplanar lines are cut by a transversal, two angles that are in similar positions on the same side of the transversal are called __?__.
4. The measure of a(n) __?__ angle of a triangle is equal to the sum of the measures of its two remote interior angles.
5. A polygon is __?__ if no diagonal contains points outside the polygon.
6. A(n) __?__ polygon has all angles congruent.
7. A(n) __?__ polygon is both equiangular and equilateral.
8. The linear equation $y - 3 = 4(x + 5)$ is written in __?__ form.
9. From the __?__ form of a linear equation, you can easily read the value of the slope and the value of the y-intercept.
10. When two coplanar lines are cut by a transversal, the angles between the two lines and on opposite sides of the transversal are called __?__.

Take It to the NET
Online vocabulary quiz at www.PHSchool.com
Web Code: afj-0351

Skills and Concepts

3-1 Objectives

▼ To identify angles formed by two lines and a transversal
▼ To prove and use properties of parallel lines

A **transversal** is a line that intersects two coplanar lines at two distinct points.
∠1 and ∠4 are **corresponding angles.**
∠3 and ∠4 are **alternate interior angles.**
∠2 and ∠4 are **same-side interior angles.**

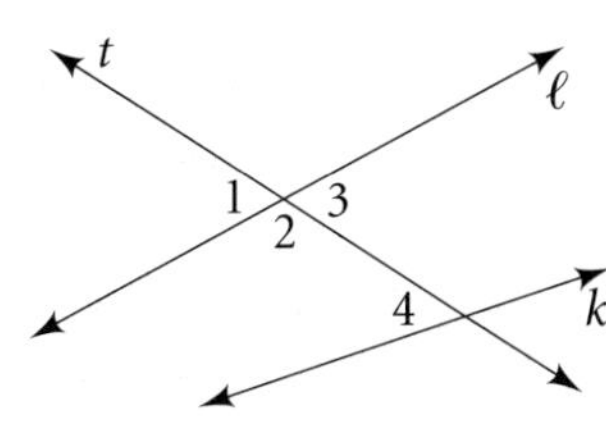

If two parallel lines are cut by a transversal, then
- corresponding angles are congruent.
- alternate interior angles are congruent.
- same-side interior angles are supplementary.

11. Suppose ℓ and k in the diagram above are parallel. If $m\angle 1 = 59$, what are the measures of $\angle 2$, $\angle 3$, and $\angle 4$?

Find $m\angle 1$ and then $m\angle 2$. Justify each answer.

12. 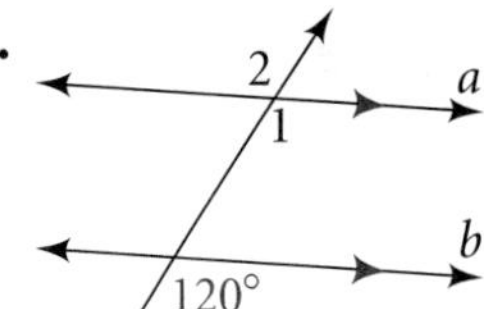

13. 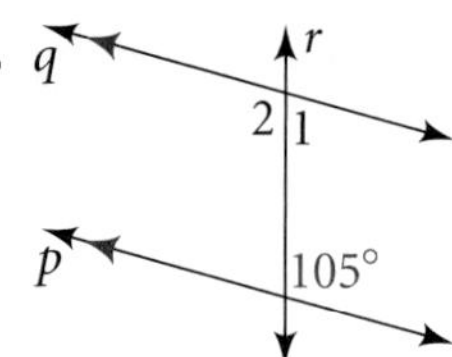

14. 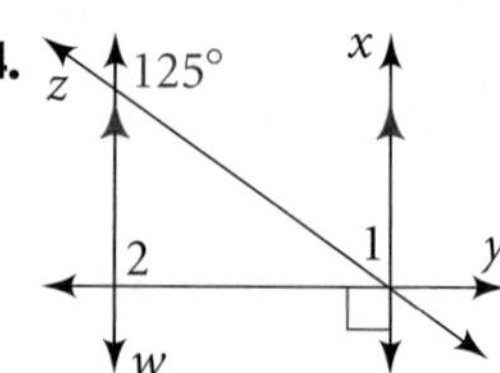

15. Writing Suppose both pairs of opposite sides of a quadrilateral are parallel. Which angles of the quadrilateral must be supplementary? Explain.

3-2 and 3-7 Objectives

- ▼ To recognize conditions that result in parallel lines
- ▼ To construct parallel lines
- ▼ To construct perpendicular lines

Two lines cut by a transversal are parallel if

- corresponding angles are congruent.
- alternate interior angles are congruent.
- same-side interior angles are supplementary.

You can construct the line parallel to a given line through a given point not on the line. You can also construct the perpendicular to a given line at a given point on the line or through a given point not on the line.

A **flow proof** uses arrows to show the logical connections between the statements. Reasons are written below the statements.

x^2 Algebra **Find the value of x for which $\ell \parallel m$.**

16. 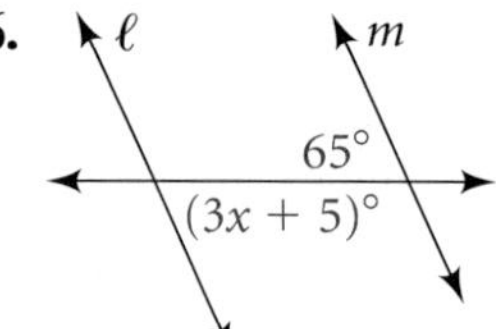

17. 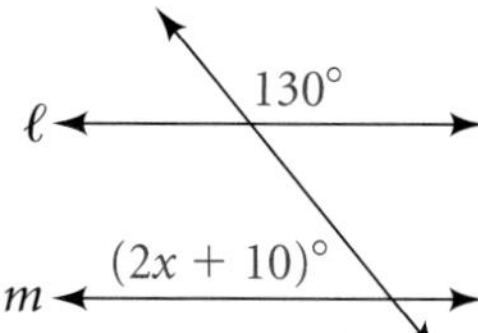

18. 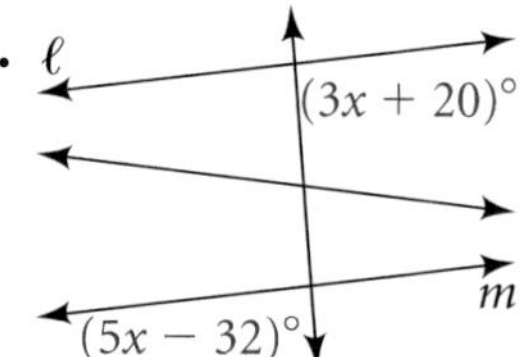

Use the segments at the right for Exercises 19 and 20.

19. Construct a rectangle with side lengths a and b.

20. Construct a quadrilateral with one pair of parallel opposite sides, each side of length $2a$.

a

b

21. To construct a line parallel to a given line m through a point not on m, you need to know how to construct __?__ angles.

3-3 Objectives

- ▼ To classify triangles and find the measures of their angles
- ▼ To relate exterior angles to the angles of a triangle

The sum of the measures of the angles of a triangle is 180. The measure of each **exterior angle** of a triangle equals the sum of the measures of its two **remote interior angles.**

You can classify triangles according to their sides and angles.

Find the values of the variables. Then classify each triangle by its sides and angles.

22. 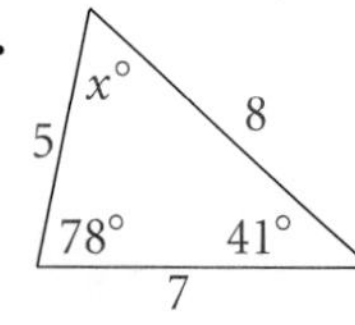

23. 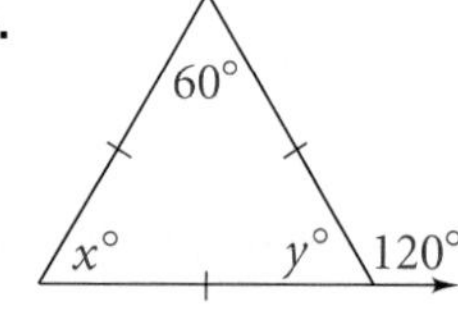

24. 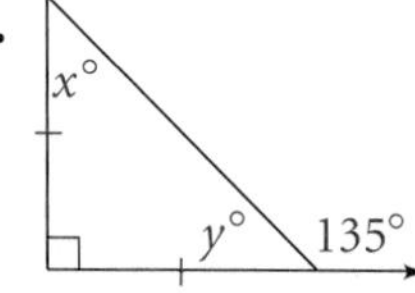

In each of Exercises 25–28, the measures of the three angles of a triangle are given. Find the value of x and then classify the triangle by its angles.

25. $x + 10, x - 20, x + 25$

26. $x, 2x, 3x$

27. $20x + 10, 30x - 2, 7x + 1$

28. $10x - 3, 14x - 20, x + 3$

29. In a right triangle, what is always true about the angles?

3-4 Objectives

- ▼ To classify polygons
- ▼ To find the sums of the measures of the interior and exterior angles of polygons

A **polygon** is a closed plane figure with at least three sides. To name a polygon, start at any vertex and list the vertices consecutively in a clockwise or counterclockwise direction. A polygon is **convex** if no diagonal contains points outside the polygon. Otherwise, it is **concave.**

An **equilateral polygon** has all sides congruent. An **equiangular polygon** has all angles congruent. A **regular polygon** is equilateral and equiangular.

The sum of the measures of the angles of an n-gon is $(n - 2)180$. The sum of the measures of the exterior angles of an n-gon, one at each vertex, is 360.

Find the measure of an interior angle and an exterior angle of each regular polygon.

30. a hexagon

31. an octagon

32. a decagon

33. a 24-gon

34. What is the sum of the measures of the exterior angles for each polygon in Exercises 30–33?

3-5 Objectives

- ▼ To graph lines given their equations
- ▼ To write equations of lines

When a linear equation is in **slope-intercept form,** $y = mx + b$, the slope m and the y-intercept b are easily identified. When a linear equation is in **point-slope form,** $(y - y_1) = m(x - x_1)$, point (x_1, y_1) and slope m can easily be identified. The equation $Ax + By = C$, where A and B are not both zero, is in **standard form.** When a linear equation is in standard form, the x- and y-intercepts are readily found.

35. Name the slope and y-intercept of $y = 2x - 1$. Graph the line.

36. Name a point on and the slope of $y - 3 = -2(x + 5)$. Graph the line.

37. Graph $y = -\frac{1}{2}$.

38. Graph $3x - 4y = 12$.

39. Write an equation for the vertical line that contains $A(6, -9)$.

3-6 Objectives

- ▼ To relate slope and parallel lines
- ▼ To relate slope and perpendicular lines

The slopes of two nonvertical parallel lines are equal. All vertical lines are parallel.

The product of the slopes of two nonvertical perpendicular lines is -1. In a plane, every vertical line is perpendicular to every horizontal line.

Determine whether $\overleftrightarrow{AB}$ and $\overleftrightarrow{CD}$ are *parallel, perpendicular,* or *neither.*

40. $A(-1, -4), B(2, 11), C(1, 1), D(4, 10)$

41. $A(2, 8), B(-1, -2), C(3, 7), D(0, -3)$

42. $A(-3, 3), B(0, 2), C(1, 3), D(-2, -6)$

43. $A(-1, 3), B(4, 8), C(-6, 0), D(2, 8)$

44. Writing For $B(4, 8)$ and $D(2, 8)$, find the slope of $\overleftrightarrow{BD}$. Explain why the slope of any horizontal line is zero.

Chapter Test

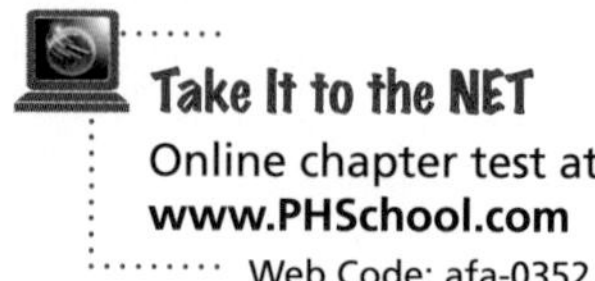

Take It to the NET
Online chapter test at
www.PHSchool.com
Web Code: afa-0352

Use a protractor and a centimeter ruler. Classify each triangle by its angles and its sides.

1. 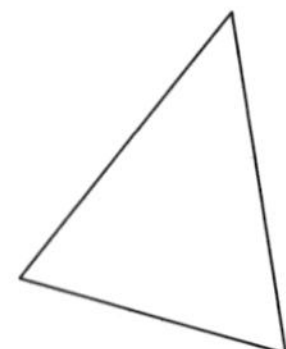

2. 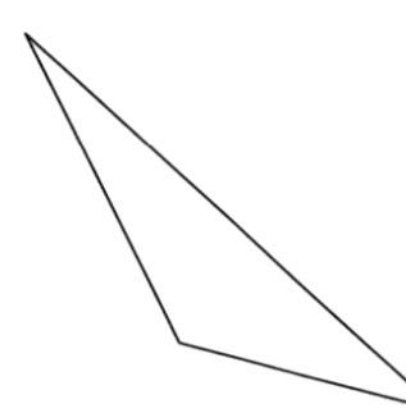

Find $m\angle 1$, then $m\angle 2$. Justify each answer.

3. 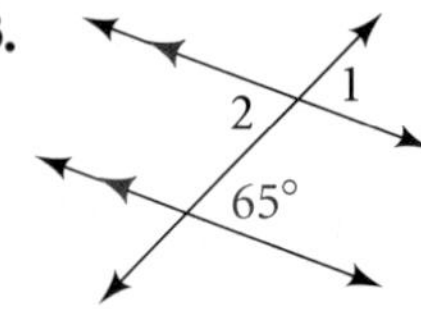

4. 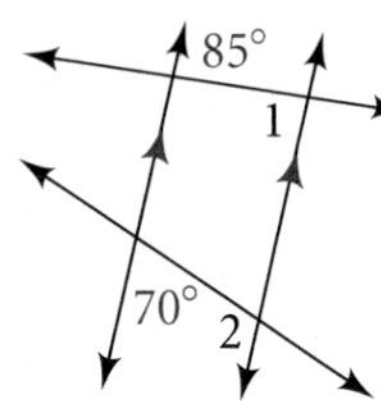

5. 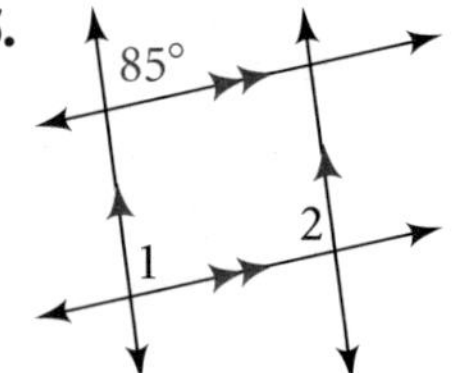

6. 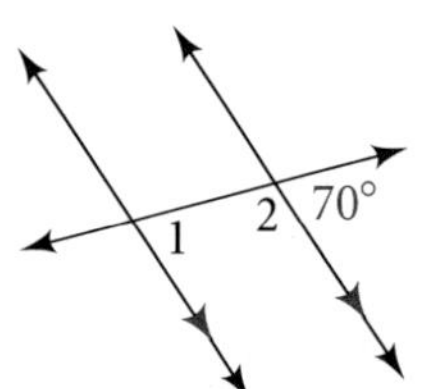

Two lines are parallel and cut by a transversal. Write *yes* or *no* to indicate whether the numbers given could be the measures of a pair of same-side interior angles.

7. 40 and 140

8. 90 and 90

9. 60 and 60

10. 27 and 27

x^2 **Algebra Find the value of x for which $\ell \parallel m$.**

11. 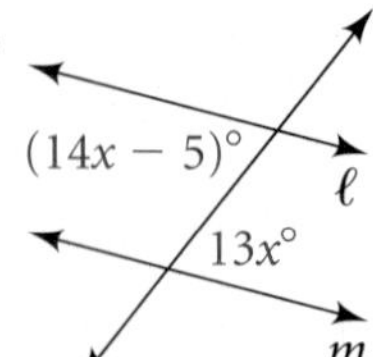

12. 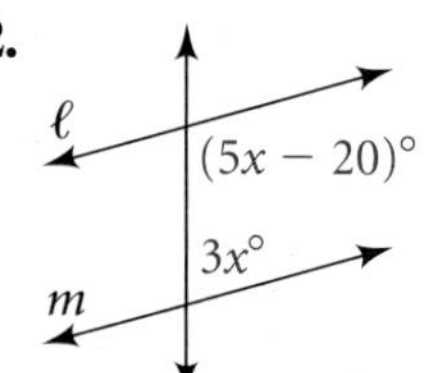

13. 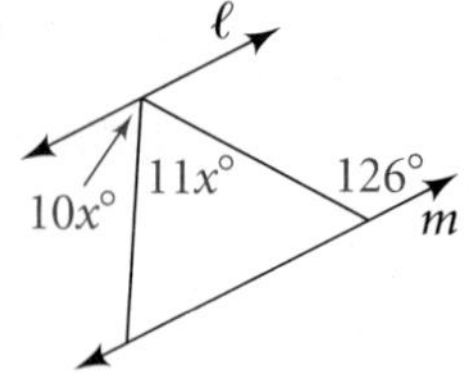

14. 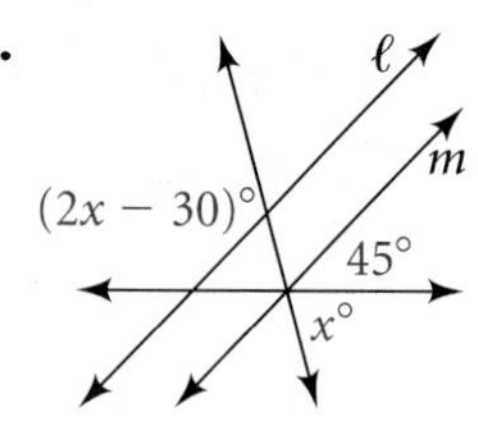

15. Draw a line m and a point T not on the line. Construct the line through T perpendicular to m.

16. Draw an angle, $\angle ABC$. Then construct line m through A so that $m \parallel \overleftrightarrow{BC}$.

17. **Open-Ended** The letter **F** illustrates a pair of same-side interior angles and a pair of corresponding angles. Find a letter that illustrates alternate interior angles.

18. **Open-Ended** Describe two corresponding angles formed by lines in your classroom.

19. Supply the reason for each step in the proof.

Given: $\ell \parallel m$ and $\angle 4 \cong \angle 2$
Prove: $n \parallel p$

1. $\ell \parallel m$	**a.** ?
2. $\angle 1 \cong \angle 2$	**b.** ?
3. $\angle 4 \cong \angle 2$	**c.** ?
4. $\angle 1 \cong \angle 4$	**d.** ?
5. $n \parallel p$	**e.** ?

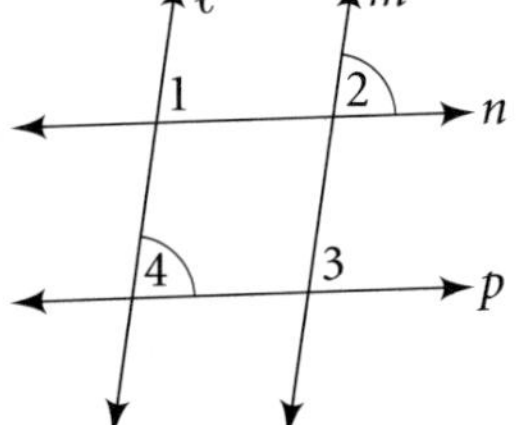

20. Write an equation of the line with slope −5 and containing $A(3, -1)$.

21. **Writing** Explain how you can determine whether a polygon is concave or convex.

Find the value of each variable.

22. 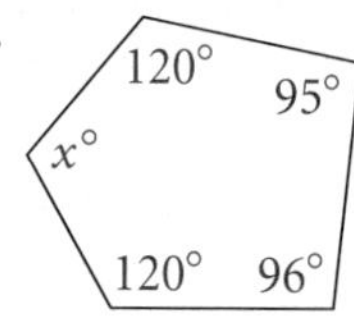

23. 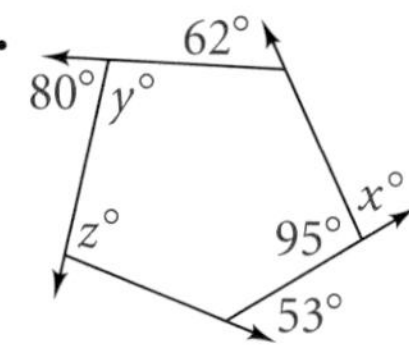

Sketch each pair of lines. Tell whether they are *parallel*, *perpendicular*, or *neither*.

24. $y = 4x + 7$
$y = -\frac{1}{4}x - 3$

25. $y = 3x - 4$
$y = 3x + 1$

26. $y = x + 5$
$y = -5x - 1$

27. $y = -3$
$x = 10$

28. What is the measure of an exterior angle of a regular 12-gon?

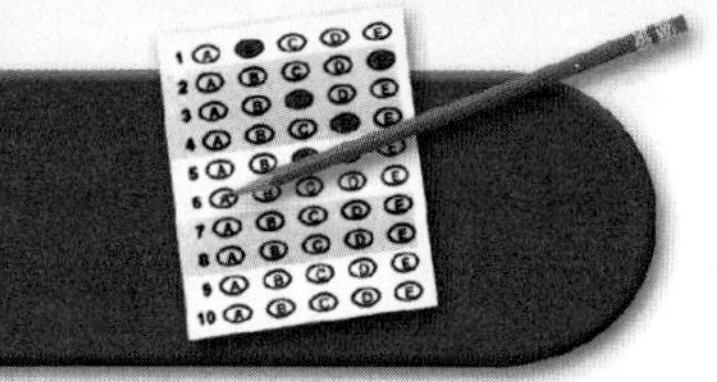

Standardized Test Prep

Reading Comprehension **Read the passage below. Then answer the questions on the basis of what is *stated* or *implied* in the passage.**

Airport Plans Civic leaders in Chicago are discussing a plan to expand O'Hare Airport and build new runways. The airport's present runways, labeled A through G in the diagram, include three pairs that are parallel. Runways B and D intersect to form right angles.

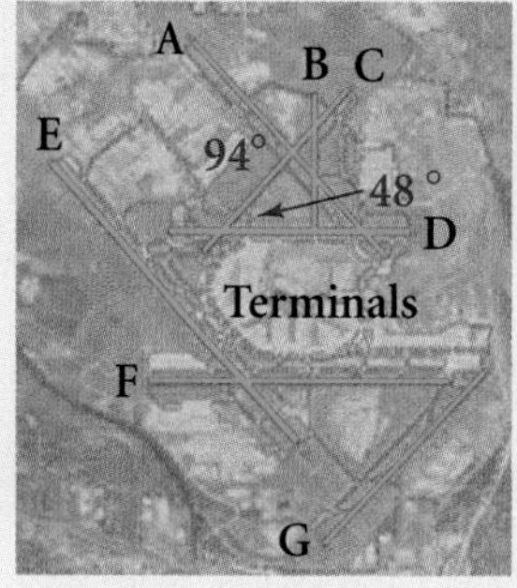

The crisscrossing layout and takeoff/landing patterns prevent the runways from being used to their full capacity. This can cause travel delays. If the planned new runways are built, then four landings and two takeoffs can happen simultaneously. The plan, however, requires an additional 292 acres of land to the south and 141 acres to the north. Taking this land would lead to the demolition of 240 apartment units and more than 300 houses and 70 businesses.

1. At present, how many runways are there?
   A. 3 **B.** 4 **C.** 6 **D.** 7

2. Which list best describes the parallel runways?
   F. A ∥ C and B ∥ D **G.** A ∥ E, C ∥ G, and D ∥ F
   H. A ∥ E and D ∥ F **I.** A ∥ C, B ∥ D, and E ∥ G

3. Which runways are perpendicular?
   A. A ⊥ E **B.** B ⊥ D **C.** C ⊥ D **D.** E ⊥ F

4. Why can runways E and G not be used to their full capacity?
   I. crisscrossing layout
   II. crisscrossing takeoff pattern
   III. crisscrossing landing pattern
   F. I only **G.** I and II only
   H. II and III only **I.** I, II, and III

5. What is the measure of the obtuse angle formed where runways B and C intersect?
   A. 42 **B.** 90 **C.** 132 **D.** 138

6. What is the measure of the acute angle formed where runways A and D intersect?
   F. 46 **G.** 48 **H.** 86 **I.** 94

7. If you extend runway C to meet runway E, what is the measure of the acute angle formed?
   A. 42 **B.** 48 **C.** 86 **D.** 90

8. If you extend runway E to meet runway G, what is the measure of the obtuse angle formed?
   F. 86 **G.** 90 **H.** 94 **I.** 104

9. At most, how many landings and takeoffs would be possible in one hour on the new runways?
   A. 4 and 2 **B.** 40 and 20
   C. 240 and 120 **D.** cannot be determined

10. How many acres larger than the current airport will the new airport be?
    F. 141 **G.** 161 **H.** 292 **I.** 433

11. Each apartment unit, house, or business is one "real estate unit." What is the average number of real estate units per acre that will be demolished in the plan? Explain your answer.

Suppose runways D and B are the *x*- and *y*-axes of a coordinate plane.

12. Which runway has a positive slope?
    A. A **B.** B **C.** C **D.** D

13. Which runway has a negative slope?
    F. F **G.** G **H.** D **I.** E

14. Which two runways have slopes whose product is approximately –1?
    A. A, G **B.** G, F **C.** F, D **D.** D, B

Where You've Been

- In Chapter 1, you learned the meanings of congruent segments and congruent angles.
- In Chapter 2, you used deductive reasoning to prove angles congruent.
- In Chapter 3, you developed relationships involving congruent angles, parallel lines, perpendicular lines, and polygons.

iTEXT Instant self-check online and on CD-ROM

Diagnosing Readiness

(For help, go to the Lesson in green.)

The Distance Formula (Lesson 1-6)

Find the lengths of the sides of $\triangle ABC$.

1. $A(3, 1), B(-1, 1), C(-1, -2)$ **2.** $A(-3, 2), B(-3, -6), C(8, 6)$ **3.** $A(-1, -2), B(6, 1), C(2, 5)$

Proving Angles Congruent (Lesson 2-5)

Draw a conclusion based on the information given.

4. $\angle A$ is supplementary to $\angle B$; $\angle C$ is supplementary to $\angle B$

5. $\angle A$ is supplementary to $\angle B$; $\angle A \cong \angle B$

6. $\angle 1$ is complementary to $\angle 2$

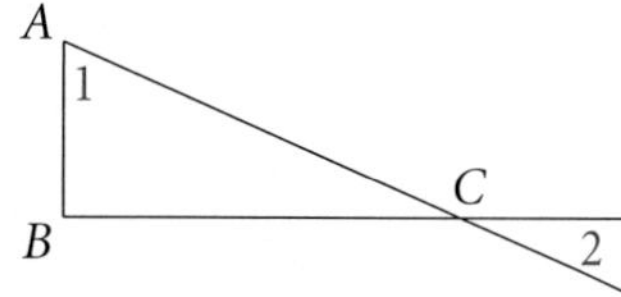

7. $\overrightarrow{FA} \perp \overrightarrow{FC}$; $\overrightarrow{FB} \perp \overrightarrow{FD}$

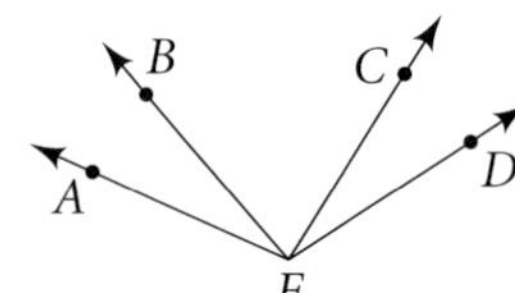

Parallel Lines and the Triangle Angle-Sum Theorem (Lesson 3-3)

What can you conclude from each diagram?

8.

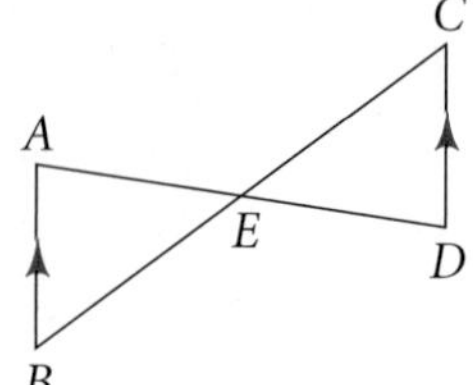

9.

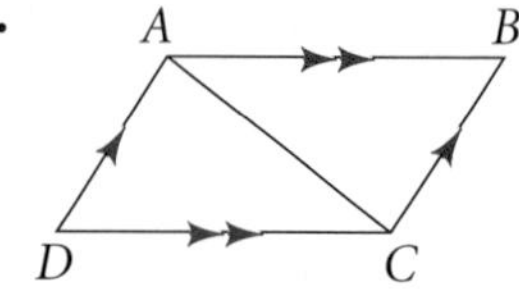

10.

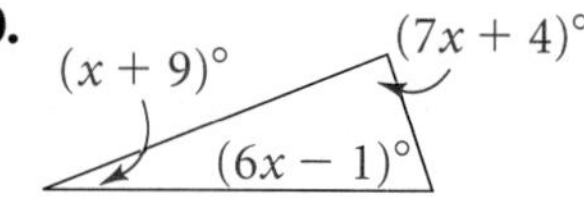

Congruent Triangles

LESSONS

Key Vocabulary

- base of an isosceles triangle (p. 211)
- base angle of an isosceles triangle (p. 211)
- congruent polygons (p. 180)
- corollary (p. 212)
- CPCTC (corresponding parts of congruent triangles are congruent) (p. 203)
- hypotenuse (p. 217)
- legs of a right triangle (p. 217)
- legs of an isosceles triangle (p. 211)
- vertex angle of an isosceles triangle (p. 211)

Where You're Going

- In this chapter, you will learn the meaning of congruent polygons.
- You will learn how to prove two triangles congruent by five different methods.
- By learning how to prove triangles congruent, you will discover properties of an isosceles triangle.
- You will also learn how to draw other conclusions, once two triangles have been proved congruent.

Real-World Snapshots You will do activities involving reflected light and congruence on pages 238 and 239.

Congruent Figures

Lesson Preview

What You'll Learn

OBJECTIVE 1 To recognize congruent figures and their corresponding parts

. . . And Why

To use corresponding parts of congruent shapes in the Space Shuttle, as in Example 2

✔ Check Skills You'll Need

(For help, go to page 24.)

Algebra **Solve each equation.**

1. $x + 6 = 25$
2. $x + 7 + 13 = 33$
3. $5x = 540$
4. $x + 10 = 2x$
5. For the triangle at the right, use the Triangle Angle-Sum Theorem to find the value of y.

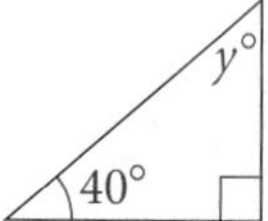

New Vocabulary • congruent polygons

Interactive lesson includes instant self-check, tutorials, and activities.

OBJECTIVE 1 Congruent Figures

Congruent figures have the same size and shape. When two figures are congruent, you can move one so that it fits exactly on the other one. Three ways to make such a move—a slide, a flip, and a turn—are shown below. You will learn much more about slides, flips, and turns in Chapter 12.

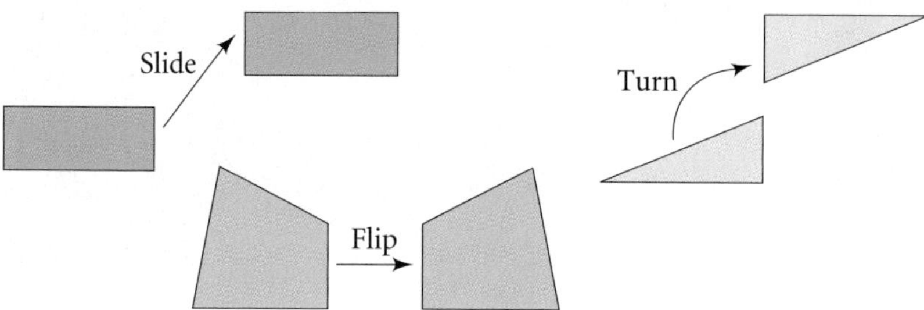

Congruent polygons have congruent corresponding parts—their matching sides and angles. Matching vertices are corresponding vertices. When you name congruent polygons, always list corresponding vertices in the same order.

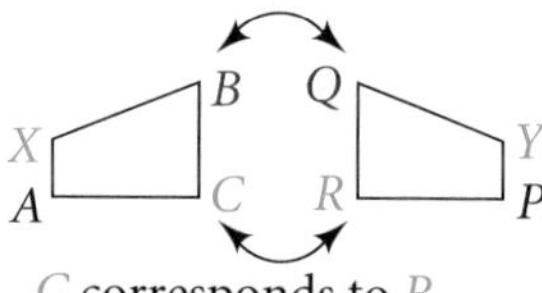

C corresponds to R.
$\angle B$ corresponds to $\angle Q$.
$\overline{AX}$ corresponds to $\overline{PY}$.
$ACBX \cong PRQY$

1 EXAMPLE Naming Congruent Parts

$\triangle TJD \cong \triangle RCF$. List the congruent corresponding parts.

Sides: $\overline{TJ} \cong \overline{RC}$ $\quad \overline{JD} \cong \overline{CF}$ $\quad \overline{DT} \cong \overline{FR}$

Angles: $\angle T \cong \angle R$ $\quad \angle J \cong \angle C$ $\quad \angle D \cong \angle F$

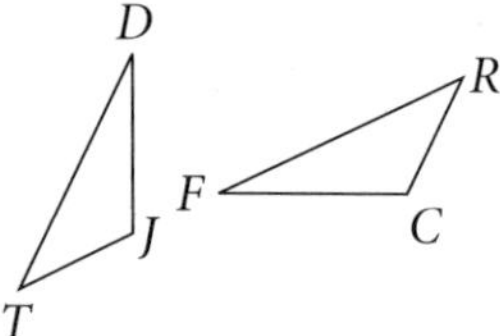

✔ Check Understanding 1 $\triangle WYS \cong \triangle MKV$. List the congruent corresponding parts. Use three letters to name each angle.

2 EXAMPLE Real-World Connection

Spacecraft The fins of the Space Shuttle suggest congruent pentagons. Find $m\angle B$.

In the congruent pentagons, B corresponds to E, so you know that $\angle B \cong \angle E$. You can find $m\angle B$ by first finding $m\angle E$.

Use the Polygon Angle-Sum Theorem. It tells you that the sum of the measures of the angles of pentagon $SPACE$ is $(5 - 2)180$, or 540.

$m\angle S + m\angle P + m\angle A + m\angle C + m\angle E = 540$	**Polygon Angle-Sum Theorem**
$88 + 90 + 90 + 132 + m\angle E = 540$	**Substitute.**
$400 + m\angle E = 540$	**Simplify.**
$m\angle E = 140$	**Subtract 400 from each side.**

$m\angle B = m\angle E$, so $m\angle B = 140$.

✓ Check Understanding **2** It is given that $\triangle WYS \cong \triangle MKV$. If $m\angle Y = 35$, what is $m\angle K$? Explain.

Two triangles are congruent when they have three pairs of congruent corresponding sides and three pairs of congruent corresponding angles.

Proof 3 EXAMPLE Finding Congruent Triangles

Developing Proof Decide whether the triangles are congruent. Justify your answer.

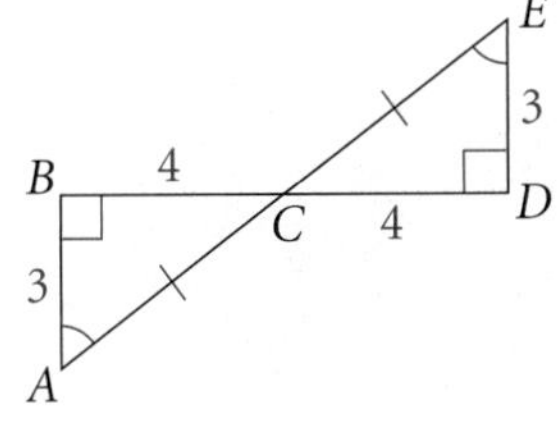

$\overline{AC} \cong \overline{EC}$	**Given**
$\overline{AB} \cong \overline{ED}$	**$AB = 3 = ED$**
$\overline{BC} \cong \overline{DC}$	**$BC = 4 = DC$**
$\angle A \cong \angle E$	**Given**
$\angle B \cong \angle D$	**All right angles are congruent.**
$\angle BCA \cong \angle DCE$	**Vertical angles are congruent.**

$\triangle ABC \cong \triangle EDC$ by the definition of congruent triangles.

✓ Check Understanding **3** Can you conclude $\triangle JKL \cong \triangle MNL$? Justify your answer.

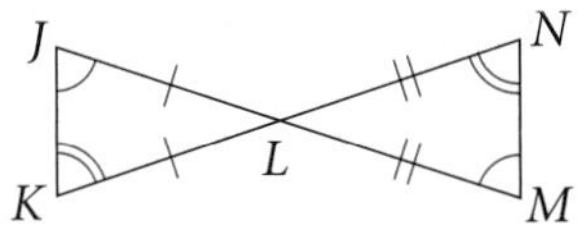

The next theorem follows from the Triangle Angle-Sum Theorem. In Exercise 45, you will explain why this theorem is true.

Key Concepts

Theorem 4-1

If two angles of one triangle are congruent to two angles of another triangle, then the third angles are congruent.

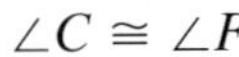

$\angle C \cong \angle F$

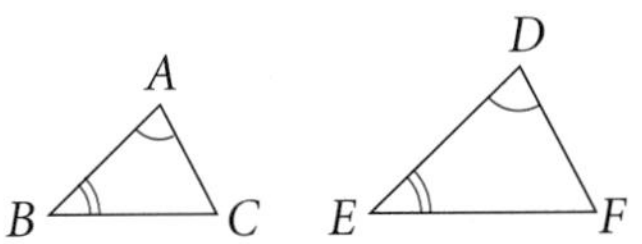

Example 4 shows typical statements that appear in a proof that two triangles are congruent. Note how you can use Theorem 4-1.

4 EXAMPLE Proving Triangles Congruent

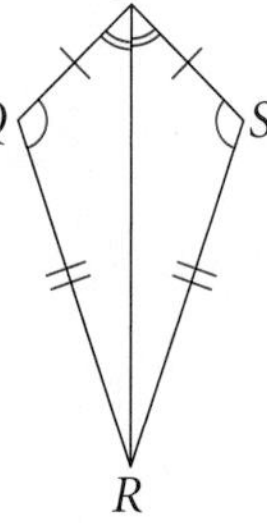

Developing Proof Use the information given in the diagram. Give a reason why each statement is true.

a. $\overline{PQ} \cong \overline{PS}, \overline{QR} \cong \overline{SR}$ — **Given**
b. $\overline{PR} \cong \overline{PR}$ — **Reflexive Property of ≅**
c. $\angle Q \cong \angle S, \angle QPR \cong \angle SPR$ — **Given**
d. $\angle QRP \cong \angle SRP$ — **Theorem 4-1**
e. $\triangle PQR \cong \triangle PSR$ — **Definition of ≅ triangles**

Check Understanding **4** Show how you can conclude that the triangles are congruent. List statements and reasons as in Example 4.

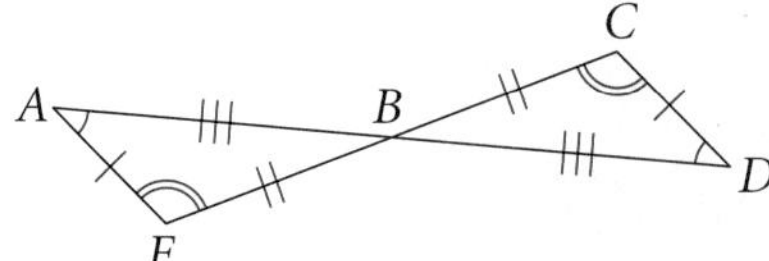

EXERCISES

For more practice, see *Extra Practice*.

Practice and Problem Solving

Practice by Example

Example 1 (page 180)

Real-World Connection

Exposed beams show the congruent triangles used in Tudor architecture.

1. Building Builders use the King Post truss, below left, for the top of a simple structure. In this truss, $\triangle ABC \cong \triangle ABD$. List the congruent corresponding parts.

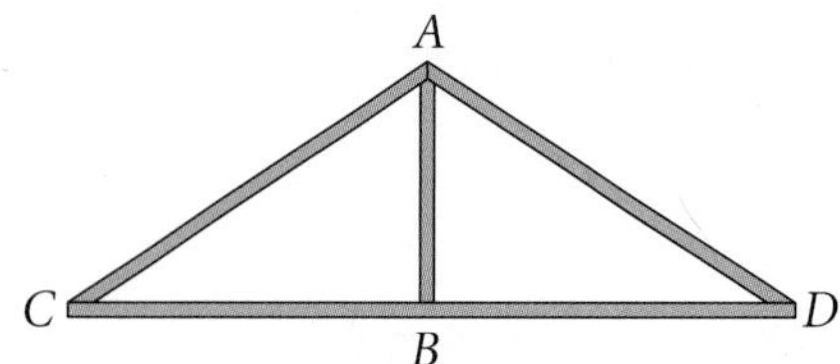

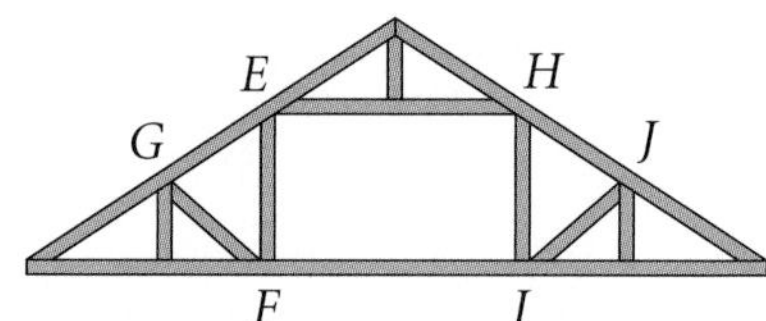

2. The Attic Frame truss, above right, provides open space in the center for storage. In this truss, $\triangle EFG \cong \triangle HIJ$. List the congruent corresponding parts.

$\triangle LMC \cong \triangle BJK$. Complete the congruence statements.

3. $\overline{LC} \cong$ ___?___   **4.** $\overline{KJ} \cong$ ___?___

5. $\overline{JB} \cong$ ___?___   **6.** $\angle L \cong$ ___?___

7. $\angle K \cong$ ___?___   **8.** $\angle M \cong$ ___?___

9. $\triangle CML \cong$ ___?___   **10.** $\triangle KBJ \cong$ ___?___

11. $\triangle MLC \cong$ ___?___   **12.** $\triangle JKB \cong$ ___?___

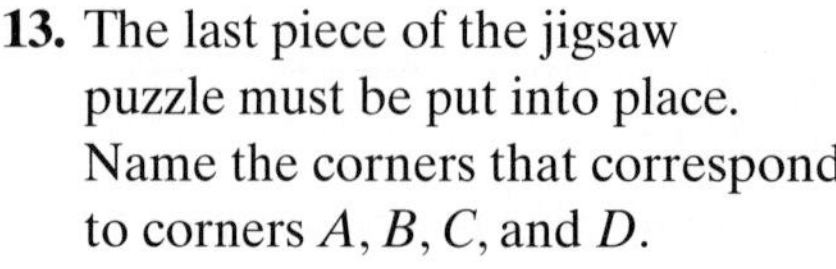

13. The last piece of the jigsaw puzzle must be put into place. Name the corners that correspond to corners A, B, C, and D.

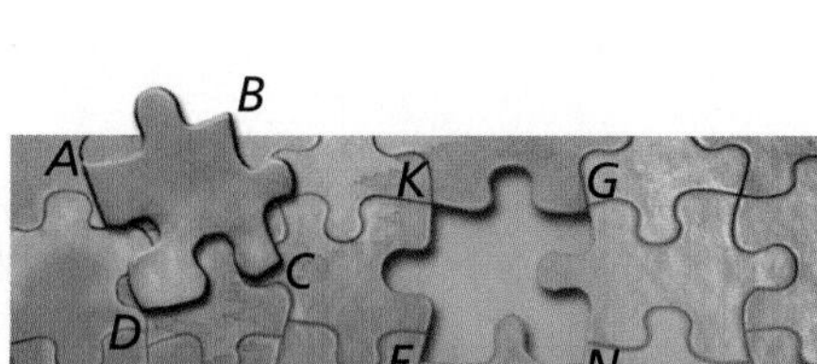

***POLY* ≅ *SIDE*. List each of the following.**

14. four pairs of congruent sides   **15.** four pairs of congruent angles

Example 2 (page 181) **In the two lifeguard chairs, $ABCD \cong FGHI$. Find the measure of the angle or the length of the side.**

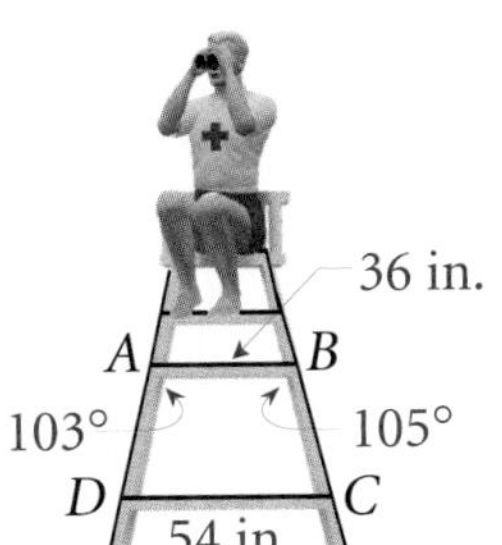

16. $\overline{AD}$
17. $\overline{HI}$
18. $\angle FGH$
19. $\angle ADC$
20. $\overline{FG}$
21. $\overline{BC}$
22. $\angle DCB$
23. $\angle IFG$

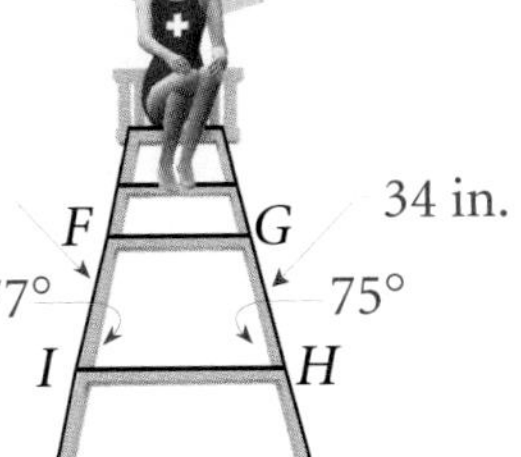

Example 3 (page 181) **Developing Proof In Exercises 24–27, can you conclude the figures are congruent? Justify each answer.**

24. $\triangle TRK$ and $\triangle TUK$

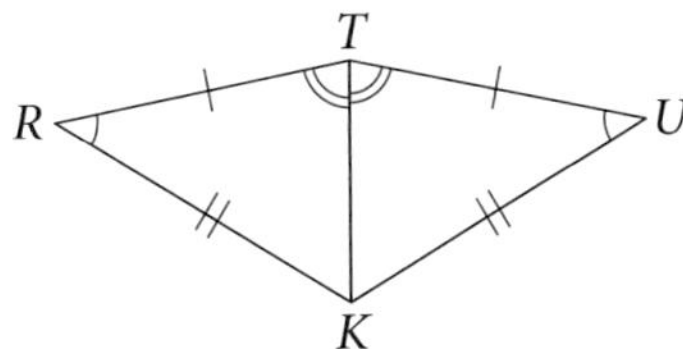

25. $\triangle SPQ$ and $\triangle TUV$

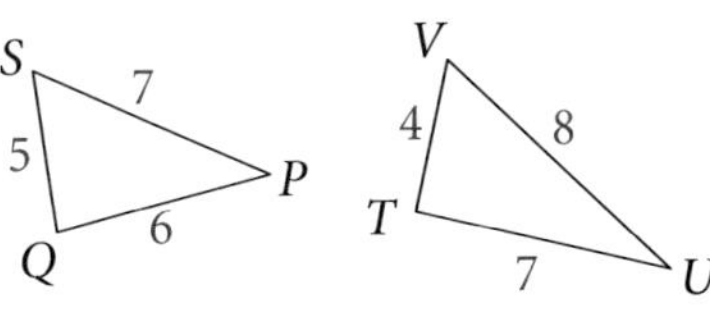

26. $\triangle XYZ$ and $\triangle XYP$

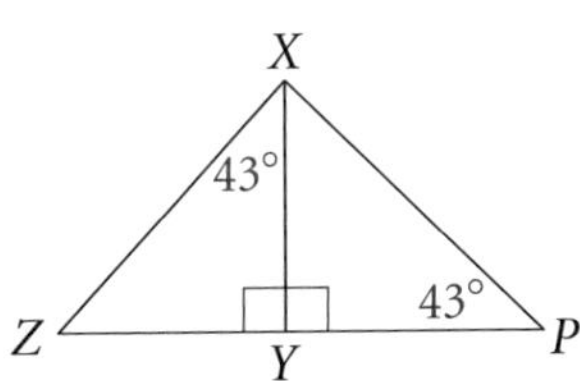

27. $HEJK$ and $GFJK$

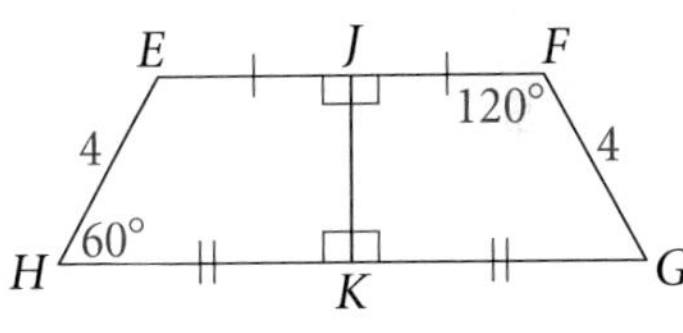

Example 4 (page 182)

28. **Developing Proof** Use the information given in the diagram. Tell why each statement is true.
    a. $\overline{AB} \parallel \overline{DC}$
    b. $\angle CAB \cong \angle ACD$
    c. $\angle B \cong \angle D$
    d. $\angle BCA \cong \angle DAC$
    e. $\overline{AC} \cong \overline{AC}$
    f. $\overline{AB} \cong \overline{DC}, \overline{BC} \cong \overline{AD}$
    g. $\triangle ABC \cong \triangle CDA$

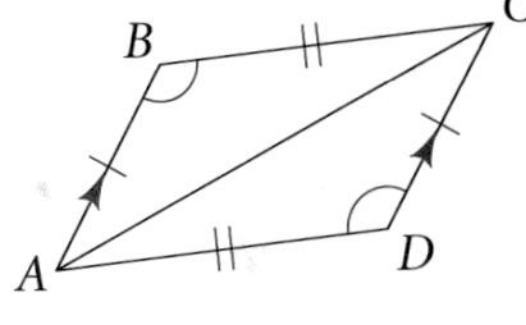

B Apply Your Skills

29. Identify the pairs of triangles that appear to be congruent.

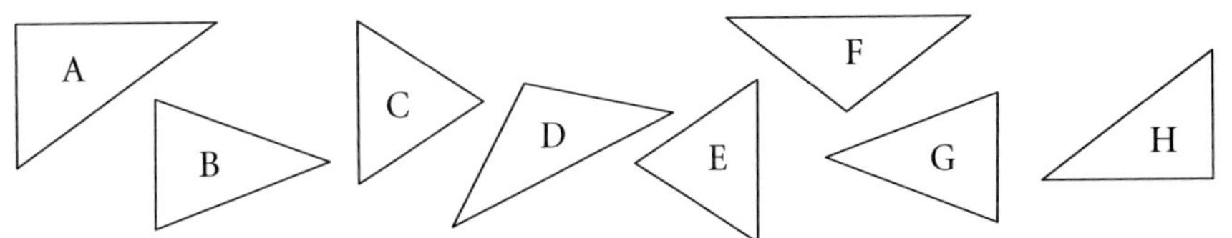

Need Help?

To review the Triangle Angle-Sum Theorem, go to Lesson 3-3.

Algebra Find the values of the variables.

30.

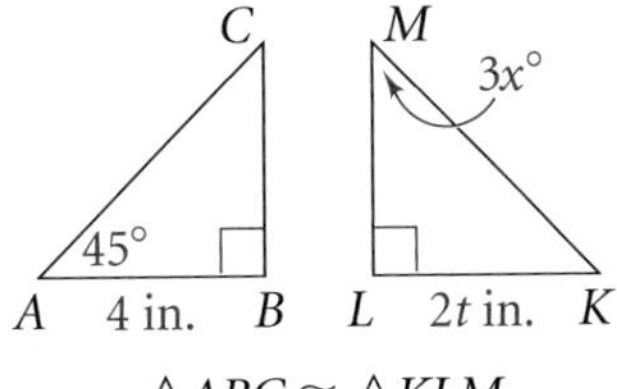

$\triangle ABC \cong \triangle KLM$

31.

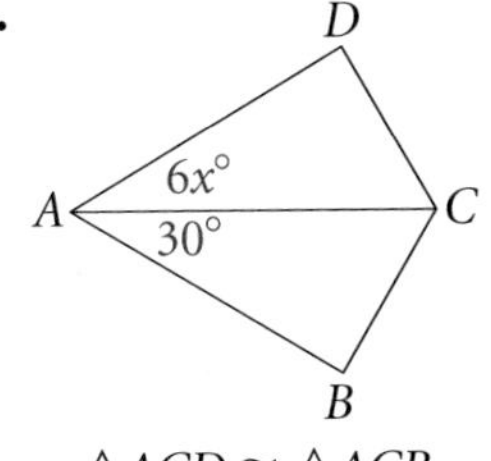

$\triangle ACD \cong \triangle ACB$

Algebra $\triangle ABC \cong \triangle DEF$. Find the measures of the given angles or the lengths of the given sides.

32. $m\angle A = x + 10, m\angle D = 2x$

33. $m\angle B = 3y, m\angle E = 21$

34. $BC = 3z + 2, EF = z + 6$

35. $AC = 7a + 5, DF = 5a + 9$

36. Parquet Floor Explain why it is important that $PACH \cong OLDE$.

37. Sports Cards The 225 cards in Tracy's sports card collection are rectangles of three different sizes. Describe how Tracy could quickly sort the cards.

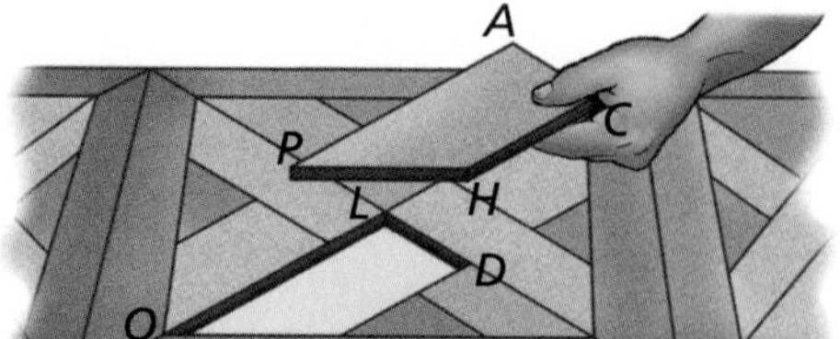

Exercise 36

Write a congruence statement for each pair of triangles.

38.

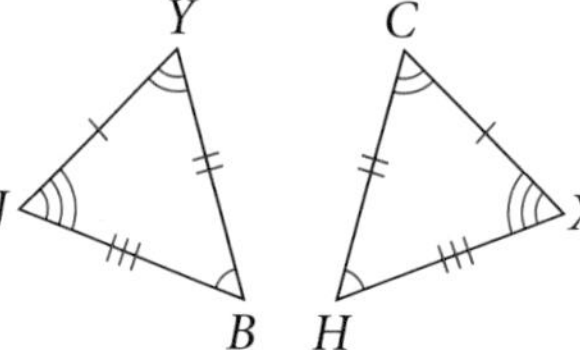

39.

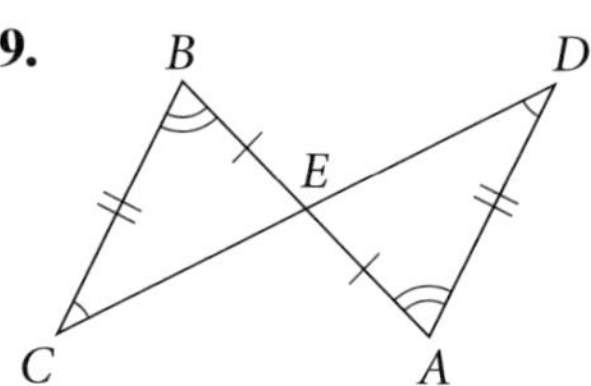

E is the midpoint of $\overline{CD}$.

40.

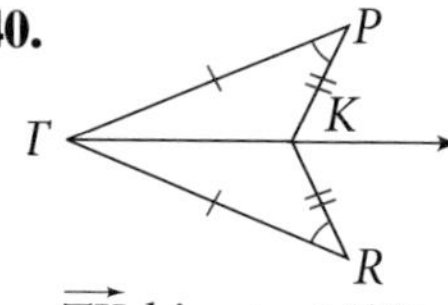

$\overrightarrow{TK}$ bisects $\angle PTR$.

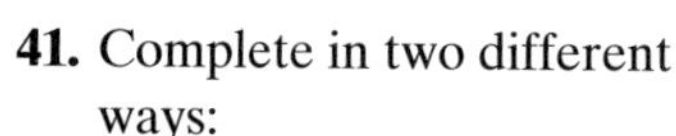

41. Complete in two different ways:

$\triangle JLM \cong$ _?_

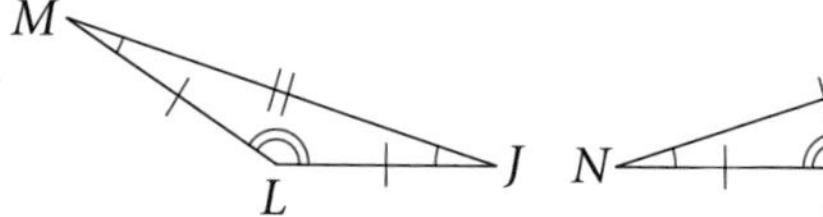

42. Writing Die-cast toys are a popular collector's item. Explain why the two die-cast toys that Pearl is studying at the left have congruent shapes.

Exercise 42

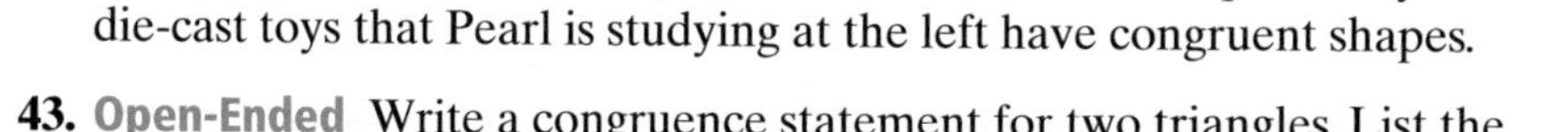

43. Open-Ended Write a congruence statement for two triangles. List the congruent sides and angles.

44. Developing Proof Use the information given in the diagram. Tell why each statement is true.

a. $\overline{PR} \parallel \overline{TQ}$

b. $\angle PRS \cong \angle QTS$

c. $\angle RPS \cong \angle TQS$

d. $\angle PSR \cong \angle QST$

e. $\overline{PR} \cong \overline{QT}, \overline{PS} \cong \overline{QS}$

f. $\overline{PQ}$ bisects $\overline{RT}$.

g. $\overline{RS} \cong \overline{TS}$

h. $\triangle PRS \cong \triangle QTS$

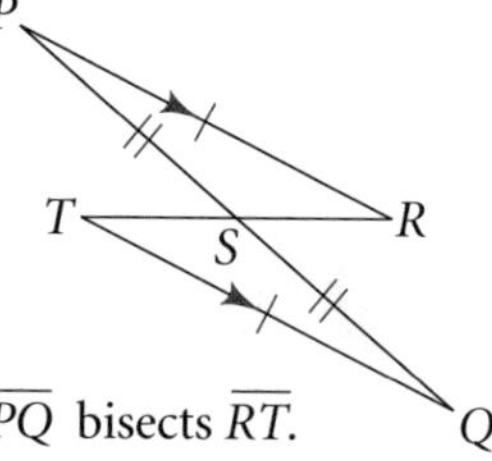

$\overline{PQ}$ bisects $\overline{RT}$.

45. Developing Proof If two angles of one triangle are congruent to two angles of another triangle, then the third angles are congruent (Theorem 4-1). Use algebra and the Triangle Angle-Sum Theorem to explain why this must be so.

C Challenge

Coordinate Geometry Vertices of $\triangle GHJ$ are $G(-2, -1), H(-2, 3)$, and $J(1, 3)$.

46. $\triangle KLM \cong \triangle GHJ$. Find KL, LM, and KM.

47. If L and M have coordinates $L(3, -3)$ and $M(6, -3)$, how many pairs of coordinates are possible for K? Find one such pair.

48. a. How many quadrilaterals (convex and concave) with different shapes or sizes can you make on a three-by-three geoboard? One is shown at the right.

b. How many quadrilaterals of each type are there?

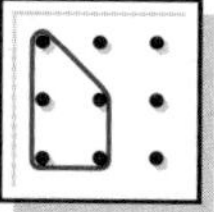

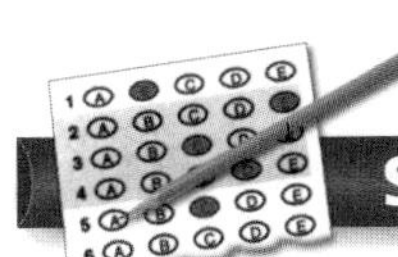

Standardized Test Prep

Gridded Response

Use the diagrams at the right for Exercises 49–51. $ABCDE \cong PFKYM$.

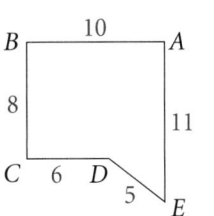

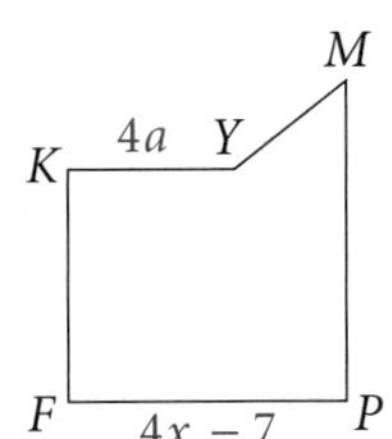

49. What is the value of a?

50. What is the value of x?

51. What is the perimeter of $PFKYM$?

52. $\triangle HLN \cong \triangle GST$, $m\angle H = 66$, and $m\angle S = 42$. What is $m\angle T$?

Take It to the NET Online lesson quiz at **www.PHSchool.com** Web Code: afa-0401

Mixed Review

Lesson 3-7 **Constructions** **For Exercises 53 and 54, construct the geometric figure.**

53. a square

54. a rectangle whose length is twice its width

Lesson 3-3 **55.** Find $m\angle A$ in the figure at the right.

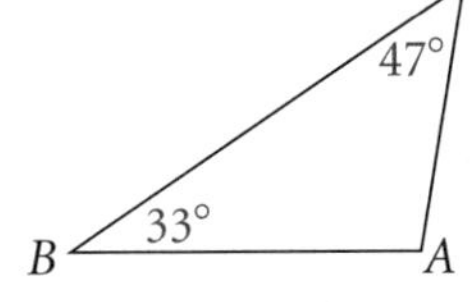

Exercise 55

Lesson 2-4 **Use the given property to complete each statement.**

56. Symmetric Property of Equality

If $PQ = RS$, then __?__.

57. Reflexive Property of Congruence

$\angle 1 \cong$ __?__

58. Addition Property of Equality

If $m\angle A - 4 = 8$, then $m\angle A =$ __?__.

59. Transitive Property of Congruence

If $\overline{AB} \cong \overline{DE}$ and $\overline{DE} \cong \overline{GH}$, then __?__.

Geometry at Work

Die Casting

Two centuries ago, people manufactured articles by hand. Each article produced was slightly different from every other. In 1800, inventor Eli Whitney recognized that he could speed up manufacturing by using congruent parts. Whitney made a die, or mold, for each part of a musket he was producing for the U.S. Army. This allowed workers to rapidly cast the parts and assemble them into standard-sized muskets. It ushered in the era of mass production.

Today, die makers are highly skilled industrial workers who shape dies out of metal, plastic, rubber, and other materials. Machines create and assemble the congruent die-cast parts into standard-sized objects, like the die-cast toy cars at the left. Other workers supply a final inspection and skilled hand finishing.

Take It to the NET For more information about die casting, go to **www.PHSchool.com**. Web Code: afb-2031

Triangle Congruence by SSS and SAS

Lesson Preview

What You'll Learn

To prove two triangles congruent using the SSS and SAS Postulates

. . . And Why

To prove that two triangles in the framework of a bridge are congruent, as in Example 1

✓ Check Skills You'll Need

(For help, go to Lesson 2-5.)

What can you conclude from each diagram?

1.

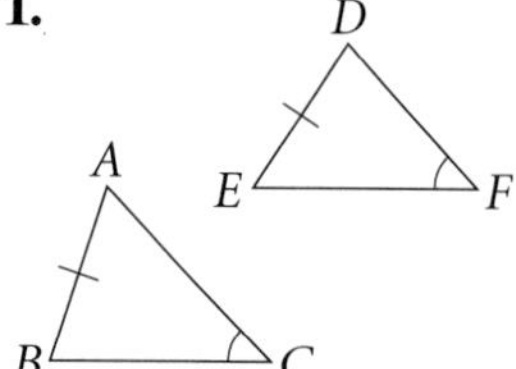

2.

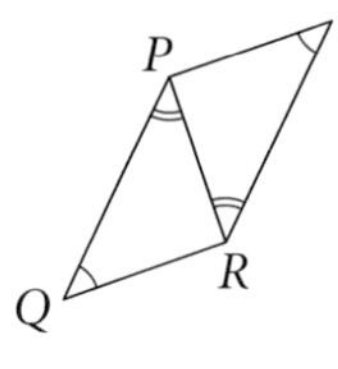

3.

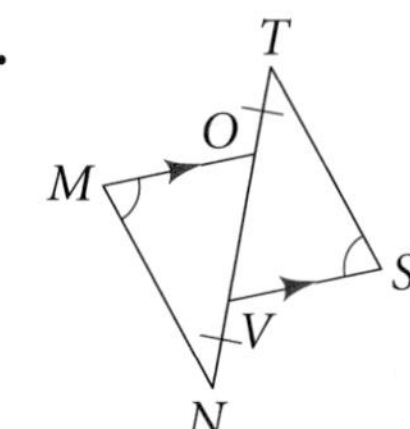

OBJECTIVE

1 Using the SSS and SAS Postulates

Interactive lesson includes instant self-check, tutorials, and activities.

Investigation: Are the Triangles Congruent?

Use straws to make a triangle with sides of 2 in., 3 in., and 4 in. Compare your triangle to the triangles made by others.

1. Make a conjecture about two triangles in which three sides of one triangle are congruent to three sides of the other triangle.
2. Support your conjecture by using three other lengths to make a different triangle. Compare your new triangle to the triangles made by others using different lengths.

In Lesson 4-1 you learned that if two triangles have three pairs of congruent corresponding angles and three pairs of congruent corresponding sides, then the triangles are congruent.

If you know this,	then you know this.
$\angle A \cong \angle X$	$\triangle ABC \cong \triangle XYZ$
$\angle B \cong \angle Y$	
$\angle C \cong \angle Z$	
$\overline{AB} \cong \overline{XY}$	
$\overline{AC} \cong \overline{XZ}$	
$\overline{BC} \cong \overline{YZ}$	

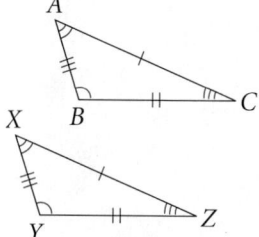

However, you do not need to know that all six corresponding parts are congruent in order to conclude that two triangles are congruent. It is enough to know only that corresponding sides are congruent.

Key Concepts

Postulate 4-1 **Side-Side-Side (SSS) Postulate**

If the three sides of one triangle are congruent to the three sides of another triangle, then the two triangles are congruent.

$\triangle GHF \cong \triangle PQR$

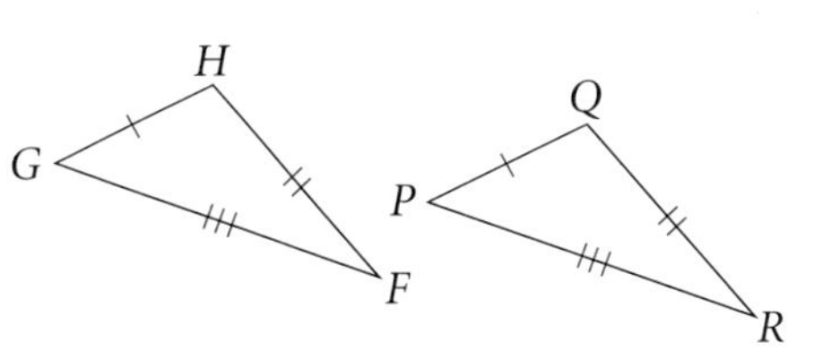

Proof **1 EXAMPLE** **Real-World Connection**

Bridge Design The bridge girders are the same size, as marked.

Given: $\overline{AB} \cong \overline{CB}$, $\overline{AD} \cong \overline{CD}$

Is this enough information to prove the two triangles are congruent? If so, write a flow proof.

Prove: $\triangle ABD \cong \triangle CBD$

Need Help?

The Reflexive Property of Congruence tells you that a figure, such as $\overline{BD}$ in this Example, is congruent to itself.

Plan: To prove the triangles congruent by the SSS Postulate, the three pairs of sides need to be congruent. Two pairs are given to be congruent. The third sides, $\overline{BD}$ in $\triangle ABD$ and $\overline{BD}$ in $\triangle CBD$, are congruent by the Reflexive Property of Congruence.

Proof:

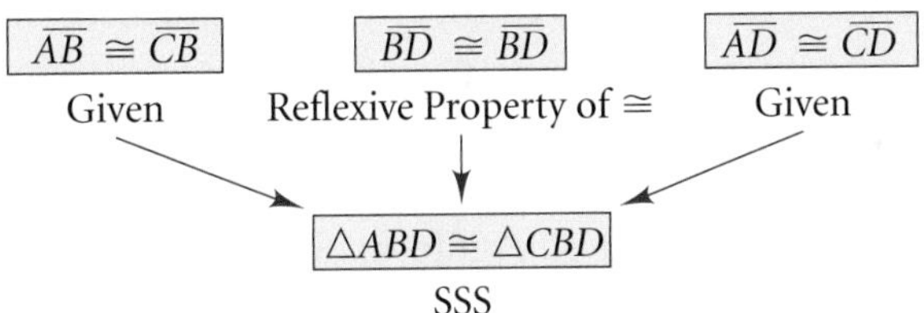

Check Understanding **1** Rewrite the proof as a paragraph proof or as a two-column proof.

The word *included* is used frequently when referring to the angles and the sides of a triangle.

$\overline{BX}$ is included between $\angle B$ and $\angle X$.

$\angle N$ is included between $\overline{NB}$ and $\overline{NX}$.

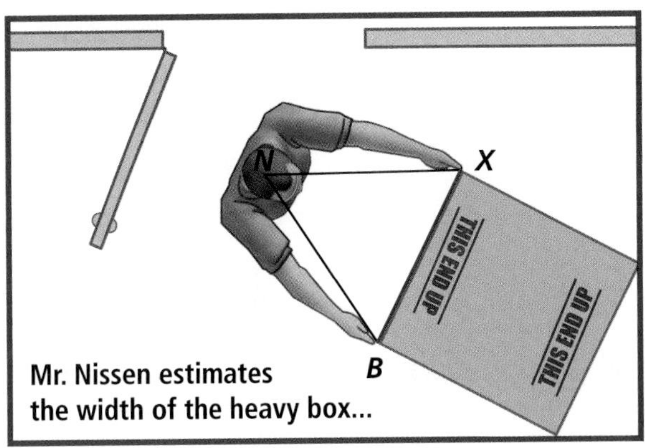

...to help decide whether the box will fit through the doorway.
THIS END UP
THIS END UP

Mr. Nissen kept his arms at a fixed angle as he moved from the box to the doorway. The triangle he used beside the box is congruent to the triangle he used beside the doorway He knows the two triangles are congruent because two sides and the included angle of one are congruent to two sides and the included angle of the other.

Key Concepts

Postulate 4-2 **Side-Angle-Side (SAS) Postulate**

If two sides and the included angle of one triangle are congruent to two sides and the included angle of another triangle, then the two triangles are congruent.

$\triangle BCA \cong \triangle FDE$

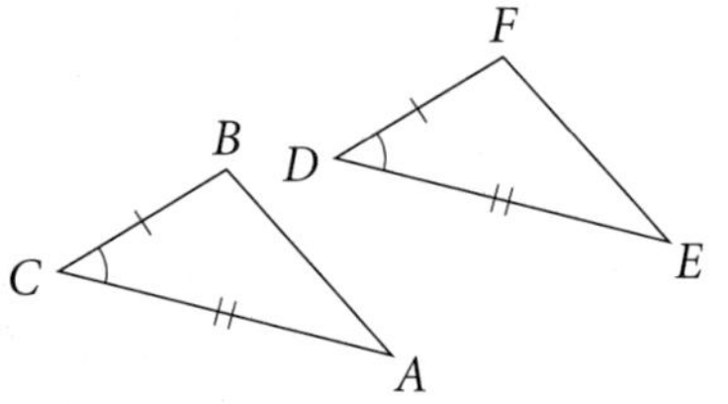

Reading Math

The abbreviations SSS and SAS give you an easy way to remember Postulates 4-1 and 4-2.

2 EXAMPLE Using SSS and SAS

Developing Proof $\overline{RS} \cong \overline{TK}$. What other information do you need to prove $\triangle RSK \cong \triangle TKS$?

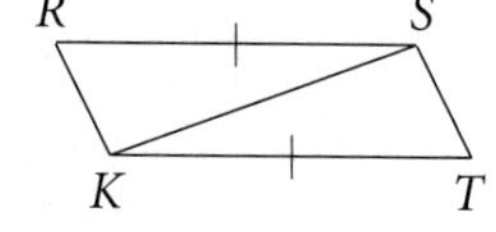

You are given $\overline{RS} \cong \overline{TK}$. Also, $\overline{KS} \cong \overline{KS}$ by the Reflexive Property of Congruence. Therefore:

Solution 1 If you know $\overline{RK} \cong \overline{TS}$, you can prove $\triangle RSK \cong \triangle TKS$ by SSS.

Solution 2 If you know $\angle RSK \cong \angle TKS$, you can prove $\triangle RSK \cong \triangle TKS$ by SAS.

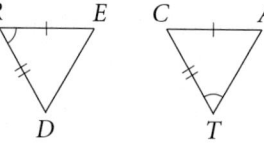

Check Understanding

2 What other information do you need to prove $\triangle ABC \cong \triangle CDA$?

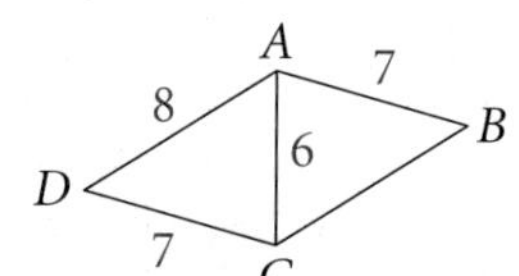

3 EXAMPLE Are the Triangles Congruent?

Developing Proof From the information given, can you prove $\triangle RED \cong \triangle CAT$? Explain.

Given: $\overline{RE} \cong \overline{CA}$, $\overline{RD} \cong \overline{CT}$, $\angle R \cong \angle T$

No, there is not enough information to prove $\triangle RED \cong \triangle CAT$. $\angle T$ is not included between $\overline{CA}$ and $\overline{CT}$. $\triangle RED$ may or may not be congruent to $\triangle CAT$.

R E C A
D T

3 From the information given, can you prove $\triangle AEB \cong \triangle DBC$? Explain.

Given: $\overline{EB} \cong \overline{CB}$, $\overline{AE} \cong \overline{DB}$

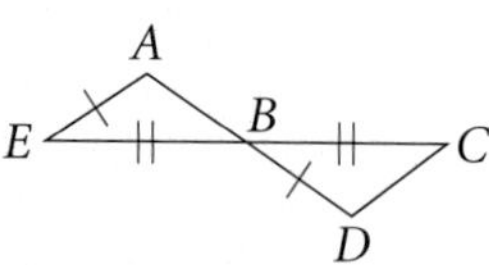

EXERCISES

For more practice, see *Extra Practice.*

Practice and Problem Solving

A Practice by Example

Examples 1, 3

(pages 187–188)

Developing Proof **Which postulate, if any, could you use to prove that the two triangles are congruent?**

1.

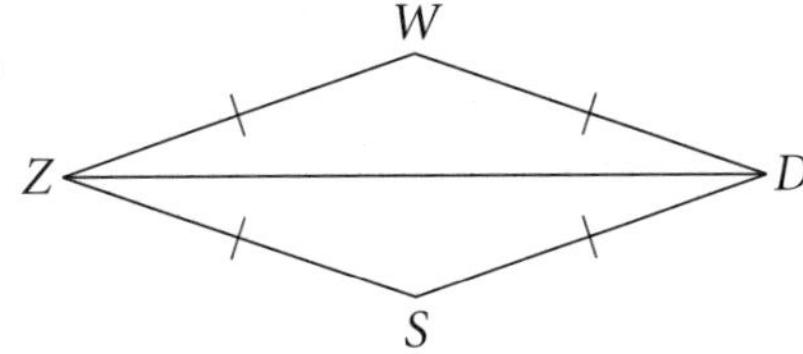

2.

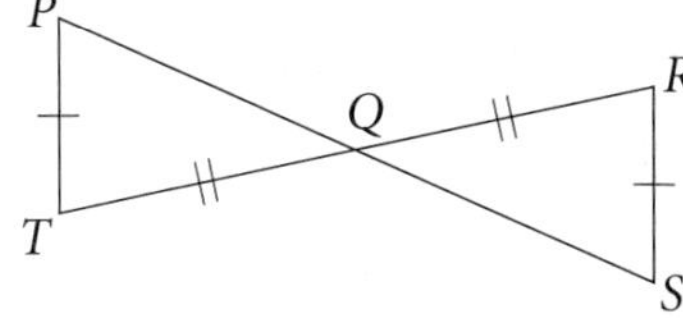

3.

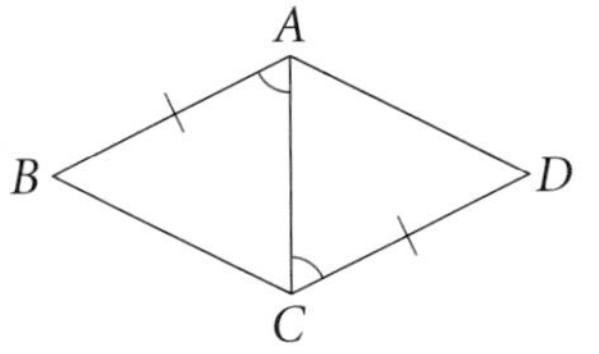

4.

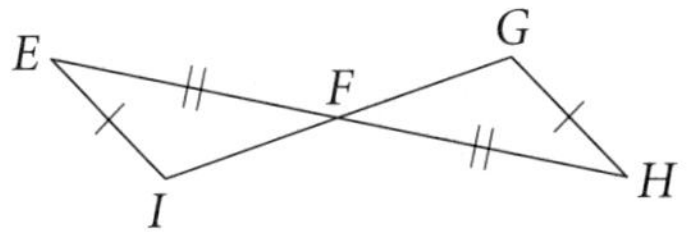

F is the midpoint of $\overline{GI}$.

Developing Proof **Is the information you are given below each photograph enough for you to prove that the two triangles are congruent? Explain.**

5.

The vertical beam $\overline{OB}$ is perpendicular to the porch roof. P, O, and R are equally spaced.

6.

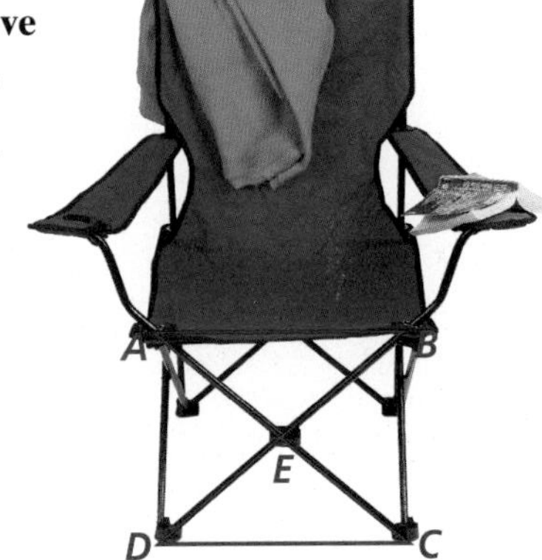

The diagonal legs have equal lengths and are joined at their midpoints.

7. Developing Proof Copy and complete the flow proof.

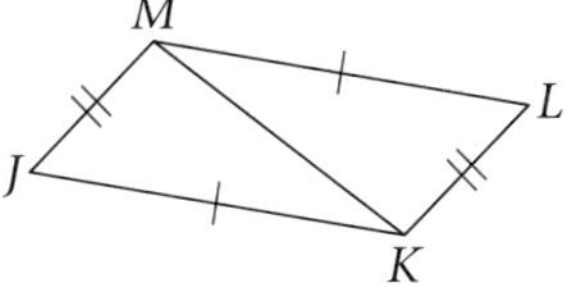

Given: $\overline{JK} \cong \overline{LM}, \overline{JM} \cong \overline{LK}$

Prove: $\triangle JKM \cong \triangle LMK$

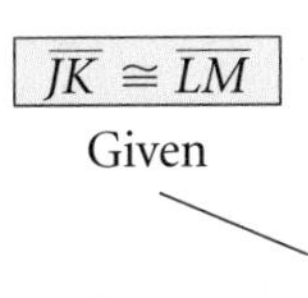

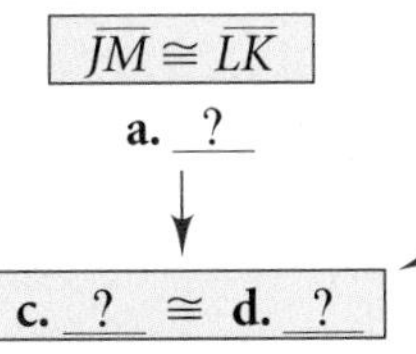

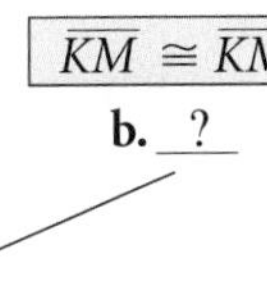

Example 2

(page 188)

Copy the triangle. Start at any vertex and label the triangle as $\triangle WVU$.

8. What sides include $\angle V$?

9. What angle is included between $\overline{WV}$ and $\overline{WU}$?

10. What angles include $\overline{UV}$?

11. What side is included between $\angle W$ and $\angle U$?

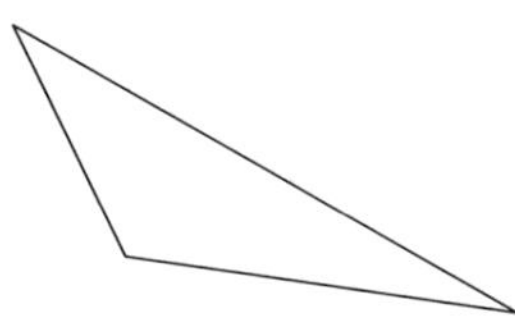

Name the indicated part(s) of $\triangle XYZ$ without drawing $\triangle XYZ$.

12. the angle included between $\overline{XY}$ and $\overline{XZ}$

13. the sides that include $\angle Z$

Developing Proof What other information, if any, do you need to prove the two triangles congruent by SSS or SAS?

14. 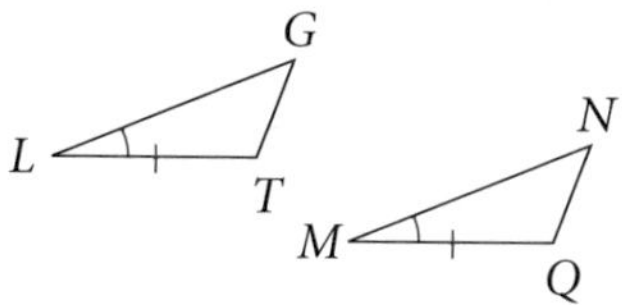

15. 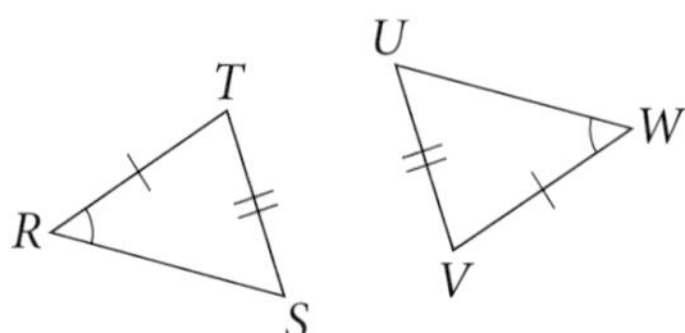

16. 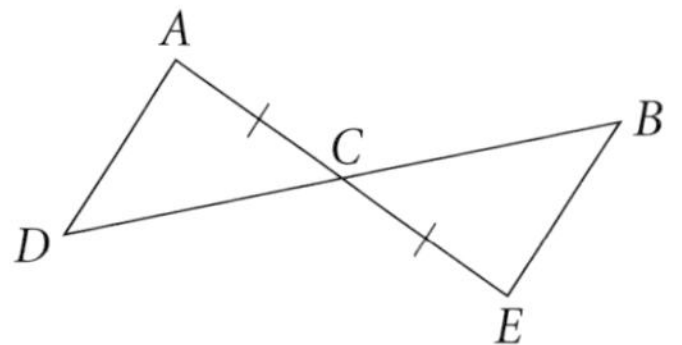

17. 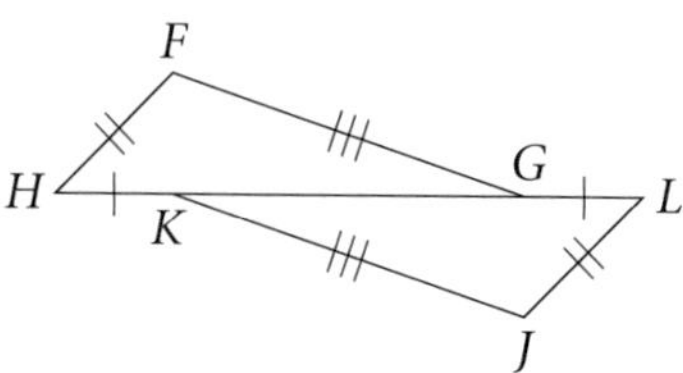

Example 3 (page 188)

Developing Proof From the information given in the diagram, can you prove that the two triangles are congruent? Explain.

18. 

19. 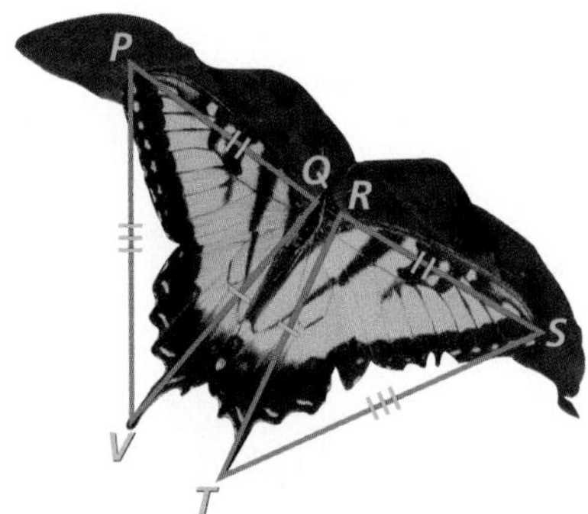

20. 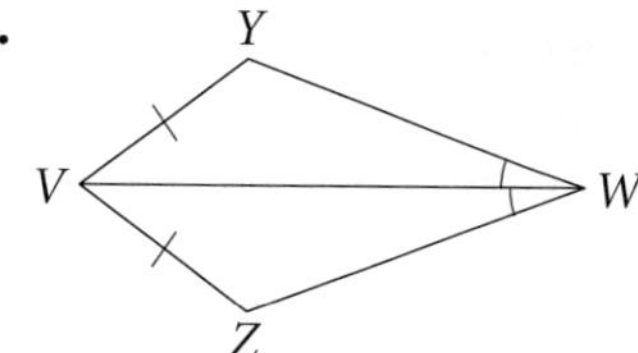

21. 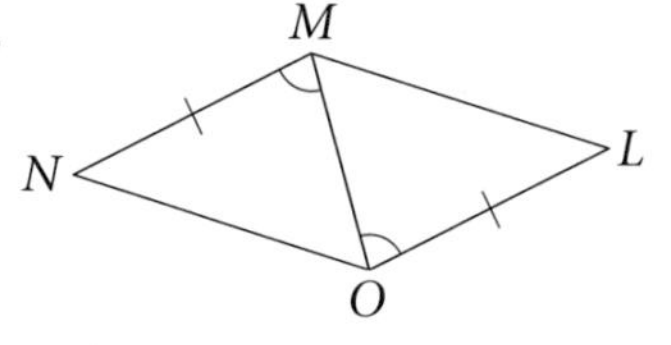

B Apply Your Skills

Developing Proof Is there enough information to prove the two triangles congruent? If so, write the congruence statement and name the postulate you would use. If not, write *not possible* and tell what other information you would need.

22. 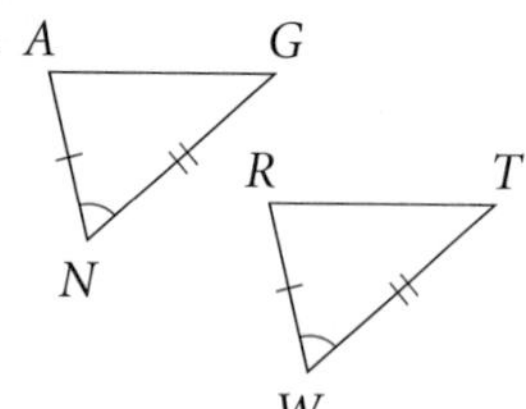

23. 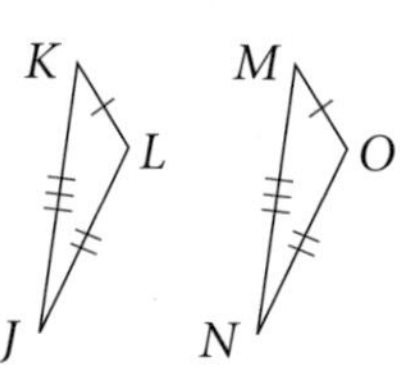

24. 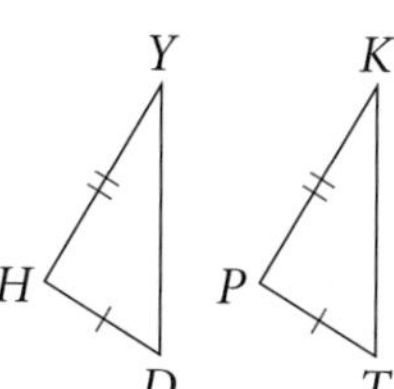

25. 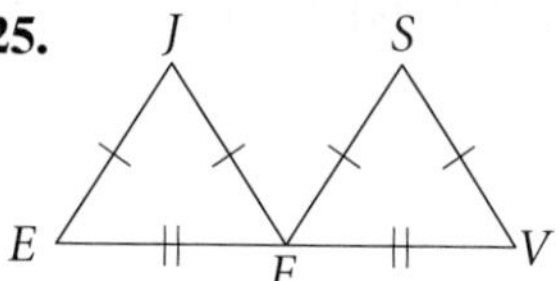

26. 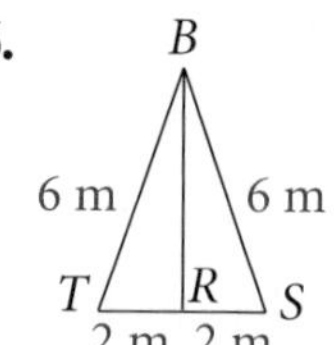

27. 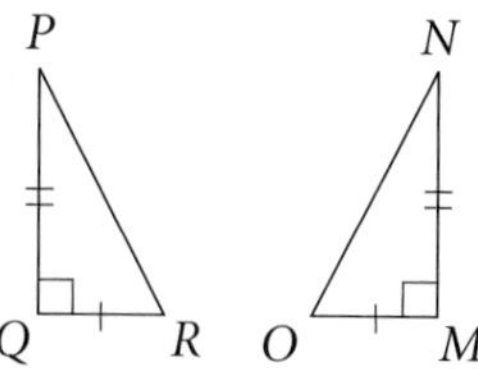

Developing Proof From the information given, can you prove the two triangles congruent? Explain.

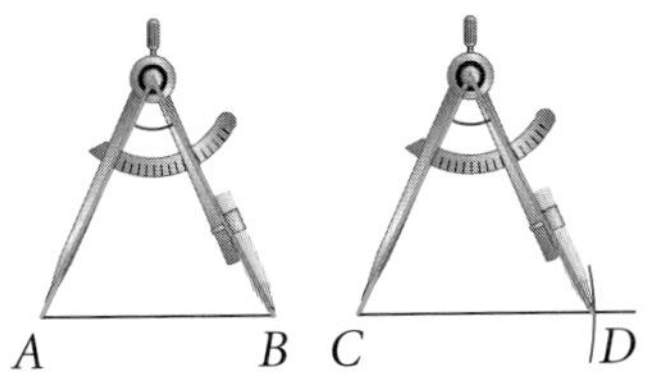

When you construct $\overline{AB} \cong \overline{CD}$, SAS tells you that the triangles outlined here are congruent.

28. $\triangle ABC$ and $\triangle DEF$ with $\angle A \cong \angle D, \angle B \cong \angle E, \angle C \cong \angle F$

29. $\triangle GHI$ and $\triangle JKL$ with $\overline{GH} \cong \overline{JK}, \overline{HI} \cong \overline{KL}, \angle I \cong \angle L$

30. $\triangle MNP$ and $\triangle QRS$ with $\overline{MN} \cong \overline{QR}, \angle N \cong \angle R, \overline{NP} \cong \overline{RS}$

Constructions Use a straightedge to draw $\triangle JKL$. Construct $\triangle MNP \cong \triangle JKL$ using the given postulate.

31. SSS **32.** SAS

33. Developing Proof Supply the reasons in this proof.

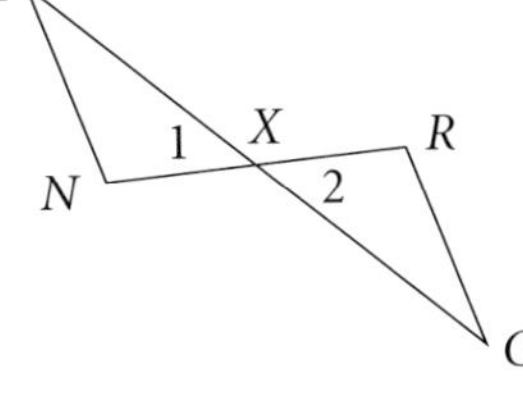

Given: X is the midpoint of $\overline{AG}$ and of $\overline{NR}$.

Prove: $\triangle ANX \cong \triangle GRX$

Statements	Reasons
1. $\angle 1 \cong \angle 2$	a. ?
2. X is the midpoint of $\overline{AG}$.	b. ?
3. $\overline{AX} \cong \overline{GX}$	c. ?
4. X is the midpoint of $\overline{NR}$.	d. ?
5. $\overline{NX} \cong \overline{RX}$	e. ?
6. $\triangle ANX \cong \triangle GRX$	f. ?

34. Error Analysis A friend conjectures that there should be an AAA Congruence Postulate since there is a SSS Congruence Postulate. Give a counterexample to disprove your friend's conjecture.

35. a. Open-Ended List three real-life uses of congruent triangles.

b. Writing For each, tell whether you think congruence is necessary and why.

Reading Math

For help with reading and solving Exercise 36, see p. 193.

Developing Proof What can you prove about $\triangle ISP$ and $\triangle OSP$ given the information in the diagram and the information below?

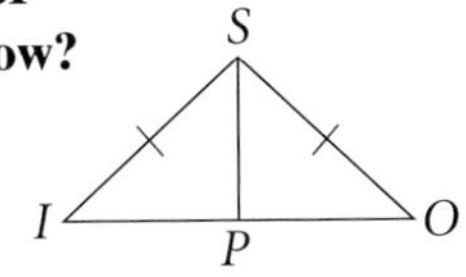

36. $\overline{SP}$ is the bisector of $\angle ISO$.

37. $\overline{SP}$ is a bisector of $\overline{IO}$.

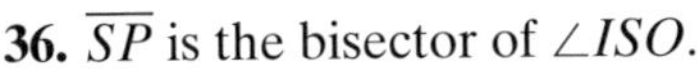

Developing Proof In $ABCD$, $\overline{AD} \parallel \overline{BC}$ and $\overline{AD} \cong \overline{BC}$. Can you prove the two triangles congruent? Explain.

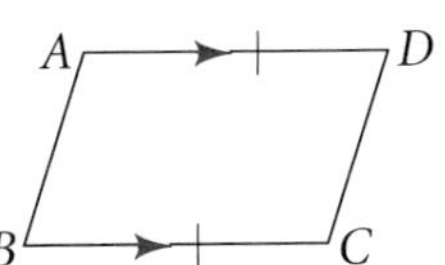

38. $\triangle ADB$ and $\triangle CBD$ **39.** $\triangle ABC$ and $\triangle CDA$

40. Critical Thinking Four sides of polygon $ABCD$ are congruent to four sides of polygon $EFGH$. Must the two quadrilaterals also be congruent? Explain.

C Challenge  **Write a proof.**

41. Given: $\overline{FG} \parallel \overline{KL}, \overline{FG} \cong \overline{KL}$

Prove: $\triangle FGK \cong \triangle KLF$

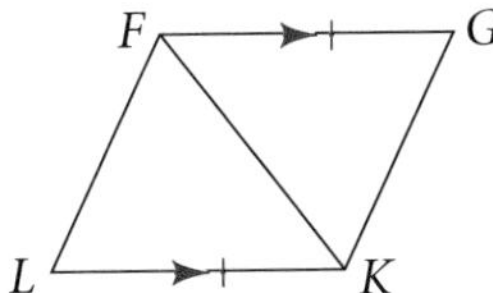

42. Given: $\overline{AE}$ and $\overline{BD}$ bisect each other.

Prove: $\triangle ACB \cong \triangle ECD$

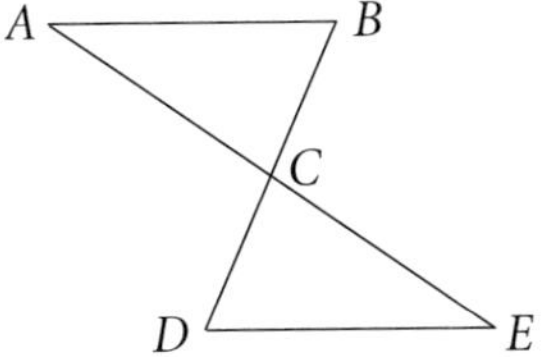

43. Given: $\overline{GK}$ bisects $\angle JGM$, $\overline{GJ} \cong \overline{GM}$.

Prove: $\triangle GJK \cong \triangle GMK$

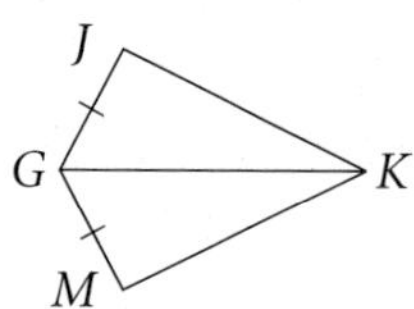

44. Given: $\overline{AB} \perp \overline{CM}$, $\overline{AB} \perp \overline{DB}$, M is the midpoint of $\overline{AB}$, $\overline{CM} \cong \overline{DB}$.

Prove: $\triangle AMC \cong \triangle MBD$

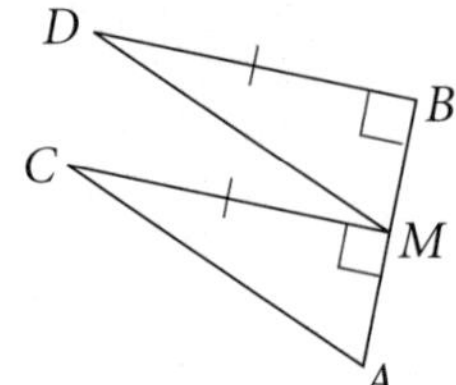

Standardized Test Prep

Multiple Choice

Use the figures at the right for Exercises 45–47.

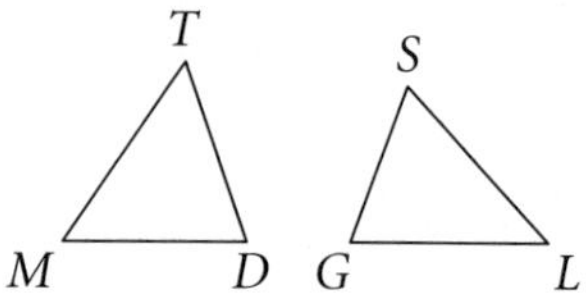

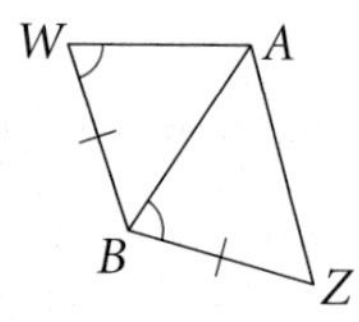

45. Suppose $\overline{TM} \cong \overline{GL}$ and $\angle M \cong \angle G$. What additional information is needed to prove $\triangle MTD \cong \triangle GLS$ by SAS?

A. $\angle T \cong \angle L$ **B.** $\angle T \cong \angle S$ **C.** $\overline{TD} \cong \overline{SL}$ **D.** $\overline{MD} \cong \overline{SG}$

46. Suppose $\overline{TD} \cong \overline{SG}$ and $\overline{MD} \cong \overline{SL}$. What additional information is needed to prove the two triangles congruent by SAS?

F. $\angle T \cong \angle S$ **G.** $\angle D \cong \angle S$ **H.** $\angle S \cong \angle L$ **I.** $\angle D \cong \angle G$

47. Suppose $TD = 10$ cm, $DM = 9$ cm, $TM = 11$ cm, $SL = 11$ cm, and $SG = 9$ cm. What else do you need to know in order to prove that the two triangles are congruent by SSS?

A. $LG = 9$ cm **B.** $TD = SL$ **C.** $GL = 10$ cm **D.** $TM = SG$

Short Response

Take It to the NET
Online lesson quiz at **www.PHSchool.com**
Web Code: afa-0402

48. In the diagram, $\overline{WB} \cong \overline{BZ}$ and $\angle W \cong \angle ABZ$.

W A B Z

a. State another conclusion you can make. Name the property that justifies your conclusion.

b. Based on the information given in the diagram, can you prove the two triangles congruent? Justify your answer.

Mixed Review

Lesson 4-1

***ABCD* ≅ *EFGH*. Name the angle or side that corresponds to the given part.**

49. $\angle A$ **50.** $\overline{EF}$ **51.** $\overline{BC}$ **52.** $\angle G$

Lesson 2-2

53. The following two statements are about lines with defined slopes. Combine them into a single biconditional.

If the product of the slopes of two lines is -1, then the lines are perpendicular.
If two lines are perpendicular, then the product of their slopes is -1.

54. Write the two conditional statements that form this biconditional:

$x = 2$ if and only if $2x = 4$.

Lesson 2-1

Write the converse of the statement. Decide whether the statement and its converse are true or false.

55. If $x = 3$ then $2x = 6$. **56.** If $x = 3$ then $x^2 = 9$.

Reading Diagrams and Words

FOR USE WITH PAGE 191, EXERCISE 36

Read the problem below and follow the discussion. Check your understanding by solving the exercise at the bottom of the page.

What can you prove about $\triangle ISP$ and $\triangle OSP$ given the information in the diagram and the information below?

$\overline{SP}$ is the bisector of $\angle ISO$.

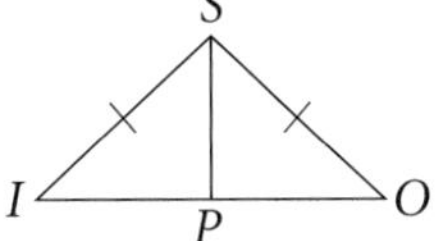

To complete this problem, you must get information from both the statement and the diagram.

The Statement

$\overline{SP}$ is the bisector of $\angle ISO$.

To "bisect" means to divide into two congruent parts.
Therefore $\angle ISP \cong \angle OSP$ by definition of an angle bisector.

The Diagram

Analyze the diagram carefully.
It may be helpful to write out in words what you see.

For example:

- There is a large triangle, $\triangle ISO$, which consists of two smaller triangles, $\triangle ISP$ and $\triangle OSP$.
- Two segments, $\overline{IS}$ and $\overline{OS}$, are marked.
  The marks show that $\overline{IS}$ and $\overline{OS}$ are congruent, or $\overline{IS} \cong \overline{OS}$.

Putting all this information together, you have $\angle ISP \cong \angle OSP$ and $\overline{IS} \cong \overline{OS}$. Look carefully at $\triangle ISP$ and $\triangle OSP$. Can you find another pair of corresponding congruent parts? Yes! They share a side, $\overline{SP}$. Clearly $\overline{SP} \cong \overline{SP}$.

Sketch your own version of the diagram to show all this information. You can use double tick marks on the segment that you cite as being congruent to itself.

Now you see that you can use SAS to prove that $\triangle ISP \cong \triangle OSP$.

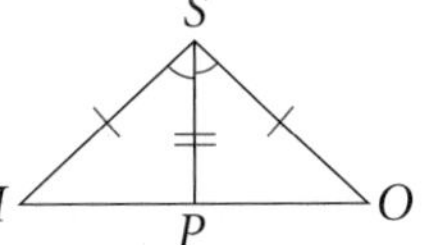

EXERCISE

What can you prove about $\triangle ABC$ and $\triangle ADC$ given the information in the diagram, and given that $\overline{AC}$ bisects $\overline{BD}$.

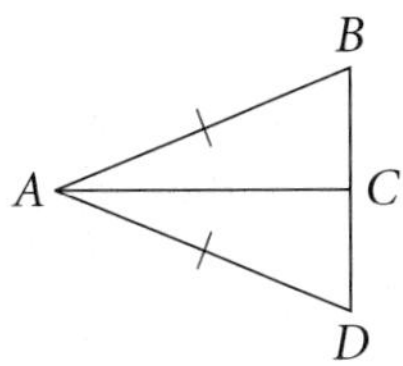

4-3 Triangle Congruence by ASA and AAS

Lesson Preview

What You'll Learn

To prove two triangles congruent using the ASA Postulate and the AAS Theorem

. . . And Why

To prove that the two sides of a lacrosse goal are congruent triangles, as in Example 2

✔ Check Skills You'll Need

(For help, go to Lesson 4-2.)

In $\triangle JHK$, which side is included between the given pair of angles?

1. $\angle J$ and $\angle H$
2. $\angle H$ and $\angle K$

In $\triangle NLM$, which angle is included between the given pair of sides?

3. $\overline{LN}$ and $\overline{LM}$
4. $\overline{NM}$ and $\overline{LN}$

Give a reason to justify each statement.

5. $\overline{PR} \cong \overline{PR}$
6. $\angle A \cong \angle D$

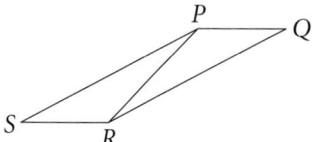

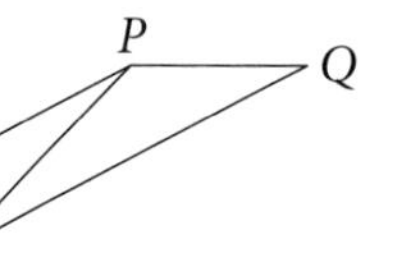

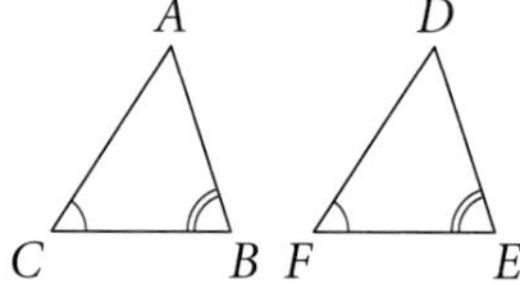

OBJECTIVE 1 Using the ASA Postulate and the AAS Theorem

Interactive lesson includes instant self-check, tutorials, and activities.

Investigation: Are the Triangles Congruent?

Draw a triangle. Label your triangle $\triangle ABC$.

- Construct $\overline{XY}$ so that $\overline{XY} \cong \overline{AB}$.
- At X, construct $\angle X$ so that $\angle X \cong \angle A$. At Y, construct $\angle Y$ so that $\angle Y \cong \angle B$. Label point Z as shown.

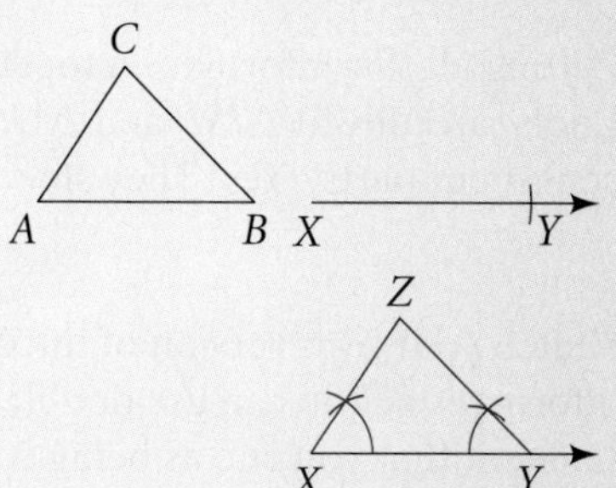

1. Cut out $\triangle ABC$ and $\triangle XYZ$. Place $\triangle ABC$ over $\triangle XYZ$ so that corresponding angles match. Are the triangles congruent? Compare your results with others.
2. Make a conjecture. What seems to be true when two angles and the included side of one triangle are congruent to two angles and the included side of another triangle?

In Lesson 4-2 you learned that two triangles are congruent if
two pairs of sides are congruent and the included angles are congruent (SAS).
The construction shown above suggests that two triangles are also congruent if
two pairs of angles are congruent and the included sides are congruent (ASA).

Key Concepts

Postulate 4-3 **Angle-Side-Angle (ASA) Postulate**

If two angles and the included side of one triangle are congruent to two angles and the included side of another triangle, then the two triangles are congruent.

$\triangle HGB \cong \triangle NKP$

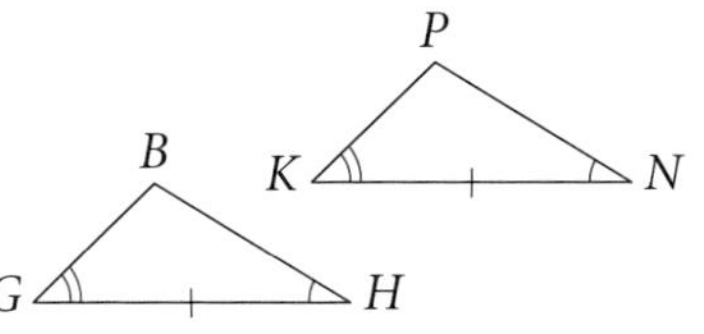

Proof 1 EXAMPLE Using ASA

Developing Proof Name two triangles that are congruent by the ASA Postulate.

$\triangle CAT \cong \triangle GDO$ because

$\angle C \cong \angle G$,

$\overline{CA} \cong \overline{GD}$,

$\angle A \cong \angle D$.

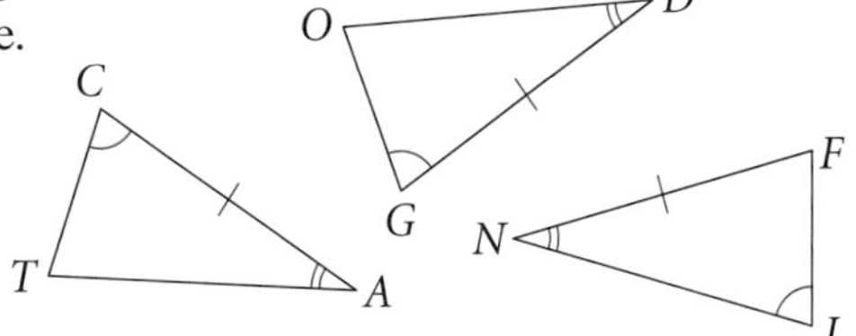

Check Understanding **1** Can you conclude that $\triangle INF$ is congruent to either of the other two triangles? Explain.

Real-World Connection

The Iroquois Nationals compete for the World Lacrosse Championship every four years.

Here is how you can use the ASA Postulate in a proof.

2 EXAMPLE Real-World Connection

Lacrosse Study what you are given and what you are to prove about the lacrosse goal. Then write a paragraph proof that uses ASA.

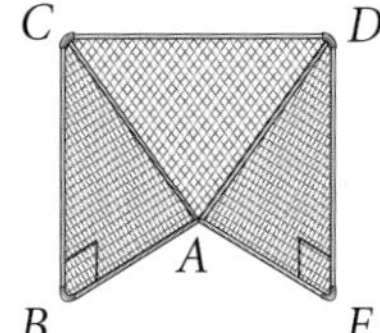

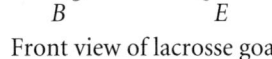

Front view of lacrosse goal

Given: $\angle CAB \cong \angle DAE$, $\overline{AB} \cong \overline{AE}$,
$\angle ABC$ and $\angle AED$ are right angles.

Prove: $\triangle ABC \cong \triangle AED$

Proof: $\angle ABC \cong \angle AED$ because all right angles are congruent. You are given that $\overline{AB} \cong \overline{AE}$ and $\angle CAB \cong \angle DAE$. Thus, $\triangle ABC \cong \triangle AED$ by ASA.

Check Understanding **2** Write a two-column proof that $\triangle ABC \cong \triangle AED$.

You can use the ASA Postulate to prove the Angle-Angle-Side Congruence Theorem. A flow proof is shown on the next page.

Key Concepts

Theorem 4-2 **Angle-Angle-Side (AAS) Theorem**

If two angles and a nonincluded side of one triangle are congruent to two angles and the corresponding nonincluded side of another triangle, then the triangles are congruent.

$\triangle CDM \cong \triangle XGT$

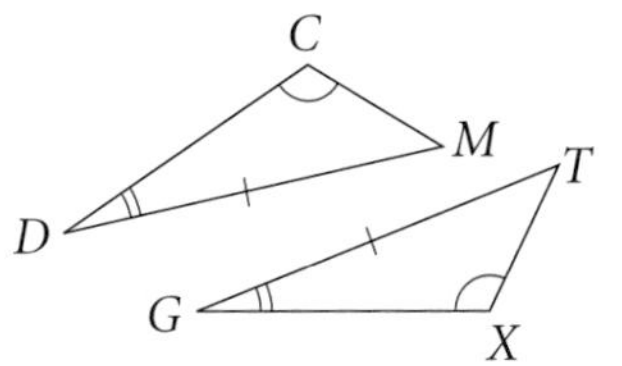

Flow Proof of the Angle-Angle-Side Theorem

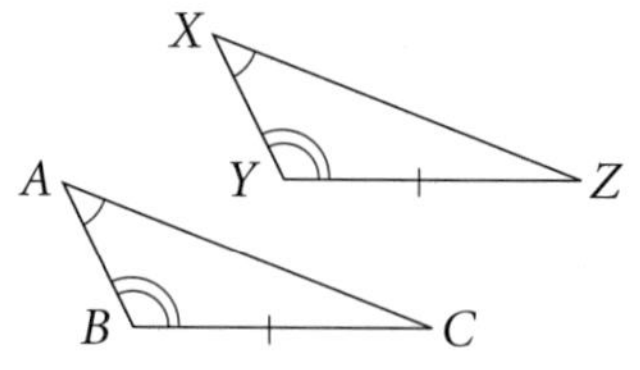

Given: $\angle A \cong \angle X$, $\angle B \cong \angle Y$,
$\overline{BC} \cong \overline{YZ}$

Prove: $\triangle ABC \cong \triangle XYZ$

Need Help?
A statement in a flow proof can be deduced from the facts that point to it.

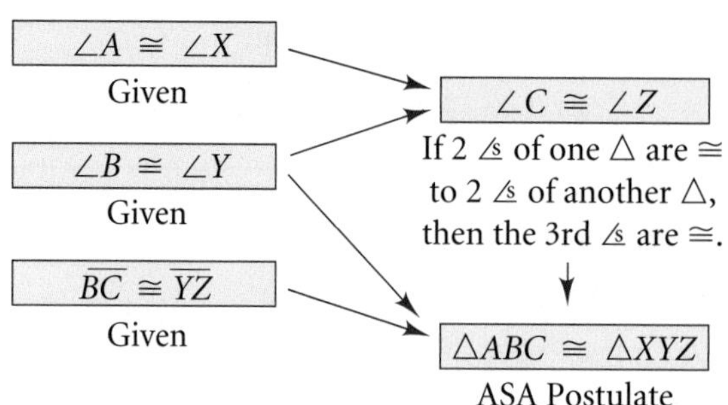

∠A ≅ ∠X
Given
∠B ≅ ∠Y
Given
BC ≅ YZ
Given
∠C ≅ ∠Z
If 2 ∠s of one △ are ≅ to 2 ∠s of another △, then the 3rd ∠s are ≅.
△ABC ≅ △XYZ
ASA Postulate

Here are two examples of how to use the AAS Theorem.

3 EXAMPLE Planning a Proof

Developing Proof Study what you are given and what you are to prove. Then plan a proof that uses AAS.

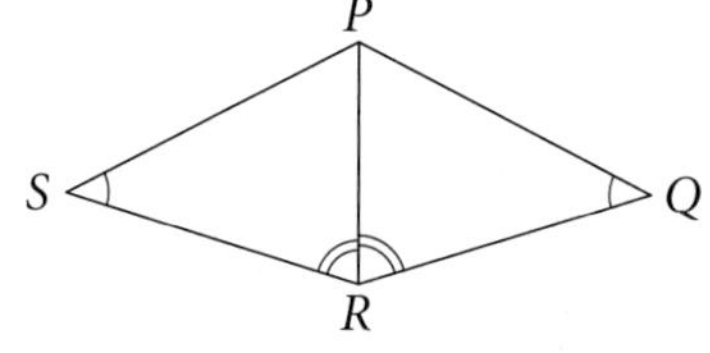

Given: $\angle S \cong \angle Q$,
$\overline{RP}$ bisects $\angle SRQ$.

Prove: $\triangle SRP \cong \triangle QRP$

Plan: $\triangle SRP \cong \triangle QRP$ by AAS
if $\overline{SP} \cong \overline{QP}$ or $\overline{RP} \cong \overline{RP}$.

The second statement is true by the Reflexive Property of Congruence.

Check Understanding 3 Use the plan from Example 3 and write a flow proof.

4 EXAMPLE Writing a Proof

Study what you are given and what you are to prove. Then write a two-column proof that uses AAS.

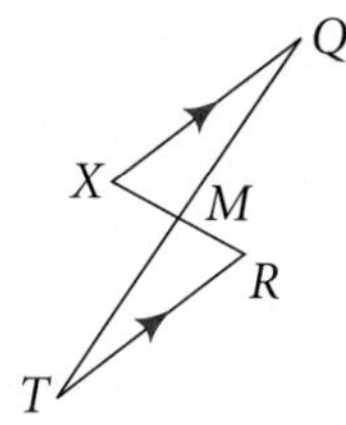

Given: $\overline{XQ} \parallel \overline{TR}$,
$\overline{XR}$ bisects $\overline{QT}$.

Prove: $\triangle XMQ \cong \triangle RMT$

Statements	Reasons
1. $\overline{XQ} \parallel \overline{TR}$	1. Given
2. $\angle Q \cong \angle T$, $\angle X \cong \angle R$	2. _?_
3. $\overline{XR}$ bisects $\overline{QT}$.	3. Given
4. $\overline{QM} \cong \overline{TM}$	4. Definition of segment bisector
5. $\triangle XMQ \cong \triangle RMT$	5. AAS

4 **a.** Supply the reason that justifies Step 2.
b. Critical Thinking Explain how you could prove $\triangle XMQ \cong \triangle RMT$ by ASA.

EXERCISES

For more practice, see *Extra Practice.*

Practice and Problem Solving

A Practice by Example

Example 1 (page 195)

Developing Proof **Name two triangles that are congruent by the ASA Postulate.**

1.

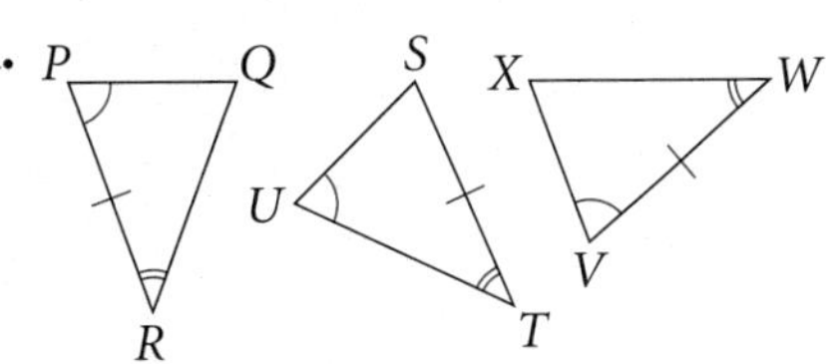

2.

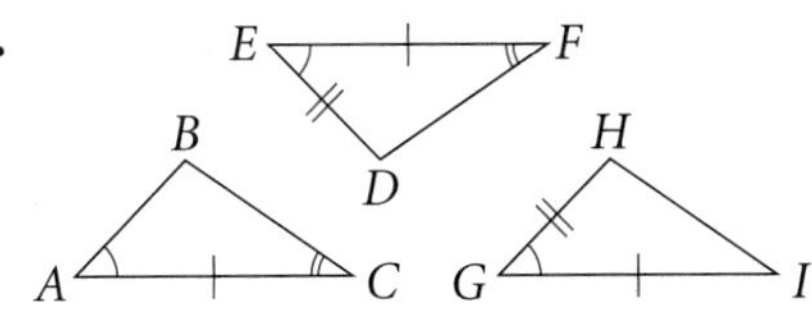

Answer each question without drawing the triangle.

3. Which side is included between $\angle R$ and $\angle S$ in $\triangle RST$?

4. Which angles include $\overline{NO}$ in $\triangle NOM$?

Example 2 (page 195)

Developing Proof **Tell whether the ASA Postulate can be used to prove the triangles congruent. If not, write *not possible.***

5.

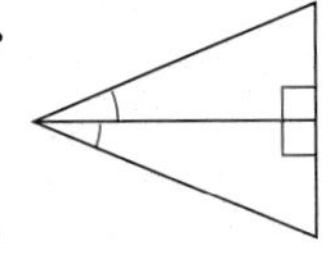

6.

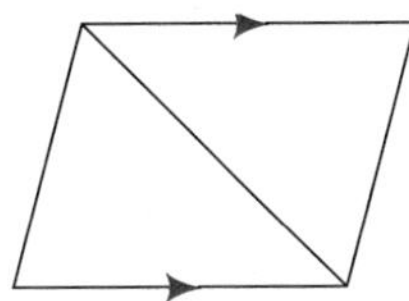

7.

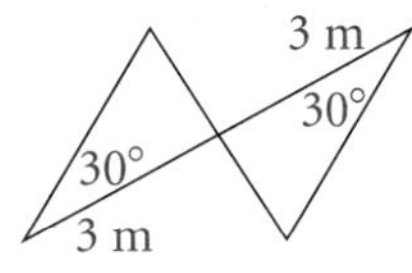

8. **Developing Proof** Complete the paragraph proof by filling in the blanks.

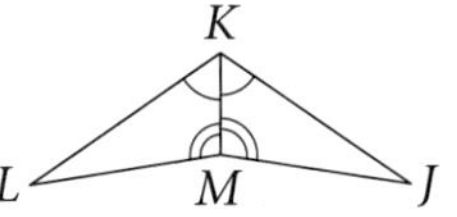

Given: $\angle LKM \cong \angle JKM$,
$\angle LMK \cong \angle JMK$

Prove: $\triangle LKM \cong \triangle JKM$

Proof: $\angle LKM \cong \angle JKM$ and $\angle LMK \cong \angle JMK$ are given. $\overline{KM} \cong \overline{KM}$ by the **a.** __?__ Property of Congruence. $\triangle LKM \cong \triangle JKM$ by the **b.** __?__ Postulate.

Example 3 (page 196)

Developing Proof **Tell whether the AAS Theorem or the ASA Postulate can be applied directly to prove the triangles congruent. If not, write *not possible.***

9.

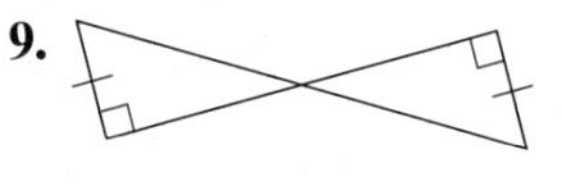

10.

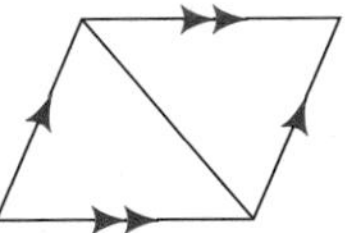

11.

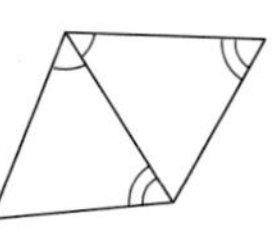

12. $\angle E \cong \angle I$ and $\overline{FE} \cong \overline{GI}$. What else must you know to prove $\triangle FDE \cong \triangle GHI$ by AAS? by ASA?

13. **Developing Proof** Complete the proof plan by filling in the blanks.

Given: $\angle UWT$ and $\angle UWV$ are right angles,
$\angle T \cong \angle V$.

Prove: $\triangle UWT \cong \triangle UWV$

U, T, W, V

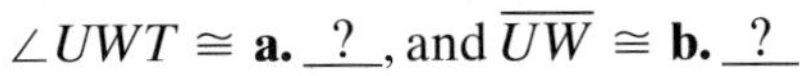

Plan: $\triangle UWT \cong \triangle UWV$ by AAS if $\angle T \cong \angle V$, $\angle UWT \cong$ **a.** __?__, and $\overline{UW} \cong$ **b.** __?__.
$\angle UWT \cong \angle UWV$ because all **c.** __?__ angles are congruent.
$\overline{UW} \cong \overline{UW}$ by the **d.** __?__ Property of Congruence.

Example 4 (page 196)

Developing Proof What else must you know to prove the triangles congruent for the reason shown?

14. AAS

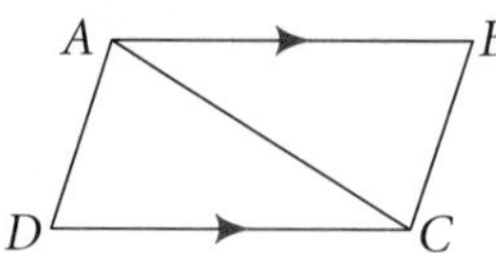

15. SAS

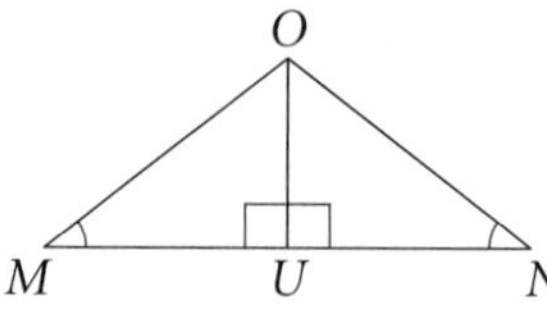

16. ASA

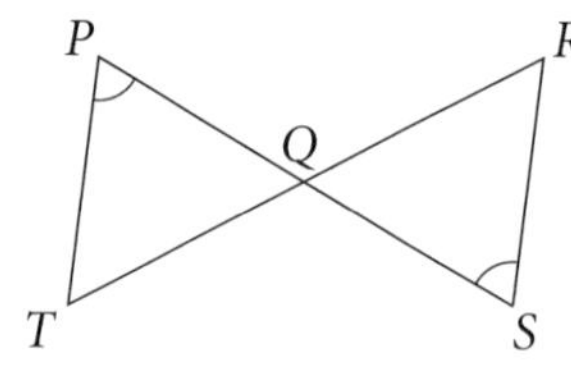

17. AAS

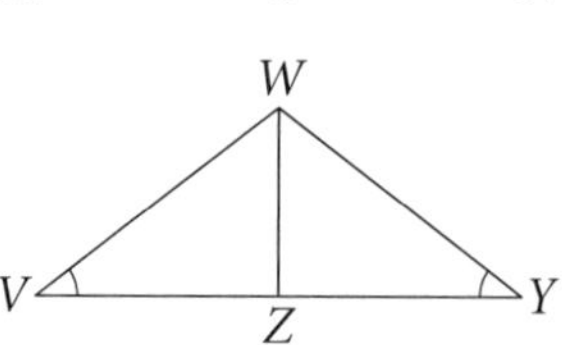

18. **Developing Proof** Complete the two-column proof by filling in the blanks.

Given: $\angle N \cong \angle S$, line ℓ bisects $\overline{TR}$ at Q.

Prove: $\triangle NQT \cong \triangle SQR$

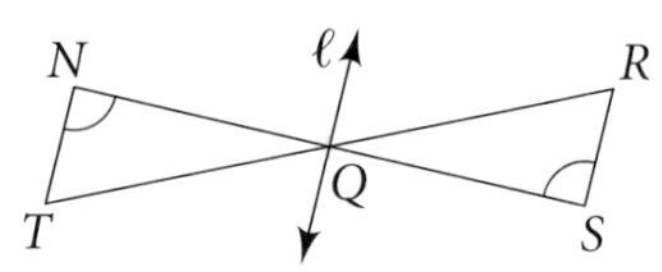

Statements	Reasons
1. $\angle N \cong \angle S$	1. Given
2. $\angle NQT \cong \angle SQR$	a. ?
3. ℓ bisects $\overline{TR}$ at Q.	b. ?
c. ?	4. Definition of bisect
5. $\triangle NQT \cong \triangle SQR$	d. ?

Developing Proof Write a congruence statement for each pair of triangles. Name the postulate or theorem that justifies your statement.

19.

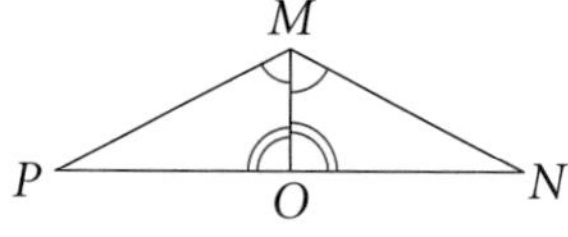

20.

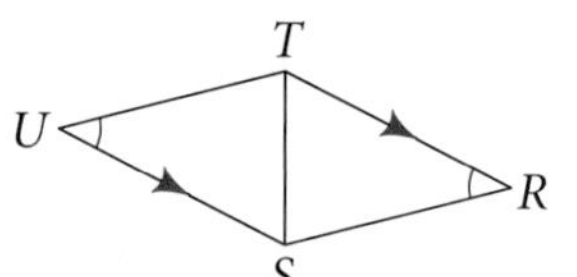

21.

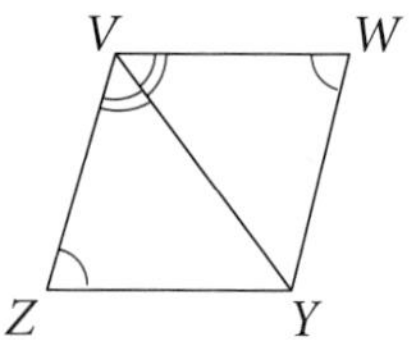

Developing Proof If the two triangles are congruent for the given conditions, write a congruence statement. Justify your conclusion.

22. $\angle D \cong \angle T, \angle E \cong \angle U, \overline{EO} \cong \overline{UX}$

23. $\angle D \cong \angle T, \angle E \cong \angle U, \angle O \cong \angle X$

24. $\overline{DO} \cong \overline{TX}, \angle D \cong \angle X, \angle O \cong \angle T$

25. $\overline{EO} \cong \overline{UX}, \angle E \cong \angle U, \overline{DO} \cong \overline{TX}$

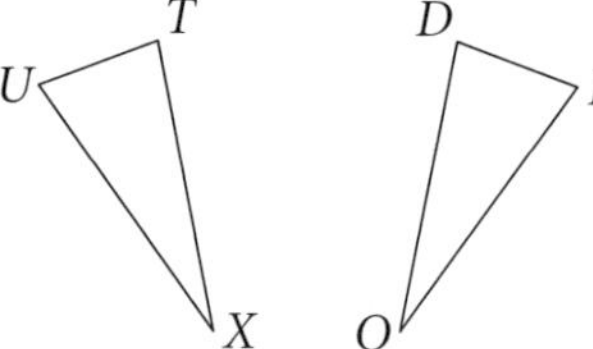

Real-World Connection

Congruent lapel and collar triangles help you look sharp.

26. **Writing** Anita says that you can rewrite any proof that uses the AAS Theorem as a proof that uses the ASA Postulate. Do you agree with Anita? Explain.

Developing Proof In Exercises 27–29, complete each proof or proof plan.

27. **Given:** $\overline{PQ} \parallel \overline{SR}$, $\angle Q \cong \angle S$

Prove: $\triangle QPR \cong \triangle SRP$

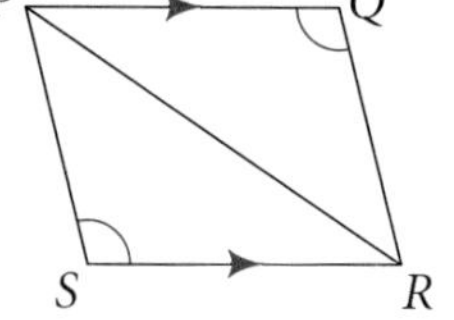

Plan: $\triangle QPR \cong \triangle SRP$ by AAS if $\angle Q \cong \angle S$, $\angle QPR \cong$ **a.** ?, and $\overline{PR} \cong$ **b.** ?. $\angle QPR \cong \angle SRP$ because they are **c.** ? angles for the given parallel lines and the transversal **d.** ?. $\overline{PR} \cong \overline{PR}$ by the **e.** ? Property of Congruence.

28. Given: $\overline{SQ}$ bisects $\angle PSR$, $\angle P \cong \angle R$.
Prove: $\triangle PSQ \cong \triangle RSQ$

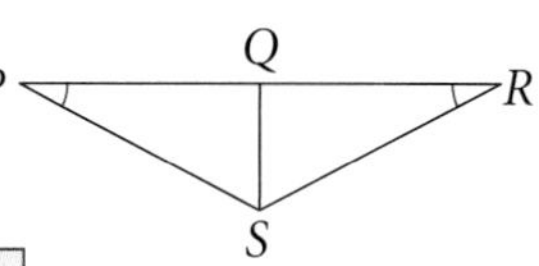

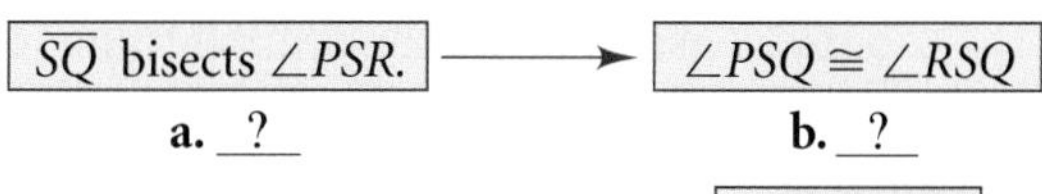

$\overline{SQ}$ bisects $\angle PSR$. → $\angle PSQ \cong \angle RSQ$

a. ? b. ?

$\angle P \cong \angle R$

c. ?

$\overline{SQ} \cong \overline{SQ}$

d. ?

→ $\triangle PSQ \cong \triangle RSQ$

e. ?

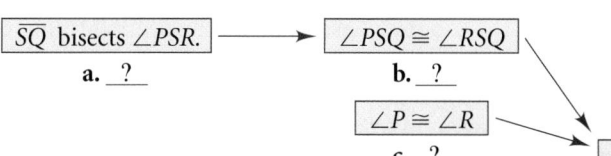

29. Given: $\overline{PQ} \perp \overline{QS}$, $\overline{RS} \perp \overline{QS}$,
T is the midpoint of $\overline{PR}$.
Prove: $\triangle PQT \cong \triangle RST$

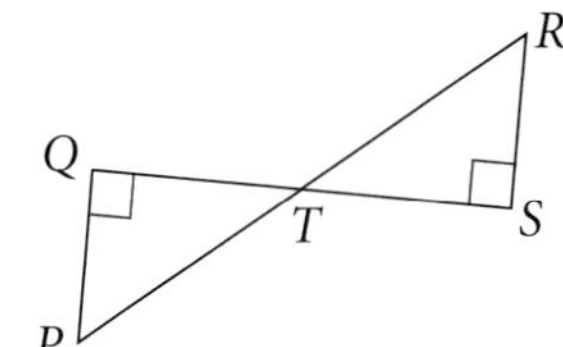

Statements	Reasons
1. $\overline{PQ} \perp \overline{QS}$, $\overline{RS} \perp \overline{QS}$	**1.** Given
2. $\angle Q$ and $\angle S$ are right angles.	**a.** ?
3. $\angle Q \cong \angle S$	**b.** ?
c. ?	**4.** Vertical angles are congruent.
5. T is the midpoint of $\overline{PR}$.	**5.** Given
6. $\overline{PT} \cong \overline{RT}$	**d.** ?
7. $\triangle PQT \cong \triangle RST$	**e.** ?

Need Help?

In Exercise 30, copy one angle, a side, and then another angle so that the copied angles include the copied side.

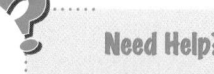

30. Constructions Using a straightedge, draw a triangle. Label it $\triangle JKL$. Construct $\triangle MNP \cong \triangle JKL$ so you know that the triangles are congruent by ASA.

Developing Proof Can you deduce the "Conclusion" from the "Given" information? Explain.

31. Given: $\angle N \cong \angle P$, $\overline{MO} \cong \overline{QO}$
Conclusion: $\triangle MON \cong \triangle QOP$

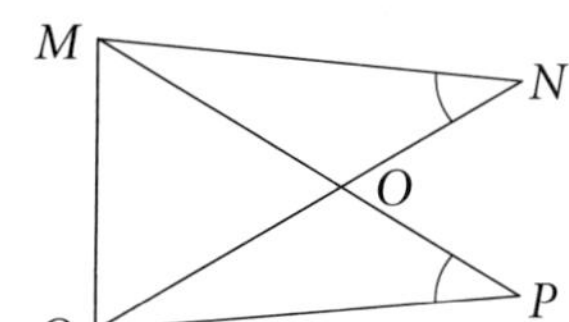

32. Given: $\angle F \cong \angle H$, $\overline{FG} \parallel \overline{JH}$
Conclusion: $\triangle FGJ \cong \triangle HJG$

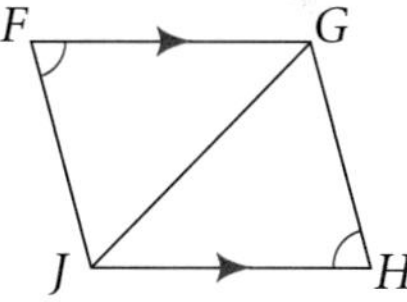

33. Given: $\overline{AE} \parallel \overline{BD}$, $\overline{AE} \cong \overline{BD}$,
$\angle E \cong \angle D$
Conclusion: $\triangle AEB \cong \triangle BDC$

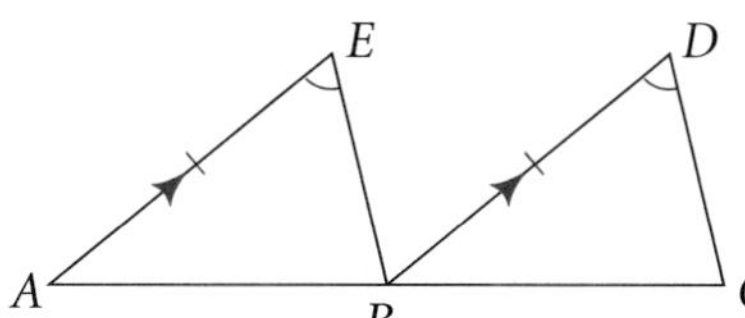

34. Given: $\overline{DH}$ bisects $\angle BDF$,
$\angle 1 \cong \angle 2$.
Conclusion: $\triangle BDH \cong \triangle FDH$

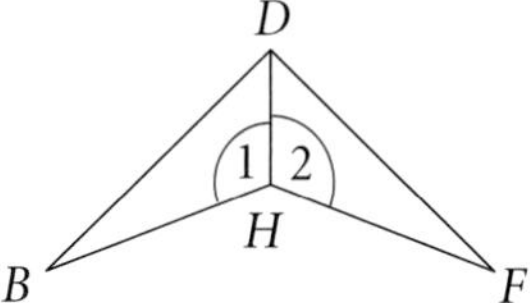

35. Reasoning If possible, draw two noncongruent triangles that have two pairs of congruent angles and one pair of congruent sides. If this is not possible, explain why.

C Challenge

36. a. **Open-Ended** Draw a triangle. Draw a second triangle that shares a common side with the first one and is congruent to it.
    b. Think about how you drew your second triangle. What postulate or theorem did you use to make the second triangle congruent to the first one?

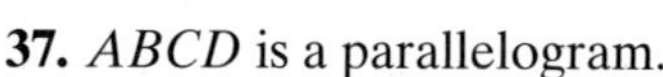

Real-World Connection

The two triangles above are congruent if just one additional condition is met.

Use the figure at the right. Name as many pairs of congruent triangles as you can for the information given.

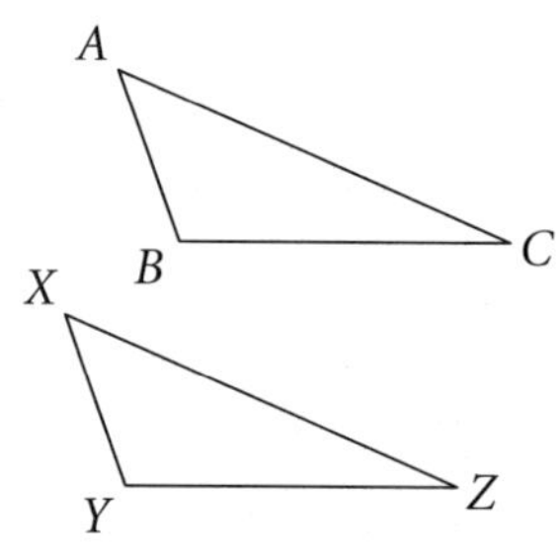

37. $ABCD$ is a parallelogram.

38. $ABCD$ is a rectangle.

39. **Reasoning** $\triangle JKL \cong \triangle MNP$. What additional information about $\overline{KQ}$ and $\overline{NR}$ will allow you to conclude that $\triangle JKQ \cong \triangle MNR$? Explain.

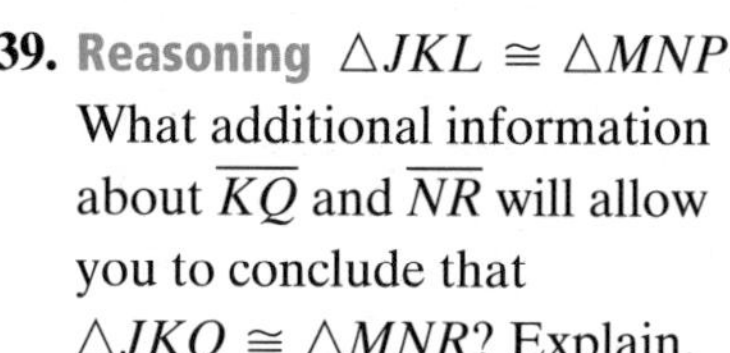

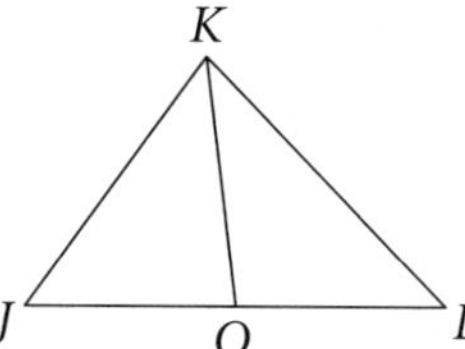

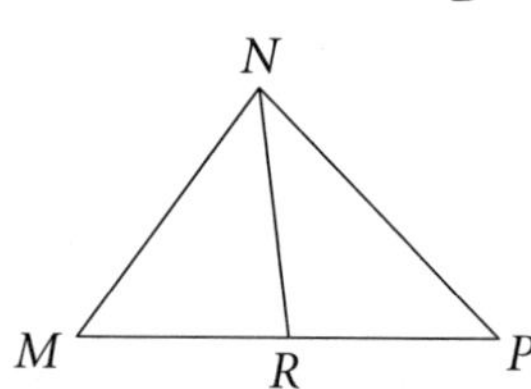

40. **Probability** Here are six congruence statements about the triangles at the right.

$\angle A \cong \angle X$ $\quad \angle B \cong \angle Y$ $\quad \angle C \cong \angle Z$

$\overline{AB} \cong \overline{XY}$ $\quad \overline{AC} \cong \overline{XZ}$ $\quad \overline{BC} \cong \overline{YZ}$

There are 20 ways to choose a group of three statements from these six. What is the probability that three statements chosen at random from the six will guarantee that the triangles are congruent?

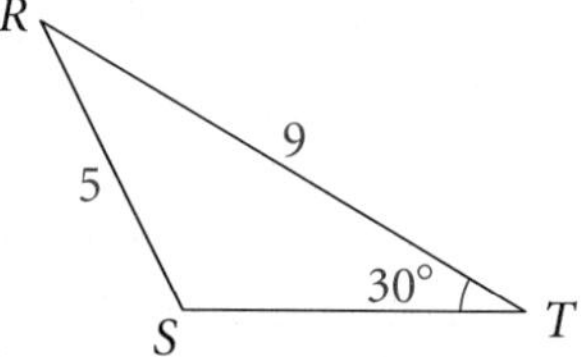

41. $\triangle RST$ at the right is with $RS = 5$, $RT = 9$, and $m\angle T = 30$. Show that there is no SSA congruence rule by constructing $\triangle UVW$ with $UV = 5$, $UW = 9$, and $m\angle W = 30$, but with $\triangle UVW \not\cong \triangle RST$.

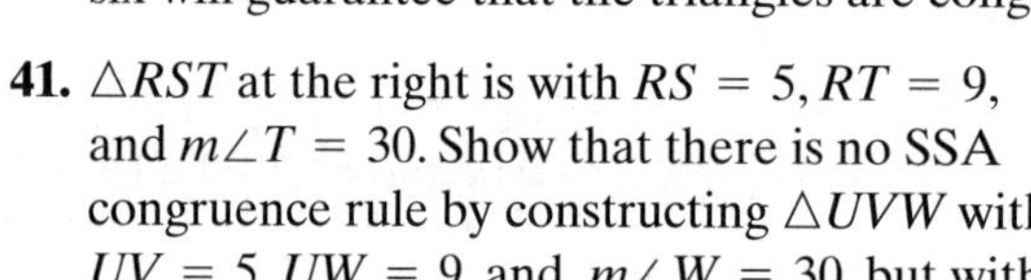

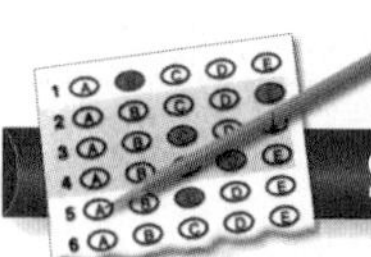

Standardized Test Prep

Multiple Choice

42. Which of the following is NOT a method used to prove triangles congruent?
    A. AAS B. ASA C. SAS D. SSA

43. Suppose $\overline{RT} \cong \overline{ND}$ and $\angle R \cong \angle N$. What additional information is needed to prove $\triangle RTJ \cong \triangle NDF$ by ASA?
    F. $\angle T \cong \angle D$ G. $\angle R \cong \angle N$ H. $\angle J \cong \angle D$ I. $\angle T \cong \angle F$

Short Response

44. $\overline{PQ}$ bisects $\angle RPS$ and $\angle RQS$. Justify each answer.
    a. Which pairs of angles, if any, are congruent?
    b. By what theorem or postulate can you prove that $\triangle PRQ \cong \triangle PSQ$?

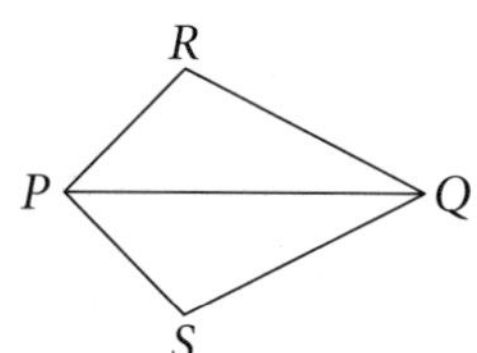

Extended Response

45. $\overline{LJ} \parallel \overline{KG}$ and M is the midpoint of $\overline{LG}$.
    a. Why is $\overline{LM} \cong \overline{GM}$?
    b. Can the two triangles be proved congruent by ASA? Explain.
    c. Can the two triangles be proved congruent by AAS? Explain.

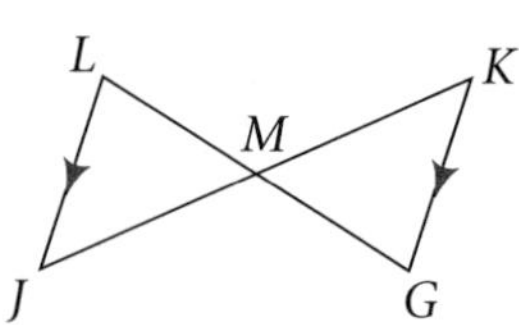

Take It to the NET
Online lesson quiz at **www.PHSchool.com**
Web Code: afa-0403

Mixed Review

Lesson 4-2

In Exercises 46 and 47, decide whether you can use the SSS Postulate or the SAS Postulate to prove the triangles congruent. If so, write the congruence statement and name the postulate. If not, write *not possible.*

46.

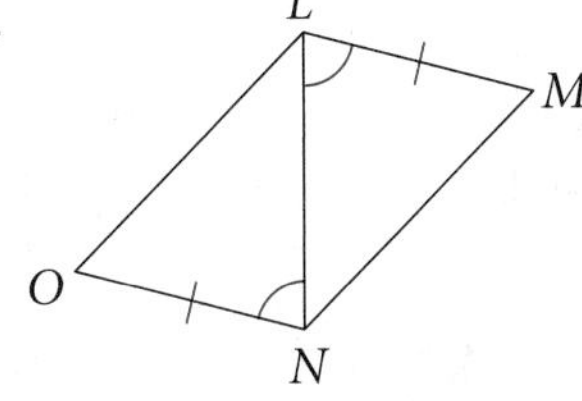

47.

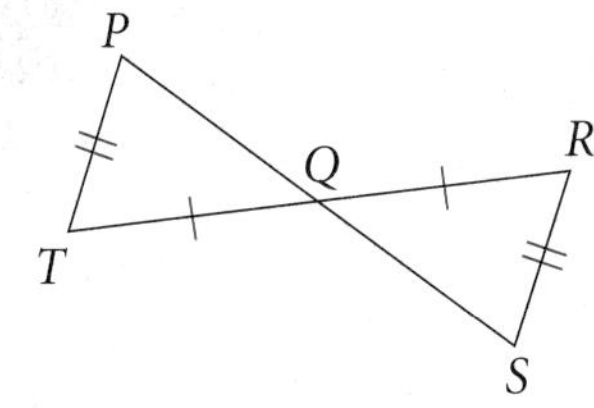

48. For any $\triangle ABC$, which sides are *not* included between $\angle A$ and $\angle B$?

Lesson 3-2

49. State the theorem or postulate that justifies the statement: If $\angle 1 \cong \angle 3$, then $a \parallel b$.

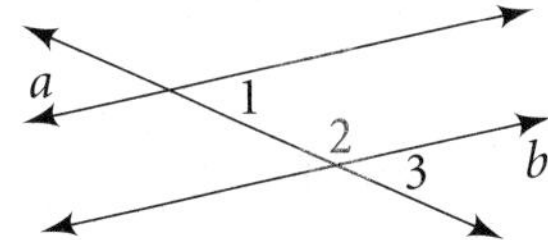

Lesson 1-7

Photography **You want to arrange class-trip photos without overlap to make a 2 ft-by-3 ft poster. You collect 3 in.-by-5 in. and 4 in.-by-6 in. photos. What is the greatest number of each type of photo that you can fit on your poster?**

50. 3 in.-by-5 in.

51. 4 in.-by-6 in.

52. What percent more paper is used for a large photo than a regular photo?

Checkpoint Quiz 1 — Lessons 4-1 through 4-3

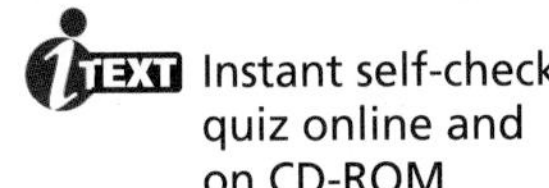

Instant self-check quiz online and on CD-ROM

1. $\triangle RST \cong \triangle JKL$. List the three pairs of congruent corresponding sides and the three pairs of congruent corresponding angles.

State the postulate or theorem you can use to prove the triangles congruent. If the triangles cannot be proven congruent, write *not possible.*

2.

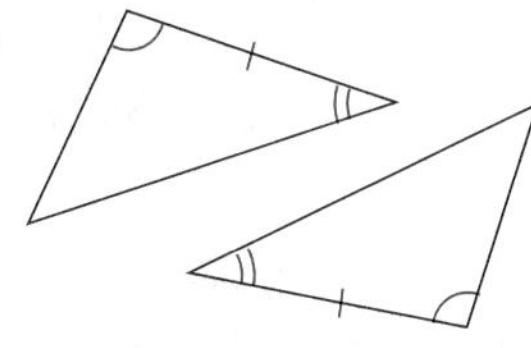

3.

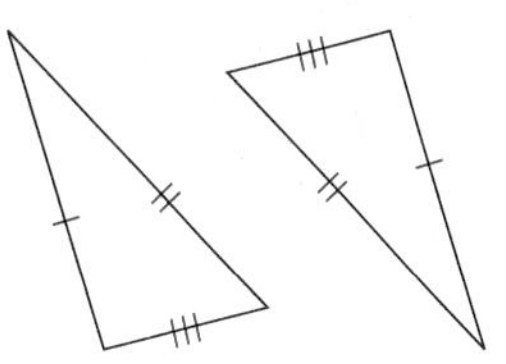

4.

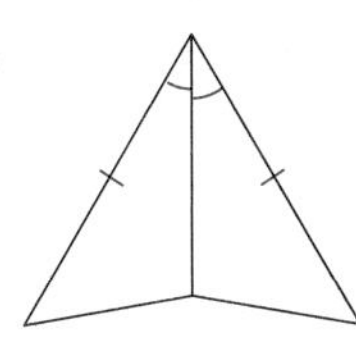

5.

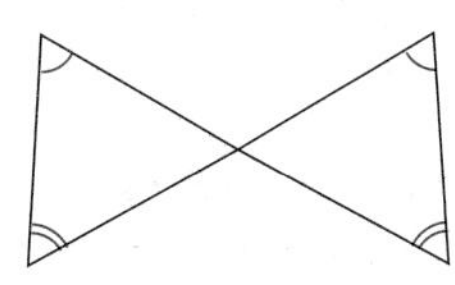

6.

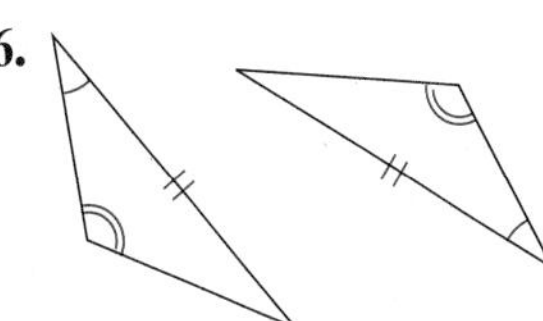

7.

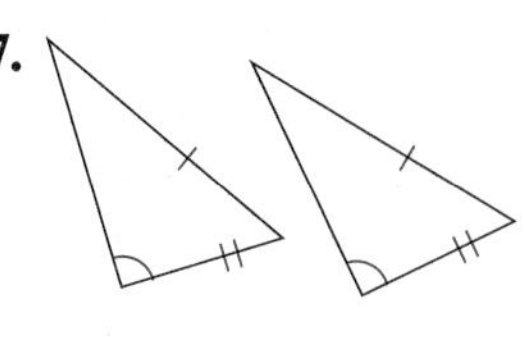

Use the information given in the diagram. Tell why each statement is true.

8. $\angle H \cong \angle K$

9. $\angle HNL \cong \angle KNJ$

10. $\triangle HNL \cong \triangle KNJ$

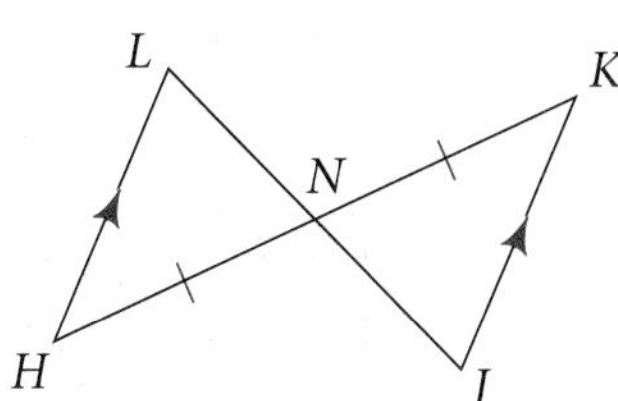

Exploring AAA and SSA

For Use With Lesson 4-3

So far, four statements allow you to conclude that two triangles are congruent. You can refer to them as SSS, SAS, ASA, and AAS. It is good mathematics to wonder about the other two possibilities, AAA and SSA.

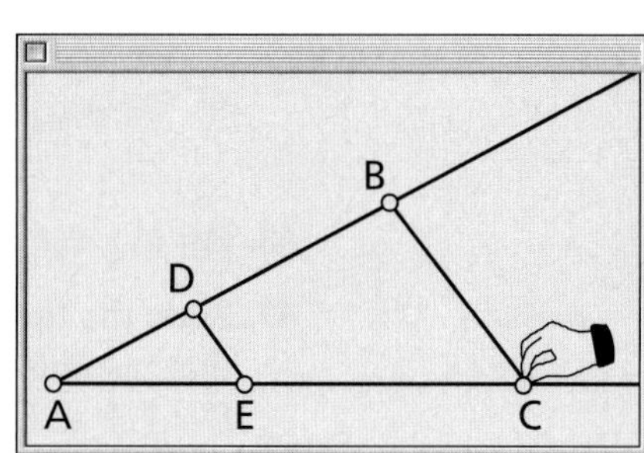

Construct

Use geometry software to construct $\overrightarrow{AB}$ and $\overrightarrow{AC}$. Construct $\overline{BC}$ to create $\triangle ABC$. Construct a line parallel to $\overline{BC}$ that intersects $\overrightarrow{AB}$ and $\overrightarrow{AC}$ at points D and E to form $\triangle ADE$.

Investigate

Are the three angles of $\triangle ABC$ congruent to the three angles of $\triangle ADE$? Manipulate the figure to change the positions of $\overline{DE}$ and $\overline{BC}$. Do the corresponding angles of the triangles remain congruent? Are the two triangles congruent? Can the two triangles be congruent?

In Exercise 1, you will be asked to make a conjecture about this investigation.

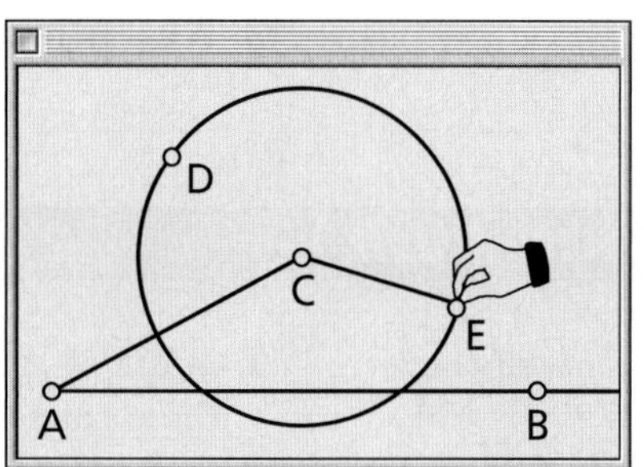

Construct

Construct $\overrightarrow{AB}$. Draw a circle with center C that intersects $\overrightarrow{AB}$ in two points. Construct $\overline{AC}$. Construct a point E on the circle and construct $\overline{CE}$.

Investigate

Move point E around the circle until E is on $\overrightarrow{AB}$ and forms $\triangle ACE$. Then move E on the circle to the other point on $\overrightarrow{AB}$ to form another $\triangle ACE$.

Compare the measures of $\overline{AC}$, $\overline{CE}$, and $\angle A$ in one triangle with the measures of $\overline{AC}$, $\overline{CE}$, and $\angle A$ in the other triangle. Are two sides and a nonincluded angle of one triangle congruent to two sides and a nonincluded angle of the other triangle? Are the two triangles congruent? Do you get the same results if you change the size of $\angle A$ and the size of the circle?

EXERCISES

1. **Make a Conjecture** Based on your first investigation above, is there an AAA congruence theorem? Explain.

For Exercises 2–4, use what you learned in your second investigation above.

2. **Make a Conjecture** Do you think there is an SSA congruence theorem? Why?
3. Manipulate the figure so that $\angle A$ is obtuse. Decide whether the circle can intersect $\overrightarrow{AB}$ twice to form two triangles. Could there be an SSA congruence theorem if the congruent angles are obtuse? Explain.
4. Suppose you are given $\overline{CE}$, $\overline{AC}$, and $\angle A$. What must be true about CE, AC, and $m\angle A$ so that you can construct exactly one $\triangle ACE$? (*Hint:* Consider cases.)

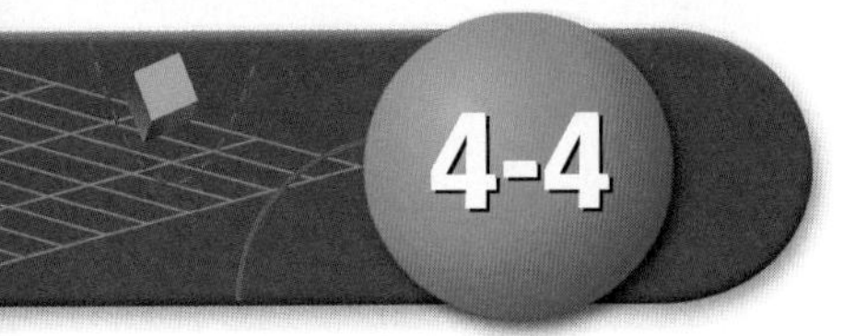

Using Congruent Triangles: CPCTC

Lesson Preview

What You'll Learn

To use triangle congruence and CPCTC to prove that parts of two triangles are congruent

. . . And Why

To measure distance indirectly, as in Example 2

✓ Check Skills You'll Need

(For help, go to Lesson 4-1.)

In the diagram, $\triangle JRC \cong \triangle HVG$.

1. List the congruent corresponding angles.
2. List the congruent corresponding sides.

You are given that $\triangle TIC \cong \triangle LOK$.

3. List the congruent corresponding angles.
4. List the congruent corresponding sides.

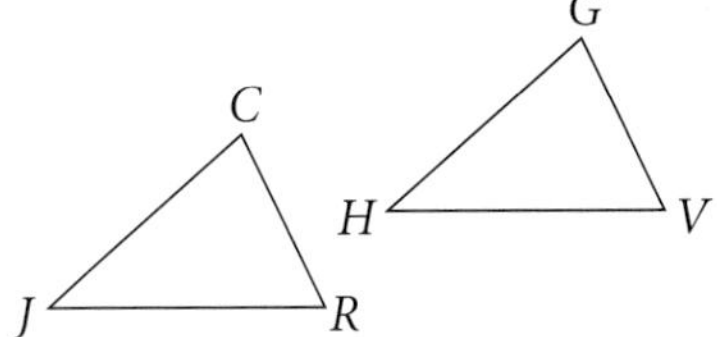

New Vocabulary • CPCTC

Interactive lesson includes instant self-check, tutorials, and activities.

OBJECTIVE 1

Proving Parts of Triangles Congruent

With SSS, SAS, ASA, and AAS, you know how to use three parts of triangles to show that the triangles are congruent. Once you have triangles congruent, you can make conclusions about their other parts because, by definition, corresponding parts of congruent triangles are congruent. You can abbreviate this as **CPCTC.**

Real-World Connection

Shapes formed by the ribs, stretchers, and shaft are congruent whether an umbrella is open or closed.

Proof

1 EXAMPLE Real-World Connection

Umbrella Frames In an umbrella frame, the stretchers are congruent and they open to angles of equal measure.

C, 3, 4, Rib, L, R, 5, 6, 1, 2, Stretcher, S, Shaft

Given: $\overline{SL} \cong \overline{SR}$,
$\angle 1 \cong \angle 2$

Prove that the angles formed by the shaft and the ribs are congruent.

Prove: $\angle 3 \cong \angle 4$

Proof: It is given that $\overline{SL} \cong \overline{SR}$ and $\angle 1 \cong \angle 2$. $\overline{SC} \cong \overline{SC}$ by the Reflexive Property of Congruence. $\triangle LSC \cong \triangle RSC$ by SAS, so $\angle 3 \cong \angle 4$ by CPCTC.

✓ Check Understanding

1 a. In Example 1, what can you say about $\angle 5$ and $\angle 6$? Explain.
b. **Critical Thinking** When fabric is stretched by the umbrella frame, do $\triangle LSC$ and $\triangle RSC$ remain congruent? Explain.

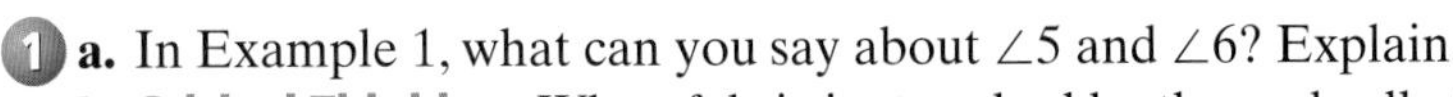

You can use congruent triangles and CPCTC to measure distances, such as the distance across a river, indirectly.

Proof **2 EXAMPLE** **Real-World Connection**

History According to legend, one of Napoleon's officers used congruent triangles to estimate the width of a river. On the riverbank, the officer stood up straight and lowered the visor of his cap until the farthest thing he could see was the edge of the opposite bank. He then turned and noted the spot on his side of the river that was in line with his eye and the tip of his visor.

Reading Math

You must read a word problem thoughtfully to find the *Given* and *Prove* information.

Given: $\angle DEG$ and $\angle DEF$ are right angles; $\angle EDG \cong \angle EDF$.

The officer then paced off the distance to this spot and declared that distance to be the width of the river! Use congruent triangles to prove that he was correct.

Prove: $\overline{EF} \cong \overline{EG}$

Statements	Reasons
1. $\angle EDG \cong \angle EDF$	1. Given
2. $\overline{DE} \cong \overline{DE}$	2. Reflexive Property of Congruence
3. $\angle DEG$ and $\angle DEF$ are right angles.	3. Given
4. $\angle DEG \cong \angle DEF$	4. All right angles are congruent.
5. $\triangle DEF \cong \triangle DEG$	5. ASA Postulate
6. $\overline{EF} \cong \overline{EG}$	6. CPCTC

Check Understanding 2 About how wide was the river if the officer stepped off 20 paces and each pace was about $2\frac{1}{2}$ ft long?

EXERCISES

For more practice, see *Extra Practice*.

Practice and Problem Solving

Practice by Example

Example 1 (page 203)

1. The diagram provides enough information for you to conclude that $\triangle QPS \cong \triangle RSP$ by AAS. What other pairs of sides and angles can you conclude are congruent by CPCTC?

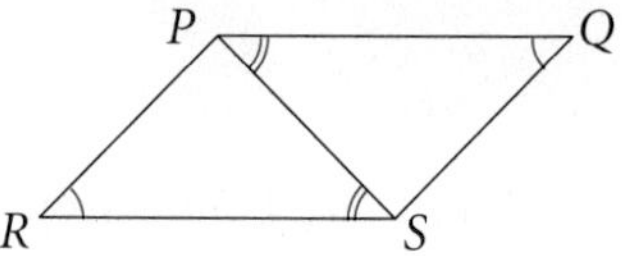

Developing Proof **State why the two triangles are congruent. Give the congruence statement. Then tell what other parts are congruent by CPCTC.**

2. 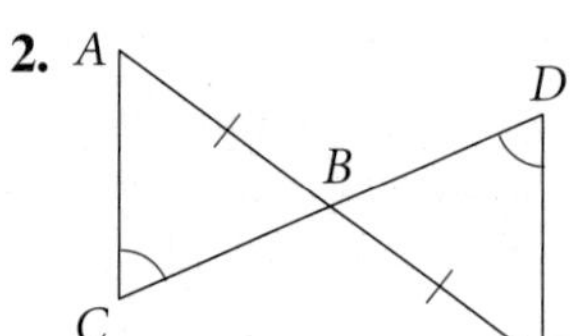

3. 

4. 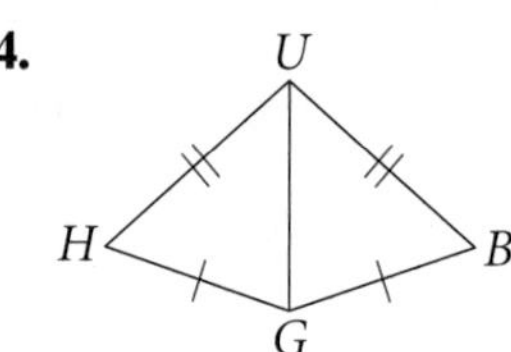

5. For $\triangle RST$ and $\triangle XYZ$, $\angle R \cong \angle X$, $\angle S \cong \angle Y$, and $\overline{ST} \cong \overline{YZ}$. What can you say about the exterior angles at T and Z? Explain.

6. **Developing Proof** Two cars of the same model have hood braces that are identical, connect to the body of the car in the same place, and fit into the same slot in the hood.

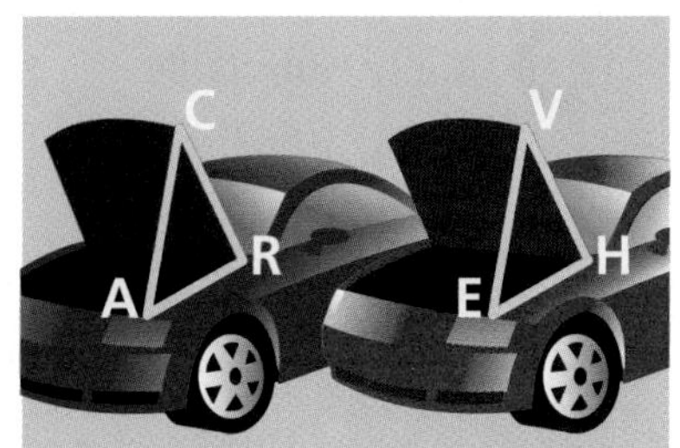

Given: $\overline{CA} \cong \overline{VE}, \overline{AR} \cong \overline{EH}, \overline{RC} \cong \overline{HV}$

Complete the proof that the hood braces hold the hoods open at the same angle.

Prove: $\angle ARC \cong \angle EHV$

Proof: It is given that the three sides of the triangles are congruent, so $\triangle ARC \cong \triangle EHV$ by **a.** __?__. Thus, $\angle ARC \cong \angle EHV$ by **b.** __?__.

Example 2 (page 204)

Developing Proof Explain how you can use SSS, SAS, ASA, or AAS with CPCTC to prove the statement true.

7. $\overline{AB} \cong \overline{CB}$

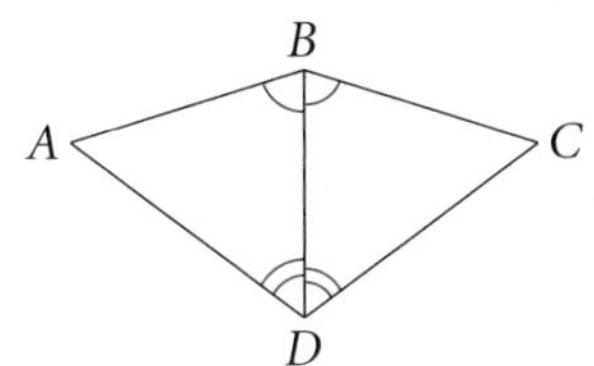

8. $\angle M \cong \angle R$

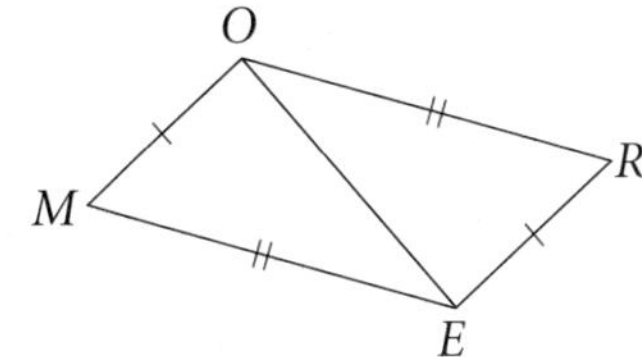

9. $\angle S \cong \angle O$

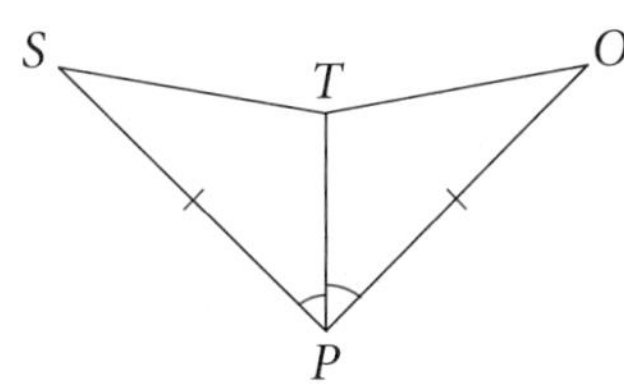

10. $\overline{KP} \cong \overline{LM}$

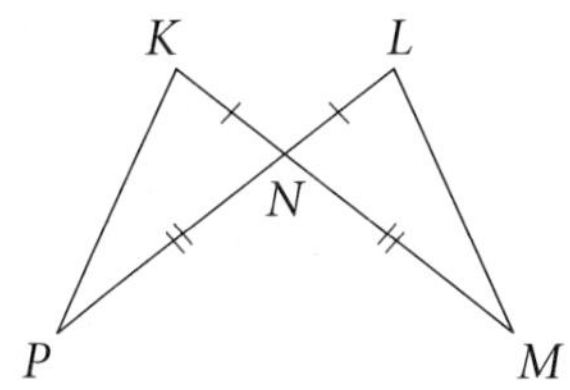

11. $\overline{CT} \cong \overline{RP}$

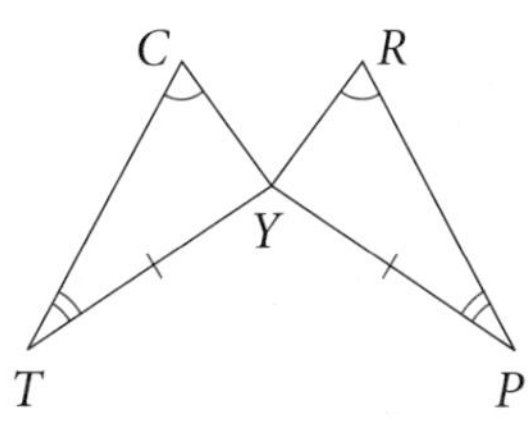

12. $\angle AMT \cong \angle RTM$

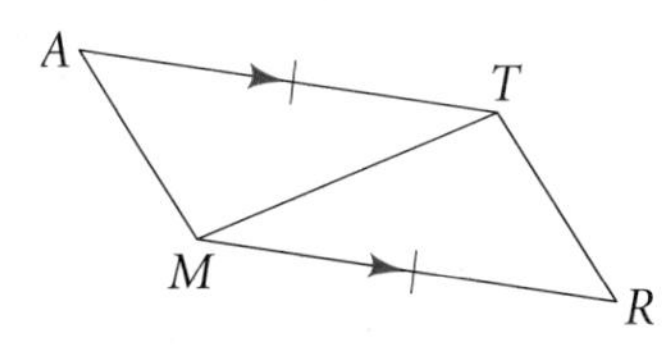

13. Karen cut this pattern for the stained glass shown here so that $AB = CB$ and $AD = CD$. Must $\angle A$ be congruent to $\angle C$? Explain.

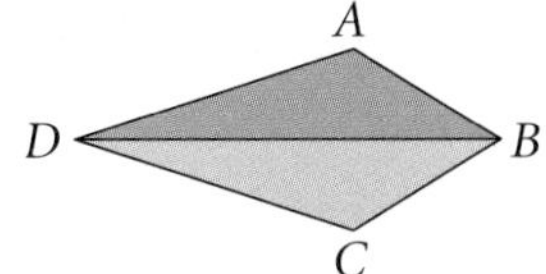

14. **Developing Proof** Complete the two-column proof by filling in the blanks.

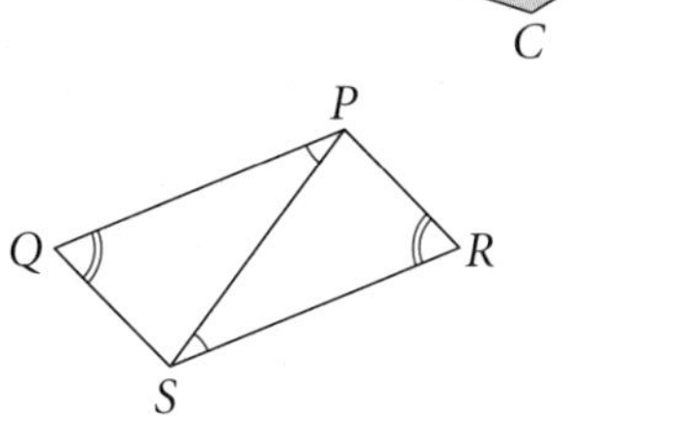

Given: $\angle QPS \cong \angle RSP, \angle Q \cong \angle R$

Prove: $\overline{PQ} \cong \overline{SR}$

Statements	Reasons
1. $\angle QPS \cong \angle RSP$	a. __?__
2. $\angle Q \cong \angle R$	b. __?__
3. $\overline{PS} \cong \overline{PS}$	c. __?__
4. $\triangle PQS \cong \triangle SRP$	d. __?__
5. $\overline{PQ} \cong \overline{SR}$	5. CPCTC

Need Help?

For Reason 4, look at Statements 1–3.

B Apply Your Skills

Developing Proof **Copy and mark the figure to show the given information. Explain how you would use SSS, SAS, ASA, or AAS with CPCTC to prove $\angle P \cong \angle Q$.**

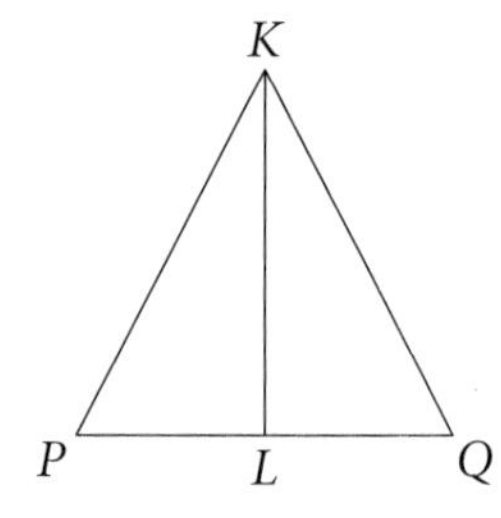

15. **Given:** $\overline{PK} \cong \overline{QK}$, $\overline{KL}$ bisects $\angle PKQ$.

16. **Given:** $\overline{KL}$ is the perpendicular bisector of $\overline{PQ}$.

17. **Given:** $\overline{KL} \perp \overline{PQ}$, $\overline{KL}$ bisects $\angle PKQ$.

18. **Earth Science** Some distances are best measured indirectly.

Sinkhole Swallows House

The large sinkhole in this photo occurred suddenly in 1981 in Winter Park, Florida, following a severe drought. Increased water consumption lowers the water table. Sinkholes form when caverns in the underlying limestone dry up and collapse.

A geometry class indirectly measured the distance across a sinkhole. The distances they measured are shown in the diagram. Explain how to use their measurements to find the distance across the sinkhole.

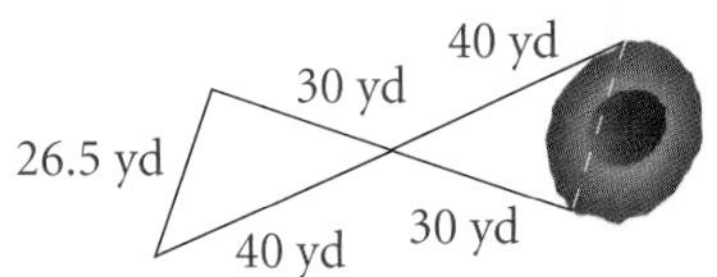

19. **Developing Proof** Complete this flow proof by filling in the blanks.

Given: $\ell \perp \overline{AB}$, ℓ bisects $\overline{AB}$ at C, P is on ℓ.

Prove: $PA = PB$

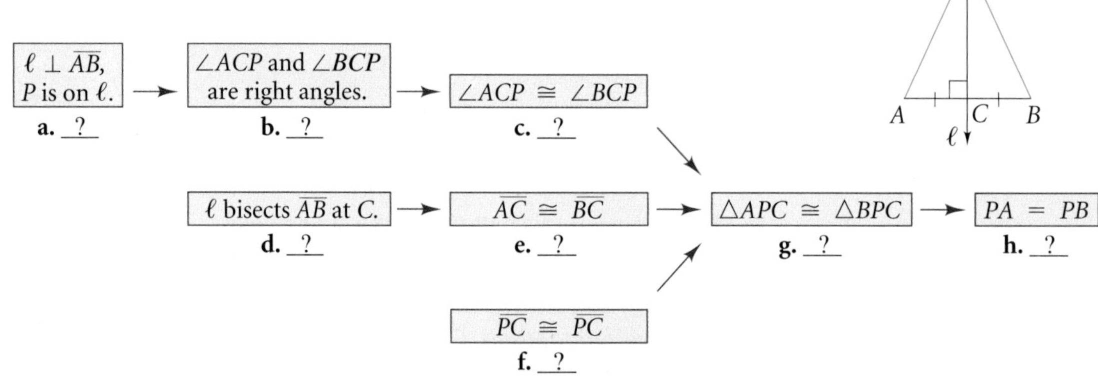

20. **Constructions** In the construction of the bisector of $\angle A$ below, $\overline{AB} \cong \overline{AC}$ because they are radii of the same circle. $\overline{BX} \cong \overline{CX}$ because both arcs had the same compass setting. Tell why you can conclude that $\overrightarrow{AX}$ bisects $\angle BAC$.

Need Help?

In the third diagram, what two triangles must be congruent, and why?

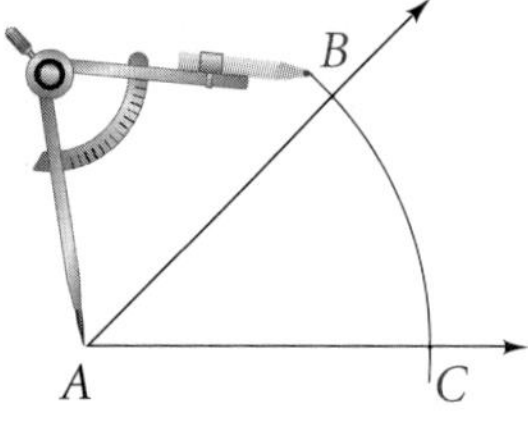

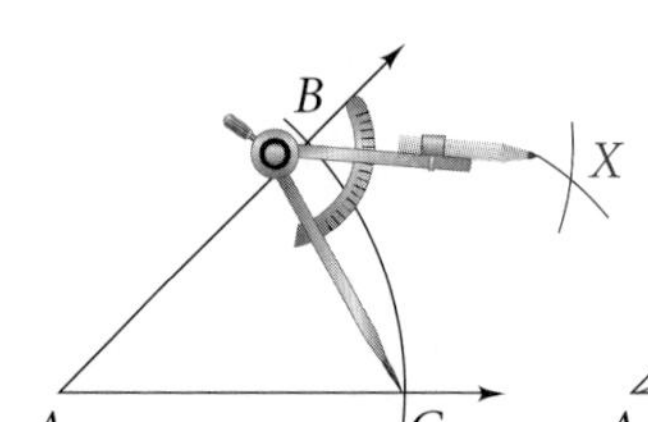

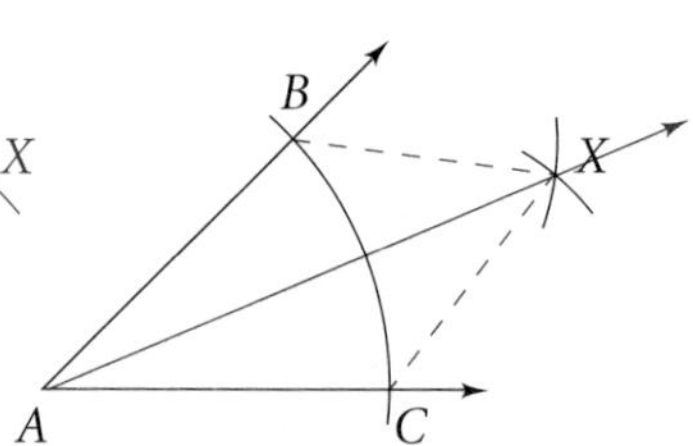

Developing Proof In Exercises 21 and 22, name two triangles you would prove congruent in order to use CPCTC. Tell how you would show them congruent.

21. **Given:** $\overline{BE} \perp \overline{AC}$, $\overline{DF} \perp \overline{AC}$, $\overline{BE} \cong \overline{DF}$, $\overline{AF} \cong \overline{EC}$

Prove: $\overline{AB} \cong \overline{DC}$

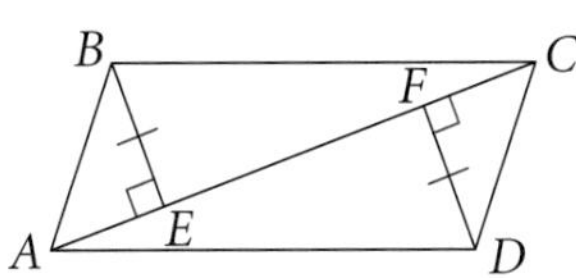

22. **Given:** $\overline{JK} \parallel \overline{QP}$, $\overline{JK} \cong \overline{QP}$

Prove: $\overline{KQ}$ bisects $\overline{JP}$.

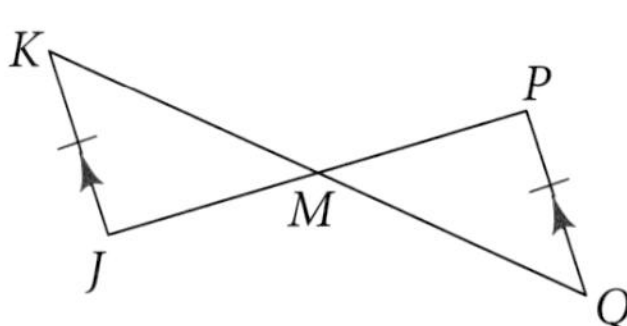

Reading Math

It is good strategy to read an exercise through to the end before trying to do it.

23. **Developing Proof** The reasons given in this proof are correct, but they are listed incorrectly. List them in the correct order.

Given: $\angle A \cong \angle C$, $\overline{BD}$ bisects $\angle ABC$.

Prove: $\overline{AB} \cong \overline{CB}$

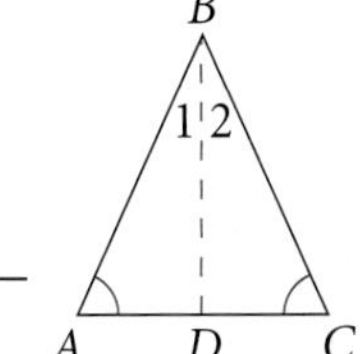

Statements	Reasons
1. $\angle A \cong \angle C$	a. CPCTC
2. $\overline{BD}$ bisects $\angle ABC$.	b. Given
3. $\angle 1 \cong \angle 2$	c. Reflexive Property of Congruence
4. $\overline{BD} \cong \overline{BD}$	d. Definition of angle bisector
5. $\triangle ABD \cong \triangle CBD$	e. Given
6. $\overline{AB} \cong \overline{CB}$	f. AAS Theorem

Proof 24. Use the plan to write a paragraph proof.

Given: $\overline{BA} \cong \overline{BC}$, $\overline{BD}$ bisects $\angle ABC$.

Prove: $\overline{BD} \perp \overline{AC}$, $\overline{BD}$ bisects $\overline{AC}$.

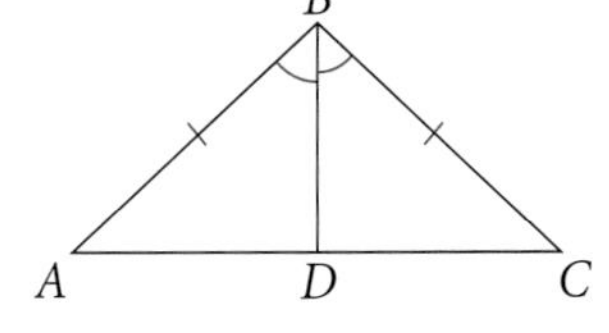

Plan: To show $\overline{BD} \perp \overline{AC}$, you can show that $\angle BDA \cong \angle BDC$ and use the fact that congruent supplementary angles are right angles. To show that $\overline{BD}$ bisects $\overline{AC}$, you can show that $\overline{AD} \cong \overline{CD}$. The desired congruent angles and segments are corresponding parts of $\triangle ABD$ and $\triangle CBD$. So, first show that $\triangle ABD \cong \triangle CBD$.

25. **Constructions** The construction of a line perpendicular to line ℓ through point P on ℓ is shown here.

a. Which lengths or distances are equal by construction?

b. Explain why you can conclude that $\overleftrightarrow{CP}$ is perpendicular to ℓ. (*Hint:* Do the construction. Then draw $\overline{CA}$ and $\overline{CB}$.)

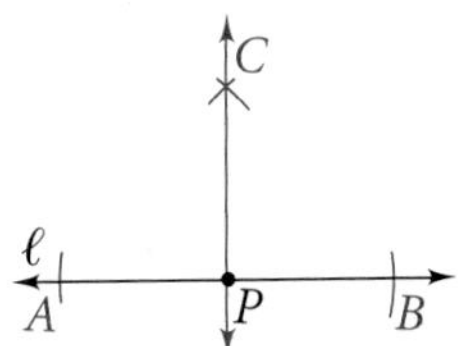

Challenge

For Exercises 26 and 27, write a proof.

Proof 26. **Given:** $\overline{PR} \parallel \overline{MG}$, $\overline{MP} \parallel \overline{GR}$

Prove: Each diagonal of $PRGM$ divides $PRGM$ into two congruent triangles.

Proof 27. **Given:** $\overline{PR} \parallel \overline{MG}$, $\overline{MP} \parallel \overline{GR}$

Prove: $\overline{PR} \cong \overline{MG}$, $\overline{MP} \cong \overline{GR}$ (*Hint:* See Exercise 26.)

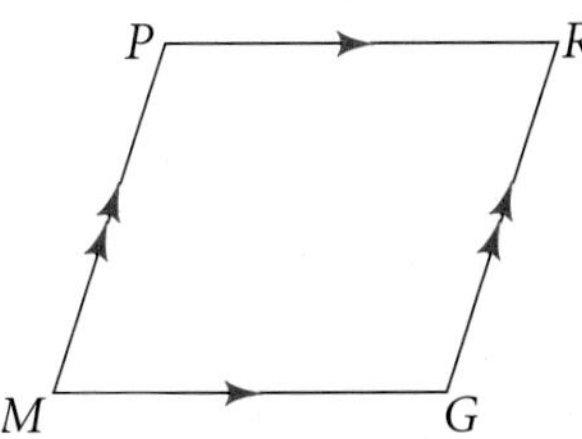

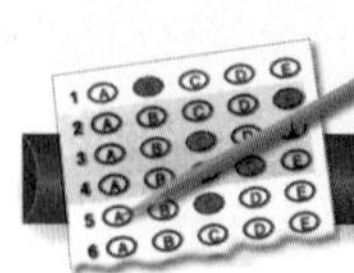

Standardized Test Prep

Multiple Choice

28. In the diagram, $\triangle RXW \cong \triangle JXT$. Which statement is NOT necessarily true?

A. $\angle J \cong \angle R$ **B.** $\angle W \cong \angle T$

C. $\overline{WX} \cong \overline{JX}$ **D.** $\overline{RW} \cong \overline{JT}$

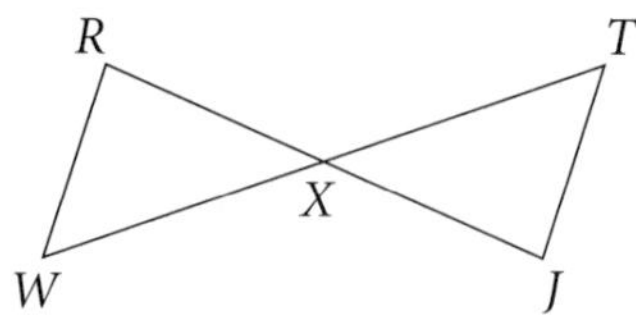

Quantitative Comparison

Compare the boxed quantity in Column A with the boxed quantity in Column B. Choose the best answer.

A. The quantity in Column A is greater.

B. The quantity in Column B is greater.

C. The two quantities are equal.

D. The relationship cannot be determined from the information given.

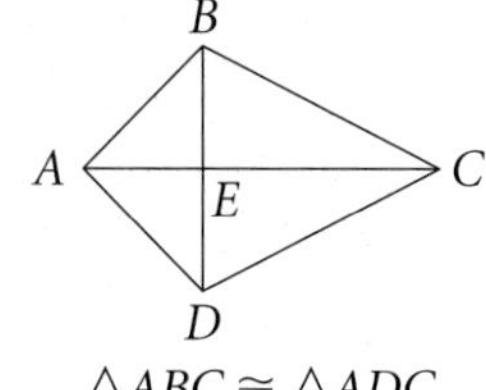

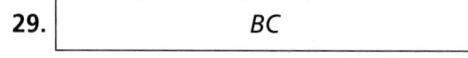

$\triangle ABC \cong \triangle ADC$

Exercises 29–32

	Column A	Column B
29.	BC	DC
30.	$m\angle ABC$	$m\angle DAB$
31.	AE	AC
32.	BE	DE

Short Response

33. In the diagram, $\overline{KB}$ bisects $\angle VKT$ and $\overline{KV} \cong \overline{KT}$.

a. What do you need to show in order to conclude $\angle KBV \cong \angle KBT$? State whether it is possible to show this and justify your answer.

b. Show that $\overline{VB} \cong \overline{TB}$.

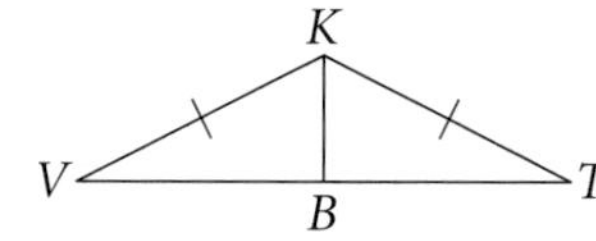

Take It to the NET

Online lesson quiz at **www.PHSchool.com**

Web Code: afa-0404

Mixed Review

Lesson 4-3

What postulate or theorem can you use to prove the triangles congruent?

34.

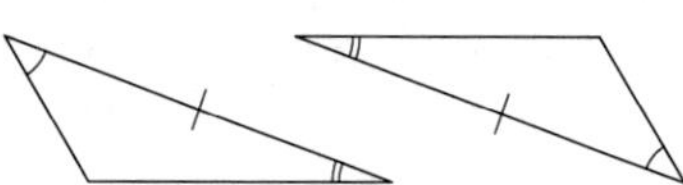

35.

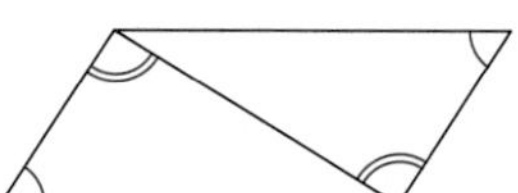

Lesson 2-5

36. The measure of an angle is 10 more than the measure of its supplement. Find the measures of both angles.

Lesson 2-3

If possible, use the Law of Detachment to draw a conclusion. If it is not possible to draw a conclusion, write *not possible.*

37. If two nonvertical lines are parallel, then their slopes are equal. Line m is nonvertical and parallel to line n.

38. If a convex polygon is a quadrilateral, then the sum of its angle measures is 360. Convex polygon $ABCDE$ has five sides.

39. If a quadrilateral is a square, then it has four congruent sides. Quadrilateral $ABCD$ has four congruent sides.

Systems of Linear Equations

For Use With Lesson 4-5

You can solve a system of equations in two variables by using substitution to create a one-variable equation.

1 EXAMPLE

Algebra Solve the system: $y = 3x + 5$
$y = x + 1$

$y = x + 1$ **Start with one equation.**

$3x + 5 = x + 1$ **Substitute $3x + 5$ for y.**

$2x = -4$ **Solve for x.**

$x = -2$

Substitute -2 for x in either equation and solve for y.

$$y = x + 1$$
$$= (-2) + 1 = -1$$

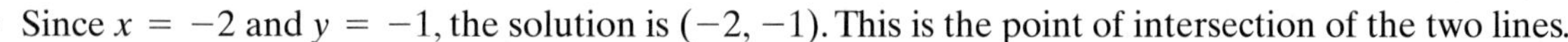

Since $x = -2$ and $y = -1$, the solution is $(-2, -1)$. This is the point of intersection of the two lines.

The graph of a linear system with *infinitely many solutions* is one line, and the graph of a linear system with *no solution* is two parallel lines.

2 EXAMPLE

Algebra Solve the system: $x + y = 3$
$4x + 4y = 8$

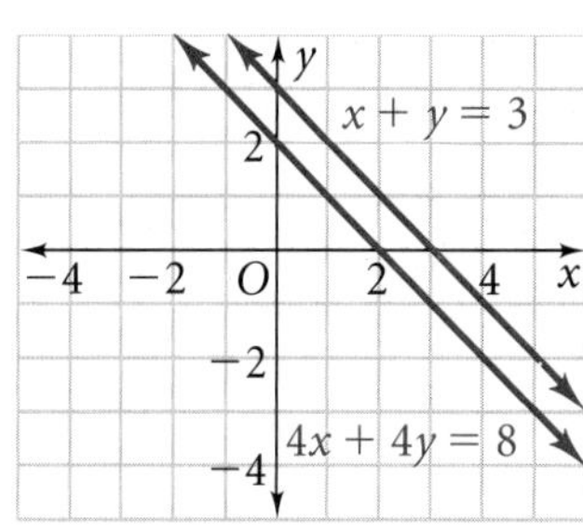

$x + y = 3$

$x = 3 - y$ **Solve the first equation for x.**

$4(3 - y) + 4y = 8$ **Substitute $3 - y$ for x in the second equation.**

$12 - 4y + 4y = 8$ **Solve for y.**

$12 = 8$ **False!**

Since $12 = 8$ is a false statement, the system has no solution.

EXERCISES

Solve each system of equations.

1. $y = x - 4$
$y = 3x + 2$

2. $2x - y = 8$
$x + 2y = 9$

3. $3x + y = 4$
$-6x - 2y = 12$

4. $2x - 3 = y + 3$
$2x + y = -3$

5. $y = x + 1$
$x = y - 1$

6. $x - y = 4$
$3x - 3y = 6$

7. $y = -x + 2$
$2y = 4 - 2x$

8. $y = 2x + 1$
$y = 3x - 7$

9. $x - y = 2$
$x + y = 1$

Isosceles and Equilateral Triangles

Lesson Preview

What You'll Learn

To use and apply properties of isosceles triangles

. . . And Why

To find the angles of a garden path, as in Example 4

✓ Check Skills You'll Need

(For help, go to Lesson 3-3.)

1. Name the angle opposite $\overline{AB}$.
2. Name the angle opposite $\overline{BC}$.
3. Name the side opposite $\angle A$.
4. Name the side opposite $\angle C$.
5. Algebra Find the value of x.

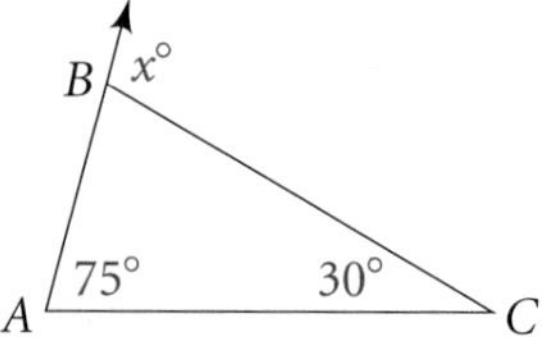

New Vocabulary
- legs of an isosceles triangle
- base of an isosceles triangle
- vertex angle of an isosceles triangle
- base angles of an isosceles triangle
- corollary

Interactive lesson includes instant self-check, tutorials, and activities.

OBJECTIVE 1

The Isosceles Triangle Theorems

Reading Math

Isosceles is derived from the Greek *isos* for equal and *skelos* for leg.

Investigation: Isosceles Triangles

Construct an isosceles triangle and then cut it out.

- Name your triangle $\triangle ABC$, with A and B opposite the congruent sides.
- Bisect $\angle C$ by folding the triangle so that the congruent sides overlap. Label the intersection of the fold line and $\overline{AB}$ as point D.
- Repeat the above steps with a different triangle. If your first triangle was acute, make your second triangle obtuse, and vice versa.

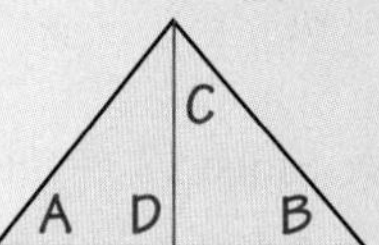

1. What do you notice about $\angle A$ and $\angle B$ in both of your triangles? Compare results with others. Make a conjecture.
2. a. What type of angle does each of $\angle CDA$ and $\angle CDB$ appear to be?

   b. What do you notice about $\overline{AD}$ and $\overline{BD}$?

   c. Use your answers to parts (a) and (b) to complete the conjecture: $\overline{CD}$ is the _?_ of $\overline{AB}$.

Isosceles triangles are common in the real world. You can find them in structures such as bridges and buildings. The congruent sides of an isosceles triangle are its **legs.** The third side is the **base.** The two congruent sides form the **vertex angle.** The other two angles are the **base angles.**

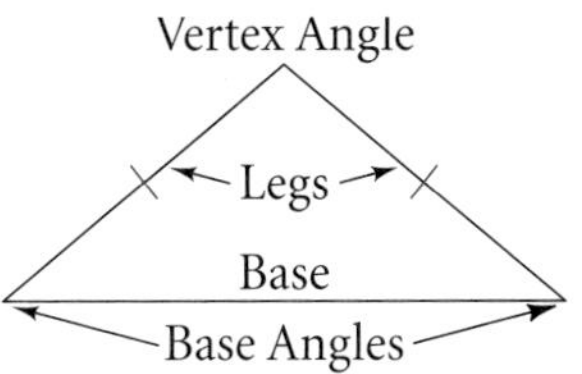

An isosceles triangle has a certain type of *symmetry* about a line through its vertex angle. This line is represented by the fold line $\overline{CD}$ in the last diagram on page 210. You can see this symmetry in the theorems below. You will learn more about this line symmetry in Lesson 12-5.

 Key Concepts

Theorem 4-3 **Isosceles Triangle Theorem**

If two sides of a triangle are congruent, then the angles opposite those sides are congruent.

$\angle A \cong \angle B$

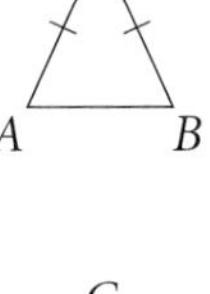

Theorem 4-4 **Converse of Isosceles Triangle Theorem**

If two angles of a triangle are congruent, then the sides opposite the angles are congruent.

$\overline{AC} \cong \overline{BC}$

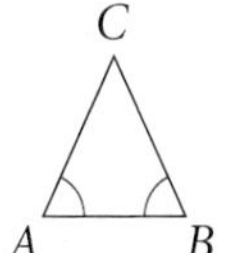

Theorem 4-5

The bisector of the vertex angle of an isosceles triangle is the perpendicular bisector of the base.

$\overline{CD} \perp \overline{AB}$ and $\overline{CD}$ bisects $\overline{AB}$.

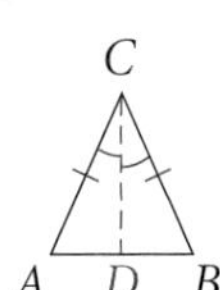

In one proof of the Isosceles Triangle Theorem, you use a special segment, the bisector of the vertex angle. Theorems 4-4 and 4-5 are proven in the Exercises.

Real-World Connection

This A-shaped roof has congruent legs and congruent base angles.

1 EXAMPLE Proving the Isosceles Triangle Theorem

Developing Proof To prove the Isosceles Triangle Theorem, begin with isosceles $\triangle XYZ$ with $\overline{XY} \cong \overline{XZ}$. Draw $\overline{XB}$, the bisector of the vertex angle $\angle YXZ$.

Given: $\overline{XY} \cong \overline{XZ}$, $\overline{XB}$ bisects $\angle YXZ$.

Show the base angles are congruent using a paragraph proof.

Prove: $\angle Y \cong \angle Z$

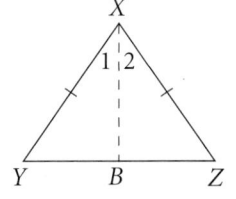

X, Y, Z, B, 1, 2

Proof: You are given that $\overline{XY} \cong \overline{XZ}$. By the definition of angle bisector, $\angle 1 \cong \angle 2$. By the Reflexive Property of Congruence, $\overline{XB} \cong \overline{XB}$. Therefore, by the SAS Postulate, $\triangle XYB \cong \triangle XZB$, and $\angle Y \cong \angle Z$ by CPCTC.

Check Understanding 1 Plan a proof, then prove the Converse of the Isosceles Triangle Theorem. (*Hint:* You can carefully parallel the proof above, but you cannot use SAS.)

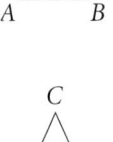

Proof

2 EXAMPLE Using the Isosceles Triangle Theorems

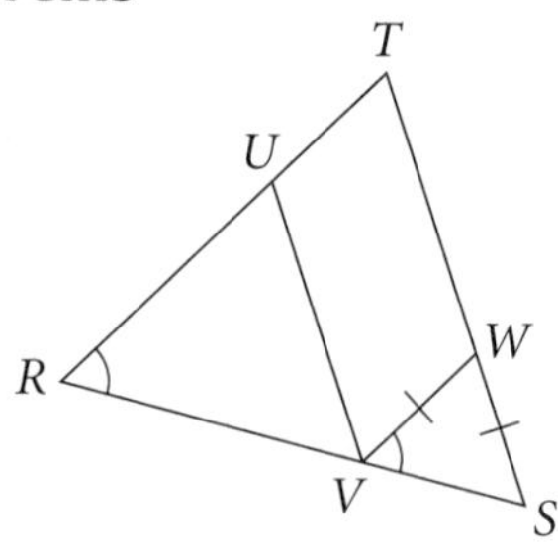

Developing Proof Explain why $\triangle RST$ is isosceles.

$\angle WVS \cong \angle S$ by the Isosceles Triangle Theorem. The diagram shows that $\angle R \cong \angle WVS$, so $\angle R \cong \angle S$ by the Transitive Property of Congruence. $\overline{TS} \cong \overline{TR}$ by the Converse of the Isosceles Triangle Theorem, and $\triangle RST$ is isosceles by the definition of isosceles triangle.

Check Understanding 2 In Example 2, can you deduce that $\triangle RUV$ is isosceles? Explain.

3 EXAMPLE Using Algebra

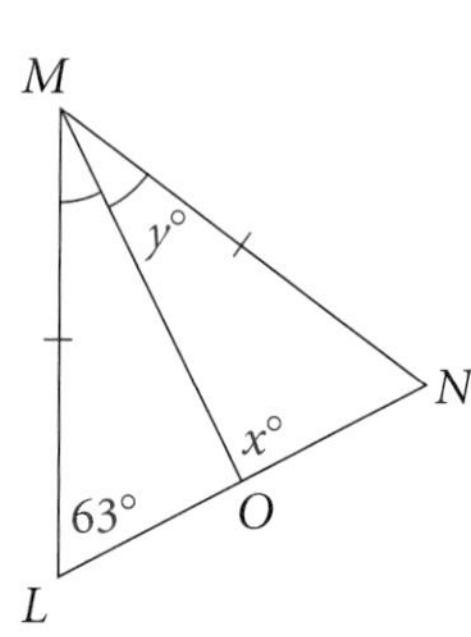

Algebra Find the values of x and y.

By Theorem 4-5, you know that $\overline{MO} \perp \overline{LN}$, so $x = 90$. $\triangle MLN$ is isosceles, so $\angle L \cong \angle N$ and $m\angle N = 63$.

$m\angle N + x + y = 180$	**Triangle Angle-Sum Theorem**
$63 + 90 + y = 180$	**Substitute for $m\angle N$ and x.**
$y = 27$	**Subtract 153 from each side.**

Check Understanding 3 Suppose $m\angle L = 43$. Find the values of x and y.

A **corollary** is a statement that follows immediately from a theorem. Here are corollaries to the Isosceles Triangle Theorem and its converse (proven in Exercise 32).

Key Concepts

Corollary **Corollary to Theorem 4-3**

If a triangle is equilateral, then the triangle is equiangular.

$$\angle X \cong \angle Y \cong \angle Z$$

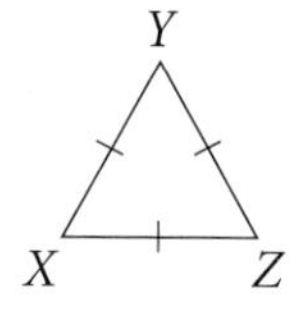

Corollary **Corollary to Theorem 4-4**

If a triangle is equiangular, then the triangle is equilateral.

$$\overline{XY} \cong \overline{YZ} \cong \overline{ZX}$$

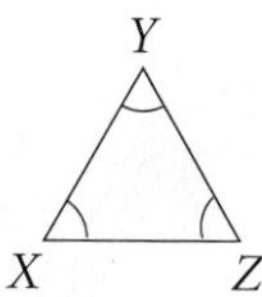

Need Help?
Equilateral: Congruent sides
Equiangular: Congruent angles

4 EXAMPLE Real-World Connection

Landscaping A landscaper uses rectangles and equilateral triangles for the path around the hexagonal garden. Find the value of x.

In a rectangle, an angle measure is 90; in an equilateral triangle, it is 60.

$$x + 90 + 60 + 90 = 360$$
$$x = 120$$

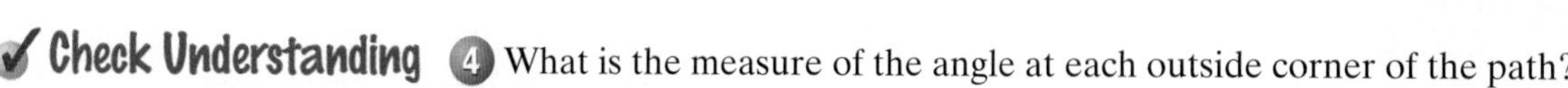

Check Understanding 4 What is the measure of the angle at each outside corner of the path?

EXERCISES

For more practice, see *Extra Practice.*

Practice and Problem Solving

A Practice by Example

Example 1 (page 211)

1. **Developing Proof** Supply the missing parts in this proof of the Converse of the Isosceles Triangle Theorem.

   Begin with $\triangle PRQ$ with $\angle P \cong \angle Q$.
   Draw **a.** _?_, the bisector of $\angle PRQ$.

   Given: $\angle P \cong \angle Q$, **b.** _?_ bisects $\angle PRQ$.
   Prove: $\overline{PR} \cong \overline{QR}$

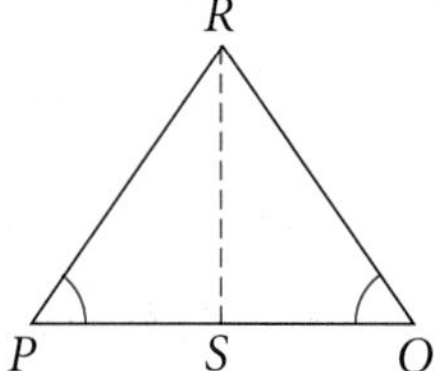

Statements	Reasons
1. $\overline{RS}$ bisects $\angle PRQ$.	c. _?_
2. $\angle PRS \cong \angle QRS$	d. _?_
3. $\angle P \cong \angle Q$	3. Given
4. $\overline{RS} \cong \overline{RS}$	e. _?_
5. $\triangle PRS \cong \triangle QRS$	f. _?_
6. $\overline{PR} \cong \overline{QR}$	6. CPCTC

2. **Developing Proof** Here is another way to prove the Isosceles Triangle Theorem. Supply the missing parts.

   Begin with isosceles $\triangle HKJ$ with $\overline{KH} \cong \overline{KJ}$.
   Draw **a.** _?_, a bisector of the base $\overline{HJ}$.

   Given: $\overline{KH} \cong \overline{KJ}$, **b.** _?_ bisects $\overline{HJ}$.
   Prove: $\angle H \cong \angle J$

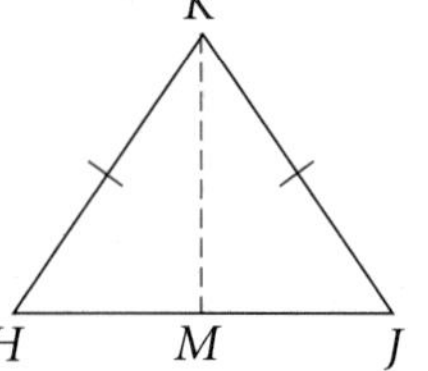

Statements	Reasons
1. $\overline{KM}$ bisects $\overline{HJ}$.	c. _?_
2. $\overline{HM} \cong \overline{JM}$	d. _?_
3. $\overline{KH} \cong \overline{KJ}$	3. Given
4. $\overline{KM} \cong \overline{KM}$	e. _?_
5. $\triangle KHM \cong \triangle KJM$	f. _?_
6. $\angle H \cong \angle J$	g. _?_

Example 2 (page 212)

Developing Proof **Complete each statement. Explain why it is true.**

3. $\overline{VT} \cong$ _?_
4. $\overline{UT} \cong$ _?_ $\cong \overline{YX}$
5. $\overline{VU} \cong$ _?_
6. $\angle VYU \cong$ _?_

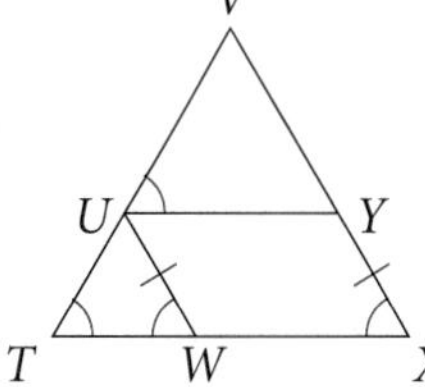

Example 3 (page 212)

x^2 **Algebra** **Find the values of x and y.**

7. 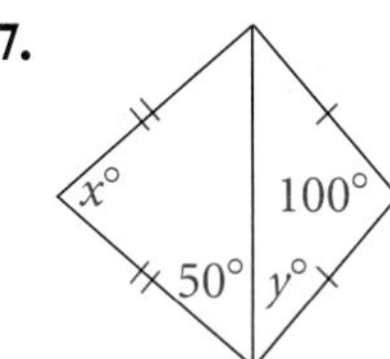

8. 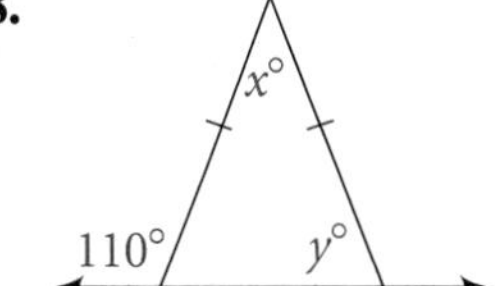

9. 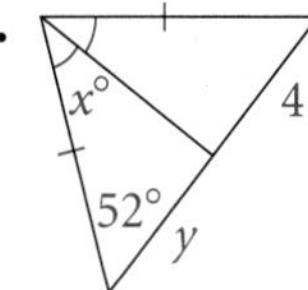

x^2 **Algebra** **Find the values of x and y.**

10.

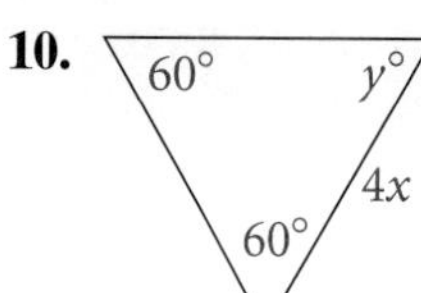

Perimeter is 54.

11.

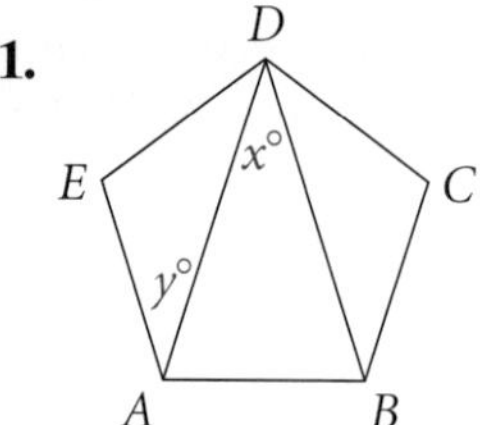

ABCDE is a regular pentagon.

12.

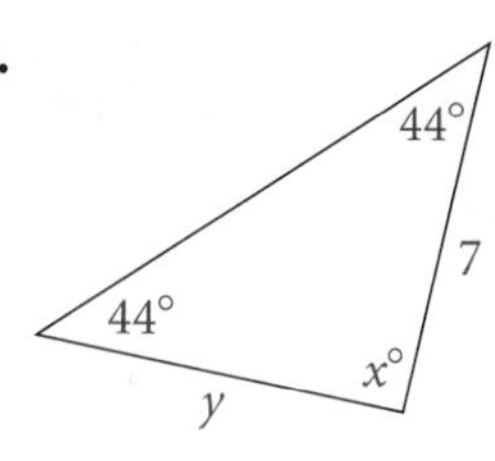

Find each value.

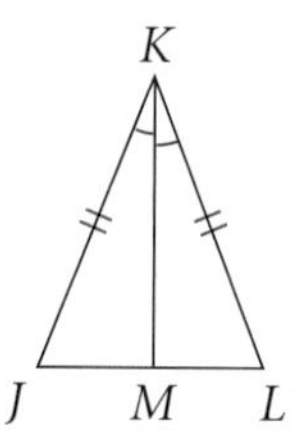

13. If $m\angle L = 58$, then $m\angle LKJ = \blacksquare$.

14. If $JL = 5$, then $ML = \blacksquare$.

15. If $m\angle JKM = 48$, then $m\angle J = \blacksquare$.

16. If $m\angle J = 55$, then $m\angle JKM = \blacksquare$.

Example 4 (page 212)

17. A square and a regular hexagon are placed so that they have a common side. Find $m\angle SHA$ and $m\angle HAS$.

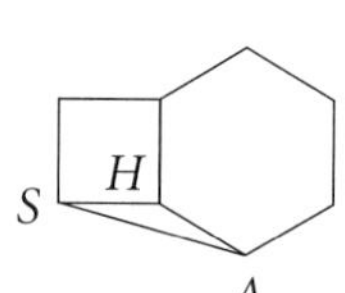

18. Five fences meet at a point to form angles with measures x, $2x$, $3x$, $4x$, and $5x$ around the point. Find the measure of each angle.

B Apply Your Skills

19. Graphic Arts The former logo for the National Council of Teachers of Mathematics is shown at the right. Trace the logo onto paper.

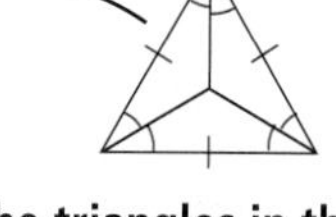

The triangles in the logo have these congruent sides and angles.

a. Highlight an obtuse isosceles triangle in the design. Then find its angle measures.

b. How many different sizes of angles can you find in the logo? What are their measures?

c. Open-Ended Design a logo using isosceles triangles. Give the measures of the angles in your logo.

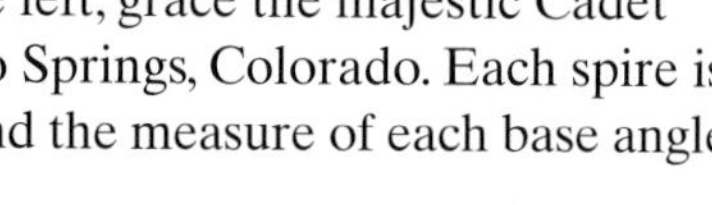

20. Architecture Seventeen spires, pictured at the left, grace the majestic Cadet Chapel at the Air Force Academy in Colorado Springs, Colorado. Each spire is an isosceles triangle with a 40° vertex angle. Find the measure of each base angle.

Exercise 20

Mental Math **Find the value of x.**

21.

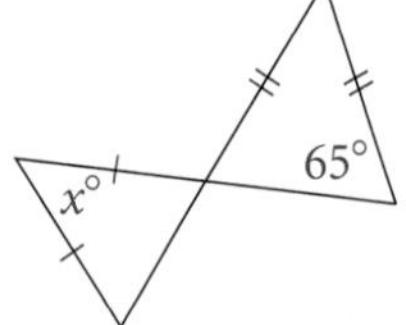

22.

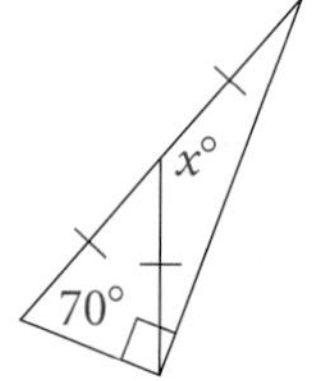

23.

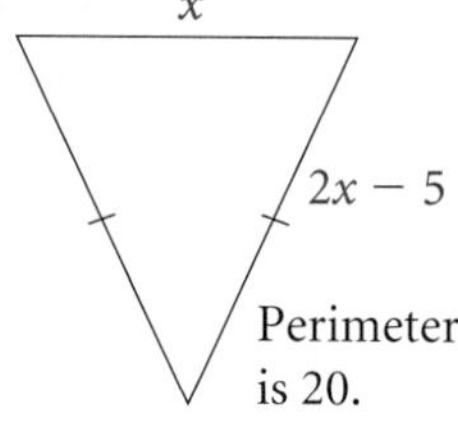

Perimeter is 20.

x^2 **Algebra** **Find the values of x and y.**

24.

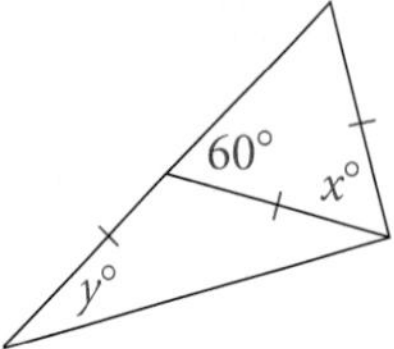

25.

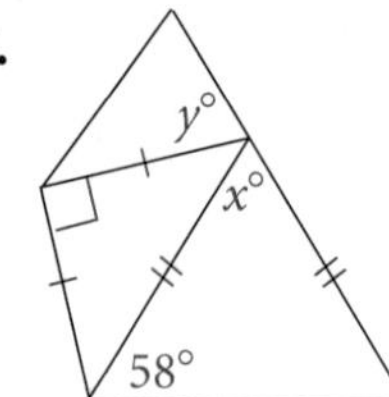

26.

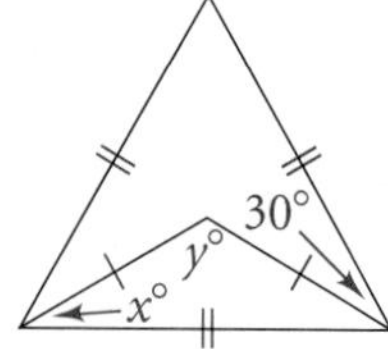

27. Write the Isosceles Triangle Theorem and its converse as a biconditional.

28. **Critical Thinking** An exterior angle of an isosceles triangle has measure 100. Find two possible sets of measures for the angles of the triangle.

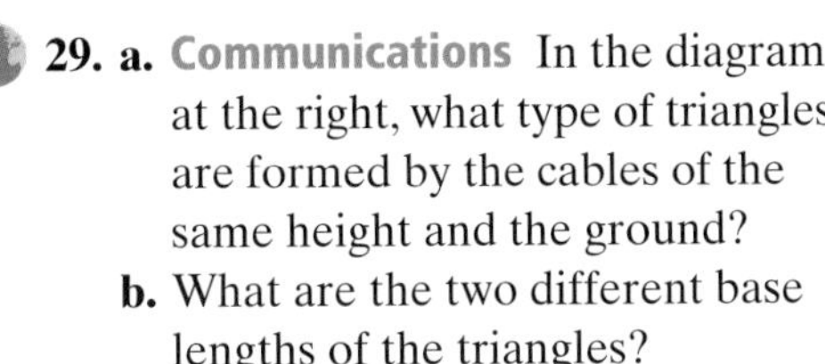

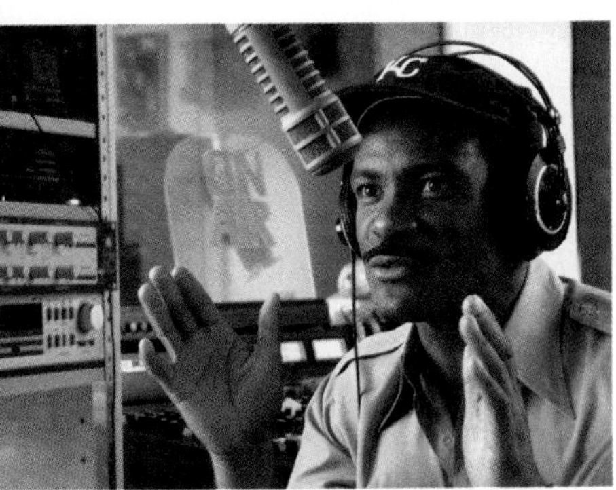

Real-World Connection

Careers Radio broadcasters must respond to opinions given by "call-in" listeners.

29. a. **Communications** In the diagram at the right, what type of triangles are formed by the cables of the same height and the ground?
 b. What are the two different base lengths of the triangles?
 c. How is the tower related to each of the triangles?

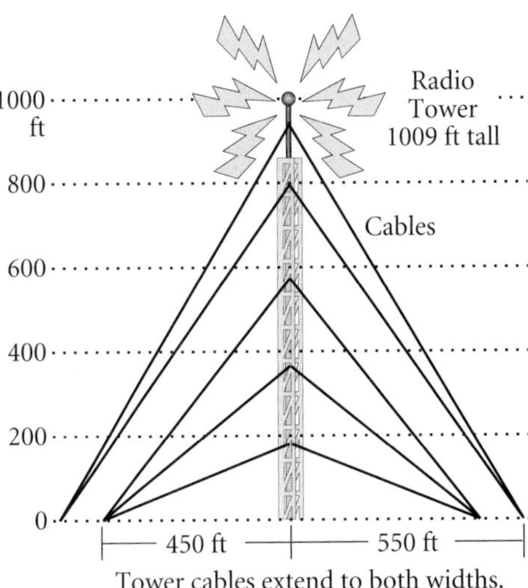

30. **Critical Thinking** Curtis defines the base of an isosceles triangle as its "bottom side." Is his definition a good one? Explain.

31. **Reasoning** What are the measures of the base angles of an isosceles right triangle? Explain.

32. **Writing** Explain how each corollary on page 212 follows from its theorem. First, write one explanation and then write the second similar to the first.

33. **Developing Proof** Copy and complete the flow proof.

Given: $\overline{AE} \cong \overline{DE}, \overline{AB} \cong \overline{DC}$

Prove: $\triangle ABE \cong \triangle DCE$

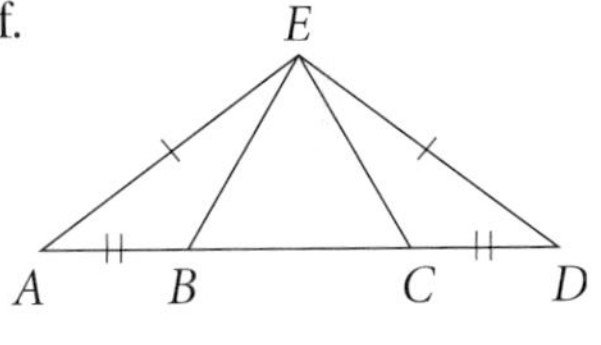

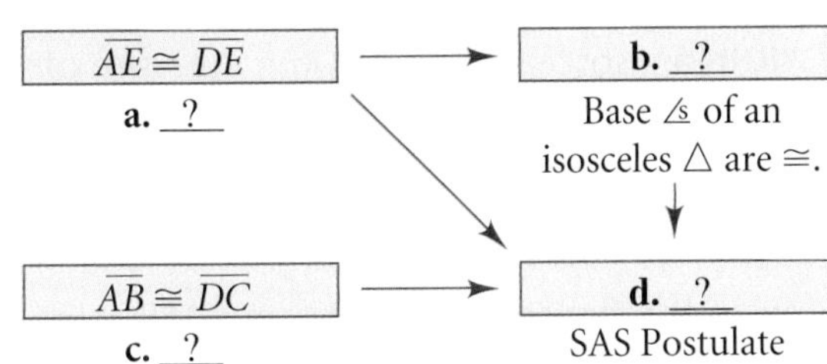

Algebra **Find the values of m and n.**

34.

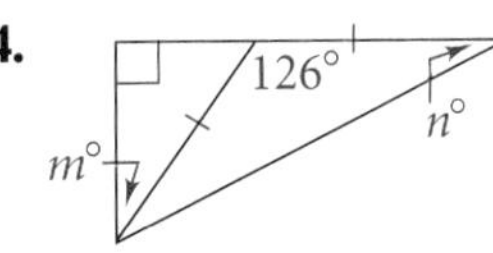

35.

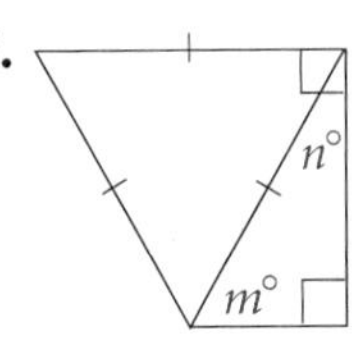

36.

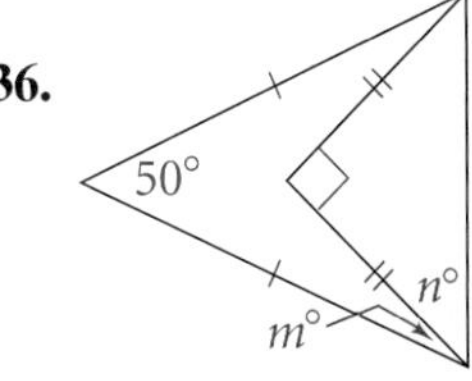

C Challenge

Coordinate Geometry **For each pair of points, there are six points that could be the third vertex of an isosceles right triangle. Find the coordinates of each point.**

37. (4, 0) and (0, 4) 38. (0, 0) and (5, 5) 39. (2, 3) and (5, 6)

40. **Algebra** A triangle has angle measures $x + 15$, $3x - 35$, and $4x$.
 a. Find the value of x. b. Find the measure of each angle.
 c. What type of triangle is it? Why?

Proof 41. Write a paragraph proof of Theorem 4-5 using the diagram next to it on page 211.

42. State the converse of Theorem 4-5. If the converse is true, write a paragraph proof. If the converse is false, give a counterexample.

Real-World Connection

The circle is a basic shape for many tile designs.

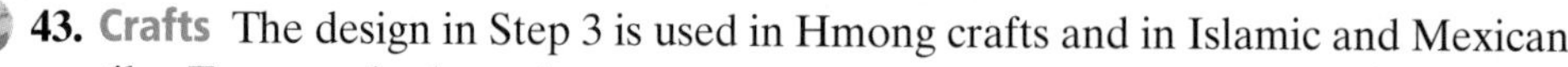

43. Crafts The design in Step 3 is used in Hmong crafts and in Islamic and Mexican tiles. To create it, the artist starts by drawing a circle and four equally spaced diameters.

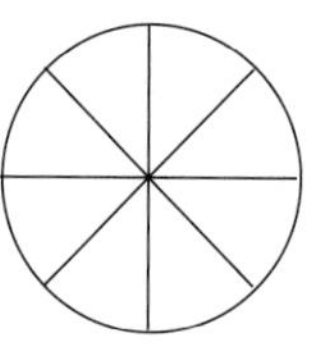

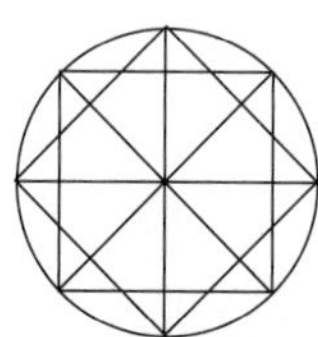

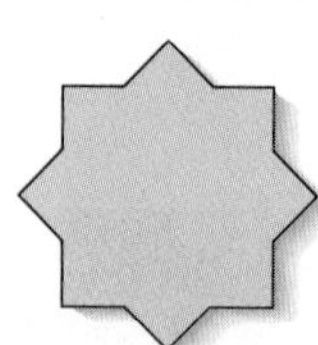

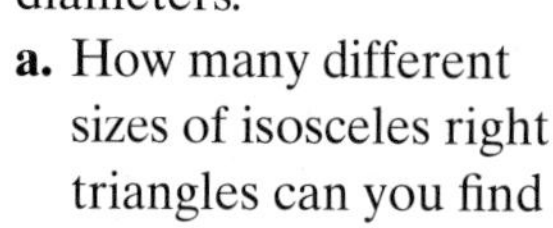

Step 1 Step 2 Step 3

a. How many different sizes of isosceles right triangles can you find in Step 2? Trace an example of each onto your paper.

b. How many times does a triangle of each size in part (a) appear in the Step 2 diagram?

Reasoning **What measures are possible for the base angles of each type of triangle? Explain.**

44. an isosceles obtuse triangle

45. an isosceles acute triangle

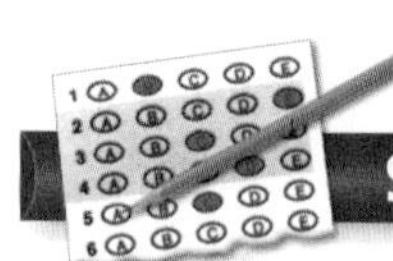

Standardized Test Prep

Multiple Choice

46. In isosceles $\triangle ABC$, the vertex angle is $\angle A$. What can be proved?

A. $AB = CB$ B. $\angle A \cong \angle B$

C. $m\angle B = m\angle C$ D. $\overline{BC} \cong \overline{AC}$

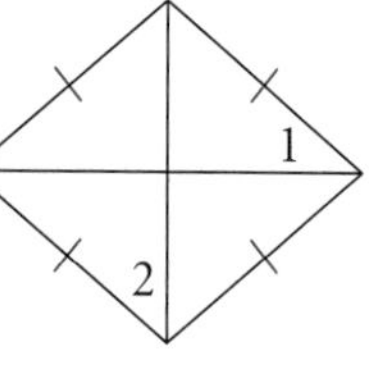

47. In the diagram at the right, $m\angle 1 = 40$. What is $m\angle 2$?

F. 40 G. 50 H. 80 I. 100

48. In an isosceles triangle, the measure of the vertex angle is $4x$. The measure of each base angle is $2x + 10$. What is the measure of the vertex angle?

A. 10 B. 20 C. 50 D. 80

Short Response

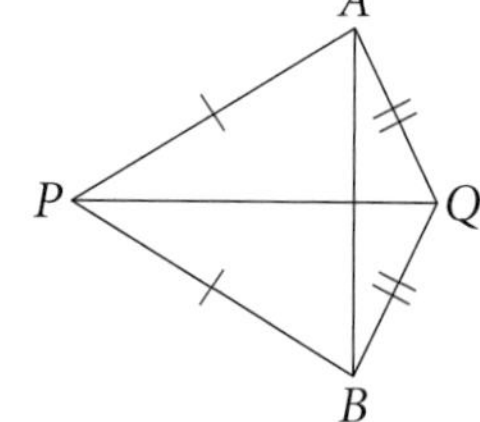

49. In the figure at the right, $m\angle APB = 60$.

a. What is $m\angle PAB$? Explain.

b. $\angle PAB$ and $\angle QAB$ are complementary. What is $m\angle AQB$? Show your work.

Take It to the NET

Online lesson quiz at **www.PHSchool.com**

Web Code: afa-0405

Mixed Review

Lesson 4-4

50. $m\angle R = 59, m\angle T = 93 = m\angle H, m\angle V = 28$, and $RT = GH$. What, if anything, can you conclude about RC and GV? Explain.

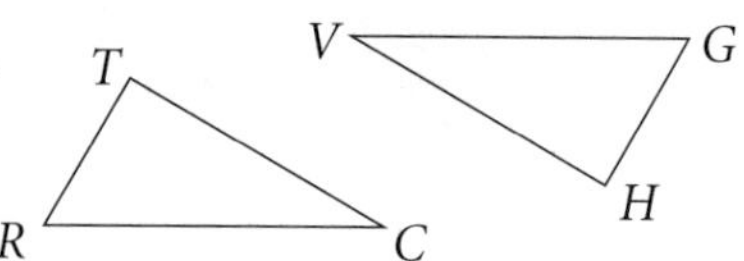

Lessons 4-2, 4-3

Which congruence statement, SSS, SAS, ASA, or AAS, would you use to conclude that the two triangles are congruent?

51.

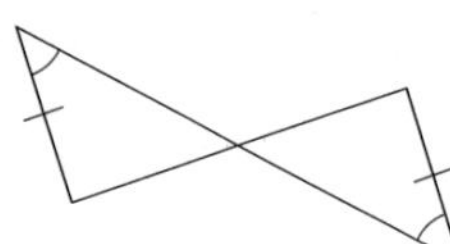

52.

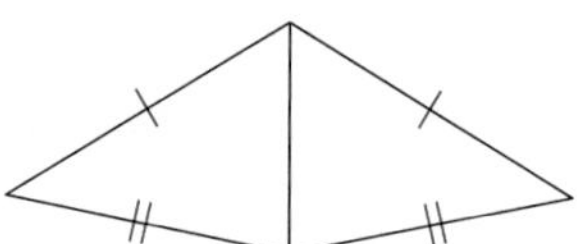

Lesson 3-4

53. How many sides are in a regular polygon whose exterior angles measure 15°?

4-6 Congruence in Right Triangles

Lesson Preview

What You'll Learn

To prove triangles congruent using the HL Theorem

. . . And Why

To show that one pattern can be used to cut the fabric for the two entrance flaps of a tent, as in Example 1

✓ Check Skills You'll Need

(For help, go to Lessons 4-2 and 4-3.)

Tell whether the abbreviation identifies a congruence statement.

1. SSS　　**2.** SAS　　**3.** SSA

4. ASA　　**5.** AAS　　**6.** AAA

Can you conclude that the two triangles are congruent? Explain.

7.

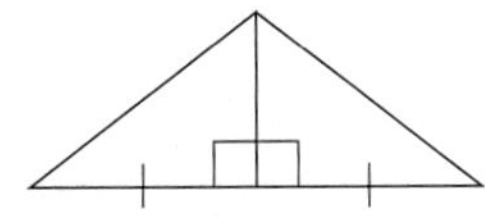

8.

New Vocabulary • hypotenuse • legs of a right triangle

Interactive lesson includes instant self-check, tutorials, and activities.

OBJECTIVE 1

The Hypotenuse-Leg Theorem

In a right triangle, the side opposite the right angle is the longest side and is called the **hypotenuse.** The other two sides are called **legs.**

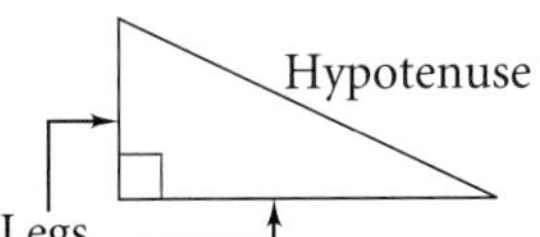

Right triangles provide a special case for which there is an SSA congruence rule. (See Lesson 4-3, Exercise 41.) It occurs when hypotenuses are congruent and one pair of legs are congruent.

Key Concepts

Theorem 4-6　Hypotenuse-Leg (HL) Theorem

If the hypotenuse and a leg of one right triangle are congruent to the hypotenuse and a leg of another right triangle, then the triangles are congruent.

Proof

Paragraph Proof of the HL Theorem

Given: $\triangle PQR$ and $\triangle XYZ$ are right triangles, with right angles Q and Y respectively. $\overline{PR} \cong \overline{XZ}$, and $\overline{PQ} \cong \overline{XY}$.

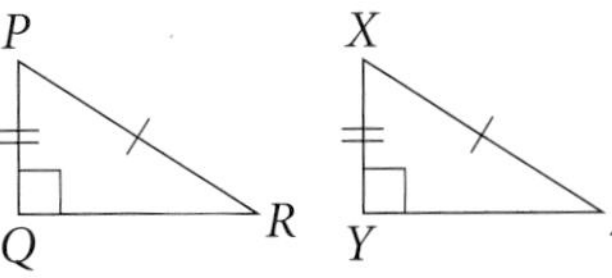

Prove: $\triangle PQR \cong \triangle XYZ$

Proof: On $\triangle XYZ$ at the right, draw $\overrightarrow{ZY}$. Mark point S as shown so that $YS = QR$. Then, $\triangle PQR \cong \triangle XYS$ by SAS. By CPCTC, $\overline{PR} \cong \overline{XS}$. It is given that $\overline{PR} \cong \overline{XZ}$, so $\overline{XS} \cong \overline{XZ}$ by the Transitive Property of Congruence.

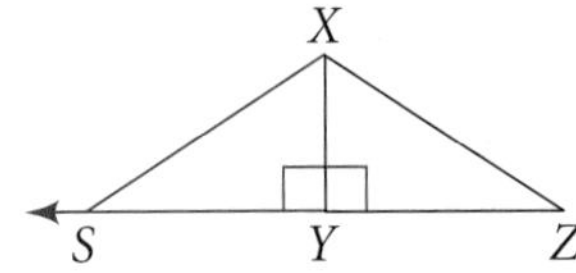

By the Isosceles Triangle Theorem, $\angle S \cong \angle Z$, so $\triangle XYS \cong \triangle XYZ$ by AAS. Therefore, $\triangle PQR \cong \triangle XYZ$ by the Transitive Property of Congruence.

1 EXAMPLE Real-World Connection

Tent Design On the tent, $\angle CPA$ and $\angle MPA$ are right angles and $\overline{CA} \cong \overline{MA}$. Write a paragraph to explain why $\triangle CPA$ and $\triangle MPA$ are congruent. Give an application of this congruence.

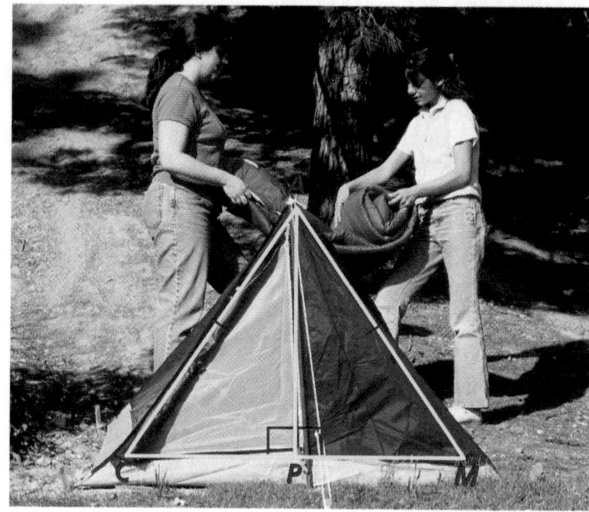

You are given that $\angle CPA$ and $\angle MPA$ are right angles. Therefore, $\triangle CPA$ and $\triangle MPA$ are right triangles. $\overline{PA}$ is a leg of both $\triangle CPA$ and $\triangle MPA$. $\overline{PA} \cong \overline{PA}$ by the Reflexive Property of Congruence. You are given that $\overline{CA} \cong \overline{MA}$. Thus, $\triangle CPA \cong \triangle MPA$ by the HL Theorem.

Application: Since the triangles are the same shape and size, you would need just one pattern to cut fabric for both flaps of the tent.

Check Understanding 1 Which two triangles are congruent by the HL Theorem? Write a correct congruence statement.

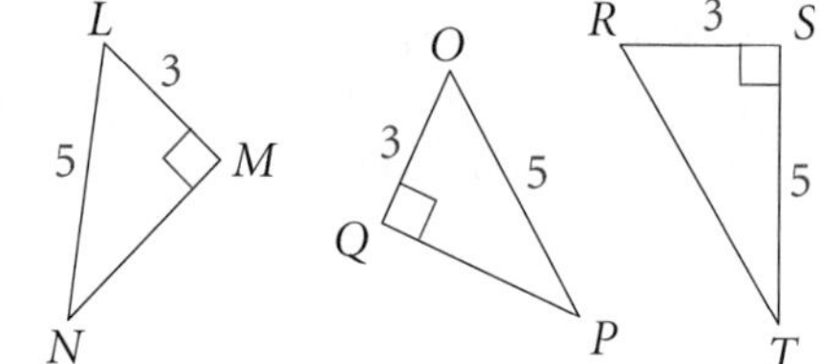

To use the HL Theorem, you must show that three conditions are met.

- There are two right triangles.
- The triangles have congruent hypotenuses.
- There is one pair of congruent legs.

Proof 2 EXAMPLE Flow Proof—Using the HL Theorem

Given: $\overline{CD} \cong \overline{EA}$, $\overline{AD}$ is the perpendicular bisector of $\overline{CE}$.

Use a flow proof to show that two triangles are congruent.

Prove: $\triangle CBD \cong \triangle EBA$.

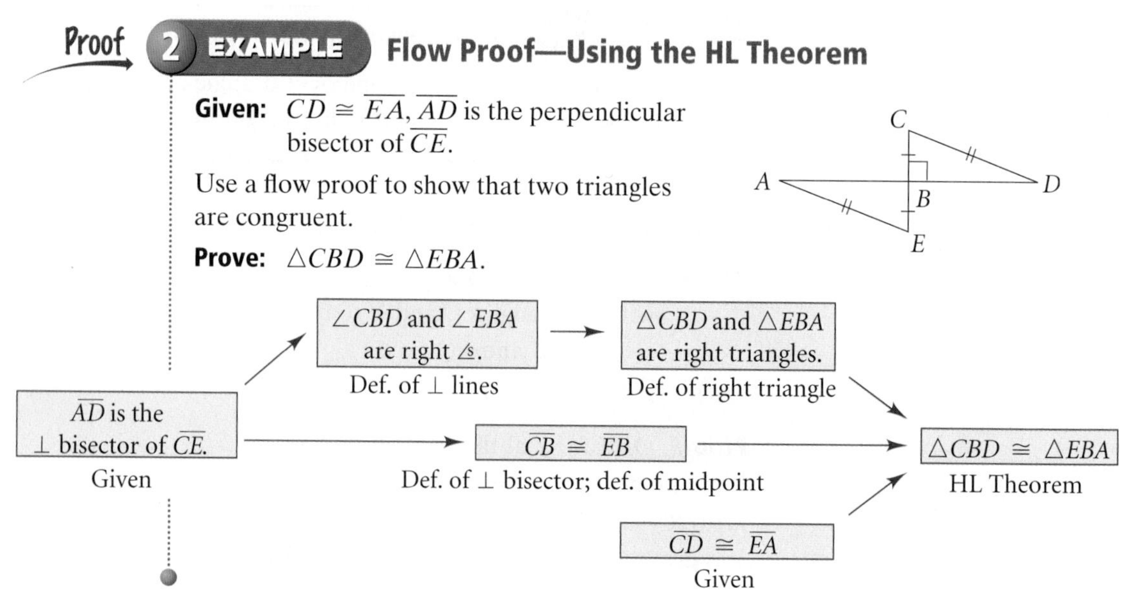

Check Understanding 2 Write a paragraph proof for Example 2.

Proof **3 EXAMPLE** **Two-Column Proof—Using the HL Theorem**

Given: $\overline{WJ} \cong \overline{KZ}$, $\angle W$ and $\angle K$ are right angles.

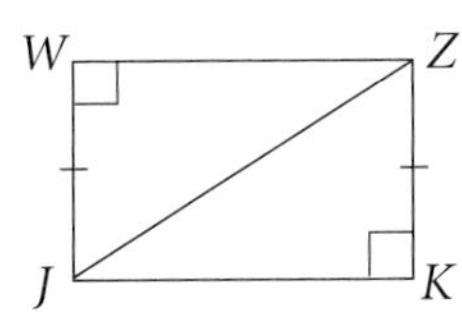

Use a two-column proof to show that two triangles are congruent.

Prove: $\triangle JWZ \cong \triangle ZKJ$

Statements	Reasons
1. $\angle W$ and $\angle K$ are right angles.	**1.** Given
2. $\triangle JWZ$ and $\triangle ZKJ$ are right triangles.	**2.** Definition of right triangle
3. $\overline{JZ} \cong \overline{JZ}$	**3.** Reflexive Property of Congruence
4. $\overline{WJ} \cong \overline{KZ}$	**4.** Given
5. $\triangle JWZ \cong \triangle ZKJ$	**5.** HL Theorem

3 **Critical Thinking** You know that two legs of one right triangle are congruent to two legs of another right triangle. Explain how to prove the triangles are congruent.

EXERCISES

For more practice, see *Extra Practice*.

Practice and Problem Solving

Practice by Example

Example 1 (page 218)

Developing Proof **Write a short paragraph to explain why the two triangles are congruent.**

1.

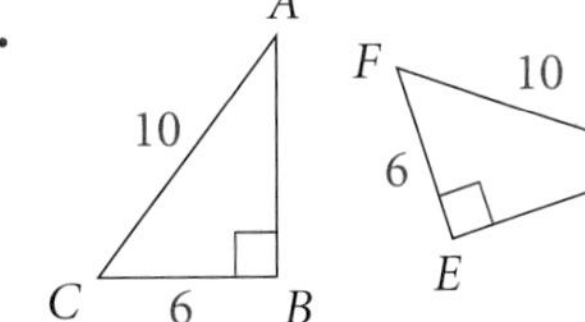

2.

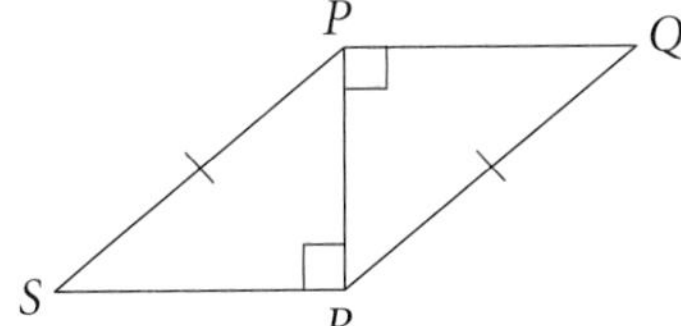

3.

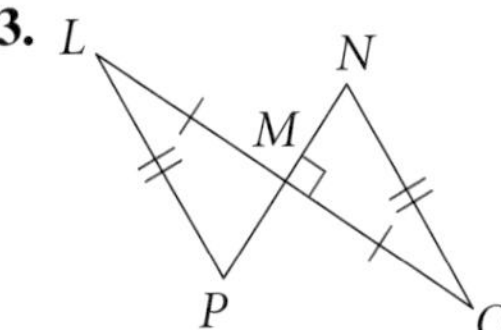

4.

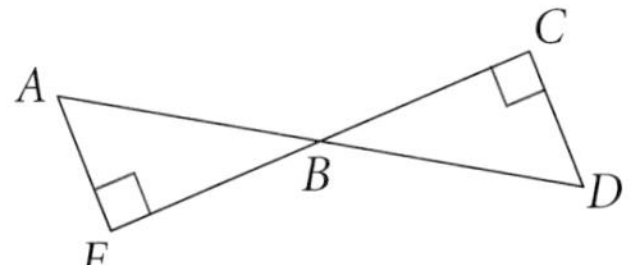

B is the midpoint of $\overline{AD}$ and $\overline{EC}$.

Developing Proof **What additional information do you need to prove the triangles congruent by the HL Theorem?**

5. $\triangle BLT$ and $\triangle RKQ$

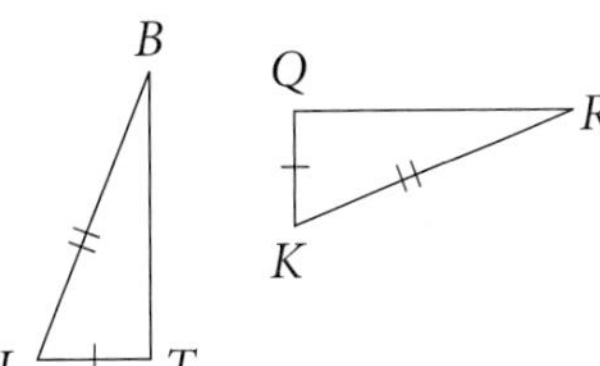

6. $\triangle XRV$ and $\triangle TRV$

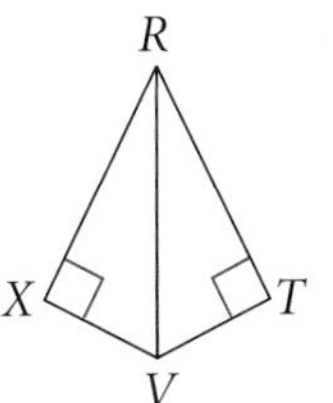

7. $\triangle TRY$ and $\triangle EYR$

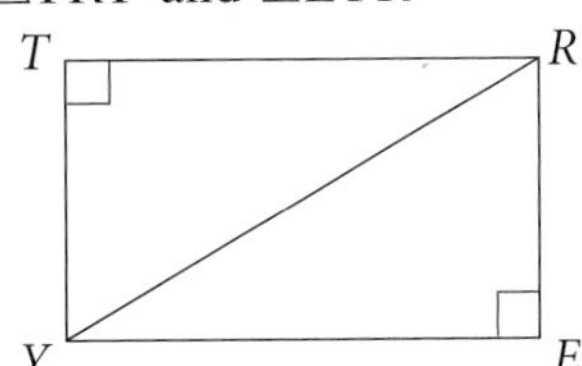

8. $\triangle ACQ$ and $\triangle GCJ$

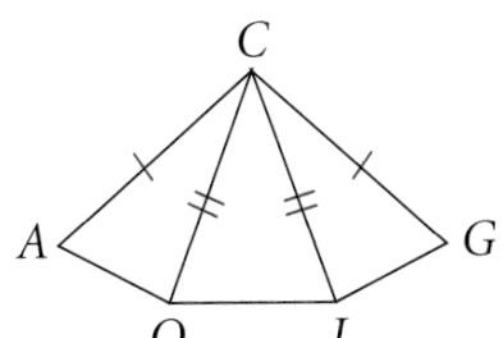

Developing Proof What additional information do you need to prove the triangles congruent by the HL Theorem?

9. $\triangle BDC$ and $\triangle FEA$

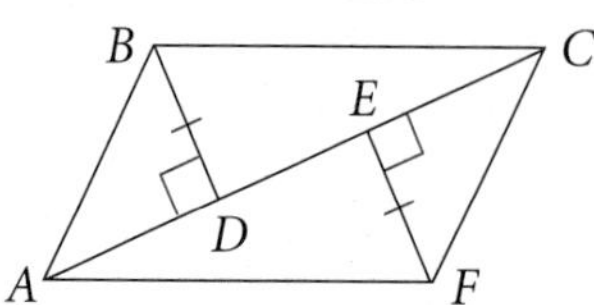

10. $\triangle STR$ and $\triangle PQN$

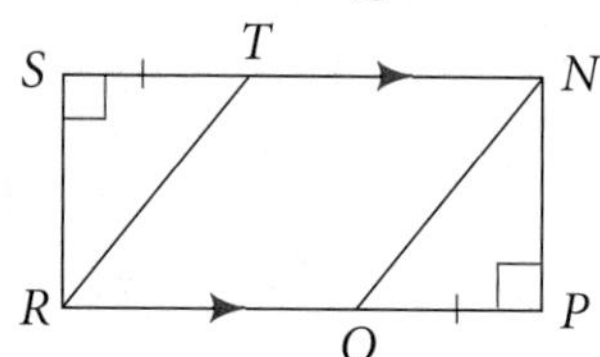

Example 2 (page 218)

Developing Proof Complete each flow proof.

11. Given: $\overline{AD} \cong \overline{CB}$, $\angle D$ and $\angle B$ are right angles.

Prove: $\triangle ADC \cong \triangle CBA$

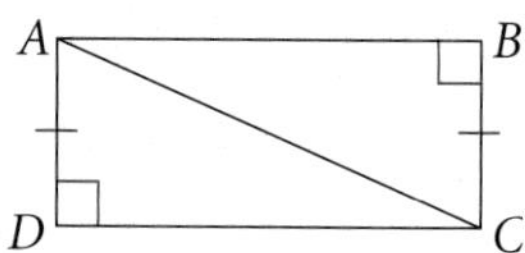

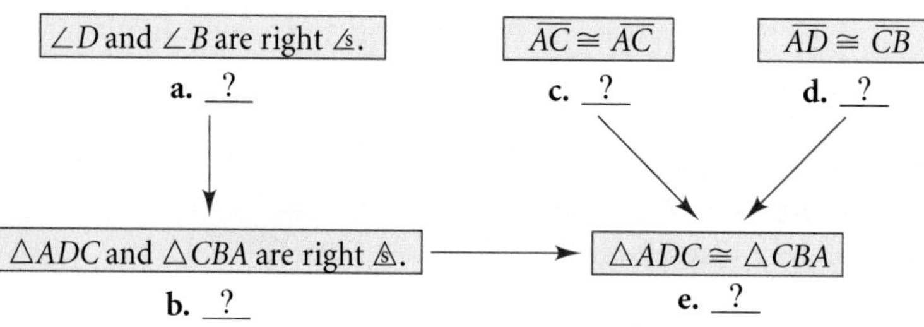

12. Given: $\overline{PS} \cong \overline{PT}$, $\angle PRS \cong \angle PRT$

Prove: $\triangle PRS \cong \triangle PRT$

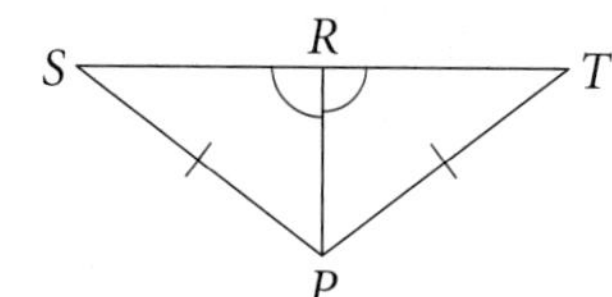

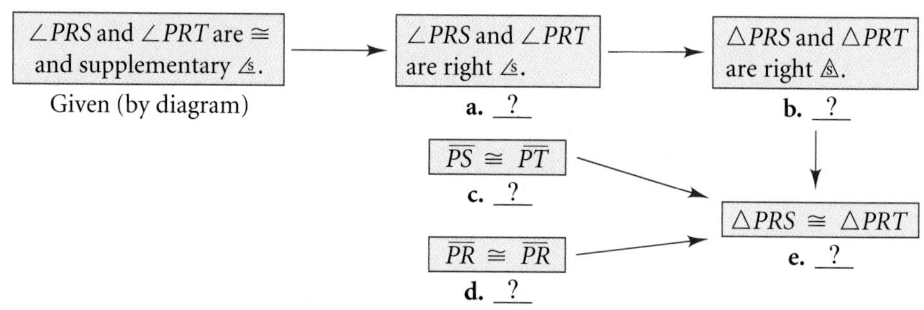

Need Help?

For Exercise 13, recall how to classify $\triangle SPT$. Then recall what is true about this type of triangle.

13. Developing Proof There is a different set of steps that will prove $\triangle PRS \cong \triangle PRT$ in Exercise 12. Decide what they are. Then write a short paragraph to explain the steps.

Developing Proof Tell whether the HL Theorem can be used to prove the two triangles congruent. If so, explain. If not, write *not possible*.

14.

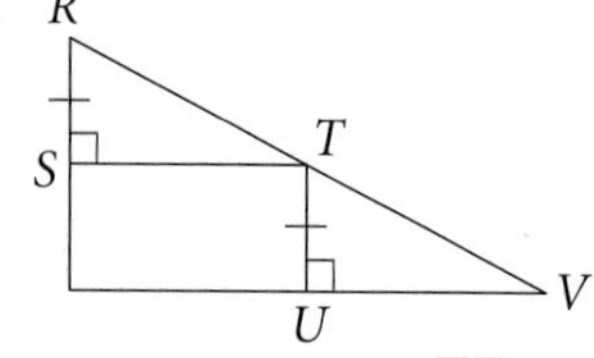

T is the midpoint of $\overline{RV}$.

15.

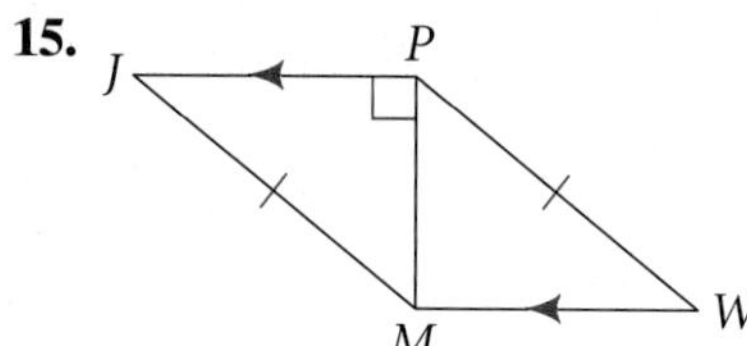

Example 3 (page 219)

Developing Proof **Complete each two-column proof.**

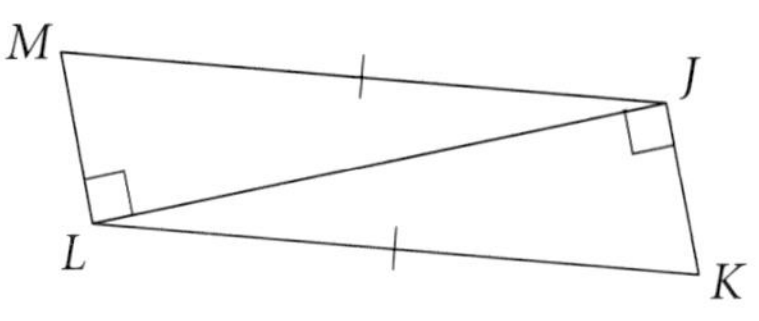

16. **Given:** $\overline{JL} \perp \overline{LM}$, $\overline{LJ} \perp \overline{JK}$, $\overline{MJ} \cong \overline{KL}$

Prove: $\triangle JLM \cong \triangle LJK$

Statements	Reasons
1. $\overline{JL} \perp \overline{LM}$ and $\overline{LJ} \perp \overline{JK}$	a. ?
2. $\angle JLM$ and $\angle LJK$ are right angles.	b. ?
c. ?	3. Definition of a right triangle
4. $\overline{MJ} \cong \overline{KL}$	d. ?
e. ?	5. Reflexive Property of Congruence
6. $\triangle JLM \cong \triangle LJK$	f. ?

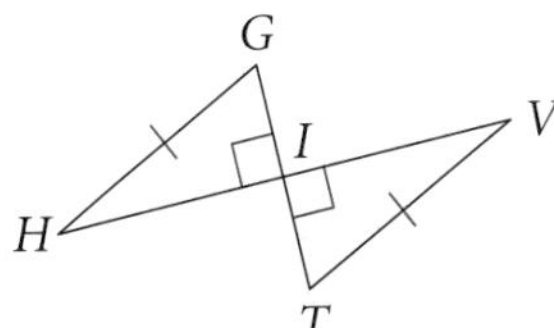

17. **Given:** $\overline{HV} \perp \overline{GT}$, $\overline{GH} \cong \overline{TV}$, I is the midpoint of $\overline{HV}$.

Prove: $\triangle IGH \cong \triangle ITV$

Statements	Reasons
1. $\overline{HV} \perp \overline{GT}$, $\overline{GH} \cong \overline{TV}$	a. ?
b. ? and $\triangle ITV$ are right triangles.	c. ?
d. ?	3. Given
4. $\overline{HI} \cong \overline{VI}$	e. ?
f. ?	5. HL Theorem

B Apply Your Skills

18. **Antiques** To repair an antique clock, a 12-toothed wheel has to be made by cutting right triangles out of a regular polygon that has twelve 4-cm sides. The hypotenuse of each triangle is a side of the regular polygon, and the shorter leg is 1 cm long. Explain why the 12 triangles must be congruent.

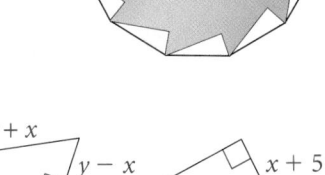

Real-World Connection

Interest in antiques and shifts in fashion have stabilized the need for dial-clock repair skills.

Algebra **In Exercises 19 and 20, for what values of x and y are the triangles congruent by HL?**

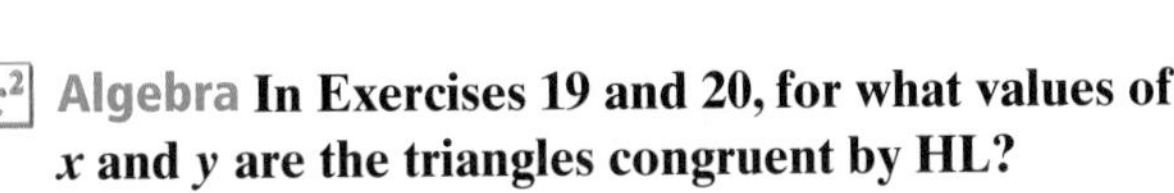

19.

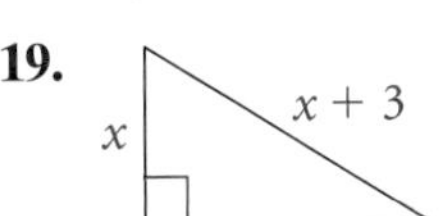

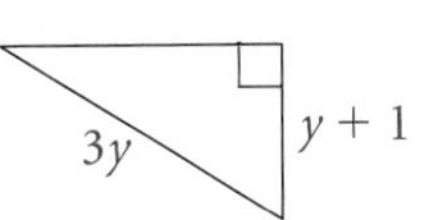

20.

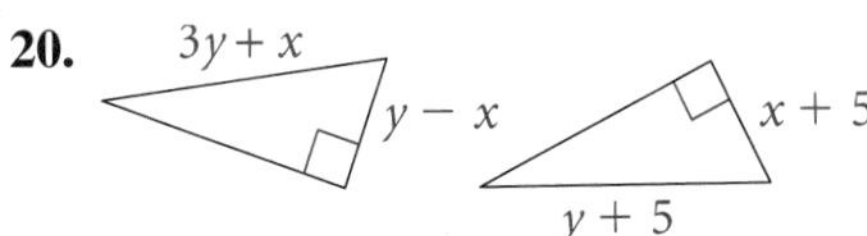

21. **Critical Thinking** While working for a landscape architect, you are told to lay out a flower bed in the shape of a right triangle with sides of 3 yd and 7 yd. Explain what else you need to know in order to make the flower bed.

22. **Reasoning** Polygon $ABCD$ has $AB = AD$, $BC = DC$, and right angles as marked. Name all the pairs of congruent right triangles in the figure. Explain why each pair is congruent.

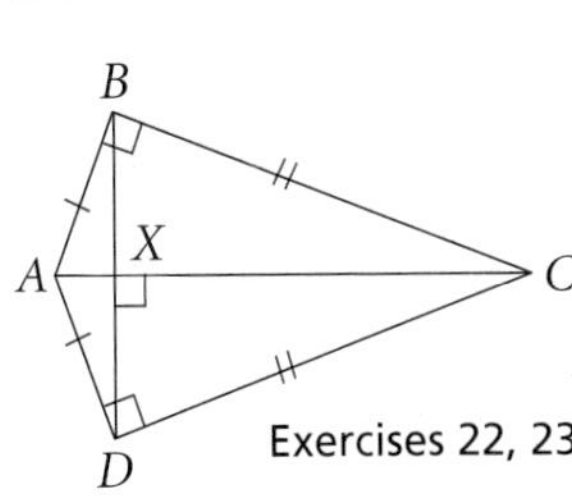

Exercises 22, 23

23. **Developing Proof** You are given what is shown in the figure, except for the right angle at X, and you are asked to prove that $\angle AXD$ is a right angle.

a. **Writing** Explain how you could complete the proof without using HL.

b. Write a paragraph proof that $\angle AXD$ must be a right angle.

Constructions **Copy the triangle and construct a triangle congruent to it using the method stated.**

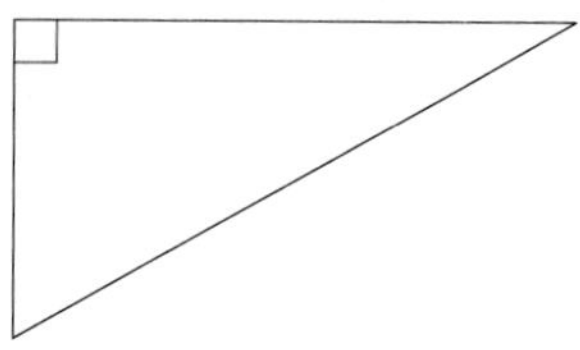

24. by SAS

25. by HL

26. by ASA

27. by SSS

Proof **Write a flow proof or a two-column proof.**

28. Given: $\overline{EB} \cong \overline{DB}$, $\angle A$ and $\angle C$ are right angles, and B is the midpoint of $\overline{AC}$.

Prove: $\triangle BEA \cong \triangle BDC$

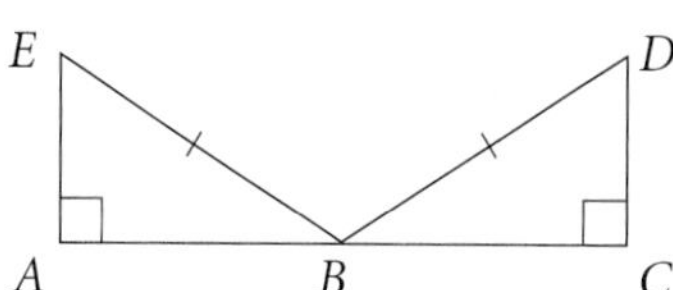

29. Given: $\overline{LO}$ bisects $\angle MLN$, $\overline{OM} \perp \overline{LM}$, and $\overline{ON} \perp \overline{LN}$.

Prove: $\triangle LMO \cong \triangle LNO$

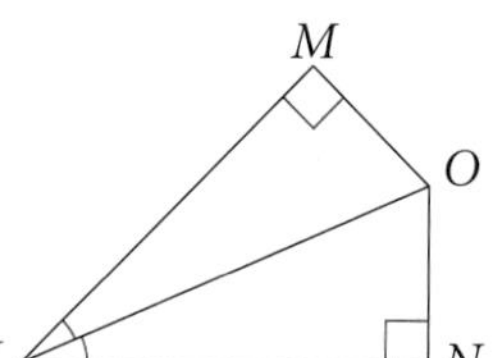

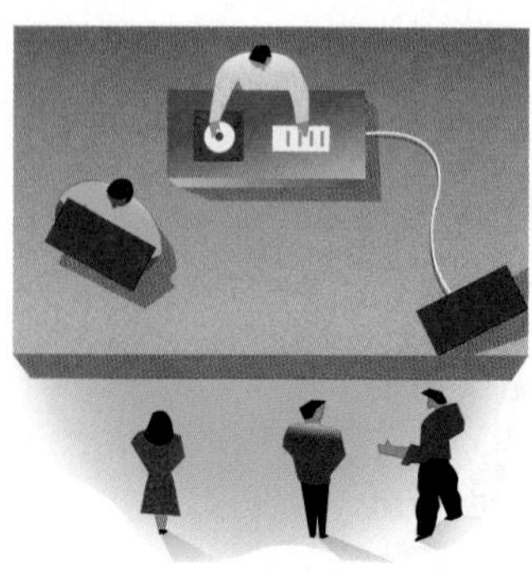

Exercise 30

30. Open-Ended You are the DJ for the school dance. To set up, you have placed one speaker in the corner of the platform. What measurement(s) could you make with a tape measure to make sure that a matching speaker is in the other corner at exactly the same angle? Explain why your method works.

31. a. Coordinate Geometry Use grid paper. Graph the points $E(-1, -1)$, $F(-2, -6)$, $G(-4, -4)$, and $D(-6, -2)$. Connect the points with segments.

b. Find the slope for each of $\overline{DG}$, $\overline{GF}$, and $\overline{GE}$.

c. Use your answer to part (b) to describe $\angle EGD$ and $\angle EGF$.

d. Use the Distance Formula to find DE and FE.

e. Write a paragraph to prove that $\triangle EGD \cong \triangle EGF$.

32. Critical Thinking "A HA!" exclaims Francis. "There is an HA Theorem . . . , something like the HL Theorem!" Explain what Francis is saying and why he is correct or incorrect.

C Challenge

Geometry in 3 Dimensions **Use the figure at the right for Exercises 33 and 34.**

Proof **33.** Write a paragraph proof.

Given: $\overline{BE} \perp \overline{EA}$, $\overline{BE} \perp \overline{EC}$, $\triangle ABC$ is equilateral.

Prove: $\triangle AEB \cong \triangle CEB$

34. Given: $\triangle AEB \cong \triangle CEB$, $\overline{BE} \perp \overline{EA}$, and $\overline{BE} \perp \overline{EC}$.
Can you prove that $\triangle ABC$ is equilateral? Explain.

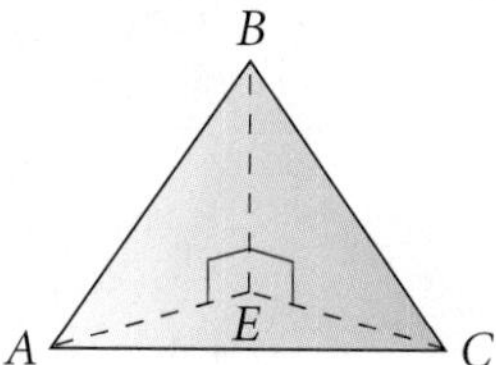

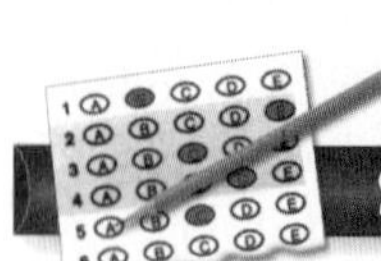

Standardized Test Prep

Multiple Choice

In Exercises 35 and 36, which additional congruence statement could you use to prove that $\triangle BJK \cong \triangle CFH$ by HL?

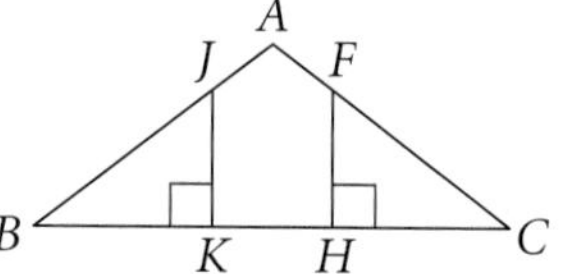

35. Given: $\overline{BJ} \cong \overline{CF}$

A. $\overline{JK} \cong \overline{FH}$ **B.** $\angle B \cong \angle C$

C. $\overline{AJ} \cong \overline{AF}$ **D.** $\angle BJK \cong \angle CFH$

36. Given: $\overline{BK} \cong \overline{CH}$

F. $\overline{JK} \cong \overline{FH}$ **G.** $\angle B \cong \angle C$ **H.** $\overline{JB} \cong \overline{FC}$ **I.** $\angle BJK \cong \angle CFH$

37. Which congruence statement can be used to prove that the two triangles are congruent?

A. SAS B. SSS
C. ASA D. HL

Short Response

38. a. Use the diagram at the right to name all the pairs of triangles you could prove congruent by using the HL Theorem.

b. Suppose you need to prove $\triangle RFW \cong \triangle RGW$. What specifically do you need to prove before you can use the HL Theorem?

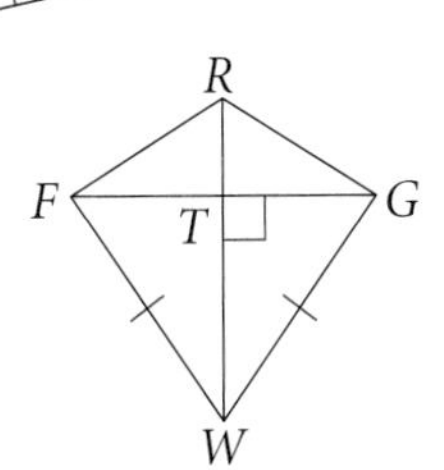

Take It to the NET
Online lesson quiz at **www.PHSchool.com**
Web Code: afa-0406

Mixed Review

Lesson 4-5

For Exercises 39 and 40, what type of triangle must $\triangle XYZ$ be?

39. $\triangle XYZ \cong \triangle ZYX$ **40.** $\triangle XYZ \cong \triangle ZXY$

Lesson 3-6

41. Connect $A(3, 3)$, $B(5, 5)$, $C(9, 1)$, and $D(9, -3)$ in order. Are any sides of the figure parallel? Are any sides perpendicular? Explain.

Lesson 3-1

State the postulate or theorem that justifies each statement.

42. $\angle 5 \cong \angle 8$ **43.** $m\angle 4 + m\angle 8 = 180$

44. $\angle 6 \cong \angle 9$ **45.** $\angle 4 \cong \angle 10$

46. $\angle 1 \cong \angle 6$ **47.** $\angle 6$ and $\angle 3$ are supplementary.

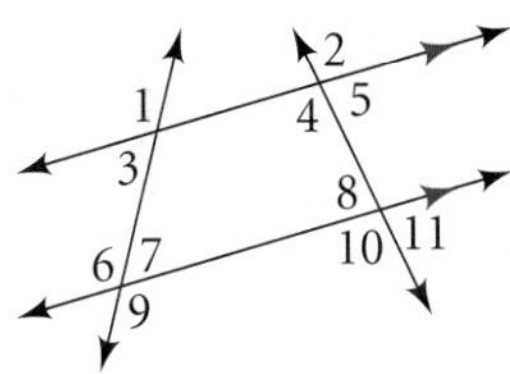

Checkpoint Quiz 2 — Lessons 4-4 Through 4-6

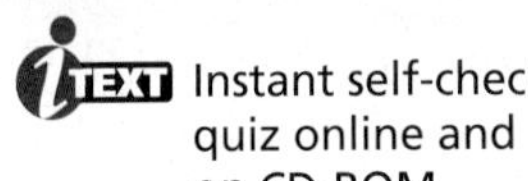
Instant self-check quiz online and on CD-ROM

1. In the diagram at the right, $\triangle PQR \cong \triangle SRQ$ by SAS. What other pairs of sides and angles can you conclude are congruent by CPCTC?

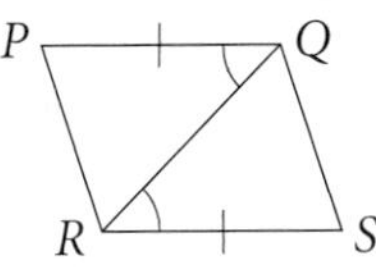

2. Complete the plan for a proof.

Given: Isosceles $\triangle JKL$ with $\overline{JK} \cong \overline{JL}$; $\overline{KM}$ and $\overline{LM}$ are bisectors of the base angles.

Prove: $\triangle KML$ is isosceles.

Plan: Since $\triangle JKL$ is isosceles, $\angle JKL \cong \angle JLK$ by the **a.** _?_ Theorem. Since $\overline{KM}$ and $\overline{LM}$ are angle bisectors, $\angle MKL$ **b.** _?_ $\angle MLK$. Therefore, $\triangle KML$ is isosceles by the **c.** _?_ Theorem.

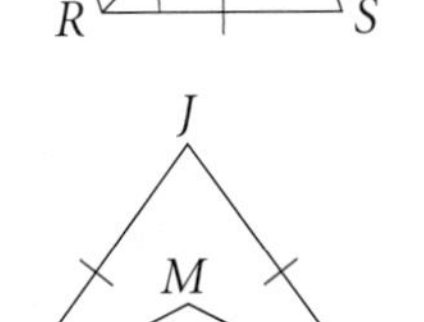

3. Six triangles are pictured in the diagram at the left. Which of the triangles are isosceles? Explain.

E
A B C D
Exercise 3

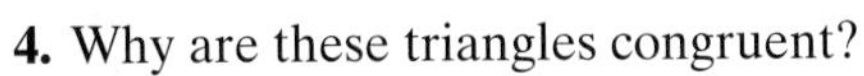

4. Why are these triangles congruent? **5.** Explain why $\overline{GW} \cong \overline{ST}$.

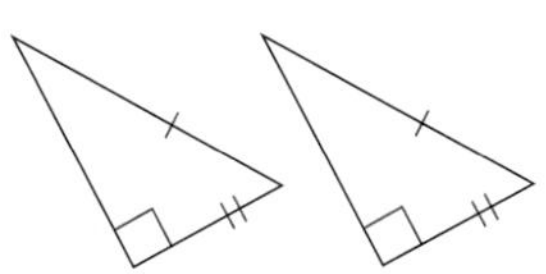

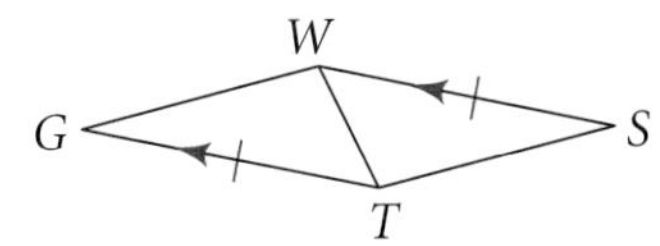

Using Corresponding Parts of Congruent Triangles

Lesson Preview

What You'll Learn

To identify congruent overlapping triangles

To prove two triangles congruent by first proving two other triangles congruent

... And Why

To identify overlapping triangles in scaffolding, as in Example 1

Check Skills You'll Need

(For help, go to Lessons 1-1 and 4-3.)

1. How many triangles will the next two figures in this pattern have?

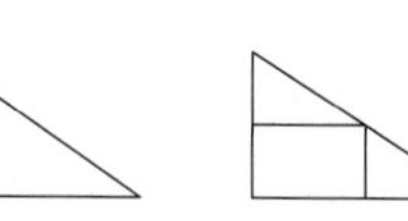

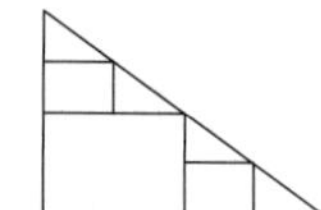

2. Can you conclude that the triangles are congruent? Explain.
   a. $\triangle AZK$ and $\triangle DRS$ b. $\triangle SDR$ and $\triangle JTN$ c. $\triangle ZKA$ and $\triangle NJT$

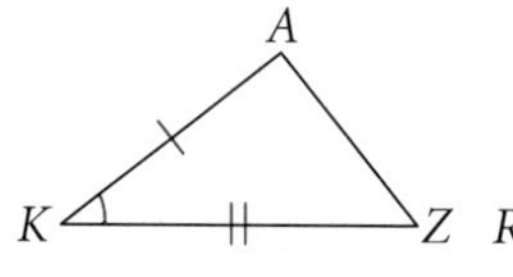

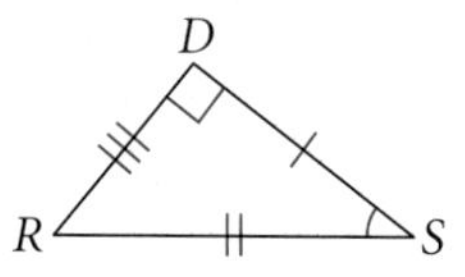

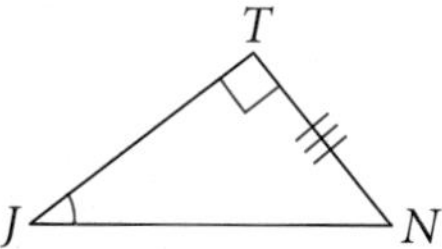

Interactive lesson includes instant self-check, tutorials, and activities.

OBJECTIVE 1

Using Overlapping Triangles in Proofs

Reading Math

Overlapping triangles share part or all of one or more sides.

Some triangle relationships are difficult to see because the triangles overlap. Overlapping triangles may have a common side or angle. You can simplify your work with overlapping triangles by separating and redrawing the triangles.

1 EXAMPLE Identifying Common Parts

Separate and redraw $\triangle DFG$ and $\triangle EHG$. Identify the common angle.

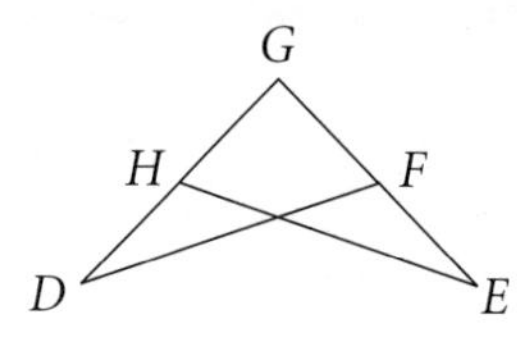

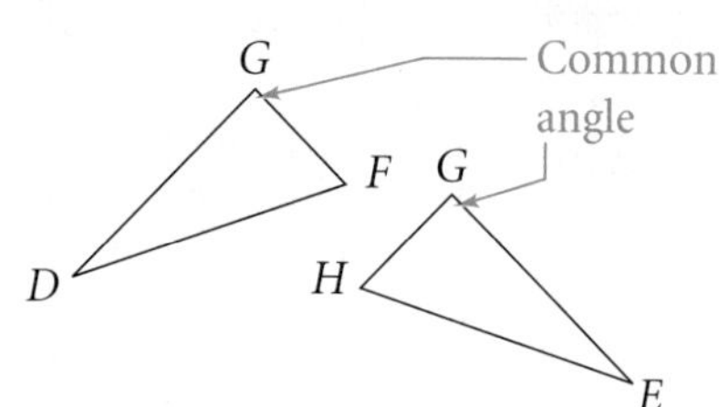

Check Understanding

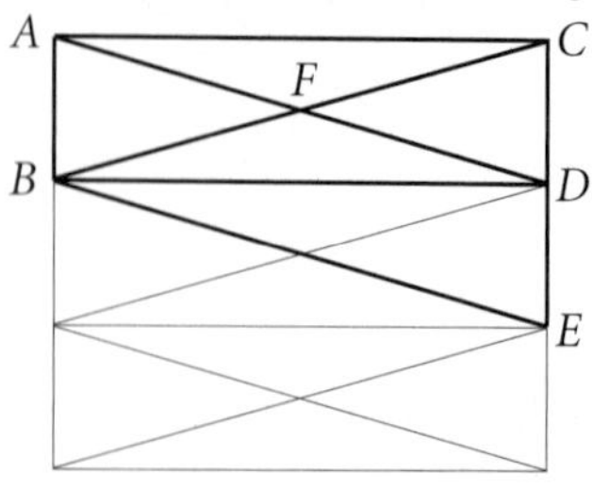

1. **Engineering** The diagram at the left shows triangles from the scaffolding that workers used when they repaired and cleaned the Statue of Liberty.
   a. Name the common side in $\triangle ADC$ and $\triangle BCD$.
   b. Name another pair of triangles that share a common side. Name the common side.

In overlapping triangles, a common side or angle is congruent to itself by the Reflexive Property of Congruence.

Proof

2 EXAMPLE Proving Two Segments Congruent

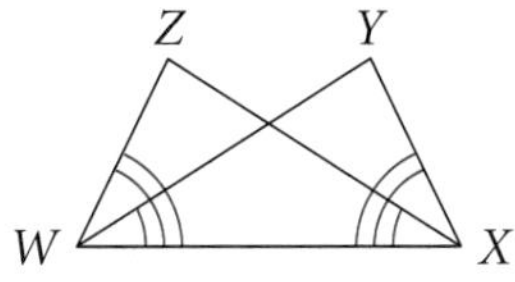

Given: $\angle ZXW \cong \angle YWX$, $\angle ZWX \cong \angle YXW$

Write a plan and then a flow proof to show that the two "outside" segments are congruent.

Prove: $\overline{ZW} \cong \overline{YX}$

Plan: First, separate the overlapping triangles. $\overline{ZW} \cong \overline{YX}$ by CPCTC if $\triangle ZXW \cong \triangle YWX$. Show this congruence by ASA.

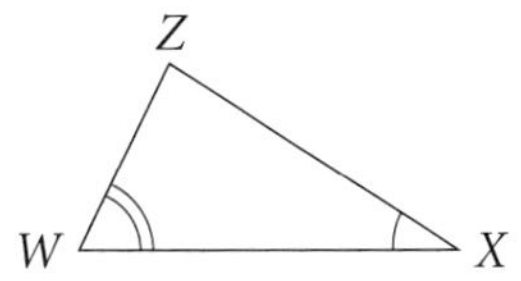

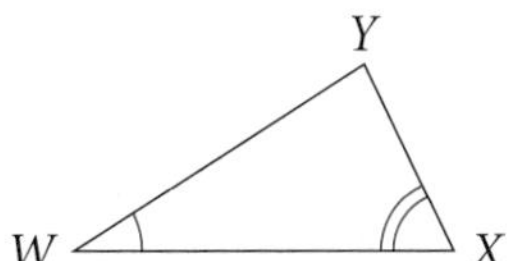

Proof:

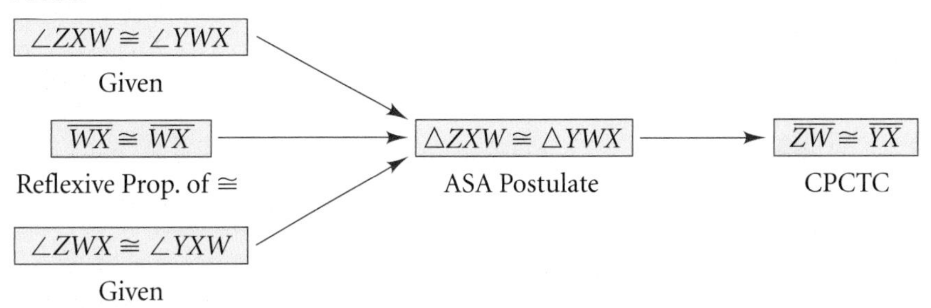

Check Understanding 2 Plan a proof. Then follow your plan and write a proof in paragraph, flow, or two-column form.

Given: $\triangle ACD \cong \triangle BDC$

Prove: $\overline{CE} \cong \overline{DE}$

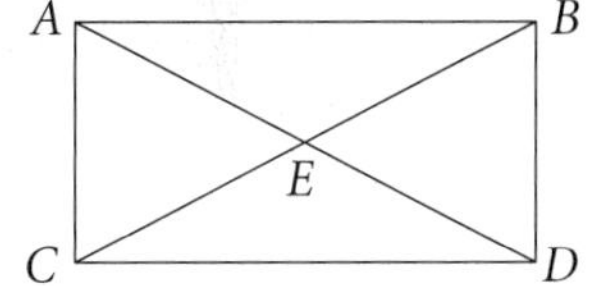

OBJECTIVE

2 Using Two Pairs of Congruent Triangles

Sometimes you can prove one pair of triangles congruent and then use their congruent corresponding parts to prove another pair congruent.

Proof

3 EXAMPLE Using SAS and Then ASA

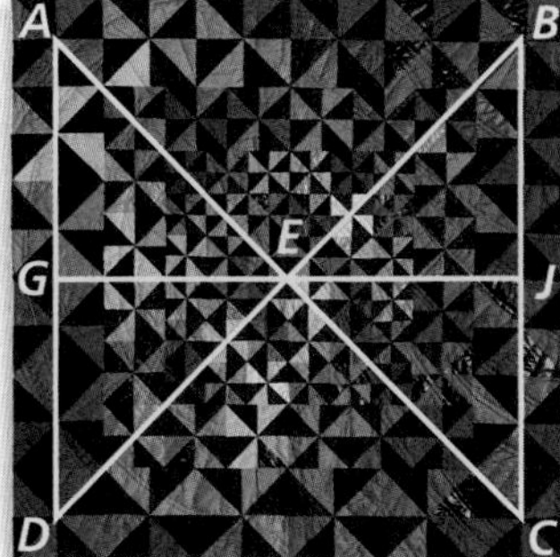

Given: In the quilt, E is the midpoint of $\overline{AC}$ and $\overline{DB}$.

Prove: $\triangle GED \cong \triangle JEB$

Write a plan and then a paragraph proof.

Plan: $\triangle GED \cong \triangle JEB$ by ASA if $\angle D \cong \angle B$. These angles are congruent by CPCTC if $\triangle AED \cong \triangle CEB$. These triangles are congruent by SAS.

Proof: E is the midpoint of $\overline{AC}$ and $\overline{DB}$, so $\overline{AE} \cong \overline{CE}$ and $\overline{DE} \cong \overline{BE}$. $\angle AED \cong \angle CEB$ because vertical angles are congruent. Therefore, $\triangle AED \cong \triangle CEB$ by SAS. $\angle D \cong \angle B$ by CPCTC, and $\angle GED \cong \angle JEB$ because they are vertical angles. Therefore, $\triangle GED \cong \triangle JEB$ by ASA.

Check Understanding 3 Plan a proof. Then follow your plan and write a proof in paragraph, flow, or two-column form.

Given: $\overline{PS} \cong \overline{RS}$, $\angle PSQ \cong \angle RSQ$

Prove: $\triangle QPT \cong \triangle QRT$

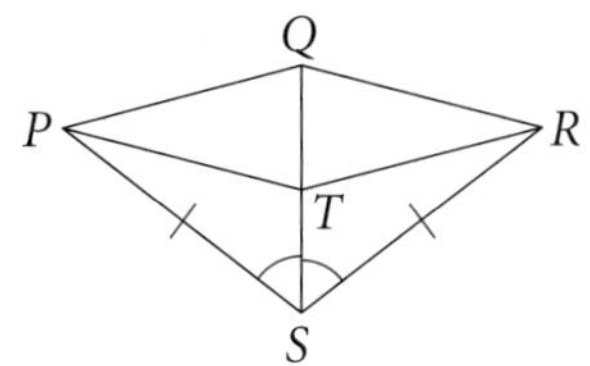

When triangles overlap, you can keep track of information by drawing other diagrams that separate the overlapping triangles.

Proof 4 EXAMPLE Separating Overlapping Triangles

Given: $\overline{CA} \cong \overline{CE}$, $\overline{BA} \cong \overline{DE}$

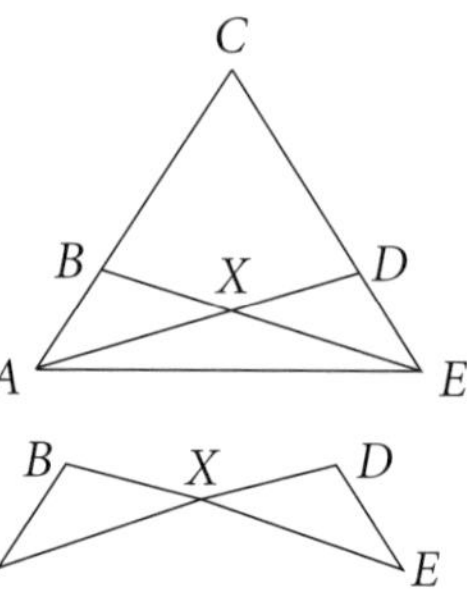

Write a plan and then a two-column proof to show that two small segments inside the triangle are congruent.

Prove: $\overline{BX} \cong \overline{DX}$

Plan: $\overline{BX} \cong \overline{DX}$ by CPCTC if $\triangle BXA \cong \triangle DXE$. This congruence holds by AAS if $\angle ABX \cong \angle EDX$. These are congruent by CPCTC in $\triangle BAE$ and $\triangle DEA$, which are congruent by SAS.

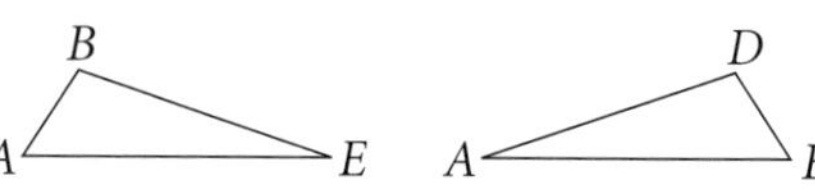

Proof:

Statements	Reasons
1. $\overline{BA} \cong \overline{DE}$	1. Given
2. $\overline{CA} \cong \overline{CE}$	2. Given
3. $\angle CAE \cong \angle CEA$	3. Isosceles Triangle Theorem
4. $\overline{AE} \cong \overline{AE}$	4. Reflexive Property of Congruence
5. $\triangle BAE \cong \triangle DEA$	5. SAS
6. $\angle ABE \cong \angle EDA$	6. CPCTC
7. $\angle BXA \cong \angle DXE$	7. Vertical angles are congruent.
8. $\triangle BXA \cong \triangle DXE$	8. AAS
9. $\overline{BX} \cong \overline{DX}$	9. CPCTC

Real-World Connection

The Japanese paper-folding art of origami involves many overlapping triangles.

Check Understanding **4** Plan a proof. Separate the overlapping triangles in your plan. Then follow your plan and write a proof.

Given: $\angle CAD \cong \angle EAD$, $\angle C \cong \angle E$

Prove: $\overline{BD} \cong \overline{FD}$

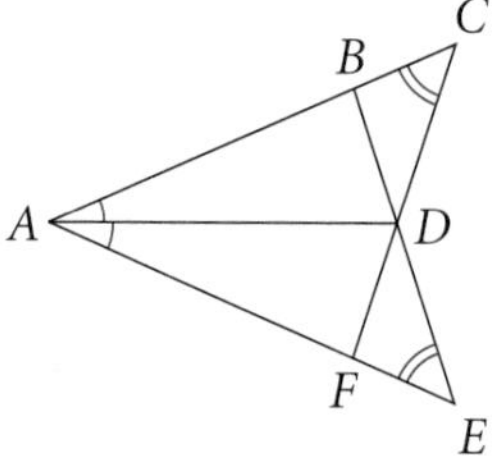

EXERCISES

For more practice, see *Extra Practice*.

Practice and Problem Solving

Practice by Example

Example 1 (page 224)

In each diagram, the red and blue triangles are congruent. Identify their common side or angle.

1. 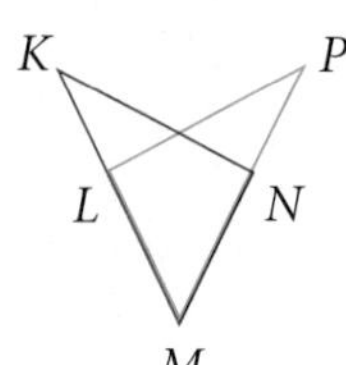

2. 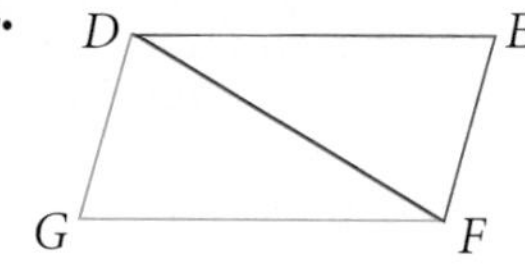

3. 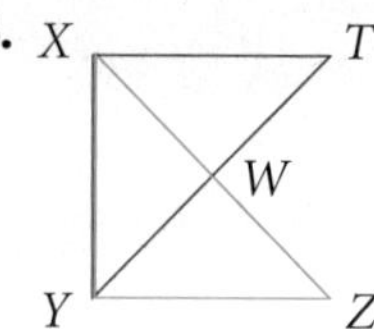

Separate and redraw the indicated triangles. Identify any common angles or sides.

4. $\triangle PQS$ and $\triangle QPR$

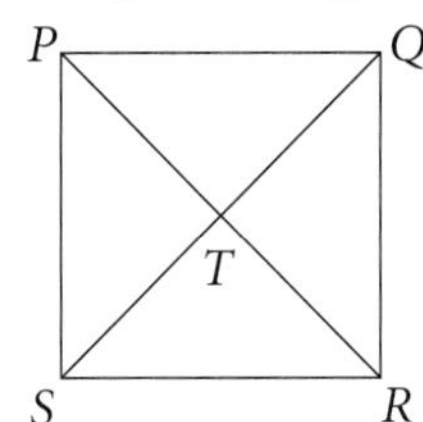

5. $\triangle ACB$ and $\triangle PRB$

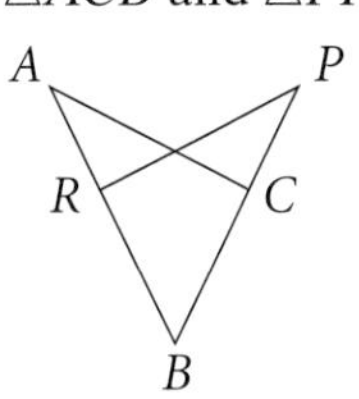

6. $\triangle TRQ$ and $\triangle PQR$

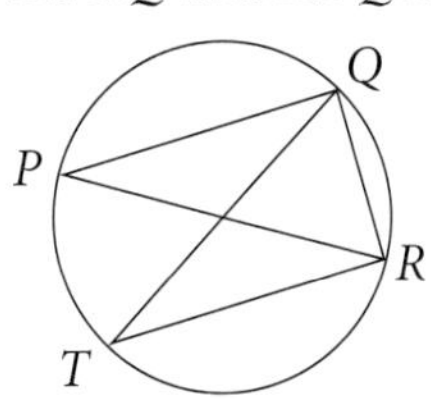

7. $\triangle ABE$ and $\triangle BAC$

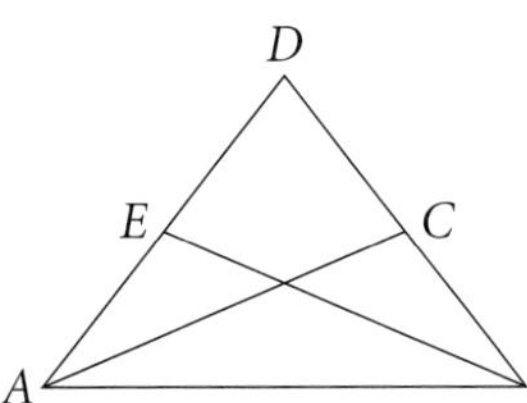

8. $\triangle JKL$ and $\triangle MLK$

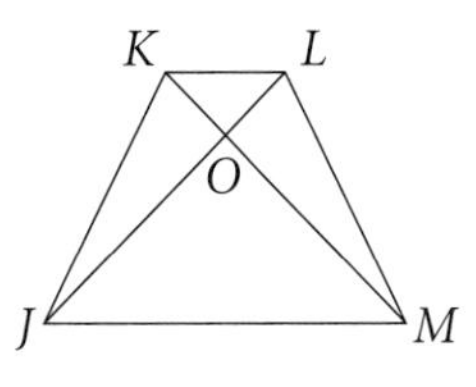

9. $\triangle PSU$ and $\triangle QVT$

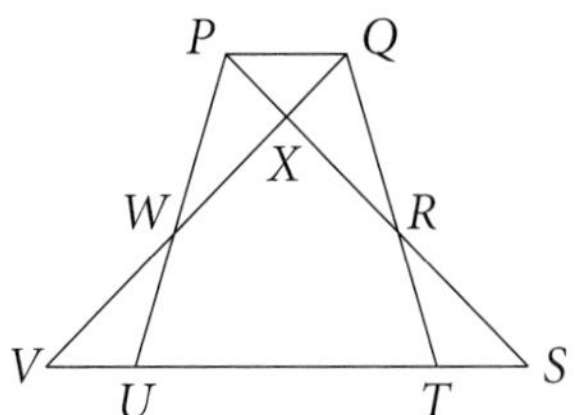

Example 2 (page 225)

10. Developing Proof Complete the flow proof.

Given: $\angle T \cong \angle R$, $\overline{PQ} \cong \overline{PV}$

Prove: $\angle PQT \cong \angle PVR$

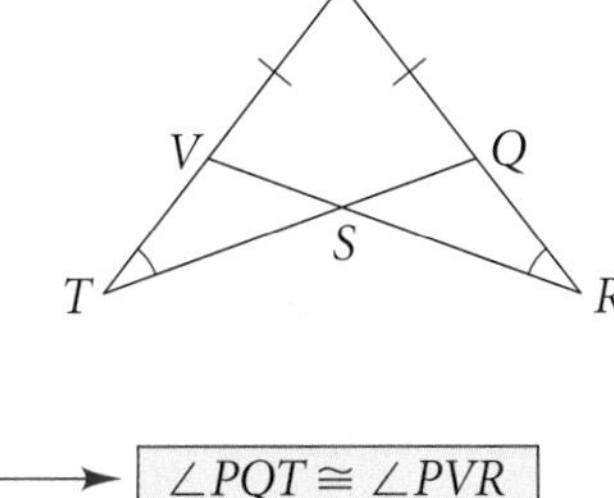

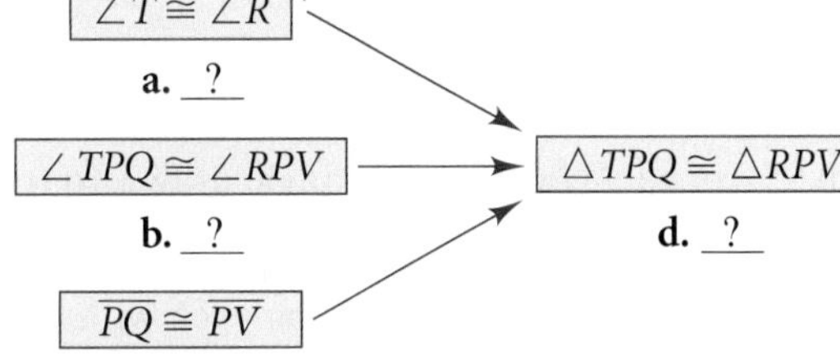

Developing Proof **Name a pair of overlapping congruent triangles in each diagram. State whether the triangles are congruent by SSS, SAS, ASA, AAS, or HL.**

11. Given: $\overline{MP} \cong \overline{QL}$, $\overline{LP} \perp \overline{LM}$, $\overline{LP} \perp \overline{PQ}$

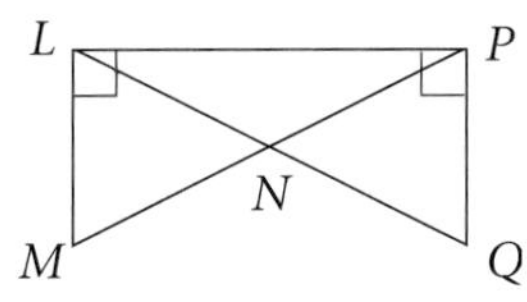

12. Given: $\overline{RS} \cong \overline{UT}$, $\overline{RT} \cong \overline{US}$

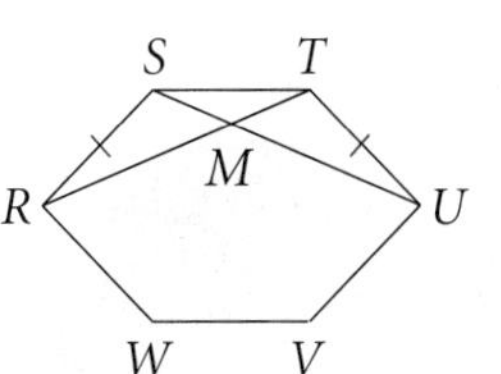

13. Given: $\overline{QD} \cong \overline{UA}$, $\angle QDA \cong \angle UAD$

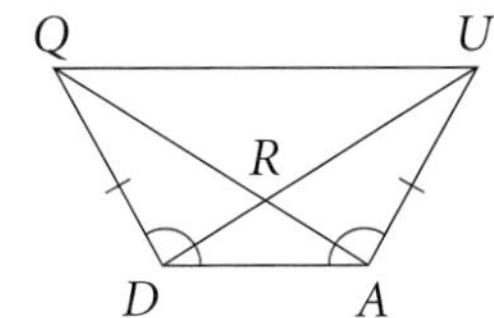

14. Given: $\overline{PQ} \parallel \overline{UR}$, $\overline{TQ} \parallel \overline{SR}$, $\overline{TQ} \cong \overline{SR}$

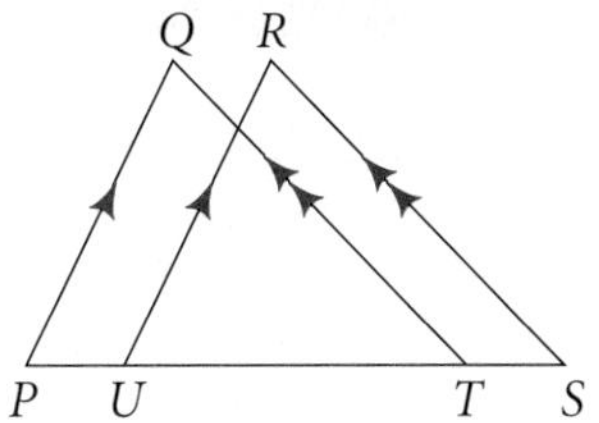

Examples 3, 4 (pages 225 and 226)

Developing Proof **Plan a proof. As part of your plan, separate the overlapping triangles you use.**

15. Given: $\overline{TE} \cong \overline{RI}$, $\overline{TI} \cong \overline{RE}$, $\angle TDI$ and $\angle ROE$ are right ∡s.

Prove: $\overline{TD} \cong \overline{RO}$

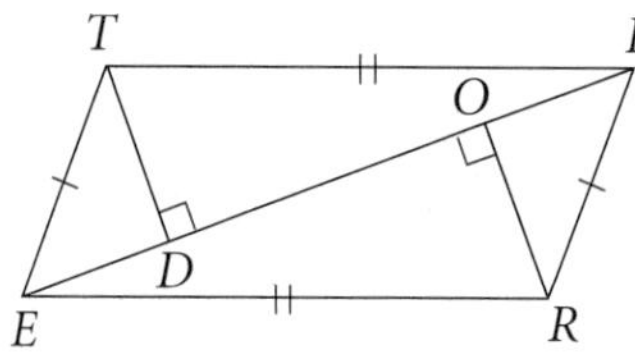

16. Given: $\overline{AB} \perp \overline{BC}$, $\overline{DC} \perp \overline{BC}$, $\overline{AC} \cong \overline{DB}$

Prove: $\overline{AE} \cong \overline{DE}$

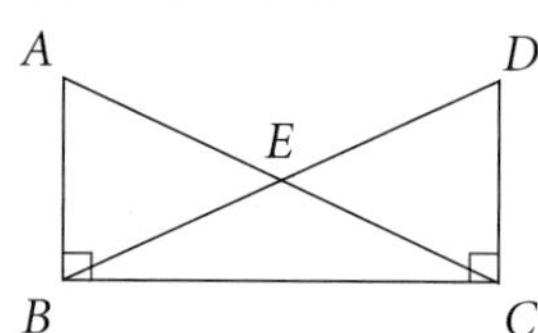

17. Given: $\angle 1 \cong \angle 2$, $\angle 3 \cong \angle 4$

Prove: $\triangle QET \cong \triangle QEU$

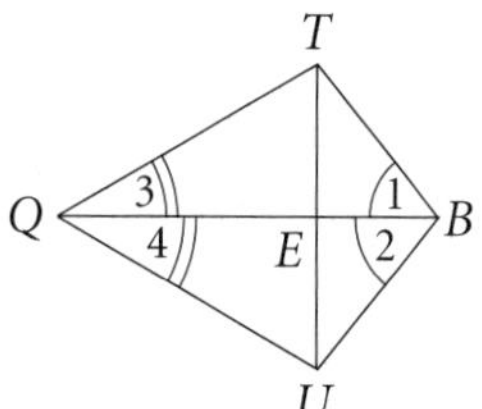

18. Given: $\overline{AD} \cong \overline{ED}$, D is the midpoint of $\overline{BF}$.

Prove: $\triangle ADC \cong \triangle EDG$

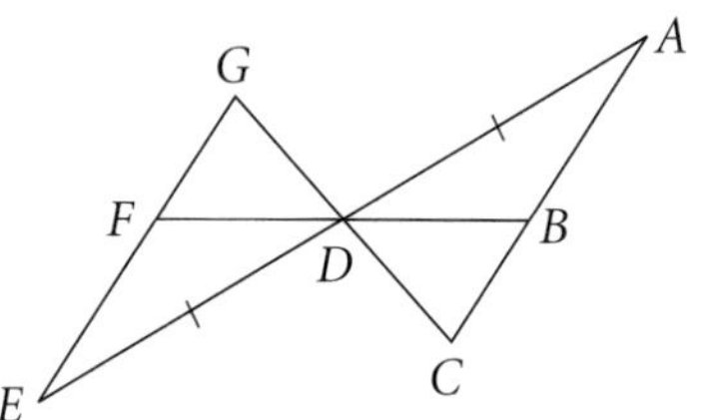

B Apply Your Skills

Open-Ended **Draw the diagram described.**

19. Draw a vertical segment on your paper. On the right side of the segment draw two triangles that share the given segment as a common side.

20. Draw an angle. On your angle draw two triangles that have the given angle as a common angle.

21. Draw two regular pentagons, each with its five diagonals.
a. In one, shade two triangles that share a common angle.
b. In the other, shade two triangles that share a common side.

22. Draw two regular hexagons and their diagonals. For these diagrams, do parts (a) and (b) of the preceding exercise.

Real-World Connection

Careers A clothing designer must carefully measure angles and segments to create a sewing pattern.

Proof **Name a pair of overlapping congruent triangles in each diagram. State whether the triangles are congruent by SSS, SAS, ASA, AAS, or HL. Plan and write a proof.**

23. Given:

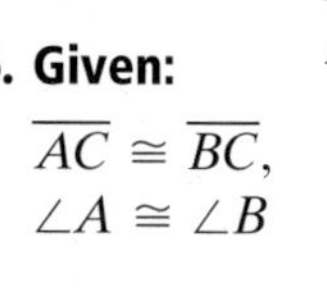

$\overline{AC} \cong \overline{BC}$, $\angle A \cong \angle B$

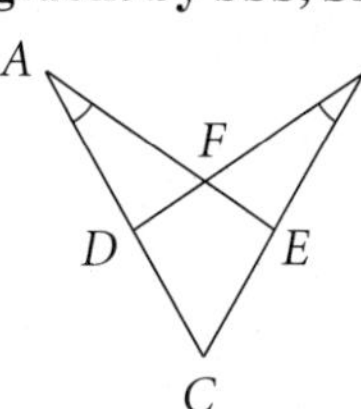

24. Given:

$\overline{WY} \perp \overline{YX}$, $\overline{ZX} \perp \overline{YX}$, $\overline{WX} \cong \overline{ZY}$

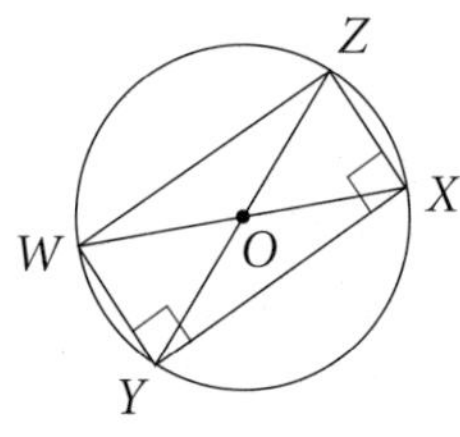

Clothes Design **The figure at the right is part of a clothing design pattern. In the figure, $\overline{AB} \parallel \overline{DE} \parallel \overline{FG}$, $\overline{AB} \perp \overline{BC}$, and $\overline{GC} \perp \overline{AC}$. $\triangle DEC$ is isosceles with base $\overline{DC}$, and $m\angle A = 56$.**

25. Find the measures of all the numbered angles in the figure.

26. $\overline{AB} \cong \overline{FC}$. Name two congruent triangles and tell how you can prove them congruent.

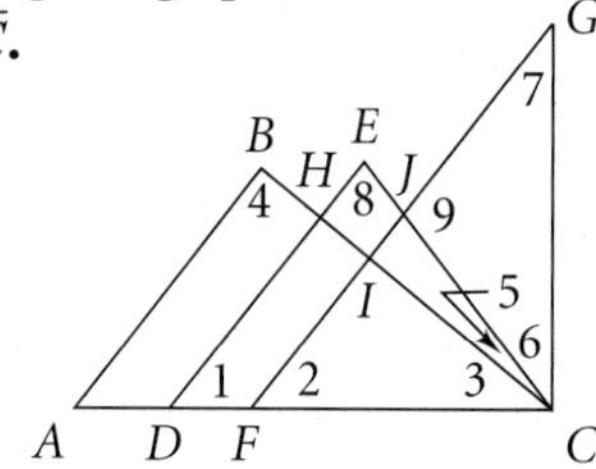

Developing Proof **Exercises 27 and 28 are proofs for Exercises 15 and 16. Copy and complete each proof. Does the proof match your plan?**

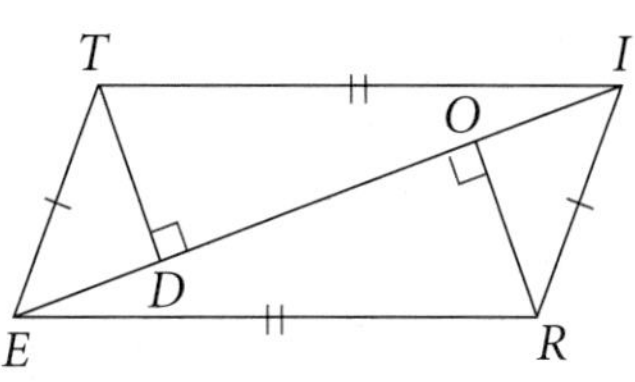

27. Given: $\overline{TE} \cong \overline{RI}, \overline{TI} \cong \overline{RE}$, $\angle TDI$ and $\angle ROE$ are right angles.

Prove: $\overline{TD} \cong \overline{RO}$

Need Help?

In each of Exercises 27 and 28, use CPCTC twice.

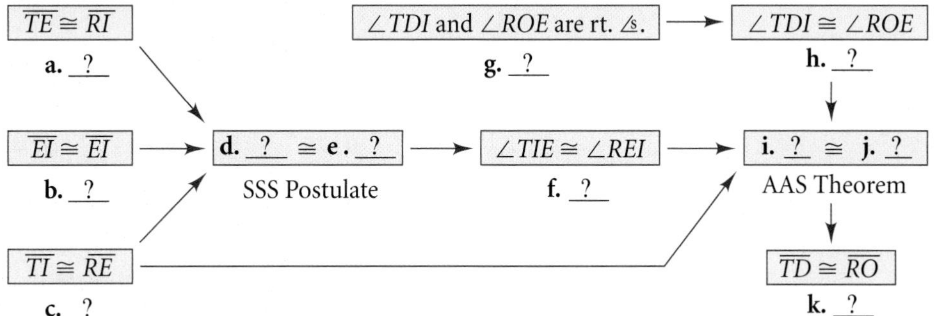

28. Given: $\overline{AB} \perp \overline{BC}$, $\overline{DC} \perp \overline{BC}$, $\overline{AC} \cong \overline{DB}$

Prove: $\overline{AE} \cong \overline{DE}$

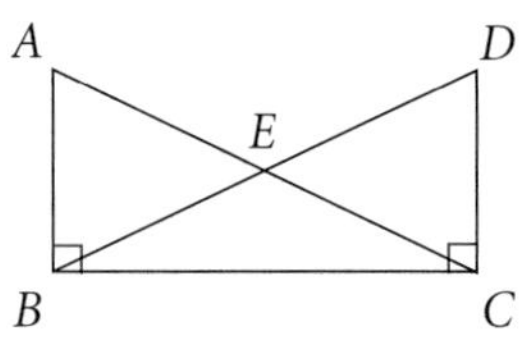

Statements	Reasons
1. $\overline{AB} \perp \overline{BC}$, $\overline{DC} \perp \overline{BC}$	a. ?
2. $\angle ABC$ and $\angle DCB$ are right angles.	b. ?
3. $\triangle ABC$ and $\triangle DCB$ are right triangles.	c. ?
4. $\overline{AC} \cong \overline{DB}$	d. ?
e. ? ≅ ?	f. ? Property of Congruence
6. $\triangle ABC \cong \triangle DCB$	g. ?
7. $\angle A \cong \angle D$, $\overline{AB} \cong \overline{DC}$	h. ?
i. $\angle AEB \cong \angle$?	j. ?
9. $\triangle ABE \cong \triangle DCE$	k. ?
l. ? ≅ ?	m. ?

Proof **Follow your plan for the given Exercise and write a proof.**

29. Exercise 17

30. Exercise 18

Challenge

31. Reasoning Draw a quadrilateral $ABCD$ with $\overline{AB} \parallel \overline{DC}$ and $\overline{AD} \parallel \overline{BC}$, and its diagonals $\overline{AC}$ and $\overline{DB}$ intersecting at E. Label your diagram to indicate the parallel sides.

a. List all the pairs of congruent segments that you can find in your diagram.

b. Writing Explain how you know that the segments you listed are congruent.

Proof **Write a proof.**

32. Given: $\overline{AC} \cong \overline{EC}, \overline{CB} \cong \overline{CD}$

Prove: $\angle A \cong \angle E$

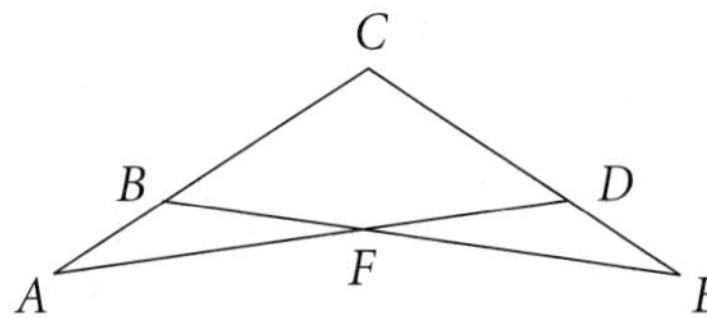

33. Given: $\overline{QT} \perp \overline{PR}$, $\overline{QT}$ bisects $\overline{PR}$, $\overline{QT}$ bisects $\angle VQS$.

Prove: $\overline{VQ} \cong \overline{SQ}$

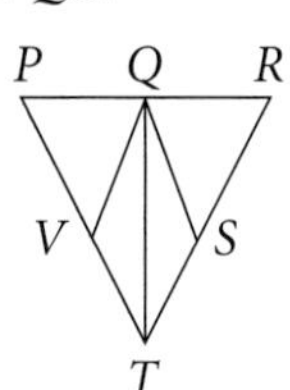

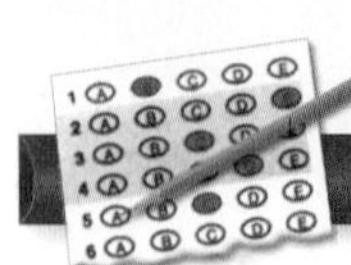

Standardized Test Prep

Multiple Choice

Use the diagram at the right for Exercises 34–36.

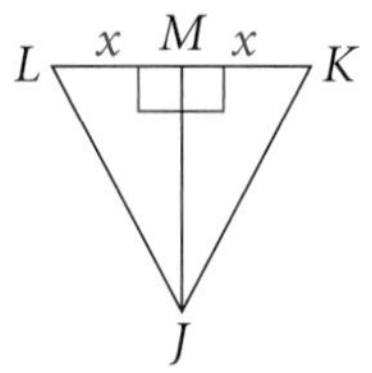

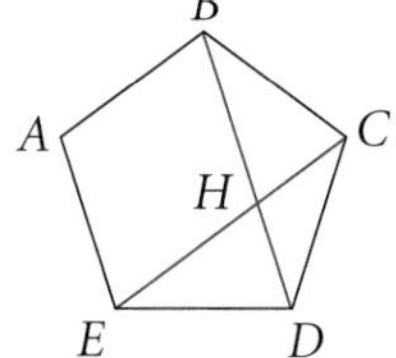

34. If $m\angle KJM = 25$, what is $m\angle LKJ$?
A. 25 **B.** 30 **C.** 65 **D.** 85

35. If $m\angle KJM = 30$ and $x = 7.4$, what is the perimeter of $\triangle LKJ$?
F. 44.4 **G.** 22.2 **H.** 14.8 **I.** 7.4

36. If $m\angle LJK = 47$, what is $m\angle LJM$?
A. 23.5 **B.** 25 **C.** 43 **D.** 47

Short Response

37. The pentagon at the right is equilateral and equiangular.
a. What two triangles must be congruent to prove $\overline{HB} \cong \overline{HE}$?
b. Plan a proof to show $\overline{HB} \cong \overline{HE}$.

B
A C
H
E D

Extended Response

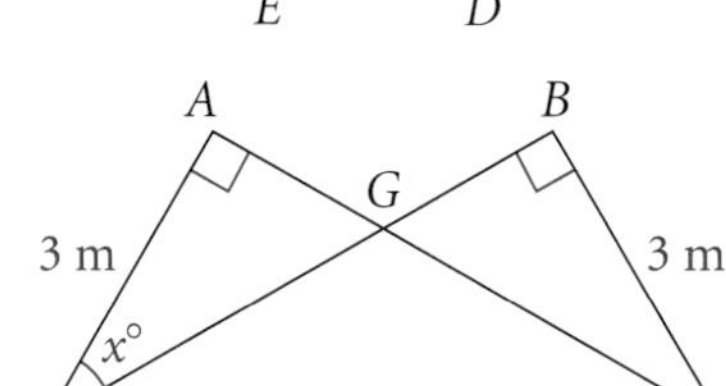

38. **a.** In the figure at the right, why is $\triangle ACD \cong \triangle BDC$?
b. Copy the figure. Mark each angle that has measure x.
c. What is the value of x? Explain how you found your answer.
d. What is $m\angle AGB$?
e. What is CD? Explain your answer.

Take It to the NET
Online lesson quiz at
www.PHSchool.com
Web Code: afa-0407

Mixed Review

Lesson 4-6

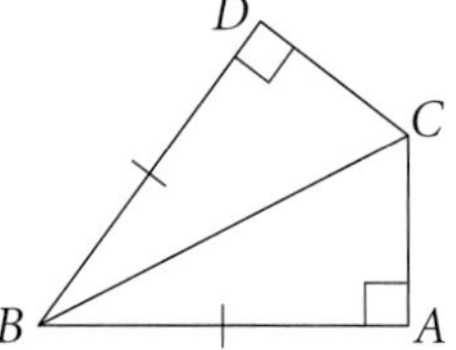

39. Complete the plan for a proof.

Given: $\angle A$ and $\angle D$ are right angles, $\overline{AB} \cong \overline{DB}$.
Prove: $\triangle ABC \cong \triangle DBC$

Plan: $\triangle ABC$ and $\triangle DBC$ are **a.** __?__ triangles with legs that are given to be **b.** __?__. The hypotenuse is congruent to itself by the **c.** __?__ Property of Congruence. $\triangle ABC \cong \triangle DBC$ by the **d.** __?__ Theorem.

Lesson 3-7

Constructions **Draw a line p and a point M not on p. Construct the described line.**

40. line n through M so that $n \perp p$ **41.** line r through M so that $r \parallel p$

Lesson 3-5

Write an equation in point-slope form of the line that contains the given point and has the given slope.

42. $P(2, -6)$; slope $\frac{1}{2}$ **43.** $Q(0, 5)$; slope 1

44. $R(-3, 6)$; slope -2 **45.** $S(0, 0)$; slope $-\frac{1}{3}$

Write an equation in point-slope form of the line that contains the given points.

46. $A(1, 4), B(0, 2)$ **47.** $E(3, -5), F(6, 0)$ **48.** $X(-4, -3), Y(2, -8)$

Extension

Writing Flow Proofs

For Use With Lesson 4-7

Proofs can get long and complex. While a two-column proof may appear more organized, a flow proof can show the logic flow better and thus be easier to follow.

To write a flow proof, sketch the logic "paths" of a proof on scratch paper. Then organize your work into a neat, easy-to-follow flow diagram, as in this Example.

EXAMPLE

Given: $\overline{KJ} \cong \overline{LM}$, $\angle KJN \cong \angle LMN$, $\overline{JN} \cong \overline{MN}$

Prove: $\overline{JL} \cong \overline{MK}$

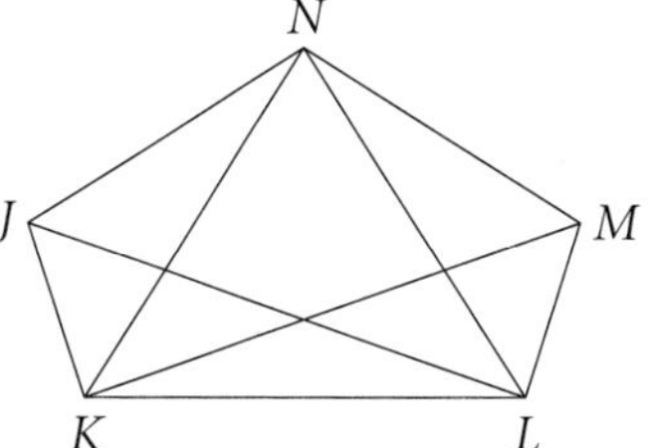

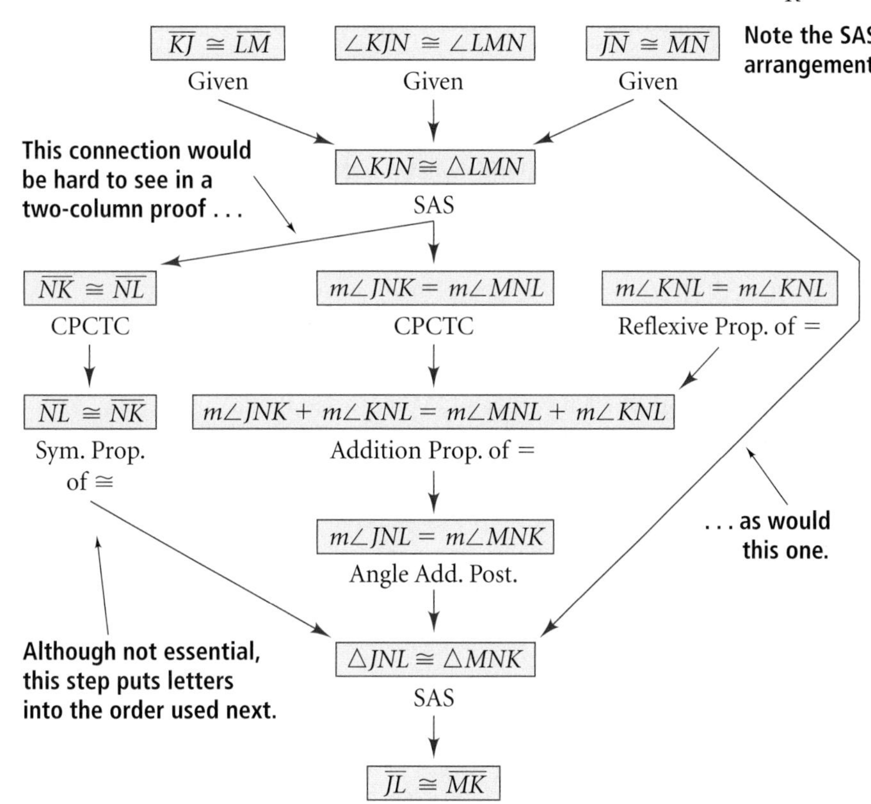

EXERCISES

Write a flow proof. Make the flow of logic as easy to follow as you can.

1. **Given:** $\overline{AB} \cong \overline{DC}$, E is the midpoint of $\overline{AD}$, and $\overline{CE} \cong \overline{BE}$.

   Prove: $\overline{AC} \cong \overline{DB}$

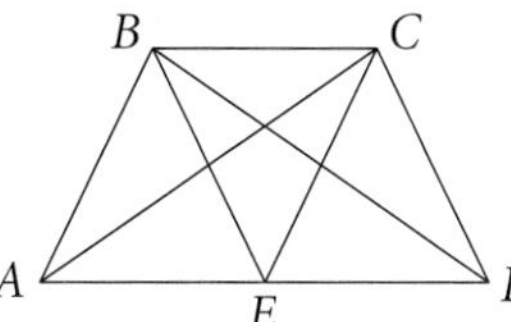

2. **Given:** $\overline{RQ} \cong \overline{RS}$, $\overline{RP} \cong \overline{RT}$, $\overline{QP} \cong \overline{ST}$

   Prove: $\overline{QT} \cong \overline{SP}$

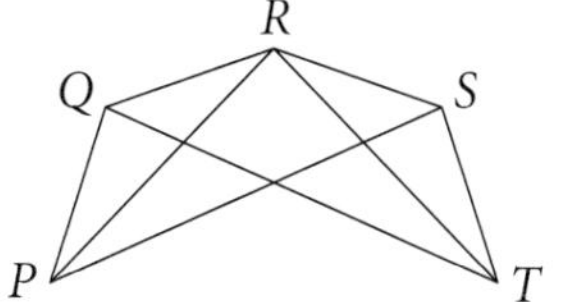

Test-Taking Strategies: Making Quantitative Comparisons

For a Quantitative Comparison test item, you must compare two given quantities. You have to decide which quantity is greater, that the two quantities are equal, or that there is not enough information to make a comparison. You must read the directions carefully and understand the two uses of each capital letter A and B.

EXAMPLE Comparing Quantities That Look Equal

Compare the boxed quantity in Column A with the boxed quantity in Column B. Choose the best answer.

A. The quantity in Column A is greater.
B. The quantity in Column B is greater.
C. The two quantities are equal.
D. The relationship cannot be determined from the information given.

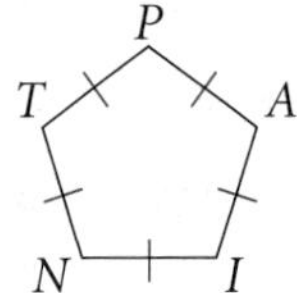

Remember: A diagram can show what *may* be true. You decide what *must* be true.

Column A	Column B
$m\angle N$	$m\angle T$

The given pentagon has congruent sides. It may have congruent angles (as the diagram suggests). However, imagine a hinge at each vertex and you can see that a pentagon can be equilateral without being equiangular. The best answer is D.

EXERCISES

x^2 Algebra **Compare the quantity in Column A with the quantity in Column B. Choose the best answer from those listed in the Example. Justify your answer.**

1.

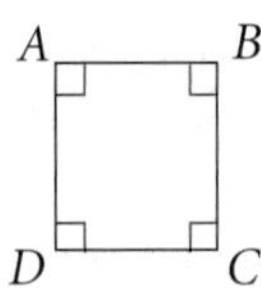

Column A	Column B
AB	BC

2.

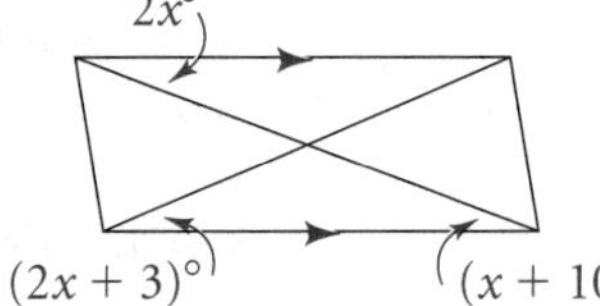

Column A	Column B
x	5

3.

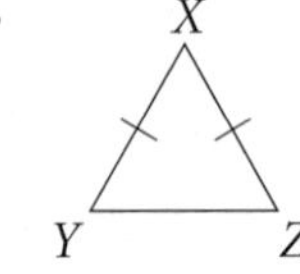

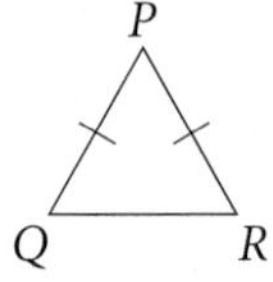

Column A	Column B
XZ	QR

4.

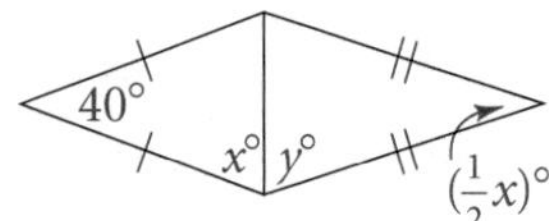

Column A	Column B
x	y

Chapter Review

Vocabulary

base of an isosceles triangle (p. 211)
base angles of an isosceles triangle (p. 211)
congruent polygons (p. 180)
corollary (p. 212)
CPCTC (corresponding parts of congruent triangles are congruent) (p. 203)
hypotenuse (p. 217)
legs of a right triangle (p. 217)
legs of an isosceles triangle (p. 211)
vertex angle of an isosceles triangle (p. 211)

Reading Math
Understanding Vocabulary

Choose the correct term to complete each sentence.

1. The two congruent sides of an isosceles triangle are the ___?___.
2. The two congruent sides of an isosceles triangle form the ___?___.
3. If you know that two triangles are congruent, then the corresponding sides and angles of the triangles are congruent because ___?___.
4. The side opposite the right angle of a right triangle is the ___?___.
5. The angles of an isosceles triangle that are not the vertex angle are called the ___?___.
6. A ___?___ to a theorem is a statement that follows immediately from the theorem.
7. The ___?___ are the two sides of a right triangle that are not the hypotenuse.
8. ___?___ have congruent corresponding parts.
9. The side of an isosceles triangle that is not a leg is called the ___?___.

Take It to the NET
Online vocabulary quiz at www.PHSchool.com
Web Code: afj-0451

Skills and Concepts

4-1 Objectives

▼ To recognize congruent figures and their corresponding parts

Congruent polygons have congruent corresponding parts. When you name congruent polygons, always list corresponding vertices in the same order.

Two triangles are congruent when they have three pairs of congruent corresponding sides and three pairs of congruent corresponding angles.

***RSTUV* ≅ *KLMNO*. Complete the congruence statements.**

10. $\overline{TS} \cong$ ___?___
11. $\angle N \cong$ ___?___
12. $\overline{LM} \cong$ ___?___
13. $VUTSR \cong$ ___?___

***WXYZ* ≅ *PQRS*. Find the measure of the angle or the length of the side.**

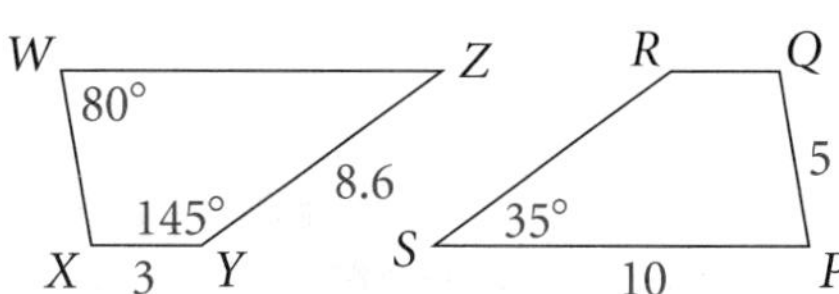

14. $\angle P$
15. $\overline{QR}$
16. $\overline{WX}$
17. $\angle Z$
18. $\angle X$

4-2 and 4-3 Objectives

- ▼ To prove two triangles congruent using the SSS and SAS Postulates
- ▼ To prove two triangles congruent using the ASA Postulate and the AAS Theorem

If three sides of one triangle are congruent to three sides of another triangle, then the two triangles are congruent by the **Side-Side-Side (SSS) Postulate.**

If two sides and the included angle of one triangle are congruent to two sides and the included angle of another triangle, then the two triangles are congruent by the **Side-Angle-Side (SAS) Postulate.**

If two angles and the included side of one triangle are congruent to two angles and the included side of another triangle, then the two triangles are congruent by the **Angle-Side-Angle (ASA) Postulate.**

If two angles and a nonincluded side of one triangle are congruent to two angles and the corresponding nonincluded side of another triangle, then the two triangles are congruent by the **Angle-Angle-Side (AAS) Theorem.**

Which postulate or theorem, if any, could you use to prove the two triangles congruent? If the triangles *cannot* be proven congruent, write *not possible.*

19.

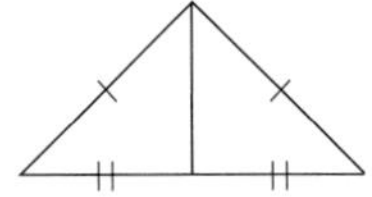

20.

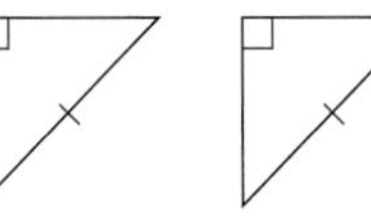

21.

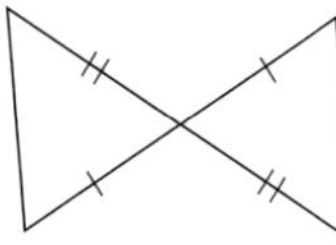

22.

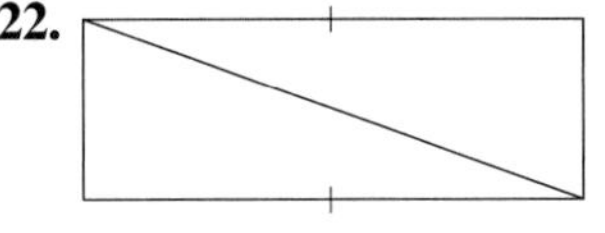

23.

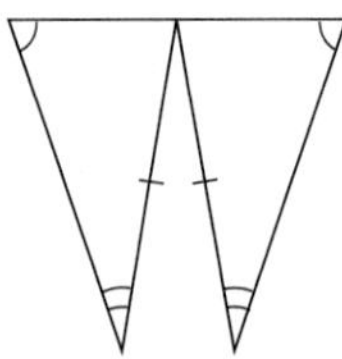

24.

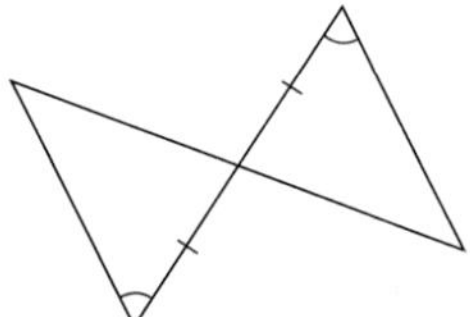

Write a congruence statement for each pair of triangles. Name the postulate or theorem that justifies your statement. If the triangles *cannot* be proven congruent, write *not possible.*

25.

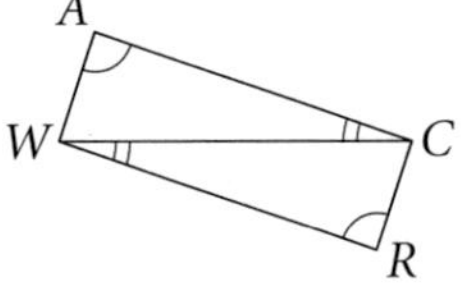

26.

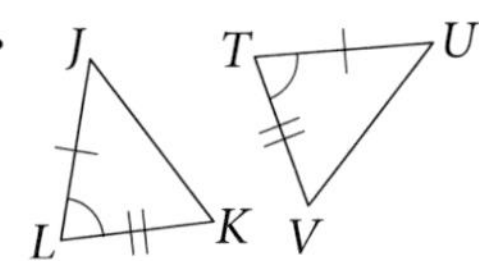

27.

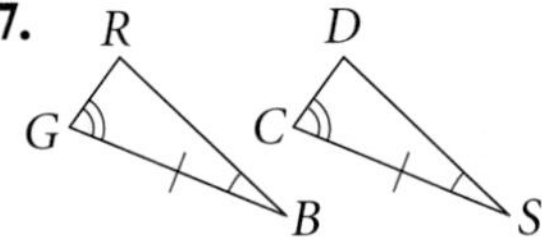

4-4 Objectives

- ▼ To use triangle congruence and CPCTC to prove that parts of two triangles are congruent

Once you know that triangles are congruent, you can make conclusions about corresponding segments and angles because, by definition, **corresponding parts of congruent triangles are congruent (CPCTC).** You can use congruent triangles in the proofs of many theorems.

Explain how you can use SSS, SAS, ASA, or AAS with CPCTC to prove the statement true.

28. $\overline{TV} \cong \overline{YW}$

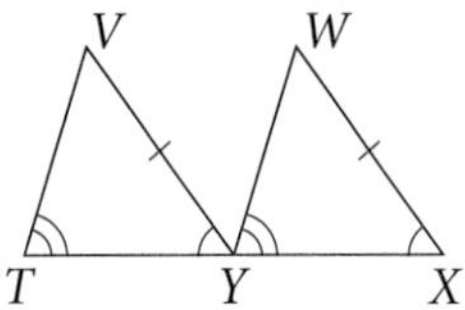

29. $\overline{BE} \cong \overline{DE}$

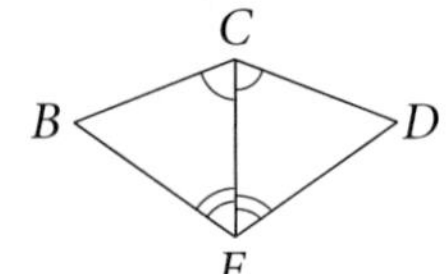

30. $\overline{KN} \cong \overline{ML}$

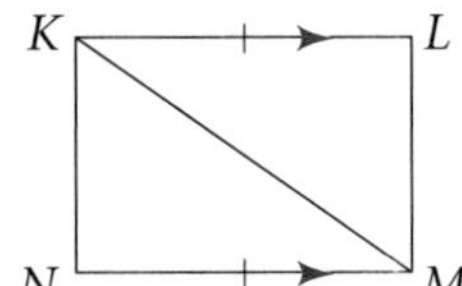

4-5 and 4-6 Objectives

- ▼ To use and apply properties of isosceles triangles
- ▼ To prove triangles congruent using the HL Theorem

If two sides of a triangle are congruent, then the angles opposite those sides are also congruent by the **Isosceles Triangle Theorem.** If two angles of a triangle are congruent, then the sides opposite the angles are congruent by the **Converse of the Isosceles Triangle Theorem.**

The bisector of the vertex angle of an isosceles triangle is the perpendicular bisector of the base.

If the hypotenuse and a leg of one right triangle are congruent to the hypotenuse and a leg of another right triangle, then the triangles are congruent by the **Hypotenuse-Leg (HL) Theorem.**

x^2 Algebra **Find the values of x and y.**

31.

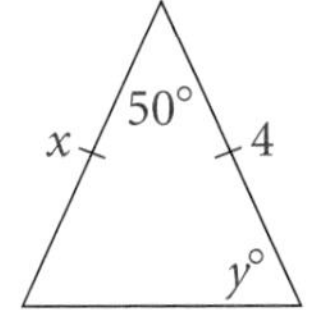

32.

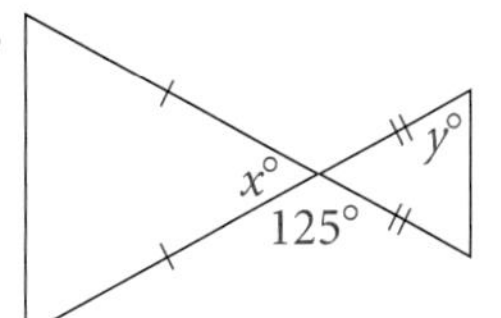

33.

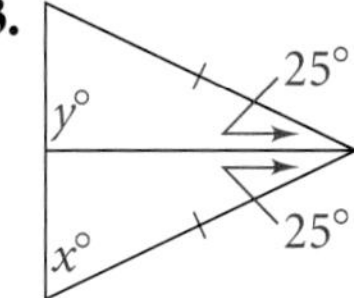

Write a paragraph explaining how to deduce what you want to prove from the given information.

34. Given: $\overline{PS} \perp \overline{SQ}, \overline{RQ} \perp \overline{QS}, \overline{PQ} \cong \overline{RS}$

Prove: $\triangle PSQ \cong \triangle RQS$

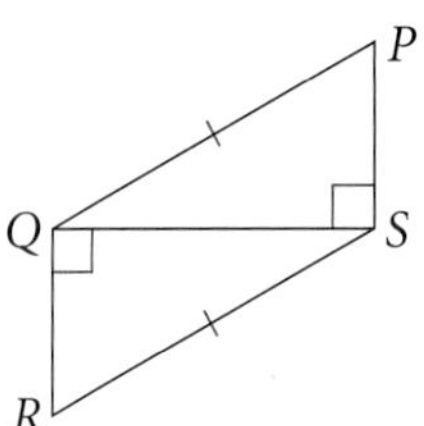

35. Given: $\overline{LN} \perp \overline{KM}, \overline{KL} \cong \overline{ML}$

Prove: $\triangle KLN \cong \triangle MLN$

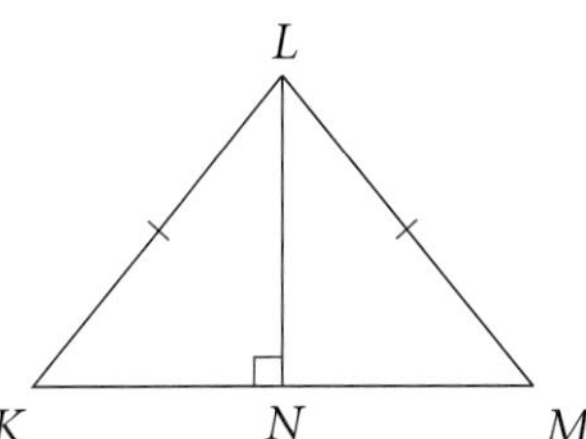

4-7 Objectives

- ▼ To identify congruent overlapping triangles
- ▼ To prove two triangles congruent by first proving two other triangles congruent

You can prove overlapping triangles congruent. You can also use the common or shared sides and angles of triangles in congruence proofs.

Name a pair of overlapping congruent triangles in each diagram. State whether the triangles are congruent by SSS, SAS, ASA, AAS, or HL.

36.

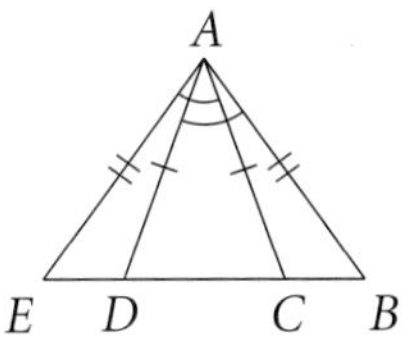

37.

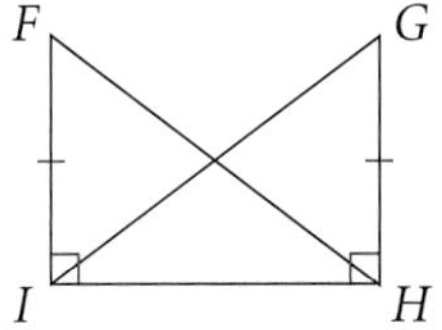

38.

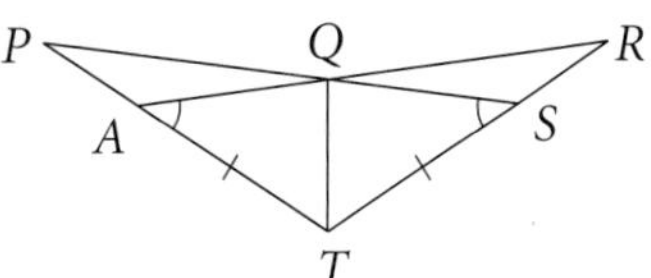

39.

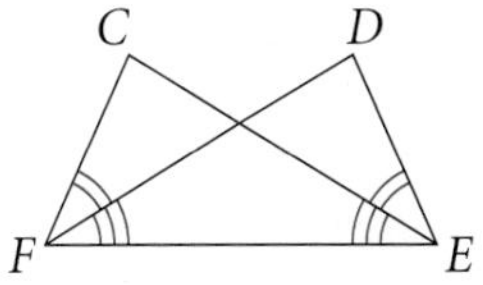

Chapter Test

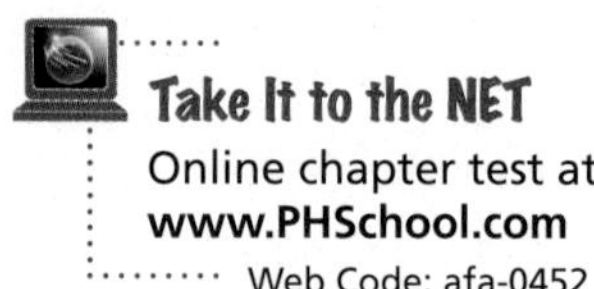

Write a congruence statement for each pair of triangles.

1.

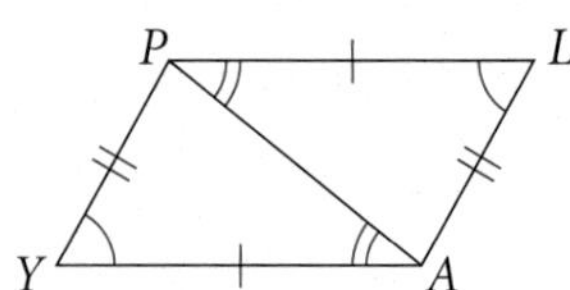

2.

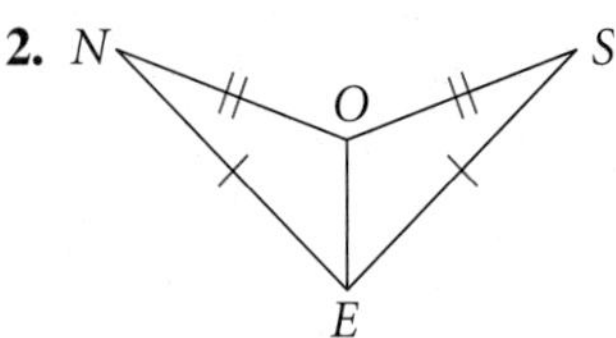

Which postulate, if any, could you use to prove the two triangles congruent? If not enough information is given, write *not possible.*

3.

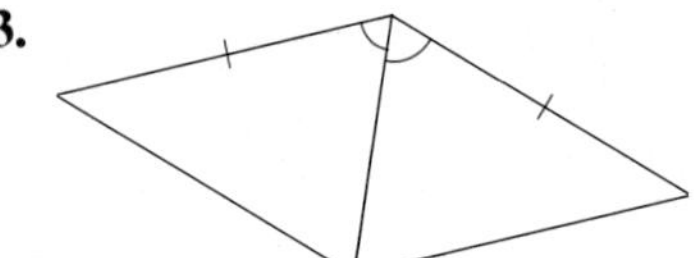

4.

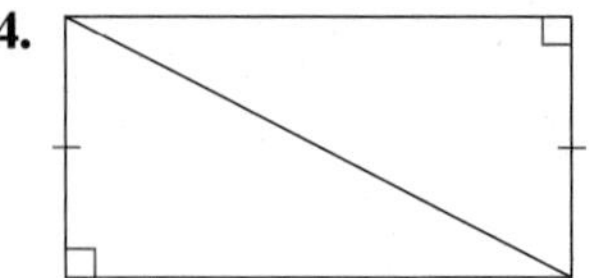

5.

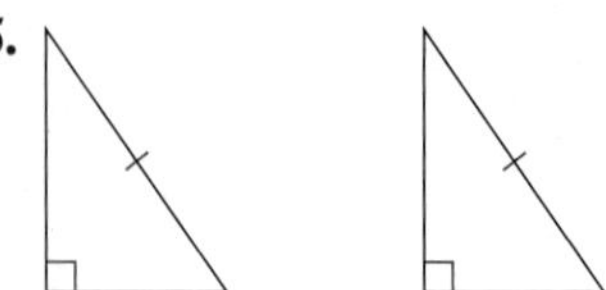

6.

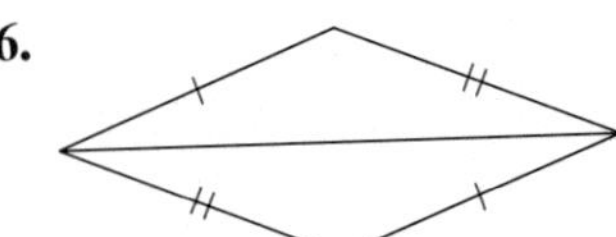

7.

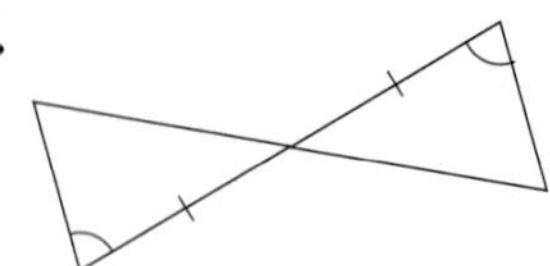

8.

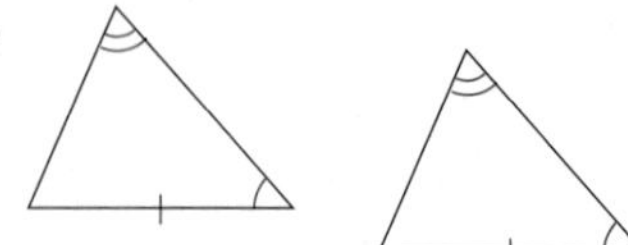

9. **Writing** Explain why you cannot use AAA to prove two triangles congruent.

10. **Open-Ended** Draw a picture to represent $\triangle CEO \cong \triangle HDF$. Name all of the pairs of corresponding congruent parts.

11. If two game boards have the same area, are the game boards congruent? Explain your answer.

12. **Algebra** Find the value of the variable.

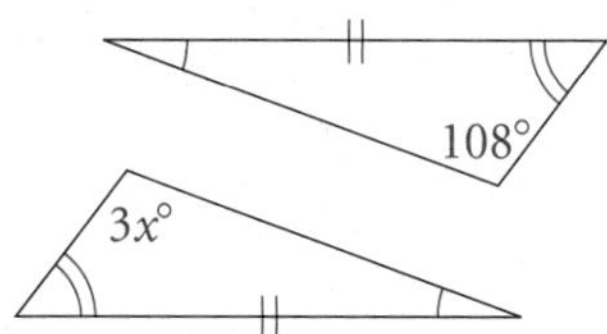

Write a paragraph explaining how to deduce what you want to prove from the given information.

13. **Given:** $\overline{AT} \cong \overline{GS}$, $\overline{AT} \parallel \overline{GS}$

Prove: $\triangle GAT \cong \triangle TSG$

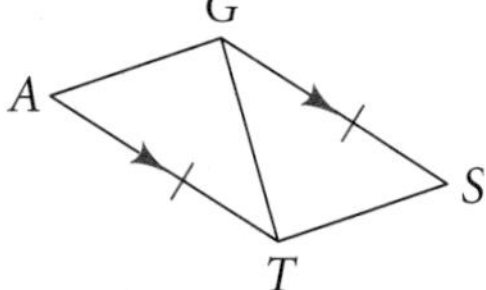

14. **Given:** $\overline{LN}$ bisects $\angle OLM$ and $\angle ONM$.

Prove: $\triangle OLN \cong \triangle MLN$

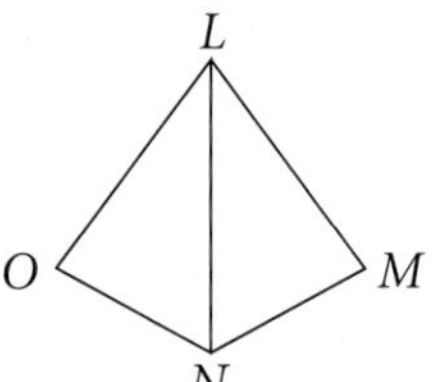

Name a pair of overlapping congruent triangles in each diagram. State whether the triangles are congruent by SSS, SAS, ASA, AAS, or HL.

15. **Given:** $\overline{CE} \cong \overline{DF}$, $\overline{CF} \cong \overline{DE}$

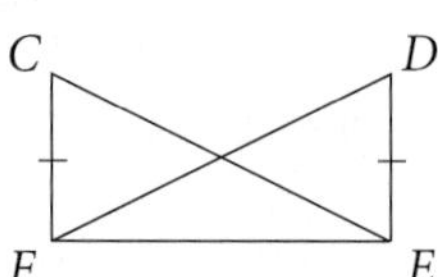

16. **Given:** $\overline{RT} \cong \overline{QT}$, $\overline{AT} \cong \overline{ST}$

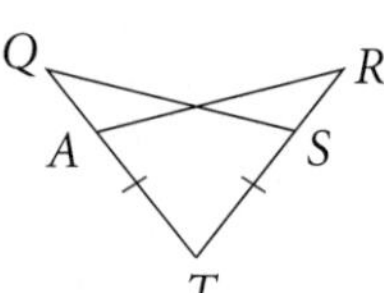

17. **Open-Ended** Draw two parallel lines and draw two parallel transversals through your parallel lines. Then draw a third transversal to create two congruent triangles. Label your triangles and write the congruence statement.

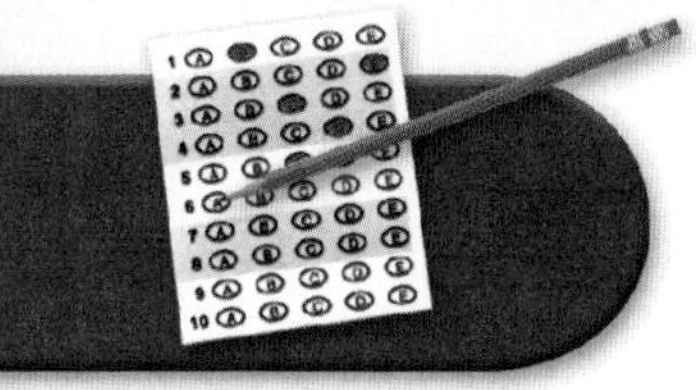

Standardized Test Prep

Multiple Choice

For Exercises 1–6, choose the correct letter.

1. What is $m\angle CDF$?

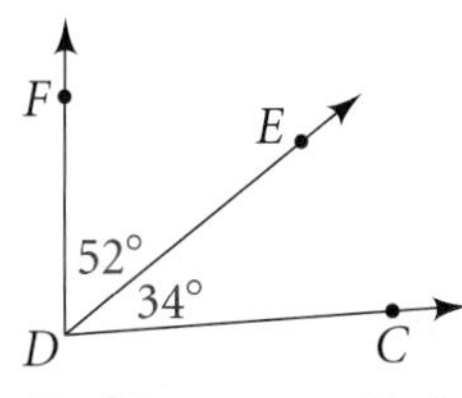

A. 18 B. 86 C. 94 D. 274

2. Which angles could an obtuse triangle have?
   I. a right angle
   II. two acute angles
   III. an obtuse angle
   IV. two vertical angles

F. I and II G. II and III
H. III and IV I. I and IV

3. What is the area in square units of a rectangle with vertices $(-2, 5)$, $(3, 5)$, $(3, -1)$, and $(-2, -1)$?
A. 56 B. 30 C. 25 D. 24

4. Quadrilateral $ABCD \cong QRST$. Which segment is congruent to $\overline{TS}$?
F. $\overline{AB}$ G. $\overline{BC}$ H. $\overline{CB}$ I. $\overline{DC}$

5. By which postulate or theorem are the triangles congruent?

A. SAS B. SSS C. ASA D. AAS

6. Which condition(s) will allow you to prove that $\ell \parallel m$?

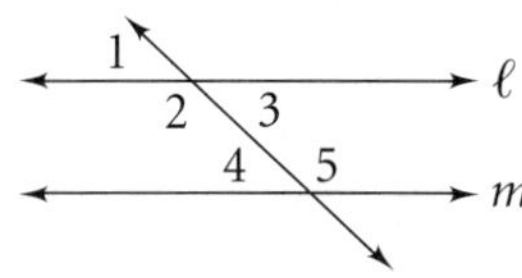

I. $\angle 1 \cong \angle 4$
II. $\angle 2 \cong \angle 5$
III. $m\angle 2 + m\angle 4 = 180$
IV. $\angle 3 \cong \angle 4$

F. III only G. I and III only
H. II and IV only I. I, II, III, and IV

Quantitative Comparison

Compare the boxed quantity in Column A with the boxed quantity in Column B. Choose the best answer.

A. The quantity in Column A is greater.
B. The quantity in Column B is greater.
C. The two quantities are equal.
D. The relationship cannot be determined from the information given.

Lines ℓ and t are nonvertical and perpendicular.

	Column A	Column B
7.	the slope of ℓ	the slope of t
8.	the product of the slopes of ℓ and t	the slope of a horizontal line

Gridded Response

9. An isosceles triangle has two angles measuring 54.5 and 71. What is the measure of the third angle?

10. What is the number of feet in the circumference of a circle with a diameter of 10 ft? Use 3.14 for π.

11. What is the measure of the complement of a 56° angle?

12. What is the measure of the supplement of a 35° angle?

Short Response

Explain your work.

13. Draw an angle. Then construct another angle congruent to the first.

14. Construct the perpendicular bisector of a segment $\overline{MN}$.

Extended Response

15. Find CD and the coordinates of the midpoint of $\overline{CD}$ if the endpoints are $C(5, 7)$ and $D(10, -5)$. Explain your work.

Real-World Snapshots

The Science of Reflection

Applying Parallel Lines When you look at the surface of a still pool of water, your reflection looks back at you. This is because the water acts like a mirror, reflecting a clear, although reversed, image. The type of reflection you see in a mirror depends on the surface of the mirror. Two flat mirrors placed at right angles to each other will seem to magnify the light hitting them by reflecting it directly back to its source.

Sir Isaac Newton

Sir Isaac Newton (1642–1727) designed and built the first reflecting telescope. His telescope used mirrors rather than glass lenses to collect and focus light. Most telescopes used by amateur astronomers are reflecting telescopes.

Replica of Newton's telescope

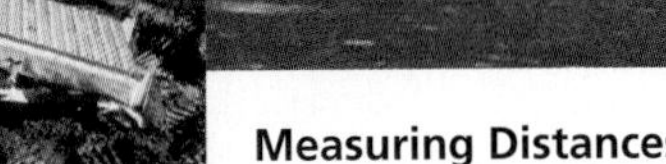

Measuring Distances

Astronauts have placed a cube-corner reflector on the surface of the moon. Each corner provides three perpendicular reflecting planes. By measuring the time it takes a laser beam to bounce back from the reflector, scientists are able to measure the distance from Earth to the moon.

Activity 1

Examine the diagram below. Notice that the mirrors are perpendicular and that each angle of reflection is congruent to the corresponding angle of incidence. Given these two facts, explain why incident and reflected rays must be parallel.

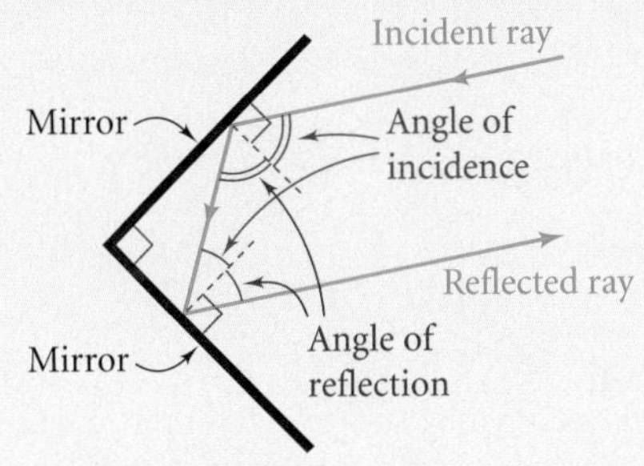

Activity 2

Materials: two flat mirrors

Arrange two flat mirrors so that they form a right angle. Look at your face in one of the mirrors and wink. Then look into the seam where the two mirrors meet, find your face, and wink. How does the reflection in the perpendicular mirrors differ from the reflection in the single mirror?

The front view sparkles.

Cut Diamonds

A cut diamond reflects most of the light that falls on its front.

The rear view is dark.

Hall of Mirrors

The Hall of Mirrors at France's Palace of Versailles is brightly lit even on a cloudy day, because each of its windows is placed opposite a mirror of the same size and shape.

Safety

A bicycle doesn't have the electric taillights that a car does, so it comes equipped with reflectors. Some helmets also have reflectors.

Take It to the NET For more information about mirrors and reflections, go to **www.PHSchool.com.**
Web Code: afe-0453

Where You've Been

- In Chapter 1, you learned how to identify segments, lines, and angles. You also learned the meaning of some important terms such as bisector, congruence, midpoint, perpendicular, and parallel.
- In Chapters 2 and 3, you made conjectures about angles, parallel lines, and perpendicular lines, and learned how to use deductive reasoning to prove the conjectures true.

Instant self-check online and on CD-ROM

Diagnosing Readiness

(For help, go to the Lesson in green.)

Inequalities (Previous Course)

x^2 **Algebra** Solve each inequality.

1. $3x + 10 \leq 22$ **2.** $4x - 1 > 2x + 14$ **3.** $30 - 5x \geq x + 24$

Basic Constructions (Lesson 1-5)

Use a compass and straightedge for the following.

4. Construct the perpendicular bisector of a segment.

5. Construct the angle bisector of an angle.

Distance Formula (Lesson 1-6)

Find the distance between each pair of points.

6. $(1, 4), (4, 8)$ **7.** $(-6, 2), (-1, 14)$ **8.** $(-3, -2), (5, -6)$

Midpoint Formula (Lesson 1-6)

Find the midpoint of the segments whose endpoints are given.

9. $(4, 11), (6, 3)$ **10.** $(-8, -3), (2, -4)$ **11.** $(-7, 15), (-2, -10)$

Slope (Algebra 1 Review, page 151)

Find the slope of the line containing each pair of points.

12. $(8, 3), (7, 12)$ **13.** $(3, -2), (0, 6)$ **14.** $(-5, 4), (-2, 4)$

Relationships Within Triangles

Chapter 5

LESSONS

Key Vocabulary

- altitude of a triangle (p. 259)
- centroid (p. 258)
- circumcenter of a triangle (p. 257)
- circumscribed about (p. 257)
- concurrent (p. 257)
- contrapositive (p. 264)
- coordinate proof (p. 244)
- distance from a point to a line (p. 250)
- equivalent statements (p. 265)
- incenter of a triangle (p. 257)
- indirect proof (p. 265)
- indirect reasoning (p. 265)
- inscribed in (p. 257)
- inverse (p. 264)
- median of a triangle (p. 258)
- midsegment (p. 243)
- negation (p. 264)
- orthocenter of a triangle (p. 259)
- point of concurrency (p. 257)

Where You're Going

- In this chapter, you will learn about geometric relationships within triangles.
- You will learn about three lines that pass through one point and find the four sets of such lines that exist for every triangle.
- You will learn about two other types of statements that are related to a conditional, as well as another type of reasoning—indirect reasoning.
- You will apply indirect reasoning to deduce information about inequalities in triangles.

Real-World Connection Applying what you learn, you will prove a basic theorem about shortcuts on page 278.

Technology

Investigating Midsegments

FOR USE WITH LESSON 5-1

Construct

Use geometry software to draw a triangle. Label it $\triangle ABC$. Construct the midpoints D and E of $\overline{AB}$ and $\overline{AC}$, respectively. Connect the midpoints with a *midsegment*.

Investigate

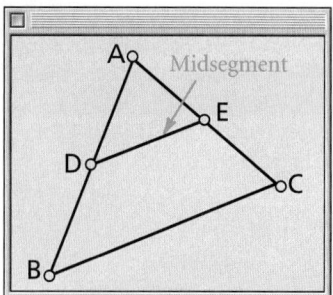

- Measure the lengths of $\overline{DE}$ and $\overline{BC}$. Calculate $\frac{DE}{BC}$.
- Measure the slopes of $\overline{DE}$ and $\overline{BC}$.
- Manipulate the triangle and observe the lengths and slopes of $\overline{DE}$ and $\overline{BC}$.

EXERCISES

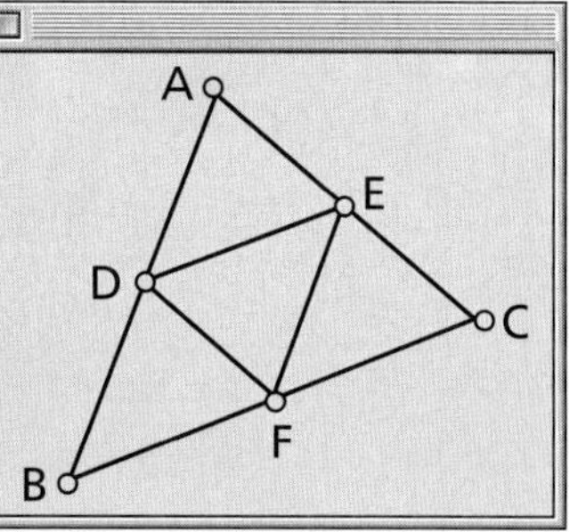

1. Make conjectures about the lengths and slopes of midsegments.
2. Construct the midpoint F of $\overline{BC}$. Then construct the other two midsegments of $\triangle ABC$. Test whether these midsegments support your conjectures in Exercise 1.
3. $\triangle ABC$ and the three midsegments form four small triangles.
   a. Measure the sides of the four small triangles and list those that you find are congruent.
   b. Use a postulate from Chapter 4 to make a conjecture about the four small triangles.

For the remaining exercises, assume your conjectures in Exercises 1 and 3 are true.

4. What can you say about the areas of the four small triangles in the window above?
5. How does $\triangle ABC$ compare to each small triangle
   a. in area?
   b. in perimeter?
6. Construct the three midsegments of $\triangle DEF$. Label this triangle $\triangle GHI$. How does $\triangle ABC$ compare to $\triangle GHI$
   a. in area?
   b. in perimeter?
   c. Suppose you construct the midsegment triangle inside $\triangle GHI$. Predict how $\triangle ABC$ would compare to this third midsegment triangle in area and perimeter.

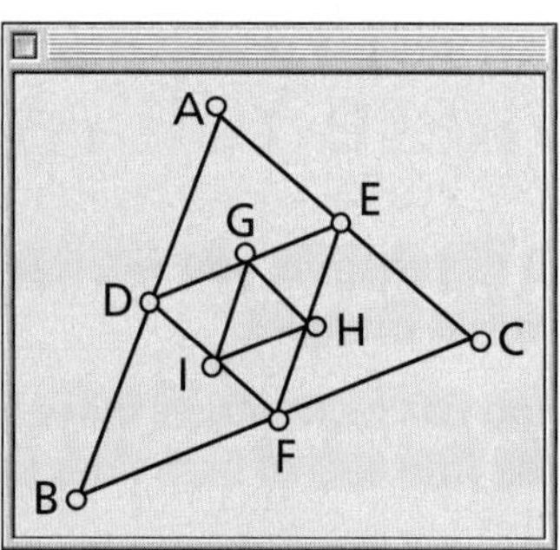

Exercise 6

7. • Draw quadrilateral $RSTU$.
   • Construct the midpoints of each side of the quadrilateral.
   • Join consecutive midpoints to form quadrilateral $YXWV$.
   • Manipulate the figure and observe the shape of quadrilateral $YXWV$.
   Make a conjecture about the sides of quadrilateral $YXWV$.

Midsegments of Triangles

Lesson Preview

What You'll Learn

To use properties of midsegments to solve problems

. . . And Why

To use indirect measurement to find the length of a lake, as in Example 3

✓ Check Skills You'll Need

(For help, go to Lesson 1-6 and page 151.)

Find the coordinates of the midpoint of each segment.

1. $\overline{AB}$ with $A(-2, 3)$ and $B(4, 1)$

2. $\overline{CD}$ with $C(0, 5)$ and $D(3, 6)$

3. $\overline{EF}$ with $E(-4, 6)$ and $F(3, 10)$

4. $\overline{GH}$ with $G(7, 10)$ and $H(-5, -8)$

Find the slope of the line containing each pair of points.

5. $A(-2, 3)$ and $B(3, 1)$

6. $C(0, 5)$ and $D(3, 6)$

7. $E(-4, 6)$ and $F(3, 10)$

8. $G(7, 10)$ and $H(-5, -8)$

New Vocabulary • midsegment • coordinate proof

Interactive lesson includes instant self-check, tutorials, and activities.

OBJECTIVE

1 Using Properties of Midsegments

Investigation: Midsegments of Triangles

Draw, label, and cut out a large scalene triangle. Do the same with other right, acute, and obtuse triangles. Label the vertices *A*, *B*, and *C*.

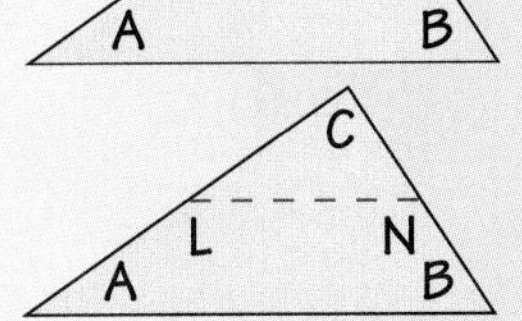

- For each triangle fold *A* onto *C* to find the midpoint of $\overline{AC}$. Do the same for $\overline{BC}$. Label the midpoints *L* and *N*, then draw $\overline{LN}$.

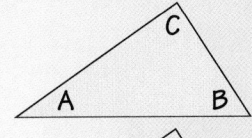

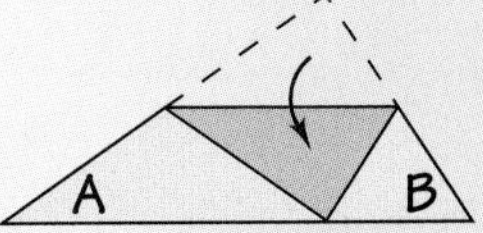

- Fold each triangle on $\overline{LN}$.
- Fold *A* to *C*. Fold *B* to *C*.

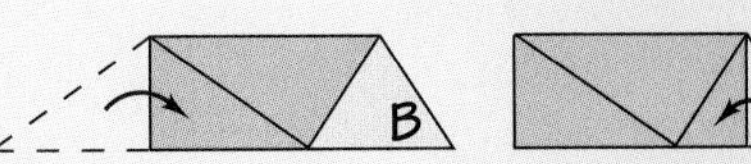

1. How does *LN* compare to *AB*? Explain.
2. Make a conjecture about how the segment joining the midpoints of two sides of a triangle is related to the third side of the triangle.

In $\triangle ABC$ above, $\overline{LN}$ is a triangle midsegment. A **midsegment** of a triangle is a segment connecting the midpoints of two sides.

Key Concepts

Theorem 5-1 **Triangle Midsegment Theorem**

If a segment joins the midpoints of two sides of a triangle, then the segment is parallel to the third side, and is half its length.

One way to prove the Triangle Midsegment Theorem is to use coordinate geometry and algebra. This style of proof is called a **coordinate proof.** You begin the proof by placing a triangle in a convenient spot on the coordinate plane. You then choose variables for the coordinates of the vertices.

Proof

Coordinate Proof of Theorem 5-1

Given: R is the midpoint of $\overline{OP}$.
S is the midpoint of $\overline{QP}$.

Prove: $\overline{RS} \parallel \overline{OQ}$ and $RS = \frac{1}{2}OQ$

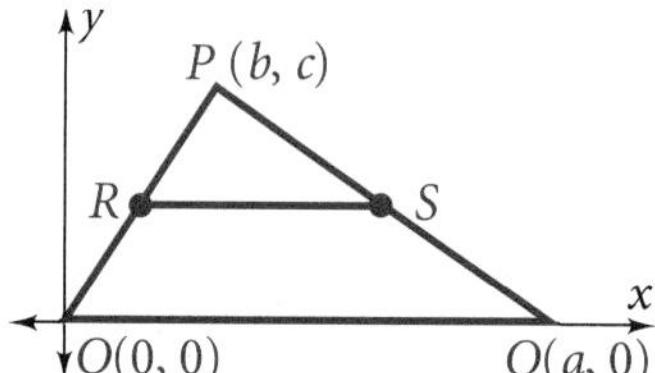

- Use the Midpoint Formula to find the coordinates of R and S.

R: $\left(\frac{0+b}{2}, \frac{0+c}{2}\right) = \left(\frac{b}{2}, \frac{c}{2}\right)$

S: $\left(\frac{a+b}{2}, \frac{0+c}{2}\right) = \left(\frac{a+b}{2}, \frac{c}{2}\right)$

Need Help?

The Midpoint Formula: $\left(\frac{x_1 + x_2}{2}, \frac{y_1 + y_2}{2}\right)$

The Distance Formula: $\sqrt{(x_2 - x_1)^2 + (y_2 - y_1)^2}$

- To prove that $\overline{RS}$ and $\overline{OQ}$ are parallel, show that their slopes are equal. Because the y-coordinates of R and S are the same, the slope of $\overline{RS}$ is zero. The same is true for $\overline{OQ}$. Therefore, $\overline{RS} \parallel \overline{OQ}$.

- Use the Distance Formula to find RS and OQ.

$$RS = \sqrt{\left(\frac{a+b}{2} - \frac{b}{2}\right)^2 + \left(\frac{c}{2} - \frac{c}{2}\right)^2}$$

$$= \sqrt{\left(\frac{a}{2} + \frac{b}{2} - \frac{b}{2}\right)^2 + 0^2} = \sqrt{\left(\frac{a}{2}\right)^2} = \frac{a}{2} = \frac{1}{2}a$$

$$OQ = \sqrt{(a-0)^2 + (0-0)^2}$$

$$= \sqrt{a^2 + 0^2} = a$$

Therefore, $RS = \frac{1}{2}OQ$.

1 EXAMPLE **Finding Lengths**

In $\triangle EFG$, H, J, and K are midpoints. Find HJ, JK, and FG.

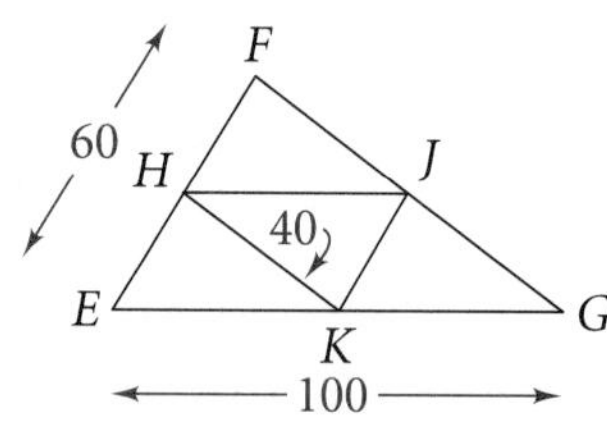

$HJ = \frac{1}{2}EG$ or $\frac{1}{2}(100)$; $HJ = 50$

$JK = \frac{1}{2}EF$ or $\frac{1}{2}(60)$; $JK = 30$

HK or $40 = \frac{1}{2}FG$; $FG = 80$

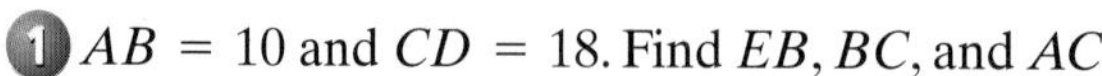

Check Understanding **1** $AB = 10$ and $CD = 18$. Find EB, BC, and AC.

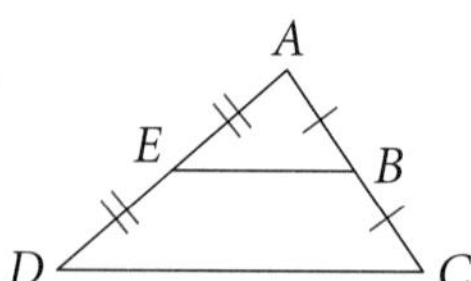

2 EXAMPLE Identifying Parallel Segments

In $\triangle DEF$, A, B, and C are midpoints. Name pairs of parallel segments.

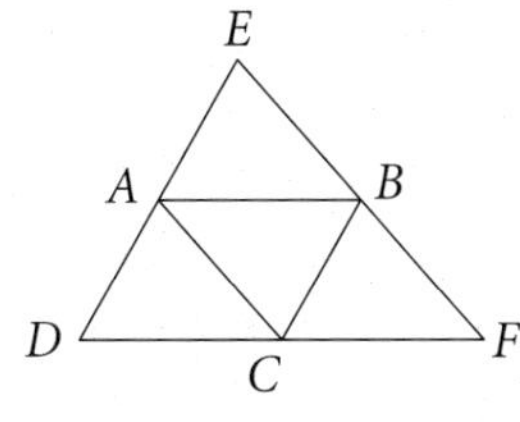

The midsegments are $\overline{AB}$, $\overline{BC}$, and $\overline{CA}$.

By the Triangle Midsegment Theorem, $\overline{AB} \parallel \overline{DF}$, $\overline{BC} \parallel \overline{ED}$, and $\overline{AC} \parallel \overline{EF}$

Check Understanding **2** **Critical Thinking** Find $m\angle VUZ$. Justify your answer.

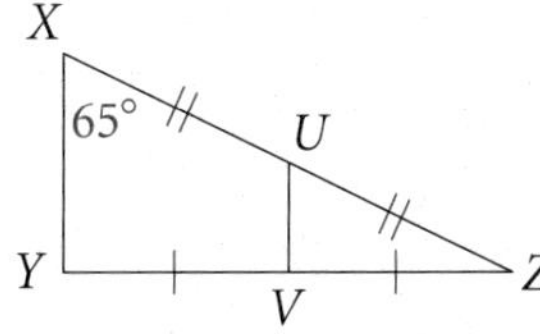

You can use the Triangle Midsegment Theorem to find lengths of segments that might be difficult to measure directly.

3 EXAMPLE Real-World Connection

Indirect Measurement Dean plans to swim the length of the lake, as shown in the photo. How far would Dean swim?

Here is what Dean does to find the distance he would swim across the lake.

Step 1: He measures his stride and adjusts it so that it averages about 3 ft.

Step 2: Then he begins at the left edge of the lake (first diagram). He paces 35 strides along the edge of the lake and sets a stake.

Step 3: He paces 35 more strides in the same direction and sets another stake.

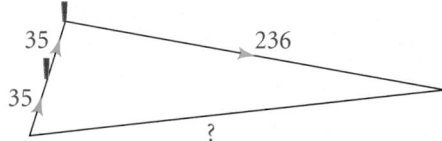

Step 4: He paces to where his swim will end at the other side of the lake, counting 236 strides.

Step 5: Then (second diagram) he paces 118 strides, or half the distance, back towards the second stake.

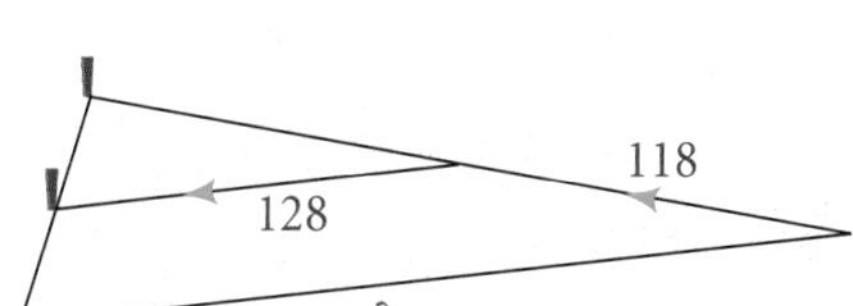

Step 6: He paces to the first stake, counting 128 strides.

Step 7: He converts strides to feet.

$$128 \text{ strides} \times \frac{3 \text{ ft}}{1 \text{ stride}} = 384 \text{ ft}$$

Step 8: He uses Theorem 5-1. The distance across the lake is twice the length of the midsegment.

$$2(384 \text{ ft}) = 768 \text{ ft}$$

Dean would swim approximately 768 ft.

Check Understanding **3** **a.** $\overline{CD}$ is a new bridge being built over a lake as shown. Find the length of the bridge.

b. How long is the bridge in miles?

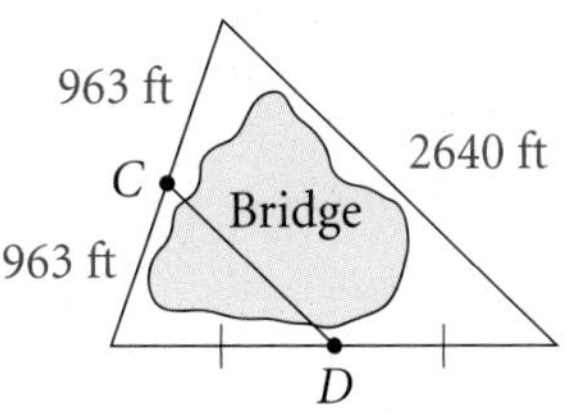

EXERCISES

For more practice, see *Extra Practice.*

Practice and Problem Solving

A Practice by Example

Example 1 (page 244)

Mental Math **Find the value of x.**

1.

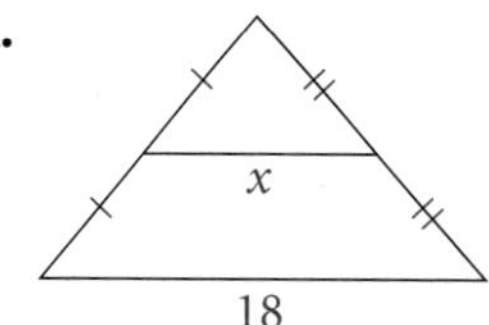

2.

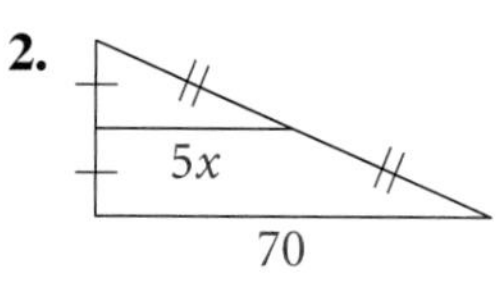

3.

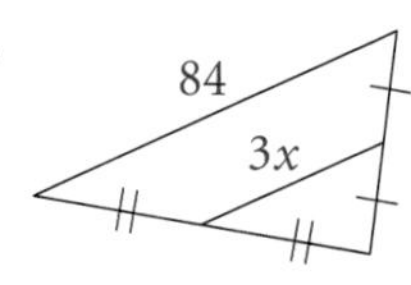

4.

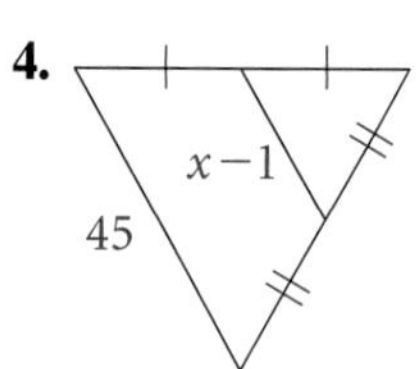

5.

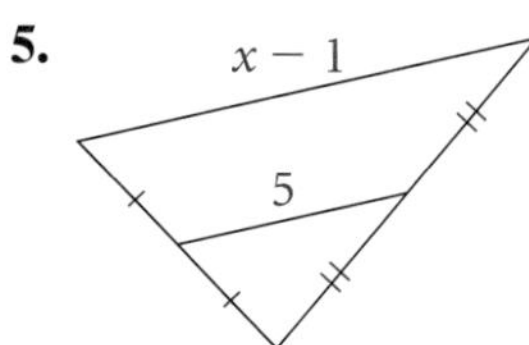

6.

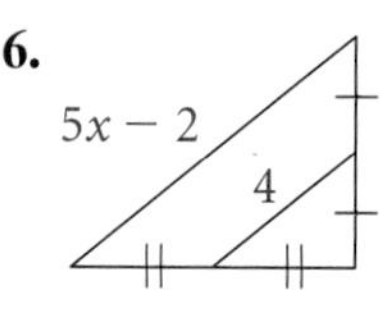

Points E, D, and H are midpoints of $\triangle TUV$. $UV = 80$, $TV = 100$, and $HD = 80$.

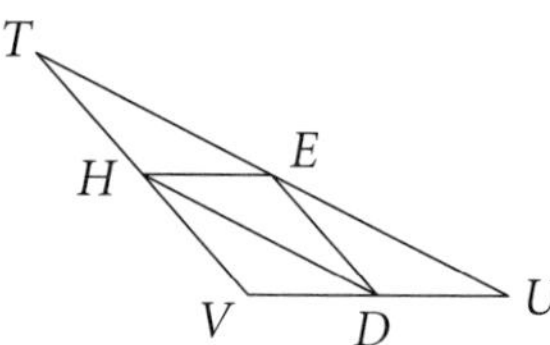

7. Find HE.

8. Find ED.

9. Find TU.

10. Find TE.

Example 2 (page 245)

Identify pairs of parallel segments in each diagram.

11.

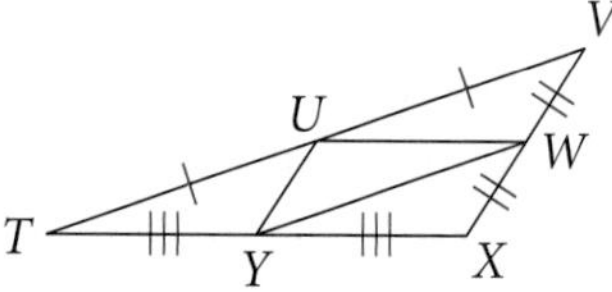

12.

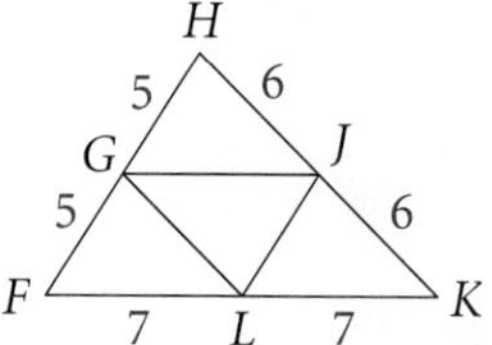

13. a. In the figure at the right, identify pairs of parallel segments.

b. If $m\angle QST = 40$, find $m\angle QPR$.

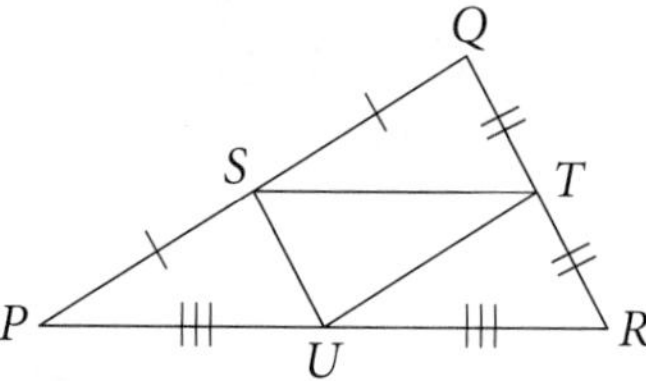

Name the segment that is parallel to the given segment.

14. $\overline{AB}$

15. $\overline{BC}$

16. $\overline{EF}$

17. $\overline{CA}$

18. $\overline{GE}$

19. $\overline{FG}$

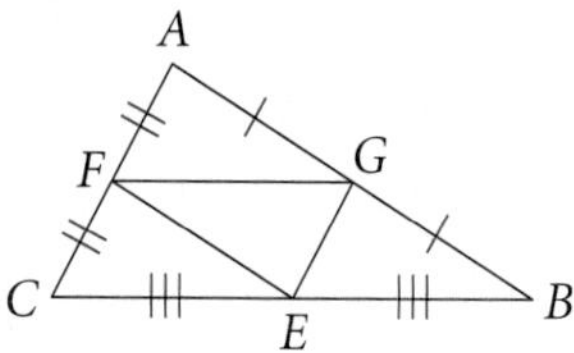

Example 3 (page 245)

20. Indirect Measurement Kate wants to paddle her canoe across the lake. To determine how far she must paddle, she paced out a triangle, counting the number of strides, as shown.

a. If Kate's strides average 3.5 ft, what is the length of the longest side of the triangle?

b. What distance must Kate paddle across the lake?

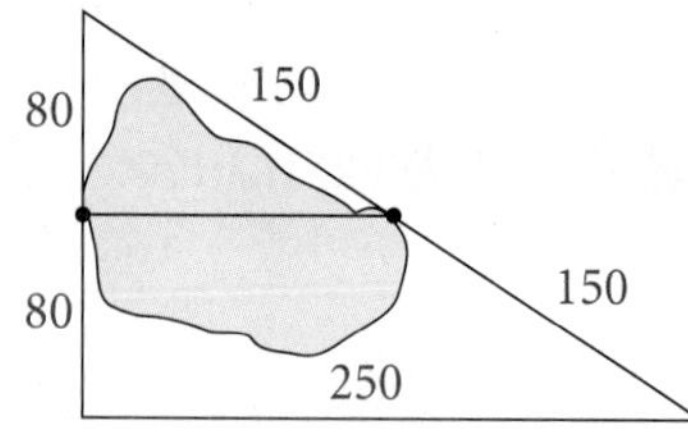

Apply Your Skills

21. a. **Architecture** The triangular face of the Rock and Roll Hall of Fame in Cleveland, Ohio, is isosceles. The length of the base is 229 ft 6 in. What is the length of the highlighted segment?

b. **Writing** Explain your reasoning.

Need Help?

The highlighted segment is halfway up the face of the Rock and Roll Hall of Fame.

X is the midpoint of $\overline{UV}$. Y is the midpoint of $\overline{UW}$.

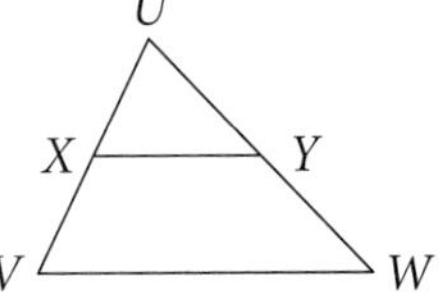

22. If $m\angle UXY = 60$, find $m\angle V$.

23. If $m\angle W = 45$ find $m\angle UYX$.

24. If $XY = 50$, find VW.

25. If $VW = 110$, find XY.

26. **Coordinate Geometry** The coordinates of the vertices of a triangle are $E(1, 2)$, $F(5, 6)$, and $G(3, -2)$.

a. Find the coordinates of H, the midpoint of $\overline{EG}$, and J, the midpoint of $\overline{FG}$.

b. Verify that $\overline{HJ} \parallel \overline{EF}$.

c. Verify that $HJ = \frac{1}{2}EF$.

$\overline{IJ}$ is a midsegment of $\triangle FGH$. $IJ = 7$, $FH = 10$, and $GH = 13$. Find the perimeter of each triangle.

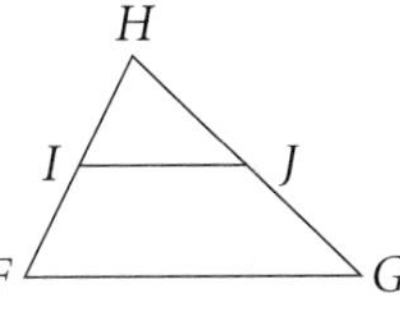

27. $\triangle IJH$

28. $\triangle FGH$

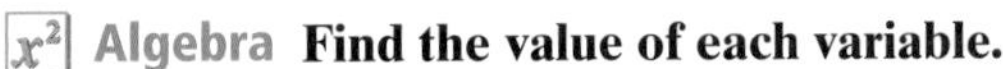

Algebra **Find the value of each variable.**

29.

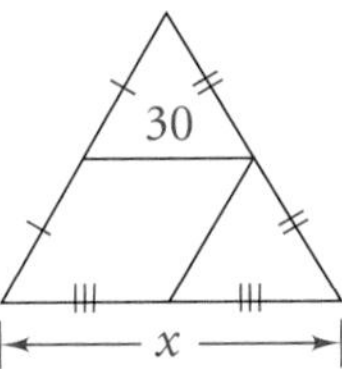

30.

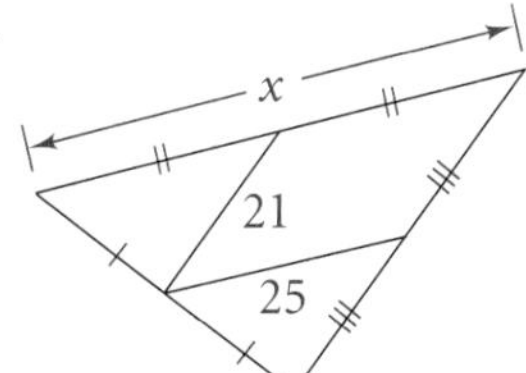

31.

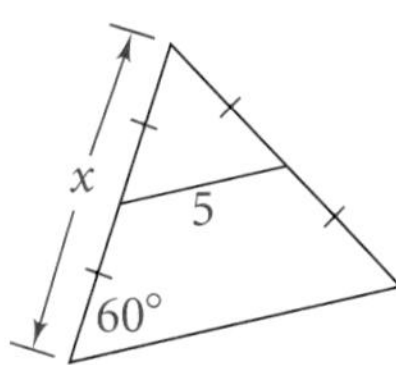

32.

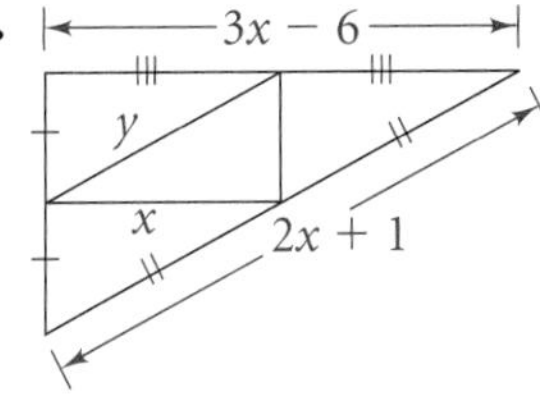

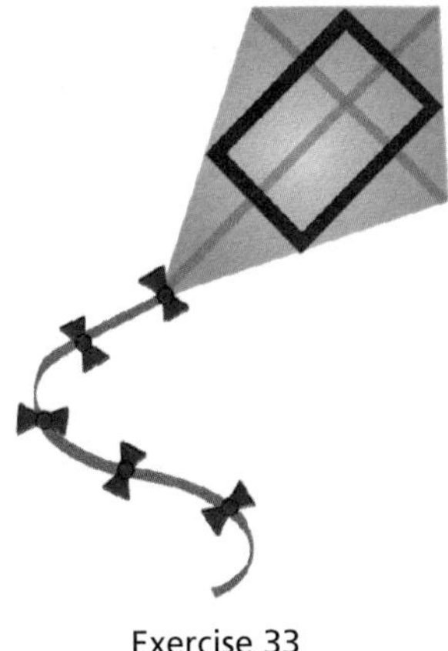

Exercise 33

33. **Kite Design** Marita is designing a kite to look like the one on the left. Its diagonals are to measure 64 cm and 90 cm. She will use ribbon to connect the midpoints of its sides. How much ribbon will Marita need?

Use the figure at the right for Exercises 34–36.

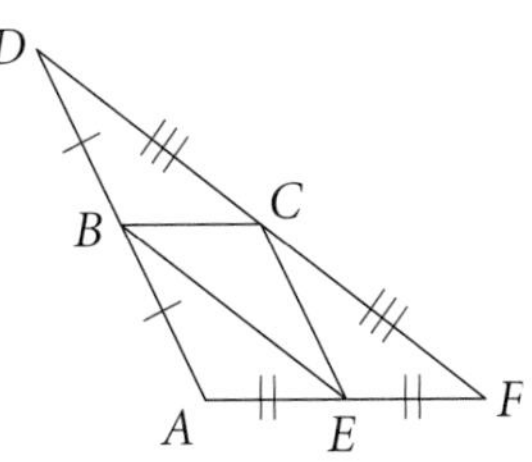

34. If $DF = 24$, $BC = 6$, and $DB = 8$, find the perimeter of $\triangle ADF$.

35. **Algebra** If $BE = 2x + 6$ and $DF = 5x + 9$, find the value of x, then find DF.

36. **Algebra** If $EC = 3x - 1$ and $AD = 5x + 7$, find the value of x, then find EC.

Challenge

37. **Open-Ended** Explain how you could use the Triangle Midsegment Theorem as the basis for this construction. Draw $\overline{CD}$. Draw point A not on $\overline{CD}$. Construct $\overline{AB}$ so that $\overline{AB} \parallel \overline{CD}$ and $AB = \frac{1}{2}CD$.

38. **Coordinate Geometry** In $\triangle GHJ$, $K(2, 3)$ is the midpoint of $\overline{GH}$, $L(4, 1)$ is the midpoint of $\overline{HJ}$, and $M(6, 2)$ is the midpoint of $\overline{GJ}$. Find the coordinates of G, H, and J.

Proof 39. Write a paragraph proof.

Given: S, T, and U are midpoints.

Prove: $\triangle YST \cong \triangle TUZ \cong \triangle SVU \cong$ __?__.

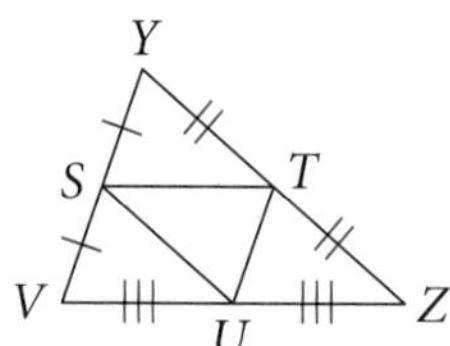

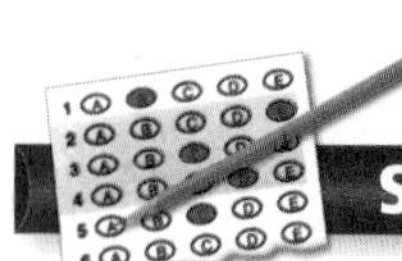

Standardized Test Prep

Gridded Response

Q and P are midpoints of the sides of $\triangle RST$.

40. What is RS?

41. What is TQ?

42. What is TS?

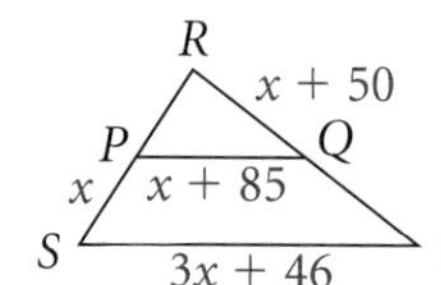

43. What is $m\angle ABC$?

44. What is $m\angle D$?

45. What is $m\angle A$?

46. What is $m\angle CBE$?

Take It to the NET
Online lesson quiz at
www.PHSchool.com
Web Code: afa-0501

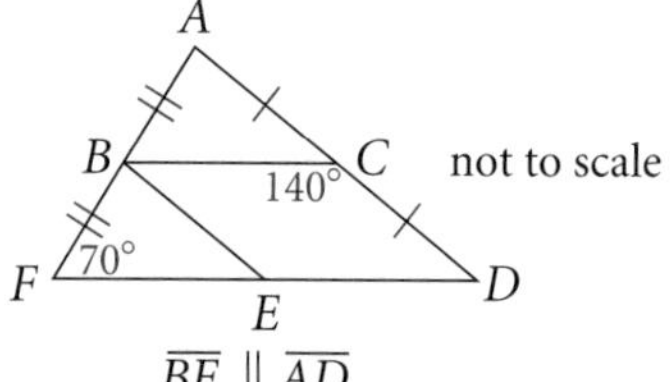

Mixed Review

Lesson 4-7 **Name a pair of overlapping congruent triangles in each diagram. State whether the triangles are congruent by SSS, SAS, ASA, AAS, or HL.**

47.

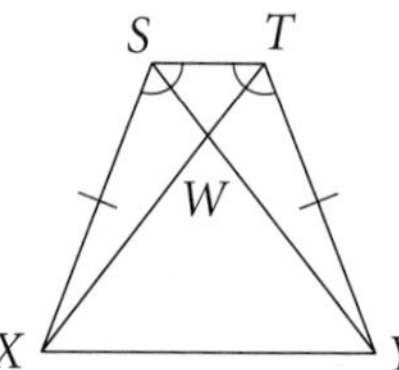

48.

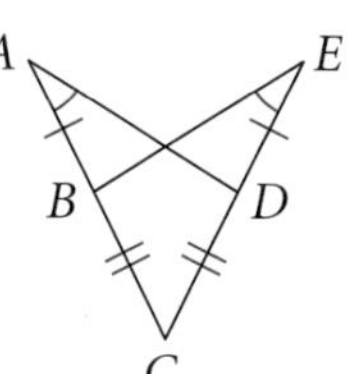

49.

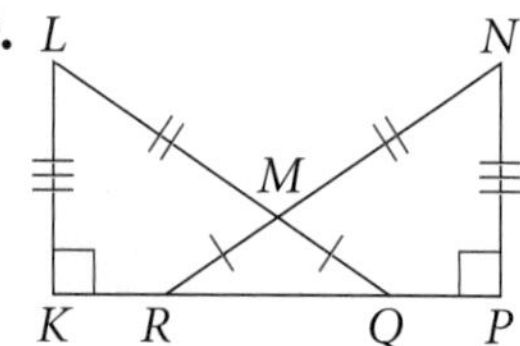

Lesson 3-5 x^2 **Algebra** **Graph each line.**

50. $y = x + 2$

51. $y = 3x - 2$

52. $y = -x - 5$

Lesson 3-2 x^2 **Algebra** **Determine the value of x for which $\ell \parallel m$.**

53.

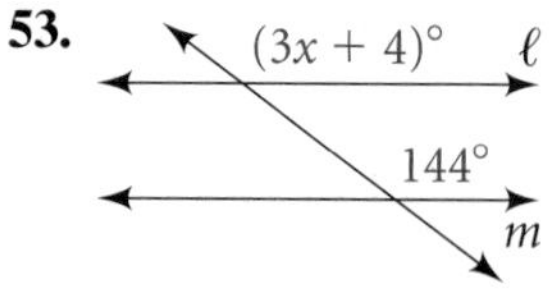

54.

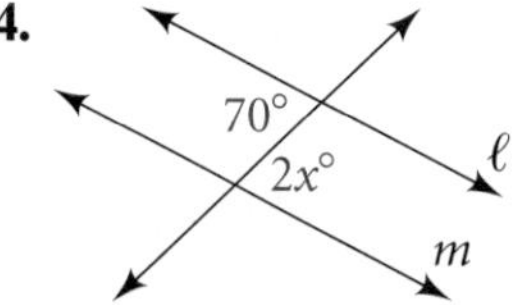

55.

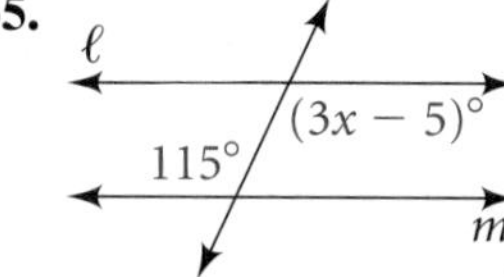

Bisectors in Triangles

Lesson Preview

What You'll Learn

To use properties of perpendicular bisectors and angle bisectors

. . . And Why

To locate places equidistant from two given points on a map, as in Example 1

✓ Check Skills You'll Need

(For help, go to Lesson 1-5.)

Use a compass and a straightedge for the following.

1. Draw a triangle, $\triangle XYZ$. Construct $\triangle STV$ so that $\triangle STV \cong \triangle XYZ$.

2. Draw acute $\angle P$. Construct $\angle Q$ so that $\angle Q \cong \angle P$.

3. Draw $\overline{AB}$. Construct a line $\overleftrightarrow{CD}$ so that $\overleftrightarrow{CD} \perp \overline{AB}$ and $\overleftrightarrow{CD}$ bisects $\overline{AB}$.

4. Draw acute angle $\angle E$. Construct the bisector of $\angle E$.

$\overrightarrow{TM}$ bisects $\angle STU$ so that $m\angle STM = 5x + 4$ and $m\angle MTU = 6x - 2$.

x^2 **5.** Algebra Find the value of x.

6. Find $m\angle STU$.

New Vocabulary • distance from a point to a line

Interactive lesson includes instant self-check, tutorials, and activities.

OBJECTIVE 1 Perpendicular Bisectors and Angle Bisectors

Triangles play a key role in relationships involving perpendicular bisectors and angle bisectors.

In the diagram below on the left, $\overleftrightarrow{CD}$ is the perpendicular bisector of $\overline{AB}$. $\overleftrightarrow{CD}$ is perpendicular to $\overline{AB}$ at its midpoint. In the diagram on the right, $\overline{CA}$ and $\overline{CB}$ are drawn to complete the triangles, $\triangle CAD$ and $\triangle CBD$.

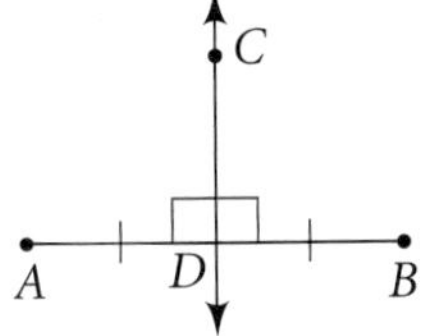

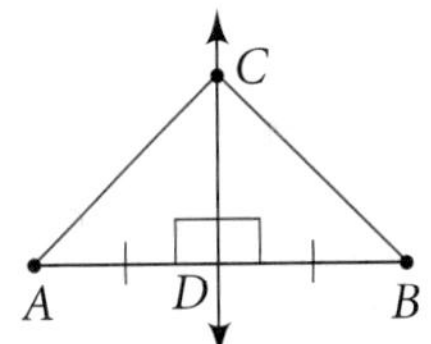

Need Help?

$\overline{CD} \cong \overline{CD}$ by the Reflexive Property and $\triangle CAD \cong \triangle CBD$ by SAS.

You should recognize from your work in Chapter 4 that $\triangle CAD \cong \triangle CBD$. Thus, you can conclude that $\overline{CA} \cong \overline{CB}$, that $CA = CB$, or simply that C is equidistant from points A and B.

This suggests a proof of Theorem 5-2 below. Its converse is also true and is stated as Theorem 5-3. You will prove these theorems in the exercises.

Key Concepts

Theorem 5-2 **Perpendicular Bisector Theorem**

If a point is on the perpendicular bisector of a segment, then it is equidistant from the endpoints of the segment.

Theorem 5-3 **Converse of the Perpendicular Bisector Theorem**

If a point is equidistant from the endpoints of a segment, then it is on the perpendicular bisector of the segment.

1 EXAMPLE Real-World Connection

National Landmarks Find the set of points on the map of Washington, D.C. that are equidistant from the Jefferson Memorial and the White House.

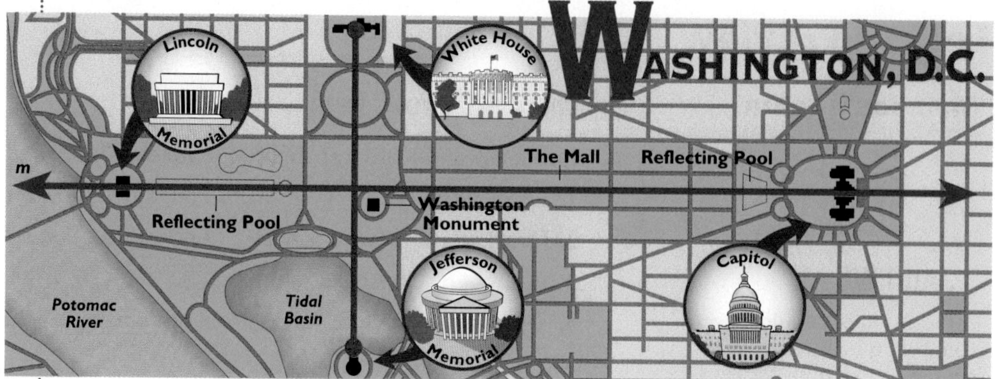

The red segment connects the Jefferson Memorial and the White House. All points on the perpendicular bisector m of this segment are equidistant from the Jefferson Memorial and the White House.

Check Understanding 1 Use the information given in the diagram. $\overleftrightarrow{CD}$ is the perpendicular bisector of $\overline{AB}$. Find CA and DB. Explain your reasoning.

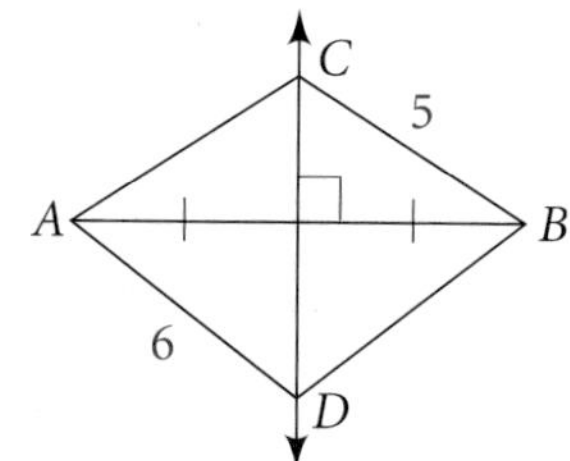

The **distance from a point to a line** is the length of the perpendicular segment from the point to the line. In the diagram, $\overrightarrow{AD}$ is the bisector of $\angle CAB$. If you measure the lengths of the perpendicular segments from D to the two sides of the angle, you will find that the lengths are equal so D is equidistant from the sides.

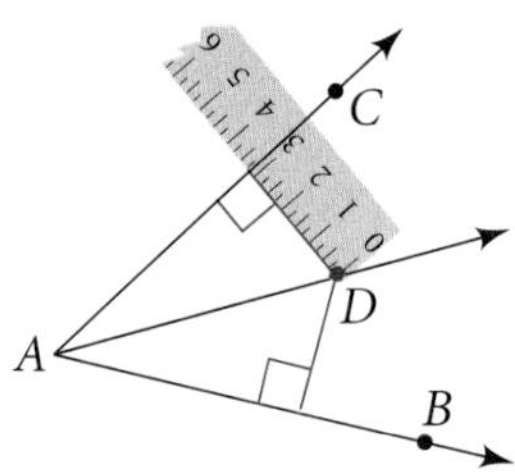

Key Concepts

Theorem 5-4 Angle Bisector Theorem

If a point is on the bisector of an angle, then the point is equidistant from the sides of the angle.

Theorem 5-5 Converse of the Angle Bisector Theorem

If a point in the interior of an angle is equidistant from the sides of the angle, then the point is on the angle bisector.

You will use congruent triangles to prove these theorems in the exercises.

You can combine Theorems 5-4 and 5-5 into a biconditional: A point in the interior of an angle is equidistant from the sides of the angle if and only if it is on the angle bisector.

2 EXAMPLE Using the Angle Bisector Theorem

Algebra Find the value of x, then find FD and FB.

From the diagram you can see that F is on the bisector of $\angle ACE$. Therefore, $FB = FD$.

$FB = FD$	
$5x = 2x + 24$	**Substitute.**
$3x = 24$	**Subtract 2x.**
$x = 8$	**Divide by 3.**
$FB = 5x = 5(8) = 40$	**Substitute.**
$FD = 40$	**Substitute.**

Check Understanding

2 **a.** According to the diagram, how far is K from $\overrightarrow{EH}$? From $\overrightarrow{ED}$?

b. What can you conclude about $\overrightarrow{EK}$?

c. Find the value of x.

d. Find $m\angle DEH$.

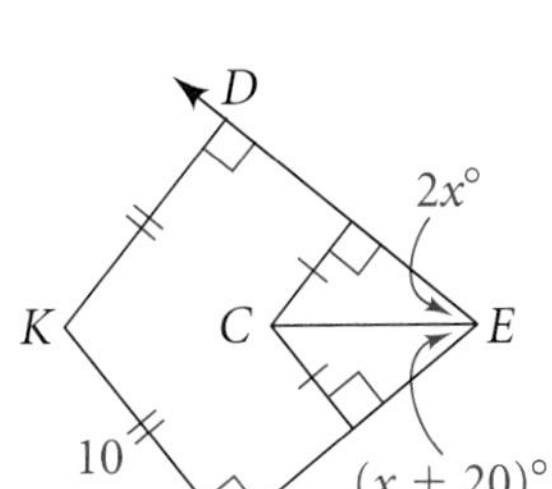

EXERCISES

For more practice, see *Extra Practice*.

Practice and Problem Solving

A Practice by Example

Example 1 (page 250)

Use the figure at the right for Exercises 1–4.

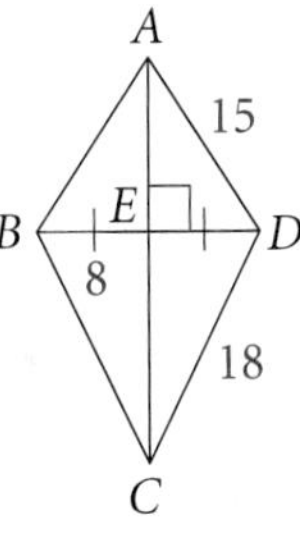

1. From the information given in the figure, how is $\overline{AC}$ related to $\overline{BD}$?

2. Find AB. **3.** Find BC. **4.** Find ED.

5. On a piece of paper, mark a point H for home and a point S for school. Describe the set of points equidistant from H and S

Example 2 (page 251)

6. Algebra Find x, JK, and JM.

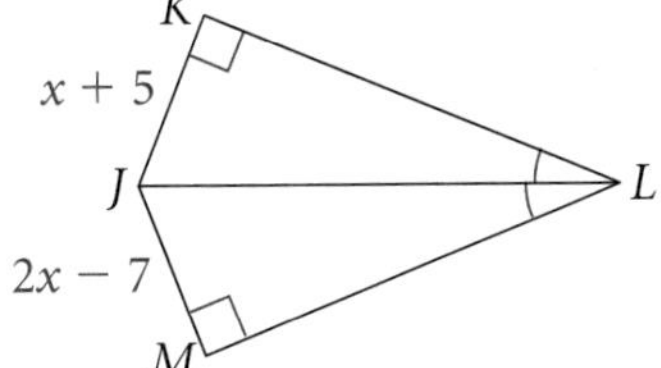

7. Algebra Find y, ST, and TU.

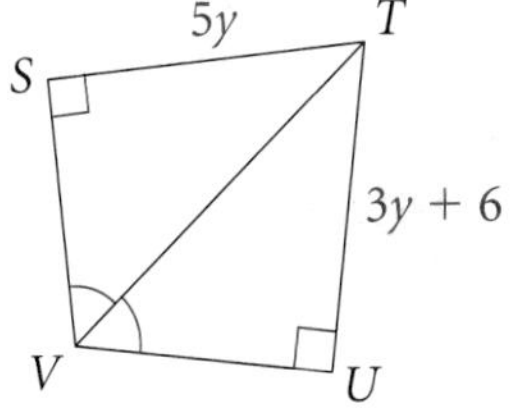

Use the figure at the right for Exercises 8–11.

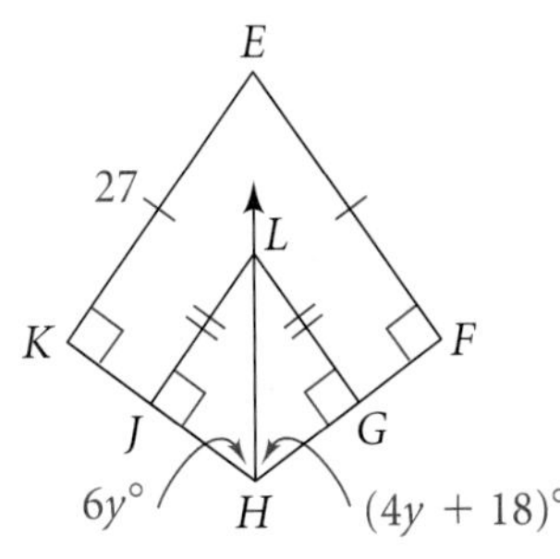

8. From the information given in the figure, how is $\overrightarrow{HL}$ related to $\angle JHG$? Explain.

9. Find the value of y, then find $m\angle FHL$ and $m\angle KHL$.

10. Find EF.

11. What can you conclude about point E?

B Apply Your Skills

x^2 **Algebra** **Use the figure, below right, for Exercises 12–16.**

12. Find the value of x.

13. Find TW.

14. Find WZ.

15. What kind of triangle is $\triangle TWZ$? Explain.

16. If R is on the perpendicular bisector of $\overline{TZ}$, then R is __?__ from T and Z, or __?__ = __?__.

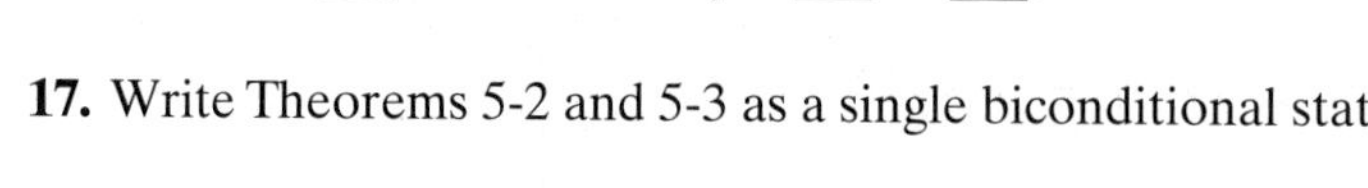

17. Write Theorems 5-2 and 5-3 as a single biconditional statement.

$\overleftrightarrow{CD}$ **is the perpendicular bisector of both $\overline{XY}$ and $\overline{ST}$, and $CY = 16$. Find each length.**

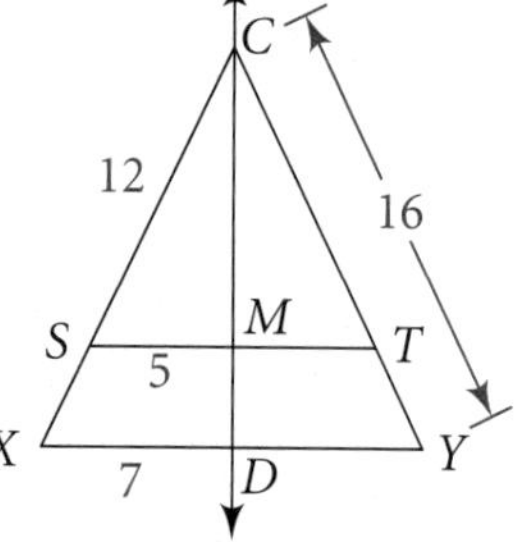

18. CT **19.** TY

20. SX **21.** CX

22. MT **23.** ST

24. DY **25.** XY

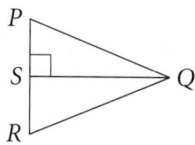

26. What kind of triangles are $\triangle SCT$ and $\triangle XCY$? Explain.

27. Error Analysis To prove that $\triangle PQR$ is isosceles, a student began by stating that since Q is on the segment perpendicular to $\overline{PR}$, Q is equidistant from the endpoints of $\overline{PR}$. What additional information does the student need in order to make that statement?

Writing **Determine whether point A must be on the bisector of $\angle TXR$. Explain.**

28.

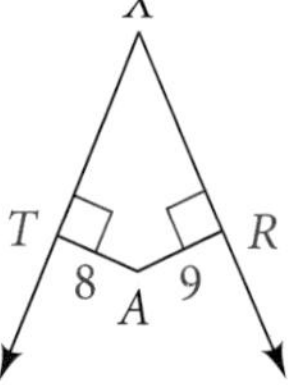

29.

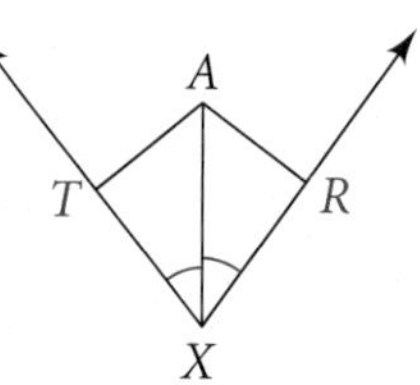

30.

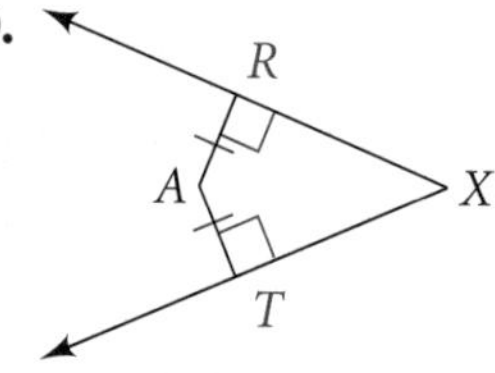

Real-World Connection

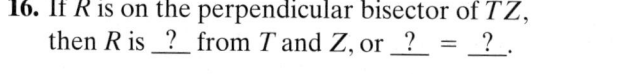

On a baseball field, second base is equidistant from the foul lines and 127 feet from home plate.

31. Baseball What is the common name for the part of a baseball field that is equidistant from the foul lines and 60 ft 6 in. from home plate?

32. a. Constructions Draw a large triangle, $\triangle CDE$. Construct the angle bisectors of each angle.

b. Make a Conjecture What appears to be true about the angle bisectors?

c. Test your conjecture with another triangle.

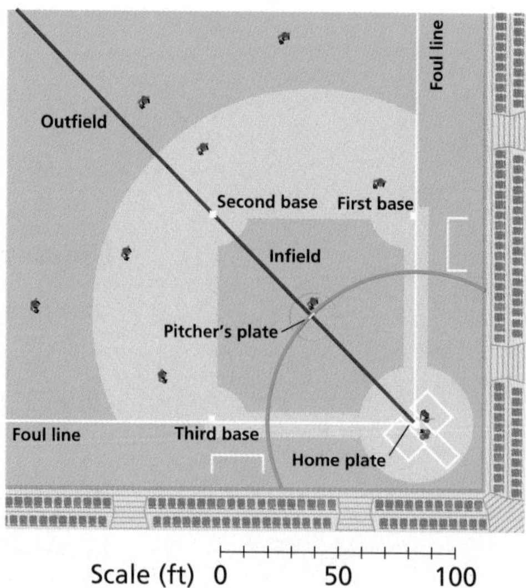

Need Help?

In Exercise 33a, your construction may suggest something but be slightly off. If so, test your conjecture *very* carefully in part (c).

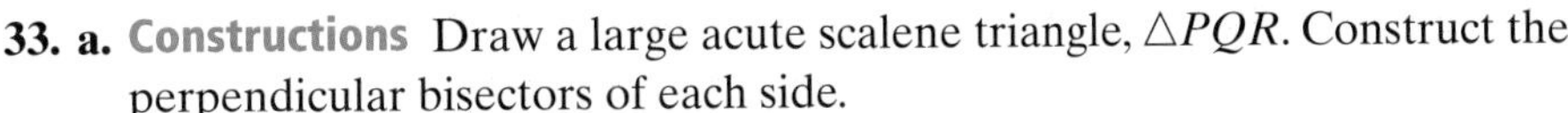

33. a. Constructions Draw a large acute scalene triangle, $\triangle PQR$. Construct the perpendicular bisectors of each side.

b. Make a Conjecture What appears to be true about the perpendicular bisectors?

c. Test your conjecture with another triangle.

Coordinate Geometry Find two points on the perpendicular bisector of $\overline{AB}$. Verify your results by showing each point is equidistant from A and B.

34. $A(0, 0), B(0,4)$ **35.** $A(0, 2), B(6, 2)$ **36.** $A(3, 3), B(3, -3)$

37. $A(3, 0), B(0,3)$ **38.** $A(3, 0), B(1, 4)$ **39.** $A(3, 0), B(2, 5)$

40. Coordinate Geometry You are given points $A(6, 8)$, $O(0, 0)$, and $B(10, 0)$.

a. Write equations of lines ℓ and m such that $\ell \perp \overleftrightarrow{OA}$ at A and $m \perp \overleftrightarrow{OB}$ at B.

b. Find the intersection C of lines ℓ and m.

c. Show that $CA = CB$.

d. Explain why C is on the bisector of $\angle AOB$.

Real-World Connection

The picture hangs straight when the hook is on the perpendicular bisector of the picture's top edge.

Proof **41. Developing Proof** Complete this paragraph proof of the Perpendicular Bisector Theorem.

Given: $\overleftrightarrow{CD} \perp \overline{AB}$, $\overleftrightarrow{CD}$ bisects $\overline{AB}$.

Prove: $DA = DB$

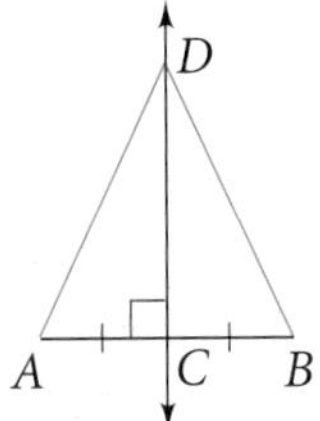

Proof: $\overline{AC} \cong \overline{BC}$ by definition of _?_.
$\overleftrightarrow{CD} \perp \overline{AB}$, so $\angle DCA$ and $\angle DCB$ are _?_ angles.
Therefore, $\angle DCA \cong \angle DCB$.
$\overline{DC} \cong \overline{DC}$ by the _?_ Property of Congruence.
Therefore, $\triangle CDA \cong \triangle CDB$ by _?_. $\overline{DA} \cong \overline{DB}$ because _?_, so $DA = DB$.

42. Developing Proof Complete the paragraph proof of the Converse of the Perpendicular Bisector Theorem.

Given: $AP = AQ$ with $\overline{AB} \perp \overline{PQ}$ at B.

Prove: $\overline{AB}$ is the perpendicular bisector of _?_.

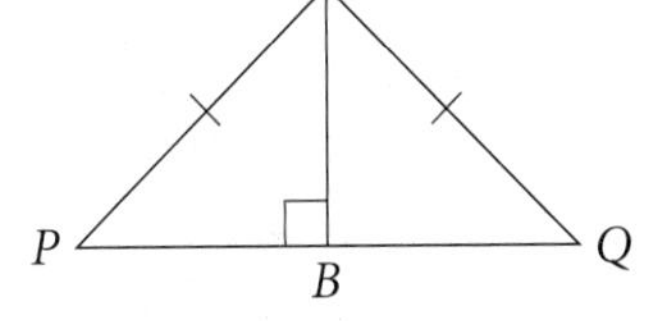

Proof: $\triangle ABP$ and $\triangle ABQ$ are right triangles with a common leg and congruent hypotenuses.
Thus $\triangle BAP \cong$ _?_ by the HL Theorem. $\overline{PB} \cong \overline{BQ}$ using _?_, so $\overline{AB}$ bisects $\overline{PQ}$ by the definition of _?_. Hence, $\overline{AB}$ is the perpendicular bisector of $\overline{PQ}$.

43. Developing Proof Use the paragraph proof from Exercise 41 or 42 to help you write a flow proof of either the Perpendicular Bisector Theorem or the Converse of the Perpendicular Bisector Theorem.

Coordinate Geometry Write an equation of the perpendicular bisector of $\overline{AB}$.

44. $A(0, 0), B(6, 0)$ **45.** $A(1, -1), B(3, 1)$ **46.** $A(-2, 0), B(2, 8)$

Challenge

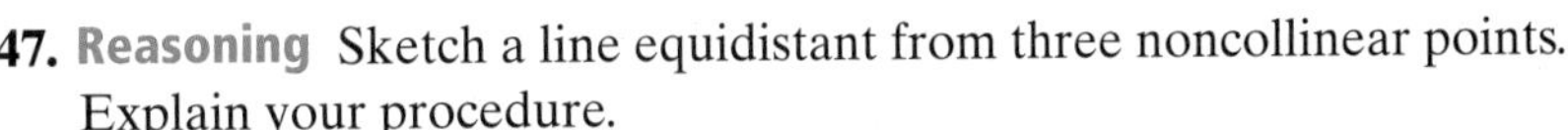

47. Reasoning Sketch a line equidistant from three noncollinear points. Explain your procedure.

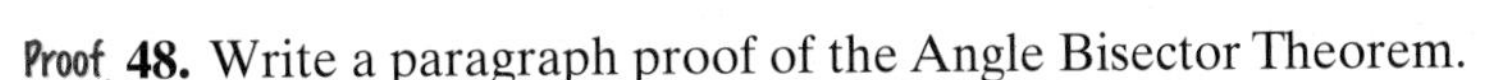

Proof **48.** Write a paragraph proof of the Angle Bisector Theorem.

Given: $\overline{PB} \perp \overrightarrow{AB}$, $\overline{PC} \perp \overrightarrow{AC}$, $\overrightarrow{AP}$ bisects $\angle BAC$.

Prove: $PB = PC$

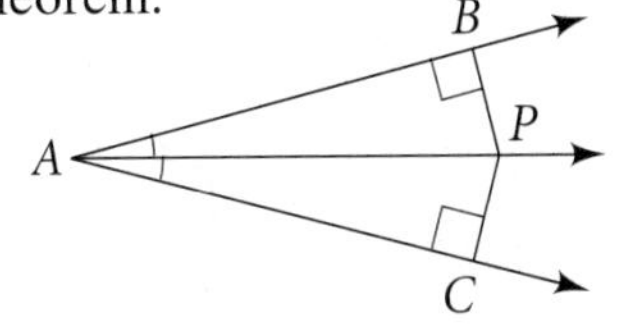

Proof **49.** Write a proof of the Converse of the Angle Bisector Theorem.

Given: $\overline{SP} \perp \overrightarrow{QP}, \overline{SR} \perp \overrightarrow{QR}, SP = SR$

Prove: $\overrightarrow{QS}$ bisects $\angle PQR$.

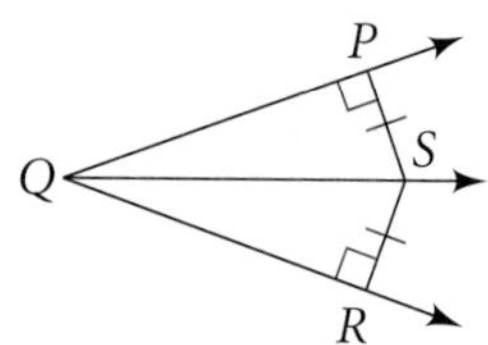

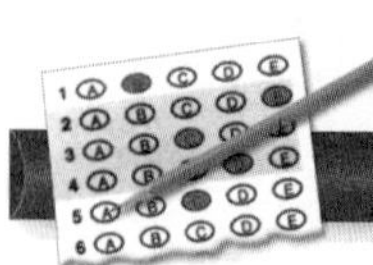

Standardized Test Prep

Multiple Choice

Use the figure at the right for Exercises 50–52.

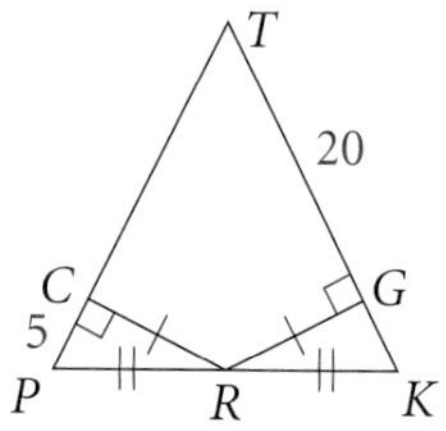

50. What is TK?

A. 4 **B.** 5 **C.** 15 **D.** 25

51. If $m\angle CTR = 27$, what is $m\angle K$?

F. 27 **G.** 54 **H.** 63 **I.** 76

52. Suppose $RK = 8$. What is the perimeter of $\triangle TPK$?

A. 25 **B.** 33 **C.** 50 **D.** 66

Take It to the NET
Online lesson quiz at
www.PHSchool.com
Web Code: afa-0502

Short Response

53. In the figure at the right, explain why $\overline{MV}$ is the angle bisector of $\angle KVR$.

Extended Response

54. In the figure at the right, explain why $\overline{MV}$ is the perpendicular bisector of $\overline{KR}$.

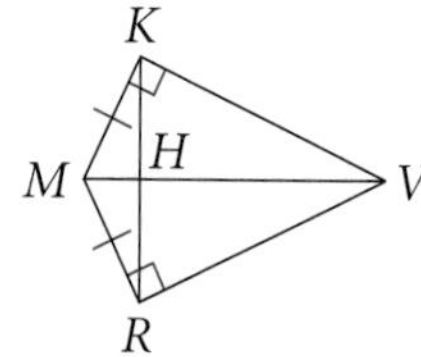

Mixed Review

Lesson 5-1 x^2 **Algebra** **Find the value of x.**

55.

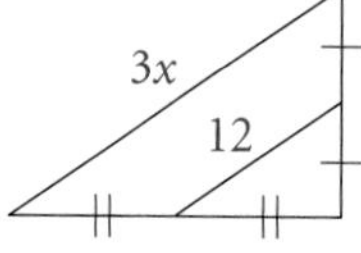

56.

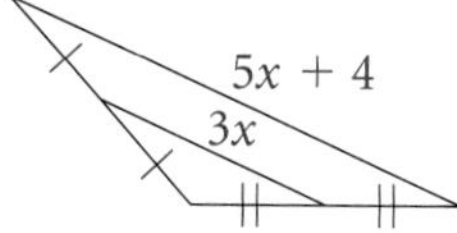

57.

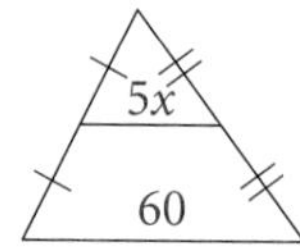

Lesson 2-4 **Name the property that justifies each statement.**

58. $AB = AB$

59. If $2x = 30$, then $x = 15$.

60. If $x = 30 - x$, then $2x = 30$.

61. $3(4x - 1) = 12x - 3$

62. If $m\angle 3 = m\angle 4$ and $m\angle 4 = m\angle 5$, then $m\angle 3 = m\angle 5$.

63. If $\angle 3 \cong \angle 4$ and $\angle 4 \cong \angle 5$, then $\angle 3 \cong \angle 5$.

Lesson 1-6 **Coordinate Geometry** **Find C the midpoint of $\overline{AB}$. Then show that $AC = CB = \frac{1}{2}AB$.**

64. $A(0, 5), B(6, 8)$ **65.** $A(-2, 8), B(2, -1)$ **66.** $A(5, 3), B(6, 7)$

Special Segments in Triangles

For Use With Lesson 5-3

Construct

Use geometry software.

- Construct a triangle and the three perpendicular bisectors of its sides.
- Construct a triangle and its three angle bisectors.
- An *altitude* of a triangle is the perpendicular segment from a vertex to the line containing the opposite side. Construct a triangle. Through a vertex of the triangle construct a line that is perpendicular to the line containing the side opposite that vertex. Next construct the altitudes from the other two vertices.

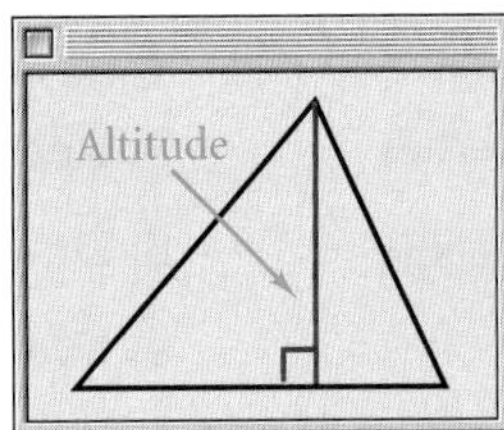

- A *median* of a triangle is the segment joining the midpoint of a side and the opposite vertex. Construct a triangle. Construct the midpoint of one side. Draw the median. Then construct the other two medians.

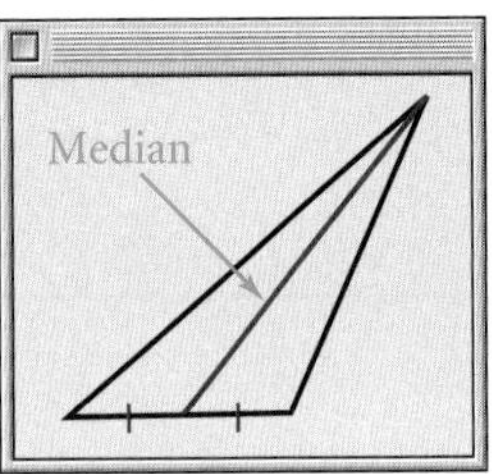

EXERCISES

1. In the constructions above, what property do the perpendicular bisectors, angle bisectors, lines containing altitudes, and medians seem to have?
2. Manipulate the triangles. Does the property still hold as you manipulate the triangles?
3. List your conjectures about the perpendicular bisectors, angle bisectors, lines containing altitudes, and medians of a triangle.

Extend

4. Copy the table. Think about acute triangles, right triangles, and obtuse triangles. Use *inside*, *on*, or *outside* to describe the location of the intersection of the segments or lines for each type of triangle.

	Perpendicular Bisectors	Angle Bisectors	Lines Containing the Altitudes	Medians
Acute Triangle				
Right Triangle				
Obtuse Triangle				

5. What observations, if any, can you make about these special segments for isosceles triangles? Equilateral triangles?
6. Your Exercise 3 conjecture should identify some special points. One of these points is equidistant from the three vertices of its triangle, no matter what shape the triangle has. Use your software. Find which special segments locate this extra-special point.

5-3 Concurrent Lines, Medians, and Altitudes

Lesson Preview

What You'll Learn

To identify properties of perpendicular bisectors and angle bisectors

To identify properties of medians and altitudes of a triangle

... And Why

To find a location in a backyard for the largest possible swimming pool, as in Example 2

✔ Check Skills You'll Need

(For help, go to Lesson 1-5.)

For Exercises 1–2, draw a large triangle. Construct each figure.

1. an angle bisector
2. a perpendicular bisector of a side
3. Draw $\overline{GH}$. Construct $\overleftrightarrow{CD} \perp \overline{GH}$ at the midpoint of $\overline{GH}$.
4. Draw $\overleftrightarrow{AB}$ with a point E not on $\overleftrightarrow{AB}$. Construct $\overleftrightarrow{EF} \perp \overleftrightarrow{AB}$.

New Vocabulary

- concurrent
- point of concurrency
- circumcenter of a triangle
- circumscribed about
- incenter of a triangle
- inscribed in
- median of a triangle
- centroid
- altitude of a triangle
- orthocenter of a triangle

Interactive lesson includes instant self-check, tutorials, and activities.

OBJECTIVE 1 Properties of Bisectors

Investigation: Paper Folding Bisectors

- Draw and cut out five different triangles: two acute, two right, and one obtuse.
- Step 1: Use paper folding to create the angle bisectors of each angle of an acute triangle. What do you notice about the angle bisectors?
- Step 2: Repeat Step 1 with a right triangle and an obtuse triangle. Does your discovery from Step 1 still hold true?

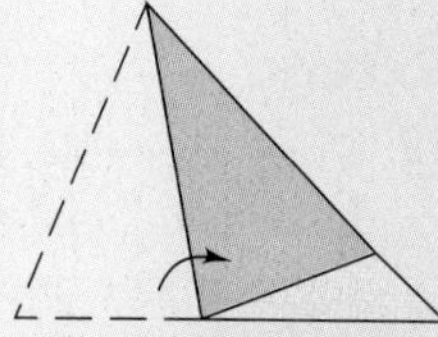

Folding an Angle Bisector

1. Make a conjecture about the bisectors of the angles of a triangle.

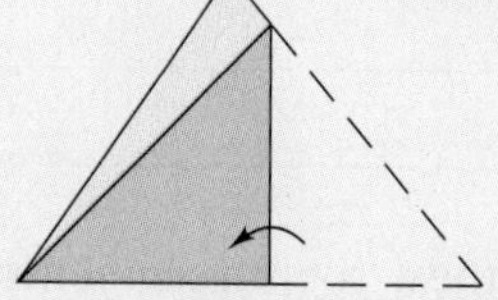

Folding a Perpendicular Bisector

- Step 3: Use paper folding to create the perpendicular bisector of each side of an acute triangle. What do you notice about the perpendicular bisectors?
- Step 4: Repeat Step 3 with a right triangle. What do you notice?

2. Make a conjecture about the perpendicular bisectors of the sides of a triangle.

When three or more lines intersect in one point, they are **concurrent.** The point at which they intersect is the **point of concurrency.** For any triangle, four different sets of lines are concurrent. Theorems 5-6 and 5-7 tell you about two of them.

Key Concepts

Theorem 5-6

The perpendicular bisectors of the sides of a triangle are concurrent at a point equidistant from the vertices.

Theorem 5-7

The bisectors of the angles of a triangle are concurrent at a point equidistant from the sides.

You will prove these theorems in the exercises.

Reading Math

The prefix *circum* is Latin for "around" or "about."

This figure shows $\triangle QRS$ with the perpendicular bisectors of its sides concurrent at C. The point of concurrency of the perpendicular bisectors of a triangle is called the **circumcenter of the triangle.**

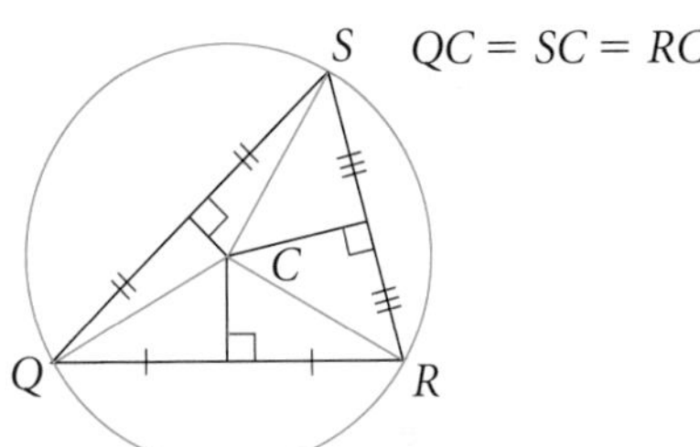

Points Q, R, and S are equidistant from C, the circumcenter. The circle is **circumscribed about** the triangle.

1 EXAMPLE Finding the Circumcenter

Coordinate Geometry Find the center of the circle that you can circumscribe about $\triangle OPS$.

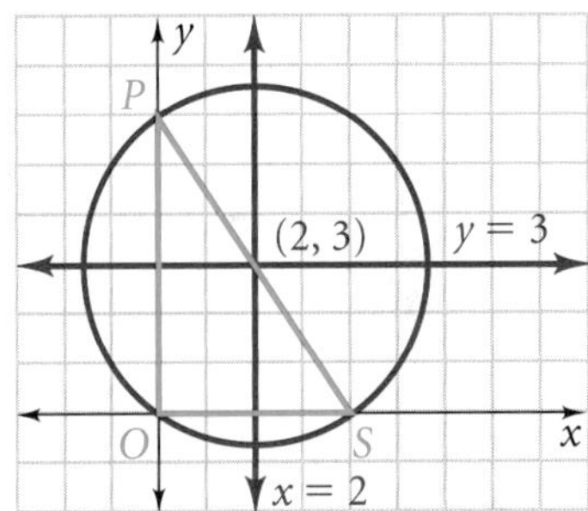

Two perpendicular bisectors of sides of $\triangle OPS$ are $x = 2$ and $y = 3$. These lines intersect at $(2, 3)$. This point is the center of the circle.

Check Understanding

1 **a.** Find the center of the circle that you can circumscribe about the triangle with vertices $(0, 0)$, $(-8, 0)$, and $(0, 6)$.

b. Critical Thinking In Example 1, explain why it is not necessary to find the third perpendicular bisector.

This figure shows $\triangle UTV$ with the bisectors of its angles concurrent at I. The point of concurrency of the angle bisectors of a triangle is called the **incenter of the triangle.**

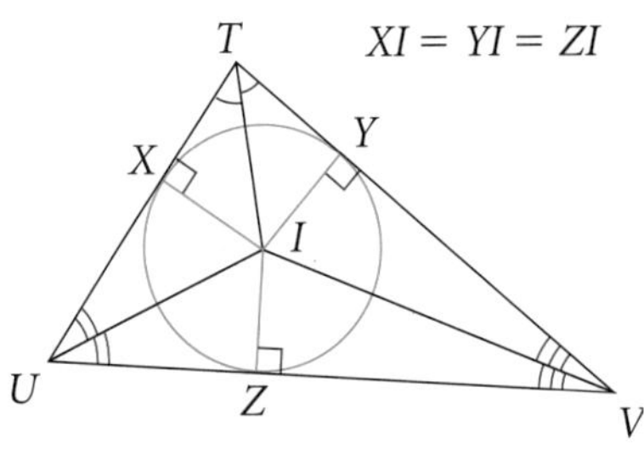

Points X, Y, and Z are equidistant from I, the incenter. The circle is **inscribed in** the triangle.

2 EXAMPLE Real-World Connection

Pools The Jacksons want to install the largest possible circular pool in their triangular backyard. Where would the largest possible pool be located?

Locate the center of the pool at the point of concurrency of the angle bisectors. This point is equidistant from the sides of the yard. If you choose any other point as the center of the pool, it will be closer to at least one of the sides of the yard, and the pool will be smaller.

Check Understanding 2 **a.** The towns of Adamsville, Brooksville, and Cartersville want to build a library that is equidistant from the three towns. Trace the diagram and show where they should build the library.

b. What theorem did you use to find the location?

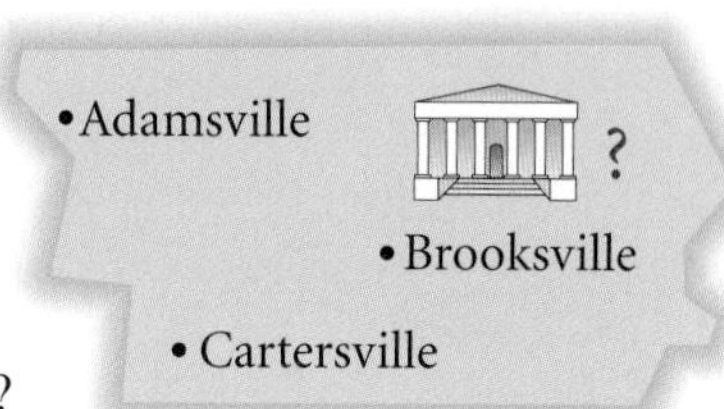

OBJECTIVE

2 Medians and Altitudes

A **median of a triangle** is a segment whose endpoints are a vertex and the midpoint of the opposite side.

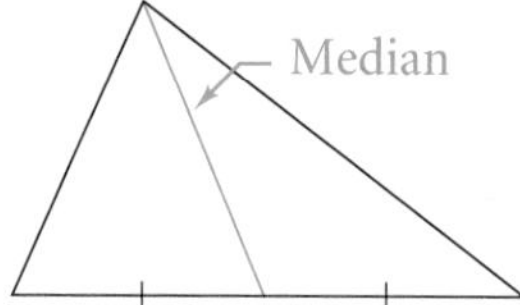

Key Concepts

Theorem 5-8

The medians of a triangle are concurrent at a point that is two thirds the distance from each vertex to the midpoint of the opposite side.

$DC = \frac{2}{3}DJ \quad EC = \frac{2}{3}EG \quad FC = \frac{2}{3}FH$

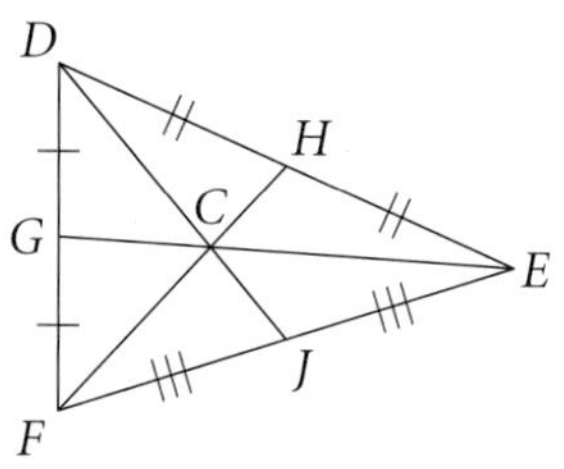

In a triangle, the point of concurrency of the medians is the **centroid.** The point is also called the center of gravity of a triangle because it is the point where a triangular shape will balance. (See Real-World Snapshots, page 345.) You will prove Theorem 5-8 in Chapter 6.

3 EXAMPLE Finding Lengths of Medians

D is the centroid of $\triangle ABC$ and $DE = 6$. Find BE.

Since D is a centroid, $BD = \frac{2}{3}BE$ and $DE = \frac{1}{3}BE$.

$\frac{1}{3}BE = DE$

$\frac{1}{3}BE = 6$ **Substitute 6 for *DE*.**

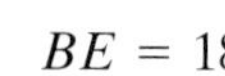

$BE = 18$

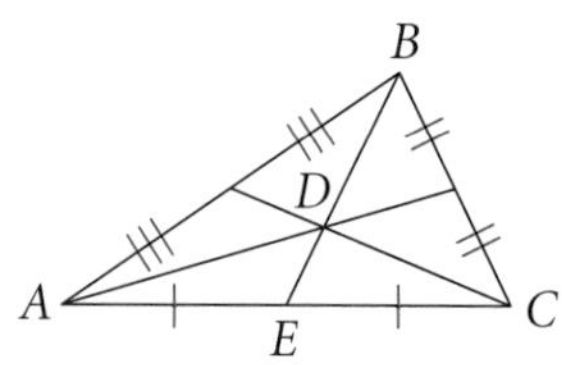

Check Understanding 3 Find BD. Check that $BD + DE = BE$.

An **altitude of a triangle** is the perpendicular segment from a vertex to the line containing the opposite side. Unlike angle bisectors and medians, an altitude of a triangle can be a side of a triangle or it may lie outside the triangle.

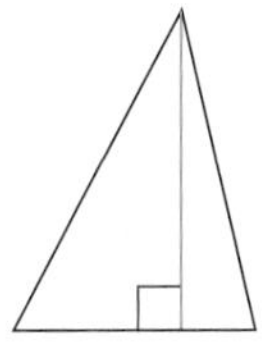

Acute Triangle:
Altitude is inside.

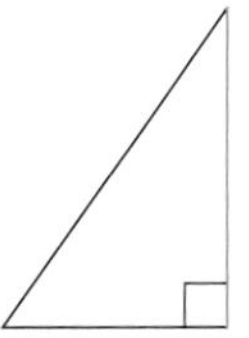

Right Triangle:
Altitude is a side.

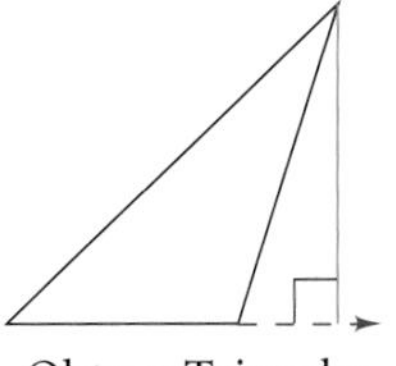

Obtuse Triangle:
Altitude is outside.

4 EXAMPLE Identifying Medians and Altitudes

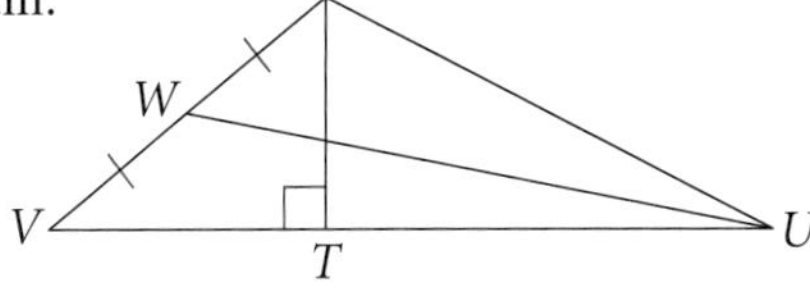

Is $\overline{ST}$ a median, an altitude, or neither? Explain.

$\overline{ST}$ is a segment extending from vertex S to the side opposite S. Also, $\overline{ST} \perp \overline{VU}$. $\overline{ST}$ is an altitude of $\triangle VSU$.

Check Understanding 4 Is $\overline{UW}$ a median, an altitude, or neither? Explain.

The lines containing the altitudes of a triangle are concurrent at the **orthocenter of the triangle.** A proof of this theorem appears in Chapter 6.

Key Concepts

Theorem 5-9

The lines that contain the altitudes of a triangle are concurrent.

EXERCISES

For more practice, see *Extra Practice.*

Practice and Problem Solving

A Practice by Example

Example 1
(page 257)

Coordinate Geometry **Find the center of the circle that you can circumscribe about each triangle.**

1.

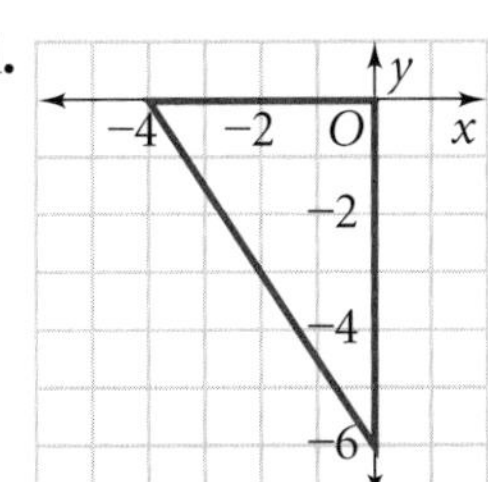

2.

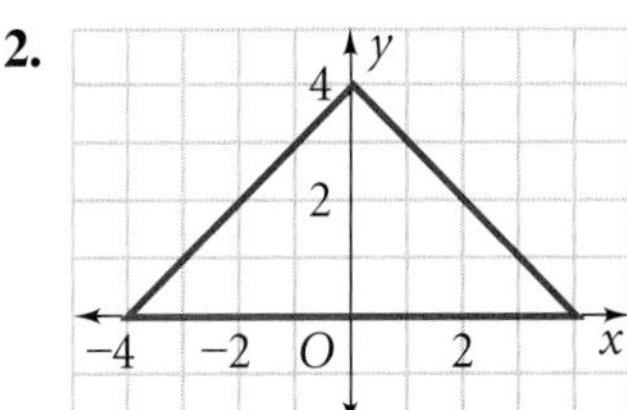

Coordinate Geometry **Find the center of the circle that you can circumscribe about $\triangle ABC$.**

3. $A(0, 0)$ $B(3, 0)$ $C(3, 2)$

4. $A(0, 0)$ $B(4, 0)$ $C(4, -3)$

5. $A(-4, 5)$ $B(-2, 5)$ $C(-2, -2)$

6. $A(-1, -2)$ $B(-5, -2)$ $C(-1, -7)$

7. $A(1, 4)$ $B(1, 2)$ $C(6, 2)$

Example 2 (page 258)

Name the point of concurrency of the angle bisectors.

8.

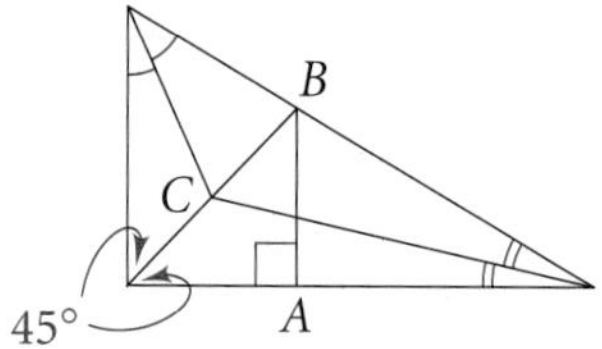

9.

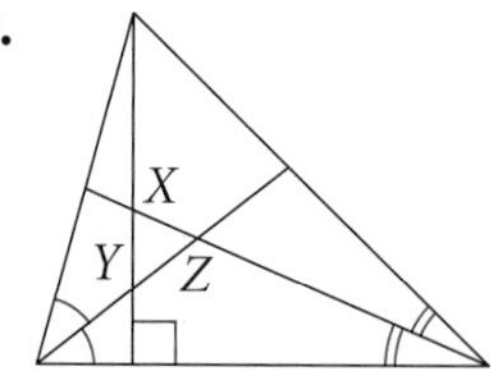

10. **City Planning** Copy the diagram of Altgeld Park. Show where park officials should place a drinking fountain so that it is equidistant from the tennis court, the playground, and the volleyball court.

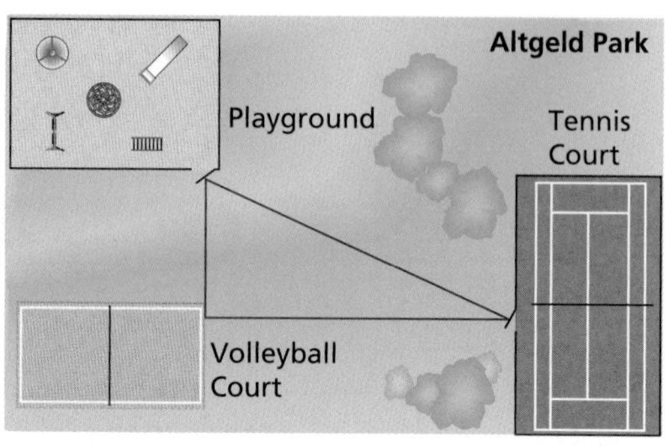

Example 3 (page 258)

In $\triangle TUV$, Y is the centroid.

11. If $YW = 9$, find TY and TW.

12. If $YU = 9$, find ZY and ZU.

13. If $VX = 9$, find VY and YX.

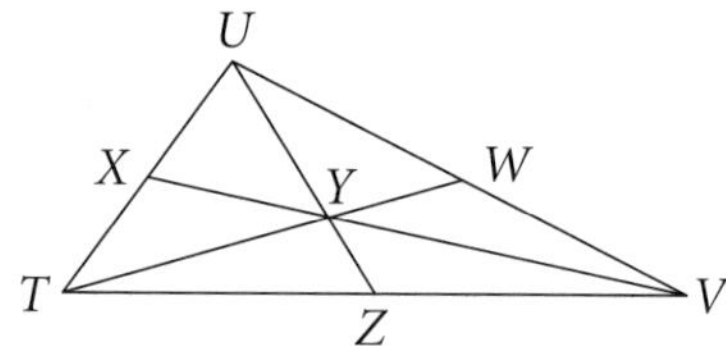

Example 4 (page 259)

Is $\overline{AB}$ a median, an altitude, or neither? Explain.

14.

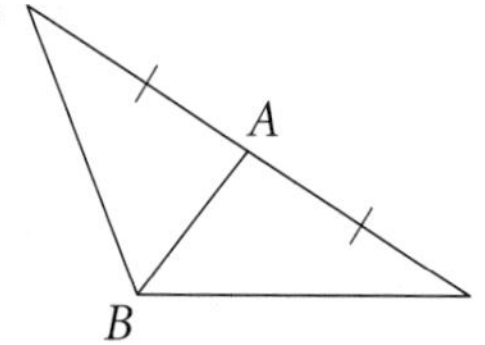

15.

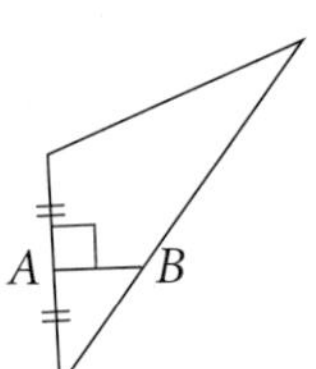

16.

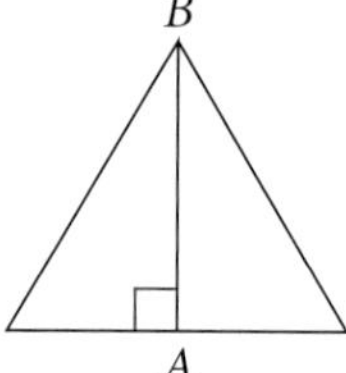

B Apply Your Skills

Constructions **Draw the triangle. Then construct the inscribed circle and the circumscribed circle.**

17. right triangle, $\triangle DEF$

18. obtuse triangle, $\triangle STU$

In Exercises 19–22, name each figure in $\triangle BDF$.

19. an angle bisector

20. a median

21. a perpendicular bisector

22. an altitude

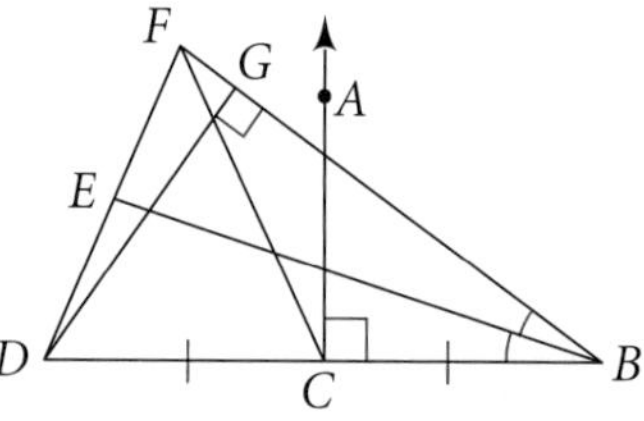

23. **Critical Thinking** A centroid separates a median into two segments. What is the ratio of the lengths of those segments?

24. **Writing** Ivars found a yellowed parchment inside an antique book. It read:

From the spot I buried Olaf's treasure, equal sets of paces did I measure; each of three directions in a line, there to plant a seedling Norway pine. I could not return for failing health; now the hounds of Haiti guard my wealth.—Karl

After searching Caribbean islands for five years, Ivars found one with three tall Norway pines. How might Ivars find where Karl buried Olaf's treasure?

The figures below show how to construct medians and altitudes by paper folding.

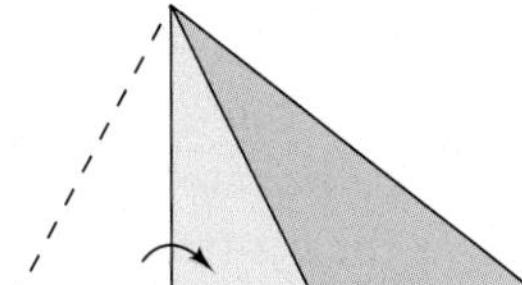

To find an altitude, fold the triangle so that a side overlaps itself and the fold contains the opposite vertex.

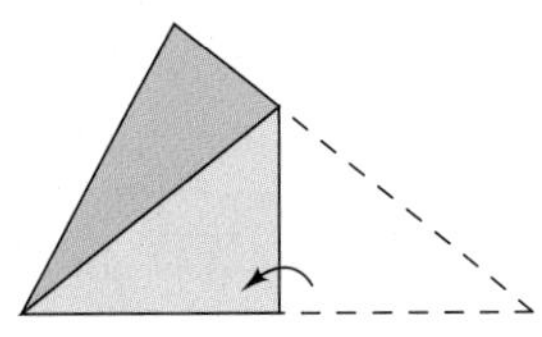

To find a median, fold one vertex to another vertex. This locates the midpoint of a side.

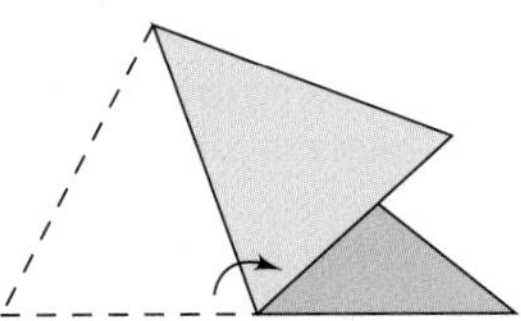

Then fold so that the fold contains the midpoint and the opposite vertex.

> **Need Help?**
> Paper-folding an altitude is the same as paper-folding the perpendicular to a line through a point not on the line.

25. Cut out a large triangle. Paper-fold very carefully to construct the three medians of the triangle and demonstrate Theorem 5-8.

26. Cut out a large acute triangle. Paper-fold very carefully to construct the three altitudes of the triangle and demonstrate Theorem 5-9.

Is $\overline{AB}$ a perpendicular bisector, an angle bisector, a median, an altitude, or none of these? Explain.

27.

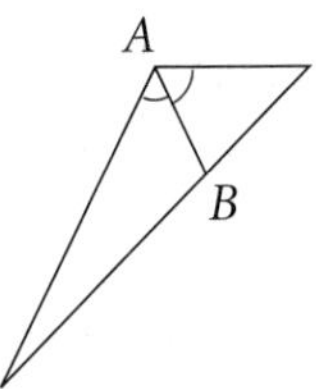

28.

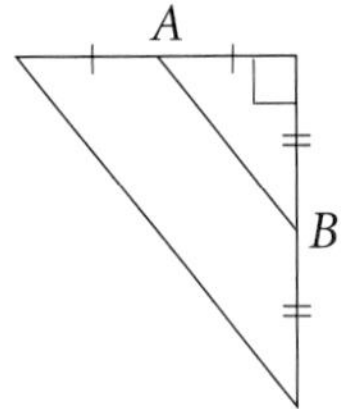

29.

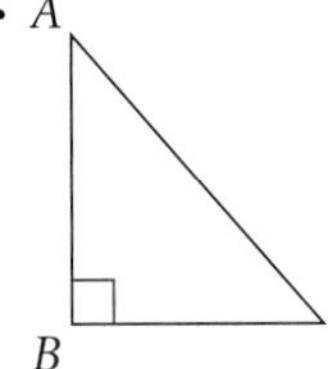

Proof **30. Developing Proof** Complete this proof of Theorem 5-6 by filling in the blanks.

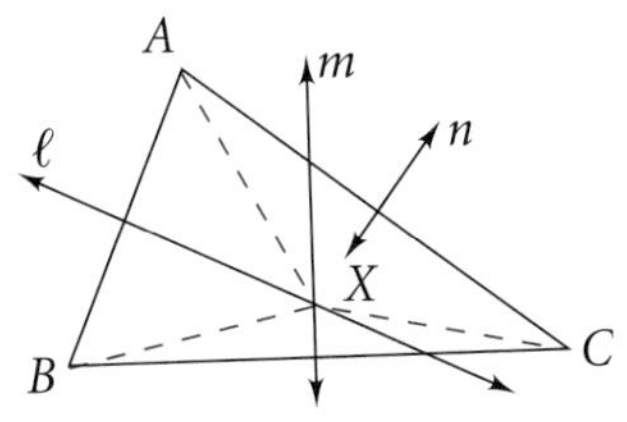

Given: Lines ℓ, m, and n are perpendicular bisectors of the sides of $\triangle ABC$. X is the intersection of lines ℓ and m.

Prove: Line n contains point X, and $XA = XB = XC$.

Proof: Since ℓ is the perpendicular bisector of **a.** _?_, $XA = XB$. Since m is the perpendicular bisector of **b.** _?_, $XB =$ **c.** _?_. Thus $XA = XB = XC$. Since $XA = XC$, X is on line n by the Converse of the **d.** _?_ Theorem.

31. Developing Proof Complete the flow proof of Theorem 5-7.

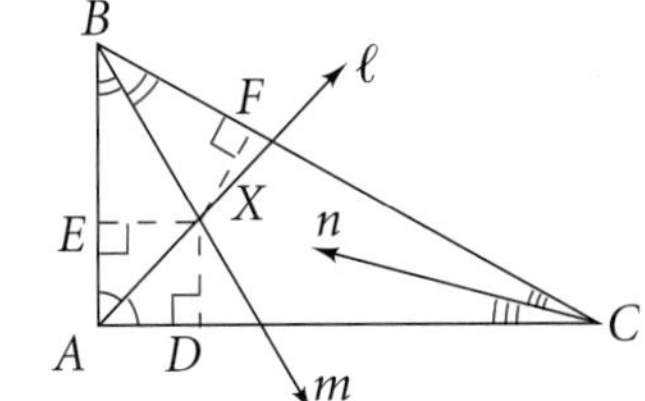

Given: Rays ℓ, m, and n are bisectors of the angles of $\triangle ABC$. X is the intersection of rays ℓ and m and $\overline{XD} \perp \overline{AC}$, $\overline{XE} \perp \overline{AB}$, $\overline{XF} \perp \overline{BC}$.

Prove: Ray n contains point X, and $XD = XE = XF$.

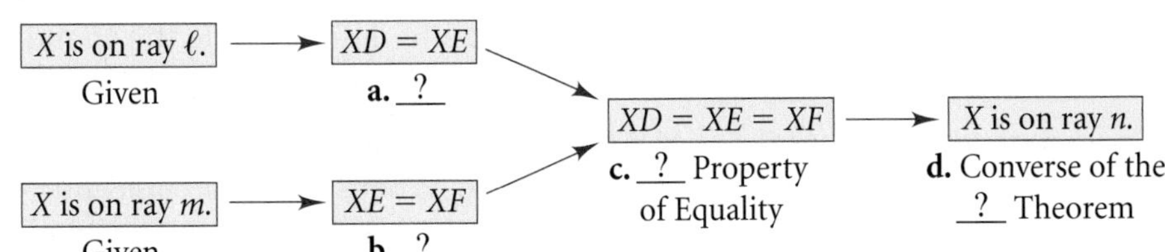

Reading Math

You can prove Theorem 5-8 for a general $\triangle ABC$ with coordinates $A(0, 0)$, $B(2b, 2d)$, and $C(2c, 0)$ by following the steps for the particular $\triangle ABC$ in Exercise 32.

32. Coordinate Geometry Complete the following steps to locate the centroid.

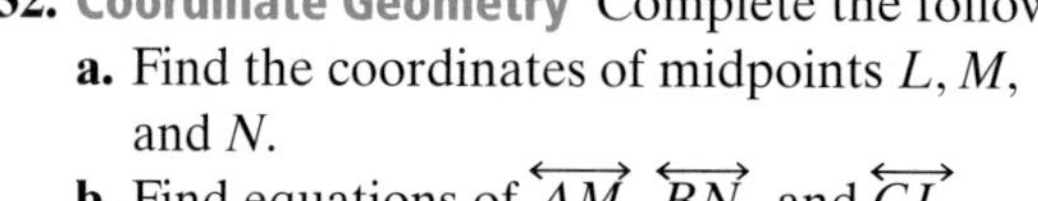

a. Find the coordinates of midpoints L, M, and N.

b. Find equations of $\overleftrightarrow{AM}$, $\overleftrightarrow{BN}$, and $\overleftrightarrow{CL}$.

c. Find the coordinates of P, the intersection of $\overleftrightarrow{AM}$ and $\overleftrightarrow{BN}$. This is the centroid.

d. Show that point P is on $\overleftrightarrow{CL}$.

e. Use the Distance Formula to show that point P is $\frac{2}{3}$ of the distance from each vertex to the midpoint of the opposite side.

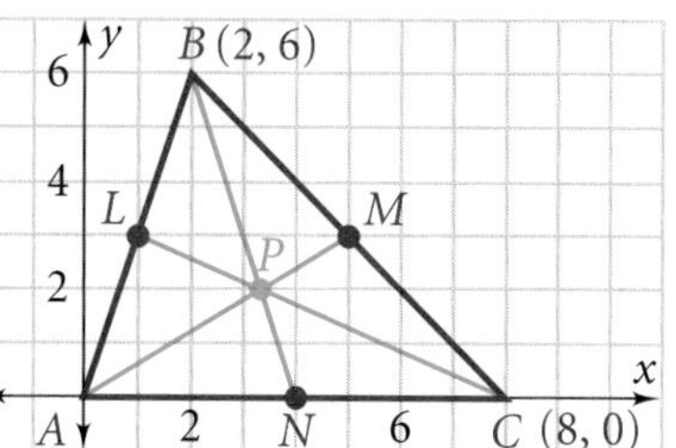

Challenge

For Exercises 33 and 34, points of concurrency have been drawn for two triangles. Match the points with the lines and segments listed in I–IV.

33.

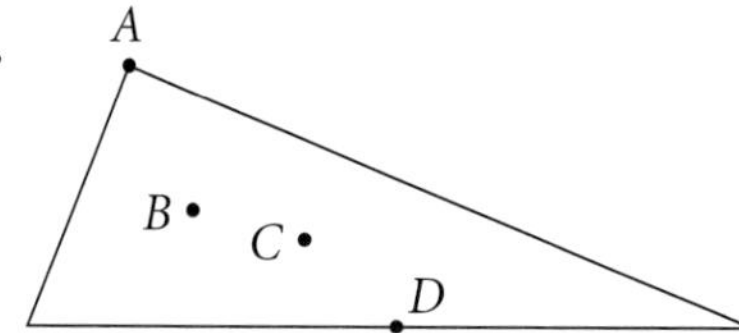

34.

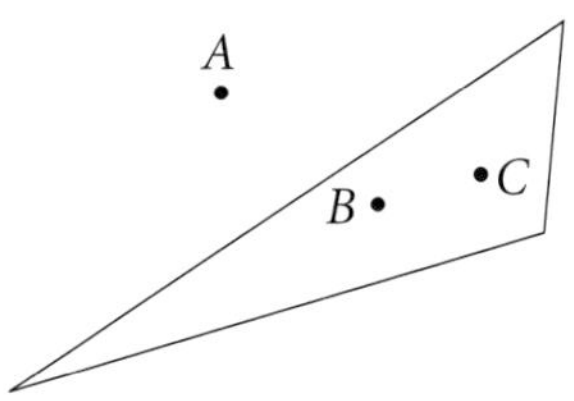

I. perpendicular bisectors of sides
II. angle bisectors
III. medians
IV. lines containing altitudes

35. In an isosceles triangle, show that the circumcenter, incenter, centroid, and orthocenter can be four different points but all four must be collinear.

36. History In 1765 Leonhard Euler proved that for any triangle, three of the four points of concurrency are collinear. The line that contains these three points is known as Euler's Line. Use Exercises 33 and 34 to determine which point of concurrency does not necessarily lie on Euler's Line.

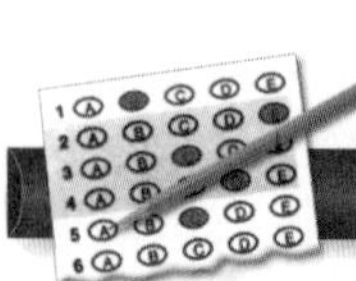

Standardized Test Prep

Multiple Choice

Use the figure at the right for Exercises 37–39.

37. What is RD if $RL = 54$ cm?

A. 81 cm B. 108 cm
C. 162 cm D. 216 cm

38. What is WL if $WJ = 210$ mm?

F. 70 mm G. 105 mm
H. 140 mm I. 157.5 mm

39. What is x if $WL = 15x$ and $LJ = 5x + 3$?

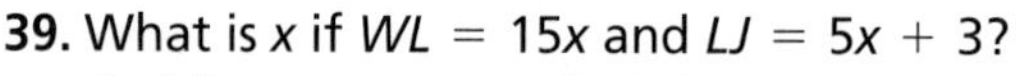

A. 0.3 B. 0.4 C. 0.6 D. 1.2

Take It to the NET

Online lesson quiz at **www.PHSchool.com**

Web Code: afa-0503

Short Response

40. Name all types of triangles for which the centroid, circumcenter, incenter, and orthocenter are all inside the triangle. Classify the triangles according to the sides as well as the angles.

Extended Response

41. The point of concurrency of the three altitudes of a triangle lies outside the triangle. Where are its circumcenter, incenter, and centroid located in relation to the triangle? Draw and label a diagram to support each of your answers.

Mixed Review

Lesson 5-2 **Determine whether point *B* must be on the bisector of $\angle T$. Explain.**

42.

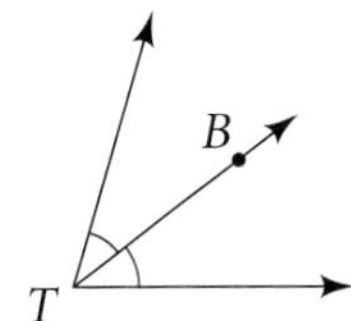

43.

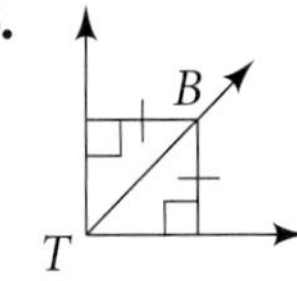

44.

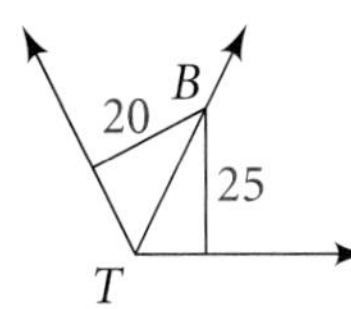

Lesson 3-3 **Classify each $\triangle JKL$ by its angles.**

45. $m\angle J = 37, m\angle K = 53, m\angle L = 90$ **46.** $m\angle J = 47, m\angle K = 98, m\angle L = 35$

Lesson 1-3 **In the figure at the right, *ABCD* is a square. Identify each of the following.**

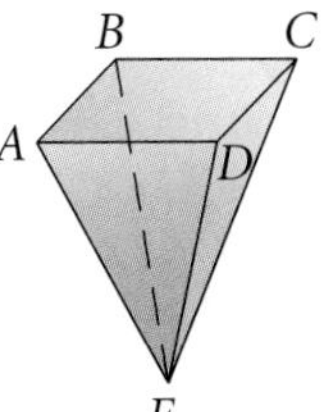

47. a line skew to $\overleftrightarrow{ED}$ **48.** a line skew to $\overleftrightarrow{EB}$

49. two intersecting planes **50.** two parallel segments

51. the intersection of plane *ABC* and plane *BCE*

Checkpoint Quiz 1 Lessons 5-1 through 5-3

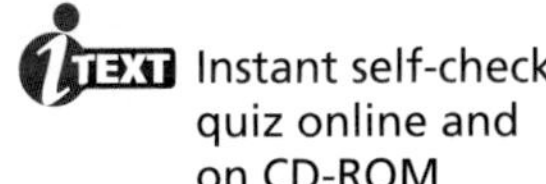
Instant self-check quiz online and on CD-ROM

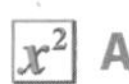
Algebra **Find the value of *x*.**

1.

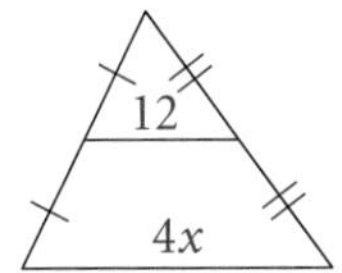

2.

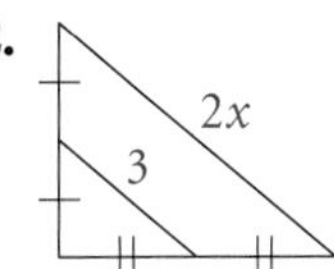

3. a. $\overline{AB}$ is a midsegment of $\triangle XYZ$. $AB = 52$. Find *YZ*.

b. $AX = 26$ and $BZ = 36$. Find the perimeter of $\triangle XYZ$.

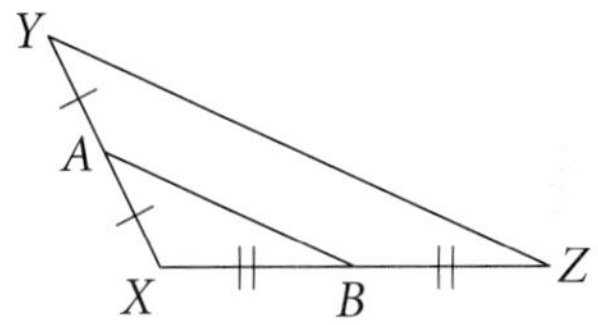

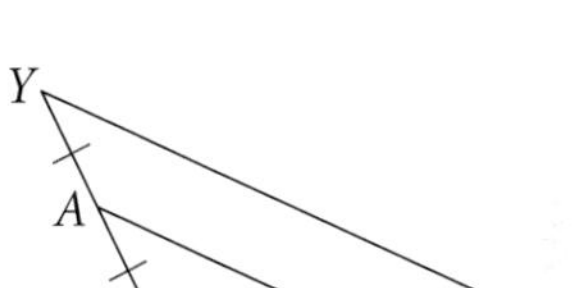

Use the diagram. What can you conclude about each of the following? Explain.

4. $\angle CDB$

5. $\triangle ABD$ and $\triangle CBD$

6. $\overline{AD}$ and $\overline{DC}$

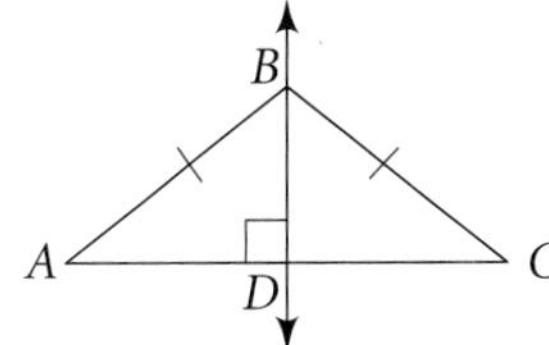

Use the figure at the right.

7. What can you conclude about $\overrightarrow{XY}$? Explain.

8. Find *XZ*. Justify your response.

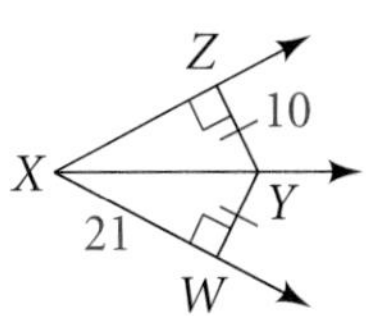

Writing **For a given triangle, describe how you can construct the following.**

9. a median **10.** an altitude

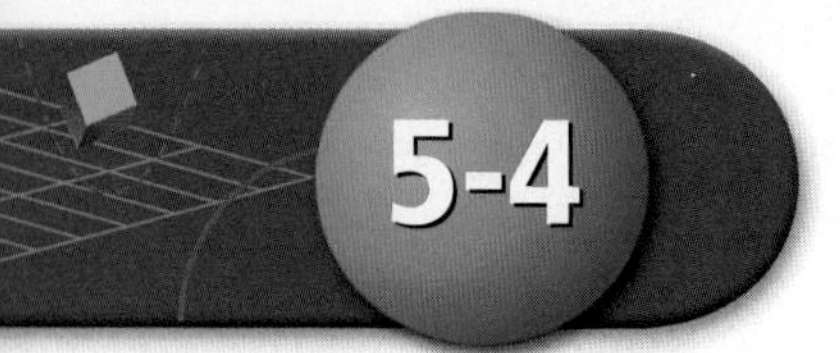

5-4 Inverses, Contrapositives, and Indirect Reasoning

Lesson Preview

What You'll Learn

OBJECTIVE 1 To write the negation of a statement and the inverse and contrapositive of a conditional statement

OBJECTIVE 2 To use indirect reasoning

. . . And Why

To describe how an advertisement can be misunderstood, as in Exercise 28

✓ Check Skills You'll Need

(For help, go to Lessons 2-1 and 2-2.)

Write the converse of each statement.

1. If it snows tomorrow, then we will go skiing.
2. If two lines are parallel, then they do not intersect.
3. If $x = -1$, then $x^2 = 1$.

Write two conditional statements that make up each biconditional.

4. A point is on the bisector of an angle if and only if it is equidistant from the sides of the angle.
5. A point is on the perpendicular bisector of a segment if and only if it is equidistant from the endpoints of the segment.
6. You will pass a geometry course if and only if you are successful with your homework.

New Vocabulary
- negation
- inverse
- contrapositive
- equivalent statements
- indirect reasoning
- indirect proof

Interactive lesson includes instant self-check, tutorials, and activities.

OBJECTIVE 1 Writing the Negation, Inverse, and Contrapositive

The statement, "Knoxville is the capital of Tennessee," is false. The **negation** of a statement has the opposite truth value. The negation, "Knoxville is not the capital of Tennessee," is true.

1 EXAMPLE Writing the Negation of a Statement

Write the negation of each statement.

a. Statement: $\angle ABC$ is obtuse.
Negation: $\angle ABC$ is not obtuse.

b. Statement: Lines m and n are not perpendicular.
Negation: Lines m and n are perpendicular.

✓ Check Understanding

1. Write the negation of each statement.
a. $m\angle XYZ > 70$.
b. Today is not Tuesday.

Reading Math
The prefix *contra* is Latin for "against."

The **inverse** of a conditional statement negates both the hypothesis and the conclusion. The **contrapositive** of a conditional switches the hypothesis and the conclusion and negates both.

"If you don't stand for something, you'll fall for anything."

—Maya Angelou, poet and author

2 EXAMPLE Writing the Inverse and Contrapositive

Write the inverse and the contrapositive of the conditional statement.

Conditional: If a figure is a square, then it is a rectangle.

Negate both.

Inverse: If a figure is not a square, then it is not a rectangle.

Conditional: If a figure is a square, then it is a rectangle.

Switch and negate both.

Contrapositive: If a figure is not a rectangle, then it is not a square.

Check Understanding 2 Write (a) the inverse and (b) the contrapositive of Maya Angelou's statement under the photo at the left.

You know that a conditional statement and its converse can have different truth values. A conditional statement and its inverse can also have different truth values. The contrapositive of a conditional statement, however, always has the same truth value as the conditional. A conditional statement and its contrapositive are equivalent. **Equivalent statements** have the same truth value.

Key Concepts

Summary Negation, Inverse, and Contrapositive Statements

Statement	Example	Symbolic Form	You Read It
Conditional	If an angle is a straight angle, then its measure is 180.	$p \rightarrow q$	If p, then q.
Negation (of p)	An angle is not a straight angle.	$\sim p$	Not p.
Inverse	If an angle is not a straight angle, then its measure is not 180.	$\sim p \rightarrow \sim q$	If not p, then not q.
Contrapositive	If an angle's measure is not 180, then it is not a straight angle.	$\sim q \rightarrow \sim p$	If not q, then not p.

OBJECTIVE

2 Using Indirect Reasoning

Suppose your brother tells you, "Susan called a few minutes ago." You think through these three steps.

Step 1 You have two friends named Susan.

Step 2 You know that one of them is at band practice.

Step 3 You conclude that the other Susan must have been the caller.

This type of reasoning is called indirect reasoning. In **indirect reasoning,** all possibilities are considered and then all but one are proved false. The remaining possibility must be true.

A proof involving indirect reasoning is an **indirect proof.** In an indirect proof, a statement and its negation often are the only possibilities.

Key Concepts

Summary **Writing an Indirect Proof**

Step 1 State as an assumption the opposite (negation) of what you want to prove.

Step 2 Show that this assumption leads to a contradiction.

Step 3 Conclude that the assumption must be false and that what you want to prove must be true.

In the first step of an indirect proof you assume as true the opposite of what you want to prove.

Proof

3 EXAMPLE The First Step of an Indirect Proof

Developing Proof Write the first step of an indirect proof.

a. Prove: Quadrilateral $QRWX$ does not have four acute angles.

Assume that quadrilateral $QRWX$ has four acute angles.

b. Prove: An integer n is divisible by 5.

Assume that the integer n is not divisible by 5.

Check Understanding 3 You want to prove each statement true. Write the first step of an indirect proof.

a. The shoes cost no more than \$20. **b.** $m\angle A > m\angle B$

Jack, 18, is a good driver. Jack concludes he will get a good insurance rate. His insurance bill is a contradiction.

To do an indirect proof, you have to be able to identify a contradiction.

4 EXAMPLE Identifying Contradictions

Developing Proof Identify the two statements that contradict each other.

I. $\triangle ABC$ is acute. II. $\triangle ABC$ is scalene. III. $\triangle ABC$ is equiangular.

A triangle can be acute and scalene. I and II do not contradict each other.

An equiangular triangle is an acute triangle. I and III do not contradict each other.

An equiangular triangle must be equilateral, so it cannot be scalene. II and III contradict each other.

Check Understanding 4 Identify the two statements that contradict each other.

I. $\overline{FG} \parallel \overline{KL}$ II. $\overline{FG} \perp \overline{KL}$ III. $\overline{FG} \cong \overline{KL}$

5 EXAMPLE Indirect Proof

Developing Proof Read the conditional statement. Think about what is given and what you are to prove. Then give the steps of an indirect proof.

If Jaeleen spends more than \$50 to buy two items at a bicycle shop, then at least one of the items costs more than \$25.

Given: The cost of two items is more than \$50.

Prove: At least one of the items costs more than \$25.

Step 1 Assume as true the opposite of what you want to prove. That is, assume that neither item costs more than $25.

Step 2 This means that each item costs $25 or less. This, in turn, means that the two items together cost $50 or less. This contradicts the given information that the amount spent is more than $50.

Step 3 Conclude that the assumption is false. One item must cost more than $25.

Check Understanding 5 **Critical Thinking** You plan to write an indirect proof showing that $\angle X$ is an obtuse angle. In the first step you assume that $\angle X$ is an acute angle. What have you overlooked?

EXERCISES

For more practice, see *Extra Practice*.

Practice and Problem Solving

A Practice by Example

Example 1 (page 264)

Write the negation of each statement.

1. Two angles are congruent.

2. You are not sixteen years old.

3. The angle is not obtuse.

4. The soccer game is on Friday.

5. The figure is a triangle.

6. $m\angle A < 90$

Example 2 (page 265)

Write (a) the inverse and (b) the contrapositive of each conditional statement.

7. If you eat all of your vegetables, then you will grow.

8. If a figure is a square, then all of its angles are right angles.

9. If a figure is a rectangle, then it has four sides.

Example 3 (page 266)

Developing Proof Write the first step of an indirect proof.

10. It is raining outside.

11. $\angle J$ is not a right angle.

12. $\triangle PEN$ is isosceles.

13. At least one angle is obtuse.

14. $\overline{XY} \cong \overline{AB}$

15. $m\angle 2 > 90$

Example 4 (page 266)

Developing Proof Identify the two statements that contradict each other.

16. I. $\triangle PQR$ is equilateral.
II. $\triangle PQR$ is a right triangle.
III. $\triangle PQR$ is isosceles.

17. I. In right $\triangle ABC, m\angle A = 60$.
II. In right $\triangle ABC, \angle A \cong \angle C$.
III. In right $\triangle ABC, m\angle B = 90$.

18. I. ℓ and m are skew.
II. ℓ and m do not intersect.
III. $\ell \parallel m$

19. I. Each of the two items that Val bought costs more than $10.
II. Val spent $34 for the two items.
III. Neither of the two items that Val bought costs more than $15.

Example 5
(page 266)

20. **Developing Proof** Fill in the blanks to prove the following statement.
If the Debate and Chess Clubs together have fewer than 20 members and the Chess Club has 10 members, then the Debate Club has fewer than 10 members.

Given: The total membership of the Debate Club and the Chess Club is fewer than 20. The Chess Club has 10 members.

Prove: The Debate Club has fewer than 10 members.

Proof: Assume that the Debate Club has 10 or more members.
This means that together the two clubs have **a.** ? members.
This contradicts the given information that **b.** ? .
The assumption is false. Therefore it is true that **c.** ? .

Reading Math
For help with reading and solving Exercise 21, see p. 271.

21. **Developing Proof** Fill in the blanks to prove the following statement.
In a given triangle, $\triangle LMN$, there is at most one right angle.

Given: $\triangle LMN$

Prove: $\triangle LMN$ has at most one right angle.

Proof: Assume that $\triangle LMN$ has more than one **a.** ? . That is, assume that both $\angle M$ and $\angle N$ are **b.** ? . If $\angle M$ and $\angle N$ are both right angles, then $m\angle M = m\angle N =$ **c.** ? . By the Triangle Angle-Sum Theorem, $m\angle L + m\angle M + m\angle N =$ **d.** ? . Use substitution to find $m\angle L +$ **e.** ? $+$ **f.** ? $= 180$. When you solve for $m\angle L$, you find that $m\angle L =$ **g.** ? . This means that there is no $\triangle LMN$, which contradicts the given statement. So the assumption that $\triangle LMN$ has **h.** ? must be false. Therefore, $\triangle LMN$ has **i.** ? .

Apply Your Skills

Write (a) the inverse and (b) the contrapositive of each statement. Give the truth value of each.

22. If you live in Sarasota, then you live in Florida.

23. If four points are collinear, then they are coplanar.

Open-Ended Write a true conditional statement for each given condition. If such a statement is not possible, tell why.

24. The inverse is false.

25. The inverse is true.

26. The contrapositive is false.

27. The contrapositive is true.

28. **Error Analysis** Angie saw an ad that stated "If you don't drink Muscle Rex, then you won't build muscles." Angie bought Muscle Rex and drank it, and nothing happened. She sent an e-mail to the company asking for her money back. The company would not refund her money. They claimed that her reasoning was faulty. Using one or more of the terms *converse*, *inverse*, or *contrapositive*, explain why Angie's reasoning was faulty.

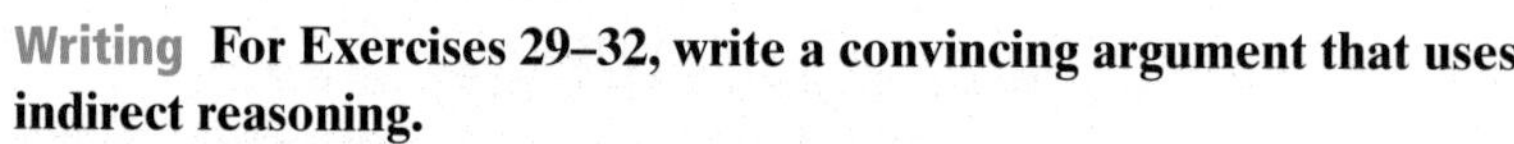
Writing For Exercises 29–32, write a convincing argument that uses indirect reasoning.

29. Fresh skid marks appear behind a green car at the scene of an accident. Show that the driver of the green car applied the brakes.

30. Ice is forming on the sidewalk in front of Toni's house. Show that the temperature of the sidewalk surface must be 32°F or lower.

31. An obtuse triangle cannot contain a right angle.

32. In a plane, a line has no more than one perpendicular at any of its points.

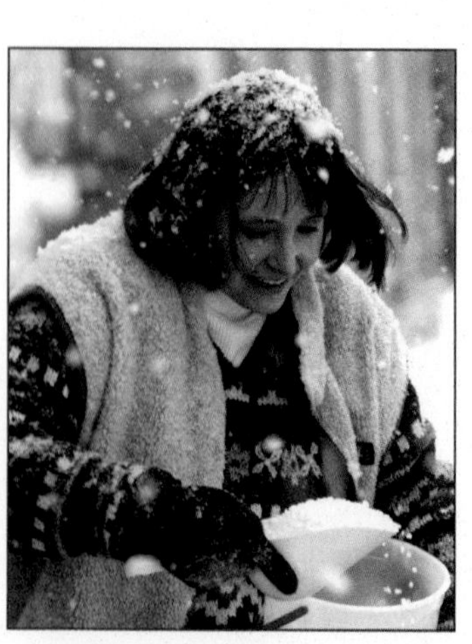

Real-World Connection
Water freezes at 32°F. Sidewalk "salt" lowers the freezing point of water.

Need Help?

To review Venn diagrams, see page 69.

Write the conditional statement illustrated by each Venn diagram. Then write its contrapositive.

33. 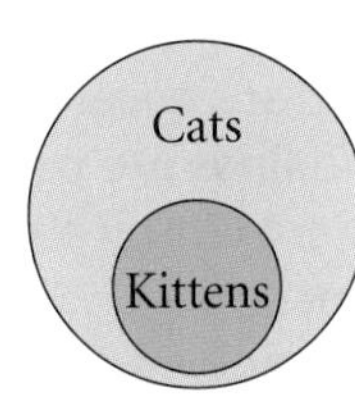

34. 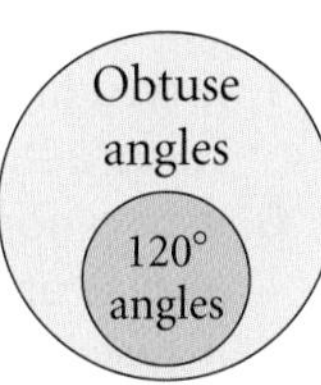

35. 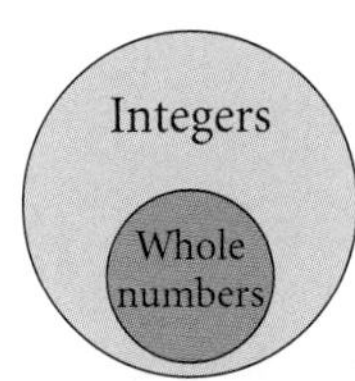

36. Open-Ended Describe a real-life situation in which you used an indirect argument to convince someone of your point of view. Outline your argument.

37. Earl lives near a noisy construction site at which work ends promptly at 5:00 each workday. Earl thinks, "Today is Tuesday. If it were before 5:00, I would hear construction noise, but I don't hear any. So it must be later than 5:00."

a. What does Earl prove? **b.** What assumption does he make?

c. What fact would contradict the assumption?

38. Literature In Arthur Conan Doyle's story "The Sign of the Four," Sherlock Holmes talks to his friend Watson about how a culprit enters a room that has only four entrances: a door, a window, a chimney, and a hole in the roof.

"You will not apply my precept," he said, shaking his head. "How often have I said to you that when you have eliminated the impossible, whatever remains, however improbable, must be the truth? We know that he did not come through the door, the window, or the chimney. We also know that he could not have been concealed in the room, as there is no concealment possible. Whence, then, did he come?"

How did the culprit enter the room? Explain.

Real-World Connection

The key to Sherlock Holmes's success is his use of deductive reasoning.

 **Challenge**

Proof **39.** Use indirect reasoning to prove the following.

Given: $\triangle ABC$ with $BC > AC$

Prove: $\angle A \not\cong \angle B$

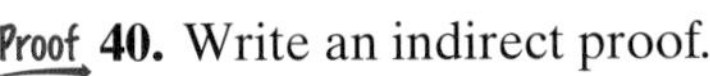

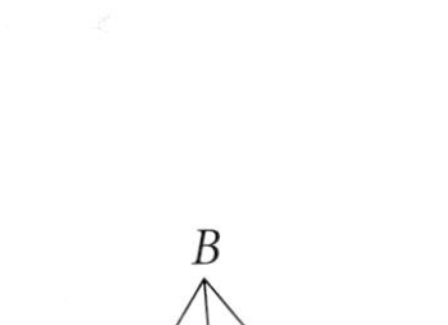

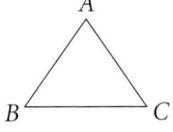

Proof **40.** Write an indirect proof.

Given: $\triangle XYZ$ is isosceles.

Prove: Neither base angle is a right angle.

Proof **41.** Write an indirect proof.

Given: $\triangle ABC$ is scalene, $m\angle ABX = 36$, and $m\angle CBX = 36$.

Prove: $\overline{XB}$ is not perpendicular to $\overline{AC}$.

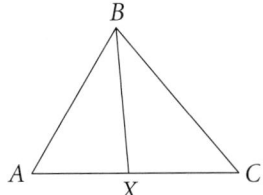

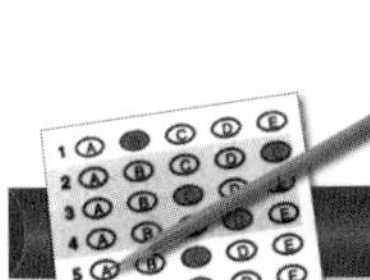

Standardized Test Prep

Multiple Choice

42. What is the negation of $x \leq 10$?

A. $x \leq -10$ **B.** $-x \leq 10$ **C.** $-x > 10$ **D.** $x > 10$

43. What is the negation of $y > 8$?

F. $y \leq -8$ **G.** $y \leq 8$ **H.** $-y > 8$ **I.** $y > 8$

44. What is the inverse of $p \to q$?

A. $q \to p$ **B.** $\sim q \to \sim p$ **C.** $p \to q$ **D.** $\sim p \to \sim q$

45. What is the contrapositive of the following statement?
If two parallel lines are cut by a transversal, then the corresponding angles are congruent.
F. If two lines are cut by a transversal and the corresponding angles are congruent, then the two lines are parallel.
G. If two nonparallel lines are cut by a transversal, then the corresponding angles are not congruent.
H. If two lines are cut by a transversal and the corresponding angles are not congruent, then the two lines are not parallel.
I. If two parallel lines are cut by a transversal, then the corresponding angles are not congruent.

Take It to the NET
Online lesson quiz at
www.PHSchool.com
Web Code: afa-0504

Short Response

46. Use indirect reasoning to give a convincing argument that an obtuse triangle has at most one obtuse angle.

Mixed Review

Lesson 5-3

Is $\overline{XY}$ a perpendicular bisector, an angle bisector, an altitude, a median, or none of these? Explain.

47.

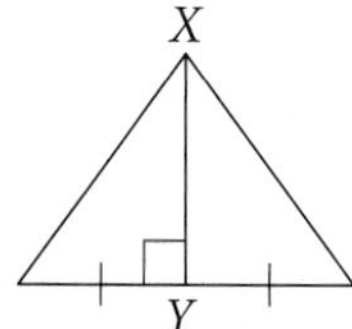

48.

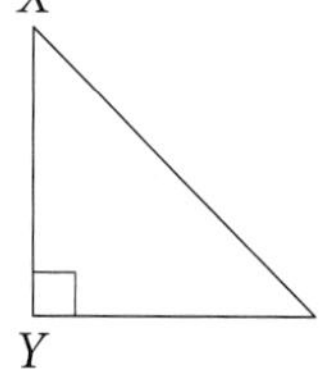

49.

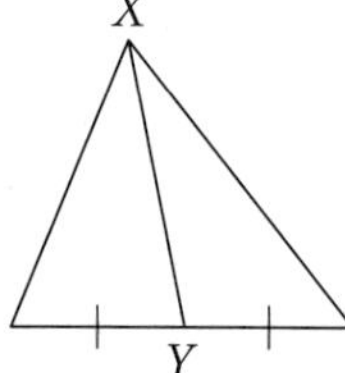

Lesson 3-1

Classify each pair of angles as *alternate interior angles*, *same-side interior angles*, or *corresponding angles*.

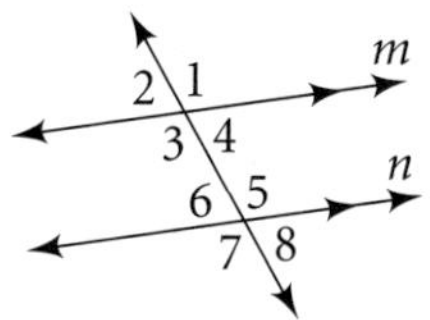

50. $\angle 1$ and $\angle 5$

51. $\angle 4$ and $\angle 5$

52. $\angle 3$ and $\angle 5$

53. $\angle 3$ and $\angle 7$

Lesson 2-4

Use the given property to complete each statement.

54. Addition Property of Equality
If $5x - 10 = 25$, then $5x = \underline{\ ?\ }$.

55. Symmetric Property of Equality
If $m\angle ABC = 45$, then $\underline{\ ?\ }$.

Geometry at Work

Industrial Designer

Industrial designers work on two-dimensional surfaces to develop products that have three-dimensional appeal to consumers. They use computer-aided design (CAD) software to create two-dimensional screen images and manipulate them for three-dimensional effects. Fashion designers use CAD to study their creations on electronic human forms from various angles and distances.

Take It to the NET For more information about industrial design go to **www.PHSchool.com**.
Web Code: afb-2031

Reading Indirect Proof

For Use With Page 268, Exercise 21

Read the problem below and then follow what Resa thinks as she solves the problem. Check your understanding by solving the exercise at the bottom of the page.

Fill in the blanks to prove the following statement.

In a given triangle, $\triangle LMN$, there is at most one right angle.

Given: $\triangle LMN$

Prove: $\triangle LMN$ has at most one right angle.

Proof: Assume that $\triangle LMN$ has more than one **a.** _?_. That is, assume that both $\angle M$ and $\angle N$ are **b.** _?_. If $\angle M$ and $\angle N$ are both right angles, then $m\angle M = m\angle N =$ **c.** _?_. By the Triangle Angle-Sum Theorem, $m\angle L + m\angle M + m\angle N =$ **d.** _?_. Use substitution to find $m\angle L +$ **e.** _?_ $+$ **f.** _?_ $= 180$. When you solve for $m\angle L$, you find that $m\angle L =$ **g.** _?_. This means that there is no $\triangle LMN$, which contradicts the information you are given. So the assumption that $\triangle LMN$ has **h.** _?_ must be false. Therefore, $\triangle LMN$ has **i.** _?_.

What Resa Thinks	What Resa Writes
To prove $\triangle LMN$ has at most one right angle, I will assume that it does not have *at most* one. This means that it has more than one.	Assume that $\triangle$LMN has more than one a. right angle.
Now I'll copy the next line in the proof. Huh? Where did $\angle M$ and $\angle N$ come from? Oh, I see. "more than one" means "at least two," so I have to choose at least two angles and assume they are right angles. The measure of a right angle is 90.	That is, assume that both $\angle$M and $\angle$N are b. right angles. If $\angle$M and $\angle$N are both right angles, then m$\angle$M = m$\angle$N = c. 90.
The Triangle Angle-Sum Theorem says that the sum of the measures of the angles in a triangle is 180. "Use substitution." I can substitute 90 for $m\angle M$ and for $m\angle N$. Solving for $m\angle L$ is easy.	m$\angle$L + m$\angle$M + m$\angle$N = d. 180. Substitute to find m$\angle$L + e. 90 + f. 90 = 180. m$\angle$L = g. 0.
But wait! How can $m\angle L = 0$? Oh! I remember. In an indirect proof, I'm looking for a contradiction. Well, I've got one! The rest is easy.	So the assumption that $\triangle$LMN has h. more than one right angle must be false. Therefore $\triangle$LMN has i. at most one right angle.

EXERCISE

Complete Exercise 20, page 268.

Algebra 1 Review

Solving Inequalities

FOR USE WITH LESSON 5-5

The solutions of an inequality are all the numbers that make the inequality true. The following chart reviews the Properties of Inequality.

Property	Properties of Inequality
	For all real numbers a, b, c, and d:
Addition Property	If $a > b$ and $c \geq d$, then $a + c > b + d$.
Multiplication Property	If $a > b$ and $c > 0$, then $ac > bc$.
	If $a > b$ and $c < 0$, then $ac < bc$.
Transitive Property	If $a > b$ and $b > c$, then $a > c$.
Comparison Property	If $a = b + c$ and $c > 0$, then $a > b$.

You use the Addition and Multiplication Properties of Inequality to solve inequalities.

EXAMPLE

Algebra Solve $-6x + 7 > 25$.

$-6x + 7 - 7 > 25 - 7$ **Add −7 to each side (or subtract 7 from each side).**

$\frac{-6x}{-6} < \frac{18}{-6}$ **Multiply each side by $-\frac{1}{6}$ (or divide each side by −6). Remember to reverse the order of the inequality.**

$x < -3$ **Simplify.**

EXERCISES

Algebra **Solve each inequality.**

1. $7x - 13 \leq -20$

2. $3x + 8 > 16$

3. $-2x - 5 < 16$

4. $8y + 2 \geq 14$

5. $5a + 1 \leq 91$

6. $-x - 2 > 17$

7. $-4z - 10 < -12$

8. $9x - 8 \geq 82$

9. $6n + 3 \leq -18$

10. $c + 13 > 34$

11. $3x - 5x + 2 < 12$

12. $x - 19 < -78$

13. $-n - 27 \leq 92$

14. $-9t + 47 < 101$

15. $8x - 4 + x > -76$

16. $2(y - 5) > -24$

17. $8b + 3 \geq 67$

18. $-3(4x - 1) \geq 15$

19. $r - 9 \leq -67$

20. $\frac{1}{2}(4x - 7) \geq 19$

21. $5x - 3x + 2x < -20$

22. $9x - 10x + 4 < 12$

23. $-3x - 7x \leq 97$

24. $8y - 33 > -1$

25. $4a + 17 \geq 13$

26. $-4(5z + 2) > 20$

27. $x + 78 \geq -284$

28. $6c \geq -12 - 24$

29. $27 - 12 < 3x$

30. $8y - 4y + 11 \leq -33$

31. $5x - 2x + 13 > -8$

32. $4(5a + 3) \leq -8$

33. $8c + 2c + 7 < -10 - 3$

5-5 Inequalities in Triangles

Lesson Preview

What You'll Learn

To use inequalities involving angles of triangles

To use inequalities involving sides of triangles

. . . And Why

To locate the largest corners on a triangular backyard deck, as in Example 2

✓ Check Skills You'll Need

(For help, go to Lessons 1-6 and 5-4.)

Graph the triangles with the given vertices. List the sides in order from shortest to longest.

1. $A(5, 0), B(0, 8), C(0, 0)$

2. $P(2, 4), Q(-5, 1), R(0, 0)$

3. $G(3, 0), H(4, 3), J(8, 0)$

4. $X(-4, 3), Y(-1, 1), Z(-1, 4)$

Recall the steps for indirect proof.

5. You want to prove $m\angle A > m\angle B$.
Write the first step of an indirect proof.

6. In an indirect proof, you deduce that $AB \geq AC$ is false. What conclusion can you make?

Interactive lesson includes instant self-check, tutorials, and activities.

OBJECTIVE 1 Inequalities Involving Angles of Triangles

When you empty a container of juice into two glasses, it is difficult to be sure that the glasses get equal amounts. You can be sure, however, that each glass holds less than the original amount in the container. This is a simple application of the Comparison Property of Inequality.

Key Concepts

Property	Comparison Property of Inequality
If $a = b + c$ and $c > 0$, then $a > b$.	

Proof

Proof of the Comparison Property

Given: $a = b + c, c > 0$

Prove: $a > b$

Statements	Reasons
1. $c > 0$	**1.** Given
2. $b + c > b + 0$	**2.** Addition Property of Inequality
3. $b + c > b$	**3.** Simplify.
4. $a = b + c$	**4.** Given
5. $a > b$	**5.** Substitute a for $b + c$ in Statement 3.

The Comparison Property of Inequality allows you to prove the following corollary to the Exterior Angle Theorem for triangles (Theorem 3-8).

Key Concepts

Corollary | **Corollary to the Triangle Exterior Angle Theorem**

The measure of an exterior angle of a triangle is greater than the measure of each of its remote interior angles.

$m\angle 1 > m\angle 2$ and $m\angle 1 > m\angle 3$

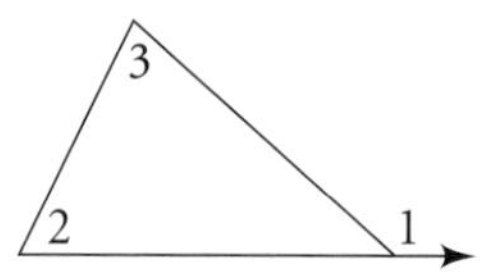

Proof

Proof of the Corollary

Given: $\angle 1$ is an exterior angle of the triangle.

Prove: $m\angle 1 > m\angle 2$ and $m\angle 1 > m\angle 3$.

Proof: By the Exterior Angle Theorem, $m\angle 1 = m\angle 2 + m\angle 3$. Since $m\angle 2 > 0$ and $m\angle 3 > 0$, you can apply the Comparison Property of Inequality and conclude that $m\angle 1 > m\angle 2$ and $m\angle 1 > m\angle 3$.

1 EXAMPLE Applying the Corollary

In the diagram, $m\angle 2 = m\angle 1$ by the Isosceles Triangle Theorem. Explain why $m\angle 2 > m\angle 3$.

By the corollary to the Exterior Angle Theorem, $m\angle 1 > m\angle 3$. So, $m\angle 2 > m\angle 3$ by substitution.

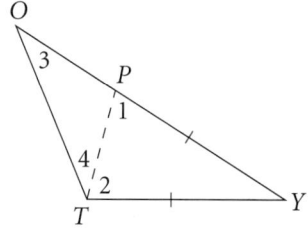

Check Understanding 1 Explain why $m\angle OTY > m\angle 3$.

You will prove the following inequality theorem in the exercises.

Key Concepts

Theorem 5-10

If two sides of a triangle are not congruent, then the larger angle lies opposite the longer side.

If $XZ > XY$, then $m\angle Y > m\angle Z$.

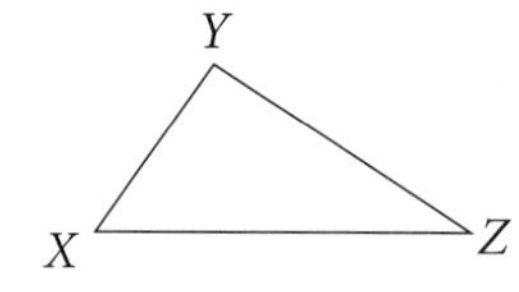

2 EXAMPLE Real-World Connection

Deck Design A landscape architect is designing a triangular deck. She wants to place benches in the two larger corners. Which corners have the larger angles?

Corners B and C have the larger angles. They are opposite the two longer sides of 27 ft and 21 ft.

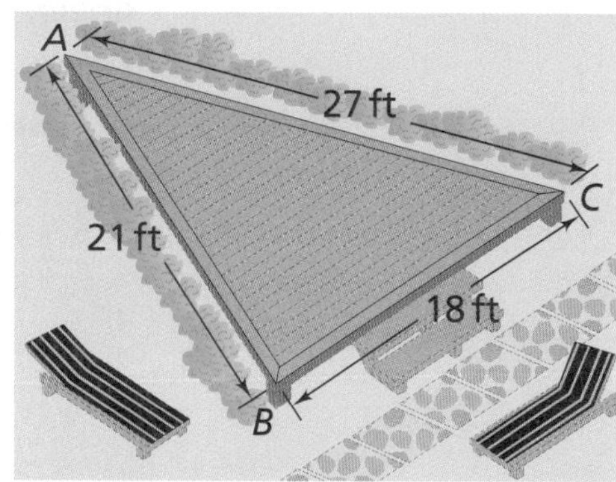

Check Understanding 2 List the angles of $\triangle ABC$ in order from smallest to largest.

Real-World Connection

Careers Landscape architects blend structures with decorative plantings.

OBJECTIVE 2

Inequalities Involving Sides of Triangles

Theorem 5-10 on the preceding page states that the larger angle is opposite the longer side. The converse is also true.

Key Concepts

Theorem 5-11

If two angles of a triangle are not congruent, then the longer side lies opposite the larger angle.

If $m\angle A > m\angle B$, then $BC > AC$.

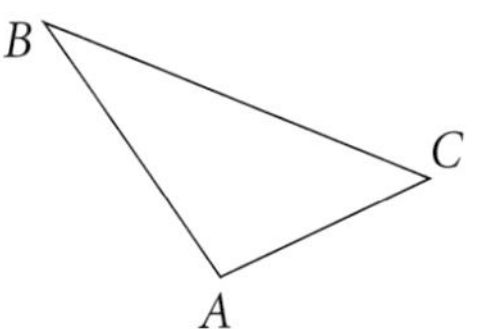

Proof

Indirect Proof of Theorem 5-11

Given: $m\angle A > m\angle B$

Prove: $BC > AC$

Need Help?
Indirect proof steps:
1. Assume the opposite.
2. Find a contradiction.
3. State a conclusion.

Step 1 Assume $BC \ngtr AC$. That is, assume $BC < AC$ or $BC = AC$.

Step 2 If $BC < AC$, then $m\angle A < m\angle B$ (Theorem 5-10). This contradicts the given fact that $m\angle A > m\angle B$. Therefore, $BC < AC$ must be false.

If $BC = AC$, then $m\angle A = m\angle B$ (Isosceles Triangle Theorem). This also contradicts $m\angle A > m\angle B$. Therefore, $BC = AC$ must be false.

Step 3 The assumption $BC \ngtr AC$ is false, so $BC > AC$.

3 EXAMPLE Using Theorem 5-11

In $\triangle TUV$, which side is shortest?

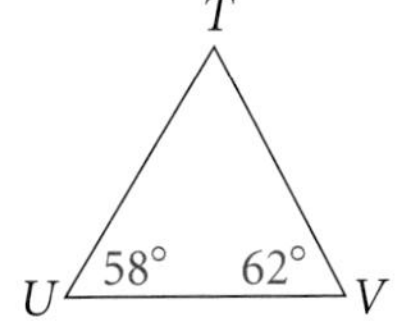

By the Triangle Angle-Sum Theorem, $m\angle T = 60$. The smallest angle in $\triangle TUV$ is $\angle U$. It follows, by Theorem 5-11, that the shortest side is $\overline{TV}$.

Check Understanding 3 List the sides of the $\triangle XYZ$ in order from shortest to longest. Explain your listing.

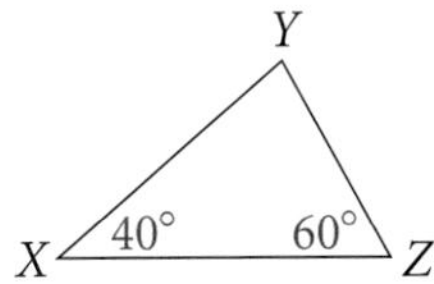

Not every set of three segments can form a triangle. The lengths of the segments must be related in a certain way.

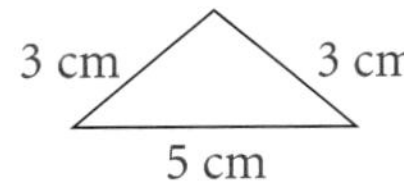

3 cm, 3 cm, 5 cm

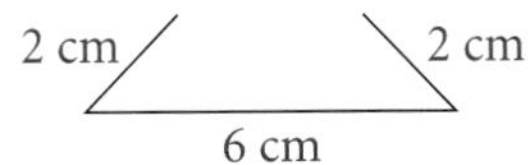

2 cm, 2 cm, 6 cm

Notice that only one of the sets of three segments above can form a triangle. The sum of the smallest two lengths must be greater than the greatest length. This is Theorem 5-12 (see next page). You will prove it in the exercises.

Key Concepts

Theorem 5-12 **Triangle Inequality Theorem**

The sum of the lengths of any two sides of a triangle is greater than the length of the third side.

$XY + YZ > XZ$

$YZ + ZX > YX$

$ZX + XY > ZY$

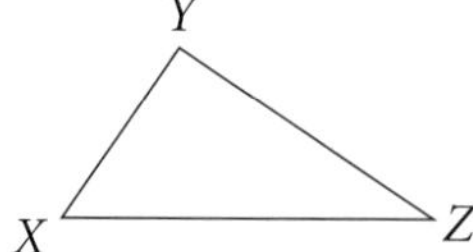

Need Help?

You may find it easier to recall this theorem as "The shortest path between two points is the straight path."

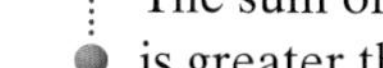

4 EXAMPLE Using the Triangle Inequality Theorem

Can a triangle have sides with the given lengths? Explain.

a. 3 ft, 7 ft, 8 ft

$3 + 7 > 8$

$8 + 7 > 3$

$3 + 8 > 7$ Yes

The sum of any two lengths is greater than the third length.

b. 3 cm, 6 cm, 10 cm

$3 + 6 \ngtr 10$ No

The sum of 3 and 6 is not greater than 10, contradicting Theorem 5-12.

Check Understanding 4 Can a triangle have sides with the given lengths? Explain.

a. 2 m, 7 m, and 9 m **b.** 4 yd, 6 yd, and 9 yd

5 EXAMPLE Finding Possible Side Lengths

Algebra A triangle has sides of lengths 8 cm and 10 cm. Describe the lengths possible for the third side.

Let x represent the length of the third side. By the Triangle Inequality Theorem,

$x + 8 > 10$	$x + 10 > 8$	$8 + 10 > x$
$x > 2$	$x > -2$	$x < 18$

The third side must be longer than 2 cm and shorter than 18 cm.

Check Understanding 5 A triangle has sides of lengths 3 in. and 12 in. Describe the lengths possible for the third side.

EXERCISES

For more practice, see *Extra Practice*.

Practice and Problem Solving

Practice by Example

Example 1 (page 274)

Explain why $m\angle 1 > m\angle 2$.

1.

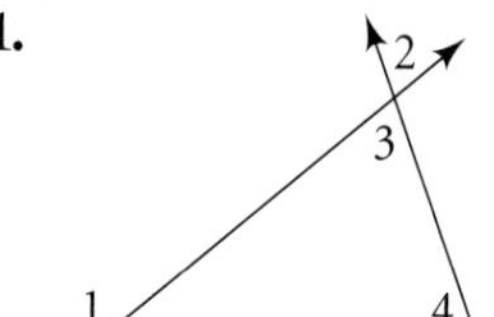

2.

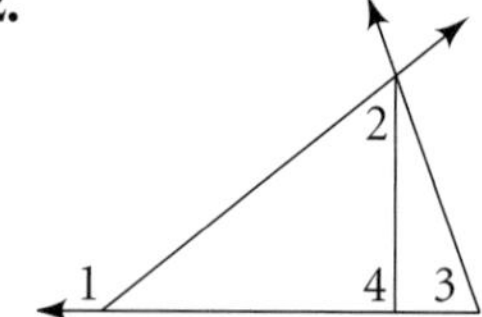

3.

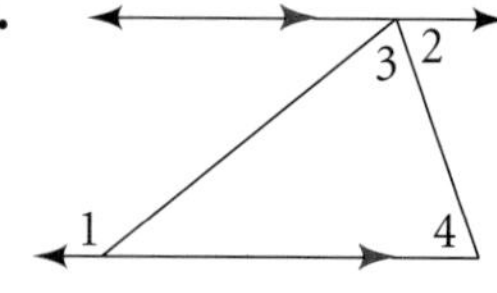

Example 2 (page 274)

List the angles of each triangle in order from smallest to largest.

4. **5.**

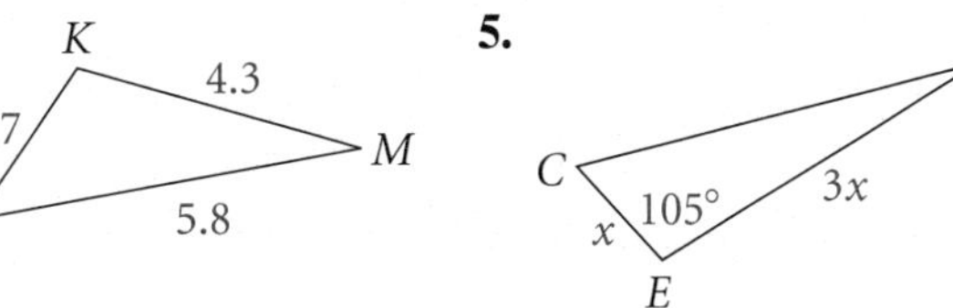

6.

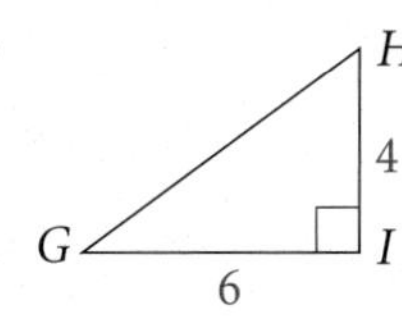

7. $\triangle ABC$, where $AB = 8$, $BC = 5$, and $CA = 7$

8. $\triangle DEF$, where $DE = 15$, $EF = 18$, and $DF = 5$

9. $\triangle XYZ$, where $XY = 12$, $YZ = 24$, and $ZX = 30$

Example 3 (page 275)

List the sides of each triangle in order from shortest to longest.

10.

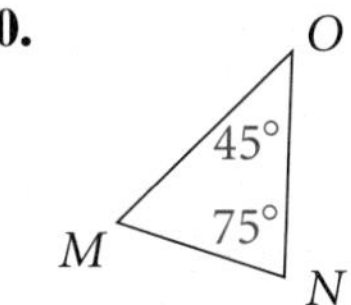

11.

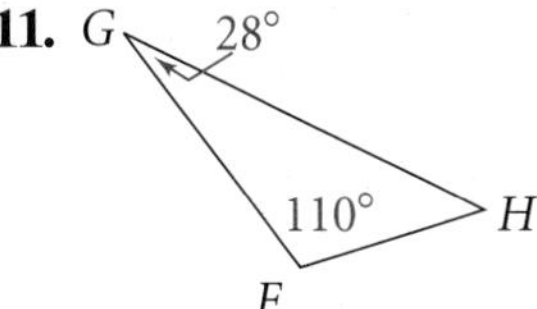

12.

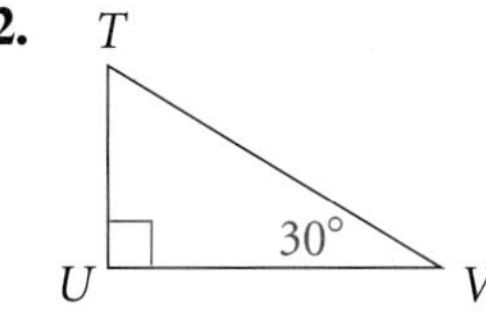

13. $\triangle ABC$, with $m\angle A = 90$, $m\angle B = 40$, and $m\angle C = 50$

14. $\triangle DEF$, with $m\angle D = 20$, $m\angle E = 120$, and $m\angle F = 40$

15. $\triangle XYZ$, with $m\angle X = 51$, $m\angle Y = 59$, and $m\angle Z = 70$

Example 4 (page 276)

Can a triangle have sides with the given lengths? Explain.

16. 2 in., 3 in., 6 in.

17. 11 cm, 12 cm, 15 cm

18. 8 m, 10 m, 19 m

19. 1 cm, 15 cm, 15 cm

20. 2 yd, 9 yd, 10 yd

21. 4 m, 5 m, 9 m

Example 5 (page 276)

x^2 Algebra **The lengths of two sides of a triangle are given. Describe the lengths possible for the third side.**

22. 8 ft, 12 ft

23. 5 in., 16 in.

24. 6 cm, 6 cm

25. 18 m, 23 m

26. 4 yd, 7 yd

27. 20 km, 35 km

B Apply Your Skills

28. Error Analysis The Shau family is crossing Kansas on Highway 70. A sign reads "Wichita 90 miles, Topeka 110 miles." Avi says, "I didn't know that it was only 20 miles from Wichita to Topeka." Explain to Avi why the distance between the cities doesn't have to be 20 miles.

Exercise 29

29. Writing Explain why the distance between the two peaks in the photograph is greater than the difference of the distances from the hiker to each of the peaks.

30. The Hinge Theorem The hypothesis of the Hinge Theorem is stated below. The conclusion is missing.

Suppose two sides of one triangle are congruent to two sides of another triangle. If the included angle of the first triangle is larger than the included angle of the second triangle, then __?__.

a. Draw a diagram to illustrate the hypothesis.

b. The conclusion of the Hinge Theorem concerns the sides opposite the two angles mentioned in the hypothesis. Write the conclusion.

c. Draw a diagram to illustrate the converse.

d. Converse of the Hinge Theorem Write the conclusion to this theorem.

Suppose two sides of one triangle are congruent to two sides of another triangle. If the third side of the first triangle is greater than the third side of the second triangle, then __?__.

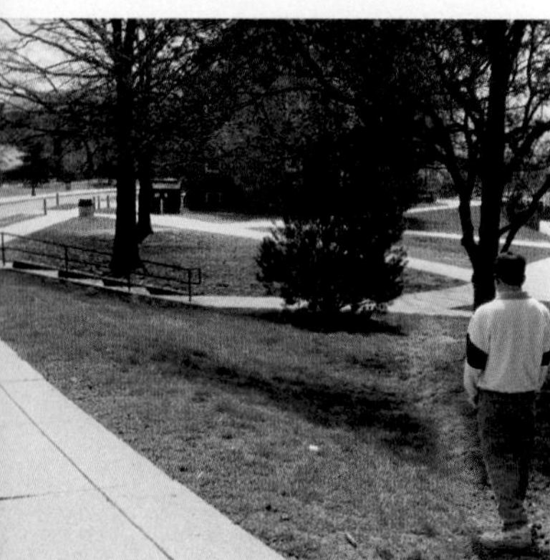

Exercise 31

31. **Shortcuts** Explain how the student in the photograph is applying the Triangle Inequality Theorem.

32. **Algebra** Find the longest side of $\triangle ABC$, if $m\angle A = 70$, $m\angle B = 2x - 10$, and $m\angle C = 3x + 20$.

Proof 33. **Developing Proof** Fill in the blanks to complete a proof of Theorem 5-10: If two sides of a triangle are not congruent, then the larger angle lies opposite the longer side.

Given: $\triangle TOY$, with $YO > YT$.

Prove: **a.** ___?___ $>$ **b.** ___?___

Mark P on $\overline{YO}$ so that $\overline{YP} \cong \overline{YT}$. Draw $\overline{TP}$.

Statements	Reasons
1. $\overline{YP} \cong \overline{YT}$	1. Ruler Post.
2. $m\angle 1 = m\angle 2$	c. ___?___
3. $m\angle OTY = m\angle 4 + m\angle 2$	d. ___?___
4. $m\angle OTY > m\angle 2$	e. ___?___
5. $m\angle OTY > m\angle 1$	f. ___?___
6. $m\angle 1 > m\angle 3$	g. ___?___
7. $m\angle OTY > m\angle 3$	h. ___?___

Need Help?

Exercise 33 plan: Get $m\angle 4 + m\angle 2 > m\angle 2$, $m\angle 2 = m\angle 1$, and $m\angle 1 > m\angle 3$.

Critical Thinking **Determine which segment is shortest in each diagram.**

34.

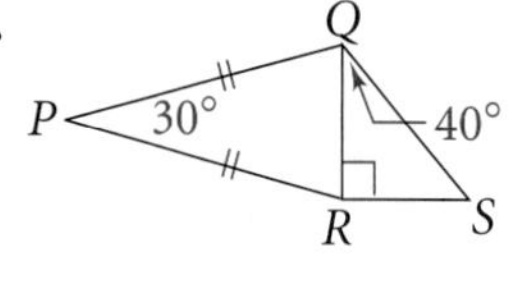

35.

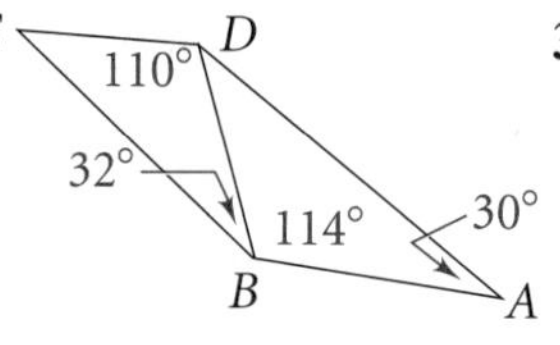

36.

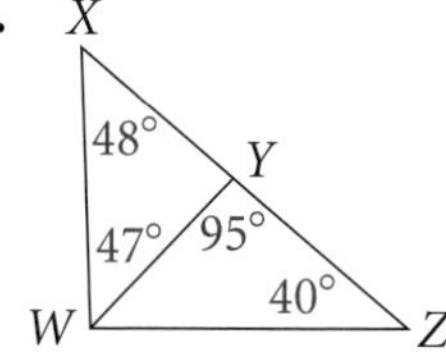

Challenge

37. **Probability** A student has two straws, one 6 cm long and the other 9 cm long. She picks a third straw at random from a group of four straws whose lengths are 3 cm, 5 cm, 11 cm, and 15 cm. What is the probability that the straw she picks will allow her to form a triangle?

For Exercises 38 and 39, x and y are whole numbers, $1 < x < 5$, and $2 < y < 9$.

38. The sides of a triangle are 5 cm, x cm, and y cm. List possible (x, y) pairs.

39. **Probability** What is the probability that you can draw an isosceles triangle that has sides 5 cm, x cm, and y cm, with x and y chosen at random?

Proof 40. Prove Theorem 5-12: The sum of the lengths of any two sides of a triangle is greater than the length of the third side.

Given: $\triangle ABC$

Prove: $AC + CB > AB$

(*Hint:* On $\overrightarrow{BC}$ mark a point D not on $\overline{BC}$, so that $DC = AC$. Draw $\overline{DA}$ and use Theorem 5-11 with $\triangle ABD$.)

41. **Reasoning** A corollary to Theorem 5-11 states: The perpendicular segment from a point to a line is the shortest segment from the point to the line. Given that $\overline{PT} \perp \overline{TA}$, show that $PA > PT$.

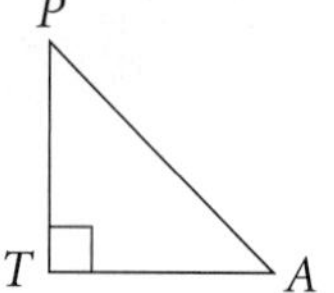

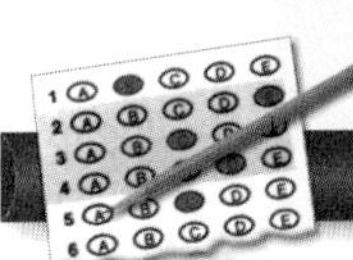

Standardized Test Prep

Multiple Choice

42. Which is the best estimate for PR?

A. 137 m **B.** 145 m
C. 163 m **D.** 187 m

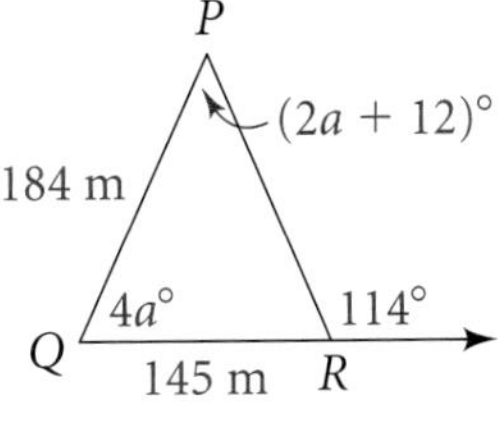

Quantitative Comparison

Compare the boxed quantity in Column A with the boxed quantity in Column B. Choose the best answer.

A. The quantity in Column A is greater.
B. The quantity in Column B is greater.
C. The two quantities are equal.
D. The relationship cannot be determined from the information given.

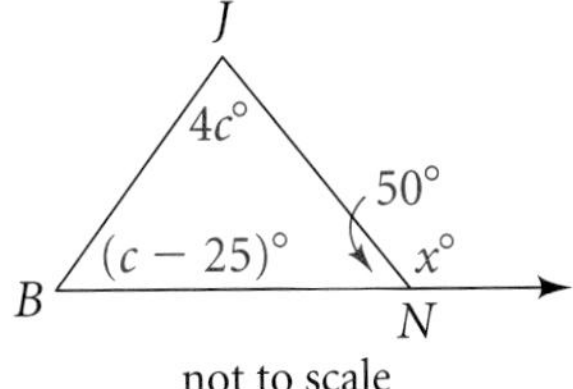

	Column A	Column B
43.	x	c
44.	JN	BN
45.	$x - 4c$	$c - 25$
46.	JB	BN

Short Response

47. In $\triangle ABC$, $m\angle A > m\angle C > m\angle B$.

a. Of $\overline{AB}$ and $\overline{AC}$, one measures 5 inches and the other measures 9 inches. Which measures 9 inches? Explain.

b. Based on your conclusion for part (a), find all possible whole-number measures for the third side. Explain.

Mixed Review

Lesson 5-4

Write the negation of each statement.

48. $m\angle A \leq m\angle B$

49. $m\angle X > m\angle B$

50. The angle is a right angle.

51. The triangle is not obtuse.

Lesson 2-5

Use the diagram. Find the measure of each angle.

52. $\angle ADH$

53. $\angle GDH$

54. $\angle CDH$

55. $\angle ADG$

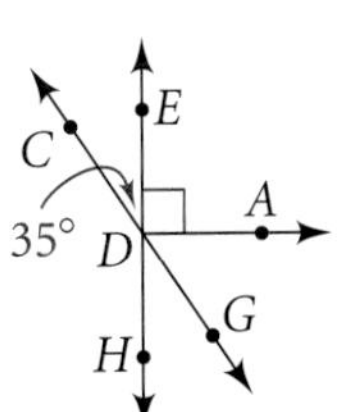

Lesson 1-7

Find to the nearest tenth of a square unit the area of each circle with the given radius *r* or diameter *d*.

56. $r = 1.6$ ft

57. $d = 35$ mm

58. $r = 0.5$ m

59. $d = 20$ mi

Test-Taking Strategies

Using a Variable

You can solve many problems by using a variable to represent an unknown quantity. You use the variable to write an equation or inequality. In the Example, Method 1 uses one variable and Method 2 uses two variables.

EXAMPLE

Algebra Points A, B, and C are collinear. BC is 6 less than twice AB, and $AC = 30$. What is the length of $\overline{BC}$?

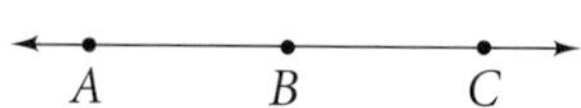

Method 1

Let $AB = x$,
then $BC = 30 - x$. **The length of $\overline{AC}$ is 30.**

BC is 6 less than twice AB,

$$30 - x = 2x - 6$$
$$36 - x = 2x \quad \textbf{Solve for } x.$$
$$36 = 3x$$
$$x = 12$$

Therefore $AB = 12$ and $BC = 30 - 12 = 18$.

Method 2

Let $AB = x$ and $BC = y$.

Since $AC = AB + BC = 30$, $x + y = 30$.

Since BC is 6 less than twice AB, $y = 2x - 6$.

$$x + (2x - 6) = 30 \quad \textbf{Substitute } 2x - 6 \textbf{ for } y.$$
$$3x - 6 = 30$$
$$3x = 36$$
$$x = 12$$

Therefore $AB = 12$ and $BC = 2(12) - 6 = 18$.

EXERCISES

x^2 **Algebra** **Write and solve an equation to answer each question.**

1. Points A, B, C, and D are collinear. AB is 15 more than BC, and CD is 8 more than BC. If AD is 5 less than twice AB, what are the lengths AB, BC, and CD?

2. $\overline{AB}$ is perpendicular to $\overline{BN}$ in the diagram at the right. What are the coordinates of point N?

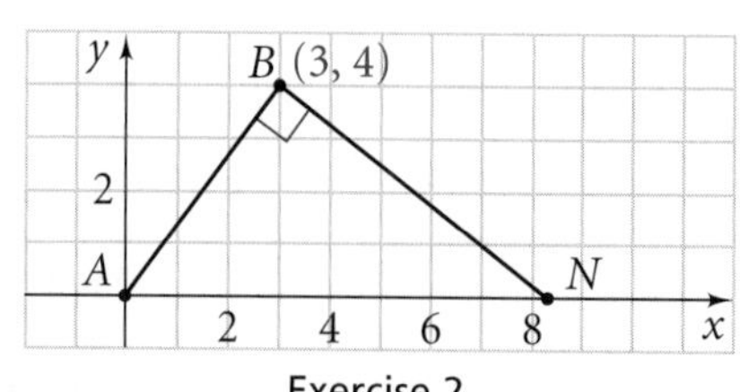

Exercise 2

3. The angles of a triangle are three consecutive even integers. What are the measures of the angles?

4. Point P is on the x-axis, 13 units from point $C(7, 5)$. What are the possible coordinates of P?

5. What are the coordinates of the point P on the x-axis such that the slope of a line from P to $A(1, 4)$ is twice the slope of a line from P to $B(9, 10)$?

Chapter Review

Vocabulary

altitude of a triangle (p. 259)
centroid (p. 258)
circumcenter of a triangle (p. 257)
circumscribed about (p. 257)
concurrent (p. 257)
contrapositive (p. 264)
coordinate proof (p. 244)
distance from a point to a line (p. 250)
equivalent statements (p. 265)
incenter of a triangle (p. 257)
indirect proof (p. 265)
indirect reasoning (p. 265)
inscribed in (p. 257)
inverse (p. 264)
median of a triangle (p. 258)
midsegment (p. 243)
negation (p. 264)
orthocenter of a triangle (p. 259)
point of concurrency (p. 257)

Reading Math
Understanding Vocabulary

Choose the correct vocabulary term to complete each sentence.

1. A *(centroid, median of a triangle)* is a segment whose endpoints are a vertex and the midpoint of the side opposite the vertex.
2. The length of the perpendicular segment from a point to a line is the *(midsegment, distance from the point to the line).*
3. If T is a point on the perpendicular bisector of $\overline{FG}$, then $TF = TG$ because of the *(Perpendicular Bisector Theorem, Angle Bisector Theorem).*
4. The *(altitude, median)* of a triangle is a perpendicular segment from a vertex to the line containing the side opposite the vertex.
5. The notation $\sim q \rightarrow \sim p$ is the *(inverse, contrapositive)* of $p \rightarrow q$.
6. To write a(n) *(indirect proof, negation)*, you start by assuming that the opposite of what you want to prove is true.
7. In $\triangle ABC$, $AB + BC > AC$ because of the *(Comparison Property of Inequality, Triangle Inequality Theorem).*
8. The *(circumcenter, incenter)* of a triangle is the point of concurrency of the angle bisectors of the triangle.
9. The *(Angle Bisector Theorem, Triangle Inequality Theorem)* says that if a point is on the bisector of an angle, then it is equidistant from the sides of the angle.
10. A point where three lines intersect is a *(point of concurrency, incenter).*

Take It to the NET
Online vocabulary quiz at **www.PHSchool.com**
Web Code: afj-0551

Skills and Concepts

5-1 and 5-2 Objectives

- ▼ To use properties of midsegments to solve problems
- ▼ To use properties of perpendicular bisectors and angle bisectors

A **midsegment** of a triangle is a segment that connects the midpoints of two sides. A midsegment is parallel to the third side, and is half its length.

In a **coordinate proof,** a figure is drawn on a coordinate plane and formulas are used to prove properties of the figure.

The **distance from a point to a line** is the length of the perpendicular segment from the point to the line. The Perpendicular Bisector Theorem together with its converse states that a point is on the perpendicular bisector of a segment if and only if it is equidistant from the endpoints of the segment. The Angle Bisector Theorem together with its converse states that a point is on the bisector of an angle if and only if it is equidistant from the sides of the angle.

x^2 **Algebra Find the value of x.**

11. 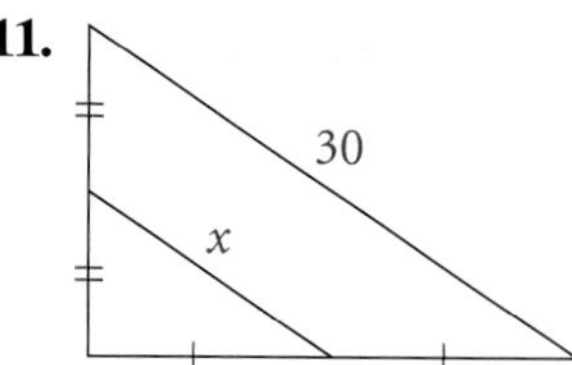

12. 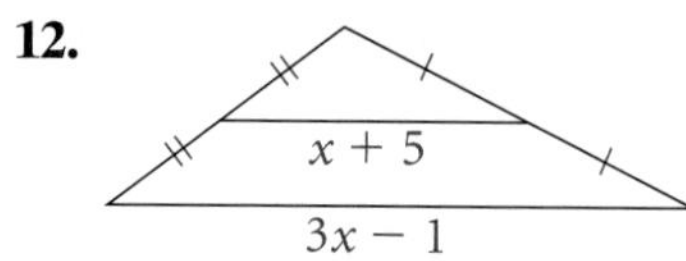

Use the figure to find each segment length or angle measure.

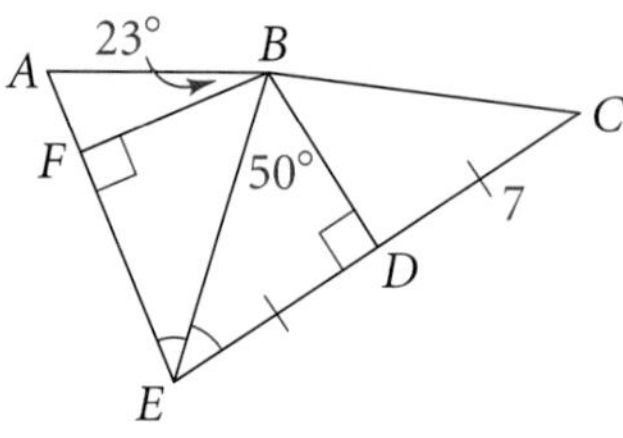

13. $m\angle BEF$

14. FE

15. EC

16. $m\angle CEA$

5-3 Objectives

▼ To identify properties of perpendicular bisectors and angle bisectors

▼ To identify properties of medians and altitudes of a triangle

When three or more lines intersect in one point, they are **concurrent**.

The **median of a triangle** is a segment whose endpoints are a vertex and the midpoint of the opposite side. The **altitude of a triangle** is a perpendicular segment from a vertex to the line containing the opposite side.

For any given triangle, special segments and lines are concurrent:

- the perpendicular bisectors of the sides at the circumcenter, the center of the circle that can be **circumscribed about** the triangle
- the bisectors of the angles at the incenter, the center of the circle that can be **inscribed in** the triangle
- the medians at the **centroid**
- the lines containing the altitudes at the **orthocenter of the triangle.**

Graph $\triangle ABC$ with vertices $A(2, 3)$, $B(-4, -3)$, and $C(2, -3)$. Find the coordinates of each point of concurrency.

17. circumcenter

18. centroid

19. orthocenter

Determine whether $\overline{AB}$ is a perpendicular bisector, an angle bisector, a median, an altitude, or none of these. Explain.

20. 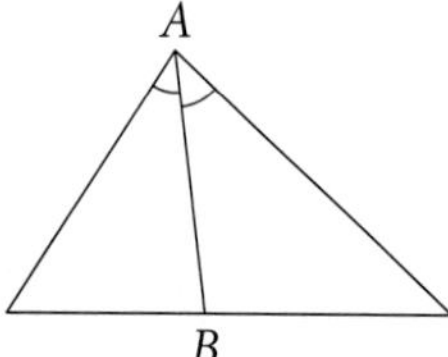

21. 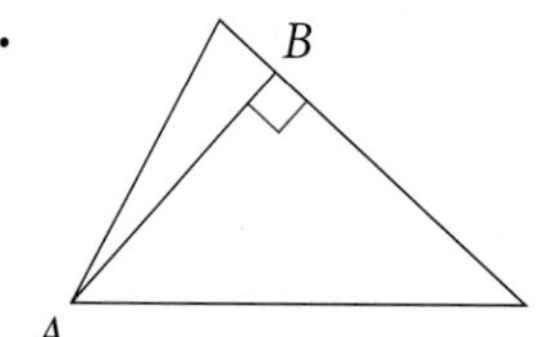

22. 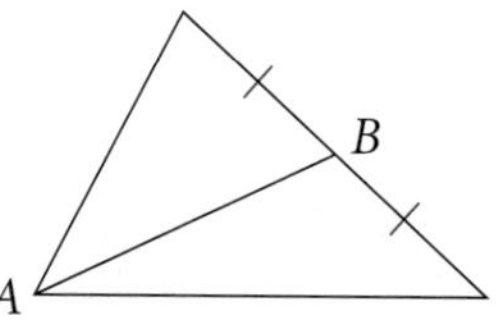

5-4 Objectives

▼ To write the negation of a statement and the inverse and contrapositive of a conditional statement

▼ To use indirect reasoning

The **negation** of a statement has the opposite truth value. The **inverse** of a conditional statement is the negation of both the hypothesis and the conclusion. The **contrapositive** of a conditional statement switches the hypothesis and the conclusion and negates both. Statements that always have the same truth value are **equivalent statements.**

To use **indirect reasoning,** consider all possibilities and then prove all but one false. The remaining possibility must be true.

The three steps of an **indirect proof** are:

Step 1 State as an assumption the opposite (negation) of what you want to prove.

Step 2 Show that this assumption leads to a contradiction.

Step 3 Conclude that the assumption must be false and that what you want to prove must be true.

Write the inverse and the contrapositive of each statement.

23. If it is snowing, then it is cold outside.

24. If an angle is obtuse, then its measure is greater than 90 and less than 180.

25. If a figure is a square, then its sides are congruent.

26. If you are in Australia, then you are south of the equator.

Write a convincing argument that uses indirect reasoning.

27. The product of two numbers is even. Show that at least one of the two numbers must be even.

28. Show that a right angle cannot be formed by the intersection of nonperpendicular lines.

29. Show that a triangle can have at most one obtuse angle.

30. Show that an equilateral triangle cannot have an obtuse angle.

5-5 Objectives

- To use inequalities involving angles of triangles
- To use inequalities involving sides of triangles

If two sides of a triangle are not congruent, then the larger angle lies opposite the longer side. The converse is also true. If two angles are not congruent, then the longer side lies opposite the larger angle.

The measure of an exterior angle of a triangle is greater than the measure of each of its remote interior angles. The sum of the lengths of any two sides of a triangle is greater than the length of the third side.

List the angles and sides in order from smallest to largest.

31.

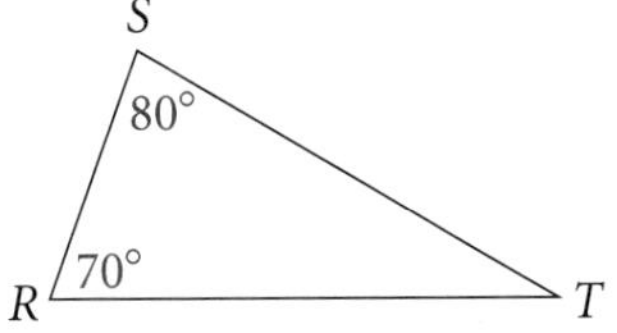

32.

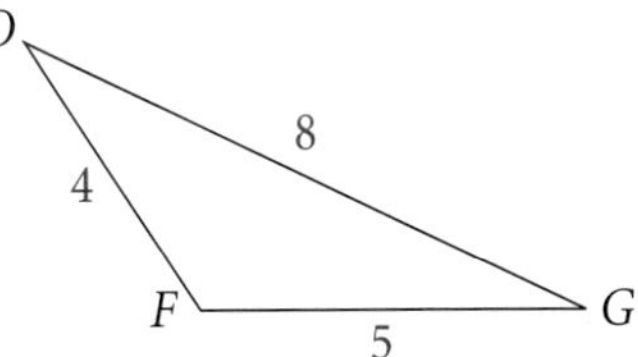

Is it possible for a triangle to have sides with the given lengths? Explain.

33. 5 in., 8 in., 15 in.

34. 10 cm, 12 cm, 20 cm

35. 20 m, 22 m, 24 m

36. 3 ft, 6 ft, 8 ft

37. 1 yd, 1 yd, 3 yd

38. 5 km, 6 km, 7 km

Two side lengths of a triangle are given. Write an inequality to show the range of values, x, for the length of the third side.

39. 4 in., 7 in.

40. 8 m, 15 m

41. 2 cm, 8 cm

42. 12 ft, 13 ft

Chapter Test

Take It to the NET
Online chapter test at
www.PHSchool.com
Web Code: afa-0552

Write (a) the inverse and (b) the contrapositive of each statement.

1. If a polygon has eight sides, then it is an octagon.
2. If it is a leap year, then it is an even-numbered year.
3. If it is snowing, then it is not summer.
4. What can you conclude from the diagram? Justify your answer.

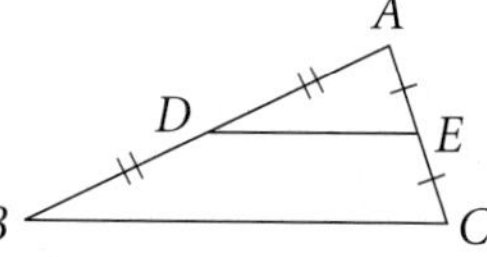

Identify the two statements that contradict each other.

5. I. $\triangle PQR$ is a right triangle.
   II. $\triangle PQR$ is an obtuse triangle.
   III. $\triangle PQR$ is scalene.
6. I. $\angle DAS \cong \angle CAT$
   II. $\angle DAS$ and $\angle CAT$ are vertical.
   III. $\angle DAS$ and $\angle CAT$ are adjacent.

List the angles of $\triangle ABC$ from smallest to largest.

7. $AB = 9, BC = 4, AC = 12$
8. $AB = 10, BC = 11, AC = 9$
9. $AB = 3, BC = 9, AC = 7$
10. **Open-Ended** Write three lengths that cannot be the lengths of the three sides of a triangle. Explain your answer.

List the sides of each triangle in order from shortest to longest.

11.

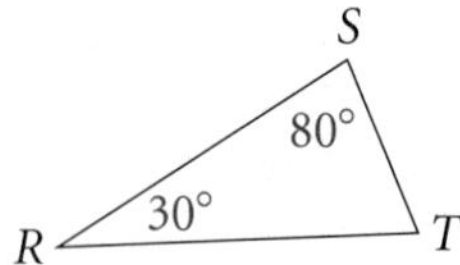

12.

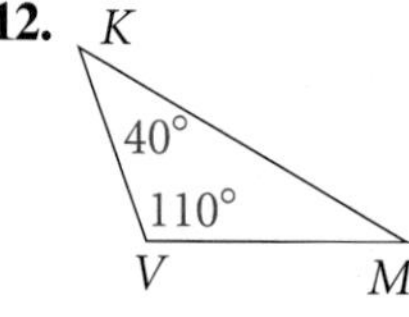

Algebra Find the value of x in each figure.

13.

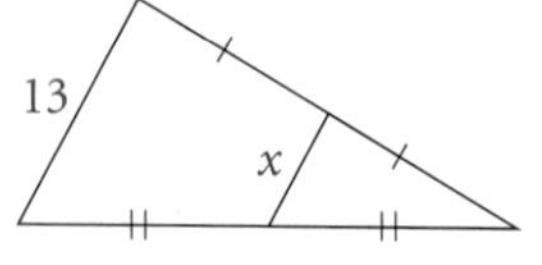

14.

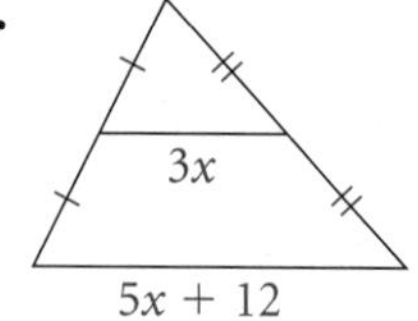

15. **Writing** Use indirect reasoning to explain why the following statement is true: If an isosceles triangle is obtuse, then the obtuse angle is the vertex angle.

Algebra Find the values of x and KM in each figure.

16.

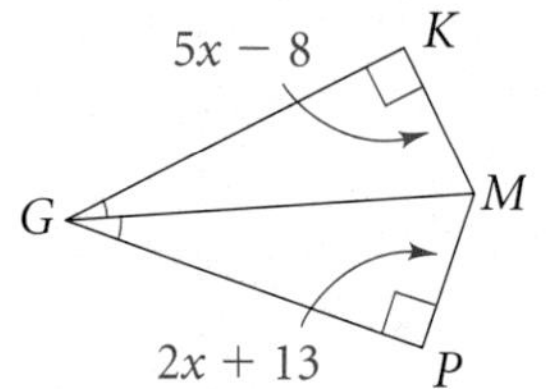

17.

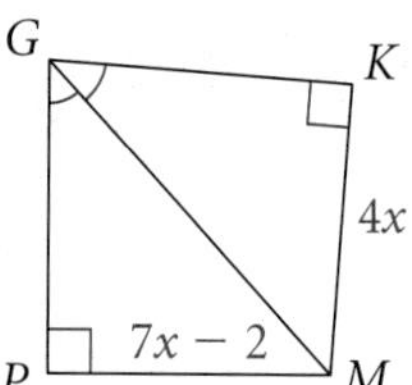

Coordinate Geometry Find the center of the circle that circumscribes $\triangle ABC$.

18. $A(0, 0), B(0, -3), C(-5, -3)$
19. $A(0, 5), B(-4, 5), C(-4, -3)$
20. $A(3, -1), B(-2, -1), C(3, -8)$
21. $\triangle ABC$ has vertices $A(2, 5), B(2, -3), C(10, -3)$. What point of concurrency is at $(6, 1)$?
22. Complete the paragraph proof below.

Given: $\overleftrightarrow{PQ}$ is the perpendicular bisector of $\overline{AB}$.
$\overleftrightarrow{QT}$ is the perpendicular bisector of $\overline{AC}$.
Prove: $QC = QB$

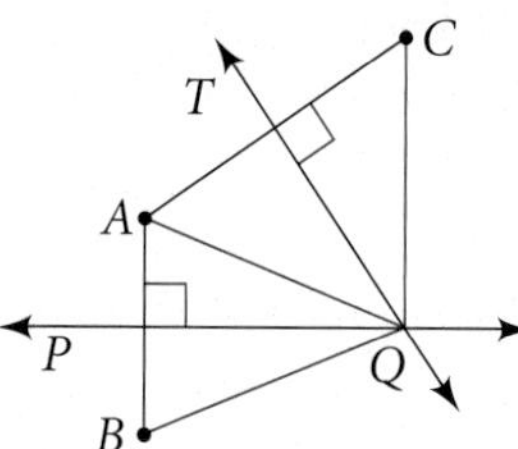

Proof: $QC =$ **a.** _?_ and **b.** _?_ $= QB$. Therefore, $QC = QB$ by the **c.** _?_.

23. What can you conclude about point Y? Explain.

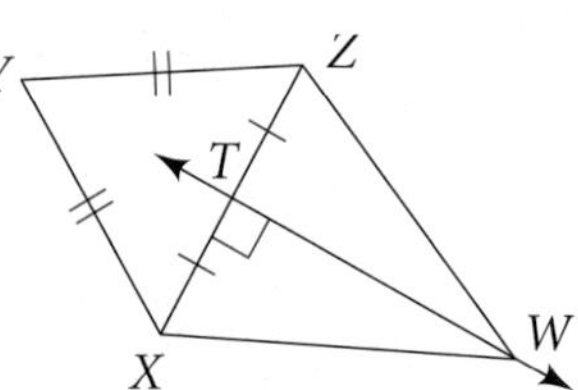

24. In the figure, $WK = KR$. What can you conclude about point A? Explain.

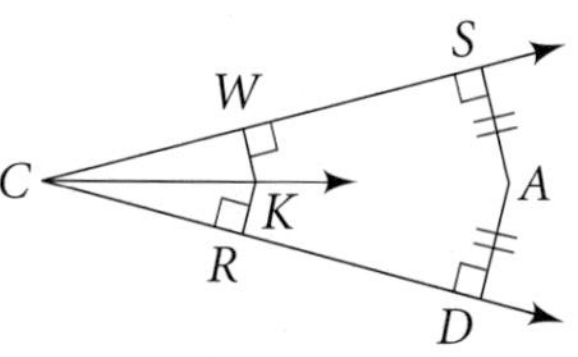

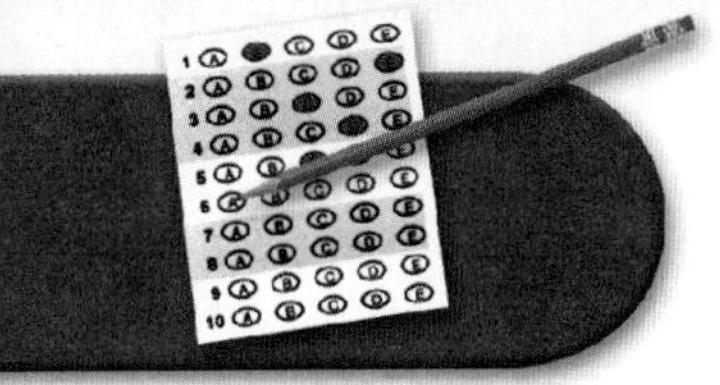

Standardized Test Prep

Reading Comprehension Read the passage below. Then answer the questions on the basis of what is *stated* or *implied* in the passage.

The Kitchen Triangle Architects, builders, and anyone who has ever prepared a full meal in a kitchen know that in most kitchen activities you go back and forth between the sink, the stove, and the refrigerator. Those three locations form what is called the "work triangle" or the "kitchen triangle."

A large apartment complex made this table of kitchen triangle dimensions for four of its units.

Kitchen Triangle Distances (cm)

Apt.	Stove to Sink	Sink to Fridge	Fridge to Stove
A	250	280	240
B	145	320	165
C	115	220	330
D	310	152	270

250 cm

240 cm

280 cm

Kitchen triangle

To have an efficient kitchen, it should be easy to traverse each side of the kitchen triangle.

1. Why are the sink, stove, and refrigerator the vertices of the kitchen triangle?
   A. Architects and builders say they are.
   B. You walk between these three appliances in most kitchen activities.
   C. Most apartments have these appliances.
   D. A sink, stove, and refrigerator form an efficient kitchen.

2. In apartment A, which appliance is at the vertex of the largest angle?
   F. the sink   **G.** the stove
   H. the refrigerator   **I.** cannot be determined

3. In apartment D, which appliance is at the vertex of the smallest angle?
   A. the sink   **B.** the stove
   C. the refrigerator   **D.** cannot be determined

4. The description of one kitchen triangle is incorrect. Which one? Justify your answer.

5. In which kitchen is it least efficient for two persons to work? Justify your answer.

In kitchen triangle A, a microwave is halfway between the stove and sink, and an electric can opener is halfway between the fridge and sink.

6. What is the distance between the microwave and the can opener? Justify your answer.
   F. 120 cm   **G.** 125 cm   **H.** 240 cm   **I.** 265 cm

7. To go from the microwave to the can opener, you must go in the direction you would travel from the stove to the refrigerator. Why?

8. Which kitchen triangle has a midsegment triangle with smallest perimeter?
   A. A   **B.** D
   C. C   **D.** cannot be determined

9. For which kitchen triangle do you need the fewest steps to go from one vertex to another and then to the third? Justify your answer.
   F. A   **G.** C
   H. D   **I.** cannot be determined

10. In Apartment D, how far is it from stove to sink by way of the refrigerator?
    A. 270 cm   **B.** 310 cm   **C.** 422 cm   **D.** 462 cm

Where You've Been

- In Chapter 3, you learned that parallel lines produce pairs of angles that are congruent or supplementary.
- In Chapter 4, you learned how to prove triangles congruent. You also learned how to use CPCTC to draw additional conclusions.
- In Chapter 5, you learned that properties of special segments of a triangle can provide additional information about a triangle.

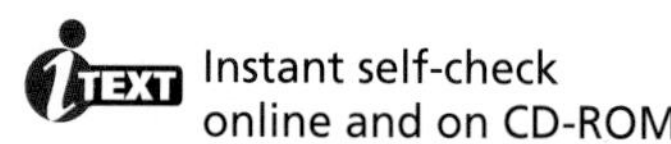

TEXT
Instant self-check online and on CD-ROM

Diagnosing Readiness

(For help, go to the Lesson in green.)

Properties of Parallel Lines (Lesson 3-1)

x^2 **Algebra** Use properties of parallel lines to find the value of x.

1. $(x + 9)°$ $(2x - 21)°$

2. $(3x - 14)°$ $(2x - 16)°$

3.

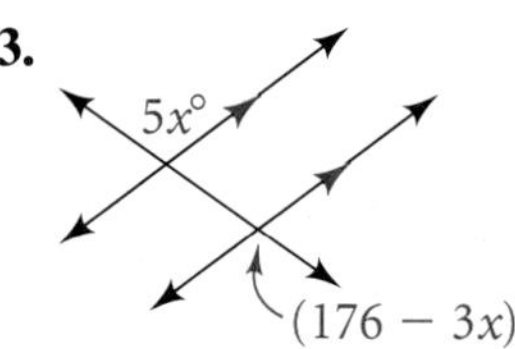

Proving Lines Parallel (Lesson 3-2)

x^2 **Algebra** Determine whether $\overleftrightarrow{AB}$ (or $\overline{AB}$) is parallel to $\overleftrightarrow{CD}$ (or $\overline{CD}$).

4.

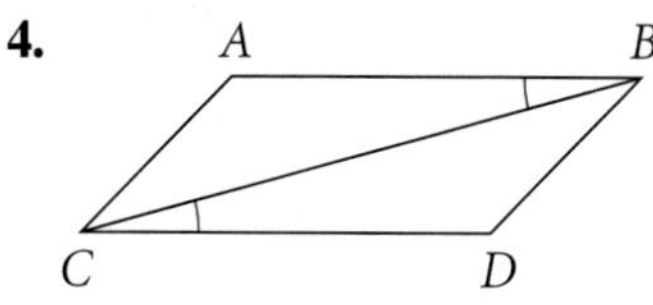

5.

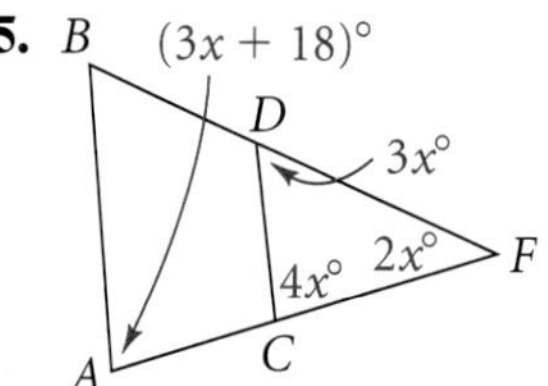

6

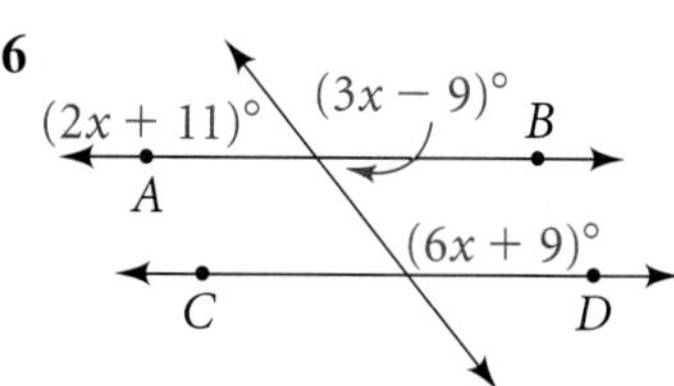

Using Slope to Determine Parallel and Perpendicular Lines (Lesson 3-6)

x^2 **Algebra** Determine whether each pair of lines is parallel, perpendicular, or neither.

7. $y = -2x; y = -2x + 4$

8. $y = -\frac{3}{5}x + 1; y = \frac{5}{3}x - 3$

9. $2x - 3y = 1; 3x - 2y = 8$

Proving Triangles Congruent (Lessons 4-2 and 4-3)

Determine the postulate or theorem that makes each pair of triangles congruent.

10.

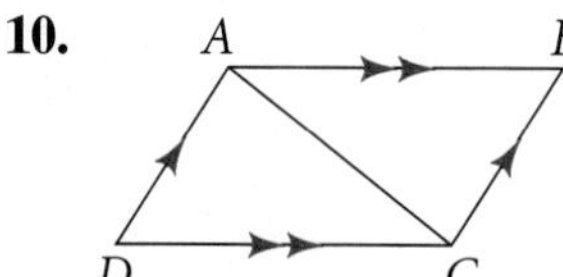

11.

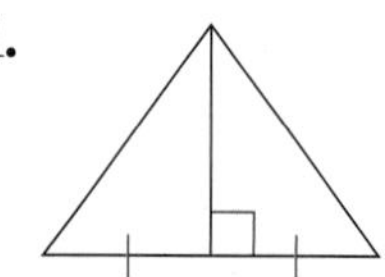

12.

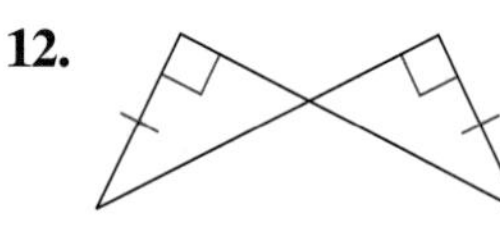

Quadrilaterals

Chapter 6

LESSONS

Key Vocabulary

- base angles of a trapezoid (p. 320)
- consecutive angles (p. 294)
- isosceles trapezoid (p. 288)
- kite (p. 288)
- midsegment of a trapezoid (p. 332)
- parallelogram (p. 288)
- rectangle (p. 288)
- rhombus (p. 288)
- square (p. 288)
- trapezoid (p. 288)

Where You're Going

- In this chapter, you will learn properties of parallelograms and other special quadrilaterals.
- You will learn properties of quadrilaterals that allow you to classify quadrilaterals.
- You will use these properties to help you place figures in the coordinate plane.
- You will verify properties of figures using coordinate techniques.

Real-World Snapshots Applying what you learn, you will do activities involving balance on pages 344 and 345.

6-1 Classifying Quadrilaterals

Lesson Preview

What You'll Learn

OBJECTIVE 1 To define and classify special types of quadrilaterals

. . . And Why

To use the properties of special quadrilaterals with a kite, as in Example 3

✓ Check Skills You'll Need

(For help, go to Lesson 1-6 and page 151.)

Find the distance between the points to the nearest tenth.

1. $M(2, -5), N(-7, 1)$ **2.** $P(-1, -3), Q(-6, -9)$ **3.** $C(-4, 6), D(5, -3)$

Find the slope of the line through each pair of points.

4. $X(0, 6), Y(4, 9)$ **5.** $R(3, 8), S(6, 0)$ **6.** $A(4, 3), B(2, 1)$

New Vocabulary • parallelogram • rhombus • rectangle • square • kite • trapezoid • isosceles trapezoid

Interactive lesson includes instant self-check, tutorials, and activities.

OBJECTIVE 1 Classifying Special Quadrilaterals

Seven important types of quadrilaterals are defined below.

Key Concepts

Definitions **Special Quadrilaterals**

A **parallelogram** is a quadrilateral with both pairs of opposite sides parallel.

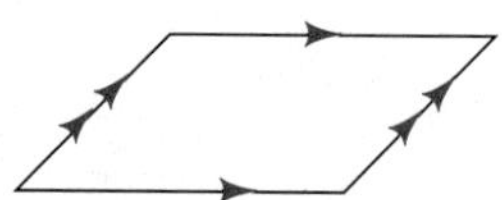

A **rhombus** is a parallelogram with four congruent sides.

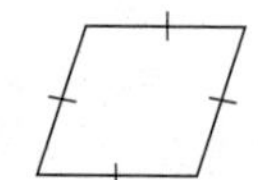

A **rectangle** is a parallelogram with four right angles.

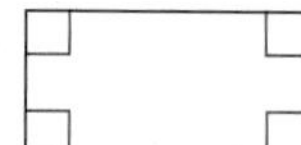

A **square** is a parallelogram with four congruent sides and four right angles.

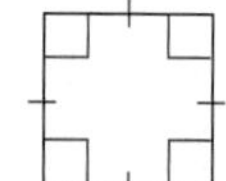

A **kite** is a quadrilateral with two pairs of adjacent sides congruent and no opposite sides congruent.

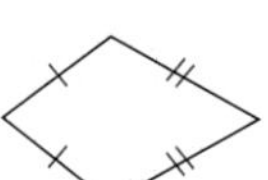

A **trapezoid** is a quadrilateral with exactly one pair of parallel sides. The **isosceles trapezoid** at the right is a trapezoid whose nonparallel opposite sides are congruent.

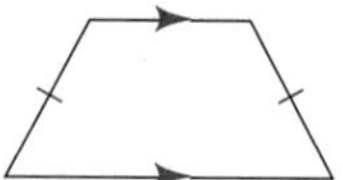

Real-World Connection

A "kite" is not the only special quadrilateral used to make a kite!

1 EXAMPLE Classifying a Quadrilateral

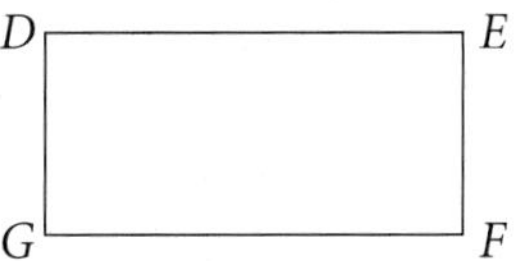

Judging by appearance, classify $DEFG$ in as many ways as possible.

$DEFG$ is a quadrilateral because it has four sides.

It is a parallelogram because both pairs of opposite sides are parallel.

It is a rectangle because it has four right angles.

Check Understanding 1 **a.** Judging by appearance, classify $WXYZ$ at the right in as many ways as possible.

b. Critical Thinking Which name gives the most information about $WXYZ$? Explain.

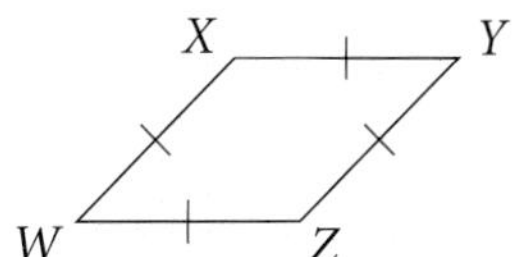

The diagram below shows the relationships among special quadrilaterals.

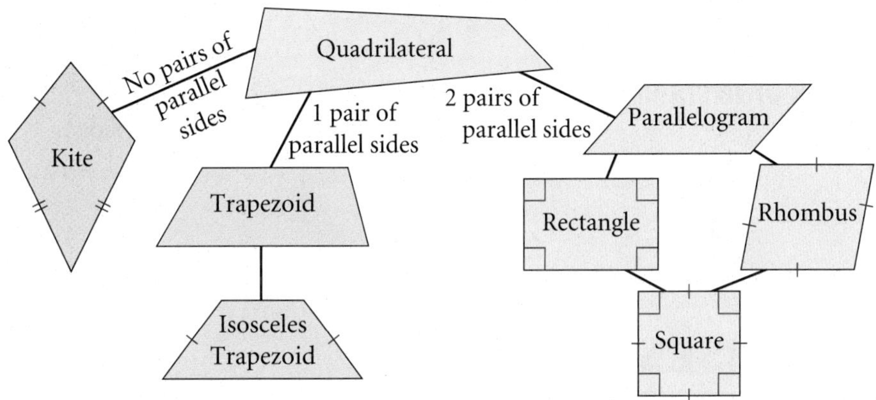

You can use what you know about slope and distance to classify a quadrilateral.

2 EXAMPLE Classifying by Coordinate Methods

Coordinate Geometry Determine the most precise name for quadrilateral $LMNP$.

Step 1 Find the slope of each side.

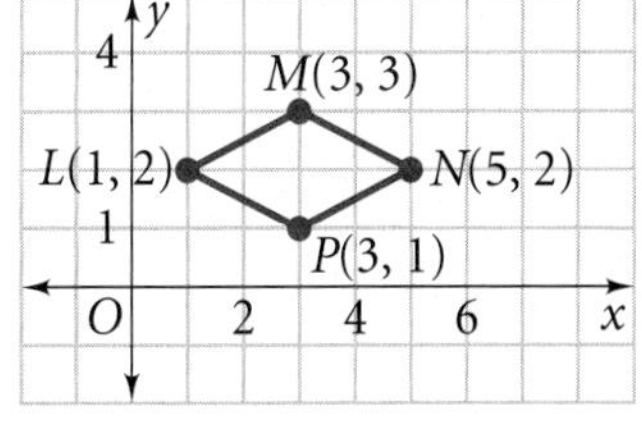

$$\text{slope of } \overline{LM} = \frac{3-2}{3-1} = \frac{1}{2}$$

$$\text{slope of } \overline{NP} = \frac{2-1}{5-3} = \frac{1}{2}$$

$$\text{slope of } \overline{MN} = \frac{3-2}{3-5} = -\frac{1}{2}$$

$$\text{slope of } \overline{LP} = \frac{2-1}{1-3} = -\frac{1}{2}$$

Both pairs of opposite sides are parallel, so $LMNP$ is a parallelogram. No sides are perpendicular, so $LMNP$ is not a rectangle.

Step 2 Use the Distance Formula to see if any pairs of sides are congruent.

$$LM = \sqrt{(3-1)^2 + (3-2)^2} = \sqrt{5} \qquad MN = \sqrt{(3-5)^2 + (3-2)^2} = \sqrt{5}$$

$$NP = \sqrt{(5-3)^2 + (2-1)^2} = \sqrt{5} \qquad LP = \sqrt{(1-3)^2 + (2-1)^2} = \sqrt{5}$$

All sides are congruent, so $LMNP$ is a rhombus.

Reading Math

Although *LMNP* is a parallelogram, rhombus is the more *precise* name because it gives more information about the quadrilateral.

Check Understanding 2 Determine the most precise name for quadrilateral $ABCD$ with vertices $A(-3, 3)$, $B(2, 4)$, $C(3, -1)$, and $D(-2, -2)$.

You can use the definitions of special quadrilaterals and algebra to find lengths of sides.

3 EXAMPLE Using the Properties of Special Quadrilaterals

Algebra Find the values of the variables for the kite.

$KB = JB$	**Definition of kite**
$3x - 5 = 2x + 4$	**Substitute.**
$x - 5 = 4$	**Subtract 2*x* from each side.**
$x = 9$	**Add 5 to each side.**
$KT = x + 6 = 15$	**Substitute 9 for *x*.**
$KT = JT$	**Definition of kite**
$15 = 2y + 5$	**Substitute.**
$10 = 2y$	**Subtract 5 from each side.**
$5 = y$	**Divide each side by 2.**

3 Find the values of the variables for the rhombus. Then find the lengths of the sides.

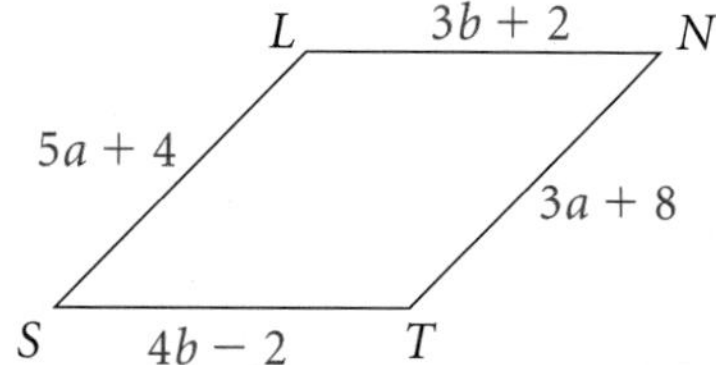

EXERCISES

For more practice, see *Extra Practice.*

Practice and Problem Solving

Practice by Example

Example 1 (page 289)

These quadrilaterals are made from a toy building set. Judging by appearance, classify each quadrilateral in as many ways as possible.

1. 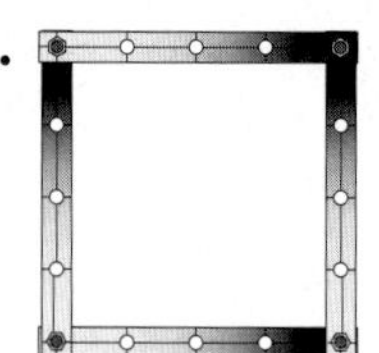

2. 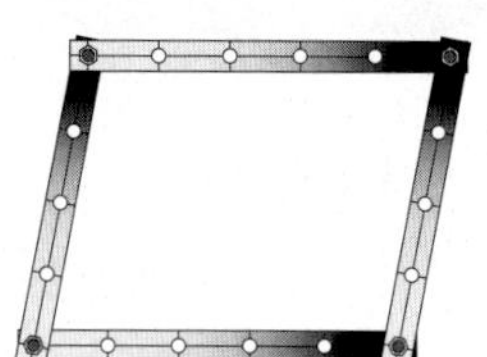

3. 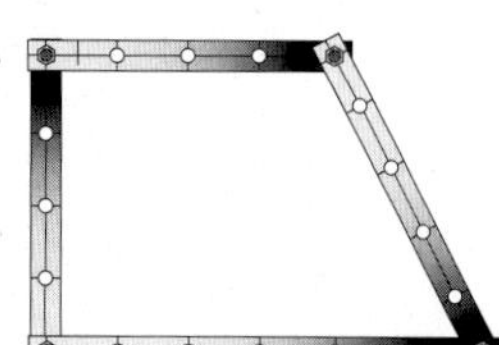

4. 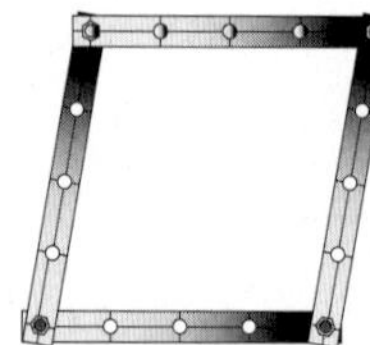

5. 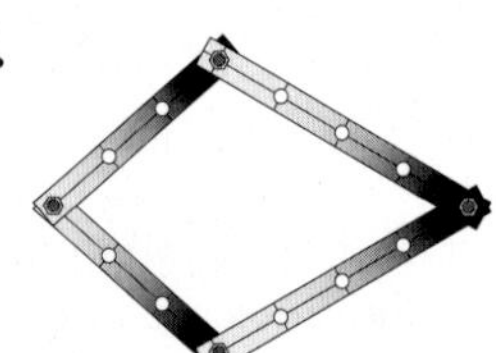

6. 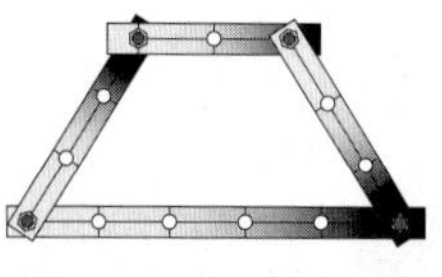

Example 2 (page 289)

Determine the most precise name for each quadrilateral.

7. 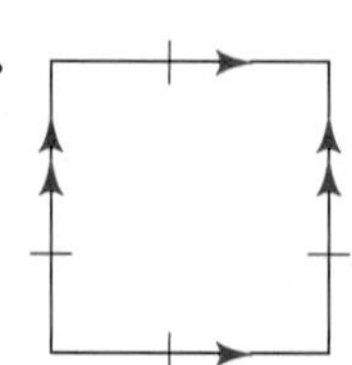

8. 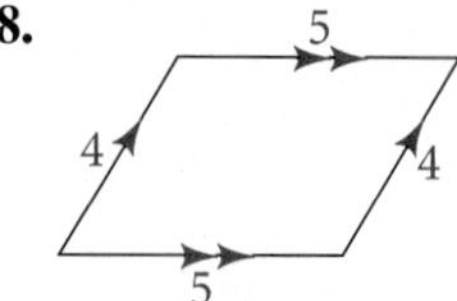

9. 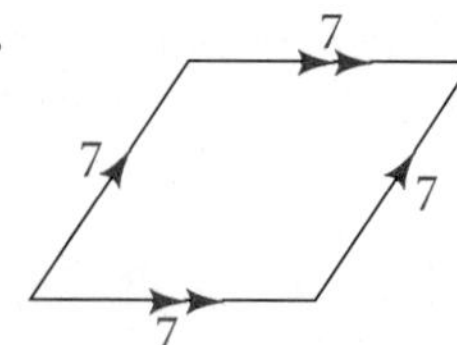

10. 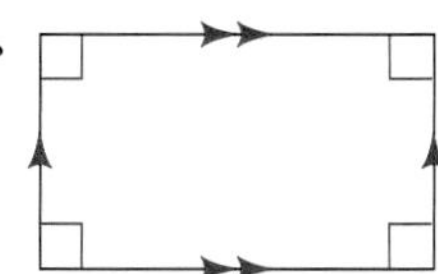

11. 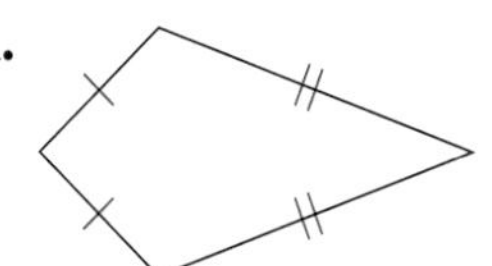

12. 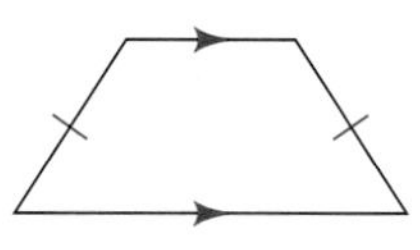

Coordinate Geometry Graph and label each quadrilateral with the given vertices. Then determine the most precise name for each quadrilateral.

13. $A(3, 5), B(7, 6), C(6, 2), D(2, 1)$

14. $W(-1, 1), X(0, 2), Y(1, 1), Z(0, -2)$

15. $J(2, 1), K(5, 4), L(7, 2), M(2, -3)$

16. $R(-2, -3), S(4, 0), T(3, 2), V(-3, -1)$

17. $N(-6, -4), P(-3, 1), Q(0, 2), R(-3, 5)$

18. $E(-3, 1), F(-7, -3), G(6, -3), H(2, 1)$

Example 3 (page 290)

 **Algebra Find the values of the variables. Then find the lengths of the sides.**

19. kite

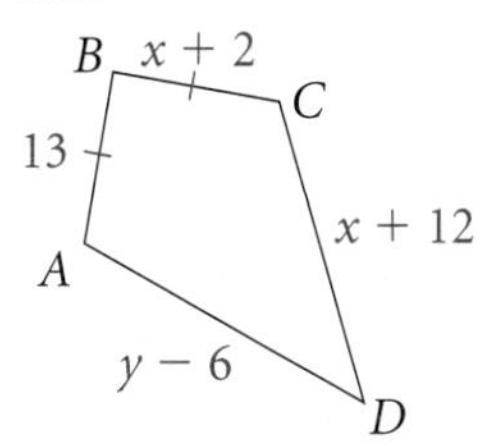

20. kite

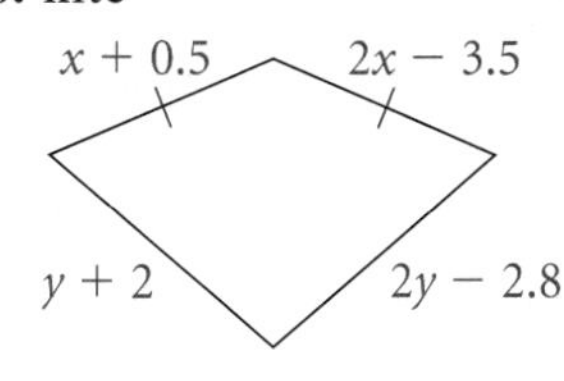

21. kite

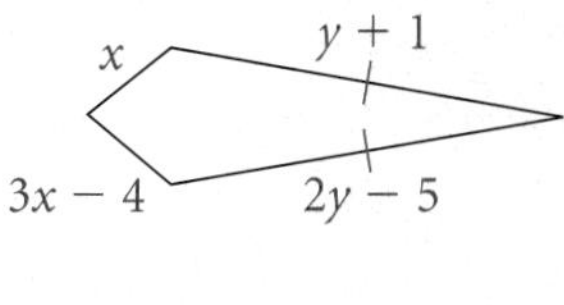

22. isosceles trapezoid

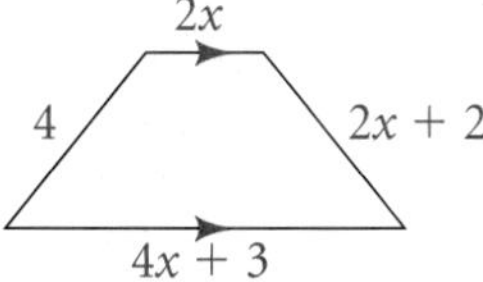

23. rhombus

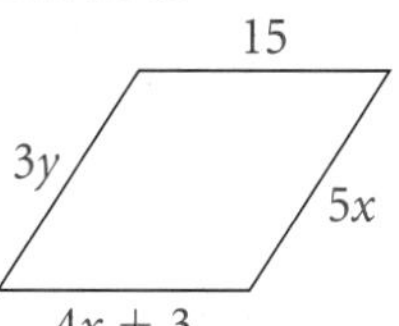

24. square

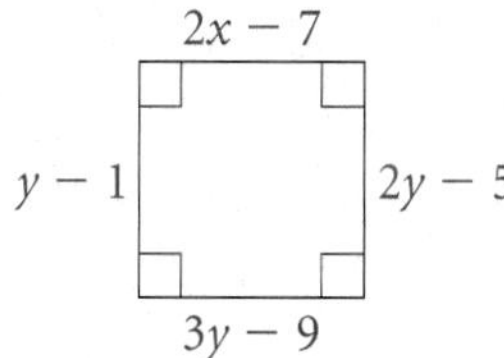

B Apply Your Skills

Algebra In each figure, find the measures of the angles and the lengths of the sides.

25. isosceles trapezoid $DEFG$

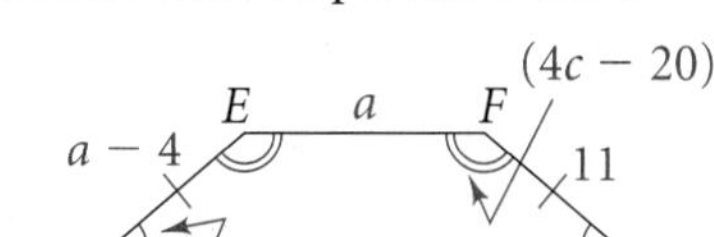

26. rhombus $HKJI$

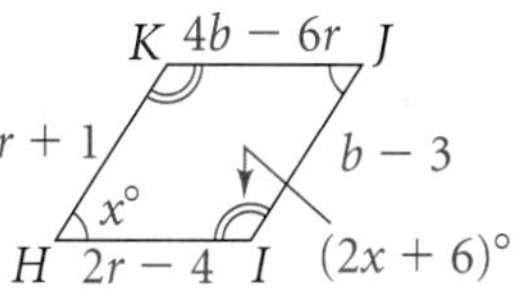

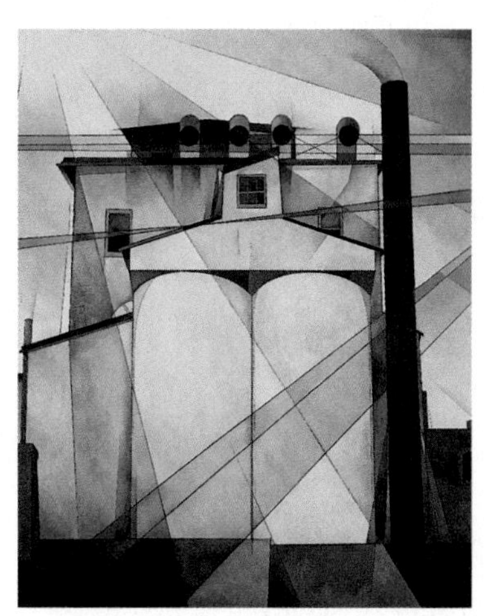
Exercise 27

27. **Art** American artist Charles Demuth created *My Egypt*, the oil painting pictured at the left. It is in an art style called Cubism, in which subjects are made of cubes and other geometric forms. Identify the types of special quadrilaterals you see in the painting.

28. Identify a parallelogram, rhombus, rectangle, square, kite, and trapezoid in your classroom. State whether your trapezoid is isosceles.

Draw each figure on graph paper. If not possible, explain.

29. a parallelogram that is neither a rectangle nor a rhombus

30. an isosceles trapezoid with vertical and horizontal congruent sides

31. a trapezoid with only one right angle

32. a trapezoid with two right angles

33. a rhombus that is not a square

34. a kite with two right angles

35. **Writing** Describe the difference between a rhombus and a kite.

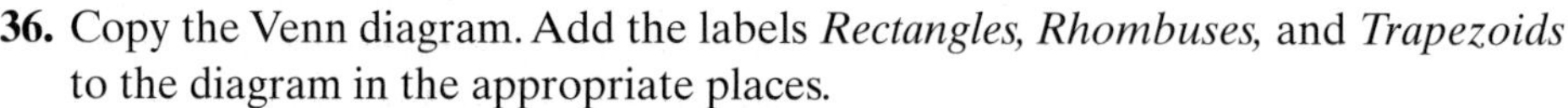

36. Copy the Venn diagram. Add the labels *Rectangles, Rhombuses,* and *Trapezoids* to the diagram in the appropriate places.

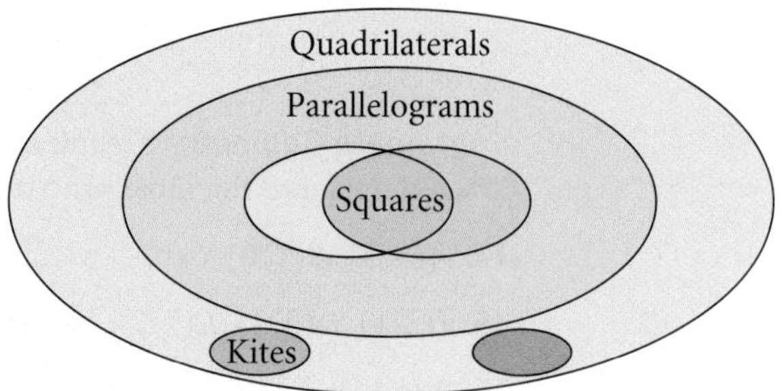

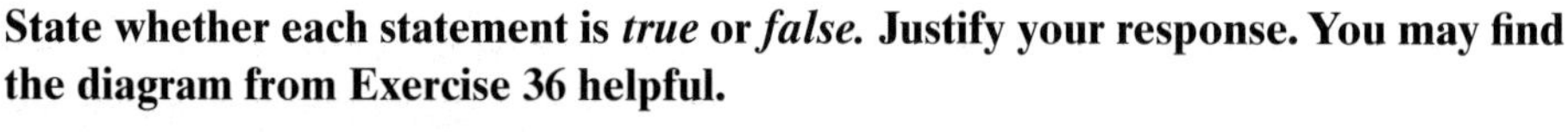

State whether each statement is *true* or *false.* Justify your response. You may find the diagram from Exercise 36 helpful.

37. All squares are rectangles.

38. A trapezoid is a parallelogram.

39. A rhombus can be a kite.

40. Some parallelograms are squares.

41. Every quadrilateral is a parallelogram.

42. All rhombuses are squares.

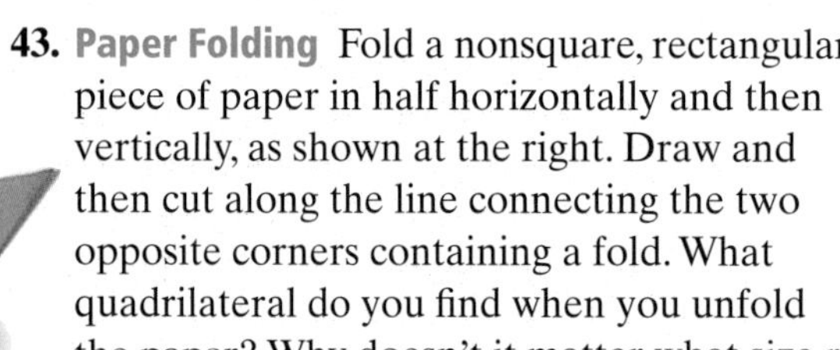

43. **Paper Folding** Fold a nonsquare, rectangular piece of paper in half horizontally and then vertically, as shown at the right. Draw and then cut along the line connecting the two opposite corners containing a fold. What quadrilateral do you find when you unfold the paper? Why doesn't it matter what size rectangle you start with?

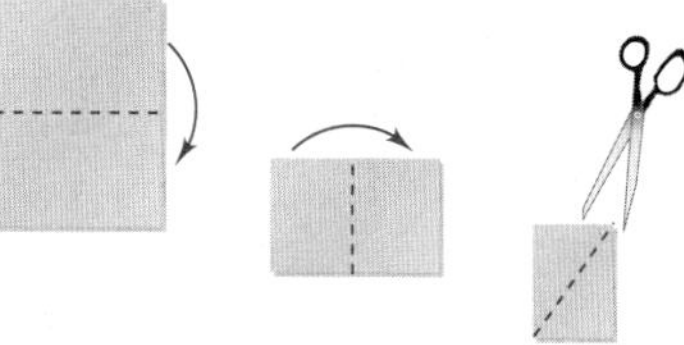

Real-World Connection

To make this butterfly, an origami square was folded first on its diagonals.

Identify a parallelogram, rhombus, rectangle, square, kite and trapezoid at each site. State whether your trapezoid is isosceles.

44. home

45. somewhere other than school and home

Name each type of special quadrilateral that can meet the given condition. Make sketches to support your answers.

46. exactly one pair of congruent sides

47. two pairs of parallel sides

48. four right angles

49. adjacent sides that are congruent

50. **Error Analysis** Lauren argues, "A parallelogram has two pairs of parallel sides, so it certainly has one pair of parallel sides. Therefore a parallelogram must also be a trapezoid." What is the error in Lauren's argument?

Name the type of special quadrilateral it appears that you can form by joining the triangles in each pair. Make sketches to support your answers.

Sample two congruent scalene triangles

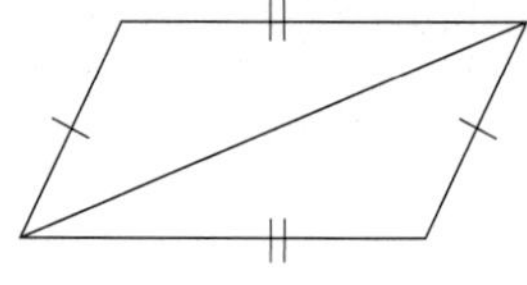

parallelogram

Need Help?

In Exercises 51–54, if you flip one of the two triangles, you may find different quadrilaterals.

51. two congruent scalene right triangles

52. two congruent equilateral triangles

53. two congruent isosceles right triangles

54. two congruent isosceles acute triangles

55. **a.** **Open-Ended** Graph and label points $K(-3, 0)$, $L(0, 2)$, and $M(3, 0)$. Find possible coordinates for point N so that $KLMN$ is a kite.
b. Explain why there is more than one possible fourth vertex.

Reasoning **A scrap of paper covers part of each quadrilateral. Name all the special quadrilaterals that each could be. Explain each choice.**

56. 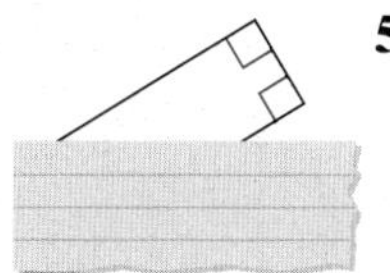 **57.** 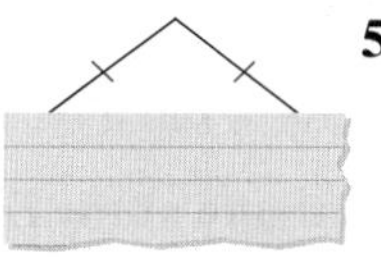 **58.** 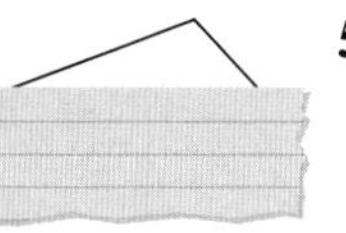 **59.** 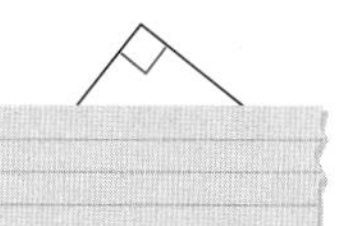

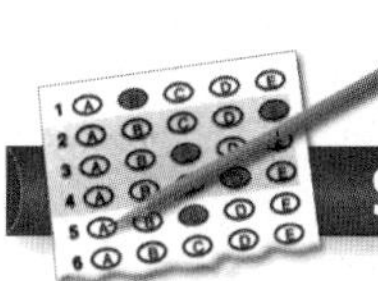

Standardized Test Prep

Multiple Choice

60. Which statement is NEVER true?
A. Square *ABCD* is a rhombus.
B. Parallelogram *PQRS* is a square.
C. Trapezoid *GHJK* is a parallelogram.
D. Square *WXYZ* is a parallelogram.

61. Which statement is true for some, but not all, rectangles?
F. Opposite sides are parallel.
G. It is a parallelogram.
H. Adjacent sides are perpendicular.
I. All sides are congruent.

62. A parallelogram has four congruent sides. Which name best describes the figure?
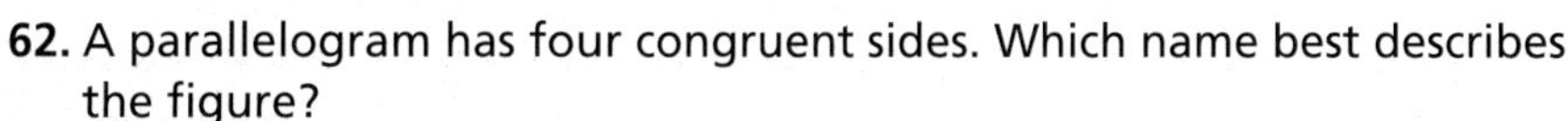
A. trapezoid **B.** parallelogram **C.** rhombus **D.** square

Take It to the NET
Online lesson quiz at **www.PHSchool.com**
Web Code: afa-0601

63. Which name best describes a parallelogram with four congruent angles?
F. kite **G.** rhombus **H.** rectangle **I.** square

Short Response

64. $A(-3, 1)$, $B(-1, -2)$, and $C(2, 1)$ are three points of quadrilateral *ABCD*. Could *ABCD* be a rectangle? Explain.

Mixed Review

Lesson 5-5

Can a triangle have sides with the given lengths? Explain.

65. 8 mm, 6 mm, 3 mm **66.** 5 ft, 20 ft, 7 ft **67.** 3 m, 5 m, 8 m

Lesson 4-1

Quadrilaterals *RSTV* and *NMQP* are congruent. Find the length of the side or the measure of the angle.

68. $\overline{MN}$ **69.** $\overline{VT}$
70. $\overline{ST}$ **71.** $\angle S$
72. $\angle V$ **73.** $\angle R$

Lesson 3-6

74. Write an equation for the line parallel to $y = -3x - 5$ that contains point $(0, 4)$.

6-2 Properties of Parallelograms

Lesson Preview

What You'll Learn

OBJECTIVE 1 To use relationships among sides and among angles of parallelograms

OBJECTIVE 2 To use relationships involving diagonals of parallelograms or transversals.

. . . And Why

To divide a blank card into three parts of equal heights without a ruler, as in Example 4

✓ Check Skills You'll Need

(For help, go to Lessons 4-1 and 4-3.)

Use the figure at the right.

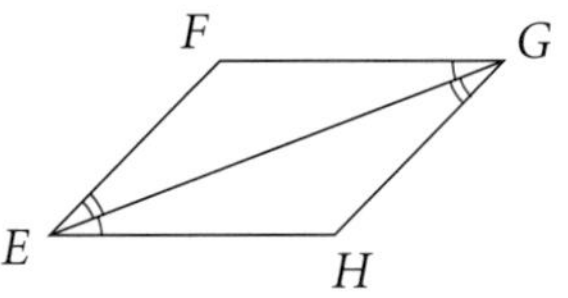

1. Name the postulate or theorem that justifies the congruence $\triangle EFG \cong \triangle GHE$.

2. Complete each statement.

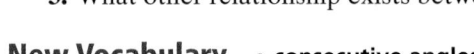

a. $\angle FEG \cong$? **b.** $\angle EFG \cong$?
c. $\angle FGE \cong$? **d.** $\overline{EF} \cong$?
e. $\overline{FG} \cong$? **f.** $\overline{GE} \cong$?

3. What other relationship exists between $\overline{FG}$ and $\overline{EH}$?

New Vocabulary • consecutive angles

Interactive lesson includes instant self-check, tutorials, and activities.

OBJECTIVE 1 Properties: Sides and Angles

You can use what you know about parallel lines and transversals to prove some theorems about parallelograms.

Key Concepts

Theorem 6-1

Opposite sides of a parallelogram are congruent.

Proof

Proof of Theorem 6-1

Given: $\square ABCD$

Prove: $\overline{AB} \cong \overline{CD}, \overline{BC} \cong \overline{DA}$

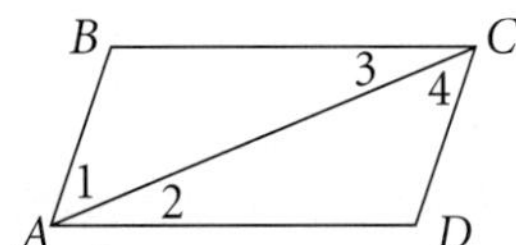

Reading Math

Read "▱" as "parallelogram." The plural is "▱s."

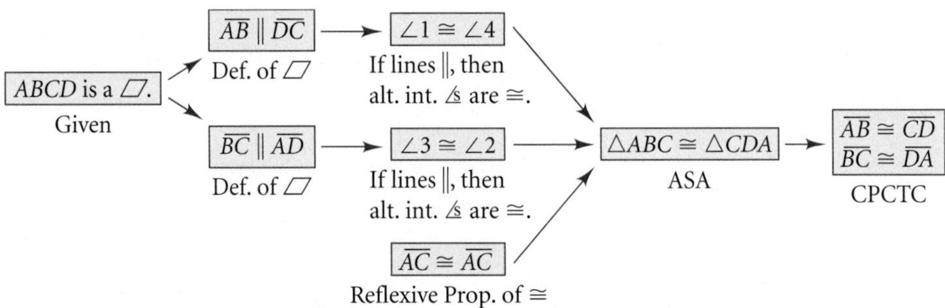

Angles of a polygon that share a side are **consecutive angles.** A parallelogram has opposite sides parallel. Its consecutive angles are same-side interior angles so they are supplementary. In $\square ABCD$, consecutive angles B and C are supplementary, as are consecutive angles C and D.

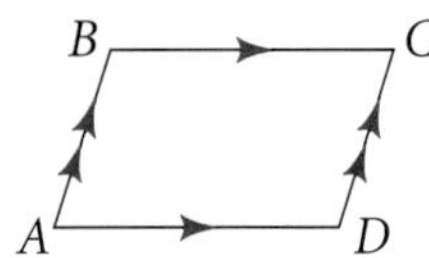

1 EXAMPLE Using Consecutive Angles

Find $m\angle S$ in ▱$RSTW$.

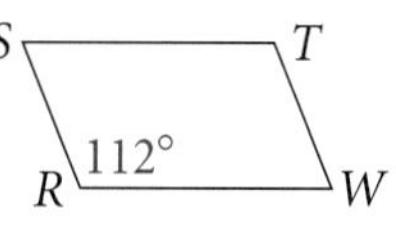

$\angle R$ and $\angle S$ are consecutive angles of a parallelogram. They are supplementary.

$m\angle R + m\angle S = 180$	**Definition of supplementary angles**
$112 + m\angle S = 180$	**Substitute.**
$m\angle S = 68$	**Subtract 112 from each side.**

✓ Check Understanding **1** **Critical Thinking** If consecutive angles of a quadrilateral are supplementary, must the quadrilateral be a parallelogram? Explain.

A proof of Theorem 6-2 uses the consecutive angles of a parallelogram, and the fact that supplements of the same angle are congruent.

Key Concepts

Theorem 6-2

Opposite angles of a parallelogram are congruent.

Real-World Connection

Opposite angles in the "cat's cradle" parallelogram (center) are congruent.

Plan for Proof of Theorem 6-2

Given: ▱$MNPQ$

Prove: $\angle M \cong \angle P$ and $\angle N \cong \angle Q$

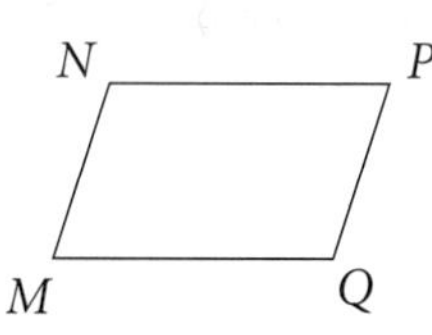

Plan: $\angle M \cong \angle P$ if they are supplements of the same angle, $\angle N$. Each is a supplement of $\angle N$ because same side interior angles are supplementary.
$\angle N \cong \angle Q$ using similar reasoning with $\angle M$.

You can complete a flow proof of Theorem 6-2 in Exercise 37. You can write another proof—also a flow proof—that follows the plan above in Exercise 38. You can use Theorems 6-1 and 6-2 along with algebra to find unknown values in parallelograms.

2 EXAMPLE Using Algebra

Algebra Find the value of x in ▱$PQRS$. Then find QR and PS.

$3x - 15 = 2x + 3$	**Opposite sides of a ▱ are congruent.**
$x - 15 = 3$	**Subtract 2x from each side.**
$x = 18$	**Add 15 to each side.**
$QR = 3x - 15 = 39$	**Substitute.**

$\overline{PS} \cong \overline{QR}$, so $PS = 39$.

✓ Check Understanding **2** Find the value of y in ▱$EFGH$. Then find $m\angle E$, $m\angle G$, $m\angle F$, and $m\angle H$.

OBJECTIVE

2 Properties: Diagonals and Transversals

The diagonals of parallelograms have a special property.

Key Concepts

Theorem 6-3

The diagonals of a parallelogram bisect each other.

Proof

Proof of Theorem 6-3

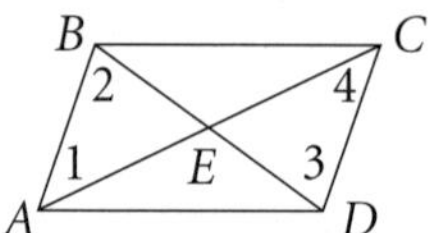

Given: $\square ABCD$

Prove: $\overline{AC}$ and $\overline{BD}$ bisect each other at E.

Statements	Reasons
1. $ABCD$ is a parallelogram.	1. Given
2. $\overline{AB} \parallel \overline{DC}$	2. Definition of parallelogram
3. $\angle 1 \cong \angle 4$; $\angle 2 \cong \angle 3$	3. Parallel lines form $\cong$ alt. int. $\angle$s.
4. $\overline{AB} \cong \overline{DC}$	4. Opposite sides of a $\square$ are $\cong$.
5. $\triangle ABE \cong \triangle CDE$	5. ASA
6. $\overline{AE} \cong \overline{CE}$; $\overline{BE} \cong \overline{DE}$	6. CPCTC
7. $\overline{AC}$ and $\overline{BD}$ bisect each other at E.	7. Definition of bisector

Real-World Connection

The railing braces are diagonals of parallelograms so they bisect each other.

You can use Theorem 6-3 to find unknown lengths in parallelograms.

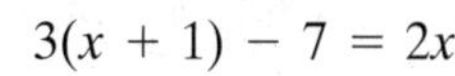

3 EXAMPLE Using Algebra

Solve a system of linear equations to find the values of x and y in $\square ABCD$. Then find AE, EC, BE, and ED.

B, C, A, D, E; $x+1$, $2x$, $3y-7$, y

① $3y - 7 = 2x$ ② $y = x + 1$	**The diagonals of a parallelogram bisect each other.**
$3(x + 1) - 7 = 2x$	**Substitute $x + 1$ for y in equation ①.**
$3x + 3 - 7 = 2x$	**Distribute.**
$3x - 4 = 2x$	**Simplify.**
$3x = 2x + 4$	**Add 4 to each side.**
$x = 4$	**Subtract $2x$ from each side.**
$3y - 7 = 2(4) = 8$ $y = 4 + 1 = 5$	**Substitute 4 for x in equations ① and ②.**

$AE = EC = 8$ and $BE = ED = 5$.

Check Understanding

3 Find the values of a and b.

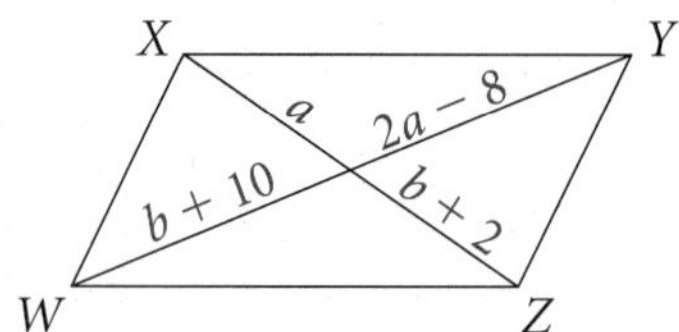

In Exercise 55, you will use Theorem 6-1, opposite sides of a parallelogram are congruent, to prove the following theorem.

Key Concepts

Theorem 6-4

If three (or more) parallel lines cut off congruent segments on one transversal, then they cut off congruent segments on every transversal.

$\overline{BD} \cong \overline{DF}$

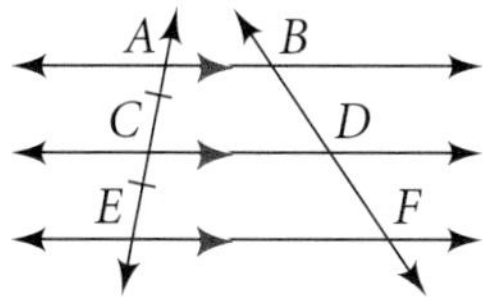

4 EXAMPLE **Real-World Connection**

Measurement Show how to separate a blank card into three strips that are the same height by using lined paper, a straightedge, and Theorem 6-4.

The lines of the paper are parallel and equally spaced. Place a corner of the top edge of the card on the first line of the paper. Place the corner of the bottom edge on the fourth line. Mark the points where the second and third lines intersect the card. The marks will be equally spaced because the edge of the card is a transversal for the equally spaced parallel lines of the paper. Repeat for the other side of the card. Connect the marks using a straightedge.

Check Understanding

4. In the figure at the right, $\overleftrightarrow{DH} \parallel \overleftrightarrow{CG} \parallel \overleftrightarrow{BF} \parallel \overleftrightarrow{AE}$, $AB = BC = CD = 2$, and $EF = 2.5$. Find EH.

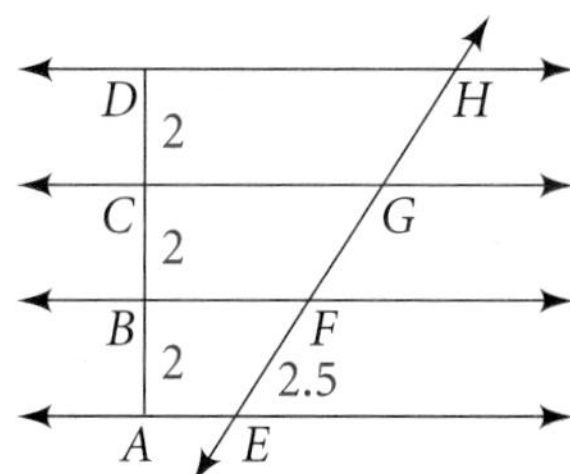

EXERCISES

For more practice, see *Extra Practice*.

Practice and Problem Solving

A Practice by Example

Example 1 (page 295)

x^2 Algebra **Find the value of x in each parallelogram.**

1.
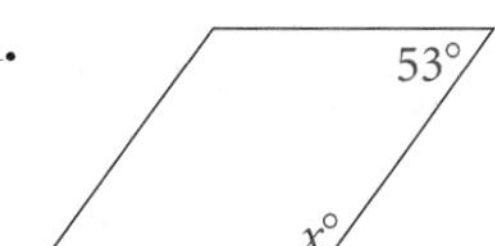

2.
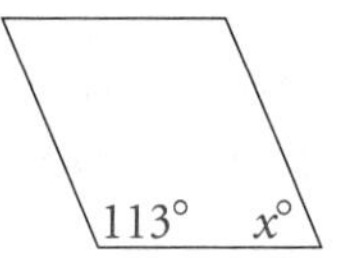

3.
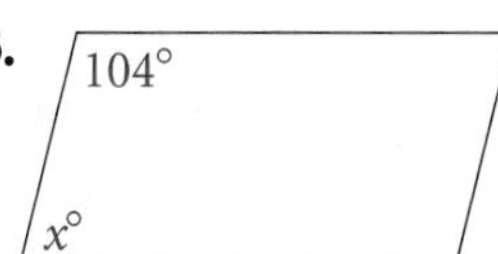

4.
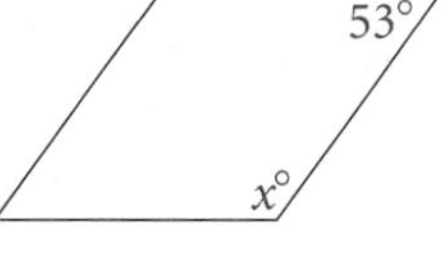

5.
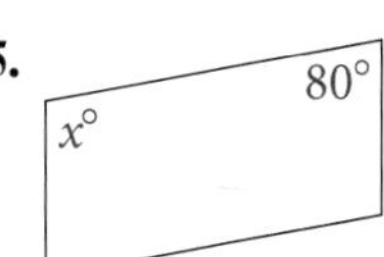

6.
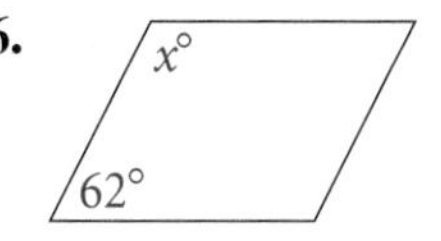

Example 2 (page 295)

x^2 Algebra **Find the value of x.**

7.
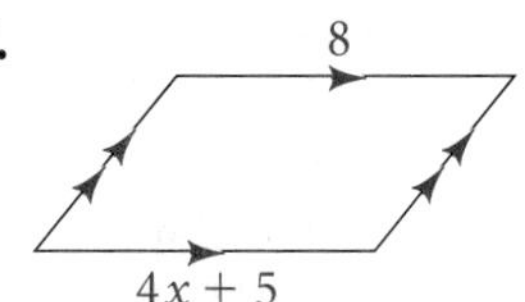

8.
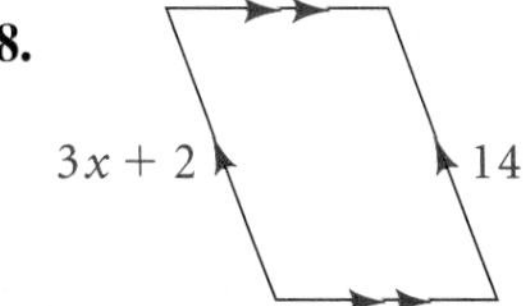

9.
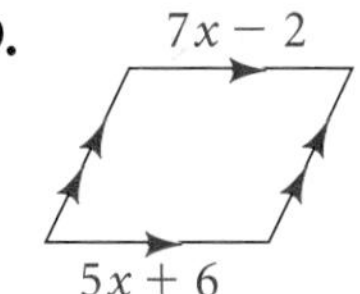

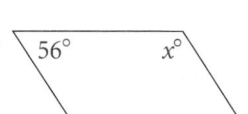

Find the value of x and the length of each side.

10. 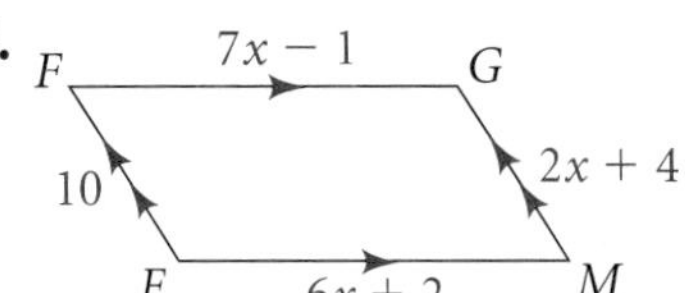

11. 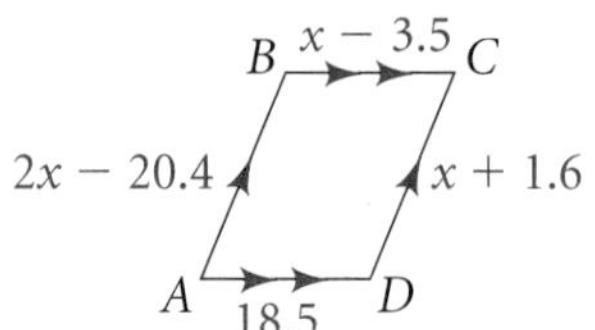

x^2 **Algebra** **Find the value of a.**

12. 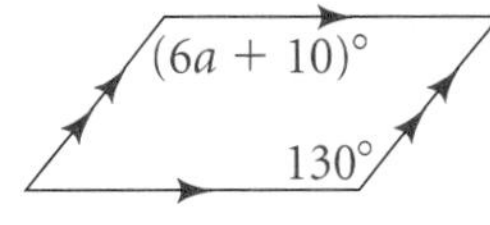

13. 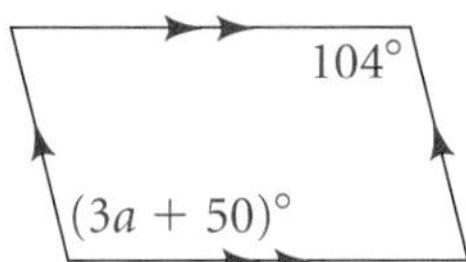

14. 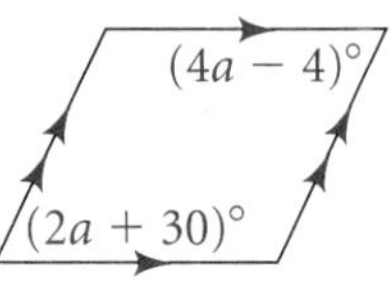

Find the value of a and the measure of each angle in each parallelogram.

15. 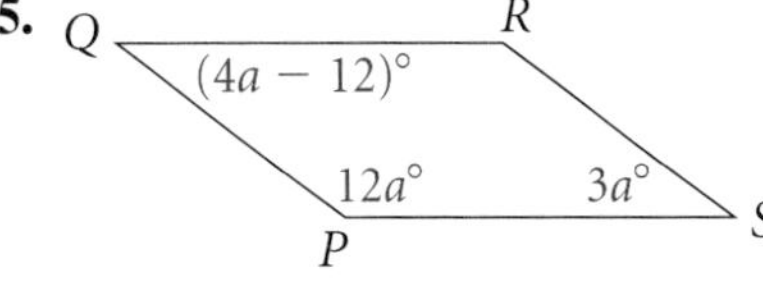

16. 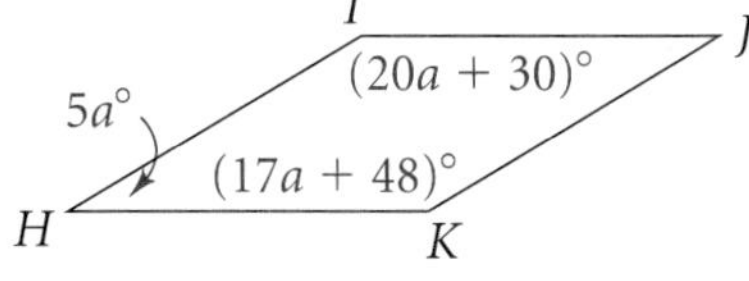

Example 3 (page 296)

x^2 **Algebra** **Find the values of x and y in $\square PQRS$.**

17. $PT = 2x, TR = y + 4, QT = x + 2, TS = y$

18. $PT = x + 2, TR = y, QT = 2x, TS = y + 3$

19. $PT = y, TR = x + 3, QT = 2y, TS = 3x - 1$

20. $PT = 2x, TR = y + 3, QT = 3x, TS = 2y$

21. $PT = 8x, TR = 6y, QT = 2x + 2, TS = 2y$

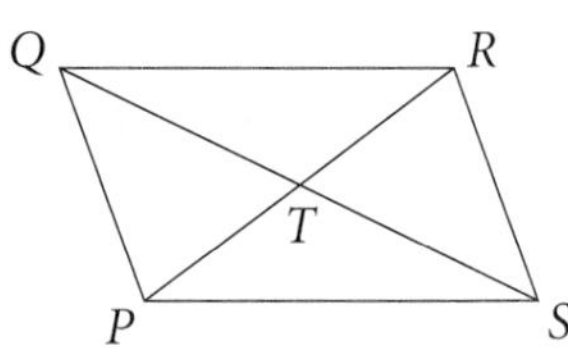

Example 4 (page 297)

22. Find ED and FD in the figure at the right.

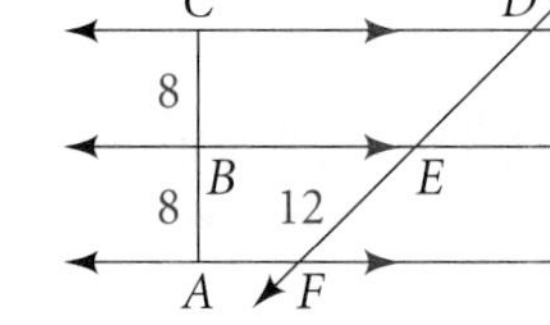

23. Sewing Suppose you don't have a ruler. Explain how to space four buttons equally on a shirt if you know where the first and last buttons must be placed and you have a large piece of lined paper.

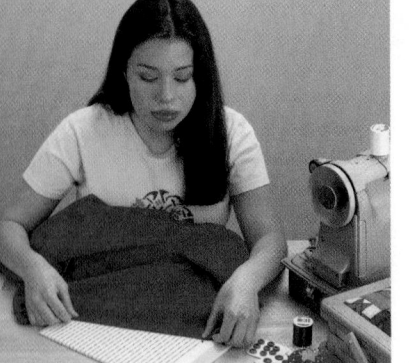

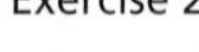
Exercise 23

In the figure, the horizontal lines are parallel and $PQ = QR = RS$. Find each length.

24. ZU **25.** XZ

26. XU **27.** TZ

28. TU **29.** XV

30. YX **31.** YV

32. WX **33.** WV

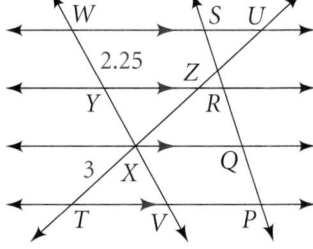

B Apply Your Skills x^2 **Algebra** **Use the given information to find the lengths of all four sides of $\square ABCD$.**

34. The perimeter is 48 in. AB is 5 in. less than BC.

35. The perimeter is 92 cm. AD is 7 cm more than twice AB.

Need Help?

Use the flow proof on p. 294.

Proof **36. Developing Proof** Complete this paragraph proof of Theorem 6-1 by filling in the blanks.

Given: $\square ABCD$

Prove: $\overline{AB} \cong \overline{CD}$ and $\overline{BC} \cong \overline{DA}$

Proof: $ABCD$ is a parallelogram, therefore $\overline{AB} \parallel$ **a.** __?__ and $\overline{BC} \parallel$ **b.** __?__. $\angle 1 \cong \angle 4$ and $\angle 3 \cong \angle 2$, because alternate interior angles are **c.** __?__. $\overline{AC} \cong \overline{AC}$ by the **d.** __?__ Property of Congruence. Therefore $\triangle ABC \cong \triangle CDA$ by **e.** __?__ . So, $\overline{AB} \cong \overline{CD}$ and $\overline{BC} \cong \overline{DA}$ because **f.** __?__.

Developing Proof Exercises 37 and 38 ask you for two different flow proofs of Theorem 6-2.

37. Complete this flow proof of Theorem 6-2 by filling in the blanks.

Given: $\square MNPQ$

Prove: $\angle NMQ \cong \angle QPN$ and $\angle MNP \cong \angle PQM$

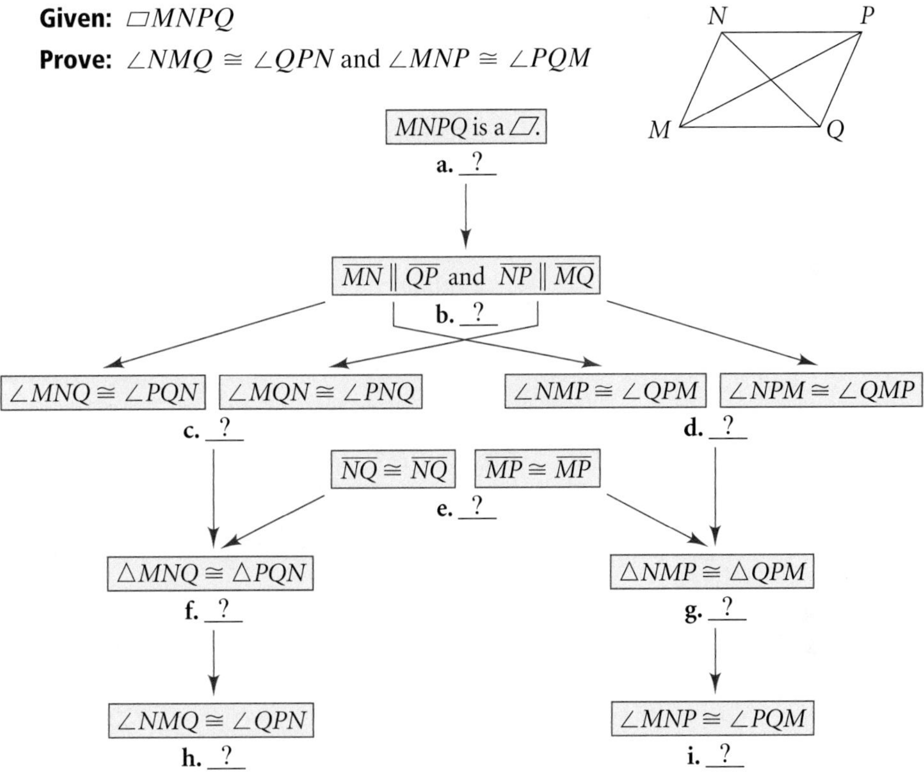

Reading Math

For help with reading and solving Exercise 38, see p. 302.

38. Write a flow proof for Theorem 6-2 that follows the plan on page 295.

Find the measures of the numbered angles for each parallelogram.

39.

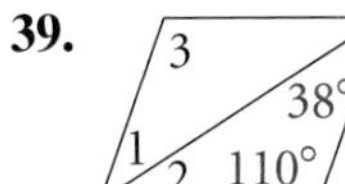

40.

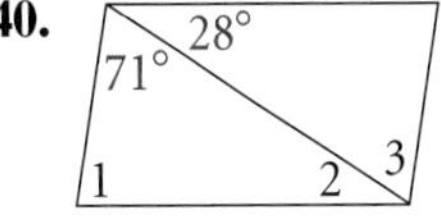

41.

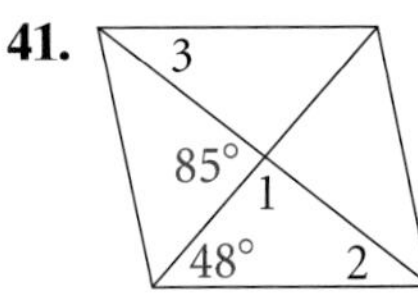

42. Error Analysis Brian states that $QV = 10$ cm in the figure at the right. Explain why Brian's statement may not be correct.

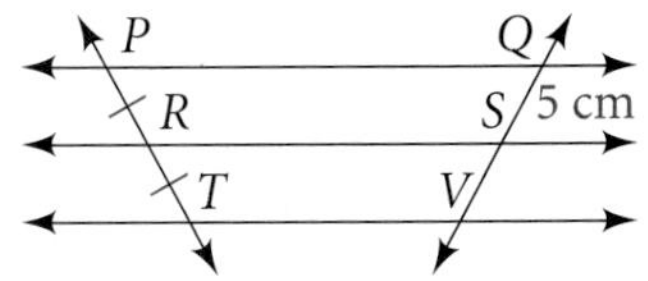

x^2 **43. Algebra** In a parallelogram one angle is 9 times the size of another. Find the measures of the angles.

Real-World Connection

As the box is flattened, the shape remains a parallelogram with opposite sides and angles congruent and consecutive angles supplementary.

Algebra **Find the value(s) of the variable(s) in each parallelogram.**

44. 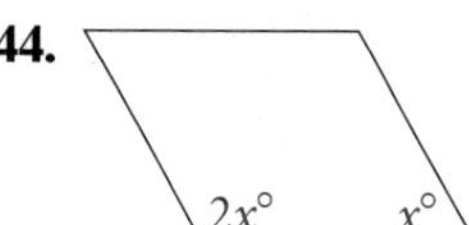

45. 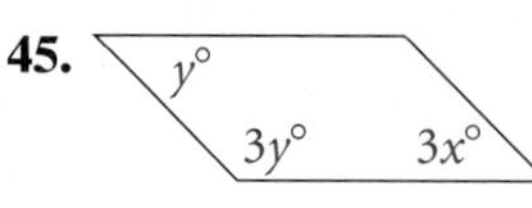

46. $x°$, $(z - 5)°$, $71°$, $(y + 21)°$

47. $(y + 16)°$, $(2x - 1)°$, $(x + 24)°$

48. 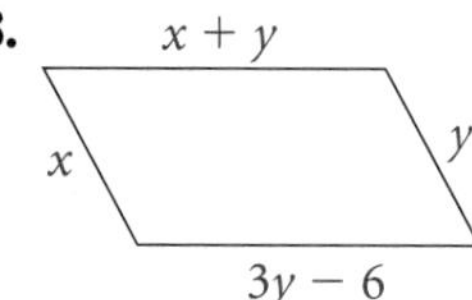

49. 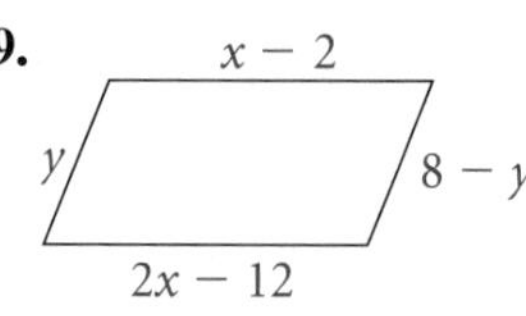

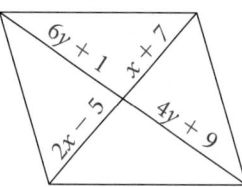

50. $6y + 1$, $x + 7$, $2x - 5$, $4y + 9$

51. $AC = 4x + 10$

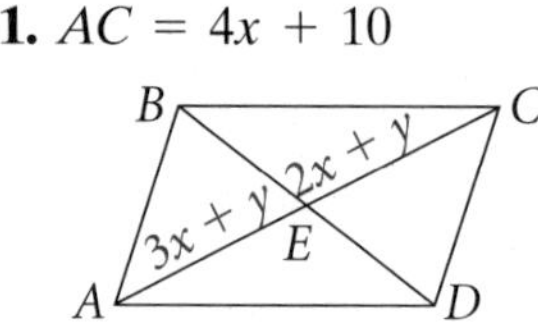

52. 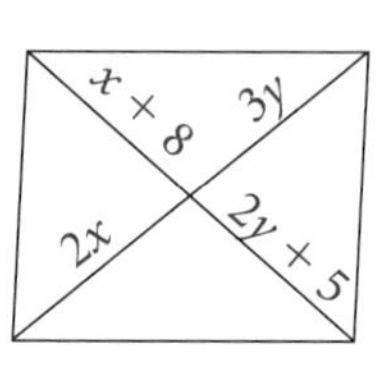

53. Writing Explain how to find the measures of the remaining three angles of a parallelogram if you already know the measure of one of the angles.

54. a. Open-Ended Sketch two parallelograms whose corresponding sides are congruent but whose corresponding angles are not congruent.

b. Critical Thinking Is there an SSSS congruence theorem for parallelograms? Explain.

55. Developing Proof A proof of Theorem 6-4 is outlined below. Supply the reasons for each step.

Given: $\overleftrightarrow{AB} \parallel \overleftrightarrow{CD} \parallel \overleftrightarrow{EF}$ and $\overline{AC} \cong \overline{CE}$

Prove: $\overline{BD} \cong \overline{DF}$

Draw lines through B and D parallel to $\overleftrightarrow{AE}$ and intersecting $\overleftrightarrow{CD}$ at G and $\overleftrightarrow{EF}$ at H.

a. $\overleftrightarrow{AB} \parallel \overleftrightarrow{CD} \parallel \overleftrightarrow{EF}$ and $\overline{AC} \cong \overline{CE}$

b. $ABGC$ and $CDHE$ are parallelograms.

c. $\overline{BG} \cong \overline{AC}$ and $\overline{DH} \cong \overline{CE}$

d. $\overline{BG} \cong \overline{DH}$

e. $\overline{BG} \parallel \overline{DH}$

f. $\angle 2 \cong \angle 1$, $\angle 1 \cong \angle 4$, $\angle 4 \cong \angle 5$, and $\angle 3 \cong \angle 6$

g. $\angle 2 \cong \angle 5$

h. $\triangle BGD \cong \triangle DHF$

i. $\overline{BD} \cong \overline{DF}$

Proof **Write a paragraph proof, a flow proof, or a two-column proof.**

Need Help?

For each of Exercises 56–58, sketch the diagram and mark it as you think through a proof.

56. Given: $\square LENS$ and $\square NGTH$

Prove: $\angle L \cong \angle T$

57. Given: $\square LENS$ and $\square NGTH$

Prove: $\overline{LS} \parallel \overline{GT}$

58. Given: $\square LENS$ and $\square NGTH$

Prove: $\angle E$ is supplementary to $\angle T$.

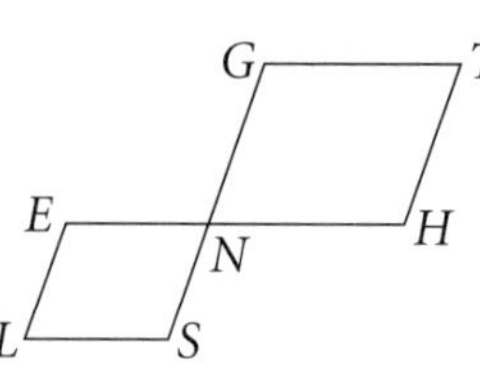

C Challenge Proof **Write a paragraph proof, a flow proof, or a two-column proof.**

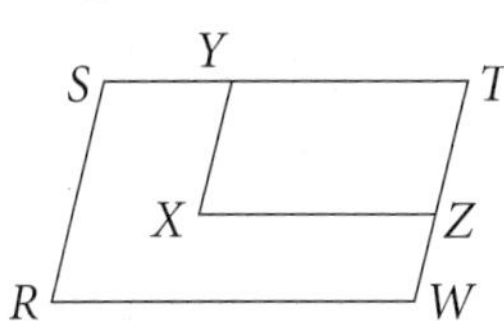

59. Given: $\square RSTW$ and $\square XYTZ$

Prove: $\angle R \cong \angle X$

60. Given: $\square RSTW$ and $\square XYTZ$

Prove: $\overline{XY} \parallel \overline{RS}$

61. Given: $\square ABCD$ and $\overline{AC}$ bisects $\angle DAB$.

Prove: $\overline{AC}$ bisects $\angle DCB$.

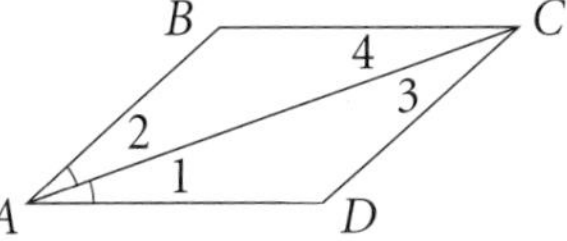

Proof **62. a.** Prove that if two sides and the included angle of one parallelogram are congruent to corresponding parts of another parallelogram, then the parallelograms are congruent. (*Hint:* Prove that all the corresponding parts of the parallelograms are congruent.)

b. Is there a theorem similar to SAS for trapezoids? Explain.

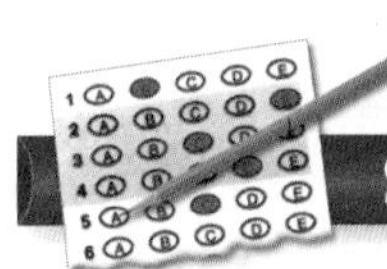

Standardized Test Prep

Gridded Response

Use the parallelogram at the right for Exercises 63–66. Find the indicated segment length or angle measure.

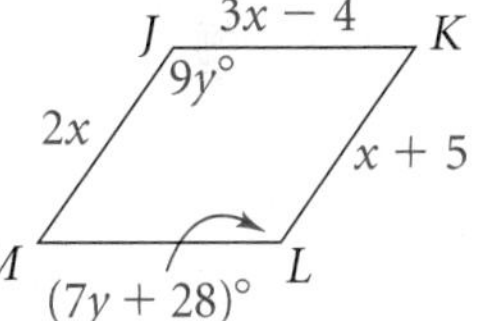

63. *JM* **64.** *ML* **65.** $m\angle L$ **66.** $m\angle J$

67. The measures of three angles in a parallelogram measure 20, 160, and 20. Find the measure of the fourth angle.

68. The measures of two angles in a parallelogram are 32 and 32. Find the measure of one of the other two angles.

69. Two consecutive angles in a parallelogram have measures $x + 5$ and $4x - 10$. Find the measure of the smaller angle.

Take It to the NET
Online lesson quiz at
www.PHSchool.com
Web Code: afa-0602

Mixed Review

Lesson 6-1 **Determine the most precise name for each figure.**

70.

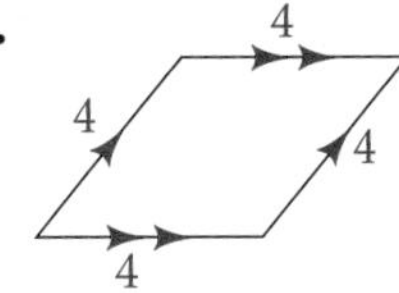

71.

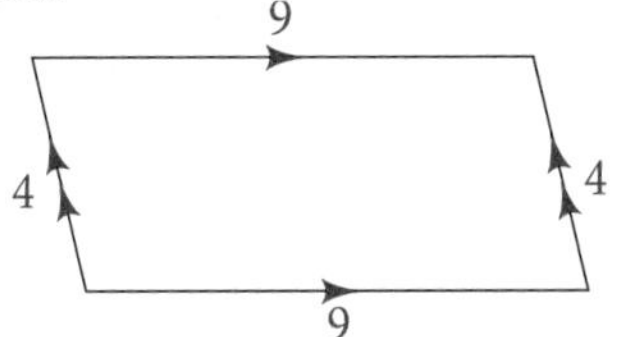

Lesson 4-6 **72.** What additional information do you need to prove $\triangle ADC \cong \triangle ABC$ by the HL Theorem?

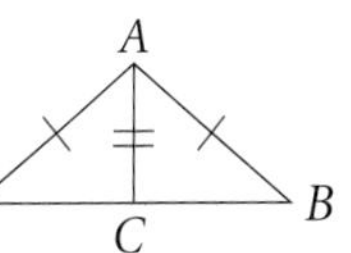

Lesson 3-1 **In the figure at the right, $\overleftrightarrow{PQ} \parallel \overleftrightarrow{RS}$. Find each measure.**

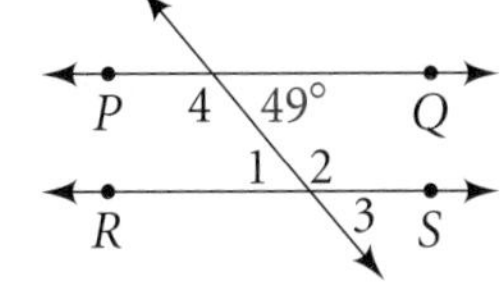

73. $m\angle 1$ **74.** $m\angle 2$ **75.** $m\angle 3$ **76.** $m\angle 4$

Reading Math

Reading a Plan for Proof

For Use With Page 299, Exercise 38

Follow along with Ravi as he writes a flow proof for Theorem 6-2 that follows the plan on page 295. Then check your understanding by solving the exercise at the bottom of the page.

Theorem 6-2 Opposite angles of a parallelogram are congruent.

Given: $\square MNPQ$

Prove: $\angle M \cong \angle P$ and $\angle N \cong \angle Q$

Plan: $\angle M \cong \angle P$ if they are supplements of the same angle, $\angle N$. Each is a supplement of $\angle N$ because same-side interior angles are supplementary. $\angle N \cong \angle Q$ using similar reasoning with $\angle M$.

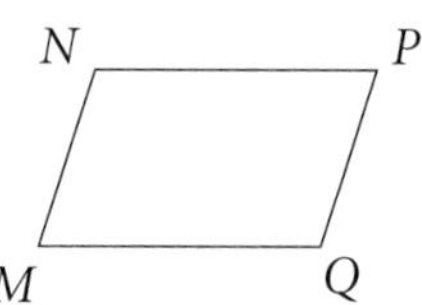

What Ravi Thinks

The second sentence of the plan is

"Each is a supplement of $\angle N$ because same-side interior angles are supplementary."

This tells me where to begin. Opposite sides of a parallelogram are parallel while the other sides act as transversals. The opposite sides and transversals form same-side interior angles.

Same-side interior angles are supplementary and supplements of the same angle are congruent.

This gives me half the proof.

The last sentence of the plan is

"$\angle N \cong \angle Q$ using similar reasoning with $\angle M$."

This tells me I can repeat the first part of the proof, but with different angles.

I have found a clever way to add this second part to my flow proof. It's in red.

What Ravi Writes

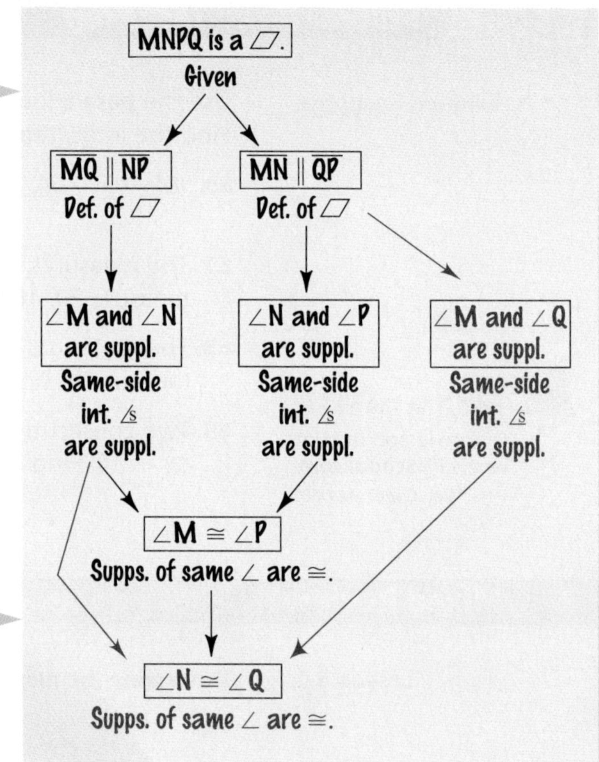

EXERCISE

For Exercise 56 on page 300, follow this plan and write a proof.

Given: $\square LENS$ and $\square NGTH$

Prove: $\angle L \cong \angle T$

Plan: $\angle L \cong \angle T$ if their opposite angles, $\angle ENS$ and $\angle HNG$, are congruent. $\angle ENS \cong \angle HNG$ because they are vertical angles.

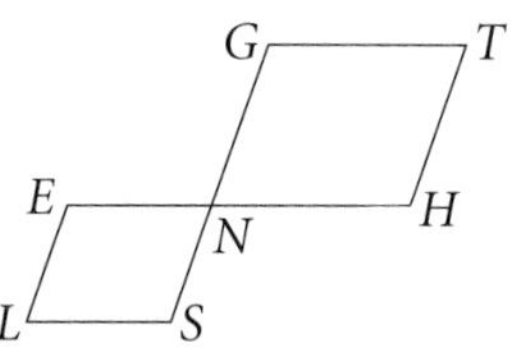

6-3 Proving That a Quadrilateral Is a Parallelogram

Lesson Preview

What You'll Learn

To determine whether a quadrilateral is a parallelogram

. . . And Why

To use a parallel rule to plot a ship's course, as in Example 3

Check Skills You'll Need

(For help, go to Lessons 1-6 and 3-6.)

Use the figure at the right.

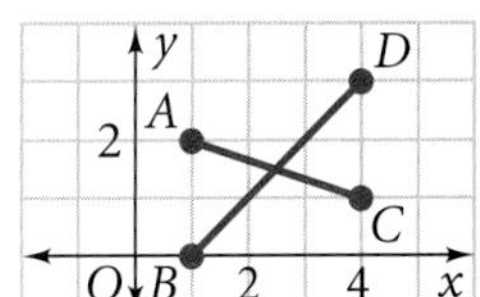

1. Find the coordinates of the midpoints of $\overline{AC}$ and $\overline{BD}$. What is the relationship between $\overline{AC}$ and $\overline{BD}$?

2. Find the slopes of $\overline{BC}$ and $\overline{AD}$. How do they compare?

3. Are $\overline{AB}$ and $\overline{DC}$ parallel? Explain.

4. What type of figure is $ABCD$?

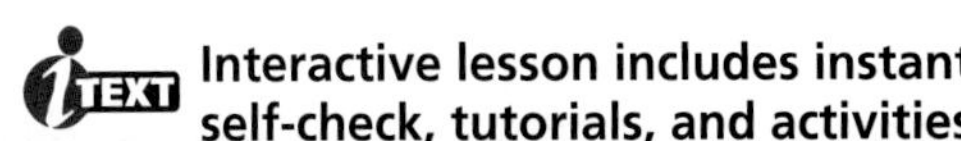

Interactive lesson includes instant self-check, tutorials, and activities.

OBJECTIVE 1

Is the Quadrilateral a Parallelogram?

Investigation: Is It a Parallelogram?

By definition, a quadrilateral is a parallelogram if both pairs of opposite sides are parallel. Use a geoboard to explore other ways to determine whether a quadrilateral is a parallelogram.

1. The segments on this geoboard bisect each other. Connect the endpoints to form a quadrilateral. Find the slopes of pairs of opposite sides and determine what type of quadrilateral it is.

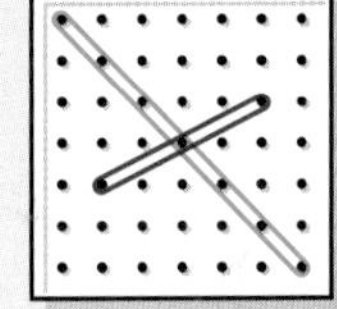

2. Make several pairs of bisecting segments on a geoboard. Join the endpoints to form quadrilaterals. Classify the quadrilaterals. Make a conjecture about quadrilaterals whose diagonals bisect each other.

3. The segments on this geoboard are congruent and parallel. Connect the endpoints to form a quadrilateral. Find the slopes of these new sides and determine what type of quadrilateral it is.

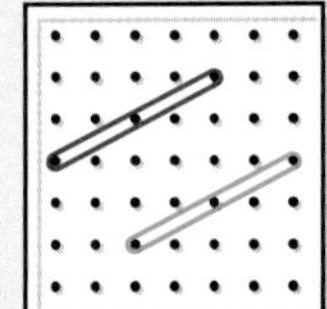

4. Make several pairs of congruent parallel segments on a geoboard. Join the endpoints to form quadrilaterals. Classify the quadrilaterals. Make a conjecture about quadrilaterals that have one pair of congruent and parallel sides.

In Lesson 6-2, you learned what you could deduce, given a parallelogram. In this lesson, you will learn how to deduce that a figure is a parallelogram.

Theorem 6-5 is the converse of Theorem 6-3 of the previous lesson.

Key Concepts

Theorem 6-5

If the diagonals of a quadrilateral bisect each other, then the quadrilateral is a parallelogram.

Proof

Proof of Theorem 6-5

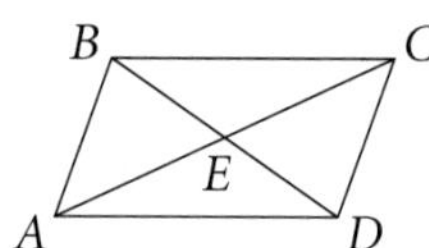

Given: $\overline{AC}$ and $\overline{BD}$ bisect each other at E.

Prove: $ABCD$ is a parallelogram.

Need Help?

Remember to mark your diagram as your proof develops.

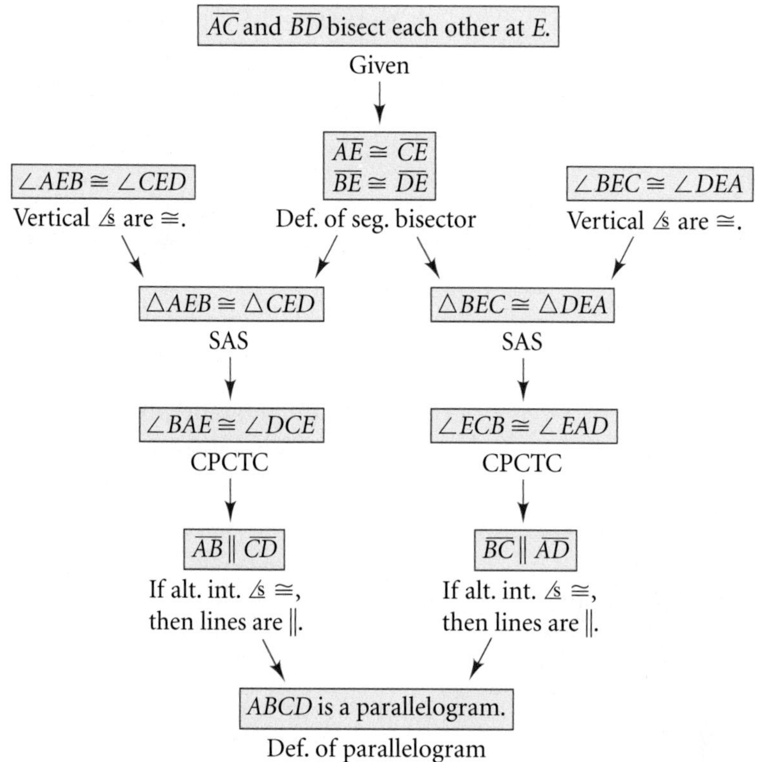

Theorem 6-6 suggests that if you keep two objects of the same length parallel, such as cross-country skis, then the quadrilateral determined by their endpoints must be a parallelogram. You will help plan a proof for Theorem 6-6 in Exercise 17.

Key Concepts

Theorem 6-6

If one pair of opposite sides of a quadrilateral is both congruent and parallel, then the quadrilateral is a parallelogram.

You can use algebra and Theorems 6-5 and 6-6 to find values for which quadrilaterals are parallelograms.

1 EXAMPLE Finding Values for Parallelograms

Algebra Find values of x and y for which $MLPN$ must be a parallelogram.

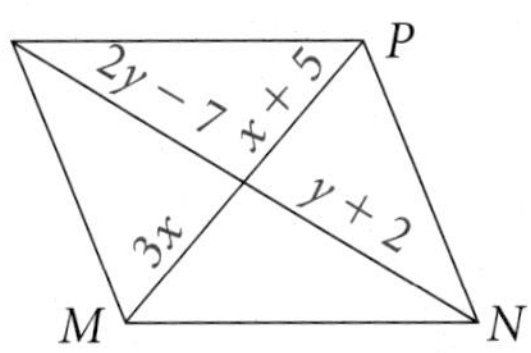

$2y - 7 = y + 2$	← **Diagonals of parallelograms bisect each other.** →	$3x = x + 5$
$y - 7 = 2$	← **Collect the variables on one side.** →	$2x = 5$
$y = 9$	← **Solve.** →	$x = \frac{5}{2}$

If $y = 9$ and $x = \frac{5}{2}$, then $MLPN$ is a parallelogram.

Check Understanding 1 Find the values of a and c for which $PQRS$ must be a parallelogram.

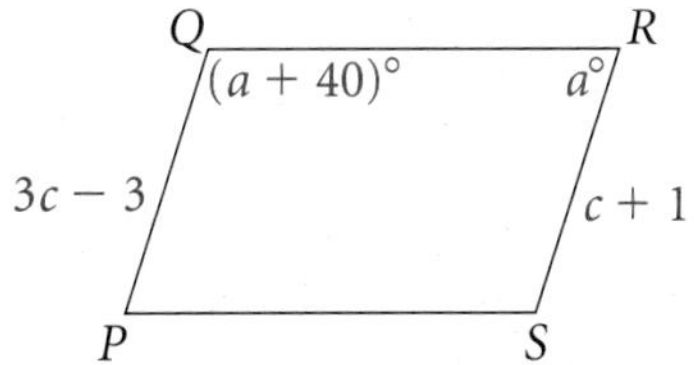

Theorems 6-7 and 6-8 are converses of Theorems 6-1 and 6-2, respectively, from the previous lesson. They provide two more ways to conclude that a quadrilateral is a parallelogram.

Key Concepts

Theorem 6-7

If both pairs of opposite sides of a quadrilateral are congruent, then the quadrilateral is a parallelogram.

Real-World Connection

The frame remains a parallelogram as it is raised and lowered, and the backboard stays vertical.

Proof of Theorem 6-7

Given: $\overline{WX} \cong \overline{ZY}$ and $\overline{XY} \cong \overline{WZ}$

Prove: $WXYZ$ is a parallelogram.

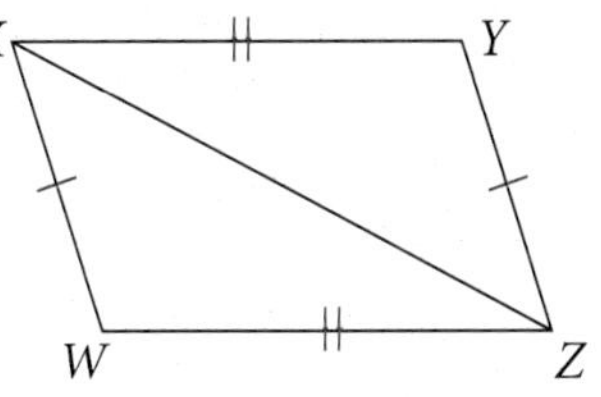

Proof: Draw diagonal $\overline{XZ}$. Since opposite sides of $WXYZ$ are congruent, $\triangle WXZ \cong \triangle YZX$ by SSS. Using CPCTC, $\angle WXZ \cong \angle YZX$, so $\overline{WX} \parallel \overline{ZY}$. Since $\overline{WX}$ and $\overline{ZY}$ are both congruent and parallel, $WXYZ$ is a parallelogram by Theorem 6-6.

You will complete a two-column proof of Theorem 6-8 in Exercise 19.

Key Concepts

Theorem 6-8

If both pairs of opposite angles of a quadrilateral are congruent, then the quadrilateral is a parallelogram.

Proof  2 EXAMPLE Is the Quadrilateral a Parallelogram?

Developing Proof Based on the information given, can you determine that the quadrilateral must be a parallelogram? Explain.

a.

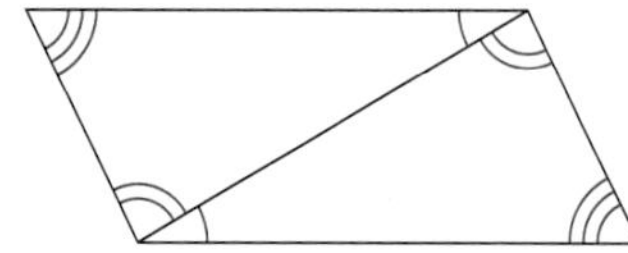

Yes, both pairs of opposite angles are congruent.

b.

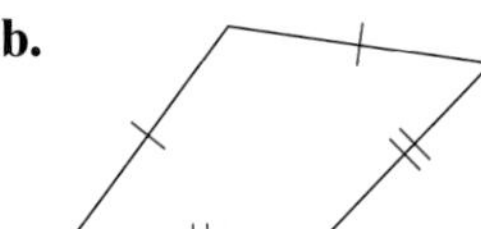

No, the figure could be a kite.

Check Understanding **2** Determine whether the quadrilateral must be a parallelogram. Explain.

a.

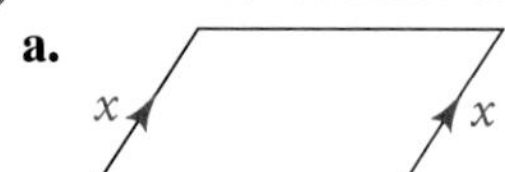

b.

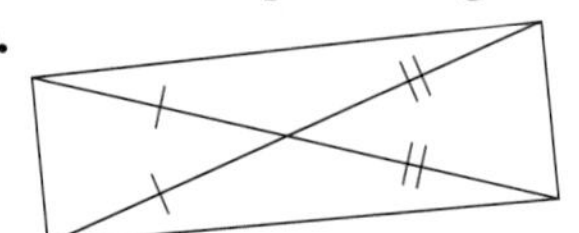

You can use the theorems of this lesson in a variety of ways.

3 EXAMPLE Real-World Connection

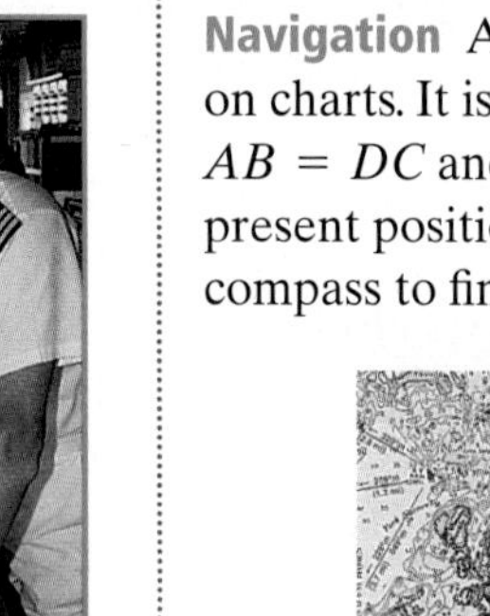

Real-World Connection

Careers A marine navigator has great responsibility for the ship, its crew, its cargo, its mission, and the surrounding natural marine environment.

Navigation A parallel rule is a navigation tool that is used to plot ship routes on charts. It is made of two rulers connected with congruent crossbars, such that $AB = DC$ and $AD = BC$. You place one ruler on the line connecting the ship's present position to its destination. Then you move the other ruler onto the chart's compass to find the direction of the route. Explain why this instrument works.

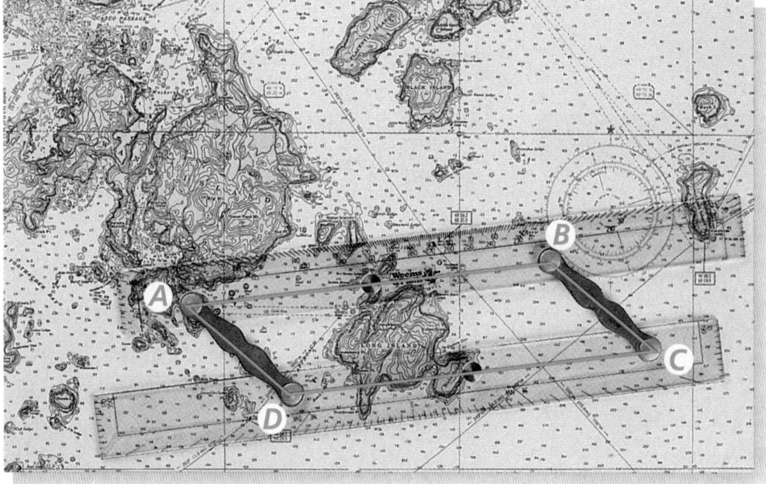

The crossbars and the sections of the rulers are congruent no matter how they are positioned. So, $ABCD$ is always a parallelogram. Since $ABCD$ is a parallelogram, the rulers are parallel. Therefore, the direction the ship should travel is the same as the direction shown on the chart's compass.

Check Understanding **3** **Critical Thinking** Suppose the ruler connecting the ship's position to its destination point gets in the way of reading the compass. How can you manipulate the tool to get the desired reading?

EXERCISES

For more practice, see *Extra Practice.*

Practice and Problem Solving

Practice by Example

 **Algebra** **Find the values of x and y for which $ABCD$ must be a parallelogram.**

Example 1 (page 305)

1. 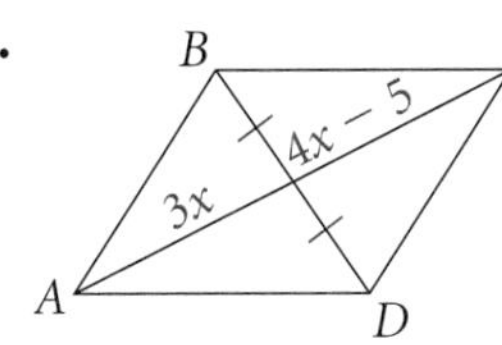

2. 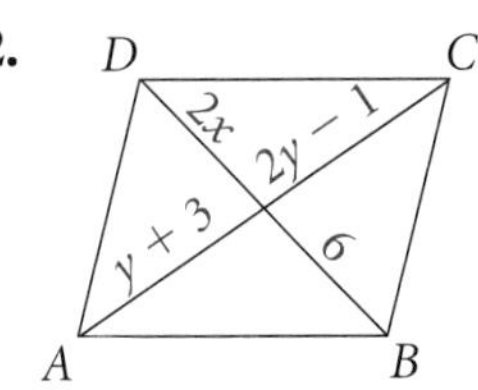

3. 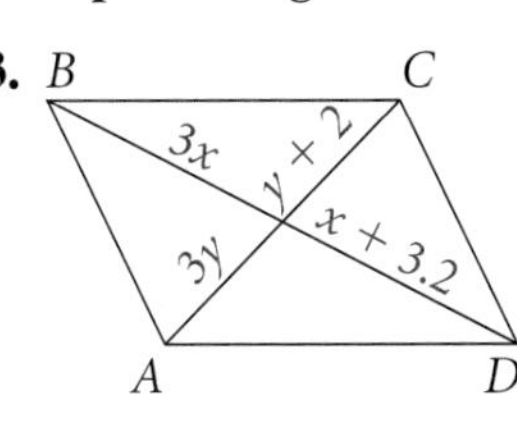

4.

5. 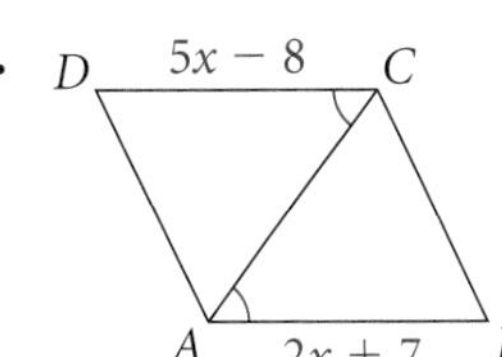

6. 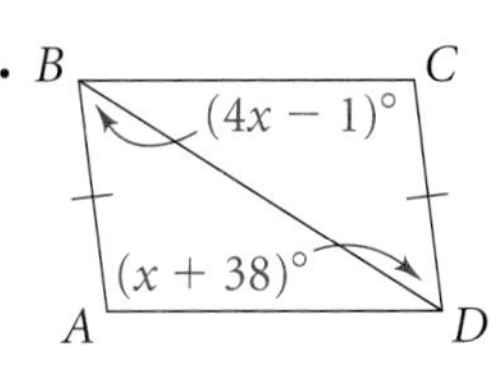

Example 2 (page 306)

Determine whether the quadrilateral must be a parallelogram. Explain.

7. 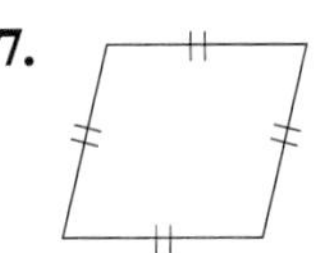

8. 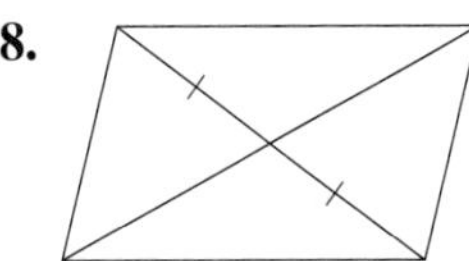

9. 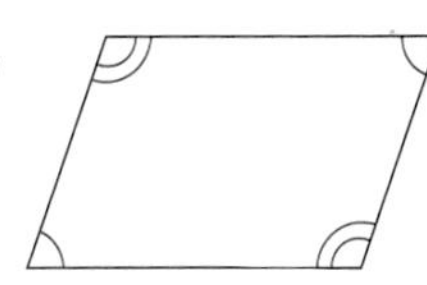

10. 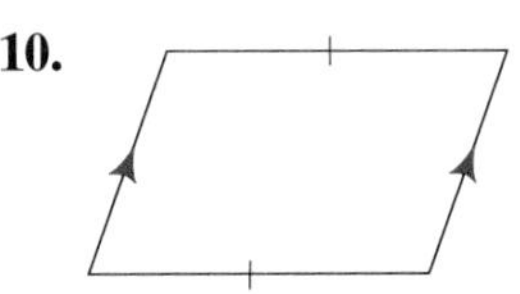

11. 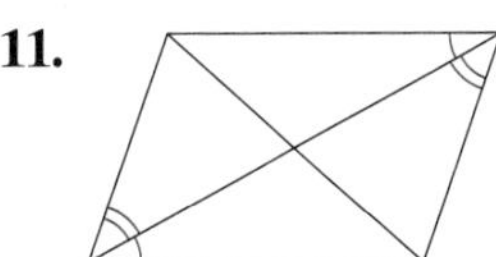

12. 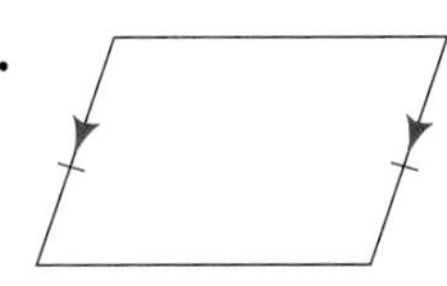

13. 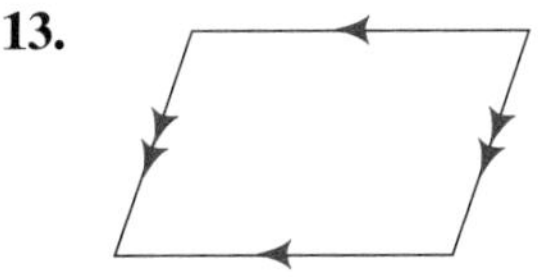

14. 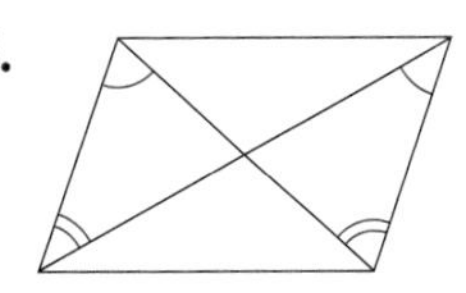

15. 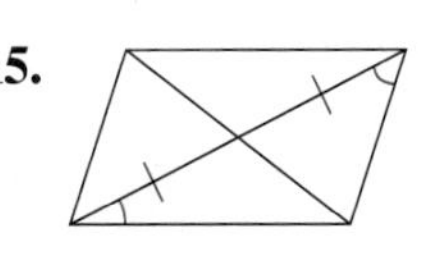

Example 3 (page 306)

16. **Fishing** Quadrilaterals are formed on on the side of this fishing tackle box by the adjustable shelves and connecting pieces. Explain why the quadrilaterals remain parallelograms no matter what position the shelves are in.

B Apply Your Skills

Proof

17. **Developing Proof** Complete this plan for a proof of Theorem 6-6.

Given: $\overline{TW} \parallel \overline{YX}$ and $\overline{TW} \cong \overline{YX}$

Prove: $TWXY$ is a parallelogram.

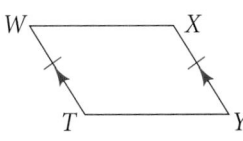

Plan: Draw diagonals $\overline{TX}$ and $\overline{WY}$ intersecting at R. Now, $TWXY$ is a parallelogram if the diagonals **a.** _?_ each other. $\overline{WR} \cong \overline{YR}$ and $\overline{TR} \cong$ **b.** _?_ by CPCTC if $\triangle TWR \cong$ **c.** _?_. These triangles are congruent by **d.** _?_ because $\overline{TW} \parallel \overline{YX}$ and **e.** _?_ angles are congruent.

Need Help?

For Exercise 18, you can review biconditionals in Lesson 2-2.

18. Combine Theorems 6-1 and 6-7 into a biconditional statement.

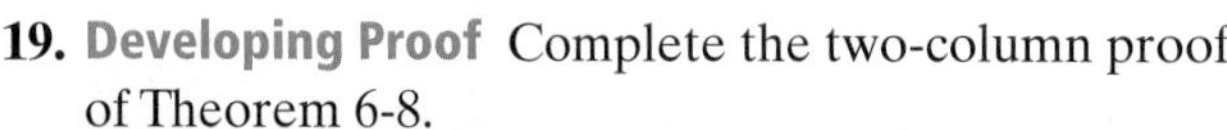

19. **Developing Proof** Complete the two-column proof of Theorem 6-8.

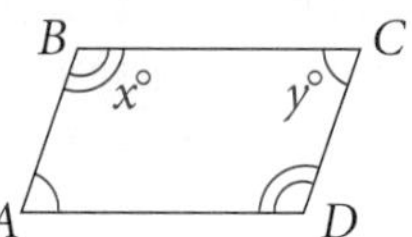

Given: $\angle A \cong \angle C$ and $\angle B \cong \angle D$

Prove: $ABCD$ is a parallelogram.

Statements	Reasons
1. $x + y + x + y = 360$	1. The sum of the measures of the angles of a quadrilateral = 360.
2. $2(x + y) = 360$	a. ?
3. $x + y = 180$	b. ?
4. $\angle A$ and $\angle B$ are supplementary. $\angle A$ and $\angle D$ are supplementary.	4. Definition of supplementary
c. ? $\parallel$?, ? $\parallel$?	d. ?
6. $ABCD$ is a parallelogram.	e. ?

Need Help?

$x + y + x + y = 2x + 2y$
$= 2(x + y)$

The last step is the Distributive Property.

Developing Proof State whether the given information is enough to conclude that *RSTW* is a parallelogram. Explain.

20. $\angle SRW \cong \angle WTS$, $\angle RST \cong \angle TWR$

21. $\angle TSZ \cong \angle RSZ$, $\angle TWZ \cong \angle RWZ$

22. $\overline{RS} \parallel \overline{WT}$, $\overline{RS} \cong \overline{WT}$

23. $\overline{RS} \parallel \overline{WT}$, $\overline{ST} \cong \overline{RW}$

24. $\overline{RS} \cong \overline{WT}$, $\overline{ST} \cong \overline{RW}$

25. $\overline{RZ} \cong \overline{TZ}$, $\overline{SZ} \cong \overline{WZ}$

Algebra Find the values of the variables for which *ABCD* must be a parallelogram.

26.

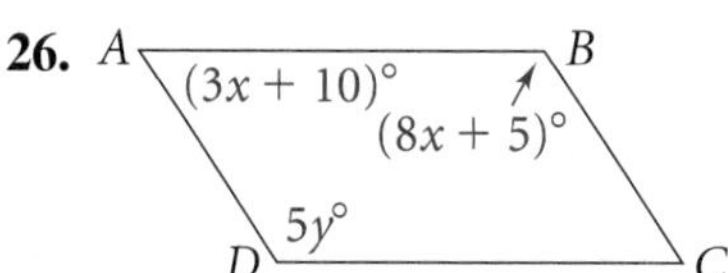

27.

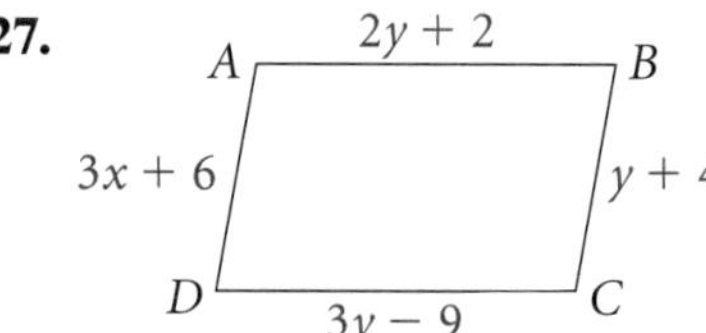

28.

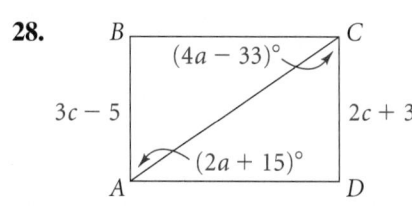

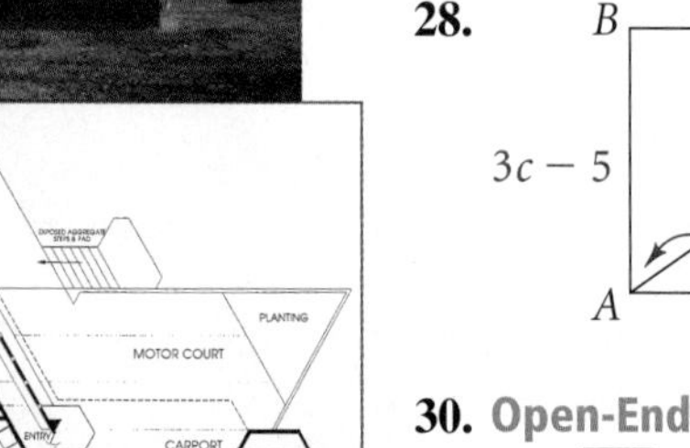

29.

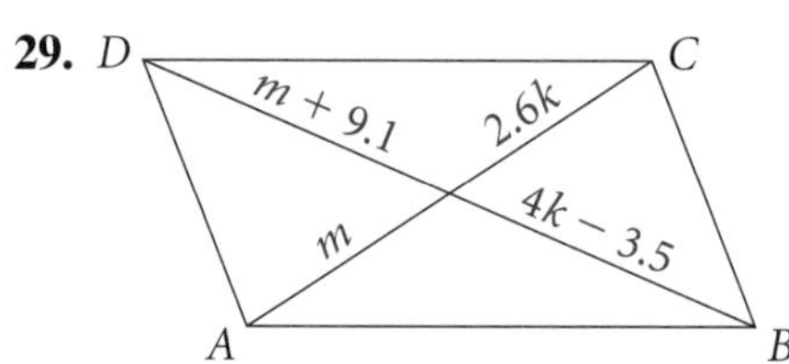

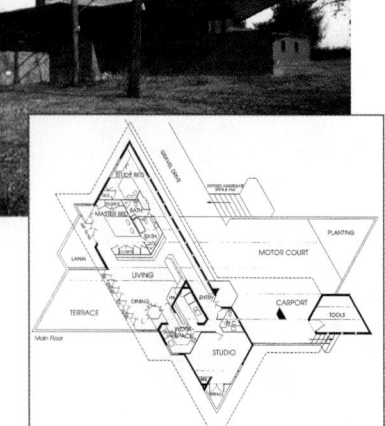

Real-World Connection

Frank Lloyd Wright, a famous architect, used parallelograms in designs of many houses, such as the Kraus House in Kirkwood, Missouri.

30. **Open-Ended** Sketch two noncongruent parallelograms $ABCD$ and $EFGH$ such that $\overline{AC} \cong \overline{EG}$ and $\overline{BD} \cong \overline{FH}$.

31. **Probability** If two opposite angles of a quadrilateral measure 120 and the measures of the other angles are multiples of 10, what is the probability that the quadrilateral is a parallelogram?

Coordinate Geometry Given points *A*, *B*, and *C* in the coordinate plane as shown, find the fourth point described below.

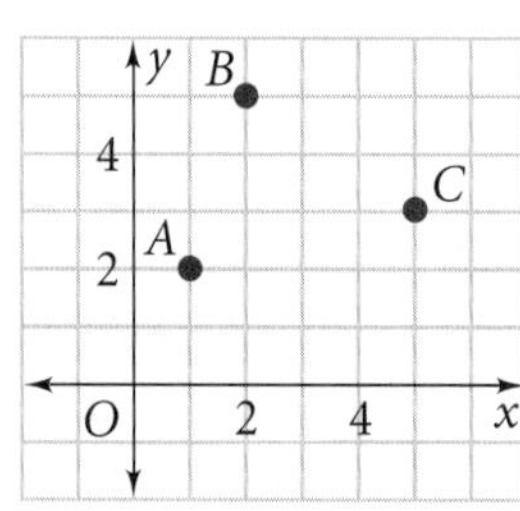

32. point D so that $ABCD$ is a parallelogram

33. point E so that $ABEC$ is a parallelogram

34. point F so that $AFBC$ is a parallelogram

35. **Writing** Summarize the ways to show that a quadrilateral is a parallelogram.

C Challenge Proof **36.** Write a paragraph proof, a flow proof, or a two-column proof.

Given: $\triangle TRS \cong \triangle RTW$

Prove: $RSTW$ is a parallelogram.

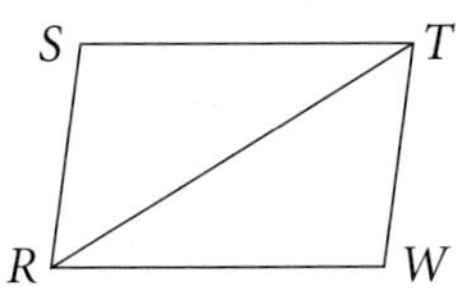

Proof **37.** In the figure at the right, point D is constructed by drawing two arcs. One has center C and radius AB. The other has center B and radius AC. Prove that $\overline{AM}$ is a median of $\triangle ABC$.

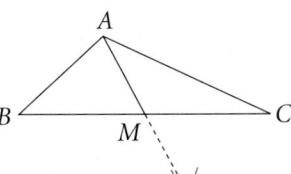

38. Coordinate Geometry The diagonals of quadrilateral $EFGH$ intersect at $D(-1, 4)$. Two vertices of $EFGH$ are $E(2, 7)$ and $F(-3, 5)$. What must be the coordinates of G and H to ensure that $EFGH$ is a parallelogram?

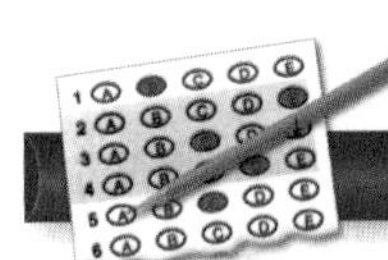

Standardized Test Prep

Multiple Choice

39. In ▱$PNWS$, what is $m\angle W$?

A. 128 **B.** 90 **C.** 52 **D.** 26

40. In ▱$PNWS$, what is $m\angle S$?

F. 128 **G.** 90 **H.** 52 **I.** 26

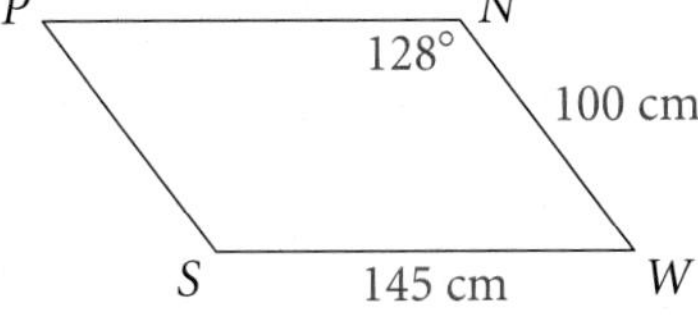

Reading Comprehension

Read the passage below, then answer the questions on the basis of what is *stated* or *implied* in the passage.

Fabric is made by weaving threads vertically (the warp) and horizontally (the weft), forming small rectangles. Pull the fabric vertically or horizontally and it will not distort. The rectangles will remain as rectangles. Pull the fabric along its diagonals and parallel threads remain parallel but form small nonrectangular parallelograms.

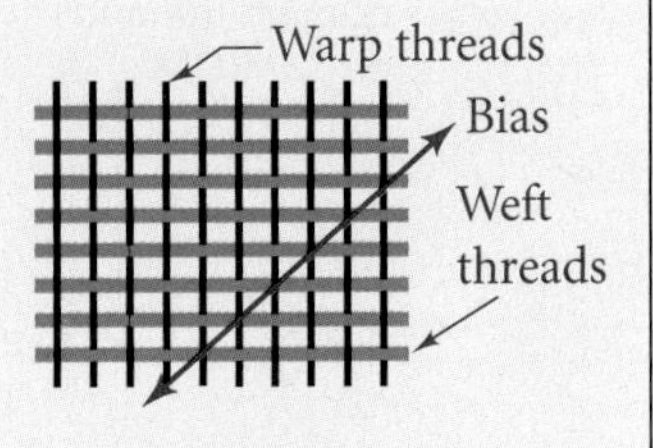

41. What is formed by the warp and the weft?

A. threads woven vertically
B. threads woven horizontally
C. small rectangles
D. nonrectangular parallelograms

42. How does pulling fabric along its diagonal affect the shape of the fabric?

F. It becomes a longer rectangle.
G. It becomes a shorter rectangle.
H. It is no longer a rectangle.
I. The shape is unchanged.

Short Response

43. Given: $\triangle NRJ \cong \triangle CPT$, $\overline{JN} \parallel \overline{CT}$

Prove: $JNTC$ is a parallelogram.

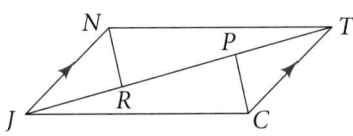

Extended Response

44. a. Write an equation and solve for x.

b. Is $\overline{AF} \parallel \overline{DE}$? Explain.

c. Is $BDEF$ a parallelogram? Explain.

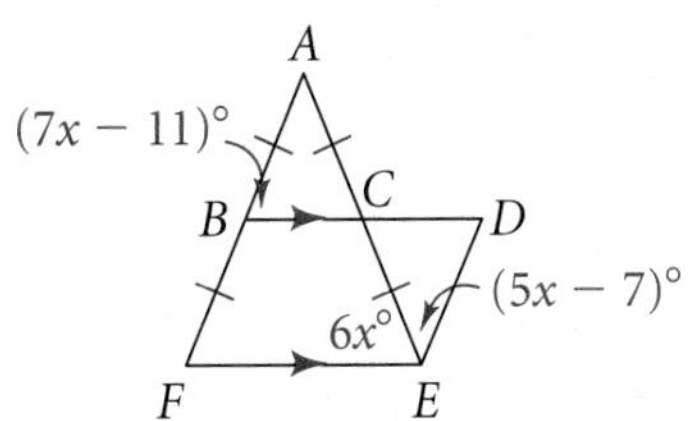

Online lesson quiz at www.PHSchool.com

Web Code: afa-0603

Mixed Review

Lesson 6-2 x^2 Algebra **Find the value of each variable in each parallelogram.**

45.

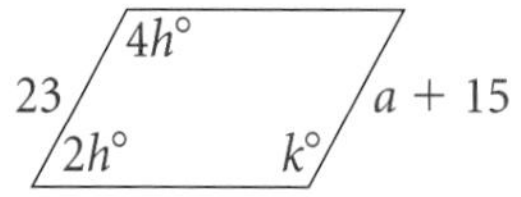

46.

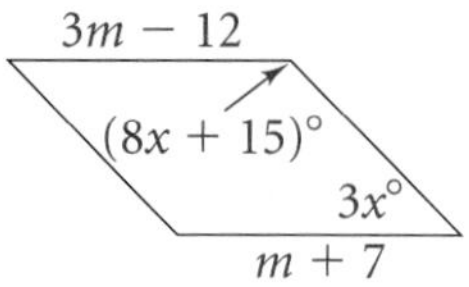

47.

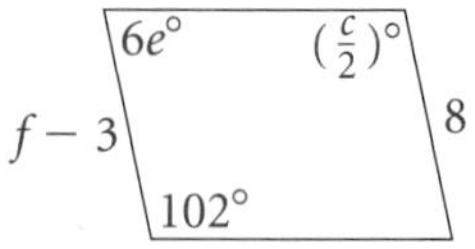

Lesson 4-7

48. Explain how you can use overlapping congruent triangles to prove $\overline{AC} \cong \overline{BD}$.

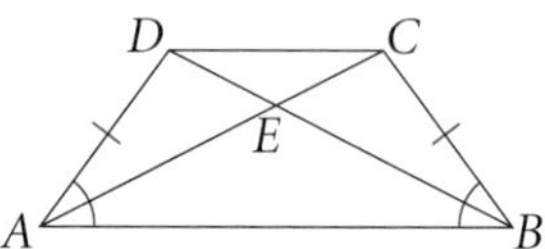

Lesson 2-2

Write the two conditional statements that make up each biconditional.

49. The diagonals of a quadrilateral bisect each other if and only if the quadrilateral is a parallelogram.

50. Two lines are parallel if and only if the two lines and a transversal form corresponding angles that are congruent.

51. Two nonvertical lines are perpendicular if and only if the product of their slopes is -1.

Checkpoint Quiz 1 — Lessons 6-1 through 6-3

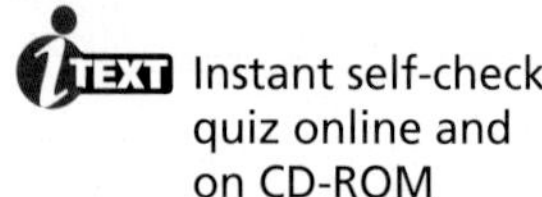

Instant self-check quiz online and on CD-ROM

Find the measures of the numbered angles for each parallelogram.

1.

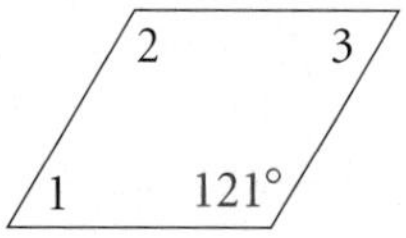

2.

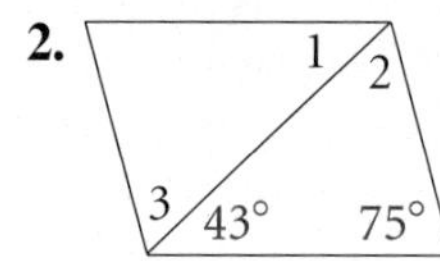

3.

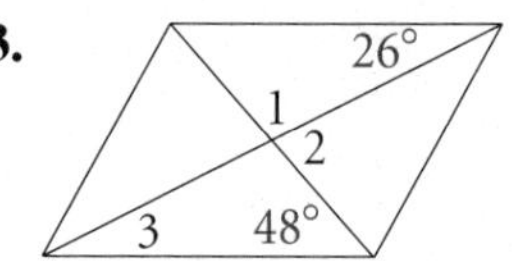

Classify each quadrilateral in as many ways as possible.

4.

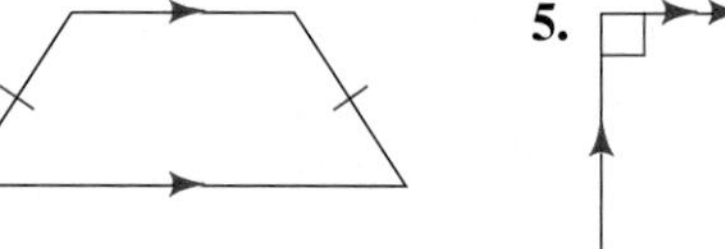

5.

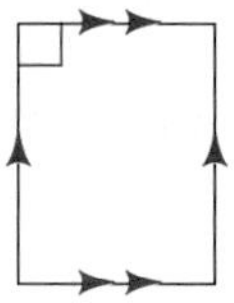

6.

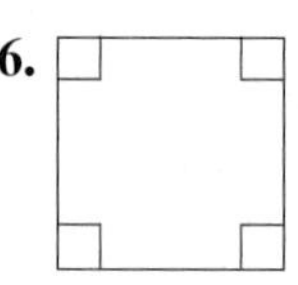

x^2 Algebra **Find the values of the variables for which *ABCD* is a parallelogram.**

7.

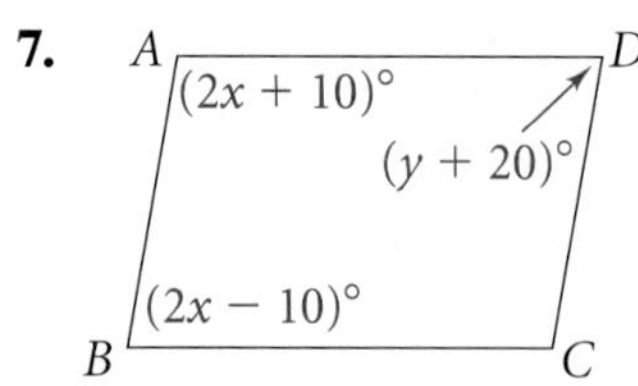

8.

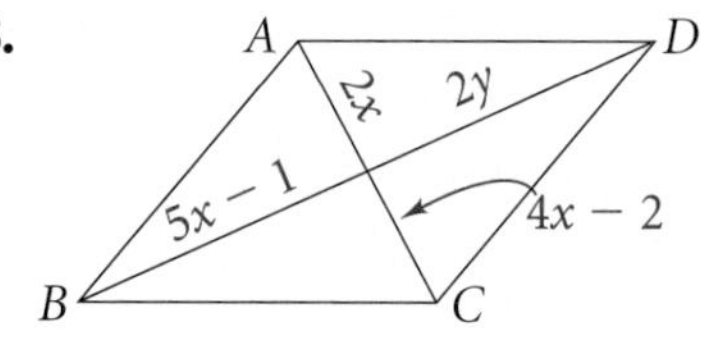

9. In the figure at the right, $\overleftrightarrow{AB} \parallel \overleftrightarrow{CD} \parallel \overleftrightarrow{EF}$. Find AE.

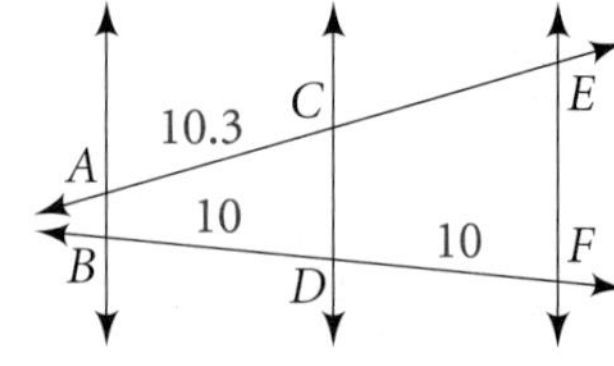

10. What is the most precise name for a quadrilateral with vertices (3, 5), (−1, 4), (3, −5), and (7, 4)?

Diagonals of Parallelograms

For Use With Lesson 6-4

Construct

Use geometry software to construct a parallelogram.

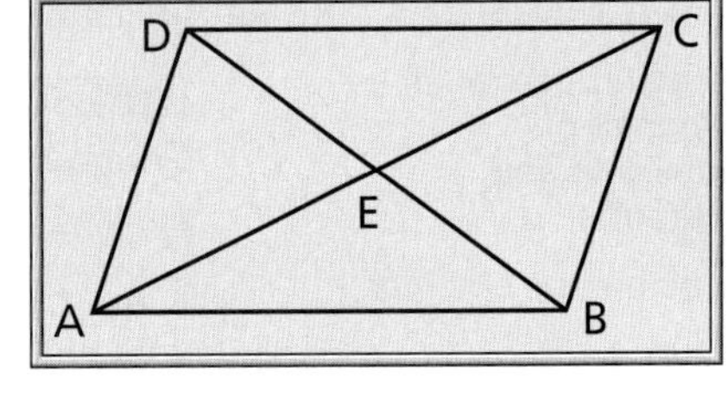

- Construct segments $\overline{AB}$ and $\overline{BC}$.
- Construct a line through C parallel to $\overline{AB}$ and a line through A parallel to $\overline{BC}$. Label the point where the two lines intersect as D.
- Hide the lines and construct $\overline{AD}$ and $\overline{CD}$.
- Construct the diagonals of $\square ABCD$ and label their point of intersection E.

Set up the following measurements. Use them where indicated.

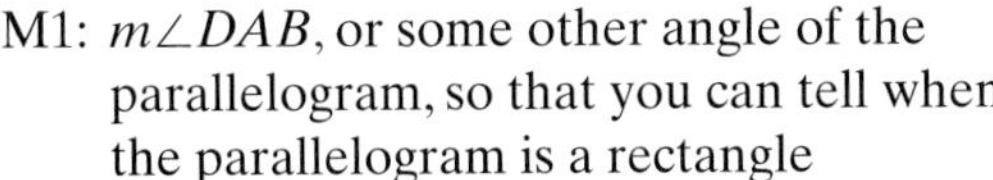

M1: $m\angle DAB$, or some other angle of the parallelogram, so that you can tell when the parallelogram is a rectangle

M2: AB and AD, or some other adjacent sides of the parallelogram, so you can tell when it is a rhombus

M3: $m\angle AED$, or some other angle at the intersection of the diagonals, so you can tell when the diagonals are perpendicular

M4: AC and DB, the diagonal lengths, so you can tell when they are equal

M5: the angles at each vertex of the parallelogram, so you can tell when the diagonals bisect the angles of the parallelogram

Investigate

- Manipulate the parallelogram to get a rectangle (M1). Make note of what appear to be any special properties of the diagonals of a rectangle. Manipulate the rectangle to check whether the properties hold (M3–5).
- Manipulate the parallelogram to get a rhombus (M2). Make note of what appear to be any special properties of the diagonals of a rhombus. Manipulate the rhombus to check whether the properties hold (M3–5).

EXERCISES

Make as many conjectures as you can about each of the following.

1. the diagonals of rectangles **2.** the diagonals of rhombuses **3.** the diagonals of squares

Extend

4. Manipulate the diagonals so they are perpendicular (M3). Make a conjecture about the type of parallelogram that is determined by perpendicular diagonals.

5. Manipulate the diagonals so they are congruent (M4). Make a conjecture about the type of parallelogram that is determined by congruent diagonals.

6. Manipulate the diagonals so they bisect the angles of the parallelogram (M5). Make a conjecture about the type of parallelogram that is determined by diagonals that bisect the angles.

7. Construct a trapezoid and then its two diagonals. Manipulate the trapezoid until the diagonals are the same length. Make a conjecture about the type of trapezoid that is determined by congruent diagonals.

6-4 Special Parallelograms

Lesson Preview

What You'll Learn

OBJECTIVE 1 To use properties of diagonals of rhombuses and rectangles

OBJECTIVE 2 To determine whether a parallelogram is a rhombus or a rectangle

. . . And Why

To lay out a rectangular patio, as in Example 4

✔ Check Skills You'll Need

(For help, go to Lesson 6-2.)

$PACE$ is a parallelogram and $m\angle PAC = 109$. Complete each of the following.

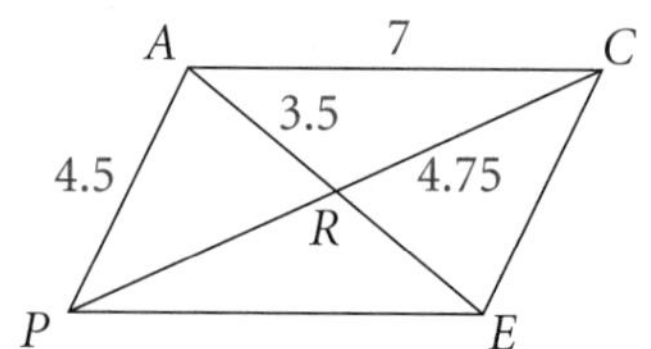

1. $EC = ■$ **2.** $EP = ■$

3. $m\angle CEP = ■$ **4.** $PR = ■$

5. $RE = ■$ **6.** $CP = ■$

7. $m\angle EPA = ■$ **8.** $m\angle ECA = ■$

9. Draw a rhombus that is not a square. Draw a rectangle that is not a square. Explain why each is not a square.

Interactive lesson includes instant self-check, tutorials, and activities.

OBJECTIVE 1

Diagonals of Rhombuses and Rectangles

If you draw two congruent isosceles triangles with base $\overline{PQ}$, you have drawn a rhombus. Note that $\angle RPQ$, $\angle SPQ$, $\angle RQP$, and $\angle SQP$ are all congruent. This suggests Theorem 6-9 and its proof.

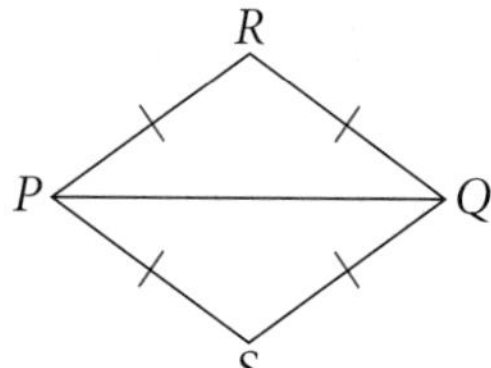

Key Concepts

Theorem 6-9

Each diagonal of a rhombus bisects two angles of the rhombus.

Proof

Proof of Theorem 6-9

Given: rhombus $ABCD$

Prove: $\overline{AC}$ bisects $\angle BAD$ and $\angle BCD$.

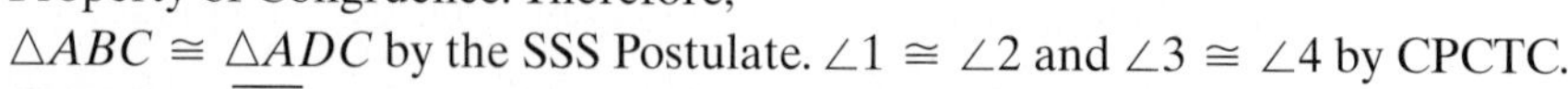

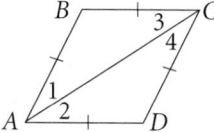

Proof: $ABCD$ is a rhombus, so its sides are all congruent. $\overline{AC} \cong \overline{AC}$ by the Reflexive Property of Congruence. Therefore, $\triangle ABC \cong \triangle ADC$ by the SSS Postulate. $\angle 1 \cong \angle 2$ and $\angle 3 \cong \angle 4$ by CPCTC. Therefore, $\overline{AC}$ bisects $\angle BAD$ and $\angle BCD$ by the definition of bisect.

You can show similarly that $\overline{BD}$ bisects $\angle ABC$ and $\angle ADC$.

Need Help?

A segment bisects an angle if and only if it divides the angle into two congruent angles.

The diagonals of a rhombus provide an interesting application of the Converse of the Perpendicular Bisector Theorem.

In the rhombus at the right, points B and D are equidistant from A and C. By the Converse of the Perpendicular Bisector Theorem, they are on the perpendicular bisector of $\overline{AC}$. This proves the next theorem. In Exercise 54, you will prove it a second way.

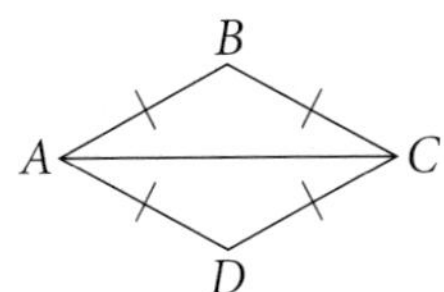

Key Concepts

Theorem 6-10

The diagonals of a rhombus are perpendicular.

$\overline{AC} \perp \overline{BD}$

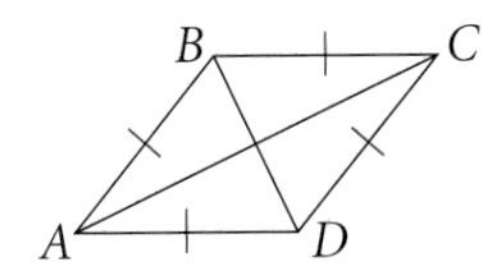

Real-World Connection

The diagonals of the rhombus formed by the pantograph stay perpendicular when the pantograph lifts or lowers.

You can use Theorems 6-9 and 6-10 to find angle measures in rhombuses.

1 EXAMPLE Finding Angle Measures

$MNPQ$ is a rhombus and $m\angle N = 120$.
Find the measures of the numbered angles.

$m\angle 1 = m\angle 3$	**Isosceles Triangle Theorem**
$m\angle 1 + m\angle 3 + 120 = 180$	**Triangle Angle-Sum Theorem**
$2(m\angle 1) + 120 = 180$	**Substitute.**
$2(m\angle 1) = 60$	**Subtract 120 from each side.**
$m\angle 1 = 30$	**Divide each side by 2.**

Therefore, $m\angle 1 = m\angle 3 = 30$. By Theorem 6-9, $m\angle 1 = m\angle 2$ and $m\angle 3 = m\angle 4$.
Therefore, $m\angle 1 = m\angle 2 = m\angle 3 = m\angle 4 = 30$.

Check Understanding

1 Find the measures of the numbered angles in the rhombus.

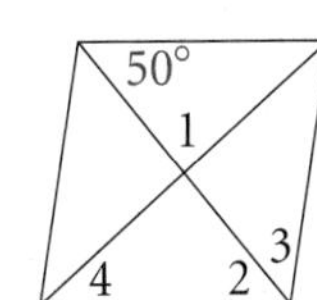

The diagonals of a rectangle, another parallelogram, also have a special property.

Key Concepts

Theorem 6-11

The diagonals of a rectangle are congruent.

Proof

Proof of Theorem 6-11

Given: Rectangle $ABCD$

Prove: $\overline{AC} \cong \overline{BD}$

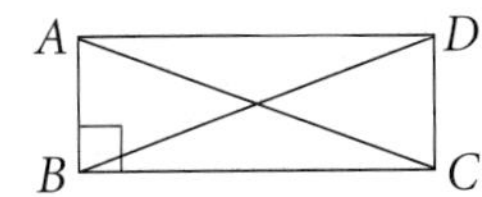

Proof: $ABCD$ is a rectangle, so it is also a parallelogram.
$\overline{AB} \cong \overline{DC}$ because opposite sides of a parallelogram are congruent.
$\overline{BC} \cong \overline{BC}$ by the Reflexive Property of Congruence.
$\angle ABC$ and $\angle DCB$ are right angles by the definition of rectangle.
$\angle ABC \cong \angle DCB$ because all right angles are congruent.
$\triangle ABC \cong \triangle DCB$ by SAS. $\overline{AC} \cong \overline{BD}$ by CPCTC.

2 EXAMPLE Finding Diagonal Length

Algebra Find the length of the diagonals of rectangle $GFED$ if $FD = 2y + 4$ and $GE = 6y - 5$.

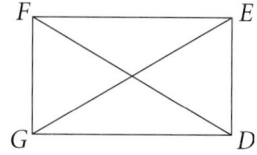

$2y + 4 = 6y - 5$ **Diagonals of a rectangle are congruent.**

$9 = 4y$ **Subtract 2y from each side and add 5 to each side.**

$\frac{9}{4} = y$ **Divide each side by 4.**

$FD = GE = 2\left(\frac{9}{4}\right) + 4 = \frac{17}{2}$, or $8\frac{1}{2}$.

2 Find the length of the diagonals of $GFED$ if $FD = 5y - 9$ and $GE = y + 5$.

OBJECTIVE 2

Is the Parallelogram a Rhombus or a Rectangle?

The following theorems are the converses of Theorems 6-9, 6-10, and 6-11 respectively. You will prove these theorems in Exercises 61–63.

Key Concepts

Theorem 6-12

If one diagonal of a parallelogram bisects two angles of the parallelogram, then the parallelogram is a rhombus.

Theorem 6-13

If the diagonals of a parallelogram are perpendicular, then the parallelogram is a rhombus.

Theorem 6-14

If the diagonals of a parallelogram are congruent, then the parallelogram is a rectangle.

You can use Theorems 6-12, 6-13, and 6-14 to classify quadrilaterals.

3 EXAMPLE Recognizing Special Parallelograms

Need Help?

Assume the quadrilateral described can be a parallelogram. Then look for an example or a contradiction.

Determine whether the quadrilateral can be a parallelogram. If not, write *impossible.*

a. The quadrilateral has congruent diagonals and one angle of 60°.

Impossible. A parallelogram with congruent diagonals is a rectangle with four right angles.

b. The quadrilateral has perpendicular diagonals and four right angles.

The figure can be a parallelogram. Perpendicular diagonals means that it would be a rhombus, and four right angles means that it would be a rectangle. Both properties together mean that it would be a square.

3 A diagonal of a parallelogram bisects two angles of the parallelogram. Is it possible for the parallelogram to have sides of lengths 5, 6, 5, and 6? Explain.

You can use properties of diagonals to construct special parallelograms.

4 EXAMPLE Real-World  Connection

A well-planned volunteer effort can frame a small house in a day.

Community Service Builders use properties of diagonals to "square up" rectangular shapes like building frames and playing-field boundaries.

Suppose you are on the volunteer building team at the right. You are helping to lay out a rectangular patio. Explain how to use properties of diagonals to locate the four corners.

To locate the corners, you can use two theorems:

- Theorem 6-5: If the diagonals of a quadrilateral bisect each other, then the quadrilateral is a parallelogram.
- Theorem 6-14: If the diagonals of a parallelogram are congruent, then the parallelogram is a rectangle.

First, cut two pieces of rope that will be the diagonals of the foundation rectangle. Cut them the same length because of Theorem 6-14. Join them at their midpoints because of Theorem 6-5. Then pull the ropes straight and taut. The ends of the ropes will be the corners of a rectangle.

 **Check Understanding** **4** Kate thinks that they can adapt this method slightly to stake off a square play area. Is she right? Explain.

EXERCISES

For more practice, see *Extra Practice*.

Practice and Problem Solving

A Practice by Example

Example 1 (page 313)

Find the measures of the numbered angles in each rhombus.

1. 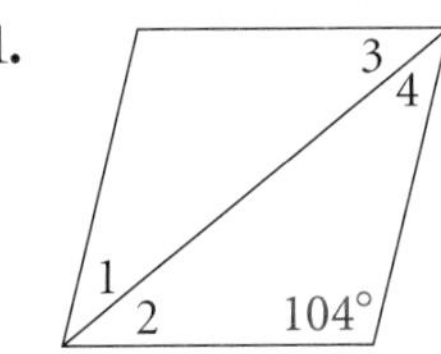

2. 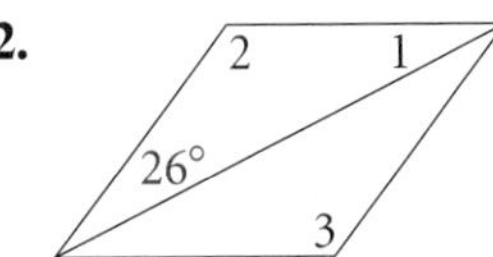

3. 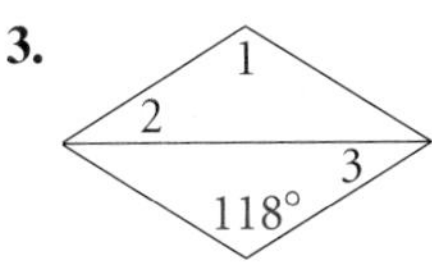

4. 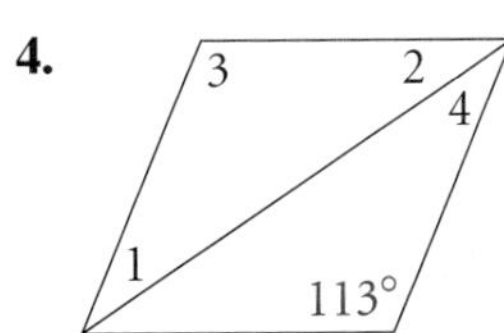

5. 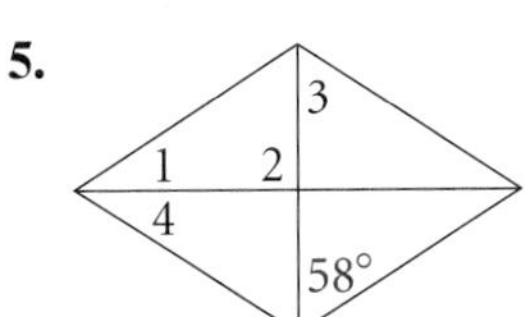

6. 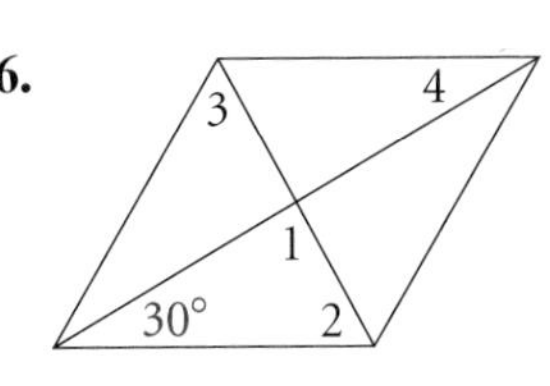

7. 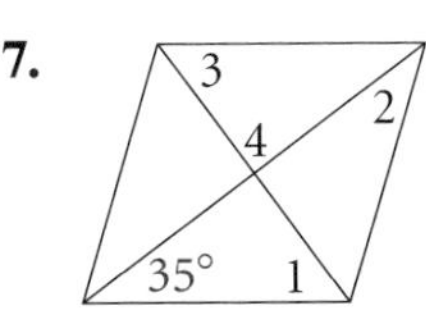

8. 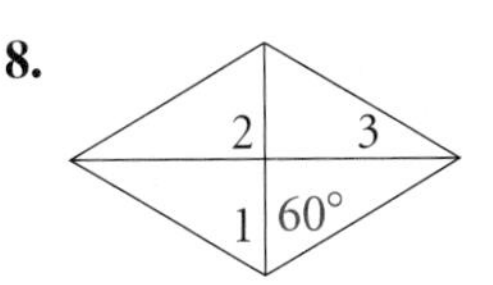

9. 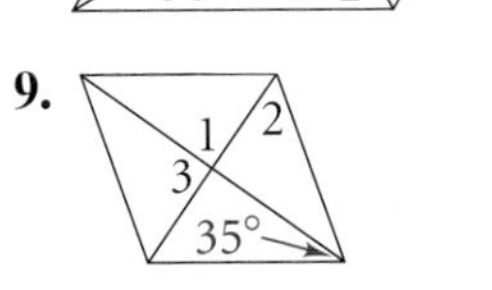

Example 2 (page 314)

Algebra ***LMNP*** **is a rectangle. Find the value of** ***x*** **and the length of each diagonal.**

10. $LN = x$ and $MP = 2x - 4$

11. $LN = 5x - 8$ and $MP = 2x + 1$

12. $LN = 3x + 1$ and $MP = 8x - 4$

13. $LN = 9x - 14$ and $MP = 7x + 4$

14. $LN = 7x - 2$ and $MP = 4x + 3$

15. $LN = 3x + 5$ and $MP = 9x - 10$

Example 3 (page 314)

Determine whether the quadrilateral can be a parallelogram. (The diagrams in Exercises 19–21 may not be to scale.) If not, write *impossible.* Explain.

16. The diagonals are congruent, but the quadrilateral has no right angles.

17. Each diagonal is 3 cm long and two opposite sides are 2 cm long.

18. Two opposite angles are right angles, but the quadrilateral is not a rectangle.

19.

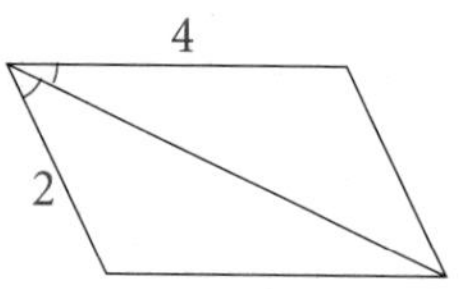

20.

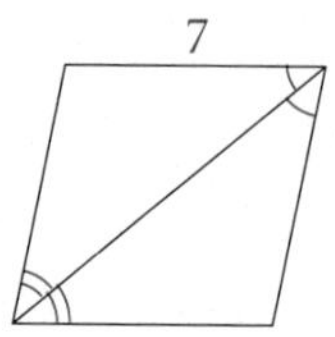

21.

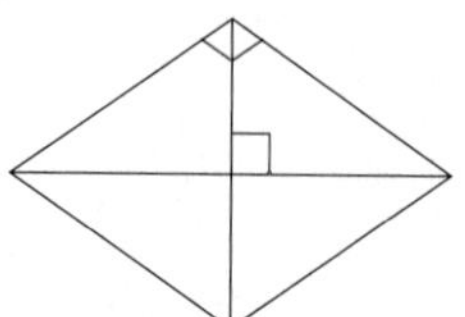

Example 4 (page 315)

22. Hardware You can use a simple device called a turnbuckle to "square up" structures that are parallelograms. For the gate pictured at the right, you tighten or loosen the turnbuckle on the diagonal cable so that the cable stays congruent to the other diagonal. Explain why a frame that normally is rectangular will, when it sags, keep the shape of a parallelogram.

Turnbuckle

23. Carpentry A carpenter is building a bookcase. How can she use a tape measure to check that the bookshelf is rectangular? Justify your answer and name any theorems used.

B Apply Your Skills

24. Reasoning Suppose the diagonals of a parallelogram are both perpendicular and congruent. What type of special quadrilateral is it? Explain your reasoning.

Using Symbols **Create your own distinctive symbols for parallelogram, rhombus, rectangle, and square. Then copy the properties in Exercises 25–34. After each property, use your symbols to list the quadrilaterals having that property.**

25. All sides are $\cong$.

26. Opposite sides are $\cong$.

27. Opposite sides are $\|$.

28. Opposite $\angle$s are $\cong$.

29. All $\angle$s are right $\angle$s.

30. Consecutive $\angle$s are supplementary.

31. Diagonals bisect each other.

32. Diagonals are $\cong$.

33. Diagonals are $\perp$.

34. Each diagonal bisects opposite $\angle$s.

Which, if any, of the properties in Exercises 25–34 can the following type of quadrilateral have? Draw diagrams to illustrate.

35. a trapezoid

36. a kite

37. a quadrilateral that is not a special quadrilateral

Reading Math

In Exercises 39–44, the "given diagonals" are two segments you draw. The constructed figures must have diagonals that match.

38. Writing Summarize the properties of squares that follow from a square being **(a)** a parallelogram, **(b)** a rhombus, and **(c)** a rectangle.

Constructions **Explain how to construct each figure, given its diagonals.**

39. parallelogram

40. rectangle

41. rhombus

42. square

43. kite

44. trapezoid

Need Help?

To review what makes a good definition, see Lesson 2-2.

Reasoning Decide whether each of these is a good definition. Justify your answer.

45. A rectangle is a quadrilateral with four right angles.

46. A rhombus is a quadrilateral with four congruent sides.

47. A square is a quadrilateral with four right angles and four congruent sides.

x^2 **Algebra Find the value(s) of the variable(s) for each parallelogram.**

48. $RZ = 2x + 5$, $SW = 5x - 20$

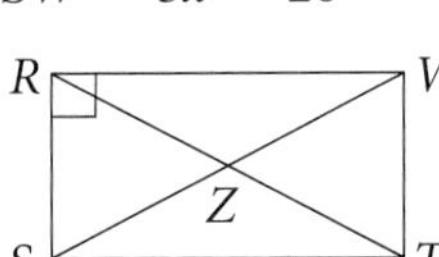

49. $m\angle 1 = 3y - 6$

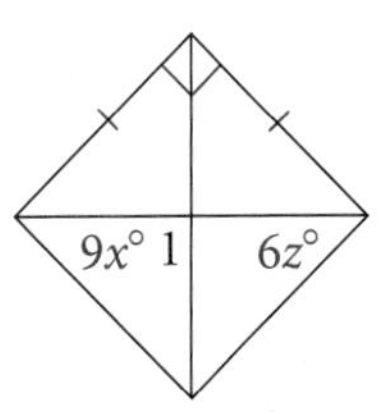

50. $BD = 4x - y + 1$

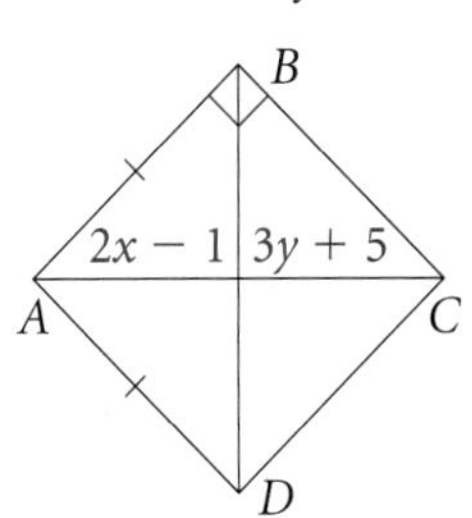

Open-Ended Given two segments with lengths a and b ($a \neq b$), what special quadrilaterals can you sketch that meet these conditions? Show each sketch.

51. Both diagonals have length a.

52. The two diagonals have lengths a and b.

53. One diagonal has length a, one side of the quadrilateral has length b.

Proof **54. Developing Proof** Complete the flow proof of Theorem 6-10.

Given: $ABCD$ is a rhombus.

Prove: $\overline{AC} \perp \overline{BD}$

B, C, E, A, D

$ABCD$ is a rhombus. — Given

→ $\overline{AB} \cong \overline{AD}$ — a. ?

→ $\overline{BE} \cong \overline{DE}$ — b. ?

→ c. ? — d. ?

→ e. ? — SSS

→ $\angle AEB \cong \angle AED$ — f. ?

$m\angle AEB + m\angle AED = 180$ — g. ?

→ h. ? — i. ?

→ $\overline{AC} \perp \overline{BD}$ — j. ?

55. Critical Thinking The hypothesis of Theorem 6-12 mentions one diagonal of a parallelogram. Why doesn't it include both diagonals?

Proof **56.** In Theorem 6-12, replace "two angles" with "one angle." Write a paragraph that proves this new statement true or show a counterexample to prove it false.

x^2 **Algebra $ABCD$ is a rectangle. Find the length of each diagonal.**

57. $AC = 2(x - 3)$ and $BD = x + 5$

58. $AC = 2(5a + 1)$ and $BD = 2(a + 1)$

59. $AC = \frac{3y}{5}$ and $BD = 3y - 4$

60. $AC = \frac{3c}{9}$ and $BD = 4 - c$

61. **Developing Proof** Fill in Steps 4–7 that are missing from this proof of Theorem 6-12. (Using more than four steps is acceptable.)

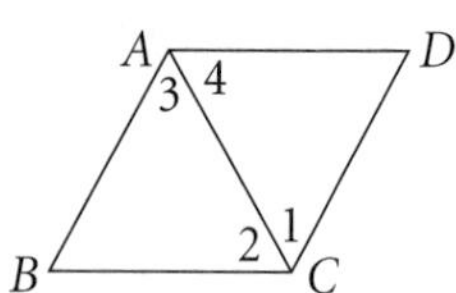

Given: $ABCD$ is a parallelogram;
$\overline{AC}$ bisects $\angle BAD$ and $\angle BCD$.

Prove: $ABCD$ is a rhombus.

Statements	Reasons
1. $ABCD$ is a parallelogram. $\overline{AC}$ bisects $\angle BAD$ and $\angle BCD$.	**1.** Given
2. $\angle 1 \cong \angle 2, \angle 3 \cong \angle 4$	**2.** Definition of bisect
3. $\overline{AC} \cong \overline{AC}$	**3.** Reflexive Property of Congruence
⋮	⋮
8. $ABCD$ is a rhombus.	**8.** Definition of rhombus

C Challenge Proof **62.** Write a paragraph proof (Thm. 6-13).

Given: $\square ABCD$; $\overline{AC} \perp \overline{BD}$ at E.

Prove: $ABCD$ is a rhombus.

63. Write a flow proof (Thm. 6-14).

Given: $\square ABCD$; $\overline{AC} \cong \overline{BD}$

Prove: $ABCD$ is a rectangle.

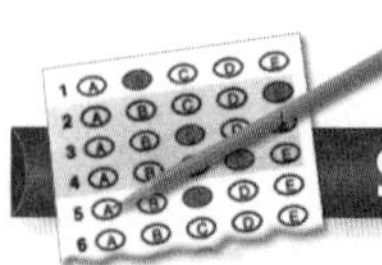

Standardized Test Prep

Multiple Choice

64. The diagonals of a quadrilateral are perpendicular bisectors of each other. What name best describes the quadrilateral?
 A. rectangle B. parallelogram C. quadrilateral D. rhombus

65. The diagonals of a quadrilateral bisect both pairs of opposite angles. What name best describes the quadrilateral?
 F. parallelogram G. quadrilateral H. rectangle I. rhombus

Take It to the NET
Online lesson quiz at **www.PHSchool.com**
Web Code: afa-0604

Short Response

66. **Given:** $QRST$ is a rhombus, $\overline{QS}$ intersects $\overline{RT}$ at P, $QR = 9$ cm, and $QP = 4.5$ cm. Find $m\angle RST$. Explain your work.

Mixed Review

Lesson 6-3

Can you conclude that the quadrilateral is a parallelogram? Explain.

67.

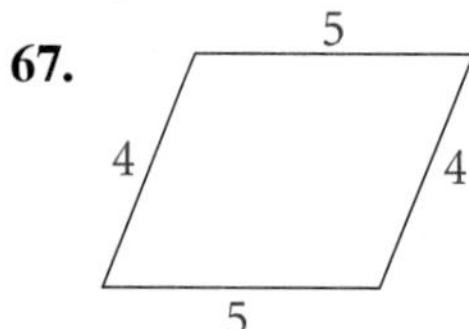

68.

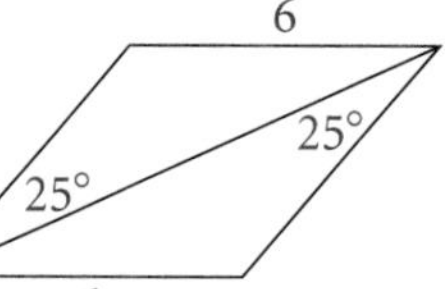

69.

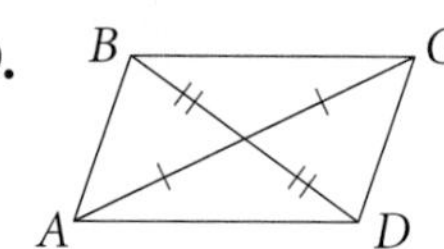

Lesson 5-1

In $\triangle PQR$, points S, T, and U are midpoints. Complete each statement.

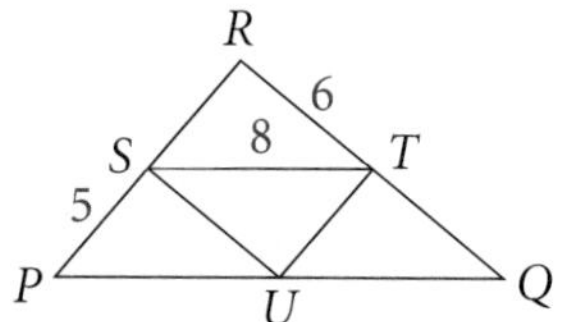

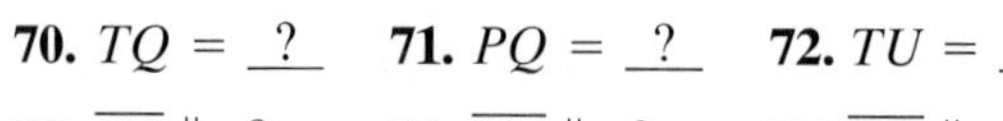

70. $TQ =$ __?__ **71.** $PQ =$ __?__ **72.** $TU =$ __?__

73. $\overline{SU} \parallel$ __?__ **74.** $\overline{TU} \parallel$ __?__ **75.** $\overline{PQ} \parallel$ __?__

Lesson 3-3 x^2 **76. Algebra** Find the value of c.

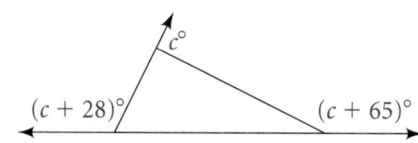

$c°$ $(c + 28)°$ $(c + 65)°$

Quadrilaterals in Quadrilaterals

For Use With Lesson 6-4

Construct

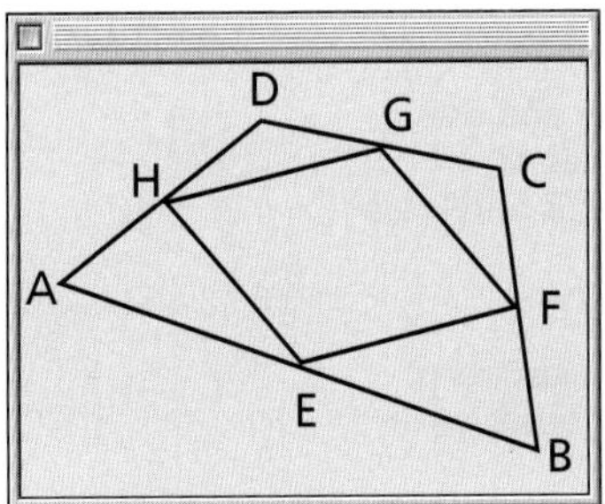

- Use geometry software to construct a quadrilateral *ABCD*.
- Construct the midpoint of each side of *ABCD*.
- Construct segments joining the midpoints, in order, to form quadrilateral *EFGH*.

Investigate

- Measure the lengths of the sides of *EFGH* and their slopes.
- Measure the angles of *EFGH*.

What kind of quadrilateral does *EFGH* appear to be?

EXERCISES

1. Manipulate quadrilateral *ABCD.*
  a. Make a conjecture about the quadrilateral whose vertices are the midpoints of the sides of a quadrilateral.
  b. Does your conjecture hold when *ABCD* is concave?
  c. Can you manipulate *ABCD* so that your conjecture doesn't hold?

Extend

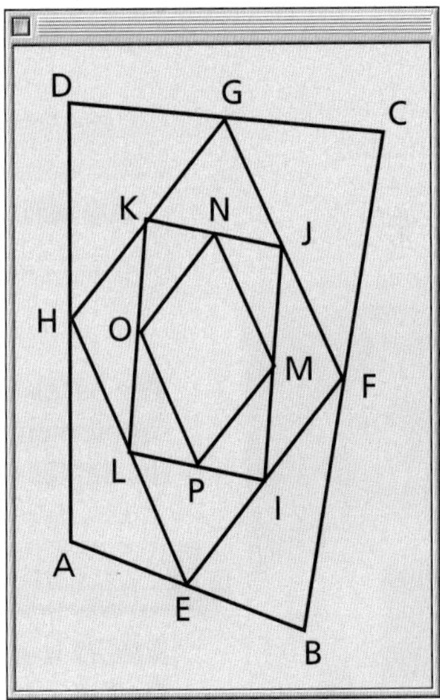

2. Draw the diagonals of *ABCD*.
  a. Describe *EFGH* when the diagonals are perpendicular.
  b. Describe *EFGH* when the diagonals are congruent.
  c. Describe *EFGH* when the diagonals are both perpendicular and congruent.

3. Construct the midpoints of *EFGH* and use them to construct quadrilateral *IJKL*. Construct the midpoints of *IJKL* and use them to construct quadrilateral *MNOP.* For *MNOP* and *EFGH*, compare the ratios of the lengths of the sides, perimeters, and areas. How are the sides of *MNOP* and *EFGH* related?

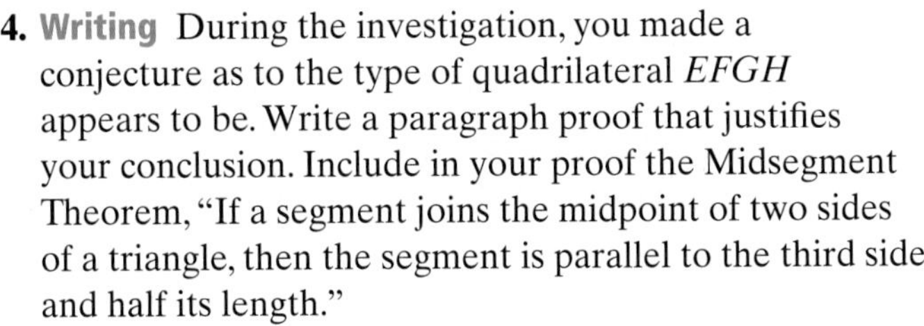

4. Writing During the investigation, you made a conjecture as to the type of quadrilateral *EFGH* appears to be. Write a paragraph proof that justifies your conclusion. Include in your proof the Midsegment Theorem, "If a segment joins the midpoint of two sides of a triangle, then the segment is parallel to the third side and half its length."

Trapezoids and Kites

Lesson Preview

What You'll Learn

OBJECTIVE 1 To verify and use properties of trapezoids and kites

. . . And Why

To find angle measures of trapezoidal windows, as in Example 2

✔ Check Skills You'll Need

(For help, go to Lesson 6-1.)

x^2 **Algebra** **Find the values of the variables. Then find the lengths of the sides.**

1.

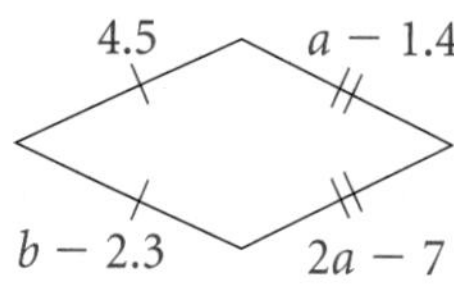

2.

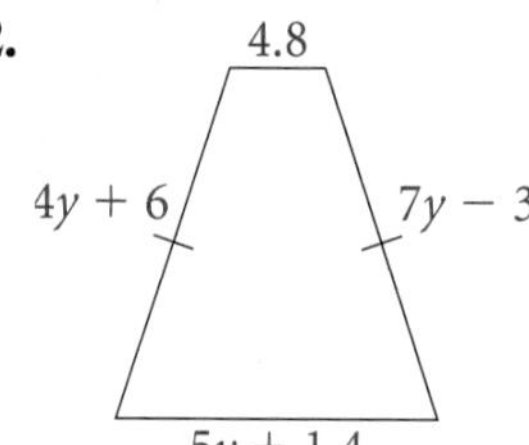

3.

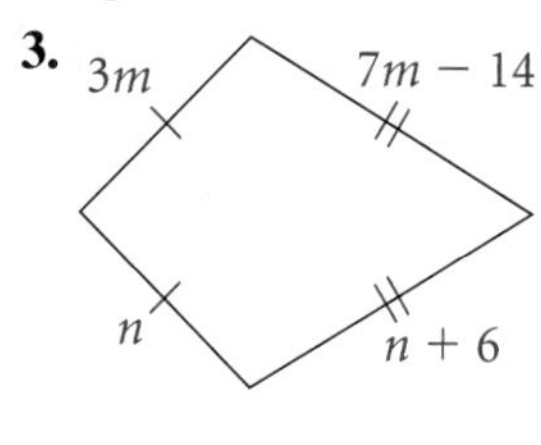

New Vocabulary • base angles of a trapezoid

Interactive lesson includes instant self-check, tutorials, and activities.

OBJECTIVE

1 Properties of Trapezoids and Kites

The parallel sides of a trapezoid are its bases. The nonparallel sides are its legs. Two angles that share a base of a trapezoid are **base angles** of the trapezoid.

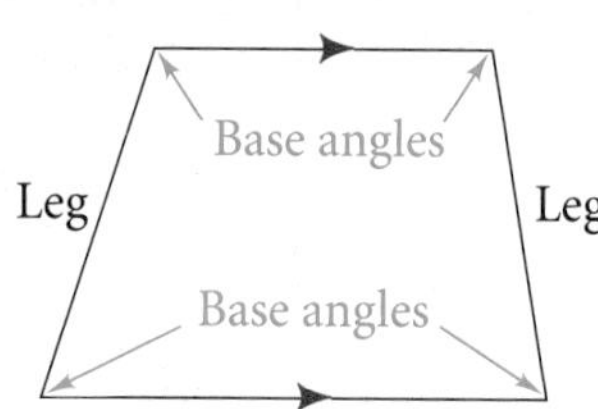

The following theorem is about each pair of base angles. You will be asked to prove it in Exercise 26.

Key Concepts

Theorem 6-15

The base angles of an isosceles trapezoid are congruent.

Real-World Connection

In the isosceles trapezoids at the top of this electric tea kettle, each pair of base angles are congruent.

The bases of a trapezoid are parallel. Therefore the two angles that share a leg are supplementary. This fact and Theorem 6-15 allow you to solve problems involving the angles of a trapezoid.

1 EXAMPLE Finding Angle Measures in Trapezoids

$ABCD$ is an isosceles trapezoid and $m\angle B = 102$. Find $m\angle A, m\angle C,$ and $m\angle D$.

$m\angle A + m\angle B = 180$	**Two angles that share a leg are supplementary.**
$m\angle A + 102 = 180$	**Substitute.**
$m\angle A = 78$	**Subtract 102 from each side.**

By Theorem 6-15, $m\angle C = m\angle B = 102$ and $m\angle D = m\angle A = 78$.

Check Understanding 1 In the isosceles trapezoid, $m\angle S = 70$. Find $m\angle P$, $m\angle Q$, and $m\angle R$.

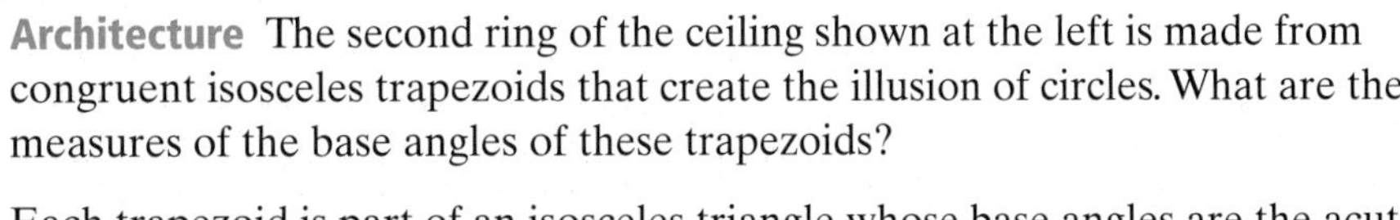

2 EXAMPLE Real-World Connection

Architecture The second ring of the ceiling shown at the left is made from congruent isosceles trapezoids that create the illusion of circles. What are the measures of the base angles of these trapezoids?

Each trapezoid is part of an isosceles triangle whose base angles are the acute base angles of the trapezoid. The isosceles triangle has a vertex angle that is half as large as an angle at the center of the ceiling.

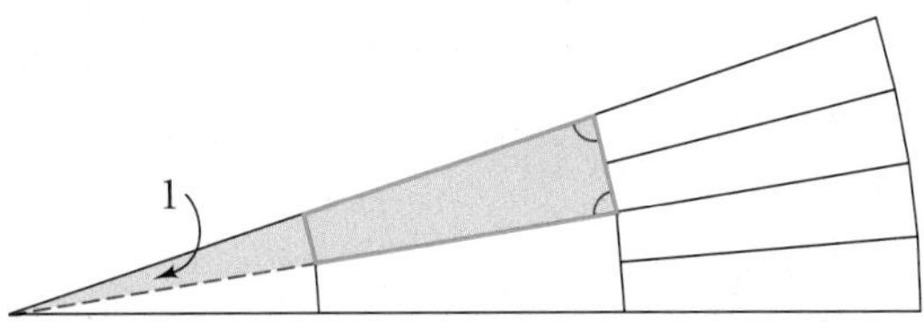

You are looking up at Harbour Centre Tower in Vancouver, Canada.

The measure of each angle at the center of the ceiling is $\frac{360}{20}$ or 18.

The measure of $\angle 1$ is $\frac{18}{2}$, or 9.

The measure of each acute base angle is $\frac{180 - 9}{2}$, or 85.5.

The measure of each obtuse base angle is $180 - 85.5$, or 94.5.

Check Understanding 2 A glass ceiling like the one above has 18 angles meeting at the center instead of 20. What are the measures of the base angles of the trapezoids in its second ring?

Like the diagonals of parallelograms, the diagonals of an isosceles trapezoid have a special property.

Key Concepts

Theorem 6-16

The diagonals of an isosceles trapezoid are congruent.

Proof

Proof of Theorem 6-16

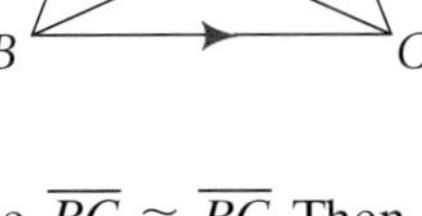

Given: Isosceles trapezoid $ABCD$ with $\overline{AB} \cong \overline{DC}$

Prove: $\overline{AC} \cong \overline{DB}$

It is given that $\overline{AB} \cong \overline{DC}$. Because the base angles of an isosceles trapezoid are congruent, $\angle ABC \cong \angle DCB$. By the Reflexive Property of Congruence, $\overline{BC} \cong \overline{BC}$. Then, by the SAS Postulate, $\triangle ABC \cong \triangle DCB$. Therefore, $\overline{AC} \cong \overline{DB}$ by CPCTC.

Another special quadrilateral that is not a parallelogram is a kite. The diagonals of a kite, like the diagonals of a rhombus, are perpendicular. A proof of this for a kite (next page) is quite like its proof for a rhombus (at the top of page 313).

Key Concepts

Theorem 6-17

The diagonals of a kite are perpendicular.

Proof

Proof of Theorem 6-17

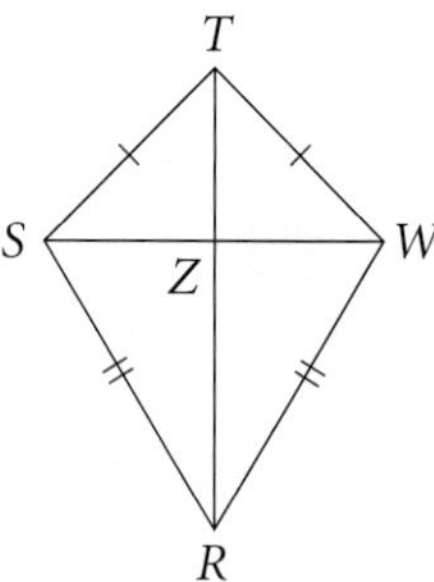

Given: Kite $RSTW$ with $\overline{TS} \cong \overline{TW}$ and $\overline{RS} \cong \overline{RW}$

Prove: $\overline{TR} \perp \overline{SW}$

Both T and R are equidistant from S and W. By the Converse of the Perpendicular Bisector Theorem, T and R lie on the perpendicular bisector of $\overline{SW}$. Since there is exactly one line through any two points (Postulate 1-1), $\overleftrightarrow{TR}$ must be the perpendicular bisector of $\overline{SW}$. Therefore, $\overline{TR} \perp \overline{SW}$.

You can use Theorem 6-17 to find angle measures in kites.

3 EXAMPLE Finding Angle Measures in Kites

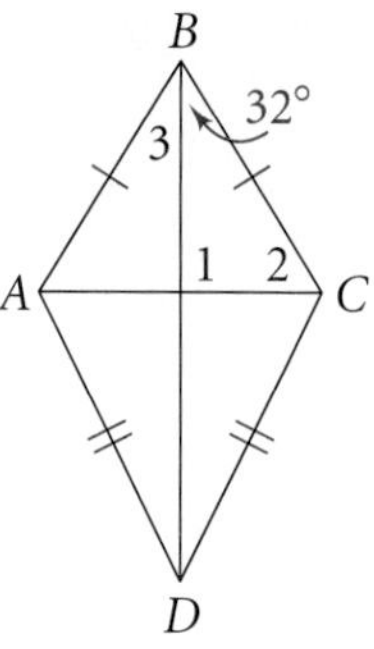

Find $m\angle 1$, $m\angle 2$, and $m\angle 3$ in the kite.

$m\angle 1 = 90$	**Diagonals of a kite are perpendicular.**
$90 + m\angle 2 + 32 = 180$	**Triangle Angle-Sum Theorem**
$122 + m\angle 2 = 180$	**Simplify.**
$m\angle 2 = 58$	**Subtract 122 from each side.**

$\triangle ABD \cong \triangle CBD$ by SSS.

By CPCTC, $m\angle 3 = m\angle DBC = 32$.

Check Understanding 3 Find $m\angle 1$, $m\angle 2$, and $m\angle 3$ in the kite.

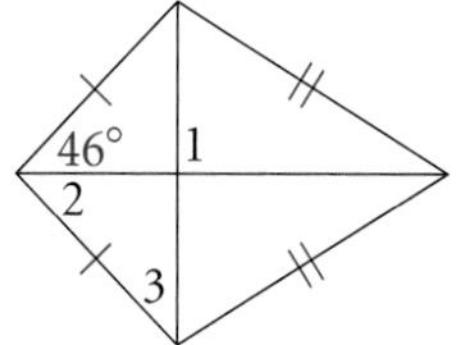

EXERCISES

For more practice, see *Extra Practice.*

Practice and Problem Solving

A Practice by Example

Example 1 (page 320)

Each trapezoid is isosceles. Find the measure of each angle.

1.

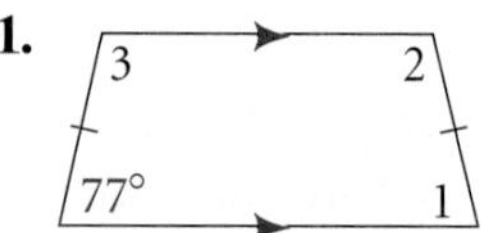

2.

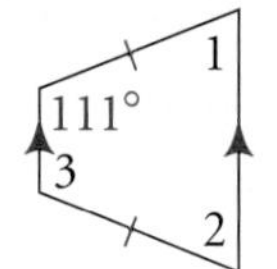

3.

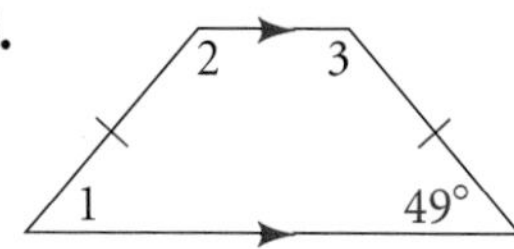

4.

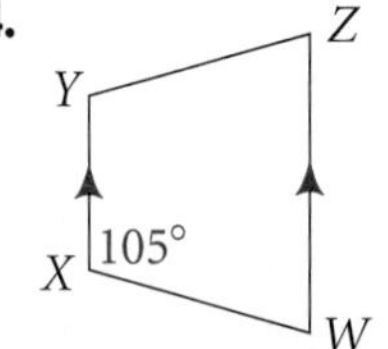

5.

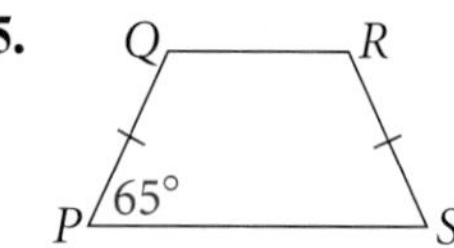

6.

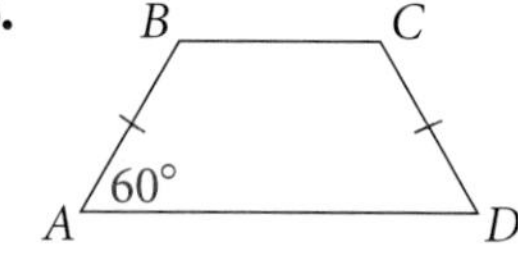

Example 2 (page 321)

7. **Design** Each patio umbrella is made of eight panels that are congruent isosceles triangles with parallel stripes. A sample panel is shown at the right. The vertex angle of the panel measures 42.
   a. Classify the quadrilaterals shown as blue stripes on the panel.
   b. Find the measures of the quadrilaterals' interior angles.

Example 3 (page 322)

Find the measures of the numbered angles in each kite.

8. 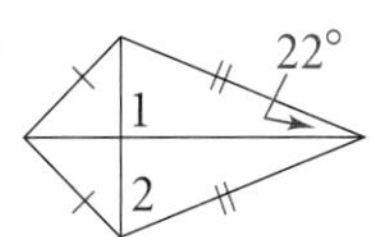

9. 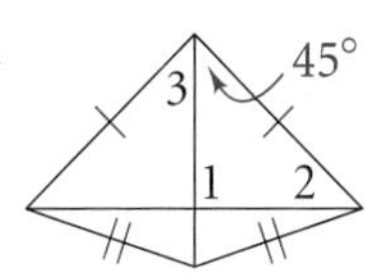

10. 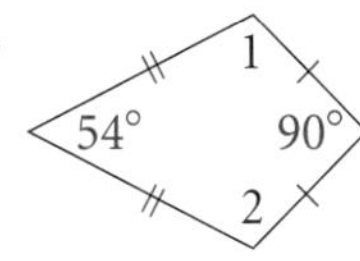

11. 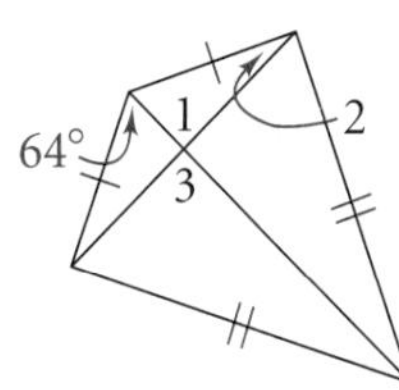

12. 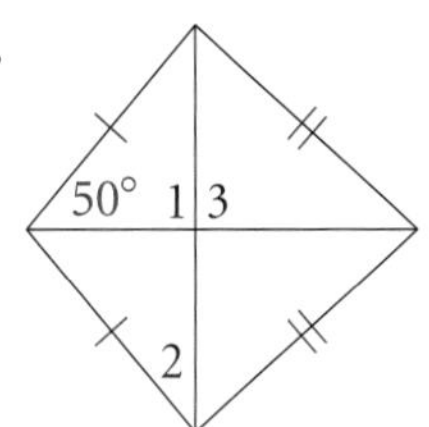

13. 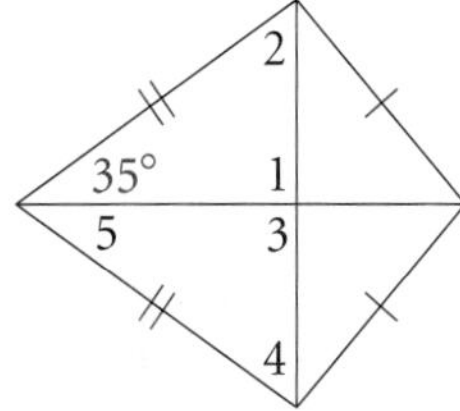

14.

15. 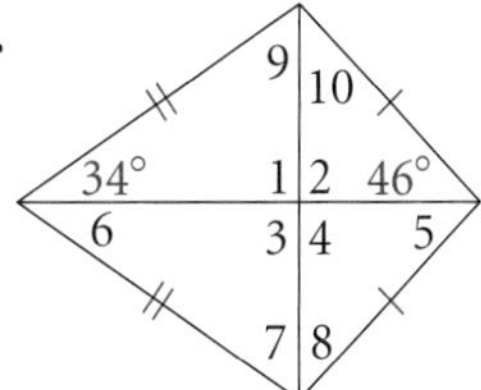

16. 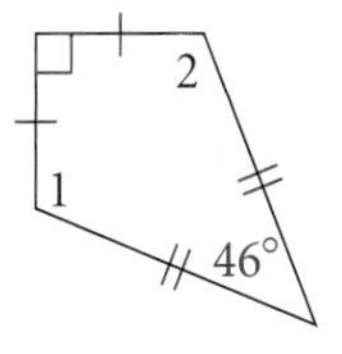

17. **Open-Ended** Sketch two kites that are not congruent, but with the diagonals of one congruent to the diagonals of the other.

18. The perimeter of a kite is 66 cm. The length of one of its sides is 3 cm less than twice the length of another. Find the length of each side of the kite.

19. **Critical Thinking** If $KLMN$ is an isosceles trapezoid, is it possible for $\overline{KM}$ to bisect $\angle LMN$ and $\angle LKN$? Explain.

B **Apply Your Skills**  **Algebra** **Find the value of the variable in each isosceles trapezoid.**

20. 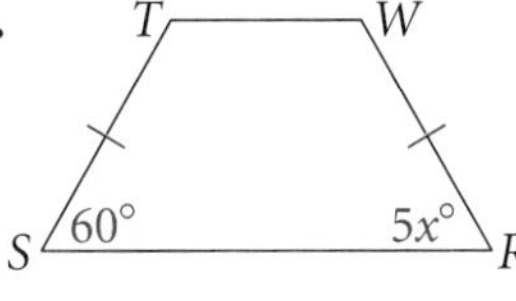

21. 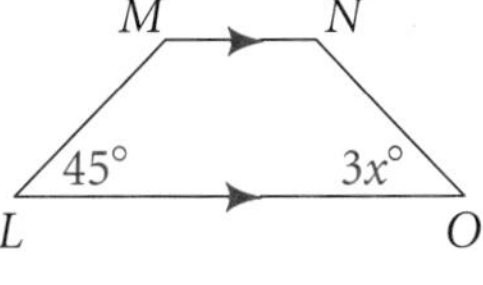

22. 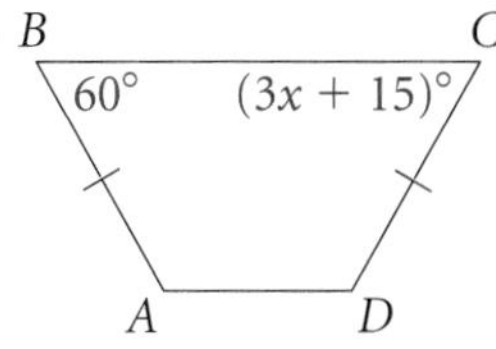

23. 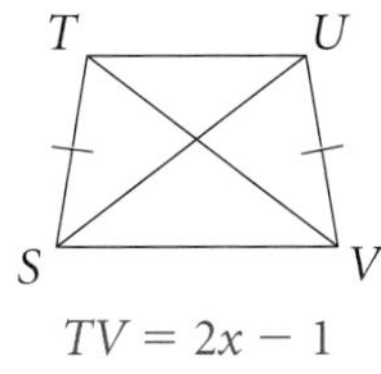

$TV = 2x - 1$
$US = x + 2$

24. 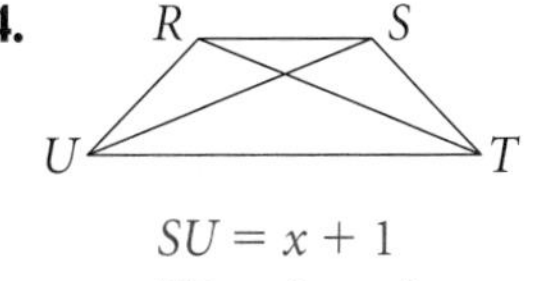

$SU = x + 1$
$TR = 2x - 3$

25. 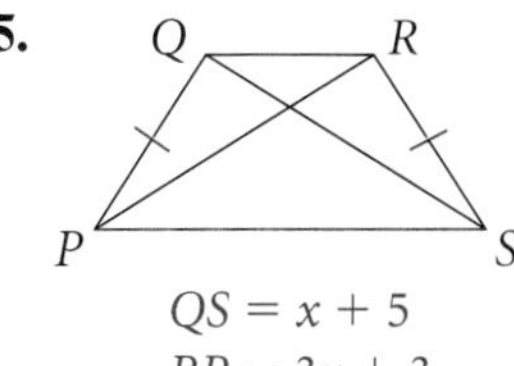

$QS = x + 5$
$RP = 3x + 3$

Proof **26. Developing Proof** The plan suggests a proof of Theorem 6-15. Follow the plan and write a paragraph, two-column, or flow proof.

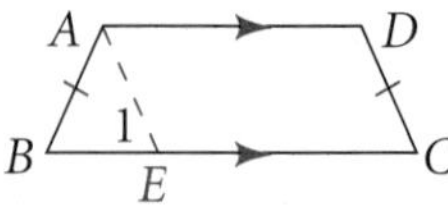

Given: Isosceles trapezoid $ABCD$ with $\overline{AB} \cong \overline{DC}$

Prove: $\angle B \cong \angle C$ and $\angle BAD \cong \angle D$

Plan: Begin by drawing $\overline{AE} \parallel \overline{DC}$ to form parallelogram $AECD$ so that $\overline{AE} \cong \overline{DC} \cong \overline{AB}$. $\angle B \cong \angle C$ because $\angle B \cong \angle 1$ and $\angle 1 \cong \angle C$. Also, $\angle BAD \cong \angle D$ because they are supplements of the congruent angles, $\angle B$ and $\angle C$.

Algebra Find the value(s) of the variable(s) in each kite.

27.

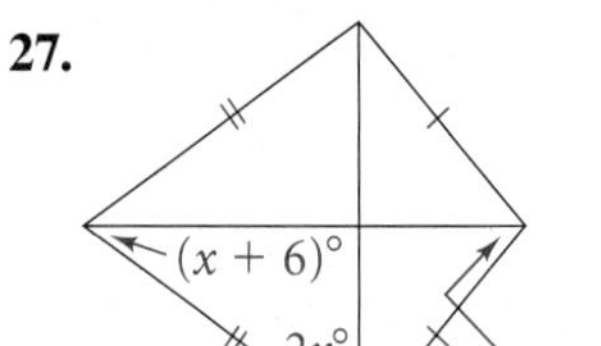

28.

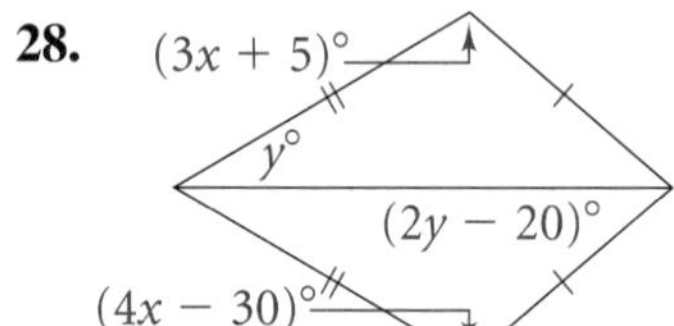

29.

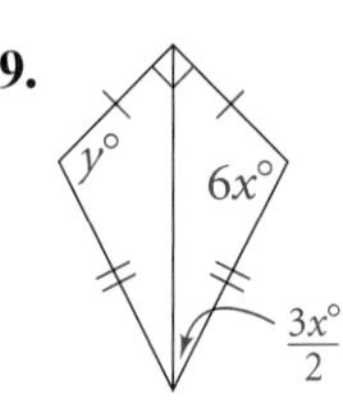

Exercises 30–31

Bridge Design A quadrilateral is formed by the beams of the bridge at the left.

30. Classify the quadrilateral. Explain your reasoning.

31. Find the measures of the other interior angles of the quadrilateral.

Critical Thinking Can two angles of a kite be as follows? Explain.

32. opposite and acute

33. consecutive and obtuse

34. opposite and supplementary

35. consecutive and supplementary

36. opposite and complementary

37. consecutive and complementary

38. Writing A kite is sometimes defined as a quadrilateral with two pairs of consecutive sides congruent. Compare this to the definition you learned in Lesson 6-1. Are parallelograms, trapezoids, rhombuses, rectangles, or squares special kinds of kites according to the changed definition? Explain.

C Challenge

39. $\overleftrightarrow{BN}$ is the perpendicular bisector of $\overline{AC}$ at N. Describe the set of points, D, for which $ABCD$ is a kite.

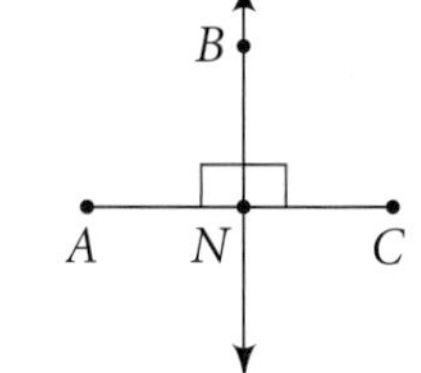

Proof **40.** Prove that the angles formed by the noncongruent sides of a kite are congruent. (*Hint:* Draw a diagonal of the kite.)

Proof **Write a proof. Use the given figure with additional lines as needed.**

41. Given: Isosceles trapezoid $TRAP$ with $\overline{TR} \cong \overline{PA}$

Prove: $\angle RTA \cong \angle APR$

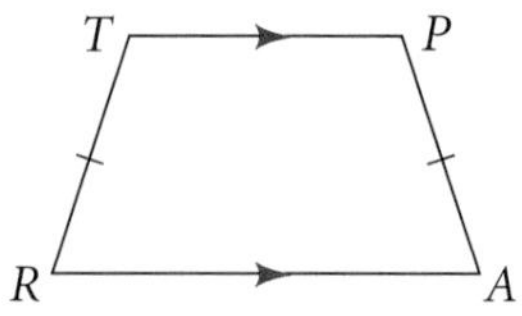

T P R A

42. Given: Isosceles trapezoid $TRAP$ with $\overline{TR} \cong \overline{PA}$; $\overline{BI}$ is the perpendicular bisector of $\overline{RA}$ intersecting $\overline{RA}$ at B and $\overline{TP}$ at I.

Prove: $\overline{BI}$ is the perpendicular bisector of $\overline{TP}$.

For a trapezoid, consider the segment joining the midpoints of the two given segments. How are its length and the lengths of the two parallel sides of the trapezoid related? Justify your answer.

43. the two nonparallel sides

44. the diagonals

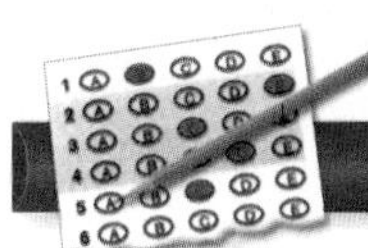

Standardized Test Prep

Multiple Choice

45. Which statement is true for every trapezoid?
A. Exactly two sides are congruent. **B.** Exactly two sides are parallel.
C. Opposite angles are supplementary. **D.** The diagonals bisect each other.

46. Which statement is true for every kite?
F. Opposite sides are congruent. **G.** At least two sides are parallel.
H. Opposite angles are supplementary. **I.** The diagonals are perpendicular.

Quantitative Comparison

Compare the boxed quantity in Column A with the boxed quantity in Column B. Choose the best answer.
A. The quantity in Column A is greater.
B. The quantity in Column B is greater.
C. The two quantities are equal.
D. The relationship cannot be determined from the information given.

Trapezoid

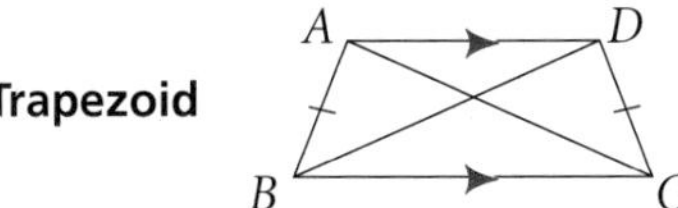

	Column A	Column B
47.	$m\angle ABC$	$m\angle BCD$
48.	AC	BD
49.	AD	BC

Take It to the NET
Online lesson quiz at **www.PHSchool.com**
Web Code: afa-0605

Short Response

50. Diagonal $\overline{RB}$ of kite *RHBW* forms an equilateral triangle with two of the sides. $m\angle BWR = 40$. Draw and label a diagram showing the diagonal and the measures of all the angles. Which angles of the kite are largest?

Mixed Review

Lesson 6-4

Find the indicated angle measures for the rhombus.

51. $m\angle 1$ **52.** $m\angle 2$ **53.** $m\angle 3$

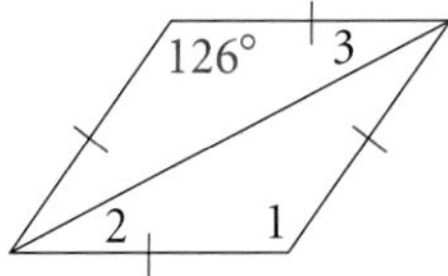

Lesson 5-2 x^2 Algebra **Find the values indicated.**

54. a. a
b. FG
c. GH

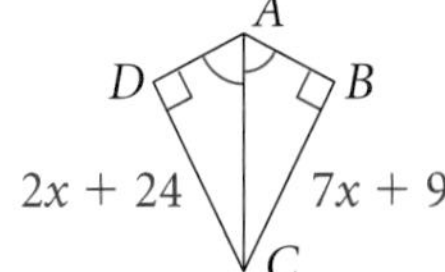

55. a. x
b. CD
c. BC

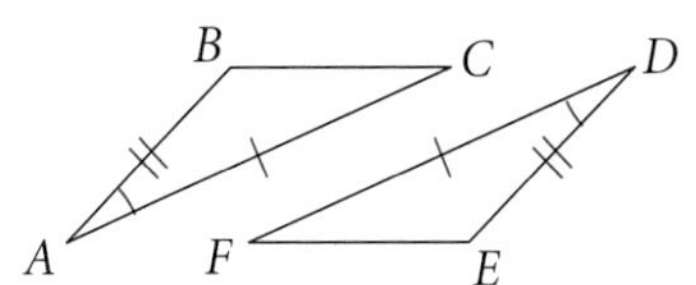

Lesson 4-2

56. State the postulate that justifies the statement $\triangle ABC \cong \triangle DEF$.

6-6 Placing Figures in the Coordinate Plane

ALGEBRA

Lesson Preview

What You'll Learn

To name coordinates of special figures by using their properties

. . . And Why

To examine a T-shirt design, as in Example 2

✓ Check Skills You'll Need

(For help, go to Lesson 6-1.)

Draw a quadrilateral with the given vertices. Then determine the most precise name for each quadrilateral.

1. $H(-5, 0), E(-3, 2), A(3, 2), T(5, 0)$
2. $S(0, 0), A(4, 0), N(3, 2), D(-1, 2)$
3. $R(0, 0), A(5, 5), I(8, 4), N(7, 1)$
4. $W(-3, 0), I(0, 3), N(3, 0), D(0, -3)$

Interactive lesson includes instant self-check, tutorials, and activities.

OBJECTIVE

1 Naming Coordinates

Investigation: Figures in the Coordinate Plane

- Use graph paper to draw a number of coordinate planes with *x*- and *y*-coordinates from −12 to 12. On each, draw one or more squares with sides 10 units long. Draw the squares in different positions, with sides on one or both axes, parallel to the axes, or not parallel to either axis. Use more than one quadrant. Label each square *ABCD*.
- On each square, record the slope of each side, the slope of each diagonal, and the coordinates of the midpoints of the diagonals.

1. Which positions for your squares made your calculations easiest? Generalize your conclusions and explain your reasons.
2. For ease of calculations in the coordinate plane, explain how you would position (a) a rectangle and (b) a parallelogram.

In the coordinate plane, the position of a figure affects the ease with which you can work with its coordinates. In coordinate proofs, it generally is good practice to center the figure on the origin, or place a vertex at the origin and one side of the figure on an axis.

1 EXAMPLE Naming Coordinates

Reading Math

A rectangle centered at the origin has opposite sides equidistant from the origin.

Algebra In the diagram, rectangle $KLMN$ is centered at the origin with sides parallel to the axes. Find the missing coordinates.

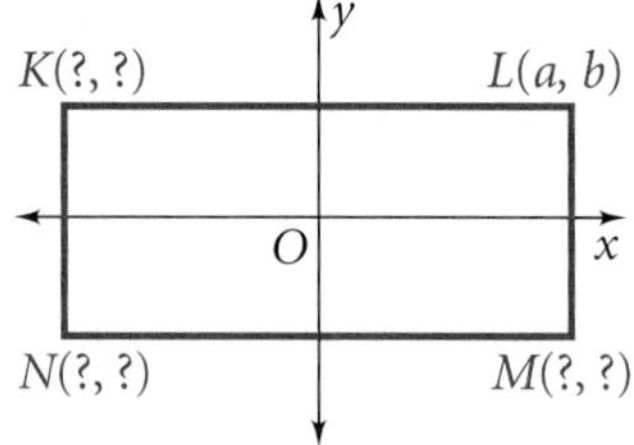

L has coordinates (a, b), so the coordinates of the other vertices are $K(-a, b)$, $M(a, -b)$, and $N(-a, -b)$.

Check Understanding **1** Use the properties of parallelogram $OPQR$ to find the missing coordinates. Do not use any new variables.

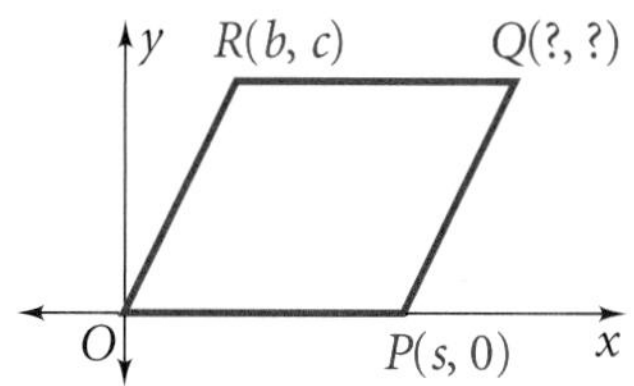

It is often convenient to use coordinates that are multiples of 2. The next example uses multiples of 2 to avoid fractions when finding midpoints.

2 EXAMPLE Real-World Connection

T-Shirt Design An art class creates T-shirt designs by drawing quadrilaterals, connecting their midpoints to form other quadrilaterals, and then coloring the regions. Tiana claims that everyone's inner quadrilateral will be a parallelogram. Is she correct? Explain.

Step 1

Draw quadrilateral $OACE$ with one vertex at the origin and one side on the x-axis. Since you are finding midpoints, use coordinates that are multiples of 2. Find the coordinates of the midpoints T, W, V, and U.

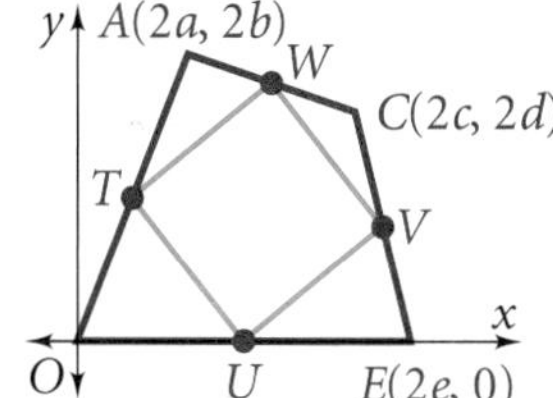

Need Help?

Use the Distributive Property.

$\frac{2a + 2c}{2} = \frac{2(a + c)}{2}$

$= a + c$

$T = \text{midpoint of } \overline{OA} = \left(\frac{2a + 0}{2}, \frac{2b + 0}{2}\right) = (a, b)$

$W = \text{midpoint of } \overline{AC} = \left(\frac{2a + 2c}{2}, \frac{2b + 2d}{2}\right) = (a + c, b + d)$

$V = \text{midpoint of } \overline{CE} = \left(\frac{2c + 2e}{2}, \frac{2d + 0}{2}\right) = (c + e, d)$

$U = \text{midpoint of } \overline{OE} = \left(\frac{0 + 2e}{2}, \frac{0 + 0}{2}\right) = (e, 0)$

Step 2

Find the slopes of the sides of $TWVU$.

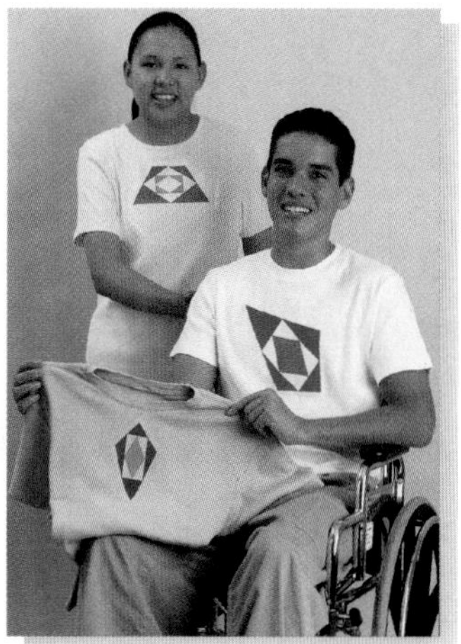

$$\text{slope of } \overline{TW} = \frac{b - (b + d)}{a - (a + c)} = \frac{d}{c}$$

$$\text{slope of } \overline{VU} = \frac{d - 0}{(c + e) - e} = \frac{d}{c}$$

The slopes are equal, so $\overline{TW} \parallel \overline{VU}$.

$$\text{slope of } \overline{WV} = \frac{(b + d) - d}{(a + c) - (c + e)} = \frac{b}{a - e}$$

$$\text{slope of } \overline{TU} = \frac{b - 0}{a - e} = \frac{b}{a - e}$$

The slopes are equal, so $\overline{WV} \parallel \overline{TU}$.

Since both pairs of opposite sides of $TWVU$ are parallel, $TWVU$ is a parallelogram, and Tiana is correct.

2 Use a different method to show that $TWVU$ is a parallelogram by finding the midpoints of the diagonals.

EXERCISES

For more practice, see *Extra Practice*.

Practice and Problem Solving

A Practice by Example

Example 1 (page 326)

Algebra **Give coordinates for points W and Z without using any new variables.**

1. rectangle

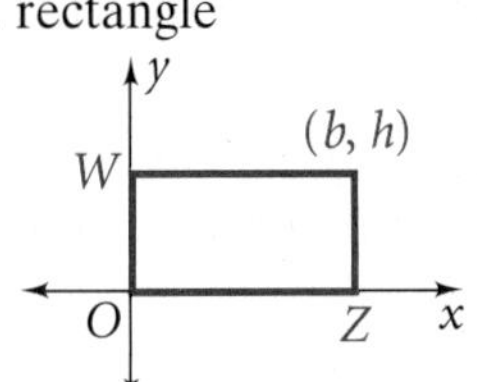

2. square

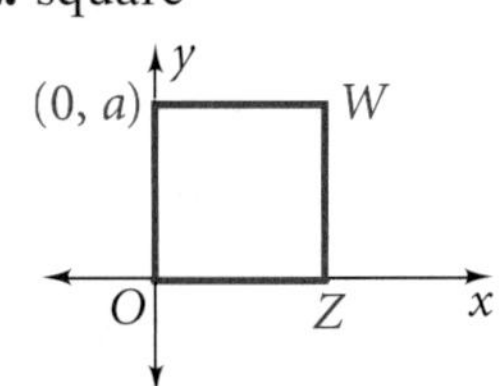

3. square

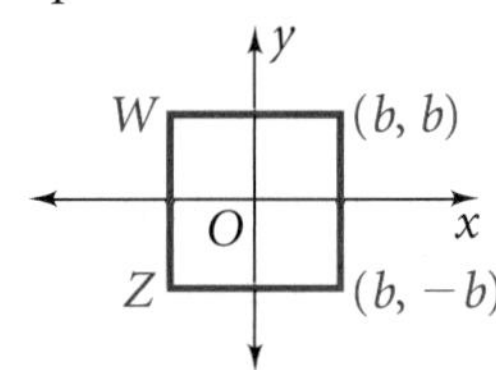

4. parallelogram

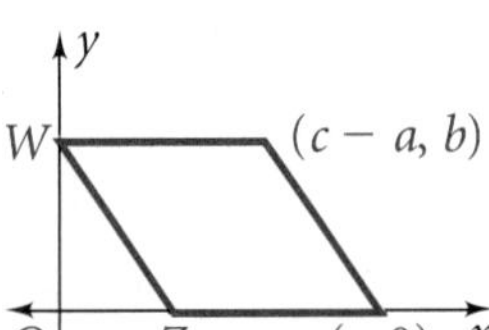

5. rhombus

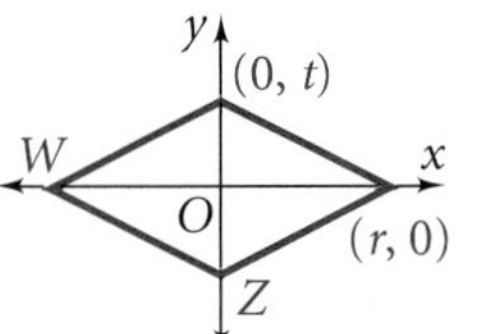

6. isosceles trapezoid

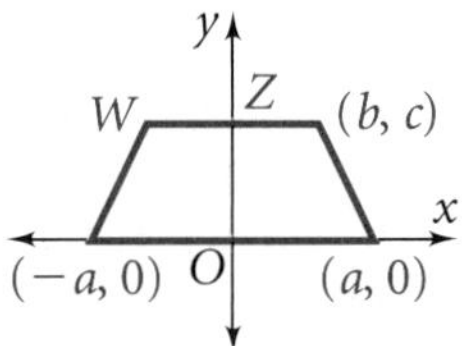

Example 2 (page 327)

In each exercise, find the coordinates of the midpoint of $\overline{WZ}$ and the slope of $\overline{WZ}$.

7. Exercise 1 **8.** Exercise 2 **9.** Exercise 3

10. Exercise 4 **11.** Exercise 5 **12.** Exercise 6

13. Developing Proof Complete the steps to show that the midpoint of the hypotenuse of a right triangle is equidistant from the vertices of the triangle.

Given: Right $\triangle ABC$ with M the midpoint of hypotenuse $\overline{AB}$

Prove: $MA = MB = MC$

Step 1: Draw right $\triangle ABC$ on a coordinate plane. Locate the right angle, $\angle C$, at the origin and leg $\overline{CA}$ on the positive x-axis.

Step 2: You seek a midpoint, so label coordinates using multiples of 2. The coordinates of point A are **a.** _?_. The coordinates of point B are **b.** _?_.

Step 3: By the Midpoint Formula, the coordinates of midpoint M are **c.** _?_.

Step 4: By the Distance Formula, $MA =$ **d.** _?_, $MB =$ **e.** _?_, and $MC =$ **f.** _?_.

Step 5: Conclusion: **g.** _?_

B Apply Your Skills

Here are coordinates for eight points in the coordinate plane ($q > p > 0$).

$A(0, 0)$, $B(p, 0)$, $C(q, 0)$, $D(p + q, 0)$, $E(0, q)$, $F(p, q)$, $G(q, q)$, $H(p + q, q)$

Which four points, if any, are the vertices for each type of figure?

14. parallelogram **15.** rhombus **16.** rectangle

17. square **18.** trapezoid **19.** isosceles trapezoid

Refer to the diagrams in Exercises 1–6. Use the coordinates given below in place of the ones shown. Then give the coordinates for points W and Z without using any new variables. The new diagram for Exercise 20 is shown here.

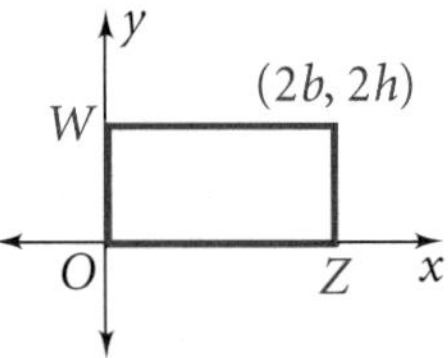

20. Ex. 1, $(2b, 2h)$ **21.** Ex. 2, $(0, 2a)$

22. Ex. 3, $(2b, 2b)$, $(2b, -2b)$ **23.** Ex. 4, $(2c, 0)$, $(2c - 2a, b)$

24. Ex. 5, $(2r, 0)$, $(0, 2t)$ **25.** Ex. 6, $(-2a, 0)$, $(2a, 0)$, $(2b, 2c)$

26. **a.** What property of a rhombus makes it convenient to place its diagonals on the x- and y-axes?

b. **Writing** Suppose a parallelogram is not a rhombus. Explain why it may not be convenient to place opposite vertices on the y-axis.

27. **Open-Ended** Choose values for r and t in Exercise 5. Find the slope and length of each side. State why the figure satisfies the definition of a rhombus.

Need Help?

In Exercise 28, draw a vertical line from P to the x-axis and a horizontal line from P to the y-axis.

Give the coordinates for point P without using any new variables.

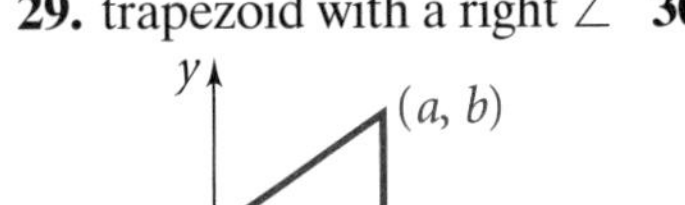

28. isosceles trapezoid

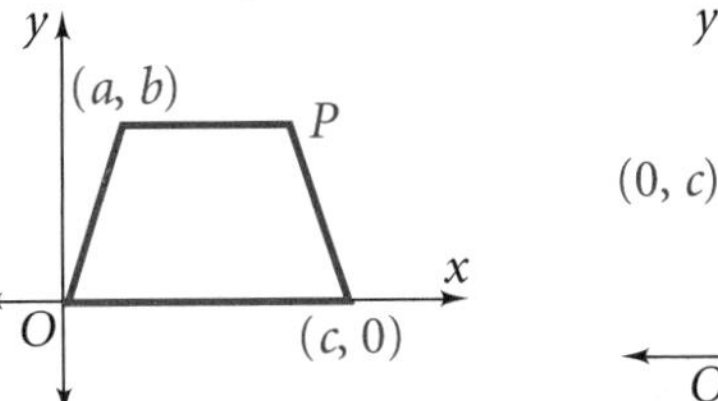

29. trapezoid with a right ∠

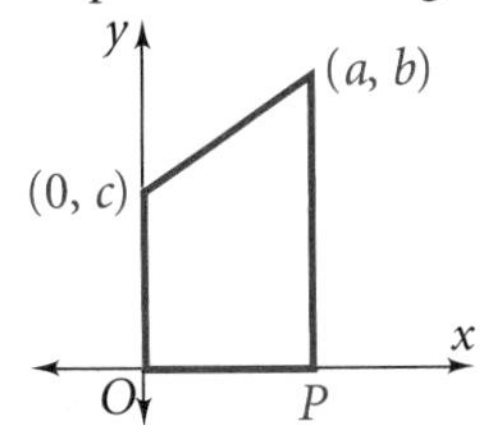

30. kite

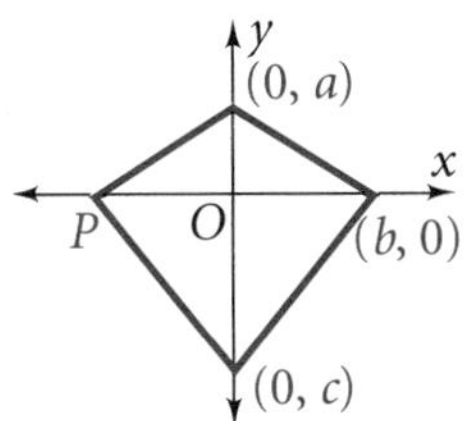

31. **a.** Draw a square whose diagonals of length $2b$ lie on the x- and y-axes.
b. Give the coordinates of the vertices of the square.
c. Compute the length of a side of the square.
d. Find the slopes of two adjacent sides of the square.
e. Do the slopes show that the sides are perpendicular? Explain.

32. Make two drawings of an isosceles triangle with base length $2b$ and height $2c$.
a. In one drawing, place the base on the x-axis with a vertex at the origin.
b. In the second, place the base on the x-axis with its midpoint at the origin.
c. Find the lengths of the legs of the triangle as placed in part (a).
d. Find the lengths of the legs of the triangle as placed in part (b).
e. How do the results of parts (c) and (d) compare?

C Challenge

33. **Marine Archaeology** Marine archaeologists sometimes use a coordinate system on the ocean floor. They record the coordinates of points where artifacts are found. Assume that each diver searches a square area and can go no farther than b units from the starting points. Draw a model for the region one diver can search. Assign coordinates to the vertices without using any new variables.

Real-World  **Connection**

Careers Underwater archaeologists also spend time on land studying historical data to locate submerged sites or ships.

Proof 34. **Coordinate Proof** Follow the steps below to prove:

If two nonvertical lines are perpendicular, the product of their slopes is -1.

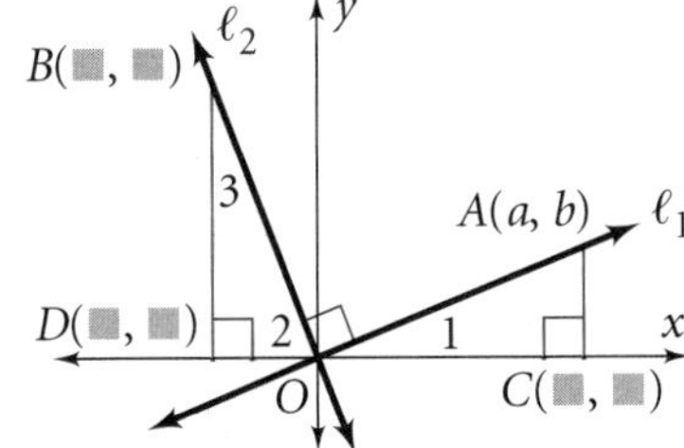

Step 1: Two nonvertical lines, ℓ_1 and ℓ_2, intersect. Which coordinate point might be the easiest to work with as the point of intersection?

Step 2: To work with the slope of a line, you need two points on the line. Choose one point $A(a, b)$ on ℓ_1. What are the coordinates of C?

Step 3: Notice that $\angle 1$ and $\angle 3$ are both complements of $\angle 2$. Why?

Step 4: This means that the two triangles pictured have congruent angles. Thus, if any pair of sides are congruent, the two triangles are congruent. Congruent triangles are desirable, so what would be a good choice for the coordinates of point D?

Step 5: If you made a choice for D so that $\triangle ACO \cong \triangle ODB$ what must be the coordinates of point B?

Step 6: Now, complete the proof that the product of slopes is -1.

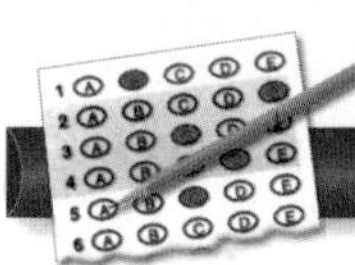

Standardized Test Prep

Multiple Choice

35. The vertices of a rhombus are located at $(a, 0)$, $(0, b)$, $(-a, 0)$, and $(0, -b)$, where $a, b > 0$. What is the midpoint of the side that is in Quadrant II?

A. $\left(\frac{a}{2}, \frac{b}{2}\right)$ **B.** $\left(-\frac{a}{2}, \frac{b}{2}\right)$ **C.** $\left(-\frac{a}{2}, -\frac{b}{2}\right)$ **D.** $\left(\frac{a}{2}, -\frac{b}{2}\right)$

36. The vertices of a kite are located at $(0, a)$, $(b, 0)$, $(0, -c)$, and $(-b, 0)$, where $a, b, c, d > 0$. What is the slope of the side in Quadrant IV?

F. $\frac{c}{b}$ **G.** $\frac{b}{c}$ **H.** $-\frac{b}{c}$ **I.** $-\frac{c}{b}$

37. The vertices of a square are located at $(a, 0)$, (a, a), $(0, a)$, and $(0, 0)$. What is the length of a diagonal?

A. a **B.** $2a$ **C.** $a\sqrt{2}$ **D.** $2\sqrt{a}$

Quantitative Comparison

Compare the boxed quantity in Column A with the boxed quantity in Column B. Choose the best answer.

A. The quantity in Column A is greater.
B. The quantity in Column B is greater.
C. The two quantities are equal.
D. The relationship cannot be determined from the information given.

The points $A(p, p + 2)$, $B(r, s)$, and $C(3p, 3p)$ are collinear, and $p \neq 0$. B is the midpoint of $\overline{AC}$.

	Column A	Column B
38.	r	$2p$
39.	s	$2p$
40.	the slope of $\overline{AC}$	$1 - \frac{1}{p}$

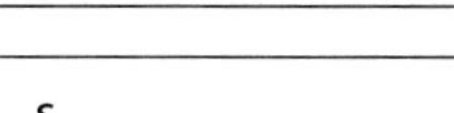

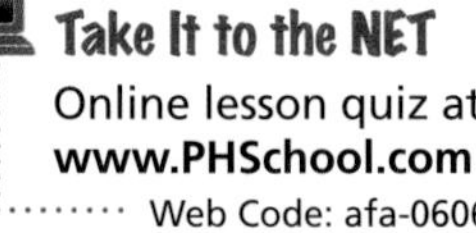

Take It to the NET
Online lesson quiz at **www.PHSchool.com**
Web Code: afa-0606

Short Response

41. The vertices of a rectangle are $(2b, 0)$, $(2b, 2a)$, $(0, 2a)$, and $(0, 0)$. What are the coordinates of the midpoint of each diagonal? What can you conclude from your answers?

Mixed Review

Lesson 6-5 x^2 **42. Algebra** Find the measure of each angle and the value of x in the isosceles trapezoid.

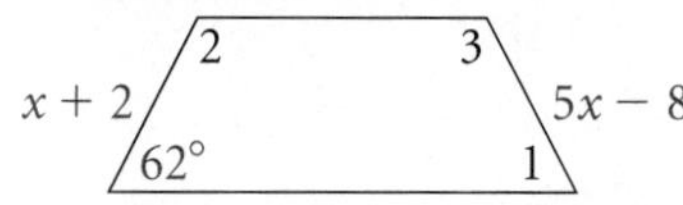

Lesson 5-3 **Find the center of the circle that circumscribes $\triangle ABC$.**

43. $A(1, 1), B(5, 3), C(5, 1)$ **44.** $A(-5, 0), B(-1, -8), C(-1, 0)$

Lesson 4-3 **45.** Supply the words that complete the paragraph proof.

Given: $\angle ACD \cong \angle ACB$ and $\angle D \cong \angle B$

Prove: $\triangle ADC \cong \triangle ABC$

$\angle ACD \cong \angle ACB$ and $\angle D \cong \angle B$. $\overline{AC} \cong \overline{AC}$ by the **a.** __?__ Property of Congruence. So, $\triangle ADC \cong \triangle ABC$ by the **b.** __?__ Theorem.

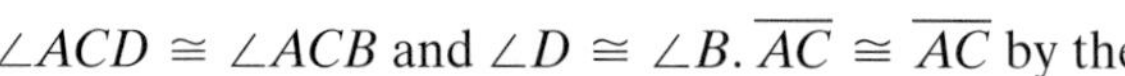

Checkpoint Quiz 2 — Lessons 6-4 through 6-6

Instant self-check quiz online and on CD-ROM

Algebra **Find the value(s) of the variable(s).**

1.
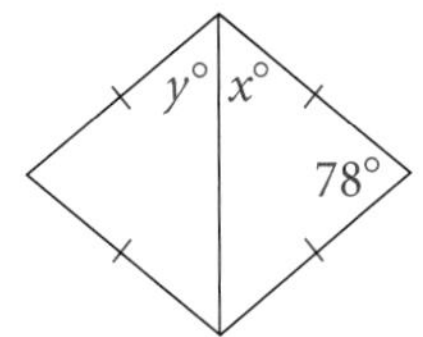

2.
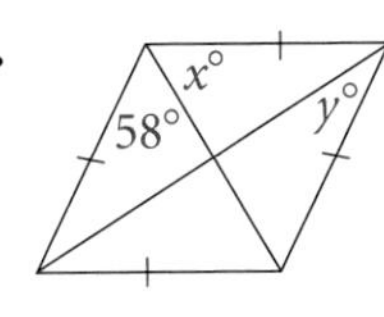

3.
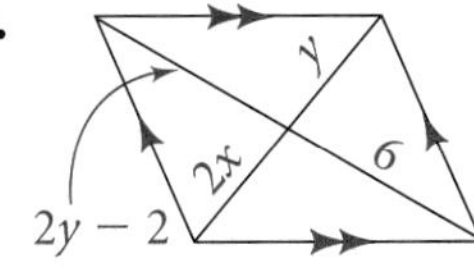

4.
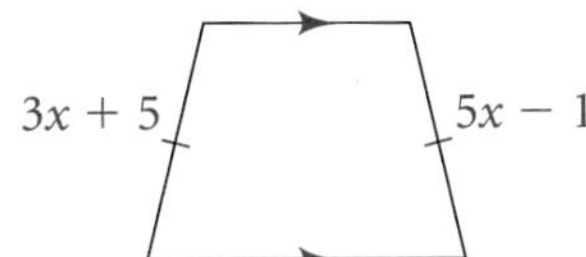

5.
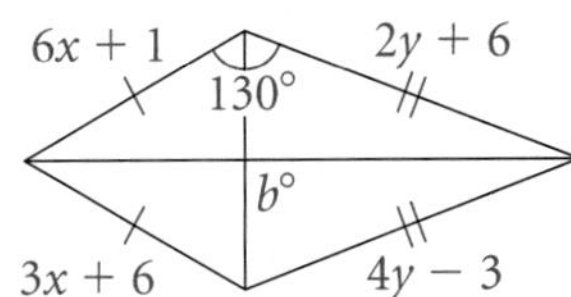

In Exercises 6–8, decide whether the statement is *true* or *false*. If true, explain why. If false, show a counterexample.

6. A quadrilateral with congruent diagonals is an isosceles trapezoid or rectangle.

7. A quadrilateral with congruent and perpendicular diagonals is a square.

8. Each diagonal of a kite bisects two angles of the kite.

Give the coordinates for point A without using any new variables.

9.
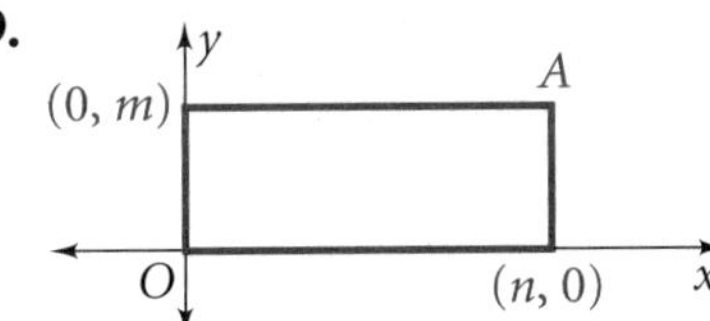

10.
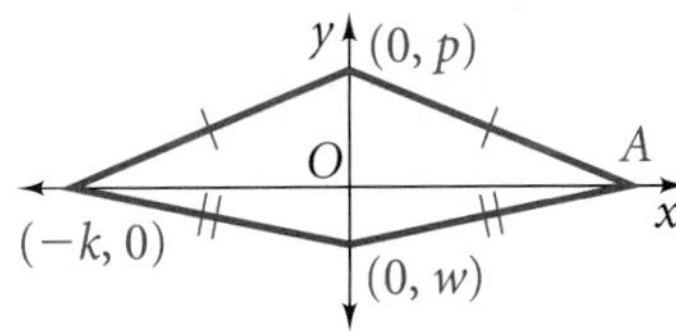

A Point in Time

400 | 200 B.C. | 0 | A.D. 200 | 2000

Many walls in ancient Egypt were decorated with reliefs. The relief in the photo was created in the year 255 B.C. First, the artist sketched the scene on papyrus overlaid with a grid. Next, the wall was marked with a grid the size of the intended sculpture. To draw each line, a tightly stretched string that had been dipped in red ochre was plucked, like a guitar string.

Using the grid squares as guides, the artist transferred the drawing to the wall. Then, a sculptor cut the background away, leaving the scene slightly raised. Finally, an artist painted the scene.

Take It to the NET For more information about Egyptian reliefs, go to **www.PHSchool.com.**
Web Code: afe-2032

6-7 Proofs Using Coordinate Geometry

ALGEBRA

Lesson Preview

What You'll Learn

OBJECTIVE 1 To prove theorems using figures in the coordinate plane

. . . And Why

To use coordinate geometry to prove that a flag design includes a rhombus, as in Example 2

✓ Check Skills You'll Need

(For help, go to Lesson 6-6.)

1. Graph the rhombus with vertices $A(2, 2)$, $B(7, 2)$, $C(4, -2)$, and $D(-1, -2)$. Then, connect the midpoints of consecutive sides to form a quadrilateral. What do you notice about the quadrilateral?

x^2 Algebra **Give the coordinates of B without using any new variables.**

2. rectangle

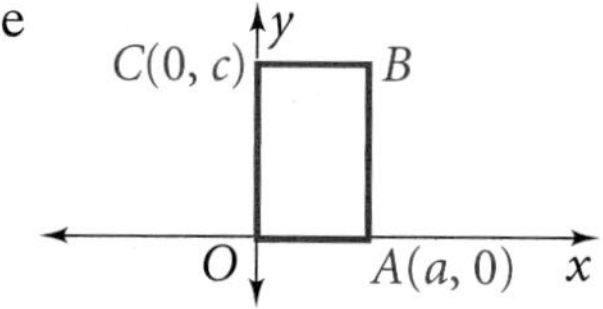

3. isosceles triangle

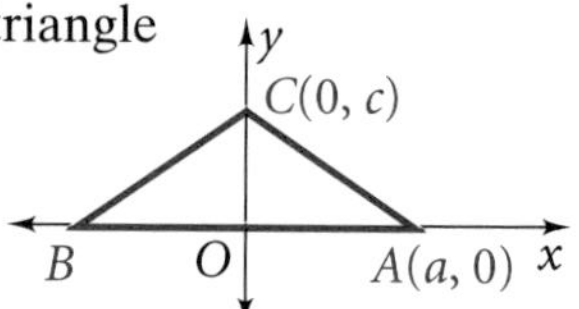

New Vocabulary • midsegment of a trapezoid

Interactive lesson includes instant self-check, tutorials, and activities.

OBJECTIVE 1 Building Proofs in the Coordinate Plane

In Lesson 5-1, you learned about midsegments of triangles. A trapezoid also has a midsegment. The **midsegment of a trapezoid** is the segment that joins the midpoints of the nonparallel opposite sides. It has two unique properties.

Key Concepts

Theorem 6-18 Trapezoid Midsegment Theorem

(1) The midsegment of a trapezoid is parallel to the bases.
(2) The length of the midsegment of a trapezoid is half the sum of the lengths of the bases.

$\overline{MN} \parallel \overline{TP}$, $\overline{MN} \parallel \overline{RA}$, and $MN = \frac{1}{2}(TP + RA)$.

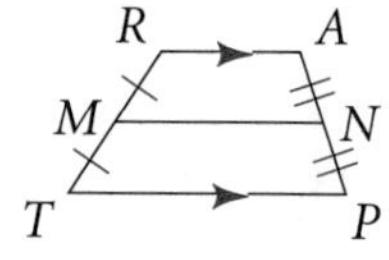

Formulas for slope, midpoint, and distance are used in a proof of Theorem 6-18.

Proof 1 EXAMPLE Planning a Coordinate Geometry Proof

Developing Proof Plan a coordinate proof of Theorem 6-18.

Given: $\overline{MN}$ is the midsegment of trapezoid $TRAP$.

Prove: $\overline{MN} \parallel \overline{TP}$, $\overline{MN} \parallel \overline{RA}$, and $MN = \frac{1}{2}(TP + RA)$.

Plan: Place the trapezoid in the coordinate plane with a vertex at the origin and a base along the x-axis. Since midpoints will be involved, use multiples of 2 to name coordinates. To show lines are parallel, check for equal slopes. To compare lengths, use the Distance Formula.

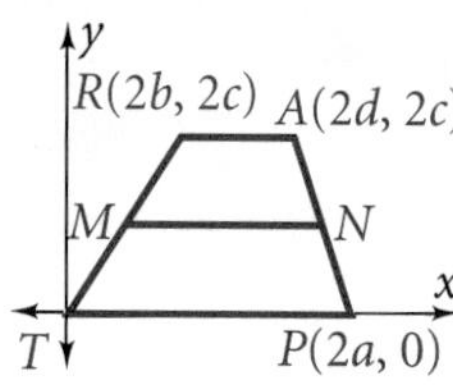

Check Understanding 1 Complete the coordinate proof of Theorem 6-18.

a. Find the coordinates of midpoints M and N. How do the multiples of 2 help?
b. Find and compare the slopes of $\overline{MN}$, $\overline{TP}$, and $\overline{RA}$.
c. Find and compare the lengths MN, TP, and RA.
d. In parts (b) and (c), how does placing a base along the x-axis help?

2 EXAMPLE Real-World Connection

Algebra The rectangular flag at the left is constructed by connecting the midpoints of its sides. Use coordinate geometry to prove that the quadrilateral formed by connecting the midpoints of the sides of a rectangle is a rhombus.

Given: $MNPO$ is a rectangle.
T, W, V, U are midpoints of its sides.

Prove: $TWVU$ is a rhombus.

Plan: Place the rectangle in the coordinate plane with two sides along the axes. Use multiples of 2 to name coordinates.
A rhombus is a parallelogram with four congruent sides. From Lesson 6-6, Example 2, you know that $TWVU$ is a parallelogram. To show $\overline{TW} \cong \overline{WV} \cong \overline{VU} \cong \overline{UT}$, use the Distance Formula.

Coordinate Proof: By the Midpoint Formula, the coordinates of the midpoints are $T(0, b)$, $W(a, 2b)$, $V(2a, b)$, and $U(a, 0)$. By the Distance Formula,

$$TW = \sqrt{(a - 0)^2 + (2b - b)^2} = \sqrt{a^2 + b^2}$$

$$WV = \sqrt{(2a - a)^2 + (b - 2b)^2} = \sqrt{a^2 + b^2}$$

$$VU = \sqrt{(a - 2a)^2 + (0 - b)^2} = \sqrt{a^2 + b^2}$$

$$UT = \sqrt{(0 - a)^2 + (b - 0)^2} = \sqrt{a^2 + b^2}$$

$\overline{TW} \cong \overline{WV} \cong \overline{VU} \cong \overline{UT}$, so parallelogram $TWVU$ is a rhombus.

Real-World Connection

A flag's length, called the *fly*, usually is greater than its width, called the *hoist*.

Check Understanding 2 **Critical Thinking** Explain why the proof using $M(0, 2b)$, $N(2a, 2b)$, $P(2a, 0)$, and $O(0, 0)$ is easier than a proof using $M(0, b)$, $N(a, b)$, $P(a, 0)$, and $O(0, 0)$.

EXERCISES

For more practice, see *Extra Practice*.

Practice and Problem Solving

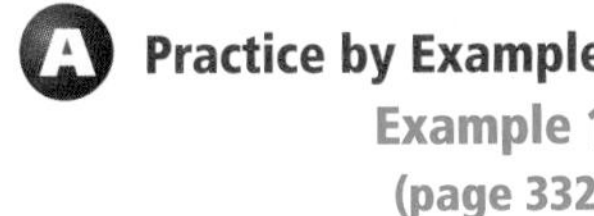

A Practice by Example
Example 1
(page 332)

1. W and Z are the midpoints of $\overline{OR}$ and $\overline{ST}$, respectively. In parts (a)–(c), find the coordinates of W and Z.

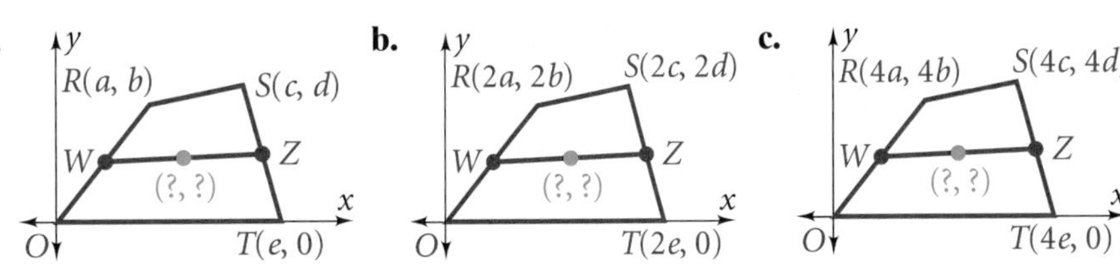

d. You are to plan a coordinate proof involving the midpoint of $\overline{WZ}$. Which of the figures (a)–(c) would you prefer to use? Explain.

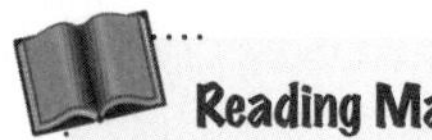

Reading Math

When you read large blocks of math text, cover all but a few lines to help you focus.

Developing Proof **Complete the plan for each coordinate proof.**

2. The diagonals of a parallelogram bisect each other (Theorem 6-3).

Given: Parallelogram $ABCD$

Prove: $\overline{AC}$ bisects $\overline{BD}$, and $\overline{BD}$ bisects $\overline{AC}$.

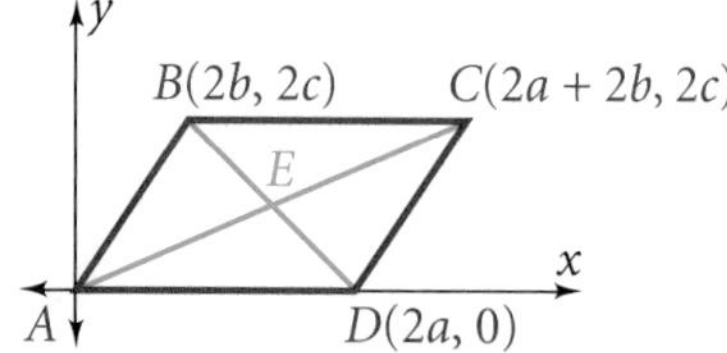

Plan: Place the parallelogram in the coordinate plane with a vertex at the **a.** __?__ and a base along the **b.** __?__. Since midpoints will be involved, use multiples of **c.** __?__ to name coordinates. To show segments bisect each other, show the midpoints have the same **d.** __?__.

3. The diagonals of an isosceles trapezoid are congruent (Theorem 6-16).

Given: Trapezoid $EFGH$ with $\overline{FE} \cong \overline{GH}$

Prove: $\overline{EG} \cong \overline{HF}$

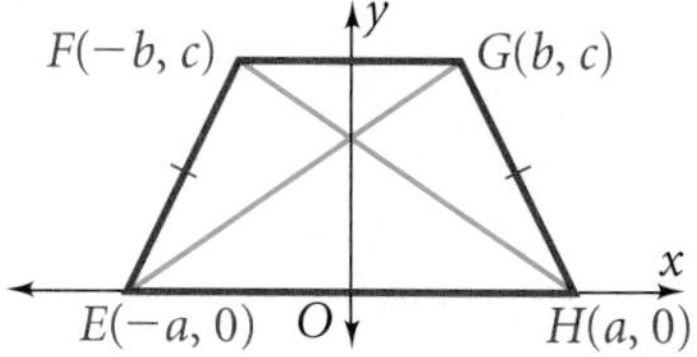

Plan: The trapezoid is isosceles, so place one base on the x-axis so that the **a.** __?__ bisects its bases. To show the diagonals are congruent, use the **b.** __?__ Formula.

4. The median to the hypotenuse of a right triangle is half the hypotenuse.

Given: $\triangle MNO$ is a right triangle with right $\angle MON$. P is the midpoint of $\overline{MN}$.

Prove: $OP = \frac{1}{2}MN$

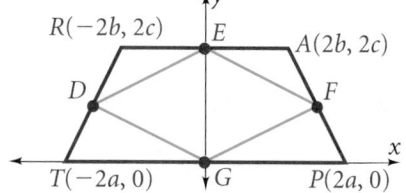

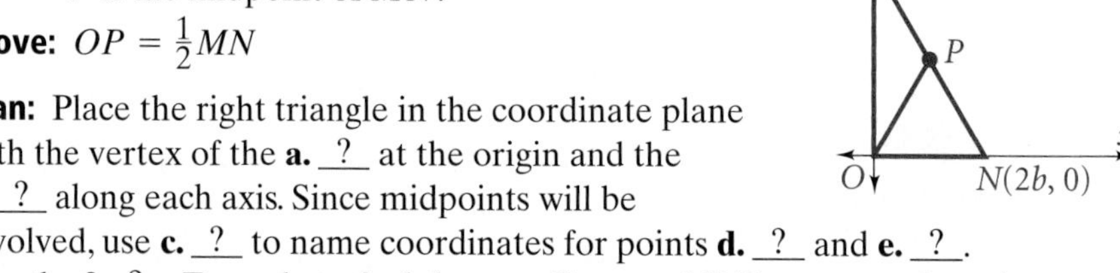

Plan: Place the right triangle in the coordinate plane with the vertex of the **a.** __?__ at the origin and the **b.** __?__ along each axis. Since midpoints will be involved, use **c.** __?__ to name coordinates for points **d.** __?__ and **e.** __?__. Use the **f.** __?__ Formula to find the coordinates of P. To compare lengths, use the **g.** __?__ Formula.

5. The segments joining the midpoints of consecutive sides of an isosceles trapezoid form a rhombus.

Given: Trapezoid $TRAP$ with $\overline{TR} \cong \overline{PA}$; D, E, F, and G are midpoints of the indicated sides.

Prove: $DEFG$ is a rhombus.

Plan: The trapezoid is **a.** __?__, so place one base on the **b.** __?__ so that the **c.** __?__ bisects its bases. Use multiples of 2 to name coordinates since **d.** __?__ will be involved. A rhombus is a parallelogram with four **e.** __?__. To show opposite sides are parallel, show that their **f.** __?__ are the same. To show sides are congruent, use **g.** __?__.

Example 2 (page 333)

Developing Proof **Follow the plans above to complete the coordinate proofs.**

6. (Exercise 3) The diagonals of an isosceles trapezoid are congruent.

Proof: By the Distance Formula, EG = **a.** __?__ and HF = **b.** __?__. Therefore, $\overline{EG} \cong \overline{HF}$ by the definition of congruence.

7. (Exercise 4) The median from the vertex of the right angle of a right triangle is half as long as the hypotenuse.

Proof: By the Distance Formula, OP = **a.** __?__ and MN = **b.** __?__. Therefore, $OP = \frac{1}{2}MN$.

8. (Exercise 5) The segments joining the midpoints of consecutive sides of an isosceles trapezoid form a rhombus.

Proof: The midpoints have coordinates **a.** $D(\underline{?}, \underline{?})$, $E(\underline{?}, \underline{?})$, $F(\underline{?}, \underline{?})$, and $G(\underline{?}, \underline{?})$. By the Distance Formula, $DE =$ **b.** ___?___, $EF =$ **c.** ___?___, $FG =$ **d.** ___?___, and $GD =$ **e.** ___?___. The slope of $DE =$ **f.** ___?___ and the slope of $FG =$ **g.** ___?___. The slope of $EF =$ **h.** ___?___ and that of $GD =$ **i.** ___?___. Thus, $DEFG$ is a parallelogram with congruent **j.** ___?___, so **k.** ___?___ is a rhombus by the definition of rhombus.

9. Use coordinate geometry to prove that the diagonals in the rectangular flag bisect each other (Theorem 6-3).

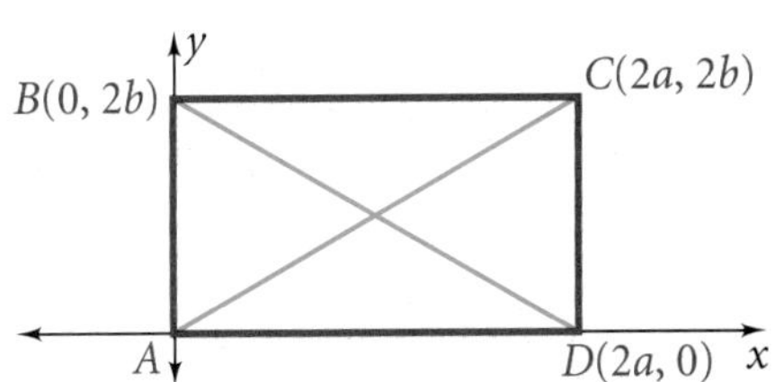

Proof: The midpoint of $\overline{AC}$ is **a.** ___?___. The midpoint of $\overline{BD}$ is **b.** ___?___. The midpoints are **c.** ___?___, so the diagonals bisect each other.

B Apply Your Skills

10. Open-Ended Give an example of a statement that you think is easier to prove with a coordinate geometry proof than with a paragraph, flow, or two-column proof. Explain your choice.

11. Developing Proof Complete the coordinate proof.

The midpoints of the sides of a kite determine a rectangle.

Given: Kite $DEFG$ with $DE = EF$ and $DG = GF$; K, L, M, and N are midpoints of the sides.

Prove: $KLMN$ is a rectangle.

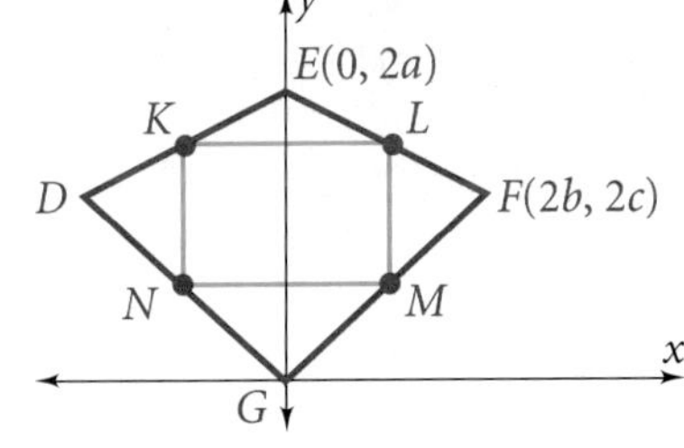

Proof: The kite has two pairs of **a.** ___?___ sides, so place congruent sides opposite each other across the y-axis. Use multiples of 2 to name coordinates since **b.** ___?___ are involved. Name E as $(0, 2a)$. Name F as $(2b, 2c)$. Then, in terms of b and c, D must be **c.** ___?___. By the Midpoint Formula, the midpoints are **d.** $L(\underline{?}, \underline{?})$, $M(\underline{?}, \underline{?})$, $N(\underline{?}, \underline{?})$, and $K(\underline{?}, \underline{?})$. Slopes for $\overline{KL}$ and $\overline{NM}$ are **e.** ___?___, so $\overline{KL}$ and $\overline{NM}$ are parallel. Slopes for $\overline{KN}$ and $\overline{LM}$ are undefined, so $\overline{KN}$ and $\overline{LM}$ are **f.** ___?___. Thus, opposite sides are **g.** ___?___ and consecutive sides are **h.** ___?___, so $KLMN$ is a rectangle.

Need Help?

Lines with undefined slope are vertical lines. All vertical lines are parallel.

State whether each type of conclusion shown here could be reached using coordinate methods. Give a reason for each answer.

12. $\overline{AB} \cong \overline{CD}$

13. $\overline{AB} \parallel \overline{CD}$

14. $\overline{AB} \perp \overline{CD}$

15. $\overline{AB}$ bisects $\overline{CD}$.

16. $\overline{AB}$ bisects $\angle CAD$.

17. $\angle A \cong \angle B$

18. $\angle A$ is a right angle.

19. $AB + BC = AC$

20. $\triangle ABC$ is isosceles.

21. $\angle A$ and $\angle B$ are supplementary.

22. $\overline{AB}$, $\overline{CD}$, and $\overline{EF}$ are concurrent.

23. A, B, and C are collinear.

24. Quadrilateral $ABCD$ is a rhombus.

A and B have coordinates -2 and 10 on a number line. Find the coordinates of the points that separate $\overline{AB}$ into the given number of congruent segments.

25. 4 **26.** 6 **27.** 10 **28.** 50 **29.** n

The endpoints of $\overline{AB}$ are $A(-3, 5)$ and $B(9, 15)$. Find the coordinates of the points that separate $\overline{AB}$ into the given number of congruent segments.

30. 4 **31.** 6 **32.** 10 **33.** 50 **34.** n

Challenge

The endpoints of $\overline{AB}$ are as given. Find the coordinates of the points that separate $\overline{AB}$ into n congruent segments.

35. A has coordinate a and B has coordinate b on a number line.

36. A has coordinates (a, c) and B has coordinates (b, d) in the coordinate plane.

37. Use the diagram at the right.

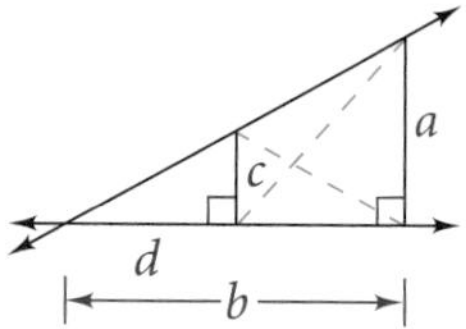

a. Explain using area why $\frac{1}{2}ad = \frac{1}{2}bc$ and hence $ad = bc$. (*Hint*: Area of triangle $= \frac{1}{2} \cdot$ base $\cdot$ height)

b. Use slope and part (a) to show: If $\frac{a}{b} = \frac{c}{d}$, then $ad = bc$.

Real-World Connection

Carefully balanced metal shapes hang from wires in the mobiles of Alexander Calder (1898–1976).

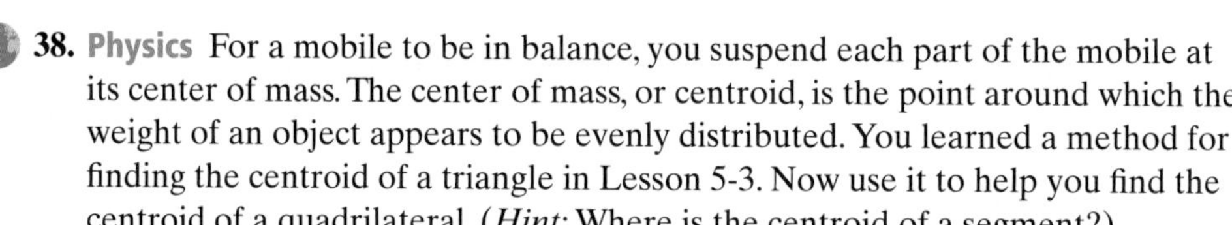

38. Physics For a mobile to be in balance, you suspend each part of the mobile at its center of mass. The center of mass, or centroid, is the point around which the weight of an object appears to be evenly distributed. You learned a method for finding the centroid of a triangle in Lesson 5-3. Now use it to help you find the centroid of a quadrilateral. (*Hint:* Where is the centroid of a segment?)

Proof **39.** You learned in Lesson 5-3 (Theorem 5-8) that the centroid of a triangle, the point where the medians meet, is $\frac{2}{3}$ of the distance from each vertex to the midpoint of the opposite side. Complete the following steps to prove this theorem.

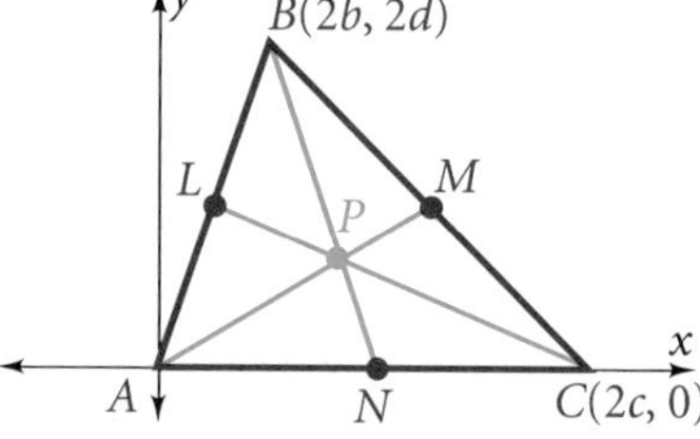

a. Find the coordinates of points L, M, and N, the midpoints of the sides of $\triangle ABC$.

b. Find equations of $\overleftrightarrow{AM}$, $\overleftrightarrow{BN}$, and $\overleftrightarrow{CL}$.

c. Find the coordinates of point P, the intersection of $\overleftrightarrow{AM}$ and $\overleftrightarrow{BN}$.

d. Show that point P is on $\overleftrightarrow{CL}$.

e. Use the Distance Formula to show that point P is $\frac{2}{3}$ of the distance from each vertex to the midpoint of the opposite side.

Need Help?

To show three lines are concurrent, you can show

1) one point is on all three lines
2) the intersection point of two lines is on the third line, or
3) the intersection of one pair of lines is the same as the intersection of another pair.

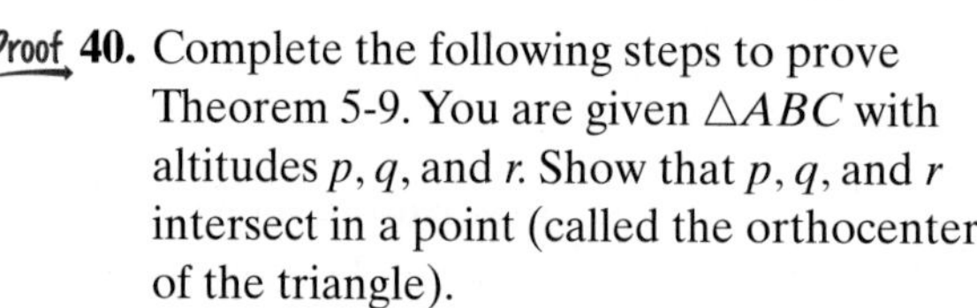

Proof **40.** Complete the following steps to prove Theorem 5-9. You are given $\triangle ABC$ with altitudes p, q, and r. Show that p, q, and r intersect in a point (called the orthocenter of the triangle).

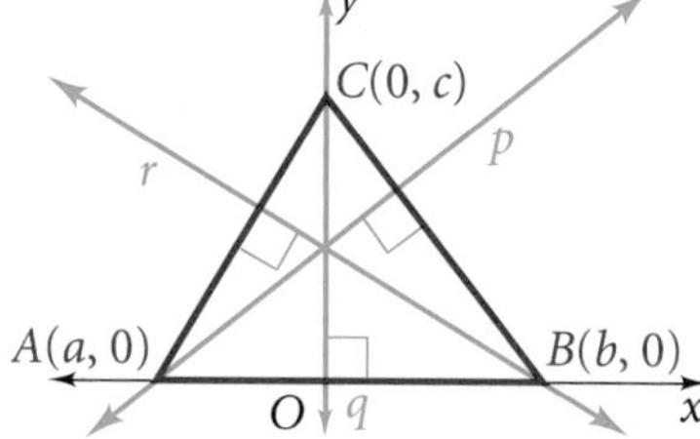

a. The slope of $\overline{BC}$ is $\frac{c}{-b}$. What is the slope of line p?

b. Show that the equation of line p is $y = \frac{b}{c}(x - a)$.

c. What is the equation of line q?

d. Show that lines p and q intersect at $\left(0, \frac{-ab}{c}\right)$.

e. The slope of $\overline{AC}$ is $\frac{c}{-a}$. What is the slope of line r?

f. Show that the equation of line r is $y = \frac{a}{c}(x - b)$.

g. Show that lines r and q intersect at $\left(0, \frac{-ab}{c}\right)$.

h. Give the coordinates of the orthocenter of $\triangle ABC$.

Proof **41.** Write a coordinate proof of the theorem:

If the slopes of two lines have product -1, the lines are perpendicular.

a. First, argue that neither line can be horizontal or vertical.
b. Then, tell why the lines must intersect. (*Hint:* Use indirect reasoning.)
c. Knowing that they do intersect, place the lines in the coordinate plane, choose a point on ℓ_1, find a related point on ℓ_2, and complete the proof.

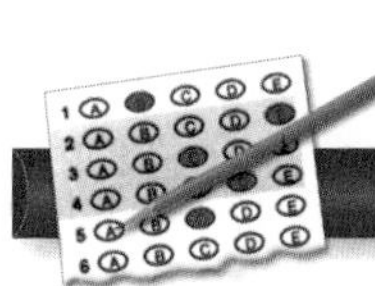

Standardized Test Prep

Multiple Choice

42. Two points on a line are $(-7, 10)$ and $(9, 2)$. Two points on a line parallel to that line are $(1, -3)$ and $(x, 4)$. What is the value of x?

A. -13 **B.** 13 **C.** 15 **D.** -15

43. Two points on a line are $(-4, 0)$ and $(8, 8)$. Two points on a line perpendicular to that line are $(8, -1)$ and $(6, y)$. What is the value of y?

F. 3 **G.** 2 **H.** $-\frac{7}{3}$ **I.** -4

Short Response

44. The endpoints of a segment are $(7, -3)$ and (a, b). The midpoint is $(3, 4)$.
a. What are the coordinates of the other endpoint? Show your work.
b. What is the length of the segment? Show your work.

Extended Response

45. Given: $\triangle ABC$; P, Q, and R are the midpoints of $\overline{AB}$, $\overline{AC}$, and $\overline{BC}$, respectively.
a. Place $\triangle ABC$ in the coordinate plane by writing coordinates for A, B, and C.
b. What are the coordinates of P, Q, and R?
c. Use coordinate geometry to prove $\triangle APQ \cong \triangle RQP$ by SSS.

Take It to the NET
Online lesson quiz at **www.PHSchool.com**
Web Code: afa-0607

Mixed Review

Lesson 6-6

46. Rectangle $LMNP$ at the right is centered at the origin. Give coordinates for point P without using any new variables.

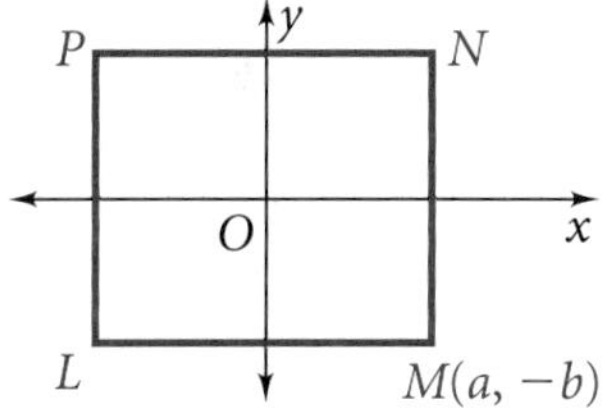

Lesson 5-4

Write (a) the inverse and (b) the contrapositive of each statement.

47. If the sum of the angles of a polygon is not 360°, then the polygon is not a quadrilateral.

48. If $x = 51$, then $2x = 102$.

49. If $a = 5$, then $a^2 = 25$.

50. If $b < -4$, then b is negative.

51. If $c > 0$, then c is positive.

Lesson 4-4

Explain how you can use SSS, SAS, ASA, or AAS with CPCTC to prove each statement true.

52. $\overline{AB} \cong \overline{CB}$

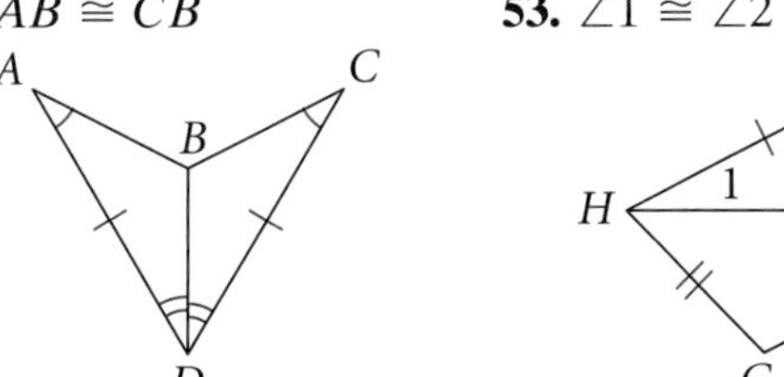

53. $\angle 1 \cong \angle 2$

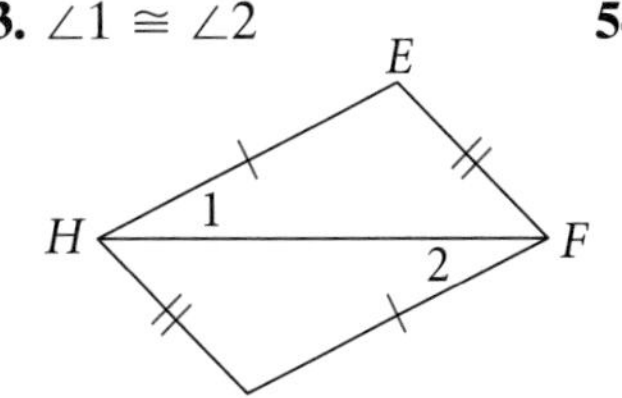

54. $\angle K \cong \angle M$

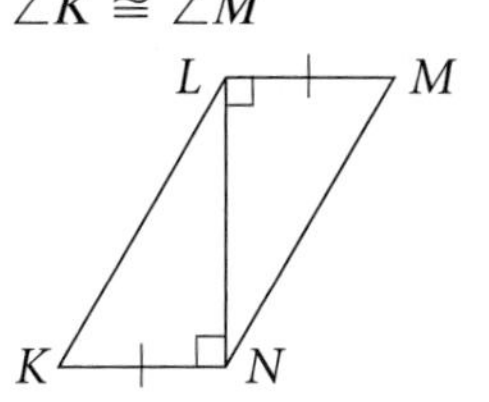

Test-Taking Strategies

Drawing a Diagram

Sometimes, if a problem does not have a diagram, you should draw one. A diagram helps you to see the given information so that you can use the information to make inferences.

1 EXAMPLE

Side $\overline{AB}$ of square $ABCD$ has endpoints $A(0, 0)$ and $B(5, 2)$. What are the possible locations of point C?

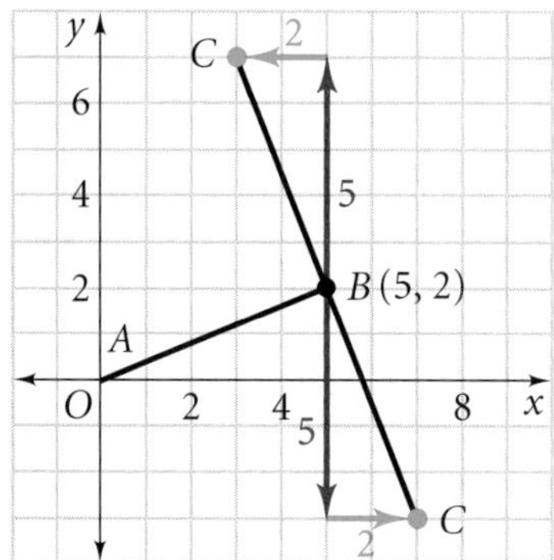

You need to draw a diagram to do this problem. Point C can be in two different locations.

First draw the segment $\overline{AB}$, and then begin the two possible squares that have $\overline{AB}$ as a side. To locate C from B you can either go up 5 units and left 2 units, or you can go down 5 units and right 2 units. The coordinates of point C can be either $(3, 7)$ or $(7, -3)$.

2 EXAMPLE

The midpoints of the sides of a rhombus are joined to form a quadrilateral. What special quadrilateral is formed? Explain.

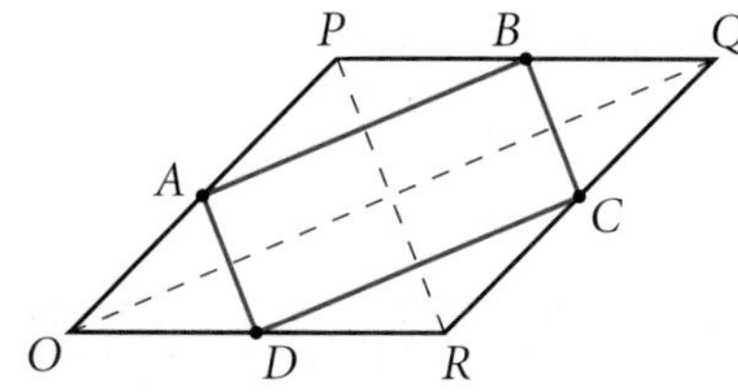

Draw a rhombus and join the midpoints of the sides. The midpoint quadrilateral is a parallelogram since both pairs of sides are parallel to a diagonal of the rhombus. The diagonals of the rhombus are perpendicular, so adjacent sides of the parallelogram are perpendicular to each other.

The quadrilateral formed is a rectangle.

EXERCISES

Draw a diagram to help you answer each question.

1. Angie says that if the diagonals of a quadrilateral are perpendicular, then the quadrilateral is a kite or a rhombus. Provide a counterexample to Angie's claim by sketching a quadrilateral with perpendicular diagonals that is neither a rhombus nor a kite.
2. Three vertices of parallelogram $ABCD$ are $A(0, 0)$, $B(5, 2)$, and $C(8, 5)$. What are the possible locations of point D?
3. Three vertices of a parallelogram are $(0, 0)$, $(5, 2)$ and $(8, 5)$. What are the possible locations of the fourth vertex?
4. The diagonal $\overline{AC}$ of square $ABCD$ has endpoints $A(0, 0)$ and $C(6, 4)$. What are the coordinates of the other two vertices of the square?
5. The midpoints of the sides of an isosceles trapezoid are joined to form a quadrilateral. What special quadrilateral is formed? Explain.

Chapter Review

Vocabulary

base angles of a trapezoid (p. 320)
consecutive angles (p. 294)
isosceles trapezoid (p. 288)
kite (p. 288)
midsegment of a trapezoid (p. 332)
parallelogram (p. 288)
rectangle (p. 288)
rhombus (p. 288)
square (p. 288)
trapezoid (p. 288)

Reading Math
Understanding Vocabulary

To complete each definition, find the appropriate word in the second column.

1. A(n) __?__ is a parallelogram with four right angles.
2. A(n) __?__ is a quadrilateral with two pairs of adjacent sides congruent and no opposite sides congruent.
3. Angles of a polygon that share a common side are __?__.
4. A(n) __?__ is a quadrilateral with exactly one pair of parallel sides.
5. A(n) __?__ is a parallelogram with four congruent sides.
6. The __?__ of a trapezoid is the segment that joins the midpoints of the nonparallel opposite sides.
7. A(n) __?__ is a quadrilateral with both pairs of opposite sides parallel.
8. A(n) __?__ is a parallelogram with four congruent sides and four right angles.
9. A(n) __?__ is a trapezoid whose nonparallel opposite sides are congruent.
10. Two angles that share a base of a trapezoid are its __?__.

A. parallelogram
B. trapezoid
C. square
D. base angles
E. isosceles trapezoid
F. rectangle
G. consecutive angles
H. kite
I. rhombus
J. midsegment

Take It to the NET
Online vocabulary quiz at **www.PHSchool.com**
Web Code: afj-0651

Skills and Concepts

6-1 Objective

▼ To define and classify special types of quadrilaterals

Special quadrilaterals are defined by their characteristics.

A **parallelogram** is a quadrilateral with both pairs of opposite sides parallel.
A **rhombus** is a parallelogram with four congruent sides.
A **rectangle** is a parallelogram with four right angles.
A **square** is a parallelogram with four congruent sides and four right angles.
A **kite** is a quadrilateral with two pairs of adjacent sides congruent and no opposite sides congruent.
A **trapezoid** is a quadrilateral with exactly one pair of parallel sides.
An **isosceles trapezoid** is a trapezoid whose nonparallel opposite sides are congruent.

Draw and label each quadrilateral with the given vertices. Then determine the most precise name for each quadrilateral.

11. $N(-1, 2), M(3, 4), L(1, -2), K(5, 0)$
12. $P(-4, 2), Q(-1, 3), R(7, 0), S(4, -1)$

Algebra **Find the values of the variables and the lengths of the sides.**

13. isosceles trapezoid $ABCD$

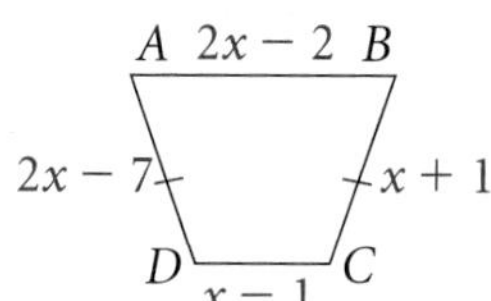

14. kite $KLMN$

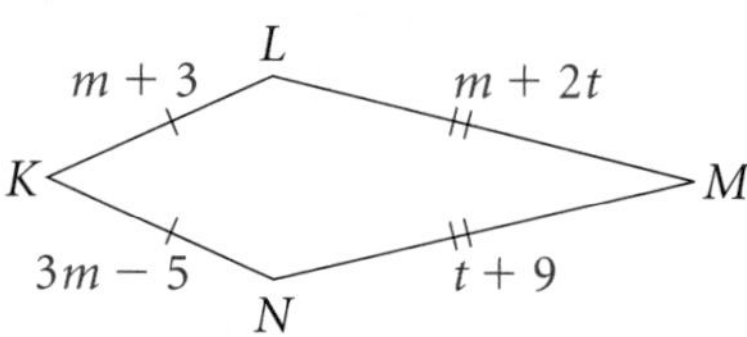

6-2 and 6-3 Objectives

- To use relationships among sides and among angles of parallelograms
- To use relationships involving diagonals of parallelograms or transversals
- To determine whether a quadrilateral is a parallelogram

Opposite sides and opposite angles of a parallelogram are congruent. The diagonals of a parallelogram bisect each other.

If three (or more) parallel lines cut off congruent segments on one transversal, then they cut off congruent segments on every transversal.

A quadrilateral is a parallelogram if any one of the following is true.
The diagonals bisect each other.
One pair of opposite sides is both congruent and parallel.
Both pairs of opposite sides are congruent.
Both pairs of opposite angles are congruent.

Find the measures of the numbered angles for each parallelogram.

15.

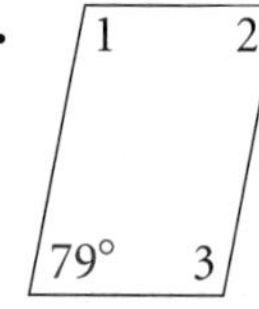

16.

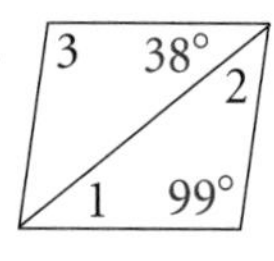

17.

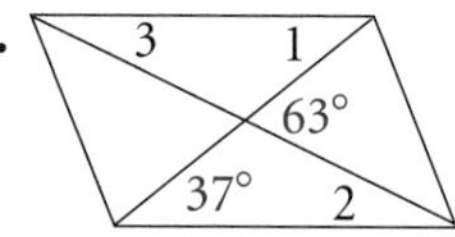

Determine whether the quadrilateral must be a parallelogram.

18.

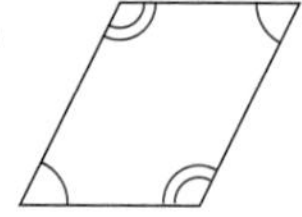

19.

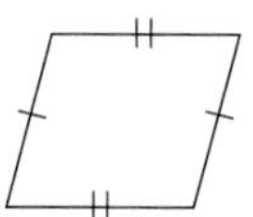

20.

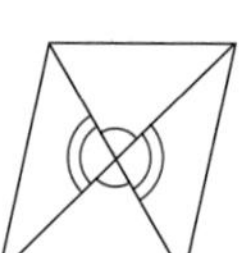

21.

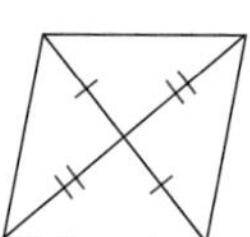

Algebra **Find the values of the variables for which *ABCD* must be a parallelogram.**

22.

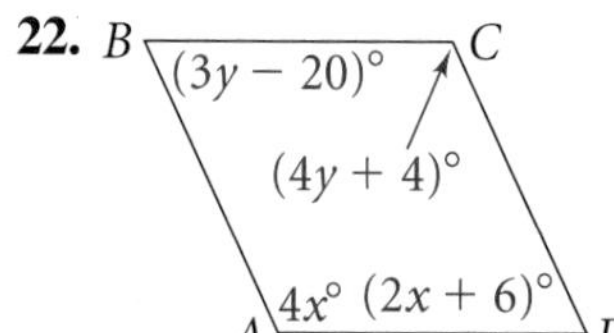

23.

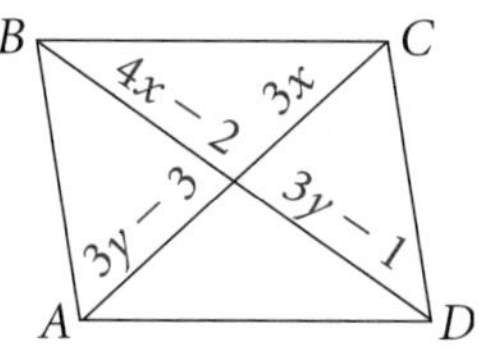

6-4 and 6-5 Objectives

- To use properties of diagonals of rhombuses and rectangles
- To determine whether a parallelogram is a rhombus or a rectangle
- To verify and use properties of trapezoids and kites

Each diagonal of a rhombus bisects two angles of the rhombus. The diagonals of a rhombus are perpendicular.

The diagonals of a rectangle are congruent.

If one diagonal of a parallelogram bisects two angles of the parallelogram, then the parallelogram is a rhombus. If the diagonals of a parallelogram are perpendicular, then the parallelogram is a rhombus. If the diagonals of a parallelogram are congruent, then the parallelogram is a rectangle.

The parallel sides of a trapezoid are its bases and the nonparallel sides are its legs. Two angles that share a base of a trapezoid are **base angles** of the trapezoid.

The base angles of an isosceles trapezoid are congruent. The diagonals of an isosceles trapezoid are congruent.

The diagonals of a kite are perpendicular.

Find the measures of the numbered angles in each quadrilateral.

24. 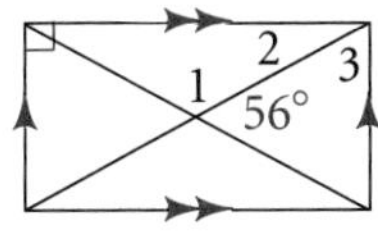

25. 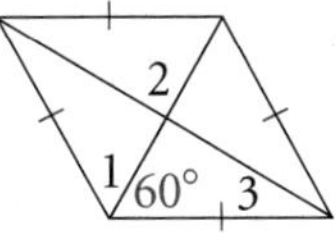

26. 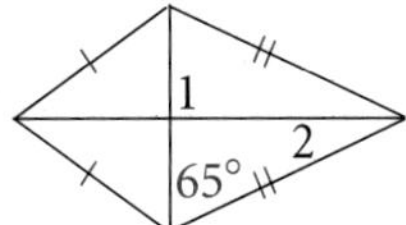

Find AC for each quadrilateral.

27. 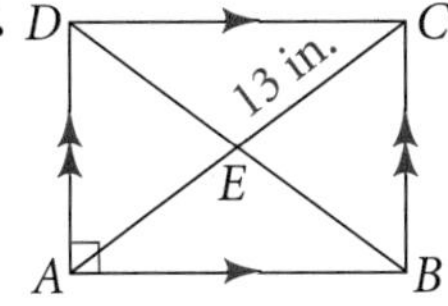

28. 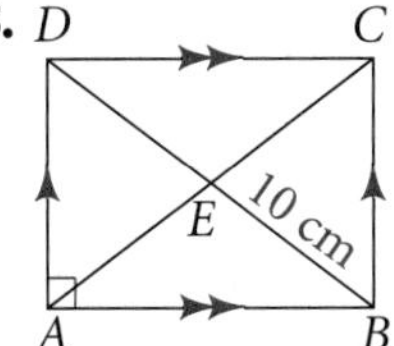

29. 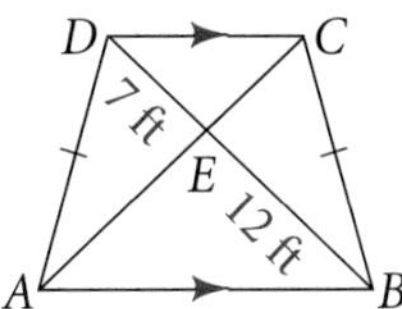

6-6 and 6-7 Objectives

- To name coordinates of special figures by using their properties
- To prove theorems using figures in the coordinate plane

In coordinate proofs, it generally is good practice to center the figure on the origin or place a vertex at the origin and one side of the figure on an axis.

The segment that joins the midpoints of the nonparallel sides of a trapezoid is the **midsegment** of the trapezoid. It is parallel to the bases and half as long as the sum of the lengths of the bases.

The formulas for slope, midpoint, and distance are used in coordinate proofs.

Give the coordinates of point P without using any new variable.

30. rectangle

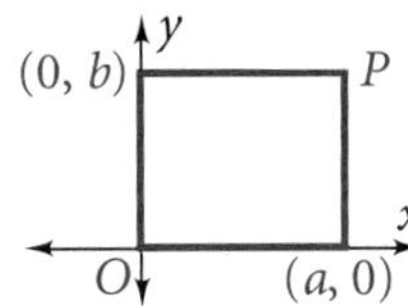

31. square

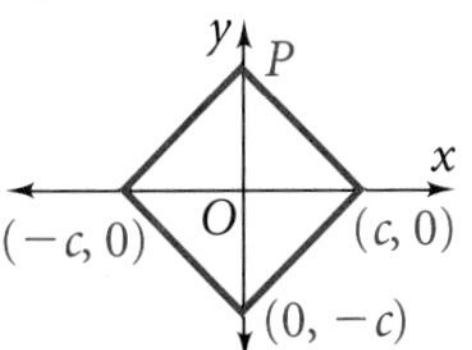

32. parallelogram

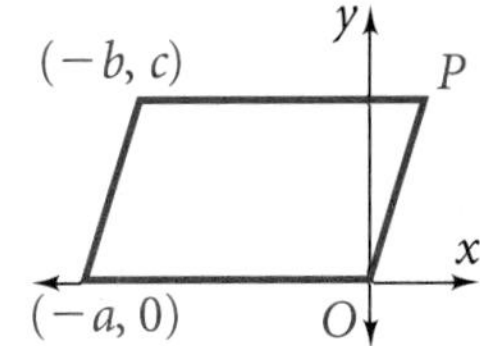

Complete each coordinate proof.

33. The diagonals of a square are perpendicular.

Given: Square $FGHI$ with vertices $I(0, 0)$, $H(a, 0)$, $G(a, a)$, and $F(0, a)$

Prove: $\overline{FH} \perp \overline{GI}$

The slope of $\overline{FH}$ is **a.** _?_. The slope of $\overline{GI}$ is **b.** _?_. $\overline{FH} \perp \overline{GI}$ because **c.** _?_.

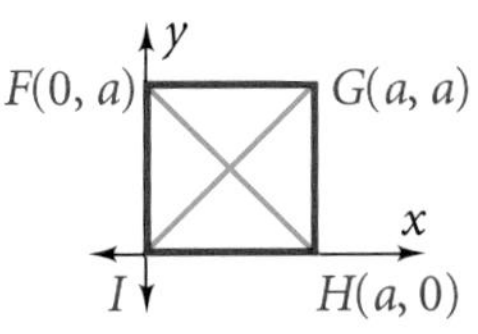

34. The diagonals of a rectangle are congruent.

Given: Rectangle $ABCD$

Prove: $\overline{AC} \cong \overline{BD}$

Vertex A is at the origin with coordinates $(0, 0)$. Name B as $(a, 0)$, C as (**a.** _?_, b), and D as **b.** _?_. AC = **c.** _?_ and BD = **d.** _?_. So, AC = **e.** _?_, and $\overline{AC} \cong \overline{BD}$.

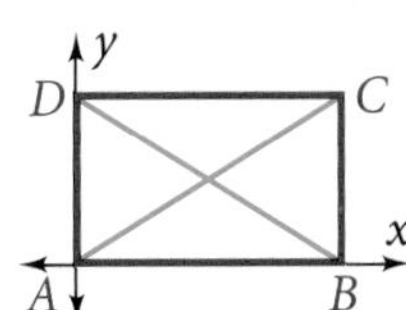

Chapter Test

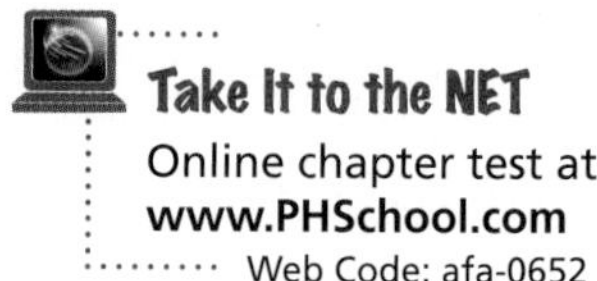

Take It to the NET
Online chapter test at
www.PHSchool.com
Web Code: afa-0652

Graph each quadrilateral *ABCD*. Then determine the most precise name for it.

1. $A(1, 2), B(11, 2), C(7, 5), D(4, 5)$
2. $A(3, -2), B(5, 4), C(3, 6), D(1, 4)$
3. $A(1, -4), B(1, 1), C(-2, 2), D(-2, -3)$

4. **Open-Ended** Write the coordinates of four points that determine each figure with the given conditions. One vertex is at the origin and one side is 3 units long.
   a. square **b.** parallelogram
   c. rectangle **d.** trapezoid

Find *AN* for each parallelogram.

5. 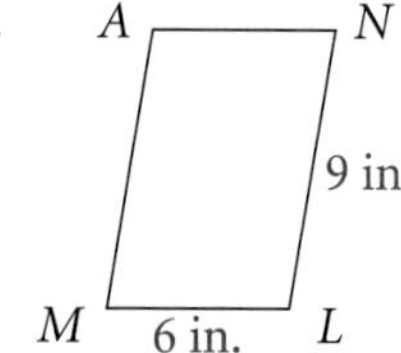

6. 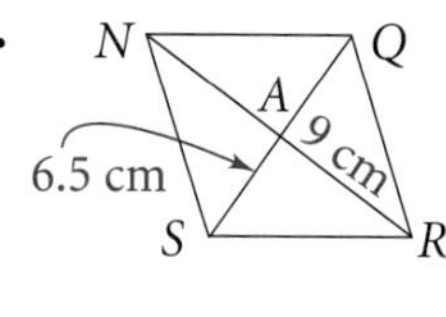

7. Sketch two noncongruent parallelograms $ABCD$ and $EFGH$ such that $\overline{AC} \cong \overline{BD} \cong \overline{EG} \cong \overline{FH}$.

 **Algebra Find the values of the variables for each parallelogram.**

8.  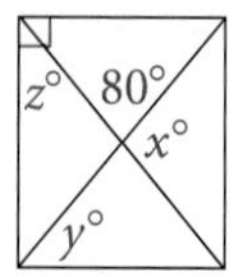

9. 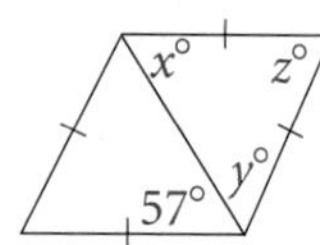

10. 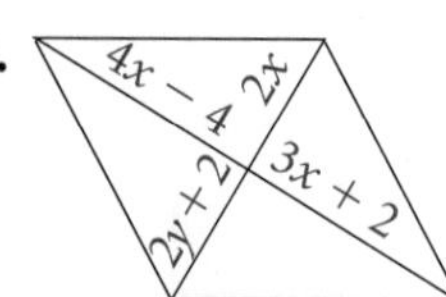

11. 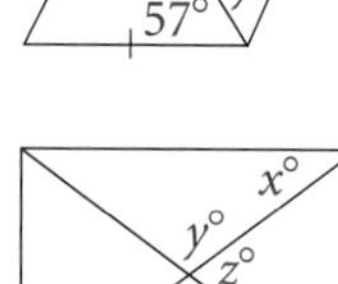

Does the information allow you to prove that *ABCD* is a parallelogram? Explain.

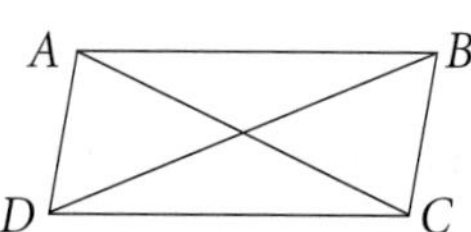

12. $\overline{AC}$ bisects $\overline{BD}$.
13. $\overline{AB} \cong \overline{DC}$; $\overline{AB} \parallel \overline{DC}$
14. $\overline{AB} \cong \overline{DC}$; $\overline{BC} \cong \overline{AD}$
15. $\angle DAB \cong \angle BCD$ and $\angle ABC \cong \angle CDA$

16. **Writing** Explain why a square cannot be a kite.

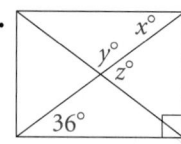

17. **Algebra** Determine the values of the variables for which $ABCD$ is a parallelogram.

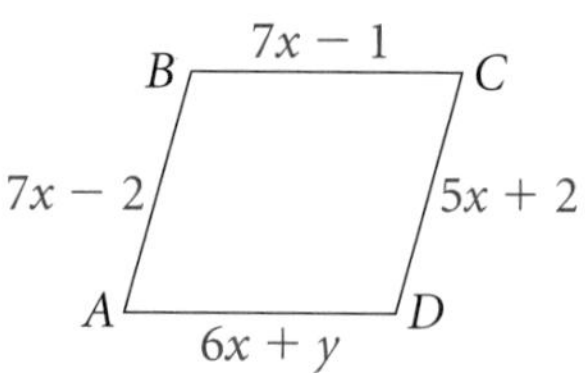

Find the measures of ∠1 and ∠2.

18. 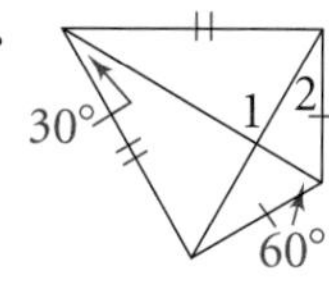

19. 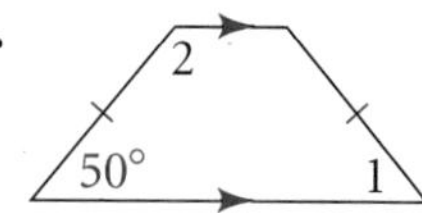

Give the coordinates for points *S* and *T* without using any new variables. Then find the midpoint and the slope of $\overline{ST}$.

20. rectangle

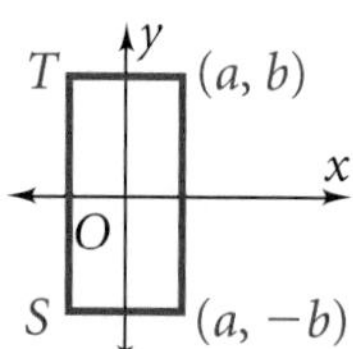

21. parallelogram

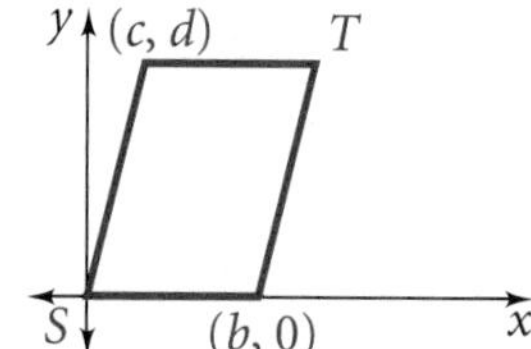

22. You want a garden border halfway between the front of your house and the city sidewalk, which are parallel to each other. You've measured those two edges. Find the length of the garden border.

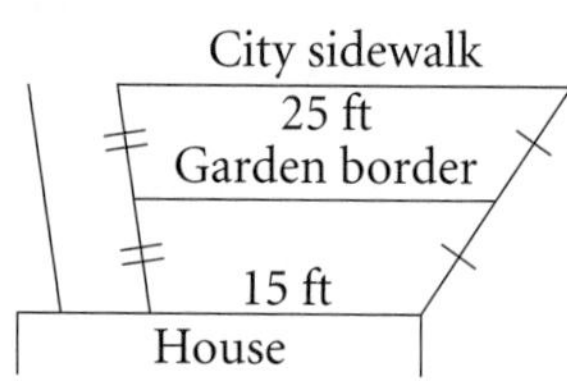

23. Complete this coordinate proof that the diagonals of a square are congruent.

Given: Square $ABCD$ with vertices $A(0, 0)$, $B(a, 0)$, $C(a, a)$, and $D(0, a)$

Prove: $\overline{AC} \cong \overline{BD}$

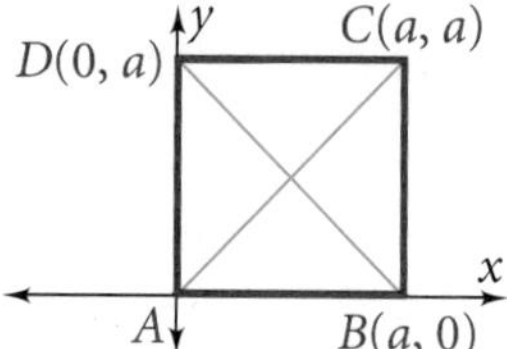

$AC =$ **a.** _?_, and $BD =$ **b.** _?_. So, **c.** _?_ $= BD$ and $\overline{AC} \cong \overline{BD}$.

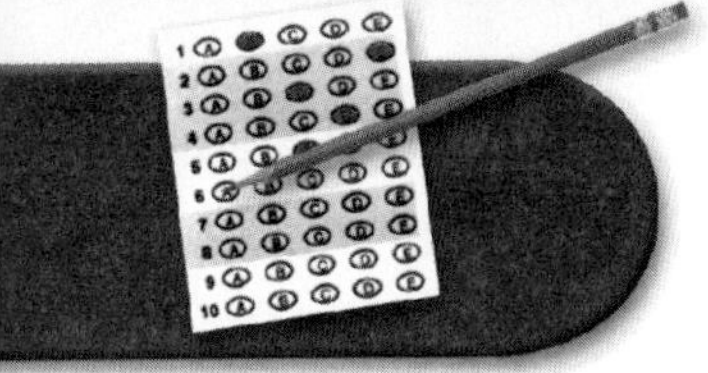

Standardized Test Prep

Multiple Choice

For Exercises 1–6, choose the correct letter.

1. What is a name for the quadrilateral below?

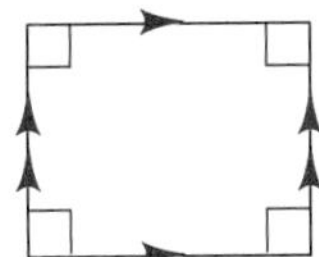

I. square
II. rectangle
III. rhombus
IV. parallelogram

A. I only **B.** IV only
C. II and IV **D.** I, II, and IV

2. An isosceles triangle has two angles measuring 48 and 84. What is the measure of the third angle?
F. 84 **G.** 51 **H.** 49 **I.** 48

3. $\overline{DE}$ is a midsegment of $\triangle ABC$. What is DE?

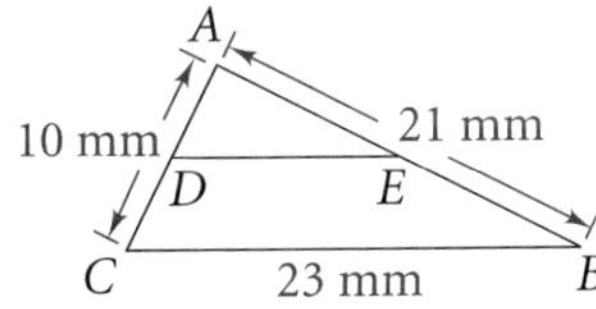

A. 11.5 mm **B.** 11 mm
C. 10.5 mm **D.** 10 mm

4. Which can you use to prove that two lines are parallel?
F. supplementary corresponding angles
G. congruent alternate interior angles
H. congruent vertical angles
I. congruent same-side interior angles

5. How can you prove that the two triangles are congruent?

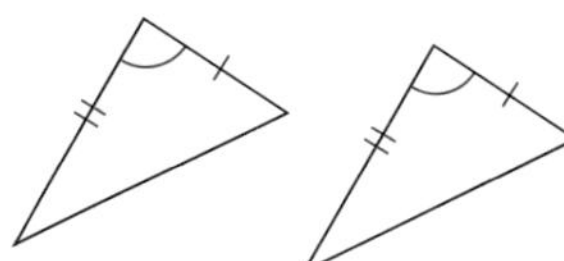

A. ASA **B.** SSS **C.** SAS **D.** CPCTC

6. What is the measure of $\angle MOQ$?

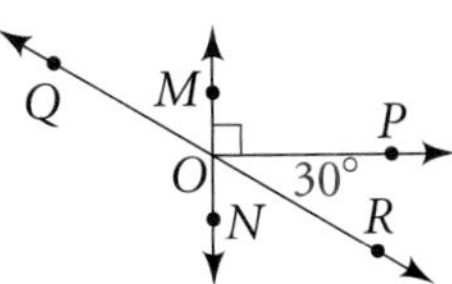

F. 15 **G.** 30 **H.** 45 **I.** 60

Quantitative Comparison

Compare the boxed quantity in Column A with the boxed quantity in Column B. Choose the best answer.

A. The quantity in Column A is greater.
B. The quantity in Column B is greater.
C. The two quantities are equal.
D. The relationship cannot be determined from the information given.

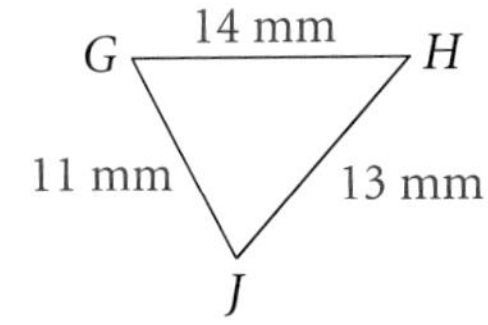

	Column A	Column B
7.	$m\angle G$	$m\angle H$
8.	$m\angle G$	 $m\angle J$
9.	$m\angle H$	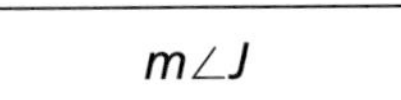 $m\angle J$

Gridded Response

10. In the parallelogram, DB is 15. What is DE?

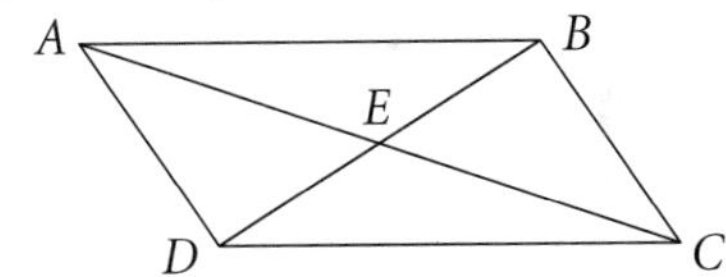

11. **Algebra** What is the value of x?

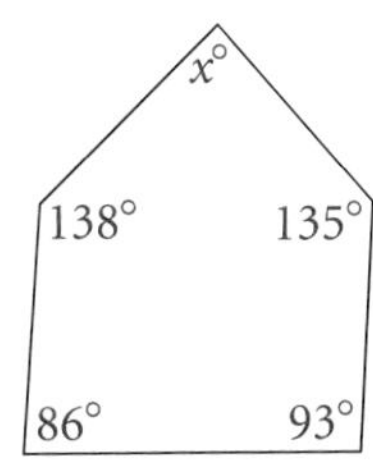

Short Response

12. In rectangle $ABCD$, $AC = 5(x - 2)$ and $BD = 3(x + 2)$. What is the value of x?

Extended Response

13. A parallelogram has vertices $L(-2, 5)$, $M(3, 3)$, $N(1, 0)$. What are possible coordinates for its fourth vertex? Explain.

Real-World Snapshots

Point of Balance

Applying Theorems About Polygons For an object to spin smoothly, its weight must be evenly distributed around its central axis. A toy top, an ice skater, and a carousel all spin around a central axis. If the spin goes slightly out of alignment, the spinning object begins to wobble and may eventually tip over.

Gyroscopes

A gyroscope is a wheel mounted in a set of rings so that the axis of the wheel can turn in any direction. When the wheel spins rapidly, a small gyroscope becomes so stable that it can balance on the tip of a pencil.

Amusing Rides

Carousels were traditionally used to train young princes in tournament riding. The more skilled the rider, the more likely he was to spear one or more of the small gold rings that hung along the outer edge. It seemed like so much fun that eventually the rest of the population wanted to ride the carousel.

The Spin

Figure skaters at the Olympic Games compete in a short program (33.3% of the total score) and a long program (66.7%). A short program can last a maximum of 2 min 40 s and must include three spins.

The Bicycle as a Gyroscope

The spinning wheels of a bicycle act as gyroscopes and help to keep the bike upright. Like all gyroscopes, the wheels tend to remain spinning in the same plane, giving the bicycle stability.

Earth as a Gyroscope

The axis of Earth is remarkably stable, but our planet does wobble slightly. It takes 25,800 years for each circular wobble. This wobble is largely caused by the gravitational pull of the sun and moon on Earth's equatorial bulge.

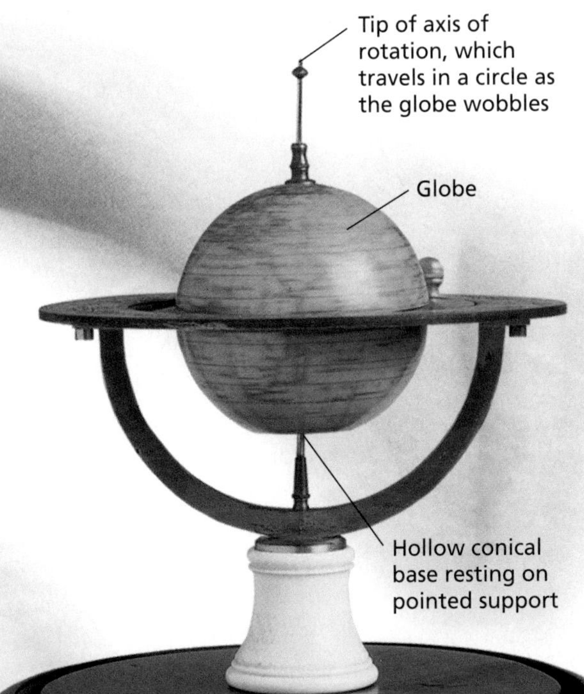

Activity

Materials: cardboard, straightedge, scissors, compass, graph paper, pencil

Draw a large triangle on the cardboard. Construct its medians. Locate the centroid, the point at which the medians meet. Cut out the triangle.

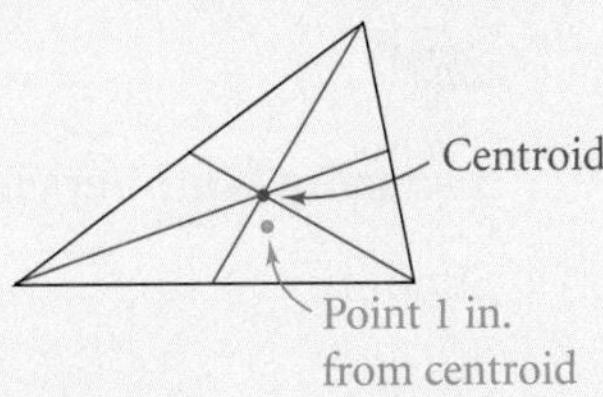

a. Balance your triangle by placing the centroid on the point of your pencil and pushing down slightly to dent the cardboard. Give your triangle a gentle spin and watch it as it moves. Describe the movement.

b. Locate a point 1 in. from the centroid. Support your triangle on your pencil at this point. Give your triangle a gentle spin and watch it as it moves. Describe any differences from its movement in part (a).

c. Suppose the coordinates of the vertices of a triangle are $(0, 0)$, $(16, 0)$, and $(20, 18)$. Find the coordinates of the centroid. Test your work by making a graph of the triangle. Glue the graph to a piece of cardboard and then cut out the triangle. Try to balance the triangle at the coordinates you calculated.

d. Draw a large convex quadrilateral on the cardboard. Locate its centroid. (See page 336, Exercise 38.) Cut out the quadrilateral and test its balance with spins as described in parts (a) and (b). Describe what you find.

Take It to the NET For more information about objects that spin, go to **www.PHSchool.com**.
Web Code: afe-0653

Where You've Been

- In Chapter 1, you learned two postulates about area and how to find the areas of rectangles and circles.
- In Chapters 3 and 6, you learned how to classify polygons, including special quadrilaterals.
- In Chapter 4, you learned conditions necessary for two polygons, particularly triangles, to be congruent.

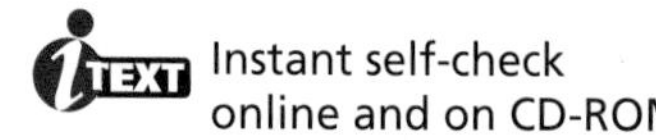

Instant self-check online and on CD-ROM

Diagnosing Readiness

(For help, go to the Lesson in green.)

Squaring Numbers and Finding Square Roots (Skills Handbook page 715)

Simplify.

1. 3^2 **2.** 8^2 **3.** 12^2 **4.** 15^2

5. $\sqrt{16}$ **6.** $\sqrt{64}$ **7.** $\sqrt{100}$ **8.** $\sqrt{169}$

Solve each quadratic equation. Round to the nearest tenth or whole number.

9. $x^2 = 36$ **10.** $a^2 = 104$ **11.** $x^2 - 48 = 0$ **12.** $b^2 - 65 = 0$

Simplifying Radicals (Skills Handbook page 717)

Simplify. Leave your answer in simplest radical form.

13. $\sqrt{8}$ **14.** $\sqrt{27}$ **15.** $\sqrt{48}$ **16.** $6\sqrt{72}$

Probability (Skills Handbook page 724)

A jar contains 3 red balls and 2 green balls. You draw one ball at random. Determine the probability of selecting a ball of the given color.

17. red **18.** green **19.** blue **20.** red or green

Classifying Quadrilaterals (Lesson 6-1)

Classify each quadrilateral as specifically as possible.

21. 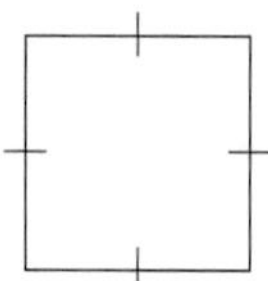

22. 

23. 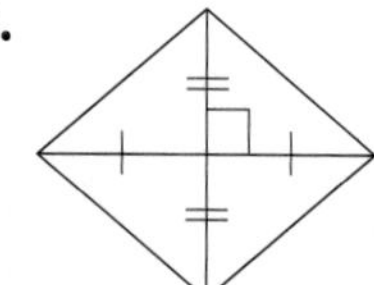

Area

LESSONS

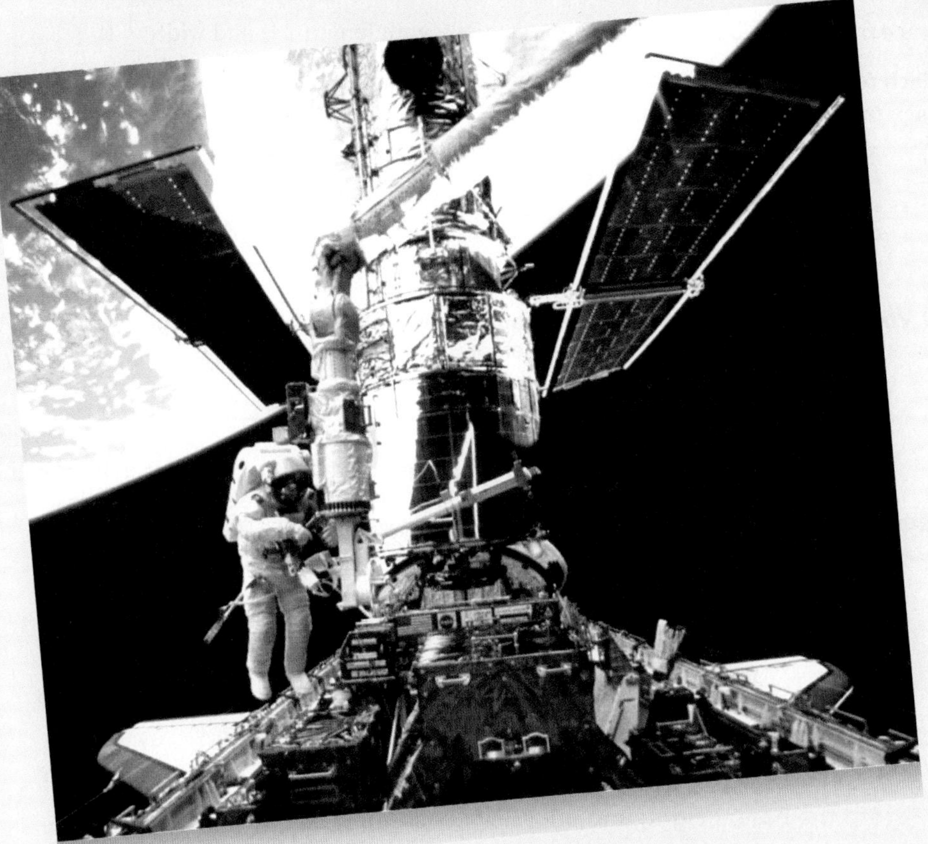

Where You're Going

- In this chapter, you will learn how finding the area of a rectangle can help you find the areas of parallelograms and triangles.
- You will learn the Pythagorean Theorem and its converse.
- You will use the Pythagorean Theorem to find relationships in special right triangles.
- You will also learn how to find the areas of special quadrilaterals and regular polygons.

Real-World Connection Applying what you learned, you will find the distance to Earth's horizon from the Hubble Space Telescope on page 363.

Key Vocabulary

- adjacent arcs (p. 387)
- apothem of a regular polygon (p. 380)
- arc length (p. 389)
- central angle (p. 386)
- circumference (p. 388)
- concentric circles (p. 388)
- congruent arcs (p. 389)
- diameter (p. 386)
- geometric probability (p. 402)
- major arc (p. 387)
- minor arc (p. 387)
- Pythagorean triple (p. 357)
- radius (p. 386)
- radius of a regular polygon (p. 380)
- sector of a circle (p. 396)
- segment of a circle (p. 397)
- semicircle (p. 387)

Areas of Parallelograms and Triangles

Lesson Preview

What You'll Learn

 To find the area of a parallelogram

 To find the area of a triangle

. . . And Why

To find the force of wind against the side of a building, as in Example 5

✓ Check Skills You'll Need

(For help, go to Lesson 1-7.)

Find the area of each figure.

1. a square with 5-cm sides

2. a rectangle with base 4 in. and height 7 in.

3. a 4.6 m-by-2.5 m rectangle

4. a rectangle with length 3 ft and width $\frac{1}{2}$ ft

Each rectangle is divided into two congruent triangles. Find the area of each triangle.

5. 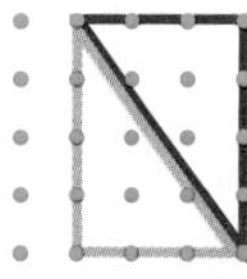

6.

7. 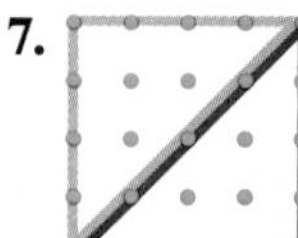

New Vocabulary
- base of a parallelogram
- altitude of a parallelogram
- height of a parallelogram
- base of a triangle
- height of a triangle

 Interactive lesson includes instant self-check, tutorials, and activities.

OBJECTIVE 1 Area of a Parallelogram

Investigation: Area of a Parallelogram

- Cut a rectangle out of centimeter grid paper by cutting along grid lines.
- Record the base, height, and area of the rectangle.
- Cut a right triangle from one end of the rectangle. Tape the triangle to the opposite end to form a parallelogram as shown below.
- Compare the original rectangle with the parallelogram formed. List the ways the rectangle and the parallelogram are the same and the ways they are different.

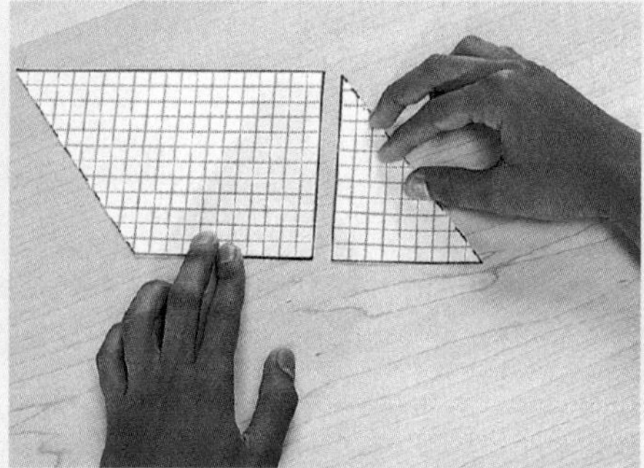

The picture on page 348 shows that a parallelogram with the same base and height as a rectangle has the same area as the rectangle.

Key Concepts

Theorem 7-1 **Area of a Rectangle**

The area of a rectangle is the product of its base and height.

$A = bh$

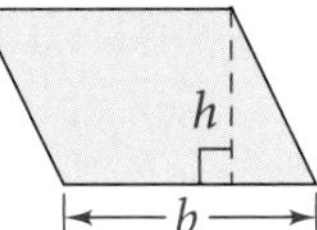

Theorem 7-2 **Area of a Parallelogram**

The area of a parallelogram is the product of a base and the corresponding height.

$A = bh$

Reading Math

The term *base* is used to represent both a segment and its length.

A **base of a parallelogram** is any of its sides. The corresponding **altitude** is a segment perpendicular to the line containing that base drawn from the side opposite the base. The **height** is the length of an altitude.

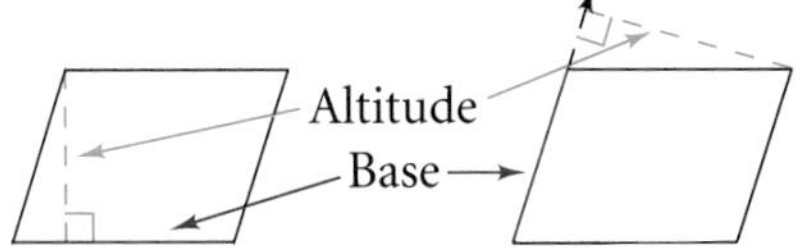

1 EXAMPLE Finding the Area of a Parallelogram

Find the area of each parallelogram.

a.

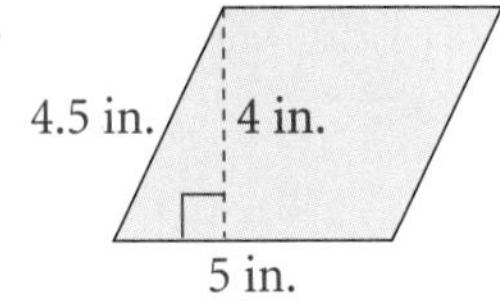

b.

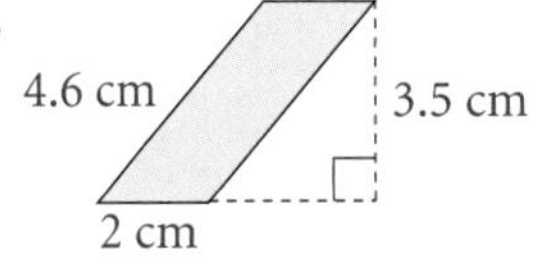

You are given each height. Choose the corresponding side to use as the base.

$A = bh$ | $A = bh$

$= 5(4) = 20$ ←**Substitute.**→ $= 2(3.5) = 7$

The area is 20 in.^{2}. | The area is 7 cm^2.

Check Understanding **1** Find the area of a parallelogram with base 12 m and height 9 m.

2 EXAMPLE Finding Area in the Coordinate Plane

Find the area of $\square PQRS$ with vertices $P(1, 2)$, $Q(6, 2)$, $R(8, 5)$, and $S(3, 5)$.

Graph $\square PQRS$. If you choose $\overline{PQ}$ as the base, then the height is 3.

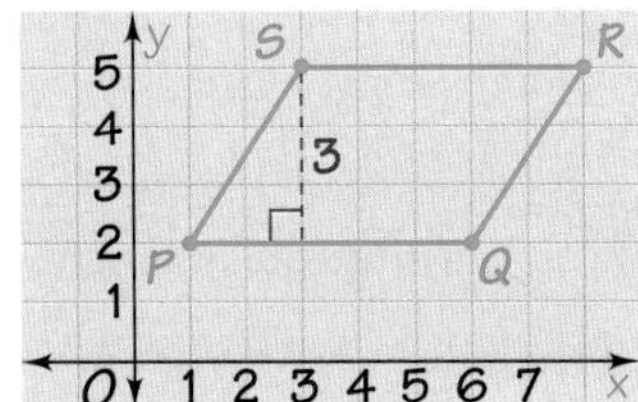

$b = PQ = 5$

$h = 3$

$A = bh = 5(3)$

$= 15$

The area of $\square PQRS$ is 15 square units.

Check Understanding **2** Find the area of $\square EFGH$ with vertices $E(-4, 3)$, $F(0, 3)$, $G(1, -2)$, and $H(-3, -2)$.

3 EXAMPLE Finding a Missing Dimension

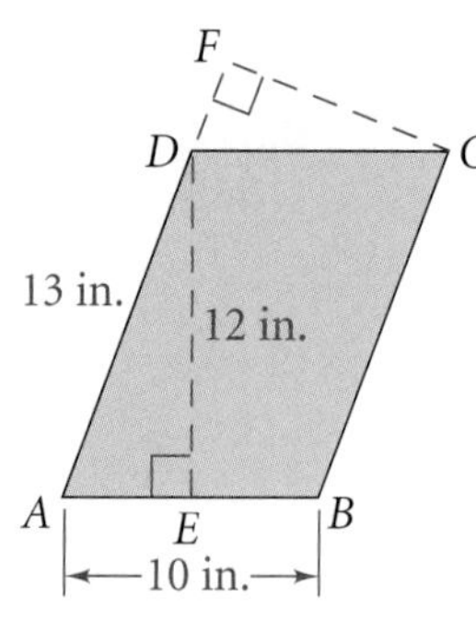

For ▱$ABCD$, find CF to the nearest tenth.

First, find the area of ▱$ABCD$. Then use the area formula a second time to find CF.

$$A = bh$$
$$= 10(12) = 120 \quad \text{Use base } AB \text{ and height } DE.$$

The area of ▱$ABCD$ is 120 in.^{2}.

$$A = bh$$
$$120 = 13(CF) \quad \text{Use base } AD \text{ and height } CF.$$
$$CF = \frac{120}{13} \approx 9.2$$

CF is about 9.2 in.

Check Understanding 3 A parallelogram has sides 15 cm and 18 cm. The height corresponding to a 15-cm base is 9 cm. Find the height corresponding to an 18-cm base.

OBJECTIVE

2 Area of a Triangle

A diagonal divides any parallelogram into two congruent triangles.

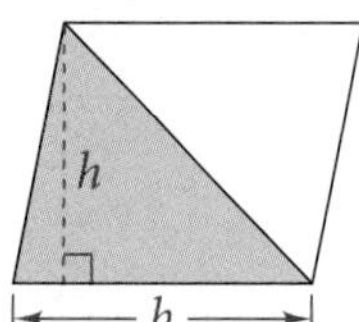

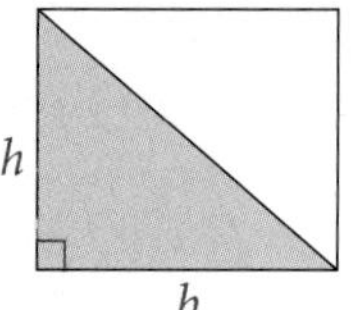

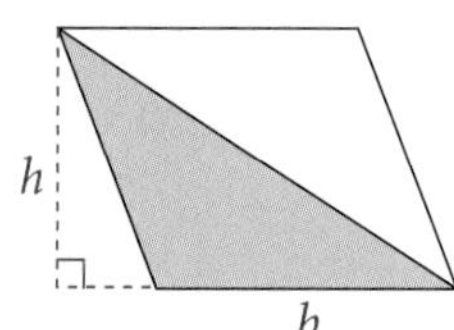

Therefore, the area of each triangle is half the area of the parallelogram.

Key Concepts

Theorem 7-3 **Area of a Triangle**

The area of a triangle is half the product of a base and the corresponding height.

$$A = \frac{1}{2}bh$$

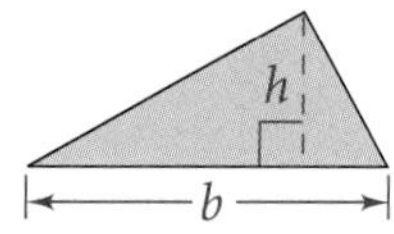

A **base of a triangle** is any of its sides. The corresponding **height** is the length of the altitude to the line containing that base.

4 EXAMPLE Finding the Area of a Triangle

Find the area of the shaded triangle at the left.

6.4 ft

10 ft 4 ft

$$A = \frac{1}{2}bh$$
$$= \frac{1}{2}(10)(6.4) = 32 \quad \text{Substitute and simplify.}$$

The area of the shaded triangle is 32 ft^2.

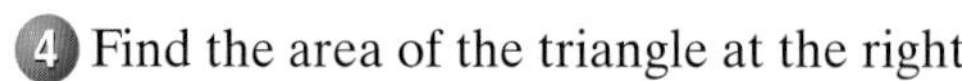

Check Understanding 4 Find the area of the triangle at the right.

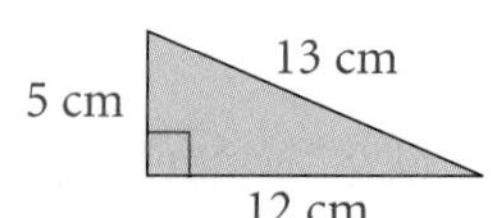

5 EXAMPLE Real-World Connection

Real-World Connection

In 1992 this building in Homestead, Florida, succumbed to the 145 mi/h winds of Hurricane Andrew.

Structural Design When designing a building, you must be sure that the building can withstand hurricane-force winds, which have a velocity of 73 mi/h or more. The formula $F = 0.004Av^2$ gives the force F in pounds exerted by a wind blowing against a flat surface. A is the area of the surface in square feet, and v is the wind velocity in miles per hour.

How much force is exerted by a 73 mi/h wind blowing directly against the side of the building shown here?

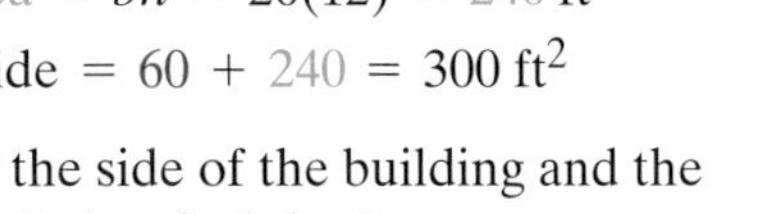

Find the area of the side of the building.

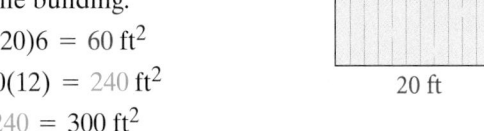

triangle area $= \frac{1}{2}bh = \frac{1}{2}(20)6 = 60 \text{ ft}^2$

rectangle area $= bh = 20(12) = 240 \text{ ft}^2$

area of the side $= 60 + 240 = 300 \text{ ft}^2$

Use the area of the side of the building and the velocity of the wind to find the force.

$F = 0.004Av^2$ **Use the formula for force.**

$= 0.004(300)(73)^2$ **Substitute 300 for *A* and 73 for *v*.**

$= 6394.8$

The force is about 6400 lb, or 3.2 tons.

Check Understanding 5 **Critical Thinking** Suppose the bases of the rectangle and triangle in the building above are doubled to 40 ft, but the height of each figure remains the same. How is the force of the wind against the side of the building affected?

EXERCISES

For more practice, see *Extra Practice*.

Practice and Problem Solving

A Practice by Example

Example 1 (page 349)

Find the area of each parallelogram.

1. 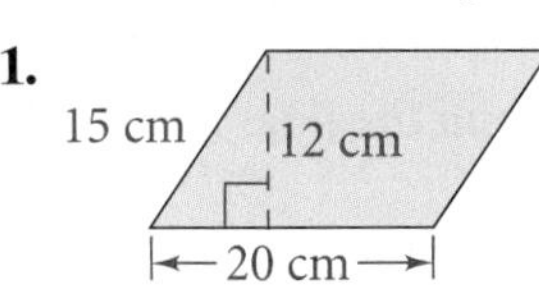

2. 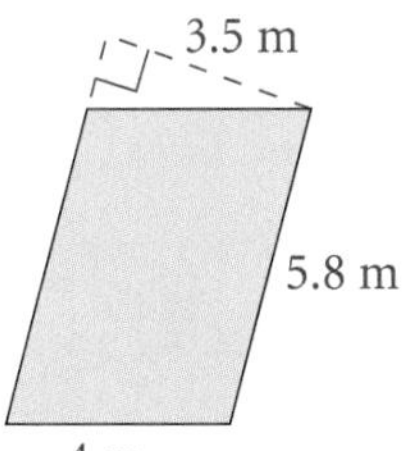

3. 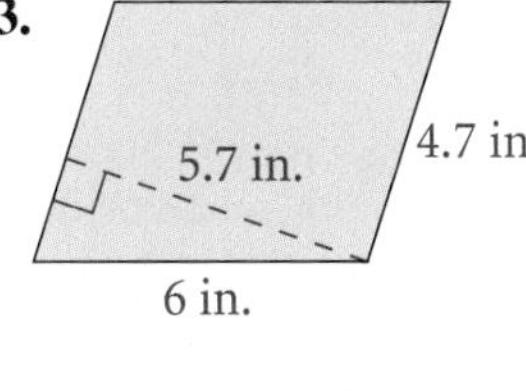

Example 2 (page 349)

Coordinate Geometry **Find the area of the parallelogram with the given vertices.**

4. $A(2, 0), B(7, 0), C(8, 4), D(3, 4)$

5. $E(-4, 0), F(-1, 0), G(1, -3), H(-2, -3)$

6. $I(2, 2), J(4, 2), K(2, -3), L(0, -3)$

7. $M(-6, -1), N(-5, 0), P(1, 0), Q(0, -1)$

Example 3 (page 350)

Find the value of *h* for each parallelogram.

8. 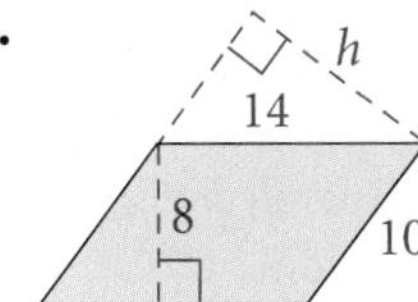

9. 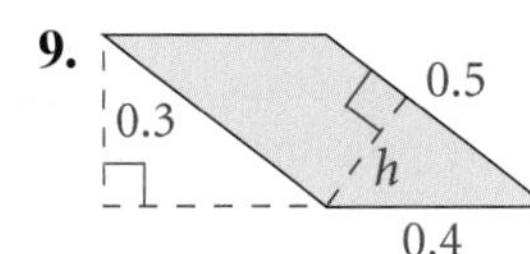

10.
13
h
12
18

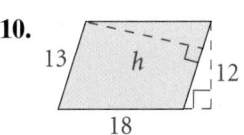

Example 4 (page 350)

Find the area of each shaded triangle.

11.

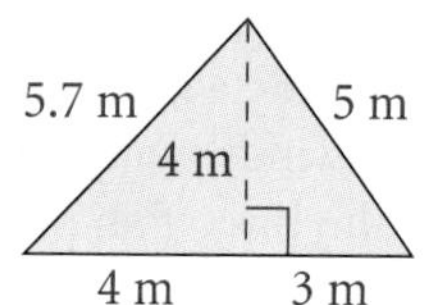

12.

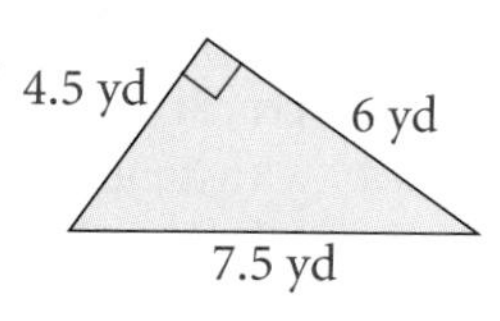

13.

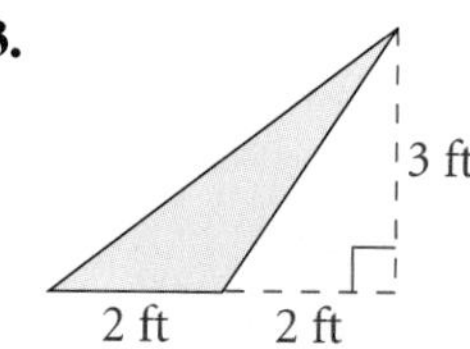

Example 5 (page 351)

14. Landscaping Taisha's Bakery has a plan for a 50 ft-by-31 ft parking lot. The four parking spaces are congruent parallelograms, the driving region is a rectangle, and the two unpaved areas for flowers are congruent triangles.

a. Find the area of the surface to be paved by adding the areas of the driving region and the four parking spaces.

b. Describe another method for finding the area of the surface to be paved.

c. Use your method from part (b) to find the area. Then compare answers from parts (a) and (b) to check your work.

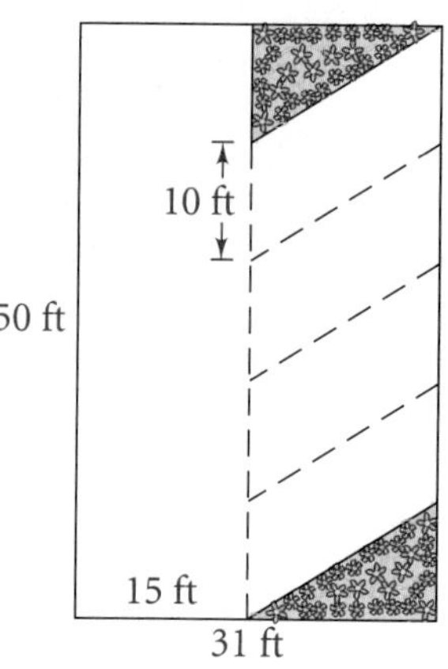

Find the area of each figure.

15. $\square ABJF$ **16.** $\triangle BDJ$

17. $\triangle DKJ$ **18.** $\square BDKJ$

19. $\square ADKF$ **20.** $\triangle BCJ$

21. $ADJF$

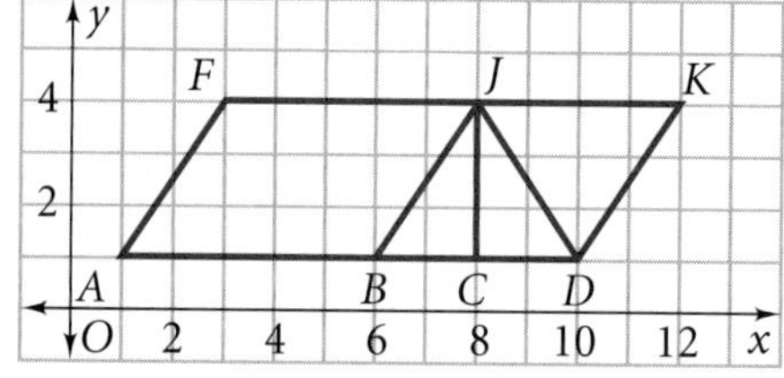

B Apply Your Skills

22. The area of a parallelogram is 24 in.^{2} and the height is 6 in. Find the corresponding base.

23. An isosceles right triangle has area of 98 cm^2. Find the length of each leg.

24. Algebra In a triangle, a base and a corresponding height are in the ratio 3 : 2. The area is 108 in.^{2}. Find the base and the corresponding height.

Need Help?

The line $x = a$ is vertical and crosses the x-axis at $x = a$.

In Exercises 25–28, (a) graph the lines and (b) find the area of the triangle enclosed by the lines.

25. $y = x, x = 0, y = 7$

26. $y = x + 2, y = 2, x = 6$

27. $y = -\frac{1}{2}x + 3, y = 0, x = -2$

28. $y = \frac{3}{4}x - 2, y = -2, x = 4$

29. Technology Ki used geometry software to create the figure at the right. She constructed $\overleftrightarrow{AB}$ and a point C not on $\overleftrightarrow{AB}$. Then she constructed line k parallel to $\overleftrightarrow{AB}$ through point C. Next, Ki constructed point D on line k as well as $\overline{AD}$ and $\overline{BD}$. She dragged point D along line k to manipulate $\triangle ABD$. How does the area of $\triangle ABD$ change? Explain.

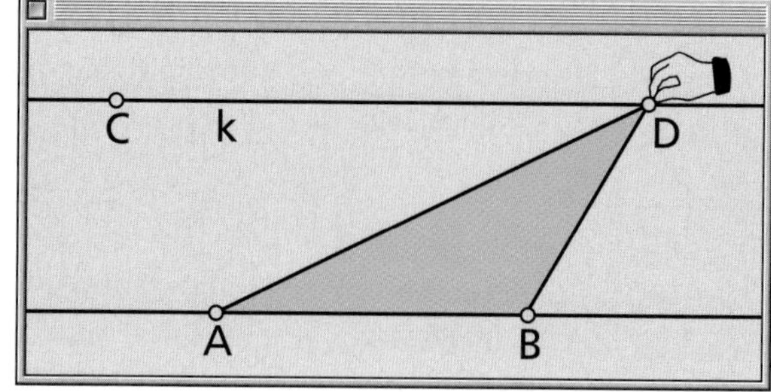

Find the area of each figure.

30. 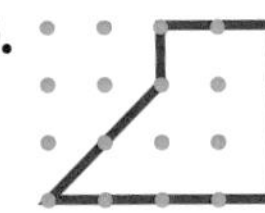

31. 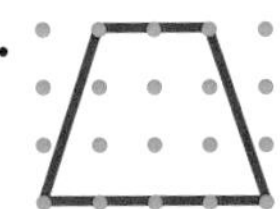

32. 

Exercise 33

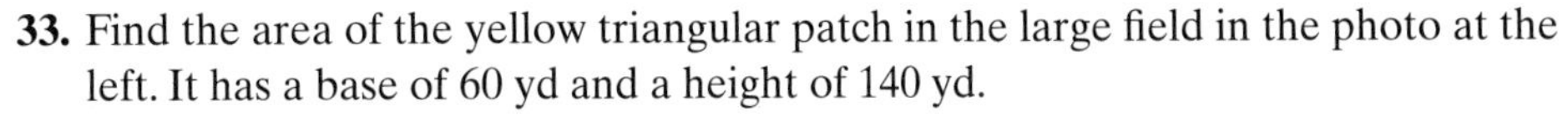

33. Find the area of the yellow triangular patch in the large field in the photo at the left. It has a base of 60 yd and a height of 140 yd.

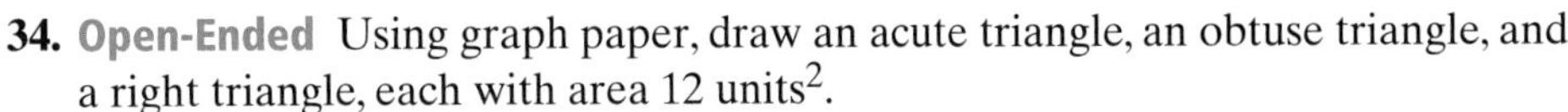

34. **Open-Ended** Using graph paper, draw an acute triangle, an obtuse triangle, and a right triangle, each with area 12 units^2.

35. **Probability** Ann drew these three figures on a grid. A fly lands at random at a point on the grid.

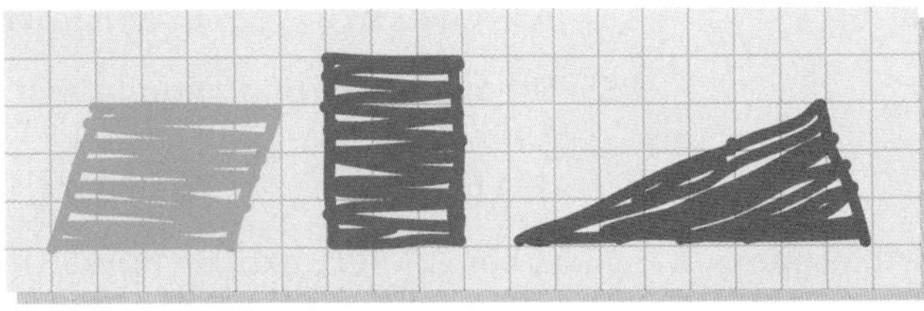

a. **Writing** Is the fly more likely to land on one of the figures or on the blank grid? Explain.

b. Suppose you know the fly lands on one of the figures. Is the fly more likely to land on one figure than on another? Explain.

Coordinate Geometry Find the area of a polygon with the given vertices.

36. $A(3, 9), B(8, 9), C(2, -3), D(-3, -3)$

37. $E(1, 1), F(4, 5), G(11, 5), H(8, 1)$

38. $M(-2, -5), L(1, -5), N(2, -2)$

39. $R(-7, 2), S(-3, -1), T(3, -1)$

40. $W(1, 2), X(1, 6), Y(4, 1)$

41. $A(-8, 0), B(-7, 4), C(-3, 3)$

42. $D(0, 0), E(2, 4), F(6, 4), G(6, 0)$

43. $K(-7, -2), L(-7, 6), M(1, 6), N(7, -2)$

Find the area of each figure.

44. 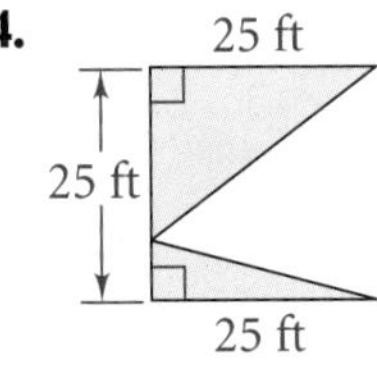

45. 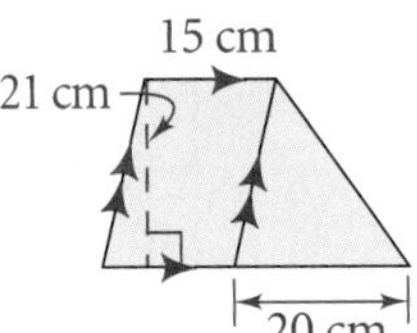

46. 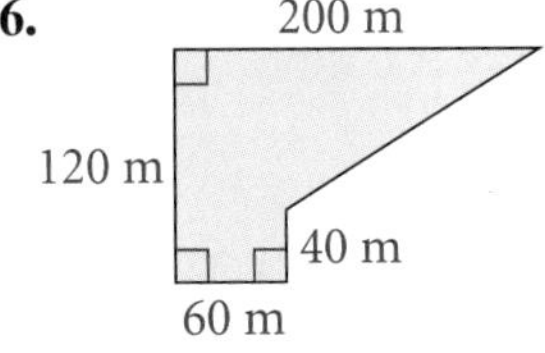

Challenge

History The ancient Greek mathematician Heron is most famous for this formula for the area of a triangle in terms of the lengths of its sides *a*, *b*, and *c*.

$$A = \sqrt{s(s-a)(s-b)(s-c)}, \text{ where } s = \tfrac{1}{2}(a+b+c)$$

Use Heron's Formula and a calculator to find the area of each triangle. Round your answer to the nearest whole number.

47. $a = 8$ in., $b = 9$ in., $c = 10$ in.

48. $a = 15$ m, $b = 17$ m, $c = 21$ m

49. $a = 6$ cm, $b = 7$ cm, $c = 11$ cm

50. $a = 10$ ft, $b = 10.2$ ft, $c = 11$ ft

51. a. Use Heron's Formula to find the area of the triangle at the right.

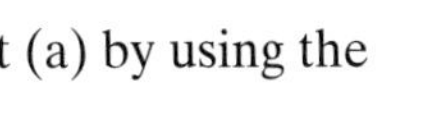

b. Verify your answer to part (a) by using the formula $A = \frac{1}{2}bh$.

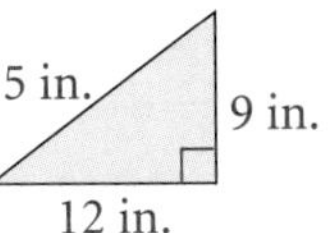

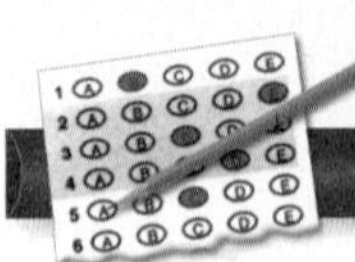

Standardized Test Prep

Multiple Choice

52. The lengths of the sides of a right triangle are 10 in., 24 in., and 26 in. What is the area of the triangle?
A. 116 in.^{2} **B.** 120 in.^{2} **C.** 130 in.^{2} **D.** 156 in.^{2}

53. What is the area of ▱*ABCD* at the right?
F. 32 in.^{2} **G.** 64 in.^{2}
H. 91.2 in.^{2} **I.** 45.6 in.^{2}

54. A parallelogram has adjacent sides of 176 ft and 312 ft. The altitude to the shorter side is 290 ft. What is the area of the parallelogram?
A. 51,040 ft^2 **B.** 51,352 ft^2 **C.** 54,912 ft^2 **D.** 55,202 ft^2

55. The perimeter of an equilateral triangle is 60 m. Its height is 17.3 m. What is its area?
F. 173 m^2 **G.** 200 m^2 **H.** 348 m^2 **I.** 1044 m^2

Short Response

56. a. For ▱*ABCD,* explain how to determine the length of an altitude drawn to base $\overline{AB}$.
b. Find the area of ▱*ABCD*.

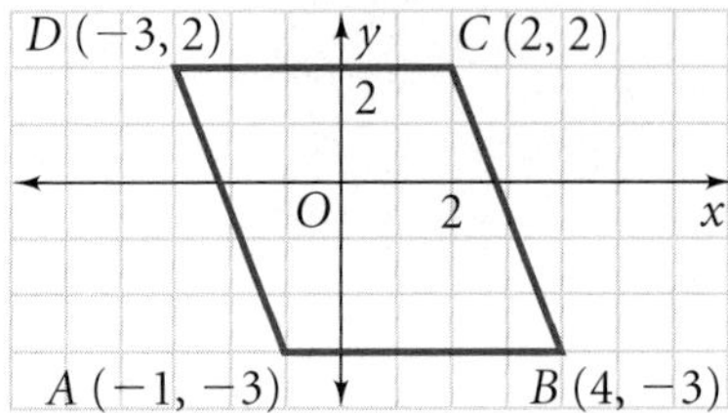

Mixed Review

Lesson 6-7

Give the coordinates for point *P* without using any new variables.

57. square

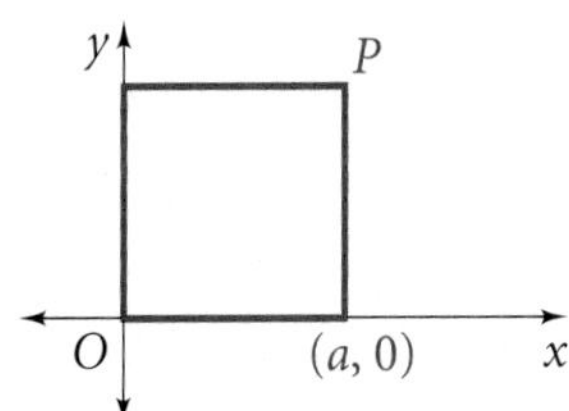

58. parallelogram

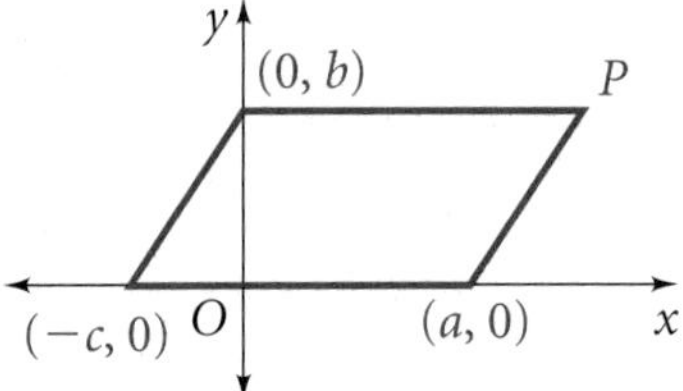

Lesson 4-5

The base of the isosceles triangle is a side of a regular pentagon *PENTA*. Find the measure of each angle.

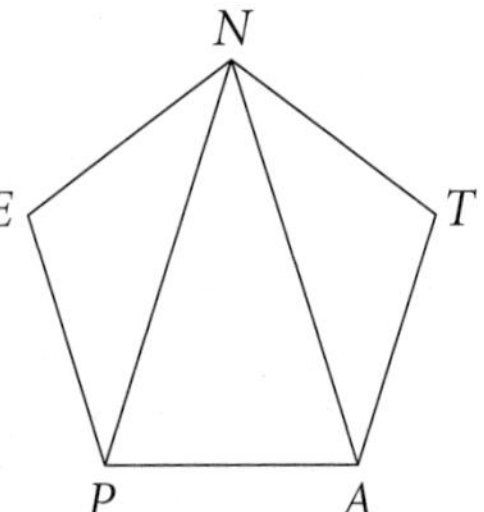

59. $\angle APE$ **60.** $\angle APN$
61. $\angle PAN$ **62.** $\angle PNA$
63. $\angle EPN$ **64.** $\angle ANT$

Lesson 3-7

Use a compass and straightedge for the following constructions.

65. Draw a segment and label it $\overline{AB}$. Construct $\overleftrightarrow{AD}$ so that $\overleftrightarrow{AD} \perp \overline{AB}$ at point A.

66. Draw a segment. Label it $\overline{EF}$. Construct a line $\overleftrightarrow{GH}$ so that $\overleftrightarrow{GH} \parallel \overline{EF}$.

67. Draw a segment and label it $\overline{KL}$. Draw a point X not on $\overleftrightarrow{KL}$. Construct a perpendicular from point X to $\overline{KL}$ (or to $\overleftrightarrow{KL}$).

Algebra 1 Review

Simplifying Radicals

For Use With Lesson 7-2

You can multiply and divide numbers that are under radical signs.

1 EXAMPLE

Simplify the expressions $\sqrt{2} \cdot \sqrt{8}$ and $\sqrt{294} \div \sqrt{3}$.

$\sqrt{2} \cdot \sqrt{8} = \sqrt{2 \cdot 8}$	← **Rewrite using one radical sign.** →	$\sqrt{294} \div \sqrt{3} = \sqrt{\frac{294}{3}}$
$= \sqrt{16}$	← **Simplify the expression under the radical.** →	$= \sqrt{98}$
$= 4$	← **Factor out perfect squares and simplify.** →	$= \sqrt{49 \cdot 2}$
		$= 7\sqrt{2}$

A radical expression is in simplest form when all the following are true.

- The number under the radical sign has no perfect square factors other than 1.
- The number under the radical sign does not contain a fraction.
- A denominator does not contain a radical expression.

2 EXAMPLE

Write $\sqrt{\frac{4}{3}}$ in simplest form.

$\sqrt{\frac{4}{3}} = \frac{\sqrt{4}}{\sqrt{3}}$ **Rewrite the single radical as a quotient.**

$= \frac{2}{\sqrt{3}}$ **Simplify the numerator.**

$= \frac{2}{\sqrt{3}} \cdot \frac{\sqrt{3}}{\sqrt{3}}$ **Multiply by a form of 1 to rationalize the denominator.**

$= \frac{2\sqrt{3}}{3}$ **Simplify.**

Check using a calculator: $\sqrt{\frac{4}{3}} \approx 1.1547005$ and $\frac{2\sqrt{3}}{3} \approx 1.1547005$.

EXERCISES

Simplify each expression.

1. $\sqrt{5} \cdot \sqrt{10}$

2. $\sqrt{243}$

3. $\sqrt{128} \div \sqrt{2}$

4. $\sqrt{\frac{125}{4}}$

5. $\sqrt{6} \cdot \sqrt{8}$

6. $\frac{\sqrt{36}}{\sqrt{3}}$

7. $\frac{\sqrt{144}}{\sqrt{2}}$

8. $\sqrt{3} \cdot \sqrt{12}$

9. $\sqrt{72} \div \sqrt{2}$

10. $\sqrt{169}$

11. $28 \div \sqrt{8}$

12. $\sqrt{300} \div \sqrt{5}$

13. $\sqrt{12} \cdot \sqrt{2}$

14. $\frac{\sqrt{24}}{\sqrt{3}}$

15. $\sqrt{\frac{75}{3}}$

16. $\sqrt{18} \cdot \sqrt{2}$

17. $\sqrt{68}$

18. $\sqrt{3} \cdot \sqrt{15}$

19. $\frac{\sqrt{20}}{\sqrt{5}}$

20. $45 \div \sqrt{3}$

21. $\sqrt{\frac{25}{20}}$

22. $\sqrt{\frac{8}{28}}$

23. $\frac{\sqrt{6} \cdot \sqrt{3}}{\sqrt{9}}$

24. $\frac{\sqrt{3} \cdot \sqrt{15}}{\sqrt{2}}$

Investigation

The Pythagorean Theorem

For Use With Lesson 7-2

The Pythagorean Theorem is introduced in Lesson 7-2. The investigation and exercises below will help you understand why the theorem works.

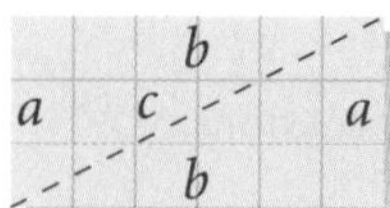

Using graph paper, draw any rectangle. Label the sides a and b. Cut four rectangles with length a and width b from the graph paper. Then cut each rectangle on its diagonal, c, forming eight congruent triangles.

Cut three squares from colored paper, one with sides of length a, one with sides of length b, and one with sides of length c.

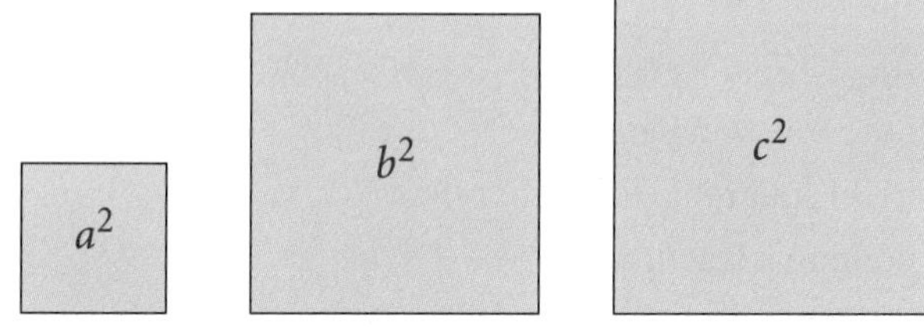

Separate the eleven pieces into groups.

Group 1: four triangles and the two smaller squares

Group 2: four triangles and the largest square

Arrange the pieces of each group to form a square.

EXERCISES

1. **a.** How do the areas of the two squares you formed in the last step above compare?
   b. Write an algebraic expression for the area of each of these squares.
   c. What can you conclude about the areas of the three squares you cut from colored paper?
2. Repeat this investigation using a new rectangle with different a and b values. What do you notice?
3. Express your conclusion as an algebraic equation.
4. Use your ruler with any rectangle to find actual measures for a, b, and c. Do these measures confirm that $a^2 + b^2 = c^2$?

Extend

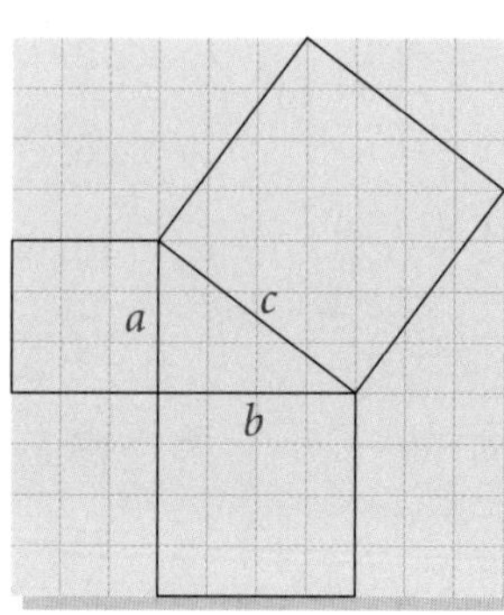

5. Explain how the diagram at the right represents your conclusion in Exercise 3.
6. Does the equation from Exercise 4 work for triangles other than right triangles? Explore and explain.

7-2 The Pythagorean Theorem and Its Converse

Lesson Preview

What You'll Learn

To use the Pythagorean Theorem

To use the Converse of the Pythagorean Theorem

. . . And Why

To find the distance between two docks on a lake, as in Example 3

✓ Check Skills You'll Need

(For help, go to the Skills Handbook, p. 715)

Square the lengths of the sides of each triangle. What do you notice?

1. 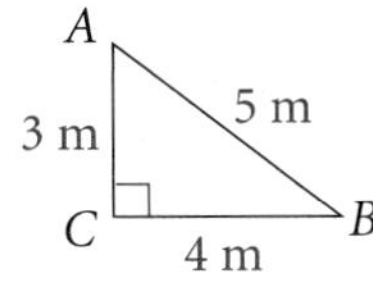

2. 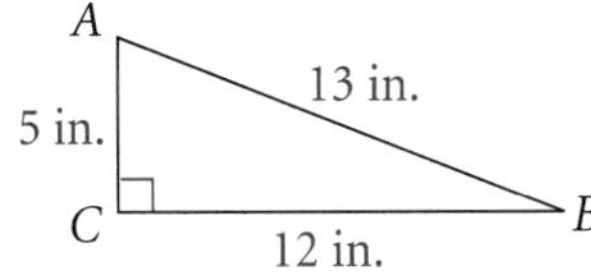

3. 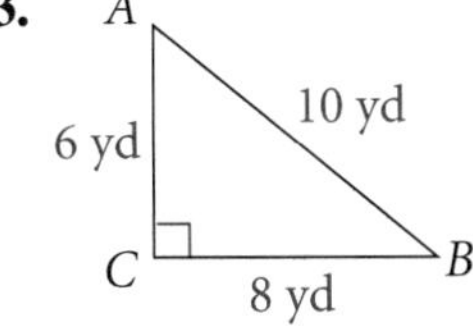

4. 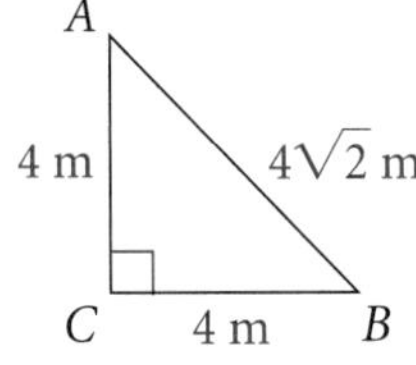

New Vocabulary • Pythagorean triple

Interactive lesson includes instant self-check, tutorials, and activities.

OBJECTIVE 1 The Pythagorean Theorem

The well-known right triangle relationship called the Pythagorean Theorem is named for Pythagoras, a Greek mathematician who lived in the sixth century B.C. We now know that the Babylonians, Egyptians, and Chinese were aware of this relationship before its discovery by Pythagoras.

There are many proofs of the Pythagorean Theorem. You will see an area proof in Exercise 60.

Key Concepts

Theorem 7-4 **Pythagorean Theorem**

In a right triangle, the sum of the squares of the lengths of the legs is equal to the square of the length of the hypotenuse.

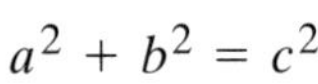

$$a^2 + b^2 = c^2$$

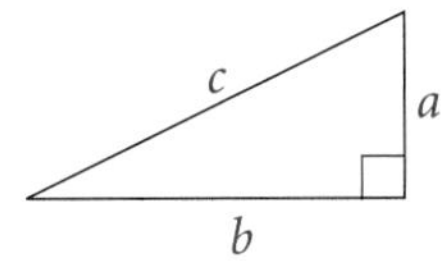

Need Help?

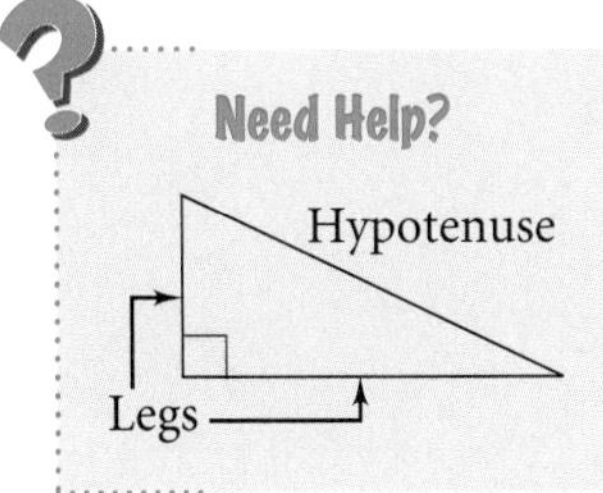

A **Pythagorean triple** is a set of nonzero whole numbers a, b, and c that satisfy the equation $a^2 + b^2 = c^2$. Here are some common Pythagorean triples.

3, 4, 5   5, 12, 13   8, 15, 17   7, 24, 25

If you multiply each number in a Pythagorean triple by the same whole number, the three numbers that result also form a Pythagorean triple.

1 EXAMPLE Pythagorean Triples

Find the length of the hypotenuse of $\triangle ABC$. Do the lengths of the sides of $\triangle ABC$ form a Pythagorean triple?

$a^2 + b^2 = c^2$	**Use the Pythagorean Theorem.**
$21^2 + 20^2 = c^2$	**Substitute 21 for *a* and 20 for *b*.**
$441 + 400 = c^2$	**Simplify.**
$841 = c^2$	
$c = 29$	**Take the square root.**

The length of the hypotenuse is 29. The lengths of the sides, 20, 21, and 29, form a Pythagorean triple because they are whole numbers that satisfy $a^2 + b^2 = c^2$.

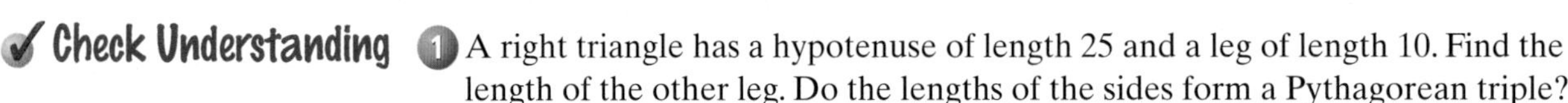

Check Understanding 1 A right triangle has a hypotenuse of length 25 and a leg of length 10. Find the length of the other leg. Do the lengths of the sides form a Pythagorean triple?

In some cases, you will write the length of a side in simplest radical form.

2 EXAMPLE Using Simplest Radical Form

Need Help?
To review simplest radical form, see page 355.

Algebra Find the value of x. Leave your answer in simplest radical form.

$a^2 + b^2 = c^2$	**Pythagorean Theorem**
$8^2 + x^2 = 20^2$	**Substitute.**
$64 + x^2 = 400$	**Simplify.**
$x^2 = 336$	**Subtract 64 from each side.**
$x = \sqrt{336}$	**Take the square root.**
$x = \sqrt{16(21)}$	**Simplify.**
$x = 4\sqrt{21}$	

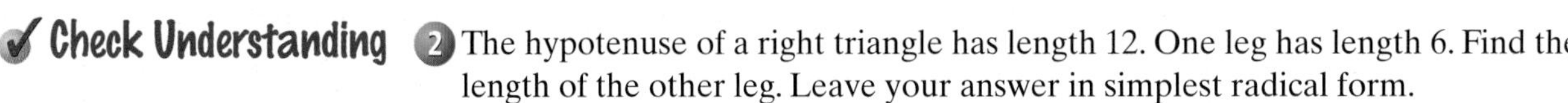

Check Understanding 2 The hypotenuse of a right triangle has length 12. One leg has length 6. Find the length of the other leg. Leave your answer in simplest radical form.

3 EXAMPLE Real-World Connection

Recreation The Parks Department rents paddle boats at docks near each entrance to the park. About how far is it to paddle from one dock to the other?

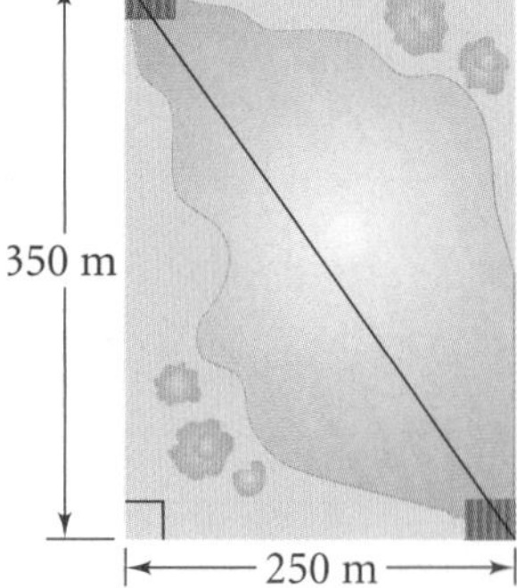

$a^2 + b^2 = c^2$	**Pythagorean Theorem**
$250^2 + 350^2 = c^2$	**Substitute.**
$185{,}000 = c^2$	**Simplify.**
$c = \sqrt{185{,}000}$	**Take the square root.**
$c = 430.11626$	**Use a calculator.**

It is about 430 m from one dock to the other.

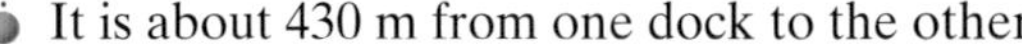

Check Understanding 3 **Critical Thinking** When you want to know how far you have to paddle a boat, why is an approximate answer more useful than an answer in simplest radical form?

You can use the Pythagorean Theorem to help you find area.

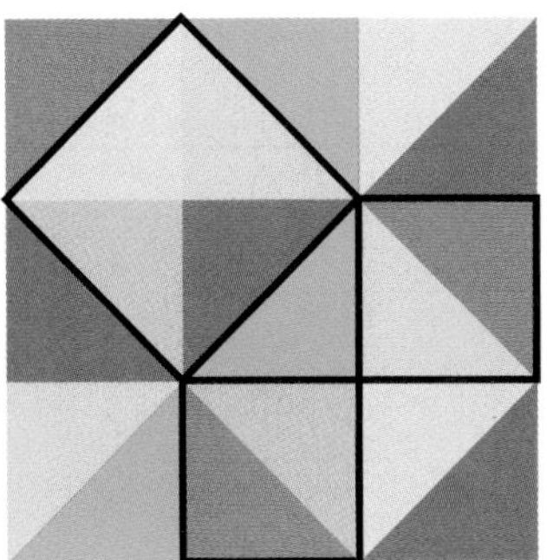

The diagram above illustrates an ancient Greek proof of the Pythagorean Theorem for an isosceles right triangle.

4 EXAMPLE Finding Area

Find the area of the triangle.

The large triangle is an isosceles triangle. The altitude to the base bisects the base and forms two right triangles. You can use the Pythagorean Theorem with the triangle at the right to find the height of the large triangle.

$10^2 + h^2 = 12^2$	
$100 + h^2 = 144$	**Simplify.**
$h^2 = 44$	**Subtract 100 from each side.**
$h = \sqrt{44}$	**Take the square root of each side.**
$h = 2\sqrt{11}$	**Write in simplest radical form.**

The large triangle has base 20 m and height $2\sqrt{11}$ m.

$A = \frac{1}{2}bh$	**Use the triangle area formula from Theorem 7-3.**
$A = \frac{1}{2}(20)(2\sqrt{11})$	**Substitute 20 for *b* and $2\sqrt{11}$ for *h*.**
$A = 20\sqrt{11}$	**Simplify.**

The area of the triangle is $20\sqrt{11}$ m^2.

Check Understanding 4 Find the area of the triangle at the right.

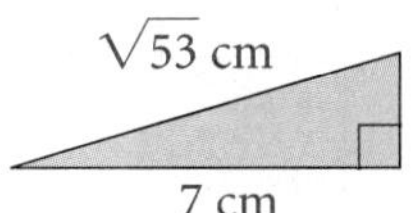

OBJECTIVE

2 The Converse of the Pythagorean Theorem

You can use the Converse of the Pythagorean Theorem to determine whether a triangle is a right triangle. You will prove Theorem 7-5 in Exercise 70.

Key Concepts

Theorem 7-5 **Converse of the Pythagorean Theorem**

If the square of the length of one side of a triangle is equal to the sum of the squares of the lengths of the other two sides, then the triangle is a right triangle.

5 EXAMPLE Is It a Right Triangle?

Is this triangle a right triangle?

$c^2 \stackrel{?}{=} a^2 + b^2$	
$85^2 \stackrel{?}{=} 13^2 + 84^2$	**Substitute the greatest length for *c*.**
$7225 \stackrel{?}{=} 169 + 7056$	**Simplify.**
$7225 = 7225$ ✓	

$c^2 = a^2 + b^2$, so the triangle is a right triangle.

Check Understanding 5 A triangle has sides of lengths 16, 48, and 50. Is the triangle a right triangle?

Suppose a triangle has sides of lengths a, b, and c, where c is the length of the longest side. If $c^2 > a^2 + b^2$, the Converse of the Pythagorean Theorem leads to the conclusion that the angle opposite side c must have measure greater than 90. Thus, the triangle is obtuse. Similarly, if $c^2 < a^2 + b^2$, the triangle is acute.

These observations are summarized in the theorems below.

Key Concepts

Theorem 7-6

If the square of the length of the longest side of a triangle is greater than the sum of the squares of the lengths of the other two sides, the triangle is obtuse.

If $c^2 > a^2 + b^2$, the triangle is obtuse.

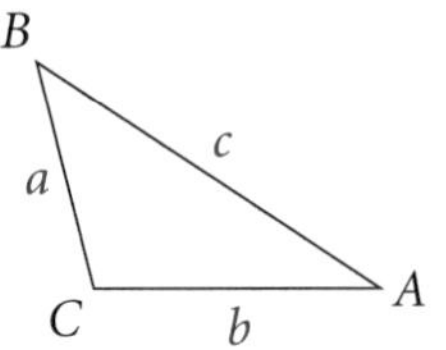

Theorem 7-7

If the square of the length of the longest side of a triangle is less than the sum of the squares of the lengths of the other two sides, the triangle is acute.

If $c^2 < a^2 + b^2$, the triangle is acute.

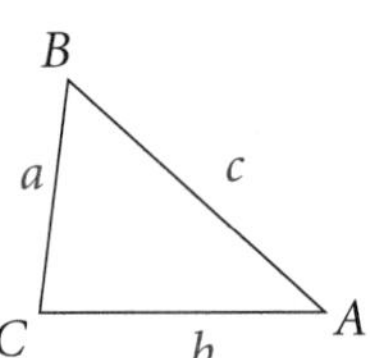

Real-World Connection

The length to the brace along each leg is 36 in. The brace is 26 in. long to guarantee that the triangle is acute.

6 EXAMPLE Classifying Triangles as Acute, Obtuse, or Right

The lengths of the sides of a triangle are given. Classify each triangle as acute, obtuse, or right.

a. 6, 11, 14

$14^2 \stackrel{?}{=} 6^2 + 11^2$ **Compare c^2 to $a^2 + b^2$. Substitute the greatest length for c.**

$196 \stackrel{?}{=} 36 + 121$

$196 > 157$

Since $c^2 > a^2 + b^2$, the triangle is obtuse.

b. 12, 13, 15

$15^2 \stackrel{?}{=} 12^2 + 13^2$ **Compare c^2 to $a^2 + b^2$. Substitute the greatest length for c.**

$225 \stackrel{?}{=} 144 + 169$

$225 < 313$

Since $c^2 < a^2 + b^2$, the triangle is acute.

Check Understanding 6 A triangle has sides of lengths 7, 8, and 9. Classify the triangle by its angles.

EXERCISES

For more practice, see *Extra Practice*.

Practice and Problem Solving

A Practice by Example Algebra **Find the value of x.**

Example 1 (page 358)

1.

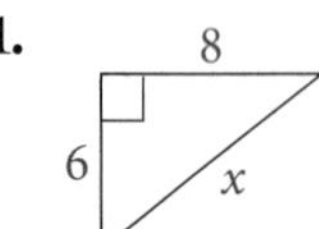

2.

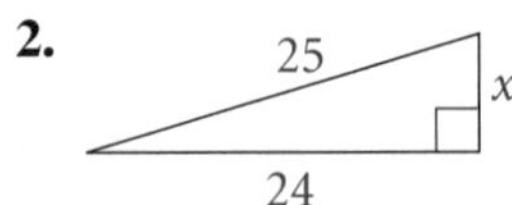

3.

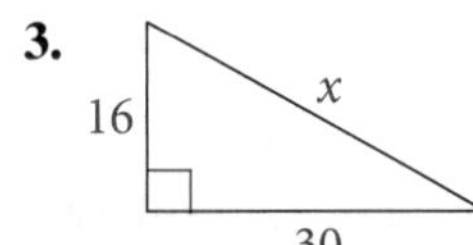

Algebra **Find the value of x.**

4.

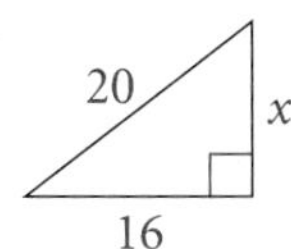

5.

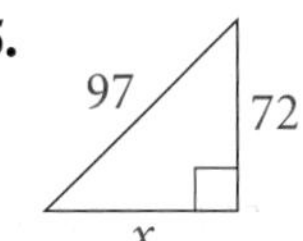

6.

15
x
17

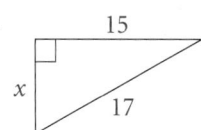

Does each set of numbers form a Pythagorean triple? Explain.

7. 4, 5, 6 **8.** 10, 24, 26 **9.** 15, 20, 25

Example 2 (page 358)

Algebra **Find the value of x. Leave your answer in simplest radical form.**

10.

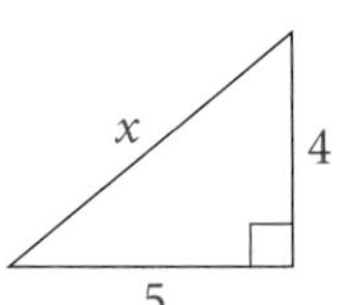

11.

x
4
7

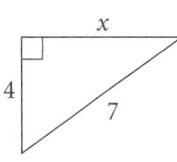

12.

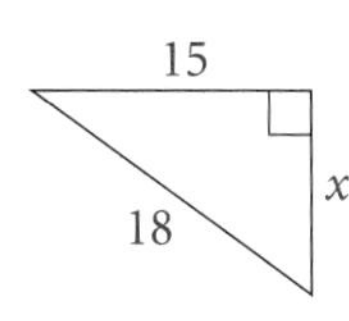

13.

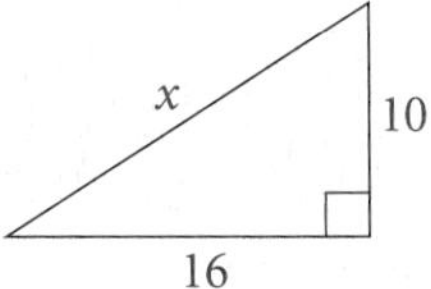

14.

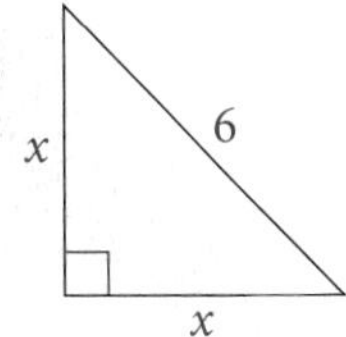

15.

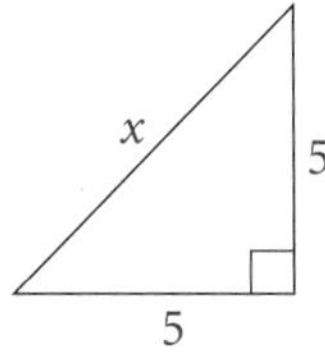

Example 3 (page 358)

16. **Home Maintenance** A painter leans a 15-ft ladder against a house. The base of the ladder is 5 ft from the house. To the nearest foot, how high on the house does the ladder reach?

17. A walkway forms the diagonal of a square playground. The walkway is 24 m long. To the nearest tenth of a meter, how long is a side of the playground?

Example 4 (page 359)

Find the area of each triangle. Leave your answer in simplest radical form.

18.

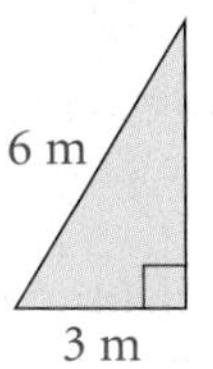

19.

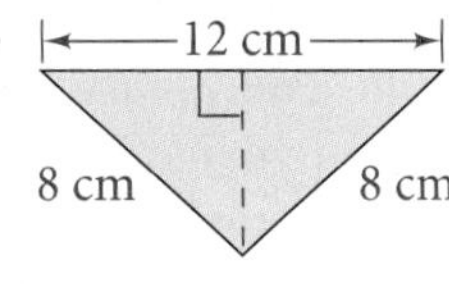

20.

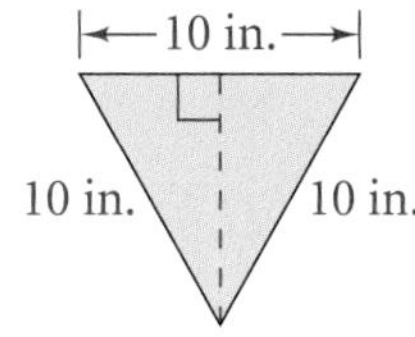

Example 5 (page 359)

Is each triangle a right triangle? Explain.

21.

20
28
19

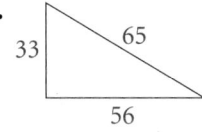

22.

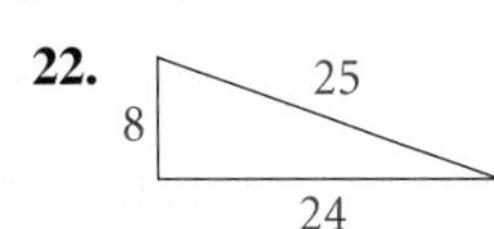

23.

33
65
56

Example 6 (page 360)

The lengths of the sides of a triangle are given. Classify each triangle as acute, right, or obtuse.

24. 15, 8, 21 **25.** 12, 16, 20 **26.** 4, 5, 6

27. 30, 34, 16 **28.** 0.3, 0.4, 0.6 **29.** 11, 12, 15

30. $\sqrt{3}, 2, 3$ **31.** 18, 80, 82 **32.** 20, 21, 28

33. 31, 23, 12 **34.** 30, 40, 50 **35.** $\sqrt{11}, \sqrt{7}, 4$

B Apply Your Skills

x^2 **Algebra** **Find the value of x. Leave your answer in simplest radical form.**

36. 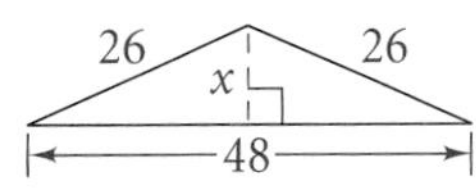

37. 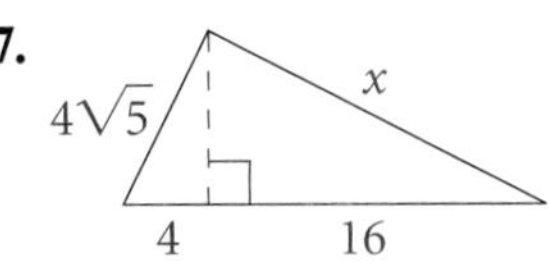

38. 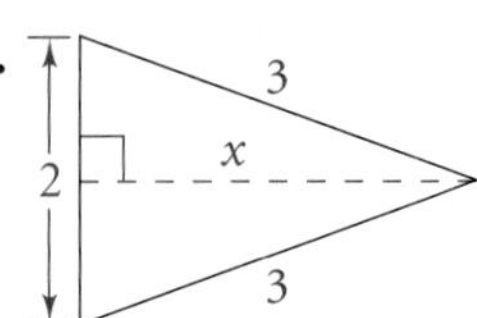

39. Writing Each year in an ancient land, a large river overflowed its banks, often destroying boundary markers. The royal surveyors used a rope with knots at 12 equal intervals to help reconstruct boundaries. Explain how a surveyor could use this rope to form a right angle. (*Hint*: Use the Pythagorean triple 3, 4, 5.)

Find the area of each figure.

40. 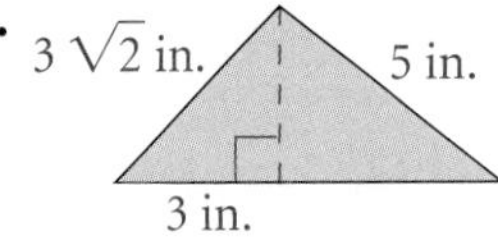

41. 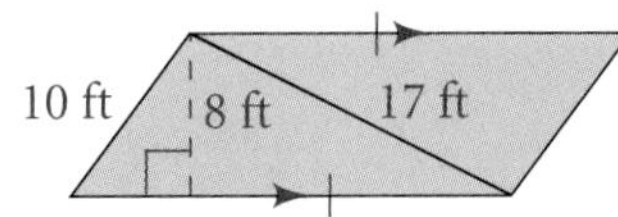

42. 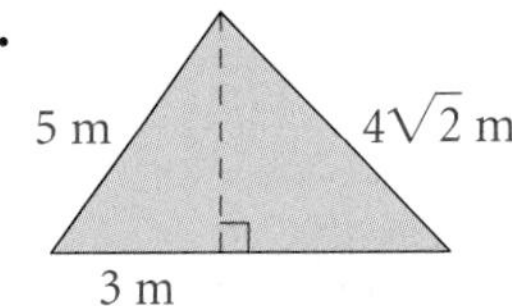

43. 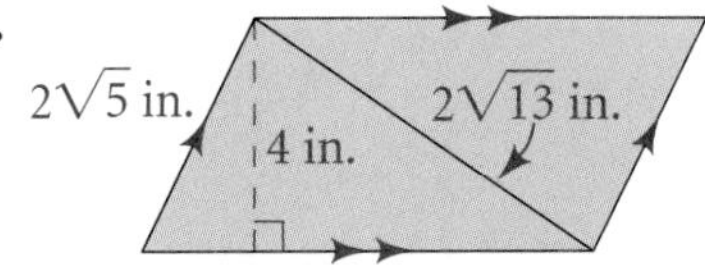

Reading Math

For help with reading and solving Exercise 44, see p. 365.

 **44. Embroidery** You want to embroider a square design. You have an embroidery hoop with a 6 in. diameter. Find the largest value of x so that the entire square will fit in the hoop. Round to the nearest tenth.

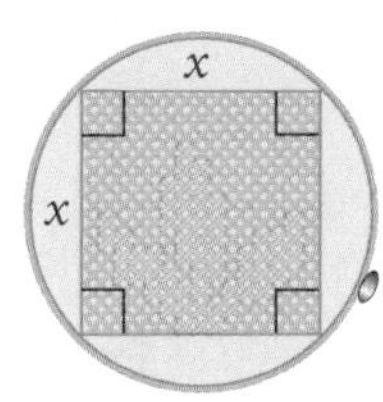

45. In parallelogram $RSTW$, $RS = 7$, $ST = 24$, and $RT = 25$. Is $RSTW$ a rectangle? Explain.

Proof **46. Coordinate Geometry** You can use the Pythagorean Theorem to prove the Distance Formula. Let points $P(x_1, y_1)$ and $Q(x_2, y_2)$ be the endpoints of the hypotenuse of a right triangle.

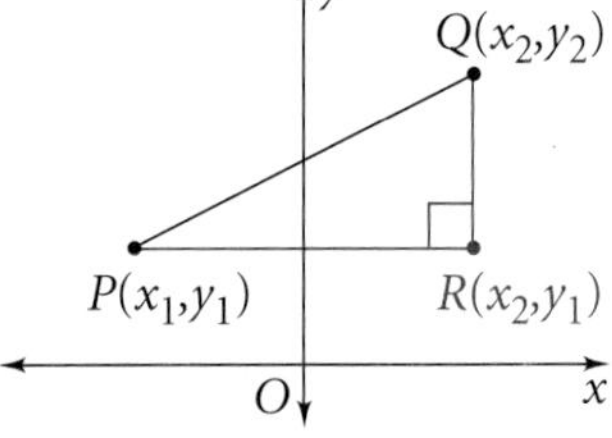

a. Write an algebraic expression to complete each of the following: $PR = \blacksquare$ and $QR = \blacksquare$.

b. By the Pythagorean Theorem, $PQ^2 = PR^2 + QR^2$. Rewrite this statement substituting the algebraic expressions you found for PR and QR in part (a).

c. Complete the proof by taking the square root of each side of the equation that you wrote in part (b).

47. Constructions Explain how to construct a segment of length $\sqrt{n}$, where n is any positive integer, and you are given a segment of length 1. (*Hint*: See the diagram.)

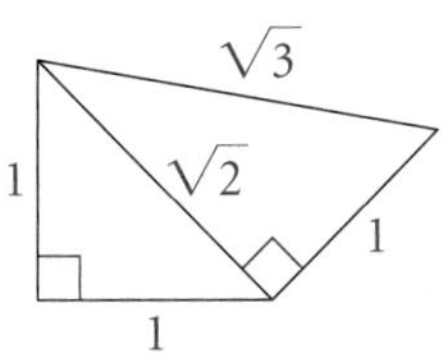

Find a third whole number so that the three numbers form a Pythagorean triple.

48. 20, 21 **49.** 14, 48 **50.** 13, 85 **51.** 12, 37

Need Help?

Remember that the sum of the lengths of any two sides of a triangle must be greater than the length of the third side.

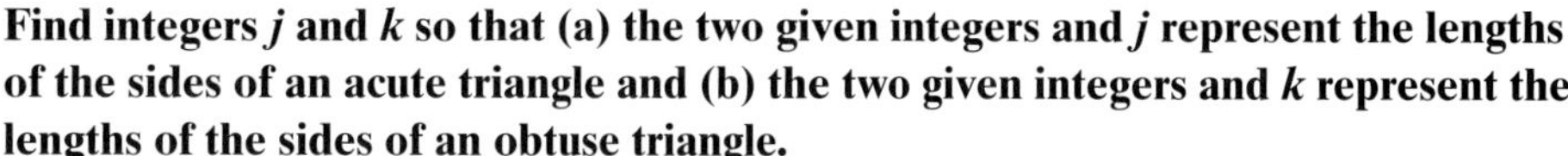

Find integers j and k so that (a) the two given integers and j represent the lengths of the sides of an acute triangle and (b) the two given integers and k represent the lengths of the sides of an obtuse triangle.

52. 4, 5 **53.** 2, 4 **54.** 6, 9 **55.** 5, 10

56. 6, 7 **57.** 9, 12 **58.** 8, 17 **59.** 9, 40

Proof **60. Reasoning** You can use the diagram at the right to prove the Pythagorean Theorem.

a. Find the area of the large square in terms of c.

b. Find the area of the large square in terms of a and b by adding the areas of the four triangles and the small square.

c. Write an equation setting your answers to part (a) and part (b) equal to each other. Simplify the equation to complete the proof.

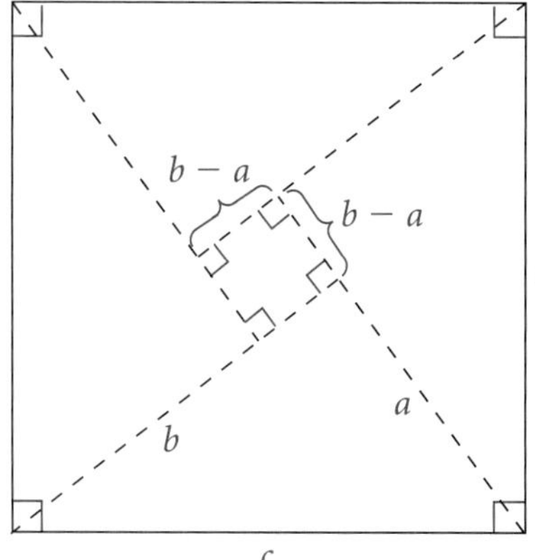

61. Astronomy The Hubble Space Telescope is orbiting Earth 600 km above Earth's surface. Earth's radius is about 6370 km. Use the Pythagorean Theorem to find the distance x from the telescope to Earth's horizon. Round your answer to the nearest ten kilometers.

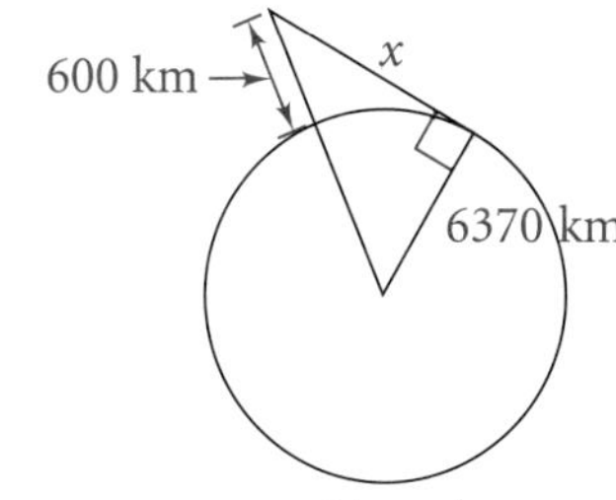

not to scale

Real-World Connection

Research by Edwin Hubble (1889–1953), here guiding a telescope in 1923, led to the Big Bang Theory of the formation of the universe.

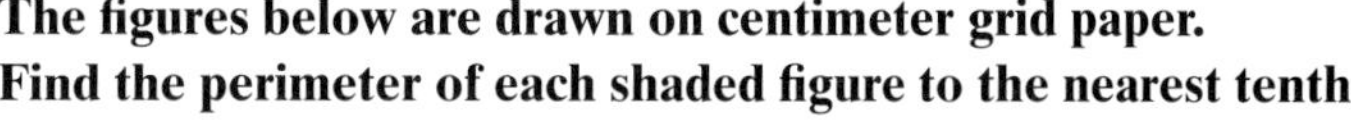

The figures below are drawn on centimeter grid paper. Find the perimeter of each shaded figure to the nearest tenth.

62.

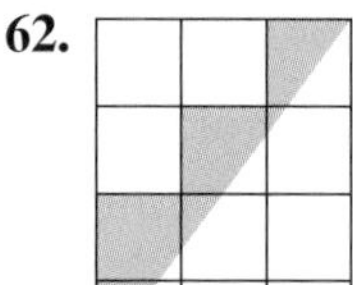

63.

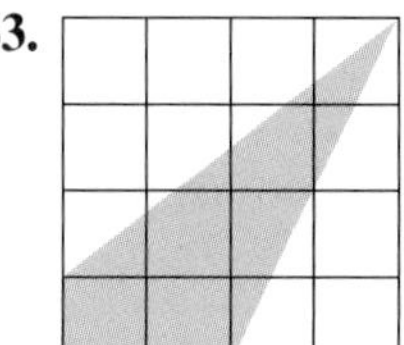

64.

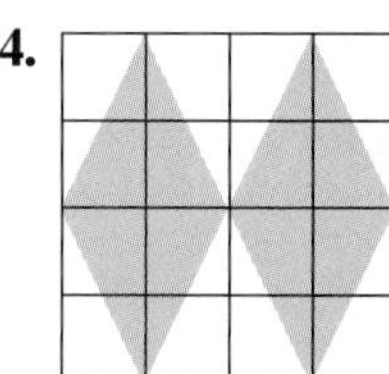

Challenge

65. a. The ancient Greek philosopher Plato used the expressions $2n$, $n^2 - 1$, and $n^2 + 1$ to produce Pythagorean triples. Choose any integer greater than 1. Substitute for n and evaluate the three expressions.

b. Verify that your answers to part (a) form a Pythagorean triple.

66. Geometry in 3 Dimensions The box at the right is a rectangular solid.

a. Use $\triangle ABC$ to find the length d_1 of the diagonal of the base.

b. Use $\triangle ABD$ to find the length d_2 of the diagonal of the box.

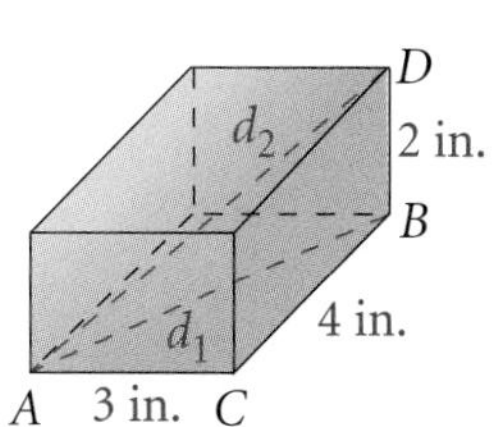

c. You can generalize the steps in parts (a) and (b). Use the facts that $AC^2 + BC^2 = d_1^2$ and $d_1^2 + BD^2 = d_2^2$ to write a one-step formula to find d_2.

d. Use the formula you wrote to find the length of the longest fishing pole you can pack in a box with dimensions 18 in., 24 in., and 16 in.

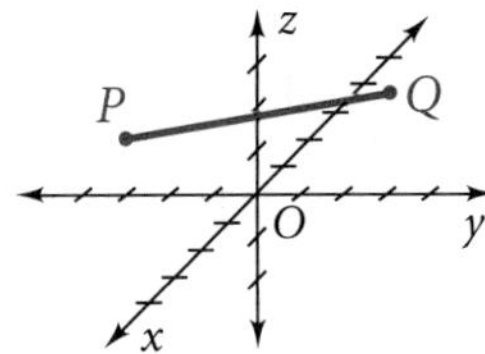

Geometry in 3 Dimensions **Points $P(x_1, y_1, z_1)$ and $Q(x_2, y_2, z_2)$ at the left are points in a three-dimensional coordinate system. Use the following formula to find PQ. Leave your answer in simplest radical form.**

$$d = \sqrt{(x_2 - x_1)^2 + (y_2 - y_1)^2 + (z_2 - z_1)^2}$$

67. $P(0, 0, 0), Q(1, 2, 3)$ **68.** $P(0, 0, 0), Q(-3, 4, -6)$ **69.** $P(-1, 3, 5), Q(2, 1, 7)$

Proof **70.** Use the plan and write a paragraph proof of Theorem 7-5, the Converse of the Pythagorean Theorem.

Given: $\triangle ABC$ with sides of length a, b, and c where $a^2 + b^2 = c^2$

Prove: $\triangle ABC$ is a right triangle.

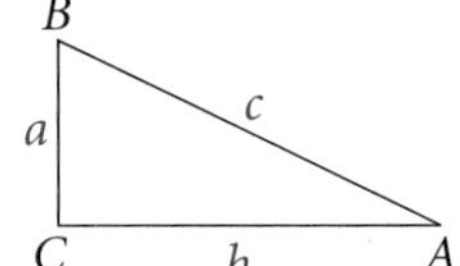

Plan: Draw a right triangle (not $\triangle ABC$) with legs of lengths a and b. Label the hypotenuse x. By the Pythagorean Theorem, $a^2 + b^2 = x^2$. Use substitution to compare the lengths of the sides of your triangle and $\triangle ABC$. Then prove the triangles congruent.

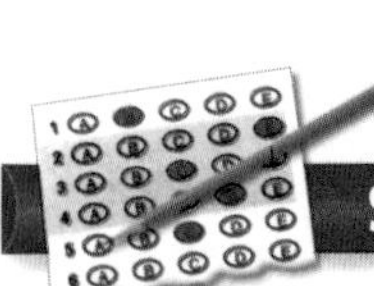

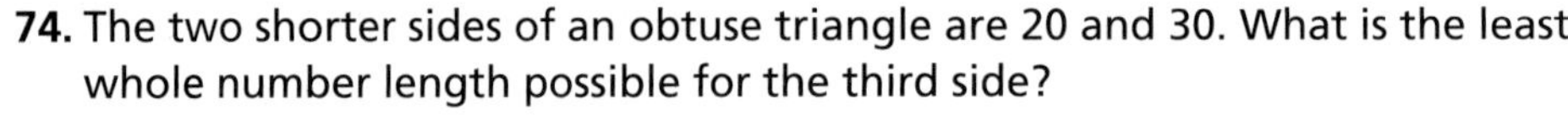

Standardized Test Prep

Gridded Response

71. The lengths of the legs of a right triangle are 17 m and 20 m. To the nearest tenth of a meter, what is the length of the hypotenuse?

72. The hypotenuse of a right triangle is 34 ft. One leg is 16 ft. Find the length of the other leg in feet.

73. What whole number forms a Pythagorean triple with 40 and 41?

74. The two shorter sides of an obtuse triangle are 20 and 30. What is the least whole number length possible for the third side?

75. Each leg of an isosceles right triangle has measure 10 cm. To the nearest tenth of a centimeter, what is the length of the hypotenuse?

Take It to the NET
Online lesson quiz at **www.PHSchool.com**
Web Code: afa-0702

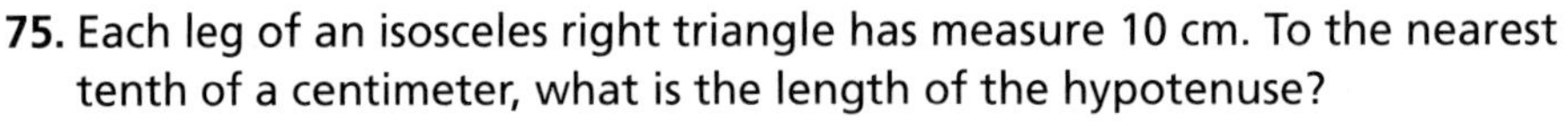

Mixed Review

Lesson 7-1

76. Find the area of an isosceles right triangle that has one leg of length 12 cm.

77. An isosceles right triangle has area of 112.5 ft^2. Find the length of each leg.

Lesson 5-2

In the figure, $\overrightarrow{PS}$ bisects $\angle RPT$. Solve for each variable. Then find RS.

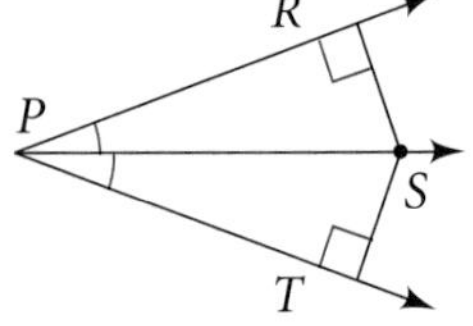

78. $RS = 2x + 19, ST = 7x - 16$; $x = ■, RS = ■$

79. $RS = 2(7y - 11), ST = 5y + 5$; $y = ■, RS = ■$

Lesson 4-1

$\triangle PQR \cong \triangle STV$. Solve for each variable.

80. $m\angle P = 4w + 5, m\angle S = 6w - 15$ **81.** $RQ = 10y - 6, VT = 5y + 9$

82. $m\angle T = 2x - 40, m\angle Q = x + 10$ **83.** $PR = 2z + 3, SV = 4z - 11$

Reading Math

Reading for Problem Solving

FOR USE WITH PAGE 362, EXERCISE 44

Read through the problem below and then follow along with what Sharleen thinks as she solves the problem. Check your understanding with the exercise at the bottom of the page.

You want to embroider a square design. You have an embroidery hoop with a 6 in. diameter. Find the largest value of x so that the entire square will fit in the hoop. Round to the nearest tenth.

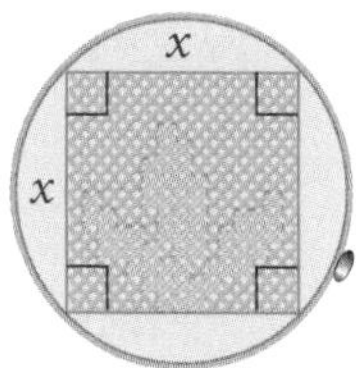

What Sharleen Thinks	What Sharleen Writes
I'll draw the diagram without the embroidery and mark in it the information I know. In particular, I'll show a 6-in. diameter that *also* happens to be a diagonal of the square.	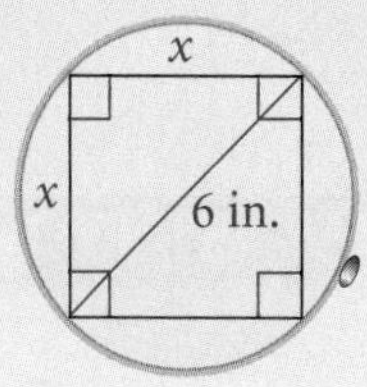
Now I have two right triangles. Each right triangle has two legs of length x in. and a hypotenuse of 6 in. I can apply the Pythagorean Theorem to find x.	Diameter = 6, so length of diagonal = 6 $a^2 + b^2 = c^2$ $a = x$, $b = x$, and $c = 6$ $x^2 + x^2 = 6^2$
Combine like terms. Divide each side by 2. Take the square root of each side. Use a calculator. Then round to the nearest tenth.	$2x^2 = 36$ $x^2 = 18$ $x = \sqrt{18}$ $x \approx 4.2426$
The largest square that you can embroider with this hoop has sides of 4.2 in. (Don't forget to include the unit of measure.)	$x \approx$ **4.2 in.**

EXERCISE

Find each measurement for $\triangle ABC$. Round to the nearest tenth.

a. the perimeter
b. the area

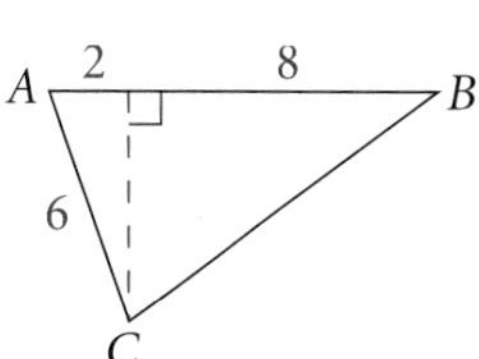

Special Right Triangles

Lesson Preview

What You'll Learn

To use the properties of 45°-45°-90° triangles

To use the properties of 30°-60°-90° triangles

. . . And Why

To find the distance from home plate to second base on a softball diamond, as in Example 3

✓ Check Skills You'll Need

(For help, go to Lesson 1-4.)

Use a protractor to find the measures of the angles of each triangle.

1.

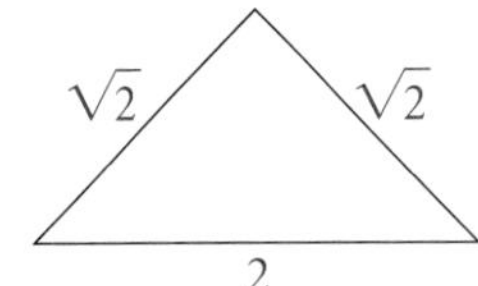

2.

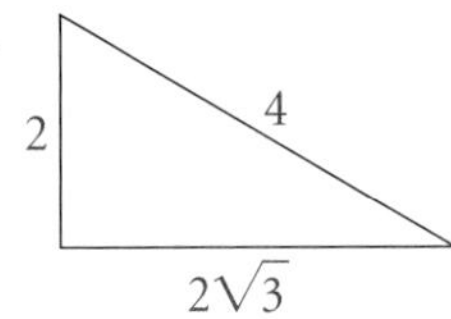

3.

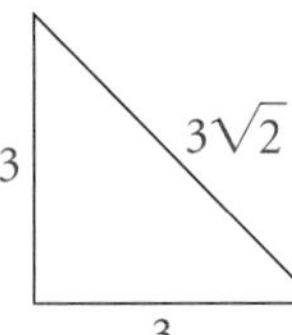

Interactive lesson includes instant self-check, tutorials, and activities.

OBJECTIVE

1 Using 45°-45°-90° Triangles

The acute angles of an isosceles right triangle are both 45° angles. Another name for an isosceles right triangle is a 45°-45°-90° triangle. If each leg has length x and the hypotenuse has length y, you can solve for y in terms of x.

$x^2 + x^2 = y^2$ **Use the Pythagorean Theorem.**

$2x^2 = y^2$ **Simplify.**

$x\sqrt{2} = y$ **Take the square root of each side.**

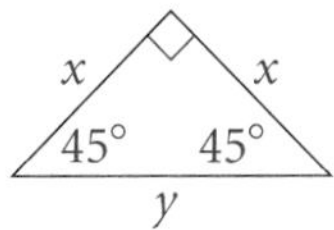

You have just proved the following theorem.

Key Concepts

Theorem 7-8 **45°-45°-90° Triangle Theorem**

In a 45°-45°-90° triangle, both legs are congruent and the length of the hypotenuse is $\sqrt{2}$ times the length of a leg.

$$\text{hypotenuse} = \sqrt{2} \cdot \text{leg}$$

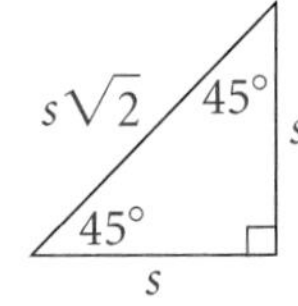

1 EXAMPLE Finding the Length of the Hypotenuse

Find the value of each variable.

a.

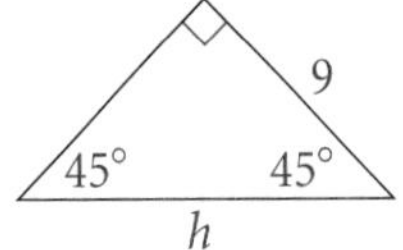

b.

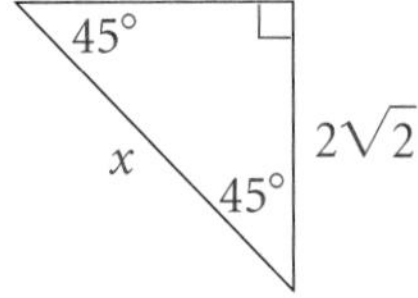

$h = \sqrt{2} \cdot 9$ ←**hypotenuse = $\sqrt{2}$ · leg**→ $x = \sqrt{2} \cdot 2\sqrt{2}$

$h = 9\sqrt{2}$ ← **Simplify.** → $x = 4$

✓ Check Understanding **1** Find the length of the hypotenuse of a 45°-45°-90° triangle with legs of length $5\sqrt{3}$.

You can use the 45°-45°-90° Triangle Theorem to find the length of a leg.

2 EXAMPLE Finding the Length of a Leg

Algebra Find the value of x.

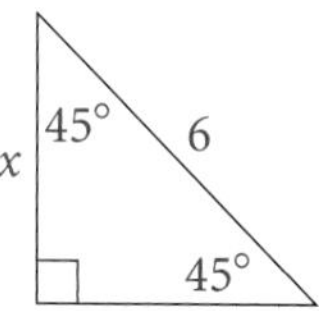

$6 = \sqrt{2} \cdot x$	**hypotenuse = $\sqrt{2}$ · leg**
$x = \frac{6}{\sqrt{2}}$	**Divide each side by $\sqrt{2}$.**
$x = \frac{6}{\sqrt{2}} \cdot \frac{\sqrt{2}}{\sqrt{2}} = \frac{6\sqrt{2}}{2}$	**Multiply by a form of 1.**
$x = 3\sqrt{2}$	**Simplify.**

✓ Check Understanding 2 Find the length of a leg of a 45°-45°-90° triangle with a hypotenuse of length 10.

Real-World Connection

Careers Opportunities for coaching in women's sports have soared since the passage of Title IX in 1972.

When you apply the 45°-45°-90° Triangle Theorem to a real-life example, you can use a calculator to evaluate square roots.

3 EXAMPLE Real-World Connection

Softball A high school softball diamond is a square. The distance from base to base is 60 ft. To the nearest foot, how far does a catcher throw the ball from home plate to second base?

The distance d from home plate to second base is the length of the hypotenuse of a 45°-45°-90° triangle.

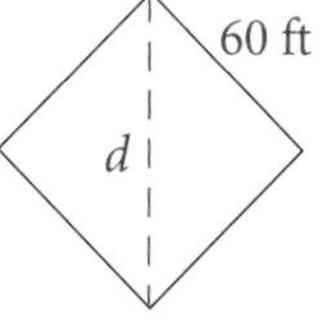

$d = 60\sqrt{2}$	**hypotenuse = $\sqrt{2}$ · leg**
$d = 84.852814$	**Use a calculator.**

On a high school softball diamond, the catcher throws the ball about 85 ft from home plate to second base.

✓ Check Understanding 3 A square garden has sides 100 ft long. You want to build a brick path along a diagonal of the square. How long will the path be? Round your answer to the nearest foot.

OBJECTIVE

2 Using 30°-60°-90° Triangles

Another type of special right triangle is a 30°-60°-90° triangle.

Key Concepts

Theorem 7-9 **30°-60°-90° Triangle Theorem**

In a 30°-60°-90° triangle, the length of the hypotenuse is twice the length of the shorter leg. The length of the longer leg is $\sqrt{3}$ times the length of the shorter leg.

hypotenuse = 2 · shorter leg

longer leg = $\sqrt{3}$ · shorter leg

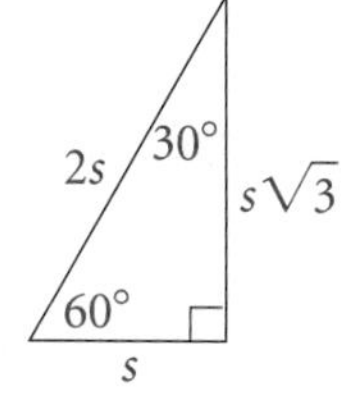

To prove Theorem 7-9, draw the a 30°-60°-90° triangle using an equilateral triangle.

Proof

Proof of Theorem 7-9

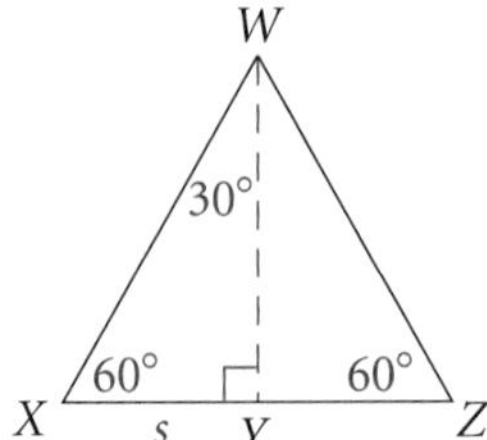

For 30°-60°-90° $\triangle WXY$ in equilateral $\triangle WXZ$, $\overline{WY}$ is the perpendicular bisector of $\overline{XZ}$. Thus, $XY = \frac{1}{2}XZ = \frac{1}{2}XW$, or $XW = 2XY = 2s$. Also,

$XY^2 + YW^2 = XW^2$	**Use the Pythagorean Theorem.**
$s^2 + YW^2 = (2s)^2$	**Substitute *s* for *XY* and 2*s* for *XW*.**
$YW^2 = 4s^2 - s^2$	**Subtract s^2 from each side.**
$YW^2 = 3s^2$	**Simplify.**
$YW = s\sqrt{3}$	**Find the square root of each side.**

Need Help?

In equilateral $\triangle WXZ$, $\overline{WY}$ is the bisector of $\angle XWZ$, the altitude and median to $\overline{XZ}$, and the perpendicular bisector of $\overline{XZ}$.

4 EXAMPLE Finding the Lengths of the Legs

Algebra Find the value of each variable.

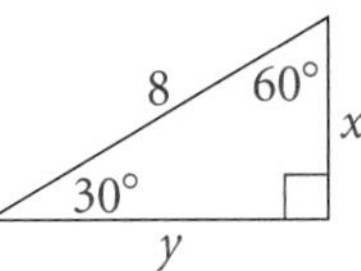

$8 = 2x$	**hypotenuse = 2 · shorter leg**
$x = 4$	**Solve for *x*.**
$y = x\sqrt{3}$	**longer leg = $\sqrt{3}$ · shorter leg**
$y = 4\sqrt{3}$	**Substitute 4 for *x*.**

Check Understanding 4 Find the lengths of the legs of a 30°-60°-90° triangle with hypotenuse of length 12.

5 EXAMPLE Using the Length of a Leg

Algebra Find the value of each variable.

d, 5, 60°, 30°, f

$5 = d\sqrt{3}$	**longer leg = $\sqrt{3}$ · shorter leg**
$d = \frac{5}{\sqrt{3}} \cdot \frac{\sqrt{3}}{\sqrt{3}} = \frac{5\sqrt{3}}{3}$	**Solve for *d*.**
$f = 2d$	**hypotenuse = 2 · shorter leg**
$f = 2 \cdot \frac{5\sqrt{3}}{3} = \frac{10\sqrt{3}}{3}$	**Substitute $\frac{5\sqrt{3}}{3}$ for *d*.**

Check Understanding 5 The shorter leg of a 30°-60°-90° triangle has length $\sqrt{6}$. What are the lengths of the other two sides? Leave your answers in simplest radical form.

You can use the properties of 30°-60°-90° triangles to find the dimensions you need to calculate area.

6 EXAMPLE Real-World Connection

Road Signs The moose warning sign at the left is an equilateral triangle. Each side is 1 m long. Find the area of the sign.

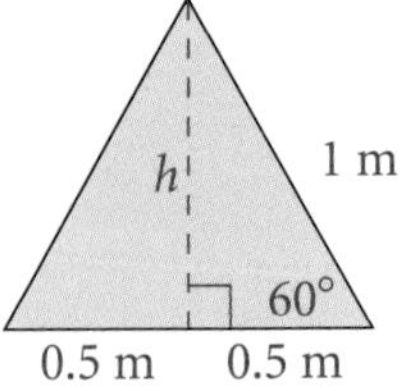

To find the area, copy the triangle, draw an altitude h and find its length. The altitude bisects the base and divides the triangle into two 30°-60°-90° triangles.

$h = 0.5\sqrt{3}$ **longer leg = $\sqrt{3}$ · shorter leg**

Use the value of h to find the area of the triangle.

$A = \frac{1}{2}bh$ **Use the formula for area of a triangle.**

$A = \frac{1}{2}(1)(0.5\sqrt{3})$ **Substitute 1 for *b* and $0.5\sqrt{3}$ for *h*.**

$A = 0.4330127$ **Use a calculator.**

The area of the sign is about 0.4 m^2.

✓ Check Understanding **6** A rhombus has 10-in. sides, two of which meet to form the indicated angle. Find the area of the rhombus. (*Hint:* Use a special right triangle to find height.)
a. a 30° angle **b.** a 60° angle

EXERCISES

For more practice, see *Extra Practice*.

Practice and Problem Solving

Practice by Example

Find the value of each variable. If your answer is not an integer, leave it in simplest radical form.

Example 1 (page 366)

1.
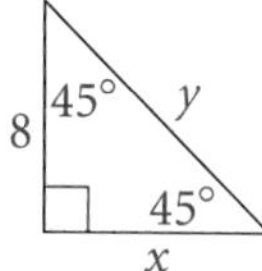

2.
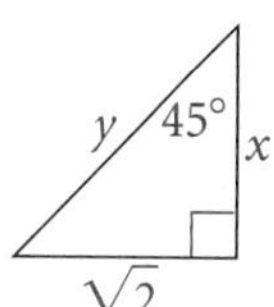

3.
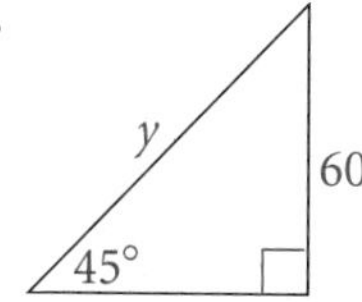

Examples 2, 3 (page 367)

4.
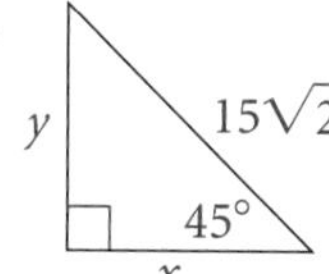

5.
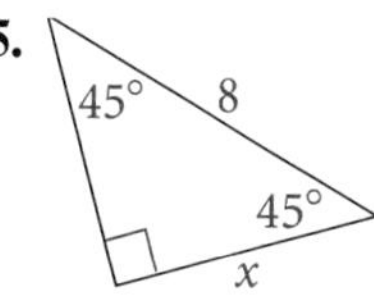

6.
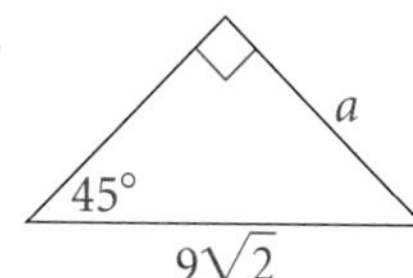

7.
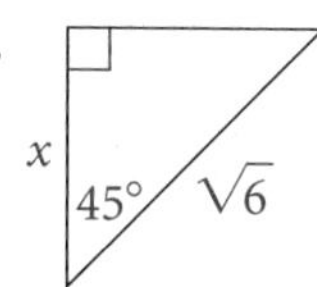

8.
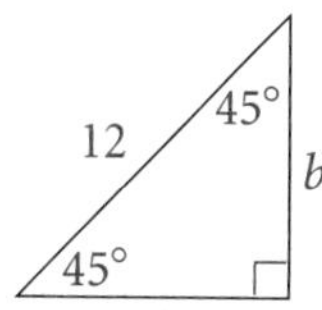

9.
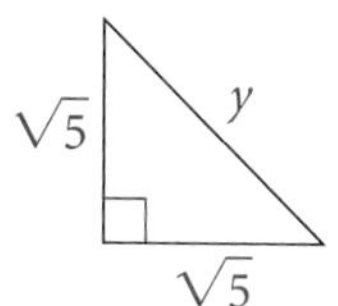

Exercise 10

10. Dinnerware Design You are designing dinnerware. What is the length of a side of the smallest square plate on which a 20-cm chopstick can fit along a diagonal without any overhang? Round your answer to the nearest tenth of a centimeter.

11. Helicopters The four blades of a helicopter meet at right angles and are all the same length. The distance between the tips of two adjacent blades is 36 ft. How long is each blade? Round your answer to the nearest tenth.

Example 4 (page 368)

Algebra **Find the value of each variable. If your answer is not an integer, leave it in simplest radical form.**

12.
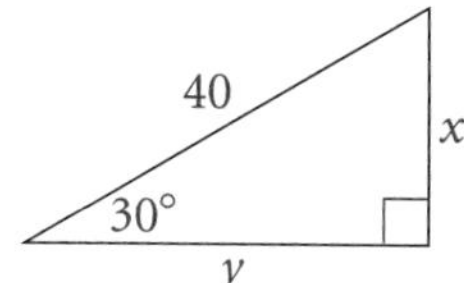

13.
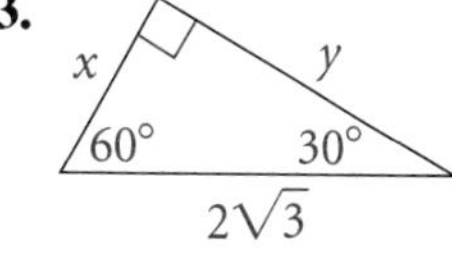

14.

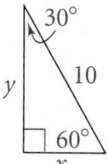

30°
y
10
60°
x

Example 5 (page 368) x^2 Algebra **Find the value of each variable. Leave your answer in simplest radical form.**

15. 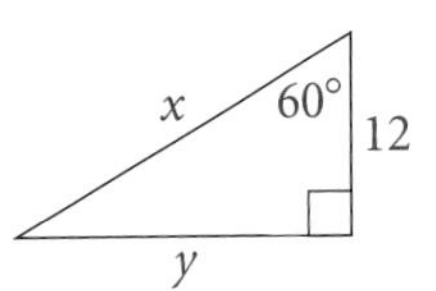

16. 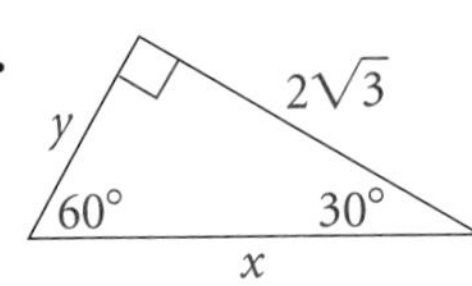

17. 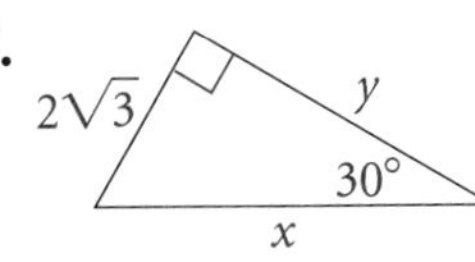

18. 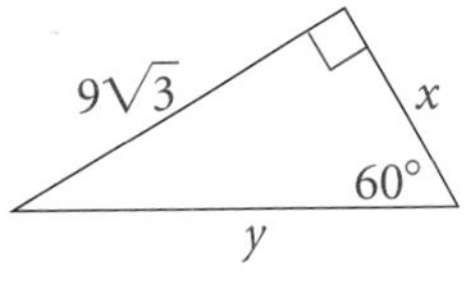

19. 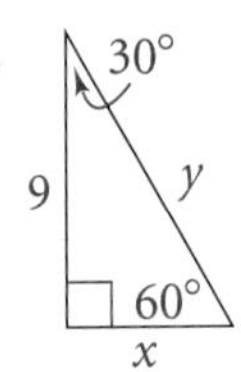

20. 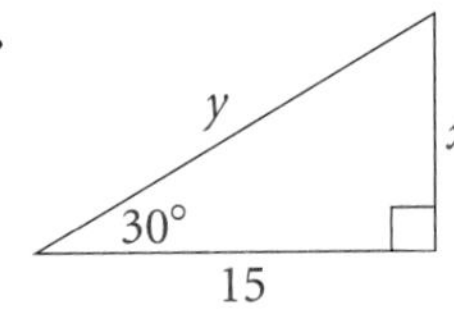

Example 6 (page 368) **Find the area of each figure. Round your answer to the nearest tenth.**

21. an equilateral triangle with sides 10 cm

22. a rhombus with a 60° angle and sides 5 cm long

23. a rhombus with a 45° angle and sides 12 m long

B Apply Your Skills

x^2 Algebra **Find the value of each variable. Leave your answer in simplest radical form.**

24. 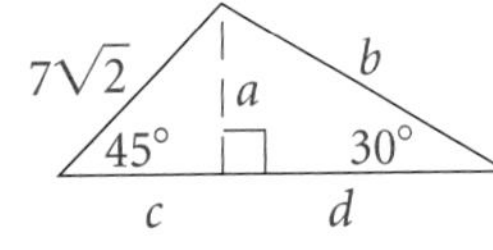

25. 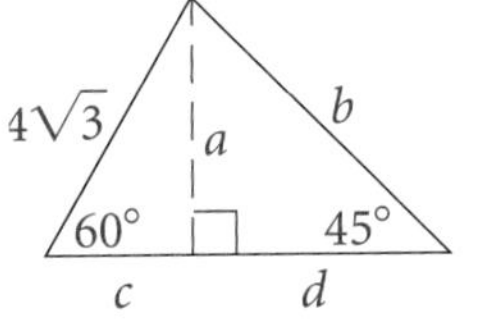

26. 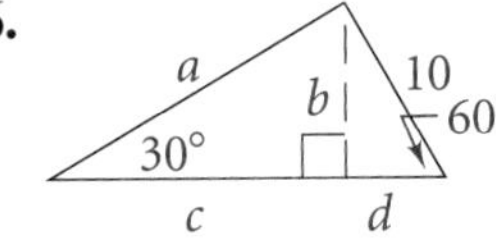

27. 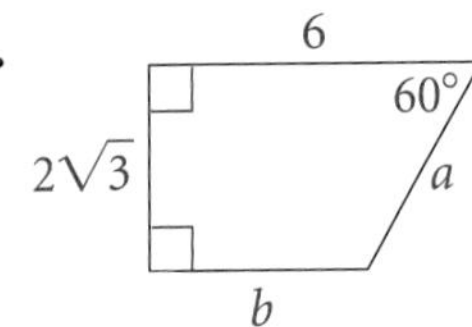

28. 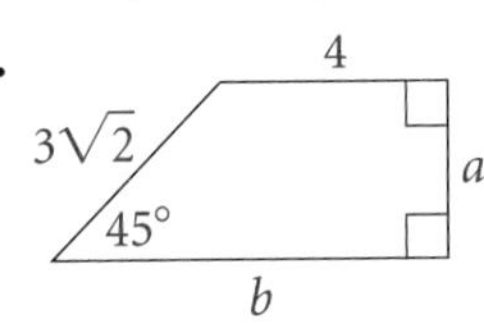

29. 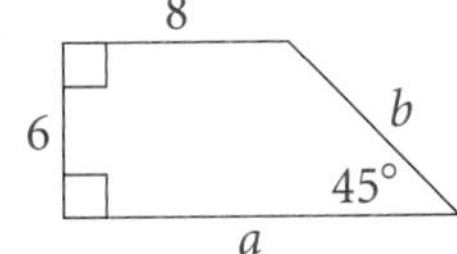

30. Error Analysis Sandra drew the triangle at the right. Rika said that the lengths couldn't be correct. With which student do you agree? Explain your answer.

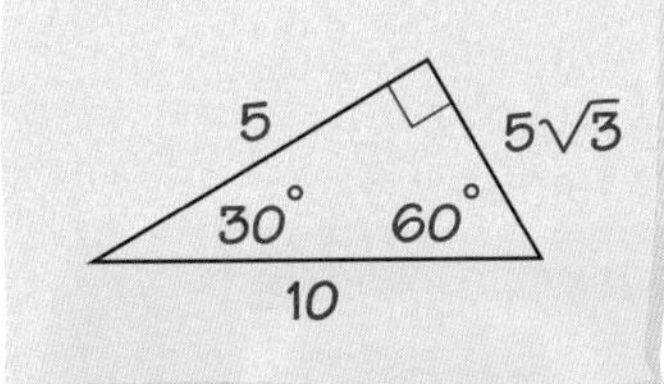

31. Open-Ended Write a real-life problem that you can solve using a 30°-60°-90° triangle with a 12 ft hypotenuse. Show your solution.

Exercise 32

32. Farming A conveyor belt carries bales of hay from the ground to the barn loft 24 ft above the ground. The belt makes a 60° angle with the ground.

a. How far does a bale of hay travel from one end of the conveyor belt to the other? Round your answer to the nearest foot.

b. The conveyor belt moves at 100 ft/min. How long does it take for a bale of hay to go from the ground to the barn loft?

33. House Repair After heavy winds damaged a farmhouse, workers placed a 6-m brace against its side at a 45° angle. Then, at the same spot on the ground, they placed a second, longer brace to make a 30° angle with the side of the house.

a. How long is the longer brace? Round your answer to the nearest tenth of a meter.

b. How much higher on the house does the longer brace reach than the shorter brace?

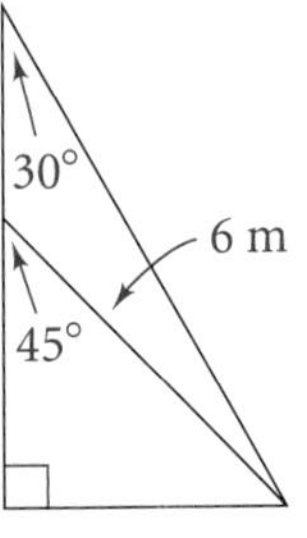

Find the area of each figure. When an answer is not a whole number, round to the nearest tenth.

34.

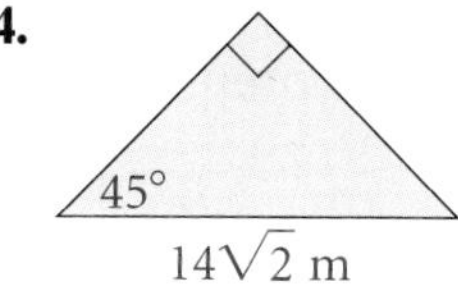

35.

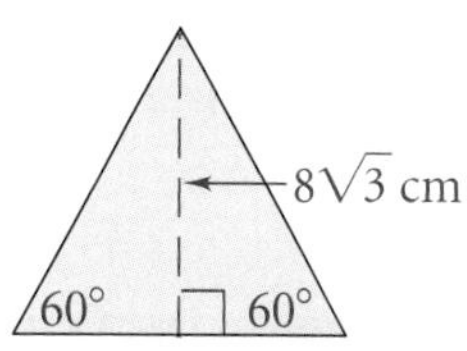

36.

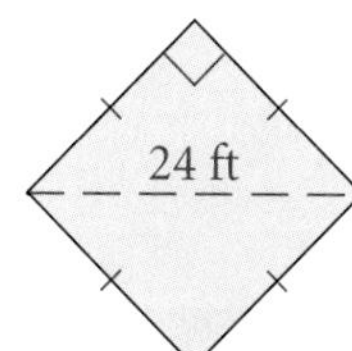

37.

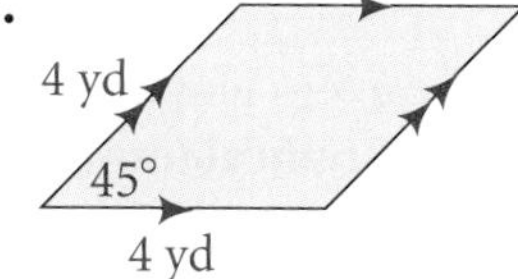

38.

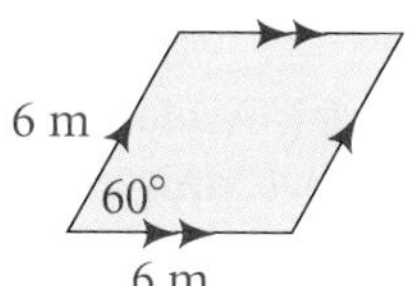

39.

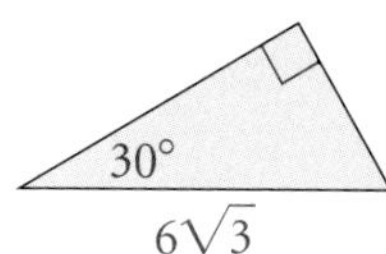

C Challenge

40. **Geometry in 3 Dimensions** Find the length d, in simplest radical form, of the diagonal of a cube with sides of the given length.

a. 1 unit **b.** 2 units **c.** s units

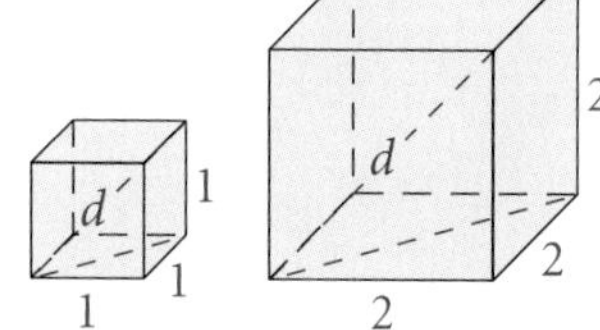

41. a. Find the area of an equilateral triangle with altitude 1 unit. Leave your answer in simplest radical form.

b. Use the relationships among the lengths of the sides in a 30°-60°-90° triangle to find a formula for the area of an equilateral triangle in terms of the length h of an altitude.

c. Use your formula from part (b) to find the area of an equilateral triangle with altitude of length 6 units.

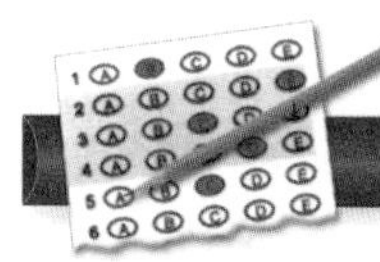

Standardized Test Prep

Quantitative Comparison

Compare the boxed quantity in Column A with the boxed quantity in Column B. Choose the best answer.

A. The quantity in Column A is greater.
B. The quantity in Column B is greater.
C. The two quantities are equal.
D. The relationship cannot be determined from the information given.

	Column A	Column B
42.	the length of the diagonal of a square with sides of length 3	the length of a leg of a 45°-45°-90° triangle with hypotenuse of length 3
43.	the length of the shorter leg of a 30°-60°-90° triangle with hypotenuse of length 4	the length of the hypotenuse of a 30°-60°-90° triangle with longer leg of length $\sqrt{3}$
44.	the length of an altitude of an equilateral triangle	the length of the shorter leg of a 30°-60°-90° triangle

Take It to the NET
Online lesson quiz at **www.PHSchool.com**
Web Code: afa-0703

Multiple Choice

45. What is the length of a diagonal of a square with sides of length 4?
A. 2 **B.** $\sqrt{2}$ **C.** $2\sqrt{2}$ **D.** $4\sqrt{2}$

Short Response

46. An isosceles right triangle has area 16 m^2.
   a. Find the length of each leg. Leave your answer in simplest radical form. Justify your answer.
   b. Find the length of the hypotenuse. Justify your answer.

Mixed Review

Lesson 7-2

An isosceles triangle has 20-cm legs and a 16-cm base. Find each of the following. Leave your answers in simplest radical form.

47. the length of the altitude to the base

48. the area of the triangle

Lesson 6-4

Determine whether each quadrilateral must be a parallelogram. If not, provide a counterexample.

49. The diagonals are congruent and perpendicular to each other.

50. Two opposite angles are right angles and two opposite sides are 5 cm long.

51. One pair of sides is congruent and the other pair of sides is parallel.

Lesson 4-3

Can you conclude that $\triangle TRY \cong \triangle ANG$ from the given conditions? If so, name the postulate or theorem that justifies your conclusion.

52. $\angle A \cong \angle T, \angle Y \cong \angle G, \overline{TR} \cong \overline{AN}$

53. $\angle T \cong \angle A, \angle R \cong \angle N, \angle Y \cong \angle G$

54. $\angle R \cong \angle N, \overline{TR} \cong \overline{AN}, \overline{TY} \cong \overline{AG}$

55. $\angle G \cong \angle Y, \angle N \cong \angle R, \overline{RY} \cong \overline{NG}$

Checkpoint Quiz 1 — Lessons 7-1 through 7-3

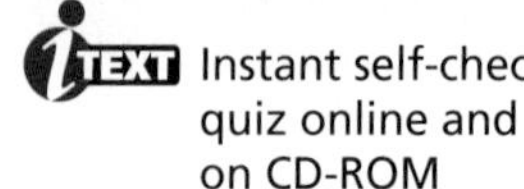

TEXT
Instant self-check quiz online and on CD-ROM

Find the area of each figure.

1.

8 in.

21 in.

2.

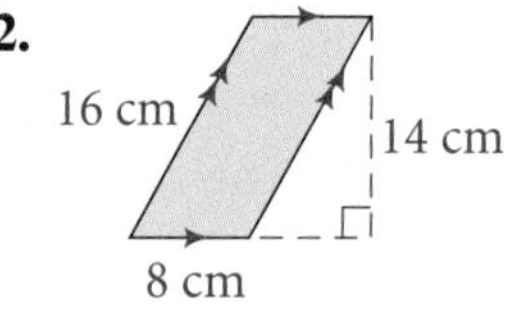

3.

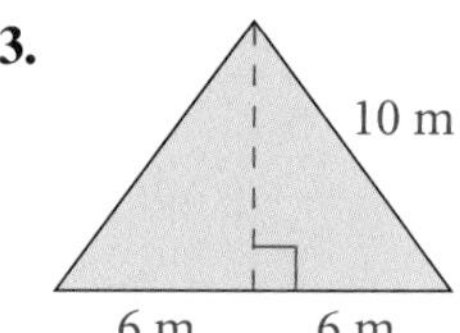

Algebra **Find the value of each variable. Leave your answer in simplest radical form.**

4.

x

15

9

5.

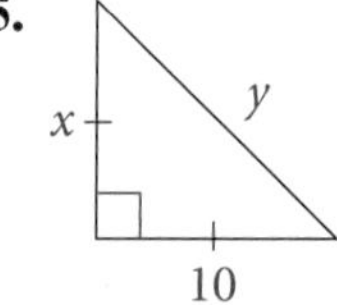

6.

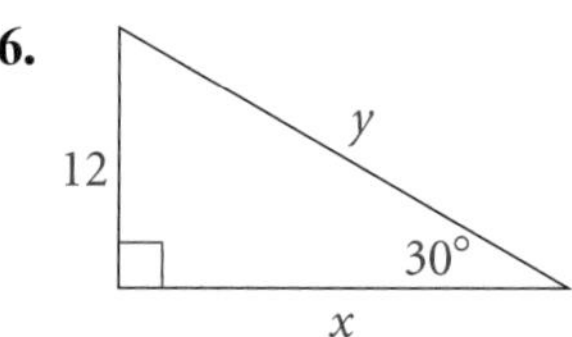

The lengths of the sides of a triangle are given. Classify each triangle as *acute*, *obtuse*, or *right*.

7. 7, 8, 9

8. 15, 36, 39

9. 10, 12, 16

10. A square has a 40-cm diagonal. How long is each side of the square? Round your answer to the nearest tenth of a centimeter.

Areas of Trapezoids, Rhombuses, and Kites

Lesson Preview

What You'll Learn

To find the area of a trapezoid

To find the area of a rhombus or a kite

. . . And Why

To use a map and the trapezoid area formula to approximate the area of Arkansas, as in Example 1

✓ Check Skills You'll Need

(For help, go to Lesson 7-1.)

Write the formula for the area of each type of figure.

1. a rectangle
2. a triangle

Find the area of each trapezoid by using the formulas for area of a rectangle and area of a triangle.

3. 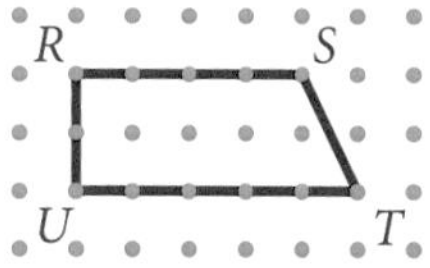 (trapezoid $RSTU$ on dot grid)
4. 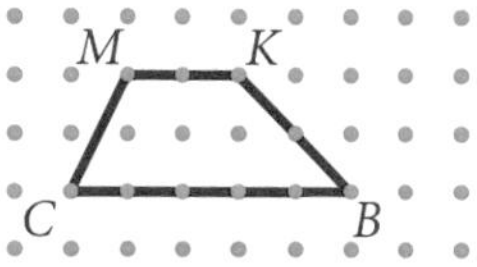 (trapezoid $MKBC$ on dot grid)
5. 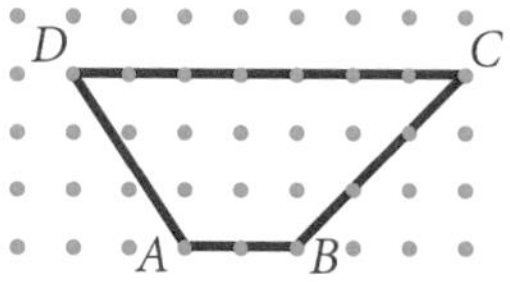 (trapezoid $DCBA$ on dot grid)

New Vocabulary • height of a trapezoid

Interactive lesson includes instant self-check, tutorials, and activities.

OBJECTIVE 1 Area of a Trapezoid

Investigation: Finding the Area of a Trapezoid

- Fold a piece of lined paper in half along one of the lines. On two lines of the folded paper, draw parallel segments of different lengths. Connect the endpoints of the segments to form a trapezoid. 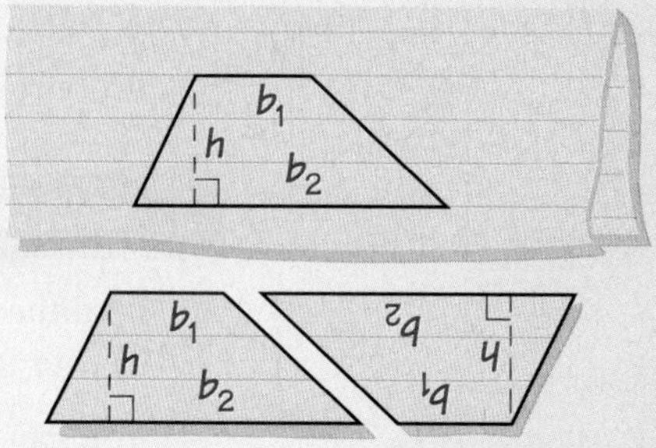
- Cut through both layers of the folded paper, so that you will have two congruent trapezoids. Label b_1, b_2, and h for each trapezoid.
- Arrange the congruent trapezoids to form a parallelogram as shown at the right above.

1. a. Write an expression for the length of the base of the parallelogram.
   b. Write an expression for the area of the parallelogram using b_1, b_2, and h.
2. How does the area of each trapezoid compare to the area of the parallelogram?
3. Use your answers to Exercises 1 and 2 to write a formula for the area of each trapezoid.

Reading Math

The term *base* can refer to either a line segment or its length.

In Lesson 6-5, you learned that the bases of a trapezoid are the parallel sides and the legs are the nonparallel sides. The **height of a trapezoid** is the perpendicular distance h between the bases.

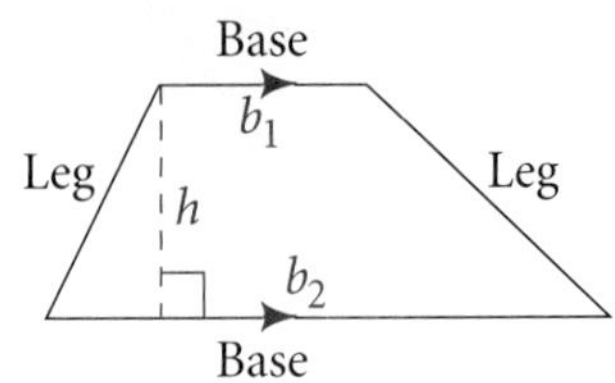

The pictures on the previous page suggest the following theorem.

Key Concepts

Theorem 7-10 **Area of a Trapezoid**

The area of a trapezoid is half the product of the height and the sum of the bases.

$$A = \frac{1}{2}h(b_1 + b_2)$$

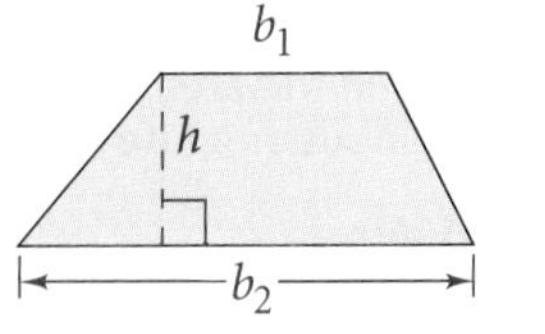

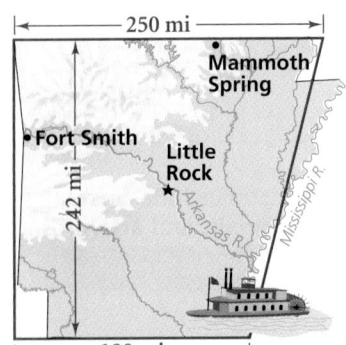

1 EXAMPLE Real-World Connection

Geography Approximate the area of Arkansas by finding the area of the trapezoid shown.

$A = \frac{1}{2}h(b_1 + b_2)$	**Use the formula for area of a trapezoid.**
$= \frac{1}{2}(242)(190 + 250)$	**Substitute 242 for h, 190 for b_1, and 250 for b_2.**
$= 53{,}240$	**Simplify.**

The area of Arkansas is about 53,240 mi^2.

Check Understanding 1 Find the area of a trapezoid with height 7 cm and bases 12 cm and 15 cm.

Properties of special right triangles can help you find the area of a trapezoid.

2 EXAMPLE Finding Area Using a Right Triangle

Find the area of trapezoid *PQRS*. Leave your answer in simplest radical form.

You can draw an altitude that divides the trapezoid into a rectangle and a 30°-60°-90° triangle. Since the opposite sides of a rectangle are congruent, the longer base of the trapezoid is divided into segments of lengths 2 m and 5 m.

Find h.

$h = 2\sqrt{3}$	**longer leg = shorter leg · $\sqrt{3}$**
$A = \frac{1}{2}h(b_1 + b_2)$	**Use the trapezoid area formula.**
$= \frac{1}{2}(2\sqrt{3})(7 + 5)$	**Substitute.**
$= 12\sqrt{3}$	**Simplify.**

The area of trapezoid *PQRS* is $12\sqrt{3}$ m^2.

Check Understanding 2 In Example 2, suppose h is made smaller so that $m\angle P = 45$ while bases and angles R and Q are unchanged. Find the area of trapezoid *PQRS*.

OBJECTIVE

2 Finding Areas of Rhombuses and Kites

Rhombuses and kites have perpendicular diagonals. This property allows you to find areas using the following theorem.

Key Concepts

Theorem 7-11 **Area of a Rhombus or a Kite**

The area of a rhombus or a kite is half the product of the lengths of its diagonals.

$$A = \frac{1}{2}d_1d_2$$

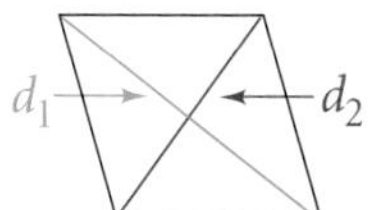

Proof

Visual Proof: The rectangle has sides d_1 and d_2 congruent to the diagonals of the kite or rhombus. Each triangle shaded blue in the diagram is congruent to the triangle shaded green that shares its hypotenuse. Thus, the area of the kite or rhombus is half the area of the rectangle.

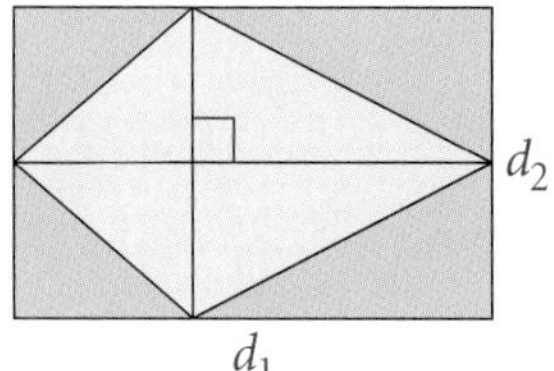

3 EXAMPLE Finding the Area of a Kite

Find the area of kite *KLMN*.

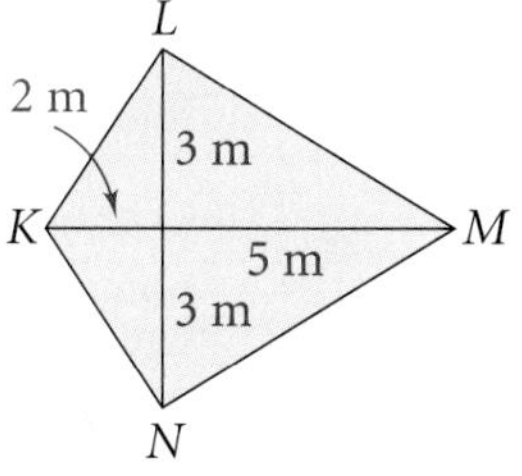

For the two diagonals, $KM = 2 + 5 = 7$ m and $LN = 3 + 3 = 6$ m.

$A = \frac{1}{2}d_1d_2$ **Use the formula for area of a kite.**

$A = \frac{1}{2}(7)(6)$ **Substitute 7 for d_1 and 6 for d_2.**

$A = 21$ **Simplify.**

The area of kite *KLMN* is 21 m^2.

Check Understanding **3** Find the area of a kite with diagonals that are 12 in. and 9 in. long.

The fact that the diagonals of a rhombus bisect each other can help you find the area.

4 EXAMPLE Finding the Area of a Rhombus

Find the area of rhombus *ABCD*.

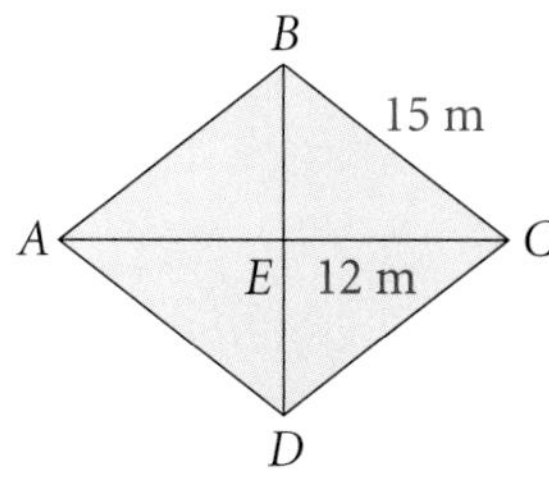

$\triangle BEC$ is a right triangle. Using a Pythagorean triple, $BE = 9$. Since the diagonals of a rhombus bisect each other, $AC = 24$ and $BD = 18$.

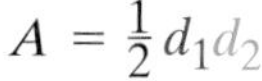

$A = \frac{1}{2}d_1d_2$ **Use the formula for area of a rhombus.**

$A = \frac{1}{2}(24)(18)$ **Substitute 24 for d_1 and 18 for d_2.**

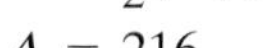

$A = 216$ **Simplify.**

The area is 216 m^2.

Check Understanding **4** **Critical Thinking** In Example 4, explain how you can use a Pythagorean triple to conclude that $BE = 9$.

EXERCISES

For more practice, see *Extra Practice.*

Practice and Problem Solving

A Practice by Example

Example 1 (page 374)

Find the area of each trapezoid.

1.

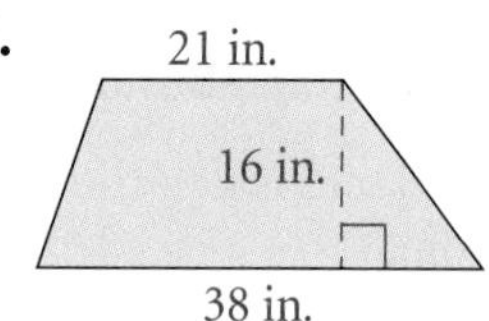

2.

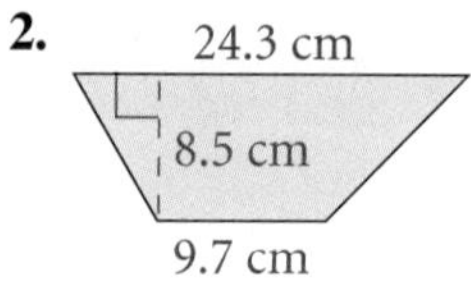

3.

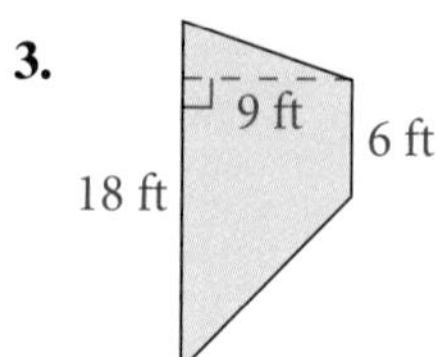

4. **Geography** Approximate the area of Nevada by finding the area of the trapezoid shown.

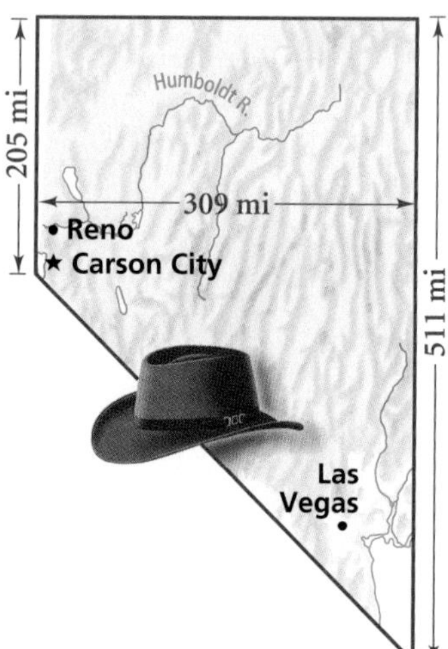

5. Find the area of a trapezoid with bases 12 cm and 18 cm and height 10 cm.

6. Find the area of a trapezoid with bases 2 ft and 3 ft and height $\frac{1}{3}$ ft.

7. **Geography** The border of Tennessee resembles a trapezoid with bases 342 mi and 438 mi, and height 111 mi. Approximate the area of Tennessee by finding the area of this trapezoid.

Example 2 (page 374)

Find the area of each trapezoid. If your answer is not an integer, leave it in simplest radical form.

8.

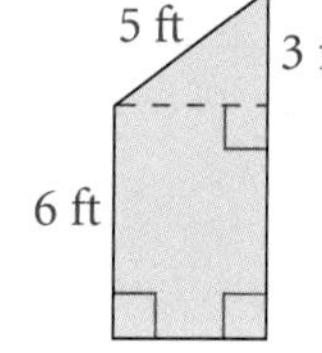

9.

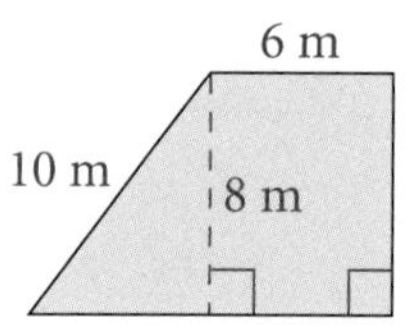

10.

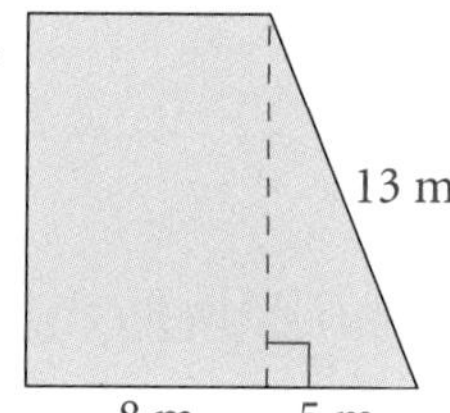

11.

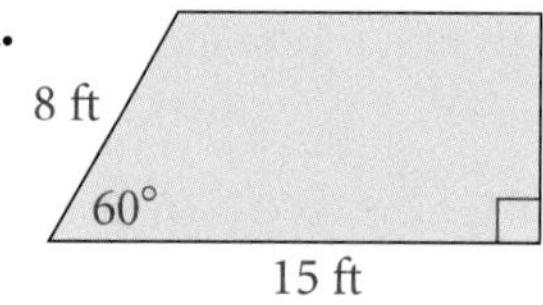

12.

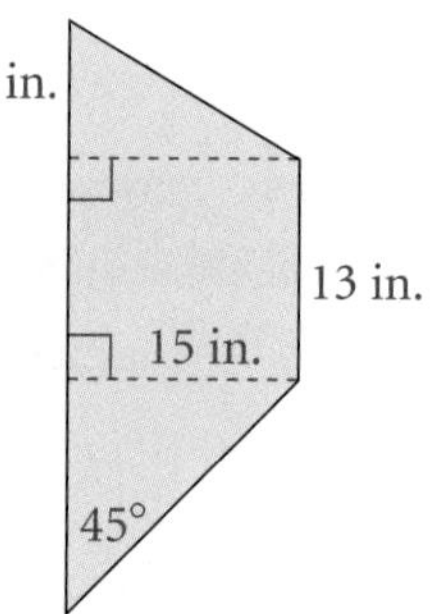

13.

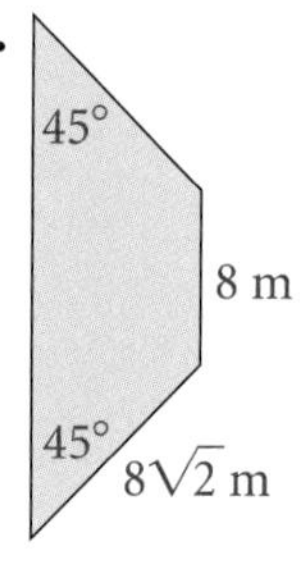

Example 3 (page 375)

Find the area of each kite.

14.

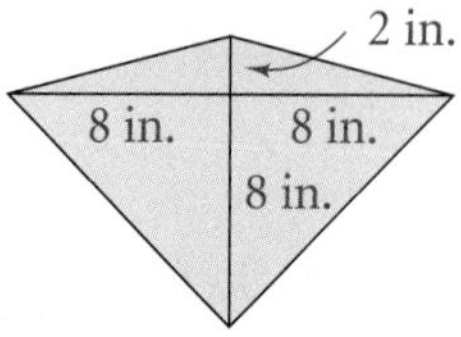

2 in.
8 in.
8 in.
8 in.

15.

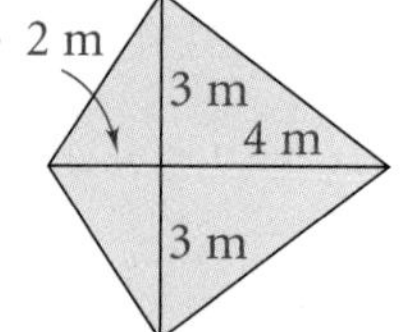

16.

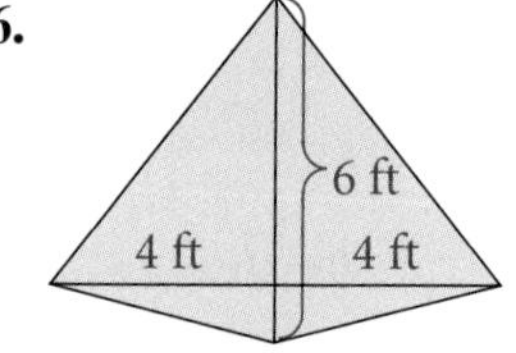

17. A kite has diagonals 7 ft and 16 ft. What is the area of the kite?

Example 4
(page 375)

Find the area of each rhombus.

18.

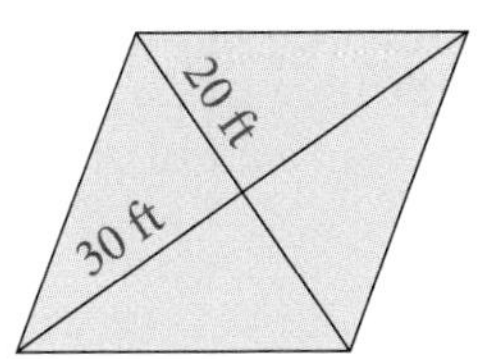

19.

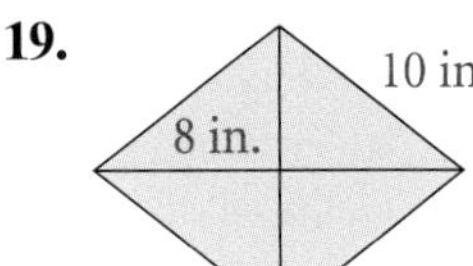

20.

6 m
5 m

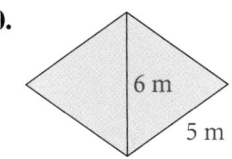

B Apply Your Skills

21. The end of the rain gutter has the shape of a trapezoid with the measurements shown. Find the area of this end.

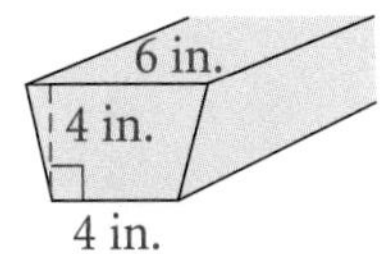

22. A trapezoid has two right angles, 12-m and 18-m bases, and 8-m height.
a. Sketch the trapezoid. **b.** Find the perimeter. **c.** Find the area.

23. Open-Ended Draw a kite. Measure the lengths of its diagonals. Find its area.

Real-World Connection

On each gold bar the four trapezoidal faces tip inwards. This simplifies the molding process.

Gold Bars **Find the area of each trapezoidal face of the gold bars.**

24. End face: bases 4 cm and 2 cm, height 3 cm.

25. Side face: bases 8 cm and 5 cm, height 3 cm.

Find the area of each trapezoid to the nearest tenth.

26.

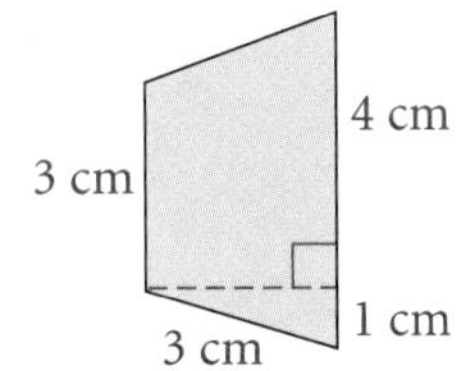

27.

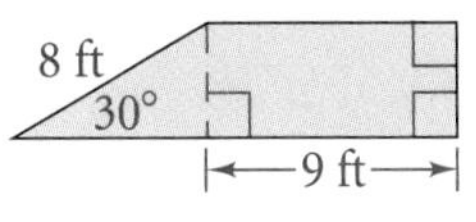

28.

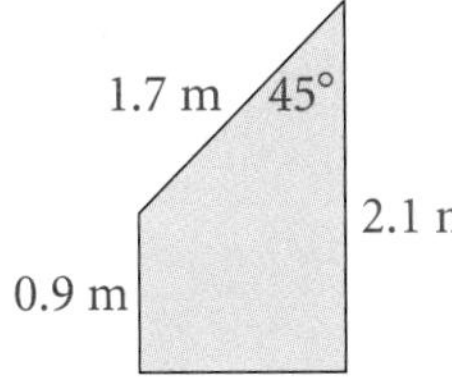

Coordinate Geometry **In Exercises 29–32, find the area of quadrilateral *QRST*.**

29.

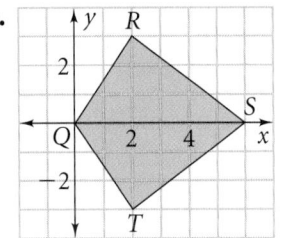

30.

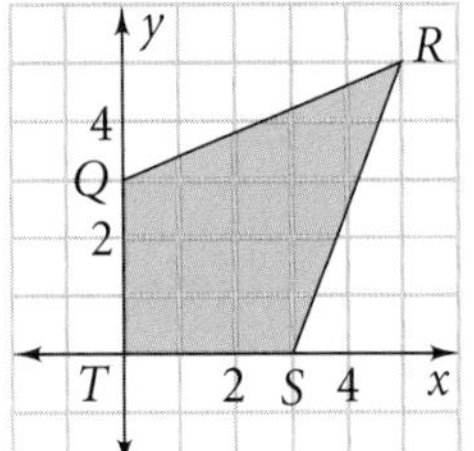

31.

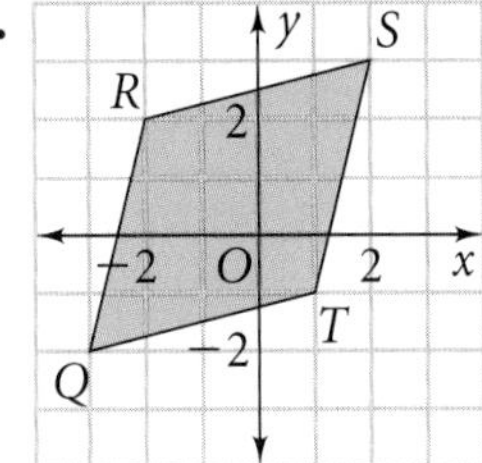

32. $QRST$ has vertices $Q(0, 0)$, $R(0, 5)$, $S(5, 5)$, and $T(7, 0)$.

33. Find the area of the kite at the right.

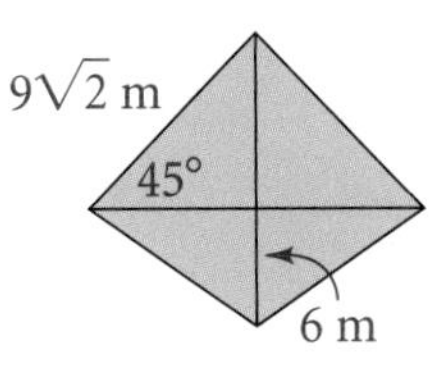

34. a. Coordinate Geometry Graph the lines $x = 0, x = 6, y = 0$, and $y = x + 4$.
b. What type of quadrilateral do the lines form?
c. Find the area of the quadrilateral.

Need Help?

In Exercises 35–37, recall what is true about the diagonals of a rhombus.

Find the area of each rhombus. Leave your answer in simplest radical form.

35.

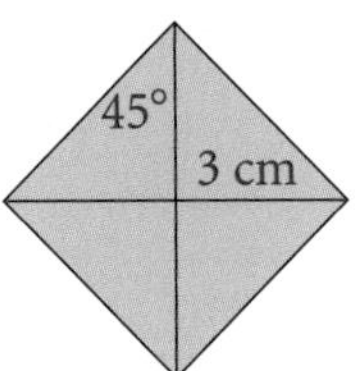

36.

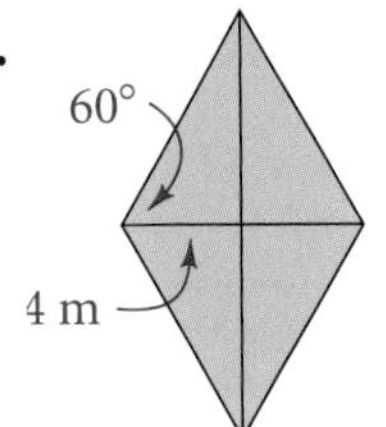

37.

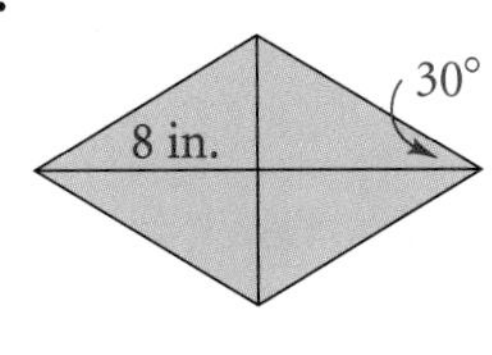

38. Draw a trapezoid. Label its bases and height b_1, b_2, and h, respectively. Then draw a diagonal of the trapezoid.

a. Write equations for the area of each of the two triangles formed.

b. **Writing** Explain how you can justify the trapezoid area formula using the areas of the two triangles.

C Challenge

39. **Algebra** One base of a trapezoid is twice the other. The height is the average of the two bases. The area is 324 cm^2. Find the height and the bases. (*Hint:* Let the smaller base be $2x$.)

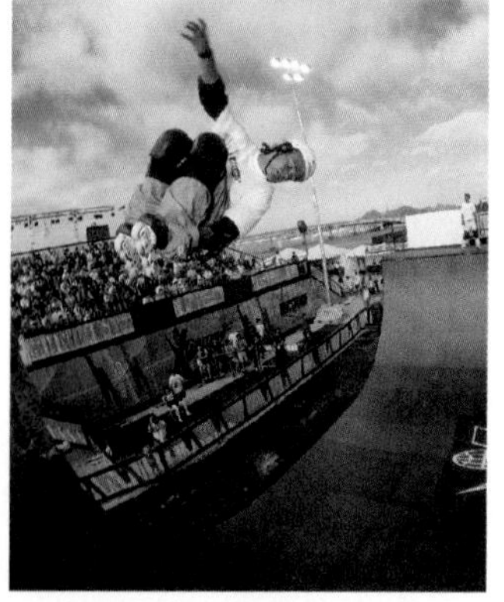

Real-World Connection

The curve of a half pipe is two quarter circles joined by a horizontal segment.

40. **Gravity Sports** Ty wants to paint one end of his homemade skateboarding ramp. The ramp is 4 m wide. Its surface is modeled by the equation $y = 0.25x^2$. Use the trapezoids and triangles shown to estimate the area to be painted.

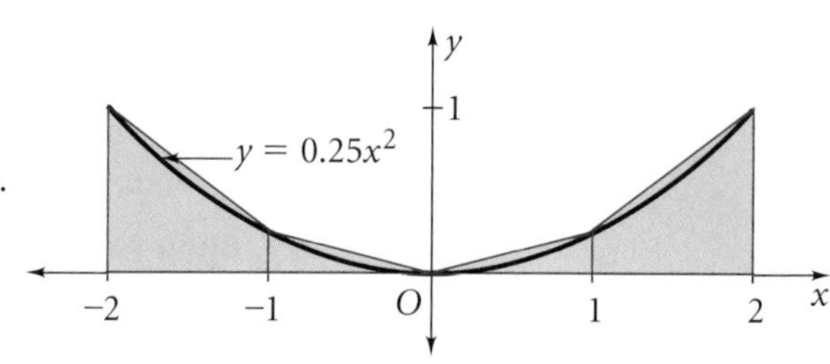

41. In trapezoid $ABCD$, $\overline{AB} \parallel \overline{DC}$. Find the area of $ABCD$.

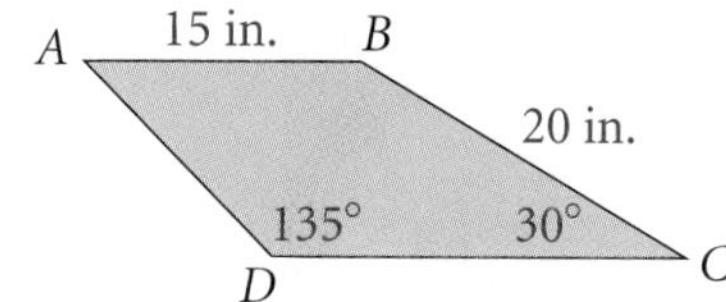

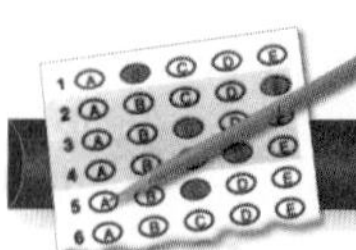

Standardized Test Prep

Multiple Choice

42. The area of a kite is 120 cm^2. The length of one diagonal is 20 cm. What is the length of the other diagonal?

A. 12 cm B. 20 cm
C. 24 cm D. 48 cm

43. What is the area of the trapezoid at the right?

F. 39 m^2 G. 60 m^2
H. 78 m^2 I. 96 m^2

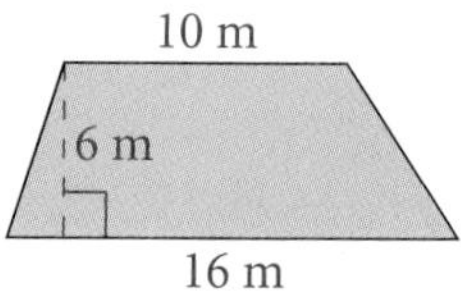

Quantitative Comparison

Compare the boxed quantity in Column A with the boxed quantity in Column B. Choose the best answer.

A. The quantity in Column A is greater.
B. The quantity in Column B is greater.
C. The two quantities are equal.
D. The relationship cannot be determined from the information given.

	Column A	Column B
44.	the area of a kite with 10-in. and 12-in. diagonals	the area of a rhombus with 10-in. and 12-in. diagonals
45.	the area of a rhombus with sides of length 5 cm	the area of a kite with 5-cm and 6-cm diagonals
46.	the area of a triangle with an 8-m base and a 10-m height	the area of a rhombus with congruent 9-m diagonals

Take It to the NET
Online lesson quiz at www.PHSchool.com
Web Code: afa-0704

Short Response

47. The area of an isosceles trapezoid is 160 cm^2. Its height is 8 cm and the length of one leg is 10 cm.
  a. Draw and label a diagram representing the given information.
  b. Find the length of each base. Show your work.

Mixed Review

Lesson 7-3

48. The hypotenuse of an isosceles right triangle has length $50\sqrt{2}$ in. Find the area of the triangle.

49. A diagonal of a square is 10 units. Find the length of a side of the square. Leave your answer in simplest radical form.

50. The area of a square is 20 cm^2. Find the length of its diagonal to the nearest tenth.

Lesson 5-3

Fill in the blank with *always, sometimes,* or *never* to form a true statement.

51. The incenter of a triangle _?_ lies inside the triangle.

52. The orthocenter of a triangle _?_ lies outside the triangle.

53. The centroid of a triangle _?_ lies on the triangle.

Lesson 3-4

54. Find the measure of an interior angle of a regular 9-gon.

A Point in Time

1500 1600 1700 1800 1900 2000

Presidents are known more often for their foreign policy than for their mathematical creativity. James Garfield, the 20th President of the United States, is an exception. In 1876, Garfield demonstrated this proof of the Pythagorean Theorem.

In the diagram, $\triangle NRM$ and $\triangle RPQ$ are congruent right triangles with sides of lengths a, b, and c. The legs of isosceles right triangle NRP have length c. The three triangles form trapezoid $MNPQ$. The sum of the areas of the three triangles equals the area of trapezoid $MNPQ$.

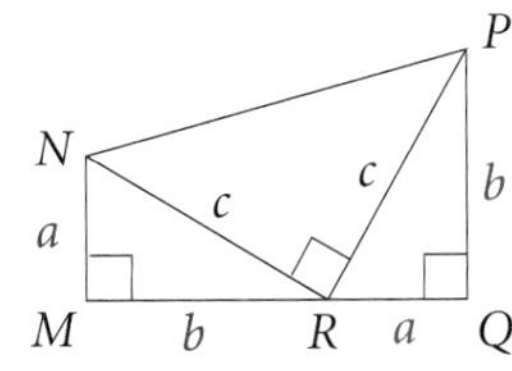

Areas of Triangles = Area of Trapezoid

$$\frac{1}{2}ab + \frac{1}{2}ab + \frac{1}{2}c^2 = \frac{1}{2}(a+b)(a+b)$$

$$ab + \frac{1}{2}c^2 = \frac{1}{2}a^2 + ab + \frac{1}{2}b^2$$

$$\frac{1}{2}c^2 = \frac{1}{2}a^2 + \frac{1}{2}b^2$$

$$c^2 = a^2 + b^2$$

Take It to the NET For more information about Pythagorean Theorem proofs, go to **www.PHSchool.com**.
Web Code: afe-2032

7-5 Areas of Regular Polygons

Lesson Preview

What You'll Learn

To find the area of a regular polygon

. . . And Why

To find the area of pieces of honeycomb material used to build boats, as in Example 3

✓ Check Skills You'll Need

(For help, go to Lesson 7-3.)

Find the area of each regular polygon. If your answer involves a radical, leave it in simplest radical form.

1. 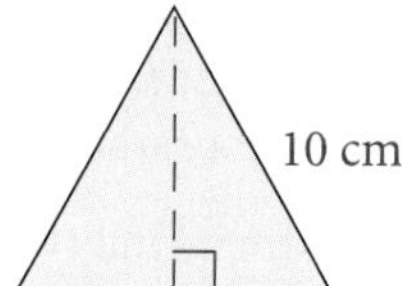

2. 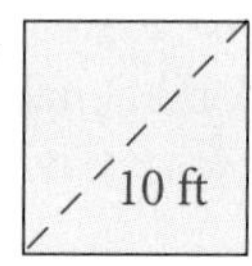

3. 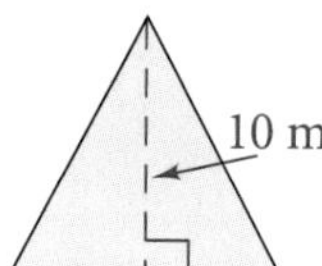

Find the perimeter of the regular polygon.

4. a hexagon with sides of 4 in.

5. an octagon with sides of $2\sqrt{3}$ cm

New Vocabulary
- center of a regular polygon
- radius of a regular polygon
- apothem of a regular polygon

Interactive lesson includes instant self-check, tutorials, and activities.

OBJECTIVE 1 Areas of Regular Polygons

Reading Math

The terms *radius* and *apothem* (AP uh them) can each refer to either a segment or its length.

You can circumscribe a circle about any regular polygon. The **center of a regular polygon** is the center of the circumscribed circle. The **radius** is the distance from the center to a vertex. The **apothem** is the perpendicular distance from the center to a side.

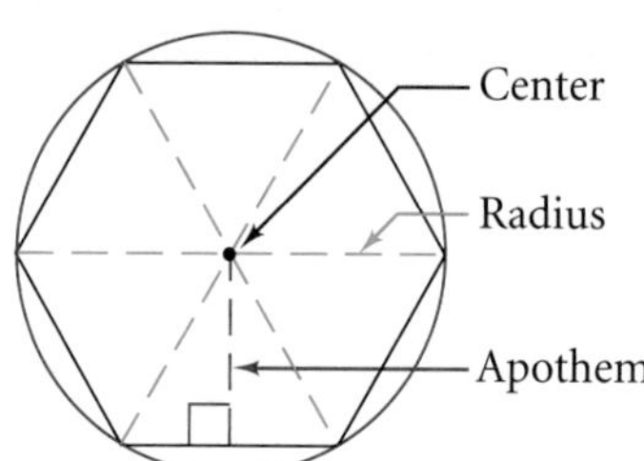

1 EXAMPLE Finding Angle Measures

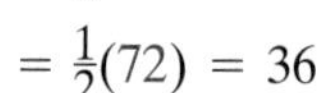

The figure at the right is a regular pentagon with radii and an apothem drawn. Find the measure of each numbered angle.

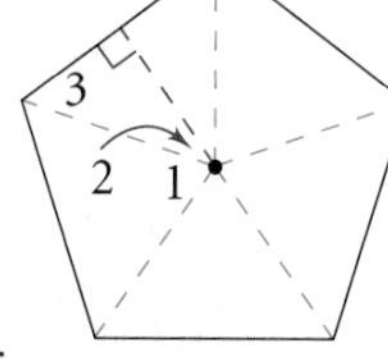

$m\angle 1 = \frac{360}{5} = 72$ **Divide 360 by the number of sides.**

$m\angle 2 = \frac{1}{2}m\angle 1$ **The apothem bisects the vertex angle of the isosceles triangle formed by the radii.**

$= \frac{1}{2}(72) = 36$

$90 + 36 + m\angle 3 = 180$ **The sum of the measures of the angles of a triangle is 180.**

$m\angle 3 = 54$

$m\angle 1 = 72, m\angle 2 = 36$, and $m\angle 3 = 54$

1 At the right, a portion of a regular octagon has radii and an apothem drawn. Find the measure of each numbered angle.

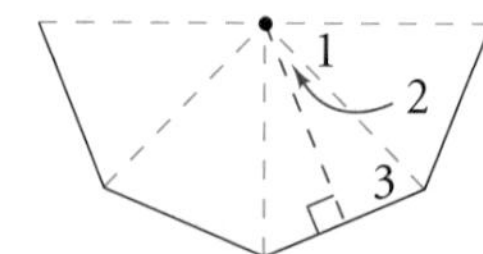

Suppose you have a regular n-gon with side s. The radii divide the figure into n congruent isosceles triangles. Each isosceles triangle has area equal to $\frac{1}{2}as$.

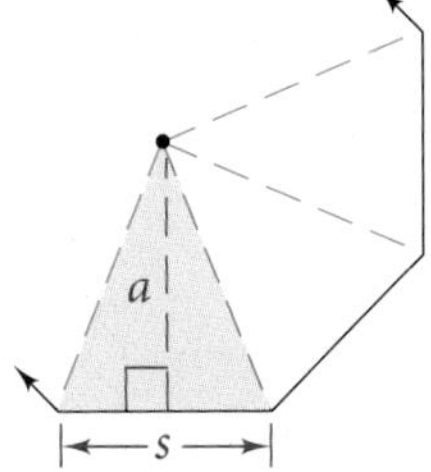

Since there are n congruent triangles, the area of the n-gon is $A = n \cdot \frac{1}{2}as$. The perimeter p of the n-gon is ns. Substituting p for ns results in a formula for the area in terms of a and p: $A = \frac{1}{2}ap$.

Key Concepts

Theorem 7-12 **Area of a Regular Polygon**

The area of a regular polygon is half the product of the apothem and the perimeter.

$$A = \frac{1}{2}ap$$

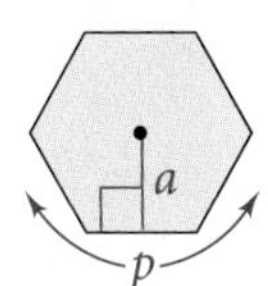

2 EXAMPLE Finding the Area of a Regular Polygon

Find the area of a regular decagon with a 12.3-in. apothem and 8-in. sides.

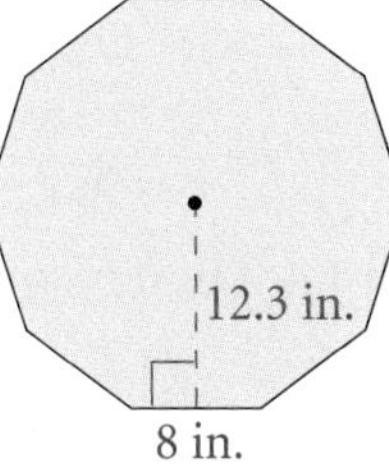

$p = ns$	**Find the perimeter.**
$= 10(8) = 80$ in.	**A decagon has 10 sides, so $n = 10$.**
$A = \frac{1}{2}ap$	**Use the formula for the area of a regular polygon.**
$= \frac{1}{2}(12.3)(80) = 492$	

The regular decagon has area 492 in.^{2}.

Check Understanding **2** Find the area of a regular pentagon with 11.6-cm sides and an 8-cm apothem.

3 EXAMPLE Real-World  Connection

Boat Racing Some boats used for racing have bodies made of a honeycomb of regular hexagonal prisms sandwiched between two layers of outer material. At the right is an end of one hexagonal cell. Find its area.

30° 60° a 10 mm 5 mm

The radii form six 60° angles at the center. You can use a 30°-60°-90° triangle to find the apothem a.

$a = 5\sqrt{3}$	**longer leg = $\sqrt{3}$ · shorter leg**
$p = ns$	**Find the perimeter of the hexagon.**
$= 6(10) = 60$	**Substitute 6 for n and 10 for s.**
$A = \frac{1}{2}ap$	**Find the area.**
$= \frac{1}{2}(5\sqrt{3})(60)$	**Substitute $5\sqrt{3}$ for a and 60 for p.**
≈ 259.80762	**Use a calculator.**

The area is about 260 mm^2.

Check Understanding **3** The side of a regular hexagon is 16 ft. Find the area of the hexagon.

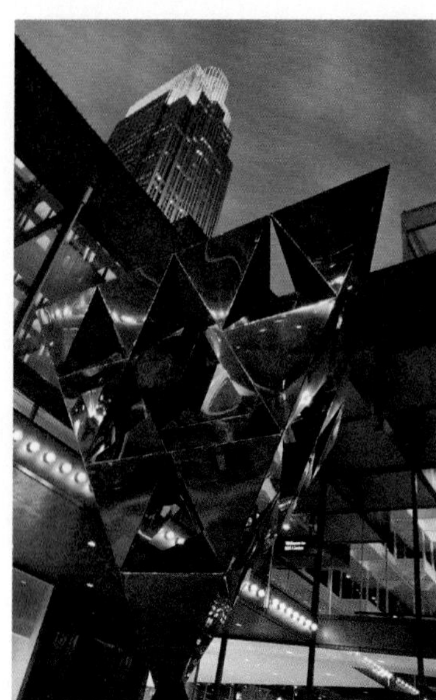

4 EXAMPLE Real-World Connection

Art The smaller triangles in the Minneapolis sculpture at the left are equilateral. Each has a 12.7-in. radius. What is the area of each to the nearest square inch?

You can use a 30°-60°-90° triangle to find the apothem a and the length s of a side.

$12.7 = 2 \cdot a$ — hypotenuse = 2 · shorter leg

$a = 6.35$

$\frac{s}{2} = 6.35\sqrt{3}$ — longer leg = $\sqrt{3}$ · shorter leg

$s = 12.7\sqrt{3}$

$p = ns$ — Find the perimeter.

$= 3(12.7\sqrt{3})$ — Substitute 3 for n and $12.7\sqrt{3}$ for s.

$= 38.1\sqrt{3}$

$A = \frac{1}{2}ap$ — Use the formula for area of a regular polygon.

$= \frac{1}{2}(6.35)(38.1\sqrt{3})$ — Substitute 6.35 for a and $38.1\sqrt{3}$ for p.

≈ 209.52186 — Use a calculator.

The area of each smaller triangle is about 210 in.^{2}.

Check Understanding **4** **Critical Thinking** In the Minneapolis sculpture, the 10 smaller triangles form a large triangle. What is the area of the large triangle?

EXERCISES

For more practice, see *Extra Practice*.

Practice and Problem Solving

A Practice by Example

Example 1 (page 380)

Each regular polygon has radii and apothem as shown. Find the measure of each numbered angle.

1. 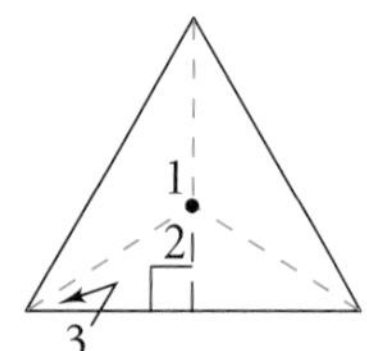

2. 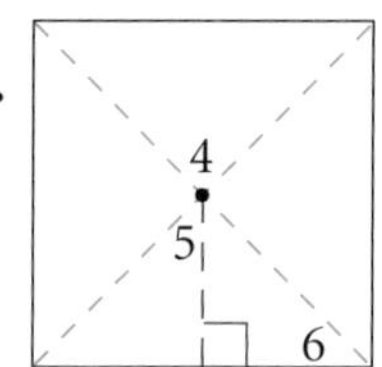

3. 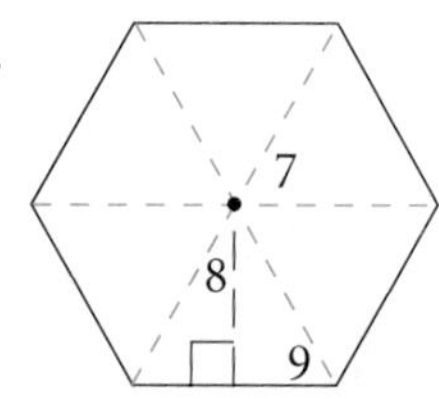

Example 2 (page 381)

Find the area of each regular polygon with the given apothem a and side length s.

4. pentagon, $a = 24.3$ cm, $s = 35.3$ cm
5. 7-gon, $a = 29.1$ ft, $s = 28$ ft
6. octagon, $a = 60.4$ in., $s = 50$ in.
7. nonagon, $a = 27.5$ in., $s = 20$ in.
8. decagon, $a = 19$ m, $s = 12.3$ m
9. dodecagon, $a = 26.1$ cm, $s = 14$ cm

Example 3 (page 381)

Find the area of each regular polygon. Round your answer to the nearest tenth.

10. 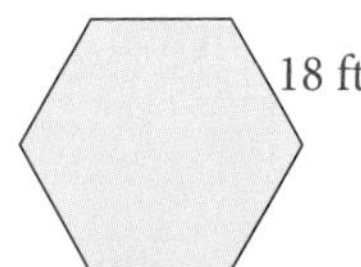

11. 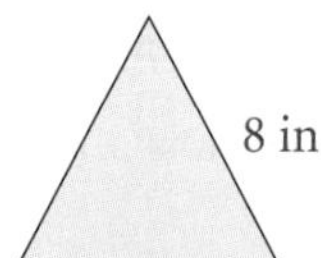

12. 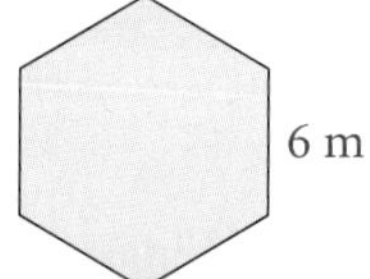

Example 4 (page 382)

Find the area of each regular polygon with the given radius or apothem. If your answer is not an integer, leave it in simplest radical form.

13. 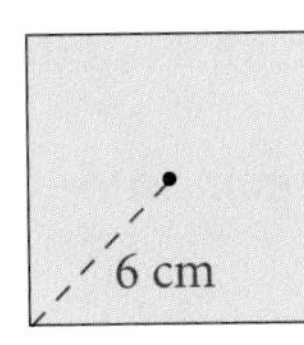

14. 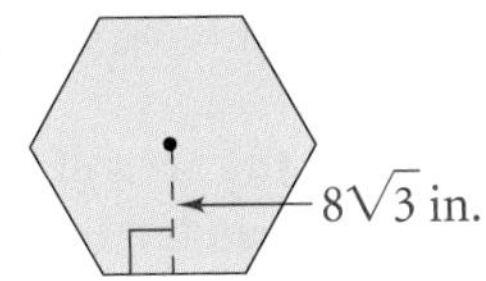

15. 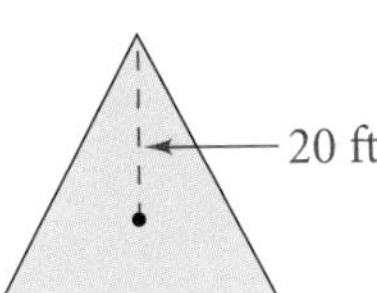

16. 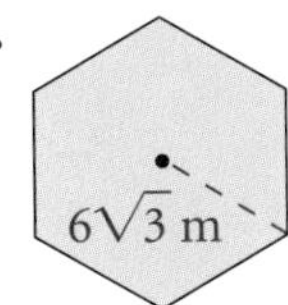

17. 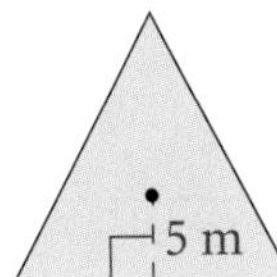

18. 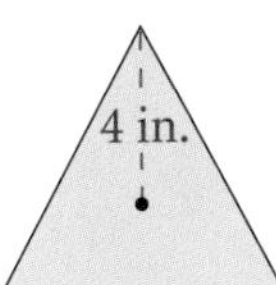

 Apply Your Skills

Find the measures of the angles formed by (a) two consecutive radii and (b) a radius and a side of the given regular polygon.

19. pentagon **20.** octagon **21.** nonagon **22.** dodecagon

23. Architecture The gazebo in the photo is built in the shape of a regular octagon. Each side is 8 ft long, and its apothem is 9.7 ft. To the nearest tenth, find the area enclosed by the gazebo.

24. The area of a regular polygon is 36 in.^{2}. Find the length of a side if the polygon has the given number of sides. Round your answer to the nearest tenth.

a. 3 **b.** 4 **c.** 6

d. Estimation Suppose the polygon is a pentagon. What would you expect the length of its side to be? Explain.

 **Need Help?**

In Exercise 25, $m\angle 1$ is what part of 360?

25. A portion of a regular decagon has radii and an apothem drawn. Find the measure of each numbered angle.

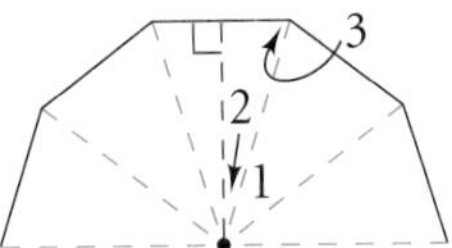

26. Writing Explain why the radius of a regular polygon is greater than the apothem.

27. Satellites One of the smallest space satellites ever developed has the shape of a pyramid. Each of the four faces of the pyramid is an equilateral triangle with sides about 13 cm long. What is the area of one equilateral triangular face of the satellite? Round your answer to the nearest whole number.

Find the area of each equilateral triangle with the given radius. Round your answers to the nearest whole number.

28. $r = 10$ in. **29.** $r = 4.6$ m **30.** $r = 8.9$ ft **31.** $r = 13$ cm

32. Constructions Use a compass to construct a circle.

a. Construct four perpendicular radii of the circle.

b. Construct radii that bisect each of the four right angles.

c. Connect the consecutive points where the radii intersect the circle. What regular polygon have you constructed?

d. Critical Thinking How can a circle help you construct a regular hexagon?

33. A regular hexagon has perimeter 120 m. Find its area.

34. **Open-Ended** Create a design using equilateral triangles and regular hexagons that have sides of the same length. Find the area of the completed design.

Find the area of each regular polygon. Show your answers in simplest radical form and rounded to the nearest tenth.

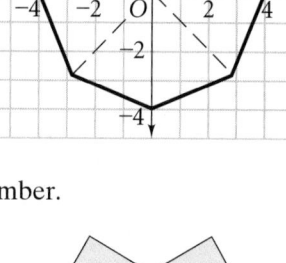

35. 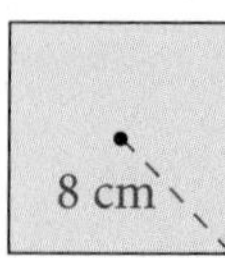

36. 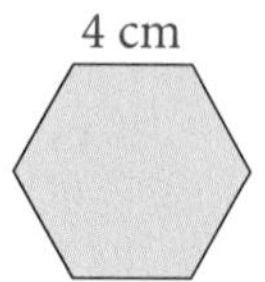

37. 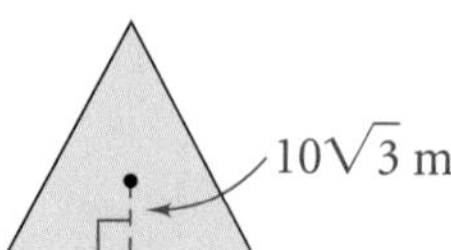

38. 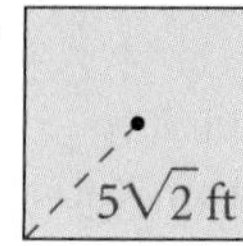

39. 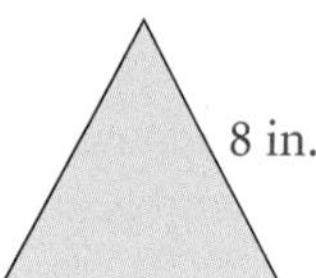

40. 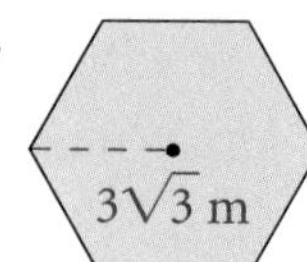

41. To find the area of an equilateral triangle, you can use the formula $A = \frac{1}{2}bh$ or $A = \frac{1}{2}ap$. A third way to find the area of an equilateral triangle is to use the formula $A = \frac{1}{4}s^2\sqrt{3}$. Verify the formula $A = \frac{1}{4}s^2\sqrt{3}$ in two ways as follows:

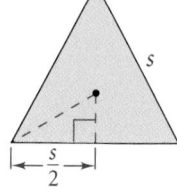

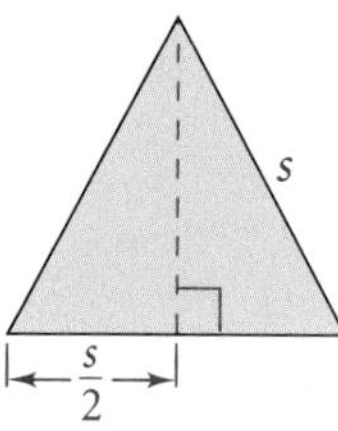

Figure 1

Figure 2

a. Find the area of Figure 1 using the formula $A = \frac{1}{2}bh$.

b. Find the area of Figure 2 using the formula $A = \frac{1}{2}ap$.

Proof 42. For Example 1 on page 380, write a proof that the apothem bisects the vertex angle of the isosceles triangle formed by the radii.

Challenge Proof 43. Prove that the bisectors of the angles of a regular polygon (given congruent sides and angles) are concurrent and that they are, in fact, radii of the polygon. (*Hint:* For regular n-gon $ABCDE\ldots$, let P be the intersection of the bisectors of $\angle ABC$ and $\angle BCD$. Show that $\overrightarrow{DP}$ must be the bisector of $\angle CDE$.)

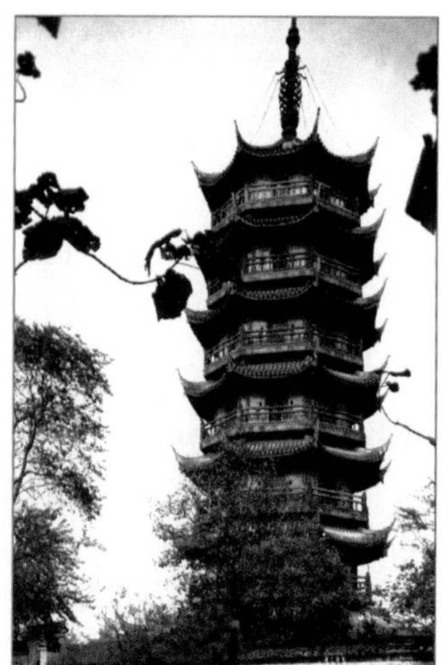

Real-World Connection

Horizontal cross sections of the Wenfeng Pagoda in Yangzhou, China, are regular octagons.

44. **Coordinate Geometry** A regular octagon with center at the origin and radius 4 is graphed in the coordinate plane.

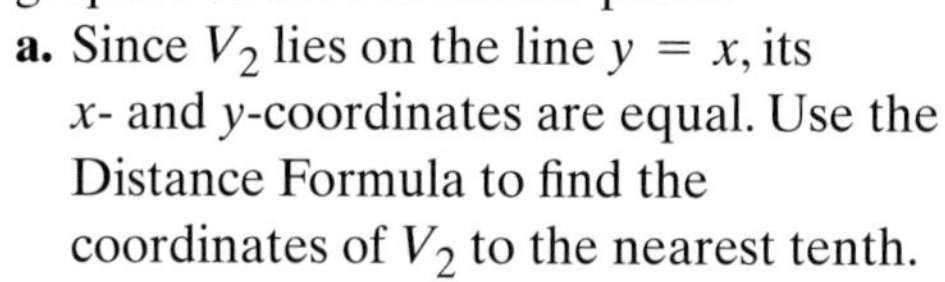

a. Since V_2 lies on the line $y = x$, its x- and y-coordinates are equal. Use the Distance Formula to find the coordinates of V_2 to the nearest tenth.

b. Use the coordinates of V_2 and the formula $A = \frac{1}{2}bh$ to find the area of $\triangle V_1OV_2$ to the nearest tenth.

c. Use your answer to part (b) to find the area of the octagon to the nearest whole number.

45. a. Find the area of the triangle if the area of each square is 10 cm^2.

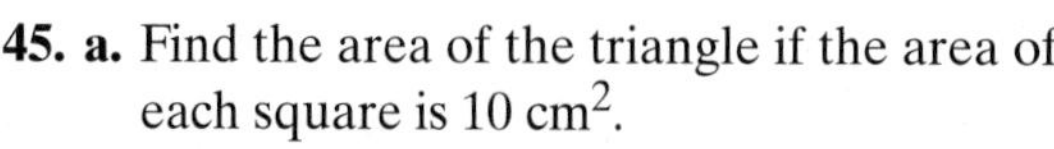

b. When a square and an equilateral triangle share a common side, what is the ratio of the area of the triangle to the area of the square? Leave your answer in simplest radical form.

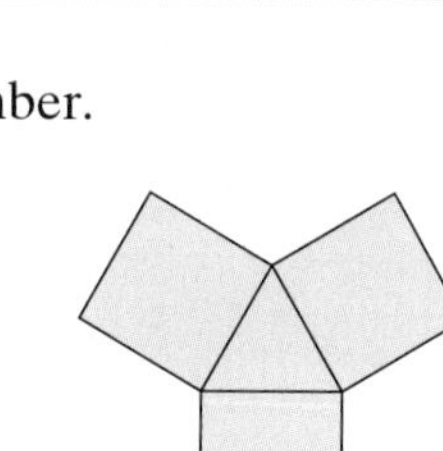

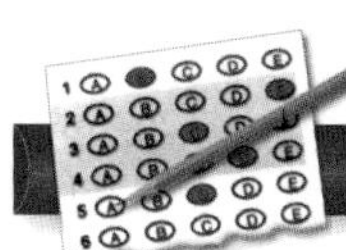

Standardized Test Prep

Multiple Choice

46. What is the area of a regular pentagon whose apothem is 25.1 mm and perimeter is 182 mm?
A. 913.6 mm^2 **B.** 2284.1 mm^2 **C.** 3654.6 mm^2 **D.** 4568.2 mm^2

47. The area of a regular octagonal garden is 1235.2 yd^2. The apothem is 19.3 yd. What is the perimeter of the garden?
F. 128 yd **G.** 154.4 yd **H.** 186.6 yd **I.** 192 yd

48. The radius of a regular hexagonal sandbox is 5 ft. What is the area to the nearest square foot?
A. 30 ft^2 **B.** 65 ft^2 **C.** 75 ft^2 **D.** 130 ft^2

Short Response

49. The perimeter of a regular decagon is 220 in. Its radius is 35.6 in.
a. Explain how to use the given information to find its area.
b. Find the area.

Extended Response

Take It to the NET
Online lesson quiz at
www.PHSchool.com
Web Code: afa-0705

50. In regular hexagon *ABCDEF*, $BC = 8\sqrt{3}$ ft.
a. Find the area of $\triangle BCG$.
b. Find the area of hexagon *ABCDEF*.
c. Describe two different methods for finding the area of hexagon *ABCDEF*.

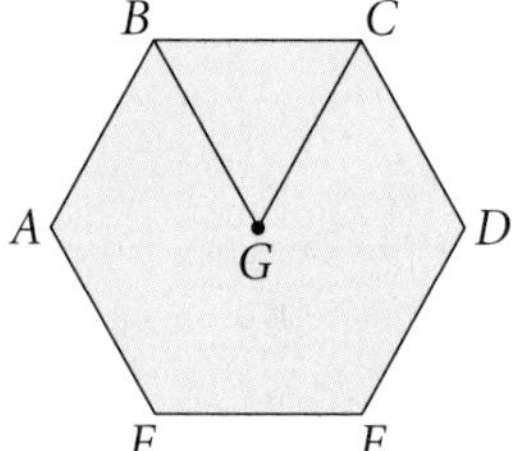

Mixed Review

Lesson 7-4

51. Find the area of a kite with diagonals 8 m and 11.5 m.

52. The area of a kite is 150 $in.^2$. The length of one diagonal is 10 in. Find the length of the other diagonal.

53. The area of a trapezoid is 42 m^2. The trapezoid has a height of 7 m and one base of 4 m. Find the length of the other base.

Lesson 4-4

Name the pairs of triangles you would have to prove congruent so that the indicated congruences are true by CPCTC.

Given: $\angle DAB \cong \angle CBA$,
$\overline{AD} \cong \overline{BC}$,
$\overline{DF}$ bisects $\angle ADB$,
$\overline{CG}$ bisects $\angle BCA$.

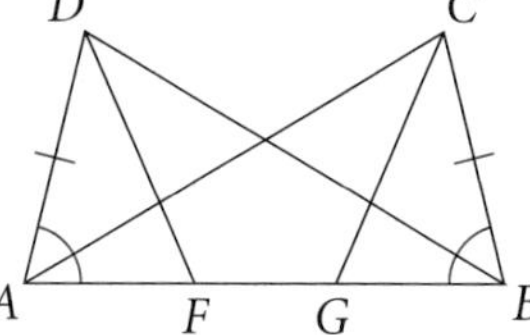

54. $\overline{AC} \cong \overline{BD}$

55. $\overline{AG} \cong \overline{BF}$

56. $\angle DFA \cong \angle CGB$

Lesson 1-7  

57. a. Biology The size of a jaguar's territory depends on how much food is available. Where there is a lot of food, such as in a forest, jaguars have circular territories about 3 mi in diameter. Use 3.14 for π to estimate the area of such a region to the nearest tenth.
b. Where food is less available, a jaguar may need up to 200 mi^2. Estimate the radius of this circular territory.

7-6 Circles and Arcs

Lesson Preview

What You'll Learn

OBJECTIVE 1: To find the measures of central angles and arcs

OBJECTIVE 2: To find circumference and arc length

. . . And Why

To use the turning radius of a car to compare the distances that its tires travel, as in Example 4

✓ Check Skills You'll Need

(For help, go to Lesson 1-7 and Skills Handbook, p. 723.)

Find the diameter or radius of each circle.

1. $r = 7$ cm, $d = ■$ **2.** $r = 1.6$ m, $d = ■$

3. $d = 10$ ft, $r = ■$ **4.** $d = 5$ in., $r = ■$

Round to the nearest whole number.

5. 9% of 360 **6.** 38% of 360 **7.** 50% of 360 **8.** 21% of 360

New Vocabulary

• circle • center • radius • congruent circles • diameter • central angle • semicircle • minor arc • major arc • adjacent arcs • circumference • pi • concentric circles • arc length • congruent arcs

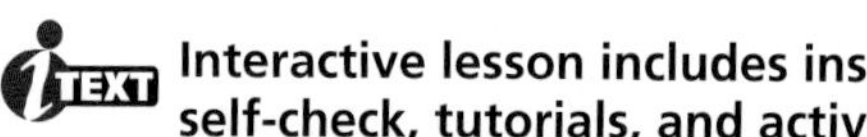

TEXT
Interactive lesson includes instant self-check, tutorials, and activities.

OBJECTIVE 1 Central Angles and Arcs

In a plane, a **circle** is the set of all points equidistant from a given point called the **center.** You name a circle by its center. Circle P ($\odot P$) is shown at the right.

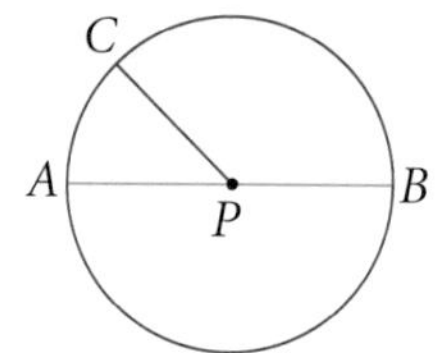

A **radius** is a segment that has one endpoint at the center and the other endpoint on the circle. $\overline{PC}$ is a radius. $\overline{PA}$ and $\overline{PB}$ are also radii. **Congruent circles** have congruent radii.

Reading Math

Diameter comes from the classical Greek words *dia*, meaning through, and *meter*, meaning measure.

A **diameter** is a segment that contains the center of a circle and has both endpoints on the circle. $\overline{AB}$ is a diameter.

A **central angle** is an angle whose vertex is the center of the circle. $\angle CPA$ is a central angle.

1 EXAMPLE Real-World Connection

Data Analysis To learn how people really spend their time, a research firm studied the hour-by-hour activities of 3600 people. The participants were between 18 and 90 years old. Each participant was sent a 24-hour recording sheet every March for three years from 2000 to 2002.

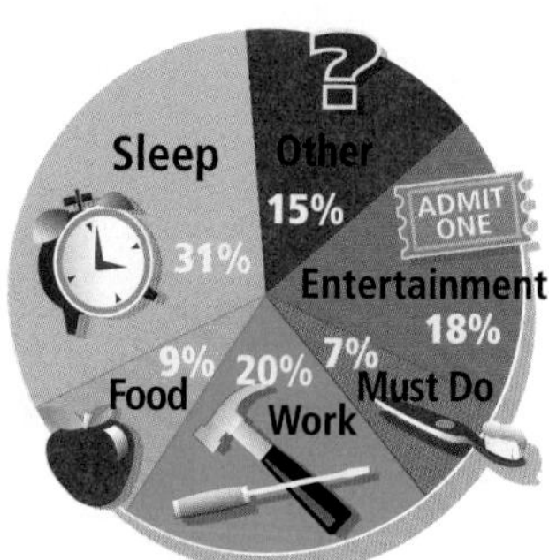

The study found that people spend most of their time sleeping, working, and watching television. Some information from the study is shown in this circle graph. Find the measure of each central angle in the circle graph.

There are 360 degrees in a circle. To find the measure of each central angle in the circle graph, find the corresponding percent of 360.

Sleep: 31% of 360 = 111.6	Other: 15% of 360 = 54
Food: 9% of 360 = 32.4	Entertainment: 18% of 360 = 64.8
Work: 20% of 360 = 72	Must Do: 7% of 360 = 25.2

Check Understanding 1 **a.** **Critical Thinking** Each section of the circle graph represents a measurable quantity. What is that quantity?
b. Each section of the circle graph represents an average. Explain.

The water line separates a circle into a major arc and a minor arc.

An arc is a part of a circle. One type of arc, a **semicircle,** is half of a circle. A **minor arc** is smaller than a semicircle. A **major arc** is greater than a semicircle.

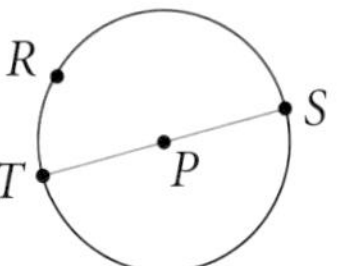

$\overparen{TRS}$ is a semicircle.
$m\overparen{TRS} = 180$

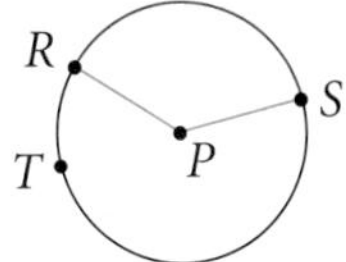

$\overparen{RS}$ is a minor arc.
$m\overparen{RS} = m\angle RPS$

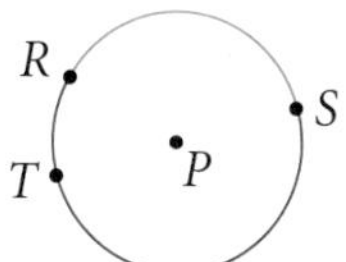

$\overparen{RTS}$ is a major arc.
$m\overparen{RTS} = 360 - m\overparen{RS}$

The measure of a semicircle is 180. The measure of a minor arc is the measure of its corresponding central angle. The measure of a major arc is 360 minus the measure of its related minor arc.

2 EXAMPLE Identifying Arcs

Identify the following in $\odot O$.

a. the minor arcs

$\overparen{AD}$, $\overparen{CE}$, $\overparen{AC}$, and $\overparen{DE}$ are minor arcs.

b. the semicircles

$\overparen{ACE}$, $\overparen{CED}$, $\overparen{EDA}$, and $\overparen{DAC}$ are semicircles.

c. the major arcs that contain point A

$\overparen{ACD}$, $\overparen{CEA}$, $\overparen{EDC}$, and $\overparen{DAE}$ are major arcs that contain point A.

Check Understanding 2 Identify the four major arcs of $\odot O$ that contain point E.

Adjacent arcs are arcs of the same circle that have exactly one point in common. You can add the measures of adjacent arcs just as you can add the measures of adjacent angles.

Key Concepts

Postulate 7-1 **Arc Addition Postulate**

The measure of the arc formed by two adjacent arcs is the sum of the measures of the two arcs.

$$m\overparen{ABC} = m\overparen{AB} + m\overparen{BC}$$

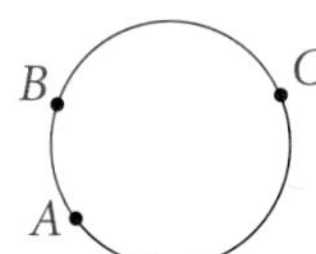

3 EXAMPLE Finding the Measures of Arcs

Find the measure of each arc.

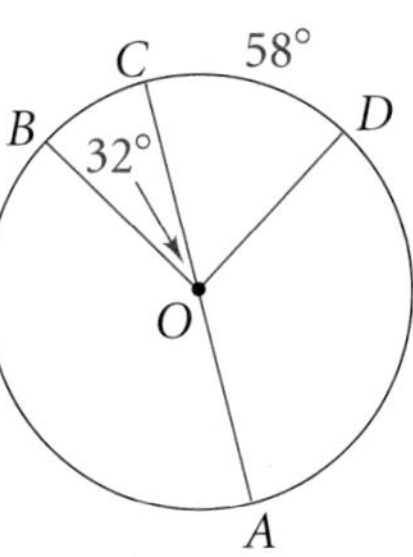

a. $\overparen{BC}$ $\quad m\overparen{BC} = m\angle BOC = 32$

b. $\overparen{BD}$ $\quad m\overparen{BD} = m\overparen{BC} + m\overparen{CD}$

$m\overparen{BD} = 32 + 58 = 90$

c. $\overparen{ABC}$ $\quad \overparen{ABC}$ is a semicircle.

$m\overparen{ABC} = 180$

d. $\overparen{AB}$ $\quad m\overparen{AB} = 180 - 32 = 148$

Check Understanding 3 Find $m\angle COD$, $m\overparen{CDA}$, $m\overparen{AD}$ and $m\overparen{BAD}$.

OBJECTIVE

2 Circumference and Arc Length

The **circumference** of a circle is the distance around the circle. The number **pi** (π) is the ratio of the circumference of a circle to its diameter.

Key Concepts

Theorem 7-13 **Circumference of a Circle**

The circumference of a circle is π times the diameter.

$$C = \pi d \text{ or } C = 2\pi r$$

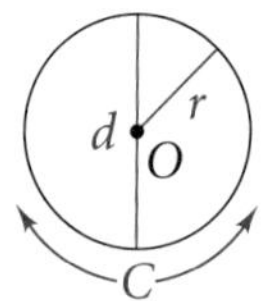

Since the number π is irrational, you cannot write it as a terminating or repeating decimal. To approximate π, you can use 3.14, $\frac{22}{7}$, or the π key on your calculator.

Circles that lie in the same plane and have the same center are **concentric circles.**

4 EXAMPLE Real-World Connection

Automobiles A car has a turning radius of 16.1 ft. The distance between the two front tires is 4.7 ft. In completing the (outer) turning circle, how much farther does a tire travel than a tire on the concentric inner circle?

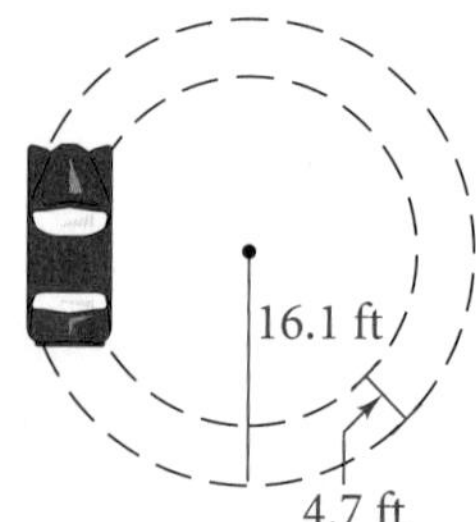

To find the radius of the inner circle, subtract 4.7 ft from the turning radius.

circumference of outer circle $= C = 2\pi r = 2\pi(16.1) = 32.2\pi$

radius of the inner circle $= 16.1 - 4.7 = 11.4$

circumference of inner circle $= C = 2\pi r = 2\pi(11.4) = 22.8\pi$

The difference in the two distances is $32.2\pi - 22.8\pi$, or 9.4π.

$9.4\pi \approx$ 29.530971 **Use a calculator.**

A tire on the turning circle travels about 29.5 ft farther than a tire on the inner circle.

Check Understanding 4 The diameter of a bicycle wheel is 22 in. To the nearest whole number, how many revolutions does the wheel make when the bicycle travels 100 ft?

The measure of an arc is in degrees while the **arc length** is a fraction of a circle's circumference. An arc of 60° represents $\frac{60}{360}$ or $\frac{1}{6}$ of the circle. Its arc length is $\frac{1}{6}$ the circumference of the circle. This observation suggests the following theorem.

Key Concepts

Theorem 7-14 **Arc Length**

The length of an arc of a circle is the product of the ratio $\frac{\text{measure of the arc}}{360}$ and the circumference of the circle.

$$\text{length of } \widehat{AB} = \frac{m\widehat{AB}}{360} \cdot 2\pi r$$

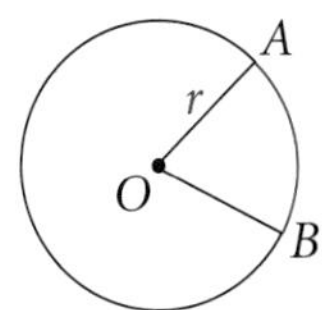

5 EXAMPLE Finding Arc Length

Find the length of each arc shown in red. Leave your answer in terms of π.

a.

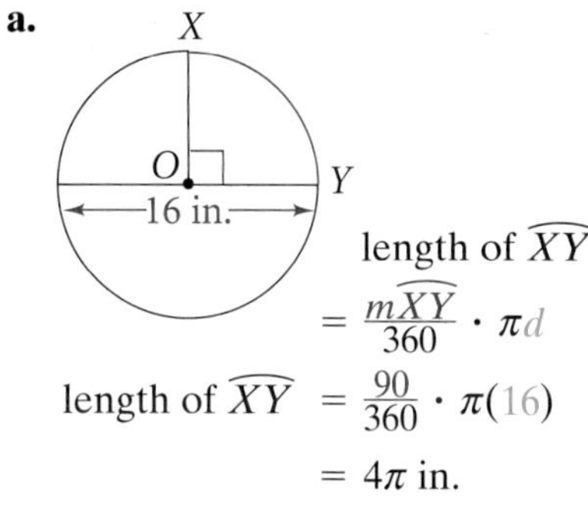

length of $\widehat{XY}$

$= \frac{m\widehat{XY}}{360} \cdot \pi d$

length of $\widehat{XY} = \frac{90}{360} \cdot \pi(16)$

$= 4\pi$ in.

b.

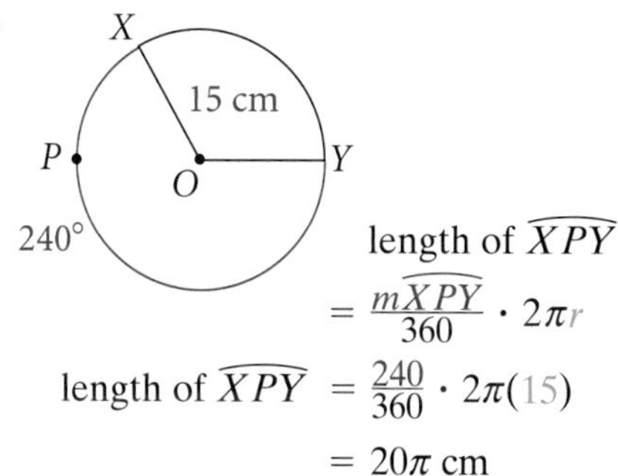

length of $\widehat{XPY}$

$= \frac{m\widehat{XPY}}{360} \cdot 2\pi r$

length of $\widehat{XPY} = \frac{240}{360} \cdot 2\pi(15)$

$= 20\pi$ cm

Check Understanding **5** Find the length of a semicircle with radius 1.3 m. Leave your answer in terms of π.

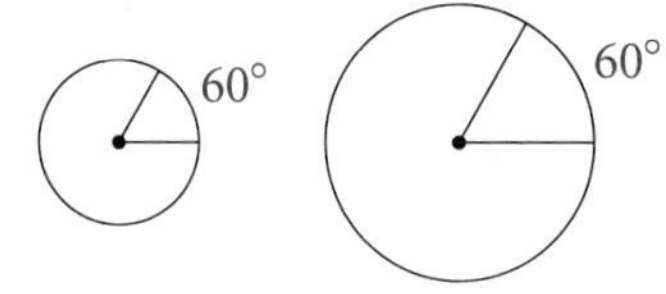

It is possible for two arcs of different circles to have the same measure but different lengths, as shown at the left. It is also possible for two arcs of different circles to have the same length but different measures. **Congruent arcs** are arcs that have the same measure *and* are in the same circle or in congruent circles.

EXERCISES

For more practice, see *Extra Practice*.

Practice and Problem Solving

Practice by Example

Example 1 **(page 386)**

Trash **The graph shows types of trash in a typical American city. Find the measure of each central angle to the nearest whole number.**

1. Glass **2.** Metals

3. Plastics **4.** Wood

5. Food Waste **6.** Yard Waste

7. Other **8.** Paper and Paperboard

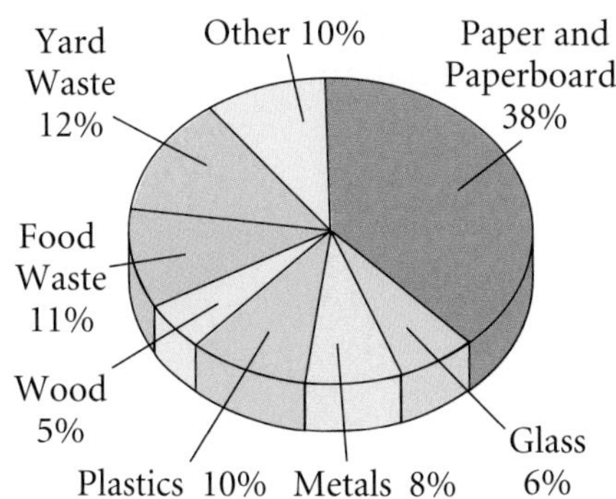

SOURCE: Environmental Protection Agency, 2001. Go to **www.PHSchool.com** for a data update. Web Code: afg-2041

Example 2 (page 387)

Identify the following in $\odot O$.

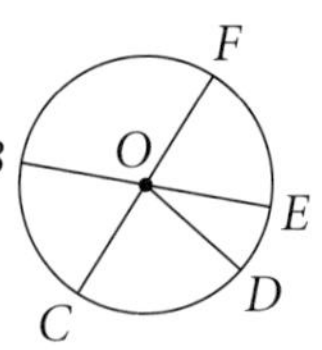

9. a minor arc
10. a major arc
11. a semicircle
12. a pair of adjacent arcs
13. an acute central angle
14. a pair of congruent angles

Example 3 (page 388)

Find the measure of each arc in $\odot P$.

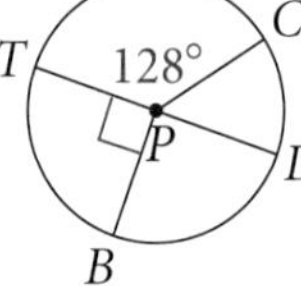

15. $\overset{\frown}{TC}$ 16. $\overset{\frown}{TBD}$ 17. $\overset{\frown}{BTC}$ 18. $\overset{\frown}{TCB}$
19. $\overset{\frown}{CD}$ 20. $\overset{\frown}{CBD}$ 21. $\overset{\frown}{TCD}$ 22. $\overset{\frown}{DB}$
23. $\overset{\frown}{TDC}$ 24. $\overset{\frown}{TB}$ 25. $\overset{\frown}{BC}$ 26. $\overset{\frown}{BCD}$

Example 4 (page 388)

Find the circumference of each circle. Leave your answer in terms of π.

27. 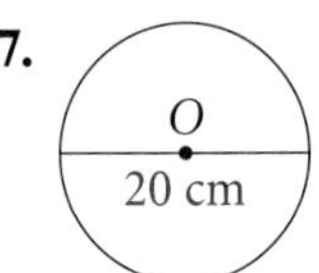

28. 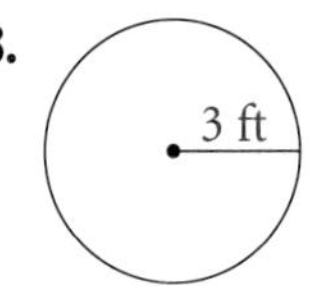

29. 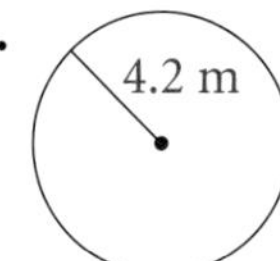

30. 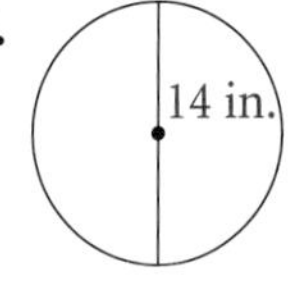

31. 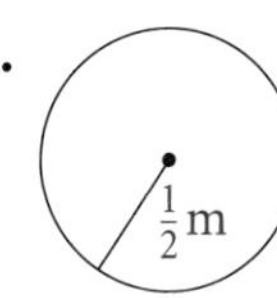

32. 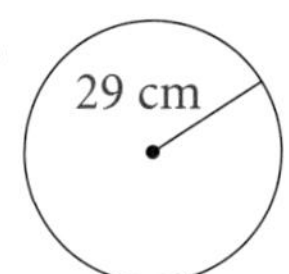

33. The wheel of an adult's bicycle has diameter 26 in. The wheel of a child's bicycle has diameter 18 in. To the nearest inch, how much farther does the larger bicycle wheel travel in one revolution than the smaller bicycle wheel?

Example 5 (page 389)

Find the length of each arc shown in red. Leave your answer in terms of π.

34. 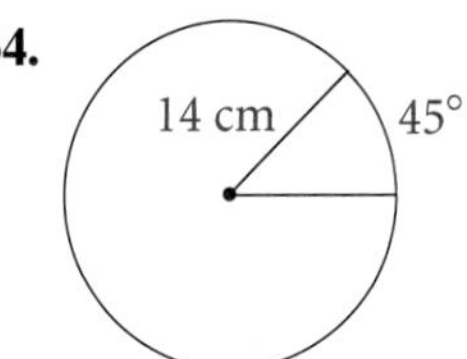

35. 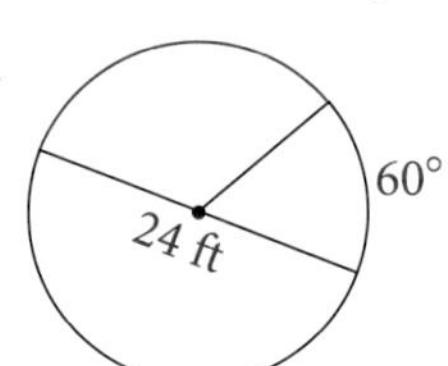

36. 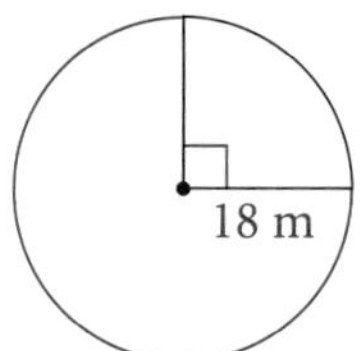

37. 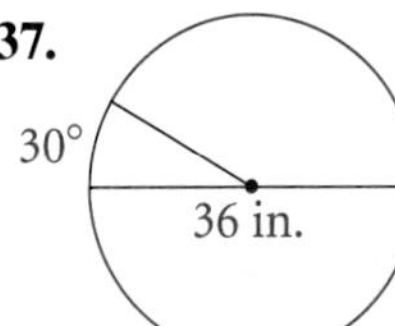

38. 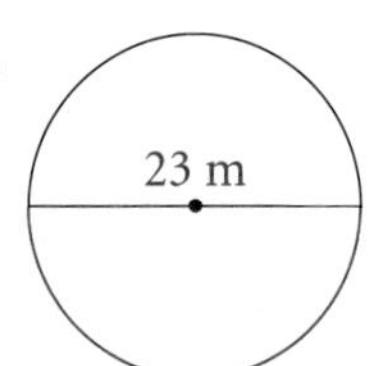

39. 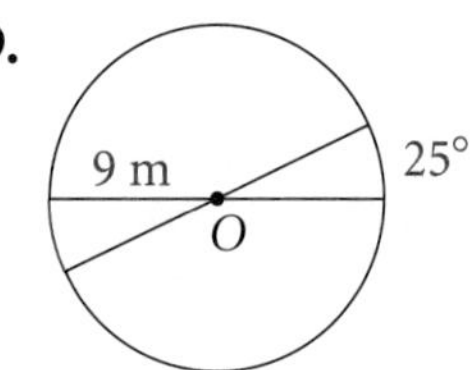

B Apply Your Skills

40. Use a compass to draw $\odot A$ and $\odot B$ with different radii. Then use a protractor to draw $\overset{\frown}{XY}$ on $\odot A$ and $\overset{\frown}{ZW}$ on $\odot B$ so that $m\overset{\frown}{XY} = m\overset{\frown}{ZW}$. Is $\overset{\frown}{XY} \cong \overset{\frown}{ZW}$?

41. **Environment** Use the data in the table to construct a circle graph.

World Carbon Dioxide Emissions from Burning Fossil Fuels
2005 Projections

Region	Percent
United States	24%
Eastern Europe and the former Soviet Union	13%
China	13%
Other Industrialized Countries	25%
Other Developing Countries	26%

SOURCE: Energy Information Admin., 2001.

Go to **www.PHSchool.com** for a data update.
Web Code: afg-2041

Real-World Connection

In 5 minutes, the tip of the minute hand of Boston's Custom House Tower travels 6 ft 10 in.

Find each indicated measure for $\odot O$.

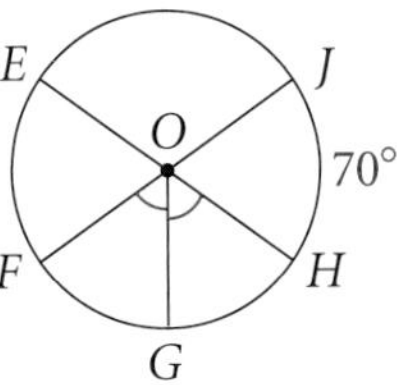

42. $m\angle EOF$ **43.** $m\widehat{EJH}$ **44.** $m\widehat{FH}$

45. $m\angle FOG$ **46.** $m\widehat{JEG}$ **47.** $m\widehat{HFJ}$

48. **Open-Ended** Make a circle graph showing how you spend a 24-hour weekday.

Time **Hands of a clock suggest an angle whose measure is continually changing.**

49. Through how many degrees does a minute hand move in each time interval?
a. 1 minute **b.** 5 minutes **c.** 20 minutes

50. Through how many degrees does an hour hand move in each time interval?
a. 1 minute **b.** 5 minutes **c.** 20 minutes

51. What is the measure of the angle formed by the hands of a clock at 7:20?

Algebra **Find the value of each variable.**

52.

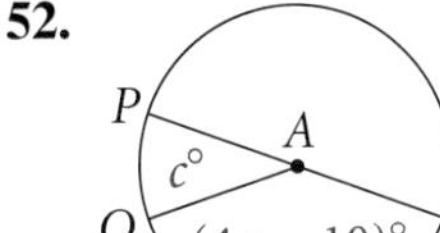
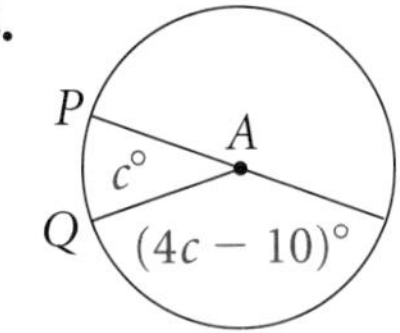

53.

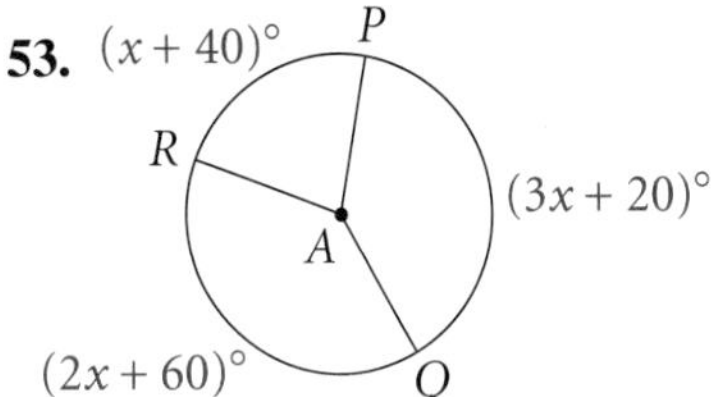

54. **Traffic** Five streets come together at a traffic circle. Vehicles travel counterclockwise around the circle. Use arc measure to give directions to someone who wants to get to East Street from Neponset Street.

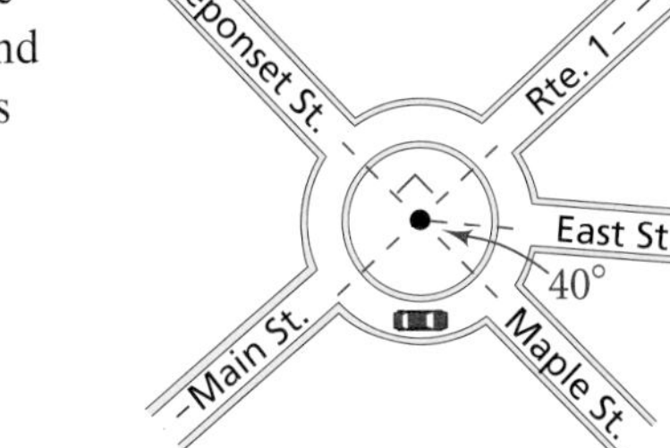

The circumference of a circle is 100π in. Find each of the following.

55. the diameter **56.** the radius

57. the length of an arc of 120°

58. A 60° arc of $\odot A$ has the same length as a 45° arc of $\odot B$. Find the ratio of the radius of $\odot A$ to the radius of $\odot B$.

Need Help?

For Exercise 58, draw $\odot A$ and $\odot B$ concentric. Draw 60° and 45° angles that share a side. To have equal arc lengths, which circle must be larger?

59. **Metalworking** Nina designed an arch made of wrought iron for the top of a mall entrance. The 11 segments between the two concentric semicircles are each 3 ft long. Find the total length of wrought iron used to make this structure. Round your answer to the nearest foot.

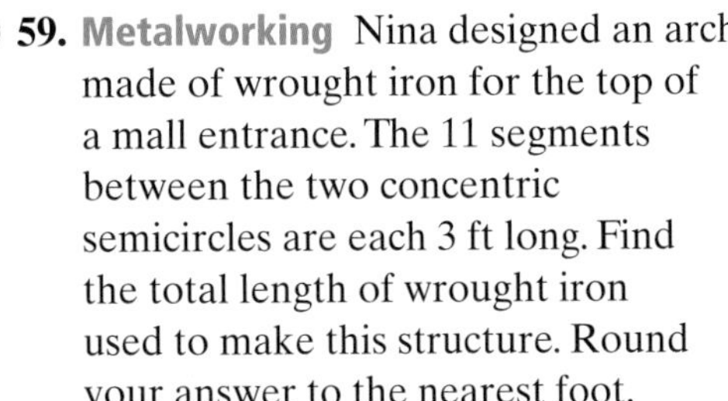
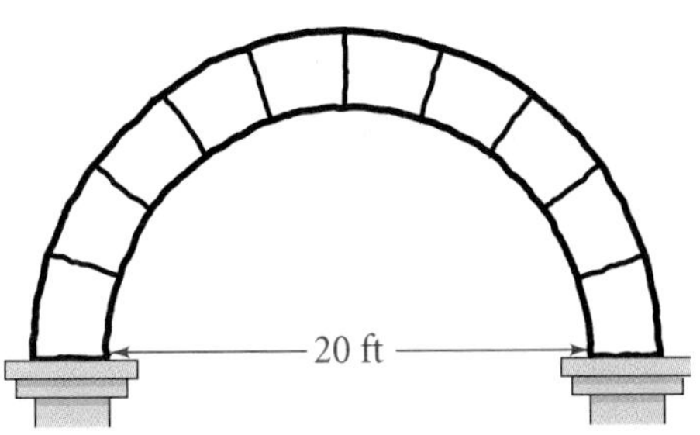

60. **History** In Exercise 24 on page 120, you learned that in 220 B.C., Eratosthenes estimated the circumference of Earth. He did so by finding that on a great circle of Earth, an arc of approximately 500 mi has a central angle of 7.2°.
a. Use Eratosthenes's measurements to estimate the circumference of Earth.
b. Compare your answer in part (a) to the actual circumference of Earth (at the equator) of 24,902 mi.

Need Help?

The Distance and Midpoint Formulas are on pages 43 and 45.

Coordinate Geometry **A diameter of a circle has endpoints $A(1, 3)$ and $B(4, 7)$. Find each of the following.**

61. the coordinates of the center

62. the circumference

Find the length of each arc shown in red. Leave your answer in terms of π.

63.

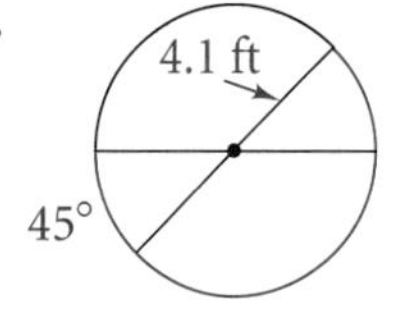

64.

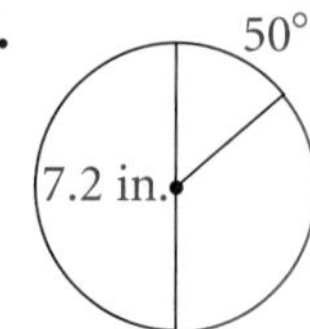

65.

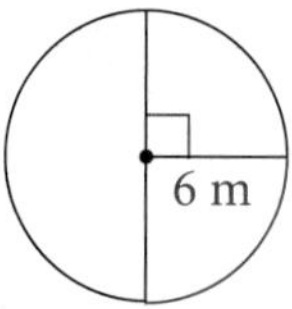

Use what you learn from Calvin's father to answer Exercises 66 and 67.

Calvin and Hobbes

by Bill Watterson

66. In one revolution, how much farther does a point 10 cm from the center of the record travel than a point 3 cm from the center? Round your answer to the nearest tenth.

67. **Writing** Kendra and her mother plan to ride the carousel. Two horses on the carousel are side by side. For a more exciting ride, should Kendra sit on the inside or the outside? Explain your reasoning.

68. In $\odot O$, the length of $\widehat{AB}$ is 6π cm and $m\widehat{AB}$ is 120. What is the diameter of $\odot O$?

69. **Coordinate Geometry** Find the length of a semicircle with endpoints $(3, 7)$ and $(3, -1)$. Round your answer to the nearest tenth.

Challenge

70. The two circles shown below are concentric.

a. Name two arcs that have the same measure.

b. Find the value of x.

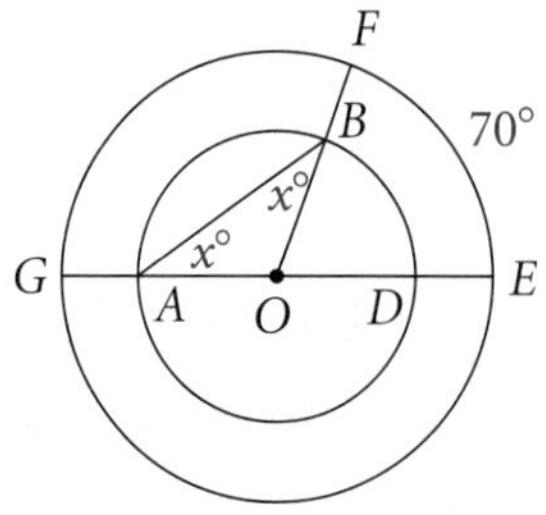

71. Find the perimeter of the shaded portion of the figure below. Leave your answer in terms of π. Explain your reasoning and state what assumptions you make.

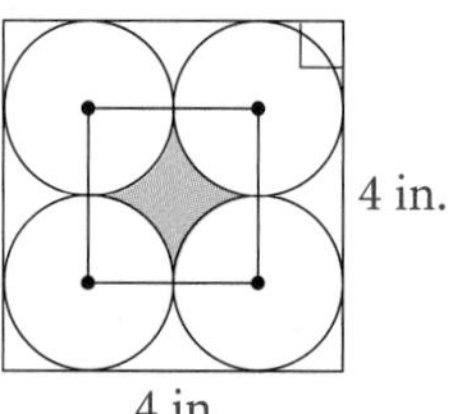

Real-World Connection

The track is longer for runners on the outside, so the start of the race is staggered.

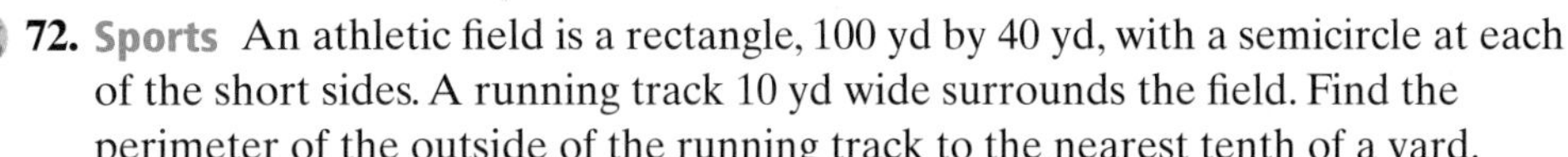

72. Sports An athletic field is a rectangle, 100 yd by 40 yd, with a semicircle at each of the short sides. A running track 10 yd wide surrounds the field. Find the perimeter of the outside of the running track to the nearest tenth of a yard.

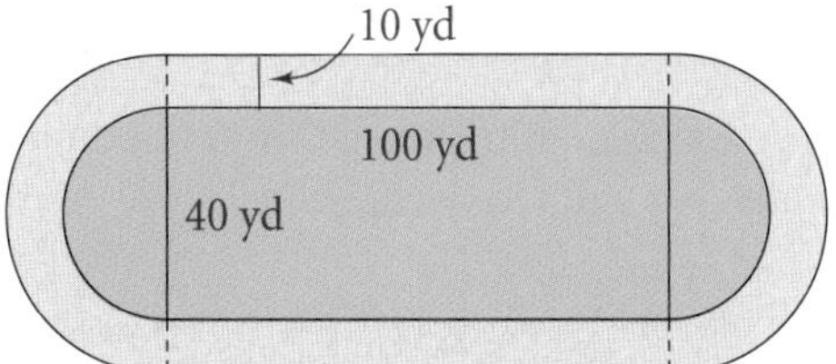

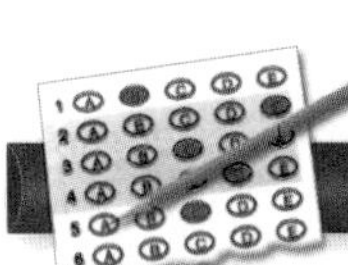

Standardized Test Prep

Multiple Choice

73. The radius of a circle is 12 cm. What is the length of a 60° arc?

A. 3π cm **B.** 4π cm **C.** 5π cm **D.** 6π cm

74. A 240° arc has length 16π ft. What is the radius of the circle?

F. 6 ft **G.** 12 ft **H.** 15 ft **I.** 24 ft

Short Response

75. Amy is constructing a curved path through a rectangular yard. She will edge the two sides of the curved path with plastic edging. Find the total length, in meters, of plastic edging she will need. Show your work or explain how you found the total.

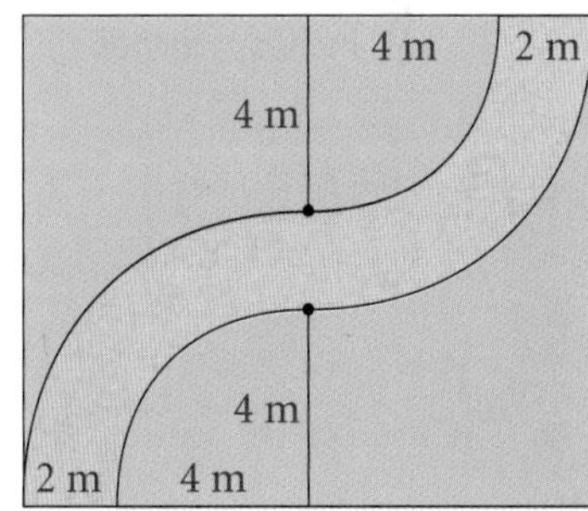

Take It to the NET
Online lesson quiz at **www.PHSchool.com**
Web Code: afa-0706

Mixed Review

Lesson 7-5

Part of a regular 12-gon is shown at the right.

76. Find the measure of each numbered angle.

77. The radius is about 19.3 mm. Each side is 10 mm. Find the apothem.

78. Find the area of the 12-gon to the nearest square millimeter.

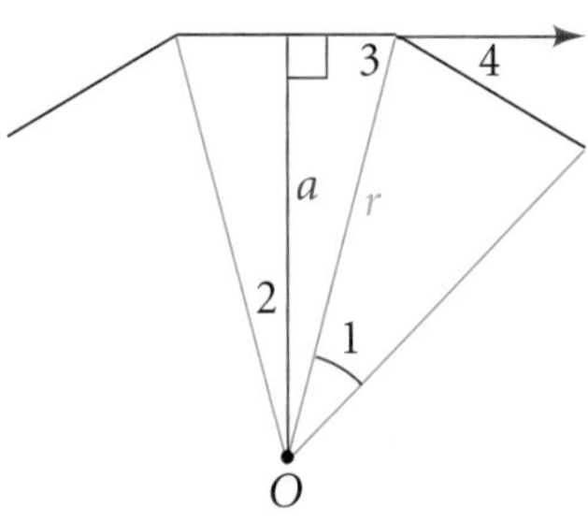

Lesson 6-3

Can you conclude that the figure is a parallelogram? Explain.

79.

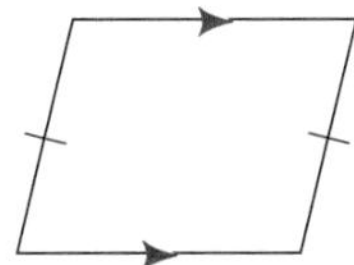

80.

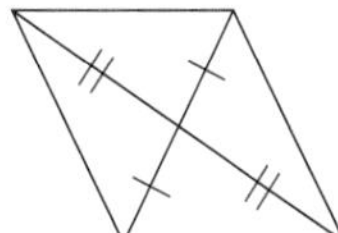

81.

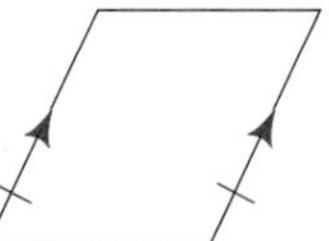

Lesson 3-6

Indicate whether each statement is *always, sometimes,* or *never* true.

82. Two nonvertical parallel lines have the same slope.

83. Two perpendicular lines have slopes that are reciprocals.

Algebra 1 Review

Dimensional Analysis

For Use With Lesson 7-7

You can use conversion factors to change from one unit of measure to another. The process of analyzing units to decide which conversion factors to use is called *dimensional analysis.*

Since 60 min = 1 h, $\frac{60\text{ min}}{1\text{ h}}$ equals 1. You can use $\frac{60\text{ min}}{1\text{ h}}$ to convert hours to minutes.

$7\cancel{\text{h}} \cdot \frac{60\text{ min}}{1\cancel{\text{h}}} = 420\text{ min}$ **The hour units cancel, and the result is minutes.**

Sometimes you need to use a conversion factor more than once.

EXAMPLE

The area of the top of a circular table is 8 ft^2. Convert the area to square inches.

You need to convert feet to inches.

feet to inches ↓ feet to inches ↓

$8\text{ ft} \cdot \text{ft} \cdot \frac{12\text{ in.}}{1\text{ ft}} \cdot \frac{12\text{ in.}}{1\text{ ft}} = 8\cancel{\text{ft}} \cdot \cancel{\text{ft}} \cdot \frac{12\text{ in.}}{1\cancel{\text{ft}}} \cdot \frac{12\text{ in.}}{1\cancel{\text{ft}}}$ **The feet units cancel. The result is square inches.**

$= 8 \cdot 12 \cdot 12\text{ in.}^2$ **Simplify.**

$= 1152\text{ in.}^2$

The area of the table top is 1152 in.^2.

EXERCISES

Choose the correct conversion factor for changing the units.

1. centimeters to meters
A. $\frac{100\text{ cm}}{1\text{ m}}$ B. $\frac{1\text{ m}}{100\text{ cm}}$

2. yards to feet
A. $\frac{3\text{ ft}}{1\text{ yd}}$ B. $\frac{1\text{ yd}}{3\text{ ft}}$

3. inches to yards
A. $\frac{36\text{ in.}}{1\text{ yd}}$ B. $\frac{1\text{ yd}}{36\text{ in.}}$

4. square feet to square inches
A. $\frac{12\text{ in.}}{1\text{ ft}}$ B. $\frac{1\text{ ft}}{12\text{ in.}}$

5. cubic meters to cubic kilometers
A. $\frac{1000\text{ m}}{1\text{ km}}$ B. $\frac{1\text{ km}}{1000\text{ m}}$

Write each quantity in the given unit.

6. 4 m = ■ cm
7. 360 in. = ■ yd
8. 9 mm = ■ cm
9. 17 yd = ■ ft
10. 2.5 ft = ■ in.
11. 35 m = ■ km
12. 2 yd = ■ in.
13. 23 cm = ■ mm
14. 2 ft^2 = ■ in.^2
15. 500 mm^2 = ■ cm^2
16. 840 in.^2 = ■ ft^2
17. 3 km^2 = ■ cm^2
18. 7 m^2 = ■ km^2
19. 360 in.^2 = ■ yd^2
20. 900 cm^3 = ■ m^3
21. 4 yd^3 = ■ ft^3
22. 75 m^2 = ■ km^2
23. 250 in.^2 = ■ yd^2
24. 3 km^3 = ■ m^3
25. 2 km^2 = ■ mm^2
26. 60 in.^2 = ■ yd^2

Areas of Circles and Sectors

Lesson Preview

What You'll Learn

To find the areas of circles, sectors, and segments of circles

. . . And Why

To compare the area of different-size pizzas, as in Example 1

✓ Check Skills You'll Need

(For help, go to Lesson 7-6.)

1. What is the radius of a circle with diameter 9 cm?
2. What is the diameter of a circle with radius 8 ft?
3. Find the circumference of a circle with diameter 12 in.
4. Find the circumference of a circle with radius 3 m.

New Vocabulary • sector of a circle • segment of a circle

Interactive lesson includes instant self-check, tutorials, and activities.

OBJECTIVE 1

Finding Areas of Circles and Parts of Circles

Investigation: Exploring the Area of a Circle

- Use a compass to draw a large circle. Fold the circle horizontally and vertically. Cut the circle into four wedges on the fold lines.

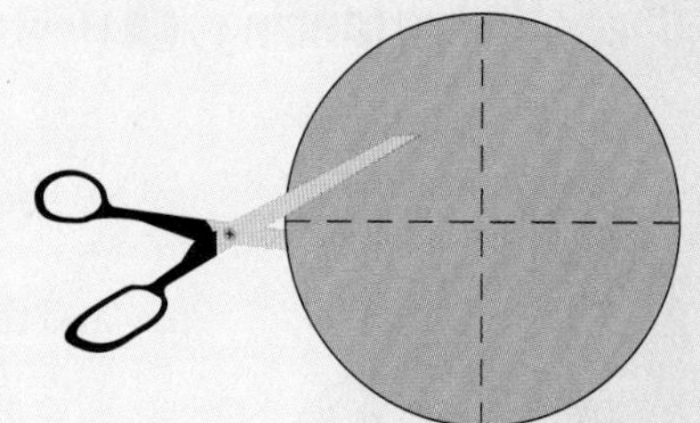

- Fold each wedge into quarters. Cut each wedge on the fold lines. You will have 16 wedges.
- Tape the wedges to a piece of paper to form the figure shown here.

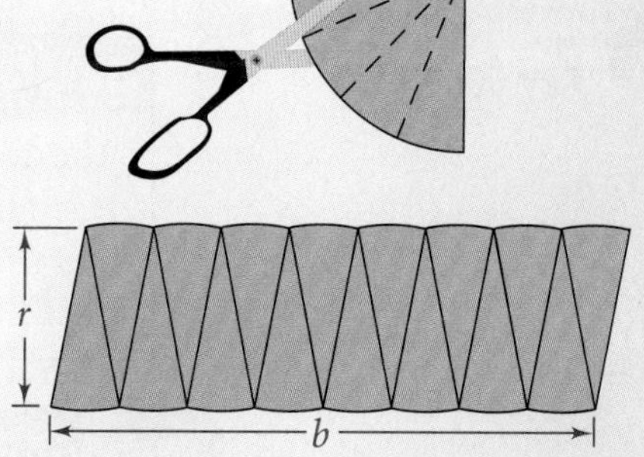

1. How does the area of the figure compare with area of the circle?
2. The base of the figure is formed by arcs of the circle. Explain how the length b relates to the circumference C of the circle.
3. Explain how the length b relates to the radius r of the circle.
4. If you increase the number of wedges, the figure you create becomes more and more like a rectangle with base b and height r. Write an expression for the area of the rectangle in terms of r.

In the diagrams on the preceding page,

area of a circle = area of a "parallelogram" $\approx b \cdot r \approx \frac{1}{2}C \cdot r = \pi r^2$,

and the approximations improve as the circle is cut into more pieces.

Key Concepts

Theorem 7-15 **Area of a Circle**

The area of a circle is the product of π and the square of the radius.

$$A = \pi r^2$$

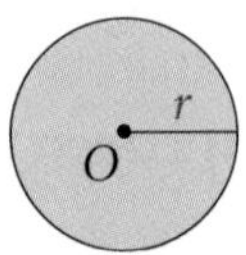

1 EXAMPLE Real-World Connection

Food How much more pizza is in a 12-in.-diameter pizza than in a 10-in. pizza?

radius of small pizza $= \frac{10}{2} = 5$

radius of medium pizza $= \frac{12}{2} = 6$ **Find the radii.**

area of small pizza $= \pi(5)^2 = 25\pi$

area of medium pizza $= \pi(6)^2 = 36\pi$ **Use the formula for area of a circle.**

difference in area $= 36\pi - 25\pi = 11\pi$

≈ 34.557519 **Use a calculator.**

There is about 35 in.^{2} more pizza in the medium pizza.

✓ Check Understanding 1 How much more pizza is in a 14-in.-diameter pizza than in a 12-in. pizza?

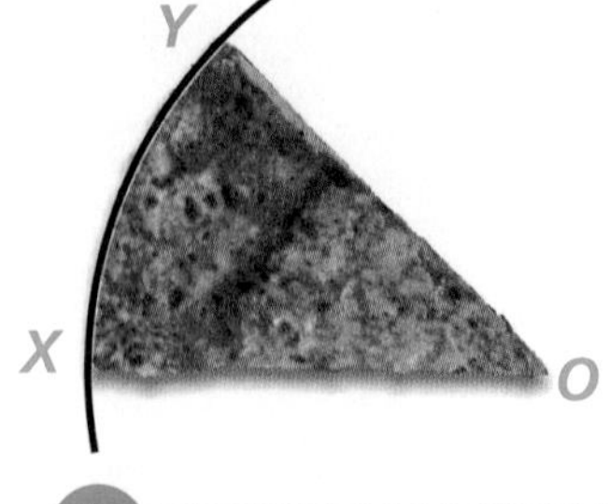

A **sector of a circle** is a region bounded by an arc of the circle and the two radii to the arc's endpoints. You name a sector using one arc endpoint, the center of the circle, and the other arc endpoint. The slice of pizza at the left is sector XOY of a circle O.

The area of a sector is a fractional part of the area of a circle. The ratio of a sector's area to a circle's area is $\frac{\text{measure of the arc}}{360}$.

Key Concepts

Theorem 7-16 **Area of a Sector of a Circle**

The area of a sector of a circle is the product of the ratio $\frac{\text{measure of the arc}}{360}$ and the area of the circle.

$$\text{Area of sector } AOB = \frac{m\overset{\frown}{AB}}{360} \cdot \pi r^2$$

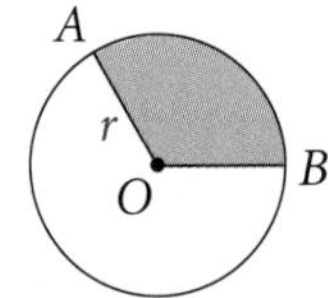

2 EXAMPLE Finding the Area of a Sector of a Circle

Find the area of sector ZOM. Leave your answer in terms of π.

$$\text{area of sector } ZOM = \frac{m\overset{\frown}{ZM}}{360} \cdot \pi r^2$$

$$= \frac{72}{360} \cdot \pi(20)^2$$

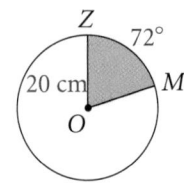

$$= 80\pi$$

Z
72°
20 cm
M
O

The area of sector ZOM is 80π cm^2.

✓ Check Understanding 2 **Critical Thinking** A circle has a diameter of 20 cm. What is the area of a sector bounded by a 208° major arc? Round your answer to the nearest tenth.

This pizza is cut into two segments.

A part of a circle bounded by an arc and the segment joining its endpoints is a **segment of a circle.** To find the area of a segment for a minor arc, draw radii to form a sector. The area of the segment equals the area of the sector minus the area of the triangle formed.

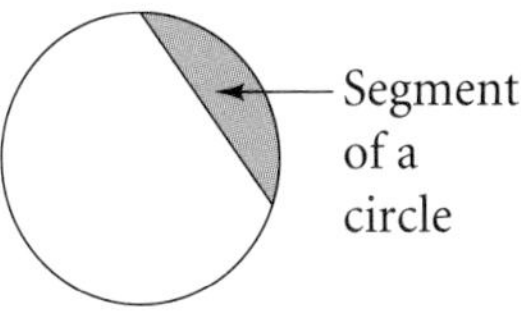

Area of sector − Area of triangle = Area of segment

3 EXAMPLE Finding the Area of a Segment of a Circle

Find the area of the shaded segment. Round your answer to the nearest tenth.

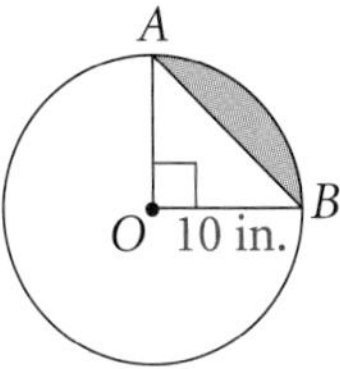

area of sector $AOB = \frac{m\widehat{AB}}{360} \cdot \pi r^2$ **Use the formula for area of a sector.**

$= \frac{90}{360} \cdot \pi(10)^2$ **Substitute.**

$= \frac{1}{4} \cdot 100\pi$

$= 25\pi$

area of $\triangle AOB = \frac{1}{2}bh$ **Use the formula for area of a triangle.**

$= \frac{1}{2}(10)(10)$ **Substitute.**

$= 50$

area of segment $= 25\pi - 50$

≈ 28.539816 **Use a calculator.**

The area of the segment is about 28.5 in.^{2}

Check Understanding **3** A circle has a radius of 12 cm. Find the area of the smaller segment of the circle determined by a 60° arc. Round your answer to the nearest tenth.

EXERCISES

For more practice, see *Extra Practice.*

Practice and Problem Solving

A Practice by Example

Example 1 (page 396)

Find the area of each circle. Leave your answer in terms of π.

1. 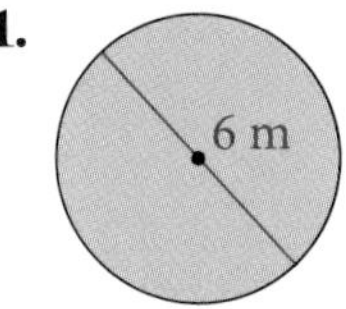

2. 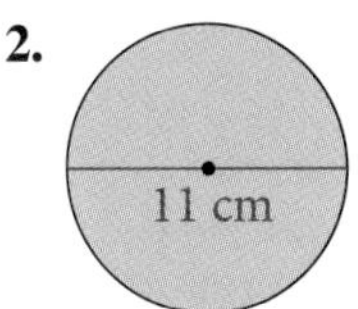

3. 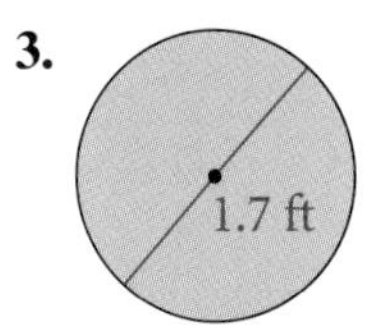

4. 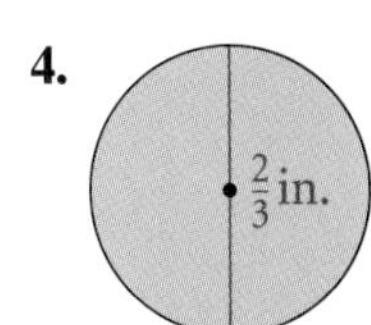

5. **Agriculture** Some farmers use a circular irrigation method. An irrigation arm acts as the radius of an irrigation circle. How much more land is covered with an irrigation arm of 300 ft than by an irrigation arm of 250 ft?

6. What is the difference in the areas of a circular table with diameter 6 ft and a circular table with diameter 8 ft?

Example 2 (page 396)

Find the area of each shaded sector of a circle. Leave your answer in terms of π.

7. 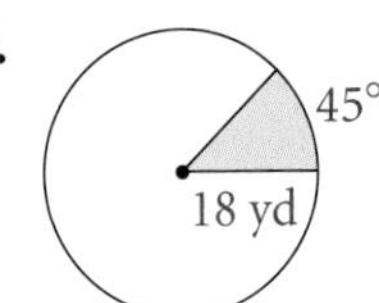

8. 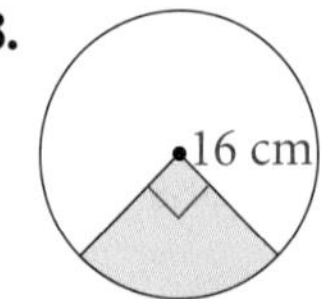

9. 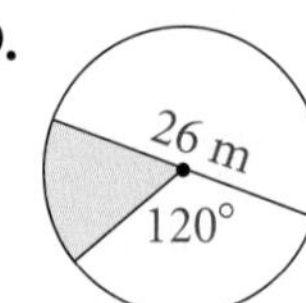

10. 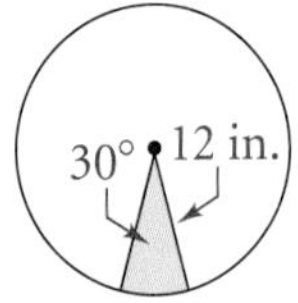

11. 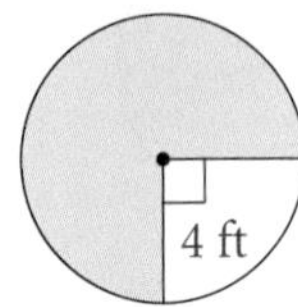

12. 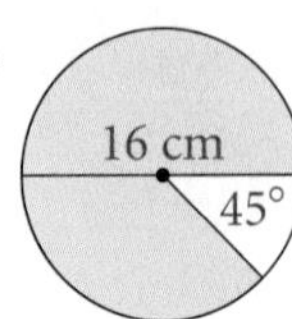

Find the area of sector *TOP* in $\odot O$ using the given information. Leave your answer in terms of π.

13. $r = 5$ m, $m\widehat{TP} = 90°$

14. $r = 6$ ft, $m\widehat{TP} = 15°$

15. $d = 16$ in., $m\widehat{PT} = 135°$

16. $d = 15$ cm, $m\widehat{PT} = 180°$

Example 3 (page 397)

Find the area of each shaded segment. Round your answer to the nearest tenth.

17. 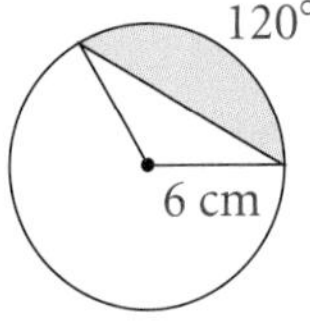

18. 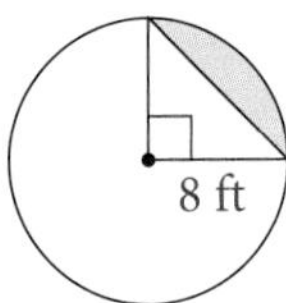

19. 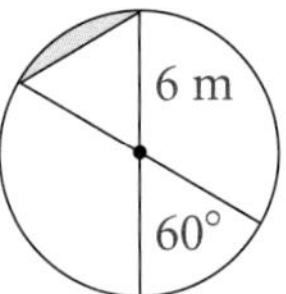

A circle has the given radius. Find the area of the smaller segment of the circle determined by an arc with the given measure. Round to the nearest tenth.

20. radius 15 m, arc 60°

21. radius 14 cm, arc 120°

B Apply Your Skills

Find the area of the shaded region. Leave your answer in terms of π and in simplest radical form.

22. 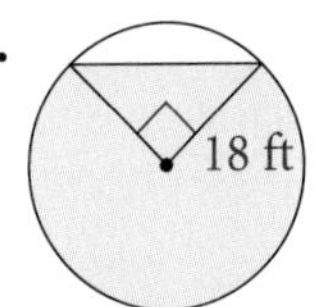

23. 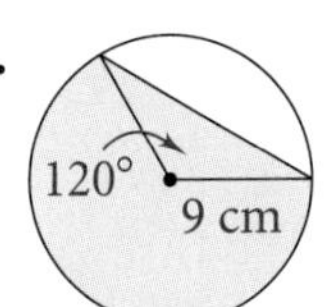

24. 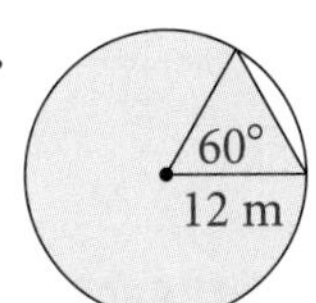

25. 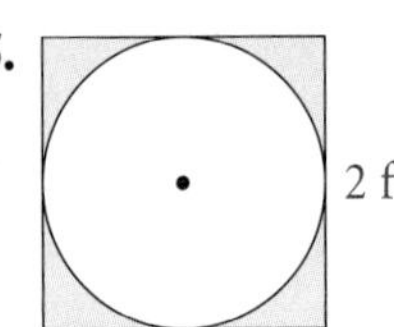

26. 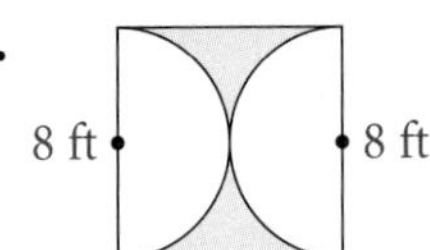

27. 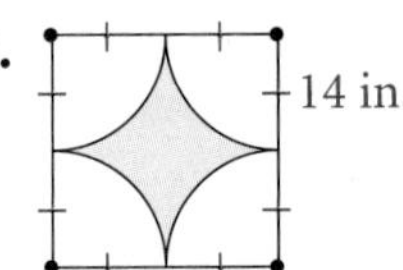

28. **Marine Biology** The diver at the right is working to bring up samples of organisms from the ocean floor. The line to the diver is 100 ft long, and the diver is working at a depth of 80 ft. What is the area of the circle that the diver can cover? Round your answer to the nearest square foot.

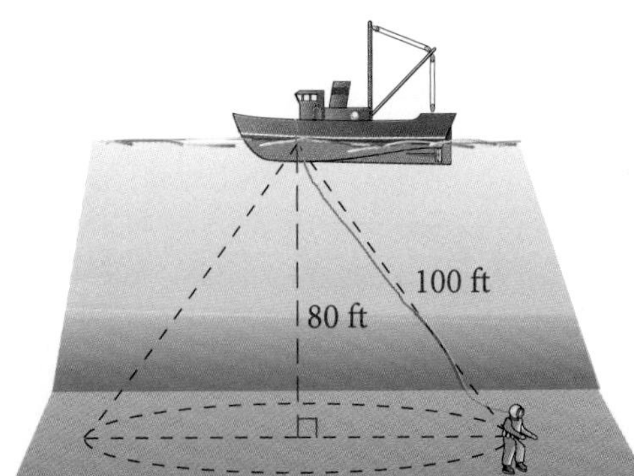

Real-World Connection

Careers Training as a pastry chef is part of the background of many executive chefs.

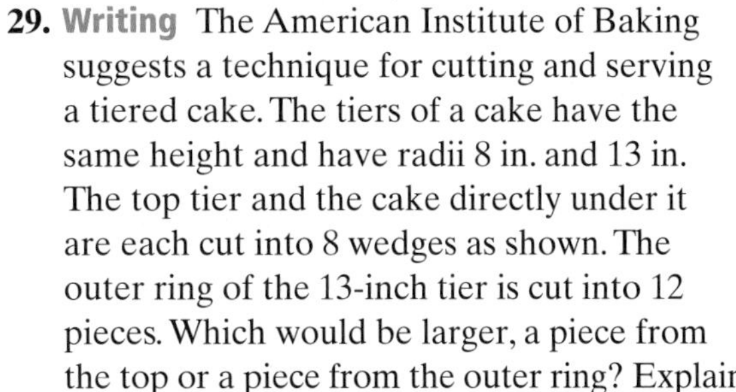

29. **Writing** The American Institute of Baking suggests a technique for cutting and serving a tiered cake. The tiers of a cake have the same height and have radii 8 in. and 13 in. The top tier and the cake directly under it are each cut into 8 wedges as shown. The outer ring of the 13-inch tier is cut into 12 pieces. Which would be larger, a piece from the top or a piece from the outer ring? Explain.

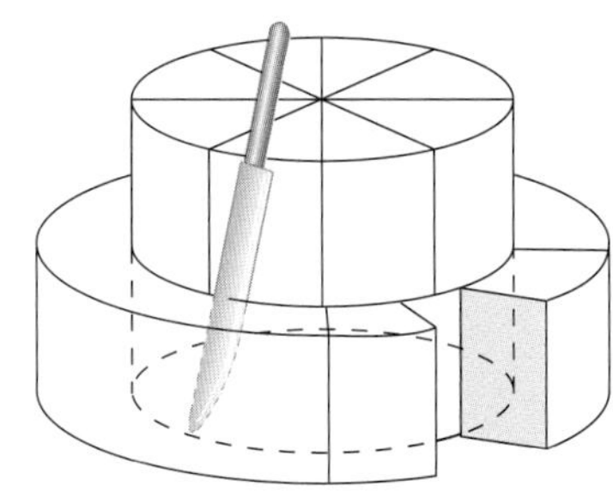

30. How many circles with radius 4 in. will have the same total area as a circle with radius 12 in.?

31. **Games** A dart board has diameter 20 in. and is divided into 20 congruent sectors. Find the area of one sector. Round your answer to the nearest tenth.

32. In a circle, a 90° sector has area 36π in.^{2}. What is the circle's radius?

33. **Open-Ended** Draw a circle and a sector so that the area of the sector is 16π cm^2. Give the radius of the circle and the measure of the arc of the sector.

34. A method for finding the area of a segment determined by a minor arc is described on page 397.
    a. Describe two ways to find the area of a segment determined by a major arc.
    b. If $m\widehat{AB} = 90$ in a circle of radius 10, find the areas of the two segments determined by $\widehat{AB}$.

C Challenge

Find the area of the shaded region. Leave your answer in terms of π.

35.

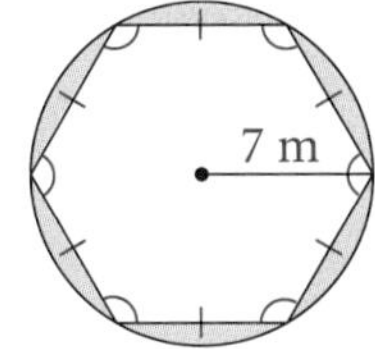

36.

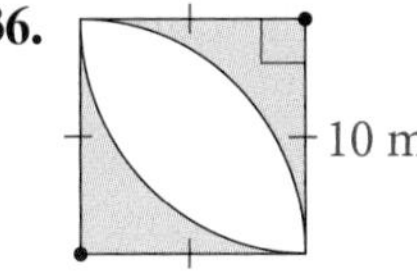

37.

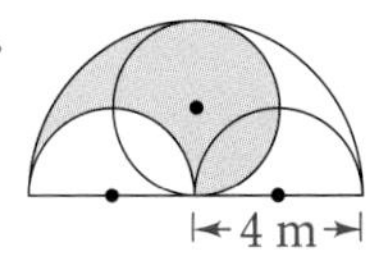

38. Circle O at the right is inscribed in square $ABCD$ and circumscribed about square $PQRS$. Which is smaller, the blue region or the yellow region? Explain.

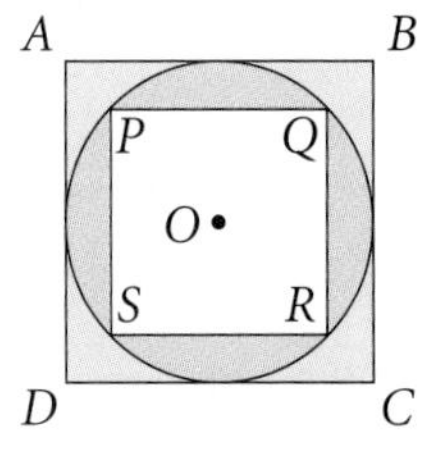

39. Circles T and U each have a radius 10 and $TU = 10$. Find the area of the region that is contained inside both circles.

Need Help?

For Exercise 39, where must T and U lie in a diagram of $\odot T$ and $\odot U$?

40. **Recreation** An 8 ft-by-10 ft floating dock is anchored in the middle of a pond. The bow of a canoe is tied to a corner of the dock with a 10-ft rope as shown in the picture below.
    a. Sketch a diagram of the region in which the bow of the canoe can travel.
    b. Write a plan for finding the area.
    c. Find the area. Round your answer to the nearest square foot.

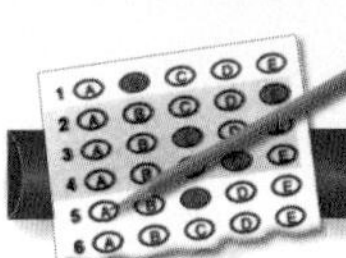

Standardized Test Prep

Multiple Choice

41. A circle has area 72π yd^2. What is the area of a 10° sector of the circle?
A. 2π yd^2 **B.** 3π yd^2 **C.** 4π yd^2 **D.** 6π yd^2

42. A sector of 90° has area π mm. What is the area of the circle?
F. 2π mm^2 **G.** 4π mm^2 **H.** 8π mm^2 **I.** 4 mm^2

Short Response

Take It to the NET
Online lesson quiz at **www.PHSchool.com**
Web Code: afa-0707

43. Each of three water sprinklers covers a semicircle of radius 2 m. The shaded region remains dry. Find the area of the shaded region to the nearest square meter. Show your work or explain how you found the area.

12 m
2 m

Mixed Review

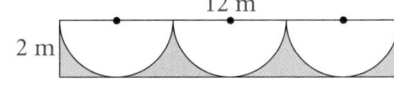

Lesson 7-6 **Find the length of $\overset{\frown}{AB}$ in each circle. Leave your answers in terms of π.**

44.

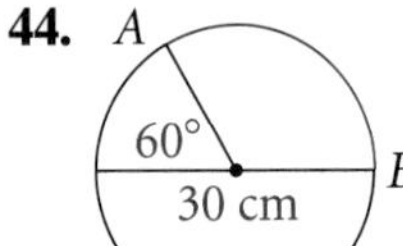

45.

B
72°
O
A
5 m

46.

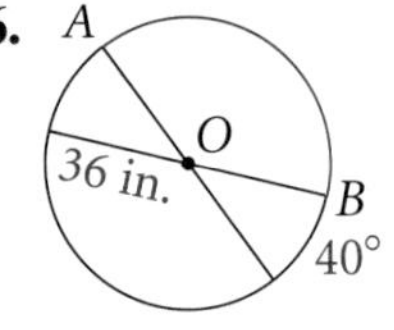

Lesson 6-5 **47.** Three sides of a trapezoid are congruent. The fourth side is 4 in. longer than each of the other three. The perimeter is 49 in. Find the length of each side.

Lesson 4-7 **48.** Write a plan for a proof. (*Hint:* First prove overlapping triangles are congruent.)

Given: $\overline{AC} \cong \overline{BC}$, $\angle A \cong \angle B$
Prove: $\triangle BDF \cong \triangle AEF$

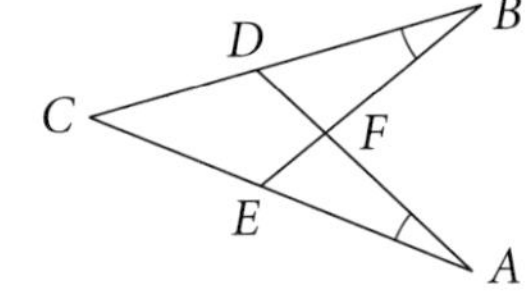

Checkpoint Quiz 2 — Lessons 7-4 through 7-7

Instant self-check quiz online and on CD-ROM

Find the area of each trapezoid, rhombus, regular polygon, circle, sector or segment. When necessary, leave answers in terms of π and in simplest radical form.

1.

12 in.
9 in.
18 in.

2.

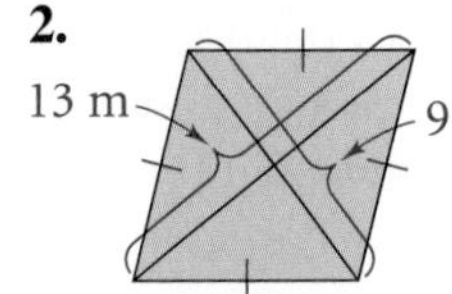

3.

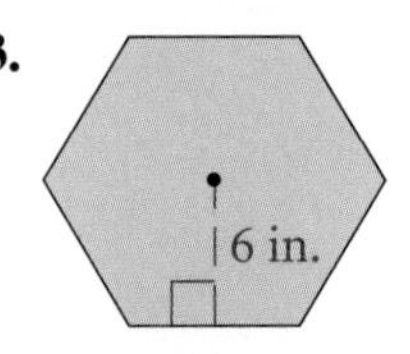

4.

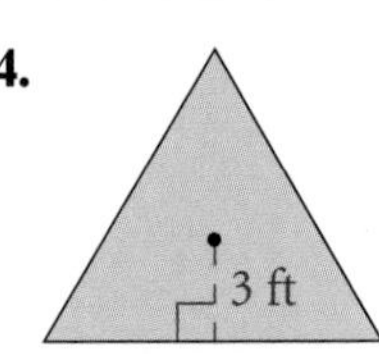

5.

4 yd

6.

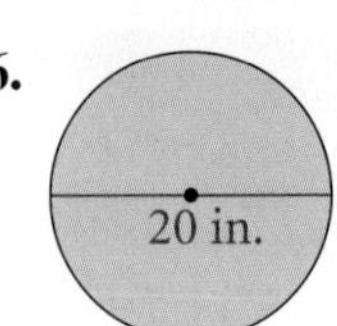

7.

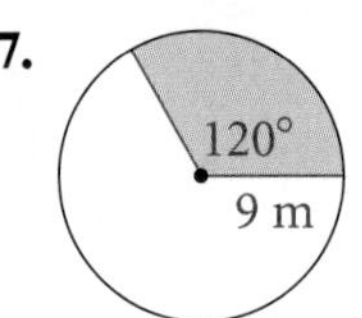

8.

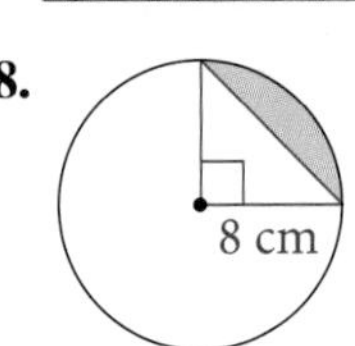

9. Find the circumference of a circle with radius 5 m. Round to the nearest tenth.

10. In a circle of radius 18 mm, $m\overset{\frown}{AB} = 45$. Find the length of $\overset{\frown}{AB}$ in terms of π.

Technology

Exploring Area and Circumference

FOR USE WITH LESSON 7-7

A polygon that is *inscribed* in a circle has all its vertices on the circle. Work in pairs or small groups. Investigate the ratios of the perimeters and areas of inscribed regular polygons to the circumference and area of the circle in which they are inscribed.

Begin by making a table like this.

Regular Polygon			Circle		Ratios	
Sides	Perimeter	Area	Circumference	Area	$\frac{\text{Perimeter}}{\text{Circumference}}$	$\frac{\text{Polygon Area}}{\text{Circle Area}}$
3						

Construct

Use geometry software to construct a circle. Find its circumference and area and record them in your table. Inscribe an equilateral triangle in the circle. Your software may be able to do this for you automatically, or you can construct three points on the circle and move them so they are approximately evenly spaced on the circle. Then draw a triangle.

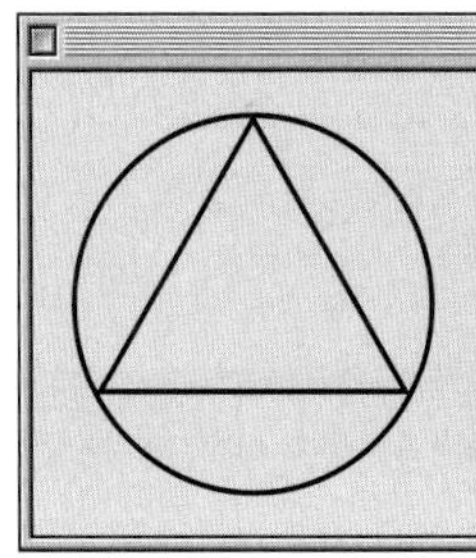

Investigate

Use your geometry software to measure the perimeter and area of the triangle and to calculate the ratios $\frac{\text{triangle perimeter}}{\text{circle circumference}}$ and $\frac{\text{triangle area}}{\text{circle area}}$. Record the results.

Manipulate the circle to change its size. Do the ratios you calculate stay the same or change?

Now inscribe a square in a circle and fill in your table for a polygon of four sides. Do the same for a regular pentagon.

EXERCISES

1. **Make a Conjecture** What will happen to the ratios $\frac{\text{perimeter}}{\text{circumference}}$ and $\frac{\text{polygon area}}{\text{circle area}}$ as you increase the number of sides of the polygon?

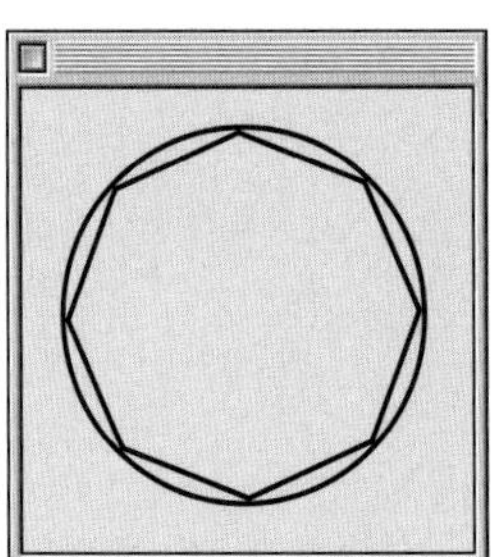

regular octagon

Extend

2. Extend your table to include polygons of 12 sides.
   a. Does your conjecture still hold?
   b. Compare the two columns of ratios in your table. How do they differ?
3. Estimate the perimeter and area of a polygon of 100 sides that is inscribed in a circle with a radius of 10 cm.

7-8

Geometric Probability

Lesson Preview

What You'll Learn

OBJECTIVE 1 To use segment and area models to find the probabilities of events

. . . And Why

To find the probability of winning a carnival game, as in Example 4

✓ Check Skills You'll Need

(For help, go to Skills Handbook pages 718 and 724.)

Find and simplify each ratio.

1. $\frac{BD}{AE}$ 2. $\frac{CE}{AF}$ 3. $\frac{AB}{BC}$

A(0), B(2), C(4), D(5), E(9), F(10) on a number line from 0 to 10

4. Two circles have radii 1 m and 2 m, respectively. What is the simplest form of the fraction with numerator equal to the area of the smaller circle and denominator equal to the area of the larger circle?

You roll a number cube. Find the probability of rolling each of the following.

5. 4
6. an odd number
7. 2 or 5
8. a prime number

New Vocabulary

- geometric probability

Interactive lesson includes instant self-check, tutorials, and activities.

OBJECTIVE 1

Using Segment and Area Models

Reading Math

P(event) is read "the probability of an event."

You may recall that the probability of an event is the ratio of the number of favorable outcomes to the number of possible outcomes.

$$P(\text{event}) = \frac{\text{favorable outcomes}}{\text{possible outcomes}}$$

Sometimes you can use a **geometric probability** model in which you let points represent outcomes. You find probabilities by comparing measurements of sets of points. For example, if points of segments represent outcomes, then

$$P(\text{event}) = \frac{\text{length of favorable segment}}{\text{length of entire segment}}.$$

1 EXAMPLE Finding Probability Using Segments

A gnat lands at a random point on the ruler's edge. Find the probability that the point is between 3 and 7.

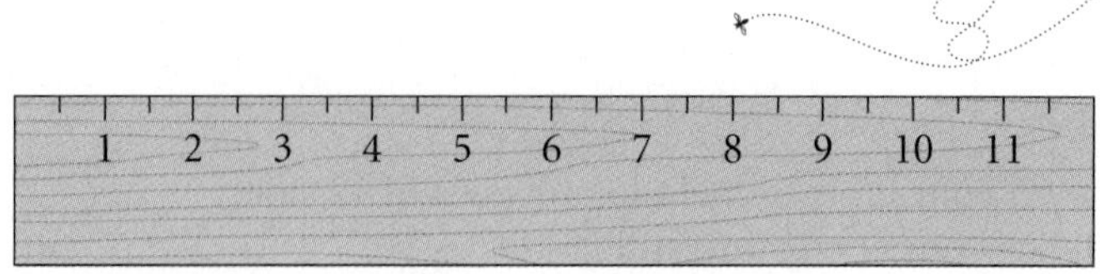

$$P(\text{landing between 3 and 7}) = \frac{\text{length of favorable segment}}{\text{length of entire segment}} = \frac{4}{12}, \text{ or } \frac{1}{3}$$

✓ Check Understanding

1. A point on $\overline{AB}$ is selected at random. What is the probability that it is a point on $\overline{CD}$?

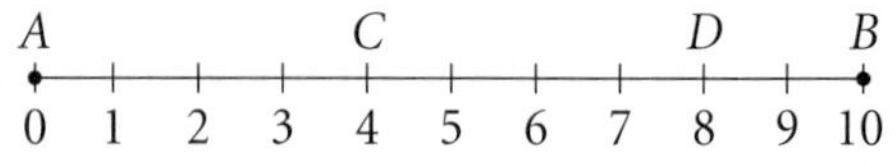

Real-World Connection

If the bus runs on schedule, Elena's average wait (Example 2) will be 12.5 min.

You can use a segment model to find the probability of how long you will wait for a bus.

2 EXAMPLE Real-World Connection

Commuting Elena's bus runs every 25 minutes. If she arrives at her bus stop at a random time, what is the probability that she will have to wait at least 10 minutes for the bus?

Assume that a stop takes very little time, and let $\overline{AB}$ represent the 25 minutes between buses.

A ... B on a number line: 0 5 10 15 20 25

If Elena arrives at any time between A and C, she has to wait at least 10 minutes until B.

A ... C ... B on a number line: 0 5 10 15 20 25

$$P(\text{waiting at least 10 min}) = \frac{\text{length of } \overline{AC}}{\text{length of } \overline{AB}} = \frac{15}{25}, \text{ or } \frac{3}{5}$$

The probability that Elena will have to wait at least 10 minutes for the bus is $\frac{3}{5}$ or 60%.

Check Understanding 2 What is the probability that Elena will have to wait no more than 10 minutes for the bus?

If the points of a region represent equally-likely outcomes, then you can find probabilities by comparing areas.

$$P(\text{event}) = \frac{\text{area of favorable region}}{\text{area of entire region}}$$

3 EXAMPLE Finding Probability Using Area

Target Game Assume that a dart you throw will land on the 1-ft square dartboard and is equally likely to land at any point on the board. Find the probability of hitting each of the blue, yellow, and red regions. The radii of the concentric circles are 1, 2, and 3 inches, respectively.

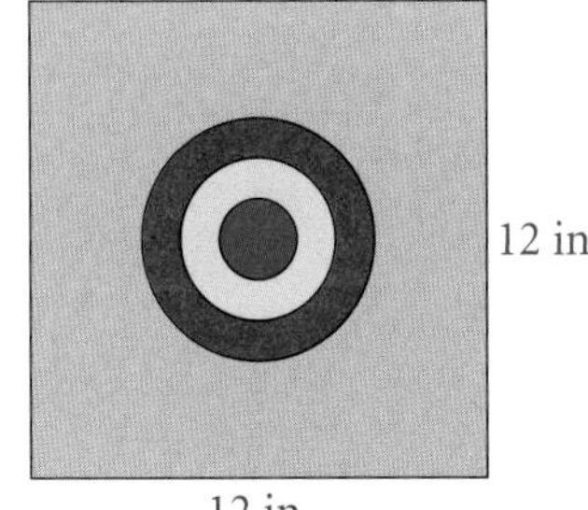

Need Help?

You can think of a probability like 0.022 as "22 times out of a thousand."

$$P(\text{blue}) = \frac{\text{area of blue region}}{\text{area of square}} = \frac{\pi(1)^2}{12^2} = \frac{\pi}{144} \approx 0.022, \text{ or } 2.2\%$$ **Use a calculator.**

$$P(\text{yellow}) = \frac{\text{area of yellow region}}{\text{area of square}} = \frac{\pi(2)^2 - \pi(1)^2}{12^2} = \frac{3\pi}{144} \approx 0.065, \text{ or } 6.5\%$$

$$P(\text{red}) = \frac{\text{area of red region}}{\text{area of square}} = \frac{\pi(3^2) - \pi(2)^2}{12^2} = \frac{5\pi}{144} \approx 0.109, \text{ or } 10.9\%$$

The probabilities of hitting the blue, yellow, and red regions are about 2.2%, 6.5%, and 10.9%, respectively.

Check Understanding 3 If you change the blue circle as indicated, how does the probability of hitting the blue circle change? Explain.

a. Double the radius.

b. Triple the radius.

As Example 3 suggests, you can apply geometric probability to some games. This can help you decide how easy or difficult it may be to win such games.

4 EXAMPLE Real-World Connection

Coin Toss To win a prize in a carnival game, you must toss a quarter so that it lands entirely within the circle as shown at the left. Find the probability of this happening on one toss. Assume that the center of a tossed quarter is equally likely to land at any point within the 8-in. square.

The radius of the circle is 1 in. The radius of a quarter is $\frac{15}{32}$ in. The favorable points are those that are less than $\frac{17}{32}$ in. from the center of the circle. They are the points within the dashed circle.

$$P(\text{quarter landing in circle}) = \frac{\text{area of dashed circle}}{\text{area of square}}$$

$$= \frac{\pi\left(\frac{17}{32}\right)^2}{8^2} \approx 0.014, \text{ or } 1.4\%$$

The probability of a quarter landing in the circle is about 1.4%.

Check Understanding 4 **Critical Thinking** Suppose you toss 100 quarters. Would you expect to win a prize? Explain.

EXERCISES

For more practice, see *Extra Practice*.

Practice and Problem Solving

Practice by Example

Example 1 (page 402)

Find the probability that a point chosen at random from $\overline{AK}$ is on the given segment.

A	B	C	D	E	F	G	H	I	J	K
0	1	2	3	4	5	6	7	8	9	10

1. $\overline{CH}$ **2.** $\overline{FG}$ **3.** $\overline{DJ}$ **4.** $\overline{EI}$ **5.** $\overline{AK}$

6. Points M and N are on $\overline{ZB}$ with $ZM = 5$, $NB = 9$, and $ZB = 20$. A point is chosen at random from $\overline{ZB}$. What is the probability that the point is on $\overline{MN}$?

Example 2 (page 403)

7. Transportation A rapid transit line runs trains every 10 minutes. Draw a geometric model and find the probability that randomly arriving passengers will not have to wait more than 4 minutes.

Traffic Patterns **Main Street intersects each street below. The traffic lights on Main follow the cycles shown. As you travel along Main and approach the intersection, what is the probability that the first color you see is green?**

8. Durham Avenue: green 30 s, yellow 5 s, red 25 s

9. Martin Luther King Boulevard: green 20 s, yellow 5 s, red 50 s

10. Yonge Street: green 40 s, yellow 5 s, red 25 s

11. International Drive: green 25 s, yellow 5 s, red 45 s

12. Tamiami Trail: green 35 s, yellow 8 s, red 32 s

13. Flutie Pass: green 50 s, yellow 4 s, red 26 s

14. During May, a certain drawbridge over the Intracoastal Waterway is raised every half hour to allow boats to pass. It remains open for 5 min. What is the probability that a motorist arriving at the bridge in May will find it raised?

Examples 3, 4 (pages 403 and 404)

Target Games **Darts are thrown at each of the boards shown below. A dart hits the board at a random point. Judging by appearances, find the probability that it will land in the shaded region.**

15. 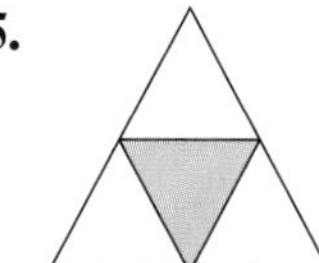

16. 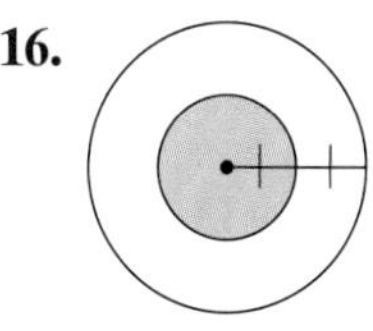

17. 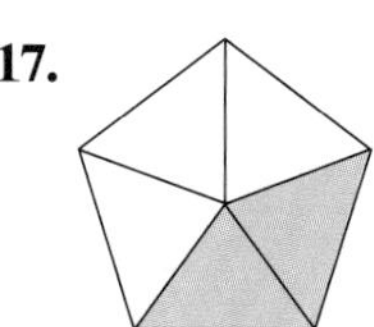

18. 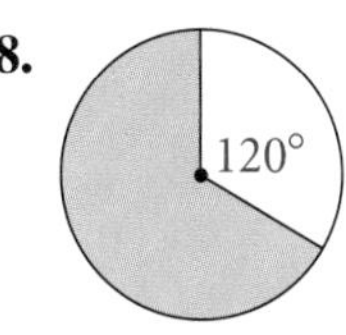

19. 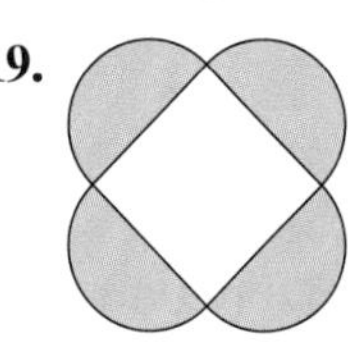

20. 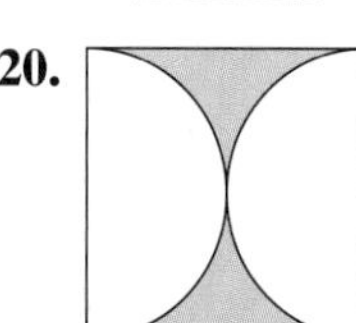

Real-World Connection

An archer receives from 1 to 10 points for an arrow that hits the target. A hit in the center zone is worth 10 points.

21. **Archery** An archery target with a radius of 61 cm has 5 scoring zones formed by concentric circles. The colors of the zones are yellow, red, blue, black, and white. The radius of the yellow circle is 12.2 cm. The width of each ring is also 12.2 cm. If an arrow hits the target at a random point, what is the probability that it hits the center yellow zone?

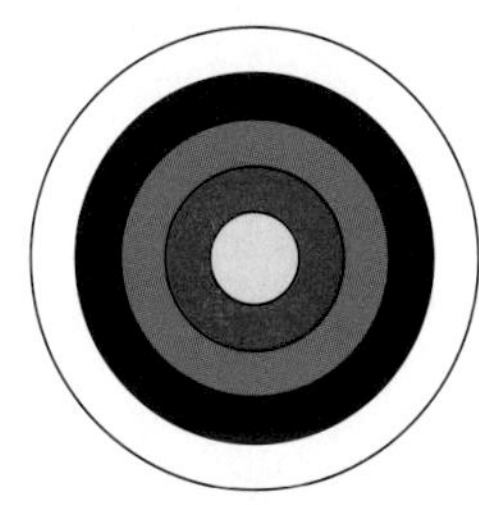

B Apply Your Skills

22. $\overline{BZ}$ contains $\overline{MN}$ and $BZ = 20$. A point is chosen at random from $\overline{BZ}$. The probability that the point is also on $\overline{MN}$ is 0.3, or 30%. Find MN.

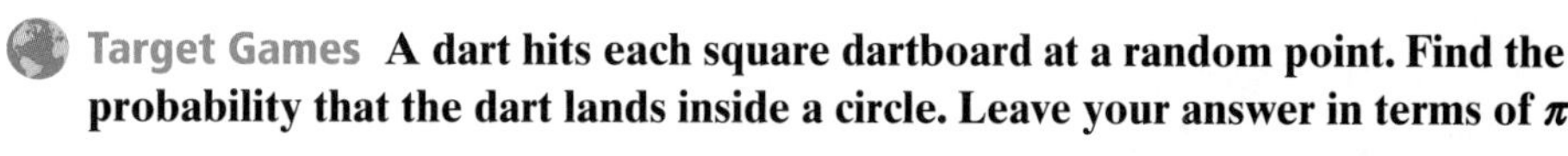

Target Games **A dart hits each square dartboard at a random point. Find the probability that the dart lands inside a circle. Leave your answer in terms of π.**

23. 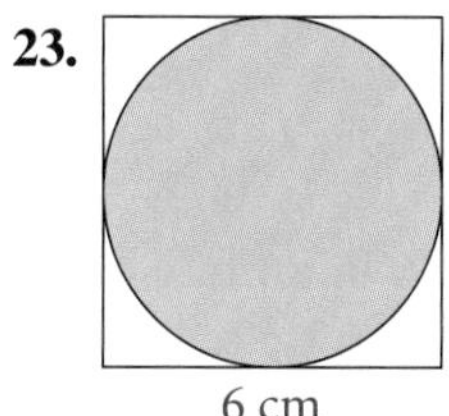

24. 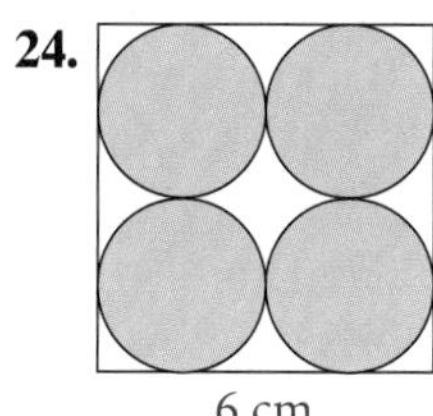

25. 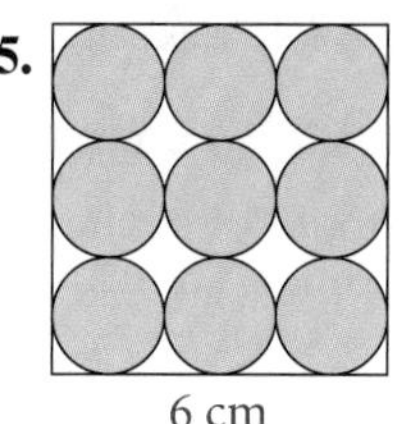

26. A dartboard is a square of radius 10 in. You throw a dart and hit the target. Find the probability that the dart lies within $\sqrt{10}$ in. of the center of the square.

27. **Critical Thinking** Use the information given in Example 4.
   a. For each 1000 quarters tossed, about how many prizes would be won?
   b. Suppose the game prize costs the carnival $10. About how much profit would the carnival expect for every 1000 quarters tossed?

Need Help?

For Exercise 28, draw a typical 25-min interval from one bus departure to the next.

28. **Commuting** Suppose a bus arrives at a bus stop every 25 min and waits 5 min before leaving. Sketch a geometric model. Use it to find the probability that a person has to wait more than 10 min for a bus to leave.

29. **Traffic Patterns** The traffic lights at Fourth and Commercial Streets repeat themselves in 60-second cycles. Ms. Li regularly has students drive on Fourth Street through the Commercial Street intersection. By experience, she knows that they will face a red light 60% of the time. Use this information to estimate how long the Fourth Street light is red during each 1-min cycle.

For Exercises 30 and 31, sketch a geometric model and solve.

30. **Astronomy** Meteoroids (mostly dust-particle size) are continually bombarding Earth. The surface area of Earth is about 65.7 million square miles. The area of the United States is about 3.7 million square miles. What is the probability that a meteoroid landing on Earth will land in the United States?

31. **Tape Recording** Amy made a tape recording of a chorus rehearsal. The recording began 21 min into the 60-min tape and lasted 8 min. Later she accidentally erased a 15-min segment somewhere on the tape.

a. In your model show the possible starting times of the erasure. Explain how you know that the erasure did not start after the 45-min mark.

b. In your model show the starting times of the erasures that would erase the entire rehearsal. Find the probability that the entire rehearsal was erased.

Need Help?

$0 \leq P(\text{event}) \leq 1$

$P(\text{event}) = 0$ means the event will not occur.

$P(\text{event}) = 1$ means the event will occur.

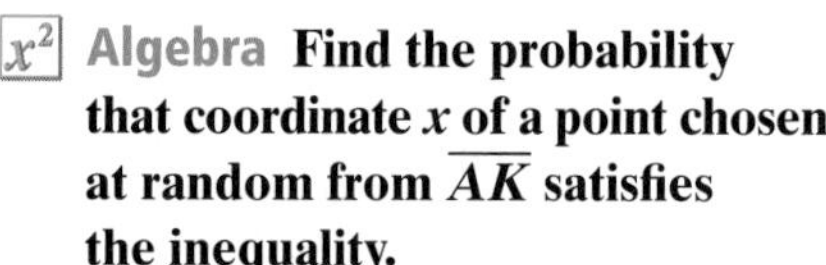

Algebra **Find the probability that coordinate x of a point chosen at random from $\overline{AK}$ satisfies the inequality.**

A B C D E F G H I J K

0 1 2 3 4 5 6 7 8 9 10

32. $2 \leq x \leq 8$ **33.** $x \geq 7$ **34.** $2x \leq 9$ **35.** $\frac{1}{2}x - 5 \geq 0$

36. $2 \leq 4x \leq 3$ **37.** $0 \leq \frac{1}{3}x + 1 \leq 5$ **38.** $|x - 6| \leq 1.5$ **39.** $\sqrt{2} \leq \pi x \leq \sqrt{10}$

Real-World Connection

A mere touch of the target by the ball triggers the dunk.

Dunk Tank **At a fund-raiser, a volunteer sits on a platform above a tank of water. She gets dunked when you throw a ball and hit the red target. The radius of the ball is 3.6 cm. What is the probability that a ball heading randomly for the given background shape would hit the given target shape?**

40 cm

10 cm

40. Background (at right): a circle 40 cm across
Target: a circle with 10-cm radius

41. Background: a square with 40-cm sides
Target: a circle with 10-cm radius

42. Background: a circle 40-cm across
Target: a square with 20-cm sides

43. Background: a square with 40-cm sides
Target: a square with 20-cm sides

44. Kimi has a 4-in. straw and a 6-in. straw. She wants to cut the 6-in. straw into two pieces so that the three pieces form a triangle.

a. If she cuts the straw to get two 3-in. pieces, can she form a triangle?

b. If the two pieces are 1 in. and 5 in., can she form a triangle?

c. If Kimi cuts the straw at a random point, what is the probability that she can form a triangle?

45. a. **Open-Ended** Design a dartboard game to be used at a charity fair. Specify the size and shape of the regions of the board.

b. **Writing** Describe the rules for using your dartboard and the prizes that winners receive. Explain how much money you would expect to raise if the game were played 100 times.

Challenge

46. **Graphing Calculator** A circular dartboard has radius 1 m and a yellow circle in the center. Assume you hit the target at a random point. For what radius of the yellow center region would $P(\text{hitting yellow})$ equal each of the following? Use the table feature of a calculator to generate all six answers. Round to the nearest centimeter.

a. 0.2 **b.** 0.4 **c.** 0.5

d. 0.6 **e.** 0.8 **f.** 1.0

47. **Target Game** A target has a central circle and three concentric rings. The diameters of the circles are 2 cm, 6 cm, 10 cm, and 14 cm. Find the probability of landing in the gray region. Compare it with the probability of landing in *either* the blue or red region.

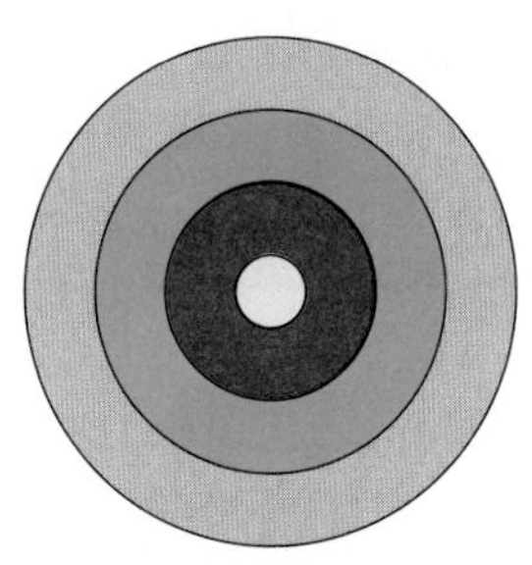

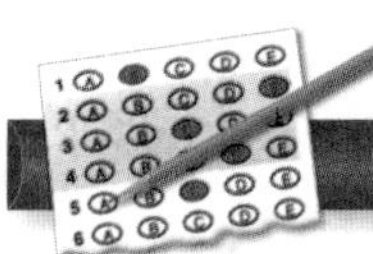

Standardized Test Prep

Multiple Choice

48. A dart hits the dartboard shown. Find the probability that it lands in the shaded region.
A. 21% **B.** 25% **C.** 50% **D.** 79%

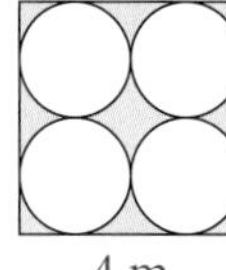

49. A dart hits the dartboard shown. Find the probability that it lands in a circle.
F. 21% **G.** 25% **H.** 50% **I.** 79%

Short Response

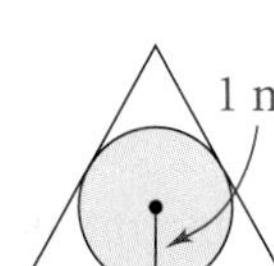

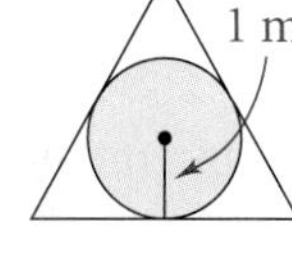

50. On this dartboard, the circle with 1-m radius is inscribed in an equilateral triangle. Find the probability that a dart that hits the board lands in the circular region. Justify your answer.

Extended Response

51. The radius of a circle is 28 m. The measure of the central angle is 120.
a. Find the area of the sector in terms of π. Justify your answer.
b. Find the area of the shaded segment to the nearest tenth. Justify your answer.

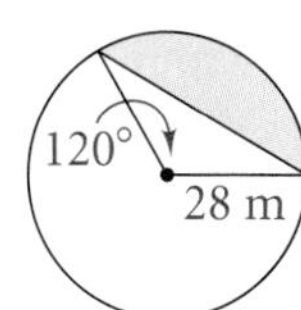

Take It to the NET
Online lesson quiz at
www.PHSchool.com
Web Code: afa-0708

Mixed Review

Lesson 7-7

52. A circle has circumference 20π ft. What is its area?

53. A circle has radius 12 cm. What is the area of a sector of the circle with a 30° central angle?

54. What is the area of a semicircle with diameter 20 ft?

Lesson 6-2 x^2 **Algebra** **Find the values of the variables in each parallelogram.**

55. 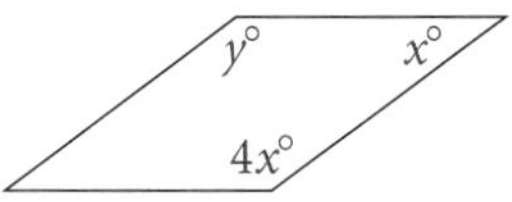

56. 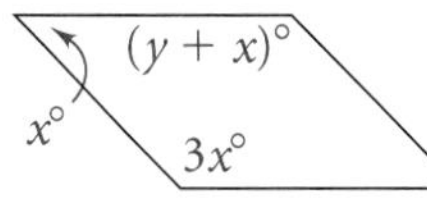

Lesson 5-1

57. The coordinates of the vertices of a triangle are $A(1, -4)$, $B(5, 6)$, and $C(-3, 2)$.
a. Find the coordinates of D, the midpoint of $\overline{AB}$, and E, the midpoint of $\overline{BC}$.
b. Find the slope of $\overline{DE}$ and the slope of $\overline{AC}$.
c. Verify that $\overline{DE} \parallel \overline{AC}$.
d. Find DE and AC.
e. Verify that $DE = \frac{1}{2}AC$.

Test-Taking Strategies

Finding Multiple Correct Answers

In Multiple-Correct-Answer questions, you have to determine whether a number of statements are true or false. As you test each statement, mark it as true or false. You then choose those that are true.

EXAMPLE

The perimeter of a rectangle is 20 cm.
Which of the following could be true?

I. One side of the rectangle is 2 cm.
II. The area of the rectangle is 24 cm^2.
III. The diagonal of the rectangle is 5 cm.

A. I and II only **B.** II and III only **C.** I and III only **D.** I, II, and III

Test each statement to see if it could be true in a rectangle with perimeter 20 cm.

Statement I is possible in a rectangle with dimensions 2-cm by 8-cm.

Statement II is possible in a rectangle with dimensions 4-cm by 6-cm.

Statement III is not possible. A diagonal is longer than each side. In any rectangle with perimeter 20 cm, at least one side has to be 5 cm or more.

Only statements I and II could be true. The correct choice is A.

EXERCISES

1. Explain why it is possible for the rectangle in the Example to have a side of length 0.1 cm. What would its area be?

2. In $\triangle ABC$, $AB = \sqrt{1}$, $BC = \sqrt{2}$, and $AC = \sqrt{3}$.
Which of the following are true?

I. The largest angle is $\angle B$.
II. The triangle is a right triangle.
III. One angle of the triangle has measure 30.

A. I only **B.** II only **C.** I and II only **D.** I, II, and III

3. A square and an equilateral triangle each have apothem of length 1 cm.
Which of the following are always true?

I. The perimeter of the square is greater than the perimeter of the triangle.
II. The area of the square is less than the area of the triangle.
III. The radius of the square is less than the radius of the triangle.

F. I only **G.** I and II only **H.** II and III only **I.** I, II, and III

4. A polygon is equilateral.
Which of the following are always true?

I. The sum of the measures of its exterior angles, one at each vertex, is 360.
II. The sum of the measures of its interior angles is divisible by 180.
III. The polygon is equiangular.

A. I only **B.** I and II only **C.** II and III only **D.** I, II, and III

Chapter Review

Vocabulary

adjacent arcs (p. 387)
altitude of a parallelogram (p. 349)
apothem of a regular polygon (p. 380)
arc length (p. 389)
base of a parallelogram (p. 349)
base of a triangle (p. 350)
center of a circle (p. 386)
center of a regular polygon (p. 380)
central angle (p. 386)
circle (p. 386)
circumference (p. 388)
concentric circles (p. 388)
congruent arcs (p. 389)
congruent circles (p. 386)
diameter (p. 386)
geometric probability (p. 402)
height of a parallelogram (p. 349)
height of a trapezoid (p. 374)
height of a triangle (p. 350)
major arc (p. 387)
minor arc (p. 387)
pi (p. 388)
Pythagorean triple (p. 357)
radius (p. 386)
radius of a regular polygon (p. 380)
sector of a circle (p. 396)
segment of a circle (p. 397)
semicircle (p. 387)

Reading Math
Understanding Vocabulary

Take It to the NET
Online vocabulary quiz at **www.PHSchool.com**
Web Code: afj-0751

Choose the correct term to complete each sentence.

1. You can use any side as the (*altitude, base*) of a triangle.
2. A (*sector, segment*) of a circle is a region bounded by two radii and the intercepted arc.
3. A segment that contains the center of a circle and has both endpoints on the circle is the (*diameter, circumference*) of a circle.
4. In a regular polygon, the perpendicular distance from the center to a side is the (*apothem, radius*) of the parallelogram.
5. Two arcs of a circle with exactly one point in common are (*congruent arcs, adjacent arcs*).

Skills and Concepts

7-1, 7-4, and 7-5 Objectives

- ▼ To find the area of a parallelogram
- ▼ To find the area of a triangle
- ▼ To find the area of a trapezoid
- ▼ To find the area of a rhombus or a kite
- ▼ To find the area of a regular polygon

You can find the area of a rectangle, a parallelogram, or a triangle if you know the **base,** b, and **height,** h. The area of a rectangle or a parallelogram is $A = bh$.

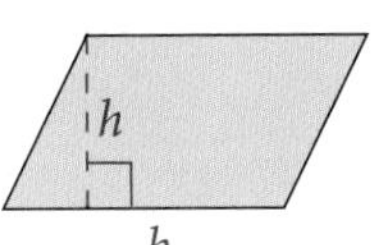

The area of a triangle is $A = \frac{1}{2}bh$.

The **height of a trapezoid,** h, is the perpendicular distance between the bases, b_1 and b_2. The area of a trapezoid is $A = \frac{1}{2}h(b_1 + b_2)$.

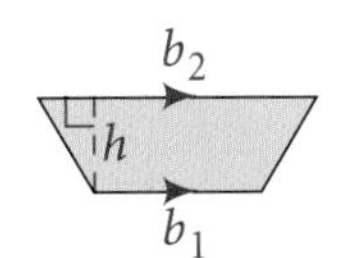

The **center of a regular polygon,** C, is the center of its circumscribed circle. The **radius,** r, is the distance from the center to a vertex. The **apothem,** a, is the perpendicular distance from the center to a side. The area of a regular polygon with apothem a and perimeter p is $A = \frac{1}{2}ap$.

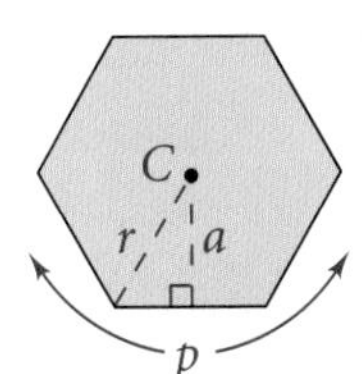

The area of a rhombus or kite is $A = \frac{1}{2}d_1d_2$.

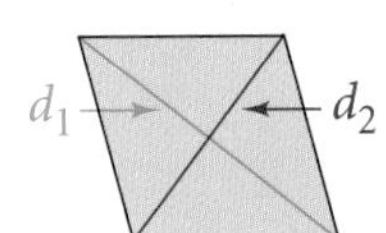

Find the area of each figure. If your answer is not an integer, leave it in simplest radical form.

6.
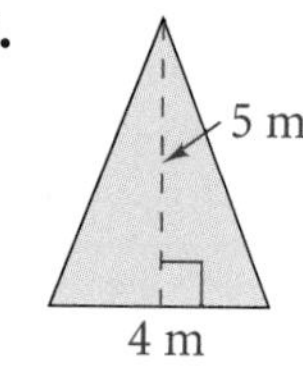

7.
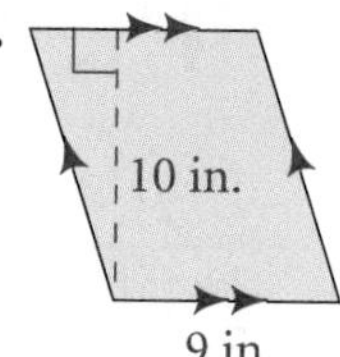

8.
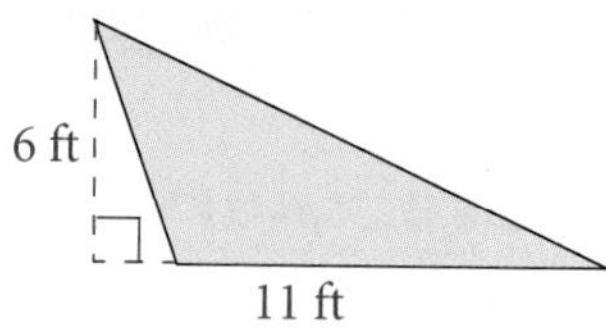

9.
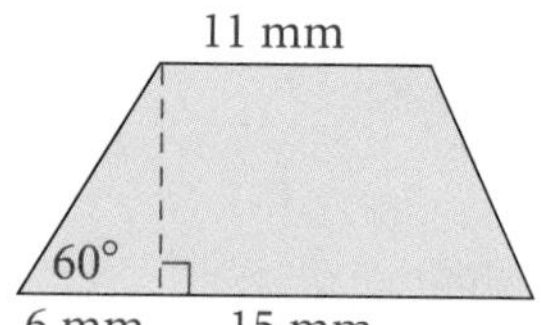

10.
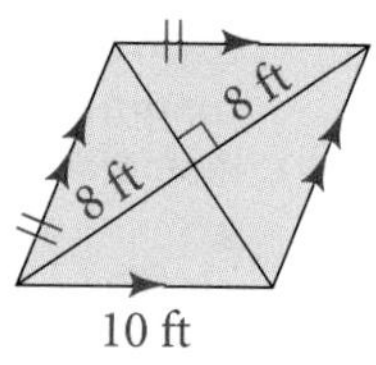

11.
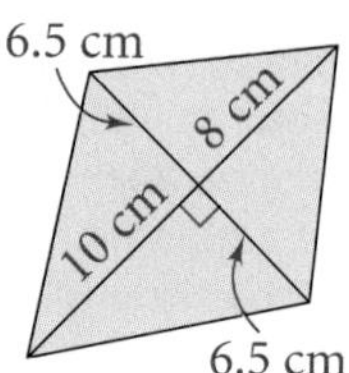

Sketch each regular polygon with the given radius. Then find its area. Round your answers to the nearest tenth.

12. triangle; radius 4 in.

13. square; radius 8 mm

14. hexagon; radius 7 cm

7-2 and 7-3 Objectives

- To use the Pythagorean Theorem
- To use the Converse of the Pythagorean Theorem
- To use properties of 45°-45°-90° triangles
- To use properties of 30°-60°-90° triangles

The **Pythagorean Theorem** states that in a right triangle, the sum of the squares of the lengths of the legs equals the square of the length of the hypotenuse, or $a^2 + b^2 = c^2$.

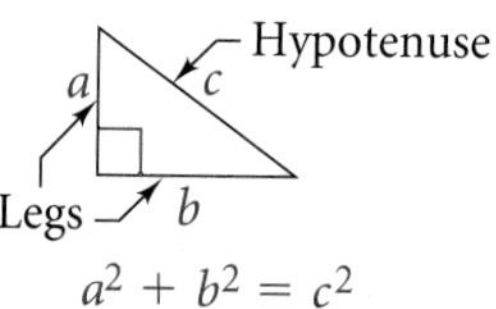

Positive integers a, b, and c form a **Pythagorean triple** if $a^2 + b^2 = c^2$.

The **Converse of the Pythagorean Theorem** states that if the square of the length of one side of a triangle is equal to the sum of the squares of the lengths of the other two sides, then the triangle is a right triangle.

In a triangle with longest side c, if $c^2 > a^2 + b^2$, the triangle is obtuse; if $c^2 < a^2 + b^2$, the triangle is acute.

In a 45°-45°-90° triangle, the legs are congruent and the length of the hypotenuse is $\sqrt{2}$ times the length of a leg.

In a 30°-60°-90° triangle, the length of the hypotenuse is twice the length of the shorter leg. The length of the longer leg is $\sqrt{3}$ times the length of the shorter leg.

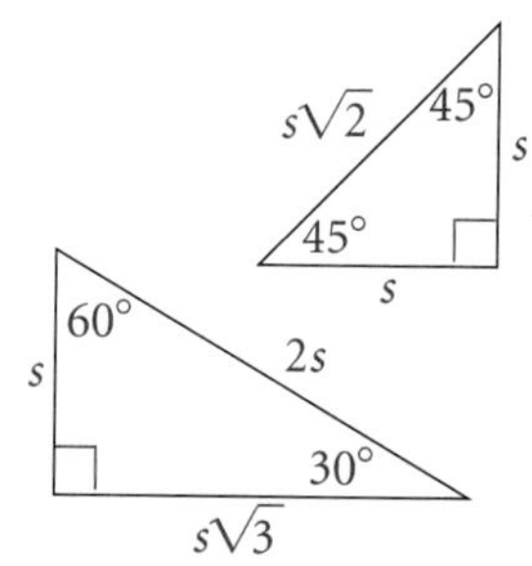

Find the value of each variable. If your answer is not an integer, leave it in simplest radical form.

15.
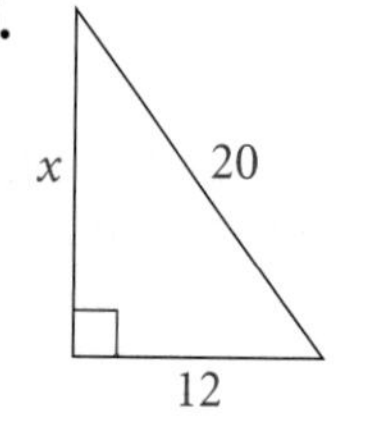

16.
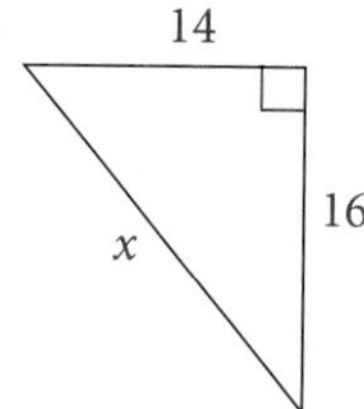

17.
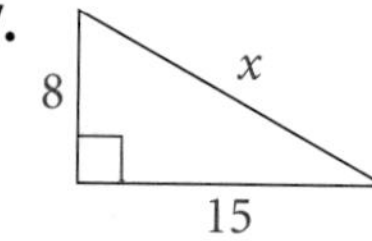

18.
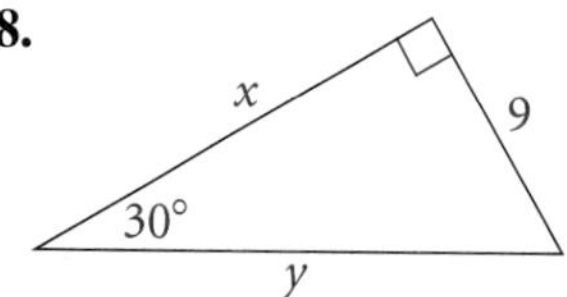

19.
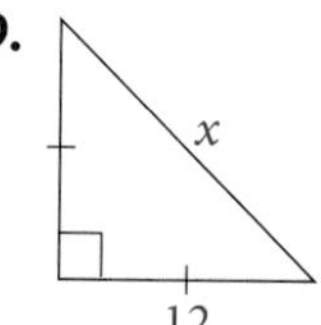

20.
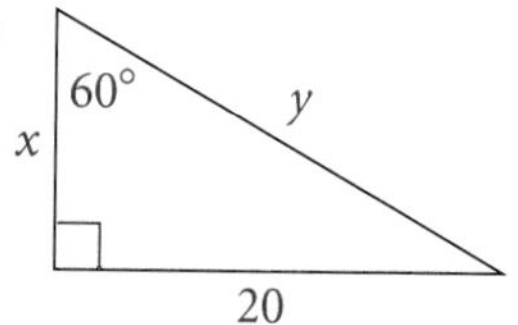

7-6 and 7-7 Objectives

- To find the measures of central angles and arcs
- To find circumference and arc length
- To find the areas of circles, sectors, and segments of circles

A **circle** is the set of all points in a plane equidistant from one point called the **center.** The measure of a **minor arc** is the measure of its corresponding central angle. The measure of a **major arc** is 360 minus the measure of its related minor arc. **Adjacent arcs** have exactly one point in common.

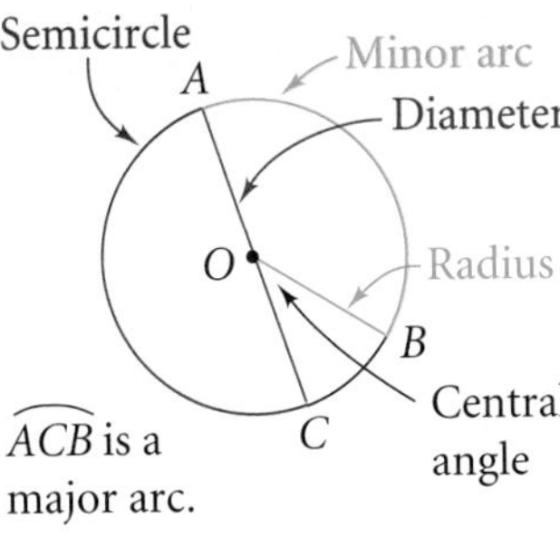

The **circumference** of a circle is $C = \pi d$ or $C = 2\pi r$. The area of a circle is $A = \pi r^2$.

Arc length is a fraction of a circle's circumference. The length of $\widehat{AB} = \frac{m\widehat{AB}}{360} 2\pi r$.

A **sector of a circle** is a region bounded by two radii and their intercepted arc.
The area of sector $APB = \frac{m\widehat{AB}}{360} \pi r^2$.

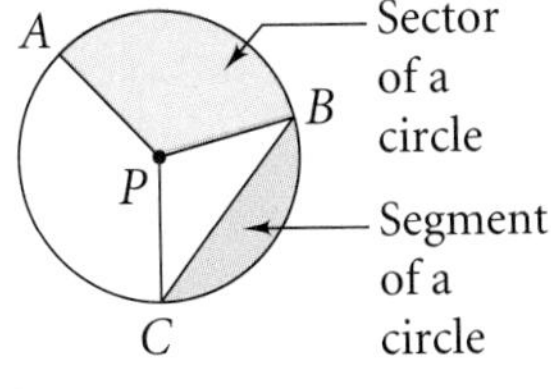

A **segment of a circle** is the part of a circle bounded by an arc and the segment joining its endpoints. The area of a segment of a circle is the difference between the areas of the related sector and the related triangle.

Find each measure.

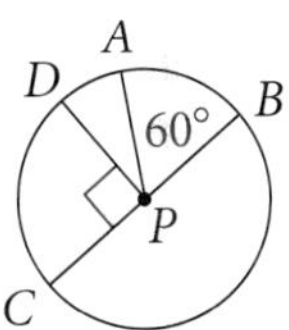

21. $m\angle APD$ **22.** $m\widehat{AC}$

23. $m\widehat{ABD}$ **24.** $m\angle CPA$

Find the length of each arc shown in red. Leave your answer in terms of π.

25.

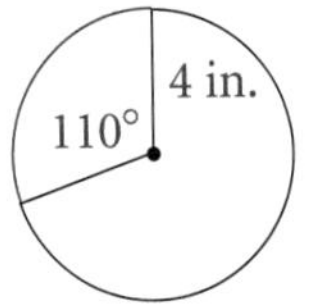

26.

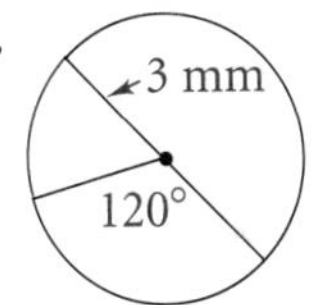

Find the area of each shaded region. Round your answer to the nearest tenth.

27.

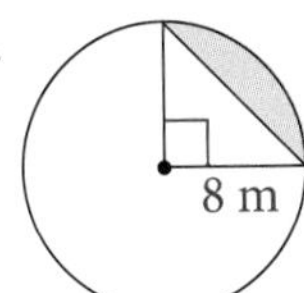

28.

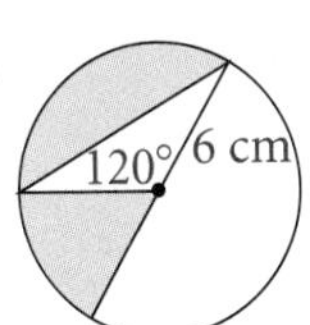

7-8 Objectives

- To use segment and area models to find the probabilities of events

Geometric probability uses geometric figures to represent occurrences of events. You can use a segment model or an area model. Compare the part that represents favorable outcomes to the whole, which represents all outcomes.

A dart hits each dartboard at a random point. Find the probability that it lands in the shaded area.

29.

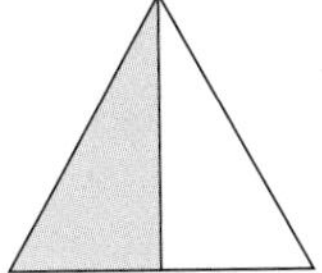

30.

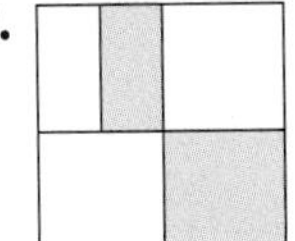

31.

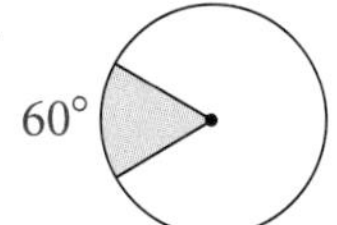

Chapter Test

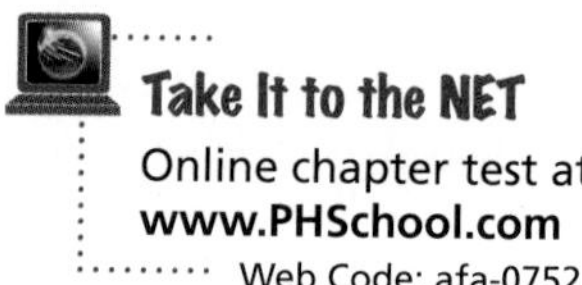

Find the area of each figure. If your answer is not an integer, round to the nearest tenth.

1. 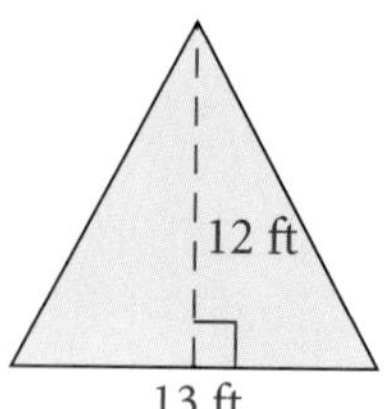

2. 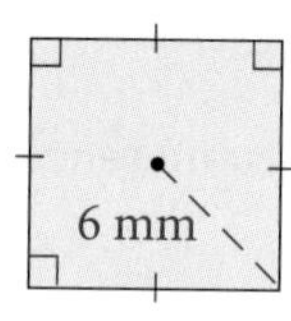

3. 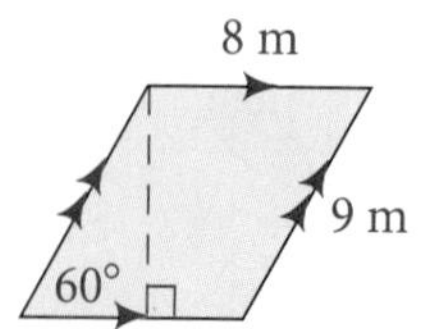

4. 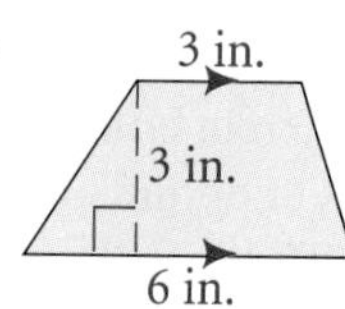

Find the area of each regular polygon. Round to the nearest tenth.

5. 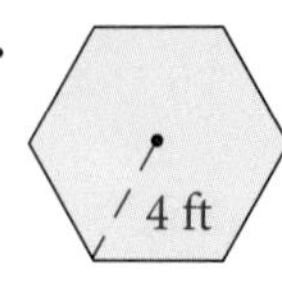

6. 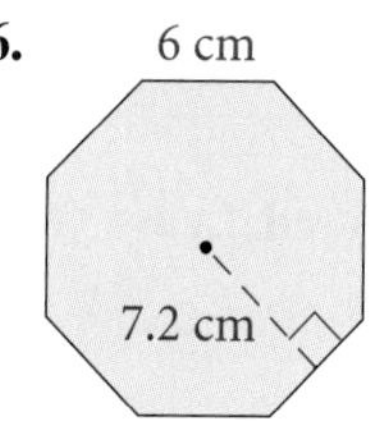

Algebra **Find the value of each variable. Leave your answer in simplest radical form.**

7. 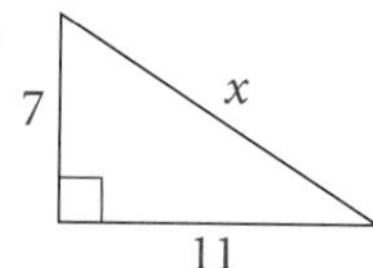

8. 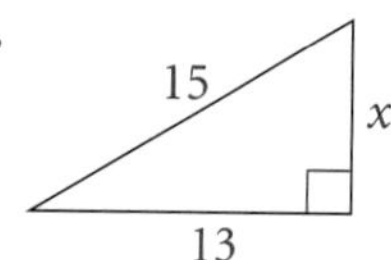

9. 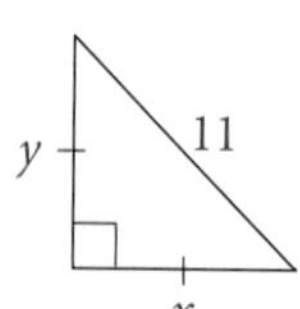

10. 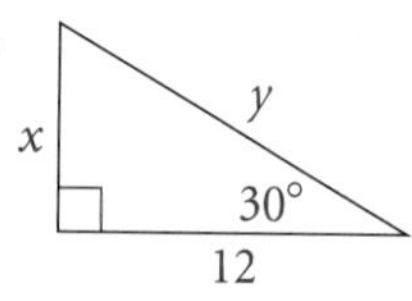

The lengths of three sides of a triangle are given. Describe each triangle as *acute, right,* or *obtuse.*

11. 9 cm, 10 cm, 12 cm

12. 8 m, 15 m, 17 m

13. 5 in., 6 in., 10 in.

14. **Writing** Explain how you can use the length of the shorter leg of a 30°-60°-90° triangle to find the lengths of the other two sides.

Find each measure for ⊙*P*.

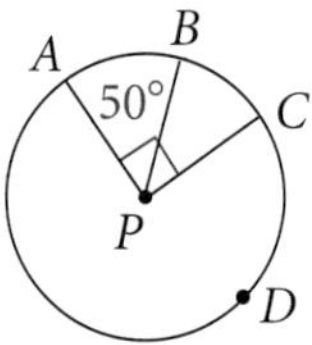

15. $m\angle BPC$
16. $m\widehat{AB}$
17. $m\widehat{ADC}$
18. $m\widehat{ADB}$

Find the length of each arc shown in red. Leave your answer in terms of π.

19. 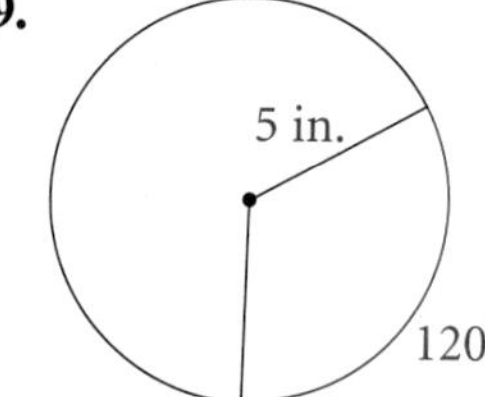

20. 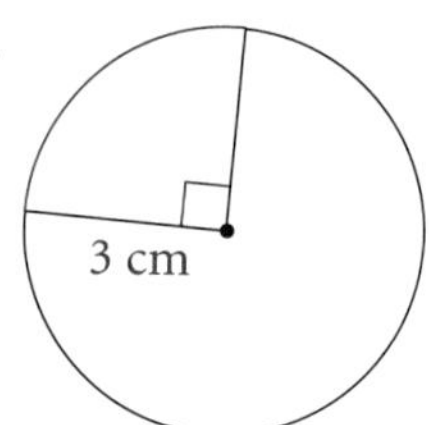

Find the area of each shaded region to the nearest hundredth.

21. 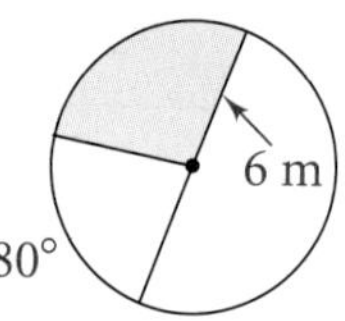

22. 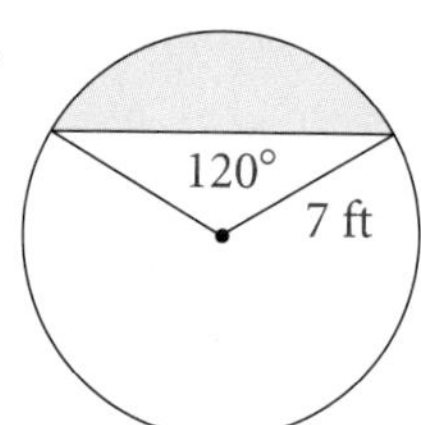

23. **Open-Ended** Use a compass to draw a circle. Shade a sector of the circle and find its area.

Find the area of each shaded region. Leave your answers in terms of π.

24. 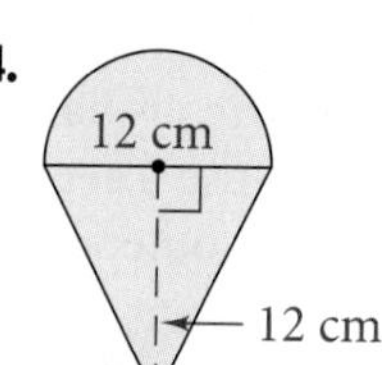

25. 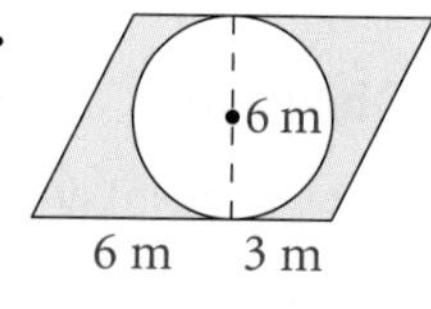

26. **Probability** Every 20 minutes from 4:00 P.M. to 7:00 P.M., a commuter train crosses Main Street. For three minutes a gate stops cars from passing as the train goes by. What is the probability that a motorist approaching the train crossing during this time interval will have to stop for the train?

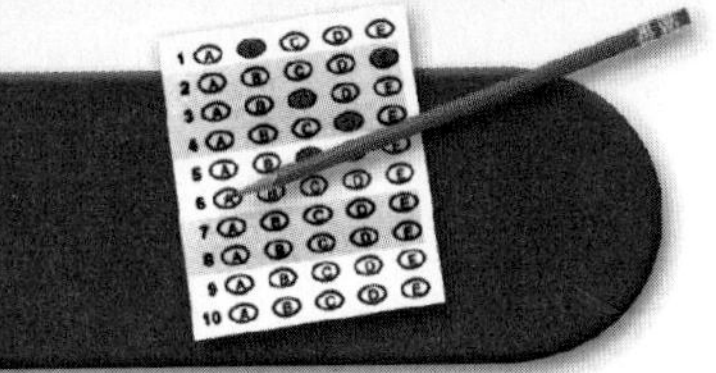

Standardized Test Prep

Reading Comprehension **Read the passage below. Then answer the questions on the basis of what is *stated* or *implied* in the passage.**

Hanging a Picture A picture has a wire from side to side across its back. Hang the picture from one hook and it can easily swing, or slide into a tilt. Use two hooks and the picture will hang level. Here is how to place two hooks on the wall to hang the picture level and precisely where you want it.

On your wall, mark two level points A and B where you want the top corners of the picture. For example, assume the back of a 21-in. wide picture is rigged as shown at the left and you want the two hooks 12 in. apart.

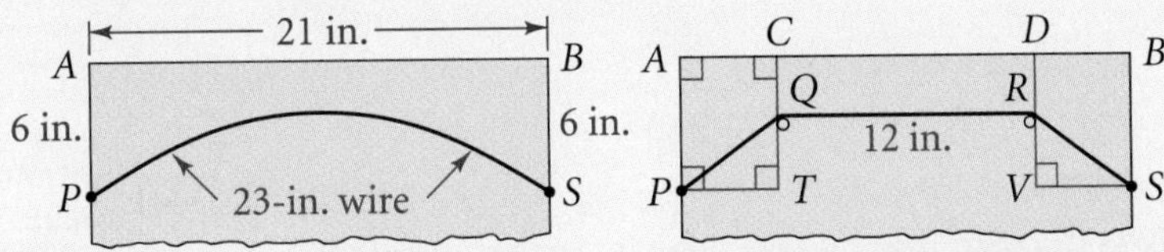

At the right, the matching diagrams in the upper corners locate points Q and R where hooks would hold the wire. Determine measurements as follows:

Calculate to find that $QP = 5.5$ in. $= RS$.
Calculate to find that $TP = 4.5$ in. $= VS$.
Then $QT = \sqrt{5.5^2 - 4.5^2} \approx 3.2$ in. $= RV$, so $CQ = 2.8$ in. $= DR$.

From points A and B on the wall, measure 4.5 in. towards each other and 2.8 in. down to find points Q and R, respectively. Attach picture hangers to support the wire at Q and R, and hang your picture perfectly!

1. From the passage, what should you learn about hanging a picture?
   - **A.** How to use one hook so that you can easily slide the picture to hang straight.
   - **B.** How to use two hooks so that the picture hangs straight and where you want it.
   - **C.** How to use one hook so that the picture can easily swing, or slide into a tilt.
   - **D.** How to use two hooks at the top corners.

2. How do you calculate QP?
   - **F.** $\frac{\text{wire length} - 12}{2}$ **G.** $\frac{PQ + RS}{2}$
   - **H.** $\frac{AB - 10}{2}$ **I.** $\frac{PT + SV + 2}{2}$

3. How do you calculate TP?
   - **A.** $\frac{\text{wire length} - 14}{2}$ **B.** $\frac{PQ + RS - 2}{2}$
   - **C.** $\frac{AB - 12}{2}$ **D.** $\frac{PT + SV}{2}$

4. Which theorem do you use to calculate QT?
   - **F.** 30°-60°-90° Triangle **G.** 45°-45°-90° Triangle
   - **H.** Pythagorean **I.** Triangle Midsegment

5. How do you calculate CQ?
   - **A.** $CQ = DR$ **B.** $CQ + QP = 8.3$
   - **C.** $CQ = 6 - CQ$ **D.** $CQ + QT = CT$

6. What kind of quadrilateral is $DBSV$? Justify your answer.

Describe how to locate the hooks for hanging.

7. A picture is 30 in. wide. The hanging wire is 34 in. long, attached at the sides of the picture, 9 in. from the top. The hooks are 14 in. apart.

8. A circular mirror has diameter 22 in. The hanging wire is 28 in. long, attached at the endpoints of a diameter. The hooks are 10 in. apart.

Where You've Been

- In Chapter 4, you learned several different methods for proving triangles congruent. You learned how to use CPCTC to find additional information about congruent triangles.
- In Chapter 5, you learned that a midsegment of a triangle is parallel to a side of the triangle and half its length.
- In Chapter 7, you learned the Pythagorean Theorem, and how to find area for triangles, quadrilaterals, and regular polygons.

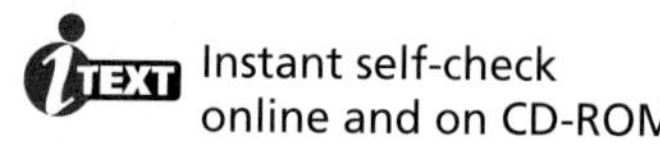

Diagnosing Readiness

(For help, go to the Lesson in green.)

Simplifying Ratios (Skills Handbook page 718)

Simplify each ratio.

1. $12 : 18$ **2.** $\frac{55}{11}$ **3.** $\frac{20a^2}{15a^5}$ **4.** $\frac{3x^2 - 12x}{x^3 - x^2}$

Polygon Angle-Sum Theorems (Lesson 3-4)

Determine the measure of an angle of each regular polygon.

5. pentagon **6.** octagon **7.** decagon **8.** 27-gon

Congruent Figures (Lesson 4-1)

$\triangle PAC \cong \triangle DHL$. Complete the congruence statements.

9. $\overline{PC} \cong$ _?_ **10.** $\angle H \cong$ _?_ **11.** $\angle PCA \cong$ _?_ **12.** $\triangle HDL \cong$ _?_

Special Right Triangles (Lesson 7-3)

x^2 **Algebra** Find the value of x. Leave your answer in simplest radical form.

13.

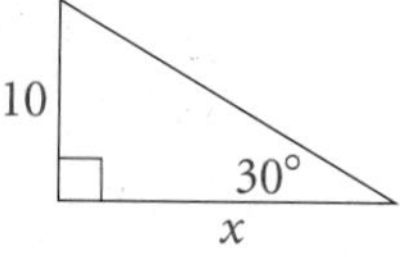

14.

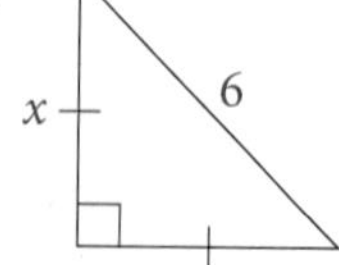

15.

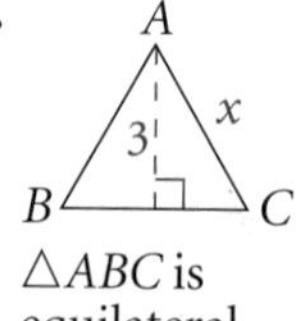

$\triangle ABC$ is equilateral.

Areas of Regular Polygons (Lesson 7-5)

Find the area of each regular polygon.

16. regular hexagon with perimeter 24 units

17. regular octagon with sides 9 units and apothem 10.9 units

Similarity

Chapter 8

LESSONS

Key Vocabulary

- Cross-Product Property (p. 417)
- extended proportion (p. 417)
- geometric mean (p. 440)
- golden ratio (p. 425)
- golden rectangle (p. 425)
- indirect measurement (p. 434)
- proportion (p. 417)
- ratio (p. 416)
- scale (p. 418)
- scale drawing (p. 418)
- similar (p. 423)
- similarity ratio (p. 423)

Where You're Going

- In this chapter, you will learn that similar polygons are polygons that have the same shape but not necessarily the same size.
- You will learn how to prove triangles similar.
- Through proving triangles similar, you will find additional relationships within triangles.
- You will also learn how the perimeters and areas of similar figures are related.

Real-World Snapshots Applying what you have learned, you will do activities on pages 466 and 467 involving views from the tops of tall structures.

ALGEBRA

8-1 Ratios and Proportions

Lesson Preview

What You'll Learn

OBJECTIVE 1 To write ratios and solve proportions

. . . And Why

To find dimensions from a scale drawing, as in Example 4

✓ Check Skills You'll Need

(For help, go to Skills Handbook p. 718 and Lesson 5-1.)

Simplify each ratio.

1. $\frac{2}{4}$ **2.** $\frac{8}{12}$ **3.** $\frac{6}{8}$ **4.** $\frac{10}{10}$

5. 20 : 30 **6.** 8 to 2 **7.** 2 to 8 **8.** 12 : 9

9. Draw a triangle. Then draw its three midsegments to form a smaller triangle. How do the lengths of the sides of the smaller triangle compare to the lengths of the sides of the larger triangle?

New Vocabulary • proportion • extended proportion • Cross-Product Property • scale drawing • scale

Interactive lesson includes instant self-check, tutorials, and activities.

OBJECTIVE 1

Using Ratios and Proportions

Reading Math

You can read $a : b$ as "the ratio a to b."

A ratio is a comparison of two quantities. You can write the ratio of a to b or $a : b$ as the quotient $\frac{a}{b}$ when $b \neq 0$. Unless otherwise stated, the terms and expressions appearing in ratios in this book are assumed to be nonzero.

1 EXAMPLE Real-World Connection

Photography A photo that is 8 in. wide and $5\frac{1}{3}$ in. high is enlarged to a poster that is 2 ft wide and $1\frac{1}{3}$ ft high. What is the ratio of the width of the photo to the width of the poster?

$$\frac{\text{width of photo}}{\text{width of poster}} = \frac{8 \text{ in.}}{2 \text{ ft}} = \frac{8 \text{ in.}}{24 \text{ in.}} = \frac{8}{24} = \frac{1}{3}$$

The ratio of the width of the photo to the width of the poster is 1 : 3 or $\frac{1}{3}$.

✓ Check Understanding **1** What is the ratio of the height of the photo to the height of the poster?

Reading Math

You can read both $\frac{a}{b} = \frac{c}{d}$ and $a : b = c : d$ as "a is to b as c is to d."

A **proportion** is a statement that two ratios are equal. You can write a proportion in these forms:

$$\frac{a}{b} = \frac{c}{d} \text{ and } a : b = c : d$$

When three or more ratios are equal, you can write an **extended proportion.** For example, you could write the following:

$$\frac{6}{24} = \frac{4}{16} = \frac{1}{4}$$

Two equations are equivalent when either can be deduced from the other using the Properties of Equality. Several equations are equivalent to a proportion. Some of them are important enough to be called Properties of Proportions.

Key Concepts

Property	Properties of Proportions	
$\frac{a}{b} = \frac{c}{d}$ is equivalent to	(1) $ad = bc$	(2) $\frac{b}{a} = \frac{d}{c}$
	(3) $\frac{a}{c} = \frac{b}{d}$	(4) $\frac{a + b}{b} = \frac{c + d}{d}$

Multiplying both sides of $\frac{a}{b} = \frac{c}{d}$ by bd results in the first property, called the **Cross-Product Property.** You may state this property as "The product of the extremes is equal to the product of the means."

means

$a : b = c : d$

extremes

$\frac{a}{b} = \frac{c}{d}$

$ad = bc$

2 EXAMPLE Properties of Proportions

Algebra If $\frac{x}{y} = \frac{5}{6}$, complete each statement.

a. $6x = \blacksquare$

$6x = 5y$

b. $\frac{y}{x} = \frac{\blacksquare}{\blacksquare}$

$\frac{y}{x} = \frac{6}{5}$

c. $\frac{x}{5} = \frac{\blacksquare}{\blacksquare}$

$\frac{x}{5} = \frac{y}{6}$

d. $\frac{x + y}{y} = \frac{\blacksquare}{\blacksquare}$

$\frac{x + y}{y} = \frac{11}{6}$

Check Understanding 2 **Critical Thinking** Write two proportions that are equivalent to $\frac{m}{4} = \frac{n}{11}$.

You solve a proportion by finding the value of the variable.

3 EXAMPLE Solving for a Variable

Algebra Solve each proportion.

a. $\frac{x}{5} = \frac{12}{7}$

$7x = 5(12)$ ← **Cross-Product Property** → $4(y + 3) = 8y$

$7x = 60$

$x = \frac{60}{7}$

b. $\frac{y + 3}{8} = \frac{y}{4}$

$4(y + 3) = 8y$

$4y + 12 = 8y$

$12 = 4y$

$y = 3$

Check Understanding 3 Solve each proportion.

a. $\frac{5}{z} = \frac{20}{3}$

b. $\frac{18}{n + 6} = \frac{6}{n}$

In a **scale drawing,** the **scale** compares each length in the drawing to the actual length. The lengths used in a scale can be in different units. A scale might be written as 1 in. to 100 mi, 1 in. = 12 ft, or 1 mm : 1 m. You can use proportions to find the actual dimensions represented in a scale drawing.

4 EXAMPLE Real-World Connection

Drafting Measure the dimensions of the bedroom in the scale drawing. Use those dimensions to find the dimensions of the actual bedroom.

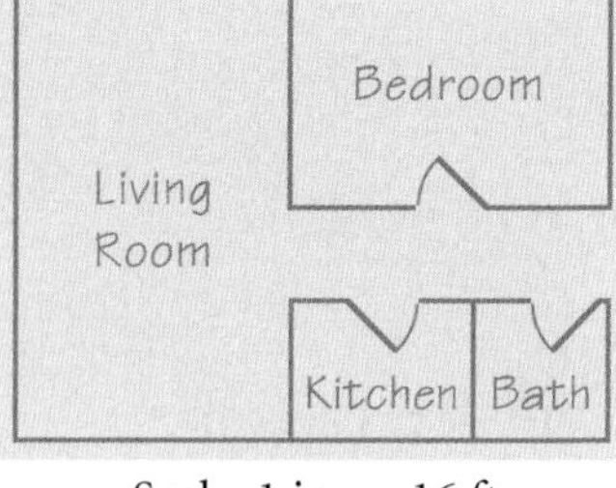

Scale: 1 in. = 16 ft

Use a ruler to find that the bedroom in the scale drawing is $\frac{7}{8}$ in. by $\frac{5}{8}$ in.

$\frac{1}{16} = \frac{\frac{7}{8}}{x}$ ← $\frac{\text{drawing length (in.)}}{\text{actual length (ft)}}$ → $\frac{1}{16} = \frac{\frac{5}{8}}{y}$

$x = 16\left(\frac{7}{8}\right)$ ← **Cross-Product Property** → $y = 16\left(\frac{5}{8}\right)$

$x = 14$ $\qquad$ $y = 10$

The actual bedroom is 14 ft by 10 ft.

Check Understanding **4** You want to make a new scale drawing with a scale of 1 in. = 4 ft. What would be the dimensions of your 14 ft-by-10 ft bedroom in this scale drawing?

EXERCISES

For more practice, see *Extra Practice.*

Practice and Problem Solving

A Practice by Example

Example 1 (page 416)

1. The base of the pyramid at the right is a square whose sides measure 0.675 m. The intent was for the sides to measure 675 m. What is the ratio of the length of a base side in the small pyramid to the length of a base side in the intended pyramid?

"We had a little problem with the decimal point."

2. **Models** The Leaning Tower of Pisa in Italy is about 185 ft tall. A model of the Leaning Tower is 6 in. tall. What is the ratio of the height of the model to the height of the real tower?

Example 2 (page 417)

Algebra If $\frac{a}{b} = \frac{3}{4}$, complete each statement.

3. $4a = \blacksquare$
4. $\frac{b}{a} = \frac{\blacksquare}{\blacksquare}$
5. $\frac{a}{3} = \frac{\blacksquare}{\blacksquare}$
6. $\frac{4}{3} = \frac{\blacksquare}{\blacksquare}$
7. $\frac{4}{b} = \frac{\blacksquare}{\blacksquare}$
8. $3b = \blacksquare$
9. $\frac{a+b}{b} = \frac{\blacksquare}{\blacksquare}$
10. $\frac{a}{a+b} = \frac{\blacksquare}{\blacksquare}$
11. $\frac{a+3}{3} = \frac{\blacksquare}{\blacksquare}$

Example 3 (page 417)

x^2 **Algebra** **Solve each proportion.**

12. $\frac{x}{2} = \frac{8}{4}$ **13.** $\frac{9}{5} = \frac{3}{x}$ **14.** $\frac{1}{3} = \frac{x}{12}$

15. $\frac{5}{x} = \frac{8}{11}$ **16.** $\frac{4}{x} = \frac{5}{9}$ **17.** $\frac{5}{6} = \frac{6}{x}$

18. $\frac{x+3}{3} = \frac{10+4}{4}$ **19.** $\frac{x+7}{7} = \frac{15}{5}$ **20.** $\frac{3}{5} = \frac{6}{x+3}$

Example 4 (page 418)

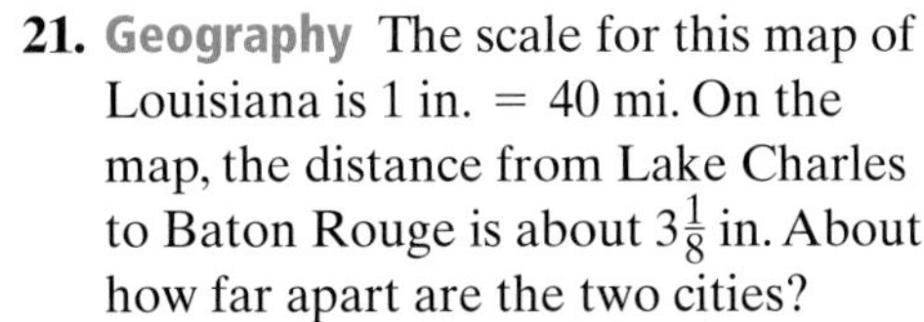

21. Geography The scale for this map of Louisiana is 1 in. = 40 mi. On the map, the distance from Lake Charles to Baton Rouge is about $3\frac{1}{8}$ in. About how far apart are the two cities?

> **Need Help?**
> In Exercise 21 and other scale problems, use mental math to estimate the answer first.

Map Reading **Measure the map distance. Then find the actual distance.**

22. Morgan City to Rayne **23.** Vinton to New Roads **24.** Kaplan to Plaquemine

25. Design You want to make a scale drawing of your bedroom to help you arrange your furniture. You decide on a scale of 3 in. = 2 ft. Your bedroom is a 12 ft-by-15 ft rectangle. What should be its dimensions in your scale drawing?

B Apply Your Skills

For each rectangle, find the ratio of the longer side to the shorter side.

26. 30 m, 65 m

27.

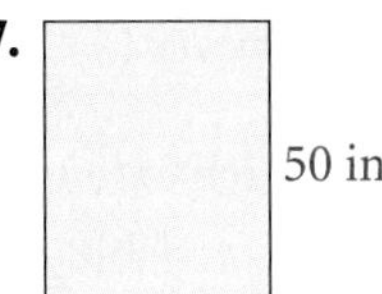

50 in., 40 in.

28.

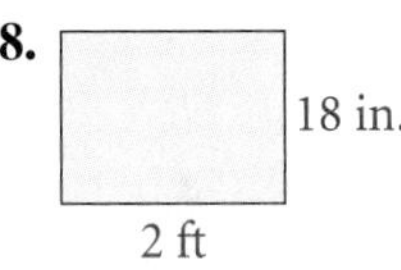

18 in., 2 ft

29. Miniatures The diameter of a dinner plate is 1 ft. In a dollhouse set, the diameter of a dinner plate is $1\frac{1}{4}$ in. What is the ratio, using whole numbers, of the diameter of the dollhouse plate to the diameter of the full-size plate?

Complete each statement.

30. If $\frac{x}{7} = \frac{y}{3}$, then $\frac{x}{y} = \frac{■}{■}$. **31.** If $4m = 9n$, then $\frac{m}{n} = \frac{■}{■}$.

32. If $\frac{30}{t} = \frac{18}{r}$, then $\frac{t}{r} = \frac{■}{■}$. **33.** If $\frac{a+5}{5} = \frac{b+2}{2}$, then $\frac{a}{5} = \frac{■}{■}$.

34. Writing Use a map in your classroom or a map from a textbook. Give the scale of the map. Explain how to use a ruler and the scale of the map to approximate an actual distance. Give an example. (If you do not have access to another map, use the map above.)

x^2 **Algebra** **Solve each proportion.**

35. $\frac{y}{10} = \frac{15}{25}$ **36.** $\frac{9}{24} = \frac{12}{n}$ **37.** $\frac{11}{14} = \frac{b}{21}$ **38.** $\frac{5}{x-3} = \frac{10}{x}$

39. $\frac{8}{n+4} = \frac{4}{n}$ **40.** $\frac{2b-1}{5} = \frac{b}{12}$ **41.** $\frac{2}{7} = \frac{x-5}{x}$ **42.** $\frac{3y-5}{y} = \frac{12}{5}$

Real-World Connection

This sandwich shop is on Museum Wharf in Boston, Massachusetts.

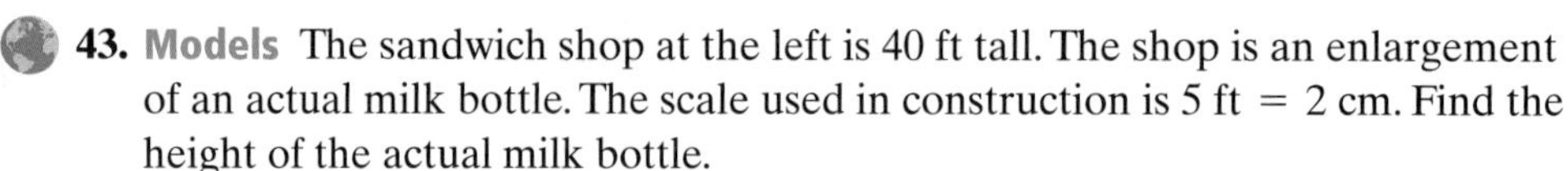

43. **Models** The sandwich shop at the left is 40 ft tall. The shop is an enlargement of an actual milk bottle. The scale used in construction is 5 ft = 2 cm. Find the height of the actual milk bottle.

44. **Geography** Students at the University of Minnesota in Minneapolis built a model globe 42 ft in diameter using a scale of 1 : 1,000,000. About how tall is Mount Everest on the model? (Mount Everest is about 29,000 ft tall.)

Complete each extended proportion.

45. $\frac{8}{12} = \frac{6}{■} = \frac{12}{■}$ 46. $\frac{■}{15} = \frac{15}{25} = \frac{■}{20}$ 47. $\frac{14}{■} = \frac{■}{12} = \frac{35}{20}$

Games **Choose a scale and make a scale drawing of the playing region.**

48. A pool table is 5 ft by 10 ft.
49. A bowling lane is 3.5 ft by 60 ft.
50. A basketball court is 92 ft by 50 ft.
51. A football field is 160 ft by 120 yd.

52. **Error Analysis** One rectangle has length 3 in. and width 4 ft. Another rectangle has length 3 ft and width 4 yd. Elaine claims that the two rectangles are similar because their corresponding angles are congruent and their corresponding sides are in proportion. Explain why Elaine's reasoning is incorrect.

If $\frac{a}{b} = \frac{c}{d}$, complete each statement.

53. $\frac{a+b}{c+d} = \frac{■}{■}$ 54. $\frac{a+c}{b+d} = \frac{■}{■}$ 55. $\frac{a+2b}{b} = \frac{■}{■}$

C Challenge x^2 **Algebra** **Justify the indicated property of proportions.**

56. Property (2): If $\frac{a}{b} = \frac{c}{d}$, then $\frac{b}{a} = \frac{d}{c}$.

57. Property (3): If $\frac{a}{b} = \frac{c}{d}$, then $\frac{a}{c} = \frac{b}{d}$.

58. Property (4): If $\frac{a}{b} = \frac{c}{d}$, then $\frac{a+b}{b} = \frac{c+d}{d}$.

Solve each extended proportion for x and y with $x > 0$ and $y > 0$.

59. $\frac{x}{6} = \frac{x+10}{18} = \frac{4x}{y}$ 60. $\frac{x}{5} = \frac{9}{y} = \frac{y}{25}$ 61. $\frac{1}{x} = \frac{4}{x+9} = \frac{7}{y}$

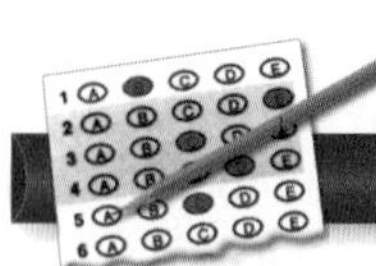

Standardized Test Prep

Multiple Choice

Solve each proportion.

62. $\frac{21}{x} = \frac{7}{3}$ A. 3 B. 7 C. 9 D. 14

63. $\frac{4}{x-1} = \frac{1}{x}$ F. −3 G. $-\frac{1}{3}$ H. $\frac{1}{3}$ I. 3

64. $\frac{x}{x+6} = \frac{2}{3}$ A. 4 B. 6 C. 8 D. 12

65. $\frac{3}{8} = \frac{x+3}{9}$ F. $3\frac{3}{8}$ G. 3 H. $\frac{3}{8}$ I. $\frac{1}{3}$

Take It to the NET
Online lesson quiz at www.PHSchool.com
Web Code: afa-0801

Short Response

66. A map of Long Island has the scale 2.75 cm = 16 km. On the map, Target Rock is 23.2 cm from Lake Montauk.
 a. Write a proportion that you can solve to determine the actual distance from Target Rock to Lake Montauk.
 b. Find the actual distance. Round your answer to the nearest kilometer.

Mixed Review

Lesson 7-8

67. **Probability** A shuttle bus to an airport terminal leaves every 20 min from a remote parking lot. Draw a geometric model and find the probability that a traveler who arrives at a random time will have to wait at least 8 min for the bus to leave the parking lot.

68. **Games** A dartboard is a circle with a 12-in. radius. You throw a dart that hits the dartboard. What is the probability that the dart lands within 6 in. of the center of the dartboard?

Lesson 6-1

Graph each quadrilateral $ABCD$. Classify $ABCD$ in as many ways as possible.

69. $A(-1, -2), B(3, -2), C(1, 4), D(-3, 4)$

70. $A(2, -1), B(6, 2), C(8, 2), D(10, -1)$

71. $A(-7, 1), B(-5, 3), C(0, -2), D(-2, -4)$

72. $A(1, 1), B(-4, 4), C(1, 7), D(6, 4)$

Lesson 5-4

In each exercise, identify two statements that contradict each other.

73. I. $\triangle PQR$ is isosceles.
II. $\triangle PQR$ is an obtuse triangle.
III. $\triangle PQR$ is scalene.

74. I. $\angle 1 \cong \angle 2$
II. $\angle 1$ and $\angle 2$ are complementary.
III. $m\angle 1 + m\angle 2 = 180$

Write (a) the inverse and (b) the contrapositive of each statement.

75. If an angle is acute, then it has measure between 0 and 90.

76. If two lines are parallel, then they are coplanar.

77. If two angles are complementary, then both angles are acute.

A Point in Time

1500 1600 1700 1800 1900 2000

In 1675, Danish astronomer Ole Römer used proportions to estimate the speed of light. He carefully measured the movements of Jupiter's moons. With Earth at point B, a moon emerged from behind Jupiter 16.6 min later than when Earth was at point A. He reasoned that it must have taken 16.6 min for the light to travel from point A to point B. Using proportions, Römer estimated the speed of light to be 150,000 mi/s. This estimate is about 81% of today's accepted value of 186,282 mi/s.

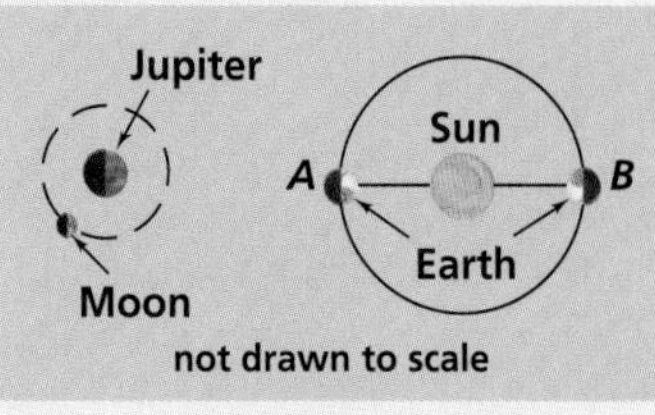

Take It to the NET For more information about the speed of light, go to **www.PHSchool.com.**
Web Code: afe-2032

Algebra 1 Review

Solving Quadratic Equations

FOR USE WITH LESSON 8-2

The *standard form* of a quadratic equation is

$$ax^2 + bx + c = 0, a \neq 0.$$

You can solve a quadratic equation by substituting the values for a, b, and c in the *Quadratic Formula.*

$$x = \frac{-b \pm \sqrt{b^2 - 4ac}}{2a}$$

1 EXAMPLE

Solve for x: $7x^2 + 6x - 1 = 0$. **The equation is in standard form.**

$a = 7, b = 6, c = -1$

$x = \frac{-6 \pm \sqrt{6^2 - 4(7)(-1)}}{2(7)}$ **Substitute in the Quadratic Formula.**

$x = \frac{-6 \pm \sqrt{36 + 28}}{14}$ **Simplify.**

$x = \frac{-6 \pm \sqrt{64}}{14}$

$x = \frac{-6 + 8}{14}$ or $x = \frac{-6 - 8}{14}$

$x = \frac{1}{7}$ or $x = -1$

Sometimes you may need a calculator to approximate the solutions.

2 EXAMPLE

Solve for x: $-3x^2 - 5x + 1 = 0$.

$a = -3, b = -5, c = 1$

$x = \frac{-(-5) \pm \sqrt{(-5)^2 - 4(-3)(1)}}{2(-3)}$ **Substitute in the Quadratic Formula.**

$x = \frac{5 \pm \sqrt{25 + 12}}{-6}$ **Simplify.**

$x = \frac{5 + \sqrt{37}}{-6}$ or $x = \frac{5 - \sqrt{37}}{-6}$

$x \approx -1.85$ or $x \approx 0.18$ **Use a calculator and round.**

EXERCISES

Solve for x. Round answers that are not integers to the nearest hundredth.

1. $x^2 + 5x - 14 = 0$ **2.** $4x^2 - 13x + 3 = 0$ **3.** $2x^2 + 7x + 3 = 0$

4. $5x^2 + 2x - 2 = 0$ **5.** $6x^2 + 10x = 5$ **6.** $1 = 2x^2 - 6x$

7. $x^2 - 6x = 27$ **8.** $2x^2 - 10x + 11 = 0$ **9.** $8x^2 - 2x - 3 = 0$

8-2 Similar Polygons

Lesson Preview

What You'll Learn

To identify similar polygons

To apply similar polygons

. . . And Why

To find the size of a video image, as in Example 4

Check Skills You'll Need

(For help, go to Lessons 4-1 and 8-1.)

1. $\triangle ABC \cong \triangle HIJ$. Name three pairs of congruent sides.

Algebra **Solve each proportion.**

2. $\frac{3}{4} = \frac{x}{8}$
3. $\frac{2}{x} = \frac{8}{24}$
4. $\frac{x}{9} = \frac{1}{3}$
5. $\frac{10}{25} = \frac{2}{x}$

New Vocabulary • similar • similarity ratio • golden rectangle • golden ratio

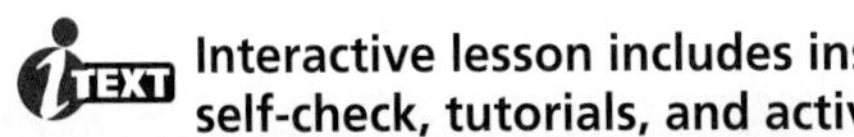

OBJECTIVE 1

Similar Polygons

Two figures that have the same shape but not necessarily the same size are similar (~). Two polygons are **similar** if (1) corresponding angles are congruent and (2) corresponding sides are proportional. The ratio of the lengths of corresponding sides is the **similarity ratio.**

1 EXAMPLE Understanding Similarity

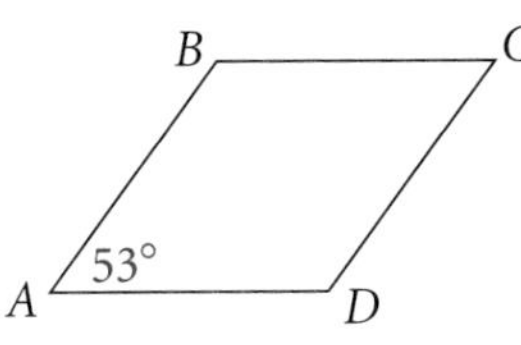

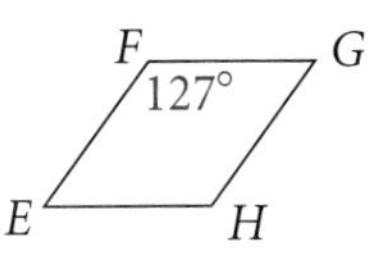

$ABCD \sim EFGH$. Complete each statement.

a. $m\angle E = \blacksquare$

$m\angle E = m\angle A = 53$ **Corresponding angles are ≅.**

b. $\frac{AB}{EF} = \frac{AD}{\blacksquare}$

$\frac{AB}{EF} = \frac{AD}{EH}$ **Corresponding sides are proportional.**

Check Understanding 1 Complete: $m\angle B = \blacksquare$ and $\frac{GH}{CD} = \frac{FG}{\blacksquare}$

2 EXAMPLE Determining Similarity

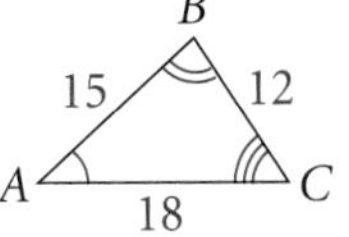

Determine whether the triangles are similar. If they are, write a similarity statement and give the similarity ratio.

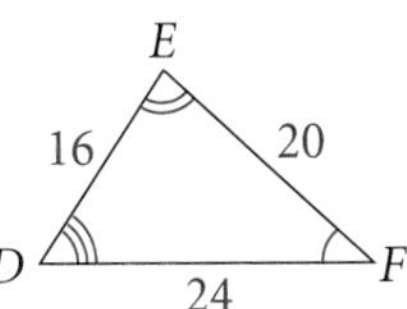

Three pairs of angles are congruent.
Also, corresponding sides are proportional.

$\frac{AC}{FD} = \frac{18}{24} = \frac{3}{4}$ $\frac{AB}{FE} = \frac{15}{20} = \frac{3}{4}$ $\frac{BC}{ED} = \frac{12}{16} = \frac{3}{4}$

$\triangle ABC \sim \triangle FED$ with a similarity ratio of $\frac{3}{4}$ or 3 : 4.

Need Help?
You can also say $\triangle FED \sim \triangle ABC$ with similarity ratio $\frac{4}{3}$.

Check Understanding 2 Sketch $\triangle XYZ$ and $\triangle MNP$ with $\angle X \cong \angle M$, $\angle Y \cong \angle N$, and $\angle Z \cong \angle P$. Also, $XY = 12$, $YZ = 14$, $ZX = 16$, $MN = 18$, $NP = 21$, and $PM = 24$. Can you conclude that the two triangles are similar? Explain.

You can use proportions to find unknown lengths in similar polygons.

3 EXAMPLE Using Similar Figures

Algebra $LMNO \sim QRST$
Find the value of x.

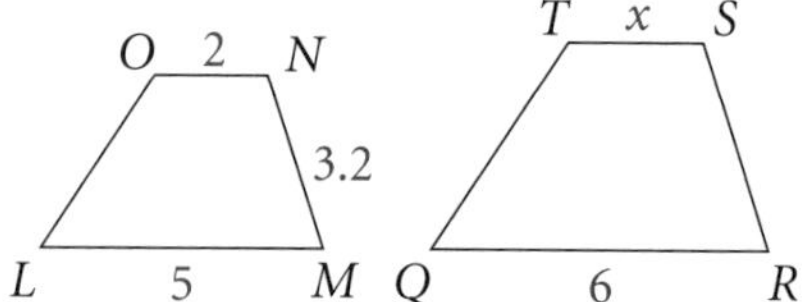

Write a proportion.

$\frac{LM}{QR} = \frac{ON}{TS}$ **Corresponding sides of ~ polygons are proportional.**

$\frac{5}{6} = \frac{2}{x}$ **Substitute.**

$5x = 12$ **Cross-Product Property**

$x = 2.4$ **Solve for *x*.**

✓ Check Understanding 3 Use the figures above. Find SR to the nearest tenth.

OBJECTIVE

2 Applying Similar Polygons

You can use similar polygons to find measures when using enlarged or reduced images.

4 EXAMPLE Real-World Connection

Technology If you have a vision problem, a magnification system can help you read. You choose a level of magnification. Then you place an image under the viewer. A similar, magnified image appears on the video screen. The video screen pictured is 16 in. wide by 12 in. tall. What is the largest complete video image possible for a block of text that is 6 in. wide by 4 in. tall?

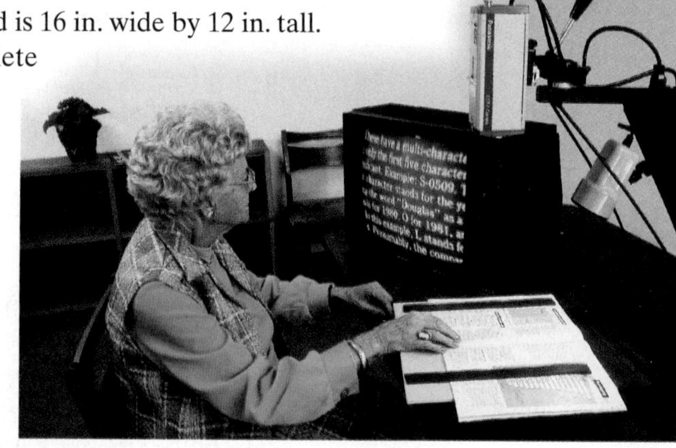

The 6-in. width can be magnified at most to a rectangle with a longer side of 16 in. Let the shorter side of the video image have length x.

$\frac{6}{16} = \frac{4}{x}$ **Corresponding sides of ~ polygons are proportional.**

$6x = 64$ **Cross-Product Property**

$x = 10\frac{2}{3}$ **Solve for *x*.**

The 4-in. height of the block of text enlarges to $10\frac{2}{3}$ in. This is less than the 12-in. height of the video screen, so the entire block of text fits on the screen.

The largest complete video image possible for the block of text is 16 in. by $10\frac{2}{3}$ in.

Need Help?
To calculate image size, estimate which screen dimension, width or height, will fill first as the image expands.

✓ Check Understanding 4 On the video screen in Example 4, what is the largest complete image possible for a photograph that is 3 in. wide by 5 in. tall?

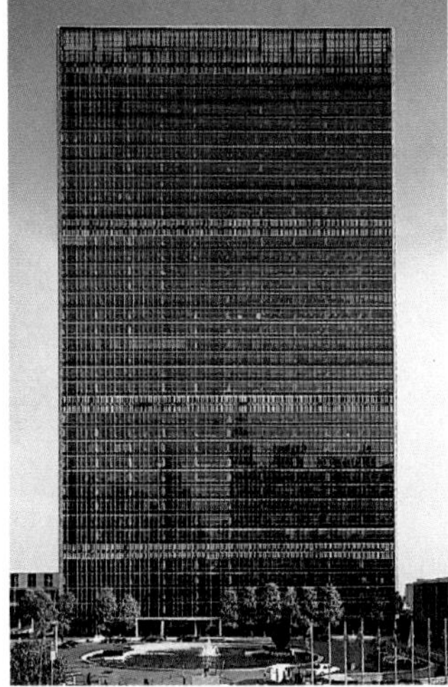

Real-World Connection

The United Nations Secretariat building in New York City suggests a golden rectangle.

A **golden rectangle** is a rectangle that can be divided into a square and a rectangle that is similar to the original rectangle. A pattern of repeated golden rectangles is shown at the right. Each golden rectangle that is formed is copied and divided again. Each golden rectangle is similar to the original rectangle.

In any golden rectangle, the length and width are in the **golden ratio** which is about 1.618 : 1. You will derive this ratio in Exercise 51.

The golden rectangle is considered pleasing to the human eye. It has appeared in architecture and art since ancient times. It has intrigued artists including Leonardo da Vinci (1452–1519). Da Vinci illustrated *The Divine Proportion,* a book about the golden rectangle.

You can apply the golden ratio to real-life design problems.

5 EXAMPLE Real-World Connection

Art An artist plans to paint a picture. He wants the canvas to be a golden rectangle with its longer horizontal sides 30 cm wide. How high should the canvas be?

Let h be the height of the canvas.

$\frac{30}{h} = \frac{1.618}{1}$	**Write a proportion.**
$1.618h = 30$	**Cross-Product Property**
$h = \frac{30}{1.618}$	**Solve for *h*.**
$h = 18.541409$	**Use a calculator.**

The canvas should be about 18.5 cm high.

Check Understanding 5 A golden rectangle has shorter sides of length 20 cm. Find the length of the longer sides.

EXERCISES

For more practice, see *Extra Practice.*

Practice and Problem Solving

A Practice by Example

Example 1 (page 423)

***JDRT ~ JHYX.* Complete the congruence and proportion statements.**

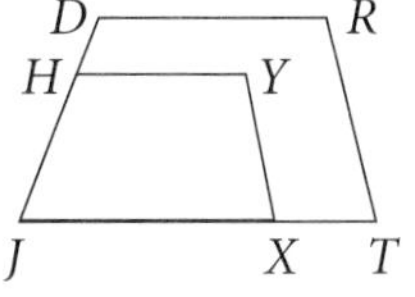

1. $\angle D \cong \underline{\ ?\ }$ **2.** $\angle Y \cong \underline{\ ?\ }$ **3.** $\angle T \cong \underline{\ ?\ }$

4. $\frac{JD}{JH} = \frac{DR}{\blacksquare}$ **5.** $\frac{RT}{YX} = \frac{\blacksquare}{JX}$ **6.** $\frac{\blacksquare}{DR} = \frac{YX}{RT}$

Example 2 (page 423)

Are the polygons similar? If they are, write a similarity statement and give the similarity ratio. If they are not, explain.

7. **8.**

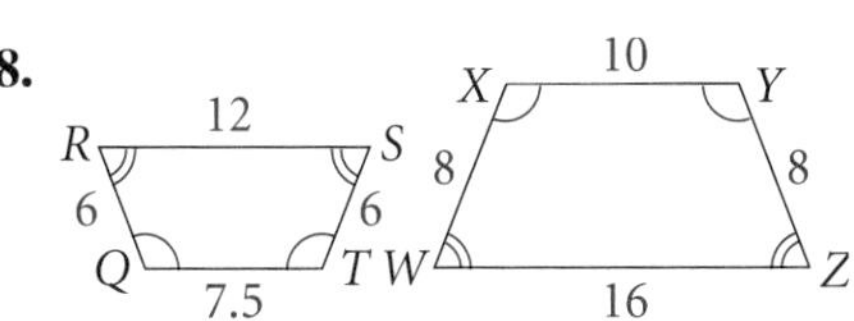

Are the polygons similar? If they are, write a similarity statement and give the similarity ratio. If they are not, explain.

9.

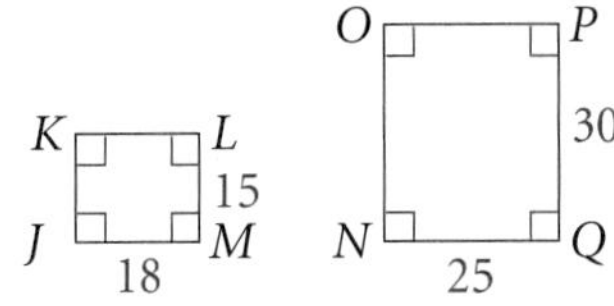

10.

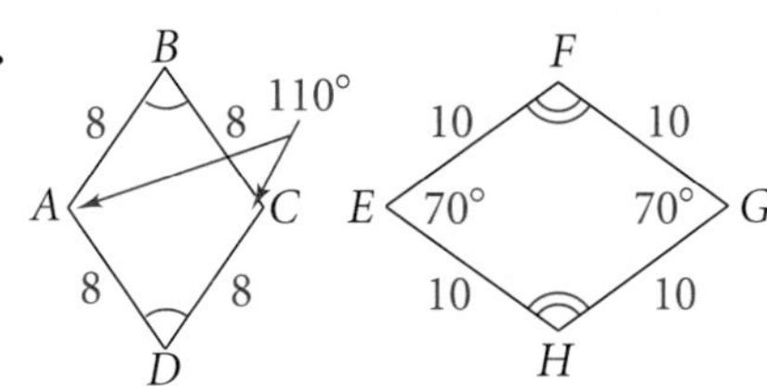

11.

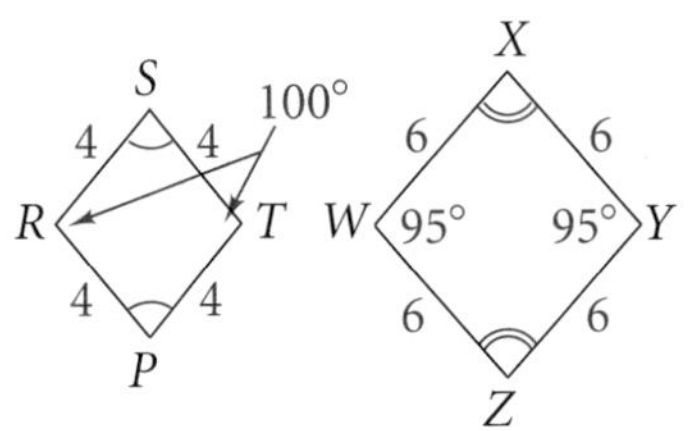

12.

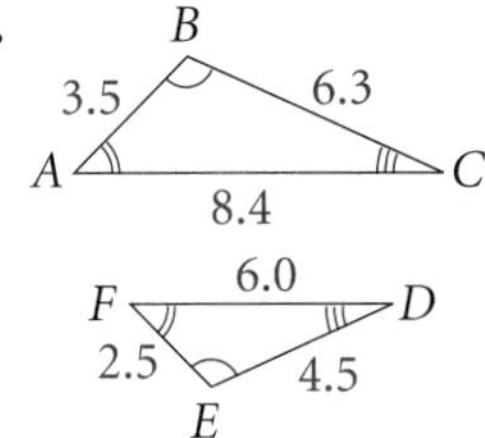

Example 3 (page 424) x^2 Algebra **The polygons are similar. Find the value of each variable.**

13.

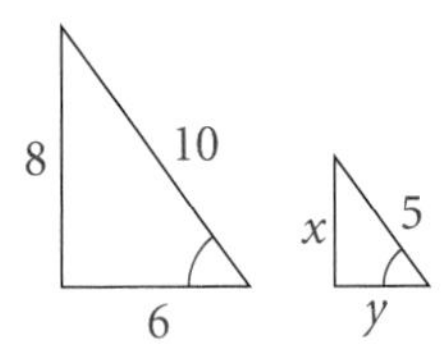

14.

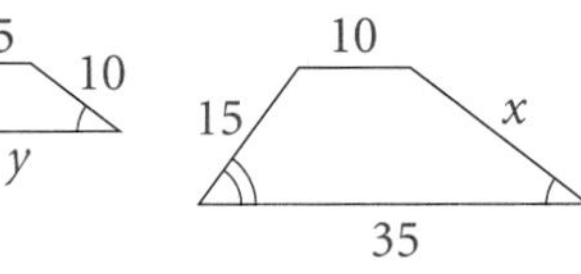

15.

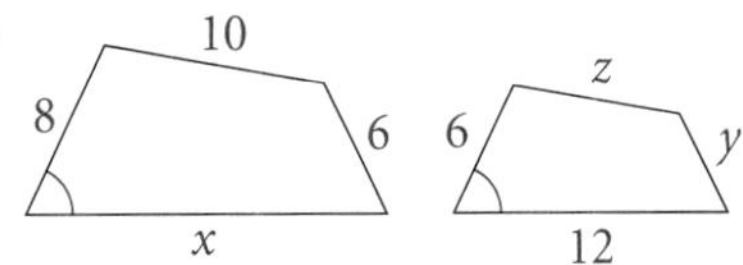

16.

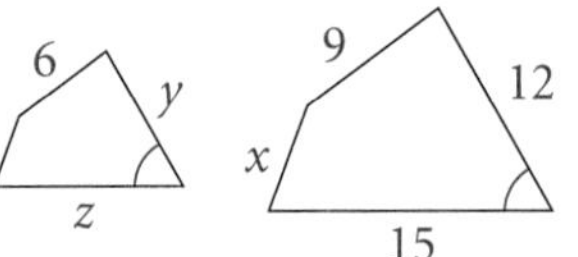

Example 4 (page 424)

17. Drawing You want to draw an enlargement of a design that is painted on a 3 in.-by-5 in. card. You plan to draw on an $8\frac{1}{2}$ in.-by-11 in. piece of paper. What are the dimensions of the largest complete enlargement you can draw?

18. A map has dimensions 9 in. by 15 in. You want to reduce the map so that it will fit on a 4 in.-by-6 in. index card. What are the dimensions of the largest possible complete map that you can fit on the index card?

Example 5 (page 425)

19. Electrical Equipment A switch plate for a standard wall switch has the shape of a golden rectangle. The longer side of the switch plate is about 114 mm. How long is the shorter side? Round your answer to the nearest millimeter.

20. Design You want the banner you are creating from one piece of cloth to be a golden rectangle. The cloth will be cut from a bolt that is 54 in. wide. What are the dimensions of the largest banner that you can make?

B Apply Your Skills

$\triangle DFG \sim \triangle HKM$. Use the diagram to find the following.

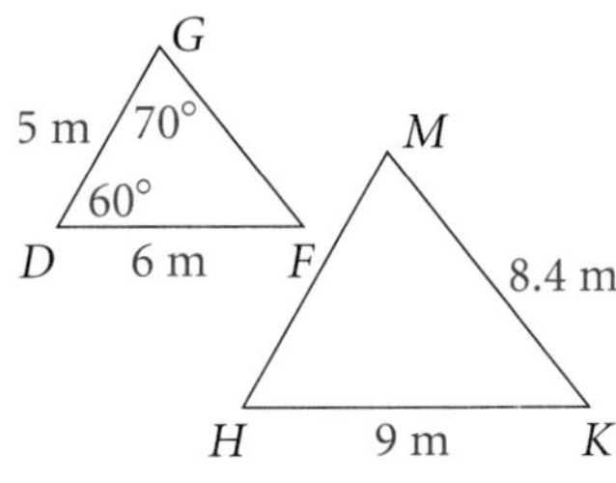

21. the similarity ratio of $\triangle DFG$ to $\triangle HKM$

22. the similarity ratio of $\triangle HKM$ to $\triangle DFG$

23. $m\angle F$ **24.** $m\angle K$ **25.** $m\angle M$

26. $\frac{DF}{HK}$ **27.** HM **28.** GF

29. Writing Are two congruent figures similar? Explain.

PEANUTS

By CHARLES SCHULZ

30. a. **Reading Math** What two symbols combine to form the congruence symbol?

b. Explain why the congruence symbol makes sense.

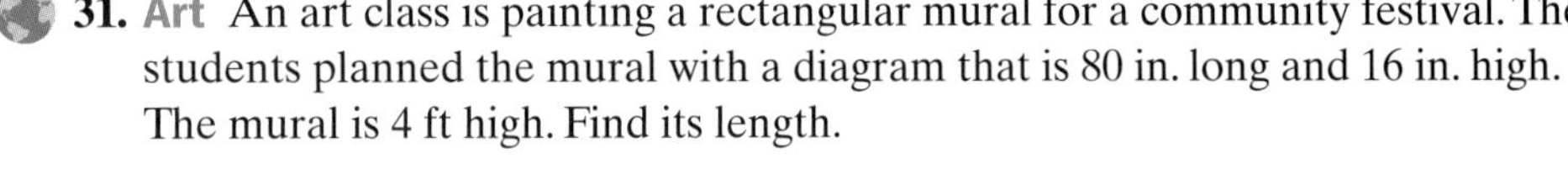

31. **Art** An art class is painting a rectangular mural for a community festival. The students planned the mural with a diagram that is 80 in. long and 16 in. high. The mural is 4 ft high. Find its length.

Real-World Connection

Murals provide a visual way to express feelings.

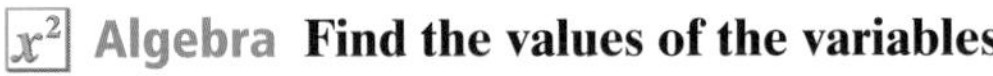

Algebra **Find the values of the variables.**

32.

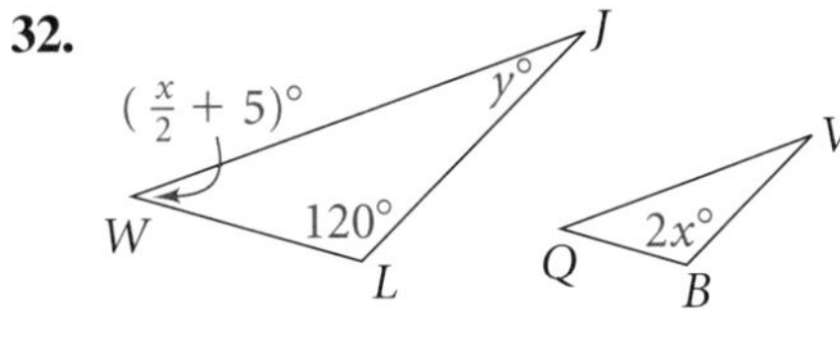

$\triangle WLJ \sim \triangle QBV$

33.

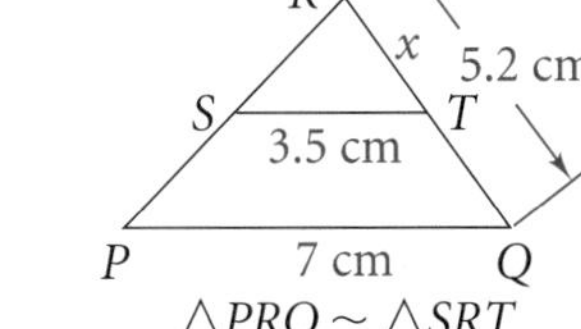

$\triangle PRQ \sim \triangle SRT$

The polygons in each exercise are similar. Find the similarity ratio of the first to the second.

34.

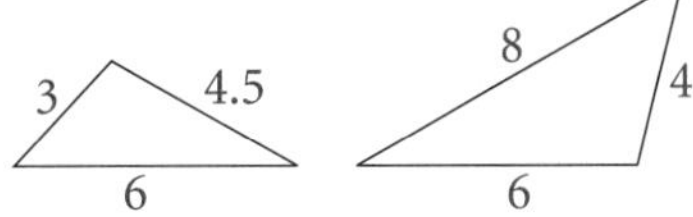

35.

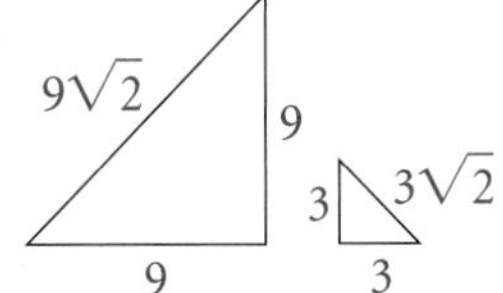

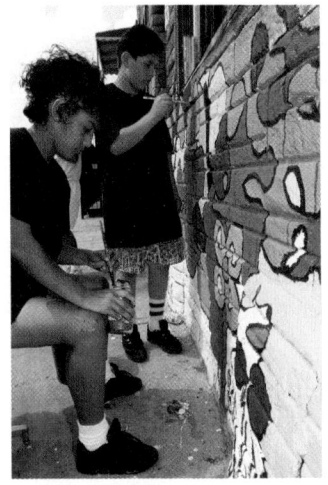

36. Exercise 13 **37.** Exercise 14 **38.** Exercise 15 **39.** Exercise 16

Reading Math

A value reduced *by* n% is reduced *to* $(100 - n)$%, and vice versa.

Logo Design **A company logo is a rhombus with 4-cm sides and angles of 60° and 120°. Find the angle measures and side lengths if the logo is changed as follows.**

40. reduced by 50% **41.** reduced to 50% **42.** reduced by 20%

43. reduced to 20% **44.** reduced by 75% **45.** reduced to 75%

Find the other side length of the golden rectangle to the nearest tenth of an inch.

46. The shorter side is 10 in. **47.** The longer side is 10 in.

48. **Money** From 1861 to 1928, U. S. paper currency measured 7.42 in. by 3.13 in. The dimensions of a current bill are shown here. Are the old and new bills similar rectangles? Explain.

49. **Critical Thinking** Are all circles similar? Explain.

50. **Open-Ended** Draw two polygons with sides in the ratio 2 : 1 that are not similar.

Challenge

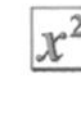

51. a. **Algebra** You know that the golden ratio is about 1.618 : 1. You can use the definition of a golden rectangle to derive this ratio. Let $ABCD$ at the left be a golden rectangle with width 1. By the definition of golden rectangle, $ABCD \sim BCFE$. Fill in the reasons in the following argument.

1. $\frac{AB}{BC} = \frac{BC}{CF}$	1. ?
2. $\frac{x}{1} = \frac{1}{x - 1}$	2. ?
3. $x^2 - x = 1$	3. ?
4. $x^2 - x - 1 = 0$	4. ?

b. Using the quadratic formula to solve the equation in part (a), you get $x = \frac{1 \pm \sqrt{5}}{2}$. Explain why $x = \frac{1 - \sqrt{5}}{2}$ does not make sense in this situation.

c. The golden ratio is the ratio $x : 1$, or $\frac{1 + \sqrt{5}}{2} : 1$. Use a calculator to find the value of $x = \frac{1 + \sqrt{5}}{2}$ to the nearest ten thousandth.

52. a. In the Fibonacci Sequence (see Lesson 1-1), each term after the first two is the sum of the two preceding terms. The first seven terms of the Fibonacci Sequence are 1, 1, 2, 3, 5, 8, and 13. Find the next seven terms.

b. Start with the second term. Here is the ratio of each term to the prior term.

$\frac{1}{1} = 1$ $\quad \frac{2}{1} = 2$ $\quad \frac{3}{2} = 1.5$ $\quad \frac{5}{3} = 1.6667$

Find the next nine ratios. Round to the nearest ten thousandth.

c. Compare the ratios that you found in part (b) to the golden ratio.

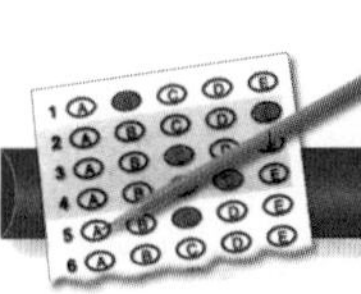

Standardized Test Prep

Quantitative Comparison

Compare the boxed quantity in Column A with the boxed quantity in Column B. Choose the best answer.

A. The quantity in Column A is greater.
B. The quantity in Column B is greater.
C. The two quantities are equal.
D. The relationship cannot be determined from the information given.

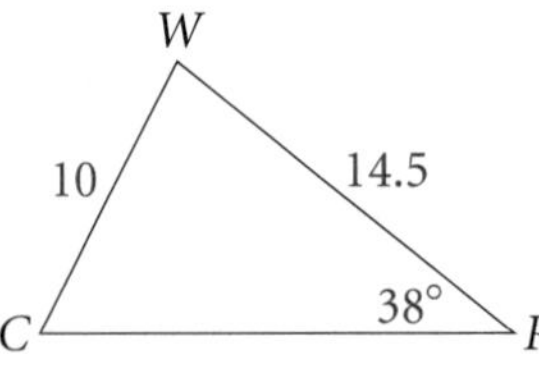

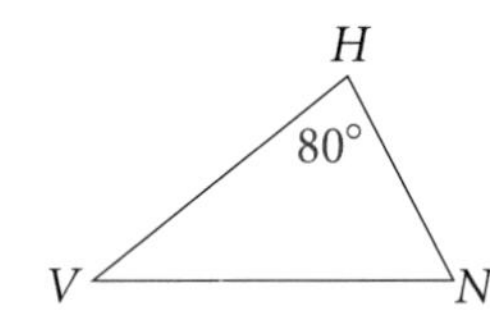

$\triangle WCP \sim \triangle HNV$

	Column A	Column B
53.	VH	WC
54.	$m\angle N$	$m\angle C$
55.	$m\angle N$	$m\angle P$

Take It to the NET
Online lesson quiz at
www.PHSchool.com
Web Code: afa-0802

Short Response

56. Quadrilateral $ABCD \sim$ quadrilateral $JKLM$ with a similarity ratio of 2 : 3.
   a. If $BC = 8$ cm, find KL.
   b. If $m\angle BCD = 38$, find $m\angle KLM$.

Mixed Review

Lesson 8-1

If $\frac{x}{7} = \frac{y}{9}$, complete each of the following using properties of proportions.

57. $9x = ■$ **58.** $\frac{x}{y} = \frac{■}{■}$ **59.** $\frac{x+7}{7} = \frac{■}{■}$

Lesson 6-3

Can you conclude that the quadrilateral is a parallelogram? Explain.

60.

61. 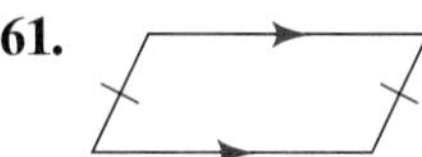

62. 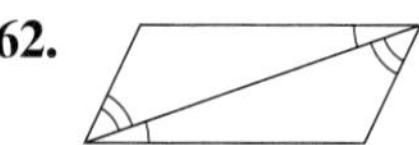

Lesson 4-5

Use the marked $\triangle CEA$ for Exercises 63–66.

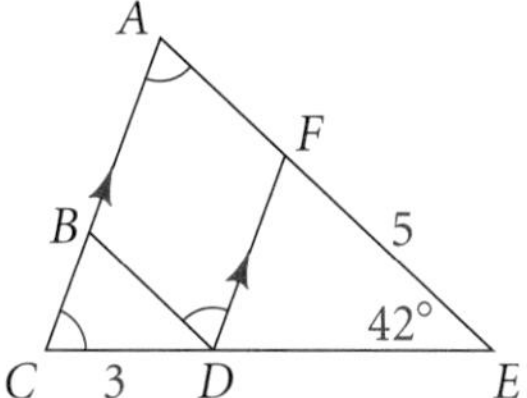

63. Name the isosceles triangles in the figure.

64. $\overline{CD} \cong$ __?__ $\cong$ __?__

Find the value of each of the following.

65. AE **66.** $m\angle A$

Checkpoint Quiz 1 — Lessons 8-1 through 8-2

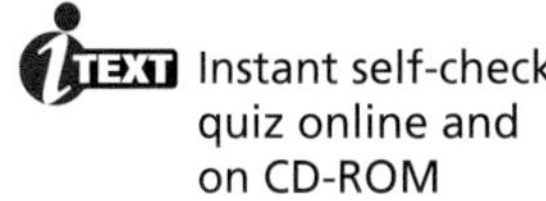

Instant self-check quiz online and on CD-ROM

1. **Models** A table is 4 ft high. A small model of the table is 6 in. high. What is the ratio of the height of the model table to the height of the real table?

2. If $\frac{a}{b} = \frac{9}{10}$, complete this statement: $\frac{a}{9} = \frac{■}{■}$

3. Are the polygons at the right similar? If so, give the similarity ratio of the first polygon to the second. If not, explain.

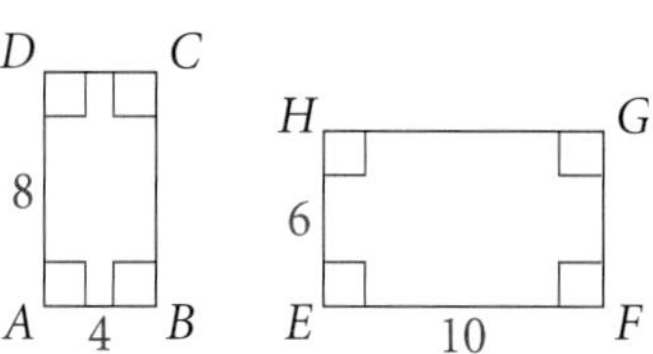

Solve each proportion.

4. $\frac{y}{6} = \frac{18}{54}$ **5.** $\frac{5}{7} = \frac{x-2}{4}$

6. The scale of a scale drawing is 2 in. = 5 ft. A room is 5 in. long on the scale drawing. Find the actual length of the room.

$\triangle ABC \sim \triangle DBF$ at the right. Complete each statement.

7. $m\angle A = m\angle$ __?__ **8.** $\frac{AB}{DB} = \frac{BC}{■}$

9. A postcard is 6 in. by 4 in. A printing shop will enlarge it so that the longer side is any length up to 3 ft. Find the dimensions of the biggest enlargement.

10. **Algebra** The polygons at the right are similar. Find the value of x.

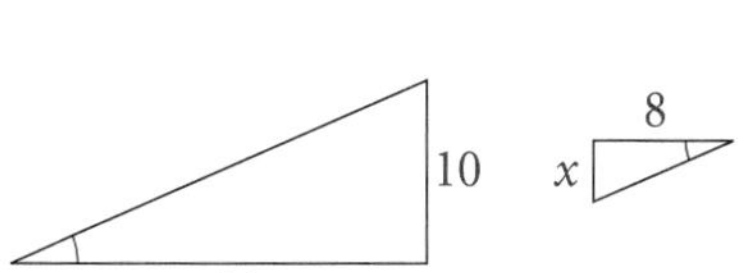

Extension Fractals

FOR USE WITH LESSON 8-2

Fractals are objects that have three important properties:

- You can form them by repeating steps—a process called *iteration*.
- They require infinitely many iterations. In practice, you can continue until the objects become too small to draw. Even then the steps could continue in your mind.
- At each stage, a portion of the object is a reduced copy of the entire object at the previous stage. This property is called *self-similarity*.

1 EXAMPLE

The segment below of length 1 unit is Stage 0 of a fractal tree. Draw Stage 1 and Stage 2 of the tree. For each stage, draw two branches from the top third of each segment.

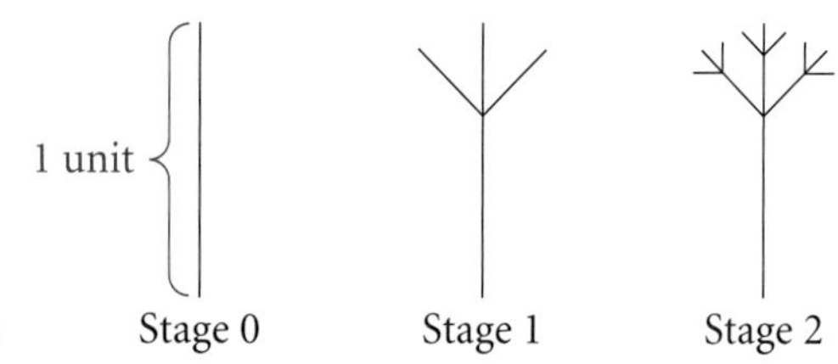

Amazingly, some fractals are used to describe natural formations such as mountain ranges and clouds. In 1904, Swedish mathematician Helge von Koch created the Koch Curve, a fractal that is used to model coastlines.

2 EXAMPLE

The segment at the right of length 1 unit is Stage 0 of a Koch Curve. Draw Stages 1–4 of the curve. For each stage, replace the middle third of each segment with two segments, both equal in length to the middle third.

- For Stage 1, replace the middle third with two segments, both $\frac{1}{3}$ unit long.
- For Stage 2, replace the middle third of each segment with two segments, both $\frac{1}{9}$ unit long.
- Continue with a third and fourth iteration.

Stages 0–4 are shown at the right.

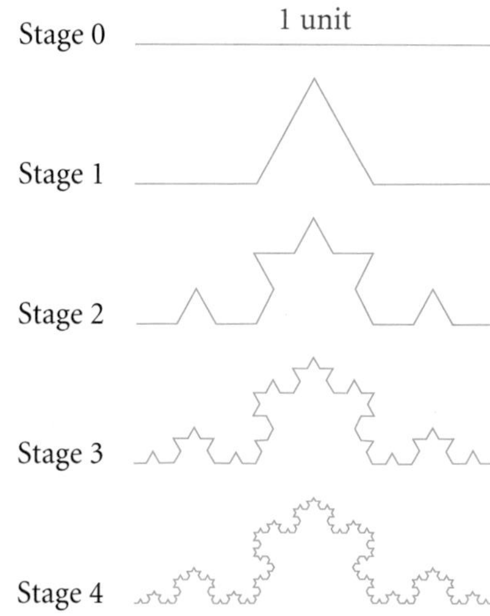

You can construct a Koch Curve on each side of an equilateral triangle and get a Koch Snowflake.

3 EXAMPLE

The equilateral triangle at the right is Stage 0 of a Koch Snowflake. Draw Stage 1.

- Draw an equilateral triangle on the middle third of each side.
- Erase the middle third of each side to get Stage 1 of the snowflake. (Continued in Exercises 5–9.)

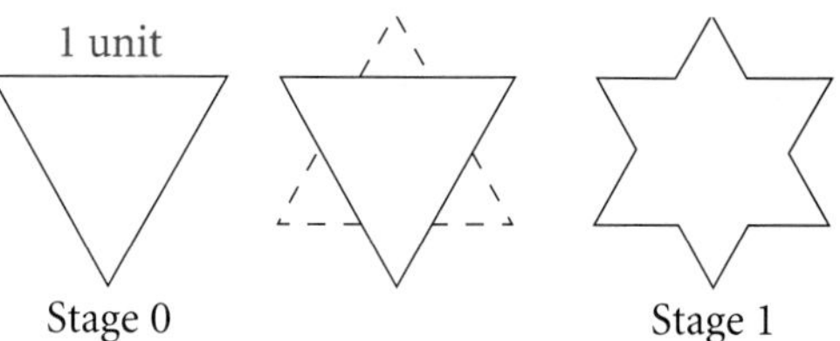

Stage 0 Stage 1

EXERCISES

1. Draw Stage 3 of the fractal tree in Example 1.

Use the Koch Curve in Example 2 for Exercises 2–4.

2. Complete the table to find the length of the Koch Curve at each stage.

Stage	0	1	2
Length	1	■	■

3. Examine the results of Exercise 2 and look for a pattern. Use this pattern to predict the length of the Koch Curve at Stage 3; at Stage 4.
4. Suppose you are able to complete a Koch Curve to Stage n.
   a. Write an expression for the length of the curve.
   b. What happens to the length of the curve as n gets large?
5. Draw Stage 2 of the Koch Snowflake in Example 3.

Stage 3 of the Koch Snowflake is shown at the right. Use it and the earlier stages to answer Exercises 6–8.

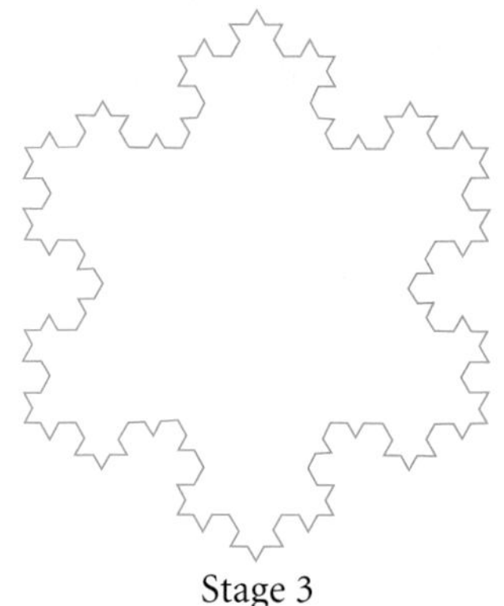
Stage 3

6. At each stage, is the snowflake equilateral?
7. **a.** Complete the table to find the perimeter at each stage.

Stage	Number of Sides	Length of a Side	Perimeter
0	3	1	3
1	■	$\frac{1}{3}$	■
2	48	■	■
3	■	■	■

   b. Predict the perimeter at Stage 4.
   c. Will there be a stage at which the perimeter is greater then 100 units? Explain.
8. What can you conclude about the area of this Koch Snowflake?
9. To draw the Sierpinski Triangle fractal, start with an equilateral triangle. For each stage, connect the midpoints of all of the triangles "pointed upwards." Stages 0–2 are shown at the right. Draw Stage 3.

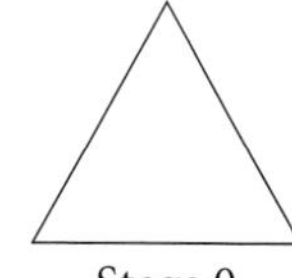
Stage 0

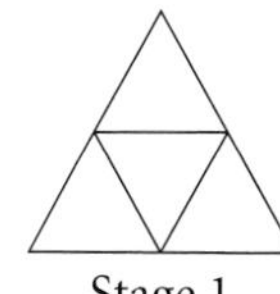
Stage 1

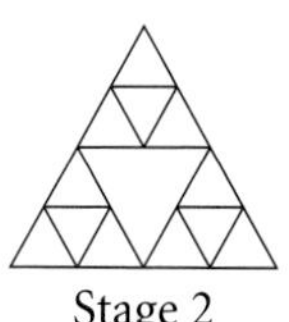
Stage 2

8-3 Proving Triangles Similar

Lesson Preview

What You'll Learn

Objective 1: To use AA, SAS, and SSS similarity statements

Objective 2: To apply AA, SAS, and SSS similarity statements

. . . And Why

To measure height indirectly, as in Example 4

Check Skills You'll Need

(For help, go to Lessons 4-2 and 4-3.)

Name the postulate or theorem you can use to prove the triangles congruent.

1. 

2.

3. 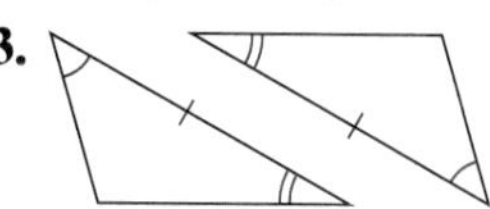

New Vocabulary

- indirect measurement

Interactive lesson includes instant self-check, tutorials, and activities.

OBJECTIVE 1

The AA Postulate and the SAS and SSS Theorems

Real-World  Connection

The gables on the historic House of the Seven Gables in Salem, Massachusetts, suggest similar triangles.

Investigation: Triangles with Two Pairs of Congruent Angles

- Draw two triangles of different sizes, each with a 50° angle and a 60° angle.
- Measure the sides of each triangle to the nearest millimeter.
- Find the ratio of the lengths of each pair of corresponding sides.

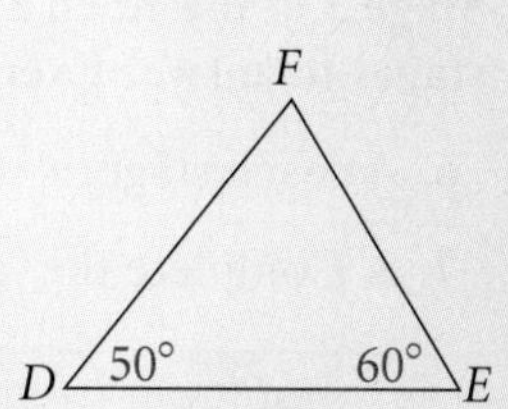

1. What conclusion can you make about the two triangles?
2. Complete this conjecture:

   If two angles of one triangle are congruent to two angles of another triangle, then the triangles are _?_.

In this lesson, you will show triangles are similar without using the definition of similar triangles. The two triangles shown above suggest the following postulate.

Key Concepts

Postulate 8-1 Angle-Angle Similarity (AA ~) Postulate

If two angles of one triangle are congruent to two angles of another triangle, then the triangles are similar.

$\triangle TRS \sim \triangle PLM$

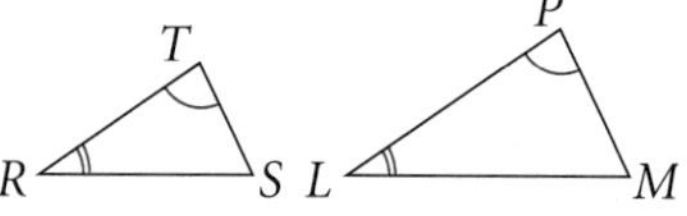

1 EXAMPLE Using the AA ~ Postulate

Explain why the triangles are similar. Write a similarity statement.

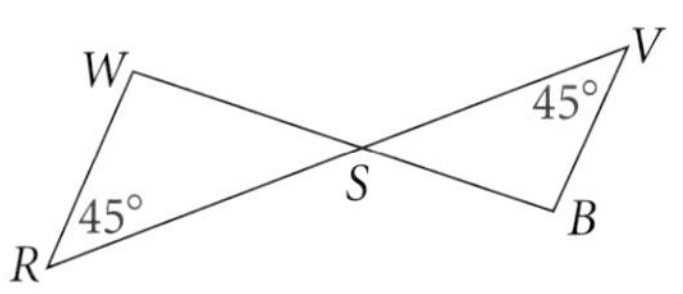

$\angle RSW \cong \angle VSB$ because vertical angles are congruent. $\angle R \cong \angle V$ because their measures are equal. $\triangle RSW \sim \triangle VSB$ by the Angle-Angle Similarity Postulate.

Check Understanding **1** **Critical Thinking** In Example 1, you have enough information to write a similarity statement. Do you have enough information to find the similarity ratio? Explain.

The next two theorems follow from the AA Similarity Postulate.

Key Concepts

Theorem 8-1 **Side-Angle-Side Similarity (SAS ~) Theorem**

If an angle of one triangle is congruent to an angle of a second triangle, and the sides including the two angles are proportional, then the triangles are similar.

Proof

Proof of Theorem 8-1

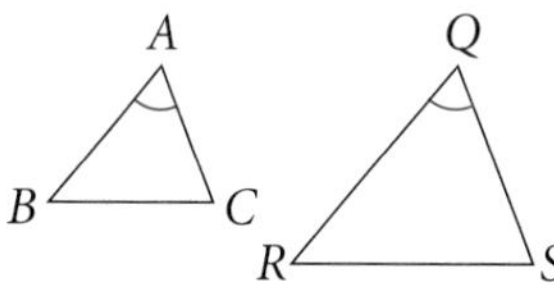

Given: $\angle A \cong \angle Q$, $\frac{AB}{QR} = \frac{AC}{QS}$

Prove: $\triangle ABC \sim \triangle QRS$

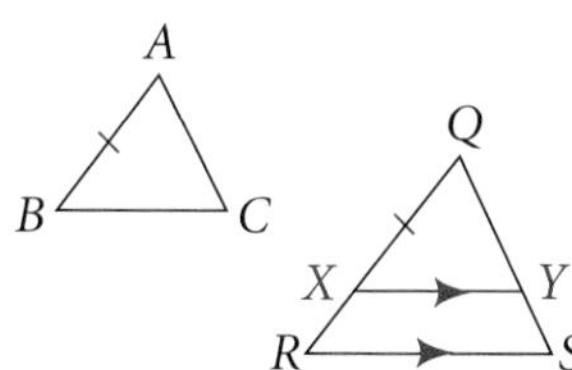

Choose X on $\overline{QR}$ so that $QX = AB$. (See figures at left.) Draw $\overline{XY} \parallel \overline{RS}$. Then $\angle QXY \cong \angle R$. By the AA ~ Postulate, $\triangle QXY \sim \triangle QRS$. Thus $\frac{QX}{QR} = \frac{QY}{QS}$. Combining this proportion, the given proportion, and the fact that $AB = QX$ shows that $\frac{AC}{QS} = \frac{QY}{QS}$. Hence, $AC = QY$.

Then $\triangle ABC \cong \triangle QXY$ by the SAS Congruence Postulate. $\angle B \cong \angle QXY$ by CPCTC, and $\angle B \cong \angle R$ by the Transitive Property. Thus, $\triangle ABC \sim \triangle QRS$ by the AA ~ Postulate.

Key Concepts

Theorem 8-2 **Side-Side-Side Similarity (SSS ~) Theorem**

If the corresponding sides of two triangles are proportional, then the triangles are similar.

Proof

Proof of Theorem 8-2

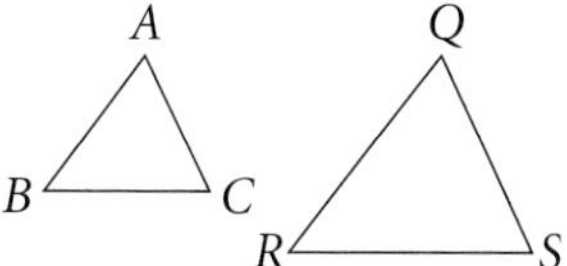

Given: $\frac{AB}{QR} = \frac{BC}{RS} = \frac{AC}{QS}$

Prove: $\triangle ABC \sim \triangle QRS$

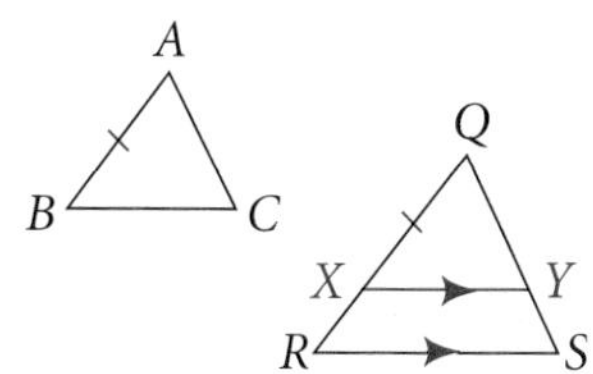

Draw $\overline{XY}$ as in the proof of Theorem 8-1. By the AA ~ Postulate, $\triangle QXY \sim \triangle QRS$. Thus $\frac{QX}{QR} = \frac{XY}{RS} = \frac{QY}{QS}$. Combining this proportion, the given proportion, and the fact that $AB = QX$ shows that $BC = XY$ and $AC = QY$.

Then $\triangle ABC \cong \triangle QXY$ by the SSS Congruence Postulate and, as in the proof above, $\triangle ABC \sim \triangle QRS$ by the AA ~ Postulate.

2 EXAMPLE Using Similarity Theorems

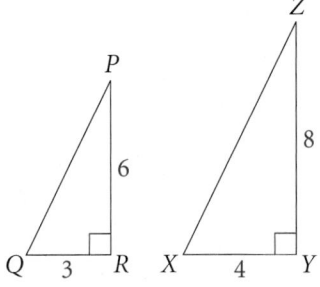

Explain why the triangles must be similar.
Write a similarity statement.

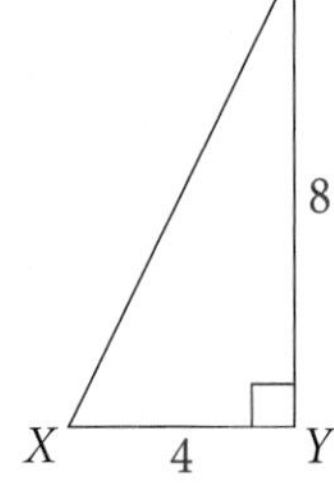

$\angle QRP \cong \angle XYZ$ because they are right angles.

$\frac{QR}{XY} = \frac{3}{4}$ and $\frac{PR}{ZY} = \frac{6}{8} = \frac{3}{4}$.

Therefore, $\triangle QRP \sim \triangle XYZ$ by the SAS $\sim$ Theorem.

✓ Check Understanding 2 Explain why the triangles must be similar.
Write a similarity statement.

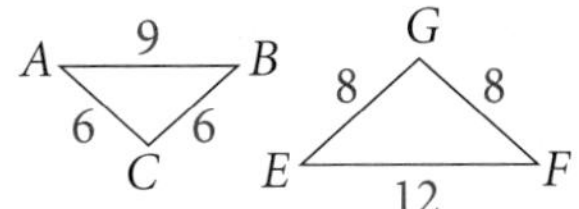

OBJECTIVE

2 Applying AA, SAS, and SSS Similarity

You can apply the AA Similarity Postulate and the SAS and SSS Similarity Theorems to find the lengths of sides in similar triangles.

3 EXAMPLE Finding Lengths in Similar Triangles

Explain why the triangles are similar.
Write a similarity statement.
Then find DE.

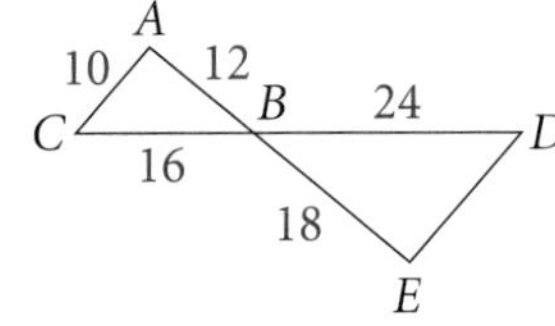

$\angle ABC \cong \angle EBD$ because vertical angles are congruent.

$\frac{AB}{EB} = \frac{12}{18} = \frac{2}{3}$ and $\frac{CB}{DB} = \frac{16}{24} = \frac{2}{3}$

Therefore, $\triangle ABC \sim \triangle EBD$ by the SAS $\sim$ Theorem.

$\frac{CA}{DE} = \frac{2}{3}$	**Corresponding sides of $\sim$ triangles are proportional.**
$\frac{10}{DE} = \frac{2}{3}$	**Substitute.**
$2DE = 30$	**Cross-Product Property**
$DE = 15$	**Solve for *DE*.**

✓ Check Understanding 3 Find the value of x in the figure at the right.

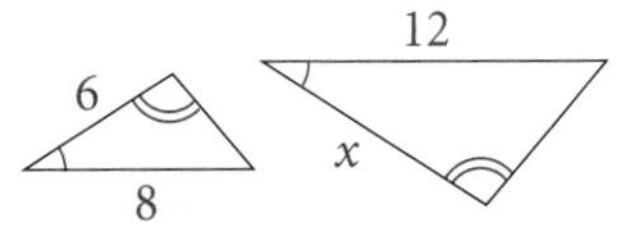

You can use similar triangles and measurements to find distances that are difficult to measure directly. This is called **indirect measurement.**

One method of indirect measurement uses the fact that light reflects off a mirror at the same angle at which it hits the mirror. A second method uses the similar triangles that are formed by certain figures and their shadows.

Both methods are illustrated in Example 4.

4 EXAMPLE Real-World Connection

Geology Ramon places a mirror on the ground 40.5 ft from the base of a geyser. He walks backwards until he can see the top of the geyser in the middle of the mirror. At that point, Ramon's eyes are 6 ft above the ground and he is 7 ft from the image in the mirror. Use similar triangles to find the height of the geyser.

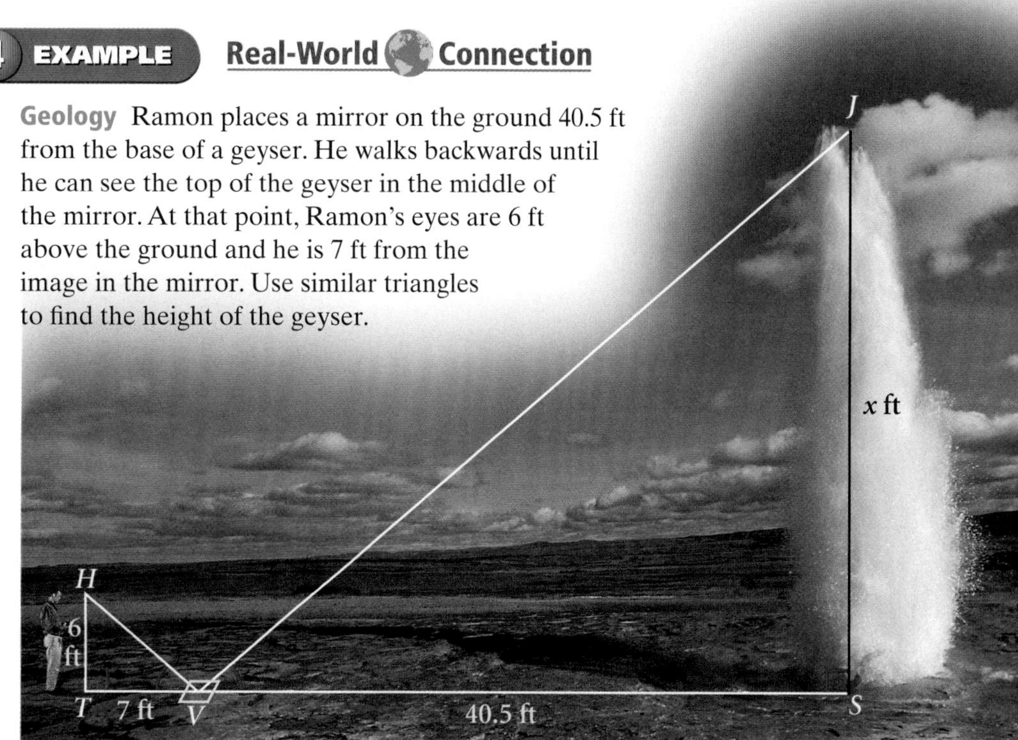

$\triangle HTV \sim \triangle JSV$	**AA ~ Postulate**
$\frac{HT}{JS} = \frac{TV}{SV}$	**Corresponding sides of ~ triangles are proportional.**
$\frac{6}{x} = \frac{7}{40.5}$	**Substitute.**
$243 = 7x$	**Cross-Product Property**
$34.7 \approx x$	**Solve for *x*.**

The geyser is about 35 ft high.

Need Help?

$\angle HVT \cong \angle JVS$ follows from the fact that the angle of incidence equals the angle of reflection. See p. 38, Exercise 18.

Check Understanding 4 In sunlight, a cactus casts a 9-ft shadow. At the same time a person 6 ft tall casts a 4-ft shadow. Use similar triangles to find the height of the cactus.

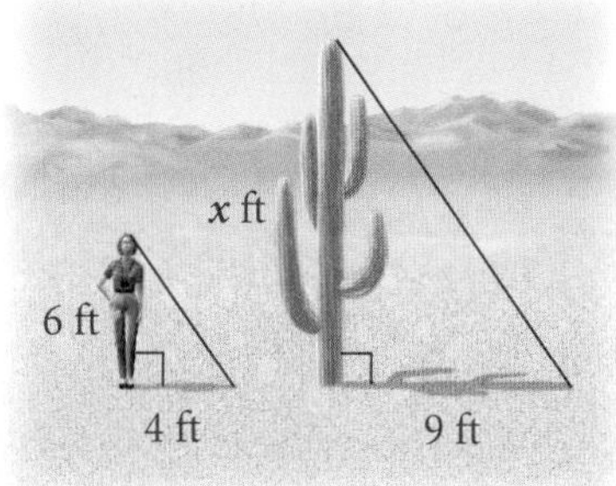

EXERCISES

For more practice, see *Extra Practice*.

Practice and Problem Solving

Practice by Example

Examples 1 and 2 (pages 433 and 434)

Can you conclude the triangles are similar? If so, write a similarity statement and name the postulate or theorem you used. If not, explain.

1. 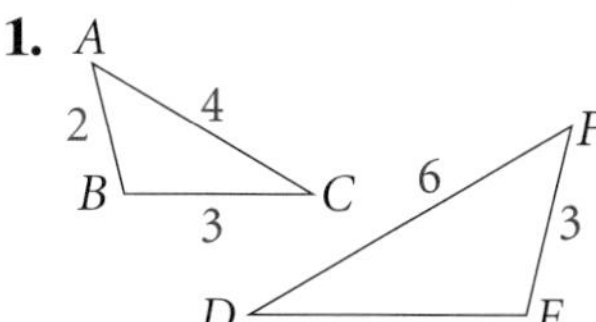

2. 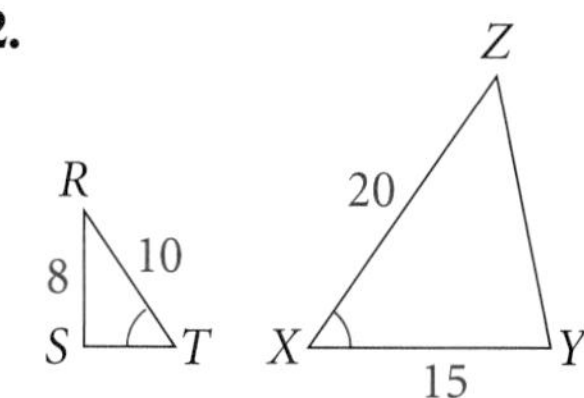

3. If possible, find the similarity ratio for each pair of similar triangles in Exercises 1 and 2. If not possible, explain.

Are the triangles similar? If so, write a similarity statement and name the postulate or theorem you used. If not, explain.

4.

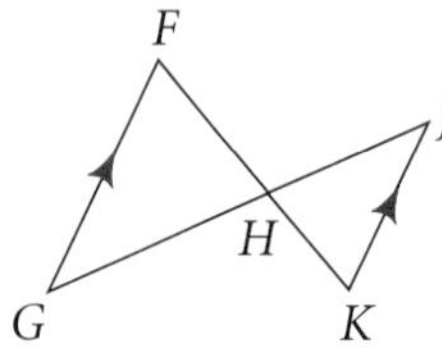

5.

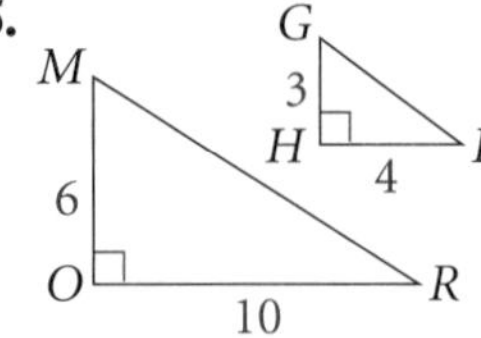

6.

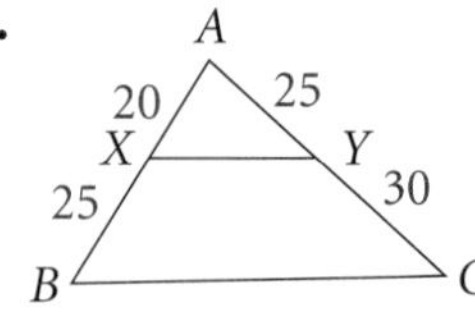

7.

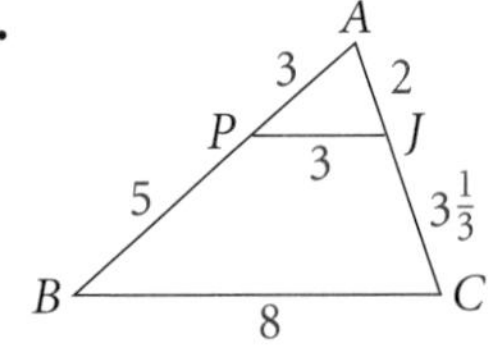

8.

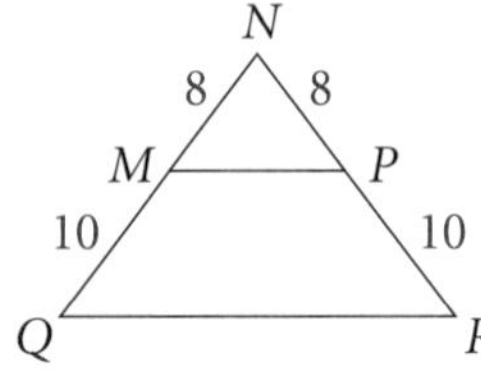

9.

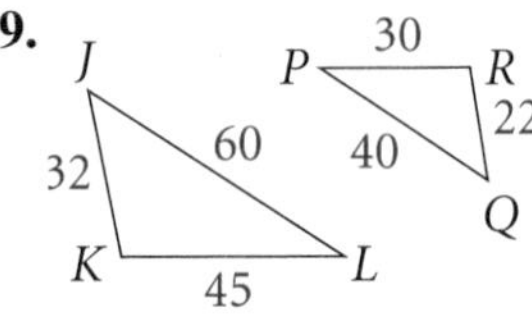

Example 3 (page 434) x^2 Algebra **Explain why the triangles are similar. Then find the value of x.**

10.

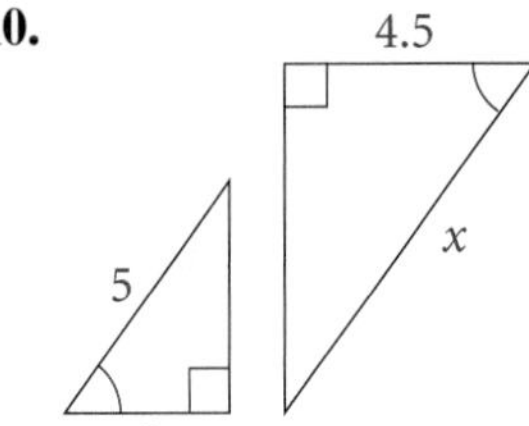

11.

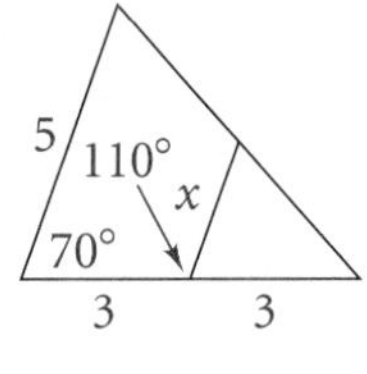

12.

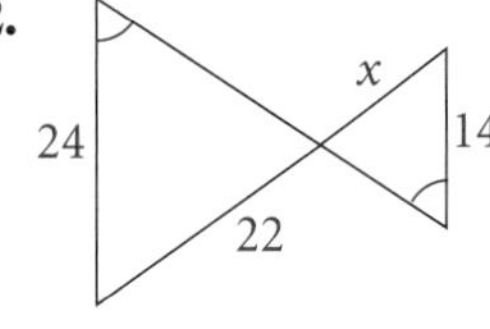

13.

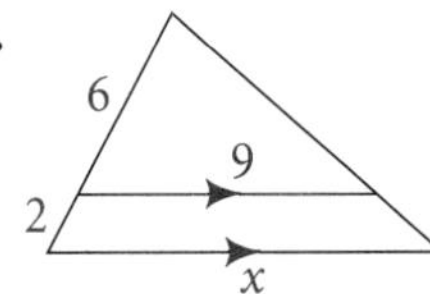

14.

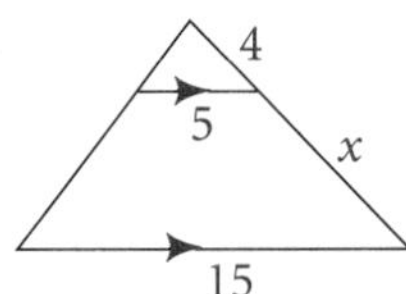

15.

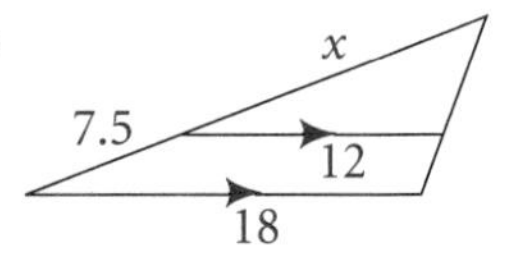

Example 4 (page 435) Indirect Measurement **Explain why the triangles are similar. Then find the distance represented by x.**

16.

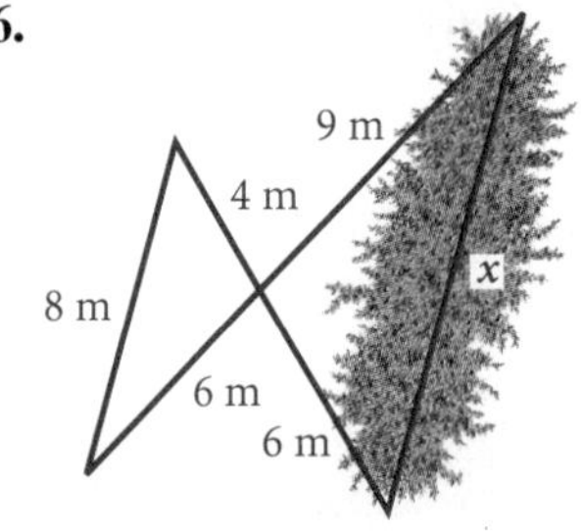

17.

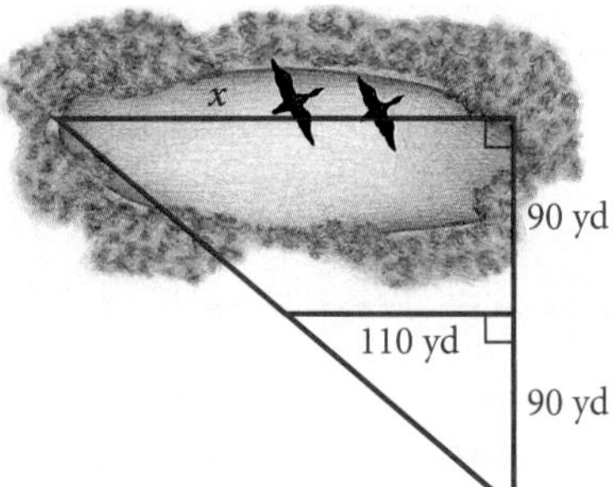

18.

19.

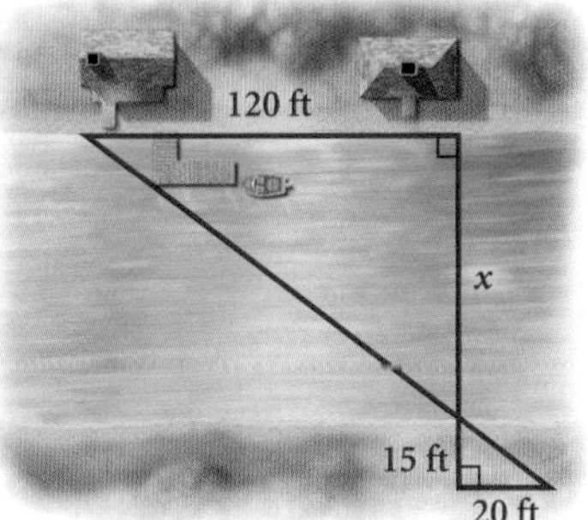

B Apply Your Skills

Skyscraper? Nein!

Hannelore Kraus of Frankfurt, Germany, stopped the development of a skyscraper because she wanted her apartment to get its fair amount of sunlight. To halt the construction she used a German law that specifies that every homeowner is entitled to sunlight.

Kraus was offered 1.6 million dollars to drop her lawsuit, but she refused. The skyscraper was scheduled to be 265 m tall and was to be built only 60 m from Kraus's apartment.

Tall Buildings **Use the news article for Exercises 20 and 21.**

20. Writing Explain how Hannelore Kraus could use indirect measurement to estimate the length of the shadow of the building at a particular time of day.

21. Indirect Measurement Suppose Ms. Kraus is 1.75 m tall. When her shadow is 1 m long, about how long would the shadow of the proposed building be?

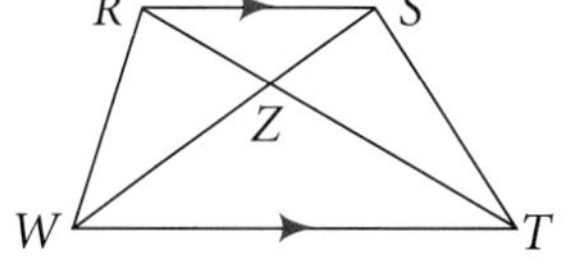

22. a. Classify $RSTW$.
b. Must any of the triangles shown be similar? Explain.

23. a. Critical Thinking Are two isosceles triangles always similar? Explain.
b. Are two isosceles right triangles always similar? Explain.

Can you conclude that the triangles are similar? If so, write a similarity statement and name the postulate or theorem you used. If not, explain.

24.

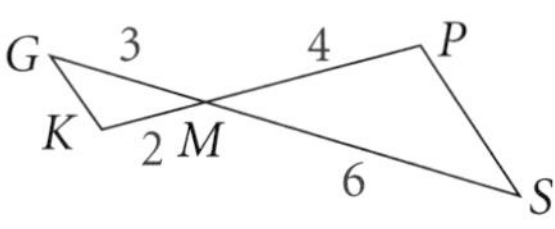

25.

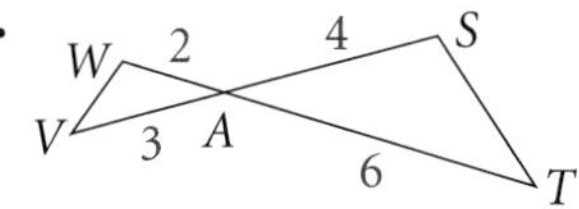

26.

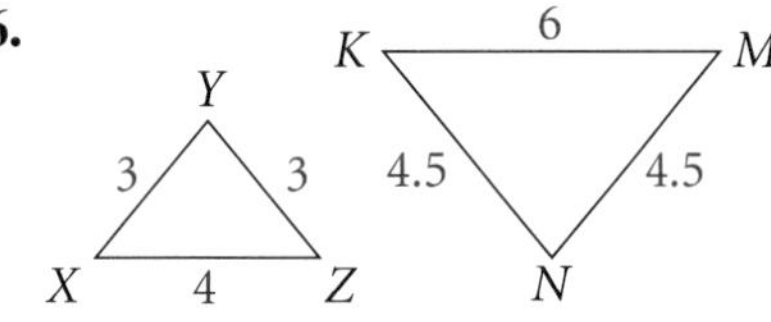

27.

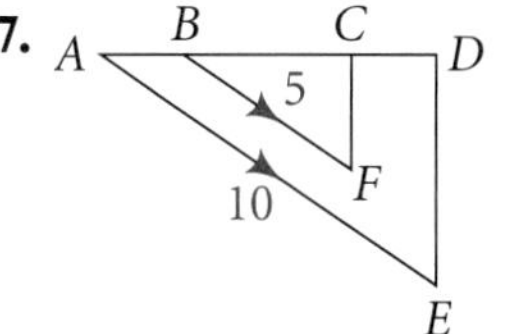

28. Indirect Measurement In sunlight, a vertical yardstick casts a 1-ft shadow at the same time that a nearby tree casts a 15-ft shadow. How tall is the tree?

29. Open-Ended Name something with a height that would be difficult to measure directly. Describe how you could measure it indirectly.

Find the similarity ratio of the larger to the smaller triangle in each exercise.

30. Ex. 10	**31.** Ex. 11	**32.** Ex. 12	**33.** Ex. 13	**34.** Ex. 14
35. Ex. 15	**36.** Ex. 16	**37.** Ex. 17	**38.** Ex. 18	**39.** Ex.19

40. Constructions Draw any $\triangle ABC$. Use a straightedge and a compass to construct $\triangle RST$ so that $\triangle ABC \sim \triangle RST$ with similarity ratio 1 : 3.

41. For each triangle at the right, find:
a. the perimeter **b.** the area
c. Critical Thinking Can you conclude that any two triangles with equal perimeters and equal areas are similar? Explain.

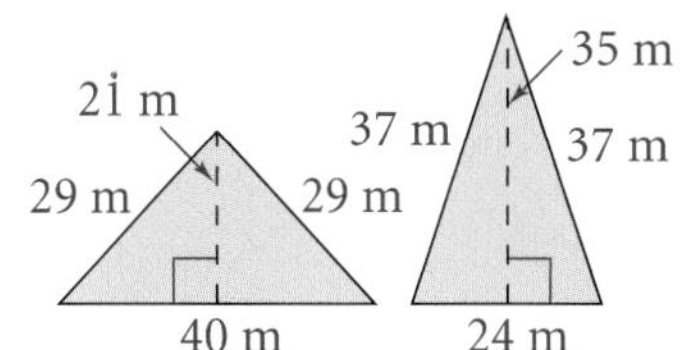

C Challenge

42. Write a proof of the following: Any two nonvertical parallel lines have equal slopes.

Given: nonvertical lines ℓ_1 and ℓ_2, $\ell_1 \parallel \ell_2$, $\overline{EF}$ and $\overline{BC} \perp$ to the x-axis

Prove: $\frac{BC}{AC} = \frac{EF}{DF}$

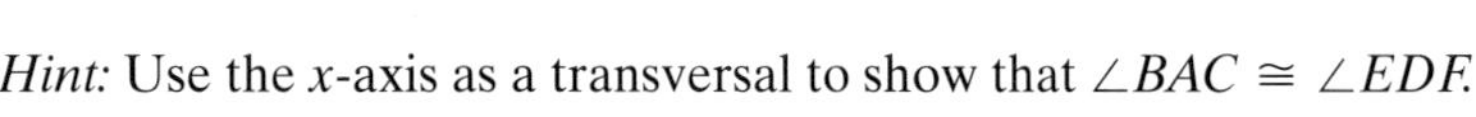

Hint: Use the x-axis as a transversal to show that $\angle BAC \cong \angle EDF$.

Proof **43.** Use the diagram in Exercise 42 on the preceding page.
Prove: Any two nonvertical lines with equal slopes are parallel.

Proof **44.** Write a proof of the following.

Given: $RT \cdot TQ = MT \cdot TS$

Prove: $\triangle RTM \sim \triangle STQ$

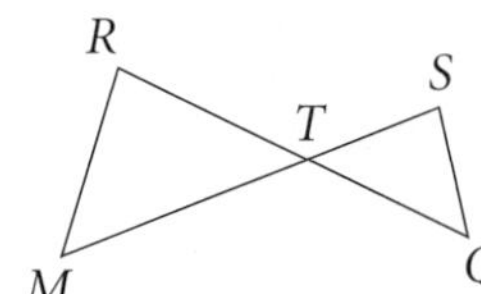

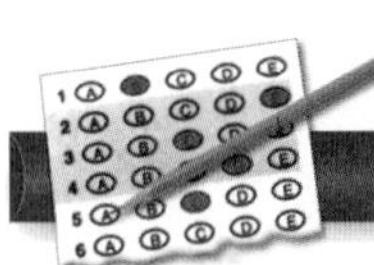

Standardized Test Prep

Multiple Choice

45. Complete the statement $\triangle ABC \sim$ __?__, and identify the reason why the triangles are similar.

A. $\triangle AKN$; SSS ~
B. $\triangle AKN$; SAS ~
C. $\triangle ANK$; SAS ~
D. $\triangle ANK$; AA ~

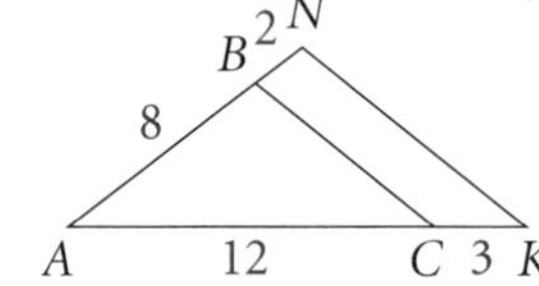

46. Complete the statement $\triangle ABC \sim$ __?__, and identify the reason why the triangles are similar.

F. $\triangle LGC$; SSS ~
G. $\triangle GLC$; SSS ~
H. $\triangle LGC$; AA ~
I. $\triangle GLC$; AA ~

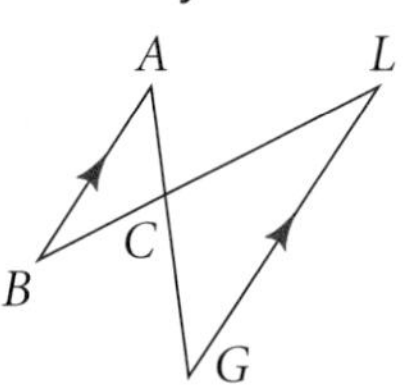

Short Response

47. Suppose $\triangle VLQ \sim \triangle PSX$.
a. Explain how you would find $m\angle X$ if $m\angle V = 48$ and $m\angle L = 80$.
b. Find $m\angle X$.

Extended Response

48. Hank is 6 ft tall. Hank measured the shadow of a tree and found it to be 30 ft long. He then measured his own shadow. It was 10 ft long.
a. Draw and label a diagram that you could use to find the height of the tree. Write a similarity statement and justify your answer.
b. Write a proportion and solve it to find the height of the tree.

Mixed Review

Lesson 8-2 ***TRAP ~ EZYD*. Complete each statement.**

49. $\angle T \cong$ __?__ **50.** $\angle D \cong$ __?__ **51.** $\angle A \cong$ __?__

52. $\frac{AP}{YD} = \frac{RA}{\blacksquare}$ **53.** $\frac{TR}{RA} = \frac{\blacksquare}{ZY}$ **54.** $\frac{DE}{PT} = \frac{\blacksquare}{AR}$

Lesson 6-6 **Give possible coordinates of points *W* and *Z* without using any new variables.**

55.

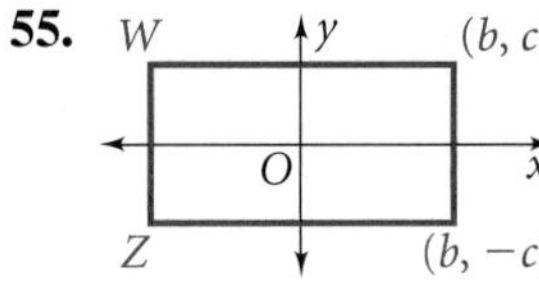

Rectangle

56.

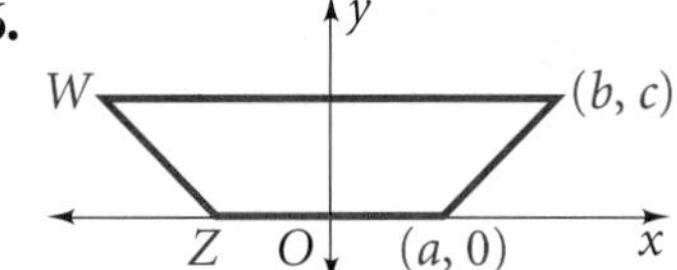

Isosceles trapezoid

Lesson 5-5 **57.** A triangle has sides with lengths 9 m and 15 m. Write an inequality that shows the range of possible lengths for the third side.

8-4 Similarity in Right Triangles

Lesson Preview

What You'll Learn

OBJECTIVE 1 To find and use relationships in similar right triangles

. . . And Why

To find a distance indirectly, as in Example 3

✔ Check Skills You'll Need

(For help, go to Lesson 8-1 and page 355.)

Algebra **Solve each proportion.**

1. $\frac{x}{8} = \frac{18}{24}$
2. $\frac{2}{3} = \frac{x}{7}$
3. $\frac{15}{4} = \frac{18}{x}$
4. $\frac{51}{x} = \frac{17}{13}$
5. $\frac{4}{10} = \frac{x}{5}$
6. $\frac{3}{m} = \frac{9}{8}$
7. $\frac{w}{2} = \frac{20}{9}$
8. $\frac{9}{6} = \frac{27}{a}$
9. Draw a right triangle. Label the triangle $\triangle ABC$ with right angle $\angle C$. Draw the altitude to the hypotenuse. Label the altitude $\overline{CD}$. Name the two smaller right triangles that are formed.

New Vocabulary • geometric mean

Interactive lesson includes instant self-check, tutorials, and activities.

OBJECTIVE 1 Using Similarity in Right Triangles

Investigation: Similarity in Right Triangles

- Draw one diagonal on a rectangular sheet of paper. Cut the paper on the diagonal to make two congruent right triangles.
- In one of the triangles, use paper folding to locate the altitude to the hypotenuse. Cut the triangle along the altitude to make two smaller right triangles.
- Label the angles of the three triangles as shown.
- Compare the angles of the three triangles by placing the angles on top of one another.

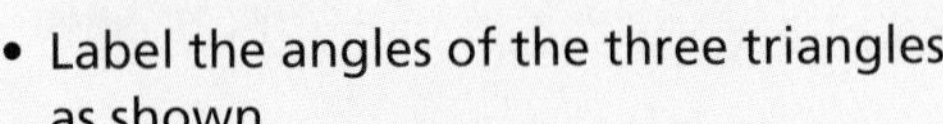

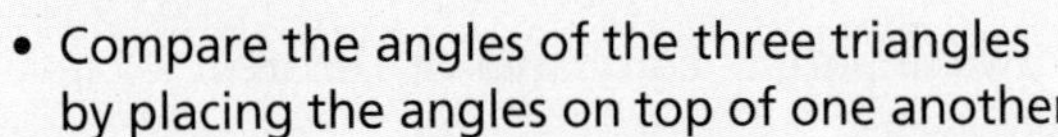

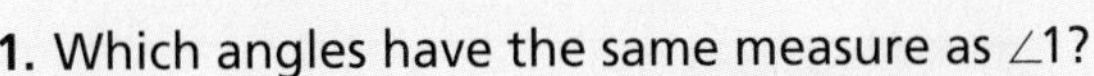

1. Which angles have the same measure as $\angle 1$?
2. Which angles have the same measure as $\angle 2$?
3. Which angles have the same measure as $\angle 3$?
4. Based on your results, what is true about the three triangles?
5. Use the diagram at the right to complete the similarity statement. $\triangle RST \sim \triangle \underline{?} \sim \triangle \underline{?}$

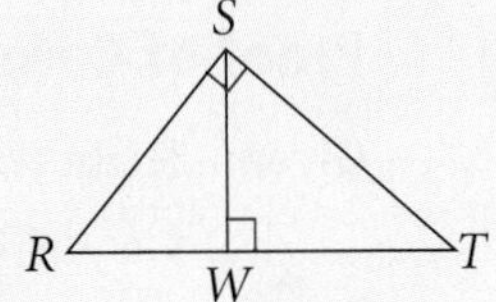

In a right triangle, the altitude to the hypotenuse yields three similar triangles.

Key Concepts

Theorem 8-3

The altitude to the hypotenuse of a right triangle divides the triangle into two triangles that are similar to the original triangle and to each other.

Proof

Proof of Theorem 8-3

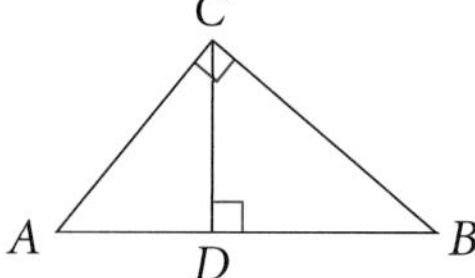

Given: Right triangle, $\triangle ABC$, with $\overline{CD}$ the altitude to the hypotenuse

Prove: $\triangle ABC \sim \triangle ACD \sim \triangle CBD$

Proof: Both smaller triangles are right triangles. Each also shares an angle with $\triangle ABC$. Thus each smaller triangle is similar to $\triangle ABC$ by the AA $\sim$ Postulate. Since both smaller triangles are similar to $\triangle ABC$, their corresponding angles are congruent. Thus they are similar to each other.

Need Help?

In the proportion $\frac{a}{b} = \frac{c}{d}$, b and c are the means.

Proportions in which the means are equal occur frequently in geometry. For any two positive numbers a and b, the **geometric mean** of a and b is the positive number x such that $\frac{a}{x} = \frac{x}{b}$. Note that $x = \sqrt{ab}$.

1 EXAMPLE Finding the Geometric Mean

Algebra Find the geometric mean of 4 and 18.

$\frac{4}{x} = \frac{x}{18}$ **Write a proportion.**

$x^2 = 72$ **Cross-Product Property**

$x = \sqrt{72}$ **Take the square root.**

$x = 6\sqrt{2}$ **Write in simplest radical form.**

The geometric mean of 4 and 18 is $6\sqrt{2}$.

✓ Check Understanding 1 Find the geometric mean of 15 and 20.

Two important corollaries of Theorem 8-3 involve a geometric mean.

Key Concepts

Corollary **Corollary 1 to Theorem 8-3**

The length of the altitude to the hypotenuse of a right triangle is the geometric mean of the lengths of the segments of the hypotenuse.

Proof

Proof of Corollary 1

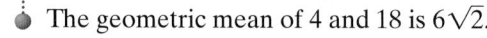

C
A D B

Given: Right triangle, $\triangle ABC$, with $\overline{CD}$ the altitude to the hypotenuse

Prove: $\frac{AD}{CD} = \frac{CD}{DB}$

Proof: By Theorem 8-3, $\triangle ACD \sim \triangle CBD$. Since corresponding sides of similar triangles are proportional, $\frac{AD}{CD} = \frac{CD}{DB}$.

Corollary | **Corollary 2 to Theorem 8-3**

The altitude to the hypotenuse of a right triangle separates the hypotenuse so that the length of each leg of the triangle is the geometric mean of the length of the adjacent hypotenuse segment and the length of the hypotenuse.

Proof

Proof of Corollary 2

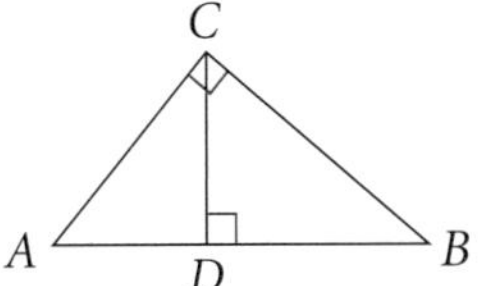

Given: Right triangle, $\triangle ABC$, with $\overline{CD}$ the altitude to the hypotenuse

Prove: $\frac{AD}{AC} = \frac{AC}{AB}$, $\frac{DB}{CB} = \frac{CB}{AB}$

Proof: By Theorem 8-3, $\triangle ACD \sim \triangle ABC$. Their corresponding sides are proportional, so $\frac{AD}{AC} = \frac{AC}{AB}$. Similarly, $\triangle CBD \sim \triangle ABC$ and $\frac{DB}{CB} = \frac{CB}{AB}$.

2 EXAMPLE Applying Corollaries 1 and 2

Algebra Solve for x and y.

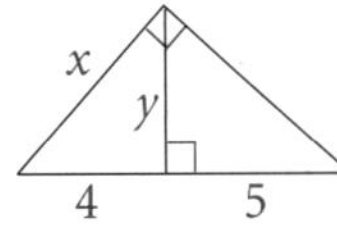

Use Corollary 2 to solve for x: | Use Corollary 1 to solve for y:

$\frac{4}{x} = \frac{x}{4+5}$	← **Write a proportion.** →	$\frac{4}{y} = \frac{y}{5}$
$x^2 = 36$	← **Cross-Product Property** →	$y^2 = 20$
$x = 6$	← **Take the square root.** →	$y = 2\sqrt{5}$

2 Solve for x and y.

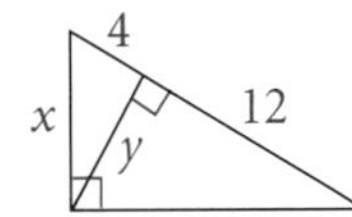

3 EXAMPLE Real-World Connection

Recreation The 300-m path to the information center and the 400-m path to the canoe rental dock meet at a right angle at the parking lot. Marla walks straight from the parking lot to the lake as shown. How far is Marla from the information center?

$\overline{CD}$, the perpendicular segment from point C to $\overline{AB}$, is the shortest path to the lake. $\triangle ABC$ is a right triangle. Using Pythagorean triples, $AB = 500$ m. To find AD, apply Corollary 2.

$\frac{AD}{AC} = \frac{AC}{AB}$ **Corollary 2**

$\frac{AD}{300} = \frac{300}{500}$ **Substitute.**

$AD = \frac{300}{500} \cdot 300$ **Solve for AD.**

$AD = 180$

Marla is 180 m from the information center.

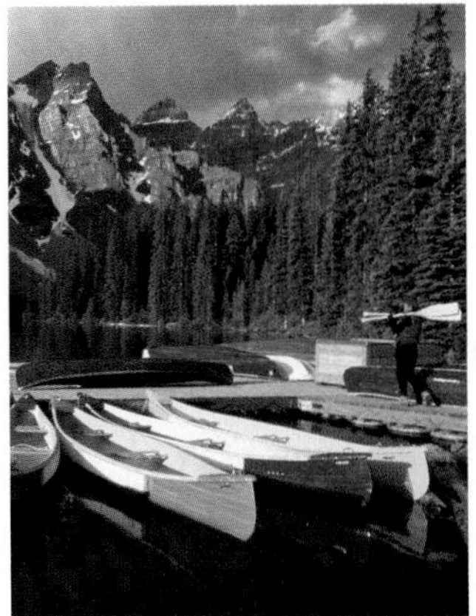

Real-World Connection

Paddling a canoe burns about 175 calories per hour.

3 How far did Marla walk from the parking lot to the lake?

EXERCISES

For more practice, see *Extra Practice.*

Practice and Problem Solving

A **Practice by Example**

Algebra **Find the geometric mean of each pair of numbers.**

Example 1 (page 440)

1. 4 and 9 **2.** 4 and 10 **3.** 4 and 12 **4.** 3 and 48

5. 7 and 56 **6.** 5 and 125 **7.** 9 and 24 **8.** 7 and 9

Example 2 (page 441)

Algebra **Refer to the figure to complete each proportion.**

9. $\frac{r}{h} = \frac{h}{\blacksquare}$ **10.** $\frac{c}{a} = \frac{a}{\blacksquare}$ **11.** $\frac{\blacksquare}{b} = \frac{b}{s}$

12. $\frac{r}{\blacksquare} = \frac{\blacksquare}{c}$ **13.** $\frac{r}{h} = \frac{\blacksquare}{s}$ **14.** $\frac{s}{b} = \frac{\blacksquare}{c}$

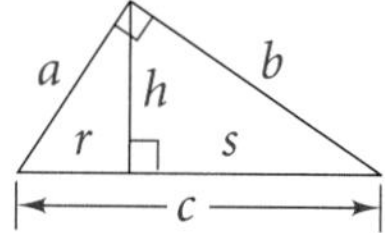

Algebra **Solve for x.**

15.

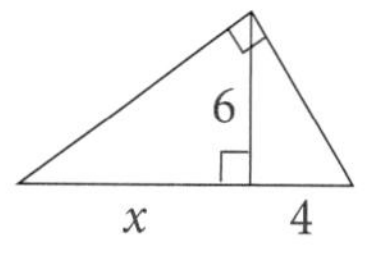

16.

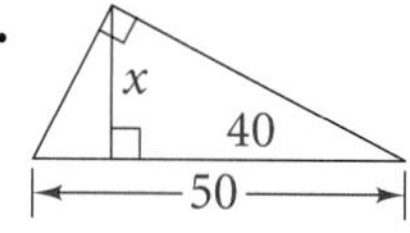

17.

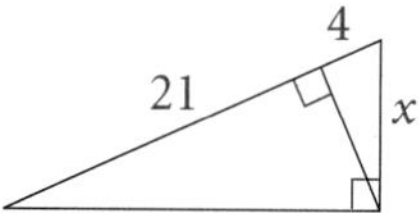

18.

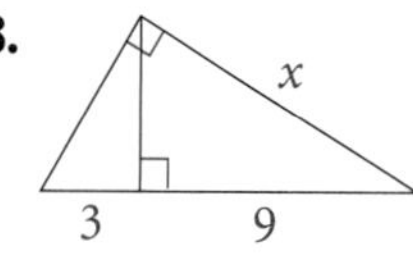

19.

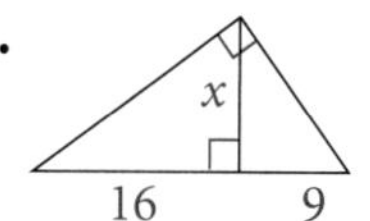

20.

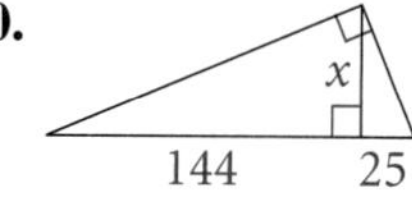

Example 3 (page 441)

21. a. Civil Engineering Study the plan at the right. A service station will be built on the highway, and a road will connect it with Cray. How far from Blare should the service station be located so that the proposed road will be perpendicular to the highway?

b. How long will the new road be?

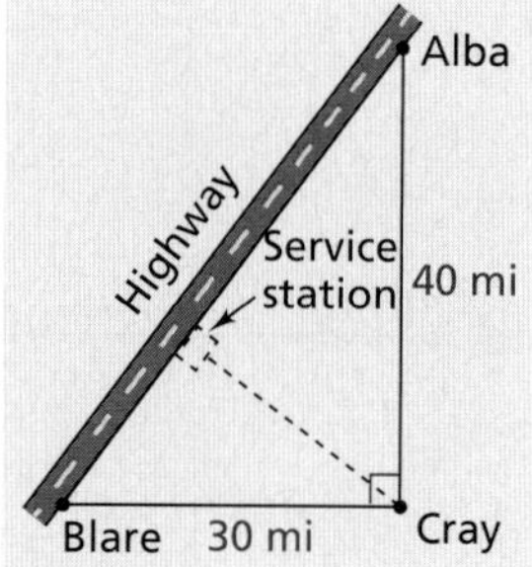

B **Apply Your Skills**

22. Complete: $\triangle JKL \sim \triangle\underline{\ ?\ } \sim \triangle\underline{\ ?\ }$

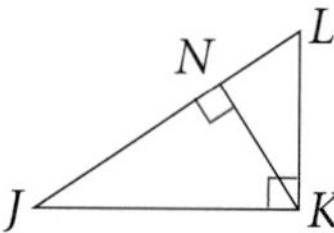

23. a. The altitude to the hypotenuse of a right triangle divides the hypotenuse into segments 2 cm and 8 cm long. Find the length h of the altitude.

b. Drawing Use the value you found for h in part (a), along with the lengths 2 cm and 8 cm, to draw the right triangle accurately.

c. Writing Explain how you drew the triangle in part (b).

24. a. Open-Ended Draw a right triangle so that the altitude from the right angle to the hypotenuse bisects the hypotenuse.

b. How does the length of the altitude compare with the lengths of the segments of the hypotenuse? Explain.

25. Coordinate Geometry $\overline{CD}$ is the altitude to the hypotenuse of right $\triangle ABC$. The coordinates of A, D, and B are $(4, 2)$, $(4, 6)$, and $(4, 15)$, respectively. Find all possible coordinates of point C.

Reading Math

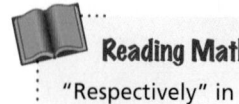

"Respectively" in Exercise 25 means you match the lists in the order named: $A(4, 2)$, $D(4, 6)$, $B(4, 15)$.

Algebra **Find the geometric mean of each pair of numbers.**

26. 3 and 16 **27.** 4 and 49 **28.** $\sqrt{8}$ and $\sqrt{2}$ **29.** $\sqrt{28}$ and $\sqrt{7}$

30. $\frac{1}{2}$ and 2 **31.** 5 and 1.25 **32.** 1 and 1000 **33.** 11 and 1331

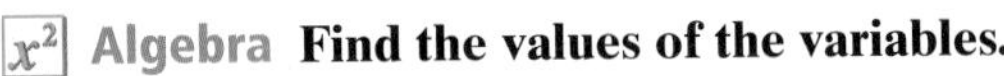

x^2 **Algebra** **Find the values of the variables.**

34.

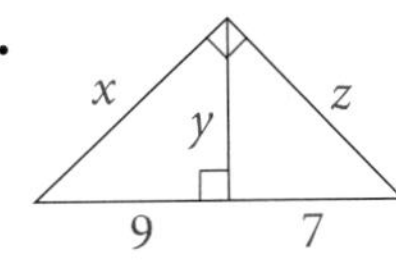

35.

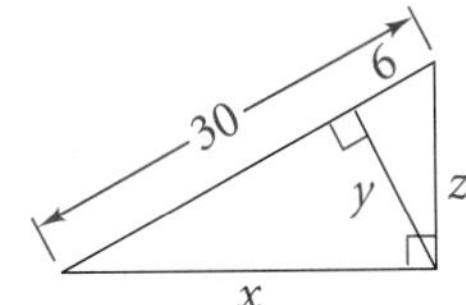

36.

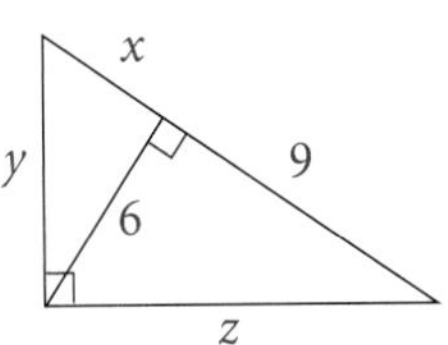

x^2 **37. Algebra** The altitude to the hypotenuse of a right triangle divides the hypotenuse into segments with lengths in the ratio 1 : 2. The length of the altitude is 8. How long is the hypotenuse?

Proof **38. Pythagorean Theorem** You can use Corollary 2 to Theorem 8-3 to prove the Pythagorean Theorem. Complete the following proof.

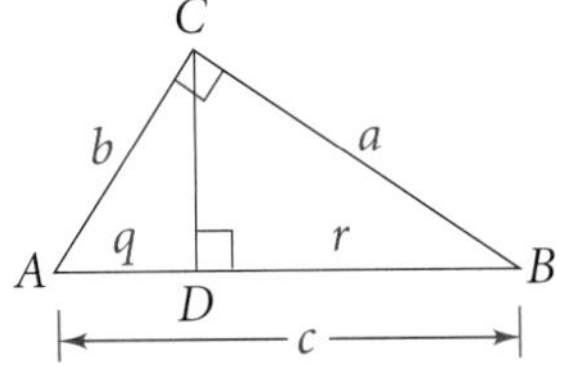

Given: Right $\triangle ABC$ with altitude $\overline{CD}$

Prove: $c^2 = a^2 + b^2$

Statements	Reasons
1. Right $\triangle ABC$ with altitude $\overline{CD}$	**a.** ?
2. $\frac{c}{a} = \frac{a}{r}, \frac{c}{b} = \frac{b}{q}$	**b.** ?
3. $cr = a^2, cq = b^2$	**c.** ?
4. $cr + cq = a^2 + b^2$	**d.** ?
5. $c(r + q) = a^2 + b^2$	**e.** ?
6. $r + q = c$	**f.** ?
7. $c^2 = a^2 + b^2$	**g.** ?

39. Indirect Measurement To estimate the height of a totem pole, Jorge uses a small square of plastic. He holds the square up to his eyes and walks backward from the pole. He stops when the bottom of the pole lines up with the bottom edge of the square and the top of the pole lines up with the top edge of the square. Jorge's eye level is about 2 m from the ground. He is about 3 m from the pole. Estimate the height of the totem pole.

3 m

2 m

Exercise 39

40. The length of the shorter leg of a 30°-60°-90° triangle is 10 cm. Find the length of the altitude to the hypotenuse.

For a right triangle, denote lengths as follows: ℓ_1 and ℓ_2 the legs, h the hypotenuse, a the altitude, and h_1 and h_2 the hypotenuse segments determined by the altitude. For the two given measures, find the other four. Use simplest radical form.

41. $\ell_1 = 3, \ell_2 = 4$ **42.** $h_1 = 4, h_2 = 9$ **43.** $a = 6, h_1 = 6$ **44.** $\ell_1 = 5, a = 4$

45. $h = 13, \ell_2 = 12$ **46.** $\ell_1 = 4, h_1 = 3$ **47.** $a = 8, h_1 = 16$ **48.** $h_1 = 3, \ell_2 = 6\sqrt{3}$

C **Challenge**

49. a. Lauren thinks she has found a new corollary: The product of the lengths of the two legs of a right triangle is equal to the product of the lengths of the hypotenuse and the altitude to the hypotenuse. Draw a figure for this corollary. Write the *Given* information and what you are to *Prove*.

b. Critical Thinking Is Lauren's corollary true? Explain.

x^2 **Algebra** **Find the value of x.**

50.

x + 3

12

x

51.

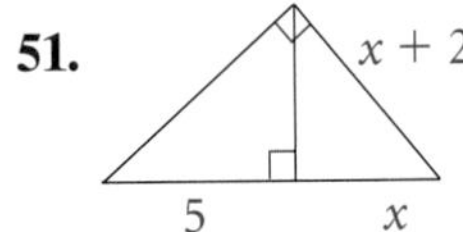

52.

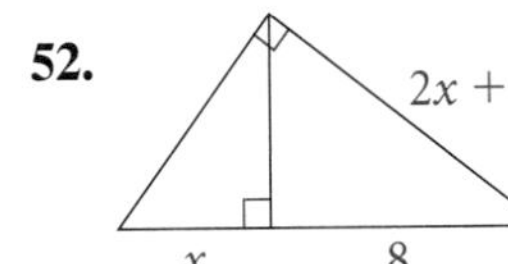

Each Pythagorean triple below represents the lengths of the sides of a right triangle. For each triangle, find the length of the altitude to the hypotenuse.

53. 3, 4, 5 **54.** 5, 12, 13 **55.** 8, 15, 17 **56.** 20, 21, 29

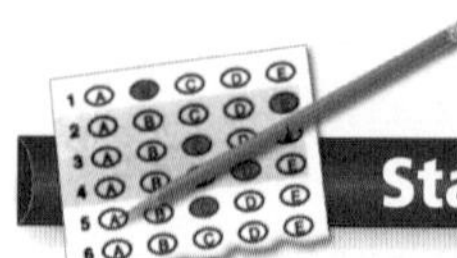

Standardized Test Prep

Multiple Choice

57. What is the geometric mean of 12 and 18?
A. 1.5 **B.** $\sqrt{6}$ **C.** 15 **D.** $6\sqrt{6}$

58. What is the geometric mean of 2 and 36?
F. 17 **G.** $6\sqrt{2}$ **H.** 38 **I.** $2\sqrt{6}$

59. Solve for m.
A. 7 **B.** 15
C. 20 **D.** 25

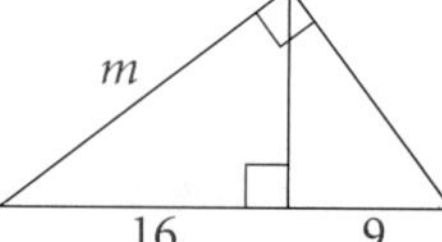

Take It to the NET
Online lesson quiz at **www.PHSchool.com**
Web Code: afa-0804

60. The altitude to the hypotenuse of a right triangle divides the hypotenuse into segments of lengths 5 and 15. What is the length of the altitude?
F. 3 **G.** 10 **H.** $5\sqrt{3}$ **I.** $5\sqrt{5}$

Short Response

61. a. Explain how you could solve for x.
b. What is the value of x?

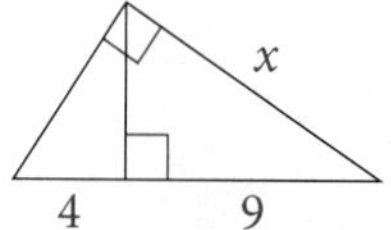

Mixed Review

Lesson 8-3 **If the triangles are similar, (a) write a similarity statement and (b) name the postulate or theorem you used. If the triangles are not similar, write *not similar*.**

62.

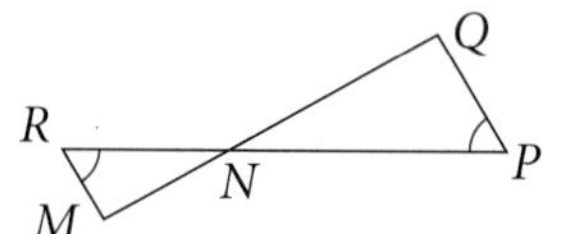

63.

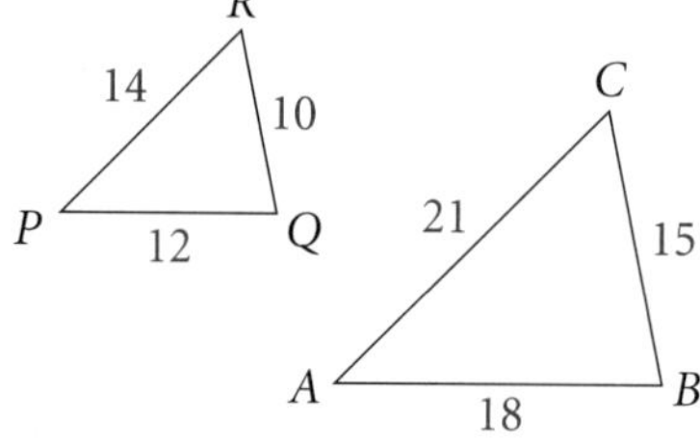

64.

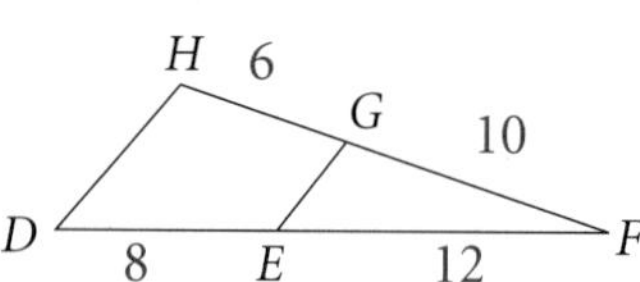

Lesson 7-1 x^2 **Algebra** **Solve for the variables in each parallelogram.**

65.

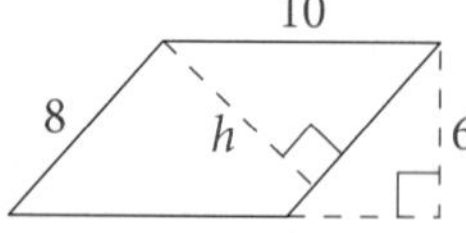

66.

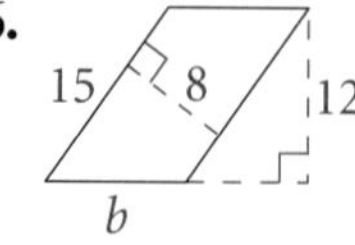

Lesson 6-2 x^2 **Algebra** **Find the values of x and y in ▱$RSTV$.**

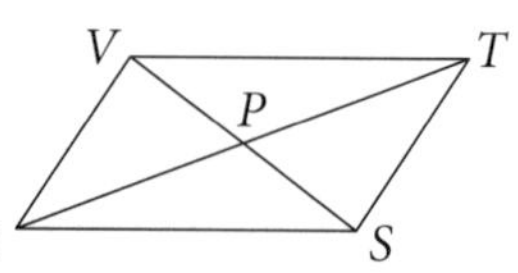

67. $RP = 2x, PT = y + 2, VP = y, PS = x + 3$

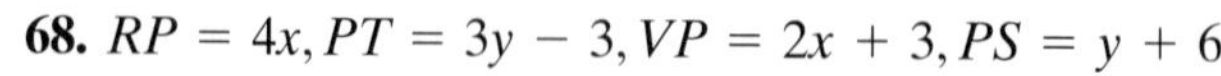

68. $RP = 4x, PT = 3y - 3, VP = 2x + 3, PS = y + 6$

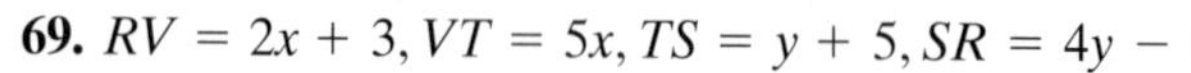

69. $RV = 2x + 3, VT = 5x, TS = y + 5, SR = 4y - 1$

Exploring Proportions in Triangles

FOR USE WITH LESSON 8-5

Construct

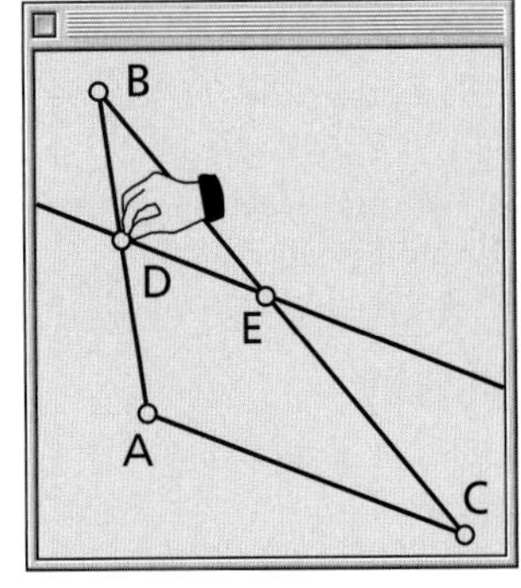

- Use geometry software. Draw $\triangle ABC$ and construct point D on $\overline{AB}$.
- Construct a line through D parallel to $\overline{AC}$.
- Construct the intersection E of the parallel line with $\overline{BC}$.

Investigate

- Measure $\overline{BD}, \overline{DA}, \overline{BE}$, and $\overline{EC}$.
- Calculate the ratios $\frac{BD}{DA}$ and $\frac{BE}{EC}$.
- Manipulate $\triangle ABC$ and observe the ratios $\frac{BD}{DA}$ and $\frac{BE}{EC}$. (Save your observations for Exercise 1.)

Construct

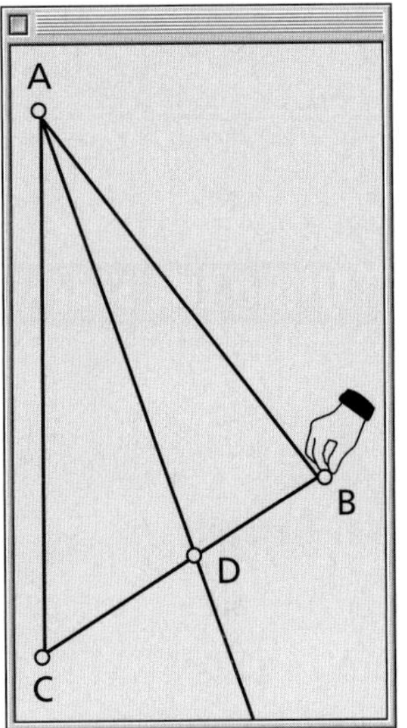

- Use geometry software. Draw $\triangle ABC$. Construct the bisector of $\angle A$. Construct point D, the intersection of the bisector and $\overline{CB}$.

Investigate

- Measure $\overline{AC}, \overline{AB}, \overline{CD}$, and $\overline{DB}$.
- Calculate the ratios $\frac{AC}{AB}$ and $\frac{CD}{DB}$.
- Manipulate $\triangle ABC$ and observe the ratios $\frac{AC}{AB}$ and $\frac{CD}{DB}$. (Save your observations for Exercise 2.)

EXERCISES

1. Suppose a line parallel to one side of a triangle intersects the other two sides. Make a conjecture about the four segments formed.

2. The bisector of an angle of a triangle divides the opposite side into two segments. Make a conjecture about the two segments and the other two sides of the triangle.

Extend

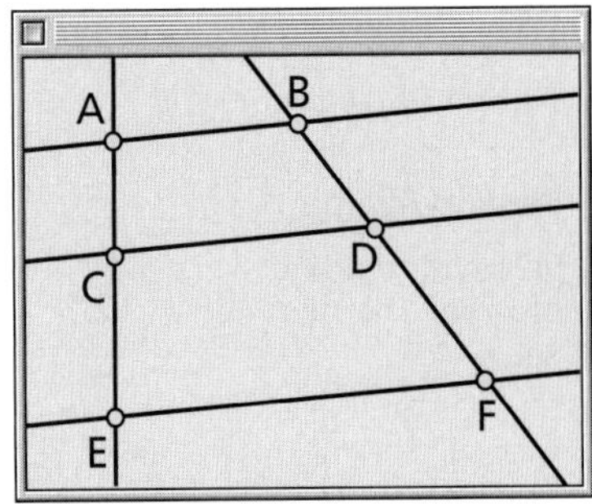

- Construct $\overleftrightarrow{AB} \parallel \overleftrightarrow{CD}$. Then construct lines $\overleftrightarrow{AC}$ and $\overleftrightarrow{BD}$.
- Construct point E on $\overleftrightarrow{AC}$.
- Construct $\overleftrightarrow{EF} \parallel \overleftrightarrow{AB}$ with point F the intersection of $\overleftrightarrow{EF}$ and $\overleftrightarrow{BD}$.
- Measure $\overline{AC}, \overline{CE}, \overline{BD}$, and $\overline{DF}$.
- Calculate the ratios $\frac{AC}{CE}$ and $\frac{BD}{DF}$.
- Manipulate the locations of A and B and observe the ratios $\frac{AC}{CE}$ and $\frac{BD}{DF}$.

3. Suppose three parallel lines intersect two transversals. Make a conjecture about the segments of the transversals.

4. Suppose that four or more parallel lines intersect two transversals. Make a conjecture about the segments of the transversals.

8-5 Proportions in Triangles

Lesson Preview

What You'll Learn

To use the Side-Splitter Theorem

To use the Triangle-Angle-Bisector Theorem

. . . And Why

To design a sail, as in Example 2

Check Skills You'll Need

(For help, go to Lesson 8-2.)

The two triangles in each diagram are similar. Find the value of x in each.

1.

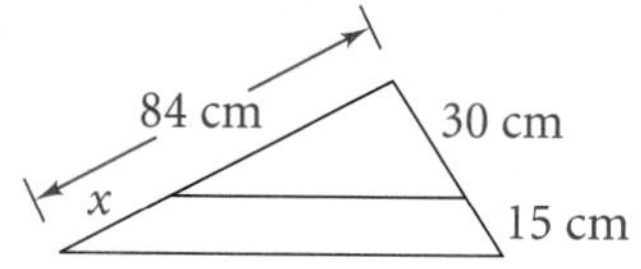

2.

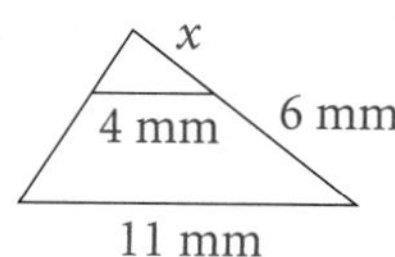

3.

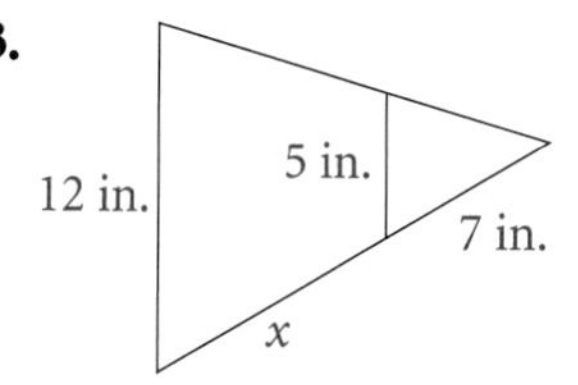

4.

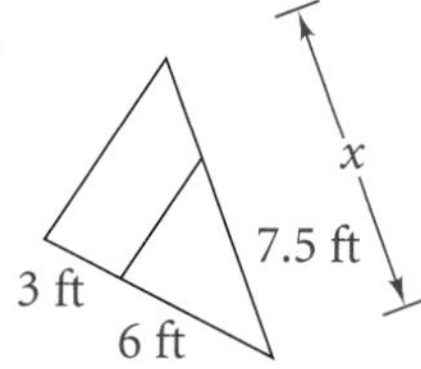

Interactive lesson includes instant self-check, tutorials, and activities.

OBJECTIVE 1 Using the Side-Splitter Theorem

You can use similar triangles to prove the following theorem.

Key Concepts

Theorem 8-4 Side-Splitter Theorem

If a line is parallel to one side of a triangle and intersects the other two sides, then it divides those sides proportionally.

Proof

Proof of Theorem 8-4

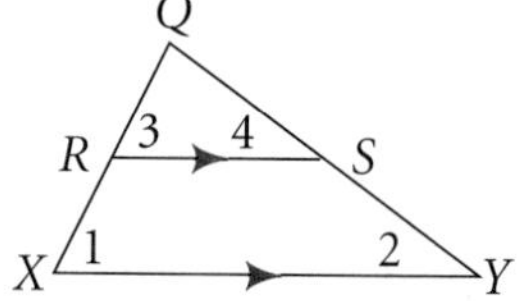

Given: $\triangle QXY$ with $\overleftrightarrow{RS} \parallel \overleftrightarrow{XY}$

Prove: $\frac{XR}{RQ} = \frac{YS}{SQ}$

Statements	Reasons
1. $\overleftrightarrow{RS} \parallel \overleftrightarrow{XY}$	**1.** Given
2. $\angle 1 \cong \angle 3, \angle 2 \cong \angle 4$	**2.** If lines are $\parallel$, then corr. $\measuredangle$s are $\cong$.
3. $\triangle QXY \sim \triangle QRS$	**3.** AA $\sim$ Postulate
4. $\frac{XQ}{RQ} = \frac{YQ}{SQ}$	**4.** Corr. sides of $\sim$ $\triangle$s are proportional.
5. $XQ = XR + RQ, YQ = YS + SQ$	**5.** Segment Addition Postulate
6. $\frac{XR + RQ}{RQ} = \frac{YS + SQ}{SQ}$	**6.** Substitute.
7. $\frac{XR}{RQ} = \frac{YS}{SQ}$	**7.** A Property of Proportions

Reading Math

For help with reading the proof of Theorem 8-4, see p. 453.

1 EXAMPLE Using the Side-Splitter Theorem

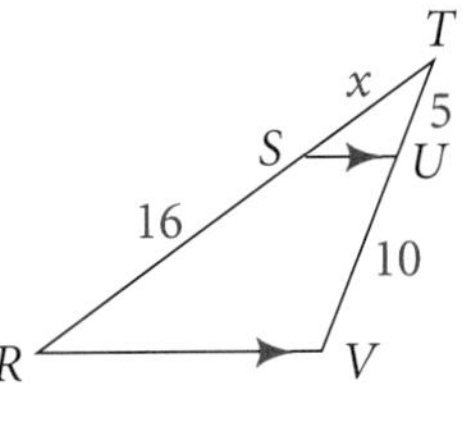

Algebra Solve for x.

$\frac{TS}{SR} = \frac{TU}{UV}$ **Side-Splitter Theorem**

$\frac{x}{16} = \frac{5}{10}$ **Substitute.**

$x = \frac{5}{10} \cdot 16$ **Solve for x.**

$x = 8$

Check Understanding **1** Use the Side-Splitter Theorem to find the value of x.

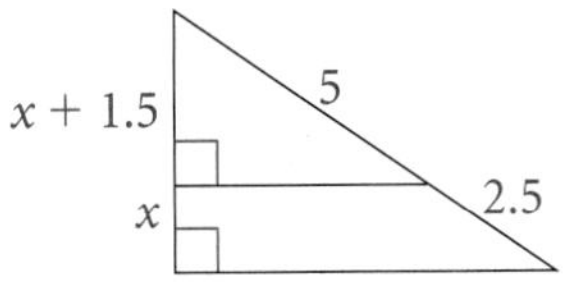

The following corollary to the Side Splitter Theorem says that parallel lines divide all transversals proportionally. You will prove this corollary in Exercise 34.

Key Concepts

Corollary **Corollary to Theorem 8-4**

If three parallel lines intersect two transversals, then the segments intercepted on the transversals are proportional.

$$\frac{a}{b} = \frac{c}{d}$$

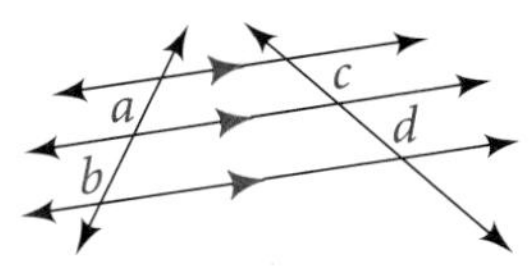

Real-World Connection

You windsurf with a large sail in light winds and a small sail in strong winds.

2 EXAMPLE Real-World Connection

Sail Making Sail makers sometimes use a computer to create a pattern for a sail. After they cut out the panels of the sail, they sew them together to form the sail.

The edges of the panels in the sail at the right are parallel. Find the lengths x and y.

$\frac{2}{x} = \frac{1.7}{1.7}$ **Side-Splitter Theorem**

$x = 2$

$\frac{3}{2} = \frac{y}{1.7}$ **Corollary to the Side-Splitter Theorem**

$\frac{3}{2}(1.7) = y$ **Solve for y.**

$2.55 = y$

Length x is 2 ft and length y is 2.55 ft.

Check Understanding **2** Solve for x and y.

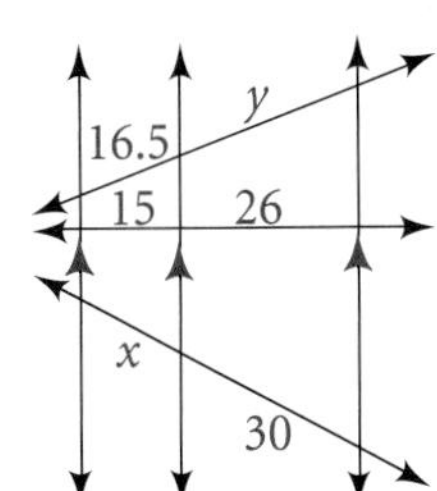

OBJECTIVE

2 Using the Triangle-Angle-Bisector Theorem

You can use the Side-Splitter Theorem to prove the following relationship.

Key Concepts

Theorem 8-5 **Triangle-Angle-Bisector Theorem**

If a ray bisects an angle of a triangle, then it divides the opposite side into two segments that are proportional to the other two sides of the triangle.

Proof

Proof of Theorem 8-5

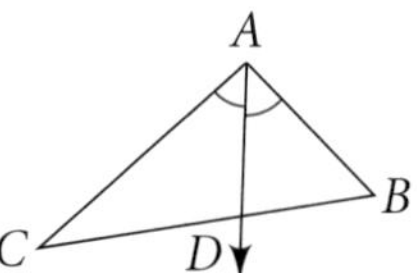

Given: $\triangle ABC$, $\overrightarrow{AD}$ bisects $\angle CAB$.

Prove: $\frac{CD}{DB} = \frac{CA}{BA}$

Need Help?

Drawing $\overleftrightarrow{BE} \parallel \overline{DA}$ sets up $\triangle BCF$ for the Side-Splitter Theorem, as well as congruent ∠s 1, 2, 3, and 4.

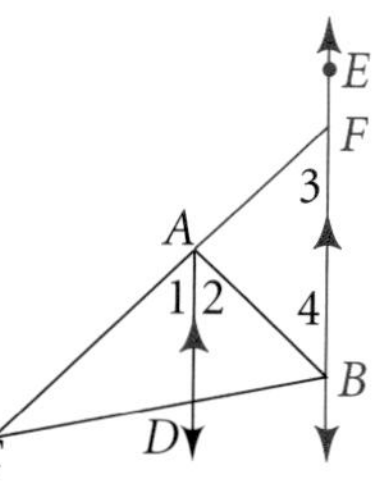

Draw $\overleftrightarrow{BE} \parallel \overline{DA}$. Extend $\overline{CA}$ to meet $\overleftrightarrow{BE}$ at point F.

Proof: By the Side-Splitter Theorem, $\frac{CD}{DB} = \frac{CA}{AF}$.
By the Corresponding Angles Postulate, $\angle 3 \cong \angle 1$.
Since $\overrightarrow{AD}$ bisects $\angle CAB$, $\angle 1 \cong \angle 2$. By the Alternate Interior Angles Theorem, $\angle 2 \cong \angle 4$. Using the Transitive Property of Congruence, you know that $\angle 3 \cong \angle 4$.
By the Converse of the Isosceles Triangle Theorem, $BA = AF$. Substituting BA for AF, $\frac{CD}{DB} = \frac{CA}{BA}$.

3 EXAMPLE Using the Triangle-Angle-Bisector Theorem

Algebra Find the value of x.

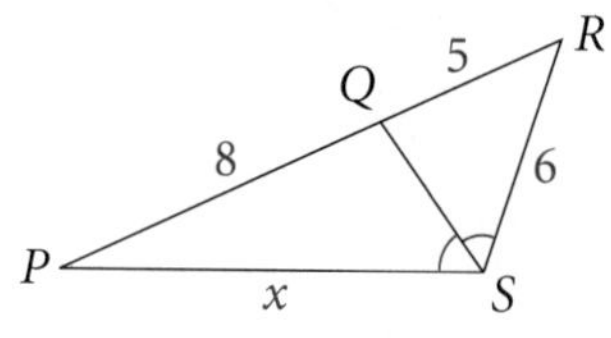

$\frac{PS}{SR} = \frac{PQ}{RQ}$	**Triangle-Angle-Bisector Theorem**
$\frac{x}{6} = \frac{8}{5}$	**Substitute.**
$5x = 48$	**Cross-Product Property**
$x = 9.6$	**Solve for x.**

Check Understanding **3** Find the value of y.

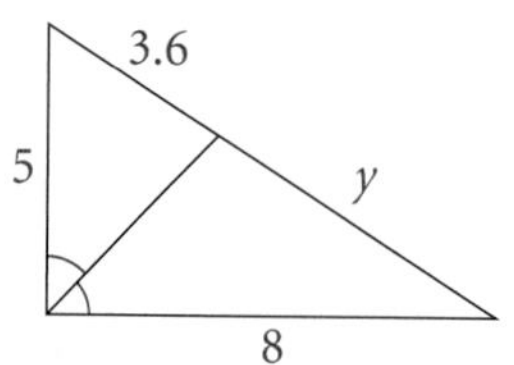

EXERCISES

For more practice, see *Extra Practice*.

Practice and Problem Solving

A **Practice by Example** x^2 **Algebra** **Solve for x.**

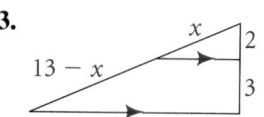

Example 1 (page 447)

1.

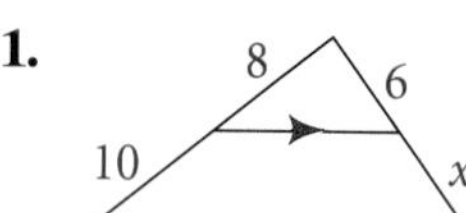

2.

3.

Example 2 (page 447)

Use the figure at the right to complete each proportion.

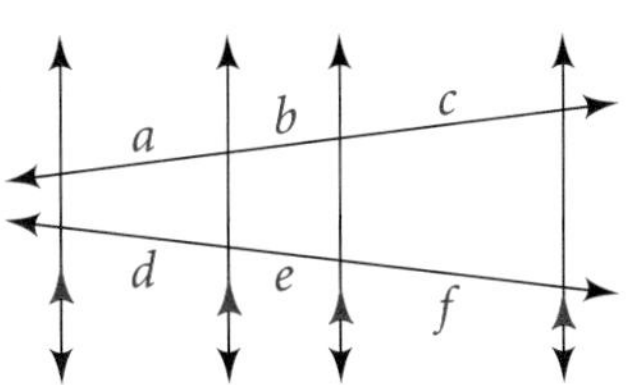

4. $\frac{a}{b} = \frac{■}{e}$
5. $\frac{b}{■} = \frac{e}{f}$
6. $\frac{f}{e} = \frac{c}{■}$
7. $\frac{a}{b + c} = \frac{■}{e + f}$

Algebra **Solve for x.**

8. 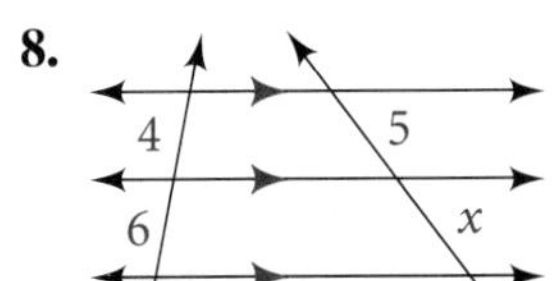

9. 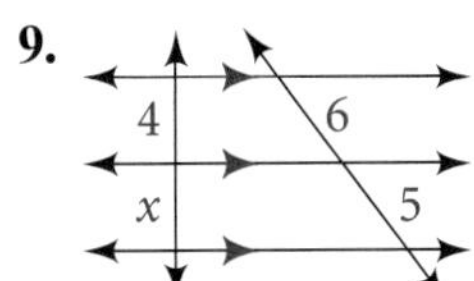

10. 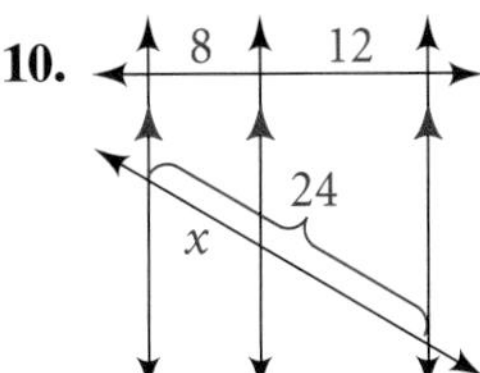

Example 3 (page 448)

Algebra **Solve for x.**

11. 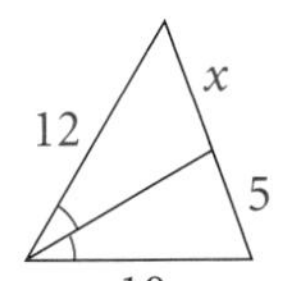

12. 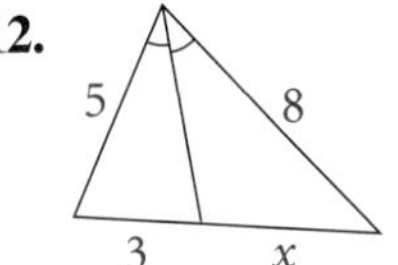

13. 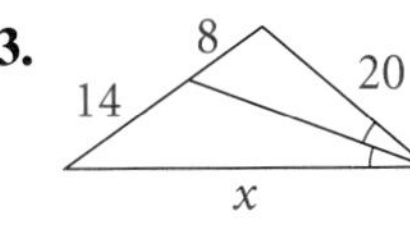

14. 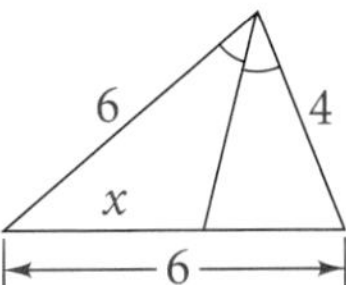

15. 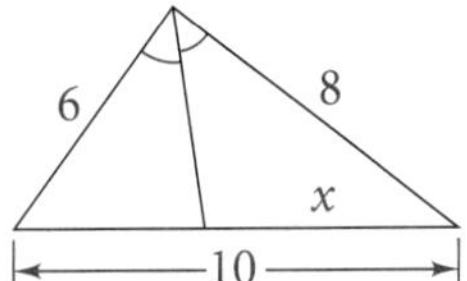

16. 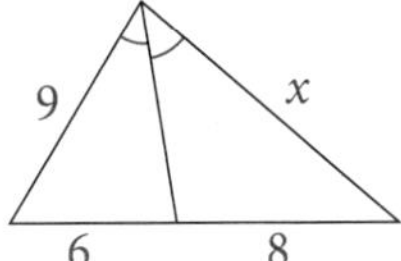

Use the figure at the right to complete each proportion.

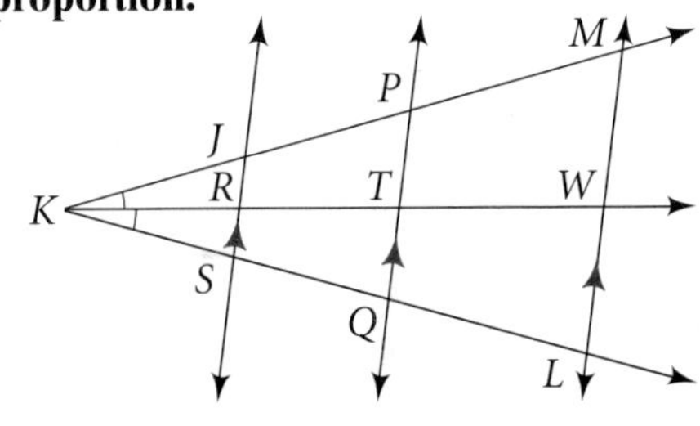

17. $\frac{RS}{■} = \frac{JR}{KJ}$
18. $\frac{KJ}{JP} = \frac{KS}{■}$
19. $\frac{QL}{PM} = \frac{SQ}{■}$
20. $\frac{PT}{■} = \frac{TQ}{KQ}$
21. $\frac{KL}{LW} = \frac{■}{MW}$
22. $\frac{■}{KP} = \frac{LQ}{KQ}$
23. $\frac{■}{SQ} = \frac{JK}{KS}$
24. $\frac{KL}{KM} = \frac{■}{MW}$

B Apply Your Skills

Urban Design **In Washington, D.C., 17th, 18th, 19th, and 20th Streets are parallel streets that intersect Pennsylvania Avenue and I Street.**

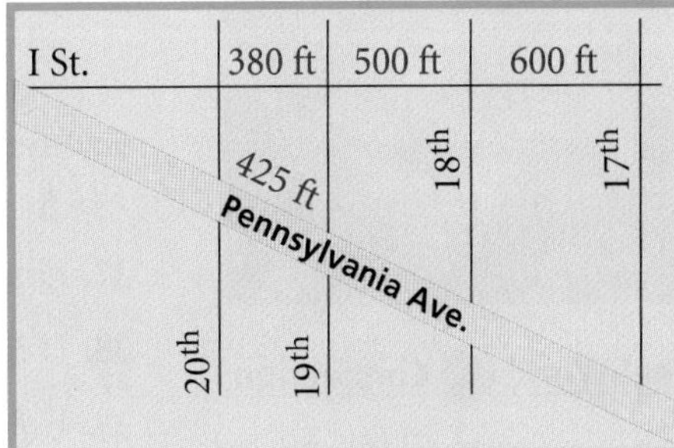

25. How long (to the nearest foot) is Pennsylvania Avenue between 19th Street and 18th Street?

26. How long (to the nearest foot) is Pennsylvania Avenue between 18th Street and 17th Street?

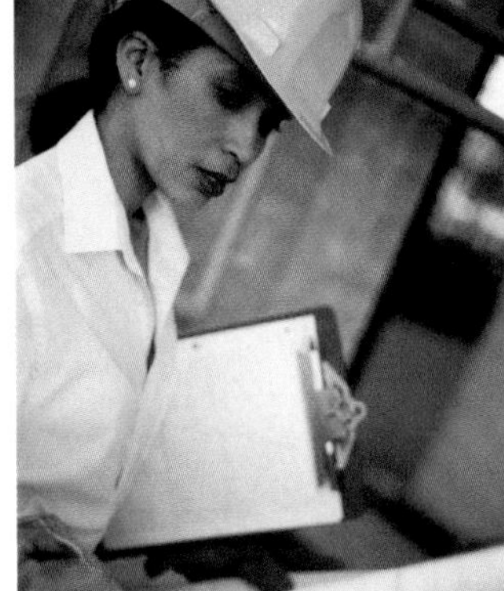

Real-World  **Connection**

Careers A master's degree in urban design is good preparation for urban planning.

27. The legs of a right triangle are 5 cm and 12 cm long. Find the lengths, to the nearest tenth, of the segments into which the bisector of the right angle divides the hypotenuse.

28. **Open-Ended** In a triangle, the bisector of an angle divides the opposite side into two segments with lengths 6 cm and 9 cm. How long could the other two sides of the triangle be? (*Caution:* Make sure the three sides satisfy the Triangle Inequality Theorem.)

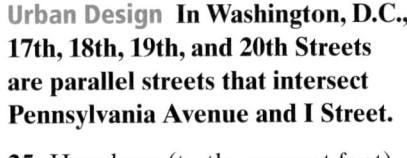

29. Surveying The perimeter of the triangular lot at the right is 50 m. The surveyor's tape bisects an angle. Find the lengths x and y.

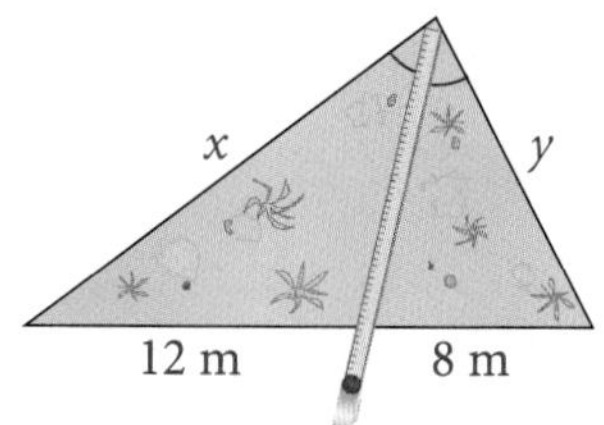

30. Critical Thinking Sharell draws $\triangle ABC$. She finds that the bisector of $\angle C$ bisects the opposite side.

a. Sketch $\triangle ABC$ and the bisector.

b. Writing What type of triangle is $\triangle ABC$? Explain your reasoning.

Algebra Solve for x.

31.

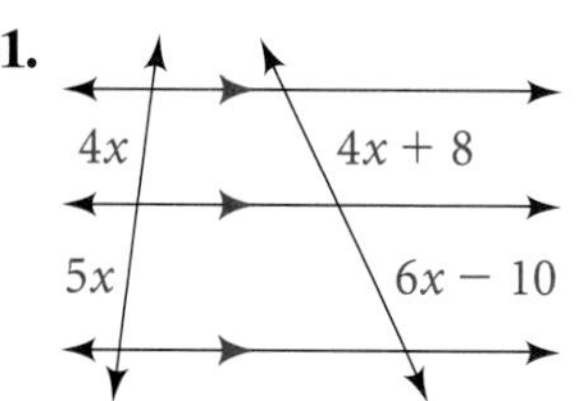

32.

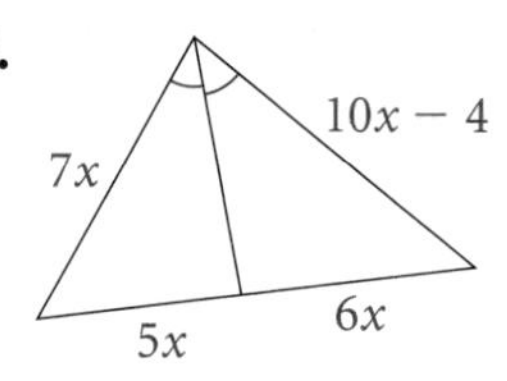

33.

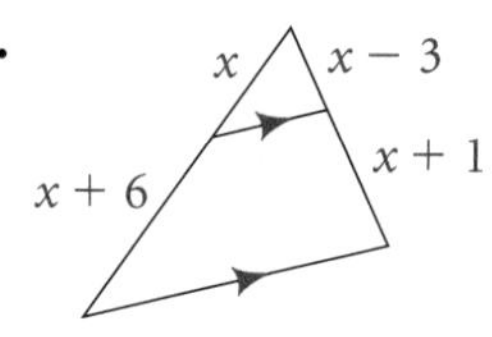

Proof **34.** Follow the steps below. Write a proof of the Corollary to the Side-Splitter Theorem found on page 447.

Given: $\overleftrightarrow{AW} \parallel \overleftrightarrow{BX} \parallel \overleftrightarrow{CY}$

Prove: $\frac{AB}{BC} = \frac{WX}{XY}$

Begin by drawing $\overleftrightarrow{WC}$, intersecting $\overline{BX}$ at point Z.

a. Apply the Side-Splitter Theorem to $\triangle ACW$: $\frac{\blacksquare}{\blacksquare} = \frac{WZ}{ZC}$.

b. Apply the Side-Splitter Theorem to $\triangle CWY$: $\frac{WZ}{ZC} = \frac{\blacksquare}{\blacksquare}$.

c. Substitute to prove the corollary.

35. Oil Spills Describe how you could use the figure at the right to find the length of the oil spill indirectly. What measurements and calculations would you use?

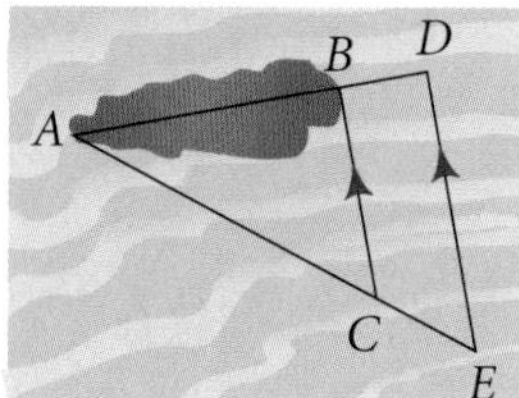

Real-World Connection

You measure an oil spill to find the size of the boom you'll need to contain it.

36. An angle bisector of a triangle divides the opposite side of the triangle into segments 5 cm and 3 cm long. A second side of the triangle is 7.5 cm long. Find all possible lengths for the third side of the triangle.

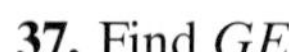

Geometry in 3 Dimensions In the figure at the right, $\overleftrightarrow{FG} \parallel \overleftrightarrow{AB}$, $\overleftrightarrow{GH} \parallel \overleftrightarrow{BC}$, $AF = 2$, $FE = 4$, and $BG = 3$.

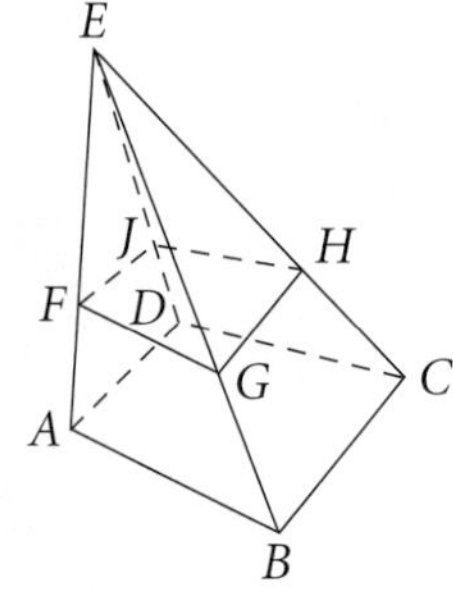

37. Find GE.

38. If $EH = 5$, find HC.

39. If $FG = 3$, find the perimeter of $\triangle ABE$.

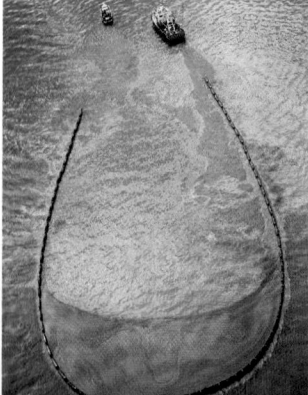

For a right triangle, denote lengths as follows: ℓ_1 and ℓ_2 the legs, h the hypotenuse, and h_1 and h_2 the hypotenuse segments determined by the bisector of the right angle. For the two given measures, find the other three to the nearest tenth.

40. $\ell_1 = 6, \ell_2 = 8$

41. $h_1 = 4, h_2 = 9$

42. $h = 13, \ell_2 = 12$

43. $\ell_1 = 5\sqrt{2}, h_1 = 5$

44. $\ell_1 = 15, \ell_2 = 8$

45. $h_1 = 4, h = 8$

Proof **46.** In a 30°-60°-90° right triangle, the right-angle bisector cuts the hypotenuse into two segments. Prove that one segment is $\sqrt{3}$ times the length of the other.

Proof **47.** Copy and complete this two-column proof of the Converse of the Side-Splitter Theorem: If a line divides two sides of a triangle proportionally, then it is parallel to the third side.

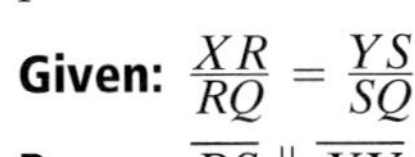

Given: $\frac{XR}{RQ} = \frac{YS}{SQ}$

Prove: $\overline{RS} \parallel \overline{XY}$

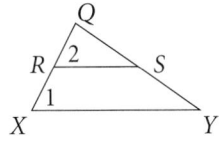

Statements	Reasons
1. $\frac{XR}{RQ} = \frac{YS}{SQ}$	a. ?
2. $\frac{XR + RQ}{RQ} = \frac{YS + SQ}{SQ}$	b. ?
3. $\frac{XQ}{RQ} = \frac{YQ}{SQ}$	c. ?
4. $\angle Q \cong \angle Q$	d. ?
5. $\triangle XQY \sim \triangle RQS$	e. ?
6. $\angle 1 \cong \angle 2$	f. ?
7. $\overline{RS} \parallel \overline{XY}$	g. ?

Real-World Connection

In this glass roof, parallel lines divide the sides of triangles proportionally.

Determine whether the red segments are parallel. Explain each answer. You can use the theorem proved in Exercise 47.

48.

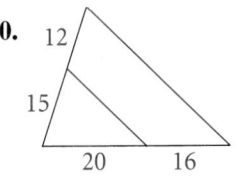

49.

50.

C Challenge Proof **51.** Use the definition in part (a) to prove the statements in parts (b) and (c).

a. Write a definition for a midsegment of a parallelogram.

b. A parallelogram midsegment is parallel to two sides of the parallelogram.

c. A parallelogram midsegment bisects the diagonals of a parallelogram.

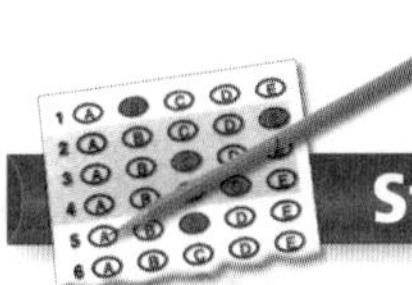

Standardized Test Prep

Multiple Choice

52. Use the figure at the right. What is x?

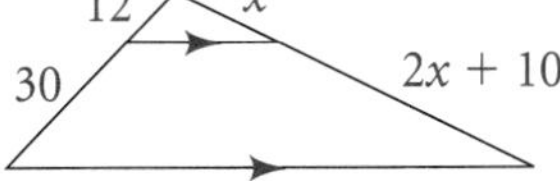

A. 5 **B.** 10

C. 15 **D.** 20

53. The legs of a right triangle have lengths 7 and 24. The bisector of the right angle divides the hypotenuse into two segments. What is the length of the shorter segment of the hypotenuse to the nearest tenth?

F. 5.6 **G.** 8.0 **H.** 19.4 **I.** 25

Short Response

54. What is n? Show your work.

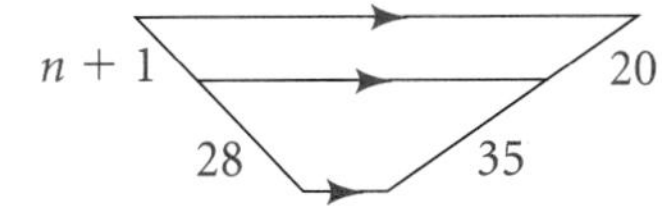

Extended Response

55. The bisectors of an angle of a triangle divide the opposite side of the triangle into segments 4 cm and 5 cm long. A second side of the triangle is 6 cm long.

a. Draw two diagrams you can use to find the two possible different lengths for the third side.

b. Use each diagram in part (a) to write a proportion. Solve for each possible length of the third side of the triangle. Show your work.

Take It to the NET

Online lesson quiz at **www.PHSchool.com**

Web Code: afa-0805

Mixed Review

Lesson 8-4 Refer to the figure to complete each proportion.

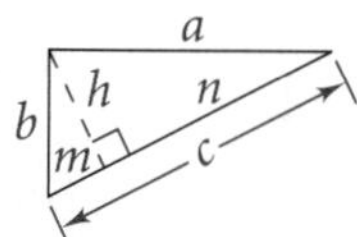

56. $\frac{n}{h} = \frac{h}{■}$

57. $\frac{■}{b} = \frac{b}{c}$

58. $\frac{n}{a} = \frac{a}{■}$

59. $\frac{m}{h} = \frac{■}{n}$

Lesson 7-3 Algebra Find the value of each variable. Leave your answer in simplest radical form.

60. 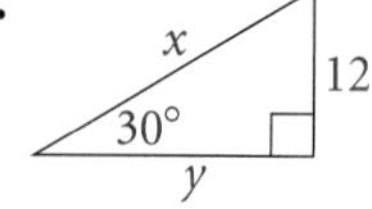

61. 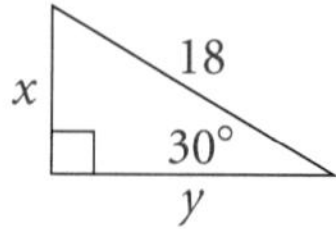

62. 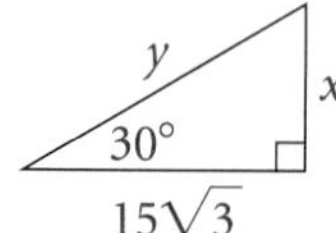

Lesson 6-4 Algebra *RSTV* is a rectangle. Find the lengths of the diagonals $\overline{RT}$ and $\overline{SV}$.

63. $RT = 5x + 8, SV = x + 32$

64. $RT = 42 - x, SV = 9x - 8$

65. $RT = 8x - 4, SV = 6x + 9$

66. $RT = 3x + 5, SV = 5x + 4$

Checkpoint Quiz 2 — Lessons 8-3 through 8-5

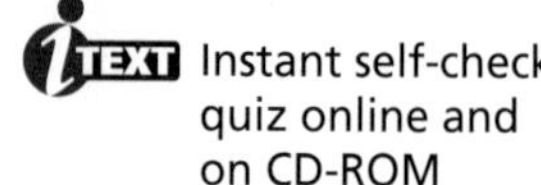

Instant self-check quiz online and on CD-ROM

Determine whether the triangles are similar. If so, write the similarity statement. Also, write the postulate or theorem that proves they are similar.

1. 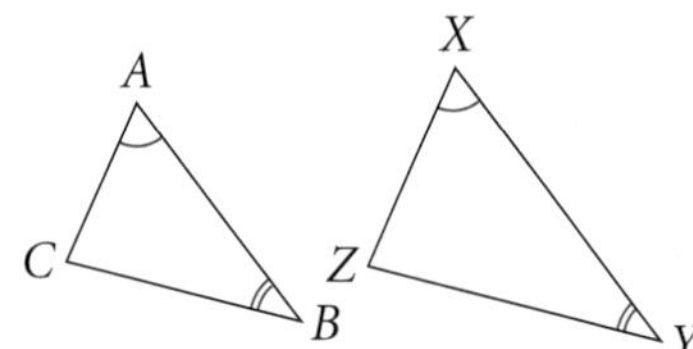

2. 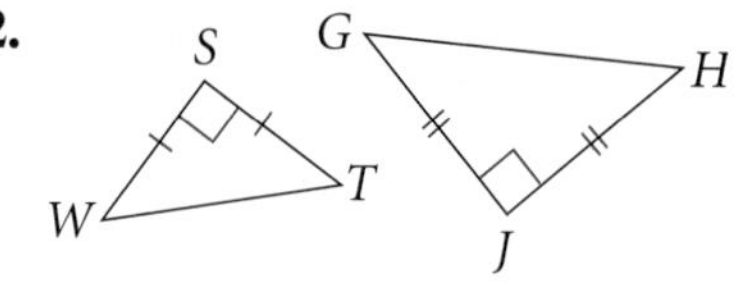

Algebra The polygons are similar. Find the value of each variable.

3. 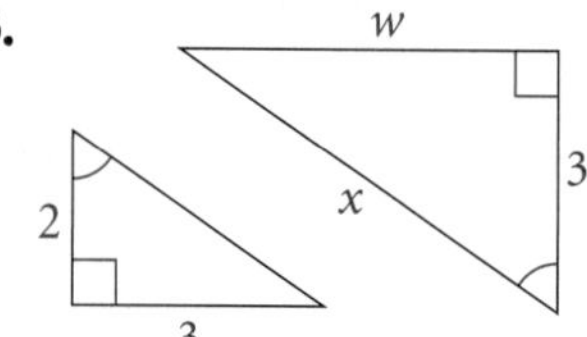

4. 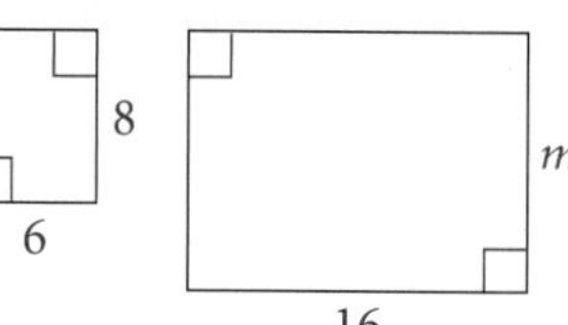

Algebra Find the value of each variable.

5. 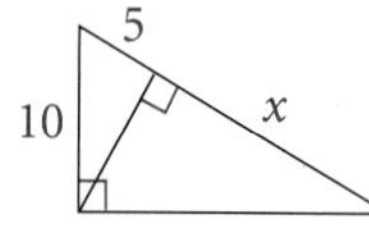

6. 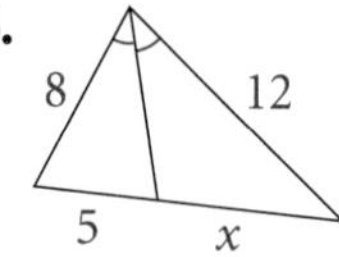

7. 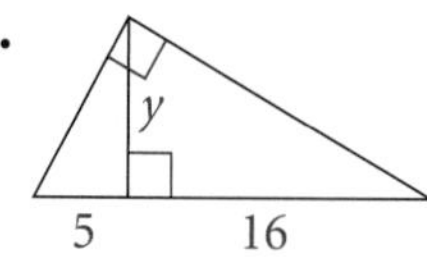

8. 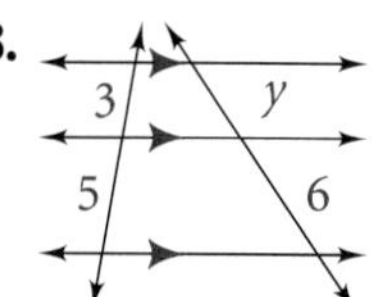

9. 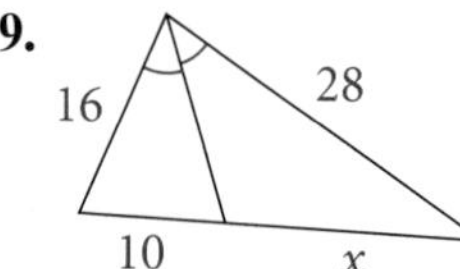

10. 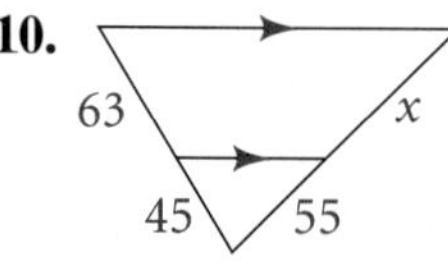

Reading a Two-Column Proof

For Use With Page 446, Theorem 8-4

Reading a two-column proof looks like it should be pretty simple. After all, the statements are numbered and it's clear which reason goes with which statement. The trick is that although the statements are listed in numerical order, it is not always true that each statement follows directly from the preceding statement.

To understand a two-column proof, you may find it helpful to copy the proof and make notes on your copy. Here are things you'll want to do:

1. Mark the diagram to keep track of what you prove.
2. Think of the statement you read as the "then" part of an if-then statement. The reason shown gives a clue to the "if" part. Write in parentheses the step (or steps) that provide the specific information needed to deduce the "then" part.
3. When you see "Substitute," write in parentheses what was substituted where.

Here is the proof of Theorem 8-4, The Side-Splitter Theorem, that a student copied and marked up.

Given: $\triangle QXY$ with $\overleftrightarrow{RS} \parallel \overleftrightarrow{XY}$

Prove: $\frac{XR}{RQ} = \frac{YS}{SQ}$

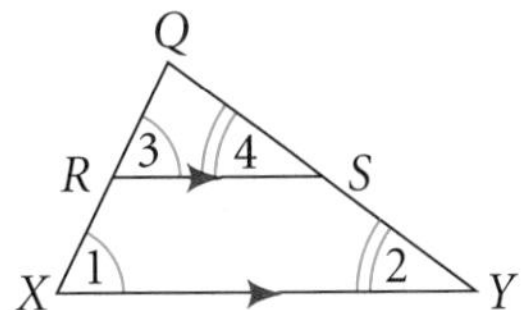

Statements	Reasons
1. $\overleftrightarrow{RS} \parallel \overleftrightarrow{XY}$	1. Given
2. $\angle 1 \cong \angle 3, \angle 2 \cong \angle 4$	2. If lines are $\parallel$, then corr. $\measuredangle$s are $\cong$. **(from step 1)**
3. $\triangle QXY \sim \triangle QRS$	3. AA $\sim$ Postulate **(from step 2)**
4. $\frac{XQ}{RQ} = \frac{YQ}{SQ}$	4. Corr. sides of $\sim$ $\triangle$s are proportional. **(from step 3)**
5. $XQ = XR + RQ$, $YQ = YS + SQ$	5. Segment Addition Postulate
6. $\frac{XR + RQ}{RQ} = \frac{YS + SQ}{SQ}$	6. Substitute. **(the two sums from step 5, into step 4)**
7. $\frac{XR}{RQ} = \frac{YS}{SQ}$	7. A Property of Proportions **(from step 6)**

In conclusion, a two-column proof has a more organized structure than a flow proof. On the other hand, the flow of logic can be harder to follow. Marking a diagram and keeping notes can be helpful.

EXERCISE

Copy the two-column proof from p. 199, Exercise 29. Fill in the missing statements and reasons. Mark your diagram and proof.

8-6 Perimeters and Areas of Similar Figures

Lesson Preview

What You'll Learn

To find the perimeters and areas of similar figures

. . . And Why

To find the expected yield of a garden, as in Example 3

✓ Check Skills You'll Need

(For help see Lesson 1-7.)

Find the perimeter and area of each figure.

1.

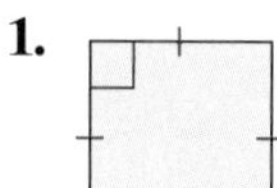

2.

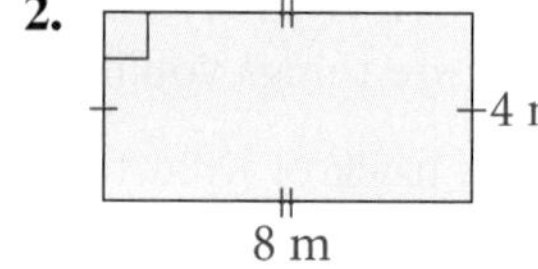

3.

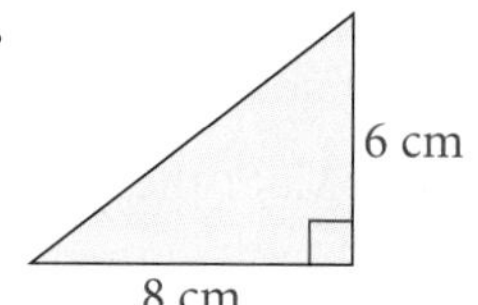

Find the perimeter and area of each rectangle with the given base and height.

4. $b = 1$ cm, $h = 3$ cm **5.** $b = 2$ cm, $h = 6$ cm **6.** $b = 3$ cm, $h = 9$ cm

Interactive lesson includes instant self-check, tutorials, and activities.

1 Finding Perimeters and Areas of Similar Figures

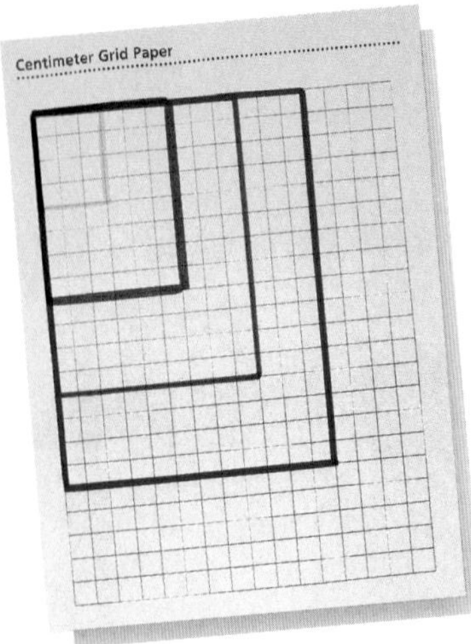

Investigation: Perimeters and Areas of Similar Rectangles

- On a piece of grid paper, draw a 3-unit by 4-unit rectangle.
- Draw three different rectangles, each similar to the original rectangle. Label them I, II, and III.

1. Use your drawings to complete a chart like this.

Rectangle	Perimeter	Area
Original		
I		
II		
III		

2. Use the information from the first chart to complete a chart like this.

Rectangle	Similarity Ratio	Ratio of Perimeters	Ratio of Areas
I to Original			
II to Original			
III to Original			

3. How do the ratios of perimeters and the ratios of areas compare with the similarity ratios?

To compare areas of similar figures, you can square the similarity ratio.

Key Concepts

Theorem 8-6 **Perimeters and Areas of Similar Figures**

If the similarity ratio of two similar figures is $\frac{a}{b}$, then
(1) the ratio of their perimeters is $\frac{a}{b}$ and
(2) the ratio of their areas is $\frac{a^2}{b^2}$.

1 EXAMPLE Finding Ratios in Similar Figures

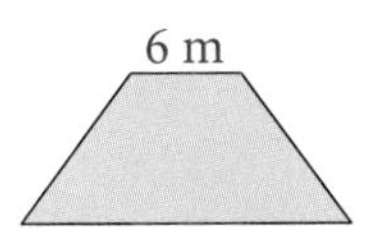

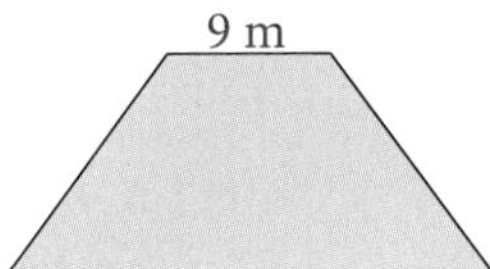

The trapezoids at the right are similar. The ratio of the lengths of corresponding sides is $\frac{6}{9}$, or $\frac{2}{3}$.

a. Find the ratio (smaller to larger) of the perimeters.

The ratio of the perimeters is the same as the ratio of corresponding sides, which is $\frac{2}{3}$.

b. Find the ratio (smaller to larger) of the areas.

The ratio of the areas is the square of the ratio of corresponding sides, which is $\frac{2^2}{3^2}$, or $\frac{4}{9}$.

Check Understanding

1 Two similar polygons have corresponding sides in the ratio 5 : 7.
a. Find the ratio of their perimeters.
b. Find the ratio of their areas.

When you know the area of one of two similar polygons, you can use a proportion to find the area of the other polygon.

2 EXAMPLE Finding Areas Using Similar Figures

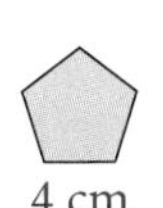

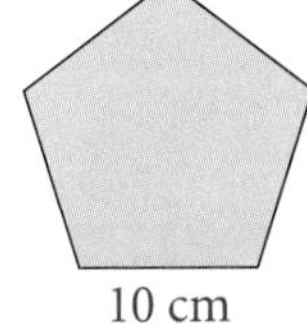

The area of the smaller regular pentagon is about 27.5 cm^2. Find the area A of the larger regular pentagon.

All regular pentagons are similar. Here the ratio of the lengths of the corresponding sides is $\frac{4}{10}$, or $\frac{2}{5}$. The ratio of the areas is $\frac{2^2}{5^2}$, or $\frac{4}{25}$.

$\frac{4}{25} = \frac{27.5}{A}$ **Write a proportion.**

$4A = 687.5$ **Cross-Product Property**

$A = \frac{687.5}{4} = 171.875$ **Solve for *A*.**

The area of the larger pentagon is about 172 cm^2.

Need Help?

Regular pentagons are similar because all angles measure 108 and all sides in each are congruent.

Check Understanding

2 The corresponding sides of two similar parallelograms are in the ratio $\frac{3}{4}$. The area of the larger parallelogram is 96 $in.^2$. Find the area of the smaller parallelogram.

You can apply what you know about the ratios of the areas of similar figures to real-world problems.

Real-World Connection

Many cities make city land available to the community for gardening.

3 EXAMPLE Real-World Connection

Community Service During the summer, a group of high school students used a plot of city land and harvested 13 bushels of vegetables that they gave to a food pantry. Their project was so successful that next summer the city will let them use a larger, similar plot of land.

In the new plot, each dimension is 2.5 times the corresponding dimension of the original plot. How many bushels can they expect to harvest next year?

The ratio of the dimensions is 2.5 : 1. So, the ratio of the areas is $(2.5)^2 : 1^2$, or 6.25 : 1. With 6.25 times as much land next year, the students can expect to harvest 6.25(13), or about 81 bushels.

Check Understanding 3 The similarity ratio of the dimensions of two similar pieces of window glass is 3 : 5. The smaller piece costs $2.50. What should be the cost of the larger piece?

When you know the ratio of the areas of two similar figures, you can work backward to find the ratio of their perimeters.

4 EXAMPLE Finding Similarity and Perimeter Ratios

The areas of two similar triangles are 50 cm^2 and 98 cm^2. What is the similarity ratio? What is the ratio of their perimeters?

Find the similarity ratio $a : b$.

$\frac{a^2}{b^2} = \frac{50}{98}$ **The ratio of the areas is $a^2 : b^2$.**

$\frac{a^2}{b^2} = \frac{25}{49}$ **Simplify.**

$\frac{a}{b} = \frac{5}{7}$ **Take square roots.**

The ratio of the perimeters equals the similarity ratio 5 : 7.

Check Understanding 4 The areas of two similar rectangles are 1875 ft^2 and 135 ft^2. Find the ratio of their perimeters.

EXERCISES

For more practice, see *Extra Practice*.

Practice and Problem Solving

A Practice by Example

Example 1 (page 455)

The figures in each pair are similar. Compare the first figure to the second. Give the ratio of the perimeters and the ratio of the areas.

1.

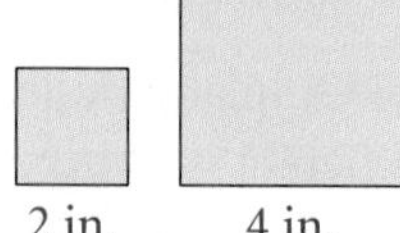

2.

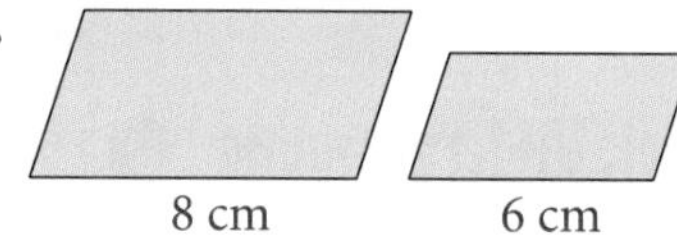

3.

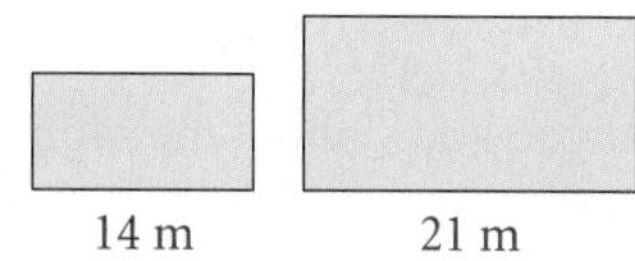

4.

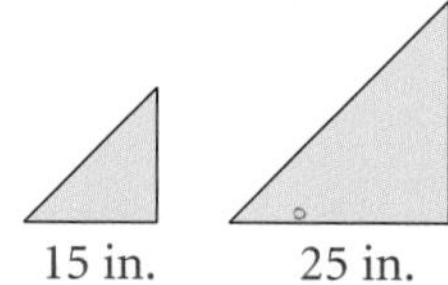

Example 2 (page 455)

The figures in each pair are similar. The area of one figure is given. Find the area of the other figure to the nearest whole number.

5.

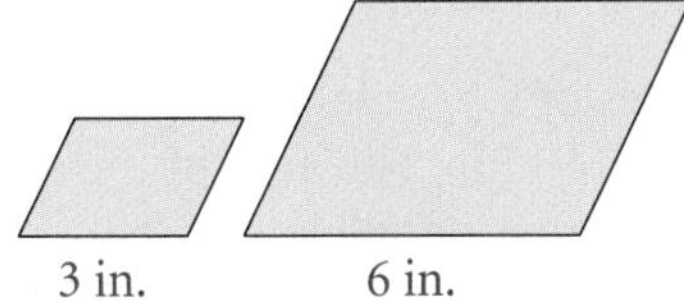

3 in. 6 in.

Area of smaller parallelogram = 6 in.^{2}

6.

12 m 18 m

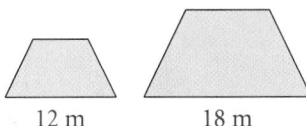

Area of larger trapezoid = 121 m^2

7.

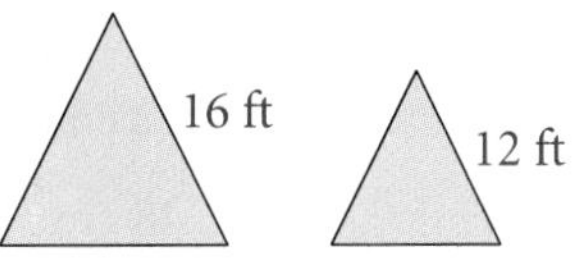

16 ft 12 ft

Area of larger triangle = 105 ft^2

8.

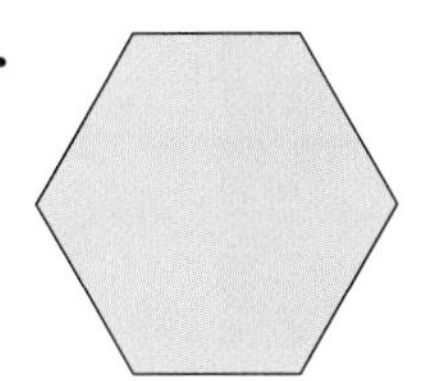

13 m 5 m

Area of smaller hexagon = 65 m^2

Example 3 (page 456)

9. Remodeling It costs a family \$216 to have a 9 ft-by-12 ft wooden floor refinished. At that rate, how much would it cost them to have a 12 ft-by-16 ft wooden floor refinished?

10. Decorating An embroidered placemat costs \$2.95. An embroidered tablecloth is similar to the placemat, but four times as long and four times as wide. How much would you expect to pay for the tablecloth?

Example 4 (page 456)

Find the similarity ratio and the ratio of perimeters for each pair of similar figures.

11. two regular octagons with areas 4 ft^2 and 16 ft^2

12. two triangles with areas 75 m^2 and 12 m^2

13. two trapezoids with areas 49 cm^2 and 9 cm^2

14. two parallelograms with areas 18 in.^{2} and 32 in.^{2}

15. two equilateral triangles with areas $16\sqrt{3}$ ft^2 and $\sqrt{3}$ ft^2

16. two circles with areas 2π cm^2 and 200π cm^2

B Apply Your Skills

The similarity ratio of two similar polygons is given. Find the ratio of their perimeters and the ratio of their areas.

17. 3 : 1 **18.** 2 : 5 **19.** $\frac{2}{3}$ **20.** $\frac{7}{4}$ **21.** 6 : 1

22. The area of a regular decagon is 50 cm^2. What is the area of a regular decagon with sides four times the length of the smaller decagon?

23. Error Analysis A reporter used the graphic below to show that the number of houses with more than two televisions had doubled in the past few years. Explain why this graphic is misleading.

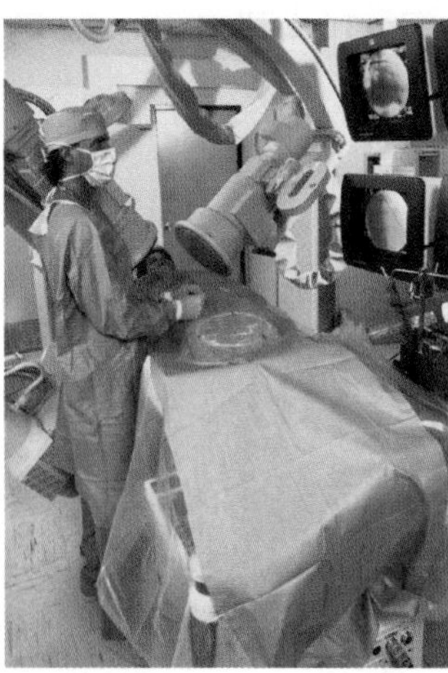

Real-World Connection

Careers Doctors use enlarged images to aid in certain medical procedures.

Need Help?

For Exercise 34, recall the length of a diagonal of a square with 2-in. sides.

24. Medicine For some medical imaging, the scale of the image is 3 : 1. That means that if an image is 3 cm long, the corresponding length on the person's body is 1 cm. Find the actual area of a lesion if its image has area 2.7 cm^2.

25. The longer sides of a parallelogram are 5 m. The longer sides of a similar parallelogram are 15 m. The area of the smaller parallelogram is 28 m^2. What is the area of the larger parallelogram?

Algebra **Find the values of x and y when the smaller triangle shown here has the given area.**

26. 3 cm^2 **27.** 6 cm^2 **28.** 12 cm^2

29. 16 cm^2 **30.** 24 cm^2 **31.** 48 cm^2

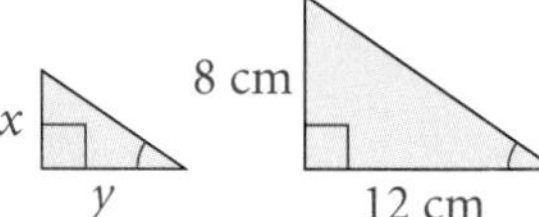

32. Two similar rectangles have areas 27 in.^{2} and 48 in.^{2}. The length of one side of the larger rectangle is 16 in. What are the dimensions of both rectangles?

33. In $\triangle RST$, $RS = 20$ m, $ST = 25$ m, and $RT = 40$ m.

a. Open-Ended Choose a convenient scale. Then use a ruler and compass to draw $\triangle R'S'T' \sim \triangle RST$.

b. Constructions Construct an altitude of $\triangle R'S'T'$ and measure its length. Find the area of $\triangle R'S'T'$.

c. Estimation Estimate the area of $\triangle RST$.

34. Drawing Draw a square with an area of 8 in.^{2}. Draw a second square with an area that is four times as large. What is the ratio of their perimeters?

Compare the blue figure to the red figure. Find the ratios of (a) their perimeters and (b) their areas.

35.

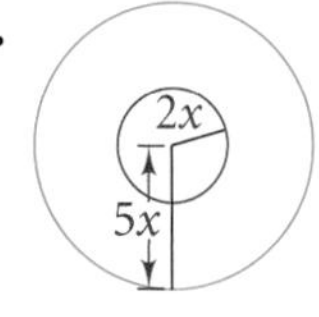

36.

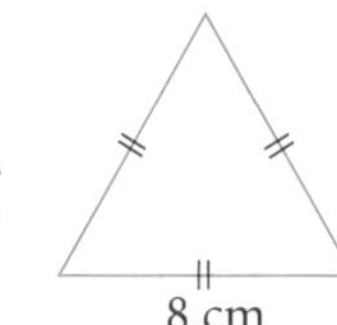

37.

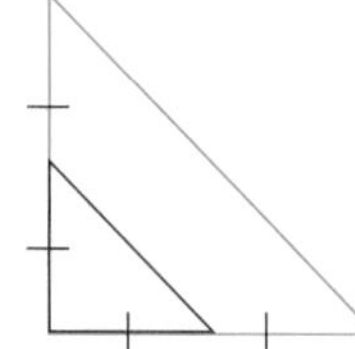

38. Writing The enrollment at an elementary school is going to increase from 200 students to 395 students. A parents' group is planning to increase the 100 ft-by-200 ft playground area to a larger area that is 200 ft by 400 ft. What would you tell the parents' group when they ask your opinion about whether the new playground will be large enough?

39. a. Surveying A surveyor measured one side and two angles of a field as shown in the diagram. Use a ruler and a protractor to draw a similar triangle.

b. Measure the sides and altitude of your triangle and find its perimeter and area.

c. Estimation Estimate the perimeter and area of the field.

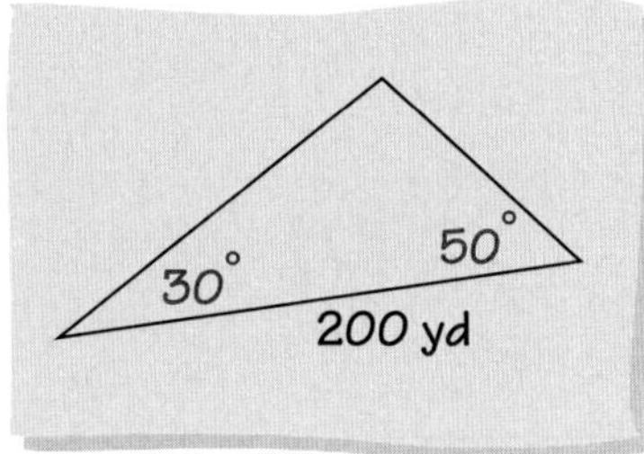

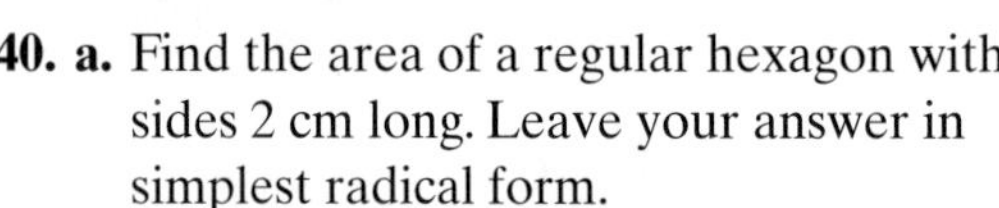

40. a. Find the area of a regular hexagon with sides 2 cm long. Leave your answer in simplest radical form.

b. Use your answer to part (a) and Theorem 8-6 to find the areas of the regular polygons shown at the right.

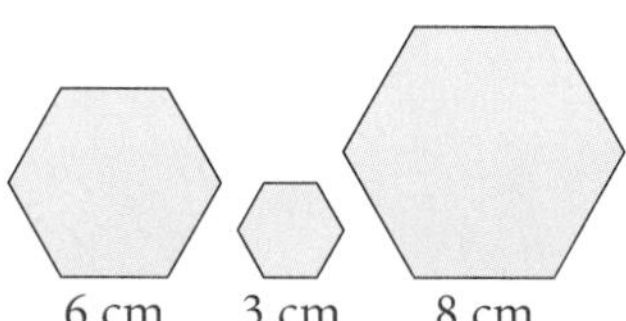

Challenge **Complete each statement with *sometimes*, *always*, or *never*. Justify your answers.**

41. Two similar rectangles with the same perimeter are _?_ congruent.

42. Two rectangles with the same area are _?_ similar.

43. Two rectangles with the same area and different perimeters are _?_ similar.

44. Similar figures _?_ have the same area.

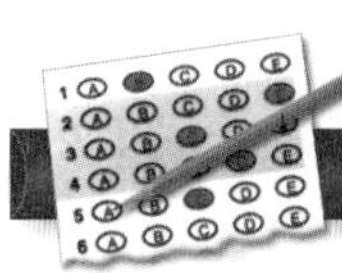

Standardized Test Prep

Gridded Response

45. Two regular hexagons have sides in the ratio 3 : 5. The area of the smaller hexagon is 81 m^2. In square meters, what is the area of the larger hexagon?

46. Two similar polygons have areas in the ratio 9 : 16. The perimeter of the larger polygon is 900. What is the perimeter of the smaller polygon?

47. The two triangles are similar. Their perimeters have the ratio 1 : 3. In square feet, what is the area of the larger triangle?

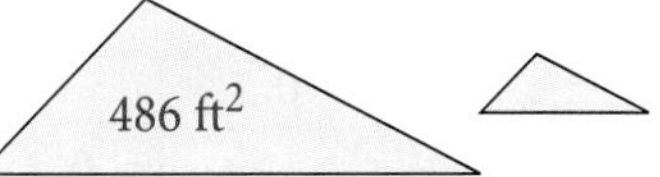

48. A rectangle has a perimeter of 192 in. A similar rectangle has a perimeter of 528 in. The area of the smaller rectangle is 2288 $in.^2$. In square inches, what is the area of the larger rectangle?

49. The area of a polygon is 3267 cm^2. The area of a similar polygon is 9075 cm^2. The perimeter of the larger polygon is 270.5 cm. In centimeters, what is the perimeter of the smaller one?

Take It to the NET
Online lesson quiz at
www.PHSchool.com
Web Code: afa-0806

Mixed Review

Lesson 8-5

50. Solve for x and y in the diagram at the right.

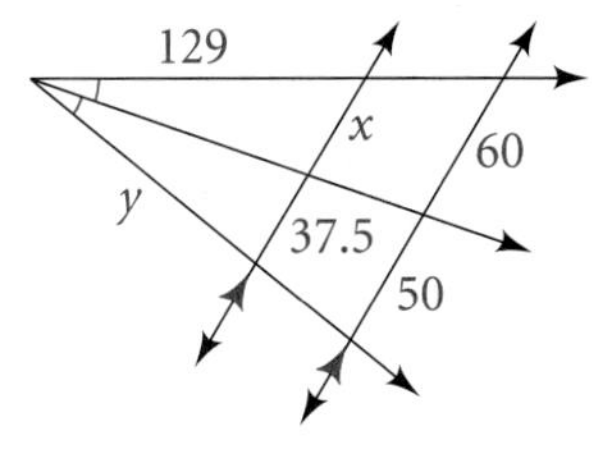

51. An angle bisector divides the opposite side of a triangle into segments 4 cm and 6 cm long. A second side of the triangle is 8 cm long. Find all possible lengths for the third side of the triangle.

Lesson 7-5 **Find the area of each regular polygon.**

52. a square with a 10-cm diagonal

53. a pentagon with apothem 13.8 and side length 20

54. an octagon with apothem 12 and side length 10

55. a 12-sided polygon with apothem 3.7 and side length 2.0

Lesson 3-5 x^2 **Algebra** **Write the equation in slope-intercept form, and graph the line.**

56. $6x - 2y = 8$ **57.** $x + y = -2$ **58.** $3x = 4y$ **59.** $2x + \frac{1}{2}y = \frac{5}{2}$

x^2 **Algebra** **Write the equation of the line described.**

60. has slope -3 and contains point $(1, -2)$

61. contains points $(3, 7)$ and $(0, -1)$

Test-Taking Strategies

Testing Multiple Choices

Your choices in a multiple-choice question include a correct answer. A strategy is to test each choice in the original problem. You may find mental math to be particularly useful for this.

EXAMPLE

Algebra What is the value of x in the diagram at the right?

A. 0 **B.** 3
C. 6 **D.** 10

The triangles are similar. The proportion $\frac{3}{5} = \frac{x}{x+4}$ is apparent in the diagram. You can test the four answer choices using mental math.

Let $x = 0$.
$\frac{x}{x+4} = \frac{0}{0+4} = 0 \neq \frac{3}{5}$
A is not the answer.

Let $x = 3$.
$\frac{x}{x+4} = \frac{3}{3+4} = \frac{3}{7} \neq \frac{3}{5}$
B is not the answer.

Let $x = 6$.
$\frac{x}{x+4} = \frac{6}{6+4} = \frac{6}{10} = \frac{3}{5}$
Yes! C is likely the answer.

To help make sure, let $x = 10$.
$\frac{x}{x+4} = \frac{10}{10+4} = \frac{10}{14} = \frac{5}{7} \neq \frac{3}{5}$
D is not the answer.

You write or mark C as your answer.

EXERCISES

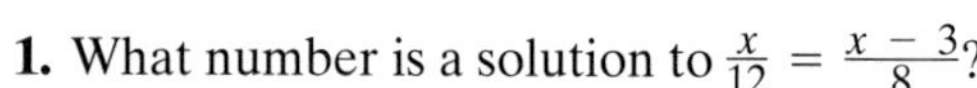

1. What number is a solution to $\frac{x}{12} = \frac{x-3}{8}$?
   A. 1 **B.** 3
   C. 6 **D.** 9

2. What number is a solution to $\frac{8}{13} = \frac{20}{a+12}$?
   F. 20.5 **G.** 31
   H. 34 **I.** 44.5

3. **Algebra** What is the value of x?
   A. 4 **B.** 6
   C. 8 **D.** 10

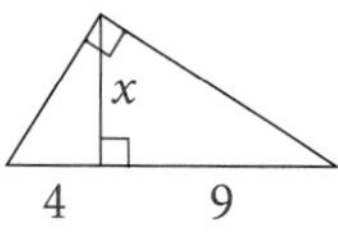

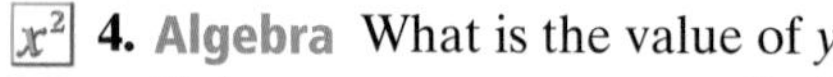

4. **Algebra** What is the value of y?
   F. 2 **G.** 4
   H. 6 **I.** 10

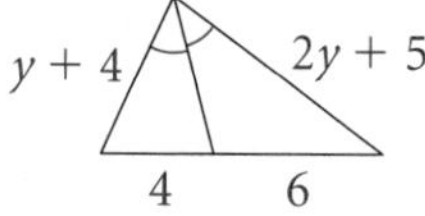

5. $AB = 2$, $CD = 4$, $FE = 10$, and $AE = 20$. What is AC?
   A. 2 **B.** 4
   C. 6 **D.** 8

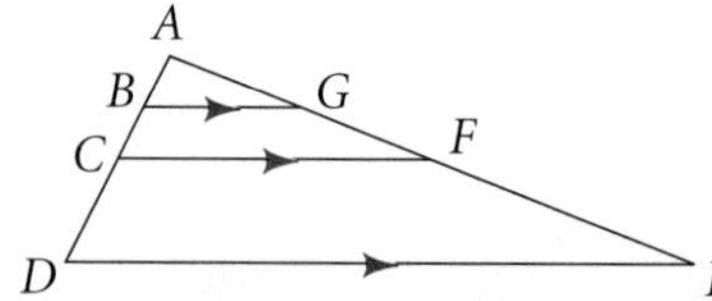

Chapter Review

Vocabulary

Cross-Product Property (p. 417)
extended proportion (p. 417)
geometric mean (p. 440)
golden ratio (p. 425)
golden rectangle (p. 425)
indirect measurement (p. 434)
proportion (p. 417)
scale (p. 418)
scale drawing (p. 418)
similar (p. 423)
similarity ratio (p. 423)

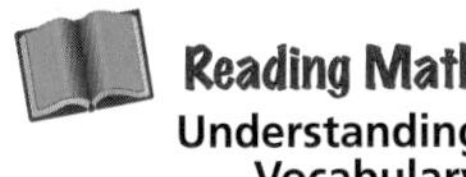

Understanding Vocabulary

Choose the correct term to complete each sentence.

1. Two polygons are _?_ if corresponding angles are congruent and corresponding sides are proportional.
2. The _?_ states that the product of the extremes is equal to the product of the means.
3. A _?_ is a rectangle that can be divided into a square and a rectangle that is similar to the original rectangle.
4. The ratio of the lengths of corresponding sides of two similar figures is the _?_.
5. A _?_ is a statement that two ratios are equal.
6. Finding distances using similar triangles is called _?_.
7. The length and width of a golden rectangle are in the _?_.

Take It to the NET
Online vocabulary quiz at **www.PHSchool.com**
Web Code: afj-0851

Skills and Concepts

8-1 Objectives

▼ To write ratios and solve proportions

A ratio is a comparison of two quantities by division. You can write the ratio of a to b or $a : b$ as the quotient $\frac{a}{b}$ when $b \neq 0$.

A **proportion** is a statement that two ratios are equal. According to the **Properties of Proportions,** $\frac{a}{b} = \frac{c}{d}$ is equivalent to

(1) $ad = bc$ (2) $\frac{b}{a} = \frac{d}{c}$ (3) $\frac{a}{c} = \frac{b}{d}$ (4) $\frac{a+b}{b} = \frac{c+d}{d}$

Property 1, above, illustrates the **Cross-Product Property,** which states that the product of the extremes is equal to the product of the means.

When three or more ratios are equal, you can write an **extended proportion.**

In a **scale drawing,** the **scale** compares each length in the drawing to the actual length being represented.

Dollhouses **Dollhouse furnishings come in different sizes depending on the size of the dollhouse. For each exercise, write a ratio of the size of the dollhouse item to the size of the larger item.**

8. dollhouse sofa: $1\frac{1}{2}$ in. long; real sofa: 6 ft long
9. dollhouse piano: $1\frac{3}{4}$ in. high real piano: 3 ft 6 in. high

If $\frac{p}{q} = \frac{2}{5}$, tell whether each equation must be true. Explain.

10. $2q = 5p$
11. $\frac{5}{2} = \frac{q}{p}$
12. $5q = 2p$
13. $\frac{p}{2} = \frac{q}{5}$

8-2 and 8-3 Objectives

- To identify and apply similar polygons
- To use AA, SAS, and SSS similarity statements
- To apply AA, SAS, and SSS similarity statements

Similar polygons have congruent corresponding angles and proportional corresponding sides. The ratio of the lengths of corresponding sides is the **similarity ratio.**

A **golden rectangle** is a rectangle that can be divided into a square and a rectangle that is similar to the original rectangle. In any golden rectangle, the length and the width are in the **golden ratio,** which is about 1.618 : 1.

If two angles of one triangle are congruent to two angles of another triangle, then the triangles are similar by the **Angle-Angle Similarity Postulate** (AA ~). If an angle of one triangle is congruent to an angle of a second triangle, and the sides including the two angles are proportional, then the triangles are similar by the **Side-Angle-Side Similarity Theorem** (SAS ~). If the corresponding sides of two triangles are proportional, then the triangles are similar by the **Side-Side-Side Similarity Theorem** (SSS ~).

Methods of **indirect measurement** use similar triangles and measurements to find distances that are difficult to measure directly.

14. If $\triangle MNP \sim \triangle RST$, which angles are congruent? Write an extended proportion to indicate the proportional corresponding sides of the triangles.

15. Art An artist is creating a stained glass window and wants it to be a golden rectangle. To the nearest inch, what should be the length if the width is 24 in.?

The triangles are similar. Find the similarity ratio of the first to the second.

16.

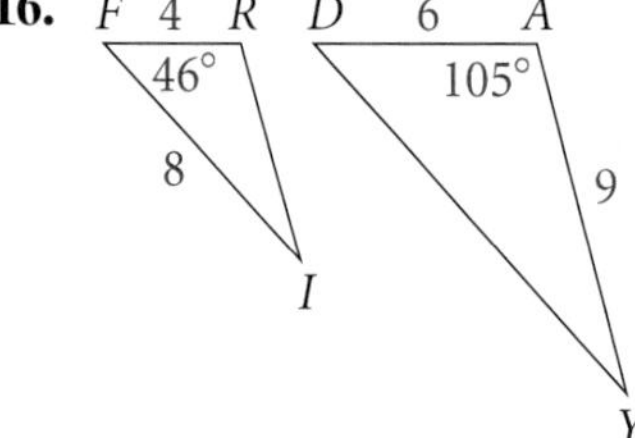

17.

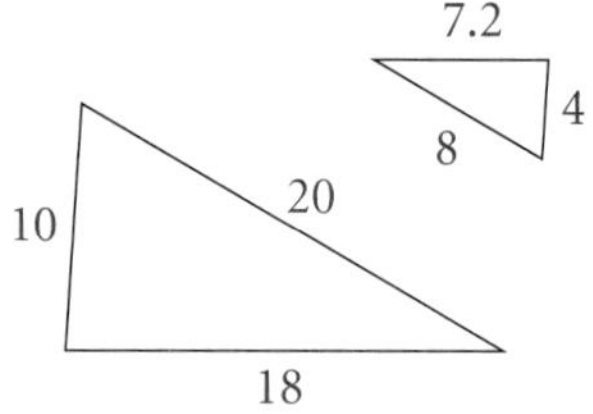

Algebra **The polygons are similar. Find the value of each variable.**

18.

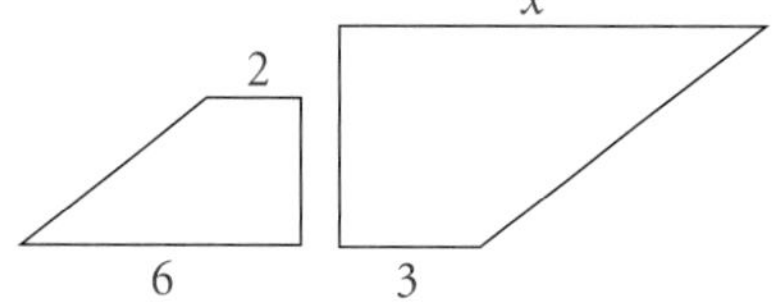

19.

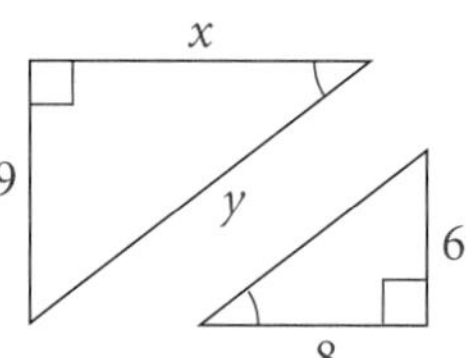

Are the triangles similar? If so, write the similarity statement and name the postulate or theorem you used. If not, explain.

20.

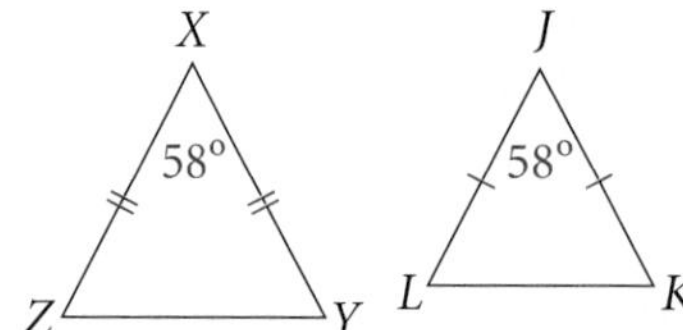

21.

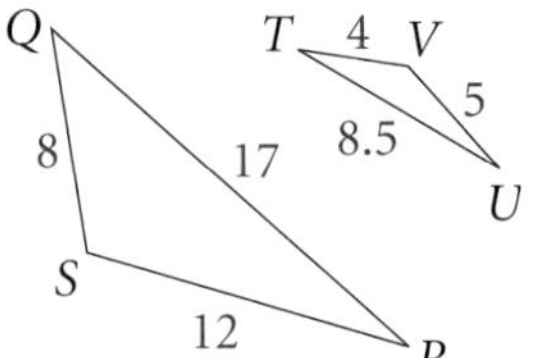

22. Two right triangles have an acute angle with the same measure. Name the theorem or postulate that is the most direct way to prove the triangles similar.

23. Indirect Measurement A crate is 1.5 ft high and casts a 2-ft shadow. At the same time, an apple tree casts an 18-ft shadow. How tall is the tree?

8-4 Objective

▼ To find and use relationships in similar right triangles

The **geometric mean** of two positive numbers a and b is the positive number x such that $\frac{a}{x} = \frac{x}{b}$.

When the altitude is drawn to the hypotenuse of a right triangle:

- the two triangles formed are similar to the original triangle and to each other;
- the length of the altitude is the geometric mean of the lengths of the segments of the hypotenuse; and
- the length of each leg is the geometric mean of the length of the adjacent hypotenuse segment and the length of the hypotenuse.

x^2 Algebra **Find the values of the variables. When an answer is not a whole number, leave it in simplest radical form.**

24. 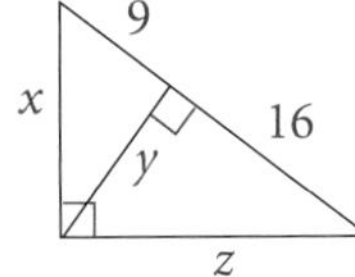

25. 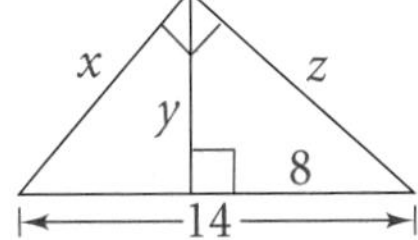

26. 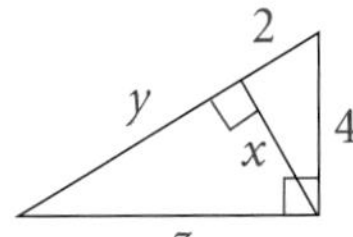

8-5 Objectives

▼ To use the Side-Splitter Theorem

▼ To use the Triangle-Angle-Bisector Theorem

The Side-Splitter Theorem states that if a line is parallel to one side of a triangle and intersects the other two sides, then it divides those sides proportionally. If three parallel lines intersect two transversals, then the segments intercepted on the transversals are proportional. The **Triangle-Angle-Bisector Theorem** states that if a ray bisects an angle of a triangle, then it divides the opposite side into two segments that are proportional to the other two sides of the triangle.

x^2 Algebra **Find the value of x.**

27. 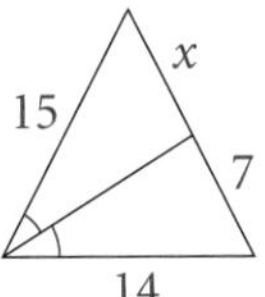

28. 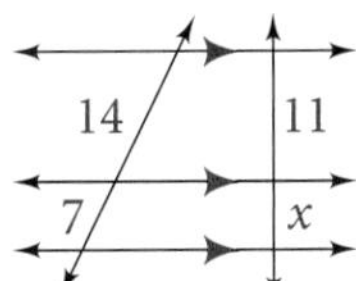

29. 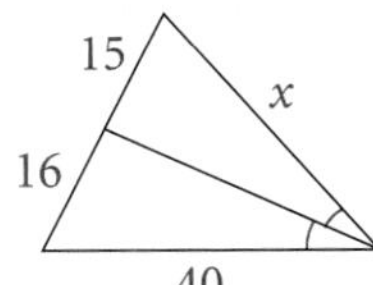

8-6 Objective

▼ To find the perimeters and areas of similar figures

If the similarity ratio of two similar figures is $\frac{a}{b}$, then the ratio of their perimeters is $\frac{a}{b}$, and the ratio of their areas is $\frac{a^2}{b^2}$.

For each pair of similar figures, find the ratio of the area of the first figure to the area of the second.

30. 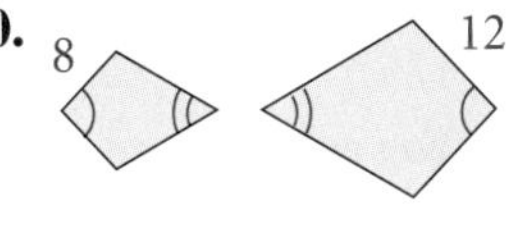

31. 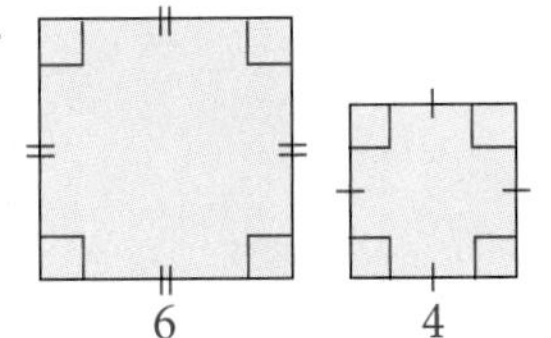

32. 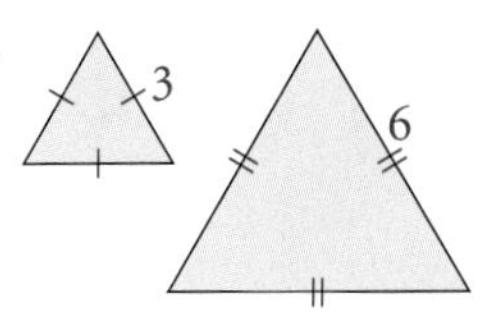

33. If the ratio of areas of two similar hexagons is 8 : 25, what is the ratio of their perimeters?

34. The similarity ratio of two similar triangles is 3 : 7. The area of the smaller triangle is 36 cm^2. What is the area of the larger triangle?

Chapter Test

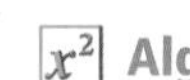 **Algebra Solve each proportion.**

1. $\frac{4}{5} = \frac{x}{20}$ 2. $\frac{6}{x} = \frac{10}{7}$ 3. $\frac{x}{3} = \frac{8}{12}$

 **Algebra The figures in each pair are similar. Find the value of each variable.**

4.
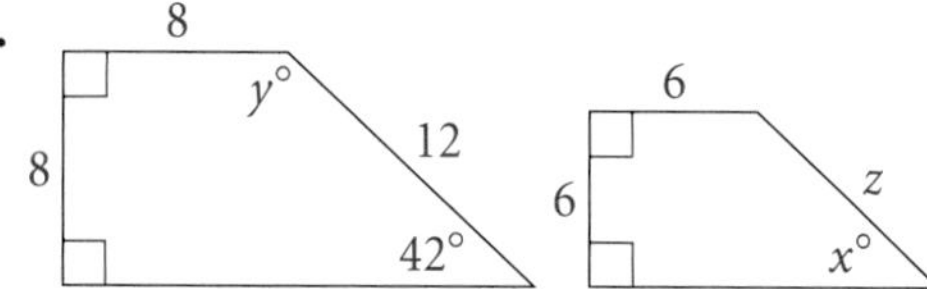

5.
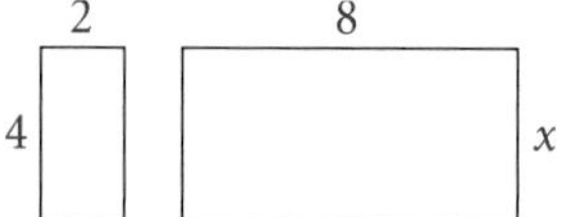

6.
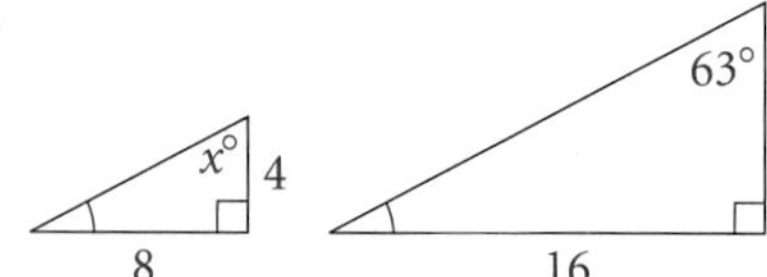

Are the triangles similar? If *yes*, write the similarity statement and name the postulate or theorem you can use to prove they are similar. If *no*, explain.

7.
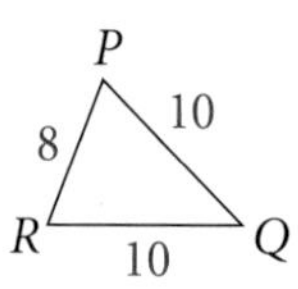

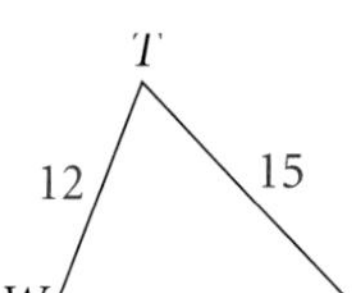

8.
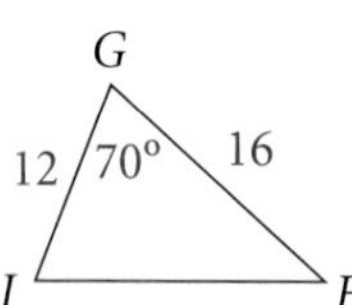

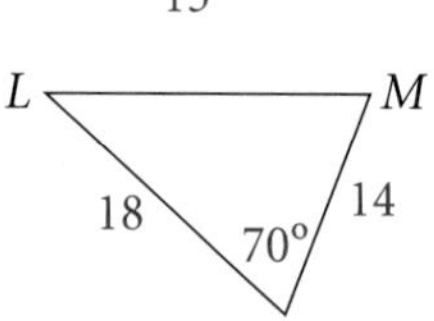

9.
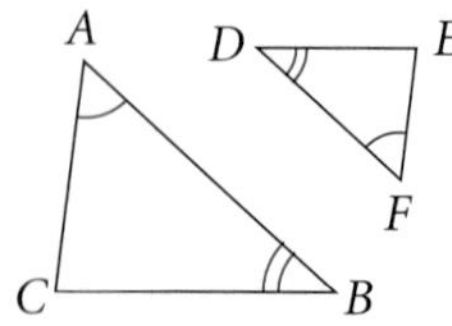

Use the information shown in the diagram and write a proportion for each triangle.

10.
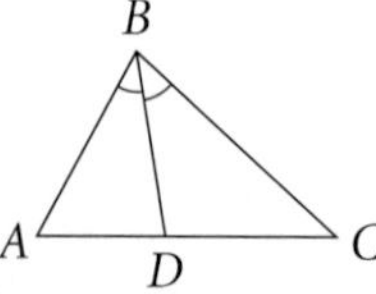

11.
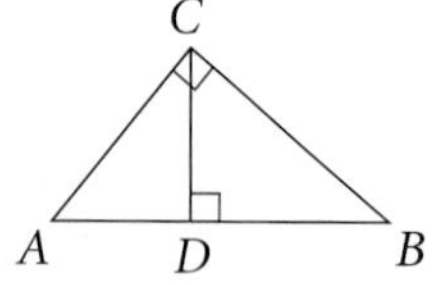

12. **Indirect Measurement** A meter stick is held perpendicular to the ground. It casts a shadow 1.5 m long. At the same time, a telephone pole casts a shadow that is 9 m long. How tall is the telephone pole?

13. **Photography** A photographic negative is 3 cm by 2 cm. If a similar print from the negative is 9 cm long on its shorter side, what is the length of its longer side?

Find the geometric mean of each pair of numbers. If the answer is not a whole number, write it in simplest radical form.

14. 10, 15 15. 4, 9 16. 6, 12

17. **Open-Ended** Draw an isosceles triangle, $\triangle ABC$. Then draw $\triangle DEF$ so that $\triangle ABC \sim \triangle DEF$. State the similarity ratio of $\triangle ABC$ to $\triangle DEF$.

Algebra Find the value of x.

18.
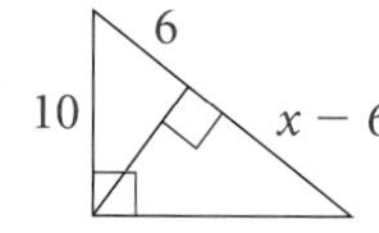

19.
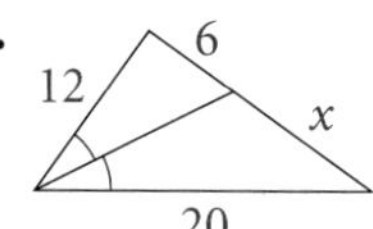

20.
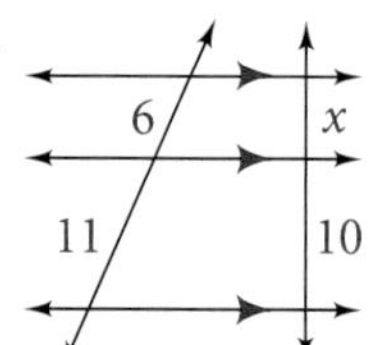

21.
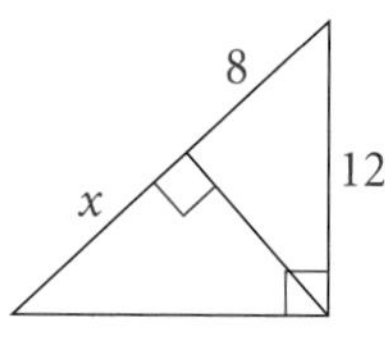

22. **Writing** Describe an object whose height or length would be difficult to measure directly. Then describe a method for measuring the object that involves using similar triangles.

For each pair of similar figures, find the ratio of the area of the first figure to the area of the second.

23.
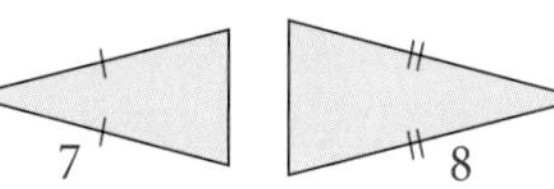

24.

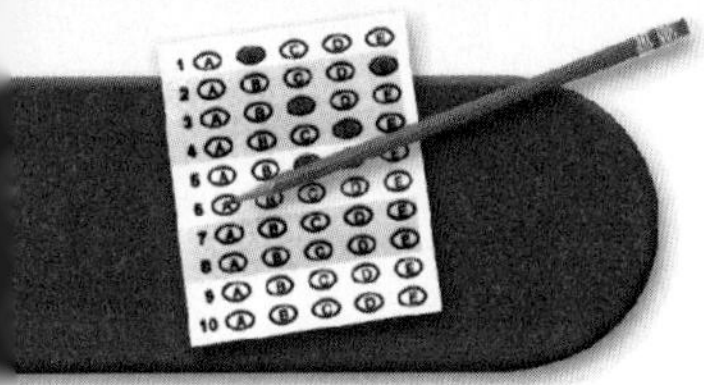

Standardized Test Prep

Multiple Choice

For Exercises 1–7, choose the correct letter.

1. What is the center of the circle that circumscribes $\triangle OMN$?
   A. (0, 0)
   B. (0, −1)
   C. (−1, 0)
   D. (−1, −1)

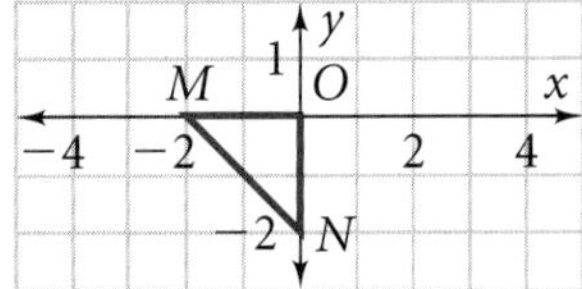

2. Which quadrilateral cannot contain four right angles?
   F. square G. trapezoid
   H. rectangle I. rhombus

3. The lengths of the hypotenuse and one leg of a right triangle are 15 and 10. What is the length of the other leg to the nearest whole number?
   A. 8 B. 9 C. 10 D. 11

4. **Algebra** For which value of x are lines g and h parallel?
   F. 12
   G. 15
   H. 18
   I. 25

$(2x + 10)°$ $(5x - 5)°$ g h

5. Which is an equation of the line that has slope 3 and contains point $P(2, 5)$?
   A. $y = x + 3$ B. $y = x - 3$
   C. $y = 3x + 1$ D. $y = 3x - 1$

6. **Algebra** What is the value of x for this kite?
   F. 48
   G. 52
   H. 62
   I. 68

22° $x°$

7. **Algebra** What is the value of x?
   A. 3.75
   B. 3.9
   C. 4
   D. 4.25

5 x 4 3

8. $\triangle ABC$ has $AB = 7$, $BC = 24$, and $CA = 25$. Which statement is true?
   F. $\triangle ABC$ is an isosceles triangle.
   G. $\triangle ABC$ is a right triangle.
   H. $\angle A$ is the largest angle.
   I. $\angle B$ is the smallest angle.

Quantitative Comparison

Compare the boxed quantity in Column A with the boxed quantity in Column B. Choose the best answer.

A. The quantity in Column A is greater.
B. The quantity in Column B is greater.
C. The two quantities are equal.
D. The relationship cannot be determined from the information given.

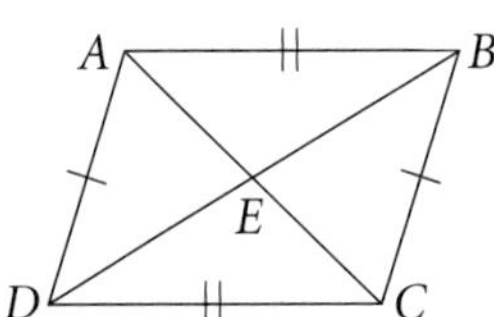

	Column A	Column B
9.	AE	EC
10.	$m\angle ACD$	$m\angle CAD$
11.	$m\angle ADB$	$m\angle CBD$

Gridded Response

12. What is the area in square centimeters of a rhombus with diagonals of lengths 20 cm and 14.2 cm?

Short Response

13. **Constructions** Draw line m with point A on it. Construct a line perpendicular to m at A.

Extended Response

14. In the diagram, $AB = FE$, $BC = ED$, and $AE = FB$.
   a. Is there enough information to prove $\triangle BCG \cong \triangle EDG$?
   b. What one additional piece of information would allow you to prove $\triangle BCD \cong \triangle EDC$?
   c. What can you conclude from the diagram that would help you prove $\triangle BAF \cong \triangle EFA$?
   d. In part (c), is $\triangle BAF \cong \triangle EFA$ by SAS or SSS?

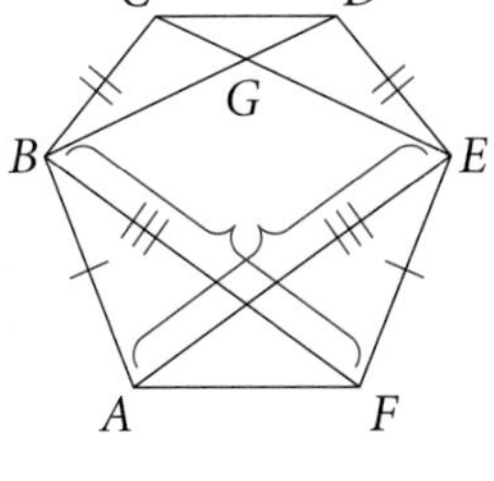

Real-World Snapshots

How Far Can You See?

Applying the Pythagorean Theorem Imagine that you're standing on an ocean beach looking out across the water. The deep blue sky is clearer than you've ever seen it, and it seems as though you can see forever! Well, you know that isn't really possible on Earth. The extent of your vision is limited by Earth's curvature. You can see to the horizon—and perhaps slightly beyond.

The Empire State Building in New York City is 1250 ft tall, not including its mast. 7000 people visit the building each day.

The Bank of China Building in Hong Kong is 1033 ft tall.

A chain of 8000 paper clips dangled from the top floor of 1 Canada Square in London would reach the ground, 797 ft below.

The Chrysler Building in New York City is 1046 ft tall.

The CN Tower in Toronto is 1815 ft tall.

The Eiffel Tower in Paris is 1052 ft tall, which is 16 times as tall as a four-story town house.

The KTHI-TV tower in North Dakota rises to 2063 ft.

Four-story town house, 66 ft tall

The *Saturn V* rocket is 364 ft tall.

Activity 1

Choose one of the structures on these pages. Imagine climbing to the very top to get a good view of the horizon. Assume that Earth is spherical and has a radius of 3963 mi. Also assume that you see a smooth horizon such as that of an ocean or desert. Find the distance from the top of the structure to the horizon. (*Hint:* Use a calculator and the Pythagorean Theorem.)

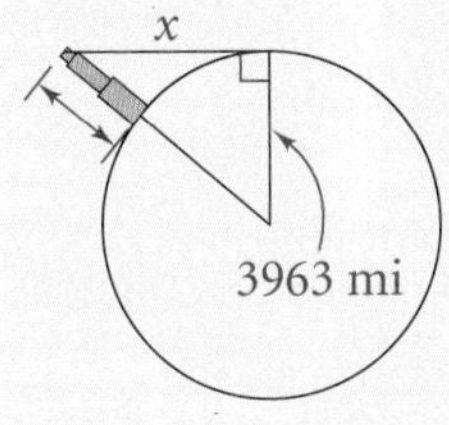

Crow's nest, lookout post for land and ships

Flag indicates ship's origin.

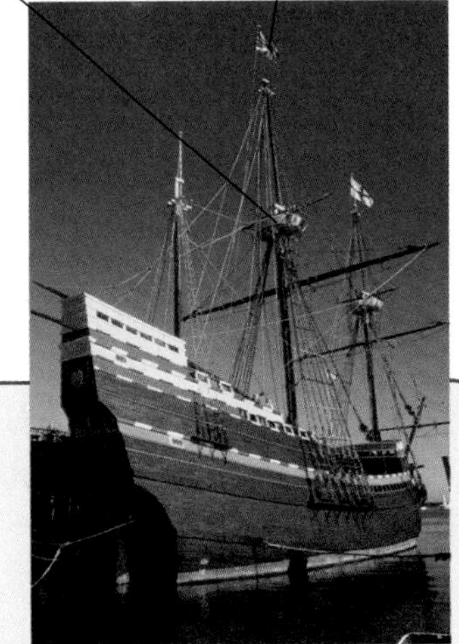

Galleon

Galleons were fighting ships, with 40 to 50 cannons on board.

Activity 2

Sailors used to climb into the crow's nest on a ship's mast so they could spot land and other ships at a greater distance than was possible on deck. Imagine that you are on watch in a crow's nest so that your eyes are 40 ft above the water.

a. Determine the farthest distance from which you could spot the top of a 50-ft tree on a sea-level island.

b. Determine the farthest distance from which you could spot the tree if you were standing on deck with your eyes 15 ft above the water.

c. Compare your answers from parts (a) and (b).

With a spyglass, distant objects appear closer.

Take It to the NET For more information about buildings, go to **www.PHSchool.com**.
Web Code: afe-0853

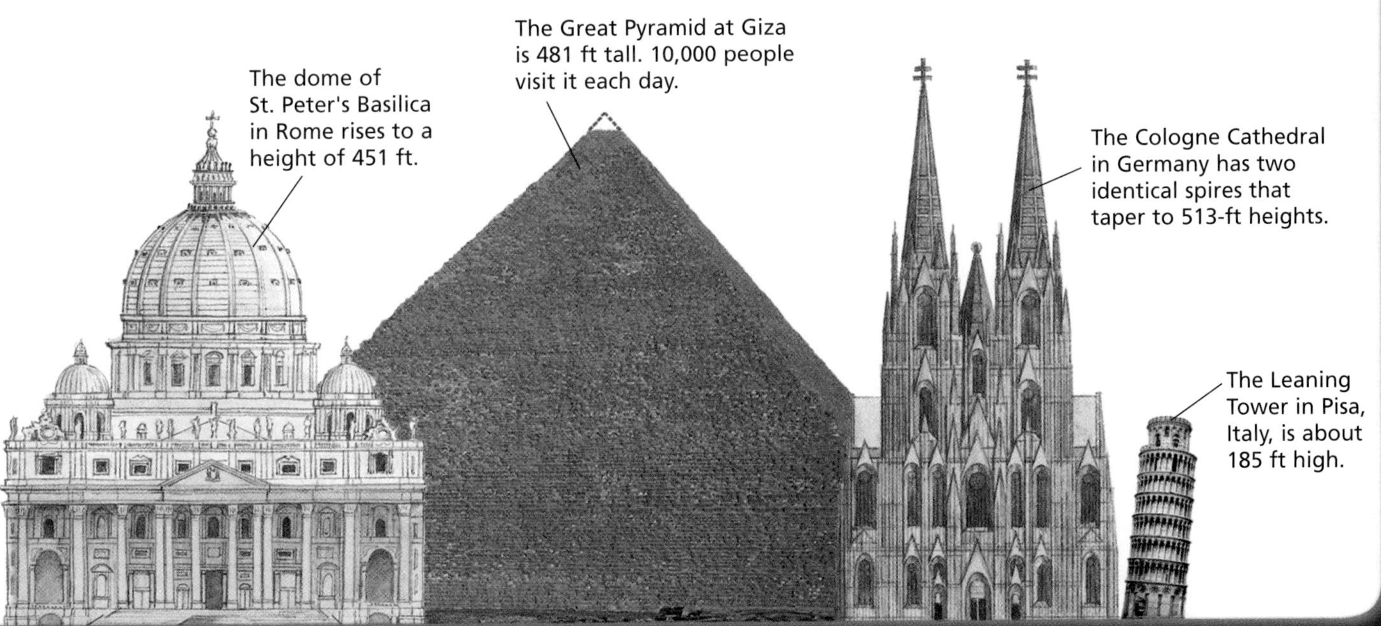

The dome of St. Peter's Basilica in Rome rises to a height of 451 ft.

The Great Pyramid at Giza is 481 ft tall. 10,000 people visit it each day.

The Cologne Cathedral in Germany has two identical spires that taper to 513-ft heights.

The Leaning Tower in Pisa, Italy, is about 185 ft high.

Where You've Been

- In Chapter 7, you learned how to use the Pythagorean Theorem to solve right triangles and to find relationships among the sides of special right triangles.
- In Chapter 8, you learned how to prove triangles similar and that corresponding sides of similar triangles are in proportion.
- In Chapter 7, you learned how to find the area of a triangle. In Chapter 8, you learned how areas of similar triangles are related.

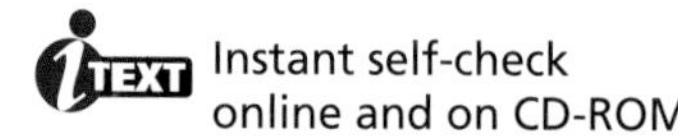

Instant self-check online and on CD-ROM

Diagnosing Readiness

(For help, go to the Lesson in green.)

Solving Proportions (Lesson 8-1)

Algebra Solve for x. Round answers to the nearest thousandth.

1. $0.2734 = \frac{x}{17}$ **2.** $0.5858 = \frac{24}{x}$ **3.** $0.8572 = \frac{5271}{x}$ **4.** $0.5 = \frac{x}{3x + 5}$

Proving Triangles Similar (Lesson 8-3)

Name the postulate or theorem that proves each pair of triangles similar.

5. $\overline{CD} \parallel \overline{AB}$

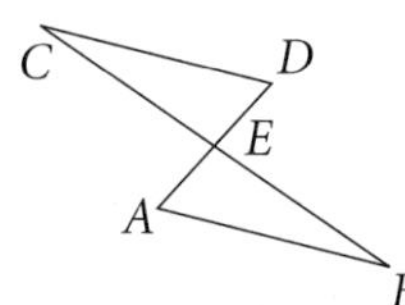

6.

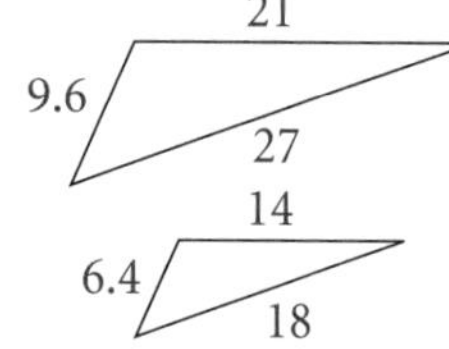

7. $\overline{JK} \perp \overline{ML}$

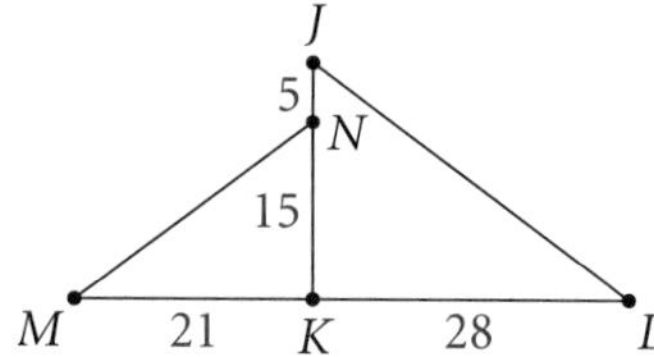

Similarity in Right Triangles (Lesson 8-4)

Algebra Find the unknown quantity in $\triangle ABC$ with right $\angle C$ and altitude $\overline{CD}$.

8.

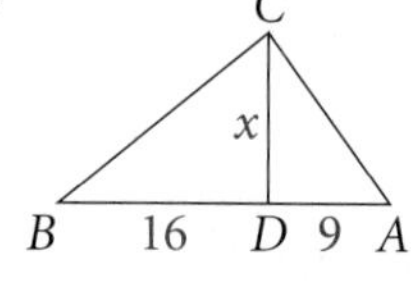

9.

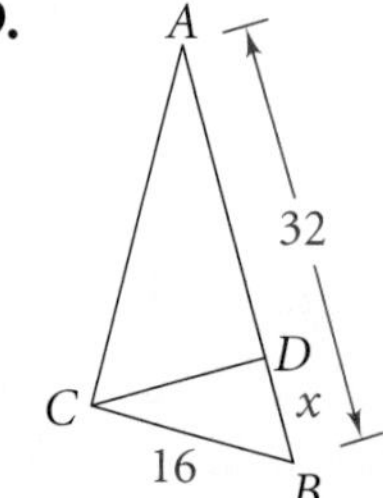

10.

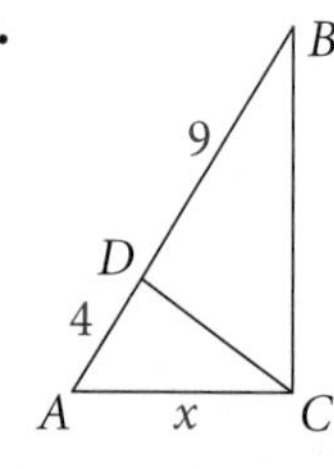

11.

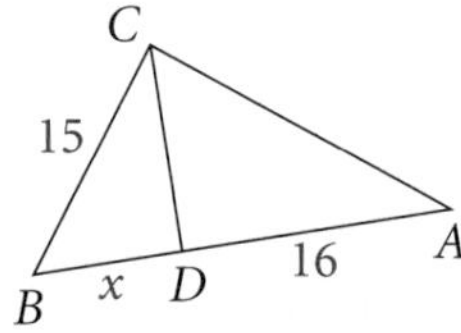

Right Triangle Trigonometry

Chapter 9

LESSONS

Key Vocabulary

- angle of depression (p. 482)
- angle of elevation (p. 482)
- cosine (p. 477)
- identity (p. 478)
- initial point (p. 490)
- magnitude (p. 490)
- resultant (p. 492)
- sine (p. 477)
- tangent (p. 470)
- terminal point (p. 490)
- vector (p. 490)

Where You're Going

- In this chapter, you will use similar right triangles to define the sine, cosine, and tangent ratios.
- With these ratios, you will solve height and distance problems using angles of elevation and angles of depression.
- You will also learn how to use vectors as a tool in other applications of trigonometry.

Real-World Connection Applying what you learn, you will find the height of a cloud layer on page 486.

The Tangent Ratio

Lesson Preview

What You'll Learn

To use tangent ratios to determine side lengths in triangles

. . . And Why

To use the tangent ratio to estimate distance to a distant object, as in Example 2

✓ Check Skills You'll Need

(For help, go to Lessons 7-3 and 8-1.)

Find the ratios $\frac{BC}{AB}$, $\frac{AC}{AB}$, and $\frac{BC}{AC}$. Round answers to the nearest hundredth.

1.

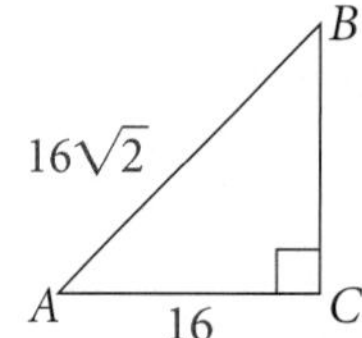

2.

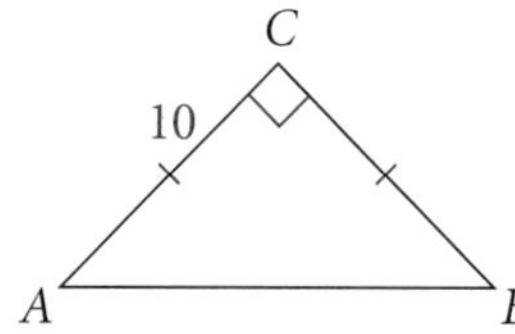

3.

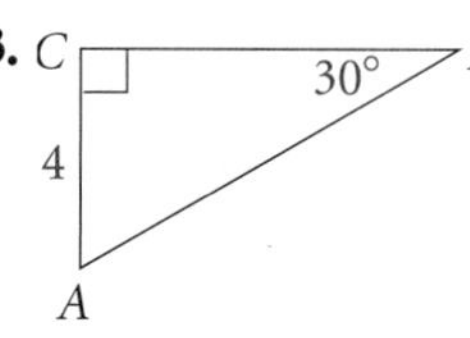

x^2 Algebra **Solve each proportion.**

4. $\frac{x}{3} = \frac{4}{7}$ **5.** $\frac{6}{11} = \frac{x}{9}$ **6.** $\frac{8}{15} = \frac{4}{x}$ **7.** $\frac{5}{x} = \frac{7}{12}$

New Vocabulary • tangent

Interactive lesson includes instant self-check, tutorials, and activities.

OBJECTIVE 1

Using Tangents in Triangles

Investigation: Tangent Ratios

Work in groups of three or four.

- Have your group select one angle measure from {10°, 20°, . . . , 80°}. Then have each member of your group draw a right triangle, $\triangle ABC$, where $\angle A$ has the selected measure. Make the triangles different sizes.
- Measure the legs of each $\triangle ABC$ to the nearest millimeter.

1. Compute the ratio $\frac{\text{leg opposite } \angle A}{\text{leg adjacent to } \angle A}$ and round to two decimal places.

2. Compare the ratios in your group. Make a conjecture.

Reading Math

Trigonometry comes from the Greek words *trigonon* and *metria* meaning "triangle measurement."

In a right triangle, $\triangle ABC$, the ratio of the length of the leg opposite $\angle A$ to the length of the leg adjacent to $\angle A$ is constant, no matter what lengths are chosen for the sides of the triangles. This trigonometric ratio is called the tangent ratio.

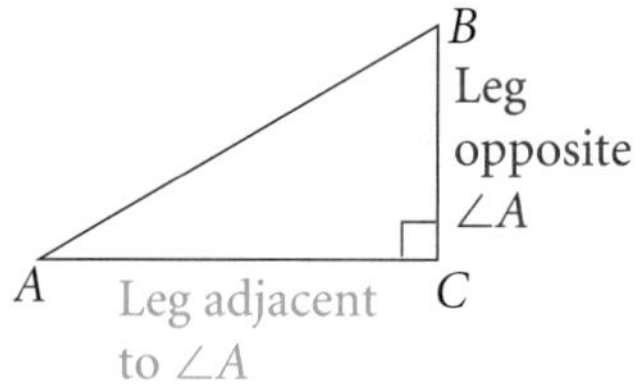

$$\textbf{tangent} \text{ of } \angle A = \frac{\text{length of leg opposite } \angle A}{\text{length of leg adjacent to } \angle A}$$

You can abbreviate this equation as $\tan A = \frac{\text{opposite}}{\text{adjacent}}$.

1 EXAMPLE Writing Tangent Ratios

Write the tangent ratios for $\angle T$ and $\angle U$.

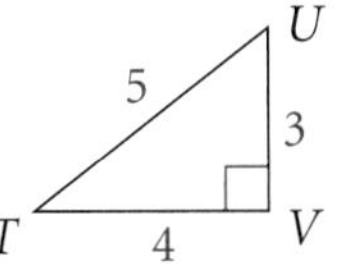

$$\tan T = \frac{\text{opposite}}{\text{adjacent}} = \frac{UV}{TV} = \frac{3}{4}$$

$$\tan U = \frac{\text{opposite}}{\text{adjacent}} = \frac{TV}{UV} = \frac{4}{3}$$

✔ Check Understanding 1 **a.** Write the tangent ratios for $\angle K$ and $\angle J$.
b. How is $\tan K$ related to $\tan J$?

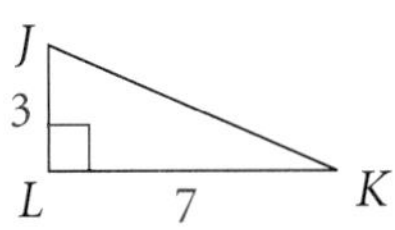

As stated on the facing page, the tangent ratio for an acute angle does not depend on leg lengths of a right triangle. To see why this is so, consider the congruent angles, $\angle T$ and $\angle T'$, in the two right triangles shown here.

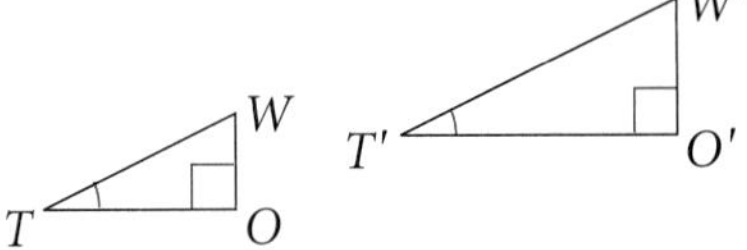

$\triangle TOW \sim T'O'W'$	**AA Similarity Postulate**
$\frac{OW}{TO} = \frac{O'W'}{T'O'}$	**Corresponding sides of ~ triangles are proportional.**
$\tan T = \tan T'$	**Substitute.**

You can use the tangent ratio to measure distances that would be difficult to measure directly.

2 EXAMPLE Real-World Connection

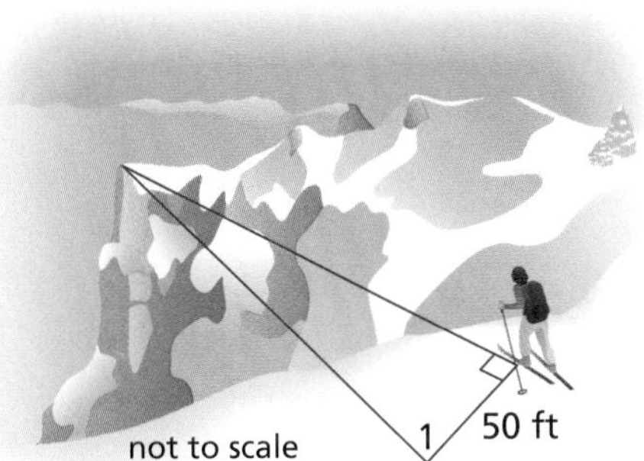

Cross-Country Skiing Your goal in Bryce Canyon National Park is the distant cliff. About how far away is the cliff?

Step 1 Point your compass at a distinctive feature of the cliff and note the reading.

Step 2 Turn 90° and stride 50 ft in a straight path.

Step 3 Turn and point the compass again at the same feature seen in Step 1. Take a reading.

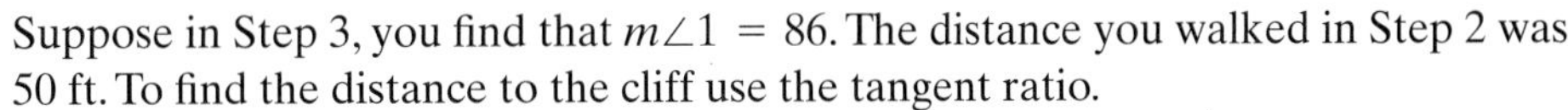

Suppose in Step 3, you find that $m\angle 1 = 86$. The distance you walked in Step 2 was 50 ft. To find the distance to the cliff use the tangent ratio.

$\tan 86^\circ = \frac{x}{50}$	**Use the tangent ratio.**
$x = 50(\tan 86^\circ)$	**Solve for *x*.**
50 TAN 86 ENTER 715.03331	**Use a calculator.**

The cliff is about 715 ft away.

✔ Check Understanding 2 Find the value of w to the nearest tenth.

a.

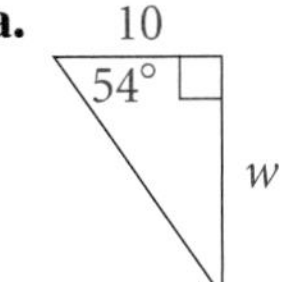

b.

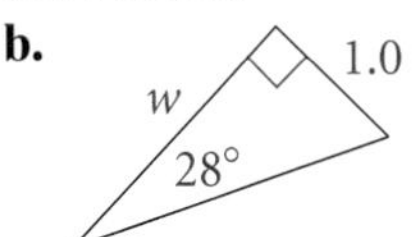

c.

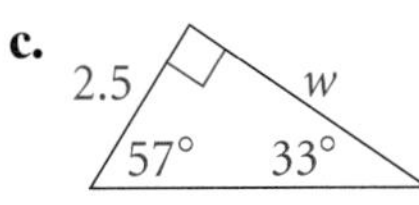

If you know leg lengths for a right triangle, you can find the tangent ratio for each acute angle. Conversely, if you know the tangent ratio for an angle, you can use inverse of tangent, $\tan^{-1}$, to find the measure of the angle.

3 EXAMPLE Using the Inverse of Tangent

The lengths of the sides of $\triangle BHX$ are given. Find $m\angle X$ to the nearest degree.

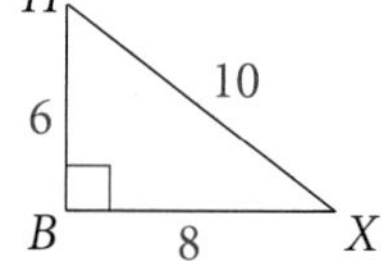

Reading Math

Think of $\tan^{-1}(0.75)$ as "the angle whose tangent is 0.75."

$\tan X = \frac{6}{8} = 0.75$ **Find the tangent ratio.**

$m\angle X = \tan^{-1}(0.75)$ **Use the inverse of tangent.**

TAN^{-1} 0.75 ENTER 36.869898 **Use a calculator.**

So $m\angle X \approx 37$.

Check Understanding 3 Find $m\angle Y$ to the nearest degree.

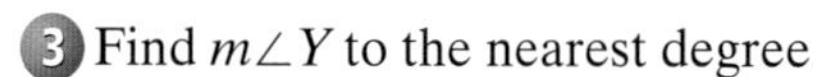

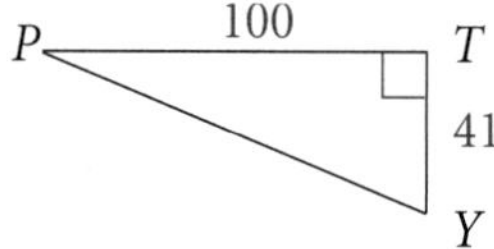

EXERCISES

For more practice, see *Extra Practice.*

Practice and Problem Solving

A Practice by Example

Example 1 (page 471)

Write the tangent ratios for $\angle A$ and $\angle B$.

1. 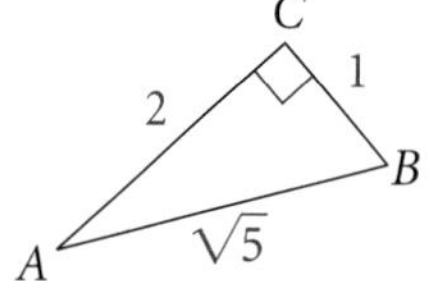

2. 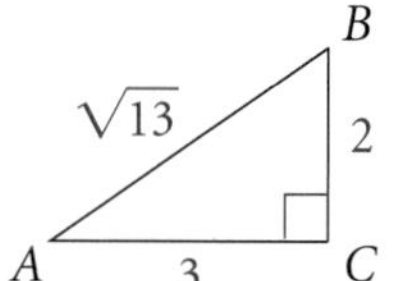

3. 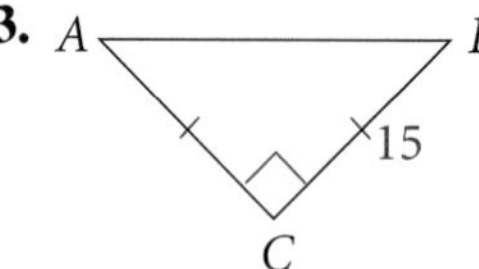

Example 2 (page 471)

Find the value of x to the nearest tenth.

4. 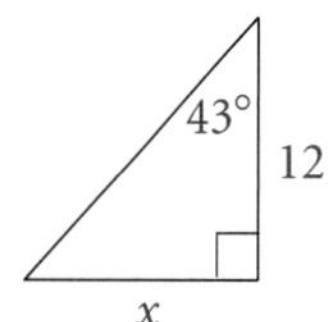

5. 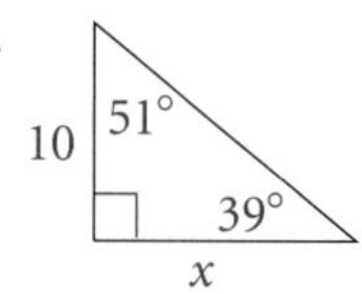

6. 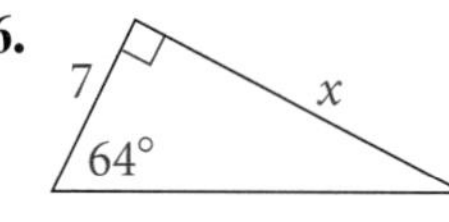

7. 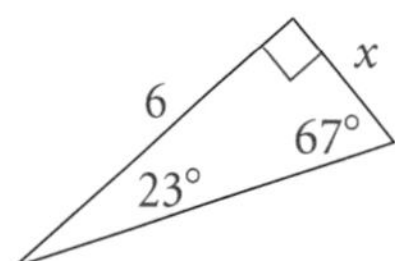

8. 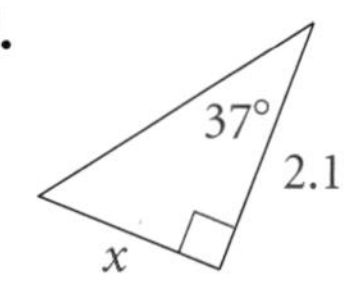

9. 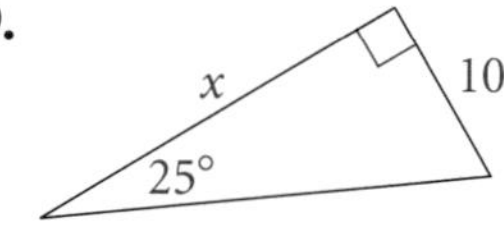

10. **Surveying** To find the distance from the boathouse on shore to the cabin on the island, a surveyor measures from the boathouse to point X as shown. He then finds $m\angle X$ with an instrument called a transit. Use the surveyor's measurements to find the distance from the boathouse to the cabin.

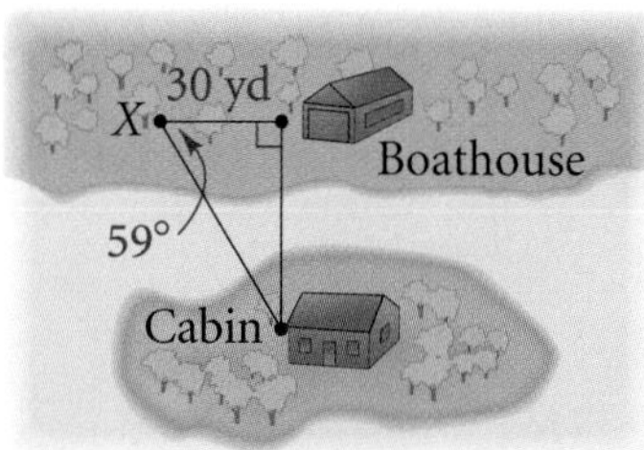

Example 3 (page 472)

Find the value of x to the nearest degree.

11. 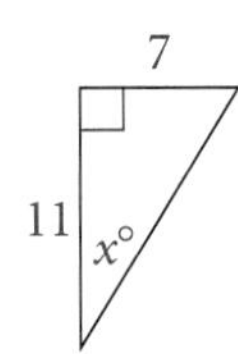

12. 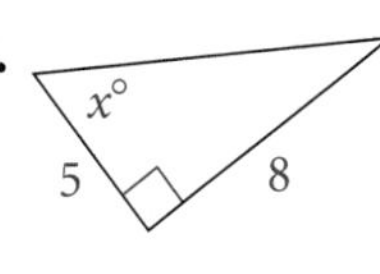

13. 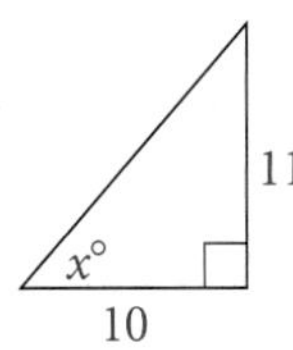

14. 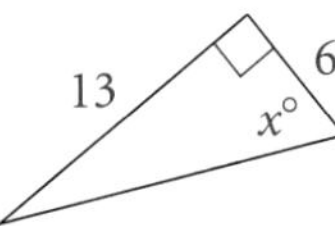

15. 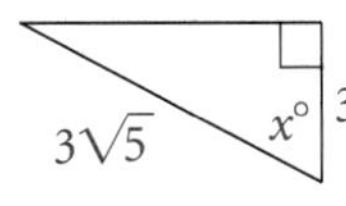

16. 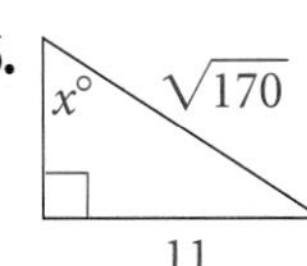

Find each missing value to the nearest tenth.

17. $\tan ■° = 3.5$ **18.** $\tan 34° = \frac{■}{20}$ **19.** $\tan 2° = \frac{4}{■}$ **20.** $\tan ■° = 90$

B Apply Your Skills

21. The lengths of the diagonals of a rhombus are 2 in. and 5 in. Find the measures of the angles of the rhombus to the nearest degree.

22. Pyramids All but two of the pyramids built by the ancient Egyptians have faces inclined at 52° angles. Suppose an archaeologist discovers the ruins of a pyramid. Most of the pyramid has eroded, but she is able to determine that the length of a side of the square base is 82 m. How tall was the pyramid, assuming its faces were inclined at 52°? Round your answer to the nearest meter.

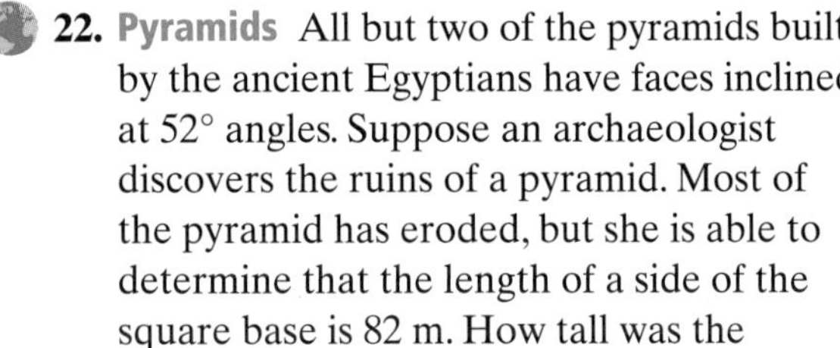

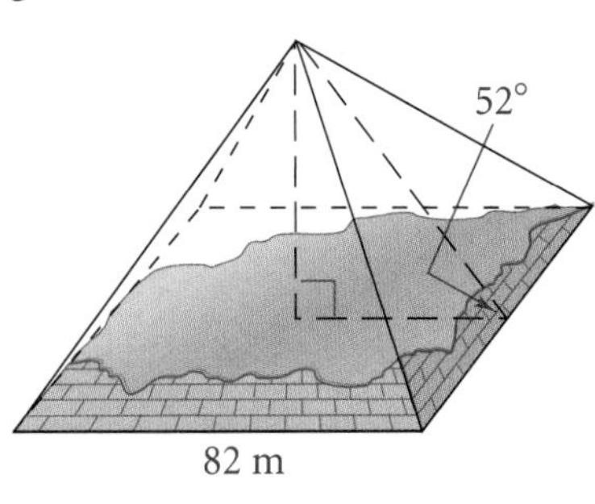

Need Help?

A Pythagorean triple is a set of three nonzero whole numbers, a, b, and c, for which $a^2 + b^2 = c^2$ (p. 357).

23. Open-Ended Select a Pythagorean triple other than a multiple of 3, 4, 5. Find the measures of the acute angles of the right triangle associated with your Pythagorean triple. Round each measure to the nearest tenth.

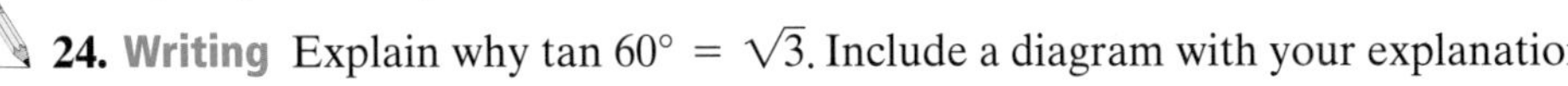

24. Writing Explain why $\tan 60° = \sqrt{3}$. Include a diagram with your explanation.

25. Explain why $\tan^{-1} \frac{\sqrt{2}}{\sqrt{2}} = 45°$.

26. A rectangle is 80 cm long and 20 cm wide. To the nearest degree, find the measures of the angles formed by the diagonals at the center of the rectangle.

Find the value of w, then x. Round lengths of segments to the nearest tenth. Round angle measures to the nearest degree.

27. 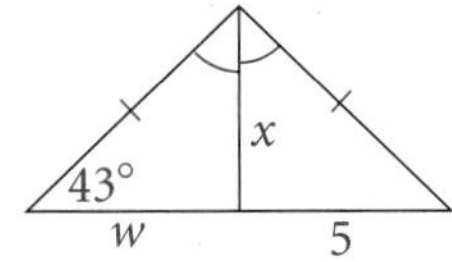

28. 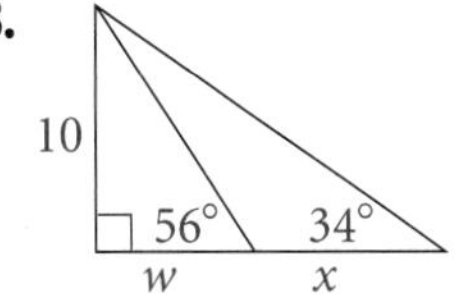

29. 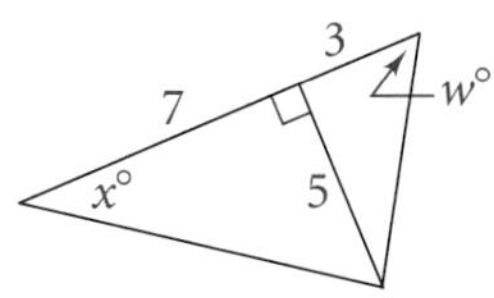

30. a. Coordinate Geometry Complete the table of values at the right. Give table entries to the nearest tenth.

b. Plot the points $(x, \tan x°)$ on the coordinate plane. Connect the points with a smooth curve.

c. What happens to the tangent ratio as the angle measure x approaches 0? Approaches 90?

d. Use your graph to estimate each value.

$\tan ■° = 7$ $\tan 68° = ■$ $\tan ■° = 3.5$

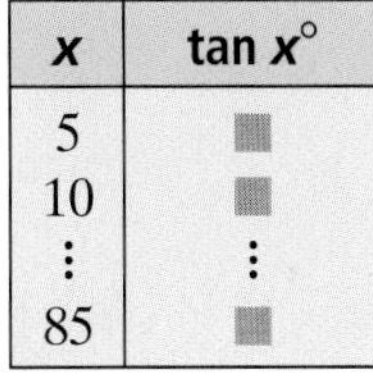

x	$\tan x°$
5	■
10	■
⋮	⋮
85	■

Real-World Connection

The world's steepest railway is the Katoomba Scenic Railway in Australia's Blue Mountains.

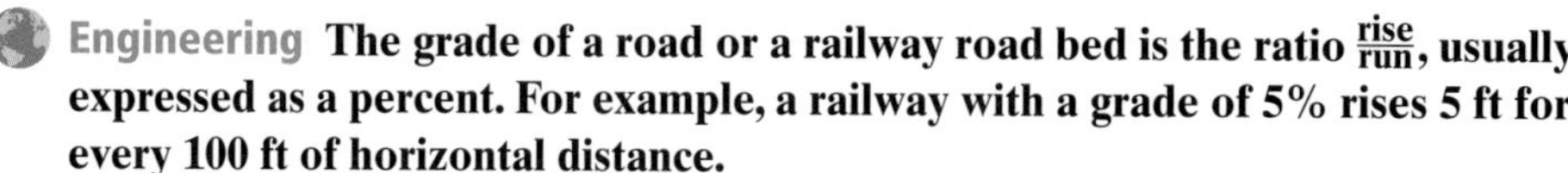

Engineering **The grade of a road or a railway road bed is the ratio $\frac{\text{rise}}{\text{run}}$, usually expressed as a percent. For example, a railway with a grade of 5% rises 5 ft for every 100 ft of horizontal distance.**

31. The Katoomba Railway, pictured at left, has a grade of 122%. What angle does its roadbed make with the horizontal?

32. The Johnstown, Pennsylvania, inclined railway was built as a "lifesaver" after the Johnstown flood of 1889. It has a 987-ft run at a 71% grade. How high does this railway lift its passengers?

33. The Fenelon Place Elevator railway in Dubuque, Iowa, lifts passengers 189 ft to the top of a bluff. It has an 83% grade. How long is this railway?

34. The Duquesne Incline Plane Company's roadway in Pittsburgh, Pennsylvania, climbs Mt. Washington, located above the mouth of the Monongahela River. It reaches a height of 400 ft with a 793-ft incline. What is its grade?

Find the missing value to the nearest tenth.

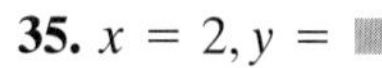

35. $x = 2, y = $ ■ **36.** $x = 2\sqrt{3}, y = $ ■ **37.** $x = 6, y = $ ■

38. $x = 6\sqrt{3}, y = $ ■ **39.** $x = $ ■$, y = 15$ **40.** $x = $ ■$, y = 30$

41. $x = $ ■, $y = 45$ **42.** $x = $ ■, $y = 60$ **43.** $x = $ ■, $y = 75$

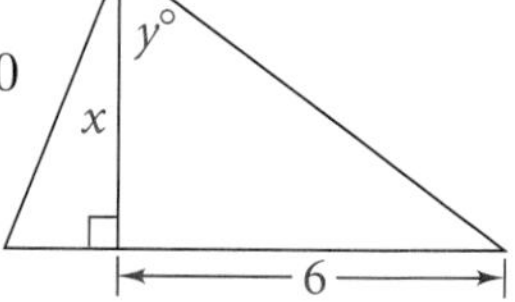

44. a. Critical Thinking Does $\tan A + \tan B = \tan(A + B)$ when $A + B < 90$? Explain.

b. Reasoning Does $\tan A - \tan B = \tan(A - B)$ when $A - B > 0$? Use part (a) and indirect reasoning to explain.

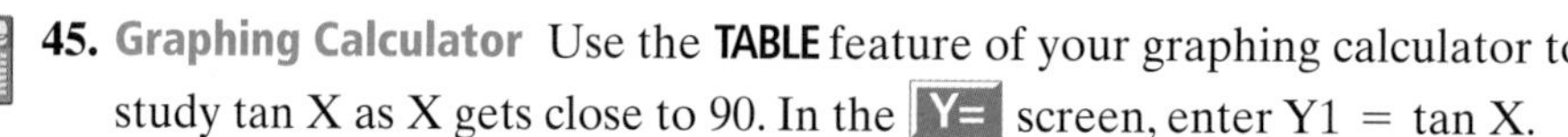

45. Graphing Calculator Use the **TABLE** feature of your graphing calculator to study tan X as X gets close to 90. In the **Y=** screen, enter Y1 = tan X.

a. Use the **TBLSET** feature so that X starts at 80 and changes by 1. Access the **TABLE**. From the table, what is tan X for X = 89?

b. Perform a "numerical zoom in." Use the **TBLSET** feature, so that X starts with 89 and changes by 0.1. What is tan X for X = 89.9?

c. Continue to numerically zoom in on values close to 90. What is the greatest value you can get for tan X on your calculator? How close is X to 90?

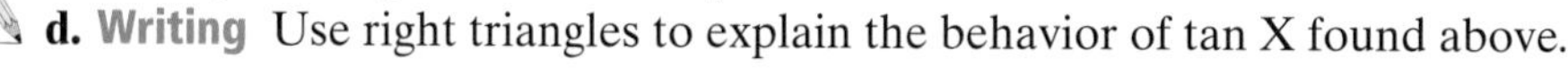

d. Writing Use right triangles to explain the behavior of tan X found above.

Take It to the NET

Graphing Calculator procedures online at **www.PHSchool.com**

Web Code: afe-2111

C Challenge

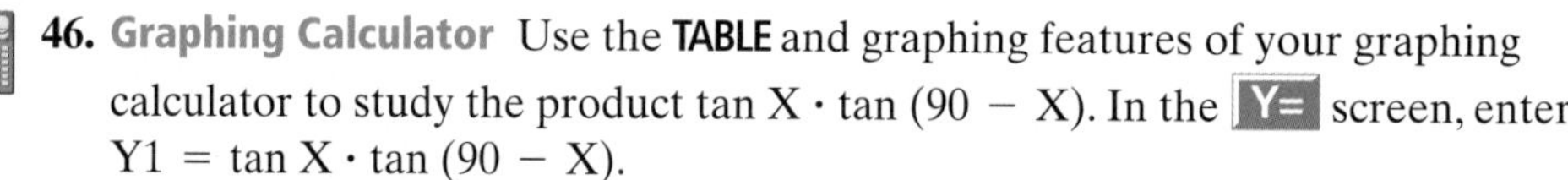

46. Graphing Calculator Use the **TABLE** and graphing features of your graphing calculator to study the product tan X · tan (90 − X). In the **Y=** screen, enter Y1 = tan X · tan (90 − X).

a. Use the **TBLSET** feature so that X starts at 1 and changes by 1. Access the **TABLE**. What do you notice?

b. Press **GRAPH**. What do you notice?

Proof **c.** Make a conjecture about tan X · tan (90 − X) based on parts (a) and (b). Write a paragraph proof of your conjecture.

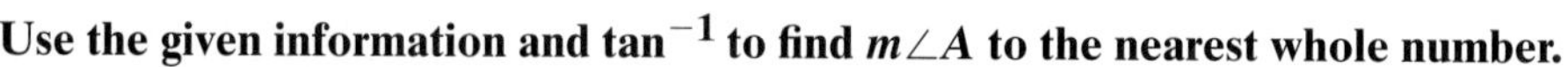

Use the given information and $\tan^{-1}$ to find $m\angle A$ to the nearest whole number.

47. $\tan 2A = 9.5144$

48. $\tan \frac{A}{3} = 0.4663$

49. $(\tan 5A)^2 = 0.3333$

50. $\frac{\tan A}{1 + \tan A} = 0.5437$

Simplify each expression. (*Hint:* Recall from p. 472 how to think of $\tan^{-1} x$.)

51. $\tan(\tan^{-1} x)$

52. $\tan^{-1}(\tan X)$

Coordinate Geometry **You can use the slope of a line to find the measure of the acute angle that the line forms with any horizontal line.**

$$\text{slope} = \frac{\text{rise}}{\text{run}} = 3$$

$$\tan A = \frac{\text{opposite}}{\text{adjacent}} = 3$$

$$m\angle A = \tan^{-1}(3) \approx 71.6$$

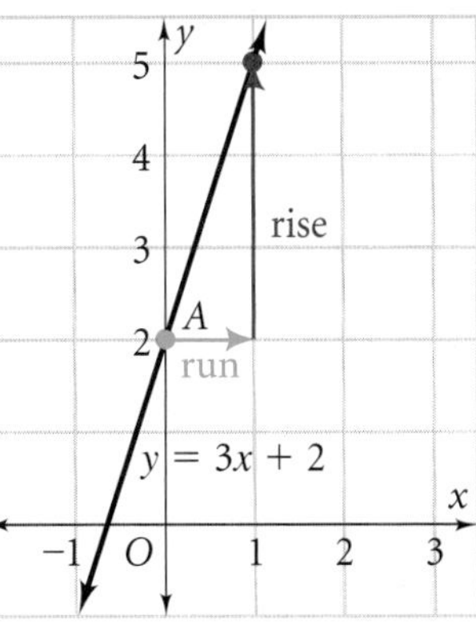

To the nearest tenth, find the measure of the acute angle that the line forms with a horizontal line.

53. $y = \frac{1}{2}x + 6$

54. $y = 6x - 1$

55. $y = 5x - 7$

56. $y = \frac{4}{3}x - 1$

57. $3x - 4y = 8$

58. $-2x + 3y = 6$

Standardized Test Prep

Gridded Response

59. What is tan 84° to the nearest tenth?

60. What is the whole number value of $\tan^{-1}\sqrt{3}$?

In Exercises 61–64 what is the value of x to the nearest tenth?

61.

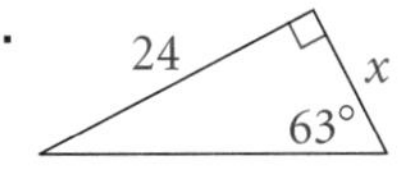

62.

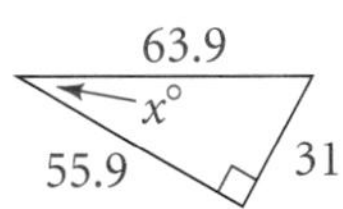

63.

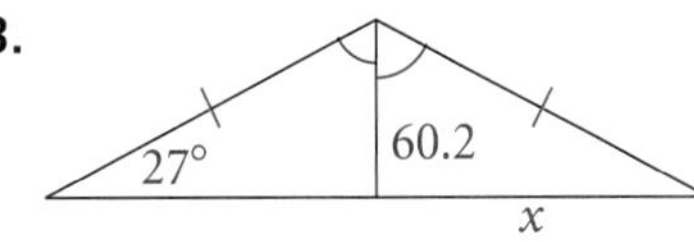

64.

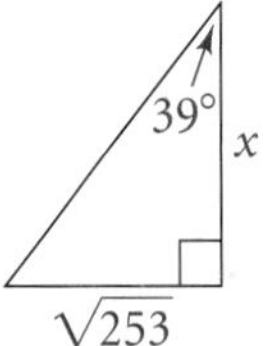

Online lesson quiz at **www.PHSchool.com**
Web Code: afa-0901

65. The tangent of an angle is 7.5. What is the measure of the angle to the nearest tenth?

Mixed Review

Lesson 8-6

66. The area of a regular octagon is 100 cm^2. Another regular octagon has sides that are three times as long. What is its area?

Lesson 7-2

The lengths of the sides of a triangle are given. Classify each triangle as *acute*, *right*, or *obtuse*.

67. 5, 8, 4

68. 15, 15, 20

69. 0.5, 1.2, 1.3

Lesson 6-7

70. For the kite pictured at the right, give the coordinates of the midpoints of its sides.

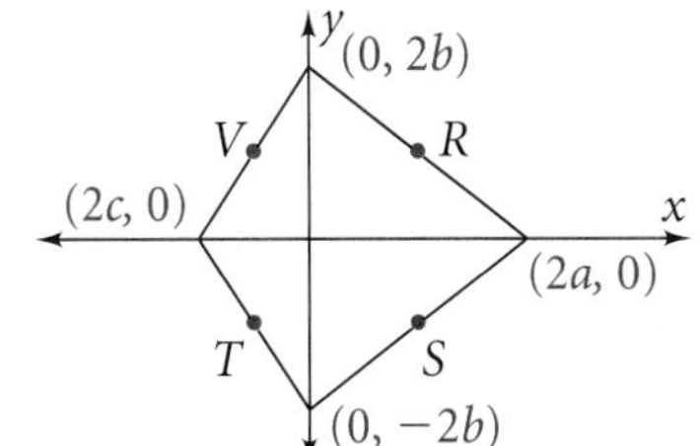

Technology Exploring Trigonometric Ratios

For Use With Lesson 9-2

Construct

Use geometry software to construct $\overrightarrow{AB}$ and $\overrightarrow{AC}$ so that $\angle A$ is acute. Through a point D on $\overrightarrow{AB}$ construct a line perpendicular to $\overrightarrow{AB}$ that intersects $\overrightarrow{AC}$ in point E. Moving point D enlarges or reduces $\triangle ADE$. Moving point C changes the size of $\angle A$.

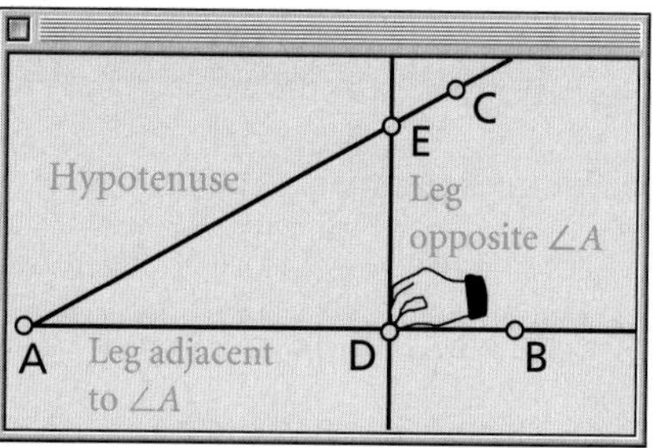

EXERCISES

1. • Measure $\angle A$.
   - Find the lengths of the sides of $\triangle ADE$.
   - Calculate the ratio $\frac{\text{leg opposite } \angle A}{\text{hypotenuse}}$, which is $\frac{ED}{AE}$.
   - Move point D to change the size of the right triangle without changing the size of $\angle A$.

   What do you observe about the ratio as the size of $\triangle ADE$ changes?

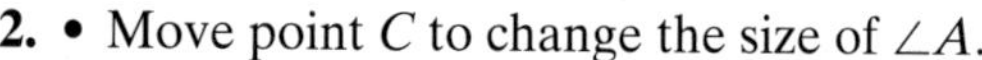

2. • Move point C to change the size of $\angle A$.

   a. What do you observe about the ratio as the size of $\angle A$ changes?

   b. What value does the ratio approach as $m\angle A$ approaches 0? As $m\angle A$ approaches 90?

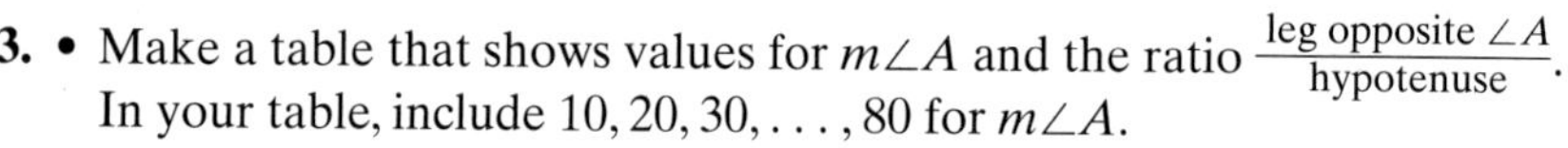

3. • Make a table that shows values for $m\angle A$ and the ratio $\frac{\text{leg opposite } \angle A}{\text{hypotenuse}}$. In your table, include 10, 20, 30, . . . , 80 for $m\angle A$.
   - Compare your table with the table of trigonometric ratios on page 731.

   Do your values for $\frac{\text{leg opposite } \angle A}{\text{hypotenuse}}$ match the values in one of the columns of the table? What is the name of this ratio in the table?

Extend

4. Repeat Exercises 1–3 for the ratio $\frac{\text{leg adjacent to } \angle A}{\text{hypotenuse}}$, which is $\frac{AD}{AE}$.
5. Repeat Exercises 1–3 for the ratio $\frac{\text{leg opposite } \angle A}{\text{leg adjacent to } \angle A}$, which is $\frac{ED}{AD}$.
6. • Choose a measure for $\angle A$ and determine the ratio $r = \frac{\text{leg opposite } \angle A}{\text{hypotenuse}}$. Record $m\angle A$ and this ratio.
   - Manipulate the triangle so that $\frac{\text{leg adjacent to } \angle A}{\text{hypotenuse}}$ has the same value r. Record this $m\angle A$ and compare it with your first value of $m\angle A$.
   - Repeat this procedure several times.
   - Look for a pattern in the two measures of $\angle A$ that you found for the different values of r.

   Make a conjecture.

9-2 Sine and Cosine Ratios

Lesson Preview

What You'll Learn

OBJECTIVE 1 To use sine and cosine to determine side lengths in triangles

. . . And Why

To use the sine ratio to estimate astronomical distances indirectly, as in Example 2

✓ Check Skills You'll Need

(For help, go to Lesson 9-1.)

For each triangle, find (a) the length of the leg opposite $\angle B$ and (b) the length of the leg adjacent to $\angle B$.

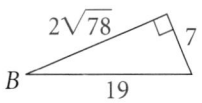

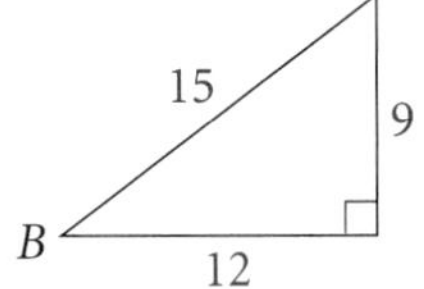

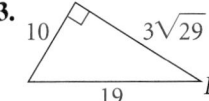

New Vocabulary

- sine
- cosine
- identity

Interactive lesson includes instant self-check, tutorials, and activities.

OBJECTIVE

1 Using Sine and Cosine in Triangles

The tangent ratio, as you have seen, involves both legs of a right triangle. The sine and cosine ratios involve one leg and the hypotenuse.

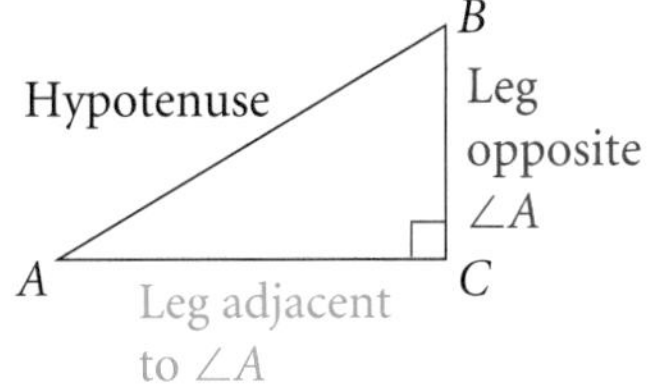

$$\textbf{sine} \text{ of } \angle A = \frac{\text{leg opposite } \angle A}{\text{hypotenuse}}$$

$$\textbf{cosine} \text{ of } \angle A = \frac{\text{leg adjacent to } \angle A}{\text{hypotenuse}}$$

These equations can be abbreviated:

$$\sin A = \frac{\text{opposite}}{\text{hypotenuse}} \qquad \cos A = \frac{\text{adjacent}}{\text{hypotenuse}}$$

Real-World Connection

For an angle of a given size, the sine and cosine ratios are constant, no matter where the angle is located.

1 EXAMPLE Writing Sine and Cosine Ratios

Use the triangle to write each ratio.

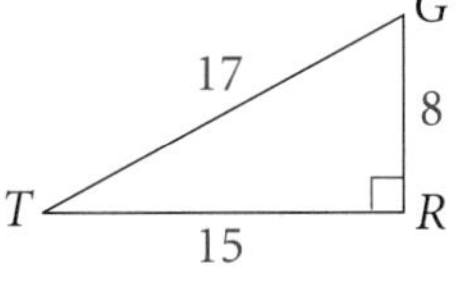

a. $\sin T$ $\quad \sin T = \frac{\text{opposite}}{\text{hypotenuse}} = \frac{8}{17}$

b. $\cos T$ $\quad \cos T = \frac{\text{adjacent}}{\text{hypotenuse}} = \frac{15}{17}$

c. $\sin G$ $\quad \sin G = \frac{\text{opposite}}{\text{hypotenuse}} = \frac{15}{17}$

d. $\cos G$ $\quad \cos G = \frac{\text{adjacent}}{\text{hypotenuse}} = \frac{8}{17}$

✓ Check Understanding

1 **a.** Write the sine and cosine ratios for $\angle X$ and $\angle Y$.

b. Critical Thinking In general, how are $\sin X$ and $\cos Y$ related? Explain.

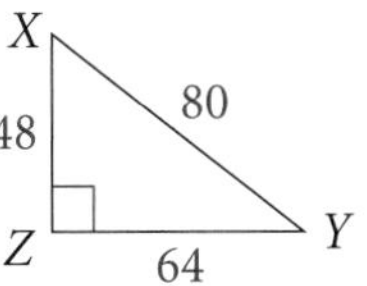

One way to describe the relationship of sine and cosine is to say that $\sin x° = \cos (90 - x)°$ for values of x between 0 and 90. This type of equation is called an **identity** because it is true for all the allowed values of the variable. You will discover other identities in the exercises.

2 EXAMPLE Real-World Connection

Astronomy The trigonometric ratios have been known for centuries by peoples in many cultures. The Polish astronomer Nicolaus Copernicus (1473–1543) developed a method for determining the sizes of orbits of planets closer to the sun than Earth. The key to his method was determining when the planets were in the position shown in the diagram, and then measuring the angle to find a.

Earth
$a°$
x
Sun
1 AU

not to scale

If $a = 22.3$ for Mercury, how far is Mercury from the sun in astronomical units (AU)? One astronomical unit is defined as the average distance from Earth to the center of the sun, about 93 million miles.

$\sin 22.3° = \frac{x}{1}$ **Use the sine ratio.**

$x = \sin 22.3°$ **Solve for x.**

SIN 22.3 ENTER .37945616 **Use a calculator.**

Mercury is about 0.38 AU from the sun.

Check Understanding 2 **a.** If $a = 46$ for Venus, how far is Venus from the sun in AU?
b. About how many miles from the sun is Venus? Mercury?

When you know the leg and hypotenuse lengths of a right triangle, you can use inverse of sine and inverse of cosine to find the measures of the acute angles.

3 EXAMPLE Using the Inverse of Cosine and Sine

Find $m\angle L$ to the nearest degree.

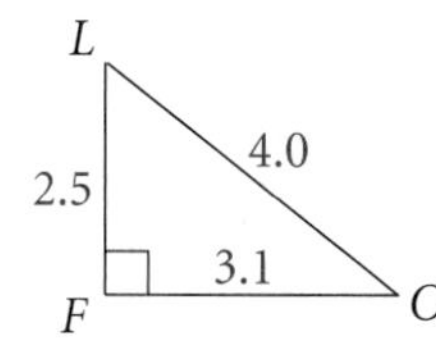

Method 1

$\cos L = \frac{2.5}{4.0} = \frac{5}{8}$ ← **Find the trigonometric ratio.** →

$m\angle L = \cos^{-1}\left(\frac{5}{8}\right)$ ← **Use the inverse.** →

COS^{-1} 5 ÷ 8 ENTER ← **Use a calculator.** →
51.317813

$m\angle L \approx 51$

Method 2

$\sin L = \frac{3.1}{4.0}$

$m\angle L = \sin^{-1}\left(\frac{3.1}{4.0}\right)$

SIN^{-1} 3.1 ÷ 4.0 ENTER
50.805033

$m\angle L \approx 51$

Reading Math

Think of $\cos^{-1}\left(\frac{5}{8}\right)$ as "the angle whose cosine is $\frac{5}{8}$," and $\sin^{-1}\left(\frac{3.1}{4.0}\right)$ as "the angle whose sine is the quotient $\frac{3.1}{4.0}$."

Check Understanding 3 Find the value of x. Round your answer to the nearest degree.

a.

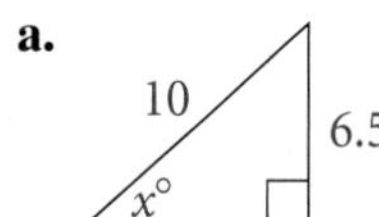

b.

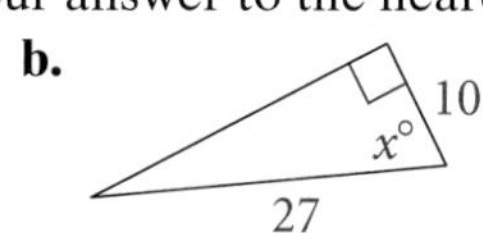

EXERCISES

For more practice, see *Extra Practice.*

Practice and Problem Solving

A Practice by Example

Example 1 (page 477)

Write the ratios for sin M and cos M.

1. 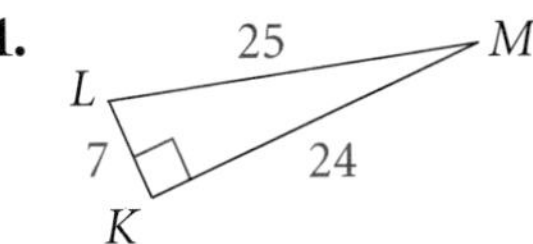

2. 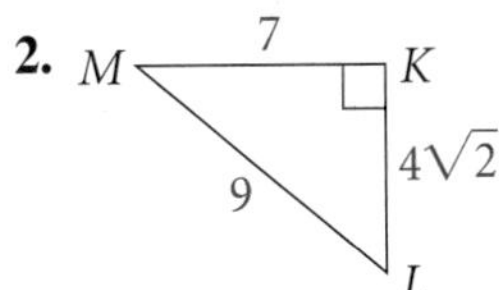

3. 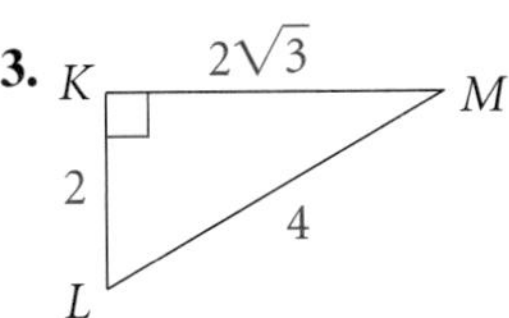

Example 2 (page 478)

Find the value of x. Round answers to the nearest tenth.

4. 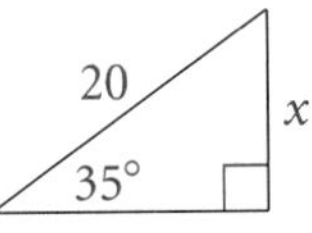

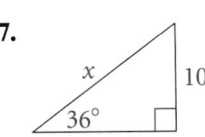

5. x, 41°, 11

6. 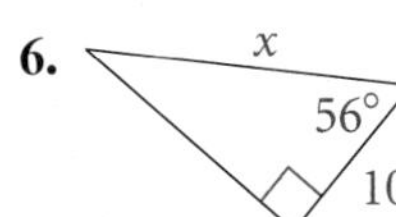

7. x, 10, 36°

8. 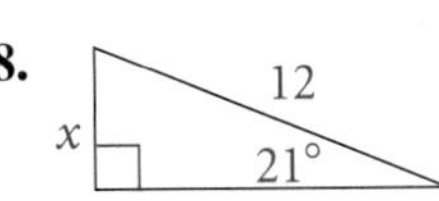

9. 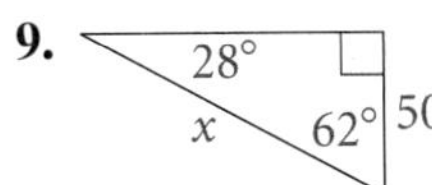

10. **Escalators** An escalator in the subway system of St. Petersburg, Russia, has a vertical rise of 195 ft 9.5 in., and rises at an angle of 10.4°. How long is the escalator? Round your answer to the nearest foot.

Example 3 (page 478)

Find the value of x. Round answers to the nearest degree.

11. 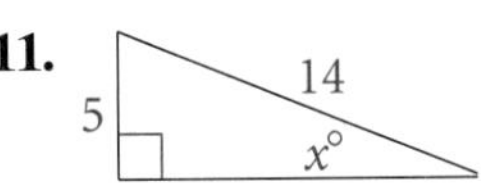

12. 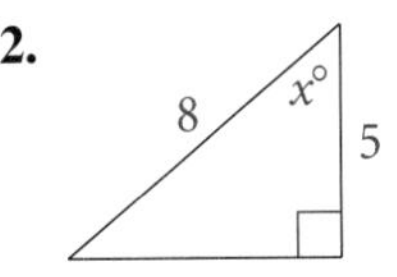

13. 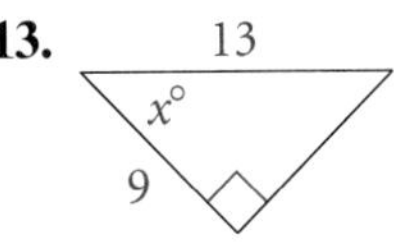

14. 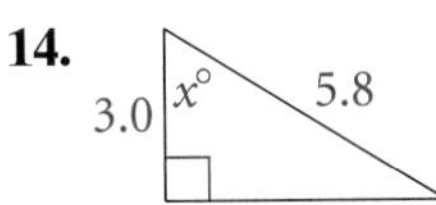

15. 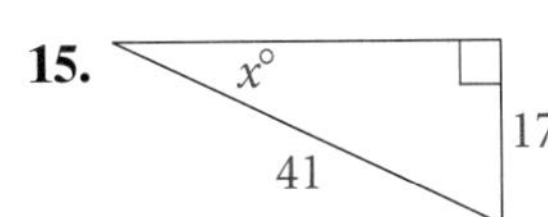

16. 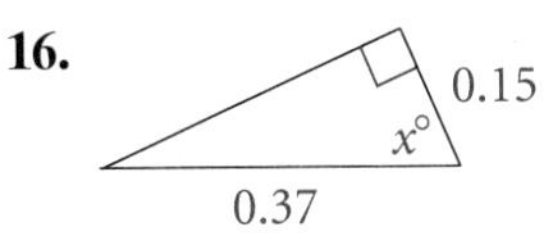

B Apply Your Skills

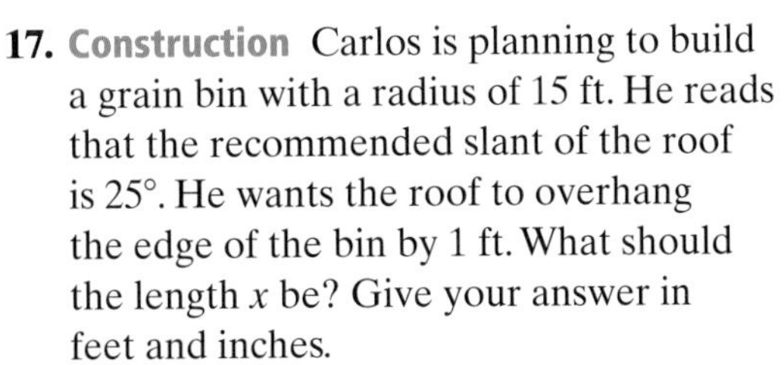

17. **Construction** Carlos is planning to build a grain bin with a radius of 15 ft. He reads that the recommended slant of the roof is 25°. He wants the roof to overhang the edge of the bin by 1 ft. What should the length x be? Give your answer in feet and inches.

x, 25°, 1 ft overhang, 15 ft

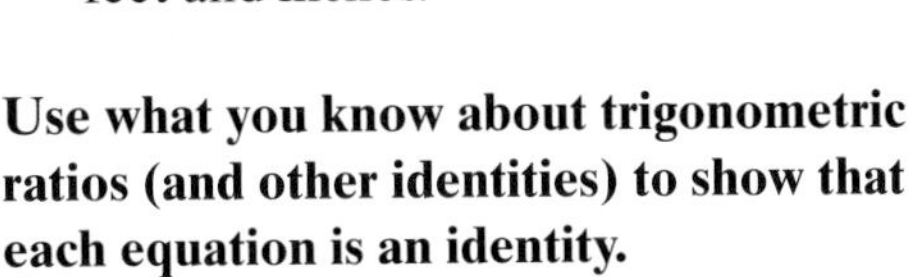

Use what you know about trigonometric ratios (and other identities) to show that each equation is an identity.

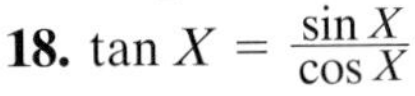

18. $\tan X = \frac{\sin X}{\cos X}$ 19. $\sin X = \cos X \cdot \tan X$ 20. $\cos X = \frac{\sin X}{\tan X}$

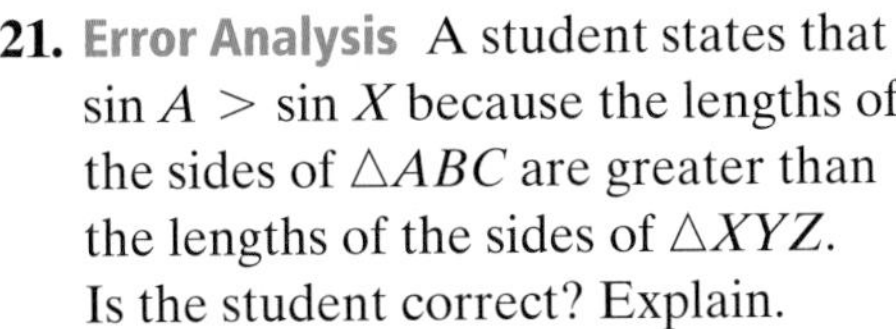

21. **Error Analysis** A student states that $\sin A > \sin X$ because the lengths of the sides of $\triangle ABC$ are greater than the lengths of the sides of $\triangle XYZ$. Is the student correct? Explain.

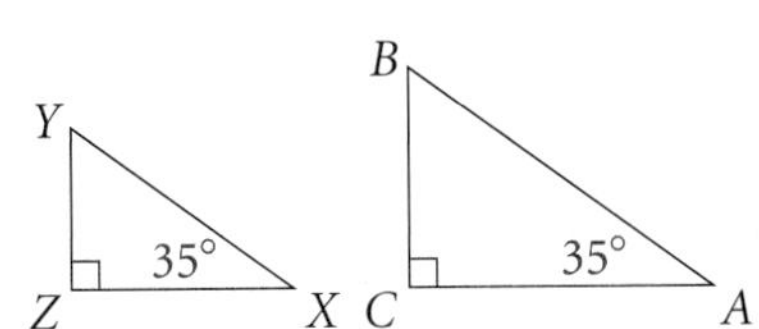

Real-World Connection

Corn that fills the bin in Exercise 17 would make 28,500 gallons of ethanol.

Find the values of w and then x. Round lengths to the nearest tenth and angle measures to the nearest degree.

22.

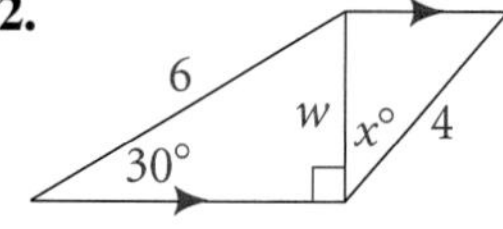

23.

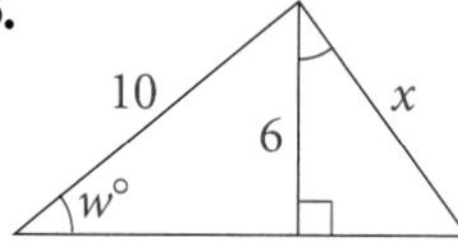

24.

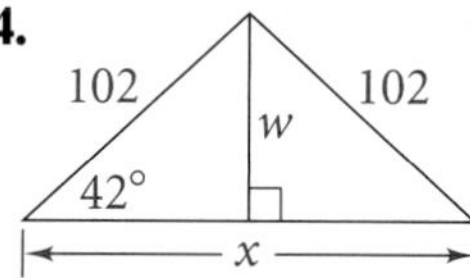

25. a. In $\triangle ABC$, how does sin A compare to cos B? Is this true for the acute angles of other right triangles?

b. Reading Math The word cosine is derived from the words *complement's sine* (see page 614). Which angle in $\triangle ABC$ is the complement of $\angle A$? Of $\angle B$?

c. Explain why the derivation of the word cosine makes sense.

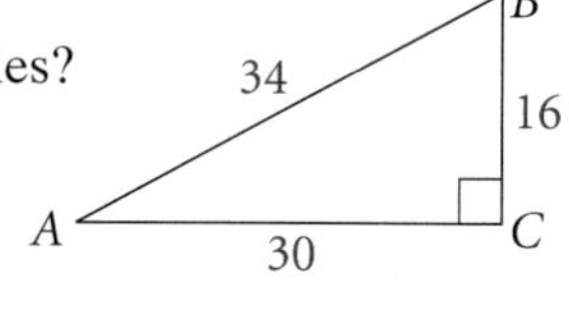

26. Find each ratio.

a. sin P **b.** cos P

c. sin R **d.** cos R

e. Make a conjecture about how the sine and cosine of a 45° angle are related.

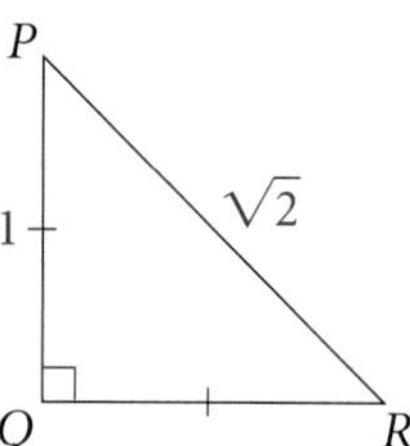

Reading Math

In Exercise 27, Leona could say, "Given a side and an acute angle of a right triangle, I can solve the triangle."

27. Writing Leona said that if she had a diagram that showed the measure of one acute angle and the length of one side of a right triangle, she could find the measure of the other acute angle and the lengths of the other sides. Is she correct? Explain.

28. Find each ratio.

a. sin S **b.** cos S

c. sin T **d.** cos T

e. Make a conjecture about how the sine and cosine of a 30° angle are related.

f. Make a conjecture about how the sine and cosine of a 60° angle are related.

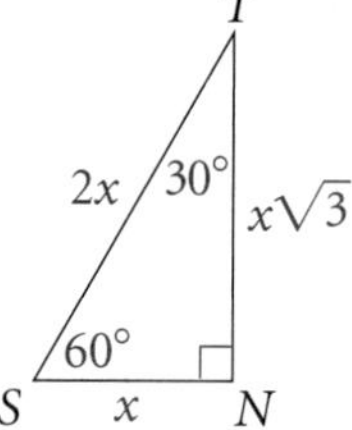

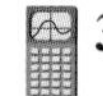

29. Write a paragraph to prove that sin $A < 1$, no matter how large $\angle A$ is in right $\triangle ABC$.

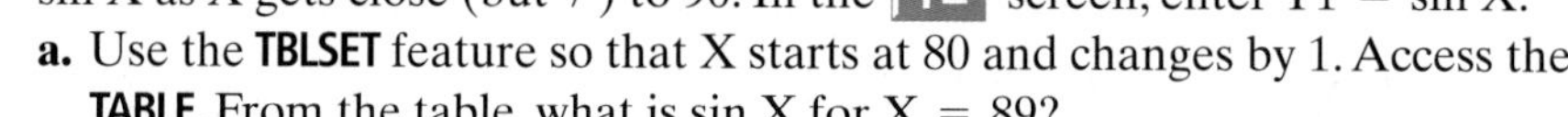

30. Graphing Calculator Use the **TABLE** feature of your graphing calculator to study sin X as X gets close (but $\neq$) to 90. In the **Y=** screen, enter Y1 = sin X.

a. Use the **TBLSET** feature so that X starts at 80 and changes by 1. Access the **TABLE**. From the table, what is sin X for X = 89?

b. Perform a "numerical zoom in." Use the **TBLSET** feature, so that X starts with 89 and changes by 0.1. What is sin X for X = 89.9?

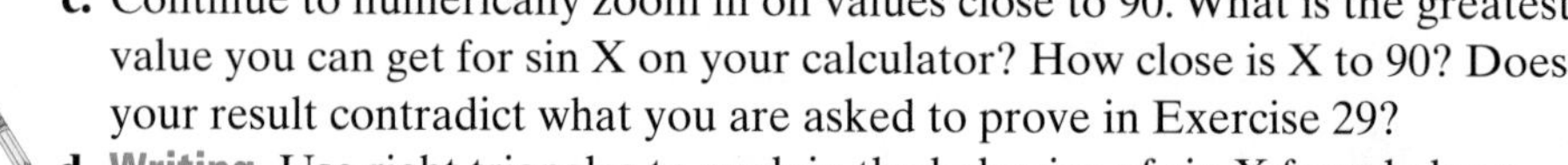

c. Continue to numerically zoom in on values close to 90. What is the greatest value you can get for sin X on your calculator? How close is X to 90? Does your result contradict what you are asked to prove in Exercise 29?

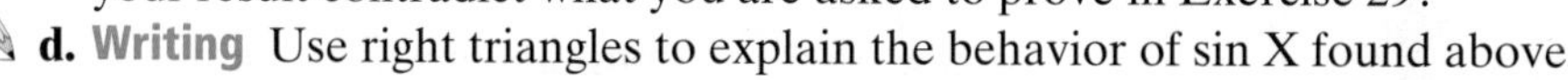

d. Writing Use right triangles to explain the behavior of sin X found above.

Take It to the NET

Graphing Calculator procedures online at **www.PHSchool.com**

Web Code: afe-2111

Challenge

Show that each equation is an identity by showing that each expression on the left simplifies to 1.

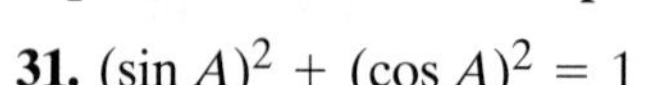

31. $(\sin A)^2 + (\cos A)^2 = 1$ **32.** $(\sin B)^2 + (\cos B)^2 = 1$

33. $\dfrac{1}{(\cos A)^2} - (\tan A)^2 = 1$ **34.** $\dfrac{1}{(\sin A)^2} - \dfrac{1}{(\tan A)^2} = 1$

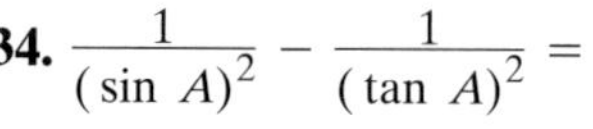

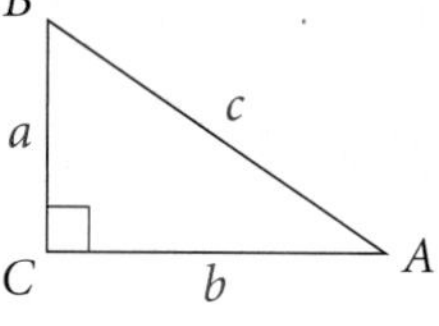

35. Show that $(\tan A)^2 - (\sin A)^2 = (\tan A)^2(\sin A)^2$ is an identity.

Real-World Connection

Poland honored Copernicus with this 1000-zloty note, last used in 1995.

36. Astronomy Copernicus devised a method different from the one in Example 2 in order to find the sizes of the orbits of planets farther from the sun than Earth. His method involved noting the number of days between the times that a planet was in the positions labeled A and B in the diagram. Using this time and the number of days in each planet's year, he calculated c and d.

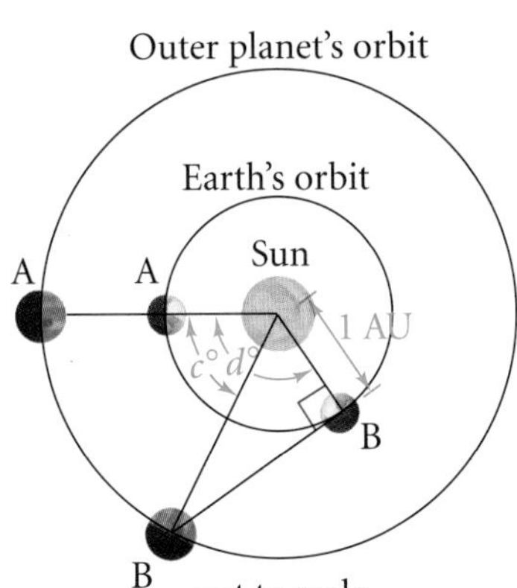

a. For Mars, $c = 55.2$ and $d = 103.8$. How far is Mars from the sun in astronomical units (AU)?

b. For Jupiter, $c = 21.9$ and $d = 100.8$. How far is Jupiter from the sun in astronomical units?

Standardized Test Prep

Multiple Choice

37. What is the value of x to the nearest whole number?

A. 2   B. 3
C. 4   D. 6

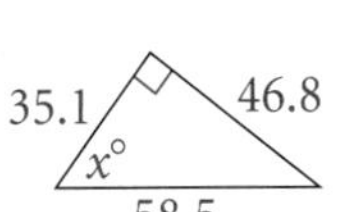

38. What is the value of y to the nearest tenth?

F. 5.4   G. 5.5
H. 5.6   I. 5.7

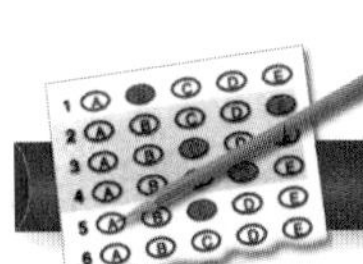

Take It to the NET
Online lesson quiz at www.PHSchool.com
Web Code: afa-0902

39. What is the value of x to the nearest whole number?

A. 53   B. 47
C. 43   D. 37

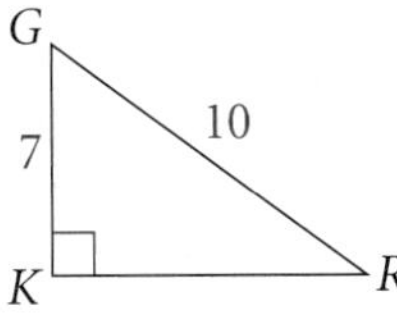

Short Response

40. Use the figure at the right.

a. Find $m\angle G$. Show your work.

b. Find $m\angle R$ by two different methods. Show your work.

Mixed Review

Lesson 9-1

Find the value of x. Round answers to the nearest tenth.

41. 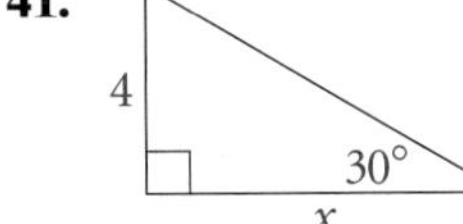

42. 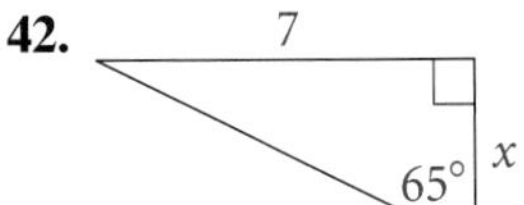

43. 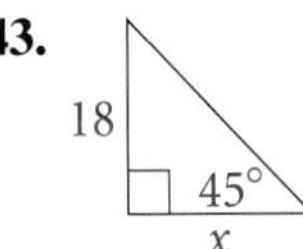

Lesson 8-2

44. The wall of a room is in the shape of a golden rectangle. If the height of the wall is 8 ft, what are the possible lengths of the wall to the nearest tenth?

Lesson 7-4

Find the area of each trapezoid. Leave your answer in simplest radical form.

45. 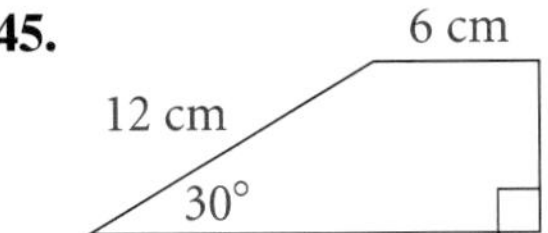

46. 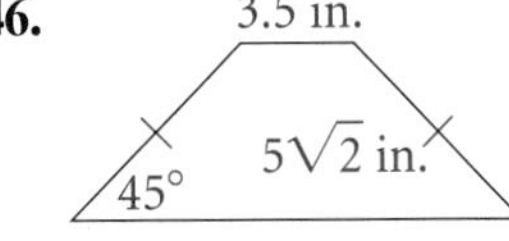

47. 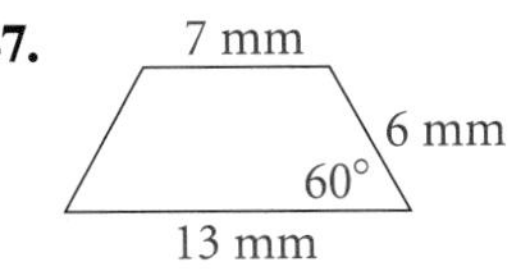

Angles of Elevation and Depression

Lesson Preview

What You'll Learn

To use angles of elevation and depression to solve problems

. . . And Why

To use the angle of elevation to calculate the height of a natural wonder, as in Example 2

✓ Check Skills You'll Need

(For help, go to Lesson 6-1.)

Refer to rectangle *ABCD* to complete the statements.

1. $\angle 1 \cong$ ▒
2. $\angle 5 \cong$ ▒
3. $\angle 3 \cong$ ▒
4. $m\angle 1 + m\angle 5 =$ ▒
5. $m\angle 10 + m\angle 3 =$ ▒
6. $\angle 10 \cong$ ▒

A, B, C, D, 10, 3, 7, 5, 11, 1, 6, 8

New Vocabulary • angle of elevation • angle of depression

Interactive lesson includes instant self-check, tutorials, and activities.

OBJECTIVE 1

Using Angles of Elevation and Depression

Suppose a person on the ground sees a hot-air balloon gondola at a 38° angle above a horizontal line.

This angle is the **angle of elevation.**

At the same time, a person in the hot-air balloon sees the person on the ground at a 38° angle below a horizontal line.

This angle is the **angle of depression.**

Examine the diagram. The angle of elevation is congruent to the angle of depression because they are alternate interior angles.

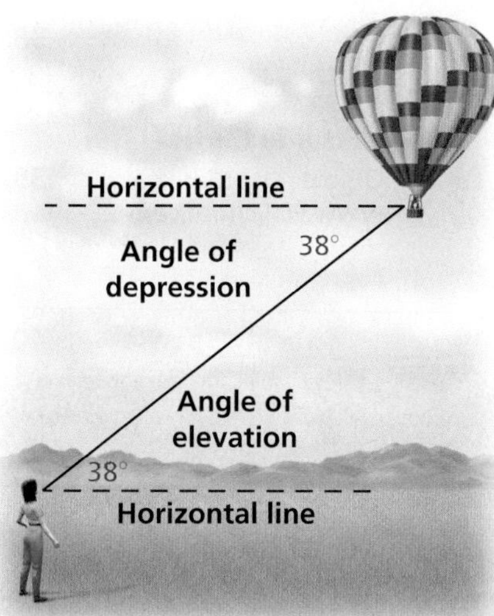

1 EXAMPLE Identifying Angles of Elevation and Depression

Describe each angle as it relates to the situation shown.

a. $\angle 1$ $\angle 1$ is the angle of depression from the peak to the hiker.

b. $\angle 4$ $\angle 4$ is the angle of elevation from the hut to the hiker.

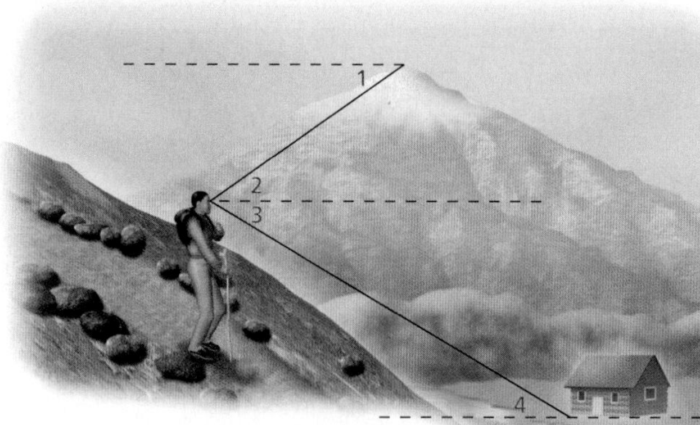

✓ Check Understanding 1 Describe each angle as it relates to the situation in Example 1.

a. $\angle 2$ **b.** $\angle 3$

Surveyors use two instruments, the transit and the theodolite, to measure angles of elevation and depression. On both instruments, the surveyor sets the horizon line perpendicular to the direction of gravity. Using gravity to find the horizon line ensures accurate measures even on sloping surfaces.

Horizon line

Pull of gravity

2 EXAMPLE Real-World Connection

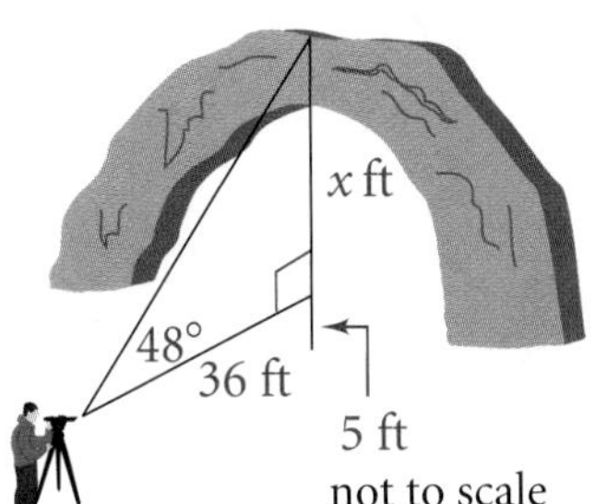

Surveying To find the height of Delicate Arch in Arches National Park in Utah, a surveyor levels a theodolite with the bottom of the arch. From there, she measures the angle of elevation to the top of the arch. She then measures the distance from where she stands to a point directly under the arch. Her results are shown in the diagram. What is the height of the arch?

$\tan 48^\circ = \frac{x}{36}$ **Use the tangent ratio.**

$x = 36(\tan 48^\circ)$ **Solve for *x*.**

36 TAN 48 ENTER 39.982051 **Use a calculator.**

So $x \approx 40$. To find the height of the arch, add the height of the theodolite. Since $40 + 5 = 45$, Delicate Arch is about 45 feet high.

✓ Check Understanding **2** You sight a rock climber on a cliff at a 32° angle of elevation. The horizontal ground distance to the cliff is 1000 ft. Find the line-of-sight distance to the rock climber.

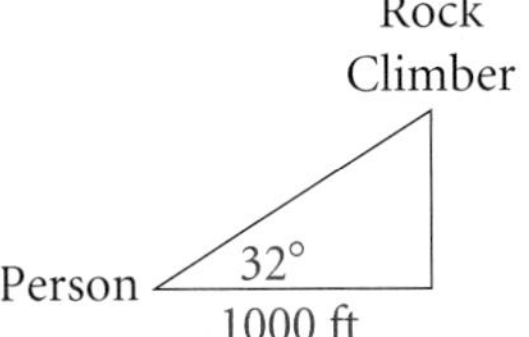

3 EXAMPLE Real-World Connection

Need Help?

A 3° descent means 3° downwards from horizontal.

Aviation To approach runway 17 of the Ponca City Municipal Airport in Oklahoma, the pilot must begin a 3° descent starting from an altitude of 2714 ft. The airport altitude is 1007 ft. How many miles from the runway is the airplane at the start of this approach?

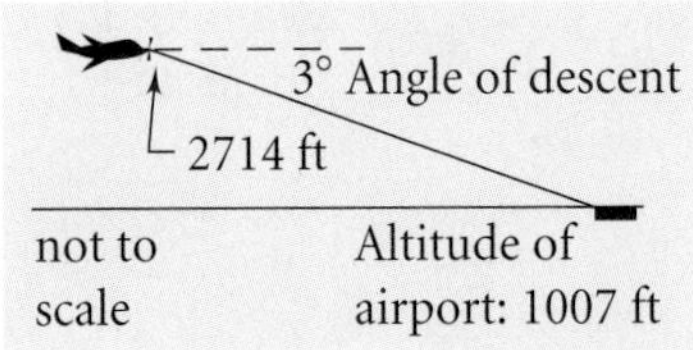

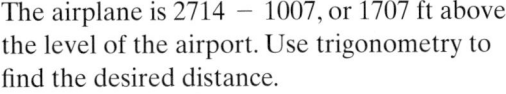

The airplane is 2714 − 1007, or 1707 ft above the level of the airport. Use trigonometry to find the desired distance.

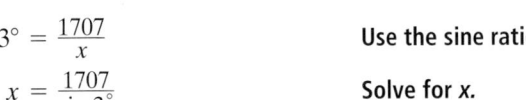

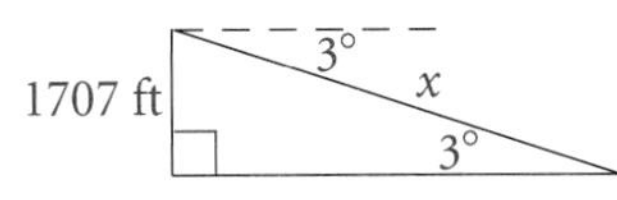

$\sin 3^\circ = \frac{1707}{x}$ **Use the sine ratio.**

$x = \frac{1707}{\sin 3^\circ}$ **Solve for *x*.**

1707 ÷ SIN 3 ENTER 32616.2 **Use a calculator.**

÷ 5280 ENTER 6.1773105 **Divide by 5280 to convert feet to miles.**

The airplane is about 6.2 mi from the runway at the start of the approach.

✓ Check Understanding **3** An airplane pilot sights a life raft at a 26° angle of depression. The airplane's altitude is 3 km. What is the airplane's surface distance *d* from the raft?

EXERCISES

For more practice, see *Extra Practice.*

Practice and Problem Solving

A **Practice by Example**

Example 1 (page 482)

Describe each angle as it relates to the situation in the diagram.

1. $\angle 1$ **2.** $\angle 2$ **3.** $\angle 3$ **4.** $\angle 4$ **5.** $\angle 5$ **6.** $\angle 6$ **7.** $\angle 7$ **8.** $\angle 8$

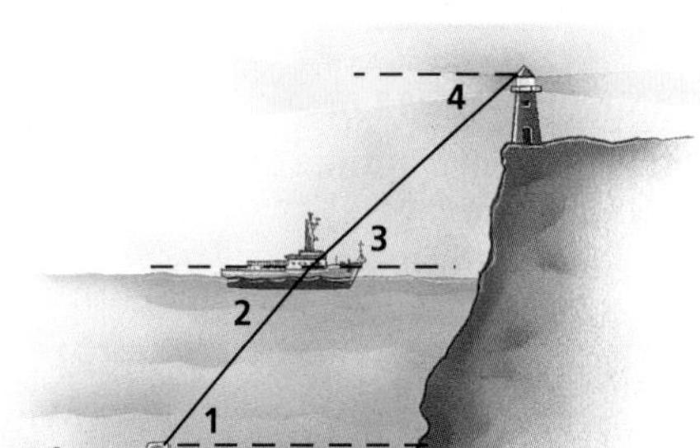

Example 2 (page 483)

Find the value of x. Round the lengths to the nearest tenth.

9.

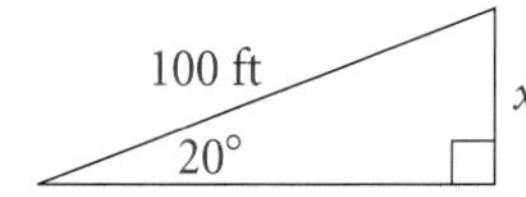

10.

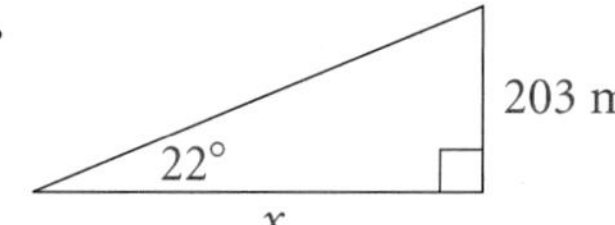

11.

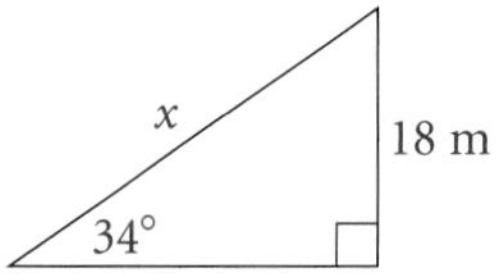

12.

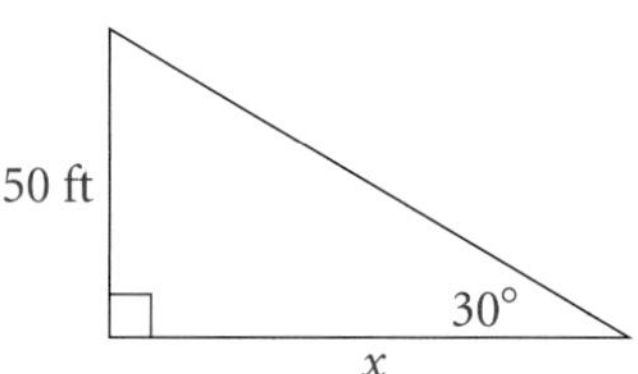

13. **Meteorology** A meteorologist measures the angle of elevation of a weather balloon as 41°. A radio signal from the balloon indicates that it is 1503 m from his location. To the nearest meter, how high above the ground is the balloon?

Example 3 (page 483)

Find the value of x. Round lengths to the nearest tenth of a unit.

14.

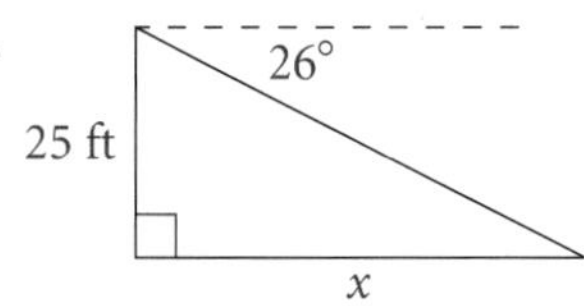

15.

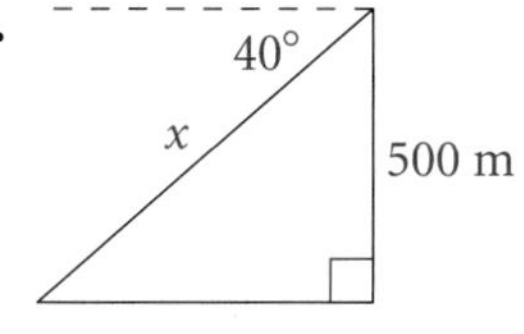

16.

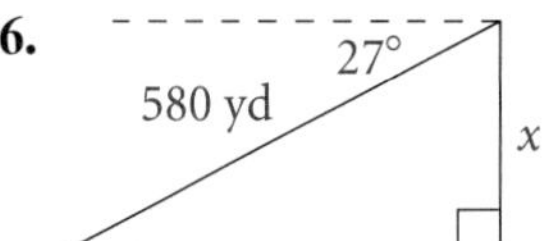

17.

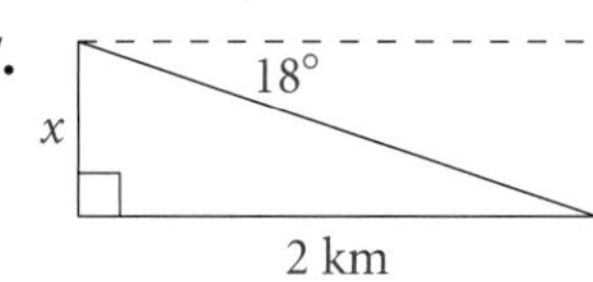

18. **Indirect Measurement** Miguel looks out from the crown of the Statue of Liberty approximately 250 ft above ground. He sights a ship coming into New York harbor and measures the angle of depression as 18°. Find the distance from the base of the statue to the ship to the nearest foot.

B **Apply Your Skills**

19. **Flagpole** The world's tallest unsupported flagpole is a 282-ft-tall steel pole in Surrey, British Columbia. The shortest shadow cast by the pole during the year is 137 ft long. To the nearest degree, what is the angle of elevation of the sun when the shortest shadow is cast?

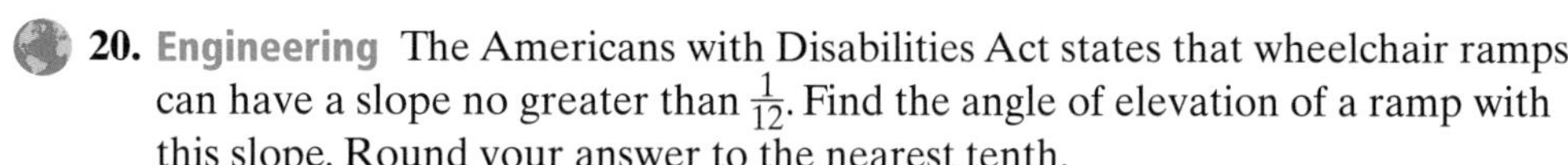

20. **Engineering** The Americans with Disabilities Act states that wheelchair ramps can have a slope no greater than $\frac{1}{12}$. Find the angle of elevation of a ramp with this slope. Round your answer to the nearest tenth.

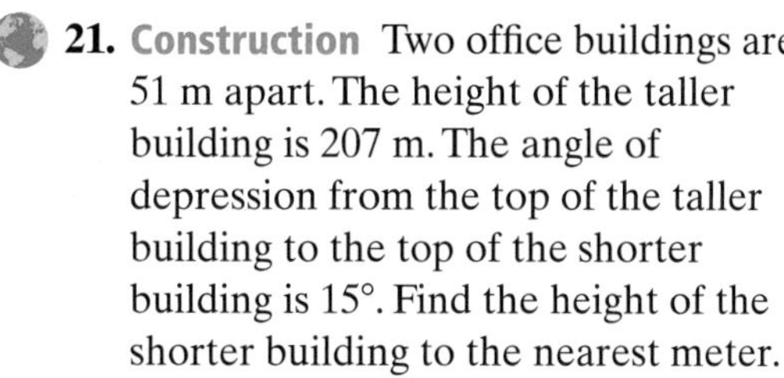

21. **Construction** Two office buildings are 51 m apart. The height of the taller building is 207 m. The angle of depression from the top of the taller building to the top of the shorter building is 15°. Find the height of the shorter building to the nearest meter.

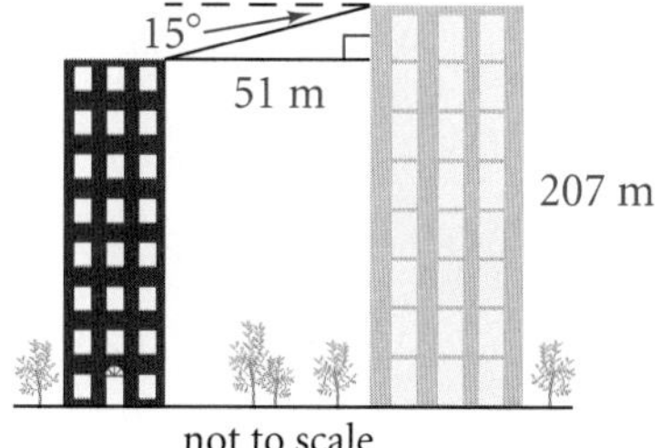

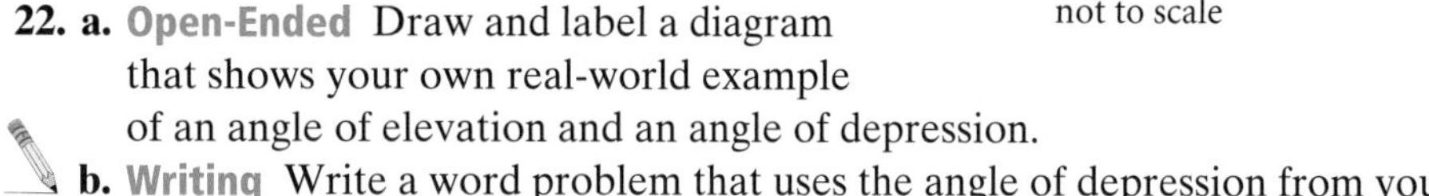

22. a. **Open-Ended** Draw and label a diagram that shows your own real-world example of an angle of elevation and an angle of depression.

b. **Writing** Write a word problem that uses the angle of depression from your diagram. Include a detailed solution to your problem.

Reading Math

For help with Exercise 23, see Reading Math on p. 489.

23. **Aerial Television** A blimp is providing aerial television views of a football game. The television camera sights the stadium at a 7° angle of depression. The blimp's altitude is 400 m. What is the line-of-sight distance from the TV camera to the stadium, to the nearest hundred meters?

Real-World Connection

The TV blimp can be $\frac{2}{3}$ the length of a football field.

Algebra The angle of elevation *e* from *A* to *B* and the angle of depression *d* from *B* to *A* are shown below. Find the measure of each angle.

24. e: $(7x - 5)°$, d: $4(x + 7)°$

25. e: $(3x + 1)°$, d: $2(x + 8)°$

26. e: $(x + 21)°$, d: $3(x + 3)°$

27. e: $5(x - 2)°$, d: $(x + 14)°$

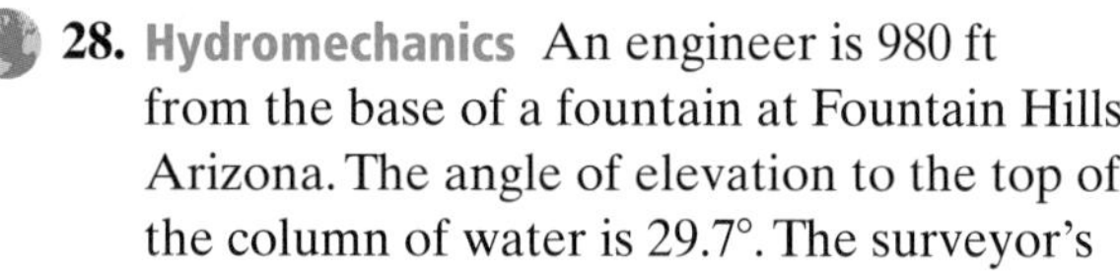

28. **Hydromechanics** An engineer is 980 ft from the base of a fountain at Fountain Hills, Arizona. The angle of elevation to the top of the column of water is 29.7°. The surveyor's angle measuring device is at the same level as the base of the fountain.

a. Find the height of the column of water to the nearest 10 ft.

b. When the top of the column of water is just half as high as in part (a), find the angle of elevation to its top.

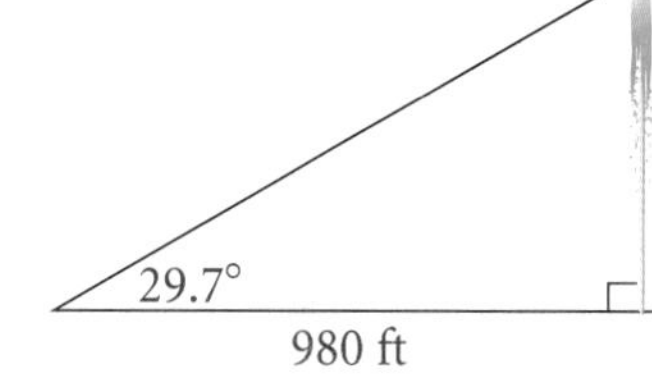

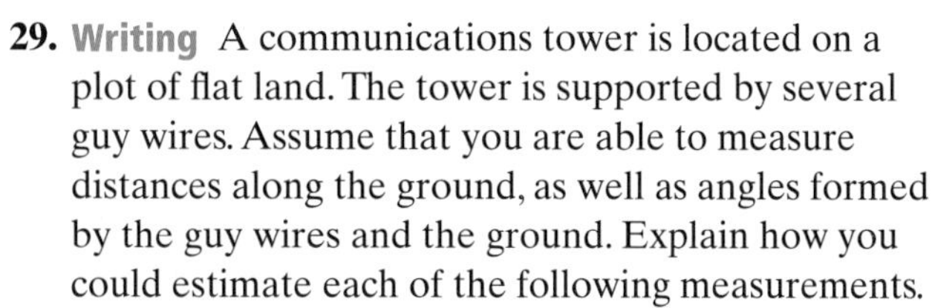

29. **Writing** A communications tower is located on a plot of flat land. The tower is supported by several guy wires. Assume that you are able to measure distances along the ground, as well as angles formed by the guy wires and the ground. Explain how you could estimate each of the following measurements.

a. the length of any guy wire

b. how high on the tower each wire is attached

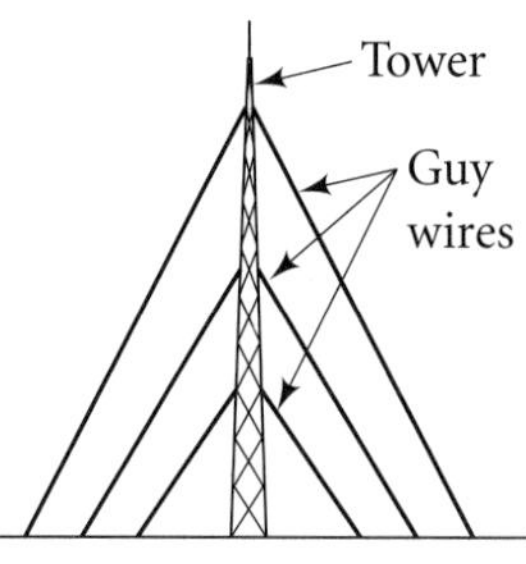

Flying An airplane at altitude *a* flies distance *d* towards you with velocity *v*. You watch for time *t* and measure its angles of elevation, $\angle E_1$ and $\angle E_2$, at the start and end of your watch. Find the missing information.

30. $a = ■$ mi, $v = 5$ mi/min, $t = 1$ min, $m\angle E_1 = 45$, $m\angle E_2 = 90$

31. $a = 2$ mi, $v = ■$ mi/min, $t = 15$ s, $m\angle E_1 = 40$, $m\angle E_2 = 50$

32. $a = 4$ mi, $d = 3$ mi, $v = 6$ mi/min, $t = ■$ min, $m\angle E_1 = 50$, $m\angle E_2 = ■$

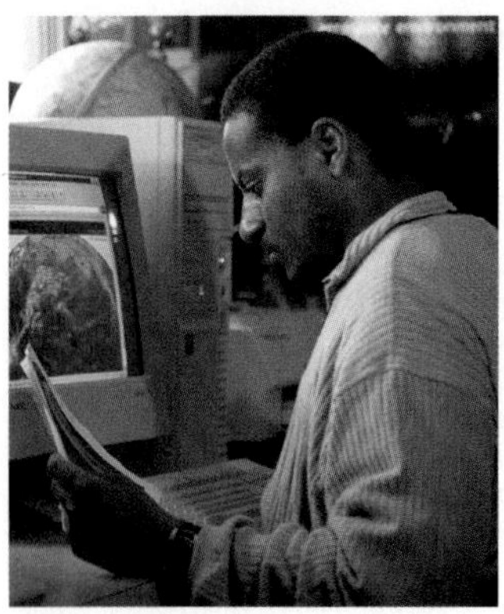

Real-World Connection

Careers Atmospheric scientists specialize by linking meteorology with another field such as agriculture.

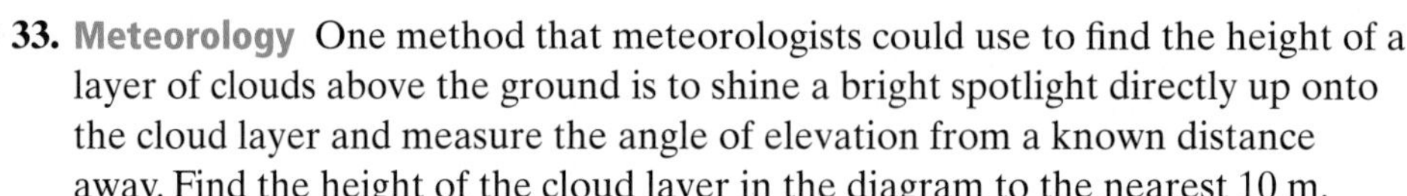

33. Meteorology One method that meteorologists could use to find the height of a layer of clouds above the ground is to shine a bright spotlight directly up onto the cloud layer and measure the angle of elevation from a known distance away. Find the height of the cloud layer in the diagram to the nearest 10 m.

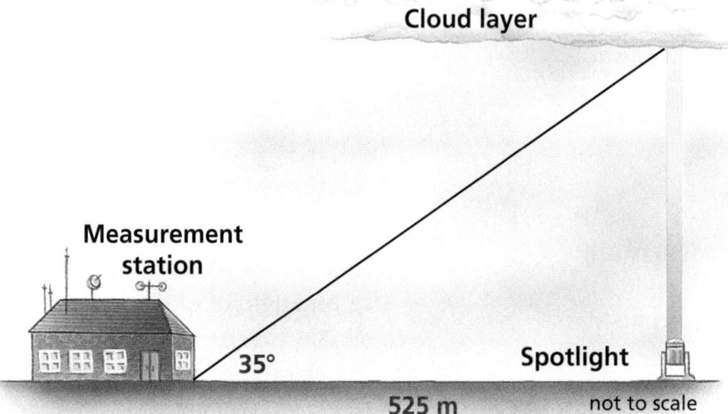

Challenge

34. Firefighting A firefighter on the ground sees fire break through a window near the top of the building. There is voice contact between the ground and firefighters on the roof. The angle of elevation to the windowsill is 28°. The angle of elevation to the top of the building is 42°. The firefighter is 75 ft from the building and her eyes are 5 ft above the ground. What roof-to-windowsill distance can she report to the firefighters on the roof?

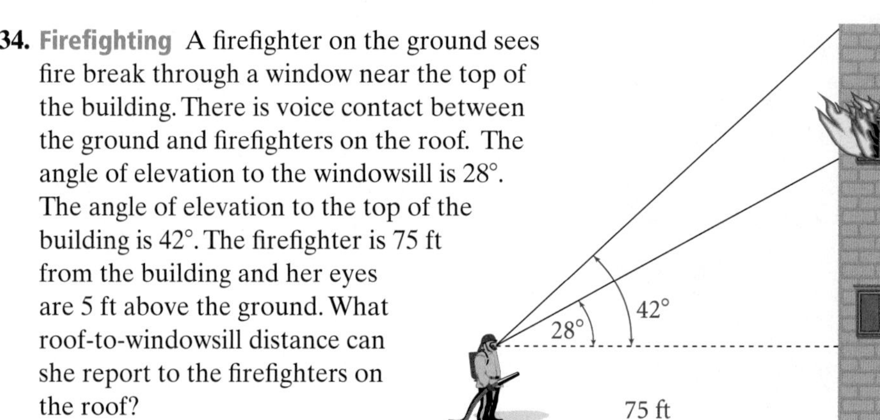

35. Indirect Measurement Here is a simple method for finding a north-south line.

Put a stick in the ground before noon and regularly mark the end of its shadow. When the shadow begins to lengthen, stop marking. The mark closest to the stick is directly north of the stick.

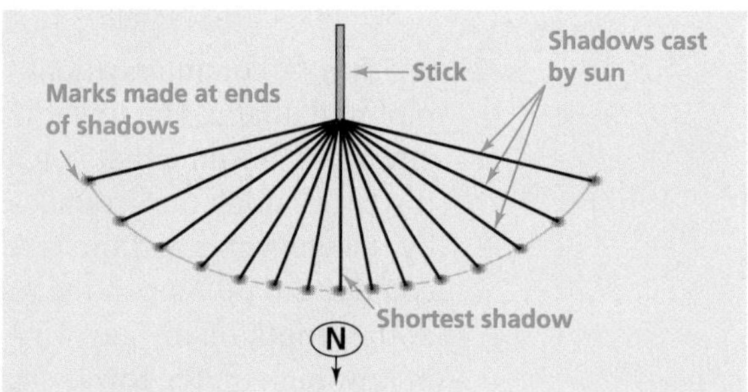

Explain how you could use this method to find the angle of elevation of the sun at noon (when the sun is highest in the sky).

36. Geography For locations in the United States, the relationship between the latitude ℓ and the greatest angle of elevation a of the sun at noon on the first day of summer is $a = 90° - \ell + 23\frac{1}{2}°$. Find the latitude of your town. Then determine the greatest angle of elevation of the sun for your town on the first day of summer.

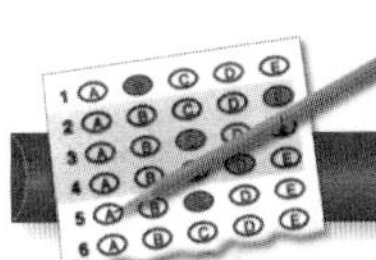

Standardized Test Prep

Multiple Choice

37. A 107-ft-tall building casts a shadow of 90 ft. To the nearest whole degree, what is the angle of elevation to the sun?
A. 33° **B.** 40° **C.** 50° **D.** 57°

38. The angle of depression of a submarine from another Navy ship is 28°. The submarine is 791 ft from the ship. About how deep is the submarine?
F. 371 ft **G.** 421 ft **H.** 563 ft **I.** 698 ft

39. A kite on a 100-ft string has an angle of elevation of 18°. The hand holding the string is 4 ft from the ground. How high above the ground is the kite?
A. 95 ft **B.** 35 ft **C.** 31 ft **D.** 22 ft

Quantitative Comparison

Compare the boxed quantity in Column A with the boxed quantity in Column B. Choose the best answer.
A. The quantity in Column A is greater.
B. The quantity in Column B is greater.
C. The two quantities are equal.
D. The relationship cannot be determined from the information given.

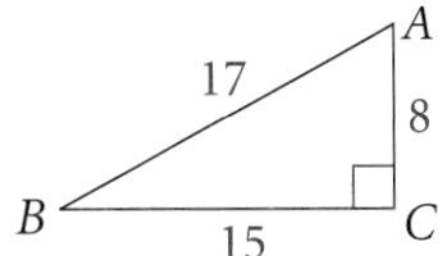

	Column A	Column B
40.	sin A	cos A
41.	sin A	cos B
42.	tan A	cos B
43.	$\frac{\sin A}{15}$	$\frac{\sin B}{8}$

Short Response

44. A 6-ft-tall man is viewing the top of a tree with an angle of elevation of 83°. He is standing 12 ft from the base of the tree.
a. Draw a sketch of the situation. Show a stick figure for the man. Label the angle of elevation, the height of the man, and the distance the man is standing from the tree.
b. Write and solve an equation to find the height of the tree. Round your answer to the nearest foot.

Online lesson quiz at **www.PHSchool.com**
Web Code: afa-0903

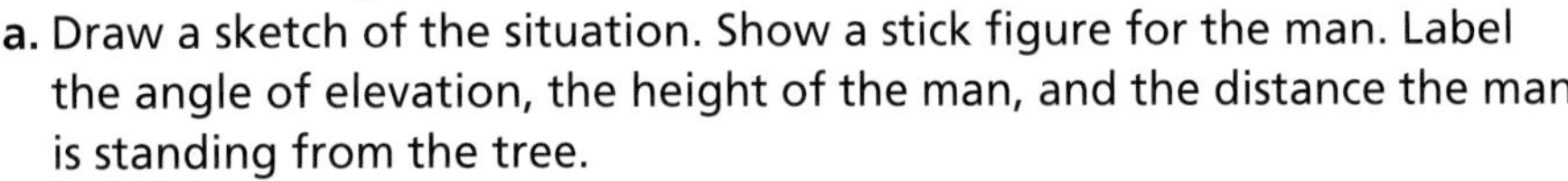

Lesson 9-2

Find the value of x. Round answers to the nearest tenth.

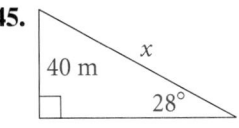

45. x, 40 m, 28°

46. 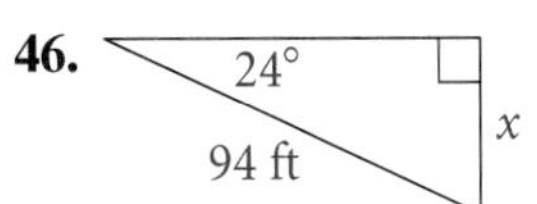

47. 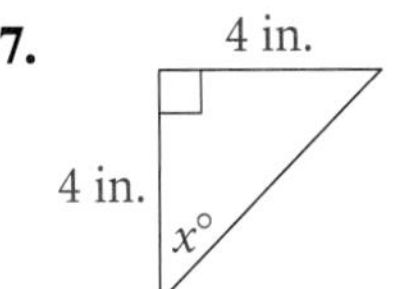

Lesson 7-6 **Find the measure of each arc in $\odot C$. $\overline{PQ}$ is a diameter.**

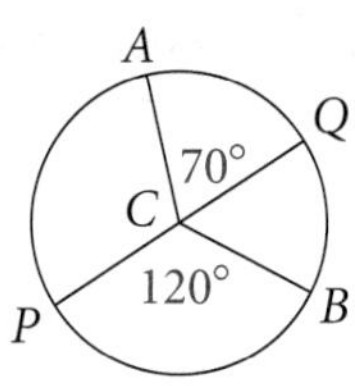

48. $\overset{\frown}{AQ}$ **49.** $\overset{\frown}{AP}$ **50.** $\overset{\frown}{BQ}$

51. $\overset{\frown}{AQB}$ **52.** $\overset{\frown}{PAB}$ **53.** $\overset{\frown}{BPA}$

Lesson 6-1 x^2 Algebra **Find the value of each variable. Then find the length of each side.**

54.

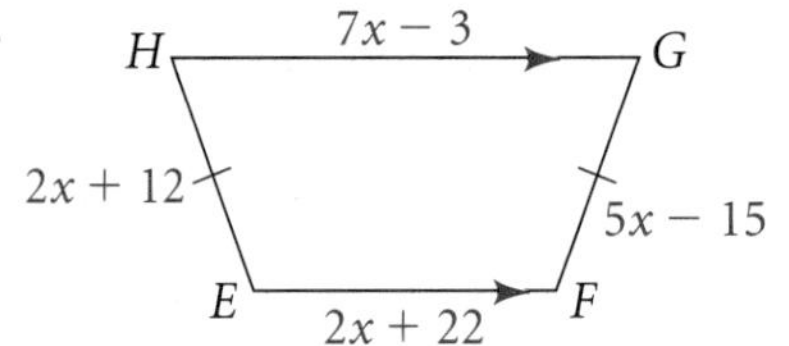

55.

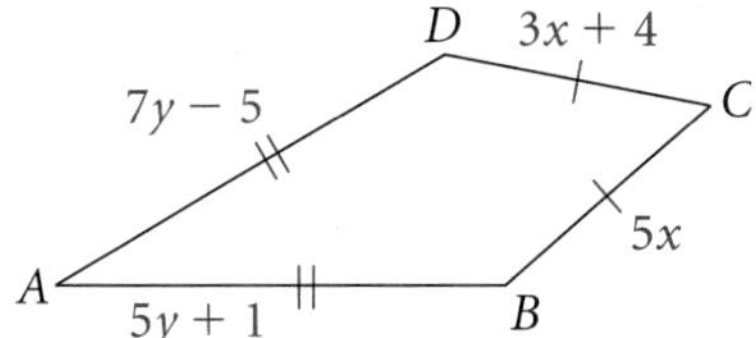

Checkpoint Quiz 1 — Lessons 9-1 through 9-3

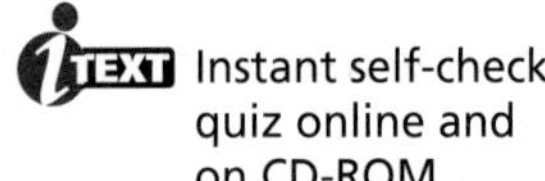
Instant self-check quiz online and on CD-ROM

Write the tangent, sine, and cosine ratios for ∠A and ∠B.

1.

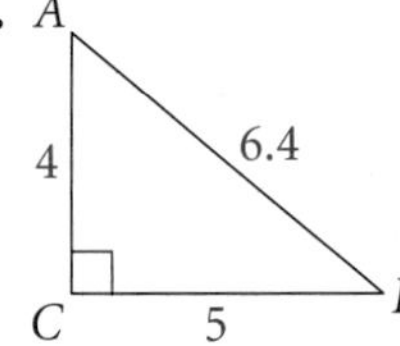

2.

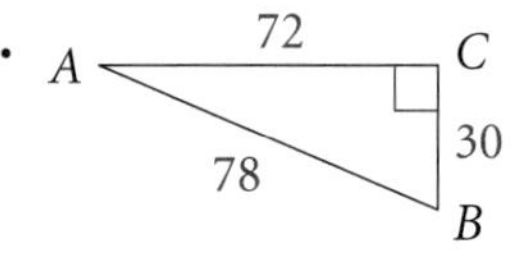

3.

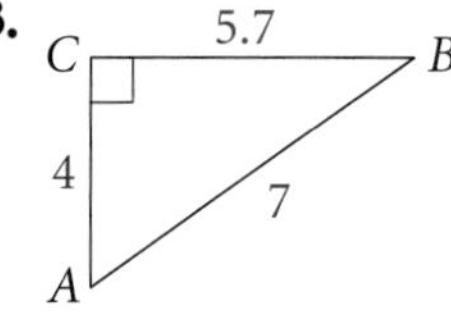

x^2 Algebra **Find the value of x. Round each segment length to the nearest tenth and each angle measure to the nearest whole number.**

4.

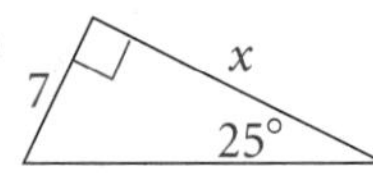

5.

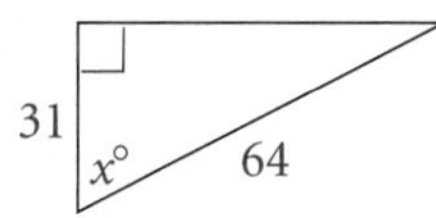

6.

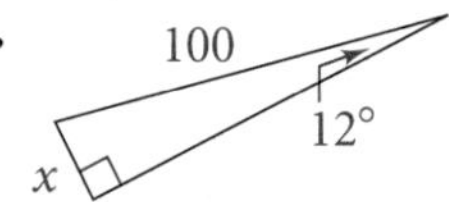

7. Landmarks The Leaning Tower of Pisa, shown at the right, reopened in 2001 after a 10-year project reduced its tilt from vertical by 0.5°. How far from the base of the tower will an object land if it is dropped the 150 ft shown in the photo?

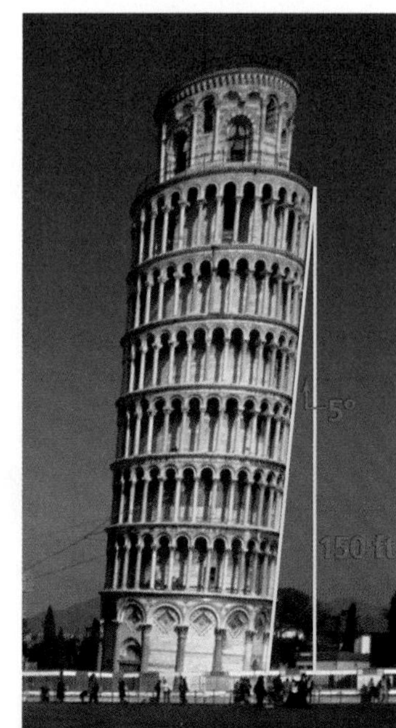

8. Navigation A captain of a sailboat sights the top of a lighthouse at a 17° angle of elevation. A navigation chart shows the height of the lighthouse to be 120 m. How far is the sailboat from the lighthouse?

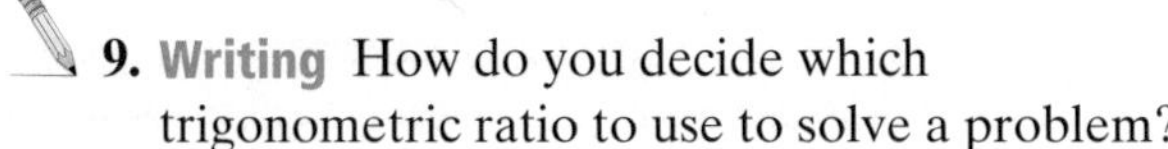

9. Writing How do you decide which trigonometric ratio to use to solve a problem?

10. Hang Gliding Students in a hang gliding class stand on the top of a cliff 70 m high. They watch a hang glider land on the beach below. The angle of depression to the hang glider is 72°. How far is the hang glider from the base of the cliff?

Reading for Problem Solving

For Use With Page 485, Exercise 23

Read the problem. Then follow along with what Curtis thinks as he solves it. Check your understanding by solving the exercise at the bottom of the page.

A blimp is providing aerial television views of a football game. The television camera sights the stadium at a 7° angle of depression. The blimp's altitude is 400 m. What is the line-of-sight distance from the TV camera to the stadium, to the nearest hundred meters?

What Curtis Thinks

To start, I'll draw and label a sketch.
Angle of depression = 7°
Altitude of blimp = 400 m

I'm supposed to find the line-of-sight distance from the TV camera to the stadium. That's the diagonal segment from the blimp's gondola to the 50-yd line. I'll label it x.

To find x, I'll probably need a trig ratio. I've labeled a leg and the hypotenuse of a right triangle 400 m and x. I can use a *sine* or *cosine* ratio if I can find one of the acute angles.

Because alternate interior angles must be congruent, the smaller acute angle is 7°.

Now I'll write an equation.

I'll solve the equation for x.

I'll use a calculator and round.

Now I can state the answer.

What Curtis Writes

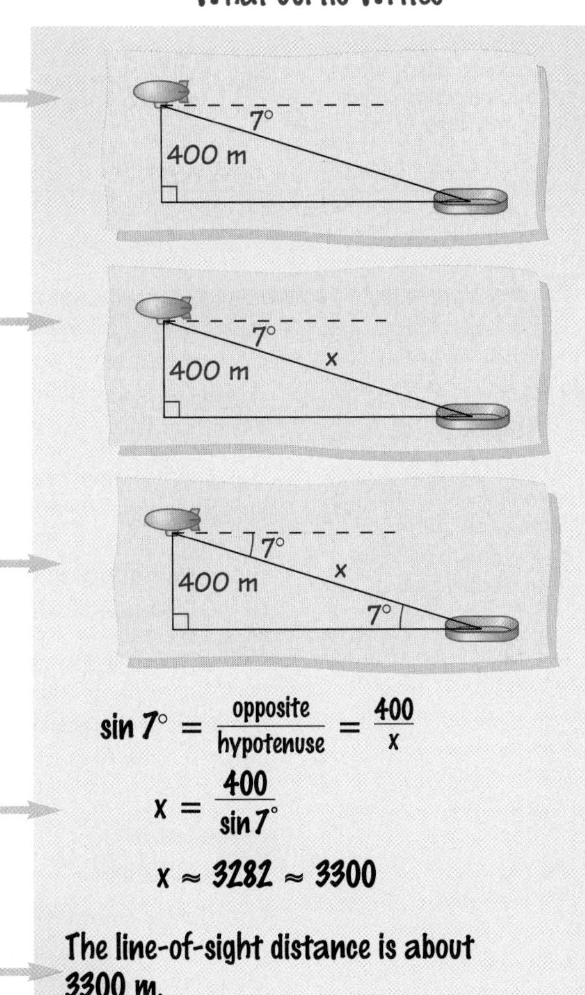

EXERCISE

A pedestrian sights the top of a building at an angle of elevation of 75°. She is standing 50 ft from the base of the building. How high above her eye level is the top of the building to the nearest foot?

Vectors

Lesson Preview

What You'll Learn

To describe vectors

To solve problems that involve vector addition

. . . And Why

To use vectors to describe the distance and direction of an airplane flight, as in Example 3

✓ Check Skills You'll Need

(For help, go to Lesson 7-2.)

x^2 **Algebra** **Find the value of x. Leave your answers in simplest radical form.**

1. 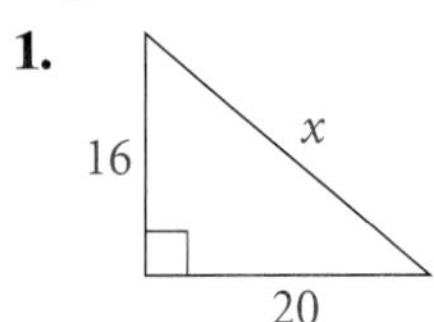

2. 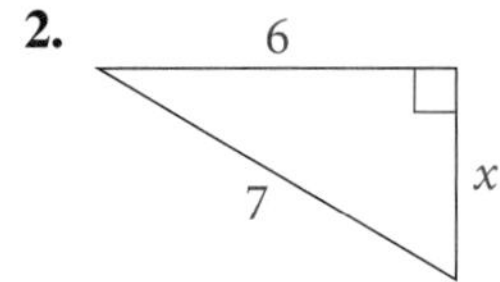

3. 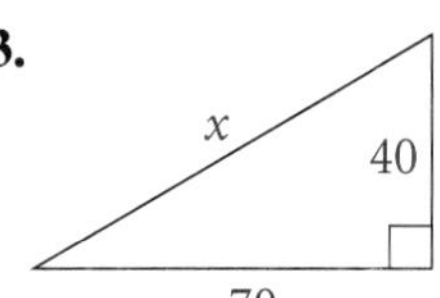

New Vocabulary • vector • magnitude • initial point • terminal point • resultant

Interactive lesson includes instant self-check, tutorials, and activities.

OBJECTIVE 1 Describing Vectors

Reading Math

You distinguish between $\overline{KW}$ and $\overrightarrow{KW}$, and between $\langle x, y\rangle$ and (x, y) by the context in which each is used.

A **vector** is any quantity with magnitude (size) and direction. There are many models for a vector.

You can use an arrow for a vector as shown by the velocity vector $\overrightarrow{KW}$ in the photo. The **magnitude** corresponds to the distance from **initial point** K to the **terminal point** W. The direction corresponds to the direction in which the arrow points.

You can also use an ordered pair $\langle x, y\rangle$ in the coordinate plane for a vector. The magnitude and direction of the vector correspond to the distance and direction of $\langle x, y\rangle$ from the origin.

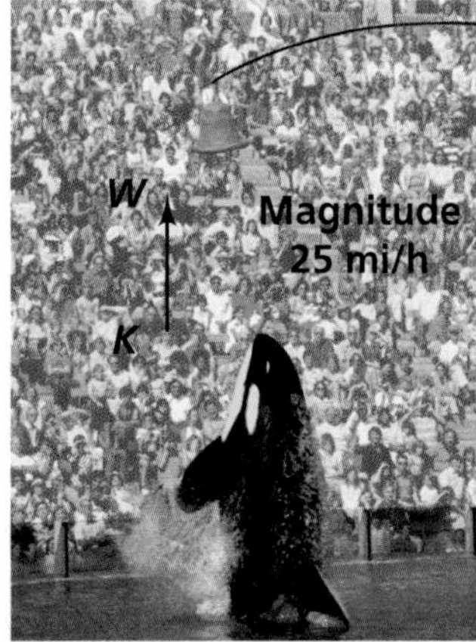

1 EXAMPLE Describing a Vector

Coordinate Geometry Describe $\overrightarrow{OL}$ as an ordered pair. Give the coordinates to the nearest tenth.

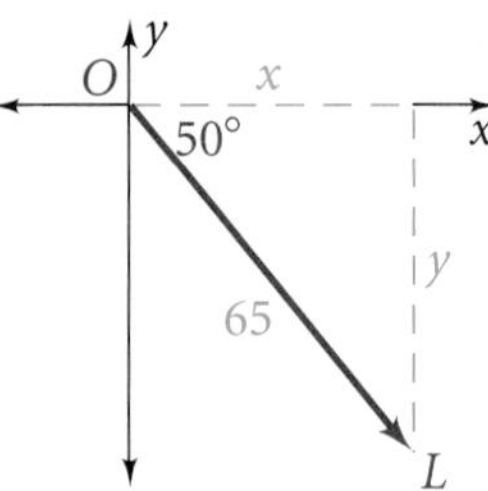

Use the sine and cosine ratios to find the values of x and y.

$\cos 50^\circ = \frac{x}{65}$	$\sin 50^\circ = \frac{y}{65}$	**Use sine and cosine.**
$x = 65(\cos 50^\circ)$	$y = 65(\sin 50^\circ)$	**Solve for the variable.**
≈ 41.78119463	≈ 49.7928888	**Use a calculator.**

L is in the fourth quadrant so the y-coordinate is negative. $\overrightarrow{OL} \approx \langle 41.8, -49.8\rangle$.

Check Understanding 1 Describe the vector at the right as an ordered pair. Give the coordinates to the nearest tenth.

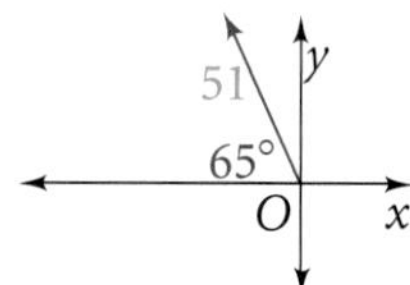

Real-World Connection

A velocity vector for a "bullet train" can have magnitude 275 km/h paired with any direction point on a compass.

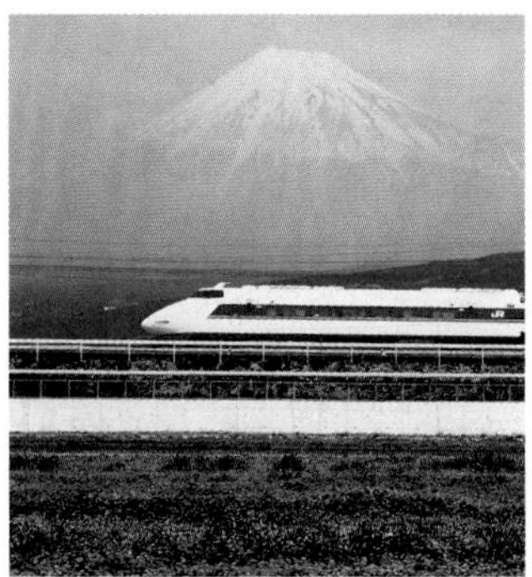

In many applications of vectors, you use the compass directions north, south, east, and west to describe the direction of a vector.

2 EXAMPLE Describing a Vector Direction

Use compass directions to describe the direction of each vector.

a.

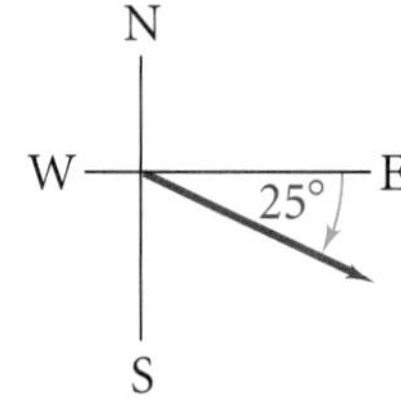

25° south of east

b.

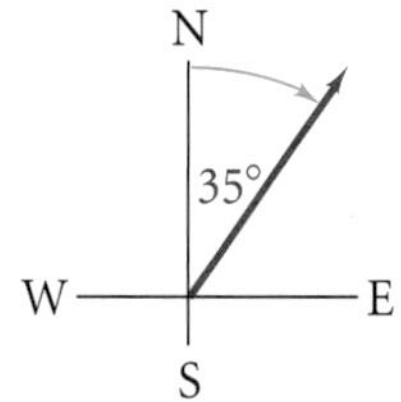

35° east of north

Check Understanding 2 **a.** Sketch a vector that has the direction 30° west of north.
b. **Critical Thinking** Give a second description for the direction of this vector.

Example 3 shows how to describe a vector's magnitude and direction when you are given its description as an ordered pair.

3 EXAMPLE Real-World Connection

Aviation An airplane lands 40 km west and 25 km south from where it took off. The result of the trip can be described by the vector $\langle -40, -25 \rangle$. Use distance (for magnitude) and direction to describe this vector a second way.

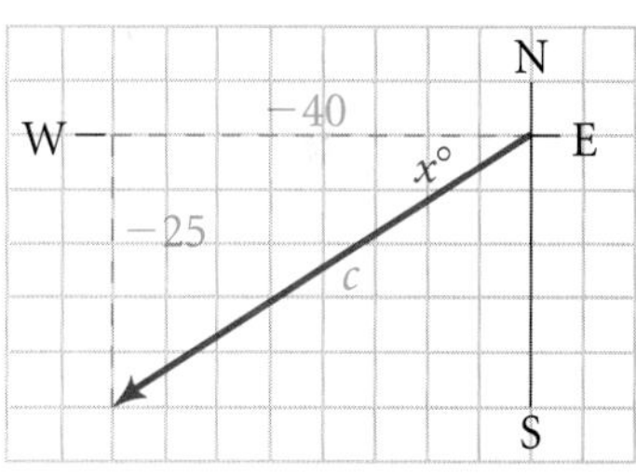

To find the distance, use the Distance Formula:

$d = \sqrt{(-40 - 0)^2 + (-25 - 0)^2}$

$d = \sqrt{1600 + 625}$ **Simplify.**

$d = \sqrt{2225}$

$d \approx 47.169906$ **Use a calculator to find the square root.**

To find the direction of the flight, find the angle of the vector south of west.

$\tan x° = \frac{25}{40}$ **Find the tangent ratio.**

$x = \tan^{-1}\left(\frac{25}{40}\right)$ **Use the inverse of tangent.**

TAN^{-1} 25 ÷ 40 ENTER 32.005383 **Use a calculator.**

The airplane flew about 47 km at 32° south of west.

Check Understanding 3 A small airplane lands at a point 246 mi east and 76 mi north of the point from which it took off. Describe the magnitude and the direction of its flight vector.

OBJECTIVE 2

Adding Vectors

You can also use a single lowercase letter, such as $\vec{u}$, to name a vector.

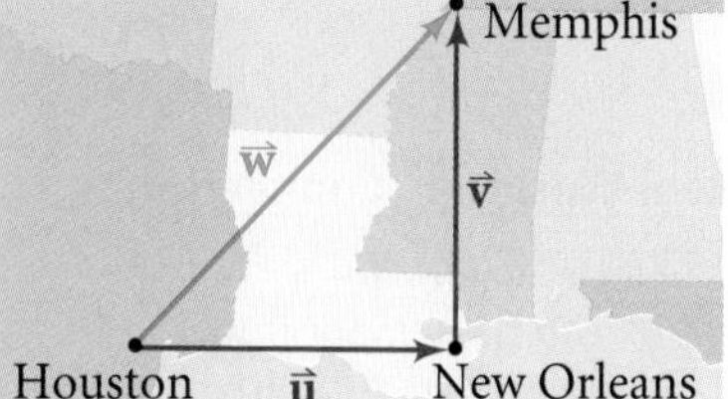

Memphis
w
v
Houston
u
New Orleans

This map shows vectors representing a flight from Houston to Memphis with a stopover in New Orleans. The vector from Houston to Memphis is called the sum, or **resultant,** of the other two vectors. You write this as

$$\vec{w} = \vec{u} + \vec{v}.$$

You can add vectors by adding their coordinates. You can also show the sum geometrically.

Key Concepts

Property	Adding Vectors
For $\vec{a} = \langle x_1, y_1 \rangle$ and $\vec{c} = \langle x_2, y_2 \rangle$, $\vec{a} + \vec{c} = \langle x_1 + x_2, y_1 + y_2 \rangle$.	

4 EXAMPLE Adding Vectors

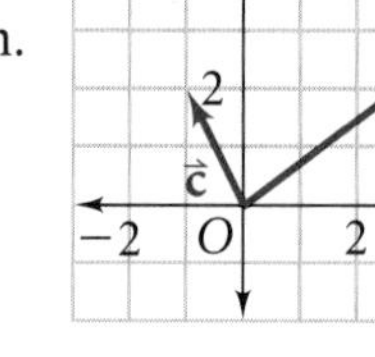

Vectors $\vec{a}\ \langle 4, 3 \rangle$ and $\vec{c}\ \langle -1, 2 \rangle$ are shown in the diagram. Write the sum of the two vectors as an ordered pair. Then draw $\vec{e}$, the sum of $\vec{a}$ and $\vec{c}$.

$\vec{a} + \vec{c} = \langle 4, 3 \rangle + \langle -1, 2 \rangle$

$= \langle 4 + (-1), 3 + 2 \rangle$ **Add the coordinates.**

$= \langle 3, 5 \rangle$ **Simplify.**

$\langle 3, 5 \rangle$ is the resultant.

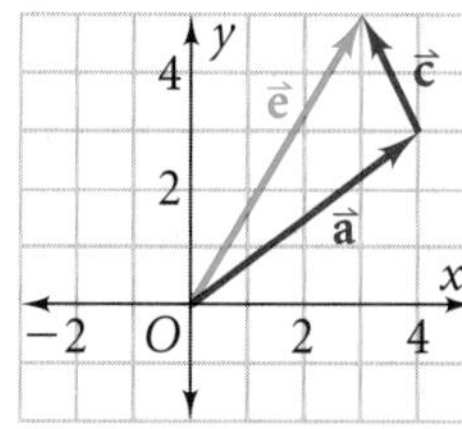

Draw $\vec{a}$ with its initial point at the origin. Then draw $\vec{c}$ with its initial point at the terminal point of $\vec{a}$. Finally, draw the resultant $\vec{e}$ from the initial point of $\vec{a}$ to the terminal point of $\vec{c}$.

Check Understanding 4 Write the sum of the two vectors $\langle 2, 3 \rangle$ and $\langle -4, -2 \rangle$ as an ordered pair.

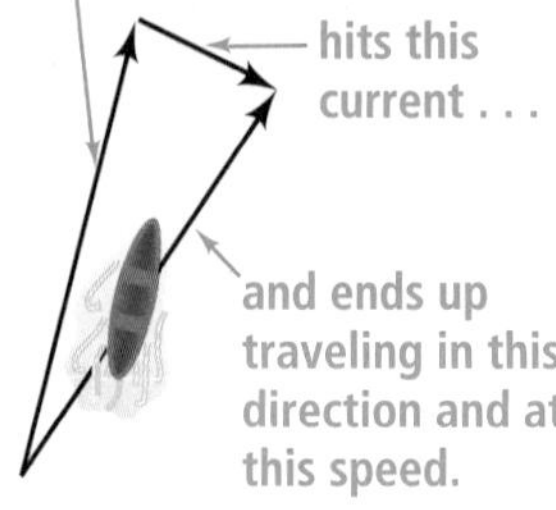

A canoe traveling in this direction and at this speed . . .
hits this current . . .
and ends up traveling in this direction and at this speed.

A vector sum can show the result of vectors that occur in sequence, such as in the airplane flight described above.

A vector sum can also show the result of vectors that act at the same time, such as when you row in a direction different from that of the current. See diagram at left.

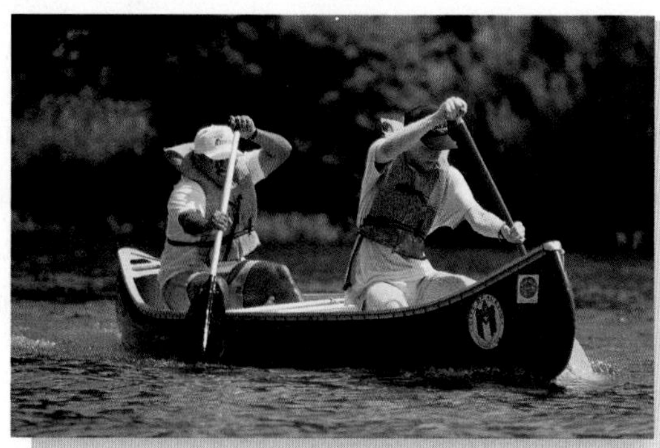

The velocity of the canoe is the vector sum of the velocities of the paddlers and the stream.

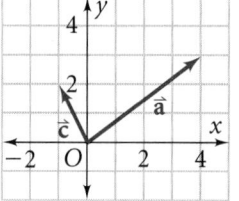

Real-World Connection

Ferry service is essential in remote regions such as on the Mackenzie River in Canada's Northwest Territories.

Navigation A ferry shuttles people from one side of a river to the other. The speed of the ferry in still water is 25 mi/h. The river flows directly south at 7 mi/h. If the ferry heads directly west, what are the ferry's resultant speed and direction?

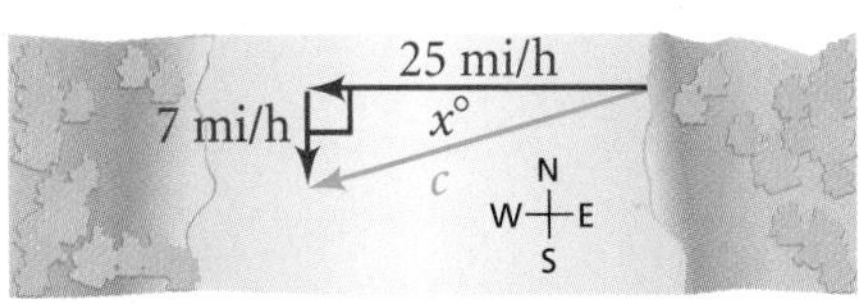

The diagram shows the sum of the two vectors. To find the ferry's resultant speed, use the Pythagorean Theorem.

$c^2 = 25^2 + 7^2$ **The lengths of the legs are 25 and 7.**

$c^2 = 674$ **Simplify.**

$c \approx 25.961510$ **Use a calculator.**

To find the ferry's resultant direction, use trigonometry.

$\tan x° = \frac{7}{25}$ **Use the tangent ratio.**

$x = \tan^{-1}\left(\frac{7}{25}\right)$ **Use the inverse of the tangent.**

$x \approx 15.642246$ **Use a calculator.**

The ferry's speed is about 26 mi/h. Its direction is about 16° south of west.

Check Understanding 5 **Critical Thinking** Use the diagram to find the angle at which the ferry must head upriver in order to travel directly across the river.

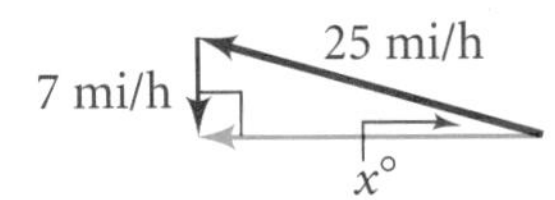

EXERCISES

For more practice, see *Extra Practice*.

Practice and Problem Solving

 **Practice by Example**

Example 1 (page 490)

Describe each vector as an ordered pair. Give the coordinates to the nearest tenth.

1.

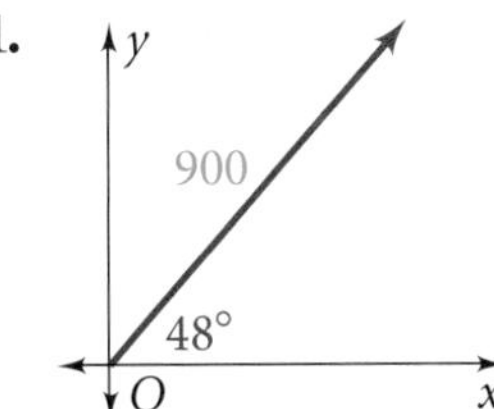

2.

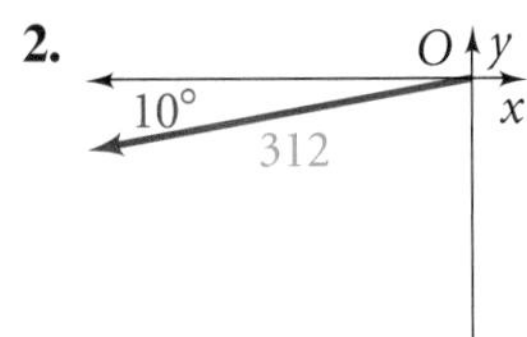

3.

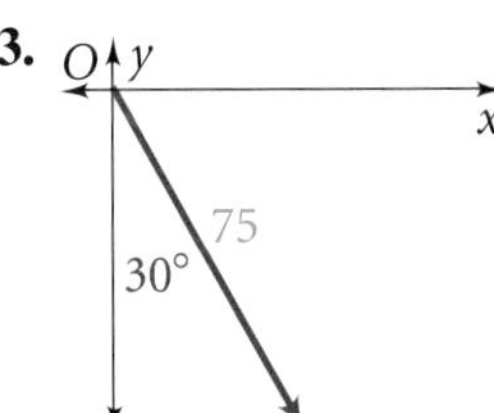

Example 2 (page 491)

Use compass directions to describe the direction of each vector.

4.

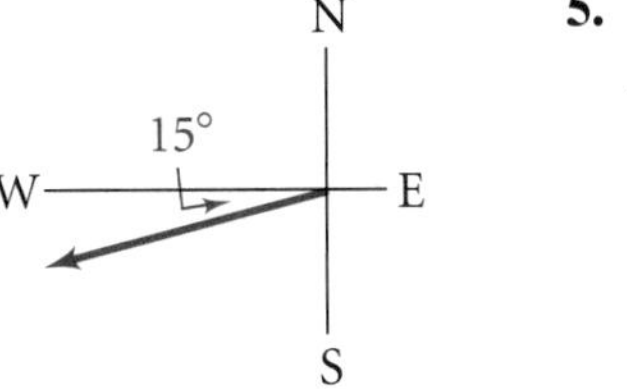

5.

6.

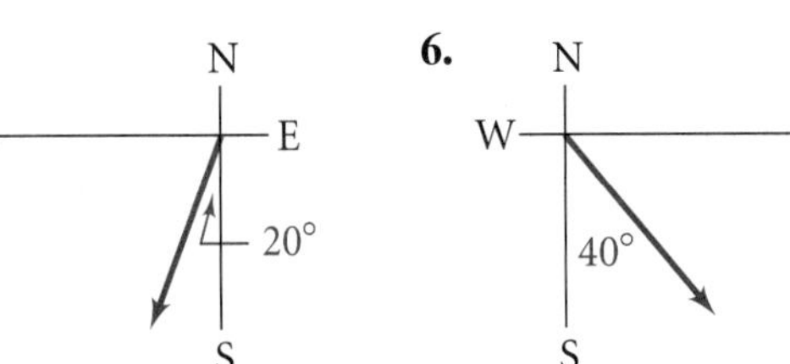

Sketch a vector that has the given direction.

7. 50° south of east
8. 20° north of west
9. 45° northeast
10. 70° west of north
11. 45° southwest
12. 10° east of south

Example 3 (page 491)

13. **History** Homing pigeons have the ability or instinct to find their way home when released hundreds of miles away from home. Homing pigeons carried news of Olympic victories to various cities in ancient Greece. Suppose one such pigeon took off from Athens and landed in Sparta, which is 73 mi west and 64 mi south of Athens. Find the distance and direction of its flight.

Find the magnitude and direction of each vector.

14.
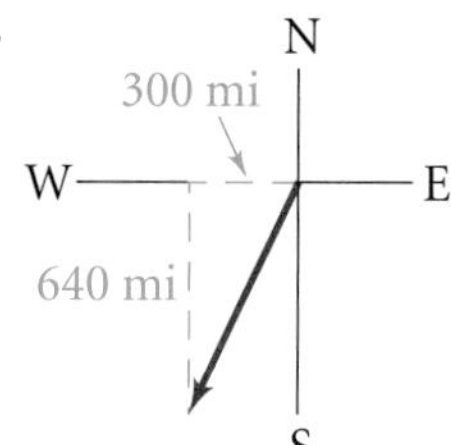

15.
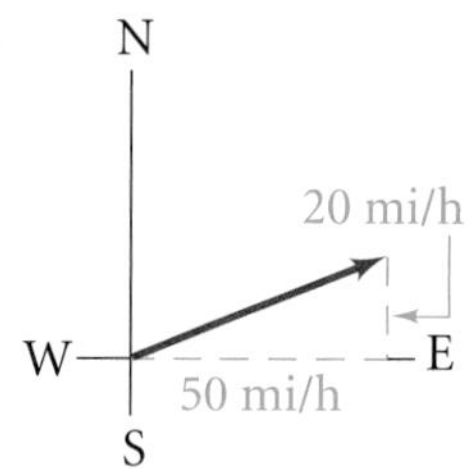

16.
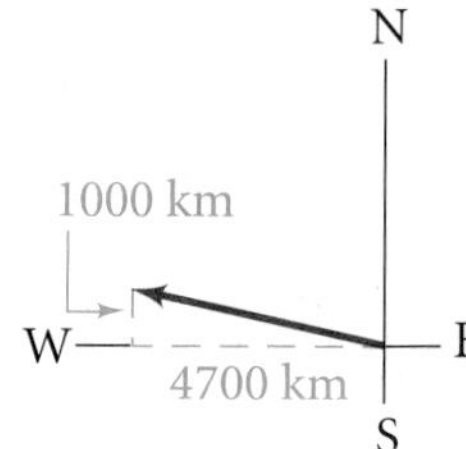

Example 4 (page 492)

In Exercises 17–22, (a) write the resultant as an ordered pair and (b) draw the resultant.

17.
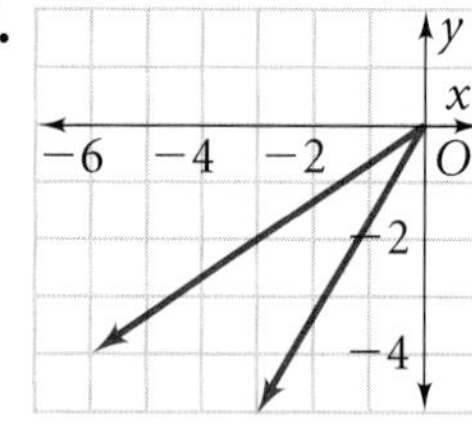

18.
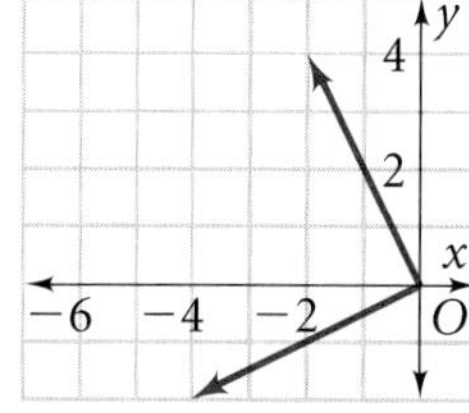

19.
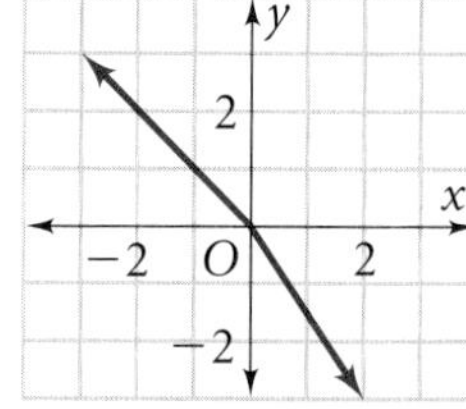

20.
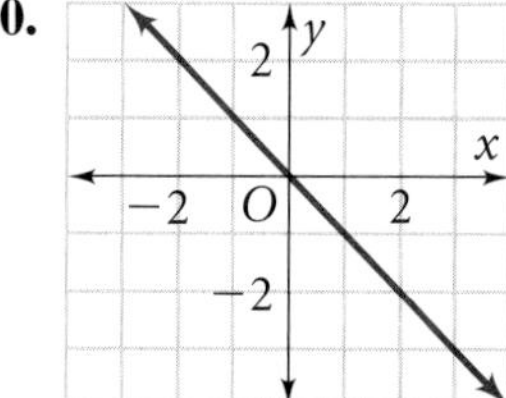

21.
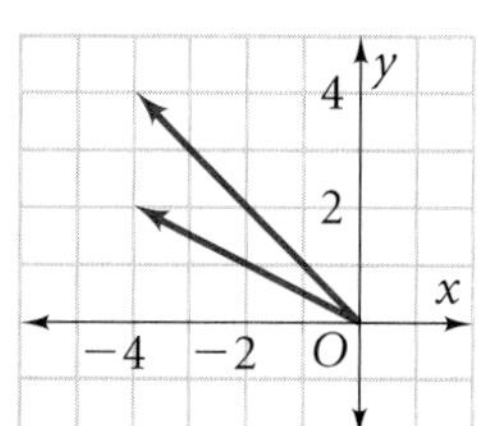

22.
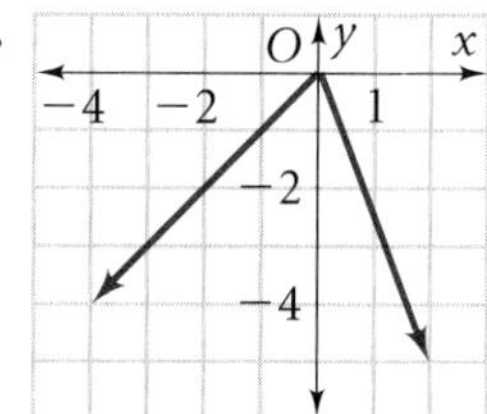

Example 5 (page 493)

Write the sum of the two vectors as an ordered pair.

23. $\langle 2, 1 \rangle$ and $\langle -3, 2 \rangle$

24. $\langle 0, 0 \rangle$ and $\langle 4, -6 \rangle$

25. $\langle -1, 1 \rangle$ and $\langle -1, 2 \rangle$

Navigation The speed of a powerboat in still water is 35 mi/h. It is traveling on a river that flows directly south at 8 mi/h.

26. The boat heads directly west across the river. What are the resulting speed and direction of the boat? Round answers to the nearest tenth.

27. At what angle should the boat head upriver in order to travel directly west?

28. **Aviation** A twin-engine airplane has a speed of 300 mi/h in still air. Suppose this airplane heads directly south and encounters a 50 mi/h wind blowing due east. Find the resulting speed and direction of the plane. Round your answers to the nearest unit.

B Apply Your Skills

29. **Critical Thinking** Valerie described the direction of a vector as 35° south of east. Pablo described it as 55° east of south. Could the two be describing the same vector? Explain.

30. **Error Analysis** Ely says that the magnitude of vector $\langle 6, 1 \rangle$ is 3 times that of vector $\langle 2, 1 \rangle$ since 6 is 3 times 2. Explain why Ely's statement is incorrect.

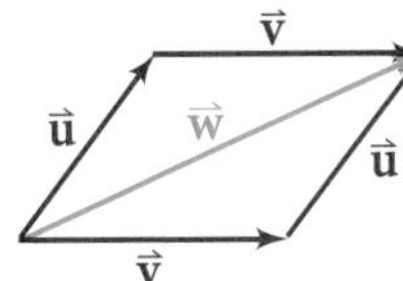

Need Help?

You can also model vector addition with the *Triangle Rule* as shown in Example 4, and by either triangular half of the diagram above.

31. The diagram at the left shows that you can add vectors in any order. That is, $\vec{u} + \vec{v} = \vec{v} + \vec{u}$. Notice also that the four vectors shown in red form a parallelogram. The resultant $\vec{w}$ is the diagonal of the parallelogram. This representation of vector addition is called *The Parallelogram Rule*.

a. Copy the diagram at the right. Draw a parallelogram that has the given vectors as adjacent sides.

b. Find the magnitude and direction of the resultant.

32. Use the diagrams below to write a definition of *equal vectors*.

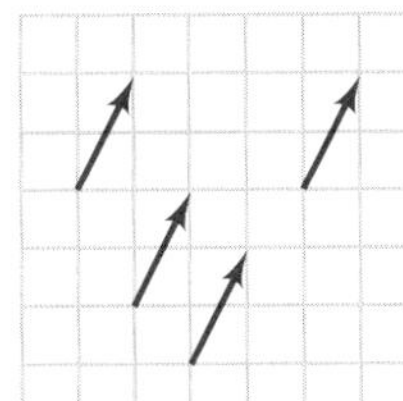

These vectors are equal.

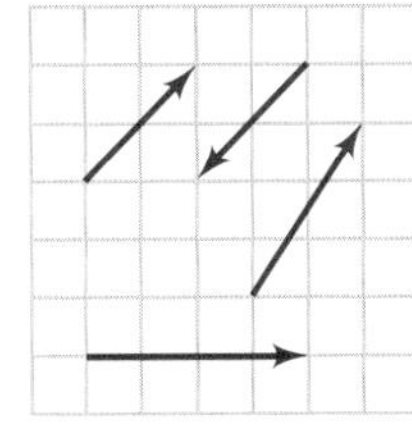

No two of these vectors are equal.

33. Use the diagrams below to write a definition of *parallel vectors*.

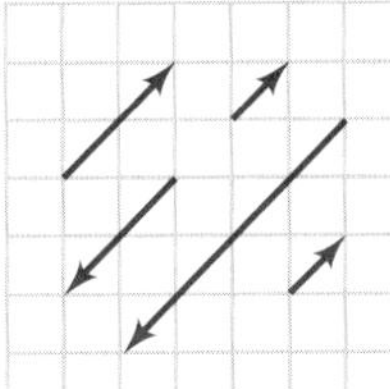

These vectors are parallel.

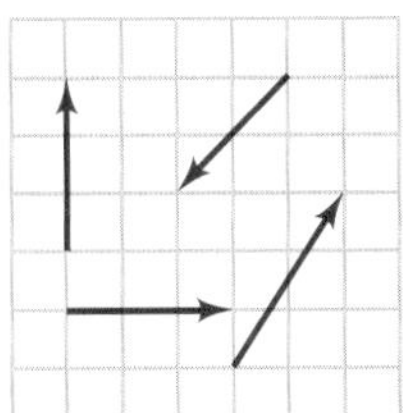

No two of these vectors are parallel.

34. Aviation A Red Cross helicopter takes off and flies 75 km at 20° south of west. There, it drops off some relief supplies. It then flies 125 km at 10° west of north to pick up three medics.

a. Make an accurate drawing of the two vectors described.

b. Draw the resultant and measure it to find the helicopter's distance from its point of origin and the direction it should head to get back.

35. a. Find the sum of $\vec{a}$ and $\vec{c}$, where $\vec{a} = \langle 45, -60 \rangle$ and $\vec{c} = \langle -45, 60 \rangle$.

b. Writing Based on your answer to part (a), how can you describe $\vec{a}$ and $\vec{c}$?

36. Aviation In still air, the WP-3D (see below) flies at 374 mi/h. Suppose that a WP-3D flies due west and meets a hurricane wind blowing due south at 95 mi/h. What are the resultant speed and direction of the airplane to the nearest unit?

Flying into a Hurricane

When most pilots hear a forecast for gale force winds, they don't think, "Time to fly." Then again, most pilots don't work for the National Oceanic and Atmospheric Administration. NOAA fly their four-engine WP-3D turboprops directly into hurricanes. These aircraft carry eight crew members, up to ten scientists, and a load of data-collection equipment. Some of this equipment is in the WP-3D's long "snout," which also serves as a lightning rod. In a routine flight, the WP-3D is struck by lightning three or four times. Surprisingly, small burn holes are the only damage from these strikes. To help overcome temporary blindness caused by lightning flashes, the pilot sets the cockpit lights at the brightest level.

The vector $\langle -5, 5\rangle$ can be written as the *column matrix* $\begin{bmatrix} -5 \\ 5 \end{bmatrix}$. Find the sum of the vectors in column matrix form.

37. $\begin{bmatrix} 2 \\ -4 \end{bmatrix} + \begin{bmatrix} -3 \\ 2 \end{bmatrix}$ **38.** $\begin{bmatrix} 8 \\ -1 \end{bmatrix} + \begin{bmatrix} 3 \\ -4 \end{bmatrix}$ **39.** $\begin{bmatrix} 4 \\ -5 \end{bmatrix} + \begin{bmatrix} -5 \\ 5 \end{bmatrix}$

Need Help?

In Exercise 40, remember that any vector is equal to one whose initial point is the origin.

40. Aviation An airplane takes off from a runway in the direction 10° east of south. When it reaches 5000 ft, it turns right 45°. It cruises at this altitude for 60 mi. Then it turns left 160°, descends, and lands. Match each vector with the appropriate portion of the flight.

I. 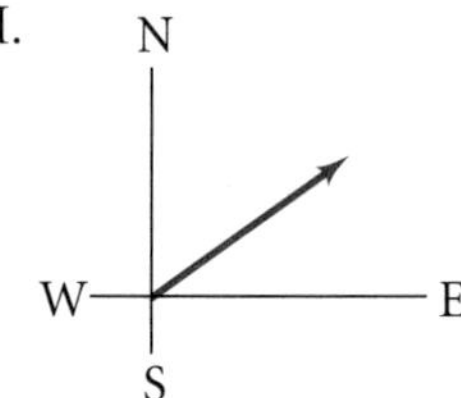

II. 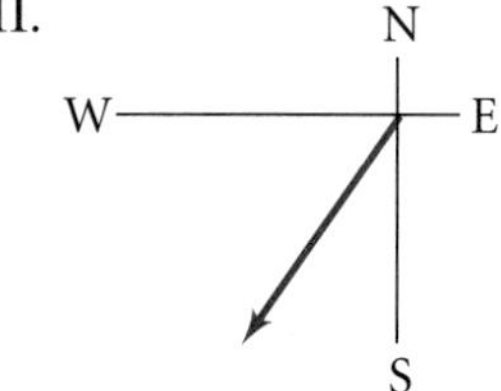

III. 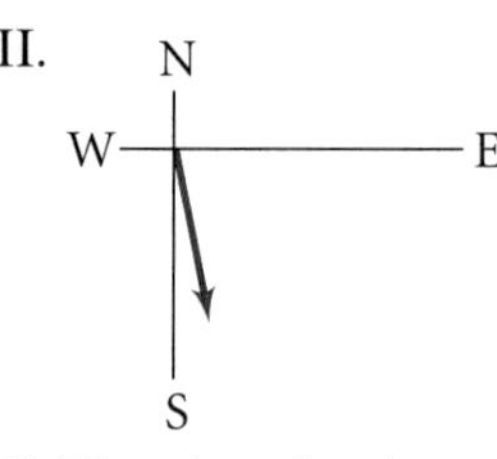

A. The plane takes off. B. The plane cruises. C. The plane lands.

41. Aviation The cruising speed of a Boeing 767 in still air is 530 mi/h. Suppose that a 767 is cruising directly east when it encounters an 80 mi/h wind blowing 40° south of west.

a. Sketch the vectors for the velocities of the airplane and the wind.

b. Express both vectors from part (a) in ordered pair notation.

c. Find the sum of the vectors from part (b).

d. Find the magnitude and direction of the vector from part (c).

Give the sum of $\vec{a}$ and $\vec{b}$. Show $\vec{a}$ and $\vec{b}$ and their sum in the coordinate plane.

42. $\vec{a}\ \langle -5, -2\rangle, \vec{b}\ \langle 2, -5\rangle$ **43.** $\vec{a}\ \langle 5, -2\rangle, \vec{b}\ \langle -5, -2\rangle$ **44.** $\vec{a}\ \langle 5, -5\rangle, \vec{b}\ \langle -2, 2\rangle$

45. Writing How are vectors $\overrightarrow{AB}$ and $\overrightarrow{BA}$ alike? How are they different?

46. Open-Ended Name four other vectors with the same magnitude as $\langle -7, -24\rangle$.

47. Navigation A fishing boat leaves its home port and travels 150 mi directly east. It then changes course and travels 40 mi due north.

a. In what direction should the boat head to return to home port?

b. How long will the return trip take if the boat averages 23 mi/h?

THE FAR SIDE® By GARY LARSON

"Well, lemme think. ... You've stumped me, son. Most folks only wanna know how to go the other way."

Exercise 45

48. Navigation A boat left dock A, traveled north for 10 miles, then 45° east of north for 20 miles, and docked at B.

a. How far north did the boat travel? How far east did it travel?

b. Find the magnitude and direction of the direct-path vector $\overrightarrow{AB}$.

Challenge

49. Geometry in 3 Dimensions A hot-air balloon traveled 2000 ft north and 900 ft east, while rising 400 ft. This trip can be described with the three-coordinate vector $\langle 2000, 900, 400\rangle$. What is the magnitude of the vector? What is the angle of elevation of the balloon from its starting point?

50. a. **Probability** You choose two of the vectors at the right at random. Find the probability that the magnitude of their resultant vector is greater than that of the third vector.

b. **Open-Ended** Draw three vectors of your own. Then do part (a) for your vectors.

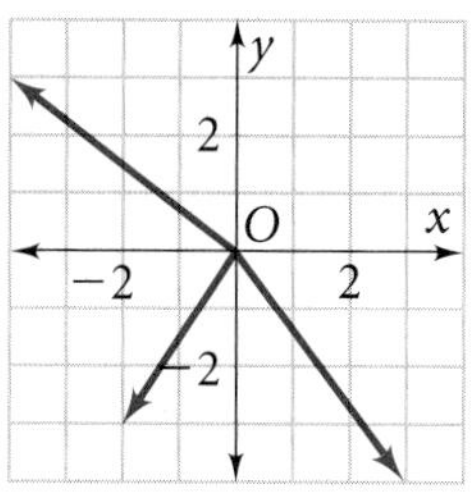

51. **Writing** Think of the number zero and its properties. Define a *zero vector* and justify your definition.

52. **Aviation** A helicopter starts at (0, 0) and makes three parts of a flight represented by the vectors ⟨10, 10⟩, ⟨5, −4⟩, and ⟨−3, 5⟩, in that order.

a. If another helicopter starts at (0, 0) and flies the same three parts in a different order, would it end in the same place? Justify your answer.

b. If yet another helicopter flew the three parts of the flight in a different order from the original trip, could the second part of the flight end at the same place as the second part of the original trip? Justify your answer.

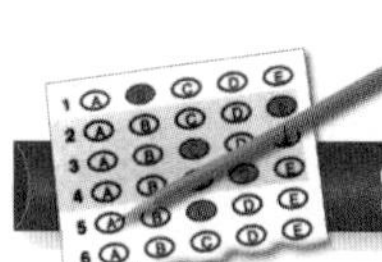

Standardized Test Prep

Multiple Choice

53. $\vec{c}$, $\vec{s}$, and $\vec{u}$ are vectors. $\vec{c} = \langle -8, 10\rangle$, $\vec{s} = \langle 0, -3\rangle$, and $\vec{u} = \vec{c} + \vec{s}$. What are the coordinates of $\vec{u}$?

A. ⟨7, −8⟩ B. ⟨−7, 8⟩ C. ⟨8, −7⟩ D. ⟨−8, 7⟩

Short Response

54. A boat heads due south directly across a river at 30 ft/min. The river is flowing east at 20 ft/min.

a. What is the resultant speed of the boat?

b. What is the resultant direction of the boat?

Extended Response

55. A small aircraft is traveling east at 400 mi/h. It encounters a 50 mi/h wind blowing 30° west of south.

a. Sketch and label vectors for the velocities of the aircraft and the wind.

b. Express both vectors in ordered pair notation.

c. Find the sum of the vectors.

d. Find the magnitude and direction of the vector from part (c).

Take It to the NET

Online lesson quiz at **www.PHSchool.com**

Web Code: afa-0904

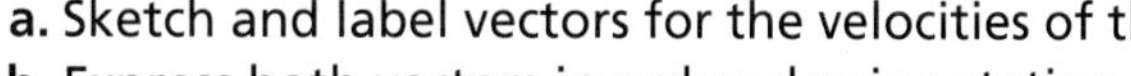

Mixed Review

Lesson 9-3

56. **Indirect Measurement** A hot-air balloon pilot sights the landing field from a height of 2000 ft. The angle of depression is 24°. To the nearest foot, what is the ground distance from the hot-air balloon to the landing field?

Lesson 7-8

Games **You toss a dart at each dartboard and hit at a random point. Find the probability that the dart hits in the red region.**

57.

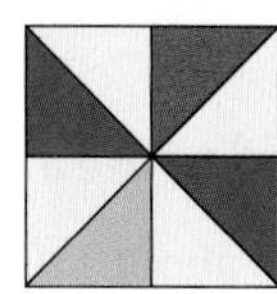

58.

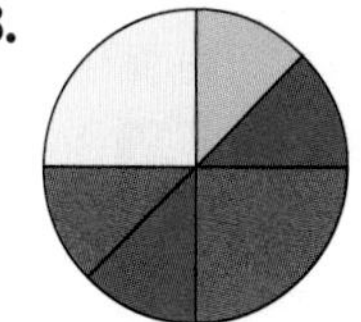

59.

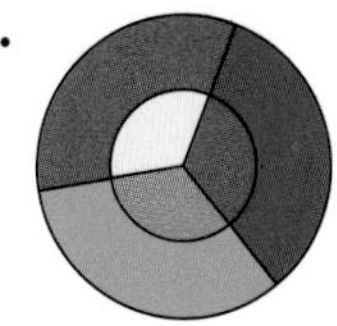

Lesson 7-1

60. Find the area of ▱$ABCD$ with vertices $A(-1, -5)$, $B(6, -5)$, $C(9, 3)$, and $D(2, 3)$.

9-5 Trigonometry and Area

Lesson Preview

What You'll Learn

To find the area of a regular polygon using trigonometry

To find the area of a triangle using trigonometry

. . . And Why

To find the area of a courtyard, as in Example 2

✓ Check Skills You'll Need

(For help, go to Lesson 7-5.)

Find the area of each regular polygon.

1.
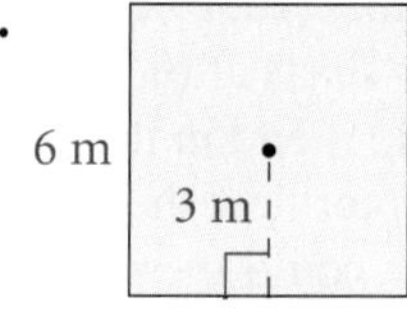

2.
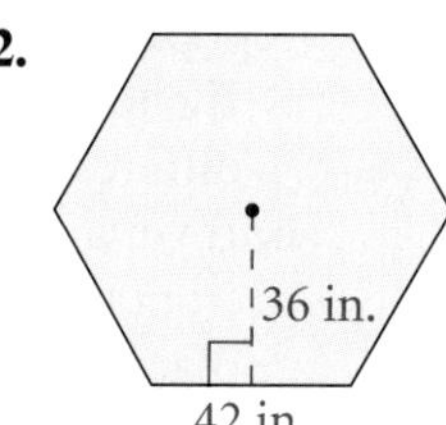

3.
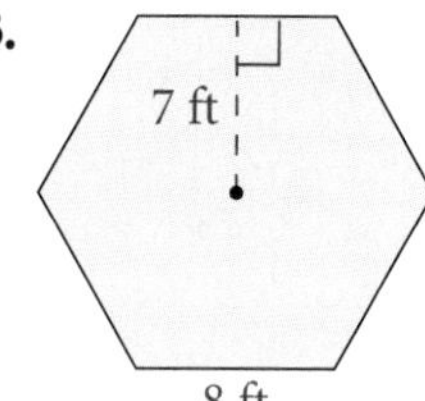

Interactive lesson includes instant self-check, tutorials, and activities.

OBJECTIVE 1 Finding the Area of a Regular Polygon

In Chapter 7, you learned to find the area of a regular polygon by using the formula $A = \frac{1}{2}ap$, where a is the apothem and p is the perimeter. By using this formula and trigonometric ratios, you can solve other types of problems.

Need Help?

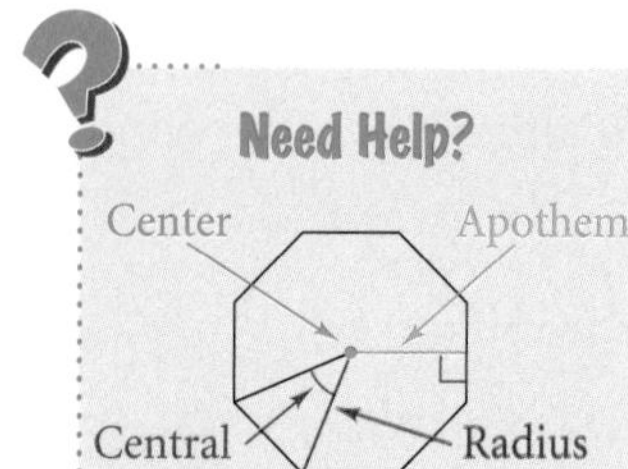

1 EXAMPLE Finding Area

Find the area of a regular pentagon with 8-cm sides.

To use the formula $A = \frac{1}{2}ap$, you need the apothem and perimeter. The perimeter is $5 \cdot 8$, or 40 cm.

To find the apothem, use trigonometry.

The measure of the central angle $\angle XCZ$ is $\frac{360}{5}$, or 72.

$m\angle XCY = \frac{1}{2}m\angle XCZ = 36$.

$XY = \frac{1}{2}XZ$, so $XY = 4$.

$\tan 36^\circ = \frac{4}{a}$ **Use the tangent ratio.**

$a = \frac{4}{\tan 36^\circ}$ **Solve for *a*.**

Now substitute into the area formula.

$A = \frac{1}{2}ap$

$= \frac{1}{2} \cdot \frac{4}{\tan 36^\circ} \cdot 40$ **Substitute for *a* and *p*.**

$= \frac{80}{\tan 36^\circ}$ **Simplify.**

80 ÷ TAN 36 ENTER 110.11055 **Use a calculator.**

The area of the regular pentagon is about 110 cm^2.

Check Understanding 1 Find the area of a regular octagon with a perimeter of 80 in. Give the area to the nearest tenth.

Sometimes you can use trigonometry to find both apothem and perimeter.

2 EXAMPLE Real-World Connection

Architecture The Castel del Monte, built on a hill in southern Italy circa 1240, makes extraordinary use of regular octagons. One regular octagon, the inner courtyard, has radius 16 m. Find the area of the courtyard.

The measure of a central angle of the octagon is $\frac{360}{8}$, or 45. So $m\angle C = \frac{1}{2}(45) = 22.5$.

Use the cosine ratio to find the apothem.

$$\cos 22.5^\circ = \frac{a}{16}$$
$$a = 16(\cos 22.5^\circ)$$

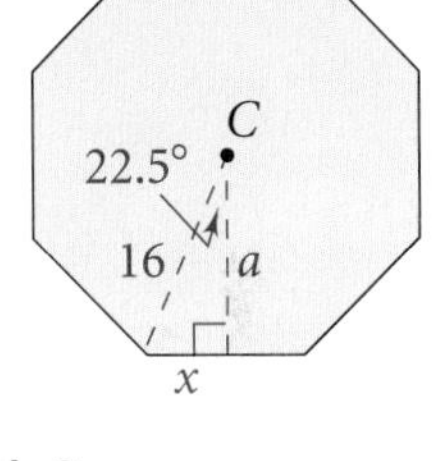

Use the sine ratio to find the perimeter.

$$\sin 22.5^\circ = \frac{x}{16}$$
$$x = 16(\sin 22.5^\circ)$$
$$p = 8 \cdot \text{length of a side}$$
$$= 8 \cdot 2x \qquad \text{The length of each side is } 2x.$$
$$= 8 \cdot 2 \cdot 16(\sin 22.5^\circ) \qquad \text{Substitute for } x.$$
$$= 256(\sin 22.5^\circ) \qquad \text{Simplify.}$$

Substitute into the area formula, $A = \frac{1}{2}ap$.

$$A = \frac{1}{2} \cdot 16(\cos 22.5^\circ) \cdot 256(\sin 22.5^\circ) \qquad \text{Substitute for } a \text{ and } p.$$
$$\approx 724.07734 \qquad \text{Use a calculator.}$$

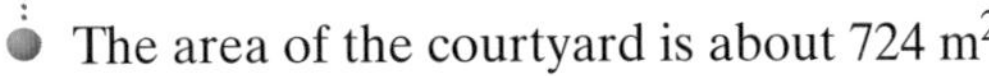

The area of the courtyard is about 724 m^2.

Check Understanding **2** **Critical Thinking** If the radius of the main structure is twice the radius of the inner courtyard, how does the area it covers compare to the area of the courtyard?

OBJECTIVE

2 Finding the Area of a Triangle

Reading Math

Before going on, learn to read the last equation as "the area of a triangle is half the product of two sides and the sine of their included angle."

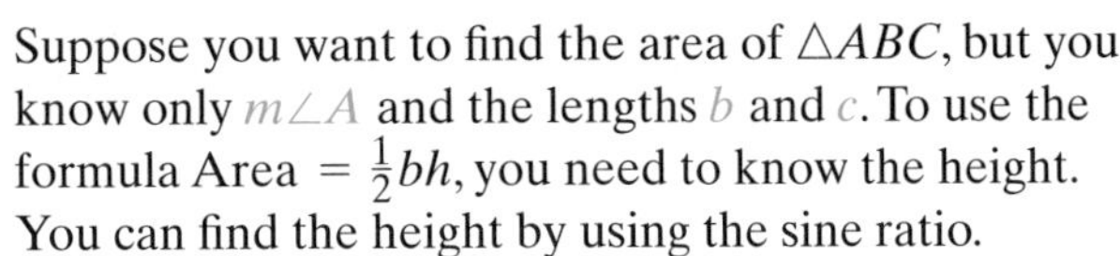

Suppose you want to find the area of $\triangle ABC$, but you know only $m\angle A$ and the lengths b and c. To use the formula Area $= \frac{1}{2}bh$, you need to know the height. You can find the height by using the sine ratio.

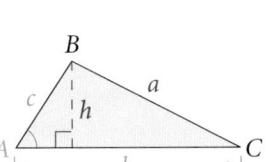

$$\sin A = \frac{h}{c} \qquad \text{Use the sine ratio.}$$
$$h = c(\sin A) \qquad \text{Solve for } h.$$

Now substitute for h in the formula Area $= \frac{1}{2}bh$.

$$\text{Area} = \frac{1}{2}bc(\sin A)$$

Your work at the bottom of page 499 completes a proof of the following theorem for the case in which $\angle A$ is acute.

Key Concepts

Theorem 9-1 **Area of a Triangle Given SAS**

The area of a triangle is one half the product of the lengths of two sides and the sine of the included angle.

$$\text{Area of } \triangle ABC = \frac{1}{2}bc(\sin A)$$

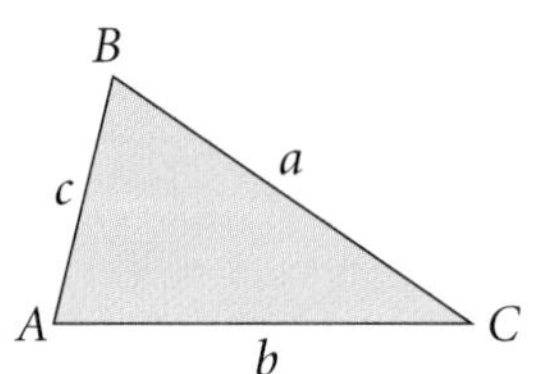

3 EXAMPLE **Real-World Connection**

Surveying The surveyed lengths of two adjacent sides of a triangular plot of land are 412 ft and 386 ft. The angle between the sides is 71°. Find the area of the plot.

$\text{Area} = \frac{1}{2} \cdot \text{side length} \cdot \text{side length} \cdot \text{sine of included angle}$

$= \frac{1}{2} \cdot 412 \cdot 386 \cdot \sin 71°$ **Substitute.**

≈ 75183.855 **Use a calculator.**

The area of the plot is approximately 75,200 ft^2.

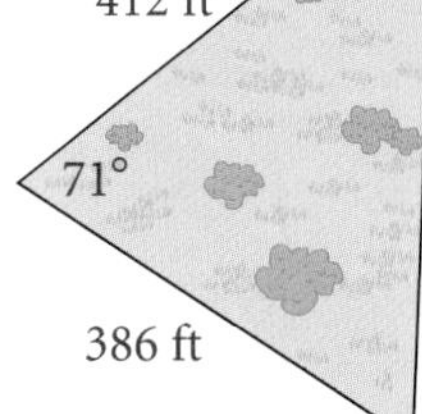

Check Understanding **3** Two sides of a triangular building plot are 120 ft and 85 ft long. They include an angle of 85°. Find the area of the building plot to the nearest square foot.

EXERCISES

For more practice, see *Extra Practice.*

Practice and Problem Solving

A Practice by Example

Example 1 (page 498)

Find the area of each regular polygon. Give answers to the nearest tenth.

1. octagon with side length 6 cm

2. pentagon with side length 7 in.

3. hexagon with perimeter 60 m

4. 15-gon with perimeter 180 yd

5. *PQRST* is a regular pentagon with center *O* and radius 10 in.

a. Find $m\angle POQ$.

b. Find $m\angle POX$.

c. Find *OX*.

d. Find *PQ*.

e. Find the perimeter.

f. Find the area.

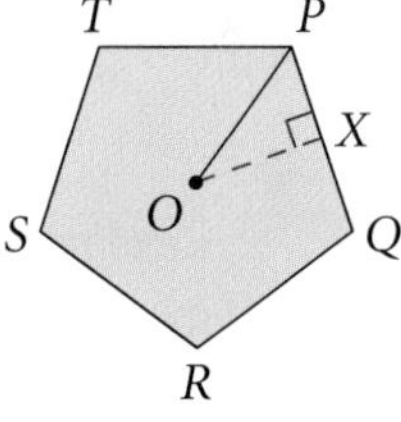

Example 2 (page 499)

Find the area of each regular polygon. Give answers to the nearest tenth.

6. hexagon with radius 10 ft

7. decagon with radius 4 in.

8. octagon with radius 20 cm

9. square with radius 2 ft

10. **Architecture** Each of the eight small towers around Castel del Monte (page 499) is a regular octagon. The radius is 7.3 m. Find the area each tower covers to the nearest square meter.

Example 3
(page 500)

Find the area of each triangle. Give answers to the nearest tenth.

11.

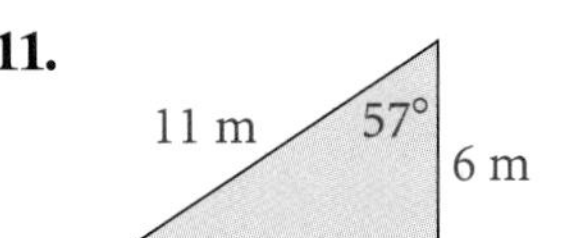

12.

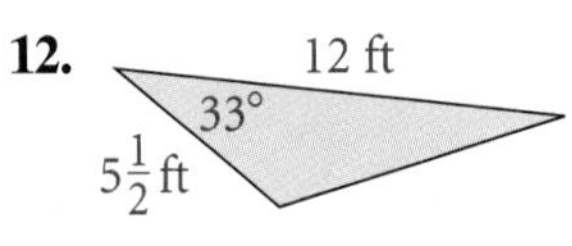

13.

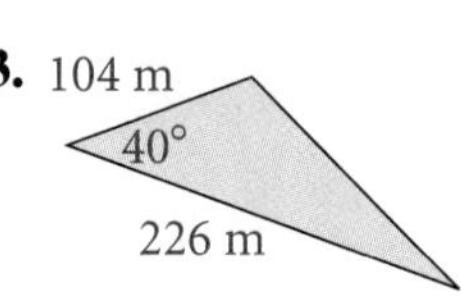

14.

34 km
28°
39 km

15.

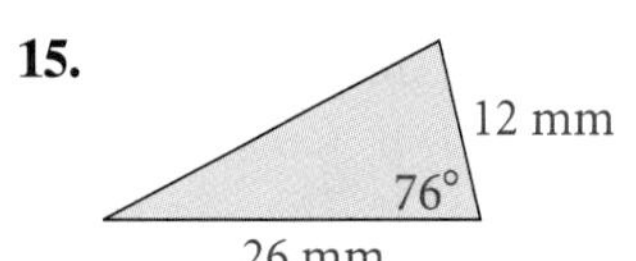

16.

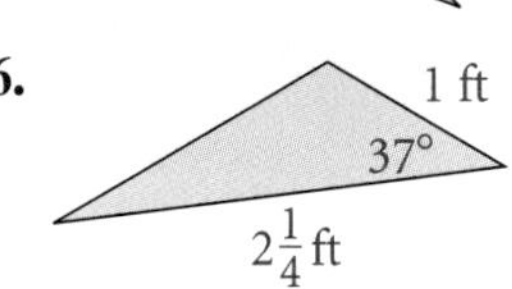

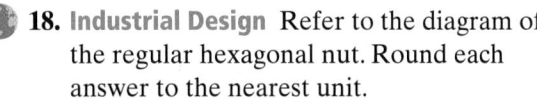

17. Surveying A surveyor marks off a triangular parcel of land. One side of the triangle extends 80 yd. A second side of 150 yd forms an angle of 67° with the first side. Determine the area of the parcel of land to the nearest square yard.

B Apply Your Skills

18. Industrial Design Refer to the diagram of the regular hexagonal nut. Round each answer to the nearest unit.

a. Find the area of the circular hole in the hexagonal nut.

b. Find the area of the hexagonal face.

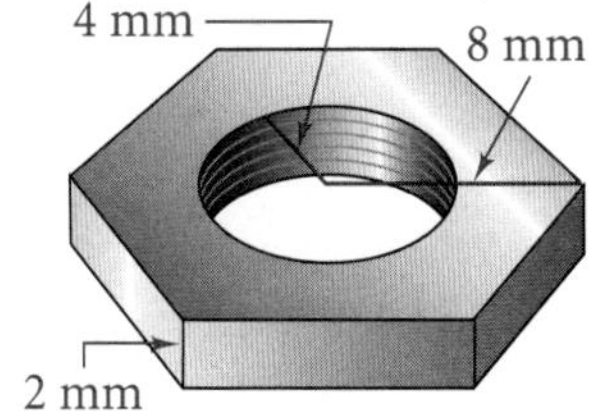

19. Writing Describe two ways to find the area of an equilateral triangle that has a 1-in. radius.

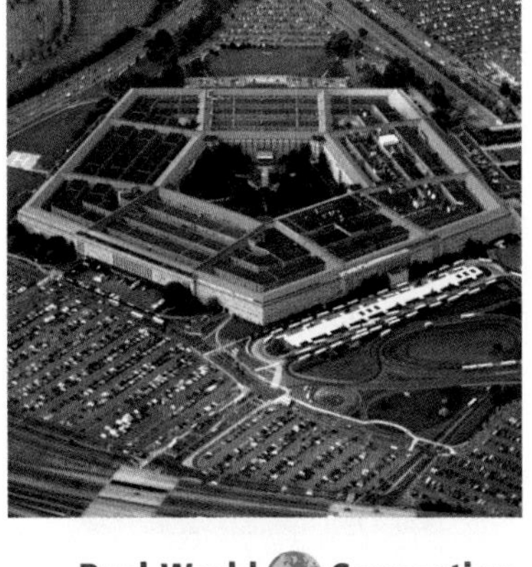

Real-World Connection

The length of each side of the Pentagon courtyard is 356 ft. A football field is 360 ft.

20. Architecture The Pentagon, in Arlington, Virginia, is one of the world's largest office buildings. It is a regular pentagon, and the length of each of its sides is 921 ft. Find the area of this pentagon to the nearest thousand square feet.

21. Windows Replacement glass for more energy efficient windows costs $\$5/\text{ft}^2$. Approximately how much will you pay for replacement glass for a regular hexagonal window with a radius of 2 ft?

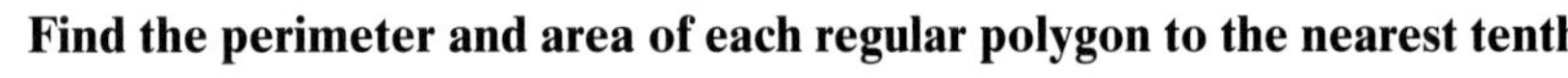

Find the perimeter and area of each regular polygon to the nearest tenth.

22.

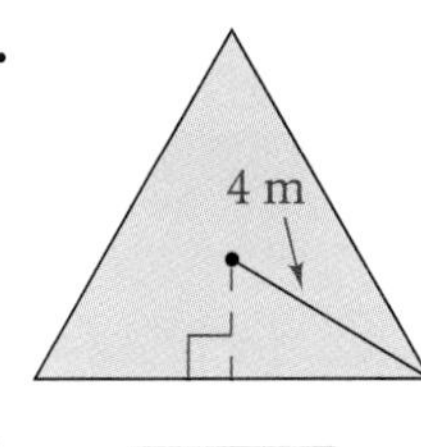

23.

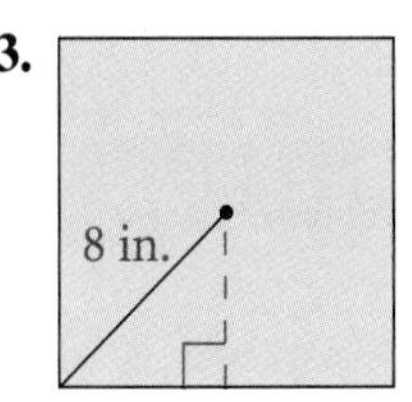

24.

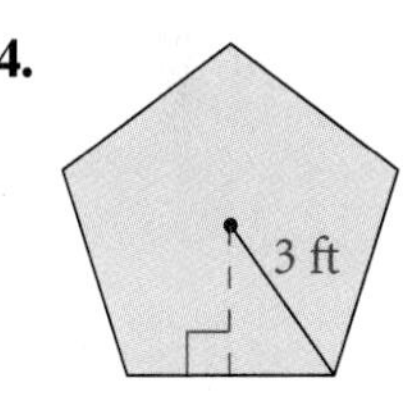

25.

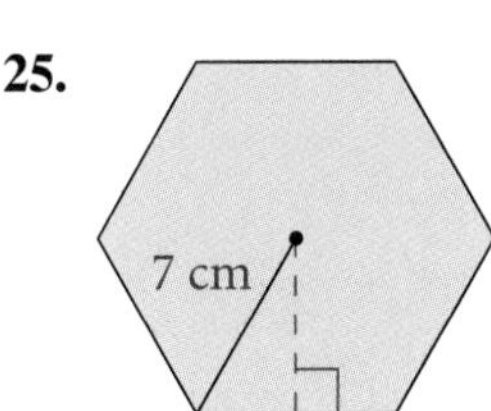

26.

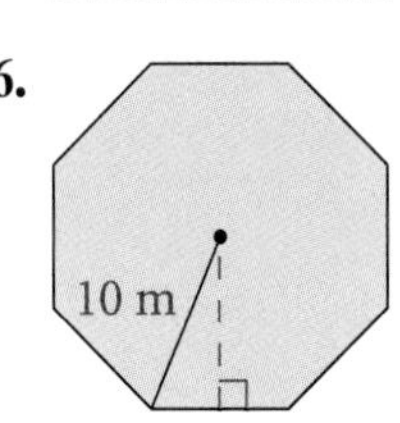

27.

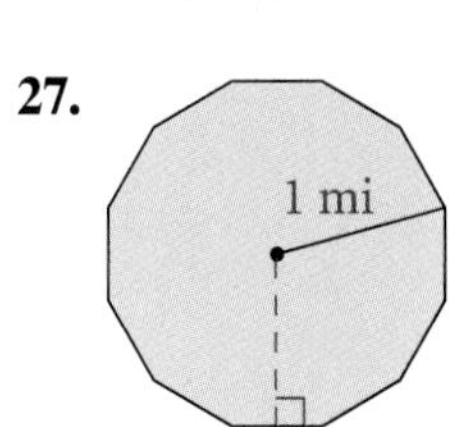

Regular polygons A and B are similar. Compare their areas.

28. The radius of square A is twice the radius of square B.

29. The apothem of pentagon A equals the radius of pentagon B.

30. The length of a side of hexagon A equals the radius of hexagon B.

31. The radius of octagon A equals the apothem of octagon B.

32. The perimeter of decagon A equals the length of a side of decagon B.

33. **Road Signs** The length of a side of the standard stop sign shown at left is 1 ft $\frac{1}{4}$ in. Find the area of the stop sign to the nearest tenth of a square foot.

34. Suppose a circle is inscribed in a regular n-gon with center C and apothem 1, as shown in the diagram. In parts (a)–(d), explain why each statement is true.

a. $m\angle C = \frac{1}{2}\left(\frac{360}{n}\right) = \frac{180}{n}$

b. $s = \tan C$

c. The perimeter of the n-gon is $2n(\tan C)$.

d. The area of the n-gon is $n\left(\tan \frac{180}{n}\right)$.

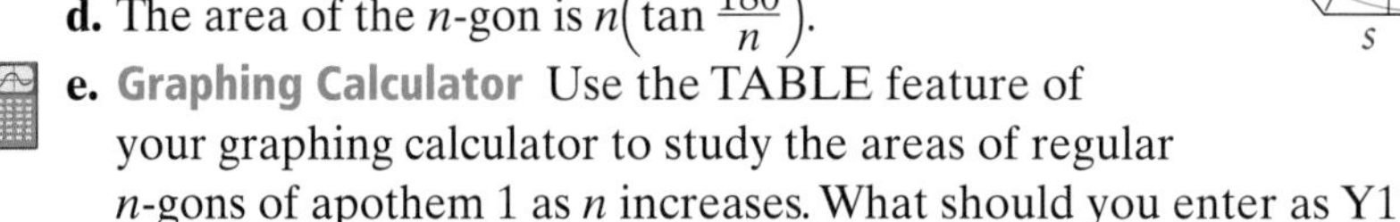

e. **Graphing Calculator** Use the TABLE feature of your graphing calculator to study the areas of regular n-gons of apothem 1 as n increases. What should you enter as Y1?

f. Use the **TBLSET** feature so that X starts at 3 and changes by 1. Access the **TABLE**. Tell what happens in the X and Y1 columns as you scroll down.

g. For what value of X does Y1 take on a new value for the last time? Explain why this is so. Also, in terms of the circle and the circumscribing regular n-gons, interpret what you observe.

Challenge

35. Suppose a circle is circumscribed about a regular n-gon with center C and radius 1. Proceed with steps similar to those in Exercise 34 to study the areas of regular n-gons inscribed in a circle as n increases.

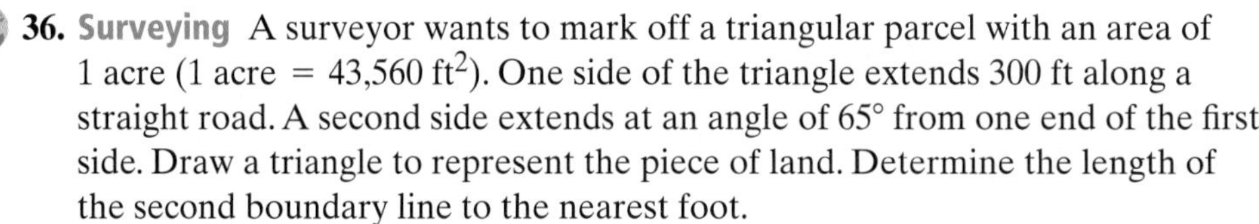

36. **Surveying** A surveyor wants to mark off a triangular parcel with an area of 1 acre (1 acre $= 43{,}560$ ft^2). One side of the triangle extends 300 ft along a straight road. A second side extends at an angle of 65° from one end of the first side. Draw a triangle to represent the piece of land. Determine the length of the second boundary line to the nearest foot.

37. Segments are drawn between the midpoints of consecutive sides of a regular pentagon to form another regular pentagon. Find, to the nearest hundredth, the ratio of the area of the smaller pentagon to the area of the larger pentagon.

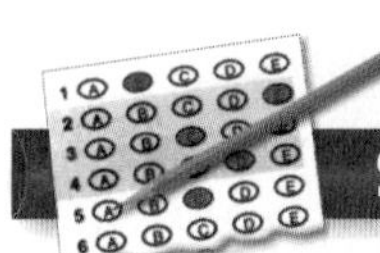

Standardized Test Prep

Multiple Choice

In Exercises 38–40, the polygons are regular.

38. The perimeter is 54 m. The apothem is $3\sqrt{3}$ m. To the nearest tenth, what is the area?

A. 46.8 m^2 **B.** 140.3 m^2 **C.** 243.0 m^2 **D.** 280.6 m^2

39. The area is 1623.8 yd^2. The perimeter is 150 yd. What is the apothem?

F. 10.8 yd **G.** 21.7 yd **H.** 32.5 yd **I.** 43.3 yd

40. The area is 100 cm^2. The apothem is 5 m. What is the perimeter?

A. 20 cm **B.** 40 cm **C.** 50 cm **D.** 100 cm

Short Response

41. Sketch all possible right triangles ABC with $m\angle A = 40$ and $AC = 10$. Find the area of each.

Extended Response

42. a. In the regular pentagon, find x. Then use x to find a.

b. Explain how you can use the perimeter of a regular polygon to find the area of the polygon.

c. Use the perimeter of the pentagon shown here to find the area to the nearest tenth. Show your work.

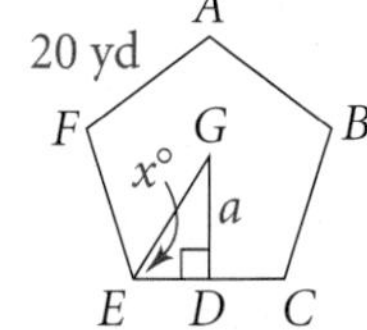

Online lesson quiz at **www.PHSchool.com** Web Code: afa-0905

Mixed Review

Lesson 9-4

43. Find the sum $\vec{a} + \vec{c}$. Give your answer as an ordered pair.

44. Describe a vector $\vec{d}$ such that $\vec{a} + \vec{d} = \vec{c}$.

45. Describe a vector $\vec{e}$ such that $\vec{c} + \vec{e} = \vec{a}$.

46. Which two vectors have $\vec{c}$ as their sum?

$\langle -2, -2 \rangle$ $\langle 2, -4 \rangle$ $\langle 4, -2 \rangle$

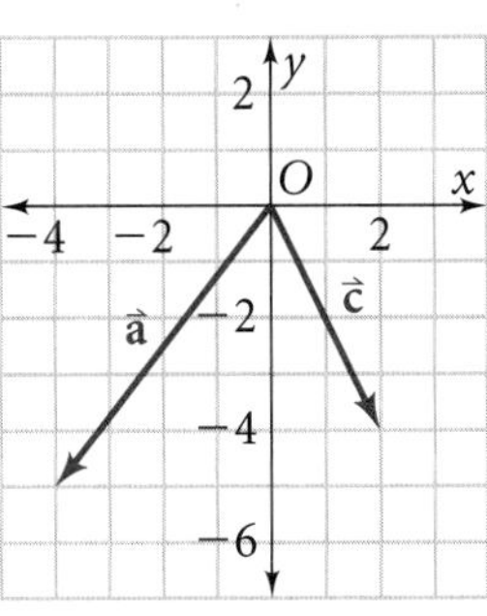

Lesson 7-7

Find the area of each shaded sector of a circle. Leave your answer in terms of π.

47.

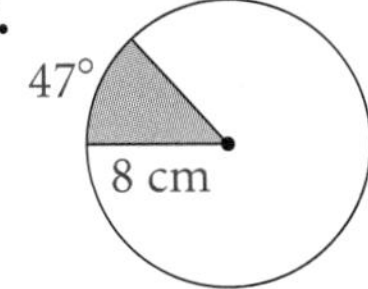

48.

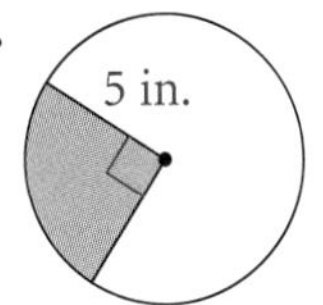

49.

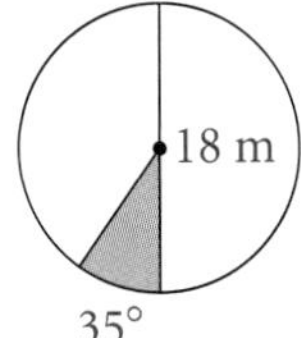

Lesson 6-6

Coordinate Geometry **Find the coordinates of the midpoint of $\overline{WZ}$. Then find WZ.**

50. rectangle

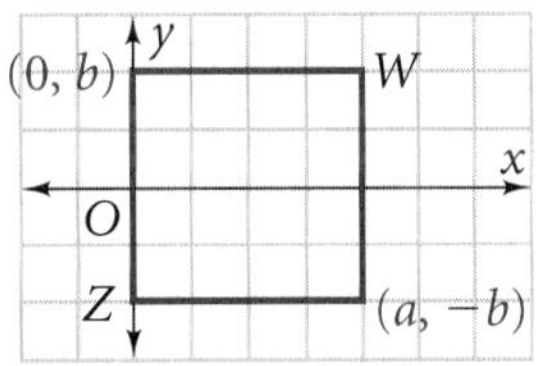

51. kite

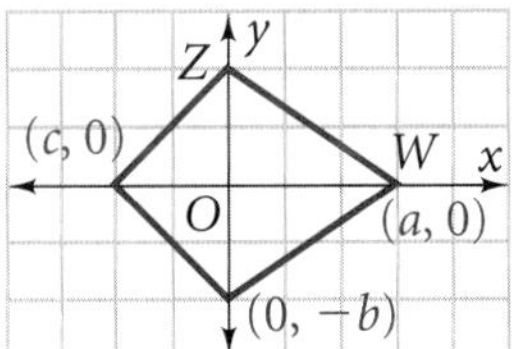

Geometry at Work

Surveyor

Surveyors calculate the locations, shapes, and areas of plots of land. A survey begins with a benchmark, a reference point whose latitude, longitude, and elevation are known. The surveyor uses a device called a transit to measure the boundary angles for the plot of land and the distances of key points from the benchmark. Using trigonometry, the surveyor finds the latitude, longitude, and elevation of each key point in the survey. These points are located on a map and an accurate sketch of the plot is drawn. Finally, the area is calculated.

One method involves dividing the plot into triangles and measuring the lengths of two sides and the included angle of each. The formula $A = \frac{1}{2}ab(\sin C)$ gives the area of each triangle. The area of the entire plot is the sum of the areas of the triangles.

Take It to the NET For more information about surveying, go to **www.PHSchool.com**.
Web Code: afb-2031

Test-Taking Strategies

Eliminating Answers

Before you begin working a problem in earnest, or if you do not know how to do a problem, you usually can eliminate some answer choices. Cross out the answers you eliminate. But do this in the test booklet, not on the answer sheet.

1 EXAMPLE

The length of a diagonal of a square is 12 cm. What is the area of the square?

A. 49 cm^2 **B.** 72 cm^2 **C.** 145 cm^2 **D.** 225 cm^2

The area of a square with side length s is s^2. Since the length of the side of the square is less than the length of the diagonal, you can eliminate answers C and D. Those areas are both larger than $12^2 = 144$. Answer A is the area of a square whose side is 7 cm, and this square does not have a diagonal whose length is 12 cm. B is the correct answer.

2 EXAMPLE

A kite at the end of a 100-ft string has an angle of elevation of 28°. The end of the string is staked to the ground. Which is the best estimate of the kite's height?

F. 38 ft **G.** 47 ft **H.** 52 ft **I.** 65 ft

Draw a diagram. Since 28° is a little less than 30°, you can estimate the answer by using a 30°-60°-90° triangle. If the angle of elevation were 30°, then the height of the kite would be 50 ft. Since the actual angle is less than 30°, you know the actual height is less than 50 ft. You can eliminate answers H and I since they are greater than 50 ft. The correct answer must be either F or G.

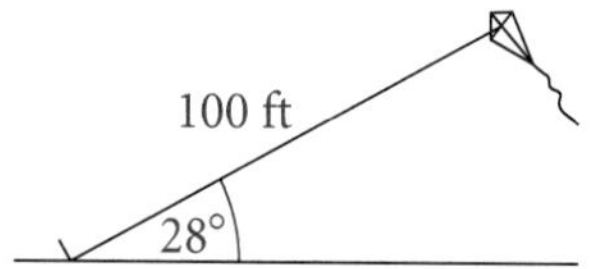

EXERCISES

1. If d is the length of a diagonal of a square, what is the area of the square in terms of d?
2. Use the sine ratio to find the height of the kite above the ground in Example 2.

Use the following question for Exercises 3–5.

The lengths of the diagonals of a rhombus are 6 cm and 10 cm. What is the measure of each acute angle of the rhombus?

A. 31.0 **B.** 45 **C.** 61.9 **D.** 118.1

3. Explain why you can immediately eliminate answer D.
4. The diagonals of a rhombus are perpendicular and bisect each other. Draw a diagram of the rhombus and its diagonals. Use the three sides of a right triangle to explain why you can eliminate answer A.
5. Explain how you now choose between B and C.

Chapter Review

Vocabulary

angle of depression (p. 482)
angle of elevation (p. 482)
cosine (p. 477)
identity (p. 478)
initial point (p. 490)
magnitude (p. 490)
resultant (p. 492)
sine (p. 477)
tangent (p. 470)
terminal point (p. 490)
vector (p. 490)

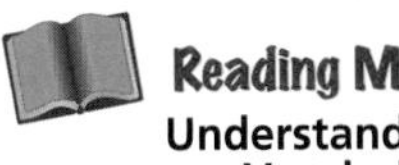

Reading Math
Understanding Vocabulary

Take It to the NET
Online vocabulary quiz at **www.PHSchool.com**
Web Code: afj-0951

Choose the correct term to complete each sentence.

1. Any quantity that has magnitude and direction is called a(n) __?__.
2. The __?__ is the angle formed by a horizontal line and the line of sight to an object above that horizontal line.
3. The __?__ of $\angle A$ is $\frac{\text{leg adjacent } \angle A}{\text{hypotenuse}}$.
4. The __?__ of $\angle A$ is $\frac{\text{leg opposite } \angle A}{\text{hypotenuse}}$.

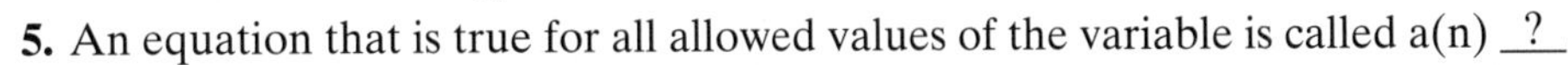

5. An equation that is true for all allowed values of the variable is called a(n) __?__.
6. The sum of two vectors is the __?__.
7. The __?__ of a vector modeled by an arrow is the distance from its __?__ to its __?__.

Skills and Concepts

9-1 and 9-2 Objectives

- To use tangent ratios to determine side lengths in triangles
- To use sine and cosine to determine side lengths in triangles

In right $\triangle ABC$,

sine of $\angle A = \sin A = \frac{\text{leg opposite } \angle A}{\text{hypotenuse}}$

cosine of $\angle A = \cos A = \frac{\text{leg adjacent to } \angle A}{\text{hypotenuse}}$

and **tangent** of $\angle A = \tan A = \frac{\text{leg opposite } \angle A}{\text{leg adjacent to } \angle A}$

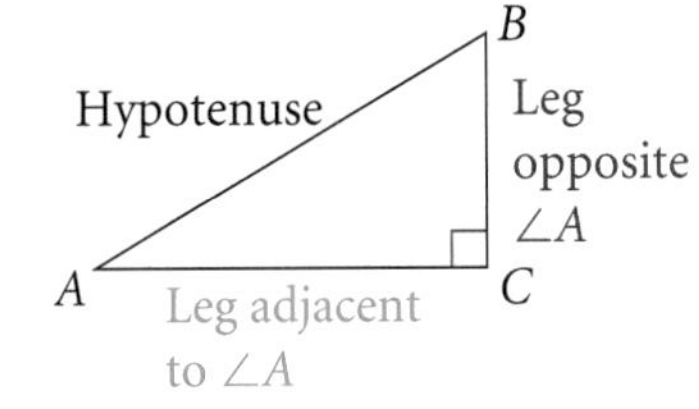

You can use the inverses of sine, cosine, and tangent to find the measures of the acute angles of a right triangle.

A trigonometric **identity** is an equation that is always true for all the allowed values of the variable.

Find each missing value to the nearest whole number.

8. $\tan \blacksquare^\circ = 0.9$
9. $\sin 17^\circ = \frac{\blacksquare}{7}$
10. $\tan 27^\circ = \frac{1}{\blacksquare}$
11. $\cos \blacksquare^\circ = 0.39$
12. $\sin \blacksquare^\circ = 0.39$
13. $\sin \blacksquare^\circ = \frac{2}{3}$
14. $\tan 76^\circ = \frac{\blacksquare}{3}$
15. $\cos 83^\circ = \frac{1}{\blacksquare}$

Express $\sin A$, $\cos A$, and $\tan A$ as ratios.

16.
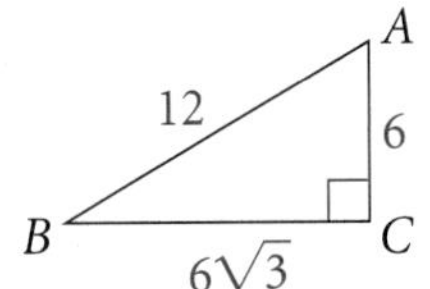

17.
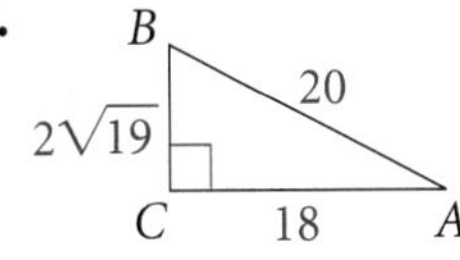

18.
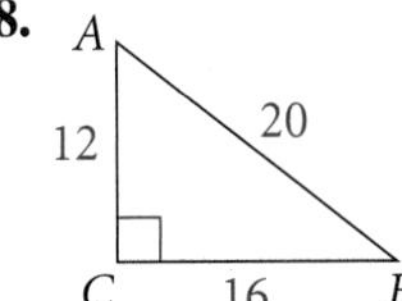

Find the value of x. Round lengths of segments to the nearest tenth. Round angle measures to the nearest degree.

19. 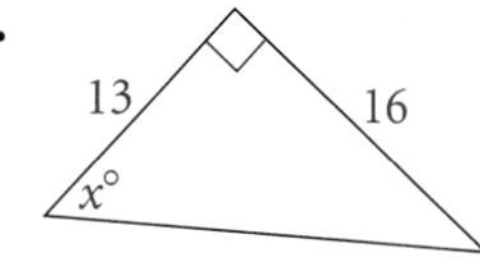

20. 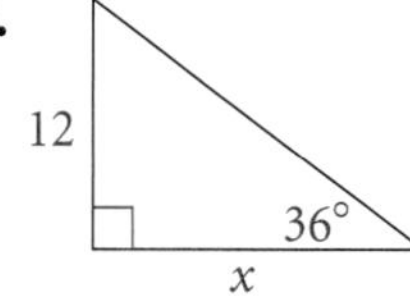

21. 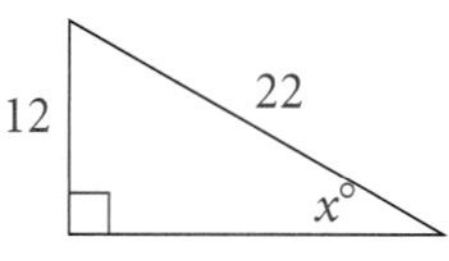

9-3 Objective

- To use angles of elevation and depression to solve problems

A horizontal line and the line of sight to an object above the horizontal line form an **angle of elevation.** A horizontal line and the line of sight to an object below that horizontal line form an **angle of depression.**

Solve each problem.

22. Elevation Two hills are 2 mi apart. The taller hill is 2707 ft high. The angle of depression from the top of the taller hill to the top of the shorter hill is 7°. Find the height of the shorter hill to the nearest foot. (1 mi = 5280 ft)

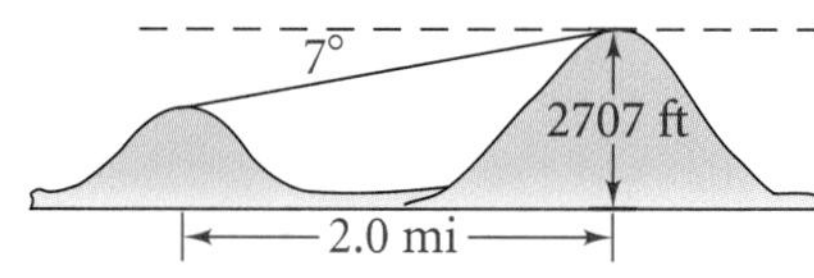

23. Surveying A surveyor is 305 ft from the base of the new courthouse. Her angle measuring device is 5 ft above the ground. The angle of elevation to the top of the courthouse is 42°. Find the height of the courthouse to the nearest foot.

24. Indirect Measurement Linda is flying a kite. She lets out 45 yd of string and anchors it to the ground. She determines that the angle of elevation of the kite is 58°. What is the height of the kite from the ground?

25. Writing Explain why in this diagram the angle of depression, $\angle 1$, and the angle of elevation, $\angle 2$, are congruent.

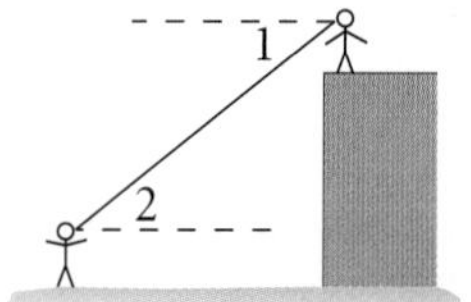

9-4 Objective

- To describe vectors
- To solve problems that involve vector addition

A **vector** is any quantity that has magnitude and direction. You can describe a vector by its horizontal and vertical change (ordered pair) or by its size and direction. Direction is often described in relation to north, south, east, and west.

The sum of two vectors is the **resultant.** Vector sums can show the result of vector actions that take place one after the other. Additionally, vector sums can show the result of two vector actions that occur at the same time. You can add vectors by adding their coordinates. You can also show the sum geometrically.

Describe each vector using ordered pair notation.

26. 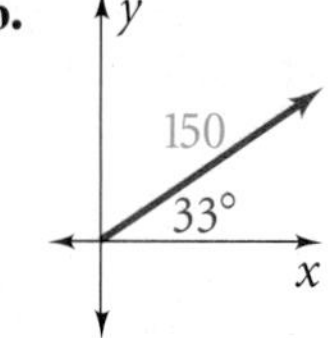

27. 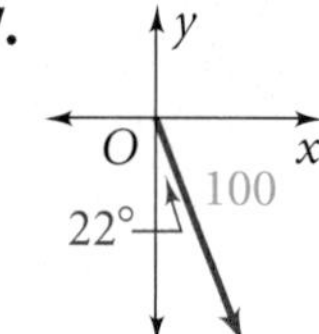

28. 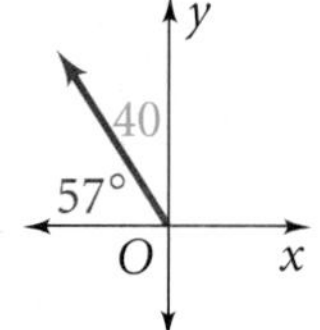

Find the magnitude and direction of each vector.

29.

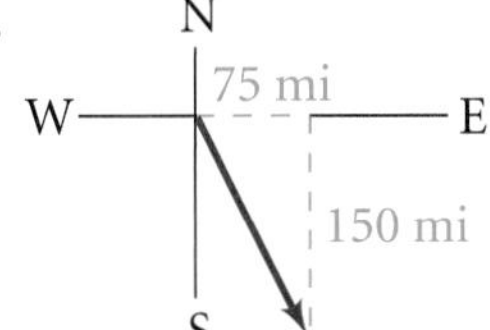

30.

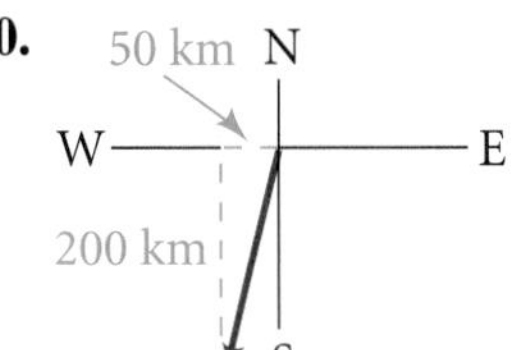

31.

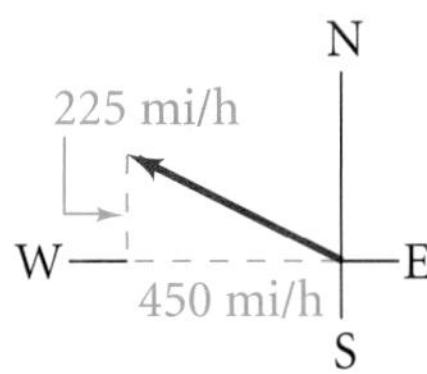

32. Open-Ended Write three vectors with the same direction as $\langle 3, 4 \rangle$. Explain how you found your answers.

Sketch a vector that has the given direction.

33. 25° east of north

34. 45° north of east

35. 60° west of south

Find the sum of each pair of vectors. Give your answers in ordered pair notation.

36.

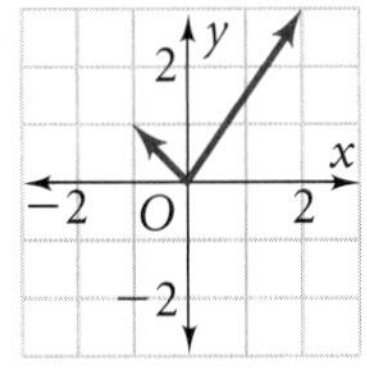

37.

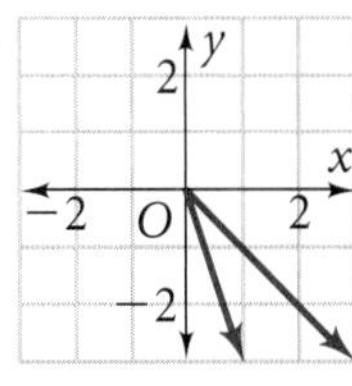

38.

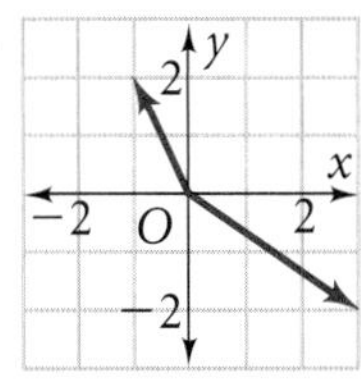

39. Navigation A whale-watching tour leaves port and travels 12 mi directly north. The tour then travels 5 mi due east.

a. In what direction should the boat head to return directly to port?

b. How long will the return trip take if the boat averages 20 mi/h?

9-5 Objectives

- To find the area of a regular polygon using trigonometry
- To find the area of a triangle using trigonometry

You can use trigonometry to find the areas of regular polygons.

You can also use trigonometry to find the area of a triangle when you know the lengths of two sides and the measure of the included angle.

Area of triangle $= \frac{1}{2} \cdot$ side length $\cdot$ side length $\cdot$ sine of included angle

Area of $\triangle ABC = \frac{1}{2}bc(\sin A)$

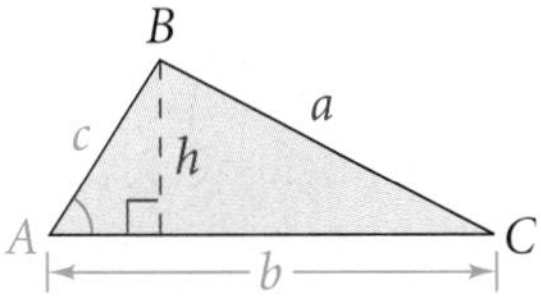

Find the area of each polygon. Round your answers to the nearest tenth.

40. regular decagon with radius 5 ft

41. regular pentagon with apothem 8 cm

42. regular hexagon with apothem 6 in.

43. regular quadrilateral with radius 2 m

44.

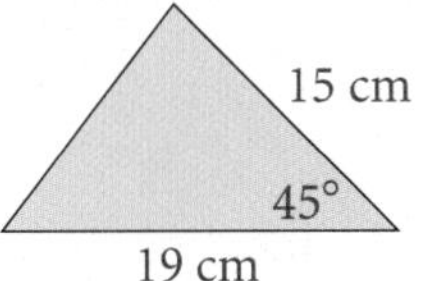

45.

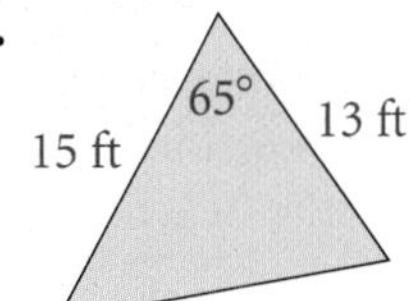

46.

12 m

78°

12 m

Chapter Test

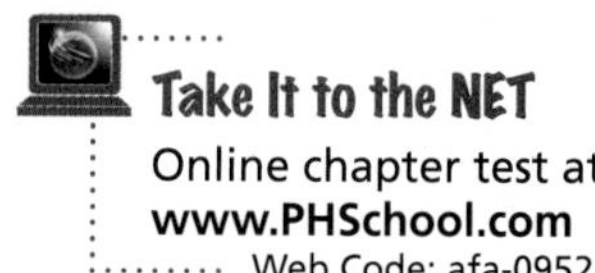

Express sin *B*, cos *B*, and tan *B* as ratios.

1. 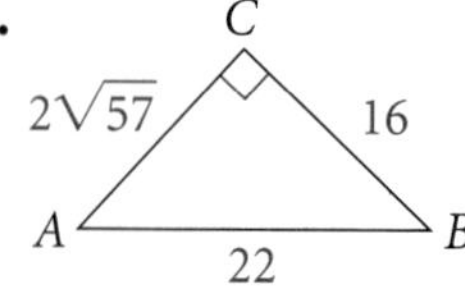

2. 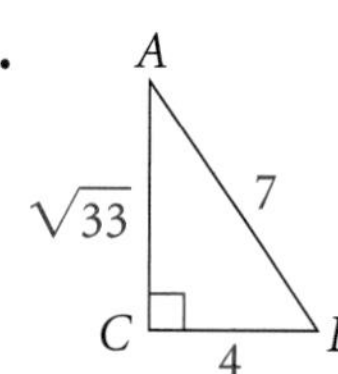

Find each missing value to the nearest tenth.

3. $\tan \blacksquare° = 1.11$

4. $\tan 18° = \frac{\blacksquare}{87}$

5. $\sin 34° = \frac{5}{\blacksquare}$

6. $\sin \blacksquare° = 0.996$

7. $\cos \blacksquare° = \frac{12}{15}$

8. $\cos 76° = \frac{\blacksquare}{24}$

Find the value of *x*. Round lengths to the nearest tenth and angle measures to the nearest degree.

9. 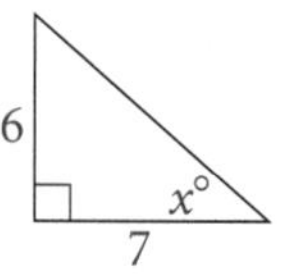

10. 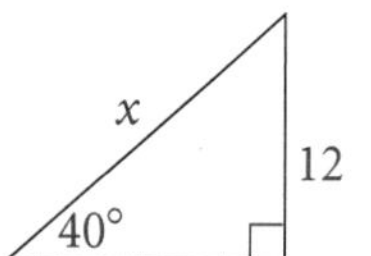

11. 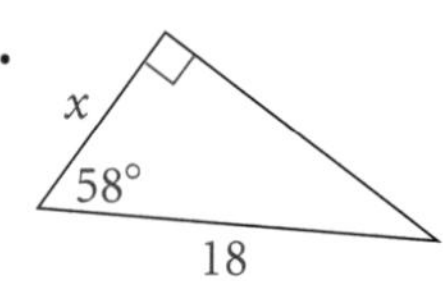

12. 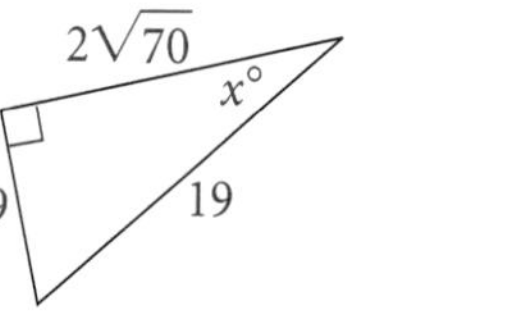

Indirect Measurement **Solve each problem.**

13. A surveyor measuring the tallest tree in a park is 100 ft from the tree. His angle-measuring device is 5 ft above the ground. The angle of elevation to the top of the tree is 48°. How tall is the tree?

14. Twenty minutes after being launched, a hot-air balloon has risen to an altitude of 300 m. The pilot can still see the starting point on the ground at a 25° angle of depression. How many meters is the balloon from the starting point?

15. A 5-foot-tall woman stands 15 ft from a statue. She must look up at an angle of 60° to see the top of the statue. How tall is the statue?

16. A family vacationed at a beach 120 mi east and 30 mi south of their home. Find the distance and the direction from their home to the beach.

17. **Writing** Explain why $\sin x° = \cos (90 - x)°$. Include a diagram with your explanation.

Describe each vector using ordered pair notation. Round the coordinates to the nearest unit.

18. 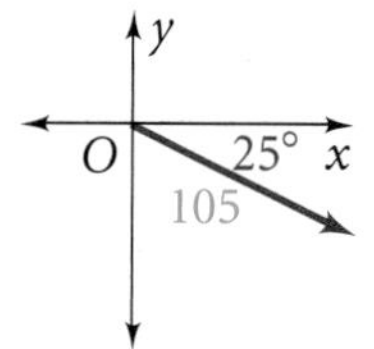

19. 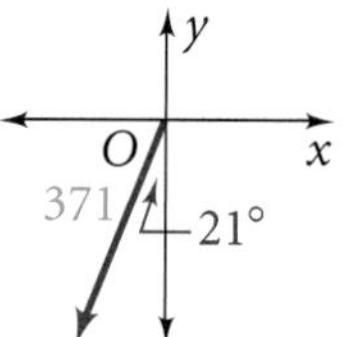

Find the magnitude and direction of each vector.

20. 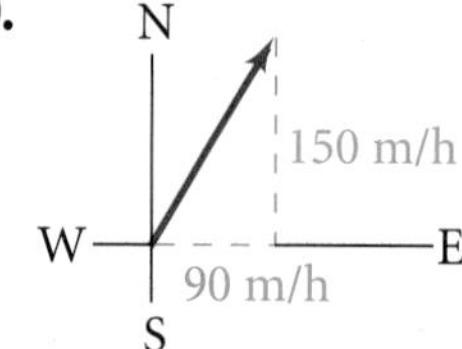

21. 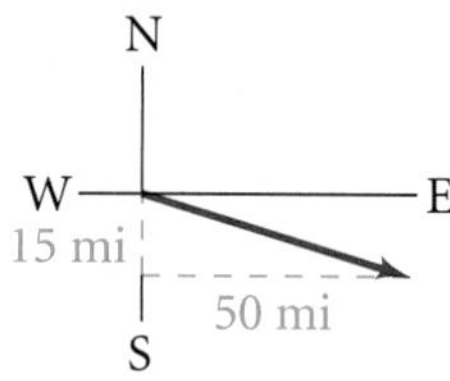

Describe the resultant as an ordered pair.

22. 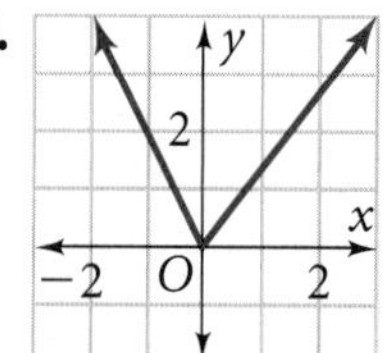

23. 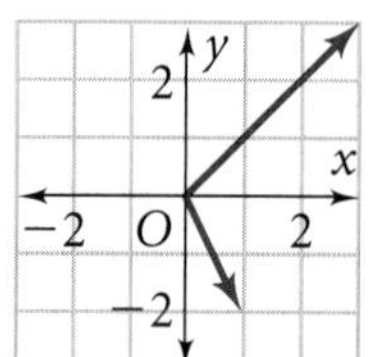

24. A canoe heading 30° west of north is being paddled at a rate of 7 mi/h. The current is pushing the canoe 20° south of west at a rate of 3 mi/h. Find the resulting speed and direction of the canoe.

25. **Open-Ended** Draw two vectors with different directions on a coordinate grid. Then draw their resultant and describe it as an ordered pair.

Find the area of each polygon to the nearest tenth.

26. 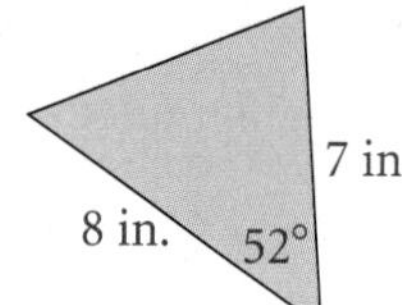

27. 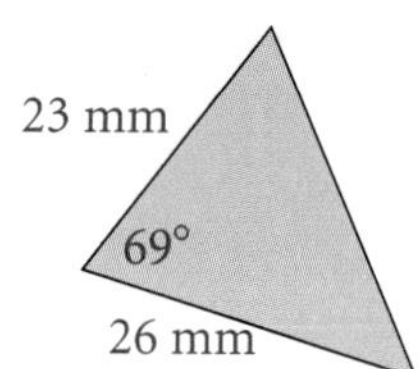

28. a regular hexagon with apothem 5 ft

29. a regular pentagon with radius 3 cm

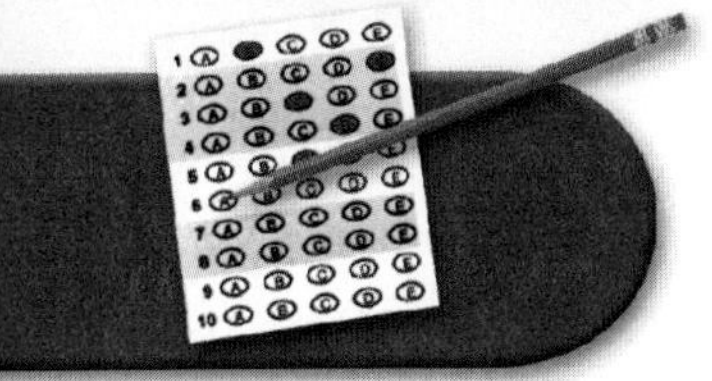

Standardized Test Prep

Reading Comprehension **Read the passage below. Then answer the questions on the basis of what is *stated* or *implied* in the passage.**

In Balance To suspend a mobile so that it balances, you need to know how to find the center of mass. If a figure has a "nice" geometric shape, you can find the center of mass, or centroid, using geometric methods. There are alternative ways to find centers of mass in figures without "nice" shapes.

Here is how one artist found the center of mass for the irregularly shaped flat sheet of metal shown at the right.

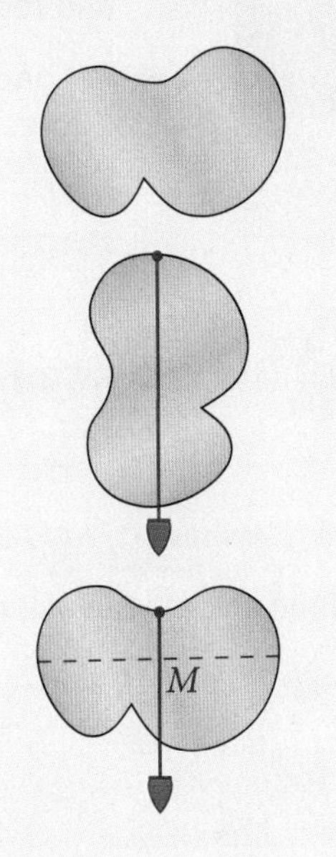

1. She suspended the shape from a point at its edge. She also suspended a *plumb line* (a weight on a string) from the same point. She traced the plumb line onto the shape.
2. She suspended the shape from another point, and again traced the plumb line. She found the center of mass of the shape at the intersection M of the two traced lines.

This method works because each traced plumb line passes through the center of mass. If you place the metal shape horizontally with a traced plumb line along the thin edge of a ruler, the shape will balance on the ruler. Since the shape balances along each traced plumb line, it will balance at the point of intersection of two such lines.

1. What should you learn how to do from the passage?
   A. suspend a mobile
   B. find a center of mass using geometric methods
   C. find the center of mass of any flat shape
   D. attach a plumb line to any flat shape

2. Why is a plumb line necessary?
   F. to show a straight line
   G. to find a vertical line
   H. to split the shape into two equal halves
   I. to suspend the shape at its center of mass

3. What geometric fact is applied in the passage?
   A. Two nonparallel planes determine a line.
   B. Two intersecting lines lie in one plane.
   C. Two nonparallel lines determine a point.
   D. Two points lie in one line.

4. Why does the shape balance when you place it on the edge of a ruler along a traced plumb line?
   F. The center of mass of the shape rests on the edge of the ruler.
   G. The traced plumb line is longer than the edge of the ruler.
   H. The shape is placed horizontally on the edge of the ruler.
   I. Half the mass of the shape is on each side of the edge of the ruler.

5. If the metal shape were an isosceles triangle, what would be other names for some traced plumb lines? Justify your answer.

6. If the metal shape were a circular ring with its inner circle cut out, where would you find the center of mass?

Where You've Been

- In Chapter 1, you learned that geometric figures can lie in a plane or be three-dimensional.
- In Chapters 7 and 9, you learned how to find the areas of certain plane figures such as triangles, special quadrilaterals, and regular polygons.
- In Chapter 8, you learned how perimeters and areas of similar figures are related.

Instant self-check online and on CD-ROM

Diagnosing Readiness

(For help, go to the Lesson in green.)

Area (Lessons 7-1, 7-4, 7-5)

Find the area of each figure. Leave your answers in simplest radical form.

1. 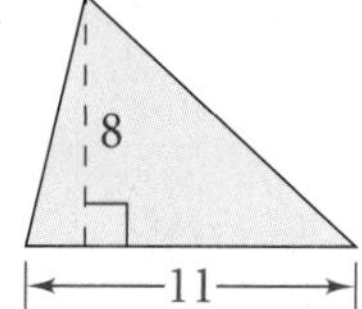

2. 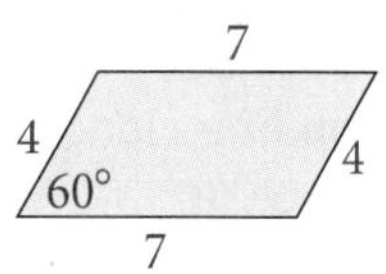

3. 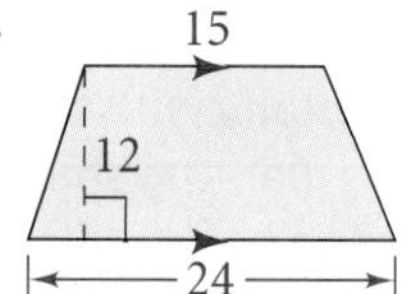

4. 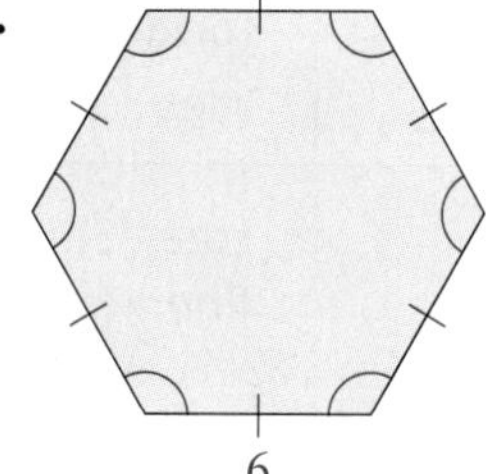

The Pythagorean Theorem (Lesson 7-2)

x^2 **Algebra** Solve for a, b, or c in right $\triangle ABC$ where a and b are the lengths of the legs and c is the length of the hypotenuse.

5. $a = 8; b = 15; c = \underline{?}$

6. $a = \underline{?}; b = 4; c = 12$

7. $a = 2\sqrt{3}; b = 2\sqrt{6}; c = \underline{?}$

Special Right Triangles (Lesson 7-3)

8. Find the length of the shorter leg of a 30°-60°-90° right triangle with hypotenuse $8\sqrt{5}$.

9. Find the length of the diagonal of a square whose perimeter is 24.

10. Find the height of an equilateral triangle with sides of length 8.

Perimeters and Areas of Similar Figures (Lesson 8-6)

11. Two similar triangles have corresponding sides in a ratio of 3 : 5. Find the perimeter of the smaller triangle if the larger triangle has perimeter 40.

12. Two regular hexagons have areas of 8 and 25. Find the ratio of corresponding sides.

Surface Area and Volume

Chapter 10

LESSONS

Where You're Going

- In this chapter, you will learn about special three-dimensional figures built from two-dimensional figures such as triangles and rectangles.
- To help you work with these space figures, you will learn how to create three-dimensional drawings on a two-dimensional sheet of paper.
- You will use what you know about finding perimeter and area to help you find surface area and volume.

Real-World Snapshots Applying what you learn, you will solve problems on pages 578 and 579 involving shapes of colossal size.

Key Vocabulary

- altitude (pp. 528, 530, 537, 539)
- base(s) (pp. 528, 537)
- cone (p. 539)
- cross section (p. 522)
- cylinder (p. 530)
- foundation drawing (p. 521)
- height (pp. 528, 530, 537, 539)
- isometric drawing (p. 520)
- net (p. 512)
- orthographic drawing (p. 521)
- prism (p. 528)
- pyramid (p. 537)
- similar solids (p. 566)
- sphere (p. 558)
- surface area (pp. 528, 530, 538)
- volume (p. 544)

Space Figures and Nets

Lesson Preview

What You'll Learn

OBJECTIVE 1 To recognize nets of space figures

. . . And Why

To see the structure of a package, as in Example 2

✓ Check Skills You'll Need

(For help, go to Lessons 1-7 and 7-5.)

Find the area of each figure. Round to the nearest tenth as needed.

1.

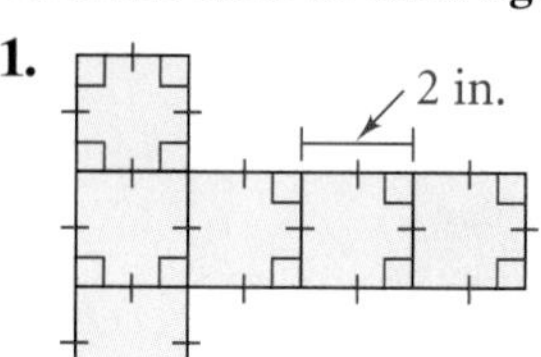

2.

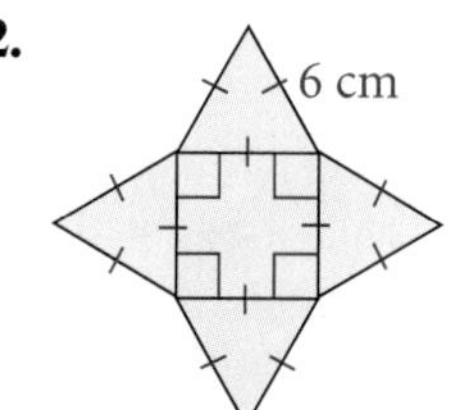

3.

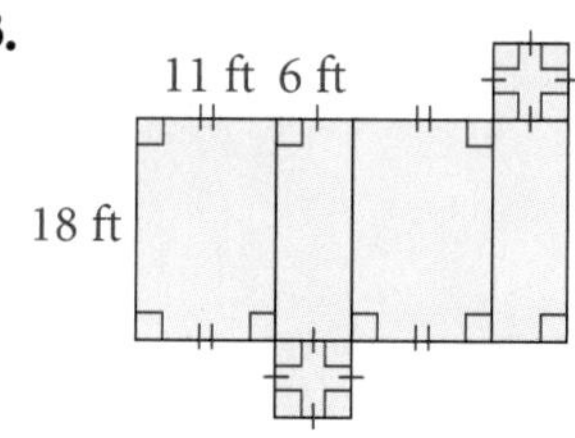

New Vocabulary • polyhedron • face • edge • vertex • net • cube

Interactive lesson includes instant self-check, tutorials, and activities.

OBJECTIVE

1 Identifying Nets of Space Figures

Reading Math

"Polyhedron" comes from the Greek *poly* for "many" and *hedron* for "side."

A **polyhedron** is a three-dimensional figure whose surfaces are polygons. Each polygon is a **face** of the polyhedron. An **edge** is a segment that is formed by the intersection of two faces. A **vertex** is a point where three or more edges intersect.

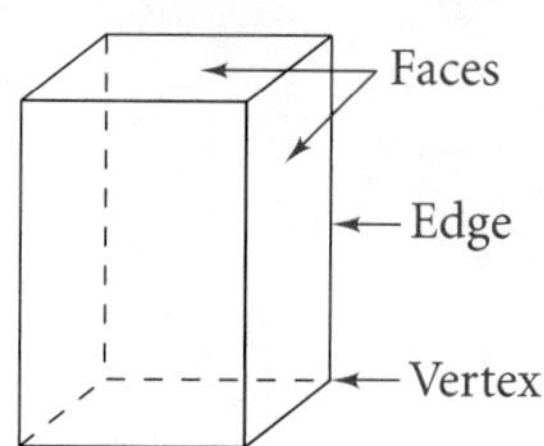

A **net** is a two-dimensional pattern that you can fold to form a three-dimensional figure. One of the simplest such figures is a **cube**—a polyhedron with six faces, each of which is a square.

1 EXAMPLE Identifying a Net

Is the pattern a net for a cube? If so, name the letters that will appear on opposite faces.

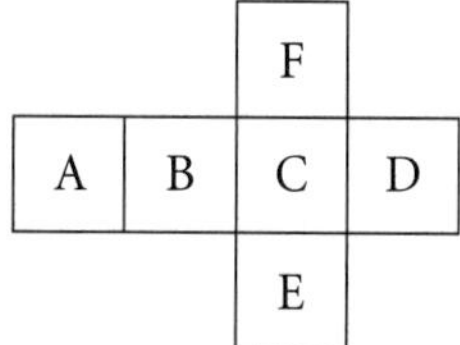

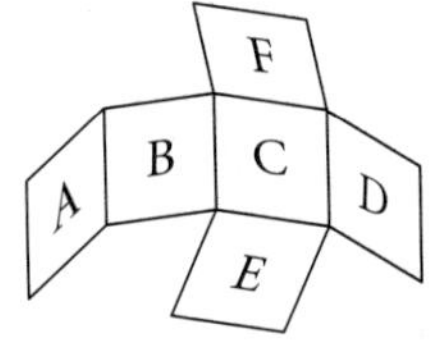

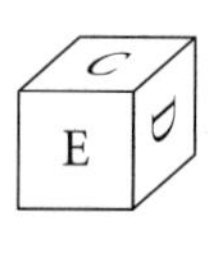

Yes, the pattern is a net because you can fold it to form a cube. A and C, B and D, and E and F are on opposite faces.

✓ Check Understanding 1 Sketch the three-dimensional figure that corresponds to the net at the right.

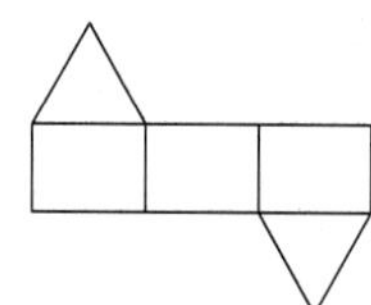

Package designers can use nets to help design containers.

2 EXAMPLE Drawing a Net

Packaging Draw a net for the graham cracker box. Label the net with its dimensions.

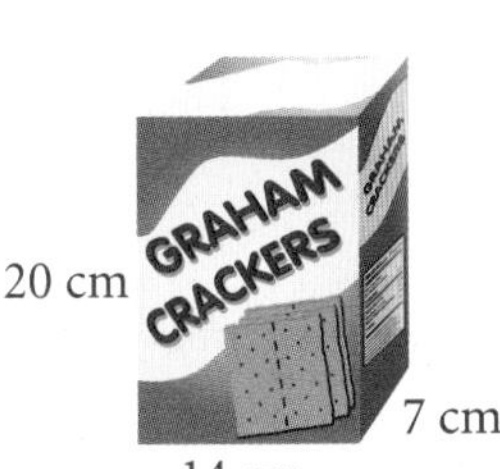

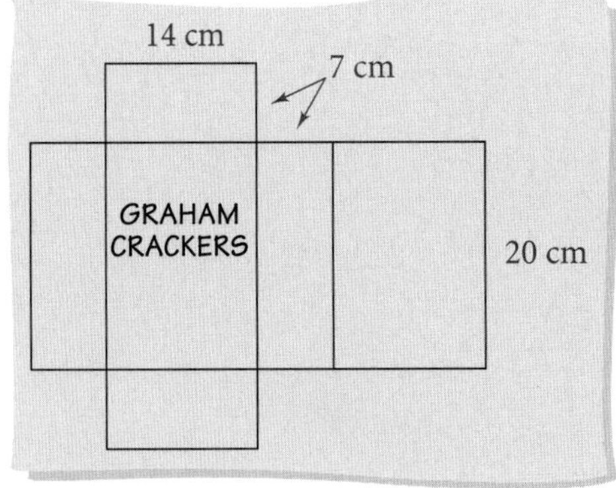

Check Understanding **2** Draw a different net for this box. Show the dimensions in your diagram.

Leonhard Euler, a Swiss mathematician, discovered a relationship among the numbers of faces, vertices, and edges of any polyhedron. The result is known as Euler's Formula.

Key Concepts

Formula **Euler's Formula**

The numbers of faces (F), vertices (V), and edges (E) of a polyhedron are related by the formula $F + V = E + 2$.

3 EXAMPLE Using Euler's Formula

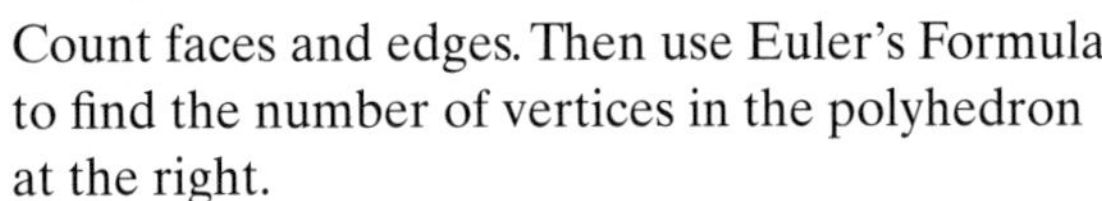

Count faces and edges. Then use Euler's Formula to find the number of vertices in the polyhedron at the right.

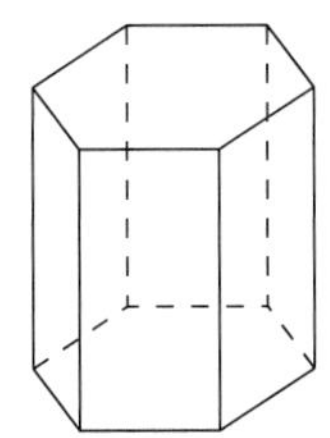

The polyhedron has 2 hexagons and 6 rectangles for a total of 8 faces.

The 2 hexagons have a total of 12 edges.
The 6 rectangles have a total of 24 edges.
If the hexagons and rectangles are joined to form a polyhedron, each edge is shared by two faces. Therefore, the number of edges in the polyhedron is one half of the total of 36, or 18.

$F + V = E + 2$	**Euler's Formula**
$8 + V = 18 + 2$	**Substitute.**
$V = 12$	**Simplify.**

Count the number of vertices in the figure to verify the result.

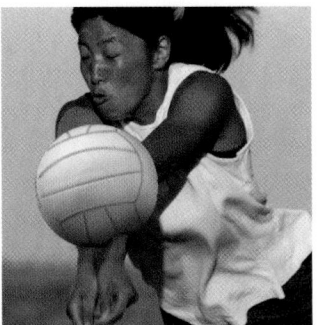

Real-World Connection

Euler's Formula applies to the polyhedron suggested by the panels on a volleyball.

Check Understanding **3** Use Euler's Formula to find the number of edges on a polyhedron with eight triangular faces.

EXERCISES

For more practice, see *Extra Practice.*

Practice and Problem Solving

Practice by Example

Example 1 (page 512)

Is each pattern below a net for a cube? If so, name the letters that will appear on opposite faces. If not, explain.

1.

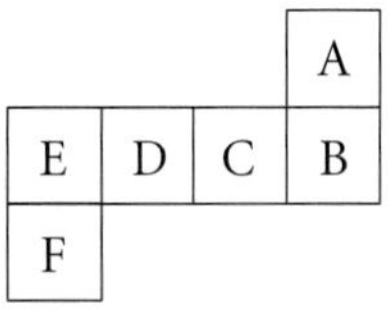

			A
E	D	C	B
F			

2.

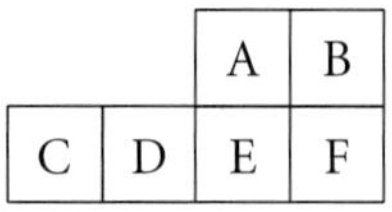

		A	B
C	D	E	F

3.

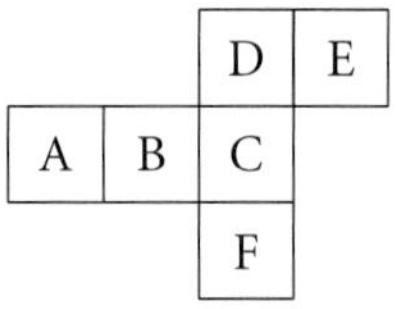

		D	E
A	B	C	
		F	

Is each pattern below a net for the three-dimensional figure at the left? Explain.

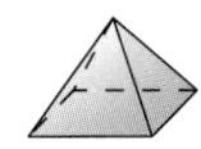

4. 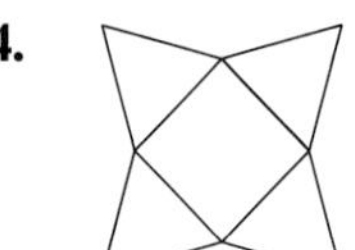

5. 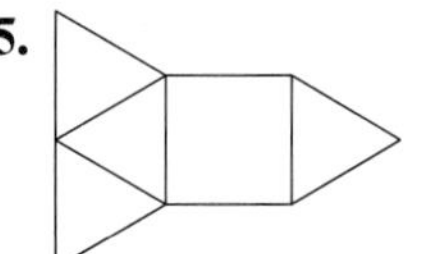

6. 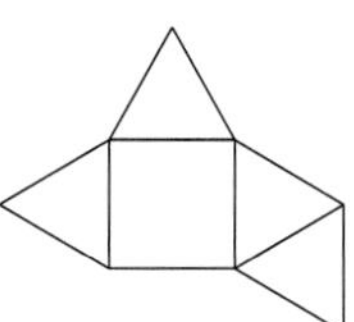

Match each three-dimensional figure with its net.

7. 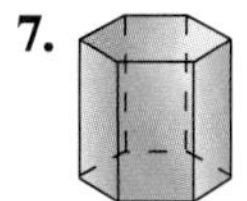

8. 

9. 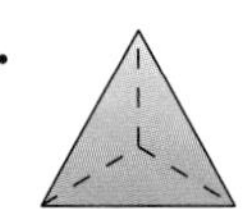

A. 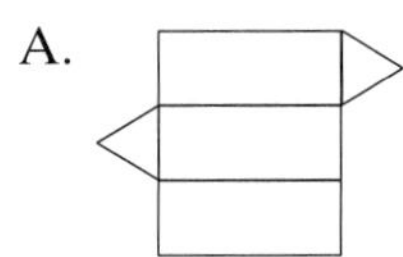

B. 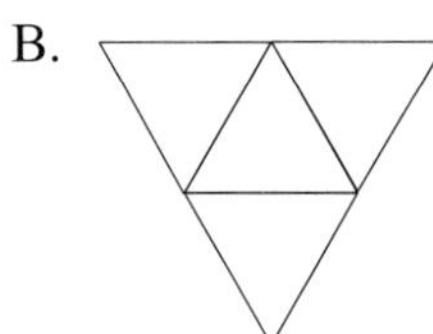

C. 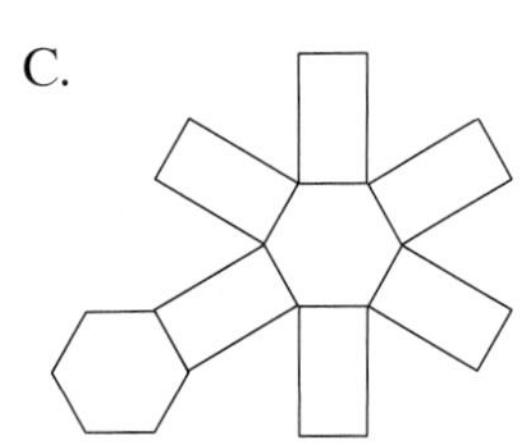

Example 2 (page 513)

Draw a net for each figure. Label the net with its dimensions.

10. 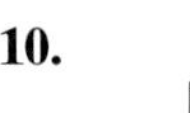
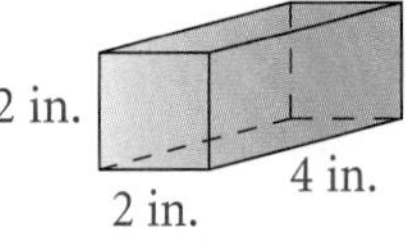

11. 
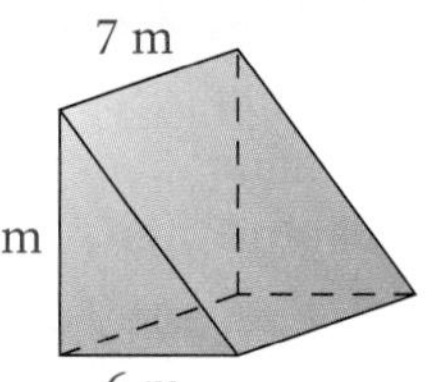

12. 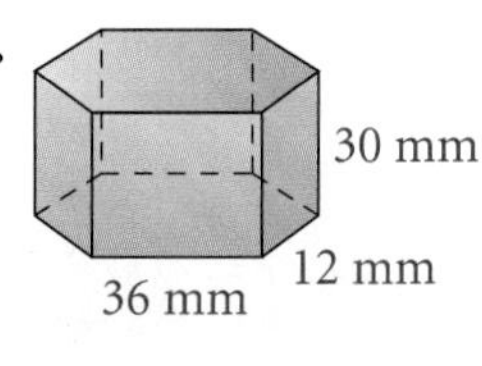

Example 3 (page 513)

Use Euler's Formula to find the missing number.

13. Faces: ■
Edges: 15
Vertices: 9

14. Faces: 8
Edges: ■
Vertices: 6

15. Faces: 20
Edges: 30
Vertices: ■

Use Euler's Formula to find the number of vertices in each polyhedron described below.

16. 6 square faces

17. 5 faces: 1 rectangle and 4 triangles

18. 9 faces: 1 octagon and 8 triangles

B Apply Your Skills

19. a. **Open-Ended** Sketch a polyhedron whose faces are all rectangles. Label the lengths of its edges.

b. Use graph paper to draw two different nets for the polyhedron.

Visualization **Think about how each net can be folded to form a cube. What is the color of the face that will be opposite the red face?**

20. 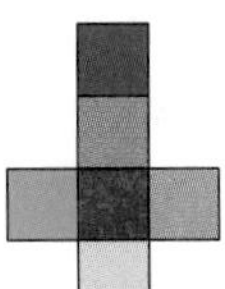 **21.** 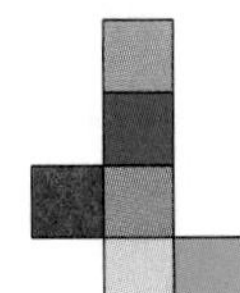 **22.** 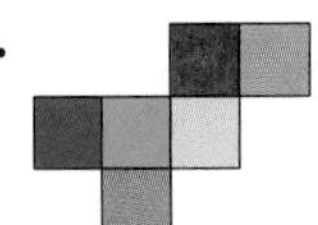  **23.** 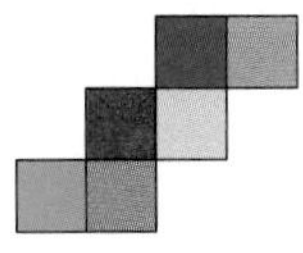

24. There are eleven different nets for a cube. Four of them are shown above.

a. Draw as many of the other seven as you can. (*Hint:* Two nets are the same if you can rotate or flip one to match the other.)

b. **Writing** If you were going to make 100 cubes for a mobile, which of the eleven nets would you use? Explain why.

25. There are eight different nets for a pyramid with a square base. Draw as many of them as you can.

Visualization **A plane region that revolves completely about a line sweeps out a *solid of revolution*. Use the sample to help you describe the solid of revolution you get by revolving each region about line ℓ.**

Sample: Revolve the rectangular region about the line ℓ and you get a cylinder as a solid of revolution.

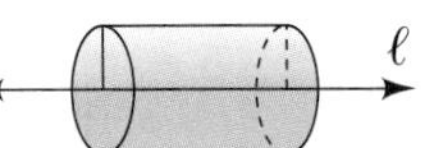

26. 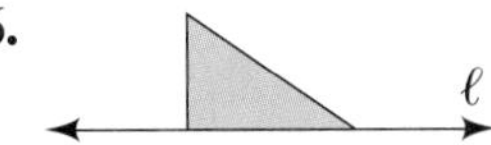

27. 

28. 

Reading Math

For help with Exercise 29, see p. 517.

29. There are five regular polyhedrons. They are called *regular* because all their faces are congruent regular polygons, and the same number of faces meet at each vertex. They are also called Platonic Solids after the Greek philosopher Plato (427–347 B.C.).

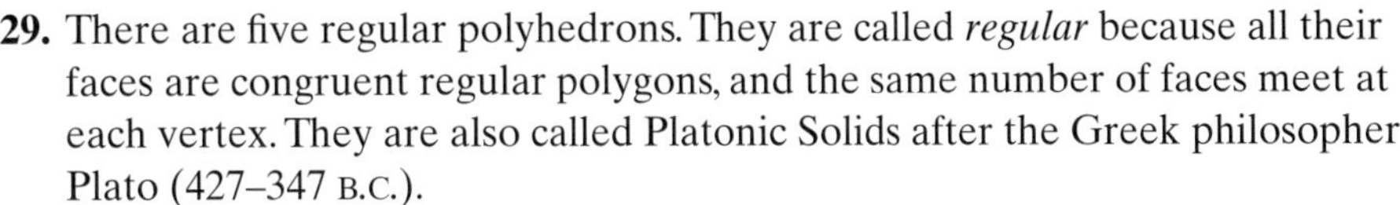

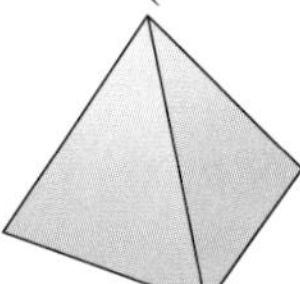

Tetrahedron

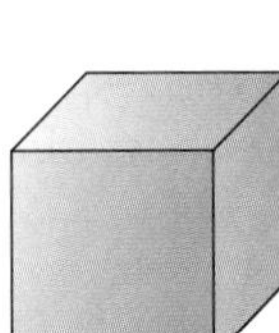

Hexahedron

Octahedron

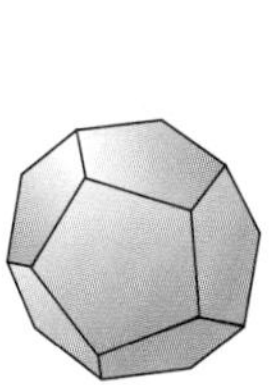

Dodecahedron

Icosahedron

a. Match each net below with a Platonic Solid.

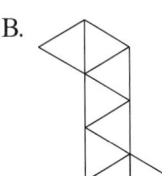

A. 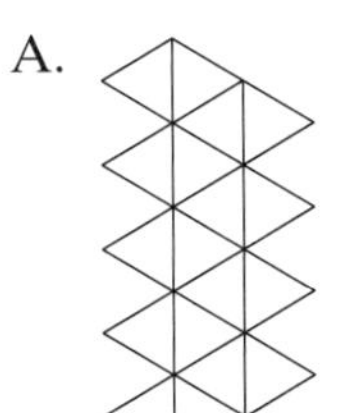 B. 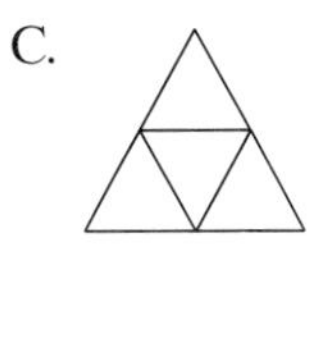 C.  D. 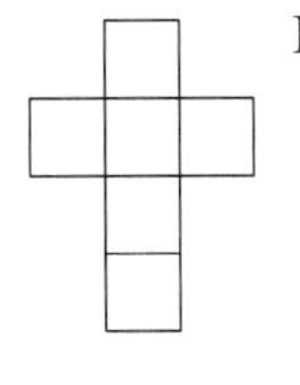 E. 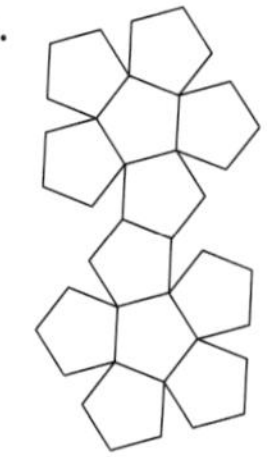

b. The first two Platonic solids have more familiar names. What are they?

c. Verify that Euler's Formula is true for the first three Platonic solids.

Real-World Connection

A fluorite crystal forms as a regular octahedron.

30. A cube has a net with area 216 in.^{2}. How long is an edge of the cube?

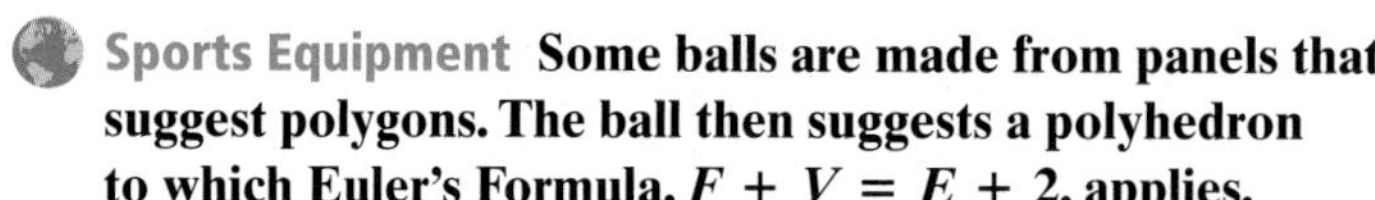

Sports Equipment **Some balls are made from panels that suggest polygons. The ball then suggests a polyhedron to which Euler's Formula, $F + V = E + 2$, applies.**

31. A soccer ball suggests a polyhedron with 20 regular hexagons and 12 regular pentagons. How many vertices does this polyhedron have?

Challenge

32. Show how Euler's Formula applies to the polyhedron suggested by the volleyball pictured on page 513. (*Hint:* It has 6 sets of 3 panels.)

33. Some older volleyballs have 6 sets of 2 panels. (See Exercise 32.) Sketch this type of volleyball and show how Euler's Formula applies.

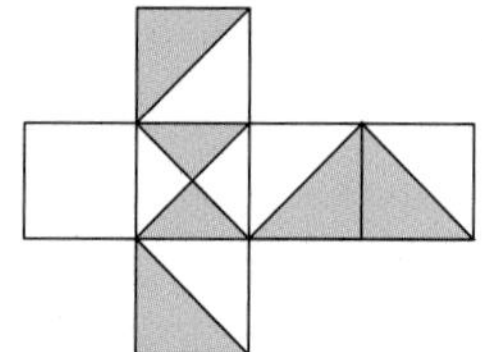

34. The net at the left is folded into a cube. Sketch the cube so that its front face is shaded as shown at the right.

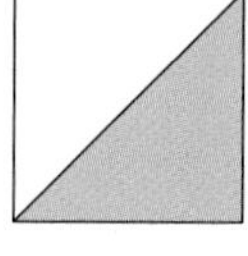

35. Refer to the Platonic Solids shown in Exercise 29.
    a. Explain why there cannot be a Platonic Solid with six equilateral triangles at each vertex.
    b. Explain why no Platonic Solid is made of polygons with more than 5 sides.

Standardized Test Prep

Multiple Choice

For Exercises 36–38, you may need Euler's Formula, $F + V = E + 2$.

36. A polyhedron has four vertices and six edges. How many faces does it have?
    A. 2 **B.** 4 **C.** 5 **D.** 10

Take It to the NET
Online lesson quiz at **www.PHSchool.com**
Web Code: afa-1001

37. A polyhedron has three rectangular faces and two triangular faces. How many vertices does it have?
    F. 5 **G.** 6 **H.** 10 **I.** 12

38. A polyhedron has 12 pentagonal faces. How many edges does it have?
    A. 12 **B.** 20 **C.** 30 **D.** 60

Short Response

39. Draw a net for the rectangular box. Label the net with its dimensions.

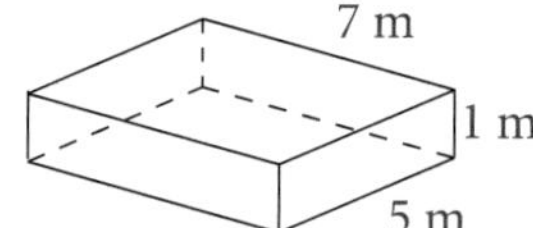

Mixed Review

Lesson 9-5

40. Find the area of a regular 12-gon with perimeter 24 cm. Give the area to the nearest tenth of a square centimeter.

Lesson 7-2

Find the length of the hypotenuse of a right triangle with the given leg lengths. Leave your answer in simplest radical form.

41. 8 cm, 9 cm
42. 3 in., 5 in.
43. 10 mm, 5 mm
44. 9 ft, 12 ft

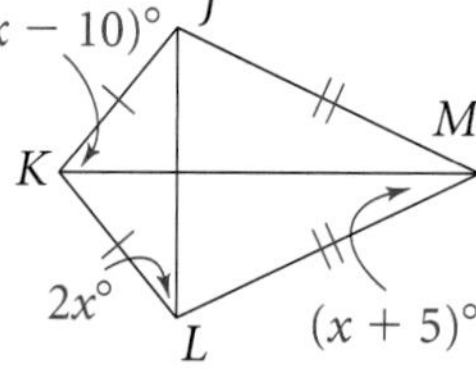

Lesson 6-5

Find each value for the kite at the right.

45. x
46. $m\angle JML$
47. $m\angle JKL$

Reading Math Vocabulary

For Use With Page 515, Exercise 29

There are five regular polyhedrons. They are called *regular* because all their faces are congruent regular polygons, and the same number of faces meet at each vertex. They are also called Platonic Solids after the Greek philosopher Plato (427–347 B.C.).

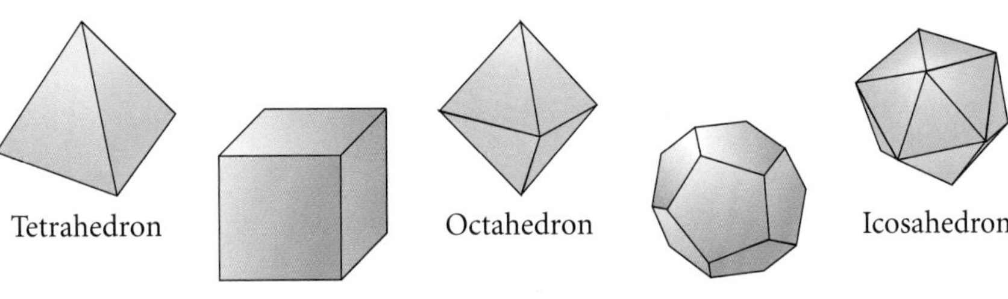

Many math vocabulary words you see in geometry have their origins in Greek. Does this mean you have to study Greek to understand these words? Of course not. Some of the terms you will learn about solids correspond to terms you already know about figures in a plane.

Plane Figures		Solid Figures	
Many angles	Polygon	Polyhedron	Many faces
All sides are ≅. All angles are ≅.	Regular Polygon	Regular Polyhedron	All faces are ≅ regular polygons. Same number of faces meet at each vertex.
_?_ sides six sides eight sides _?_ sides	Tetragon Hexagon Octagon Dodecagon	Tetrahedron Hexahedron Octahedron Dodecahedron	four faces six faces eight faces _?_ faces

EXERCISES

1. A tetrahedron has four faces.
  a. How many sides does a tetragon have?
  b. What is another name for a tetragon?

2. Dodeca comes from a combination of the Greek words "duo," meaning "two," and "deca," meaning "ten." Dodeca = duo + deca.
  a. Find two other words that begin with "deca."
  b. How many sides does a dodecagon have?
  c. How many faces does a dodecahedron have?

3. Icosa, as in icosahedron, comes from the Greek "eikosi." What number does "eikosi" stand for?

Extension

Perspective Drawing

For Use With Lesson 10-1

You can create a three-dimensional space figure with a two-dimensional *perspective drawing*. Suppose two lines are parallel in three dimensions but recede from the viewer. You draw them—and create perspective—so that they meet at a *vanishing point* on a *horizon line*.

1 EXAMPLE

Draw a cube in one-point perspective.

Step 1: Draw a square. Then draw a horizon line and a vanishing point on the line.

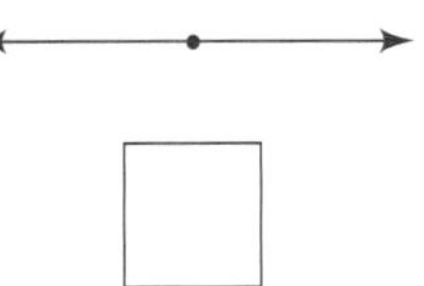

Step 2: Lightly draw segments from the vertices of the square to the vanishing point.

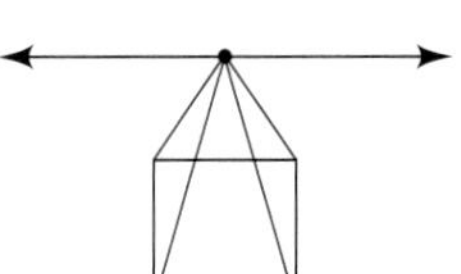

Step 3: Draw a square for the back of the cube. Each vertex should lie on a segment you drew in Step 2.

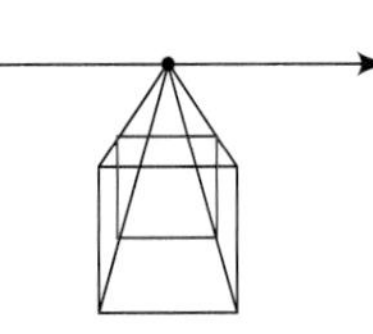

Step 4: Complete the figure by using dashes for hidden edges of the cube. Erase unneeded lines.

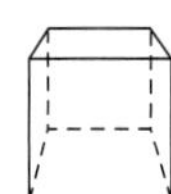

Two-point perspective involves the use of two vanishing points.

2 EXAMPLE

Draw a box in two-point perspective.

Step 1: Draw a vertical segment. Then draw a horizon line and two vanishing points on the line.

Step 2: Lightly draw segments from the endpoints of the vertical segment to each vanishing point.

Step 3: Draw two vertical segments between the segments of Step 2.

Step 4: Draw segments from the endpoints of the segments you drew in Step 3 to the vanishing points.

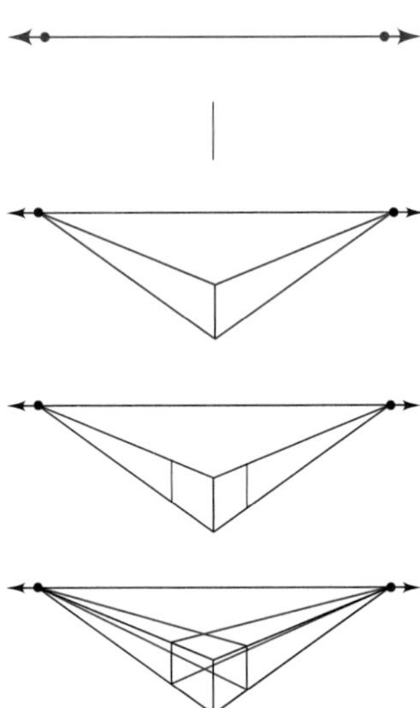

Step 5: Complete the figure by using dashes for hidden edges of the figure. Erase unneeded lines.

EXERCISES

Is each object drawn in one- or two-point perspective?

1. 

2. 

3. 

4. 

5. 

6. 

Draw each object in one-point perspective and then in two-point perspective.

7. a shoe box

8. a building in your town that sits on a street corner

Draw each container using one-point perspective. Show a base at the front.

9. triangular carton

10. hexagonal box

Copy each figure and locate the vanishing point(s).

11. 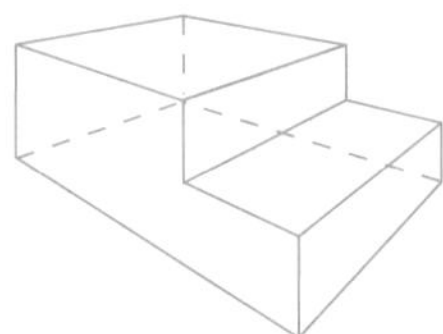

12. 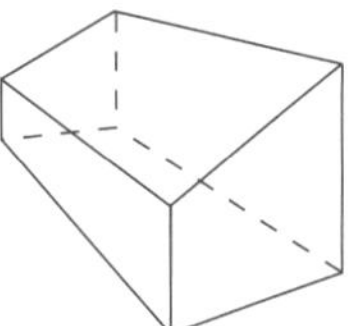

13. 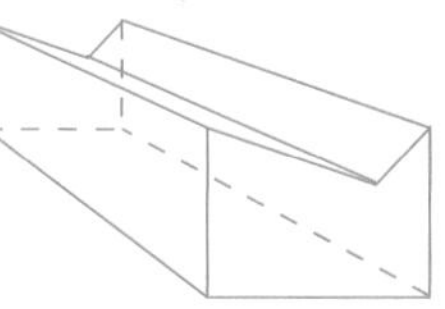

Optical Illusions **What is the optical illusion? Explain how each illusion relates to concepts on these pages.**

14. 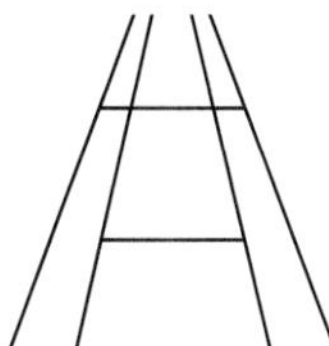

15. 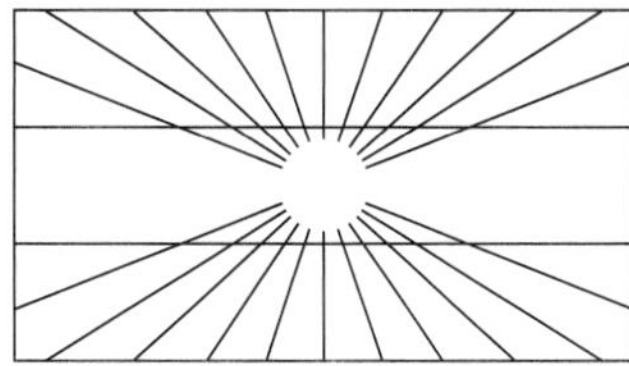

16. Open Ended You can draw block letters in either one-point perspective or two-point perspective. Write your initals in block letters using one-point perspective and two-point perspective.

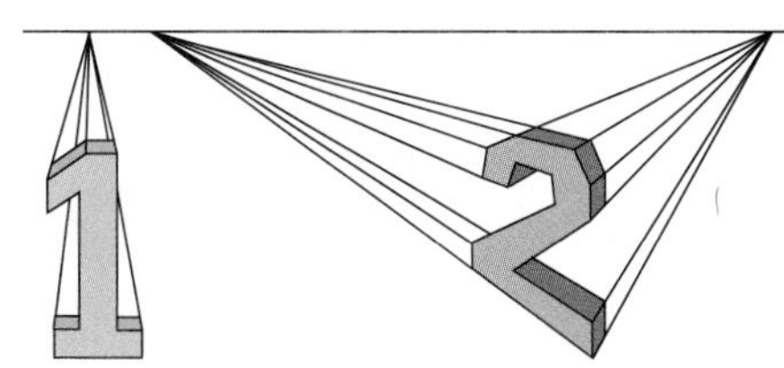

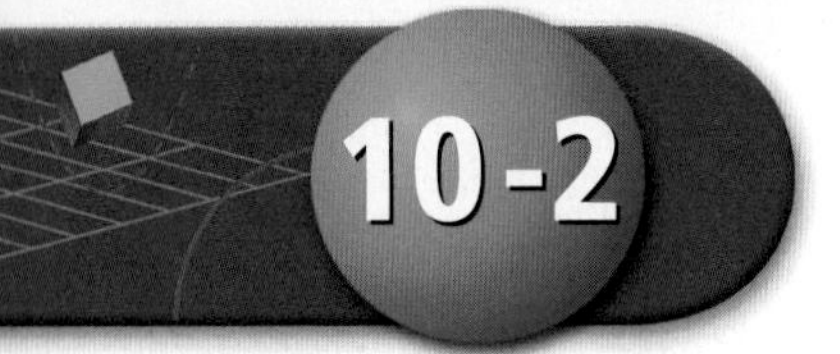

Space Figures and Drawings

Lesson Preview

What You'll Learn

To make isometric and orthographic drawings

To describe cross sections of three-dimensional figures

. . . And Why

To make a foundation drawing, as in Example 3

✓ Check Skills You'll Need

(For help, go to Lesson 1-2.)

For each exercise, make a copy of the cube at the right. Shade the plane that contains the indicated points.

1. A, B, and C
2. A, B, and G
3. A, C, and G
4. A, D, and G
5. F, D, and G
6. B, D, and G
7. the midpoints of $\overline{AD}$, $\overline{CD}$, $\overline{EH}$, and $\overline{GH}$

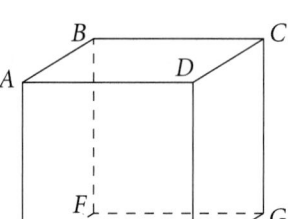

New Vocabulary • isometric drawing • orthographic drawing • foundation drawing • cross section

Interactive lesson includes instant self-check, tutorials, and activities.

OBJECTIVE 1 Drawing Isometric and Orthographic Views

Reading Math

In Greek, *isos* means "equal" and *metron* means "measure." In an isometric drawing, all 3-D measurements are scaled equally.

There are different ways to show a three-dimensional figure on a two-dimensional surface. On a computer screen, you can manipulate the figure for a virtual view of it from any direction. On isometric dot paper, you can make an **isometric drawing** to show three sides of the figure from a corner view.

1 EXAMPLE Isometric Drawing

Make an isometric drawing of the cube structure at the left.

Isometric drawing:

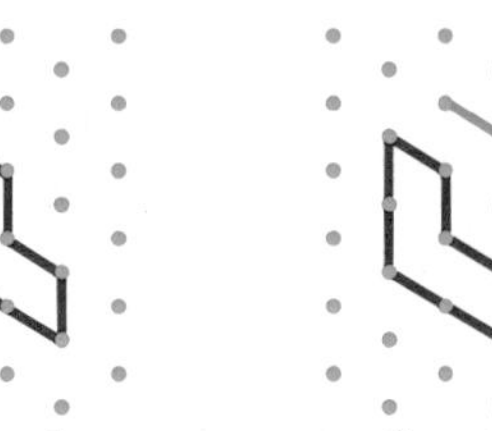

Step 1 Step 2

Step 3

✓ Check Understanding 1 Make an isometric drawing of a structure that can be made using 4 cubes.

An **orthographic drawing** is another way to show a three-dimensional figure. It shows a top view, front view, and right-side view.

2 EXAMPLE Orthographic Drawing

Need Help?
Use dashed segments for "hidden" edges.

Make an orthographic drawing from the isometric drawing at the left.

Isometric drawing:

Orthographic drawing:

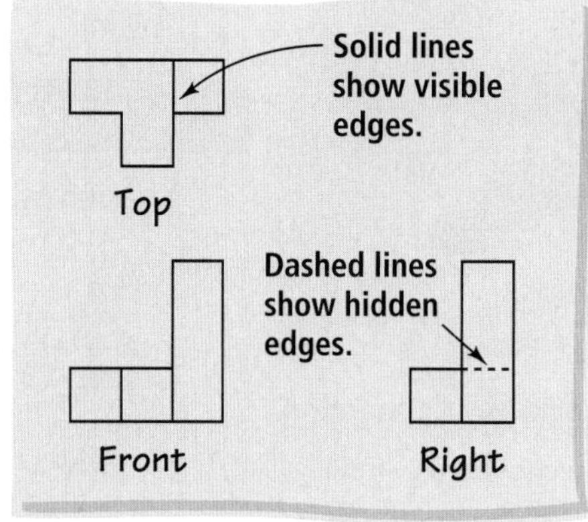

✓ Check Understanding 2 Make an orthographic drawing from this isometric drawing.

Isometric drawing:

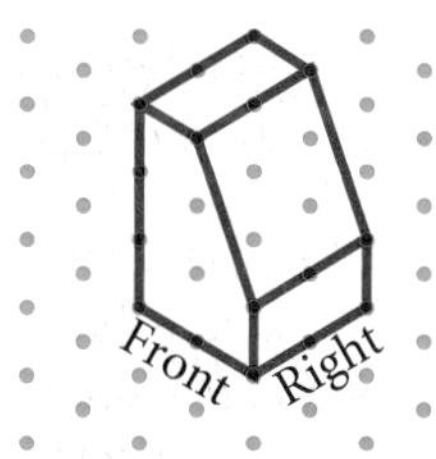

A **foundation drawing** shows the base of a structure and the height of each part. A foundation drawing of the Sears Tower is shown at the right.

49	89	65
109	109	89
65	89	49

The Sears Tower is made up of nine sections. The numbers tell how many stories tall each section is.

Real-World Connection
The foundation drawing shows four heights in the nine sections of the Sears Tower in Chicago, Illinois.

3 EXAMPLE Foundation Drawing

Make a foundation drawing for the isometric drawing at the left.

Isometric drawing:

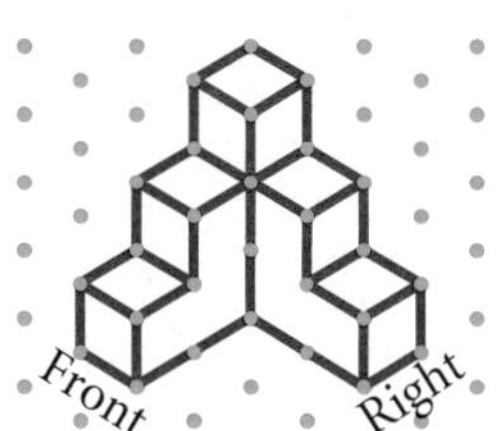

Foundation drawing:

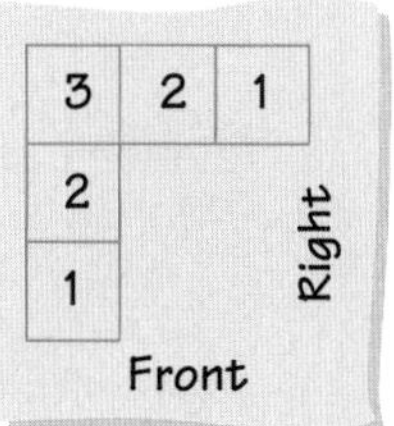

✓ Check Understanding 3 **a.** How many cubes would you use to make the structure in Example 3?

b. Critical Thinking Which drawing did you use to answer part (a), the foundation drawing or the isometric drawing? Explain.

OBJECTIVE 2

Describing Cross Sections

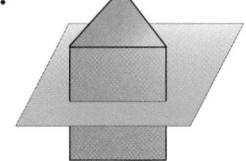

Real-World Connection

A cross section of a cylinder can be a circle.

A **cross section** is the intersection of a solid and a plane. You can think of a cross section as a very thin slice of the solid.

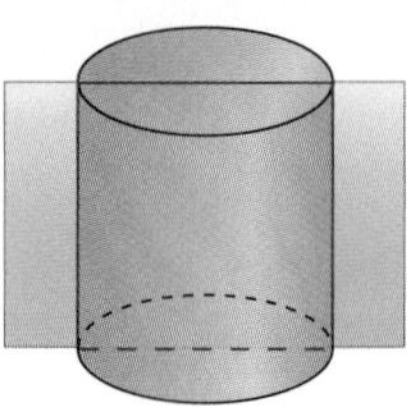

4 EXAMPLE Describing a Cross Section

Describe each cross section.

a.

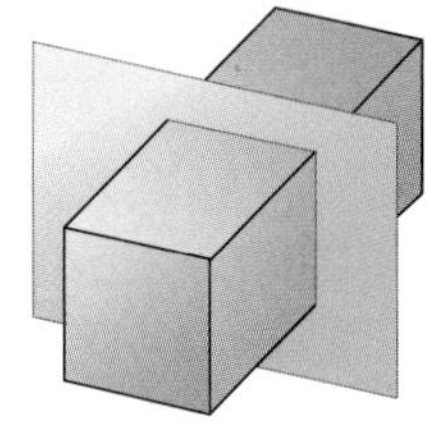

The cross section is a square.

b.

The cross section is a triangle.

✓ **Check Understanding** 4 Describe this cross section of a sphere.

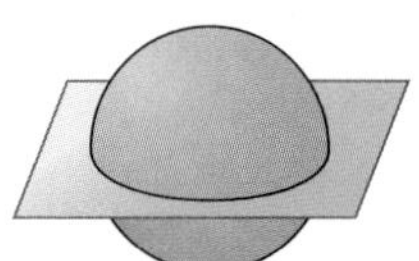

To draw a cross section, you can sometimes use the idea from Postulate 1-3 that the intersection of two planes is exactly one line.

5 EXAMPLE Drawing a Cross Section

Visualization Draw and describe a cross section formed by a vertical plane intersecting the front and right faces of the cube.

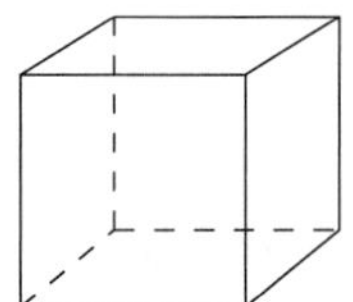

A vertical plane cuts the vertical faces of the cube in parallel segments.

Draw the parallel segments.

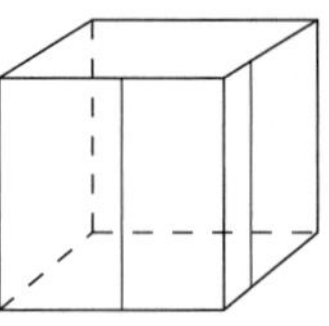

Join their endpoints. Shade the cross section.

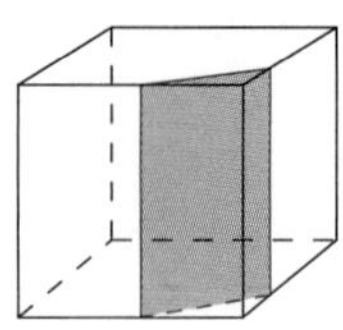

The cross section is a rectangle.

✓ **Check Understanding** 5 Draw and describe the cross section formed by a horizontal plane intersecting the left and right faces of the cube.

EXERCISES

For more practice, see *Extra Practice.*

Practice and Problem Solving

Practice by Example

Example 1 (page 520)

Make an isometric drawing of each cube structure.

1. 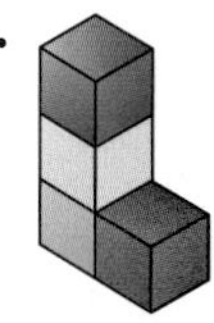

2. 

3. 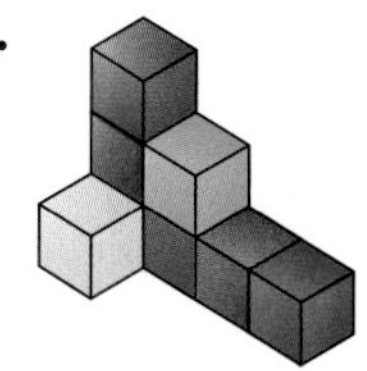

Example 2 (page 521)

Match each isometric drawing with the correct orthographic drawing.

4. 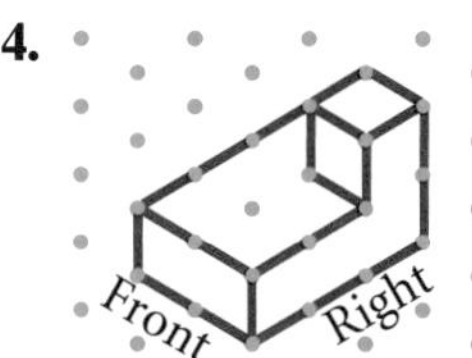

5. 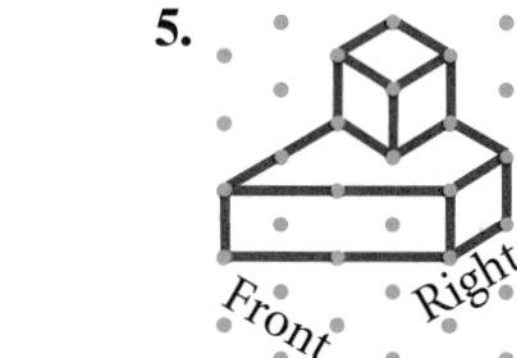

6. 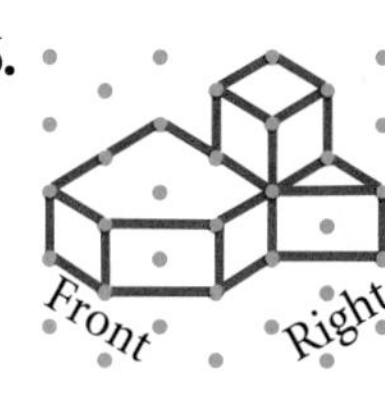

A. 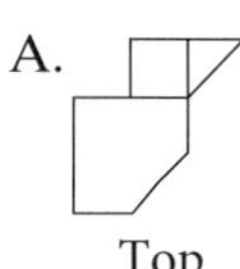

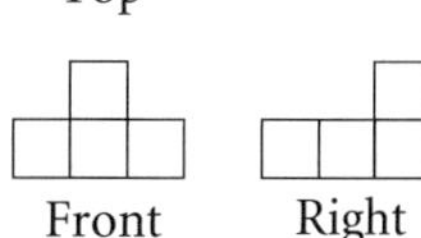

B. 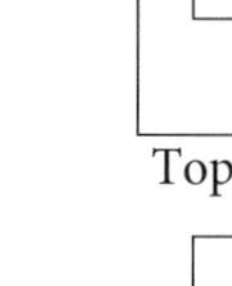

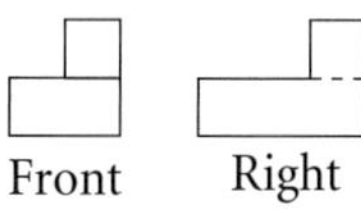

C. 

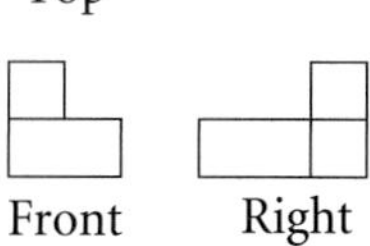

Make an orthographic drawing for each isometric drawing.

7. 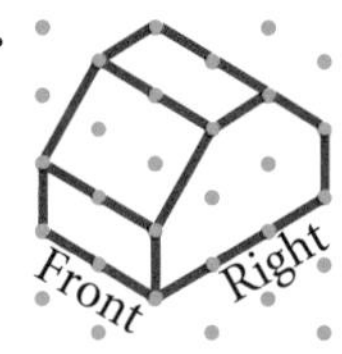

8. 

9. 

Examples 2, 3 (page 521)

For each figure, make (a) a foundation drawing, and (b) an orthographic drawing.

10. 

11. 

12. 

How many cubes would you use to make each of the following?

13. the structure in Exercise 10

14. the structure in Exercise 11

15. the structure in Exercise 12

16. a model of the Sears Tower on page 521

Example 4
(page 522)

Describe each cross section.

17. 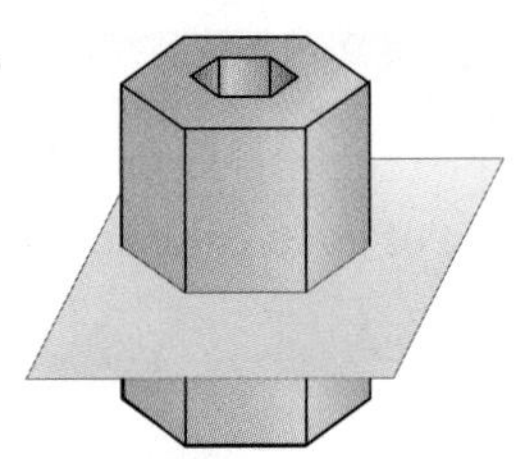

18. 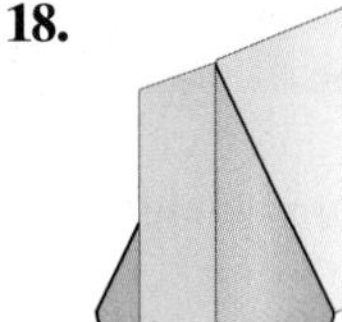

19. 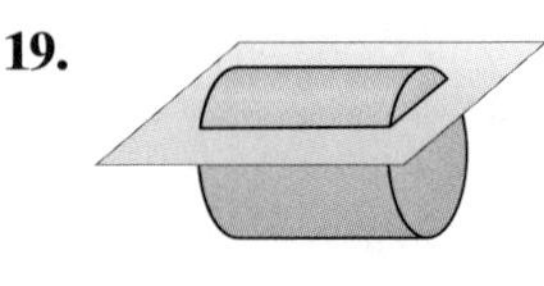

Example 5
(page 522)

Visualization **Draw and describe a cross section formed by a vertical plane intersecting the cube as follows.**

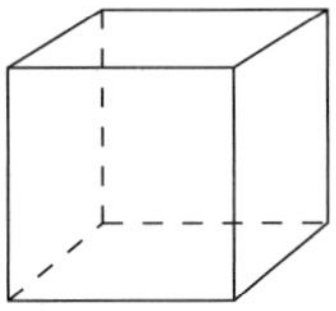

20. The vertical plane intersects the front and left faces of the cube.

21. The vertical plane intersects opposite faces of the cube.

22. The vertical plane contains opposite edges of the cube.

Apply Your Skills

23. a. **Open-Ended** Make an isometric drawing of a structure that can be built using 8 cubes.

b. Make an orthographic drawing of this structure.

c. Make a foundation drawing for this structure.

For each foundation drawing, make (a) an isometric drawing on dot paper, and (b) an orthographic drawing.

24.

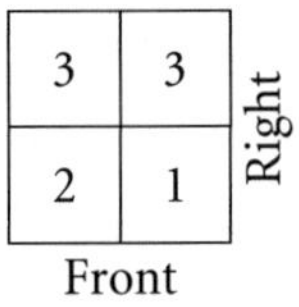

3	3
2	1

Front; Right

25. 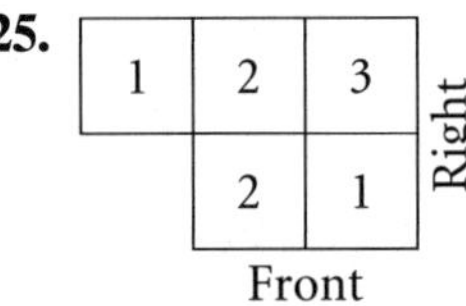

26. 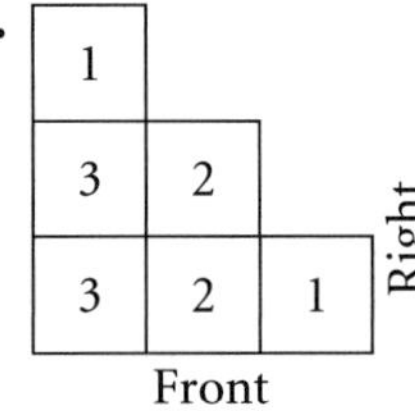

Need Help?
Two cube stuctures are the same if you can rotate one to match the other.

A two-by-two foundation drawing shows a positive integer in each of its four squares. How many different cube structures are possible if the sum of the numbers is as given?

27. 4

28. 5

29. 6

30. 7

Read the comic strip and complete Exercises 31 and 32.

SHOE by Jeff MacNelly

31. What type of drawing that you've studied in this lesson is a "bird's-eye view"?

32. **Writing** Photographs of the Washington Monument are typically not taken from a bird's-eye view. Describe a situation in which you would want a photo showing a bird's-eye view.

33. Engineering Engineers use engineering layouts to describe structures. A complete layout includes three orthographic views and an isometric view. Make a complete engineering layout for a cube structure suggested by the foundation plan below.

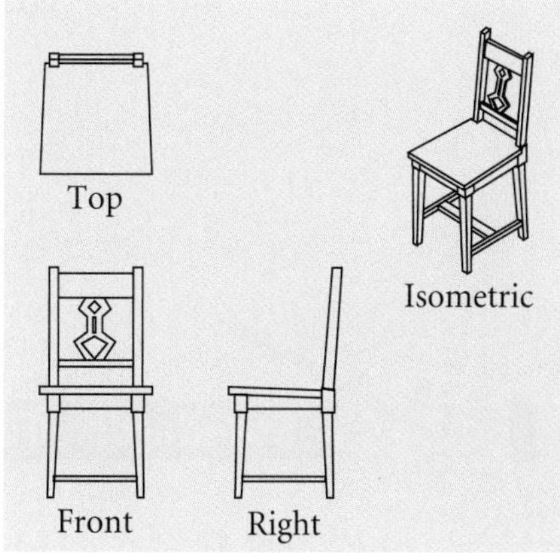

4	3	2
3	2	1
2	1	

Front (bottom), Right (right side)

34. Probability Mark made the structure at the left using 27 wooden cubes. He painted four of the faces blue and left the top and bottom unpainted. Then he took the structure apart and placed the cubes in a bag.

Leah closes her eyes, reaches into the bag, and pulls out a cube.

a. What is the probability that the cube is unpainted?
b. What is the probability that two of its faces are blue?
c. What is the probability that only one of its faces is blue?

For each figure, make (a) a foundation drawing and (b) an orthographic drawing. Assume there are no cubes hidden behind the structures.

35.

36.

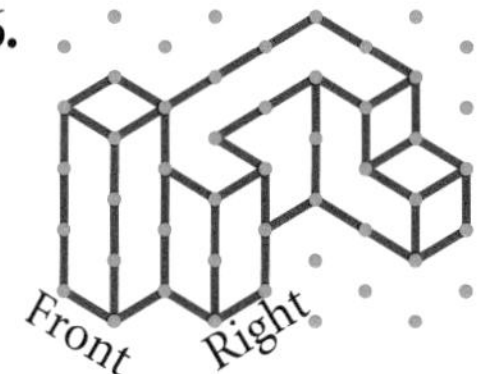

Visualization **Draw and describe a cross section formed by a plane intersecting the cube as follows.**

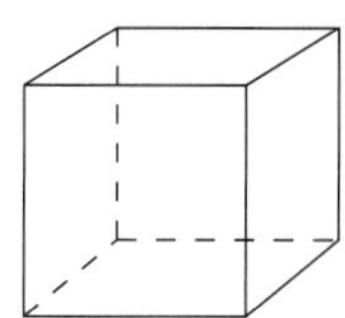

37. The plane is tilted and intersects the left and right faces of the cube.

38. The plane contains opposite horizontal edges of the cube.

39. The plane cuts off a corner of the cube.

Describe the cross section shown.

40.

41.

42.

Challenge

Visualization **Draw a plane intersecting a cube to get the cross section indicated.**

43. scalene triangle	**44.** isosceles triangle	**45.** equilateral triangle
46. trapezoid	**47.** isosceles trapezoid	**48.** parallelogram
49. rhombus	**50.** pentagon	**51.** hexagon

52. **Visualization** Use the orthographic drawing at the right.
   a. Make an isometric drawing of the structure.
   b. Make an isometric drawing of the structure from part (a) after it has been turned on its base 90° counterclockwise.
   c. Make an orthographic drawing of the stucture from part (b).
   d. Turn the structure from part (a) 180°. Repeat parts (b) and (c).

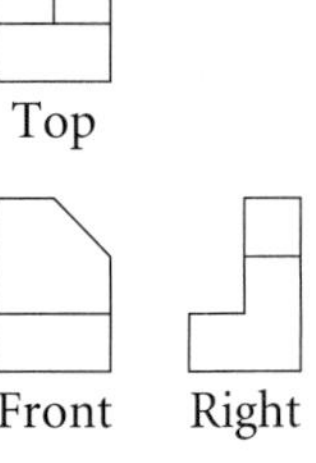

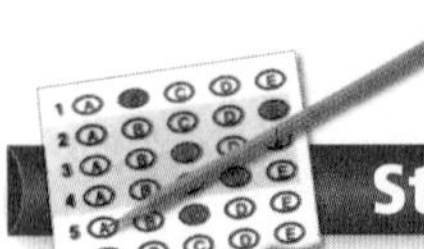

Standardized Test Prep

Multiple Choice

53. The plane is horizontal. What best describes the shape of the cross section?
   A. rhombus B. trapezoid
   C. parallelogram D. square

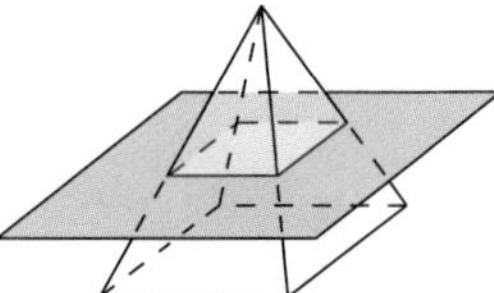

Take It to the NET
Online lesson quiz at **www.PHSchool.com**
Web Code: afa-1002

54. The plane is vertical. What best describes the shape of the cross section?
   F. pentagon G. square
   H. rectangle I. triangle

Short Response

55. Draw and describe a cross section formed by a plane intersecting a cube as follows.
   a. The plane is parallel to a horizontal face of the cube.
   b. The plane cuts off two corners of the cube.

Extended Response

56. Make drawings to show the top view, the front view, and the right-side view of the figure at the right.

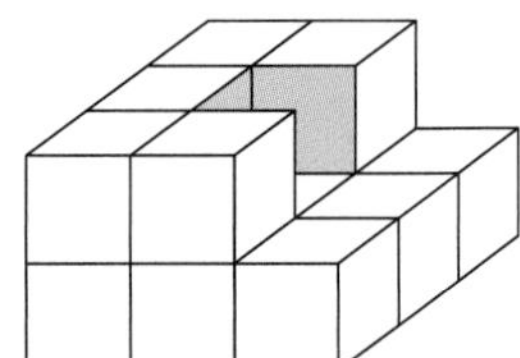

Mixed Review

Lesson 10-1

Draw a net for each space figure. Label the net with its dimensions.

57. a rectangular box with height 5 cm and a base 3 cm by 4 cm

58. a cube with 2-in. sides

Lesson 9-1

Find the value of x to the nearest tenth.

59.

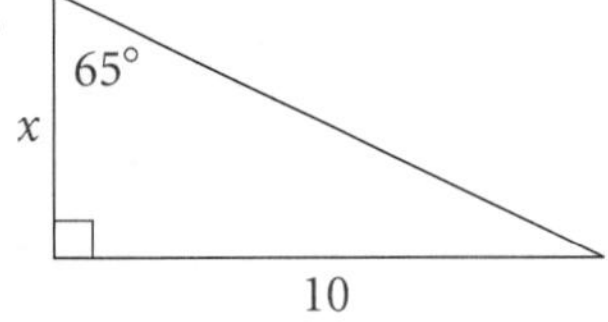

60.

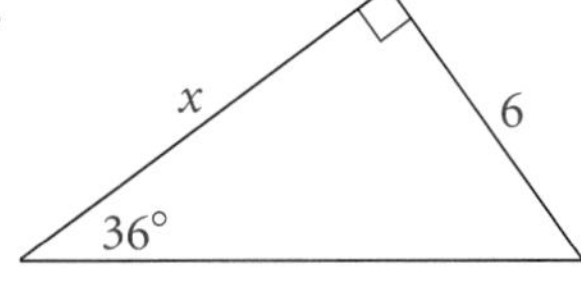

61. The lengths of the diagonals of a rhombus are 4 cm and 6 cm. Find the measures of the angles of the rhombus to the nearest degree.

Lesson 7-5

Find the area of each equilateral triangle with the given measure. Leave answers in simplest radical form.

62. side 2 ft 63. apothem 8 cm 64. radius 100 in.

Literal Equations

FOR USE WITH LESSON 10-3

A *literal equation* is an equation involving two or more variables. A formula is a special type of literal equation. You can transform a formula by solving for one variable in terms of the others.

1 EXAMPLE

Algebra The formula for the volume of a cylinder is $V = \pi r^2 h$. Find a formula for the height in terms of the radius and volume.

$V = \pi r^2 h$

$\frac{V}{\pi r^2} = \frac{\pi r^2 h}{\pi r^2}$ **Divide each side by πr^2, $r \neq 0$.**

$\frac{V}{\pi r^2} = h$ **Simplify.**

The formula for the height is $h = \frac{V}{\pi r^2}$.

Solving literal equations also allows you to build other formulas.

2 EXAMPLE

Algebra Find a formula for the area of a square in terms of its perimeter.

$P = 4s$ **Use the formula for perimeter.**

$\frac{P}{4} = s$ **Solve for *s* in terms of *P*.**

$A = s^2$ **Use the formula for area.**

$A = \left(\frac{P}{4}\right)^2$ **Substitute.**

$A = \frac{P^2}{16}$ **Simplify.**

The formula for the area is $A = \frac{P^2}{16}$.

EXERCISES

Algebra Solve each equation for the variable in red.

1. $C = 2\pi r$
2. $A = \frac{1}{2}bh$
3. $A = \pi r^2$

Algebra Solve for the variable in red. Then solve for the variable in blue.

4. $P = 2w + 2\ell$
5. $\tan A = \frac{y}{x}$
6. $A = \frac{1}{2}(b_1 + b_2)h$

Find a formula as stated.

7. the circumference of a circle in terms of its area
8. the area of an isosceles right triangle in terms of the hypotenuse
9. the apothem of a regular hexagon in terms of the area of the hexagon

10-3 Surface Areas of Prisms and Cylinders

Lesson Preview

What You'll Learn

OBJECTIVE 1: To find the surface area of a prism

OBJECTIVE 2: To find the surface area of a cylinder

. . . And Why

To find the area covered by a drum on a roller used in road construction, as in Example 4

✔ Check Skills You'll Need

(For help, go to Lessons 1-7 and 7-5.)

Find the area of each net.

1.

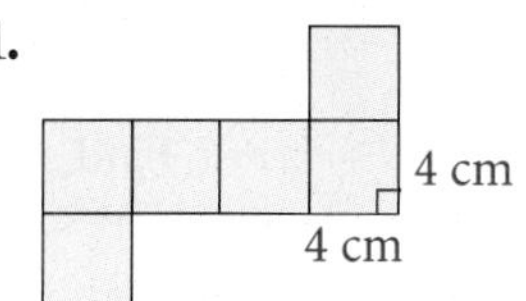

2.

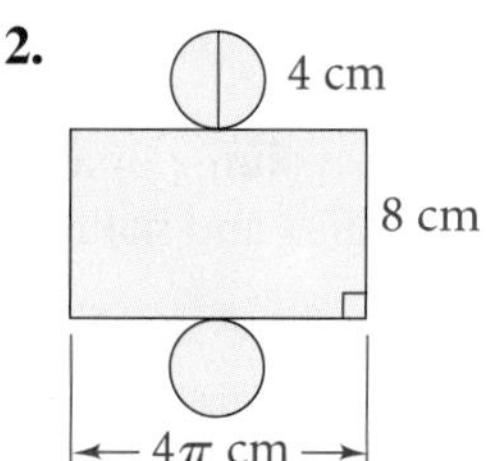

3.

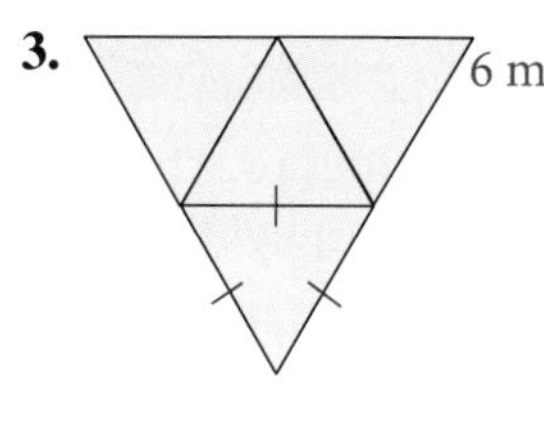

New Vocabulary • prism • bases, lateral faces, altitude, height, lateral area, surface area (of a prism) • right prism • oblique prism • cylinder • bases, altitude, height, lateral area, surface area (of a cylinder) • right cylinder • oblique cylinder

Interactive lesson includes instant self-check, tutorials, and activities.

OBJECTIVE 1

Finding Surface Area of a Prism

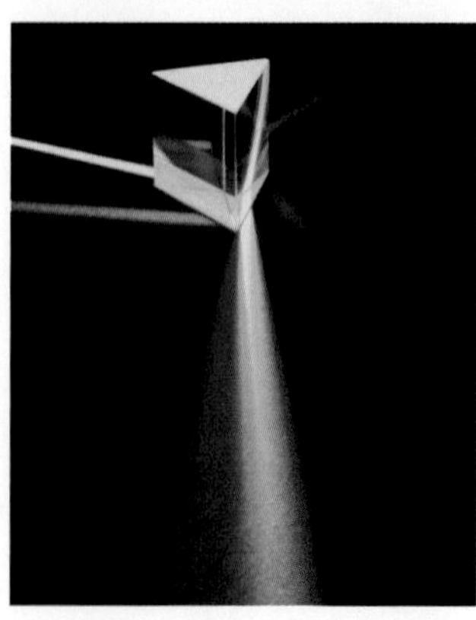

Real-World Connection

A triangular prism breaks white light into rainbow colors.

A **prism** is a polyhedron with exactly two congruent, parallel faces, called **bases.** Other faces are **lateral faces.** You name a prism by the shape of its bases.

An **altitude** of a prism is a perpendicular segment that joins the planes of the bases. The **height** h of the prism is the length of an altitude.

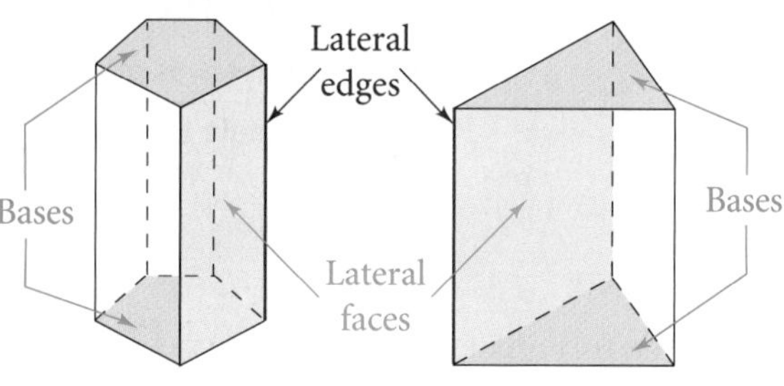

A prism may either be right or oblique.

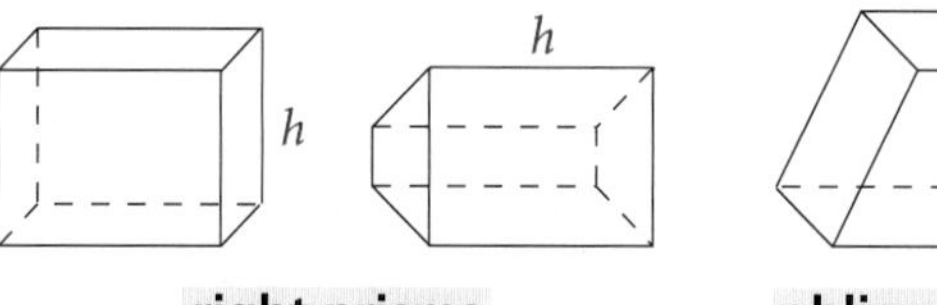

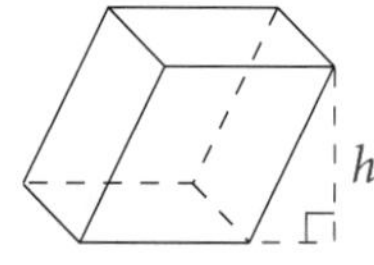

In a right prism the lateral faces are rectangles and a lateral edge is an altitude. In this book you may assume that a prism is a right prism unless stated or pictured otherwise.

The **lateral area** of a prism is the sum of the areas of the lateral faces. The **surface area** is the sum of the lateral area and the area of the two bases.

1 EXAMPLE Finding Surface Area of a Prism

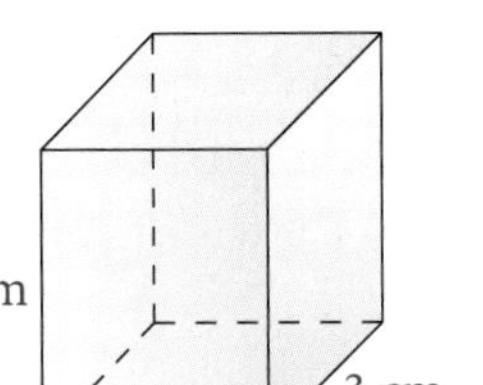

Use a net to find the surface area of the prism at the left.

Surface Area = Lateral Area + area of bases
= sum of areas of lateral faces + area of bases
$= (5 \cdot 4 + 5 \cdot 3 + 5 \cdot 4 + 5 \cdot 3) + 2(3)(4)$
$= 70 + 24$
$= 94$

The surface area of the prism is 94 cm^2.

1 Use a net to find the surface area of the triangular prism.

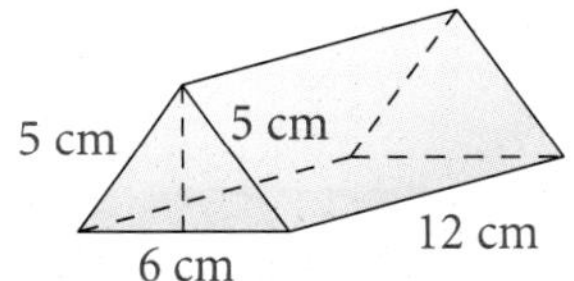

You can find formulas for lateral and surface areas by looking at a net for a prism.

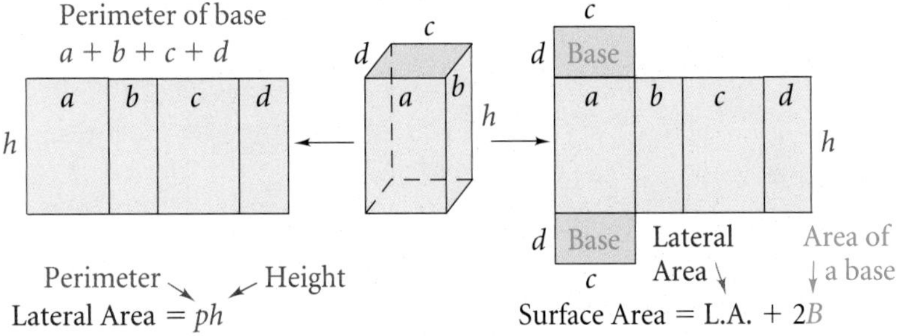

You can use the formulas with any right prism.

2 EXAMPLE Using Formulas to Find Surface Area

Use formulas to find the lateral area and surface area of the prism.

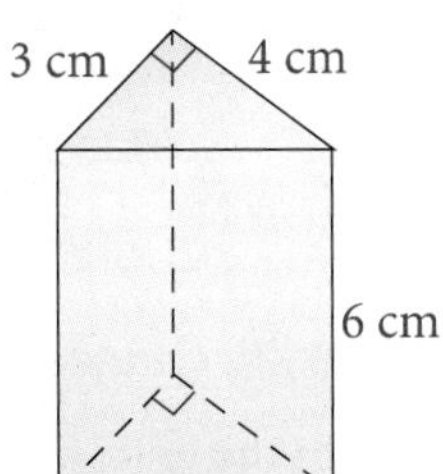

By the Pythagorean Theorem, the hypotenuse of the triangular base is 5 cm.

L.A. $= ph$ **Use the formula for lateral area.**
$= 12 \cdot 6$ **$p = 3 + 4 + 5 = 12$ cm**
$= 72$

The lateral area of the prism is 72 cm^2.

Now use the formula for surface area.

S.A. = L.A. + $2B$
$= 72 + 2(6) = 84$ **$B = \frac{1}{2}(3 \cdot 4) = 6$ cm^2**

The surface area of the prism is 84 cm^2.

Check Understanding

2 Use formulas to find the lateral area and surface area of the prism.

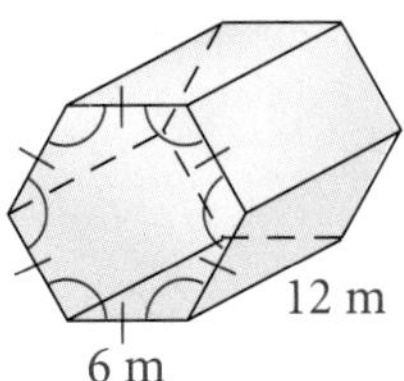

The formulas are summarized at the top of the next page.

Key Concepts

Theorem 10-1 **Lateral and Surface Areas of a Prism**

The lateral area of a right prism is the product of the perimeter of the base and the height.

$$\text{L.A.} = ph$$

The surface area of a right prism is the sum of the lateral area and the areas of the two bases.

$$\text{S.A.} = \text{L.A.} + 2B$$

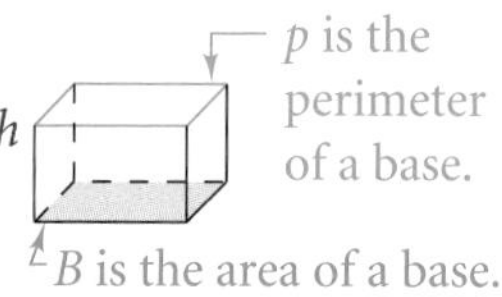

OBJECTIVE

2 Finding Surface Area of a Cylinder

Like a prism, a **cylinder** has two congruent parallel **bases.** However, the bases of a cylinder are circles. An **altitude** of a cylinder is a perpendicular segment that joins the planes of the bases. The **height** h of a cylinder is the length of an altitude.

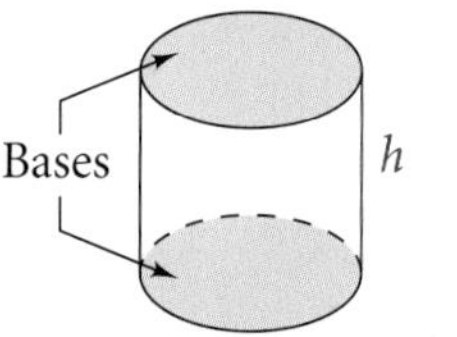

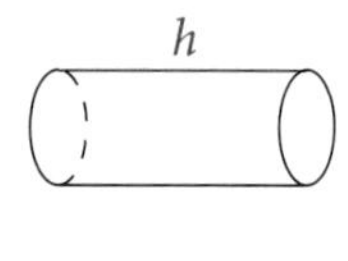

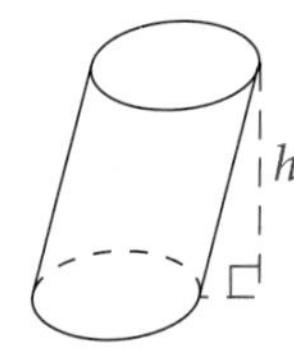

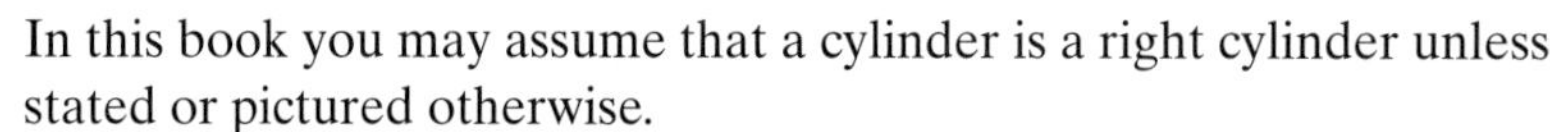

Real-World Connection

A full turn of the roller inks a rectangle with area equal to the roller's lateral area.

In this book you may assume that a cylinder is a right cylinder unless stated or pictured otherwise.

To find the area of the curved surface of a cylinder, visualize "unrolling" it. The area of the resulting rectangle is the **lateral area** of the cylinder. The **surface area** of a cylinder is the sum of the lateral area and the areas of the two circular bases. You can find formulas for these areas by looking at a net for a cylinder.

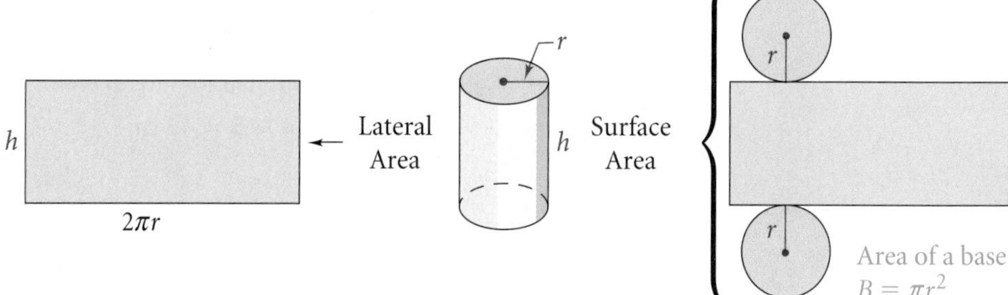

Key Concepts

Theorem 10-2 **Lateral and Surface Areas of a Cylinder**

The lateral area of a right cylinder is the product of the circumference of the base and the height of the cylinder.

$$\text{L.A.} = 2\pi rh, \text{ or L.A.} = \pi dh$$

The surface area of a right cylinder is the sum of the lateral area and the areas of the two bases.

$$\text{S.A.} = \text{L.A.} + 2B, \text{ or S.A.} = 2\pi rh + 2\pi r^2$$

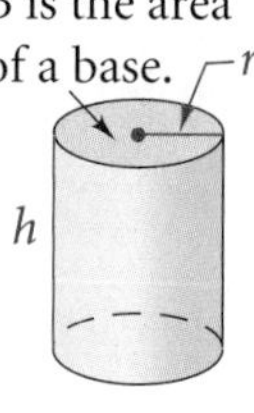

3 EXAMPLE Finding Surface Area of a Cylinder

The radius of the base of a cylinder is 4 in. and its height is 6 in. Find the surface area of the cylinder in terms of π.

S.A. $= \text{L.A.} + 2B$	**Use the formula for surface area of a cylinder.**
$= 2\pi rh + 2(\pi r^2)$	**Substitute the formulas for lateral area and area of a circle.**
$= 2\pi(4)(6) + 2\pi(4^2)$	**Substitute 4 for *r* and 6 for *h*.**
$= 48\pi + 32\pi$	**Simplify.**
$= 80\pi$	

The surface area of the cylinder is 80π in.^{2}.

Check Understanding 3 Find the surface area of a cylinder with height 10 cm and radius 10 cm in terms of π.

4 EXAMPLE Real-World Connection

Machinery The drums of the roller at the left are cylinders of length 3.5 ft. The diameter of the large drum is 4.2 ft. What area does the large drum cover in one full turn? Round your answer to the nearest square foot.

The area covered is the lateral area of a cylinder that has a diameter of 4.2 ft and a height of 3.5 ft.

L.A. $= \pi dh$	**Use the formula for lateral area of a cylinder.**
$= \pi(4.2)(3.5)$	**Substitute.**
$= 46.181412$	**Use a calculator.**

In one full turn, the large drum covers about 46 ft^2.

Check Understanding 4 The small drum has diameter 3 ft.
a. To the nearest square foot, what area does the small drum cover in one turn?
b. **Critical Thinking** What area does the small drum cover in one turn of the large drum?

EXERCISES

For more practice, see *Extra Practice*.

Practice and Problem Solving

A Practice by Example

Example 1 (page 529)

Use a net to find the surface area of each prism.

1. 

2. 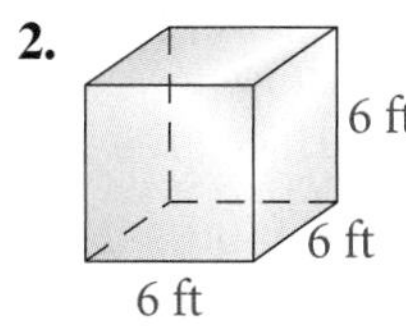

3. 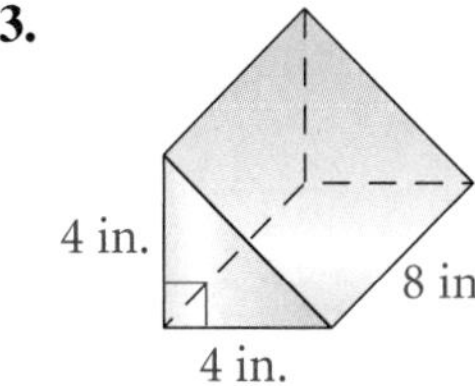

4. **a.** Classify the prism.
b. Find the lateral area of the prism.
c. The bases are regular hexagons. Find the sum of their areas.
d. Find the surface area of the prism.

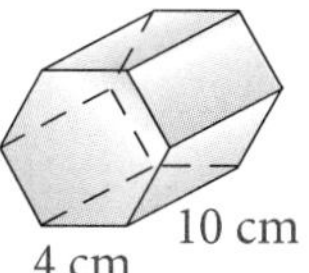

Example 2 (page 529)

Use formulas to find the lateral area and surface area of each prism. Show your answer to the nearest whole number.

5.

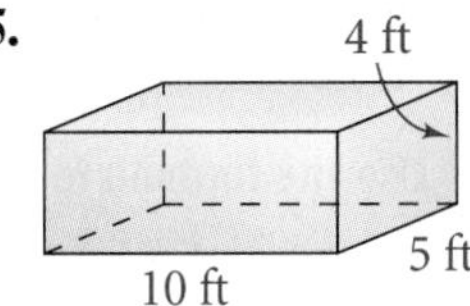

6.

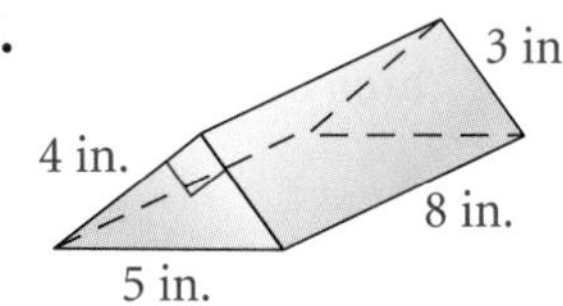

7.

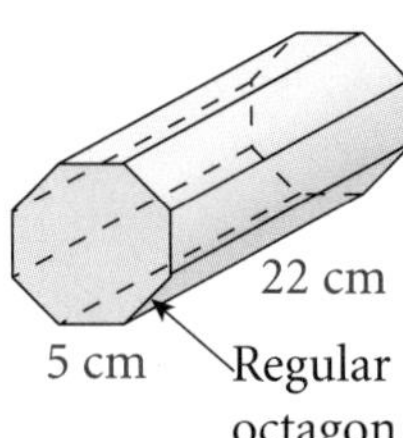

Example 3 (page 531))

Find the surface area of each cylinder in terms of π.

8.

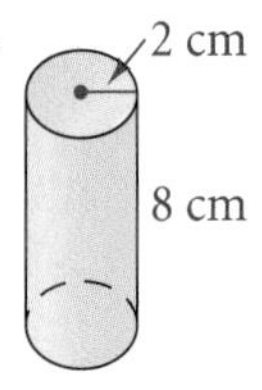

9.

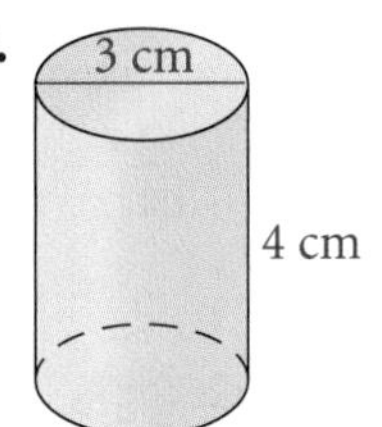

10.

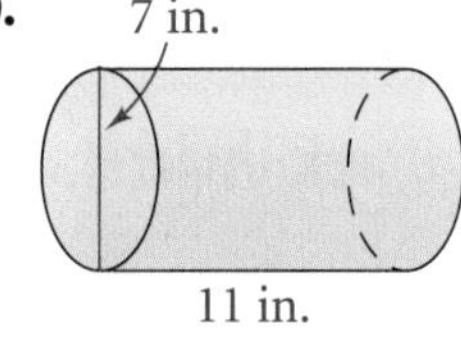

11. A standard drinking straw is 19.5 cm long and has a diameter of 0.6 cm. How many square centimeters of plastic are used in one straw? Round your answer to the nearest tenth.

Example 4 (page 531)

12. **Packaging** A cylindrical carton of oatmeal with radius 3.5 in. is 9 in. tall. If all surfaces except the top are made of cardboard, how much cardboard is used to make the oatmeal carton? Round your answer to the nearest square inch.

Find the surface area of each cylinder to the nearest whole number.

13.

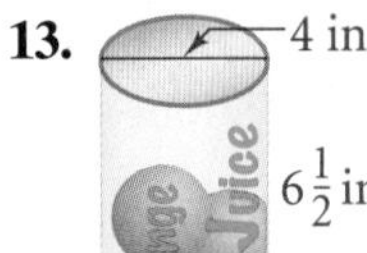

14.

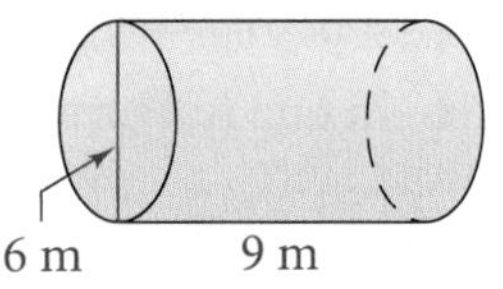

15.

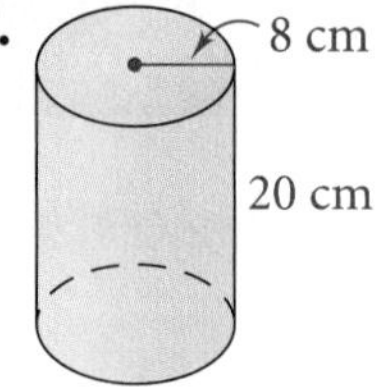

B Apply Your Skills

16. A triangular prism has base edges 4 cm, 5 cm, and 6 cm long. Its lateral area is 300 cm^2. What is the height of the prism?

17. **Estimation** Estimate the surface area of a cube with edges 4.95 cm long.

18. **Writing** Explain how a cylinder and a prism are alike and how they are different.

19. A hexagonal pencil is a hexagonal prism. A base edge of the pencil has length 4 mm. The pencil (without eraser) has height 170 mm. How much surface area of a hexagonal pencil gets painted?

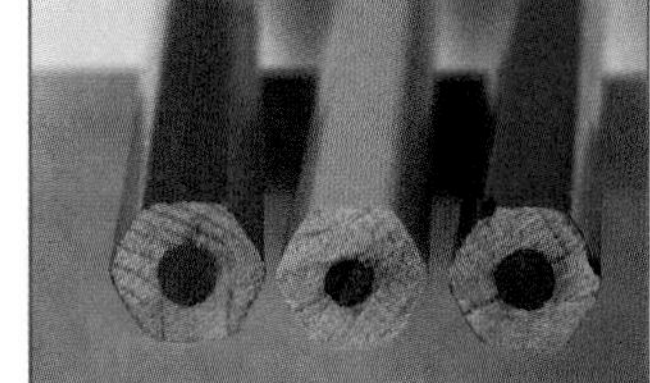

20. **Open-Ended** Draw a net for a rectangular prism with a surface area of 220 cm^2.

21. Consider a box with dimensions 3, 4, and 5.

a. Find its surface area.

b. Double each dimension and then find the new surface area.

c. Find the ratio of the new surface area to the original surface area.

d. Repeat parts (a)–(c) for a box with dimensions 6, 9, and 11.

e. **Make a Conjecture** How does doubling the dimensions of a rectangular prism affect the surface area?

22. The surface area of a cube is 726 $in.^2$. What is the length of each lateral edge of the cube?

23. **Pest Control** A flour moth trap has the shape of a triangular prism that is open on both ends. An environmentally safe chemical draws the moth inside the prism, which is lined with an adhesive. Find the surface area of the trap.

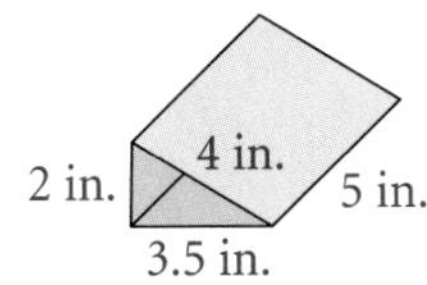

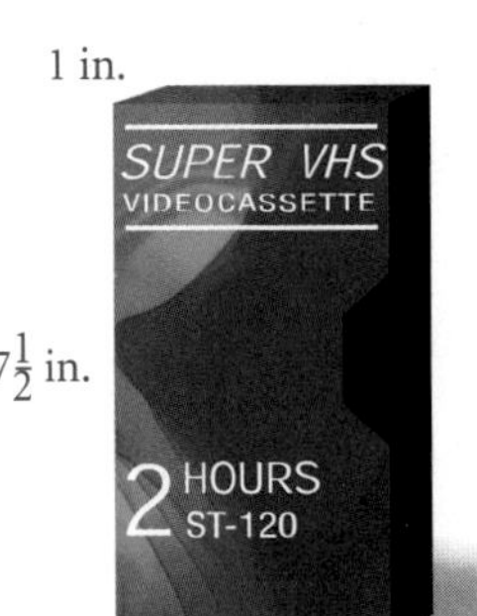

Exercise 24

24. **Packaging** A typical box for a videocassette tape is open on one side as pictured at the left. How many square inches of cardboard are in a typical box for a videocassette tape?

25. Suppose that a cylinder has a radius of r units, and that the height of the cylinder is also r units. The lateral area of the cylinder is 98π square units.

a. **Algebra** Find the value of r.

b. Find the surface area of the cylinder.

26. a. **Geometry in 3 Dimensions** Find the three coordinates of each vertex A, B, C, and D of the rectangular prism.

b. Find AB.

c. Find BC.

d. Find CD.

e. Find the surface area of the prism.

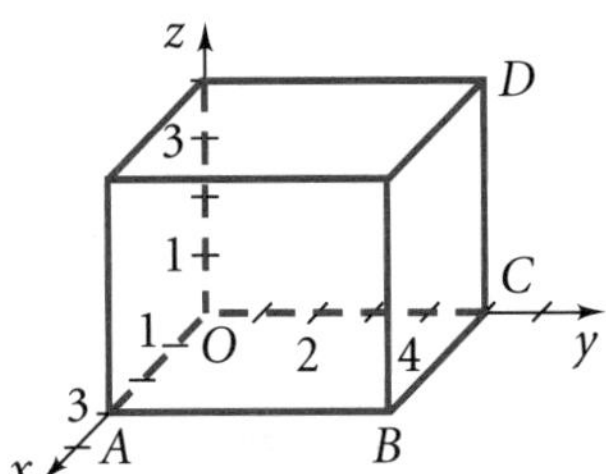

Visualization **The plane region is revolved completely about the given line to sweep out a solid of revolution. Describe the solid and find its surface area in terms of π.**

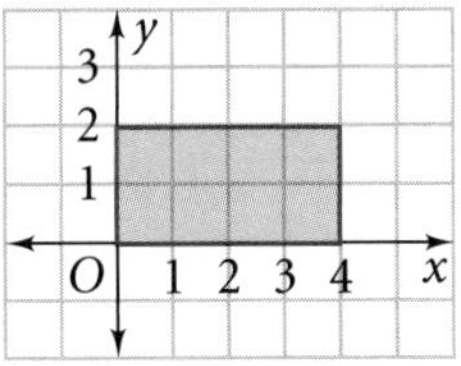

27. the y-axis

28. the x-axis

29. the line $y = 2$

30. the line $x = 4$

31. a. **Critical Thinking** Suppose you double the radius of a right cylinder. How does that affect the lateral area?

b. How does that affect the surface area?

c. Use the formula for surface area of a right cylinder to explain why the surface area in part (b) was not doubled.

Need Help?

In Exercise 32, the slanted sides of the parallelogram form a spiral seam about the biscuit cylinder. The horizontal sides form circular bases.

32. a. **Packaging** The wrapper for a container of biscuits is a parallelogram with base 7.5 in. and height 6 in. Find the radius and height of the container.

b. Find the surface area of the container of biscuits.

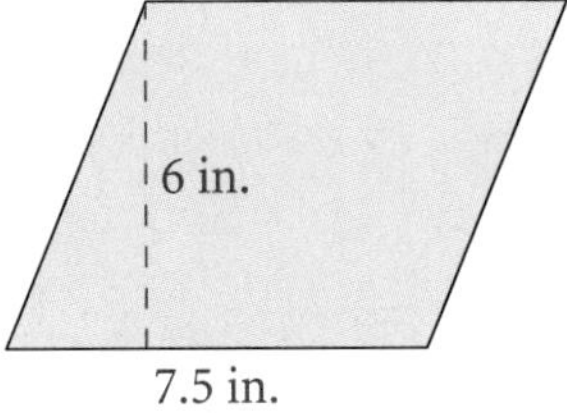

Challenge

Judging by appearances, what is the surface area of each solid?

33.

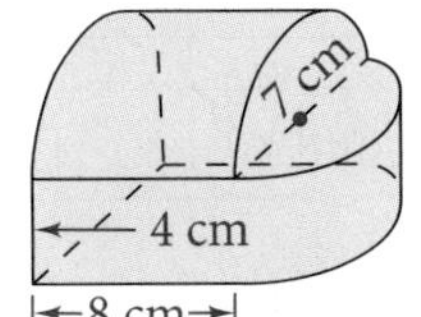

34.

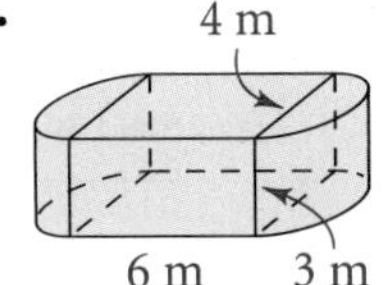

35.

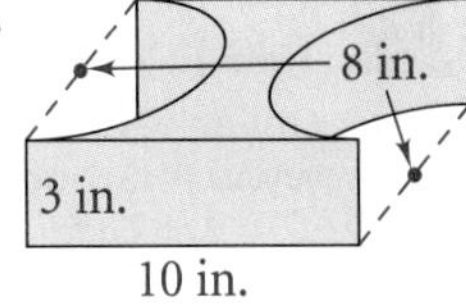

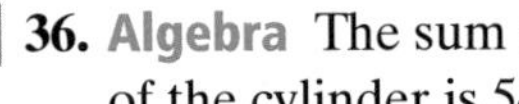

36. **Algebra** The sum of the height and radius of a cylinder is 9 m. The surface area of the cylinder is 54π m^2. Find the height and the radius.

37. Each edge of the large cube at the right is 12 inches long. The cube is painted on the outside, and then cut into 27 smaller cubes. Answer these questions about the 27 cubes.

a. How many are painted on 4, 3, 2, 1, and 0 faces?

b. What is the total surface area that is unpainted?

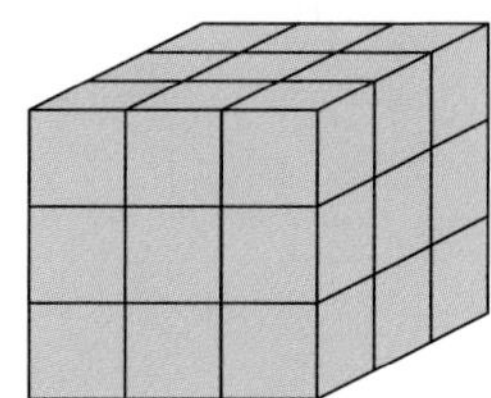

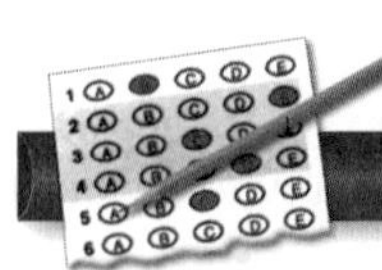

Standardized Test Prep

Multiple Choice

38. What is the surface area of the figure to the nearest tenth?

A. 335.7 m^2 **B.** 411.6 m^2

C. 671.5 m^2 **D.** 721.2 m^2

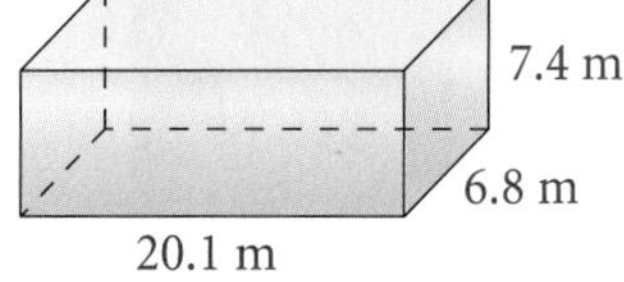

39. If the radius and height of a cylinder are both doubled, then the surface area is __?__.

F. the same **G.** doubled **H.** tripled **I.** quadrupled

40. A cylinder of radius r sits snugly inside a cube. Which expression represents the difference of their lateral areas?

A. $2r^2(8 - \pi)$ **B.** $2r(\pi - 2)$ **C.** $2r(4 - \pi)$ **D.** $4r^2(4 - \pi)$

Quantitative Comparison

Compare the boxed quantity in Column A with the boxed quantity in Column B. Choose the best answer.

A. The quantity in Column A is greater.

B. The quantity in Column B is greater.

C. The two quantities are equal.

D. The relationship cannot be determined from the information given.

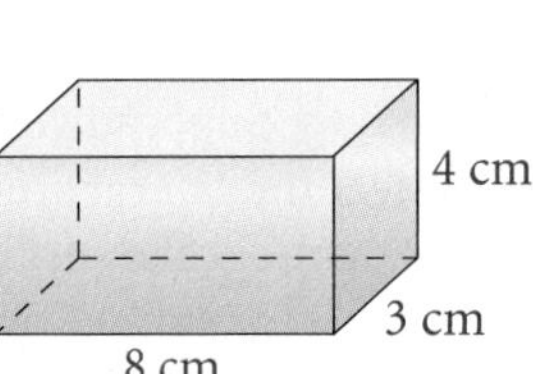

Figure 1

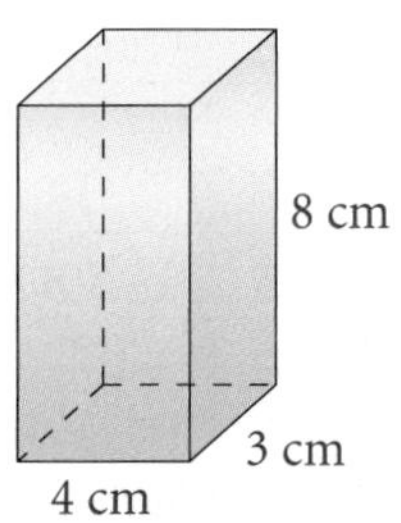

Figure 2

	Column A	Column B
41.	perimeter of the base in Figure 1	perimeter of the base in Figure 2
42.	lateral area in Figure 1	lateral area in Figure 2
43.	surface area in Figure 1	surface area in Figure 2

Take It to the NET
Online lesson quiz at **www.PHSchool.com**
Web Code: afa-1003

Short Response

44. The sides of a base of a right triangular prism are 6 in., 8 in., and 10 in. The lateral area of the prism is 48 $in.^2$.

a. Find the height of the prism. Explain your reasoning.

b. What is the surface area of the prism?

Mixed Review

Lesson 10-2

Make each type of drawing from the foundation drawing at the right.

2	3
1	1

Front; Right

45. an isometric drawing

46. an orthographic drawing

47. Draw sketches to show how three planes can intersect a cube to form three different rectangular cross sections.

Lesson 7-7

Find the area of each part of the circle to the nearest tenth.

P, Q, O, 120°, 6 cm

48. sector QOP

49. the segment of the circle bounded by $\overline{QP}$ and $\overset{\frown}{QP}$

Lesson 6-7

50. In the kite at the right $AB = AD$ and $CB = CD$. Points P, Q, R, and S are midpoints.

a. Determine the coordinates of the midpoints.

b. $RQ = \blacksquare$; $SP = \blacksquare$; $PQ = \blacksquare$; $SR = \blacksquare$

c. Use your answers to part (b) to explain why $PQRS$ must be a parallelogram.

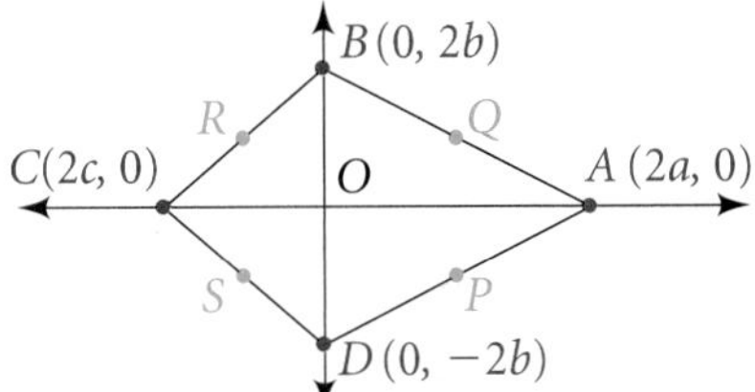

Checkpoint Quiz 1

Lessons 10-1 through 10-3

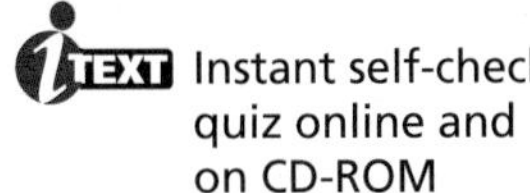
Instant self-check quiz online and on CD-ROM

Draw a net for each figure. Label the net with its dimensions.

1.

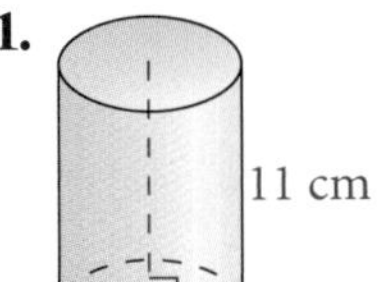

2.

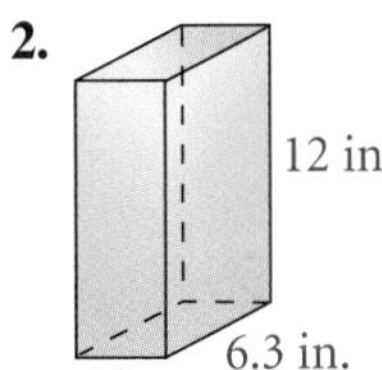

3. Find the surface area of the cylinder in Exercise 1.

4. Find the surface area of the prism in Exercise 2.

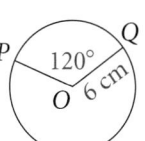

5. Space Exploration A space shuttle brings a docking module to a space station. The module is a cylinder with a 24-m diameter and a 46-m height. What is the surface area of the docking module to the nearest tenth?

6. Open-Ended Draw a net for a regular hexagonal prism.

7. Writing Explain how the formulas for the lateral area of a prism and the lateral area of a cylinder are alike and how they are different.

8. Create an isometric drawing of a figure that can be constructed with 5 cubes.

Draw a cube. Shade the cube to show each cross section.

9. a rectangle

10. a trapezoid

Technology

Exploring Surface Area

For Use With Lesson 10-3

At room temperature, 1 L, 1000 mL, and 1000 cm^3 all represent the same amount of water. Thus, one type of model for a liter is any square prism that holds 1000 cm^3. The best model, perhaps, is a 10-cm cube as shown here. But there are many others.

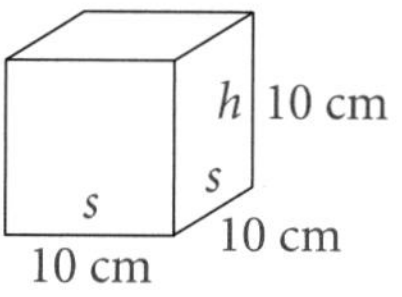

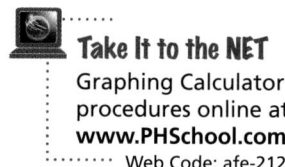

Take It to the NET
Graphing Calculator procedures online at **www.PHSchool.com**
Web Code: afe-2121

You can use graphing calculator lists to study how height (h) and surface area (S.A.) of a 1-L square prism change as the length (s) of each side of a base changes.

The volume of a prism equals the area of a base times its height ($V = Bh$ or $V = s^2h$). You can solve for h in each equation to find $h = \frac{V}{B} = \frac{V}{s^2}$. The surface area equals two times the area of a base plus four times the area of a face, or

$$\text{S.A.} = 2B + 4sh = 2s^2 + 4sh$$

$$= 2s^2 + 4s\frac{V}{s^2} \quad \textbf{Substitute.}$$

$$= 2s^2 + \frac{4V}{s} \quad \textbf{Simplify.}$$

Use the commands shown on the screens below to create lists L_1, L_2, and L_3, for s, h, and S.A., respectively. The fourth screen shows the lists after they have been created.

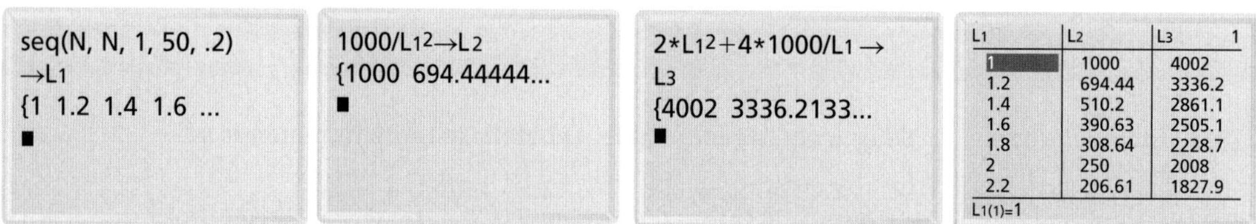

EXERCISES

Create the lists (shown above) on your graphing calculator. Scroll down to study them.

1. How small can the surface area be? How large can it be?

2. a. Which dimensions give a very large surface area?
b. Which dimensions give the smallest surface area?
c. How do s and h compare in the prism with the smallest surface area?
d. What is the shape of the prism that has the smallest surface area?

Extend

3. If a square prism must have a volume of 100 cm^3, what dimensions would give the smallest surface area?

4. A cereal manufacturer is designing a cereal box that has a capacity of 3000 cm^3. Surface area should be large to provide space for advertising. What else should be considered for the box design? Use a graphing calculator as needed to support your conclusions.

10-4 Surface Areas of Pyramids and Cones

Lesson Preview

What You'll Learn

To find the surface area of a pyramid

To find the surface area of a cone

. . . And Why

To find the lateral area of the Great Pyramid of Egypt, as in Example 2

✔ Check Skills You'll Need

(For help, go to Lesson 7-2.)

Find the length of the hypotenuse in simplest radical form.

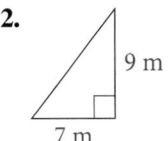

1. 8 in., 13 in.

2. 9 m, 7 m

3. 13 cm, 12 cm

New Vocabulary • pyramid • base, lateral faces, vertex, altitude, height, slant height, lateral area, surface area (of a pyramid) • regular pyramid • cone • base, altitude, vertex, height, slant height, lateral area, surface area (of a cone) • right cone

Interactive lesson includes instant self-check, tutorials, and activities.

OBJECTIVE 1

Finding Surface Area of a Pyramid

Need Help?

If the base is a hexagon, the pyramid is a hexagonal pyramid.

A **pyramid** is a polyhedron in which one face (the **base**) can be any polygon and the other faces (the **lateral faces**) are triangles that meet at a common vertex (called the **vertex** of the pyramid).

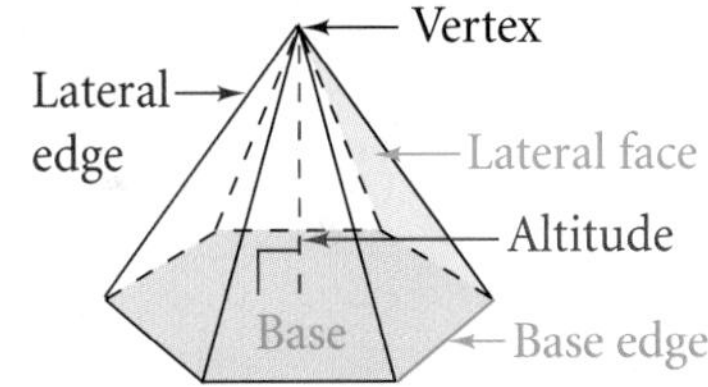

You can name a pyramid by the shape of its base. The **altitude** of a pyramid is the perpendicular segment from the vertex to the plane of the base. The length of the altitude is the **height** h of the pyramid.

A **regular pyramid** is a pyramid whose base is a regular polygon and whose lateral faces are congruent isosceles triangles. The **slant height** ℓ is the length of the altitude of a lateral face of the pyramid.

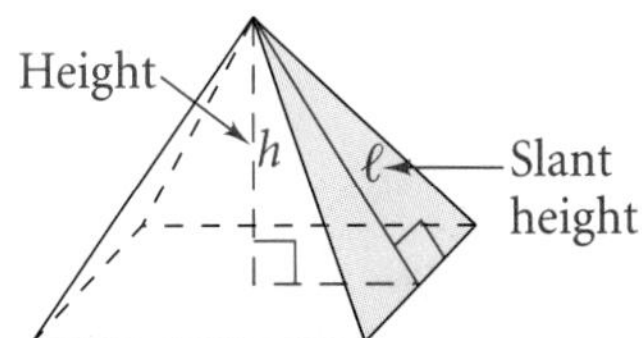

In this book, you can assume that a pyramid is regular unless stated otherwise.

The **lateral area** of a pyramid is the sum of the areas of the congruent lateral faces. You can find a formula for the lateral area of a pyramid by looking at its net.

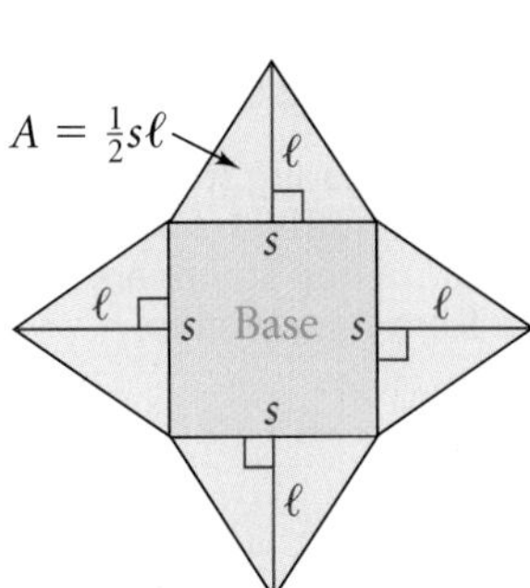

$\text{L.A.} = 4\left(\frac{1}{2}s\ell\right)$	The area of each lateral face is $\frac{1}{2}s\ell$.
$= \frac{1}{2}(4s)\ell$	Commutative and Associative Properties of Multiplication
$= \frac{1}{2}p\ell$	The perimeter p of the base is $4s$.

To find the **surface area** of a pyramid, add the area of its base to its lateral area.

Key Concepts

Theorem 10-3 **Lateral and Surface Areas of a Regular Pyramid**

The lateral area of a regular pyramid is half the product of the perimeter of the base and the slant height.

$$\text{L.A.} = \frac{1}{2}p\ell$$

The surface area of a regular pyramid is the sum of the lateral area and the area of the base.

$$\text{S.A.} = \text{L.A.} + B$$

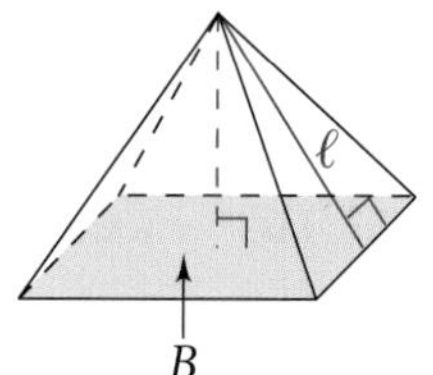

1 EXAMPLE Finding Surface Area of a Pyramid

Find the surface area of the hexagonal pyramid at the left.

$\text{S.A.} = \text{L.A.} + B$	**Use the formula for surface area.**
$= \frac{1}{2}p\ell + \frac{1}{2}ap$	**Substitute the formulas for L.A. and *B*.**
$= \frac{1}{2}(36)(9) + \frac{1}{2}(3\sqrt{3})(36)$	**Substitute.**
≈ 255.53074	**Use a calculator.**

The surface area of the pyramid is about 256 in.^{2}.

Check Understanding 1 Find the surface area of a square pyramid with base edges 5 m and slant height 3 m.

Sometimes the slant height of a pyramid is not given. You must calculate it before you can find the lateral or surface area.

2 EXAMPLE Real-World Connection

Social Studies The Great Pyramid at Giza, Egypt, pictured at the left, was built about 2580 B.C. as a final resting place for Pharaoh Khufu. At the time it was built, its height was about 481 ft. Each edge of the square base was about 756 ft long. What was the lateral area of the Great Pyramid?

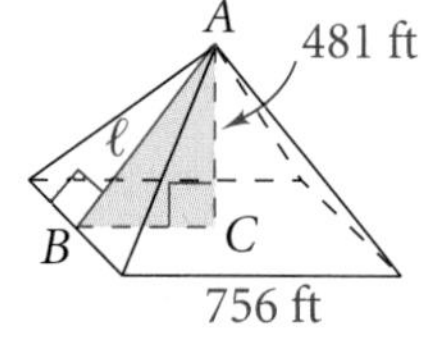

The legs of right $\triangle ABC$ are the height of the pyramid and the apothem of the base. The height of the pyramid was 481 ft. The apothem of the base was $\frac{756}{2}$, or 378 ft. You can use the Pythagorean Theorem to find the slant height ℓ.

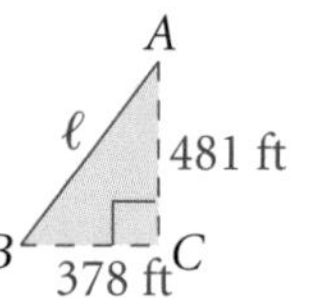

$\text{L.A.} = \frac{1}{2}p\ell$	**Use the formula for lateral area.**
$= \frac{1}{2}(4s)\sqrt{a^2 + b^2}$	**Substitute the formulas for *p* and ℓ.**
$= \frac{1}{2}(4 \cdot 756)\sqrt{378^2 + 481^2}$	**Substitute.**
≈ 924974.57	**Use a calculator.**

The lateral area of the Great Pyramid was about 925,000 ft^2.

Real-World Connection

Today, most casing stones (used to smooth the sides) and some of the top stones are gone from this pyramid.

Check Understanding 2 Find the surface area of the Great Pyramid to the nearest square foot.

OBJECTIVE 2

Finding Surface Area of a Cone

A **cone** is "pointed" like a pyramid, but its **base** is a circle. In a **right cone,** the **altitude** is a perpendicular segment from the **vertex** to the center of the base. The **height** h is the length of the altitude. The **slant height** ℓ is the distance from the vertex to a point on the edge of the base.

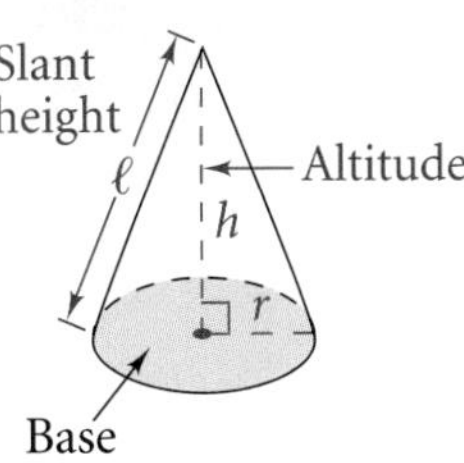

As with a pyramid, the **lateral area** is $\frac{1}{2}$ the perimeter (circumference) of the base times the slant height. The formulas for the lateral area and **surface area** of a cone are similar to those for a pyramid.

Key Concepts

Need Help?

Circumference of base = $2\pi r$

Theorem 10-4 **Lateral and Surface Areas of a Cone**

The lateral area of a right cone is half the product of the circumference of the base and the slant height.

$$\text{L.A.} = \frac{1}{2} \cdot 2\pi r \cdot \ell, \text{ or L.A.} = \pi r\ell$$

The surface area of a right cone is the sum of the lateral area and the area of the base.

$$\text{S.A.} = \text{L.A.} + B$$

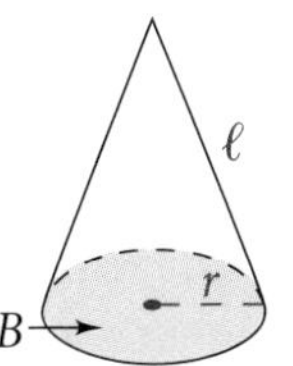

In this book, you can assume that a cone is a right cone unless stated or pictured otherwise.

3 EXAMPLE Finding Surface Area of a Cone

Find the surface area of the cone in terms of π.

$\text{S.A.} = \text{L.A.} + B$	**Use the surface area formula.**
$= \pi r\ell + \pi r^2$	**Substitute the formulas for L.A. and *B*.**
$= \pi(15)(25) + \pi(15)^2$	**Substitute.**
$= 375\pi + 225\pi$	**Simplify.**
$= 600\pi$	

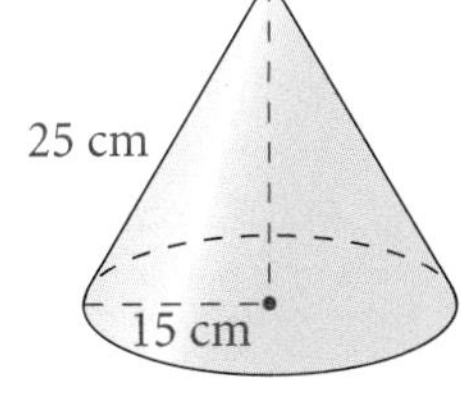

The surface area of the cone is 600π cm^2.

Check Understanding 3 The radius of the base of a cone is 16 m. Its slant height is 28 m. Find the surface area in terms of π.

By cutting a cone and laying it out flat, you can see how the formula for lateral area of a cone $\left(\text{L.A.} = \frac{1}{2} \cdot C_{\text{base}} \cdot \ell\right)$ resembles that for the area of a triangle $\left(A = \frac{1}{2}bh\right)$.

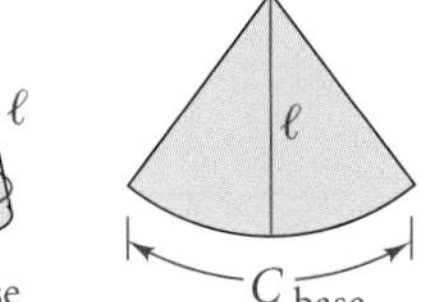

Careers Successful chemists attend to detail, persevere, and work independently.

4 EXAMPLE Real-World Connection

Chemistry The funnel is in the shape of a cone. How much filter paper do you need to line the funnel?

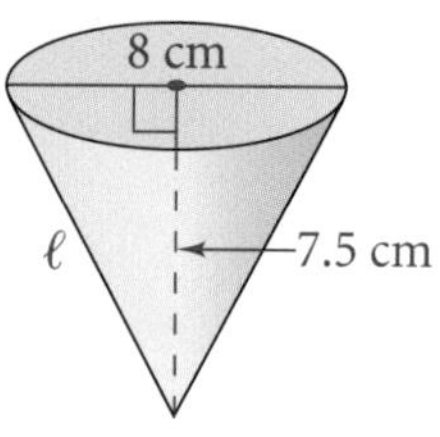

The area covered is the lateral area of a cone that has a diameter of 8 cm and a height of 7.5 cm.

Use the formula for the lateral area of a cone.

$$\text{L.A.} = \pi r \ell$$
$$= \pi r\left(\sqrt{a^2 + b^2}\right) \quad \textbf{To find the slant height use the Pythagorean Theorem.}$$
$$= \pi(4)\left(\sqrt{4^2 + 7.5^2}\right) \quad \textbf{Substitute. If } d = 8, \textbf{ then } r = 4.$$
$$= 106.81415 \quad \textbf{Use a calculator.}$$

You need about 107 cm^2 of filter paper to line the funnel.

 **Check Understanding** 4 Find the lateral area of a cone with radius 15 in. and height 20 in.

EXERCISES

For more practice, see *Extra Practice.*

Practice and Problem Solving

A Practice by Example

Example 1 (page 538)

Find the surface area of each pyramid to the nearest whole number.

1. 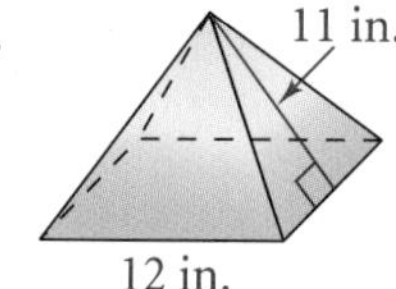

2. 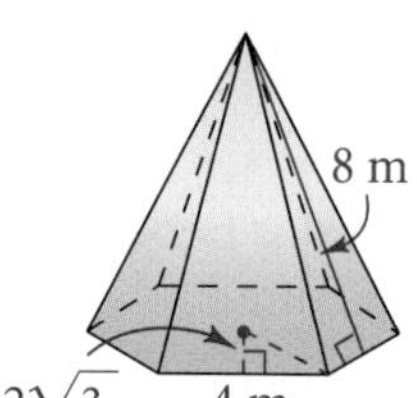

3. 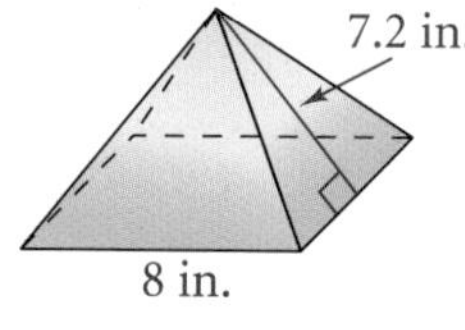

Example 2 (page 538)

Find the slant height ℓ of each pyramid to the nearest whole number.

4. 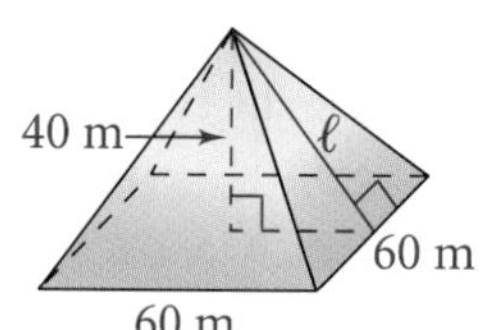

5. 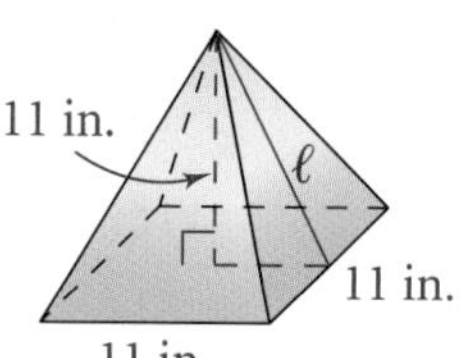

6. 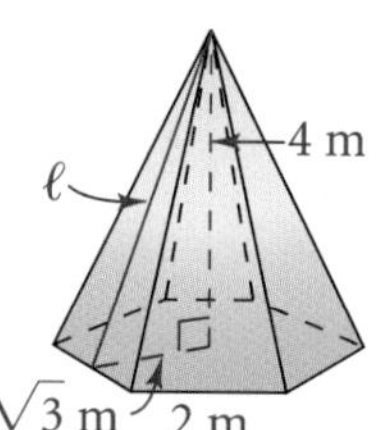

Find the lateral area of each pyramid to the nearest whole number.

7. 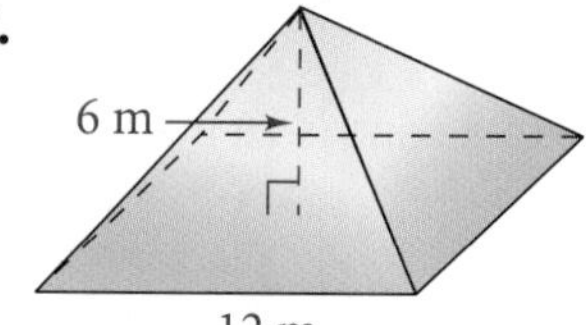

8. 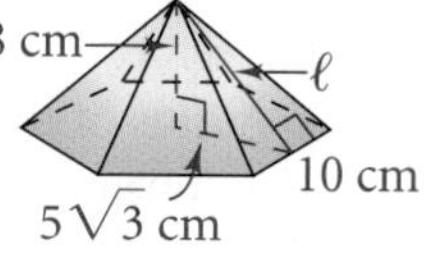

9. 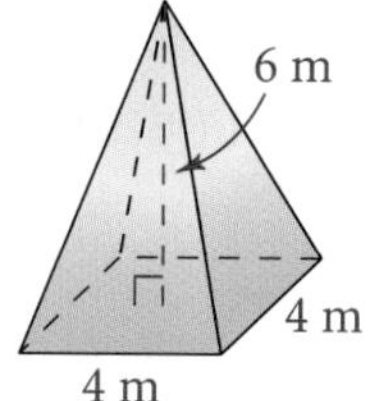

10. **Social Studies** The original height of the pyramid built for Khafre, next to the Great Pyramid, was about 471 ft. Each side of its square base was about 708 ft. What is the lateral area to the nearest foot of a pyramid with those dimensions?

11. **Construction** The roof of a tower is a square pyramid with side length 10 ft. The height of the pyramid is 6 ft. To the nearest square foot, find the area of the roofing material needed to cover the roof.

Example 3 (page 539)

Find the surface area of each cone in terms of π.

12. 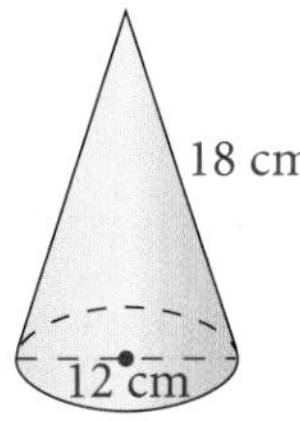

13. 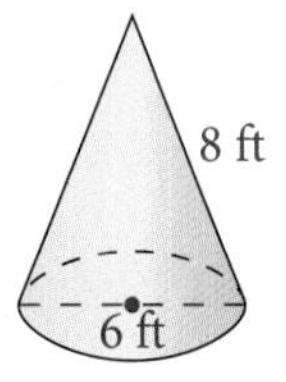

14. 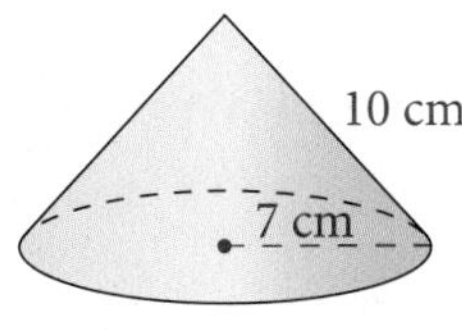

Example 4 (page 540)

Find the slant height ℓ of each cone to the nearest whole number.

15. 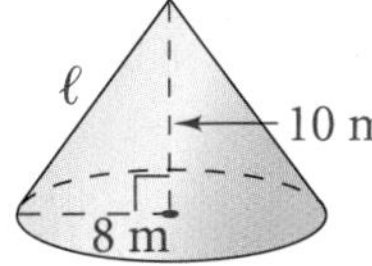

16. 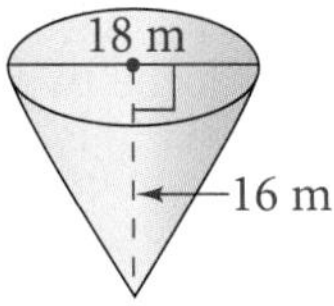

17. 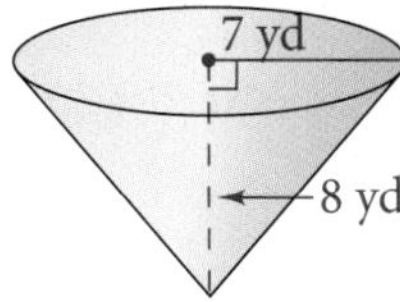

Find the lateral area of each cone to the nearest whole number.

18. 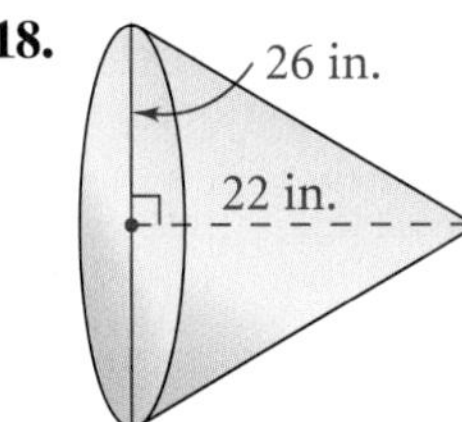

19. 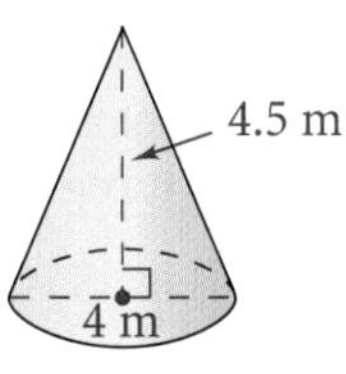

20. 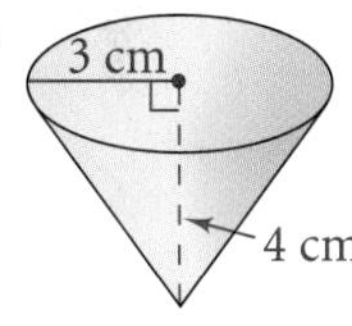

B Apply Your Skills

Need Help?

In Exercise 21, explain why $\overline{PT}$ is shorter than $\overline{PR}$, and then why $\overline{PR}$ is shorter than $\overline{PC}$.

21. **Writing** Explain why the altitude $\overline{PT}$ in the pyramid at the right must be shorter than each edge $\overline{PA}$, $\overline{PB}$, $\overline{PC}$, and $\overline{PD}$.

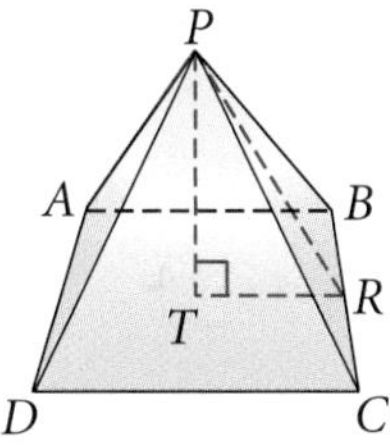

22. **Reasoning** Suppose you could climb to the top of the Great Pyramid in Egypt. Which route would be shorter, a route along a lateral edge or along the altitude of a side? Which of these routes is steeper? Explain your answers.

23. A square pyramid has base edges 10 in. long and height 4 in. Sketch the pyramid and find its surface area. Round your answer to the nearest tenth.

24. **Algebra** The lateral area of a pyramid with a square base is 240 ft^2. Its base edges are 12 ft long. Find the height of the pyramid.

Find the surface area to the nearest whole number.

25. 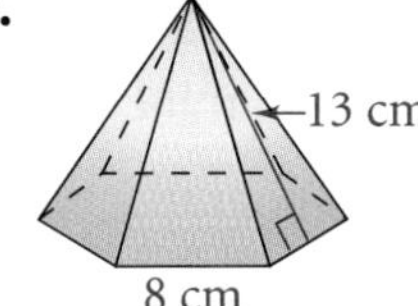

26. 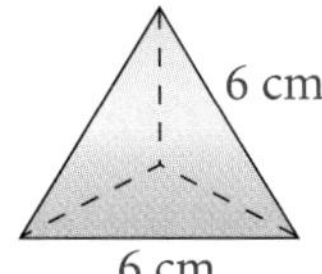

27. 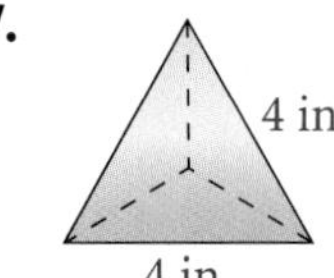

28. The lateral area of a cone is 48π in.^{2}. The radius is 12 in. Find the slant height.

29. **Open-Ended** Draw a square pyramid with a lateral area of 48 cm^2. Label its dimensions. Then find its surface area.

Exercise 30

30. **Architecture** The roof of a tower in a castle is shaped like a cone. The height of the roof is 30 ft and the radius of the base is 15 ft. What is the area of the roof? Round your answer to the nearest tenth.

Find the surface area to the nearest whole number.

31. 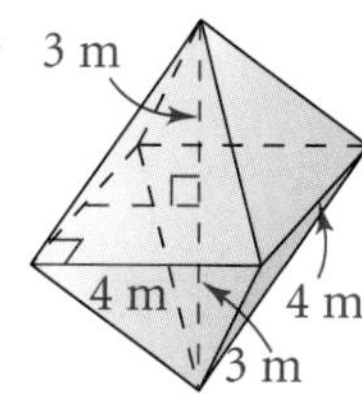

32. 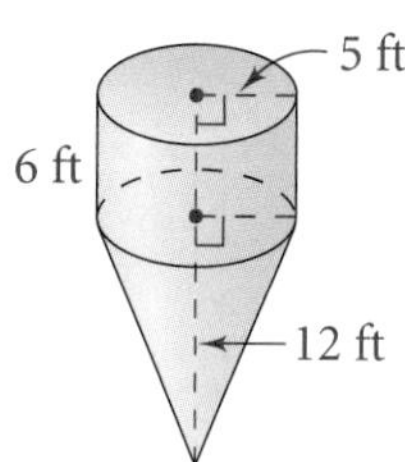

33. 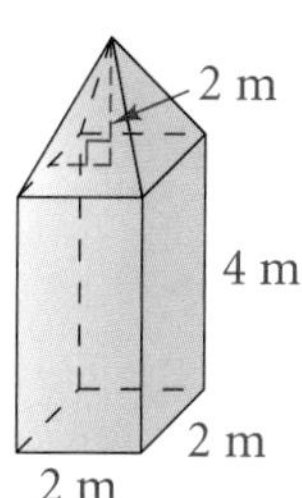

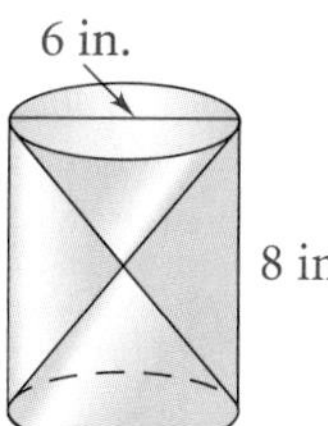

34. The hourglass shown at the right is made by connecting two glass cones inside a glass cylinder. Which has more glass, the two cones or the cylinder? Explain.

35. You can use the formula S.A. $= (\ell + r) r\pi$ to find the surface area of a cone. Explain why this formula works. Also, explain why you may prefer to use this formula when finding surface area with a calculator.

The length of a side of the base (s), slant height, height, lateral area, and surface area are measurements of a square pyramid. Given two of the measurements, find the other three to the nearest tenth.

36. $s = 3$ in., S.A. $= 39$ in.^{2}

37. $h = 8$ m, $\ell = 10$ m

38. $\ell = 5$ ft, L.A. $= 20$ ft^2

39. L.A. $= 118$ cm^2, S.A. $= 182$ cm^2

Circumference, radius, slant height, lateral area, and surface area are measurements of a cone. Given two of the measurements, find the other three to the nearest tenth.

40. $r = 3$ ft, S.A. $= 50$ ft^2

41. $r = 4$ m, L.A. $= 81.7$ m^2

42. $C = 44$ in., L.A. $= 176$ in.^{2}

43. $\ell = 10.6$ ft, L.A. $= 33.3$ ft^2

44. A cone with radius 9 cm has the same surface area as a cylinder with radius 6 cm and height 18 cm. What is the height of the cone to the nearest tenth?

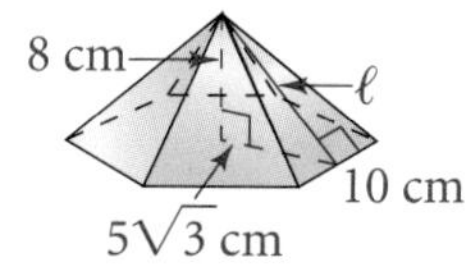

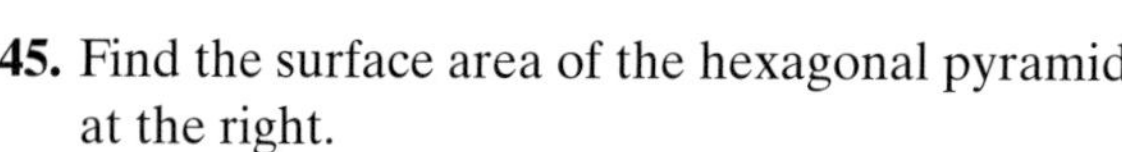

45. Find the surface area of the hexagonal pyramid at the right.

Visualization **The plane region is revolved completely about the given line to sweep out a solid of revolution. Describe the solid. Then find its surface area in terms of π.**

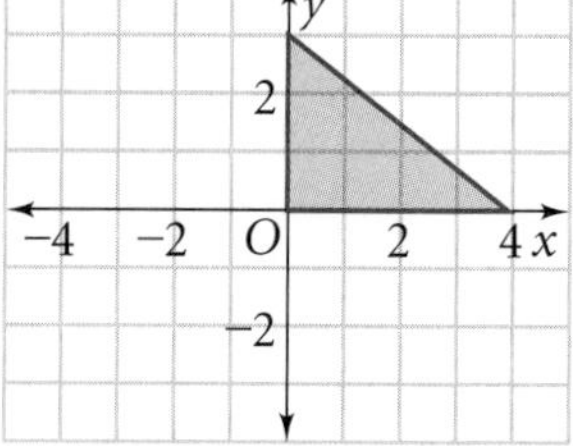

46. about the y-axis

47. about the x-axis

C Challenge

48. about the line $x = 4$

49. about the line $y = 3$

The given figure fits inside a 10-cm cube. The figure's base is in one face of the cube and is as large as possible. The figure's vertex is in the opposite face of the cube. Draw a sketch and find the lateral and surface areas of the figure.

50. a square pyramid

51. a cone

52. A sector has been cut out of the disk. The radii of the part that remains are taped together, without overlapping, to form the cone. The cone has a lateral area of 64π cm^2. Find the measure of the central angle of the cut-out sector.

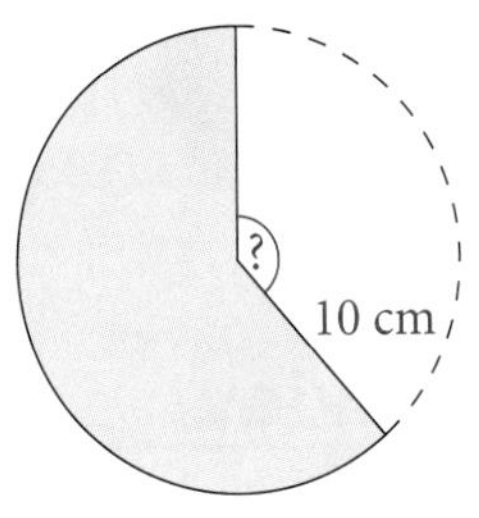

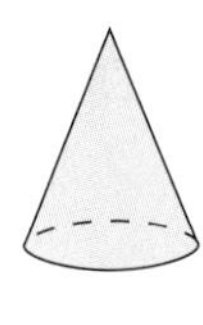

 **53. Archaeology** Find out about ancient Mexican and Egyptian pyramids. How are they alike and different? Summarize your findings in a short report.

54. The lateral area of a cone is three fifths the surface area. Find the ratio of the radius to the slant height.

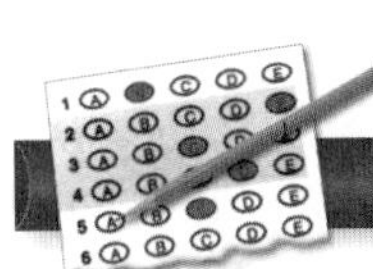

Standardized Test Prep

Multiple Choice

55. To the nearest whole number, what is the surface area of a cone with diameter 27 m and slant height 19 m?
A. 1378 m^2 **B.** 1951 m^2 **C.** 2757 m^2 **D.** 3902 m^2

56. To the nearest whole number, what is the surface area of a cone with radius 14 cm and slant height 18 cm?
F. 448 cm^2 **G.** 836 cm^2 **H.** 1012 cm^2 **I.** 1407 cm^2

57. To the nearest whole number, what is the surface area of a square pyramid with each side of the base 30 yd and slant height 42 yd?
A. 900 yd^2 **B.** 2520 yd^2 **C.** 3420 yd^2 **D.** 3600 yd^2

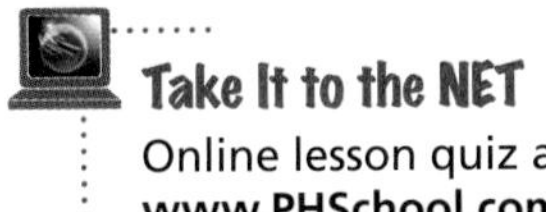

Take It to the NET
Online lesson quiz at **www.PHSchool.com**
Web Code: afa-1004

58. A cylinder and a cone each have height 1 and radius $\sqrt{3}$. How does the cylinder's lateral area x compare with the cone's lateral area y?
F. $x = y$ **G.** $x = 2y$ **H.** $x > 2y$ **I.** $x < 2y$

Short Response

59. A square pyramid is 8 m on each side. Its surface area is 240 m^2. What is its slant height? Show your work and explain your reasoning.

Extended Response

60. The lateral area of a cone is twice the area of its base.
a. What is its slant height in terms of the radius r? Show your work.
b. What is the lateral area to the nearest tenth if the radius is 6 centimeters? Show your work.

Mixed Review

Lesson 10-3

61. How much cardboard do you need to make a closed box that is 4 ft by 5 ft by 2 ft?

62. How much posterboard do you need to make a cylinder, open at each end, with height 9 in. and diameter $4\frac{1}{2}$ in.? Round your answer to the nearest square inch.

Lesson 9-3

63. A TV camera views a tall building 400 m away with a 35° angle of elevation to the top. How tall is the building if the camera lens is 160 cm off the ground?

Lesson 7-4

64. The area of a rhombus is 714 cm^2. One diagonal is 42 cm long. Find the length of the other diagonal.

65. A kite with area 195 in.^{2} has a 15-in. diagonal. How long is the other diagonal?

10-5 Volumes of Prisms and Cylinders

Lesson Preview

What You'll Learn

OBJECTIVE 1: To find the volume of a prism

OBJECTIVE 2: To find the volume of a cylinder

. . . And Why

To estimate the volume of a backpack, as in Example 4

✓ Check Skills You'll Need

(For help, go to Lessons 1-7 and 7-1.)

Find the area of each figure. For answers that are not whole numbers, round to the nearest tenth.

1. a square with side length 7 cm
2. a circle with diameter 15 in.
3. a circle with radius 10 mm
4. a rectangle with length 3 ft and width 1 ft
5. a rectangle with base 14 in. and height 11 in.
6. a triangle with base 11 cm and height 5 cm
7. an equilateral triangle that is 8 in. on each side

New Vocabulary • volume • composite space figure

Interactive lesson includes instant self-check, tutorials, and activities.

OBJECTIVE 1 Finding Volume of a Prism

Investigation: Finding Volume

Explore the volume of a prism with unit cubes.

- Make a one-layer rectangular prism that is 4 cubes long and 2 cubes wide. The prism will be 4 units by 2 units by 1 unit.

1. How many cubes are in the prism?
2. Add a second layer to your prism to make a prism 4 units by 2 units by 2 units. How many cubes are in this prism?

3. Add a third layer to your prism to make a prism 4 units by 2 units by 3 units. How many cubes are in this prism?
4. How many cubes would be in the prism if you added two additional layers of cubes for a total of 5 layers?
5. How many cubes would be in the prism if there were 10 layers?

Volume is the space that a figure occupies. It is measured in cubic units such as cubic inches (in.^{3}), cubic feet (ft^3), or cubic centimeters (cm^3). The volume of a cube is the cube of the length of its edge, or $V = e^3$.

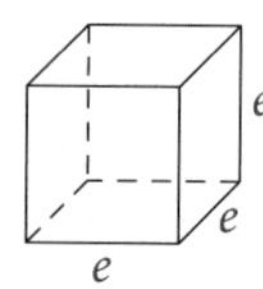

Both stacks of paper below contain the same number of sheets.

The first stack forms a right prism. The second forms an oblique prism. The stacks have the same height. The area of every cross section parallel to a base is the area of one sheet of paper. The stacks have the same volume. These stacks illustrate the following principle.

Key Concepts

Theorem 10-5 **Cavalieri's Principle**

If two space figures have the same height and the same cross-sectional area at every level, then they have the same volume.

The area of each shaded cross section below is 6 cm^2. Since the prisms have the same height, their volumes must be the same by Cavalieri's Principle.

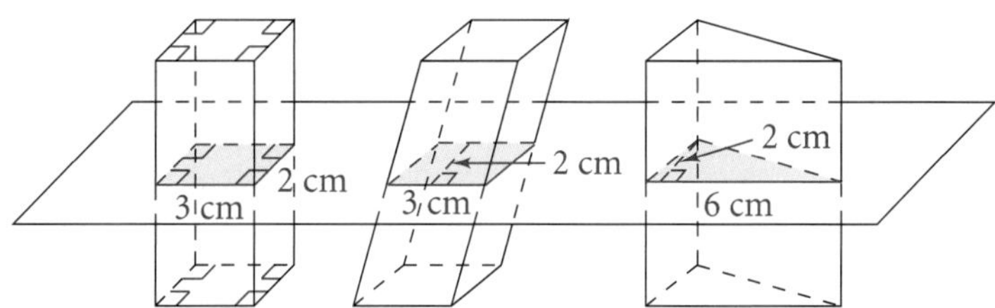

You can find the volume of a right prism by multiplying the area of the base by the height. Cavalieri's Principle lets you extend this idea to any prism.

Key Concepts

Theorem 10-6 **Volume of a Prism**

The volume of a prism is the product of the area of a base and the height of the prism.

$$V = Bh$$

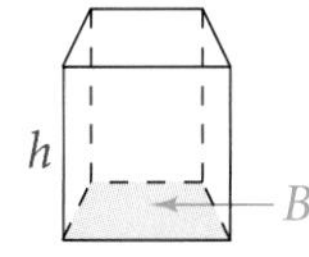

1 EXAMPLE Finding Volume of a Rectangular Prism

Find the volume of the prism at the right.

$V = Bh$	**Use the formula for volume.**
$= 480 \cdot 10$	**$B = 24 \cdot 20 = 480$ cm^2**
$= 4800$	**Simplify.**

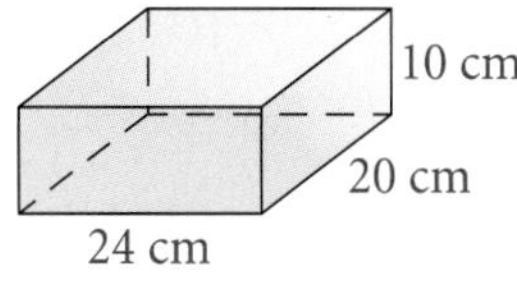

The volume of the rectangular prism is 4800 cm^3.

Check Understanding 1 **Critical Thinking** Suppose the prism in Example 1 is turned so that the base is 20 cm by 10 cm and the height is 24 cm. Explain why the volume does not change.

2 EXAMPLE Finding Volume of a Triangular Prism

Find the volume of the triangular prism at the right.

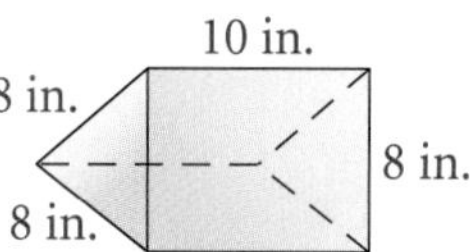

Each base of the triangular prism is an equilateral triangle. An altitude of the triangle divides it into two 30°-60°-90° triangles. The area of the base is $\frac{1}{2} \cdot 8 \cdot 4\sqrt{3}$, or $16\sqrt{3}$ in.^{2}.

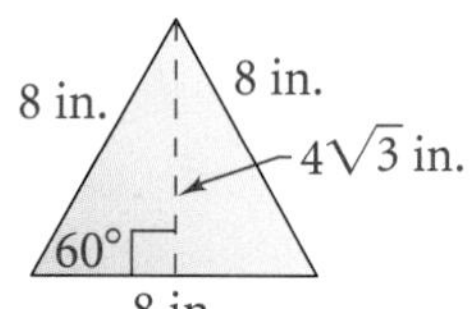

$V = Bh$ **Use the formula for the volume of a prism.**

$= 16\sqrt{3} \cdot 10$ **Substitute.**

$= 160\sqrt{3}$ **Simplify.**

The volume of the triangular prism is $160\sqrt{3}$ in.^{3}.

Check Understanding 2 Find the volume of the triangular prism at the right.

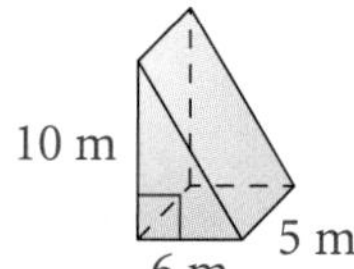

OBJECTIVE

2 Finding Volume of a Cylinder

To find the volume of a cylinder, you use the same formula $V = Bh$ that you use to find the volume of a prism. Now, however, B is the area of the circle, so you use the formula $B = \pi r^2$ to find its value.

Key Concepts

Theorem 10-7 **Volume of a Cylinder**

The volume of a cylinder is the product of the area of the base and the height of the cylinder.

$$V = Bh, \text{ or } V = \pi r^2 h$$

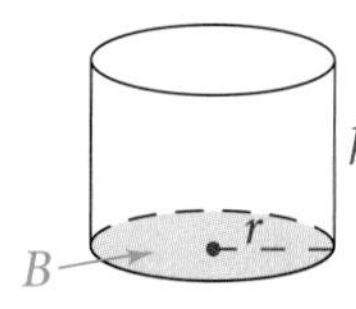

3 EXAMPLE Finding Volume of a Cylinder

Find the volume of the cylinder at the right. Leave your answer in terms of π.

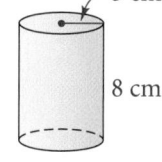

$V = \pi r^2 h$ **Use the formula for the volume of a cylinder.**

$= \pi(3)^2(8)$ **Substitute.**

$= \pi(72)$ **Simplify.**

The volume of the cylinder is 72π cm^3.

3 The cylinder at the right is oblique.

a. Find its volume in terms of π.

b. Find its volume to the nearest tenth of a cubic meter.

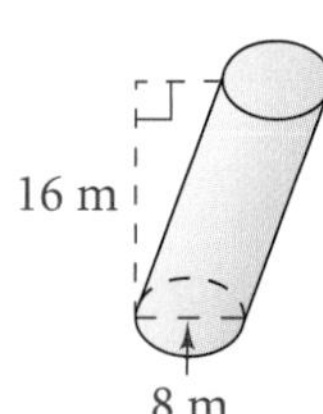

A **composite space figure** is a three-dimensional figure that is the combination of two or more simpler figures. A space probe, for example, might begin as a composite figure—a cylindrical rocket engine in combination with a nose cone.

You can find the volume of a composite space figure by adding the volumes of the figures that are combined.

4 EXAMPLE Finding Volume of a Composite Figure

Estimation Use a composite space figure to estimate the volume of the backpack shown at the left.

Step 1: You can use a prism and half of a cylinder to approximate the shape, and therefore the volume, of the backpack.

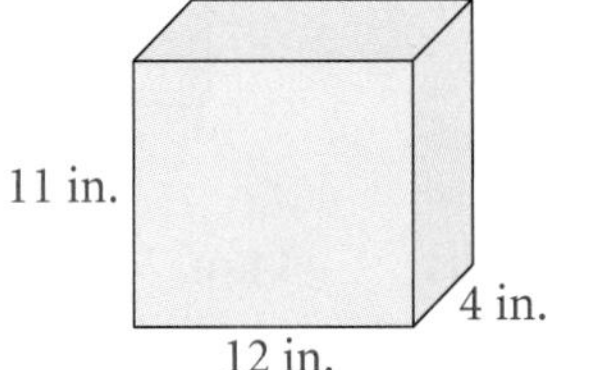

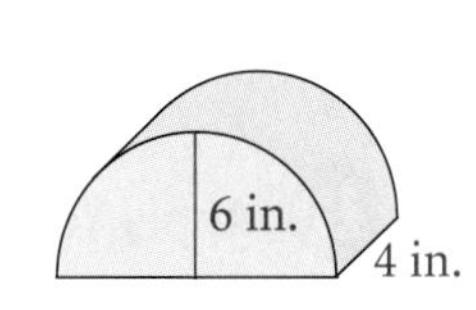

Step 2: Volume of the prism $= Bh = (12 \cdot 4)11 = 528$

Step 3: Volume of the half cylinder $= \frac{1}{2}(\pi r^2 h) = \frac{1}{2}\pi(6)^2(4)$

$= \frac{1}{2}\pi(36)(4) \approx 226$

Step 4: Sum of the two volumes $= 528 + 226 = 754$

The approximate volume of the backpack is 754 in.^{3}.

4 Find the volume of the composite space figure.

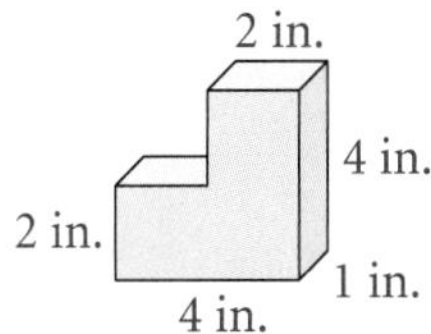

EXERCISES

For more practice, see *Extra Practice.*

Practice and Problem Solving

Practice by Example

Example 1 (page 545)

In Exercises 1–8, find the volume of each prism.

1.

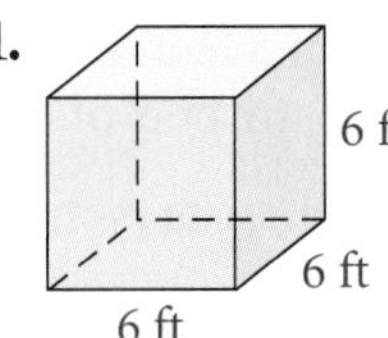

2.

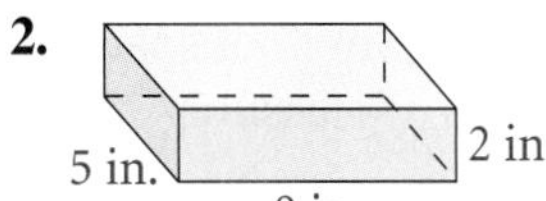

3.

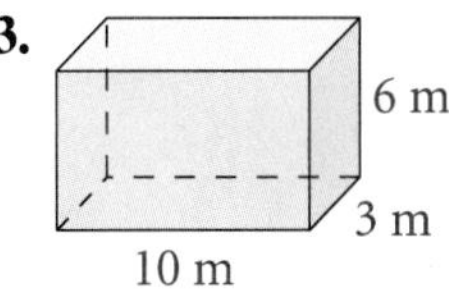

4. The base is a square, 2 cm on a side. The height is 3.5 cm.

Example 2 (page 546)

5.

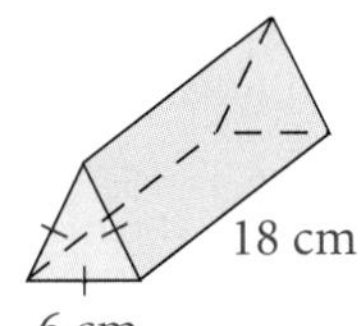

6.

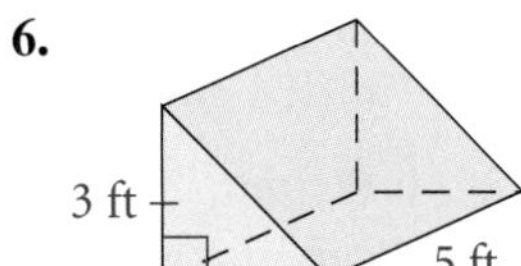

7.

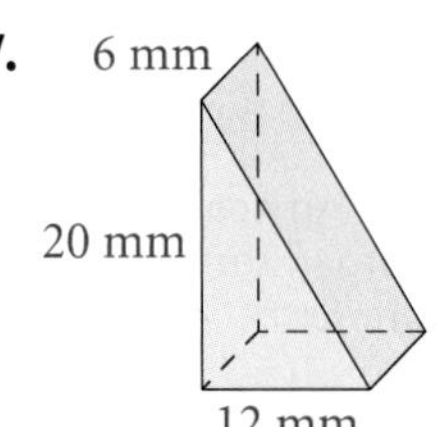

8. The base is a 45°-45°-90° triangle with a leg of 5 in. The height is 1.8 in.

Example 3
(page 546)

Find the volume of each cylinder in terms of π and to the nearest tenth.

9. 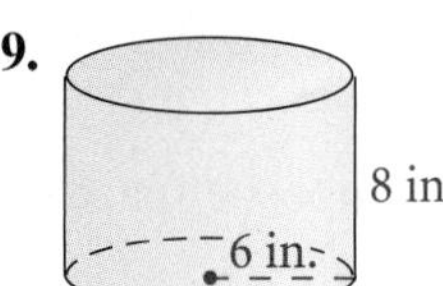

10. 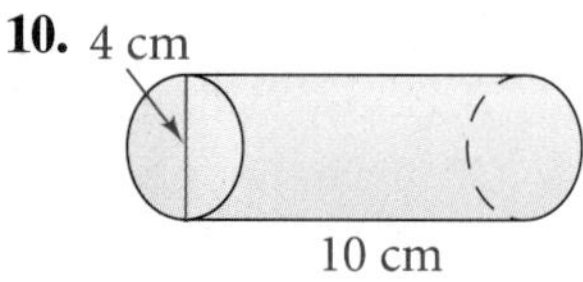

11. 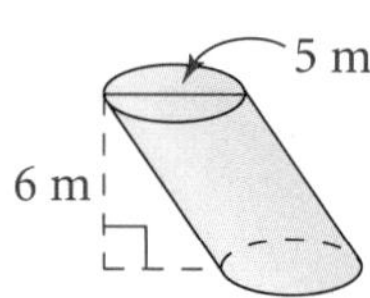

Example 4
(page 547)

Find the volume of each composite space figure to the nearest whole number.

12. 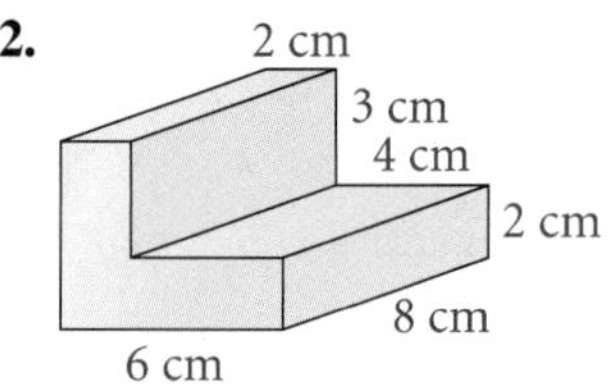

13. 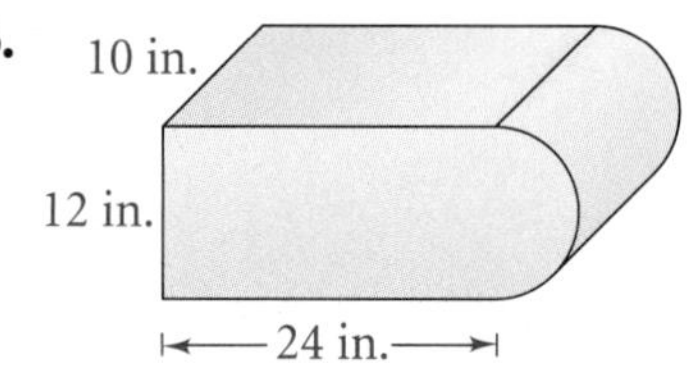

B Apply Your Skills

14. **a.** What is the volume of a waterbed mattress that is 7 ft by 4 ft by 1 ft?
b. To the nearest pound, what is the weight of the water in a full mattress? (Water weighs 62.4 lb/ft^3.)

15. Find the volume of the lunch box shown at the right to the nearest cubic inch.

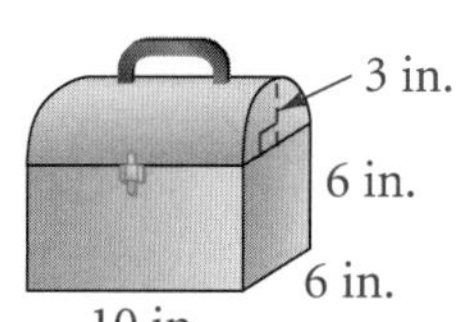

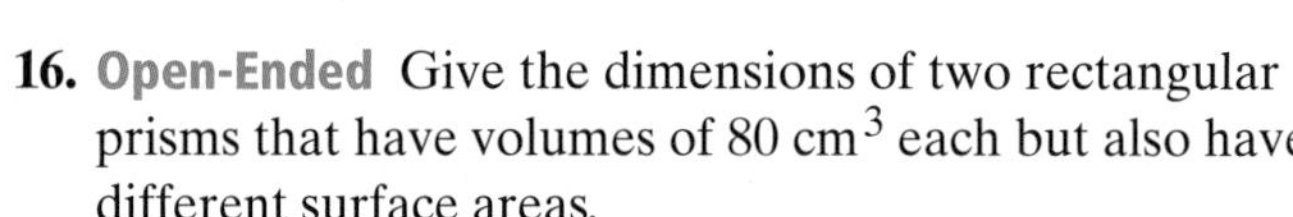

16. **Open-Ended** Give the dimensions of two rectangular prisms that have volumes of 80 cm^3 each but also have different surface areas.

Find the height of each figure with the given volume.

17. 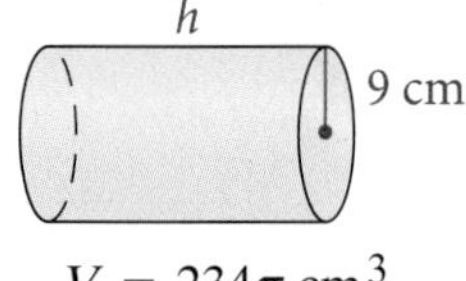

18. 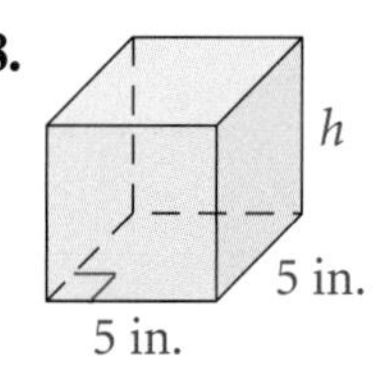

19. 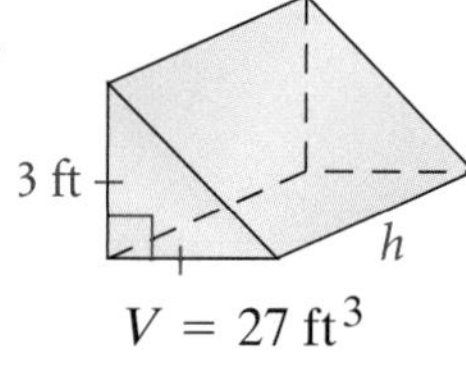

Careers An ecologist studies living organisms and their environments.

20. **Ecology** The isolation cube at the left measures 27 in. on each side. What is its volume in cubic feet?

21. **Environmental Engineering** A scientist suggests keeping indoor air relatively clean as follows: Provide two or three pots of flowers for every 100 square feet of floor space under a ceiling of 8 feet. If your classroom has an 8-ft ceiling and measures 35 ft by 40 ft, how many pots of flowers should it have?

22. Find the volume of the oblique prism pictured at the right.

6 ft
4 ft

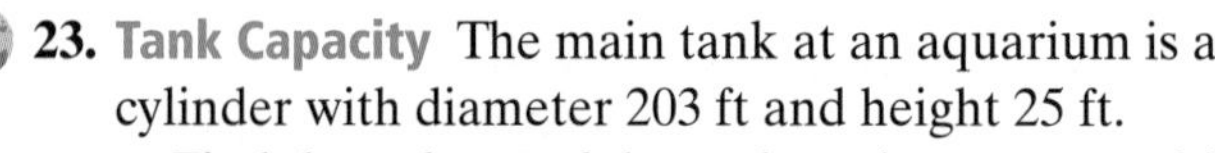

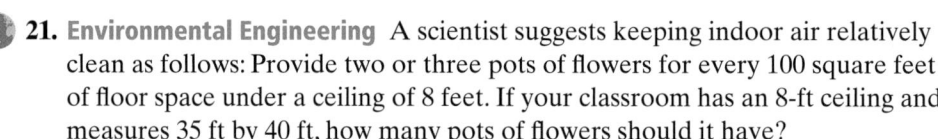

23. **Tank Capacity** The main tank at an aquarium is a cylinder with diameter 203 ft and height 25 ft.
a. Find the volume of the tank to the nearest cubic foot.
b. Convert your answer to part (a) to cubic inches.
c. If 1 gallon $\approx$ 231 in.^{3}, about how many gallons does the tank hold?

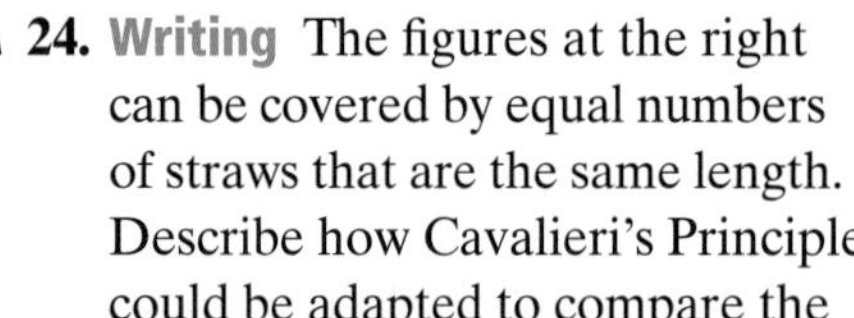

24. **Writing** The figures at the right can be covered by equal numbers of straws that are the same length. Describe how Cavalieri's Principle could be adapted to compare the areas of these figures.

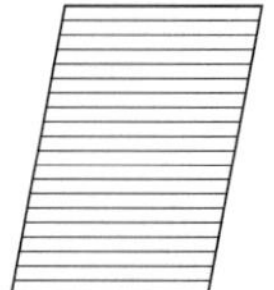

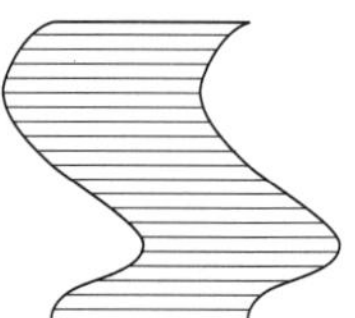

Need Help?

In Exercise 25, find the length, width, and height along the axes.

25. **Coordinate Geometry** Find the volume of the rectangular prism at the right.

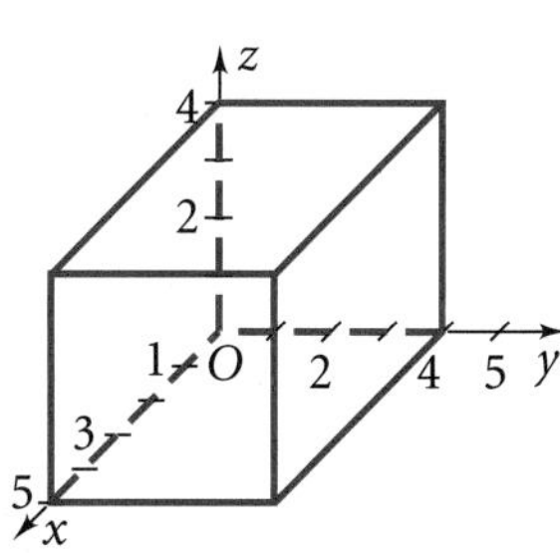

26. The volume of a cylinder is 600π cm^3. The radius of a base of the cylinder is 5 cm. What is the height of the cylinder?

27. The volume of a cylinder is 135π cm^3. The height of the cylinder is 15 cm. What is the radius of a base of the cylinder?

28. **Landscaping** To landscape her 70 ft-by-60 ft rectangular backyard, Joy is planning first to put down a 4-in. layer of topsoil. She can buy bags of topsoil at \$2.50 per 3-ft^3 bag, with free delivery. Or, she can buy bulk topsoil for \$22.00/yd^3, plus a \$20 delivery fee. Which option is less expensive? Explain.

Visualization **The plane region is revolved completely about the given line to sweep out a solid of revolution. Describe the solid and find its volume in terms of π.**

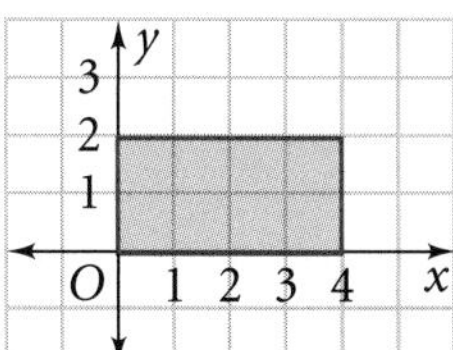

29. the x-axis

30. the y-axis

31. the line $y = 2$

32. the line $x = 5$

A cylinder has been cut out of each solid. Find the volume of the remaining solid. Round your answer to the nearest tenth.

33.

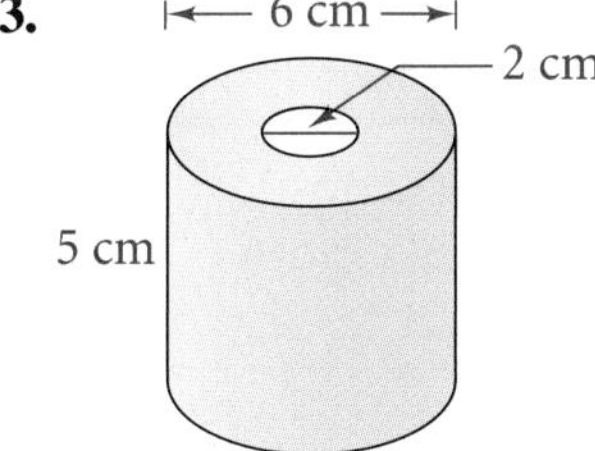

34.

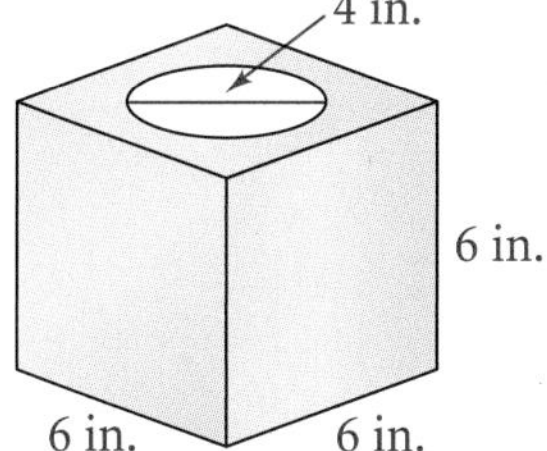

35. A closed box is 9 in. by 14 in. by 6 in. on the inside and 11 in. by 16 in. by 7 in. on the outside. Find each measurement.

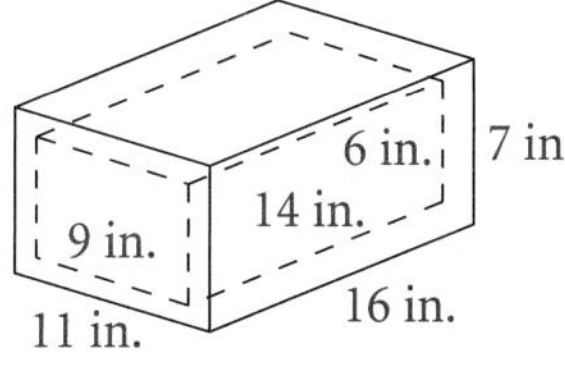

a. the outside surface area
b. the inside surface area
c. the inside volume
d. the volume of the material needed to make the box

C Challenge

36. Any rectangular sheet of paper can be rolled into a right cylinder in two ways.
a. Use ordinary sheets of paper to model the two cylinders. Compute the volume of each cylinder. How do they compare?
b. Of all sheets of paper with perimeter 39 in., which size can be rolled into a right cylinder with greatest volume? (*Hint:* See Exploration, page 536.)

37. The outside diameter of a pipe is 5 cm. The inside diameter is 4 cm. The pipe is 4 m long. What is the volume of the material used for this length of pipe? Round your answer to the nearest cubic centimeter.

38. A cube has a volume of $2M$ cubic units and a total surface area of $3M$ square units. Find the length of an edge of the cube.

39. The radius of cylinder B is twice the radius of cylinder A. The height of cylinder B is half the height of cylinder A. Compare their volumes.

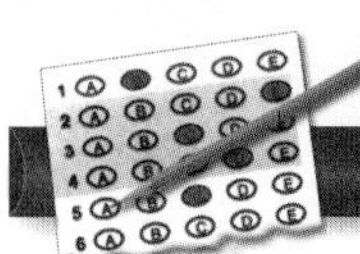

Standardized Test Prep

Multiple Choice

40. What is the volume of a rectangular prism whose edges measure 2 ft, 2 ft, and 3 ft?

A. 7 ft^3 **B.** 12 ft^3 **C.** 14 ft^3 **D.** 16 ft^3

41. One gallon fills about 231 $in.^3$. A right cylindrical carton is 12 in. tall and holds 9 gal when full. Find the radius of the carton to the nearest tenth of an inch.

F. 0.5 in. **G.** 7.4 in. **H.** 37.7 in. **I.** 55.1 in.

Quantitative Comparison

Compare the boxed quantity in Column A with the boxed quantity in Column B. Choose the best answer.

A. The quantity in Column A is greater.
B. The quantity in Column B is greater.
C. The two quantities are equal.
D. The relationship cannot be determined from the information given.

	Column A	Column B
42.	volume of a cylinder whose radius is 50 cm and whose height is 10 cm	volume of a cylinder whose radius is 10 cm and whose height is 50 cm
43.	volume of a cube having a side measuring 18 in.	volume of a rectangular prism having sides of 12, 18, and 27 in.
44.	height of a cylinder whose volume is 100 ft^3 and whose diameter is 8 ft	height of a prism whose volume is 100 ft^3 and whose base area is 25 ft^2

Take It to the NET
Online lesson quiz at
www.PHSchool.com
Web Code: afa-1005

Short Response

45. How is the formula for finding the lateral area of a cylinder like the formula for finding the area of a rectangle?

Mixed Review

Lesson 10-4

Find the lateral area of each figure to the nearest tenth.

46. a right circular cone with height 12 mm and radius 5 mm

47. a regular hexagonal pyramid with base edges 9.2 ft long and slant height 17 ft

Lesson 8-3

48. You want to find the height of a tree near your school. Your shadow is three-fourths of your height. The tree's shadow is 57 feet. How tall is the tree?

Lesson 7-6 x^2 **Algebra** **Find the value of each variable and the measure of each labeled angle.**

49.

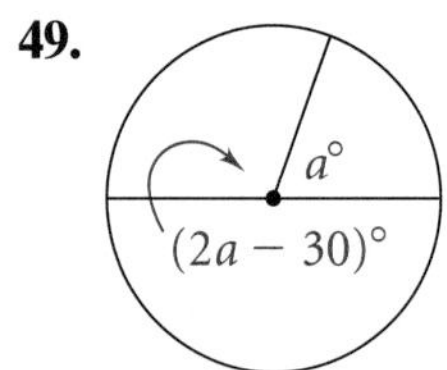

50.

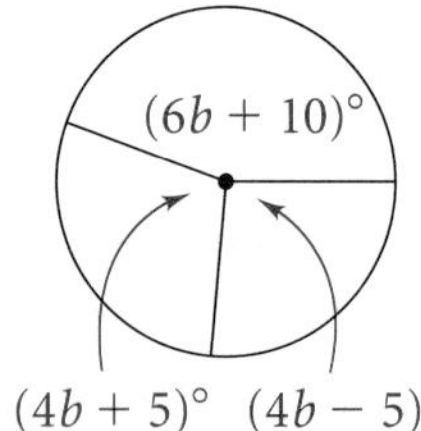

51.

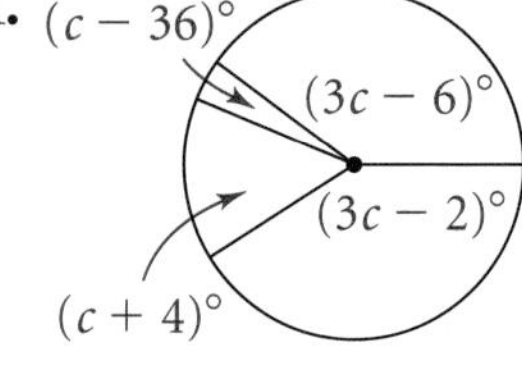

10-6 Volumes of Pyramids and Cones

Lesson Preview

What You'll Learn

To find the volume of a pyramid

To find the volume of a cone

. . . And Why

To find the volume of a structure in the shape of a pyramid, as in Example 1

✓ Check Skills You'll Need

(For help, go to Lesson 7-2.)

Use the Pythagorean Theorem to find the value of the variable.

1. 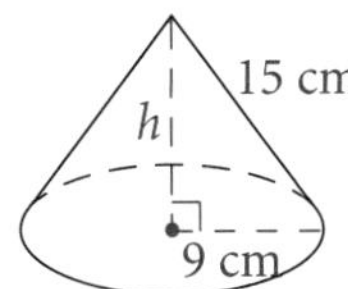

2. 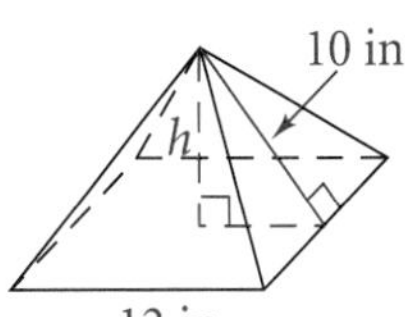

3. 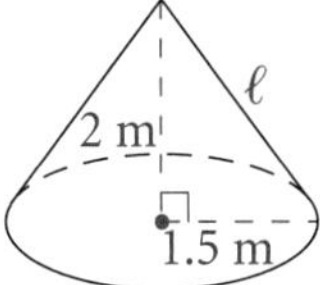

Interactive lesson includes instant self-check, tutorials, and activities.

OBJECTIVE

1 Finding Volume of a Pyramid

Investigation: Finding Volume

You know how to find the volume of a prism. Use the following to explore finding the volume of a pyramid.

- Draw the nets shown at the right on cardboard.
- Cut out the nets and tape them together to make a cube and a regular square pyramid. Each model will have one open face.

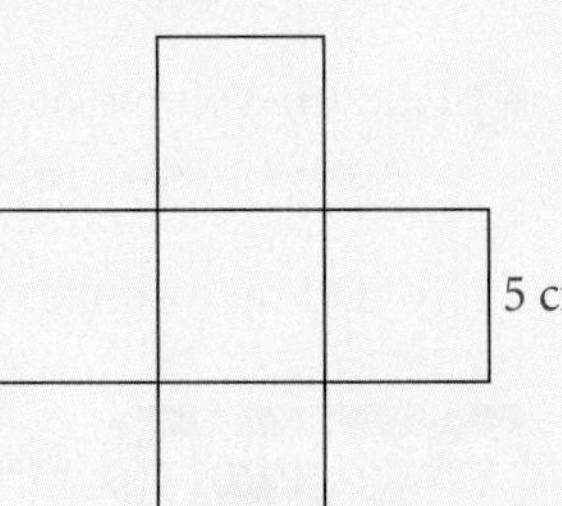

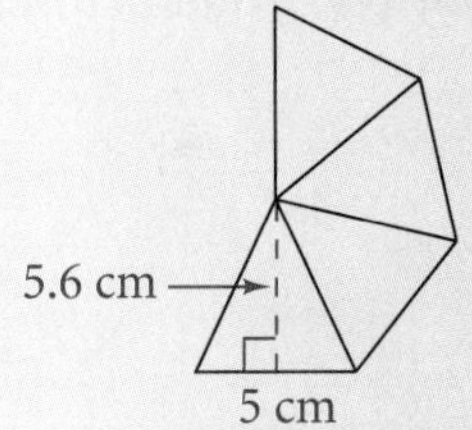

1. How do the areas of the bases of the cube and the pyramid compare?
2. How do the heights of the cube and pyramid compare?
3. Fill the pyramid with rice or other material. Then pour the rice from the pyramid into the cube. How many pyramids full of rice does the cube hold?
4. The volume of the pyramid is what fractional part of the volume of the cube?

The volume of a pyramid is a particular fraction of the volume of a prism that has the same base and height as the pyramid. The fraction is shown and this fact is stated as Theorem 10-8 at the top of the next page.

Key Concepts

Theorem 10-8 **Volume of a Pyramid**

The volume of a pyramid is one third the product of the area of the base and the height of the pyramid.

$$V = \frac{1}{3}Bh$$

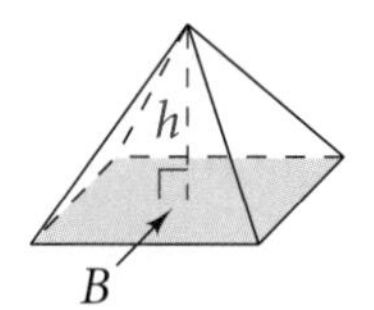

Need Help?
You can find Cavalieri's Principle on page 545.

Because of Cavalieri's Principle, the volume formula is true for all pyramids, including oblique pyramids. The height h of an oblique pyramid is the length of the perpendicular segment from the vertex to the plane of the base.

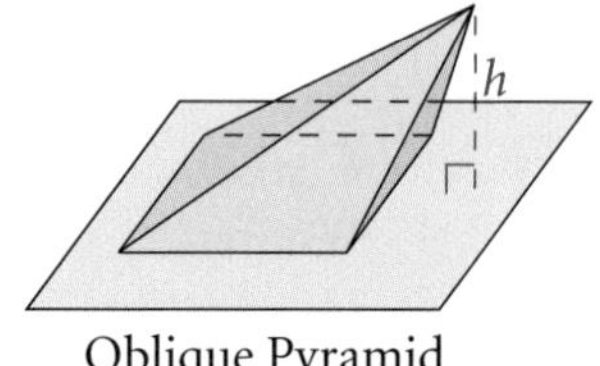

Oblique Pyramid

1 EXAMPLE Real-World Connection

Architecture The Pyramid is an arena in Memphis, Tennessee. The area of the base of The Pyramid is about 300,000 ft^2. Its height is 321 ft. What is the volume of The Pyramid?

$V = \frac{1}{3}Bh$ **Use the formula for volume of a pyramid.**

$= \frac{1}{3}(300{,}000)(321)$ **Substitute.**

$= 32{,}100{,}000$ **Simplify.**

The volume is about 32,100,000 ft^3.

Check Understanding 1 Find the volume of a square pyramid with base edges 12 in. and height 8 in.

To find the volume of a pyramid you may first need to find its height.

2 EXAMPLE Finding Volume of a Pyramid

Find the volume of a square pyramid with base edges 40 ft and slant height 25 ft.

Step 1: Find the height of the pyramid.

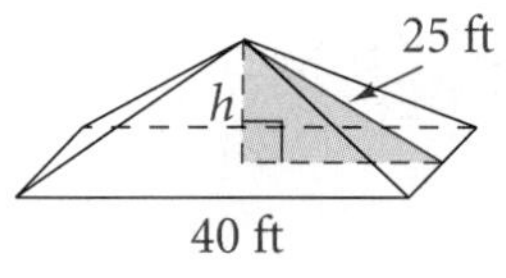

$25^2 = h^2 + 20^2$ **Use the Pythagorean Theorem.**

$625 = h^2 + 400$ **Simplify.**

$h^2 = 225$ **Solve for h^2.**

$h = 15$ **Take square roots.**

Step 2: Find the volume of the pyramid.

$V = \frac{1}{3}Bh$ **Use the formula for volume of a pyramid.**

$= \frac{1}{3}(40 \cdot 40)15$ **Substitute.**

$= 8000$ **Simplify.**

The volume of the pyramid is 8000 ft^3.

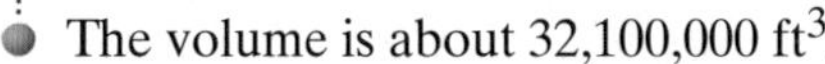

Check Understanding 2 Find the volume of a square pyramid with base edges 24 m and slant height 13 m.

OBJECTIVE

2 Finding Volume of a Cone

You have seen that the volume of a pyramid is one third the volume of a prism with the same base and height. Similarly, the volume of a cone is one third the volume of a cylinder with the same base and height.

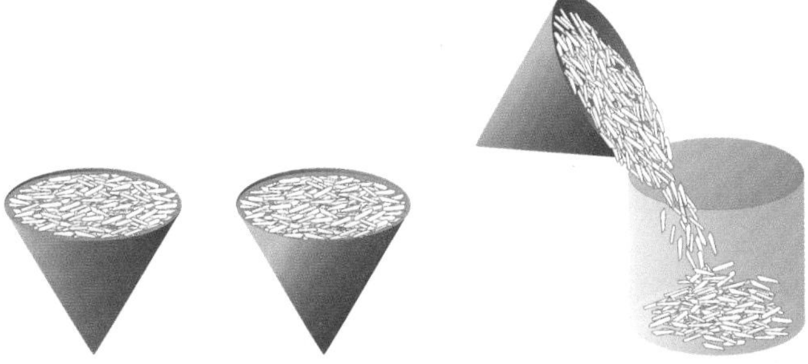

The cones and the cylinder have the same base and height. It takes three cones full of rice to fill the cylinder.

Key Concepts

Theorem 10-9 **Volume of a Cone**

The volume of a cone is one third the product of the area of the base and the height of the cone.

$$V = \frac{1}{3}Bh, \text{ or } V = \frac{1}{3}\pi r^2 h$$

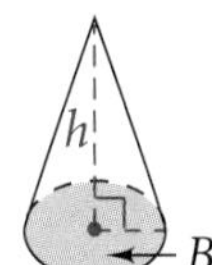

This volume formula applies to all cones, including oblique cones.

3 EXAMPLE Finding Volume of an Oblique Cone

Find the volume of an oblique cone with diameter 30 ft and height 25 ft. Give your answer in terms of π and also rounded to the nearest cubic foot.

$V = \frac{1}{3}\pi r^2 h$ **Use the formula for volume of a cone.**

$= \frac{1}{3}\pi(15)^2 25$ **Substitute 15 for *r* and 25 for *h*.**

$= 1875\pi$ **Simplify.**

≈ 5890.4862 **Use a calculator.**

The volume of the cone is 1875π ft^3, or about 5890 ft^3.

25 ft

30 ft

Check Understanding

3 Find the volume of each cone in terms of π and also rounded as indicated.

a. to the nearest cubic meter

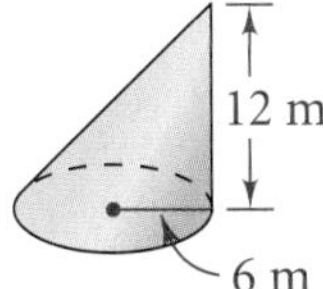

b. to the nearest cubic millimeter

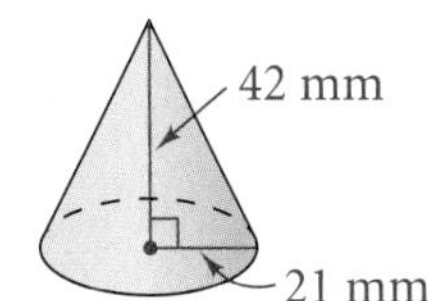
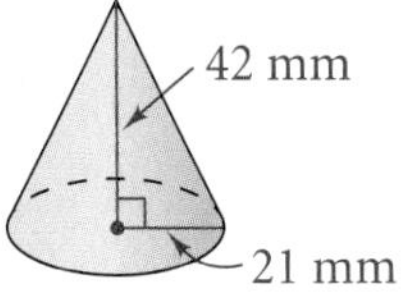

A cone-shaped structure can be particularly strong, as downward forces at the vertex are distributed to all points in its circular base.

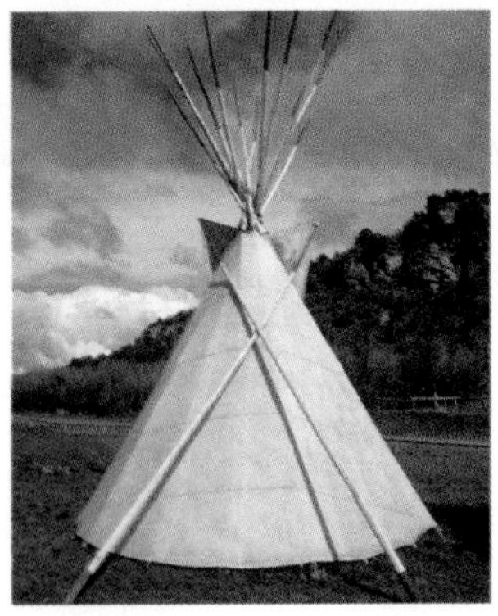

4 EXAMPLE **Real-World Connection**

Dwelling The covering on a teepee rests on poles that come together like concurrent lines. The resulting structure approximates a cone. If the teepee pictured is 12 ft. high with a base diameter 14 ft, estimate its volume.

$V = \frac{1}{3}\pi r^2 h$ **Use the formula for the volume of a cone.**

$V = \frac{1}{3}\pi(7)^2(12)$ **Substitute; $r = \frac{1}{2}(14) = 7$.**

$= 615.75216$ **Use a calculator.**

The volume of the teepee is approximately 616 ft^3.

4 A small child's teepee is 6 ft tall and 7 ft in diameter. Find the volume of the teepee to the nearest cubic foot.

EXERCISES

For more practice, see *Extra Practice.*

Practice and Problem Solving

A Practice by Example

Example 1 (page 552)

1. The entrance to the Louvre Museum in Paris, France is a pyramid. The height of the pyramid is about 70 ft and the area of its base is about 10,000 ft^2. What is the volume of the pyramid?

Find the volume of a square pyramid with the following dimensions.

2. base edges 10 cm, height 6 cm

3. base edges 18 in., height 12 in.

4. base edges 5 m, height 6 m

Find the volume of each square pyramid.

5.

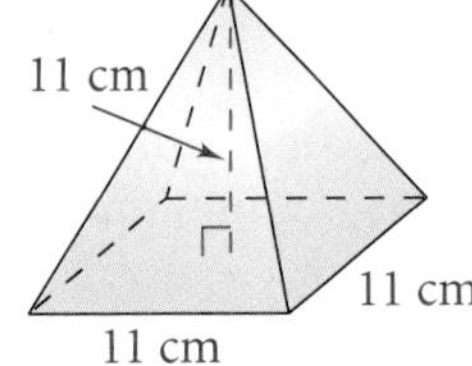

6.

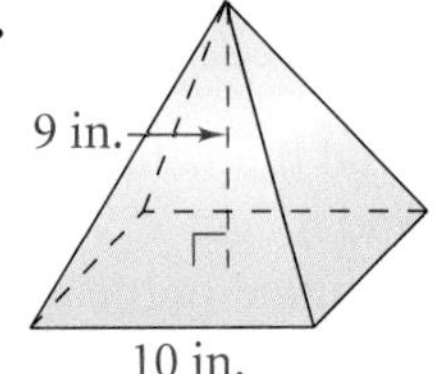

7.

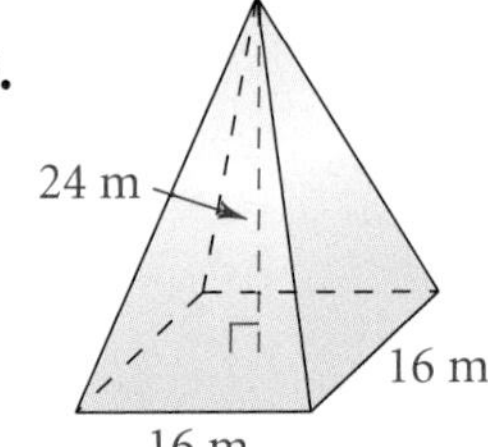

Example 2 (page 552)

8.

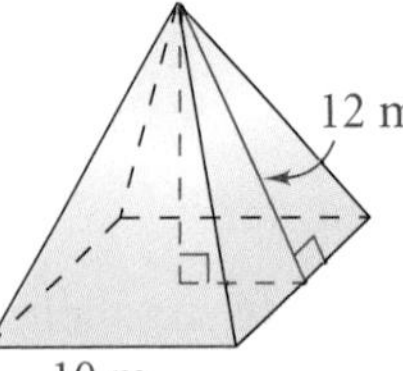

9.

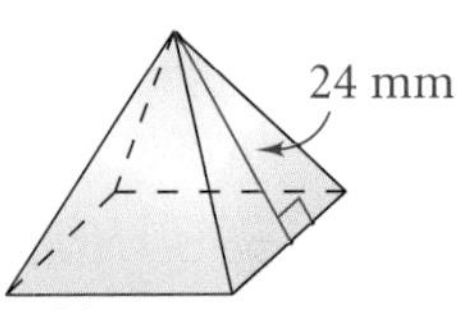

10.

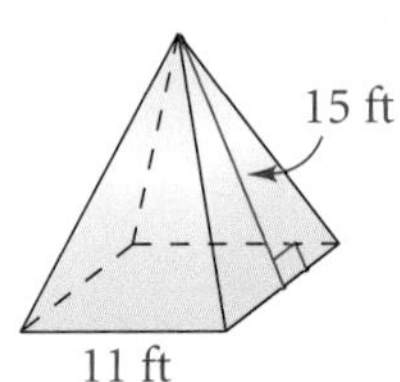

Example 3 (page 553)

Find the volume of each cone in terms of π and also rounded as indicated.

11. nearest cubic foot

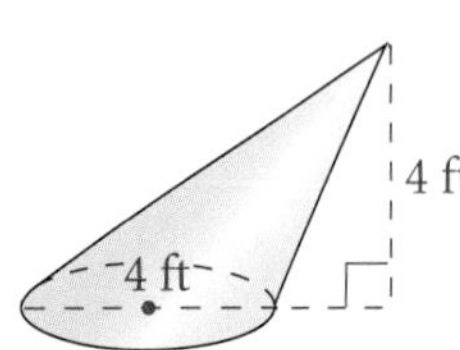

12. nearest cubic inch

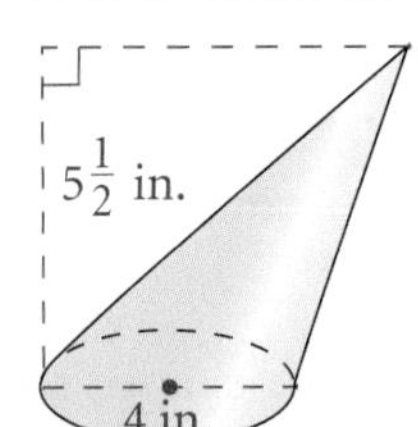

13. nearest cubic inch

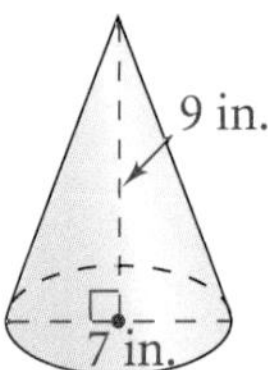

Example 4 (page 554)

14. **Chemistry** In a chemistry lab you use a filter paper cone to filter a liquid. The diameter of the cone is 6.5 cm and its height is 6 cm. How much liquid will the cone hold when it is full?

15. **Chemistry** This funnel has a filter that was being used to remove impurities from a solution but became clogged and stopped draining. The remaining solution is represented by the shaded region. How many cubic centimeters of the solution remain in the funnel?

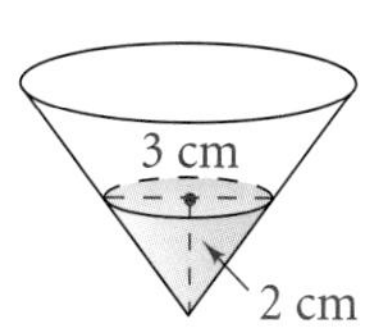

Apply Your Skills

Find the volume to the nearest whole number.

16.
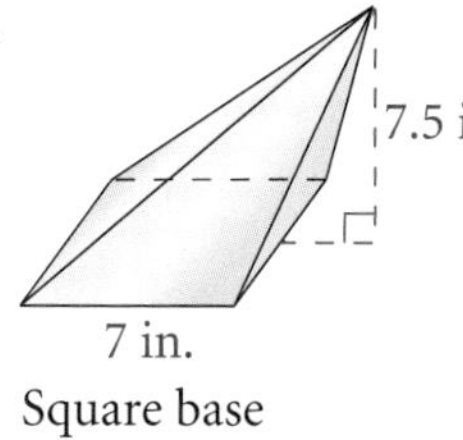

Square base

17.
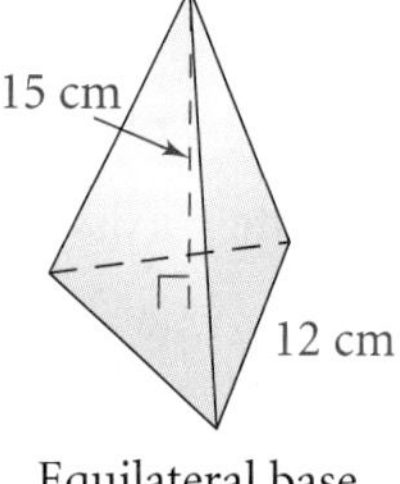

Equilateral base

18.
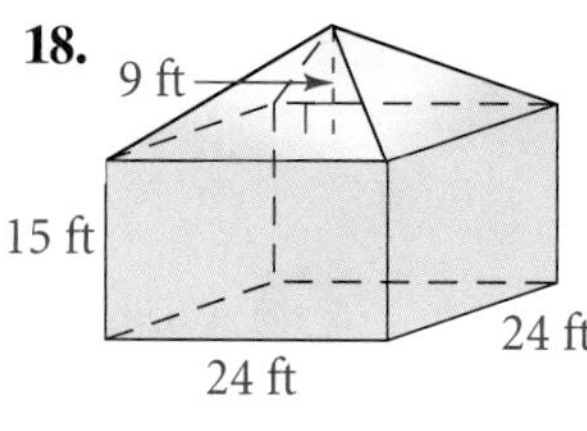

Square base

19. **Writing** The two cylinders pictured at the right are congruent. How does the volume of the larger cone compare to the total volume of the two smaller cones? Explain.

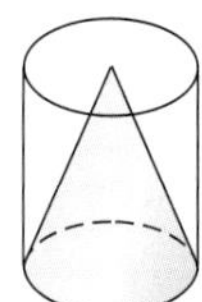
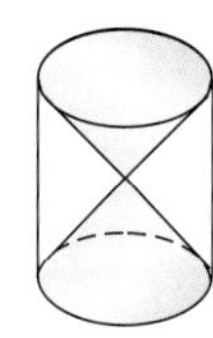

Exercise 20

20. **Architecture** The Transamerica Pyramid in San Francisco (see photo at left) is 853 ft tall with a square base that is 149 ft on each side.
   a. What is its volume to the nearest thousand cubic feet?
   b. Imagine, in place of the Transamerica Pyramid, a building in the shape of a prism with the same square base as the Pyramid. How tall would this building have to be to have the same volume as the Pyramid?

x^2 **Algebra** **Find the value of the variable in each figure. Leave answers in simplest radical form. The diagrams are not to scale.**

21.
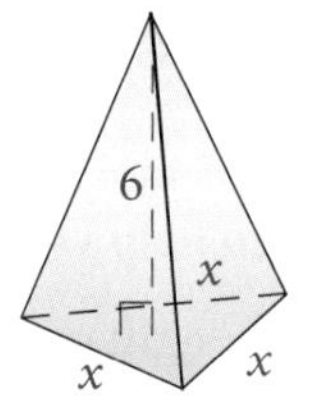

Volume = $18\sqrt{3}$

22.
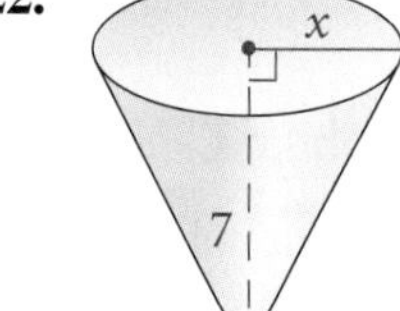

Volume = 21π

23.
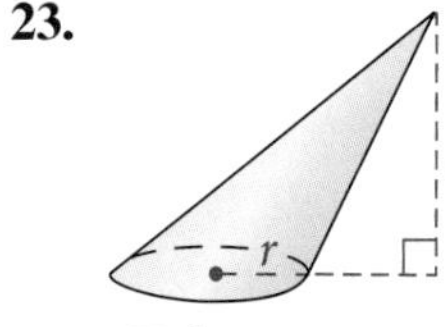

Volume = 24π

24. **Hardware** Builders use a plumb bob to find a vertical line. The plumb bob shown combines a regular hexagonal prism with a pyramid. Find its volume to the nearest cubic centimeter.

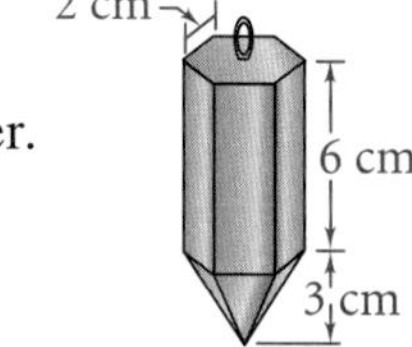

25. **Open-Ended** A cone has a volume of 600π in.^{3}. Find two possible sets of dimensions for its height and radius.

26. A cone with radius 1 fits snugly inside a square pyramid which fits snugly inside a cube. What are the volumes of the three figures?

27. A cone with radius 3 ft and height 10 ft has a volume of 30π ft^3. What is the volume of the cone formed when the following happens to the original cone?
   a. The radius is doubled. **b.** The height is doubled.
   c. The radius and the height are both doubled.

28. List the volumes of the cone, prism, and pyramid in order from least to greatest.

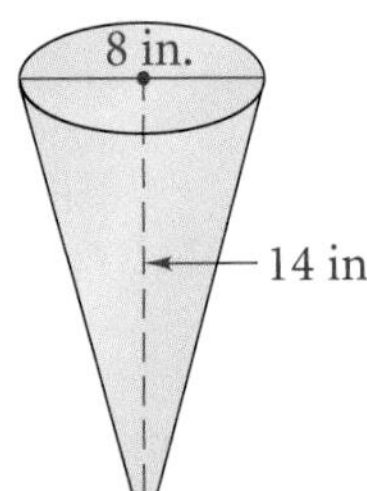

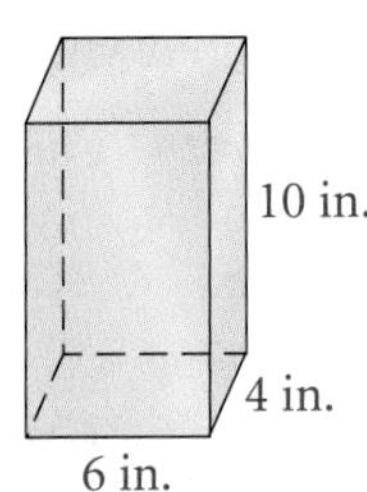

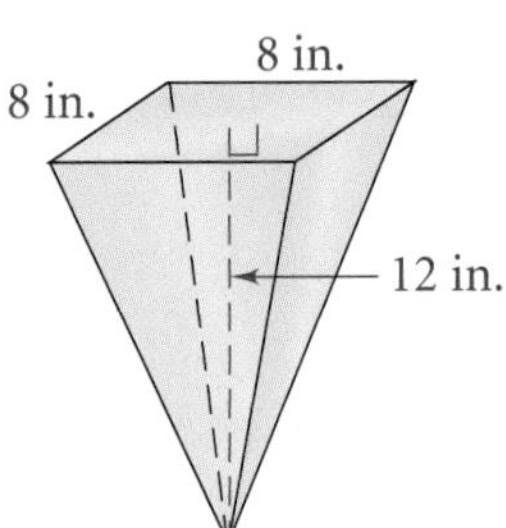

Visualization The plane region is revolved completely about the given line to sweep out a solid of revolution. Describe the solid. Then find its volume in terms of π.

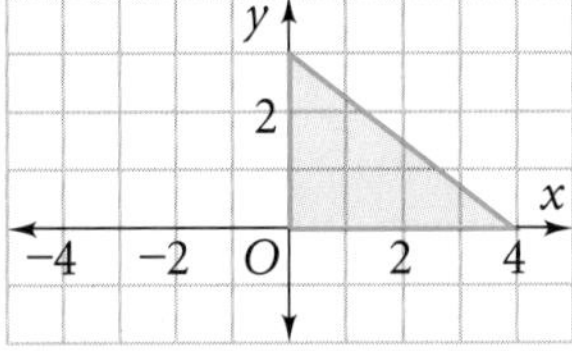

29. the y-axis

30. the x-axis

Challenge

31. the line $x = 4$

32. the line $y = -1$

33. A *frustum* of a cone is the part that remains when the vertex is cut off by a plane parallel to the base.
   a. Explain how to use the formula for the volume of a cone to find the volume of a frustum of a cone.
    b. **Containers** A 9-in. tall popcorn container is the frustum of a cone. Its small radius is 4.5 in. and its large radius is 6 in. What is its volume?

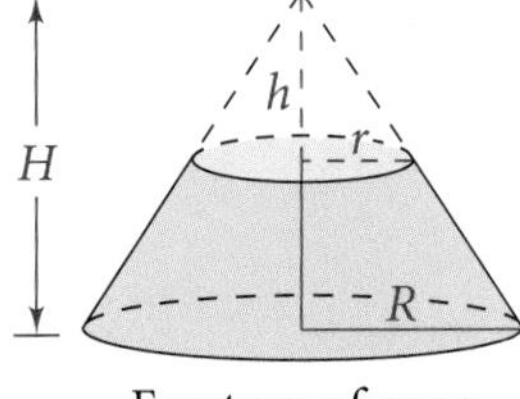

Frustum of cone

34. A disk has radius 10 m. A 90° sector is cut away, and a cone is formed.
   a. What is the circumference of the base of the cone?
   b. What is the area of the base of the cone?
   c. What is the volume of the cone? (*Hint:* Use the slant height and the radius of the base to find the height.)

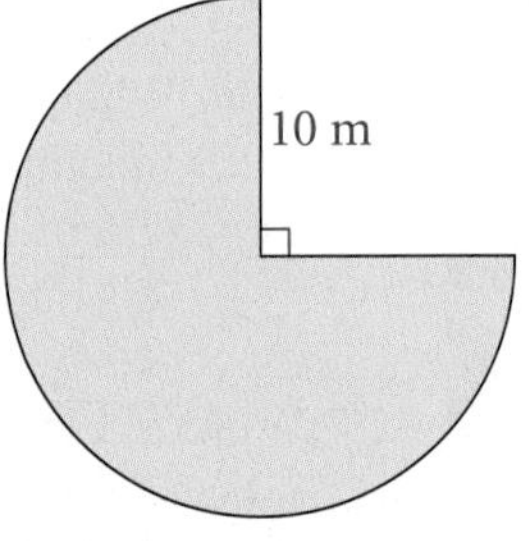

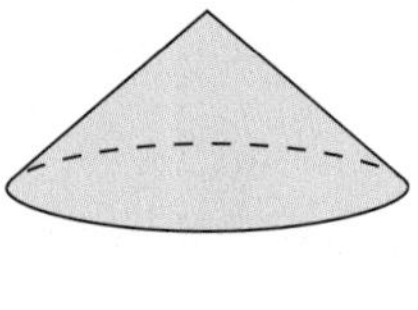

Graphing Calculator In Exercises 35 and 36, the volume of the solid is 1000 cm^3. Use the Exploration on page 536 to help you complete each exercise.

35. For a square pyramid, find the length of a side of the base for which the lateral area is as small as possible.

36. For a cone, find the radius for which the lateral area is as small as possible.

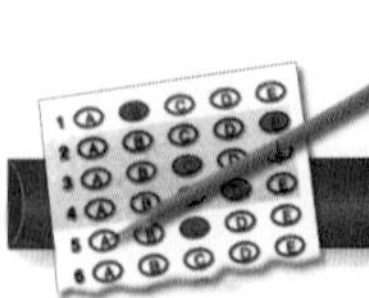

Standardized Test Prep

Multiple Choice

37. What is the volume of a 6-ft high square pyramid with base edges 8 ft?
   A. 128 ft^3 B. 192 ft^3 C. 256 ft^3 D. 384 ft^3

38. What is the volume of a cone with diameter 21 m and height 4 m?
   F. 147π m^3 G. 220.5π m^3 H. 294π m^3 I. 441π m^3

39. What is the volume of an oblique cone with radius 9 cm and height 12 cm?
   A. 324π cm^3 B. 486π cm^3 C. 648π cm^3 D. 972π cm^3

Take It to the NET
Online lesson quiz at
www.PHSchool.com
Web Code: afa-1006

40. What is the volume of the square pyramid at the right?
 F. 1568 m^3 G. 1633 m^3
 H. 2352 m^3 I. 2450 m^3

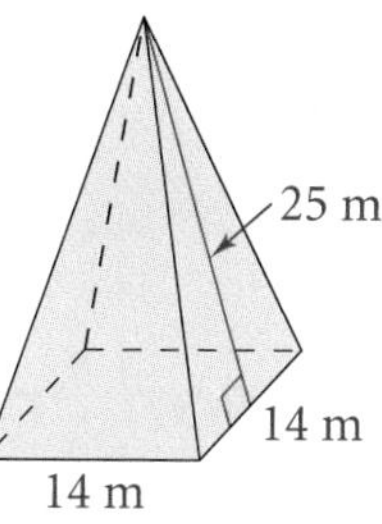

41. What is the volume of an oblique square pyramid with base edges 25 in. and height 24 in.?
 A. 5000 $in.^3$ B. 7500 $in.^3$
 C. 10,000 $in.^3$ D. 15,000 $in.^3$

Short Response

42. The volume of a cone is $82{,}418\pi$ cm^3. Its diameter is 203 cm. What is its height? Show all your work, including any formulas that you use.

Mixed Review

Lesson 10-5

43. **Sports** A cylindrical hockey puck is 1 in. high and 3 in. in diameter. What is its volume in cubic inches? Round your answer to the nearest tenth.

44. A triangular prism has height 30 cm. Its base is a right triangle with legs 10 cm and 24 cm. Find the volume of the prism.

Lesson 9-5

45. Find the area of a regular pentagon with a radius 5 in. Give your answer to the nearest tenth of a square inch.

Lesson 7-3

Find the area of each equilateral triangle to the nearest tenth of a square unit.

46. The triangle has 12 cm sides.

47. The triangle has 10-in. altitudes.

48. Find the area of a 30°-60°-90° triangle with shorter leg of length 4 cm.

Geometry at Work

Package Designer

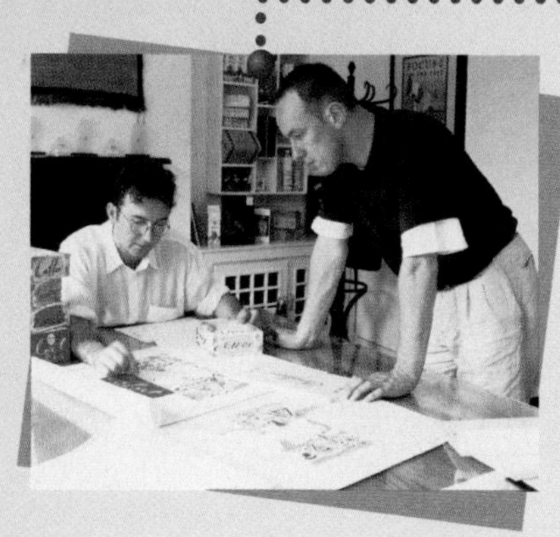

Each year, more than one trillion dollars in manufactured goods are packaged in containers. To create each new box, bag, or carton, package designers must balance such factors as safety, environmental impact, and attractiveness against cost of production.

Consider the three boxes of dishwasher detergent. All three boxes have standard volumes of 108 $in.^3$. The boxes have different shapes, however, and different surface areas. The box on the left has the greatest surface area and therefore costs the most to produce. Despite the higher cost, the box on the left has become standard. In this case, the least expensive package on the right is too difficult for a consumer to pick up and pour.

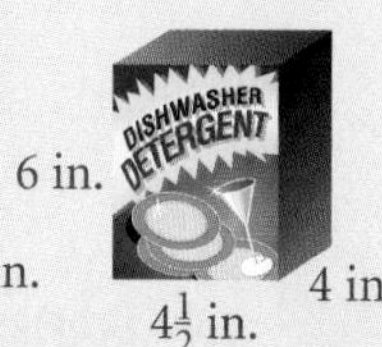

Take It to the NET For more information about package design, go to **www.PHSchool.com**.
Web Code: afb-2031

10-7 Surface Areas and Volumes of Spheres

Lesson Preview

What You'll Learn

To find the surface area and volume of a sphere

. . . And Why

To approximate the surface area of Earth, as in Example 2

✓ Check Skills You'll Need

(For help, go to Lesson 1-7.)

Find the area and circumference of a circle with the given radius. Round your answers to the nearest tenth.

1. 6 in. **2.** 5 cm **3.** 2.5 ft

4. 1.2 m **5.** 15 yd **6.** 12 mm

New Vocabulary • sphere • center, radius, diameter, circumference (of a sphere) • great circle • hemisphere

Interactive lesson includes instant self-check, tutorials, and activities.

OBJECTIVE

1 Finding Surface Area and Volume of a Sphere

Real-World Connection

The diameter of the Hayden Sphere in New York City is 87 ft.

A **sphere** is the set of all points in space equidistant from a given point called the **center.** A **radius** is a segment that has one endpoint at the center and the other endpoint on the sphere. A **diameter** is a segment passing through the center with endpoints on the sphere.

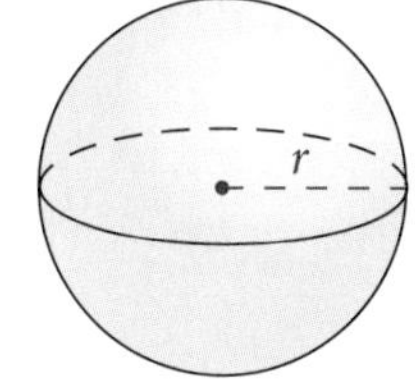

The *length r* is *the* radius of the sphere. $2r$ is *the* diameter.

When a plane and a sphere intersect in more than one point, the intersection is a circle. If the center of the circle is also the center of the sphere, the circle is called a **great circle** of the sphere. The circumference of a great circle is the **circumference** of the sphere. A great circle divides a sphere into two **hemispheres.**

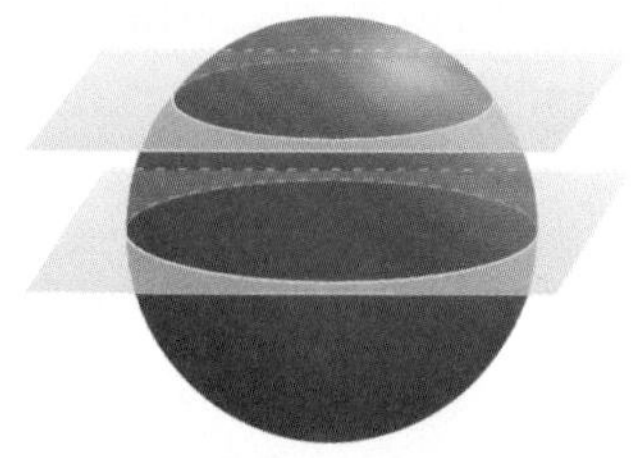

A baseball is a model of a sphere. To approximate its surface area, you can take apart its covering. Each of the two sections suggests a pair of circles with radius r approximately the radius of the ball. The area of the four circles, $4\pi r^2$, suggests the surface area of the ball.

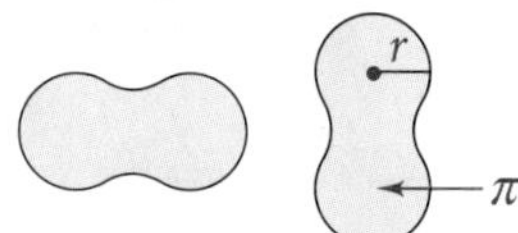

Key Concepts

Theorem 10-10 **Surface Area of a Sphere**

The surface area of a sphere is four times the product of π and the square of the radius of the sphere.

$$\text{S.A.} = 4\pi r^2$$

1 EXAMPLE Finding Surface Area

Find the surface area of this sphere. Leave your answer in terms of π.

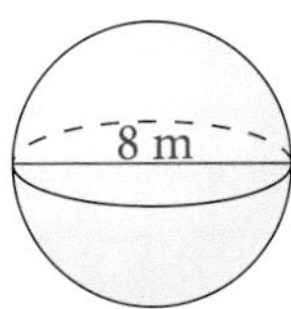

S.A. $= 4\pi r^2$ **Use the formula for surface area.**

$= 4\pi 4^2$ **Substitute $r = \frac{8}{2} = 4$.**

$= 64\pi$ **Simplify.**

The surface area is 64π m^2.

Check Understanding 1 Find the surface area of a sphere with $d = 14$ in. Give your answer two ways, in terms of π and rounded to the nearest square inch.

You can use spheres to approximate the surface areas of real-world objects.

2 EXAMPLE Real-World Connection

Geography Earth's equator is about 24,902 mi long. Approximate the surface area of Earth by finding the surface area of a sphere with circumference 24,902 mi.

Step 1 Find the radius.

$C = 2\pi r$ **Use the formula for circumference.**

$24{,}902 = 2\pi r$ **Substitute.**

$\frac{24{,}902}{2\pi} = r$ **Solve for *r*.**

$r = 3963.2764$ **Use a calculator.**

Step 2 Use the radius to find the surface area.

S.A. $= 4\pi r^2$ **Use the formula for surface area.**

$= 4\pi$ ANS x^2 ENTER **Use a calculator.**

$= 197387020$

The surface area of Earth is about 197,400,000 mi^2.

Take It to the NET Graphing Calculator procedures online at **www.PHSchool.com** Web Code: afe-2101

Check Understanding 2 Find the surface area of a melon with circumference 18 in. Round your answer to the nearest ten square inches.

The following model suggests a formula for the volume of a sphere.

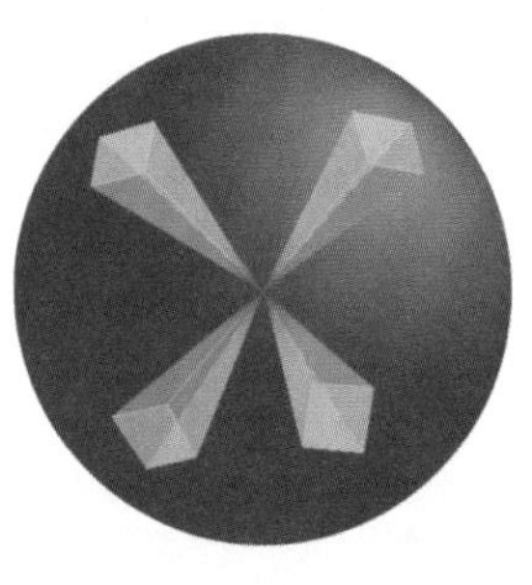

Fill a sphere with a large number n of small pyramids. The vertex of each pyramid is the center of the sphere. The height of each pyramid is approximately the radius r of the sphere. The sum of the areas of the bases of the n pyramids approximates the surface area of the sphere. The sum of the volumes of the n pyramids should approximate the volume of the sphere.

Volume of each pyramid $= \frac{1}{3}Bh$

Sum of the volumes of n pyramids $\approx n \cdot \frac{1}{3}Br$ **Substitute *r* for *h*.**

$= \frac{1}{3} \cdot (nB) \cdot r$

$\approx \frac{1}{3} \cdot (4\pi r^2) \cdot r$ **Replace *nB* with the surface area of a sphere.**

$= \frac{4}{3}\pi r^3$

It is reasonable to conjecture that the volume of a sphere is $\frac{4}{3}\pi r^3$.

Key Concepts

Theorem 10-11 **Volume of a Sphere**

The volume of a sphere is four thirds the product of π and the cube of the radius of the sphere.

$V = \frac{4}{3}\pi r^3$

3 EXAMPLE Finding Volume

Find the volume of the sphere. Leave your answer in terms of π.

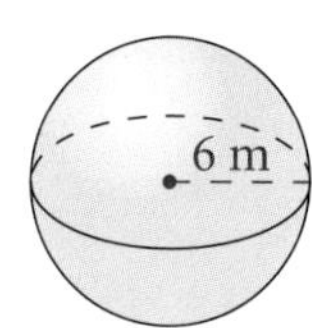

$V = \frac{4}{3}\pi r^3$ **Use the formula for volume.**

$= \frac{4}{3}\pi 6^3$ **Substitute.**

$= 288\pi$

The volume of the sphere is 288π m^3.

Check Understanding 3 Find the volume to the nearest cubic inch of a sphere with diameter 60 in.

If you know the volume of a sphere, you can find its surface area.

4 EXAMPLE Using Volume to Find Surface Area

The volume of a sphere is 5000 m^3. What is the surface area of the sphere?

Step 1 Find the radius r.

$V = \frac{4}{3}\pi r^3$ **Use the formula for volume of a sphere.**

$5000 = \frac{4}{3}\pi r^3$ **Substitute.**

$5000\left(\frac{3}{4\pi}\right) = r^3$ **Solve for r^3.**

$\sqrt[3]{5000\left(\frac{3}{4\pi}\right)} = r$ **Take cube roots.**

$r = 10.607844$ **Use a calculator.**

Step 2 Find the surface area of the sphere.

S.A. $= 4\pi r^2$ **Use the formula for the surface area of a sphere.**

$= 4\pi$ ANS x^2 ENTER **Use a calculator.**

$= 1414.0479$

The surface area of the sphere is about 1414 m^2.

Need Help?

The cube root of x, $\sqrt[3]{x}$, is the number whose third power is x.

Check Understanding 4 The volume of a sphere is 4200 ft^3. Find the surface area to the nearest tenth.

EXERCISES

For more practice, see *Extra Practice*.

Practice and Problem Solving

Practice by Example

Example 1 (page 559)

Find the surface area of the sphere with the given diameter or radius. Leave your answer in terms of π.

1. $d = 30$ m **2.** $r = 10$ in. **3.** $d = 32$ mm **4.** $r = 100$ yd

Find the surface area of each ball. Leave each answer in terms of π.

5. 

$d = 68$ mm

6. 

$d = 24$ cm

7. 

$d = 2\frac{3}{4}$ in.

Example 2 (page 559)

Use the given circumference to find the surface area of each spherical object. Round your answer to the nearest whole number.

8. a grapefruit with $C = 14$ cm
9. a bowling ball with $C = 27$ in.
10. a pincushion with $C = 8$ cm
11. a head of lettuce with $C = 22$ in.

Example 3 (page 560)

Find the volume of each sphere. Give each answer in terms of π and rounded to the nearest cubic unit.

12. 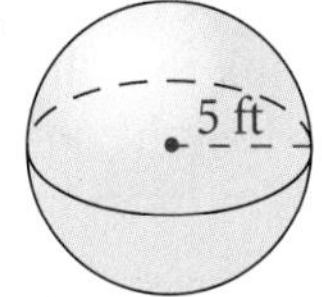

13. 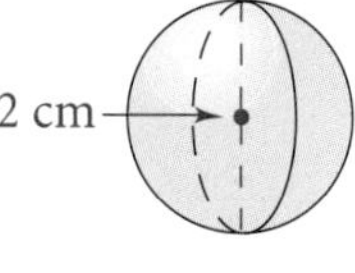

14. 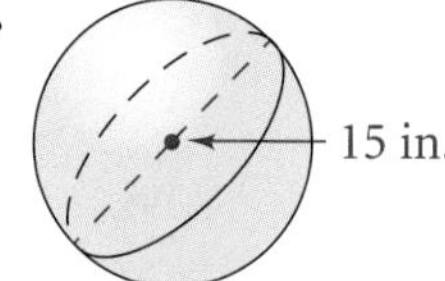

15. 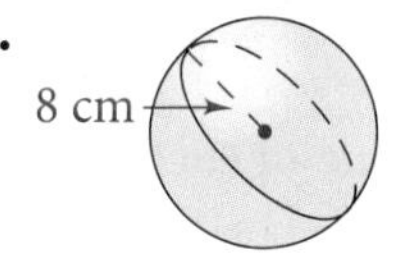

16. 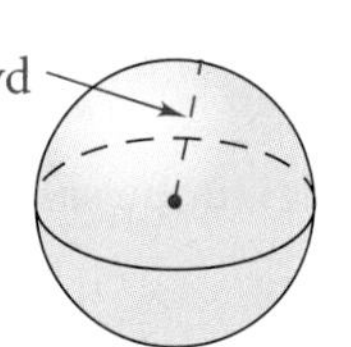

17. 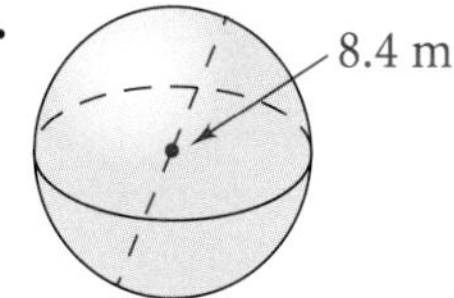

Example 4 (page 560)

A sphere has the volume given. Find its surface area to the nearest whole number.

18. $V = 900$ in.^{3}
19. $V = 3000$ m^3
20. $V = 140$ cm^3

21. **Mental Math** Use $\pi \approx 3$ to estimate the surface area and volume of a sphere with radius 3 cm.

22. **Visualization** The region enclosed by the semicircle at the right is revolved completely about the x-axis.
 a. Describe the solid of revolution that is formed.
 b. Find its volume in terms of π.
 c. Find its surface area in terms of π.

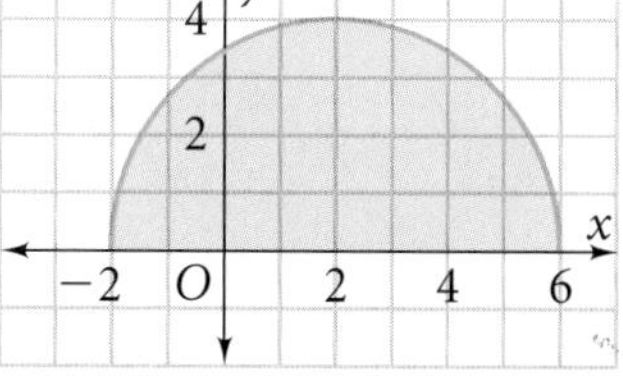

23. **Food** A sphere of frozen yogurt was pressed into the cone as shown at the left. If the yogurt melts into the cone, would the cone overflow? Explain.

24. The sphere at the right fits snugly inside a cube with 6-in. edges.
 a. What is the radius of the sphere?
 b. What is the volume of the space between the sphere and cube, to the nearest tenth?

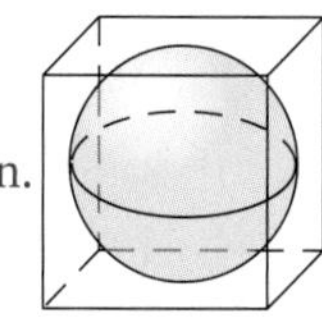

Geometry in 3 Dimensions **A sphere has center (0, 0, 0) and radius 5.**

25. Name the coordinates of six points on the sphere.

26. Tell whether each of the following points is inside, outside, or on the sphere. $A(0, -3, 4)$, $B(1, -1, -1)$, $C(4, -6, -10)$

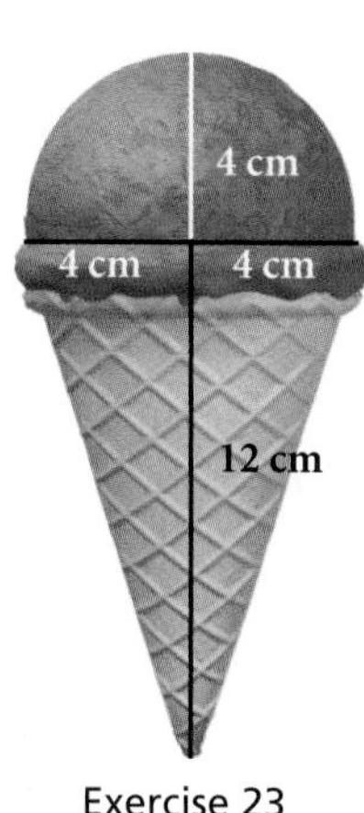

Exercise 23

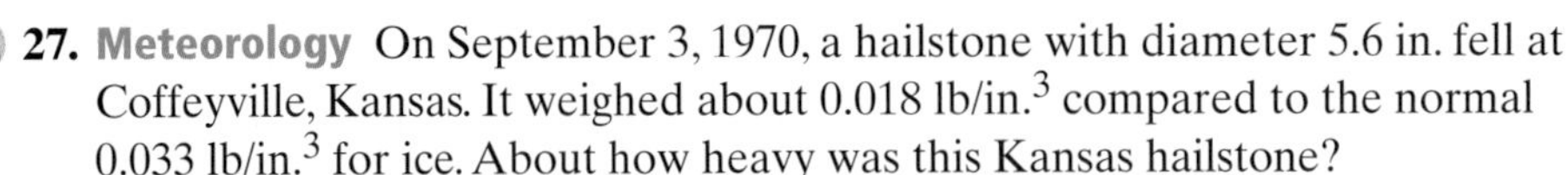

Real-World Connection

Hail with diameter about an inch larger than shown here broke this windshield.

27. Meteorology On September 3, 1970, a hailstone with diameter 5.6 in. fell at Coffeyville, Kansas. It weighed about 0.018 lb/in.^{3} compared to the normal 0.033 lb/in.^{3} for ice. About how heavy was this Kansas hailstone?

28. Critical Thinking Which is greater, the total volume of three spheres, each of which has diameter 3 in., or the volume of one sphere that has diameter 8 in.?

Find the volume in terms of π of each sphere with the given surface area.

29. 4π m^2	**30.** 36π in.^{2}	**31.** 9π ft^2	**32.** 100π mm^2
33. 25π yd^2	**34.** 144π cm^2	**35.** 49 m^2	**36.** 225π mi^2

37. A balloon has a 14-in. diameter when it is fully inflated. Half of the air is let out of the balloon. Assume that the balloon is a sphere.

a. Find the volume of the fully-inflated balloon in terms of π.

b. Find the volume of the half-inflated balloon in terms of π.

c. What is the diameter of the half-inflated balloon to the nearest inch?

38. Sports Equipment The golf ball diameter is 1.68 in.

a. Approximate the surface area of the golf ball.

b. Critical Thinking Do you think that the value you found in part (a) is greater or less than the actual surface area of the golf ball? Explain.

39. Open-Ended Give the dimensions of a cylinder and a sphere that have the same volume.

Find the surface area and volume of each figure.

40.

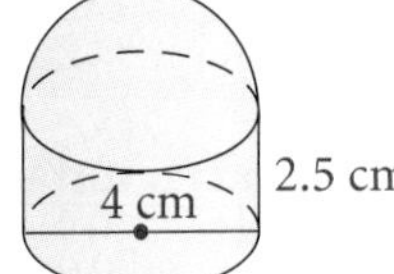

41.

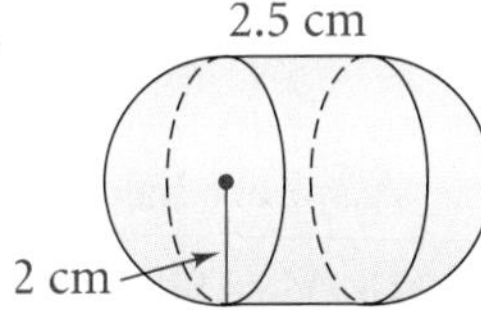

42.

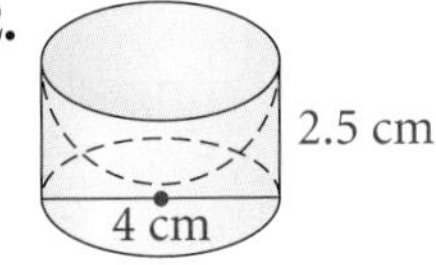

43. Science The density of steel is about 0.28 lb/in.^{3}. Could you lift a solid steel ball with radius 4 in.? With radius 6 in.? Explain.

44. A cube with edges 6 in. long fits snugly inside the sphere. The diagonal of the cube is the diameter of the sphere.

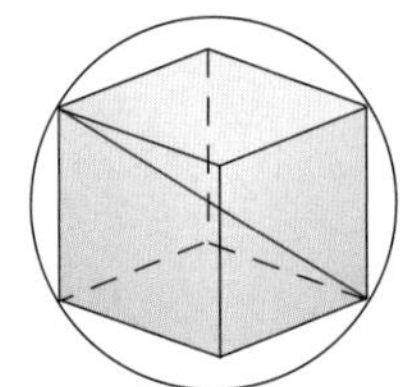

a. Find the length of the diagonal and the radius of the sphere. Leave your answers in simplest radical form.

b. What is the volume of the space between the sphere and the cube to the nearest tenth?

Challenge

Graphing Calculator **The sphere has a 10-cm radius. Of all the cylinders that fit snugly inside the sphere, such as the one shown here, find the dimensions of the one with the greatest measure indicated. (*Hint:* Use the Exploration on page 536.)**

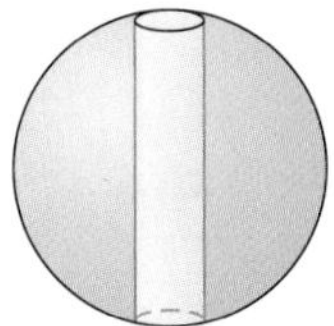

45. lateral area

46. volume

47. A plane intersects a sphere to form a circular cross section. The radius of the sphere is 17 cm and the plane comes to within 8 cm of the center. Draw a sketch and find the area of the cross section, to the nearest whole number.

48. Suppose a cube and a sphere have the same volume.

a. Which has the greater surface area? Explain.

b. Writing Explain why spheres are rarely used for packaging.

Find the radius of a sphere with the given property.

49. The number of square meters of surface area equals the number of cubic meters of volume.

50. The ratio of surface area in square meters to volume in cubic meters is 1 : 5.

51. History The sphere fits snugly inside the cylinder. Archimedes (c. 287–212 B.C.) asked that such a figure be put on his gravestone along with the ratio of their volumes, a finding that he regarded as his greatest. What is that ratio?

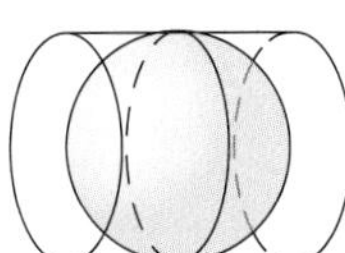

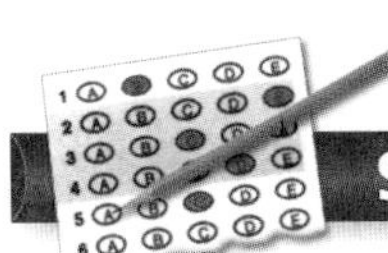

Standardized Test Prep

Reading Comprehension

Read the passage below, then answer Exercises 52–54 based on what is stated in the passage.

Believe It Or Not

J.C. Payne, a Texas farmer, is the world champion string collector. The ball of string he wound over a three-year period has a circumference of 41.5 ft. It weighs 13,000 lb.

Listed in the Guinness Book of World Records, the ball of string is now in a museum devoted to oddities. It took almost a dozen men with fork-lift trucks to load the ball onto a truck to move it there.

52. What is the radius of the ball of string to the nearest tenth of a foot?
A. 3.3 ft **B.** 6.6 ft **C.** 13.2 ft **D.** 20.75 ft

53. Which is the best approximation of the volume of the ball of string?
F. 300 ft^3 **G.** 600 ft^3 **H.** 1200 ft^3 **I.** 2400 ft^3

54. If Mr. Payne wound the same amount of string each year, which is the best estimate of the radius after one year?
A. 2.2 ft **B.** 2.3 ft **C.** 4.4 ft **D.** 4.6 ft

Multiple Choice

55. What is the surface area of a sphere whose radius is 7.5 m?
F. 75π m^2 **G.** 112.5π m^2 **H.** 225π m^2 **I.** 562.5π m^2

56. What is the volume of a sphere whose radius is 6 ft?
A. 48π ft^3 **B.** 144π ft^3 **C.** 288π ft^3 **D.** 324π ft^3

Take It to the NET
Online lesson quiz at **www.PHSchool.com**
Web Code: afa-1007

57. The volume of a sphere is $26{,}244\pi$ cm^3. What is its surface area?
F. 1070π cm^2 **G.** 1402π cm^2 **H.** 2448π cm^2 **I.** 2916π cm^2

58. The surface area of a sphere is 576π in.^{2}. What is its diameter?
A. 1 ft **B.** 1.7 ft **C.** 2 ft **D.** 3.5 ft

Short Response

59. The surface area of a sphere is 36π ft^2.
a. What is the radius of the sphere? Show your work.
b. What is the volume of the sphere? Show your work.

Mixed Review

Lesson 10-6 **Find the volume of each figure to the nearest cubic unit.**

60. 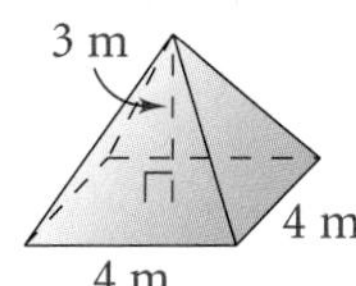

61. 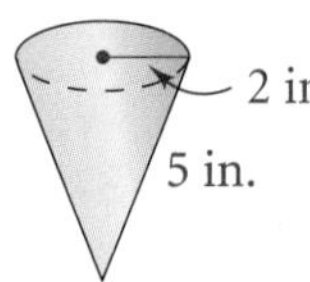

62. 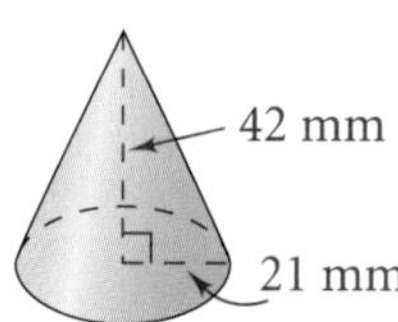

Lesson 9-2

63. A leg of a right triangle measures 4 cm and the hypotenuse measures 7 cm. Find the measure of each acute angle of the triangle to the nearest degree.

64. The length of each side of a rhombus is 16. The longer diagonal has length 26. Find the measures of the angles of the rhombus to the nearest degree.

Lesson 8-6 **The similarity ratio of a pair of similar isosceles trapezoids is 2 : 3. A diagonal of the smaller figure has length 7 cm.**

65. Find the length of a diagonal in the larger trapezoid.

66. The perimeter of the larger trapezoid is 40.5 cm. What is the perimeter of the smaller trapezoid?

67. The area of the smaller trapezoid is 30 cm^2. What is the area of the larger trapezoid?

Checkpoint Quiz 2 — Lessons 10-4 through 10-7

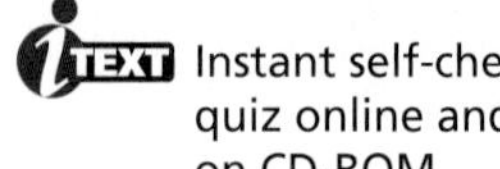

Instant self-check quiz online and on CD-ROM

Find the surface area and volume of each figure to the nearest tenth.

1. 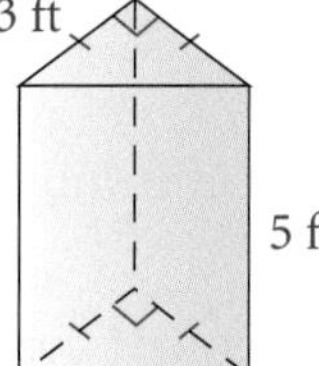

2. 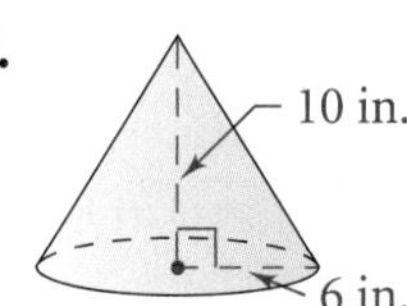

3. 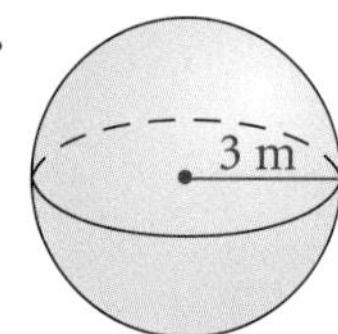

4. 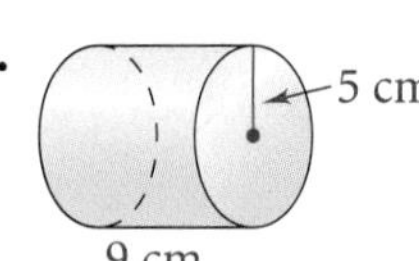

5. 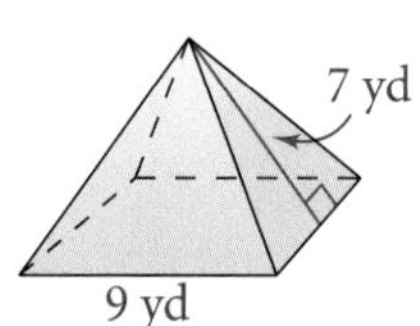

6. 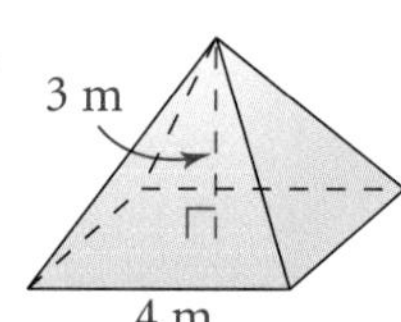

7. 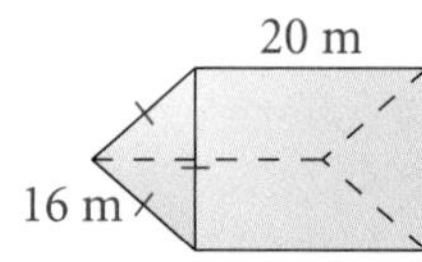

8. 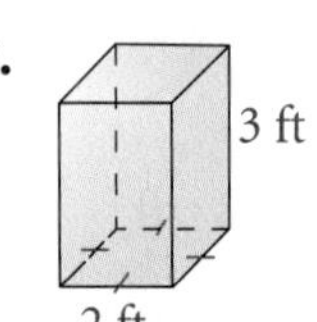

9. 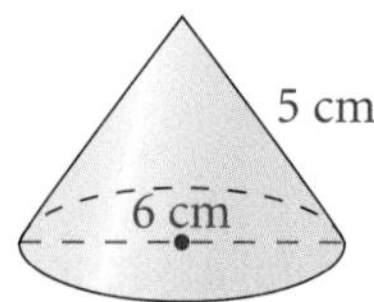

10. **Critical Thinking** Tennis balls fit snugly inside a cylinder as shown. Which is greater, the volume of the three tennis balls or the volume of the space around the balls? Explain.

Technology

Exploring Similar Solids

For Use With Lesson 10-8

To explore the surface areas and volumes of similar rectangular prisms, you can set up a spreadsheet like the one below. You choose the numbers for the length, width, height, and similarity ratio. The computer will use formulas to calculate all the other numbers.

	A	B	C	D	E	F	G	H	I
1					Surface		Similarity		
2		Length	Width	Height	Area	Volume	Ratio (II : I)	Ratio of	Ratio of
3	Rectangular Prism I	6	4	23	508	552	2	Surface	Volumes
4								Areas (II : I)	(II : I)
5	Similar Prism II	12	8	46	2032	4416		4	8

In cell E3 enter the formula =2*(B3*C3+B3*D3+C3*D3).
This will calculate the sum of the areas of the six faces of Prism I.
In cell F3 enter the formula =B3*C3*D3. This will calculate the volume of Prism I.

In cells B5, C5, and D5 enter the formulas =G3*B3, =G3*C3, and =G3*D3, respectively. These will calculate the dimensions of similar Prism II. Copy the formulas from E3 and F3 into E5 and F5 to calculate the surface area and volume of Prism II.

In cell H5 enter the formula =E5/E3 and in cell I5 enter the formula =F5/F3. These will calculate the ratios of the surface areas and volumes.

Investigate

In row 3, enter numbers for the length, width, height, and similarity ratio. Change those numbers to investigate how the ratio of the surface areas and the ratio of the volumes are each related to the similarity ratio.

EXERCISES

Make a Conjecture **State a relationship that seems to be true about the similarity ratio and each given ratio.**

1. the ratio of volumes

2. the ratio of surface areas

Extend

Set up spreadsheets that allow you to investigate the following ratios. State a conclusion from each investigation.

3. the volumes of similar cylinders

4. the lateral areas of similar cylinders

5. the surface areas of similar cylinders

6. the volumes of similar square pyramids

7. the lateral areas of similar square pyramids

8. the surface areas of similar square pyramids

Areas and Volumes of Similar Solids

Lesson Preview

What You'll Learn

To find relationships between the ratios of the areas and volumes of similar solids

. . . And Why

To use similarity ratios to find the weight of an object, as in Example 4

✓ Check Skills You'll Need

(For help, go to Lessons 8-2 and 10-5.)

Are the figures similar? Explain. Include the similarity ratio as appropriate.

1. two squares, one with 3-in. sides and the other with 1-in. sides
2. two isosceles right triangles, one with a 3-cm hypotenuse and the other with a 1-cm leg

Find the volume of each space figure.

3. a cube with a 3-in. edge
4. a 3 m-by-5 m-by-9 m rectangular prism
5. a cylinder with radius 4 cm and height 8 cm

New Vocabulary • similar solids • similarity ratio

Interactive lesson includes instant self-check, tutorials, and activities.

Finding Relationships in Area and Volume

Similar solids have the same shape, and all their corresponding dimensions are proportional. The ratio of corresponding linear dimensions of two similar solids is the **similarity ratio.** Any two cubes are similar, as are any two spheres.

These Russian nesting dolls suggest similar solids.

1 EXAMPLE Identifying Similar Solids

Are the two rectangular prisms similar? If so, give the similarity ratio.

a.

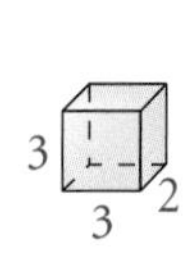

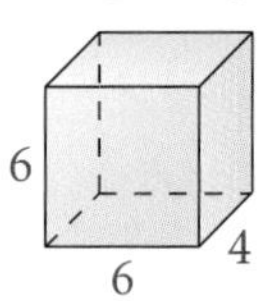

$\frac{3}{6} = \frac{3}{6} = \frac{2}{4}$

The rectangular prisms are similar because the ratios of the corresponding linear dimensions are equal.

The similarity ratio is $\frac{1}{2}$.

b.

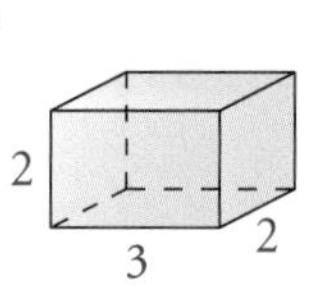

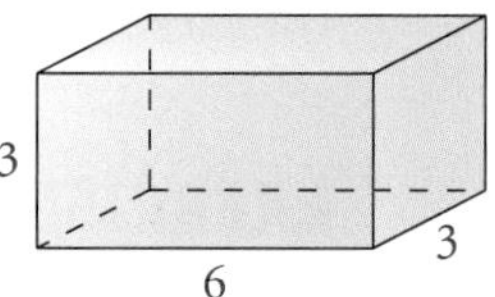

$\frac{2}{3} \neq \frac{3}{6}$

The rectangular prisms are not similar because the ratios of corresponding linear dimensions are not equal.

✓ Check Understanding

1. Are the two cylinders similar? If so, give the similarity ratio.

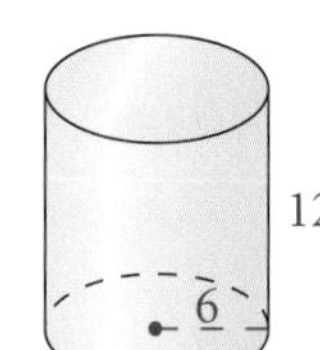

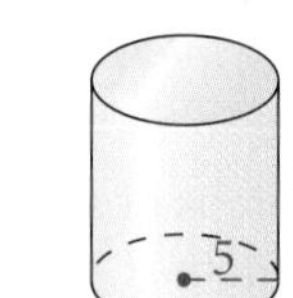

The two similar prisms shown here suggest two important relationships for similar solids.

The ratio of the side lengths is 1 : 2.
The ratio of the surface areas is 22 : 88, or 1 : 4.
The ratio of the volumes is 6 : 48, or 1 : 8.

The ratio of the surface areas equals the square of the similarity ratio. The ratio of the volumes equals the cube of the similarity ratio. These two facts apply to all similar solids.

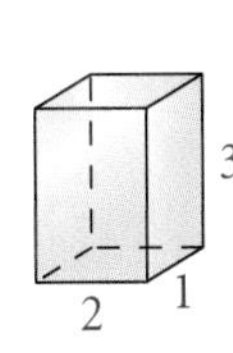

S.A. = 22 m^2
V = 6 m^3

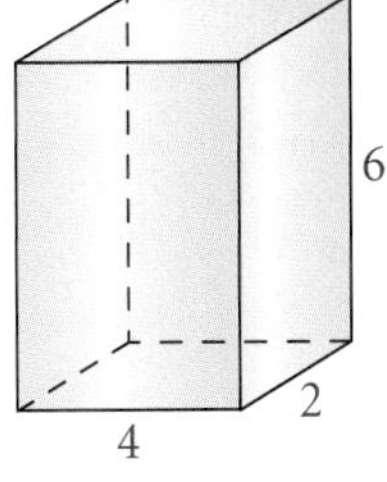

S.A. = 88 m^2
V = 48 m^3

Key Concepts

Theorem 10-12 **Areas and Volumes of Similar Solids**

If the similarity ratio of two similar solids is $a : b$, then
(1) the ratio of their corresponding areas is $a^2 : b^2$, and
(2) the ratio of their volumes is $a^3 : b^3$.

2 EXAMPLE Finding the Similarity Ratio

Find the similarity ratio of two cubes with volumes of 729 cm^3 and 1331 cm^3.

$\frac{a^3}{b^3} = \frac{729}{1331}$ **The ratio of the volumes is $a^3 : b^3$.**

$\frac{a}{b} = \frac{9}{11}$ **Take cube roots.**

The similarity ratio is 9 : 11.

✓ Check Understanding **2** Find the similarity ratio of two similar prisms with surface areas 144 m^2 and 324 m^2.

3 EXAMPLE Using a Similarity Ratio

Paint Cans The lateral areas of two similar paint cans are 1019 cm^2 and 425 cm^2. The volume of the small can is 1157 cm^3. Find the volume of the large can.

First find the similarity ratio $a : b$.

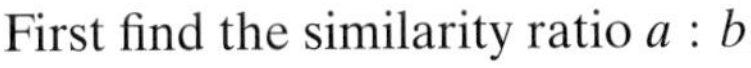

$\frac{a^2}{b^2} = \frac{1019}{425}$ **The ratio of the surface areas is $a^2 : b^2$.**

$\frac{a}{b} = \frac{\sqrt{1019}}{\sqrt{425}}$ **Take square roots.**

Reading Math

V_{large} and V_{small} are the volumes of the large and small cans, respectively.

Use the similarity ratio to find the volume.

$\frac{V_{large}}{V_{small}} = \frac{\sqrt{1019}^3}{\sqrt{425}^3}$ **The ratio of the volumes is $a^3 : b^3$.**

$\frac{V_{large}}{1157} = \frac{\sqrt{1019}^3}{\sqrt{425}^3}$ **Substitute 1157 for V_{small}.**

$V_{large} = 1157 \cdot \frac{\sqrt{1019}^3}{\sqrt{425}^3}$ **Solve for V_{large}.**

$V_{large} \approx 4295$ **Use a calculator.**

The volume of the large paint can is about 4295 cm^3.

✓ Check Understanding **3** The volumes of two similar solids are 128 m^3 and 250 m^3. The surface area of the larger solid is 250 m^2. What is the surface area of the smaller solid?

The weights of solid objects made of the same material are proportional to their volumes.

4 EXAMPLE **Real-World Connection**

Paperweights A marble paperweight shaped like a pyramid weighs 0.15 lb. How much does a similarly shaped marble paperweight weigh if each dimension is three times as large?

The similarity ratio is 1 : 3. The ratio of the volumes, and hence the ratio of the weights, is $1^3 : 3^3$, or 1 : 27.

$\frac{1}{27} = \frac{0.15}{x}$ **Let x = the weight of the larger paperweight.**

$x = 27(0.15)$ **Use the Cross Product Property.**

$x = 4.05$

The larger paperweight weighs about 4 lb.

Check Understanding 4 Find the weight of a marble bead that is similar to the paperweight in Example 4 but has dimensions half as large.

EXERCISES

For more practice, see *Extra Practice*.

Practice and Problem Solving

A Practice by Example

Example 1 (page 566)

Are the two figures similar? If so, give the similarity ratio.

1.

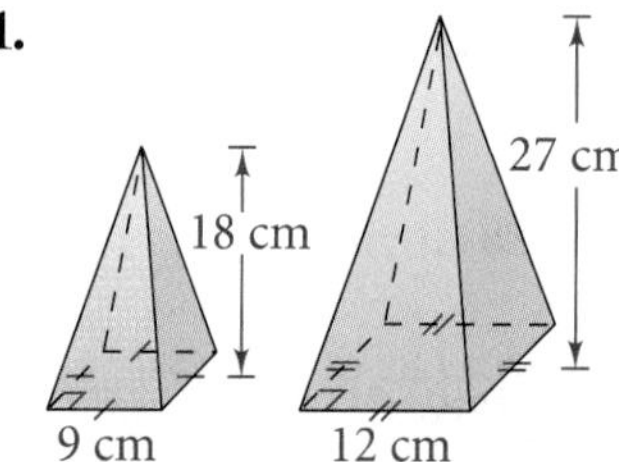

2.

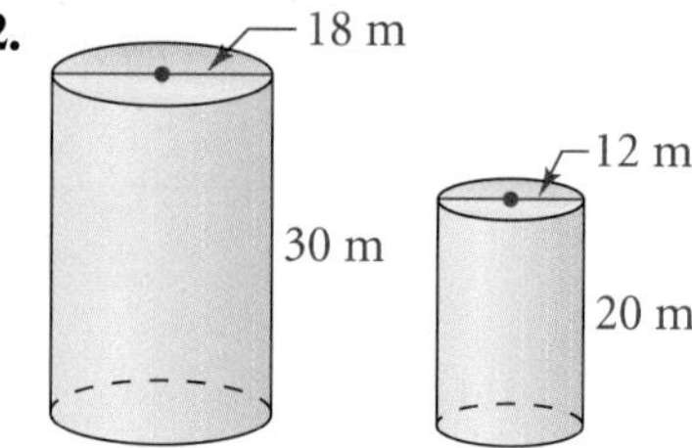

3.

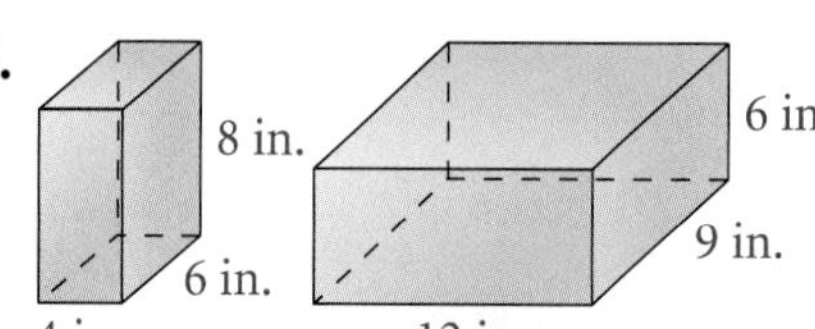

4.

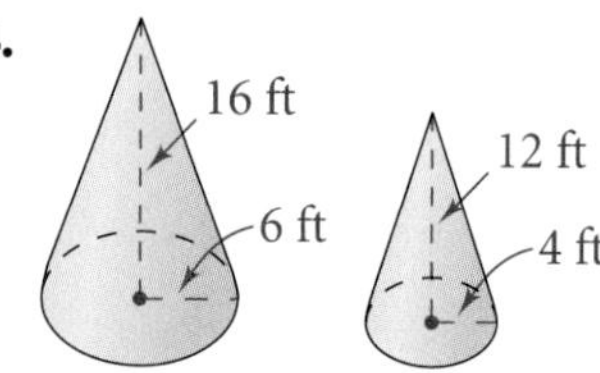

5. two cubes, one with 3-cm edges, the other with 4.5-cm edges

6. a cylinder and a square prism each with 3-in. radii and 1-in. heights

Example 2 (page 567)

Each pair of figures is similar. Use the given information to find the similarity ratio of the smaller figure to the larger figure.

7.

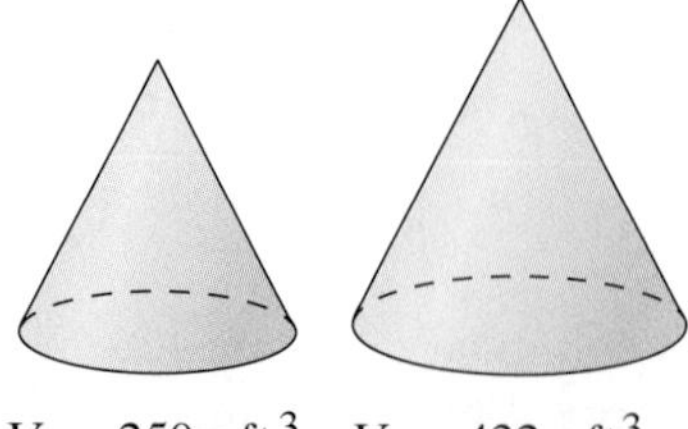

$V = 250\pi \text{ ft}^3$ $V = 432\pi \text{ ft}^3$

8.

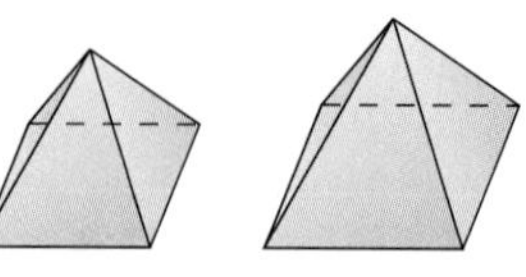

$V = 216 \text{ in.}^3$ $V = 343 \text{ in.}^3$

9.

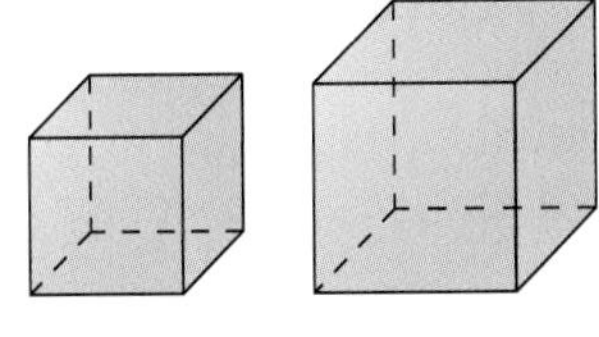

S.A. = 18 m^2 S.A. = 32 m^2

10.

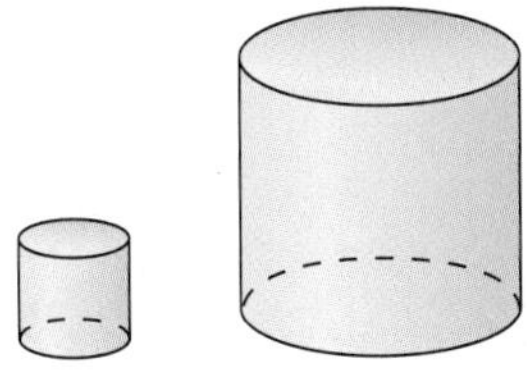

S.A. = 20π yd^2 S.A. = 125π yd^2

Example 3 (page 567)

The surface areas of two similar figures are given. The volume of the larger figure is given. Find the volume of the smaller figure.

11. S.A. = 18 in.^{2}
S.A. = 98 in.^{2}
V = 343 in.^{3}

12. S.A. = 192 m^2
S.A. = 1728 m^2
V = 4860 m^3

13. S.A. = 52 ft^2
S.A. = 208 ft^2
V = 192 ft^3

The volumes of two similar figures are given. The surface area of the smaller figure is given. Find the surface area of the larger figure.

14. V = 27 in.^{3}
V = 125 in.^{3}
S.A. = 63 in.^{2}

15. V = 5 m^3
V = 40 m^3
S.A. = 4 m^2

16. V = 54 yd^3
V = 128 yd^3
S.A. = 18 yd^2

Example 4 (page 568)

17. **Packaging** There are 750 toothpicks in a regular-sized box. If a jumbo box is made by doubling all the dimensions of the regular-sized box, how many toothpicks will the jumbo box hold?

18. **Packaging** A cylinder 4 in. in diameter and 6 in. high holds 1 lb of oatmeal. To the nearest ounce, how much oatmeal will a similar 10-in.-high cylinder hold? (*Hint:* 1 lb = 16 oz)

19. A regular pentagonal solid prism has 9-cm base edges. A larger, similar solid prism of the same material has 36-cm base edges. How does each indicated measurement for the larger prism compare to the same measurement for the smaller prism?
a. the volume **b.** the weight

Apply Your Skills

20. Two similar prisms have heights 4 cm and 10 cm.
a. What is their similarity ratio?
b. What is the ratio of their surface areas?
c. What is the ratio of their volumes?

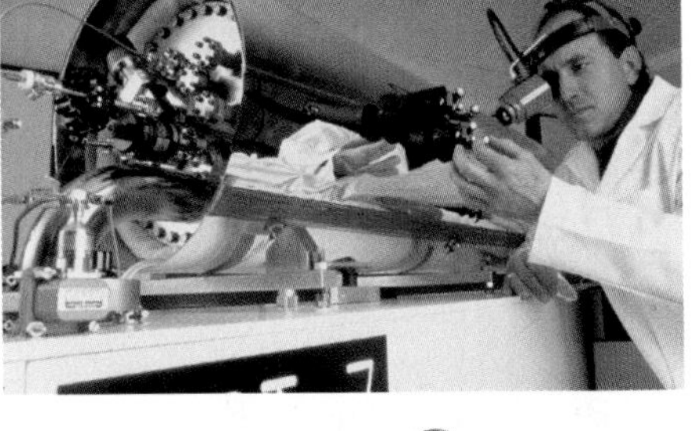

Real-World Connection

The time scale of an atomic clock is based on vibrations of atoms and molecules.

21. **Atomic Clock** A company announced that it had developed the technology to reduce the size of its atomic clock, which is used in electronic devices that transmit data. The company claims that the smaller clock will be similar to the existing clock made of the same material. It will be $\frac{1}{10}$ the size of its existing atomic clocks and $\frac{1}{100}$ the weight. Do these ratios make sense? Explain.

22. Is there a value of x for which the rectangular prisms below are similar? Explain.

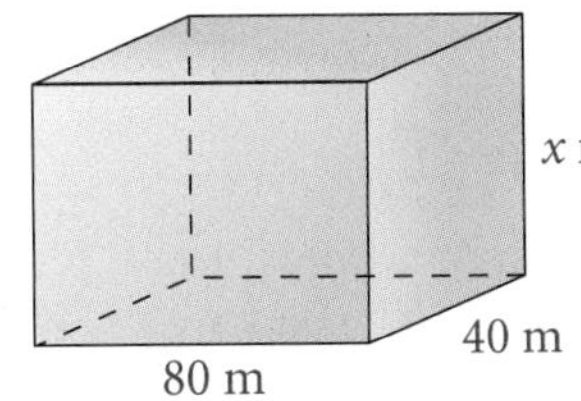

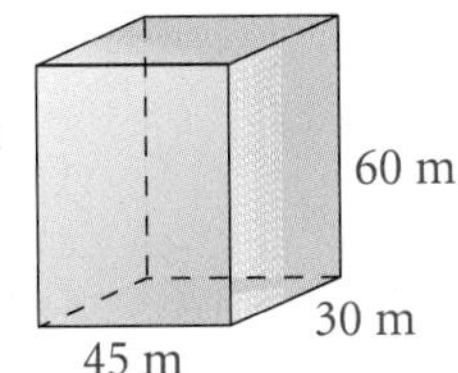

23. The volume of a spherical balloon with radius 3.1 cm is about 125 cm^3. Estimate the volume of a similar balloon with radius 6 cm.

24. **Critical Thinking** A carpenter is making a blanket chest based on an antique chest. Both chests have the shape of a rectangular prism. The length, width, and height of the new chest will all be 4 in. greater than the respective dimensions of the antique. Will the chests be similar? Explain.

25. **Writing** Explain why all spheres are similar.

26. Two similar pyramids have lateral area 8 ft^2 and 18 ft^2. The volume of the smaller pyramid is 32 ft^3. Find the volume of the larger pyramid.

27. The volumes of two spheres are 729 in.^{3} and 27 in.^{3}.
   a. Find the ratio of their radii.
   b. Find the ratio of their surface areas.

28. The volumes of two similar pyramids are 1331 cm^3 and 2744 cm^3.
   a. Find the ratio of their heights.
   b. Find the ratio of their surface areas.

29. A clown's face on a balloon is 4 in. high when the balloon holds 108 in.^{3} of air. How much air must the balloon hold for the face to be 8 in. high?

Copy and complete the table for the similar solids.

	Similarity Ratio	Ratio of Surface Areas	Ratio of Volumes
30.	1 : 2	■ : ■	■ : ■
31.	3 : 5	■ : ■	■ : ■
32.	■ : ■	49 : 81	■ : ■
33.	■ : ■	■ : ■	125 : 512

34. **Literature** In *Gulliver's Travels* by Jonathan Swift, Gulliver first traveled to Lilliput. The Lilliputian average height was one twelfth of Gulliver's height.
   a. How many Lilliputian coats could be made from the material in Gulliver's coat? *(Hint:* Use the ratio of surface areas.)
   b. How many Lilliputian meals would be needed to make a meal for Gulliver? (*Hint:* Use the ratio of volumes.)

C Challenge

35. **Indirect Reasoning** Some stories say that Paul Bunyan was ten times as tall as the average human. Assume that Paul Bunyan's bone structure was proportional to that of ordinary people.
   a. Strength of bones is proportional to the area of their cross section. How many times as strong as the average person's bones would Paul Bunyan's bones be?
   b. Weights of objects made of like material are proportional to their volumes. How many times the average person's weight would Paul Bunyan's weight be?
   c. Human leg bones can support about 6 times the average person's weight. Use your answers to parts (a) and (b) to explain why Paul Bunyan could not exist with a bone structure that was proportional to that of ordinary people.

36. Square pyramids A and B are similar. In pyramid A, each base edge is 12 cm. In pyramid B, each base edge is 3 cm and the volume is 6 cm^3.
   a. Find the volume of pyramid A.
   b. Find the ratio of the surface area of A to the surface area of B.
   c. Find the surface area of each pyramid.

Need Help?

A frustum of a cone is defined on page 556.

37. The cone is cut by a plane parallel to its base. The small cone on top is similar to the large cone. The ratio of the slant heights of the cones is 1 : 2. Find the ratio indicated.

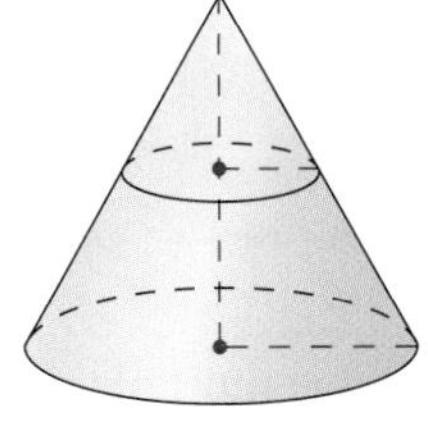

a. the surface area of the large cone to that of the small cone; the volume of the large cone to that of the small cone

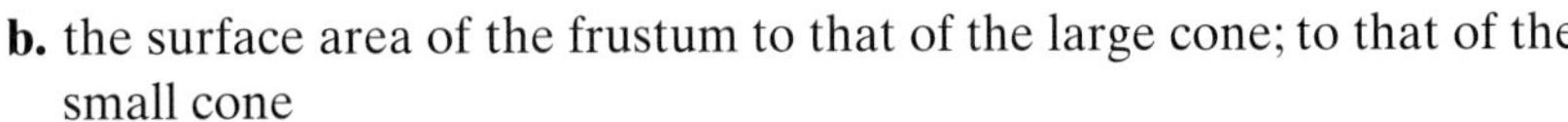

b. the surface area of the frustum to that of the large cone; to that of the small cone

c. the volume of the frustum to that of the large cone; to that of the small cone

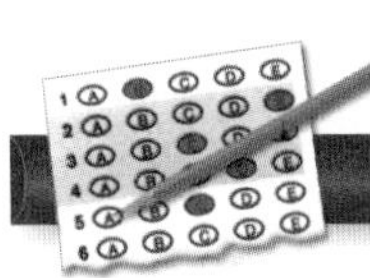

Standardized Test Prep

Gridded Response

38. The slant heights of two similar pyramids are in the ratio 1 : 5. The volume of the smaller pyramid is 60 m^3. What is the volume in cubic meters of the larger pyramid?

39. A lawn chair weighs 8 lb. A child's lawn chair has dimensions exactly one half those of the larger chair. How many pounds does the child's chair weigh?

40. A model of a historical home has dimensions that are one fifteenth the dimensions of the actual home. The area of a window in the model is 2 cm^2. What is the area in square centimeters of the corresponding window in the actual home?

41. The volumes of two similar rectangular prisms are 64 cm^3 and 1000 cm^3. The surface area of the smaller figure is 112 cm^2. What is the surface area in square centimeters of the larger figure?

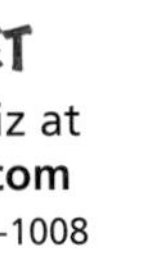

Take It to the NET

Online lesson quiz at **www.PHSchool.com**

Web Code: afa-1008

42. The surface areas of two similar cylinders are 54 ft^2 and 96 ft^2. The volume of the smaller cylinder is 216 ft^3. What is the volume in cubic feet of the larger cylinder?

Mixed Review

Lesson 10-7

43. Sports Equipment The circumference of a regulation basketball is between 75 cm and 78 cm. What are the smallest and the largest surface areas that a basketball can have? Give your answers to the nearest whole unit.

Find the volume and surface area of each sphere to the nearest tenth.

44. diameter = 6 in. **45.** circumference = 2.5π m **46.** radius = 6 in.

Lesson 8-4

47. The altitude to the hypotenuse of a right triangle ABC divides the hypotenuse into 12-mm and 16-mm segments. Find the length of each of the following.

a. the altitude to the hypotenuse

b. the shorter leg of $\triangle ABC$

c. the longer leg of $\triangle ABC$

Lesson 8-1 x^2 **Algebra** **Solve each proportion.**

48. $\frac{25}{16} = \frac{x}{16}$ **49.** $\frac{21}{x} = \frac{8}{5}$ **50.** $\frac{3}{8} = \frac{n}{n + 4}$

Test-Taking Strategies: Choosing "Cannot Be Determined"

Some multiple-choice questions do not contain enough information. In such cases, you will not be able to find an answer, and one of the answer choices should be "cannot be determined." If, however, you see "cannot be determined" before reading the question, don't assume that you cannot answer the question. You still have to try to answer it on its own merits.

EXAMPLE

The rectangular prism is inscribed in the cylinder. The diameter and height of the cylinder are both s. What is the ratio of the volume of the prism to the volume of the cylinder?

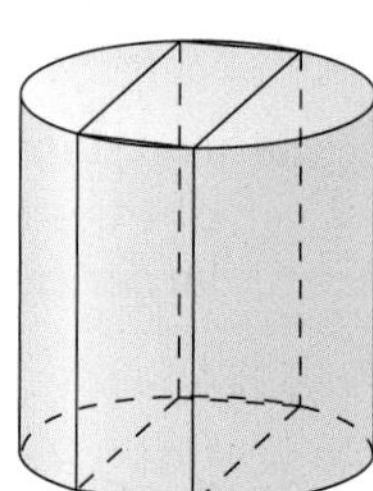

A. $\frac{2}{\pi}$ **B.** $\frac{1}{\pi}$

C. $\frac{1}{2}$ **D.** cannot be determined

To find the ratio of the volumes, you need to find the volume of each solid. The volume of a cylinder is $V = \pi r^2 h$. You know that the height of this cylinder is s and its radius is one half the diameter, or $\frac{s}{2}$. The volume of this cylinder is $V = \pi r^2 h = \pi\left(\frac{s}{2}\right)^2 \cdot s = \frac{\pi s^3}{4}$.

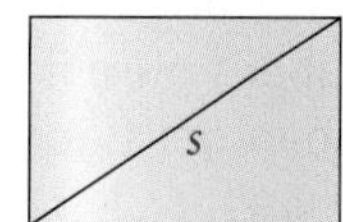

The volume of the prism is $V = Bh$ where B is the area of the base and h is the height. The height of the prism is s, but what is the area of the base? The only thing you know about the base is that it is a rectangle whose diagonal is s. Since the length of the diagonal of a rectangle does not fix the dimensions of the rectangle, there is not enough information about the base to find its area.

There is not enough information to determine the volume of the prism. The correct answer choice is D, "cannot be determined."

EXERCISES

Can the answer to each exercise be determined? If *yes*, state the answer. If *no*, explain.

1. The sum of the circumference and height of a cylinder is 20 cm. What is the surface area of the cylinder?
2. **a.** The surface area of a cylinder is 44 cm^2. What is the volume of the cylinder?
   b. The surface area of a sphere is 44 cm^2. What is the volume of the sphere?
3. A polyhedron has 10 faces and the number of edges is 8 more than the number of vertices. What is the number of edges of the polyhedron?
4. An equilateral triangle has an area of 100 $in.^2$. What is the length of a side?

Chapter Review

Vocabulary

altitude (pp. 528, 530, 537, 539)
base(s) (pp. 528, 530, 537, 539)
center of a sphere (p. 558)
circumference of a sphere (p. 558)
composite space figure (p. 547)
cone (p. 539)
cross section (p. 522)
cube (p. 512)
cylinder (p. 530)
diameter of a sphere (p. 558)
edge (p. 512)
face (p. 512)
foundation drawing (p. 521)
great circle (p. 558)
height (pp. 528, 530, 537, 539)
hemisphere (p. 558)
isometric drawing (p. 520)
lateral area (pp. 528, 530, 537, 539)
lateral faces (pp. 528, 537)
net (p. 512)
oblique cylinder (p. 530)
oblique prism (p. 528)
orthographic drawing (p. 521)
polyhedron (p. 512)
prism (p. 528)
pyramid (p. 537)
radius of a sphere (p. 558)
regular pyramid (p. 537)
right cone (p. 539)
right cylinder (p. 530)
right prism (p. 528)
similar solids (p. 566)
similarity ratio (p. 566)
slant height (p. 537, 539)
sphere (p. 558)
surface area (pp. 528, 530, 538, 539)
vertex (pp. 512, 537, 539)
volume (p. 544)

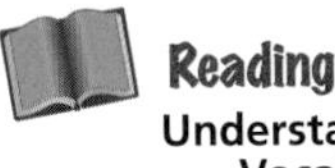

Reading Math
Understanding Vocabulary

Take It to the NET
Online vocabulary quiz at **www.PHSchool.com**
Web Code: afj-1051

Choose the correct term to complete each sentence.

1. A set of points in space equidistant from a given point is called a (*circle, sphere*).
2. A(n) (*orthographic drawing, net*) is a two-dimensional pattern that you can fold to form a three-dimensional figure.
3. A (*pyramid, prism*) is a polyhedron in which one face can be any polygon and the lateral faces are triangles that meet at a common vertex.
4. If you slice a prism with a plane, the intersection of the prism and the plane is a (*lateral area, cross section*) of the prism.
5. In a(n) (*right, oblique*) prism, the lateral faces are rectangles and a lateral edge is an altitude.

Skills and Concepts

10-1 and 10-2 Objectives

- To recognize nets of space figures
- To make isometric and orthographic drawings
- To describe cross sections of three-dimensional figures

A **polyhedron** is a three-dimensional figure whose surfaces are polygons. The polygons are **faces** of the polyhedron. An **edge** is a segment that is the intersection of two faces. A **vertex** is a point where three or more edges intersect. A **net** is a two-dimensional pattern that folds to form a three-dimensional figure.

Draw a net for each three-dimensional figure.

6. 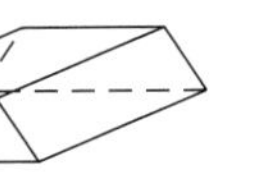

7. 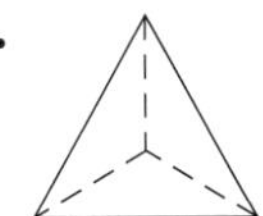

8. 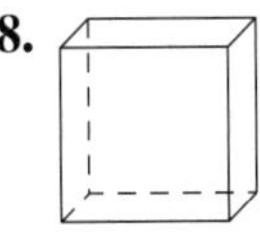

The number of faces (F), vertices (V), and edges (E) of a polyhedron are related by Euler's Formula $F + V = E + 2$.

Use Euler's Formula to find the missing number.

9. $F = 5, V = 5, E = ■$
10. $F = 6, V = ■, E = 12$

An **isometric drawing** is a two-dimensional drawing of a three-dimensional object that shows three sides of the object in one drawing. An **orthographic drawing** shows the top, front, and right-side views of an object. A **foundation drawing** shows the base of a structure and the height of each part. A **cross section** is the intersection of a solid and a plane.

11. a. Use the isometric drawing at the right to make an orthographic drawing.
b. Make a foundation drawing.

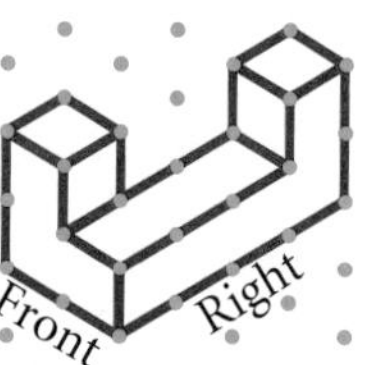

12. Sketch a cube with an equilateral triangle cross section.

10-3 and 10-5 Objectives

- To find the surface area of a prism
- To find the surface area of a cylinder
- To find the volume of a prism
- To find the volume of a cylinder

The **lateral area** of a **right prism** is the product of the perimeter of the base and the height. The **lateral area** of a **right cylinder** is the product of the circumference of the base and the height of the cylinder. The **surface area** of each solid is the sum of the lateral area and the areas of the bases.

The **volume** of a space figure is the space that the figure occupies. Volume is measured in cubic units. The **volume** of a **prism** and the **volume** of a **cylinder** are the product of the area of a base and the height of the solid.

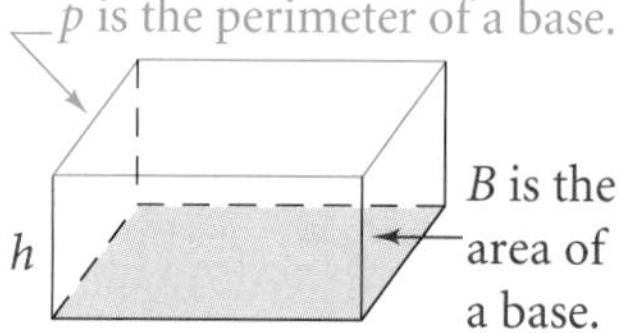

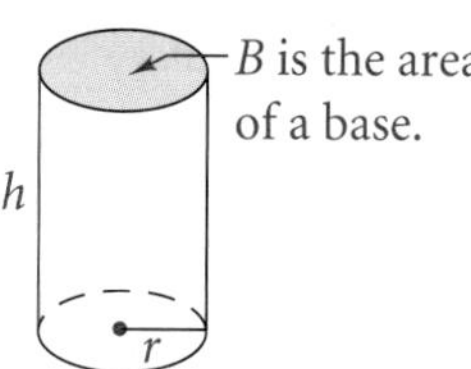

L.A. (prism) $= ph$
S.A. $=$ L.A. $+ 2B$
$V = Bh$

L.A. (cylinder) $= 2\pi rh$ or πdh
S.A. $=$ L.A. $+ 2B$
$V = Bh$

Find the surface area and volume of each figure. Leave your answers in terms of π.

13.

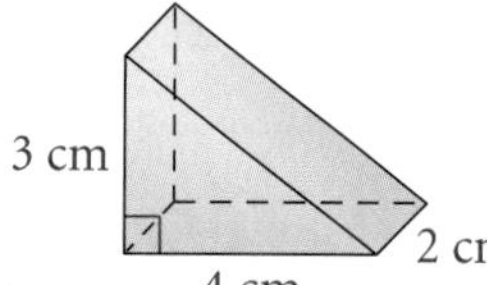

14.

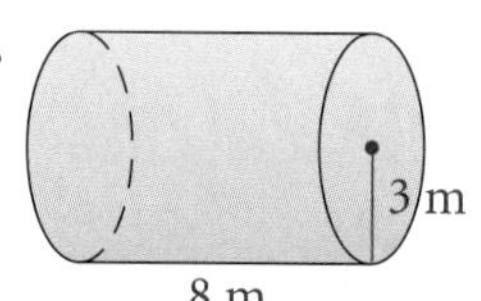

15.

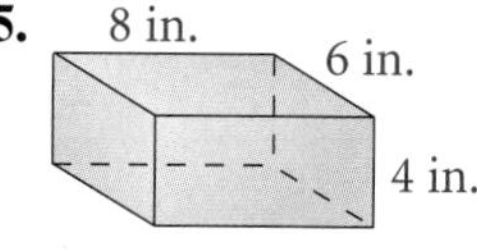

10-4 and 10-6 Objectives

- To find the surface area of a pyramid
- To find the surface area of a cone
- To find the volume of a pyramid
- To find the volume of a cone

The **lateral area** of a **regular pyramid** is half the product of the perimeter of the base and the slant height.

The **surface area** of a pyramid is the sum of the lateral area and the area of the base.

The **volume** of a pyramid is one third the product of the area of the base and the height of the solid.

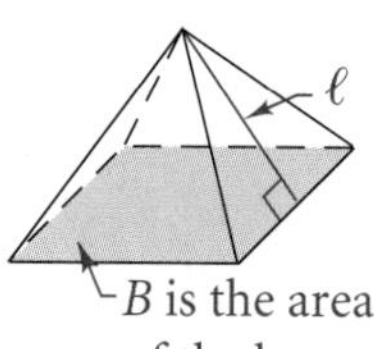

L.A. (pyramid) $= \frac{1}{2}p\ell$
S.A. $=$ L.A. $+ B$
$V = \frac{1}{3}Bh$

The **lateral area** of a **right cone** is half the product of the circumference of the base and the slant height.

The **surface area** of a cone is the sum of the lateral area and the area of the base.

The **volume** of a cone is one third the product of the area of the base and the height of the solid.

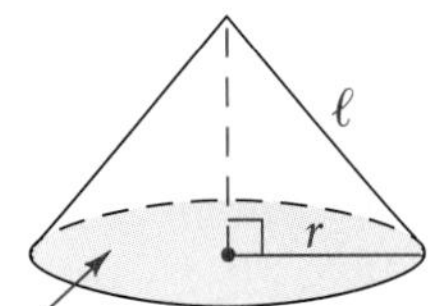

B is the area of the base.

$$\text{L.A. (cone)} = \pi r \ell$$

$$\text{S.A.} = \text{L.A.} + B$$

$$V = \frac{1}{3}Bh$$

Find the surface area and volume of each figure. Leave your answers in terms of π.

16.
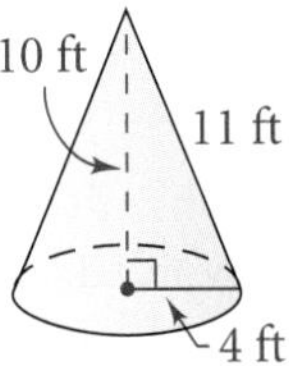

17.
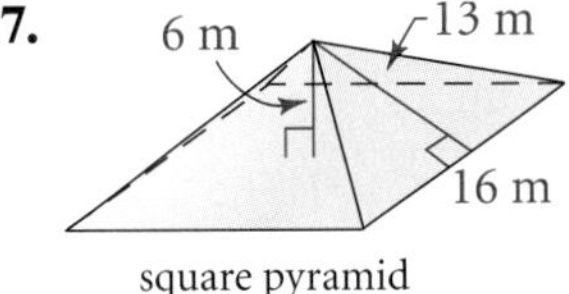

square pyramid

18.
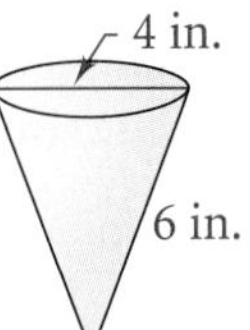

10-7 Objectives

▼ To find the surface area and volume of a sphere

The **surface area of a sphere** is four times the product of π and the square of the radius of the sphere. The **volume of a sphere** is $\frac{4}{3}$ the product of π and the cube of the radius of the sphere.

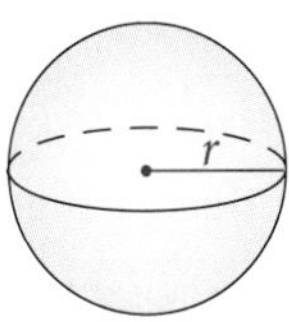

Find the surface area and volume of a sphere with the given radius or diameter. Round answers to the nearest tenth.

19. $r = 5$ in. **20.** $d = 7$ cm **21.** $d = 4$ ft **22.** $r = 0.8$ ft

23. Sports Equipment The circumference of a lacrosse ball is 8 in. Find its volume to the nearest tenth of a cubic inch.

10-8 Objectives

▼ To find relationships between the ratios of the areas and volumes of similar solids

Similar solids have the same shape and all their corresponding dimensions are proportional.

If the **similarity ratio** of two similar solids is $a : b$, then the ratio of their corresponding surface areas is $a^2 : b^2$, and the ratio of their volumes is $a^3 : b^3$.

24. Open-Ended Sketch two similar solids whose surface areas are in the ratio 16 : 25. Include dimensions.

For each pair of similar solids, find the ratio of the volume of the first figure to the volume of the second.

25.
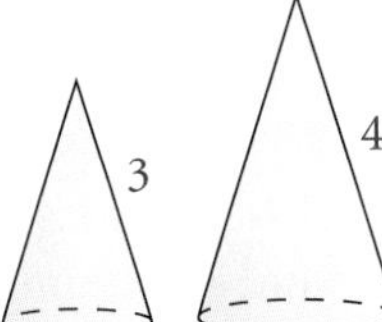

26. 12 9

Chapter Test

Draw a net for each figure. Label the net with appropriate dimensions.

1.

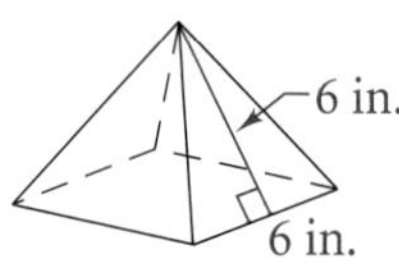

2.

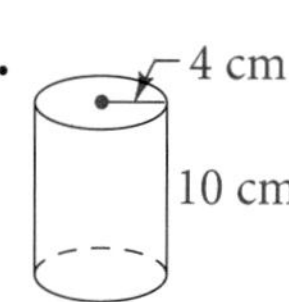

Use the foundation drawing at the right for Exercises 3 and 4.

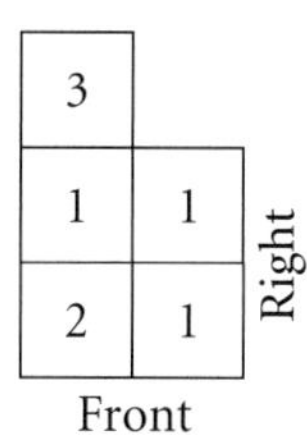

3. Create an isometric drawing.

4. Create an orthographic drawing.

5. Find the number of edges in a pyramid with seven faces.

Describe the cross section formed in each diagram.

6.

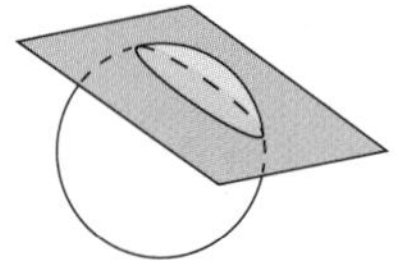

7.

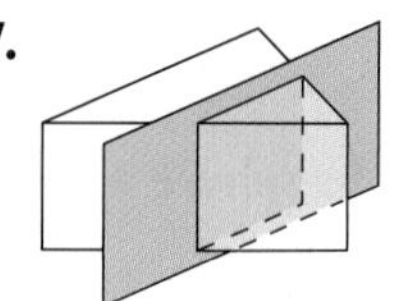

Aviation **The "black box" data recorders on commercial airliners are rectangular prisms.**

8. The base of a recorder is 15 in. by 8 in. Its height ranges from 15 in. to 22 in. What are the largest and smallest possible volumes for the recorder?

9. New flight data recorders are smaller and record more data. A new recorder might be 8 in. by 8 in. by 13 in. What is its volume?

Find the volume and surface area of each figure to the nearest tenth.

10.

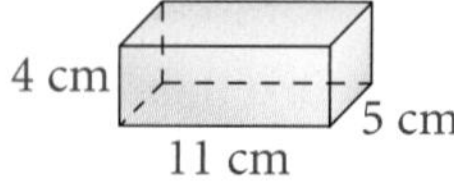

11.

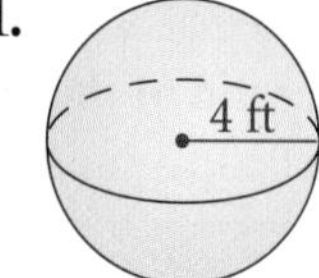

12.

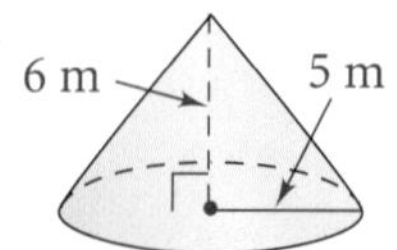

13.

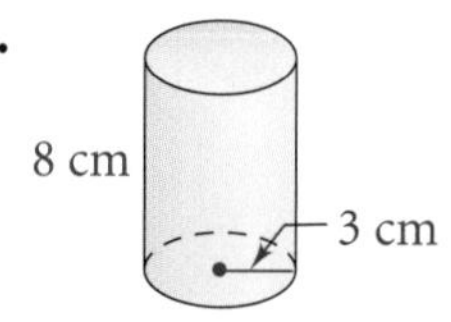

14.

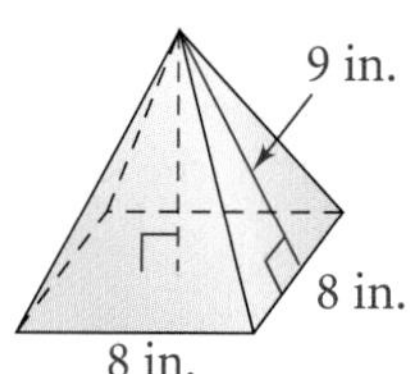

15.

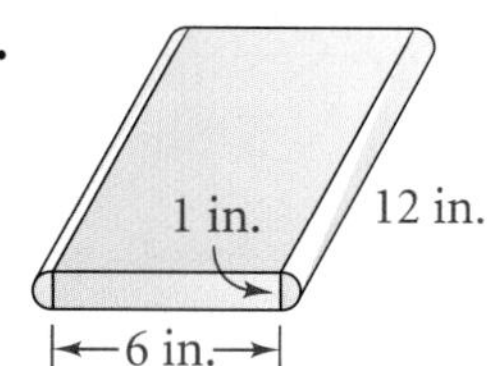

16. **Open-Ended** Draw two different space figures that have a volume of 100 in.^{3}. Label the dimensions of each figure.

17. **Visualization** The triangle is revolved completely about the y-axis.

a. Describe the solid of revolution that is formed.

b. Find its lateral area and volume in terms of π.

18. **Painting** The floor of a bedroom is 12 ft by 15 ft and the walls are 7 ft high. One gallon of paint covers about 450 ft^2. How many gallons of paint do you need to paint the walls of the bedroom?

19. List these space figures in order from the one with least volume to the one with greatest volume.

A. cube with an edge of 5 cm

B. cylinder with radius 4 cm and height 4 cm

C. square pyramid with base sides of 6 cm and height 6 cm

D. cone with radius 4 cm and height 9 cm

E. rectangular prism with a 5 cm-by-5 cm base and height 6 cm

20. **Writing** Describe a real-world situation in which you would need to know the volume of an object. Then describe another situation in which you would need to know the lateral area of an object.

21. The two solids are similar. Find the ratio of the volume of the first figure to the volume of the second.

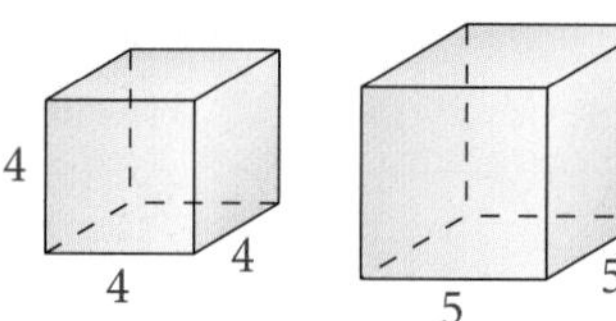

22. The volumes of two spheres are 327π mm^3 and 8829π mm^3. What is the ratio of their surface areas?

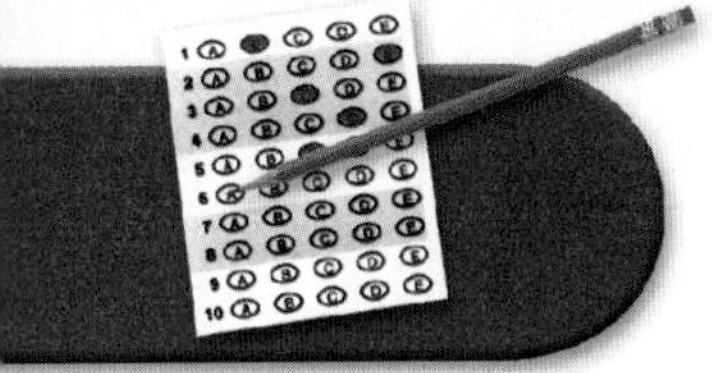

Standardized Test Prep

Multiple Choice

For Exercises 1–7, choose the correct letter.

1. One leg of an isosceles right triangle is 3 in. long. What is the length of the hypotenuse?
   A. 3 in. **B.** $3\sqrt{2}$ in. **C.** $3\sqrt{3}$ in. **D.** 6 in.

2. What is the ratio of the volumes of similar solids whose similarity ratio is 4 : 9?
   F. 2 : 3 **G.** 8 : 27 **H.** 16 : 81 **I.** 64 : 729

3. What is the most precise name of the figure?

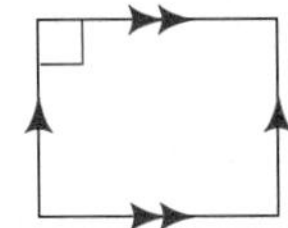

   A. quadrilateral **B.** parallelogram
   C. rectangle **D.** square

4. For what value of x will the two triangles be similar?

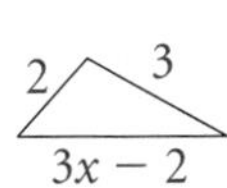

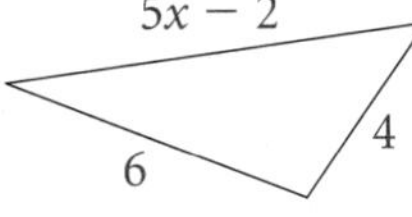

   F. 10 **G.** 8 **H.** 4 **I.** 2

5. What is the surface area of the cylinder?

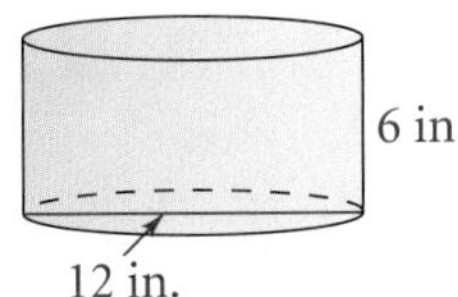

   A. 96π in.^{2} **B.** 144π in.^{2}
   C. 192π in.^{2} **D.** 216π in.^{2}

6. Find the surface area of a sphere with radius 6 in.
   F. 36π in.^{2} **G.** 144π in.^{2}
   H. 216π in.^{2} **I.** 288π in.^{2}

7. Which ordered pair describes the vector?
   A. $\langle 50\sqrt{2}, 50\rangle$
   B. $\langle 50, 50\sqrt{2}\rangle$
   C. $\langle 50, 50\sqrt{3}\rangle$
   D. $\langle 50\sqrt{3}, 50\rangle$

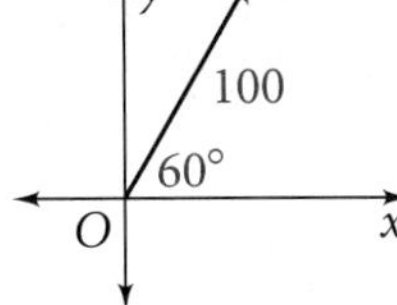

Quantitative Comparison

Compare the boxed quantity in Column A with the boxed quantity in Column B. Choose the best answer.

A. The quantity in Column A is greater.
B. The quantity in Column B is greater.
C. The two quantities are equal.
D. The relationship cannot be determined from the information given.

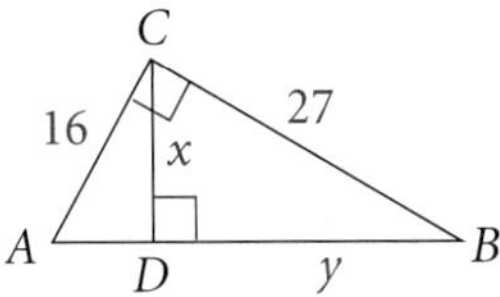

	Column A	Column B
8.	x	y
9.	$m\angle ACD$	$m\angle B$

Gridded Response

10. Find the area in square centimeters of a regular pentagon with side length 4 cm. Round your answer to the nearest tenth.

Short Response

11. Find the circumference of the circle shown below and then the length of $\widehat{AB}$. Leave your answers in terms of π.

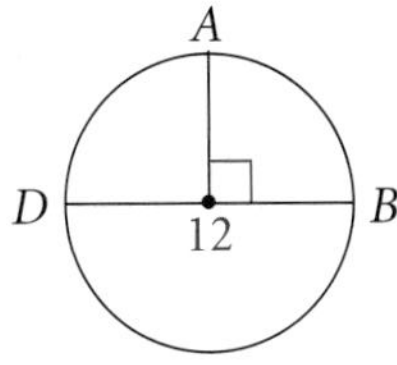

Extended Response

12. Find the area of the shaded figure. Leave your answer in terms of π. Explain your work.

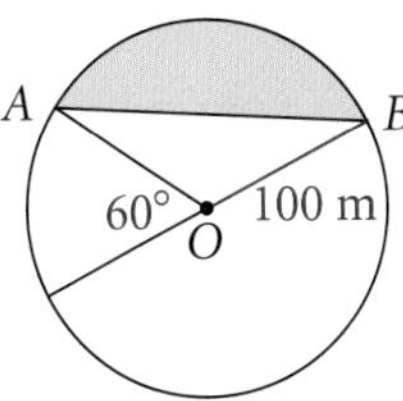

Real-World Snapshots

A Colossal Task

Applying Volume The Statue of Liberty stands in New York harbor, welcoming people to the United States. A similar giant statue once stood at the entrance to the harbor of the Greek island of Rhodes. A stone base and an iron framework supported the bronze statue, which took 12 years to construct. The statue remained standing for only about 66 years, falling to the ground after a violent earthquake weakened its knees.

The Colossus of Rhodes

The Colossus is believed to have included 12.9 tons of bronze and 7.7 tons of iron. Some historians believe that the sculptor modeled the head of the Colossus on that of Alexander the Great.

Activity 1

Materials: ruler, paper and pencil

a. Measure the height of one person attaching bronze plates to the shin of the Colossus. Estimate the probable height of the finished statue.

b. Using the painting of the Colossus (above left) as a guide, sketch the statue. Use proportions to determine at least eight dimensions on the statue. Add these dimensions to your sketch.

The Sculptor

Chares of Lindos (in red robes) probably made small models and scaled them up to get correct proportions.

Artist's rendition

Activity 2

a. The dimensions of the larger block are twice the dimensions of the smaller block. Calculate the ratio of the larger block's volume to the smaller block's volume.

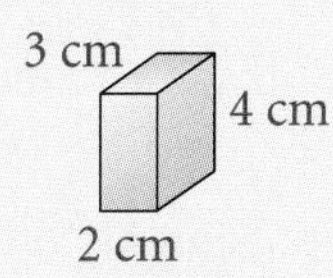

b. Determine what the volume ratio would be if the larger block's dimensions were 10 times the smaller block's dimensions.

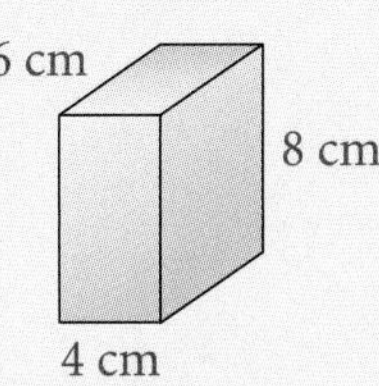

The Statue of Liberty

French sculptor Frederic-Auguste Bartholdi used his mother as the model for the Statue of Liberty. The statue was built in France and shipped to New York in 350 pieces. The seven spikes on the crown symbolize the seven seas and seven continents.

Activity 3

Materials: newspaper or Internet

Suppose the residents in your area have decided to honor you, a friend, or a local hero by building a 100-ft solid-gold statue in the center of town. Draw a sketch of the statue. Estimate the weight and cost.

Hints:

- Use what you learned in Activity 2 to estimate the ratio of the statue's volume to its subject's volume.
- Think about how the weight ratio relates to the volume ratio.
- You'll need to find the density of gold. You'll also need to compare the density of gold to that of a person. Keep in mind that our bodies are mostly water.
- Research the current price of gold.

Light Lady Liberty

From heel to top of head, the Statue of Liberty is about 1.3 times as long as a mature blue whale but only about 1.6 times as heavy. The statue weighs less than you'd think because, rather than being solid, it is a thin layer of copper over an iron framework.

A fully grown blue whale weighs about 143 tons.

Take It to the NET For more information about statues, go to **www.PHSchool.com.**
Web Code: afe-1053

Where You've Been

- In Chapters 1 and 7, you learned how to find the circumference and area of a circle.
- In Chapters 4 and 5, you learned relationships involving congruent triangles, corresponding parts of congruent triangles, and special segments within a triangle.
- In Chapter 7, you learned special properties of right triangles, including the Pythagorean Theorem.

Instant self-check online and on CD-ROM

Diagnosing Readiness

(For help, go to the Lesson in green.)

Solving Equations (Skills Handbook Page 720)

Algebra Solve for x.

1. $\frac{1}{2}(x + 42) = 62$ **2.** $(5 + 3)8 = (4 + x)6$ **3.** $(9 + x)2 = (12 + 4)3$

Distance Formula (Lesson 1-6)

Find the distance between each pair of points.

4. $(13, 7), (6, 31)$ **5.** $(-4, 4), (2, -4)$ **6.** $(-3, -1), (0, 3)$ **7.** $(2\sqrt{3}, 5), (-\sqrt{3}, 2)$

Isosceles and Equilateral Triangles (Lesson 4-5)

Algebra Find the value of x.

8.

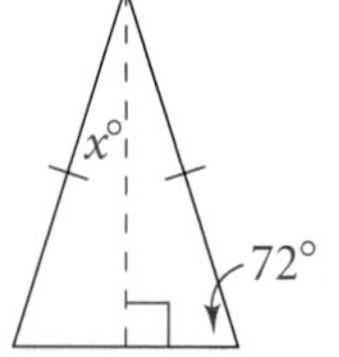

9.

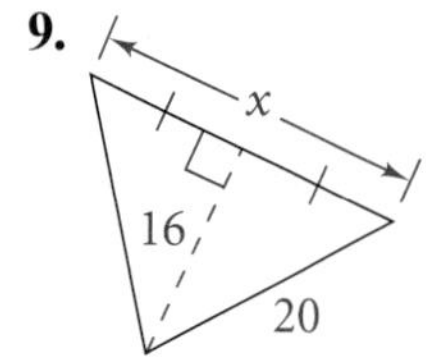

10.

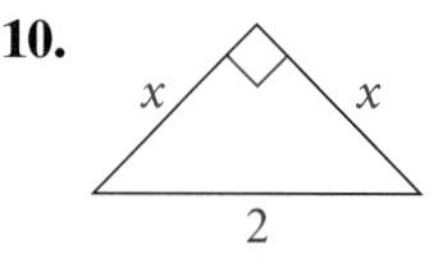

11.

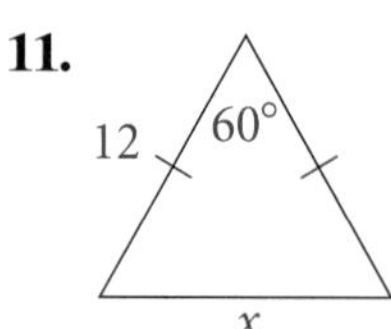

The Pythagorean Theorem (Lesson 7-2)

Algebra Find the value of x. Leave your answer in simplest radical form.

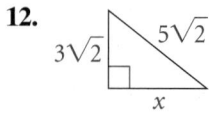

12. $3\sqrt{2}$, $5\sqrt{2}$, x

13.

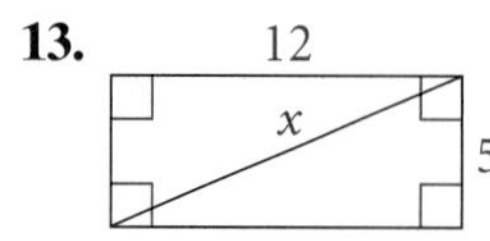

14.

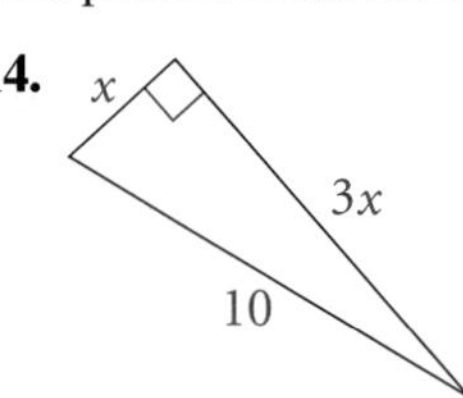

15.

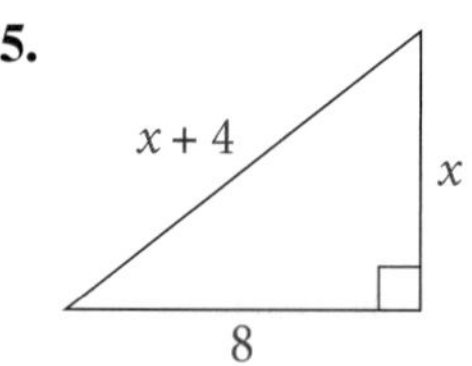

Circles

Chapter 11

LESSONS

Key Vocabulary

- chord (p. 590)
- circumscribed about (p. 585)
- inscribed angle (p. 598)
- inscribed in (p. 585)
- intercepted arc (p. 598)
- locus (p. 621)
- point of tangency (p. 582)
- secant (p. 607)
- standard form of an equation of a circle (p. 615)
- tangent to a circle (p. 582)

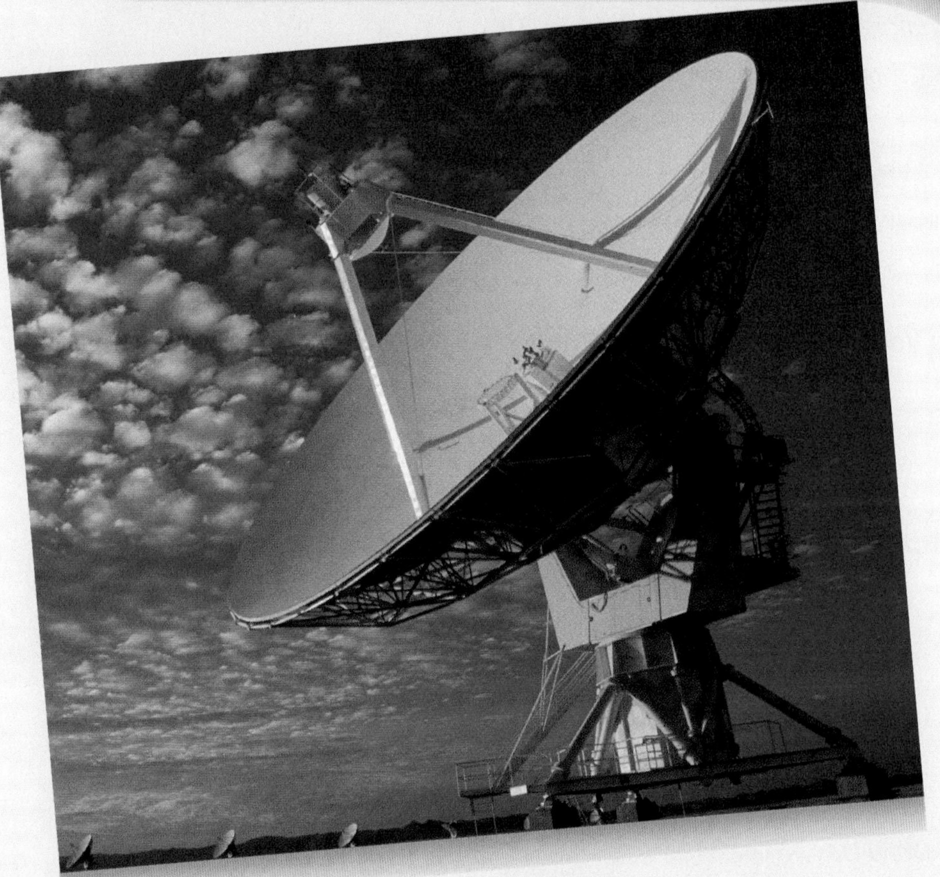

Where You're Going

- In this chapter, you will learn the many properties of circles and of lines and segments that intersect circles.
- When these lines and segments meet to form angles, you will learn how the angles are related to the arcs they intercept on a circle.
- You will also learn how to describe a set of points as a locus.

Real-World Connection Applying what you learn, you will describe on page 625 the locus of points in space that are equidistant from the points of a circle.

Tangent Lines

Lesson Preview

What You'll Learn

To use the relationship between a radius and a tangent

To use the relationship between two tangents from one point

. . . And Why

To find the distance between the centers of two dirt bike gears, as in Example 2

✓ Check Skills You'll Need

(For help, go to Skills Handbook page 716 and Lesson 7-2.)

Find each product.

1. $(p + 3)^2$ **2.** $(w + 10)^2$ **3.** $(m - 2)^2$

x^2 Algebra **Find the value of x. Leave your answer in simplest radical form.**

4.
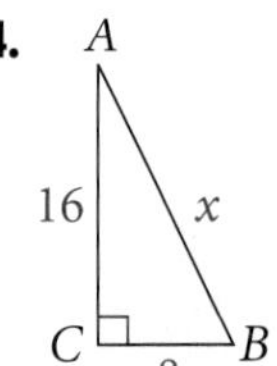

5.
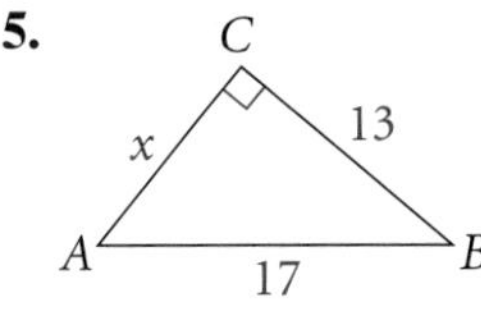

6.
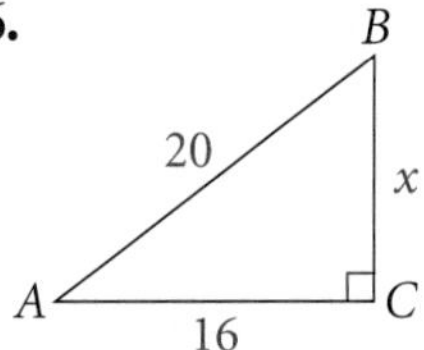

New Vocabulary • tangent to a circle • point of tangency • inscribed in • circumscribed about

Interactive lesson includes instant self-check, tutorials, and activities.

OBJECTIVE 1 Using the Radius-Tangent Relationship

Investigation: Exploring Properties of Tangents

- Use a compass to draw a circle. Label the center O.
- Use a straightedge to draw a line (not a line segment) that intersects the circle in only one point. Label the point A.
- Draw $\overline{OA}$.

1. What seems to be true about the angles with side $\overline{AO}$?
2. Compare your results with others in your class. Make a conjecture about the relationship between a line that intersects a circle in only one point and the radius to that point.

In Chapter 9, you studied the tangent ratio in right triangles. The tangents you will study here relate to circles.

Reading Math

The word "tangent" may refer to a line, ray, or segment.

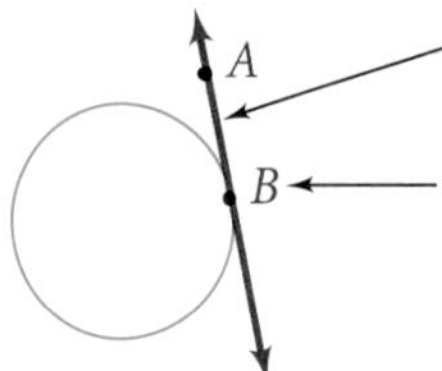

A **tangent to a circle** is a line in the plane of the circle that intersects the circle in exactly one point.

The point where a circle and a tangent intersect is the **point of tangency.**

$\overrightarrow{BA}$ is a tangent ray and $\overline{BA}$ is a tangent segment.

Theorem 11-1 relates a tangent and a radius in a given circle.

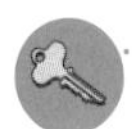

Key Concepts

Theorem 11-1

If a line is tangent to a circle, then the line is perpendicular to the radius drawn to the point of tangency.

$\overleftrightarrow{AB} \perp \overline{OP}$

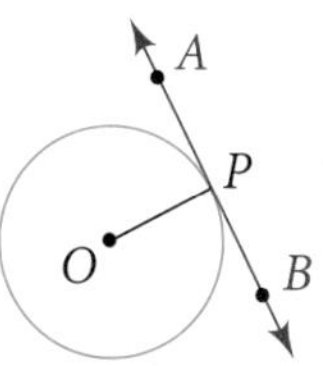

Proof

Indirect Proof of Theorem 11-1

Given: line n is tangent to $\odot O$ at P.

Prove: line $n \perp \overline{OP}$

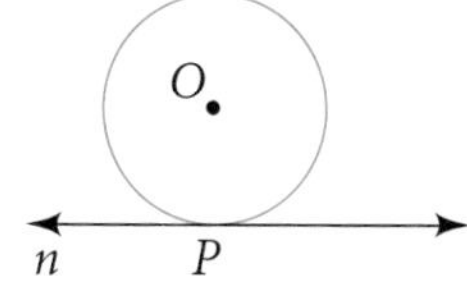

Step 1 Assume the opposite.
Assume that line n is not perpendicular to $\overline{OP}$.

Step 2 Find a contradiction.
If line n is not perpendicular to $\overline{OP}$, some other segment $\overline{OL}$ must be perpendicular to line n. Also there is a point K on $\overrightarrow{PL}$ as shown in the diagram such that $\overline{LK} \cong \overline{LP}$. $\angle OLK$ and $\angle OLP$ are right angles by the definition of perpendicular.
$\angle OLK \cong \angle OLP$ and $\overline{OL} \cong \overline{OL}$.
$\triangle OLK \cong \triangle OLP$ by SAS, so $\overline{OK} \cong \overline{OP}$ by CPCTC. Thus, both K and P are on $\odot O$. For two points of line n to also be on $\odot O$ contradicts the given fact that line n is tangent to $\odot O$ at P.

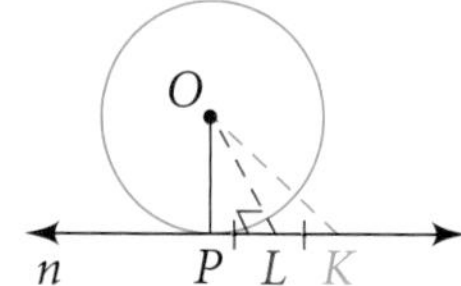

Step 3 State a conclusion.
The assumption that line n is not perpendicular to $\overline{OP}$ must be false. Therefore, line $n \perp \overline{OP}$ must be true.

Real-World Connection

The tire and its shadow suggest a circle and a tangent line.

You can use Theorem 11-1 to solve problems involving tangents to circles.

1 EXAMPLE Finding Angle Measures

Algebra $\overline{ML}$ and $\overline{MN}$ are tangent to $\odot O$. Find the value of x.

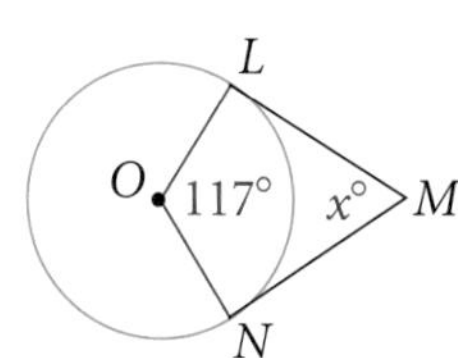

Since $\overline{ML}$ and $\overline{MN}$ are tangent to $\odot O$, $\angle L$ and $\angle N$ are right angles. $LMNO$ is a quadrilateral whose angle measures have a sum of 360.

$$m\angle L + m\angle M + m\angle N + m\angle O = 360$$

$90 + x + 90 + 117 = 360$ **Substitute.**

$297 + x = 360$ **Simplify.**

$x = 63$ **Solve.**

Check Understanding 1 $\overline{ED}$ is tangent to $\odot O$. Find the value of x.

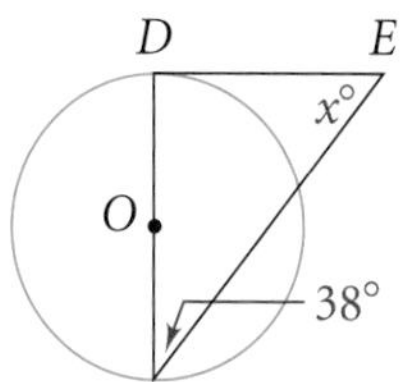

2 EXAMPLE Real-World  Connection

Real-World Connection

This motorcycle and many other two-wheeled vehicles have chain-drive systems like the one shown in Example 2.

Dirt Bikes A dirt bike chain fits tightly around two gears. The chain and gears form a figure like the one at the right. Find the distance between the centers of the gears.

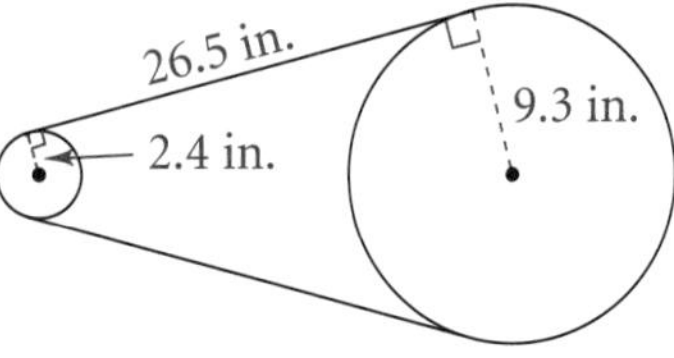

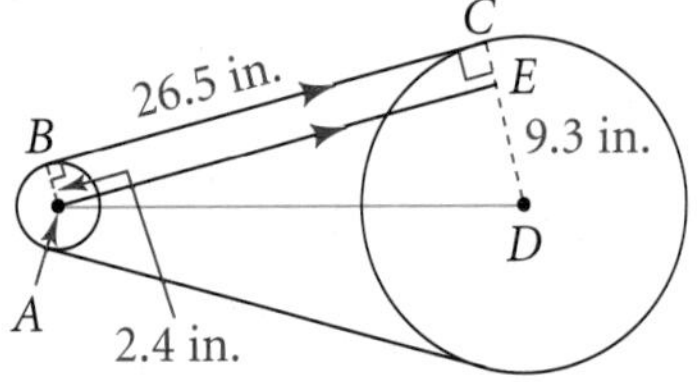

Label the diagram.

Draw $\overline{AE}$ parallel to $\overline{BC}$.

$ABCE$ is a rectangle. $\triangle AED$ is a right triangle with $AE = 26.5$ in. and $ED = 9.3 - 2.4 = 6.9$ in.

$AD^2 = AE^2 + ED^2$ **Pythagorean Theorem**

$AD^2 = 26.5^2 + 6.9^2$ **Substitute.**

$AD^2 = 749.86$ **Simplify.**

$AD \approx 27.383572$ **Use a calculator to find the square root.**

The distance between the centers is about 27.4 in.

Check Understanding 2 A belt fits tightly around two circular pulleys, as shown at the right. Find the distance between the centers of the pulleys.

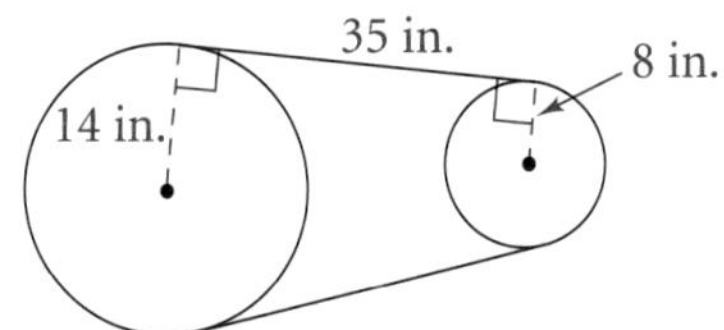

Theorem 11-2 is the converse of Theorem 11-1. You can use it to prove that a segment is tangent to a circle. You can also use Theorem 11-2 to construct a tangent to a circle (see Exercise 32). You will prove this theorem in Exercise 38.

Key Concepts

Theorem 11-2

If a line in the plane of a circle is perpendicular to a radius at its endpoint on the circle, then the line is tangent to the circle.

$\overleftrightarrow{AB}$ is tangent to $\odot O$.

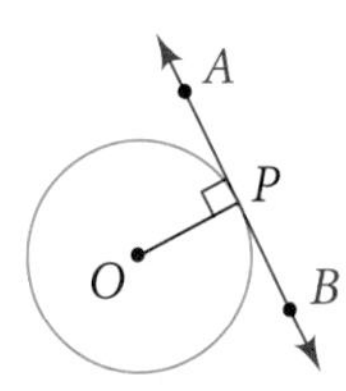

3 EXAMPLE Finding a Tangent

Is $\overline{ML}$ tangent to $\odot N$ at L? Explain.

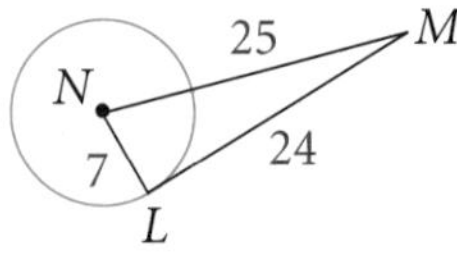

$NL^2 + LM^2 \stackrel{?}{=} NM^2$ **Is $\triangle MLN$ a right triangle?**

$7^2 + 24^2 \stackrel{?}{=} 25^2$ **Substitute.**

$625 = 625$ ✓ **Simplify.**

By the Converse of the Pythagorean Theorem, $\triangle MLN$ is a right triangle with right $\angle L$. Therefore $\overline{ML} \perp \overline{NL}$, and $\overline{ML}$ is tangent to $\odot N$ at L by Theorem 11-2.

Check Understanding 3 If $NL = 4$, $LM = 7$, and $NM = 8$, is $\overline{ML}$ tangent to $\odot N$ at L? Explain.

OBJECTIVE 2

Using Multiple Tangents

In Chapter 5 you learned that a circle is circumscribed about a triangle if all vertices of the triangle lie on the circle. In that case, the triangle is **inscribed in** the circle.

Similarly, when a circle is inscribed in a triangle, as in the diagram at the right, the triangle is **circumscribed about** the circle. Each side of the triangle is tangent to the circle.

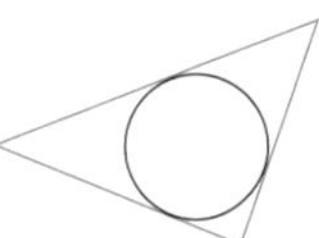

Theorem 11-3 will help you solve problems about polygons that circumscribe circles. You will prove this theorem in Exercise 40.

Key Concepts

Theorem 11-3

The two segments tangent to a circle from a point outside the circle are congruent.

$\overline{AB} \cong \overline{CB}$

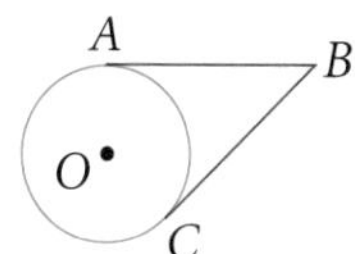

4 EXAMPLE Using Theorem 11-3

The diagram represents a chain drive system on a bicycle. Give a convincing argument that $BC = GF$.

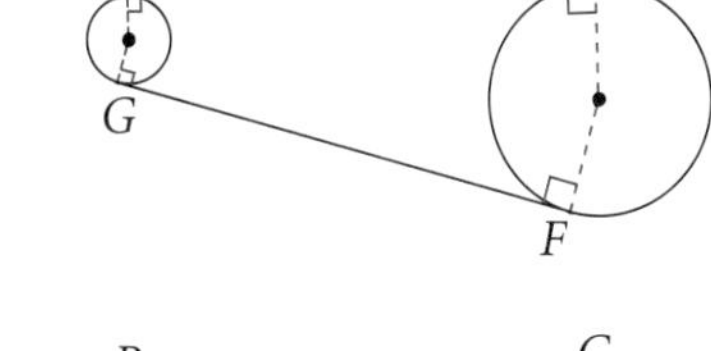

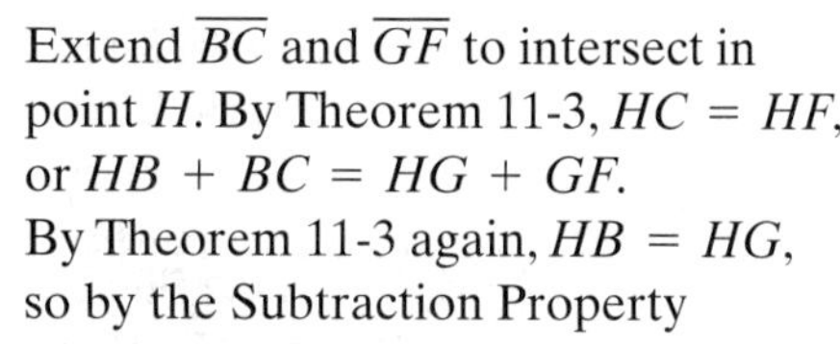

Extend $\overline{BC}$ and $\overline{GF}$ to intersect in point H. By Theorem 11-3, $HC = HF$, or $HB + BC = HG + GF$. By Theorem 11-3 again, $HB = HG$, so by the Subtraction Property of Equality, $BC = GF$.

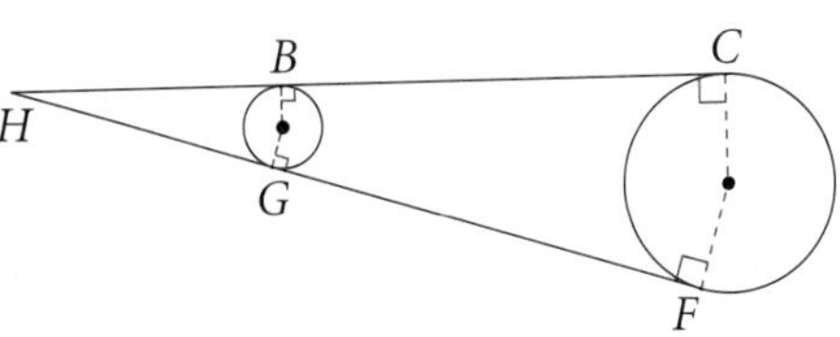

Check Understanding **4** **Critical Thinking** Give a convincing argument that $BC = GF$ above if you know that $\overleftrightarrow{BC}$ and $\overleftrightarrow{GF}$ never intersect.

5 EXAMPLE Circles Inscribed in Polygons

$\odot O$ is inscribed in $\triangle ABC$. Find the perimeter of $\triangle ABC$.

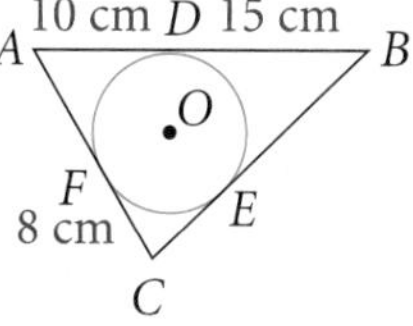

$AD = AF = 10$ cm — **The two segments tangent to a circle from a point outside the circle are congruent.**
$BD = BE = 15$ cm
$CF = CE = 8$ cm

$p = AB + BC + CA$ — **Definition of perimeter p**
$= AD + DB + BE + EC + CF + FA$ — **Segment Addition Postulate**
$= 10 + 15 + 15 + 8 + 8 + 10$ — **Substitute.**
$= 66$

The perimeter is 66 cm.

Check Understanding **5** $\odot O$ is inscribed in $\triangle PQR$. $\triangle PQR$ has a perimeter of 88 cm. Find QY.

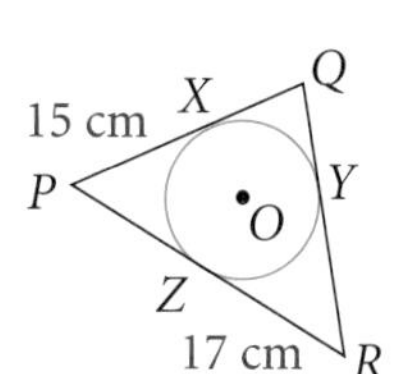

EXERCISES

For more practice, see *Extra Practice.*

Practice and Problem Solving

Practice by Example

Example 1 (page 583)

Algebra **Assume that lines that appear to be tangent are tangent. O is the center of each circle. Find the value of x.**

1.

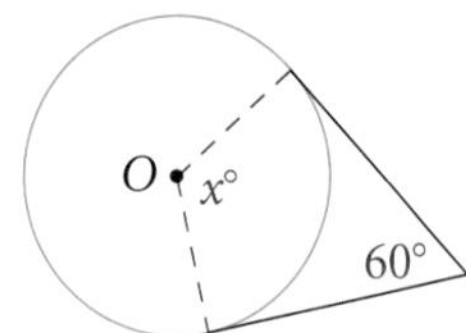

2.

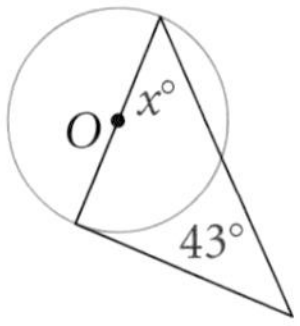

3.

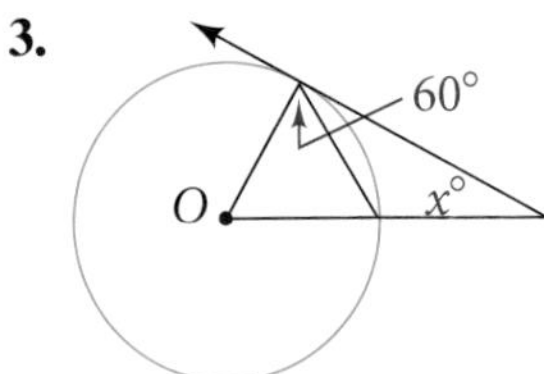

Examples 2, 4 (pages 584, 585)

A belt fits snugly around the two circular pulleys shown.

4. Find the distance between the centers of the pulleys. Round to the nearest hundredth.

5. Give a convincing argument why the belt lengths RS and QP are equal.

Reading Math

$\overline{RS}$ and $\overline{QP}$ are *common tangents.*

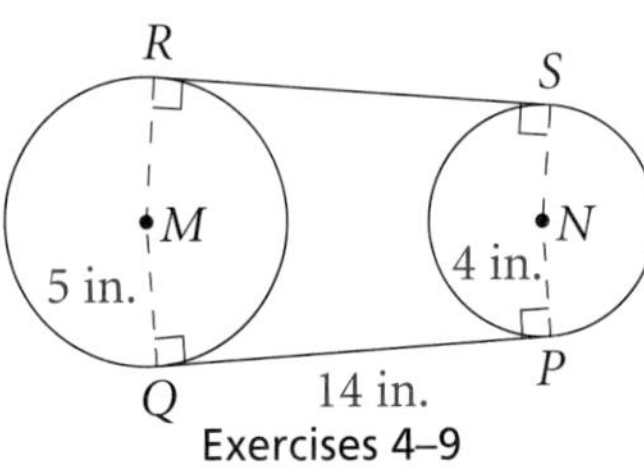

Exercises 4–9

For the pulley system shown, use the lengths given below. Find the missing length to the nearest tenth.

6. $MQ = 10$ cm, $NP = 4$ cm, $QP = 14$ cm, $MN = ■$ cm

7. $MQ = 5$ in., $NP = 4$ in., $QP = 20$ in., $MN = ■$ in.

8. $MQ = 5$ in., $NP = 4$ in., $MN = 14$ in., $QP = ■$ in.

9. $MQ = 10$ cm, $NP = 4$ cm, $MN = 14$ cm, $RS = ■$ cm

Example 3 (page 584)

Determine whether a tangent line is shown in each diagram. Explain.

10.

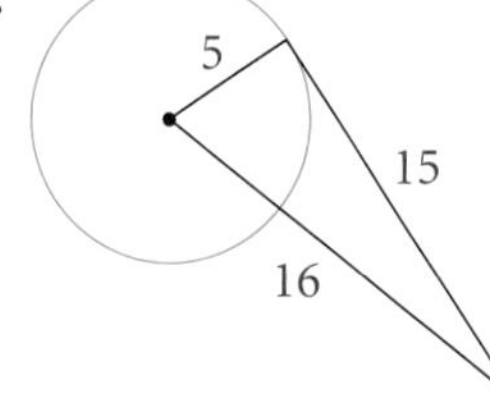

11.

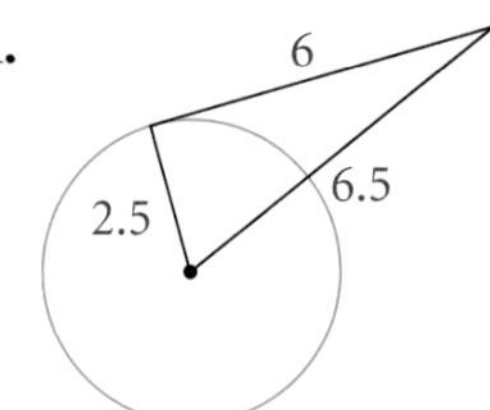

12.

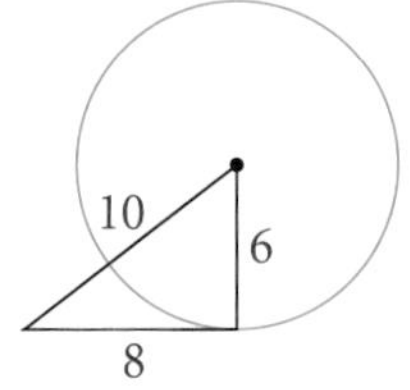

Example 5 (page 585)

Tell whether each polygon is inscribed in or circumscribed about the circle.

13.

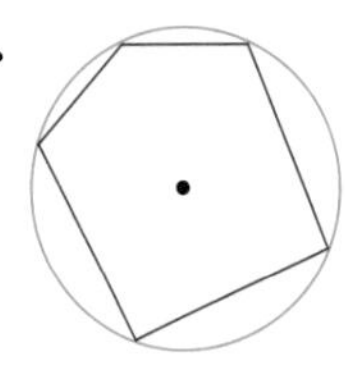

14.

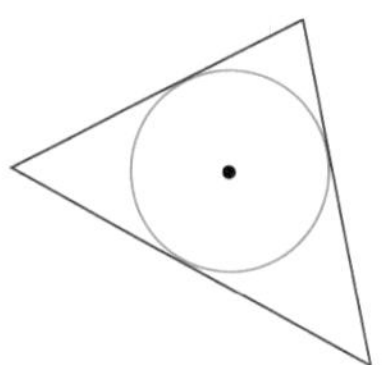

15.

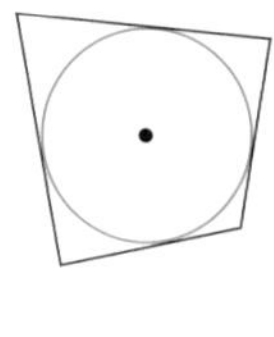

Each polygon circumscribes a circle. Find the perimeter of the polygon.

16.

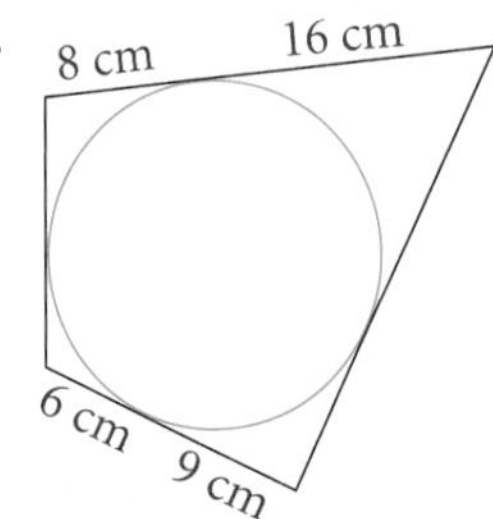

17.

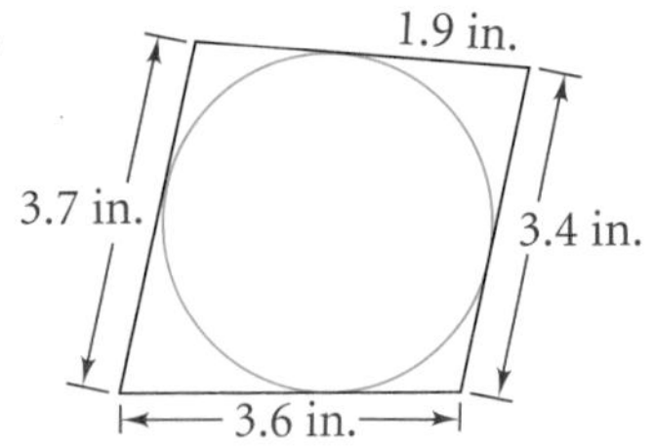

18.

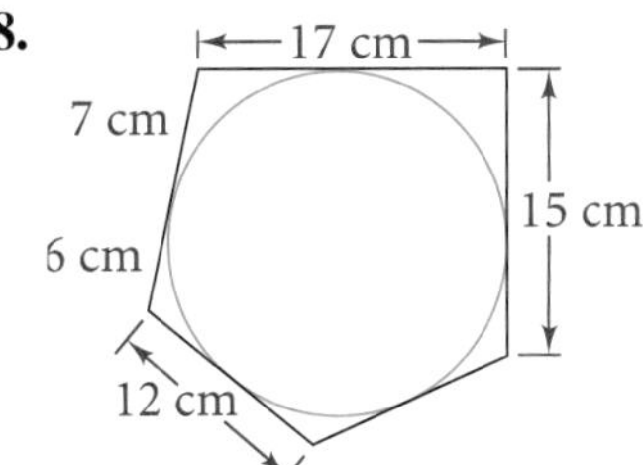

19.

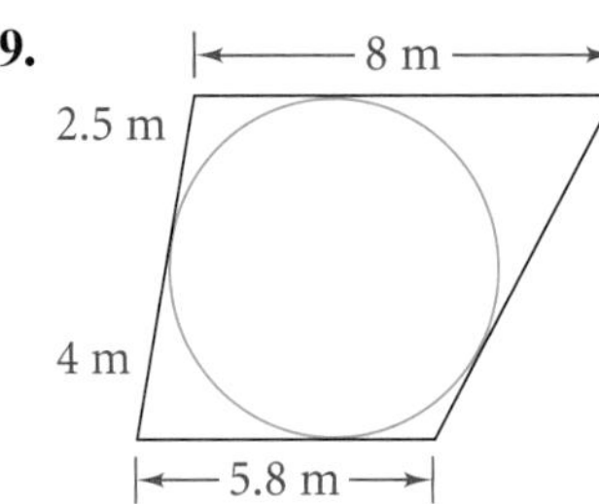

B Apply Your Skills

x^2 Algebra **Assume that lines that appear to be tangent are tangent. *O* is the center of each circle. Find the value of *x* to the nearest tenth.**

20.

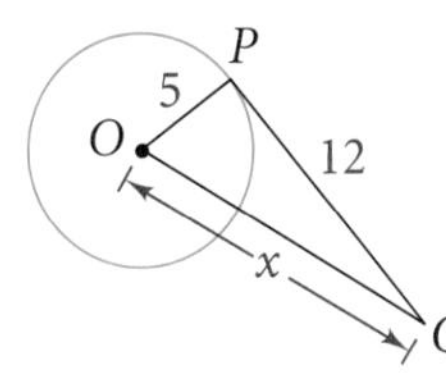

21.

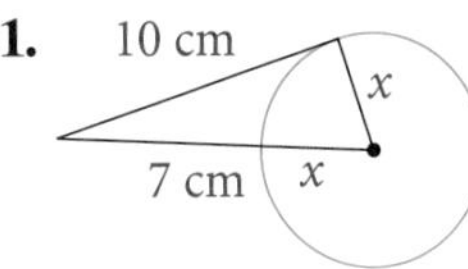

22.

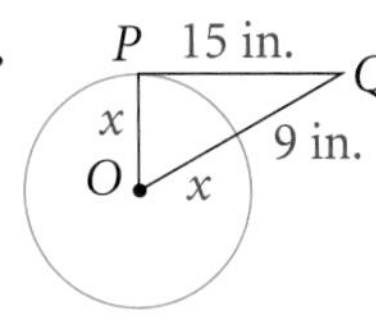

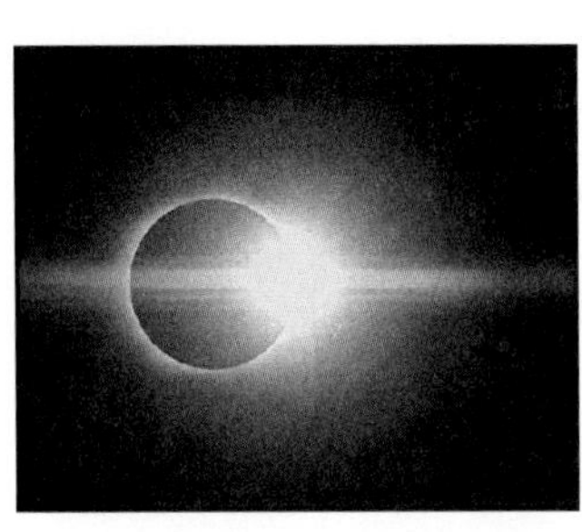

Real-World Connection

This "diamond ring" effect in a solar eclipse may be seen by a person on Earth at the end of a common external tangent of the sun and moon. (See diagram at right.)

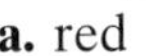

23. **Solar Eclipse** Common tangents to two circles may be *internal* or *external.* If you draw a segment joining the centers of the circles, a common internal tangent will intersect the segment. A common external tangent will not.

For this cross-sectional diagram of the sun, moon, and Earth during a solar eclipse, use the terms above to describe the types of tangents of each color.

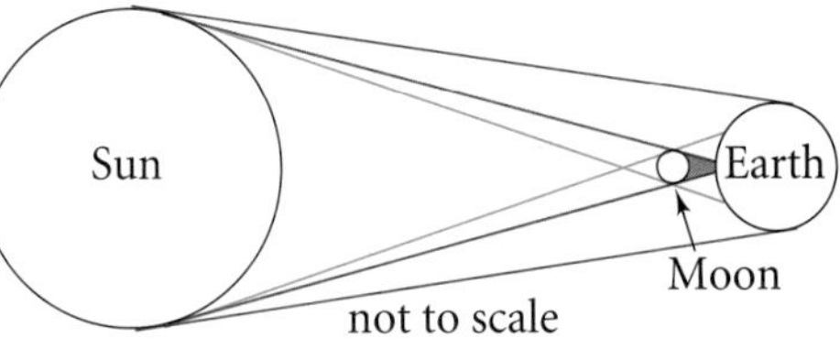

a. red **b.** blue **c.** green

d. Which tangents show the extent on Earth's surface of total eclipse? Of partial eclipse?

e. Reasoning In general, does every pair of circles have common tangents of both types? Explain.

Earth **The circle at the right represents Earth. The radius of Earth is about 6400 km. Find the distance *d* that a person can see on a clear day from each of the following heights *h* above Earth. Round your answer to the nearest tenth of a kilometer.**

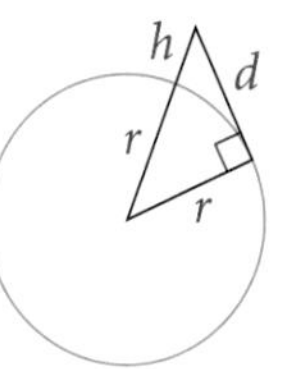

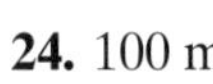

24. 100 m **25.** 500 m **26.** 1 km

27. $\overline{BD}$ and $\overline{CK}$ at the right are diameters of $\odot A$. $\overline{BP}$ and $\overline{QP}$ are tangents to $\odot A$. What is $m\angle CDA$?

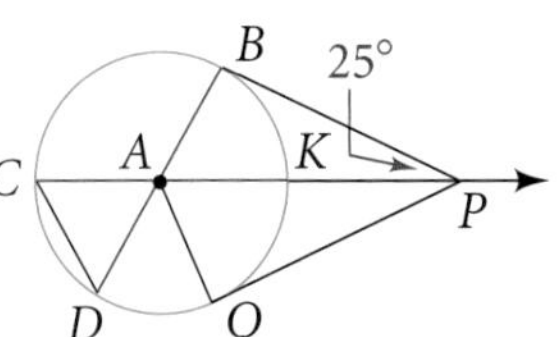

Need Help?

For Exercise 28(a), you must make a sketch for what da Vinci meant, *not* merely for what he said.

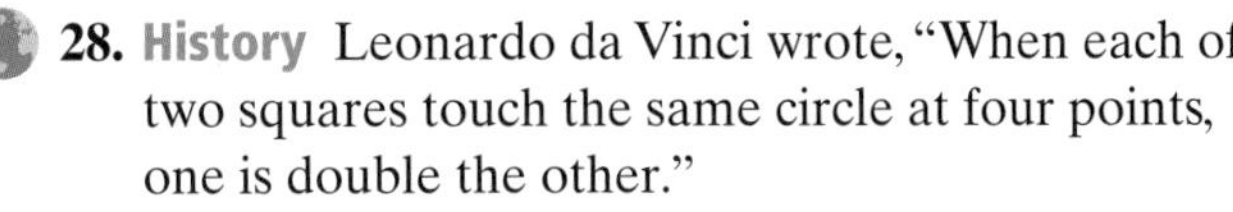

28. History Leonardo da Vinci wrote, "When each of two squares touch the same circle at four points, one is double the other."

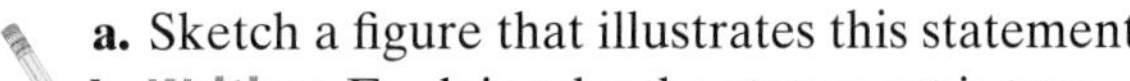

a. Sketch a figure that illustrates this statement.

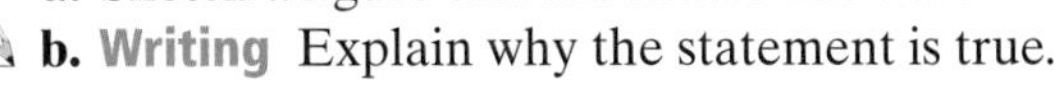

b. Writing Explain why the statement is true.

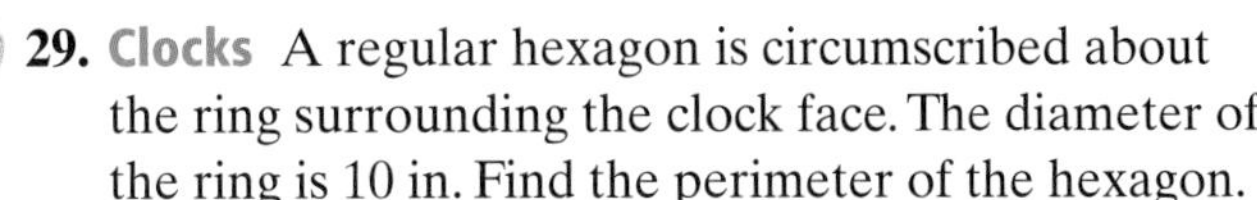

29. Clocks A regular hexagon is circumscribed about the ring surrounding the clock face. The diameter of the ring is 10 in. Find the perimeter of the hexagon.

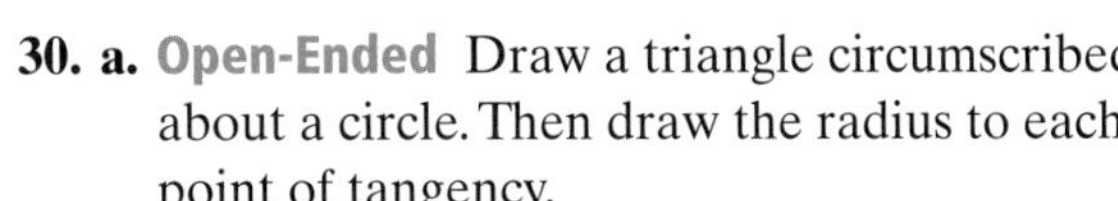

30. a. Open-Ended Draw a triangle circumscribed about a circle. Then draw the radius to each point of tangency.

b. How many quadrilaterals are in the figure you drew in part (a)?

c. Classify these special quadrilaterals. Explain.

31. **Critical Thinking** A nickel, a dime, and a quarter are touching as shown. Tangents are drawn from point A to both sides of each coin. What can you conclude about the four tangent segments? Explain.

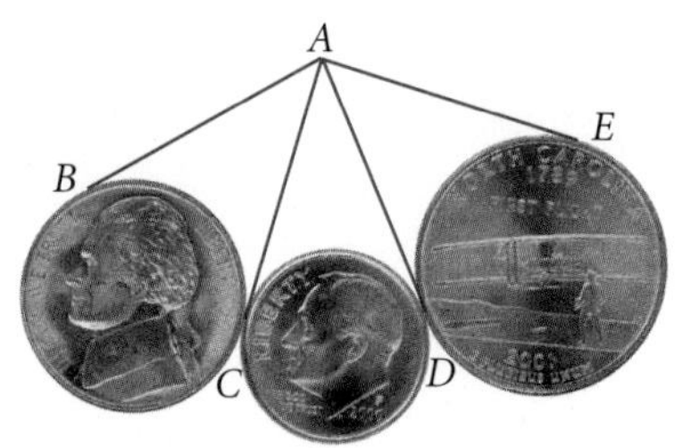

32. **Constructions** Draw a circle. Label the center T. Locate a point on the circle and label it R. Construct a tangent to $\odot T$ at R.

$\overline{AC}$ is tangent to $\odot O$ at A, and $m\angle 1 = 70$.

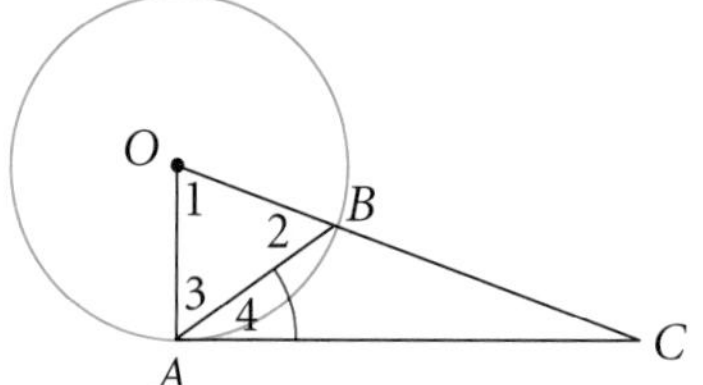

33. Find $m\angle 4$.

34. Let $m\angle 1 = x$. Find $m\angle 4$ in terms of x. What is the relationship between $\angle 1$ and $\angle 4$?

35. **Coordinate Geometry** Graph the equation $x^2 + y^2 = 9$. Then draw a segment from $(0, 5)$ tangent to the circle. Find the length of the segment.

Real-World Connection

Careers HVAC technicians often specialize in either installation or maintenance and repair of heating, ventilation, and air conditioning systems.

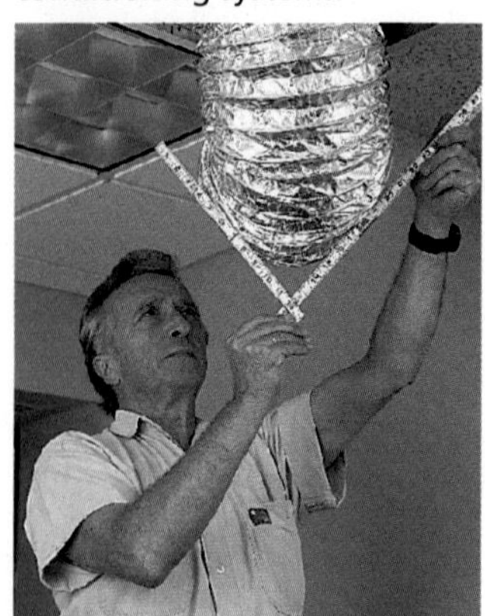

36. **Maintenance** Mr. Gonzales is replacing a cylindrical air-conditioning duct. He estimates the radius of the duct by folding a ruler to form two 6-in. tangents to the duct. The tangents form an angle. Mr. Gonzales measures the angle bisector from the vertex to the duct. It is about $2\frac{3}{4}$ in. long. What is the radius of the duct?

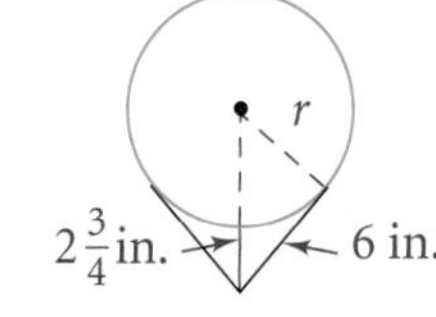

37. a. Construct two nonintersecting circles, $\odot O$ and $\odot P$, of different sizes on the same sheet of paper. Neither circle should be inside the other.
    b. Carefully draw tangents from the center of $\odot O$ to $\odot P$. Label the points of intersection of the tangent lines with $\odot P$ as A and B.
    c. Carefully draw tangents from the center of $\odot P$ to $\odot O$. Label the points of intersection of the tangent lines with $\odot O$ as C and D.
    d. **Make a Conjecture** What seems to be true about $\overline{AB}$ and $\overline{CD}$? Give a convincing argument to support your conjecture. (*Hint:* Draw $\overline{OP}$.)

C Challenge

Proof 38. Write an indirect proof of Theorem 11-2.

Given: $\overleftrightarrow{AB} \perp \overline{OP}$ at P.

Prove: $\overleftrightarrow{AB}$ is tangent to $\odot O$.

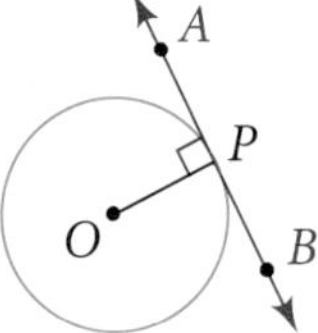

39. $\overline{PR}$ is tangent to $\odot O$ at R, $OP = 17$ cm, and $RP = 15$ cm. Find the area of $\triangle QPR$ to the nearest tenth of a square centimeter.

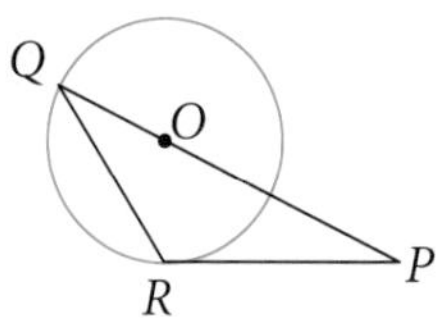

Proof **In Exercises 40–42, write a two-column proof, paragraph proof, or flow proof.**

40. Prove Theorem 11-3.

Given: $\overline{BA}$ and $\overline{BC}$ are tangent to $\odot O$ at A and C, respectively.

Prove: $\overline{BA} \cong \overline{BC}$

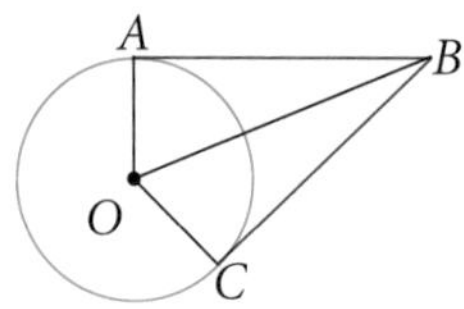

41. Given: $\overline{BC}$ is tangent to $\odot A$ at D.
$\overline{DB} \cong \overline{DC}$
Prove: $\overline{AB} \cong \overline{AC}$

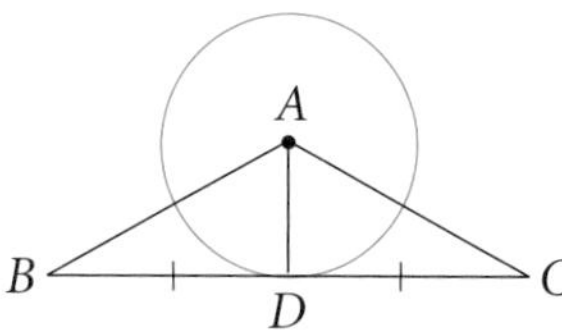

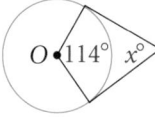

42. Given: $\odot A$ and $\odot B$ with common tangents $\overline{DF}$ and $\overline{CE}$
Prove: $\triangle GDC \sim \triangle GFE$

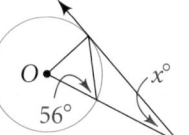

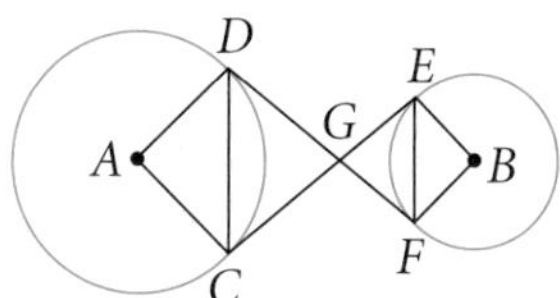

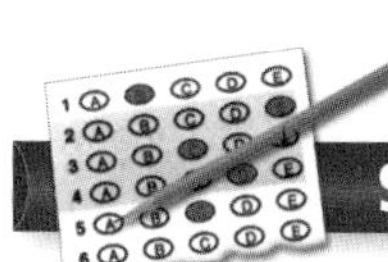

Standardized Test Prep

Multiple Choice

Point O is the center of each circle. Assume the lines that appear tangent are tangent. What is the value of the variable?

43. O 114° x°

A. 26
B. 57
C. 66
D. 114

44. O 56° x°

F. 22
G. 28
H. 34
I. 40

45. O 9 x 8

A. 8
B. 9
C. 15
D. 17

46. O 12 x 8

F. 2
G. 3
H. 4
I. 5

Short Response

47. Find the value of x. Show your work.

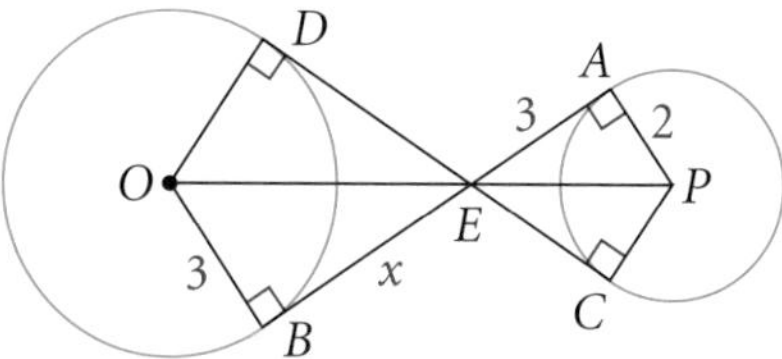

Take It to the NET
Online lesson quiz at
www.PHSchool.com
Web Code: afa-1101

Mixed Review

Lesson 10-8

Two cubes have heights 6 in. and 8 in. Find each ratio.

48. similarity ratio
49. ratio of surface areas
50. ratio of volumes

Lesson 9-1 **Algebra** **Find the value of x. Round answers to the nearest tenth.**

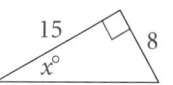

51. 5, 9, x°

52. 15, 8, x°

53.

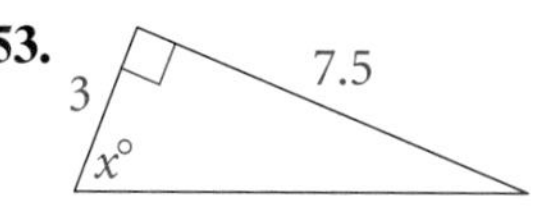

Lesson 8-2

The polygons are similar. (a) State the similarity ratio and (b) find the values of the variables.

54. m, 11.9, 7, 2.6, 5.4, n

55.

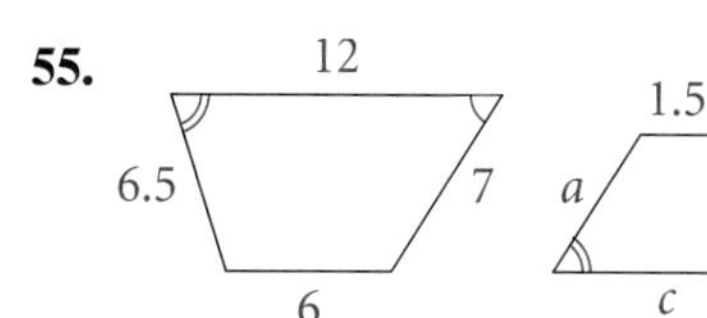

11-2 Chords and Arcs

Lesson Preview

What You'll Learn

To use congruent chords, arcs, and central angles

To recognize properties of lines through the center of a circle

. . . And Why

To see how an archaeologist finds the center and radius of the rim of a jar, as in Exercise 20

✔ Check Skills You'll Need

(For help, go to Lesson 7-3.)

Find the value of each variable. Leave your answer in simplest radical form.

1.

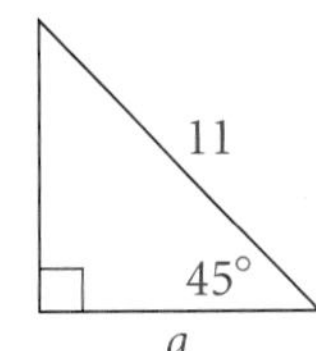

2. (right triangle with hypotenuse $5\sqrt{2}$, angle 45°, leg c)

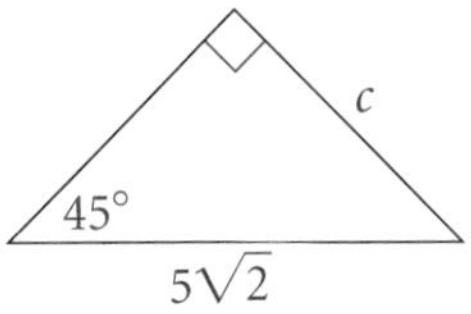

3.

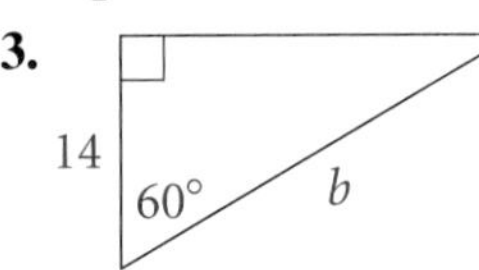

New Vocabulary • chord

Interactive lesson includes instant self-check, tutorials, and activities.

OBJECTIVE 1

Using Congruent Chords, Arcs, and Central Angles

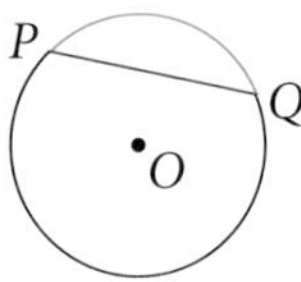

A segment whose endpoints are on a circle is called a **chord.** The diagram shows the related chord and arc, $\overline{PQ}$ and $\overset{\frown}{PQ}$.

The following theorem is about related central angles, chords, and arcs. It says, for example, that if two central angles in a circle are congruent, then so are the two chords and two arcs that the angles intercept.

Key Concepts

Theorem 11-4

Within a circle or in congruent circles

(1) Congruent central angles have congruent chords.

(2) Congruent chords have congruent arcs.

(3) Congruent arcs have congruent central angles.

You will prove Theorem 11-4 in Exercises 23, 24, and 35.

1 EXAMPLE Using Theorem 11-4

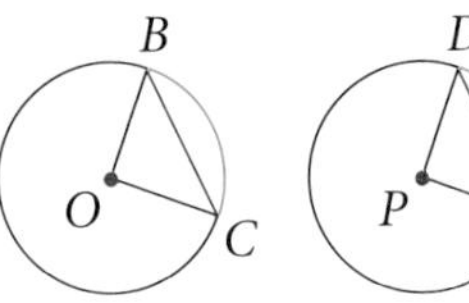

In the diagram, $\odot O \cong \odot P$. Given that $\overset{\frown}{BC} \cong \overset{\frown}{DF}$, what can you conclude?

By Theorem 11-4, $\angle O \cong \angle P$ and $\overline{BC} \cong \overline{DF}$.

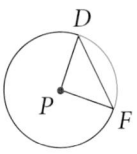

Check Understanding

1 If you are instead given that $\overline{BC} \cong \overline{DF}$, what can you conclude?

The following theorem shows a relationship between two chords and their distances from the center of a circle. A proof of part (1) is given below. You will prove part (2) in Exercise 37.

Key Concepts

Theorem 11-5

Within a circle or in congruent circles

(1) Chords equidistant from the center are congruent.

(2) Congruent chords are equidistant from the center.

Proof

Need Help?

In a circle, the distance from the center to a chord is the length of the perpendicular segment from the center to the chord.

Proof of Theorem 11-5, Part (1)

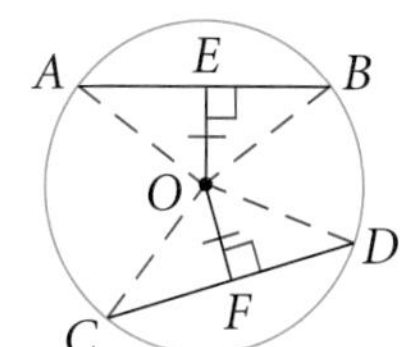

Given: $\odot O, \overline{OE} \cong \overline{OF}$, $\overline{OE} \perp \overline{AB}, \overline{OF} \perp \overline{CD}$

Prove: $\overline{AB} \cong \overline{CD}$

Statements	Reasons
1. $\overline{OA} \cong \overline{OB} \cong \overline{OC} \cong \overline{OD}$	**1.** Radii of a circle are congruent.
2. $\overline{OE} \cong \overline{OF}, \overline{OE} \perp \overline{AB}, \overline{OF} \perp \overline{CD}$	**2.** Given
3. $\angle AEO$ and $\angle CFO$ are right angles.	**3.** Def. of perpendicular segments
4. $\triangle AEO \cong \triangle CFO$	**4.** HL Theorem
5. $\angle A \cong \angle C$	**5.** CPCTC
6. $\angle B \cong \angle A, \angle C \cong \angle D$	**6.** Isosceles Triangle Theorem
7. $\angle B \cong \angle D$	**7.** Transitive Property of Congruence
8. $\angle AOB \cong \angle COD$	**8.** If two ∠s of a △ are ≅ to two ∠s of another △, then the third ∠s are ≅.
9. $\overline{AB} \cong \overline{CD}$	**9.** ≅ central angles have ≅ chords.

Real-World Connection

Steel beams model congruent chords equidistant from the center to give the illusion of a circle.

You can use Theorem 11-5 to find missing lengths in circles.

2 EXAMPLE Using Theorem 11-5

Find the value of a in the circle.

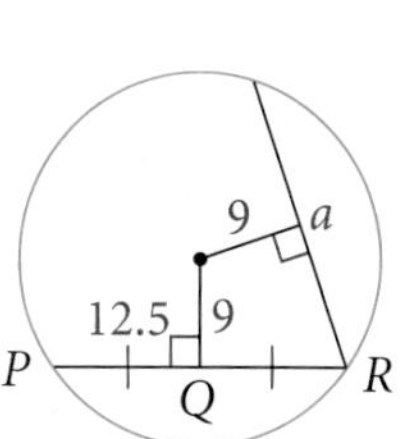

$PQ = QR = 12.5$ **Given**

$PQ + QR = PR$ **Segment Addition Postulate**

$25 = PR$ **Substitute.**

$a = PR$ **Chords equidistant from the center of a circle are congruent.**

$a = 25$ **Substitute.**

Check Understanding **2** Find the value of x in the circle.

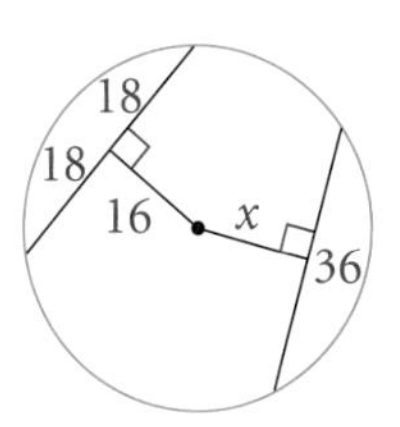

OBJECTIVE

2 Lines Through the Center of a Circle

The Converse of the Perpendicular Bisector Theorem from Lesson 5-2 has special applications to a circle and its diameters, chords, and arcs.

Key Concepts

Theorem 11-6

In a circle, a diameter that is perpendicular to a chord bisects the chord and its arcs.

Theorem 11-7

In a circle, a diameter that bisects a chord (that is not a diameter) is perpendicular to the chord.

Theorem 11-8

In a circle, the perpendicular bisector of a chord contains the center of the circle.

Proof

Proof of Theorem 11-7

Given: $\odot T$ with diameter $\overline{QR}$ bisecting $\overline{SU}$ at V.

Prove: $\overline{QR} \perp \overline{SU}$

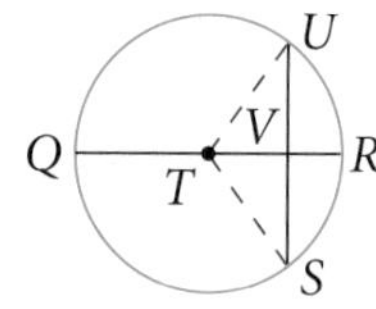

Proof: $TS = TU$ because the radii of a circle are congruent. $VS = VU$ by the definition of bisect. Thus, T and V are equidistant from S and U. By the Converse of the Perpendicular Bisector Theorem, T and V are on the perpendicular bisector of $\overline{SU}$. Since two points determine one line, $\overleftrightarrow{TV}$ is the perpendicular bisector of $\overline{SU}$. Another name for $\overleftrightarrow{TV}$ is $\overline{QR}$. Thus, $\overline{QR} \perp \overline{SU}$.

You will prove Theorems 11-6 and 11-8 in Exercises 25 and 36, respectively.

3 EXAMPLE Using Diameters and Chords

Real-World Connection

The center of the tire is located on the perpendicular bisector of the flat part.

Algebra Find each missing length to the nearest tenth.

a.

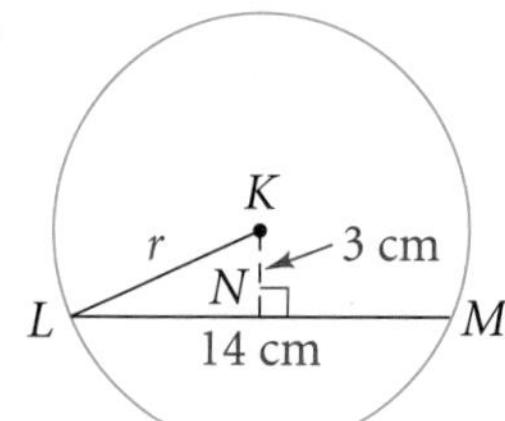

$LN = \frac{1}{2}(14) = 7$ — A diameter $\perp$ to a chord bisects the chord.

$r^2 = 3^2 + 7^2$ — Use the Pythagorean Theorem.

$r \approx 7.6$ — Find the square root of each side.

b.

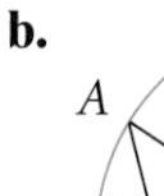

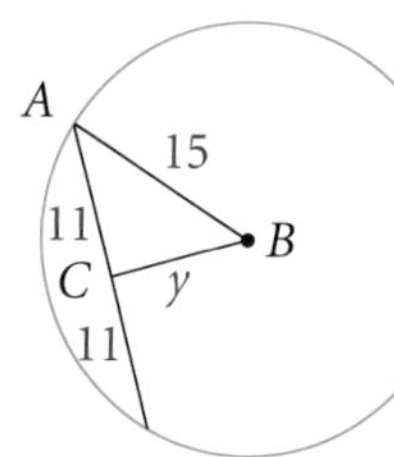

$\overline{BC} \perp \overline{AC}$ — A diameter that bisects a chord that is not a diameter is $\perp$ to the chord.

$y^2 + 11^2 = 15^2$ — Use the Pythagorean Theorem.

$y^2 = 104$ — Solve for y^2.

$y \approx 10.2$ — Find the square root of each side.

✓ Check Understanding **3** Use the circle at the right.

a. Find the length of the chord.

b. Find the distance from the midpoint of the chord to the midpoint of its minor arc.

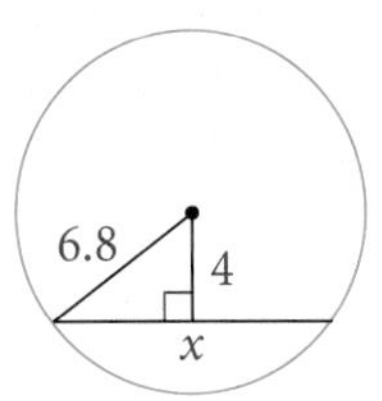

EXERCISES

For more practice, see *Extra Practice.*

Practice and Problem Solving

Practice by Example

Example 1 (page 590)

In Exercises 1 and 2, the circles are congruent. What can you conclude?

1.

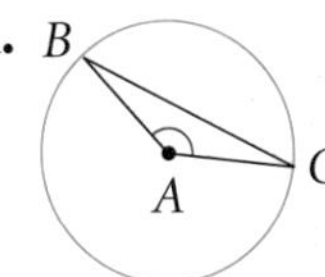

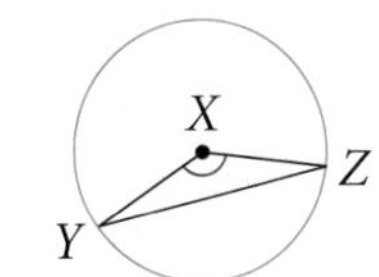

2.

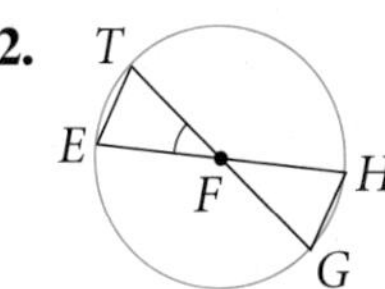

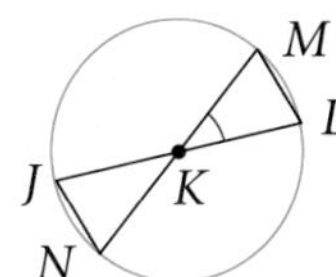

Example 2 (page 591)

Find the value of *x*.

3.

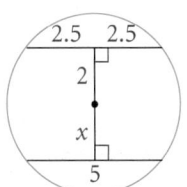

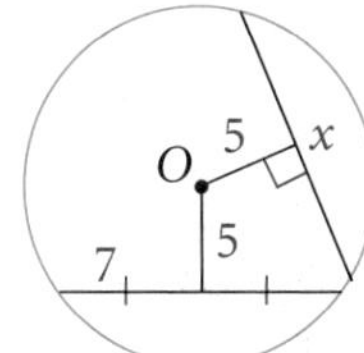

4. 2.5 2.5 2 x 5

5.

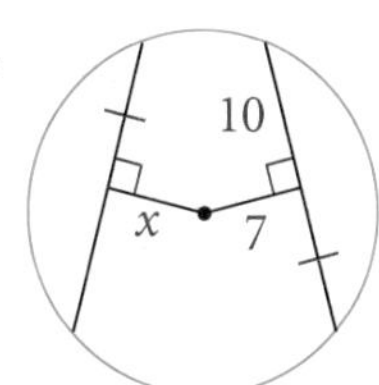

6. 25 18 18 x

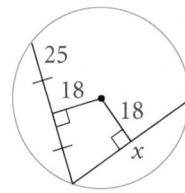

7.

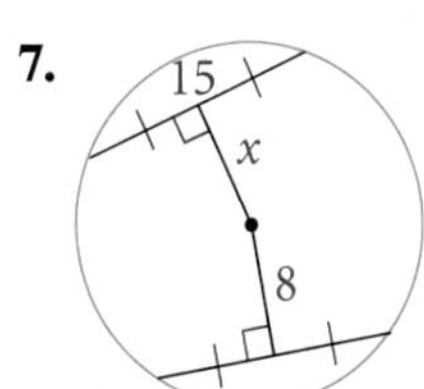

8.

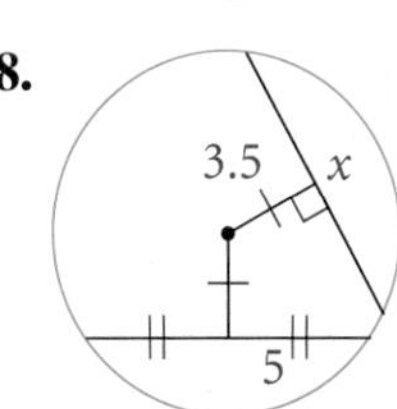

Example 3 (page 592)

Use the diagram at the right to complete Exercises 9 and 10.

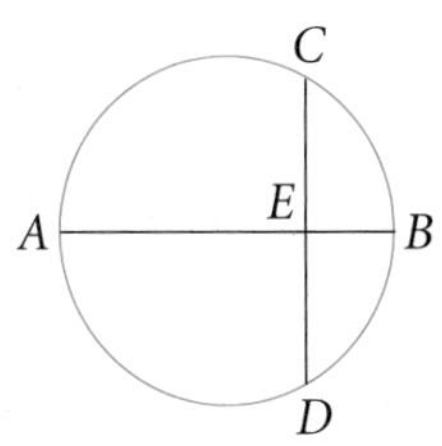

9. Given that $\overline{AB}$ is a diameter of the circle and $\overline{AB} \perp \overline{CD}$, then **a.** _?_ ≅ **b.** _?_ and **c.** _?_ ≅ **d.** _?_.

10. Given that $\overline{AB}$ is the perpendicular bisector of $\overline{CD}$, then $\overline{AB}$ contains _?_.

Algebra Find the value of *x* to the nearest tenth.

11.

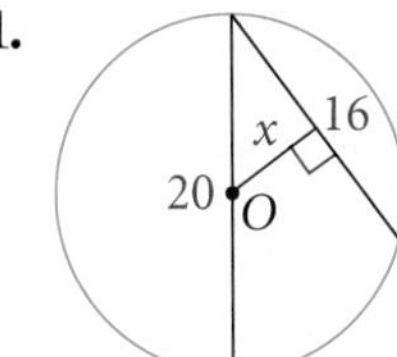

12.

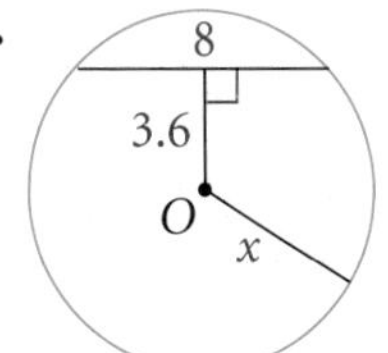

13.

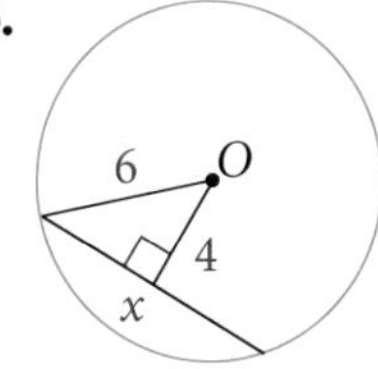

14.

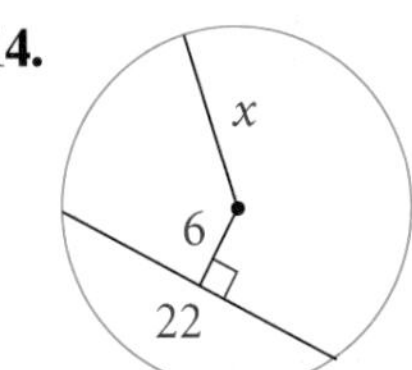

15.

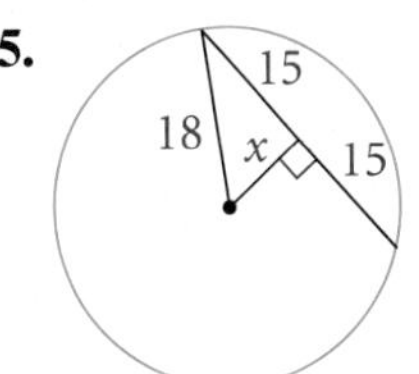

16.

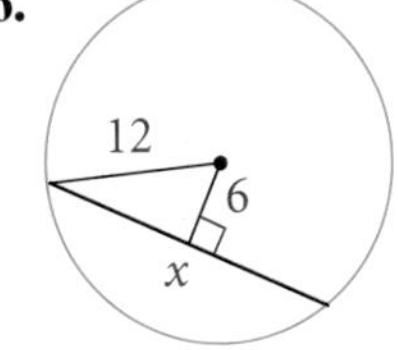

B Apply Your Skills

Find $m\widehat{AB}$. (*Hint:* You will need to use trigonometry in Exercise 19.)

17.

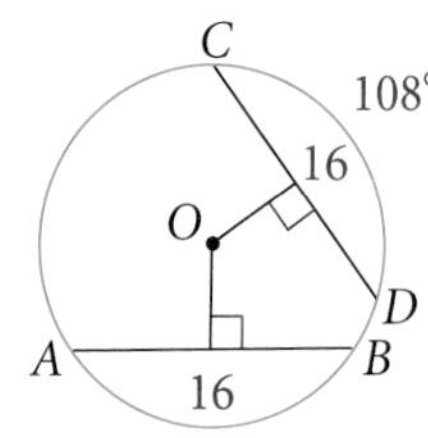

18.

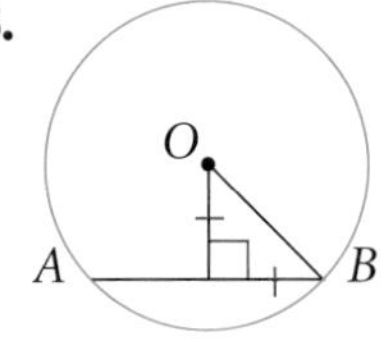

19.

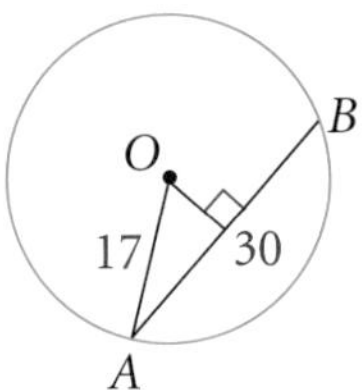

Real-World Connection

Careers Field archaeologists analyze artifacts to provide glimpses of life in the past.

20. Archaeology An archaeologist found several jar fragments including a large piece of the circular rim. How can she find the center and radius of the rim to help her reconstruct the jar?

21. Geometry in 3 Dimensions In the figure at the right, sphere O with radius 13 cm is intersected by a plane 5 cm from center O. Find the radius of cross section $\odot A$.

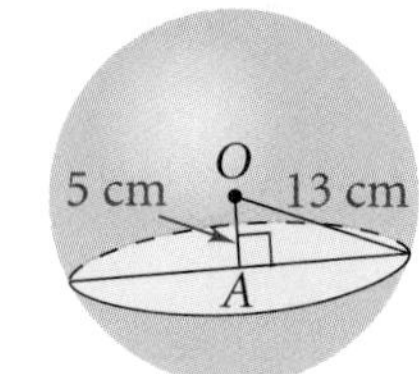

22. Geometry in 3 Dimensions A plane intersects a sphere that has radius 10 in. forming cross section $\odot B$ with radius 8 in. How far is the plane from the center of the sphere?

23. Complete the paragraph proof of Theorem 11-4, Part (1).

Given: $\odot P$ with $\angle KPM \cong \angle LPN$

Prove: $\overline{KM} \cong \overline{LN}$

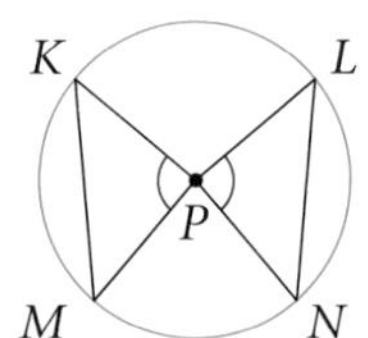

Proof: $\overline{KP} \cong$ **a.** ___?___ $\cong$ **b.** ___?___ $\cong \overline{NP}$ because **c.** ___?___. $\triangle KPM \cong$ **d.** ___?___ by **e.** ___?___. $\overline{KM} \cong \overline{LN}$ by **f.** ___?___.

24. Complete the flow proof of Theorem 11-4, Part (2).

Given: $\odot E$ with congruent chords $\overline{AB}$ and $\overline{CD}$

Prove: $\widehat{AB} \cong \widehat{CD}$

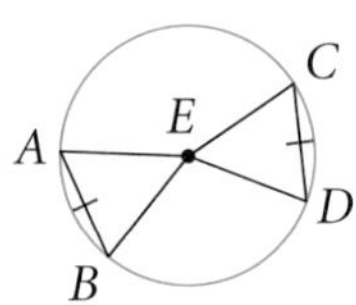

Need Help?

Recall that in a circle congruent central angles intercept congruent arcs.

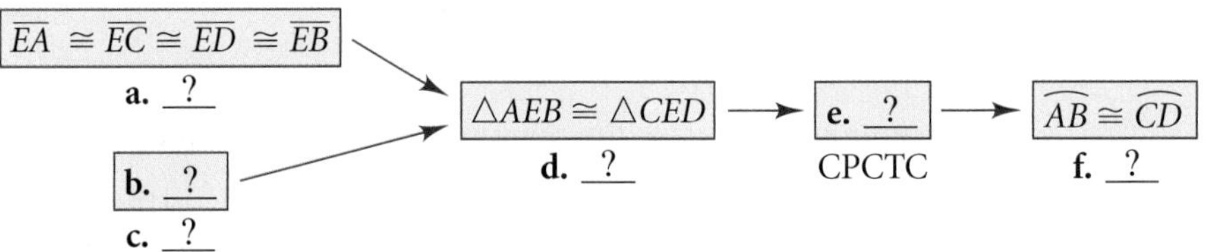

25. Complete the two-column proof of Theorem 11-6.

Given: $\odot O$ with diameter $\overline{ED} \perp \overline{AB}$ at C

Prove: $\overline{AC} \cong \overline{BC}$ and $\widehat{AD} \cong \widehat{BD}$

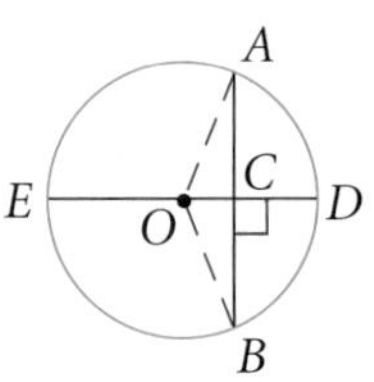

Begin by drawing $\overline{OA}$ and $\overline{OB}$.

Statements	Reasons
1. $\overline{OA} \cong \overline{OB}$	a. ___?___
2. $\overline{ED} \perp \overline{AB}$	b. ___?___
3. $\angle ACO$ and $\angle BCO$ are right angles.	c. ___?___
4. $\overline{OC} \cong \overline{OC}$	d. ___?___
5. $\triangle AOC \cong \triangle BOC$	e. ___?___
6. $\overline{AC} \cong \overline{BC}$	f. ___?___
7. $\angle AOC \cong \angle BOC$	g. ___?___
8. $\widehat{AD} \cong \widehat{BD}$	h. ___?___

Reading Math

For help with reading and solving Exercise 26, see p. 597.

26. Two concentric circles have radii of 4 cm and 8 cm. A segment tangent to the smaller circle is a chord of the larger circle. What is the length of the segment?

27. **Error Analysis** Scott looks at this figure and concludes that $\overline{ST} \cong \overline{PR}$. What is wrong with Scott's conclusion?

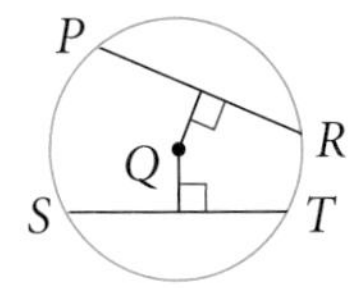

28. **Open-Ended** Use a circular object such as a can or a saucer to draw a circle. Construct the center of the circle.

29. **Writing** Theorems 11-4 and 11-5 both begin with the phrase "Within a circle or in congruent circles." Explain why "congruent" is essential for both theorems.

$\odot A$ and $\odot B$ are congruent. $\overline{CD}$ is a chord of both circles.

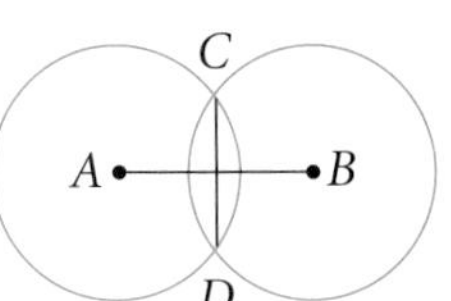

30. $AB = 8$ in., $CD = 6$ in. How long is a radius?

31. $AB = 24$ cm, radius $= 13$ cm. How long is $\overline{CD}$?

32. radius $= 13$ ft, $CD = 24$ ft. How long is $\overline{AB}$?

33. **Coordinate Geometry** Find the length of the chord of the circle $x^2 + y^2 = 25$ that is formed by the line $x = 3$.

34. **Critical Thinking** The diameter of a circle is 20 cm. Two chords parallel to the diameter are 6 cm and 16 cm long. What are the possible distances between the chords to the nearest tenth of a centimeter?

Proof **Write a two-column proof, paragraph proof, or flow proof.**

35. Prove Theorem 11-4, Part (3).

Given: $\odot P$ with $\overset{\frown}{QS} \cong \overset{\frown}{RT}$

Prove: $\angle QPS \cong \angle RPT$

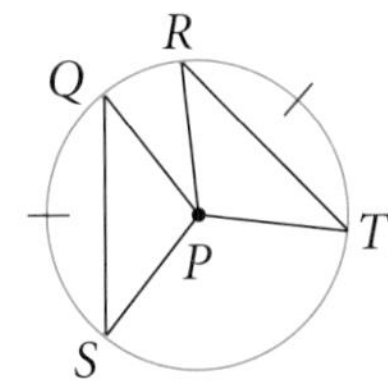

36. Prove Theorem 11-8.

Given: ℓ is the $\perp$ bisector of $\overline{WY}$.

Prove: ℓ contains the center of $\odot X$.

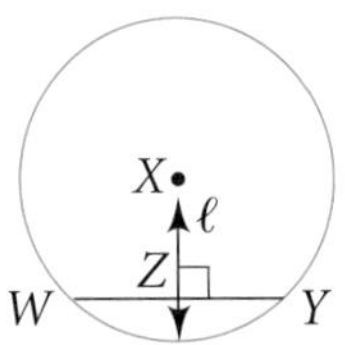

C Challenge Proof **Write a two-column proof, paragraph proof, or flow proof.**

Real-World Connection

The cylinders used on milk tank trucks lie on the lateral surface and have a vertical base at each end.

37. Prove Theorem 11-5, Part (2).

Given: $\odot O$ with $\overline{AB} \cong \overline{CD}$

Prove: $\overline{OE} \cong \overline{OF}$

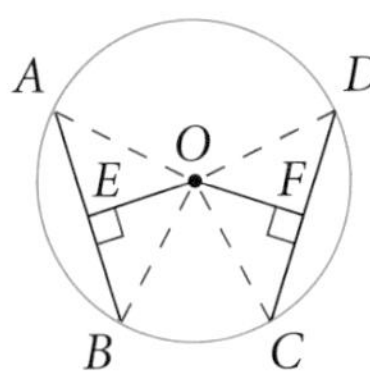

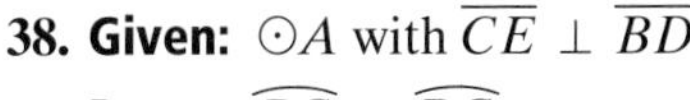

38. **Given:** $\odot A$ with $\overline{CE} \perp \overline{BD}$

Prove: $\overset{\frown}{BC} \cong \overset{\frown}{DC}$

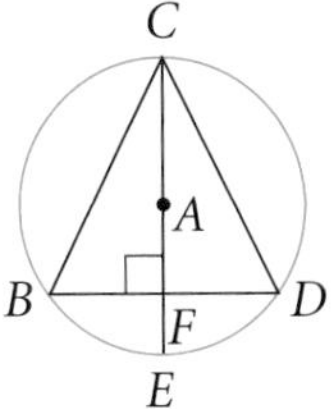

39. **Dairy** The diameter of the base of a cylindrical milk tank is 59 in. The length of the tank is 470 in. You estimate that the depth of the milk in the tank is 20 in. Find the number of gallons of milk in the tank to the nearest gallon. (1 gal $= 231$ in.^{3})

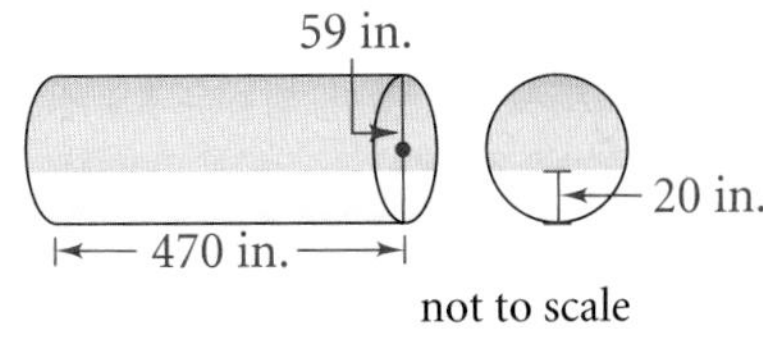

40. If two circles are concentric and a chord of the larger circle is tangent to the smaller circle, prove that the point of tangency is the midpoint of the chord.

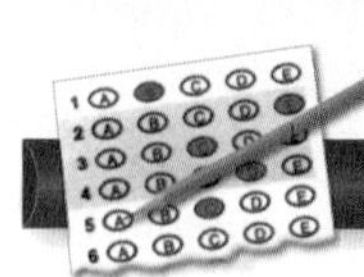

Standardized Test Prep

Multiple Choice

41. The diameter of a circle is 25 cm and a chord of the same circle is 16 cm. To the nearest tenth, what is the distance of the chord from the center of the circle?

A. 9.0 cm **B.** 9.6 cm **C.** 18.0 cm **D.** 19.2 cm

42. In the figure at the right, what is the value of x to the nearest tenth?

F. 3.0 **G.** 6.2
H. 6.8 **I.** 9.0

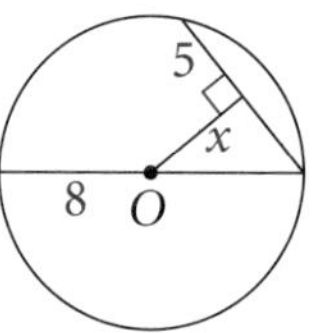

Quantitative Comparison

Compare the boxed quantity in Column A with the boxed quantity in Column B. Choose the best answer.

A. The quantity in Column A is greater.
B. The quantity in Column B is greater.
C. The two quantities are equal.
D. The relationship cannot be determined from the information given.

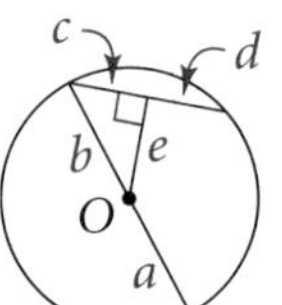

	Column A	Column B
43.	a	b
44.	d	e
45.	$b + d$	$a + c$

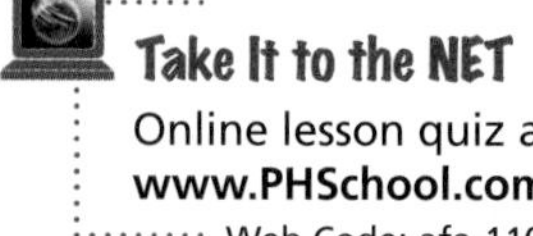

Take It to the NET
Online lesson quiz at **www.PHSchool.com**
Web Code: afa-1102

Short Response

46. Circles M and N are congruent with radii measuring 13 cm. $\overline{PQ}$ is a chord of both circles and $PQ = 18$ cm. To the nearest tenth, find MN. Justify your answer.

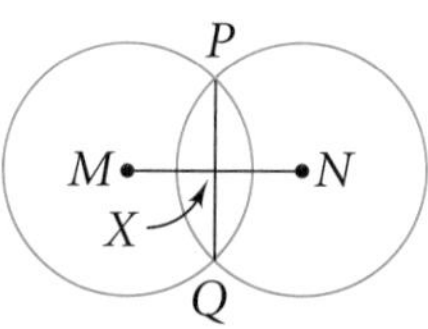

Mixed Review

Lesson 11-1

Assume that lines that appear to be tangent are tangent. *O* is the center of each circle. Find the value of *x* to the nearest tenth.

47.

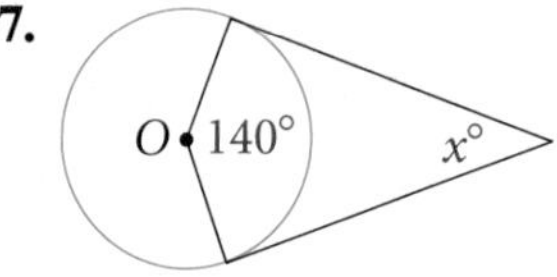

48.

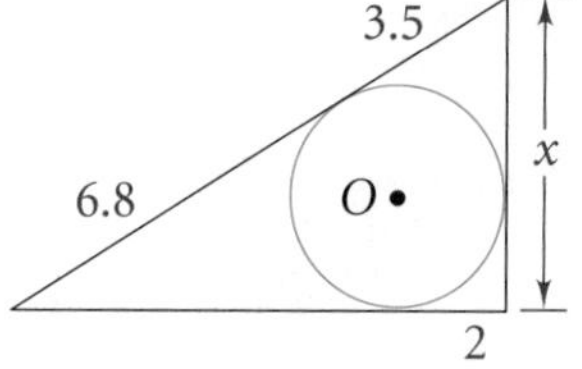

Lesson 9-3

49. From the top of a building you look down at an object on the ground. If your eyes are 50 feet above the ground and the angle of depression is 50°, how far is the object on the ground from the base of the building?

Lesson 8-5

50. The legs of a right triangle are 10 in. and 24 in. long. Find the lengths, to the nearest tenth, of the segments into which the bisector of the right angle divides the hypotenuse.

Reading for Problem Solving

FOR USE WITH PAGE 595, EXERCISE 26

Read the problem below and then follow along with what Jamal thinks as he solves the problem. Check your understanding by solving the exercise at the bottom of the page.

x^2 **Algebra** Two concentric circles have radii of 4 cm and 8 cm. A segment tangent to the smaller circle is a chord of the larger circle. What is the length of the segment?

What Jamal Thinks	What Jamal Writes
I need a picture to understand what this is about. I'll make a sketch. Concentric circles have the same center, like circles in a bull's eye. The larger circle has radius 8 cm. The smaller circle has radius 4 cm.	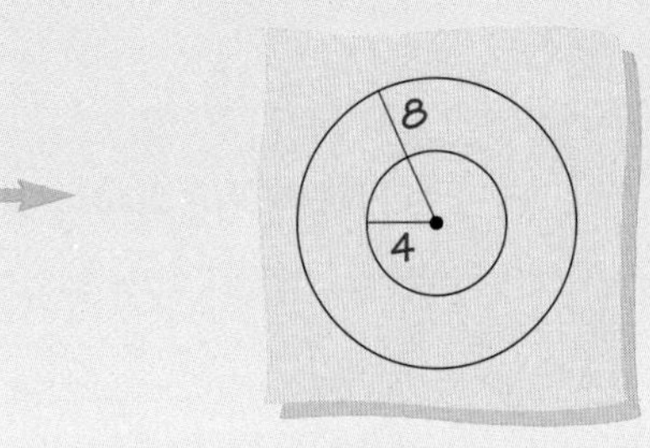
I need to draw a segment tangent to the smaller circle with both ends on the larger circle.	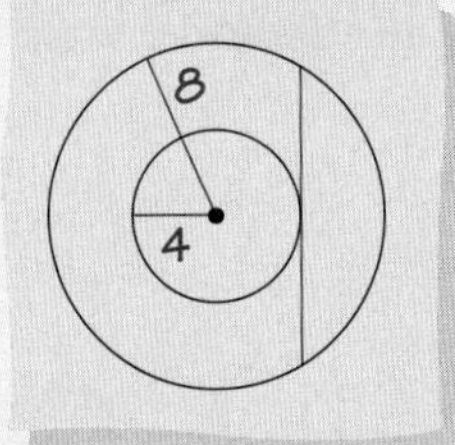
Now I need to find a relationship between these segments. I'll redo my sketch; move things around. Is a right triangle possible for my sketch so I can use the Pythagorean Theorem? Yes! Theorem 11-1 says a tangent to a circle and the radius to the point of tangency are perpendicular.	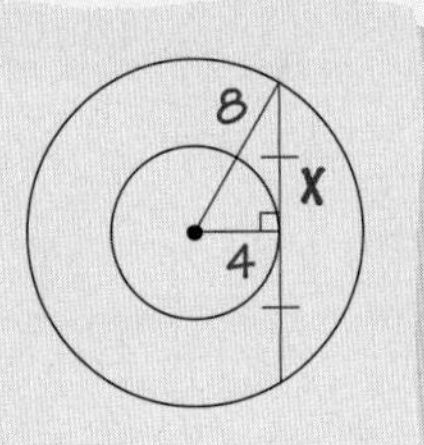
I'll use the Pythagorean Theorem . . . . . . and a calculator to find $\sqrt{48}$.	$4^2 + x^2 = 8^2$ $x^2 = 64 - 16$ $x = \sqrt{48} \approx 6.9$
To find the length of the chord, I multiply 6.9 by 2 because Theorem 11-6 says that a diameter perpendicular to a chord bisects the chord.	**The chord is about 13.8 cm long.**

EXERCISE

x^2 **Algebra** Two parallel chords of a circle are each 24 cm long. The distance between them is 10 cm. Find the circumference of the circle.

Inscribed Angles

Lesson Preview

What You'll Learn

To find the measure of an inscribed angle

To find the measure of an angle formed by a tangent and a chord

. . . And Why

To use theorems and corollaries to find missing lengths in circles, as in Example 3

✓ Check Skills You'll Need

(For help, go to Lesson 7-6.)

Identify the following in ⊙P at the right.

1. a semicircle
2. a minor arc
3. a major arc
4. a central angle

Find the measure of each arc in ⊙P.

5. $\overset{\frown}{ST}$
6. $\overset{\frown}{STQ}$
7. $\overset{\frown}{RST}$
8. $\overset{\frown}{TQ}$

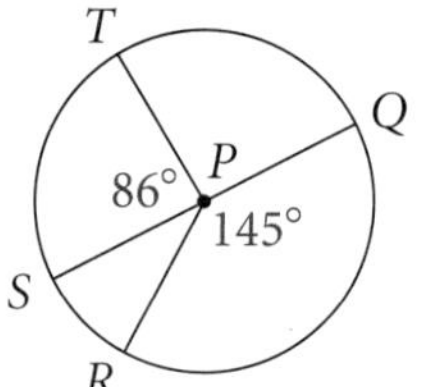

New Vocabulary • inscribed angle • intercepted arc

Interactive lesson includes instant self-check, tutorials, and activities.

OBJECTIVE 1

Finding the Measure of an Inscribed Angle

Investigation: Exploring Inscribed Angles

- Draw two large circles with a compass. Label the centers X and Y.
- On the circles, use a straightedge and copy the diagrams shown.

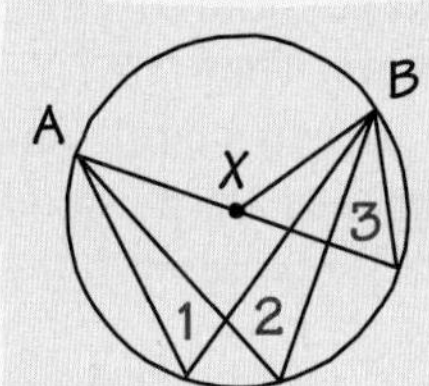

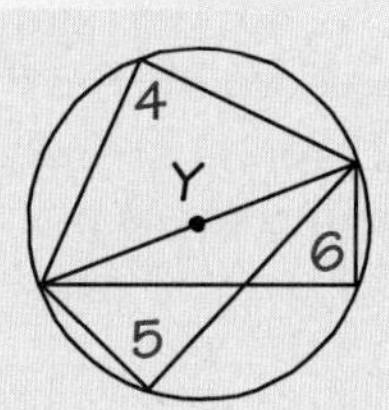

1. a. **Patterns** In ⊙X, use a protractor to measure $\angle AXB$ and each numbered angle. Determine $m\overset{\frown}{AB}$. Record your results and look for patterns. Compare your results with others.
   b. Write a conjecture about the relationship between $m\angle 1$ and $m\overset{\frown}{AB}$.
   c. Write a conjecture about the measures of $\angle 1$, $\angle 2$, and $\angle 3$.
2. a. **Patterns** Use a protractor to measure the numbered angles in ⊙Y. Record your results and look for patterns. Compare your results.
   b. Write a conjecture about an angle whose vertex is on a circle and whose sides intersect the endpoints of a diameter of the circle.

At the right, the vertex of $\angle C$ is on ⊙O, and the sides of $\angle C$ are chords of the circle. $\angle C$ is an **inscribed angle.** $\overset{\frown}{AB}$ is the **intercepted arc** of $\angle C$.

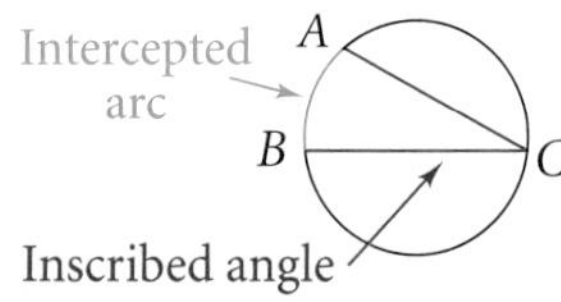

Theorem 11-9 describes the relationship between an inscribed angle and its intercepted arc.

Key Concepts

Theorem 11-9 **Inscribed Angle Theorem**

The measure of an inscribed angle is half the measure of its intercepted arc.

$$m\angle B = \frac{1}{2}m\overset{\frown}{AC}$$

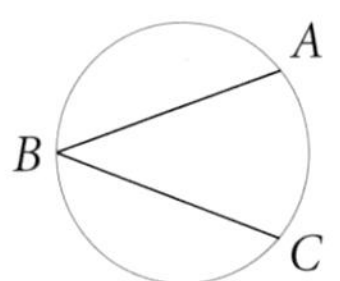

Reading Math

When different conditions are possible, each possibility can be called a case. You can prove a theorem by proving it for all possible cases.

To prove Theorem 11-9, there are three cases to consider.

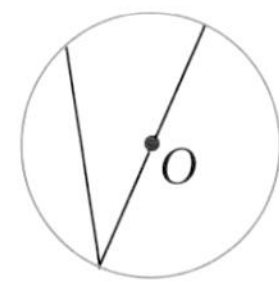

I: The center is on a side of the angle.

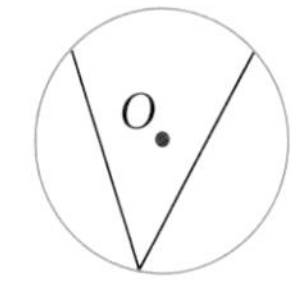

II: The center is inside the angle.

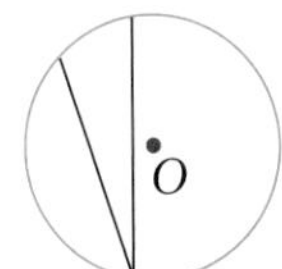

III: The center is outside the angle.

A proof of Case I is below. You will prove Cases II and III in Exercises 40 and 41.

Proof

Proof of Theorem 11-9, Case I

Given: $\odot O$ with inscribed $\angle B$ and diameter $\overline{BC}$

Prove: $m\angle B = \frac{1}{2}m\overset{\frown}{AC}$

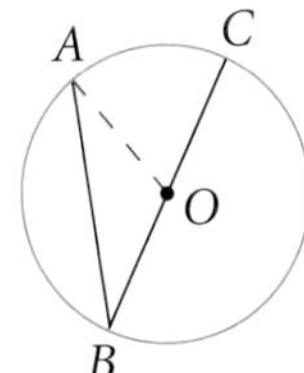

Draw radius $\overline{OA}$ to form isosceles $\triangle AOB$ with $OA = OB$ and, hence, $m\angle A = m\angle B$.

$m\overset{\frown}{AC} = m\angle AOC$	**Definition of $m\overset{\frown}{AC}$**
$= m\angle A + m\angle B$	**Triangle Exterior Angle Theorem**
$= 2m\angle B$	**Substitute and simplify.**
$\frac{1}{2}m\overset{\frown}{AC} = m\angle B$	**Solve for $m\angle B$.**

You can use the Inscribed Angle Theorem to find missing measures in circles.

1 EXAMPLE Using the Inscribed Angle Theorem

Find the values of a and b.

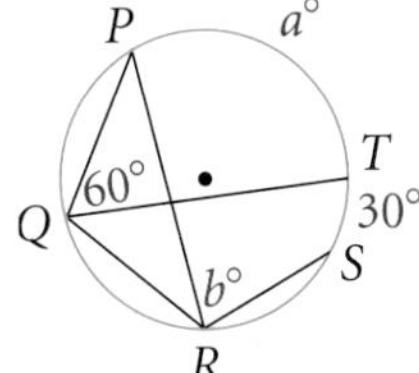

$m\angle PQT = \frac{1}{2}m\overset{\frown}{PT}$	**Inscribed Angle Theorem**
$60 = \frac{1}{2}a$	**Substitute.**
$120 = a$	**Solve for a.**

$m\angle PRS = \frac{1}{2}m\overset{\frown}{PS}$	**Inscribed Angle Theorem**
$b = \frac{1}{2}(m\overset{\frown}{PT} + m\overset{\frown}{TS})$	**Arc Addition Postulate**
$= \frac{1}{2}(120 + 30)$	**Substitute.**
$b = 75$	**Simplify.**

Check Understanding

1 Find $m\angle PQR$ if $m\overset{\frown}{RS} = 60$.

You will use three corollaries to the Inscribed Angle Theorem to find measures of angles in circles. You will justify these corollaries in Exercises 42, 43, and 44.

Key Concepts

Corollaries — **Corollaries to the Inscribed Angle Theorem**

1. Two inscribed angles that intercept the same arc are congruent.
2. An angle inscribed in a semicircle is a right angle.
3. The opposite angles of a quadrilateral inscribed in a circle are supplementary.

2 EXAMPLE Using Corollaries to Find Angle Measures

Find the measure of the numbered angle.

a.

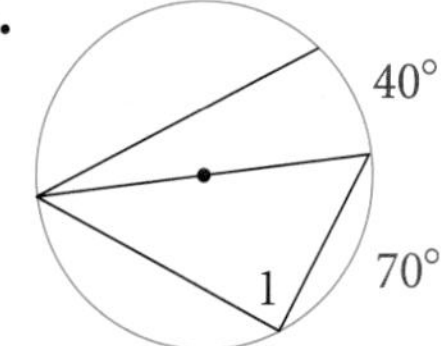

$\angle 1$ is inscribed in a semicircle.
By Corollary 2, $\angle 1$ is a right angle.
$m\angle 1 = 90$

b.

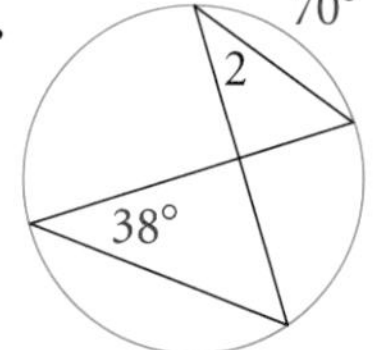

$\angle 2$ and the 38° angle intercept the same arc. By Corollary 1, the angles are congruent, so $m\angle 2 = 38$.

Check Understanding

2 For the diagram at the right, find the measure of each numbered angle.

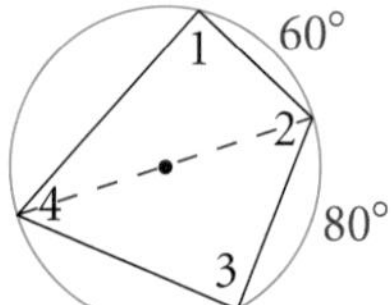

OBJECTIVE

2 The Angle Formed by a Tangent and a Chord

In the diagram, B and C are fixed points, and point A moves along the circle. From the Inscribed Angle Theorem, you know that as A moves, $m\angle A$ remains the same and is $\frac{1}{2}m\widehat{BC}$. As the last diagram suggests, this is also true when A and C coincide.

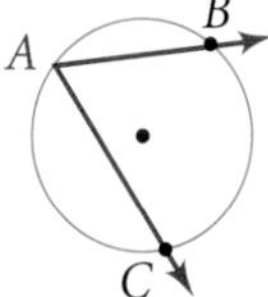

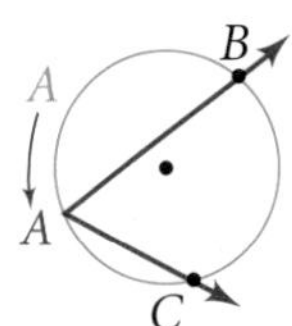

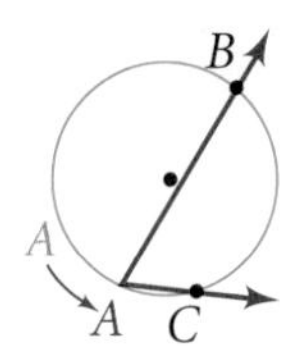

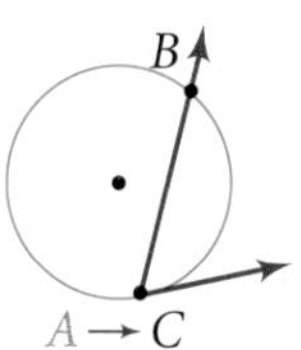

Key Concepts

Theorem 11-10

The measure of an angle formed by a tangent and a chord is half the measure of the intercepted arc.

$$m\angle C = \frac{1}{2}m\widehat{BDC}$$

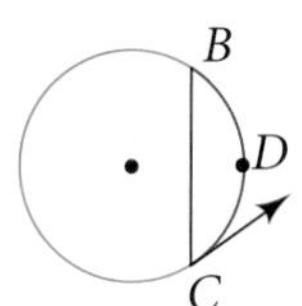

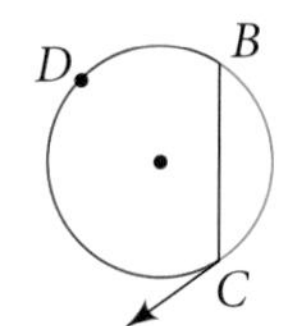

You will prove Theorem 11-10 in Exercise 45.

3 EXAMPLE Using Theorem 11-10

In the diagram at the right, $\overrightarrow{KJ}$ is tangent to the circle at J. Find the values of x and y.

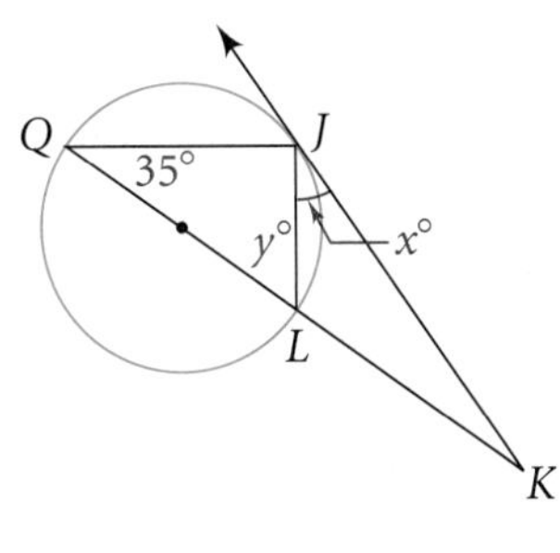

$x = \frac{1}{2}m\widehat{JL}$	**Theorem 11-10**
$= m\angle Q$	**Inscribed Angle Theorem**
$= 35$	**Substitution**
$y = \frac{1}{2}m\widehat{QJ}$	**Theorem 11-10**
$= \frac{1}{2}(m\widehat{QJL} - m\widehat{JL})$	**Arc Addition Postulate**
$= \frac{1}{2}(180 - 70)$	**Substitute.**
$= 55$	**Simplify.**

✓ Check Understanding 3 Describe two ways to find $m\angle QJK$ using Theorem 11-10.

EXERCISES

For more practice, see *Extra Practice*.

Practice and Problem Solving

A Practice by Example

Example 1 (page 599)

Identify the inscribed angle and its intercepted arc.

1. 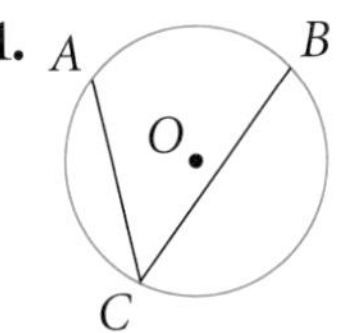

2. 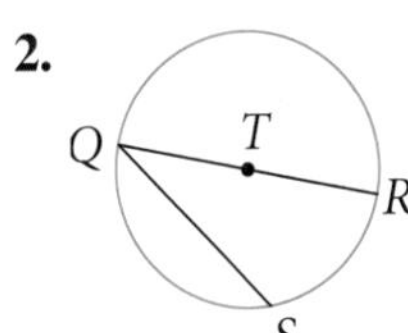

3. 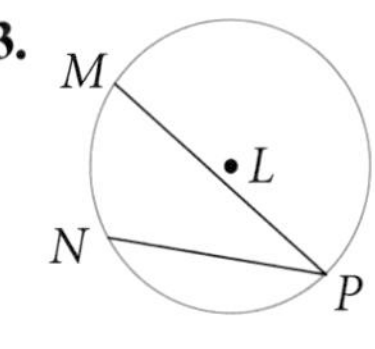

4. **a.** Name the four inscribed angles and their intercepted arcs.
   b. Which angles appear to intercept major arcs? What kind of angles do these appear to be?

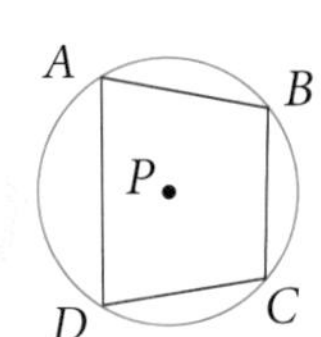

Find the value of each variable.

5. 116° $a°$

6. 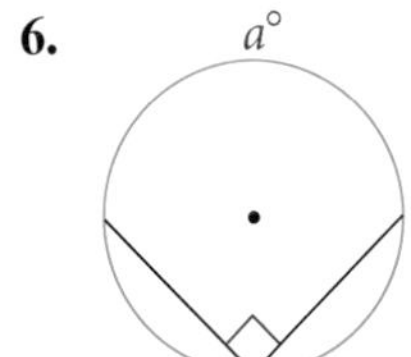

7. 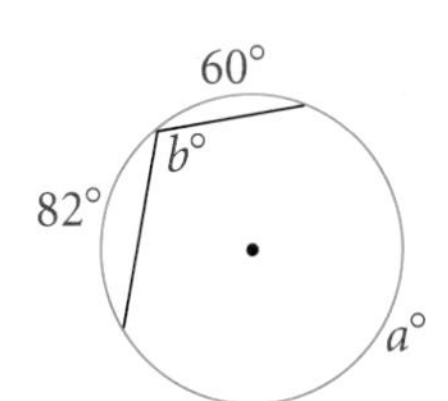

8. 60° $a°$ $b°$ $c°$ 108°

9. 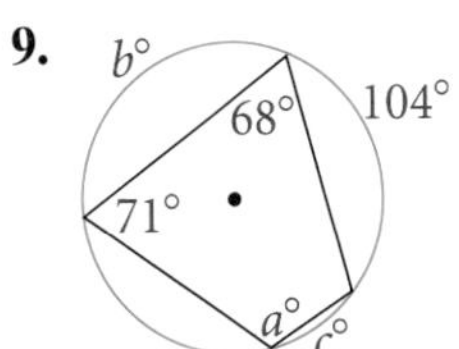

10. 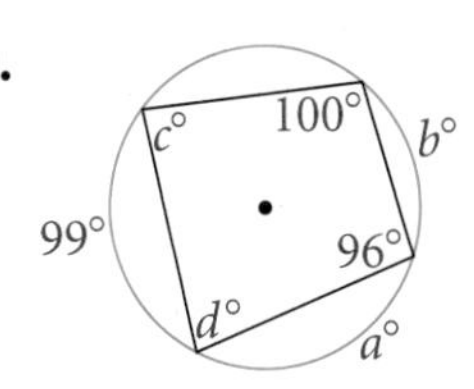

Example 2 (page 600)

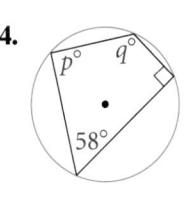

11. 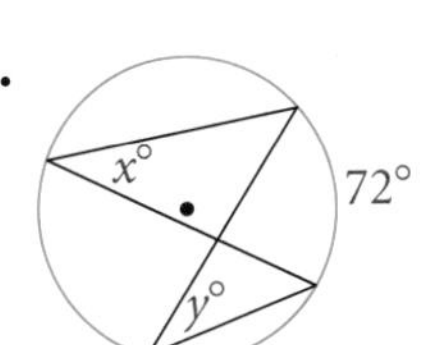

12. 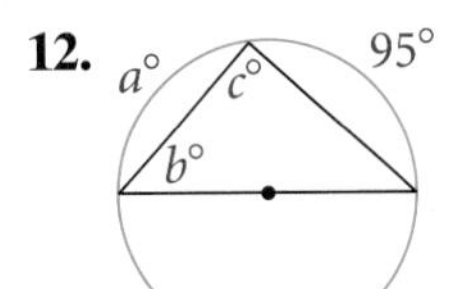

13. 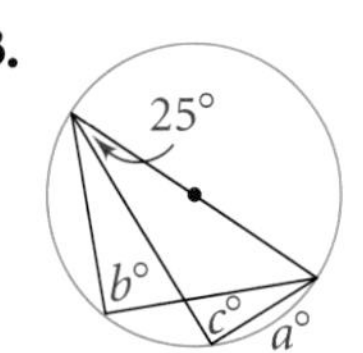

14. $p°$ $q°$ 58°

Example 3 (page 601)

Find the value of each variable. You may assume that rays that appear to be tangent are tangent.

15.

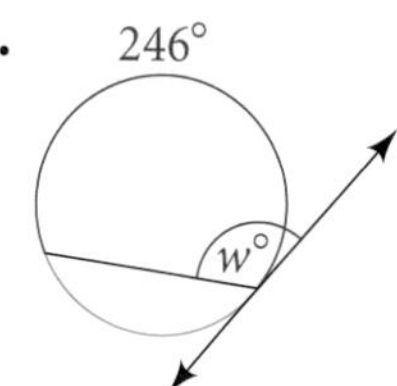

16.

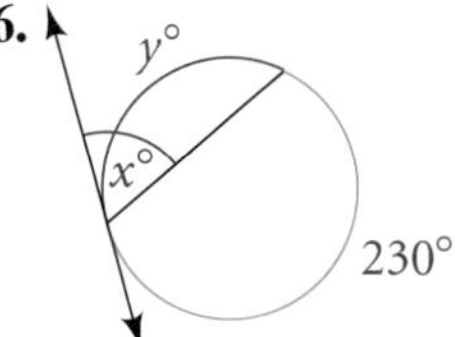

17.

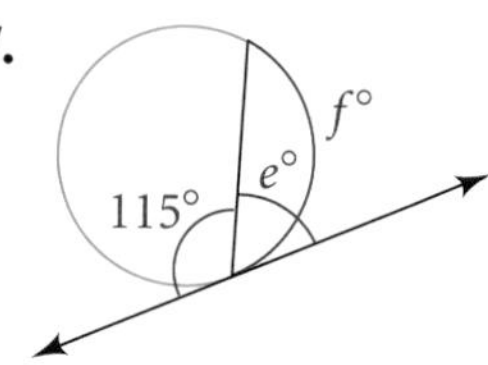

18.

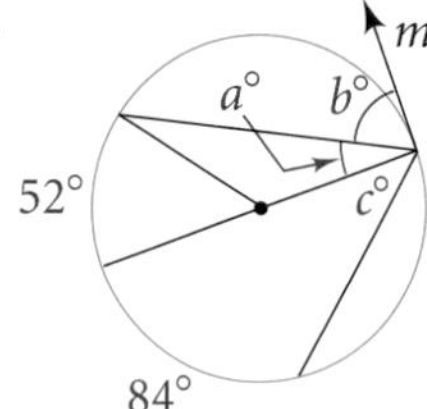

19.

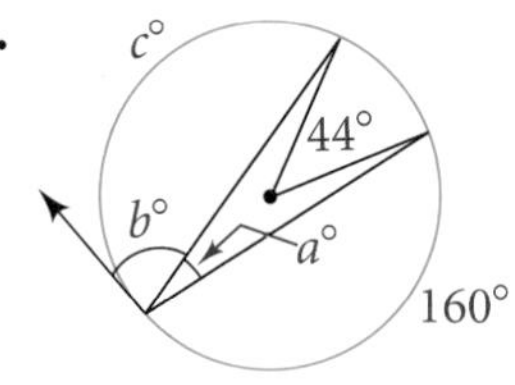

20.

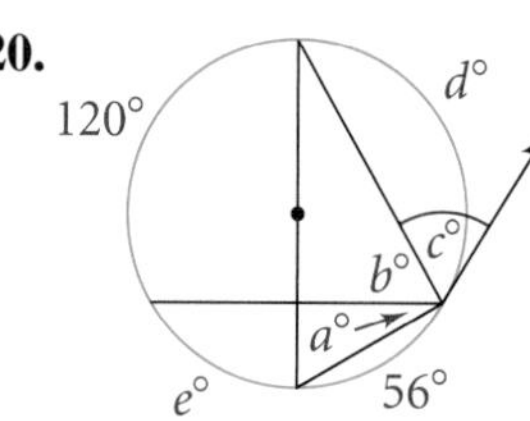

B Apply Your Skills

Find each indicated measure for ⊙O.

21. a. $m\widehat{BC}$
b. $m\angle B$
c. $m\angle C$
d. $m\widehat{AB}$

22. a. $m\angle A$
b. $m\widehat{CE}$
c. $m\angle C$
d. $m\angle D$
e. $m\angle ABE$

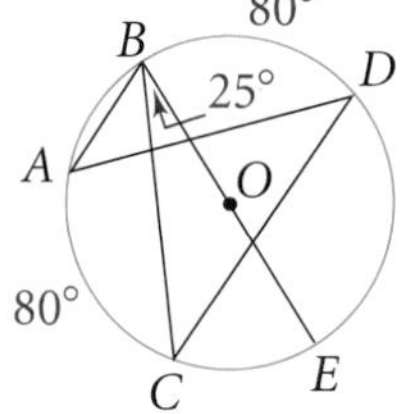

23. a. $m\widehat{EA}$
b. $m\widehat{BC}$
c. $m\angle A$
d. $m\angle B$
e. $m\angle BCD$
f. $m\angle D$

24. a. $m\widehat{DC}$
b. $m\widehat{BD}$
c. $m\angle BCD$
d. $m\angle BDC$
e. $m\angle ABC$
f. $m\angle ADB$

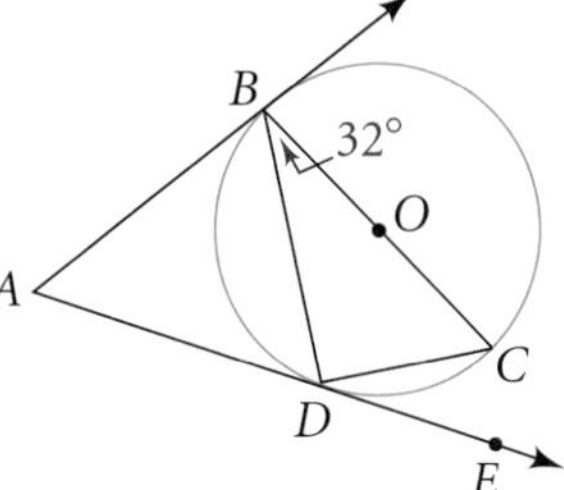

25. Writing Copy the diagram at the right on your paper. Draw chord $\overline{RQ}$. Explain why $m\widehat{PR} = m\widehat{QS}$.

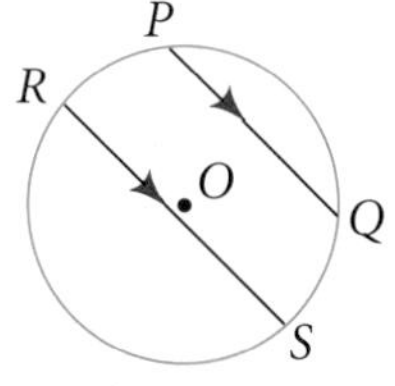

26. a. **Open-Ended** Sketch a trapezoid inscribed in a circle. Repeat several times using different circles.
b. **Make a Conjecture** What kind of trapezoid can be inscribed in a circle? Justify your response.

Need Help?

A *regular star* (Exercise 27) has congruent sides. Also, the angles "pointing out" are congruent, as are the angles "pointing in."

27. Landscape Architecture Some circular English gardens, like the one shown here, have paths in the shape of an inscribed regular star.
a. Find the measure of an inscribed angle formed by the star in the garden shown here.
b. What is the measure of an inscribed angle in a garden with a five-pointed star?

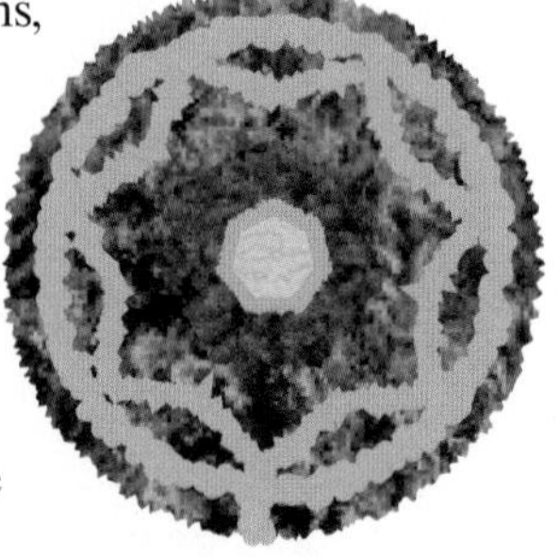

28. Critical Thinking A parallelogram inscribed in a circle must be what kind of parallelogram? Explain.

Graphing Calculator **The diameter of a circle is 10 cm. Find the dimensions of the largest figure of each type that can be inscribed in the circle. (*Hint:* Use techniques demonstrated in the Exploration on page 536.)**

29. a rectangle **30.** a triangle **31.** a right triangle

Real-World Connection

A big red "tally light" on each camera tells this anchorman which camera is "hot" (on the air).

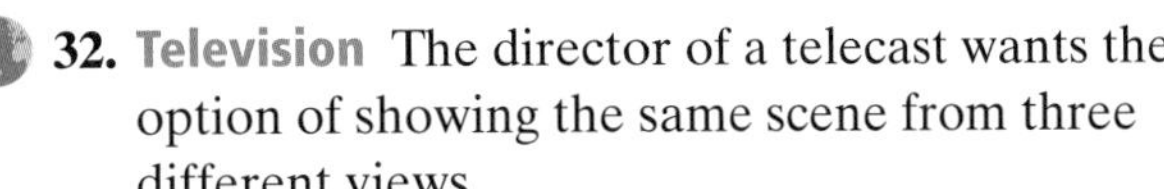

32. Television The director of a telecast wants the option of showing the same scene from three different views.

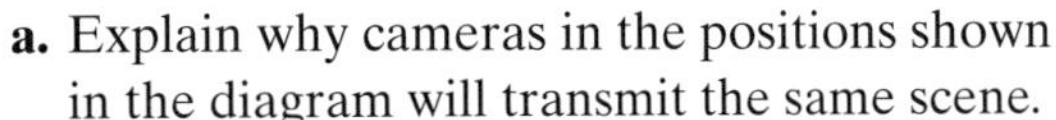

a. Explain why cameras in the positions shown in the diagram will transmit the same scene.

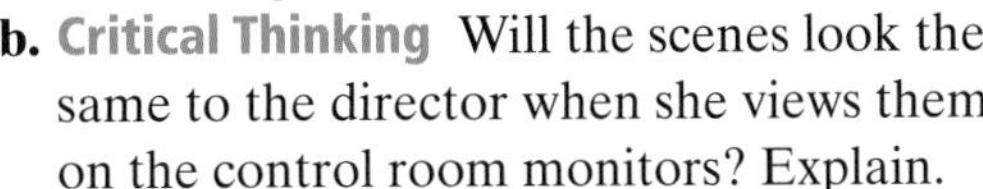

b. Critical Thinking Will the scenes look the same to the director when she views them on the control room monitors? Explain.

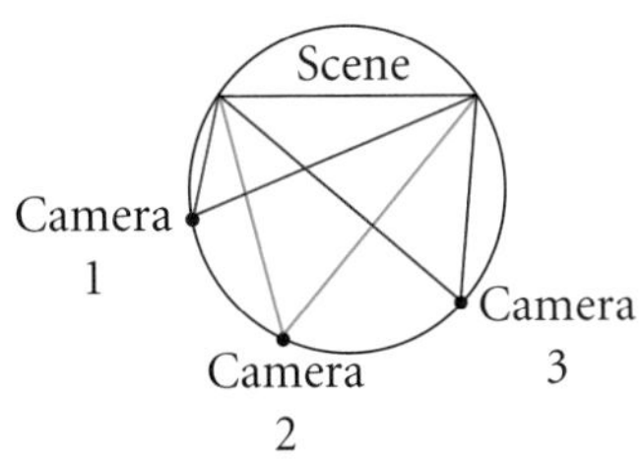

Critical Thinking Decide whether each statement is true or false. Give a counterexample for each false statement.

33. If two angles inscribed in a circle are congruent, then they intercept the same arc.

34. If an inscribed angle is a right angle, then it is inscribed in a semicircle.

35. A circle can always be circumscribed about a quadrilateral whose opposite angles are supplementary.

36. Constructions The diagrams below show the construction of a tangent to a circle from a point outside the circle. Explain why $\overleftrightarrow{BC}$ must be tangent to $\odot A$. (*Hint:* Copy the third diagram and draw $\overline{AC}$.)

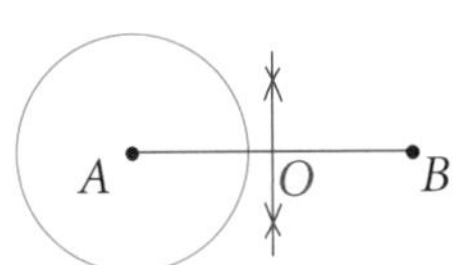

Given: $\odot A$ and point B. Construct the midpoint of $\overline{AB}$. Label the point O.

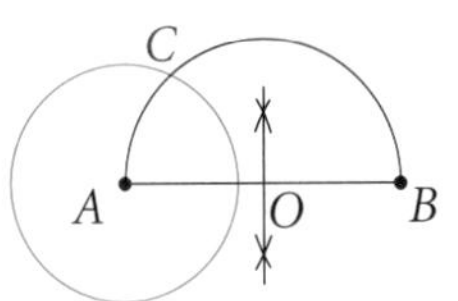

Construct a semicircle with radius OA and center O. Label its intersection with $\odot A$ as C.

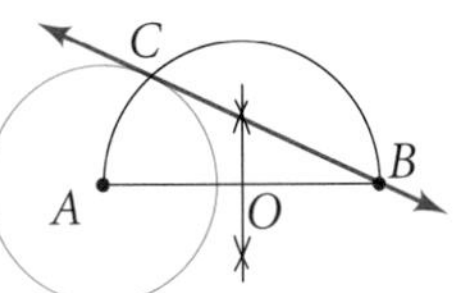

Draw $\overleftrightarrow{BC}$.

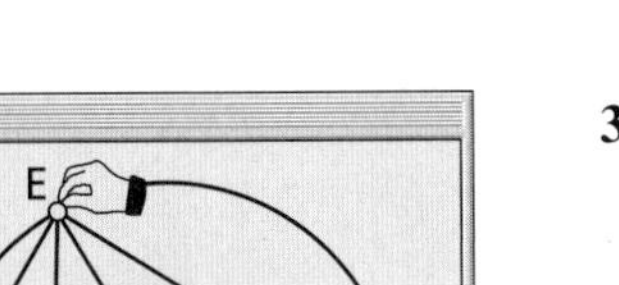

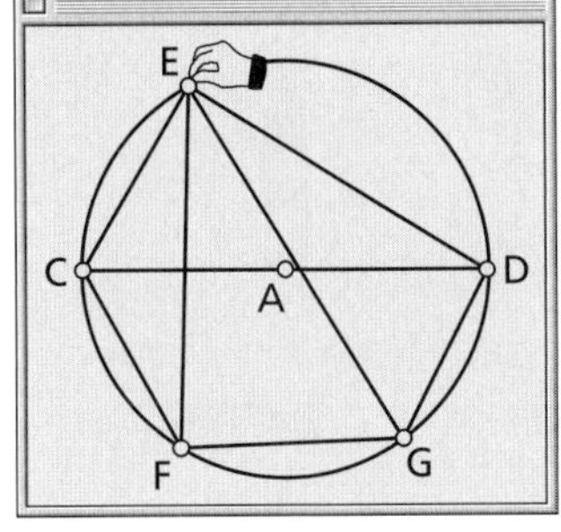

37. Technology Construct $\odot A$ and the chords shown with geometry software.

a. As you move E on $\overset{\frown}{CED}$ between C and D, which inscribed angles remain congruent?

b. Which inscribed angle remains a right angle?

c. Which inscribed angles remain supplementary in quadrilateral $EFGD$?

38. Constructions Use Corollary 2 of Theorem 11-9 to construct a right triangle given one leg and the hypotenuse.

39. Constructions Draw two segments. Label their lengths x and y. Construct the geometric mean of x and y. (*Hint:* Construct a circle with diameter $x + y$. Then find a right triangle whose altitude to the hypotenuse has the length you seek.)

C Challenge Proof **Write a two-column proof, paragraph proof, or flow proof.**

40. Inscribed Angle Theorem, Case II

Given: $\odot O$ with inscribed $\angle ABC$

Prove: $m\angle ABC = \frac{1}{2}m\overset{\frown}{AC}$

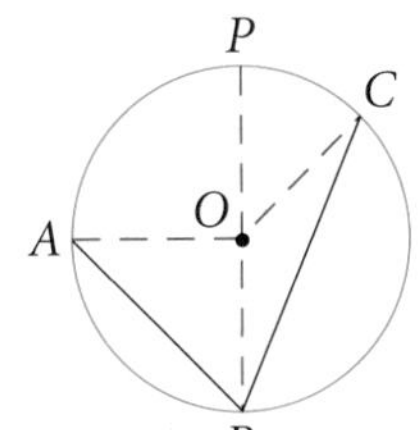

Hint: Use the Inscribed Angle Theorem, Case I.

41. Inscribed Angle Theorem, Case III

Given: $\odot S$ with inscribed $\angle PQR$

Prove: $m\angle PQR = \frac{1}{2}m\overset{\frown}{PR}$

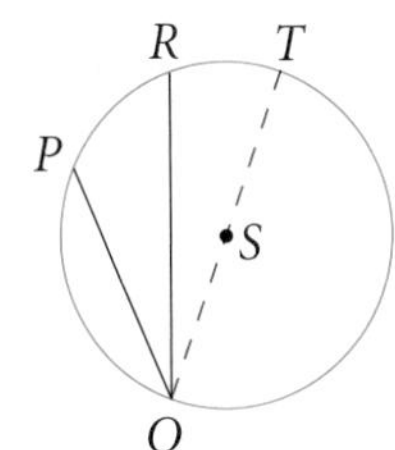

Hint: Use the Inscribed Angle Theorem, Case I.

42. Inscribed Angle Theorem, Cor. 1

Given: $\odot O$; $\angle A$ intercepts $\overset{\frown}{BC}$, and $\angle D$ intercepts $\overset{\frown}{BC}$.

Prove: $\angle A \cong \angle D$

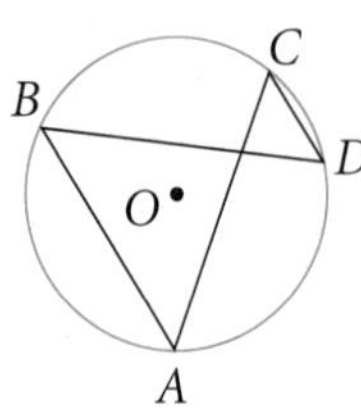

43. Inscribed Angle Theorem, Cor. 2

Given: $\odot O$ with $\angle CAB$ inscribed in a semicircle

Prove: $\angle CAB$ is a right angle.

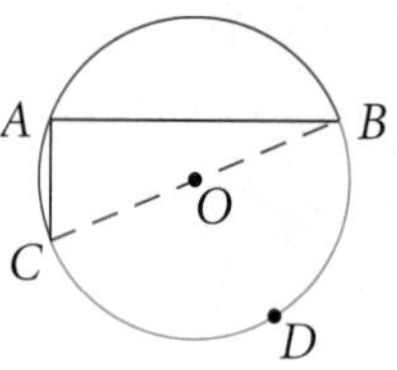

Need Help?

In Exercise 45, let $\overline{GH}$ first be a diameter.

44. Inscribed Angle Theorem, Cor. 3

Given: quadrilateral $ABCD$ inscribed in $\odot O$

Prove: $\angle A$ and $\angle C$ are supplementary. $\angle B$ and $\angle D$ are supplementary.

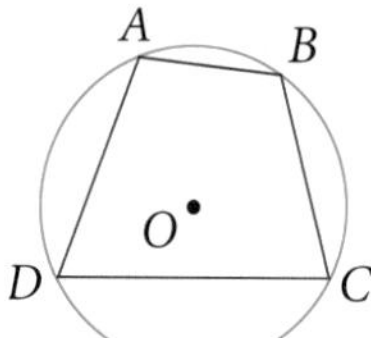

45. Theorem 11-10

Given: $\overline{GH}$ and tangent ℓ intersecting at H on $\odot E$

Prove: $m\angle GHI = \frac{1}{2}m\overset{\frown}{GFH}$

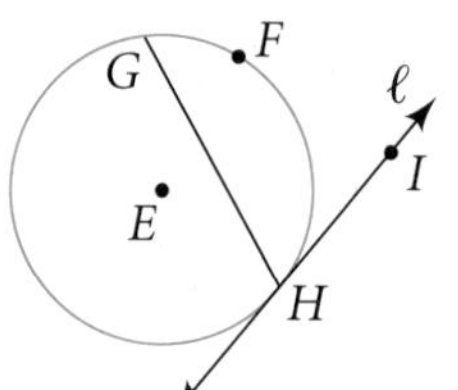

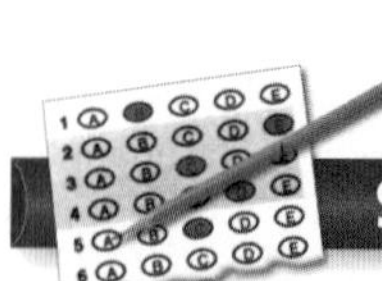

Standardized Test Prep

Multiple Choice

In Exercises 46 and 47, what is the value of each variable?

46.

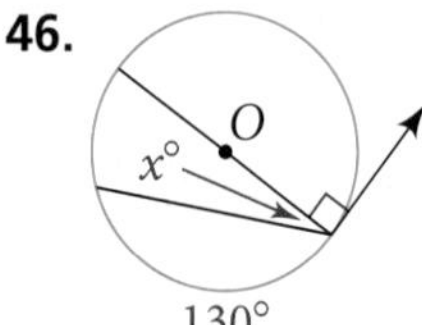

A. 25
B. 35
C. 45
D. 65

47. 60°, $y°$, O

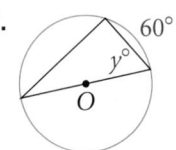

F. 20
G. 30
H. 50
I. 60

Take It to the NET

Online lesson quiz at **www.PHSchool.com**

Web Code: afa-1103

48. In the figure at the right, a square is circumscribed about $\odot A$. What is the area of the square?

A. 64 in.^{2} **B.** 192 in.^{2}
C. 256 in.^{2} **D.** $(256 + 16\sqrt{3})$ in.^{2}

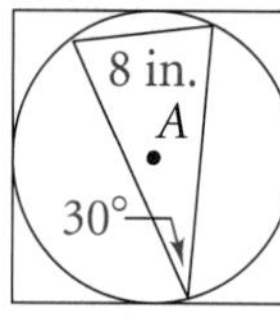

Short Response

49. **a.** Explain how you can find $m\angle XYZ$.
b. Find $m\angle XYZ$.

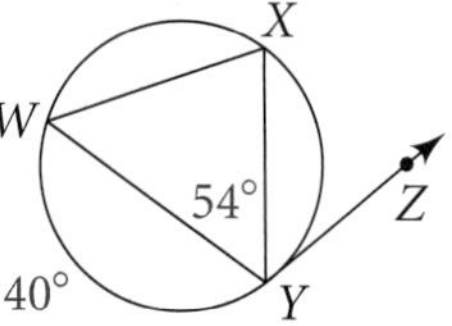

Extended Response

50. Use the figure at the right.
a. What is $m\angle D$? Explain.
b. What is $m\angle ACB$? Explain.
c. Use an equation to find the value of x.

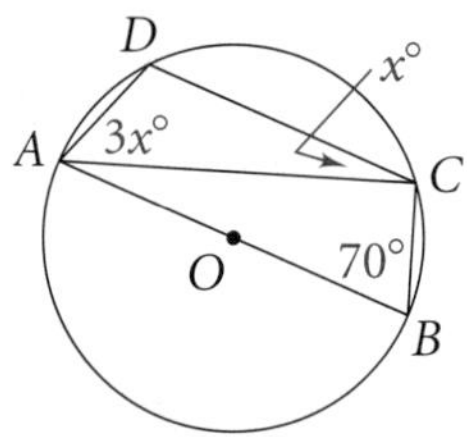

Mixed Review

Lesson 11-2 Algebra **Find the value of x to the nearest tenth.**

51.
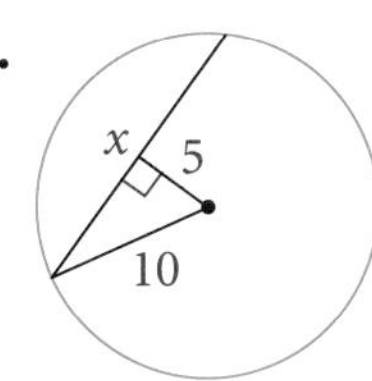

52.
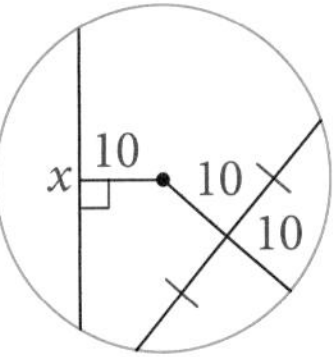

53.
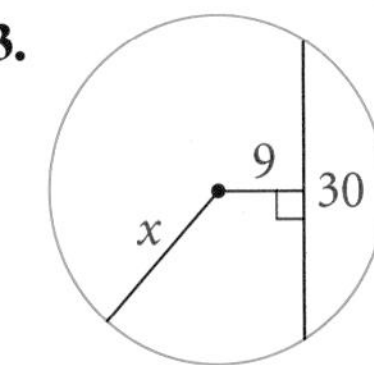

Lesson 9-5 **Find the area of each triangle. Give answers to the nearest tenth.**

54.
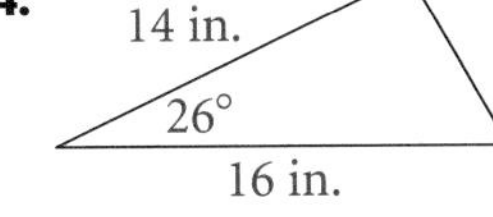

55.
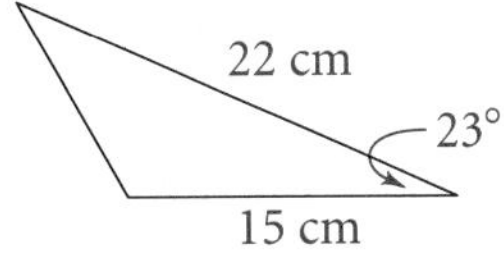

56.
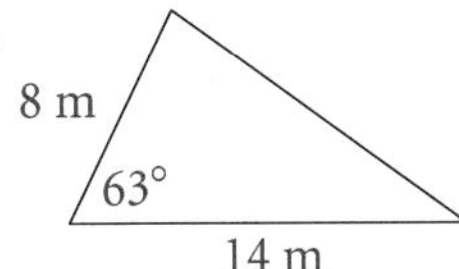

Lesson 8-3 **Indirect Measurement** To find the width of a river, you have made the measurements shown in the sketch.

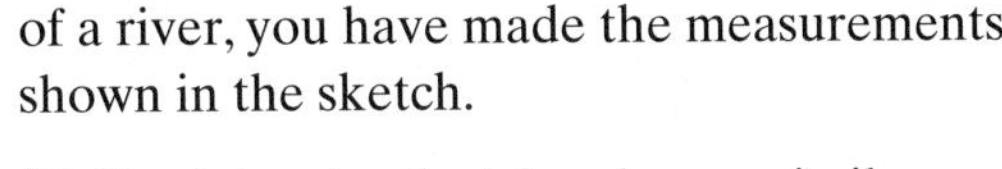

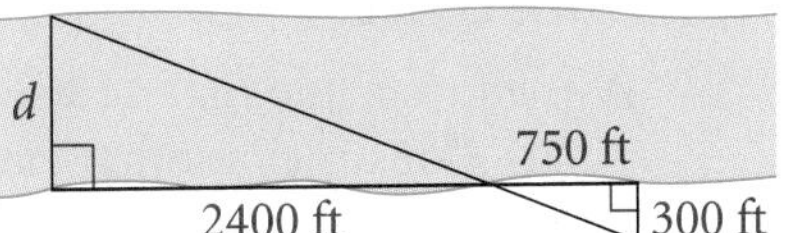

57. Explain why the triangles are similar.

58. a. Find the width of the river in feet.
b. Find the width of the river in miles.

Checkpoint Quiz 1

Lessons 11-1 through 11-3

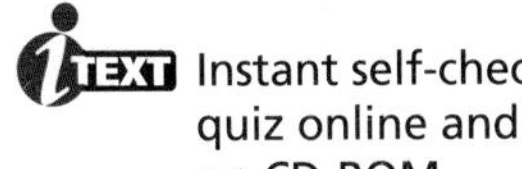

Instant self-check quiz online and on CD-ROM

Each polygon below circumscribes the circle. Find the perimeter of the polygon.

1.
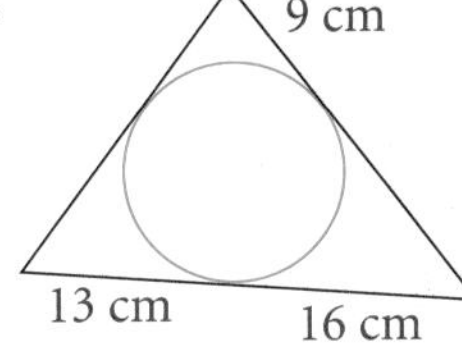

2.
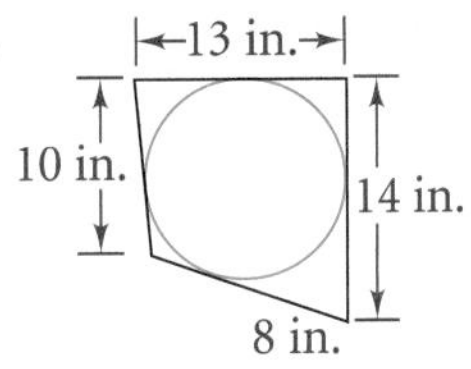

3.
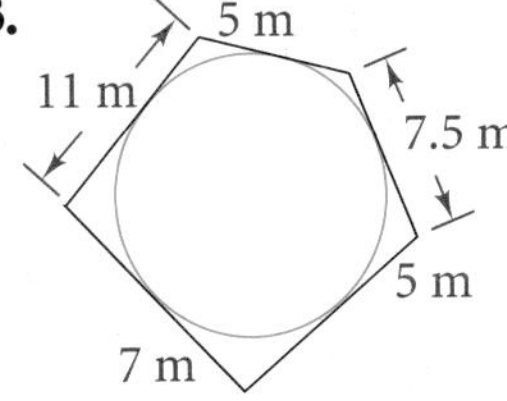

Algebra **Find the value of x.**

4.

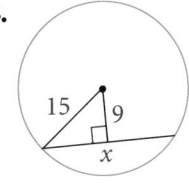

15
9
x

5.
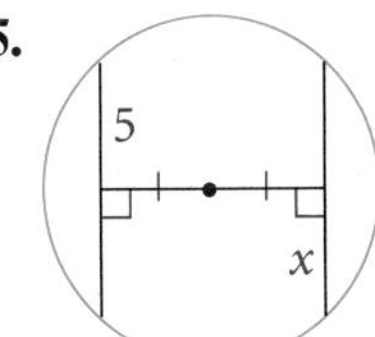

6.
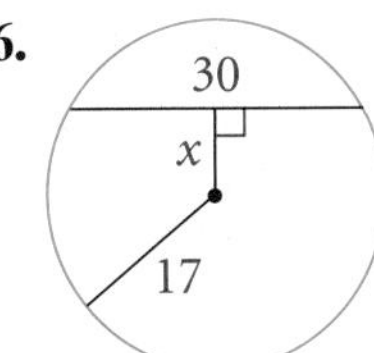

Algebra **Find the value of each variable. Lines that appear to be tangent are tangent.**

7.
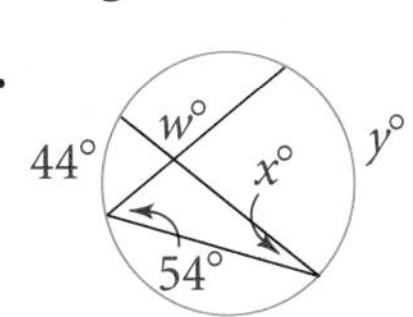

8.
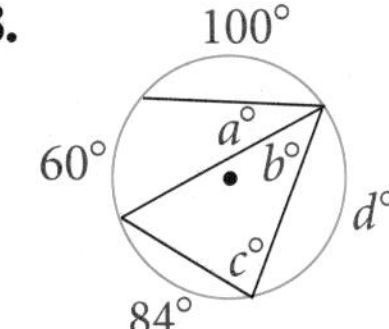

9.
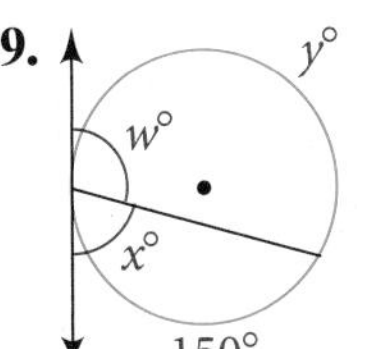

10.
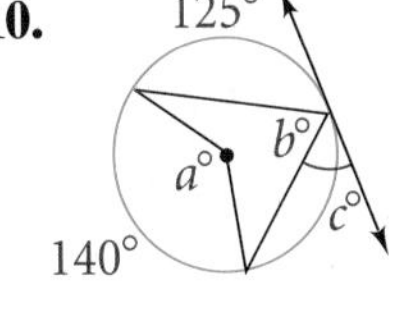

Exploring Chords and Secants

For Use With Lesson 11-4

Construct

Construct a circle with center A and two chords $\overline{BC}$ and $\overline{DE}$ that intersect each other at F.

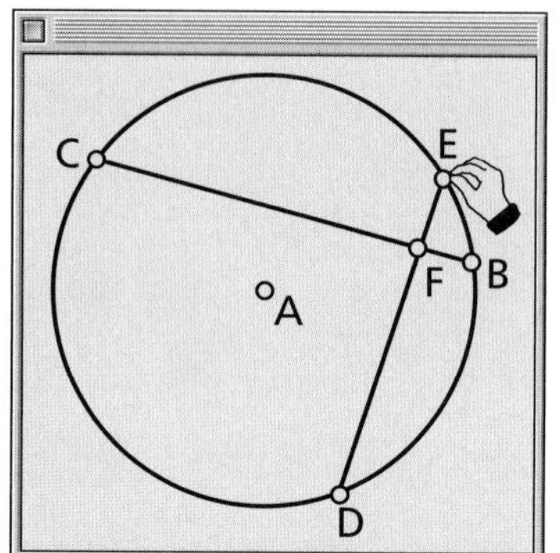

Investigate

Measure $\overline{BF}$, $\overline{FC}$, $\overline{EF}$, and $\overline{FD}$. Use the calculator program of your software to find the products $BF \cdot FC$ and $EF \cdot FD$. Manipulate your construction and observe the products. What do you discover? Use your discovery to answer Exercise 1.

Construct

A *secant* is a line that intersects a circle in two points. Construct another circle and two secants that intersect in a point outside the circle. Label your construction as shown in the diagram.

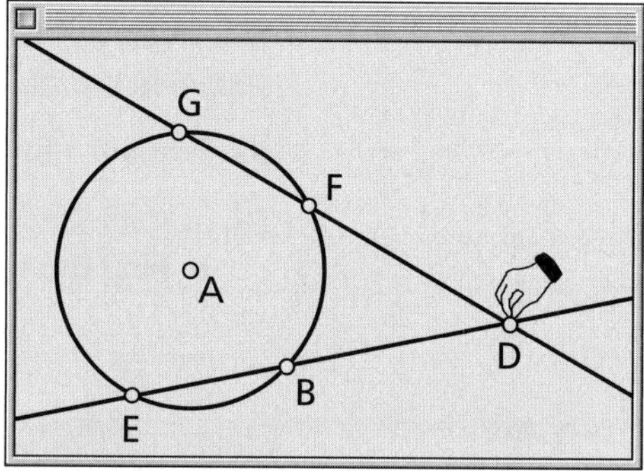

Investigate

Measure $\overline{DG}$, $\overline{DF}$, $\overline{DE}$, and $\overline{DB}$. Calculate the products $DG \cdot DF$ and $DE \cdot DB$. Manipulate your construction and observe the products. What do you discover? Use your discovery to answer Exercise 2.

EXERCISES

Use results from your two investigations above. Make conjectures about the products of the lengths of the segments to a circle from the point of intersection of the figures given below.

1. two chords inside a circle
2. two secants outside a circle

Extend

3. Construct circle A with radius $\overline{AG}$ as shown. Construct a segment $\overline{DG}$ perpendicular to radius $\overline{AG}$. Then construct a secant $\overline{DE}$ that does not cross $\overline{AG}$. Hide $\overline{AG}$. Measure $\overline{DG}$, $\overline{DE}$, and $\overline{DB}$. Calculate DG^2 and the product $DE \cdot DB$. What is true about the products you calculated? Can you explain how this special case is related to the case of two secants?

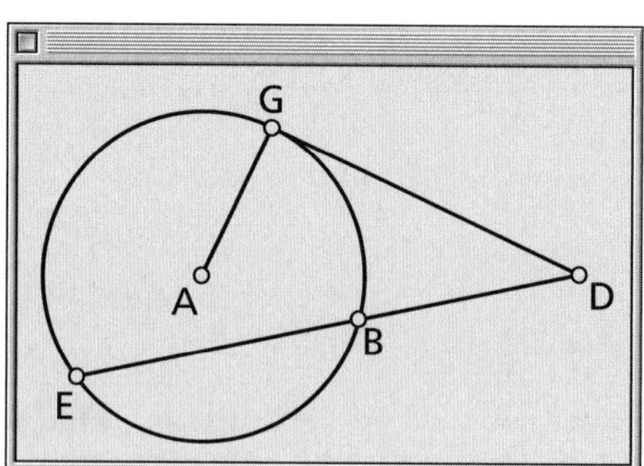

4. Combine conjectures from Exercises 1–3 into a conjecture about any two intersecting lines, each of which also intersects a circle.

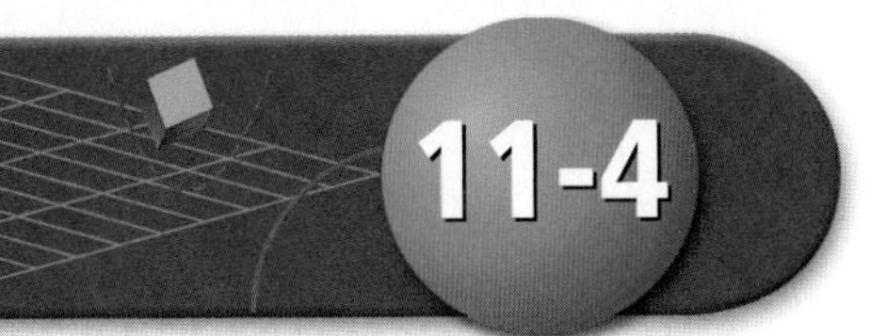

11-4 Angle Measures and Segment Lengths

Lesson Preview

What You'll Learn

OBJECTIVE 1 To find the measures of angles formed by chords, secants, and tangents

OBJECTIVE 2 To find the lengths of segments associated with circles

. . . And Why

To find the measure of an arc of a circular basin, as in Example 2

✓ Check Skills You'll Need

(For help, go to Lessons 11-1 and 11-3.)

In the diagram at the right, $\overline{FE}$ and $\overline{FD}$ are tangents to $\odot C$. Find each arc measure, angle measure, or length.

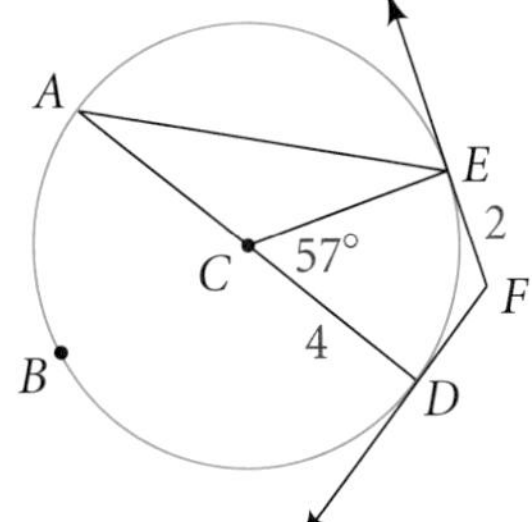

1. $m\widehat{DE}$ **2.** $m\widehat{AED}$ **3.** $m\widehat{EBD}$

4. $m\angle EAD$ **5.** $m\angle AEC$ **6.** CE

7. DF **8.** CF **9.** $m\angle EFD$

New Vocabulary

• secant

Interactive lesson includes instant self-check, tutorials, and activities.

OBJECTIVE 1

Finding Angle Measures

Reading Math

The word "secant" may refer to a line, ray, or segment.

A **secant** is a line that intersects a circle at two points. $\overrightarrow{AB}$ is a secant ray, and $\overline{AB}$ is a secant segment.

Angles formed by secants, tangents and chords intercept arcs on circles. The measures of the intercepted arcs can help you find the measures of the angles.

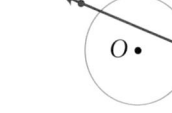

Key Concepts

Theorem 11-11

The measure of an angle formed by two lines that

(1) intersect inside a circle is half the sum of the measures of the intercepted arcs.

$$m\angle 1 = \frac{1}{2}(x + y)$$

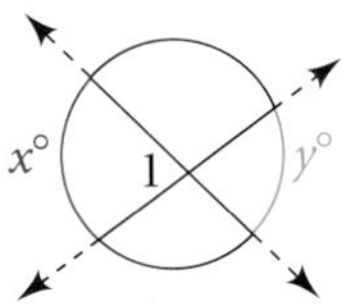

(2) intersect outside a circle is half the difference of the measures of the intercepted arcs.

$$m\angle 1 = \frac{1}{2}(x - y)$$

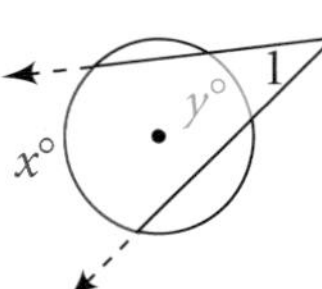

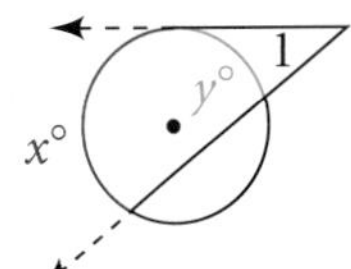

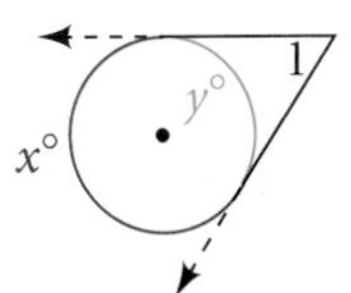

Part (1) is proved on the next page. The three cases of Part (2) are proved in Exercises 29 and 30.

Proof

Proof of Theorem 11-11, Part (1)

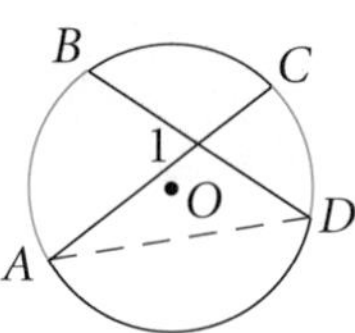

Given: $\odot O$ with intersecting chords $\overline{AC}$ and $\overline{BD}$

Prove: $m\angle 1 = \frac{1}{2}\left(m\widehat{AB} + m\widehat{CD}\right)$

Begin by drawing $\overline{AD}$ as shown in the diagram.

$m\angle BDA = \frac{1}{2}m\widehat{AB}$, and $m\angle CAD = \frac{1}{2}m\widehat{CD}$
Inscribed Angle Theorem

$m\angle 1 = m\angle BDA + m\angle CAD$
Exterior Angle Theorem

$m\angle 1 = \frac{1}{2}m\widehat{AB} + \frac{1}{2}m\widehat{CD}$
Substitute.

$m\angle 1 = \frac{1}{2}(m\widehat{AB} + m\widehat{CD})$
Distributive Property

You can use Theorem 11-11 to find the measures of angles and intercepted arcs.

1 EXAMPLE Finding Angle Measures

Algebra Find the value of each variable.

a.

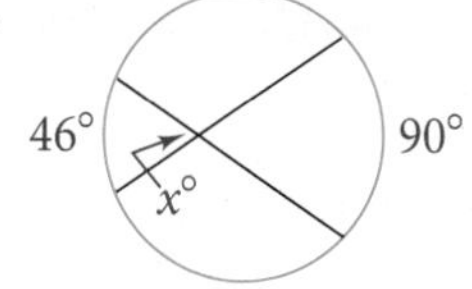

$x = \frac{1}{2}(46 + 90)$ **Theorem 11-11 (1)**

$x = 68$ **Simplify.**

b. 95°

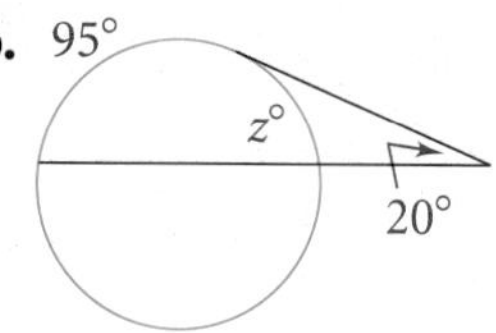

$20 = \frac{1}{2}(95 - z)$ **Theorem 11-11 (2)**

$40 = 95 - z$ **Solve for z.**

$z = 55$

Check Understanding **1** Find the value of each variable.

a.

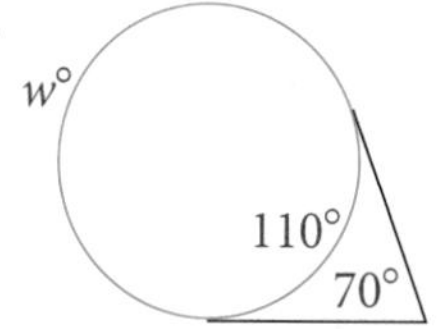

b.

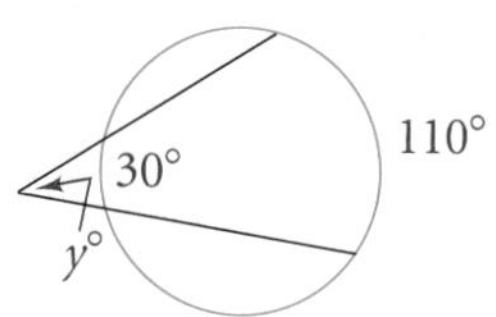

Real-World Connection

Line-of-sight tangents to this fountain basin form a larger angle than do those to the distant basin.

2 EXAMPLE Real-World Connection

Photography You focus your camera on a fountain. Your camera is at the vertex of the angle formed by tangents to the fountain. You estimate that this angle is 40°.

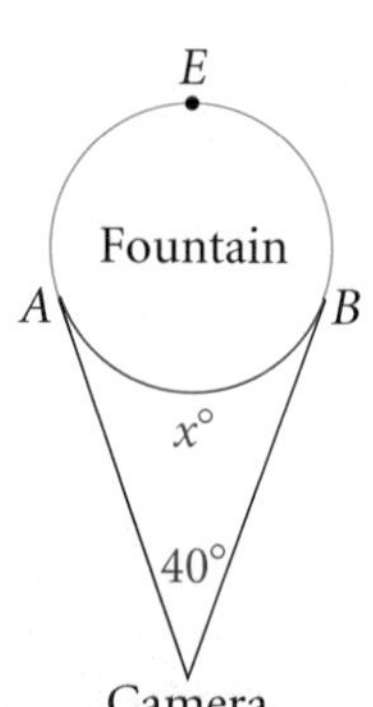

What is the measure of the arc of the circular basin of the fountain that will be in the photograph?

Let $m\widehat{AB} = x$.

Then $m\widehat{AEB} = 360 - x$.

$40 = \frac{1}{2}(m\widehat{AEB} - m\widehat{AB})$ **Theorem 11-11 (2)**

$40 = \frac{1}{2}[(360 - x) - x]$ **Substitute.**

$40 = \frac{1}{2}(360 - 2x)$ **Simplify.**

$40 = 180 - x$ **Distribute.**

$x = 140$ **Solve for *x*.**

A 140° arc will be in the photograph.

Check Understanding **2** **Critical Thinking** To photograph a 160° arc of the basin, should you move towards or away from the fountain? What angle should the tangents form?

OBJECTIVE

2 Finding Segment Lengths

From a given point P, you can draw two segments to a circle along infinitely many lines. For example, $\overline{PA_1}$ and $\overline{PB_1}$ lie along one such line. Theorem 11-12 states the surprising result that, no matter which line you use, the product $PA \cdot PB$ remains constant.

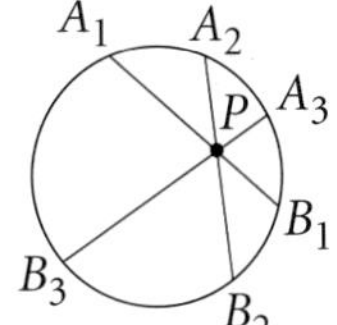

$PA_i \cdot PB_i$ is constant.

Key Concepts

Theorem 11-12

For a given point and circle, the product of the lengths of the two segments from the point to the circle is constant along any line through the point and circle.

I.

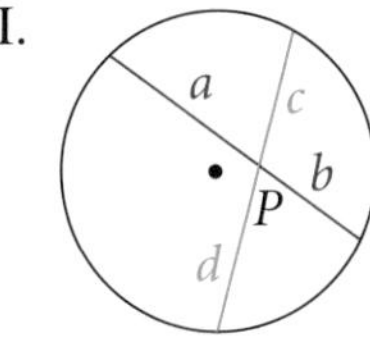

$a \cdot b = c \cdot d$

II.

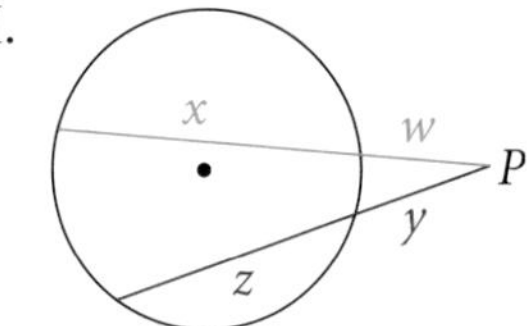

$(w + x)w = (y + z)y$

III.

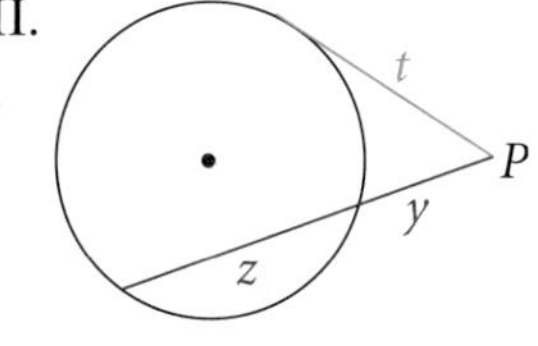

$(y + z)y = t^2$

Reading Math

The two segments to a circle along a secant are called *secant segments.*

Note in Case III that the tangent segment is used twice.

Here is a proof for Case I. You will prove II and III in Exercises 31 and 32.

Proof

Proof of Theorem 11-12 (I)

Given: a circle with chords $\overline{AB}$ and $\overline{CD}$ intersecting at P

Prove: $a \cdot b = c \cdot d$

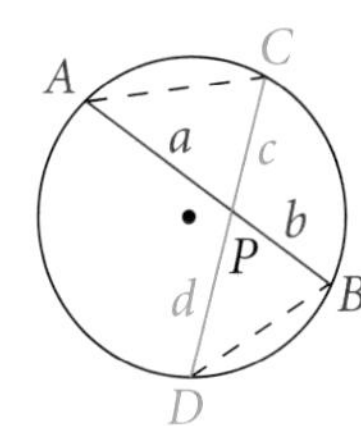

Draw $\overline{AC}$ and $\overline{BD}$. $\angle A \cong \angle D$ and $\angle C \cong \angle B$ because they are inscribed angles and each pair intercept the same arc. Thus, $\triangle APC \sim \triangle DPB$ by the Angle-Angle Similarity Postulate. The lengths of corresponding sides of similar triangles are proportional, so $\frac{a}{d} = \frac{c}{b}$. Therefore, $a \cdot b = c \cdot d$.

You can use Theorem 11-12 to find lengths of segments in circles.

3 EXAMPLE Finding Segment Lengths

Algebra Find the value of the variable. If the answer is not a whole number, round to the nearest tenth.

a.

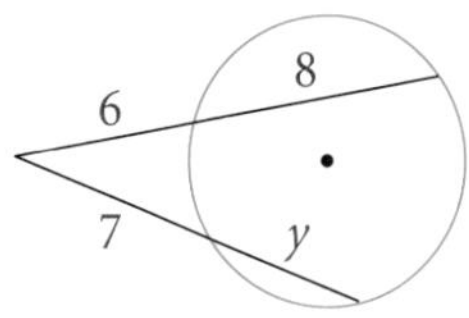

b.

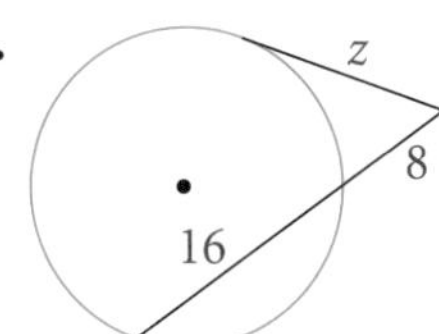

$(6 + 8)6 = (7 + y)7$ **Thm. 11-12 (II)**

$84 = 49 + 7y$ **Solve for *y*.**

$35 = 7y$

$5 = y$

$(8 + 16)8 = z^2$ **Thm. 11-12 (III)**

$192 = z^2$ **Solve for *z*.**

$13.9 \approx z$

✓ Check Understanding 3 Find the value of the variable to the nearest tenth.

a.

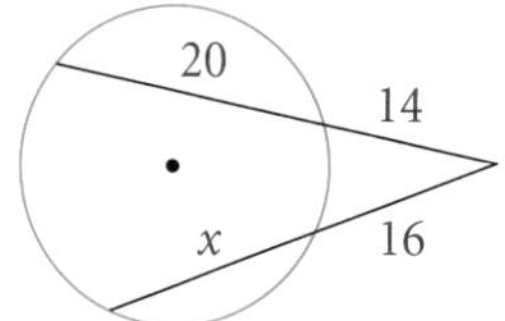

b.

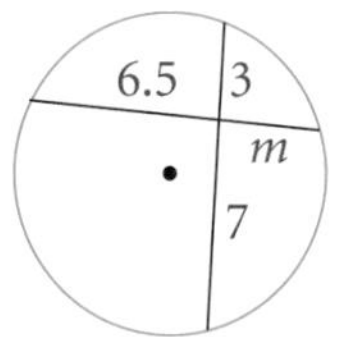

4 EXAMPLE Real-World Connection

Real-World Connection

The Taiko Bashi is a pedestrian bridge in the Japanese Tea Garden in San Francisco's Golden Gate Park.

Bridge Design The arch of the Taiko Bashi is an arc of a circle. A 14-ft chord is 4.8 ft from the edge of the circle. Find the radius of the circle.

Draw a diagram that shows a 14-ft chord 4.8 ft below the top of a circle. Let x represent the length of the part of the diameter from the chord to the bottom of the circle. Use x and Theorem 11-12 to find the radius.

$4.8x = 7 \cdot 7$ **Theorem 11-12 (I)**

$4.8x = 49$ **Solve for *x*.**

$x \approx 10.2$

diameter $\approx 10.2 + 4.8 = 15$ ft **Add the segment lengths.**

radius ≈ 7.5 ft

The radius is about 7.5 ft.

✓ Check Understanding 4 The basis of a design of a rotor for a Wankel engine is an equilateral triangle. Each side of the triangle is a chord to an arc of a circle. The opposite vertex of the triangle is the center of the arc. In the diagram at the right, each side of the equilateral triangle is 8 in. long.

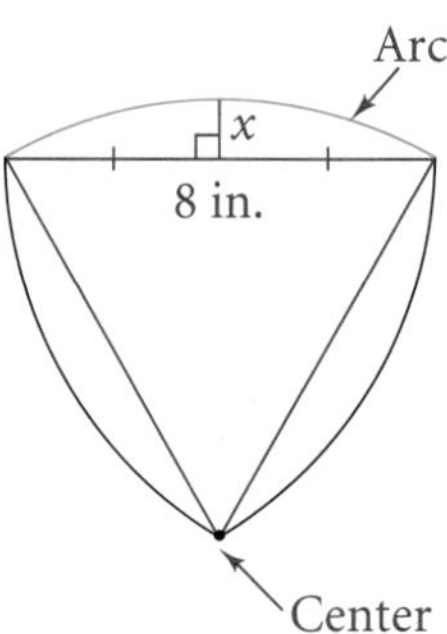

a. Use what you know about equilateral triangles and find the value of x.

b. **Critical Thinking** Copy the diagram and complete the circle with the given center. Then use Theorem 11-12 to find the value of x. Show that your answers to parts (a) and (b) are equal.

EXERCISES

For more practice, see *Extra Practice.*

Practice and Problem Solving

A Practice by Example  Algebra **Find the value of each variable.**

Example 1 (page 608)

1. 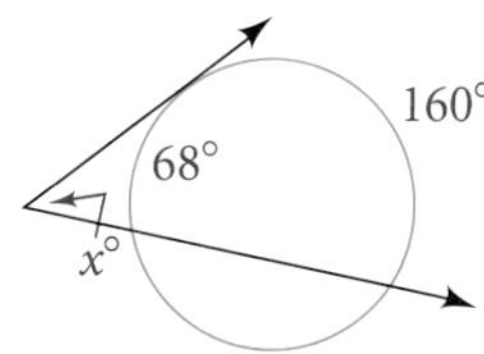

2.
130°
30°
$x°$

3. 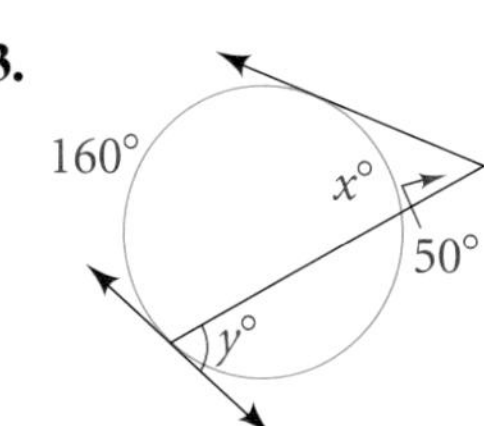

4. 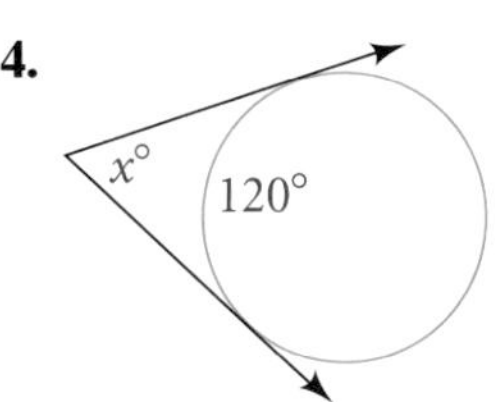

5. 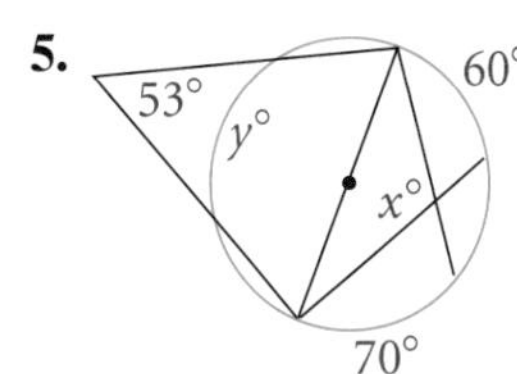

6. 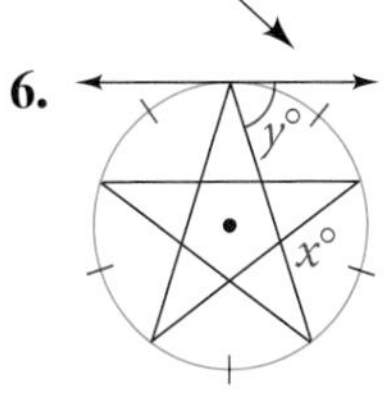

Example 2 (pages 608–609)

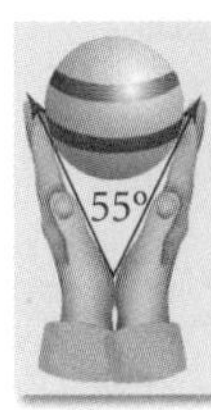

7. Astroscience A departing space probe sends back a picture of Earth as it crosses the plane of Earth's equator. The angle formed by the two tangents to the equator is 20°. What arc of the equator is visible to the space probe?

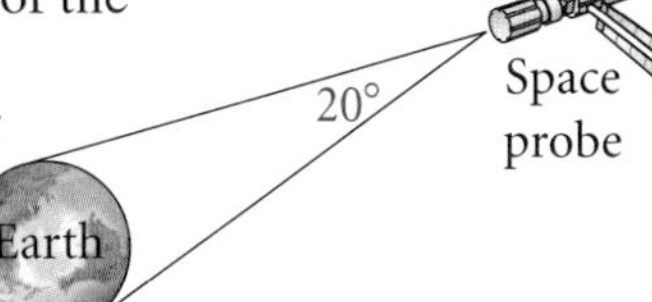

8. At the left, the cross section of the ball is a circle. About how many degrees is the arc of the circle that is below the points of contact with the hands?

Example 3 (page 610)

x^2 Algebra **Find the value of each variable using the given chord, secant, and tangent lengths. If the answer is not a whole number, round to the nearest tenth.**

9.
20
8
6
x

10. 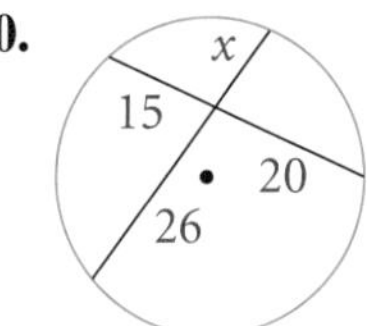

11. 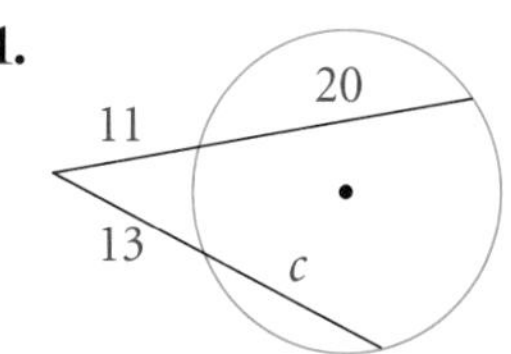

12.
6
x
3
7

13. 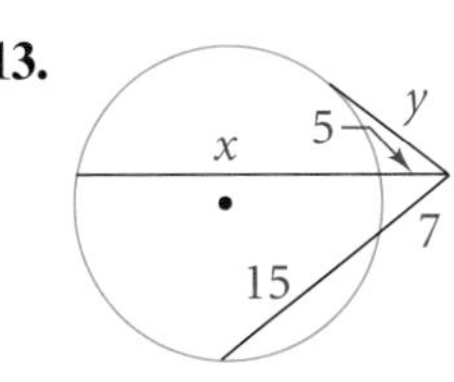

14. 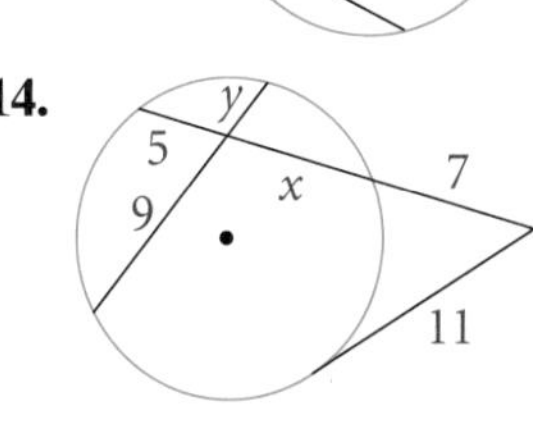

Example 4 (page 610)

Geology This natural arch, in Arches National Park, Utah, is an arc of a circle.

15. Find the diameter of the circle.

16. The chord length shown is rounded. It could range from 165 ft to 175 ft. Find the corresponding range for the diameter.

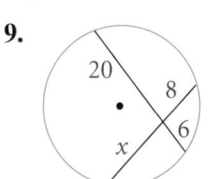 Apply Your Skills 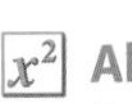 Algebra **$\overline{CA}$ and $\overline{CB}$ are tangents to $\odot O$. Write an expression for each arc or angle in terms of the given variable.**

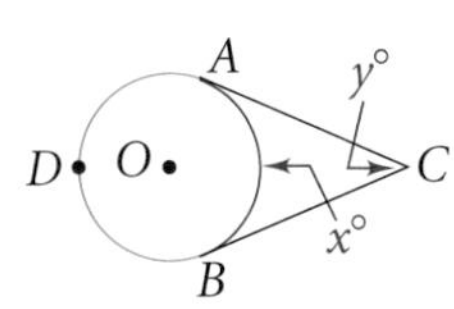

17. $m\widehat{ADB}$ using x **18.** $m\angle C$ using x **19.** $m\widehat{AB}$ using y

Find the diameter of $\odot O$. If your answer is not a whole number, round it to the nearest tenth.

20.

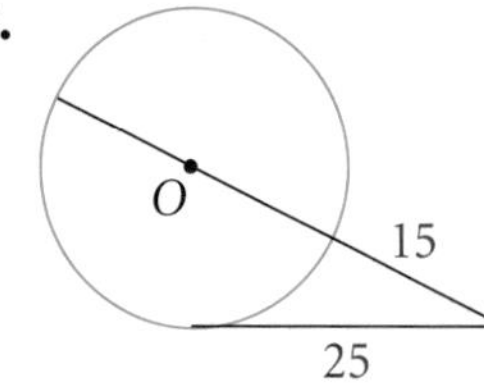

21.

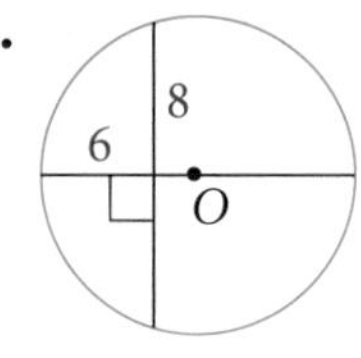

22.

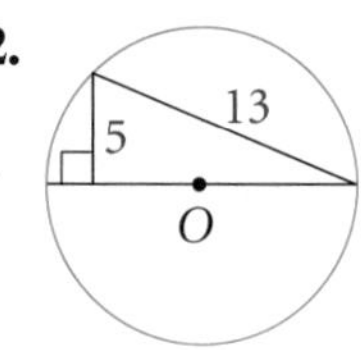

Algebra **Find the values of x and y using the given chord, secant, and tangent lengths. If your answer is not a whole number, round it to the nearest tenth.**

23.

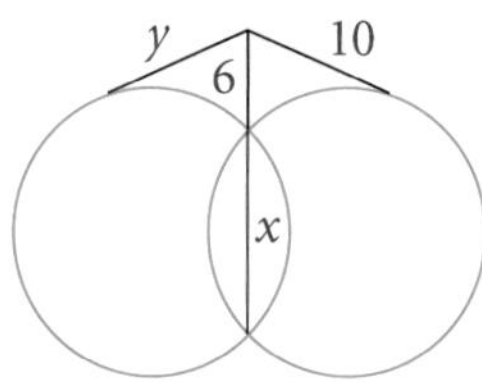

24.

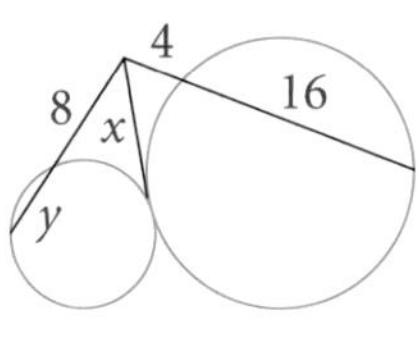

25.

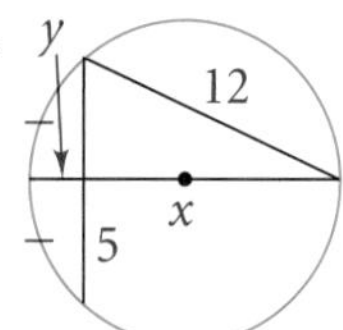

26. Error Analysis To find the value of x, a student wrote the equation $(7.5)6 = x^2$. What error did the student make?

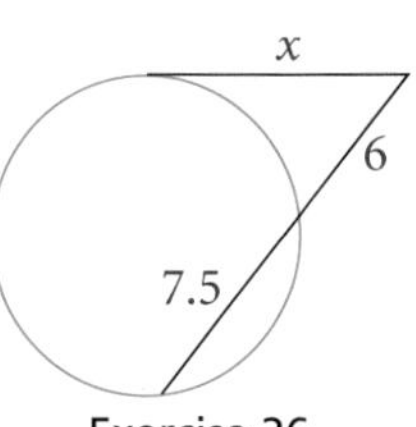

Exercise 26

27. A circle is inscribed in a quadrilateral whose four angles have measures 85, 76, 94, and 105. Find the measures of the four arcs between consecutive points of tangency.

28. Navigation The map at the left shows that the waters within $\widehat{AXB}$, a 300° arc, are unsafe. Here are what the letters represent.

A: a lighthouse B: a lighthouse X: locations of a ship on $\odot O$
Y: locations of a ship inside $\odot O$ Z: locations of a ship outside $\odot O$

a. Critical Thinking What measures are possible for $\angle X$? For $\angle Y$? For $\angle Z$?

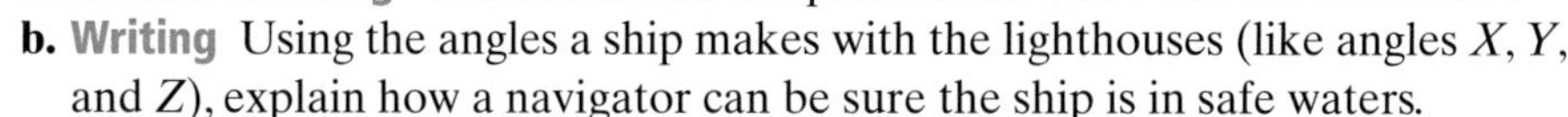

b. Writing Using the angles a ship makes with the lighthouses (like angles X, Y, and Z), explain how a navigator can be sure the ship is in safe waters.

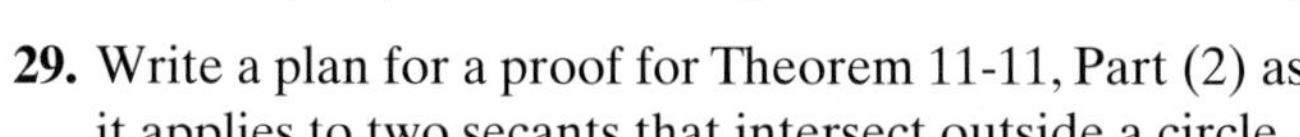

29. Write a plan for a proof for Theorem 11-11, Part (2) as it applies to two secants that intersect outside a circle.

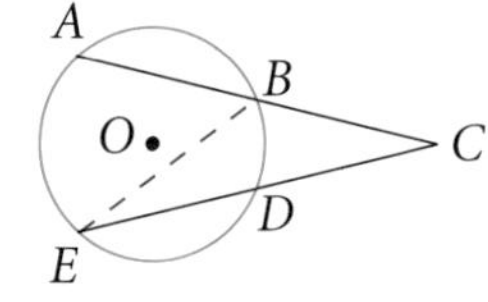

Given: $\odot O$ with secants $\overline{CA}$ and $\overline{CE}$ intersecting at C

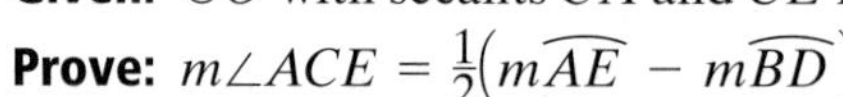

Prove: $m\angle ACE = \frac{1}{2}(m\widehat{AE} - m\widehat{BD})$

Proof **30.** Prove the other two cases of Theorem 11-11, Part (2). (See Exercise 29.)

Proof **For Exercises 31 and 32, write proofs that use similar triangles.**

31. Prove Theorem 11-12 (II). **32.** Prove Theorem 11-12 (III).

33. Explain why Theorem 11-12 is true when the given point is on the circle.

Challenge Proof **In Exercises 34–37, prove each statement or theorem.**

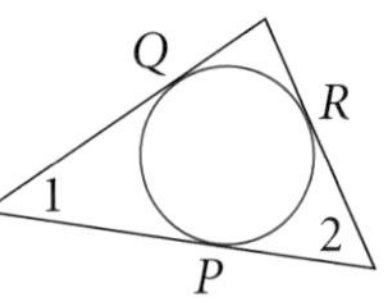

Exercises 34, 35

34. $m\angle 1 + m\widehat{PQ} = 180$ **35.** $m\angle 1 + m\angle 2 = m\widehat{QR}$

36. the Pythagorean Theorem (Use the diagram at the right and the theorems of this lesson.)

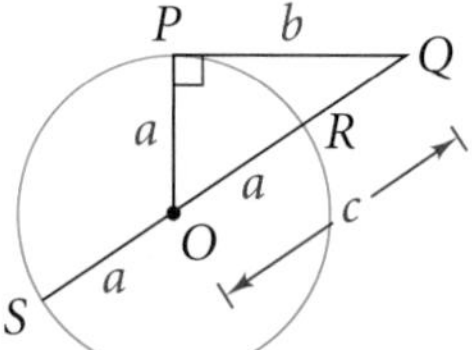

37. The tangents to a circle at the vertices of an inscribed equilateral triangle form an equilateral triangle.

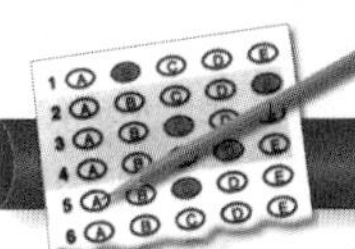

Standardized Test Prep

Gridded Response

Take It to the NET Online lesson quiz at **www.PHSchool.com** Web Code: afa-1104

38. If $m\widehat{AE} = 86$ and $m\widehat{BD} = 40$, find $m\angle BKD$.
39. If $AK = 14$, $EK = 17$, and $BK = 7$, find DK.
40. If $BC = 6$, $DC = 5$, and $CE = 12$, find AC.
41. If $m\angle C = 14$ and $m\widehat{AE} = 140$, find $m\widehat{BD}$.
42. If $m\widehat{AB} = 110$ and $m\widehat{DE} = 130$, find $m\angle AKE$.

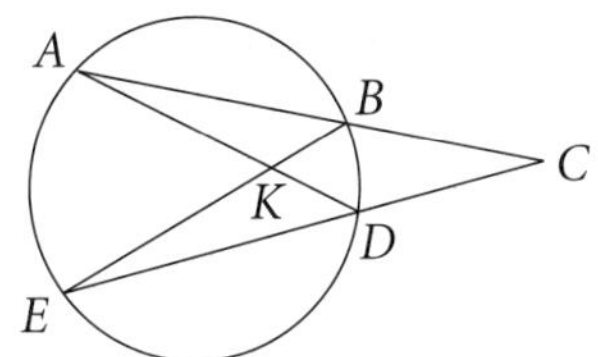

Mixed Review

Lesson 11-3 **Find the value of each variable.**

43.

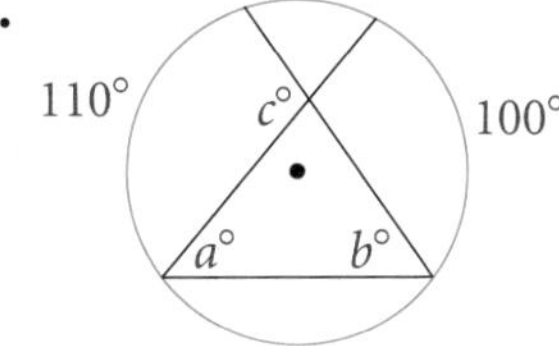

44.

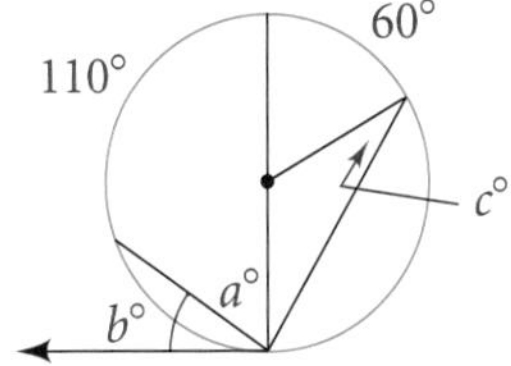

Lesson 9-2 **Find the value of x to the nearest degree.**

45.

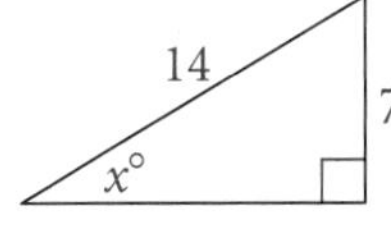

46.

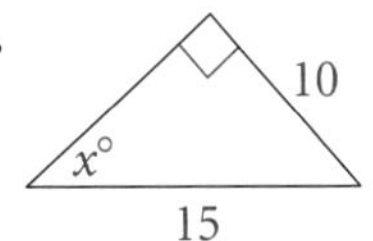

47.

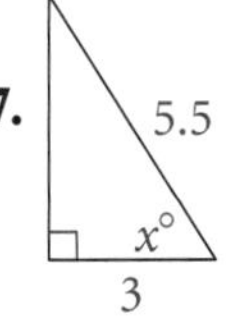

Lesson 8-6 **48.** The areas of two similar parallelograms are 20 cm^2 and 3.2 cm^2. Find the similarity ratio of the larger parallelogram to the smaller parallelogram.

Geometry at Work

Aerospace Engineer

Aerospace engineers design and build all types of spacecraft, from the low-orbit space shuttle to interplanetary probes. Much of today's work involves communications satellites that relay television, telephone, computer, and other signals all over the world. The portion of Earth's surface that can communicate with a satellite increases as the height of the orbit increases.

Earth has a radius of about 3960 miles. The figure at the right shows a satellite 12,000 miles above Earth. $\widehat{AB}$ is the arc of Earth that is in the range of the satellite. You can find $m\widehat{AB}$ by finding $m\angle AEB$, which is twice $m\angle AES$.

S
12,000 mi
A
3960 mi
E
B
Earth

$$m\widehat{AB} = m\angle AEB = 2m\angle AES = 2 \cdot \cos^{-1}\left(\frac{3960}{3960 + 12{,}000}\right) \approx 151.3$$

The measure of the arc of Earth in the range of the satellite is about 151.3.

Take It to the NET For more information about aerospace careers, go to **www.PHSchool.com.** Web Code: afb-2031

Extension

Tangent Lines, Tangent Ratios

For Use With Lesson 11-4

You learned about tangent ratios in Chapter 9 and tangent lines in this chapter. Are the two related? Yes, indeed! In fact, there are six trigonometric ratios that you can study in advanced mathematics.

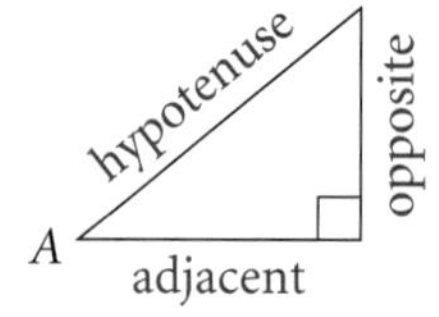

$$\text{sine } \angle A = \frac{\text{opposite}}{\text{hypotenuse}} \qquad \text{cosine } \angle A = \frac{\text{adjacent}}{\text{hypotenuse}} \qquad \text{tangent } \angle A = \frac{\text{opposite}}{\text{adjacent}}$$

$$\text{cosecant } \angle A = \frac{\text{hypotenuse}}{\text{opposite}} \qquad \text{secant } \angle A = \frac{\text{hypotenuse}}{\text{adjacent}} \qquad \text{cotangent } \angle A = \frac{\text{adjacent}}{\text{opposite}}$$

Each of these is related to the geometry of a unit circle, the circle shown in both figures below. Sine A, tangent A, and secant A are the segment lengths highlighted in Figure 1. Cosine A, cotangent A, and cosecant A are highlighted in Figure 2.

Figure 1:

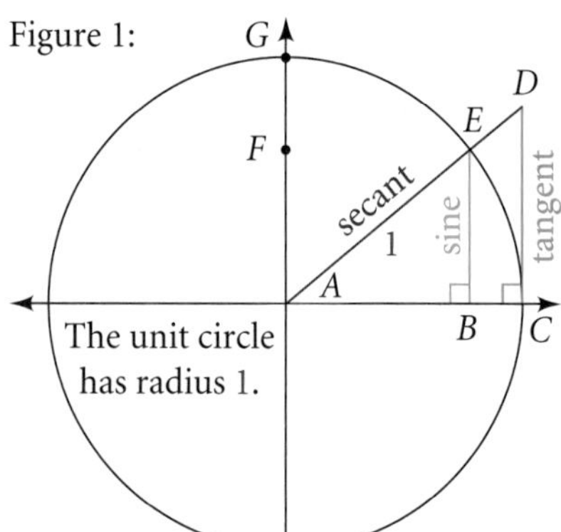

Figure 2:

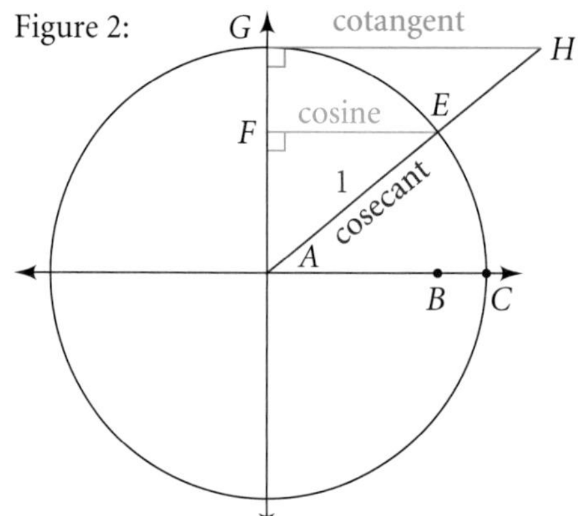

EXERCISES

1. For the four triangles shown above, complete these similarity statements: $\triangle ABE \sim \triangle$ _?_ $\sim \triangle$ _?_ $\sim \triangle$ _?_.
2. Explain why the sine A, tangent A, and secant A ratios have the same values as the segment lengths highlighted in Figure 1.
3. Explain why the cosine A, cotangent A, and cosecant A ratios have the same values as the segment lengths highlighted in Figure 2.

Describe the connection between each of the following.

4. the tangent A ratio and a tangent segment
5. the secant A ratio and a secant segment
6. $\angle EAB$ in Figure 1 and $\angle EAF$ in Figure 2; what are the first two letters in a word that is commonly used to describe this connection?

Show that each equation is true.

7. $(\text{tangent } A)^2 = (\text{secant } A)^2 - 1$
8. $\text{tangent } A = \frac{\text{sine } A}{\text{cosine } A}$
9. $\text{cotangent } A = \frac{1}{\text{tangent } A}$
10. $(\text{sine } A)^2 + (\text{cosine } A)^2 = 1$
11. $\text{secant } A = \frac{1}{\text{cosine } A}$
12. $\text{cosecant } A = \frac{1}{\text{sine } A}$

Circles in the Coordinate Plane

Lesson Preview

What You'll Learn

To write an equation of a circle

To find the center and radius of a circle

. . . And Why

To describe the position and range of three cellular telephone towers, as in Example 4

Check Skills You'll Need

(For help, go to Lesson 1-6.)

Find the length of each segment to the nearest tenth.

1.

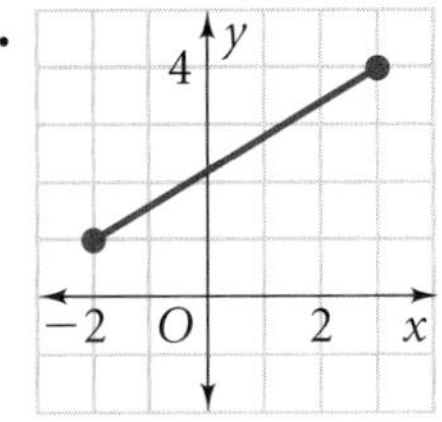

2.

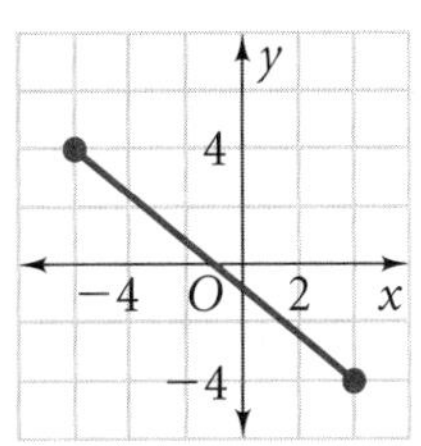

3.

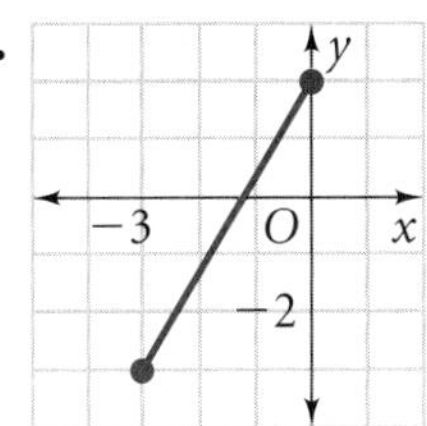

New Vocabulary • standard form of an equation of a circle

Interactive lesson includes instant self-check, tutorials, and activities.

OBJECTIVE 1

Writing an Equation of a Circle

You can use the Distance Formula to find an equation of a circle with center (h, k) and radius r. Let (x, y) be any point on the circle. Then the radius r is the distance from (h, k) to (x, y).

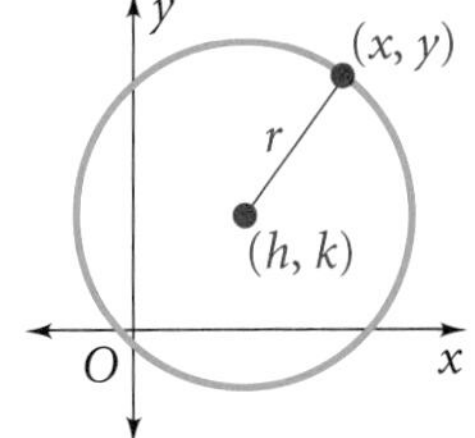

$r = \sqrt{(x - h)^2 + (y - k)^2}$ **Distance Formula**

$r^2 = (x - h)^2 + (y - k)^2$ **Square both sides.**

This essentially proves the following theorem.

Key Concepts

Theorem 11-13

An equation of a circle with center (h, k) and radius r is $(x - h)^2 + (y - k)^2 = r^2$.

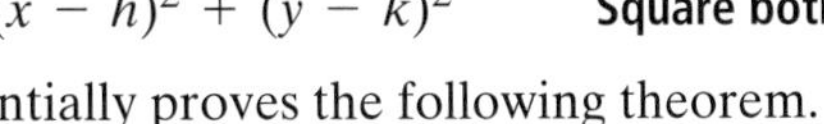

The equation $(x - h)^2 + (y - k)^2 = r^2$ is in **standard form.** You may also call it the *standard equation* of a circle.

1 EXAMPLE Writing the Equation of a Circle

Write the standard equation of the circle with center (5, −2) and radius 7.

$(x - h)^2 + (y - k)^2 = r^2$ **Use standard form.**

$(x - 5)^2 + [y - (-2)]^2 = 7^2$ **Substitute (5, −2) for (h, k), and 7 for r.**

$(x - 5)^2 + (y + 2)^2 = 49$ **Simplify.**

Check Understanding **1** Write the standard equation of each circle.

a. center (3, 5); radius 6

b. center (−2, −1); radius $\sqrt{2}$

If you know the center of a circle and a point on the circle, you can write the standard equation of the circle.

2 EXAMPLE Using the Center and a Point on a Circle

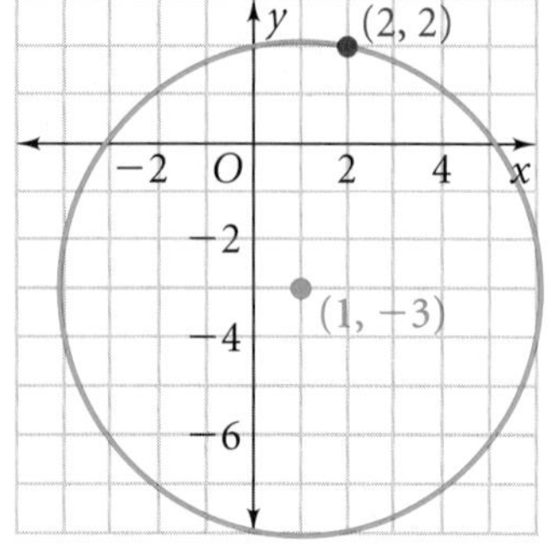

Write the standard equation of the circle with center $(1, -3)$ that passes through the point $(2, 2)$.

$r = \sqrt{(x - h)^2 + (y - k)^2}$ **Use the Distance Formula to find *r*.**

$= \sqrt{(2 - 1)^2 + (2 - (-3))^2}$ **Substitute (1, −3) for (*h*, *k*), and (2, 2) for (*x*, *y*).**

$= \sqrt{1 + 25} = \sqrt{26}$ **Simplify.**

$(x - h)^2 + (y - k)^2 = r^2$ **Use standard form.**

$(x - 1)^2 + [y - (-3)^2] = (\sqrt{26})^2$ **Substitute (1, −3) for (*h*, *k*), and $\sqrt{26}$ for *r*.**

$(x - 1)^2 + (y + 3)^2 = 26$ **Simplify.**

Check Understanding 2 Write the standard equation of the circle with center $(2, 3)$ that passes through the point $(-1, 1)$.

OBJECTIVE

2 Finding the Center and Radius of a Circle

If you know the standard equation of a circle, you can describe the circle by naming its center and radius. Then you can use this information to graph the circle.

3 EXAMPLE Graphing a Circle Given its Equation

Need Help?

Standard form requires that $y + 2$ be written with a minus sign.

Find the center and radius of the circle with equation $(x - 7)^2 + (y + 2)^2 = 64$. Then graph the circle.

$(x - 7)^2 + (y + 2)^2 = 64$

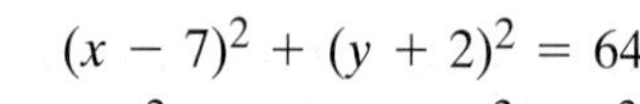

$(x - 7)^2 + (y - (-2))^2 = 8^2$ **Use standard form.**

↑ h ↑ k ↑ r

The center is $(7, -2)$ and the radius is 8.

To graph the circle, place the compass point at the center $(7, -2)$ and draw a circle with radius 8.

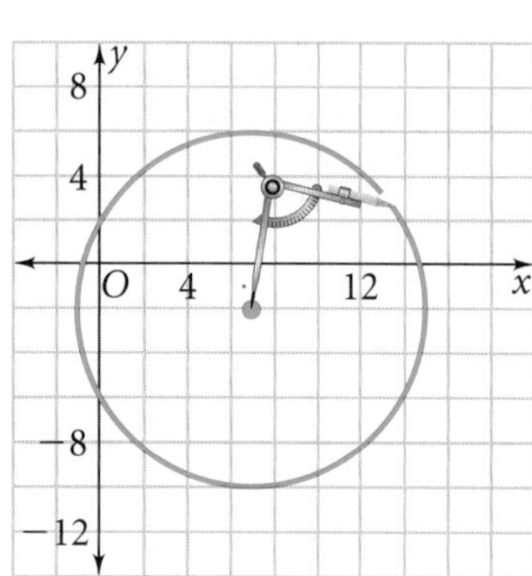

Check Understanding 3 Find the center and radius of the circle with equation $(x - 2)^2 + (y - 3)^2 = 100$. Then graph the circle.

You can use equations of circles to model real-world situations.

4 EXAMPLE Real-World Connection

Real-World Connection

To blend into the landscape, cellular phone towers can be disguised as trees.

Communications When you make a call on a cellular phone, a tower receives the call. In the diagram, the centers of circles O and A are locations of cellular telephone towers.

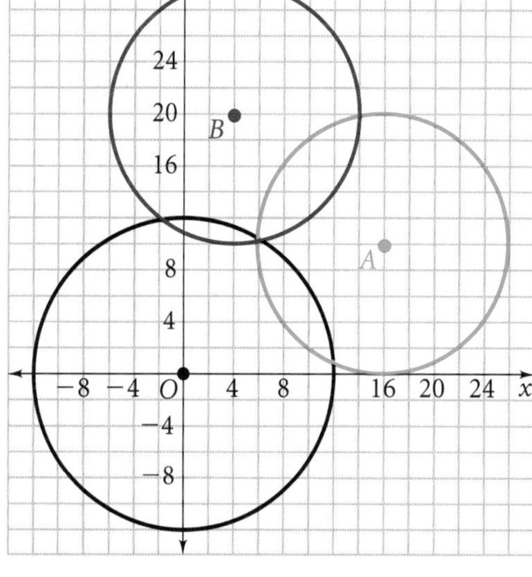

a. The equation $(x - 16)^2 + (y - 10)^2 = 100$ models the position and range of Tower A. Describe the position and range of Tower A.

$(x - 16)^2 + (y - 10)^2 = 10^2$ is in standard form. It shows that tower A is located at (16, 10) and has a range of 10 units.

b. A new tower is to be built at B with range indicated in the graph. Write an equation that describes the position and range of this tower.

$\odot B$ has center (4, 20) and radius 10. Substitute these into the standard equation.

$(x - h)^2 + (y - k)^2 = r^2$

$(x - 4)^2 + (y - 20)^2 = 10^2$ **Substitute.**

$(x - 4)^2 + (y - 20)^2 = 100$ **This is an equation for Tower *B*.**

Check Understanding 4 Write an equation that describes the position and range of Tower O.

EXERCISES

For more practice, see *Extra Practice*.

Practice and Problem Solving

A Practice by Example

Example 1 (page 615)

Write the standard equation of each circle.

1. center $(2, -8)$; $r = 9$ **2.** center $(0, 3)$; $r = 7$ **3.** center $(0.2, 1.1)$; $r = 0.4$

4. center $(5, -1)$; $r = 12$ **5.** center $(-6, 3)$; $r = 8$ **6.** center $(-9, -4)$; $r = \sqrt{5}$

7. center $(0, 0)$; $r = 4$ **8.** center $(-4, 0)$; $r = 3$ **9.** center $(-1, -1)$; $r = 1$

Example 2 (page 616)

Write the standard equation of the circle with the given center that passes through the given point.

10. center $(-2, 6)$; point $(-2, 10)$ **11.** center $(1, 2)$; point $(0, 6)$

12. center $(7, -2)$; point $(1, -6)$ **13.** center $(-10, -5)$; point $(-5, 5)$

14. center $(6, 5)$; point $(0, 0)$ **15.** center $(-1, -4)$; point $(-4, 0)$

Example 3 (page 616)

Find the center and radius of the circle with the given equation. Then graph the circle.

16. $(x + 7)^2 + (y - 5)^2 = 16$ **17.** $(x - 3)^2 + (y + 8)^2 = 100$

18. $(x + 4)^2 + (y - 1)^2 = 25$ **19.** $x^2 + y^2 = 36$

20. $(x - 0.3)^2 + y^2 = 0.04$ **21.** $(x + 5)^2 + (y + 2)^2 = 48$

Example 4
(page 617)

Use the diagram at the right. Write an equation that describes the position and radius of each circle.

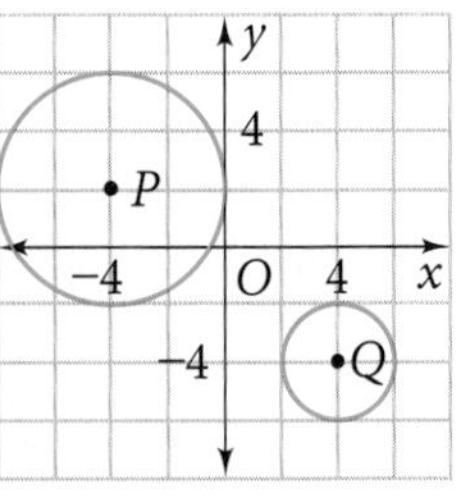

22. $\odot P$ **23.** $\odot Q$

24. **Communications** The plotted location of a cellular phone tower on a coordinate grid is $(-3, 2)$ and the range is 5 units. Write an equation that describes the position and range of the tower.

Each equation models the position and range of a tornado alert siren. Describe the position and range of each.

25. $(x - 5)^2 + (y - 7)^2 = 81$ **26.** $(x + 4)^2 + (y - 9)^2 = 144$

B Apply Your Skills

Write the standard equation of each circle.

27.

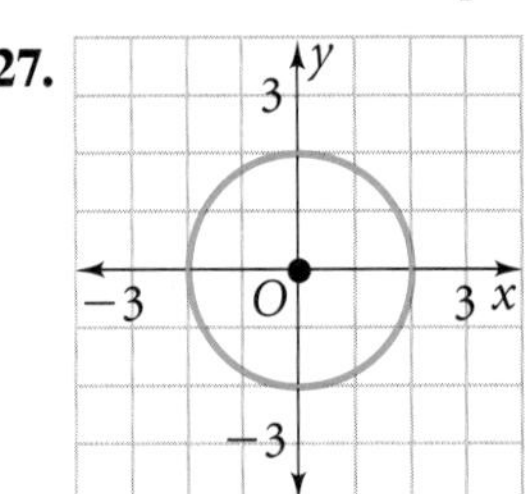

28.

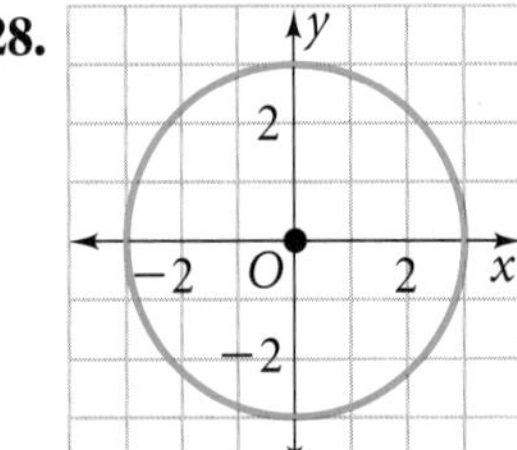

29.

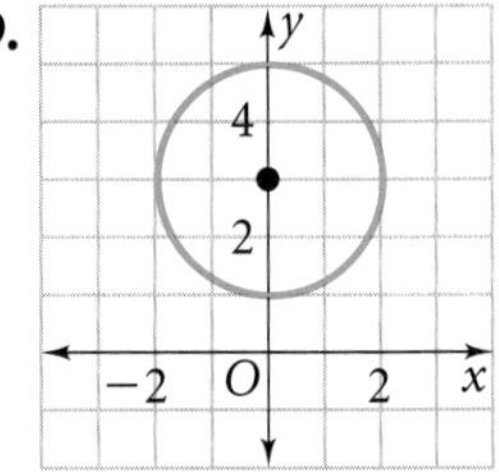

30.

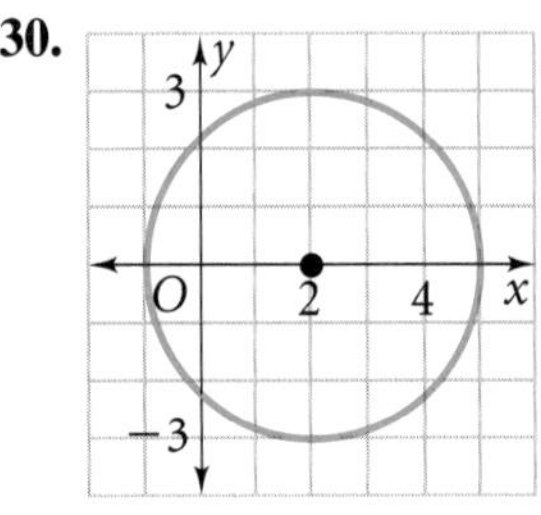

31.

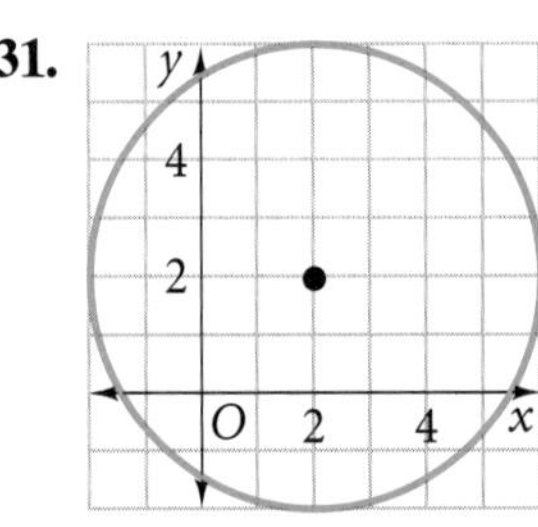

32.

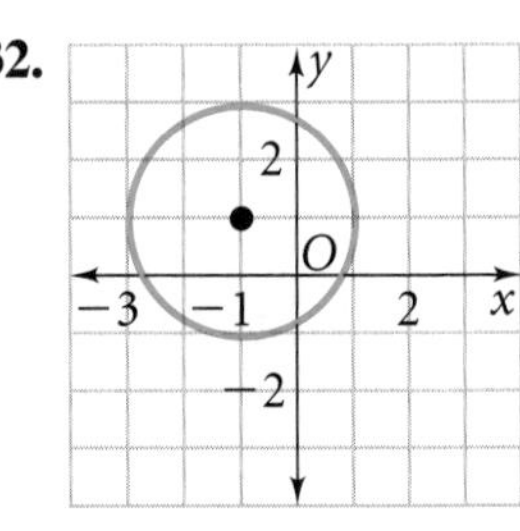

Need Help?
In Exercises 33–38, use the Midpoint Formula (p. 45) to find centers.

Write an equation of a circle with diameter $\overline{AB}$.

33. $A(0, 0), B(8, 6)$ **34.** $A(3, 0), B(7, 6)$ **35.** $A(1, 1), B(5, 5)$

36. $A(-1, 0), B(-5, -3)$ **37.** $A(-3, 1), B(0, 9)$ **38.** $A(-2, 3), B(6, -7)$

39. The *unit circle* has center $(0, 0)$ and radius 1. Write an equation for this circle.

40. **Critical Thinking** Describe the graph of $x^2 + y^2 = r^2$ when $r = 0$.

41. **Open-Ended** On graph paper, make a design that includes at least three circles. Write the standard equations of your circles.

Determine whether each equation is an equation of a circle. If not, explain.

42. $(x - 1)^2 + (y + 2)^2 = 9$ **43.** $x + y = 9$ **44.** $x + (y - 3)^2 = 9$

45. Find the circumference and area of the circle whose equation is $(x - 9)^2 + (y - 3)^2 = 64$. Leave your answers in terms of π.

46. Write an equation of a circle with area 36π and center $(4, 7)$.

47. What are the x- and y-intercepts of the line tangent to the circle $(x - 2)^2 + (y - 2)^2 = 5^2$ at the point $(5, 6)$?

48. For $(x - h)^2 + (y - k)^2 = r^2$, show that $y = \sqrt{r^2 - (x - h)^2} + k$, or $y = -\sqrt{r^2 - (x - h)^2} + k$.

Take It to the NET
Graphing Calculator procedures online at **www.PHSchool.com**
Web Code: afe-2110

Graphing Calculator **Use a graphing calculator to graph each circle. (*Hint:* See Exercise 48.) View the plotting in both sequential mode and simultaneous mode.**

49. $(x - 3)^2 + (y - 2)^2 = 9$

50. $(x + 5)^2 + (y - 8)^2 = 1$

51. circle with center $(0, 0)$ and radius 7

52. circle with center $(-6, -3)$ and radius 2

Find all points of intersection of each pair of graphs. Make a sketch.

53. $x^2 + y^2 = 13$, $y = -x + 5$

54. $x^2 + y^2 = 17$, $y = -\frac{1}{4}x$

55. $x^2 + y^2 = 8$, $y = 2$

56. $x^2 + y^2 = 20$, $y = -\frac{1}{2}x + 5$

57. $(x + 1)^2 + (y - 1)^2 = 18$, $y = x + 8$

58. $(x - 2)^2 + (y - 2)^2 = 10$, $y = -\frac{1}{3}x + 6$

Graphing Calculator **Use a graphing calculator to convince yourself that the given line is not tangent to the circle $x^2 + y^2 = 25$. Explain what you did.**

59. $y = -5x + 26$

60. $3x + 5y = 29$

61. Writing Explain why it is not possible to conclude that a line and a circle are tangent by viewing their graphs.

Challenge

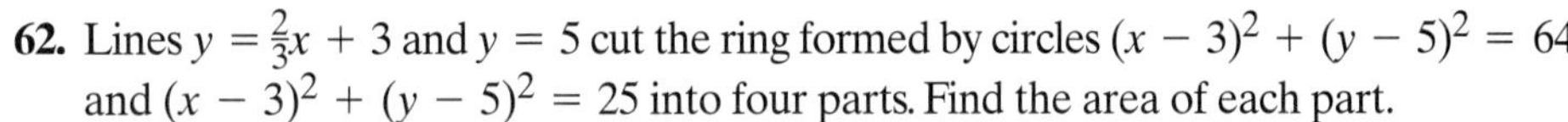

62. Lines $y = \frac{2}{3}x + 3$ and $y = 5$ cut the ring formed by circles $(x - 3)^2 + (y - 5)^2 = 64$ and $(x - 3)^2 + (y - 5)^2 = 25$ into four parts. Find the area of each part.

63. Nautical Distance The radius of Earth's equator is about 3960 miles.

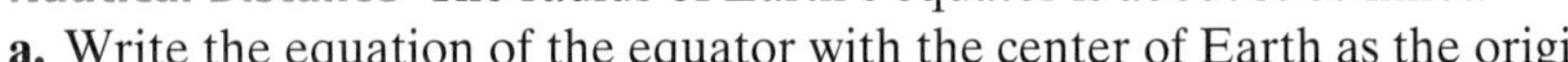

a. Write the equation of the equator with the center of Earth as the origin.
b. Find the length of a 1° arc on the equator to the nearest tenth of a mile.
c. A 1° arc along the equator is 60 nautical miles long. How many miles are in a nautical mile? Round to the nearest tenth.
d. History Columbus planned his trip to the East by going west. He thought each 1° arc was 45 miles long. He estimated that the trip would take 21 days. Use your answer to part (b) to find a better estimate.

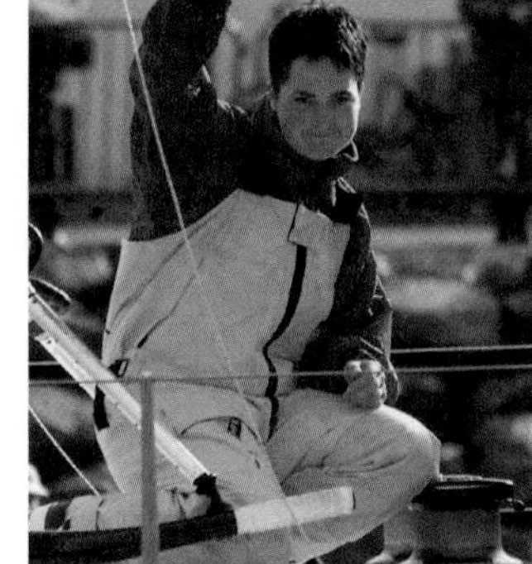

Real-World Connection

In 2001, Ellen MacArthur, age 24, sailed solo around the world in 94.2 days.

64. Geometry in 3 Dimensions The equation of a sphere is similar to the equation of a circle. The equation of a sphere with center (h, j, k) and radius r is

$$(x - h)^2 + (y - j)^2 + (z - k)^2 = r^2.$$

a. $M(-1, 3, 2)$ is the center of a sphere passing through $T(0, 5, 1)$. What is the radius of the sphere?
b. Write an equation of the sphere.

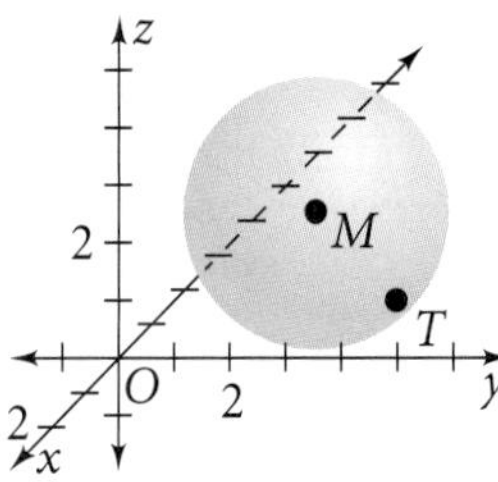

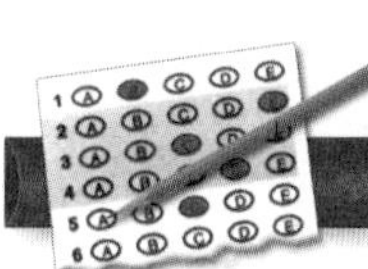

Standardized Test Prep

Multiple Choice

65. What is an equation of a circle with radius 16 and center (2, −5)?

A. $(x - 2)^2 + (y + 5)^2 = 16$
B. $(x + 2)^2 + (y - 5)^2 = 256$
C. $(x + 2)^2 + (y - 5)^2 = 4$
D. $(x - 2)^2 + (y + 5)^2 = 256$

66. What are the coordinates of the center of the circle whose equation is $(x - 9)^2 + (y + 4)^2 = 1$?

F. (3, −2) **G.** (−3, 2) **H.** (−9, 4) **I.** (9, −4)

Take It to the NET
Online lesson quiz at **www.PHSchool.com**
Web Code: afa-1105

67. What is the diameter of the circle with equation $(x - 1)^2 + (y + 1)^2 = 4$?

A. 1 **B.** 2 **C.** 4 **D.** 16

Short Response

68. Show how to find the radius of the circle whose equation is $x^2 + (y + 8)^2 = 25$.

Extended Response

69. The line represented by the equation $y = -\frac{4}{3}x + 11$ is tangent to a circle at (6, 3). The center of the circle is on the x-axis. Write an equation of the circle. Show your work.

Mixed Review

Lesson 11-4

Find the value of each variable. Assume that lines that appear tangent are tangent.

70.

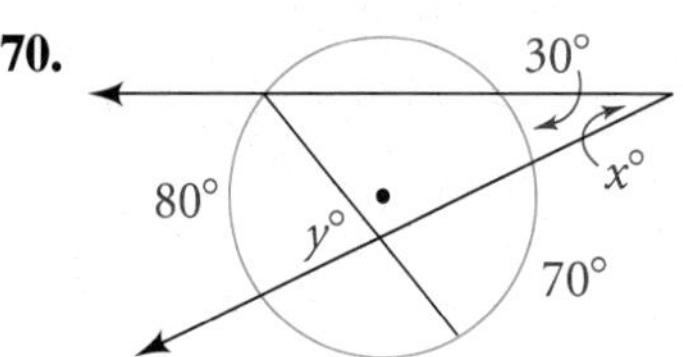

71.

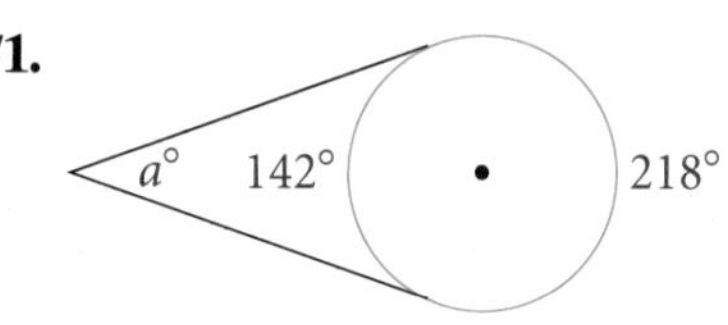

Lesson 9-4

For the given vectors $\vec{a}$ and $\vec{c}$, write the sum $\vec{a} + \vec{c}$ as an ordered pair.

72. $\vec{a} = \langle -2, 5 \rangle$ and $\vec{c} = \langle 8, 7 \rangle$

73. $\vec{a} = \langle -3, -4 \rangle$ and $\vec{c} = \langle -2, 6 \rangle$

74. $\vec{a} = \langle 3, 1 \rangle$ and $\vec{c} = \langle 1, 3 \rangle$

75. $\vec{a} = \langle 9, -6 \rangle$ and $\vec{c} = \langle 2, -1 \rangle$

Lesson 8-4

Find the geometric mean of each pair of numbers in simplest radical form.

76. 3 and 12

77. 9 and 27

78. 4 and 18

79. $\sqrt{3}$ and $\sqrt{27}$

80. $\sqrt{3}$ and $\sqrt{12}$

81. $\frac{3}{8}$ and $\frac{3}{2}$

Checkpoint Quiz 2 — Lessons 11-4 through 11-5

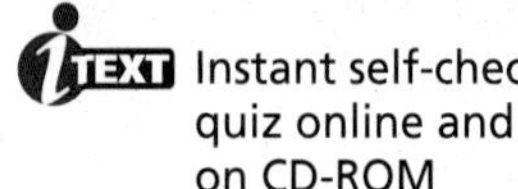

Instant self-check quiz online and on CD-ROM

Find the value of each variable. Assume that lines that appear tangent are tangent.

1. 170°, 56°, x°

2.

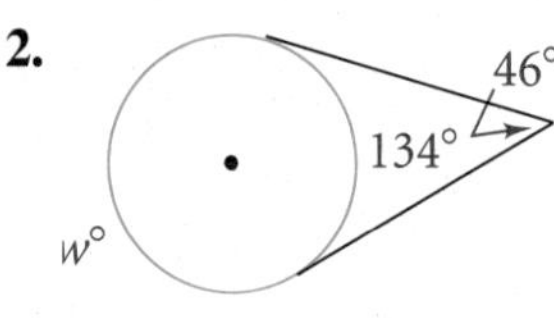

3.

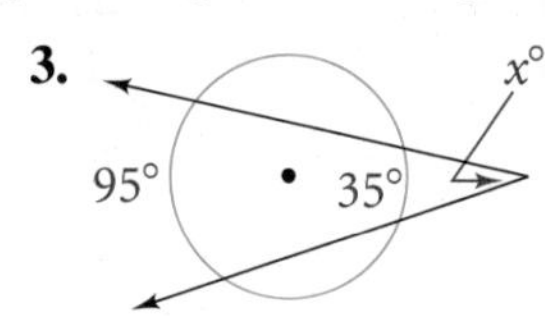

4. 4, 5.5, c, 5.9

5.

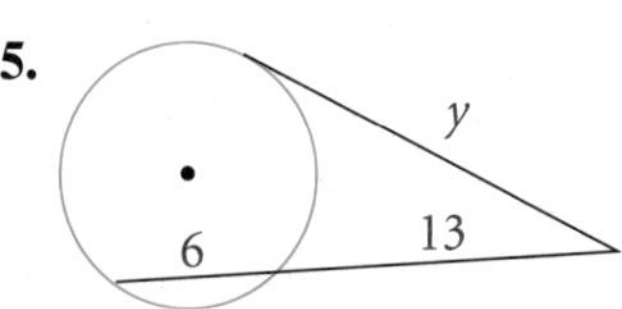

6. In the circle at the right, what is $m\overparen{BF}$?

7. Writing Explain the difference between a chord and a secant. Include a diagram.

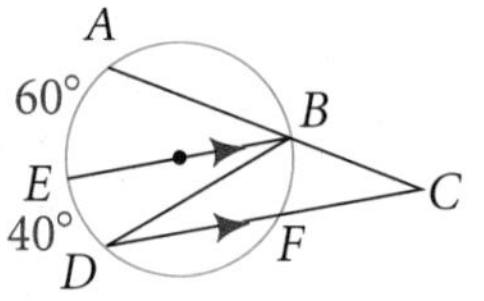

The endpoints of a diameter are given. Write an equation of the circle.

8. (3, 1) and (0, 0)

9. (−2, 5) and (9, −3)

10. (−4, −8) and (1, 0)

Locus: A Set of Points

Lesson Preview

What You'll Learn

To draw and describe a locus

. . . And Why

To interpret a locus description of a geometric figure, as in Example 3

Check Skills You'll Need

(For help, go to Lessons 1-5 and 3-7.)

Sketch each of the following.

1. the perpendicular bisector of $\overline{CD}$

2. $\angle EFG$ bisected by $\overrightarrow{FH}$

3. line k parallel to line m and perpendicular to line w, all in plane N

New Vocabulary

• locus

Interactive lesson includes instant self-check, tutorials, and activities.

OBJECTIVE

1 Drawing and Describing a Locus

A **locus** is a set of points, all of which meet a stated condition. To sketch a locus, draw points of the locus until you see a pattern.

1 EXAMPLE Describing a Locus in a Plane

a. Draw and describe the locus: In a plane, the points 1 cm from a given point C.

Draw a point C.
Sketch several points 1 cm from C.
Keep doing so until you see a pattern.
Draw the figure the pattern suggests.

The locus is a circle with center C and radius 1 cm.

b. Draw and describe the locus: In a plane, the points 1 cm from a segment $\overline{AB}$.

The locus is
- two segments parallel to $\overline{AB}$ and
- two semicircles centered at A and B

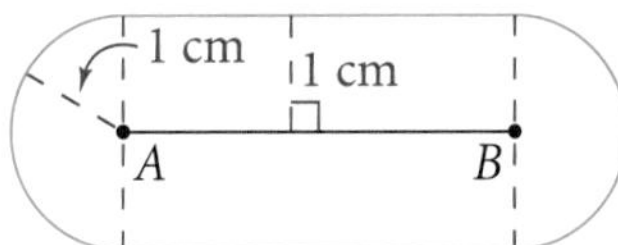

Real-World Connection

The locus of footprints of children pushing the merry-go-round is a circle.

Check Understanding

1 Draw and describe the locus: In a plane, the points 2 cm from a line $\overleftrightarrow{XY}$.

You can use locus descriptions for geometric terms.

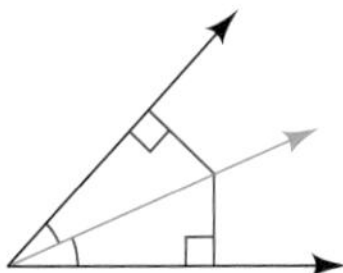

An angle bisector: The points in the interior of the angle that are equidistant from the sides of the angle.

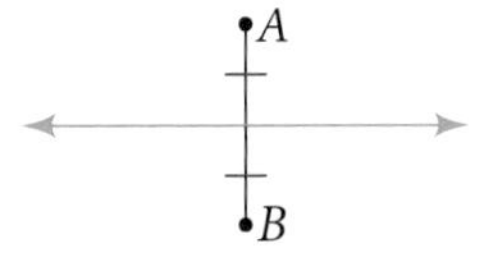

A perpendicular bisector of a segment: In a plane, the points that are equidistant from the segment endpoints.

Reading Math

The word "locus" comes from the Latin word for "location." Its plural is *loci* (LOH sy).

Sometimes a locus is described by two conditions. You can draw the locus by first drawing the points that satisfy each condition. Then find their intersection.

2 EXAMPLE Drawing a Locus for Two Conditions

Draw the locus: In a plane, the points equidistant from two lines k and m and 5 cm from the point where k and m intersect.

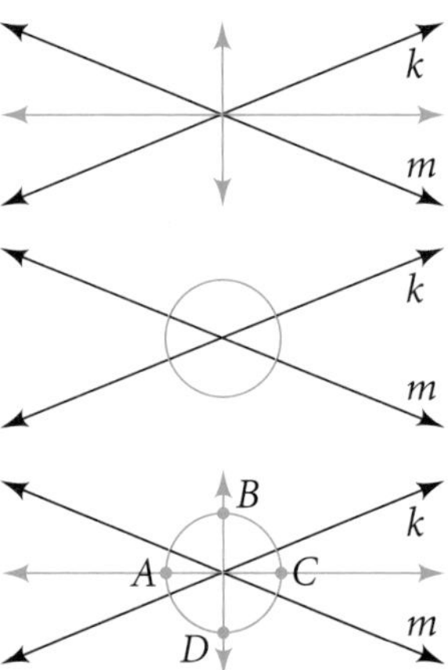

The points in a plane equidistant from lines k and m are two lines that bisect the vertical angles formed by k and m.

The points in a plane 5 cm from the point where k and m intersect is a circle.

The locus that satisfies both conditions is the set of points A, B, C, and D.

✓ Check Understanding 2 Draw the locus: In a plane, the points equidistant from two points X and Y and 2 cm from the midpoint of $\overline{XY}$.

A locus in a plane and a locus in space can be quite different.

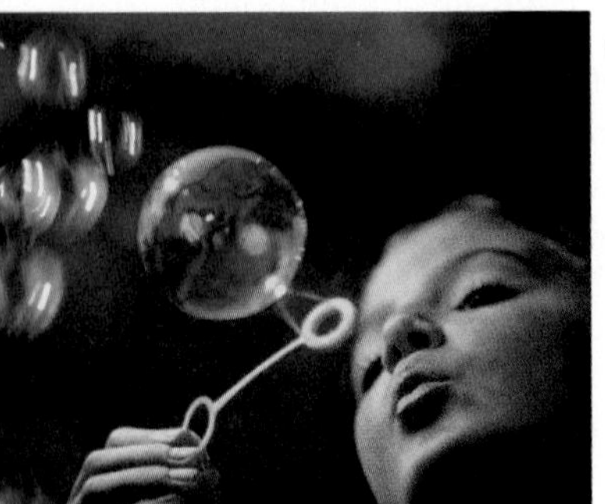

Real-World Connection

A soap bubble is a sphere, a locus of points in space that are a given distance from a given point.

3 EXAMPLE Describing a Locus in Space

a. Draw and describe the locus: In space, the points that are c units from a point D.

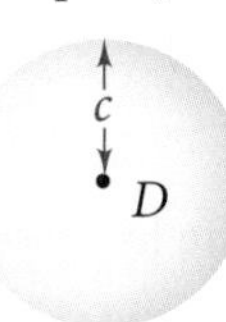

The locus is a sphere with center at point D and radius c.

b. Draw and describe the locus: In space, the points that are 3 cm from a line ℓ.

The locus is an endless cylinder with radius 3 cm and center-line ℓ.

✓ Check Understanding 3 Draw and describe each locus.
a. In a plane, the points that are equidistant from two parallel lines.
b. In space, the points that are equidistant from two parallel planes.

You can also think of a locus as a path. For example, the locus of the tip of a hand of a clock each day is the circle traced by the tip as it travels around the clock face. The locus of a point on the handle of a sliding-glass door when you enter a room is the line segment along which the point travels as the door slides back and forth.

EXERCISES

For more practice, see *Extra Practice.*

Practice and Problem Solving

A Practice by Example

Example 1 (page 621)

Draw and describe each locus in a plane.

1. points 4 cm from a point X
2. points 2 in. from a segment $\overline{UV}$
3. points 3 mm from a line $\overleftrightarrow{LM}$
4. points 1 in. from a circle with radius 3 in.
5. points equidistant from the endpoints of $\overline{PQ}$
6. points in the interior of $\angle ABC$ and equidistant from the sides of $\angle ABC$
7. points equidistant from two perpendicular lines
8. midpoints of radii of a circle with radius 2 cm

Example 2 (page 622)

In a plane, draw the locus whose points satisfy the given conditions.

9. equidistant from points M and N and on a circle with center M and radius $= \frac{1}{2}MN$
10. 3 cm from $\overline{GH}$ and 5 cm from G, where $GH = 4.5$ cm
11. equidistant from the sides of $\angle PQR$ and on a circle with center P and radius PQ
12. equidistant from both points A and B and points C and D
13. equidistant from the sides of $\angle JKL$ and on $\odot C$

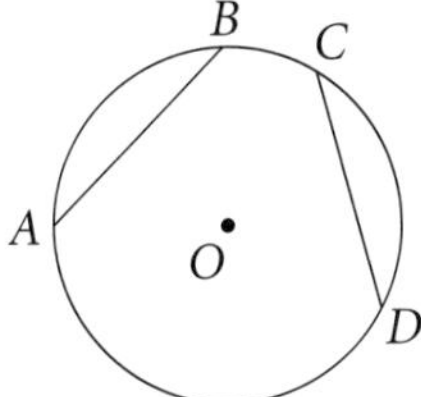

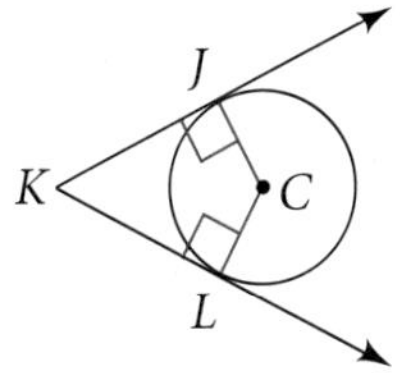

Example 3 (page 622)

Draw and describe each locus in space.

14. points 3 cm from a point F
15. points 4 cm from a line $\overleftrightarrow{DE}$
16. points 1 in. from plane M
17. points 5 mm from $\overrightarrow{PQ}$

B Apply Your Skills

Describe the locus that each blue figure represents.

18.

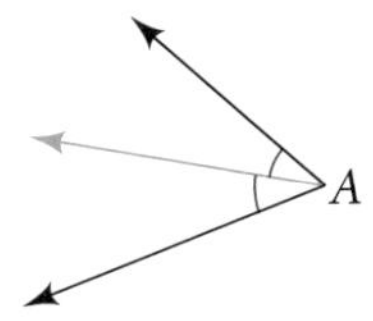

19.

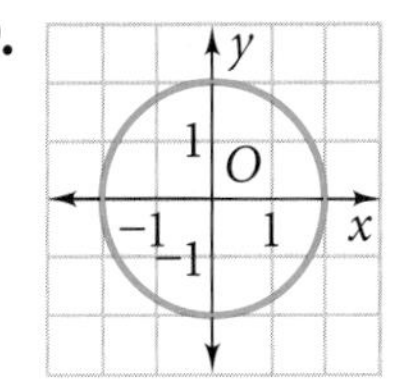

20.

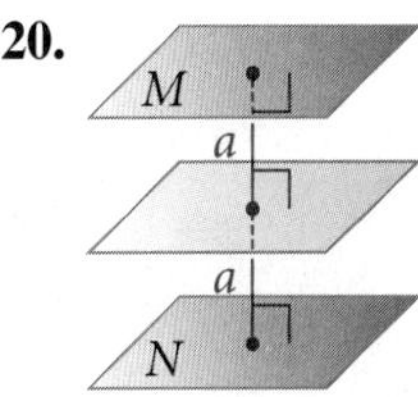

21. **Open-Ended** Give two examples of loci from everyday life, one in a plane and one in space.
22. **Reasoning** Rosie says that it is impossible to find a point equidistant from three collinear points. Is she correct? Explain.

Real-World Connection

A fingertip of the skater traces a locus as she twirls.

Coordinate Geometry Write an equation for the locus: In the plane, the points equidistant from the two given points.

23. $A(0, 2)$ and $B(2, 0)$
24. $P(1, 3)$ and $Q(5, 1)$
25. $T(2, -3)$ and $V(6, 1)$

26. **Coordinate Geometry** Complete the following locus description of the points highlighted in blue at the right: in the coordinate plane, the points 2 units from the _?_ and 1 unit from the _?_-axis.

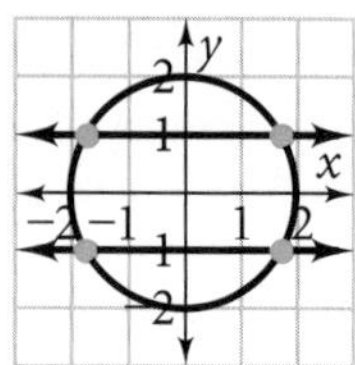

Make a drawing of each locus.

27. the path of a doorknob as a door opens

28. the path of a knot in the middle of a jump rope as it is being used

29. the path of the tip of your nose as you turn your head

30. the path of a fast-pitched softball

31. Jack and Julie Wilson take new jobs in Shrevetown and need a place to live. Jack says, "Let's try to move somewhere equidistant from both of our offices." Julie says, "Let's try to stay within three miles of downtown." Where on the map should the Wilsons look for a home?

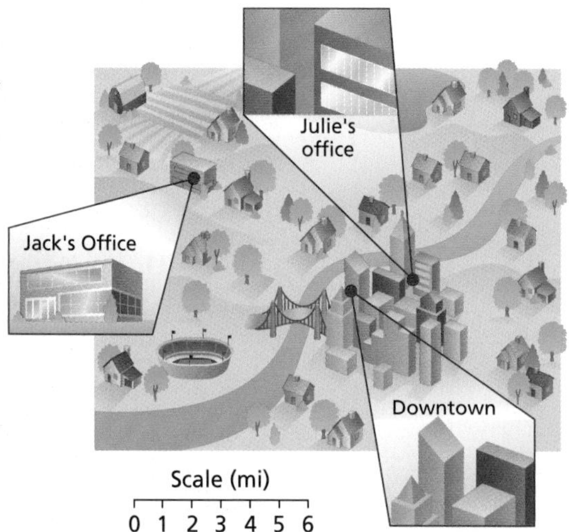

32. **Critical Thinking** Points A and B are 5 cm apart. Do the following loci in a plane have any points in common?

    the points 3 cm from A

    the points 4 cm from B

    Illustrate with a sketch.

Coordinate Geometry **Draw each locus on the coordinate plane.**

33. all points 3 units from the origin

34. all points 2 units from $(-1, 3)$

35. all points 4 units from the y-axis

36. all points 5 units from $x = 2$

37. all points equidistant from $y = 3$ and $y = -1$

38. all points equidistant from $x = 4$ and $x = 5$

39. all points equidistant from the x- and y-axes

40. all points equidistant from $x = 3$ and $y = 2$

Real-World Connection

An anemometer measures wind speed.

Meteorology **In an anemometer, there are three cups mounted on an axis. Imagine a point on the edge of one of the cups.**

41. Describe the locus that this point traces as the cup spins in the wind.

42. Suppose the distance of the point from the axis of the anemometer is 2 in. Write an equation for the locus of part (a). Use the axis as the origin.

43. Robert draws a segment to use as the base of an isosceles triangle.
    a. Draw a segment to represent Robert's base. Locate three points that could be the vertex of the isosceles triangle.
    b. Describe the locus of possible vertices for Robert's isosceles triangle.
    c. **Writing** Explain why points in the locus you described are the only possibilities for the vertex of Robert's triangle.

44. Describe the locus: The points in space equidistant from the points of a circle.

Challenge Playground Equipment **Think about the path of a child on each piece of playground equipment. Draw the path from (a) a top view, (b) a front view, and (c) a side view.**

45. a swing **46.** a straight slide **47.** a corkscrew slide

48. a merry-go-round **49.** a firefighters' pole

50. In the diagram, three students are seated at uniform distances around a circular table. Copy the diagram. Shade the points on the table that are closer to Moesha than to Jan or Leandra.

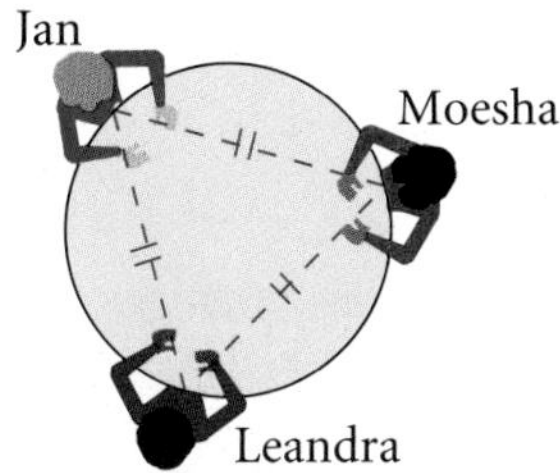

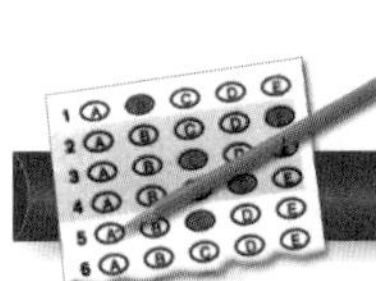

Standardized Test Prep

Multiple Choice

51. Which graph shows the locus: The points in a plane 1 unit from the intersection of the lines $x + y = 2$ and $x - y = 4$?

A. / **C.**

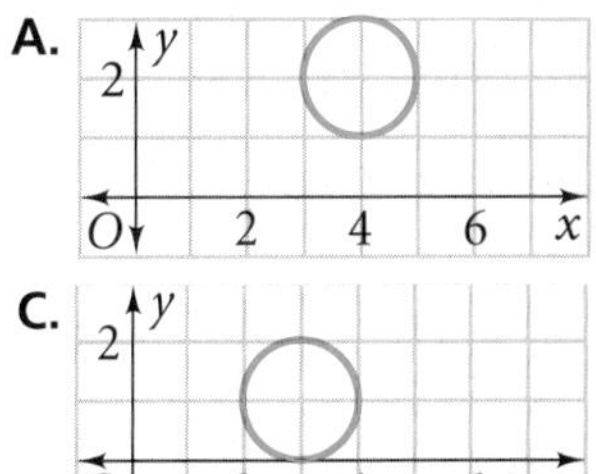

B.

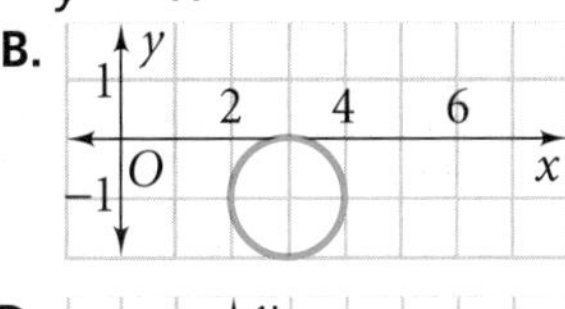

D.

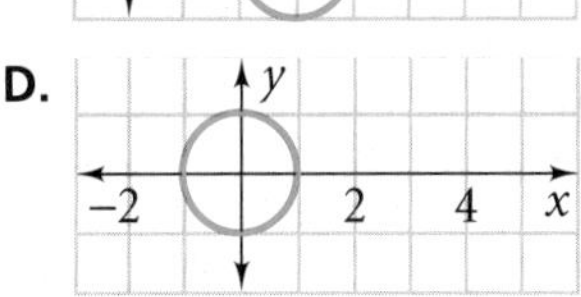

Take It to the NET
Online lesson quiz at **www.PHSchool.com**
Web Code: afa-1106

52. Which equation describes the locus: The points in the coordinate plane that are 5 units from the y-axis?

F. $|y| = 5$ **G.** $|x| = 5$ **H.** $x + y = 5$ **I.** $x^2 + y^2 = 25$

Short Response

53. Margie's cordless telephone can transmit up to 0.5 mile from her home. Carol's cordless telephone can transmit up to 0.25 mile from her home. Carol and Margie live 0.25 mile from each other. Can Carol's telephone work in a region that Margie's cannot? Sketch and label a diagram.

Mixed Review

Lesson 11-5 **Write an equation of the circle with center C and radius r.**

54. $C(6, -10), r = 5$ **55.** $C(1, 7), r = 6$ **56.** $C(-8, 1), r = \sqrt{13}$

Lesson 10-3 **Find the surface area of each figure to the nearest tenth.**

57.

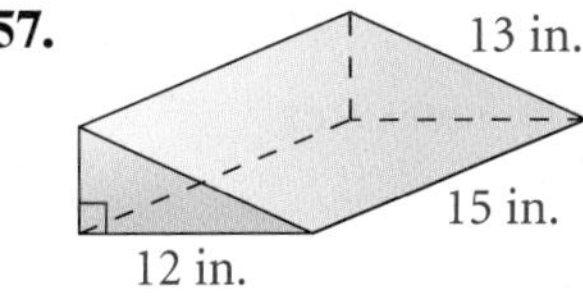

58.

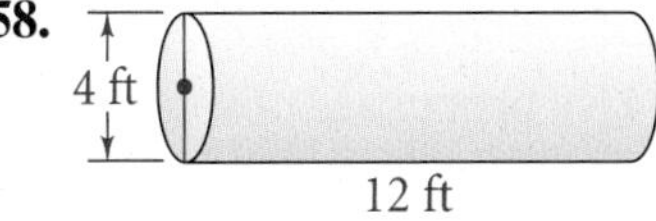

Lesson 7-7 **In $\odot O$, find the area of sector AOB. Leave your answer in terms of π.**

59. $OA = 4, m\overset{\frown}{AB} = 90$ **60.** $OA = 8, m\overset{\frown}{AB} = 72$ **61.** $OA = 10, m\overset{\frown}{AB} = 36$

Test-Taking Strategies

Using Estimation

Estimation may help you find answers, check an answer, or eliminate one or more answer choices. Here are some decimal approximations that can be helpful. The symbol $\approx$ means "is approximately equal to."

$\pi \approx 3$ $\qquad \frac{1}{\pi} \approx \frac{1}{3} \approx 0.3$ $\qquad \sqrt{2} \approx 1.4$ $\qquad \sqrt{3} \approx 1.7$

EXAMPLE

Two circles have the same center O. The radius of the larger circle is twice the radius of the smaller circle, and chord $\overline{DB}$ is tangent to the smaller circle at C. Which of the following is the greatest?

A. DB **B.** OA

C. length of $\widehat{XCY}$ **D.** length of $\widehat{AB}$

Let $OY = 1$ and $YA = 1$. Therefore $OA = 2$.

The length of $\widehat{XCY}$ is one-half the circumference of the small circle.
The length of $\widehat{XCY} = \frac{1}{2}(2\pi r) = \pi \approx 3$. Thus, choice C is greater than choice B.

Draw $\overline{OC}$. $\triangle ODC$ has a right angle at C with $OD = 2$ and $OC = 1$.
By the Pythagorean Theorem, $DC = \sqrt{3}$. Therefore $DB = 2\sqrt{3} \approx 2(1.7) = 3.4$.
So, choice A is greater than choice C.

$\triangle OCD$ is a 30°-60°-90° triangle, so $m\widehat{AB} = 60$.
Thus, the length of $\widehat{AB}$ is $\frac{1}{6}$ the circumference of the larger circle.
The length of $\widehat{AB} = \frac{1}{6}(2\pi r) = \frac{1}{6}(4\pi) = \frac{2}{3}\pi \approx 2$, which is less than DB (choice A).

Therefore the greatest quantity is DB. The correct answer is A.

EXERCISES

1. Use the approximations above to estimate the value of each number.
   a. 2π **b.** $\frac{\pi}{2}$ **c.** $\frac{1}{\sqrt{2}}$ **d.** $\frac{1}{\sqrt{3}}$ **e.** $\sqrt{8}$
2. Which number is greatest? (*Hint:* Use estimation.)
   A. π **B.** $2\sqrt{3}$ **C.** $3\sqrt{2}$ **D.** $\sqrt{3} + \sqrt{2}$
3. A student used a calculator to find the value of $\sqrt{8} + \sqrt{15}$ and got 4.796. Use estimation to explain why this answer is incorrect.
4. Which is the best estimate for sin A?
   A. 0.32 **B.** 0.42 **C.** 0.52 **D.** 0.62
5. Which is the best estimate for tan A?
   A. 0.14 **B.** 0.24 **C.** 0.34 **D.** 0.44
6. Use properties of special triangles to estimate the measures of $\angle X$ and $\angle Y$ in $\triangle XYZ$.

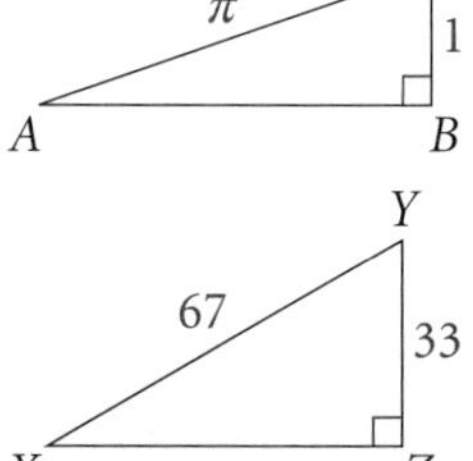

Chapter Review

Vocabulary

chord (p. 590)
circumscribed about (p. 585)
inscribed angle (p. 598)
inscribed in (p. 585)
intercepted arc (p. 598)
locus (p. 621)
point of tangency (p. 582)
secant (p. 607)
standard form of an equation of a circle (p. 615)
tangent to a circle (p. 582)

Reading Math
Understanding Vocabulary

Take It to the NET
Online vocabulary quiz at **www.PHSchool.com**
Web Code: afj-1151

Use the figure to choose the correct term to complete each sentence.

1. $\overline{CB}$ is *(a secant of, tangent to)* $\odot X$.
2. $\overline{DF}$ is a *(chord, locus)* of $\odot X$.
3. $\triangle DEF$ is *(inscribed in, circumscribed about)* $\odot X$.
4. $\angle DEF$ is an *(intercepted arc, inscribed angle)* of $\odot X$.
5. The set of "all points equidistant from the endpoints of $\overline{CB}$" is a *(locus, tangent)*.

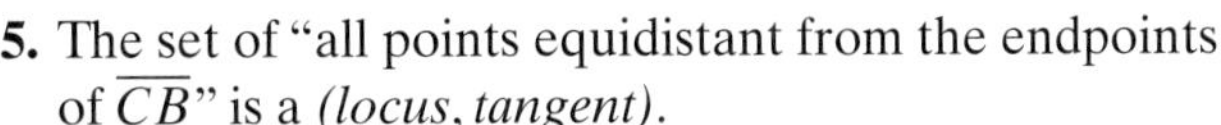

Skills and Concepts

11-1 Objectives

▼ To use the relationship between a radius and a tangent

▼ To use the relationship between two tangents from one point

A **tangent to a circle** is a line, ray, or segment in the plane of the circle that intersects the circle in exactly one point, the **point of tangency**. Two segments tangent to a circle from a point outside the circle are congruent. If a line is tangent to a circle, then the line is perpendicular to the radius drawn to the point of tangency. The converse is also true.

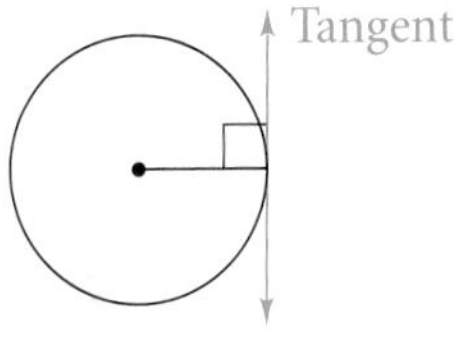

A triangle is **inscribed in** a circle if all of the vertices lie on the circle. When a triangle is **circumscribed about** a circle, each side is tangent to the circle.

Each polygon circumscribes a circle. Find the perimeter of the polygon.

6.
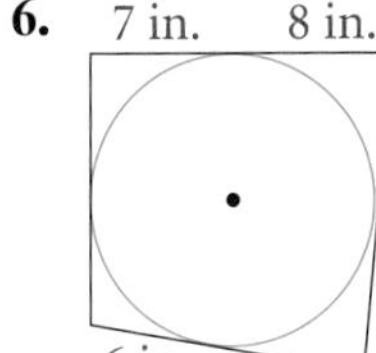

7.
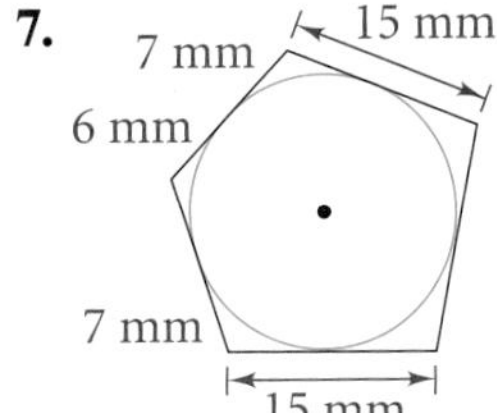

8.
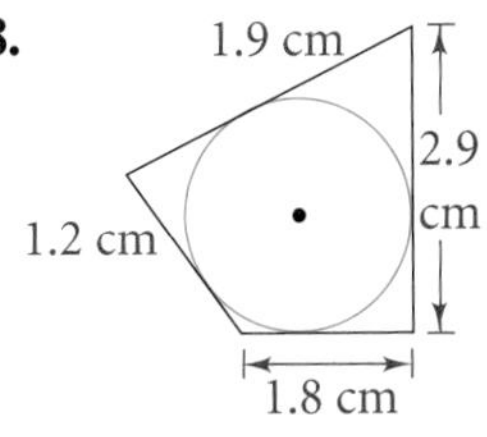

11-2 Objectives

▼ To use congruent chords, arcs, and central angles

▼ To recognize properties of lines through the center of a circle

Segments with endpoints on a circle are called **chords**. Within a circle or in congruent circles,

- congruent central angles have congruent chords.
- congruent chords have congruent arcs.
- congruent arcs have congruent central angles.

- chords equidistant from the center are congruent.
- congruent chords are equidistant from the center.

A diameter that is perpendicular to a chord bisects the chord and its arcs. A diameter that bisects a chord that is not a diameter is perpendicular to the chord. The perpendicular bisector of a chord contains the center of the circle.

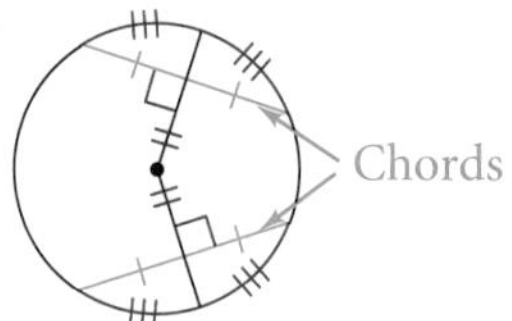

Find the value of *x* to the nearest tenth.

9. 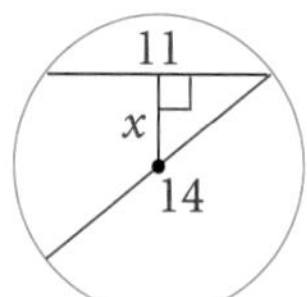

10. 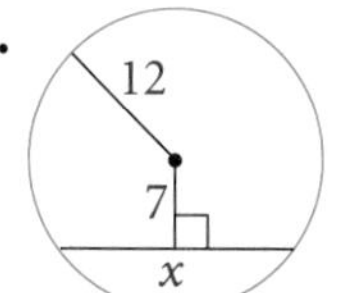

11. 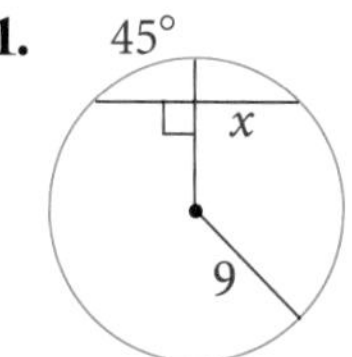

12. 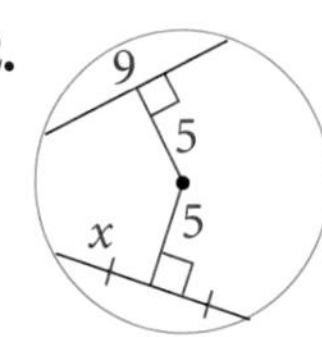

11-3 Objectives

- ▼ To find the measure of an inscribed angle
- ▼ To find the measure of an angle formed by a tangent and a chord

An angle is an **inscribed angle** if the vertex is on a circle and sides of the angle are chords of the circle. Its **intercepted arc** is the arc whose endpoints are on the sides of the angle and whose remaining points lie in the interior of the angle.

The measure of an inscribed angle is half the measure of its intercepted arc. The measure of an angle formed by a tangent and a chord that intersect on a circle is half the measure of the intercepted arc.

Two inscribed angles that intercept the same arc are congruent. An angle inscribed in a semicircle is a right angle. The opposite angles of a quadrilateral inscribed in a circle are supplementary.

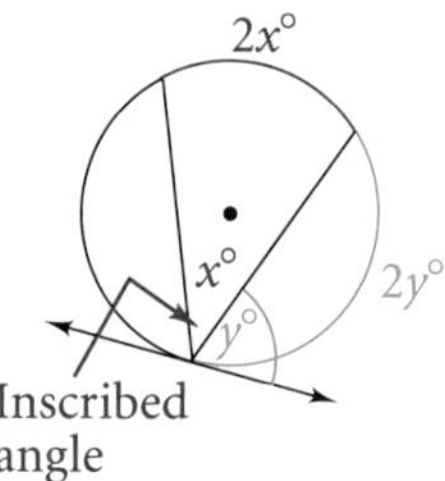

Assume that lines that appear tangent are tangent. Find the value of each variable.

13. 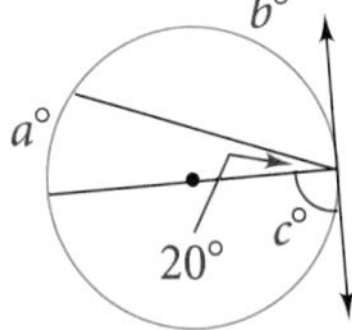

14. 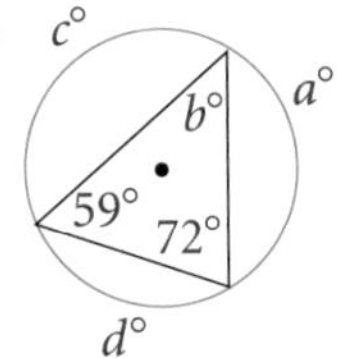

15. 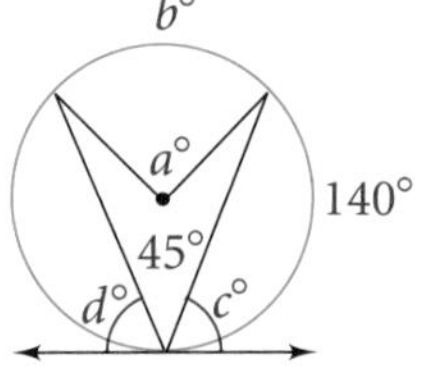

11-4 Objectives

- ▼ To find the measures of angles formed by chords, secants, and tangents
- ▼ To find the lengths of segments associated with circles

A **secant** is a line, ray, or segment that intersects a circle at two points.

The measure of an angle formed by two chords that intersect in a circle is half the sum of the measures of the intercepted arcs.

The measure of an angle formed by two secants, two tangents, or a secant and a tangent drawn from a point outside the circle is half the difference of the measures of the intercepted arcs.

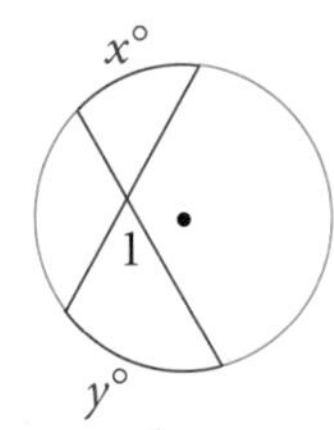

$m\angle 1 = \frac{1}{2}(x + y)$

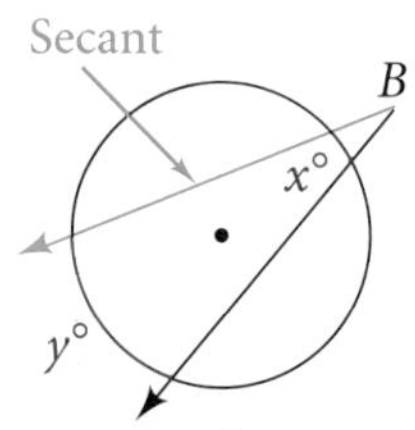

$m\angle B = \frac{1}{2}(y - x)$

For a given point and circle, the product of the lengths of the two segments from the point to the circle is constant along any line through the point and circle.

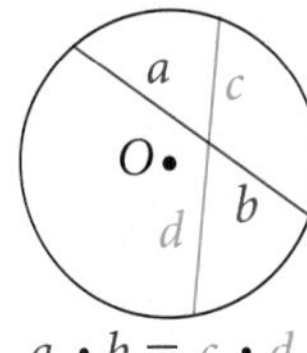

$a \cdot b = c \cdot d$

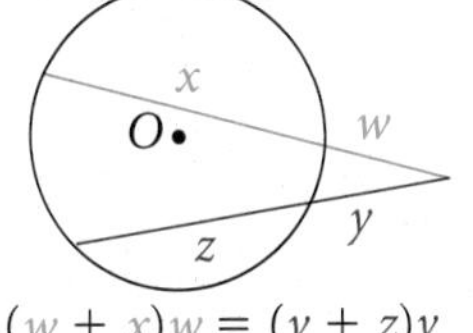

$(w + x)w = (y + z)y$

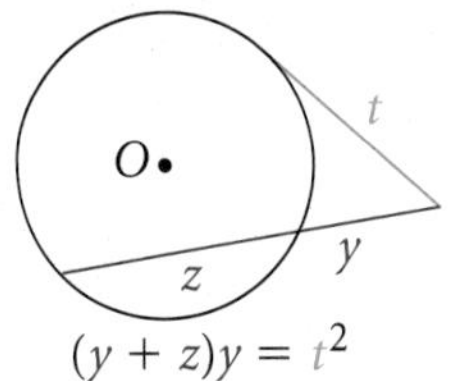

$(y + z)y = t^2$

Assume that lines that appear tangent are tangent. Find the value of each variable.

16.

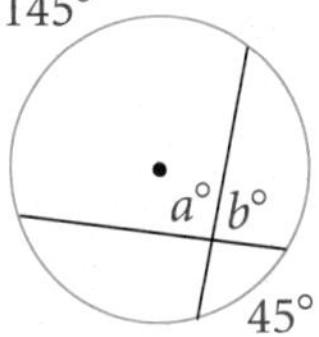

17.

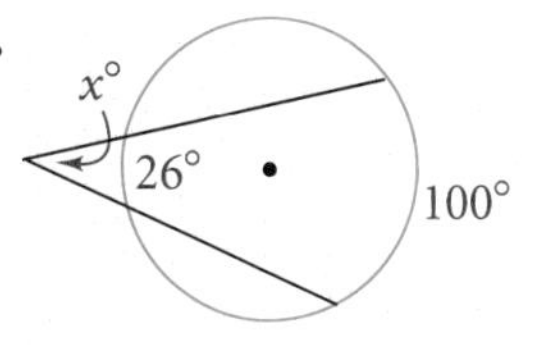

18.

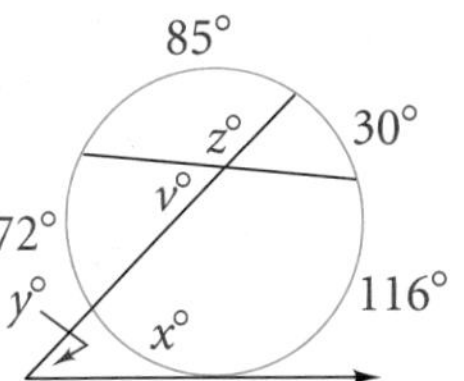

x^2 Algebra **Find the value of each variable using the given chords, secants, and tangents. If your answer is not an integer, round to the nearest tenth.**

19.

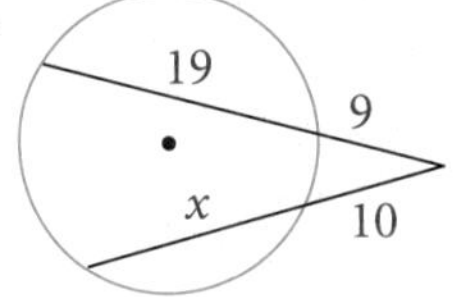

20.

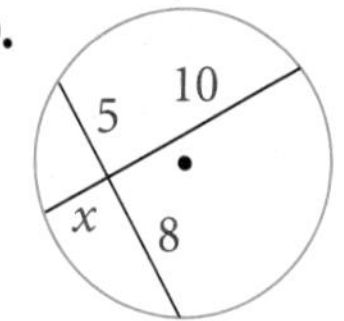

21.

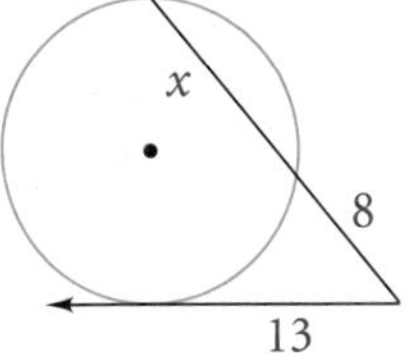

11-5 and 11-6 Objectives

- To write an equation of a circle
- To find the center and radius of a circle
- To draw and describe a locus

The equation $(x - h)^2 + (y - k)^2 = r^2$ is in **standard form.** You may also call it the *standard equation* of a circle.

If you know the center and a point on a circle, you can write the standard equation of the circle. Use the Distance Formula to find the radius. Then substitute the coordinates of the center for (h, k) and the radius for r in the equation of a circle. If you know the equation of a circle, you can identify the center and radius.

A set of points that meet a stated condition is a **locus**. Sometimes you can describe a figure as a locus.

Write the standard equation of the circle with center C and radius r.

22. $C(2, 5); r = 3.5$ **23.** $C(-3, 1); r = \sqrt{5}$ **24.** $C(9, -4); r = 4$

Write the standard equation of the circle with center C passing through point P.

25. $C(0, 1); P(4, 9)$ **26.** $C(-2, 3); P(4, -4)$ **27.** $C(10, 7); P(-8, -5)$

Describe the circle with the given equation.

28. $x^2 + (y - 8)^2 = 49$ **29.** $(x - 5)^2 + (y + 9)^2 = 40$ **30.** $(x + 1)^2 + y^2 = 9$

Sketch and label each locus.

31. all points in a plane 2 cm from a circle with radius 1 cm

32. all points in a plane equidistant from two points

33. all points in space a distance a from $\overline{DS}$

Chapter Test

Algebra **Assume that lines that appear tangent are tangent. Find the value of x.**

1. 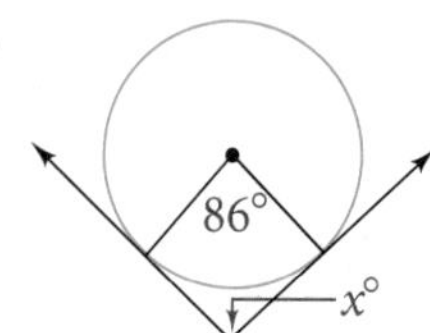

2. 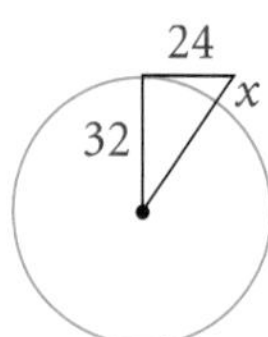

3. a. **Open-Ended** Draw a circle with two congruent chords that form an inscribed angle.
   b. **Constructions** Construct the bisector of the inscribed angle. What do you notice?

Algebra **Find the value of x. If your answer is not an integer, round to the nearest tenth.**

4. 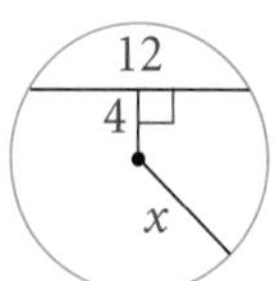

5. 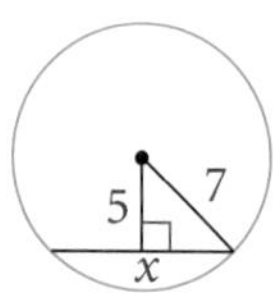

6. **Coordinate Geometry** An equation of a circle is $(x - 4)^2 + (y - 3)^2 = 25$. Find the center and radius of the circle. Then graph the circle.

Find $m\widehat{AB}$.

7. 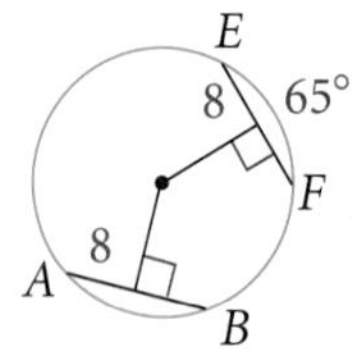

8. 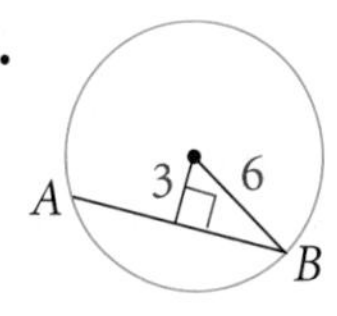

9. Find the value of z.

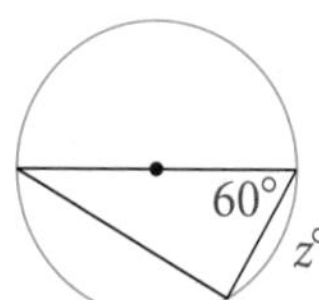

10. **Writing** What is special about a rhombus inscribed in a circle? Justify your answer.

11. A chord of a circle has length 4.2 cm and is 8 cm from the center of the circle. What is the radius of the circle to the nearest hundredth?

Find the center and radius of each circle.

12. $(x + 3)^2 + (y - 2)^2 = 9$

13. $x^2 + (y - 9)^2 = 225$

Algebra **For Exercises 14–19, lines that appear tangent are tangent. Find the value of each variable. If your answer is not an integer, round to the nearest tenth.**

14. 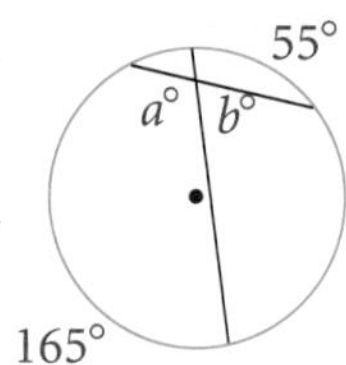

15. 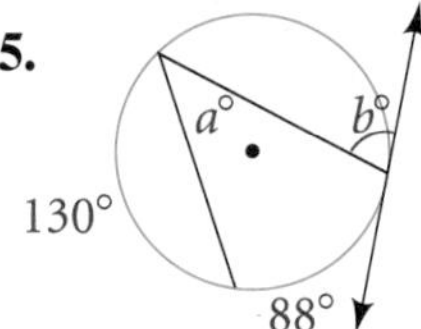

16. 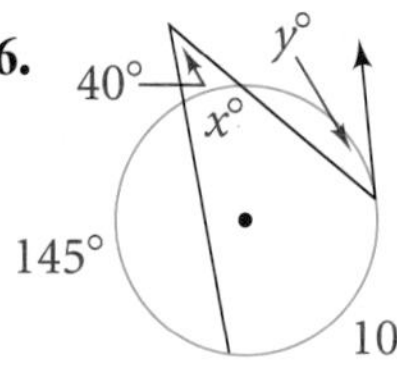

17. 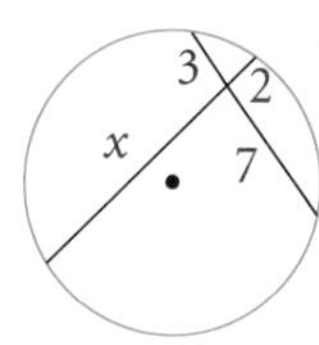

18. 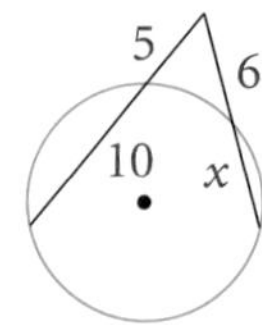

19. 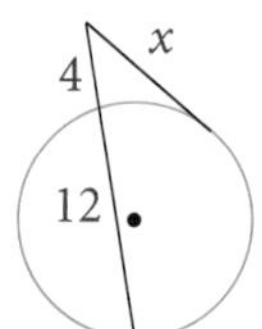

Write the standard equation of each circle.

20. 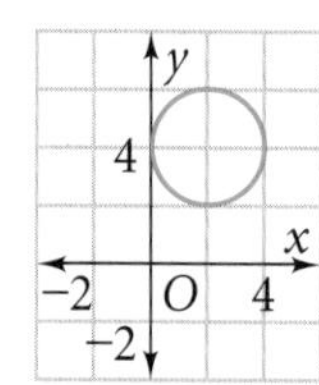

21. 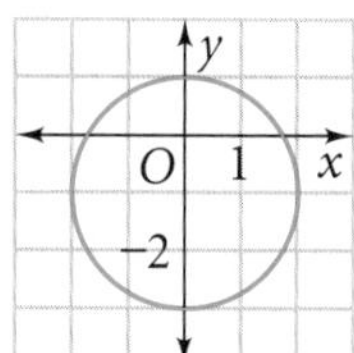

22. Write the equation of the circle with center (3, 0) that passes through point (−2, −4).

23. Find the circumference and area of the circle whose equation is $(x - 2)^2 + (y - 7)^2 = 81$. Round to the nearest tenth.

24. Write an equation for the locus: Points in the coordinate plane that are 4 units from (−5, 2).

Coordinate Geometry **Sketch each locus on a coordinate plane.**

25. all points 6 units from the origin

26. all points 3 units from the line $y = -2$

27. all points equidistant from points (2, 4) and (0, 0)

28. all points equidistant from the axes

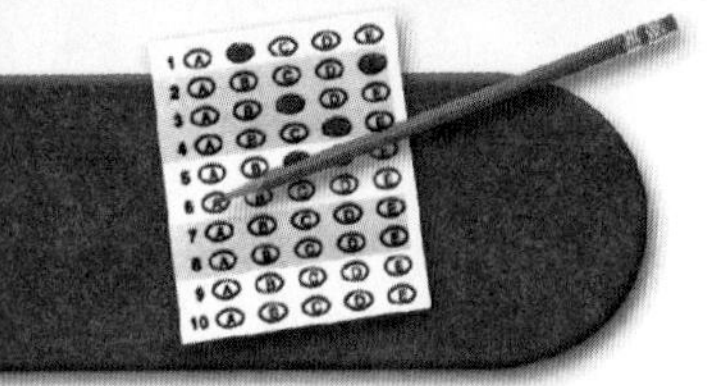

Standardized Test Prep

Reading Comprehension **Read the passage below. Then answer the questions on the basis of what is *stated* or *implied* in the passage.**

Packaging In the cosmetics section of a department store you can see many unusual and eye-catching geometric shapes. There are star-shaped perfume sprayers, gourd-shaped bath-oil bottles, and hexagonal jars of skin cream. In general, the easiest way to package and ship such items is to use rectangular boxes.

Suppose a bar of soap has a "footprint" that is a parallelogram with sides of lengths 3 and 4. There are two ways to "box" the parallelogram (shown in red and blue at the right) so that the box aligns with one side of the parallelogram and otherwise wastes no space.

The red box has base $4 \cdot \sin X$ and height $3 + 4 \cdot \cos X$. Its area is $4 \cdot \sin X \cdot (3 + 4 \cdot \cos X)$, or $12 \cdot \sin X + 16 \cdot \sin X \cdot \cos X$.

The blue box has base $4 + 3 \cdot \cos X$ and height $3 \cdot \sin X$. Its area is $3 \cdot \sin X \cdot (4 + 3 \cdot \cos X)$, or $12 \cdot \sin X + 9 \cdot \sin X \cdot \cos X$.

Thus the area of the red box is $7 \cdot \sin X \cdot \cos X$ greater than the area of the blue box. This value is greatest when $X = 45$.

It can also be shown that the perimeter of the red box exceeds the perimeter of the blue box by $2 \cdot \sin X + 2 \cdot \cos X - 2$, which is also greatest when $X = 45$.

Clearly the blue box is a better design for packaging the parallelogram.

1. Why is it important to design rectangular boxes for packages with unusual shapes?
   A. for easy arrangement on store shelves
   B. to disguise the contents
   C. for easy shipment
   D. so the packages don't rattle around inside

2. In the passage, why is the blue box a better design for packaging the parallelogram?
   F. In the blue box the parallelogram has base 4.
   G. The blue box is horizontal.
   H. The parallelogram fits perfectly inside the blue box.
   I. The blue box requires less package materials.

3. With how many different rectangles can you box an equilateral triangle so that the box contains one side of the triangle and otherwise wastes no space?
   A. 1 **B.** 2 **C.** 3 **D.** infinitely many

With how many different rectangles can you box the given shape so that the box contains at least one side of the shape and otherwise wastes no space? Justify each answer.

4. a scalene triangle
5. a rhombus
6. an isosceles trapezoid
7. a regular hexagon

8. Which fact below allows you to express the dimensions of both rectangles in terms of X?
   F. The red and blue triangles are congruent.
   G. Sine equals cosine of the complement.
   H. Vertical angles are congruent.
   I. All right angles are congruent.

9. Explain how you can check that $7 \cdot \sin X \cdot \cos X$ is greatest when $X = 45$.

10. For the boxes above, the red box has the greater perimeter. Show that it exceeds the perimeter of the blue box by $2 \cdot \sin X + 2 \cdot \cos X - 2$.

Where You've Been

- In Chapter 4, you learned that you can move one of two congruent figures so that it can fit exactly on the other one.
- In Chapter 9, you learned how vectors can be used to represent distance and direction.
- In Chapter 11, you learned to use the relationship between central angles and arcs on a circle.

Instant self-check online and on CD-ROM

Diagnosing Readiness

(For help, go to the Lesson in green.)

Regular Polygons (Lesson 3-4)

Determine the measure of an angle of the given regular polygon.

1. pentagon **2.** octagon **3.** decagon **4.** 18-gon

Congruent Figures (Lesson 4-1)

The triangles are congruent. Complete the congruence statement, $\triangle ABC \cong$ ___?___.

5.

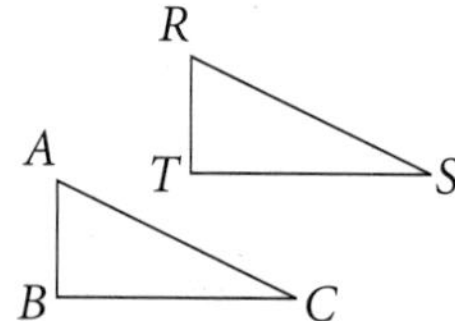

6.

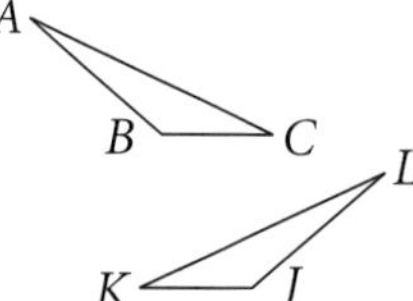

7.

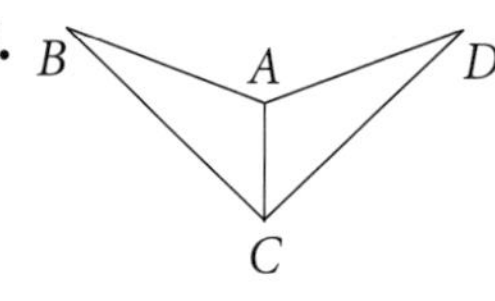

8.

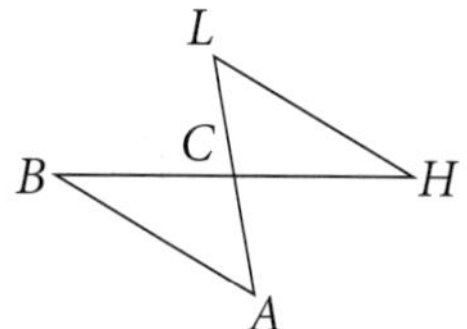

Quadrilaterals (Lessons 6-2, 6-4, and 6-5)

Determine whether a diagonal of the given quadrilateral *always, sometimes,* or *never* produces congruent triangles.

9. rectangle **10.** isosceles trapezoid **11.** kite **12.** parallelogram

Similar Figures (Lesson 8-6)

Determine the similarity ratio for each pair of similar polygons.

13. triangles with perimeters 45 and 72 **14.** squares with areas 16 and 64

Vectors (Lesson 9-4)

Write the sum of the two vectors as an ordered pair.

15. $\langle 3, 1\rangle$ and $\langle -2, 4\rangle$ **16.** $\langle -1, 2\rangle$ and $\langle -5, 0\rangle$ **17.** $\langle 0, 0\rangle$ and $\langle -6, 3\rangle$

Transformations

Chapter 12

LESSONS

Key Vocabulary

- composition (p. 642)
- dilation (p. 674)
- enlargement (p. 674)
- glide reflection (p. 656)
- glide reflectional symmetry (p. 668)
- image (p. 634)
- isometry (p. 634)
- line symmetry (p. 662)
- point symmetry (p. 663)
- preimage (p. 634)
- reduction (p. 674)
- reflection (p. 635)
- reflectional symmetry (p. 662)
- rotation (p. 648)
- rotational symmetry (p. 663)
- scalar multiplication (p. 675)
- symmetry (p. 662)
- tessellation (p. 667)
- tiling (p. 667)
- transformation (p. 634)
- translation (p. 641)
- translational symmetry (p. 668)

Where You're Going

- In this chapter, you will learn how to use transformations known as reflections, translations, and rotations to create a congruent image of a given shape.
- You will learn to use transformations for relating two given congruent shapes to each other.
- You will learn the effects of applying two transformations, one after the other.
- By learning about transformations, you will understand such terms as *symmetry* and *tessellation*.

Real-World Snapshots Applying what you learn, you will do activities on pages 688 and 689 involving transformations in three dimensions.

12-1 Reflections

Lesson Preview

What You'll Learn

To identify isometries

To find reflection images of figures

. . . And Why

To minimize distances in construction, as in Example 4

Check Skills You'll Need

(For help, go to Lesson 4-1.)

$\triangle ABC \cong \triangle EFG$.
Complete the congruence statements.

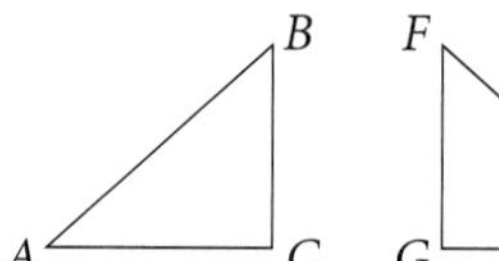

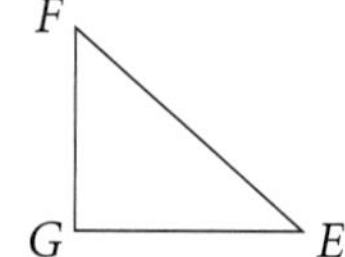

1. $\overline{AB} \cong$ _?_ **2.** $\overline{EG} \cong$ _?_
3. $\overline{FG} \cong$ _?_ **4.** $\angle C \cong$ _?_
5. $\angle E \cong$ _?_ **6.** $\angle B \cong$ _?_

7. Complete: If $\triangle KTQ \cong \triangle LGR$, then $\overline{TK} \cong$ _?_ and $\angle TQK \cong$ _?_.

New Vocabulary • transformation • preimage • image • isometry • reflection

Interactive lesson includes instant self-check, tutorials, and activities.

OBJECTIVE 1

Identifying Isometries

Reading Math

In general, the word *transformation* can refer to any kind of change in appearance.

A **transformation** of a geometric figure is a change in its position, shape, or size. When you assemble a jigsaw puzzle, you often move the puzzle pieces by flipping them, sliding them, or turning them. Each move is a type of transformation. The photos below illustrate some basic transformations that you will study.

The figure flips.

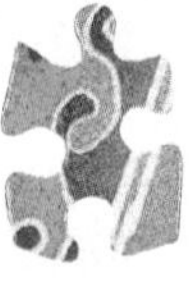

The figure slides.

The figure turns.

The original figure is the **preimage.** The resulting figure is an **image.** An **isometry** is a transformation in which the preimage and image are congruent. Each transformation above is an isometry.

1 EXAMPLE Identifying Isometries

Does the transformation appear to be an isometry? Explain.

No, this transformation involves a change in size. The sides of the preimage square and the sides of its image are not congruent.

Preimage Image

Check Understanding

1. Does the transformation appear to be an isometry? Explain.

a.

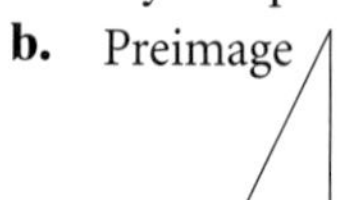

b. Preimage Image

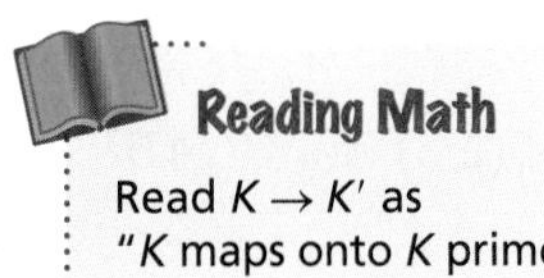

Read $K \rightarrow K'$ as "K maps onto K prime."

A transformation maps a figure onto its image and may be described with arrow ($\rightarrow$) notation. Prime ($'$) notation is sometimes used to identify image points. In the diagram at the right, K' is the image of K ($K \rightarrow K'$).

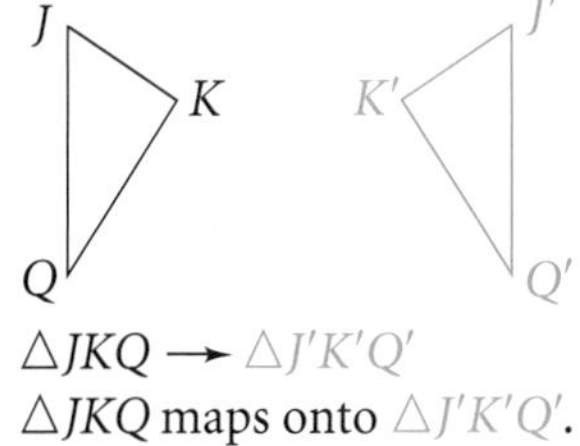

$\triangle JKQ \rightarrow \triangle J'K'Q'$

$\triangle JKQ$ maps onto $\triangle J'K'Q'$.

Notice that you list corresponding points of the preimage and image in the same order, as you do for corresponding points of congruent or similar figures.

2 EXAMPLE Naming Images and Corresponding Parts

In the diagram, $E'F'G'H'$ is an image of $EFGH$.

a. Name the images of $\angle F$ and $\angle H$.

$\angle F'$ is the image of $\angle F$.
$\angle H'$ is the image of $\angle H$.

b. List all pairs of corresponding sides.

$\overline{EF}$ and $\overline{E'F'}$; $\overline{FG}$ and $\overline{F'G'}$;
$\overline{EH}$ and $\overline{E'H'}$; $\overline{GH}$ and $\overline{G'H'}$

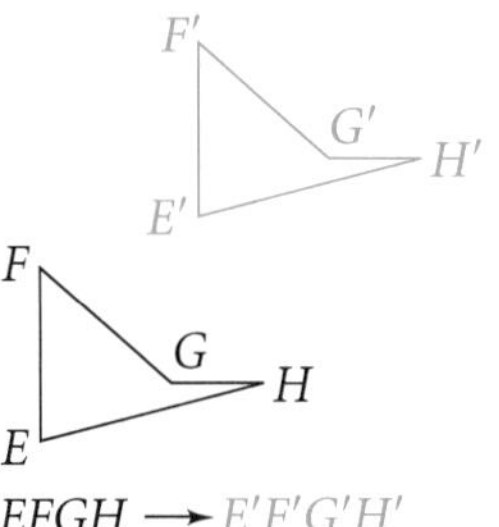

$EFGH \rightarrow E'F'G'H'$

2 In the diagram, $NID \rightarrow SUP$.

a. Name the images of $\angle I$ and point D.

b. List all pairs of corresponding sides.

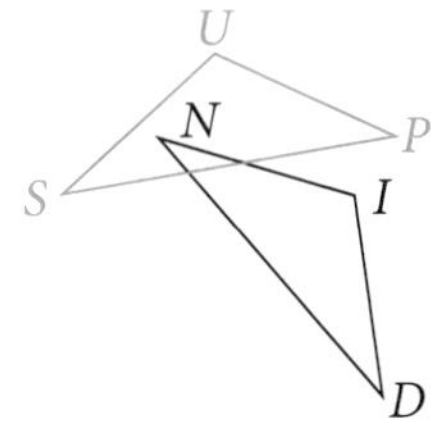

OBJECTIVE

2 Finding Reflection Images

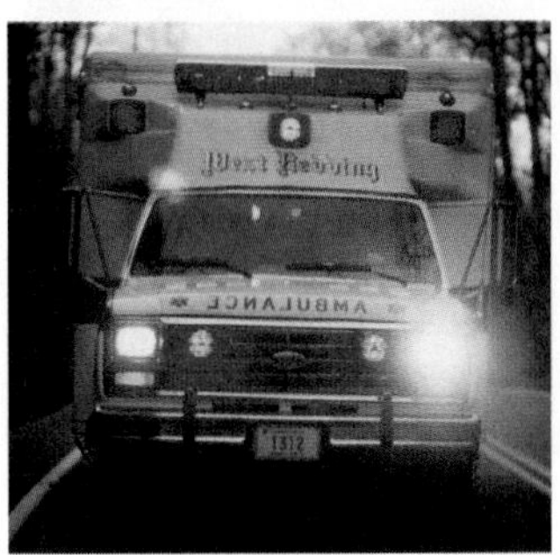

Real-World Connection

In your rear-view mirror you see the reflection "AMBULANCE."

A reflection (or *flip*) is an isometry in which a figure and its image have opposite orientations. Thus, a reflected image in a mirror appears "backwards." In the diagram at the right, $\triangle BUG$ is reflected in a line to produce $\triangle B'U'G'$. Since the reflection is an isometry, $\triangle BUG \cong \triangle B'U'G'$.

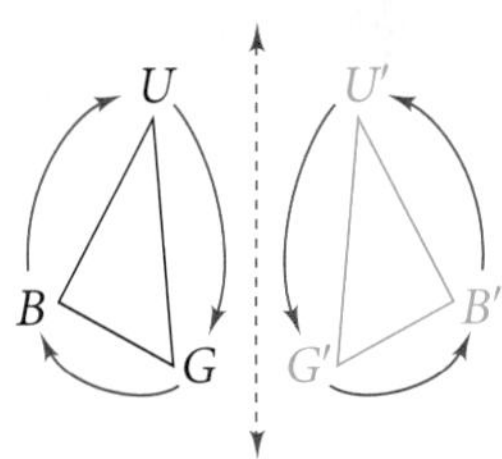

Using the diagram below, a **reflection** in line r is a transformation for which the following are true.

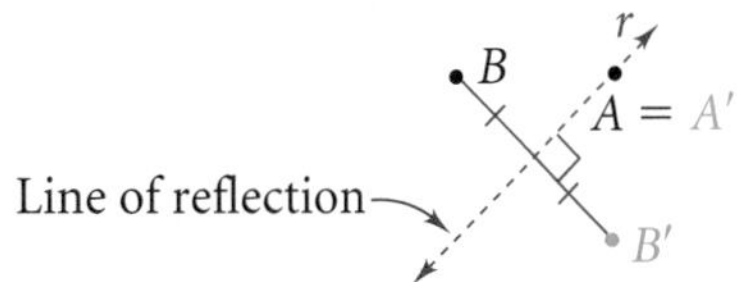

- If a point A is on line r, then the image of A is A itself (that is, $A' = A$).
- If a point B is not on line r, then r is the perpendicular bisector of $\overline{BB'}$.

You can use these properties to find and draw reflection images.

3 EXAMPLE Drawing Reflection Images

Coordinate Geometry Given points $A(-3, 4)$, $B(0, 1)$, and $C(2, 3)$, draw $\triangle ABC$ and its reflection image in each line.

a. the x-axis

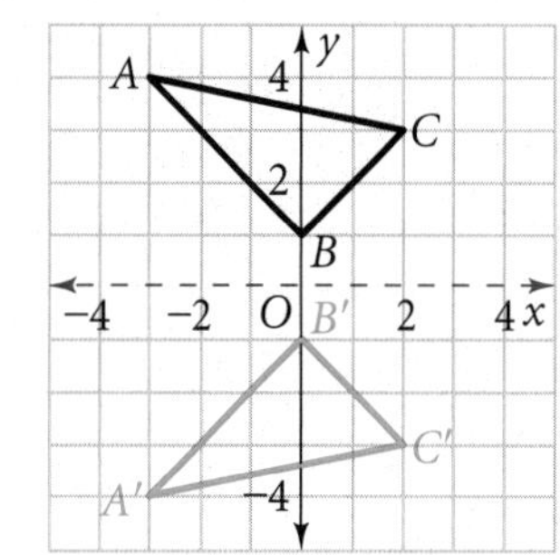

Locate points A', B', and C' such that the line of reflection is the perpendicular bisector of $\overline{AA'}$, $\overline{BB'}$, and $\overline{CC'}$.

b. the y-axis

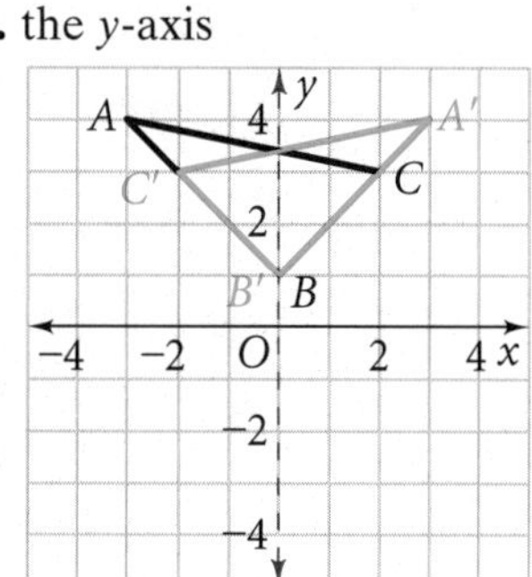

Check Understanding 3 Draw $\triangle ABC$ of Example 3. Then draw its reflection image in the line $x = 3$.

You can use the properties of reflections to solve real-world problems.

4 EXAMPLE Real-World Connection

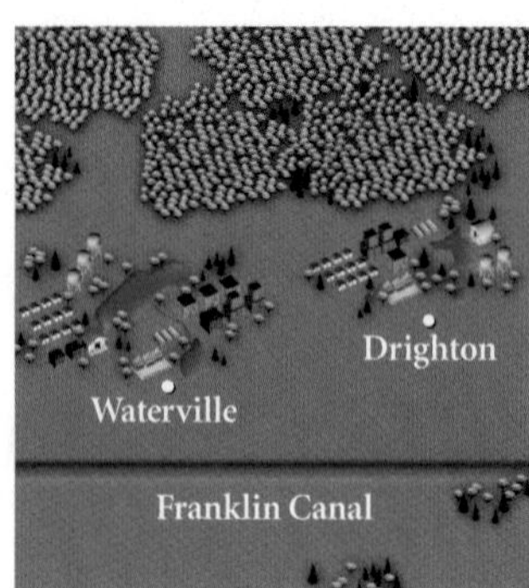

Engineering Town officials in Waterville and Drighton (see aerial view at left) are planning to construct a water pumping station along the Franklin Canal. The station will provide both towns with water. Where along the canal should the officials build the pumping station to minimize the amount of pipe needed?

You need to find the point P on ℓ such that $WP + PD$ is as small as possible. Locate D', the reflection image of D in ℓ. Because a reflection is an isometry, $PD = PD'$, and $WP + PD = WP + PD'$. By the Triangle Inequality Theorem, the sum $WP + PD'$ is smallest when W, P, and D' are collinear. So, the pump should be located at the point P where $\overline{WD'}$ intersects ℓ.

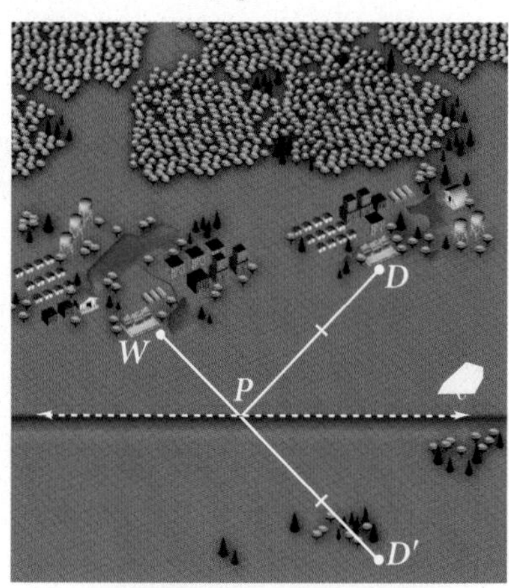

Check Understanding 4 **Critical Thinking** Angela began to solve the problem above by reflecting point W in line ℓ. Will her method work? Explain.

EXERCISES

For more practice, see *Extra Practice*.

Practice and Problem Solving

A Practice by Example

Example 1 (page 634)

State whether the transformation appears to be an isometry. Explain.

1.

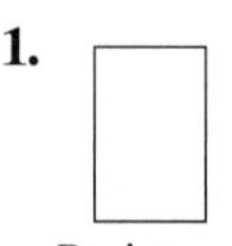

2.

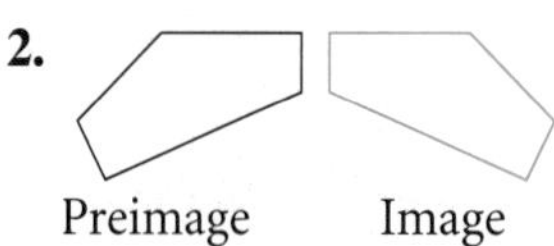

3. Preimage Image

Example 2 (page 635)

In each diagram, the blue figure is an image of the black figure.
(a) Choose an angle or point from the preimage and name its image.
(b) List all pairs of corresponding sides.

4.

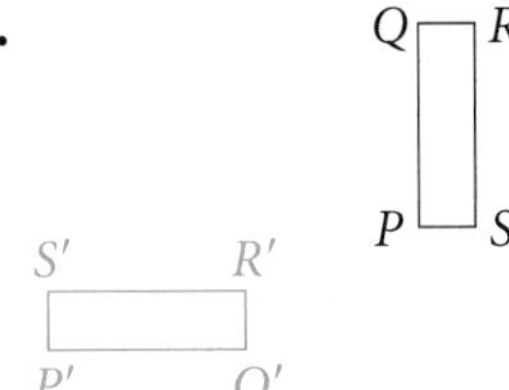

5.

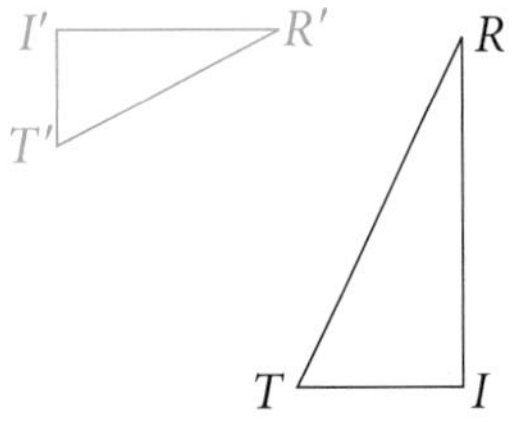

6.

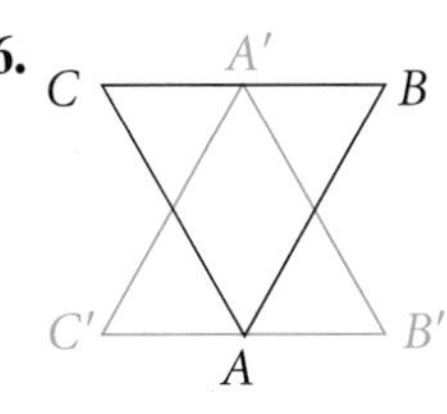

7.

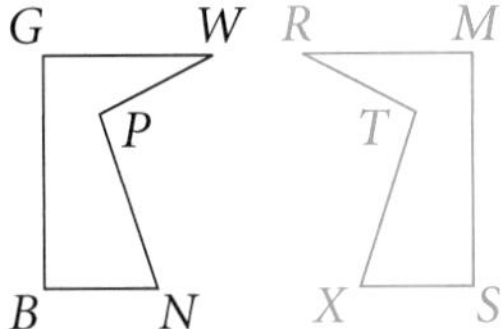

8.

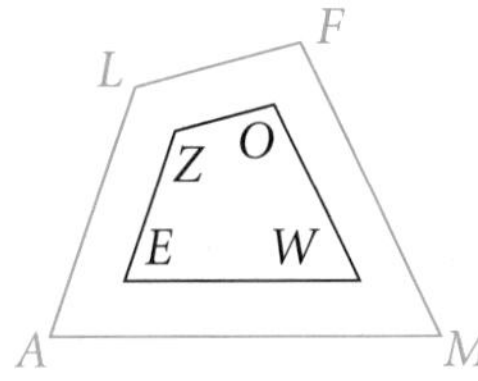

9.

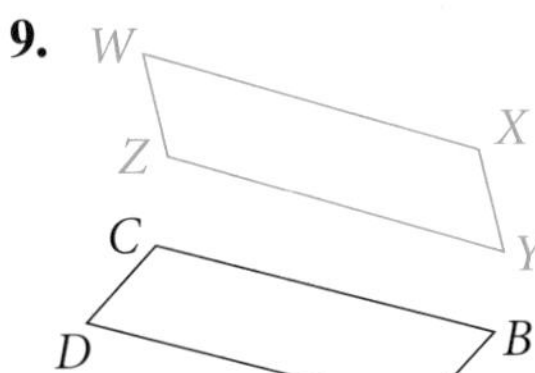

Example 3 (page 636)

Coordinate Geometry **Given points $J(1, 4)$, $A(3, 5)$, and $R(2, 1)$, draw $\triangle JAR$ and its reflection image in each line.**

10. the x-axis
11. the y-axis
12. $y = 2$
13. $y = 5$
14. $x = -1$
15. $x = 2$
16. $y = -x$
17. $y = x - 3$

Example 4 (page 636)

18. Trail Building A hiking club is building a new trail system. They want to build trails to the Overlook and Balance Rock that will connect at a point on Summit Trail. Working under a tight budget, they want to minimize the total length of these trails. If the trails cover similar terrain, at what point should they meet on Summit Trail?

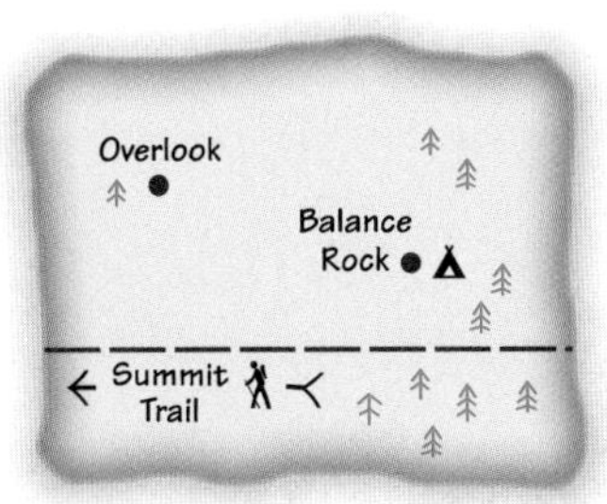

19. Security You are installing a security camera. At what point on the mirrored wall should you aim camera C in order to videotape door D?

Mirrored wall

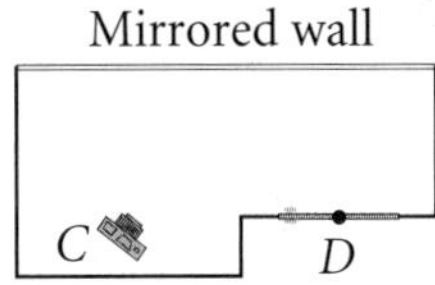

B Apply Your Skills

Copy each figure and line ℓ. Then draw each figure's reflection image in line ℓ.

20.

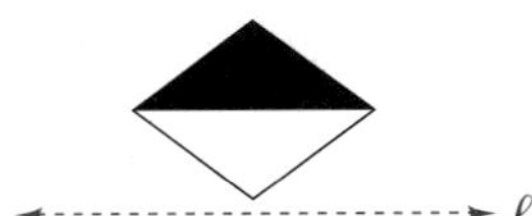

21.

Copy each pair of figures. Then draw the line of reflection you can use to map one figure onto the other.

22.

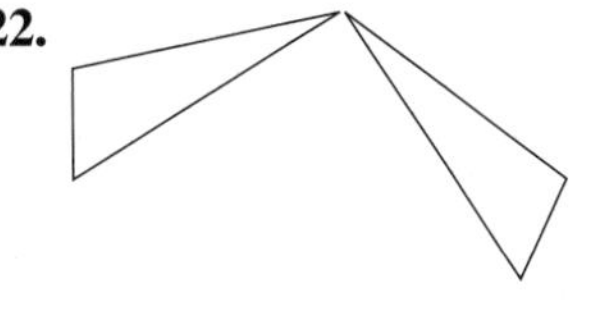

23.

24.

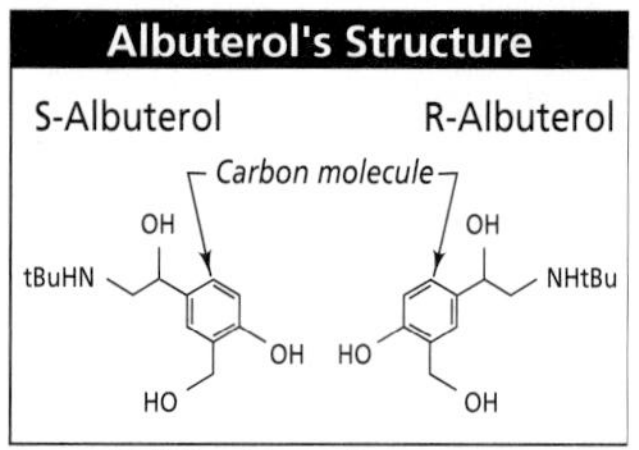

SOURCE: *Wall Street Journal*

The *R-isomer* of the drug albuterol relieves asthma. Its twin has been shown to increase the chances of having future attacks.

25. **Pharmaceuticals** Most drugs are made of two versions of the same molecule, each a mirror image of the other. One version is known as an *R-isomer* and the other as an *S-isomer*. While one isomer can help with what ails you, the other can create unwanted side effects. Models of two isomers are shown above. For this drug to cure an illness, it needs to fit into the "receptor molecule." Which isomer will cure the illness?

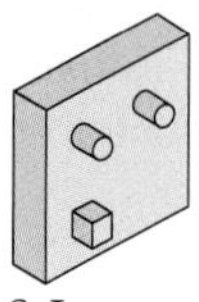

S-Isomer

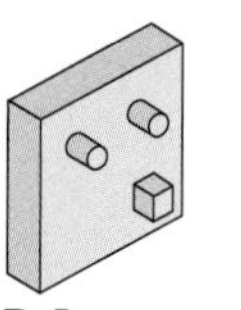

R-Isomer

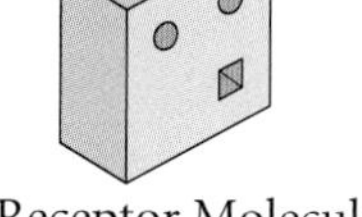

Receptor Molecule

26. **Open-Ended** Give three examples from everyday life of objects that come in a left-handed version and a right-handed version.

Coordinate Geometry **A point is reflected in the given line. How are the coordinates of the point and its image related? Explain.**

27. x-axis

28. y-axis

29. the line $y = x$

30. **History** The work of artist and scientist Leonardo da Vinci (1452–1519) has an unusual characteristic. His handwriting is a mirror image of normal handwriting.

a. Write the mirror image of the sentence, "Leonardo da Vinci was left-handed." Use a mirror to check how well you did.

b. Explain why the fact about da Vinci in part (a) might have made mirror writing seem natural to him.

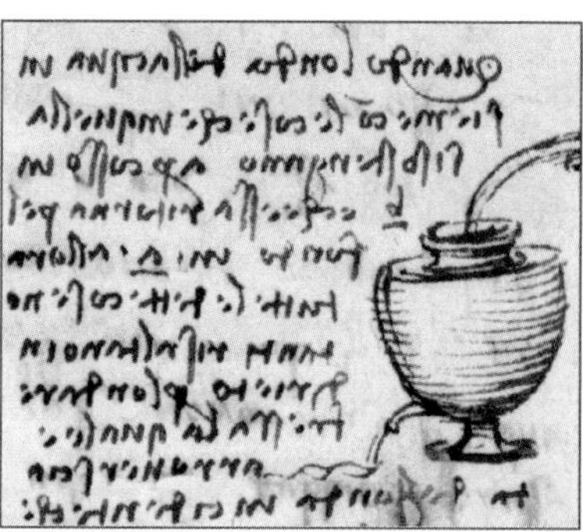

Write an equation for the image of the given circle after a reflection in line ℓ.

31. $x^2 + y^2 = 49, \ell: y\text{-axis}$

32. $x^2 + y^2 = 4, \ell: y = 2$

33. $(x - 2)^2 + (y + 3)^2 = 9, \ell: x = 1$

34. $(x + 3)^2 + (y + 4)^2 = 16, \ell: x\text{-axis}$

35. $x^2 + (y + 3)^2 = 36, \ell: y = -3$

36. $(x + 1)^2 + (y - 5)^2 = 25, \ell: y = x$

Find the image of $O(0, 0)$ after two reflections, first in ℓ_1 and then in ℓ_2.

37. $\ell_1: y = 3, \ell_2: x\text{-axis}$

38. $\ell_1: x = -2, \ell_2: y\text{-axis}$

39. $\ell_1: x\text{-axis}, \ell_2: y\text{-axis}$

40. $\ell_1: x = -2, \ell_2: y = 3$

41. $\ell_1: y = 3, \ell_2: x = -2$

42. $\ell_1: x = -2, \ell_2: y = x$

43. $\ell_1: x = a, \ell_2: y = b$

44. $\ell_1: x = a, \ell_2: y = x$

45. $\ell_1: y = b, \ell_2: y = x$

46. **Critical Thinking** Given that the transformation $\triangle ABC \rightarrow \triangle A'B'C'$ is an isometry, list everything you know about the two figures.

C **Challenge**

Writing **Can the given type of quadrilateral be described in terms of reflections? Explain.**

47. parallelogram

48. isosceles trapezoid

49. kite

50. rhombus

51. rectangle

52. square

53. **Coordinate Geometry** Show that $B(b, a)$ is the reflection image of $A(a, b)$ in the line $y = x$. (*Hint:* Show that $y = x$ is the perpendicular bisector of $\overleftrightarrow{AB}$.)

54. **Coordinate Geometry** Find the line of reflection that maps $A(a, b)$ to $C(c, d)$.

55. Use the diagram at the right. Find the coordinates of the given point in the given line.

a. A', the reflection image of A in the line $y = x$

b. A'', the reflection image of A' in the line $y = -x$

c. A''', the reflection image of A'' in the line $y = x$

d. A'''', the reflection image of A''' in the line $y = -x$

e. How are A and A'''' related?

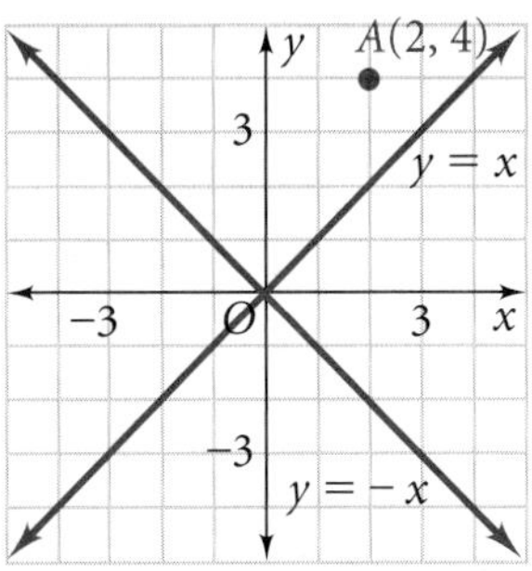

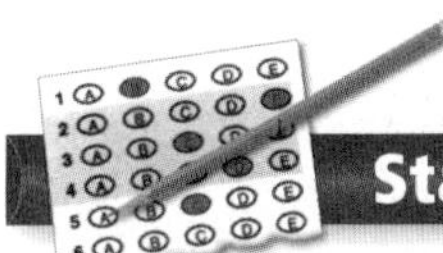

Standardized Test Prep

Multiple Choice

56. What is the reflection image of (5, −3) in the y-axis?
A. (5, 3) **B.** (−5, 3) **C.** (−5, −3) **D.** (−3, 5)

57. What is the reflection image of (5, −3) in the line $y = -x$?
F. (−3, 5) **G.** (−3, −5) **H.** (3, −5) **I.** (3, 5)

Quantitative Comparison

Compare the boxed quantity in Column A with the boxed quantity in Column B. Choose the best answer.

A. The quantity in Column A is greater.
B. The quantity in Column B is greater.
C. The two quantities are equal.
D. The relationship cannot be determined from the information given.

(−7, −1) reflected in the x-axis has image (x_1, y_1).
(−7, −1) reflected in the y-axis has image (x_2, y_2).

	Column A	Column B
58.	x_1	x_2
59.	y_1	y_2
60.	$\lvert y_1 \rvert$	$\lvert y_2 \rvert$

Take It to the NET
Online lesson quiz at www.PHSchool.com
Web Code: afa-1201

Short Response

61. A point is reflected in the line $y = x$. Its image is in Quadrant III. In which quadrant is the preimage? Explain.

Mixed Review

Lesson 11-6

62. Write an equation for the locus: The points equidistant from (1, 4) and (5, −2).

Lesson 10-8

63. **Sports Equipment** The circumference of a softball is 12 in. and the circumference of a field hockey ball is 9 in.

a. Find the similarity ratio of the softball to the field hockey ball.

b. Find the ratio of the volumes: softball to field hockey ball.

Lesson 8-1

64. **Maps** A map of Alberta, Canada, is drawn to the scale 1 cm = 25 km. On the map, the distance from Calgary to Edmonton is about 11.1 cm.

a. About how far apart are the two cities?

b. If 1 km = 0.62 mi, about how many miles apart are the cities?

Algebra 1 Review

Matrices

FOR USE WITH LESSON 12-2

A *matrix* is a rectangular arrangement of numbers. You can display a matrix by writing it between brackets as shown at the right. You identify the size of a matrix by how many rows and columns it has. This matrix has two rows and three columns, so it is a 2×3 (two-by-three) matrix. Each number in a matrix is called an *entry*. This matrix has six entries.

$$\begin{bmatrix} -1 & 4 & 9 \\ 3 & -5 & 7 \end{bmatrix}$$

You can add or subtract matrices if they are the same size. You do this by adding or subtracting corresponding entries.

EXAMPLE

Add $\begin{bmatrix} 6 & -5 \\ 0 & 3 \end{bmatrix} + \begin{bmatrix} 1 & 8 \\ -2 & 10 \end{bmatrix}$.

$$\begin{bmatrix} 6 & -5 \\ 0 & 3 \end{bmatrix} + \begin{bmatrix} 1 & 8 \\ -2 & 10 \end{bmatrix} = \begin{bmatrix} 6+1 & -5+8 \\ 0+(-2) & 3+10 \end{bmatrix}$$

$$= \begin{bmatrix} 7 & 3 \\ -2 & 13 \end{bmatrix}$$

EXERCISES

Add or subtract each pair of matrices.

1. $\begin{bmatrix} 3 & 8 \\ 1 & 5 \end{bmatrix} + \begin{bmatrix} 8 & 2 \\ 0 & 7 \end{bmatrix}$

2. $\begin{bmatrix} -6 & 3 \\ -8 & 1 \end{bmatrix} - \begin{bmatrix} -4 & -9 \\ 3 & 5 \end{bmatrix}$

3. $\begin{bmatrix} 1 & -6 \\ 2 & -7 \end{bmatrix} + \begin{bmatrix} \frac{1}{2} & -1 \\ \frac{2}{3} & -2 \end{bmatrix}$

4. $\begin{bmatrix} \frac{1}{3} & \frac{3}{4} \\ \frac{1}{2} & \frac{2}{5} \end{bmatrix} - \begin{bmatrix} -\frac{1}{6} & \frac{1}{4} \\ -\frac{3}{5} & \frac{2}{3} \end{bmatrix}$

5. $\begin{bmatrix} 2 & 9 \\ 6 & 7 \end{bmatrix} + \begin{bmatrix} 6 & 2.3 \\ 9 & 4.1 \end{bmatrix}$

6. $\begin{bmatrix} 3 & -7 & 4 \\ 0 & -4 & 9 \end{bmatrix} + \begin{bmatrix} -9 & 4 & 10 \\ 3 & -11 & 2 \end{bmatrix}$

7. $\begin{bmatrix} 5 & -3.5 \\ 10 & 14 \\ -5 & 4.7 \end{bmatrix} + \begin{bmatrix} -6.1 & 0.8 \\ 7 & -5 \\ 8.3 & 9 \end{bmatrix}$

8. $\begin{bmatrix} 4 & 2 & 9 \\ -11 & 20 & 5 \\ -18 & 21 & -2 \end{bmatrix} - \begin{bmatrix} 8 & 17 & 4 \\ -34 & 26 & -9 \\ 3 & 0 & 17 \end{bmatrix}$

9. Use matrix addition to find the total number of Greenfield students per grade involved in each activity.

Greenfield High School North

	Sports	Drama	Debate
9th	146	5	11
10th	201	15	4
11th	205	11	7
12th	176	19	13

Greenfield High School South

	Sports	Drama	Debate
9th	301	13	9
10th	345	8	6
11th	245	11	11
12th	220	11	9

12-2

Translations

Lesson Preview

What You'll Learn

To describe translations using vectors

To find translation images using matrix and vector sums

. . . And Why

To determine a position after a composition of translations, as in Example 4

✓ Check Skills You'll Need

(For help, go to Lesson 9-4 and page 640.)

Write the sum of the two vectors as an ordered pair.

1. $\langle 12, -3 \rangle$ and $\langle -8, 6 \rangle$

2. $\langle -1, -5 \rangle$ and $\langle -6, 10 \rangle$

Add each pair of matrices.

3. $\begin{bmatrix} -2 & 3 \\ 1 & 8 \end{bmatrix} + \begin{bmatrix} -5 & 0 \\ -2 & 5 \end{bmatrix}$

4. $\begin{bmatrix} -1 & -2 & -3 \\ -7 & -6 & -5 \end{bmatrix} + \begin{bmatrix} 2 & 2 & 2 \\ 3 & 3 & 3 \end{bmatrix}$

New Vocabulary • translation • composition

Interactive lesson includes instant self-check, tutorials, and activities.

OBJECTIVE 1

Translations Using Vectors

Real-World Connection

It is easier to check parts when each is a translation image of the others.

A translation (or *slide*) is an isometry that maps all points of a figure the same distance in the same direction. Thus you can use a vector to describe a translation.

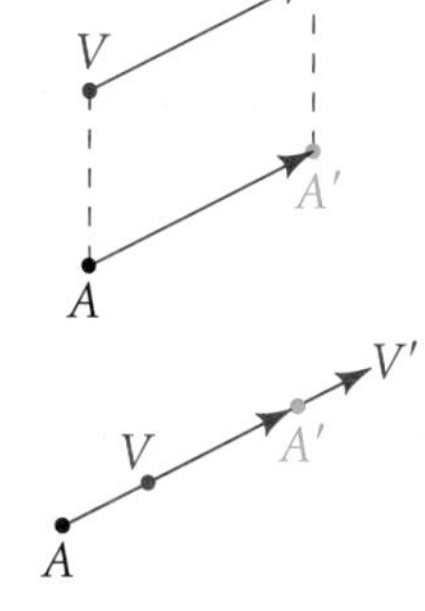

Using the diagram at the right, a **translation** described by $\overrightarrow{VV'}$ is a transformation that maps point A to A' so that the following are true.

- $AA'V'V$ is a parallelogram if A, V, and V' are noncollinear.
- $AA' = VV'$ and $AV = A'V'$ if A, V, and V' are collinear.

For the coordinate plane, recall that you use an ordered pair $\langle x, y \rangle$ for a vector. In this notation, x represents horizontal change and y represents vertical change from the initial point to the terminal point.

1 EXAMPLE Translations Using Vectors

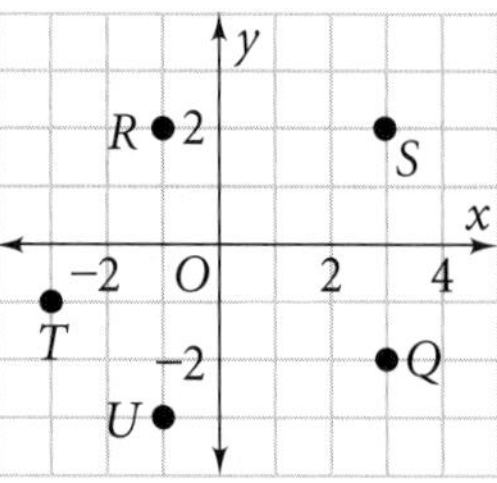

a. Find the image of T under the translation described by the vector $\langle 2, 3 \rangle$.

$\langle 2, 3 \rangle$ is a translation right 2 units and up 3 units. The image of T under $\langle 2, 3 \rangle$ is R.

b. Find the vector that describes the translation $S \rightarrow U$.

To go from S to U, you move left 4 units and down 5 units. The translation vector is $\langle -4, -5 \rangle$.

✓ Check Understanding

1 Refer to the diagram in Example 1.

a. Find the image of Q under the translation described by the vector $\langle -4, 4 \rangle$.

b. Find the vector that describes the translation $T \rightarrow S$.

Using variables, you can say that the vector $\langle a, b \rangle$ maps each (x, y) pair to $(x + a, y + b)$. Symbolically, $(x, y) \rightarrow (x + a, y + b)$.

2 EXAMPLE Writing a Rule to Describe a Translation

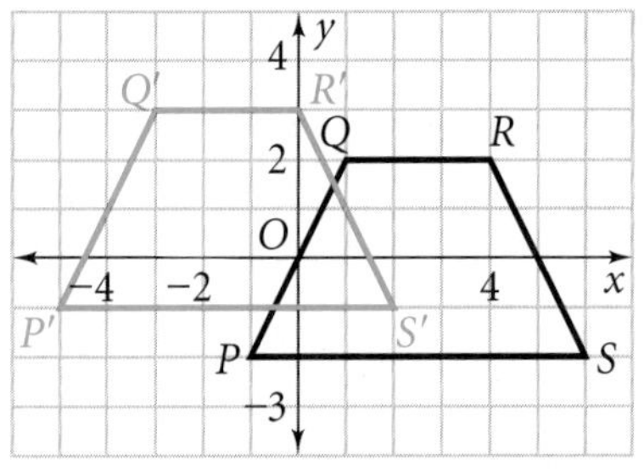

Write a rule to describe the translation $PQRS \rightarrow P'Q'R'S'$.

Use $P(-1, -2)$ and its image $P'(-5, -1)$.

Horizontal change: $-5 - (-1) = -4$
Vertical change: $-1 - (-2) = 1$

The vector is $\langle -4, 1 \rangle$.

The rule is $(x, y) \rightarrow (x - 4, y + 1)$.

Check Understanding **2** Use the rule $(x, y) \rightarrow (x + 7, y - 1)$ to find the translation image of $\triangle LMN$.

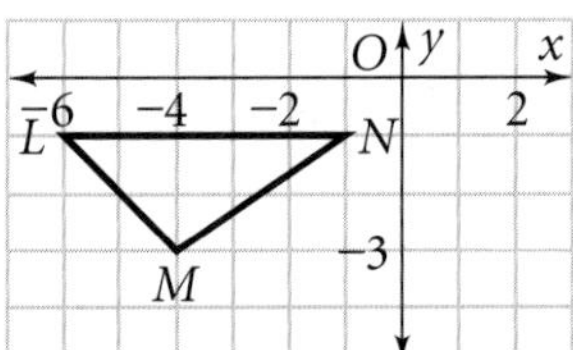

OBJECTIVE 2 Translations Using Matrix and Vector Sums

You can use matrices to find translation images of several points at once. To translate a triangle, you need a matrix for the three vertices and a matrix that shows the translation vector three times.

3 EXAMPLE Using Matrices to Find Images

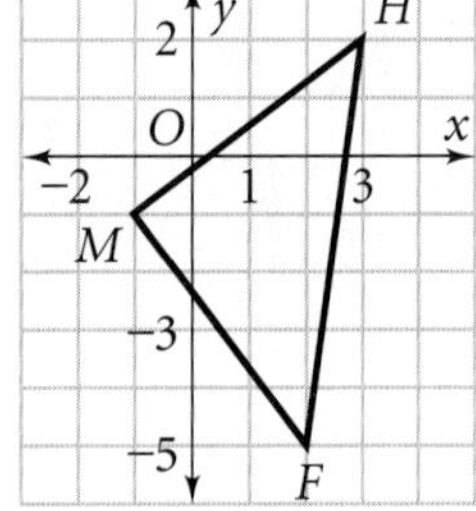

Use matrices to find the image of $\triangle MFH$ under the translation $\langle 4, -5 \rangle$.

$$\begin{matrix} & M & F & H \\ x\text{-coordinate} & \multirow{2}{*}{} -1 & 2 & 3 \\ y\text{-coordinate} & -1 & -5 & 2 \end{matrix} \quad \text{Write a matrix for } \triangle MFH.$$

$$\begin{bmatrix} 4 & 4 & 4 \\ -5 & -5 & -5 \end{bmatrix} \quad \text{Write the translation matrix.}$$

$$\begin{bmatrix} -1 & 2 & 3 \\ -1 & -5 & 2 \end{bmatrix} + \begin{bmatrix} 4 & 4 & 4 \\ -5 & -5 & -5 \end{bmatrix} = \begin{bmatrix} 3 & 6 & 7 \\ -6 & -10 & -3 \end{bmatrix} \quad \text{Add the matrices.}$$

The image of $\triangle MFH$ is $\triangle M'F'H'$ with $M'(3, -6)$, $F'(6, -10)$, and $H'(7, -3)$.

Check Understanding **3** Use matrices to find the image of $\triangle MFH$ under the translation $\langle 2, 8 \rangle$.

A **composition** of transformations is a combination of two or more transformations. In a composition, each transformation is performed on the image of the preceding transformation.

In a knight's move on a chessboard, the translation indicated in blue is the composition of two translations indicated in red.

In general, the composition of any two translations is a translation.

4 EXAMPLE Real-World Connection

Tourism Yolanda Perez is visiting San Francisco. From her hotel near Union Square, she walks 4 blocks east and 4 blocks north to the Wells Fargo History Museum to see a stagecoach and relics of the Gold Rush. Then she walks 5 blocks west and 3 blocks north to the Cable Car Barn Museum. Now how many blocks is she from her hotel?

The vector $\langle 4, 4 \rangle$ represents a walk of 4 blocks east and 4 blocks north. The vector $\langle -5, 3 \rangle$ represents her second walk. Yolanda's current position is the sum of the vectors. $\langle 4, 4 \rangle + \langle -5, 3 \rangle = \langle -1, 7 \rangle$, so Yolanda is 1 block west and 7 blocks north of her hotel.

Check Understanding 4 Yolanda next walks to a restaurant 2 blocks east and 4 blocks south of the Cable Car Barn Museum. Now how many blocks is she from her hotel?

EXERCISES

For more practice, see *Extra Practice*.

Practice and Problem Solving

Practice by Example

Example 1 (page 641)

Describe in words the translation represented by each vector.

1. $\langle 2, 5 \rangle$ **2.** $\langle 4, 1 \rangle$ **3.** $\langle -3, 8 \rangle$ **4.** $\langle 7, -2 \rangle$ **5.** $\langle -1, -6 \rangle$

Describe each translation using an ordered pair.

6. 0 units to the right, 4 units up

7. 2 units to the left, 1 unit down

8. 3 units to the left, 6 units down

9. 8 units to the right, 10 units up

In the diagram, find the image of F under the translation described by the given vector.

10. $\langle -1, 4 \rangle$ **11.** $\langle 4, -1 \rangle$ **12.** $\langle 4, 1 \rangle$

13. $\langle 1, 4 \rangle$ **14.** $\langle 5, 5 \rangle$ **15.** $\langle -4, -1 \rangle$

Find the vector that describes each translation.

16. $G \rightarrow H$ **17.** $B \rightarrow E$ **18.** $I \rightarrow C$

19. $H \rightarrow G$ **20.** $E \rightarrow B$ **21.** $C \rightarrow I$

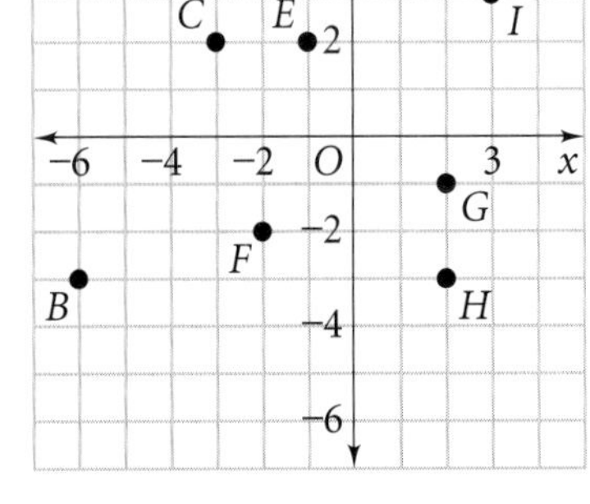

Example 2 (page 642)

In Exercises 22–25, the blue figure is a translation image of the red figure. Write a rule to describe each translation.

22.

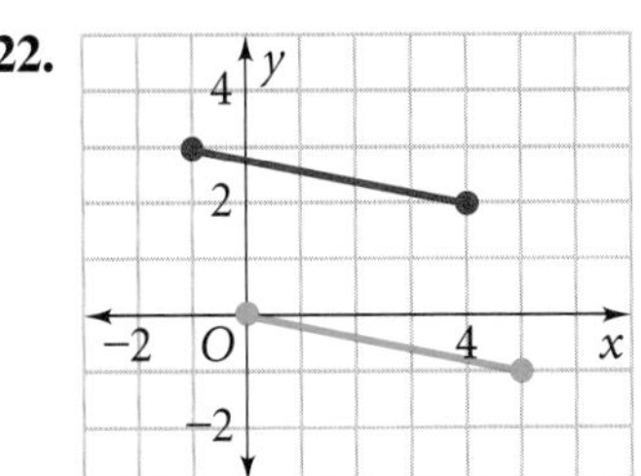

23.

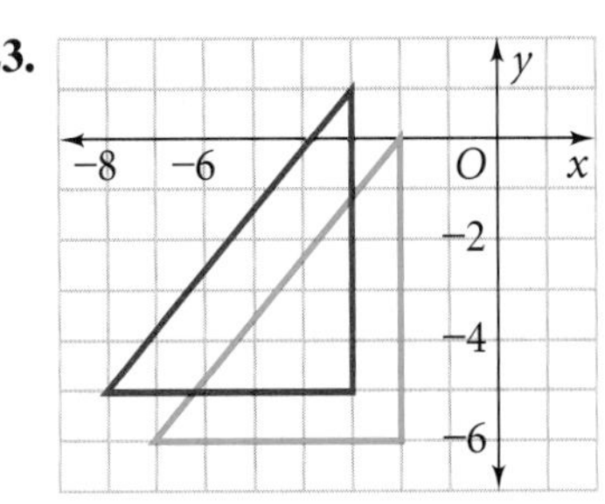

24.

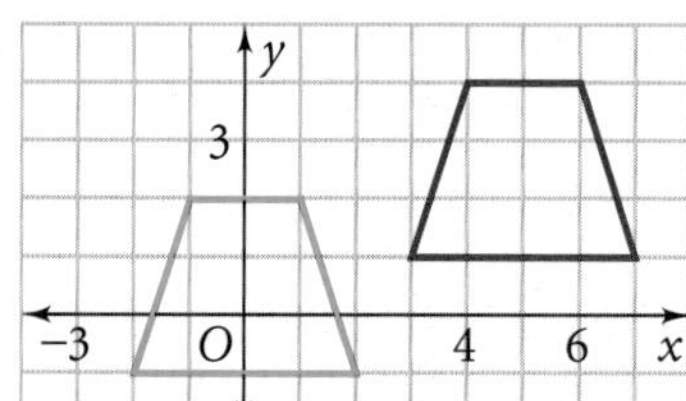

25.

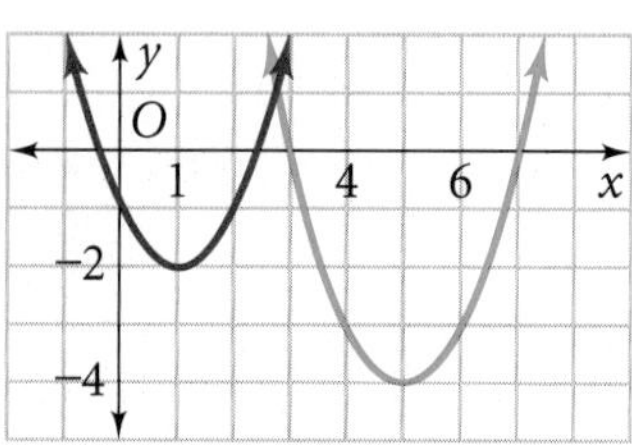

Example 3 (page 642)

Use matrices to find the image of each figure under the given translation.

26. translation $\langle 3, 2\rangle$

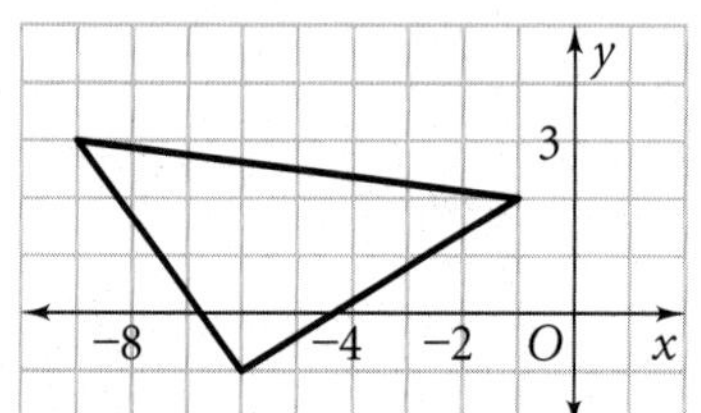

27. translation $\langle 5, -1\rangle$

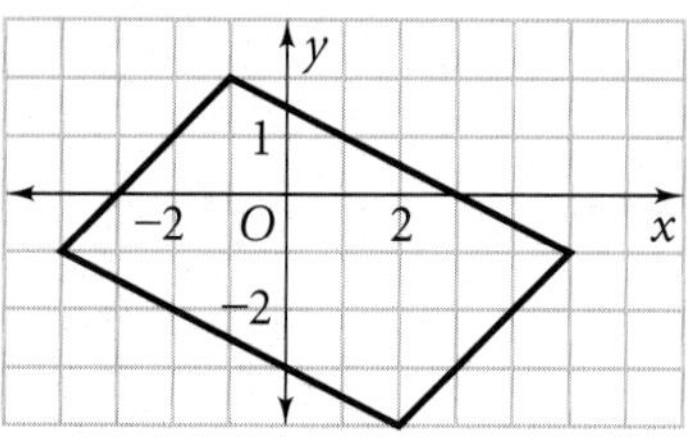

28. translation $\langle -2, 5\rangle$

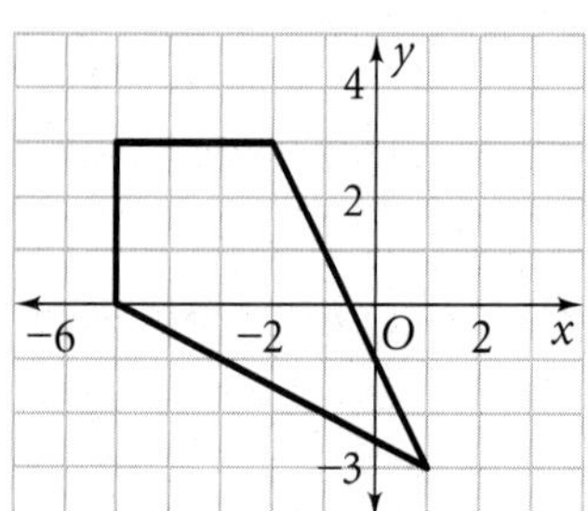

29. translation $\langle -4, 3\rangle$

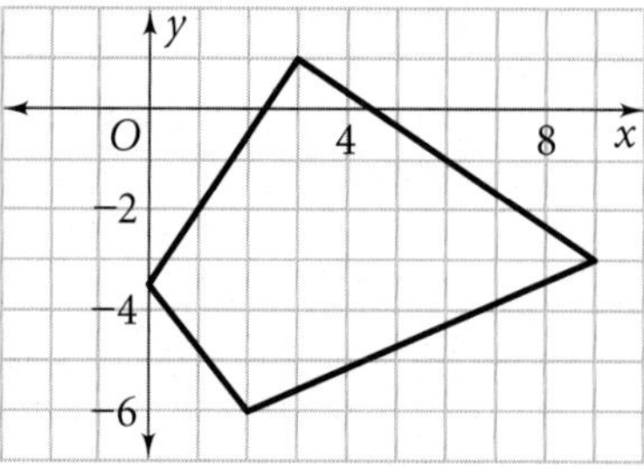

30. $\triangle ACE$ with vertices $A(7, 2)$, $C(-8, 5)$, $E(0, -6)$; translation: $\langle -9, 4\rangle$

31. $\triangle PUN$ with vertices $P(1, 0)$, $U(4, 6)$, $N(-5, 8)$; translation: $\langle 11, -13\rangle$

32. $\square PLAT$ with vertices $P(-2, 0)$, $L(-1, 1)$, $A(0, 1)$, $T(-1, 0)$; translation: $\langle 1, 0\rangle$

33. $\square NILE$ with vertices $N(2, -5)$, $I(2, 2)$, $L(-3, 4)$, $E(-3, -3)$; translation: $\langle -3, -4\rangle$

Example 4 (page 643)

34. Emily left Galveston Bay at the east jetty and sailed 4 km north to an oil rig. She then sailed 5 km west to Redfish Island. Finally, she sailed 3 km southwest to Spinnaker Restaurant.
a. Draw vectors on graph paper that show her journey.
b. Describe where Spinnaker Restaurant is from where Emily started.

35. Nakesha and her parents are visiting colleges. They leave their home in Enid, Oklahoma, and drive to Tulsa, which is 107 mi east and 18 mi south of Enid. From Tulsa, they go to Norman, 83 mi west and 63 mi south of Tulsa. Draw a diagram to show their trip. Then, tell where Norman is in relation to Enid.

B Apply Your Skills

The orange figure is a translation image of the red figure. Write a rule to describe each translation.

36.

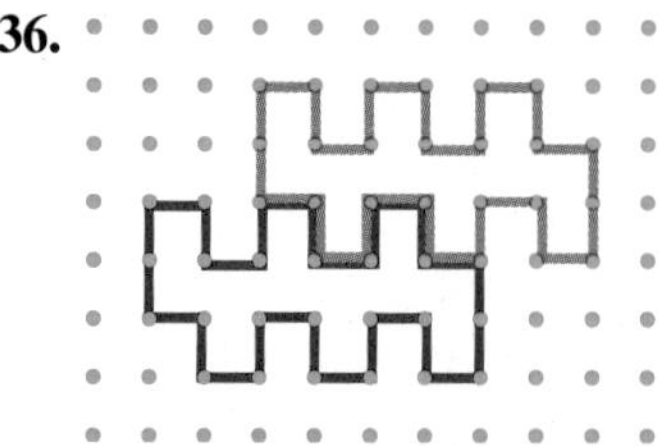

37.

Real-World Connection

A time-lapse photo captures translations of different points of the truck.

38. Photography When you snap a photograph, a shutter opens to expose the film to light. The amount of time that the shutter remains open is known as the shutter speed. For the photograph at the left, the photographer used a long shutter speed. It created an image that suggests a translation. Draw a picture of your own that suggests a translation.

39. Coordinate Geometry $\triangle MUG$ has coordinates $M(2, -4)$, $U(6, 6)$, and $G(7, 2)$. A translation maps point M to $M'(-3, 6)$. Find the coordinates of U' and G' under this translation.

40. Coordinate Geometry $\square ABCD$ has vertices $A(3, 6)$, $B(5, 5)$, $C(4, 2)$, and $D(2, 3)$. The figure is translated so that the image of point C is the origin.

a. Find the vector that describes the translation.

b. Graph $\square ABCD$ and its image.

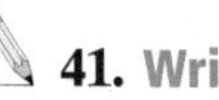

41. Writing Is the transformation at the right, $\triangle HYP \rightarrow \triangle H'Y'P'$, a translation? Explain.

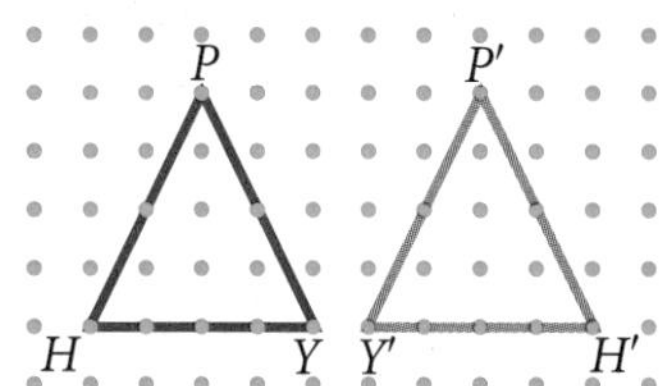

Find a single translation that has the same effect as each composition of translations.

42. $\langle 2, 5 \rangle$ followed by $\langle -4, 9 \rangle$

43. $\langle -3, 7 \rangle$ followed by $\langle 3, -7 \rangle$

44. $\langle 1, -3 \rangle$ followed by $\langle 5, 2 \rangle$

45. $\langle 12, 0.5 \rangle$ followed by $\langle 1, -3 \rangle$

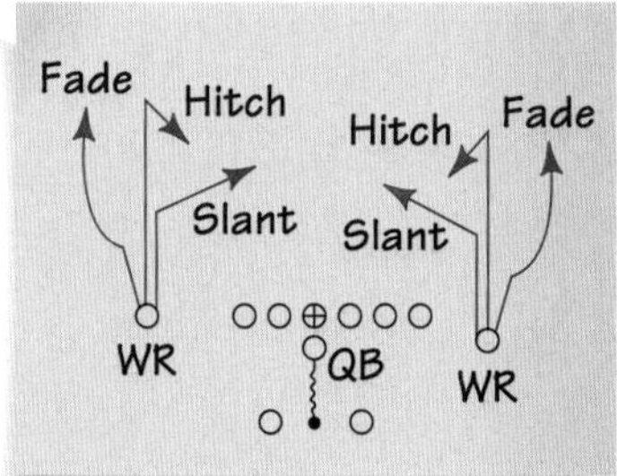

46. Football The play chart at the left shows routes that a wide receiver (WR) can choose to run when the team is in the "red zone" (within 20 yards of the goal line). The quarterback (QB) drops back two steps to make the pass to the wide receiver.

a. Suppose a wide receiver runs a slant. Describe the two translations involved and the composition of those two translations.

b. Describe the two intended translations of the football during the play, and the composition of the translations.

c. What is the intended outcome of the two compositions in parts (a) and (b)?

Geometry in 3 Dimensions **Use each figure, graph paper, and the given vector to draw a three-dimensional figure.**

SAMPLE Use the rectangle and vector $\langle 3, 1 \rangle$ to draw a box.

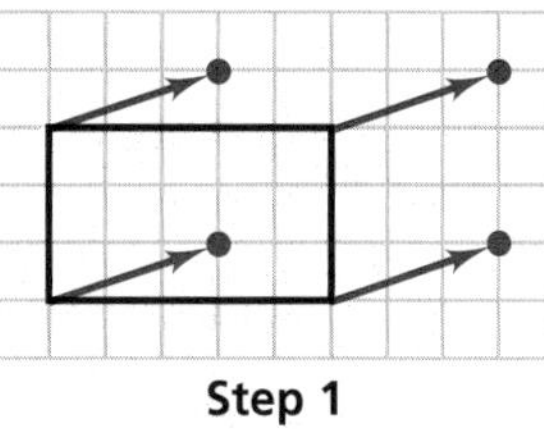

Step 1

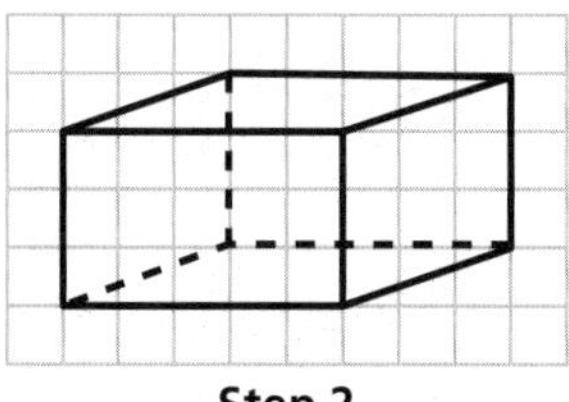

Step 2

47.

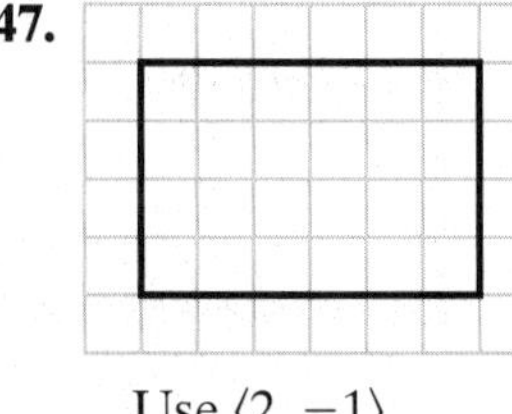

Use $\langle 2, -1 \rangle$.

48.

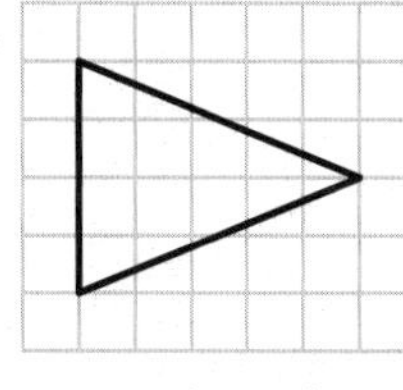

Use $\langle -2, 2 \rangle$.

49.

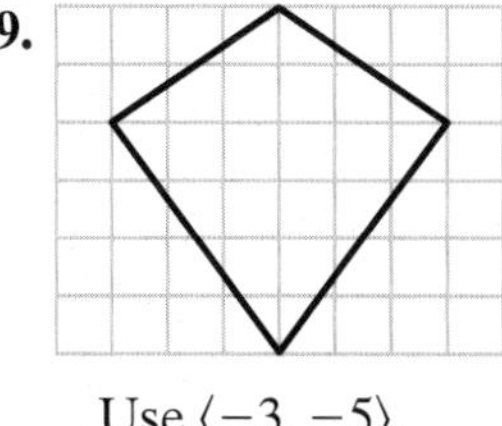

Use $\langle -3, -5 \rangle$.

50. Open-Ended You work for a company that specializes in creating unique, artistic designs for business stationery. One of your clients is Totter Toy Co. You have been assigned to create a border design for the top of their stationery. Create a design that involves translations to present to your client.

Challenge

51. a. $\triangle ABC$ has vertices $A(-2, 5)$, $B(-4, -1)$, and $C(2, -3)$. Find the image of $\triangle ABC$ under the translation $\langle 4, 2 \rangle$.

b. Show that the images of the midpoints of the sides of $\triangle ABC$ are the midpoints of $\triangle A'B'C'$.

52. Writing Explain how a parallelogram could be defined in terms of translations.

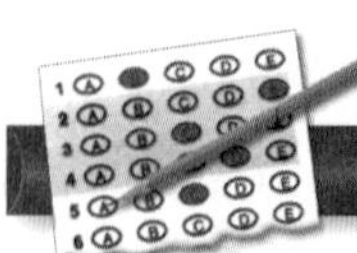

Standardized Test Prep

Multiple Choice

53. What is the image of (6, −2) under the translation ⟨−5, −8⟩?
A. (14, 3) B. (−2, −7) C. (11, 6) D. (1, −10)

54. The point (5, −9) is the image under the translation ⟨3, 2⟩. What is the preimage?
F. (2, −11) G. (8, −7) H. (2, −7) I. (8, −11)

55. What vector describes the translation of 4 units up and 12 units left?
A. ⟨12, 4⟩ B. ⟨−12, 4⟩ C. ⟨−12, −4⟩ D. ⟨12, −4⟩

56. What vector describes the translation from (0, −3) to (9, 5)?
F. ⟨−9, −8⟩ G. ⟨−9, 8⟩ H. ⟨9, −8⟩ I. ⟨9, 8⟩

Take It to the NET
Online lesson quiz at www.PHSchool.com
Web Code: afa-1202

57. $\triangle XYZ$ has vertices $X(-5, 2)$, $Y(0, -4)$, and $Z(3, 3)$. What are the vertices of the image of $\triangle XYZ$ under the translation ⟨7, −5⟩?
A. $X'(2, -3)$, $Y'(7, -9)$, $Z'(10, -2)$ B. $X'(-12, 7)$, $Y'(-7, 1)$, $Z'(-4, 8)$
C. $X'(-12, -3)$, $Y'(-7, -9)$, $Z'(-4, -2)$ D. $X'(2, -3)$, $Y'(10, -2)$, $Z'(7, -9)$

Short Response

58. $\triangle ABC$ has coordinates $A(0, -3)$, $B(-4, -2)$, and $C(2, 1)$. A translation maps point B to (10, −3).
a. What vector describes the translation?
b. What are the images of A and C under this translation?

Mixed Review

Lesson 12-1

$\triangle BIG$ has vertices $B(-4, 2)$, $I(0, -3)$, and $G(1, 0)$. Draw $\triangle BIG$ and then its reflection image in the given line.

59. the y-axis **60.** the x-axis **61.** $x = 4$

Lesson 10-5

Find the volume of each cylinder in terms of π.

62.
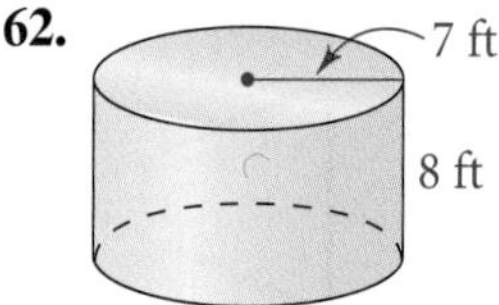

63.
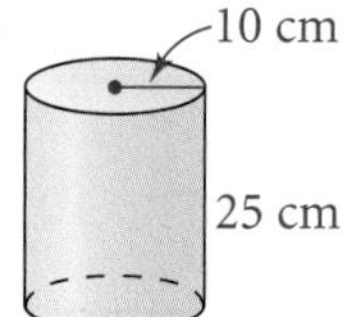

64.
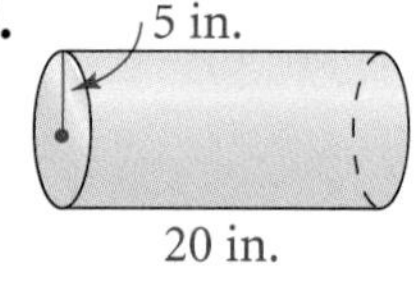

Lesson 8-5

Solve for x.

65.
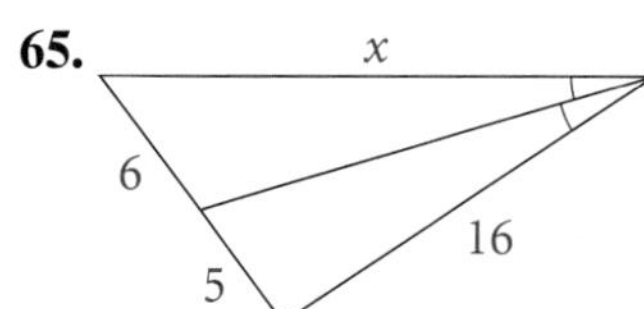

66.
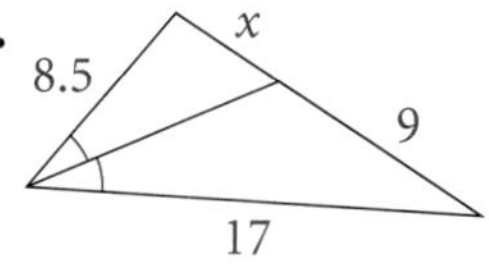

Rotations

Lesson Preview

What You'll Learn

To draw and identify rotation images of figures

. . . And Why

To identify rotation images in art designs, as in Example 3

✓ Check Skills You'll Need

(For help, go to Lesson 7-5.)

Find the measure of the angle formed by two consecutive radii in each regular polygon.

1. triangle
2. quadrilateral
3. pentagon
4. hexagon
5. octagon
6. decagon

New Vocabulary • rotation

Interactive lesson includes instant self-check, tutorials, and activities.

OBJECTIVE

1 Drawing and Identifying Rotation Images

Investigation: Making Designs With Rotations

You will need at least three pieces of tracing paper for this Investigation.

Step 1 Place a piece of paper over the figure at the right. Trace the six points on the circle, the center of the circle, and the triangle.

Step 2 Place the point of your pencil on the center of the circle and then rotate the paper until the six points align again. Trace the triangle in its new location.

Step 3 Repeat Step 2 until there are six triangles on your paper. Compare your drawings to others to be sure that your results look the same.

Step 4 Now it's your turn to be creative. Place a piece of paper over the figure above, trace the six points on the circle and the center of the circle, and then draw your own triangle on the paper.

Step 5 Place the paper from Step 4 on your desk. On a blank piece of paper, repeat Steps 1–3. Color your drawing to make a design.

Turn the above diagram 60° about the center of the circle and each dot on the circle maps to the next dot on the circle. This is an example of a type of transformation known as a rotation (or *turn*).

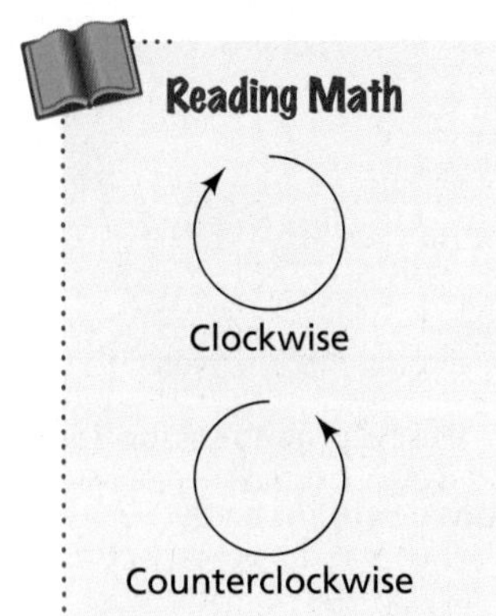

To describe a rotation, you need to know the center of rotation (a point), the angle of rotation (a positive number of degrees), and whether the rotation is clockwise or counterclockwise. Unless stated otherwise, rotations in this book are counterclockwise.

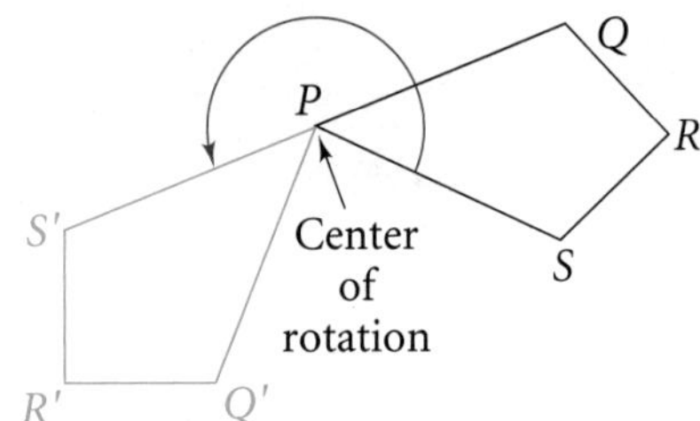

In general, a **rotation** of $x°$ about a point R is a transformation for which the following are true.

- The image of R is itself (that is, $R' = R$).
- For any point V, $RV' = RV$ and $m\angle VRV' = x$.

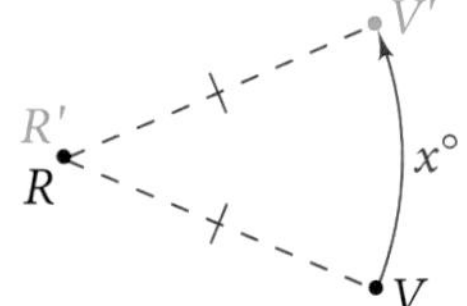
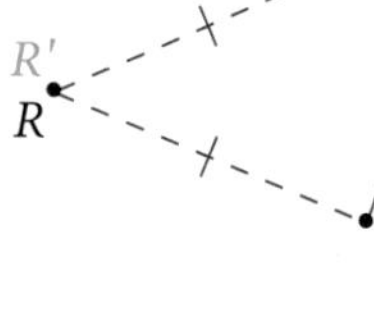

1 EXAMPLE Drawing a Rotation Image

Draw the image of $\triangle LOB$ for a 100° rotation about C.

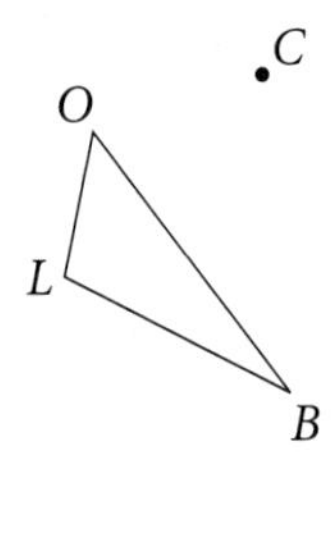

Step 1
Use a protractor to draw a 100° angle with vertex C and side $\overline{CO}$.

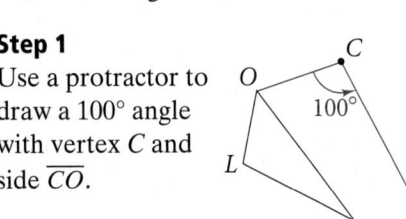

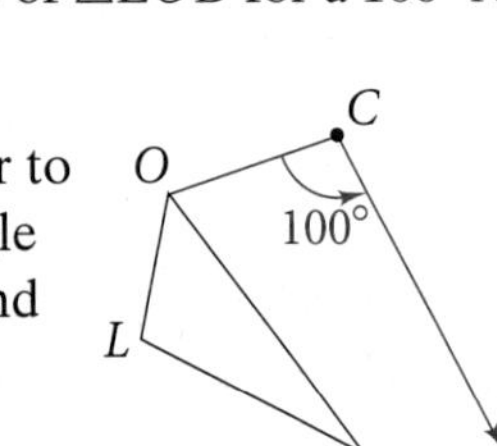

Step 2
Use a compass to construct $\overline{CO'} \cong \overline{CO}$.

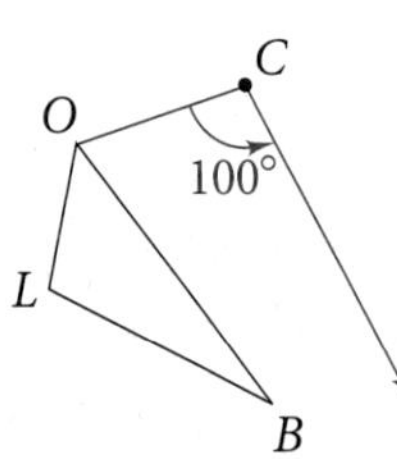
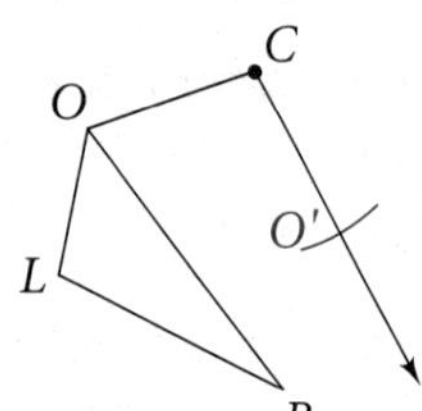

Step 3
Locate B' and L' in a similar manner. Draw $\triangle L'O'B'$.

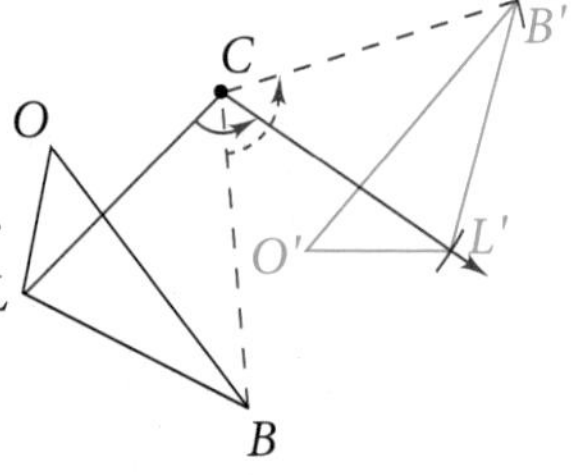

Check Understanding 1 Draw the image of $\triangle LOB$ from Example 1 for a 50° rotation about B. Label the vertices of the image.

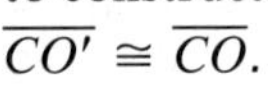

You can use what you know about regular polygons to identify images for a given angle of rotation.

2 EXAMPLE Identifying a Rotation Image

Regular pentagon $PENTA$ is divided into five congruent triangles.

a. Name the image of E for a 72° rotation about X.

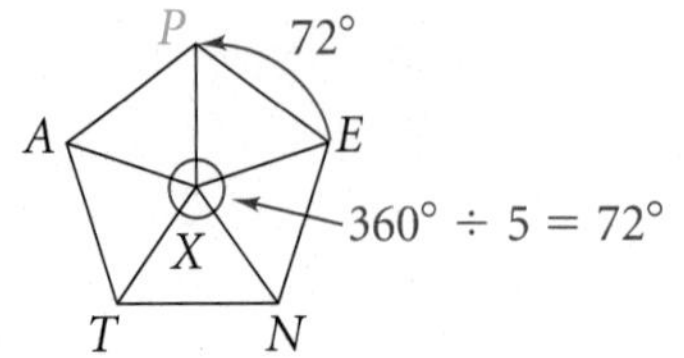

P is the image of E.

b. Name the image of P for a 216° rotation about X.

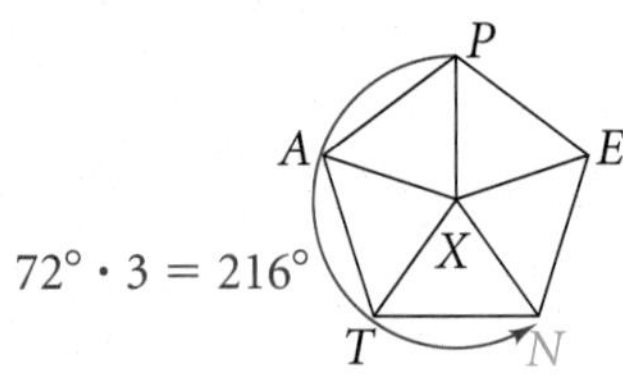

N is the image of P.

Check Understanding 2 Name the image of T for a 144° rotation about X.

Figures that are rotation images of themselves have a special beauty that you will study more closely in Lesson 12-5.

3 EXAMPLE Real-World Connection

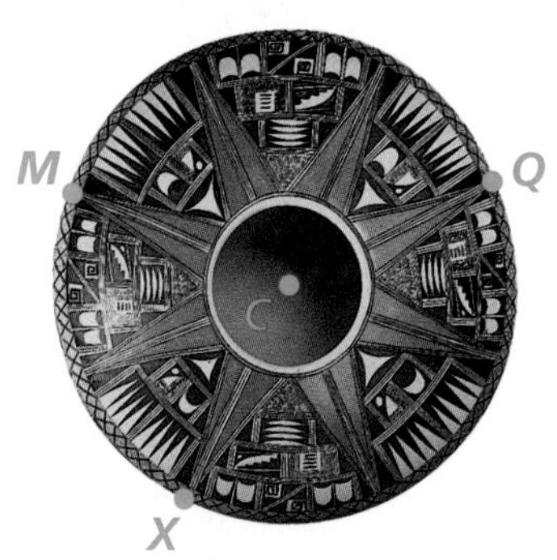

Native American Art You can find circular designs with rotation images in some types of Native American art. In the design pictured, find the angle of rotation about C that maps Q to X.

The eight-pointed star in the design divides the circle into eight congruent parts. $360 \div 8 = 45$, so each part has a 45° central angle. The angle of rotation that maps Q to X is $5 \cdot 45$, or 225°.

Check Understanding 3 In the design above, find the angle of rotation about C that maps Q to M.

A composition of rotations about the same point is itself a rotation about that point. To sketch the image, add the angles of rotation to find the total rotation.

4 EXAMPLE Compositions of Rotations

K

Draw the image of the kite at the left for a composition of a 30° rotation and a 60° rotation, both about point K.

The total rotation is 90°. Draw the kite. Locate image points of the vertices for a 90° rotation. Use the image points to sketch the entire image.

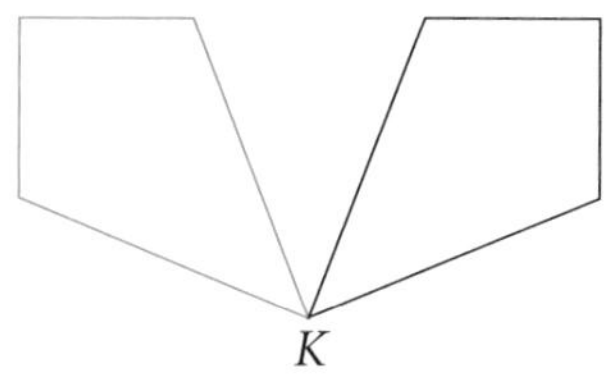

Check Understanding 4 Draw the kite at the left. Then draw its image for a composition of two 90° rotations about point K.

EXERCISES

For more practice, see *Extra Practice*.

Practice and Problem Solving

A Practice by Example

Example 1 (page 648)

Copy each figure and point P. Draw the image of each figure for the given rotation about P. Label the vertices of the image.

1. 60°

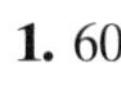

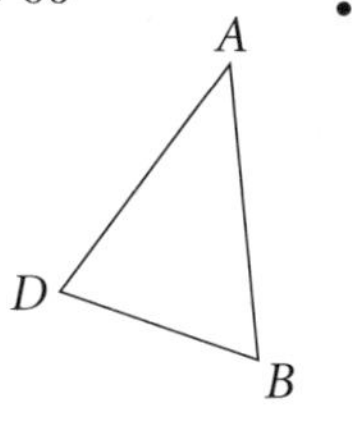

2. 90°

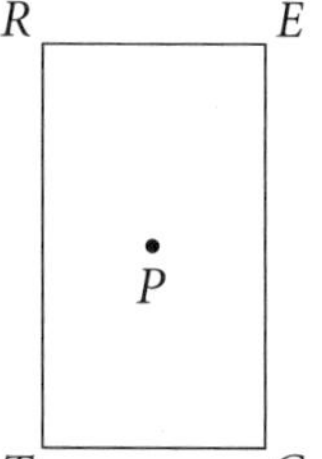

3. 90°

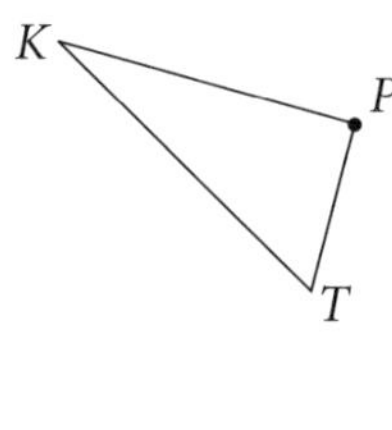

4. 180°

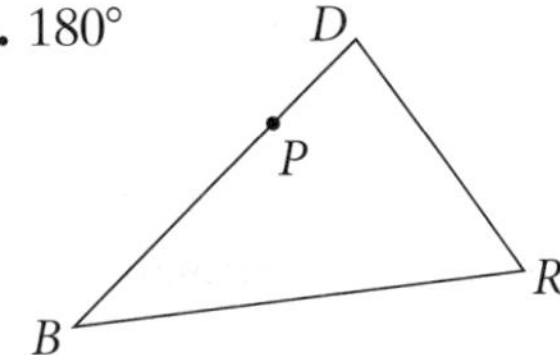

5. 140°

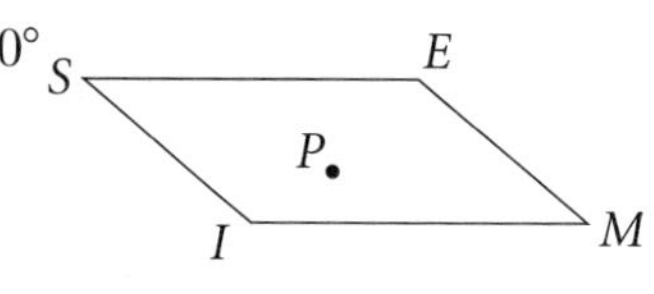

Copy each figure. Then draw the image of $\overline{JK}$ for a 180° rotation about *P*.

6. J P K

7. K J P

8. J K P

9. K J = P

Example 2 (page 648)

The large triangle, quadrilateral, and hexagon are regular. Find the image of each point or segment for the given rotation. (*Hint:* Green segments form 30° angles.)

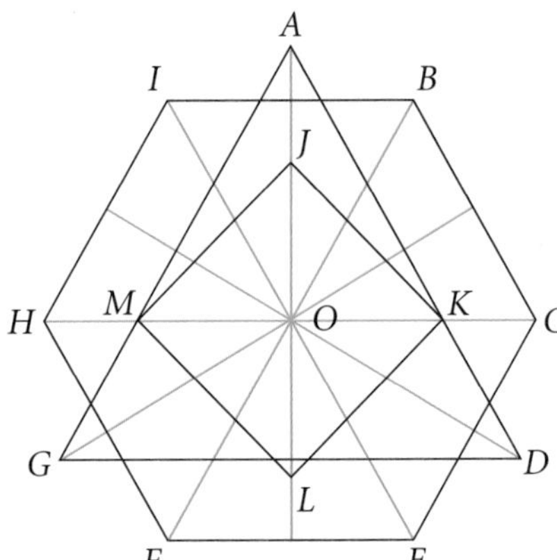

10. 120° rotation of *B* about *O*

11. 270° rotation of *L* about *O*

12. 60° rotation of *E* about *O*

13. 300° rotation of $\overline{IB}$ about *O*

14. 240° rotation of *G* about *O*

15. 180° rotation of $\overline{JK}$ about *O*

16. 120° rotation of *F* about *H*

17. 270° rotation of *M* about *L*

Example 3 (page 649)

Native American Art **Find the angle of rotation about *C* that (a) maps *Q* to *X* and (b) maps *X* to *Q*.**

18.

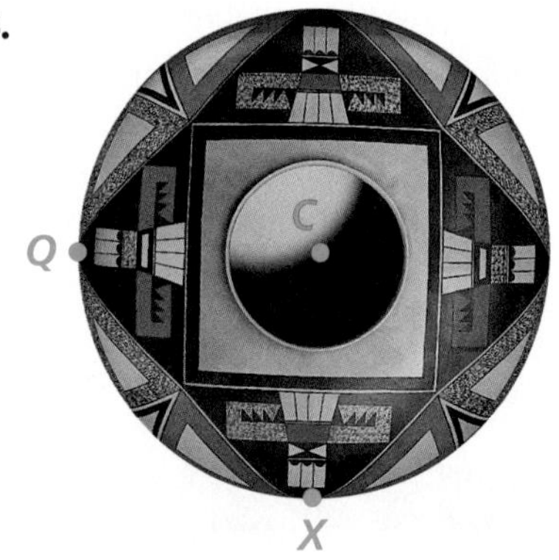

19.

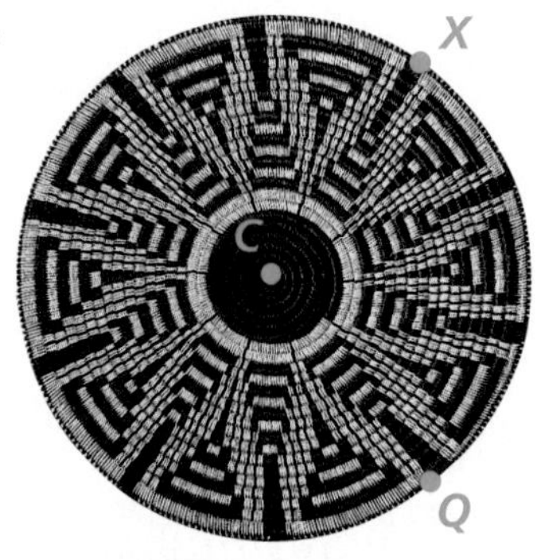

Example 4 (page 649)

For each of Exercises 20–25, copy $\triangle XYZ$. Draw the image of $\triangle XYZ$ for the given composition of rotations about the given point.

Y X Z

20. 45°, then 45°; *X*

21. 45°, then 45°; *Y*

22. 30°, then 30°; *Z*

23. 20°, then 160°; *Z*

24. 135°, then 135°; *Y*

25. 180°, then 180°; *X*

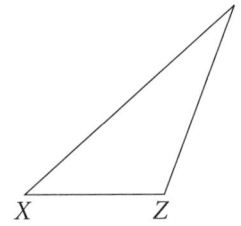

B Apply Your Skills

26. $\overline{M'N'}$ is the rotation image of $\overline{MN}$ about point *E*. Name all pairs of congruent angles and all pairs of congruent segments in the diagram.

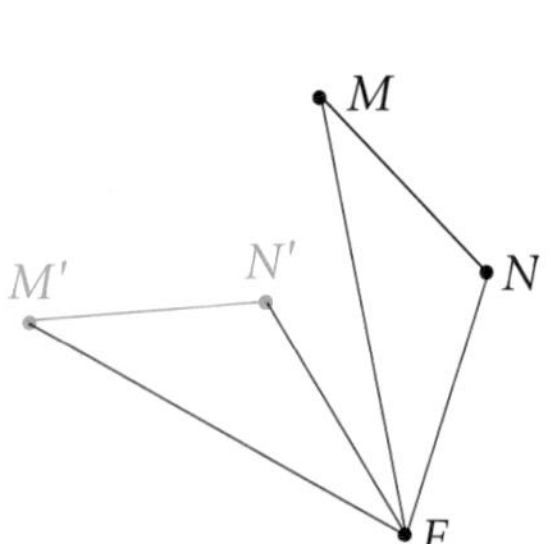

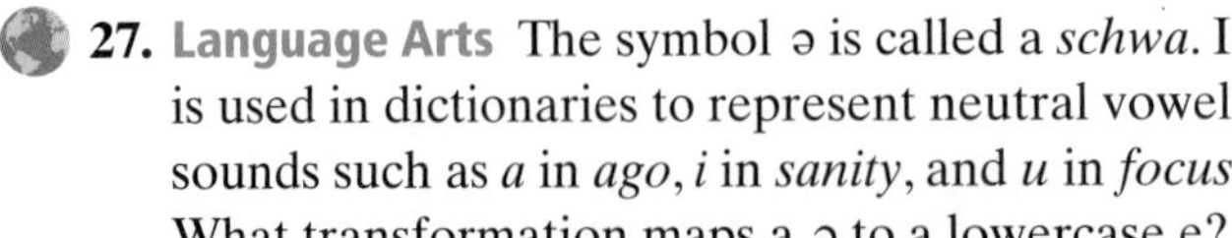

27. **Language Arts** The symbol ə is called a *schwa*. It is used in dictionaries to represent neutral vowel sounds such as *a* in *ago*, *i* in *sanity*, and *u* in *focus*. What transformation maps a ə to a lowercase e?

Find the angle of rotation about C that maps the black figure onto the blue figure.

28.

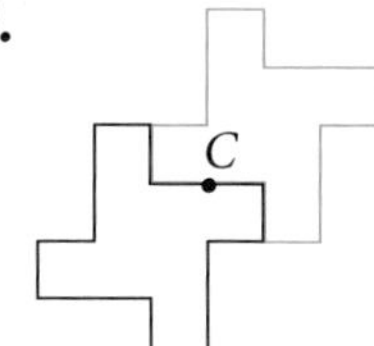

29.

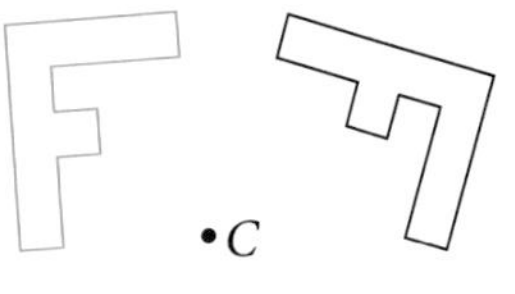

30.

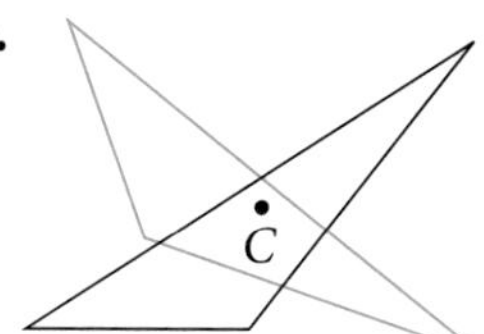

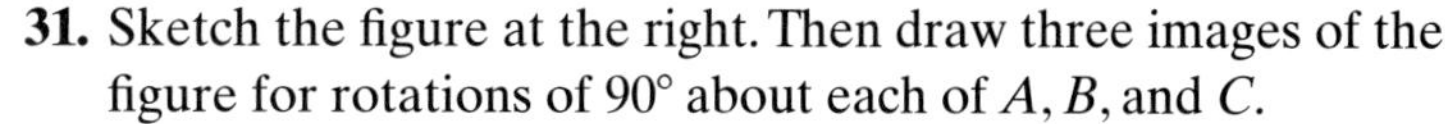

31. Sketch the figure at the right. Then draw three images of the figure for rotations of 90° about each of A, B, and C.

Reading Math

For help with reading and solving Exercise 32, see p. 653.

32. **Reasoning** If you are given a figure and a rotation image of the figure, how can you find the center and angle of rotation?

33. **Writing** Describe compositions of rotations that have the same effect as a 360° rotation about a point X.

Challenge

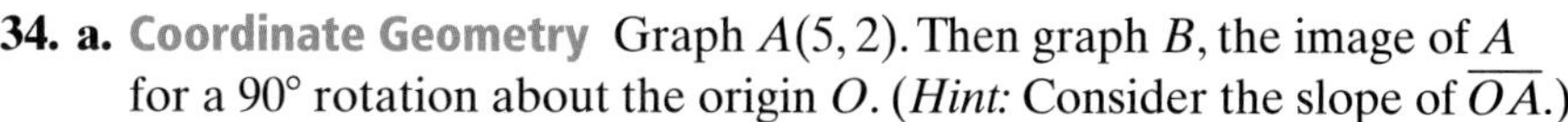

34. a. **Coordinate Geometry** Graph $A(5, 2)$. Then graph B, the image of A for a 90° rotation about the origin O. (*Hint:* Consider the slope of $\overline{OA}$.)

b. Graph C, the image of A for a 180° rotation about O.

c. Graph D, the image of A for a 270° rotation about O.

d. What type of quadrilateral is $ABCD$? Explain.

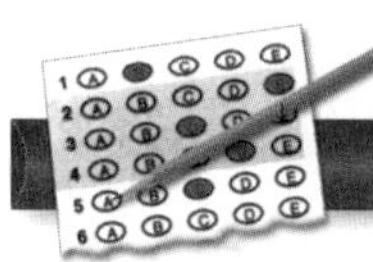

Standardized Test Prep

Multiple Choice

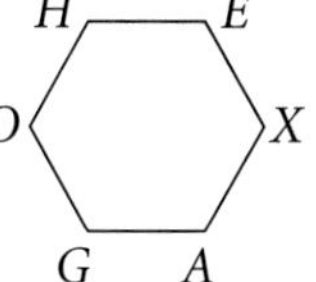

35. Name the image of X for a 240° counterclockwise rotation about the center of the regular hexagon.

A. A **B.** G **C.** O **D.** H

36. What is the image of (1, −6) for a 90° counterclockwise rotation about the origin?

F. (6, 1) **G.** (−1, 6) **H.** (−6, −1) **I.** (−1, −6)

Reading Comprehension

Read the passage below. Then answer the questions on the basis of what is *stated* or *implied* in the passage.

The same hemisphere of the moon always faces Earth. Thus, the motion of the moon about Earth for a given time interval can be modeled by a rotation. The center of the rotation is the center of Earth. The angle of rotation is determined by the time interval, given that one journey of the moon around Earth takes about $27\frac{1}{3}$ days.

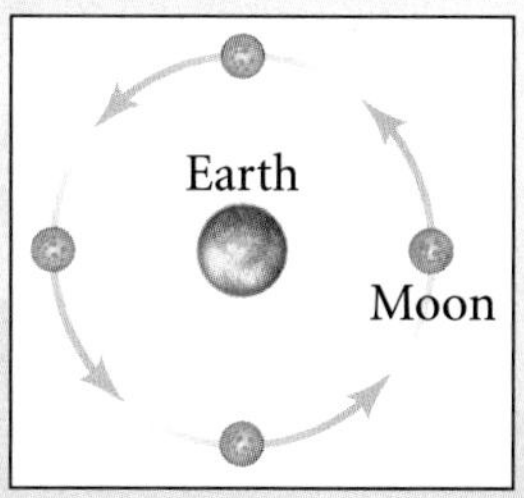

Take It to the NET

Online lesson quiz at **www.PHSchool.com**

Web Code: afa-1203

37. What rotation is modeled by the motion of the moon?

A. a circle rotating about its center **B.** a circle rotating about a point

C. 2 circles rotating around each other **D.** a circle rotating around a circle

38. In how many days does the moon complete a 90° angle of rotation?

F. about 4 **G.** about 7 **H.** about 14 **I.** about 27

Short Response

39. $\triangle XYZ$ has vertices $X(1, 2)$, $Y(0, 5)$, and $Z(-8, 0)$.

a. Graph $\triangle XYZ$ and its image after a 270° rotation about the origin.

b. Name the coordinates of each vertex of the image.

Mixed Review

Lesson 12-2

In each diagram, the blue figure is the translation image of the red figure. Write a rule to describe each translation.

40.

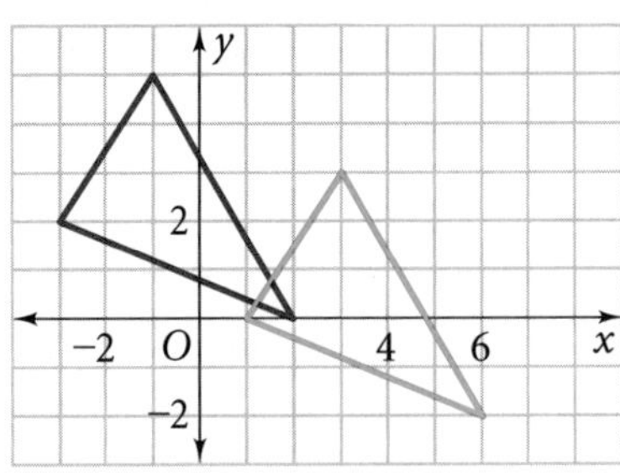

41.

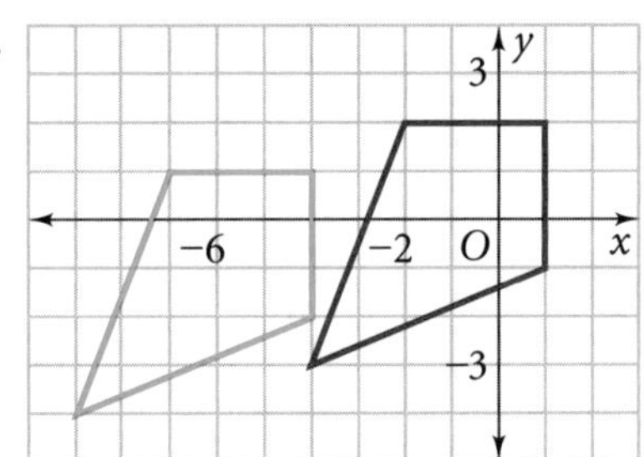

Lesson 10-7  **42. Geography** The United States has about 3,540,000 mi^2 of land. Earth is approximately a sphere with radius 3960 miles. What percent, to the nearest tenth, of the surface area of Earth is the land area of the United States?

Lesson 9-4 **43. Navigation** An airplane lands at a point 100 km east and 420 km south from where it took off. Describe the magnitude and the direction of its flight vector.

Checkpoint Quiz 1 Lessons 12-1 through 12-3

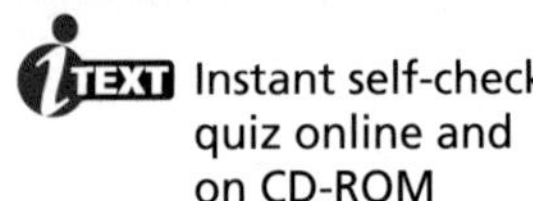

Instant self-check quiz online and on CD-ROM

State whether the transformation appears to be an isometry. Explain.

1.

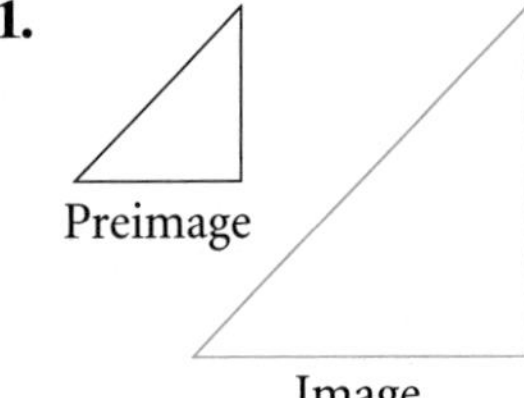

2.

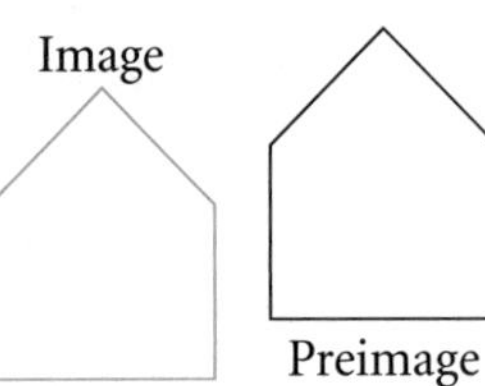

3.

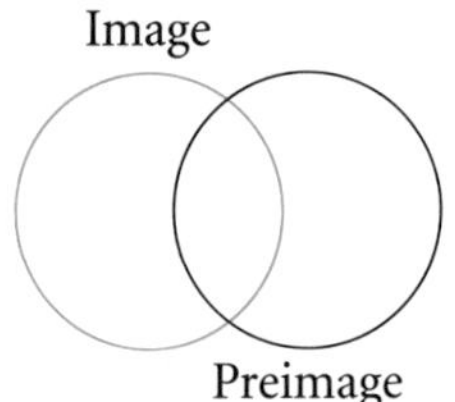

4. Describe in words the translation represented by the vector $\langle -3, 5\rangle$.

5. Use an ordered pair to describe a translation 5 units left and 10 units up.

6. Describe in words the result of the translation $\langle 7, -2\rangle$ followed by the translation $\langle -3, 2\rangle$.

Sketch each figure and point *A*. Draw the image of each figure for the given angle of rotation about *A*. Label the vertices of the image.

7. 40°

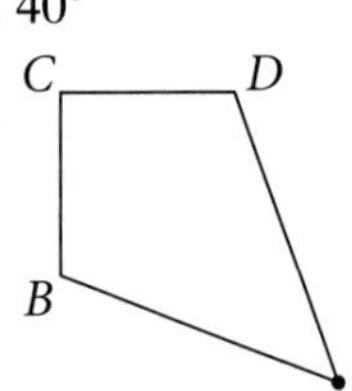

8. 90°

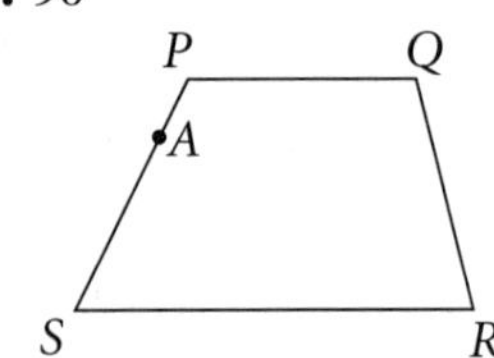

9. 180°

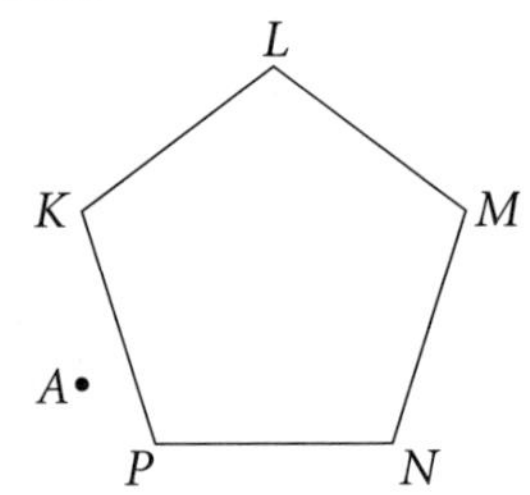

10. $\triangle WXY$ has vertices $W(-4, 1)$, $X(2, -7)$, and $Y(0, -3)$. Find its image for the translation $\langle -2, 5\rangle$.

Reading for Problem Solving

For Use With Page 651, Exercise 32

Read the problem below and then follow along with what Kate thinks as she solves the problem. Check your understanding by solving the exercise at the bottom of the page.

If you are given a figure and a rotation image of the figure, how can you find the center and angle of rotation?

What Kate Thinks	What Kate Draws
I'll use tracing paper and draw two congruent figures that have the same orientation. I like the letter K, so I think I'll use it. I'll tilt one K so that it's not a translation image.	
I think I see a rotation. It will rotate the left K counterclockwise onto the right K. It will rotate point A to point A' and point B to point B'.	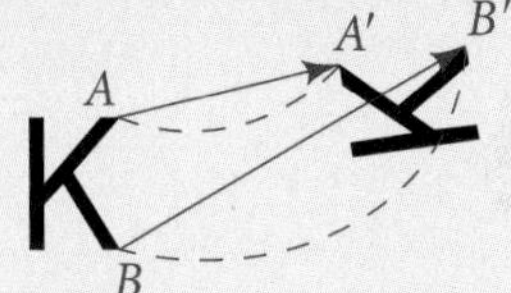
That means that A and A' are on a circle whose center is the center of rotation. The same is true for B and B'. The perpendicular bisectors of both $\overline{AA'}$ and $\overline{BB'}$ go through the center. I'll use blue to construct the perpendicular bisectors. Point C must be a center of rotation. I can check this using tracing paper.	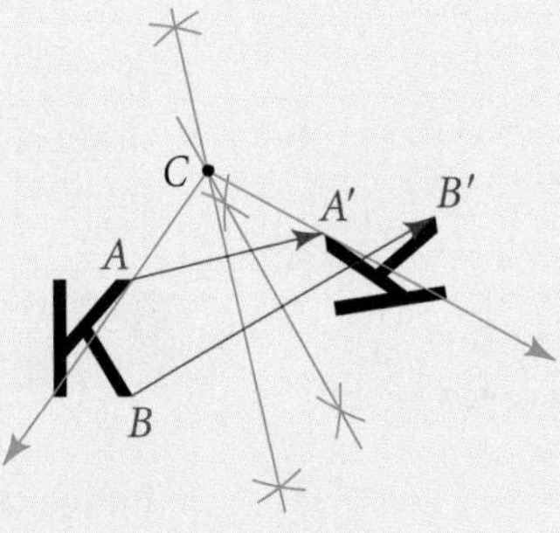
To find the angle of rotation, I just have to draw $\angle ACA'$ and measure it.	The center of rotation is C. The angle of rotation is 98°.

EXERCISE

In a newspaper or magazine that you can cut, find two large identical letters that are the same size and type. Cut them out and place them at random on a large piece of paper. Then find the center and angle of rotation that maps one onto the other.

Compositions of Reflections

Lesson Preview

What You'll Learn

OBJECTIVE 1 To use a composition of reflections

OBJECTIVE 2 To identify glide reflections

. . . And Why

To classify isometries, as in Example 5

Check Skills You'll Need

(For help, go to Lessons 12-1 and 12-2.)

Given points $R(-1, 1)$, $S(-4, 3)$, and $T(-2, 5)$, draw $\triangle RST$ and its reflection image in each line.

1. the y-axis **2.** the x-axis **3.** $y = 1$

Draw $\triangle RST$ described above and its translation image for each translation vector.

4. $\langle 0, -3 \rangle$ **5.** $\langle 4, 0 \rangle$ **6.** $\langle 2, -5 \rangle$

7. Copy the figure. Draw images of the figure for a reflection in $\overleftrightarrow{DG}$ and for the translation vector $\overrightarrow{FG}$.

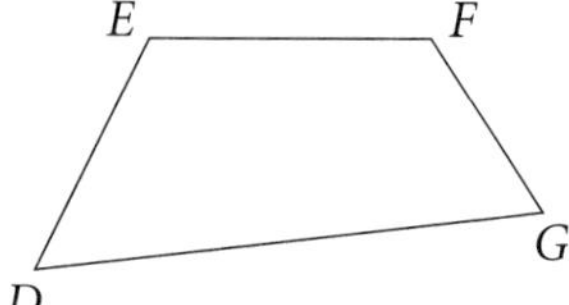

New Vocabulary

- glide reflection

Interactive lesson includes instant self-check, tutorials, and activities.

OBJECTIVE 1 Compositions of Reflections

Need Help?

You know a reflection is involved if a figure and its image have opposite orientations.

If two figures are congruent, there is a transformation that maps one onto the other. If no reflection is involved, then the figures are either translation or rotation images of each other.

1 EXAMPLE Recognizing the Transformation

The two figures are congruent. Is one figure a translation image of the other, a rotation image, or neither? Explain.

The orientations of these congruent figures do not appear to be opposite, so one is a translation image or a rotation image of the other. Clearly, it's not a translation image, so it must be a rotation image.

Check Understanding

1 The two figures are congruent. Is one figure a translation image of the other, a rotation image, or neither? Explain.

Any translation or rotation can be expressed as the composition of two reflections.

Key Concepts

Theorem 12-1

A translation or rotation is a composition of two reflections.

The examples that illustrate Theorems 12-2 and 12-3 suggest a proof of Theorem 12-1 (how to find two reflections for a given translation or rotation).

Theorems 12-2 and 12-3 together form the converse of Theorem 12-1.

Key Concepts

Theorem 12-2

A composition of reflections in two parallel lines is a translation.

Theorem 12-3

A composition of reflections in two intersecting lines is a rotation.

Real-World Connection

Each mirror shows a reverse image. But bend the mirrors like this /‾\ and you get compositions of reflections.

2 EXAMPLE Composition of Reflections in Parallel Lines

Find the image of R or a reflection in line ℓ followed by a reflection in line m. Describe the resulting translation.

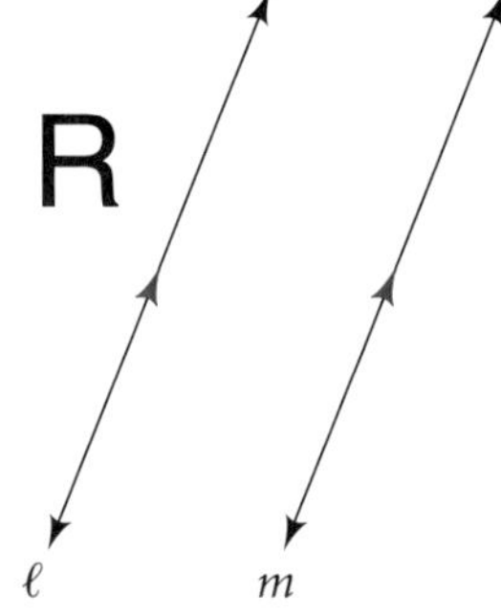

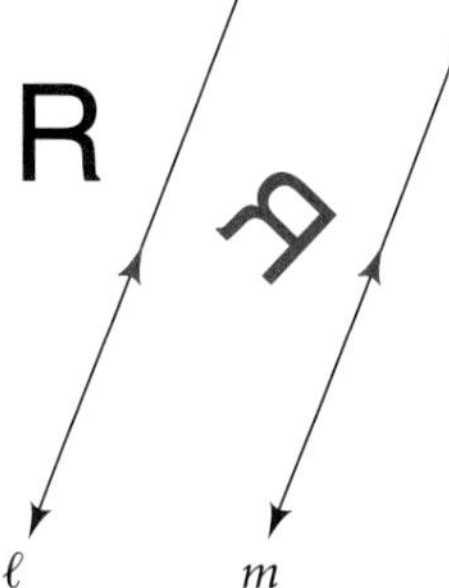

Reflect in ℓ.

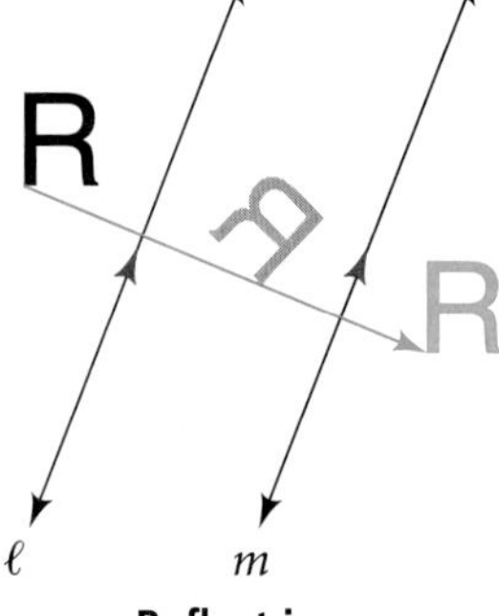

Reflect in *m*.

R is translated the distance and direction shown by the green arrow. The arrow is perpendicular to lines ℓ and m with length equal to twice the distance from ℓ to m.

Check Understanding 2 Draw lines ℓ and m as shown above. Draw R between ℓ and m. Find the image of R for a reflection in line ℓ and then in line m. Describe the resulting translation.

3 EXAMPLE Composition of Reflections in Intersecting Lines

Lines a and b intersect in point C and form acute $\angle 1$ with measure 35. Find the image of R for a reflection in line a and then a reflection in line b. Describe the resulting rotation.

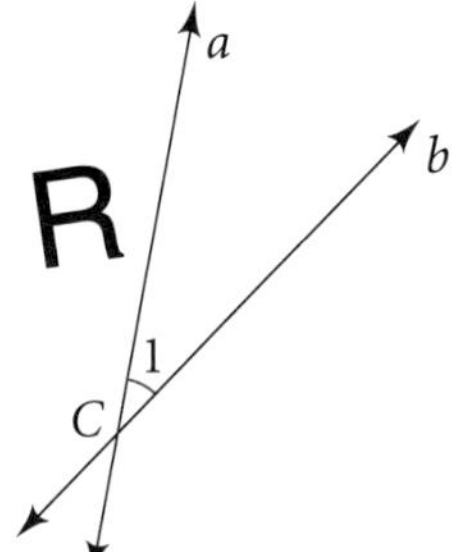

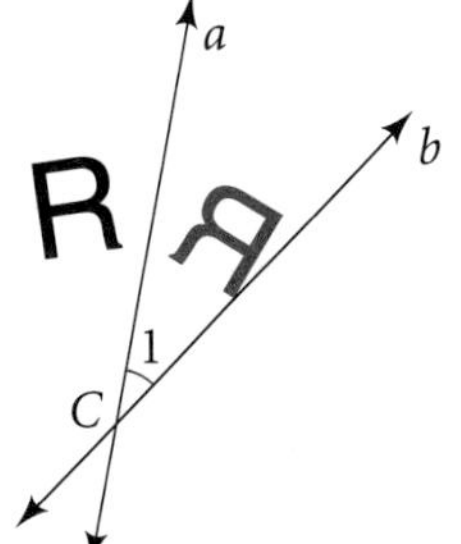

Reflect in *a*.

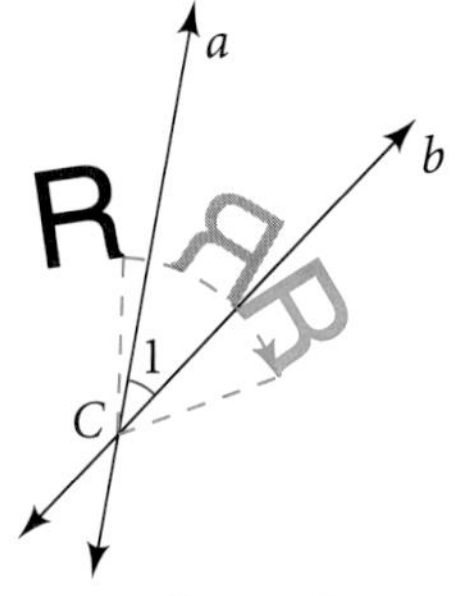

Reflect in *b*.

R rotates clockwise through the angle shown by the green arrow. The center of rotation is C and the measure of the angle is twice $m\angle 1$, or 70.

Check Understanding 3 Repeat Example 3, but begin with R in a different position.

OBJECTIVE

2 Glide Reflections

Two plane figures A and B can be congruent with opposite orientations. Reflect A and you get a figure A′ that has the same orientation as B. Thus, B is a translation or rotation image of A′. By Theorem 12-1, two reflections map A′ to B. The net result is that three reflections map A to B.

This is summarized in what is sometimes called the Fundamental Theorem of Isometries.

Key Concepts

Theorem 12-4 **Fundamental Theorem of Isometries**

In a plane, one of two congruent figures can be mapped onto the other by a composition of at most three reflections.

Real-World Connection

A computer can translate an image and then reflect it, or vice versa. The two rabbit images are glide reflection images of each other.

If two figures are congruent and have opposite orientations (but are not simply reflections of each other), then there is a slide and a reflection that will map one onto the other. A **glide reflection** is the composition of a glide (translation) and a reflection in a line parallel to the glide vector.

4 EXAMPLE Finding a Glide Reflection Image

Coordinate Geometry Find the image of $\triangle TEX$ for a glide reflection where the glide vector is $\langle 0, -5 \rangle$ and the reflection line is $x = 0$.

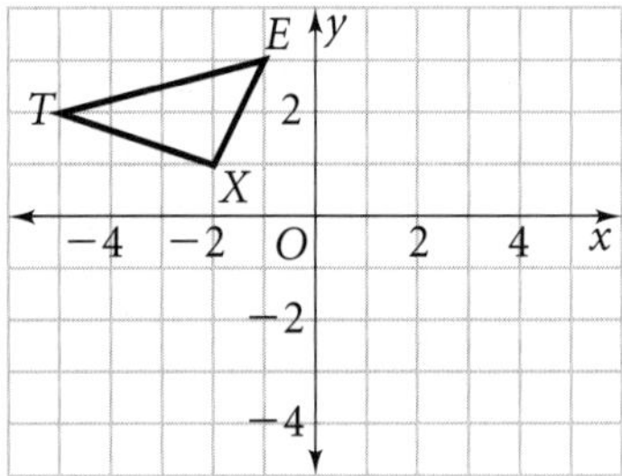

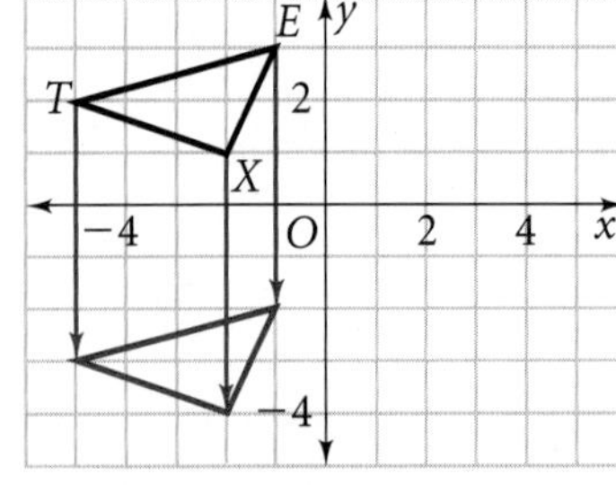

Translate $\triangle TEX$ by $\langle 0, -5 \rangle$.

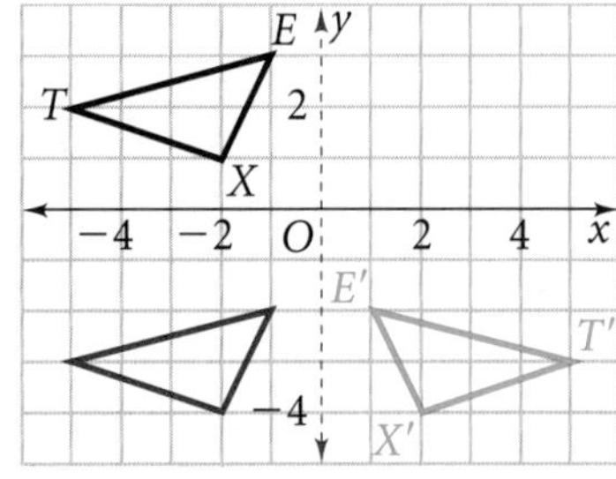

Reflect the image in $x = 0$.

Check Understanding 4 Use $\triangle TEX$ from Example 4 above.

a. Find the image of $\triangle TEX$ under a glide reflection where the glide vector is $\langle 1, 0 \rangle$ and the reflection line is $y = -2$.

b. Critical Thinking Would the result of part (a) be the same if you reflected $\triangle TEX$ first, and then translated it? Explain.

You can map one of any two congruent figures onto the other by a single reflection, translation, rotation, or glide reflection. Thus, you are able to classify any isometry.

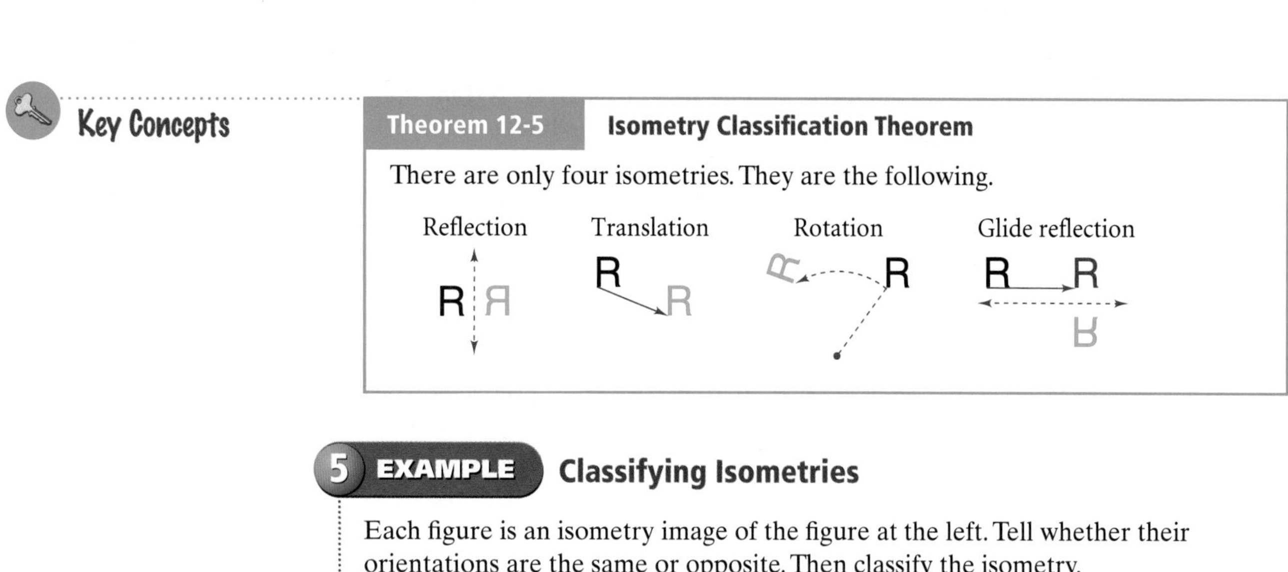

Key Concepts

Theorem 12-5 Isometry Classification Theorem

There are only four isometries. They are the following.

5 EXAMPLE Classifying Isometries

Each figure is an isometry image of the figure at the left. Tell whether their orientations are the same or opposite. Then classify the isometry.

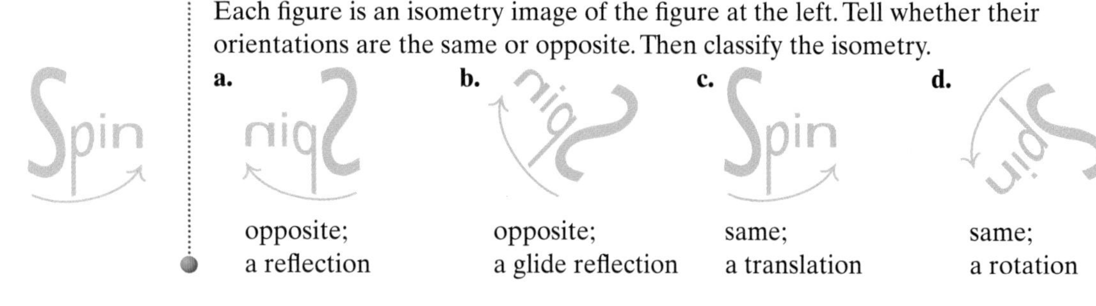

a. opposite; a reflection

b. opposite; a glide reflection

c. same; a translation

d. same; a rotation

Check Understanding 5 Classify the isometry. 45

EXERCISES

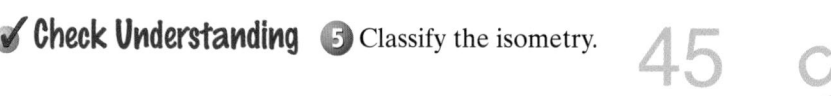

For more practice, see *Extra Practice*.

Practice and Problem Solving

A Practice by Example

Example 1 (page 654)

The two figures in each pair are congruent. Is one figure a translation image of the other, a rotation image, or neither? Explain.

1. F

2. bye bye

3. tu

Example 2 (page 655)

Find the image of each letter through a reflection in line ℓ and then a reflection in line m. Describe the resulting translation or rotation.

4. 5. 6.

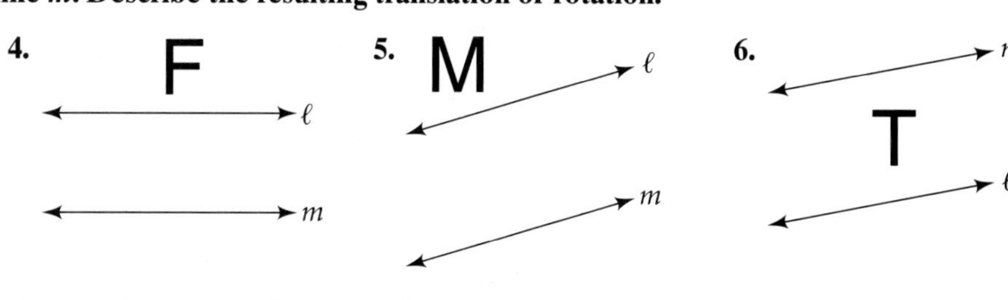

Example 3 (page 655)

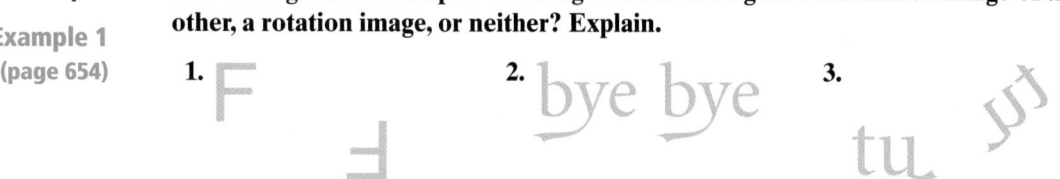

7. 8.

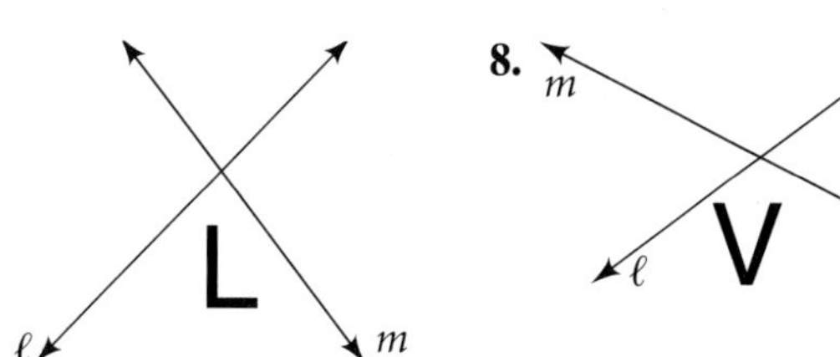

9.

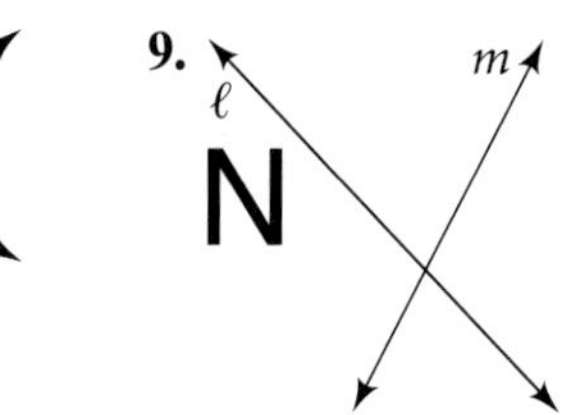

Example 4 (page 656)

Find the glide reflection image of $\triangle PNB$ for the given glide vector and reflection line.

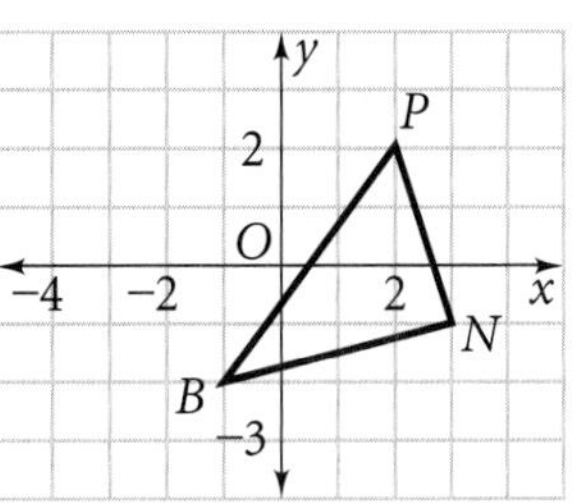

10. $\langle 2, 0\rangle$ and $y = 3$

11. $\langle 0, -3\rangle$ and $x = 0$

12. $\langle 0, 3\rangle$ and $x = -2$

13. $\langle -2, 0\rangle$ and $y = -1$

14. $\langle 2, 2\rangle$ and $y = x$

15. $\langle -1, 1\rangle$ and $y = -x$

16. $\langle 0, -2\rangle$ and $x = 2$

17. $\langle -2, -2\rangle$ and $y = x$

Example 5 (page 657)

Each figure is an isometry image of the figure at the left. Tell whether their orientations are the same or opposite. Then classify the isometry.

18. 

19. 

20. 

21. 

22.  

23. 

24. 

25. 

B Apply Your Skills

The two figures are congruent. Name the isometry that maps one onto the other.

26. 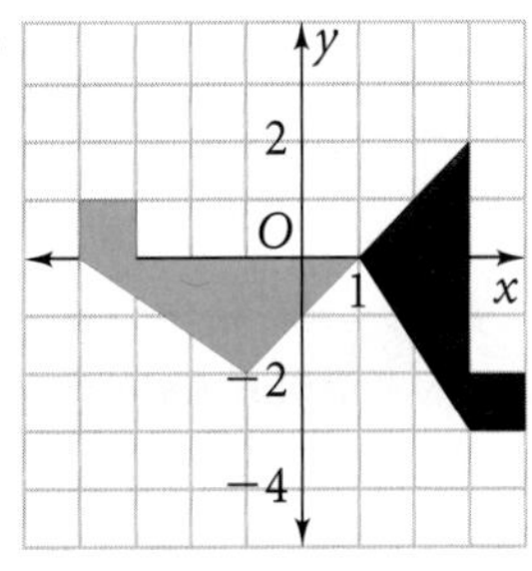

27. 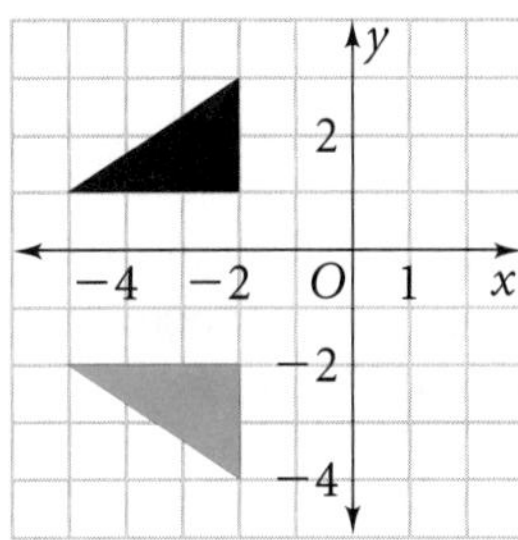

28. 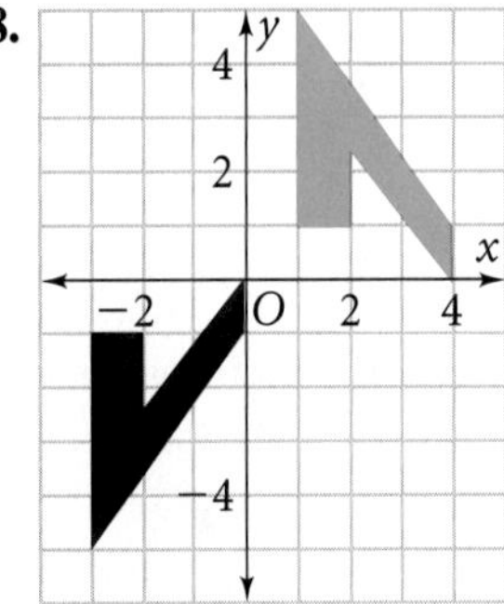

29. 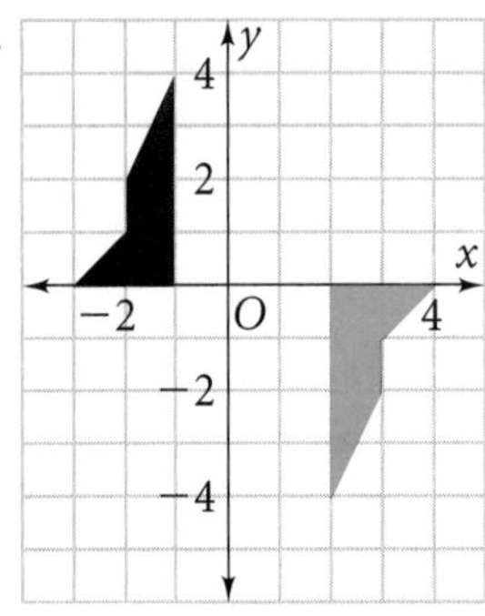

30. **Writing** Reflections and glide reflections are *odd isometries*, while translations and rotations are *even isometries*. Use what you learned in this lesson to explain why these categories make sense.

31. **Open-Ended** Draw $\triangle ABC$. Then, describe a reflection, a translation, a rotation, and a glide reflection, and draw the image of $\triangle ABC$ for each transformation.

32. For center of rotation P, does an $x°$ rotation followed by a $y°$ rotation give the same image as a $y°$ rotation followed by an $x°$ rotation? Explain.

33. Does an $x°$ rotation about a point P followed by a reflection in a line ℓ give the same image as a reflection in ℓ followed by an $x°$ rotation about P? Explain.

Need Help?

To learn more about kaleidoscopes, see p. 661.

Kaleidoscopes **The vibrant images of a kaleidoscope are produced by compositions of reflections in intersecting mirrors. Determine the angle between the mirrors in each kaleidoscope image.**

34.

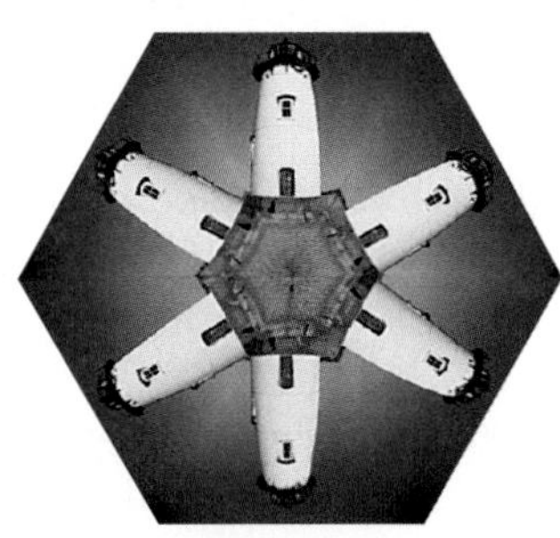

35.

36.

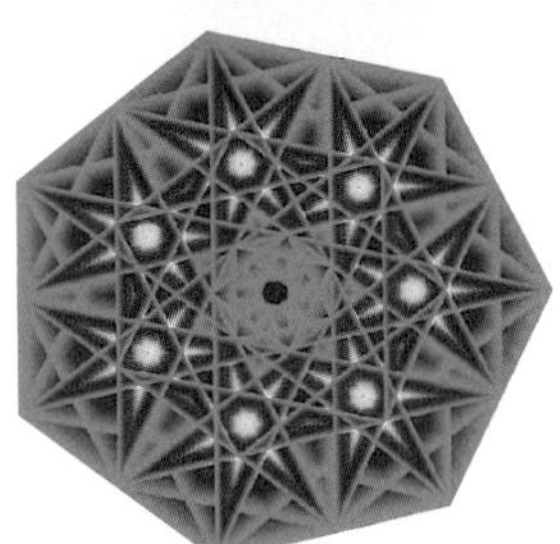

37.

Identify each mapping as a reflection, translation, rotation, or glide reflection. Find the reflection line, translation vector, center and angle of rotation, or glide vector and reflection line.

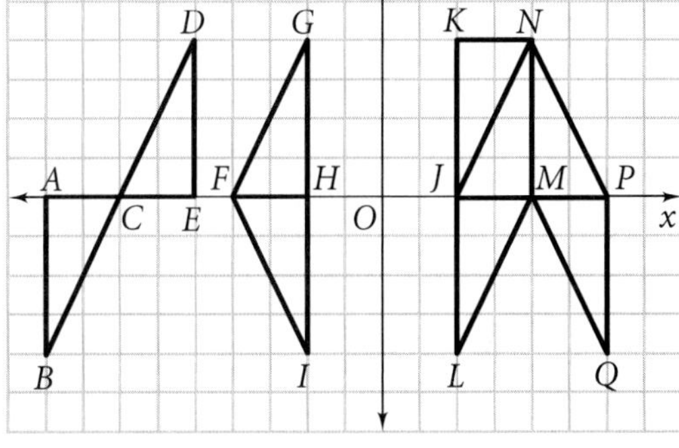

38. $\triangle ABC \rightarrow \triangle EDC$

39. $\triangle EDC \rightarrow \triangle PQM$

40. $\triangle MNJ \rightarrow \triangle EDC$

41. $\triangle HIF \rightarrow \triangle HGF$

42. $\triangle PQM \rightarrow \triangle JLM$

43. $\triangle MNP \rightarrow \triangle EDC$

44. $\triangle JLM \rightarrow \triangle MNJ$

45. $\triangle PQM \rightarrow \triangle KJN$

46. $\triangle KJN \rightarrow \triangle ABC$

47. $\triangle HGF \rightarrow \triangle KJN$

Challenge

48. Describe a glide and a reflection that maps the red R to the blue R.

For the given transformation mapping $\overline{XY}$ to $\overline{X'Y'}$, give a convincing argument why $\overline{XY} \cong \overline{X'Y'}$.

49. a reflection

50. a translation

51. a rotation

52. The definition states that a glide reflection is the composition of a translation and a reflection. Explain why these can occur in either order.

53. For lines of reflection r and s, does a reflection in r followed by a reflection in s give the same image as a reflection in s followed by a reflection in r? Explain.

$P \rightarrow P'(3, -1)$ for the given glide vector and reflection line. Find the coordinates of P.

54. glide $\langle -3, 0 \rangle$, reflection line $y = 2$

55. glide $\langle 0, -3 \rangle$, reflection line $x = 2$

56. glide $\langle -3, -3 \rangle$, reflection line $y = x$

57. glide $\langle 4, -4 \rangle$, reflection line $y = -x$

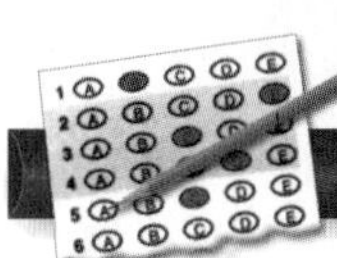

Standardized Test Prep

Multiple Choice

58. Find the image of $P(11, -5)$ for the translation $\langle -12, -6 \rangle$ followed by a reflection in $x = 0$.

A. (1, −11) **B.** (−1, 11) **C.** (1, 11) **D.** (−1, −11)

59. A reflection in the y-axis followed by a reflection in the x-axis does NOT give the same result as which of the following transformations?

F. a reflection in the x-axis followed by a reflection in the y-axis
G. a rotation of 180°
H. a rotation of 90° followed by a reflection in the x-axis
I. a reflection in the line $y = x$ followed by a reflection in the line $y = -x$

Short Response

60. Find the image of $\triangle VTY$ for the given glide reflection. Show all your steps.
glide vector: $\langle 3, -3 \rangle$
reflection line: $y = -x$

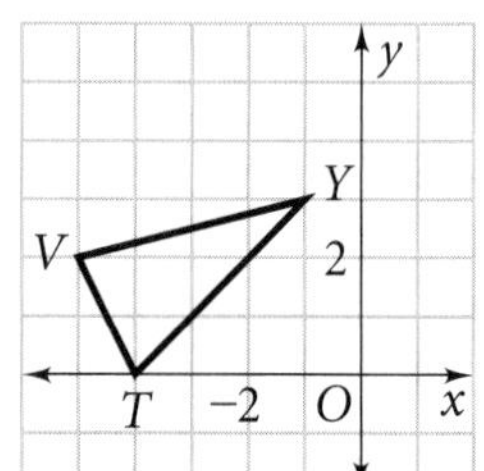

Extended Response

Take It to the NET
Online lesson quiz at
www.PHSchool.com
Web Code: afa-1204

61. Copy the diagram with $s \parallel t$.

a. Draw the image of F for a composition of two reflections. Reflect first in line s and then in line t.

b. Explain why the resulting image is the same image as found by translating F in a direction parallel to $\overline{PQ}$ through a distance $2 \cdot PQ$.

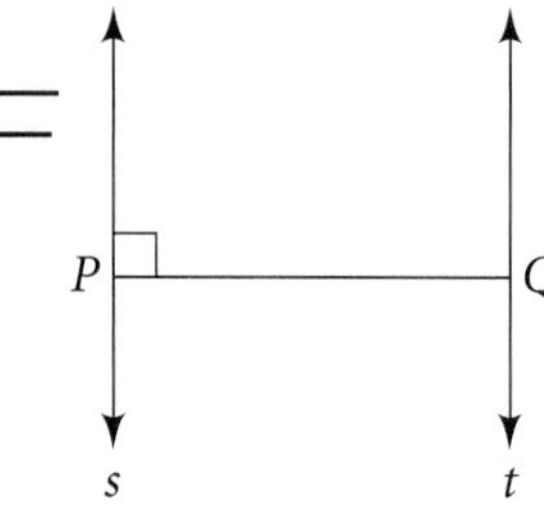

Mixed Review

Lesson 12-3

62. Which capital letters of the alphabet are rotation images of themselves? Draw each letter and give an angle of rotation (< 360°).

Lesson 11-3

Find the value of *a*.

63.

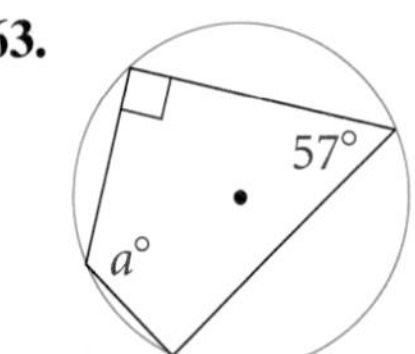

64.

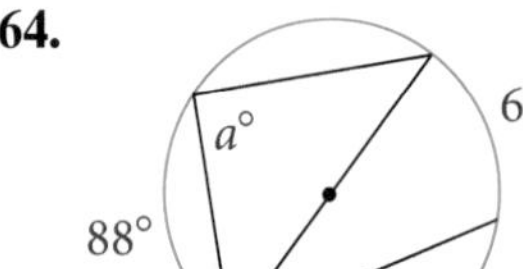

65.

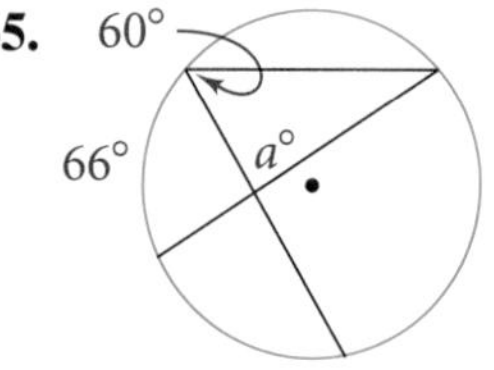

66. Diameter $\overline{AB}$ and chord $\overline{AC}$ of $\odot O$ form an inscribed angle with measure 48.

a. How many arcs do A, B, and C determine on the circle?

b. What is the measure of each arc?

Lesson 10-4

Find the slant height of each cone.

67.

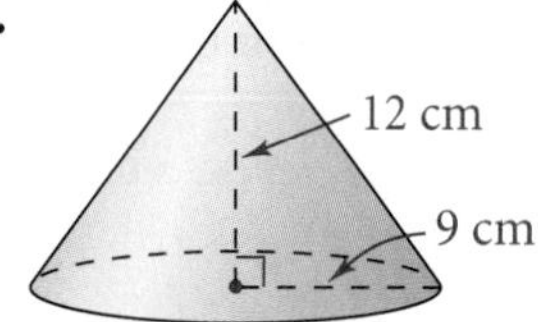

68.

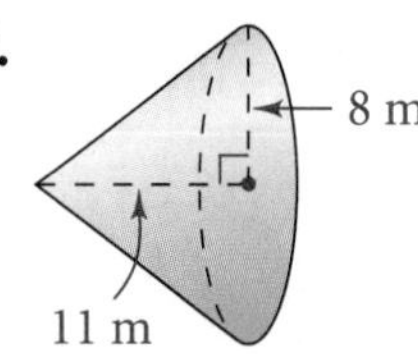

69. cone with a base radius of 4 m and a lateral area of 22π m^2

Kaleidoscopes

For Use With Lesson 12-4

The mirrors in a kaleidoscope provide compositions of reflections to create a *symmetrical* design. You can create your own kaleidoscope.

Construct

- Use geometry software. Draw a line and construct a point on the line. Rotate the line 60° about the point and repeat to get a third line.
- Construct a polygon in the interior of an angle, as shown. Reflect the polygon in the closest line, then in the next line, and so on until the kaleidoscope is filled and you have a symmetrical design. Then hide the lines of reflection.

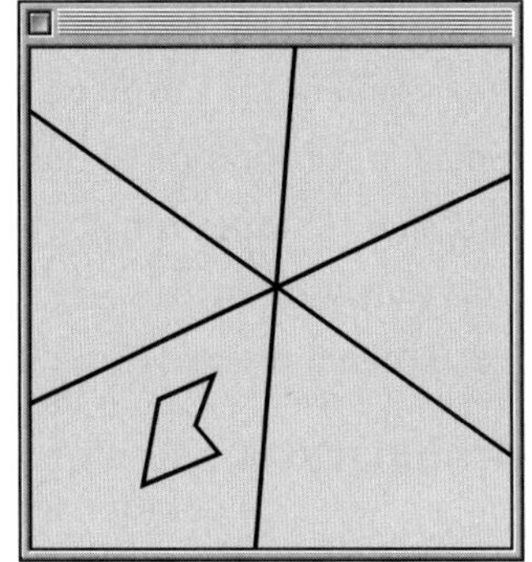

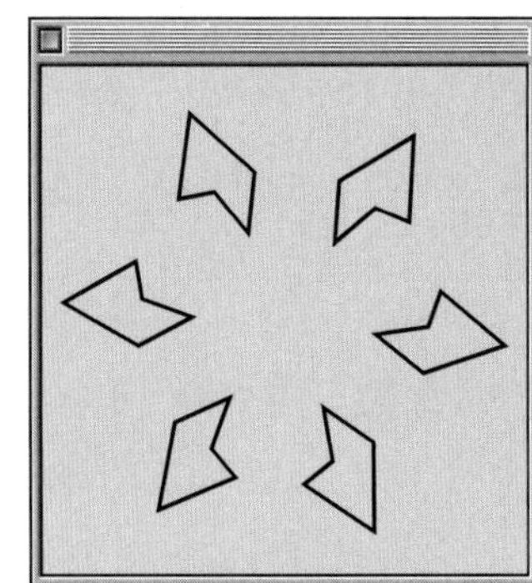

Investigate

- Manipulate the original figure by dragging any of its vertices or selecting and moving it. As you manipulate the figure, what happens to the images? Does the design remain symmetrical? Continue manipulating the original figure until you are satisfied with your design. Print the design and color it.
- Now add other figures beside the original polygon. Reflect these figures to create a more interesting design, as shown at the right. (You may need to temporarily show the lines of reflection.) Print your design and color it.

EXERCISES

1. Create a kaleidoscope with four lines of reflection. Draw a line and construct a point on the line. Rotate the line 45° about the point and repeat two more times to get four lines. Add a figure to the interior of an angle and reflect it as described above.

A *tessellation* is another type of interesting design that can be constructed using geometry software. An example is shown in Exercise 2 and tessellations are explained more fully in Lesson 12-6.

2. Construct a regular hexagon. Translate the hexagon several times to create the tessellation shown. Can you make a similar tessellation with other regular polygons? Can you find two or more polygons that, when placed together repeatedly, form a tessellation?

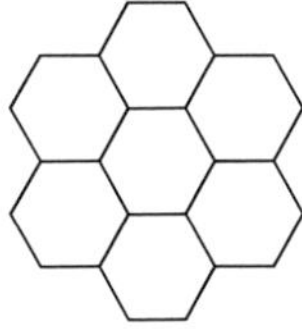

Symmetry

Lesson Preview

What You'll Learn

To identify the type of symmetry in a figure

. . . And Why

To identify types of symmetry in real-life objects, as in Example 3

Check Skills You'll Need

(For help, go to Lessons 12-1 and 12-3.)

The regular octagon at the right is divided into eight congruent triangles. Find the image of the given point or segment for the given rotation or reflection.

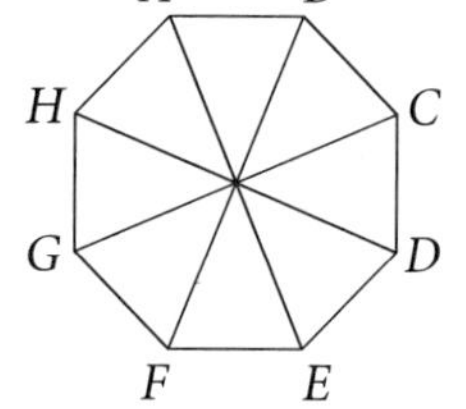

1. point A; a 90° rotation about the center
2. point H; a 180° rotation about the center
3. $\overline{AB}$; a reflection in $\overleftrightarrow{AE}$
4. $\overline{GH}$; a reflection in $\overleftrightarrow{AE}$

New Vocabulary
- symmetry
- reflectional symmetry
- line symmetry
- rotational symmetry
- point symmetry

Interactive lesson includes instant self-check, tutorials, and activities.

OBJECTIVE

1 Identifying Types of Symmetry in Figures

Reading Math

If a figure maps onto itself by some type of isometry, the figure has that type of symmetry.

A figure has **symmetry** if there is an isometry that maps the figure onto itself. If the isometry is the reflection of a plane figure, the figure has **reflectional symmetry** or **line symmetry.** One half of the figure is a mirror image of its other half. Fold the figure along the line of symmetry and the halves match exactly.

The image of the Inuit sculpture at the right has reflectional symmetry about a vertical line down the middle of the face.

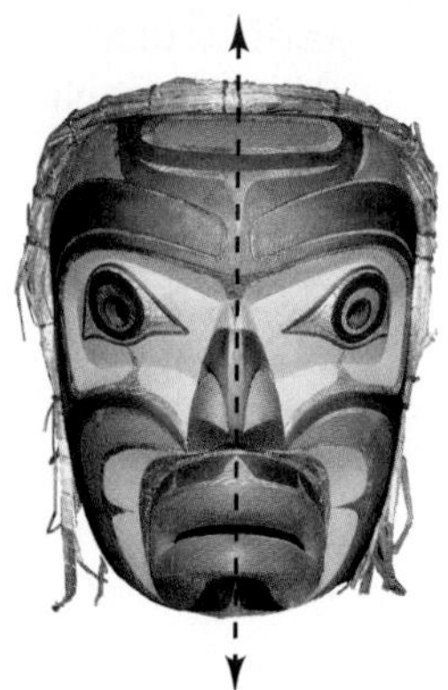

It is possible for a figure to have more than one line of symmetry.

1 EXAMPLE Identifying Lines of Symmetry

Draw all lines of symmetry for a regular hexagon.

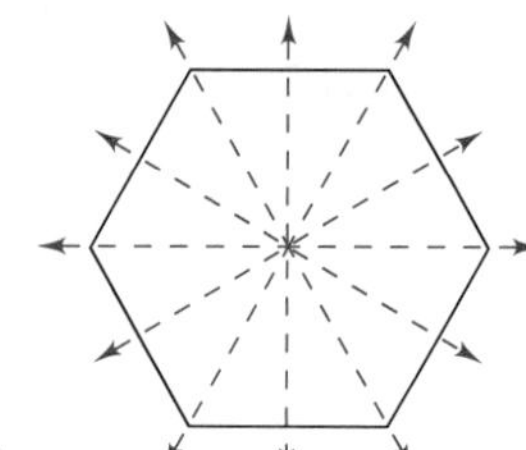

Draw a regular hexagon.

Then draw lines on the hexagon that make mirror-image congruent halves.

There are 6 lines of symmetry.

Check Understanding 1 Draw a rectangle and all of its lines of symmetry.

A figure that has **rotational symmetry** is its own image for some rotation of 180° or less. A figure that has **point symmetry** has 180° rotational symmetry. A square has 90° and 180° rotational symmetry with the center of rotation at the center of the square. Thus, a square also has point symmetry.

2 EXAMPLE Identifying Rotational Symmetry

Reading Math

The angle of rotation for rotational symmetry is the smallest angle needed for the figure to rotate onto itself.

Judging from appearance, tell whether each triangle has rotational symmetry. If so, give the angle of rotation.

a.

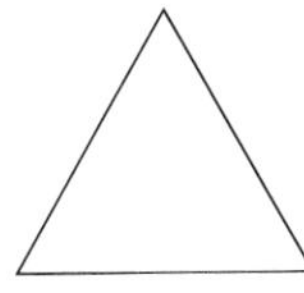

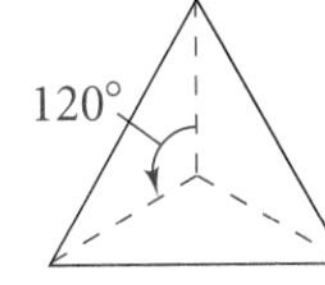

The equilateral triangle has rotational symmetry. The angle of rotation is 120°.

b.

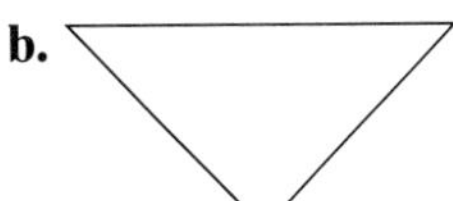

This isosceles triangle does not have rotational symmetry.

Check Understanding 2 **a.** Judging from appearance, tell whether the figure at the right has rotational symmetry. If so, give the angle of rotation.
b. Does the figure have point symmetry?

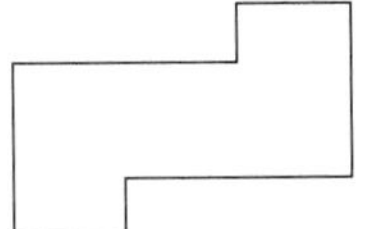

Three-dimensional objects can have various types of symmetry, including rotational symmetry about a line and reflectional symmetry in a plane.

3 EXAMPLE Real-World Connection

Symmetric Design Tell whether each object has rotational symmetry about a line and/or reflectional symmetry in a plane.

a.

The paddle has both rotational and reflectional symmetry.

b.

The cup has reflectional symmetry.

Check Understanding 3 Tell whether the umbrella has rotational symmetry about a line and/or reflectional symmetry in a plane.

EXERCISES

For more practice, see *Extra Practice.*

Practice and Problem Solving

Practice by Example

Examples 1, 2 (pages 662, 663)

Tell what type(s) of symmetry each figure has. If it has line symmetry, sketch the figure and the line(s) of symmetry. If it has rotational symmetry, state the angle of rotation.

1. 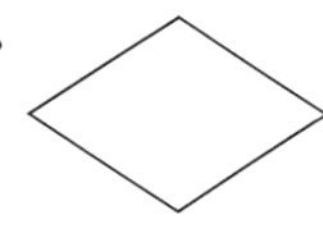

2. 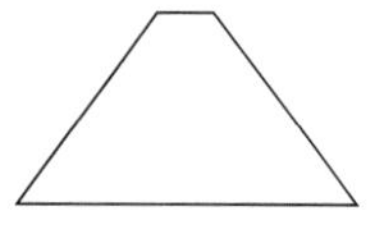

3. 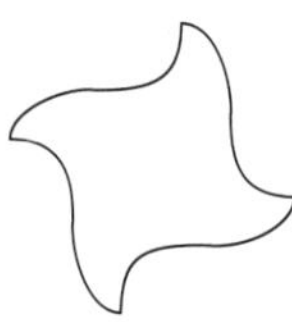

4. 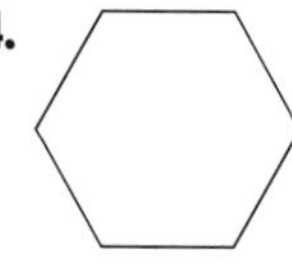

5. 

6. 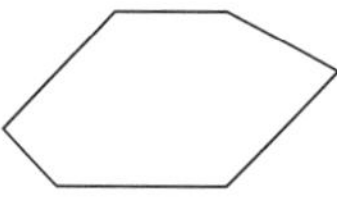

7. 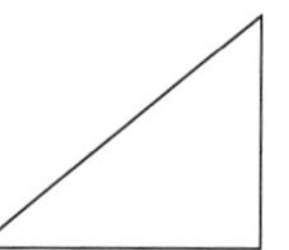

8. 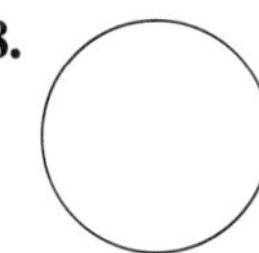

9. 

10. 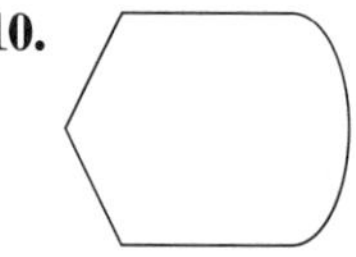

11. 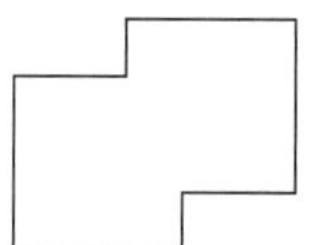

12. 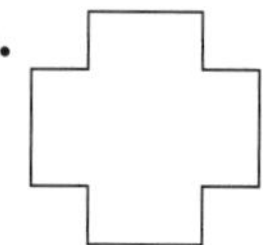

Draw each quadrilateral. Then draw all of its lines of symmetry.

13. rhombus **14.** kite **15.** square **16.** parallelogram

Example 3 (page 663)

Tell whether each three-dimensional object has rotational symmetry about a line and/or reflectional symmetry in a plane.

17. 

18. 

B Apply Your Skills

19. Open-Ended The word CHECKBOOK has a horizontal line of symmetry. Find two other words for which this is true.

20. Open-Ended Stack the letters of MATH vertically and upright, and you can find a vertical line of symmetry. Find two other words for which this is true.

21. a. Alphabets Copy the chart. Use it to classify the letters of the English and Greek alphabets below. You will list some letters in more than one category.

b. Which alphabet can you say is more symmetrical? Explain.

Type of Symmetry

Language	Horizontal Line	Vertical Line	Point
English			
Greek			

English: ABCDEFGHIJKLMNOPQRSTUVWXYZ

Greek: ΑΒΓΔΕΖΗΘΙΚΛΜΝΞΟΠΡΣΤΥΦΧΨΩ

Tell what type(s) of symmetry each image has. For line symmetry, sketch the image and the line(s) of symmetry. For rotational symmetry, state the angle of rotation.

22. 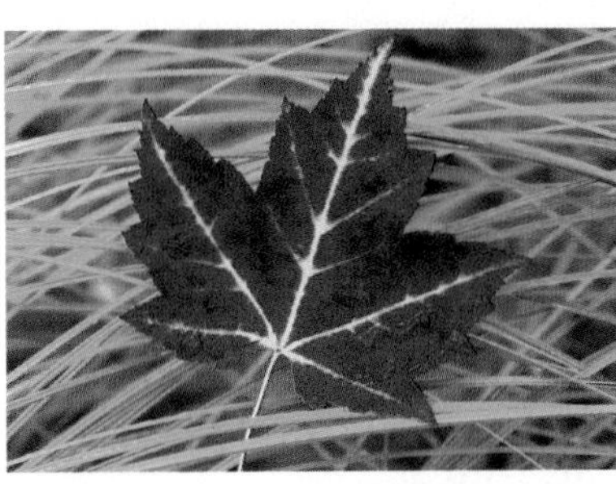

23. 

24. **Open-Ended** The equation $\frac{10}{10} - 1 = 0 \div \frac{83}{83}$ is not only true, but also symmetrical (horizontally). Write four other equations or inequalities that are both true and symmetrical.

Logos **Describe the types of symmetry, if any, of each automobile logo.**

25. 

26. 

27. 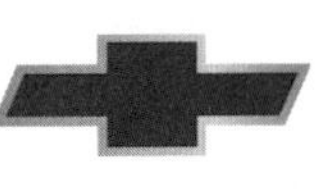

28. 

29. 

30. 

31. 

32. 

Need Help?

In Exercises 33–35, you can conclude a statement is false by finding a counterexample.

33. Is the line that contains the bisector of an angle a line of symmetry of the angle? Explain.

34. Is the line that contains the bisector of an angle of a triangle a line of symmetry of the triangle? Explain.

35. Is a bisector of a segment a line of symmetry of the segment? Explain.

36. **Writing** Use what you learned in Lesson 12-4 to explain why a figure with two or more lines of symmetry also has rotational symmetry.

Coordinate Geometry **A figure has a vertex at (3, 4). If the figure has the given type of symmetry, state the coordinates of another vertex of the figure.**

37. line symmetry about the y-axis

38. line symmetry about the x-axis

39. point symmetry about the origin

40. line symmetry about the line $y = x$

Coordinate Geometry **Graph each equation. Describe the symmetry of each graph.**

41. $y = x$

42. $y = x^2$

43. $x = y^2$

44. $x^2 + y^2 = 9$

C Challenge

45. $y = (x + 2)^2$

46. $y = x^3$

47. $y = |x|$

48. $x = |y|$

For each three-dimensional figure, draw a net that has rotational symmetry and a net that has 1, 2, or 4 lines of symmetry.

49. 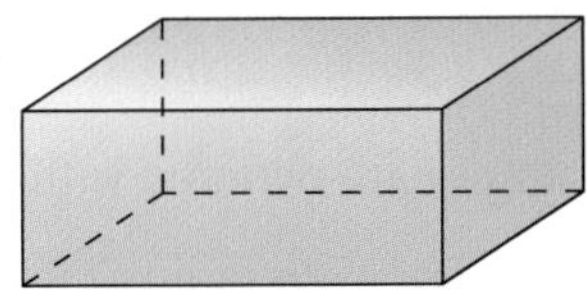

50. 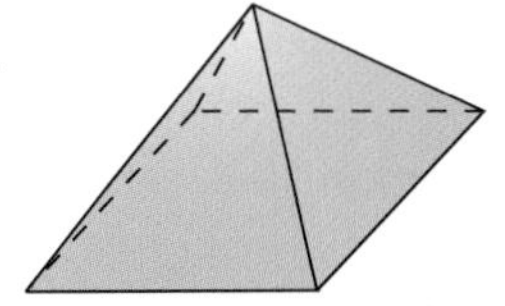

Square pyramid

Standardized Test Prep

Multiple Choice

51. Which figure does NOT have rotational symmetry?

A. 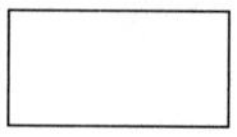
B. 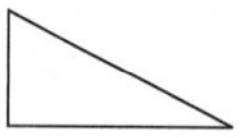
C. 

D. 

52. Which figure, in general, has exactly two lines of symmetry?
F. pentagon **G.** circle **H.** square **I.** rectangle

Quantitative Comparison

Compare the boxed quantity in Column A with the boxed quantity in Column B. Choose the best answer.
A. The quantity in Column A is greater.
B. The quantity in Column B is greater.
C. The two quantities are equal.
D. The relationship cannot be determined from the information given.

	Column A	Column B
53.	the smallest angle of rotational symmetry for an equilateral triangle	the smallest angle of rotational symmetry for a regular hexagon
54.	the number of lines of symmetry for a nonrectangular parallelogram	the number of lines of symmetry for a nonrectangular quadrilateral
55.	the number of lines of symmetry for a regular pentagon	the number of lines of symmetry for a regular octagon

Take It to the NET
Online lesson quiz at **www.PHSchool.com**
Web Code: afa-1205

Short Response

56. Use the figure at the right to answer the questions below.
a. Does the figure have rotational symmetry? If so, identify the angle of rotation.
b. Does the figure have reflectional symmetry? If so, how many lines of symmetry does it have?

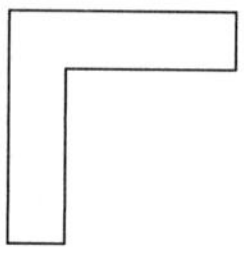

Mixed Review

Lesson 12-4

57. A triangle has vertices $A(3, 2)$, $B(4, 1)$, and $C(4, 3)$. Find the coordinates of the images of A, B, and C for a glide reflection with glide vector $\langle 0, 1 \rangle$ and reflection line $x = 0$.

Lesson 11-4

Find the value of each variable using the given chords, secants, and tangents. If your answer is not an integer, round it to the nearest tenth.

58. 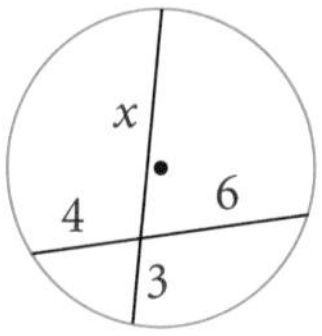

59. 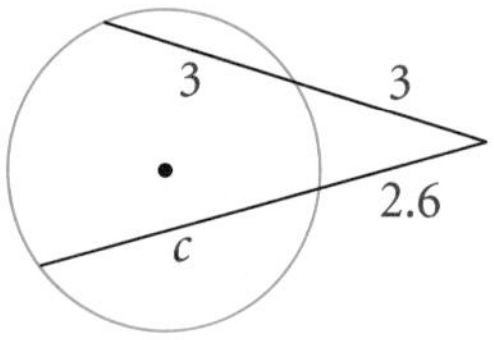

60. 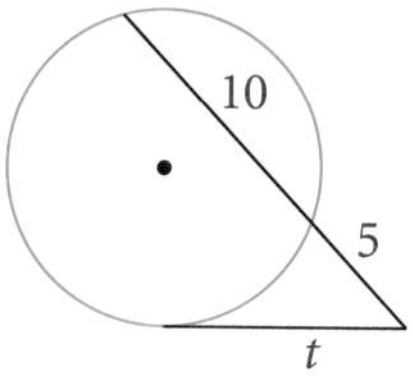

Lesson 10-6

61. Find the volume of a square pyramid with height 8 cm and base edges 5 cm.

62. Find the volume of a cone with radius 7 in. and height 10 in.

12-6 Tessellations

Lesson Preview

What You'll Learn

To identify transformations in tessellations, and figures that will tessellate

To identify symmetries in tessellations

. . . And Why

To identify a tessellation in art, as in Example 1

✔ Check Skills You'll Need

(For help, go to Lesson 3-4.)

Classify the polygon with the given number of sides.

1. five **2.** eight **3.** twelve

Find the measure of an angle of each regular polygon.

4. triangle **5.** quadrilateral **6.** hexagon

7. octagon **8.** decagon **9.** 14-gon

New Vocabulary • tessellation • tiling • translational symmetry • glide reflectional symmetry

Interactive lesson includes instant self-check, tutorials, and activities.

OBJECTIVE 1 Identifying Transformations in Tessellations

Reading Math

A figure that creates a tessellation is said *to tessellate*.

A **tessellation,** or **tiling,** is a repeating pattern of figures that completely covers a plane, without gaps or overlaps. You can create tessellations with translations, rotations, and reflections. You can find tessellations in art (see below), nature (cells in a honeycomb), and everyday life (tiled floors).

1 EXAMPLE Identifying the Transformation in a Tessellation

Art Identify a transformation and the repeating figures in this tessellation.

Repeating figures

The arrow shows a translation.

✔ Check Understanding

1 Identify a transformation and the repeating figures in each tessellation below.

a.

b.

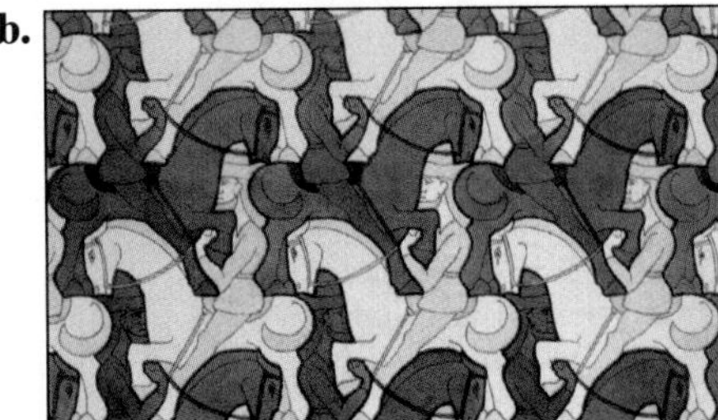

Because the figures in a tessellation do not overlap or leave gaps, the sum of the measures of the angles around any vertex must be 360°. If the angles around a vertex are all congruent, then the measure of each angle must be a factor of 360.

2 EXAMPLE Determining Figures That Will Tessellate

Determine whether a regular 18-gon tessellates a plane.

$a = \frac{180(n - 2)}{n}$ **Use the formula for the measure of an angle of a regular polygon.**

$a = \frac{180(18 - 2)}{18}$ **Substitute 18 for *n*.**

$a = 160$ **Simplify.**

Since 160 is not a factor of 360, the 18-gon will not tessellate.

Check Understanding 2 Explain why you can tessellate a plane with an equilateral triangle.

A figure does not have to be a regular polygon to tessellate.

Key Concepts

Theorem 12-6

Every triangle tessellates.

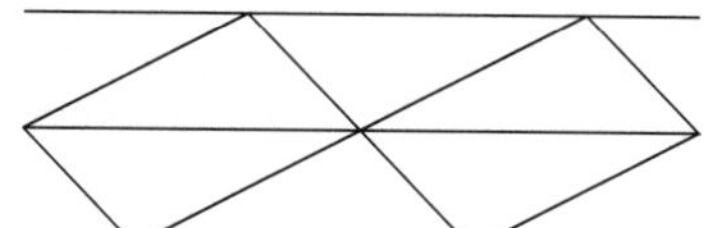

Theorem 12-7

Every quadrilateral tessellates.

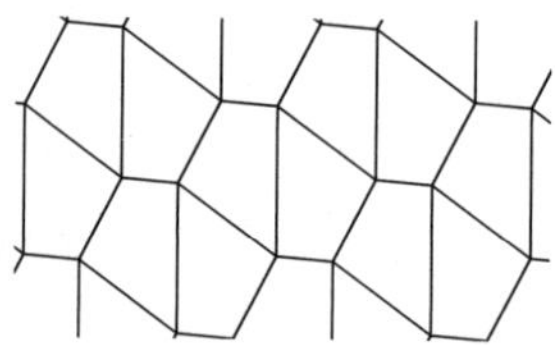

OBJECTIVE

2 Identifying Symmetries in Tessellations

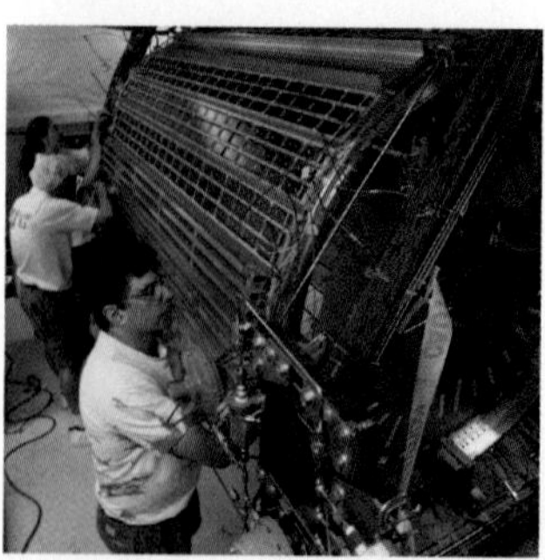

Real-World Connection

Careers Physicists apply the symmetries of tessellations to study subatomic particles. Here they use a particle detector to study quarks.

The tessellation with regular hexagons at the right has reflectional symmetry in each of the blue lines. It has rotational symmetry centered at each of the red points. The tessellation also has translational symmetry and glide reflectional symmetry, as shown below.

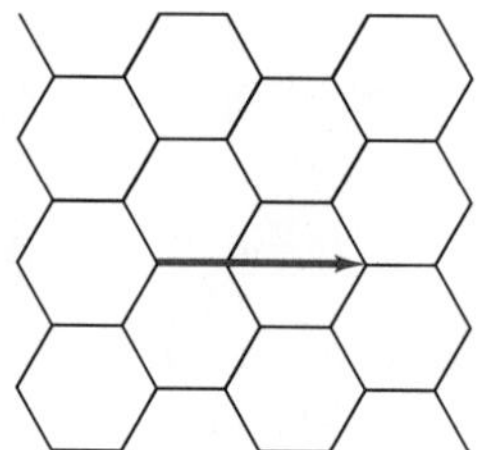

Translational Symmetry

A translation maps the tessellation onto itself.

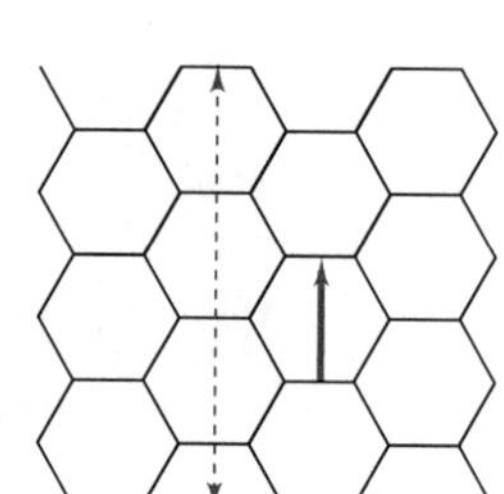

Glide Reflectional Symmetry

A glide reflection maps the tessellation onto itself.

3 EXAMPLE Identifying Symmetries in Tessellations

List the symmetries in the tessellation.

Rotational symmetry centered at each red point
Translational symmetry (blue arrow)

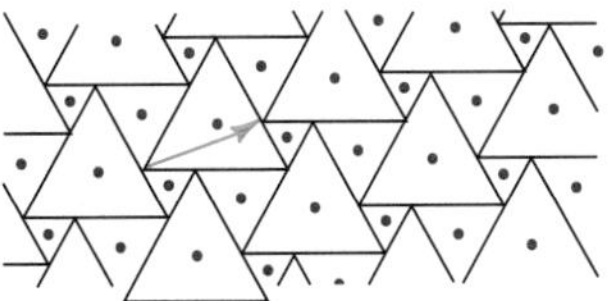

✓ Check Understanding 3 List the symmetries in the tessellation at the right.

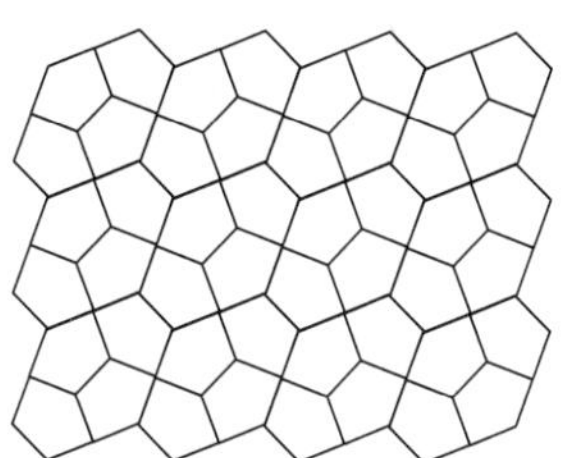

The following Investigation shows the steps for making creative tessellations.

Investigation: Creating Tessellations

- Draw a 1.5-inch square on a blank piece of paper and cut it out.
- Draw a curve joining two consecutive vertices.

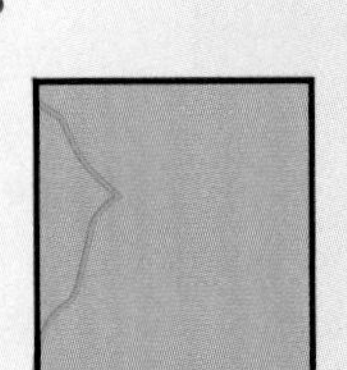

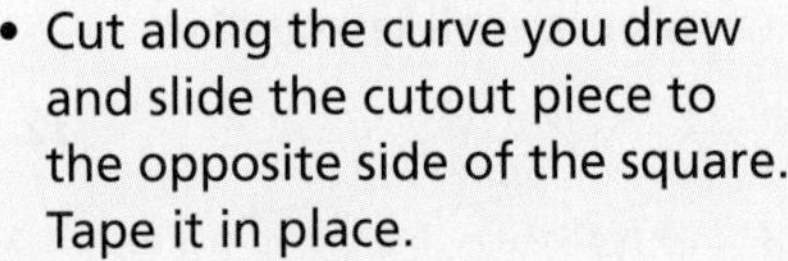

- Cut along the curve you drew and slide the cutout piece to the opposite side of the square. Tape it in place.

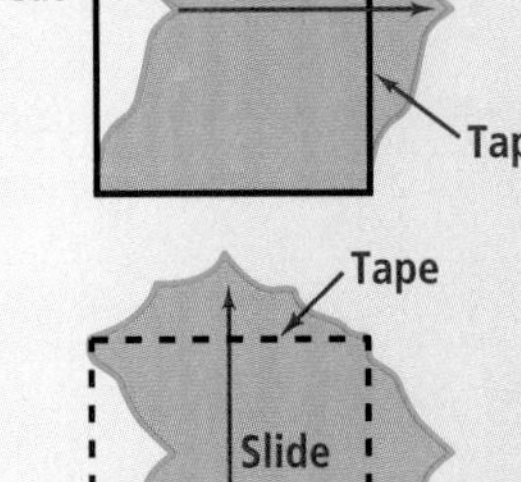

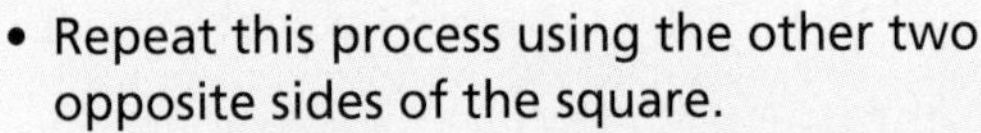

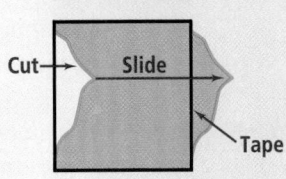

- Repeat this process using the other two opposite sides of the square.
- Rotate the resulting figure. What does your imagination suggest it looks like? Is it a penguin wearing a hat or a knight on horseback? Could it be a dog with floppy ears? Draw the image on your figure.
- Create a tessellation using your figure.

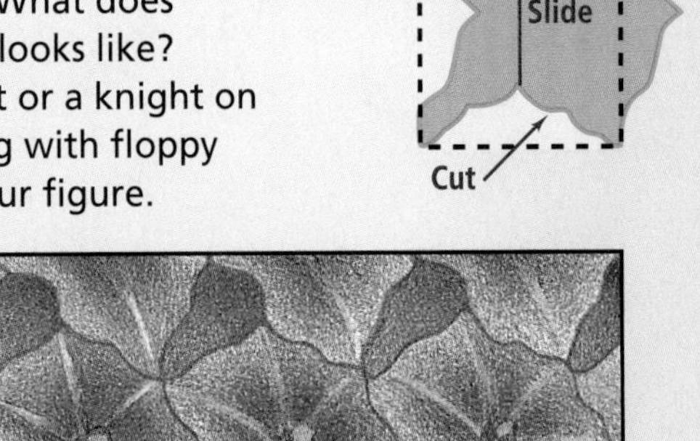

EXERCISES

For more practice, see *Extra Practice.*

Practice and Problem Solving

Practice by Example

Example 1 (page 667)

Does the picture show a tessellation of repeating figures? If so, identify a transformation and the repeating figure.

1. 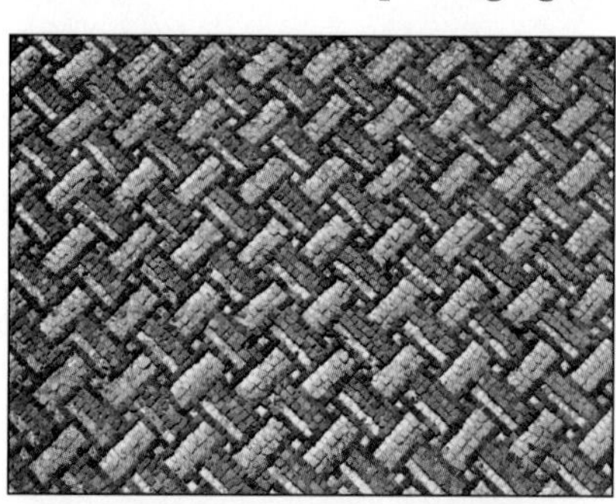

2. 

3. 

4. 

Example 2 (page 668)

Determine whether each figure will tessellate a plane.

5. equilateral triangle **6.** square **7.** regular pentagon

8. regular heptagon **9.** regular octagon **10.** regular nonagon

Example 3 (page 669)

List the symmetries in each tessellation.

11. 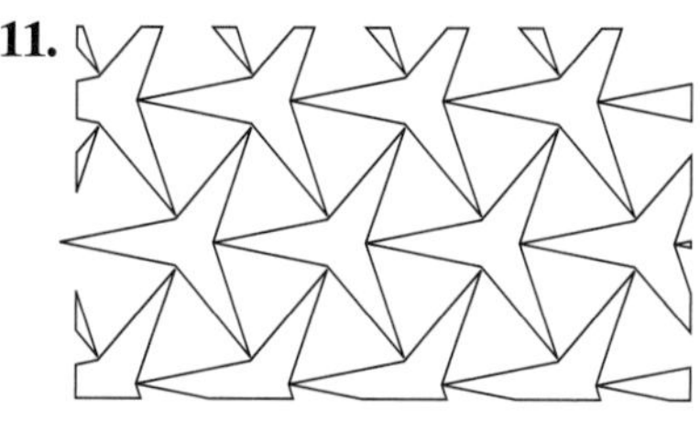

12. 

13. 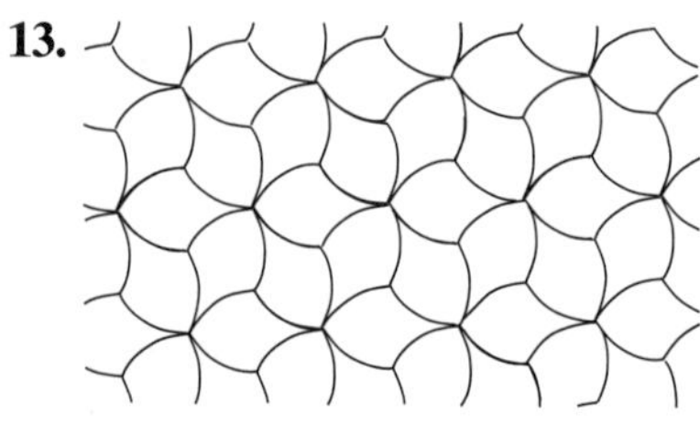

14. 

15. 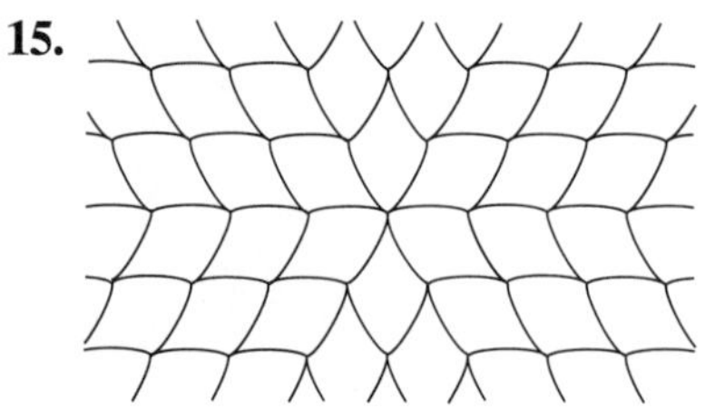

16. 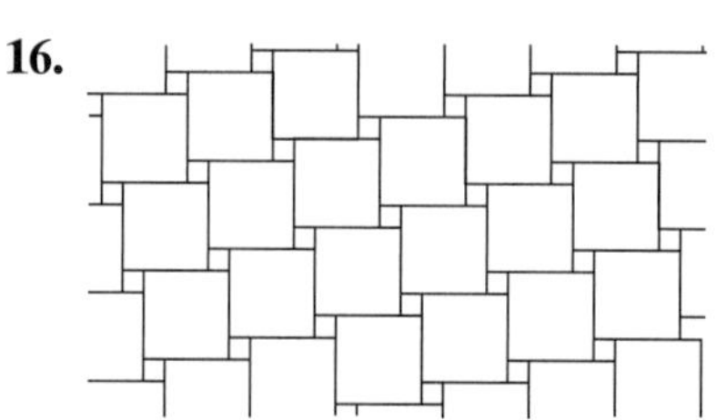

B Apply Your Skills

Use each figure to create a tessellation on dot paper.

17.

18. 

19. 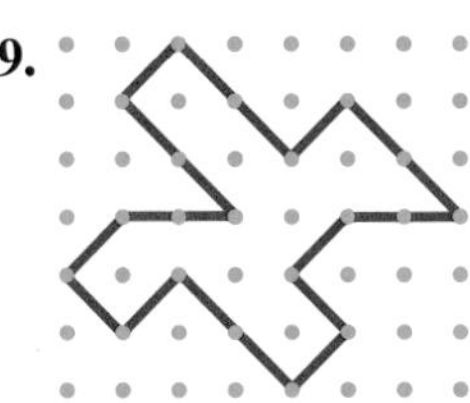

Show how to tessellate with each figure described below. Try to draw two different tessellations. If you think that two are not possible, explain.

20. a scalene triangle

21. the pentagon at the right

22. a quadrilateral with no sides parallel or congruent

23. Writing A *pure tessellation* is a tessellation made up of congruent copies of one figure. Explain why there are three, and only three, pure tessellations that use regular polygons. (*Hint:* See Exercises 5–10.)

A *semiregular tessellation* is made from two or more regular polygons.

Decide whether a semiregular tessellation (see photo) is possible using the given pair of regular polygons. If so, draw a sketch.

24.

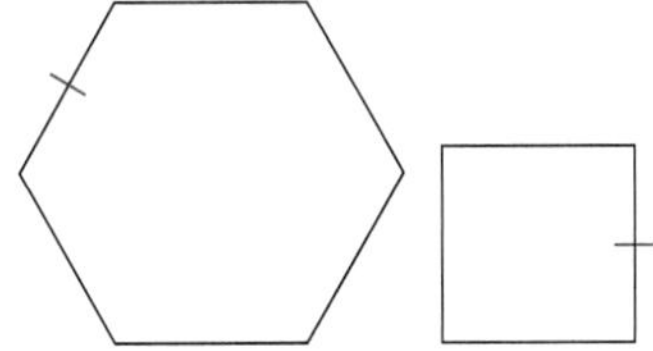

25.

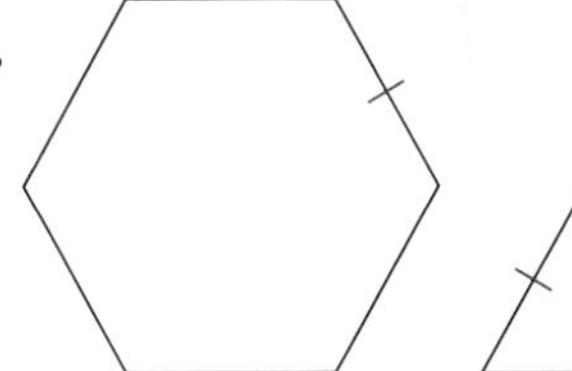

Can each set of polygons be used to create a tessellation? If so, draw a sketch.

26.

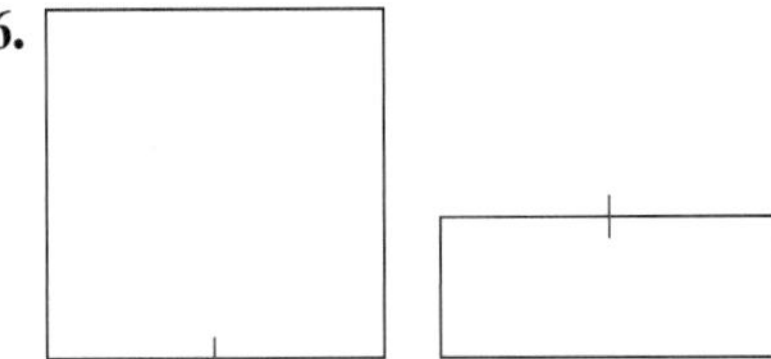

27.

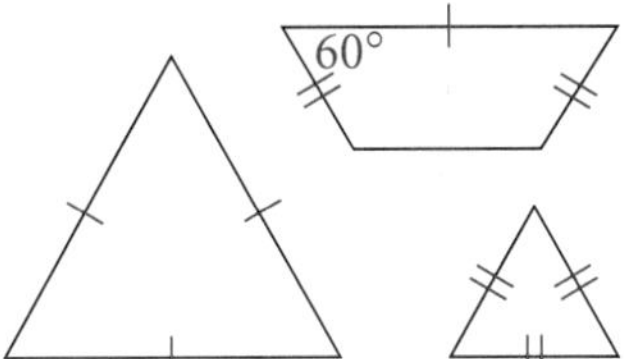

Challenge

Copy the Venn diagram. Write each exercise number in the correct region of the diagram.

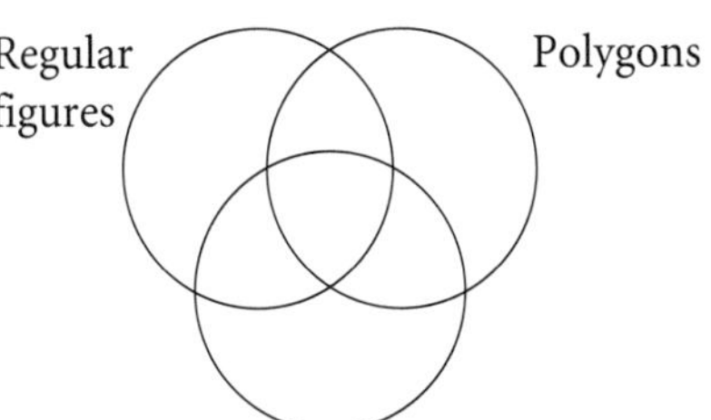

28. scalene triangle

29. obtuse triangle

30. equilateral △

31. isosceles △

32. kite

33. rhombus

34. square

35. regular pentagon

36. regular hexagon

37. regular octagon

38. On graph paper, draw quadrilateral $ABCD$ with no two sides congruent. Locate M, the midpoint of $\overline{AB}$, and N, the midpoint of $\overline{BC}$.

a. Draw the image of $ABCD$ under a 180° rotation about M.

b. Draw the image of $ABCD$ under a 180° rotation about N.

c. Draw the image of $ABCD$ under the translation that maps D to B.

d. Make a conjecture about whether your quadrilateral tessellates, using the pattern in parts (a)–(c). Justify your answer.

39. List steps (like those in Exercise 38) that suggest a way to tessellate with any scalene triangle. Then list a second set of steps that suggest another way.

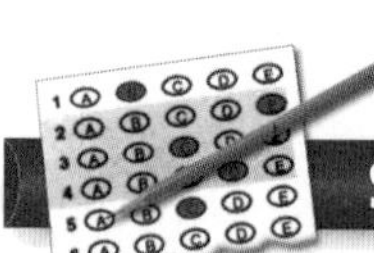

Standardized Test Prep

Multiple Choice

40. Which figure will NOT tessellate a plane?

A.  B. 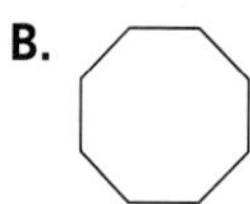 C.  D. 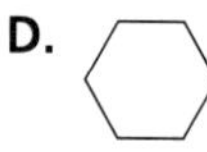

41. You can tessellate a plane using a regular octagon together with which other type of regular polygon?

F. triangle G. square H. pentagon I. hexagon

Take It to the NET
Online lesson quiz at
www.PHSchool.com
Web Code: afa-1206

42. Which is NOT a symmetry for the tessellation?

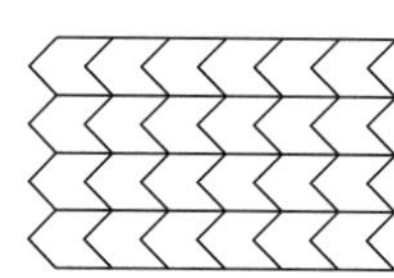

A. line symmetry
B. translational symmetry
C. rotational symmetry
D. glide reflectional symmetry

Short Response

43. Is it possible to tile a plane with regular pentagons? Justify your answer.

Extended Response

44. Unit squares form this tessellation. Tell whether this tessellation has each type of symmetry (line, point, rotational, translational, or glide reflectional). Explain.

Mixed Review

Lesson 12-5

Coordinate Geometry **A figure has a vertex at $(-2, 7)$. If the figure has the given type of symmetry, state the coordinates of another vertex of the figure.**

45. line symmetry about the x-axis

46. line symmetry about the y-axis

47. point symmetry about the origin

48. line symmetry about the line $y = x$

Lesson 11-5

Write the standard equation of each circle.

49. 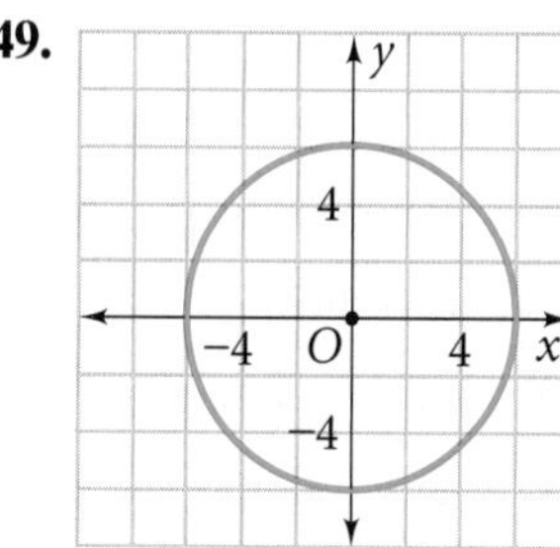

50. 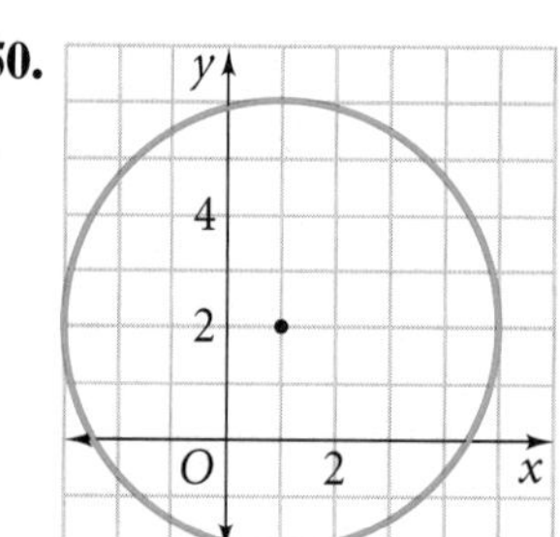

51. the circle with center $(-1, 0)$ and radius 3

Lesson 10-1

Use Euler's Formula, $F + V = E + 2$, to find the missing number.

52. Faces: ■
Edges: 16
Vertices: 9

53. Faces: 12
Edges: ■
Vertices: 20

54. Faces: 7
Edges: 12
Vertices: ■

Checkpoint Quiz 2 — Lessons 12-4 through 12-6

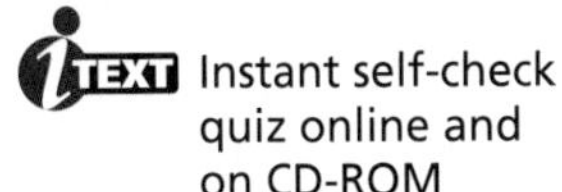

Instant self-check quiz online and on CD-ROM

The two figures in each pair are congruent. Is one figure a translation image, a rotation image, or a reflection image of the other? Explain.

1. 

2. oS So

Tell what type(s) of symmetry (line, rotational, or point) each figure has. For line symmetry, sketch the figure and the line(s) of symmetry. For rotational symmetry, state the angle of rotation.

3.

4. 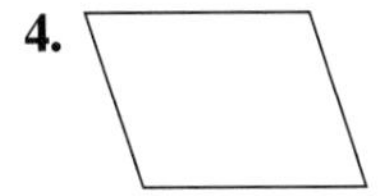

5. 

6. 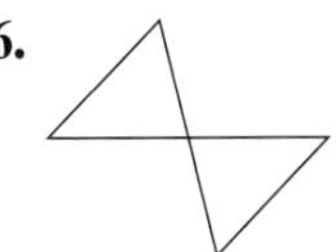

List the symmetries of each tessellation.

7. 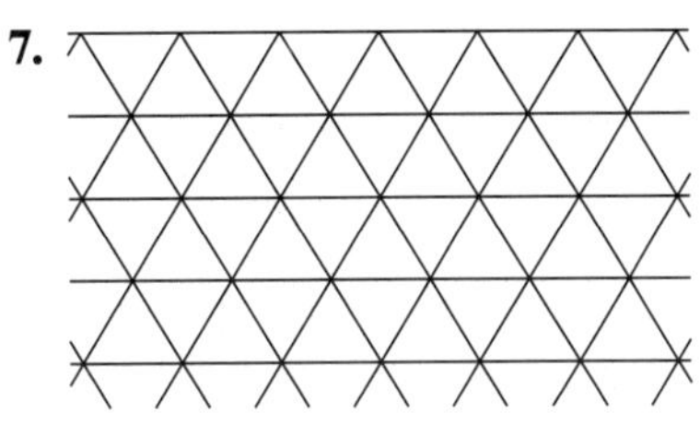

8. 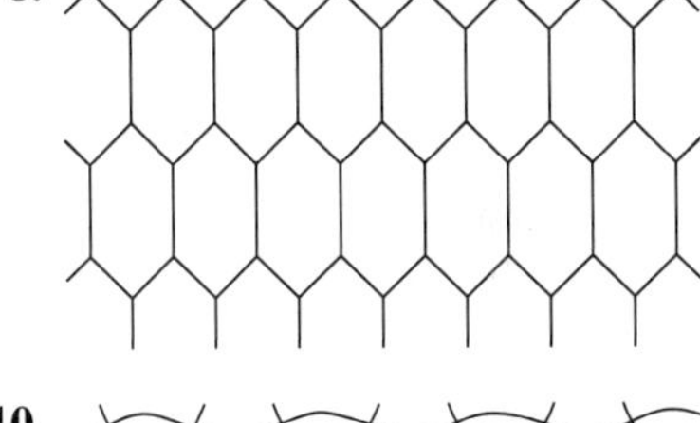

9. 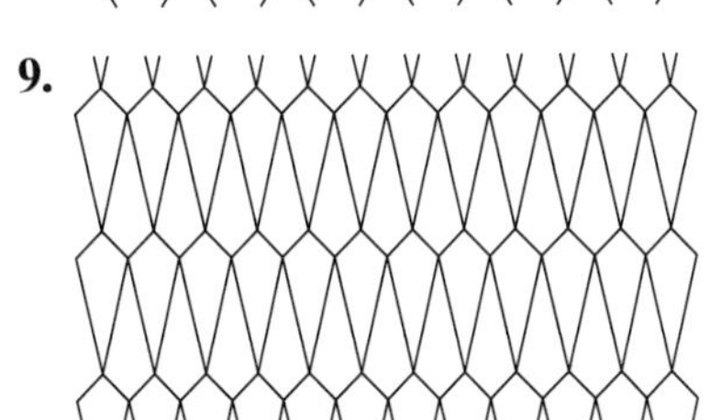

10. 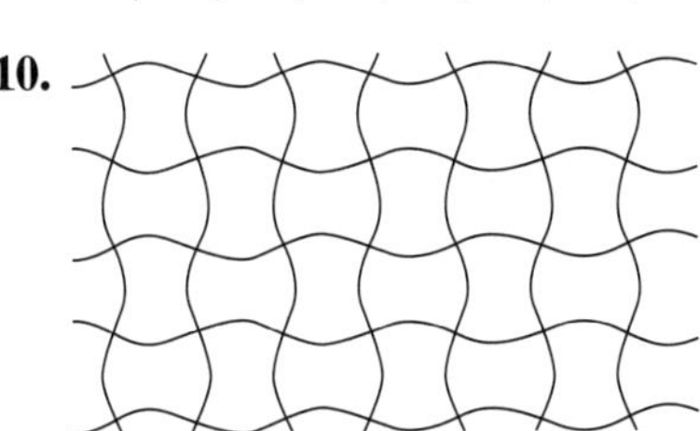

A Point in Time

1500 1600 1700 1800 1900 2000

A **mosaic** is a picture or design made by setting tiny pieces of glass, stone, or other materials in clay or plaster. A mosaic may be a tessellation. Most mosaics, however, do not have a repeating pattern of figures. Mosaics go back at least 6000 years to the Sumerians, who used tiles to both decorate and reinforce walls.

During 100 and 200 A.D., Roman architects used two million tiles to create the magnificent mosaic of Dionysus in Germany. In the years 1941–1951 Mexican artist Juan O'Gorman covered all four sides of a 10-story library in Mexico with 7.5 million stones—the largest mosaic ever. It depicts Mexico's cultural history.

Take It to the NET For more information about mosaics, go to **www.PHSchool.com**.
Web Code: afe-2032

12-7 Dilations

Lesson Preview

What You'll Learn

OBJECTIVE 1 To locate dilation images of figures

. . . And Why

To find the dimensions of a car using the dimensions of its model, as in Example 2

✓ Check Skills You'll Need

(For help, go to Lesson 8-1.)

Determine the scale drawing dimensions of a room using a scale of $\frac{1}{4}$ in. = 1 ft.

1. kitchen: 12 ft by 16 ft

2. bedroom: 8 ft by 10 ft

3. laundry room: 6 ft by 9 ft

4. bathroom: 5 ft by 7 ft

New Vocabulary
- dilation
- enlargement
- reduction
- scalar multiplication

Interactive lesson includes instant self-check, tutorials, and activities.

OBJECTIVE

1 Locating Dilation Images

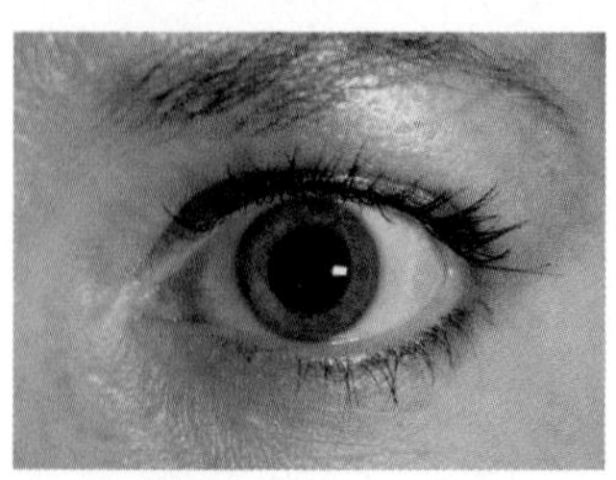

Real-World Connection

Look closely at your pupil in a mirror, and you can watch it dilate.

A dilation is a transformation whose preimage and image are similar. Thus, a dilation is a similarity transformation. It is *not*, in general, an isometry.

Every dilation has a center and a scale factor n, $n > 0$. The scale factor describes the size change from the original figure to the image.

In general, a **dilation** with center C and scale factor n is a transformation for which the following are true.

- The image of C is itself (that is, $C' = C$).
- For any point R, R' is on $\overrightarrow{CR}$ and $CR' = n \cdot CR$.

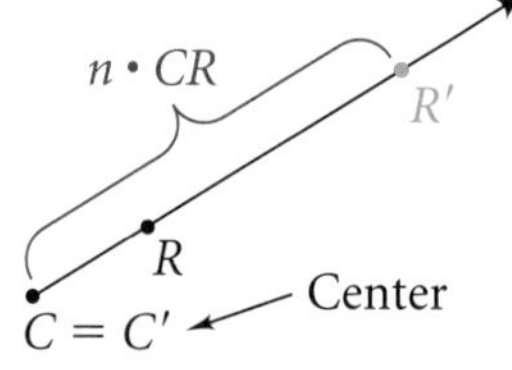

The dilation is an **enlargement** if the scale factor is greater than 1. The dilation is a **reduction** if the scale factor is between 0 and 1.

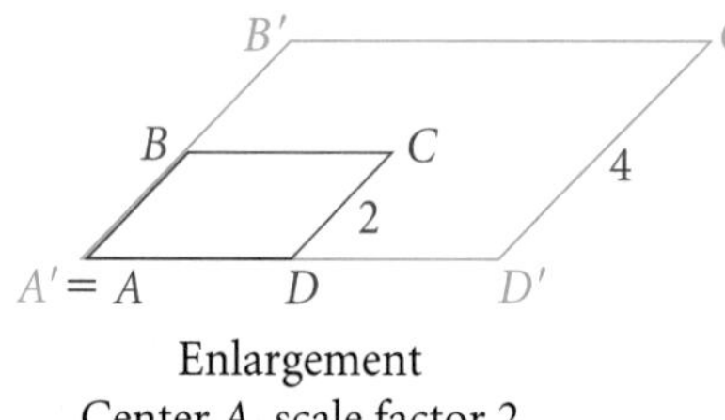

Enlargement
Center A, scale factor 2

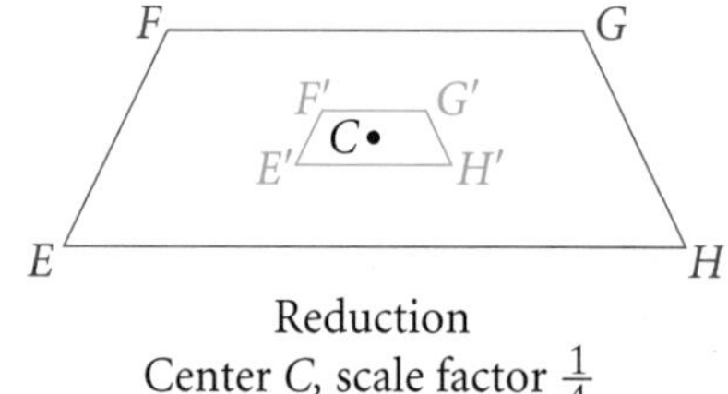

Reduction
Center C, scale factor $\frac{1}{4}$

1 EXAMPLE Finding a Scale Factor

The blue triangle is a dilation image of the red triangle. Describe the dilation.

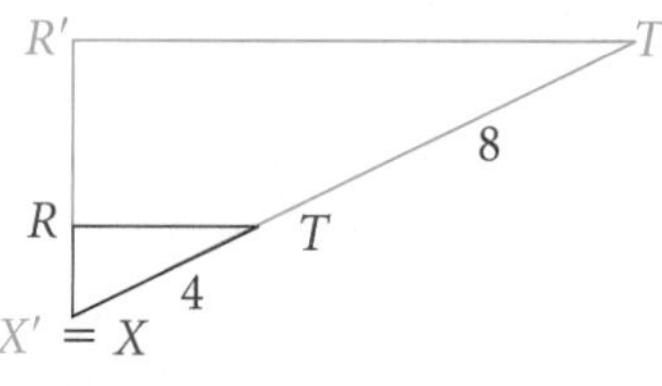

The center is X. The image is larger than the preimage, so the dilation is an enlargement.

$$\frac{X'T'}{XT} = \frac{4 + 8}{4} = 3$$

The dilation has center X and scale factor 3.

✓ Check Understanding **1** The blue quadrilateral is a dilation image of the red quadrilateral. Describe the dilation.

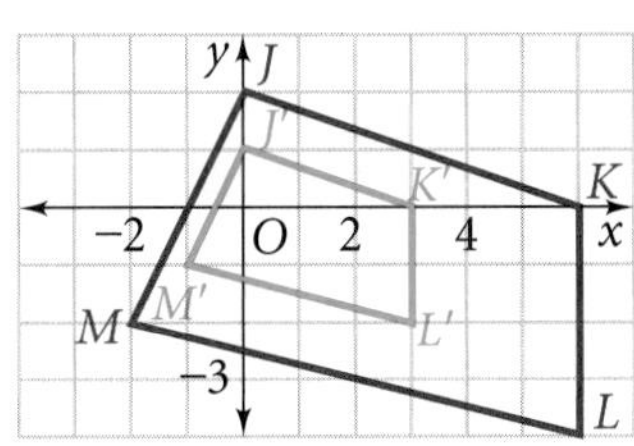

Scale factors help you understand scale models, both large and small.

2 EXAMPLE Real-World Connection

Scale Models The packaging lists a model car's length as 7.6 cm. It also gives the scale as 1 : 63. What is the length of the actual car?

To "enlarge" the model car to the actual car, use the scale factor 63. Multiply 7.6 cm by 63 to get 478.8 cm, or about 4.8 m, for the length of the actual car.

✓ Check Understanding **2** The height of a tractor-trailer truck is 4.2 m. The scale factor for a model of the truck is $\frac{1}{54}$. Find the height of the model to the nearest centimeter.

Suppose a dilation is centered at the origin. You can find the dilation image of a point by multiplying its coordinates by the scale factor.

Scale factor 4, $(x, y) \longrightarrow (4x, 4y)$

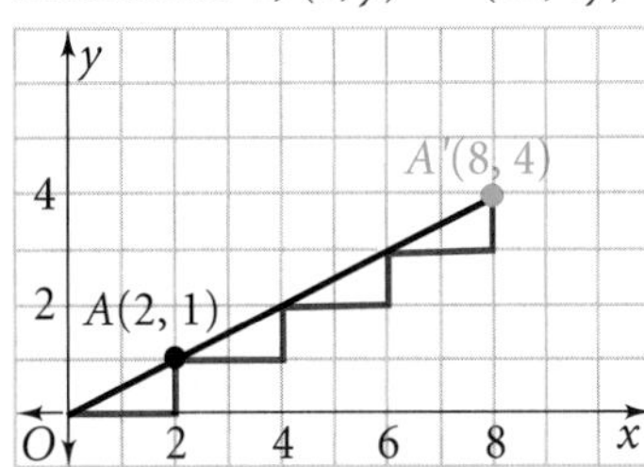

Scale factor $\frac{1}{3}$, $(x, y) \longrightarrow \left(\frac{1}{3}x, \frac{1}{3}y\right)$

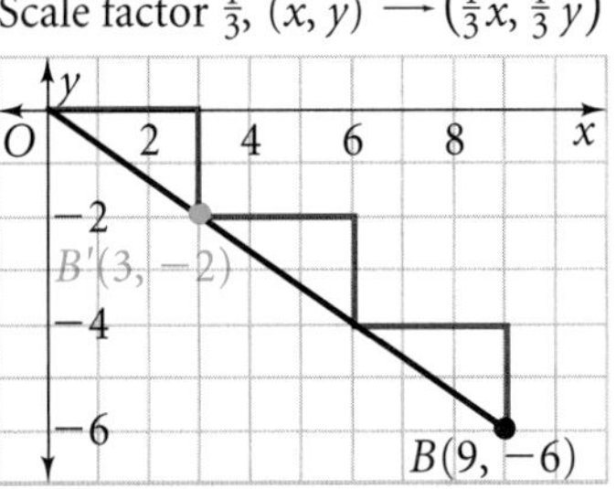

To dilate a triangle from the origin, find the dilation images of its vertices. Enter all six vertex coordinates in a matrix, and then multiply each matrix entry by the scale factor. Multiplying a matrix by a *scalar* in this way is called **scalar multiplication.**

3 EXAMPLE Using Scalar Multiplication

$\triangle PZG$ has vertices $P(2, 0)$, $Z\left(-1, \frac{1}{2}\right)$, and $G(1, -2)$. Use scalar multiplication to find the image of $\triangle PZG$ for a dilation with center (0, 0) and scale factor 3. Draw the enlargement.

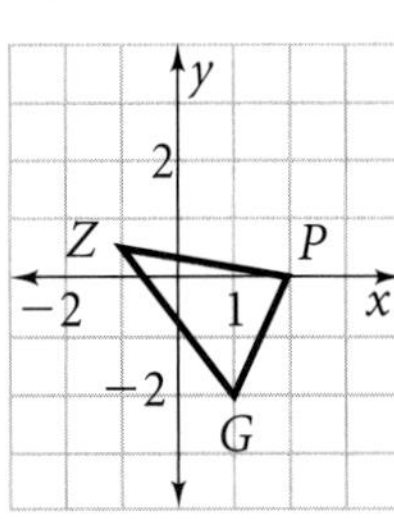

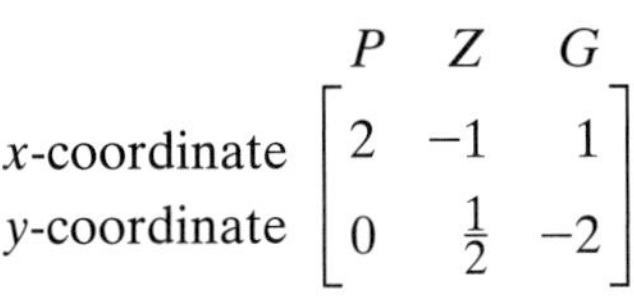

$$\begin{array}{l} \\ x\text{-coordinate} \\ y\text{-coordinate} \end{array} \begin{array}{c} \begin{array}{ccc} P & Z & G \end{array} \\ \begin{bmatrix} 2 & -1 & 1 \\ 0 & \frac{1}{2} & -2 \end{bmatrix} \end{array}$$

Write a matrix for △PZG.

$$3 \cdot \begin{bmatrix} 2 & -1 & 1 \\ 0 & \frac{1}{2} & -2 \end{bmatrix} = \begin{bmatrix} 6 & -3 & 3 \\ 0 & \frac{3}{2} & -6 \end{bmatrix}$$

Multiply entries by the scale factor 3.

The vertices of the enlargement at the left are $P'(6, 0)$, $Z'\left(-3, \frac{3}{2}\right)$, and $G'(3, -6)$.

✓ Check Understanding **3** Use scalar multiplication to find the image of $\triangle PZG$ for a dilation with center (0, 0) and scale factor $\frac{1}{2}$. Draw the reduction.

EXERCISES

For more practice, see *Extra Practice*.

Practice and Problem Solving

Practice by Example

Example 1 (page 674)

The blue figure is a dilation image of the red figure. Describe the dilation.

1. 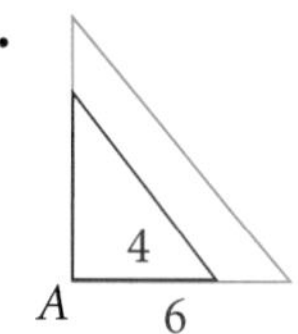

2.
C
3
9

3. 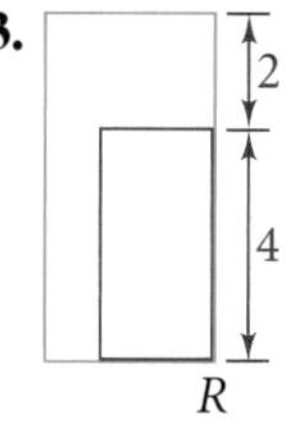

4. 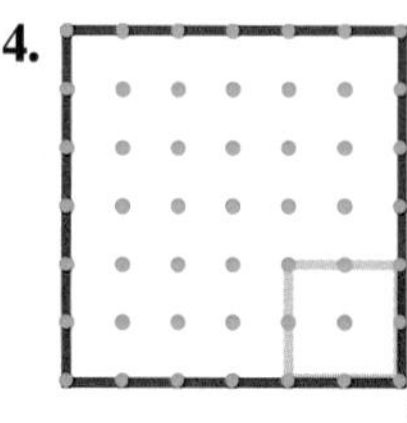

5. 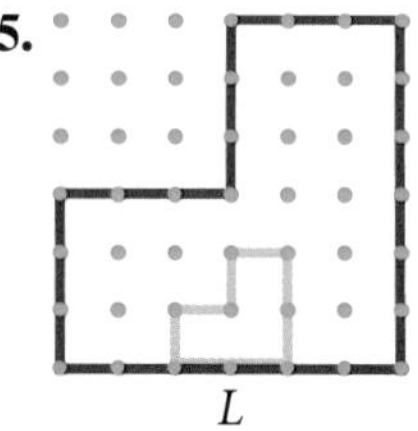

6. 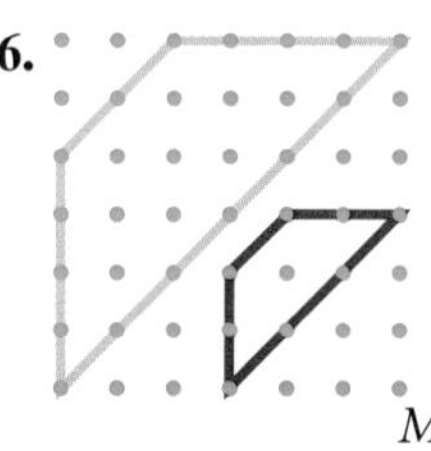

7. 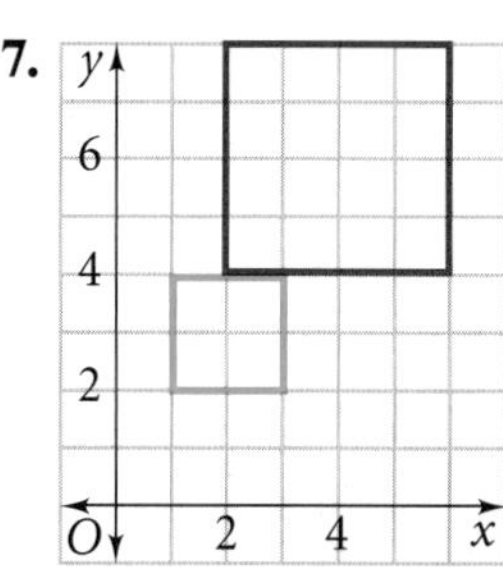

8. 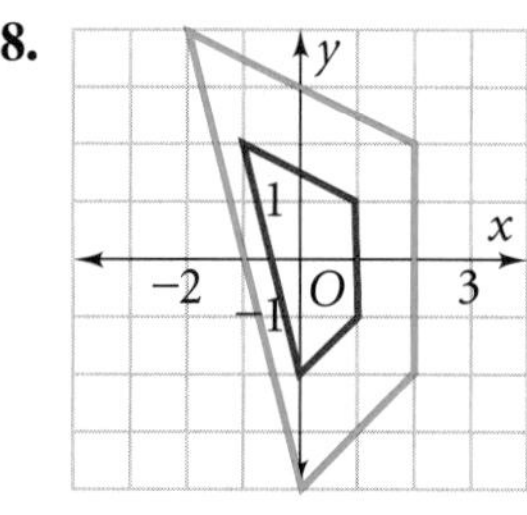

9. 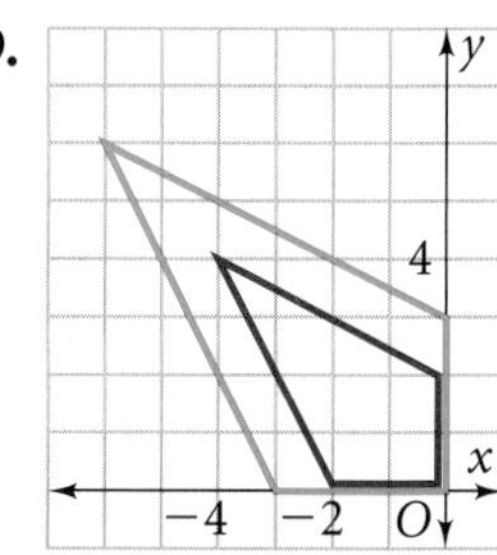

Example 2 (page 675)

Model Railroads The table shows scales for different types of model railroads. For each model in Exercises 10–12, what would be the actual measurement?

Model Railroad Scales

Scale Name	Scale Ratio
N	1 : 160
HO	1 : 87.1
S	1 : 64
O	1 : 48
G	1 : 22.5

10. An HO-scale tank car is 1.4 in. high.
11. An S-scale boxcar has length 8 in.
12. A model of an engineer in a G-scale model train layout is 3 in. tall.
13. A diesel engine is 60 feet long. How long is its O-scale model?
14. Actual railroad tracks are 4 ft 8.5 in. apart. How far apart are N-scale tracks?

Example 3 (page 675)

Use a matrix and scalar multiplication. Find the image of $\triangle PQR$ for a dilation with center (0, 0) and the scale factor given. Draw the image.

15. 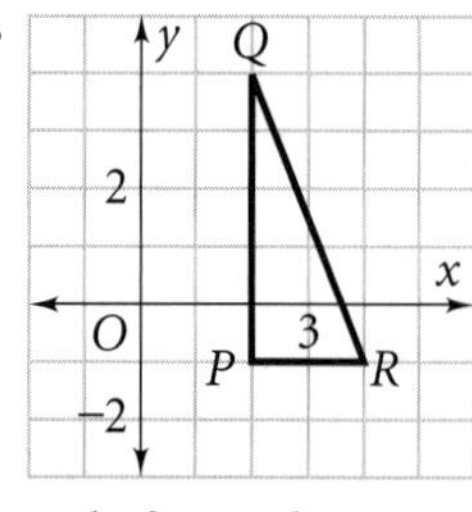

scale factor 3

16. 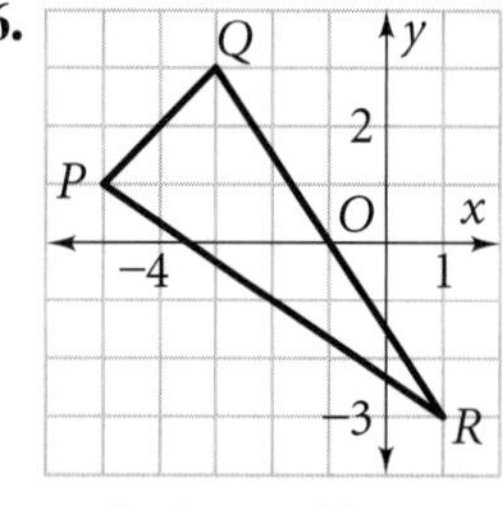

scale factor 10

17. 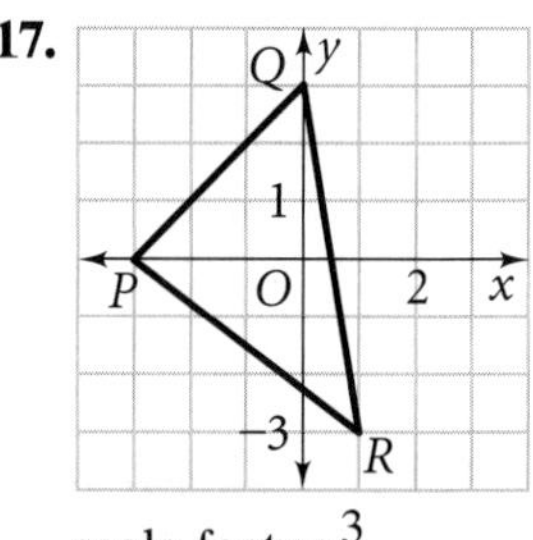

scale factor $\frac{3}{4}$

A dilation has center (0, 0). Find the image of each point for the scale factor given.

18. $D(1, -5); 2$ **19.** $L(-3, 0); 5$ **20.** $A(-6, 2); 1.5$

21. $T(0, 6); 3$ **22.** $M(0, 0); 10$ **23.** $N(-4, -7); 0.1$

Use scalar multiplication to find the image of $\triangle ABC$ for a dilation with center (0, 0) and the scale factor given. Draw $\triangle ABC$ and its image.

24.
$$\begin{array}{l} \\ x\text{-coordinate} \\ y\text{-coordinate} \end{array} \begin{array}{c} \begin{matrix} A & B & C \end{matrix} \\ \begin{bmatrix} 1 & 3 & 5 \\ 0 & 2 & 1 \end{bmatrix} \end{array}$$
scale factor 2

25.
$$\begin{array}{l} \\ x\text{-coordinate} \\ y\text{-coordinate} \end{array} \begin{array}{c} \begin{matrix} A & B & C \end{matrix} \\ \begin{bmatrix} -2 & 1 & 1 \\ -2 & 1 & -1 \end{bmatrix} \end{array}$$
scale factor $\frac{1}{4}$

26.
$$\begin{array}{l} \\ x\text{-coordinate} \\ y\text{-coordinate} \end{array} \begin{array}{c} \begin{matrix} A & B & C \end{matrix} \\ \begin{bmatrix} 3 & -6 & 12 \\ 1 & -9 & -3 \end{bmatrix} \end{array}$$
scale factor $\frac{1}{3}$

27.
$$\begin{array}{l} \\ x\text{-coordinate} \\ y\text{-coordinate} \end{array} \begin{array}{c} \begin{matrix} A & B & C \end{matrix} \\ \begin{bmatrix} -2 & -4 & -3 \\ 0 & -3 & 0 \end{bmatrix} \end{array}$$
scale factor 5

B Apply Your Skills

Use scalar multiplication to find the image of $QRTW$ for a dilation with center (0, 0) and the scale factor given.

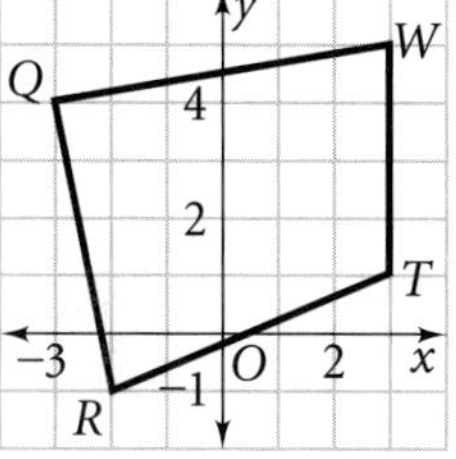

28. 3 **29.** 2 **30.** $\frac{1}{2}$ **31.** $\frac{1}{4}$

32. 0.6 **33.** 0.9 **34.** 10 **35.** 100

36. Writing An equilateral triangle has 4-in. sides. Describe its image for a dilation with scale factor 2.5. Explain.

Coordinate Geometry Graph $MNPQ$ and its image $M'N'P'Q'$ for a dilation with center (0, 0) and the scale factor given.

37. $M(-1, -1), N(1, -2), P(1, 2), Q(-1, 3)$; scale factor 2

38. $M(1, 3), N(-3, 3), P(-5, -3), Q(-1, -3)$; scale factor 3

39. $M(0, 0), N(4, 0), P(6, -2), Q(-2, -2)$; scale factor $\frac{1}{2}$

40. $M(2, 6), N(-4, 10), P(-4, -8), Q(-2, -12)$; scale factor $\frac{1}{4}$

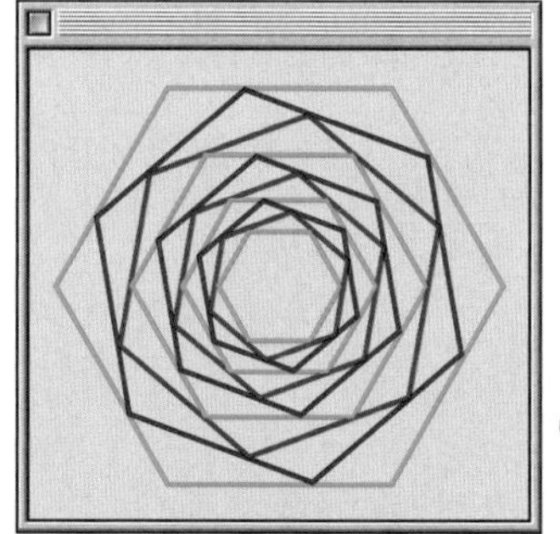

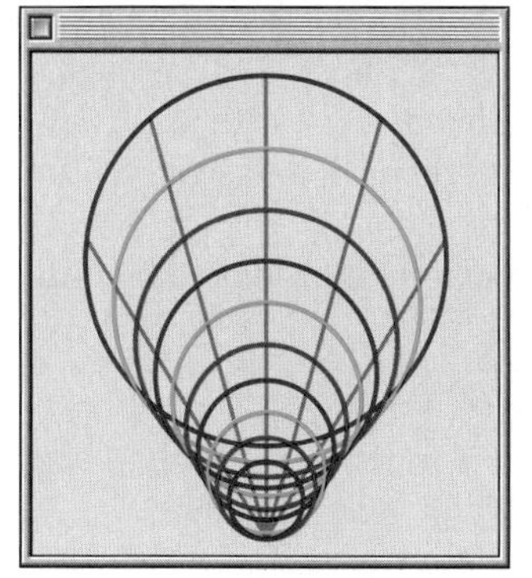

Exercise 41

41. Open-Ended Use the dilation command in geometry software or drawing software to create a design that involves repeated dilations. The software will prompt you to specify a center of dilation and a scale factor. Print your design and color it. Feel free to use other transformations along with dilations.

42. Copy Reduction Your copy of your family crest is 4.5 in. wide. You need a reduced copy for the front page of the family newsletter. The copy must fit in a space 1.8 in. wide. What scale factor should you use on the copy machine?

A dilation maps $\triangle HIJ$ to $\triangle H'I'J'$. Find the missing values.

43.	**44.**	**45.**
$HI = 8$ in.	$HI = 7$ cm	$HI = \blacksquare$ ft
$IJ = 5$ in.	$IJ = 7$ cm	$IJ = 30$ ft
$HJ = 6$ in.	$HJ = \blacksquare$ cm	$HJ = 24$ ft
$H'I' = 16$ in.	$H'I' = 5.25$ cm	$H'I' = 8$ ft
$I'J' = \blacksquare$ in.	$I'J' = \blacksquare$ cm	$I'J' = \blacksquare$ ft
$H'J' = \blacksquare$ in.	$H'J' = 9$ cm	$H'J' = 6$ ft

46. Error Analysis Brendan says that when a rectangle with length 6 cm and width 4 cm is dilated by a scale factor of 2, the perimeter and area of the rectangle are doubled. Explain what is incorrect about Brendan's statement.

The diagram at the right shows $\triangle LMN$ and its image $\triangle L'M'N'$ for a dilation with center P.

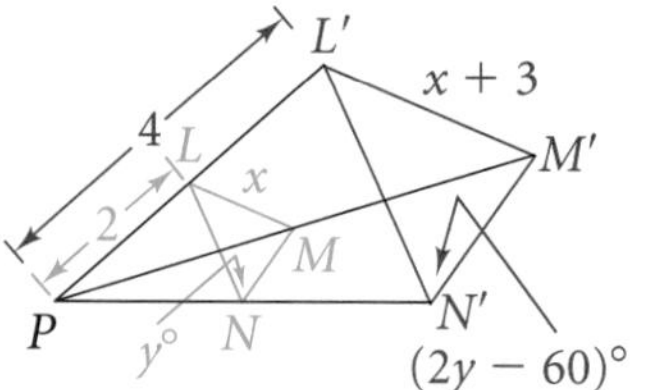

 **47.** Algebra Find the values of x and y.

48. How does the area of $\triangle L'M'N'$ compare with the area of $\triangle LMN$?

Copy $\triangle TBA$ and point O for each of Exercises 49–52. Draw the dilation image $\triangle T'B'A'$ for the given center and scale factor.

49. center O, scale factor $\frac{1}{2}$

50. center B, scale factor 3

51. center T, scale factor $\frac{1}{3}$

52. center O, scale factor 2

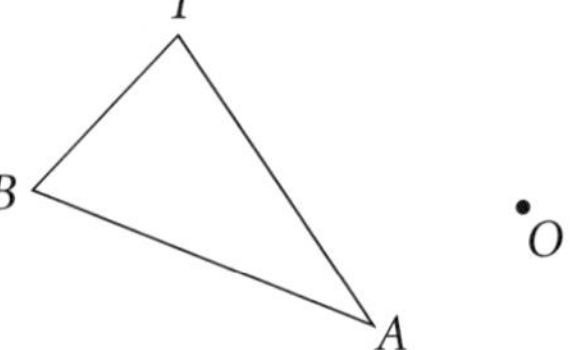

Real-World Connection

An overhead projection is a dilation only when the mirror in the head is tilted at a 45° angle. Turning the head distorts the images.

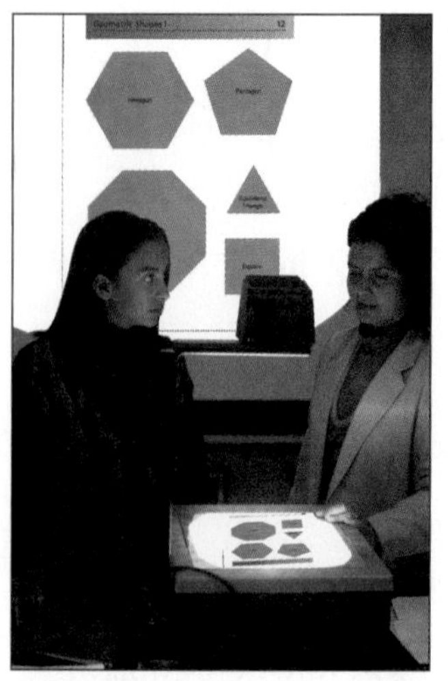

53. Constructions Copy $\triangle GHI$ and point X onto your paper. Use a compass and straightedge to construct the image of $\triangle GHI$ for a dilation with center X and scale factor 2.

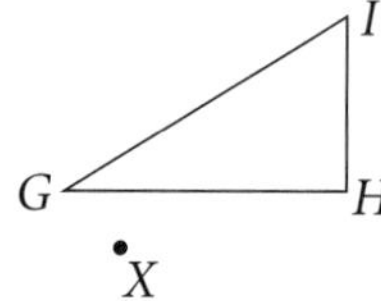

Overhead Projection **An overhead projector can dilate figures on transparencies.**

54. A segment on a transparency is 2 in. long. Its image on the screen is 2 ft long. What is the scale factor of the dilation?

55. The height of a parallelogram on the transparency is 4 cm. The scale factor is 15. What is the height of the parallelogram on the screen?

56. The area of a triangle on the screen is 9 ft^2. The scale factor is 16. What is the area of the triangle on the transparency?

Write *true* or *false* for Exercises 57–61. Explain your answers.

57. A dilation is an isometry.

58. A dilation changes orientation.

59. A dilation with a scale factor greater than 1 is a reduction.

60. For a dilation, corresponding angles of the image and preimage are congruent.

61. A dilation image cannot have any points in common with its preimage.

Challenge

62. A flashlight projects an image of rectangle $ABCD$ on a wall so that each vertex of $ABCD$ is 3 ft away from the corresponding vertex of $A'B'C'D'$. The length of $\overline{AB}$ is 3 in. The length of $\overline{A'B'}$ is 1 ft. How far from each vertex of $ABCD$ is the light?

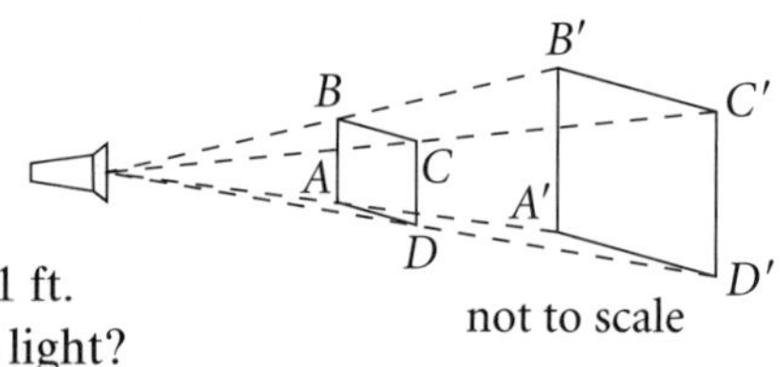

63. Critical Thinking You are given $\overline{AB}$ and its dilation image $\overline{A'B'}$ with A, B, A', and B' noncollinear. Explain how to find the center of dilation and scale factor.

Coordinate Geometry **In the coordinate plane you can extend dilations to include scale factors that are negative numbers.**

64. a. Graph $\triangle PQR$ with vertices $P(1, 2)$, $Q(3, 4)$, and $R(4, 1)$.

b. For a dilation centered at the origin with a scale factor of -3, multiply the coordinates in part (a) by -3. List the results as P', Q', and R'.

c. Graph $\triangle P'Q'R'$ on the same set of axes.

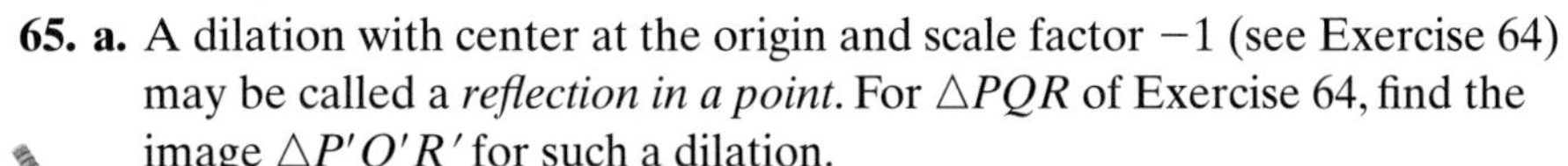

Need Help?
For Exercise 65(b), recall the meaning of reflection in a line.

65. a. A dilation with center at the origin and scale factor -1 (see Exercise 64) may be called a *reflection in a point*. For $\triangle PQR$ of Exercise 64, find the image $\triangle P'Q'R'$ for such a dilation.

b. Writing Explain why the dilation described in part (a) may be called a *reflection in a point*. Extend your explanation to a new definition of point symmetry. Compare your new definition with the definition given on page 663.

66. Constructions Draw acute $\triangle ABC$. Construct square $DEFG$ so that $\overline{DG}$ is on $\overline{AC}$, and E and F are on the other two sides of $\triangle ABC$. (*Hint:* First, try the special case with a right angle at A and use a dilation.)

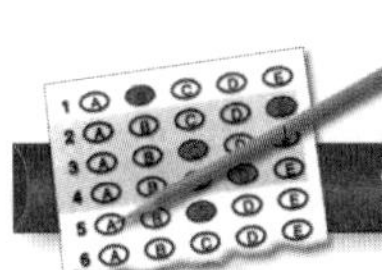

Standardized Test Prep

Gridded Response

67. A dilation maps $\triangle ABC$ onto $\triangle A'B'C'$ with a scale factor of 0.3. If $A'B' = 3126$ m, what is AB in meters?

68. A dilation maps $\triangle CDE$ onto $\triangle C'D'E'$. If $CD = 7.5$ ft, $CE = 15$ ft, $D'E' = 3.75$ ft, and $C'D' = 2.5$ ft, what is DE in feet?

69. A dilation maps $\triangle XYZ$ onto $\triangle X'Y'Z'$. If $XY = 24$ m, $YZ = 29$ m, $X'Z' = 8.7$ m, and $Y'Z' = 29.145$ m, what is $X'Y'$ in meters?

Take It to the NET
Online lesson quiz at **www.PHSchool.com**
Web Code: afa-1207

70. The center of dilation of quadrilateral $ABCD$ is point X, as shown at the right. The length of a side of quadrilateral $A'B'C'D'$ is what percent of the length of the corresponding side of quadrilateral $ABCD$?

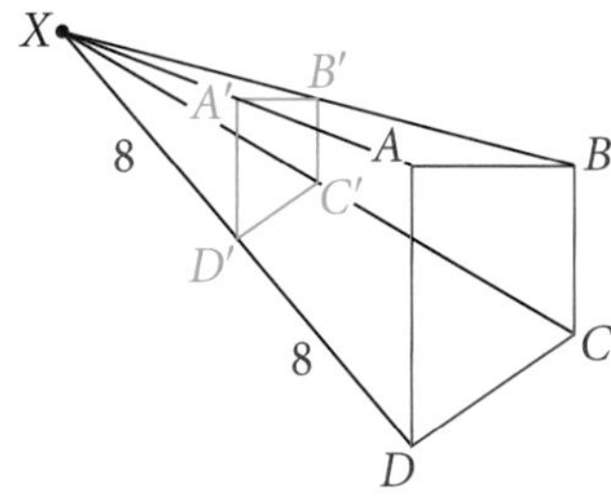

71. A dilation maps $\triangle JKL$ onto $\triangle J'K'L'$. If $JK = 28$ cm, $KL = 52$ cm, $JL = 40.2$ cm, and $J'K' = 616$ cm, what is the scale factor?

Mixed Review

Lesson 12-6 **Determine whether the polygons described could tessellate a plane.**

72. congruent regular hexagons
73. squares and regular triangles
74. congruent regular octagons
75. congruent kite figures

Lesson 11-6 **Give another description of each locus.**

76. all points in a plane equidistant from three noncollinear points

77. all points in space 3 inches from a sphere with a 3-inch radius

Lesson 11-2 x^2 **Algebra** **Find the value of *a*.**

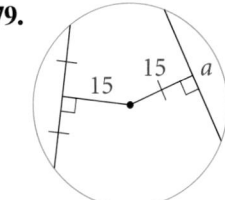

78.

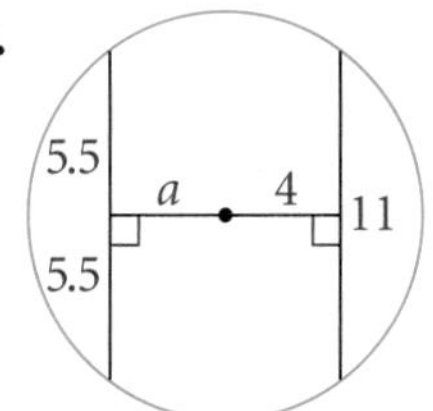

79.

Test-Taking Strategies

Answering the Question Asked

When answering a question, be sure to answer the question that is asked. Read the question carefully and identify the quantity that you are asked to find. Some answer choices are answers to related questions, so you have to be careful.

1 EXAMPLE

The point $L(a, b)$ in Quadrant I is rotated 90° about the origin and is then reflected in the y-axis. What is the x-coordinate of the image?

A. a **B.** $-b$ **C.** b **D.** $-a$

The question asks for the x-coordinate of the image. The x-coordinate of the preimage is a. After the 90° rotation about the origin, the x-coordinate is $-b$. After a reflection in the y-axis, the x-coordinate of the image is b.

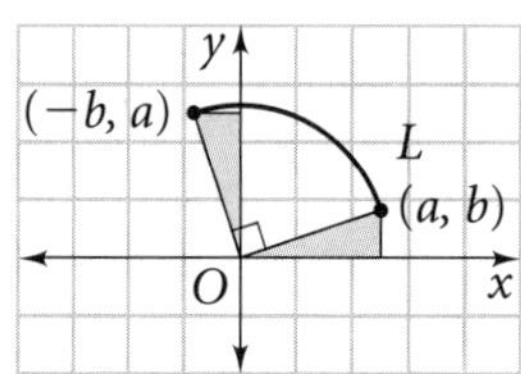

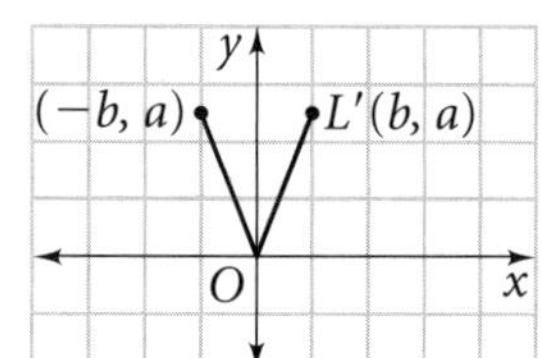

The correct answer is C. Choice A is the y-coordinate of the image, but that is not what is asked for.

2 EXAMPLE

What is the image of $M(4, 3)$ for the translation $\langle -2, 1\rangle$ followed by a reflection in the line $x = -1$?

F. $(2, -6)$ **G.** $(-4, 4)$ **H.** $(0, 4)$ **I.** $(-8, 4)$

The translation $\langle -2, 1\rangle$ puts the point at $(2, 4)$. A reflection in $x = -1$ then puts the point at $(-4, 4)$. The correct answer is G.

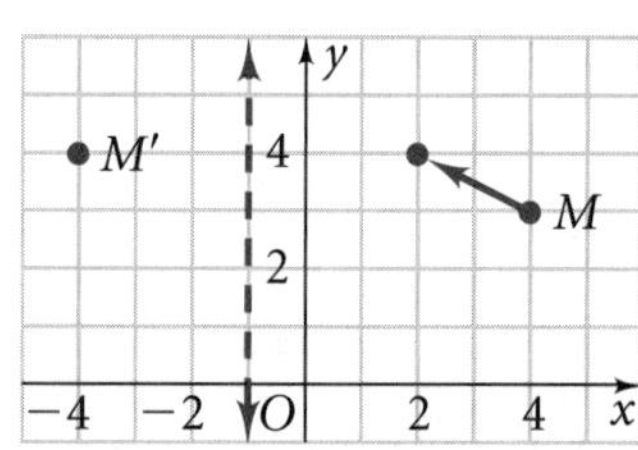

Answers F and H result from the translation $\langle -2, 1\rangle$ followed by a reflection in a line other than $x = -1$. In fact, if you reflect $(2, 4)$ in $x = 1$, which is one unit in the negative direction from $(2, 4)$, you get $(0, 4)$, or choice H, as your answer. If you do the steps in the wrong order, you will get answer I.

EXERCISES

Answer the question. Then ask a related question that would lead to an incorrect choice.

1. The point $K(4, 3)$ is rotated 90° about the origin. What is the sum of the x- and y-coordinates of the image?

   A. -7 **B.** -1 **C.** 1 **D.** 7

2. The point $P(1, 3)$ is rotated 180° about the origin, and then reflected in the line $y = 0$. What is the y-coordinate of the image?

   F. -3 **G.** -1 **H.** 1 **I.** 3

3. The point $T(5, -1)$ is reflected in the y-axis. What is the distance between the image and the preimage?

   A. 1 **B.** 2 **C.** $\sqrt{26}$ **D.** 10

Chapter Review

Vocabulary

composition (p. 642)	**point symmetry** (p. 663)	**symmetry** (p. 662)
dilation (p. 674)	**preimage** (p. 634)	**tessellation** (p. 667)
enlargement (p. 674)	**reduction** (p. 674)	**tiling** (p. 667)
glide reflection (p. 656)	**reflection** (p. 635)	**transformation** (p. 634)
glide reflectional symmetry (p. 668)	**reflectional symmetry** (p. 662)	**translation** (p. 641)
image (p. 634)	**rotation** (p. 648)	**translational symmetry** (p. 668)
isometry (p. 634)	**rotational symmetry** (p. 663)	
line symmetry (p. 662)	**scalar multiplication** (p. 675)	

Reading Math
Understanding Vocabulary

To complete each definition, find the appropriate word in the second column.

1. A(n) _?_ is a change in position, shape, or size of a figure.
2. A(n) _?_ is a transformation in which the preimage and its image are congruent.
3. A _?_ is an isometry in which a figure and its image have opposite orientations.
4. A _?_ is an isometry in which all points of a figure move the same distance in the same direction.
5. A(n) _?_ is a translation followed by a reflection in a line parallel to the translation vector.
6. A(n) _?_ is a repeating pattern of figures that completely covers a plane, without gaps or overlaps.
7. A(n) _?_ is a transformation that proportionally reduces or enlarges a figure.

A. dilation
B. glide reflection
C. tessellation
D. isometry
E. reflection
F. transformation
G. translation

Take It to the NET
Online vocabulary quiz at **www.PHSchool.com**
Web Code: afj-1251

Skills and Concepts

12-1 and 12-2 Objectives

- ▼ To identify isometries
- ▼ To find reflection images of figures
- ▼ To describe translations using vectors
- ▼ To find translation images using matrix and vector sums

A **transformation** of a geometric figure is a change in its position, shape, or size. An **isometry** is a transformation in which the **preimage** and **image** are congruent. A transformation maps a figure onto its image. The diagram shows a **reflection** of B to B' in line r. A reflection is an isometry in which a figure and its image have opposite orientations.

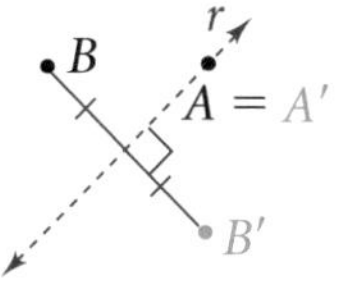

A **translation** is an isometry that maps all points of a figure the same distance in the same direction. A translation is an isometry that does not change orientation. You can use vectors and matrices to describe a translation.

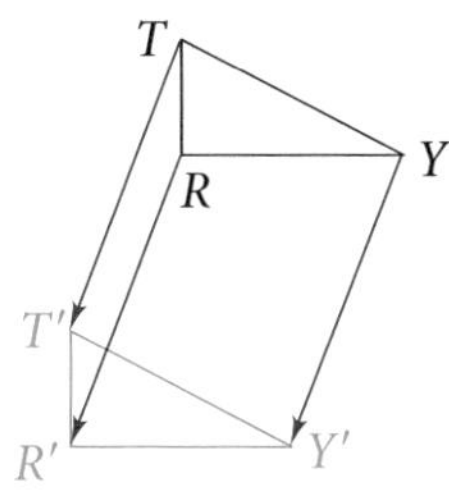

A **composition** of transformations is a combination of two or more transformations. Each transformation is performed on the image of the preceding transformation.

Given points $A(6, 4)$, $B(-2, 1)$, and $C(5, 0)$, draw $\triangle ABC$ and its reflection image in each line.

8. the x-axis **9.** $x = 4$ **10.** $y = x$

Use matrices to find the image of each triangle for the given translation.

11. $\triangle ABC$ with vertices $A(5, 9)$, $B(6, 3)$, $C(1, 2)$; translation: $\langle 2, 3 \rangle$

12. $\triangle RST$ with vertices $R(0, -4)$, $S(-2, -1)$, $T(-6, 1)$; translation: $\langle -4, 7 \rangle$

Find a single translation that has the same effect as each composition of translations.

13. $\langle -5, -7 \rangle$ followed by $\langle 3, 6 \rangle$ **14.** $\langle 10, -9 \rangle$ followed by $\langle 1, 5 \rangle$

12-3 and 12-4 Objectives

- ▼ To draw and identify rotation images of figures
- ▼ To use a composition of reflections
- ▼ To identify glide reflections

The diagram shows a rotation of point V about point R through $x°$. A **rotation** is an isometry that does not change orientation.

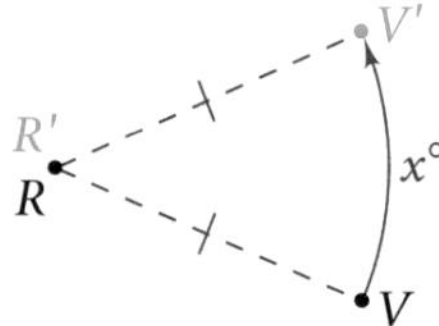

A composition of reflections in two parallel lines is a translation. A composition of reflections in two intersecting lines is a rotation. A **glide reflection** is the composition of a glide (translation) and a reflection in a line parallel to the translation vector. The only four isometries are reflection, translation, rotation, and glide reflection.

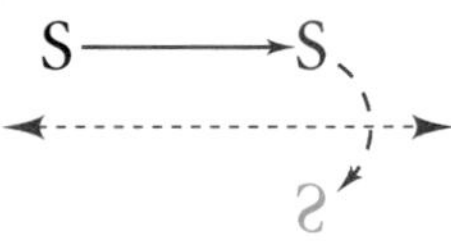

Copy each figure and point *P*. Draw the image of each figure for the given rotation about *P*. Label the vertices of the image.

15. 180°

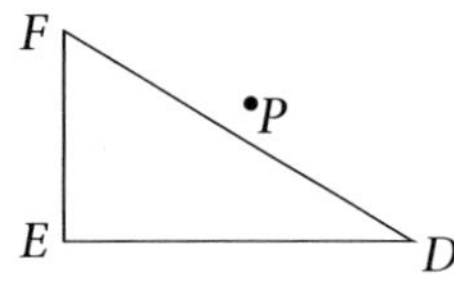

16. 60°

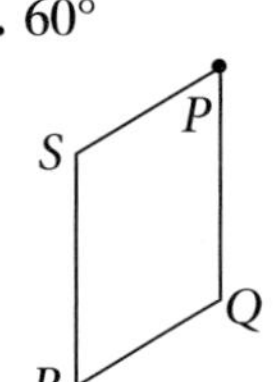

17. 90°

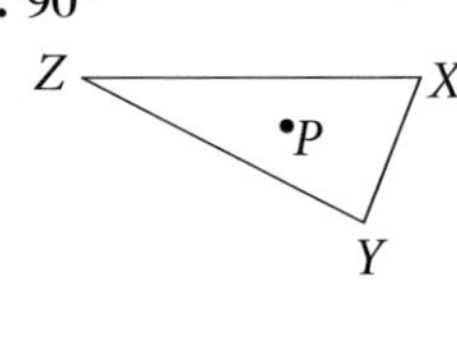

Find the image of each point for a 90° rotation about the origin.

18. $(5, 2)$ **19.** $(0, 3)$ **20.** $(-4, 1)$ **21.** $(7, 0)$ **22.** $(-2, -8)$

For each figure at the left below, four isometry images are shown. Tell whether orientations are the same or opposite. Then classify the isometry.

23. 

24. 

25. 

26. 

ine

27. 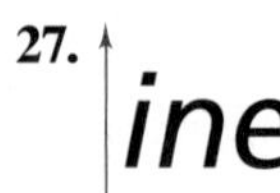

28. 

29. ine

30. 

31. $\triangle TAM$ has vertices $T(0, 5)$, $A(4, 1)$, and $M(3, 6)$. Find the image of $\triangle TAM$ where the glide vector is $\langle -4, 0 \rangle$ and the reflection is in the line $y = -2$.

12-5 and 12-6 Objectives

- To identify the type of symmetry in a figure
- To identify transformations in tessellations and figures that will tessellate
- To identify symmetries of tessellations

A figure has **symmetry** if there is an isometry that maps the figure onto itself. A plane figure has **reflectional symmetry,** or **line symmetry,** if one half of the figure is a mirror image of its other half. A figure that has **rotational symmetry** is its own image for some rotation of 180° or less. A figure that has **point symmetry** has 180° rotational symmetry.

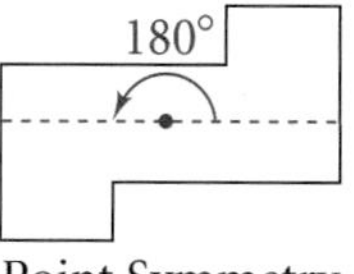

Point Symmetry

Tell what type(s) of symmetry each figure has. If it has rotational symmetry, state the angle of rotation.

32.

33.

A **tessellation,** or **tiling,** is a repeating pattern of figures that completely covers a plane, without gaps or overlaps. A tessellation can have **translational symmetry** if there is a translation that maps the tessellation onto itself. If a tessellation can be mapped onto itself by a glide reflection, then the tessellation has **glide reflectional symmetry**.

For each tessellation, (a) identify a transformation and the repeating figures, and (b) list the symmetries.

34. 

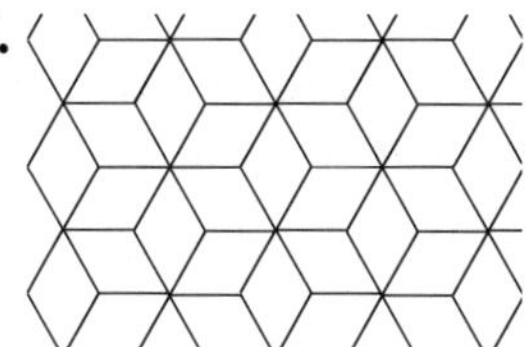

35.

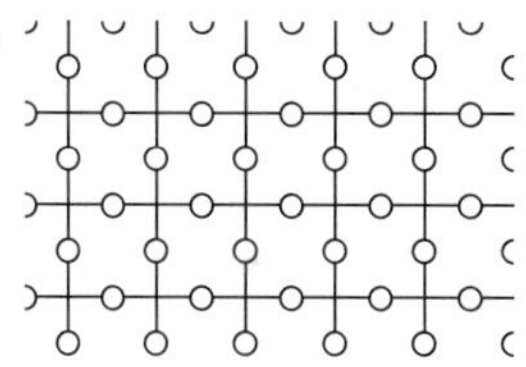

12-7 Objective

- To locate dilation images of figures

The diagram shows a **dilation** with center C and scale factor n. A dilation is a similarity transformation because its preimage and image are similar figures. When the scale factor is greater than 1, the dilation is an **enlargement.** When the scale factor is between 0 and 1, the dilation is a **reduction.** In the coordinate plane, you can use **scalar multiplication** to find the image of a figure under a dilation centered at the origin.

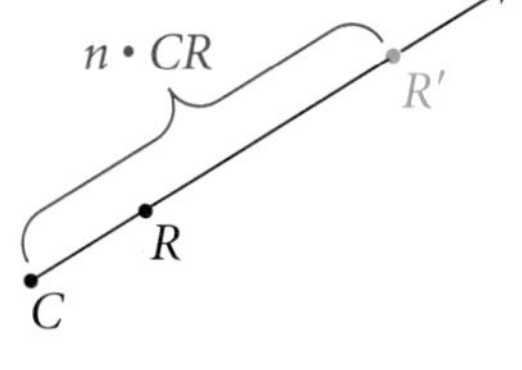

A dilation has center (0, 0). Find the image of each point for the scale factor given.

36. $A(0, 3); 4$ **37.** $B(-2, 6); 0.5$ **38.** $C(1.5, -2); 10$

Use matrices to find the image of each set of points for a dilation with center at the origin and the scale factor given.

39. $M(-3, 4), A(-6, -1), T(0, 0), H(3, 2)$; scale factor 5

40. $F(-4, 0), U(5, 0), N(-2, -5)$; scale factor $\frac{1}{2}$

Chapter Test

Take It to the NET
Online chapter test at
www.PHSchool.com
Web Code: afa-1252

Find the coordinates of the vertices of the image of *ABCD* for each transformation.

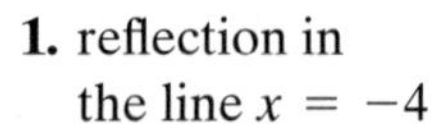

1. reflection in the line $x = -4$

2. translation $\langle -6, 8 \rangle$
3. rotation of 90º about the point $(0, 0)$
4. dilation centered at $(0, 0)$ with scale factor $\frac{2}{3}$
5. glide reflection with glide vector $\langle 0, 3 \rangle$ and reflection in the line $x = 0$
6. reflection in the line $y = x$
7. rotation of 270º about $(0, 0)$
8. dilation centered at the origin with scale factor 5
9. glide reflection with glide vector $\langle -2, 0 \rangle$ and reflection in the line $y = 5$
10. translation 3 units right and 1 unit down

What type of transformation has the same effect as each composition of transformations?

11. translation $\langle 4, 0 \rangle$ followed by a reflection in the line $y = -4$
12. translation $\langle 4, 8 \rangle$ followed by $\langle -2, 9 \rangle$
13. reflection in the line $y = 7$, and then in the line $y = 3$
14. reflection in the line $y = x$, and then in the line $y = 2x + 5$

Open-Ended **Draw a figure that has each type of symmetry.**

15. reflectional
16. rotational
17. point

What type(s) of symmetry does each figure have?

18.

19.

20. **Writing** Line m intersects $\overline{UH}$ at N, and $UN = NH$. Must H be the reflection image of U in line m? Explain.
21. Describe the symmetries of this tessellation. Copy a portion of the tessellation and draw any centers of rotational symmetry or lines of symmetry.

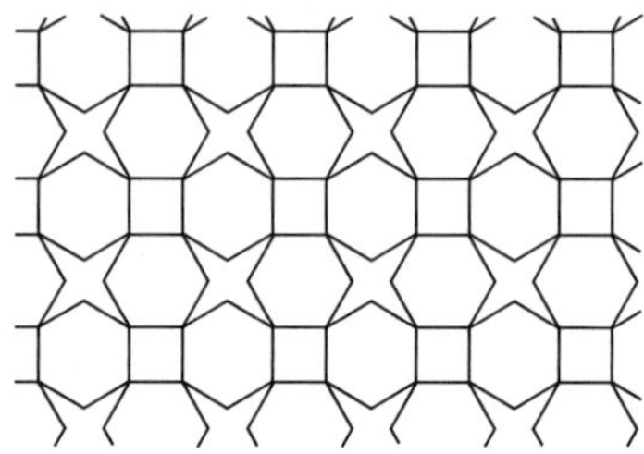

Does each letter tessellate? If so, sketch a tessellation. If not, explain why it cannot tessellate.

22.

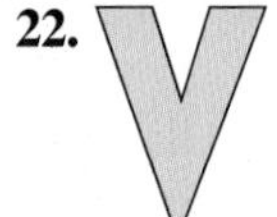

23.

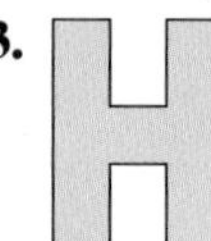

24.

Find the image of $\triangle ABC$ for a dilation with center (0, 0) and the scale factor given.

25. $A(-2, 2), B(2, -2), C(3, 4)$; scale factor 3
26. $A(0, 0), B(-3, 2), C(1, 7)$; scale factor $\frac{1}{2}$
27. The blue figure is a translation image of the red figure. Write a rule to describe the translation.

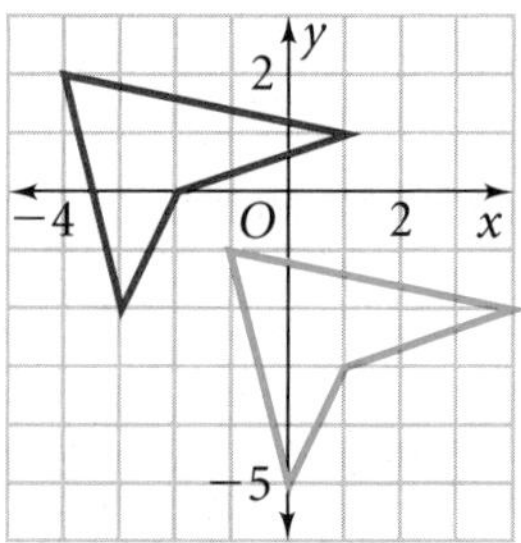

28. A dilation with center $(0, 0)$ and scale factor 2.5 maps $(4, -10)$ to (a, b). Find the values of a and b.
29. A dilation maps $\triangle LMN$ to $\triangle L'M'N'$. Find the missing values.

    $LM = 36$ ft, $LN = 26$ ft, and $MN = 45$ ft;
    $L'M' = 9$ ft, $L'N' = ■$ ft, and $M'N' = ■$ ft;
    scale factor $= ■$
30. A dilation with scale factor 4 maps square A onto square B. The area of square B is 25. Find the area of square A.

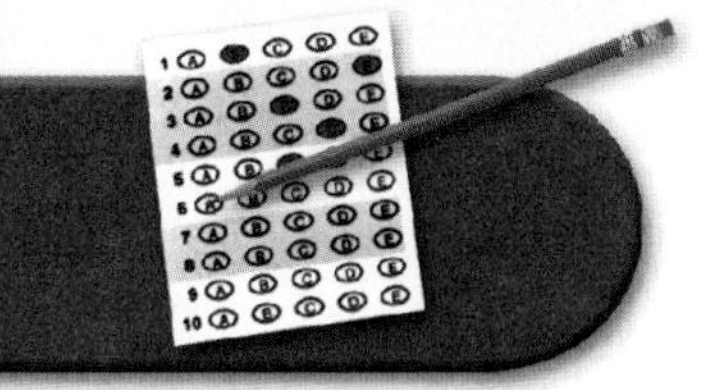

Standardized Test Prep

Take It to the NET
Online end-of-course test at **www.PHSchool.com**
Web Code: afa-1354

Multiple Choice

For Exercises 1–31, choose the correct letter.

1. Which word(s) best describes the triangle at the right?

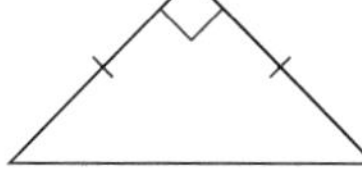

A. equilateral
B. isosceles
C. right
D. isosceles right

2. What are the coordinates of the midpoint of $\overline{QS}$ with endpoints $Q(-2, -5)$ and $S(3, -8)$?

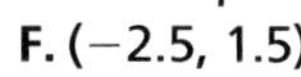

F. $(-2.5, 1.5)$ **G.** $(-2.5, 6.5)$
H. $(0.5, -6.5)$ **I.** $(0.5, 1.5)$

3. What is the volume of the figure?

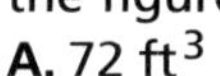

A. 72 ft^3
B. 72π ft^3
C. $(18 + 72\pi)$ ft^3
D. $(72 + 18\pi)$ ft^3

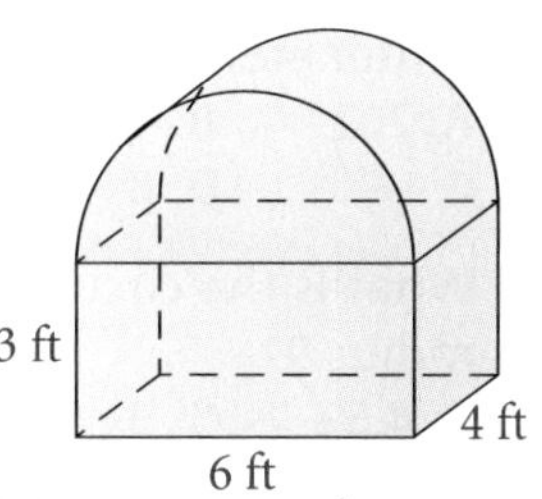

4. Which of the following statements can be derived from the biconditional statement "The day is long if and only if it is summer"?

F. If the day is long, then it is summer.
G. If it is summer, then the day is long.
H. If the day is not long, then it is not summer.
I. all of the above

5. Which line or lines are perpendicular to the line $y = 4x - 1$?

I. $y = 4x + 7$ II. $y = \frac{1}{4}x + 3$
III. $y = -\frac{1}{4}x - 5$ IV. $x + 4y = 16$

A. I only **B.** II only
C. III only **D.** III and IV

6. Which solid has the least volume?

F.

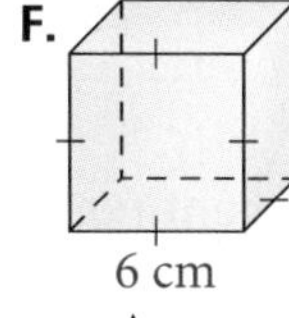

G.

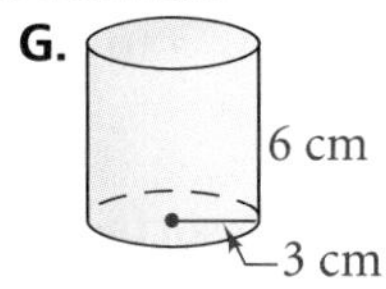

H.

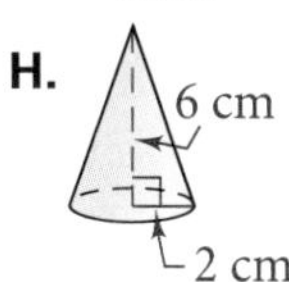

I.

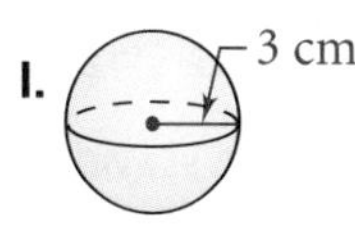

7. Which figure below is the reflection in the x-axis of the figure at the right?

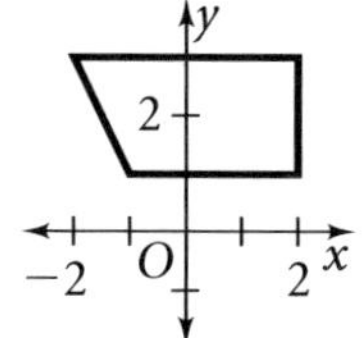

A.

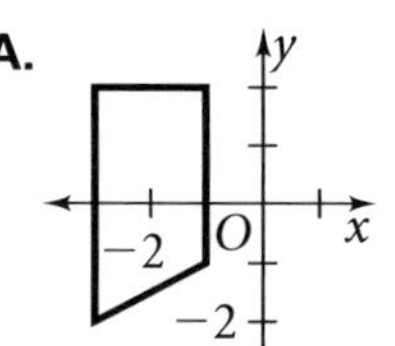

B.

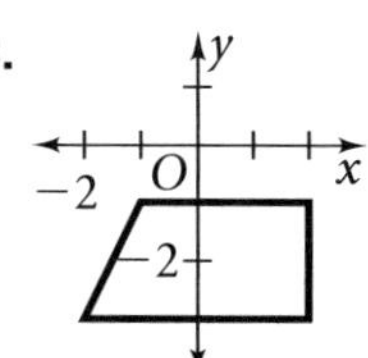

C.

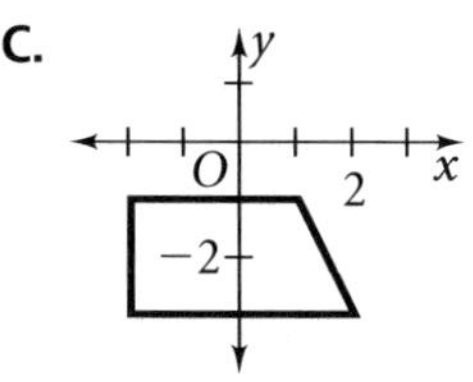

D.

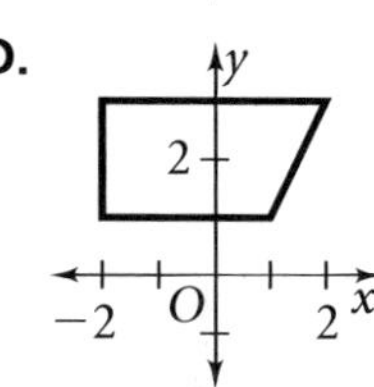

8. Which conditions allow you to conclude that a quadrilateral is a parallelogram?

F. one pair of sides congruent, the other pair parallel
G. perpendicular congruent diagonals
H. congruent bisecting diagonals
I. one diagonal bisecting opposite angles

9. Which triangle is drawn with its medians?

A.

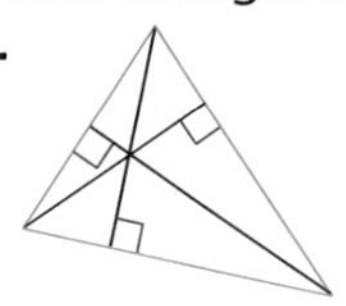

B.

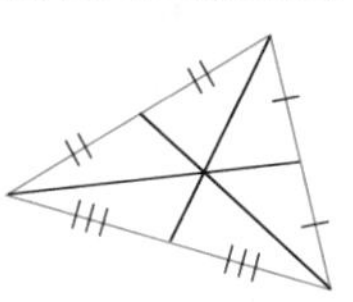

C.

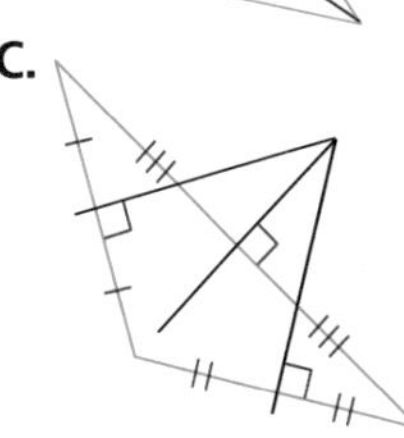

D.

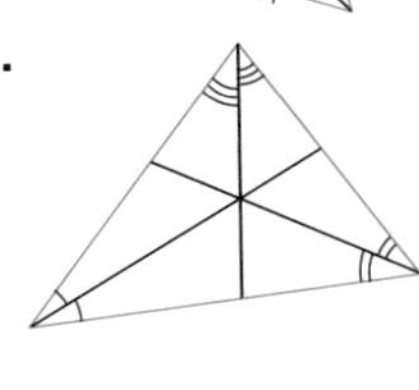

10. What kind of symmetry does the figure have?

F. 60° rotational symmetry
G. 90° rotational symmetry
H. line symmetry
I. point symmetry

11. What is the surface area in square centimeters of a sphere with radius 7 cm?

A. 196π **B.** $\frac{196}{3}\pi$ **C.** 49π **D.** 14π

12. In $\triangle RST$, $RS = 4$, $ST = 5$, and $RT = 6$. Which angle is largest?
F. $\angle R$ G. $\angle S$ H. $\angle T$
I. cannot be determined

13. Which is true for both a rhombus and a kite?
A. The diagonals are congruent.
B. Opposite sides are congruent.
C. The diagonals are perpendicular.
D. Opposite sides are parallel.

14. To the nearest tenth, what is the value of x?
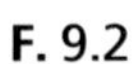
F. 9.2
G. 13.6
H. 15.0
I. 20.6

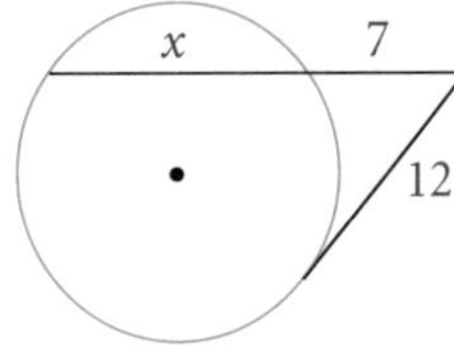

15. If $\frac{m}{n} = \frac{1}{3}$, which of the following must be true?
I. $3m = n$ II. $m = 3n$
III. $m + 1 = \frac{n+3}{3}$ IV. $mn = 3$
A. I only B. I and II only
C. I and III only D. I and IV only

16. The length of the hypotenuse of an isosceles right triangle is 8 in. What is the length of one leg?
F. $8\sqrt{2}$ in. G. $4\sqrt{2}$ in. H. 4 in. I. 2 in.

17. Which equation is that of a line that contains the point $P(5, 6)$ and has slope $-\frac{1}{3}$?
A. $y = -\frac{1}{3}x + \frac{3}{23}$ B. $y = -\frac{1}{3}x - \frac{3}{23}$
C. $y = -\frac{1}{3}x - \frac{23}{3}$ D. $y = -\frac{1}{3}x + \frac{23}{3}$

18. Which of the following must be true?
I. $\angle BAC \cong \angle B$
II. $\angle B \cong \angle C$
III. $\overline{AD} \cong \overline{AB}$
IV. $\overline{BD} \cong \overline{CD}$
F. I and II only G. I and III only
H. II and IV only I. III and IV only

19. What is the area of the trapezoid?
A. 75 in.^{2}
B. 43 in.^{2}
C. 79.5 in.^{2}
D. 159 in.^{2}

20. $\overleftrightarrow{AB}$ is tangent to $\odot C$ at point B. Which of the following can you NOT conclude is true? F
F. $m\angle CAB < m\angle ACB$
G. $AB^2 + BC^2 = AC^2$
H. $\angle CAB$ and $\angle ACB$ are complements.
I. $\overleftrightarrow{AB} \perp \overleftrightarrow{BC}$

21. Sphere B has 4 times the surface area of sphere A. How many times the volume of sphere A is the volume of sphere B?
A. 4 B. 8 C. 4π D. 8π

22. What is the value of x?
F. $\sqrt{30}$
G. $\sqrt{39}$
H. $3\sqrt{13}$
I. $\sqrt{130}$

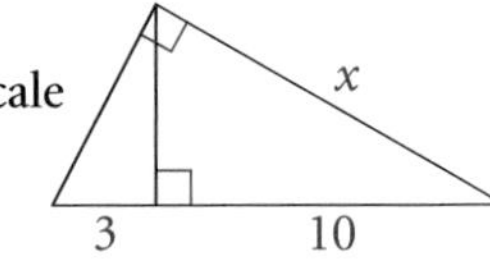

23. What is the ratio of the surface areas of similar solids whose similarity ratio is 3 : 5?
A. 6 : 10 B. 9 : 15 C. 9 : 25 D. 27 : 125

24. What are the values of x and y?
F. $x = 56$, $y = 68$
G. $x = 68$, $y = 56$
H. $x = 57$, $y = 66$
I. $x = 66$, $y = 57$

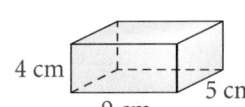

25. What is the volume of the prism in cubic centimeters?
A. 202 B. 180
C. 99 D. 81

26. What is the circumference of a circle with radius 9?
F. 4.5π G. 9π H. 18π I. 81π

27. Which information CANNOT be used to prove that two triangles are congruent?
A. SAS B. ASA C. AAS D. AAA

28. Which figure does NOT have an area of 15 ft^2?
F. G.

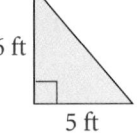

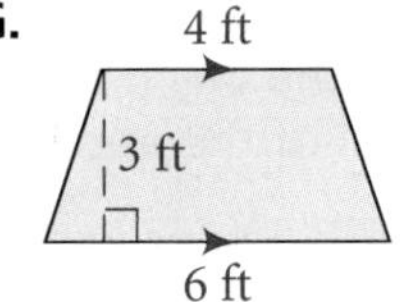

H. I.

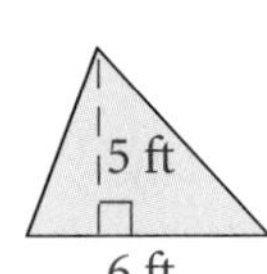

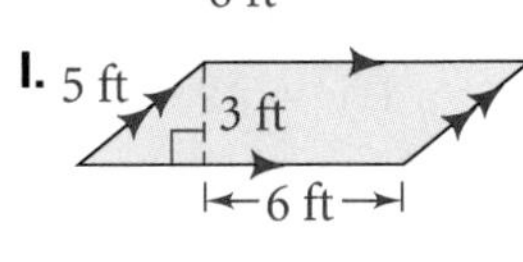

29. Which is greatest in $\triangle ABC$?
A. $\sin A$ B. $\cos A$
C. $\tan A$ D. $\tan B$

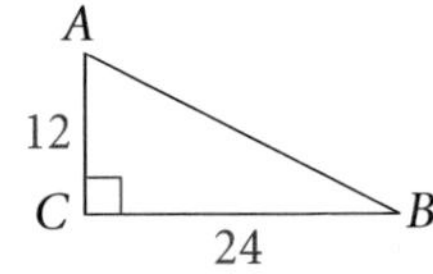

30. What is the surface area in square centimeters of a rectangular prism 9 cm by 8 cm by 10 cm?
F. 240 G. 242 H. 484 I. 720

31. What is the standard equation of a circle with center $(-2, 0)$ and radius 4?
A. $(x - 2)^2 + y^2 = 4$ B. $(x + 2)^2 + y^2 = 16$
C. $x^2 + (y - 2)^2 = 2^2$ D. $x^2 + (y + 2)^2 = 16$

Quantitative Comparison

Compare the boxed quantity in Column A with the boxed quantity in Column B. Choose the best answer.

A. The quantity in Column A is greater.
B. The quantity in Column B is greater.
C. The two quantities are equal.
D. The relationship cannot be determined from the information given.

	Column A	Column B
32.	the magnitude of $\langle 5, 1 \rangle$	the magnitude of $\langle 4, -2 \rangle$
33.	the distance between (7, 3) and (10, −2)	the distance between (3, −1) and (0, 4)
34.	in a circle, the measure of an inscribed angle that intercepts a 78° arc	in a circle, the measure of a central angle that intercepts a 78° arc
35.	the number of pairs of corresponding angles formed by two parallel lines and a transversal	the number of pairs of alternate interior angles formed by three parallel lines and a transversal

$\angle R$ is a supplement of $\angle S$.

36.	$m\angle R$	$m\angle S$

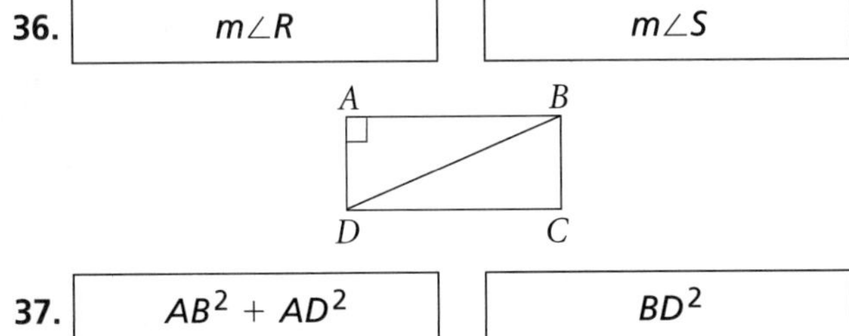

37. C	$AB^2 + AD^2$	BD^2

Gridded Response

38. A diagonal of a rectangular field makes a 70° angle with a side of the field that is 100 ft long. To the nearest whole number of square feet, what is the area of the rectangle?

39. You are making a scale model of a building. The front of the actual building is 60 ft wide and 100 ft tall. The front of your model is 3 ft by 5 ft. What is the scale factor of the reduction?

40. You are 5 ft 6 in. tall. When your shadow is 6 ft long, the shadow of a sculpture is 30 ft long. How tall is the sculpture?

41. What is the surface area in square centimeters of a right cone with slant height 5 cm and radius 3 cm? Use 3.14 for π.

42. At 8 o'clock, what is the degree measure of the angle formed by the two hands of the clock?

Short Response

Show your work.

43. What is the area of an isosceles right triangle whose hypotenuse is $5\sqrt{2}$ m long?

44. The coordinates of the endpoints of $\overline{CD}$ are $C(5, 2.5)$ and $D(0, -9.5)$. Find the length of $\overline{CD}$ and the coordinates of the midpoint of $\overline{CD}$.

45. Write an equation of a line parallel to the line $y = 6x + 4$. Then write an equation of a line perpendicular to the line $y = 6x + 4$.

46. $\triangle DEB$ has vertices $D(3, 7)$, $E(1, 4)$, and $B(-1, 5)$. In which quadrant(s) is the image of $\triangle DEB$ for a 90° rotation about the origin?

Extended Response

Show your work.

47. Draw an angle. Then construct another angle congruent to the first.

48. Quadrilateral $ABCD$ has vertices $A(-1, -3)$, $B(4, -2)$, $C(3, 7)$, and $D(-7, 0)$. Find the vertices of the image of quadrilateral $ABCD$ under the translation $\langle -4, -1 \rangle$.

49. When airplane pilots make a visual sighting of an object outside the airplane, they often refer to the face of a dial clock to help locate the object. For example, an object at 12 o'clock is straight ahead, an object at 3 o'clock is 90° to the right, and so on.

Suppose that two pilots flying two airplanes in the same direction spot the same object. One pilot reports the object at 1 o'clock; the other pilot reports the object at 2 o'clock. At the same time the first pilot reports seeing the other airplane at 9 o'clock.

Draw a diagram showing the possible locations of the two planes and the object.

Real-World Snapshots

How'd They Do That?

Applying Translations and Rotations To create computer-generated characters and objects, computer animators and designers first define every point of a wire-frame model within a three-dimensional coordinate system. To make the model move and rotate, the animators must move and rotate its points.

Wire-frame wings stretch out in flight or fold in close to the dragon's body.

Activity

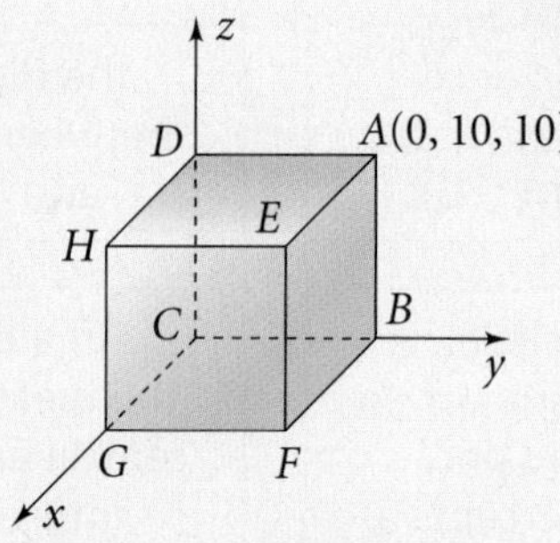

Use the diagram at the right.

a. Write the coordinates of all eight vertices of the cube.

b. Suppose the cube rotates 90° clockwise about the z-axis (looking down from the positive z-axis). Find the new coordinates of vertices A–H.

c. Starting from the cube's position at the end of part (b), rotate the cube 90° clockwise about the x-axis (looking toward the origin from the positive x-axis). Find the new coordinates of vertices A–H.

d. Describe a composition of rotations that will move point E from its original location to $(-10, -10, -10)$.

e. **Open-Ended** You can also find a composition of translations, each parallel to an axis, to move point E from its original location to the original location of point C, $(0, 0, 0)$. Describe compositions of rotations (about axes) and translations (parallel to axes) that move point E to the locations of two vertices of the cube. Let each composition include at least one translation and one rotation.

f. Suppose the cube returns to its original position and then rotates 30° clockwise about the y-axis (looking toward the origin from the positive y-axis). Find the new coordinates of the eight vertices. (*Hint:* Use trigonometric ratios.)

Dragon Lore

Unlike European dragons, which breathe fire and wreak havoc across the countryside, Asian dragons are peace-loving protectors of the heavens.

Tail shape changes as points move and lines stretch.

Muscle structure added to frame

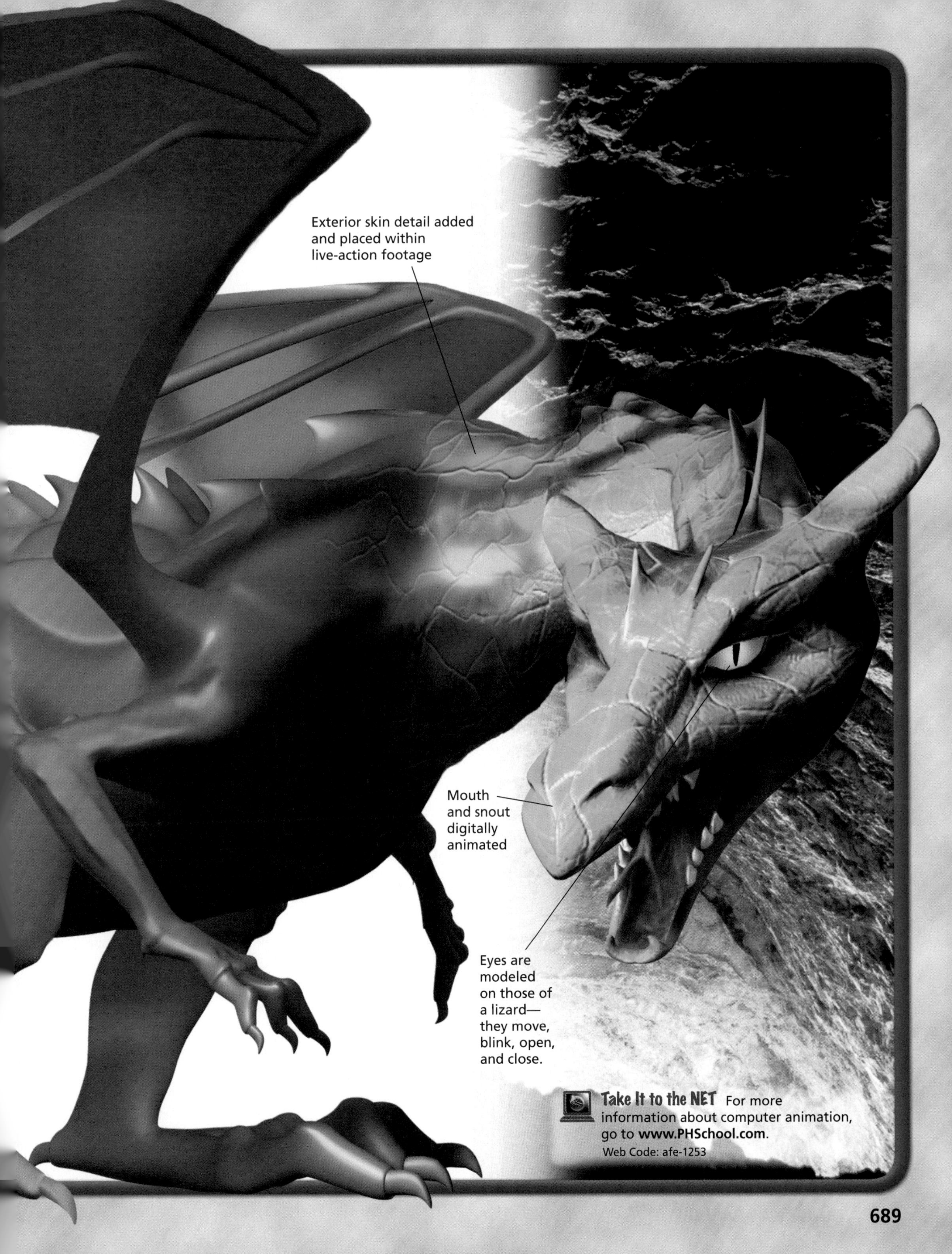

Exterior skin detail added and placed within live-action footage
Mouth and snout digitally animated
Eyes are modeled on those of a lizard—they move, blink, open, and close.

Take It to the NET For more information about computer animation, go to **www.PHSchool.com**.
Web Code: afe-1253

Chapter 1 Extra Practice

Lesson 1-1 Find the next two terms in each sequence.

1. 12, 17, 22, 27, 32, . . .

2. 1, 1.1, 1.11, 1.111, 1.1111, . . .

3. 5000, 1000, 200, 40, . . .

4. 1, 12, 123, 1234, . . .

5. 3, 0.3, 0.03, 0.003, . . .

6. 1, 4, 9, 16, 25, . . .

Lessons 1-2 and 1-3 Write *true* or *false*.

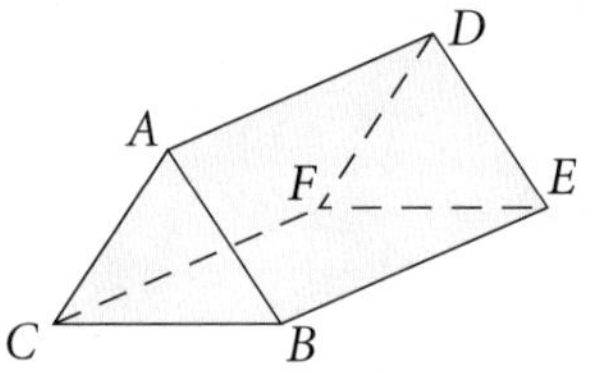

7. A, D, F are coplanar.

8. $\overleftrightarrow{AC}$ and $\overleftrightarrow{FE}$ are coplanar.

9. A, B, E are coplanar.

10. D, A, B, E are coplanar.

11. $\overleftrightarrow{FC} \parallel \overleftrightarrow{EF}$

12. plane $ABC \parallel$ plane FDE

13. $\overleftrightarrow{BC}$ and $\overleftrightarrow{DF}$ are skew lines.

14. $\overleftrightarrow{AD}$ and $\overleftrightarrow{EB}$ are skew lines.

15. $\overleftrightarrow{DE} \parallel \overleftrightarrow{CF}$

16. D, E, and B are collinear.

Lessons 1-4 and 1-5 Use the figure at the right for Exercises 17–22.

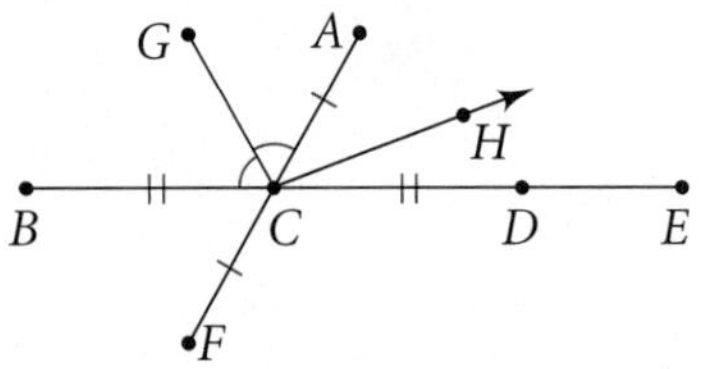

17. If $BC = 12$ and $CE = 15$, then $BE =$ ■.

18. ■ is the angle bisector of ■.

19. Algebra $BC = 3x + 2$ and $CD = 5x - 10$. Solve for x.

20. Algebra If $AC = 5x - 16$ and $CF = 2x - 4$, then $AF =$ ■.

21. $m\angle BCG = 60$, $m\angle GCA =$ ■, and $m\angle BCA =$ ■.

22. $m\angle ACD = 60$ and $m\angle DCH = 20$. Find $m\angle HCA$.

Lesson 1-5 Make a diagram larger than the given one. Then do the construction.

23. Construct the perpendicular bisector of $\overline{AB}$.

24. Construct $\angle A$ so that $m\angle A = m\angle 1 + m\angle 2$.

25. Construct the angle bisector of $\angle 1$.

26. Construct $\overline{FG}$ so that $FG = AB + CD$.

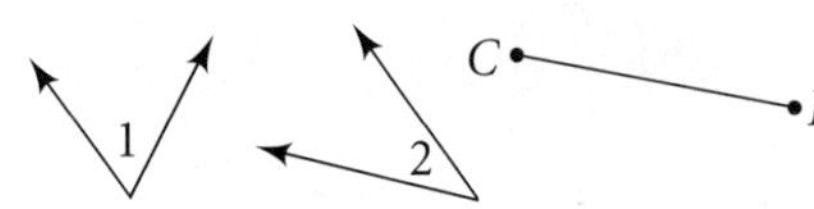

Lesson 1-6 (a) Find the distance between the points to the nearest tenth.
(b) Find the coordinates of the midpoint of the segments with the given endpoints.

27. $A(2, 1), B(3, 0)$

28. $R(5, 2), S(-2, 4)$

29. $Q(-7, -4), T(6, 10)$

30. $C(-8, -1), D(-5, -11)$

31. $J(0, -5), N(3, 4)$

32. $Y(-2, 8), Z(3, -5)$

Lesson 1-7 Find the perimeter (or circumference) and area of each figure.

33.

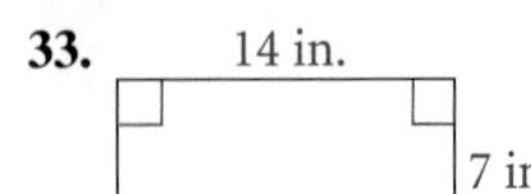

34.

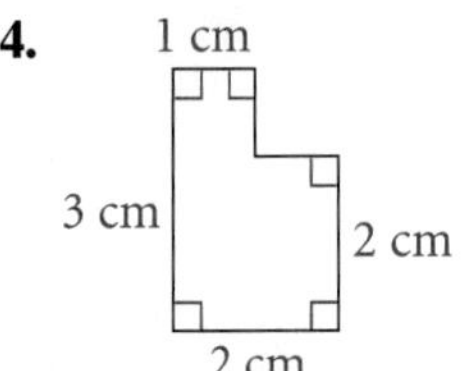

35.

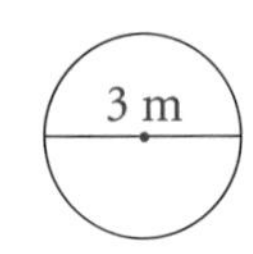

36.

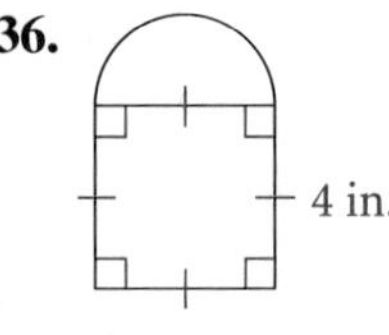

Extra Practice

Lessons 2-1 and 2-2 For each of the statements, write the conditional form and then the converse of the conditional. If the converse is true, combine the statements as a biconditional.

1. The number one is the smallest positive square.

2. Rectangles have four sides.

3. A square with area 100 m^2 has sides that measure 10 m.

4. Two numbers that add up to be less than 12 have a product less than 37.

5. Three points on the same line are collinear.

Lesson 2-2 Is each statement a good definition? If not, find a counterexample.

6. A circle with center O and radius r is defined by the set of points in a plane a distance r from the point O.

7. A plane is defined by two lines.

8. Segments with the same length are congruent.

Lesson 2-3 Using the statements below, apply the Law of Detachment or the Law of Syllogism to draw a conclusion.

9. If Jorge can't raise money, he can't buy a new car. Jorge can't raise money.

10. If Shauna is early for her meeting, she will gain a promotion. If Shauna wakes up early, she will be early for her meeting. Shauna wakes up early.

11. If Linda's band wins the contest, they will win \$500. If Linda practices, her band will win the contest. Linda practices.

12. If Brendan learns the audition song, he will be selected for the chorus. If Brendan stays after school to practice, he will learn the audition song. Brendan stays after school to practice.

Lesson 2-4 Algebra You are given that $2c^2 = 2bc + \frac{ac}{2}$ with $c \neq 0$. Show that $4b = 4c - a$ by filling in the blanks.

13. a. $2c^2 = 2bc + \frac{ac}{2}$ — **a.** Given

b. $4c^2 = 4bc + ac$ — **b.** __?__ and __?__

c. $4c = 4b + a$ — **c.** __?__ and Distributive Property

d. __?__ — **d.** Subtraction Property

e. $4b = 4c - a$ — **e.** __?__

Lesson 2-5 Algebra Find the value of x.

14.

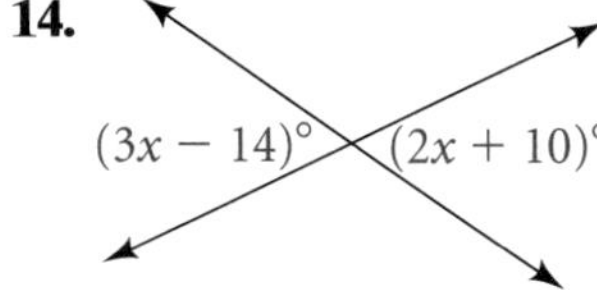

15.

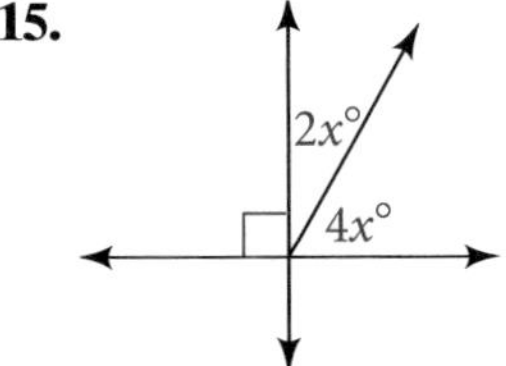

16.

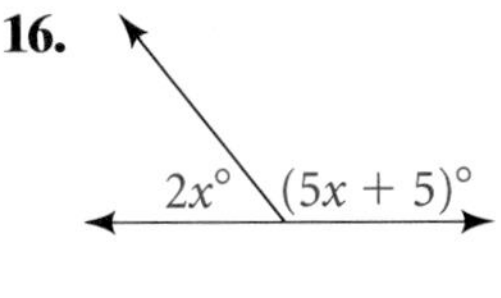

Chapter 3 Extra Practice

Lesson 3-1 **Find $m\angle 1$ and then $m\angle 2$. State the theorems or postulates that justify your answers.**

1. 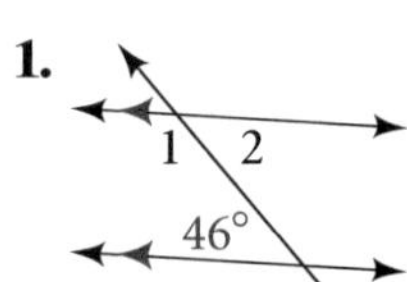

2. 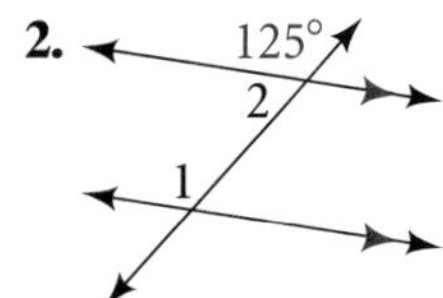

3. 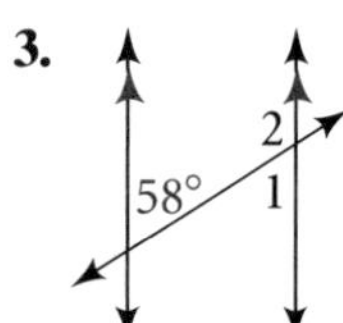

4. 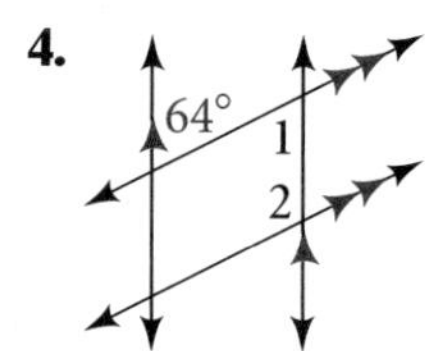

Lesson 3-2 **Refer to the diagram at the right. Use the given information to determine which lines, if any, must be parallel. If any lines are parallel, use a theorem or postulate to tell why.**

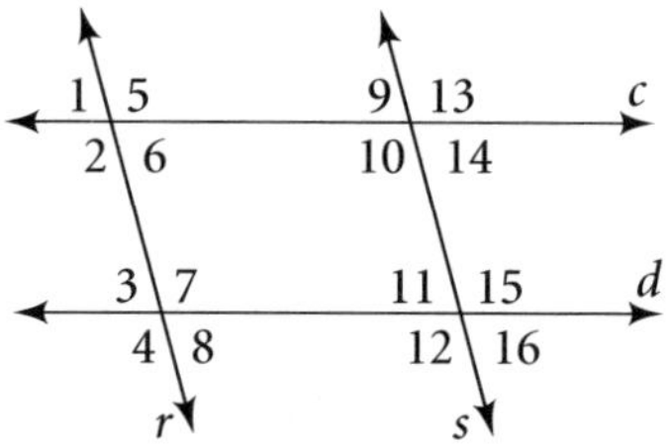

5. $\angle 9 \cong \angle 14$

6. $\angle 1 \cong \angle 9$

7. $\angle 2$ is supplementary to $\angle 3$.

8. $\angle 7 \cong \angle 14$

9. $m\angle 6 = 60, m\angle 13 = 120$

10. $\angle 4 \cong \angle 13$

11. $\angle 3$ is supplementary to $\angle 10$.

12. $\angle 10 \cong \angle 15$

Lesson 3-3 **Use a protractor and a centimeter ruler to measure the angles and the sides of each triangle. Classify each triangle by its angles and sides.**

13. 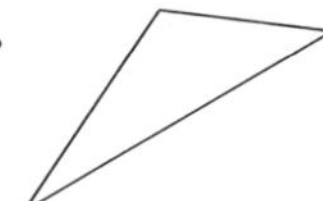

14.  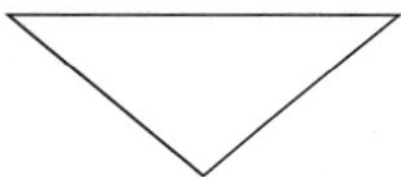

15. 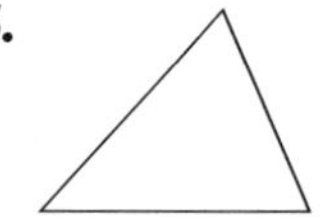

16. 

Lessons 3-3 and 3-4 **Algebra** **Find the value of each variable.**

17. 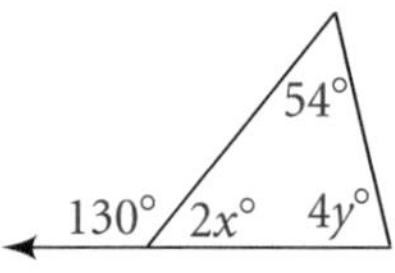

18.

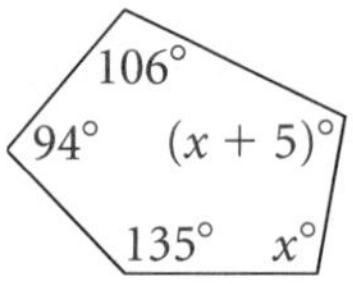

19. 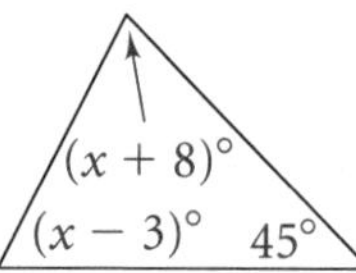

20. 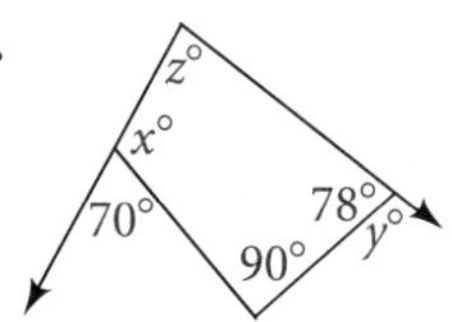

Lessons 3-5 **Write an equation in point-slope form of the line that contains the given points.**

21. $A(4, 2), B(6, -3)$

22. $C(-1, -1), D(1, 1)$

23. $F(3, -5), G(-5, 3)$

24. $K(5, 0), L(-5, 2)$

Lessons 3-5 and 3-6 **Algebra** **Graph each pair of lines and state whether they are parallel, perpendicular, or neither. Explain.**

25. $y = 4x - 8$
$y = 4x - 2$

26. $13y - x = 7$
$7 - \frac{y}{2} = x$

27. $y = \frac{-4}{3}x + 2$
$\frac{4}{3}y = x - 1$

28. $\frac{3}{5}y = -x + \frac{3}{2}$
$3x - \frac{15}{3}y = 0$

Lesson 3-7 **Use the segments for each construction.**

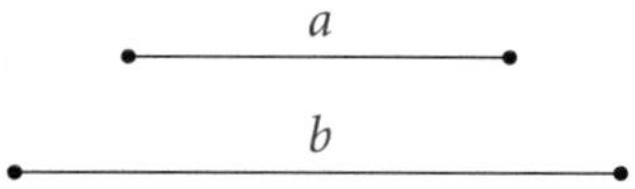

29. Construct a square with side length $2a$.

30. Construct a quadrilateral with one pair of parallel sides each of length $2b$.

31. Construct a rectangle with sides b and a.

Extra Practice

Lesson 4-1 **$\triangle SAT \cong \triangle GRE$. Complete each congruence statement.**

1. $\angle S \cong$? **2.** $\overline{GR} \cong$? **3.** $\angle E \cong$?

4. $\overline{AT} \cong$? **5.** $\triangle ERG \cong$? **6.** $\overline{EG} \cong$?

7. $\triangle REG \cong$? **8.** $\angle R \cong$?

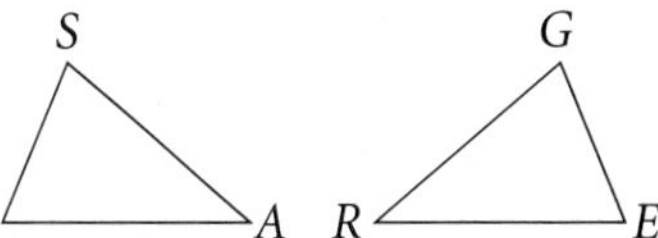

State whether the figures are congruent. Justify each answer.

9. $\triangle ABF$; $\triangle EDC$

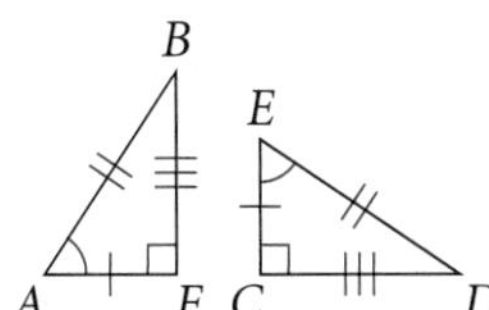

10. $\triangle TUV$; $\triangle UVW$

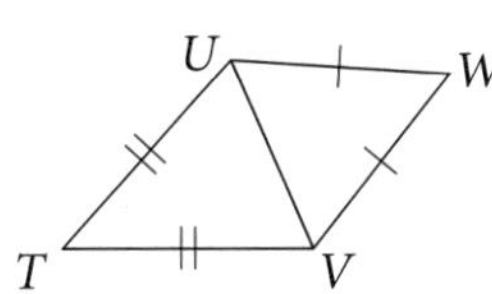

11. $\square XYZV$; $\square UTZV$

T U Y Z 120° 60° X V

12. $\triangle ABD$; $\triangle EDB$

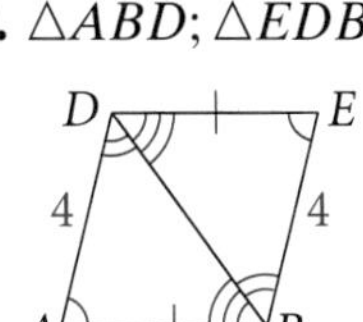

Lessons 4-2 and 4-3 **Where possible, explain how you would use SSS, SAS, ASA, or AAS to prove the triangles congruent. If not possible, write *not possible.***

13.

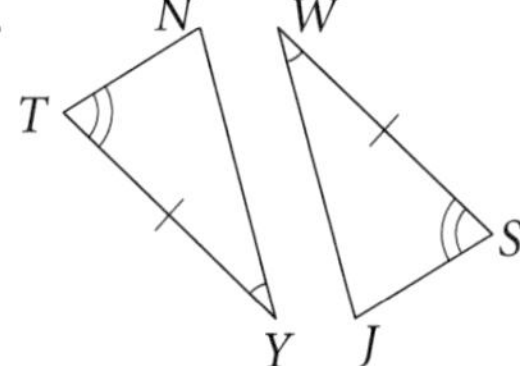

14.

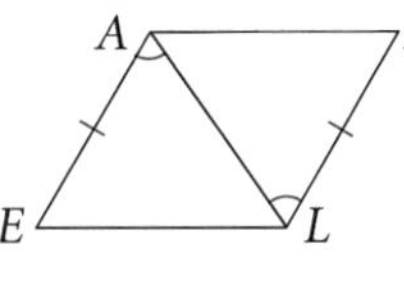

15.

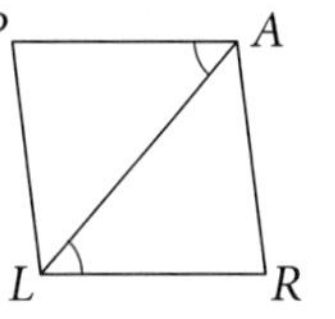

16.

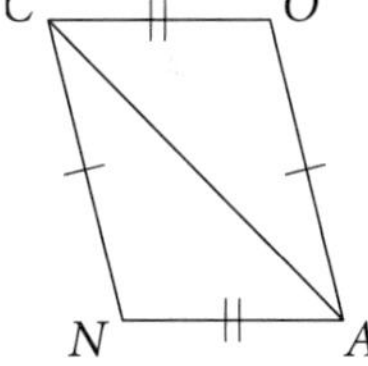

Lesson 4-4 **Explain how you would use SSS, SAS, ASA, or HL with CPCTC to prove each statement.**

17. $\angle MLN \cong \angle ONL$

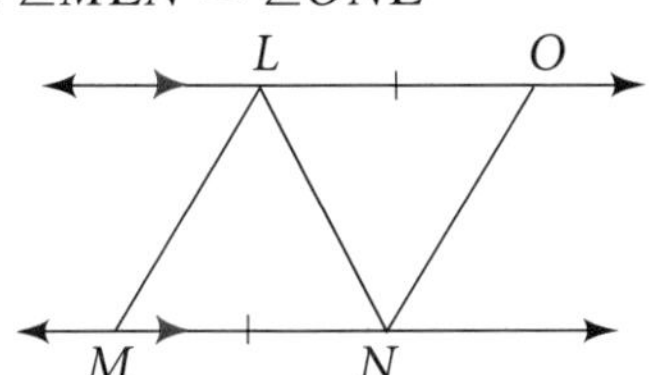

18. $\overline{TO} \cong \overline{ES}$

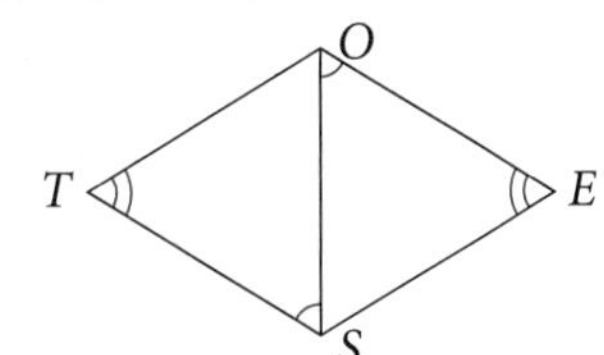

19. $\overline{MB} \cong \overline{RI}$

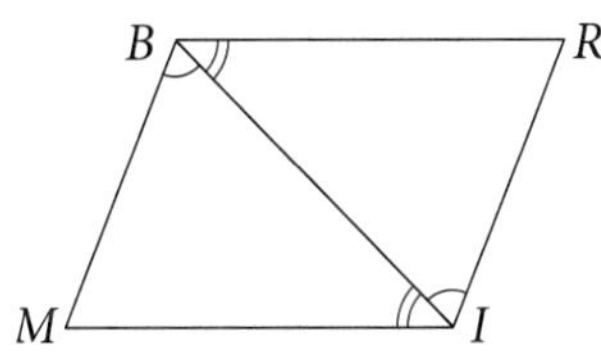

Lessons 4-5 and 4-6 **Algebra** **Find the value of each variable.**

20.

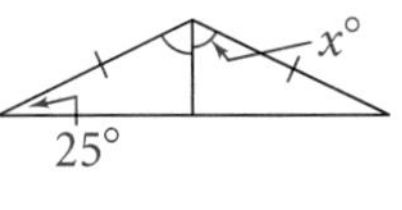

21.

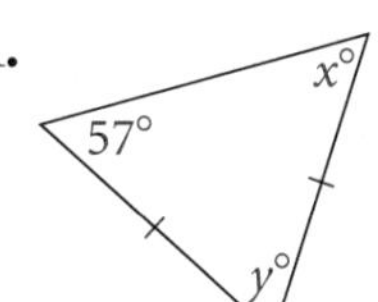

22.

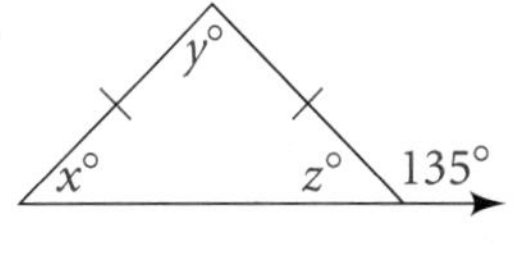

23.

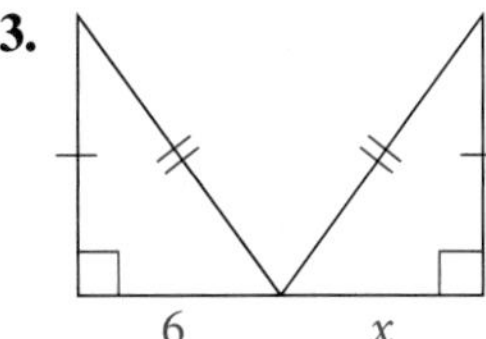

Lesson 4-7 **Name a pair of overlapping congruent triangles in each diagram. State whether the triangles are congruent by SSS, SAS, ASA, AAS, or HL.**

24.

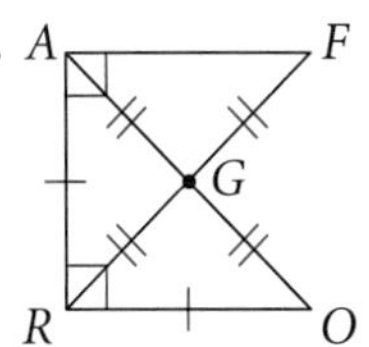

25.

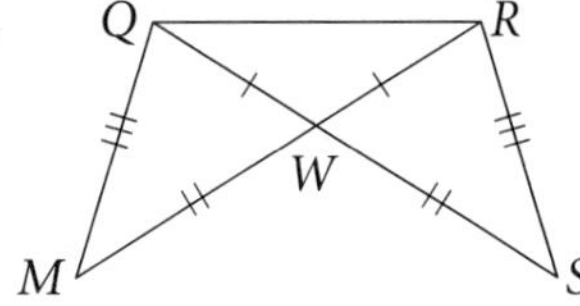

26.

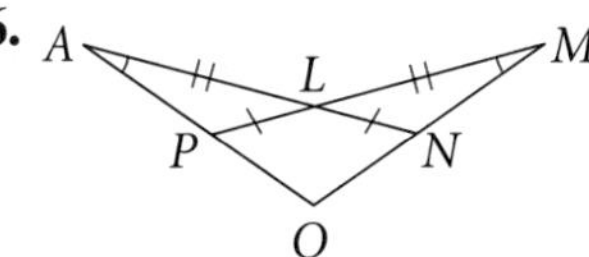

Chapter 5

Extra Practice

Lesson 5-1 Algebra Find the value of *x*.

1. 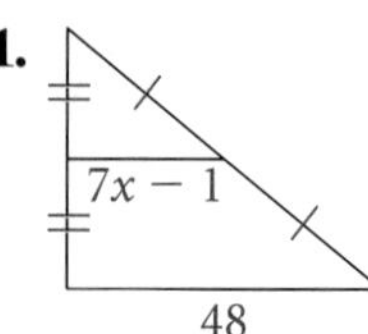

2. 48

3x

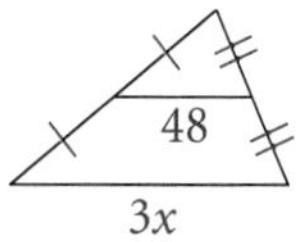

3. 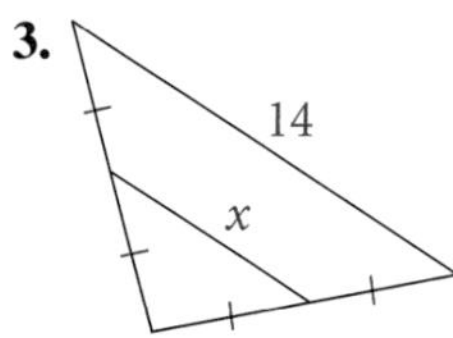

4. 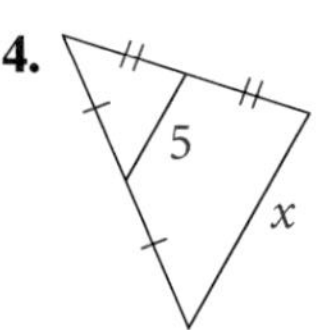

Lessons 5-1 and 5-2 Algebra Use the figure at the right.

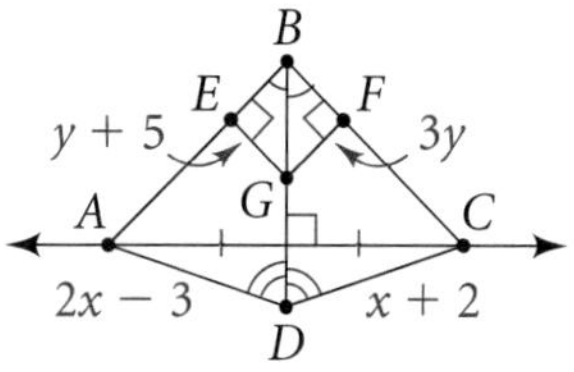

B E F y + 5 3y A G C 2x − 3 x + 2 D

5. Find the value of x.

6. Find the length of $\overline{AD}$.

7. Find the value of y.

8. Find the length of $\overline{EG}$.

Lesson 5-3 Find the center of the circle that you can circumscribe about $\triangle ABC$.

9. $A(2, 8)$ $B(0, 8)$ $C(2, 2)$

10. $A(-3, 6)$ $B(-3, -2)$ $C(7, 6)$

11. $A(4, 3)$ $B(-4, -3)$ $C(4, -3)$

12. $A(-10, -2)$ $B(-2, -2)$ $C(-2, -10)$

Is $\overline{AB}$ an angle bisector, altitude, median, or perpendicular bisector?

13. 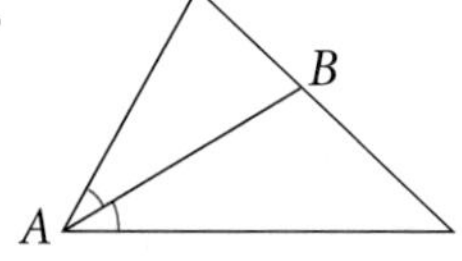

14. 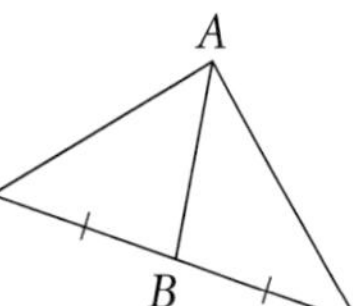

15. 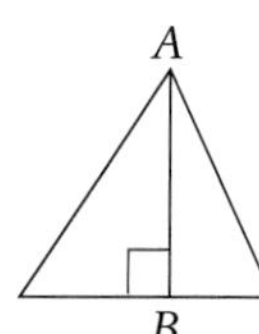

16. 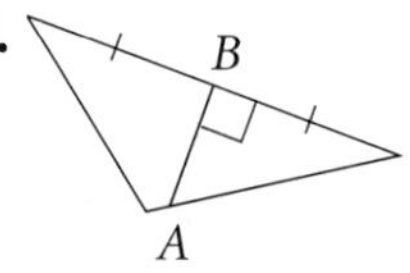

Lesson 5-4 Write (a) the inverse and (b) the contrapositive of each statement.

17. If two angles are vertical, then they are congruent.

18. If figures are similar, then their side lengths are proportional.

19. If a car is blue, then it has no doors.

Write the first step of an indirect proof of each statement.

20. $\triangle ABC$ is a right triangle.

21. Points J, K, and L are collinear.

22. Lines ℓ and m are not parallel.

23. $\square XYZV$ is a square.

Lesson 5-5 List the sides of each triangle in order from shortest to longest.

24. 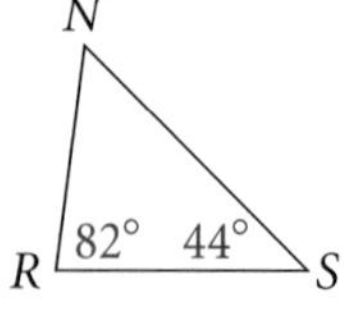

25. 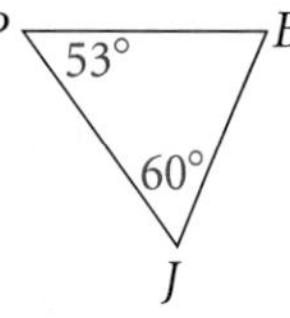

26. 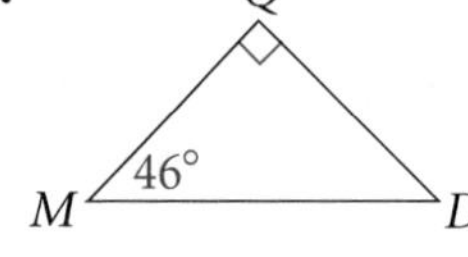

27. 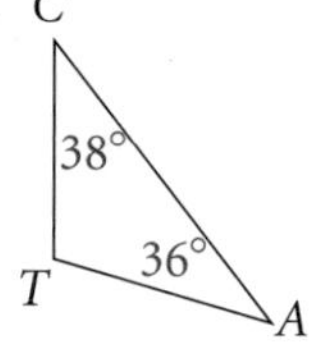

Can a triangle have sides with the given lengths? Explain.

28. 2 in., 3 in., 5 in.

29. 9 cm, 11 cm, 15 cm

30. 8 ft, 9 ft, 18 ft

Chapter 6

Extra Practice

Lesson 6-1 **Graph the given points. Use slope and the Distance Formula to determine the most precise name for quadrilateral *ABCD*.**

1. $A(3, 5), B(6, 5), C(2, 1), D(1, 3)$

2. $A(-1, 1), B(3, -1), C(-1, -3), D(-5, -1)$

3. $A(2, 1), B(5, -1), C(4, -4), D(1, -2)$

4. $A(-4, 5), B(-1, 3), C(-3, 0), D(-6, 2)$

Lesson 6-2 **Algebra** **Find the values of the variables in each parallelogram.**

5.

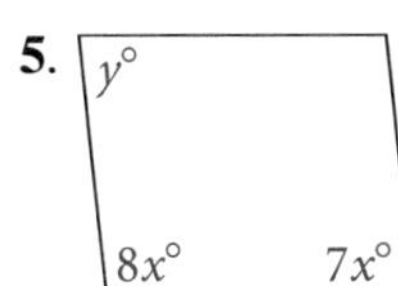

6.

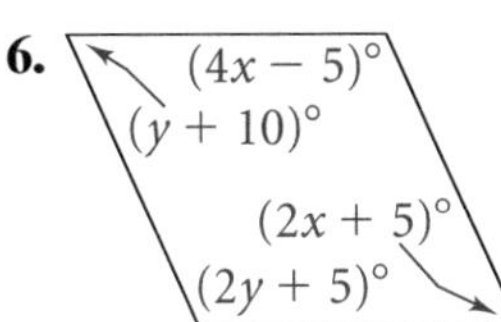

7.

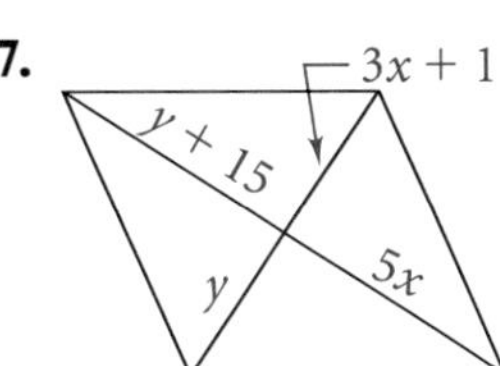

8.

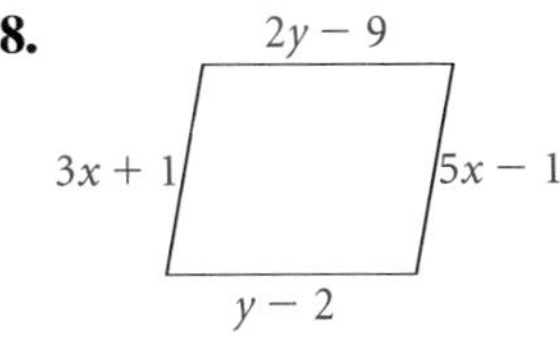

Lesson 6-3 **Based on the markings, decide whether each figure must be a parallelogram.**

9. 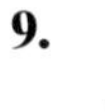

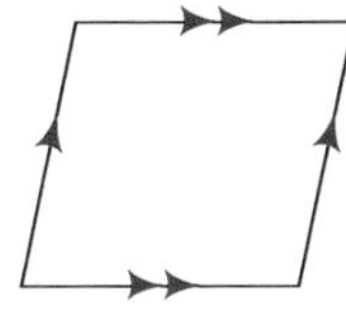

10. 

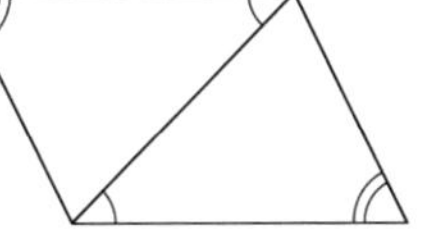

11. 

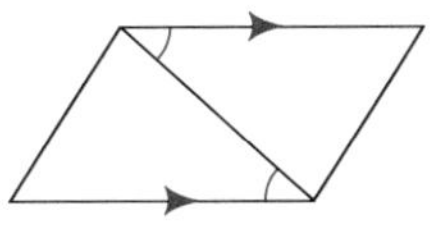

12. 

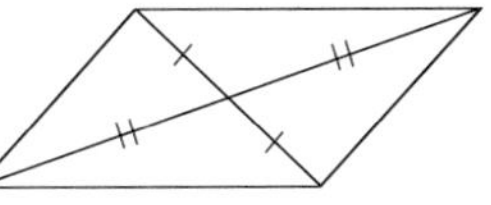

Lesson 6-4 **For each parallelogram, determine the most precise name and find the measures of the numbered angles.**

13.

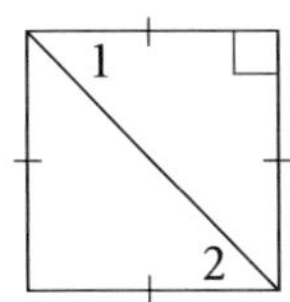

14.

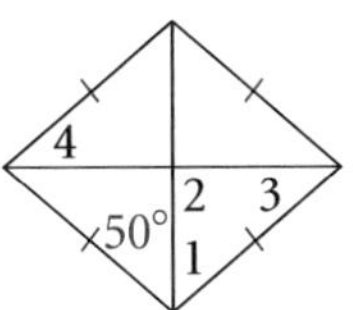

15.

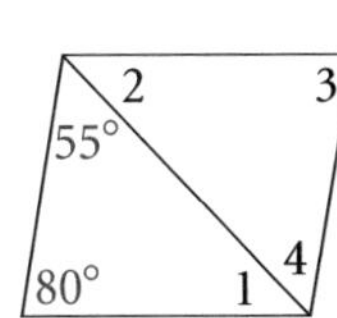

16.

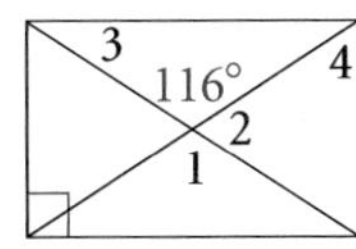

Lesson 6-5 **Find $m\angle 1$ and $m\angle 2$.**

17.

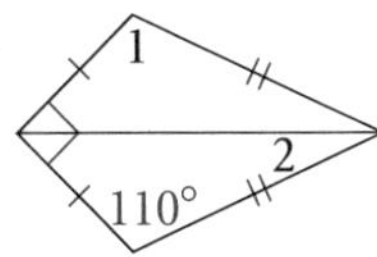

18.

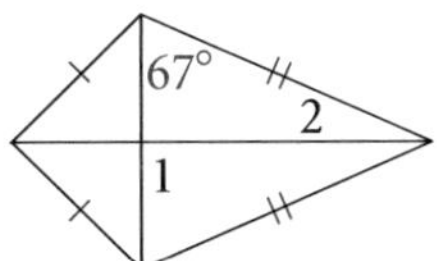

19.

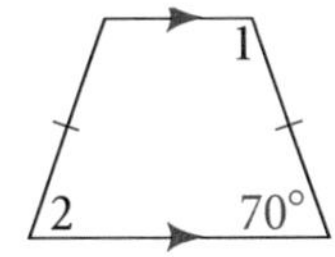

20.

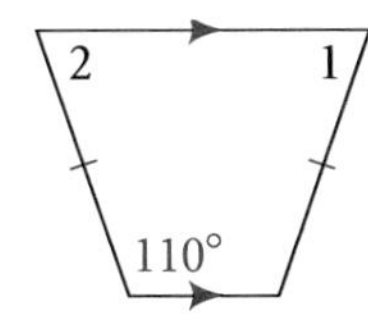

Lesson 6-6 **Give coordinates for points *D* and *S* without using any new variables.**

21. rectangle

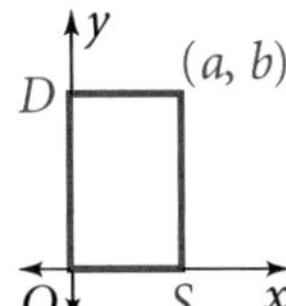

22. parallelogram

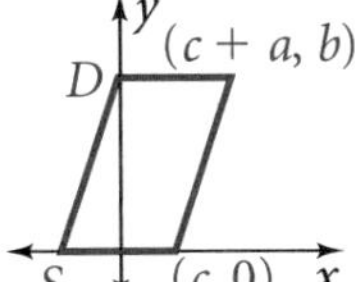

23. rhombus

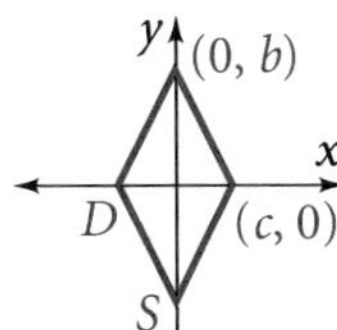

24. square

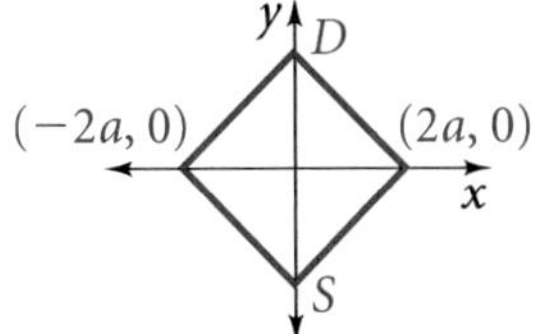

Lesson 6-7

25. For the figure in Exercise 24, use coordinate geometry to prove that the midpoints of the sides of a square determine a square.

Chapter 7

Extra Practice

Lesson 7-1 Find the perimeter and area of each figure.

1.
4.33 ft
5 ft
5 ft

2. 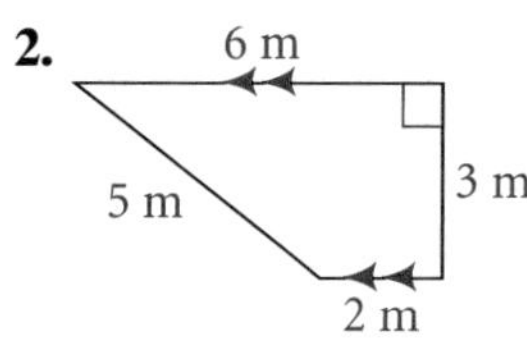

3. 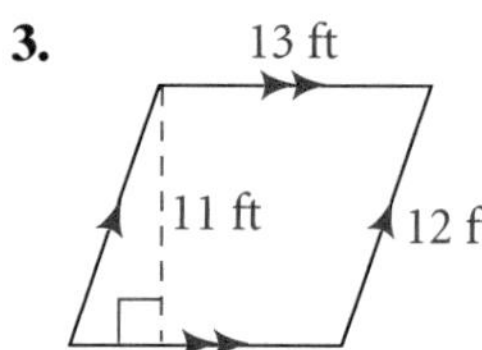

4. 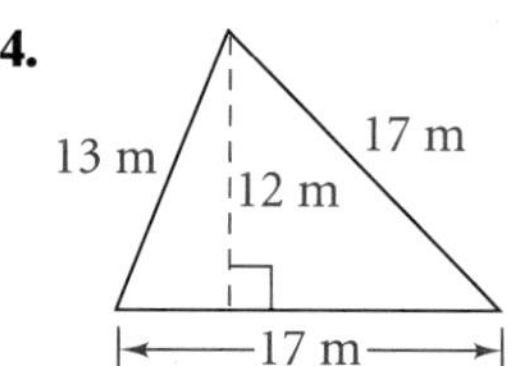

Lessons 7-2 and 7-3 Find the value of x. If your answer is not a whole number, leave it in simplest radical form.

5. 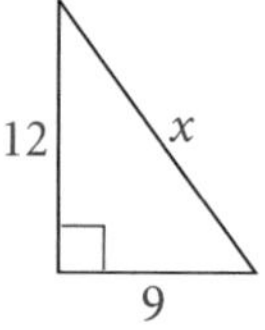

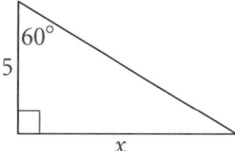

6.
60°
5
x

7.
9
x
6

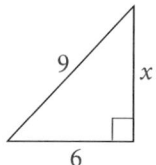

8. 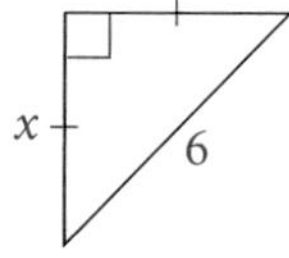

Lessons 7-4 and 7-5 Find the area of each trapezoid or regular polygon. Leave your answer in simplest radical form.

9. 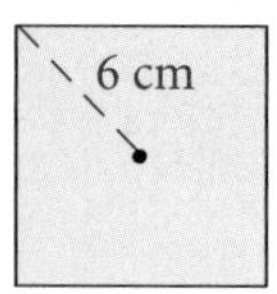

10. 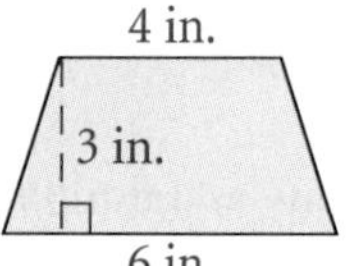

11. 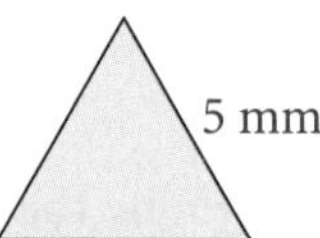

12. 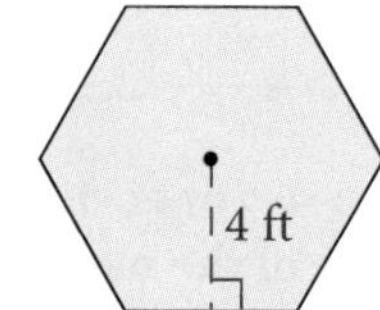

Lesson 7-6 (a) Find the circumference of each circle. (b) Find the length of the arc shown in red. Leave your answers in terms of π.

13. 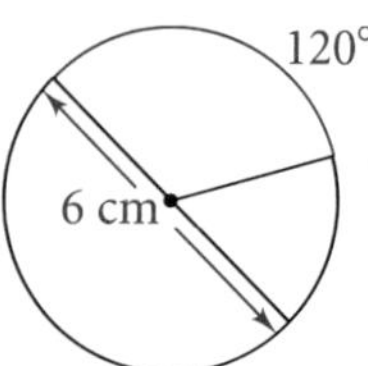

14. 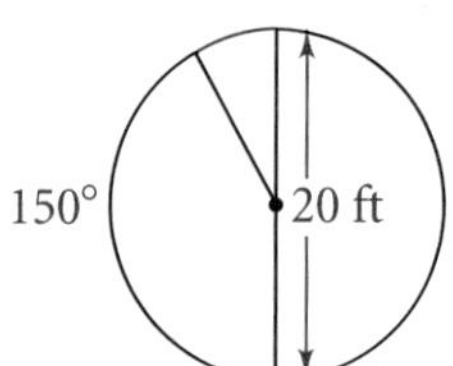

15. 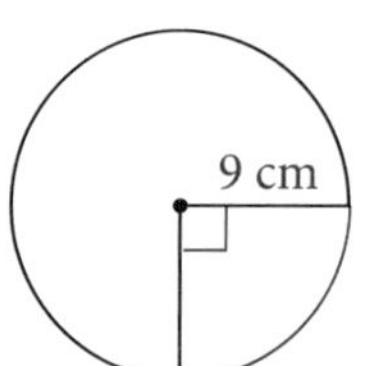

16. 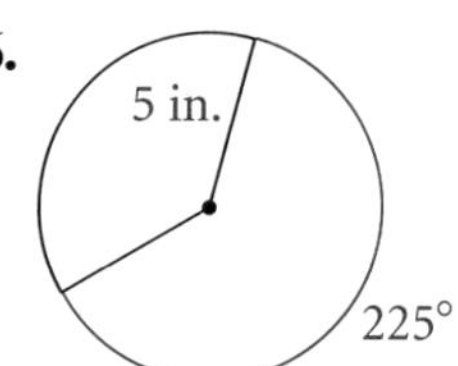

Lesson 7-7 Find the area of each shaded sector or segment. Leave your answers in terms of π.

17. 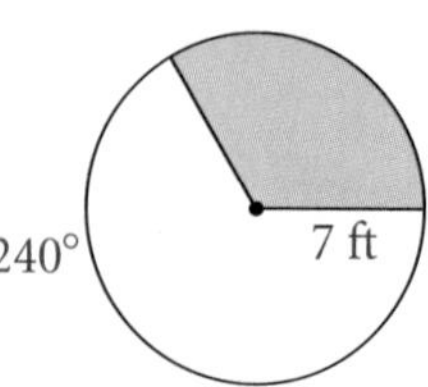

18. 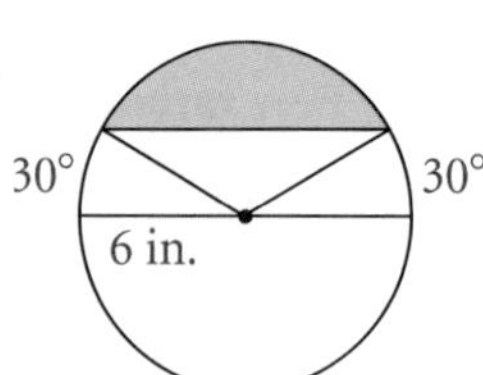

19. 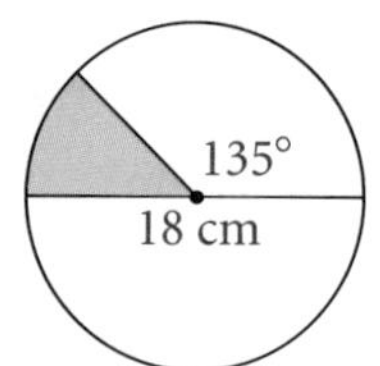

20. 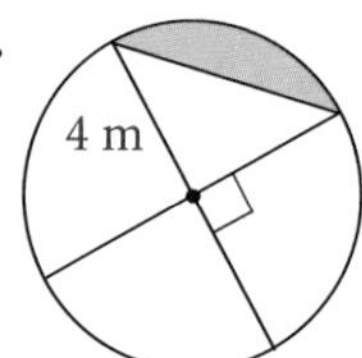

Lesson 7-8 Darts are thrown at random at each of the boards shown. If a dart hits the board, find the probability that it will land in the shaded area.

21. 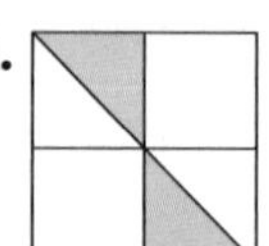

22. 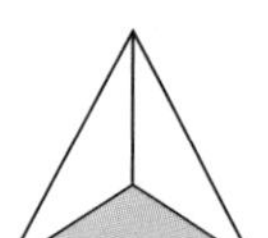

23. 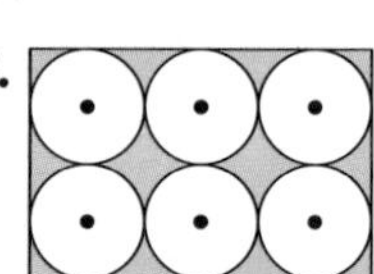

24. 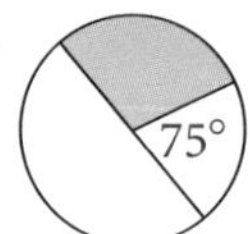

Chapter 8 Extra Practice

Lesson 8-1 Algebra Solve each proportion.

1. $\frac{2}{3} = \frac{x}{15}$
2. $\frac{4}{9} = \frac{16}{x}$
3. $\frac{x}{4} = \frac{6}{12}$
4. $\frac{2}{x} = \frac{3}{9}$
5. $\frac{3}{4} = \frac{x}{6}$
6. $\frac{3}{7} = \frac{9}{x}$

Lesson 8-2 Algebra The polygons are similar. Find the values of the variables.

7. 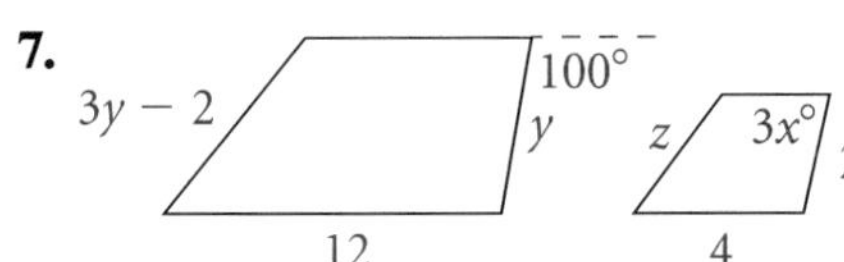

8. 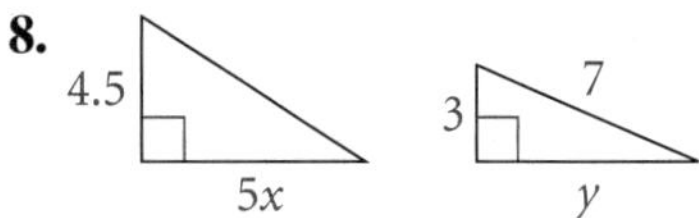

9. 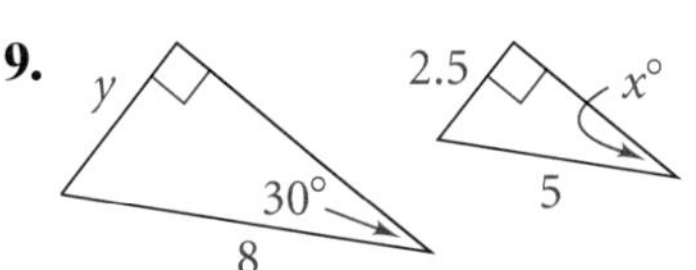

10. 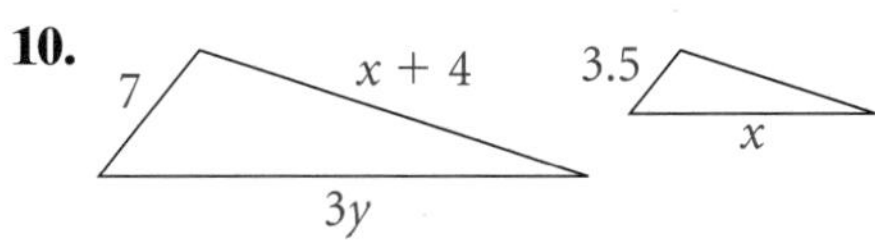

Lesson 8-3 Can you prove that the triangles are similar? If so, write a similarity statement and tell whether you would use AA~, SAS~, or SSS~.

11. 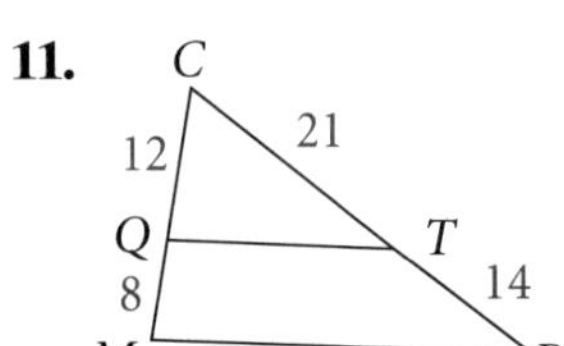

12. 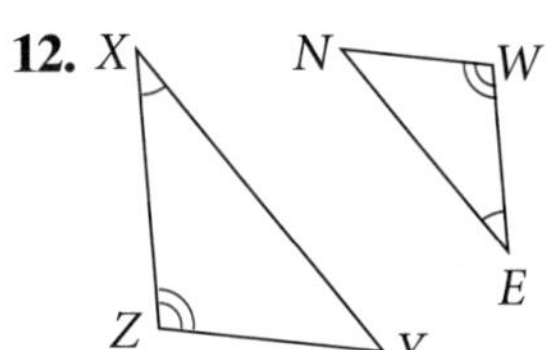

13. 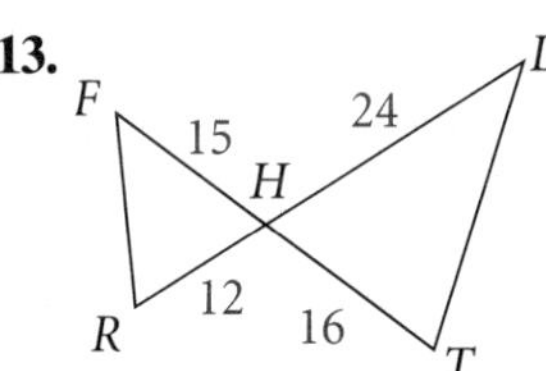

Lessons 8-4 and 8-5 Algebra Find the value of each variable. If an answer is not a whole number, leave it in simplest radical form.

14. 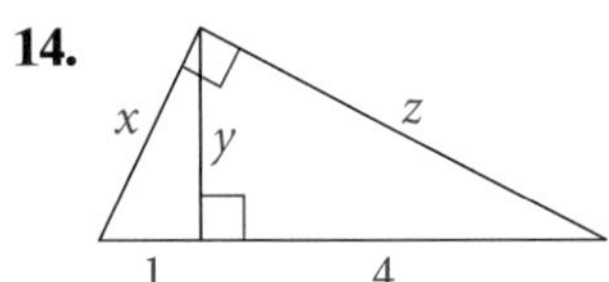

15. 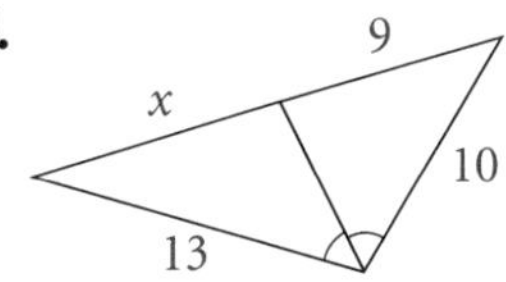

16. 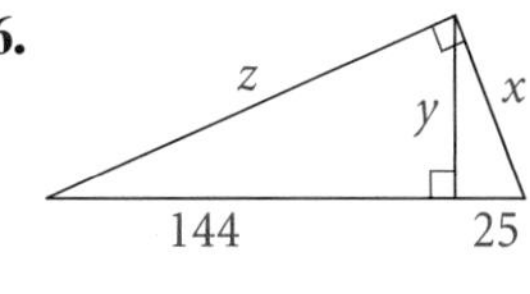

17. 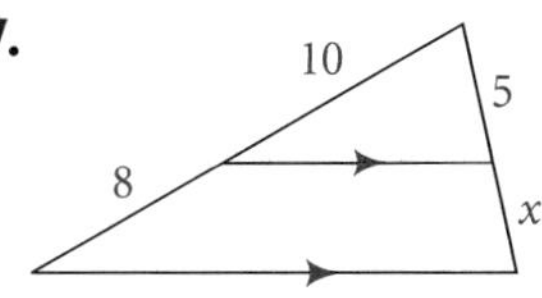

18. 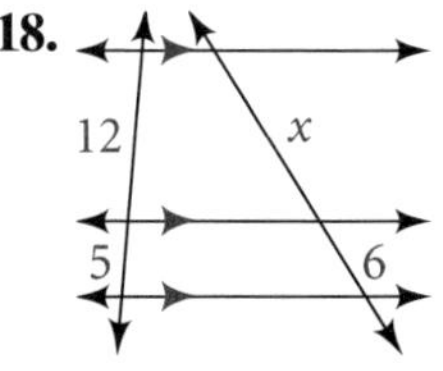

19. 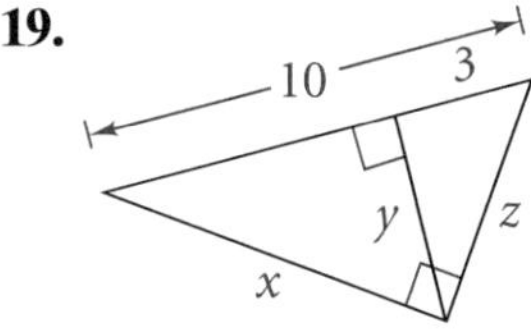

20. 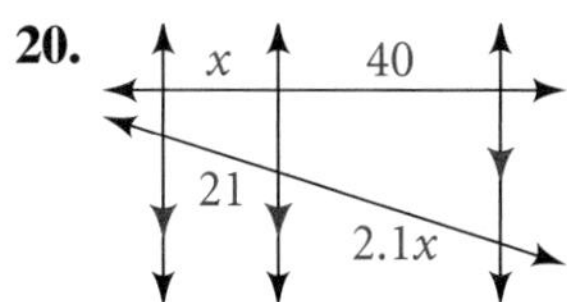

21. 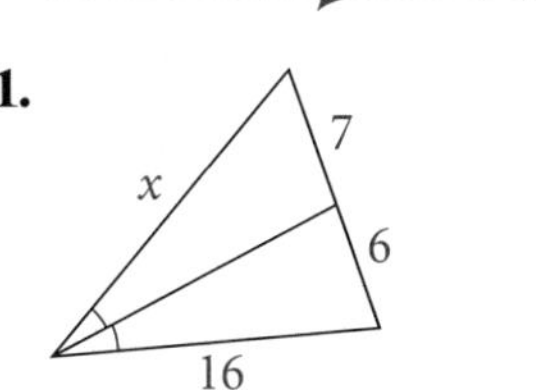

Lesson 8-6 Find the ratio of the perimeters and the ratio of the areas of the blue figure to the red figure.

22. 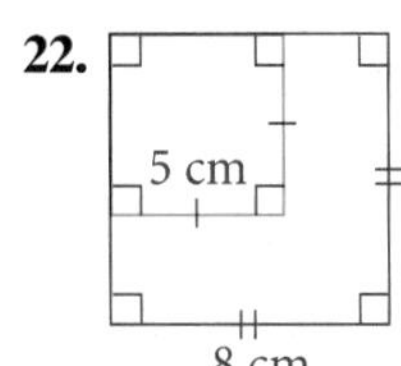

23. 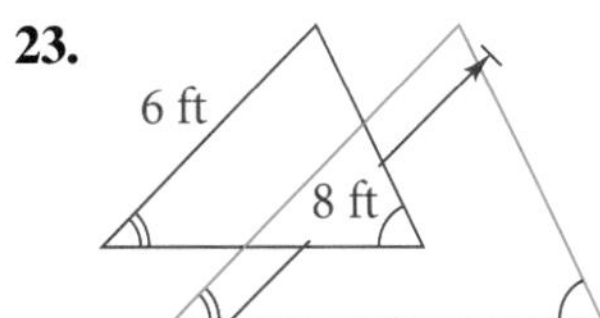

24. 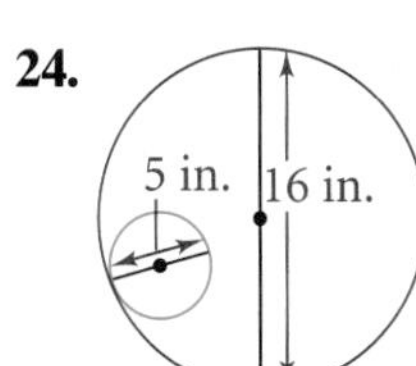

Chapter 9 Extra Practice

Lessons 9-1 and 9-2 Find the value of *x*. Round lengths of segments to the nearest tenth and angle measures to the nearest degree.

1. 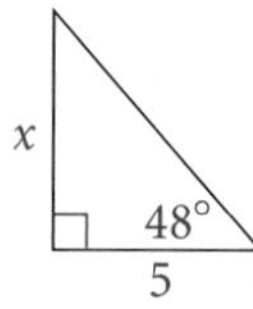

2. 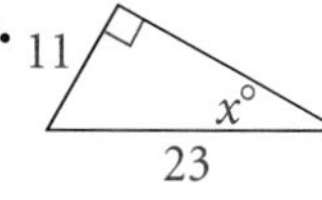

3. 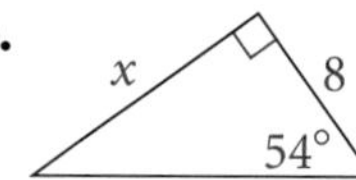

4. 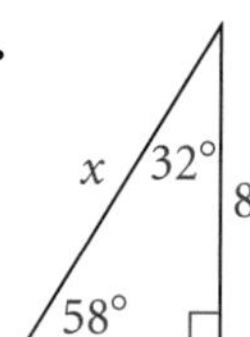

5. 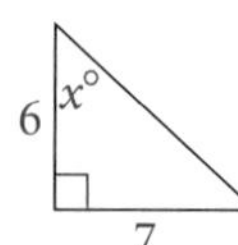

6. 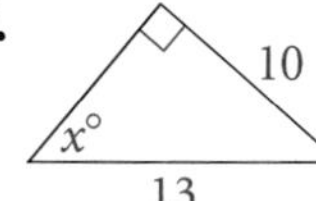

7. 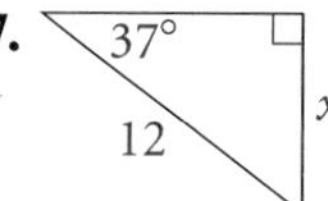

8. 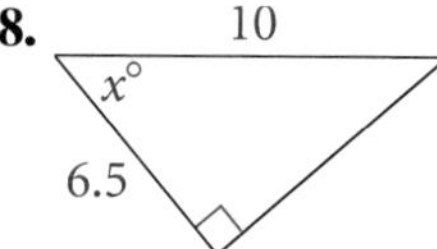

Lesson 9-3 Solve each problem. Round your answers to the nearest foot.

9. A couple is taking a balloon ride. After 25 minutes aloft, they measure the angle of depression from the balloon to its launch place as 16°. They are 180 ft above ground. Find the distance from the balloon to its launch place.

10. A surveyor is 300 ft from the base of an apartment building. The angle of elevation to the top of the building is 24°, and her angle-measuring device is 5 ft above the ground. Find the height of the building.

11. Oriana is flying a kite. She lets out 105 ft of string and anchors it to the ground. She determines that the angle of elevation of the kite is 48°. Find the height the kite is from the ground.

12. A plane flying at 10,000 ft spots a hot air balloon in the distance. The balloon is 9000 ft above ground. The angle of depression from the plane to the balloon is 30°. Find the distance from the plane to the balloon.

Lesson 9-4 (a) Describe each vector as an ordered pair. Give the coordinates to the nearest unit. (b) Write the resultant of each pair of vectors as an ordered pair.

13. 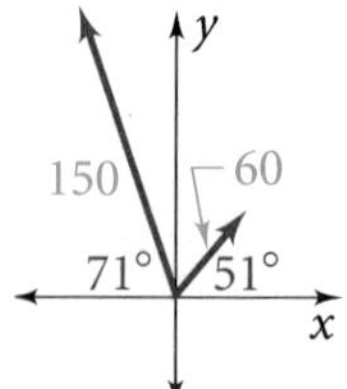

14. 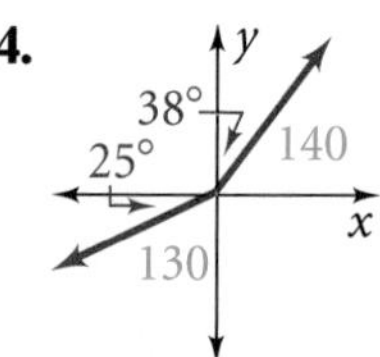

15. 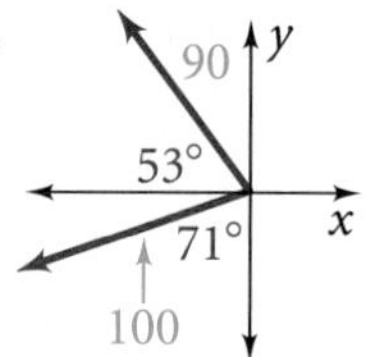

16. 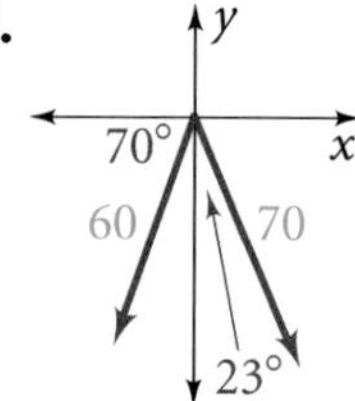

Lesson 9-5 Find the area of each polygon. Round your answers to the nearest tenth.

17. 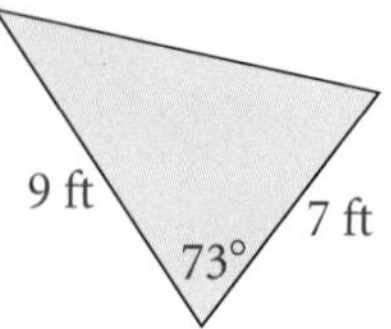

18. 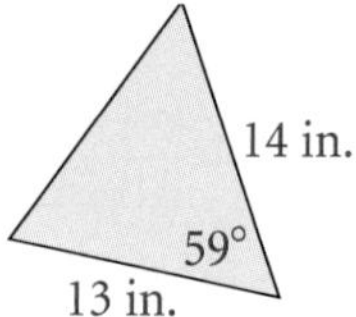

19. 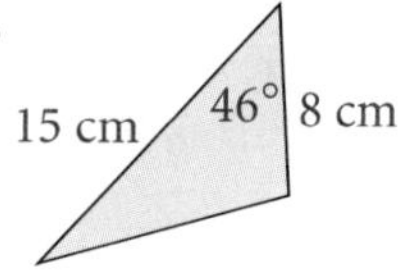

20. 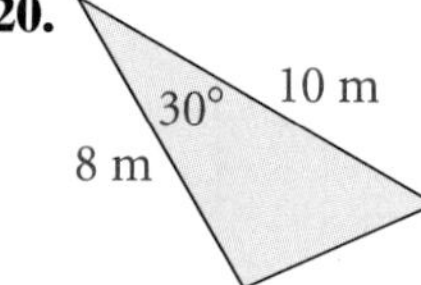

21. a regular hexagon with an apothem of 3 ft

22. a regular octagon with radius 5 ft

Chapter 10 Extra Practice

Lesson 10-1 **Name the space figure that can be formed by folding each net.**

1. 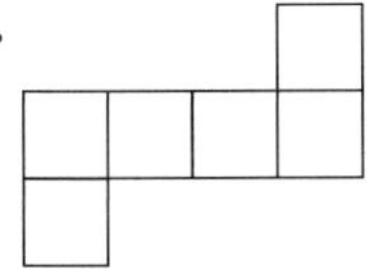

2. 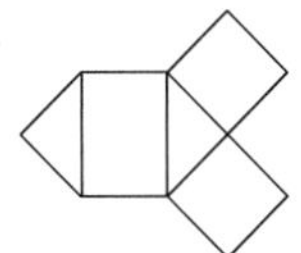

3. 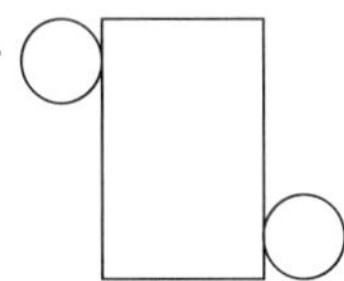

4. 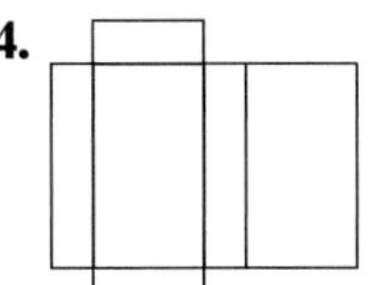

Lesson 10-2 **Create (a) an isometric drawing and (b) an orthographic drawing for each foundation drawing.**

5. 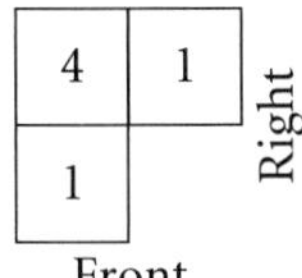

6.

3	3
1	2

Right
Front

7. 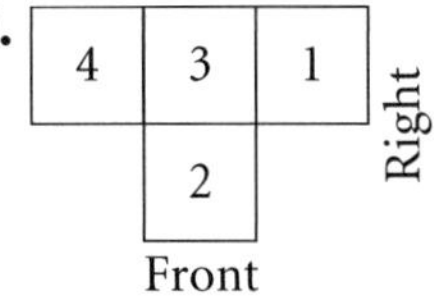

8. 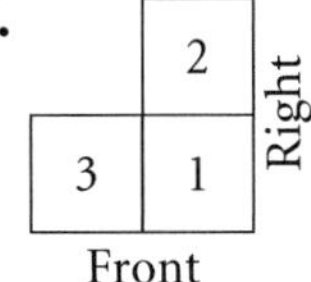

Lessons 10-3 and 10-4 **Find the (a) lateral area and (b) surface area of each figure. Leave your answers in terms of π or in simplest radical form.**

9. 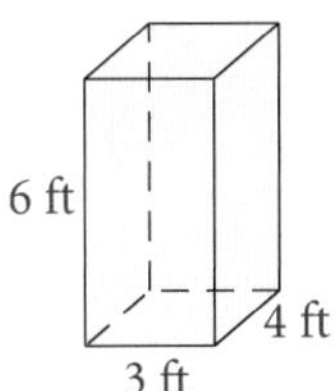

10. 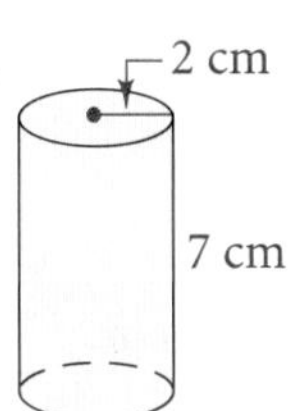

11. 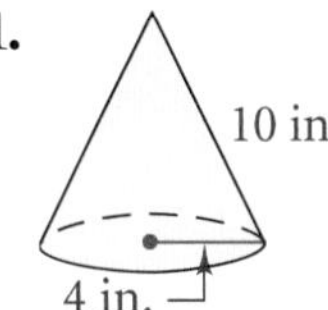

12. 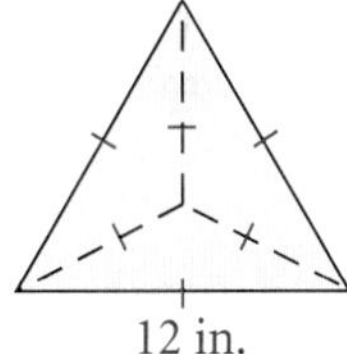

Lessons 10-5 and 10-6 **Find the volume of each figure.**

13. 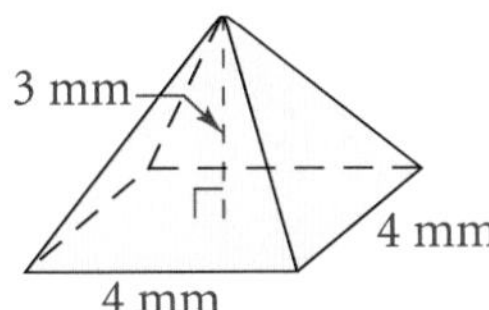

14. 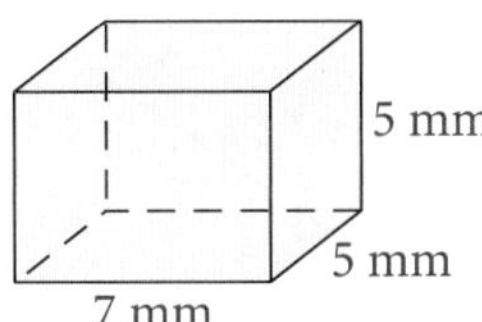

15. 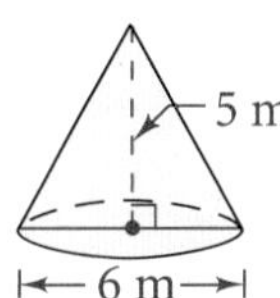

16. 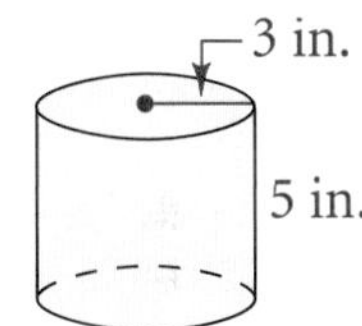

Lesson 10-7 **Find the volume and surface area of a sphere with the given radius or diameter. Give each answer in terms of π and rounded to the nearest whole number.**

17. $r = 5$ cm **18.** $r = 3$ ft **19.** $d = 8$ in.

20. $d = 2$ ft **21.** $r = 0.5$ in. **22.** $d = 9$ m

The surface area of each sphere is given. Find the volume of each sphere in terms of π.

23. 64π m^2 **24.** 16π in^2 **25.** 49π ft^2

Lesson 10-8 **Copy and complete for three similar solids.**

	Similarity Ratio	Ratio of Surface Areas	Ratio of Volumes
26.	2 : 3	■ : ■	■ : ■
27.	■ : ■	25 : 64	■ : ■
28.	■ : ■	■ : ■	27 : 64

Chapter 11 Extra Practice

Lesson 11-1 **Assume that lines that appear to be tangent are tangent. *P* is the center of each circle. Find the value of *x*.**

1. 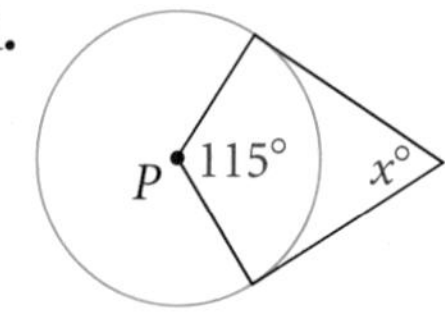

2. 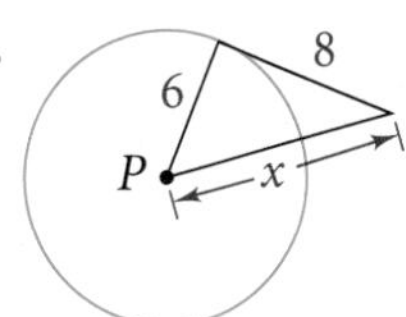

3. 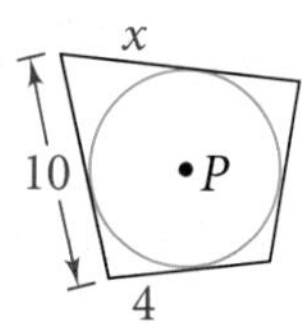

4. 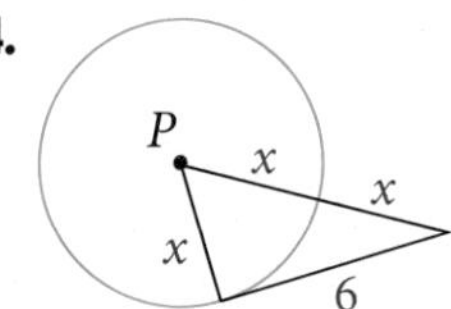

Lessons 11-2 and 11-3 **Algebra** **Find the value of each variable. If your answer is not a whole number, round it to the nearest tenth.**

5. 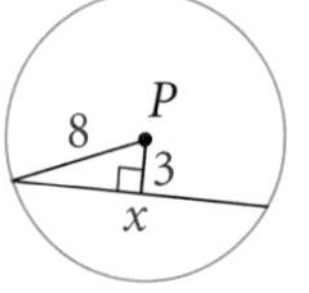

6. 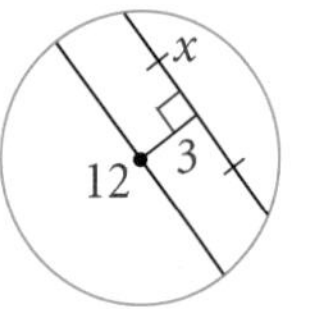

7. 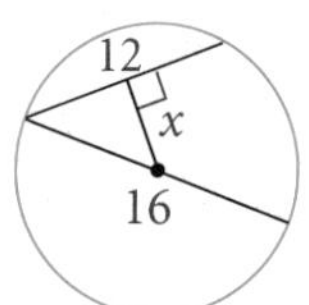

8. 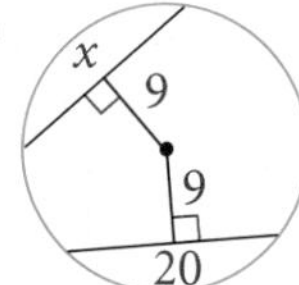

9. 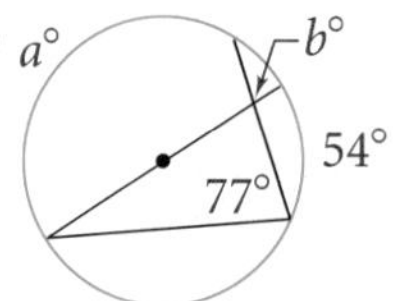

10. 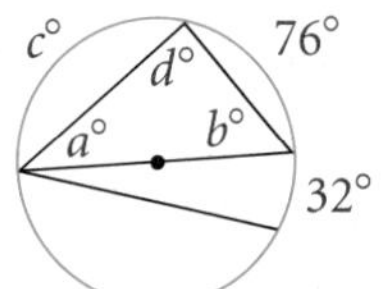

11. 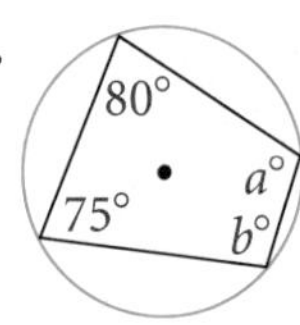

12. 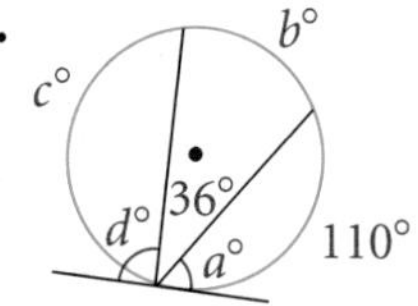

Lesson 11-4 **Algebra** **Assume that lines that appear to be tangent are tangent. Find the value of each variable. If your answer is not a whole number, round it to the nearest tenth.**

13. 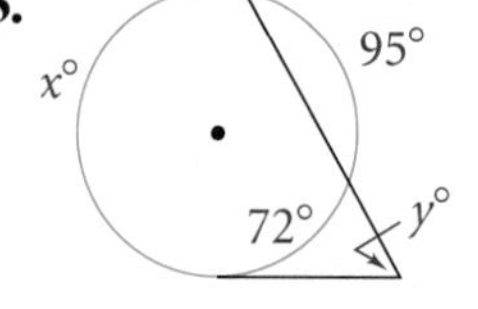

14. 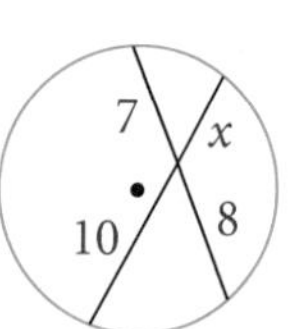

15. 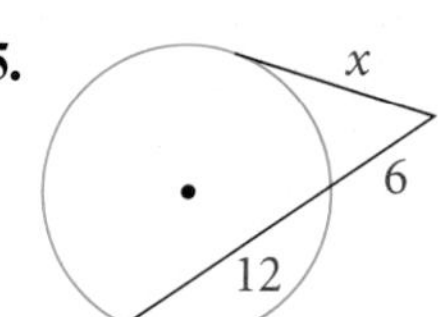

16. 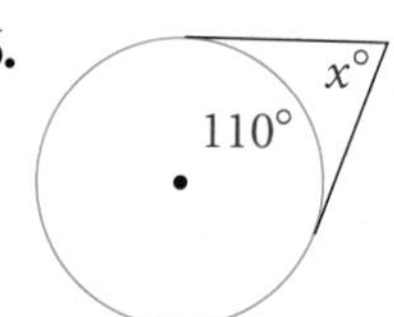

17. 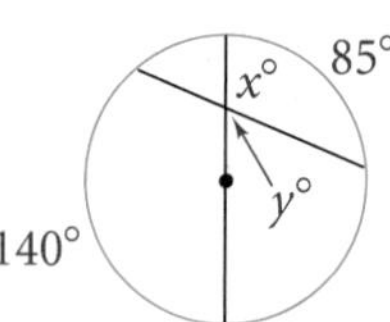

18. 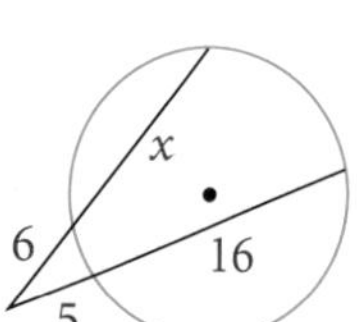

19. 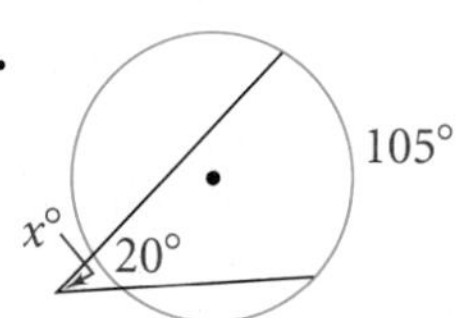

20. 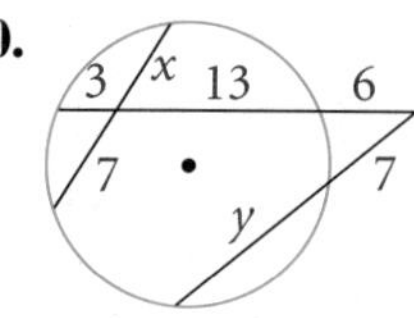

Lesson 11-5 **Write the standard equation for each circle with center *P*.**

21. $P = (0, 0); r = 4$

22. $P = (0, 5); r = 3$

23. $P = (9, -3); r = 7$

24. $P = (-4, 0)$; through $(2, 1)$

25. $P = (-6, -2)$; through $(-8, 1)$

26. $P = (-1, -3); r = 3$

Lesson 11-6 **Draw and describe each locus.**

27. all points in a plane 2 cm from $\overrightarrow{AB}$

28. all points in a plane 3 cm from a circle with $r = 2$ cm

29. all points in space 1.5 in. from a point Q

Chapter 12 Extra Practice

Lesson 12-1 Given points $S(6, 1)$, $U(2, 5)$, and $B(-1, 2)$, draw $\triangle SUB$ and its reflection image in each line.

1. $y = 5$ **2.** $x = 7$ **3.** $y = -1$ **4.** the x-axis

5. $y = x$ **6.** $x = -1$ **7.** $y = 3$ **8.** the y-axis

Lesson 12-2 In Exercises 9–14, refer to the figure at the right.

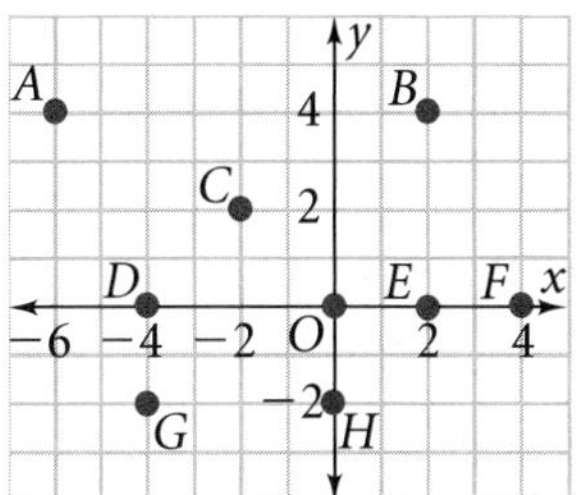

9. What is the image of C under the translation $\langle 4, -2\rangle$?

10. What vector describes the translation $F \rightarrow B$?

11. What is the image of H under the translation $\langle -2, 4\rangle$?

12. What vector describes the translation $D \rightarrow H$?

13. What is the image of C under the translation $\langle -2, -4\rangle$?

14. What vector describes the translation $B \rightarrow A$?

Use matrices to find the image of each figure under the given translation.

15. $\triangle ABC$ with vertices $A(-3, 4)$, $B(-1, -2)$, $C(1, 5)$; translation: $\langle -2, 5\rangle$

16. $\triangle EFG$ with vertices $E(0, 3)$, $F(6, -1)$, $G(4, 2)$; translation: $\langle 1, -3\rangle$

17. $\triangle PQR$ with vertices $P(-9, -4)$, $Q(-5, 1)$, $R(2, 8)$; translation: $\langle -6, -7\rangle$

Lesson 12-3 Copy each figure and point P. Draw the image of each figure for the given rotation about P. Label the vertices of the image.

18. 60°

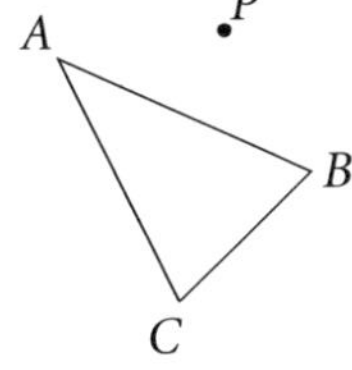

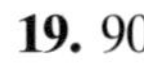
19. 90°

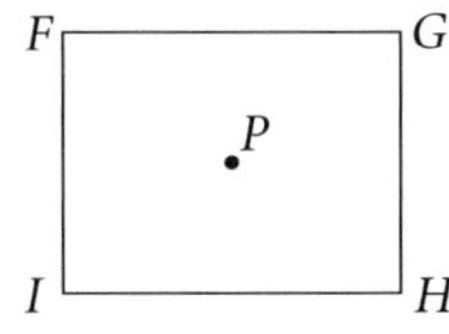

20. 45°

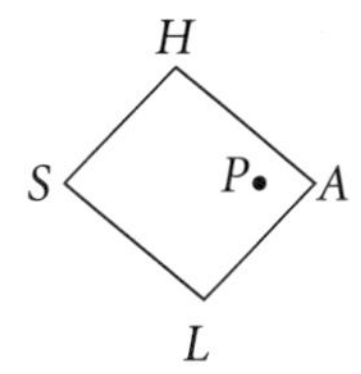

21. 180°

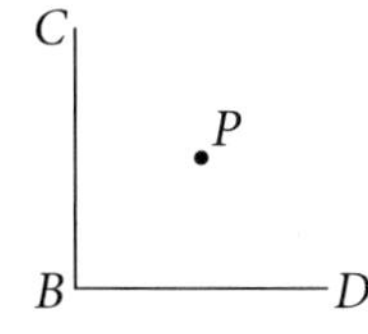

Lessons 12-4 and 12-7 The blue figure is the image of the gray figure. State whether the mapping is a reflection, rotation, translation, glide reflection, or dilation.

22.

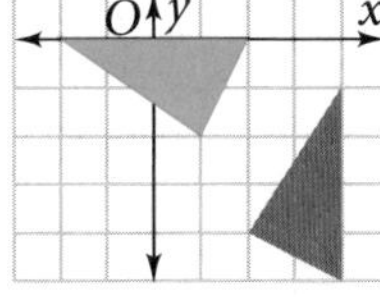

23.

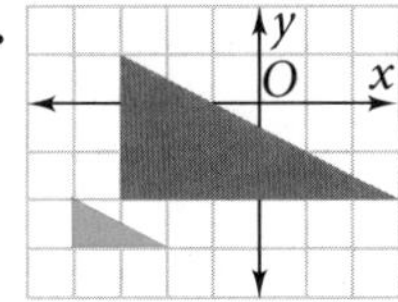

24.

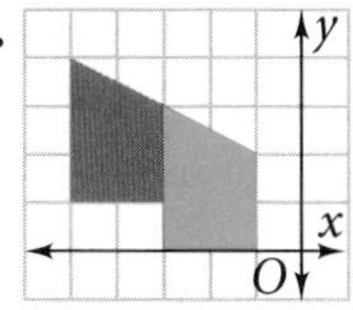

25.

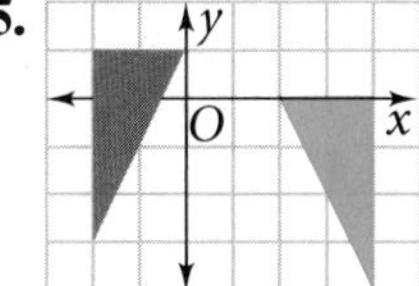

Lessons 12-5 and 12-6 (a) State what kind of symmetry each figure has. (b) State whether each figure tessellates.

26.

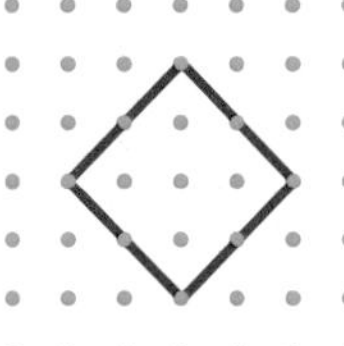

27.

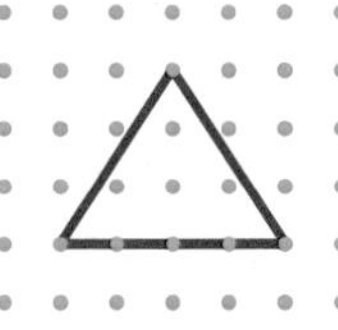

28.

29.

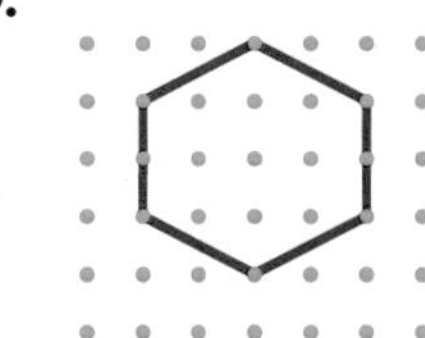

Skills Handbook

Problem Solving Strategies

You may find one or more of these strategies helpful in solving a word problem.

Strategy	When to Use it
Draw a Diagram	You need help in visualizing the problem.
Try, Check, Revise	Solving the problem directly is too complicated.
Make a Table	The problem has data that need organizing.
Look for a Pattern	The problem describes a relationship.
Solve a Simpler Problem	The problem is complex or has numbers that are too unmanageable to use at first.
Use Logical Reasoning	You need to reach a conclusion from some given information.
Work Backward	You undo various operations to arrive at the answer.

Problem Solving: Draw a Diagram

EXAMPLE

Antoine is 1.91 m tall. He measures his shadow and finds that it is 2.34 m long. He then measures the length of the shadow of a flagpole and finds that it is 13.2 m long. How tall is the flagpole?

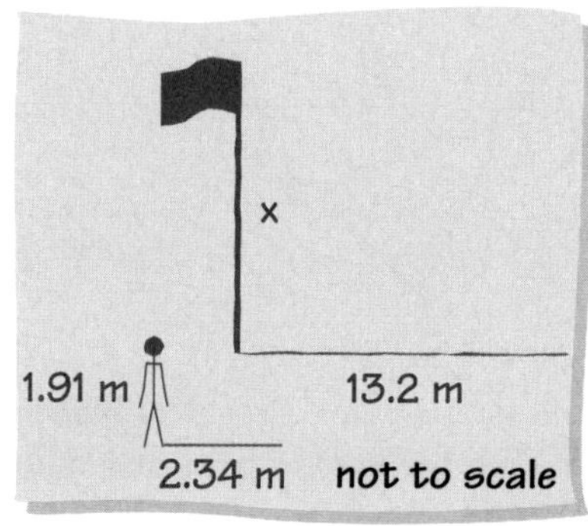

Start by drawing a diagram showing the given information. The diagram shows that you can solve the problem by using a proportion.

$\frac{1.91}{2.34} = \frac{x}{13.2}$ **Write a proportion.**

$x \approx 10.77$ **Solve for *x*.**

The flagpole is about 10.8 m tall.

EXERCISES

1. Five people meet and shake hands with one another. How many handshakes are there in all?

2. Three tennis balls fit snugly in an ordinary, cylindrical tennis ball container. Which is greater, the circumference of a ball or the height of the container?

3. Three lines that all intersect a circle can determine at most 7 regions within the circle, as shown in the diagram. What is the greatest number of regions that can be determined by 5 lines?

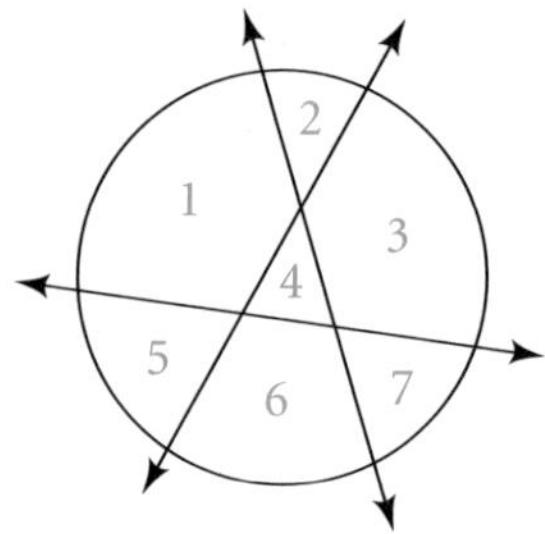

4. A triangle has vertices (1, 3), (2, 3), and (7, 5). Find its area.

Problem Solving: Try, Check, Revise

Have you ever weighed yourself on a balance scale at a doctor's office? You start by guessing your weight, and then you see if the scale balances. If it doesn't, you slide the weights back and forth until the scale does balance. This is an example of the *Try, Check, Revise* strategy, a strategy helpful for solving many types of problems.

EXAMPLE

You have 100 ft of fencing and want to build a fence in the shape of a rectangle to enclose the largest possible area. What should be the dimensions of the rectangle?

Try 1:	10 ft wide by 40 ft long $10 \cdot 40 = 400$ ft^2	**Make an initial try with a perimeter of 100 ft. Find the area.**
Try 2:	20 ft wide by 30 ft long $20 \cdot 30 = 600$ ft^2	**Try again and find the area. The area is larger than the initial try.**
Try 3:	35 ft wide by 15 ft long $35 \cdot 15 = 525$ ft^2	**Continue trying and testing areas. This area is smaller than the last try.**
Try 4:	22 ft wide by 28 ft long $22 \cdot 28 = 616$ ft^2	**Notice that the areas are larger when the width and length are closer together.**
Try 5:	25 ft wide by 25 ft long $25 \cdot 25 = 625$ ft^2	**Choose dimensions that are as close together as possible.**

The dimensions of your rectangle should be 25 ft by 25 ft.

EXERCISES

1. The product of three consecutive even integers is 480. Find the integers.

2. The combined ages of a father and his twin daughters are 54 years. The father was 24 years old when the twins were born. How old is each of the three people?

3. What numbers can x represent in the rectangle?

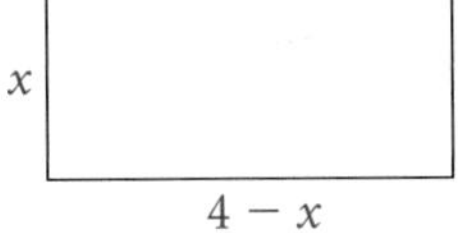

4. Alexandra has a collection of dimes and quarters. The number of dimes equals the number of quarters. She has a total of \$2.80. How many of each coin does Alexandra have?

Use the Try, Check, Revise strategy to find the value of each variable.

5. $2a + 5 = 1$ **6.** $10 - 3c = -2$ **7.** $\frac{w}{-3} + 12 = -6$

8. $5y - 32 = 28$ **9.** $12b + 11 = 14$ **10.** $0.5x - 15 = -7$

11. Ruisa bought 7 rolls of film to take 192 pictures on a field trip. Some rolls had 36 exposures and the rest had 24 exposures. How many of each type did Ruisa buy?

12. The sum of five consecutive integers is 5. Find the integers.

13. Paul buys a coupon for \$20 from a local theater that allows him to see movies for half price over the course of one year. The cost of seeing a movie is normally \$7.50. What is the least number of movies Paul would have to see to pay less than the normal price per movie?

Problem Solving: Make a Table and Look for a Pattern

There are two important ways that making a table can help you solve a problem. First, a table is a handy method of organizing information. Second, once the information is in a table, it is easier for you to find patterns.

EXAMPLE

The squares below are made of toothpicks. How many toothpicks are in the square with 7 toothpicks on a side?

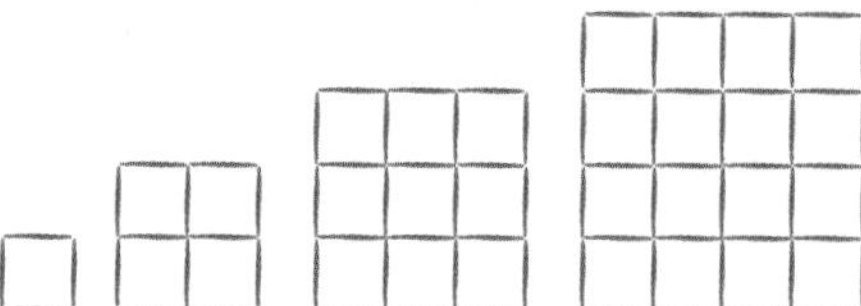

Use a table to organize the information.

Notice the pattern in the increases in the numbers of toothpicks in the squares. For each increase of 1 toothpick on a side, the increase increases by 4. The number of toothpicks in the 5th square is 40 + 20, or 60. The number in the 6th square is 60 + 24, or 84, and the number in the 7th square is 84 + 28, or 112.

Toothpicks on a side	1	2	3	4
Toothpicks in the square	4	12	24	40

+8 +12 +16

EXERCISES

1. The triangles are made of toothpicks. How many toothpicks are in Figure 10?

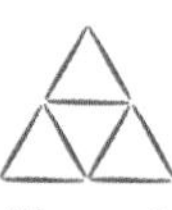

Figure 1

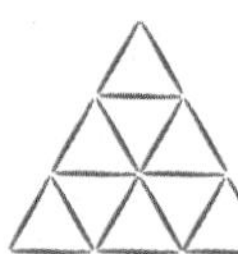

Figure 2

Figure 3

2. In each figure, the vertices of the smallest square are midpoints of the sides of the next larger square. Find the area of the ninth shaded square.

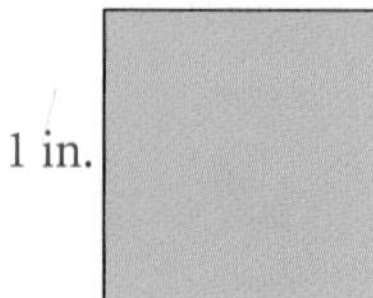

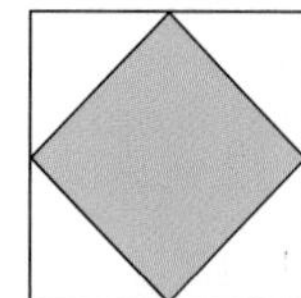

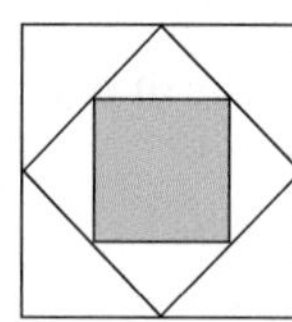

3. In each figure, the midpoints of the sides of the unshaded triangles are used as vertices of the shaded triangles. Find the total number of shaded triangles in Figure 8.

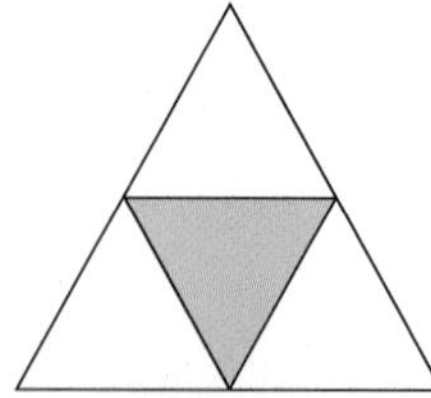

Figure 1

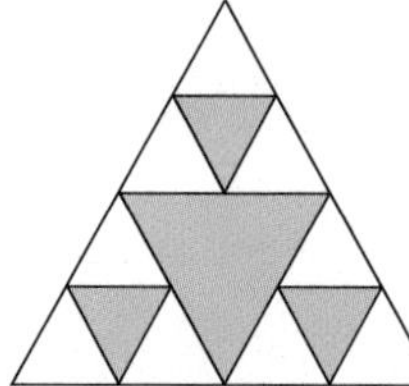

Figure 2

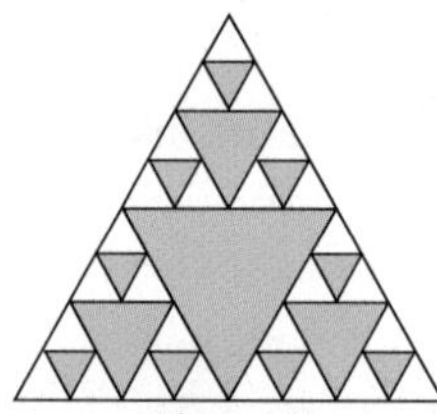

Figure 3

Problem Solving: Solve a Simpler Problem

Looking at a simpler version of a problem can be helpful in suggesting a problem solving approach.

EXAMPLE

A fence along the highway is 570 m long. There is a fence post every 10 m. How many fence posts are there?

You may be tempted to divide 570 by 10, getting 57 as an answer, but looking at a simpler problem suggests that this answer isn't right. Suppose you have just 10 or 20 m of fencing.

10 m — two fence posts

20 m — three fence posts

These easier problems suggest that there is always *one more* fence post than one tenth the length. So for a 570-m fence, there are $\frac{570}{10} + 1$, or 58 fence posts.

EXERCISES

1. A farmer wishes to fence in a square lot 70 yards by 70 yards. He will install a fence post every 10 yards. How many fence posts will he need?
2. A snail is trying to escape from a well 10 ft deep. The snail can climb 2 ft each day, but each night it slides back 1 ft. How many days will the snail take to climb out of the well?
3. Janette is planning to walk from her house to her friend Barbara's house. How many different paths can she take to get there? Assume that she walks only east and south (along the grid lines).

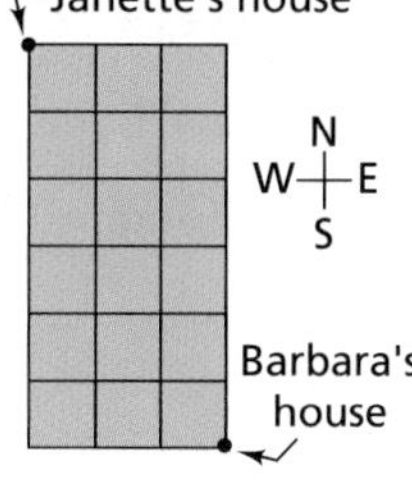

4. A square table can seat four people. For a banquet, a long rectangular table is formed by placing 14 such tables edge to edge in a straight line. How many people can sit at the long table?
5. Find the sum of the whole numbers from 1 to 999.
6. How many trapezoids are in the figure below? (*Hint:* Solve several simpler problems, and then look for a pattern.)

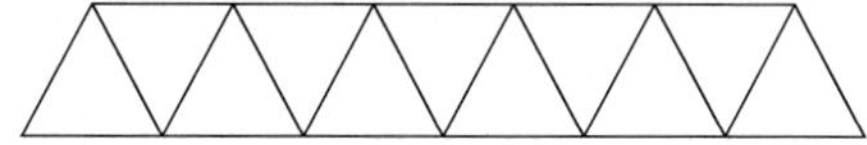

7. At a business luncheon, 424 handshakes took place. No two people shook hands with each other more than once. What is the least number of people in attendance at the luncheon?
8. On the occasion of his 50th birthday, the President was honored with a 21-gun salute. The sound of each gunshot lasted 1 second, and 4 seconds elapsed between shots. How long did the salute last?
9. In a tennis tournament, each athlete plays one match against each of the other athletes. There are 14 athletes scheduled to play in the tournament. How many matches will be played?

Problem Solving: Use Logical Reasoning

Some problems can be solved without the use of numbers. They can be solved by the use of logical reasoning, given some information.

EXAMPLE

Anna, Bill, Carla, and Doug are siblings. Each lives in a different state beginning with W. Use these clues to determine where each sibling lives:

(1) Neither sister lives in a state containing two words.

(2) Bill lives to the west of his sisters.

(3) Anna doesn't cross the Mississippi River when she visits Doug.

Make a table to organize what you know. Use an initial for each name.

State	A	B	C	D
West Virginia	✗	✗	✗	
Wisconsin		✗		
Wyoming		✗		
Washington	✗	✓	✗	✗

From clue 1, you know that neither Anna nor Carla lives in West Virginia.

Using clues 1 and 2, you know that Bill must live in Washington if he lives to the west of his sisters.

Use logical reasoning to complete the table.

State	A	B	C	D
West Virginia	✗	✗	✗	✓
Wisconsin	✓	✗	✗	✗
Wyoming	✗	✗	✓	✗
Washington	✗	✓	✗	✗

Doug lives in West Virginia because no other sibling does.

From clue 3, you know that Anna must live in Wisconsin.

Carla, therefore, lives in Wyoming.

EXERCISES

1. Harold has a dog, a parrot, a goldfish, and a hamster. Their names are J. T., Izzy, Arf, and Blinky. Izzy has neither feathers nor fins. Arf can't bark. J. T. weighs less than the four-legged pets. Neither the goldfish nor the dog has the longest name. Arf and Blinky don't get along well with the parrot. What is each pet's name?

2. At the state basketball championship tournament, 31 basketball games are played to determine the winner of the tournament. After each game, the loser is eliminated from the tournament. How many teams are in the tournament?

3. The sophomore class has 124 students. Of these students, 47 are involved in musical activities: 25 in band and 36 in choir. How many students are involved in both band and choir?

4. Tina's height is between Kimiko's and Ignacio's. Ignacio's height is between Jerome's and Kimiko's. Tina is taller than Jerome. List the people in order from shortest to tallest.

Problem Solving: Work Backward

In some situations it is easier to start with the end result and work backward to find the solution. You work backward in order to solve linear equations. The equation $2x + 3 = 11$ means "double x and add 3 to get 11." To find x, you "undo" those steps in reverse order.

$$2x + 3 = 11$$

$$2x = 8 \quad \textbf{Subtract 3 from each side.}$$

$$x = 4 \quad \textbf{Divide each side by 2.}$$

Another time it is convenient to work backward is when you want to "reverse" a set of directions.

EXAMPLE

Algebra Sandy spent $\frac{1}{10}$ of the money in her purse for lunch. She then spent \$23.50 for a gift for her brother, then half of what she had left on a new CD. If Sandy has \$13 left in her purse, how much money did she have in it before lunch?

Start with the \$13 that Sandy has left in her purse.
She spent half of what she had before the \$13 on a new CD, so she must have had twice \$13, or \$26, before she bought the CD.

She spent \$23.50 on a gift for her brother, so add \$23.50 to \$26. Before buying the gift for her brother, she had \$49.50.

She spent $\frac{1}{10}$ of the money for lunch and was left with \$49.50. That means $\frac{9}{10}$ of what she had is \$49.50. Set up an equation.

$$\frac{9}{10}x = 49.50$$

$$x = 55$$

Sandy had \$55 in her purse before lunch.

EXERCISES

1. To go from Bedford to Worcester, take Route 4 south, then Route 128 south, and then Route 90 west. How do you get from Worcester to Bedford?
2. Algae are growing on a pond's surface. The area covered doubles each day. It takes 24 days to cover the pond completely. After how many days will the pond be half covered with algae?
3. Don sold $\frac{1}{5}$ as many raffle tickets as Carlita. Carlita sold 3 times as many as Ranesha. Ranesha sold 7 fewer than Russell. If Russell sold 12 tickets, how many did Don sell?
4. At 6% interest compounded annually, the balance in a bank account will double about every 12 years. If such an account has a balance of \$16,000 now, how much was deposited when the account was opened 36 years ago?
5. Solve the puzzle that Yuan gave to Inez: I am thinking of a number. If I triple the number and then halve the result, I get 12. What number am I thinking of?
6. Carlos paid a \$14.60 taxi fare from a hotel to the airport, including a \$2.00 tip. Green Cab Co. charges \$1.20 per passenger plus \$0.20 for each additional $\frac{1}{5}$ mile. How many miles is the hotel from the airport?

Using a Ruler and Protractor

Knowing how to use a ruler and protractor is crucial for success in geometry.

EXAMPLE

Draw a triangle that has sides of length 5.2 cm and 3.0 cm and a 68° angle between these two sides.

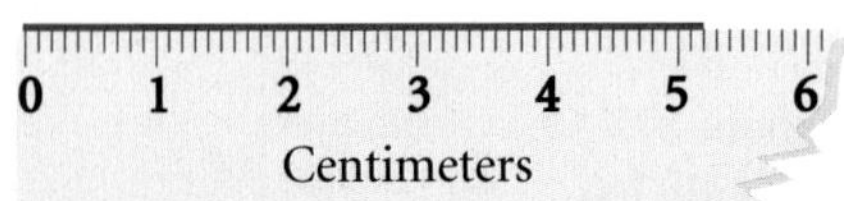

Step 1 Use a ruler to draw a segment 5.2 cm long.

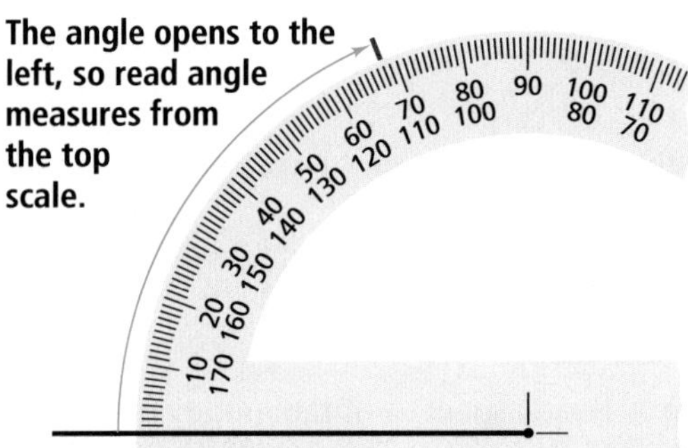

The angle opens to the left, so read angle measures from the top scale.

Step 2 Place the crosshairs of a protractor at one endpoint of the segment. Make a small mark at the 68° position along the protractor.

Step 3 Align the ruler along the small mark and the endpoint you used in Step 2. Place the zero point of the ruler at the endpoint. Draw a segment 3.0 cm long.

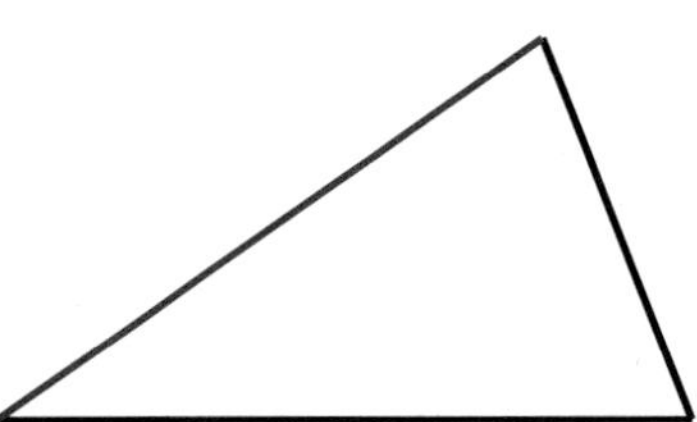

Step 4 Complete the triangle by connecting the endpoints of the first and second segments.

EXERCISES

1. Measure sides $\overline{AB}$ and $\overline{BC}$ to the nearest millimeter.
2. Measure each angle of $\triangle ABC$ to the nearest degree.
3. Draw a triangle that has sides of length 4.8 cm and 3.7 cm and a 34° angle between these two sides.
4. Draw a triangle that has 43° and 102° angles and a side of length 5.4 cm between these two angles.
5. Draw a rhombus that has sides of length $2\frac{1}{4}$ in., and 68° and 112° angles.
6. Draw an isosceles trapezoid that has one pair of 48° base angles and a base of length 2 in. between these two base angles.
7. Draw an isosceles triangle that has two congruent sides $3\frac{1}{2}$ in. long and a 134° vertex angle.

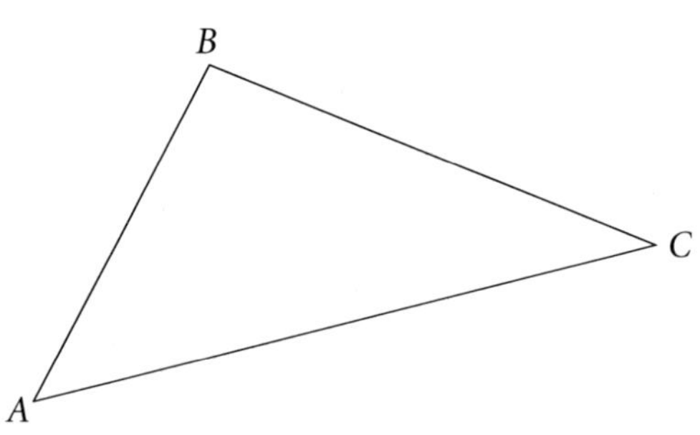

Measurement Conversions

To convert from one unit of measure to another, you multiply by a conversion factor in the form of a fraction. The numerator and denominator are in different units, but they represent the same amount. So, you can think of this as multiplying by 1.

An example of a conversion factor is $\frac{1 \text{ ft}}{12 \text{ in.}}$. You can create other conversion factors using the table on page 728.

1 EXAMPLE

Complete each statement.

a. 88 in. = ■ ft

$88 \text{ in.} \cdot \frac{1 \text{ ft}}{12 \text{ in.}} = \frac{88}{12} \text{ ft} = 7\frac{1}{3} \text{ ft}$

b. 5.3 m = ■ cm

$5.3 \text{ m} \cdot \frac{100 \text{ cm}}{1 \text{ m}} = 5.3(100) \text{ cm} = 530 \text{ cm}$

c. 3700 mm = ■ cm

$3700 \text{ mm} \cdot \frac{1 \text{ cm}}{10 \text{ mm}} = 370 \text{ cm}$

d. 90 in. = ■ yd

$90 \text{ in.} \cdot \frac{1 \text{ ft}}{12 \text{ in.}} \cdot \frac{1 \text{ yd}}{3 \text{ ft}} = \frac{90}{36} \text{ yd} = 2\frac{1}{2} \text{ yd}$

Area is always in square units, and volume is always in cubic units.

3 ft

1 yd = 3 ft

3 ft

3 ft

$1 \text{ yd}^2 = 9 \text{ ft}^2$

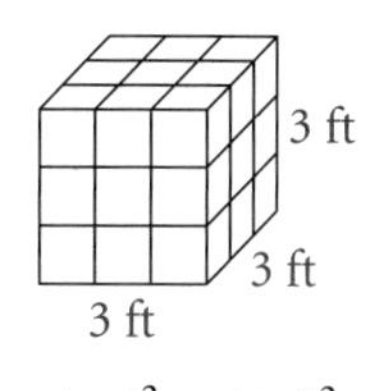

$1 \text{ yd}^3 = 27 \text{ ft}^3$

2 EXAMPLE

Complete each statement.

a. 300 in.^{2} = ■ ft^2

$1 \text{ ft} = 12 \text{ in., so } 1 \text{ ft}^2 = (12 \text{ in.})^2 = 144 \text{ in.}^2$

$300 \text{ in.}^2 \cdot \frac{1 \text{ ft}^2}{144 \text{ in.}^2} = 2\frac{1}{12} \text{ ft}^2$

b. 200,000 cm^3 = ■ m^3

$1 \text{ m} = 100 \text{ cm, so } 1 \text{ m}^3 = (100 \text{ cm})^3 = 1{,}000{,}000 \text{ cm}^3$

$200{,}000 \text{ cm}^3 \cdot \frac{1 \text{ m}^3}{1{,}000{,}000 \text{ cm}^3} = 0.2 \text{ m}^3$

EXERCISES

Complete each statement.

1. 40 cm = ■ m
2. 1.5 kg = ■ g
3. 60 cm = ■ mm
4. 200 in. = ■ ft
5. 28 yd = ■ in.
6. 1.5 mi = ■ ft
7. 42 fl oz = ■ qt
8. 430 mg = ■ g
9. 34 L = ■ mL
10. 1.2 m = ■ cm
11. 43 mm = ■ cm
12. 3600 s = ■ min
13. 15 g = ■ mg
14. 12 qt = ■ c
15. 0.03 kg = ■ mg
16. 14 gal = ■ qt
17. 4500 lb = ■ t
18. 234 min = ■ h
19. 12 mL = ■ L
20. 2 pt = ■ fl oz
21. 20 m/s = ■ km/h
22. 3 ft^2 = ■ in.^{2}
23. 108 m^2 = ■ cm^2
24. 2100 mm^2 = ■ cm^2
25. 1.4 yd^2 = ■ ft^2
26. 0.45 km^2 = ■ m^2
27. 1300 ft^2 = ■ yd^2
28. 1030 in.^{2} = ■ ft^2
29. 20,000,000 ft^2 = ■ mi^2
30. 1000 cm^3 = ■ m^3

Measurement, Rounding Error, and Reasonableness

There is no such thing as an *exact* measurement. Measurements are always approximate. No matter how precise it is, a measurement actually represents a range of values.

1 EXAMPLE

Chris's height, to the nearest inch, is 5 ft 8 in. Find the range of values this measurement represents.

The height is given to the nearest inch, so the error is $\frac{1}{2}$ in. Chris's height, then, is between 5 ft $7\frac{1}{2}$ in. and 5 ft $8\frac{1}{2}$ in., or 5 ft 8 in. $\pm \frac{1}{2}$ in. Within this range are all measures which, when rounded to the nearest inch, equal 5 ft 8 in.

As you calculate with measurements, errors can accumulate.

2 EXAMPLE

Jean drives 18 km to work each day. The distance is given to the nearest kilometer.

a. Find the range of values this measurement represents.

The driving distance is between 17.5 and 18.5 km, or 18 ± 0.5 km.

b. Find the error in the round-trip distance.

Double the lower limit, 17.5, and the upper limit, 18.5. Thus, the round trip can be anywhere between 35 and 37 km, or 36 ± 1 km. The error for the round trip is double the error of a single leg of the trip.

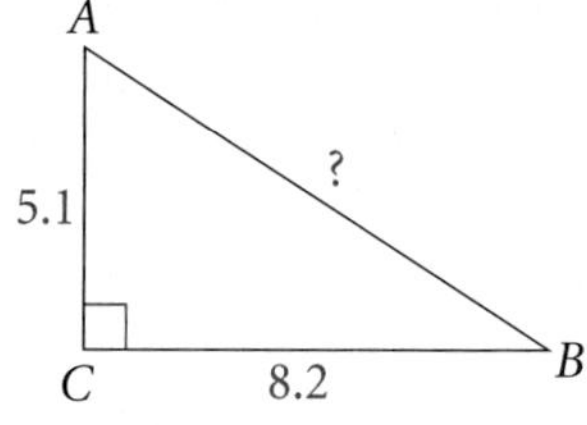

So that your answers will be reasonable, keep precision and error in mind as you calculate. For example, in finding AB, the length of the hypotenuse of $\triangle ABC$, it would be inappropriate to give the answer as 9.6566 if the sides are given to the nearest tenth. Round your answer to 9.7.

EXERCISES

Each measurement is followed by its unit of greatest precision. Find the range of values that each measurement represents.

1. 24 ft (ft)

2. 124 cm (cm)

3. 340 mL (mL)

4. $5\frac{1}{2}$ mi. $\left(\frac{1}{2}\text{ mi}\right)$

5. 73.2 mm (0.1 mm)

6. 34 yd^2 (yd^2)

7. 5.4 mi (0.1 mi)

8. 6 ft 5 in. (0.5 in.)

9. $15\frac{1}{2}$ yd $\left(\frac{1}{2}\text{ yd}\right)$

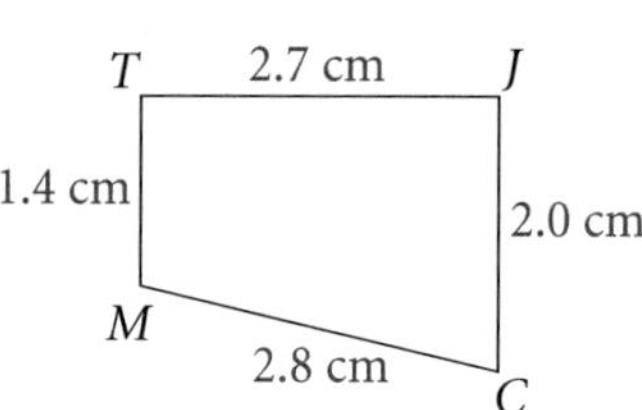

10. The lengths of the sides of $TJCM$ are given to the nearest tenth of a centimeter. Find the range of values for the figure's perimeter.

11. To the nearest degree, two angles of a triangle are 49° and 73°. What is the range of values for the measure of the third angle?

12. The lengths of the legs of a right triangle are measured as 131 m and 162 m. You use a calculator to find the length of the hypotenuse. The calculator display reads 208.33867. What should your answer be?

The Effect of Measurement Errors on Calculations

Measurements are always approximate, and calculations with these measurements produce error. Percent error is a measure of accuracy of a measurement or calculation. It is the ratio of the greatest possible error to the measurement.

$$\text{percent error} = \frac{\text{greatest possible error}}{\text{measurement}}$$

EXAMPLE

The dimensions of a box are measured as 18 in., 12 in., and 9 in. Find the percent error in calculating its volume.

The measurements are to the nearest inch, so the greatest possible length error is one half of one inch, or 0.5 in.

as measured	maximum value	minimum value
$V = \ell \cdot w \cdot h$	$V = \ell \cdot w \cdot h$	$V = \ell \cdot w \cdot h$
$= 18 \cdot 12 \cdot 9$	$= 18.5 \cdot 12.5 \cdot 9.5$	$= 17.5 \cdot 11.5 \cdot 8.5$
$= 1944$, or 1944 in.^{3}	≈ 2196.9, or 2196.9 in.^{3}	≈ 1710.6, or 1710.6 in.^{3}

Possible Error:

maximum − measured: $2196.9 - 1944 = 252.9$

measured − minimum: $1944 - 1710.6 = 233.4$

$$\begin{aligned}\text{percent error} &= \frac{\text{greatest possible error}}{\text{measurement}}\\ &= \frac{252.9}{1944}\\ &\approx 0.1300926\\ &\approx 13\%\end{aligned}$$

The percent error is about 13%.

EXERCISES

Find the percent error in calculating the volume of each box given its dimensions. Round to the nearest percent.

1. 10 cm by 5 cm by 20 cm

2. 12 in. by 6 in. by 2 in.

3. 1.2 mm by 5.7 mm by 2.0 mm

4. 7.5 m by 6.4 m by 2.7 m

5. 22.5 cm by 16.4 cm by 26.4 cm

6. 1.24 cm by 4.45 cm by 5.58 cm

7. $8\frac{1}{4}$ in. by $17\frac{1}{2}$ in. by 5 in.

8. $7\frac{3}{4}$ in. by $22\frac{1}{8}$ in. by $6\frac{1}{4}$ in.

Find the percent error in calculating the perimeter of each figure.

9.

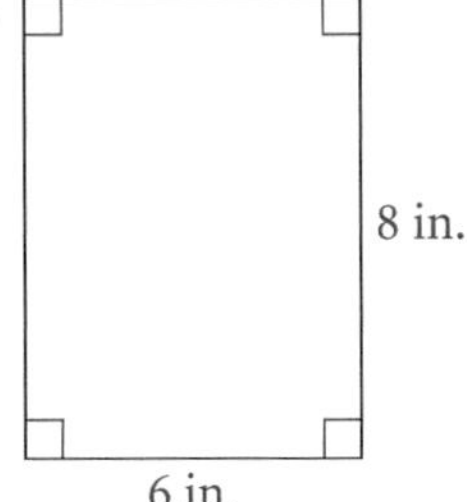

10.

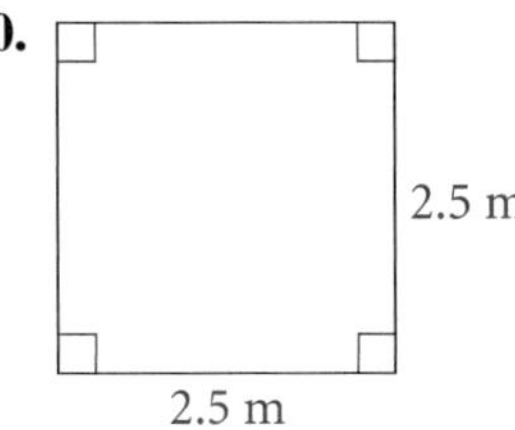

11.

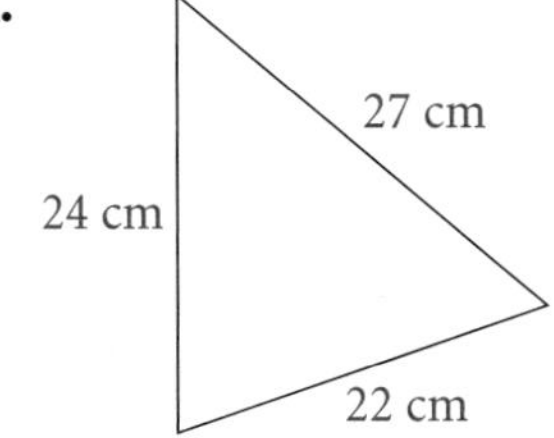

Mean, Median, and Mode

Measures of central tendency, such as mean, median, and mode, are numbers that describe a set of data.

The mean, sometimes called the average, is the sum of the data items divided by the number of data items.

The median is the middle number when data items are placed in order and there are an odd number of data items. For an even number of data items, the median is the mean of the middle two numbers.

The mode is the data item that appears most frequently.
A set of data may have more than one mode or no modes.

EXAMPLE

Eighteen students were asked to measure the angle formed by the three objects in the diagram. Their answers, in order from least to greatest, are as follows:

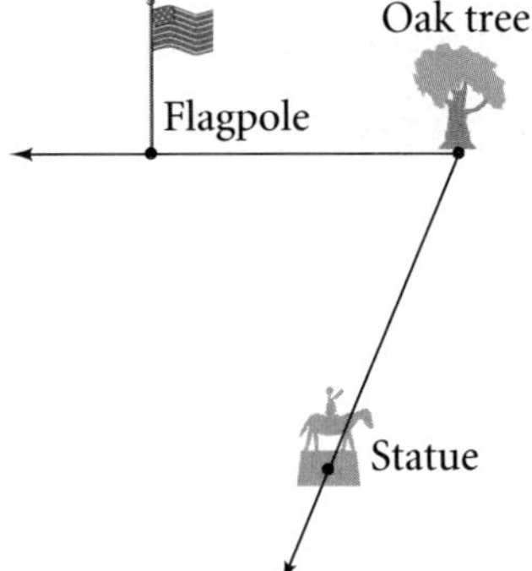

65, 66, 66, 66, 66, 66, 66, 67, 67, 67, 67, 67, 68, 68, 69, 70, 74, 113

Find the mean, median, and mode of the data.

Mean: $\frac{\text{sum of the 18 measures}}{18} = \frac{1258}{18} = 69\frac{8}{9}$

Median:
This data list is already ordered. The two middle numbers—the ninth and the tenth numbers on the list—are both 67. So the median is 67.

Mode:
There are more 66's than any other number, so the mode is 66.

EXERCISES

Find the mean, median, and mode of each set of data.

1. Numbers of students per school in Newtown: 234, 341, 253, 313, 273, 301, 760
2. Lunch expenses: \$4.50, \$3.26, \$5.02, \$3.58, \$1.25, \$3.05, \$4.24, \$3.56, \$3.31
3. Salaries at D. B. Widget & Co.: \$15,000; 18,000; \$18,000; \$21,700; \$26,500; \$27,000; \$29,300; \$31,100; \$43,000; \$47,800; \$69,000; \$140,000
4. Population of towns in Brower County: 567, 632, 781, 902, 1034, 1100, 1598, 2164, 2193, 3062, 3074, 3108, 3800, 3721, 4104
5. In Exercise 3, which measure or measures of central tendency do you think best represent the data? Explain.
6. Find the mean, median, and mode of the exam scores at the right.
7. In the example, the student who reported the angle measure as 113 most likely made an error. If this measure is dropped from the list, what are the mean, median, and mode of the remaining 17 scores?
8. In the example, if the measurement 65 were instead 51, would the mean decrease? Would the median? Would the mode?
9. In the example, if the two students who measured the angle at 68 both reduced their measurements to 67, would the mode be affected? How?

Final Exam Scores
34, 47, 53, 56, 57, 62, 62, 64, 67, 70, 74, 74, 74, 78, 82, 85, 85, 85, 85, 86, 88, 92, 93, 93, 94, 95, 97

Bar Graphs and Line Graphs

Data displayed in a table can be very useful, but a table is not always as easy to interpret as a graph. Bar graphs and line graphs can show the same data, but sometimes one type of graph has advantages over the other.

EXAMPLE

Make a bar graph and a line graph showing the data in the table at the right.

Bar Graph

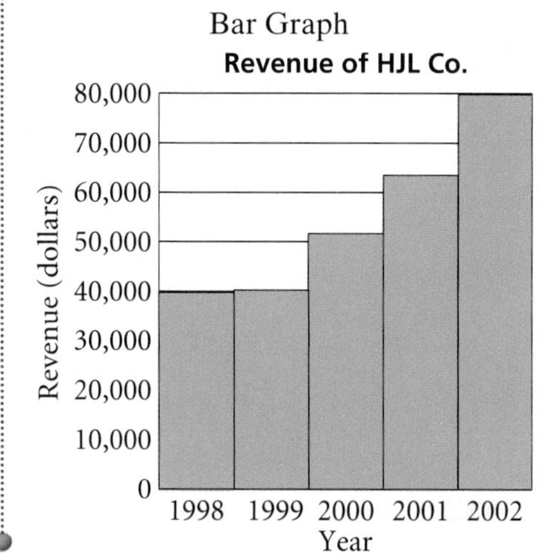

Line Graph

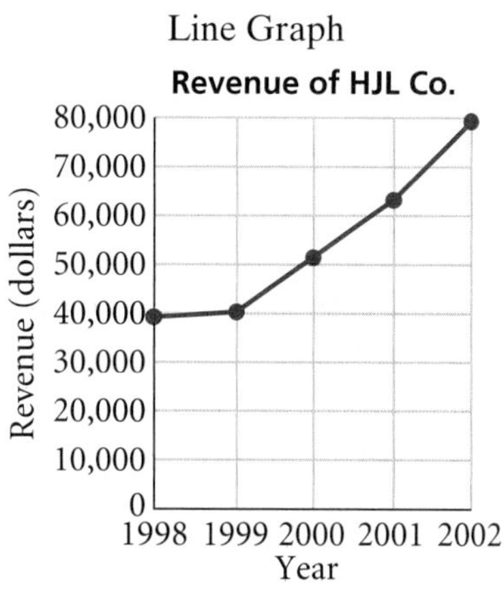

Revenue of HJL Co.

Year	Revenue
1998	$39,780
1999	$40,019
2000	$51,772
2001	$63,444
2002	$79,855

Bar graphs are useful when you wish to compare amounts. In the example above, the tallest bar is clearly twice the height of the shortest bar. At a glance, it is evident that in four years the revenue approximately doubled.

Line graphs allow you to see how a set of data changes over time. In the example, the slope of the line shows that revenue has increased at a steady rate since 1999.

Did revenue increase from 1998 to 1999? It is difficult to tell by looking at either graph; for that information, you should look back at the table.

EXERCISES

1. Create a bar graph and a line graph to display the data in the table below.

Sales of Rock Music (in millions of dollars)

Year	1995	1996	1997	1998	1999	2000
Sales	$4127	$4086	$3977	$3527	$3675	$3552

SOURCE: Recording Industry Association of America.
Go to **www.PHSchool.com** for a data update.
Web Code: afg-2041

For Exercises 2–6, refer to the line graph at the right.

Temperatures in Grand Island, Nebraska, on February 2

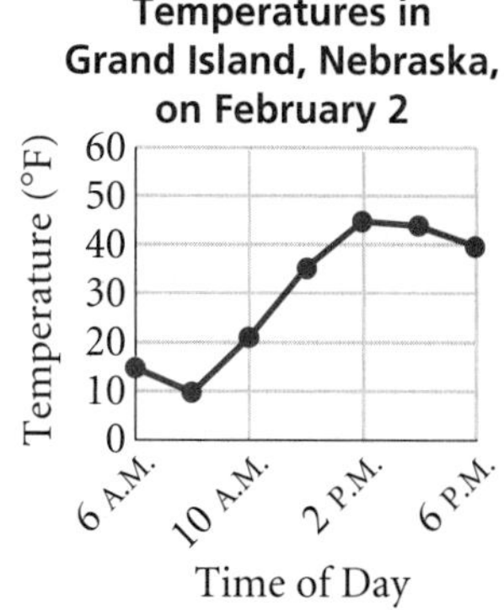

2. What was the lowest temperature recorded between 6 A.M. and 6 P.M.?

3. During which time periods did the temperature appear to increase?

4. Estimate the temperature at 11 A.M. and at 5 P.M.

5. Can you tell from the graph what the actual maximum and minimum temperatures were between 6 A.M. and 6 P.M.? Explain.

6. The same data could be presented in a bar graph. Which presentation is better for these data, a line graph or a bar graph? Explain why.

Box-and-Whisker Plots

A *box-and-whisker plot* is a way to display data on a number line. It provides a picture of how tightly the data cluster around the median and how wide a range the data have. The diagram below shows the various points associated with a box-and-whisker plot.

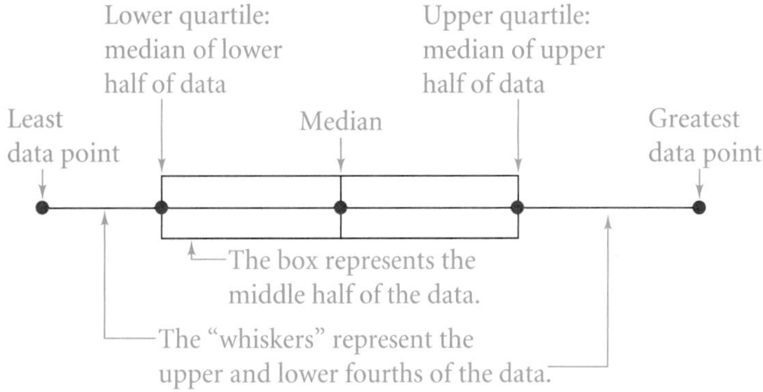

EXAMPLE

The heights, in inches, of 23 geometry students are as follows.

58, 61, 63, 63, 63, 64, 64, 65, 65, 65, 67, 68, 68, 68, 69, 70, 70, 70, 72, 72, 72, 74, 75

Draw a box-and-whisker plot.

The heights range from 58 in. to 75 in. Show 58 and 75 as endpoints on a line segment. The median is 68, so locate 68 in relation to 58 and 75. The lower quartile (the median of the lower eleven heights) is 64. The upper quartile (the median of the upper eleven heights) is 70. Locate 64 and 70 and draw a box enclosing them. Draw a vertical segment inside the box through the median.

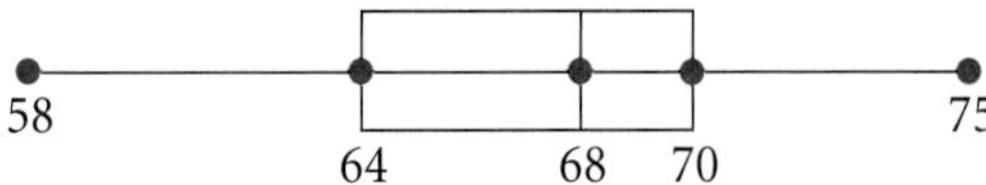

EXERCISES

1. All of the physical education students at Martin Luther King, Jr., High School were timed sprinting the 100-meter dash. The box-and-whisker plot below summarizes the data. Use it to find the following.
   a. median **b.** lower quartile **c.** upper quartile

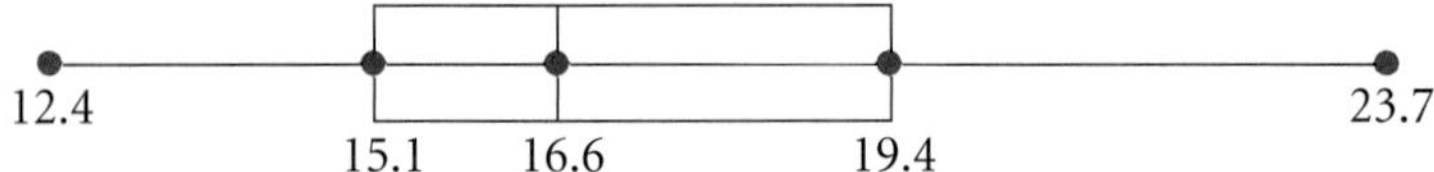

2. Make a box-and-whisker plot for the following data set, which lists the weights, in pounds, of the students trying out for the wrestling team at Benjamin Banneker High School.

   104, 121, 122, 130, 130, 131, 140, 144, 147, 147, 148, 155, 160, 163, 171

3. Make a box-and-whisker plot for the following set of data, which lists the numbers of pages in a set of books. (*Hint:* Order the data from smallest to largest.)

   205, 198, 312, 254, 185, 268, 297, 242, 356, 262

Squaring Numbers and Finding Square Roots

The square of a number is found by multiplying the number by itself. An exponent of 2 is used to indicate that a number is being squared.

1 EXAMPLE

Simplify.

a. 5^2

$5^2 = 5 \cdot 5$

$= 25$

b. $(-3.5)^2$

$(-3.5)^2 = (-3.5) \cdot (-3.5)$

$= 12.25$

c. $(\frac{2}{7})^2$

$(\frac{2}{7})^2 = \frac{2}{7} \cdot \frac{2}{7}$

$= \frac{4}{49}$

The square root of a number is itself a number that, when squared, results in the original number. A radical symbol ($\sqrt{\ }$) is used to represent the positive square root of a number.

2 EXAMPLE

Simplify. Round to the nearest tenth if necessary.

a. $\sqrt{36}$

$\sqrt{36} = 6$ since $6^2 = 36$

b. $\sqrt{174}$

$\sqrt{174} \approx 13.2$ since $13.2^2 \approx 174$

You can solve equations that include squared numbers.

3 EXAMPLE

Algebra Solve.

a. $x^2 = 144$

$x = 12$ or -12

b. $a^2 + 3^2 = 5^2$

$a^2 + 9 = 25$

$a^2 = 16$

$a = 4$ or -4

EXERCISES

Simplify.

1. 11^2 **2.** 16^2 **3.** $(-14)^2$ **4.** $(-21)^2$

5. 5.1^2 **6.** $(\frac{3}{7})^2$ **7.** $(\frac{8}{5})^2$ **8.** -6^2

Simplify. Round to the nearest tenth if necessary.

9. $\sqrt{100}$ **10.** $\sqrt{169}$ **11.** $\sqrt{74}$ **12.** $\sqrt{50}$

13. $\sqrt{400}$ **14.** $\sqrt{289}$ **15.** $\sqrt{\frac{4}{9}}$ **16.** $\sqrt{\frac{49}{81}}$

Algebra **Solve. Round to the nearest tenth if necessary.**

17. $x^2 = 49$ **18.** $a^2 = 9$ **19.** $y^2 + 7 = 8$ **20.** $5 + x^2 = 11$

21. $8^2 + b^2 = 10^2$ **22.** $5^2 + 4^2 = c^2$ **23.** $p^2 + 12^2 = 13^2$ **24.** $20^2 = 15^2 + a^2$

Evaluating and Simplifying Expressions

You evaluate an expression with variables by substituting a number for each variable. Then simplify the expression using the order of operations. Be especially careful with exponents and negative signs. For example, the expression $-x^2$ always yields a negative or zero value, and $(-x)^2$ is always positive or zero.

Order of Operations

1. Perform any operation(s) inside grouping symbols.
2. Simplify any term with exponents.
3. Multiply and divide in order from left to right.
4. Add and subtract in order from left to right.

1 EXAMPLE

Algebra Evaluate each expression for $r = 4$.

a. $-r^2$

$-r^2 = -(4^2) = -16$

b. $-3r^2$

$-3r^2 = -3(4^2) = -3(16) = -48$

c. $(-3r)^2$

$(-3r)^2 = (-3 \cdot 4)^2 = (-12)^2 = 144$

To simplify an expression, you eliminate any parentheses and combine like terms.

2 EXAMPLE

Algebra Simplify each expression.

a. $5r - 2r + 1$

Combine like terms.
$5r - 2r + 1 = 3r + 1$

b. $\pi(3r - 1)$

Use the distributive property.
$\pi(3r - 1) = 3\pi r - \pi$

c. $(r + \pi)(r - \pi)$

Multiply polynomials.
$(r + \pi)(r - \pi) = r^2 - \pi^2$

EXERCISES

Algebra **Evaluate each expression for $x = 5$ and $y = -3$.**

1. $-2x^2$ **2.** $-y + x$ **3.** $-xy$ **4.** $(x + 5y) \div x$

5. $x + 5y \div x$ **6.** $(-2y)^2$ **7.** $(2y)^2$ **8.** $(x - y)^2$

9. $\frac{x + 1}{y}$ **10.** $y - (x - y)$ **11.** $-y^x$ **12.** $\frac{2(1 - x)}{y - x}$

13. $x \cdot y - x$ **14.** $x - y \cdot x$ **15.** $\frac{y^3 - x}{x - y}$ **16.** $-y(x - 3)^2$

17. Which expression gives the area of the shaded figure at the right?

A. $\pi(r - s)^2$ **B.** $\pi(r^2 - s^2)$
C. $\pi(s^2 - r^2)$ **D.** $\pi r^2 - 2\pi s$

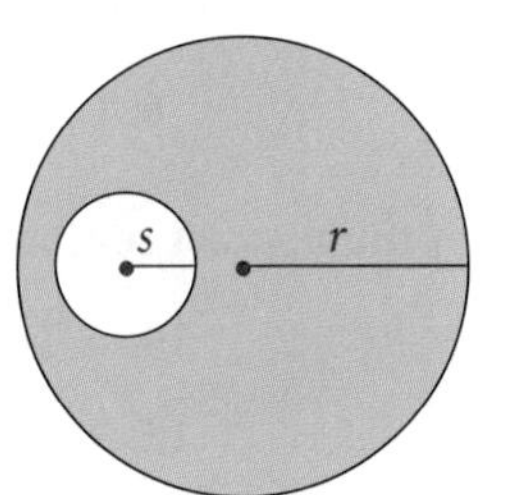

Algebra **Simplify.**

18. $6x - 4x + 8 - 5$ **19.** $2(\ell + w)$ **20.** $-(4x + 7)$

21. $-4x(x - 2)$ **22.** $3x - (5 + 2x)$ **23.** $2t^2 + 4t - 5t^2$ **24.** $(r - 1)^2$

25. $(1 - r)^2$ **26.** $(y + 1)(y - 3)$ **27.** $4h + 3h - 4 + 3$ **28.** $\pi r - (1 + \pi r)$

29. $(x + 4)(2x - 1)$ **30.** $2\pi h(1 - r)^2$ **31.** $3y^2 - (y^2 + 3y)$ **32.** $-(x + 4)^2$

Simplifying Radicals

A radical expression is in its simplest form when all three of the following statements are true.

1. The expression under the radical sign contains no perfect square factors (other than 1).
2. The expression under the radical sign does not contain a fraction.
3. The denominator does not contain a radical expression.

1 EXAMPLE

Simplify.

a. $\sqrt{\frac{4}{9}}$

$\sqrt{\frac{4}{9}} = \frac{\sqrt{4}}{\sqrt{9}} = \frac{2}{3}$

b. $\sqrt{12}$

$\sqrt{12} = \sqrt{4} \cdot \sqrt{3} = 2\sqrt{3}$

2 EXAMPLE

Find the length of the diagonal of rectangle *HJKL*.

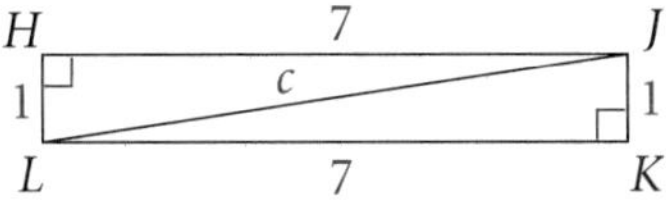

$c^2 = 7^2 + 1^2$	**Use the Pythagorean Theorem.**
$c^2 = 50$	**Simplify the right side.**
$c = \sqrt{50}$	**Find the square root of each side.**
$= \sqrt{25 \cdot 2}$	**Find a perfect square factor of 50.**
$= 5\sqrt{2}$	**Simplify the radical.**

3 EXAMPLE

Simplify $\frac{1}{\sqrt{3}}$.

$\frac{1}{\sqrt{3}} \cdot \frac{\sqrt{3}}{\sqrt{3}} = \frac{\sqrt{3}}{3}$ **Multiply by $\frac{\sqrt{3}}{\sqrt{3}}$, or 1, to eliminate the radical in the denominator.**

EXERCISES

Simplify each radical expression.

1. $\sqrt{27}$ **2.** $\sqrt{24}$ **3.** $\sqrt{150}$ **4.** $\sqrt{\frac{1}{9}}$ **5.** $\sqrt{\frac{72}{9}}$

6. $\frac{\sqrt{228}}{\sqrt{16}}$ **7.** $\sqrt{\frac{2}{5}}$ **8.** $\sqrt{\frac{27}{75}}$ **9.** $\frac{3}{\sqrt{8}}$ **10.** $\frac{6\sqrt{18}}{\sqrt{48}}$

x^2 Algebra **Find the value of x. Leave your answer in simplest radical form.**

11.
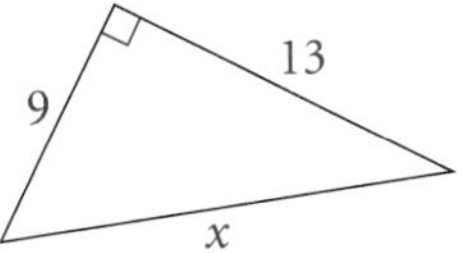

12.
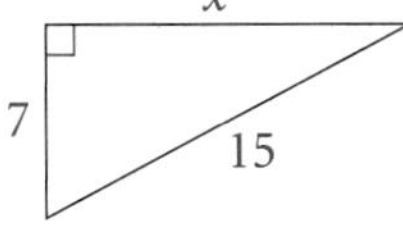

13.
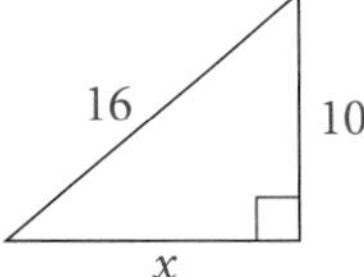

14.
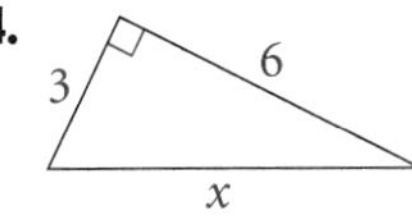

15.
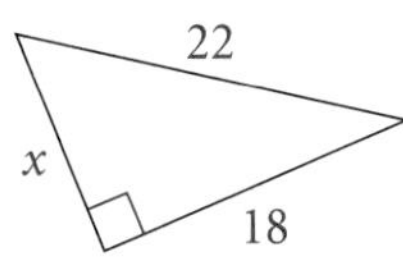

16.
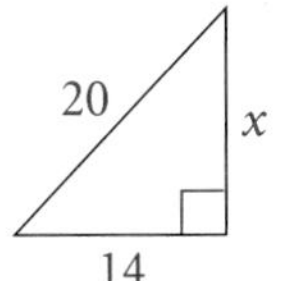

17.
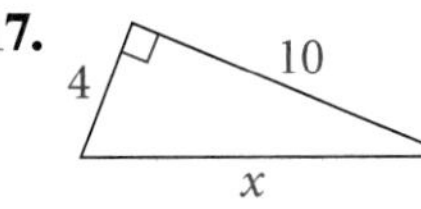

18.
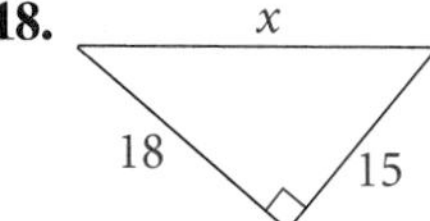

Simplifying Ratios

The ratio of the length of the shorter leg to the length of the longer leg for this right triangle is 4 to 6. This ratio can be written in several ways.

4 to 6 $\qquad \frac{4}{6} \qquad$ 4 : 6

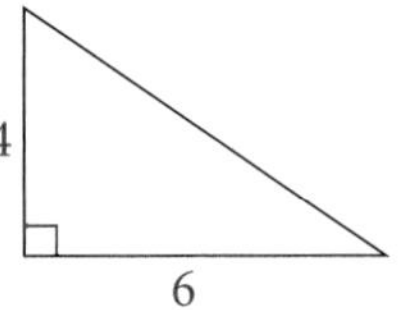

EXAMPLE

Algebra Simplify each ratio.

a. 4 to 6

$$4 \text{ to } 6 = \frac{4}{6} = \frac{2 \cdot 2}{2 \cdot 3} = \frac{2}{3}$$

← **Find and remove the common factor.** →

b. $3ab : 27ab$

$$3ab : 27ab = \frac{3ab}{27ab} = \frac{3ab}{9 \cdot 3ab} = \frac{1}{9}$$

c. $\frac{4a + 4b}{a + b}$

$$\frac{4a + 4b}{a + b} = \frac{4(a + b)}{a + b} = 4$$

Factor the numerator. The denominator cannot be factored. Remove the common factor $(a + b)$.

EXERCISES

Algebra Simplify each ratio.

1. 25 to 15
2. 6 : 9
3. $\frac{36}{54}$
4. 0.8 to 2.4
5. $\frac{7}{14x}$
6. $\frac{12c}{14c}$
7. $22x^2$ to $35x$
8. $0.5ab : 8ab$
9. $\frac{4xy}{0.25x}$
10. $1\frac{1}{2}x$ to $5x$
11. $\frac{x^2 + x}{2x}$
12. $\frac{1}{4}r^2$ to $6r$
13. $0.72t : 7.2t^2$
14. $(2x - 6) : (6x - 4)$
15. $12xy : 8xy$
16. $(9x - 9y)$ to $(x - y)$
17. $\frac{\pi r}{r^2 + \pi r}$
18. $\frac{8ab}{32xy}$

Express each ratio in simplest form.

19. shorter leg : longer leg
20. hypotenuse to shorter leg
21. $\frac{\text{shorter leg}}{\text{hypotenuse}}$
22. hypotenuse : longer leg
23. longer leg to shorter leg
24. $\frac{\text{longer leg}}{\text{hypotenuse}}$

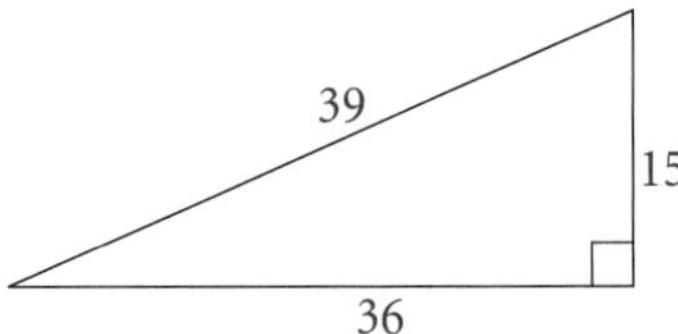

Algebra Write an expression in simplest form for $\frac{\text{area of shaded figure}}{\text{area of blue figure}}$.

25.

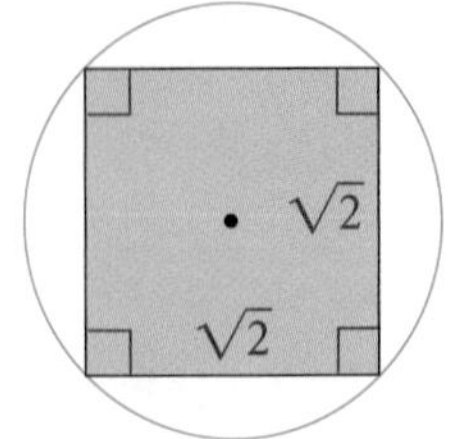

26.

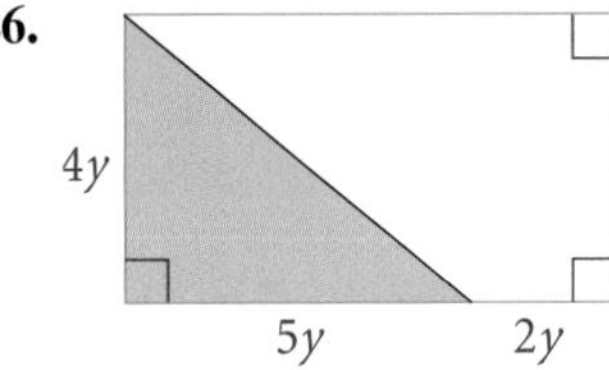

27.

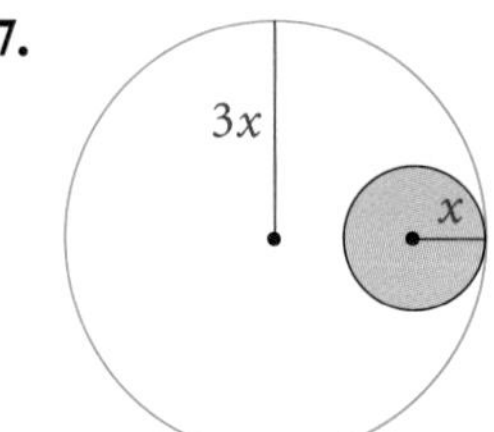

Absolute Value

Absolute value is used to represent the distance of a number from 0 on a number line. Since distance is always referred to as a nonnegative number, the absolute value of an expression is nonnegative.

On the number line at the right, both 4 and -4 are four units from zero. Therefore, $|4|$ and $|-4|$ are both equal to four.

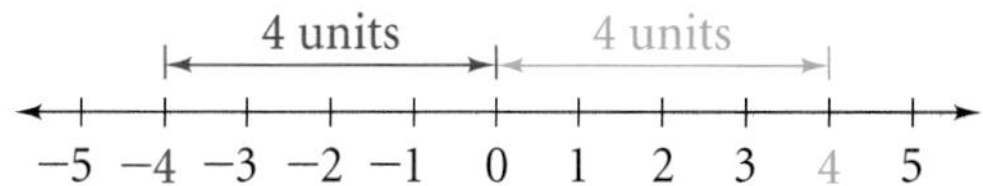

1 EXAMPLE

Simplify each expression.

a. $|-7|$

$|-7| = 7$

b. $|15|$

$|15| = 15$

c. $|4| + |-19|$

$|4| + |-19| = 4 + 19 = 23$

When working with more complicated expressions, always remember to simplify within absolute value symbols first.

2 EXAMPLE

Simplify each expression.

a. $|4 - 8|$

$|4 - 8| = |-4|$

$= 4$

b. $-3|-7 - 4|$

$-3|-7 - 4| = -3|-11|$

$= -3 \cdot 11$

$= -33$

To solve an equation involving absolute value, remember that absolute value symbols cause both negative and positive values to become positive.

3 EXAMPLE

Algebra Solve.

a. $|x| = 7$

$x = 7$ or -7

b. $|x| - 3 = 22$

$|x| - 3 = 22$

$|x| = 25$

$x = -25$ or 25

EXERCISES

Simplify each expression.

1. $|-8|$ **2.** $|11|$ **3.** $|16|$ **4.** $|-23|$

5. $|-7| + |15|$ **6.** $|-12| - |-12|$ **7.** $|5| - |10|$ **8.** $|4| + |2|$

9. $10 - |-20|$ **10.** $|-9 - 11|$ **11.** $2|-21 + 16|$ **12.** $-8|-9 + 4|$

x^2 **Algebra Solve.**

13. $|x| = 16$ **14.** $2 = |x|$ **15.** $|x| + 7 = 27$ **16.** $|x| - 9 = 15$

Solving and Writing Linear Equations

To solve a linear equation, use the properties of equality and properties of real numbers to find the value of the variable that satisfies the equation.

1 EXAMPLE

Algebra Solve each equation.

a. $5x - 3 = 2$

$5x - 3 = 2$

$5x = 5$ **Add 3 to each side.**

$x = 1$ **Divide each side by 5.**

b. $1 - 2(x + 1) = x$

$1 - 2(x + 1) = x$

$1 - 2x - 2 = x$ **Use the Distributive Property.**

$-1 - 2x = x$ **Simplify the left side.**

$-1 = 3x$ **Add $2x$ to each side.**

$-\frac{1}{3} = x$ **Divide each side by 3.**

You will sometimes need to translate word problems into equations. Look for words that suggest a relationship or some type of mathematical operation.

2 EXAMPLE

Algebra A student has grades of 80, 65, 78, and 92 on four tests. What is the minimum grade she must earn on her next test to ensure an average of 80?

Relate average of 80, 65, 78, 92, and next test, is 80 **Pull out the key words and numbers.**

Define Let x = the grade on the next test. **Let a variable represent what you are looking for.**

Write $\frac{80 + 65 + 78 + 92 + x}{5} = 80$ **Write an equation.**

$\frac{315 + x}{5} = 80$ **Combine like terms.**

$315 + x = 400$ **Multiply each side by 5.**

$x = 85$ **Subtract 315 from each side.**

The student must earn 85 on the next test for an average of 80.

EXERCISES

Algebra **Solve each equation.**

1. $3n + 2 = 17$

2. $5a - 2 = -12$

3. $2x + 4 = 10$

4. $3(n - 4) = 15$

5. $4 - 2y = 8$

6. $-6z + 1 = 13$

7. $6 - (3t + 4) = -17$

8. $7 = -2(4n - 4.5)$

9. $(w + 5) - (2w + 5) = 5$

10. $\frac{5}{7}p - 10 = 30$

11. $\frac{m}{-2} - 3 = 1$

12. $5k + 2(k + 1) = 23$

Algebra **Write an equation and solve the problem.**

13. Twice a number subtracted from 35 is 9. What is the number?

14. A new tenant pays the landlord the amount of the first month's rent, the same amount for the last month's rent, and half a month's rent for a security deposit. The total is $2437.50. How much is the monthly rent?

15. The Johnsons pay $9.95 a month plus $0.035 per minute for local phone service. Last month, they paid $12.75. How many minutes of local calls did they make?

Solving Literal Equations

An equation with two or more variables is called a literal equation. It is often necessary to solve a literal equation for a particular variable.

1 EXAMPLE

Algebra The formula $P = 2(\ell + w)$ gives the perimeter P of a rectangle with length ℓ and width w. Solve the equation for ℓ.

$$P = 2(\ell + w)$$

$$P = 2\ell + 2w \quad \text{Use the Distributive Property.}$$

$$P - 2w = 2\ell \quad \text{Subtract } 2w \text{ from each side.}$$

$$\frac{P - 2w}{2} = \ell \quad \text{Divide each side by 2.}$$

2 EXAMPLE

Algebra The formula $A = \frac{1}{2}(b_1 + b_2)h$ gives the area A of a trapezoid with bases b_1 and b_2 and height h. Solve for h.

$$A = \tfrac{1}{2}(b_1 + b_2)h$$

$$2A = h(b_1 + b_2) \quad \text{Multiply each side by 2.}$$

$$\frac{2A}{b_1 + b_2} = h \quad \text{Divide each side by } (b_1 + b_2).$$

3 EXAMPLE

Algebra The formula for converting from degrees Celsius C to degrees Fahrenheit F is $F = \frac{9}{5}C + 32$. Solve for C.

$$F = \tfrac{9}{5}C + 32$$

$$F - 32 = \tfrac{9}{5}C \quad \text{Subtract 32 from each side.}$$

$$\tfrac{5}{9}(F - 32) = C \quad \text{Multiply each side by } \tfrac{5}{9}.$$

EXERCISES

Algebra **Solve each equation for the variable in red.**

1. Perimeter of rectangle: $P = 2w + 2\ell$
2. Volume of prism: $V = \ell wh$
3. Surface area of sphere: $S = 4\pi r^2$
4. Lateral area of cylinder: $A = 2\pi rh$
5. Area of kite or rhombus: $A = \frac{1}{2}d_1d_2$
6. Area of circle: $A = \pi r^2$
7. Area of regular polygon: $A = \frac{1}{2}ap$
8. Volume of cylinder: $V = \pi r^2h$
9. Area of triangle: $A = \frac{1}{2}bh$
10. Tangent of $\angle A$: $\tan A = \frac{y}{x}$
11. Euler's Formula: $F + V = E + 2$
12. Circumference of circle: $C = 2\pi r$
13. Cosine of $\angle A$: $\cos A = \frac{b}{c}$
14. Volume of cone: $V = \frac{1}{3}\pi r^2h$
15. Surface area of right cone: $S = \pi r^2 + \pi r\ell$
16. Area of trapezoid: $A = \frac{1}{2}(b_1 + b_2)h$
17. Volume of pyramid: $V = \frac{1}{3}Bh$
18. Pythagorean Theorem: $a^2 + b^2 = c^2$
19. Surface area of regular pyramid: $S = B + \frac{1}{2}p\ell$
20. Surface area of right cylinder: $S = 2\pi r^2 + 2\pi rh$

Systems of Linear Equations

Normally, there are many ordered pairs that satisfy a given equation. For example, (3, 4), (4, 5), (5, 6), and infinitely many other pairs all satisfy the equation $y = x + 1$. In solving a system of two linear equations, however, you need to find ordered pairs that satisfy both equations at once. Ordinarily, there is just one such ordered pair; it is the point where the graphs of the two lines intersect.

One method you can always use to solve a system of linear equations is the substitution method.

EXAMPLE

Algebra Solve the system. $2x - y = -10$
$-3x - 2y = 1$

Solve one of the equations for a variable. Looking at the two equations, it seems easiest to solve the first equation for *y*.

$2x - y = -10$

$-y = -2x - 10$ **Subtract 2*x* from each side.**

$y = 2x + 10$ **Multiply each side by −1.**

Now substitute $2x + 10$ for *y* in the other equation.

$-3x - 2y = 1$ **Write the other equation.**

$-3x - 2(2x + 10) = 1$ **Substitute (2*x* + 10) for *y*.**

$-3x - 4x - 20 = 1$ **Use the Distributive Property.**

$-7x = 21$ **Simplify and add 20 to each side.**

$x = -3$ **Divide each side by −7.**

So $x = -3$. To find *y*, substitute -3 for *x* in either equation.

$2x - y = -10$ **Write one of the equations.**

$2(-3) - y = -10$ **Substitute −3 for *x*.**

$-6 - y = -10$ **Simplify.**

$-y = -4$ **Add 6 to each side.**

$y = 4$ **Multiply each side by −1.**

So the solution is $x = -3$ and $y = 4$, or $(-3, 4)$. If you graph $2x - y = -10$ and $-3x - 2y = 1$, you'll find that the lines intersect at $(-3, 4)$.

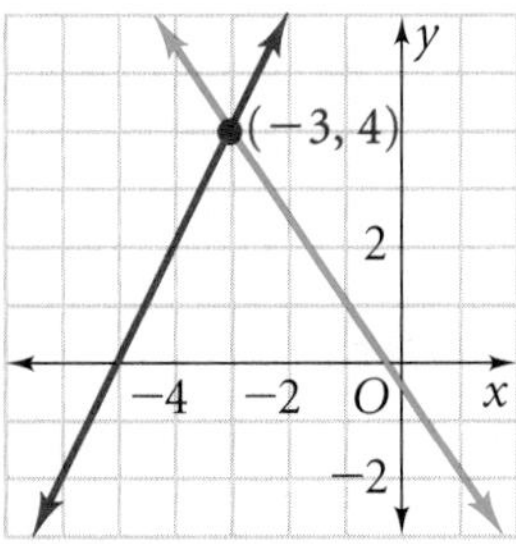

EXERCISES

Algebra Solve each system.

1. $x + y = 3$
   $x - y = 5$
2. $y - x = 4$
   $x + 3 = y$
3. $y = 1$
   $5x - 2y = 18$
4. $3x - y = 5$
   $x = -2$
5. $4y - x = -3$
   $2x - 6 = 8y$
6. $8x - 1 = 4y$
   $3x = y + 1$
7. $2x + 2y = -4$
   $-x + 3y = 6$
8. $12y - 3x = 11$
   $x - 2y = -2$
9. $5x + 7y = 1$
   $4x - 2y = 16$
10. Give an example of a system of linear equations with no solution. What do you know about the slopes of the lines of such a system?

Percents

A percent is a ratio in which a number is compared to 100. For example, the expression *60 percent* means "60 out of 100." The symbol % stands for "percent."

A percent can be written in decimal form by first writing it in ratio form, and then writing the ratio as a decimal. For example, 25% is equal to the ratio $\frac{25}{100}$ or $\frac{1}{4}$. As a decimal, $\frac{1}{4}$ is equal to 0.25. Note that 25% can also be written directly as a decimal by moving the decimal point two places to the left.

1 EXAMPLE

Convert each percent to a decimal.

a. 42%	**b.** 157%	**c.** 12.4%	**d.** 4%
42% = 0.42	157% = 1.57	12.4% = 0.124	4% = 0.04

To calculate a percent of a number, write the percent as a decimal and multiply.

2 EXAMPLE

Simplify. Where necessary, round to the nearest tenth.

a. 30% of 242

$$\begin{aligned} 30\% \text{ of } 242 &= 0.3 \cdot 242 \\ &= 72.6 \end{aligned}$$

b. 7% of 38

$$\begin{aligned} 7\% \text{ of } 38 &= 0.07 \cdot 38 \\ &= 2.66 \approx 2.7 \end{aligned}$$

For a percent problem, it is a good idea to check that your answer is reasonable by estimating it.

3 EXAMPLE

Estimate 23% of 96.

$23\% \approx 25\%$ and $96 \approx 100$. $25\% \left(\text{or } \frac{1}{4}\right)$ of $100 = 25$. A reasonable estimate is 25.

EXERCISES

Convert each percent to a decimal.

1. 50%	**2.** 75%	**3.** 27%	**4.** 6%
5. 32.5%	**6.** 84.6%	**7.** 9%	**8.** 2.5%

Simplify. Where necessary, round to the nearest tenth.

9. 21% of 40	**10.** 45% of 200	**11.** 6% of 120	**12.** 2% of 54
13. 80.4% of 52	**14.** 23.8% of 176	**15.** 7.5% of 32	**16.** 9.25% of 89

Estimate.

17. 12% of 70	**18.** 48% of 87	**19.** 73% of 64	**20.** 77% of 42

Probability

Probability is a measure of the likelihood of an event occurring. All probabilities range from 0 to 1 where 0 is the probability of an event that cannot happen and 1 is the probability of an event that is certain to happen. An event with probability 0.5 or 50% has an equal chance of happening or not happening.

The formula $P(E) = \frac{\text{number of favorable outcomes}}{\text{number of possible outcomes}}$ is used to calculate the probability of event E.

1 EXAMPLE

The numbers 2 through 21 are written on pieces of paper and placed in a hat. One piece of paper is drawn at random. Determine the probability of selecting a perfect square.

The total number of outcomes, 2, 3, 4, . . . , 21, for this event is 20.

There are 3 favorable outcomes: 4, 9, 16.

$P(\text{selecting a perfect square}) = \frac{3}{20}$

2 EXAMPLE

Determine the probability of getting exactly two heads when two coins are tossed.

The total number of outcomes, (H, H), (H, T), (T, H), (T, T), for this event is 4.

There is 1 favorable outcome, (H, H).

$P(\text{two heads}) = \frac{1}{4}$

EXERCISES

A jar contains 3 white balls, 7 red balls, and 4 green balls. A ball is selected at random from the jar. Determine the probability of selecting a ball with the given color.

1. red
2. white
3. green
4. green or white

5. A red ball is removed from the jar. Determine the probability that the next ball selected will be green.

6. Two green balls are removed from the jar. Determine the probability that the next ball selected will be green.

You roll a 12-sided polyhedron with the numbers 1–12 on its congruent faces. Determine the probability of each outcome.

7. rolling a 2
8. rolling a 4 or a 5
9. rolling an even number
10. rolling an odd number
11. rolling a prime number
12. rolling a factor of 8

A coin is flipped three times. Determine the probability of each outcome.

13. exactly two tails
14. two heads and one tail
15. no more than two tails
16. no more than one head
17. at least one tail
18. all tails or all heads

Tables

Table 1 Reading Math Symbols

Symbol	Meaning	Page
$\ldots$	and so on	p. 4
$=$	is equal to, equality	p. 4
$\times, \cdot$	times (multiplication)	p. 4
n^2	square of n	p. 4
$+$	plus (addition)	p. 5
$-a$	opposite of a	p. 6
$\overline{AB}$	segment with endpoints A and B	p. 7
$\overrightarrow{AB}$	ray with endpoint A and through point B	p. 7
$^\circ$	degree(s)	p. 7
$(\ )$	parentheses for grouping	p. 8
$-$	minus (subtraction)	p. 10
$\overleftrightarrow{AB}$	line through points A and B	p. 11
$\parallel$	is parallel to	p. 18
AB	length of $\overline{AB}$	p. 25
$\lvert a \rvert$	absolute value of a	p. 25
$\cong$	is congruent to	p. 25
$\angle A$	angle with vertex A	p. 27
$\angle ABC$	angle with sides $\overrightarrow{BA}$ and $\overrightarrow{BC}$	p. 27
$m\angle A$	measure of angle A	p. 27
$\urcorner$	right angle symbol	p. 28
$\perp$	is perpendicular to	p. 35
d	distance	p. 43
(a, b)	ordered pair with x-coordinate a and y-coordinate b	p. 43
A	area	p. 52
s	length of a side	p. 52
b	base length	p. 52
h	height	p. 52
$\approx$	is approximately equal to	p. 52
d	diameter	p. 52
r	radius	p. 52
P	perimeter	p. 52
π	pi, ratio of the circumference of a circle to its diameter	p. 52
C	circumference	p. 52
$\{\ \}$	set brackets	p. 68
$\rightarrow$	maps to	p. 71
$>$	is greater than	p. 73
$<$	is less than	p. 73
$\leftrightarrow$	if and only if	p. 76
$\neq$	is not equal to	p. 90
$\angle$s	angles	p. 121
$\triangle ABC$	triangle with vertices A, B, and C	p. 132
n-gon	polygon with n sides	p. 144
m	slope of a linear function	p. 152
b	y-intercept of a linear function	p. 152
$[\ ]$	brackets for grouping	p. 154
$\ncong$	is not congruent to	p. 200
$\triangle$s	triangles	p. 220
$\sim$	not	p. 265
$\geq$	is greater than or equal to	p. 272
$\leq$	is less than or equal to	p. 272
$\ngtr$	is not greater than	p. 275
$\nless$	is not less than	p. 275
$\square ABCD$	parallelogram with vertices A, B, C, and D	p. 294
$\square$s	parallelograms	p. 294
$\sqrt{x}$	nonnegative square root of x	p. 355
$\stackrel{?}{=}$	Is this statement true?	p. 359
b_1, b_2	bases of a trapezoid	p. 374
d_1, d_2	lengths of diagonals	p. 375
a	apothem	p. 381
$\odot A$	circle with center A	p. 386
$\%$	percent	p. 386
$\overset{\frown}{AB}$	arc with endpoints A and B	p. 387
$\overset{\frown}{ABC}$	arc with endpoints A and C and containing B	p. 387
$m\overset{\frown}{AB}$	measure of $\overset{\frown}{AB}$	p. 387
P(event)	probability of the event	p. 402
$a:b, \frac{a}{b}$	ratio of a to b	p. 416
$\pm$	plus or minus	p. 422
$\sim$	is similar to	p. 423
A'	image of A, A prime	p. 432
$\tan A$	tangent of $\angle A$	p. 470
$\sin A$	sine of $\angle A$	p. 477
$\cos A$	cosine of $\angle A$	p. 477
$\overrightarrow{AB}$	vector with initial point A and terminal point B	p. 490
$\langle x, y \rangle$	ordered pair notation for a vector	p. 490
$\vec{\mathbf{v}}$	vector $\mathbf{v}$	p. 492
B	area of a base	p. 529
h	length of an altitude	p. 529
L.A.	lateral area	p. 529
S.A.	surface area	p. 529
ℓ	slant height	p. 537
V	volume	p. 544
$\begin{bmatrix} 1 & 2 \\ 3 & 4 \end{bmatrix}$	matrix	p. 640

Table 2 Formulas

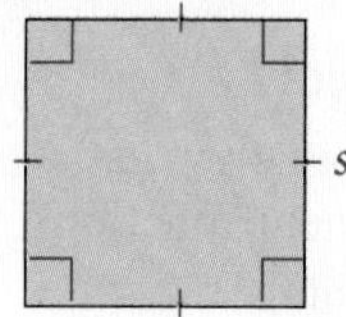

$P = 4s$
$A = s^2$

Square

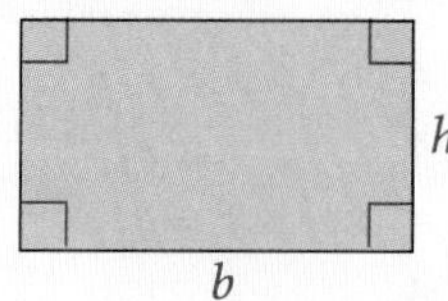

$P = 2b + 2h$
$A = bh$

Rectangle

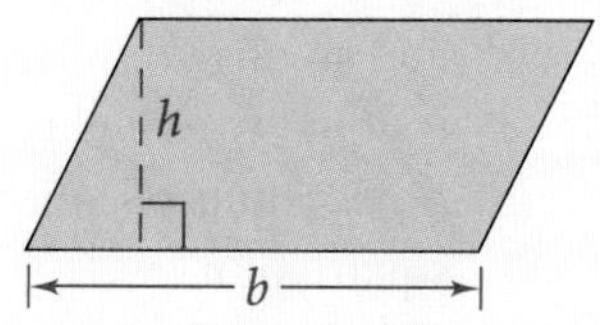

$A = bh$

Parallelogram

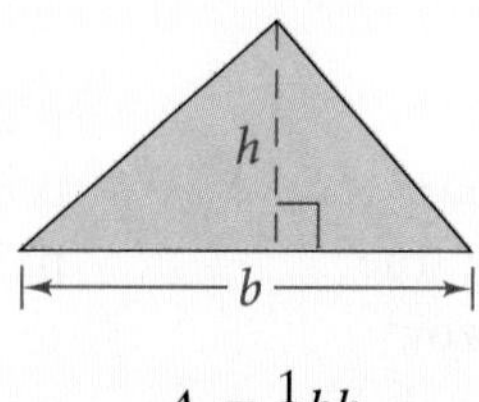

$A = \frac{1}{2}bh$

Triangle

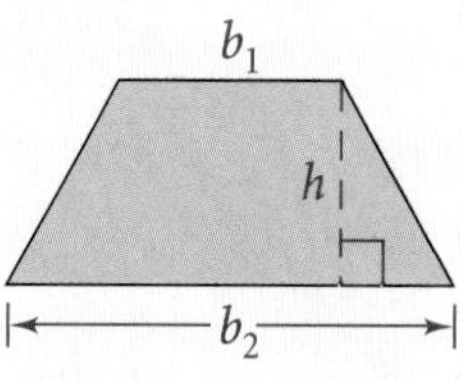

$A = \frac{1}{2}h(b_1 + b_2)$

Trapezoid

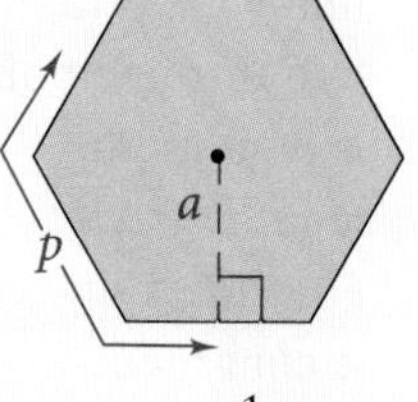

$A = \frac{1}{2}ap$

Regular Polygon

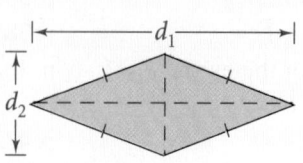

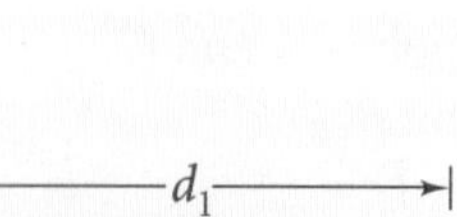

$A = \frac{1}{2}d_1d_2$

Rhombus

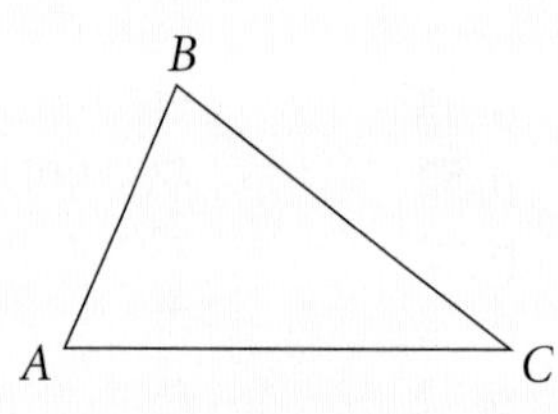

$m\angle A + m\angle B + m\angle C = 180$

Triangle Angle Sum

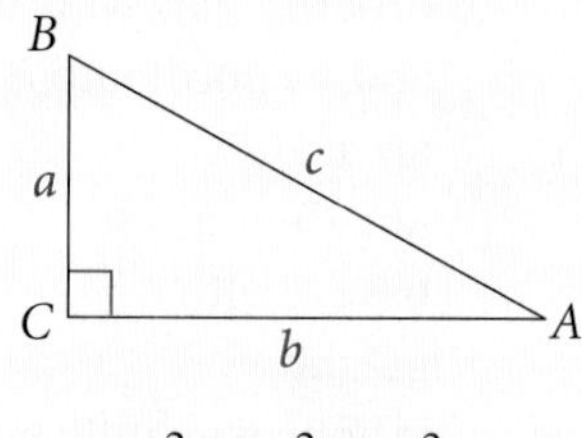

$a^2 + b^2 = c^2$

Pythagorean Theorem

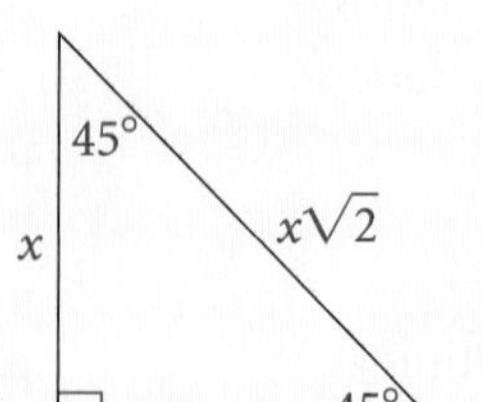

Ratio of sides $= 1:1:\sqrt{2}$

45°-45°-90° Triangle

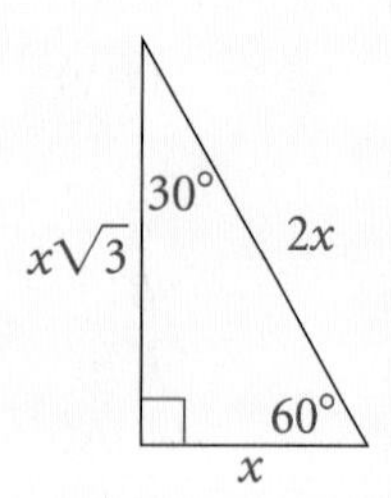

Ratio of sides $= 1:\sqrt{3}:2$

30°-60°-90° Triangle

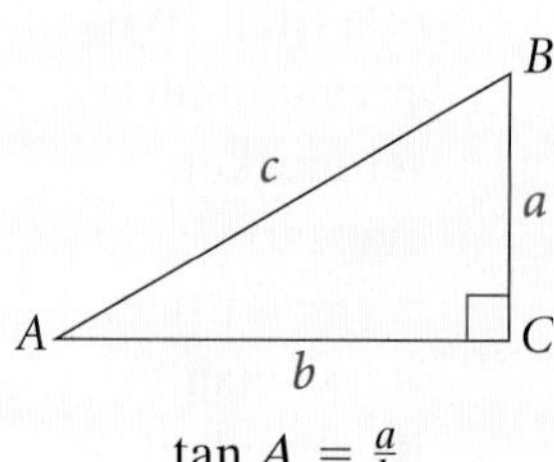

$\tan A = \frac{a}{b}$

$\sin A = \frac{a}{c}$ $\cos A = \frac{b}{c}$

Trigonometric Ratios

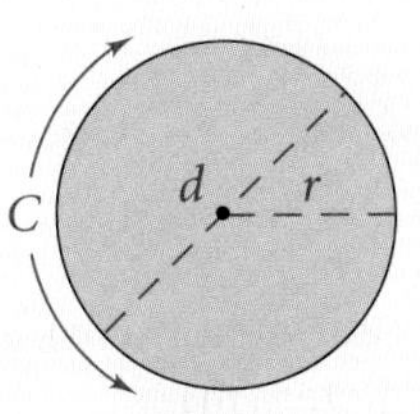

$C = \pi d$ or $C = 2\pi r$
$A = \pi r^2$

Circle

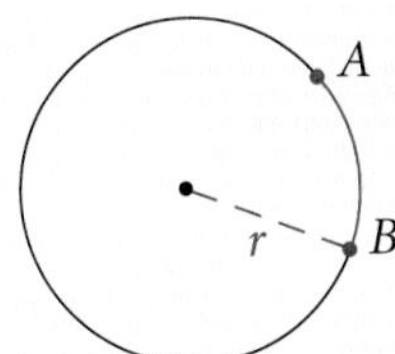

Length of $\widehat{AB} = \dfrac{m\widehat{AB}}{360} \cdot 2\pi r$

Arc

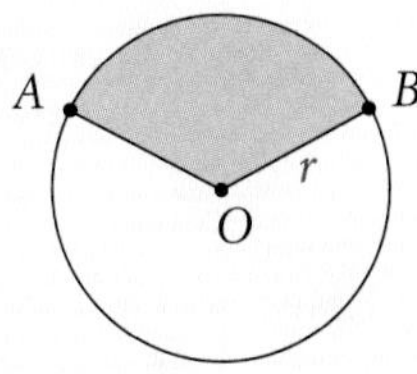

Area of sector $AOB = \dfrac{m\widehat{AB}}{360} \cdot \pi r^2$

Sector of a Circle

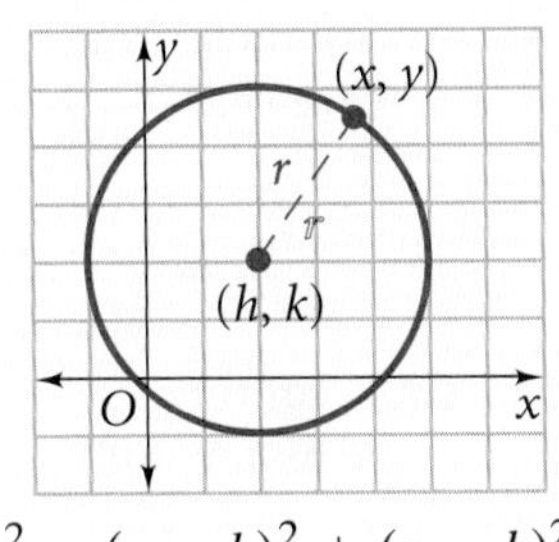

$r^2 = (x - h)^2 + (y - k)^2$

Equation of Circle

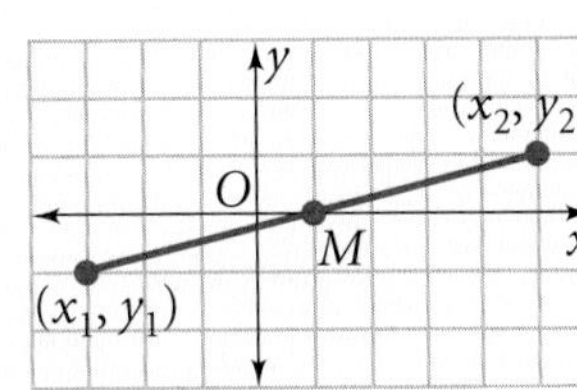

$d = \sqrt{(x_2 - x_1)^2 + (y_2 - y_1)^2}$

$M = \left(\dfrac{x_1 + x_2}{2}, \dfrac{y_1 + y_2}{2}\right)$

Distance and Midpoint

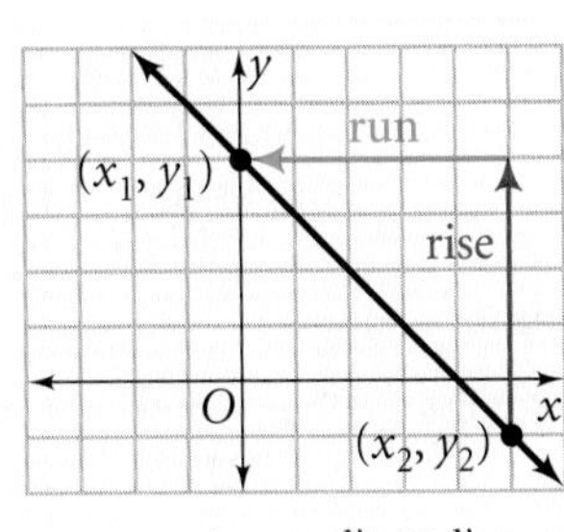

$m = \dfrac{\text{rise}}{\text{run}} = \dfrac{y_2 - y_1}{x_2 - x_1}$

Slope

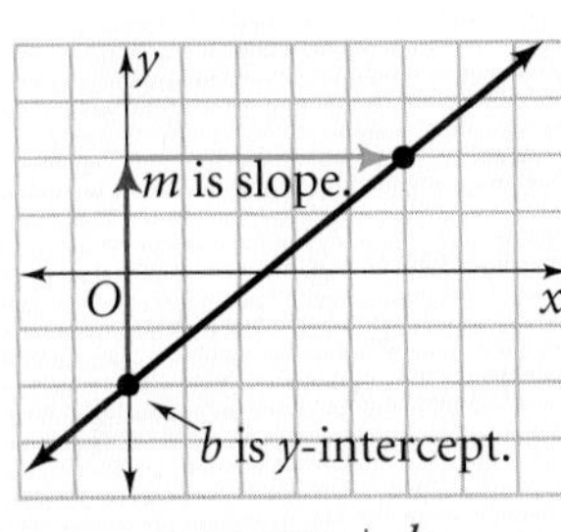

$y = mx + b$

Slope-intercept Form of a Linear Equation

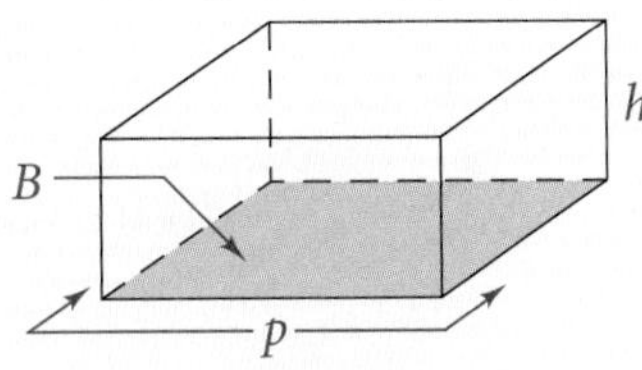

L.A. $= ph$
S.A. $=$ L.A. $+ 2B$
$V = Bh$

Right Prism

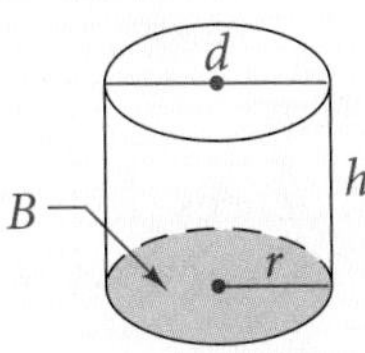

L.A. $= 2\pi rh$ or L.A. $= \pi dh$
S.A. $=$ L.A. $+ 2B$
$V = Bh$ or $V = \pi r^2 h$

Right Cylinder

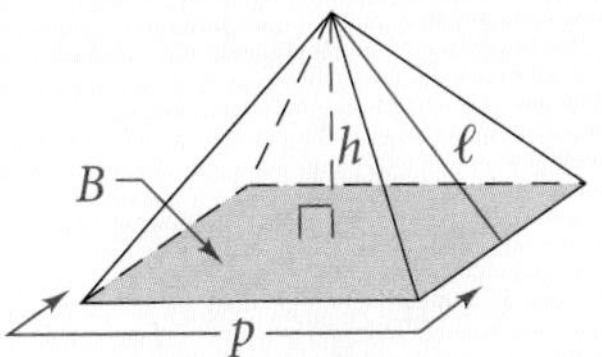

L.A. $= \frac{1}{2}p\ell$
S.A. $=$ L.A. $+ B$
$V = \frac{1}{3}Bh$

Regular Pyramid

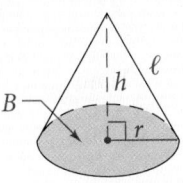

L.A. $= \pi r\ell$
S.A. $=$ L.A. $+ B$
$V = \frac{1}{3}Bh$ or $V = \frac{1}{3}\pi r^2 h$

Right Cone

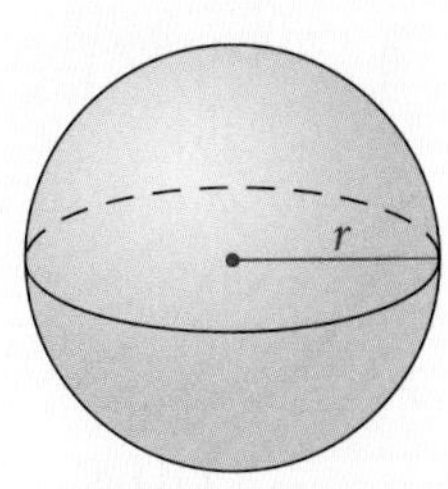

S.A. $= 4\pi r^2$
$V = \frac{4}{3}\pi r^3$

Sphere

Tables

Table 3 Measures

United States Customary	Metric
Length	
12 inches (in.) = 1 foot (ft)	10 millimeters (mm) = 1 centimeter (cm)
36 in. = 1 yard (yd)	100 cm = 1 meter (m)
3 ft = 1yard	1000 mm = 1 meter
5280 ft = 1 mile (mi)	1000 m = 1 kilometer (km)
1760 yd = 1 mile	
Area	
144 square inches (in.^2) = 1 square foot (ft^2)	100 square millimeters (mm^2) = 1 square centimeter (cm^2)
9 ft^2 = 1 square yard (yd^2)	10,000 cm^2 = 1 square meter (m^2)
43,560 ft^2 = 1 acre	10,000 m^2 = 1 hectare (ha)
4840 yd^2 = 1 acre	
Volume	
1728 cubic inches (in.^3) = 1 cubic foot (ft^3)	1000 cubic millimeters (mm^3) = 1 cubic centimeter (cm^3)
27 ft^3 = 1 cubic yard (yd^3)	1,000,000 cm^3 = 1 cubic meter (m^3)
Liquid Capacity	
8 fluid ounces (fl oz) = 1 cup (c)	1000 milliliters (mL) = 1 liter (L)
2 c = 1 pint (pt)	1000 L = 1 kiloliter (kL)
2 pt = 1 quart (qt)	
4 qt = 1 gallon (gal)	
Weight or Mass	
16 ounces (oz) = 1 pound (lb)	1000 milligrams (mg) = 1 gram (g)
2000 pounds = 1 ton (t)	1000 g = 1 kilogram (kg)
	1000 kg = 1 metric ton
Temperature	
32°F = freezing point of water	0°C = freezing point of water
98.6°F = normal body temperature	37°C = normal body temperature
212°F = boiling point of water	100°C = boiling point of water

Time	
60 seconds (s) = 1 minute (min)	365 days = 1 year (yr)
60 minutes = 1 hour (h)	52 weeks (approx.) = 1 year
24 hours = 1 day (d)	12 months = 1 year
7 days = 1 week (wk)	10 years = 1 decade
4 weeks (approx.) = 1 month (mo)	100 years = 1 century

Table 4 Properties of Real Numbers

Unless otherwise stated, *a, b, c,* and *d* are real numbers.

Identity Properties

Addition $a + 0 = a$ and $0 + a = a$

Multiplication $a \cdot 1 = a$ and $1 \cdot a = a$

Commutative Properties

Addition $a + b = b + a$

Multiplication $a \cdot b = b \cdot a$

Associative Properties

Addition $(a + b) + c = a + (b + c)$

Multiplication $(a \cdot b) \cdot c = a \cdot (b \cdot c)$

Inverse Properties

Addition

The sum of a number and its *opposite,* or *additive inverse,* is zero.

$a + (-a) = 0$ and $-a + a = 0$

Multiplication

The reciprocal, or multiplicative inverse, of a rational number $\frac{a}{b}$ is $\frac{b}{a}$ $(a, b \neq 0)$.

$a \cdot \frac{1}{a} = 1$ and $\frac{1}{a} \cdot a = 1$ $(a \neq 0)$

Distributive Properties

$a(b + c) = ab + ac$ $(b + c)a = ba + ca$

$a(b - c) = ab - ac$ $(b - c)a = ba - ca$

Properties of Equality

Addition If $a = b$, then $a + c = b + c$.

Subtraction If $a = b$, then $a - c = b - c$.

Multiplication If $a = b$, then $a \cdot c = b \cdot c$.

Division If $a = b$ and $c \neq 0$, then $\frac{a}{c} = \frac{b}{c}$.

Substitution If $a = b$, then b can replace a in any expression.

Reflexive $a = a$

Symmetric If $a = b$, then $b = a$.

Transitive If $a = b$ and $b = c$, then $a = c$.

Properties of Proportions

$\frac{a}{b} = \frac{c}{d}$ $(a, b, c, d \neq 0)$ is equivalent to

(1) $ad = bc$ (2) $\frac{b}{a} = \frac{d}{c}$

(3) $\frac{a}{c} = \frac{b}{d}$ (4) $\frac{a + b}{b} = \frac{c + d}{d}$

Zero-Product Property

If $ab = 0$, then $a = 0$ or $b = 0$.

Properties of Inequality

Addition If $a > b$ and $c \geq d$, then $a + c > b + d$.

Multiplication If $a > b$ and $c > 0$, then $ac > bc$. If $a > b$ and $c < 0$, then $ac < bc$.

Transitive If $a > b$ and $b > c$, then $a > c$.

Comparison If $a = b + c$ and $c > 0$, then $a > b$.

Properties of Exponents

For any nonzero numbers a and b, any positive number c, and any integers m and n,

Zero Exponent $a^0 = 1$

Negative Exponent $a^{-n} = \frac{1}{a^n}$

Product of Powers $a^m \cdot a^n = a^{m+n}$

Quotient of Powers $\frac{a^m}{a^n} = a^{m-n}$

Power to a Power $(c^m)^n = c^{mn}$

Product to a Power $(ab)^n = a^n b^n$

Quotient to a Power $\left(\frac{a}{b}\right)^n = \frac{a^n}{b^n}$

Properties of Square Roots

For any nonnegative numbers a and b, and any positive number c,

Product of Square Roots $\sqrt{a} \cdot \sqrt{b} = \sqrt{ab}$

Quotient of Square Roots $\frac{\sqrt{a}}{\sqrt{c}} = \sqrt{\frac{a}{c}}$

Tables

Table 5 Squares and Square Roots

Number n	Square n^2	Positive Square Root $\sqrt{n}$	Number n	Square n^2	Positive Square Root $\sqrt{n}$	Number n	Square n^2	Positive Square Root $\sqrt{n}$
1	1	1.000	**51**	2601	7.141	**101**	10,201	10.050
2	4	1.414	**52**	2704	7.211	**102**	10,404	10.100
3	9	1.732	**53**	2809	7.280	**103**	10,609	10.149
4	16	2.000	**54**	2916	7.348	**104**	10,816	10.198
5	25	2.236	**55**	3025	7.416	**105**	11,025	10.247
6	36	2.449	**56**	3136	7.483	**106**	11,236	10.296
7	49	2.646	**57**	3249	7.550	**107**	11,449	10.344
8	64	2.828	**58**	3364	7.616	**108**	11,664	10.392
9	81	3.000	**59**	3481	7.681	**109**	11,881	10.440
10	100	3.162	**60**	3600	7.746	**110**	12,100	10.488
11	121	3.317	**61**	3721	7.810	**111**	12,321	10.536
12	144	3.464	**62**	3844	7.874	**112**	12,544	10.583
13	169	3.606	**63**	3969	7.937	**113**	12,769	10.630
14	196	3.742	**64**	4096	8.000	**114**	12,996	10.677
15	225	3.873	**65**	4225	8.062	**115**	13,225	10.724
16	256	4.000	**66**	4356	8.124	**116**	13,456	10.770
17	289	4.123	**67**	4489	8.185	**117**	13,689	10.817
18	324	4.243	**68**	4624	8.246	**118**	13,924	10.863
19	361	4.359	**69**	4761	8.307	**119**	14,161	10.909
20	400	4.472	**70**	4900	8.367	**120**	14,400	10.954
21	441	4.583	**71**	5041	8.426	**121**	14,641	11.000
22	484	4.690	**72**	5184	8.485	**122**	14,884	11.045
23	529	4.796	**73**	5329	8.544	**123**	15,129	11.091
24	576	4.899	**74**	5476	8.602	**124**	15,376	11.136
25	625	5.000	**75**	5625	8.660	**125**	15,625	11.180
26	676	5.099	**76**	5776	8.718	**126**	15,876	11.225
27	729	5.196	**77**	5929	8.775	**127**	16,129	11.269
28	784	5.292	**78**	6084	8.832	**128**	16,384	11.314
29	841	5.385	**79**	6241	8.888	**129**	16,641	11.358
30	900	5.477	**80**	6400	8.944	**130**	16,900	11.402
31	961	5.568	**81**	6561	9.000	**131**	17,161	11.446
32	1024	5.657	**82**	6724	9.055	**132**	17,424	11.489
33	1089	5.745	**83**	6889	9.110	**133**	17,689	11.533
34	1156	5.831	**84**	7056	9.165	**134**	17,956	11.576
35	1225	5.916	**85**	7225	9.220	**135**	18,225	11.619
36	1296	6.000	**86**	7396	9.274	**136**	18,496	11.662
37	1369	6.083	**87**	7569	9.327	**137**	18,769	11.705
38	1444	6.164	**88**	7744	9.381	**138**	19,044	11.747
39	1521	6.245	**89**	7921	9.434	**139**	19,321	11.790
40	1600	6.325	**90**	8100	9.487	**140**	19,600	11.832
41	1681	6.403	**91**	8281	9.539	**141**	19,881	11.874
42	1764	6.481	**92**	8464	9.592	**142**	20,164	11.916
43	1849	6.557	**93**	8649	9.644	**143**	20,449	11.958
44	1936	6.633	**94**	8836	9.695	**144**	20,736	12.000
45	2025	6.708	**95**	9025	9.747	**145**	21,025	12.042
46	2116	6.782	**96**	9216	9.798	**146**	21,316	12.083
47	2209	6.856	**97**	9409	9.849	**147**	21,609	12.124
48	2304	6.928	**98**	9604	9.899	**148**	21,904	12.166
49	2401	7.000	**99**	9801	9.950	**149**	22,201	12.207
50	2500	7.071	**100**	10,000	10.000	**150**	22,500	12.247

Table 6 Trigonometric Ratios

Angle	Sine	Cosine	Tangent
1°	0.0175	0.9998	0.0175
2°	0.0349	0.9994	0.0349
3°	0.0523	0.9986	0.0524
4°	0.0698	0.9976	0.0699
5°	0.0872	0.9962	0.0875
6°	0.1045	0.9945	0.1051
7°	0.1219	0.9925	0.1228
8°	0.1392	0.9903	0.1405
9°	0.1564	0.9877	0.1584
10°	0.1736	0.9848	0.1763
11°	0.1908	0.9816	0.1944
12°	0.2079	0.9781	0.2126
13°	0.2250	0.9744	0.2309
14°	0.2419	0.9703	0.2493
15°	0.2588	0.9659	0.2679
16°	0.2756	0.9613	0.2867
17°	0.2924	0.9563	0.3057
18°	0.3090	0.9511	0.3249
19°	0.3256	0.9455	0.3443
20°	0.3420	0.9397	0.3640
21°	0.3584	0.9336	0.3839
22°	0.3746	0.9272	0.4040
23°	0.3907	0.9205	0.4245
24°	0.4067	0.9135	0.4452
25°	0.4226	0.9063	0.4663
26°	0.4384	0.8988	0.4877
27°	0.4540	0.8910	0.5095
28°	0.4695	0.8829	0.5317
29°	0.4848	0.8746	0.5543
30°	0.5000	0.8660	0.5774
31°	0.5150	0.8572	0.6009
32°	0.5299	0.8480	0.6249
33°	0.5446	0.8387	0.6494
34°	0.5592	0.8290	0.6745
35°	0.5736	0.8192	0.7002
36°	0.5878	0.8090	0.7265
37°	0.6018	0.7986	0.7536
38°	0.6157	0.7880	0.7813
39°	0.6293	0.7771	0.8098
40°	0.6428	0.7660	0.8391
41°	0.6561	0.7547	0.8693
42°	0.6691	0.7431	0.9004
43°	0.6820	0.7314	0.9325
44°	0.6947	0.7193	0.9657
45°	0.7071	0.7071	1.0000
46°	0.7193	0.6947	1.0355
47°	0.7314	0.6820	1.0724
48°	0.7431	0.6691	1.1106
49°	0.7547	0.6561	1.1504
50°	0.7660	0.6428	1.1918
51°	0.7771	0.6293	1.2349
52°	0.7880	0.6157	1.2799
53°	0.7986	0.6018	1.3270
54°	0.8090	0.5878	1.3764
55°	0.8192	0.5736	1.4281
56°	0.8290	0.5592	1.4826
57°	0.8387	0.5446	1.5399
58°	0.8480	0.5299	1.6003
59°	0.8572	0.5150	1.6643
60°	0.8660	0.5000	1.7321
61°	0.8746	0.4848	1.8040
62°	0.8829	0.4695	1.8807
63°	0.8910	0.4540	1.9626
64°	0.8988	0.4384	2.0503
65°	0.9063	0.4226	2.1445
66°	0.9135	0.4067	2.2460
67°	0.9205	0.3907	2.3559
68°	0.9272	0.3746	2.4751
69°	0.9336	0.3584	2.6051
70°	0.9397	0.3420	2.7475
71°	0.9455	0.3256	2.9042
72°	0.9511	0.3090	3.0777
73°	0.9563	0.2924	3.2709
74°	0.9613	0.2756	3.4874
75°	0.9659	0.2588	3.7321
76°	0.9703	0.2419	4.0108
77°	0.9744	0.2250	4.3315
78°	0.9781	0.2079	4.7046
79°	0.9816	0.1908	5.1446
80°	0.9848	0.1736	5.6713
81°	0.9877	0.1564	6.3138
82°	0.9903	0.1392	7.1154
83°	0.9925	0.1219	8.1443
84°	0.9945	0.1045	9.5144
85°	0.9962	0.0872	11.4301
86°	0.9976	0.0698	14.3007
87°	0.9986	0.0523	19.0811
88°	0.9994	0.0349	28.6363
89°	0.9998	0.0175	57.2900
90°	1.0000	0.0000	

Postulates, Theorems, and Constructions

Chapter 1: Tools of Geometry

Postulate 1-1
Through any two points there is exactly one line. (p. 12)

Postulate 1-2
If two lines intersect, then they intersect in exactly one point. (p. 12)

Postulate 1-3
If two planes intersect, then they intersect in exactly one line. (p. 12)

Postulate 1-4
Through any three noncollinear points there is exactly one plane. (p. 13)

Postulate 1-5
Ruler Postulate
The points of a line can be put into one-to-one correspondence with the real numbers so that the distance between any two points is the absolute value of the difference of the corresponding numbers. (p. 25)

Postulate 1-6
Segment Addition Postulate
If three points A, B, and C are collinear and B is between A and C, then $AB + BC = AC$. (p. 26)

Postulate 1-7
Protractor Postulate
Let $\overrightarrow{OA}$ and $\overrightarrow{OB}$ be opposite rays in a plane. $\overrightarrow{OA}$, $\overrightarrow{OB}$, and all the rays with endpoint O that can be drawn on one side of $\overleftrightarrow{AB}$ can be paired with the real numbers from 0 to 180 so that

a. $\overrightarrow{OA}$ is paired with 0 and $\overrightarrow{OB}$ is paired with 180.

b. If $\overrightarrow{OC}$ is paired with x and $\overrightarrow{OD}$ is paired with y, then $m\angle COD = |x - y|$. (p. 28)

Postulate 1-8
Angle Addition Postulate
If point B is in the interior of $\angle AOC$, then $m\angle AOB + m\angle BOC = m\angle AOC$.
If $\angle AOC$ is a straight angle, then $m\angle AOB + m\angle BOC = 180$. (p. 28)

The Distance Formula
The distance d between two points $A(x_1, y_1)$ and $B(x_2, y_2)$ is $d = \sqrt{(x_2 - x_1)^2 + (y_2 - y_1)^2}$. (p. 43)
- Proof on p. 362, Exercise 46

The Midpoint Formula
The coordinates of the midpoint M of $\overline{AB}$ with endpoints $A(x_1, y_1)$ and $B(x_2, y_2)$ are the following.
$M\left(\frac{x_1 + x_2}{2}, \frac{y_1 + y_2}{2}\right)$ (p. 45)

The Distance Formula (Three Dimensions)
In a three-dimensional coordinate system, the distance between two points (x_1, y_1, z_1) and (x_2, y_2, z_2) can be found using this extension of the Distance Formula.
$d=\sqrt{(x_2 - x_1)^2 + (y_2 - y_1)^2 + (z_2 - z_1)^2}$ (p. 48)

Postulate 1-9
If two figures are congruent, then their areas are equal. (p. 54)

Postulate 1-10
The area of a region is the sum of the areas of its nonoverlapping parts. (p. 54)

Chapter 2: Reasoning and Proof

Law of Detachment
If a conditional is true and its hypothesis is true, then its conclusion is true. In symbolic form: If $p \rightarrow q$ is a true statement and p is true, then q is true. (p. 83)

Law of Syllogism
If $p \rightarrow q$ and $q \rightarrow r$ are true statements, then $p \rightarrow r$ is a true statement. (p. 83)

Properties of Congruence
Reflexive Property
$\overline{AB} \cong \overline{AB}$ and $\angle A \cong \angle A$
Symmetric Property
If $\overline{AB} \cong \overline{CD}$, then $\overline{CD} \cong \overline{AB}$.
If $\angle A \cong \angle B$, then $\angle B \cong \angle A$.
Transitive Property
If $\overline{AB} \cong \overline{CD}$ and $\overline{CD} \cong \overline{EF}$, then $\overline{AB} \cong \overline{EF}$.
If $\angle A \cong \angle B$ and $\angle B \cong \angle C$, then $\angle A \cong \angle C$. (p. 91)

Theorem 2-1
Vertical Angles Theorem
Vertical angles are congruent. (p. 98)
- Proof on p. 98, Example 3

Theorem 2-2
Congruent Supplements Theorem
If two angles are supplements of the same angle (or of congruent angles), then the two angles are congruent. (p. 99)
- Proofs on p. 99; p. 102, Exercise 55

Theorem 2-3
Congruent Complements Theorem
If two angles are complements of the same angle (or of congruent angles), then the two angles are congruent. (p. 99)
- Proofs on p. 100, Exercise 19; p. 102, Exercise 56

Theorem 2-4
All right angles are congruent. (p. 99)
- Proof on p. 101, Exercise 31

Theorem 2-5
If two angles are congruent and supplementary, then each is a right angle. (p. 99)
- Proof on p. 101, Exercise 35

Chapter 3: Parallel and Perpendicular Lines

Postulate 3-1
Corresponding Angles Postulate
If a transversal intersects two parallel lines, then corresponding angles are congruent. (p. 116)

Theorem 3-1
Alternate Interior Angles Theorem
If a transversal intersects two parallel lines, then alternate interior angles are congruent. (p. 116)
- Proof on p. 117

Theorem 3-2
Same-Side Interior Angles Theorem
If a transversal intersects two parallel lines, then same-side interior angles are supplementary. (p. 116)
- Proof on p. 117, Example 3

Postulate 3-2
Converse of the Corresponding Angles Postulate
If two lines and a transversal form corresponding angles that are congruent, then the two lines are parallel. (p. 122)

Theorem 3-3
Converse of the Alternate Interior Angles Theorem
If two lines and a transversal form alternate interior angles that are congruent, then the two lines are parallel. (p. 123)
- Proof on p. 123, Example 1

Theorem 3-4
Converse of the Same-Side Interior Angles Theorem
If two lines and a transversal form same-side interior angles that are supplementary, then the two lines are parallel. (p. 123)
- Proofs on p. 126, Exercise 17 and p. 128, Exercise 47

Theorem 3-5
If two lines are parallel to the same line, then they are parallel to each other. (p. 124)
- Proof on p. 127, Exercise 26

Theorem 3-6
In a plane, if two lines are perpendicular to the same line, then they are parallel to each other. (p. 124)
- Proofs on p. 124, Example 3; p. 126, Exercise 16

Theorem 3-7
Triangle Angle-Sum Theorem
The sum of the measures of the angles of a triangle is 180. (p. 131)
- Proof on p. 132

Theorem 3-8
Triangle Exterior Angle Theorem
The measure of each exterior angle of a triangle equals the sum of the measures of its two remote interior angles. (p. 133)
- Proof on p. 137, Exercise 49

  Corollary
  The measure of an exterior angle of a triangle is greater than the measure of either of its remote interior angles. (p. 274)
  - Proof on p. 274

Parallel Postulate
Through a point not on a line, there is one and only one line parallel to a given line. (p. 140)

Spherical Geometry Parallel Postulate
Through a point not on a line, there is no line parallel to the given line. (p. 140)

Theorem 3-9
Polygon Angle-Sum Theorem
The sum of the measures of the angles of an n-gon is $(n - 2)180$. (p. 145)
- Proof on p. 149, Exercise 54

Theorem 3-10
Polygon Exterior Angle-Sum Theorem
The sum of the measures of the exterior angles of a polygon, one at each vertex, is 360. (p. 146)
- Proofs on p. 142 (using a computer) and p. 148, Exercise 46

Slopes of Parallel Lines
If two nonvertical lines are parallel, their slopes are equal. If the slopes of two distinct nonvertical lines are equal, the lines are parallel. Any two vertical lines are parallel. (p. 158)
- Proofs on p. 437, Exercises 42, 43

Slopes of Perpendicular Lines
If two nonvertical lines are perpendicular, the product of their slopes is -1. If the slopes of two lines have a product of -1, the lines are perpendicular. Any horizontal line and vertical line are perpendicular. (p. 159)
- Proofs on p. 329, Exercise 34 and p. 337, Exercise 41

Chapter 4: Congruent Triangles

Theorem 4-1
If the two angles of one triangle are congruent to two angles of another triangle, then the third angles are congruent. (p. 181)
- Proof on p. 184, Exercise 45

Postulate 4-1
Side-Side-Side (SSS) Postulate
If the three sides of one triangle are congruent to the three sides of another triangle, then the two triangles are congruent. (p. 187)

Postulate 4-2
Side-Angle-Side (SAS) Postulate
If two sides and the included angle of one triangle are congruent to two sides and the included angle of another triangle, then the two triangles are congruent. (p. 188)

Postulate 4-3
Angle-Side-Angle (ASA) Postulate
If two angles and the included side of one triangle are congruent to two angles and the included side of another triangle, then the two triangles are congruent. (p. 195)

Theorem 4-2
Angle-Angle-Side (AAS) Theorem
If two angles and a nonincluded side of one triangle are congruent to two angles and the corresponding nonincluded side of another triangle, then the triangles are congruent. (p. 195)
- Proof on p. 196

Theorem 4-3
Isosceles Triangle Theorem
If two sides of a triangle are congruent, then the angles opposite those sides are congruent. (p. 211)
- Proofs on p. 211, Example 1; p. 213, Exercise 2

Corollary
If a triangle is equilateral, then the triangle is equiangular. (p. 212)
- Proof on p. 215, Exercise 32

Theorem 4-4
Converse of the Isosceles Triangle Theorem
If two angles of a triangle are congruent, then the sides opposite the angles are congruent. (p. 211)
- Proofs on p. 211, Question 1; p. 213, Exercise 1

Corollary
If a triangle is equiangular, then the triangle is equilateral. (p. 212)
- Proof on p. 215, Exercise 32

Theorem 4-5
The bisector of the vertex angle of an isosceles triangle is the perpendicular bisector of the base. (p. 211)
- Proof on p. 215, Exercise 41

Theorem 4-6
Hypotenuse-Leg (HL) Theorem
If the hypotenuse and a leg of one right triangle are congruent to the hypotenuse and a leg of another right triangle, then the triangles are congruent. (p. 217)
- Proof on p. 217

Chapter 5: Relationships Within Triangles

Theorem 5-1
Triangle Midsegment Theorem
If a segment joins the midpoints of two sides of a triangle, then the segment is parallel to the third side, and is half its length. (p. 244)
- Proof on p. 244

Theorem 5-2
Perpendicular Bisector Theorem
If a point is on the perpendicular bisector of a segment, then it is equidistant from the endpoints of the segment. (p. 249)
- Proof on p. 253, Exercise 41

Theorem 5-3
Converse of the Perpendicular Bisector Theorem
If a point is equidistant from the endpoints of a segment, then it is on the perpendicular bisector of the segment. (p. 249)
- Proof on p. 253, Exercise 42

Theorem 5-4
Angle Bisector Theorem
If a point is on the bisector of an angle, then the point is equidistant from the sides of the angle. (p. 250)
- Proof on p. 253, Exercise 48

Theorem 5-5
Converse of the Angle Bisector Theorem
If a point in the interior of an angle is equidistant from the sides of the angle, then the point is on the angle bisector. (p. 250)
- Proof on p. 254, Exercise 49

Theorem 5-6
The perpendicular bisectors of the sides of a triangle are concurrent at a point equidistant from the vertices. (p. 257)
- Proof on p. 261, Exercise 30

Theorem 5-7
The bisectors of the angles of a triangle are concurrent at a point equidistant from the sides. (p. 257)
- Proof on p. 261, Exercise 31

Theorem 5-8
The medians of a triangle are concurrent at a point that is two thirds the distance from each vertex to the midpoint of the opposite side. (p. 258)
- Proof on p. 336, Exercise 39

Theorem 5-9
The lines that contain the altitudes of a triangle are concurrent. (p. 259)
- Proof on p. 336, Exercise 40

Comparison Property of Inequality
If $a = b + c$ and $c > 0$, then $a > b$. (p. 273)
- Proof on p. 273

Theorem 5-10
If two sides of a triangle are not congruent, then the larger angle lies opposite the longer side. (p. 274)
- Proof on p. 278, Exercise 33

Theorem 5-11
If two angles of a triangle are not congruent, then the longer side lies opposite the larger angle. (p. 275)
- Proof on p. 275

Theorem 5-12
Triangle Inequality Theorem
The sum of the lengths of any two sides of a triangle is greater than the length of the third side. (p. 276)
- Proof on p. 278, Exercise 40

Chapter 6: Quadrilaterals

Theorem 6-1
Opposite sides of a parallelogram are congruent. (p. 294)
- Proofs on p. 294; p. 299, Exercise 36

Theorem 6-2
Opposite angles of a parallelogram are congruent. (p. 295)
- Proofs on p. 299, Exercises 37, 38

Theorem 6-3
The diagonals of a parallelogram bisect each other. (p. 296)
- Proofs on p. 296; p. 334, Exercise 2

Theorem 6-4
If three (or more) parallel lines cut off congruent segments on one transversal, then they cut off congruent segments on every transversal. (p. 297)
- Proof on p. 300, Exercise 55

Theorem 6-5
If the diagonals of a quadrilateral bisect each other, then the quadrilateral is a parallelogram. (p. 304)
- Proof on p. 304

Theorem 6-6
If one pair of opposite sides of a quadrilateral are both congruent and parallel, then the quadrilateral is a parallelogram. (p. 304)
- Proof on p. 307, Exercise 17

Theorem 6-7
If both pairs of opposite sides of a quadrilateral are congruent, then the quadrilateral is a parallelogram. (p. 305)
- Proof on p. 305

Theorem 6-8
If both pairs of opposite angles of a quadrilateral are congruent, then the quadrilateral is a parallelogram. (p. 305)
- Proof on p. 308, Exercise 19

Theorem 6-9
Each diagonal of a rhombus bisects two angles of the rhombus. (p. 312)
- Proof on p. 312

Theorem 6-10
The diagonals of a rhombus are perpendicular. (p. 313)
- Proof on p. 317, Exercise 54

Theorem 6-11
The diagonals of a rectangle are congruent. (p. 313)
- Proof on p. 313

Theorem 6-12
If one diagonal of a parallelogram bisects two angles of the parallelogram, then the parallelogram is a rhombus. (p. 314)
- Proof on p. 318, Exercise 61

Theorem 6-13
If the diagonals of a parallelogram are perpendicular, then the parallelogram is a rhombus. (p. 314)
- Proof on p. 318, Exercise 62

Theorem 6-14
If the diagonals of a parallelogram are congruent, then the parallelogram is a rectangle. (p. 314)
- Proof on p. 318, Exercise 63

Theorem 6-15
The base angles of an isosceles trapezoid are congruent. (p. 320)
- Proof on p. 324, Exercise 26

Theorem 6-16
The diagonals of an isosceles trapezoid are congruent. (p. 321)
- Proofs on p. 321; p. 334, Exercise 3

Theorem 6-17
The diagonals of a kite are perpendicular. (p. 322)
- Proof on p. 322

Theorem 6-18
(1) The midsegment of a trapezoid is parallel to the bases.
(2) The length of a midsegment of a trapezoid is half the sum of the lengths of the bases. (p. 332)
- Proof on p. 333, Question 1

Chapter 7: Area

Theorem 7-1
Area of a Rectangle
The area of a rectangle is the product of its base and height.
$A = bh$ (p. 349)

Theorem 7-2
Area of a Parallelogram
The area of a parallelogram is the product of a base and the corresponding height.
$A = bh$ (p. 349)

Theorem 7-3
Area of a Triangle
The area of a triangle is half the product of a base and the corresponding height.
$A = \frac{1}{2}bh$ (p. 350)

Theorem 7-4
Pythagorean Theorem
In a right triangle, the sum of the squares of the lengths of the legs is equal to the square of the length of the hypotenuse.
$a^2 + b^2 = c^2$ (p. 357)
- Proofs on p. 356; p. 363, Exercise 60; p. 379; p. 443, Exercise 38; p. 612, Exercise 36

Theorem 7-5
Converse of the Pythagorean Theorem
If the square of the length of one side of a triangle is equal to the sum of the squares of the lengths of the other two sides, then the triangle is a right triangle. (p. 359)
- Proof on p. 364, Exercise 70

Theorem 7-6
If the square of the length of the longest side of a triangle is greater than the sum of the squares of the lengths of the other two sides, the triangle is obtuse. (p. 360)

Theorem 7-7
If the square of the length of the longest side of a triangle is less than the sum of the squares of the lengths of the other two sides, the triangle is acute. (p. 360)

Theorem 7-8
45°-45°-90° Triangle Theorem
In a 45°-45°-90° triangle, both legs are congruent and the length of the hypotenuse is $\sqrt{2}$ times the length of a leg.
hypotenuse $= \sqrt{2} \cdot$ leg (p. 366)
- Proof on p. 366

Theorem 7-9
30°-60°-90° Triangle Theorem
In a 30°-60°-90° triangle, the length of the hypotenuse is twice the length of the shorter leg. The length of the longer leg is $\sqrt{3}$ times the length of the shorter leg.
hypotenuse $= 2 \cdot$ shorter leg
longer leg $= \sqrt{3} \cdot$ shorter leg (p. 367)
- Proof on p. 368

Theorem 7-10

Area of a Trapezoid

The area of a trapezoid is half the product of the height and the sum of the bases.

$A = \frac{1}{2}h(b_1 + b_2)$ (p. 374)

Theorem 7-11

Area of a Rhombus or a Kite

The area of a rhombus or a kite is half the product of the lengths of its diagonals.

$A = \frac{1}{2}d_1d_2$ (p. 375)

- Proof on p. 375

Theorem 7-12

Area of a Regular Polygon

The area of a regular polygon is half the product of the apothem and the perimeter.

$A = \frac{1}{2}ap$ (p. 381)

Postulate 7-1

Arc Addition Postulate

The measure of the arc formed by two adjacent arcs is the sum of the measures of the two arcs. (p. 387)

Theorem 7-13

Circumference of a Circle

The circumference of a circle is π times the diameter.
$C = \pi d$ or $C = 2\pi r$ (p. 388)

Theorem 7-14

Arc Length

The length of an arc of a circle is the product of the ratio $\frac{\text{measure of the arc}}{360}$ and the circumference of the circle.

length of $\widehat{AB} = \frac{m\widehat{AB}}{360} \cdot 2\pi r$ (p. 389)

Theorem 7-15

Area of a Circle

The area of a circle is the product of π and the square of the radius.
$A = \pi r^2$ (p. 396)

Theorem 7-16

Area of a Sector of a Circle

The area of a sector of a circle is the product of the ratio $\frac{\text{measure of the arc}}{360}$ and the area of the circle.

Area of sector $AOB = \frac{m\widehat{AB}}{360} \cdot \pi r^2$ (p. 396)

Chapter 8: Similarity

Postulate 8-1

Angle-Angle Similarity (AA ~) Postulate

If two angles of one triangle are congruent to two angles of another triangle, then the triangles are similar. (p. 432)

Theorem 8-1

Side-Angle-Side Similarity (SAS ~) Theorem

If an angle of one triangle is congruent to an angle of a second triangle, and the sides including the two angles are proportional, then the triangles are similar. (p. 433)

- Proof on p. 433

Theorem 8-2

Side-Side-Side Similarity (SSS ~) Theorem

If the corresponding sides of two triangles are proportional, then the triangles are similar. (p. 433)

- Proof on p. 433

Theorem 8-3

The altitude to the hypotenuse of a right triangle divides the triangle into two triangles that are similar to the original triangle and to each other. (p. 440)

- Proof on p. 440

Corollary 1

The length of the altitude to the hypotenuse of a right triangle is the geometric mean of the lengths of the segments of the hypotenuse. (p. 440)

- Proof on p. 440

Corollary 2

The altitude to the hypotenuse of a right triangle separates the hypotenuse in such a way that the length of each leg of the triangle is the geometric mean of the length of the adjacent hypotenuse segment and the length of the hypotenuse. (p. 441)

- Proof on p. 441

Theorem 8-4

Side-Splitter Theorem

If a line is parallel to one side of a triangle and intersects the other two sides, then it divides those sides proportionally. (p. 446)

- Proof on p. 446

Corollary

If three parallel lines intersect two transversals, then the segments intercepted on the transversals are proportional. (p. 447)

- Proof on p. 450, Exercise 34

Converse

If a line divides two sides of a triangle proportionally, then it is parallel to the third side.

- Proof on p. 451, Exercise 47

Theorem 8-5
Triangle-Angle-Bisector Theorem
If a ray bisects an angle of a triangle, then it divides the opposite side into two segments that are proportional to the other two sides of the triangle. (p. 448)
- Proof on p. 448

Theorem 8-6
Perimeters and Areas of Similar Figures
If the similarity ratio of two similar figures is $\frac{a}{b}$, then
(1) the ratio of their perimeters is $\frac{a}{b}$ and
(2) the ratio of their areas is $\frac{a^2}{b^2}$. (p. 455)

Chapter 9: Right Triangle Trigonometry

Theorem 9-1
Area of a Triangle Given SAS
The area of a triangle is one half the product of the lengths of two sides and the sine of the included angle.
Area of $\triangle ABC = \frac{1}{2}bc(\sin A)$ (p. 500)
- Proof on p. 499

Chapter 10: Surface Area and Volume

Theorem 10-1
Lateral and Surface Areas of a Prism
The lateral area of a right prism is the product of the perimeter of the base and the height.
$\text{L.A.} = ph$

The surface area of a right prism is the sum of the lateral area and the areas of the two bases.
$\text{S.A.} = \text{L.A.} + 2B$ (p. 530)

Theorem 10-2
Lateral and Surface Areas of a Cylinder
The lateral area of a right cylinder is the product of the circumference of the base and the height of the cylinder.
$\text{L.A.} = 2\pi rh$, or $\text{L.A.} = \pi dh$

The surface area of a right cylinder is the sum of the lateral area and the areas of the two bases.
$\text{S.A.} = \text{L.A.} + 2B$, or $\text{S.A.} = 2\pi rh + 2\pi r^2$ (p. 530)

Theorem 10-3
Lateral and Surface Areas of a Regular Pyramid
The lateral area of a regular pyramid is half the product of the perimeter of the base and the slant height.
$\text{L.A.} = \frac{1}{2}p\ell$

The surface area of a regular pyramid is the sum of the lateral area and the area of the base.
$\text{S.A.} = \text{L.A.} + B$ (p. 538)

Theorem 10-4
Lateral and Surface Areas of a Cone
The lateral area of a right cone is half the product of the circumference of the base and the slant height.
$\text{L.A.} = \frac{1}{2} \cdot 2\pi r\ell$, or $\text{L.A.} = \pi r\ell$

The surface area of a right cone is the sum of the lateral area and the area of the base.
$\text{S.A.} = \text{L.A.} + B$ (p. 539)

Theorem 10-5
Cavalieri's Principle
If two space figures have the same height and the same cross-sectional area at every level, then they have the same volume. (p. 545)

Theorem 10-6
Volume of a Prism
The volume of a prism is the product of the area of a base and the height of the prism.
$V = Bh$ (p. 545)

Theorem 10-7
Volume of a Cylinder
The volume of a cylinder is the product of the area of the base and the height of the cylinder.
$V = Bh$, or $V = \pi r^2 h$ (p. 546)

Theorem 10-8
Volume of a Pyramid
The volume of a pyramid is one third the product of the area of the base and the height of the pyramid.
$V = \frac{1}{3}Bh$ (p. 552)

Theorem 10-9
Volume of a Cone
The volume of a cone is one third the product of the area of the base and the height of the cone.
$V = \frac{1}{3}Bh$, or $V = \frac{1}{3}\pi r^2 h$ (p. 553)

Theorem 10-10
Surface Area of a Sphere
The surface area of a sphere is four times the product of π and the square of the radius of the sphere.
$\text{S.A.} = 4\pi r^2$ (p. 558)

Theorem 10-11
Volume of a Sphere
The volume of a sphere is four thirds the product of π and the cube of the radius of the sphere.
$V = \frac{4}{3}\pi r^3$ (p. 560)

Theorem 10-12
Areas and Volumes of Similar Solids
If the similarity ratio of two similar solids is $a : b$, then (1) the ratio of their corresponding areas is $a^2 : b^2$, and (2) the ratio of their volumes is $a^3 : b^3$. (p. 567)

Chapter 11: Circles

Theorem 11-1
If a line is tangent to a circle, then the line is perpendicular to the radius drawn to the point of tangency. (p. 583)
- Proof on p. 583

Theorem 11-2
If a line in the plane of a circle is perpendicular to a radius at its endpoint on the circle, then the line is tangent to the circle. (p. 584)
- Proof on p. 588, Exercise 38

Theorem 11-3
The two segments tangent to a circle from a point outside the circle are congruent. (p. 585)
- Proof on p. 588, Exercise 40

Theorem 11-4
Within a circle or in congruent circles
(1) Congruent central angles have congruent chords.
(2) Congruent chords have congruent arcs.
(3) Congruent arcs have congruent central angles. (p. 590)
- Proofs on p. 594, Exercises 23, 24; p. 595, Exercise 35

Theorem 11-5
Within a circle or in congruent circles
(1) Chords equidistant from the center are congruent.
(2) Congruent chords are equidistant from the center. (p. 591)
- Proofs on p. 591; p. 595, Exercise 37

Theorem 11-6
In a circle, a diameter that is perpendicular to a chord bisects the chord and its arcs. (p. 592)
- Proof on p. 594, Exercise 25

Theorem 11-7
In a circle, a diameter that bisects a chord (that is not a diameter) is perpendicular to the chord. (p. 592)
- Proof on p. 592

Theorem 11-8
In a circle, the perpendicular bisector of a chord contains the center of the circle. (p. 592)
- Proof on p. 595, Exercise 36

Theorem 11-9
Inscribed Angle Theorem
The measure of an inscribed angle is half the measure of its intercepted arc. (p. 599)
- Proofs on p. 599; p. 603, Exercises 40, 41

Corollary 1
Two inscribed angles that intercept the same arc are congruent. (p. 600)
- Proof on p. 604, Exercise 42

Corollary 2
An angle inscribed in a semicircle is a right angle. (p. 600)
- Proof on p. 604, Exercise 43

Corollary 3
The opposite angles of a quadrilateral inscribed in a circle are supplementary. (p. 600)
- Proof on p. 604, Exercise 44

Theorem 11-10
The measure of an angle formed by a tangent and a chord is half the measure of the intercepted arc. (p. 600)
- Proof on p. 604, Exercise 45

Theorem 11-11
The measure of an angle formed by two lines that
(1) intersect inside a circle is half the sum of the measures of the intercepted arcs.
(2) intersect outside a circle is half the difference of the measures of the intercepted arcs. (p. 607)
- Proofs on p. 608; p. 612, Exercises 29, 30

Theorem 11-12
For a given point and circle, the product of the lengths of the two segments from the point to the circle is constant along any line through the point and circle. (p. 609)
- Proofs on p. 609; p. 612, Exercises 31–33

Theorem 11-13
An equation of a circle with center (h, k) and radius r is $(x - h)^2 + (y - k)^2 = r^2$. (p. 615)

Chapter 12: Transformations

Theorem 12-1
A translation or rotation is a composition of two reflections. (p. 654)

Theorem 12-2
A composition of reflections in two parallel lines is a translation. (p. 655)

Theorem 12-3
A composition of reflections in two intersecting lines is a rotation. (p. 655)

Theorem 12-4
Fundamental Theorem of Isometries
In a plane, one of two congruent figures can be mapped onto the other by a composition of at most three reflections. (p. 656)

Theorem 12-5
Isometry Classification Theorem
There are only four isometries. They are reflection, translation, rotation, and glide reflection. (p. 657)

Theorem 12-6
Every triangle tessellates. (p. 668)

Theorem 12-7
Every quadrilateral tessellates. (p. 668)

Constructions

Construction 1
Congruent Segments
Construct a segment congruent to a given segment. (p. 34)

Construction 2
Congruent Angles
Construct an angle congruent to a given angle. (p. 35)

Construction 3
Perpendicular Bisector
Construct the perpendicular bisector of a segment. (p. 36)

Construction 4
Angle Bisector
Construct the bisector of an angle. (p. 37)

Construction 5
Parallel Through a Point Not on a Line
Construct a line parallel to a given line and through a given point that is not on the line. (p. 165)

Construction 6
Perpendicular Through a Point on a Line
Construct the perpendicular to a given line at a given point on the line. (p. 166)

Construction 7
Perpendicular Through a Point Not on a Line
Construct the perpendicular to a given line through a given point not on the line. (p. 167)

English/Spanish Illustrated Glossary

A

EXAMPLES

Acute angle (p. 28) An acute angle is an angle whose measure is between 0 and 90.

Ángulo agudo (p. 28) Un ángulo agudo es un ángulo que mide entre 0 y 90 grados.

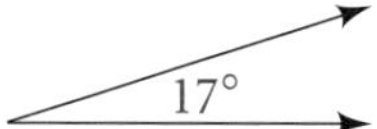

Acute triangle (p. 133) An acute triangle has three acute angles.

Triángulo acutángulo (p. 133) Un triángulo acutángulo tiene los tres ángulos agudos.

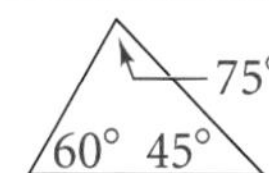

Adjacent angles (p. 96) Adjacent angles are two coplanar angles that have a common side and a common vertex but no common interior points.

Ángulos adyacentes (p. 96) Los ángulos adyacentes son dos ángulos coplanares que tienen un lado común y el mismo vértice, pero no tienen puntos interiores comunes.

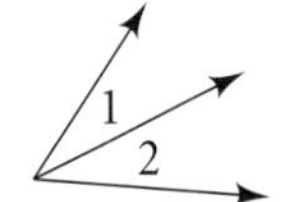

$\angle 1$ and $\angle 2$ are adjacent.

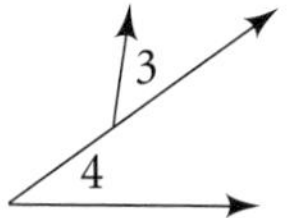

$\angle 3$ and $\angle 4$ are *not* adjacent.

Adjacent arcs (p. 387) Adjacent arcs are on the same circle and have exactly one point in common.

Arcos adyacentes (p. 387) Los arcos adyacentes están en el mismo círculo y tienen exactamente un punto en común.

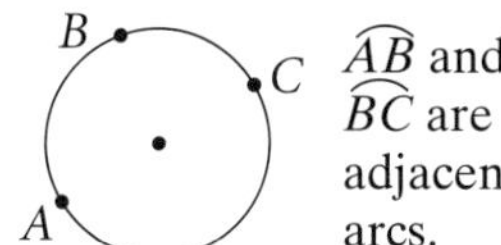

$\widehat{AB}$ and $\widehat{BC}$ are adjacent arcs.

Alternate interior angles (p. 115) Alternate interior angles are nonadjacent interior angles that lie on opposite sides of the transversal.

Ángulos alternos internos (p. 115) Dadas dos rectas y una transversal, los ángulos alternos internos son ángulos internos no adyacentes situados en lados opuestos de la transversal.

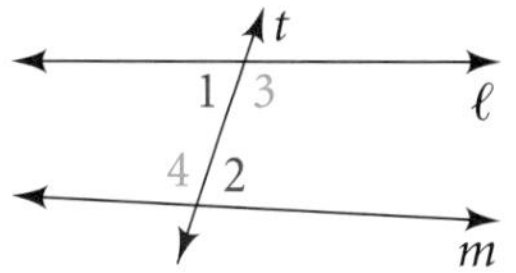

$\angle 1$ and $\angle 2$ are alternate interior angles, as are $\angle 3$ and $\angle 4$.

Altitude *See* **cone; cylinder; parallelogram; prism; pyramid; trapezoid; triangle.**

Altura *Ver* **cone; cylinder; parallelogram; prism; pyramid; trapezoid; triangle.**

Altitude of a triangle (p. 259) An altitude of a triangle is a perpendicular segment from a vertex to the line containing the side opposite that vertex.

Altura de un triángulo (p. 259) Una altura de un triángulo es el segmento perpendicular que va desde un vértice hasta la recta que contiene el lado opuesto a ese vértice.

English/Spanish Glossary

EXAMPLES

Angle (p. 27) An angle is formed by two rays with the same endpoint. The rays are the *sides* of the angle and the common endpoint is the *vertex* of the angle.

Ángulo (p. 27) Un ángulo está formado por dos rayos que convergen en un mismo punto llamado *vértice*. Los rayos son los *lados* del ángulo.

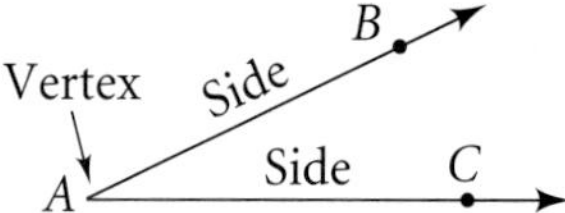

This angle could be named $\angle A$, $\angle BAC$, or $\angle CAB$.

Angle bisector (p. 36) An angle bisector is a ray that divides an angle into two congruent angles.

Bisectriz de un ángulo (p. 36) La bisectriz de un ángulo es un rayo que divide al ángulo en dos ángulos congruentes.

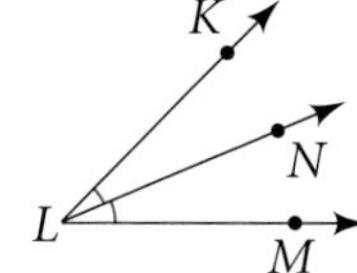

$\overrightarrow{LN}$ bisects $\angle KLM$.
$\angle KLN \cong \angle NLM$.

Angle of elevation or depression (p. 482) An angle of elevation (depression) is the angle formed by a horizontal line and the line of sight to an object above (below) the horizontal line.

Ángulo de elevación o depresión (p. 482) Un ángulo de elevación (depresión) es el ángulo formado por una línea horizontal y la recta que va de esa línea a un objeto situado arriba (debajo) de ella.

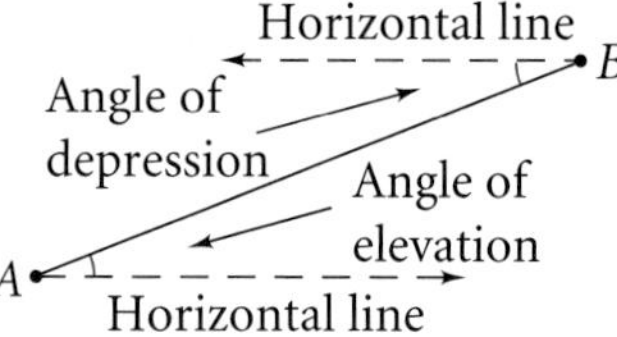

Apothem (p. 380) The apothem of a regular polygon is the distance from the center to a side.

Apotema (p. 380) La apotema de un polígono regular es la distancia desde el centro hasta un lado.

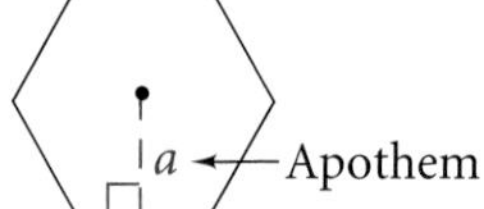

Arc *See* **major arc; minor arc.** *See also* **arc length; measure of an arc; semicircle.**

Arco *Ver* **major arc; minor arc.** *Ver también* **arc length; measure of an arc; semicircle.**

Arc length (p. 389) The length of an arc of a circle is the product of the ratio $\frac{\text{measure of the arc}}{360}$ and the circumference of the circle.

Longitud de un arco (p. 389) La longitud del arco de un círculo es el producto del cociente $\frac{\text{medida del arco}}{360}$ por la circunferencia del círculo.

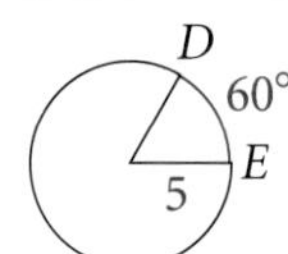

Length of $\widehat{DE} = \frac{60}{360} \cdot 2\pi(5) = \frac{5\pi}{3}$

Area (pp. 348–351, 373–375, 381, 396, 401) The area of a plane figure is the number of square units enclosed by the figure. A list of area formulas is on pp. 726–727.

Área (pp. 348–351, 373–375, 381, 396, 401) El área de una figura plana es de unidades cuadradas que contiene la figura. Una lista de fórmulas para calcular áreas está en las págs. 726–727.

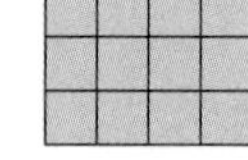

The area of the rectangle is 12 square units, or 12 units^2.

EXAMPLES

Axes (p. 43) *See* **coordinate plane.**

Ejes (p. 43) *Ver* **coordinate plane**.

Axiom (p. 12) *See* **postulate.**

Axioma (p. 12) *Ver* **postulate.**

B

Base(s) *See* **cone; cylinder; isosceles triangle; parallelogram; prism; pyramid; trapezium; triangle.**

Base(s) *Ver* **cone; cylinder; isosceles triangle; parallelogram; prism; pyramid; trapezium; triangle.**

Base angles *See* **isosceles trapezoid; isosceles triangle.**

Ángulos de base *Ver* **isosceles trapezoid; isosceles triangle.**

Biconditional (p. 75) A biconditional statement is the combination of a conditional statement and its converse. A biconditional contains the words "if and only if."

This biconditional statement is true: Two angles are congruent *if and only if* they have the same measure.

Bicondicional (p. 75) Un enunciado bicondicional es la combinación de un enunciado condicional y su recíproco. El enunciado bicondicional incluye las palabras "si y solo si".

Bisector *See* **segment bisector; angle bisector.**

Bisectriz *Ver* **segment bisector; angle bisector.**

C

Center *See* **circle; dilation; regular polygon; sphere.**

Centro *Ver* **circle; dilation; regular polygon; sphere.**

Central angle of a circle (p. 386) A central angle of a circle is an angle whose vertex is the center of the circle.

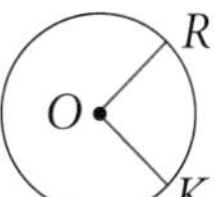

$\angle ROK$ is a central angle of $\odot O$.

Ángulo central de un círculo (p. 386) Un ángulo central de un círculo es un ángulo cuyo vértice es el centro del círculo.

English/Spanish Glossary

EXAMPLES

Central angle of a regular polygon (p. 498) A central angle of a regular polygon is an angle formed by two consecutive radii.

Ángulo central de un polígono regular (p. 498) Un ángulo central de un polígono regular es el ángulo formado por dos radios consecutivos.

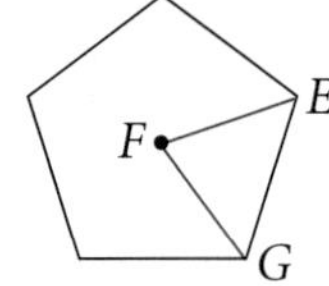

$\angle EFG$ is a central angle of the regular pentagon.

Centroid (p. 258) The centroid of a triangle is the point of intersection of the medians of that triangle.

P is the centroid of $\triangle ABC$.

Centroide (p. 258) El centroide de un triángulo es el punto de intersección de las medianas del triángulo.

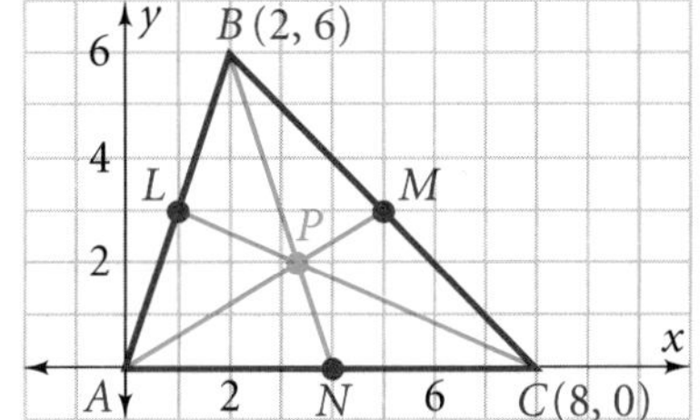

Chord (p. 590) A chord of a circle is a segment whose endpoints are on the circle.

Cuerda (p. 590) Una cuerda de un círculo es un segmento cuyos extremos son dos puntos del círculo.

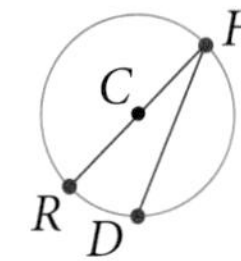

$\overline{HD}$ and $\overline{HR}$ are chords of $\odot C$.

Circle (pp. 386, 615) A circle is the set of all points in a plane that are a given distance, the *radius*, from a given point, the *center*. The standard form for an equation of a circle with center (h, k) and radius r is $(x - h)^2 + (y - k)^2 = r^2$.

Círculo (pp. 386, 615) Un círculo es el conjunto de todos los puntos de un plano situados a una distancia dada, el *radio*, de un punto dado, el *centro*. La fórmula normal de la ecuación de un círculo con centro (h, k) y radio r es $(x - h)^2 + (y - k)^2 = r^2$.

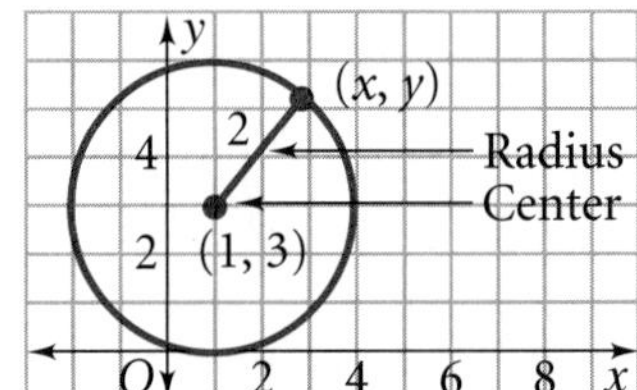

The equation of the circle whose center is (1, 3) and whose radius is 2 is $(x - 1)^2 + (y - 3)^2 = 4$.

Circumcenter (p. 257) A circumcenter is the point of concurrency of the perpendicular bisectors of a triangle.

Circuncentro (p. 257) El circuncentro es el punto de intersección de las tres mediatrices de un triángulo.

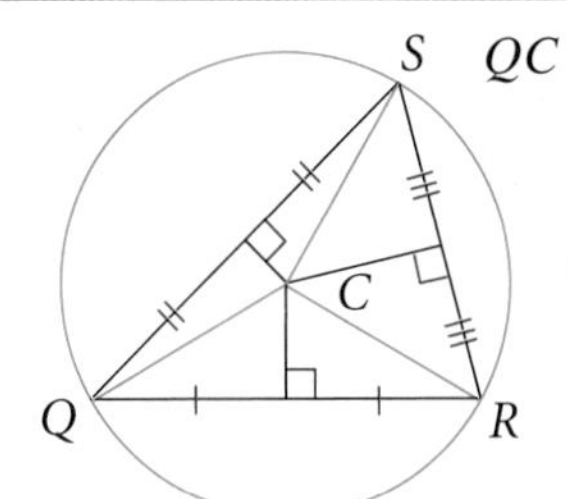

$QC = SC = RC$

C is the circumcenter.

Circumference (p. 388) The circumference of a circle is the distance around the circle. Given the radius r of a circle, you can find its circumference C by using the formula $C = 2\pi r$.

Circunferencia (p. 388) La circunferencia de un círculo es la distancia alrededor del círculo. Dado el radio r de un círculo, se puede hallar la circunferencia C usando la fórmula $C = 2\pi r$.

$$C = 2\pi r = 2\pi(4) = 8\pi$$

4

Circumference is the distance around the circle.

EXAMPLES

Circumference of a sphere (p. 558) *See* **sphere.**

Circunferencia de una esfera (p. 558) *Ver* **sphere.**

Circumscribed about (pp. 257, 585) A circle is circumscribed about a polygon if the vertices of the polygon are on the circle. A polygon is circumscribed about a circle if all the sides of the polygon are tangent to the circle.

Circunscrito en (pp. 257, 585) Un círculo está circunscrito en un polígono si los vértices del polígono están en el círculo. Un polígono está circunscrito en un círculo si todos los lados del polígono son tangentes al círculo.

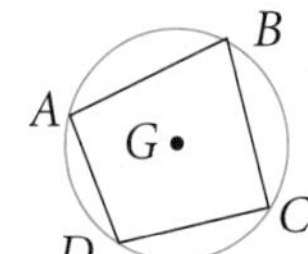

⊙G is circumscribed about $ABCD$.

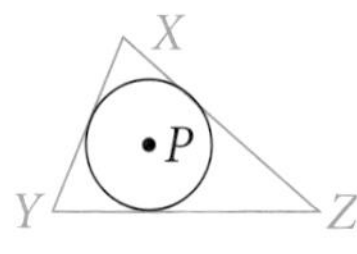

$\triangle XYZ$ is circumscribed about ⊙P.

Collinear points (p. 11) Collinear points lie on the same line.

Puntos colineales (p. 11) Los puntos colineales son los que están sobre la misma recta.

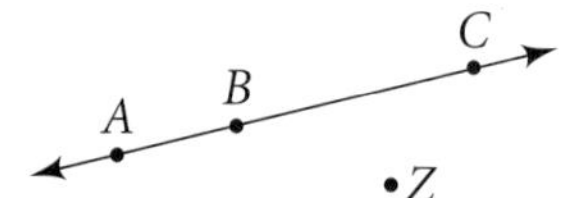

Points A, B, and C are collinear, but points A, B, and Z are noncollinear.

Compass (p. 34) A compass is a geometric tool used to draw circles and parts of circles, called arcs.

Compás (p. 34) El compás es un instrumento usado para dibujar círculos y partes de círculos, llamados arcos.

Complementary angles (p. 96) Two angles are complementary angles if the sum of their measures is 90.

Ángulos complementarios (p. 96) Dos ángulos son complementarios si la suma de sus medidas es igual a 90.

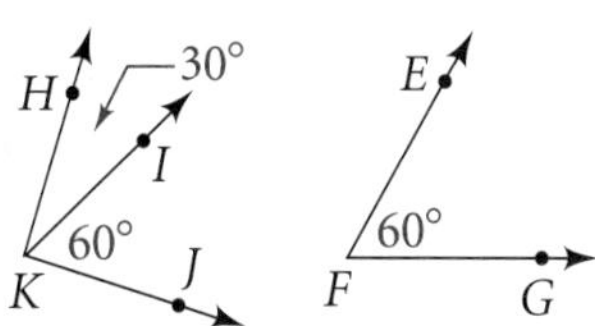

$\angle HKI$ and $\angle IKJ$ are complementary angles, as are $\angle HKI$ and $\angle EFG$.

Composite space figures (p. 547) A composite space figure is the combination of two or more figures into one object.

Figuras geométricas compuestas (p. 547) Una figura geométrica compuesta es la combinación de dos o más figuras en un mismo objeto.

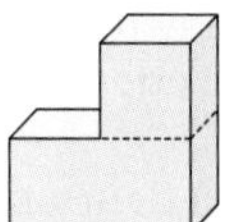

Composition of transformations (p. 642) A composition of two transformations is a transformation in which a second transformation is performed on the image of a first transformation.

Composición de transformaciones (p. 642) Una composición de dos transformaciones es una transformación en la cual una segunda transformación se realiza sobre la imagen de una primera.

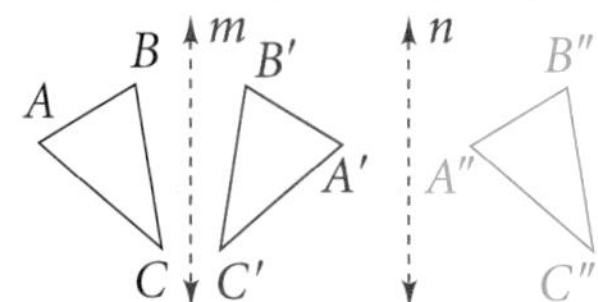

If you reflect $\triangle ABC$ in line m to get $\triangle A'B'C'$ and then reflect $\triangle A'B'C'$ in line n to get $\triangle A''B''C''$, you perform a composition of transformations.

English/Spanish Glossary

EXAMPLES

Concave polygon (p. 144) *See* **polygon.**

Polígono cóncavo (p. 144) *Ver* **polygon.**

Concentric circles (p. 388) Concentric circles lie in the same plane and have the same center.

Círculos concéntricos (p. 388) Los círculos concéntricos están en el mismo plano y tienen el mismo centro.

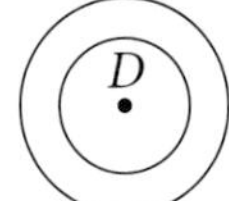

The two circles both have center D and are therefore concentric.

Conclusion (p. 68) The conclusion is the part of an *if-then* statement (conditional) that follows *then.*

Conclusión (p. 68) La conclusión es lo que sigue a la palabra *entonces* en un enunciado condicional (*Si..., entonces...*).

In the statement, "If it rains, then I will go outside," the *conclusion* is "I will go outside."

Concurrent lines (p. 257) Concurrent lines are three or more lines that meet in one point. The point at which they meet is the *point of concurrency*.

Rectas concurrentes (p. 257) Las rectas concurrentes son tres o más rectas que se unen en un punto. El punto en que se unen es el *punto de concurrencia.*

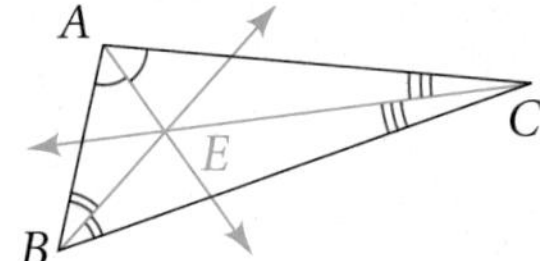

Point E is the point of concurrency of the bisectors of the angles of $\triangle ABC$. The bisectors are concurrent.

Conditional (p. 68) A conditional is an *if-then* statement.

Condicional (p. 68) Un enunciado condicional es del tipo *si..., entonces...*

If you act politely, *then* you will earn respect.

Cone (p. 539) A cone is a three-dimensional figure that has a circular *base,* a *vertex* not in the plane of the circle, and a curved lateral surface, as shown in the diagram. The *altitude* of a cone is the perpendicular segment from the vertex to the plane of the base. The *height* is the length of the altitude. In a *right cone,* the altitude contains the center of the base. The *slant height* of a right cone is the distance from the vertex to the edge of the base.

Cono (p. 539) Un cono es una figura tridimensional que tiene una *base* circular, un *vértice* que no está en el plano del círculo y una superficie lateral curvada (indicada en el diagrama). La *altura* de un cono es el segmento perpendicular desde el vértice hasta el plano de la base. La *altura*, por extensión, es la longitud de la altura. Un *cono recto* es un cono cuyo altura contiene el centro de la base. *La longitud de la generatriz* de un cono recto es la distancia desde el vértice hasta el borde de la base.

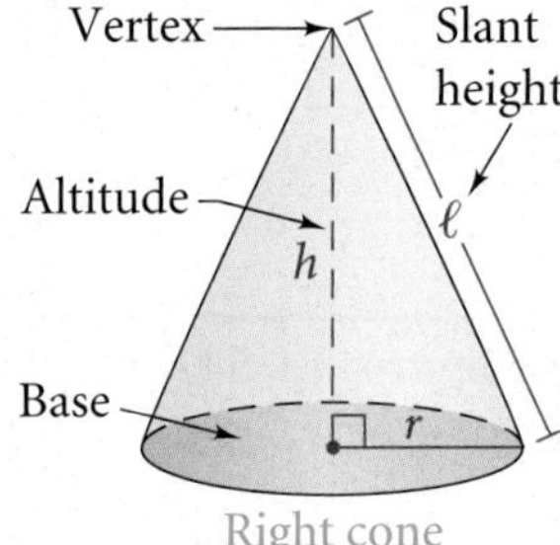

Right cone

Congruence transformation (p. 634) *See* **isometry.**

Transformación de congruencia (p. 634) *Ver* **isometry.**

EXAMPLES

Congruent angles (p. 29) Congruent angles are angles that have the same measure.

Ángulos congruentes (p. 29) Los ángulos congruentes son ángulos que tienen la misma medida.

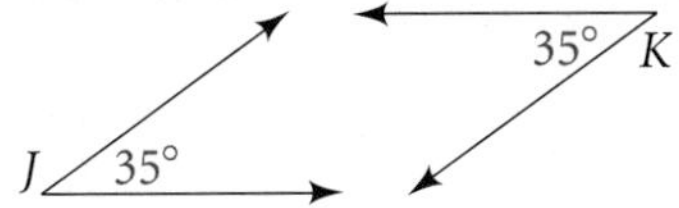

$m\angle J = m\angle K$, so $\angle J \cong \angle K$.

Congruent arcs (p. 389) Congruent arcs are arcs that have the same measure and are in the same circle or congruent circles.

Arcos congruentes (p. 389) Arcos congruentes son arcos que tienen la misma medida y están en el mismo círculo o en círculos congruentes.

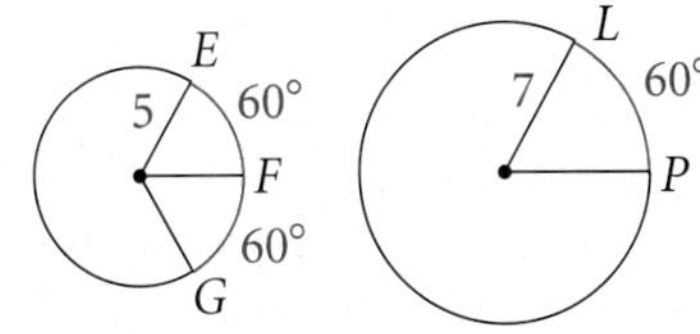

$\widehat{EF} \cong \widehat{FG}$ $\widehat{EF} \ncong \widehat{LP}$

Congruent circles (p. 386) Congruent circles are circles whose radii are congruent.

Círculos congruentes (p. 386) Los círculos congruentes son círculos cuyos radios son congruentes.

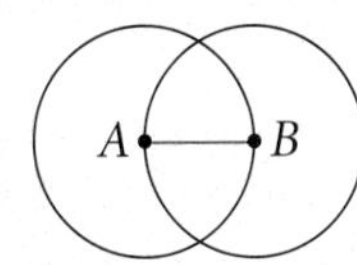

$\odot A$ and $\odot B$ have the same radius, so $\odot A \cong \odot B$.

Congruent polygons (p. 180) Congruent polygons are polygons that have corresponding sides congruent and corresponding angles congruent.

Polígonos congruentes (p. 180) Los polígonos congruentes son polígonos cuyos lados correspondientes son congruentes y cuyos ángulos correspondientes son congruentes.

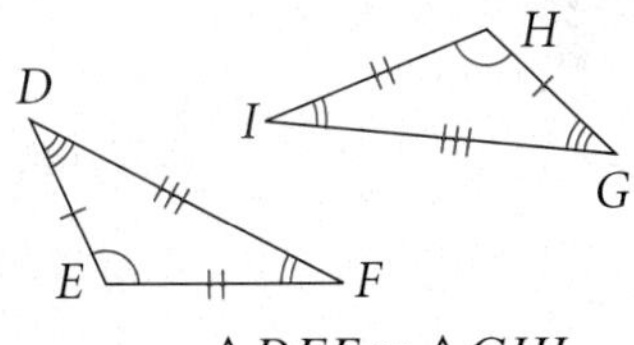

$\triangle DEF \cong \triangle GHI$

Congruent segments (p. 25) Congruent segments are segments that have the same length.

Segmentos congruentes (p. 25) Los segmentos congruentes son segmentos que tienen la misma longitud.

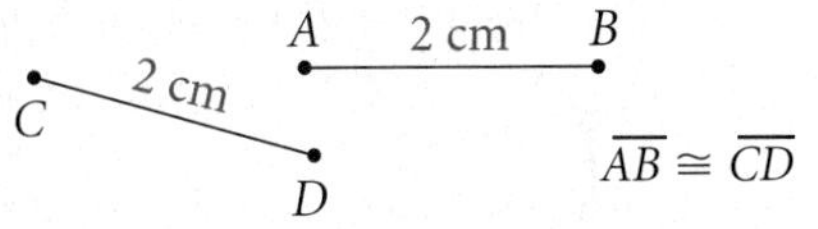

$\overline{AB} \cong \overline{CD}$

Conjecture (p. 5) A conjecture is a conclusion reached by using inductive reasoning.

Conjetura (p. 5) Una conjetura es una conclusión obtenida usando el razonamiento inductivo.

As you walk down the street, you see many people holding unopened umbrellas. You conjecture that the forecast must call for rain.

Consecutive angles (p. 295) Consecutive angles of a polygon share a common side.

Ángulos consecutivos (p. 295) Los ángulos consecutivos de un polígono tienen un lado común.

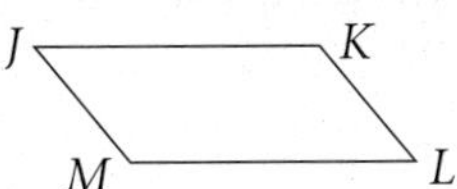

In $\square JKLM$, $\angle J$ and $\angle M$ are consecutive angles, as are $\angle J$ and $\angle K$. $\angle J$ and $\angle L$ are *not* consecutive.

EXAMPLES

Construction (p. 34) A construction is a geometric figure made with only a straightedge and compass.

Construcción (p. 34) Una construcción es una figura geométrica trazada solamente con una regla sin graduación y un compás.

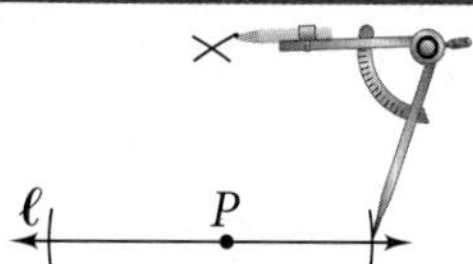

The diagram shows the construction (in progress) of a line perpendicular to a line ℓ through a point P on ℓ.

Contrapositive (p. 264) The contrapositive of the conditional "if p, then q" is the conditional "if not q, then not p." A conditional and its contrapositive always have the same truth value.

Contrapositivo (p. 264) El contrapositivo del condicional "si p, entonces q" es el condicional "si no q, entonces no p." Un condicional y su contrapositivo siempre tienen el mismo valor verdadero.

Conditional: If a figure is a triangle, then it is a polygon.
Contrapositive: If a figure is not a polygon, then it is not a triangle.

Converse (p. 69) The converse of the conditional "if p, then q" is the conditional "if q, then p."

Recíproco (p. 69) El recíproco del condicional "si p, entonces q" es el condicional "si q, entonces p."

Conditional: If you live in Cheyenne, then you live in Wyoming.
Converse: If you live in Wyoming, then you live in Cheyenne.

Convex polygon (p. 144) *See* **polygon.**

Polígono convexo (p. 144) *Ver* **polygon.**

Coordinate(s) of a point (pp. 25, 43) The coordinate of a point is its distance and direction from the origin of a number line. The coordinates of a point on a coordinate plane are in the form (x, y), where x is the x-coordinate and y is the y-coordinate.

Coordenada(s) de un punto (pp. 25, 43) La coordenada de un punto es su distancia y dirección desde el origen en una recta numérica. Las coordenadas de un punto en un plano de coordenadas se expresan como (x, y), donde x es la coordenada x y y es la coordenada y.

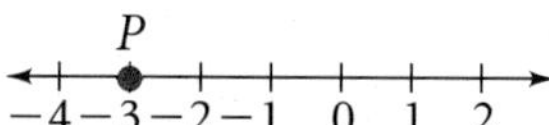

The coordinate of P is -3.

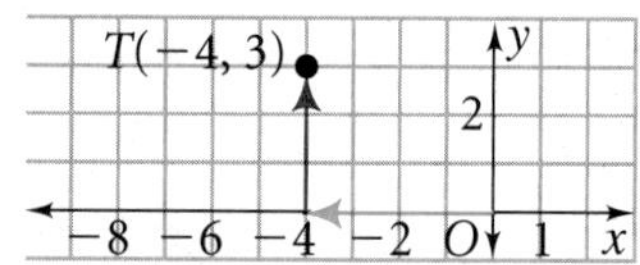

The coordinates of T are $(-4, 3)$.

Coordinate plane (p. 43) The coordinate plane is formed by two number lines, called the axes, intersecting at right angles. The x-axis is the horizontal axis, and the y-axis is the vertical axis. The two axes meet at the origin, $O(0, 0)$. The axes divide the plane into four quadrants.

Plano de coordenadas (p. 43) El plano de coordenadas se forma con dos rectas numéricas, llamadas ejes, que se cortan en ángulos rectos. El eje x es el eje horizontal y el eje y es el eje vertical. Los dos ejes se unen en el origen, $O(0, 0)$. Los ejes dividen el plano de coordenadas en cuatro cuadrantes.

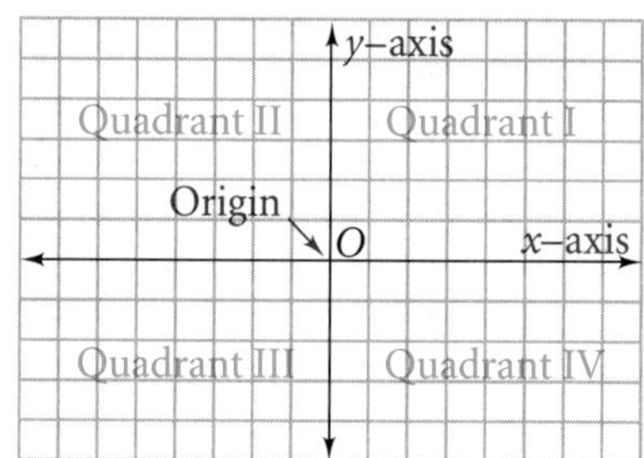

EXAMPLES

Coordinate proof (p. 244) *See* **proof.**

Prueba de coordenadas (p. 244) *Ver* **proof.**

Coplanar figures (p. 11) Coplanar figures are figures in the same plane.

Figuras coplanares (p. 11) Las figuras coplanares son las figuras que estan localizados en el mismo plano.

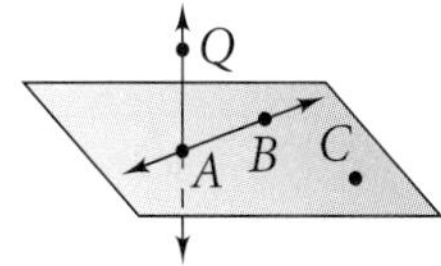

Point C and $\overleftrightarrow{AB}$ are coplanar but points A, B, C, and Q are noncoplanar.

Corollary (p. 212) A corollary is a statement that follows directly from a theorem.

Corolario (p. 212) Un corolario es un enunciado que procede directamente de un teorema.

Theorem: If two sides of a triangle are congruent, then the angles opposite those sides are congruent.
Corollary: If a triangle is equilateral, then it is equiangular.

Corresponding angles (p. 115) Corresponding angles lie on the same side of the transversal t and in corresponding positions relative to ℓ and m.

Ángulos correspondientes (p. 115) Los ángulos correspondientes están en el mismo lado de la transversal t y en las correspondientes posiciones relativas a ℓ y m.

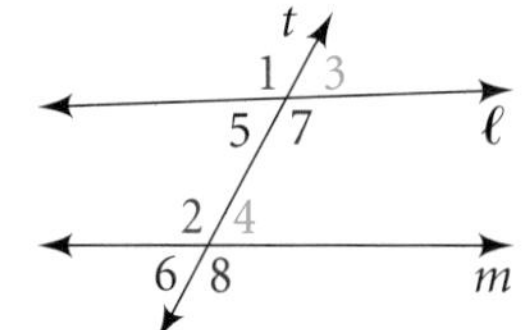

$\angle 1$ and $\angle 2$ are corresponding angles, as are $\angle 3$ and $\angle 4$, $\angle 5$ and $\angle 6$, and $\angle 7$ and $\angle 8$.

Cosine ratio (p. 477) *See* **trigonometric ratios.**

Razón coseno (p. 477) *Ver* **trigonometric ratios.**

Counterexample (pp. 5, 69) A counterexample to a statement is a particular example or instance of the statement that makes the statement false.

Contraejemplo (pp. 5, 69) Un contraejemplo a un enunciado es un ejemplo particular o caso que demuestra que el enunciado no es verdadero.

Statement: If the name of a state begins with W, then that state does not border an ocean.
Counterexample: Washington

CPCTC (p. 203) CPCTC is an abbreviation for "corresponding parts of congruent triangles are congruent."

EXAMPLE By the SAS Congruence Postulate, $\triangle KLM \cong \triangle QPR$. By CPCTC, you also know that $\angle L \cong \angle P$, $\angle M \cong \angle R$, and $\overline{LM} \cong \overline{PR}$.

CPCTC (p. 203) CPCTC es una abreviatura para "partes correspondientes de triángulos congruentes son congruentes."

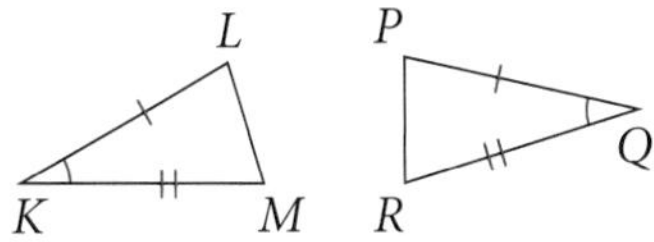

English/Spanish Glossary

EXAMPLES

Cross-Product Property (p. 417) The product of the extremes of a proportion is equal to the product of the means.

Propiedad del producto en equis (p. 417) El producto de los extremos de una proporción es igual al producto de los medios.

If $\frac{x}{3} = \frac{12}{21}$, then $21x = 3 \cdot 12$.

Cross section (p. 522) A cross section is the intersection of a solid and a plane.

Sección de corte (p. 522) Una sección de corte es la intersección de un plano y un sólido.

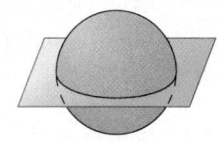

The cross section is a circle.

Cube (p. 512) A cube is a polyhedron with six faces, each of which is a square.

Cubo (p. 512) Un cubo es un poliedro de seis caras, cada una de las caras es un cuadrado.

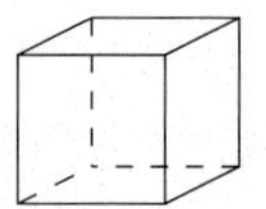

Cylinder (p. 530) A cylinder is a three-dimensional figure with two congruent circular *bases* that lie in parallel planes. An *altitude* of a cylinder is a perpendicular segment that joins the planes of the bases. Its length is the *height* of the cylinder. In a *right cylinder,* the segment joining the centers of the bases is an altitude. In an *oblique cylinder,* the segment joining the centers of the bases is not perpendicular to the planes containing the bases.

Cilindro (p. 530) Un cilindro es una figura tridimensional con dos *bases* congruentes circulares en planos paralelos. Una *altura* de un cilindro es un segmento perpendicular que une los planos de las bases. Su longitud es, por extensión, la *altura* del cilindro. En un *cilindro recto,* el segmento que une los centros de las bases es una altura. En un *cilindro oblicuo,* el segmento que une los centros de las bases no es perpendicular a los planos que contienen las bases.

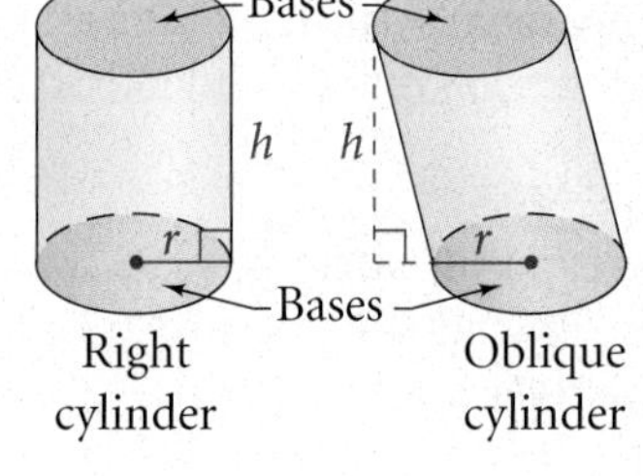

Decagon (p. 144) A decagon is a polygon with ten sides.

Decágono (p. 144) Un decágono es un polígono de diez lados.

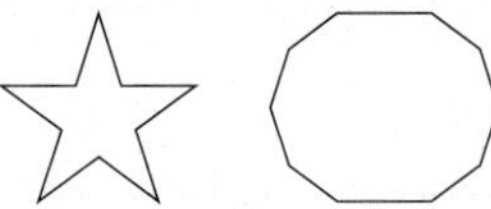

Deductive reasoning (p. 82) Deductive reasoning is a process of reasoning logically from given facts to a conclusion.

Razonamiento deductivo (p. 82) El razonamiento deductivo es un proceso de razonmiento lógico que parte de hechos dados hasta llegar a una conclusión.

Based on the fact that the sum of any two even numbers is even, you can deduce that the product of any whole number and any even number is even.

Diagonal (p. 144) *See* **polygon.**

Diagonal (p. 144) *Ver* **polygon.**

Diameter of a circle (p. 386) A diameter of a circle is a segment that contains the center of the circle and whose endpoints are on the circle. The term *diameter* can also mean the length of this segment.

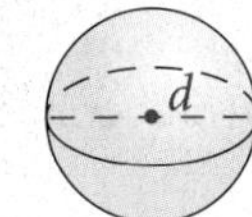

$\overline{DM}$ is a diameter of $\odot C$.

Diámetro de un círculo (p. 386) Un diámetro de un círculo es un segmento que contiene el centro del círculo y cuyos extremos están en el círculo. El término *diámetro* también puede referirse a la longitud de este segmento.

Diameter of a sphere (p. 558) The diameter of a sphere is a segment passing through the center, with endpoints on the sphere.

Diámetro de una esfera (p. 558) El diámetro de una esfera es un segmento que contiene el centro de la esfera y cuyos extremos están en la esfera.

Dilation (p. 674) A dilation, or *similarity transformation,* is a transformation that has *center C* and *scale factor n,* where $n > 0$, and maps a point R to R' in such a way that R' is on $\overrightarrow{CR}$ and $CR' = n \cdot CR$. The center of a dilation is its own image. If $n > 1$, the dilation is an *enlargement,* and if $0 < n < 1$, the dilation is a *reduction.*

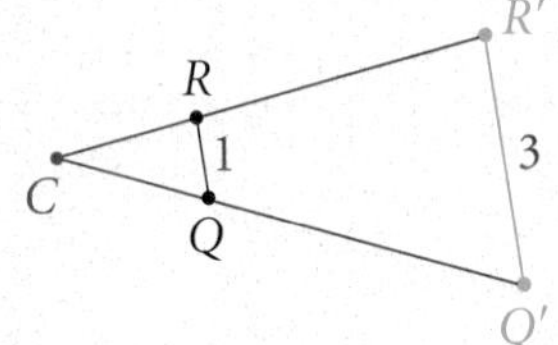

$\overline{R'Q'}$ is the image of $\overline{RQ}$ under a dilation with center C and scale factor 3.

Dilatación (p. 674) Una dilatación, o *transformación de semejanza,* tiene *centro C* y *factor de escala n* para $n > 0$, y asocia un punto R a R' de tal modo que R' está en $\overrightarrow{CR}$ y $CR' = n \cdot CR$. El centro de una dilatación es su propia imagen. Si $n > 1$, la dilatación es un *aumento,* y si $0 < n < 1$, la dilatación es una *reducción.*

Direction of a vector (p. 490) *See* **vector.**

Dirección de un vector (p. 490) *Ver* **vector.**

Distance from a point to a line (p. 250) The distance from a point to a line is the length of the perpendicular segment from the point to the line.

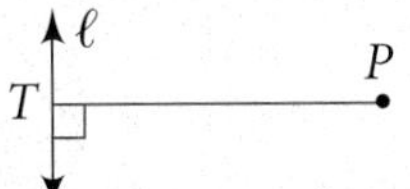

The distance from point P to a line ℓ is PT.

Distancia desde un punto hasta una recta (p. 250) La distancia desde un punto hasta una recta es la longitud del segmento perpendicular que va desde el punto hasta la recta.

Dodecagon (p. 144) A dodecagon is a polygon with twelve sides.

Dodecágono (p. 144) Un dodecágono es un polígono de doce lados.

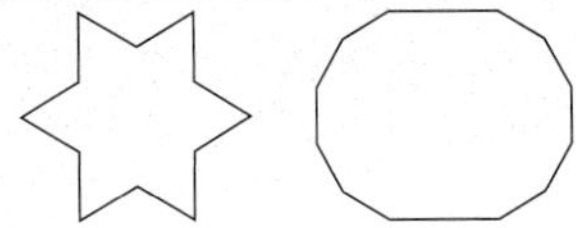

Edge (p. 512) *See* **polyhedron.**

Arista (p. 512) *Ver* **polyhedron.**

Endpoint (p. 17) *See* **ray; segment.**

Extremo (p. 17) *Ver* **ray; segment.**

Enlargement (p. 674) *See* **dilation.**

Aumento (p. 674) *Ver* **dilation.**

Equiangular triangle or polygon (pp. 133, 146) An equiangular triangle (polygon) is a triangle (polygon) whose angles are all congruent.

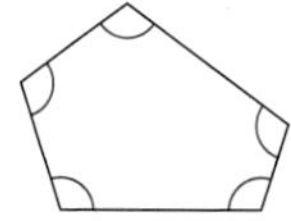

Each angle of the pentagon is a 108° angle.

Triángulo o polígono equiángulo (pp. 133, 146) Un triángulo (polígono) equiángulo es un triángulo (polígono) cuyos ángulos son todos congruentes.

Equilateral triangle or polygon (pp. 133, 146) An equilateral triangle (polygon) is a triangle (polygon) whose sides are all congruent.

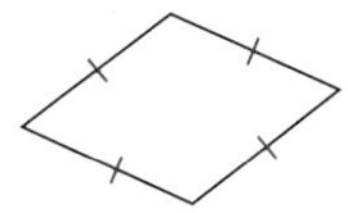

Each side of the quadrilateral is 1.2 cm long.

Triángulo o polígono equilátero (pp. 133, 146) Un triángulo (polígono) equilátero es un triángulo (polígono) cuyos lados son todos congruentes.

Equivalent statements (p. 265) Equivalent statements are statements with the same truth value.

Enunciados equivalentes (p. 265) Los enunciados equivalentes son enunciados con el mismo valor verdadero.

The following statements are equivalent:
If a figure is a square, then it is a rectangle.
If a figure is not a rectangle, then it is not a square.

Euclidean geometry (p. 140) Euclidean geometry is a geometry of the plane in which Euclid's Parallel Postulate is accepted as true.

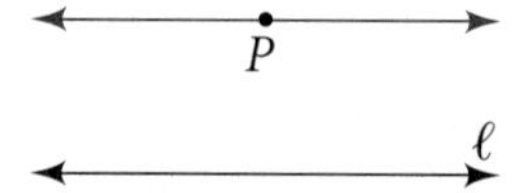

In Euclidean geometry, there is exactly one line parallel to line ℓ through point P.

Geometría euclidiana (p. 140) La geometría euclidiana es una geometría del plano en donde el postulado paralelo de Euclides es verdadero.

Extended proportion (p. 417) *See* **proportion.**

Proporción por extensión (p. 417) *Ver* **proportion.**

EXAMPLES

Exterior angle of a polygon (p. 133) An exterior angle of a polygon is an angle formed by a side and an extension of an adjacent side.

Ángulo exterior de un polígono (p. 133) El ángulo exterior de un polígono es un ángulo formado por un lado y una extensión de un lado adyacente.

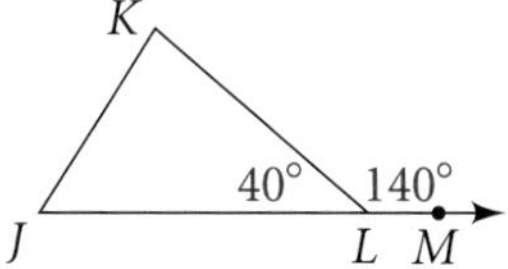

$\angle KLM$ is an exterior angle of $\triangle JKL$.

F

Face (p. 512) *See* **polyhedron.**

Cara (p. 512) *Ver* **polyhedron.**

Flip (p. 635) *See* **reflection.**

Flow proof (p. 123) *See* **proof.**

Prueba de flujo (p. 123) *Ver* **proof.**

Foundation drawing (p. 521) A foundation drawing shows the base of a structure and the height of each part.

Dibujo de fundación (p. 521) Un dibujo de fundación muestra la base de una estructura y la altura de cada parte.

3	2
2	1

Front Right

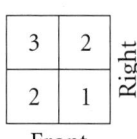

The first drawing is a foundation drawing, and the second is an isometric drawing based on the foundation drawing.

G

Geometric mean (p. 440) The geometric mean is the number x such that $\frac{a}{x} = \frac{x}{b}$, where a, b and x are positive numbers.

Media geométrica (p. 440) La media geométrica es el número x tanto que $\frac{a}{x} = \frac{x}{b}$, donde a, b y x son números positivos.

The geometric mean of 6 and 24 is 12.

$\frac{6}{x} = \frac{x}{24} \rightarrow x^2 = 144 \rightarrow x = 12$

Geometric probability (p. 402) Geometric probability is a probability that uses a geometric model in which points represent outcomes.

Probabilidad geométrica (p. 402) La probabilidad geométrica es una probabilidad que utiliza un modelo geométrico donde es usan puntos para representar resultados.

EXAMPLES

Glide reflection (p. 656) A glide reflection is the composition of a translation followed by a reflection in a line parallel to the translation vector.

Reflexión deslizada (p. 656) Una reflexión deslizada es la composición de una traslación seguida de una reflexión en una recta paralela al vector de traslación.

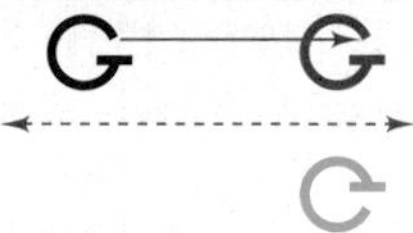

The blue G in the diagram is a glide reflection image of the black G.

Glide reflectional symmetry (p. 668) Glide reflectional symmetry is the type of symmetry for which there is a glide reflection that maps a figure onto itself.

Simetría por reflexión deslizada (p. 668) La simetría por reflexión deslizada es un típo de simetriá en la que una reflexión deslizada vuelve a trazar una figura sobre sí misma.

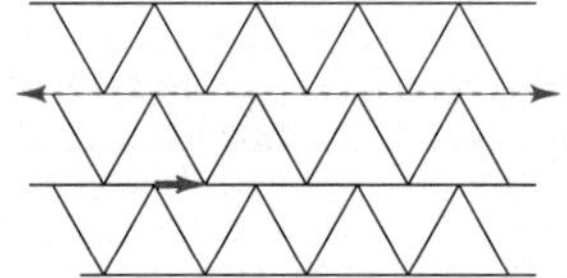

The tessellation shown can be mapped onto itself by a glide reflection in the given glide vector and reflection line.

Golden rectangle, Golden ratio (p. 425) A *golden rectangle* is a rectangle that can be divided into a square and a rectangle that is similar to the original rectangle. The *golden ratio* is the ratio of the length of a golden rectangle to its width. The value of the golden ratio is $\frac{1 + \sqrt{5}}{2}$, or about 1.62.

Rectángulo áureo, razón áurea (p. 425) Un *rectángulo áureo* es un rectángulo que se puede dividir en un cuadrado y un rectángulo semejante al rectángulo original. La *razón áurea* es la razón de la longitud de un rectángulo áureo en relación a su ancho. El valor de la razón áurea es $\frac{1 + \sqrt{5}}{2}$ o aproximadamente 1.62.

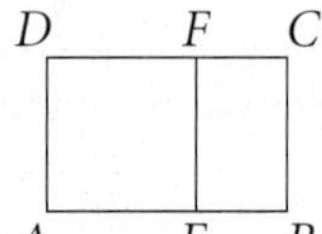

$ABCD$ is a rectangle.
$ADFE$ is a square.

$ABCD \sim BCFE$

Great circle (p. 558) A great circle is the intersection of a sphere and the plane containing the center of the sphere. A great circle divides a sphere into two hemispheres.

Círculo máximo(p. 558) Un círculo máximo es la intersección de una esfera y un plano que contiene el centro de la esfera. Un círculo máximo divide una esfera en dos hemisferios.

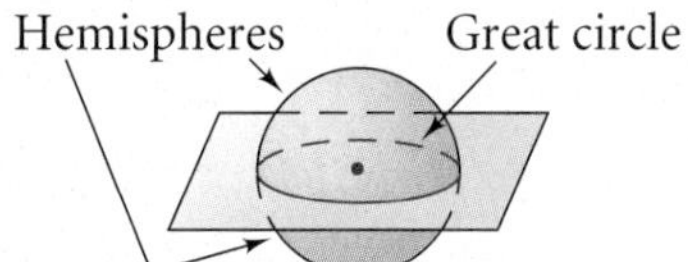

Height *See* **cone; cylinder; parallelogram; prism; pyramid; trapezoid; triangle.**

Altura *Ver* **cone; cylinder; parallelogram; prism; pyramid; trapezoid; triangle.**

EXAMPLES

Hemisphere (p. 558) *See* **great circle.**

Hemisferio (p. 558) *Ver* **great circle.**

Heptagon (p. 144) A heptagon is a polygon with seven sides.

Heptágono (p. 144) Un heptágono es un polígono de siete lados.

Heron's Formula (p. 353) Heron's Formula is a formula for finding the area of a triangle given the lengths of its sides.

Fórmula de Herón (p. 353) La fórmula de Herón se usa para hallar el área de un triángulo, dadas las longitudes de sus lados.

$A = \sqrt{s(s - a)(s - b)(s - c)}$, where s is half the perimeter (semi-perimeter) of the triangle and a, b, and c are the lengths of its sides.

Hexagon (p. 144) A hexagon is a polygon with six sides.

Hexágono (p. 144) Un hexágono es un polígono de seis lados.

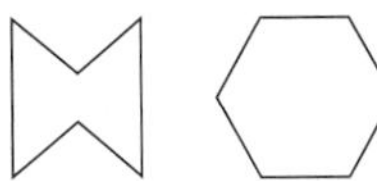

Hypotenuse (p. 217) *See* **right triangle.**

Hipotenusa (p. 217) *Ver* **right triangle.**

Hypothesis (p. 68) The hypothesis is the part that follows *if* in an *if-then* statement (conditional).

Hipótesis (p. 68) La hipótesis es lo que sigue a la palabra *si* en un *enunciado condicional* (*si..., entonces...*).

In the statement "If she leaves, then I will go with her," the hypothesis is "she leaves."

I

Identity (p. 478) An identity is an equation that is true for all allowed values of the variable.

Identidad (p. 478) Una identidad es una ecuación que es verdadera para todos los valores posibles de las variables.

$\sin x° = \cos(90 - x)°$

Incenter of a triangle (p. 257) The incenter of a triangle is the point of concurrency of the angle bisectors of the triangle.

Incentro de un triángulo (p. 257) El incentro de un triángulo es el punto donde concurren las tres bisectrices de los ángulos del triángulo.

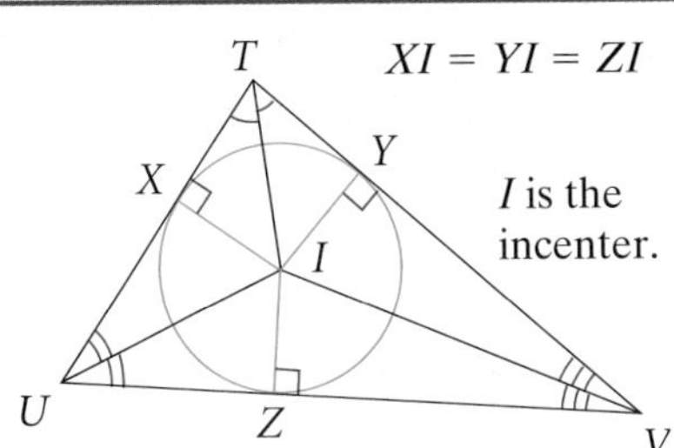

EXAMPLES

Indirect measurement (p. 434) Indirect measurement is a way of measuring things that are difficult to measure directly.

EXAMPLE By measuring the distances shown in the diagram and using proportions of similar figures, you can find the height of the taller tower. $\frac{196}{540} = \frac{x}{1300} \rightarrow x \approx 472$ ft

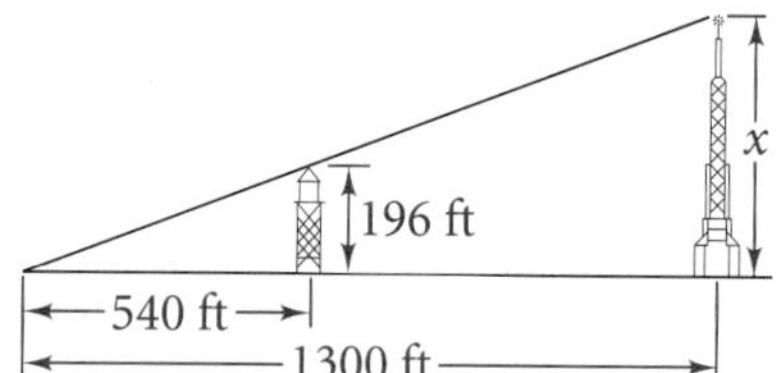

Medición indirecta (p. 434) La medición indirecta es un modo de medir cosas difíciles de medir directamente.

Indirect proof (p. 265) *See* **indirect reasoning; proof.**

Prueba indirecta (p. 265) *Ver* **indirect reasoning; proof.**

Indirect reasoning (p. 265) Indirect reasoning is a type of reasoning in which all possibilities are considered and then all but one are proved false. The remaining possibility must be true.

Razonamiento indirecto (p. 265) El razonamiento indirecto es un tipo de razonamiento en el que todas las posibilidades se consideran, y luego todas menos una resultan falsas. La posibilidad que queda debe ser verdadera.

Eduardo spent more than \$60 on two books at a store. Prove that at least one book costs more than \$30.
Proof: Suppose neither costs more than \$30. Then he spent no more than \$60 at the store. Since this contradicts the given information, at least one book costs more than \$30.

Inductive reasoning (p. 4) Inductive reasoning is a type of reasoning that reaches conclusions based on a pattern of specific examples or past events.

Razonamiento inductivo (p. 4) El razonamiento inductivo es un tipo de razonamiento en el cual se llega a conclusiones con base en un patrón de ejemplos específicos o sucesos pasados.

You see four people walk into a building. Each person emerges with a small bag containing hot food. You use inductive reasoning to conclude that this building contains a restaurant.

Initial point of a vector (p. 488) *See* **vector.**

Punto inicial de un vector (p. 488) *Ver* **vector.**

Inscribed in (pp. 257, 585) A circle is inscribed in a polygon if the sides of the polygon are tangent to the circle. A polygon is inscribed in a circle if the vertices of the polygon are on the circle.

Inscrito en (pp. 257, 585) Un círculo está inscrita en un polígono si los lados del polígono son tangentes al círculo. Un polígono está inscrito en un círculo si los vértices del polígono están en el círculo.

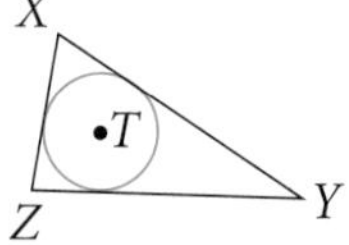

$\odot T$ is inscribed in $\triangle XYZ$.

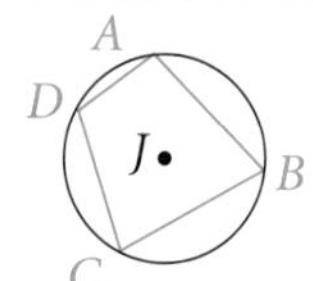

ABCD is inscribed in $\odot J$.

Inscribed angle (p. 598) An angle is inscribed in a circle if the vertex of the angle is on the circle and the sides of the angle are chords of the circle.

Ángulo inscrito (p. 598) Un ángulo está inscrito en un círculo si el vértice del ángulo está en el círculo y los lados del ángulo son cuerdas del círculo.

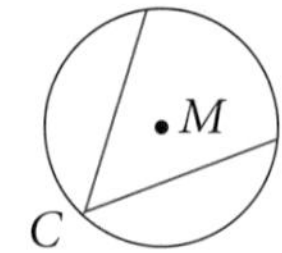

$\angle C$ is inscribed in $\odot M$.

EXAMPLES

Intercepted arc (p. 598) An intercepted arc is an arc of a circle having endpoints on the sides of an inscribed angle, and its other points in the interior of the angle.

Arco interceptor (p. 598) Un arco interceptor es un arco de un círculo cuyos extremos están en los lados de un ángulo inscrito y los puntos restantes están en el interior del ángulo.

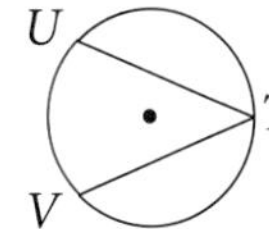

$\overset{\frown}{UV}$ is the intercepted arc of inscribed angle $\angle T$.

Inverse (p. 264) The inverse of the conditional "if *p*, then *q*" is the conditional "if not *p*, then not *q*."

Inverso (p. 264) El inverso del condicional "si *p*, entonces *q*," es el condicional "si no *p*, entonces no *q*."

Conditional: If a figure is a square, then it is a parallelogram.
Inverse: If a figure is not a square, then it is not a parallelogram.

Isometric drawing (p. 520) An isometric drawing of a three-dimensional object shows a corner view of a figure. It is not drawn in perspective and distances are not distorted.

Dibujo isométrico (p. 520) Un dibujo isométrico de un objeto tridimensional muestra una vista desde una esquina de la figura. No se muestra en perspectiva y las distancías no aparacen distorcionades.

Isometry (p. 634) An isometry, also known as a *congruence transformation,* is a transformation in which an original figure and its image are congruent.

Isometría (p. 634) Una isometría, conocida también como una *transformación de congruencia,* es una transformación en donde una figura original y su imagen son congruentes.

The four isometries are reflections, rotations, translations, and glide reflections.

Isosceles trapezoid (p. 288) An isosceles trapezoid is a trapezoid whose nonparallel opposite sides are congruent.

Trapecio isósceles (p. 288) Un trapecio isósceles es un trapecio cuyos lados opuestos no paralelos son congruentes.

Isosceles triangle (pp. 133, 211) An isosceles triangle is a triangle that has at least two congruent sides. If there are two congruent sides, they are called *legs.* The *vertex angle* is between them. The third side is called the *base* and the other two angles are called the *base angles.*

Triángulo isósceles (pp. 133, 211) Un triángulo isósceles es un triángulo que tiene por lo menos dos lados congruentes. Si tiene dos lados congruentes, éstos se llaman *catetos*. Entre ellos se encuentra el *ángulo de vértice*. El tercer lado se llama *base* y los otras dos ángulos se llaman *ángulos de base.*

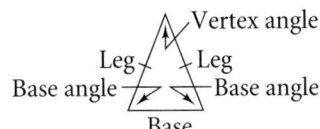

Vertex angle
Leg
Leg
Base angle
Base angle
Base

EXAMPLES

Kite (p. 288) A kite is a quadrilateral with two pairs of congruent adjacent sides and no opposite sides congruent.

Cometa (p. 288) Una cometa es un cuadrilátero con dos pares de lados congruentes adyacentes, pero sin lados opuestos congruentes.

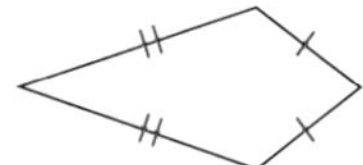

Lateral area (pp. 529, 530, 537, 539) The lateral area of a prism or pyramid is the sum of the areas of the lateral faces. The lateral area of a cylinder or cone is the area of the curved surface. A list of lateral area formulas is on p. 727.

Área lateral (pp. 529, 530, 537, 539) El área lateral de un prisma o pirámide es la suma de las áreas de sus caras laterales. El área lateral de un cilindro o de un cono es el área de la superficie curvada. Una lista de las fórmulas de áreas laterales está en la p. 727.

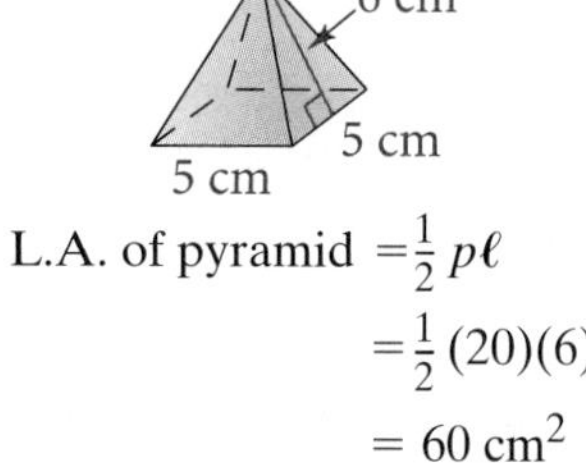

L.A. of pyramid $= \frac{1}{2} p\ell$

$= \frac{1}{2}(20)(6)$

$= 60 \text{ cm}^2$

Lateral face *See* **prism; pyramid.**

Cara lateral *Ver* **prism; pyramid.**

Leg *See* **isosceles triangle; right triangle; trapezoid.**

Cateto *Ver* **isosceles triangle; right triangle; trapezoid.**

Line (pp. 11, 140) In Euclidean geometry, a line is undefined. You can think of a line as a series of points that extend in two directions without end. In spherical geometry, you can think of a line as a great circle of a sphere.

Línea (pp. 11, 140) En la geometría euclidiana, una recta es indefinido. Puedes imaginarte a una recta como una serie de puntos que se extienden en dos direcciones sin fin. En la geometría esférica, puedes imaginarte a una recta como un círculo máximo de una esfera.

Line symmetry (p. 662) *See* **reflectional symmetry.**

Simetría lineal (p. 662) *Ver* **reflectional symmetry.**

Locus (p. 621) A locus is a set of points, all of which meet a stated condition.

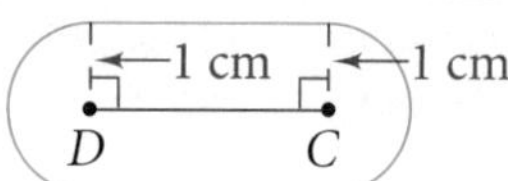

Lugar geométrico (p. 621) Un lugar geométrico es un conjunto de puntos de que todos cumplen una condición dada.

The points in blue are the locus of points in a plane 1 cm from $\overline{DC}$.

EXAMPLES

Magnitude of a vector (p. 490) *See* **vector.**

Magnitud de un vector (p. 490) *Ver* **vector.**

Major arc (p. 387) A major arc of a circle is an arc that is larger than a semicircle.

Arco mayor (p. 387) Un arco mayor de un círculo es cualquier arco más grande que un semicírculo.

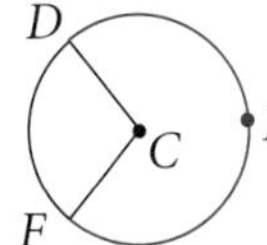

$\widehat{DEF}$ is a major arc of $\odot C$.

Map (p. 635) *See* **transformation.**

Trazar (p. 635) *Ver* **transformation.**

Matrix (p. 640) A matrix is a rectangular array of numbers. Each number in a matrix is called an *entry*.

Matriz (p. 640) Una matriz es un conjunto de números dispuestos en forma de rectángulo. Cada número de una matriz se llama *elemento* de la matriz.

The matrix $\begin{bmatrix} 1 & -2 \\ 0 & 13 \end{bmatrix}$ has dimensions 2×2. The number 1 is the entry in the first row and first column.

Measure of an angle (p. 27) The measure of an angle is a number of degrees greater than 0 and less than or equal to 180. An angle can be measured with a protractor.

Medida de un ángulo (p. 27) La medida de un ángulo es un número de grados mayor de 0 y menor o igual a 180. Un ángulo se puede medir con un transportador.

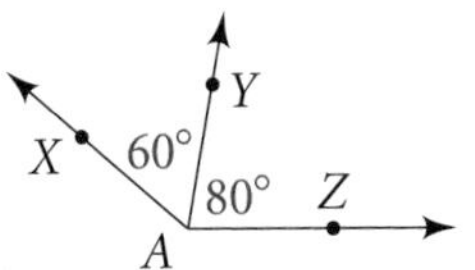

$m\angle ZAY = 80$, $m\angle YAX = 60$, and $m\angle ZAX = 140$.

Measure of an arc (p. 387) The measure of a minor arc is the measure of its central angle. The measure of a major arc is 360 minus the measure of its related minor arc.

Medida de un arco (p. 387) La medida de un arco menor es la medida de su ángulo central. La medida de un arco mayor es 360 menos la medida en grados de su arco menor correspondiente.

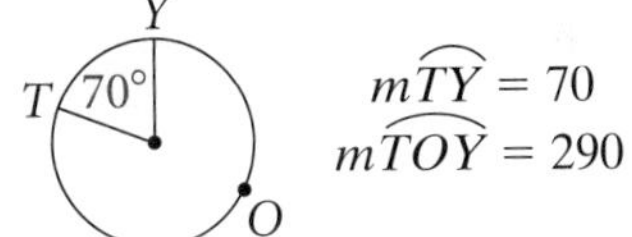

$m\widehat{TY} = 70$
$m\widehat{TOY} = 290$

Median of a triangle (p. 258) A median of a triangle is a segment that has as its endpoints a vertex of the triangle and the midpoint of the opposite side.

Mediana de un triángulo (p. 258) Una mediana de un triángulo es un segmento que tiene en su extremo el vértice del triángulo y el punto medio del lado opuesto.

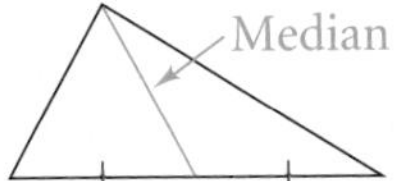

Midpoint of a segment (p. 26) A midpoint of a segment is the point that divides the segment into two congruent segments.

Punto medio de un segmento (p. 26) El punto medio de un segmento es el punto que divide el segmento en dos segmentos congruentes.

Midpoint of $\overline{AB}$

A M B

English/Spanish Glossary

EXAMPLES

Midsegment of a trapezoid (p. 332) The midsegment of a trapezoid is the segment that joins the midpoints of the nonparallel opposite sides of a trapezoid.

Segmento medio de un trapecio (p. 332) El segmento medio de trapecio es el segmento que une los puntos medios de los lados paralelos de un trapecio.

Midsegment of a triangle (p. 243) A midsegment of a triangle is the segment that joins the midpoints of two sides of the triangle.

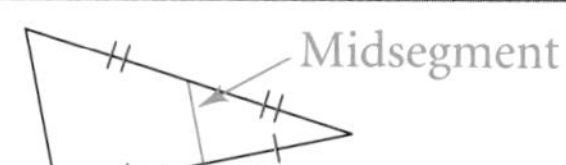

Segmento medio de un triángulo (p. 243) Un segmento medio de un triángulo es el segmento que une los puntos medios de dos lados del triángulo.

Minor arc (p. 387) A minor arc is an arc that is smaller than a semicircle.

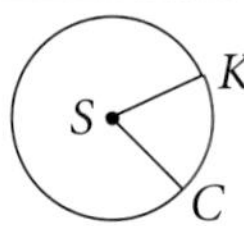

$\widehat{KC}$ is a minor arc of $\odot S$.

Arco menor (p. 387) Un arco menor de un círculo es un arco más corto que un semicírculo.

N

Negation (p. 264) A negation of a statement has the opposite meaning of the original statement.

Statement: The angle is obtuse.
Negation: The angle is not obtuse.

Negación (p. 264) La negación de un enunciado tiene el sentido opuesto del enunciado original.

Net (p. 512) A net is a two-dimensional pattern that you can fold to form a three-dimensional figure.

Patrón (p. 512) Un patrón es una figura bidimensional que se puede doblar para formar una figura tridimensional.

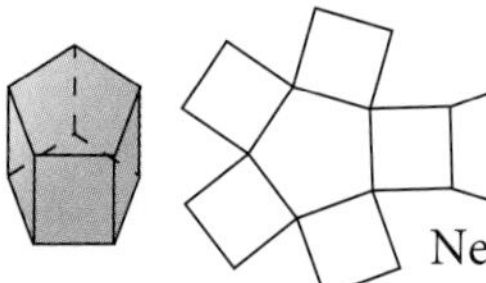

The net shown can be folded into a prism with pentagonal bases.

***n*-gon (p. 144)** An n-gon is a polygon with n sides.

***n*-ágono (p. 144)** Un n-ágono es un polígono de n lados.

Nonagon (p. 144) A nonagon is a polygon with nine sides.

Nonágono (p. 144) Un nonágono es un polígono de nueve lados.

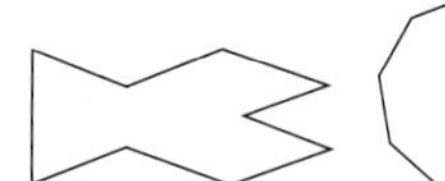

EXAMPLES

Oblique cylinder or prism *See* **cylinder; prism.**

Cilindro oblicuo o prisma *Ver* **cylinder; prism.**

Obtuse angle (p. 28) An obtuse angle is an angle whose measure is between 90 and 180.

Ángulo obtuso (p. 28) Un ángulo obtuso es un ángulo que mide entre 90 y 180.

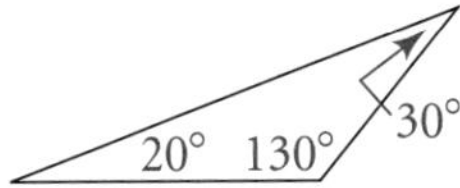

Obtuse triangle (p. 133) An obtuse triangle has one obtuse angle.

Triángulo obtusángulo (p. 133) Un triángulo obtusángulo tiene un ángulo obtuso.

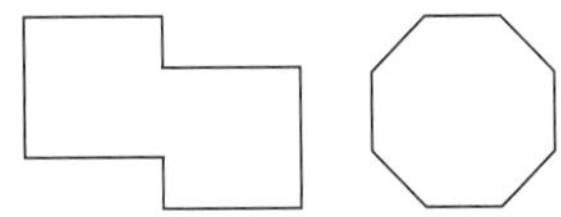

Octagon (p. 144) An octagon is a polygon with eight sides.

Octágono (p. 144) Un octágono es un polígono de ocho lados.

Opposite rays (p. 18) Opposite rays are collinear rays with the same endpoint. They form a line.

Rayos opuestos (p. 18) Los rayos opuestos son rayos colineales con el mismo extremo. Forman una recta.

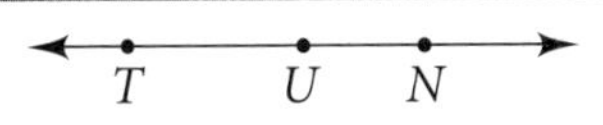

$\overrightarrow{UT}$ and $\overrightarrow{UN}$ are opposite rays.

Orientation (p. 635) Two congruent figures have *opposite* orientation if a reflection is needed to map one onto the other. If a reflection is not needed to map one figure onto the other, the figures have the same orientation.

Orientación (p. 635) Dos figuras congruentes tienen orientación *opuesta* si una reflexión es necesaria para trazar una sobre la otra. Si una reflexión no es necesaria para trazar una figura sobre la otra, las figuras tiene la misma orientación.

R Я The two R's have opposite orientation.

Origin (p. 43) *See* **coordinate plane.**

Origen (p. 43) *Ver* **coordinate plane.**

Orthocenter (p. 259) The orthocenter of a triangle is the point of intersection of the lines containing the altitudes of the triangle.

Ortocentro (p. 259) El ortocentro de un triángulo es el punto donde concurren las tres alturas del triángulo.

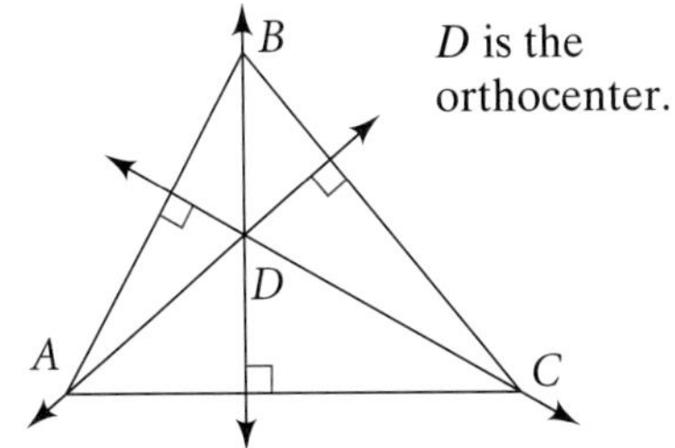

D is the orthocenter.

English/Spanish Glossary

EXAMPLES

Orthographic drawing (p. 521) An orthographic drawing is the top view, front view, and right-side view of a three-dimensional figure.

EXAMPLE The diagram shows an isometric drawing (upper right) and the three views that make up an orthographic drawing.

Dibujo ortográfico (p. 521) Un dibujo ortográfico es la vista desde arriba, la vista de frente y la vista del lado derecho de una figura tridimensional.

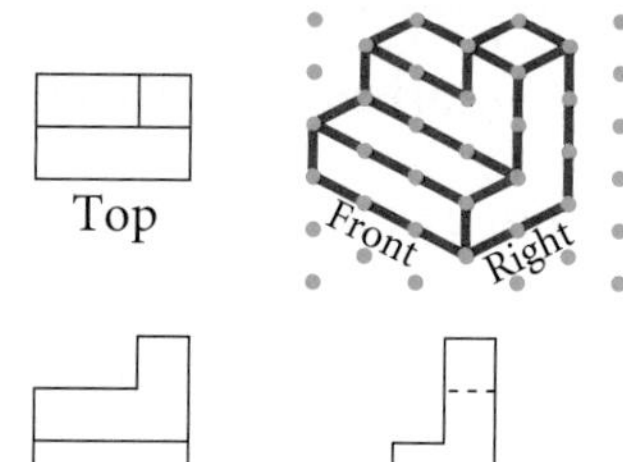

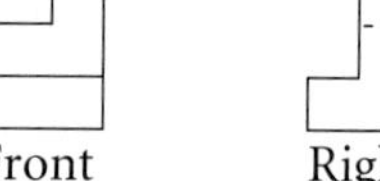

Paragraph proof (p. 100) *See* **proof.**

Prueba de párrafo (p. 100) *Ver* **proof.**

Parallel lines (pp. 18, 115) Two lines are parallel if they lie in the same plane and do not intersect. The symbol ∥ means "is parallel to."

Rectas paralelas (pp. 18, 115) Dos rectas son paralelas si están en el mismo plano y no se cortan. El símbolo ∥ significa "es paralelo a."

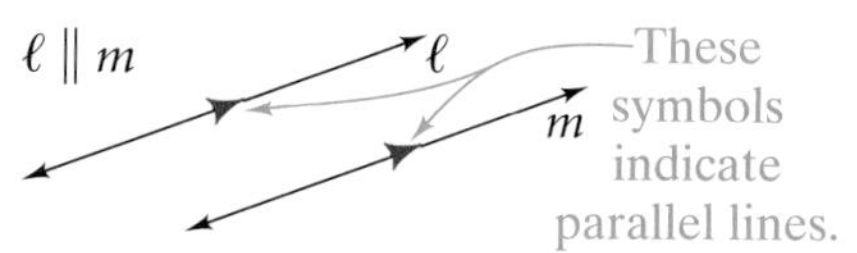

Parallelogram (p. 288) A parallelogram is a quadrilateral with two pairs of parallel sides. You can choose any side to be the *base.* An *altitude* is any segment perpendicular to the line containing the base drawn from the side opposite the base. The *height* is the length of an altitude.

Paralelogramo (p. 288) Un paralelogramo es un cuadrilátero con los dos pares de lados paralelos. Se puede escoger cualquier lado como la *base.* Una *altura* es un segmento perpendicular a la recta que contiene la base, trazada desde el lado opuesto a la base. La *altura*, por extensión, es la longitud de una altura.

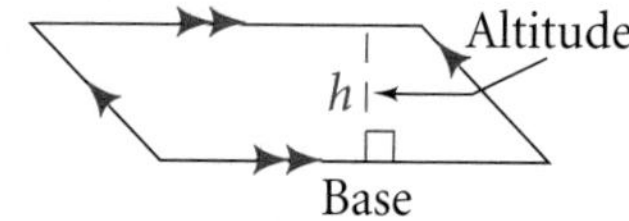

Parallel planes (p. 19) Parallel planes are planes that do not intersect.

Planos paralelos (p. 19) Planos paralelos son planos que no se cortan.

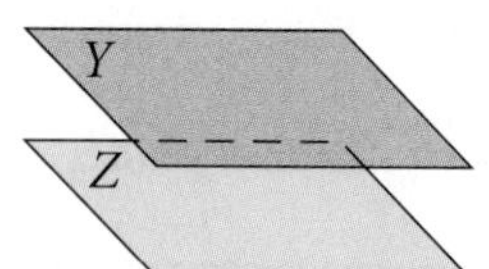

Planes Y and Z are parallel.

Pentagon (p. 144) A pentagon is a polygon with five sides.

Pentágono (p. 144) El pentágono es un polígono de cinco lados.

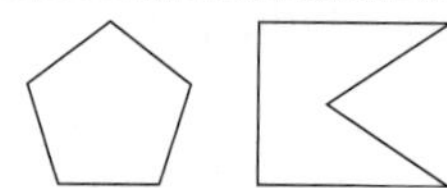

Perimeter of a polygon (p. 51) The perimeter of a polygon is the sum of the lengths of its sides.

Perímetro de un polígono (p. 51) El perímetro de un polígono es la suma de las longitudes de sus lados.

4 in.

4 in. 3 in.

5 in.

$P = 4 + 4 + 5 + 3$
$= 16$ in.

EXAMPLES

Perpendicular bisector (p. 35) The perpendicular bisector of a segment is a line, segment, or ray that is perpendicular to the segment at its midpoint.

Mediatriz (p. 35) La mediatriz de un segmento es una recta, segmento, o rayo que es perpendicular al segmento en su punto medio.

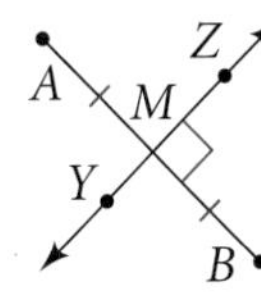

$\overleftrightarrow{YZ}$ is the perpendicular bisector of $\overline{AB}$. It is perpendicular to $\overline{AB}$ and intersects $\overline{AB}$ at midpoint M.

Perpendicular lines (p. 35) Perpendicular lines are lines that intersect and form right angles. The symbol $\perp$ means "is perpendicular to."

Rectas perpendiculares (p. 35) Las rectas perpendiculares son rectas que se cortan y forman ángulos rectos. El símbolo $\perp$ significa "es perpendicular a".

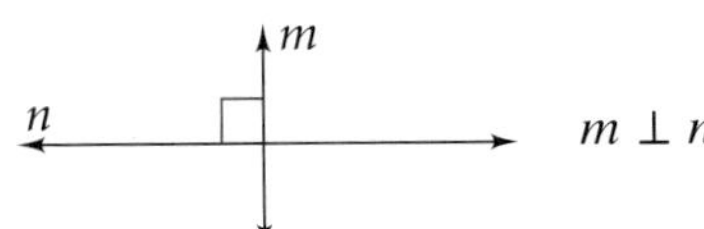

Perspective drawing (p. 518) Perspective drawing is a way of drawing objects on a flat surface so that they look the same way as they appear to the eye. In *one-point perspective,* there is one *vanishing point.* In *two-point perspective,* there are two vanishing points.

Dibujar en perspectiva (p. 518) Dibujar en perspectiva es una manera de dibujar objetos en una superficie plana de modo que se vean como los percibe el ojo humano. En la *perspectiva de un punto* hay un *punto de fuga.* En la *perspectiva de dos puntos* hay dos puntos de fuga.

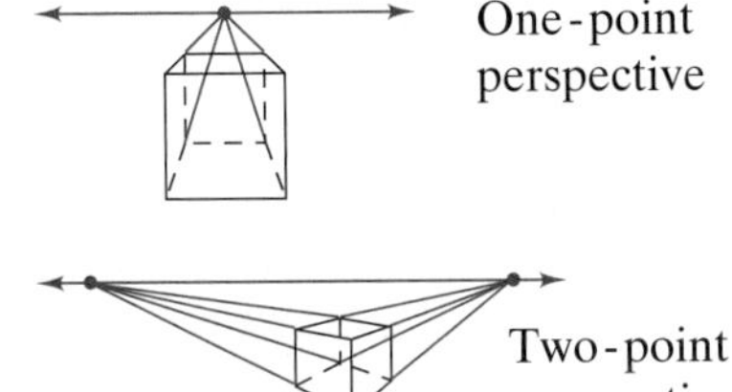

One-point perspective

Two-point perspective

Pi (p. 388) Pi (π) is the ratio of the circumference of any circle to its diameter. The number π is irrational and is approximately 3.14159.

Pi (p. 388) Pi (π) es la razón de la circunferencia de cualquier círculo en relación a su diámetro. El número π es irracional y se aproxima a $\pi \approx 3.14159$.

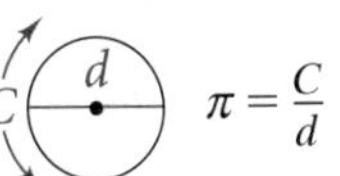

Plane (p. 11) In Euclidean geometry, a plane is undefined. You can think of a plane as a flat surface that has no thickness. A plane contains many lines and extends without end in the directions of its lines.

Plano (p. 11) En la geometría euclidiana, un plano es indefinido. Puedes imaginarte a un plano como una superficie plana que no tiene grosor. Un plano tiene muchas rectas y se extiende sin fin en la misma dirección que todas las rectas.

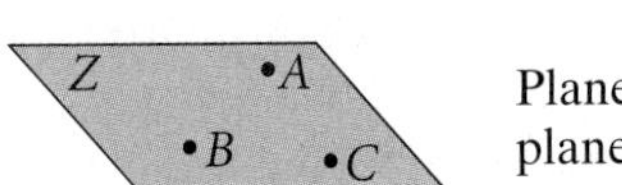

Plane ABC or plane Z

Point (p. 11) In Euclidean geometry, a point is undefined. You can think of a point as a location. A point has no size.

Punto (p. 11) En la geometría euclidiana, un punto es indefinido. Puedes imaginarte a un punto como un lugar. Un punto no tiene dimensión.

Point of concurrency (p. 257) *See* **concurrent.**

Punto de concurrencia (p. 257) *Ver* **concurrent.**

English/Spanish Glossary

EXAMPLES

Point of tangency (p. 582) *See* **tangent to a circle.**

Punto de tangencia (p. 582) *Ver* **tangent to a circle.**

Point symmetry (p. 663) Point symmetry is the type of symmetry for which there is a rotation of 180° that maps a figure onto itself.

Simetría central (p. 663) La simetría central es un tipo de simetría en la que una figura se ha rotado 180° sobre sí misma.

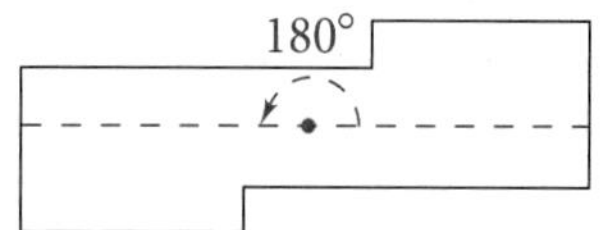

Point-slope form (p. 154) The point-slope form for a nonvertical line with slope m and through point (x_1, y_1) is $y - y_1 = m(x - x_1)$.

Forma punto-pendiente (p. 154) La forma punto-pendiente para una línea no vertical con pendiente m y que pasa por el punto (x_1, y_1) es $y - y_1 = m(x - x_1)$.

$y + 1 = 3(x - 4)$

In this equation, the slope is 3 and (x_1, y_1) is $(4, -1)$.

Polygon (p. 143) A polygon is a closed plane figure with at least three *sides* that are segments. The sides intersect only at their endpoints and no two adjacent sides are collinear. The *vertices* of the polygon are the endpoints of the sides. A *diagonal* is a segment that connects two nonconsecutive vertices. A polygon is *convex* if no diagonal contains points outside the polygon. A polygon is *concave* if a diagonal contains points outside the polygon.

Polígono (p. 143) Un polígono es una figura plana cerrada de, por lo menos, tres *lados.* Los lados se cortan solo en los extremos. No hay dos lados adyacentes que sean colineales. Los *vértices* del polígono son los extremos de los lados. Una *diagonal* es un segmento que une dos vértices no consecutivos. Un polígono es *convexo* si ninguna diagonal contiene puntos fuera del polígono. Un polígono es *cóncavo* si una diagonal contiene puntos fuera del polígono.

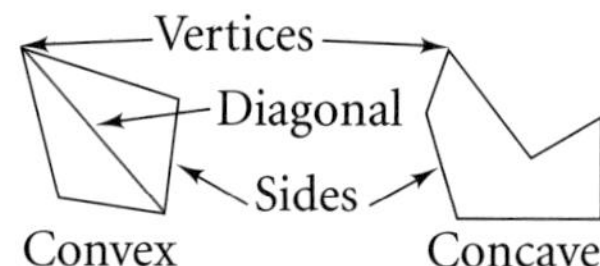

Polyhedron (p. 512) A polyhedron is a three-dimensional figure whose surfaces, or *faces,* are polygons. The vertices of the polygons are the *vertices* of the polyhedron. The intersections of the faces are the *edges* of the polyhedron.

Poliedro (p. 512) Un poliedro es una figura tridimensional cuyas superficies, o *caras,* son polígonos. Los vértices de los polígonos son los *vértices* del poliedro. Las intersecciones de las caras son las *aristas* del poliedro.

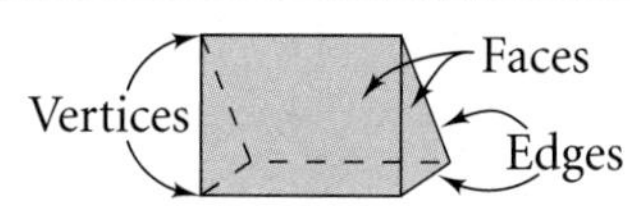

Postulate (p. 12) A postulate, or *axiom,* is an accepted statement of fact.

Postulado (p. 12) Un postulado, o *axioma,* es un enunciado que se acepta como un hecho.

Postulate: Through any two points there is exactly one line.

Preimage (p. 634) *See* **transformation.**

Preimagen (p. 634) *Ver* **transformation.**

Prime notation (p. 635) *See* **transformation.**

Notación prima (p. 635) *Ver* **transformation.**

Prism (p. 528) A prism is a polyhedron with two congruent and parallel faces, which are called the *bases.* The other faces, which are parallelograms, are called the *lateral faces.* An *altitude* of a prism is a perpendicular segment that joins the planes of the bases. Its length is the *height* of the prism. A *right prism* is one whose lateral faces are rectangular regions and a lateral edge is an altitude. In an *oblique prism,* some or all of the lateral faces are nonrectangular.

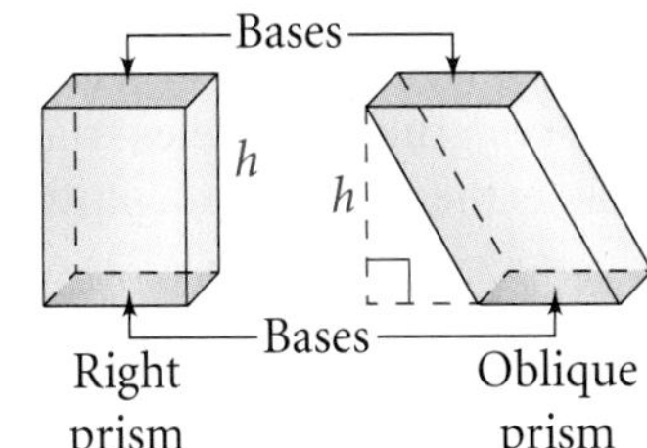

Prisma (p. 528) Un prisma es un poliedro con dos caras congruentes paralelas llamadas *bases.* Las otras caras son paralelogramos llamados *caras laterales.* La *altura* de un prisma es un segmento perpendicular que une los planos de las bases. Su longitud es también la *altura* del prisma. En un *prisma recto,* las caras laterales son rectangulares y una de las aristas laterales es la altura. En un *prisma oblicuo,* algunas o todas las caras laterales no son rectangulares.

Proof (pp. 100, 117, 123, 242, 263) A proof is a convincing argument that uses deductive reasoning. A proof can be written in many forms. In a *two-column proof,* the statements and reasons are aligned in columns. In a *paragraph proof,* the statements and reasons are connected in sentences. In a *flow proof,* arrows show the logical connections between the statements. In a *coordinate proof,* a figure is drawn on a coordinate plane and the formulas for slope, midpoint, and distance are used to prove properties of the figure. An *indirect proof* involves the use of indirect reasoning.

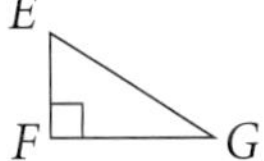

Given: $\triangle EFG$, with right angle $\angle F$

Prove: $\angle E$ and $\angle G$ are complementary.

Paragraph Proof: Because $\angle F$ is a right angle, $m\angle F = 90$. By the Triangle Angle-Sum Theorem, $m\angle E + m\angle F + m\angle G = 180$. By substitution, $m\angle E + 90 + m\angle G = 180$. Subtracting 90 from each side yields $m\angle E + m\angle G = 90$. $\angle E$ and $\angle G$ are complementary by definition.

Prueba (pp. 100, 117, 123, 242, 263) Una prueba es un argumento convincente en el cual se usa el razonamiento deductivo. Una prueba se puede escribir de varias maneras. En una *prueba de dos columnas,* los enunciados y las razones se alinean en columnas. En una *prueba de párrafo,* los enunciados y razones están unidos en oraciones. En una *prueba de flujo,* hay flechas que indican las conexiones lógicas entre enunciados. En una *prueba de coordenadas,* se dibuja una figura en un plano de coordenadas y se usan las fórmulas de la pendiente, punto medio y distancia para probar las propiedades de la figura. Una *prueba indirecta* incluye el uso de razonamiento indirecto.

Proportion (p. 417) A proportion is a statement that two ratios are equal. An *extended proportion* is a statement that three or more ratios are equal.

$\frac{x}{5} = \frac{3}{4}$ is a proportion.

$\frac{9}{27} = \frac{3}{9} = \frac{1}{3}$ is an extended proportion.

Proporción (p. 417) Una proporción es un enunciado en el cual dos razones son iguales. Una *proporción extendida* es un enunciado que dice que tres razones o más son iguales.

EXAMPLES

Pyramid (p. 537) A pyramid is a polyhedron in which one face, the *base,* is a polygon and the other faces, the *lateral faces,* are triangles with a common vertex, called the *vertex* of the pyramid. An *altitude* of a pyramid is the perpendicular segment from the *vertex* to the plane of the base. Its length is the *height* of the pyramid. A *regular pyramid* is a pyramid whose base is a regular polygon and whose lateral faces are congruent isosceles triangles. The *slant height* of a regular pyramid is the length of an altitude of a lateral face.

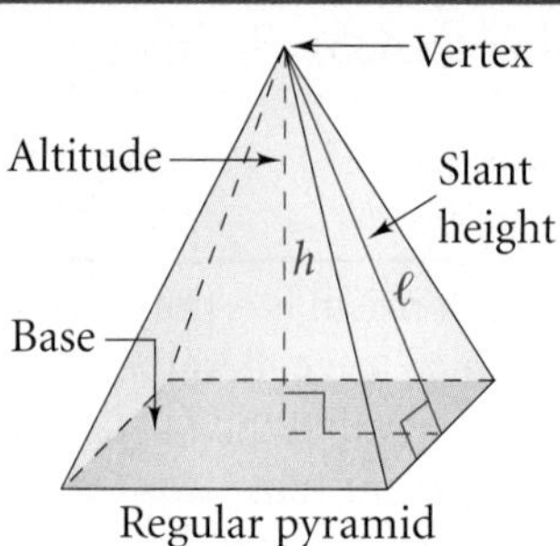

Regular pyramid

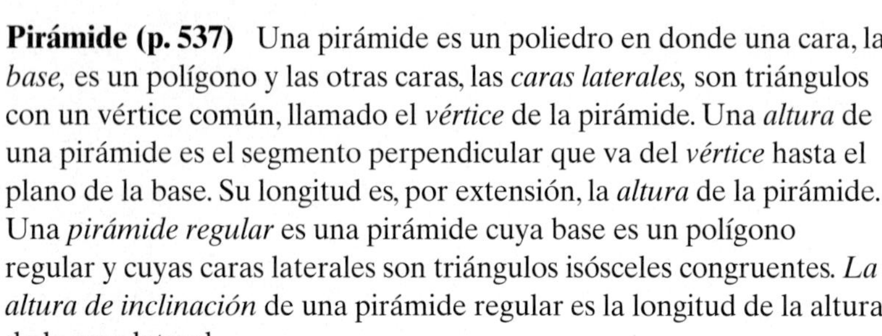

Pirámide (p. 537) Una pirámide es un poliedro en donde una cara, la *base,* es un polígono y las otras caras, las *caras laterales,* son triángulos con un vértice común, llamado el *vértice* de la pirámide. Una *altura* de una pirámide es el segmento perpendicular que va del *vértice* hasta el plano de la base. Su longitud es, por extensión, la *altura* de la pirámide. Una *pirámide regular* es una pirámide cuya base es un polígono regular y cuyas caras laterales son triángulos isósceles congruentes. *La altura de inclinación* de una pirámide regular es la longitud de la altura de la cara lateral.

Pythagorean triple (p. 357) A Pythagorean triple is a set of three nonzero whole numbers a, b, and c, that satisfy the equation $a^2 + b^2 = c^2$.

The numbers 5, 12, and 13 form a Pythagorean triple because $5^2 + 12^2 = 13^2 = 169$.

Triple de Pitágoras (p. 357) Un triple de Pitágoras es un conjunto de tres números enteros positivos a, b, and c que satisfacen la ecuación $a^2 + b^2 = c^2$.

Quadrant (p. 43) *See* **coordinate plane.**

Cuadrante (p. 43) *Ver* **coordinate plane.**

Quadrilateral (p. 144) A quadrilateral is a polygon with four sides.

Cuadrilátero (p. 144) Un cuadrilátero es un polígono de cuatro lados.

Radius of a circle (p. 386) A radius of a circle is any segment with one endpoint on the circle and the other endpoint at the center of the circle. *Radius* can also mean the length of this segment.

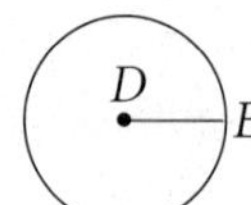

$\overline{DE}$ is a radius of $\odot D$.

Radio de un círculo (p. 386) Un radio de un círculo es cualquier segmento con un extremo en el círculo y el otro extremo en el centro del círculo. *Radio* también se refiere a la longitud de este segmento.

EXAMPLES

Radius of a regular polygon (p. 380) The radius of a regular polygon is the distance from the center to a vertex.

Radio de un polígono regular (p. 380) El radio de un polígono regular es la distancia desde el centro hasta un vértice.

Radius

Radius of a sphere (p. 558) The radius of a sphere is a segment that has one endpoint at the center and the other endpoint on the sphere.

Radio de una esfera (p. 558) El radio de una esfera es un segmento con un extremo en el centro y otro en la superficie esférica.

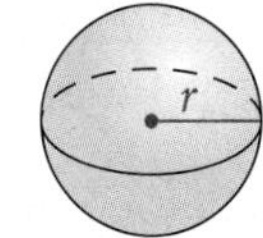

Ratio (p. 416) A ratio is the comparison of two quantities by division.

Razón (p. 416) Una razón es la comparación de dos cantidades por medio de una división.

5 to 7

5 : 7

$\frac{5}{7}$

Ray (p. 17) A ray is the part of a line consisting of one *endpoint* and all the points of the line on one side of the endpoint.

Rayo (p. 17) Un rayo es una parte de una recta que contiene un *extremo* y todos los puntos de la recta a un lado del extremo.

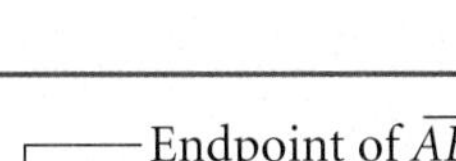

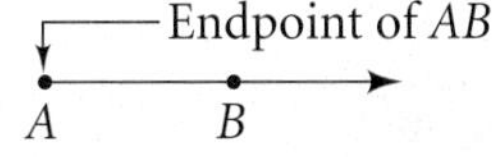

Rectangle (p. 288) A rectangle is a parallelogram with four right angles.

Rectángulo (p. 288) Un rectángulo es un paralelogramo con cuatro ángulos rectos.

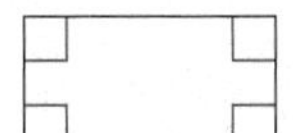

Reduction (p. 674) *See* **dilation.**

Reducción (p. 674) *Ver* **dilation.**

Reflection (p. 635) A reflection in (or *flip* across) line r is a transformation such that if a point A is on line r, then the image of A is itself, and if a point B is not on line r, then its image B' is the point such that r is the perpendicular bisector of $\overline{BB'}$.

Reflexión (p. 635) Una reflexión en la recta r es una transformación tal que si un punto A está en la recta r, entonces la imagen de A es ella misma, y si un punto B no está en la recta r, entonces su imagen B' es el punto tal que r es la mediatriz de $\overline{BB'}$.

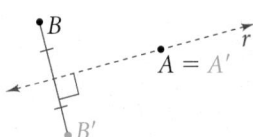

B

A = A′

r

B′

Reflectional symmetry (p. 662) Reflectional symmetry, or *line symmetry,* is the type of symmetry for which there is a reflection that maps a figure onto itself. The reflection line is the line of symmetry.

Simetría por reflexión (p. 662) La simetría por reflexión, o simetría línea, es un tipo de simetría en la que la reflexión vuelve a trazar la figura sobre sí misma. La recta de reflexión es la recta de simetría.

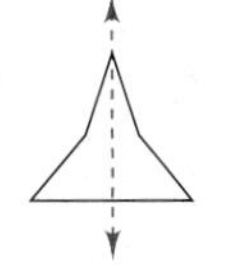

A reflection in the given line maps the figure onto itself.

EXAMPLES

Regular polygon (p. 146) A regular polygon is a polygon that is both equilateral and equiangular. Its *center* is the center of the circumscribed circle.

Polígono regular (p. 146) Un polígono regular es un polígono que es equilátero y equiángulo. Su *centro* es el centro del círculo circunscrito.

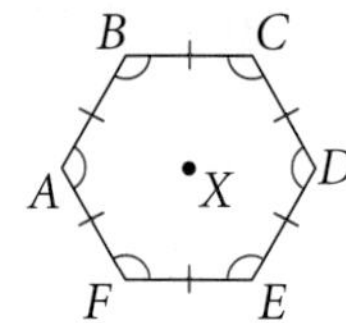

$ABCDEF$ is a regular hexagon. Point X is its center.

Regular pyramid (p. 537) *See* **pyramid.**

Pirámide regular (p. 537) *Ver* **pyramid.**

Remote interior angles (p. 133) Remote interior angles are the two nonadjacent interior angles corresponding to each exterior angle of a triangle.

Ángulos interiores remotos (p. 133) Las ánglos interiores remotes son los dos angulos interiores no adyacentes que corresponden a cada ángulo exterior de un triángulo.

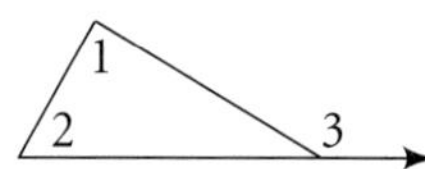

$\angle 1$ and $\angle 2$ are remote interior angles of $\angle 3$.

Resultant vector (p. 490) The sum of two vectors is a resultant.

Vector resultante (p. 490) La suma de dos vectores es el vector resultante.

$\vec{w}$ is the resultant of $\vec{u} + \vec{v}$.

Rhombus (p. 288) A rhombus is a parallelogram with four congruent sides.

Rombo (p. 288) Un rombo es un paralelogramo de cuatro lados congruentes.

Right angle (p. 28) A right angle is an angle whose measure is 90.

Ángulo recto (p. 28) Un ángulo recto es un ángulo que mide 90.

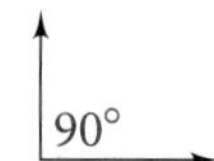

This symbol indicates a right angle.

Right cone (p. 539) *See* **cone.**

Cono recto (p. 539) *Ver* **cone.**

Right cylinder (p. 530) *See* **cylinder.**

Cilindro recto (p. 530) *Ver* **cylinder.**

Right prism (p. 528) *See* **prism.**

Prisma recto (p. 528) *Ver* **prism.**

EXAMPLES

Right triangle (pp. 133, 217) A right triangle contains one right angle. The side opposite the right angle is the *hypotenuse* and the other two sides are the *legs.*

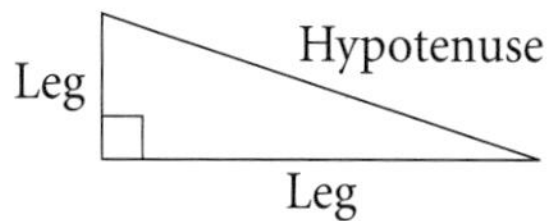

Triángulo rectángulo (pp. 133, 217) Un triángulo rectángulo contiene un ángulo recto. El lado opuesto del ángulo recto es la *hipotenusa* y los otros dos lados son los *catetos.*

Rotation (p. 648) A rotation (*turn*) of $x°$ about a point R is a transformation such that for any point V, its image is the point V', where $RV = RV'$ and $m\angle VRV' = x$. The image of R is itself.

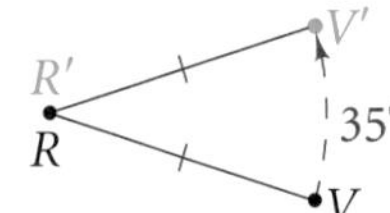

Rotación (p. 648) Una rotación de $x°$ alrededor de un punto R es una transformación de modo que para cualquier punto V, su imagen es el punto V', donde $RV = RV'$ y $m\angle VRV' = x$. La imagen de R es R misma.

Rotational symmetry (p. 663) Rotational symmetry is the type of symmetry for which there is a rotation of 180° or less that maps a figure onto itself.

The figure has 120° rotational symmetry.

Simetría rotacional (p. 663) La semetría rotacional es un tipo de simetría en la que una rotación de 180° o menos vuelve a trazar una figura sobre sí misma.

Same-side interior angles (p. 115) Same side interior angles lie on the same side of the transversal t and between ℓ and m.

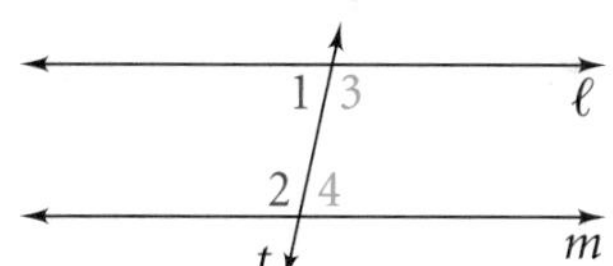

$\angle 1$ and $\angle 2$ are same-side interior angles, as are $\angle 3$ and $\angle 4$.

Ángulos internos del mismo lado (p. 115) Los ángulos internos del mismo lado están en el mismo lado de la transversal t y entre ℓ y m.

Scalar multiplication (p. 675) Scalar multiplication is the multiplication of each entry in a matrix by the same number, the *scalar.*

$$2 \cdot \begin{bmatrix} 1 & 0 \\ -2 & 3 \end{bmatrix} = \begin{bmatrix} 2(1) & 2(0) \\ 2(-2) & 2(3) \end{bmatrix}$$
$$= \begin{bmatrix} 2 & 0 \\ -4 & 6 \end{bmatrix}$$

Multiplicación escalar (p. 675) La multiplicación escalar es cada elemento de una matriz la multiplicación de por el mismo número, el *escalar.*

Scale (p. 418) A scale is the ratio of any length in a scale drawing to the corresponding actual length. The lengths may be in different units.

1 cm to 1 ft
1 cm = 1 ft
1 cm : 1 ft

Escala (p. 418) Una escala es la razón de cualquier longitud en un dibujo a escala en relación a la correspondiente longitud verdadera.

EXAMPLES

Scale drawing (p. 418) A scale drawing is a drawing in which all lengths are proportional to corresponding actual lengths.

Living Room | Bedroom | Bath

Scale: 1 in. = 30 ft

Dibujo a escala (p. 418) Un dibujo a escala es un dibujo en el que todas las longitudes son proporcionales a las correspondientes longitudes verdaderas.

Scale factor (p. 674) The scale factor of a dilation is the number that describes the size change from an original figure to its image. *See also* **dilation.**

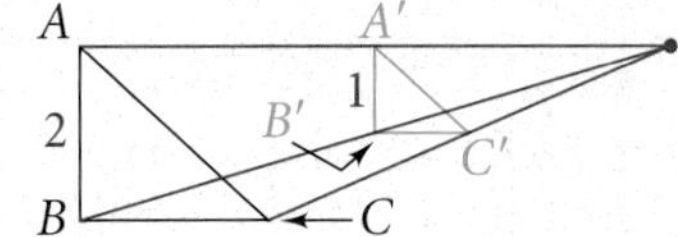

Factor de escala (p. 674) El factor de escala de una dilatación es el número que describe el cambio de tamaño de una figura original a su imagen. *Ver también* **dilation.**

The scale factor of the dilation that maps $\triangle ABC$ to $\triangle A'B'C'$ is $\frac{1}{2}$.

Scalene triangle (p. 133) A scalene triangle has no sides congruent.

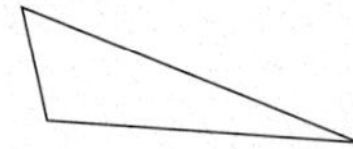

Triángulo escaleno (p. 133) Un triángulo escaleno no tiene lados congruentes.

Secant (p. 607) A secant is a line, ray, or segment that intersects a circle at two points.

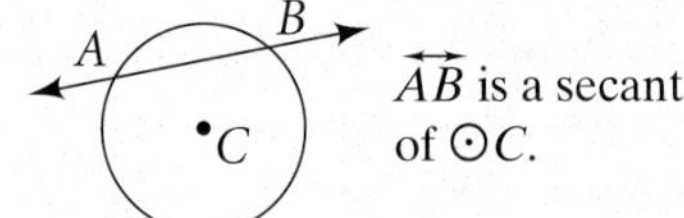

$\overleftrightarrow{AB}$ is a secant of $\odot C$.

Secante (p. 607) Un secante es una recta, rayo o segmento que corta un círculo en dos puntos.

Sector of a circle (p. 396) A sector of a circle is the region bounded by two radii and their intercepted arc.

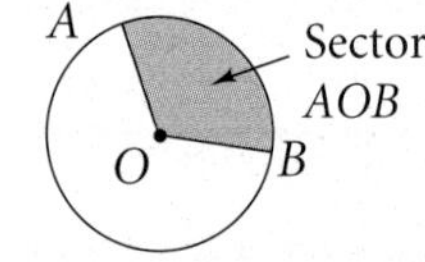

Sector de un círculo (p. 396) Un sector de un círculo es la región limitada por dos radios y el arco abarcado por ellos.

Segment (p. 17) A segment is the part of a line consisting of two points, called *endpoints,* and all points between them.

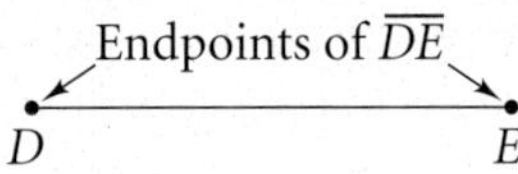

Segmento (p. 17) Un segmento es una parte de una recta que consiste en dos puntos, llamados *extremos,* y todos los puntos entre los extremos.

Segment bisector (p. 26) A segment bisector is a line, segment, ray, or plane that intersects a segment at its midpoint.

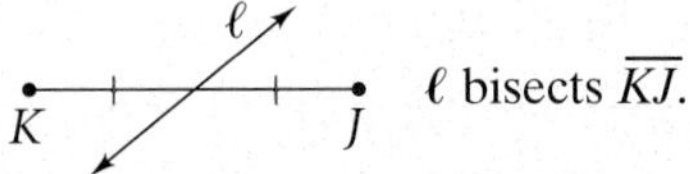

ℓ bisects $\overline{KJ}$.

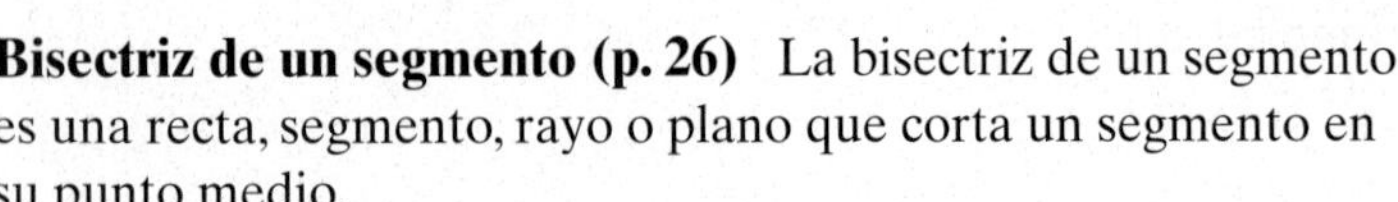

Bisectriz de un segmento (p. 26) La bisectriz de un segmento es una recta, segmento, rayo o plano que corta un segmento en su punto medio.

EXAMPLES

Segment of a circle (p. 397) A segment of a circle is the part of a circle bounded by an arc and the segment joining its endpoints.

Segmento de un círculo (p. 397) Un segmento de un círculo es la parte de un círculo bordeada por un arco y el segmento que une sus extremos.

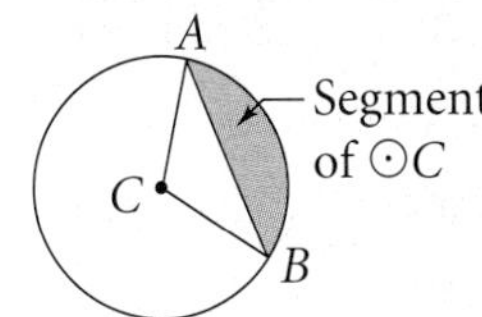

Semicircle (p. 387) A semicircle is half a circle.

Semicírculo (p. 387) Un semicírculo es la mitad de un círculo.

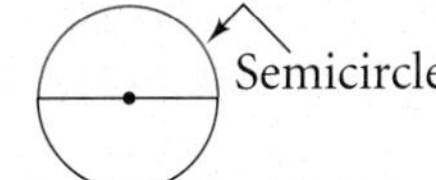

Side *See* **angle; polygon.**

Lado *Ver* **angle; polygon.**

Similarity ratio (pp. 423, 566) The similarity ratio is the ratio of the lengths of corresponding sides of similar polygons.

Razón de semejanza (pp. 423, 566) La razón de semejanza es la razón de la longitud de los lados correspondientes de polígonos semejantes.

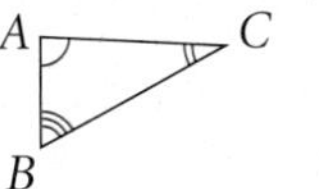

$\frac{AB}{DE} = \frac{BC}{EF} = \frac{CA}{FD}$

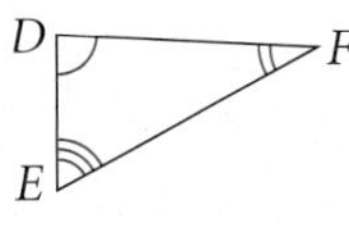

$\triangle ABC \sim \triangle DEF$

Similarity transformation (p. 674) *See* **dilation.**

Transformación de semejanza (p. 674) *Ver* **dilation.**

Similar polygons (p. 423) Similar polygons are polygons having corresponding angles congruent and corresponding sides proportional. You denote similarity by ~.

Polígonos semejantes (p. 423) Los polígonos semejantes son polígonos cuyos ángulos correspondientes son congruentes y los lados correspondientes son proporcionales. El símbolo ~ significa "es semejante a".

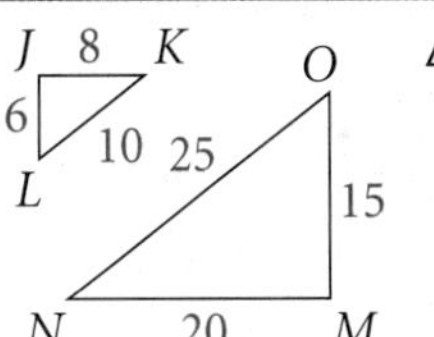

$\triangle JKL \sim \triangle MNO$

Similarity ratio $= \frac{2}{5}$

Similar solids (p. 566) Similar solids have the same shape and have all their corresponding dimensions proportional.

Cuerpos geométricos semejantes (p. 566) Los cuerpos geométricos semejantes tienen la misma forma y todas sus dimensiones correspondientes son proporcionales.

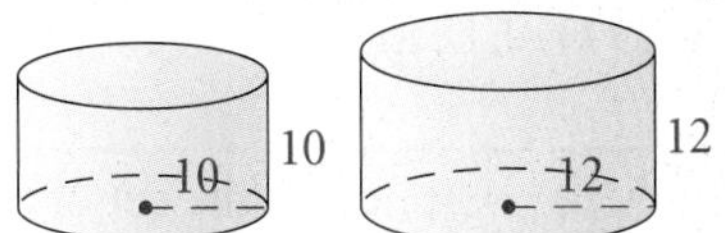

Sine ratio (p. 477) *See* **trigonometric ratios.**

Razón seno (p. 477) *Ver* **trigonometric ratios.**

EXAMPLES

Skew lines (p. 18) Skew lines are lines that do not lie in the same plane.

Rectas cruzadas (p. 18) Las rectas cruzadas son rectas que no están en el mismo plano.

$\overleftrightarrow{AB}$ and $\overleftrightarrow{EF}$ are skew.

Slant height *See* **cone; pyramid.**

Altura de inclinación *Ver* **cone; pyramid.**

Slide (p. 641) *See* **translation.**

Slope-intercept form (p. 152) The slope-intercept form of a linear equation is $y = mx + b$, where m is the slope of the line and b is the y-intercept.

Fórmula pendiente-intercepto (p. 152) La fórmula pendiente-intercepto es la ecuación lineal $y = mx + b$, en la que m es la pendiente de la recta y b es el punto de intersección de esa recta con el eje y.

$y = \frac{1}{2}x - 3$

In this equation, the slope is $\frac{1}{2}$ and the y-intercept is -3.

Slope of a line (p. 151) The slope of a line is the ratio of its vertical change in the coordinate plane to the corresponding horizontal change. If (x_1, y_1) and (x_2, y_2) are points on a nonvertical line, then the slope is $\frac{y_2 - y_1}{x_2 - x_1}$. The slope of a horizontal line is 0 and the slope of a vertical line is undefined.

Pendiente de una recta (p. 151) La pendiente de una recta es la razón del cambio vertical en el plano de coordenadas en relación a al cambio horizontal correspondiente. Si (x_1, y_1) y (x_2, y_2) son puntos en una recta no vertical, entonces la pendiente es $\frac{y_2 - y_1}{x_2 - x_1}$. La pendiente de una recta horizontal es 0, y la pendiente de una recta vertical es indefinida.

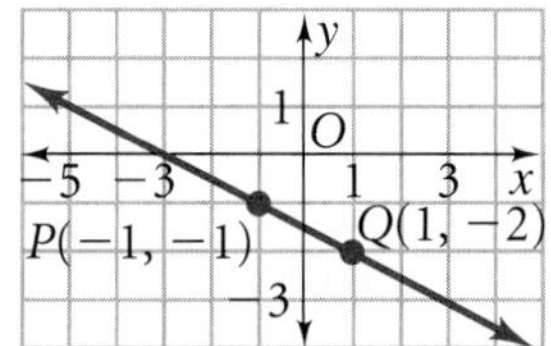

The line containing $P(-1, -1)$ and $Q(1, -2)$ has slope

$\frac{-2 - (-1)}{1 - (-1)} = \frac{-1}{2} = -\frac{1}{2}$.

Space (p. 11) Space is the set of all points.

Espacio (p. 11) El espacio es el conjunto de todos los puntos.

Sphere (p. 558) A sphere is the set of all points in space a given distance r, the *radius,* from a given point C, the *center.* A *great circle* is the intersection of a sphere with a plane containing the center of the sphere. The *circumference* of a sphere is the circumference of any great circle of the sphere.

Esfera (p. 558) Una esfera es el conjunto de los puntos del espacio que están a una distancia dada r, el *radio,* de un punto dado C, el *centro.* Un *círculo máximo* es la intersección de una esfera y un plano que contiene el centro de la esfera. La *circunferencia* de una esfera es la circunferencia de cualquier círculo máximo de la esfera.

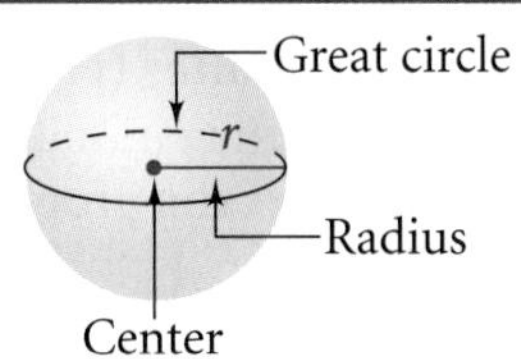

EXAMPLES

Spherical geometry (p. 140) In spherical geometry, a plane is considered to be the surface of a sphere and a line is considered to be a great circle of the sphere. In spherical geometry, through a point not on a given line there is no line parallel to the given line.

Geometría esférica (p. 140) En la geometría esférica, un plano es la superficie de una esfera y una recta es un círculo máximo de la esfera. En la geometría esférica, a través de un punto que no está en una recta dada, no hay recta paralela a la recta dada.

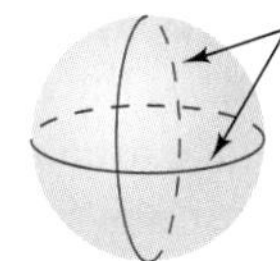

In spherical geometry, lines are represented by great circles of a sphere.

Square (p. 288) A square is a parallelogram with four congruent sides and four right angles.

Cuadrado (p. 288) Un cuadrado es un paralelogramo con cuatro lados congruentes y cuatro ángulos rectos.

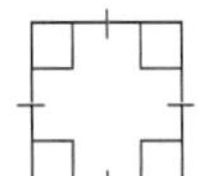

Standard form of a linear equation (p. 153) The standard form of a linear equation is $Ax + By = C$, where A, B, and C are integers and A and B are not both zero.

Fórmula normal de una ecuación lineal (p. 153) La fórmula normal de una ecuación lineal es $Ax + By = C$, donde A, B, y C son números reales, y donde A y B no son ambos iguales a cero.

$6x - y = 3$

Standard form of an equation of a circle (p. 615) The standard form of an equation of a circle is $(x - h)^2 + (y - k)^2 = r^2$, where (h, k) is the center of the circle.

Fórmula normal de la ecuación de un círculo (p. 615) La fórmula normal de la ecuación de un círculo es $(x - h)^2 + (y - k)^2 = r^2$, donde (h, k) son las coordenadas del centro del círculo.

In $(x + 5)^2 + (y + 2)^2 = 48$, $(-5, -2)$ is the center of the circle.

Straight angle (p. 28) A straight angle is an angle whose measure is 180.

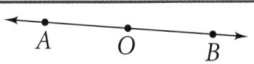

Ángulo llano (p. 28) Un ángulo llano es un ángulo que mide 180.

A O B

$m\angle AOB = 180$

Straightedge (p. 34) A straightedge is a ruler with no markings on it.

Regla sin graduación (p. 34) Una regla que sólo sirve para trazar rectas.

Supplementary angles (p. 96) Two angles are supplementary if the sum of their measures is 180.

Ángulos suplementarios (p. 96) Dos ángulos son suplementarios cuando sus medidas suman 180.

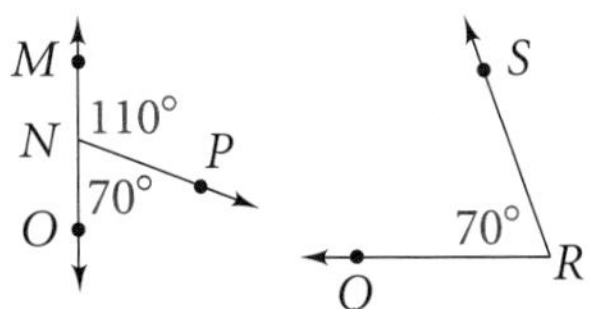

$\angle MNP$ and $\angle ONP$ are supplementary, as are $\angle MNP$ and $\angle QRS$.

EXAMPLES

Surface area (pp. 529, 530, 538, 539, 558) The surface area of a prism, cylinder, pyramid, or cone is the sum of the lateral area and the areas of the bases. The surface area of a sphere is four times the area of a great circle. A list of surface area formulas is on p. 727.

Área (pp. 529, 530, 538, 539, 558) El área de un prisma, pirámide, cilindro o cono es la suma del área lateral y las áreas de las bases. El área de una esfera es igual a cuatro veces el área de un círculo máximo. Una lista de fórmulas de áreas está en la p. 727.

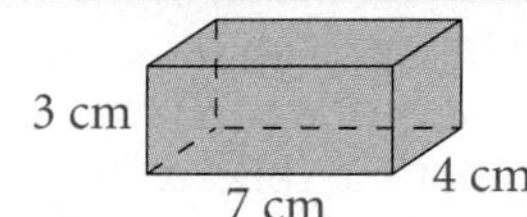

S.A. of prism $= \text{L.A.} + 2B$
$= 66 + 2(28)$
$= 122 \text{ cm}^2$

Symmetry (pp. 662, 663, 668) A figure has symmetry if there is an isometry that maps the figure onto itself. *See* **glide reflectional symmetry; point symmetry; reflectional symmetry; rotational symmetry; translational symmetry.**

Simetría (pp. 662, 663, 668) Una figura tiene simetría si hay una isometría que traza la figura sobre sí misma. *Ver* **glide reflectional symmetry; point symmetry; reflectional symmetry; rotational symmetry; translational symmetry.**

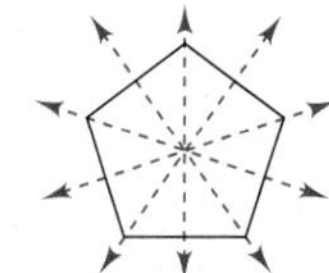

A regular pentagon has reflectional symmetry and 72° rotational symmetry.

Tangent ratio (p. 470) *See* **trigonometric ratios.**

Razón tangente (p. 470) *Ver* **trigonometric ratios.**

Tangent to a circle (p. 582) A tangent to a circle is a line, segment, or ray in the plane of the circle that intersects the circle in exactly one point. That point is the *point of tangency.*

Tangente de un círculo (p. 582) Un tangente de un círculo es una recta, segmento o rayo en el plano del círculo que corta el círculo en exactamente un punto. Ese punto es el *punto de tangencia.*

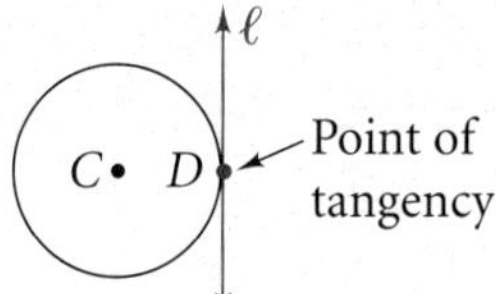

Line ℓ is tangent to $\odot C$. Point D is the point of tangency.

Terminal point of a vector (p. 490) *See* **vector.**

Punto terminal de un vector (p. 490) *Ver* **vector.**

Tessellation (p. 667) A tessellation, or *tiling,* is a repeating pattern of figures that completely covers a plane without gaps or overlap. A *pure tessellation* is a tessellation that consists of congruent copies of one figure.

Teselado (p. 667) Un teselado o *reticulado* es un patrón repetitivo de figuras que cubre completamente una superficie plana sin dejar espacios vacíos ni traslaparse. Un *teselado puro* consiste en copias congruentes de una figura.

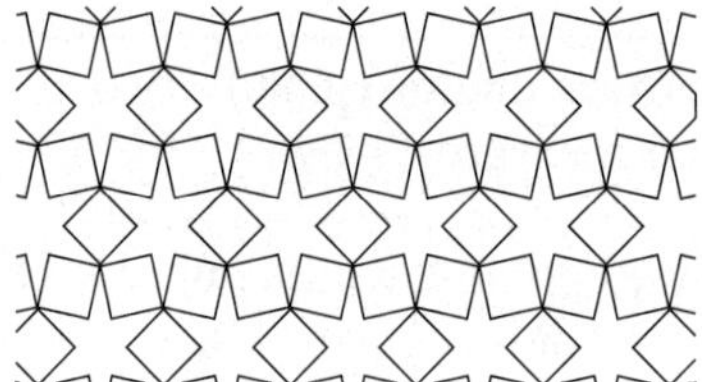

EXAMPLES

Theorem (p. 98) A theorem is a conjecture that is proven.

Teorema (p. 98) Un teorema es una conjetura que se demuestra.

The theorem "Vertical angles are congruent" can be proven by using postulates, definitions, properties, and previously stated theorems.

Tiling (p. 667) *See* **tessellation.**

Reticulado (p. 667) *Ver* **tessellation.**

Transformation (p. 634) A transformation is a change in the position, size, or shape of a geometric figure. The given figure is called the *preimage* and the resulting figure is called the *image.* A transformation *maps* a figure onto its image. *Prime notation* is sometimes used to identify image points. In the diagram, X' (read "X prime") is the image of X.

Transformación (p. 634) Una transformación es un cambio en la posición, tamaño o forma de una figura. La figura dada se llama la *preimagen* y la figura resultante se llama la *imagen.* Una transformación *traza* la figura sobre su propia imagen. La *notación prima* a veces se utiliza para identificar los puntos de la imagen. En el diagrama de la derecha, X' (leído prima X) es la imagen de X.

Preimage Image

X Y Y' X'

Z Z'

$\triangle XYZ \rightarrow \triangle X'Y'Z'$

Translation (p. 641) A translation (*slide*)is a transformation that moves points the same distance and in the same direction. A translation in the coordinate plane is described by a vector.

Translación (p. 641) Una translación es la transformación que mueve puntos a la misma distancia y en la misma dirección. Un vector puede describir la translación en un plano de coordenadas.

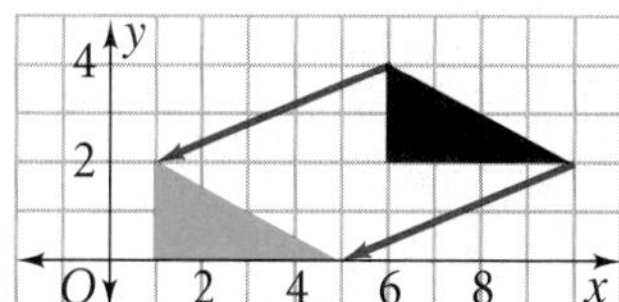

The blue triangle is the image of the black triangle under the translation $\langle -5, -2 \rangle$.

Translational symmetry (p. 668) Translational symmetry is the type of symmetry for which there is a translation that maps a figure onto itself.

Simetría translacional (p. 668) La simetría translacional es un tipo de simetría en la que la translación vuelve a trazar la figura sobre sí misma.

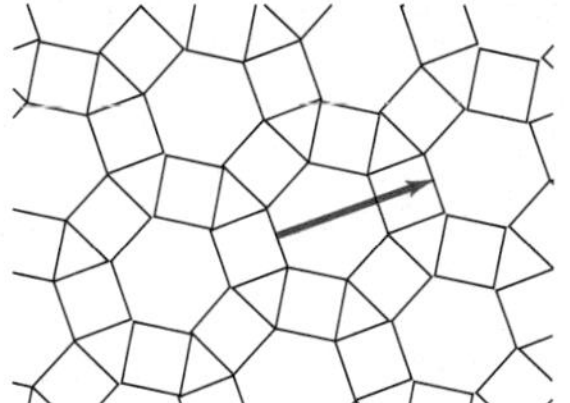

The tessellation shown can be mapped onto itself by the given translation.

Transversal (p. 115) A transversal is a line that intersects two coplanar lines in two points.

Transversal (p. 115) Una transversal es una recta que corta dos rectas coplanares en dos puntos.

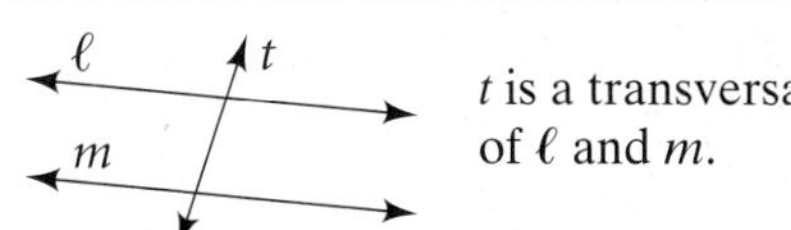

t is a transversal of ℓ and m.

EXAMPLES

Trapezoid (pp. 288, 322) A trapezoid is a quadrilateral with exactly one pair of parallel sides, the *bases.* The nonparallel sides are called the *legs* of the trapezoid. Each pair of angles adjacent to a base are *base angles* of the trapezoid. An *altitude* of a trapezoid is a perpendicular segment from one base to the line containing the other base. Its length is called the *height* of the trapezoid.

Trapecio (pp. 288, 322) Un trapecio es un cuadrilátero con exactamente un par de lados paralelos, las *bases.* Los lados no paralelos se llaman los *catetos* del trapecio. Cada par de ángulos adyacentes a la base son *ángulos de base* del trapecio. Una *altura* del trapecio es un segmento perpendicular que va de una base a la recta que contiene la otra base. Su longitud se llama, por extensión, la *altura* del trapecio.

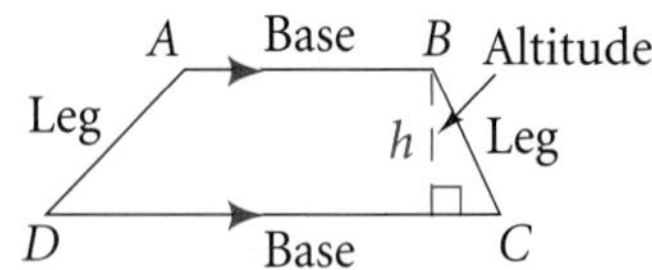

In trapezoid $ABCD$, $\angle ADC$ and $\angle BCD$ are one pair of base angles, and $\angle DAB$ and $\angle ABC$ are the other.

Triangle (p. 143) A triangle is a polygon with three sides. You can choose any side to be a *base.* The *height* is the length of the altitude drawn to the line containing that base.

Triángulo (p. 143) Un triángulo es un polígono con tres lados. Se puede escoger cualquier lado como *base.* La *altura,* entonces, es la longitud de la altura trazada hasta la recta que contiene la base.

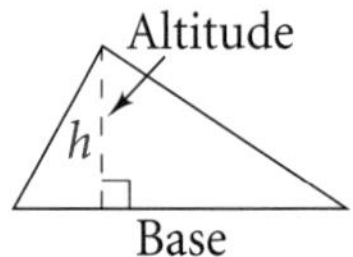

Trigonometric ratios (pp. 470, 477) In right triangle $\triangle ABC$ with acute angle $\angle A$

$$\text{sine } \angle A = \sin A = \frac{\text{leg opposite } \angle A}{\text{hypotenuse}}$$

$$\text{cosine } \angle A = \cos A = \frac{\text{leg adjacent } \angle A}{\text{hypotenuse}}$$

$$\text{tangent } \angle A = \tan A = \frac{\text{leg opposite } \angle A}{\text{leg adjacent } \angle A}$$

Razones trigonométricas (pp. 468, 475) En un triángulo rectángulo $\triangle ABC$ con ángulo agudo $\angle A$

$$\text{seno } \angle A = \text{sen } A = \frac{\text{cateto opuesto a } \angle A}{\text{hipotenusa}}$$

$$\text{coseno } \angle A = \cos A = \frac{\text{cateto adyecente a } \angle A}{\text{hipotenusa}}$$

$$\text{tangente } \angle A = \tan A = \frac{\text{cateto opuesto a } \angle A}{\text{cateto adyecente a } \angle A}$$

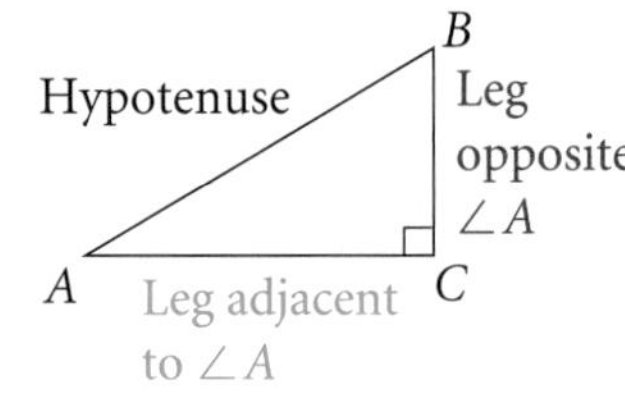

Truth value (p. 69) The truth value of a statement is "true" or "false" according to whether the statement is true or false, respectively.

Valor verdadero (p. 69) El valor verdadero de un enunciado es "verdadero" o "falso" según el enunciado sea verdadero o falso, respectivamente.

The truth value of the statement "If a figure is a triangle, then it has four sides" is *false*.

Turn (p. 648) *See* **rotation.**

Two-column proof (p. 117) *See* **proof.**

Prueba de dos columnas (p. 117) *Ver* **proof.**

Vector (p. 490) A vector is any quantity that has magnitude (size) and direction. You can represent a vector as an arrow that starts at one point, the *initial point,* and points to a second point, the *terminal point.* A vector can be described by *ordered pair notation* $\langle x, y \rangle$, where x represents horizontal change from the initial point to the terminal point and y represents vertical change from the initial point to the terminal point.

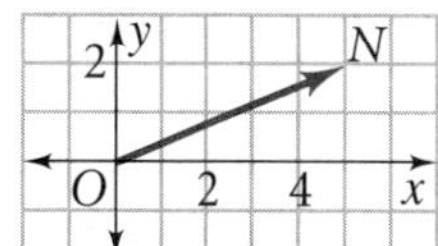

Vector ON has initial point O and terminal point N. The ordered pair notation for the vector is $\langle 5, 2 \rangle$.

Vector (p. 490) Un vector es cualquier cantidad que tiene magnitud (tamaño) y dirección. Se puede representar un vector como una flecha que empieza en un punto, el *punto inicial,* y se dirige a un segundo punto, el *punto terminal.* Un vector se puede describir mediante la *notación de pares ordenados* $\langle x, y \rangle$, donde x representa el cambio horizontal desde el punto inicial hasta el punto final, y y representa el cambio vertical desde el punto inicial hasta el punto final.

Vertex *See* **angle; cone; polygon; polyhedron; pyramid.** The plural form of *vertex* is *vertices.*

Vértice *Ver* **angle; cone; polygon; polyhedron; pyramid.**

Vertex angle (p. 211) *See* **isosceles triangle.**

Ángulo del vértice (p. 211) *Ver* **isosceles triangle.**

Vertical angles (p. 96) Vertical angles are two angles whose sides form two pairs of opposite rays.

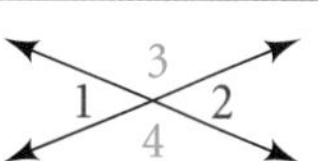

$\angle 1$ and $\angle 2$ are vertical angles, as are $\angle 3$ and $\angle 4$.

Ángulos opuestos por el vértice (p. 96) Dos ángulos son ángulos opuestos por el vértice si sus lados son rayos opuestos.

Volume (p. 544) Volume is a measure of the space a figure occupies. A list of volume formulas is on p. 727.

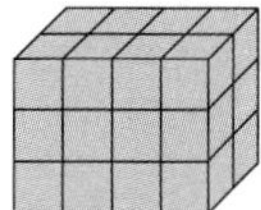

The volume of this prism is 24 cubic units, or 24 units^3.

Volumen (p. 544) El volumen es una medida del espacio que ocupa una figura. Una lista de las fórmulas de volumen está en la p. 727.

Answers to Instant Check System™

Chapter 1

Diagnosing Readiness p. 2

1. 9 **2.** 16 **3.** 121 **4.** 37 **5.** 78.5 **6.** 13 **7.** 1 **8.** $-\frac{3}{5}$ **9.** 5 **10.** 8 **11.** 4 **12.** 3 **13.** 3 **14.** 6 **15.** 1

Lesson 1-1 pp. 4–6

Check Skills You'll Need **1.** 2, 4, 6, 8, 10, . . . **2.** 1, 3, 5, 7, 9, . . . **3.** $1^2 = 1, 2^2 = 4, 3^2 = 9, 4^2 = 16, 5^2 = 25, 6^2 = 36, 7^2 = 49, 8^2 = 64, 9^2 = 81, 10^2 = 100$ **4.** It is odd.

Check Understanding **1a.** 29, 37 **b.** Thursday, Friday **c.**

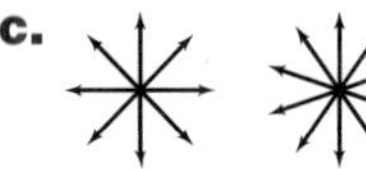

2. The sum of the first 35 odd numbers is 35^2, or 1225.

3. Answers may vary. Sample: True; the product of 5 and any odd number is odd. False; the product of 5 and any number ends in 5. **4a.** 39 skateboards **b.** Not confident; December is too far away.

Lesson 1-2 pp. 10–13

Check Skills You'll Need **1.** (1, 6) **2.** (3, 2) **3.** (5, 10)

4.

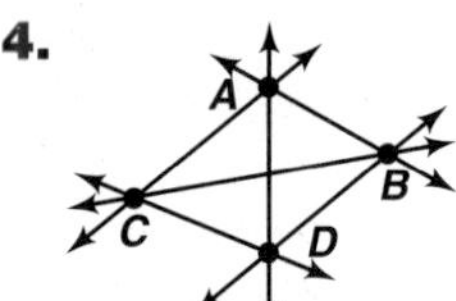

Check Understanding **1a.** no **b.** Answers may vary. Sample: $\overleftrightarrow{EF}$, $\overleftrightarrow{FC}$, $\overleftrightarrow{CE}$ **c.** Arrowheads are used to show that the line extends in opposite directions without end. **2.** Answers may vary. Sample: *HEF*, *HEFG*, *FGH* **3.** *ABF* and *CBF* **4a.** *D* **b.** *B*

Lesson 1-3 pp. 17–19, 23

Check Skills You'll Need **1.** no **2.** yes **3.** no **4–9.** Answers may vary. Samples are given. **4.** *NMR* **5.** *PQL* **6.** *NKL* **7.** *PQR* **8.** *PKN* **9.** *LQR*

Check Understanding **1.** No, they do not have the same endpoint. **2a.** $\overline{HI}$, $\overline{DN}$ **b.** $\overline{AB}$, $\overline{CD}$, $\overline{CH}$ **c.** $\overline{DN}$, $\overline{HI}$; $\overline{DN}$, $\overline{HC}$ **3a.** *PSWT* ∥ *RQVU*, *PRUT* ∥ *SQVW*, *PSQR* ∥ *TWVU* **b.** $\overleftrightarrow{TV}$ **c.** Answers may vary. Sample: $\overleftrightarrow{PS}$

Checkpoint Quiz 1 **1.** 29, 31.5 **2.** 3.45678, 3.456789 **3.** For 1: Add 2.5. For 2: Extend the decimal to one more place with a digit that is 1 more than the one to its left. **4.** yes, plane *AEF* **5.** yes, plane *DCEF* **6.** No; *H*, *G*, and *F* are in the front plane, *B* is not. **7.** No; *A*, *E*, and *B* are in the top plane, *C* is not. **8.** $\overline{CD}$, $\overline{AB}$, $\overline{EF}$ **9.** Answers may vary. Sample: $\overleftrightarrow{AE}$ and $\overleftrightarrow{BC}$ **10.** *H*

Lesson 1-4 pp. 25–29

Check Skills You'll Need **1.** 6 **2.** 3.5 **3.** 3 **4.** 6 **5.** 2 **6.** 9 **7.** 4 **8.** 9 **9.** $\frac{1}{3}$

Check Understanding **1a.** $CD = DE$ **b.** yes; $|-5-(-8)| = |3| = 3$ **2.** 15; $EF = 40$, $FG = 60$ **3.** 13.5 **4a.** ∠2, ∠*DEC* **b.** No; 3 ∠s have *E* for a vertex, so you need more info. in the name to distinguish them from one another. **5a.** 30; acute **b.** 90; right **c.** 140; obtuse **6.** 35

Lesson 1-5 pp. 34–37

Check Skills You'll Need **1.** C D **2.** G H **3.** A B **4.** m **5.** A B C **6.** X Y S T **7.** 10 **8.** 60° **9.** 120°

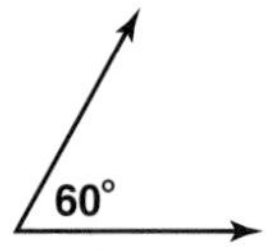

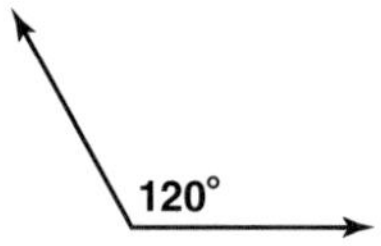

Check Understanding **1.** X Y R S **2.** B F **3.** S T **4.** 50; 100

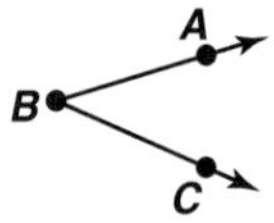

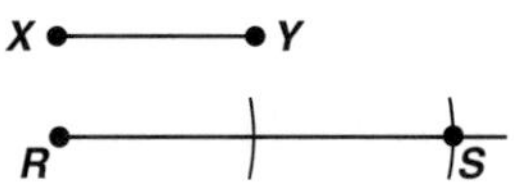

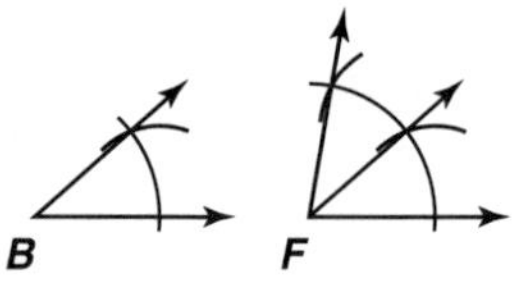

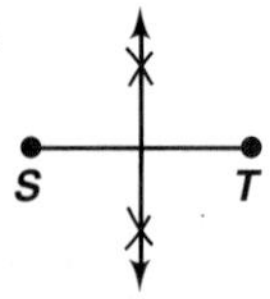

5a. X P Y Z **b.** Measure ∠*XYP* and ∠*PYZ* to see that they are ≅.

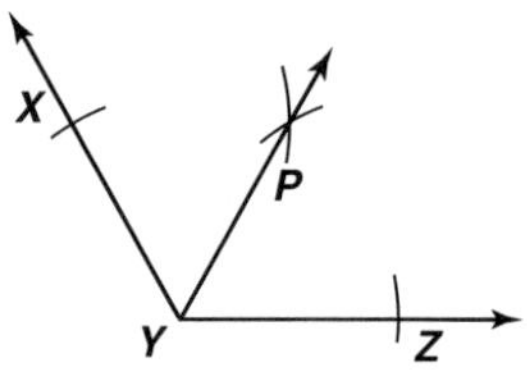

Lesson 1-6 pp. 43–45, 49

Check Skills You'll Need **1.** 5.0 **2.** 4.1 **3.** 11.1 **4.** 100 **5.** 100 **6.** 58 **7.** 196 **8.** 10 **9.** −1

Check Understanding **1a.** 8.6 **b.** Yes; the differences are opposites, and the square of a number and the square of its opposite are the same. **2a.** about 8.9 mi **b.** about 3.2 mi **3.** (4, 4) **4.** (6, −9)

Checkpoint Quiz 2 **1.** 17 **2.** 110 **3.** 140 **4a.** 90 **b.** 60 **5.** $\angle APT \cong \angle RPT$ **6.** 45

7. 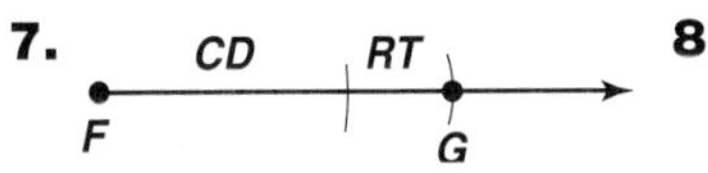

8. 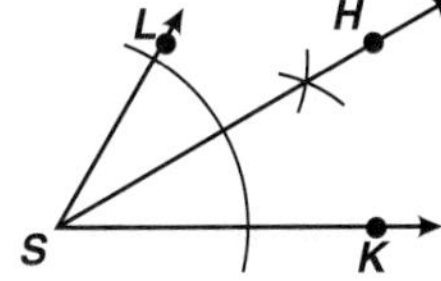

9. 12.2 units **10.** (1, 1.5)

Lesson 1-7 pp. 51–54

Check Skills You'll Need **1.** 4 **2.** 15 **3.** 8 **4.** 6.7 **5.** 3.2 **6.** 7.8 **7.** 4.5 **8.** 13.0 **9.** 7.8

Check Understanding **1a.** 26 in. **b.** 30 in. **2a.** 36π m **b.** 56.5 m **3.** 20 units

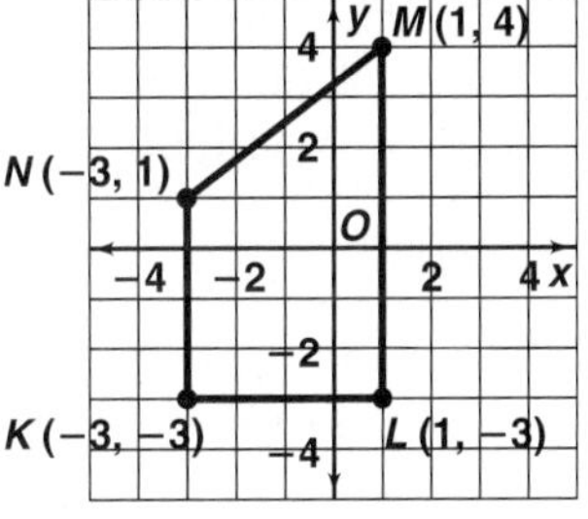

4. $9\frac{1}{3}$ yd^2; $9\frac{1}{3}$ is one ninth of 84.

5a. $\frac{25}{4}\pi$ ft^2 **b.** 19.6 ft^2

6. 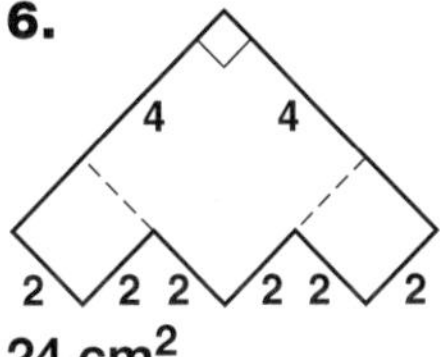

24 cm^2

Chapter 2

Diagnosing Readiness p. 66

1. 50 **2.** −3 **3.** $25\frac{1}{2}$ **4.** 10.5 **5.** 15 **6.** 11 **7.** 20 **8.** −5 **9.** −4 **10.** 5 **11.** 6 **12.** 7 **13.** 18 **14.** $\angle ACD$, $\angle DCA$ **15.** C **16.** 3 **17.** $\angle ADB$ or $\angle BDA$ **18.** $\overline{CD}$ **19.** 45 **20.** 48, 42

Lesson 2-1 pp. 68–70

Check Skills You'll Need **1.** −1 **2.** −2, 2 **3.** 2 **4.** −4, **5.** 0 **6.** −1

Check Understanding **1.** Hypothesis: $y - 3 = 5$, Conclusion: $y = 8$ **2a.** If an integer ends with 0, then it is divisible by 5. **b.** If a figure is a square, then it has 4 congruent sides. **3.** The conditional is false; New Mexico is a counterexample.

4. 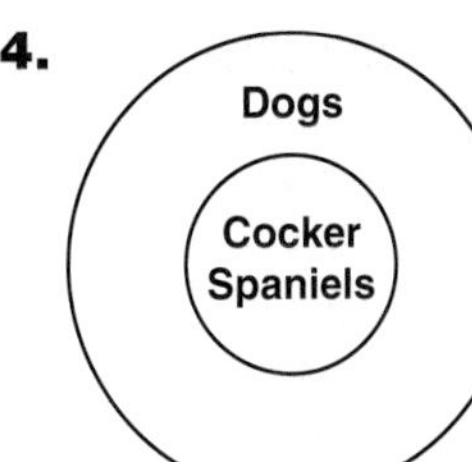

5. If two lines are skew, then they are not parallel and do not intersect. **6a.** If two lines are parallel, then they do not intersect. The conditional is false and the converse is true. **b.** If $|x| = 2$, then $x = 2$. The conditional is true and the converse is false. **7.** Answers may vary. Sample: The statement "I breathe when I sleep" can be rewritten as "If I sleep, then I breathe." The statement "I sleep when I breathe" can be rewritten as "If I breathe, then I sleep." The two statements are converses, and do not have the same meaning.

Lesson 2-2 pp. 75–77

Check Skills You'll Need **1.** Hypothesis: $x > 10$, Conclusion: $x > 5$ **2.** Hypothesis: You live in Milwaukee. Conclusion: You live in Wisconsin. **3.** If a figure is a square, then it has four sides. **4.** If something is a butterfly, then it has wings. **5.** If we go on a picnic, then the sun shines. **6.** If two lines do not intersect, then they are skew. **7.** If $x^3 = -27$, then $x = -3$.

Check Understanding **1.** If three points lie on the same line, then they are collinear. The converse is also true. Three points are collinear if and only if they lie on the same line. **2.** If a number is prime, then it has only two distinct factors, 1 and itself. If a number has only two distinct factors, 1 and itself, then it is prime. **3.** Conditional: If an angle is a right angle, then its measure is 90. Converse: If an angle has measure 90, then it is a right angle. The two statements are true. An angle is a right angle if and only if its measure is 90. **4.** It is not a good definition because a rectangle has four right angles and is not necessarily a square.

Lesson 2-3 pp. 82–84, 88

Check Skills You'll Need **1.** If your grades suffer, then you don't sleep enough. **2.** If you must start early, then you want to arrive on time. **3.** If a year is a leap year, then it has 366 days. **4.** If students do not complete their homework, then they will have lower grades. **5.** If two lines are perpendicular, then they meet to form right angles. **6.** If a person is 16 years old, then that person is a teenager.

Check Understanding **1.** No, there could be other things wrong with the car, such as a faulty starter. **2.** Answers may vary. Sample: Vladimir Nuñez should not pitch a complete game on Tuesday.

3. Not possible; you do not know that the hypothesis is true. **4a.** If a number ends in 0, then it is divisible by 5. **b.** Not possible; the conclusion of one statement is not the hypothesis of the other statement. **5.** The Volga River is less than 2300 miles long. The Volga River is not one of the world's ten longest rivers.

Checkpoint Quiz 1 **1.** Hypothesis: $x > 5$, Conclusion: $x^2 > 25$ **2.** If something is a rose, then it is a beautiful flower. **3.** If an integer is divisible by 2, then the integer ends with 0. **4.** Answers may vary. Sample: 42 is divisible by 2, but it does not end with 0. **5.** If an angle is an acute angle, then its measure is between 0 and 90. If an angle's measure is between 0 and 90, then it is an acute angle. **6.** Points are collinear if and only if they lie on the same line. **7.** Answers may vary. Sample: A graphing calculator has a keyboard and a memory. **8.** Theresa has passing grades. **9.** If a student studies geometry, then the student's mind is expanded. **10.** not possible

Lesson 2-4 pp. 89–91

Check Skills You'll Need **1.** $\angle AOB$, $\angle BOA$ **2.** O **3.** $\overrightarrow{OB}$ **4.** 45 **5.** $\overrightarrow{OA}$ and $\overrightarrow{OC}$

Check Understanding **1.** Subst. Prop.; Subtr. Prop. of =; Div. Prop. of = **2.** $AB = 12$; $BC = 9$; $AB + BC = 12 + 9 = 21$ **3a.** Reflexive Prop. of ≅ **b.** Transitive or Subst. Prop. of ≅

Lesson 2-5 pp. 96–99

Check Skills You'll Need **1.** 50 **2.** 90 **3.** 35 **4.** right ⦤s **5.** vertex

Check Understanding **1a.** Answers may vary. Sample: $\angle AFB$ and $\angle BFC$; $\angle BFD$ and $\angle DFE$ **b.** 153 **2a.** Yes; the ≅ segments are marked. **b.** No; there are no markings. **c.** No; there are no markings. **d.** No; there are no markings. **e.** Yes; the ≅ segments are marked. **3.** No; no; the size of the ⦤s does not affect the proof or the truth value of the thm. **4a.** 140 **b.** 40 **c.** $140 + 40 = 180$

Chapter 3

Diagnosing Readiness p. 112

1. 72 **2.** 1260 **3.** 2700 **4.** 4 **5.** 15 **6.** −24

7. $2x + x + x = 180$; 45, 45, 90

8. $\frac{1}{2}x + x + x = 180$; 36, 72, 72

9. 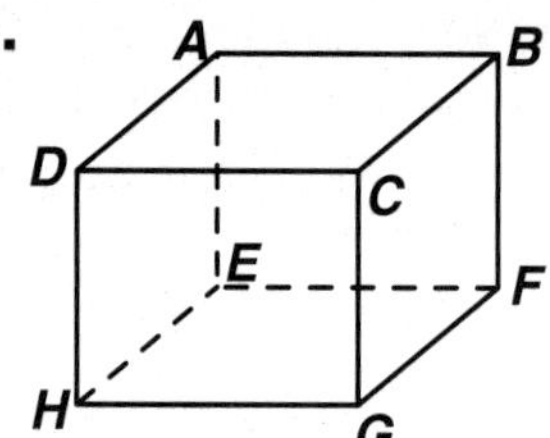

$\overleftrightarrow{AB}$ and $\overleftrightarrow{GH}$; $\overleftrightarrow{AE}$ and $\overleftrightarrow{EF}$

10–12. Check students' work.

Lesson 3-1 pp. 115–118

Check Skills You'll Need **1.** 30 **2.** 30 **3.** 60 **4.** 9 **5.** $m\angle 1 + 2(90 - m\angle 1) = 146$; $m\angle 1 = 34$ **6.** 72 and 108

Check Understanding **1.** ∠5 and ∠4; ∠6 and ∠2; ∠3 and ∠8 **2.** same-side int. ⦤s **3.** 1. $a \parallel b$ (Given) 2. $m\angle 3 + m\angle 2 = 180$ (∠ Add. Post.) 3. $m\angle 1 = m\angle 3$ (Corr. ⦤s Post.) 4. $m\angle 1 + m\angle 2 = 180$ (Subst.) 5. ∠1 and ∠2 are suppl. (Def. of Suppl. ⦤s) **4a.** 130; corr. ⦤s are ≅. **b.** 130; vert. ⦤s are ≅. **c.** 50; alt. int. ⦤s are ≅. **d.** 50; alt. int. ⦤s are ≅. **e.** 130; same-side int. ⦤s are suppl. **f.** 50; corr. ⦤s are ≅ or vert. ⦤s are ≅. **5.** $x = 45$, $y = 115$; 90, 90, 115, 65

Lesson 3-2 pp. 122–125

Check Skills You'll Need **1.** 11 **2.** 4 **3.** 26 **4.** 6 **5.** If a △ has a 90° ∠, then it is a right △; true. **6.** If two ⦤s are ≅, then they are vert. ⦤s; false. **7.** If two ⦤s are suppl., then they are same-side int. ⦤s; false.

Check Understanding **1.** If corr. ⦤s are ≅, then the lines are ∥. **2.** $\overleftrightarrow{EC} \parallel \overleftrightarrow{DK}$; Conv. of Corr. ⦤s Post. **3.** no **4.** 18; $7 \cdot 18 - 8 = 118$, and $62 + 118 = 180$. **5.** By def. of ⊥, all ⦤s formed are 90°. So, the sum of the measures of each pair of same-side int. ⦤s is 180, making them suppl. By the Conv. of the Same-Side Int. ⦤s Thm., the lines are ∥.

Lesson 3-3 pp. 131–134, 139

Check Skills You'll Need **1.** right **2.** acute **3.** acute **4.** 60 **5.** 20 **6.** 32 **7.** 58

Check Understanding **1a.** 32 **b.** The sum of the measures of the ⦤s of a △ is 180. If you subtract the measure of the right ∠ from 180, you get 90. The sum of the other two ⦤s is 90, so they are compl. **2.** For △GFH, $65 + (39 + 21) + z = 180$. Then $125 + z = 180$ and $z = 55$.

3a. 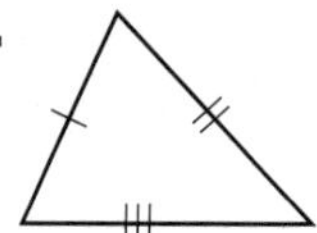 **b.** **c.** Not possible; an equilateral △ has all acute ⦤s.

4a. 90 **b.** If the acute ⦤s of a △ are compl., then the △ is a right △. True because the two compl. ⦤s add to 90, leaving 90 for the third ∠. **5a.** 130 **b.** Answers may vary. Sample: Find the measure of the third ∠ of the △. Subtract this from 180.

Checkpoint Quiz 1 **1.** Corr. ∠s Post. **2.** Conv. of Corr. ∠s Post. **3.** Same-Side Int. ∠s Thm. **4.** Conv. of the Alt. Int. ∠s Thm. **5.** Vert. ∠s Thm. **6.** Alt. Int. ∠s Thm. **7.** Conv. of Corr. ∠s Post. **8.** Corr. ∠s Post. **9.** Conv. of Same-Side Int. ∠s Thm. **10.** 38, 55, 87; acute, 55, 26, 99; obtuse

Lesson 3-4 pp. 143–146

Check Skills You'll Need **1.** $m\angle DAB = 77$; $m\angle B = 65$; $m\angle BCD = 131$; $m\angle D = 87$ **2.** $m\angle D = m\angle B = 60$; $m\angle DAB = m\angle DCB = 120$ **3.** $m\angle A = 70$; $m\angle ABC = 85$; $m\angle C = 125$; $m\angle ADC = 80$

Check Understanding **1.** *ABE*; sides: $\overline{AB}, \overline{BE}, \overline{EA}$; ∠s: $\angle A, \angle ABE, \angle BEA$; *BCDE*; sides: $\overline{BC}, \overline{CD}, \overline{DE}, \overline{EB}$; ∠s: $\angle EBC, \angle C, \angle D, \angle DEB$; *ABCDE*; sides: $\overline{AB}, \overline{BC}, \overline{CD}, \overline{DE}, \overline{EA}$; ∠s: $\angle A, \angle ABC, \angle C, \angle D, \angle AED$ **2a.** hexagon; convex **b.** octagon; concave **c.** 24-gon; concave **3a.** 1980 **b.** You can solve the equation $(n - 2)180 = 720$. **4.** 108 **5.** 30; no, it is not formed by extending one side of the polygon.

Lesson 3-5 pp. 152–154

Check Skills You'll Need **1.** $-\frac{2}{3}$ **2.** $\frac{5}{3}$ **3.** 0 **4.** undefined or no slope **5.** $\frac{2}{3}$ **6.** $\frac{3}{2}$ **7.** $\frac{4}{5}$ **8.** −1

Check Understanding

1. 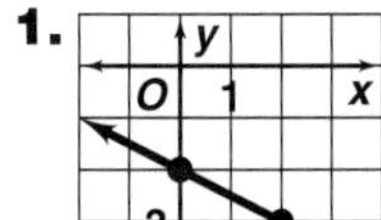

2. 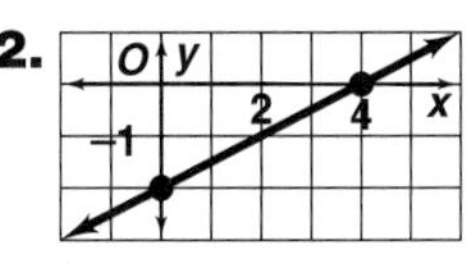

3. 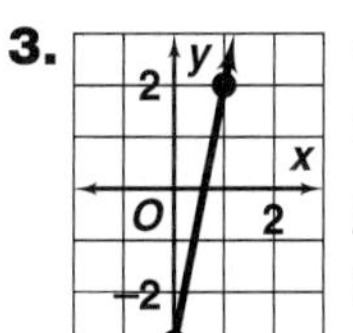

4. $y + 4 = -1(x - 2)$
5. $y - 0 = -\frac{3}{2}(x - 5)$ or $y + 3 = -\frac{3}{2}(x - 7)$
6. $y = -1$; $x = 5$

Lesson 3-6 pp. 158–161, 164

Check Skills You'll Need **1.** $\frac{1}{2}$ **2.** $\frac{5}{2}$ **3.** −5 **4.** 2 **5.** −1 **6.** $\frac{2}{3}$ **7.** 1 **8.** 0 **9.** $\frac{2}{3}$

Check Understanding **1.** No; the slope of $\ell_3 = -\frac{1}{7}$, and the slope of $\ell_4 = -\frac{1}{6}$. **2a.** Yes; each line has a slope of $-\frac{1}{2}$, and the *y*-intercepts are different. **b.** No; the lines have the same slope and *y*-intercept, so they are the same line. **3.** $y - 5 = -1(x + 2)$ **4.** No; the slope of $\ell_3 = \frac{4}{9}$, and the slope of $\ell_4 = -\frac{7}{3}$, and $\frac{4}{9} \cdot -\frac{7}{3} \neq -1$. **5.** $y + 4 = -5(x - 15)$ **6.** $y - 8 = \frac{3}{2}(x - 2)$ or $y = \frac{3}{2}x + 5$

Checkpoint Quiz 2 **1.** octagon; $n = 125$ **2.** hexagon; $x = 122$; $w = 90$ **3.** quad.; $a = 105$; $m = 116$

4. 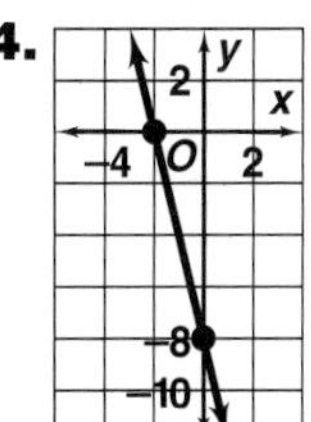

5. 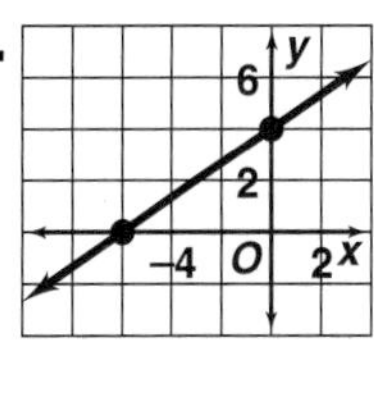

6. 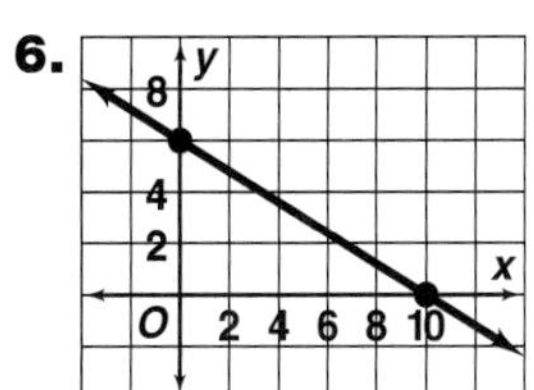

7. slope of $\overleftrightarrow{RS} = -\frac{2}{5}$; slope of $\overleftrightarrow{TV} = \frac{3}{5}$; neither
8. slope of $\overleftrightarrow{RS} = 1$; slope of $\overleftrightarrow{TV} = -1$; ⊥

9. slope of $\overleftrightarrow{RS} = -\frac{5}{4}$; slope of $\overleftrightarrow{TV} = \frac{4}{5}$; ⊥
10. slope of $\overleftrightarrow{RS} = \frac{2}{9}$; slope of $\overleftrightarrow{TV} = \frac{2}{9}$; ∥

Lesson 3-7 pp. 165–167

Check Skills You'll Need **1.** $\overline{AB} \cong \overline{CD}$

A B

C D

2. 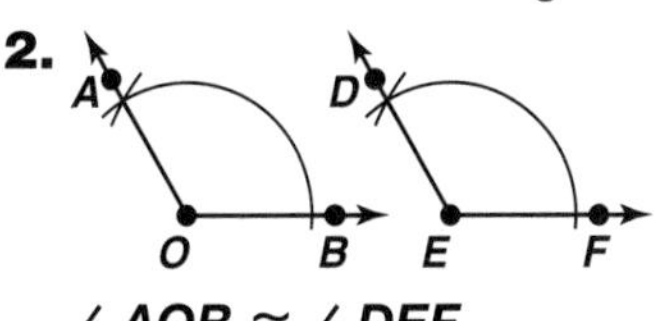

$\angle AOB \cong \angle DEF$

3. 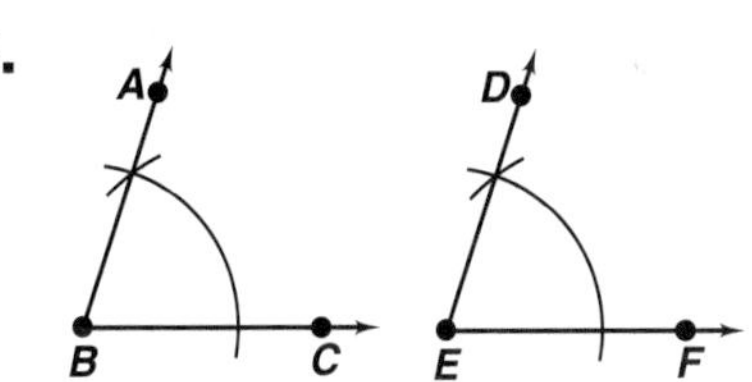

$\angle ABC \cong \angle DEF$

4. **5.** 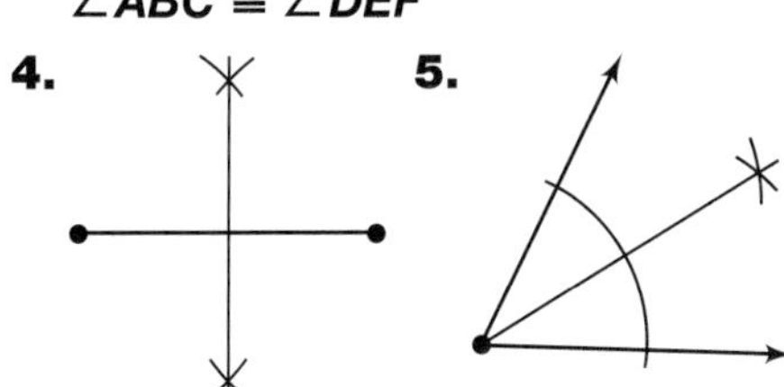

6. 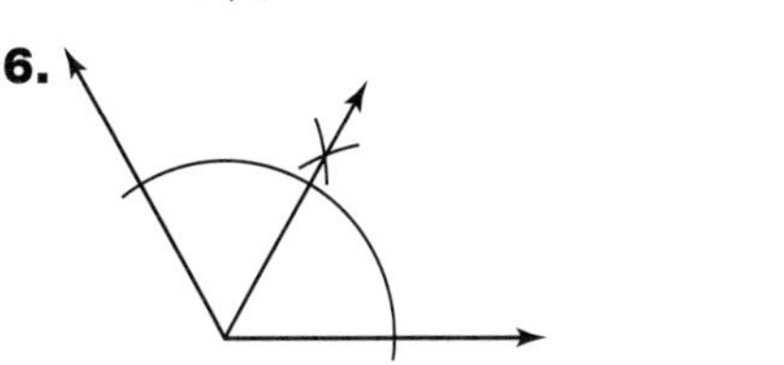

Check Understanding **1.** If corr. ∠s are ≅, the lines are ∥ by the Conv. of Corr. ∠s Post.

Instant Check System™ Answers

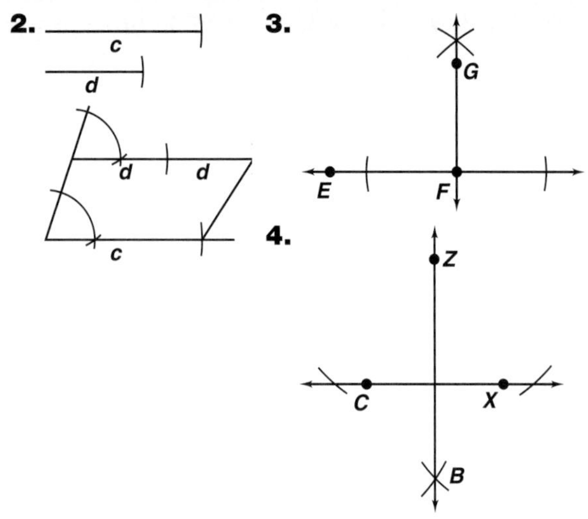

Check Understanding **1.** No; the $\cong$ side is not the included side. **2.** 1. $\angle CAB \cong \angle DAE$; $\overline{AB} \cong \overline{AE}$ (Given) 2. $\angle ABC$ and $\angle AED$ are right $\angle$s. (Given) 3. $\angle ABC \cong \angle AED$ (All right $\angle$s are $\cong$.) 4. $\triangle ABC \cong \triangle AED$ (ASA)

3.

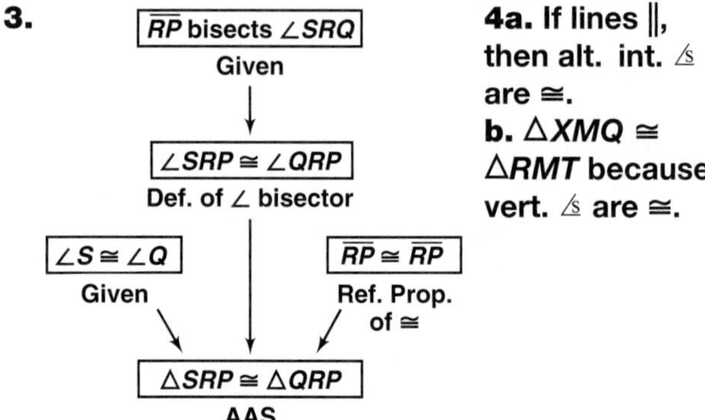

4a. If lines $\parallel$, then alt. int. $\angle$s are $\cong$. **b.** $\triangle XMQ \cong \triangle RMT$ because vert. $\angle$s are $\cong$.

Chapter 4

Diagnosing Readiness p. 178

1. $AB = 4, BC = 3, AC = 5$ **2.** $AB = 8, BC = \sqrt{265}, AC = \sqrt{137}$ **3.** $AB = \sqrt{58}, BC = 4\sqrt{2}, AC = \sqrt{58}$ **4.** $\angle A \cong \angle C$ **5.** $m\angle A = 90 = m\angle B$ or $\angle A$ and $\angle B$ are rt. $\angle$s. **6.** $\angle B$ is a rt. $\angle$. **7.** $\angle AFB \cong \angle DFC$ **8.** $\angle A \cong \angle D$ and $\angle B \cong \angle C$ **9.** $\angle ACD \cong \angle CAB$ and $\angle DAC \cong \angle BCA$ **10.** $x = 12$

Lesson 4-1 pp. 180–182

Check Skills You'll Need **1.** 19 **2.** 13 **3.** 108 **4.** 10 **5.** 50

Check Understanding **1.** $\angle WSY \cong \angle MVK$; $\angle SWY \cong \angle VMK$; $\angle WYS \cong \angle MKV$; $\overline{WY} \cong \overline{MK}$; $\overline{WS} \cong \overline{MV}$; $\overline{YS} \cong \overline{KV}$ **2.** $m\angle K = 35$; corr. $\angle$s are $\cong$. **3.** No; corr. sides are not necessarily $\cong$. **4a.** $\angle A \cong \angle D$; $\angle E \cong \angle C$ (Given) **b.** $\angle ABE \cong \angle DBC$ (Vert. $\angle$s are $\cong$.) **c.** $\overline{AE} \cong \overline{CD}$; $\overline{AB} \cong \overline{BD}$; $\overline{EB} \cong \overline{BC}$ (Given) **d.** $\triangle ABE \cong \triangle DBC$ (Def. of $\cong$ $\triangle$s)

Lesson 4-2 pp. 186–188

Check Skills You'll Need **1.** $\overline{AB} \cong \overline{DE}$; $\angle C \cong \angle F$ **2.** $\angle Q \cong \angle S$; $\angle QPR \cong \angle SRP$; $\overline{PR} \cong \overline{PR}$ **3.** $\angle M \cong \angle S$; $\angle MON \cong \angle SVT$; $\overline{TO} \cong \overline{NV}$; $\overline{MO} \parallel \overline{VS}$

Check Understanding **1.** You are given that $\overline{AB} \cong \overline{CB}$ and $\overline{AD} \cong \overline{CD}$. $\overline{BD} \cong \overline{BD}$ by the Refl. Prop. of $\cong$, so $\triangle ABD \cong \triangle CBD$ by SSS. **2.** $\angle DCA \cong \angle BAC$ or $CB = 8$ **3.** No; you don't know that $\angle E \cong \angle DBC$ or that $\overline{AB} \cong \overline{DC}$.

Lesson 4-3 pp. 194–196, 201

Check Skills You'll Need **1.** $\overline{JH}$ **2.** $\overline{HK}$ **3.** $\angle L$ **4.** $\angle N$ **5.** Reflexive Prop. of $\cong$ **6.** If 2 $\angle$s of a $\triangle$ are $\cong$ to 2 $\angle$s of another $\triangle$, the third $\angle$s are $\cong$.

Checkpoint Quiz 1 **1.** $\overline{RS} \cong \overline{JK}$; $\overline{ST} \cong \overline{KL}$; $\overline{RT} \cong \overline{JL}$; $\angle R \cong \angle J$; $\angle S \cong \angle K$; $\angle T \cong \angle L$ **2.** ASA **3.** SSS **4.** SAS **5.** not possible **6.** AAS **7.** not possible **8.** If $\parallel$ lines, then alt. int. $\angle$s are $\cong$. **9.** Vert. $\angle$s are $\cong$. **10.** ASA or AAS

Lesson 4-4 pp. 203–204

Check Skills You'll Need **1.** $\angle J \cong \angle H$; $\angle R \cong \angle V$; $\angle C \cong \angle G$ **2.** $\overline{JR} \cong \overline{HV}$; $\overline{RC} \cong \overline{VG}$; $\overline{JC} \cong \overline{HG}$ **3.** $\angle T \cong \angle L$; $\angle I \cong \angle O$; $\angle C \cong \angle K$ **4.** $\overline{TI} \cong \overline{LO}$; $\overline{IC} \cong \overline{OK}$; $\overline{TC} \cong \overline{LK}$

Check Understanding **1a.** They are $\cong$ because suppl. of $\cong$ $\angle$s are $\cong$. **b.** As point S is moved toward point C, $\angle LSC$ and $\angle RSC$ change shape, but they are always $\cong$ to each other. **2.** 50 ft

Lesson 4-5 pp. 210–212

Check Skills You'll Need **1.** $\angle C$ **2.** $\angle A$ **3.** $\overline{BC}$ **4.** $\overline{BA}$ **5.** 105

Check Understanding **1.** Draw $\overline{XB}$, the bisector of $\angle YXZ$. Then, since $\angle Z \cong \angle Y$ and $\overline{XB} \cong \overline{XB}$ by the Reflexive Prop. of $\cong$, $\triangle ZXB \cong \triangle YXB$ by AAS. Then $\overline{XZ} \cong \overline{XY}$ by CPCTC. **2.** No; neither $\angle RVU$ nor $\angle RUV$ can be shown $\cong$ to $\angle R$. **3.** $x = 90$; $y = 47$ **4.** 150

Lesson 4-6 pp. 217–219, 223

Check Skills You'll Need **1.** yes **2.** yes **3.** no **4.** yes **5.** yes **6.** no **7.** yes; SAS **8.** yes; SAS

Check Understanding **1.** $\triangle LMN \cong \triangle OQP$ **2.** $\overline{CB} \cong \overline{EB}$ and $m\angle CBD = m\angle EBA$ because $\overline{AD}$ is the $\perp$ bis. of $\overline{CE}$. It is given that $\overline{CD} \cong \overline{EA}$. $\triangle CBD \cong \triangle EBA$ by HL. **3.** The $\triangle$s are $\cong$ by SAS.

Checkpoint Quiz 2 **1.** $\overline{PR} \cong \overline{SQ}$; $\angle P \cong \angle S$; $\angle PRQ \cong \angle SQR$ **2a.** Isosc. $\triangle$ **b.** $\cong$ **c.** Converse of the Isosc. $\triangle$ Thm. **3.** $\triangle AED$; $\angle EAB \cong \angle EDC$ (Given), $\triangle EBC$; $\angle EBC \cong \angle ECB$ (Suppl. of $\cong$ $\angle$s are $\cong$.) **4.** HL **5.** $\triangle GTW \cong \triangle SWT$ by SAS since $\overline{WT} \cong \overline{WT}$, $\angle WTG \cong \angle TWS$, and $\overline{GT} \cong \overline{SW}$. So $\overline{GW} \cong \overline{ST}$ by CPCTC.

Lesson 4-7 pp. 224–226

Check Skills You'll Need **1.** 15; 31 **2a.** yes; SAS **b.** yes; AAS **c.** yes; Trans. Prop. of $\cong$

Check Understanding **1a.** $\overline{CD}$ **b.** Answers may vary. Sample: $\triangle ABD$ and $\triangle CBD$; $\overline{BD}$ **2.** 1. $\triangle ACD \cong \triangle BDC$ (Given) 2. $\angle ADC \cong \angle BCD$ (CPCTC) 3. $\overline{CE} \cong \overline{DE}$ (If base $\angle$s are $\cong$, the opp. sides are $\cong$.) **3.** 1. $\overline{PS} \cong \overline{RS}$; $\angle PSQ \cong \angle RSQ$ (Given) 2. $\overline{QS} \cong \overline{QS}$ (Reflexive Prop. of $\cong$) 3. $\triangle PSQ \cong \triangle RSQ$ (SAS) 4. $\overline{PQ} \cong \overline{RQ}$ (CPCTC) 5. $\angle PQT \cong \angle RQT$ (CPCTC) 6. $\overline{QT} \cong \overline{QT}$ (Reflexive Prop. of $\cong$) 7. $\triangle PQT \cong \triangle RQT$ (SAS) **4.** 1. $\angle CAD \cong \angle EAD$; $\angle C \cong \angle E$ (Given) 2. $\overline{AD} \cong \overline{AD}$ (Reflexive Prop. of $\cong$) 3. $\triangle ACD \cong \triangle AED$ (AAS) 4. $\overline{CD} \cong \overline{ED}$ (CPCTC) 5. $\angle BDC \cong \angle FDE$ (Vert. $\angle$s are $\cong$.) 6. $\triangle BDC \cong \triangle FDE$ (ASA) 7. $\overline{BD} \cong \overline{FD}$ (CPCTC)

Chapter 5

Diagnosing Readiness p. 240

1. $x \le 4$ **2.** $x > \frac{15}{2}$ **3.** $x \le 1$

4.

A B

5.

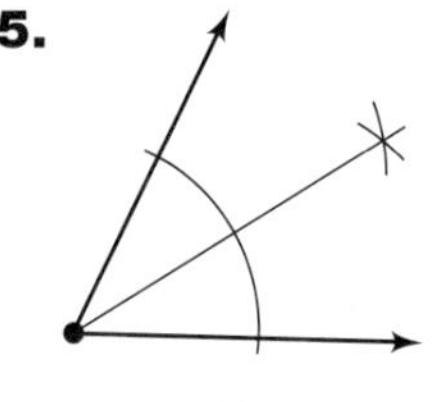

6. 5 **7.** 13 **8.** $4\sqrt{5}$ **9.** (5, 7) **10.** $\left(-3, -\frac{7}{2}\right)$ **11.** $\left(-\frac{9}{2}, \frac{5}{2}\right)$ **12.** -9 **13.** $-\frac{8}{3}$ **14.** 0

Lesson 5-1 pp. 243–245

Check Skills You'll Need **1.** (1, 2) **2.** $\left(\frac{3}{2}, \frac{11}{2}\right)$ **3.** $\left(-\frac{1}{2}, 8\right)$ **4.** (1, 1) **5.** $-\frac{2}{5}$ **6.** $\frac{1}{3}$ **7.** $\frac{4}{7}$ **8.** $\frac{3}{2}$

Check Understanding **1.** $EB = 9$; $BC = 10$; $AC = 20$ **2.** 65; the lines are $\parallel$ so $\angle VUZ$ and $\angle YXZ$ are corr. and $\cong$. **3a.** 1320 ft **b.** $\frac{1}{4}$ mi

Lesson 5-2 pp. 249–251

Check Skills You'll Need

1.

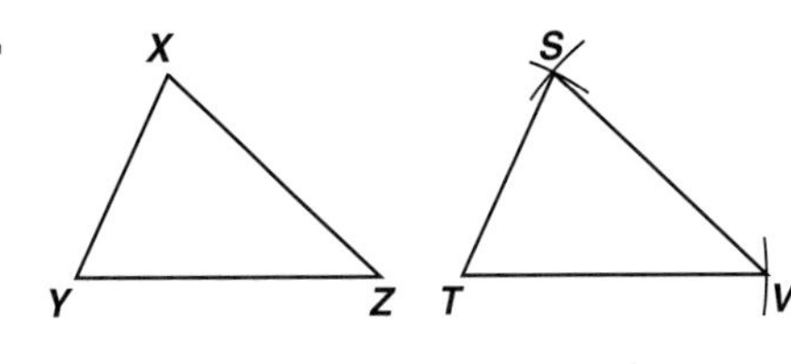

2.

P Q

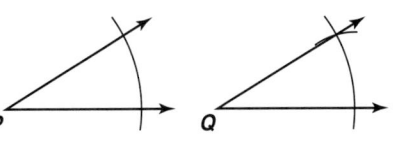

3. **4.**

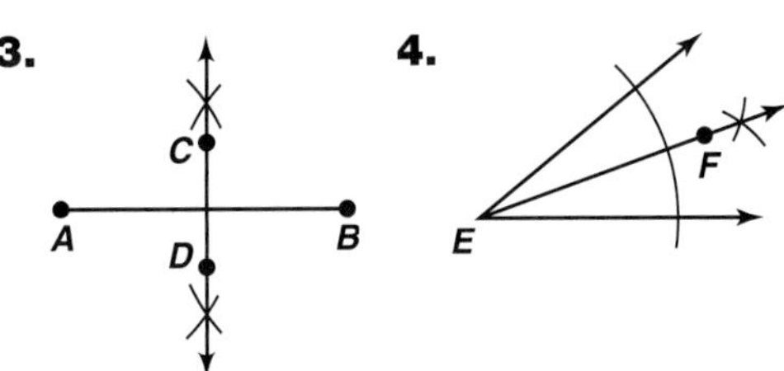

5. 6 **6.** 68

Check Understanding **1.** $CA = 5$; $DB = 6$; $\overleftrightarrow{CD}$ is the $\perp$ bis. of $\overline{AB}$; therefore $CA = CB$ and $DA = DB$. **2a.** 10; 10 **b.** $\overrightarrow{EK}$ is on the $\angle$ bis. of $\angle DEH$. **c.** 20 **d.** 80

Lesson 5-3 pp. 256–258, 263

Check Skills You'll Need

1–2.

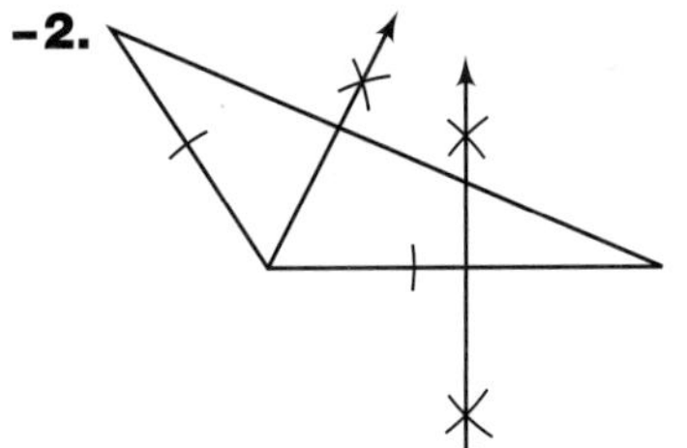

3.

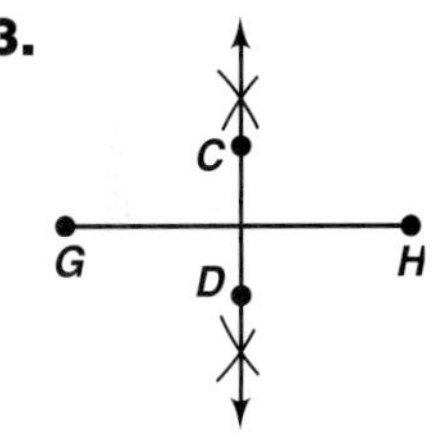

4.

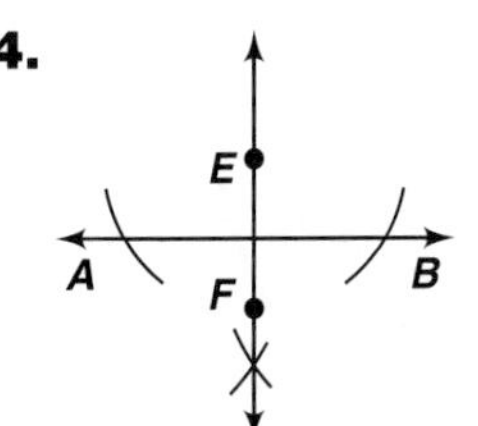

Check Understanding **1a.** $(-4, 3)$ **b.** Thm. 5-6: All of the $\perp$ bis. of the sides of a $\triangle$ are concurrent. **2a.** Draw segments connecting the towns. Build the library at the inters. pt. of the $\perp$ bisectors of the segments. **b.** The $\perp$ bisectors of the sides of a $\triangle$ are concurrent at a point equidistant from the vertices. **3.** 12 **4.** Median; $\overline{UW}$ is a segment from vertex U to the midpt. of the opp. side.

Checkpoint Quiz 1 **1.** 6 **2.** 3 **3a.** 104 **b.** 228 **4.** right ∠; suppl. to $\angle ADB$ **5.** $\triangle ABD \cong \triangle CBD$; HL **6.** $\overline{AD} \cong \overline{DC}$; CPCTC **7.** $\overrightarrow{XY}$ bisects $\angle ZXW$; Y is equidist. from $\overrightarrow{XZ}$ and $\overrightarrow{XW}$. **8.** 21; $\triangle XYZ \cong \triangle XYW$ by HL, so $XZ = 21$ by CPCTC. **9.** Answers may vary. Sample: Bisect a side of a △. Connect the opp. vertex with the midpt. **10.** Use the procedure for constructing a ⊥ to a line from a point not on the line.

Lesson 5-4 pp. 264–267

Check Skills You'll Need **1.** If we go skiing, then it snows tomorrow. **2.** If 2 lines do not intersect, then they are parallel. **3.** If $x^2 = 1$, then $x = -1$. **4.** If a point is on the bisector of an angle, then it is equidistant from the sides of the angle. If a point is equidistant from the sides of an angle, then it is on the bisector of the angle. **5.** If a point is on the ⊥ bis. of a segment, then it is equidistant from the endpoints of the segment. If a point is equidistant from the endpoints of a segment, then it is on the ⊥ bis. of the segment. **6.** If you will pass a geometry course, then you are successful with your homework. If you are successful with your homework, then you will pass a geometry course.

Check Understanding **1a.** The measure of $\angle XYZ$ is not more than 70. **b.** Today is Tuesday. **2a.** If you stand for something, you won't fall for anything. **b.** If you won't fall for anything, then you stand for something. **3a.** Assume that the shoes cost more than $20. **b.** Assume that $m\angle A \leq m\angle B$. **4.** I and II **5.** $\angle X$ could be a right ∠.

Lesson 5-5 pp. 273–276

Check Skills You'll Need

1.

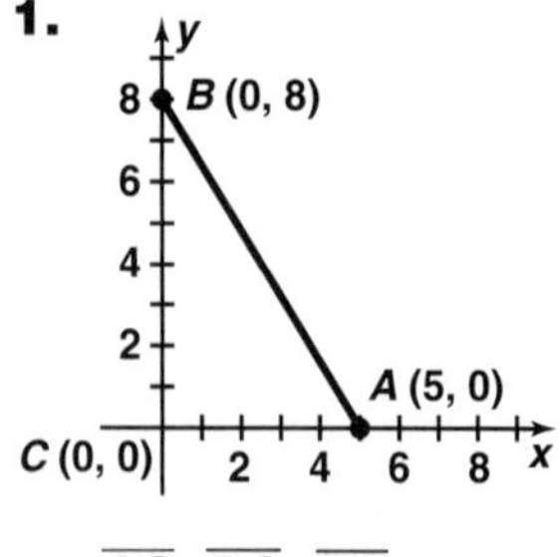

$\overline{AC}, \overline{BC}, \overline{AB}$

2.

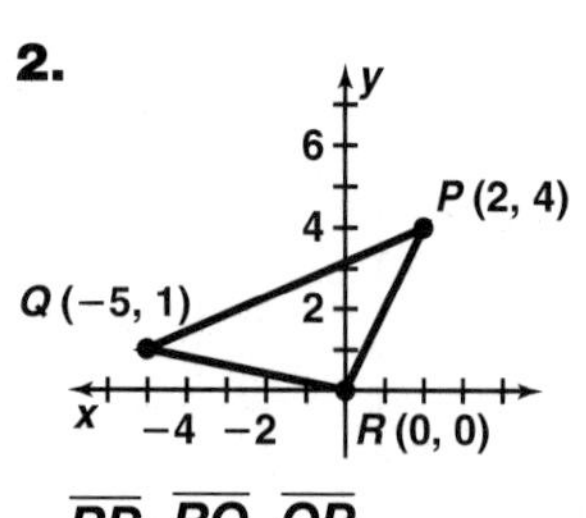

$\overline{RP}, \overline{RQ}, \overline{QP}$

3. **4.**

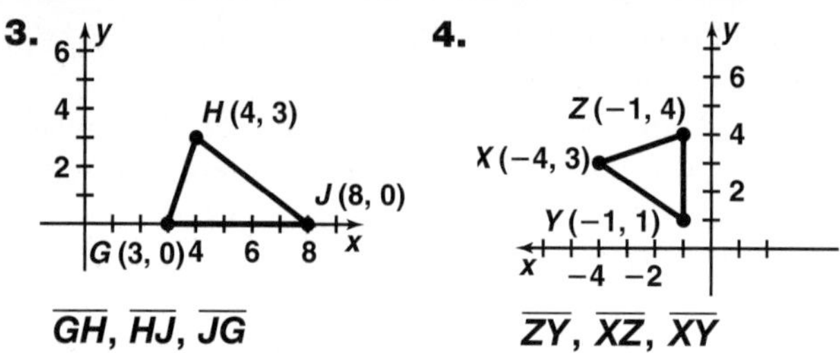

$\overline{GH}, \overline{HJ}, \overline{JG}$ $\overline{ZY}, \overline{XZ}, \overline{XY}$

5. Assume that $m\angle A \leq m\angle B$. **6.** $AB < AC$

Check Understanding **1.** $m\angle OTY > m\angle 2$ by the Comparison Prop. of Ineq. Since it was proven that $m\angle 2 > m\angle 3$, then by the Trans. Prop. $m\angle OTY > m\angle 3$. **2.** $\angle A, \angle C, \angle B$ **3.** $\overline{YZ}, \overline{XY}, \overline{XZ}$; $m\angle Y = 80$. **4a.** No; $2 + 7 \not> 9$. **b.** Yes; $4 + 6 > 9$; $6 + 9 > 4$; $4 + 9 > 6$. **5.** $9 < x < 15$

Chapter 6

Diagnosing Readiness p. 286

1. 30 **2.** 42 **3.** 22 **4.** yes **5.** no **6.** yes **7.** parallel **8.** perpendicular **9.** neither **10.** ASA **11.** SAS **12.** AAS

Lesson 6-1 pp. 288–290

Check Skills You'll Need **1.** 10.8 **2.** 7.8 **3.** 12.7 **4.** $\frac{3}{4}$ **5.** $-\frac{8}{3}$ **6.** 1

Check Understanding **1a.** quad., ▱, rhombus **b.** Rhombus; it is a ▱ and quad. with 4 sides that are ≅. **2.** square **3.** $a = 2, b = 4$; $LN = ST = NT = SL = 14$

Lesson 6-2 pp. 294–297

Check Skills You'll Need **1.** ASA **2a.** $\angle HGE$ **b.** $\angle GHE$ **c.** $\angle HEG$ **d.** $\overline{GH}$ **e.** $\overline{HE}$ **f.** $\overline{EG}$ **3.** They are ∥.

Check Understanding **1.** Yes; by the Converse of the Same-Side Int. ∠s Thm., both pairs of opp. sides are ∥. **2.** 11; $m\angle E = 70$, $m\angle G = 70$, $m\angle F = 110$, $m\angle H = 110$ **3.** $a = 16, b = 14$ **4.** 7.5

Lesson 6-3 pp. 303–306, 310

Check Skills You'll Need **1.** $\left(\frac{5}{2}, \frac{3}{2}\right)$, $\left(\frac{5}{2}, \frac{3}{2}\right)$; they bisect each other. **2.** Slope of $\overline{BC} = \frac{1}{3}$, slope of $\overline{AD} = \frac{1}{3}$. The slopes are =. **3.** Yes; they are vertical lines. **4.** parallelogram

Check Understanding **1.** 70, 2 **2a.** Yes; a pair of opp. sides are ∥ and ≅. **b.** No; the figure could be a trapezoid. **3.** Once in place, both rulers show the direction and remain ∥. Keep the second ruler in place and move the first ruler to get the compass reading.

Checkpoint Quiz 1 **1.** $m\angle 1 = 59$, $m\angle 2 = 121$, $m\angle 3 = 59$ **2.** $m\angle 1 = 43$, $m\angle 2 = 62$, $m\angle 3 = 62$ **3.** $m\angle 1 = 106$, $m\angle 2 = 74$, $m\angle 3 = 26$ **4.** trapezoid, isos. trapezoid **5.** rectangle, ▱ **6.** rectangle, ▱ **7.** $x = 45$, $y = 60$ **8.** $x = 1$, $y = 2$ **9.** 20.6 **10.** kite

Lesson 6-4 pp. 312–315

Check Skills You'll Need **1.** 4.5 **2.** 7 **3.** 109 **4.** 4.75 **5.** 3.5 **6.** 9.5 **7.** 71 **8.** 71

9.

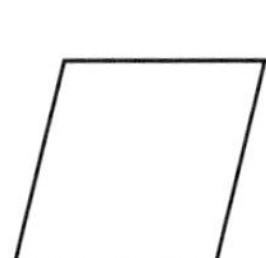

The rhombus is not a square because it has no right ⊿s. The rectangle is not a square because all 4 sides aren't ≅.

Check Understanding **1.** $\angle 1 = 90$, $\angle 2 = 50$, $\angle 3 = 50$, $\angle 4 = 40$ **2.** $8\frac{1}{2}$ **3.** No; if one diagonal bisects two ⊿s, then the figure is a rhombus and cannot have noncongruent sides. **4.** Yes; if the ropes are ⊥ to each other, then the endpoints of the ropes determine a square.

Lesson 6-5 pp. 320–322

Check Skills You'll Need **1.** $a = 5.6$, $b = 6.8$; 4.5, 4.2, 4.5, 4.2 **2.** 3; 4.8, 16.4, 18, 18 **3.** $m = 5$, $n = 15$; 15, 15, 21, 21

Check Understanding **1.** 110, 110, 70 **2.** 85, 95 **3.** 90, 46, 44

Lesson 6-6 pp. 326–327, 331

Check Skills You'll Need

1.

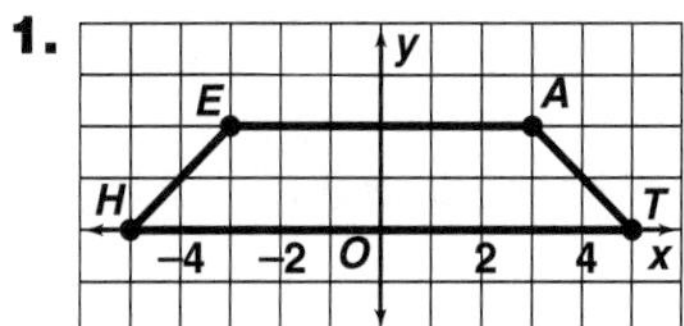

isosc. trapezoid

2.

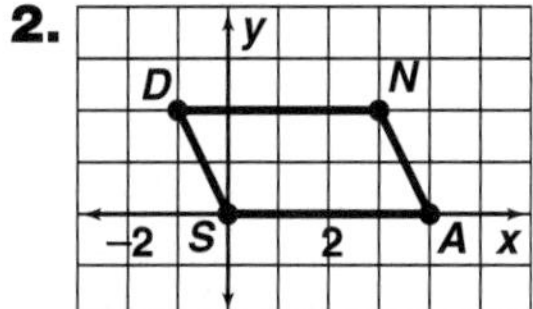

parallelogram

3.

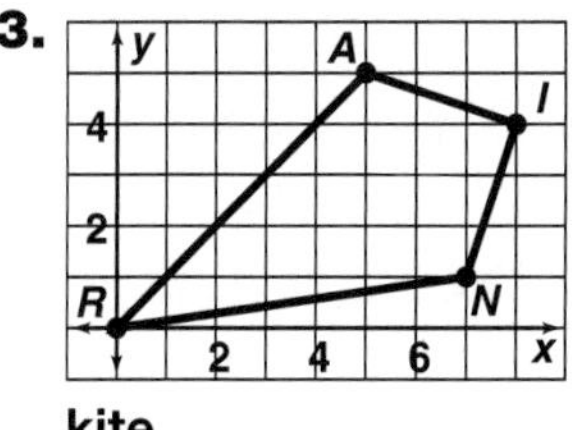

kite

4.

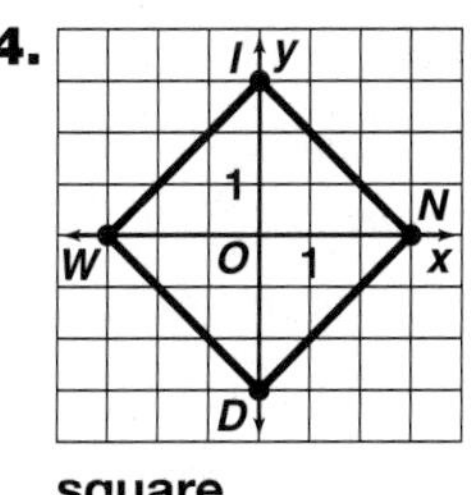

square

Check Understanding **1.** $Q(s + b, c)$ **2.** Midpoint of $\overline{TV} = \left(\frac{a + c + e}{2}, \frac{b + d}{2}\right)$ = midpoint of $\overline{UW}$. So, the diagonals bisect each other and $TWVU$ is a ▱.

Checkpoint Quiz 2 **1.** $x = 51$, $y = 51$ **2.** $x = 58$, $y = 32$ **3.** $x = 2$, $y = 4$ **4.** 3 **5.** $x = \frac{5}{3}$, $y = \frac{9}{2}$, $b = 90$ **6–8.** Counterexamples may vary.

6. false;

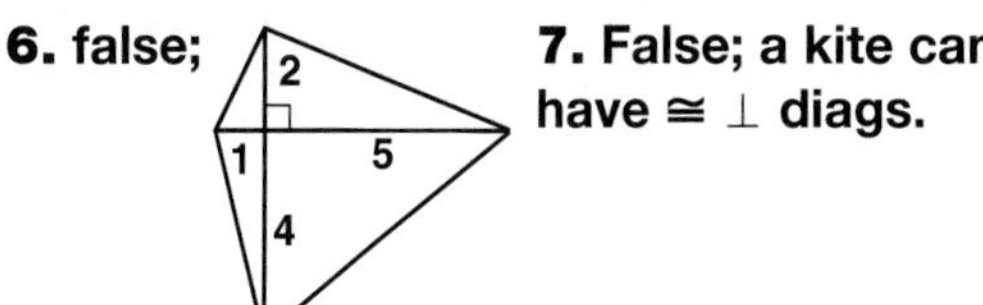

7. False; a kite can have ≅ ⊥ diags.

8. false

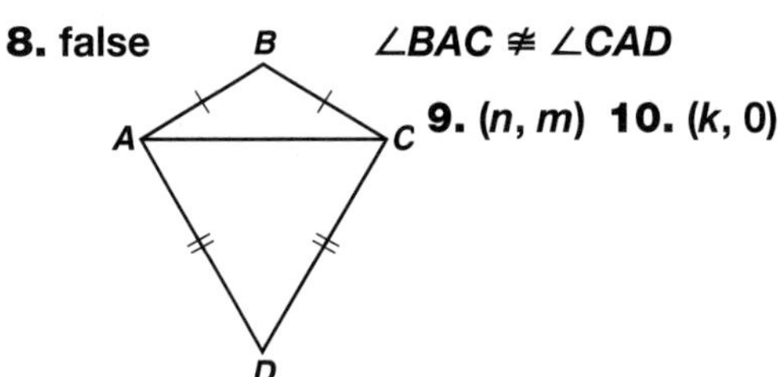

$\angle BAC \not\cong \angle CAD$

9. (n, m) **10.** $(k, 0)$

Lesson 6-7 pp. 332–333

Check Skills You'll Need **1.** The quad. is a rectangle. **2.** (a, c) **3.** $(-a, 0)$

Check Understanding **1a.** $M(b, c)$, $N(a + d, c)$; by starting with multiples of 2 you eliminate fractions when using the midpoint formula. **b.** 0, 0, 0; they are =. **c.** $MN = d + a - b$, $TP = 2a$, $RA = 2d - 2b$; so $RA + TP = 2d + 2a - 2b$ which is twice MN. So the midsegment is half the sum of the lengths of the bases. **d.** The base along the x-axis allows us to calculate length by subtracting x-values. **2.** Using multiples of 2 in the coordinates for M, N, P, and O eliminates the use of fractions when finding midpoints since finding midpoints requires division by 2.

Chapter 7

Diagnosing Readiness p. 346

1. 9 **2.** 64 **3.** 144 **4.** 225 **5.** 4 **6.** 8 **7.** 10 **8.** 13 **9.** ±6 **10.** ±10.2 **11.** ±6.9 **12.** ±8.1 **13.** $2\sqrt{2}$ **14.** $3\sqrt{3}$ **15.** $4\sqrt{3}$ **16.** $36\sqrt{2}$ **17.** $\frac{3}{5}$ **18.** $\frac{3}{10}$ **19.** 0 **20.** 1 **21.** rhombus **22.** parallelogram **23.** rhombus

Lesson 7-1 pp. 348–351

Check Skills You'll Need **1.** 25 cm^2 **2.** 28 $in.^2$ **3.** 11.5 m^2 **4.** $\frac{3}{2}$ ft^2 **5.** 6 $units^2$ **6.** 2 $units^2$ **7.** 8 $units^2$

Check Understanding **1.** 108 m^2 **2.** 20 $units^2$ **3.** 7.5 cm **4.** 30 cm^2 **5.** The force is doubled.

Lesson 7-2 pp. 357–360

Check Skills You'll Need **1.** $3^2 + 4^2 = 5^2$ **2.** $5^2 + 12^2 = 13^2$ **3.** $6^2 + 8^2 = 10^2$ **4.** $4^2 + 4^2 = (4\sqrt{2})^2$

Check Understanding **1.** $5\sqrt{21}$; no **2.** $6\sqrt{3}$ **3.** You want to know the nearest whole number value, which may not be apparent in a radical expression. **4.** 7 cm^2 **5.** no **6.** acute

Lesson 7-3 pp. 366–369, 372

Check Skills You'll Need **1.** 45, 45, 90 **2.** 30, 60, 90 **3.** 45, 45, 90

Check Understanding **1.** $5\sqrt{6}$ **2.** $5\sqrt{2}$ **3.** 141 ft **4.** 6; $6\sqrt{3}$ **5.** $3\sqrt{2}$; $2\sqrt{6}$ **6a.** 50 $in.^2$ **b.** $50\sqrt{3}$ $in.^2$

Checkpoint Quiz 1 **1.** 84 $in.^2$ **2.** 112 cm^2 **3.** 48 m^2 **4.** 12 **5.** $x = 10$; $y = 10\sqrt{2}$ **6.** $x = 12\sqrt{3}$; $y = 24$ **7.** acute **8.** right **9.** obtuse **10.** 28.3 cm

Lesson 7-4 pp. 373–375

Check Skills You'll Need **1.** $A = bh$ or $A = \ell w$ **2.** $A = \frac{1}{2}bh$ **3.** 9 $units^2$ **4.** 7 $units^2$ **5.** 13.5 $units^2$

Check Understanding **1.** 94.5 cm^2 **2.** 12 m^2 **3.** 54 $in.^2$ **4.** $9^2 + 12^2 = 15^2$

Lesson 7-5 pp. 380–382

Check Skills You'll Need **1.** $25\sqrt{3}$ cm^2 **2.** 50 ft^2 **3.** $\frac{100\sqrt{3}}{3}$ m^2 **4.** 24 in. **5.** $16\sqrt{3}$ cm

Check Understanding **1.** $m\angle 1 = 45$; $m\angle 2 = 22.5$; $m\angle 3 = 67.5$ **2.** 232 cm^2 **3.** $384\sqrt{3}$ ft^2 **4.** about 3352 $in.^2$

Lesson 7-6 pp. 386–389

Check Skills You'll Need **1.** 14 cm **2.** 3.2 m **3.** 5 ft **4.** 2.5 in. **5.** 32 **6.** 137 **7.** 180 **8.** 76

Check Understanding **1a.** number of hours spent doing an activity **b.** Each section represents the average of the 3600 participants' answers. **2.** $\overset{\frown}{CEA}$, $\overset{\frown}{DAE}$, $\overset{\frown}{ACD}$, $\overset{\frown}{EDC}$ **3.** 58; 180; 122; 270 **4.** 17 revolutions **5.** 1.3π m

Lesson 7-7 pp. 395–397, 400

Check Skills You'll Need **1.** 4.5 cm **2.** 16 ft **3.** 12π or about 37.7 in. **4.** 6π or about 18.8 m

Check Understanding **1.** about 41 $in.^2$ **2.** 181.5 cm^2 **3.** 13.0 cm^2

Checkpoint Quiz 2 **1.** 135 $in.^2$ **2.** 58.5 m^2 **3.** $72\sqrt{3}$ $in.^2$ **4.** $27\sqrt{3}$ ft^2 **5.** 32 yd^2 **6.** 100π $in.^2$ **7.** 27π m^2 **8.** $(16\pi - 32)$ cm^2 **9.** 31.4 m **10.** $\frac{9\pi}{2}$ mm

Lesson 7-8 pp. 402–404

Check Skills You'll Need **1.** $\frac{1}{3}$ **2.** $\frac{1}{2}$ **3.** 1 **4.** $\frac{1}{4}$ **5.** $\frac{1}{6}$ **6.** $\frac{1}{2}$ **7.** $\frac{1}{3}$ **8.** $\frac{1}{2}$

Check Understanding **1.** $\frac{2}{5}$ **2.** $\frac{2}{5}$ **3a.** It becomes about 8.7%, or about 4 times greater. **b.** It becomes 19.6%, or about 9 times greater. **4.** Yes; theoretically you should win 1.4 times out of 100.

Chapter 8

Diagnosing Readiness p. 414

1. $\frac{2}{3}$ **2.** 5 **3.** $\frac{4}{3a^3}$ **4.** $\frac{3x - 12}{x^2 - x}$ **5.** $\overline{DL}$ **6.** $\angle A$ **7.** $\angle DLH$ **8.** $\triangle APC$ **9.** 108 **10.** 135 **11.** 144 **12.** $166\frac{2}{3}$ **13.** $10\sqrt{3}$ **14.** $3\sqrt{2}$ **15.** $2\sqrt{3}$ **16.** $24\sqrt{3}$ $units^2$ **17.** 392.4 $units^2$

Lesson 8-1 pp. 416–418

Check Skills You'll Need **1–5.** Answers may vary. Samples are given. **1.** $\frac{1}{2}$ **2.** $\frac{2}{3}$ **3.** $\frac{3}{4}$ **4.** 1 **5.** $\frac{2}{3}$ **6.** 4 **7.** $\frac{1}{4}$ **8.** $\frac{4}{3}$ **9.** Each side of the smaller $\triangle$ is $\frac{1}{2}$ the length of a side of the larger $\triangle$.

Check Understanding **1.** 1 : 3 **2.** Answers may vary. Sample: $\frac{4}{m} = \frac{11}{n}$, $\frac{m+4}{4} = \frac{n+11}{11}$ **3a.** 0.75 **b.** 3 **4.** $3\frac{1}{2}$ in. by $2\frac{1}{2}$ in.

Lesson 8-2 pp. 423–425, 429

Check Skills You'll Need **1.** $\overline{AB} \cong \overline{HI}$; $\overline{BC} \cong \overline{IJ}$; $\overline{AC} \cong \overline{HJ}$ **2.** 6 **3.** 6 **4.** 3 **5.** 5

Check Understanding **1.** $m\angle F = 127$; BC **2.** Yes; corr. ∡ are ≅ and corr. sides are prop. **3.** 3.8 **4.** 7.2 in. by 12 in. **5.** about 32.4 cm

Checkpoint Quiz 1 **1.** 1 : 8 **2.** $\frac{b}{10}$ **3.** no; $\frac{4}{6} \neq \frac{8}{10}$ **4.** 2 **5.** $\frac{34}{7}$ **6.** 12.5 ft **7.** $\angle BDF$ **8.** BF **9.** 3 ft by 2 ft **10.** $3\frac{1}{3}$

Lesson 8-3 pp. 432–435

Check Skills You'll Need **1.** SSS **2.** SAS **3.** ASA

Check Understanding **1.** No; none of the side lengths are known. **2.** $\frac{AC}{EG} = \frac{CB}{GF} = \frac{AB}{EF} = \frac{3}{4}$, so the ⊿ are ~ by SSS ~ Thm.; $\triangle ABC \sim \triangle EFG$. **3.** 9 **4.** 13.5 ft

Lesson 8-4 pp. 439–441

Check Skills You'll Need **1.** 6 **2.** $\frac{14}{3}$ **3.** $\frac{24}{5}$ **4.** 39 **5.** 2 **6.** $\frac{8}{3}$ **7.** $\frac{40}{9}$ **8.** 18

9. Sample: $\triangle ADC$ and $\triangle BCD$

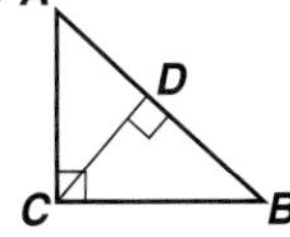

Check Understanding **1.** $10\sqrt{3}$ **2.** $x = 8$; $y = 4\sqrt{3}$ **3.** 240 m

Lesson 8-5 pp. 446–448, 452

Check Skills You'll Need **1.** 28 cm **2.** $3\frac{3}{7}$ mm **3.** 9.8 in. **4.** 11.25 ft

Check Understanding **1.** 1.5 **2.** $x = \frac{225}{13}$; $y = 28.6$ **3.** 5.76

Checkpoint Quiz 2 **1.** $\triangle ABC \sim \triangle XYZ$; AA ~ Post. **2.** $\triangle WST \sim \triangle HJG$; SAS ~ Thm. **3.** $x = \frac{3\sqrt{13}}{2}$; $w = 4.5$ **4.** 12 **5.** 15 **6.** 7.5 **7.** $4\sqrt{5}$ **8.** 3.6 **9.** 17.5 **10.** 77

Lesson 8-6 pp. 454–456

Check Skills You'll Need **1.** 28 in.; 49 in.^{2} **2.** 24 m; 32 m^2 **3.** 24 cm; 24 cm^2 **4.** 8 cm; 3 cm^2 **5.** 16 cm; 12 cm^2 **6.** 24 cm; 27 cm^2

Check Understanding **1a.** 5 : 7 **b.** 25 : 49 **2.** 54 in.^{2} **3.** \$6.94 **4.** $5\sqrt{5} : 3$

Chapter 9

Diagnosing Readiness p. 468

1. 4.648 **2.** 40.970 **3.** 6149.090 **4.** −5 **5.** AA~ Post. **6.** SSS~ Thm. **7.** SAS~ Thm. **8.** 12 **9.** 8 **10.** $2\sqrt{13}$ **11.** 9

Lesson 9-1 pp. 470–472

Check Skills You'll Need **1.** 0.71, 0.71, 1 **2.** 0.71; 0.71; 1.00 **3.** 0.87; 0.5; 1.73 **4.** $\frac{12}{7}$ **5.** $\frac{54}{11}$ **6.** $\frac{15}{2}$ **7.** $\frac{60}{7}$

Check Understanding **1a.** $\frac{3}{7}$; $\frac{7}{3}$ **b.** They are reciprocals. **2a.** 13.8 **b.** 1.9 **c.** 3.8 **3.** 68

Lesson 9-2 pp. 477–478

Check Skills You'll Need **1a.** 9 **b.** 12 **2a.** 7 **b.** $2\sqrt{78}$ **3a.** 10 **b.** $3\sqrt{29}$

Check Understanding **1a.** $\sin X = \frac{64}{80}$; $\cos X = \frac{48}{80}$; $\sin Y = \frac{48}{80}$; $\cos Y = \frac{64}{80}$ **b.** $\sin X = \cos Y$ when $\angle X$ and $\angle Y$ are complementary. **2a.** about 0.72 AU **b.** 66,960,000 mi; 35,340,000 mi **3a.** 41 **b.** 68

Lesson 9-3 pp. 482–483, 488

Check Skills You'll Need **1.** $\angle 7$ **2.** $\angle 11$ **3.** $\angle 6$ **4.** 90 **5.** 180 **6.** $\angle 8$

Check Understanding **1a.** $\angle$ of elevation **b.** $\angle$ of depression **2.** about 1179 ft **3.** about 6.2 km

Checkpoint Quiz 1 **1.** $\tan A = \frac{5}{4}$; $\sin A = \frac{25}{32}$; $\cos A = \frac{5}{8}$; $\tan B = \frac{4}{5}$; $\sin B = \frac{5}{8}$; $\cos B = \frac{25}{32}$ **2.** $\tan A = \frac{5}{12}$; $\sin A = \frac{5}{13}$; $\cos A = \frac{12}{13}$; $\tan B = \frac{12}{5}$; $\sin B = \frac{12}{13}$; $\cos B = \frac{5}{13}$ **3.** $\tan A = \frac{57}{40}$; $\sin A = \frac{57}{70}$; $\cos A = \frac{4}{7}$; $\tan B = \frac{40}{57}$; $\sin B = \frac{4}{7}$; $\cos B = \frac{57}{70}$ **4.** 15.0 **5.** 61 **6.** 20.8 **7.** about 13.1 ft **8.** about 393 m **9.** Answers may vary. Sample: Identify the unknown you want to find in a right triangle. Then find two pieces of known information that will let you write a trigonometric-ratio equation you can solve for the unknown. **10.** about 22.7 m

Lesson 9-4 pp. 490–493

Check Skills You'll Need **1.** $4\sqrt{41}$ **2.** $\sqrt{13}$ **3.** $10\sqrt{65}$

Check Understanding **1.** $\langle -21.6, 46.2 \rangle$

2a.

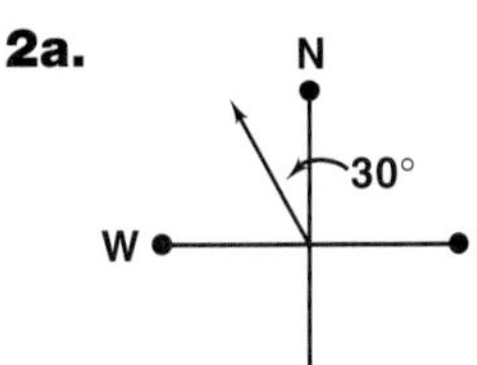

b. 60° north of west **3.** about 257 mi at 17° north of east **4.** $\langle -2, 1 \rangle$ **5.** about 16° north of west

Lesson 9-5 pp. 498–500

Check Skills You'll Need **1.** 36 m^2 **2.** 4536 in.^{2} **3.** 168 ft^2

Check Understanding **1.** 482.8 in.^{2} **2.** It is 4 times as large. **3.** 5081 ft^2

Chapter 10

Diagnosing Readiness p. 510

1. 44 units^2 **2.** $14\sqrt{3}$ units^2 **3.** 234 units^2 **4.** $54\sqrt{3}$ units^2 **5.** 17 **6.** $8\sqrt{2}$ **7.** 6 **8.** $4\sqrt{5}$ **9.** $6\sqrt{2}$ **10.** $4\sqrt{3}$ **11.** 24 **12.** $2\sqrt{2} : 5$

Lesson 10-1 p. 511–513

Check Skills You'll Need **1.** 24 in.^{2} **2.** 98.4 cm^2 **3.** 684 ft^2

Check Understanding

1. 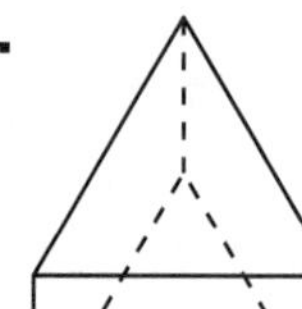

2. Answers may vary. Sample:

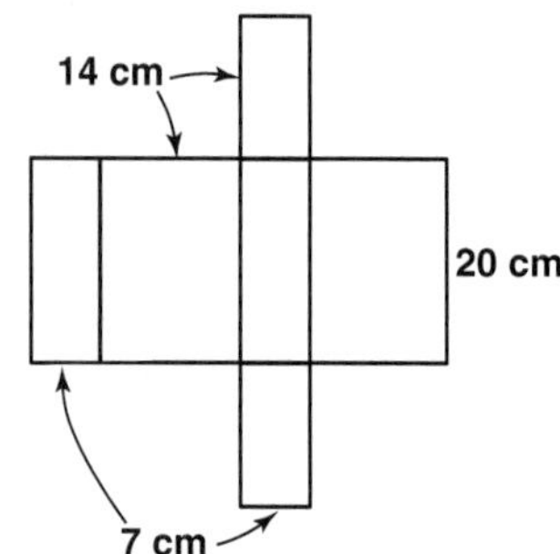

3. 12 edges

Lesson 10-2 pp. 520–522

Check Skills You'll Need

1. 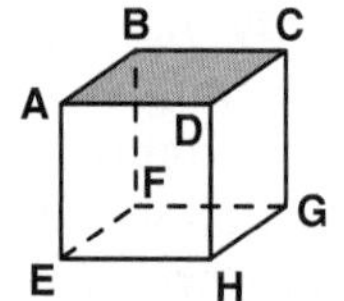

2. 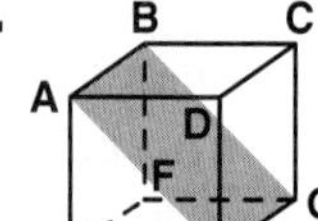

3. 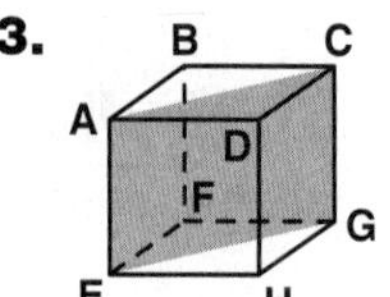

4. 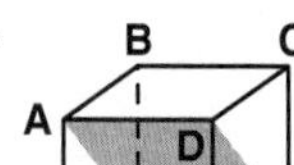

5. 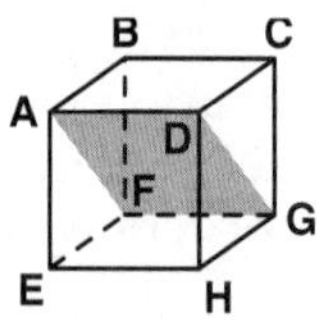

6. 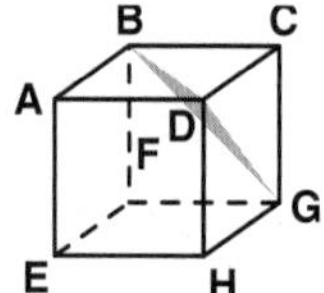

7. 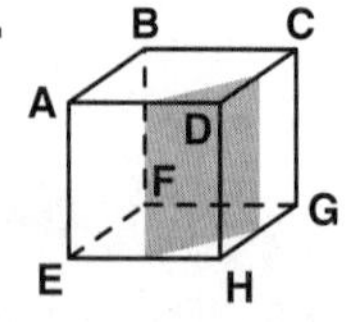

Check Understanding

1. Answers may vary. Sample: 

2. 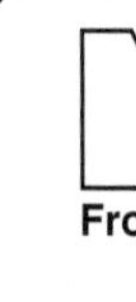

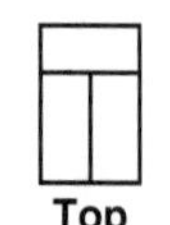

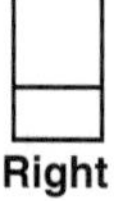

3a. 9 cubes **b.** Answers may vary. Sample: The foundation drawing; you can just add the five numbers. **4.** circle **5.** square

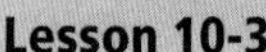

Lesson 10-3 pp. 528–531, 535

Check Skills You'll Need **1.** 96 cm^2 **2.** 40π cm^2 **3.** $36\sqrt{3}$ m^2

Check Understanding

1. 216 cm^2

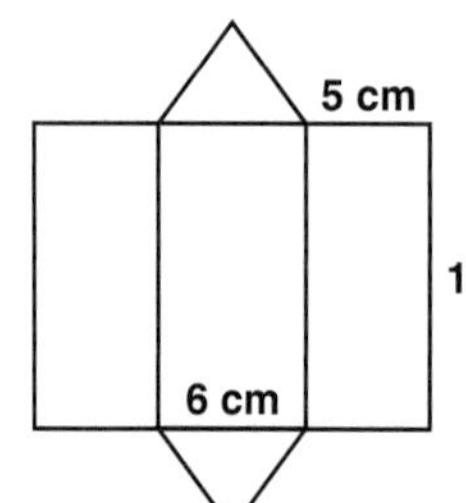

2. 432 m^2; about 619 m^2
3. 400π cm^2
4a. 33 ft^2
b. same as large drum (about 46 ft^2)

Checkpoint Quiz 1

1. 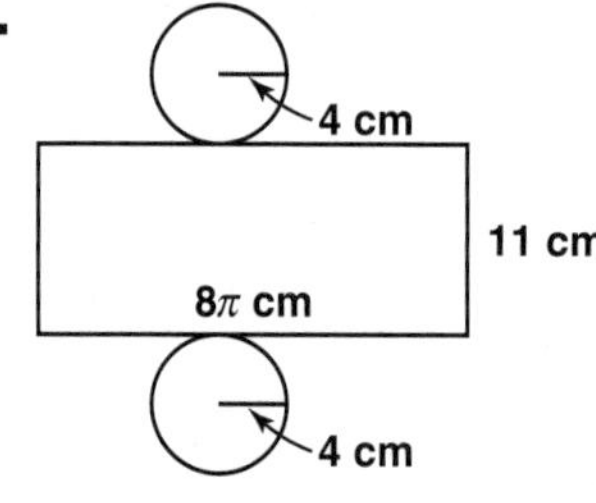

2. 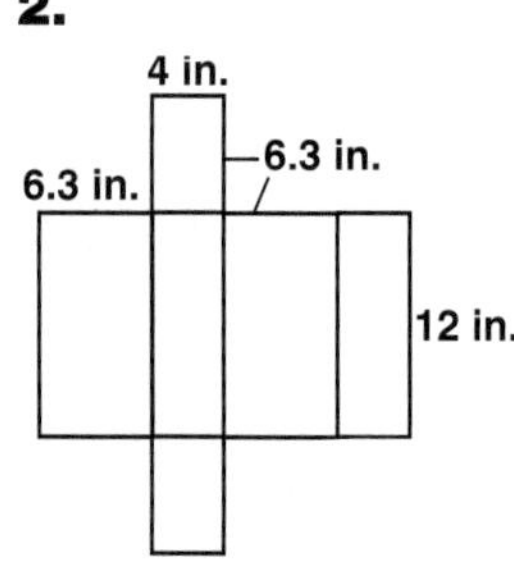

3. 120π cm^2 **4.** 297.6 in.^2 **5.** 4373.1 m^2

6. Answers may vary. Sample:

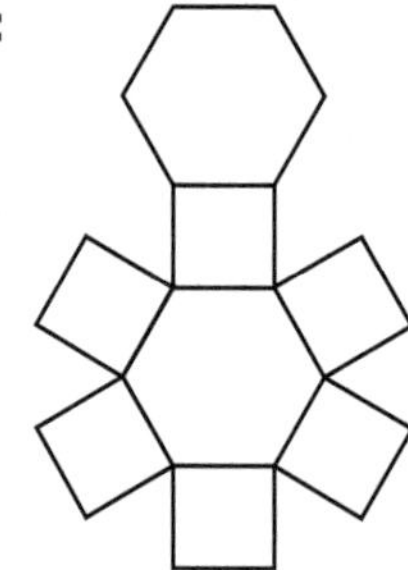

7. Both formulas involve multiplying perimeter of the base by the height. For a cylinder, the base is a circle so π is always in the formula.

8–10. Answers may vary. Samples:

8. 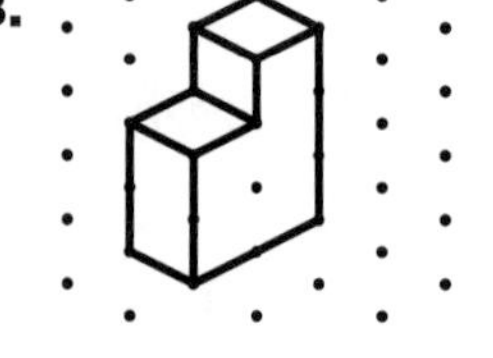

9. 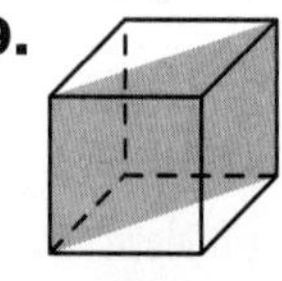

10. 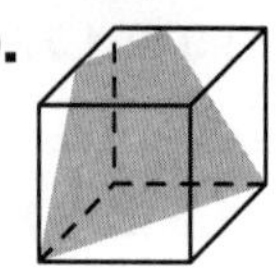

Lesson 10-4 pp. 537–540

Check Skills You'll Need **1.** $\sqrt{233}$ in. **2.** $\sqrt{130}$ m **3.** $\sqrt{313}$ cm

Check Understanding **1.** 55 m^2 **2.** 1,496,511 ft^2 **3.** 704π m^2 **4.** 1178 $in.^2$

Lesson 10-5 pp. 544–547

Check Skills You'll Need **1.** 49 cm^2 **2.** 176.7 $in.^2$ **3.** 314.2 mm^2 **4.** 3 ft^2 **5.** 154 $in.^2$ **6.** 27.5 cm^2 **7.** 27.7 $in.^2$

Check Understanding **1.** Answers may vary. Sample: Multiplication is commutative. **2.** 150 m^3 **3a.** 256π m^3 **b.** 804.2 m^3 **4.** 12 $in.^3$

Lesson 10-6 pp. 551–554

Check Skills You'll Need **1.** 12 cm **2.** 8 in. **3.** 2.5 m

Check Understanding **1.** 384 $in.^3$ **2.** 960 m^3 **3a.** 144π m^3; 452 m^3 **b.** 6174π mm^3; 19,396 mm^3 **4.** 77 ft^3

Lesson 10-7 pp. 558–560, 564

Check Skills You'll Need **1.** 113.1 $in.^2$; 37.7 in. **2.** 78.5 cm^2; 31.4 cm **3.** 19.6 ft^2; 15.7 ft **4.** 4.5 m^2; 7.5 m **5.** 706.9 yd^2; 94.2 yd **6.** 452.4 mm^2; 75.4 mm

Check Understanding **1.** 196π $in.^2$; 616 $in.^2$ **2.** 100 $in.^2$ **3.** 113,097 $in.^3$ **4.** 1258.9 ft^2

Checkpoint Quiz 2 **1.** 60.2 ft^2; 22.5 ft^3 **2.** 332.9 $in.^2$; 377.0 $in.^3$ **3.** 113.1 m^2; 113.1 m^3 **4.** 439.8 cm^2; 706.9 cm^3 **5.** 207 yd^2; 144.8 yd^3 **6.** 44.8 m^2; 16 m^3 **7.** 181.7 m^2; 2217.0 m^3 **8.** 32 ft^2; 12 ft^3 **9.** 75.4 cm^2; 37.7 cm^3 **10.** The balls; the volume of the space is $2\pi r^3$ and the volume of the balls is $4\pi r^3$.

Lesson 10-8 pp. 566–568

Check Skills You'll Need **1.** Yes; all corr. $\triangle$s are $\cong$ and corr. sides are prop.; 3 : 1. **2.** Yes; all corr. $\triangle$s are $\cong$ and corr. sides are prop.; $3:\sqrt{2}$. **3.** 27 $in.^3$ **4.** 135 m^3 **5.** 402.1 cm^3

Check Understanding **1.** yes; 6 : 5 **2.** 2 : 3 **3.** 160 m^2 **4.** 0.01875 lb

Chapter 11

Diagnosing Readiness

1. 82 **2.** $6\frac{2}{3}$ **3.** 15 **4.** 25 **5.** 10 **6.** 5 **7.** 6 **8.** 18 **9.** 24 **10.** $\sqrt{2}$ **11.** 12 **12.** $4\sqrt{2}$ **13.** 13 **14.** $\sqrt{10}$ **15.** 6

Lesson 11-1 pp. 582–585

Check Skills You'll Need **1.** $p^2 + 6p + 9$ **2.** $w^2 + 20w + 100$ **3.** $m^2 - 4m + 4$ **4.** $8\sqrt{5}$ **5.** $2\sqrt{30}$ **6.** 12

Check Understanding **1.** 52 **2.** about 35.5 in. **3.** No; $4^2 + 7^2 \neq 8^2$ **4.** If $\overleftrightarrow{BC}$ and $\overleftrightarrow{GF}$ never intersect, then *BCFG* is a rectangle. **5.** 12 cm

Lesson 11-2 pp. 590–593

Check Skills You'll Need **1.** $\frac{11\sqrt{2}}{2}$ **2.** 5 **3.** 28

Check Understanding **1.** $\angle O \cong \angle P$; $\widehat{BC} \cong \widehat{DF}$ **2.** 16 **3a.** about 11 **b.** 2.8

Lesson 11-3 pp. 598–601, 605

Check Skills You'll Need **1–3.** Answers may vary. Samples are given. **1.** $\widehat{STQ}$ **3.** $\widehat{RTQ}$ **5.** 86 **7.** 121

Check Understanding **1.** 90 **2.** $m\angle 1 = 105, m\angle 2 = 101$ **3.** $m\angle QJK = m\angle LJK + m\angle QJL = 35 + 90 = 125$ $m\angle QJK + \frac{1}{2}m\widehat{QLJ} = \frac{1}{2}(70 + 180) = 125$

Checkpoint Quiz 1 **1.** 76 cm **2.** 48 in. **3.** 51 m **4.** 24 **5.** 5 **6.** 8 **7.** $w = 104; x = 22; y = 108$ **8.** $a = 30; b = 42; c = 80; d = 116$ **9.** $w = 105; x = 75; y = 210$ **10.** $a = 140; b = 70; c = 47.5$

Lesson 11-4 pp. 607–610

Check Skills You'll Need **1.** 57 **2.** 180 **3.** 303 **4.** 28.5 **5.** 28.5 **6.** 4 **7.** 2 **8.** about 4.5 **9.** 123

Check Understanding **1a.** 250 **b.** 40 **2.** away; 20° **3a.** 13.8 **b.** 3.2 **4a.** $(8 - 4\sqrt{3})$ in. **b.** $\frac{16}{8 + 4\sqrt{3}}$ in.

Lesson 11-5 pp. 615–617, 620

Check Skills You'll Need **1.** 5.8 **2.** 12.8 **3.** 5.8

Check Understanding **1a.** $(x - 3)^2 + (y - 5)^2 = 36$ **b.** $(x + 2)^2 + (y + 1)^2 = 2$ **2.** $(x - 2)^2 + (y - 3)^2 = 13$ **3.** center: (2, 3); radius: 10

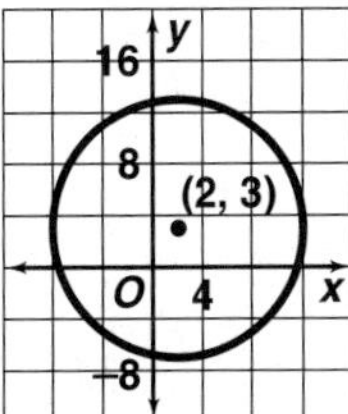

4. $(x - 0)^2 + (y - 0)^2 = x^2 + y^2 = 144$

Instant Check System™ Answers

Checkpoint Quiz 2 **1.** 58 **2.** 226 **3.** 30 **4.** about 3.0 **5.** about 15.7 **6.** 40 **7.** A chord is a segment whose endpoints are on the circle. A secant is a line, ray, or segment that intersects a circle at two points.

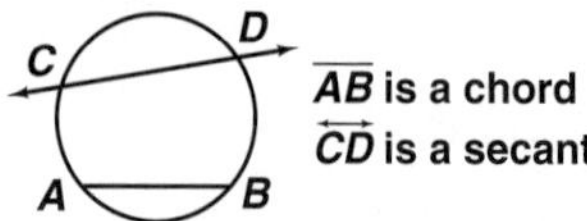

$\overline{AB}$ is a chord
$\overleftrightarrow{CD}$ is a secant

8. $(x - 1.5)^2 + (y - 0.5)^2 = 2.5$
9. $(x - 3.5)^2 + (y - 1)^2 = 46.25$
10. $(x + 1.5)^2 + (y + 4)^2 = 22.25$

Lesson 11-6 pp. 621–622

Check Skills You'll Need

1.

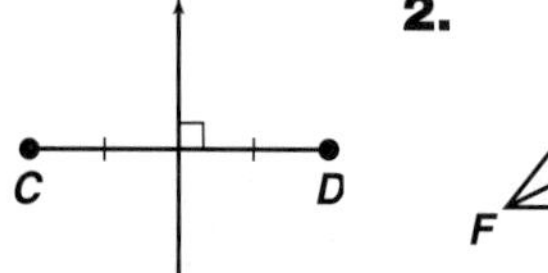

2.

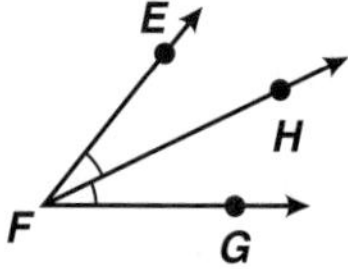

3.

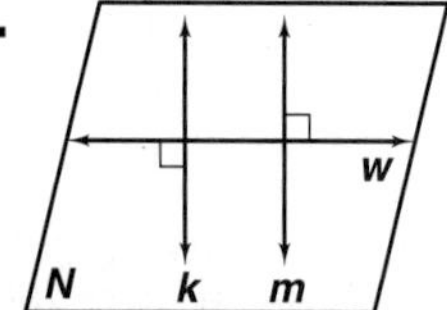

Check Understanding **1.** Two lines ∥ to $\overleftrightarrow{XY}$, each 2 cm from $\overleftrightarrow{XY}$.

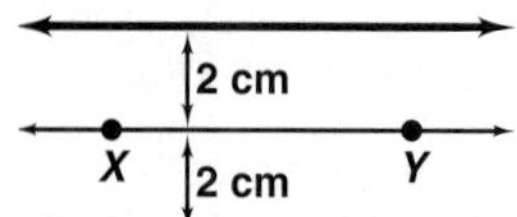

2.

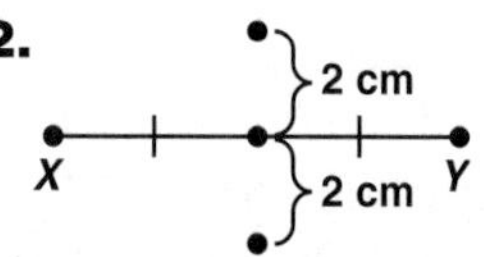

3a. Consider two ∥ lines in a plane. The locus is the line ∥ to and equidist. from the ∥ lines.

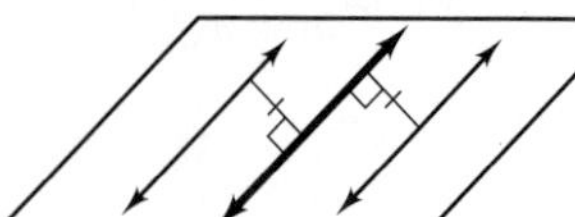

b.

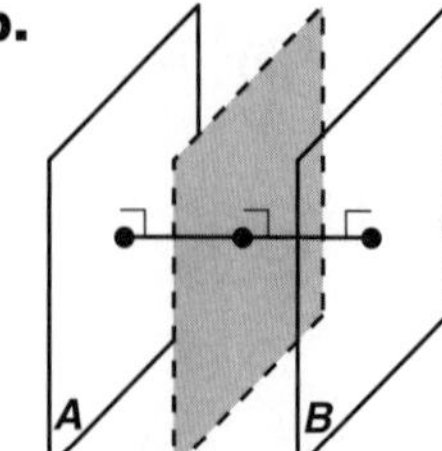

Consider a segment ⊥ to both planes, with one endpoint on plane *A* and the other on plane *B*. The locus is the set of points ⊥ to this segment and through its midpoint.

Chapter 12

Diagnosing Readiness p. 632

1. $\triangle RTS$ **2.** $\triangle LJK$ **3.** $\triangle ADC$ **4.** $\triangle LHC$ **5.** always **6.** never **7.** sometimes **8.** always **9.** $\langle 1, 5 \rangle$ **10.** $\langle -6, 2 \rangle$ **11.** $\langle -6, 3 \rangle$ **12.** 108 **13.** 135 **14.** 144 **15.** 160 **16.** 5 : 8 **17.** 1 : 2

Lesson 12-1 pp. 634–636

Check Skills You'll Need **1.** $\overline{EF}$ **2.** $\overline{AC}$ **3.** $\overline{BC}$ **4.** $\angle G$ **5.** $\angle A$ **6.** $\angle F$ **7.** $\overline{GL}$; $\angle GRL$

Check Understanding **1a.** Yes; the figures are ≅ by a flip. **b.** Yes; the figures are ≅ by a flip and a slide. **2a.** $\angle U$; *P* **b.** $\overline{NI}$ and $\overline{SU}$; $\overline{ID}$ and $\overline{UP}$; $\overline{ND}$ and $\overline{SP}$

3.

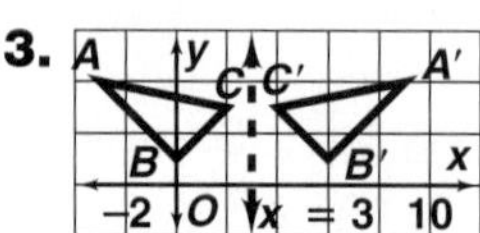

4. Yes; the intersection of $\overline{DW'}$ and *l* is the point for the location of the pump.

Lesson 12-2 pp. 641–643

Check Skills You'll Need **1.** $\langle 4, 3 \rangle$ **2.** $\langle -7, 5 \rangle$

3. $\begin{bmatrix} -7 & 3 \\ -1 & 13 \end{bmatrix}$ **4.** $\begin{bmatrix} 1 & 0 & -1 \\ -4 & -3 & -2 \end{bmatrix}$

Check Understanding **1a.** *R* **b.** $\langle 6, 3 \rangle$ **2.** L' (1, −2), M'(3, −4), N'(6, −2) **3.** M' (1, 7), F' (4, 3), H' (5, 10) **4.** 1 block east and 3 blocks north of her hotel

Lesson 12-3 pp. 647–649, 652

Check Skills You'll Need **1.** 120 **2.** 90 **3.** 72 **4.** 60 **5.** 45 **6.** 36

Check Understanding

1.

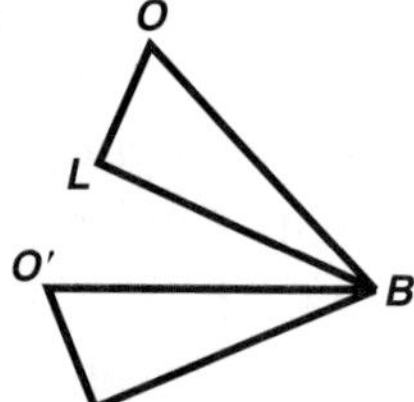

2. *E* **3.** 135°

4.

Checkpoint Quiz 1 **1.** No; the figures are not ≅. **2.** Yes; the figures are ≅ and the transf. is a translation. **3.** Yes; the figures are ≅ and the transf. is a translation or reflection. **4.** $\langle -3, 5 \rangle$ is a translation of 3 units left, 5 units up. **5.** $\langle -5, 10 \rangle$ **6.** $\langle 4, 0 \rangle$, a translation 4 units right

7.

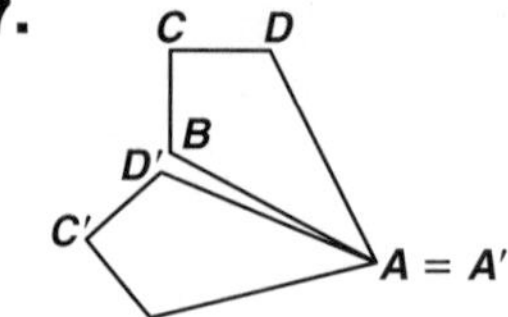

8.

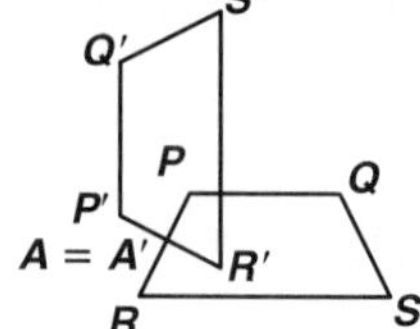

9.

10. $W'(-6, 6)$, $X'(0, -2)$, $Y'(-2, 2)$

Lesson 12-4 pp. 654–657

Check Skills You'll Need

1.

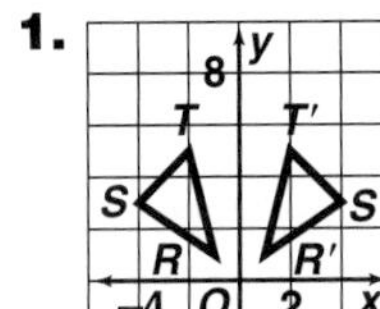

2.

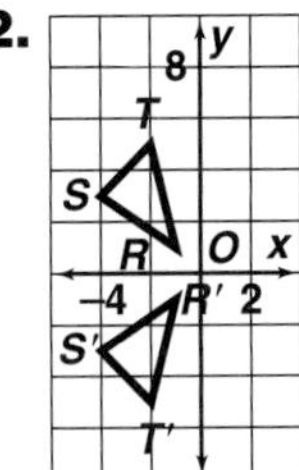

3.

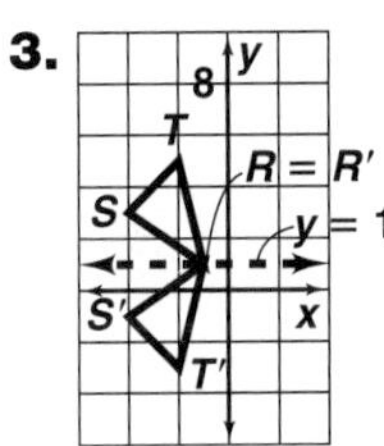

4.

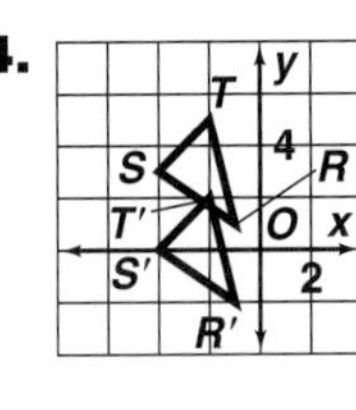

5.

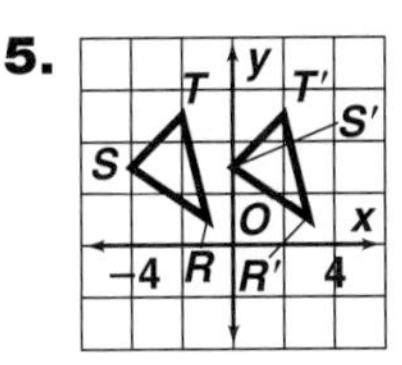

6.

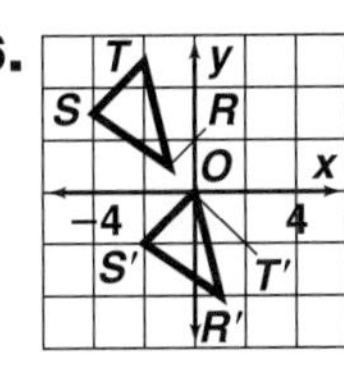

7.

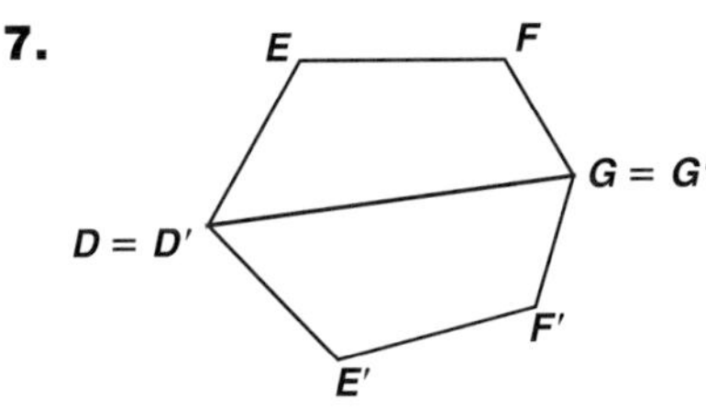

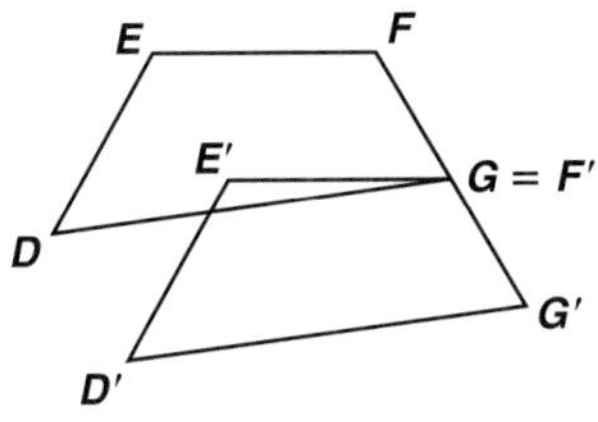

Check Understanding **1.** Neither; the figures do not have the same orientation.

2.

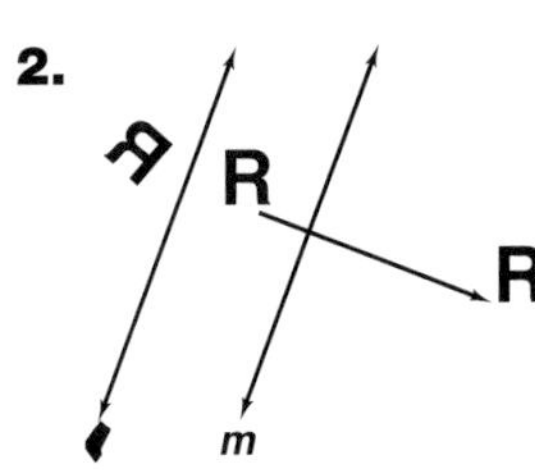

R is translated the distance and direction shown by the arrow. The length of the arrow is twice the distance between ℓ and *m*.

3. Answers may vary. Sample:

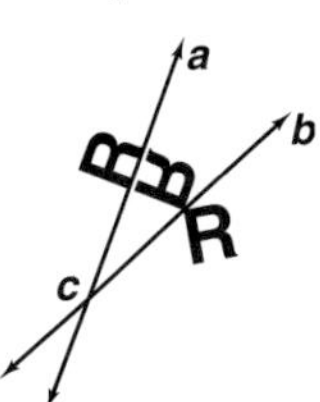

4a.

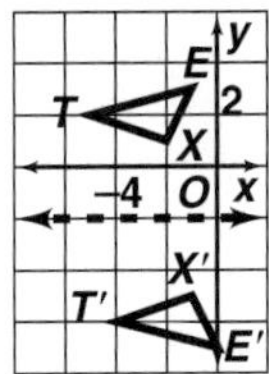

b. Yes; if you reflected it then moved it right, the result would be the same.

5. rotation

Lesson 12-5 pp. 662–663

Check Skills You'll Need **1.** *G* **2.** *D* **3.** $\overline{AH}$ **4.** $\overline{CB}$

Check Understanding

1.

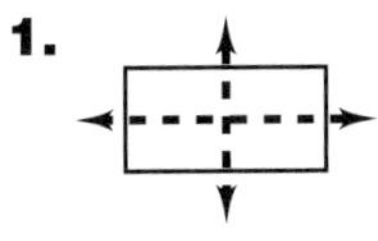

2a. yes; 180° **b.** yes **3.** rotational and reflectional symmetry

Lesson 12-6 pp. 667–669, 673

Check Skills You'll Need **1.** pentagon **3.** dodecagon

Check Understanding **1a.** rotation; one fish **b.** translation; horse and rider **2.** The interior ∠s of an equilateral △ measure 60. 60 divides 360, so it will tessellate. **3.** line symmetry, rotational symmetry, glide reflectional symmetry, translational symmetry

Checkpoint Quiz 2 **1.** Rotation; the image appears rotated ≈ 90°. **2.** reflection; reverse orientation

3. line, point **4.** point **5.** line, rotational: 120

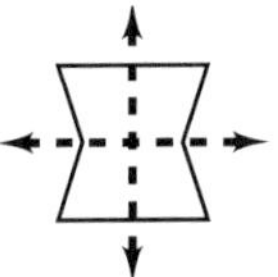

6. point **7.** rotational, reflectional, glide reflectional, and translational **8.** rotational, point, reflectional, glide reflectional, and translational **9.** reflectional, glide reflectional, and translational **10.** rotational, point, reflectional, glide reflectional, and translational

Lesson 12-7 pp. 674–675

Check Skills You'll Need **1.** 3 in. by 4 in. **2.** 2 in. by $2\frac{1}{2}$ in. **3.** $1\frac{1}{2}$ in. by $2\frac{1}{4}$ in. **4.** $1\frac{1}{4}$ in. by $1\frac{3}{4}$ in.

Check Understanding **1.** The dilation is a reduction with center (0, 0) and scale factor $\frac{1}{2}$. **2.** 8 cm

3. $P'(1, 0)$, $Z'(-\frac{1}{2}, \frac{1}{4})$, $G'(\frac{1}{2}, -1)$

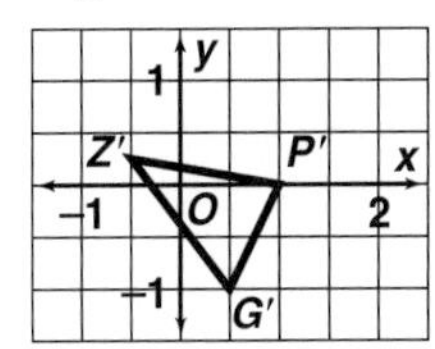

Selected Answers

Chapter 1

Lesson 1-1 pp. 7–9

EXERCISES **1.** 80, 160 **3.** −3, 4 **17.** 

19. The sum of the first 6 pos. even numbers is 6 · 7, or 42. **21.** The sum of the first 100 pos. even numbers is 100 · 101, or 10,100. **23.** 555,555,555 **25–27.** Answers may vary. Samples are given. **25.** 8 + (−5) = 3 and 3 ≯ 8 **27.** −6 − (−4) = −2 and −2 ≮ −4 **29.** 75°F **31.** 31, 43

33. 0.0001, 0.00001 **43.** 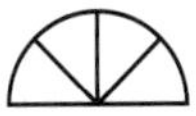 **45.** 

60–67. 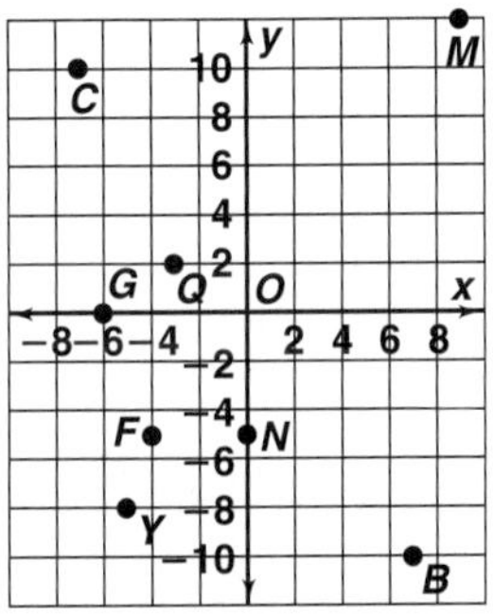

69. *N*

Lesson 1-2 pp. 13–16

EXERCISES **1.** no **3.** yes; line *n* **11.** *ABCD* **13.** *ABHF* **17.** $\overleftrightarrow{RS}$ **19.** $\overleftrightarrow{UV}$ **21.** planes *QUX* and *QUV* **23.** planes *UXT* and *WXT*

25. 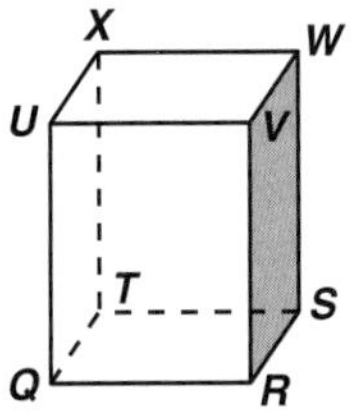

27. 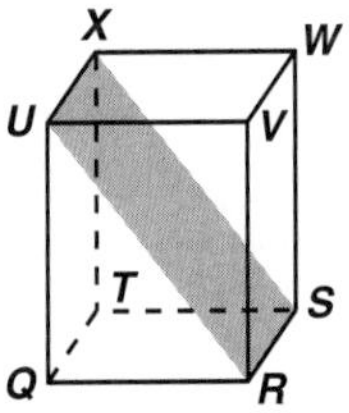

31. *X* **33.** *Q* **35.** no **37.** no **39.** coplanar **41.** coplanar **49.** not possible **51.** not possible

53. 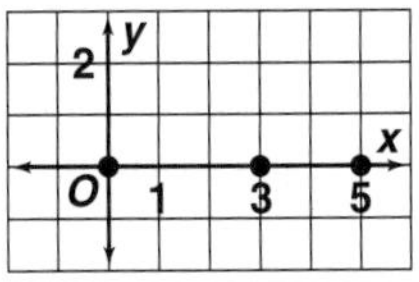

yes **61.** never **63.** always

67. 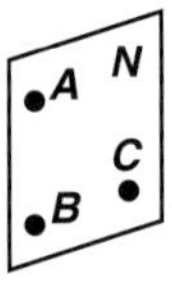

Post. 1-4: Through three noncollinear points there is exactly one plane. **69.** *A*, *B*, and *D*

73. 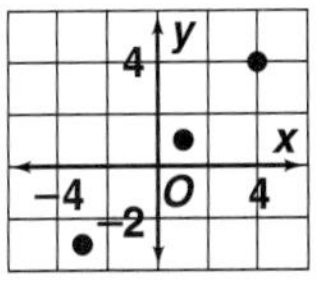

yes **91.** I, K **93.** 1024, 4096 **95.** 34

Lesson 1-3 pp. 19–23

EXERCISES **1.** 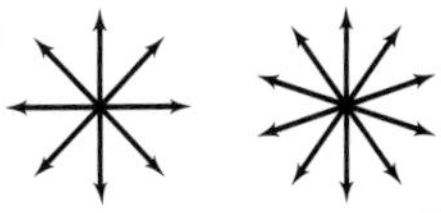 **3.** 

5. $\overline{RS}$, $\overline{RT}$, $\overline{RW}$, $\overline{ST}$, $\overline{SW}$, $\overline{TW}$ **7a.** $\overrightarrow{TS}$ or $\overrightarrow{TR}$, $\overrightarrow{TW}$ **b.** $\overrightarrow{SR}$, $\overrightarrow{ST}$ **9.** Answers may vary. Sample: 2; $\overrightarrow{YS}$ or $\overrightarrow{YR}$, $\overrightarrow{YT}$ or $\overrightarrow{YW}$ **11.** $\overline{DF}$ **13.** $\overline{BE}$, $\overline{CF}$ **15.** $\overline{AD}$, $\overline{AB}$, $\overline{AC}$ **17.** *ABC* ∥ *DEF* **19.** Answers may vary. Sample: $\overleftrightarrow{CF}$, $\overleftrightarrow{DE}$ **21.** $\overleftrightarrow{FG}$ **23.** Answers may vary. Sample: $\overleftrightarrow{BG}$, $\overleftrightarrow{DH}$, $\overleftrightarrow{CL}$ **25.** true **27.** true **33.** Yes; both name the segment with endpoints *X* and *Y*. **35.** Yes; both are the line through pts. *X* and *Y*. **37.** always **39.** always **49a.** Answers may vary. Sample: northeast and southwest, east and west **b.** Answers may vary. Sample: northwest and southeast **53.** Answers may vary. Sample: $\overleftrightarrow{XY}$ and $\overleftrightarrow{ZW}$ intersect at *R*. **71–73.** Answers may vary. Samples are given. **71.** $\overleftrightarrow{EF}$ **73.** *C*

79. 

81. 

Lesson 1-4 pp. 29–33

EXERCISES **1.** 9; 9; yes **3.** 11; 13; no **5.** *XY* = *ZW* **7.** *YZ* < *XW* **9.** 25 **11a.** 7 **b.** *RS* = 60, *ST* = 36, *RT* = 96 **13.** 33 **15.** 130 **17.** ∠*MCP*, ∠*PCM*, ∠*C*, or ∠1 **19.** ∠*CBD*, ∠*DBC* **21–23.** Drawings may vary. **21.** 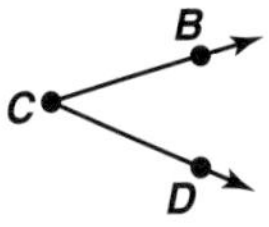

23. 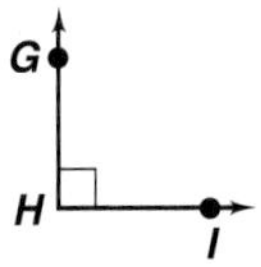

25. 90; right **27.** 34 **29.** *Q* **31.** −4 **33.** −2.5, 2.5 **35.** −6, −1, 1, 6 **43.** false; *BD* = 9, *CD* = 2 **45.** true; *AC* = 9, *CD* = 2, *AD* = 11, and 9 + 2 = 11 **47.** 115 **55.** about 42° **59–61.** Answers may vary. Samples are given. **59.** 180 **61.** 30 **65.** 125 **67–69.** Answers may vary. Samples are given. **67.** ∠*QVM* and ∠*VPN* **69.** ∠*MQV* and ∠*PNQ* **71.** *y* = 15; *AC* = 24, *DC* = 12 **73a.** Answers may vary. Sample: The two rays come together at a sharp point. **b.** Answers may vary. Sample: Molly had an *acute* pain in her knee. **75.** 12; *m*∠*AOC* = 82, *m*∠*AOB* = 32, *m*∠*BOC* = 50 **77.** 18; *m*∠*AOB* = 28, *m*∠*BOC* = 52, *m*∠*AOD* = 108 **87.** never **89.** always **91.** always **93.** always **95.** 25, 30 **97.** 30, 34

Lesson 1-5 pp. 37–40

EXERCISES 1.

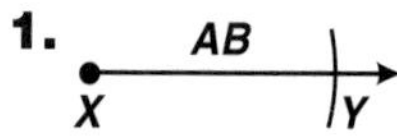

3.

TR PS
D E

5. **7.**

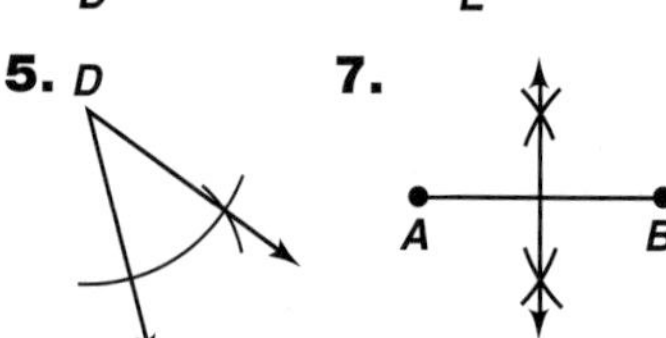

A B

9a. 11; 30 **b.** 30 **c.** 60 **11.** 15; 48

13. **15.**

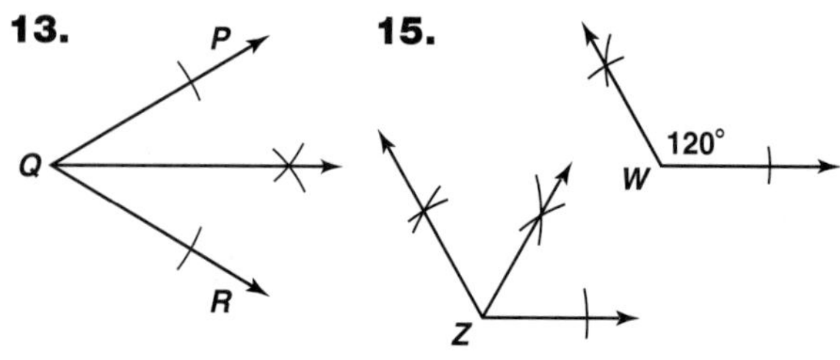

17. Find a segment on $\overleftrightarrow{SQ}$ so that you can construct $\overleftrightarrow{SP}$ as its ⊥ bisector. Then bisect ∠*PSQ*.

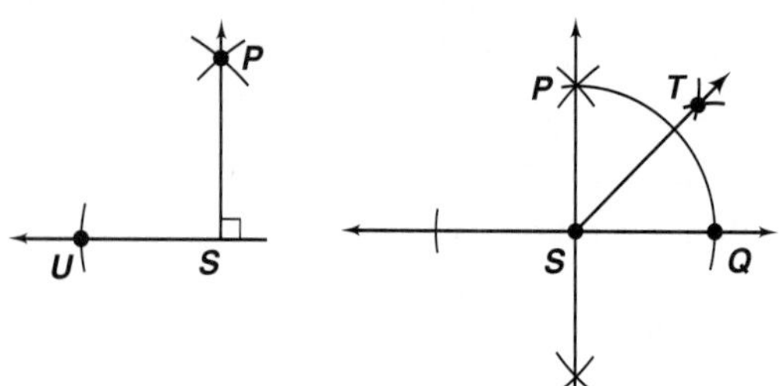

23. **29.**

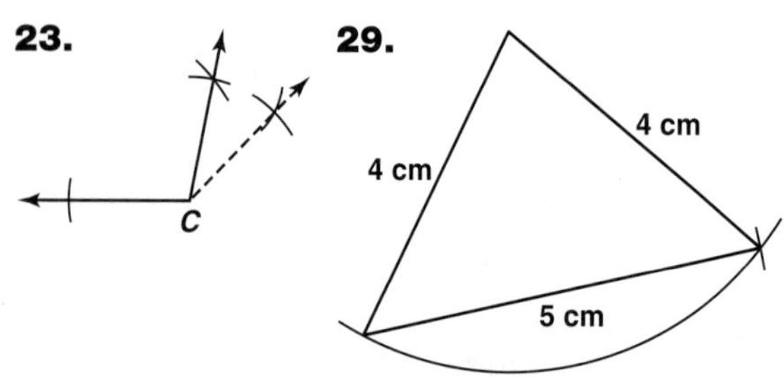

31. impossible; the short segments are not long enough to form a △. **41.** 6 **43.** 4 **49.** No; they do not have the same endpt.

Technology p. 41

1b. Answers may vary. Sample: Construction is exact and drawing is not. **3b.** no

Lesson 1-6 pp. 46–49

EXERCISES 1. 6 **3.** 8 **11.** about 4.5 mi **13.** 6.4 **15.** 15.8 **19.** (3, 1) **21.** (6, 1) **25.** (5, −1) **27.** (12, −24) **31.** (4, −11) **33.** 5.8; (1.5, 0.5) **41.** IV **45.** 10.8 units; (3, −4) **47.** *Z*; about 12 units **49.** 934 mi **51.** 2693 mi **53–55.** Answers may vary. Samples are given. **53.** (3, 6), (0, 4.5) **55.** (1, 0), (−1, 4)

71.

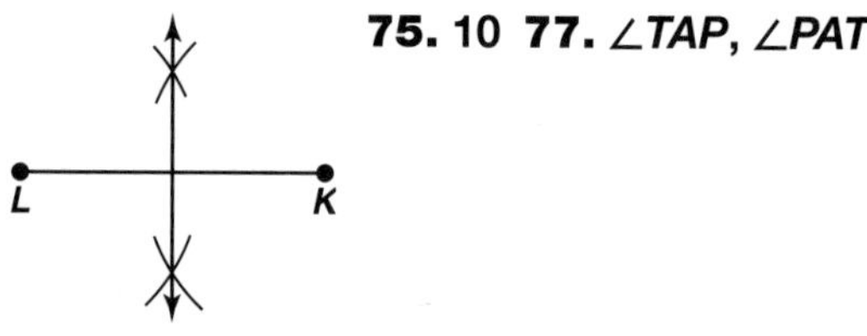

75. 10 **77.** ∠*TAP*, ∠*PAT*

Lesson 1-7 pp 55–58

EXERCISES 1. 22 in. **3.** 56 in. **5.** 120 m **9.** 10π ft **11.** $\frac{1}{2}\pi$ m **13.** 22.9 m **15.** 351.9 cm

17.

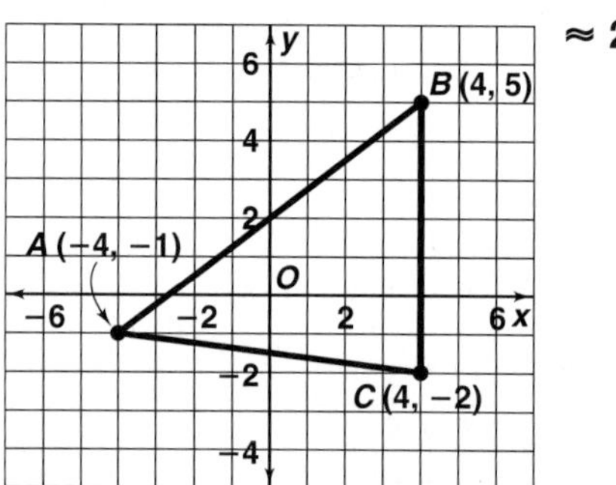

≈ 25.1 units

21. 4320 in.^{2}, or $3\frac{1}{3}$ yd^2 **23.** 8000 cm^2, or 0.8 m^2 **27.** 400π m^2 **29.** $\frac{9}{64}\pi$ in.^{2} **33.** 153.9 ft^2 **35.** 452.4 cm^2 **37.** 310 m^2 **39.** 24 cm^2 **41a.** 144 in.^{2} **b.** 1 ft^2 **43.** 3289 m^2 **45–47.** Answers may vary. Check students' work. Samples are given. **45.** 39 in.; 93.5 in.^{2} **47.** 8 ft; 3.75 ft^2

55.

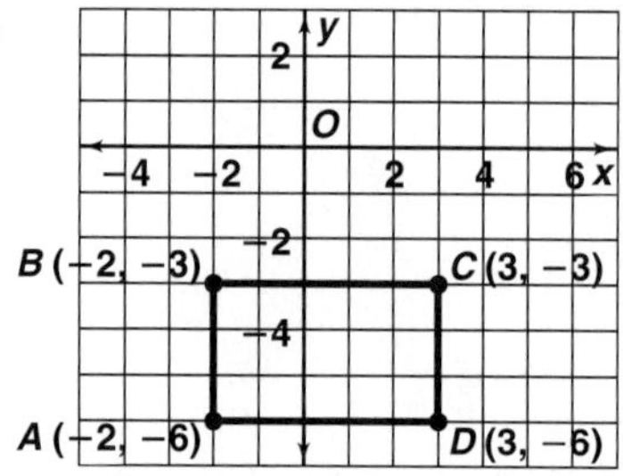

perimeter = 16 units, area = 15 units^2
57. 54 units^2 **59.** 30 m **61.** Area; the wall is a surface. **63.** Perimeter; the fence must fit the perimeter of the garden. **79.** 8.5 units; (5.5, 5) **81.** 13.9 units; (3, 5.5) **85.** 90 **87.** 62 units **89.** 6 units

Technology p. 59

1. square **3a.** Answers may vary. Sample: 25 ft by 36 ft; *P* = 122 ft, 30 ft by 30 ft; *P* = 120 ft, 10 ft by 90 ft; *P* = 200 ft **b.** 30 ft-by-30 ft square

Chapter Review pp. 61–63

1. coplanar **2.** segment **3.** congruent **4.** midpoint **5.** angle bisector **6.** conjecture **7.** postulate or axiom **8.** Parallel lines **9.** obtuse angle **10.** perpendicular bisector **11.** subtract 5; 20, 15 **12.** Answers may vary. Sample: mult. by −1; 5, −5 **13.** subtr. 7; −1, −8 **14.** mult. by 4; 1536, 6144 **15.** mult. by 2; 64, 128 **16.** alternate adding 1 and 3; 10, 13 **17.** **18–23.** Answers may vary. Samples are given. **18.** $\overleftrightarrow{AQ}$ and $\overleftrightarrow{QR}$ **19.** $\overleftrightarrow{AQ}$ and $\overleftrightarrow{BC}$ **20.** *A*, *Q*, *R* **21.** *A*, *Q*, *R*, *S* **22.** *AQTD* and *BRSC* **23.** $\overleftrightarrow{AD}$, $\overleftrightarrow{TD}$, $\overleftrightarrow{CD}$ **24.** always **25.** sometimes **26.** never **27.** never **28.** always **29.** always **30.** −7, 3 **31.** 0.5 **32.** 15 **33.** 31 **34.** $\overline{AB} \cong \overline{CD}$, $\overline{AC} \cong \overline{BD} \cong \overline{CE}$, $\overline{BC} \cong \overline{DE}$ **35.** ∠1: ∠*WXY*, ∠*YXW*; ∠2: ∠*YXZ*, ∠*ZXY*

36. **37a–b.**

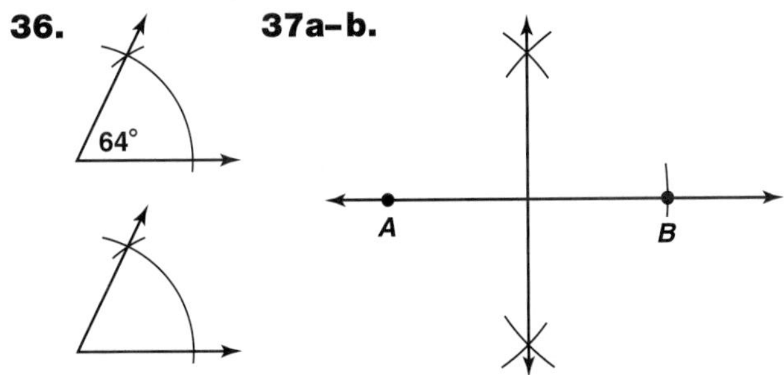

38. 1.4 units **39.** 7.6 units **40.** 14.4 units **41.** (0, 0) **42.** 7.2 units **43.** $P = 32$ cm, $A = 64$ cm^2 **44.** $P = 38$ ft, $A = 78$ ft^2 **45.** $P = 32$ in., $A = 40$ in.^{2} **46.** $C = 18.85$ in., $A = 28.27$ in.^{2} **47.** $C = 47.12$ m, $A = 176.71$ m^2 **48.** $C = 163.36$ m, $A = 2123.72$ m^2

Chapter 2

Lesson 2-1 pp. 71–74

EXERCISES **1.** Hypothesis: You send in the proof-of-purchase. Conclusion: They send you a get-well card. **3.** Hypothesis: $x + 20 = 32$, Conclusion: $x = 12$ **9.** If an object is glass, then it is fragile. **11.** If a whole number has 2 as a factor, then it is even. **15.** Sunday **17.** Mexico

19.

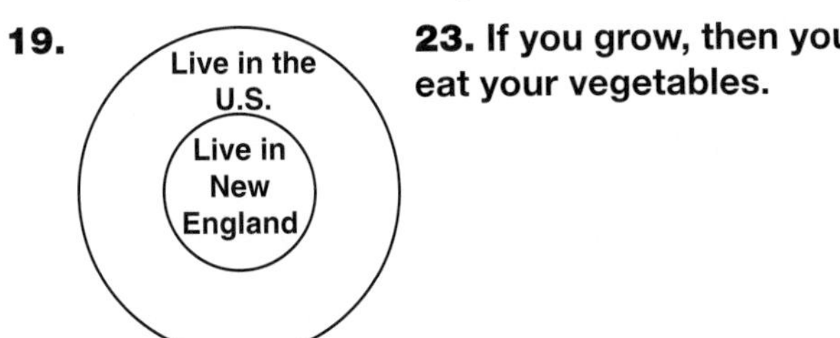

23. If you grow, then you eat your vegetables. **25.** If two segments have the same length, then they are congruent. **27.** Converse: If you have a passport, then you travel from the United States to Kenya. The original conditional is true and the converse is false. **29.** Converse: If the chemical formula for a substance is H_2O, then it is water. Both statements are true. **33.** If a person is an Olympian, then that person is an athlete. **35.** If something is a whole number, then it is an integer. **37–39.** Answers may vary. Samples are given. **37.** If $x = 1$, then $2x = 2$. **39.** If $x = 3$, then $x^2 = 6$. **41.** If a work is great, then it is made out of a combination of obedience and liberty. **43.** If $x = 18$, then $x - 3 = 15$; true. **51.** If a figure has four congruent angles, then it is a square; false; a rectangle that is not a square. **55–57.** Answers may vary. Samples are given. **55.** If two planes intersect, then they meet in exactly one line. **57.** If two points are given, then there is exactly one line through them. **69.** 21 cm **71.** 23.2 m or 2320 cm **73.** 5 **75.** 9.2 **77.** Subtract 3 from the previous term; −7, −10.

Lesson 2-2 pp. 78–81

EXERCISES **1.** If two segments are congruent, then they have the same length. It is true. Two segments have the same length if and only if they are congruent. **3.** If a number is even, then it is divisible by 20. It is false since 4 is even but not divisible by 20. **7.** If a line bisects a segment, then the line intersects the segment only at its midpoint. If a line intersects a segment only at its midpoint, then it bisects the segment. **9.** If you live in Washington, D.C., then you live in the capital of the United States. If you live in the capital of the United States, then you live in Washington, D.C. **13.** A line, segment, or ray is a perpendicular bisector of a segment if and only if it is perpendicular to the segment at its midpoint. **15.** not reversible **19–21.** Answers may vary. Samples are given. **19.** No; it is not reversible; a cat is a counterexample. **21.** No; it is not reversible; skew lines are not parallel. **29.** Yes; ∠1 and ∠2 share a side and a vertex, and are suppl. **31.** No; ∠1 and ∠2 do not share a side, and are not suppl. **33.** The converse is false. $x = -3$ is a counterexample. **35.** $x^3 = 125$ if and only if $x = 5$. **37.** *V* is a counterexample. **39.** good definition **41.** Angles are congruent if and only if they have equal measure. **43.** A number is a whole number if and only if it is a nonnegative integer. **45.** If ∠*A* has measure between 0 and 90, then ∠*A* is an acute angle. **55.** If a whole number ends in 0, then it is even. **57.** If a day is Sunday, then it is a weekend day.

59.

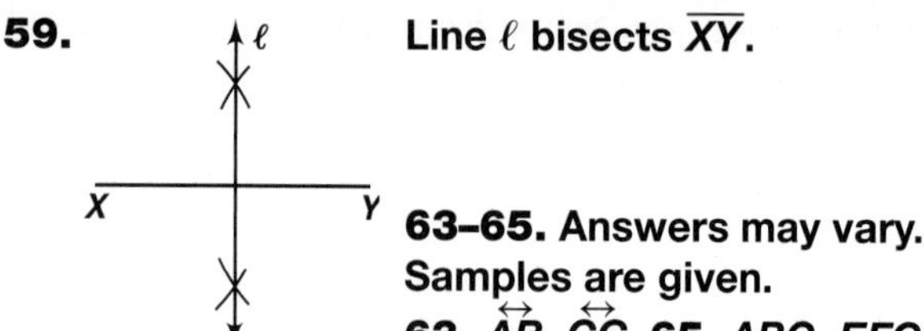

Line ℓ bisects $\overline{XY}$.

63–65. Answers may vary. Samples are given.
63. $\overleftrightarrow{AB}$, $\overleftrightarrow{CG}$ **65.** *ABC, EFG*

Lesson 2-3 pp. 84–87

EXERCISES **1.** Felicia will pass the music theory course. **3.** Line ℓ and line m do not intersect. **5.** Figure *ABCD* has two pairs of parallel sides. **7.** Points *X, Y,* and *Z* are collinear. **11.** If two planes are not parallel, then they intersect in a line. **13.** If you are studying botany, then you are studying a science. **15.** Answers may vary. Sample: If you live in Little Rock, then you live in the 25th state to enter the Union. Levon lives in the 25th state to enter the Union. **17.** Must be true; by (E) and (A), it is breakfast time. Then by (C), Curtis drinks water. **19.** Is not true; by (E) and (A), it is breakfast time. By (C), Curtis drinks water and nothing else. **23.** If you are in Key West, Florida, then the temperature is always above 32°F; not possible. **25.** If a figure is a square, then it is a rectangle; *ABCD* is a rectangle. **27.** No; red cars can never park. **29.** yes **39.** good definition **41.** Answers may vary. Sample: $\frac{1}{2}$ **43.** never

Lesson 2-4 pp. 91–94

EXERCISES **1a.** ∠ Add. Post. **b.** Subst. Prop. **c.** Simplify. **d.** Subtr. Prop. of = **e.** Div. Prop. of = **3a.** Mult. Prop. of = **b.** Distr. Prop. **c.** Add. Prop. of = **5.** Reflexive Prop. of ≅ **7.** Div. Prop. of = **17.** $5x$ **19.** $\angle K$ **27a.** Given **b.** Def. of midpoint **c.** Subst. Prop. of = **d.** Subtr. Prop. of = **e.** Div. Prop. of = **29a.** $m\angle GFE + m\angle EFI = m\angle GFI$ (∠ Add. Post.) $9x - 2 + 4x = 128$ (Subst. Prop.) $13x - 2 = 128$ (Simplify.) $13x = 130$ (Add. Prop. of =) $x = 10$ (Div. Prop. of =) **b.** 40 **43.** Elena's teacher is concerned. **45.** 80 **47.** 65 **51.** 3.45678, 3.456789 **53.** $\frac{1}{2}, -\frac{1}{4}$

Lesson 2-5 pp. 100–103

EXERCISES **1.** $\angle AOB$ or $\angle DOC$ **3.** $\angle EOC$ **7.** 30 **9.** 30 **11.** No; there are no markings. **13.** No; there are no markings. **19a.** 90 **b.** 90 **c.** Subst. **d.** $m\angle 3$ **21.** $x = 25, y = 105$ **23.** 60, 60 **25.** 120, 120 **29.** 15; 25, 25 **31a.** rt. ∠ **b.** $m\angle Y$ **33.** $\angle EIG \cong \angle FIH$ since all rt. ∠s are ≅; $\angle EIF \cong \angle HIG$ since they are compl. of the same ∠. **35a.** *V* **b.** 180 **c.** Division **d.** right **39.** 9; 36 **41.** 18; 54, 36 **43.** Suppl. of ≅ ∠s are ≅.

45. 45, 45 **47.** $m\angle A = 72, m\angle B = 18$ **49.** $m\angle A = 60, m\angle B = 30$ **67.** 12 **69.** $3 + NP = 15$ **71.** ∠1 and ∠2 are ≅. **73.** If you live south of the equator, then you live in Australia.

Chapter Review pp. 105–107

1. Reflexive **2.** hypothesis **3.** adjacent **4.** Transitive **5.** complementary **6.** biconditional **7.** vertical angles **8.** converse **9.** Symmetric **10.** supplementary **11a.** If you are younger than 20, then you are a teenager. **b.** conditional: true, converse: false **12a.** If an angle has measure greater than 90 and less than 180, then it is obtuse. **b.** conditional: true, converse: true **c.** An angle is obtuse if and only if it has measure greater than 90 and less than 180. **13a.** If a figure has four sides, then it is a square. **b.** conditional: true, converse: false **14.** If something is a flower, then it is beautiful. **15.** Rico's definition is not reversible. A magazine is a counterexample. You read a magazine, but it is not a book. **16.** A phrase is an oxymoron if and only if it contains contradictory terms. **17.** If two angles are complementary, then the sum of their measures is 90. If the sum of the measures of two angles is 90, then the angles are complementary. **18.** Lucy will become a better player. **19.** Lines ℓ and m intersect to form right angles. **20.** The sum of the measures of ∠1 and ∠2 is 180. **21.** If Kate studies, then she will graduate. **22.** If *a*, then *c*. **23.** If the weather is wet, then Nathan can stop at the ice cream shop. **24a.** Segment Add. Post. **b.** Subst. Prop. **c.** Simplify. **d.** Subtr. Prop. of Equality **e.** Div. Prop. of Equality **25.** 8 **26.** *BY* **27.** $m\angle Y$ **28.** $RS = XY$ **29.** y **30.** 10 **31.** $p - 2q$ **32.** $\overline{NM}$ **33.** 18 **34.** 31 **35.** 20 **36.** $m\angle KJD + m\angle DJH = m\angle KJH$ by the ∠ Add. Post.; $m\angle KJD = m\angle DJH$ by the markings; $\overrightarrow{JD}$ bisects $\angle KJH$ by the def. of ∠ bisector. **37.** $AB = CD$ by the markings; $AC = BD$ by the Add. Prop. of = and the Seg. Add. Post. **38.** ∠1 ≅ ∠4 by the markings; ∠1 ≅ ∠2 and ∠3 ≅ ∠4 because vert. ∠s are ≅; ∠2 ≅ ∠3 by the Trans. Prop. of ≅.

Chapter 3

Technology p. 114

1. ∠2 ≅ ∠4 ≅ ∠6 ≅ ∠8; ∠1 ≅ ∠3 ≅ ∠5 ≅ ∠7; When a transversal intersects two ∥ lines, the ∠s formed have one of two measures; ∠s between the ∥ lines on opp. sides of the transversal are ≅; ∠s between the ∥ lines on the same side of the transversal are supp. **3.** a right ∠ **5a.** If the same-side int. ∠s are suppl., then the lines are ∥. **b.** The other conjecture is the converse.

Lesson 3-1 pp. 118–121

EXERCISES **1.** $\overleftrightarrow{PQ}$ and $\overleftrightarrow{SR}$ with transversal $\overleftrightarrow{SQ}$; alt. int. $\angle$s **3.** $\overleftrightarrow{PS}$ and $\overleftrightarrow{QR}$ with transversal $\overleftrightarrow{PQ}$; same-side int. $\angle$s **5.** $\angle 1$ and $\angle 2$: corr. $\angle$s, $\angle 3$ and $\angle 4$: alt. int. $\angle$s, $\angle 5$ and $\angle 6$: corr. $\angle$s **7.** $\angle 1$ and $\angle 2$: corr. $\angle$s, $\angle 3$ and $\angle 4$: same-side int. $\angle$s, $\angle 5$ and $\angle 6$: alt. int. $\angle$s **9a.** 2 **b.** $\angle 1$ **c.** corr. **11.** $m\angle 1 = 75$ because corr. $\angle$s of $\parallel$ lines are $\cong$; $m\angle 2 = 105$ because same-side int. $\angle$s of $\parallel$ lines are suppl. **13.** $m\angle 1 = 100$ because same-side int. $\angle$s of $\parallel$ lines are suppl.; $m\angle 2 = 70$ because alt. int. $\angle$s of $\parallel$ lines have = measure. **15.** 25; 65, 65 **17.** $m\angle 1 = m\angle 3 = m\angle 6 = m\angle 8 = m\angle 9 = m\angle 11 = m\angle 13 = m\angle 15 = 52$; $m\angle 2 = m\angle 4 = m\angle 5 = m\angle 7 = m\angle 10 = m\angle 12 = m\angle 14 = 128$ **19.** two **21.** two **23.** 32 **25.** $x = 135, y = 45$ **29a.** alt. int. $\angle$s **b.** He knew that alt. int. $\angle$s of $\parallel$ lines are $\cong$. **43.** 59 **45.** (0.5, 7) **47.** (3, 3) **49.** multiply by -2; 16, -32

Lesson 3-2 pp. 125–129

EXERCISES **1.** $\overleftrightarrow{BE} \parallel \overleftrightarrow{CG}$; Conv. of Corr. $\angle$s Post. **3.** $\overline{JO} \parallel \overline{LM}$; if two lines and a transversal form same-side int. $\angle$s that are suppl., then the lines are $\parallel$. **5.** $a \parallel b$; if two lines and a transversal form same-side int. $\angle$s that are suppl., then the lines are $\parallel$. **7.** none **17a.** $\angle 1$ **b.** $\angle 1$ **c.** $\angle 2$ **d.** $\angle 3$ **e.** Conv. of Corr. $\angle$s **19.** 50 **21.** 31 **25.** The corr. $\angle$s are $\cong$, so the lines are $\parallel$ by the Conv. of Corr. $\angle$s Post. **27.** 10; $m\angle 1 = m\angle 2 = 70$ **29.** 2.5; $m\angle 1 = m\angle 2 = 30$ **31.** The corr. $\angle$s he draws are $\cong$. **33.** $\overline{PL} \parallel \overline{NA}$ by Conv. of Same-Side Int. $\angle$s Thm. **35.** $\overline{PN} \parallel \overline{LA}$ by Conv. of Same-Side Int. $\angle$s Thm. **39.** The corr. $\angle$s are $\cong$, and the oars are $\parallel$ by the Conv. of Corr. $\angle$s Post. **57.** $m\angle 1 = 66$ because alt. int. $\angle$s are $\cong$. $m\angle 2 = 180 - 94 = 86$ because same-side int. $\angle$s are suppl. **59.** If a circle has a radius of 4 cm, then it has a diameter of 8 cm. Both are true. **61.** If you form the past tense of a verb, then you add *ed* to the verb. Original statement is false, converse is false. **63.** 201.1 in.^{2} **65.** 63.6 ft^2

Lesson 3-3 pp. 134–139

EXERCISES **1.** 30 **3.** 90 **7.** $t = 60$; $w = 60$ **9.** 70 **13.** acute, equiangular, equilateral **15.** obtuse, isosceles **17.** Not possible; a right $\triangle$ will always have one longest side opp. the right $\angle$.

19.

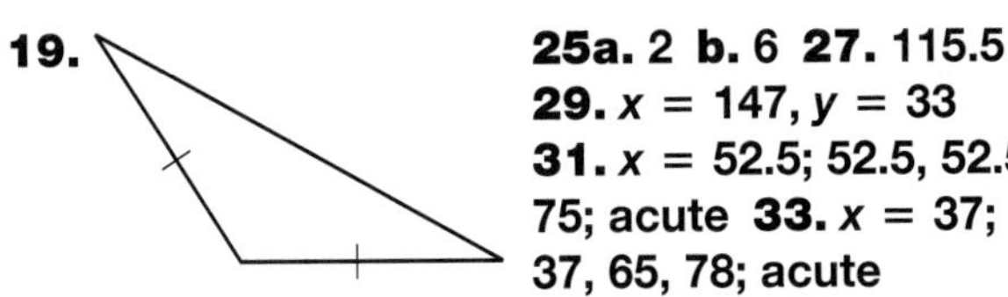

25a. 2 **b.** 6 **27.** 115.5 **29.** $x = 147, y = 33$ **31.** $x = 52.5$; 52.5, 52.5, 75; acute **33.** $x = 37$; 37, 65, 78; acute **37.** 60; $180 \div 3 = 60$ **43a.** 40, 60, 80 **b.** acute **45.** 100 **47.** 32 **53.** 120 or 60 **55.** 90 **71.** 46

73.

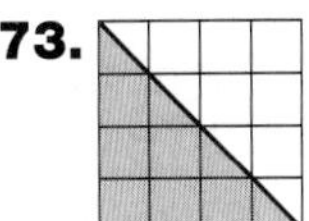

Extension pp. 140–141

1. Answers may vary. Sample:

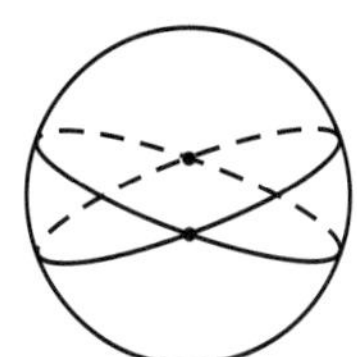

In Euclidean geometry, there is only one line through two points.

3. Answers may vary. Sample:

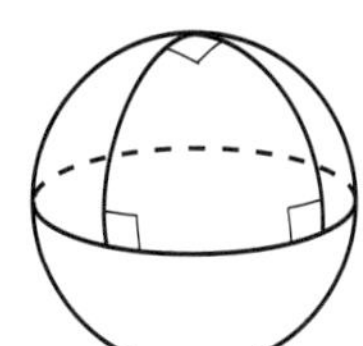

In Euclidean geometry, the only possible equiangular $\triangle$ has 60° $\angle$s.

5. Answers may vary. Sample:

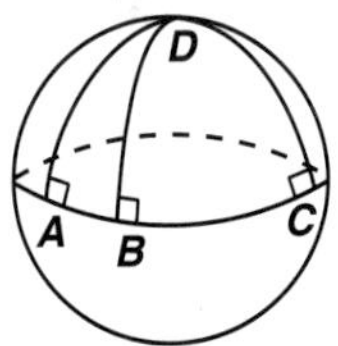

$\angle ADB \ncong \angle ADC$

7. The top circle is not a line, so a piece of the top circle cannot be a line segment.

9. true

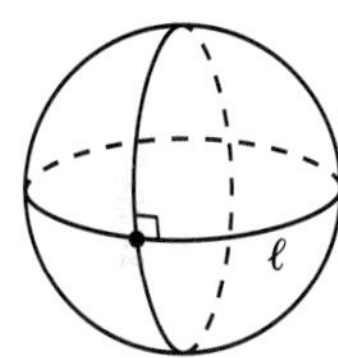

Technology p. 142

1. The sum of the measures of the ext. $\angle$s of a convex polygon is always 360. **3.** The sum of the measures of the five $\angle$s meeting at one point is 360.

Lesson 3-4 pp. 147–150

EXERCISES **1.** yes **3.** No; it is not a plane figure. **5.** *MWBFX*; sides: $\overline{MW}, \overline{WB}, \overline{BF}, \overline{FX}, \overline{XM}$; $\angle$s: $\angle M, \angle W, \angle B, \angle F, \angle X$ **7.** *HEPTAGN*; sides: $\overline{HE}, \overline{EP}, \overline{PT}, \overline{TA}, \overline{AG}, \overline{GN}, \overline{NH}$; $\angle$s: $\angle H, \angle E, \angle P, \angle T, \angle A, \angle G, \angle N$ **9.** decagon; concave **11.** 1080 **13.** 1440 **17.** 103 **19.** 37 **23.** 150; 30 **25.** 176.4; 3.6

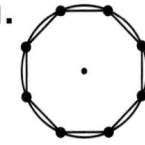

27.

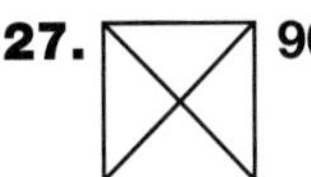

90 **29.** **31.**

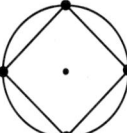

33. 8 **35.** 18 **37.** octagon; $m\angle 1 = 135$; $m\angle 2 = 45$ **39.** 20-80-80; 50-50-80 **41.** 144; 10 **43.** 150; 12 **45.** $\frac{4}{5}$ **47.** $y = 103$; $z = 70$; quad. **49.** $x = 36$, $2x = 72$, $3x = 108$, $4x = 144$; quad. **71.** 120, 25 **73.** 104, 76, 35, 69 **75.** Subst. Prop. **77.** Symm. Prop. of ≅ **81.** $\angle BRT$, $\angle BRK$ **83.** Answers may vary. Sample: $\angle BRM$

Lesson 3-5 pp. 155–157

EXERCISES

1.

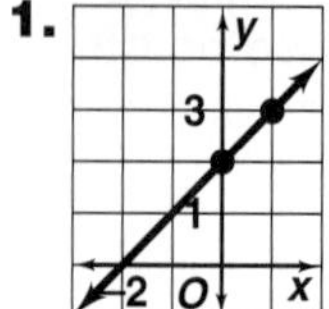

3.

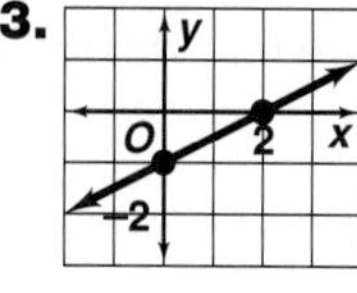

5.

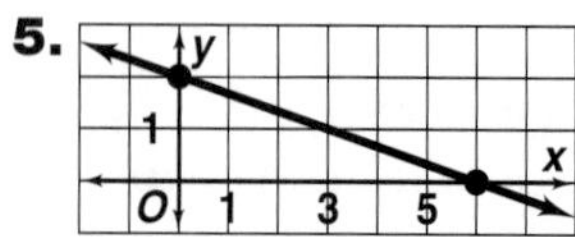

11.

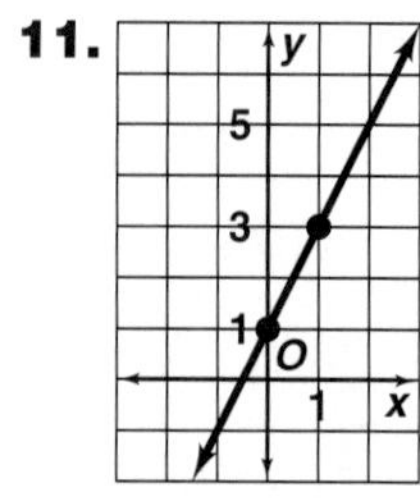

$y = 2x + 1$

13a. $y = -2x + 4$
17. $y - 3 = 2(x - 2)$
19. $y - 5 = -1(x + 3)$
23–25. Equations may vary from the pt. chosen. Samples are given.
23. $y - 5 = \frac{3}{5}(x - 0)$
25. $y - 6 = 1(x - 2)$ **29a.** $y = 7$
b. $x = 4$ **31a.** $y = -1$ **b.** $x = 0$

33.

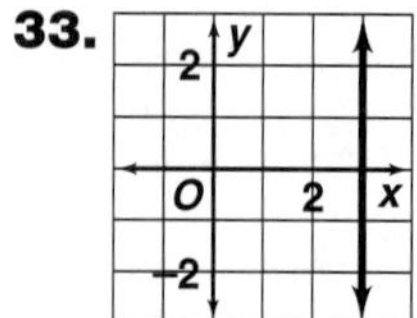

35.

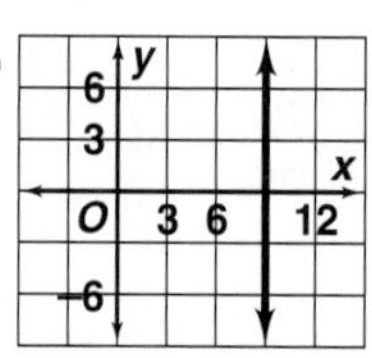

39. No; a line with no slope is a vertical line. 0 slope is a horizontal line. **41a.** Undefined; it is a vertical line. **b.** $x = 0$

49.

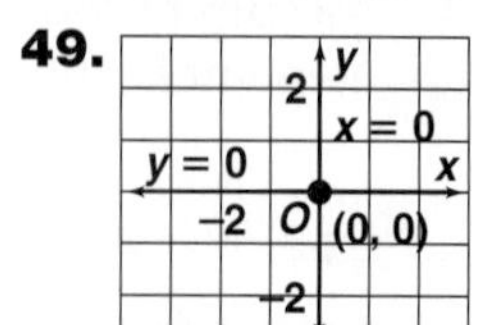

51.

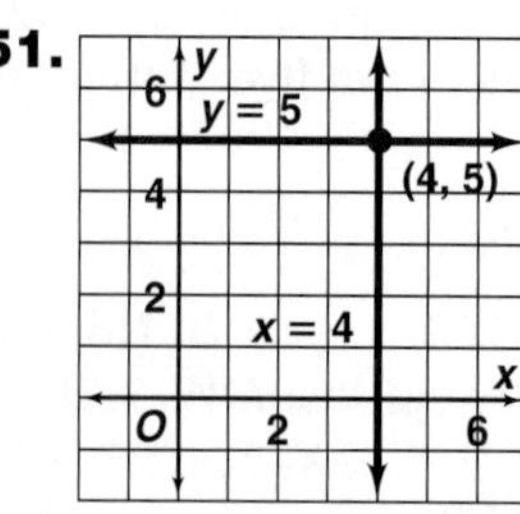

57. Yes; the slope of $\overline{AB}$ = the slope of $\overline{BC}$.
59. Yes; the slope of $\overline{GH}$ = the slope of $\overline{HI}$.
61. $y - 2 = 3(x + 2)$; $3x - y = -8$
63. $y - 6 = \frac{2}{3}(x - 2)$; $2x - 3y = -14$ **71.** 540
73. 2160 **75.** No; ∥ lines never intersect, but they are not skew. **77.** $a = 5$; $m\angle MPR = 30$
79. $a = 2$; $m\angle QPR = 8$

Lesson 3-6 pp. 161–164

EXERCISES **1.** Yes; both slopes $= -\frac{1}{2}$. **3.** No; the slope of $\ell_1 = \frac{3}{2}$, and the slope of $\ell_2 = 2$. **7.** Yes; the lines both have a slope of $\frac{3}{4}$ but different y-intercepts. **9.** No; one slope = 7 and the other slope = −7. **13.** $y - 0 = \frac{1}{3}(x - 6)$ or $y = \frac{1}{3}(x - 6)$ **15.** $y + 2 = -\frac{3}{2}(x - 6)$ **17.** Yes; the slope of $\ell_1 = -\frac{3}{2}$, and the slope of $\ell_2 = \frac{2}{3}$; $-\frac{3}{2} \cdot \frac{2}{3} = -1$. **19.** Yes; the slope of $\ell_1 = -1$, and the slope of $\ell_2 = 1$; $-1 \cdot 1 = -1$. **21–23.** Answers may vary. Samples are given. **21.** $y = -2(x - 4)$ **23.** $y = \frac{4}{5}x$ **25.** No; $\frac{1}{2} \cdot 2 \neq -1$. **27.** Yes; one is vertical and the other is horizontal. **31.** slope of $\overline{AB}$ = slope of $\overline{CD} = \frac{2}{3}$; $\overline{AB} \parallel \overline{CD}$ slope of $\overline{BC}$ = slope of $\overline{AD} = -3$; $\overline{BC} \parallel \overline{AD}$ **33.** slope of $\overline{AB} = \frac{1}{2}$; slope of $\overline{CD} = \frac{1}{4}$; $\overline{AB} \nparallel \overline{CD}$; slope of $\overline{BC} = -1$; slope of $\overline{AD} = -\frac{1}{2}$; $\overline{BC} \nparallel \overline{AD}$ **39.** The lines will have the same slope. **41a.** $y + 20 = \frac{3}{4}(x - 35)$ **b.** because you are given a point and can quickly find the slope **43.** ⊥ **45.** ⊥ **55.** $y - 3 = -\frac{1}{2}(x - 0)$ or $y - 3 = -\frac{1}{2}x$ **57.** $y + 2 = \frac{3}{4}(x - 3)$ **59.** Mult. Prop. of = **61.** Symm. Prop. of ≅ **63.** If you travel to Switzerland, then you have a passport.

Lesson 3-7 pp. 168–170

1.

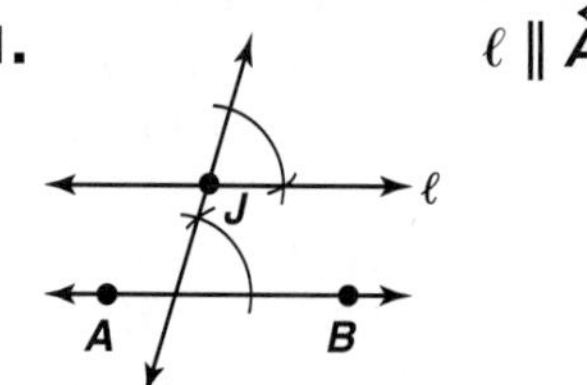

$\ell \parallel \overleftrightarrow{AB}$

For Exercise 5, constructions may vary. Sample using the following segments is shown:

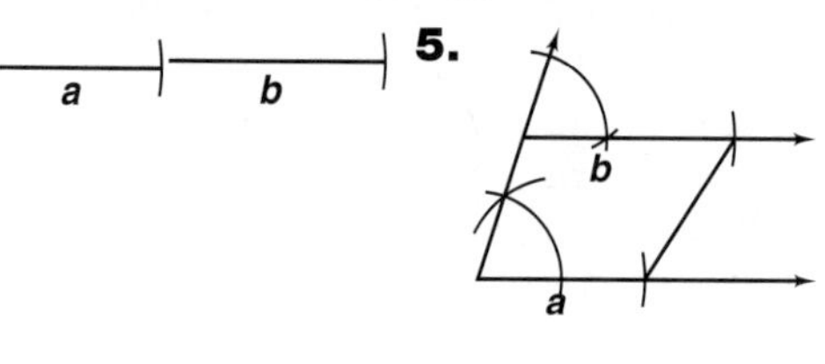

9. **11.**

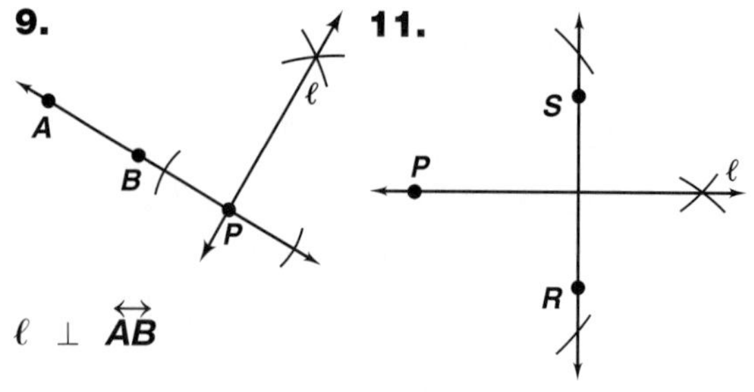

$\ell \perp \overleftrightarrow{AB}$

$\ell \perp \overleftrightarrow{RS}$

For Exercises 17–19, constructions may vary. Samples are given.

17. **19.**

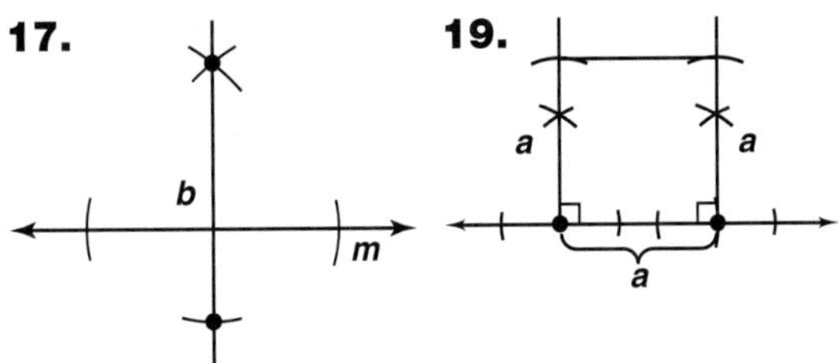

41. No; the slopes are different. **43.** Yes; the slopes are both $-\frac{1}{3}$. **45.** 8.9 **47.** $\overleftrightarrow{DF}$

Chapter Review pp. 173–175

1. acute **2.** obtuse **3.** corr. ∠s **4.** exterior **5.** convex **6.** equiangular **7.** regular **8.** point-slope **9.** slope-int. **10.** alt. int. ∠s **11.** $m\angle 2 = 121$, $m\angle 3 = 59$, $m\angle 4 = 59$ **12.** $m\angle 1 = 120$; corr. ∠s are ≅. $m\angle 2 = 120$; vert. ∠s are ≅. **13.** $m\angle 1 = 75$; same side int. ∠s are suppl. $m\angle 2 = 105$; alt. int. ∠s are ≅ or two ∠s that form a straight ∠ are suppl. **14.** $m\angle 1 = 55$; same side int. ∠s are suppl. $m\angle 2 = 90$; alt. int. ∠s are ≅. **15.** Pairs of consec. ∠s are suppl. because the sides of the quad. are transversals and the int. ∠s are on the same side of a transversal. **16.** 20 **17.** 20 **18.** 24

19. **20.**

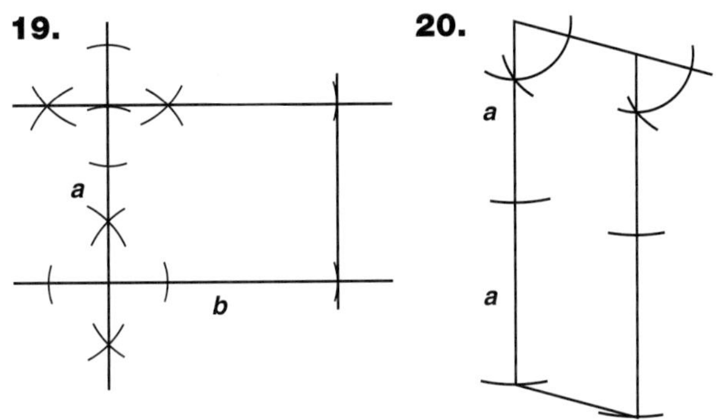

21. ≅ **22.** 61; scalene, acute **23.** $x = 60$; $y = 60$; equilateral, acute **24.** $x = 45$; $y = 45$; isosc., right **25.** 55; acute **26.** 30; right **27.** 3; acute **28.** 8; obtuse **29.** One ∠ is 90; the remaining 2 ∠s are compl. **30.** 120; 60 **31.** 135; 45 **32.** 144; 36 **33.** 165; 15 **34.** 360

35. $m = 2$; y-int. $= -1$

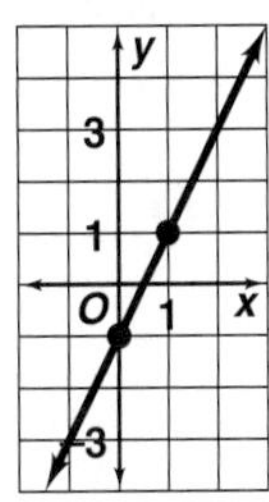

36. $m = -2$; point $= (-5, 3)$

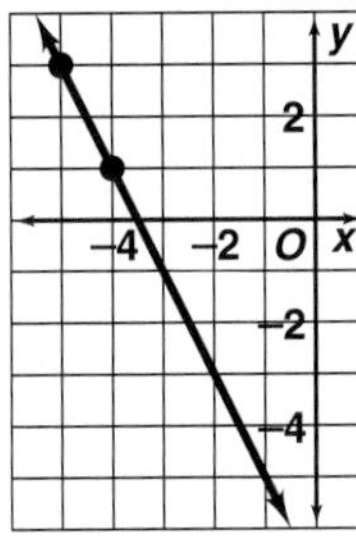

37.

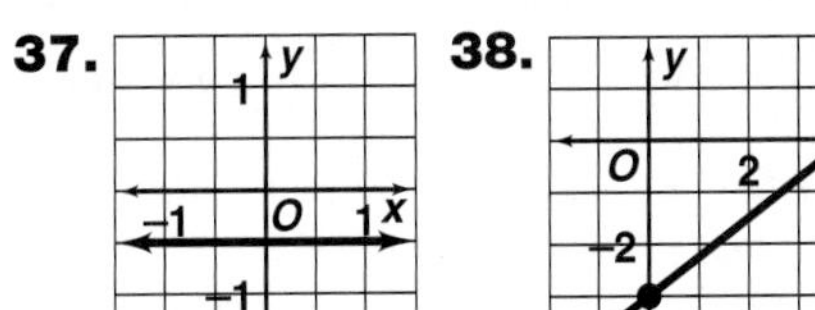

38.

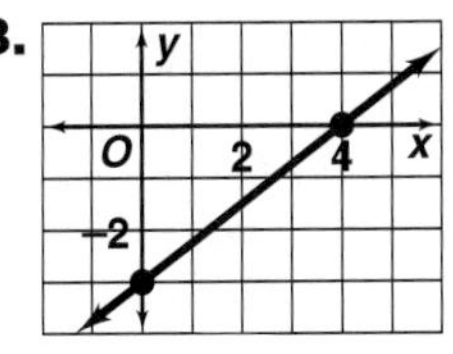

39. $x = 6$ **40.** neither **41.** ∥ **42.** ⊥ **43.** ∥ **44.** 0; the difference of y-coordinates is always zero.

Chapter 4

Lesson 4-1 pp. 182–185

EXERCISES **1.** $\angle CAB \cong \angle DAB$; $\angle C \cong \angle D$; $\angle ABC \cong \angle ABD$; $\overline{AC} \cong \overline{AD}$; $\overline{AB} \cong \overline{AB}$; $\overline{CB} \cong \overline{DB}$ **3.** $\overline{BK}$ **5.** $\overline{ML}$ **9.** $\triangle KJB$ **11.** $\triangle JBK$ **15.** $\angle P \cong \angle S$; $\angle O \cong \angle I$; $\angle L \cong \angle D$; $\angle Y \cong \angle E$ **17.** 54 in. **19.** 77 **25.** No; the corr. sides are not ≅. **27.** Yes; all corr. sides and ∠s are ≅. **29.** A and H; B and G; C and E; D and F **31.** 5 **33.** $m\angle B = m\angle E = 21$ **35.** $AC = DF = 19$ **39.** $\triangle BCE \cong \triangle ADE$ **41.** $\triangle JLM \cong \triangle NRZ$; $\triangle JLM \cong \triangle ZRN$

53. Answers may vary.

Sample:

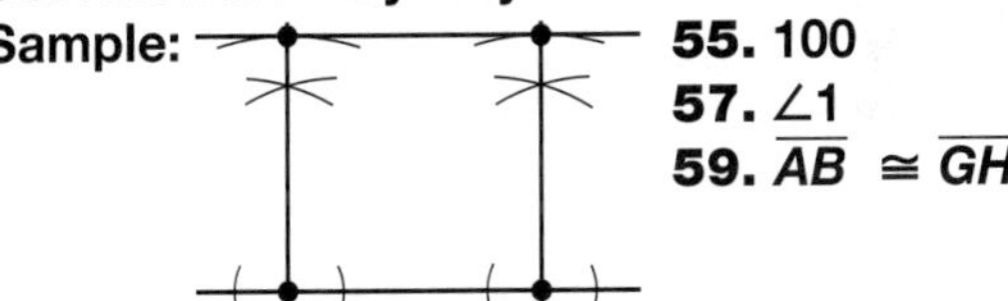

55. 100 **57.** $\angle 1$ **59.** $\overline{AB} \cong \overline{GH}$

Lesson 4-2 pp. 189–192

EXERCISES **1.** SSS **3.** SAS **5.** Yes; $\overline{OB} \cong \overline{OB}$ by Refl. Prop.; $\angle BOP \cong \angle BOR$ since all rt. ∠s are ≅; $\overline{OP} \cong \overline{OR}$ (Given); the △s are ≅ by SAS. **7a.** Given **b.** Reflexive **c.** $\triangle JKM$ **d.** $\triangle LMK$ **9.** $\angle W$ **11.** $\overline{WU}$ **13.** $\overline{XZ}$, $\overline{YZ}$ **15.** $\angle T \cong \angle V$ or $\overline{RS} \cong \overline{WU}$ **17.** additional information not needed **19.** Yes; $\triangle PVQ \cong \triangle STR$ by SSS. **21.** Yes; $\triangle NMO \cong \triangle LOM$ by SAS. **23.** $\triangle KLJ \cong \triangle MON$; SSS **25.** $\triangle JEF \cong \triangle SVF$ or $\triangle JEF \cong \triangle SFV$; SSS **29.** No; you would need $\angle H \cong \angle K$ or $\overline{GI} \cong \overline{JL}$.

31.

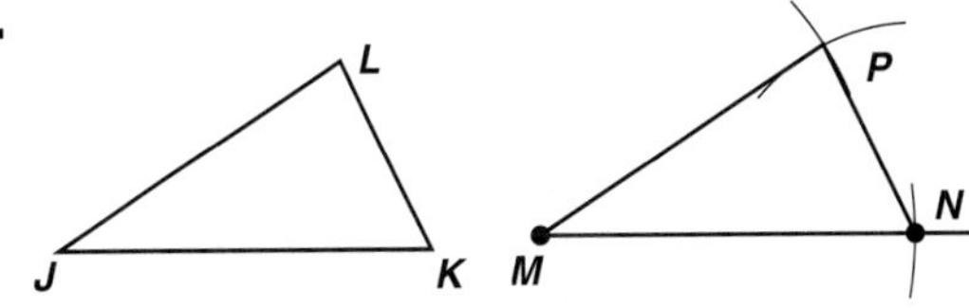

33a. Vertical ∠s are ≅. **b.** Given **c.** Def. of midpt. **d.** Given **e.** Def. of midpt. **f.** SAS **37.** $\overline{IP} \cong \overline{PO}$; $\triangle ISP \cong \triangle OSP$ by SSS. **39.** Yes; $\triangle ABC \cong \triangle CDA$ by SAS; $\angle DAC \cong \angle ACB$ because if ∥ lines, then alt. int. ∠s are ≅. **49.** $\angle E$ **51.** $\overline{FG}$ **53.** The product of the slopes of two lines is −1 if and only if the lines are ⊥. **55.** If $2x = 6$, then $x = 3$. The statement and the converse are both true.

Lesson 4-3 pp. 197–201

EXERCISES **1.** $\triangle PQR \cong \triangle VXW$ **3.** $\overline{RS}$ **5.** yes **7.** yes **9.** AAS **11.** not possible **13a.** $\angle UWV$ **b.** $\overline{UW}$ **c.** right **d.** Reflexive **15.** $\overline{MU} \cong \overline{UN}$ **17.** $\angle WZV \cong \angle WZY$ **19.** $\triangle PMO \cong \triangle NMO$; ASA **21.** $\triangle ZVY \cong \triangle WVY$; AAS **23.** The $\triangle$s are not $\cong$ because no sides are $\cong$. **25.** The $\triangle$s are not $\cong$ because the $\cong$ $\angle$s are not included $\angle$s. **27a.** $\angle SRP$ **b.** $\overline{PR}$ **c.** alt. int. **d.** $\overline{PR}$ **e.** Reflexive **29a.** Def. of $\perp$ **b.** All right $\angle$s are $\cong$. **c.** $\angle QTP \cong \angle STR$ **d.** Def. of midpt. **e.** AAS **31.** Yes; by AAS since $\angle MON \cong \angle QOP$. **33.** Yes; by ASA, since $\angle EAB \cong \angle DBC$ because $\parallel$ lines have $\cong$ corr. $\angle$s. **47.** not possible **49.** If corr. $\angle$s are $\cong$, then the lines are $\parallel$. **51.** 36 photos

Technology pp. 202

1. No; there are many noncongruent $\triangle$s with all 3 pairs of $\angle$s $\cong$. **3.** No; the circle intersects $\overrightarrow{AB}$ just once, so only one $\triangle$ is formed. If the $\cong$ $\angle$s are obtuse, then there could be an SSA congruency since a $\triangle$ can have only one obtuse $\angle$.

Lesson 4-4 pp. 204–208

EXERCISES **1.** $\angle PSQ \cong \angle SPR$; $\overline{SQ} \cong \overline{RP}$; $\overline{PQ} \cong \overline{SR}$ **3.** SAS; $\triangle KLJ \cong \triangle OMN$; $\angle K \cong \angle O$; $\angle J \cong \angle N$; $\overline{KJ} \cong \overline{ON}$ by CPCTC. **7.** $\triangle ABD \cong \triangle CBD$ by ASA because $\overline{BD} \cong \overline{BD}$ by Reflexive Prop. of $\cong$; $\overline{AB} \cong \overline{CB}$ by CPCTC. **9.** $\triangle SPT \cong \triangle OPT$ by SAS because $\overline{TP} \cong \overline{TP}$ by Refl. Prop. of $\cong$; $\angle S \cong \angle O$ by CPCTC. **15.** $\angle PKL \cong \angle QKL$ by def. of $\angle$ bisect., and $\overline{KL} \cong \overline{KL}$ by Refl. Prop. of $\cong$, so the $\triangle$s are $\cong$ by SAS. **17.** $\angle KLP \cong \angle KLQ$ because all rt. $\angle$s are $\cong$, $\overline{KL} \cong \overline{KL}$ by Refl. Prop. of $\cong$; and $\angle PKL \cong \angle QKL$ by def. of $\angle$ bisect; the $\triangle$s are $\cong$ by ASA. **21.** Prove $\triangle ABE \cong \triangle CDF$ by SAS since $\overline{AE} \cong \overline{FC}$ by subtr. **23.** b or e, b or e, d, c, f, a **35.** AAS **37.** The slope of line m is the same as the slope of line n.

Lesson 4-5 pp. 213–216

EXERCISES **1a.** $\overline{RS}$ **b.** $\overline{RS}$ **c.** Given **d.** Def. of $\angle$ bisector **e.** Reflexive Prop. of $\cong$ **f.** AAS **3.** $\overline{VX}$; Conv. of the Isosc. $\triangle$ Thm. **5.** $\overline{VY}$; $VT = VX$ (Ex. 3) and $UT = YX$ (Ex. 4), so $VU = VY$ by the Subtr. Prop. of =. **7.** $x = 80$; $y = 40$ **9.** $x = 38$; $y = 4$ **11.** $x = 36$; $y = 36$ **13.** 64 **15.** 42 **17.** 150; 15

19a.

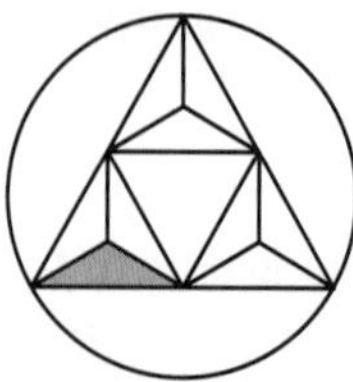

30, 30, 120 **b.** 5; 30, 60, 90, 120, 50 **21.** 50 **23.** 6 **25.** $x = 64$; $y = 71$ **27.** Two sides of a $\triangle$ are $\cong$ if and only if the $\angle$s opp. those sides are $\cong$. **35.** $m = 60$; $n = 30$ **51.** AAS **53.** 24 sides

Lesson 4-6 pp. 219–223

EXERCISES **1.** $\triangle ABC \cong \triangle DEF$ by HL. Both $\triangle$s are rt. $\triangle$s, $\overline{AC} \cong \overline{DF}$, and $\overline{CB} \cong \overline{FE}$. **3.** $\triangle LMP \cong \triangle OMN$ by HL. Both $\triangle$s are rt. $\triangle$s because vert. $\angle$s are $\cong$; $\overline{LP} \cong \overline{NO}$, and $\overline{LM} \cong \overline{OM}$. **5.** $\angle T$ and $\angle Q$ are rt. $\angle$s. **7.** $\overline{TY} \cong \overline{ER}$ or $\overline{RT} \cong \overline{YE}$ **9.** $\overline{BC} \cong \overline{FA}$ **11a.** Given **b.** Def. of rt. $\triangle$ **c.** Reflexive Prop. of $\cong$ **d.** Given **e.** HL **15.** Yes; $\overline{PM} \cong \overline{PM}$ and $\angle PMW$ is a rt. $\angle$ since $\overline{JP} \parallel \overline{MW}$. **17a.** Given **b.** $\triangle IGH$ **c.** Def. of rt. $\triangle$ **d.** I is the midpt. of $\overline{HV}$. **e.** Def. of midpt. **f.** $\triangle IGH \cong \triangle ITV$ **19.** $x = 3$; $y = 2$ **21.** whether the 7-yd side is the hyp. or a leg **25.** **27.**

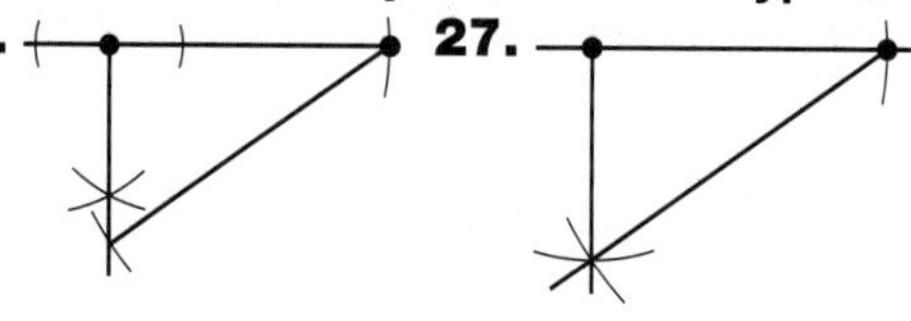

29. 1. $\overline{LO}$ bisects $\angle MLN$, $\overline{OM} \perp \overline{LM}$, $\overline{ON} \perp \overline{LN}$ (Given) 2. $\angle M$ and $\angle N$ are rt. $\angle$s (Def. of $\perp$) 3. $\angle MLO \cong \angle NLO$ (Def. of $\angle$ bis.) 4. $\angle M \cong \angle N$ (All rt. $\angle$s are $\cong$.) 5. $\overline{LO} \cong \overline{LO}$ (Reflexive Prop. of $\cong$) 6. $\triangle LMO \cong \triangle LNO$ (AAS) **39.** isosceles **41.** $\overline{BC} \parallel \overline{AD}$ because each slope $= -1$. $\overline{BT} \perp \overline{BA}$, $\overline{BA} \perp \overline{AS}$ because product of slopes is -1. **43.** If two lines are $\parallel$, then same-side int. $\angle$s are suppl. **45.** If two lines are $\parallel$, then corr. $\angle$s are $\cong$.

Lesson 4-7 pp. 226–230

EXERCISES **1.** $\angle M$ **3.** $\overline{XY}$

5. **7.**

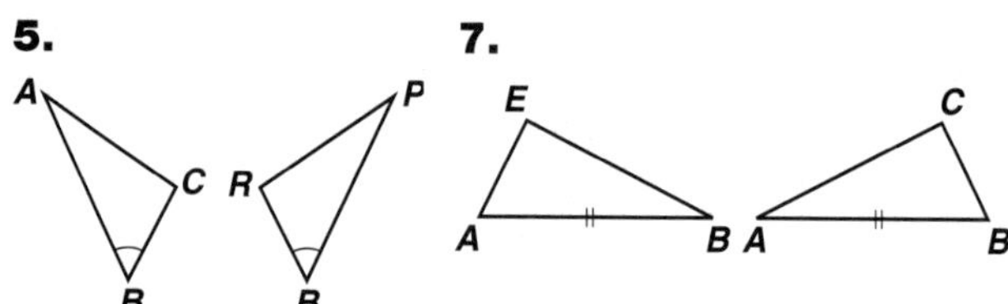

9.

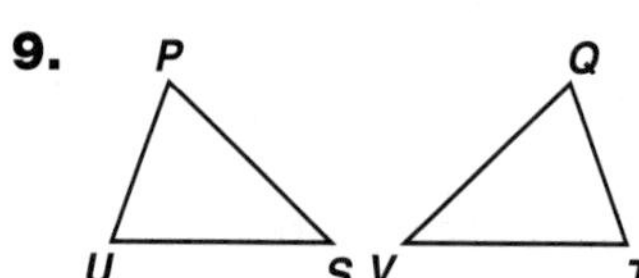

11. $\triangle LQP \cong \triangle PML$; HL **13.** $\triangle QDA \cong \triangle UAD$; SAS **15.** $\overline{TD} \cong \overline{RO}$ if $\triangle TDI \cong \triangle ROE$ by AAS. $\angle TID \cong \angle REO$ if $\triangle TEI \cong \triangle RIE$. $\triangle TEI \cong \triangle RIE$ by SSS. **17.** $\triangle QET \cong \triangle QEU$ by SAS if $\overline{QT} \cong \overline{QU}$. $\overline{QT}$ and $\overline{QU}$ are corr. parts of $\triangle QTB$ and $\triangle QUB$ which are $\cong$ by ASA. **19–21.** Answers may vary. Samples are given. **19.** **21a.**

b.

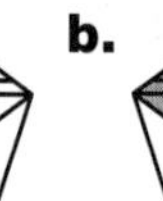

23. $\triangle ACE \cong \triangle BCD$ by ASA; $\overline{AC} \cong \overline{BC}$, $\angle A \cong \angle B$ (Given) $\angle C \cong \angle C$ (Reflexive Prop. of $\cong$) $\triangle ACE \cong \triangle BCD$ (ASA)

25. $m\angle 1 = 56$; $m\angle 2 = 56$; $m\angle 3 = 34$; $m\angle 4 = 90$; $m\angle 5 = 22$; $m\angle 6 = 34$; $m\angle 7 = 34$; $m\angle 8 = 68$; $m\angle 9 = 112$ **29.** Proofs may vary. Sample: It is given that $\angle 1 \cong \angle 2$ and $\angle 3 \cong \angle 4$. Since $\overline{QB} \cong \overline{QB}$ by the Reflexive Prop. of $\cong$, $\triangle QTB \cong \triangle QUB$ by ASA. So $\overline{QT} \cong \overline{QU}$ by CPCTC. Since $\overline{QE} \cong \overline{QE}$ by the Reflexive Prop. of $\cong$, then $\triangle QET \cong \triangle QEU$ by SAS. **39a.** right **b.** $\cong$ **c.** Reflexive **d.** HL

41.

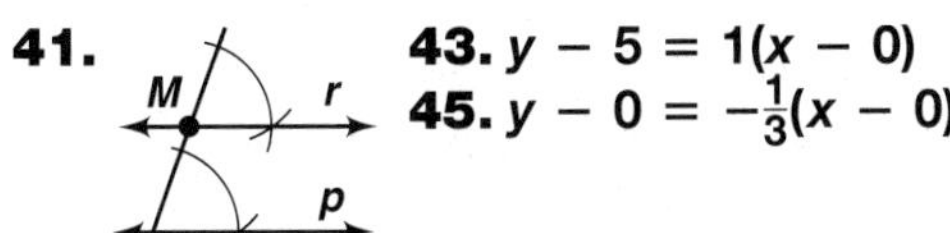

43. $y - 5 = 1(x - 0)$
45. $y - 0 = -\frac{1}{3}(x - 0)$

47. Eq. may vary, depending on pt. chosen. Sample: $y + 5 = \frac{5}{3}(x - 3)$

Chapter Review pp. 233–235

1. legs **2.** vertex angle **3.** CPCTC **4.** hypotenuse **5.** base angles **6.** corollary **7.** legs **8.** Congruent polygons **9.** base **10.** $\overline{ML}$ **11.** $\angle U$ **12.** $\overline{ST}$ **13.** *ONMLK* **14.** 80 **15.** 3 **16.** 5 **17.** 35 **18.** 100 **19.** SSS **20.** not possible **21.** SAS **22.** not possible **23.** AAS **24.** ASA **25.** $\triangle AWC \cong \triangle RCW$; AAS **26.** $\triangle JKL \cong \triangle UVT$; SAS **27.** $\triangle RGB \cong \triangle DCS$; ASA **28.** $\triangle VTY \cong \triangle WYX$ by AAS so $\overline{TV} \cong \overline{YW}$ by CPCTC. **29.** $\triangle BCE \cong \triangle DCE$ by ASA so $\overline{BE} \cong \overline{DE}$ by CPCTC. **30.** $\triangle KNM \cong \triangle MLK$ by SAS so $\overline{KN} \cong \overline{ML}$ by CPCTC. **31.** $x = 4, y = 65$ **32.** $x = 55, y = 62.5$ **33.** $x = 65, y = 90$ **34.** Since $\overline{PS} \perp \overline{SQ}$ and $\overline{RQ} \perp \overline{QS}$, $\triangle PSQ$ and $\triangle RQS$ are rt. ⩟. $\overline{PQ} \cong \overline{RS}$ and $\overline{QS} \cong \overline{SQ}$ so $\triangle PSQ \cong \triangle RQS$ by HL. **35.** Since $\overline{LN} \perp \overline{KM}$, $m\angle LNK = m\angle LNM = 90$. $\overline{KL} \cong \overline{ML}$ and $\overline{LN} \cong \overline{LN}$ so $\triangle KLN \cong \triangle MLN$ by HL. **36.** $\triangle AEC \cong \triangle ABD$ by SAS. **37.** $\triangle FIH \cong \triangle GHI$ by SAS. **38.** $\triangle PTS \cong \triangle RTA$ by ASA. **39.** $\triangle CFE \cong \triangle DEF$ by ASA.

Chapter 5

Technology p. 242

1. Midsegments have slopes that are the same as the slopes of the third side, and lengths that are $\frac{1}{2}$ the length of the third side. **3b.** The 4 ⩟ are $\cong$ by Post. 4-1: If 3 sides of one $\triangle$ are $\cong$ to 3 sides of another $\triangle$, the ⩟ are $\cong$. **5a.** The area of $\triangle ABC$ is 4 times the area of each small $\triangle$. **b.** The perimeter of $\triangle ABC$ is 2 times the perimeter of each small $\triangle$.

Lesson 5-1 pp. 246–248

EXERCISES **1.** 9 **3.** 14 **7.** 40 **9.** 160 **11.** $\overline{UW} \parallel \overline{TX}$; $\overline{UY} \parallel \overline{VX}$; $\overline{YW} \parallel \overline{TV}$ **13a.** $\overline{ST} \parallel \overline{PR}$; $\overline{SU} \parallel \overline{QR}$; $\overline{UT} \parallel \overline{PQ}$ **b.** $m\angle QPR = 40$ **15.** $\overline{FG}$ **17.** $\overline{EG}$

21a. 114 ft 9 in. **b.** Answers may vary. Sample: The highlighted segment is a midsegment of the triangular face of the building. **23.** 45 **25.** 55 **27.** $18\frac{1}{2}$ **29.** 60 **31.** 10 **35.** $x = 3$; $DF = 24$ **47.** $\triangle SXT \cong \triangle TYS$; SAS **49.** $\triangle KLQ \cong \triangle PNR$; HL

51.

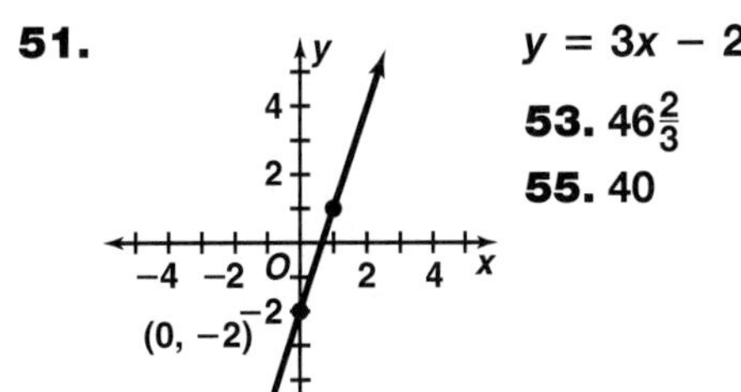

53. $46\frac{2}{3}$
55. 40

Lesson 5-2 pp. 251–254

EXERCISES **1.** $\overline{AC}$ is the $\perp$ bis. of $\overline{BD}$. **3.** 18 **7.** $y = 3$; $ST = 15$; $TU = 15$ **9.** $y = 9$; $m\angle FHL = 54$; $m\angle KHL = 54$ **11.** Point *E* is on the bisector of $\angle KHF$. **13.** 10 **15.** Isosceles; it has 2 $\cong$ sides. **19.** 4 **21.** 16 **27.** Answers may vary. Sample: The student needs to know that $\overline{QS}$ bisects $\overline{PR}$. **31.** the pitcher's plate **35.** $C(3, 2)$, $D(3, 0)$; $AC = BC = 3$, $AD = BD = \sqrt{13}$ **37.** $C(0, 0)$, $D(1, 1)$; $AC = BC = 3$, $AD = BD = \sqrt{5}$ **41.** bisector; right; Reflexive; SAS; CPCTC **55.** 8 **57.** 6 **59.** Div. Prop. of = **61.** Distr. Prop. **65.** $C\left(0, \frac{7}{2}\right)$; $AB = \sqrt{97}$, $AC = BC = \frac{\sqrt{97}}{2}$

Technology p. 255

1. Each set of 3 lines intersect in one point. **3.** Each set of 3 lines, $\angle$ bisectors, $\perp$ bisectors, lines containing altitudes, and the medians of a $\triangle$ meet in one point. **5.** Since isosc. ⩟ can be acute, right, or obtuse, the special segments are as seen in the table. Since all equil. ⩟ are acute, all special segments intersect inside.

Lesson 5-3 pp. 259–263

EXERCISES **1.** $(-2, -3)$ **3.** $\left(1\frac{1}{2}, 1\right)$ **9.** *Z* **11.** $TY = 18$; $TW = 27$ **13.** $VY = 6$; $YX = 3$ **15.** Neither; it's not a segment drawn from a vertex.

17.

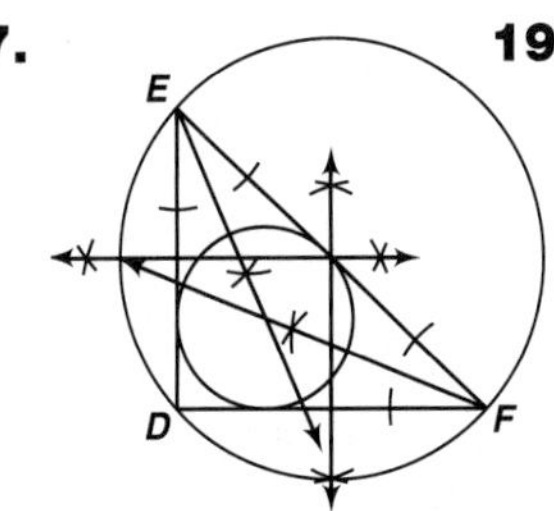

19. $\overline{BE}$ **21.** $\overrightarrow{CA}$ **23.** 1 : 2 or 2 : 1 **27.** $\angle$ bisector; it bisects an $\angle$. **29.** Altitude; $\overline{AB}$ is $\perp$ to a side from a vertex. **31a.** $\angle$ Bis. Thm. **b.** $\angle$ Bis. Thm. **c.** Trans. **d.** $\angle$ Bis. **43.** Yes; point *B* is equidistant from the sides. **45.** right **47–49.** Answers may vary. Samples are given.

47. $\overleftrightarrow{AB}$ **49.** *ABC* and *ADE*

Lesson 5-4 pp. 267–270

EXERCISES **1.** Two angles are not congruent. **3.** The angle is obtuse. **7a.** If you don't eat all of your vegetables, then you won't grow. **b.** If you won't grow, then you don't eat all of your vegetables. **9a.** If a figure isn't a rectangle, then it doesn't have four sides. **b.** If a figure doesn't have four sides, then it isn't a rectangle. **11.** Assume that $\angle J$ is a right angle. **13.** Assume that none of the angles is obtuse. **17.** I and II **19.** II and III **21a.** right angle **b.** right angles **c.** 90 **d.** 180 **e.** 90 **f.** 90 **g.** 0 **h.** more than one right angle **i.** at most one right angle **23a.** If four points aren't collinear, then they aren't coplanar; false **b.** If four points aren't coplanar, then they aren't collinear; true **25–27.** Answers may vary. Samples are given. **25.** If today is Sunday, then tomorrow is Monday. **27.** If two sides of a triangle are congruent, then the triangle is isosceles. **33.** If the animal is a kitten, then it is a cat. If the animal isn't a cat, then it's not a kitten. **35.** If a number is a whole number, then it is an integer. If a number isn't an integer, then it isn't a whole number. **37a.** Earl proves that it's later than 5:00. **b.** He starts with the assumption that it is before 5:00. **c.** It is not noisy. **51.** same-side int. ⦣s **53.** corr. ⦣s **55.** $45 = m\angle ABC$

Lesson 5-5 pp. 273–276

EXERCISES **1.** $\angle 3 \cong \angle 2$ because they are vertical ⦣s and $m\angle 1 > m\angle 3$ by Corollary to the Ext. ∠ Thm. So, $m\angle 1 > m\angle 2$ by subst. **3.** $m\angle 1 > m\angle 4$ by Corollary to the Ext. ∠ Thm. and $\angle 4 \cong \angle 2$ because if ∥ lines, then alt. int. ⦣s are ≅. **5.** $\angle D, \angle C, \angle E$ **7.** $\angle A, \angle B, \angle C$ **9.** $\angle Z, \angle X, \angle Y$ **11.** $\overline{FH}, \overline{GF}, \overline{GH}$ **13.** $\overline{AC}, \overline{AB}, \overline{CB}$ **17.** Yes; $11 + 12 > 15$; $12 + 15 > 11$; $11 + 15 > 12$. **19.** Yes; $1 + 15 > 15$; $15 + 15 > 1$. **23.** $11 < s < 21$ **25.** $5 < s < 41$ **31.** Answers may vary. Sample: The shortcut across the grass is shorter than the sum of the two paths. **35.** $\overline{CD}$ **49.** $m\angle X \leq m\angle B$ **51.** The triangle is obtuse. **53.** 35 **55.** 55 **57.** 962.1 mm^2 **59.** 314.2 mi^2

Chapter Review pp. 281–283

1. median of a △ **2.** distance from the point to the line **3.** ⊥ Bis. Thm. **4.** altitude **5.** contrapositive **6.** indirect proof **7.** △ Ineq. Thm. **8.** incenter **9.** ∠ Bis. Thm. **10.** point of concurrency **11.** 15 **12.** 11 **13.** 40 **14.** 7 **15.** 14 **16.** 80 **17.** (−1, 0) **18.** (0, −1) **19.** (2, −3) **20.** ∠ bisector, it bisects an ∠. **21.** altitude; it is ⊥ to a side. **22.** median; it goes through a midpoint. **23.** Inverse: If it is not snowing, then it is not cold outside. Contrapositive: If it is not cold outside, then it is not snowing. **24.** Inverse: If an angle is not obtuse, then its measure is not greater than 90 and less than 180. Contrapositive: If an angle's measure is not greater than 90 and less than 180, then it is not obtuse. **25.** Inverse: If a figure is not a square, then its sides are not congruent. Contrapositive: If a figure's sides are not congruent, then it is not a square. **26.** Inverse: If you are not in Australia, then you are not south of the equator. Contrapositive: If you are not south of the equator, then you are not in Australia. **27.** Assume that both numbers are odd. The product of 2 odd numbers is always odd, which contradicts that the product is even. Therefore, at least one number must be even. **28.** Assume a right ∠ can be formed by non-perp. lines. Then by the def. of ⊥, the lines are ⊥. Therefore, the assumption is false. **29.** Assume that an △ has 2 obtuse ⦣s. Then these ⦣s by def. are greater than 90, which makes their sum greater than 180. But the sum of the measures of the ⦣s of a △ = 180, so the assumption must be false. **30.** Assume an ∠ is obtuse, and therefore has measure greater than 90. Since the △ is equilateral, it is equiangular, and each ∠ measures 60. **31.** $\angle T, \angle R, \angle S$; $\overline{RS}$, $\overline{TS}$, $\overline{TR}$ **32.** $\angle G, \angle O, \angle F$; $\overline{OF}$, $\overline{FG}$, $\overline{OG}$ **33.** No; $5 + 8 \not> 15$. **34.** Yes; each pair > 3rd. **35.** Yes; each pair > 3rd. **36.** Yes; each pair > 3rd. **37.** No; $1 + 1 \not> 3$. **38.** Yes; each pair > 3rd. **39.** $3 < x < 11$ **40.** $7 < x < 23$ **41.** $6 < x < 10$ **42.** $1 < x < 25$

Chapter 6

Lesson 6-1 pp. 288–293

EXERCISES **1.** ▱, rectangle, rhombus, square **3.** trapezoid **7.** rhombus **9.** rhombus

13. rhombus

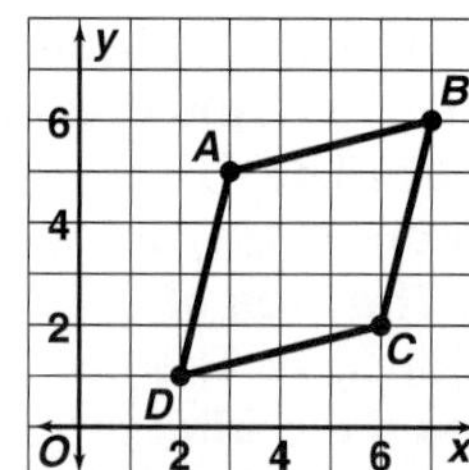

15. trapezoid **19.** $x = 11, y = 29$; 13, 13, 23, 23 **21.** $x = 2, y = 6$; 2, 7, 7, 2 **25.** 40, 40, 140, 140; 11, 11, 15, 32 **27.** rectangle, square, trapezoid

29–31. Answers may vary. Samples are given.

29.

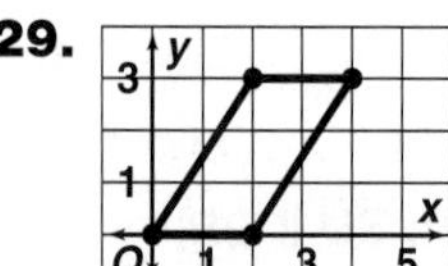

31. Impossible; a trapezoid with one rt. ∠ must have another, since two sides are ∥.

37. True; a square is both a rectangle and a rhombus. **39.** False; a kite does not have ≅ opp. sides. **43.** Rhombus; all 4 sides are ≅ because they come from the same cut. **51.** rectangle, ▱, kite **53.** square, rhombus, ▱ **65.** Yes; the sum of the lengths of any 2 sides is greater than the third side. **67.** No; $3 + 5 \not> 8$. **69.** 16 mm **71.** 82

Lesson 6-2 pp. 297–301

EXERCISES **1.** 127 **3.** 76 **7.** $\frac{3}{4}$ **9.** 4 **11.** 22; 18.5, 23.6, 23.6 **13.** 18 **15.** 12; $m\angle Q = m\angle S = 36$, $m\angle P = m\angle R = 144$ **17.** $x = 6, y = 8$ **19.** $x = 7$, $y = 10$ **25.** 3 **27.** 6 **35.** $BC = AD = 33$ cm; $AB = CD = 13$ cm **37a.** Given **b.** Def. of ▱ **c.** If 2 lines are ∥, then alt. int. $\angle$s are ≅. **d.** If 2 lines are ∥, then alt. int. $\angle$s are ≅. **e.** Reflexive Prop. of ≅ **f.** ASA **g.** ASA **h.** CPCTC **i.** CPCTC **39.** 38, 32, 110 **41.** 95, 37, 37 **43.** 18, 162 **45.** $x = 15, y = 45$ **47.** $x = 25, y = 115$ **57.** Answers may vary. Sample: In ▱s *LENS* and *NGTH*, $\overline{GT} \parallel \overline{EH}$ and $\overline{EH} \parallel \overline{LS}$ by the def. of a ▱. Therefore $\overline{LS} \parallel \overline{GT}$ because if 2 lines are ∥ to the same line then they are ∥ to each other. **71.** parallelogram **73.** 49 **75.** 49

Lesson 6-3 pp. 307–310

EXERCISES **1.** 5 **3.** $x = 1.6, y = 1$ **7.** Yes; both pairs of opp. sides are ≅. **9.** Yes; both pairs of opp. $\angle$s are ≅. **17a.** bisect **b.** $\overline{XR}$ **c.** $\triangle XYR$ **d.** ASA **e.** alt. interior **21.** No; the figure could be a kite. **23.** No; the figure could be a trapezoid. **27.** $x = 3, y = 11$ **29.** $k = 9, m = 23.4$ **31.** $\frac{1}{6}$ **33.** (6, 6) **47.** $e = 13, f = 11$, $c = 204$ **49.** If a quad. is a ▱, then the diagonals bisect each other; if the diagonals of a quad. bisect each other, then it is a ▱. **51.** If the prod. of the slopes of two nonvertical lines is −1, then they are ⊥; if two nonvertical lines are ⊥, then the prod. of their slopes is −1.

Technology p. 311

1. Diagonals of a rectangle are ≅. **3.** Diagonals of a square are both ≅ and ⊥, and bisect the $\angle$s. **5.** Diagonals that are ≅ yield a rectangle.

Lesson 6-4 pp. 315–318

EXERCISES **1.** 38, 38, 38, 38 **3.** 118, 31, 31 **11.** 3; $LN = MP = 7$ **13.** 9; $LN = MP = 67$ **17.** Yes; ≅ diagonals in a ▱ mean it can be a rectangle with 2 opp. sides 2 cm long. **19.** Impossible; if the figure is a ▱, then the ∠ opp. the bisected ∠ is also bisected, and the figure is a rhombus. But the sides are not ≅. **23.** After measuring the sides, she can measure the diagonals. If the diagonals are ≅, then the figure is a rectangle by Thm. 6-14. **25–27.** Symbols may vary. Sample: parallelogram: ▱; rhombus: Ⓡ▱; rectangle: ▭; square: Ⓢ **25.** Ⓡ▱, Ⓢ **27.** ▱, Ⓡ▱, ▭, Ⓢ

37. 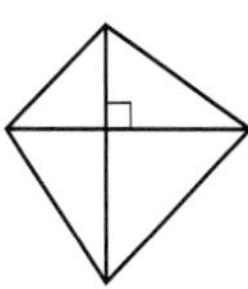 Diag. are ≅, diag. are ⊥. **39–41.** Answers may vary. Samples are given. **39.** Draw diag. 1, and construct its midpt. Draw a line through the midpt. Construct segments of length diag. 2 in opp. directions from mdpt. Then, bisect these segments. Connect these mdpts. with the endpoints of diag. 1. **41.** Same as 39, but construct a ⊥ line at the midpt. of diag. 1. **45.** Yes; since all right $\angle$s are ≅, the opp. $\angle$s are ≅ and it is a ▱. Since it has all right $\angle$s, it is a rectangle. **47.** Yes; a quad. with 4 ≅ sides is a ▱ and a ▱ with 4 ≅ sides and 4 right $\angle$s is a square. **49.** $x = 5, y = 32, z = 7.5$ **57.** 16, 16 **59.** 1, 1 **61.** 4. $\triangle ABC \cong \triangle ADC$ (ASA) 5. $\overline{AB} \cong \overline{AD}$ (CPCTC) 6. $\overline{AB} \cong \overline{DC}$, $\overline{AD} \cong \overline{BC}$ (Opp. sides of a ▱ are ≅.) 7. $\overline{AB} \cong \overline{BC} \cong \overline{CD} \cong \overline{AD}$ (Trans. Prop. of ≅) **67.** Yes; both pairs of opp. sides are ≅. **69.** Yes; the diag. bisect each other. **71.** 16 **73.** $\overline{RQ}$

Technology p. 319

3. For *MNOP* and *EFGH*, the ratio of the sides and perimeters is 1 : 2 and the ratios of the areas is 1 : 4. The sides of *MNOP* and *EFGH* are ∥.

Lesson 6-5 pp. 322–325

EXERCISES **1.** 77, 103, 103 **3.** 49, 131, 131 **7a.** isosc. trapezoids **b.** 69, 69, 111, 111 **9.** 90, 45, 45 **11.** 90, 26, 90 **19.** No; explanations may vary. Sample: If both $\angle$s are bisected, then this combined with $\overline{KM} \cong \overline{KM}$ by the Reflexive Prop. means $\triangle KLM \cong \triangle KNM$ by SAS. So by CPCTC, opp. $\angle$s *L* and *N* are ≅, so it is not an isos. trapezoid. **21.** 15 **23.** 3 **27.** 28 **29.** $x = 18$, $y = 108$ **31.** 112, 68, 68 **33.** Yes, the ≅ $\angle$s can be obtuse, as well as one other ∠. **37.** No; if two consecutive $\angle$s were compl., then the kite would be concave. **51.** 126 **53.** 27 **55a.** 3 **b.** 30 **c.** 30

Lesson 6-6 pp. 328–330

EXERCISES **1.** $W(0, h)$; $Z(b, 0)$ **3.** $W(-b, b)$; $Z(-b, -b)$ **7.** $\left(\frac{b}{2}, \frac{h}{2}\right)$; $-\frac{h}{b}$ **9.** $(-b, 0)$; undefined **13a.** $(2a, 0)$ **b.** $(0, 2b)$ **c.** (a, b) **d.** $\sqrt{b^2 + a^2}$ **e.** $\sqrt{b^2 + a^2}$ **f.** $\sqrt{b^2 + a^2}$ **g.** $MA = MB = MC$ **15–17.** Answers may vary. Samples are given.

15. B, D, H, F **17.** A, C, G, E **21.** $W(2a, 2a)$; $Z(2a, 0)$ **23.** $W(0, b)$; $Z(2a, 0)$ **29.** $(a, 0)$

31a.

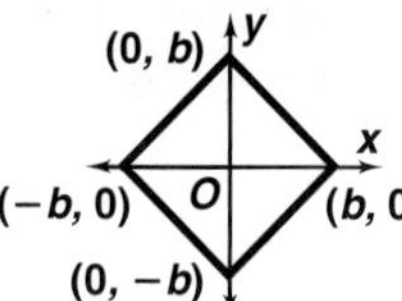

b. $(-b, 0), (0, b), (b, 0), (0, -b)$ **c.** $b\sqrt{2}$ **d.** 1, −1 **e.** Yes, because the product of the slopes is −1. **43.** (3, 2) **45a.** Reflexive **b.** AAS

Lesson 6-7 pp. 333–337

EXERCISES **1a.** $W(\frac{a}{2}, \frac{b}{2})$; $Z(\frac{c+e}{2}, \frac{d}{2})$ **b.** $W(a, b)$; $Z(c + e, d)$ **c.** $W(2a, 2b)$; $Z(2c + 2e, 2d)$; c; it uses multiples of 2 to name the coordinates of W and Z. **3a.** y-axis **b.** Distance **5a.** isos. **b.** x-axis **c.** y-axis **d.** Midpoints **e.** ≅ sides **f.** slopes **g.** the Distance Formula **7a.** $\sqrt{a^2 + b^2}$ **b.** $2\sqrt{a^2 + b^2}$ **9a.** (a, b) **b.** (a, b) **c.** the same point **11a.** ≅ **b.** midpts. **c.** $(-2b, 2c)$ **d.** $L(b, a + c), M(b, c), N(-b, c), K(-b, a + c)$ **e.** 0 **f.** vertical lines **g.** ∥ **h.** ⊥ **13–15.** Answers may vary. Samples are given. **13.** yes; same slope **15.** no; may not have intersection pt. **25.** 1, 4, 7 **27.** −0.8, 0.4, 1.6, 2.8, 4, 5.2, 6.4, 7.6, 8.8 **31.** $(-1, 6\frac{2}{3}), (1, 8\frac{1}{3}), (3, 10), (5, 11\frac{2}{3}), (7, 13\frac{1}{3})$ **33.** (−2.76, 5.2), (−2.52, 5.4), (−2.28, 5.6), . . . , (8.52, 14.6), (8.76, 14.8) **47a.** If the sum of the ∠s of a polygon is 360°, then the polygon is a quad. **b.** If a polygon is a quad., then the sum of its ∠s is 360°. **49a.** If $a \neq 5$, then $a^2 \neq 25$. **b.** If $a^2 \neq 25$, then $a \neq 5$. **53.** $\overline{HE} \cong \overline{FG}$, $\overline{EF} \cong \overline{GH}$, and $\overline{HF} \cong \overline{HF}$ by the Reflexive Prop. of ≅, so $\triangle HEF \cong \triangle FGH$ by SSS. Then by CPCTC $\angle 1 \cong \angle 2$.

Chapter Review pp. 339–341

1. F **2.** H **3.** G **4.** B **5.** I **6.** J **7.** A **8.** C **9.** E **10.** D

11.

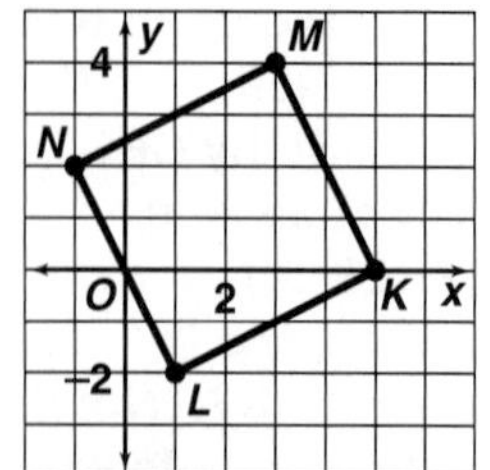

square

12. parallelogram

13. $x = 8$; 9, 14, 9, 7 **14.** $m = 4, t = 5$; 7, 14, 14, 7 **15.** 101, 79, 101 **16.** 38, 43, 99 **17.** 37, 26, 26 **18.** yes **19.** yes **20.** no **21.** yes **22.** $x = 29$, $y = 28$ **23.** $x = 4, y = 5$ **24.** 124, 28, 62 **25.** 60, 90, 30 **26.** 90, 25 **27.** 26 in. **28.** 20 cm **29.** 19 ft **30.** (a, b) **31.** $(0, c)$ **32.** $(a - b, c)$ **33a.** −1 **b.** 1 **c.** The prod. of the slopes is −1. **34a.** a **b.** $(0, b)$ **c.** $\sqrt{a^2 + b^2}$ **d.** $\sqrt{a^2 + b^2}$ **e.** BD

Chapter 7

Lesson 7-1 pp. 351–354

EXERCISES **1.** 240 cm^2 **3.** 26.79 in.^{2} **5.** 9 units^2 **7.** 6 units^2 **9.** 0.24 **11.** 14 m^2 **13.** 3 ft^2 **15.** 15 units^2 **17.** 6 units^2 **23.** 14 cm

25a.

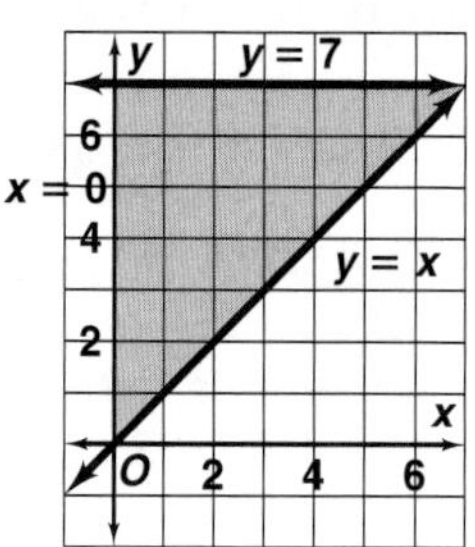

b. 24.5 units^2 **27b.** 16 units^2 **29.** The area does not change; the height and base AB do not change. **31.** 9 units^2 **33.** 4200 yd^2 **35a.** Blank grid; area is 84 units^2 while figures are 36 units^2. **b.** No; the figures have the same area. **37.** 28 units^2 **39.** 9 units^2 **45.** 525 cm^2 **57.** (a, a) **59.** 108 **61.** 72 **65.**

D

A B

Lesson 7-2 pp. 360–364

EXERCISES **1.** 10 **3.** 34 **5.** 65 **7.** No; $4^2 + 5^2 \neq 6^2$. **9.** Yes; $15^2 + 20^2 = 25^2$. **11.** $\sqrt{33}$ **13.** $2\sqrt{89}$ **17.** 17.0 m **19.** $12\sqrt{7}$ cm^2 **21.** No; $19^2 + 20^2 \neq 28^2$. **23.** Yes; $33^2 + 56^2 = 65^2$. **25.** right **27.** right **37.** $8\sqrt{5}$ **41.** 168 ft^2 **43.** 32 in.^{2} **45.** Yes; $7^2 + 24^2 = 25^2$, so $\angle RST$ is a rt. ∠. **49.** 50 **51.** 35 **53–55.** Answers may vary. Samples are given. **53.** 4; 5 **55.** 11; 12 **61.** 2830 km **63.** 12.5 cm **77.** 15 ft **79.** 3; 20 **81.** 3 **83.** 7

Lesson 7-3 pp. 369–372

EXERCISES **1.** $x = 8; y = 8\sqrt{2}$ **3.** $y = 60\sqrt{2}$ **5.** $4\sqrt{2}$ **7.** $\sqrt{3}$ **11.** 25.5 ft **13.** $x = \sqrt{3}; y = 3$ **15.** $x = 24; y = 12\sqrt{3}$ **17.** $x = 4\sqrt{3}; y = 6$ **21.** 43.3 cm^2 **23.** 101.8 m^2 **25.** $a = 6; b = 6\sqrt{2}$; $c = 2\sqrt{3}; d = 6$ **27.** $a = 4; b = 4$ **33a.** 8.5 m **b.** 3.1 m **35.** 110.9 cm^2 **37.** 11.3 yd^2 **47.** $4\sqrt{21}$ cm

49. no

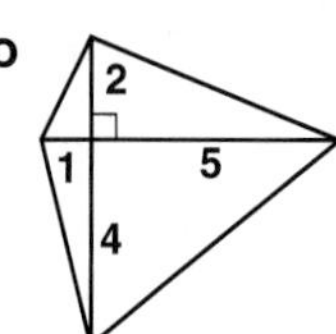

51. no; an isosceles trapezoid **53.** no **55.** yes; ASA Post.

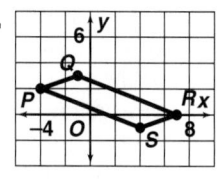

Lesson 7-4 pp. 376–379

EXERCISES **1.** 472 in.^{2} **3.** 108 ft^2 **5.** 150 cm^2 **7.** about 43,290 mi^2 **9.** 72 m^2 **11.** $52\sqrt{3}$ ft^2 **15.** 18 m^2 **17.** 56 ft^2 **19.** 96 in.^{2} **21.** 20 in.^{2} **25.** 19.5 cm^2 **27.** 49.9 ft^2 **29.** 18 units^2 **31.** 15 units^2 **33.** 135 m^2 **35.** 18 cm^2 **37.** $\frac{128\sqrt{3}}{3}$ in.^{2} **49.** $5\sqrt{2}$ units **51.** always **53.** never

Lesson 7-5 pp. 382–385

EXERCISES **1.** $m\angle 1 = 120$; $m\angle 2 = 60$; $m\angle 3 = 30$ **3.** $m\angle 7 = 60$; $m\angle 8 = 30$; $m\angle 9 = 60$ **5.** 2851.8 ft^2 **7.** 2475 in.^{2} **11.** 27.7 in.^{2} **13.** 72 cm^2 **15.** $300\sqrt{3}$ ft^2 **19a.** 72 **b.** 54 **21a.** 40 **b.** 70 **23.** 310.4 ft^2 **25.** $m\angle 1 = 36$; $m\angle 2 = 18$; $m\angle 3 = 72$ **27.** 73 cm^2 **29.** 27 m^2 **31.** 220 cm^2 **33.** $600\sqrt{3}$ m^2 **35.** 128 cm^2 **37.** $900\sqrt{3}$ m^2; 1558.8 m^2 **41a.** $b = s$; $h = \frac{\sqrt{3}}{2}s$; $A = \frac{1}{2}bh = \frac{1}{2}s \cdot \frac{\sqrt{3}}{2}s = \frac{1}{4}s^2\sqrt{3}$ **b.** apothem $= \frac{s\sqrt{3}}{6}$; $A = \frac{1}{2}ap = \frac{1}{2}\left(\frac{s\sqrt{3}}{6}\right)(3s) = \frac{1}{4}s^2\sqrt{3}$ **51.** 46 m^2 **53.** 8 m **55.** $\triangle ACG$ and $\triangle BDF$ **57a.** 7.1 mi^2 **b.** about 8 mi

Lesson 7-6 pp. 389–393

EXERCISES **1.** 25 **3.** 32 **9–11.** Answers may vary. Samples are given. **9.** $\overset{\frown}{ED}$ **11.** $\overset{\frown}{BFE}$ **15.** 128 **17.** 218 **27.** 20π cm **29.** 8.4π m **33.** 25 in. **35.** 8π ft **37.** 33π in. **43.** 180 **45.** 55 **49a.** 6 **b.** 30 **c.** 120 **51.** 100 **53.** 40 **55.** 100 in. **57.** $\frac{100\pi}{3}$ in. **59.** 105 ft **61.** (2.5, 5) **63.** 5.125π ft **65.** 3π m **69.** 12.6 units **77.** 18.6 mm **79.** No; it could be an isosc. trap. **81.** Yes; if one pair of sides is both $\cong$ and $\parallel$, it is a ▱. **83.** never

Lesson 7-7 pp. 397–400

EXERCISES **1.** 9π m^2 **3.** 0.7225π ft^2 **5.** about 86,394 ft^2 **7.** 40.5π yd^2 **9.** $\frac{169\pi}{6}$ m^2 **13.** $\frac{25\pi}{4}$ m^2 **15.** 24π in.^{2} **17.** 22.1 cm^2 **19.** 3.3 m^2 **21.** 120.4 cm^2 **23.** $(54\pi + 20.25\sqrt{3})$ cm^2 **25.** $(4 - \pi)$ ft^2 **31.** 15.7 in.^{2} **35.** $(49\pi - 73.5\sqrt{3})$ m^2 **37.** 4π m^2 **45.** 2π m **47.** $11\frac{1}{4}$ in., $11\frac{1}{4}$ in., $11\frac{1}{4}$ in., $15\frac{1}{4}$ in.

Technology p. 401

1. Each ratio will approach 1. **3.** about 63 cm; about 314 cm^2

Lesson 7-8 pp. 404–407

EXERCISES **1.** $\frac{1}{2}$ **3.** $\frac{3}{5}$ **7.** $\frac{2}{5}$ or 40%

0 1 2 3 4 5 6 7 8 9 10

9. $\frac{4}{15}$ or about 27% **11.** $\frac{1}{3}$ or about 33% **15.** $\frac{1}{4}$ or 25% **17.** $\frac{2}{5}$ or 40% **21.** 4% **23.** $\frac{\pi}{4}$ **25.** $\frac{\pi}{4}$ **27a.** 14 prizes **b.** \$110 **29.** 36 s **31a.**

0 10 20 30 40 50 60

If it starts after 45 min, you cannot erase 15 min of a 60 min tape. **b.** $\frac{7}{45}$ or about 16% **33.** $\frac{3}{10}$ **35.** 0 **41.** about 36% **43.** about 46% **53.** 12π cm^2 **55.** $x = 36$; $y = 144$ **57a.** $D(3, 1)$; $E(1, 4)$ **b.** slope $\overline{DE} = -\frac{3}{2}$; slope $\overline{AC} = -\frac{3}{2}$

Chapter Review pp. 409–411

1. base **2.** sector **3.** diameter **4.** apothem **5.** adjacent arcs **6.** 10 m^2 **7.** 90 in.^{2} **8.** 33 ft^2 **9.** $96\sqrt{3}$ mm^2 **10.** 96 ft^2 **11.** 117 cm^2 **12.** 20.8 in.^{2} **13.** 128 mm^2

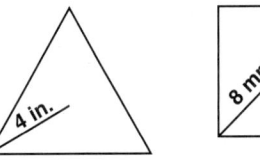

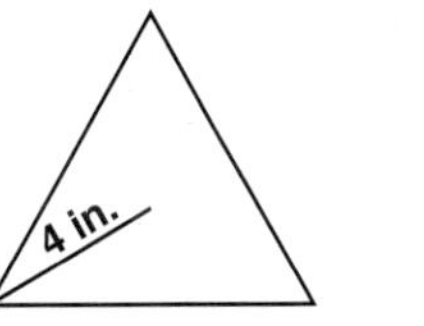

8 mm

14. 127.3 cm^2

7cm

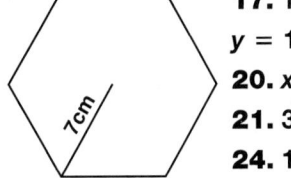

15. 16 **16.** $2\sqrt{113}$ **17.** 17 **18.** $x = 9\sqrt{3}$; $y = 18$ **19.** $12\sqrt{2}$ **20.** $x = \frac{20\sqrt{3}}{3}$; $y = \frac{40\sqrt{3}}{3}$ **21.** 30 **22.** 120 **23.** 330 **24.** 120 **25.** $\frac{22}{9}\pi$ in. **26.** π mm **27.** 18.3 m^2 **28.** 41.0 cm^2 **29.** $\frac{1}{2}$ or 50% **30.** $\frac{3}{8}$ or 37.5% **31.** $\frac{1}{6}$ or about 16.7%

Chapter 8

Lesson 8-1 pp. 418–421

EXERCISES **1.** 1 : 1000 **3–5.** Answers may vary. Samples are given. **3.** $3b$ **5.** $\frac{b}{4}$ **13.** $1\frac{2}{3}$ **15.** 6.875 **21.** 125 mi **23.** about 135 mi **27.** 5 : 4 **29.** $\frac{5}{48}$ **31.** $\frac{9}{4}$ **33.** $\frac{b}{2}$ **35.** 6 **37.** 16.5 **45.** 9; 18 **47.** 8; 21 **49–51.** Answers may vary. Samples are given.

49.

Scale 1 cm = 10 ft

51. 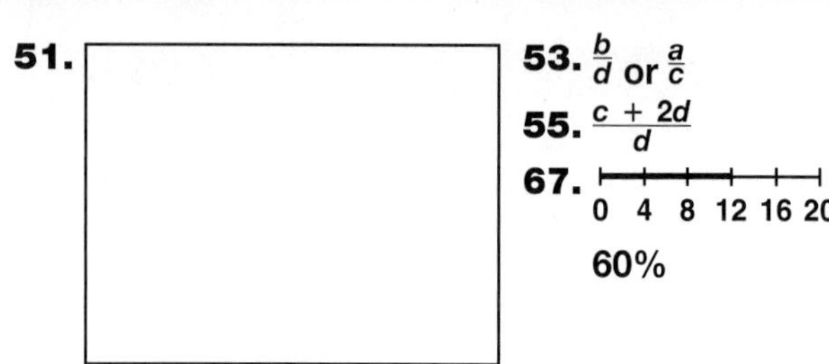

53. $\frac{b}{d}$ or $\frac{a}{c}$

55. $\frac{c + 2d}{d}$

67. 0 4 8 12 16 20

60%

69. **71.** 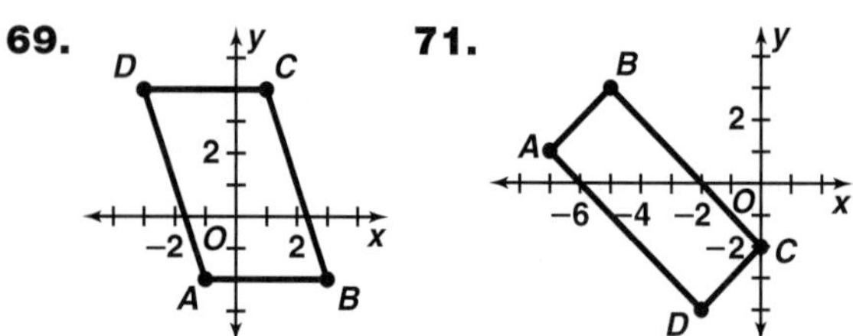

parallelogram rectangle, parallelogram

73. I and III **75a.** If an ∠ is not acute, then it does not have measure between 0 and 90. **b.** If an ∠ does not have measure between 0 and 90, then it is not acute. **77a.** If two ∠s are not compl., then the ∠s are not both acute. **b.** If two ∠s are not both acute, then they are not compl.

Lesson 8-2 pp. 425–429

EXERCISES **1.** ∠*JHY* **3.** ∠*JXY* **7.** no; $\frac{20}{30} \neq \frac{36}{52}$ **9.** yes; *KLMJ* ~ *PQNO*; $\frac{3}{5}$ **11.** No; corr. ∠s are not ≅. **13.** $x = 4$; $y = 3$ **15.** $x = 16$; $y = 4.5$; $z = 7.5$ **17.** 3.6 in. by 6 in. **19.** 70 mm **21.** 2 : 3 **33.** 2.6 cm **35.** 3 : 1 **37.** 1 : 2 **39.** 2 : 3 **41.** sides of 2 cm; ∠s of 60° and 120° **43.** sides of 0.8 cm; ∠s of 60° and 120° **47.** 6.2 in. **57.** $7y$ **59.** $\frac{y + 9}{9}$ **61.** no; only one pair of ∥ sides **63.** △*CEA*, △*FED*, △*BCD* **65.** 8

Extension pp. 430–431

1. **3.** $\frac{64}{27}$; $\frac{256}{81}$ **5.** **9.**

Lesson 8-3 pp. 435–438

EXERCISES **1.** Yes; △*ABC* ~ △*FED*; SSS ~ Thm. **3.** Ex. 1: $\frac{2}{3}$ (for △*ABC* to △*FED*); Ex. 2: Not possible; the △s aren't similar. **5.** No; $\frac{6}{3} \neq \frac{10}{4}$. **7.** Yes; △*APJ* ~ △*ABC*; SSS ~ Thm. or SAS ~ Thm. **11.** AA ~ Post.; 2.5 **13.** AA ~ Post.; 12 **17.** AA ~ Post.; 220 yd **19.** AA ~ Post.; 90 ft **21.** 151 m **23a.** No; the corr. ∠s may not be ≅. **b.** Yes; every isosc. rt. △ is a 45°-45°-90° △. Therefore, by AA ~ Thm. they are all ~. **25.** Yes; △*AWV* ~ △*AST*; SAS ~ Thm. **27.** No; there is only one pair of ≅ ∠s. **31.** 2 : 1 **33.** 4 : 3 **41a.** 98 m; 98 m **b.** 420 m^2; 420 m^2 **c.** No; the △s given are a counterexample to this conjecture, since the sides are not in proportion. **49.** ∠*E* **51.** ∠*Y* **55.** *x*-values may vary. Sample: $W(-b, c)$; $Z(-b, -c)$ **57.** $6 < x < 24$

Lesson 8-4 pp. 442–444

EXERCISES **1.** 6 **3.** $4\sqrt{3}$ **9.** *s* **11.** *c* **15.** 9 **17.** 10 **21a.** 18 mi **b.** 24 mi **23a.** 4 cm

23b. 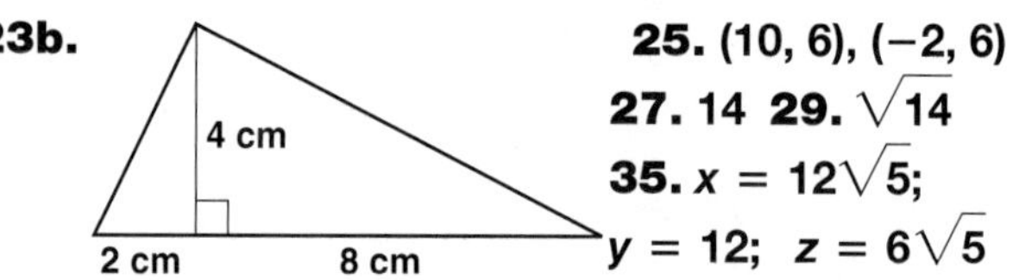

25. (10, 6), (−2, 6) **27.** 14 **29.** $\sqrt{14}$ **35.** $x = 12\sqrt{5}$; $y = 12$; $z = 6\sqrt{5}$

37. $12\sqrt{2}$ **39.** about 6.5 m **41.** $h = 5$, $a = \frac{12}{5}$, $h_1 = \frac{9}{5}$, $h_2 = \frac{16}{5}$ **43.** $\ell_1 = \ell_2 = 6\sqrt{2}$, $h = 12$, $h_2 = 6$ **63a.** △*PRQ* ~ △*ACB* **b.** SSS ~ Thm. **65.** 7.5 **67.** $x = 5$; $y = 8$ **69.** $x = 3$; $y = 4$

Technology p. 445

1. It divides the sides into prop. segments. **3.** The corr. segment ratios are =.

Lesson 8-5 pp. 448–452

EXERCISES **1.** 7.5 **3.** 5.2 **5.** *c* **7.** *d* **9.** $3\frac{1}{3}$ **11.** 6 **13.** 35 **19.** *JP* **21.** *KM* **25.** 559 ft **27.** 3.8 cm and 9.2 cm **29.** $x = 18$ m; $y = 12$ m **31.** 20 **33.** 9 **37.** 6 **39.** 19.5 **41.** $h = 13.0$, $\ell_1 = 5.3$, $\ell_2 = 11.9$ **43.** $\ell_2 = 7.1$, $h_2 = 5.0$, $h = 10.0$ **49.** No; $\frac{28}{12} \neq \frac{24}{10}$. **57.** *m* **59.** *h* **61.** $x = 9$; $y = 9\sqrt{3}$ **63.** $RT = SV = 38$ **65.** $RT = SV = 48$

Lesson 8-6 pp. 456–459

EXERCISES **1.** 1 : 2; 1 : 4 **3.** 2 : 3; 4:9 **5.** 24 in.^{2} **7.** 59 ft^2 **9.** $384 **11.** 1 : 2; 1 : 2 **13.** 7 : 3; 7 : 3 **17.** 3 : 1; 9 : 1 **19.** 2 : 3; 4 : 9 **27.** $x = 2\sqrt{2}$ cm, $y = 3\sqrt{2}$ cm **29.** $x = \frac{8\sqrt{3}}{3}$ cm, $y = 4\sqrt{3}$ cm **35a.** $\frac{5}{2}$ **b.** $\frac{25}{4}$ **37a.** $\frac{2}{1}$ **b.** $\frac{4}{1}$ **51.** $5\frac{1}{3}$ cm; 12 cm **53.** 690 units^2 **55.** 44.4 units^2

57. $y = -x - 2$;

1 y x −3 O 1 3 −3 −5

61. Answers may vary. Sample: $y + 1 = \frac{8}{3}x$

Chapter Review pp. 461–463

1. similar **2.** Cross-Product Property **3.** golden rectangle **4.** similarity ratio **5.** proportion **6.** indirect measurement **7.** golden ratio **8.** 1 : 48 **9.** 1 : 24 **10.** True; use the Cross-Product Prop. **11.** True; the cross product is equivalent to the original proportion. **12.** False; the cross product is *not* equivalent to the original proportion. **13.** True; the cross product is equivalent to the original proportion. **14.** $\angle M \cong \angle R$, $\angle N \cong \angle S$, $\angle P \cong \angle T$; $\frac{MN}{RS} = \frac{MP}{RT} = \frac{NP}{ST}$ **15.** 39 in. **16.** 2 : 3 **17.** 2.5 : 1 or 5 : 2 **18.** 9 **19.** $x = 12$; $y = 15$ **20.** $\triangle XYZ \sim \triangle JKL$; SAS ~ Thm. **21.** No; corr. sides are not in prop. **22.** AA ~ Post. **23.** 13.5 ft **24.** $x = 15$; $y = 12$; $z = 20$ **25.** $x = 2\sqrt{21}$; $y = 4\sqrt{3}$; $z = 4\sqrt{7}$ **26.** $x = 2\sqrt{3}$; $y = 6$; $z = 4\sqrt{3}$ **27.** 7.5 **28.** 5.5 **29.** 37.5 **30.** 4 : 9 **31.** 9 : 4 **32.** 1 : 4 **33.** $2\sqrt{2}$: 5 **34.** 196 cm^2

Chapter 9

Lesson 9-1 pp. 472–475

EXERCISES **1.** $\frac{1}{2}$; 2 **3.** 1; 1 **5.** 12.3 **7.** 2.5 **9.** 21.4 **11.** 32 **13.** 48 **17.** 74.1 **19.** 114.5 **21.** 44 and 136 **27.** $w = 5$; $x = 4.7$ **29.** $w = 59$; $x = 36$ **31.** about 51° **33.** about 296 ft **35.** 71.6 **37.** 45.0 **47.** 42 **49.** 6 **51.** x **53.** 26.6 **55.** 78.7 **67.** obtuse **69.** right

Technology p. 476

1. It doesn't change. **3.** yes; sine **5.** It doesn't change; the ratio becomes larger as the angle becomes larger; 0; a large number; the values match tangent.

Lesson 9-2 pp. 479–481

EXERCISES **1.** $\frac{7}{25}$; $\frac{24}{25}$ **3.** $\frac{1}{2}$; $\frac{\sqrt{3}}{2}$ **5.** 8.3 **7.** 17.0 **11.** 21 **13.** 46 **19.** $\cos X \cdot \tan X = \frac{\text{adj.}}{\text{hyp.}} \cdot \frac{\text{opp.}}{\text{adj.}} = \frac{\text{opp.}}{\text{hyp.}} = \sin X$ **21.** No; the △ are ~ and the sine ratio for 35° is constant. **23.** $w = 37$; $x = 7.5$ **41.** 6.9 **43.** 18 **45.** $(36 + 18\sqrt{3})$ cm^2 **47.** $30\sqrt{3}$ mm^2

Lesson 9-3 pp. 484–488

EXERCISES **1.** ∠ of elevation from sub to boat **3.** ∠ of elevation from boat to lighthouse **9.** 34.2 ft **11.** 32.2 m **15.** 777.9 m **17.** 0.6 km **19.** 64° **21.** about 194 m **23.** 3300 m **25.** 46, 46 **27.** 20, 20 **31.** about 2.8 **33.** 370 m **45.** 85.2 m **47.** 45 **49.** 110 **55.** $y = 3$, $x = 2$; 16, 10, 10, 16

Lesson 9-4 pp. 493–497

EXERCISES **1.** ⟨602.2, 668.8⟩ **3.** ⟨37.5, −65.0⟩ **5.** 20° west of south

7. N, W, E, S, 50°

13. about 97 mi at 41° south of west **15.** about 54 mi/h; 22° north of east

17a. ⟨−9, −9⟩

b.

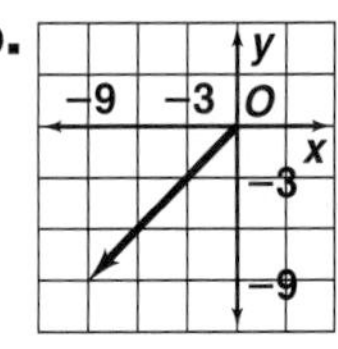

23. ⟨−1, 3⟩ **25.** ⟨−2, 3⟩ **27.** about 13.2° north of west **29.** Yes; both vectors have the same direction, but could have diff. mag.

31a.

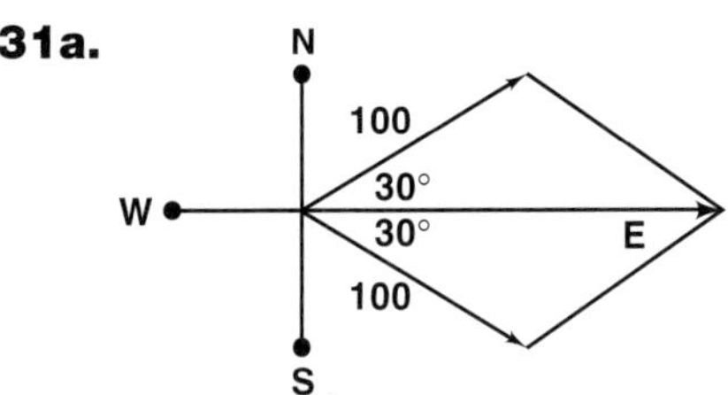

b. about 173 due east **33.** Vectors are ∥ if they have the same or opp. directions. **35a.** ⟨0, 0⟩ **b.** $\vec{a}$ and $\vec{c}$ have = mag. and opp. direction.

37. $\begin{bmatrix} -1 \\ -2 \end{bmatrix}$ **39.** $\begin{bmatrix} -1 \\ 0 \end{bmatrix}$ **43.** ⟨0, −4⟩

45. The vectors have the same mag.; the vectors have opp. directions. **47a.** 15° south of west **b.** about 6.7 h **57.** $\frac{1}{8}$ **59.** $\frac{1}{3}$

Lesson 9-5 pp. 500–503

EXERCISES **1.** 173.8 cm^2 **3.** 259.8 m^2 **7.** 47.0 $in.^2$ **9.** 8 ft^2 **11.** 27.7 m^2 **13.** 7554.0 m^2 **17.** 5523 yd^2 **21.** \$51.96 **23.** 45.3 in.; 128 $in.^2$ **29.** (area of pent. A) ≈ 1.53 · (area of pent. B) **31.** (area of oct. B) ≈ 1.17 · (area of oct. A) **33.** 5.0 ft^2 **43.** ⟨−2, −9⟩ **45.** ⟨−6, −1⟩ **47.** $\frac{376\pi}{45}$ cm^2 **49.** $\frac{63\pi}{8}$ m^2 **51.** $\left(\frac{a}{2}, \frac{b}{2}\right)$; $\sqrt{a^2 + b^2}$

Chapter Review pp. 505–507

1. vector **2.** angle of elevation **3.** cosine **4.** sine **5.** identity **6.** resultant vector **7.** magnitude; initial point; terminal point **8.** 42 **9.** 2 **10.** 2 **11.** 67 **12.** 23 **13.** 42 **14.** 12 **15.** 8 **16.** $\frac{\sqrt{3}}{2}$, $\frac{1}{2}$, $\sqrt{3}$ **17.** $\frac{\sqrt{19}}{10}$, $\frac{9}{10}$, $\frac{\sqrt{19}}{9}$ **18.** $\frac{4}{5}$, $\frac{3}{5}$, $\frac{4}{3}$ **19.** 51 **20.** 16.5 **21.** 33

22. 1410 ft **23.** 280 ft **24.** about 38.2 yd **25.** They are alt. int. ∆s to ∥ lines. **26.** ⟨125.8, 81.7⟩ **27.** ⟨37.5, −92.7⟩ **28.** ⟨−21.8, 33.5⟩ **29.** about 167.7 mi; about 26.6° east of south **30.** about 206.2 km; about 14.0° west of south **31.** about 503.1 mi/h; about 26.6° north of west **32.** ⟨6, 8⟩, ⟨9, 12⟩, ⟨30, 40⟩; ⟨*x*, *y*⟩ and ⟨*nx*, *ny*⟩ have the same direction for $n > 0$.

33. N, 25°, W, E, S **34.** N, 45°, W, E, S

35. N, 60°, W, E, S

36. ⟨1, 4⟩ **37.** ⟨4, −6⟩ **38.** ⟨2, 0⟩ **39a.** about 67.4° south of west **b.** about 39 min **40.** 73.5 ft^2 **41.** 232.5 cm^2 **42.** 124.7 in.^{2} **43.** 8 m^2 **44.** 100.8 cm^2 **45.** 88.4 ft^2 **46.** 70.4 m^2

Chapter 10

Lesson 10-1 pp. 514–516

EXERCISES **1.** yes; *E* and *C*, *B* and *D*, *A* and *F* **3.** yes; *A* and *C*, *B* and *E*, *D* and *F* **5.** Yes; the faces only share one edge. **7.** C **9.** B **11.** Answers may vary. Sample:

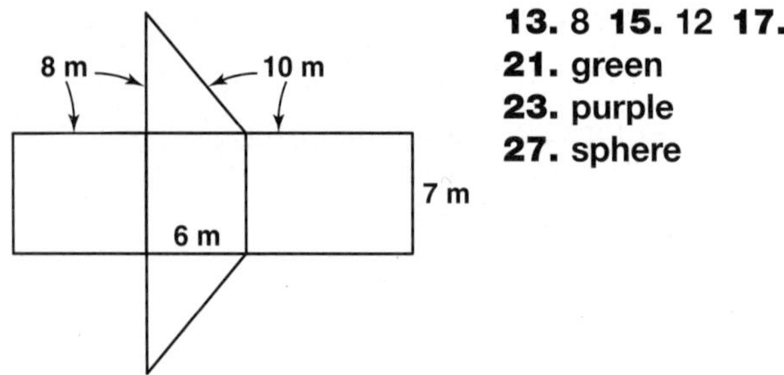

13. 8 **15.** 12 **17.** 5 **21.** green **23.** purple **27.** sphere

29a. A. icosahedron B. octahedron C. tetrahedron D. hexahedron E. dodecahedron **b.** reg. triangular pyramid, cube **c.** $4 + 4 = 6 + 2$; $6 + 8 = 12 + 2$; $8 + 6 = 12 + 2$ **31.** 60 **41.** $\sqrt{145}$ cm **43.** $5\sqrt{5}$ mm **45.** 20 **47.** 105

Extension p. 519

1. two-point **3.** one-point

7.

9.

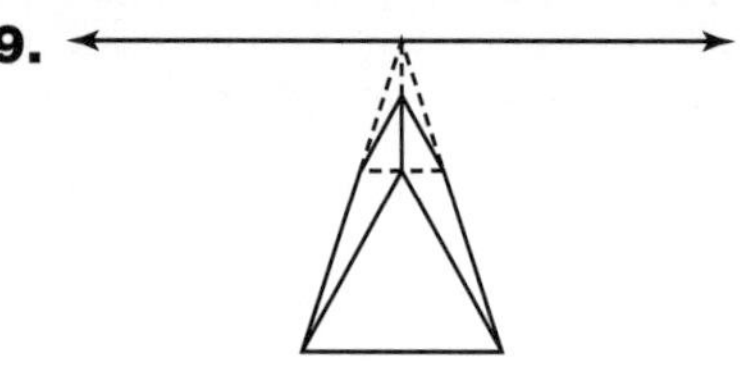

15. Answer may vary. Sample: The horizontal lines appear to be curved; the slanted lines that would meet at the vanishing pt. create a cylinder effect.

Lesson 10-2 pp. 523–526

EXERCISES

1. **3.**

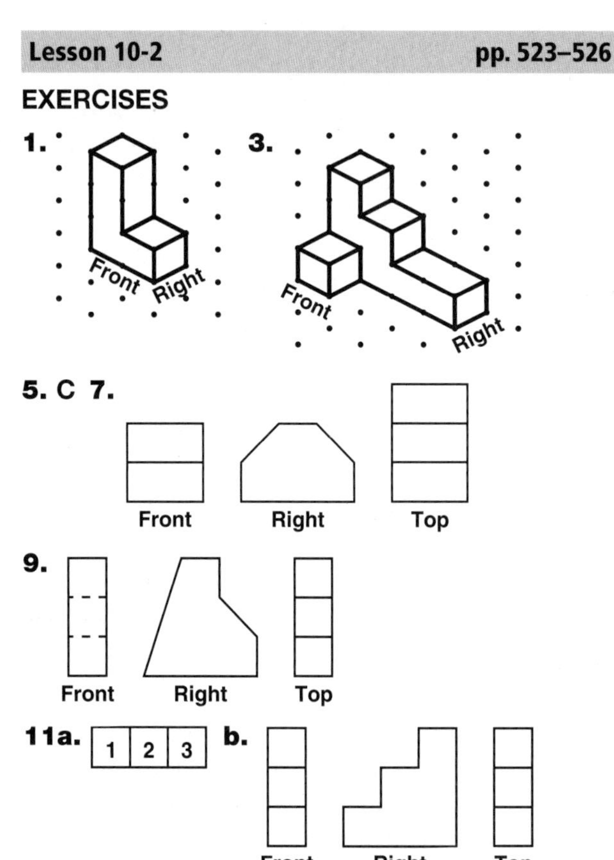

5. C **7.**

9.

11a. **b.**

13. 6 **15.** 8 **17.** regular hexagon with hexagonal hole **19.** rectangle **21.** square

25a.

b.

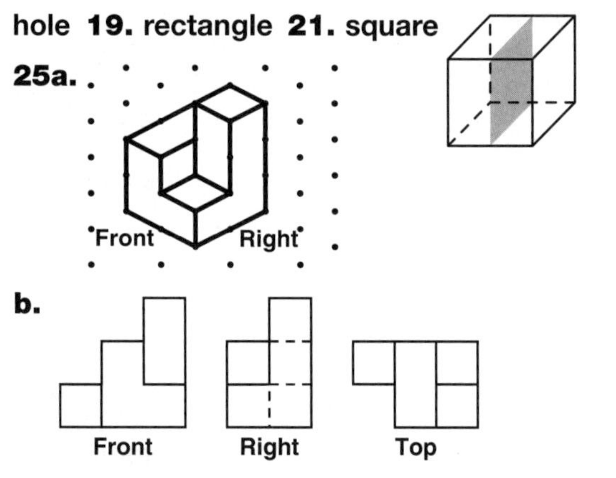

27. 1 **29.** 3 **31.** orthographic top view

33.

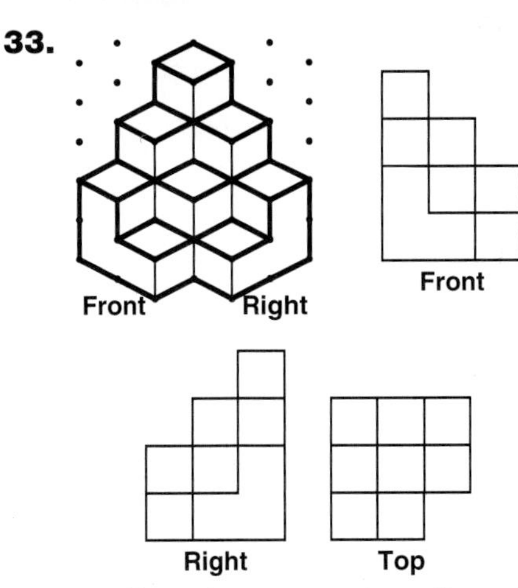

35–39. Drawings may vary. Samples are given.

35a.

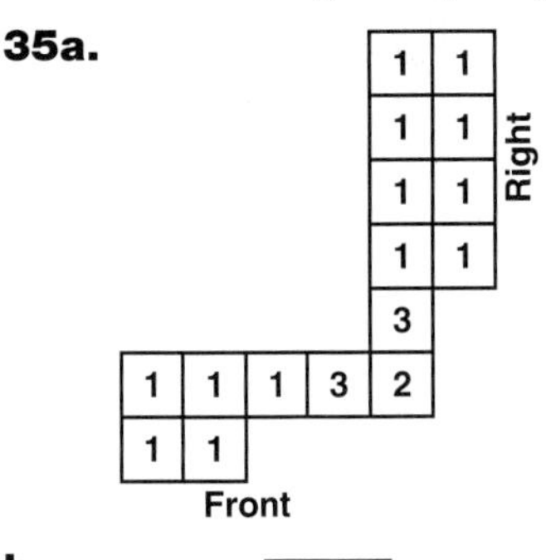

b.

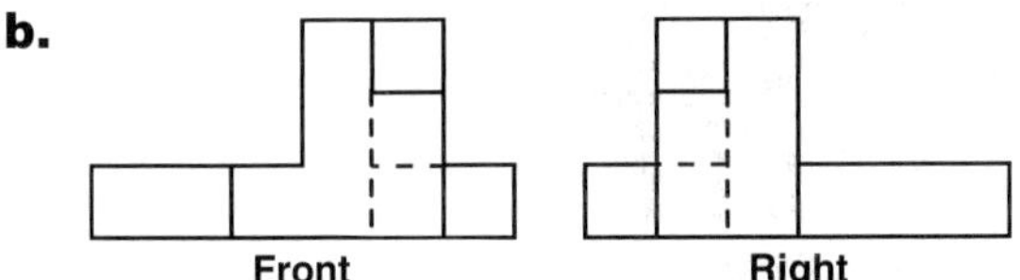

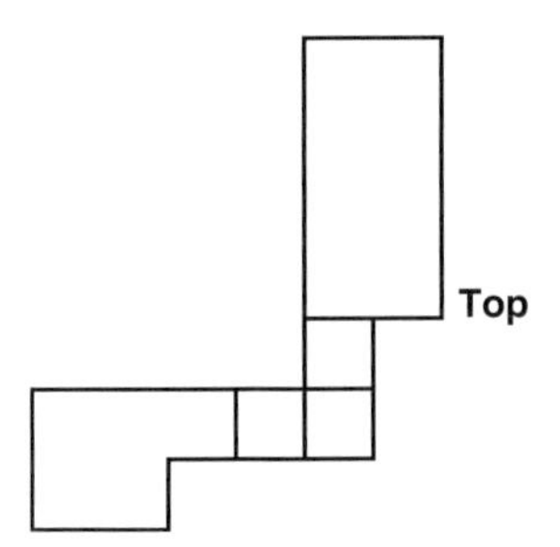

37. rectangle **39.** triangle

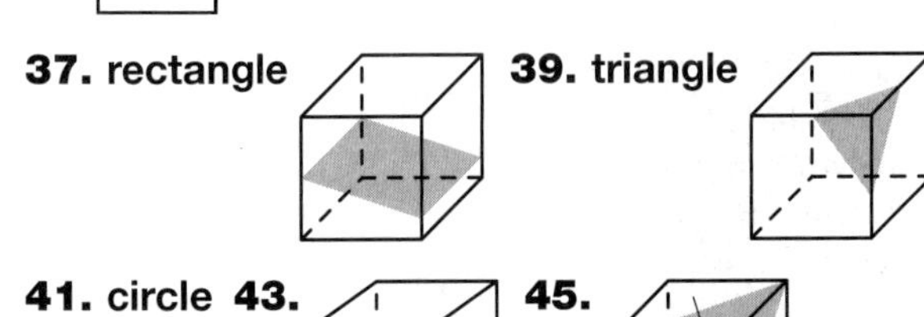

41. circle **43.** **45.**

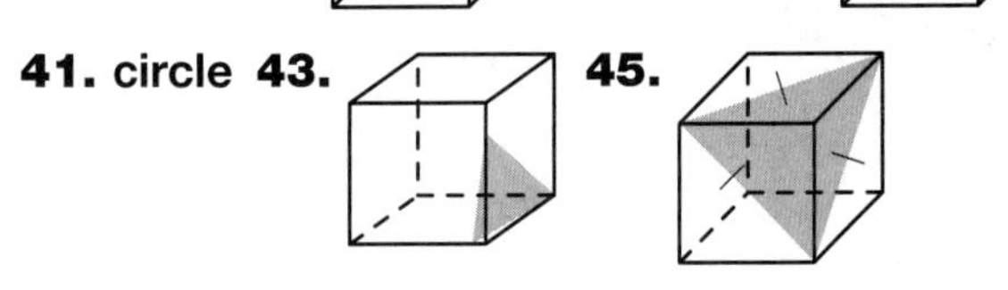

57. Answers may vary. Sample:

3 cm, 4 cm, 4 cm, 5 cm, 3 cm

59. 4.7 **61.** 67 and 113 **63.** $192\sqrt{3}$ cm^2

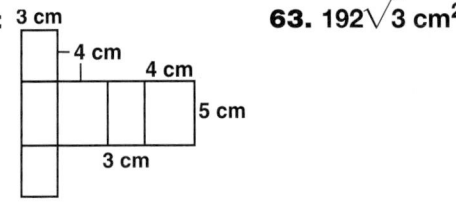

Lesson 10-3 pp. 531–535

EXERCISES **1.** 1726 cm^2 **3.** 125.6 in.^{2}

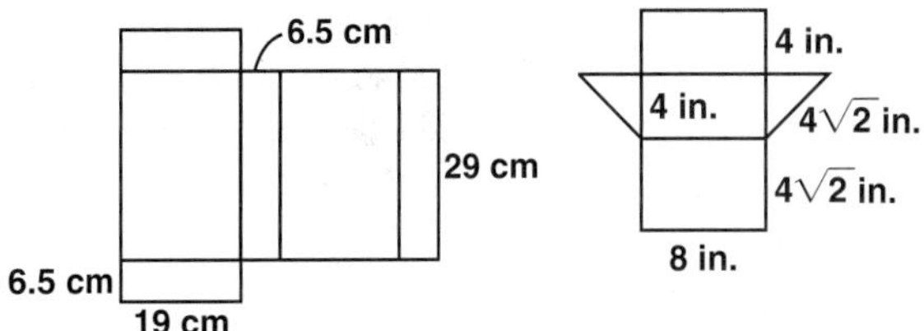

5. 120 ft^2; 220 ft^2 **7.** 880 cm^2; 1121 cm^2 **9.** 16.5π cm^2 **11.** 36.8 cm^2 **13.** 107 in.^{2} **15.** 1407 cm^2 **17.** 150 cm^2 **19.** 4080 mm^2 **23.** 47.5 in.^{2} **25a.** 7 units **b.** 196π units^2 **27.** cylinder of radius 4 and height 2; 48π units^2 **29.** cylinder of radius 2 and height 4; 24π units^2

45.

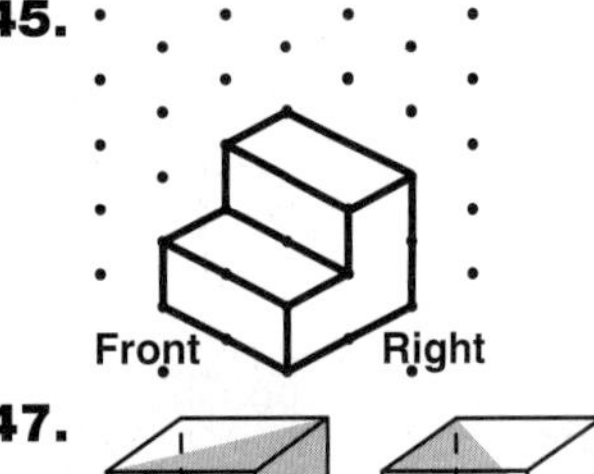

47.

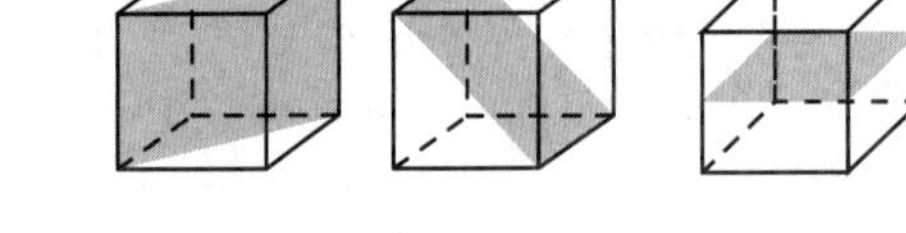

49. 22.1 cm^2

Technology p. 536

1–3. Answers may vary. Samples are given.

1. 600 cm^2; 5080 cm^2 **3.** about 4.64 cm by 4.64 cm by 4.64 cm

Lesson 10-4 pp. 540–543

EXERCISES **1.** 408 in.^{2} **3.** 179 in.^{2} **5.** 12 in. **7.** 204 m^2 **9.** 51 m^2 **11.** 156 ft^2 **13.** 33π ft^2 **15.** 13 m **17.** 11 yd **19.** 31 m^2 **23.** 228.1 in.^{2}

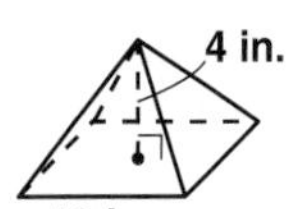

25. 478 cm^2 **27.** 28 in.^{2} **31.** 58 m^2 **33.** 45 m^2

37. $s = 12$ m, L.A. = 240 m^2, S.A. = 384 m^2
39. $s = 8$ cm, $\ell = 7.4$ cm, $h = 6.2$ cm
41. $\ell = 6.5$ m, $C = 25.1$ m, S.A. = 132.0 m^2
43. $r = 1.0$ ft, S.A. = 36.4 ft^2, $C = 6.3$ ft
47. cone with $r = 3$ and $h = 4$; 24π
61. 76 ft^2 **63.** about 281.7 m **65.** 26 in.

Lesson 10-5 pp. 547–550

EXERCISES **1.** 216 ft^3 **3.** 180 m^3 **5.** about 280.6 cm^3 **7.** 720 mm^3 **9.** 288π in.^{3}, 904.8 in.^{3} **11.** 37.5π m^3, 117.8 in.^{3} **13.** 3445 in.^{3} **15.** 501 in.^{3} **17.** $\frac{26}{9}$ cm **19.** 6 ft **21.** 28–42 pots **25.** 80 units^3 **27.** 3 cm **29.** cylinder with $r = 2$ and $h = 4$; 16π units^3 **31.** cylinder with $r = 2$ and $h = 4$; 16π units^3 **33.** 125.7 cm^3 **47.** 469.2 ft^2 **49.** 70; 110, 70 **51.** 50; 14, 144, 148, 54

Lesson 10-6 pp. 554–557

EXERCISES **1.** about 233,333 ft^3 **3.** 1296 in.^{3} **5.** about 443.7 cm^3 **7.** 2048 m^3 **9.** about 3714.5 mm^3 **11.** $\frac{16}{3}\pi$ ft^3; 17 ft^3 **13.** 36.75π in.^{3}; 115 in.^{3} **15.** $\approx$ 4.7 cm^3 **17.** 312 cm^3 **19.** They are equal; both volumes are $\frac{1}{3}\pi r^2 h$. **21.** 6 **23.** $3\sqrt{2}$ **27a.** 120π ft^3 **b.** 60π ft^3 **c.** 240π ft^3 **29.** cone with $r = 4$ and $h = 3$; 16π **43.** 7.1 in.^{3} **45.** 59.4 in.^{2} **47.** 57.7 in.^{2}

Lesson 10-7 pp. 560–564

EXERCISES **1.** 900π m^2 **3.** 1024π mm^2 **5.** 4624π mm^2 **7.** $\frac{121}{16}\pi$ in.^{2} **9.** 232 in.^{2} **11.** 154 in.^{2} **13.** 288π cm^3; 905 cm^3 **15.** $\frac{2048}{3}\pi$ cm^3; 2145 cm^3 **19.** 1006 m^2 **21.** S.A. $\approx$ 108 cm^2, $V \approx$ 108 cm^3 **27.** 1.7 lb **29.** $\frac{4}{3}\pi$ m^3 **31.** $\frac{9}{2}\pi$ ft^3 **41.** 26π cm^2; $\frac{62}{3}\pi$ cm^3 **61.** 19 in.^{3} **63.** 35, 55 **65.** 10.5 cm **67.** 67.5 cm^2

Technology p. 565

1. The ratio of volumes is the similarity ratio cubed. **3.** The ratio of volumes is the similarity ratio cubed. **5.** The ratio of surface areas is the similarity ratio squared.

Lesson 10-8 pp. 568–571

EXERCISES **1.** no **3.** yes; 2 : 3 **7.** 5 : 6 **9.** 3 : 4 **11.** 27 in.^{3} **13.** 24 ft^3 **15.** 16 m^2 **17.** 6000 toothpicks **19a.** It is 64 times the smaller prism. **b.** It is 64 times the smaller prism. **23.** about 1000 cm^3 **27a.** 3 : 1 **b.** 9 : 1 **29.** 864 in.^{3} **31.** 9 : 25; 27 : 125 **33.** 5 : 8; 25 : 64 **43.** 1790 cm^2 and 1937 cm^2 **45.** 8.2 m^2; 19.6 m^2 **47a.** $8\sqrt{3}$ mm 809 **b.** $4\sqrt{21}$ mm **c.** $8\sqrt{7}$ mm **49.** 13.125

Chapter Review pp. 573–575

1. sphere **2.** net **3.** pyramid **4.** cross section **5.** right

6. **7.**

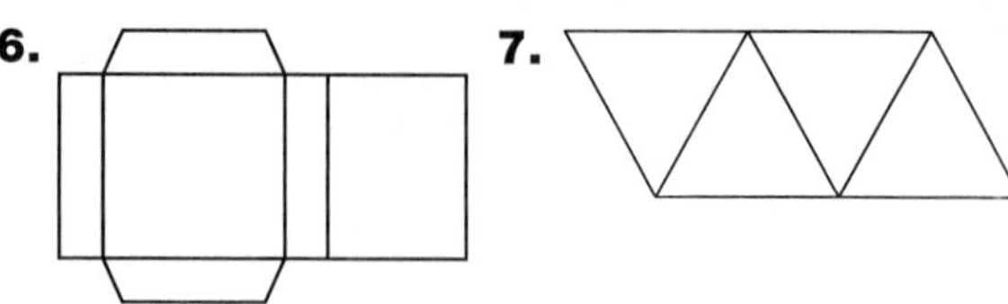

8. **9.** 8 **10.** 8

11a.

Front Right

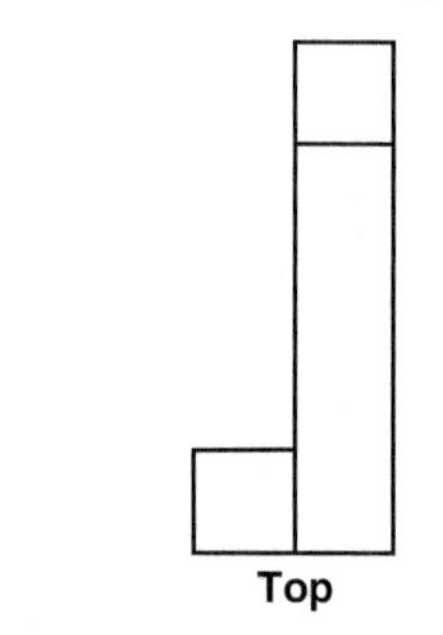

Top

b.

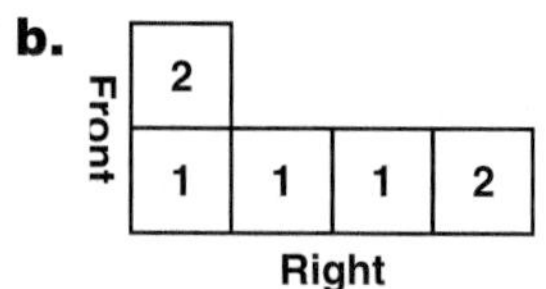

Right

12.

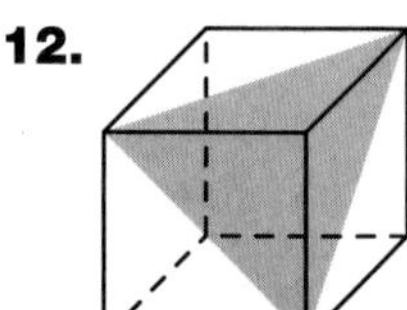

13. 36 cm^2; 12 cm^3 **14.** 66π m^2; 72π m^3 **15.** 208 in.^{2}; 192 in.^{3} **16.** 60π ft^2; $\frac{160}{3}\pi$ ft^3

17. 672 m^2; 512 m^3 **18.** 16π in.^{2}; $\frac{16\sqrt{2}}{3}\pi$ in.^{3} **19.** 314.2 in.^{2}; 523.6 in.^{3} **20.** 153.9 cm^2; 179.6 cm^3 **21.** 50.3 ft^2; 33.5 ft^3 **22.** 8.0 ft^2; 2.1 ft^3 **23.** 8.6 in.^{3} **24.** Answers may vary. Sample:

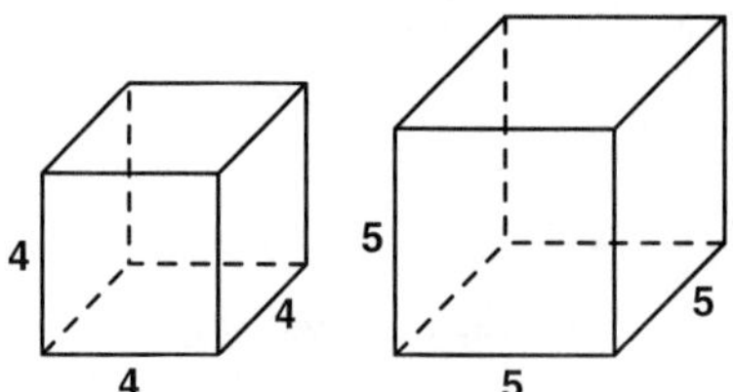

25. 27 : 64 **26.** 64 : 27

Chapter 11

Lesson 11-1 pp. 586–589

EXERCISES **1.** 120 **3.** 30 **7.** 20.0 in. **9.** 19.1 cm **11.** Yes; $2.5^2 + 6^2 = 6.5^2$ **13.** inscribed in **15.** circumscribed about **17.** 14.2 in. **21.** 3.6 cm **25.** 80.0 km **27.** 57.5 **29.** about 34.6 in. **33.** 35 **37.** a–c.

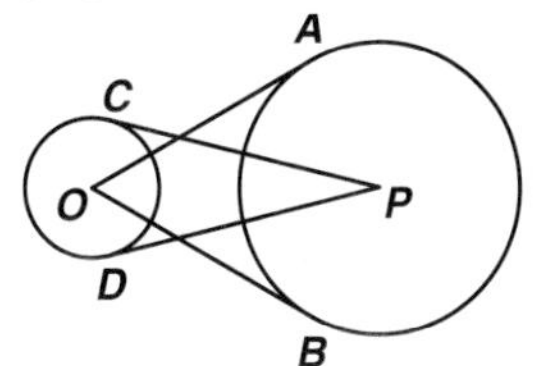

d. $\overline{AB} \parallel \overline{CD}$; arguments may vary.

49. 9:16 **51.** 29.1 **53.** 68.2 **55a.** 4:1 **b.** $a = 1.625$; $b = 1.75$, $c = 3$

Lesson 11-2 pp. 593–596

EXERCISES **1.** $\widehat{BC} \cong \widehat{YZ}$; $\overline{BC} \cong \overline{YZ}$ **3.** 14 **5.** 7 **9.** Answers may vary. Samples are given. **a.** $\overline{CE}$ **b.** $\overline{DE}$ **c.** $\angle CEB$ **d.** $\angle DEA$ **11.** 6 **13.** 8.9 **17.** 108 **19.** about 123.9 **21.** 12 cm **31.** 10 cm **33.** 8 **47.** 40 **49.** about 42 ft

Lesson 11-3 pp. 601–605

EXERCISES **1.** $\angle ACB$; $\widehat{AB}$ **3.** $\angle MPN$; $\widehat{MN}$ **5.** 58 **7.** $a = 218$; $b = 109$ **11.** $x = 36$; $y = 36$ **13.** $a = 50$; $b = 90$; $c = 90$ **15.** $w = 123$ **17.** $e = 65$; $f = 130$ **21a.** 96 **b.** 55 **c.** 77 **d.** 154 **23a.** 30 **b.** 78 **c.** 95 **d.** 105 **e.** 85 **f.** 75 **27a.** $77\frac{1}{7}°$ **b.** 36° **29.** about 7.1 cm by 7.1 cm **31.** about 7.1 cm legs, and a 10 cm base

33. false

35. true

37a. $\angle CEF$, $\angle FEG$, $\angle GFD$ and $\angle GED$ **b.** $\angle CED$ **c.** $\angle EFG$ and $\angle EDG$; $\angle FED$ and $\angle FGD$ **51.** 17.3 **53.** 17.5 **55.** 64.5 cm^2 **57.** Both have rt. ∡ and the vertical ∡ are ≅, so ▵ are ~ by AA ~ Post.

Technology pp. 606

1. The prod. of the lengths of the segments of one chord = the prod. of the lengths of the segments of the other chord.

3. The products are =. For $\overline{DG}$, the secant segment and its external segment are the same.

Lesson 11-4 pp. 611–613

EXERCISES **1.** 46 **3.** $x = 60$; $y = 70$ **7.** 160° **9.** 15 **11.** 13.2 **15.** about 270.8 ft **17.** $360 - x$ **19.** $180 - y$ **21.** 16.7 **23.** $x \approx 10.7$; $y = 10$ **25.** $x \approx 10.9$; $y \approx 2.3$ **27.** 95, 104, 86, 75 **29.** Answers may vary. Sample: Since they are inscribed ∡: $m\angle BED = \frac{1}{2}m\widehat{BD}$ and $m\angle ABE = \frac{1}{2}m\widehat{AE}$. Apply the Ext. ∠ Thm. to $\triangle BCE$ to prove that $m\angle C = \frac{1}{2}(m\widehat{AE} - m\widehat{BD})$. **31.** Given: a circle with secant segments $\overline{XV}$ and $\overline{ZV}$; Prove: $XV \cdot WV = ZV \cdot YV$.

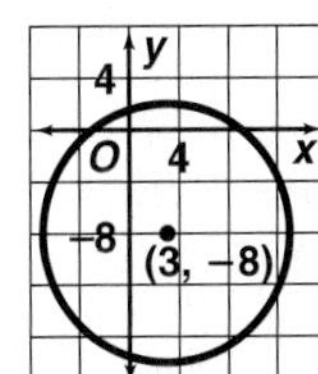

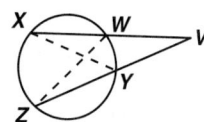

1. Construct $\overline{XY}$ and $\overline{ZW}$. **2.** $\angle XVY \cong \angle ZVW$ (Reflexive Prop. of ≅) **3.** $\angle VXY \cong \angle WZV$ (2 inscribed ∡ that intercept the same arc are ≅.) **4.** $\triangle XVY \sim \triangle ZVW$ (AA~) **5.** $\frac{XV}{ZV} = \frac{YV}{WV}$ (In similar figures, corr. sides are proport.) **6.** $XV \cdot WV = YV \cdot ZV$ (Prop. of Proport.) **43.** $a = 50$; $b = 55$; $c = 105$ **45.** 30 **47.** 57

Extension p. 614

1. *ACD*; *HGA*; *EFA* **3.** The radius of the circle is 1, which is the denominator in each of the ratios. **5.** On the unit circle, secant $A = \frac{\text{hyp.}}{1} = \text{hyp.} =$ length of $\overline{DA}$, the secant segment. **7.** $(\text{tangent } A)^2 = \left(\frac{DC}{CA}\right)^2 = \left(\frac{EB}{BA}\right)^2 = \frac{(EB)^2}{(BA)^2} = \frac{(EA)^2 - (BA)^2}{(BA)^2} = \frac{(EA)^2}{(BA)^2} - 1 = (\text{secant } A)^2 - 1$ **9.** $\text{cotangent } A = \frac{HG}{GA} = \frac{CA}{CD} = \frac{1}{\frac{CD}{CA}} = \frac{1}{\text{tangent } A}$ **11.** $\text{secant } A = \frac{EA}{AB} = \frac{EA}{EF} = \frac{1}{\frac{EF}{EA}} = \frac{1}{\text{cosine } A}$

Lesson 11-5 pp. 617–620

EXERCISES **1.** $(x - 2)^2 + (y + 8)^2 = 81$ **3.** $(x - 0.2)^2 + (y - 1.1)^2 = 0.16$ **11.** $(x - 1)^2 + (y - 2)^2 = 17$ **13.** $(x + 10)^2 + (y + 5)^2 = 125$ **17.** center: (3, −8); radius: 10

23. $(x - 4)^2 + (y + 4)^2 = 4$ **25.** position: (5, 7); range: 9 units **27.** $x^2 + y^2 = 4$ **29.** $x^2 \pm (y - 3)^2 \neq 4$ **33.** $(x - 4)^2 + (y - 3)^2 = 25$ **35.** $(x - 3)^2 + (y - 3)^2 = 8$ **39.** $x^2 + y^2 = 1$ **43.** No; the *x* and *y* terms are not squared. **45.** circumference: 16π; area: 64π

49. 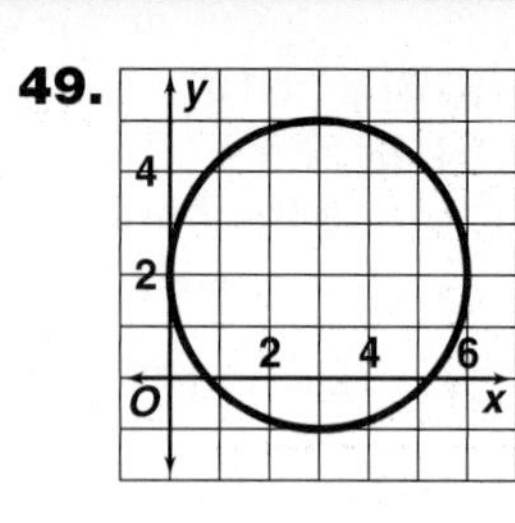

53. (3, 2); (2, 3)

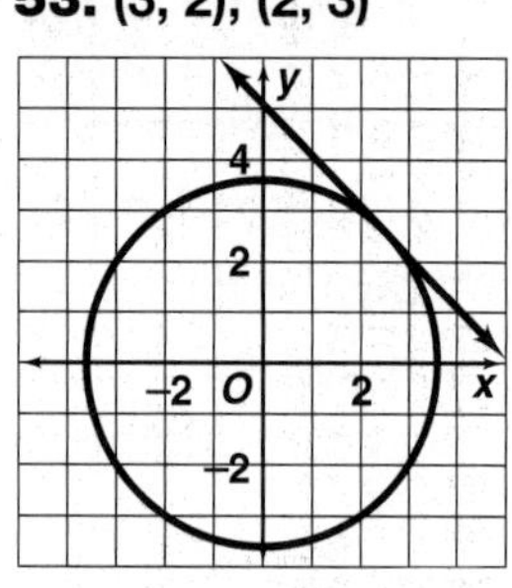

71. 38 **73.** $\langle -5, 2\rangle$ **75.** $\langle 11, -7\rangle$ **77.** $9\sqrt{3}$ **79.** 3

Lesson 11-6 pp. 623–625

EXERCISES 1. a circle of radius 4 cm with center *X*

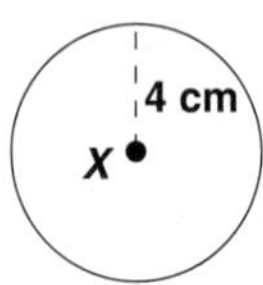

3. two distinct lines ∥ to $\overleftrightarrow{LM}$ and 3 mm from $\overleftrightarrow{LM}$

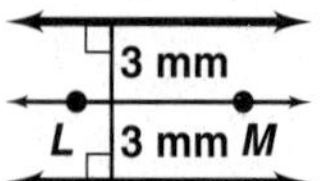

9. the single pt. *L* **11.** the single pt. *N*

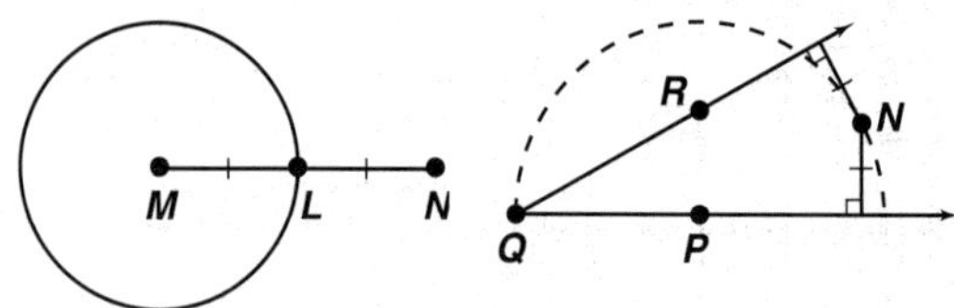

15. an endless cylinder with radius 4 cm and center-line $\overleftrightarrow{DE}$

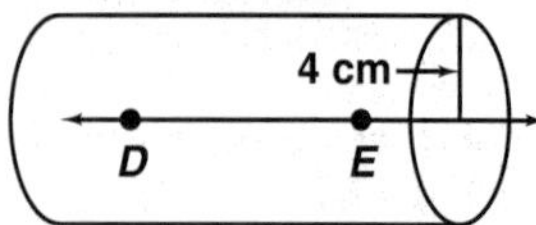

17. an endless cylinder with radius 5 mm and center-ray $\overrightarrow{PQ}$ and a hemisphere of radius 5 mm centered at *P*

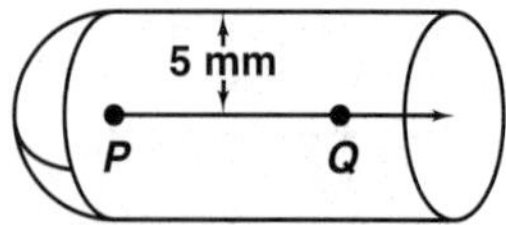

19. the set of all points 2 units from the origin
23. $y = x$ **25.** $y = -x + 3$

27. **29.** **33.**

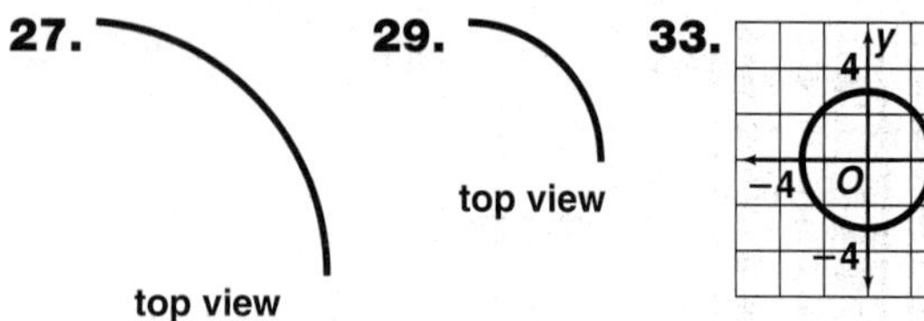

35. 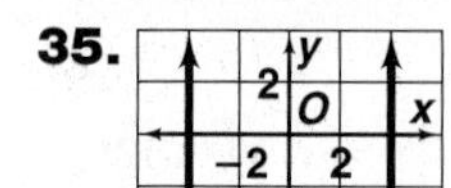

41. a circle **55.** $(x - 1)^2 + (y - 7)^2 = 36$ **57.** 510 in.^{2} **59.** 4π **61.** 10π

Chapter Review pp. 627–629

1. tangent to **2.** chord **3.** inscribed in **4.** inscribed angle **5.** locus **6.** 57 in. **7.** 72 mm **8.** 9.8 cm **9.** 4.3 **10.** 19.5 **11.** 6.4 **12.** 4.5 **13.** $a = 40$; $b = 140$; $c = 90$ **14.** $a = 118$; $b = 49$; $= 144$; $d = 98$ **15.** $a = 90$; $b = 90$; $c = 70$; $d = 65$ **16.** $a = 95$; $b = 85$ **17.** 37 **18.** $x = 57$; $y = 44.5$; $z = 129$; $v = 51$ **19.** 17.1 **20.** 4 **21.** 21.1 **22.** $(x - 2)^2 + (y - 5)^2 = 12.25$ **23.** $(x + 3)^2 + (y - 1)^2 = 5$ **24.** $(x - 9)^2 + (y + 4)^2 = 16$ **25.** $x^2 + (y - 1)^2 = 80$ **26.** $(x + 2)^2 + (y - 3)^2 = 85$ **27.** $(x - 10)^2 + (y - 7)^2 = 468$ **28.** center = (0, 8); $r = 7$ **29.** center = (5, −9); $r = 2\sqrt{10}$ **30.** center = (−1, 0); $r = 3$

31. a circle of radius 3 cm **32.** the ⊥ bis. of the segment between the pts.

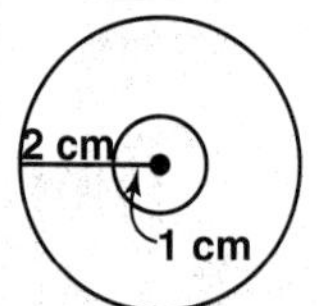

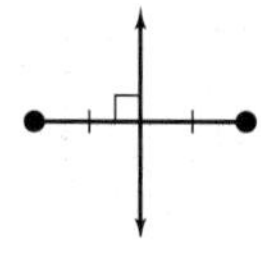

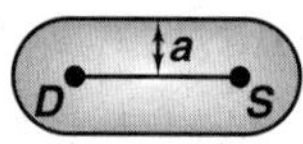

33. a cylinder with hemispherical ends

Chapter 12

Lesson 12-1 pp. 636–639

EXERCISES 1. Yes; the trans. is a slide. **3.** No; the figures are not ≅. **5a.** Answers may vary. Sample: $\angle R \rightarrow \angle R'$ **b.** $\overline{RI}$ and $\overline{R'I'}$; $\overline{IT}$ and $\overline{I'T'}$; $\overline{RT}$ and $\overline{R'T'}$ **7a.** Answers may vary. Sample: $G \rightarrow M$ **b.** $\overline{GW}$ and $\overline{MR}$; $\overline{WP}$ and $\overline{RT}$; $\overline{PN}$ and $\overline{TX}$; $\overline{NB}$ and $\overline{XS}$; $\overline{BG}$ and $\overline{SM}$

11. 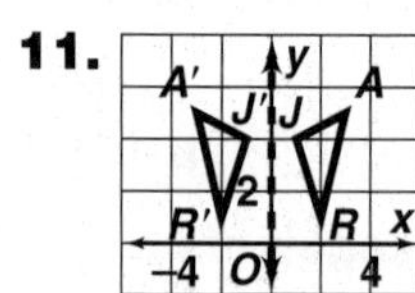

13. 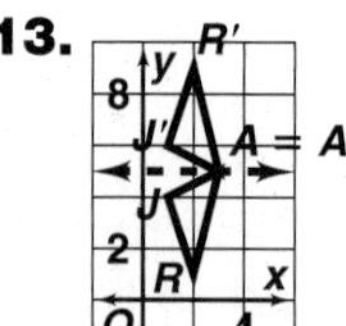

19. Reflect point *D* over the mirrored wall. Connect this point and *C*. The intersection of the segment and the wall is the point to focus the camera.

21. 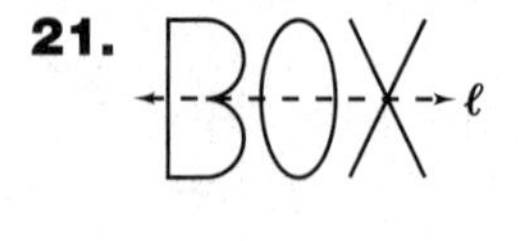

23. 

25. S-Isomer **27.** (x, y) has image $(x, -y)$. **29.** (x, y) has image (y, x). **31.** $x^2 + y^2 = 49$ **33.** $x^2 + (y + 3)^2 = 9$ **37.** $(0, -6)$ **39.** $(0, 0)$ **63a.** 4 : 3 **b.** 64 : 27

Lesson 12-2 pp. 643–646

EXERCISES **1.** $\langle 2, 5 \rangle$ is a translation of 2 units to the right and 5 units up. **3.** $\langle -3, 8 \rangle$ is a translation of 3 units to the left and 8 units up. **7.** $\langle -2, -1 \rangle$ **9.** $\langle 8, 10 \rangle$ **11.** *H* **13.** *E* **17.** $\langle 5, 5 \rangle$ **19.** $\langle 0, -2 \rangle$ **23.** $(x, y) \rightarrow (x + 1, y - 1)$ **25.** $(x, y) \rightarrow (x + 4, y - 2)$ **27.** (1, −2), (4, 1), (10, −2), (7, −5) **29.** (−4, −0.5), (−2, −3), (−1, 4), (5, 0)

35.

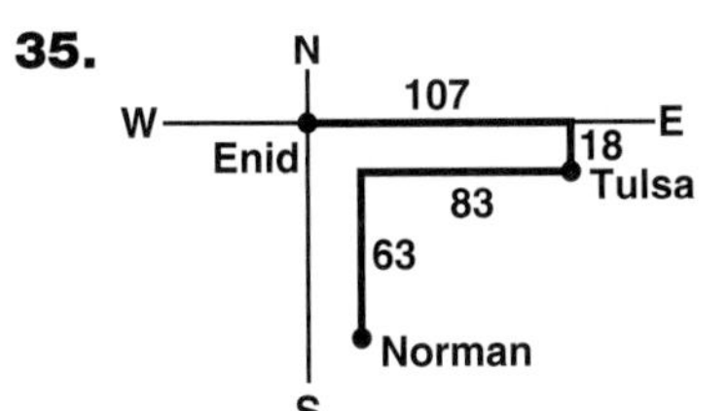

Norman is 24 mi east and 81 mi south of Enid.

37. $(x, y) \rightarrow (x - 3, y + 1)$ **39.** $U'(1, 16)$, $G'(2, 12)$ **43.** $\langle 0, 0 \rangle$ **45.** $\langle 13, -2.5 \rangle$

47.

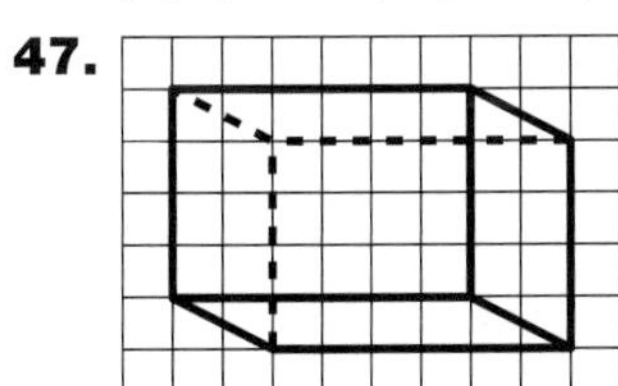

49.

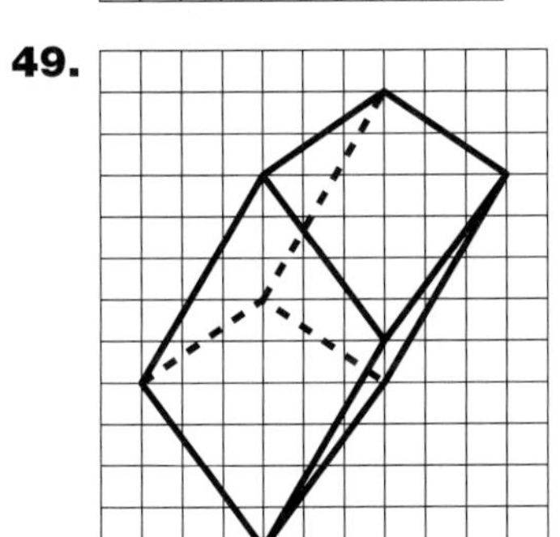

Lesson 12-3 pp. 649–652

EXERCISES

1.

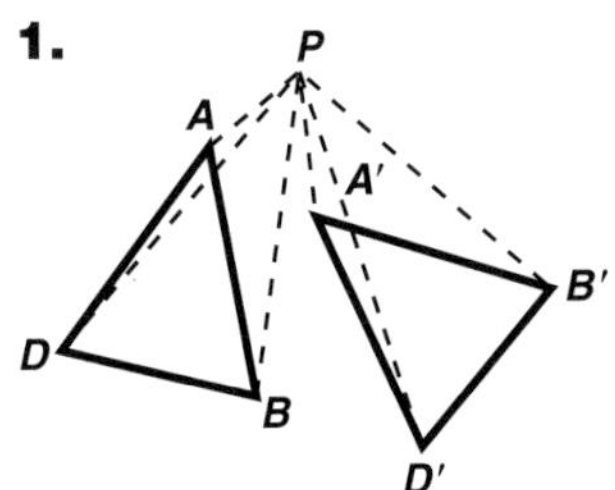

3.

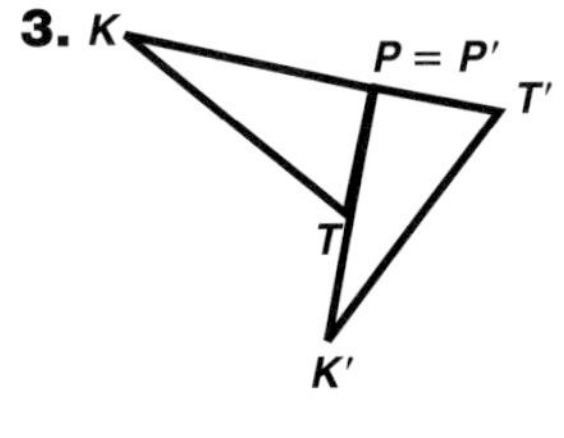

5. **7.**

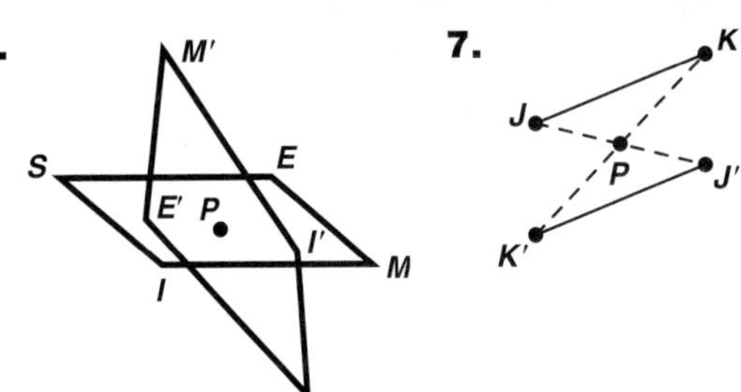

9.

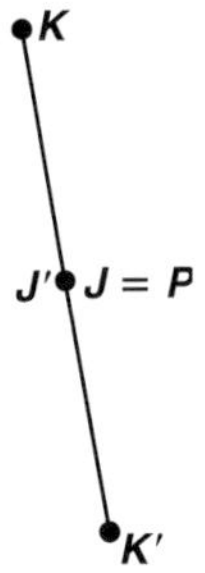

11. *M* **13.** $\overline{BC}$ **19.** 108°; 252°

21.

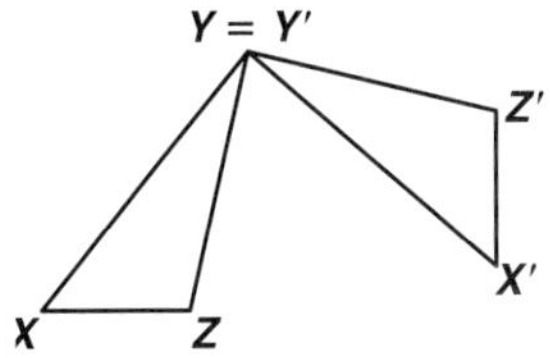

23.

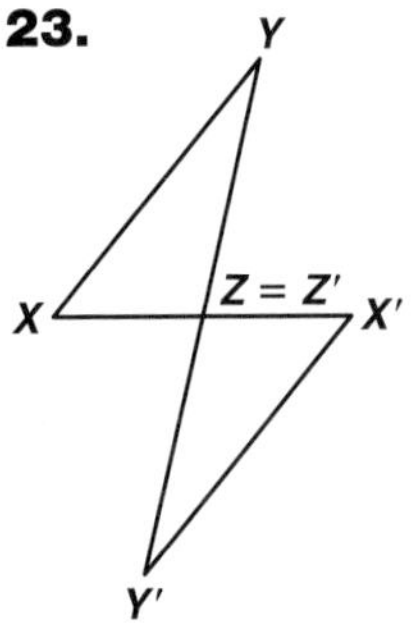

27. 180° rotation about its center **29.** Answers may vary. Sample: 110

31.

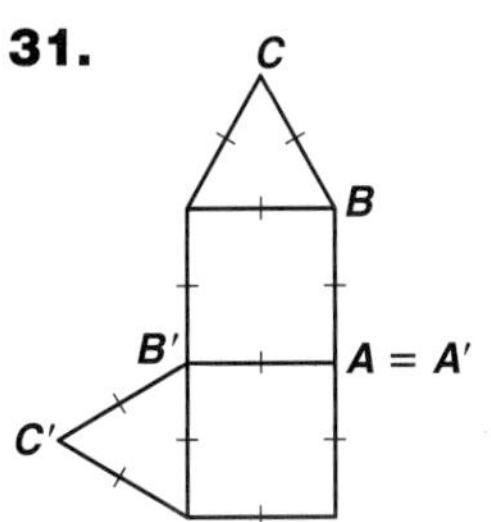

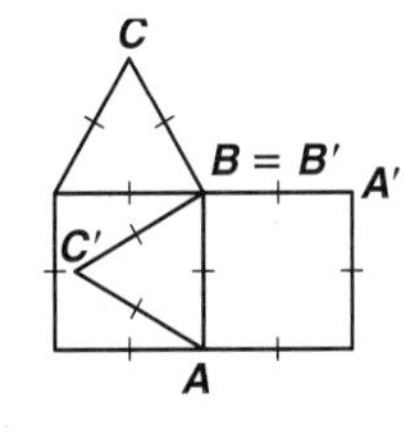

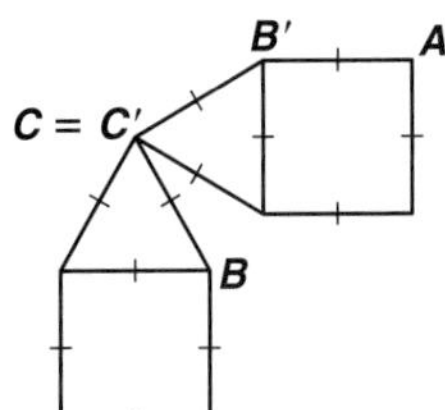

41. $(x, y) \rightarrow (x - 5), (y - 1)$ **43.** about 431.7 mi at 76.6° south of east

Lesson 12-4 pp. 657–660

EXERCISES **1.** rotation **3.** Neither; the figures do not have the same orientation.

5.

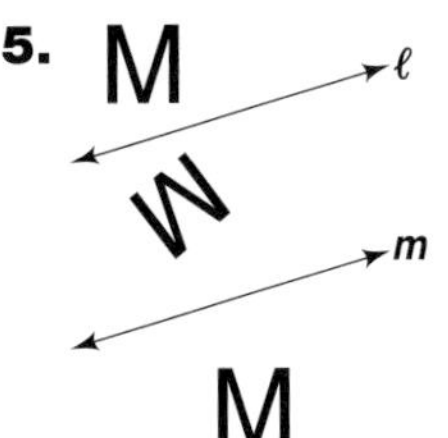

M is translated across line *m* twice the distance between ℓ and *m*.

Selected Answers

7. 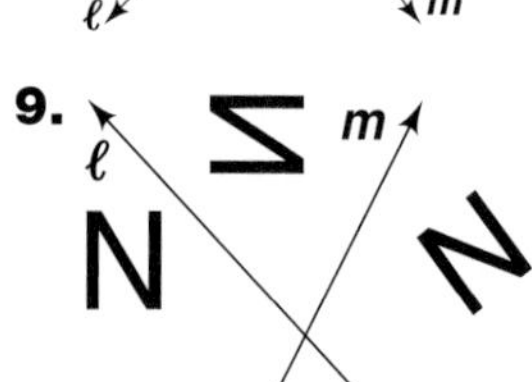

L is rotated clockwise about 180°.

9. 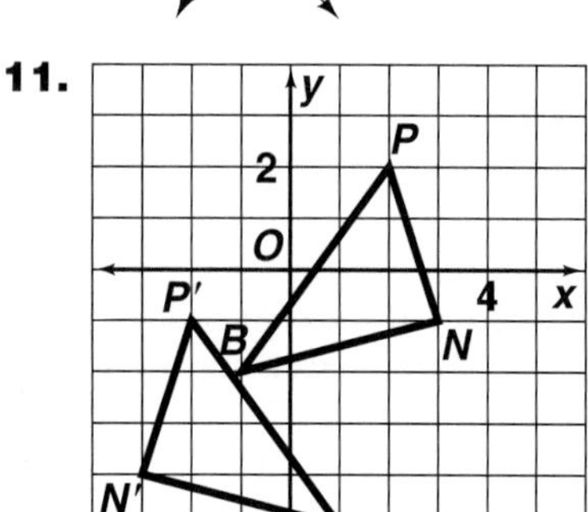

N is rotated clockwise about 160°.

11. 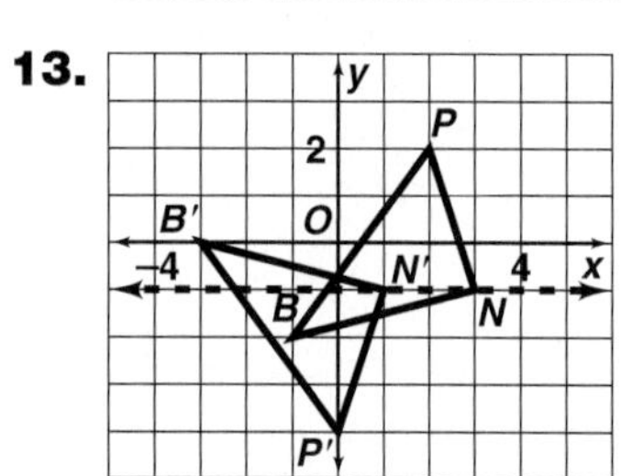

13.

19. opp.; glide reflection **21.** same; rotation **27.** reflection **29.** rotation **35.** 60 **37.** 30 **39.** glide reflection; $\langle 11, 0\rangle$, $y = 0$ **41.** reflection; $y = 0$ **63.** 123 **65.** 87 **67.** 15 cm **69.** 5.5 m

Lesson 12-5 pp. 664–666

EXERCISES

1. line

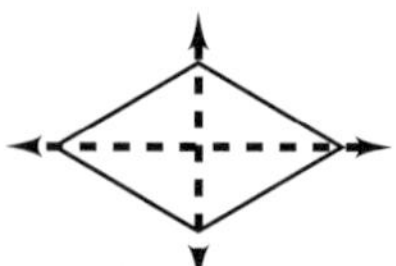

3. rotational: 90°

13.

15. 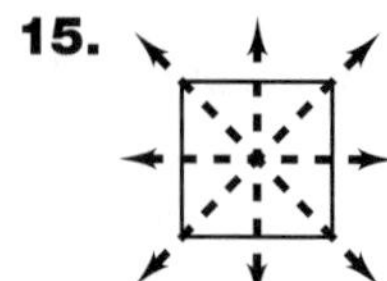

17. rotational and reflectional **19.** Answer may vary. Samples: CODE, HOOD, DOCK

21a.

Language	Horiz. line	Vert. line	Point
English	B, C, D, E, H, I, K, O, X	A, H, I, M, O, T, U, V, W, X, Y	H, I, N, O S, X, Z
Greek	B, E, H, Θ I, K, Ξ, O, Σ, Φ, X	A, Δ, H, Θ, I, Λ, M, Ξ, O, Π, T, Υ, Φ, X, Ψ, Ω	Z, H, Θ, I, N, Ξ, O, Φ, X

b. Sample: Greek; Greek alphabet has more letters with at least one kind of symmetry and more letters with multiple symmetries. **23.** rotational, reflectional **25.** reflectional; rotational **27.** point **29.** reflectional; rotational **33.** Yes; the bisector divides the ∠ into 2 ≅ ∠s with one side of the ∠ being the reflection of the other. **35.** Not necessarily; the bisector divides the segment into 2 ≅ parts but one part cannot be the reflection of the other unless the bisector is the ⊥ bisector. **37.** (−3, 4) **39.** (−3, −4)

41. point symmetry about any pt. on the line; reflectional in any member of the family of lines $y = -x + b$

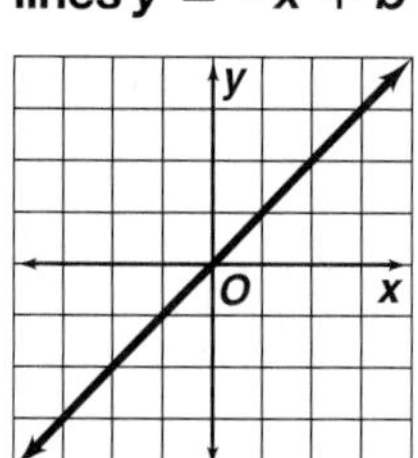

43. reflectional in x-axis

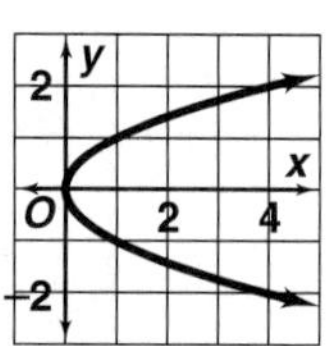

45. reflectional in $x = -2$

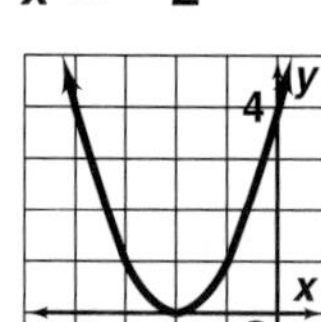

47. reflectional in y-axis

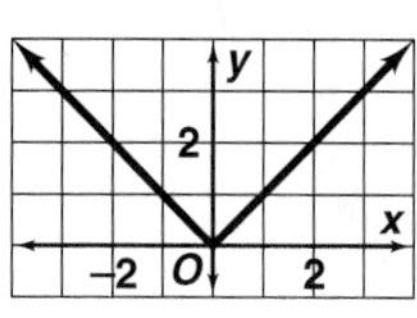

49. Sample:

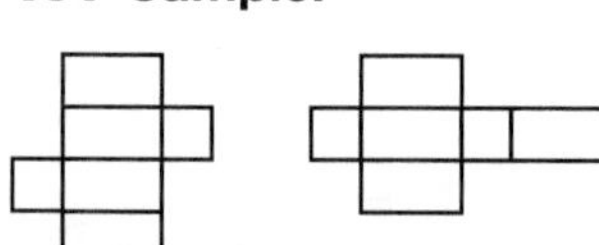

57. $A'(-3, 3)$, $B'(-4, 2)$, $C'(-4, 4)$ **59.** 4.3 **61.** $66\frac{2}{3}$ cm^3

Lesson 12-6 pp. 670–672

EXERCISES **1–3.** Answers may vary. Samples are given. **1.** yes; translation; two ⊥ rectangles **3.** rotation; four rectangles in a square shape **5.** yes **7.** no **11.** rotational, reflectional, glide reflectional, and translational **13.** rotational, reflectional, glide reflectional, and translational

17. 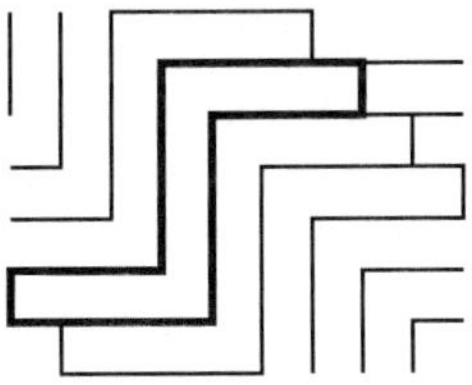 **19.** 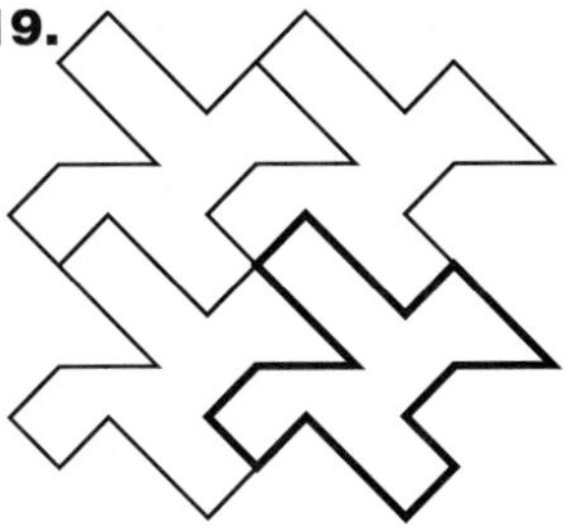

21. Answers may vary. Sample is given.

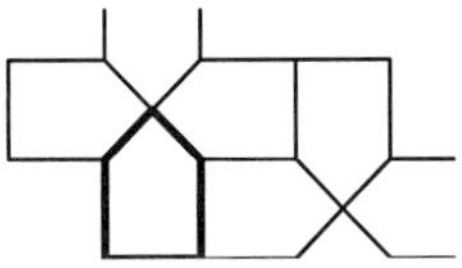 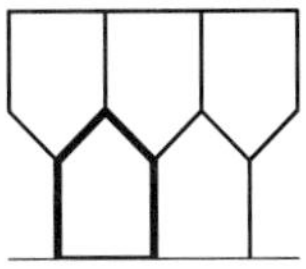

25. yes; **27.** yes;

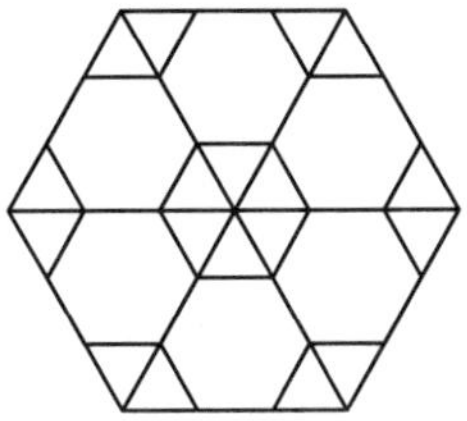 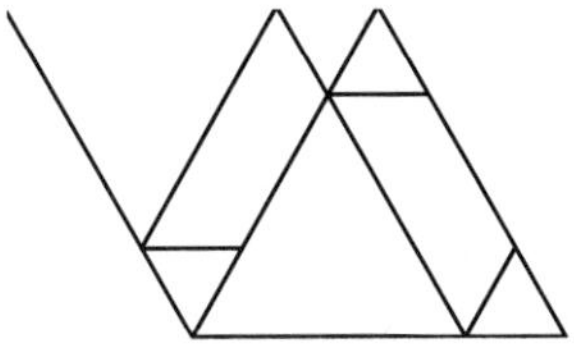

45. (−2, −7) **47.** (2, −7) **49.** $x^2 + y^2 = 36$
51. $(x + 1)^2 + y^2 = 9$ **53.** 30

Lesson 12-7 pp. 676–679

EXERCISES **1.** enlargement; center *A*, scale factor $\frac{3}{2}$ **3.** enlargement; center *R*, scale factor $\frac{3}{2}$
11. 512 in. **13.** 1.25 ft
15. *P*′(6, −3), *Q*′(6, 12), *R*′(12, −3)

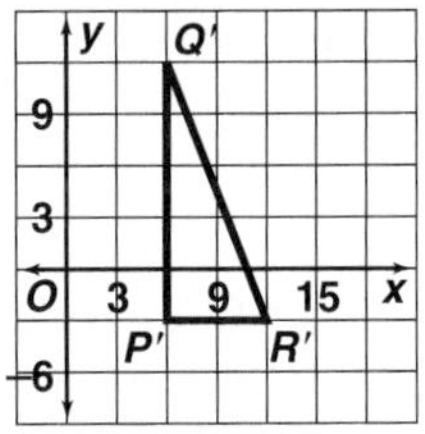

19. *L*′(−15, 0)
21. *T*′(0, 18)

25. $A'\left(-\frac{1}{2}, -\frac{1}{2}\right), B'\left(\frac{1}{4}, \frac{1}{4}\right), C'\left(\frac{1}{4}, -\frac{1}{4}\right)$

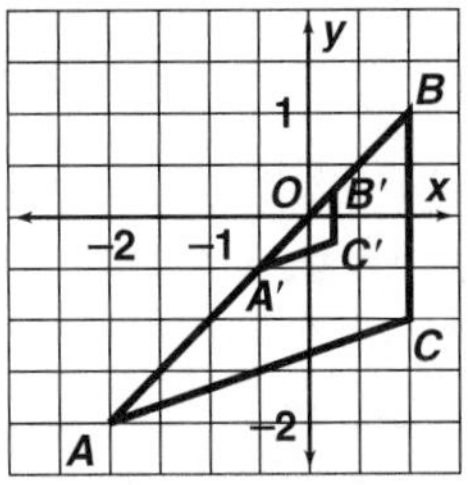

29. *Q*′(−6, 8), *W*′(6, 10), *T*′(6, 2), *R*′(−4, −2)
31. $Q'\left(-\frac{3}{4}, 1\right), W'\left(\frac{3}{4}, \frac{5}{4}\right), T'\left(\frac{3}{4}, \frac{1}{4}\right), R'\left(-\frac{1}{2}, -\frac{1}{4}\right)$

37. 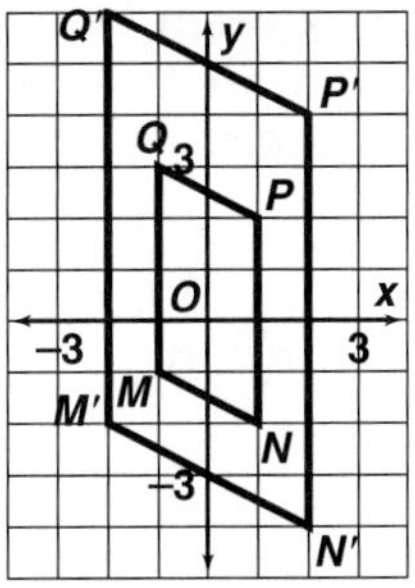

43. *I*′*J*′ = 10; *H*′*J*′ = 12
45. *HI* = 32; *I*′*J*′ = 7.5
47. *x* = 3; *y* = 60
49. 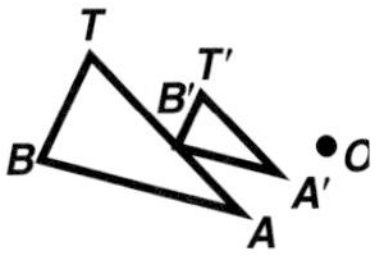

55. 60 cm **57.** False; a dilation doesn't map a segment to a ≅ segment unless the scale factor is 1. **59.** False; a dilation with a scale factor greater than 2 is an enlargement. **73.** yes **75.** yes **77.** a sphere with a 6-in. radius, concentric with the given sphere, and the center of the spheres **79.** 30

Chapter Review pp. 681–683

1. F **2.** D **3.** E or B **4.** G **5.** B **6.** C **7.** A

8. 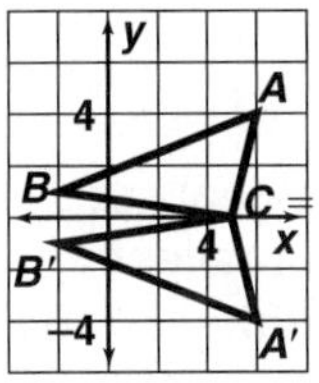 **9.** 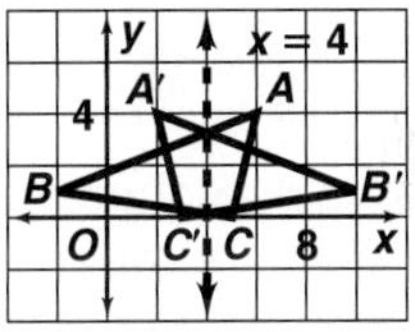

10. 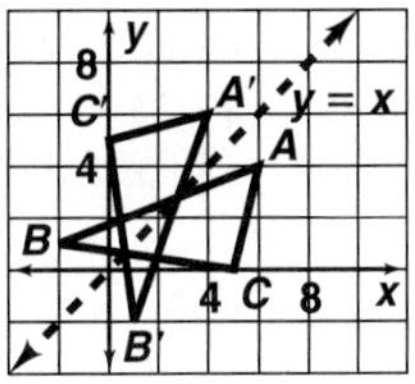

11. *A*′(7, 12), *B*′(8, 6), *C*′(3, 5) **12.** *R*′(−4, 3), *S*′(−6, 6), *T*′(−10, 8)
13. ⟨−2, −1⟩ **14.** ⟨11, −4⟩

15. 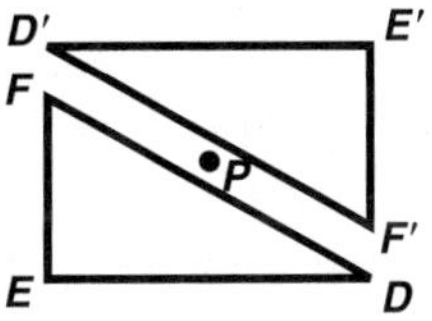 **16.** 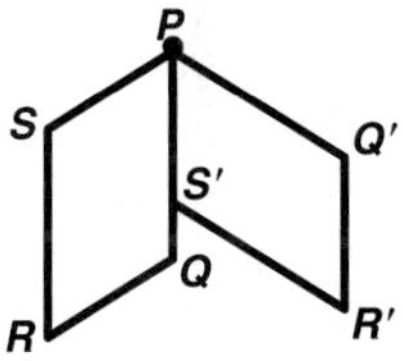

17. 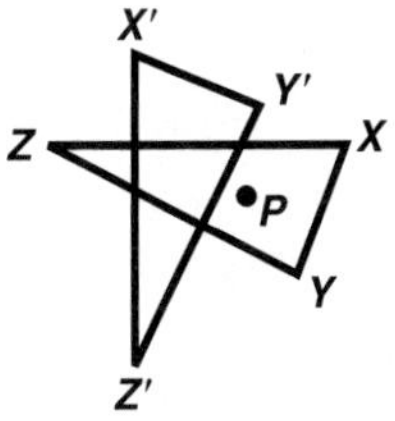

18. (−2, 5) **19.** (−3, 0) **20.** (−1, −4) **21.** (0, 7) **22.** (8, −2) **23.** same; rotation **24.** opposite; reflection **25.** same; translation **26.** opposite; glide reflection

27. same; translation **28.** opposite; glide reflection **29.** same; rotation **30.** opposite; reflection **31.** *T*′(−4, −9), *A*′(0, −5), *M*′(−1, −10)
32. reflectional **33.** rotational; 72°

34a. 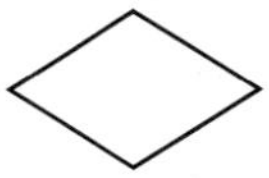

b. rotational, point, reflectional, translational, glide reflectional

35a. and b. rotational, point, reflectional, translational, glide reflectional

36. $A'(0, 12)$ 37. $B'(-1, 3)$
38. $C'(15, -20)$ 39. $M'(-15, 20)$, $A'(-30, -5)$, $T'(0, 0)$, $H'(15, 10)$ 40. $F'(-2, 0)$, $U'\left(\frac{5}{2}, 0\right)$, $N'\left(-1, -\frac{5}{2}\right)$

Extra Practice

Chapter 1

1. 37, 42 3. 8, $\frac{8}{5}$ 7. true 9. true 17. 27 19. 6

23.

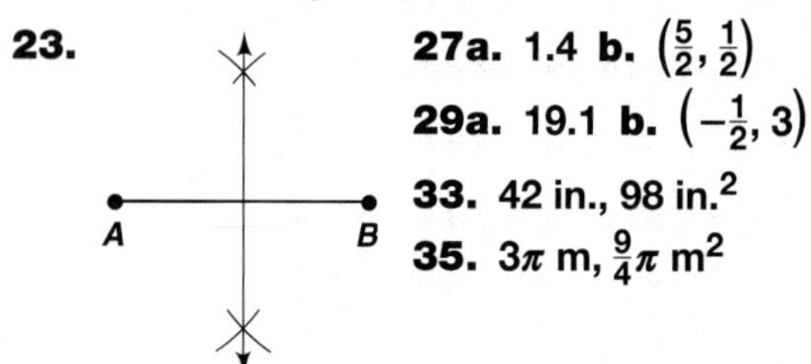

27a. 1.4 b. $\left(\frac{5}{2}, \frac{1}{2}\right)$
29a. 19.1 b. $\left(-\frac{1}{2}, 3\right)$
33. 42 in., 98 in.^{2}
35. 3π m, $\frac{9}{4}\pi$ m^2

Chapter 2

1. If a number is one, then it is the smallest positive square. If a number is the smallest positive square, then it is one. A number is one if and only if it is the smallest positive square.
7. No; two skew lines are a counterexample.
9. Jorge can't buy a new car. 11. Linda's band will win $500. 13b. Mult. Prop. of =, Distr. Prop.
c. Mult. Prop. of = d. $4c - a = 4b$
e. Symm. Prop. of = 15. 15

Chapter 3

1. $m\angle 1 = 134$; Same-Side Int. ∠s Thm. $m\angle 2 = 46$; Alt. Int. ∠ Thm. 3. $m\angle 1 = 58$; Alt. Int. ∠ Thm. $m\angle 2 = 122$; Same-Side Int. ∠s Thm.
5. none 7. $c \parallel d$, Conv. of Same-Side Interior ∠s Thm. 13. obtuse; scalene 15. isosceles; acute
17. $x = 25$; $y = 19$ 19. 65
21. $y - 2 = -\frac{5}{2}(x - 4)$ or $y + 3 = -\frac{5}{2}(x - 6)$
23. $y + 5 = -1(x - 3)$ or $y - 3 = -1(x + 5)$
25. ∥; same slope 27. perp.; $m_1 \cdot m_2 = -1$

29.

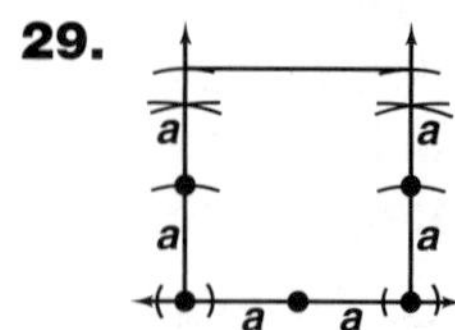

Chapter 4

1. $\angle G$ 3. $\angle T$ 9. Yes; corr. sides and corr. ∠s are ≅. 11. Yes; corr. sides and corr. ∠s are ≅. 13. $\angle T \cong \angle S$, $\angle Y \cong \angle W$ and included sides $\overline{TY} \cong \overline{SW}$; ASA 15. not possible
17. $\overleftrightarrow{OL} \parallel \overleftrightarrow{MN}$, so $\angle OLN \cong \angle MNL$. $\overline{LN} \cong \overline{LN}$ by the Reflexive Prop. of ≅. Since $\overline{LO} \cong \overline{MN}$, $\triangle MLN \cong \triangle ONL$ by SAS, and $\angle MLN \cong \angle ONL$ by CPCTC.
19. $\overline{BI} \cong \overline{BI}$ by the Reflexive Prop. of ≅. Since $\angle MBI \cong \angle RIB$ and $\angle MIB \cong \angle RBI$, $\triangle MBI \cong \triangle RIB$ by ASA, and $\overline{MB} \cong \overline{RI}$ by CPCTC.
21. $x = 57$; $y = 66$ 23. 6 25. $\triangle RQM \cong \triangle QRS$; SSS

Chapter 5

1. $\frac{25}{7}$ 3. 7 5. 5 7. $\frac{5}{2}$ 9. (1, 5) 11. (0, 0)
13. ∠ bisector 15. altitude 17a. If two ∠s are not vert., then they are not ≅. b. If two ∠s are not ≅, then they are not vert. 19a. If a car is not blue, then it has doors. b. If a car has doors, then it is not blue. 21. Assume points J, K, and L are not collinear. 23. Assume ▱$XYZV$ is not a square. 25. $\overline{JB}$, $\overline{PB}$, $\overline{PJ}$ 27. $\overline{CT}$, $\overline{TA}$, $\overline{CA}$
29. Yes; $9 + 11 > 15$.

Chapter 6

1.

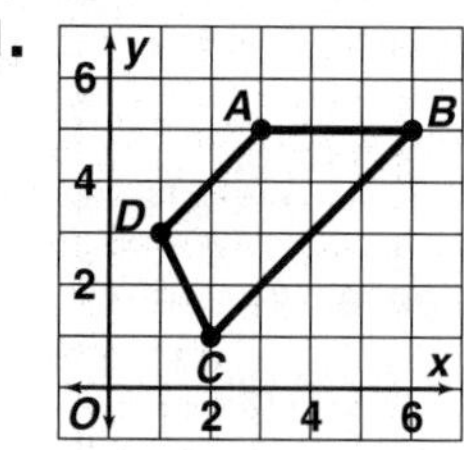

trapezoid

5. $x = 12$, $y = 84$ 7. $x = 8$, $y = 25$ 9. yes 11. no
13. square; $m\angle 1 = 45$, $m\angle 2 = 45$ 15. ▱; $m\angle 1 = 45$, $m\angle 2 = 45$, $m\angle 3 = 80$, $m\angle 4 = 55$ 17. $m\angle 1 = 110$, $m\angle 2 = 25$

19. $m\angle 1 = 110$, $m\angle 2 = 70$ 21. $D(0, b)$; $S(a, 0)$
23. $D(-c, 0)$; $S(0, -b)$

Chapter 7

1. 15 ft; 10.825 ft^2 3. 50 ft; 143 ft^2 5. 15 7. $3\sqrt{5}$
9. 72 cm^2 11. $\frac{25}{4}\sqrt{3}$ mm^2 13a. 6π cm b. 2π cm
15a. 18π cm b. $\frac{9}{2}\pi$ cm 17. $\frac{49}{3}\pi$ ft^2 19. $\frac{81}{8}\pi$ cm^2
21. $\frac{1}{4}$ 23. $1 - \frac{\pi}{4}$

Chapter 8

1. 10 3. 2 7. $x = \frac{80}{3}$; $y = 6$; $z = \frac{16}{3}$ 9. $x = 30$; $y = 4$ 11. Yes; $\triangle QCT \sim \triangle MCP$ by SAS~.
13. no 15. $\frac{117}{10}$ 17. 4 23. 3 : 4; 9 : 16

Chapter 9

1. 5.6 3. 11.0 9. 653 ft 11. 78 ft
13a. $\langle -49, 142 \rangle$, $\langle 38, 47 \rangle$ b. $\langle -11, 189 \rangle$
15a. $\langle -54, 72 \rangle$, $\langle -95, -33 \rangle$ b. $\langle -149, 39 \rangle$
17. 30.1 ft^2 19. 43.2 cm^2 21. 31.2 ft^2

Chapter 10

1. cube **3.** cylinder

5.

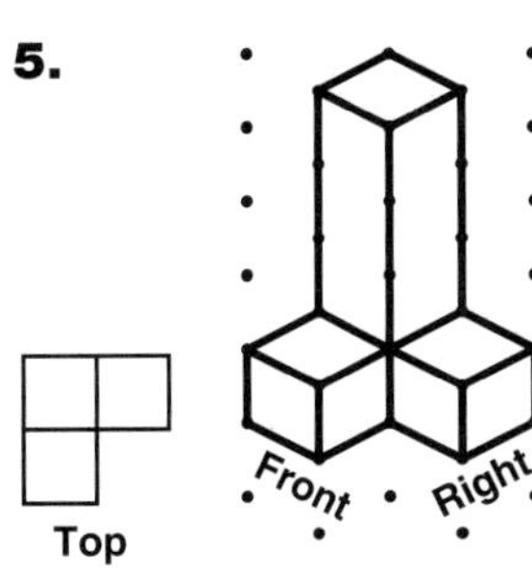

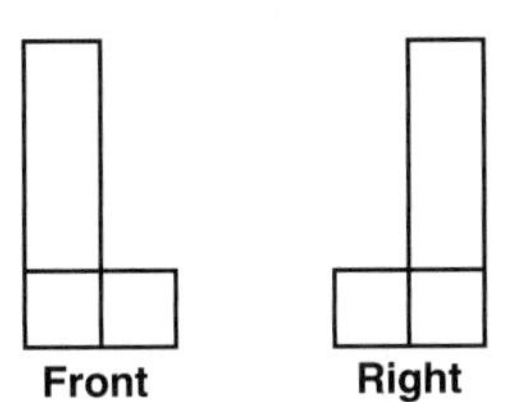

27. 5 : 8; 125 : 512

9. 84 ft^2; 108 ft^2
11. 40π in.^{2}; 56π in.^{2}
13. 16 mm^3
15. 15π m^3
17. $\frac{500\pi}{3}$ cm^3, 524 cm^3; 100π cm^2, 314 cm^2
19. $\frac{256\pi}{3}$ in.^{3}, 268 in.^{3}; 64π in.^{2}, 201 in.^{2}
21. $\frac{\pi}{6}$ in.^{3}, 1 in.^{3}; π in.^{2}, 3 in.^{2}
23. $\frac{256\pi}{3}$ m^3
25. $\frac{343\pi}{6}$ ft^3

Chapter 11

1. 65 **3.** 6 **5.** 14.8 **7.** 5.3 **13.** $x = 193$; $y = 60.5$
15. $x \approx 10.4$ **21.** $x^2 + y^2 = 16$
23. $(x - 9)^2 + (y + 3)^2 = 49$

27. two rays ∥ to and 2 cm from $\overrightarrow{AB}$, and the semicircle of radius 2 with center A, opp. pt. B.

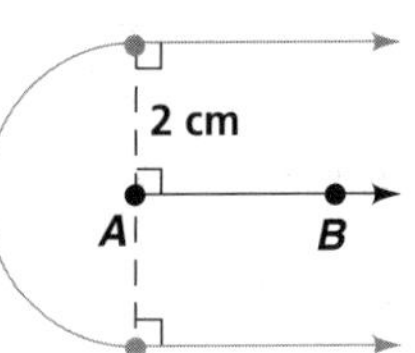

Chapter 12

1.

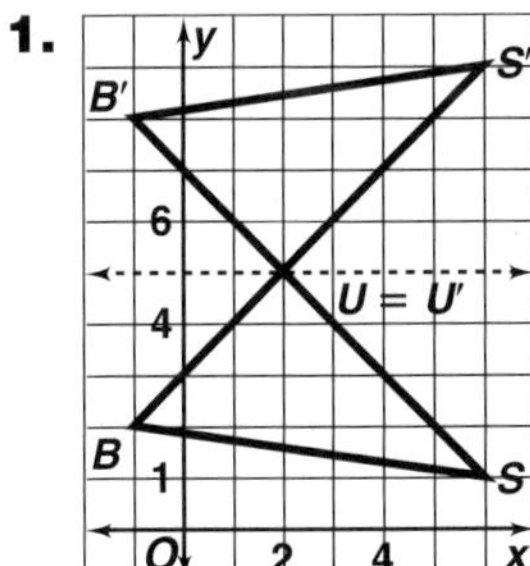

9. E **11.** C **15.** $A'(-5, 9)$, $B'(-3, 3)$, $C'(-1, 10)$
17. $P'(-15, -11)$, $Q'(-11, -6)$, $R'(-4, 1)$

19.

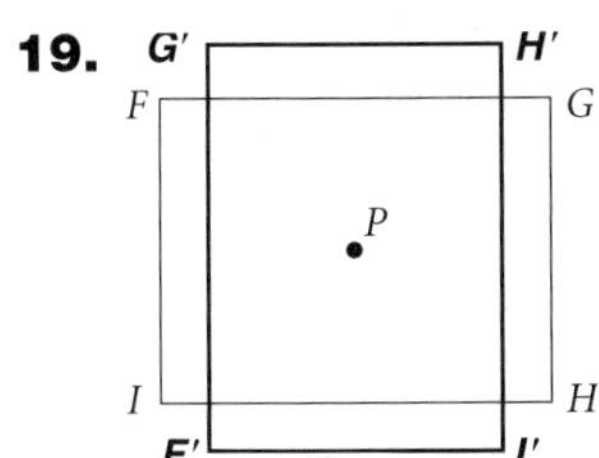

23. dilation
25. glide reflection
27a. line **b.** yes
29a. line, rotation, point **b.** yes

Skills Handbook

p. 702 **1.** 10 handshakes **3.** 16 regions

p. 703 **1.** 6, 8, 10 **3.** any pos. number less than 4 **5.** –2 **7.** 54

p. 704 **1.** 165 toothpicks **3.** 3280 triangles

p. 705 **1.** 28 posts **3.** 84 paths

p. 706 **1.** J.T. is the parrot; Izzy is the dog; Arf is the goldfish; Blinky is the hamster. **3.** 14 students

p. 707 **1.** Route 90 east, Route 128 north, Route 4 north **3.** 3 tickets

p. 708 **1.** Answers may vary slightly. Sample: 35 mm; 46 mm

3.

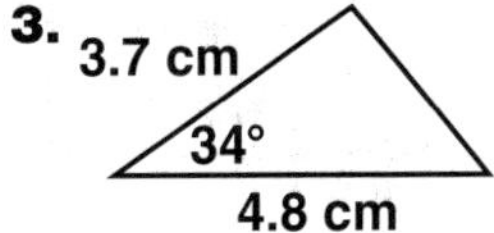

p. 709 **1.** 0.4 **3.** 600

p. 710 **1.** $23\frac{1}{2}$ ft to $24\frac{1}{2}$ ft **3.** $339\frac{1}{2}$ mL to $340\frac{1}{2}$ mL

p. 711 **1.** 18% **3.** 8% **9.** ≈7% **11.** ≈2%

p. 712 **1.** 353.6; 301; no mode **3.** $40,533; $28,150; $18,000

p. 713 **1.**

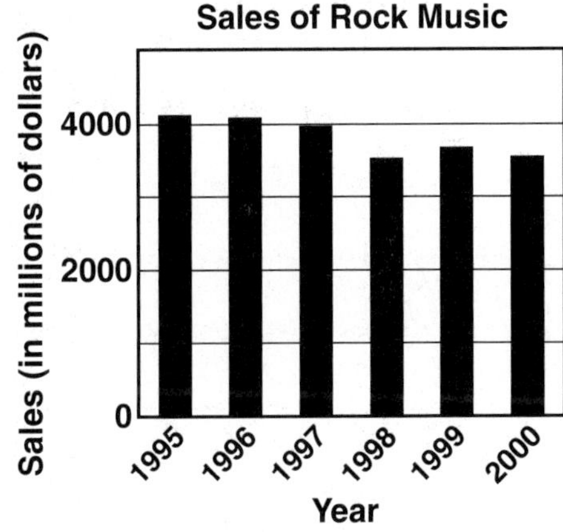

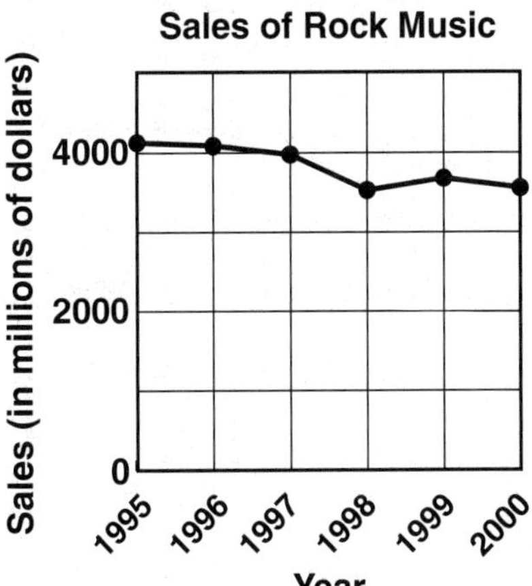

3. 8 A.M.–2 P.M.

p. 714 **1a.** 16.6 **b.** 15.1 **c.** 19.4

3.

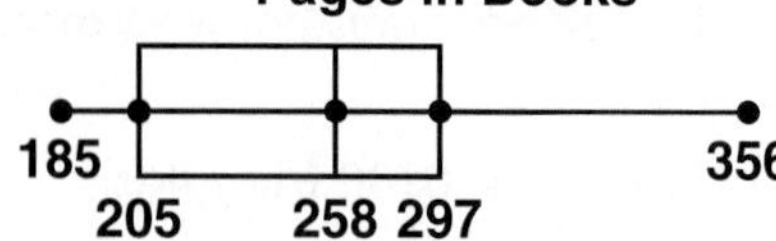

p. 715 **1.** 121 **3.** 196 **9.** 10 **11.** 8.6 **17.** ±7 **19.** ±1

p. 716 **1.** −50 **3.** 15 **19.** $2\ell + 2w$ **21.** $-4x^2 + 8x$

p. 717 **1.** $3\sqrt{3}$ **3.** $5\sqrt{6}$ **11.** $5\sqrt{10}$ **13.** $2\sqrt{39}$

p. 718 **1.** $\frac{5}{3}$ **3.** $\frac{2}{3}$ **19.** $\frac{5}{12}$ **21.** $\frac{5}{13}$ **25.** $\frac{2}{\pi}$ **27.** $\frac{1}{9}$

p. 719 **1.** 8 **3.** 16 **13.** −16 or 16 **15.** −20 or 20

p. 720 **1.** 5 **3.** 3 **13.** $35 - 2x = 9$; 13
15. $\$9.95 + \$0.035m = \$12.75$; 80 min

p. 721 **1.** $w = \frac{P - 2\ell}{2}$ **3.** $r = \frac{1}{2}\sqrt{\frac{S}{\pi}} = \frac{\sqrt{\pi S}}{2\pi}$

p. 722 **1.** (4, −1) **3.** (4, 1)

p. 723 **1.** 0.5 **3.** 0.27 **9.** 8.4 **11.** 7.2
17–19. Answers may vary. Samples are given.
17. 7 **19.** 45

p. 724 **1.** $\frac{1}{2}$ **3.** $\frac{2}{7}$ **7.** $\frac{1}{12}$ **9.** $\frac{1}{2}$ **13.** $\frac{3}{8}$ **15.** $\frac{7}{8}$

Index

A

B

C

J

K

L

M

N

O

Q

R

S

Index

Acknowledgments

Staff Credits

The people who made up the High School Mathematics team—representing design services, editorial, editorial services, market research, marketing services, online services & multimedia development, production services, project office, and publishing processes—are listed below. Bold type denotes the core team members.

Leora Adler, Carolyn Artin, Stephanie Bradley, Amy D. Breaux, **Peter Brooks,** Judith Buice, Ronit Carter, **Lisa J. Clark,** Bob Cornell, Sheila DeFazio, Marian DeLollis, Jo DiGiustini, Delphine Dupee, Emily Ellen, Janet Fauser, Debby Faust, Suzanne Feliciello, Frederick Fellows, Steve Fenton, Jonathan Fisher, **Paula Foye,** Paul Frisoli, Patti Fromkin, Melissa Garcia, Jonathan Gorey, Jennifer Graham, Barbara Hardt, Daniel R. Hartjes, Richard Heater, Kerri Hoar, Jayne Holman, Karen Holtzman, Angela Husband, Kevin Jackson-Mead, Albert Jacobson, Misty-Lynn Jenese, Carolyn Lock, Diahanne Lucas, Catherine Maglio, Cheryl Mahan, Barry Maloney, Meredith Mascola, Ann McSweeney, **Eve Melnechuk,** Sandy Morris, **Cindy Noftle,** Marsha Novak, **Marie Opera,** Jill Ort, Michael Oster, Steve Ouellette, Dorothy M. Preston, Rashid Ross, Donna Russo, **Malti Sharma, Dennis Slattery,** Kathryn Smith, Lisa Smith-Ruvalcaba, Emily Soltanoff, **Deborah Sommer,** Mark Tricca, Nate Walker, Diane Walsh, **Joe Will,** Amy Winchester, Carol Zacny

Cover Design
Brainworx Studio

Cover Photos
Zebras, Art Wolfe/Stone/Getty Images, Inc.; **Glass Dome,** John McAnulty/Corbis.

Technical Illustration
Network Graphics

Illustration
Andrea G. Maginnis: 32
John Edwards: 18, 120, 182, 188, 274
JB Woolsey: 15, 76, 148, 183, 212, 315, 376, 435, 436, 482
Dennis Harms: 8, 47, 204, 205, 222, 258, 386, 457
Function through Form: 42, 250, 513, 531, 561, 643
Leo Abbett: 80, 519 All
Stephanie Bradley: 247, 525
Roberta Warshaw: 533, 545, 557
Jim Delapine: 399, 558, 559
Seymour Levy: 563
Kenneth Batelman: 443, 471, 570, 621, 624
Christine Graham: 602, 651
Roberta Warshaw: 611, 637
Peter Bollinger: 633, 688, 689
Brucie Rosch: 59, 69, 253, 636, 642
Linda Johnson: 665
Gary Torrisi: 484 all, 486
Lois Leonard Stock: 669
Ortelius Design, Inc.: 374
Gary Phillips: 28, 32

Photography

Page vii, Johnny Johnson/DRK Photo; **viii,** Andy Sacks/Stone/Getty Images, Inc.; **ix,** Peter Menzel/Stock Boston; **x,** Russ Lappa; **xi,** Timothy Hursley/SuperStock, Inc.; **xii,** Kunio Owaki/Corbis Stock Market; **xiii,** Russ Lappa; **xiv,** David Young-Wolff/PhotoEdit; **xv,** Scott T. Smith/Corbis; **xvi,** Felicia Martinez/PhotoEdit; **xvii,** Reza Estakhrian/Stone/Getty Images, Inc.; **xviii,** Roy Ooms/Masterfile Corporation.

Chapter 1: Pages 2, 3, SeaWorld; **4,** Julie Houck/Stock Boston; **6,** Brett Froomer/Image Bank/Getty Images, Inc.; **7,** Stone/Getty Images, Inc.; **9,** PhotoDisc, Inc./Getty Images, Inc.; **13,** Russ Lappa; **14,** Johnny Johnson/DRK Photo; **17,** Daryl Benson/Masterfile Corporation; **18,** Stacy Pick/Stock Boston; **21 bl,** Dave Bartruff/Stock Boston; **21 inset,** SuperStock, Inc.; **21 tr,** Tim O'Hara/Index Stock Imagery, Inc.; **27,** Bill Nation/Corbis Sygma; **27 inset,** Chad Slattery/Stone/Getty Images, Inc.; **29,** Corbis; **31,** William Sallaz/Duomo; **32,** Cameramann/The Image Works; **35,** Jon Feingersh/Corbis Stock Market; **36,** Tim Panell/Corbis; **38 t,** ©1997 Richard Megna/Fundamental Photographs, NYC; **38 b,** *Peanuts* reprinted by permission of United Feature Syndicate, Inc.; **40,** Dan McCoy/Corbis Stock Market; **45,** Michael Newman/PhotoEdit; **47,** Laura Dwight/PhotoEdit; **48,** Richard Eller/Aerial Images Photography; **53,** Gail Mooney/Corbis; **56,** Hans Georg Roth/Corbis; **57,** Michael Rosenfeld/Stone/Getty Images, Inc.

Chapter 2: Pages 66, 67, Stewart Cohen/Stone/Getty Images, Inc.; **70,** Jon Chomitz; **71 t,** ©1977 NEA, Inc.; **71 bl,** AP Photo/Richard Drew; **71 br,** Tony Vaccaro/Archive Photos/Getty Images, Inc.; **73 t,** Hulton-Deutsch Collection/Corbis; **73 b,** Mug Shots/Corbis Stock Market; **77,** Richard Haynes; **79 l,** Russ Lappa; **79 r,** National Association for the Deaf; **80 l,** Andy Sacks/Stone/Getty Images, Inc.; **80 r,** C. Squared Studios/PhotoDisc, Inc./PictureQuest; **82,** Tony Freeman/PhotoEdit; **84,** InterNetwork Media/PhotoDisc, Inc./PictureQuest; **85,** Damian Strohmey/Sports Illustrated; **86 t,** Fotopic/Omni-Photo Communications, Inc.; **86 m,** *The Far Side* by John McPherson/ Dist. by Universal Press Syndicate. Reprinted with permission. All rights reserved.; **86 b,** Gregory Scott/Index Stock Imagery, Inc.; **88 l,** Courtesy of WGBH; **88 r,** ©King Collection/Retna, Ltd.; **92 l,** PhotoDisc, Inc./Getty Images, Inc.; **92 r,** Tony Freeman/PhotoEdit; **93 t,** The Granger Collection, NY; **93 m,** John Lopinot/Black Star Publishing/PictureQuest; **93 b,** Neal Preston-Andy Kent/Still Bill Productions; **97 l,** Joe Bator/Corbis Stock Market; **97 r,** Telegraph Colour Library/FPG International/Getty Images, Inc.; **101,** Corbis Digital Images/PictureQuest; **102,** Paul A. Souder/Corbis; **110 hands and pan,** David Murray and Jules Selmes/Dorling Kindersley Ltd.; **110 the rest,** Dorling Kindersley Ltd.; **111 pizza cutter,** Russ Lappa; **111 grater, baking tin, mortar and pestle,** Christ Graham and Nick Nichols/Dorling Kindersley Ltd.; **111 the rest,** Dorling Kindersley Ltd.

Chapter 3: Pages 112, 113, Imtek Imagineering/Masterfile Corporation; **116 composite,** Joe Towers/Corbis Stock Market and H.P. Merten/Corbis Stock Market; **119,** Peter Menzel/Stock Boston; **122,** Gary Kufner/Corbis; **125,** Jon Chomitz; **126,** John M. Roberts/Corbis Stock Market; **127 both,** Jon Chomitz; **128,** Richard Pasley/Stock Boston; **133,** Chuck Pefley/Stone/Getty Images, Inc.; **134,** Stewart Cohen /Stone/Getty Images, Inc.; **136,** John Coletti/The Picture Cube/Index Stock Imagery, Inc.;

137 both, Jerry Jacka Photography; **143,** Jim Cummins/FPG International/Getty Images, Inc.; **144,** Arthur ThÈvenart/Corbis; **146,** Ken O'Donoghue; **147 l,** Russ Lappa; **147 m,** Nawrocki Stock Photo/Picture Perfect; **147 r,** Russ Lappa; **148,** Courtesy of the Theatre in the Round Players, Inc., Minneapolis, MN; **149,** Michael Newman/PhotoEdit; **155,** NASA; **156,** Michael Newman/PhotoEdit; **158,** Bob Daemmrich/Stock Boston; **161,** PhotoDisc, Inc./Getty Images, Inc.; **163,** Getty Images Sport Services; **165,** Michael Newman/PhotoEdit; **167,** Addison Gallery of Art at Phillips Acadamy; **169 all,** Jon Chomitz.

Chapter 4: Pages 178, 179, Peter Willi/SuperStock, Inc.; **181,** NASA; **182,** John Elk III/Stock Boston; **184,** Richard Haynes; **185,** Hans Gregory Roth/Corbis; **187,** Tom Alexander/Stone/Getty Images, Inc.; **189 l,** Tony Freeman Photography; **189 r,** Russ Lappa; **190 both,** Prentice Hall; **195,** Mike Greenlar Photography; **198,** Richard Haynes; **200,** Photo Researchers, Inc.; **203,** Russ Lappa; **206,** Leif Skoogfors/Woodfin Camp & Associates; **211,** Pat O'Hara/Corbis; **214,** Fernando Serna/Department of the Air Force; **215,** Richard Hutchins/PhotoEdit; **216,** Corbis; **218,** Tony Freeman Photography; **221,** Jeff Greenberg/Omni-Photo Communications, Inc.; **224,** Jim Rudnick/Corbis Stock Market; **225,** Miriam Nathan-Roberts; **226 t,** Russ Lappa; **226 b,** Walter Hodges/Stone/Getty Images, Inc.; **228,** Corbis Stock Market; **238 Isaac Newton,** Science Museum Photo Library/Dorling Kindersley Ltd.; **238 the rest,** Dorling Kindersley Ltd.; **239 cube-corner reflector,** NASA; **239 Hall of Mirrors,** Max Alexander/Dorling Kindersley Ltd.; **239 the rest,** Dorling Kindersley Ltd.

Chapter 5: Pages 240, 241, Jeff Greenberg/PhotoEdit; **245,** Clyde Lockwood/Animals Animals/Earth Scenes; **247,** Timothy Hursley/SuperStock, Inc.; **252,** Jim Cummins/Corbis Stock Market; **265,** AP/Wide World Photos; **266,** Michael Newman/PhotoEdit; **268,** AP/Wide World Photos; **269,** Corbis; **270,** Tom Pantages; **273,** Russ Lappa; **274,** David Young-Wolff/PhotoEdit; **277,** Dave Schiefelbein /Stone/Getty Images, Inc.; **278,** Fred Wood/Summer Productions.

Chapter 6: Pages 286, 287, Complete Sportswear; **288,** The Image Works; **291,** Photograph copyright ©1996: Whitney Museum of American Art, New York. Photography by Sheldan C. Collins; **292,** Russ Lappa; **295,** Richard Haynes; **296,** Tony Freeman/PhotoEdit; **298, 300,** Richard Haynes; **303,** Ken O'Donoghue; **305,** Tony Freeman Photography; **306 l,** Dave Bartruff/Stock Boston; **306 r,** Mark Thayer; **307,** Russ Lappa; **308 t,** Photo of Russell W.M. and Ruth Kraus residence, S.340 in *The Architecture of Frank Lloyd Wright: A Complete Catalog,* 3rd Edition, ©2002/William Allin Storrer, PhD; **308 b,** Plan of Russell W.M. and Ruth Kraus residence, S.340 in *The Frank Lloyd Wright Companion,* ©1973/William Allin Storrer, PhD; **313,** Walter Bibikow/Index Stock Imagery, Inc.; **315,** Ron Sherman/Stone/Getty Images, Inc.; **316,** Tony Freeman Photography; **316 inset,** Russ Lappa; **320,** archivebroehandesign.com, New York; **321,** Carl Purcell/Corbis; **323,** Mark E. Gibson/Visuals Unlimited; **324,** Wallace Garrison/Index Stock Imagery, Inc.; **327,** Richard Haynes; **329,** ©National Park Service, photo by Bill Hudson, Biscayne National Park; **331 both,** Geoffrey Clifford/Woodfin Camp; **333,** SuperStock, Inc.; **336,** Kunio Owaki/Corbis Stock Market; **344–345 skater,** Index Stock Imagery, Inc./PictureQuest; **344, 345 the rest,** Dorling Kindersley Ltd.

Chapter 7: Pages 346, 347, AP Photo/NASA; **348,** Mark Thayer; **351,** Roessler/SuperStock, Inc.; **353,** Larry Lefever/Grant Heilman Photography, Inc.; **360,** Tom Tracy/FPG International/Getty Images, Inc.; **363,** The Observatories of the Carnegie Institution of Washington; **367,** Rhoda Sidney/PhotoEdit; **368,** Stephen Saks/ Index Stock Imagery, Inc./PictureQuest; **369,** Russ Lappa; **370,** Macduff Everton/Corbis; **377,** Simon Battensby/Stone/Getty Images, Inc.; **378,** Tony Donaldson/SportsChrome-USA; **379,** The Granger Collection, NY; **381,** Photo courtesy of NidaCore; **382,** Richard Cummins/Corbis; **383,** G. Ross/FPG International/Getty Images, Inc.; **384,** F. Dewey Webster/Sovfoto/Eastfoto/ PictureQuest; **387,** PhotoDisc, Inc./Getty Images, Inc.; **391,** Bill Horsman/Stock Boston; **392,** *Calvin and Hobbs* ©Watterson. Dist. by Universal Press Syndicate. Reprinted with permission. All rights reserved.; **393,** Bob Daemmrich/Stock Boston; **396,** Russ Lappa; **397,** Russ Lappa; **399,** Bill Bachmann/Photo Network/PictureQuest; **403,** David Young-Wolff/PhotoEdit; **405,** Frank Fournier/Corbis Stock Market; **406,** AP/Wide World Photos.

Chapter 8: Pages 414, 415, David Maenza /SuperStock, Inc.; **416,** both David Young-Wolff/PhotoEdit; **418,** Prentice Hall; **419,** ©AAA reprinted with permission.; **420,** Michael Dwyer/Stock Boston; **421,** NASA; **424,** Miro Vintoniv/Stock Boston; **425,** Telegraph Colour Library/FPG International/Getty Images, Inc.; **427 t,** *Peanuts* reprinted by permission of United Feature Syndicate, Inc.; **427 m,** Ralf-Finn Hestoft/Index Stock Imagery, Inc.; **427 b,** Russ Lappa; **432,** Lee Snider/Photo Images; **435,** Francis Lepine/Animals Animals/Earth Scenes; **437,** AP/Wide World Photos; **441,** Paul Chesley/Stone/Getty Images, Inc.; **443,** Kevin Miller/Stone/Getty Images, Inc.; **447,** Corbis Digital Stock; **449,** Vincent Hobbs/SuperStock, Inc.; **450,** David Woodfall/Stone/Getty Images, Inc.; **451,** Mark Richards/PhotoEdit; **454,** Russ Lappa; **456,** David Young-Wolff/PhotoEdit; **458,** Bob Daemmrich/Stock Boston/PictureQuest; **466 both,** Dorling Kindersley Ltd.; **467 t,** Corbis Digital Stock; **467 m,** Ryan McVay/PhotoDisc, Inc./PictureQuest; **467 bl,** Dorling Kindersley Ltd.; **467 br,** Corbis Images/PictureQuest.

Chapter 9: Pages 468, 469, Peter Hendrie/Image Bank/Getty Images, Inc.; **471,** Scott T. Smith/Corbis; **474,** Katoomba Scenic Railway; **477,** Richard Hamilton/Corbis; **479,** David Young Wolff/PhotoEdit; **481 both,** Tom Pantages; **483,** Tom Carroll Photography; **485,** The Goodyear Tire & Rubber Company; **486,** Dwayne Newton/PhotoEdit; **488,** Giulio Andreini/Liaison Agency/Getty Images, Inc.; **490,** Lowell Georgia/Corbis; **491,** Stone/Getty Images, Inc.; **492,** Bob Daemmrich/Stock Boston; **493,** William J. Weber/Visuals Unlimited; **495,** NOAA; **496,** *The Far Side* ® by Gary Larson © 1993 Farworks, Inc. All rights reserved. Used with permission; **497,** Joe Towers/Corbis Stock Market; **499,** George Gerster/Photo Researchers, Inc.; **501,** Corbis; **502,** PhotoDisc, Inc./Getty Images, Inc.; **503,** Ralph Cowan/FPG International/Getty Images, Inc.

Chapter 10: Pages 510, 511, Dorling Kindersley Ltd.; **513,** Michael Kevin Daly/Corbis Stock Market; **515,** Breck P. Kent; **516,** PhotoDisc, Inc./Getty Images, Inc.; **520,** Mark Thayer; **521,** Barry Durand/Odyssey/Chicago; **522,** Richard Haynes; **524,** Reprinted by Permission of Tribune Media Services; **525 all,** Russ Lappa; **528,** Uniphoto, Inc./Pictor International; **530,** Russ Lappa; **531,** Tony Freeman/PhotoEdit; **532,** Russ Lappa; **538,** Will & Deni McIntyre/Stone/Getty Images, Inc.; **540,** Roger Allyn Lee/SuperStock, Inc.; **542,** Michael Busselle/Corbis; **544 both,** Russ Lappa; **548,** James King-Holmes/Science Photo Library/Photo Researchers, Inc.; **551,** Ken O'Donoghue; **552,** Pictor International; **554,** Carolyn Ross/Index Stock Imagery, Inc.; **555,** John Elk/StockBoston/PictureQuest; **556,** Phil Martin/PhotoEdit; **557,** Alan Klehr/Stone/Getty Images, Inc.; **558,** Rafael Macia/Photo Researchers, Inc.; **561 l,** Richard Hutchings/Photo Researchers, Inc.; **561 m,** Mark C. Burnett/Photo Researchers, Inc.; **561 r,** Tony Freeman/PhotoEdit; **562,** Gene Moore/Phototake/PictureQuest; **564,** Ken O'Donoghue; **566,** Felicia

Martinez/PhotoEdit; **567,** Russ Lappa; **569,** U.S. Department of Commerce **579 t,** Dorling Kindersley Ltd.; **579 b, 467 bl,** Mick Roessler/Index Stock Imagery, Inc./PictureQuest.

Chapter 11: Pages 580, 581, Ray Ooms/Masterfile Corporation; **583,** Jose Carrillo; **584,** Patrick Ward/Corbis; **587 t,** Carl F. Romney; **587 b, 588 both,** Russ Lappa; **591,** Steve Vidler/SuperStock, Inc.; **592,** Tony Freeman Photographs; **594,** Robert Frerck/Stone/Getty Images, Inc.; **595,** Grant Heilman Photography, Inc.; **603,** AP/Wide World Photos; **608,** Shaun Egan/Stone/Getty Images, Inc.; **610,** Carol Simowitz; **611,** Stone/Getty Images, Inc.; **613,** Rosenfeld Images Ltd./Science Photo Library/Photo Researchers, Inc.; **617,** Tony Freeman Photographs; **619,** AFP/Corbis; **622,** Reza Estakhrian/Stone/Getty Images, Inc.; **623,** Steven E. Sutton/Duomo; **624,** Christian Grzimek/Okapia/Photo Researchers, Inc.

Chapter 12: Page 634 l, Tom Rosenthal /SuperStock, Inc.; **634 r,** Russ Lappa; **635,** Gabe Palmer/Corbis Stock Market; **638,** Seth Joel/Corbis; **641,** Adam Smith Productions/Corbis; **645,** Roy Ooms/Masterfile Corporation; **649, 650 both,** Jerry Jacka Photography; **655,** Michael Newman/PhotoEdit; **656,** PhotoDisc, Inc./Getty Images, Inc.; **659 tl,** Viviane Moos/Corbis Stock Market; **659 bl,** Paul Jablonka/International Stock Photo; **659 tr,** Alfred Pasieka/SPL/Photo Researchers, Inc.; **659 br,** Adam Peirport/Corbis Stock Market; **662,** Brian Parker/Tom Stack & Associates, Inc.; **663 both,** Prentice Hall; **664 l,** Andrew J. Martinez ©1993/Photo Researchers, Inc.; **664 r,** Guido Alberto Rossi/Image Bank/Getty Images, Inc.; **665 l,** Tom Salyer/ Stock Connection/PictureQuest; **665 r,** Stone/Getty Images, Inc.; **667 t,** ©1996 M.C. Escher Heirs/Cordon Art, Baarn, Holland. All rights reserved.; **667 bl,** ©2001 Cordon Art, Baarn, Holland. All rights reserved.; **667 br,** Symmetry Drawing E67 by M.C. Escher. ©2002 Cordon Art, Baarn, Holland. All rights reserved.; **668,** Syracuse Newspapers/The Image Works; **670 tl,** Ira Kirschenbaum/Stock Boston; **670 bl,** Margaret Courtney-Clarke/Corbis; **670 tr,** Suzanne Murphy-Larronde; **670 br,** M. Angelo/Corbis; **671,** From *The Grammar of Ornament* by Owen Jones, 1856 Edition/1998 Octavo Corporation; **673,** Robert Frerck/Odyssey/Chicago; **674,** Frank T. Awbrey/Visuals Unlimited; **678,** David Young/Wolff/PhotoEdit; **683 l,** Patti Murray/Animals Animals/Earth Scenes; **683 r,** Russ Lappa; **684 l,** Don & Pat Valenti/DRK Photo; **684 r,** Jeff Foott/DRK Photo; **689,** Stone/Getty Images, Inc.